4TH EDITION
AMMO ENCYCLOPEDIA

BY MICHAEL BUSSARD
EDITED BY JOHN B. ALLEN, DAVID KOSOWSKI, AND CHARLES F. PRIORE, JR.

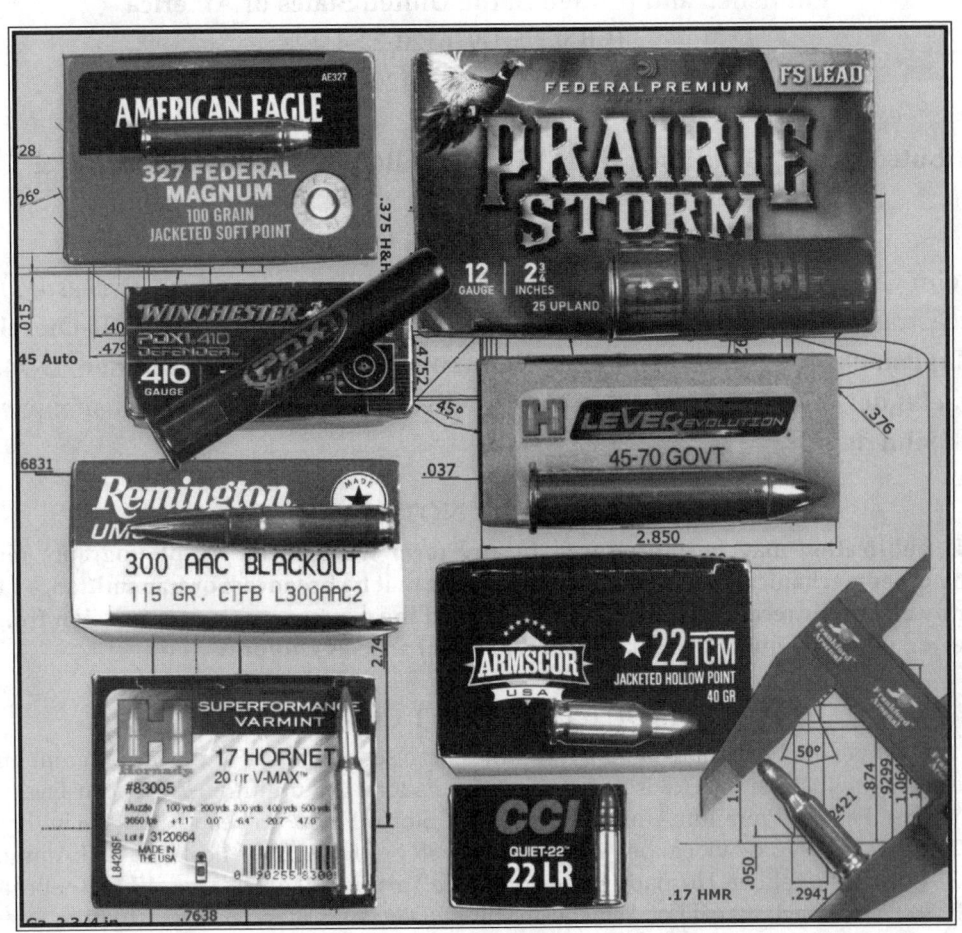

$34.95
PUBLISHER'S SUGGESTED LIST PRICE

PUBLISHER'S LIMITED EDITION HARDCOVER SUGGESTED LIST PRICE
$59.95
(limited quantities)

PUBLISHER'S NOTE:

This book is the result of continuous firearms ammunition research by the author obtained by getting information and data directly from the factories, attending and/or participating in trade shows, gun shows, and also communicating with collectors, company historians, reloading experts and other knowledgeable industry professionals worldwide.

All Rights Reserved
Copyright 2012

Blue Book Publications, Inc.
8009 34th Avenue South, Suite 250
Minneapolis, MN 55425 U.S.A.
Orders Only: 800-877-4867, ext. 3 (domestic only)
Phone No.: 952-854-5229
Fax No.: 952-853-1486
General Email: support@bluebookinc.com
Web site: www.bluebookofgunvalues.com

Published and printed in the United States of America
ISBN 10: 1-936120-22-4
ISBN 13: 978-1-936120-22-2

Distributed in part to the book trade by Ingram Book Company and Baker & Taylor.

Distributed throughout Europe by:

Gustav Jehn GmbH	*Visier GmbH*	*Deutsches Waffen Journal*
Josefkirchstrasse 3	Wipsch 1	Rudolf-Diesel-Strasse 46
59557 Lippstadt	Bad Ems, Germany D-56130	Blaufelden, D-74572 Germany
www.jehn.de	www.vsmedien.de	Website: www.dwj.de
gustav@jehn.de		

COPYRIGHT NOTICE:

ABOUT THE FRONT COVER:

Pictured on the front cover are boxes and sample cartridges representing some of the more recent offerings from the ammunition industry. They include (clockwise from top left): Federal Ammunition American Eagle 100 gr. JSP .327 Federal Magnum caliber, Federal Premium Ammunition Prairie Storm 1¼ oz. FS Lead 5 Shot 2¾ in. 12 gauge, Hornady LeverEvolution 325 gr. FTX .45–70 Govt. caliber, Armscor USA 40 gr. JHP, .22TCM caliber, CCI Ammunition Quiet-22 .40 gr. Lead RN . 22 Long Rifle caliber, Hornady Superformance Varmint 20 gr. V–Max .17 Hornet caliber, Remington UMC 115 gr. CTFB .300 AAC Blackout caliber, Winchester Elite PDX1 410 Defender 3 in. 410 Bore.

ABOUT THE BACK COVER:

Boxes of older ammunition and airgun pellets include (clockwise from top left): Dynamit Nobel RWS Special Match Meisterkugeln .177 caliber, Remington Kleanbore Police Targetmaster Lubricated .22 Long Rifle caliber, Browning 35 Power ½ oz. 6 shot 2½ in. 410 Bore, Winchester-Western Division Super X 29 gr. Lubaloy SX22S .22 Short caliber, Winchester Supreme Black Talon 230 gr. SXT .45 Auto caliber, Federal 55 gr. SP .22–250 Rem. Caliber.

CREDITS:

Design & layout – S.P. Fjestad, Clint H. Schmidt, and John B. Allen
Printing – Bang Printing, Brainerd, MN

TABLE OF CONTENTS

TABLE OF CONTENTS

GENERAL INFORMATION

While many of you have probably dealt with our company for years, it may be helpful for you to know a little bit more about our operation, including information on how to contact us regarding our various titles and other informational services.

Blue Book Publications, Inc.
8009 34th Avenue South, Suite 250
Minneapolis, MN 55425 USA
GPS Coordinates: N44° 51 28.44, W93° 13.1709

Phone No.: 952-854-5229 • Orders Only (domestic and Canada): 800-877-4867
Fax No.: 952-853-1486 (available 24 hours a day)
Web site: www.bluebookofgunvalues.com

General Email: support@bluebookinc.com - we check our email at 9am, 12pm, and 4pm M - F (excluding major U.S. holidays). Please refer to individual email addresses listed below with phone extension numbers.

To find out the latest information on our products, including availability and pricing, consumer related services, and up-to-date industry information (blogs, trade show recaps with photos/captions, upcoming events, feature articles, etc.), please check our website, as it is updated on a regular basis. Surf us - you'll have fun!

Since our phone system is equipped with voice mail, you may also wish to know extension numbers, which have been provided below:

Extension 10 - Beth Schreiber	beths@bluebookinc.com	Extension 17 - Zachary R. Fjestad	zachf@bluebookinc.com
Extension 11 - Katie Sandin	katies@bluebookinc.com	Extension 18 - Tom Stock	toms@bluebookinc.com
Extension 12 - John Andraschko	johnand@bluebookinc.com	Extension 19 - Cassandra Faulkner	cassandraf@bluebookinc.com
Extension 13 - S.P. Fjestad	stevef@bluebookinc.com	Extension 20 - Adam Burt	adamb@bluebookinc.com
Extension 15 - Clint H. Schmidt	clints@bluebookinc.com	Extension 22 - Kelsey Fjestad	kelseyf@bluebookinc.com
Extension 16 - John Allen	johna@bluebookinc.com		

Office hours are: 8:30am - 5:00pm CST, Monday - Friday.

Additionally, an after-hours message service is available for ordering. All orders are processed within 24 hours of receiving them, assuming payment and order information is correct. Depending on the product, we typically ship Fed Ex, UPS, Media Mail, or Priority Mail. Expedited shipping services are also available domestically for an additional charge. Please contact us directly for an expedited shipping quotation.

All correspondence regarding technical information/values on guns or guitars is answered in a FIFO (first in, first out) system. That means that letters, faxes, and email are answered in the order in which they are received, even though some people think that their emails take preference over everything else.

Online subscriptions and informational services are available for the *Blue Book of Gun Values, Blue Book of Modern Black Powder Arms, Ammo Encyclopedia, American Gunsmiths, Blue Book of Airguns, Ammo Encyclopedia, Blue Book of Electric Guitars, Blue Book of Acoustic Guitars,* and the *Blue Book of Guitar Amplifiers.*

We would like to thank all of you for your business in the past – you are the reason we are successful. Our goal remains the same – to give you the best products, the most accurate and up-to-date information for the money, and the highest level of customer service available in today's marketplace. If something's right, tell the world over time. If something's wrong, please tell us immediately – we'll make it right.

MEET THE STAFF

Many of you may want to know what the person on the other end of the telephone/fax/email looks like, so here are the faces that go with the voices and emails.

S.P. Fjestad
Publisher

John B. Allen
Primary Editor

Charles F. Priore, Jr.
Editor (non-employee)

David Kosowski
Editor (non-employee)

Adam Burt
Business
Development Officer

Cassandra Faulkner
Executive Editor

Lisa Beuning
Manuscript Input/Proofing

Tom Stock
CFO

Clint H. Schmidt
Art Director

John Andraschko
Technology Director

Zachary R. Fjestad
Author/Editor Guitar &
Amp Division

Beth Schreiber
Operations Manager

Katie Sandin
Operations

Kelsey Fjestad
Operations/Proofing

FOREWORD

This newest 4th Edition of the *Ammo Encyclopedia* by Michael Bussard has now established itself as the primary reference source on both current and obsolete ammunition. Along with the *Blue Book of Gun Values*, Blue Book Publications, Inc. is very proud to publish the two most comprehensive and up-to-date publications on both firearms and ammunition.

The 1st Edition, published in 2008 with 792 pages, quickly sold out. The 2nd Edition was published in 2010, and the 3rd Edition followed a year later – all were well received and are now also sold out. This new 4th Edition has been expanded to almost 1,000 pages with over 100 chapters. An invaluable new addition is the 12-page color section on pages 289-300 (Chapter 51) depicting over 265 current rimfire/centerfire cartridges and shotshells in actual size. Cartridge profiles/drawings and ballistics charts have been updated to include all the new factory cartridges. Some airgun enthusiasts have indicated that they would like to see information on pellets, so charts and related information have also been included on the wide variety of airgun pellets available for today's adult airguns.

Certainly a publication of this size and scope takes a lot of work and effort. I'd like to thank the author for all the hours he has spent both putting together and upgrading this large database. Michael is a tenured senior spokesman for the ammunition industry and has almost 40 years of experience with a variety of ammunition companies. He is a virtual walking encyclopedia on ammunition and regardless how hard or obscure our questions to him might seem, his answer(s) will be faster and more accurate than anything found in a Google search!

Most of the cartridge drawings and profiles within this 4th Edition were created in the software program QuickDESIGN. Initially, we contemplated using camera-provided images for the color section, but it would have been very time consuming and also difficult to maintain an up-to-date cartridge image bank. That's when Michael suggested using QuickDESIGN for the color section also, and I am really glad we did. Mr. Ed Dillon from NECOS was nice enough to allow Blue Book Publications to use this color application from QuickDESIGN to create almost 3-dimensional line art images for rimfire/centerfire cartridges, in addition to shotshells – see pages 289-300.

The International Ammunition Association (IAA) was also kind enough to allow us to use some of their Cartridge of the Month images from their website, cartridgecollectors.org. These will appear throughout the book, and the information and facts they provide might

Roy G. Jinks (c), Smith & Wesson's long time historian and chef extraordinaire takes a little time at the recent NRA Annual Meeting & Convention to stop by the BBP booth and entertain author Michael Bussard (r) and publisher S.P. Fjestad.

surprise you. If you're interested in older ammunition, I would certainly recommend joining their organization. For more information, please look at their ad on the inside back cover or visit cartridgecollectors.org.

Once again, Clint H. Schmidt, Blue Book Publications' talented art director, and primary editor John B. Allen get most of the credit for ensuring this large manuscript is everything it can be once it's published. David Kosowski and Charles F. Priore, Jr. also helped immensely with corrections, revisions, and proofing. Critical additional in-house proofing was also provided by Kelsey Fjestad and Cassandra Faulkner. This was no easy task – especially when taking into consideration the complexity of drawings, charts, graphs, profiles, and related miscellaneous information that all needed to be formatted correctly so users can easily find the information they are looking for quickly.

The biggest thank you goes out to all you readers who have supported this project over the years. Remember, this book is also available online – please visit www.bluebookofgunvalues.com, where good information never sleeps! As Oliver Cromwell so eloquently put it over 350 years ago, "Keep your head down and your powder dry."

Sincerely,

S.P. Fjestad
Publisher
Blue Book Publications, Inc.

Technology has always been the major force driving ammunition development. The historical record shows that long periods of ennui pass while technological advancements are made, collected, and digested. Suddenly, the accumulated new technology reaches critical mass and a Golden Age of intense development occurs as the knowledge is collectively applied and absorbed into accepted ammunition science.

The first Golden Age (1807-1885) began with Rev. Alexander Forsyth's discovery of percussion ignition in 1807. There followed a 78 year-long struggle to perfect Forsyth's discovery. It was during this period of time that Gen. Hiram Berdan perfected his Berdan primer and Col. Edward Boxer perfected his Boxer primer. Along the way, LeFaucheux developed the pinfire cartridge in 1836, followed by Horace Smith and Daniel Wesson's rimfire cartridge in 1856. These inventions made the self-contained cartridge as we know it today a reality. Ammunition manufacturers of the day answered the call with such classics as the .22 Short, .44-40 Winchester, .45 Colt, and .45-70 Government – all of which remain in production to this day.

The Second Golden Age began with Paul Vieille's perfection of smokeless powder manufacture in 1886. The significance of his discovery was grasped immediately by the armies and ammunition manufacturers of most major countries. It touched off a race to develop new military and sporting small arms cartridges to take full advantage of the new propellants. On the sporting side, these efforts included transitioning some existing black powder cartridges to the new smokeless propellants. Efforts to exploit the potential of smokeless propellant for military cartridges continued into the 1970s. However, the two World Wars slowed commercial cartridge development until the late 1960s.

Michael Bussard, a licensed "ammo-cologist" and author of the *Ammo Encyclopedia*, takes a little time to sit down in the Blue Book Publications booth during a recent NRA Show. This newest 4th Edition has been expanded to almost 1,000 pages!

In 2000, the Third Golden Age of ammunition development arrived. It is being driven by an avalanche of technical advancements in materials, propellants, metallurgy, ballistics, market analysis, and quality control. For example, new high strength polymers finally make it possible to mold a centerfire rifle cartridge case of this material fully capable of replacing the familiar metal cartridge case. Non-toxic composites are replacing lead in bullet cores and shotshells without sacrificing ballistic performance. Low drag bullet designs and supercavitating tips will soon be entering the market. High energy propellants allow increased muzzle velocities without increasing pressures. Modern, computer-controlled, high speed manufacturing equipment coming online will reduce costs and increase output. Advanced measuring and detection devices on loading machines check every cartridge component while laser and optical scanning machines inspect every finished cartridge! All major ammunition manufacturers are busy adding to their product line in an effort to leave no niche market unfilled.

Have you noticed? The pace of development in ammunition technology is speeding up. The periods between critical masses is shortening and the absorption pace of new technology between them more intense.

We will be covering these exciting developments in future editions of *The Ammo Encyclopedia* – stay tuned!

It will be interesting.

Sincerely,

Michael Bussard

Michael Bussard
Author – *Ammo Encyclopedia*

ACKNOWLEDGEMENTS

The author would like to extend a special thank you to John B. Allen, David Kosowski, and Charles F. Priore, Jr. for taking this book to the next level in terms of being thorough and more complete. Also, Clint H. Schmidt deserves special recognition for spending a lot of time making sure all the images, graphics, and overall design turned out as well as they did. This was a long, hard, uphill climb again, but at the end, all of us felt good once we reached the summit.

Dimensional drawings by QuickDESIGN© program available from NECONOS (Nostalgia Enterprises Company) at www.neconos.com.

The following people and companies also deserve special mention.

S.P. Fjestad (Publisher & Cover Design)
Kenneth A. Alexander
Mike Bitler
Ed Dillon - NECONOS
Hartmut Broemel – NECONOS (Germany)
Steve Sanetti - NSSF

Randy Bimson – SAAMI
Pepper Burruss – IAA
Steve Hornady
Lawrence Wales
Bob Metz
Bob Hodgdon
Bill Woodin
R.T. Lunger, Jr.

Evan Marshall
Heather Clark
Paul Shipley
Audra Calloway
Joe Chamberlain
Mike Haas at ammoguide.com

Andrew Chamberlain – Chamberlain Development Publishing
Alvin Olson - MWCA
Pat McKune – Sporting Collectibles
Jan Shrader

*T*he *Ammo Encyclopedia* is intended to be a broad, practical reference work on sporting and military small arms ammunition. This book is not a reloading manual and contains no reloading data. Readers seeking such data are referred to the many excellent books on this subject published by bullet and powder manufacturers. With the volume and diversity of information included, it became obvious this 4th Edition needed to be completely reorganized to make it possible for you to locate the information you are looking for as fast as possible. A quick look in the Table of Contents and you will see how the book is divided into 18 sections and 102 Chapters. On the first page of most chapters you will find a gray box with Chapter Highlights so at a glance you know what is included in the chapter. We have expanded and improved the Cartridge Index to include both the Industry Standard Cartridge Names and all the Alternate Cartridge Names that some of you find more recognizable. Also new in this index we have included a letter suffix after each cartridge name, (C) for Commercial Ammunition or (M) for Military Ammunition.

Sections I-VIII: Chapters 1-45 contain detailed information on the history, nomenclature, manufacture, application, and ballistics of small arms ammunition that guides and supports readers' understanding of the core material. To aid in placing the core material and technical data in a practical context, these sections also contain chapters on world ammunition markets, domestic and foreign manufacturers, governing bodies, and production volumes. Be sure not to miss the very important chapters on safety (Chapters 37-41).

Sample cartridge illustration with description: See page 10 for explanations per numeral listings.

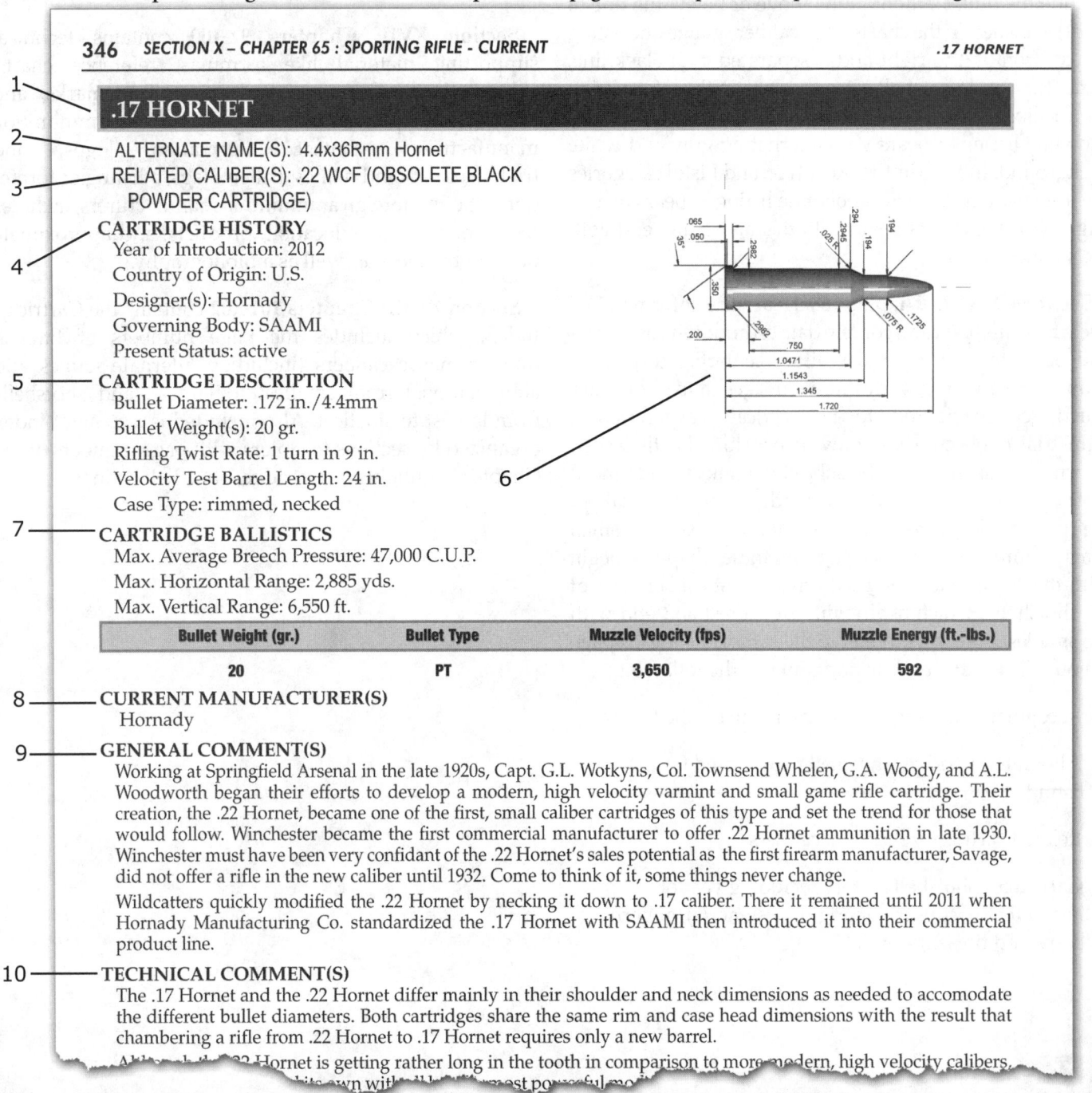

345 SECTION X – CHAPTER 65 : SPORTING RIFLE - CURRENT | .17 HORNET

1 — **.17 HORNET**

2 — ALTERNATE NAME(S): 4.4x36Rmm Hornet

3 — RELATED CALIBER(S): .22 WCF (OBSOLETE BLACK POWDER CARTRIDGE)

4 — **CARTRIDGE HISTORY**
Year of Introduction: 2012
Country of Origin: U.S.
Designer(s): Hornady
Governing Body: SAAMI
Present Status: active

5 — **CARTRIDGE DESCRIPTION**
Bullet Diameter: .172 in./4.4mm
Bullet Weight(s): 20 gr.
Rifling Twist Rate: 1 turn in 9 in.
Velocity Test Barrel Length: 24 in.
Case Type: rimmed, necked

6 —

7 — **CARTRIDGE BALLISTICS**
Max. Average Breech Pressure: 47,000 C.U.P.
Max. Horizontal Range: 2,885 yds.
Max. Vertical Range: 6,550 ft.

Bullet Weight (gr.)	Bullet Type	Muzzle Velocity (fps)	Muzzle Energy (ft.-lbs.)
20	PT	3,650	592

8 — **CURRENT MANUFACTURER(S)**
Hornady

9 — **GENERAL COMMENT(S)**
Working at Springfield Arsenal in the late 1920s, Capt. G.L. Wotkyns, Col. Townsend Whelen, G.A. Woody, and A.L. Woodworth began their efforts to develop a modern, high velocity varmint and small game rifle cartridge. Their creation, the .22 Hornet, became one of the first, small caliber cartridges of this type and set the trend for those that would follow. Winchester became the first commercial manufacturer to offer .22 Hornet ammunition in late 1930. Winchester must have been very confidant of the .22 Hornet's sales potential as the first firearm manufacturer, Savage, did not offer a rifle in the new caliber until 1932. Come to think of it, some things never change.

Wildcatters quickly modified the .22 Hornet by necking it down to .17 caliber. There it remained until 2011 when Hornady Manufacturing Co. standardized the .17 Hornet with SAAMI then introduced it into their commercial product line.

10 — **TECHNICAL COMMENT(S)**
The .17 Hornet and the .22 Hornet differ mainly in their shoulder and neck dimensions as needed to accomodate the different bullet diameters. Both cartridges share the same rim and case head dimensions with the result that chambering a rifle from .22 Hornet to .17 Hornet requires only a new barrel.

Although the .22 Hornet is getting rather long in the tooth in comparison to more modern, high velocity calibers, it holds its own with all but the most powerful modern...

HOW TO USE THIS BOOK

Section IX: Chapters 46-64 contain the new ballistic charts and a color section of current cartridge images. These cartridge images where created using the QuickDESIGN metallic cartridge designer software. They are printed on a one to one scale and as close to actual size as possible. They provide a visual representation of the cartridges that you have interest in and also can be used to visually compare one cartridge with another on a one to one basis. The color on some of the bullets and cartridge cases may vary somewhat, but if you lay your cartridge over the image you will see how close the actual size is. Each ballistic chart begins with the smallest and ends with the largest calibers and includes (for most of the cartridges) the cartridge's recognized name along with its bullet weights, types, styles, velocity in FPS, energy in FT.-LBS., and some charts include the bullet's flight path (above or below the line of sight) in inches. In the charts, each caliber/gauge line listing is read from left to right and is separated by a black line. In the Rifle and Shotshell categories, when the information on a caliber/gauge reads continually across both pages, each line listing appears with alternating gray and white background. In the Rimfire, Revolver, and Pistol categories the information for each caliber line listing appears on one page. Shotshell charts begin with the largest and end with the smallest bore.

Sections X-XVI: Chapters 65-91 are the informational "heart" of this book and contain data on hundreds of current and obsolete sporting and military centerfire cartridges, proprietary cartridges, rimfire cartridges, and shotshells. Cartridges considered to be wildcats, experimental, industrial, or obscure have only been included with limited information as these are the subject of books for advanced cartridge collectors. Military cartridges above .60 caliber are not included here since they are not considered small arms ammunition. The listings in these chapters begin with the smallest and end with the largest calibers except for shotshells, which begin with the largest and end with the smallest bore. If you refer to the sample listing on page 9, you will see that each listing contains the following:

1. Recognized cartridge/shotshell name for the listing

2. Alternate cartridge/shotshell names used for the listing

3. Related cartridge/shotshell calibers

4. Cartridge/Shotshell history including year of introduction, country of origin, designer(s), governing body, and present status

5. Cartridge/Shotshell description including bullet diameter and weight, rifling twist rate and test barrel length, case type and material it is made of, and primer size

6. Cartridge/Shotshell dimensional drawing

7. Cartridge/Shotshell ballistics including max. average breech pressure, max. horizontal and vertical range, and a chart

8. Current manufacturers list (if any)

9. General comment(s) about how, when, where, or why a cartridge/shotshell came to be

10. Technical comment(s)

Section XVII: Chapters 92-100 contains technical supporting material like formulas, reference charts, abbreviations, Glossary, Addresses, Trademarks and Brands, an alphabetical listing of current ammunition manufacturers' contact information, logos, and trademarks/brand names. Fallen Flags, a listing of former domestic and foreign ammunition manufacturers, includes the company name, location, products, and approximate dates of business, as well as a Bibliography.

Section XVIII: Chapters 101-102 contains the Cartridge Index, which includes the page numbers of English unit or metric calibers (including alternate names and abbreviations) from smallest to largest, and shotshells from largest to smallest. Also included is a General Index organized by sections/chapters with page numbers of the Chapter Highlights or cartridge/shotshell listings.

SECTION I – DEFINING A CARTRIDGE
CHAPTER 1 : WHAT IS A CARTRIDGE?

CHAPTER 1 HIGHLIGHTS:

- TECHNICAL DEFINITION OF A FIREARM
- TECHNICAL DEFINITION OF A CARTRIDGE
- WHAT DOES A CARTRIDGE DO?
- DEFINITION OF AMMUNITION
- ROOTS OF ORDNANCE-RELATED WORDS IN ENGLISH
- A CARTRIDGE IS NOT A BULLET

In the configurations you see today, modern cartridges are the culmination of over 760 years of persistent scientific development by thousands of individuals, companies, and governments in diverse scientific disciplines such as metallurgy, chemistry, mathematics, measurement, ballistics, engineering, and manufacturing. This is the longest thread of technical development in recorded history!

However, before we define a cartridge, we first must define a firearm in purely technical terms. By doing so, we will be able to better understand and define a cartridge.

TECHNICAL DEFINITION OF A FIREARM

A firearm is a heat engine that converts the chemically stored energy in the propellant into kinetic energy by accelerating the bullet or shot pellets to high velocity.

There are two basic types of cartridges—modern and antique (muzzle loading). Modern cartridges are self-contained assemblies that contain all the components a firearm requires to function as a projectile launching device—cartridge case, primer, propellant, and bullet. Antique cartridges are containers holding a lubricated bullet and a pre-measured charge of black powder. Such cartridges do not contain a primer and do not have a cartridge case.

TECHNICAL DEFINITION OF A CARTRIDGE

MODERN: A cartridge is a complete round of self-contained ammunition consisting of, at minimum, a case, primer, propellant powder, and bullet or shot charge.

ANTIQUE (Muzzle Loading): A muzzle loading cartridge is a paper, gutta percha, or other non-metallic material container which holds a pre-measured charge of black powder and a lubricated projectile (a conical bullet or a round ball).

Modern cartridges and their components are mass produced to exacting standards in dedicated factories. In the modern technical lexicon for ammunition, the word "cartridge" refers to centerfire and rimfire ammunition. Shotgun shells are cartridges, although

they are normally called shotshells.

Paper cartridges for muzzle loading firearms were made commercially until the late 1800s. As a cartridge material, paper is cheap, but fragile and offers slight protection against moisture or rough handling. Muzzle loading cartridges made of wood or other materials are heavy, but sturdy and reusable. Such cartridges were, and still are, handmade by the shooter.

Muzzle Loading Cartridge

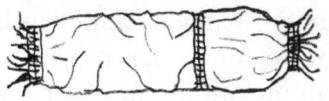

Self-Contained Cartridge

The word "cartridge" derives from the early French word "carta" meaning a container to hold a substance that is troublesome or difficult to handle. By 1550, "cartage" had become "cartouche" in French. In the early 1600s, "cartouche" entered the English language as "cartridge."

WHAT DOES A CARTRIDGE DO?

MODERN: A modern cartridge provides all components necessary for a firearm to convert stored chemical energy into kinetic energy and transfer that kinetic energy, via the projectile, on/into the target.

ANTIQUE (Muzzle Loading): An antique cartridge speeds up the loading process for a muzzle loading firearm by providing the shooter with an efficiently manipulated ready to use container of pre-measured powder and projectile, versus a "bulk" powder container and another container of projectiles.

Ordnance terms for self-contained ammunition have become firmly embedded in the English language and are often used to describe products with no firearms or ballistic functionality. For example, pre-loaded ink containers for printers and ball point pens are called ink cartridges. Other examples include cassette tape cartridges, toner cartridges, and typewriter ribbon cartridges.

DEFINITION OF AMMUNITION

The word ammunition is a synonym for cartridges. Cartridges are ammunition and ammunition consists of cartridges.

ROOTS OF ORDNANCE-RELATED WORDS IN ENGLISH

The English word "ammunition" comes from the French word "munition" circa 1600. The French word derives from the Latin word "munitio" which means fortification.

In modern English, the word "ammunition" has entered the lexicon as more than just a technical term. It can convey a sense of stored potential power in terms of quantity. For example, someone might exclaim, "I need more ammunition to finish this project," or, "I want to build up our ammo supply for the big sales push." During World War II, ammunition entered the lexicon through a famous phrase that went on to become the title of a popular song.

> *"Praise the Lord and pass the ammunition!"*
>
> - Chaplain Howell Forgy, USN aboard the USS New Orleans on December 7, 1941, during the Japanese attack on Pearl Harbor.

Recently, anti-gun groups have declared all-out war on all ordnance terms in the modern lexicon. Using the mantle of political correctness, they encourage teachers to eliminate all references to firearms and ammunition in American educational institutions and to punish students who persist in using them. This is a culture war which anti-gun groups will lose.

A CARTRIDGE IS NOT A BULLET

A cartridge often is mistakenly referred to as a bullet. For example: "I loaded the magazine with 10 bullets." This is incorrect as a bullet is only one of the component parts of a cartridge.

A STRAIGHT SHOOTER
To become a skilled shooter takes practice and concentration. Today an honest and reliable person is said to be a "straight shooter".

SPORTING REVOLVER CARTRIDGE SUPERLATIVES

SMALLEST CALIBER
SPORTING REVOLVER CARTRIDGE

.224 in. dia. 40-gr. bullet, MV 2,460 fps, ME 535 ft.-lbs.

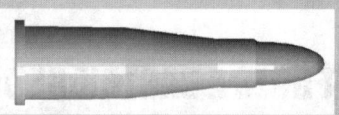

.22 Remington Jet Magnum

HIGHEST VELOCITY
SPORTING REVOLVER CARTRIDGE

.4525 in. dia. 200-gr. bullet, MV 2,300 fps, ME 2,350 ft.-lbs.

.460 S&W Magnum

LARGEST AND MOST POWERFUL
SPORTING REVOLVER CARTRIDGE

.500 in. dia. 440-gr. bullet, MV 1,625 fps, ME 2,580 ft.-lbs.

.500 S&W Magnum

CHAPTER 2 : BASIC TYPES OF CARTRIDGES

CHAPTER 2 HIGHLIGHTS:
- THE THREE BASIC TYPES OF MODERN, SELF-CONTAINED CARTRIDGES
- CENTERFIRE CARTRIDGE DEFINED AND ILLUSTRATED
- RIMFIRE CARTRIDGE DEFINED AND ILLUSTRATED
- SHOTSHELL DEFINED AND ILLUSTRATED

There are three basic types of modern, self-contained cartridges: centerfire, rimfire, and shotshell.

THE THREE BASIC TYPES OF MODERN, SELF-CONTAINED CARTRIDGES

1. Centerfire

2. Rimfire

3. Shotshell

RELATIVE SIZES OF CARTRIDGES TO SCALE

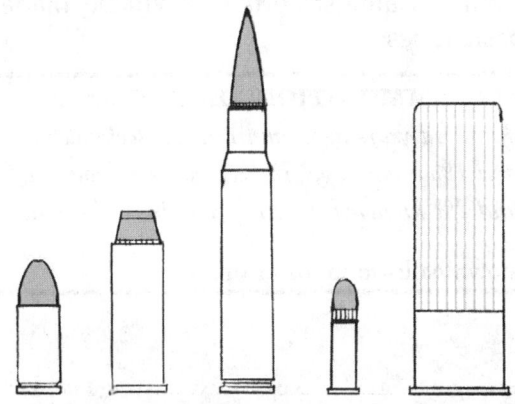

Each modern cartridge type has been designed for a broad set of specific applications, and advances in metallurgy, propellants, and bullet construction provide the flexibility for new applications as they arise. Examples of this include increasing maximum average breech pressure, using bullets heavier or lighter than the "standard" for that caliber, steel or other non-toxic shot, match grade ammunition, and using new materials for components.

CENTERFIRE CARTRIDGE DEFINED AND ILLUSTRATED

A centerfire cartridge is a self-contained assembly of four component parts:

1. Bullet

2. Cartridge case

3. Propellant powder

4. Primer

Centerfire cartridges are made in many different sizes and shapes for use in firearms of that specific caliber.

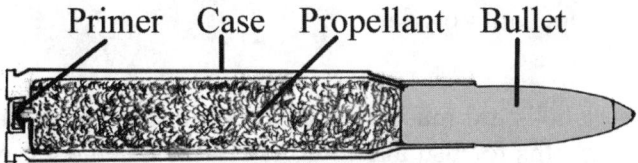

Primer   Case   Propellant   Bullet

CUES FOR IDENTIFYING A TYPICAL CENTERFIRE CARTRIDGE

- Heavy brass, steel, or aluminum cartridge case
- Case may be rimmed, semi-rimmed, rimless, belted, or rebated
- Visible primer in center of case head
- Headstamp on case head around primer
- Cartridge substantially longer and larger than rimfire

RIMFIRE CARTRIDGE DEFINED AND ILLUSTRATED

A rimfire cartridge is a self-contained assembly of three component parts:

1. Bullet

2. Metallic cartridge case with an integral primer inside its rim

3. Propellant powder

Rimfire cartridges are made in a limited number of sizes and shapes for use in firearms of that specific caliber.

Primer   Case   Propellant   Bullet

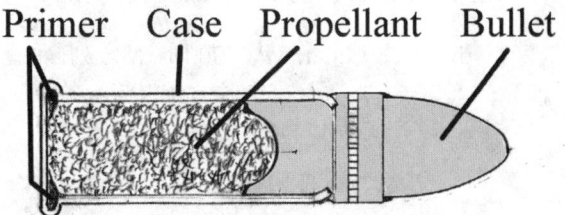

CUES FOR IDENTIFYING A RIMFIRE CARTRIDGE

- Rimmed, brass cartridge case
- No visible primer in case head
- Headstamp in center of case head
- Case mouth heavily crimped into bullet
- Much shorter and lighter than centerfire

SHOTSHELL DEFINED AND ILLUSTRATED

A shotshell is a self-contained assembly of five component parts:

1. Shot charge or single projectile (e.g. rifled slug)
2. Wad column
3. Hull (cartridge case)
4. Propellant powder
5. Primer

Shotshells are made in a limited number of gauges and lengths for use in shotguns of that specific gauge and shell length.

Note: Gauge is an indicator of shotshell diameter but it is not the "caliber" of the shotshell or the shotgun.

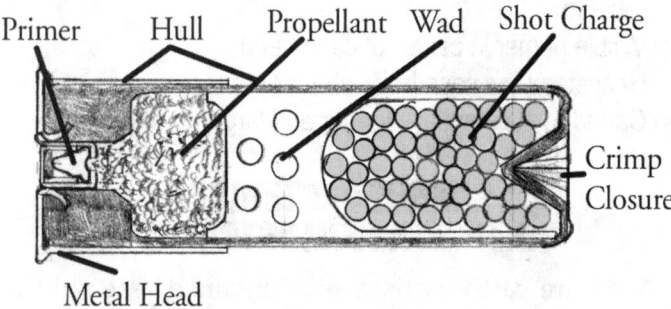

CUES FOR IDENTIFYING A TYPICAL SHOTSHELL

- Rimmed metal head with colored plastic or paper body
- Battery cup primer in center of case head
- Six or eight fold crimp or rolled closure on hull mouth

- Shot charge of multiple pellets or single projectile
- Printing on paper or plastic section of hull
- May have gauge or other headstamp around primer

Ammunition technology development is not static and much remains to be done. Inventors, engineers, and ballisticians continue to "think outside the box" as so many of their predecessors have done over the centuries. Examples of modern developments include caseless, telescoped, folded, rocket, and combustible cartridges. While these types may well become common in the future, at present they are experimental and outside the scope of this book.

Individual cartridge designs and applications also will change according to regulation, customer taste, advances in materials, new production methods, and better tooling. Despite this, future changes and improvements almost certainly will be made to the three basic types.

AMMUNITION TECHNOLOGY

"One hundred years ago, ammunition technology was 99% guess and 1% knowledge. Today, we have progressed to 98% guess and 2% knowledge. Much remains to be done!"

- Unknown ballistic engineer in 2000.

"A .22"

In referring to "a .22" you must distinguish between a .22 rimfire and a .22 centerfire rifle cartridge. They are dimensionally, ballistically, and functionally very different.

SPORTING PISTOL CARTRIDGE SUPERLATIVES

SMALLEST CALIBER
SPORTING PISTOL CARTRIDGE

.107 in. dia. 3-gr. bullet, MV 700 fps, ME 3 ft.-lbs.

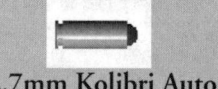

2.7mm Kolibri Auto

HIGHEST VELOCITY
SPORTING PISTOL CARTRIDGE

.311 in. dia. 87-gr. bullet, MV 1,705 fps, ME 552 ft.-lbs.

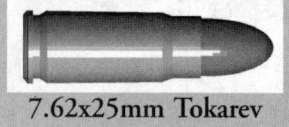

7.62x25mm Tokarev

LARGEST AND MOST POWERFUL
SPORTING PISTOL CARTRIDGE

.500 in. dia. 300-gr. bullet, MV 1,550 fps, ME 1,600 ft.-lbs.

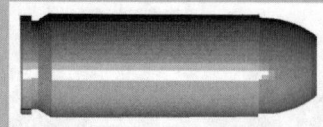

.50 Action Express

CHAPTER 3 : CARTRIDGE FAMILIES

WHAT IS A CARTRIDGE FAMILY?

A cartridge family is a group of related cartridge designs all based on the head diameter and rim configuration of a single parent or "basic" cartridge.

Centerfire cartridge cases may be divided into broad families according to their base diameter and rim type. These families exist because production tooling is expensive and maximum use must be made of tooling for economic reasons. It is inexpensive and easy to make a variation of a basic or parent cartridge by simply changing the case length, bullet diameter, neck, or other dimensions.

There are a surprisingly limited number of cartridge families. In addition to case length and bullet diameter, variations may have revised body taper, shoulder position, neck length, or neck angle. There are numerous variations and sub-variants, but just when it appears there are no further possible combinations, new variants are introduced.

Cartridge variants from commercial manufacturers are intended to fill market niches, and therefore are designed to meet specific size, velocity level, application, and numerous other requirements. However, customer taste and demand are the overarching reasons.

WHAT IS THE LARGEST CENTERFIRE SPORTING CARTRIDGE?

Without doubt this is the .700 Nitro Express. This cartridge fires a 1,200 grain bullet at a muzzle velocity of 1,900 FPS and generates 9,618 ft.-lbs. of energy.

WHAT IS THE SMALLEST CENTERFIRE CARTRIDGE?

The winner in this category is the 2.7mm Kolibri pistol cartridge designed in Europe and introduced in 1914. This pipsqueak fires a 3 grain full metal jacket bullet at a muzzle velocity of approximately 700 FPS to generate just over 3 ft.-lbs of energy. Not surprisingly, this impractical cartridge was not a commercial success and ammunition in this caliber is no longer made. The Kolibri company still exists, but is no longer in the firearms and ammunition business.

Leading the charge in this respect are the individuals called wildcatters who experiment endlessly with cartridge case shapes in an attempt to improve performance or adapt the case to a new application for regulatory, performance, or technical reasons. Although wildcat cartridges will not be covered completely in this book, some of them have become so popular they have become standard calibers in ammunition manufacturers product lines. Examples of these include: .22 Hornet, .22-250 Remington, .25-06 Remington, and .35 Whelen.

DEFINITION OF A WILDCAT CARTRIDGE

A wildcat cartridge is an experimental cartridge design created from a standard parent cartridge by individual experimenters seeking to improve ballistic performance or adapt the cartridge to meet specific requirements. Typically, a wildcat cartridge embodies changes in some or all of these features: case length, body taper, shoulder location, shoulder angle, neck length, neck diameter, and rim diameter.

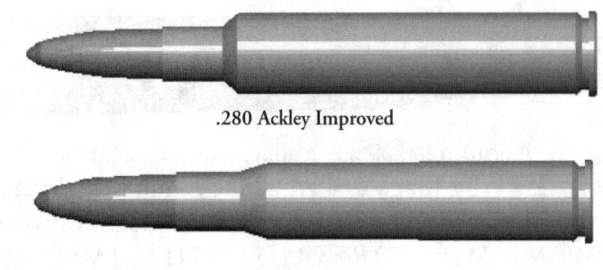

.280 Ackley Improved

.30-'06 Springfield

Here follows an ABRIDGED list of founder or parent cartridges and their offspring.

LIST OF POPULAR CARTRIDGE FAMILIES

Family Name	Founding Date

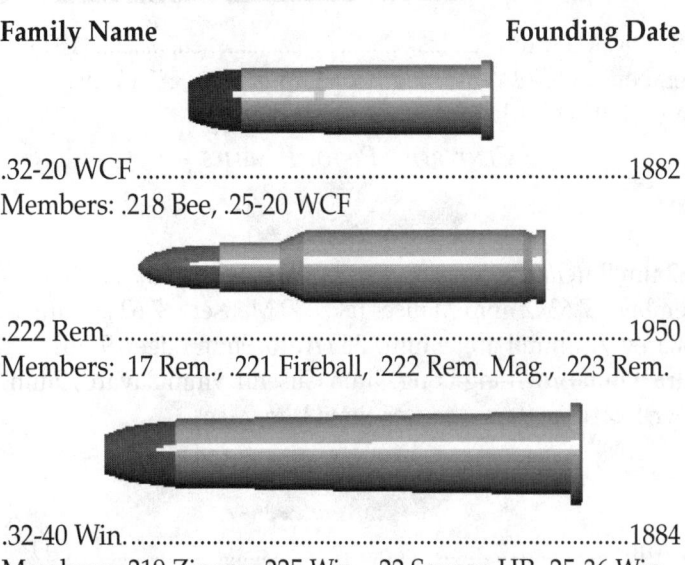

.32-20 WCF 1882
Members: .218 Bee, .25-20 WCF

.222 Rem. 1950
Members: .17 Rem., .221 Fireball, .222 Rem. Mag., .223 Rem.

.32-40 Win. 1884
Members: .219 Zipper, .225 Win., .22 Savage HP, .25-36 Win., 7-30 Waters, .30-30 Win., .32 Spec., .38-55 Win., .375 Win.

Family Name	Founding Date

.236 U.S. Navy..1895
Members: .220 Swift, .220 Russ., .22 PPC, 6mm PPC,
7.62x39mm

8x57mmJ Mauser..1888
Members: .22-250 Rem., .243 Win., 6mm Rem., .257 Rob'ts.,
.250-3000 Sav., .260 Rem., .25-'06 Rem., .270 Win., 7mm-08
Rem., .280 Rem., .300 Sav., .308 Win., .30-'06 Spr., .35 Whelen,
5.6x57mm RWS, 6x57mm Mauser, 6.5x55mm Swedish,
6.5x57mm Mauser, 7x57mm Mauser, 7x64mm Brenneke,
7.65x53mm Argentine, 7.7x58mm Japanese, 9.3x57mm Mauser,
9.3x62mm Mauser

.300 H & H Magnum 1912
Members: .257 Wby. Mag., .264 Win. Mag., 7mm Rem. Mag.,
7mm Wby. Mag., .300 Wby. Mag., 8mm Rem. Mag., .338 Win.
Mag., .340 Wby. Mag., .350 Rem. Mag., .375 H & H Mag., .416
Rem. Mag., .458 Win. Mag.

378 Wby. Magnum 1953
Members: .30-378 Wby. Mag., .338 Lapua Mag., .416 Wby.
Mag., .460 Wby. Mag.

Centerfire Pistol Families

7.62mm Borchardt...1893
Members: 7.63x25mm Mauser (aka .30 Mauser), 7.62x25mm
Tokarev, 7.65mm Parabellum, .380 Auto, 9mm Luger, 9mm
Ultra, 9mm Browning Long, 9mm Glisenti, 9mm Bayard, 9mm
Steyr, 9x21mm, 9mm Mauser, 9mm Win. Mag.

.32 Auto..1899
Members: 7.65mm MAS

Family Name	Founding Date

10mm Auto...1983
Members: .40 S & W, .357 SIG

.45 Auto...1905
Members: .45 Short, .45 Win. Mag., .45 GAP

Centerfire Revolver Families

.32 S & W 1878
Members: .32 S & W Long, .32 Colt New Police, .32-44 Target,
.32 H & R Mag.

.38 S & W 1877
Members: .38 Colt New Police, .38 Long Colt, .380 Revolver,
.38 Special, .357 Magnum, .357 Maximum

.44 S & W Russian 1870
Members: .44 Colt, .44 S & W Special, .44 S & W Magnum

.45 Colt...1873
Members: .45 Schofield, .454 Casull,.450 Revolver

Rimfire Families

.22 Short 1856
Members: .17 Aguila, .17 Mach2, .22 Long, .22 Long Rifle

.22 WRF...1890
Members: .17 HRM, .22 Rem. Auto, .22 WMR

SECTION II – CARTRIDGE AND COMPONENT NOMENCLATURE
CHAPTER 4 : CARTRIDGE NAMES

CHAPTER 4 HIGHLIGHTS:

- DEFINITION OF CALIBER
- CENTERFIRE NAMING CONVENTIONS
- WHAT'S IN A NAME?
- RIMFIRE NAMING CONVENTIONS
- SHOTSHELL NAMING CONVENTIONS
- DEFINITION OF SHOTSHELL GAUGE
- THE UNIQUE CASE OF THE .410 "GAUGE"
- HOW TO READ A CARTRIDGE OR SHOTSHELL

DEFINITION OF CALIBER

In modern ammunition, caliber is a numerical expression of the approximate diameter of the bullet in English or metric units. It is an integral part of cartridge nomenclature.

Each cartridge is unique. As ammunition technology developed, thousands of cartridges in different shapes and sizes have been designed and manufactured. As many cartridges are visually similar and may use the same diameter bullet, each cartridge configuration must be given a unique identity for convenience, reliable identification, and safety. This is exactly what cartridge nomenclature systems are intended to do.

While this sounds straightforward enough, cartridge nomenclature systems incorporate equal parts identity, hubris, merchandising, technology, and nostalgia with results that have been called, appropriately, "borderline chaos." For example, there are five centerfire nomenclatural systems, of which three are modern (SAAMI-sporting, CIP-sporting, and MIL SPEC-military) and two are obsolescent (American and British black powder). However, obsolescent systems nostalgically refuse to die and new cartridges are regularly christened with names outside any nomenclatural system.

Adding to the confusion, many centerfire cartridges have two or more "official" designations—one from each of the SAAMI, CIP, or MILSPEC systems—and numerous abbreviations. As if this were not enough, nomenclature systems used to identify rimfire cartridges and shotshells are different from those used for centerfire cartridges.

Ammunition manufacturers have formed two industry groups which provide standardized names for sporting cartridges. In the U.S., this group is called the "Sporting Arms and Ammunition Manufacturers' Institute" (SAAMI). In Europe, a similar group of manufacturers has been formed called the "Commission Internationale Permanente Pour L'epreuve Des Armes À Feu Portatives" (C.I.P.). Despite their efforts, hubris and merchandising continue to trump convention when many a new cartridge is named. MIL SPEC (military) ammunition is

identified by the armed forces of the country which uses it. For example NATO members use a common MILSPEC system to identify military ammunition.

CENTERFIRE NAMING CONVENTIONS

Centerfire sporting cartridge nomenclature rests on two firm goal posts – caliber and name. Using these two elements, nearly all centerfire cartridges can be reliably identified.

CENTERFIRE CARTRIDGE CALIBERS

Centerfire nomenclature systems are based on the concept of caliber.

In turn, caliber is determined by the approximate bore diameter of the barrel as measured across the tops of the barrel's lands or bottom of the grooves. This measurement is then used to determine the caliber of a given cartridge. Caliber takes the form of a number or numbers placed at the left of a cartridge name. Different calibers of centerfire cartridges are normally listed in ascending order, i.e. .22 Hornet is listed before .308 Winchester. Rifle, pistol, and revolver cartridges are normally listed in separate groups.

Caliber may be expressed in one of two ways: English units or metric units.

Most cartridges of American or British origin express their caliber in English units using two or three digit numbers. Calibers expressed in English units may or may not place a decimal point in front of the first digit. Most cartridges of European origin express their caliber in metric units using one or two digits. However, there are many exceptions to both these rules. In addition, American manufacturers have recently started using the metric system to describe the caliber of some new cartridges.

A caliber designation may be supplemented by additional numbers containing two or three digits and/or letters. These are typically separated from the caliber by an x, a hyphen (-), or a slash (/). Supplemental numbers and letters are used to convey additional information such as:

- **Case length and rim type**

Metric cartridges may have a lower case x after the caliber followed by two digits reflecting the approximate case length in millimeters. One or two additional letters immediately following the case length indicate rim type. For example:

- No letter designates a rimless case, i.e. 7x57mm
- R designates a rimmed case, i.e. 9.3x74Rmm
- SR designates a semi-rimmed case, i.e. 6.5x50SRmm
- RB designates a rebated rim case i.e. 10.75x63RBmm

Two additional letters are used exclusively for the 8x57mm Mauser and some other German 8mm cartridges:

- J or I to indicate a .318" diameter bullet, i.e. 8x57mmJ or 8x57RmmJ
- S indicating a .323" diameter bullet, i.e. 8x57mmJS or 8x57RmmJS

Obsolescent British or American cartridges which have a case length designation do so in English fractions immediately after the caliber and propellant charge weight designation, i.e. .500 3¼" or .50-110 3½".

- **Year of adoption**

A hyphen followed by a contraction designating the year of adoption, i.e. .30-'06 Springfield.

- **Muzzle velocity or black powder charge weight**

A hyphen followed by a two or three digit number to designate one of the following:

- Muzzle velocity in feet per second, i.e. .250-3000 (3000 fps MV)
- Charge weight of black powder, i.e..50-110 (except .30-30 Win.)

- **Origin of parent cartridge**

A slash (/) or dash (-) followed by a two or three digit number to designate the original cartridge from which the present one was derived. This designation system was typically employed for large British calibers, i.e. .577/450, or 7mm-08.

CENTERFIRE CARTRIDGE NAMES

A name(s) and/or designation(s) must be added to the caliber to fully identify a specific cartridge.

While there is no rigorous convention for cartridge names, they tend to fall into one of four categories:

- **Original manufacturer or developer**, i.e. .270 Winchester, .300 Savage, .35 Remington

- **Inventor's name**, i.e. 8x57mm Mauser, .300 Weatherby Magnum, .35 Whelen

- **Application**, i.e. 7.62x51mm NATO, .500/450 No. 1 Musket

- **Action word**, i.e. .221 Fireball, .220 Swift, 7mm Firehawk

WHAT'S IN A NAME?

Centerfire and rimfire cartridge nomenclature consists of two parts:

1. **The caliber (with or without supplements) expressed in English or metric units.**

2. **A name or names reflecting its origin, inventor, application, or action.**

In many instances, a centerfire cartridge designation will have one or more additional words following the basic name. Such words usually are one of the following:

- **Magnum (Mag.)**

This suffix is commonly used to denote a cartridge offering higher ballistic performance than standard cartridges, i.e. .300 H&H Magnum.

- **Express (Exp.)**

A nearly obsolete suffix denoting a cartridge loaded to above normal muzzle velocity, i.e. .577 Nitro Express.

- **Ultra Magnum; and Short-Action Ultra Magnum**

A new designation coined in the early 2000s by Remington to identify a series of new high performance magnum rifle cartridges of their design, i.e. .375 Remington Ultra Magnum (RUM).

- **Light Magnum, Heavy Magnum**

A description introduced by Hornady Manufacturing Co. in the 1990s to identify their loadings which offer magnum performance in non-magnum caliber rifle cartridges, i.e. .308 Light Magnum, 7mm Remington Heavy Magnum.

- **Short Magnum**

A term applied by Winchester to their new line of short magnum rifle cartridges, i.e. .270 Winchester Short Magnum (WSM).

- **Super Short Magnum**

Another term from Winchester to denote their new line of super short magnum rifle cartridges, i.e. .243 Winchester Super Short Magnum (WSSM).

- **High Energy**

Federal offers a line of rifle cartridges in standard and magnum calibers loaded to higher ballistic performance levels with this designation, i.e. 30-'06 Springfield High Energy (H.E.).

- **Supreme**

A trademark used by Winchester for their line of rifle or handgun cartridges loaded to higher muzzle velocity levels with premium bullets, i.e. .30-30 Winchester Supreme, .357 Magnum Supreme.

- **Super**

A suffix sometimes applied to old or new cartridges upgraded to provide added performance, i.e. 7x61mm S & H Super, .38 Super Auto +P.

- **Subsonic**

Cartridges loaded to a muzzle velocity below the speed of sound (approx. 1,150 fps) often carry this suffix, i.e. 9mm Luger Subsonic.

- **Managed-Recoil**

A new term used by Remington for their line of rifle cartridges loaded to a lower velocity (not subsonic) to reduce recoil, i.e. .30-'06 Springfield Managed Recoil.

- **High Velocity, Hi-Power (H.V., H-P)**

A self-explanatory suffix used frequently in the past, i.e. .22 Savage Hi-Power. While the term "Hi-Power" is a Federal/ATK trademark, the suffix "high velocity" is a generic term used mainly with centerfire handgun and rimfire ammunition to indicate that the cartridge is loaded to above normal muzzle velocity.

- **Shot**

A descriptive label applied to handgun cartridges loaded with shot instead of a single bullet, i.e. .44 Magnum Shot, .45 ACP Shot.

- **Cowboy**

A recent suffix applied to lead bullet rifle and handgun ammunition in classic black powder calibers loaded to original muzzle velocity specifications, i.e. .45 Colt Cowboy.

- **+P**

A suffix added to modern versions of some older handgun cartridges for safety reasons to identify them as having been loaded to increased breech pressures and higher muzzle velocity, i.e. .38 Special +P, .38 Super Auto +P.

From the number of newly minted suffixes on this list, it is obvious that the development and application of action words for cartridge names continues to move forward at a frantic pace. Indeed, such activities have become a popular sport of one-upmanship in which everyone can participate.

> **THE FIRST MAGNUM CARTRIDGE**
> The first magnum cartridge was the .375 Holland & Holland Magnum introduced in 1912. The high brow Holland & Holland firm borrowed the term from extra large "magnum" bottles of champagne.

CENTERFIRE CARTRIDGE PROLIFERATION

The increasing number of cartridges which have the same English or metric caliber but differ significantly in case configuration and dimensions has become a growing problem. For example, there are no less than 22 different 7mm cartridges and 10 different .300 Magnum cartridges. As new cartridges are introduced and older cartridges remain in production, the problem will only become more serious.

Due to cartridge proliferation within calibers it has never been more important when referring to a cartridge to be clear, precise, and complete. Not doing so can lead to confusion and safety issues. As very few cartridges are interchangeable, attempting to fire a cartridge of one caliber in a firearm chambered for another could result in serious personal injury. For further information on this subject, see Dangerous Combinations in Chapter 39: Shooting Safety.

EXAMPLES OF CENTERFIRE CARTRIDGE CALIBER PROLIFERATION

Although the following centerfire calibers all fire the same 7mm diameter bullet, they are not interchangeable due to differences in case length, width, volume, and configuration. For this reason, it is very important to correctly and fully describe a given cartridge by its caliber and full name.

7x33mm Finnish
7mm Remington BR
7-30 Waters
7mm-08 Remington
7x61mm Sharp & Hart Super

7x57mm Mauser

7x57Rmm Mauser

7x64mm Brenneke

7x64Rmm Brenneke

.280 Remington

.284 Winchester

7mm Dakota

7mm Shooting Times Easterner (STE)

7mm Shooting Times Westerner (STW)

7mm Firehawk

7.21mm Firebird

7.21mm Tomahawk

7mm Remington Magnum

7mm Remington Short Action-Ultra Magnum

7mm Remington Ultra Magnum

7mm Winchester Short Magnum

7mm Weatherby Magnum

DISSECTING MILITARY TYPE CLASSED AMMUNITION

Military cartridge nomenclature systems are used by the armed forces of individual nations to precisely identify their military ammunition caliber and type. Today, the armed forces of most countries adhere in whole or in part to the nomenclature systems developed by treaty organizations such as NATO and the ex-Warsaw Pact to ensure interoperability.

These systems use one to three numbers to indicate the caliber in millimeters (mm) followed by an x and two or three numbers indicating the case length in mm. Following this is the name of the country that first adopted the cartridge or the treaty organization writing the specifaction. Modern examples of such systems include: 5.56x45mm NATO, 7.62x51mm NATO, and 7.62x39mm Soviet. Following this, the year of adoption is sometimes indicated such as 7.62x39mm Soviet M43.

From this point, modern military type classification nomenclature systems further identify the nature and variant of the cartridge. Examples of the nature may include Ball, Tracer, Armor Piercing, Blank, Match, Subsonic, Proof, Incendiary, Grenade Launching, etc. Lastly, a series of numbers and/or letters identifies the variant, for example: 7.62x51mm NATO Ball M80, 7.62x39mm Soviet Ball M43 Type XXX, or 5.56x45mm NATO Ball M855A1.

Prior to 1950, most nations used individual military type classification systems which were confusing and often complicated. These systems used English units or metric units to define caliber followed by a dizzying array of unique systems to express nature, variants, and models. In some countries, several different systems were in use at the same time as new calibers were introduced but old calibers remained in service. Examples include: .303 British Mark 8Z, .30-'06 Ball M2, 7.62x54Rmm Russian Type LPS and 7.9x57mmJS Mauser sS Geschoss mit Eisenkern.

RIMFIRE NAMING CONVENTIONS

In broad terms, rimfire cartridges predominantly follow the nomenclature system of their centerfire brethren in that there are two firm nomenclatural goal posts –caliber and name. As it must encompass a far fewer number of different cartridges, rimfire nomenclature is less complex than centerfire conventions. One major difference is that rimfire names may indicate case length or muzzle velocity.

RIMFIRE CARTRIDGE CALIBERS

Rimfire cartridge nomenclature is based on the concept that the barrel's bore diameter, rather than actual bullet diameter, determines caliber. All rimfire cartridges express their caliber using a two digit number. Most modern rimfire cartridges are .17 caliber or .22 caliber, however, many obsolete rimfire cartridges were made in larger calibers.

While rimfire calibers may be expressed in metric units, such designations are uncommon as both American and European shooters routinely use English units when referring to rimfire cartridges. Rimfire cartridge caliber numbers may have supplements.

RIMFIRE CARTRIDGE NAMES

Rimfire cartridge names fall into two groups:

• **Names based on case length, i.e.: .22 Short, .22 Long, .22 Long Rifle**

• **Names of origin, i.e.: .17 Hornady Magnum Rimfire, .17 Aguila, .22 Winchester Magnum Rimfire**

Rimfire cartridge names in the .22 Short-Long-Long Rifle group typically have suffixes to indicate intended use or muzzle velocity level, i.e. Rifle Match, Pistol Match, Silhouette, Blank, Shot; or Target Velocity, Subsonic, Standard Velocity, High Velocity, Hyper Velocity. In some instances, the type of bullet may be indicated such as Solid, Hollow Point, or shot size.

Rimfire cartridge name suffixes are often arranged as follows: .22 Long Rifle Standard Velocity, .22 Long Rifle Subsonic HP, .22 Long Rifle Pistol Match, .22 Long Rifle High Velocity HP.

Magnum rimfire cartridge origin or source names typically have a designating suffix, i.e.: .22 Winchester Magnum Rimfire, .17 Hornady Magnum Rimfire.

Caliber proliferation in rimfire has not been a problem.

**THE OLDEST CARTRIDGE
STILL IN PRODUCTION**

This honor goes to the humble .22 Short rimfire introduced in 1856 and still in production over 150 years later.

SHOTSHELL NAMING CONVENTIONS

Shotshell nomenclature is completely different from centerfire or rimfire nomenclature. Because shotshell nomenclature is not based directly on caliber and no names are attached for differentiation, on the surface it may seem simpler and easier to comprehend. However, in many ways its rules are more arcane and complex.

DEFINITION OF SHOTSHELL GAUGE

Shotshell bore sizes are referred to as gauges. Gauge is normally expressed in two digits followed by a hyphen and the word gauge. While centerfire and rimfire calibers are arranged in ascending order of bore/caliber diameter, the opposite is true for shotshell gauges - the smaller the gauge number, the larger the shotshell. Under the gauge system, a 10-gauge shotshell is larger than a 12-gauge shotshell and a 20-gauge shotshell is larger than a 28-gauge shotshell. Of course, shotgun bores and chambers have specific diameters, however the gauge system is commonly used when referring to shotshell sizes.

Gauge as it refers to shotshells is an indicator of shotgun bore diameter. A gauge is equal to the number of unalloyed lead balls of a given bore diameter in one pound of lead. Shotshells below 50 gauge are specified by bore diameter.

Shotshells between 1 and 2 gauge and above 1 gauge are specified by letters. See Chapter 96: Reference Material for a full listing of gauges with their corresponding bore sizes.

While most centerfire cartridges have an abbreviated caliber designation stamped into the case head for identification, many shotshells have no indication of their gauge on the case head. However, some manufacturers color-code the hulls of some shotshells for identification.

For example, Federal uses the following system:
10-gauge brown
12-gauge red
16-gauge purple
20-gauge yellow
28-gauge red
.410 bore red

Safety is the major reason for shotshell color coding. Shotshells of different gauges often look identical on cursory examination in the field or on the range. Color-coding serves as an important identifier for safety in such cases.

Here it is important to note that not all manufacturers adhere to the above shotshell color-coding system. Some use their own color-coding systems while others use none at all. An additional complication is that for marketing purposes shotshell manufacturers often produce shells with tube colors which are not included in their normal color-coding system. For these reasons, experienced shooters should expect to encounter shotshell tubes of nearly every color in the palette, including clear.

SHOTSHELL TUBE LENGTHS

When referring to a specific gauge of shotshell, it is customary to list the length of the tube after the gauge in inches or millimeters, i.e. 12-gauge 3" or 20-gauge 70mm. Here it is important to remember that the length is measured on an uncrimped shell. Many gauges of shotshell are offered with different tube lengths to accommodate various loads. An important reason for determining tube length is to prevent inadvertently firing a longer shell in a shorter chamber.

SHOTSHELL TUBE LENGTHS BY GAUGE	
Gauge	Tube Lengths
10	2 5/8"-67mm (obsolete)
	2 7/8"-73mm (obsolete)
	3½"-89mm
12	2"-51mm (British)
	2½"-63.5mm (European)
	2¾"-70mm
	3"-76mm
	3½"-89mm (U.S.)
16	2¾"-70mm
20	2¾"-70mm
	3"-76mm
28	2¾"-70mm
.410 Bore (68-ga.)	2½"-63.5mm
	3"-76mm

SHOTSHELL LOADS

Many shotshell manufacturers print the type of load on the plastic tube. As the printing is in ink, it is not permanent and can easily wear off. After the printing wears off, it is very difficult to determine the load level, shot charge weight, shot size, and shot type of a given shotshell.

The information printed on the tube may consist of

some or all of the following four elements:

1. Type of load

The type of load normally is expressed as one of the following: Light Target, Heavy Target, Handicap, Game, Light Field, Heavy Field, High Velocity, Short Magnum, Magnum, Buckshot, Slug, Rifled Slug, or other types.

2. Dram equivalent (D.E.)

If indicated, the dram equivalent usually is expressed in whole numbers and fractions, i.e. 2¾, 3, 3¾, 4, or Max., and indicates the muzzle velocity of the load.

Shotshell Dram Equivalent

Dram equivalent (DE) is an archaic method of indicating the muzzle velocity of a given smokeless powder shotshell load by comparing it to a black powder load of similar muzzle velocity. Due to its complexities, the dram equivalent system has been dropped by many manufacturers.

A dram is an English unit of weight equal to 1/16 of an ounce or 27.3 grains. Drams were the standard unit of weight used in loading shotguns with black powder. A dram is NOT a unit of measure for weighing smokeless propellants!

3. Shot charge weight

U.S. shotshell manufacturers normally list shot charge weights in ounces and fractions of an ounce. Countries using the metric system commonly express shot charge weight in grams. Buckshot loads normally list the number of pellets instead of a shot charge weight. Slug projectile weight is expressed in ounces and fractions of an ounce, and/or grains (like rifle or handgun bullet weights).

4. Pellet size and type

Pellet size (diameter) may be indicated by letters or numbers, sometimes followed by a word denoting pellet material, i.e. No. 4 steel, No. 6 copper (plated lead), No. BB. Buckshot is normally described on shotshell tubes by one or two digits and or one or two letters indicating pellet size followed by the word buck, i.e. 9 pellet 00 buck. For a full listing of pellet sizes by type see Chapter 96: Reference Material.

On many shotshells, some or all of this information may be absent. A complete description printed on a shotshell tube might appear as: 3¾-1¼-6 meaning 3¾ dram equivalent-1¼ ounce-No. 6 shot. Shortened variations might read: High Velocity 1¼-6 or High Velocity No. 6 or even simply 1 1/4-6. Today, a growing practice is to eliminate all references to dram equivalent on the shotshell tube.

> ### LARGEST SHOTSHELL LEGAL FOR HUNTING
> In 1918, the Migratory Waterfowl Act outlawed shotshells larger than 10-gauge for hunting such birds in the U.S. Prior to that date, many waterfowl hunters used 8-gauge or larger shotguns. Despite this, the 8-gauge remains in full production for industrial use in kiln guns.

THE UNIQUE CASE OF THE .410 "GAUGE"

The .410 shotshell is an exception to the gauge nomenclatural system. For this diminutive shotshell, the numbers refer to the bore diameter much like a centerfire cartridge. For this reason, the .410 shotshell is properly called the .410 Bore, not .410 Gauge. Although sometimes incorrectly called the 36 gauge, the .410 bore is actually a 68 gauge shell.

HOW TO READ A LISTING FOR CARTRIDGE OR SHOTSHELL

Centerfire

Step 1.

Use the format of the full cartridge name to identify which of the nomenclatural systems and units is being used.

  a. SAAMI in English or metric units, i.e. .243 Winchester, 7mm Remington Magnum
  b. CIP in metric units, i.e. 7x5mm Mauser
  c. Black powder American in English units, i.e. .50-110 Sharps
  d. British in English units, i.e. .577/450 Martini-Henry

Step 2.

Use the numbers on the left side to determine the caliber of the cartridge, i.e. .22, 6mm, .300, 9mm, .45.

Step 3.

Note any supplements to the caliber and their meaning, i.e. .22-250 Remington, .30-'06 Springfield, 8x57RmmJS Mauser.

Step 4.

Note all names after the supplement(s), i.e. Winchester, Savage, Mauser, Remington.

Step 5.

Note any suffixes after the name(s) and their meaning, i.e. magnum, express, +P, high velocity.

Rimfire

Step 1.

Use the numbers on the left side to determine the caliber of the cartridge, i.e. , .17, .22.

Step 2.
Note the name(s) of the cartridge after the caliber, i.e. Short, Long, Long Rifle, Hornady, Winchester, CCI, Stinger.

Step 3.
Note any suffixes after the name and their meaning, i.e. rifle match, high velocity, magnum, Stinger, HP.

SHOTSHELL

Step 1.
Note the gauge of the shell, i.e. 10, 12, 16, 20, 28, or .410 bore.

Step. 2
Note the tube length of the shotshell, i.e. 2¾, 3, 3½, 70mm.

Step. 3
Note the load type and/or dram equivalent of the shell, i.e. target, field, magnum, 3¾ Dram Equiv.

Step. 4
Note the shot charge or slug weight in the shell, i.e. 1¼ ozs., 28 grams, 437 grains, 9 pellets.

Step 5.
Note the shot size and composition, i.e. No. 6, No. BB, buck, steel, copper plated, slug.

ORDER OF LISTING

Lists of centerfire pistol and revolver cartridges are arranged according to the following rules:

1.) All Metric cartridges
    a. First in ascending numerical order of approximate caliber designation,
    b. Then in alphabetical order

2.) Followed by American cartridges
    a. First in ascending numerical order of approximate caliber designation,
    b. Then alphabetical order

3.) Within each of the above groups, cartridges are arranged in order of:
    a. 2-digit numbers
    b. 2-digit numbers and a hyphen followed by more numbers
    c. 3-digit numbers

Who Designed the Winchester Trademark Horse and Rider?

Phillip R. Goodwin (1881-1935) was an aspiring young artist in late 1890s New York City when he was introduced to Charles M. Russell, the famous western artist. The two became good friends and spent much time together in the American West. Goodwin put his talents to good use illustrating calendars, posters, stationery, and ads for arms and ammunition companies such as Peters, Marlin, Remington, and Winchester. Goodwin designed the famous Winchester horse and rider trademark in 1919. It remains one of the most recognized trademarks in the world to this day.

CHAPTER 5 : CARTRIDGE NOMENCLATURE

CHAPTER 5 HIGHLIGHTS:

• RIMFIRE   • CENTERFIRE   • SHOTSHELL
All drawings by Author, unless otherwise noted.

RIMFIRE

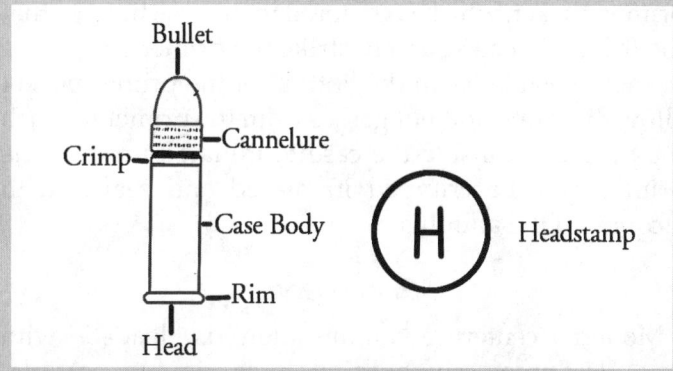

CHARACTERISTICS OF A RIMFIRE CARTRIDGE
- Bullet
- Cannelure
- Crimp
- Cartridge Case
- Rim
- Headstamp

Drawing by Author

A rimfire cartridge is a four part assembly consisting of: a bullet, a cartridge case, propellant, and priming.

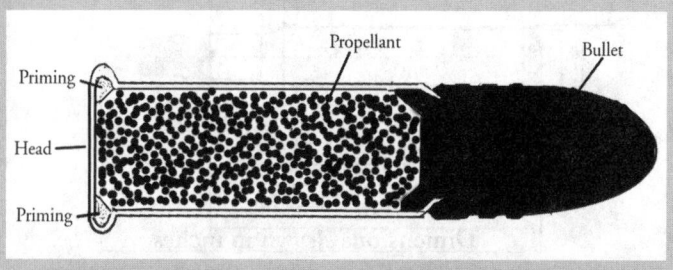

CUTAWAY VIEW OF A RIMFIRE CARTRIDGE
A rimfire cartridge is an assembly of four parts:

- Bullet
- Cartridge Case
- Propellant
- Priming

Drawing by author

BULLET

Rimfire bullets are lead and may be plain, copper-plated or jacketed. Both plain lead and copper-plated rimfire bullets are coated on their exterior surface with a wax lubricant to prevent lead build up in the rifle's bore. The lubricant is not the same as is used on centerfire bullets.

Note the heavy crimp applied to plain lead and copper-plated rimfire bullets. This is necessary to increase bullet pull as rimfire priming is weak and considerable shot start resistance is required to ignite the propellant.

CARTRIDGE CASE

All rimfire cartridge cases are rimmed with a one-piece, drawn brass body. Note that the .22 WMR and .22 WRF cartridge cases differ from the .22 Long Rifle in a variety of ways although they look very similar.

Rimfire cartridge cases cannot be reloaded for all practical purposes. However, spent cartridge brass commands a premium price from scrap metal dealers, so most empty cases can be recycled.

PRIMING

In a rimfire design, the priming compound is held in the entire circumference of the hollow rim. There is no anvil or cup.

PROPELLANT

Modern rimfire ammunition typically is loaded with fast burning, double-base propellants in the form of balls or flakes specifically formulated for ease of ignition due to the weak priming system. Such propellants are special "production powders" not available to hand loaders.

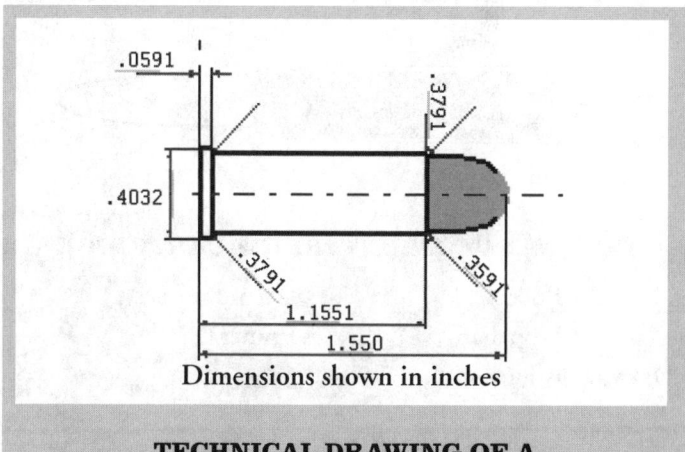

Dimensions shown in inches

**TECHNICAL DRAWING OF A
TYPICAL RIMFIRE CARTRIDGE**
Drawing courtesy of Hartmut Broemel

CENTERFIRE

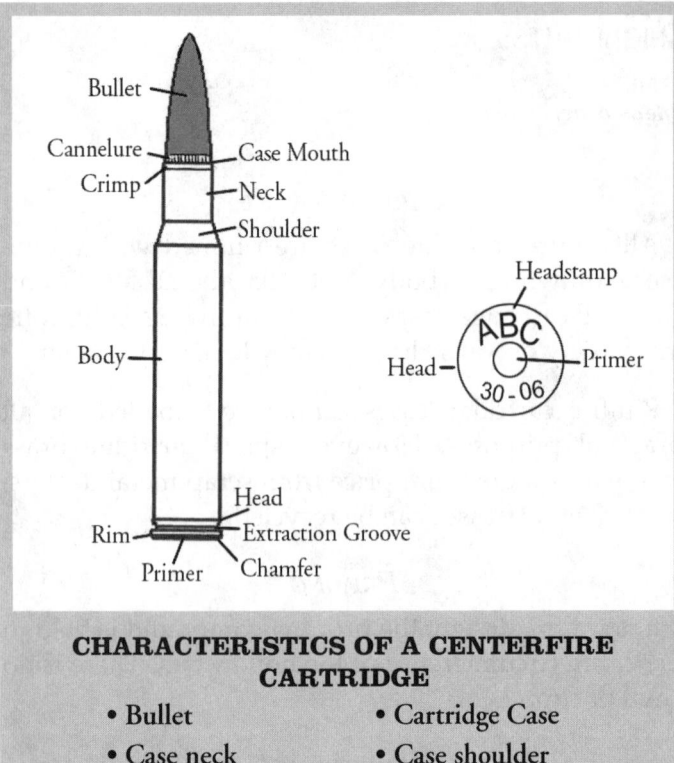

CHARACTERISTICS OF A CENTERFIRE CARTRIDGE

- Bullet
- Cartridge Case
- Case neck
- Case shoulder
- Extraction groove
- Rim
- Primer
- Headstamp

Drawing by author

Centerfire ammunition is a four part assembly consisting of: a bullet, a cartridge case, propellant, and primer.

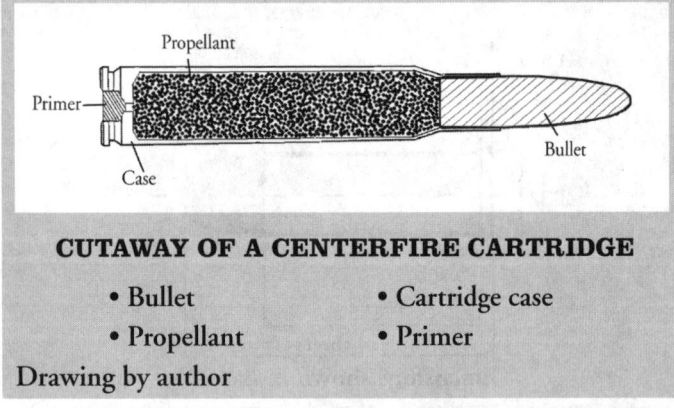

CUTAWAY OF A CENTERFIRE CARTRIDGE

- Bullet
- Cartridge case
- Propellant
- Primer

Drawing by author

BULLET

Centerfire cartridges may be loaded with a wide variety of plain lead, monolithic (cast, molded, sintered, or swaged metal alloy or composite), or jacketed bullets configured according to their intended purpose. For most shooters, bullet selection is one of the most important considerations when purchasing ammunition.

CARTRIDGE CASE

Modern centerfire cartridge cases are constructed of drawn brass, steel, or aluminum alloy with a thick head, a solid internal web, and a centrally located pocket for the primer. Centerfire primers may be small or large in size depending on cartridge size. Case heads may be rimmed, semi-rimmed, rimless, or rebated.

PRIMER

The primer is held by an interference fit in the tapered primer pocket, which is centered in the case head so that the firing pin can squarely strike the primer's cap. One or more flash holes in the bottom of the primer pocket allow the flame and hot gasses from the primer to reach the propellant inside the case to initiate burning. The primer may be crimped in placed and sealed with lacquer on the annulus.

PROPELLANT

Modern centerfire ammunition is loaded with smokeless progressive burning single-, double-, or triple-base propellants which are carefully tested and matched to each caliber and bullet weight. The propellant charge may or may not completely fill the case.

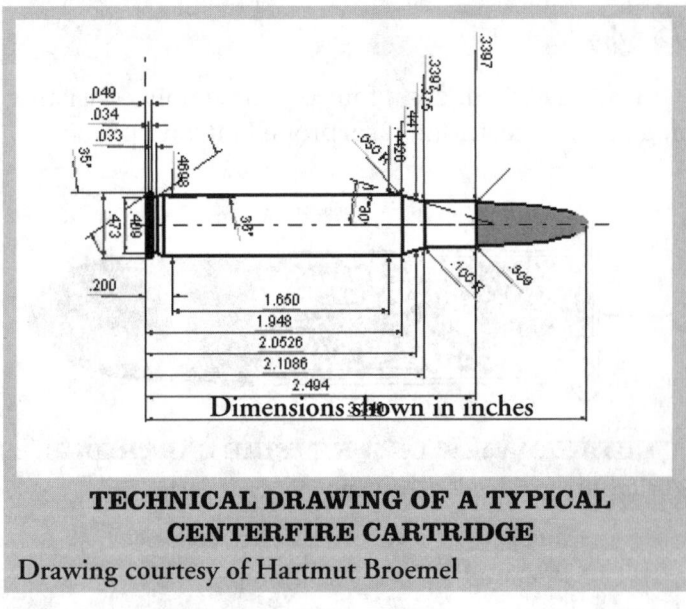

Dimensions shown in inches

TECHNICAL DRAWING OF A TYPICAL CENTERFIRE CARTRIDGE

Drawing courtesy of Hartmut Broemel

"Those who hammer their guns into plows will plow for those who do not."

- Thomas Jefferson

"Those who trade liberty for security will have neither."

- John Adams

CHAPTER 6 : BULLET NOMENCLATURE

CHAPTER 6 HIGHLIGHTS:

- DEFINITION OF A BULLET
- PARTS OF A BULLET
- BULLET MATERIALS
- CATEGORIES OF BULLETS BY USE
- BULLET TYPES
- BULLET CONFIGURATIONS

All drawings by Author, unless otherwise noted.

DEFINITION OF A BULLET

PRACTICAL

A bullet is the component part of a cartridge which is accelerated down the gun barrel and flies through the air to strike the intended target.

In popular use, a bullet is an elongated projectile or missile intended to be fired from a rifled barrel. A large spherical projectile is called a round ball while smaller spheres are called pellets. Elongated projectiles for shotguns are called slugs.

SCIENTIFIC

A bullet is a round or elongated body which, after being accelerated down a gun barrel, continues in motion by its own inertia.

PARTS OF A BULLET

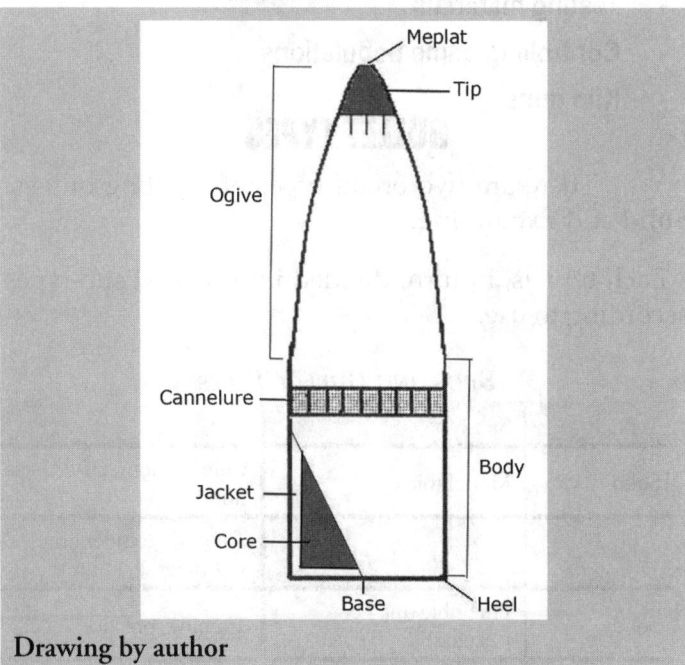

Drawing by author

The parts of a typical bullet are:

Meplat
» The small flat surface at the bullet's tip

Tip
» The front end of the bullet

Ogive
» The tapering portion of the bullet from the forward end of the body to the tip

Body
» The constant diameter portion aft of the ogive, which engages and is engraved by the barrel's rifling

Cannelure
» A circumferential groove on the bullet's body; for crimping or other uses

Groove
» A shallow circumferential cut or depression on a lead bullet's body; usually for holding bullet lubricant

Core
» The interior of a bullet

Heel
» The portion of the bullet where the body transitions into the base

Base
» The rear end of a bullet

Each of these parts will be found in a wide variety of major and minor variations.

BULLET MATERIALS

There are two general categories of bullets: **Monolithic** and **Built-up.**

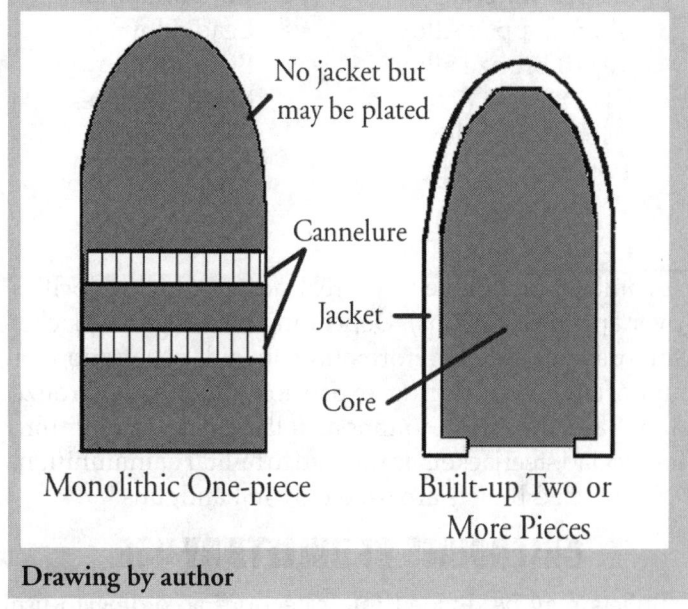

Monolithic One-piece   Built-up Two or More Pieces

Drawing by author

MONOLITHIC

Monolithic bullets are cast, swaged, injection molded, sintered, extruded, or turned to full bullet diameter using one of the following materials.

Material	Manufacturing System(s)	Comments
Lead alloy	Cast, swaged	Most common material
Iron	Sintering	For lead free frangible bullets
Copper/ bronze alloy	Swaged, turned, extruded	For lead-free bullets
Metal Composites	Molded, sintered	For lead-free frangible bullets
Plastic, Wax	Molded, extruded	For short range
Paper	Molded	For blanks
Wood	Turned	For blanks

Although monolithic lead bullets are not jacketed, they may be plated with a thin coating of copper or polymer. Monolithic lead bullets normally are lubricated on their outer surface.

Lead alloys have been used to make bullets for centuries. Lead is easy to cast, soft, and dense. Copper or bronze alloys have become popular recently due to efforts to reduce lead in the environment. Composite bullets are also environmentally-friendly and lead-free. Typically, they are frangible types designed to readily disintegrate into small particles on impact with a hard surface. Plastic or wax bullets are suitable for short range practice at low velocities.

BUILT-UP (JACKETED)

A built-up bullet consists of two, three, or more parts; at minimum, a core and a jacket. The jacket may be made of a separate piece of drawn, machined, or swaged metal alloy or electro-plated onto the core. Polymer jackets are heat-fused to the core surface. Bullet jackets and cores are made of the following materials:

Jacket Materials
95/5 Copper Alloy
90/10 Bronze alloy
Clad Steel
Aluminum alloy
Polymer
Paper (historic)

Core Materials
Lead alloy
Bismuth alloy
Metal Composites
Aluminum
Polymer
Steel
Sintered iron

A bullet jacket prevents barrel leading at high velocities (over approx. 1,500 fps). Depending on design, the jacket can prevent bullet deformation to aid penetration or support the core during expansion. Copper or bronze alloys are the most common, followed by aluminum. Today, clad steel jackets are limited to military ammunition. Polymer clad bullets are used only in handguns.

CATEGORIES OF BULLETS BY USE

Bullets may be divided into categories according to use and type. There are five general categories of use for bullets:

1. Sporting
- **Instruction, training, qualification**
- **Plinking**
- **Hunting**
- **Personal defense**

2. Competition
- **Practice, training, qualification**
- **Informal competition**
- **Formal competition**

3. Military
- **Training, practice, qualification**
- **Competition**
- **Combat**

4. Law Enforcement
- **Training, practice, qualification**
- **Duty**

5. Industrial
- **Proofing firearms**
- **Testing firearms**
- **Testing materials**
- **Controlling game populations**
- **Kiln guns**

BULLET TYPES

There are two broad types of sporting bullets: **Solid** and **Expanding**.

Each type is, in turn, divided into several sub-types according to use.

SPORTING BULLET TYPES

Type	Sub-type	Use
Solid	Monolithic	Competition, self-defense, hunting
Solid	Full Metal Jacket	Training, competition, self-defense, hunting
Solid	Frangible (may be jacketed)	Training, practice
Pellets	Shot	Pests, rodents
Expanding	Hollow Point-monolithic	Self-defense, hunting
Expanding	Jacketed Soft Point	Hunting, self-defense
Expanding	Jacketed Hollow Point	Hunting, self-defense, competition
Expanding	Jacketed Soft/Hollow Point	Self-defense, hunting
Expanding	Tipped, Capped	Hunting

MILITARY BULLET TYPES

Military small arms bullet types are more varied and include:

Military Type	Use
Ball/full metal jacket	Combat, training, qualification
Hollow point	Match competition
Tracer	Observing and adjusting fire
Spotting	Observation
Explosive	Anti-materiel
Armor piercing	Defeating hardened targets
Incendiary	Igniting flammable targets
Armor piercing-incendiary	Combines features of both types
Military Type	Use
Armor piercing-tracer	Combines features of both types
Armor piercing-incendiary-tracer	Combines features of three types
Frangible	Close quarters combat training
Short range	Training
Subsonic	For suppressed weapons
Shot	Survival

BULLET CONFIGURATIONS

HANDGUN BULLET TIP CONFIGURATIONS

1. Metal cased/Full metal jacket
2. Soft point
3. Hollow point
4. Hollow soft point
5. Tipped or capped

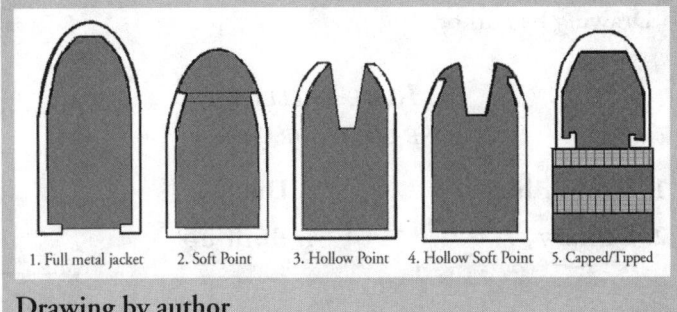

1. Full metal jacket 2. Soft Point 3. Hollow Point 4. Hollow Soft Point 5. Capped/Tipped

Drawing by author

HANDGUN BULLET OGIVE/POINT CONFIGURATIONS

1. Round ball
2. Round nose
3. Wadcutter
4. Semi-wadcutter
5. Cutaway
6. Flat nose
7. Cone point
8. Truncated cone
9. Pointed

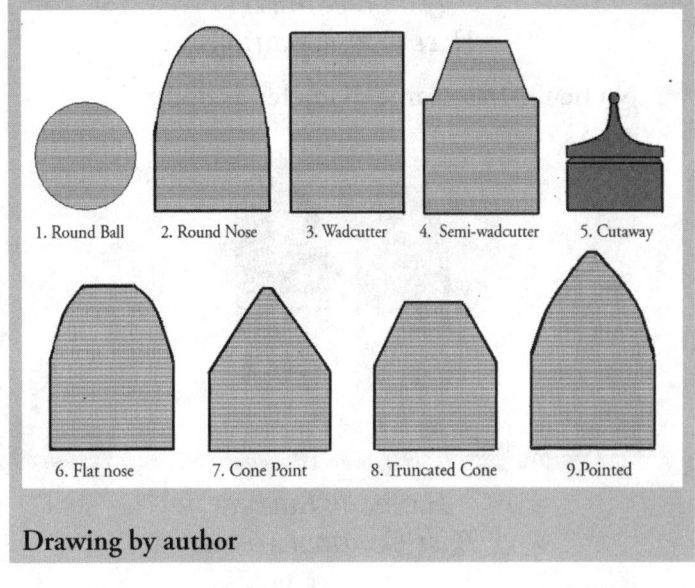

1. Round Ball 2. Round Nose 3. Wadcutter 4. Semi-wadcutter 5. Cutaway

6. Flat nose 7. Cone Point 8. Truncated Cone 9. Pointed

Drawing by author

HANDGUN BULLET BODY CONFIGURATIONS

1. Monolithic
   - Smooth
   - Cannelured
   - Grooved
2. Jacketed
   - Smooth-half jacket
   - Smooth

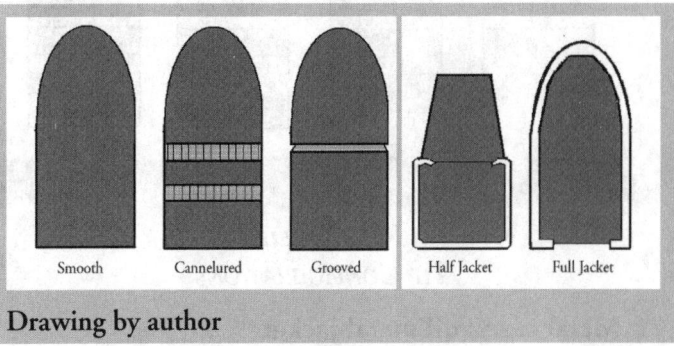

Smooth Cannelured Grooved Half Jacket Full Jacket

Drawing by author

HANDGUN BULLET CORE CONFIGURATIONS-JACKETED

1. Unitary
2. Dual
3. Built-up—dissimilar materials

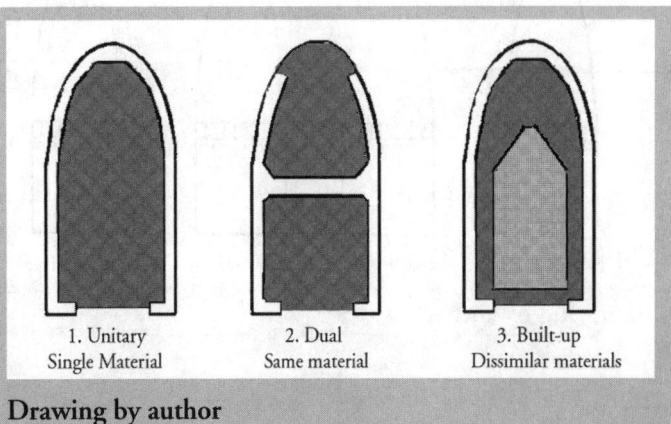

1. Unitary Single Material 2. Dual Same material 3. Built-up Dissimilar materials

Drawing by author

HANDGUN BULLET
HEEL CONFIGURATIONS

1. No heel—base same diameter as body

2. Heeled

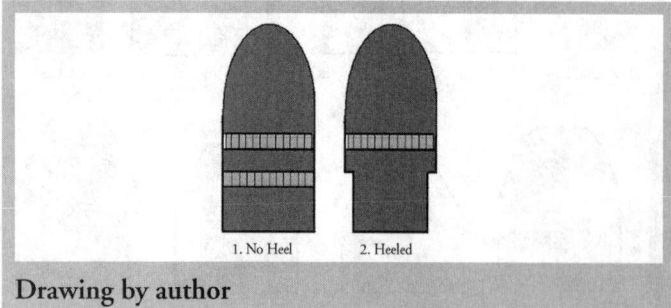

1. No Heel   2. Heeled

Drawing by author

HANDGUN BULLET
BASE CONFIGURATIONS

1. Recessed   2. Flat

  - Hollow base   - Plain

  - Cupped base   - Gas check

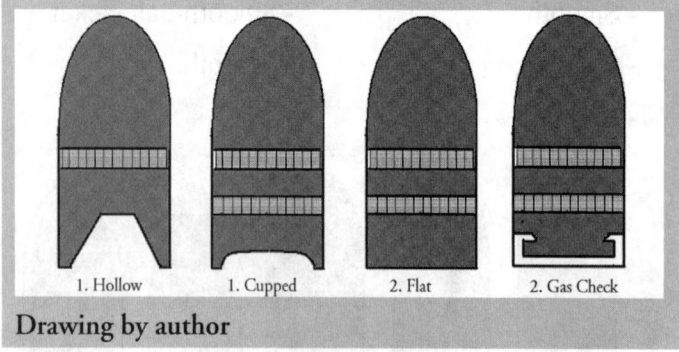

1. Hollow   1. Cupped   2. Flat   2. Gas Check

Drawing by author

RIFLE BULLET
TIP CONFIGURATIONS

1. Metal case/Full metal jacket

2. Soft-point

3. Hollow point

4. Tipped or capped

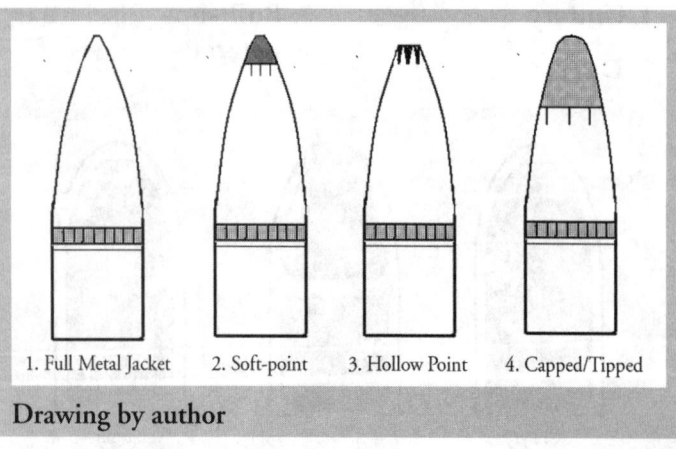

1. Full Metal Jacket   2. Soft-point   3. Hollow Point   4. Capped/Tipped

Drawing by author

RIFLE BULLET
OGIVE CONFIGURATIONS

1. Cone   4. Semi-round nose
2. Secant   5. Round nose
3. Tangent   6. Flat nose

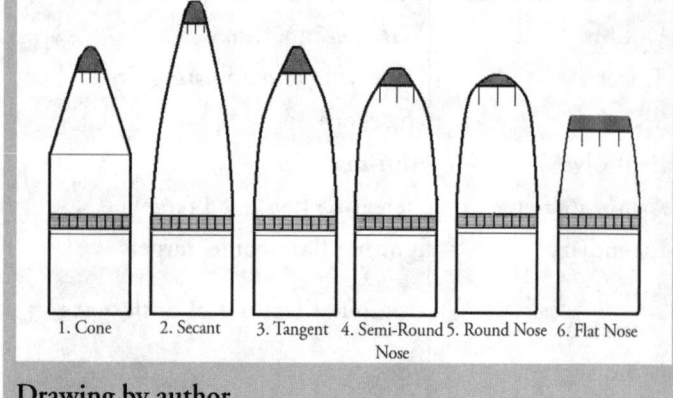

1. Cone   2. Secant   3. Tangent   4. Semi-Round Nose   5. Round Nose   6. Flat Nose

Drawing by author

RIFLE BULLET
BODY CONFIGURATIONS

1. Smooth   4. Stepped

2. Smooth w/cannelure   5. Belted

3. Smooth w/groove   6. Wasp waist (not shown)

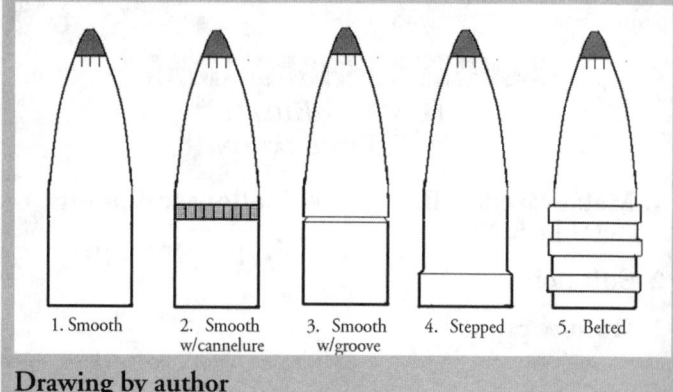

1. Smooth   2. Smooth w/cannelure   3. Smooth w/groove   4. Stepped   5. Belted

Drawing by author

RIFLE BULLET
CORE CONFIGURATIONS

1. Monolithic   3. Dual

2. Unitary   4. Built-up

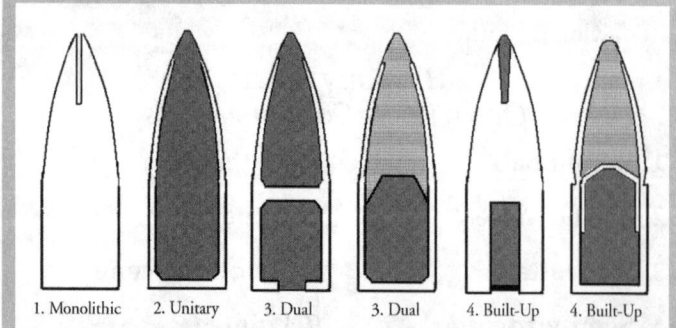

1. Monolithic   2. Unitary   3. Dual   3. Dual   4. Built-Up   4. Built-Up

Drawing by author

RIFLE BULLET
HEEL CONFIGURATIONS

1. No heel

2. Vestigial boat-tail

3. Rebated boat-tail

4. Full boat-tail

RIFLE BULLET
BASE CONFIGURATIONS

1. Flat

2. Recessed

3. Hemispherical

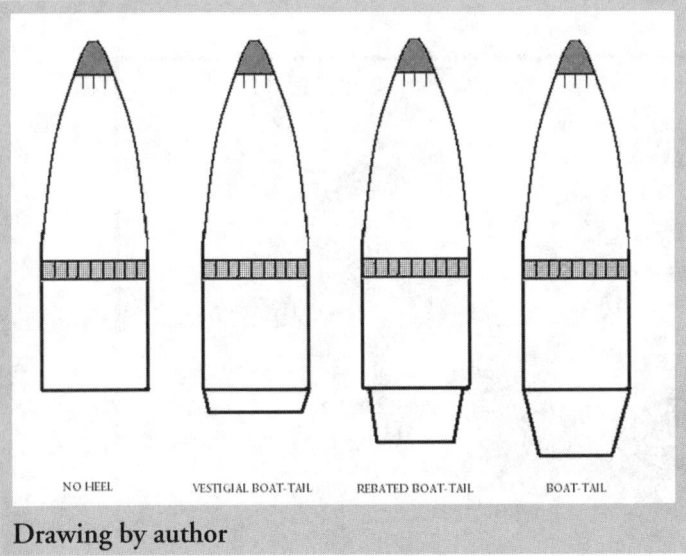

Drawing by author

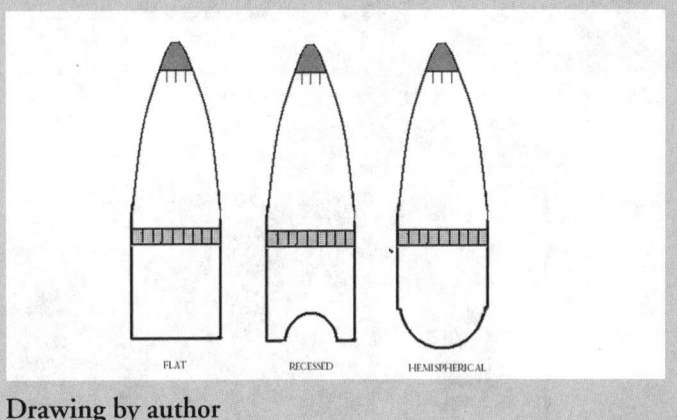

Drawing by author

He Is A High Speed, Low Drag Individual

This modern term is used often to describe an exceptionally capable, hard-working individual who is a reliable self-starter. The ballistic comparison to a high velocity boat tail bullet is obvious. This is yet another example of how shooting terms continue to enter our language.

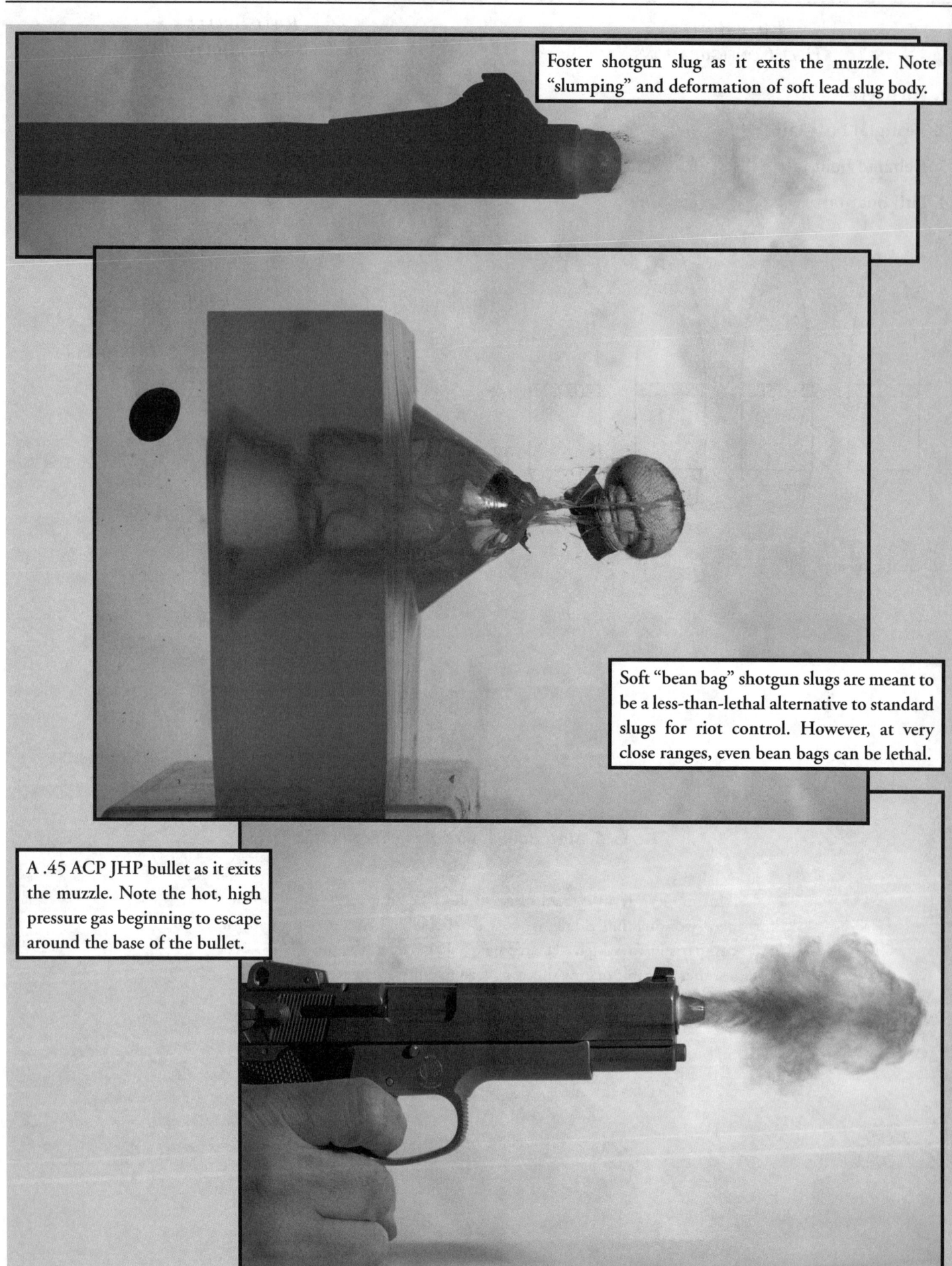

Foster shotgun slug as it exits the muzzle. Note "slumping" and deformation of soft lead slug body.

Soft "bean bag" shotgun slugs are meant to be a less-than-lethal alternative to standard slugs for riot control. However, at very close ranges, even bean bags can be lethal.

A .45 ACP JHP bullet as it exits the muzzle. Note the hot, high pressure gas beginning to escape around the base of the bullet.

CHAPTER 7 : CARTRIDGE CASE NOMENCLATURE

CHAPTER 7 HIGHLIGHTS:

- **THE CARTRIDGE CASE**
- **RIMFIRE**
- **CENTERFIRE**

All drawings by Author, unless otherwise noted.

THE CARTRIDGE CASE

The cartridge case serves three purposes:

- **Hold the component parts of the cartridge securely in position**
- **Protect the component parts during shipping, handling, and loading**
- **Seal the chamber to prevent the escape of high pressure propellant gasses**

While the concept seems simple enough, developing the technology for the modern cartridge case of today required over five centuries of effort! And, development continues.

In holding the primer, propellant, and bullet or shot charge securely in position, the assembly becomes a self-contained cartridge in that all components are present to fire that round of ammunition in a suitable firearm.

CARTRIDGE CASE TYPES

There are three different types of cartridge cases:

- Rimfire
- Centerfire
- Shotshell

THREE TYPES OF CARTRIDGE CASE

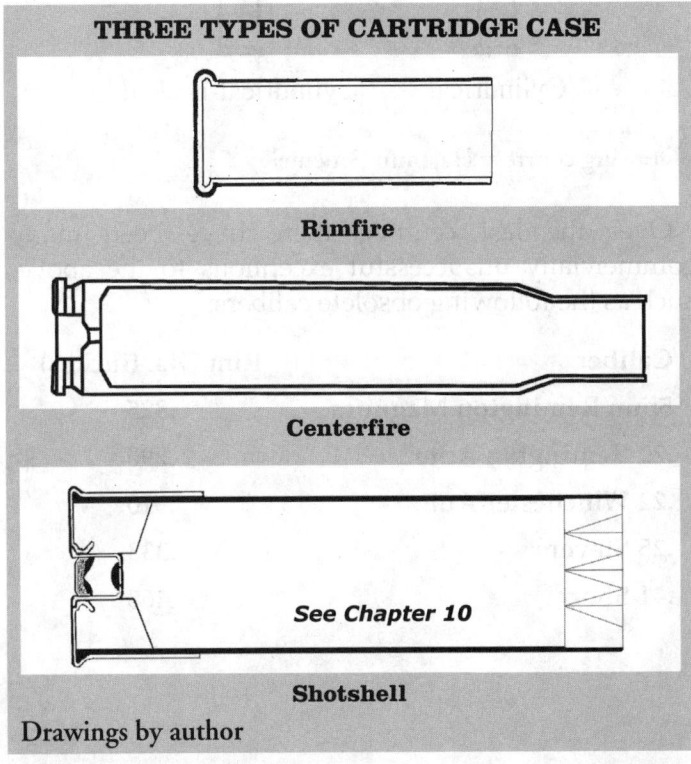

Rimfire

Centerfire

See Chapter 10

Shotshell

Drawings by author

Each type is unique and configured for a purpose. However, within each type are a wide assortment of subtypes which vary according to:

- **Size**
- **Body configuration**
- **Head configuration**
- **Primer type**
- **Materials**

With the large number of possible cartridge combinations due entirely to cartridge case configuration, one can begin to appreciate the importance of a complete caliber designation.

RIMFIRE

If one purposely set out to design a cartridge which would be extremely difficult to manufacture, the .22 Long Rifle rimfire cartridge would serve that purpose very well indeed. Some of the problems with the basic rimfire design include:

- **Weak case design**
- **Inherently weak ignition**
- **Low breech pressure limits**
- **Bullet diameter same as the cartridge case**
- **Bullet lubrication problems**

In spite of these shortcomings, the humble .22 rimfire cartridge soldiers on due to its low price, dependable quality, and widespread availability. With annual world rimfire production quantities exceeding five billion rounds, ammunition manufacturers spend considerable time and money to increase their rimfire capacity, lower cost, and upgrade quality.

When you add all this up, the .22 rimfire truly is a cartridge for the 21st century.

CUTAWAY OF TYPICAL RIMFIRE CARTRIDGE CASE

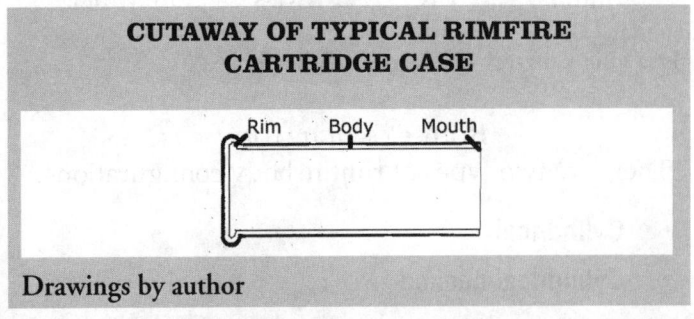

Rim   Body   Mouth

Drawings by author

SIZE

Most shooters are familiar with the ubiquitous .22 rimfire cartridge. In fact, when the word "rimfire" is mentioned, most shooters visualize a .22 Long Rifle cartridge. At just under an inch in overall length, the diminutive .22 Long Rifle cartridge with its blunt 40 grain bullet does not make much of an impression. But, it was not always so!

During the golden era of rimfire from 1855 to 1890, rimfire ammunition was offered in calibers as large as .58 (the .58 Miller). During the Civil War, Spencer carbines chambered various .56 caliber rimfire cartridges which were very popular in the Union Army. In 1920, RWS introduced the 4mm/.157 caliber zimmerstutzen rimfire for indoor training and practice. Both a short and a long version were produced!

The fatal flaw of the rimfire cartridge hinges on the weak case design which limits breech pressures to relatively low levels, thus limiting ballistic performance. When centerfire cartridge cases and smokeless propellants combined to offer a quantum increase in ballistic performance about 1900, the rimfire cartridge was doomed to small calibers where the weak cartridge case was not a limitation.

RIMFIRE CARTRIDGE SIZES
THE LONG, THE SHORT AND THE WIDE

4mm Z   .22 LR   .41 Swiss   .58 Miller

Drawing courtesy of Hartmut Broemel

BODY CONFIGURATION

There are two types of rimfire body configurations:

*   **Cylindrical**

*   **Cylindrical-necked**

The vast majority of rimfire cartridges have cylindrical cases. Historically, there have been very few necked rimfire case designs. Recently however, interest in such designs has increased with the introduction of the .17 HMR and several other .17 caliber rimfire cartridges.

HEAD CONFIGURATION

All modern rimfire cartridges have a rimmed case head. This is a requirement of the basic design. In fact, all modern rimfire cartridges are made on one of two different rim diameters:

*   **Standard Rim (.275" dia.)**
    *   » .17 Mach 2/Aguila
    *   » .22 BB Cap and CB Cap
    *   » .22 Short
    *   » .22 Long
    *   » .22 Long Rifle
    *   » .22 LR Shotshell

*   **Magnum Rim (.291" dia.)**
    *   » .17 HMR
    *   » .22 WRF
    *   » .22 WMR

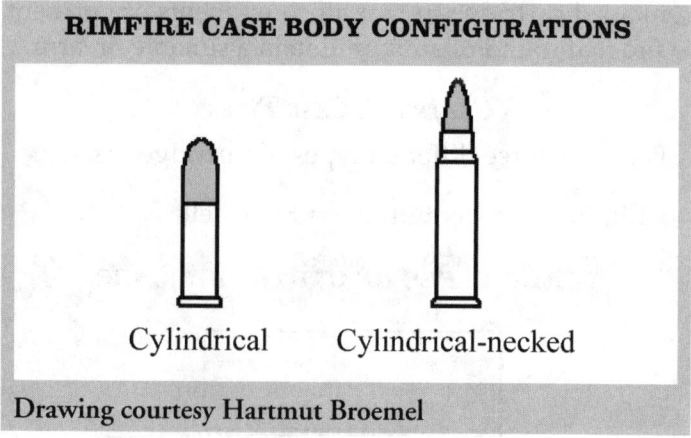

RIMFIRE CASE BODY CONFIGURATIONS

Cylindrical   Cylindrical-necked

Drawing courtesy Hartmut Broemel

Over the last century, there have been many commercially unsuccessful exceptions to the above, such as the following obsolete calibers:

Caliber	Rim Dia. (inches)
5mm Remington Magnum	.325
.22 Remington Auto	.290
.22 Winchester Auto	.310
.25 Stevens	.333
.41 Short	.468

PRIMER TYPE

In modern rimfire cartridges, the priming is contained inside the hollow rim of the cartridge case. During manufacture, the wet (and therefore inert) priming mixture is forced into the rim by a combination of hydraulic pressure and centrifugal force applied by metal spindles rotating at approximately 10,000 rpm. This is not an exact process and regularly leaves priming compound smeared on the interior case walls for a considerable height.

The ignition sequence begins when the firing pin of the gun strikes the rim of the cartridge, crushing the priming mixture between the two inside surfaces of the hollow rim.

As there is no anvil, the rimfire priming mixture must be fortified with ground glass as a frictioning agent. To further assist ignition, manufacturers must heavily crimp the bullet into the cartridge case. As there is no primer cap or flash hole to focus the hot gasses squarely into the propellant, rimfire ignition is weak, and often a considerable amount of unburned powder is blown out of the barrel upon firing.

MATERIALS

Rimfire cartridge cases typically are made of drawn brass alloy consisting of approximately 85% copper and 15% zinc. Efforts to develop other metal alloys based on aluminum, zinc, or steel for rimfire cartridge cases have been unsuccessful. While steel case rimfire ammunition will be found occasionally from foreign manufacturers, these are suitable only for use in bolt-action rifles as such ammunition will cause extraction problems in semi-automatic guns.

Some rimfire cartridge cases are nickel-plated for identification or sales appeal, however the plating serves no ballistic purpose.

As ammunition manufacturers try to meet consumer demand for increased ballistic performance from rimfire ammunition, they have approached the limits of rimfire case strength.

CENTERFIRE

Unlike rimfire and shotshell cartridge cases which are all of rimmed design, centerfire cartridge cases are made in a wide variety of head and body configurations. Despite repeated efforts to reduce the number and variety of centerfire calibers, new designs are constantly being introduced and old favorites refuse to die and may even come back to life. For this reason, it has become very difficult to declare a once popular centerfire cartridge obsolete, even if it has been out of production

for decades and the existing demand is small. Just when the ax of obsolescence seems certain, someone introduces a competitive sport or style of hunting supporting the hoary caliber and demand is renewed. Examples of this phenomenon include the .45-70 Government and the .44-40 WCF. Of course these were supported by the large number of old firearms in this caliber still in use. And, we all know that old firearms never wear out!

Here it is important to note that obsolete is not the same as obscure. After introduction, many new cartridges do not become commercially successful. Frequently, commercial failure becomes apparent to the manufacturer in the short space of a year or two, and the cartridge is dropped from the lists. It then becomes obscure because such small quantities were made, there is no possibility of revival as the pool of firearms chambered in that caliber is also so small. Does anyone remember the .307 Winchester or the 9mm Federal?

Although centerfire rifle cartridges are staple goods for hunters, production and expenditure of centerfire handgun cartridges exceed that of centerfire rifle by a substantial margin. Despite this dichotomy in manufacturing, the number of different centerfire rifle cartridges exceeds the number of centerfire handgun cartridges by a factor of five to one. This poses an interesting question: What is it about centerfire rifle cartridges that causes a shooter, gunsmith, firearms maker, military ordnance officer, or police firearms instructor to believe he has discovered a ballistic breakthrough by changing a cartridge case body or head configuration? After all, the entire panoply of hunting, competition, law enforcement, and military service could be covered with just five or six different calibers. But this would remove a key aspect of hunting and shooting, as the variety of calibers itself is a major attraction.

While shotshells are technically centerfire cartridges, they are considered to be a distinct type due to their unique features.

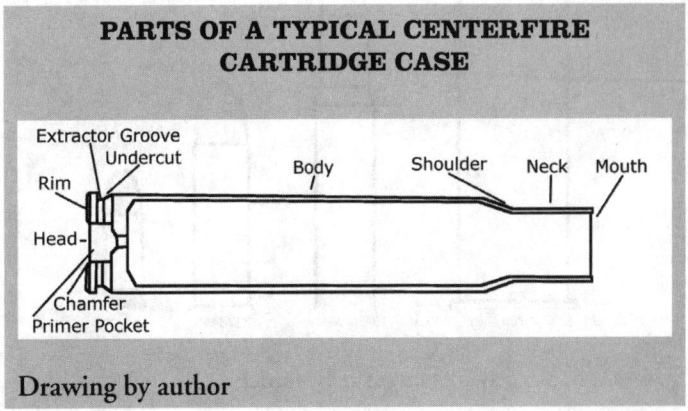

PARTS OF A TYPICAL CENTERFIRE CARTRIDGE CASE

Drawing by author

SIZE

When the first centerfire cartridges appeared in the mid-1870s, most of them were rimmed designs. An excellent example of this type is the venerable .44-40 Winchester (WCF). In short order, larger and longer cartridge cases were designed for rifles such as the famous Sharps models. Nearly all of them were rimmed head types with straight or necked body styles. By 1885, a great number of centerfire cartridge variations filled ammunition manufacturers' catalogs.

The advent of smokeless propellants circa 1890 resulted in massive changes in cartridge case design. The more powerful propellants and smaller bullet diameters allowed the size of centerfire rifle cartridge cases to be reduced. At the same time, the substantially higher breech pressures of smokeless propellants required stronger cartridge cases. Almost overnight, many of the large black powder cartridge cases became obsolete.

However, smokeless propellants spurred innovation as cartridge designers moved to exploit the advantages of the new technological order. A pivotal point was reached in the late 1880s when the German 8x57mmJ Mauser cartridge was introduced. This cartridge's rimless head and necked body design proved nearly ideal. The 8x57mmJ Mauser cartridge went on to become the basis for a wide variety of new smokeless powder cartridge variations including the popular .30-'06 Springfield.

SIZES OF CENTERFIRE CARTRIDGES

(NOT ACTUAL SIZE)   700 N.E.   .30-30 WIN   .357 MAG   .32 ACP

Drawing courtesy of Hartmut Broemel

BODY CONFIGURATION

The case body is the part that extends forward from the head to the case mouth. It is the case mouth that holds the bullet in place. The internal space created by the case sidewalls holds the propellant. The case sidewalls are normally tapered with the thinnest part at the case mouth.

There are four types of centerfire body configuration:

- **Conical - tapered**
- **Cylindrical - straight**
- **Conical - necked**
- **Cylindrical - necked**

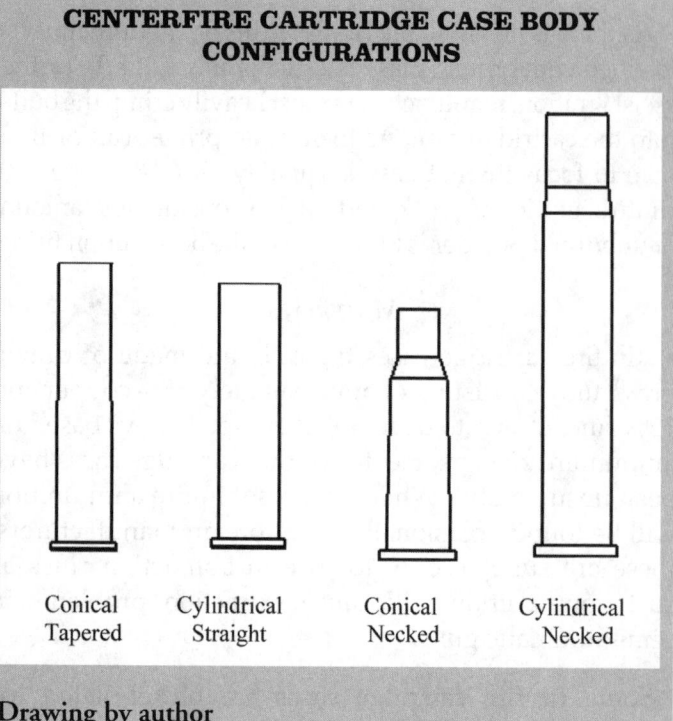

CENTERFIRE CARTRIDGE CASE BODY CONFIGURATIONS

Conical Tapered   Cylindrical Straight   Conical Necked   Cylindrical Necked

Drawing by author

The conical tapered and cylindrical straight case body styles vary by length and diameter, but have no neck. Necked cases have a tapered shoulder near the case mouth and a reduced diameter, straight-walled "neck" which holds the bullet.

All cartridge cases belong to one of a dozen or so different dimensional families of headed, cylindrical "basic" case designs. It is from one of these "basic" dimensional case families that nearly all caliber variations originate. (see Chapter 3: Cartridge Families)

Within a given dimensional family, the major differences between cartridge calibers are in the body length, taper, and neck dimensions. For example, members of the .30-'06 Springfield family include: .25-06 Remington, .270 Winchester, and .35 Whelen. The

.38 Long Colt family members include: .38 Special, .357 Magnum, and .357 Maximum. From the .30 Mauser parent we have the: .30 Luger, .380 ACP, 9mm Luger, 9mm Steyr, 9mm Bergmann-Bayard, 9mm Mauser, 9x21mm, and 9mm Winchester Magnum.

If a cylindrical cartridge case requires the fewest number of production steps, why not make more centerfire cartridge cases in such a configuration? The reason is geometric. A neck allows the internal volume (powder capacity) of a cartridge case to be increased without increasing its length.

Manufacturers pay particular attention to the concentricity of the case mouth. The purpose of this is to insure a chambered cartridge's bullet is aligned concentrically with the firearm's bore axis. A misaligned bullet will not be accurate. Match-grade cartridge cases should have a total run out of no more than five or six ten thousandths of an inch at the case mouth. Standard ammunition is considered acceptable at just over twice that amount.

Necking and tapering a cartridge case builds stress in the neck which embrittles the brass. A case neck which has not been annealed will often split from these stresses long after the cartridge has reached the customer. For this reason, all centerfire rifle cartridge case necks are annealed (softened) using heat from flame or electric induction. The annealing process leaves a bluish-black deposit or "iris" on the outer surface of the case neck and shoulder which commercial manufacturers remove as unsightly and military contractors leave in place as an inspection indicator to prove the annealing process has been done.

CENTERFIRE CARTRIDGE CASE HEAD CONFIGURATIONS

| Rimmed | Rimless | Semi-rimmed | Rebated | Belted |

Drawing by author

HEAD CONFIGURATION

Located at the rear end of the cartridge case, the head is the thickest and strongest part of the case body. The head incorporates a rim, a circumferential extractor groove (or undercut), a centrally located primer pocket, and a solid internal web.

There are five different head configurations for centerfire cartridge cases:

- **Rimmed**
- **Rimless**
- **Semi-rimmed**
- **Rebated**
- **Belted**

Here it must be noted that all of the above configurations have a rim on the back end of the cartridge case. They differ in rim diameter and case head configuration directly in front of the rim.

In rimmed case head designs, rim diameter is greater than body diameter with only a small undercut on the head. Although rimmed designs work well in single-shot and tubular fed repeating arms, they are difficult to feed from box magazines (and machine gun belts) and reduce magazine capacity. This led to the development of the rimless head design.

On a rimless cartridge, the rim diameter is equal to the body diameter and there is a deep extractor groove cut into the case head directly in front of the rim. The main purpose of this is to assure reliable and stoppage-free cartridge feeding from vertical internal or external magazines, or machine gun belts.

The features of a semi-rimmed cartridge are very similar to those of a rimless configuration except the rim extends purposely beyond the body diameter. The intended purpose of this is better control of the cartridge during chambering and stronger extraction.

The rebated head is basically a rimless design with a body diameter greater than the rim. The purpose of this is to increase case capacity without increasing cartridge length or altering head dimensions.

The belted head configuration is a rimless design with the addition of a belt of greater diameter than the case body in front of the extractor groove. The intended purpose of the belt is to augment the strength of the head. For this reason, belted cartridges are often used for magnum calibers.

PRIMER TYPE

There are two types of centerfire primer—Boxer and Berdan (see Chapter 9: Primer Nomenclature). The predominant type of primer in domestic and foreign sporting ammunition is the Boxer type. Although U.S. military small arms ammunition is loaded exclusively with Boxer primers, Berdan primers predominate in foreign military ammunition.

Each type of primer requires a dedicated pocket design centrally located in the case head. Boxer primer pockets are simple depressions in the case head with a single, central flash hole through the web. The Berdan type of primer pocket is more complex as it incorporates an anvil in the bottom of the pocket with one or more offset flash holes.

A hybrid primer pocket is a recent variation of the Boxer type with two or more offset flash holes replacing the single central flash hole. The purpose of this arrangement is to make the fired cartridge case very difficult to reload.

Normally, military primers are crimped in place in order to assure functioning in machine guns. This crimp may take one of several forms. The most common is a shallow, circumferential depression around the primer pocket rim. Other types include stab crimps that appear as three or more indentations on the primer pocket rim. While the crimped primer serves a military requirement, it makes removal (decapping) of primers more difficult when reloading military cartridges. The primers of sporting ammunition are not crimped.

MATERIALS

Based on years of experience, brass has been found to be the best metal alloy for centerfire cartridge cases. It offers a nearly ideal combination of characteristics such as:

- **Worldwide availability**
- **Low cost of copper and zinc**
- **Excellent metallurgical characteristics**
- **Ease of manufacture**
- **Reloadable**

Cartridge case brass is a metal alloy containing 80 to 85% copper and 15 to 20% zinc. These alloys are often referred to simply as 85/15, 83/17 and etc. Cartridge case brass differs from bullet jacket brass which is 95/5 or 90/10 alloy.

Some brass cases are nickel-plated. Beyond any sales appeal or identification purpose, this process serves two legitimate functions: nickel plating facilitates fired case extraction and prevents the acids in leather cartridge belt loops from attacking the brass.

During war time, copper becomes a strategic metal in short supply. For this reason, considerable effort has been expended over the years to develop a suitable substitute for brass in cartridge cases. Some of the materials tried with varying success include: steel, aluminum, zinc, plastic, and hybrids.

STEEL

During World War I, Germany successfully pioneered

and developed steel cartridge cases out of strategic necessity. Although steel cartridge cases did not reach German troops until War's end, steel case technology had been proven to work. After World War I, Russia used steel for its cartridge cases. Both Russia and Germany fought World War II with steel case small arms ammunition.

Steel is an attractive cartridge case material because it is strong, not a strategic metal, and relatively cheap. However, steel does require different tooling and more production steps than brass. Perhaps the biggest problem with steel cartridge cases is corrosion or rust. To prevent this, steel cases must be protected with some type of coating. Of course copper, brass, nickel, or even chromium works nicely for this purpose, but leads directly back to the strategic metal supply problem. After much research, German scientists found a variety of suitable lacquer coatings which worked well. In the U.S., phosphate coatings were found acceptable for steel case ammunition. Despite this, brass remains the preferred metal for cartridge cases, especially for sporting ammunition. Today, steel cases are made by Russia, China, and several ex-Warsaw Pact nations for military service.

ALUMINUM

Aluminum based alloys are attractive as a cartridge case metal due to their light weight, low cost, and compatibility with existing manufacturing techniques. The low cost characteristic may appear dubious because aluminum is more expensive than brass, however there is a greater cubic volume of aluminum than brass for unit of weight. This allows ammunition manufacturers to make three times more cartridge cases from a given weight of aluminum than brass.

However, aluminum has two fatal flaws for cartridge case manufacture. First, it can become a strategic metal during wartime. Second is a phenomenon called "burnout". This occurs when an aluminum alloy cartridge case head fails, allowing hot propellant gasses to leak into the firearm's action. The high temperature of the gasses causes the aluminum to ignite, the burning aluminum adding substantially to the damaging effects of the gasses themselves. In most cases, a burnout not only completely destroys the gun, it severely injures the shooter as well. Efforts to solve the burnout problem have proven to be technically feasible, but not economical.

Fortunately, burnout does not occur at the lower breech pressures of handgun cartridges, making some aluminum alloys suitable for that application. Aluminum alloy cartridge cases also are suitable for use in military aircraft weapons, where weight is a primary concern and burnout does not pose a problem.

ZINC

Zinc is a cheap, non-strategic metal with widespread availability. Zinc lends itself to precision die casting techniques, a potentially attractive method of manufacturing cartridge cases. Unfortunately, zinc alloys do not have the strength or metallurgical characteristics required of cartridge case material—even for low pressure handgun cartridges. In the 1950s, efforts were made in Europe to develop zinc shotshells. Although not unsafe, they did not prove a commercial success. Later efforts in the U.S. to develop zinc handgun cartridge cases failed also.

PLASTIC

Plastic is the holy grail of centerfire cartridge case technology. The attractions are many and obvious—cheap feedstock material, mature technology, corrosion-free, and injection moldable. Plastic has been used successfully in shotshell tubes and wad columns for decades, thus providing a pool of experience and technical knowledge of the material. In addition, ammunition makers developed drawn plastic shotshells which have been a commercial success. Despite these advantages, a successful plastic centerfire cartridge case has eluded ammunition engineers.

Problems with plastic cartridge cases include:

- **Weak rims which fracture when extracted after being fired in semi-auto guns**
- **Primer pockets which will not hold a primer in place**
- **Case necks which will not hold a bullet in place**
- **Insufficient bullet pull and push**

As the technology of plastics steadily advances toward ever stronger materials and improved manufacturing methods, ammunition manufacturers may be able to develop a suitable plastic centerfire cartridge case in the future. But for now, there are hybrids.

HYBRIDS

A hybrid centerfire cartridge case addresses the problems of plastic centerfire cartridge cases by employing several different materials to assemble a suitable "built-up" case in much the same manner as a shotshell. A recent example used a stub metal head inserted in an injection molded plastic body. The stub metal head solves problems with extraction and primer retention while a blow-out plastic web under the bullet solves bullet push and shot start requirements. The case is molded around the bullet thus eliminating bullet pull difficulties. The cartridge works and has been sold commercially. However, the type and number of pieces involved in such an assembly are not economical and have technical problems of their own (such as bullet concentricity).

While hybrid cases may seem attractive, currently they cannot be profitably manufactured. However, hybrids do advance the gunner's art and may point the way to the future.

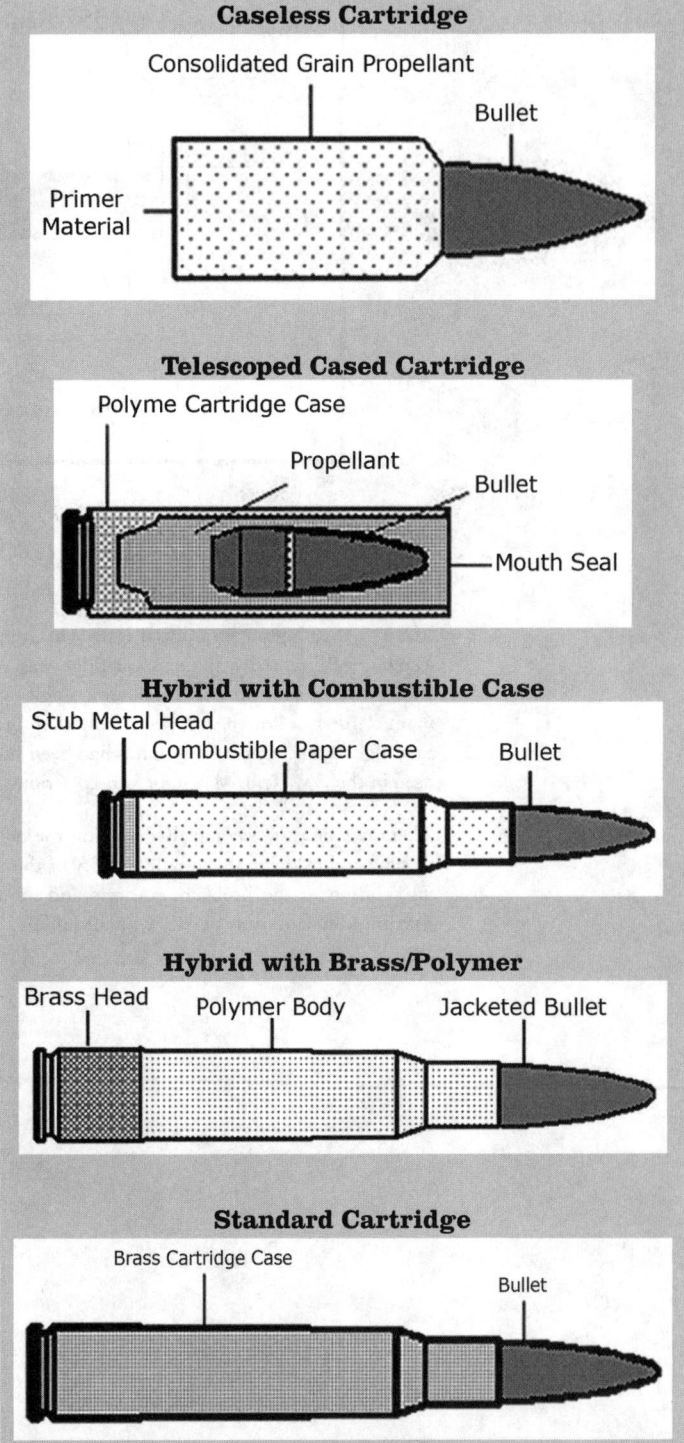

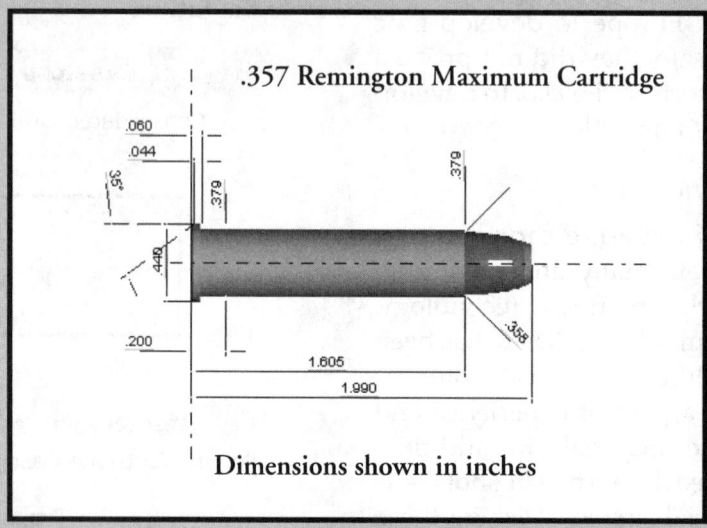

.357 Remington Maximum Cartridge

Dimensions shown in inches

THE .357 REMINGTON MAXIMUM STORY

In 1983, Remington introduced a new magnum revolver cartridge called the .357 Remington Maximum. Essentially, the new cartridge was an enlongated .357 Magnum. At the same time, Ruger offered their seminal Blackhawk single-action revolver in the new caliber. Other handgun manufacturers followed suit. It was only then that a serious problem was discovered with the new cartridge. By the time 1,000 rounds had been fired, the hot gasses from the heavy powder charges used in the .357 Rem. Maximum caused serious gas cutting on the top strap of revolver frames.

There was no easy way out. Redesigning the metal frame of such revolvers was not economically feasible and reducing the muzzle velocity of the cartridge eliminated its reason for existence. With no solution to the problem, firearms and ammunition manufacturers allowed the .357 Rem. Maximum to fade away quietly without fanfare.

CHAPTER 8 : PROPELLANT NOMENCLATURE

All drawings by Author, unless otherwise noted.

WHAT IS A PROPELLANT?

A propellant is a flammable solid which, when confined and ignited, rapidly completes an exothermic reaction (deflagrates) which releases its stored chemical energy in the form of hot, expanding gasses. As a heat engine, a firearm converts this chemical energy to kinetic energy using the propellant as the fuel.

THE DIFFERENCE BETWEEN PROPELLANTS AND EXPLOSIVES

When propellants deflagrate and explosives detonate, they undergo a chemical reaction which rearranges their atoms. There are three requirements for this:

1. The reaction must take place quickly
2. The reaction must be exothermic (gives off energy)
3. As many products as possible must be gasses

Both propellants and explosives contain stored chemical energy. While the amount of chemical energy stored in a propellant or explosive may be great, it is technically valuable only because all the energy can be released in a short period of time. It is the speed of energy release which sets a propellant apart from an explosive.

There is no agreed upon reaction speed dividing propellants from explosives. Propellants deflagrate in milliseconds producing pressures of up to 100,000 psi, allowing them to be used to safely accelerate objects down gun barrels. On the other hand, explosives detonate in microseconds, creating pressures up to 3,910,000 psi with a shattering effect that is useful for mining, construction, and warfare, but too fast for use in firearms.

As a flammable solid, propellants will burn vigorously in the open, but release their energy more quickly when confined such as in the chamber of a firearm. Explosives will also burn vigorously in the open, but will detonate if sufficient pressure, temperature, or shock is applied.

Both propellants and explosives are inefficient and expensive sources of energy. Only a small part of their stored energy is usefully employed doing work.

CARTRIDGE EFFICIENCY

As a heat engine, a firearm's efficiency may be measured by the amount of stored chemical energy in the propellant which is converted into kinetic energy. In practice, the efficiency of the conversion process is poor with the norm being about 25-30%. Where does the remaining 70% of the energy go? Here is a breakdown of average losses:

2%   Unburned propellant

3%   Gas friction on the bore walls

25% Heat transfer to barrel

40% Unused energy in the gas escaping at muzzle

As the conversion efficiency is so low, most smokeless powders have a progressive burning rate in an effort to boost efficiency.

PROPELLANT BURNING CHARACTERISTICS

Propellants create gas by burning only on their surface. For this reason, the size and shape of the propellant granules are important factors in controlling the burning rate and amount of gas production.

Burning rate is proportional to the amount of propellant free to burn. This is measured in two ways:

1. Linear Burning Rate

This is the speed at which the flame front advances through the propellant granules and it is determined by the rate the powder granules receive heat from surrounding combustion.

2. Mass Burning Rate

This is the total amount of time taken for a given mass of propellant to burn completely.

RELATIVE QUICKNESS

Relative quickness is the speed at which a flame front moves through the propellant granules. This is determined by closed bomb laboratory tests under standard conditions. The results are compared to control propellants and expressed as a number which enables a given propellant to be compared to other propellants (See Chapter 96: Reference Material).

Propellant burning rates are characterized into three types:

1. Degressive burning - a short, inefficient push

As the surface area of the granules burns away, their area decreases and gas production falls off rapidly. Such propellants are inefficient and leave very little area under their pressure-time curve.

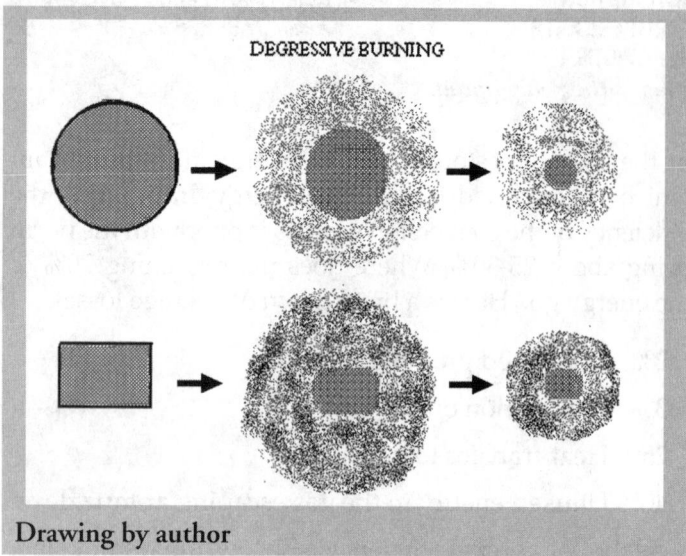

Drawing by author

2. Neutral burning - a longer, but still inefficient push

Neutral burning propellants are more efficient than degressive propellants as the size and shape of the powder granules holds gas production steady for a longer time than degressive propellants. This produces a greater area under their pressure-time curve. However, neutral burning powders still waste much of the energy in the propellant.

3. Progressive burning - a sustained push for maximum efficiency

This is the most efficient type of smokeless propellant. As the surface area of the powder granules decrease as they burn, production of gasses increases. Such propellants provide the maximum amount of area under the pressure-time curve to create a sustained push.

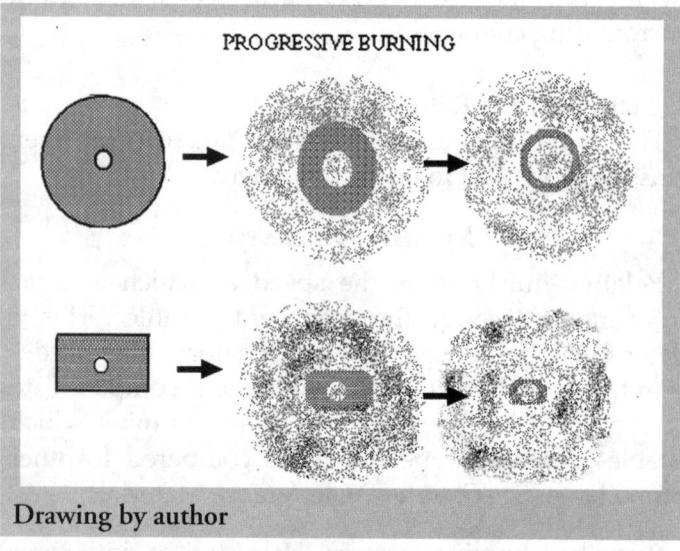

Drawing by author

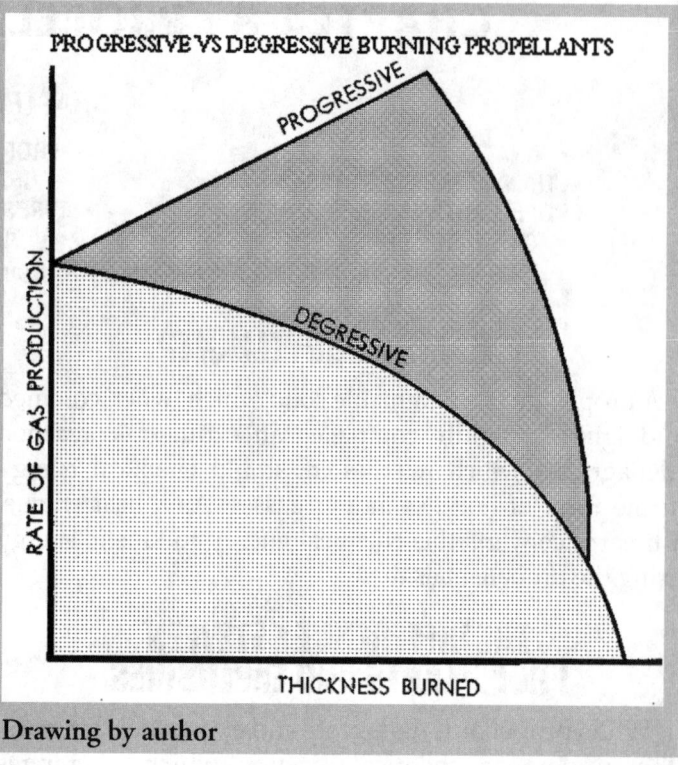

Drawing by author

Powder Volume

As many smokeless propellants are dense, they occupy very little volume inside the cartridge case. This is an excellent characteristic for modern calibers with small cartridge case volumes such as 9mm Luger and .223 Remington. However, it is a problem in older cases having a large volume, especially those originally designed for black powder such as the .45 Colt, .38 Special, and .45-70 Gov't. In such spacious cases, the position of a small charge of dense propellant, within the case at the instant it is ignited, can cause hang fires, erratic muzzle velocities, pressure excursions, and poor accuracy. In answer to these problems, powder manufacturers have introduced "bulk" powders which occupy more space inside the cartridge case.

TYPES OF PROPELLANTS

There are four basic types of small arms propellants:

- **Black powder**
- **Brown powder**
- **Semi-smokeless powder**
- **Smokeless powder**
  - » Bulk
  - » Single-base
  - » Double-base
  - » Triple-base

BLACK POWDER

Black powder is a mechanical mixture of three finely-divided natural ingredients which do not undergo chemical change during manufacture: potassium nitrate (KNO), charcoal (C), and sulfur (S). Tests conducted in the late 1800s confirmed the ideal ratio of the components by weight to be: 74% potassium nitrate, 15 ½ % charcoal and 10 ½ % sulfur.

When ignited, black powder begins an exothermic reaction (deflagrates) which releases stored energy in the form of hot, rapidly expanding gasses. These gasses are produced by potassium nitrate oxidizing the sulfur and charcoal in a complex series of reactions to form carbon monoxide, carbon dioxide, and nitrogen; and three solids: potassium carbonate, potassium sulphate, and potassium sulfide. Taken together, the three gasses constitute approximately 45% of the products of combustion while the remaining 55% are solids which make up the smoke and residue left in the gun barrel. Potassium sulphide is the cause of the stench in black powder smoke.

As the gasses are generated, they expand to a volume over 3,600 times greater than the black powder, releasing heat and creating pressure on the order of 20 tons per square inch. Black powder will burn equally well in a vacuum as the potassium nitrate provides the oxygen for the reaction. In its normal form of randomly shaped grains, black powder burns degressively.

ADVANTAGES OF BLACK POWDER

- **Very easy to ignite**
- **Very quick burning**
- **Good ballistic stability**
- **Ingredients are cheap and readily available**
- **Generates low breech pressures**

DISADVANTAGES OF BLACK POWDER

- **Smoky**
- **Hygroscopic (absorbs moisture)**
- **Leaves heavy corrosive residue in gun barrel**
- **Grain size has only minor effect on degressive burn rate**
- **Dangerous to manufacture, ship, and store**

BROWN POWDER

Black powder can be made without or with very small amounts of sulfur. Such powders are called brown powders after their appearance. Brown powder was developed in Germany and consisted of a mixture of 80% potassium nitrate, 18% charcoal made from partially burnt rye straw and 2-3% sulfur. When they appeared briefly during the 1880s, brown powders were the epitome of black powder development and rivaled the ballistic performance of early single-base smokeless propellants. Within ten years, brown powder was made redundant by smokeless propellants and so had very little impact on ammunition development.

Brown powder burns degressively like black powder, producing carbon dioxide gas, nitrogen gas, and potassium in the process. However the amounts of carbon oxisulfide and carbon disulphide produced by brown powders are considerably reduced compared to black powder due to the low sulfur content. Smoke and bore fouling are also reduced, but not eliminated. Brown powder smoke does not have the stench of black powder smoke.

The key ingredient in brown powder performance was the charcoal made from partially burnt rye straw. This material was found to offer far superior burning characteristics than charcoal made from other materials.

ADVANTAGES OF BROWN POWDER

- **Can be made using procedures and machinery for black powder**
- **Uses similar raw materials as black powder**
- **Energy content rivals single-base smokeless propellants**
- **Not as smoky as black powder**
- **Cleaner burning than black powder**

DISADVANTAGES OF BROWN POWDER

- **Hard to ignite**
- **Harder to incorporate**
- **Still corrosive**
- **Degressive burning**
- **Still smoky**

SEMI-SMOKELESS POWDER

Essentially, semi-smokeless propellants were a mechanical mixture of black powder with a small percentage of smokeless propellant to reduce smoke and fouling to acceptable levels.

Although smokeless powders were common by 1900, some rimfire shooters insisted there was no substitute for black powder in .22 rimfire match ammunition. To appease this group of target shooters, in the 1920s powder manufacturers developed semi-smokeless powders. By the early 1930s, the advantages of smokeless propellants in rimfire ammunition had become completely evident and cartridges loaded with semi-smokeless powder disappeared.

ADVANTAGES OF SEMI-SMOKELESS POWDER

- **Maintains steady push of black powder**
- **Easy to ignite**
- **Cleaner burning than black powder**
- **Bulk fills rimfire cartridge case**
- **Not as smoky as black powder**

DISADVANTAGES OF SEMI-SMOKELESS PROPELLANTS

- **Leaves corrosive residue**
- **More smoke than smokeless propellants**
- **Expensive hybrid**
- **No real ballistic advantage**

SMOKELESS POWDER

Smokeless powder is a mixture of ingredients which undergo chemical change during manufacture through a process called nitration. This process adds nitrogen and oxygen atoms to cellulose molecules, substantially increasing their stored chemical energy.

Smokeless propellants have considerably more stored chemical energy than black powders. As they burn, smokeless propellants release energy in the form of hot expanding gasses containing carbon monoxide, carbon dioxide, nitrogen, hydrogen, and water (steam). Unlike black powder, smokeless propellants convert nearly all of their constituents into gas leaving little residue. The shape of smokeless propellant grains is a major factor in obtaining a specific progressive burning rate.

BURNING TEMPERATURE

Black powders burn at a temperature of approximately 3,900° F. Single-base smokeless propellants burn at a temperature of about 4,000° F. and double-base propellants up to 5,600° F.

SMOKELESS PROPELLANT ADDITIVES

Most smokeless propellants contain additives designed to confer specific advantages. Of course, some additives are common while others are rarely used and no smokeless propellant contains all of these additives.

- **Solvents**

Although powder manufacturers try to remove solvents from finished powder, small amounts often remain. Typically these are alcohol, ether, acetic acid, and nitroglycerine. The ether-like odor from a container of fresh powder is caused by solvents.

- **Stabilizers**

A common formulation for this purpose is dyphenalamine. The purpose of a stabilizer is to help prevent deterioration in storage.

- **Flash Inhibitors**

Normally, potassium sulphate is added for this purpose. Flash inhibitors are required in military propellants but seldom added to sporting powders.

- **Deterrent Coatings**

These coatings help control burning rate. Graphite is a common deterrent coating, however dinitrotoluene (DNT) and diethyldiphenylurea (Centralite) also are common deterrent coatings. They are used in small amounts (2-3%).

- **Anti-static Coatings**

These coatings are intended to reduce static electricity for safety. Graphite commonly is used for this purpose and gives powder its black, shiny appearance.

- **Identity Markers**

These are small, inert, colored granules to differentiate propellants which otherwise may look similar. They are not always used and when they are, only in sporting powders.

- **Decoppering Agents**

A small amount of tin (2%) may be used to reduce copper fouling in the bore.

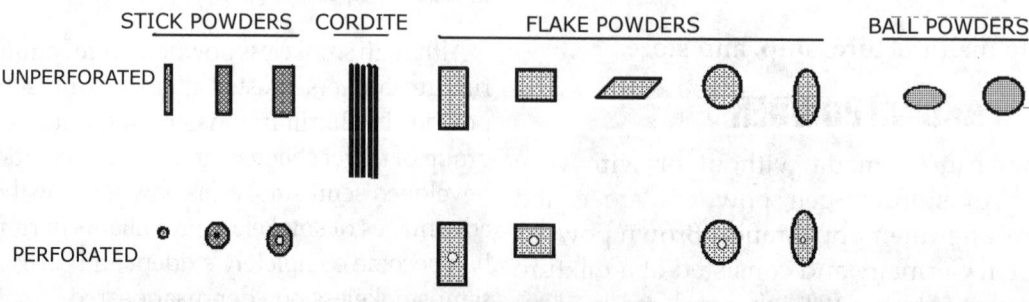

PROPELLANT CONFIGURATIONS

STICK POWDERS   CORDITE   FLAKE POWDERS   BALL POWDERS

UNPERFORATED

PERFORATED

• **Wear Inhibitors**

Titanium dioxide powder placed in front of the propellant charge is used for this purpose. As the propellant burns, the titanium dioxide forms a cool gas along the bore surface to reduce heat transfer from the hot propellant gasses to the barrel. Plastic disks have also been used for this purpose. Centralite also reduces barrel wear. Mineral jelly was used in Cordite for this purpose. Wear inhibitors are common in artillery propellants but seldom used in small arms powders.

TYPES OF SMOKELESS PROPELLANTS

There are four types of smokeless propellants:

* **Bulk**
* **Single-base**
* **Double-base**
* **Triple-base**

BULK POWDERS

Bulk powders are single-base, smokeless propellants made from wood cellulose with a low level of nitration and energy content. Introduced in the late 1800s, their application was mainly in shotshells where bulk powders could be substituted on a dram-for-dram basis for black powders. Ballistic performance was similar to the same charge of black powder.

Bulk powders remained popular until the late 1930s when World War II ended their manufacture. Bulk powders are now obsolete and old stocks should not be used.

SINGLE-BASE SMOKELESS PROPELLANTS

Single-base smokeless propellants use highly nitrated cellulose as their main energetic ingredient. Nitrocellulose is made by the nitration of wood or cotton cellulose using hot, concentrated nitric acid and sulfuric acid. Prolonged treatment yields a product called guncotton containing 13.3% nitrogen. Weaker acids at lower temperatures combined with a shorter treatment time will produce collodion or pyroxylin with a nitrogen content of 8-12%. Next, the acids are removed by pulping, boiling in alkali, and washing with water. The nitrated cellulose or guncotton is then dissolved in a mixture of ether and alcohol to form a colloid paste that can be rolled into sheets or extruded into rods, then cut into flakes or tubes. Introduced in 1914, the DuPont series of Improved Military Rifle (IMR) powders are all of single-base chemistry.

ADVANTAGES OF SINGLE-BASE PROPELLANTS

• **Very little bore erosion due to lower flame temperature**

• **Ballistically unaffected by temperature changes**
• **Easily made to burn progressively**

DISADVANTAGES OF SINGLE-BASE PROPELLANTS

• **Lower energy content requires larger charge weight**
• **Somewhat hygroscopic**
• **Somewhat hard to ignite with weak primers**

DOUBLE-BASE SMOKELESS PROPELLANTS

Double-base smokeless propellants use two energetic ingredients as their base—nitrocellulose and nitroglycerine. Double-base propellants begin life as single-base propellants. Instead of using a mixture of alcohol and ether as a plasticizer, double-base propellants are dissolved in nitroglycerine to form a colloid paste.

This paste is pressed between two hot rollers, then extruded and cut into flakes. A double-base propellant may contain from 7% to 40% nitroglycerine which boosts the stored chemical energy in the propellant.

Cordite is a type of double-base propellant containing approximately 65% nitrocellulose, 30% nitroglycerine and 5% mineral jelly colloided with acetone. Extruded into strands, Cordite was cut to the length of the powder chamber of the cartridge. Manufacture of Cordite was discontinued in the early 1990s.

Ball powders are double-base propellants. They also begin life as a single-base propellant. After washing, the nitrocellulose is not colloided. Rather, it is completely dissolved and the resulting liquid agitated to form small spheres of different diameters. These are treated with nitroglycerine to boost their energy content. The balls may be flattened or left spherical. Ball propellants are inherently safe to manufacture and work well for recycling the nitrocellulose from old propellants. However, ball propellants have a degressive burn rate and depend heavily on suitable deterrent coatings and mixing various sizes to adjust burning rates.

ADVANTAGES OF DOUBLE-BASE PROPELLANTS

• **Easy and cheap to manufacture**
• **Easy to ignite**
• **High energy content allows smaller powder charges**
• **Non-hygroscopic**

DISADVANTAGES OF DOUBLE-BASE PROPELLANTS

• **Bore erosion due to high flame temperature**
• **Temperature sensitive**
• **Not suitable for some calibers**

Necessity is the Mother of Invention

After Japanese military forces occupied the Philippine Islands in 1942, many Filipino citizens began active resistance using ex-U.S. military weapons and ammunition. In short order, Filipino resistance forces began running low on .30-'06 Springfield ammunition. With no possibility of resupply, the only solution was to setup reloading operations on a semi-industrial scale.

Guerrilla forces carefully saved their empty brass cartridge cases after each battle, thus insuring a steady supply of cases. But, they had to improvise components such as primers, propellant, and bullets.

A suitable propellant was made from the high explosives in Japanese sea mines. Swimmers sawed off the chains anchoring these mines, then guided them ashore where they were cut open and the explosive removed. The burning speed of the explosive was slowed by mixing it with saw dust or other inert substances to make it suitable for firearms use.

Fired primers were carefully removed, disassembled and cleaned. The indent from the firing pin was flattened out using a hammer and punch. Next, a priming compound made from the heads of strike anywhere matches was compressed into the primer cap, the anvil was replaced, and the primer inserted back into the cartridge case.

Bullets were made by cutting brass curtain rods into appropriate lengths, and pointed by filing.

This crudely loaded ammunition actually worked very well. Breech pressure was certainly much higher than normal as the guerrillas reported that the high velocity and flat trajectory of these powerful loads made windage adjustments unnecessary.

When American submarines eventually began delivering supplies of new ammunition, the guerrillas preferred their reloads which were substantially more powerful than the new ammunition!

TRIPLE-BASE POWDERS

Triple-base propellants use three energetic ingredients as their base—nitrocellulose, nitroglycerine, and nitroguanidine. Triple-base propellants begin life as single-base, then double-base propellants in similar processes to those outlined above. To further boost energy content, nitroguanidine, a nitrated organic compound, is added to the propellant.

As triple-base propellants are expensive, they are seldom used in small arms ammunition.

ADVANTAGES OF TRIPLE-BASE PROPELLANTS

- **Easy to ignite**
- **Fast burning**
- **Non-hygroscopic**
- **Very stable**
- **Low charge weights**

DISADVANTAGES OF TRIPLE-BASE PROPELLANTS

- **Expensive to manufacture**
- **Nitroguanidine in short supply**

CANISTER VS. PRODUCTION POWDERS

Most smokeless propellants exist in two forms: canister and production.

A canister powder is one which is packaged in small containers and sold to reloaders. As handloaders have no way of measuring breech pressure, there can be only one acceptable burning rate for a canister powder. For this reason, manufacturers make every effort to assure the consistency of a given canister powder from one lot to the next.

Production powders are made in a wide variety of burning rates. In many cases, a given production propellant will be available in eight to twelve different burning speeds. Production propellants are sold in bulk to ammunition manufacturers and government arsenals. As these plants can measure breech pressure, manufacturers and arsenals can select the propellant and burning speed which best matches their ballistic requirements for a specific load.

"No one was ever killed by a quick, loud noise!"

- Bill Jordan on combat handgun accuracy

Common Propellant Shapes
(Enlarged to show detail)

Flake   **Tubular**

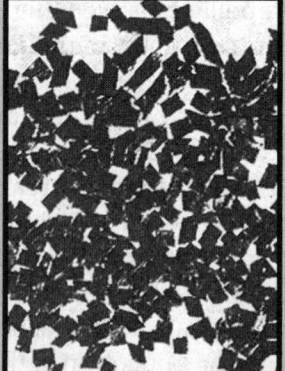

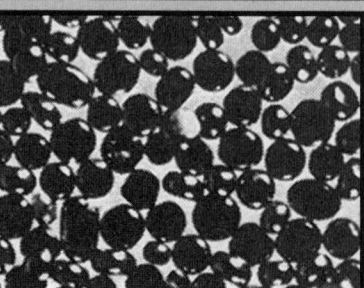

Ball

HODGDON/WINCHESTER HYBRID PROPELLANT

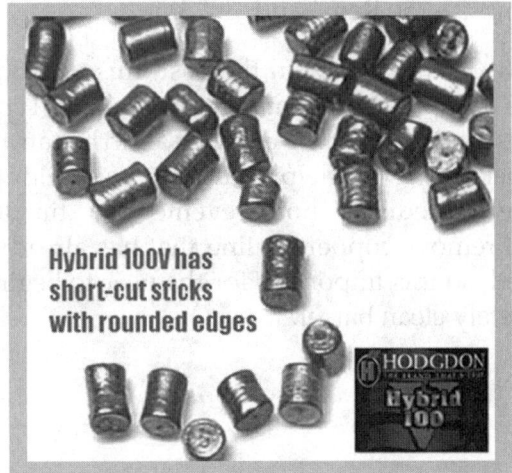

Hybrid 100V has short-cut sticks with rounded edges

"What is a hybrid propellant?" you ask, and "What are the uses and advantages of such a propellant?"

Hybrid propellants were developed at the St. Marks plant in Florida, which is well known for its Winchester brand of Ball powders. Basically, the new St. Marks Hybrid powder combines the chemistry of a Ball propellant with the particle geometry of an extruded, perforated stick powder. As Ball powder is double-base, so is the new Hybrid propellant. St. Marks offers hybrid propellant as Winchester 780 or Hodgdon 100V.

As a high energy propellant, Hodgdon 100V Hybrid can offer:

- **A 10% reduction in charge weight for equivalent muzzle velocity**

- **Low muzzle flash**

- **Low barrel erosion**

- **Higher loading densities**

- **Excellent progressivity**

- **Consistent performance at temperatures between -40° F. and 145° F.**

The new Hodgdon 100V Hybrid rifle powder has a short, perforated stick configuration with rounded ends for smooth metering. Burning speed is approximately half way between their familiar H4350 and H4831 single-base rifle propellants making it a good choice for .270 Win., .30-'06 Spr., 7mm Rem. Mag., and .300 Win. Mag. applications.

Hybrid stick propellant can be made with one, seven, or nineteen perforations. Burning temperatures can vary from 2,000-3,500 °K. Better yet, St. Marks hybrid propellant is naturally plastic allowing it to

be consolidated to significantly increase load density over loose powder. Tests made under the High Density Propellant Charge technology program have shown a 30% increase in load density with a 22% increase in muzzle velocity!

VIHTAVUORI TIN STAR

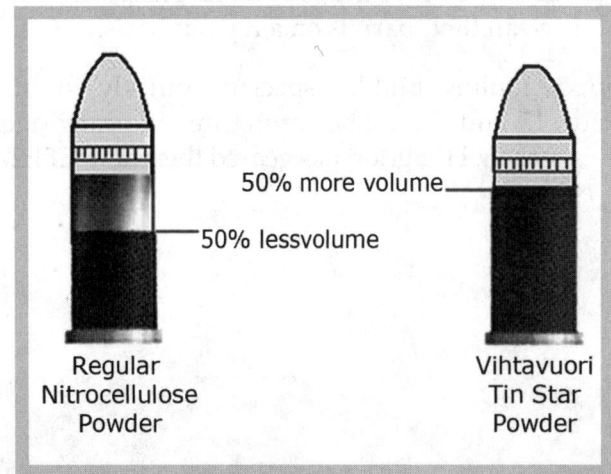

50% more volume

50% less volume

Regular Nitrocellulose Powder — Vihtavuori Tin Star Powder

Today, many older black powder revolver cartridges remain in service since reproduction handguns in these nostalgic calibers are popular. Such calibers include: .38 Special, .38-40 WCF, .44-40 WCF, .44 Special, .44 Russian, .45 Colt, and .45 Schofield among others.

The problem is these old codgers have large case volumes designed for heavy charges of black powder. They were also designed for low maximum average pressures and modest muzzle velocities using lubricated lead bullets. Loading these calibers with smokeless propellants can present a problem as their density means they occupy a small percentage of the available case volume.

What does this mean? Small charges of smokeless propellants in large volume cases can cause extreme variations in maximum average pressure and muzzle velocity depending on the position of the propellant in the case at the time of ignition. For example, with the powder charge at the bullet, pressure and velocity will be lower. If the powder is at the back end of the case, the pressure and muzzle velocity will be higher. In extreme cases, a bullet may become lodged in the barrel.

Shooters do not like "musical" loads such as these. To solve this problem, Vihtavuori of Finland has introduced a single-base smokeless propellant with approximately the bulk of black powder but none of its drawbacks. This means you can load these old favorites with a propellant that will take up most of the volume in these cases without the music.

Hodgdon CFE223 223 Propellant

CFE stands for "copper fouling eraser". It has been specially formulated to reduce copper fouling in rifle barrels. As any bench rest shooter, rifle competitor, or varmint shooter will attest, as copper fouling builds up in a rifle barrel it adversely affects accuracy. In addition, copper fouling is very hard to remove. This is why such shooters clean their barrels on a regular basis.

Copper fouling builds especially quickly in high velocity .17 and .22 caliber centerfire rifle cartridges. For this reason, Hodgdon has geared their new CFE223

Ball propellant for such calibers as .17 Rem., .204 Ruger, .223 Rem., .22-250 Rem., and .308 Win.

So how do they do it? In the past, this was done by adding a decoppering agent to the propellant. Typically, additives like tin dioxide were used as tin has an affinity for copper which will help reduce copper buildup. The key here is "reduce," not prevent. Also, tin dioxide does not remove copper fouling that has already been deposited, so it is important for the user to begin with a completely clean barrel.

MASSIVE EXPLOSION DESTROYS TEXAS CITY, TX
APRIL 16, 1947

On April 16, 1947, the 472-foot long, ex-Liberty ship Grandcamp was docked in Texas City, TX, where it was being loaded with 3,800 tons of 38% ammonium nitrate fertilizer and small arms ammunition. Berthed about 600 ft. down the pier was the SS High Flyer loaded with 961 tons of ammonium nitrate. At approximately 8:00 am, a fire broke out in the hold of the Grandcamp. All efforts to put out the fire were in vain, and at 9:12 am, the entire load of ammonium nitrate blew up in a huge explosion. The ship disintegrated, throwing 6,350 tons of steel shrapnel into the air and creating a 15-foot high tidal wave. The ship's 2- ton anchor was thrown 1.62 miles creating a ten foot crater on landing.

The blast flattened the entire dock area, leveled the adjacent Monsanto Chemical Company plant, and ignited chemical tanks all along the waterfront. Fires spread to the nearby SS High Flyer, which blew up 15 hours later, increasing the devastation. The High Flyer's propeller was thrown over a mile inland.

The official death toll was at least 581 (most were never found) and 5,000 injured. Over 1,000 buildings, 1,100 vehicles, and 362 railroad cars were obliterated. Ten miles away in Galveston, people were knocked down by the blast; windows were shattered as far away as Houston (40 miles).

CHAPTER 9 : PRIMER NOMENCLATURE

CHAPTER 9 HIGHLIGHTS:

- WHAT IS A PRIMER
- HOW A PRIMER WORKS
- PRIMER CONFIGURATIONS
- PRIMER SIZES
- PRIMER APPLICATIONS
- PRIMER CHEMISTRY

All drawings by Author, unless otherwise noted.

WHAT IS A PRIMER?

Practical

A primer is the small cap in the center of a cartridge case head. When struck by the firing pin of the firearm, the priming compound explodes, igniting the propellant powder.

Technical

A primer is a percussion ignition system for firearms. Most primers are an assembly of three or more parts including a metal cap, an anvil, and a small amount of explosive compound.

HOW A PRIMER WORKS

When the firing pin of the gun strikes the metal primer cap, the impact crushes the explosive compound inside the primer between the metal primer cap and the tip of the anvil inside. This causes the explosive to detonate, sending a stream of hot expanding gasses into the propellant. These gasses raise the temperature and the pressure inside the cartridge case, causing the propellant to ignite.

PRIMER CONFIGURATIONS

There are four modern primer configurations for small arms:

- Rimfire
- Boxer (for centerfire cartridges)
- Berdan (for centerfire cartridges)
- Battery cup (for shotguns)

RIMFIRE

The priming compound of a rimfire cartridge is held in the hollow rim of the cartridge case. As there is no anvil, the priming mix contains ground glass as a frictioning agent. When the firing pin strikes the rim of the cartridge case, the priming compound is crushed between the two sides of the hollow rim. This causes the priming compound to explode, igniting the propellant.

Rimfire priming is weak and large amounts of unburned powder are common despite the use of fast burning propellants and a heavy crimp on the bullet.

ADVANTAGES OF RIMFIRE IGNITION

- **Easy and cheap to manufacture**
- **No anvil, foil, or sealer needed**
- **Waterproof when bullet is properly crimped**

DISADVANTAGES OF RIMFIRE IGNITION

- **Weak ignition**
- **Additional cost and manufacturing steps for ground glass additive**
- **Leaves a lot of unburned powder**
- **Unsuitable for high pressure cartridges**

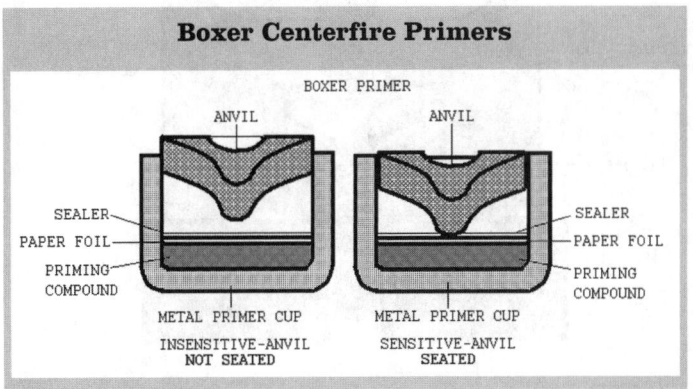

Boxer Centerfire Primers

BOXER PRIMER

ANVIL — ANVIL

SEALER — SEALER
PAPER FOIL — PAPER FOIL
PRIMING COMPOUND — PRIMING COMPOUND

METAL PRIMER CUP — METAL PRIMER CUP

INSENSITIVE-ANVIL NOT SEATED — SENSITIVE-ANVIL SEATED

BOXER

This primer configuration is named after its inventor, Col. Edward M. Boxer, who was Superintendent of the British Royal Laboratory at Woolwich Arsenal in the 1860s. Boxer primers have become the most popular type in the world. They are the dominant primer used in the manufacture of sporting centerfire ammunition and many types of military ammunition.

Boxer centerfire primers are an assembly of three or more parts consisting of: a U-shaped, brass primer cup, a brass or steel anvil, and an explosive compound with a paper foil cover and lacquer sealer. The anvil's legs project beyond the open end of the cup after assembly.

This desensitizes the primer by holding the tip of the anvil away from the priming compound. Seating the primer in the cartridge case also seats the anvil so that its tip contacts the explosive compound and sensitizes the primer.

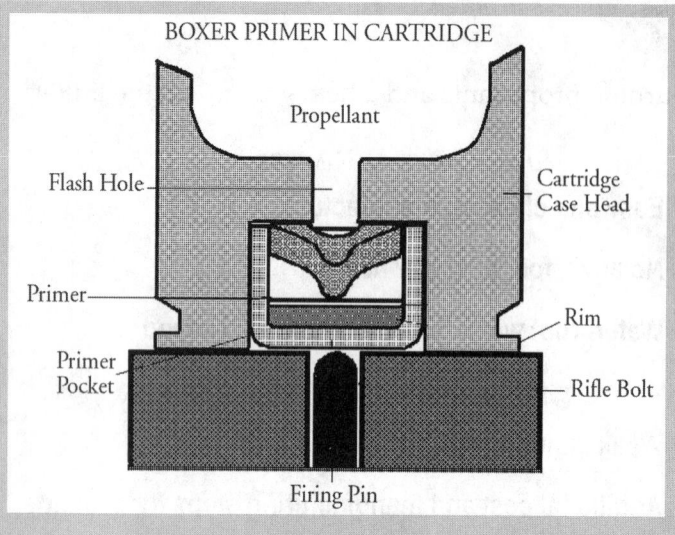

BOXER PRIMER IN CARTRIDGE

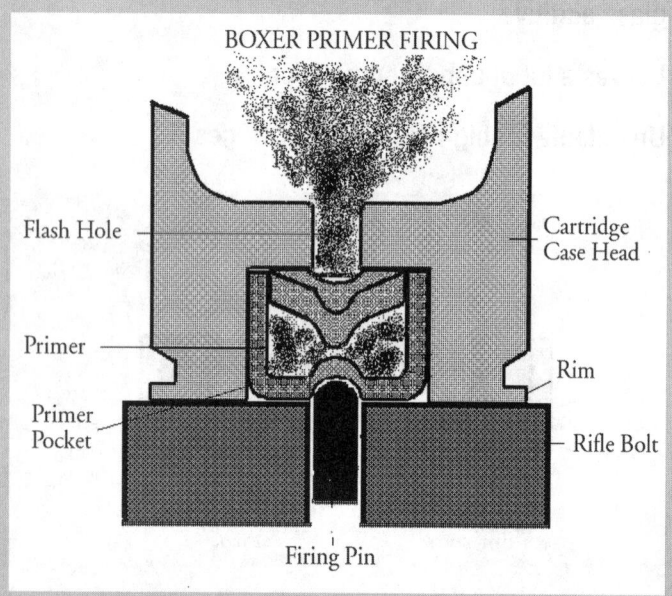

BOXER PRIMER FIRING

Primer pockets for Boxer primers are depressions in the rear face of the cartridge case head with a single central hole through the case web into the propellant chamber. The central flash hole makes it easy to decap a fired Boxer primed cartridge case for handloading.

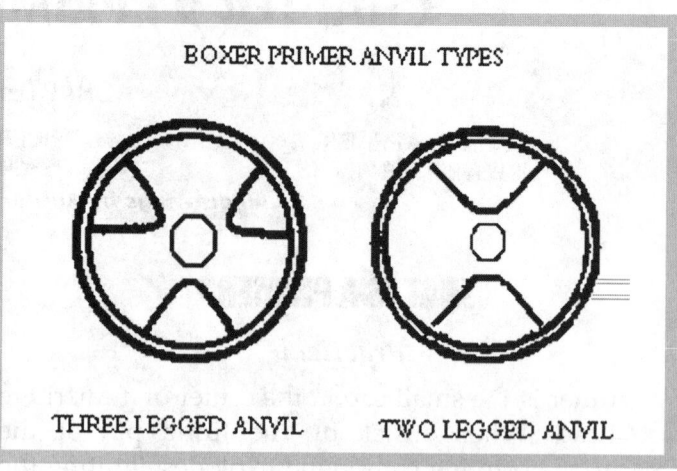

BOXER PRIMER ANVIL TYPES

THREE LEGGED ANVIL   TWO LEGGED ANVIL

ADVANTAGES OF BOXER PRIMER

- **Primer insensitive until seated in cartridge case**

- **Cartridge case does not incorporate anvil**

- **Reloading easier due to central flash hole**

DISADVANTAGES OF BOXER PRIMER

- **More parts increases difficulty of manufacture**

- **More expensive to manufacture**

BERDAN

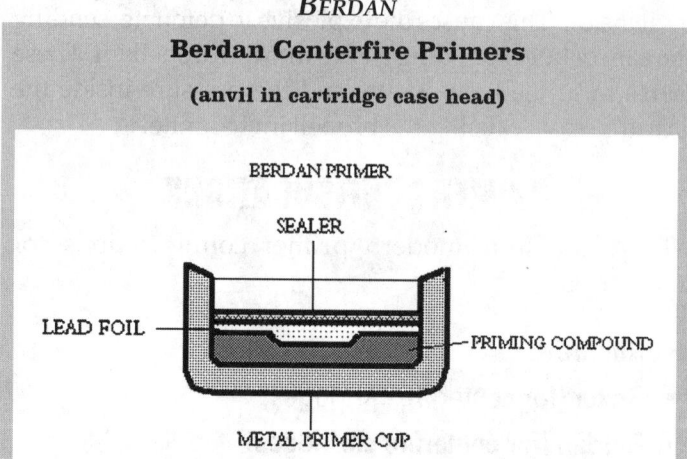

Berdan Centerfire Primers

(anvil in cartridge case head)

The Berdan centerfire primer was patented by an American, Gen. Hiram Berdan, in 1866. For many years after its introduction, the Berdan primer remained a popular rival to its Boxer competitor. Today, Berdan primers are used mainly in military ammunition by some overseas government arsenals. Most modern sporting ammunition is loaded with Boxer primers. Some European commercial ammunition manufacturers offer Berdan primers for handloading.

Unlike a Boxer primer, the anvil for a Berdan primer is not a "part" of the assembled primer. A Berdan primer is a simple, U-shaped brass cup with the priming compound inside, covered by foil and sealed with lacquer. This simplicity is somewhat negated as a Berdan cartridge case is more complex than a Boxer type because its primer pocket incorporates the anvil. As the flash hole(s) of a Berdan primer are offset to accommodate the centrally located anvil, depriming a Berdan primed case is difficult. For this reason, hand loading Berdan primed cases is not popular.

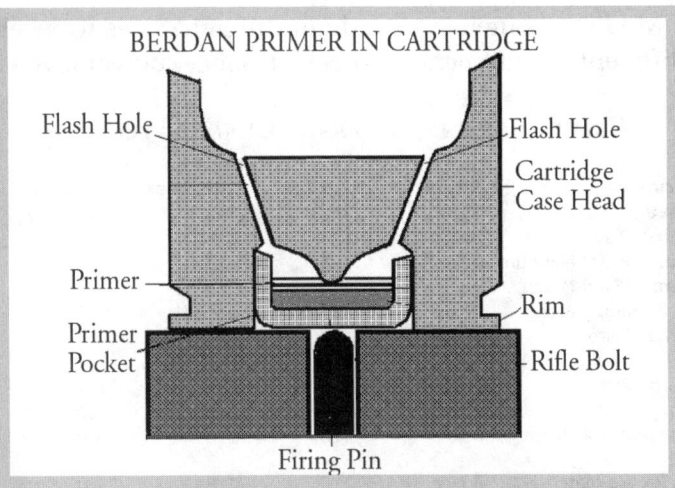

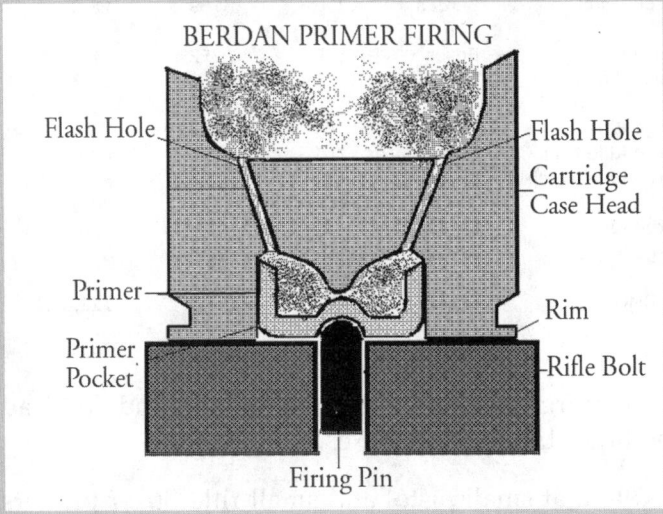

ADVANTAGES OF BERDAN PRIMER

- **Simple to manufacture, primer is one piece and not an assembly**

- **Inexpensive**

- **Anvil is positively located in case head**

DISADVANTAGES OF BERDAN PRIMER

- **Cartridge cases more difficult and expensive to make**

- **Difficult to reload**

BATTERY CUP

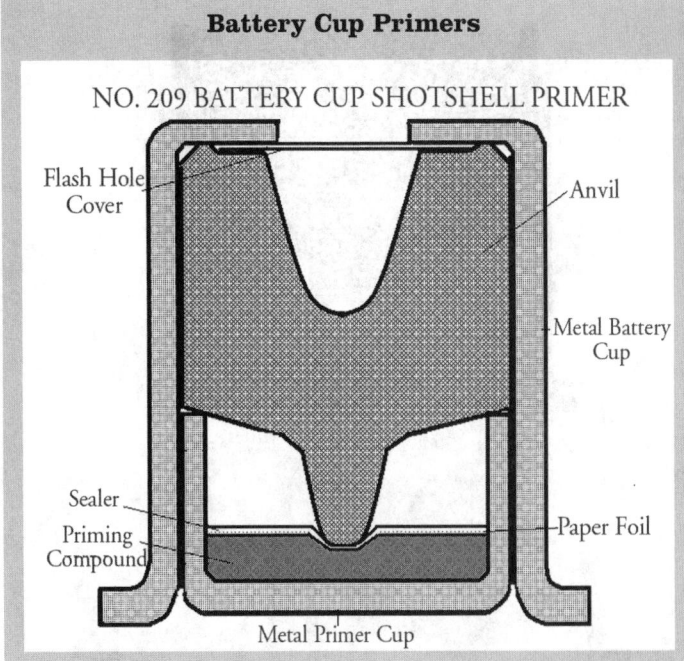

Development of the battery cup primer is attributed to an American military officer, Brigadier General Stephen Vincent Benet, in 1868. The inventor intended battery cup primers to be used in rifle cartridges. However, the battery cup primer found its main application in modern shotshells where it has supplanted all other types, except for all-metal shotshells which use Boxer centerfire primers. Because shotshell case heads are "built-up," they cannot hold a Boxer or Berdan primer securely in place. For this reason, the battery cup primer is the best design for shotshells. The battery cup and anvil shoulders hold the primer cup securely in position, while the battery cup provides plenty of bearing surface for the shotshell head to hold the entire assembly in place.

A battery cup primer is an assembly of five pieces: a brass primer cup, priming compound, brass anvil, brass cup body, and flash hole cover. While manufacturers offer shotshell primers for a variety of applications, every shotshell primer has the same external dimension. Therefore, only one primer size is used in all shotshells.

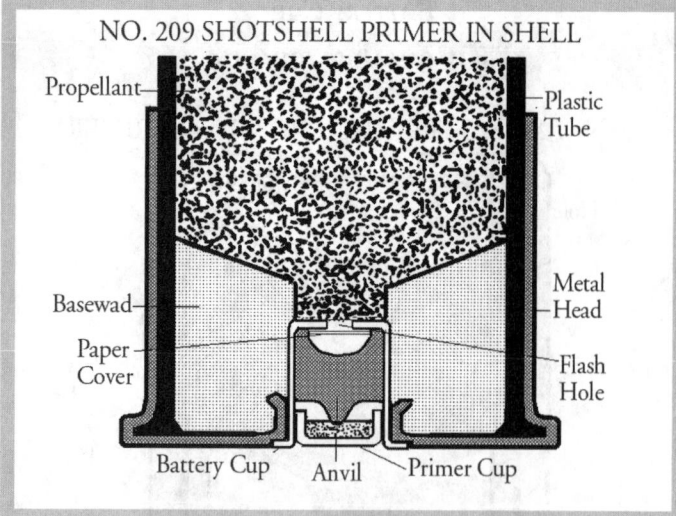

NO. 209 SHOTSHELL PRIMER IN SHELL

Propellant — Plastic Tube — Metal Head — Flash Hole — Basewad — Paper Cover — Battery Cup — Anvil — Primer Cup

NO. 209 SHOTSHELL PRIMER FIRING

In recent years, a variation of the battery cup design called the IABC has been used for some types of light shotshell loads, Essentially, the IABC primer is a simplified cheaper battery cup primer. The main difference is that the IABC type forms the battery cup body and anvil from a single drawn piece with a blow-out panel instead of a flash hole. This design reduces the number of parts from five to three, however, it is suitable only for light loads.

ADVANTAGES OF BATTERY CUP PRIMER

- Holds primer securely in place in shotshell head

- Flash hole cover prevents powder grains from migrating into battery cup

- Easy to remove and replace in shotshell

DISADVANTAGES OF BATTERY CUP PRIMER

- Complex assembly of four of more parts.

- Expensive to manufacture

- Suitable only for shotshells.

PRIMER SIZES

Modern primers are made in different sizes to meet different requirements and performance/power levels.

PRIMER SIZES AND AVERAGE CHARGE WEIGHTS

Primer Size	Primer Type	Cup Dia. (ins)	Bottom Thickness (ins.)	Avg Chg Wgt.(mgs)
Small Pistol	Boxer	.175	.0165	21.7
Small Pistol Magnum	Boxer	.175	.0165	25.0
Small Pistol Match	Boxer	.175	.0165	21.7
S. P. Mag. Match	Boxer	.175	.0165	25.0
Small Pistol	Berdan	.177	.0157	21.2
Large Pistol	Boxer	.210	.0169	28.8
Large Pistol Magnum	Boxer	.210	.0169	31.0
Large Pistol Match	Boxer	.210	.0169	28.8
L. P. Mag Match	Boxer	.210	.0169	31.0
Large Pistol	Berdan	.200	.0169	28.8
Small Rifle	Boxer	.175	.0252	21.7
Small Rifle Match	Boxer	.175	.0252	21.7
Large Rifle	Boxer	.210	.0252	37.3
Large Rifle Magnum	Boxer	.210	.0252	40.0
Large Rifle Match	Boxer	.210	.0252	37.3
L. R. Mag. Match	Boxer	.210	.0252	40.0
Large Rifle	Berdan	.2165	.02755	39.0
Large Rifle	Berdan	.2165	.0303	39.0
50 BMG	Boxer	.317	.0343	122.0
Shotshell	Battery Cup	.210	.0185	54.0

All charge weights are approximate, and for lead styphnate base primer mixes.

Note that small pistol and small rifle Boxer primers have identical diameters, and this is the case with large pistol/large rifle also. However, they are NOT interchangeable! The bottom of the metal primer cup is substantially thicker in rifle primers and the amount of priming compound may be heavier. Loading a pistol primer in a rifle case may result in a pierced primer and leakage of high pressure propellant gas into the rifle action. Rifle primers can be loaded into pistol cartridges, however rifle primers are not as sensitive as pistol primers and using them for handgun cartridges may result in misfires.

PRIMER APPLICATIONS

RIMFIRE

Modern rimfire primers are based on one of two case sizes: .22 Long Rifle, and .22 Magnum. The difference is in the amount of priming compound inserted in the case. This differs from one manufacturer to the next. Older rimfire designs of larger caliber are obsolete.

CENTERFIRE

Each caliber of centerfire cartridge is designed for one of the four Boxer primer sizes. The primer pocket in the case head is dimensioned accordingly. In general, handgun cartridges from .25 ACP through the .357/.38 calibers, and the .40 S&W, are designed for small pistol primers. Handgun cartridges from .38-40 WCF on up are designed for large pistol primers. A similar pattern exists for centerfire rifle cartridges. Rifle cartridges from .17 Rem. to .30 Carbine use a small rifle primer while larger calibers use the large rifle primer (see Chapter 96: Reference Material for a complete listing).

Magnum primers offer additional ignition potential for large capacity cartridge cases. In general, this includes magnum rifle or handgun calibers with maximum loads of slow burning propellant. Magnum primers can be used in standard calibers, however there is no ballistic advantage in doing so.

Match primers are dimensionally identical to standard primers. However, additional care and quality control procedures are taken in their manufacture to insure the highest possible consistency. While this is of minor concern to hunters, it is of major importance to target shooters seeking maximum accuracy.

FACTORS IN DETERMINING PRIMER APPLICATIONS

A wide variety of factors must be considered in determining the exact priming mix to be used for a particular application. A few of them are listed below:

- **Primer size**
- **Applications (military, sporting, competition)**
- **Cartridge case capacity**
- **Propellant type and burning rate**
- **Breech pressures**
- **Bullet caliber and weight**
- **Flash hole diameter**
- **Barrel lengths**
- **Corrosive residue**
- **Stability**
- **Cost**
- **Safety**

There are no rules for this. Rather it is the experience of the chemist dealing in the explosive arts which enables a choice to be made.

PRIMER CHEMISTRY

There are four chemical types of explosive initiator in priming compounds:

- **Mercury fulminate (obsolete)**
- **Potassium chlorate (obsolete)**
- **Lead styphnate**
- **Diazodinitrophenol**

MERCURY FULMINATE

This is the original priming compound used by Rev. Alexander Forsyth to develop explosive ignition in the early 1800s. This type of priming mix remained in use until 1947, but is now obsolete.

ADVANTAGES OF MERCURY FULMINATE PRIMERS

- **Easy to manufacture from commonly available raw materials**
- **Excellent sensitivity to impact**
- **Powerful ignition potential (especially good for black powder)**
- **Dry mixture**

DISADVANTAGES OF MERCURY FULMINATE PRIMERS

- **Short shelf life**
- **Sensitive to high temperatures**
- **Corrosive effects on brass cases and barrels**

POTASSIUM CHLORATE
(Non-mercuric, but corrosive) (Semi-obsolete)

When the U.S. Army discontinued using mercuric primers in the 1890s, they adopted a chlorate-based primer developed at Frankford Arsenal called H-48. This primer was used until 1917. The U.S. military then used the FA 70 chlorate primer until the mid-1950s. Commercial manufacturers discontinued the use of mercuric primers and switched to chlorate-based primers in the early 1900s as well. They replaced corrosive chlorate-based primers in the early 1930s with non-corrosive lead styphnate primers.

ADVANTAGES OF POTASSIUM CHLORATE PRIMERS

- **Insensitive during wet handling and assembly**
- **Stable at high temperatures**
- **Easy to manufacture**

DISADVANTAGES OF CHLORATE PRIMERS

- **Leaves corrosive residue in bore**

LEAD STYPHNATE
(MODERN, NON-CORROSIVE)

Lead styphnate priming compounds were developed and patented in Germany in the 1920s. Both Remington and Winchester purchased a license to manufacture it in the early 1930s. Nearly all sporting and some military ammunition now has non-corrosive lead styphnate priming.

There are two types of lead styphnate used for primers - normal and basic. Federal Cartridge is the sole manufacturer of basic lead styphnate primers. Basic and normal lead styphnate differ in a number of subtle ways:

Basic lead styphnate	Normal lead styphnate
* Crystals small and regular	* Crystals large and irregular
* When wet does not attack primer cup	* Acidic when wet-will attack primer cup
* More needed at low temperatures	* Better at low temperatures
* Better for match, magnum applications	* Better for low temperatures and rimfire applications

In practice, both basic and normal work equally well for average applications. It is in specialized applications that the differences between the two become apparent.

DIAZODINITROPHENOL
(DDNP, HEAVY METAL-FREE)

Primers based on this type of chemistry are not new, having been developed prior to World War II. However, efforts to reduce airborne lead levels in indoor shooting ranges have led to renewed interest in this type due to the absence of heavy metals. Several problems have slowed widespread use of this type of primer, namely:

- **Short storage life**

- **Sensitivity to high temperatures**

- **Requires larger flash hole diameters**

- **Reduced ignition potential**

Efforts are being made to remedy these shortcomings and progress has been made. For example, Dynamit Nobel/RWS in Germany has succeeded in formulating a heavy metal free DDNP primer that meets all NATO requirements for military ammunition. American ammunition manufacturers have developed and load DDNP primers for some lead-free handgun loads.

ADDITIONAL PRIMER MIX COMPONENTS

In addition to the base explosive initiators listed above, priming compounds may also contain:

Explosive Boosters

- **Tetrazene**

- **TNT**

- **Lead Thiocyanate**

- **PETN**

Small amounts of these high explosives are added to increase brisance or power.

Solid Fuels

- **Calcium Silicide**

- **Antimony Sulphide**

- **Aluminum powder**

- **Titanium powder**

Solid fuels are added to priming compounds to improve ignition. The exploding primer compound ignites the small particles in the solid fuel. These burning particles are carried by the hot primer gasses into the powder charge where they aid ignition.

Oxidizers

- **Barium Nitrate**

- **Lead Dioxide**

- **Lead Nitrate**

- **Potassium Chlorate**

- **Potassium Nitrate**

- **Zinc Peroxide**

Oxidizers enhance the potential of the priming compound and solid fuels.

Binders

- **Gelatine**

- **Gum Arabic**

- **Gum Tragacanth**

Binding agents are used to hold the priming compounds together.

Sealers

- **Lacquer**
- **Shellac**
- **Lead foil**
- **Paper**

The priming compound must be protected from moisture and dust. For this purpose, a paper or metal foil cover is placed over the priming mix after it has been pressed into the metal primer cup. A drop of lacquer or shellac seals the foil in place and adds an additional layer of protection. The lacquer may be color coded to differentiate among primer sizes.

Other

- **Ground glass as a frictioning agent (typically for rimfire)**
- **Paper cover over battery cup flash hole**
- **Lacquer sealer around primer annulus after seating in cartridge case**

SAFETY

Always handle primers with safety and respect. Despite their small size, they are quite powerful and can cause serious personal injury when mishandled. See Chapter 37: Handling Safety and Chapter 38: Storage Safety for more information.

Electric Primers Are Not New

One early attempt at designing and manufacturing an electrically-primed rifle was made in 1866, by LeBaron and Dumas of Paris, France. A dry cell battery in the butt stock powered the system. It was not a commercial success and the company disappeared into the mists of history.

Closer to home, in 1884 the American Electric Arms And Ammunition Company of New York patented and produced a sporting rifle with electric ignition. The special primers were made by Samuel Russel in Brooklyn, New York. A battery in the stock powered the system. Pulling the trigger closed a circuit allowing current to flow to the primer through a platinum wire. The resulting glow on the tip of the wire was intended to ignite the primer. The design was complex and heavy for the time and was not a commercial success.

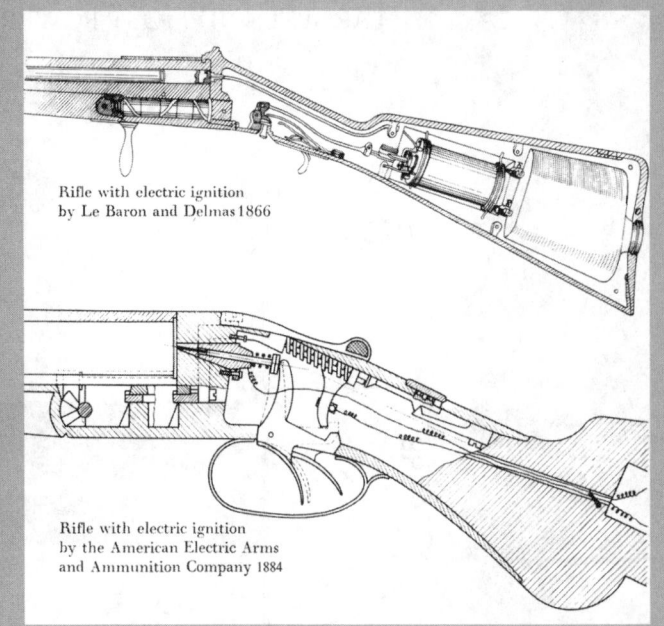

Rifle with electric ignition by Le Baron and Delmas 1866

Rifle with electric ignition by the American Electric Arms and Ammunition Company 1884

SPORTING RIFLE CARTRIDGE SUPERLATIVES

SMALLEST CALIBER SPORTING RIFLE CARTRIDGE

.172 in. dia. 20-gr. bullet, MV 4,000 fps, ME 710 ft.-lbs.

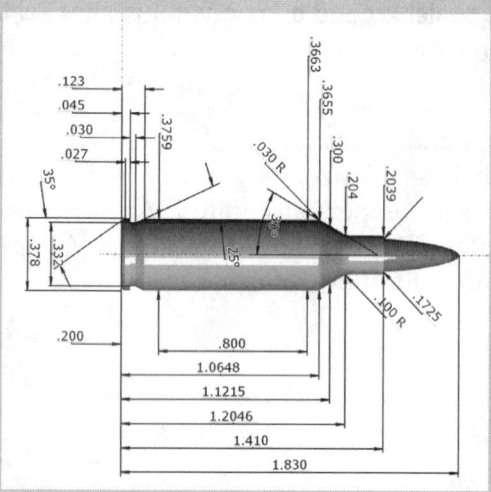

.17 Remington Fireball

SPORTING RIFLE CARTRIDGE WITH HIGHEST MUZZLE VELOCITY

.224 in. dia. 35-gr. bullet, MV 4,450 fps, ME 1,539 ft.-lbs.

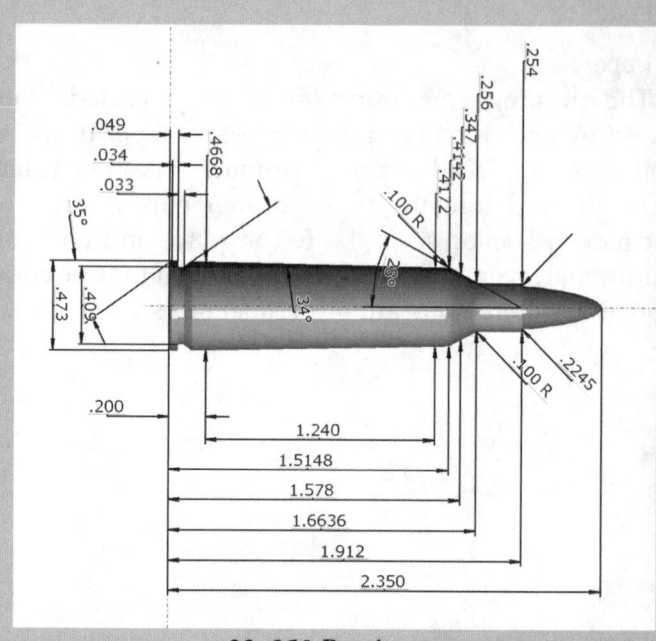

.22–250 Remington

LARGEST AND MOST POWERFUL SPORTING RIFLE CARTRIDGE

.700 in. dia. 1,000-gr. bullet, MV 2,000 fps, ME 8,900 ft.-lbs.

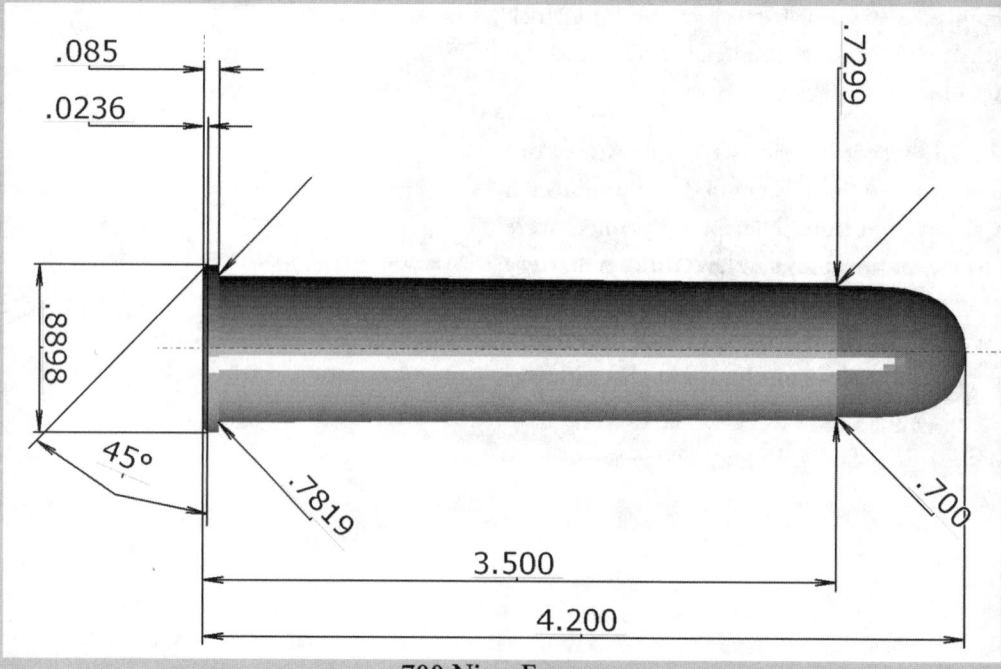

.700 Nitro Express

CHAPTER 10 : SHOTSHELL NOMENCLATURE

CHAPTER 10 HIGHLIGHTS:

- SHOTSHELL
- SHOTGUN WAD COLUMNS
- WAD MATERIALS
- WAD COLUMN TYPES
- OTHER WAD MATERIALS
- DEFINITION OF A SHOTGUN PELLET
- DEFINITION OF A SHOTGUN SLUG

All drawings by Author, unless otherwise noted.

SHOTSHELL

Most shotshells are of "built up" design containing six or more parts including: a paper or plastic tube, a metal head, a base wad, a primer, a wad column (may be one or more pieces), and a shot charge or slug. An attractive visual feature of shotshells is the variety of plastic tube colors ranging from translucent to black.

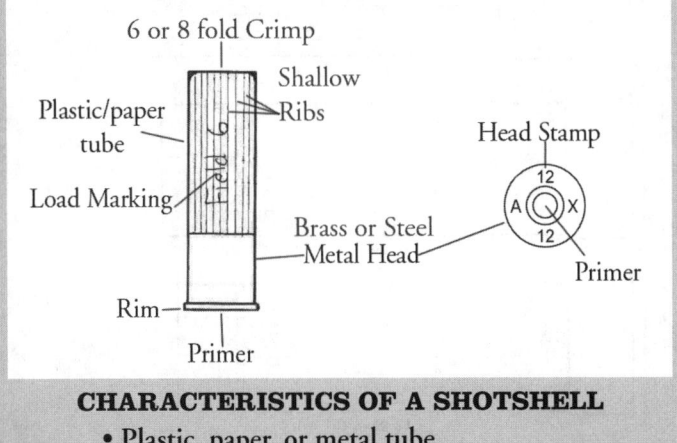

CHARACTERISTICS OF A SHOTSHELL

- Plastic, paper, or metal tube
- Crimp closure
- Metal head
- Primer
- Headstamp

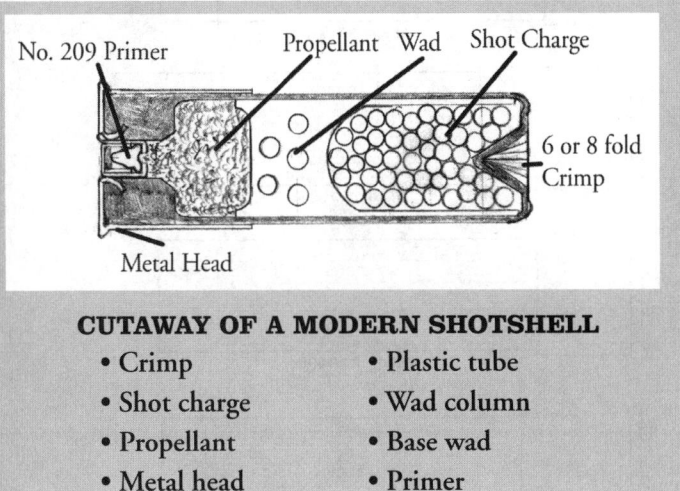

CUTAWAY OF A MODERN SHOTSHELL

- Crimp
- Shot charge
- Propellant
- Metal head
- Plastic tube
- Wad column
- Base wad
- Primer

SHOT AND SLUG

A typical shotshell contains a charge of round balls or pellets of a particular size, however shot charges of two or more different sizes in layers may be encountered. The pellets may be of lead, steel, other metals, or composites. A single large projectile with or without a sabot can be loaded in lieu of a shot charge.

WAD COLUMN

All loaded shotshells contain a wad column made of plastic, paper, felt, or a combination of these. There are a wide variety of wad column designs, however all of them are designed to seal the shot charge from the hot propellant gases, cushion the shot charge on acceleration, and adjust the volume inside the shell to the components.

TUBE

Shotshell tubes may be of molded, extruded, or drawn high density polyethylene plastic, wound paper, or drawn metal. The crimp closure at the front of the tube may be rolled (to secure a top wad disk or a slug) or folded with six or eight segments.

HEAD

A metal head is crimped on the rear of the plastic or paper tubes. The head may be of brass, steel, or aluminum and is designed to provide a strong surface for the extractor, not reinforce the tube against breech pressure.

PRIMING

Modern shotshells are loaded with No. 209 battery cup primers. No. 209 denotes a size (external configuration and dimensions) only; there may be variations in the design and/or composition of components.

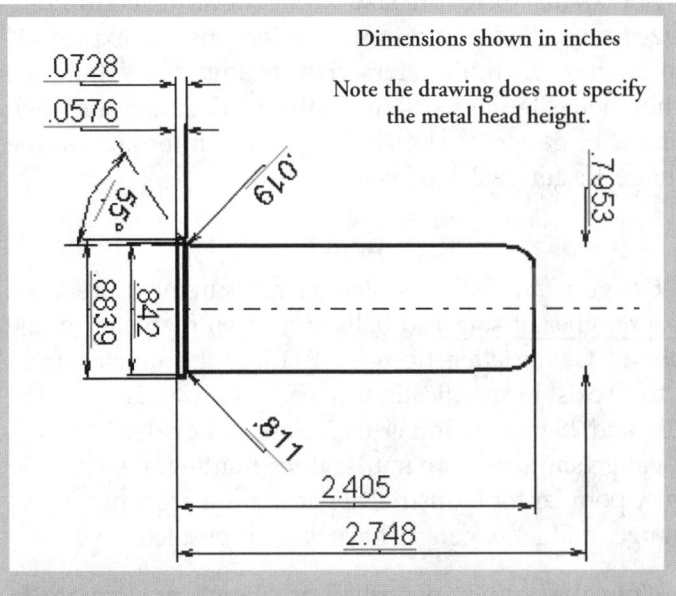

TECHNICAL DRAWING OF A TYPICAL SHOTSHELL

Drawing courtesy of Hartmut Broemel

PROPELLANT

A fast burning single- or double-base smokeless propellant is typically used for most shotshells.

There are three types of shotshell that differ according to construction:

- **Built up with separate base wad**
- **Built up with integral base wad**
- **Monolithic**

PARTS OF A SHOTSHELL

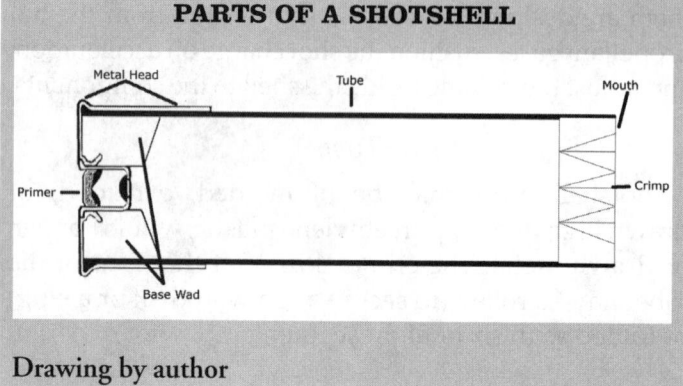

Drawing by author

A built up shotshell with a separate base wad is an assembly of four parts: tube, base wad, metal head and primer. An integral base wad design incorporates the tube and base wad as a single piece thus reducing the number of separate parts by one. A monolithic shotshell consists of a one piece hull made of drawn brass or molded plastic. The built up shotshell has become the dominant type due to low cost and excellent performance.

SIZE

Shotshells differ in size and length. The different sizes are called gauges and the lengths are expressed in inches or millimeters. For example, a 10-gauge shotshell is larger in diameter than a 12 gauge shotshell and a 12-gauge 3" shotshell has more internal volume that a 12-gauge 2 3/4" shell.

GAUGE

Gauge is an ancient system of measurement based on the number of soft lead balls of a given diameter in one pound. Gauge letters from A to P and gauge numbers from 1 to 50 exist in specification; in reality, only 8-, 10-, 12-, 16-, 20-, and 28-gauges and .410 bore are still made. Although 8-gauge shotshells are not legal for hunting, they remain very popular for industrial applications. Larger numerical gauges and letter gauges have become obsolete.

Note the .410 is described as "bore" not gauge. In terms of gauge, the .410 bore is a 67-gauge. However, the gauge measurement system only goes to 50, so the "bore" designation is correct.

POPULAR SHOTSHELL GAUGES BY SIZE

10-ga 3 1/2"/89 mm

12-ga. 3 1/2"/89 mm

12-ga. 3"/76 mm

12-ga. 2 3/4"/70 mm

12-ga. 2"/51 mm

16-ga. 2 3/4"/70 mm

20-ga. 3"/76 mm

20-ga. 2 "/70 mm

28-ga. 2 3/4"/70 mm

410 bore 3"/76 mm

410 bore 2 1/2"/63.5 mm

Drawing by Author

Body and Head Configuration

Unlike centerfire ammunition, shotshells are all of a single head and body configuration—rimmed and cylindrical.

Some domestic shotshell manufacturers adhere to a voluntary color-coding system to denote shotshell gauge. For example, 12-gauge tubes are red, 16-gauge tubes are purple and 20-gauge tubes are yellow. This system is intended for safety identification to help prevent inserting a smaller gauge shotshell in the chamber of a larger gauge shotgun. The smaller shotshell can fall through the chamber and become lodged in the barrel creating a bore obstruction with catastrophic results if a shell of the correct gauge is then fired. Unfortunately, many shotshell makers do not adhere to a colorcoding system while those who do often bend this convention for sales appeal purposes. And, metal shotshells are not easily or inexpensively color-coded.

The mouth of the tube must be closed with a crimp to prevent the shot charge from spilling out. There are two types of mouth crimp—rolled with a top wad, and folded.

A folded crimp on a plastic tube may be of six segments (hunting loads) or eight segments (target loads). All paper tubes have a six segment fold. For eight segment crimps, the mouth of the tube normally is skived (thinned) to provide a better looking product. Hunting loads do not have skived tube mouths as they do not need it. Folded crimps have several advantages over rolled crimps. Their major advantage is they do not require a top wad. However, folded crimps use up more tube length (typically about 5-7mm) than rolled crimps (typically 3-4mm). This can become a serious problem in volume-hungry loads such as those using steel shot.

Early, shotshells nearly all had a rolled crimp closure with a paper top wad. Rolled crimps fell into disuse as the top wad interfered with pattern quality. Most metal shotshells require a top wad, as they cannot be roll or fold crimped. A rolled crimp is used on all modern slug loads as they do not require a top wad, and it leaves the nose of the slug exposed for identification purposes.

Most shotshells have the shot charge weight and shot size printed on the tube.

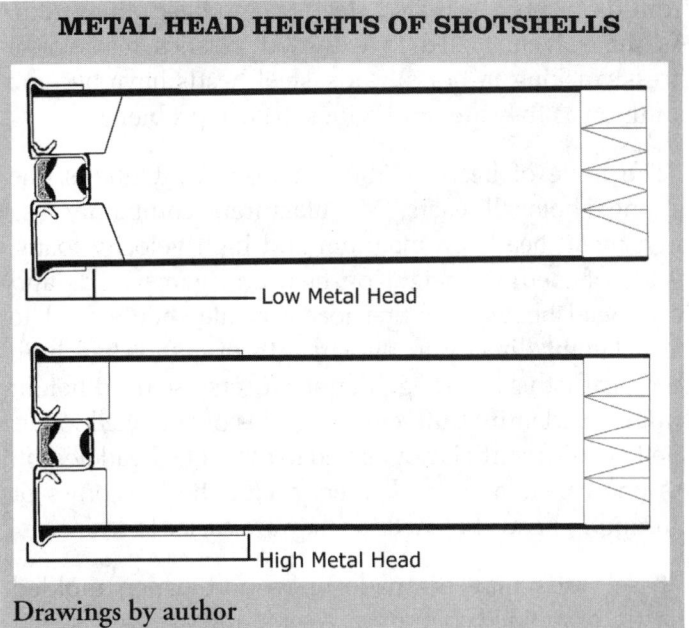

METAL HEAD HEIGHTS OF SHOTSHELLS

Low Metal Head

High Metal Head

Drawings by author

Primers

All modern shotshells use a No. 209 battery cup primer (see Chapter 9: Primer Nomenclature) with the exception of a few monolithic metal shells which use centerfire rifle primers.

Materials

Built-up shotshell tubes may be of extruded high density polyethylene plastic or wound paper. Both plastic and paper tubes are colored. Monolithic shotshell tubes may be of steel, brass, aluminum, zinc, or injection molded plastic. Although drawn brass shotshells were developed in the late 1800s, they have become semi-obsolete due to high cost, special wad requirements, and the advent of cheaper paper and plastic tube shotshells. Recently, shotshells having plated steel tubes have been imported from Russia to indifferent customer response. Aluminum shotshell tubes are rare and seldom seen.

As with centerfire ammunition, considerable efforts have been made to develop a monolithic molded plastic shotshell. These efforts have centered on preventing rim failures during extraction from semi-auto shotguns. Metal disks molded inside the shell, metal rings crimped on the rim and other methods have proven technically successful but sales failures.

Extruded plastic tubes often have shallow ribs on their outer surface while metal and molded or drawn plastic tubes are smooth. Modern paper tube shotshells have smooth outer surfaces, although some early paper tube shotshells had ribbed outer surfaces. In a built-up shotshell with a separate base wad, the bottom rim of the tube is crimped to the head inside the rim.

The metal heads on built-up shotshells may be made

from drawn brass, plated steel, or anodized aluminum. As the solvents used in extruded plastics may cause stress cracking in brass heads, steel heads have become common as they are impervious to such problems.

The issue of head height remains a contentious one among shotshell users. Manufacturers commonly use high metal heads on magnum and high velocity loads, heads of medium height on field and game loads and low metal heads on target loads. While shooters relate head height directly to the strength of a shotshell hull, technically this is wrong. Manufacturers use head height simply to identify different categories of shotshell loads; shell head strength is not related to the metal head height. As one can imagine, reloaders prefer the low brass or aluminum head shotshells as they are easier to resize.

Base wads may be made of wound paper, molded plastic, or molded composite. A separate base wad is held in place by crimping it inside the rim of the metal head. A central flash hole allows the primer flame and gasses to reach the propellant.

SHOTSHELL BASEWAD TYPES

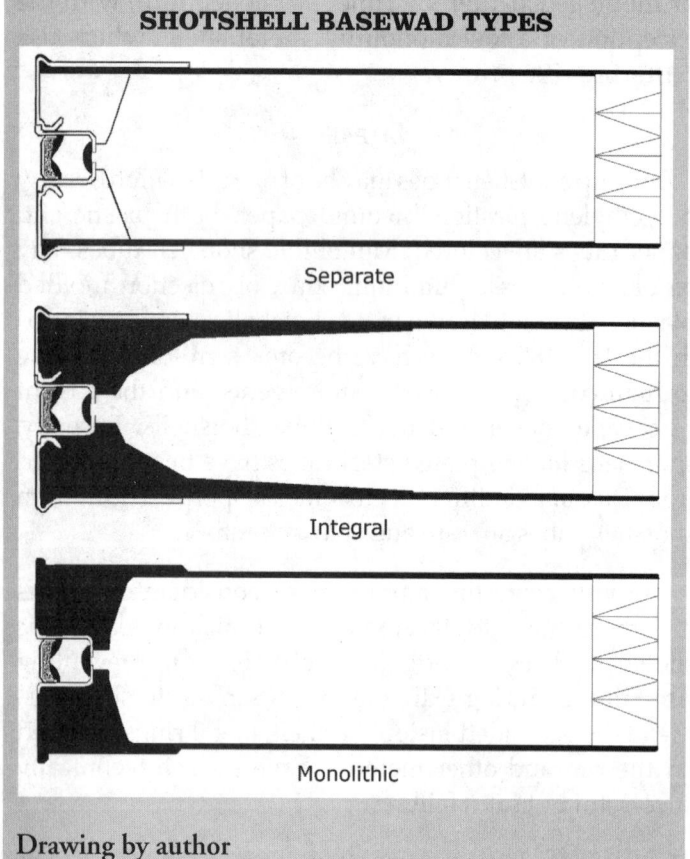

Separate

Integral

Monolithic

Drawing by author

A wad column is functionally a sabot which is launched with the shot charge, then falls away (cleanly it is hoped). There are two types of wad columns—unitary and multi-piece. Within these parameters, wad designs exist in a profusion of different styles and materials.

Historic wad columns have been multi-piece types built up of card disks called nitro wads and waxed felt spacer wads. Nitro wads of different thickness were used on top of the powder charge to seal off the hot propellant gasses and as top wads for shotshells with rolled crimps. The nitro and felt wad columns came in a variety of thicknesses which could be combined to nearly any desired length. The problem with such wad columns was that they were heavy and did not seal the propellant gasses well. In more recent times, the cost of felt became prohibitive for wad column use causing various substitutes such as pressed paper to be used. Plastic over powder wads which were more efficient at sealing replaced nitro cards for that purpose. Shot charges were prevented from scrubbing on the bore surfaces by plastic shot protectors in the form of band-aids or cups. Built-up wad columns are no longer used for shot loads, but are still common in many slug loads.

Most modern shotshells are loaded with unitary wads molded from low density (for lead shot) or high density (for steel shot) polyethylene plastic. Such wads are cheap, light, easy to load, and come in various sizes and gauges. Most have a flanged base for sealing the powder gasses, a cushioned mid-section and an integral shot cup to prevent the pellets from scrubbing on the bore surfaces. Such wads produce better patterns and fall cleanly away after exiting the muzzle. Recent developments in plastic additives have made wad column plastic more biodegradable.

Many plastic wads are color coded as to length and shot charge weight.

SHOTGUN WAD COLUMNS

PRACTICAL

A shotshell wad column is a bore diameter plug made of fiber or plastic which seals the propellant gasses and pushes the shot charge down the barrel.

TECHNICAL

A shotshell wad column is a type of discarding, pusher sabot which performs five functions:

- **It takes up excess space in a shotshell**
- **It seals the propellant gasses**
- **It cushions the shot charge against the forces of acceleration**
- **It pushes the shot charge down the barrel**
- **It protects the pellets from contacting the bore**

After exiting the muzzle, the wad column falls away.

WAD MATERIALS

Wad columns are built up from the following types of materials:

• Hard card disks of .030", .075", and .135" thickness

These wads are used as over powder wads to seal powder gasses and as over shot wads to seal rolled crimps. They are now obsolete for both purposes. Their main use today is as spacers and as pusher disks under rifled slugs.

• Hard clear plastic disks .080" thick

These wads were used to seal rolled crimped shotshells. They are now obsolete.

• Fiber cushion filler wads of felt, cork, or fiber of 1/4", 3/8", and 1/2" thickness

Fiber cushion wads served to take up space inside the shotshell and cushion the shot pellets during acceleration. Different thicknesses could be combined to achieve nearly any desired wad column height. Often they were waxed to prevent bore leading. Felt and cork are seldom used today as they are heavy and have become expensive.

Fiber wads still are used in some modern loads in combination with plastic. Fiber wads are very heavy and increase recoil.

• Low density injection molded plastic

This is the material typically used for the modern one-piece wad column for lead shot. A pouch on the front protects the pellets from contacting the bore. Low density plastic is light weight, tough, and flexible. As such, it is an excellent material for wad columns. Plastic wad columns are made in different lengths to accommodate different shot charge weights.

• High density injection molded plastic

Steel and hard composite shot pellets require extra protection from bore contact which low density plastic wads cannot offer. For this application, high density plastic wads are used to prevent scrubbing. These wads have no cushion in their base as the very hard pellets are not deformed during acceleration. The bottom of the shot pouch is convex to prevent stacking.

WAD COLUMN TYPES

There are four types of wad column:

• Traditional

This type is a combination of card and fiber cushion wads. It is now obsolete.

• Semi-traditional

During the early days of plastic wads in the late 1950s, these hybrid wad columns were common. As one-piece plastic wads were not yet available, they allowed wad column length to be adjusted easily by combining a plastic gas sealing wad and plastic shot pouch with traditional card and fiber cushion wads. While better than traditional wad columns, these hybrids were heavy and are now obsolete.

• Semi-modern

Another advance over semi-traditional wad columns, this type is also a hybrid which combines a multi-function one-piece modern plastic wad with a traditional fiber cushion wad spacer. This combination allowed variations in wad column height before the advent of modern, one-piece plastic wads. This type of wad column is semi-obsolete.

• Modern

Modern injection molded plastic wad columns are specifically designed for a given shot charge weight and gauge. Nearly all plastic wad columns are of one-piece construction incorporating a shot pouch, cushion, and gas sealer. Within brands, they are often color-coded. These wad columns are light, flexible, and tough. Adding 5% corn starch to their mixture substantially increases biodegradability.

OTHER WAD MATERIALS

• Grex Fillers

Grex is a finely ground plastic used as a buffer/filler in some premium lead shot loads. The grex particles serve as an additional cushion for the shot pellets during acceleration and provide a noticeably better pattern for improved performance. In some loads, grex has been used as a cushion wad.

• Spreaders

A spreader is sometimes added to a lead shot charge to open the pattern faster than the normal choke would produce. Spreaders normally take the form of a paper X inserted vertically into the shot charge. Layered card disks are another variation.

• Inserts

Smaller gauge card or fiber cushion wads are sometimes used as inserts in the shot pouch of plastic wads columns to take up excess space.

• Two-piece plastic wad designs

Plastic two-piece wads have been used in factory loaded shotshells. The lower gas sealing part of the wad is molded of high density plastic with a stalk on the front face that can be rolled to different lengths and collapses on acceleration. The upper portion of the wad is a plastic shot pouch. A variation on this concept combines a high density gas sealing bottom with an H-shaped top to form an air chamber to cushion the shot.

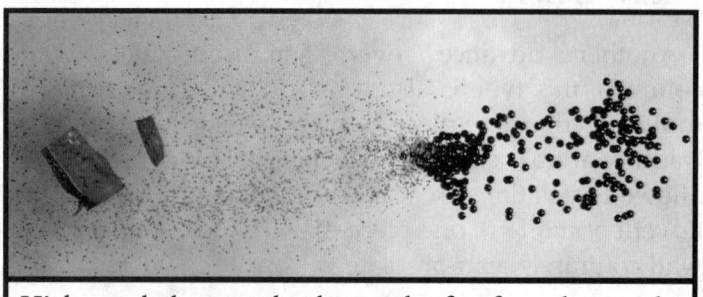

High speed photograph taken twelve feet from the muzzle, of a traditional wad and lead shot string.

DEFINITION OF A SHOTGUN PELLET

PRACTICAL

A shotgun pellet is a small round ball made of lead or other material, fired from a shotshell. The pellets create a random pattern in flight.

SCIENTIFIC

A shotgun pellet is a spherical, metal body that is bulk-loaded into a shotshell. After being accelerated down the barrel by the wad column and exiting the muzzle, the pellets continue by their own inertia and are randomly distributed within the pattern "cone" during their flight.

PELLET TYPES

Shotgun pellets may be divided into two types based on the materials from which they are made:

TOXIC	NON-TOXIC
• Lead	• Bismuth alloy
	• Soft steel
	• Soft composites
	• Hard composites

In an effort to reduce lead poisoning of migratory waterfowl, lead shot has been banned in many areas. In such areas, non-toxic shot must be used. Approved non-toxic materials include: bismuth alloys, soft steel, soft composites, and hard composites.

MATERIALS

Shotgun pellets are made from the following materials:

SHOTSHELL WAD CONFIGURATIONS

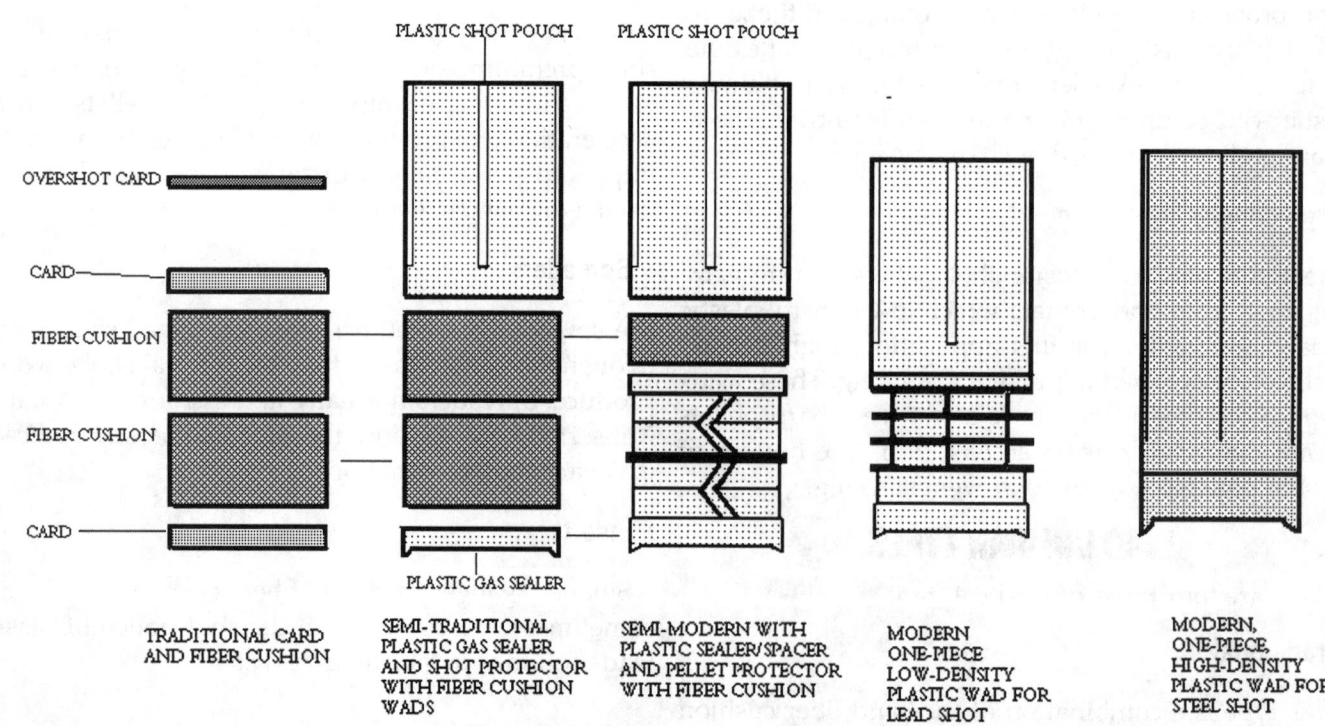

OVERSHOT CARD

CARD

FIBER CUSHION

FIBER CUSHION

CARD

PLASTIC SHOT POUCH   PLASTIC SHOT POUCH

PLASTIC GAS SEALER

TRADITIONAL CARD AND FIBER CUSHION

SEMI-TRADITIONAL PLASTIC GAS SEALER AND SHOT PROTECTOR WITH FIBER CUSHION WADS

SEMI-MODERN WITH PLASTIC SEALER/SPACER AND PELLET PROTECTOR WITH FIBER CUSHION

MODERN ONE-PIECE LOW-DENSITY PLASTIC WAD FOR LEAD SHOT

MODERN, ONE-PIECE, HIGH-DENSITY PLASTIC WAD FOR STEEL SHOT

1. Lead alloy

Lead alloy is the classic material for making shotgun pellets. Most lead pellets are hardened to some extent by adding antimony. Hard pellets produce better patterns. Small pellets may contain up to 6% antimony while larger pellets may contain up to 3% antimony. Lead shot may be copper- or nickel-plated. Environmental concerns have caused lead shot to be banned for hunting migratory waterfowl.

2. Bismuth alloy

Bismuth is a metal about 83% the density of lead. As a shot pellet, bismuth is alloyed with about 2% cobalt to prevent shattering. Although slightly more expensive than lead, bismuth shot is non-toxic allowing it to be used in areas where lead shot is banned. Unlike steel pellets, bismuth shot does not require hardened chokes, and can be loaded with lead shot wad columns.

3. Soft steel

This material remains the most popular cost effective non-toxic substitute for lead shot. It is more expensive than lead and substantially lighter. Steel also requires special high-density plastic wad columns and hardened chokes to prevent damage to shotgun barrels. Steel shot may be plated with copper, nickel, or zinc to prevent corrosion.

4. Soft composites

Soft composite pellets are made from proprietary mixtures of powdered metals such as copper, tin, iron, and tungsten held in a polymer binder. Such pellets can be loaded with lead shot wads and do not require high density wad columns or hardened chokes. The density of such pellets approaches that of lead, but they are more expensive.

5. Hard composites

Hard composite pellets are sintered from mixtures of powdered metals such as copper, iron, steel, tungsten, and tin. Such pellets equal or even exceed the density of lead pellets, but are very expensive. Hard composite pellets must be loaded with steel shot wad columns and fired only through hardened chokes.

6. Other materials

Other materials which have been tried without success for making shotgun pellets include: zinc (toxic), copper (toxic and expensive), tin (expensive), plastic (too light), and tungsten (hard and expensive). Rubber has been used successfully for less-than-lethal buckshot and slug loads.

CONFIGURATIONS

Shotgun pellets may be divided into two broad categories according to size:

- **Small shot or bird shot-diameters from 0.050 to 0.230 in.**

- **Buckshot- diameters from 0.240 to .360 in.**

Smaller sizes of shot are numbered from 12 (the smallest) to FF (the largest). Buckshot sizes begin with No. 4 Buck (the smallest) and end with OOO (the largest). For a complete listing of shot sizes and the number of pellets per ounce, see Chapter 96: Reference Material.

Experience has shown that each pellet size has a range of practical uses.

See Chapter 36: Shotshell Recommendations for further information.

Popular Shot Sizes

SHOT SIZES	12	9	8½	8	7½	6	5	4	2	BB
PELLET DIAMETER										
(IN.)	.050	.080	.085	.090	.095	.110	.120	.130	.150	.180
(MM)	1.27	2.03	2.16	2.29	2.41	2.79	3.05	3.30	3.81	4.57

BUCKSHOT SIZES	No. 4	No. 3	No. 2	No. 1	No. 0	No. 00	No. 000
PELLET DIAMETER							
(IN.)	.24	.25	.27	.30	.32	.33	.36
(MM)	6.10	6.35	6.86	7.62	8.13	8.38	9.14

DEFINITION OF A SHOTGUN SLUG

PRACTICAL

A shotgun slug is a single spherical or elongated projectile fired from a shotgun.

SCIENTIFIC

A shotgun slug is a spherical or elongated, self-stabilized or spin-stabilized, full-caliber or sabotted sub-caliber projectile that, after being accelerated down a shotgun barrel, continues in motion by its own inertia.

SLUG MATERIALS

Modern shotgun slugs may be monolithic or built-up. Monolithic slugs and built-up slug cores are made of the following materials:

1. **Lead alloy**
2. **Copper alloy**
3. **Bismuth alloy**
4. **Composites (frangible)**
5. **Steel (military)**
6. **Plastic (for law enforcement)**
7. **Rubber (for law enforcement)**
8. **Soft materials (for law enforcement)**
9. **Zinc (for kiln guns)**
10. **Tungsten alloys (military)**

CATEGORIES

Shotgun slugs are used for:

1. Hunting at close ranges (100 yards or less)

2. Law enforcement

3. Military

4. Industrial (for kilns)

TYPES OF SHOTGUN SLUGS

1. Full Bore Type

2. Subcaliber Sabot Types

3. Hybrid Types

PARTS OF A FULL BORE SHOTGUN SLUG

- Tip
- Ogive
- Body
- Base
- Sabot
- Wad column

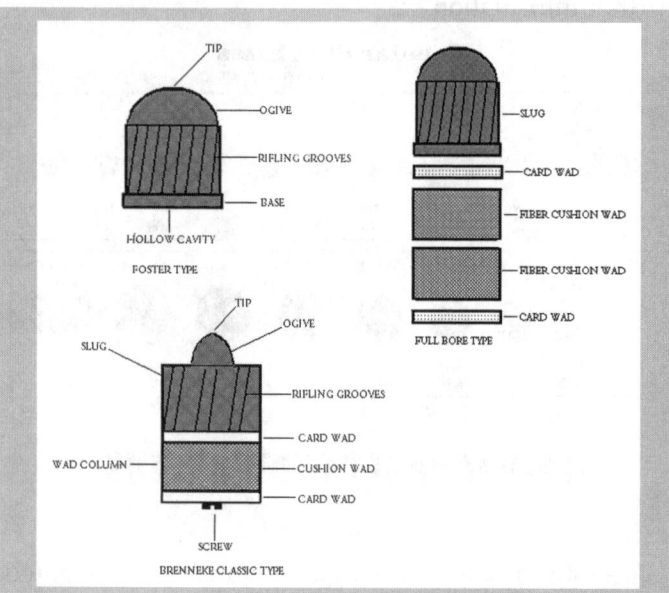

PARTS OF A SUBCALIBER SABOT SHOTGUN SLUG

- Tip
- Ogive
- Body
- Base
- Sabot
- Wad column

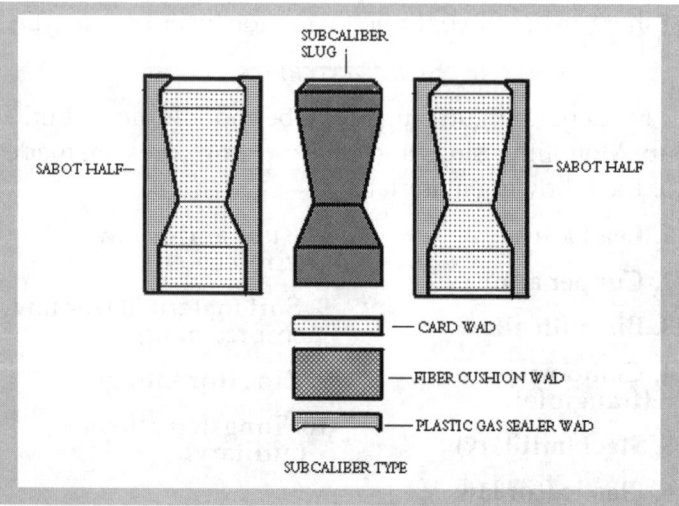

Shotgun slugs are much heavier than rifle bullets, consequently their weight is often expressed in ounces such as 1 ounce (437.5 grains) or 1 ¼ ounce (547 grains). The muzzle velocity of shotgun slugs is about 50% less than that of a typical rifle bullet. However, as shotgun slugs are intended for use only at close ranges, slug weight and diameter make up for the lack of muzzle velocity. Recoil from shotguns slugs is heavy.

SLUG CONFIGURATIONS

TIP	OGIVE
1. Solid	**1. Round nose**
2. Hollow point	**2. Flat nose**
3. Tipped	**3. Pointed**

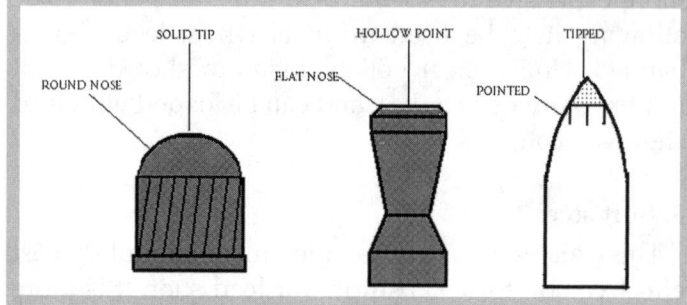

BODY	BASE
1. Smooth	**1. Hollow**
2. Rifled/grooved	**2. Flat**
3. Tapered	**3. Posted**
4. Hollow	

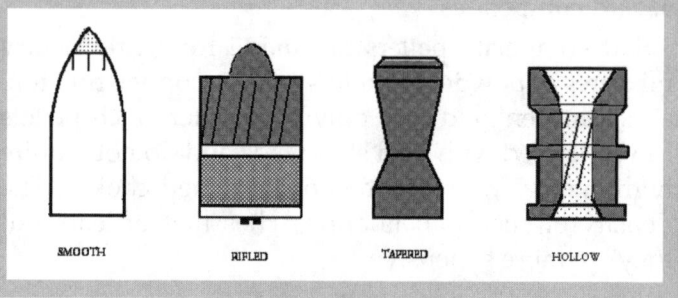

SLUG STABILIZATION

Shotgun slugs are stabilized in flight by one of two methods:

- **Self-stabilization**

- **Spin-stabilization**

1. Self-stabilized full-bore slugs

This is accomplished by locating the center of mass in front of the center of aerodynamic pressure in much the same manner as a badminton bird. This may take the form of a simple nose heavy or U-shaped design (Foster) or a sophisticated design which keeps the wad column and slug together in flight (Brenneke).

Sloped surfaces or pre-engraved rifling grooves on the slug body may be used to supplement stabilization by inducing slow rotation. Experience has shown that the ideal groove angle is about nine degrees.

Although the slow rotation is not sufficient to completely stabilize the slug, tests have shown that accuracy is improved.

2. Spin-stabilized full-bore slugs

Sufficient spin to stabilize a full-bore shotgun slug can be imparted by rifling in the barrel, or aerodynamically.

Most manufacturers of rifled shotgun barrels use a rifling twist rate of 1 turn in 24-, 26-, or 28". For best accuracy, special full-bore slugs must be designed for this application.

Aerodynamically spin-stabilized shotgun slugs are designed to be fired from smooth bore barrels. They depend on the airflow striking angled surfaces on the slug body or wad to impart the necessary spin. Methods of doing this include tubular slugs with interior fins, finned wad columns or slugs, and grooved/angled surfaces.

3. Self-stabilized, sub-caliber, sabot slugs

This type of slug is designed to be fired from a smooth bore barrel. The slug is of similar self-stabilizing design to the others described above, only sub-caliber in diameter. Aerodynamic pressure causes the sabot to fall away after exit from the barrel.

4. Spin-stabilized, sub-caliber, sabot slugs

Slugs of this type must be fired from a rifled barrel. They depend on the rotation imparted by the rifling in the barrel to strip the sabot from the slug after it exits the muzzle and to impart sufficient spin for stabilization. The sub-caliber slugs offer a much better coefficient of drag than full-bore slugs thus extending effective range by 50% (to 100 yards).

Rifled shotgun barrels offer better accuracy with full-bore slugs and with sub-caliber sabot slugs especially designed for a rifled barrel. Smooth bore barrels work best with self-stabilizing shotgun slugs designed for them. It is safe to fire either type in either barrel, however accuracy will be very poor with such combinations and cannot be recommended.

WAD COLUMNS

All shotgun slugs use wad columns to seal the propellant gasses which push the slug down the barrel. Traditional wad columns used stacks of heavy card and felt wads under the slug. These gave way to plastic over powder wads with fiber spacer wads on top. Today, all but the most basic shotgun slugs have plastic wad columns and plastic sabots.

Wad columns may be of the discarding type or the fixed type. The discarding types fall away from the slug after exiting the muzzle. Fixed types remain attached to the slug. The advantage of this type is that the weight of the wad column is added to the weight of the slug which substantially increases striking energy with no interior ballistic weight penalty.

FULL BORE SHOTGUN SLUG TYPES WITH WAD COLUMNS

FOSTER   DIABOLO   ROUND BALL   BLONDEAU   STRELA

BRENNEKE-OLD   BRENNEKE-NEW   BRENNEKE K.O.   REMINGTON BUCKHAMMER   LIGHTFIELD HYBRID

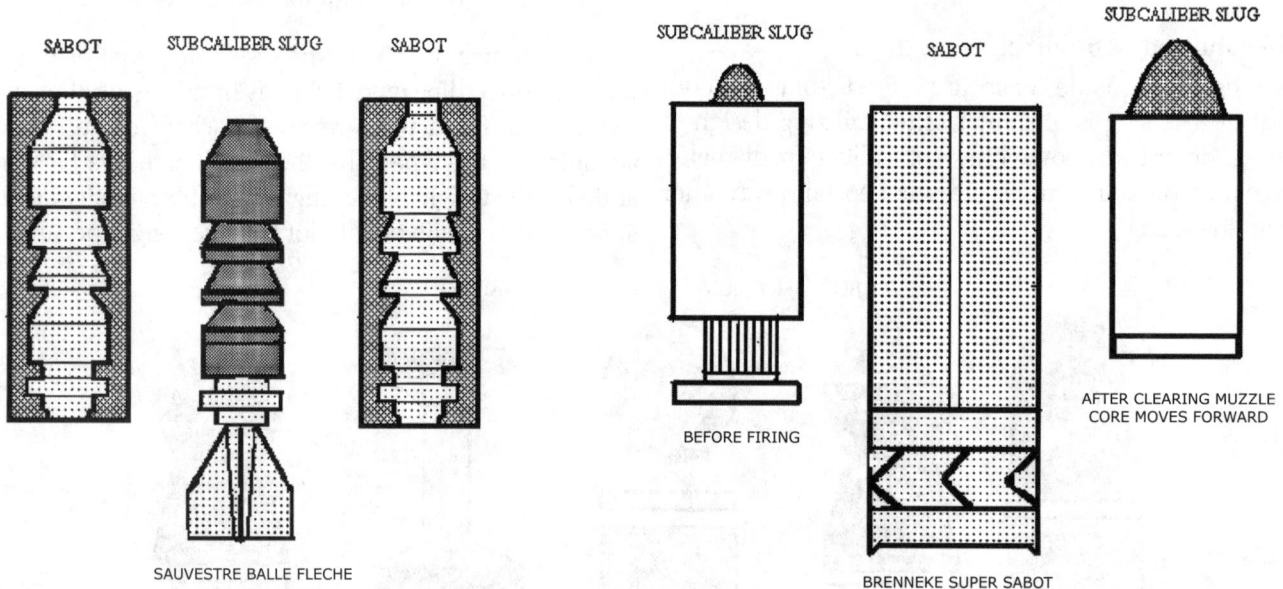

SHOTGUN SLUG SUBCALIBER SABOT TYPES

SABOT HALF   SUBCALIBER SLUG   SABOT HALF   SUBCALIBER SLUG   SABOT

CARD WAD

FIBER CUSHION WAD   FIBER CUSHION WAD

PLASTIC GAS SEALING WAD   PLASTIC GAS SEALING WAD

BRI SUBCALIBER SLUG   HORNADY SST SUBCALIBER SLUG

SHOTGUN SLUG SUBCALIBER TYPES

SABOT   SUBCALIBER SLUG   SABOT   SUBCALIBER SLUG   SABOT   SUBCALIBER SLUG

BEFORE FIRING   AFTER CLEARING MUZZLE CORE MOVES FORWARD

SAUVESTRE BALLE FLECHE   BRENNEKE SUPER SABOT

RELOADING

Most shooters simply discard fired cartridge cases. Fortunately for shooting ranges, scrap metal dealers regard cartridge brass as prime material and will pay premium prices for it. Shooting ranges usually provide containers dedicated for collecting empty cartridge cases which may be sold to reloaders or recyclers. In the field, courtesy to the land owner demands that hunters pocket their fired cartridge cases for later disposal.

Some centerfire cartridge cases and shotshells can be reloaded. In general, a brass centerfire cartridge case can be reloaded up to 40 or more times depending on the type of load used (light loads extend case life). Nickel plating normally reduces the reloading life of revolver cartridge cases substantially. Paper tube shotshells will survive three or four reloading cycles while plastic tube shotshells can be reloaded ten to fifteen times on average.

About 5-7% of shooters are hand loaders. A major reason for reloading is economy, especially for competitive target shooters for whom ammunition can be a major outlay. However, reducing overall cost is not the only reason for handloading. Many centerfire rifle shooters reload to squeeze that last little bit of accuracy from a firearm or to develop loads not sold by ammunition manufacturers. While handgun cartridges account for the largest number of reloaded centerfire cartridges, most of this is done by commercial reloaders for resale through gun stores and shooting ranges.

SECTION III – HISTORY OF AMMUNITION DEVELOPMENT
CHAPTER 11 : HISTORICAL PERSPECTIVE

CHAPTER 11 HIGHLIGHTS:

- ALCHEMY (850-1300)
- ART (1301-1503)
- SCIENCE (1504-1650)
- STASIS AND FORMALITY (1651-1807)
- INVENTION (1808-1885)
- SMOKELESS (1886-1913)
- WAR, PEACE, WAR (1914-1945)
- THE MODERN ERA (1946-2000)
- THE FUTURE (2001-2100)

Mankind has always been fascinated by objects that fly through the air. Beyond human curiosity, there was a practical reason for such interest. If man could harness the power of such objects, enemies could be kept at a safe distance.

In the early mists of human history, an inquisitive *homo sapien* picked up a rock and threw it. He soon learned that by throwing rocks, he could strike enemies at a distance. This led directly from the Mark I throwing rock, to the spear and the bow. Yet, all these weapons suffered from one major flaw—they depended on human muscle for power. Thus, their range and effectiveness were limited.

The discovery of gunpowder in China around 850 BC forever changed the human condition. From that beginning, man instinctively understood that gunpowder offered a powerful new source of energy if he could find ways to harness its potential. Because man did not understand how or why gunpowder behaved as it did, development lurched forward slowly in fits and starts.

Although gunpowder was not invented for guns and the first guns did not appear until 400 years after gunpowder had been discovered, man's instincts proved correct.

In the future, weapons would no longer depend on human muscle for power, and personal defense would no longer depend on size or strength. It is this instinct that has driven the 1,150 year development of firearms, the longest thread of technological development in recorded history.

> *"The invention of gunpowder hath quite altered the condition of Martial Affairs over the world by sea and by land."*
> - Robert Boyle, Anno 1664

ALCHEMY (850-1300)

FROM CHINA TO MELILLA

Alchemy is a medieval pseudo-science driven by speculative philosophy. Alchemists used purification, observation, and systematic trial and error to study how the five basic elements—earth, metal, wood, fire, and water—interacted in various ways. Substances with unique properties such as sulfur, the stone that burns, were of particular interest. Western alchemists focused on attempting to transmute base metals into gold. Chinese alchemists' principal aim was to discover an elixir to infinitely prolong life.

China and its culture were already old when gunpowder was discovered there about 850 BC. While the name of the man who discovered gunpowder has been lost to history, his discovery was almost certainly the accidental result of alchemy experiments. Due to gunpowder's propensity to burn quickly when exposed to heat, the Chinese called gunpowder the "fire drug."

Fire Drug

The principal goal of Chinese alchemists was to find an elixir for eternal life. As many such elixirs contained saltpeter, they burned vigorously when exposed to heat. The Chinese labeled these "fire drugs" for this reason. For centuries, this label was applied to gunpowder in China as guns had not yet been invented. Below are listed the traditional Chinese characters for fire drug and gunpowder.

火 fire   藥 elixir (drug)   槍 gun   粉 powder

火藥 fire drug   槍粉 gun powder

A more important question is what did the Chinese do with their discovery? In China, gunpowder found its first use as a pyrotechnic in the form of fireworks. These were used for frightening demons and celebratory spectacles.

Contrary to Western opinion, the Chinese were very interested in gunpowder for military purposes. Their first efforts in this field were incendiary devices. By 904 AD, the Chinese were using gunpowder explosives in warfare and by 1268 they had developed mortars with metal tubes. By the 14th century, the Chinese had developed a portable incendiary device called the "fire-lance". This was a metal tube on the end of a wooden pole. The tube was filled with gunpowder to provide the incendiary effect. As gunpowder continued to improve, firing a projectile soon replaced the incendiary purpose of these devices. In Europe, such devices were called "hand cannons."

Early hand guns were little more than a metal tube lashed to a wooden pole and fired with a match (left). Compare this to the sophisticated handguns we have today (right).

Left: Tunis drawing/Right: US Army photo, Pg. 246 ROTCM 145-30 Individual Weapons and Marksmanship July 1958

Around 1200, the formula for making gunpowder traveled from China to Europe. The first reference to gunpowder in Western civilization comes from the legendary Greek writer Marcus Graecus who recorded a formula for gunpowder in *Liber Ignum* (Book of Fires) written about 1225.

> *"Take 1 lb. of native sulphur, 2 lbs. of linden or willow charcoal, 6 lbs. of native salpetre, which three things are very finely powdered on a marble slab. Then put as much powder as desired into a case to make flying fire or thunder."*
> - Marcus Graecus, *Book Of Fires*, Anno Circa 1225

The first written record of gunpowder in Europe occurred in 1234 when an English monk named Roger Bacon, recorded the formula in his manuscript *De Nulliate Magiae* (The Nullity of Magic).

> *"But however of stone of Tagus (saltpeter), take seven parts, five parts of young hazelwood (charcoal) and five parts vapor of pearl (sulfur), and so you will make thunder and lightning…"*
> - Roger Bacon, *De Secretis Operibus Artis Et Naturae Et De Nulliate Magiae*, Anno Circa 1248

Technical efforts to harness the power of gunpowder now gained momentum in both China and Europe. By the late 1200s, the first guns appeared in China as small cannon. In 1259, cannon were used to defend the city of Melilla in North Africa.

At this time, gunpowder was made by crushing each of the three dry components (potassium nitrate, charcoal and sulfur) separately using a mortar and pestle. When they reached a flour-like consistency, the dry powders were then ground together by hand or in a stamping mill, a dangerous process. This type of gunpowder was weak, erratic, and left heavy deposits in the bore. For good reason, it was called "serpentine".

With the serpentine boom and smoke from the first cannon shot at Melilla, gunpowder's age of alchemy closed. It had taken 409 years to get this far.

ART (1301-1503)

FROM SERPENTINE TO CORNED POWDER

To the medieval mind of 1300, guns were diabolical instruments of the devil and gunners his executive agents. Gunpowder was the devil's meal and the sulfurous, foul smelling smoke the devil's breath. Repeated attempts by the Catholic Church to stem the spread of gunpowder went unheeded. It might be magic, but medieval military men knew a good thing when they saw it.

At this time, gunpowder was a rare and exotic substance which few people knew how to make and fewer still understood how to handle safely. Early guns were small cannon with limited power and short range. Because guns plainly had military potential, in 1300 the tactics for their use were quickly being developed. And just fifty years later, gunners were firing cannon at the walls of castles and gunners on castle walls were firing back with their own cannon. In large part, these developments were due to Edward III, King of England and a strong proponent of guns. It was he who placed the first cannon on ships in 1340 and he who took two small cannon to the Battle of Crecy in 1346.

Origin of the Word "Cannon"

The modern English word "cannon" is derived from the Latin word "canna" which means reed. As guns were closed at one end and open at the other, they closely resembled a reed. In French, this became "cannone" and in Middle English "canon". In German, the word is derived from "canneken" meaning a drinking vessel.

European monarchs of this age could not afford to maintain a trained body of full-time, professional gunners. As a result, gunners organized into companies of professional mercenaries selling their expertise to whoever could pay them. To maintain their value, gunners closely guarded their trade craft.

Patron Saint of Shooters

Santa Barbara (Saint Barbara) is the patron saint of shooters. According to legend, Barbara was born in the third or fourth century AD into a wealthy family living in what is now eastern Turkey. To protect his very beautiful daughter, Barbara's father locked her in a tower. Looking out her window, Barbara saw the beautiful trees and animals. Realizing these were the handiwork of God, Barbara became a Christian. When her father found out, he fell into a rage and killed her. Shortly after, he was struck by lightning and killed during a storm. The just retribution of the lightning served as the basis for Barbara to become the patron saint of shooters. In her memory, a feast day is celebrated every December 4.

Typical employment for mercenary gunners included besieging or defending cities, castles, and fortresses. Before gunpowder, sieges often took years. Now, the large cannon of the professional gunners could demolish fortress walls in a matter of hours. As metal was scarce and expensive during this era, mercenary gunners normally claimed a defeated city's church bells which they used to cast more cannon.

Nobles could no longer challenge the king's authority. Monarchs could hire mercenary gunners to bring nobles quickly to heel. The feudal system began to disintegrate and kings began to build nations with themselves holding authority. In 1435, King Charles VII of France hired gunners Jean and Gaspard Bureau to create the world's first full time professional artillery organization in monarchial service.

By 1300, Chinese "fire lances" and European hand cannon had become smaller, lighter, and more powerful. However, despite these improvements, effective range was still limited and they remained clumsy, difficult to aim, and slow to load. Given the variable quality of gunpowder during that era, ignition and firing was a 50-50 proposition.

Origin of the Word "Gun"

Geoffrey Chaucer initiated the use of the word "gonne" into Middle English vernacular in the late 1300s during his tenure as an administrator for King Richard III of England:

*"As swift as a pillet out of a gonne
When fire is in the pouder ronne."*
- Geoffrey Chaucer, *House of Fame b. ii*, Anno circa 1373

Improvements to hand cannon came quickly with the aim of making them the central focus of infantry tactics. Handling improved dramatically when the crude pole was replaced by a wooden stock designed to fit the shooter's shoulder. Ballistics improved by lengthening the barrel and using high quality gunpowder made especially for the purpose. The addition of a matchlock ignition system substantially improved the odds for a successful shot. By the early 1400s, the results of these improvements became the arquebus, a 25 lb. gun designed to be loaded and fired by a single soldier. The arquebus was designed initially for defensive fire from fortress walls. For this type of shooting, it was fitted with a wall hook to steady the shooter's aim. By replacing the wall hook with a wooden stick on which to rest the fore-end, an arquebus could be fired in the field. While the arquebus was replaced in European military service in the mid 1600s, the Chinese continued to employ such guns well into the late 19th century by continually updating them.

ARQUEBUSIER AND HELPER

This arquebusier is in the act of firing his matchlock. Note the smoking match in the match lock. The helper is molding lead balls, a task normally done before a battle.

When loaded with small bits of metal or rocks, early

hand cannon and fire lances were effective only at very close range. Obviously, a single heavier projectile would increase the effective range. As quarrels (small finned bolts) launched from crossbows had proven very effective, it seemed logical to fire these from guns. However, the finned bolts had to be wrapped in leather so as to be supported in the bore snugly. This made loading cumbersome and did nothing to improve accuracy.

Eventually, the best projectiles were found to be cast lead balls just under bore diameter. Casting these balls provided a reliable size and weight. While the effective range of these balls was short, their lethality was such that no armored knight was safe from an arquebusier or musketeer. This development caused the feudal social system to unravel.

At this time, gunners had scant understanding of ballistics. For example, what path did a ball travel after it left the barrel and what forces acted on it? Most gunners intuitively believed a ball traveled in a straight line after leaving the barrel, then dropped to the ground at the end of its travel. A young Italian math teacher named Niccolo Tartaglia disagreed, asserting that a ball traveled along a curve at all times. Tartaglia conducted various experiments in an unsuccessful attempt to decipher the laws governing such motion. In the end, he failed. Galileo Galilei took up the challenge in the late 1500s.

However, Galileo also failed as he did not take into account the air resistance on the ball.

Origin of the Word "Arquebus"

In German, "hake" means hook and "busse" means gun. Used together, a "hakebusse" or "hakenbusse" describes a heavy, but portable, matchlock gun with a hook under the barrel. In use, the hook was slipped over the edge of a wall to steady the gun when fired. In French, the word became "harquebuse" further shortened to "arquebus". The word arquebus entered Middle English in the late 15th century.

About 1430, a new method of incorporating the components of gunpowder using water was developed. Called the "wet" method of incorporation, this process was safer and produced a consistent, cleaner burning, more powerful propellant. In 1450, it was determined that different sizes of gunpowder granules allowed better control of the burning rate. This resulted in a second technical innovation in gunpowder manufacture called "corning". After the dry cake of powder was crushed, sieves were used to separate the various grain sizes. The grain sizes were then matched or blended according to the type of firearm they would be used in.

Dumpling and Corn

In 1400, powder makers found that by adding a small amount of water when incorporating the three ingredients, they could form the dough-like powder into loaves, balls or mounds. After drying, these powder "knollen" or "dumplings" could be safely transported to the battle site and ground into powder there thus saving considerable effort.

However, when the powder "dumplings" were ground up, gunners found that leaving chunks or kernels of different sizes in the powder significantly increased the burning rate often resulting in burst barrels. Such "corned" powder burned three times faster than the best serpentine. Experiments showed that by using various sizes of powder kernels, the burning rate of the powder could be varied to suit the requirement. The result was dubbed "corned" powder.

These two technical achievements combined to elevate the hand held gun to a central role in military service for the first time in 1503 when small arms made their first significant military impact at the Battle of Cerignola in Spain. From then on, small arms development seized center stage in the march of firearms technology. In 203 years, gunpowder had progressed from a diabolical instrument of the devil to the central focus of military tactics. Gunnery was becoming a science.

SCIENCE (1504-1650)

FROM CHIVALRY TO THE FLINTLOCK

Renaissance gunnery blended science with art. The science was composed of a complex mix of chemistry, metallurgy, engineering, physics, mathematics, ballistics, and tactics. Tempering this, the gunner's art provided the ability to interpolate between the known and the unknown borders of science, relying on experience and judgment. Acquiring these attributes required study, experience, and training. This is why, throughout history, gunners have considered themselves as a professional elite quite apart from regular military personnel.

What it Takes to be a "Gunner"

"A gunner ought to be sober, wakefull (sic), lusty, hardy, patient, prudent and a quick-spirited man, he ought also to have good eyesight, a good judgment and perfect knowledge to select a convenient place on the day of service, to plant his ordnance where he may do the utmost hurt unto enemies and be least annoyed by them…"
- Nicolo Tartaglia, *La Nova Sciento Invento*, Anno 1537

Hoisted On His Own Petard

A petard is a squat iron container filled with gunpowder. During a siege, petards would be exploded against gates and doors in an effort to blow holes in them. It took a brave man to place a petard properly, light the fuse and take cover before the explosion. Of course the defenders made stringent efforts to prevent him from doing this, making petard placement a risky business. Often, the individual placing the petard would be wounded by the defenders after lighting the fuse thus preventing him from escaping the blast. In this manner, he was "hoisted on his own petard".

The word "petard" was adapted from the French word of the same spelling meaning "to break wind, or to fart". Shakespeare first used the phrase in Hamlet.

The nobility blamed gunpowder for the demise of chivalry. However, the real causes were the societal changes brought on by gunpowder. Firearms put into the hands of commoners a lethal equalizer. In turn, this reduced the importance of chivalric hand-to-hand combat. Equipping soldiers with firearms was so expensive that only kings could afford it, thus speeding up unraveling of the feudal system.

In 1586, the invention of the paper cartridge significantly advanced the technology of ammunition. Prior to this, arquebusiers and musketeers carried pre-measured charges of powder in small wood or bone containers fastened to their belt. To load an arquebus, the soldier removed the tightly fitting top of the container and poured the powder charge carefully down the barrel. Next, he dropped a lead ball down the barrel and seated it firmly against the powder charge using his ramrod. After priming the ignition system, he was ready to fire once again. An experienced arquebusier could fire two or three shots per minute.

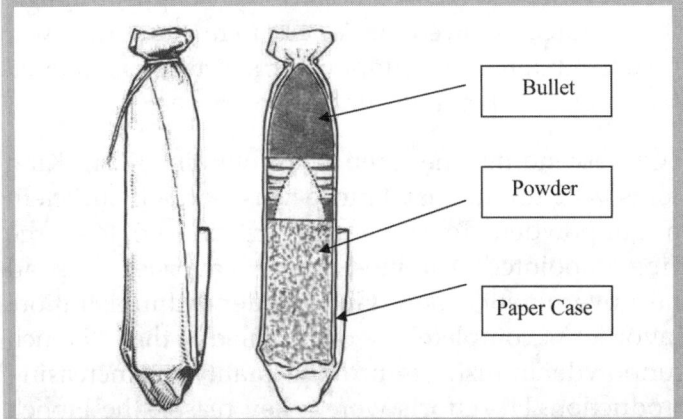

This is a paper cartridge typical of the type used during the American Civil War. In use, the soldier tears the back end open and pours the powder down the barrel followed by the bullet. The paper is discarded.

The paper cartridge substantially reduced the time needed for reloading which increased the rate of fire. A paper cartridge consisted of a pre-measured charge of powder and a bullet in a paper container. The container was closed at both ends and the paper was treated to resist moisture. To load, the shooter tore off the end of the cartridge holding the powder, poured the powder down the barrel and followed this with the bullet. The paper was then discarded or rammed home on top of the bullet to prevent it from rolling out the end of the barrel. Paper cartridges were rapidly adopted by most European armies with the Swedish Army of Gustavus Adolphus leading the way in the early 1600s.

In 1610, Marin Le Bourgeoys in France invented the flintlock. This simple, inexpensive, and reliable mechanism revolutionized ignition systems. By 1650, flintlocks were in common use.

When the Age of Science ended in 1650, gunpowder had become the key instrument kings used to demolish the feudal system and build nations with strong central governments. It was an instrument of social change that made men equal, but also made the battlefield a more deadly place. Gunnery had become equal part art and science. This period began with the wheel lock and ended 147 years later with the paper cartridge and flintlock.

STASIS AND FORMALITY (1651-1807)

FROM THE FLINTLOCK TO FULMINATE—SLOWLY

Although a well trained musketeer with a flintlock could fire a shot every fifteen seconds, the inherent inaccuracy of the smoothbore musket gave soldiers only a 50-50 chance of hitting a man-sized target at 100 yards. For this reason, the bayonet was considered the principal infantry weapon and military tactics changed to accommodate this. Massed ranks of infantry were marched to within 50 feet or even less of the enemy before firing one or more volleys. They then charged the enemy survivors at bayonet point. As volley fire was not aimed at individual targets, muskets had no sights. Officers commanded: Ready! Level! Fire!

Chivalry now transformed itself into a courteous military ritual with numerous formalities being exchanged before the fighting began. These theatrical forms of military etiquette were intended to civilize the slaughter that had reached unprecedented levels.

A reliable source for saltpeter now became critical to national security. Most European governments reacted by regulating or participating in gunpowder manufacture.

Charcoal and sulfur were abundant. The real problem

was to find a secure source of potassium nitrate (saltpetre). European monarchs chartered "saltpetre men" to collect the substance from farmers' cellars, barns, stock pens, latrines, and from whatever other source they could find. The saltpetre men had a blanket license to enter private property to search for or dig saltpetre. When large deposits of saltpetre were found, for example in India, the mineral was treated like gold.

What Do Demons Prefer?

By the early 1500s, rifled barrels were common. Shooters immediately noted that rifled barrels were more accurate than smoothbore barrels. Why? No one knew. One popular theory held that demons rode the profane spinning balls fired from rifled barrels and guided them to their target.

In March 1547, the Sharpshooters' Guild of Mainz, Germany decided to put the matter to a test. They prepared 20 profane (unblessed) lead balls and 20 sacred, thrice blessed silver balls having a small cross molded on their surface. Everyone knew that demons could never ride a sacred silver ball. All balls were then fired from the same rifle at a target 200 yards away. The issue was decided when 19 of the profane balls were demon-guided to the target, but none of the silver.

Gunpowder played a major role in the American Revolution. In 1774, Lieutenant General Thomas Gage, supreme British military commander in North America, quickly realized that supplies of gunpowder would be critical to the rebel cause as there were no gunpowder mills in the colonies. Accordingly, Gage set into motion a plan to bring all gunpowder supplies in the colonies under the control of the Crown. On September 1, 1774, Gage sent a company of Redcoats to the Boston powder storage house where they removed 250 barrels of powder and two pieces of artillery. Next, Gage confiscated all gunpowder supplies held by Boston merchants. In October of that same year, King George issued a decree banning all imports of gunpowder into the colonies.

Why Paul Revere Rode 50 Miles

"The British are coming!"
- Paul Revere 1774

Why did Paul Revere ride fifty miles through a raging snow storm to warn the citizens of Portsmouth, New Hampshire that the British were coming? General Thomas Gage, the Supreme British Military Commander in North American, knew that the American rebels were desperately short of gunpowder. Gage sent a British Army column to Portsmouth to secure the 100 barrels of gunpowder stored at Fort William and Mary. Revere's warning gave the 400 local militiamen time to haul away the sorely needed powder before the British column arrived.

In response, the rebels seized the military gunpowder stores in Newport, Providence, and New London. Gage then ordered a secret operation in which British soldiers would stage a surprise raid on Concord to seize the large stocks of military gunpowder held there. When the British column reached the town, they were confronted by the rebel militia. Shots were fired. Now the insurrection began in earnest.

Sound Advice at Bunker Hill

"Don't fire until you see the whites of their eyes!"
- Col. William Prescott at the Battle of Bunker Hill, June 17, 1775 during the Revolutionary War

---

Col. Prescott's words were composed of pure desperation. His men only had enough gunpowder to fire two volleys. This was clearly not enough to defend his position, but Prescott was determined to make the British pay dearly to take the hill. Prescott admonished his men hold their fire until the range was so close they could make every shot count with their smoothbore muskets. About 50 feet or so is the distance at which the whites of an enemy's eyes can be seen. Prescott's first volley sent the British reeling down the hill. After regrouping, the British attacked the hill again. Another devastating volley at close range from Prescott's men drove the British back again. The third British charge up the hill forced Prescott's men to abandon their position as they were out of powder and without bayonets. However, the British Army suffered over 1,100 casualties to seize Bunker Hill.

By August 1775, General Washington reported that he had less than one half pound of gunpowder per man and could anticipate no further shipments. The only way to solve the problem was to import gunpowder. In this effort, France and the Netherlands were happy to oblige. These sources allowed the American revolutionary war to succeed, although gunpowder shortages hampered Washington's operations until the very end.

On ascending the French throne in 1774, King Louis XVI found that France was not self-sufficient in gunpowder. To solve this critical problem, the King appointed Antoine-Laurent Lavoisier to head the government's new Gunpowder Administration. Lavoisier completely overhauled the French gunpowder industry, improving quality and increasing production. His efforts were a key reason the French government was able to supply gunpowder to the American rebels.

By 1789, revolutionary fever struck France. As the social turmoil grew, Bernard de Launay, the Governor of the Bastille in Paris, ordered gunpowder stored in the nearby arsenal moved into the fortress. On July 14, hundreds of armed French citizens gathered near the Bastille intent on seizing the gunpowder stored there. After a desultory siege lasting most of the day, de Launay surrendered the fortress to the mob. Lavoisier welcomed the French Revolution and continued to serve France. However, in 1793 during the Terror, he was arrested and went to the guillotine.

On March 13, 1800, E.C. Howard, an amateur scientist and avid experimenter with explosives published a report detailing his discovery of a new explosive substance—fulminate of mercury.

Meanwhile in Scotland, Rev. Alexander Forsyth became frustrated when the flash from the priming pan on his flintlock shotgun gave waterfowl sufficient warning to flare before his gun fired. Resolving to do something about this, Forsyth began experimenting with various impact sensitive ignition materials. Forsyth found that a mixture of potassium chlorate, charcoal, and sulfur in a small metal container held near the flash hole provided ignition when struck by the hammer. Forsyth obtained a patent on his idea in 1807 (the pill lock). Forsyth's idea was so far superior to previous ignition systems that his system quickly became very popular with British hunters.

An Old Adage

"Pistols for two, champagne for one."
- Old saying about duels

In 1800, Pierre Samuel du Pont de Nemours and his son Irenee´ emigrated from France to America, thus single-handedly bringing his adopted country's persistent shortage of gunpowder to an abrupt end. Du Pont and his family were experts in the manufacture of gunpowder. By 1804, the E.I. du Pont de Nemours & Company was making gunpowder in Delaware.

After 156 years of status quo, Forsyth's invention propelled firearms technology forward at breakneck speed.

INVENTION (1808-1885)

A FAST TRACK FROM THE
PERCUSSION CAP TO SMOKELESS POWDER

Three developments during first half of this period allowed firearms technology to take several giant steps forward. These were: the percussion cap, the combustible cartridge, and the conical bullet.

Building on Forsyth's work, an American, Joshua Shaw, invented the percussion cap in 1814. Shaw

placed the priming compound in a soft metal cap that was placed on the nipple of the lock system. When the hammer struck the cap, the priming compound ignited and sent flame and hot gas down a passage igniting the propellant. Shaw's invention dramatically improved reliability, reloading speed, and ballistic performance. European armies were not slow to recognize the advantages of percussion ignition. The British Army adopted percussion in 1839, the French and American in 1840, and the Austrian in 1841. In short order, all earlier ignition systems quickly became obsolete.

Building on the development of percussion ignition, two French inventors advanced the art further when Flobert developed the BB cap in 1835 and LeFaucheux the pin fire cartridge in 1836. Dr. Edward Maynard, an American dentist, followed with his tape primer system in 1845 and Christian Sharps patented his disc primer system in 1852. A milestone was reached in 1866 when Col. Hiram Berdan patented the primer that bears his name in the U.S. and Col. Edward Boxer patented the primer bearing his name in England in 1869.

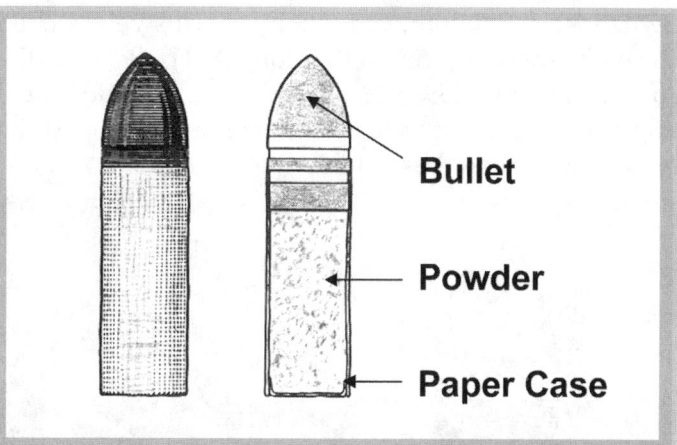

Bullet

Powder

Paper Case

A combustible cartridge considerably decreased the amount of time needed to reload a rifle. In use, the entire cartridge was simply rammed down the barrel and fired. The paper was treated so as to burn up on firing.

Circa 1812, the combustible cartridge appeared. Basically, the combustible cartridge was an improvement on existing paper cartridges. Paper, linen, or skin was highly nitrated, making it very flammable. The nitrated material was then formed into a tube closed at one end. After coating with varnish or collodion to resist moisture, the tube was filled with a pre-measured charge of gunpowder. Finally, a bullet was glued into the open end of the tube, sealing the cartridge. In use, the entire cartridge was simply rammed down the barrel and fired. However, paper cartridges remained fragile and susceptible to moisture. A water resistant self-contained cartridge was sorely needed. Case technology was creeping up on just such a cartridge. In 1812, a Swiss inventor named M. Pauli added a metal head with a primer to a combustible cartridge case making the first self-contained centerfire cartridge. In 1847, M. Houllier, a French gunsmith, patented a metal cartridge case with various types of primer. A milestone was reached in 1854 when Horace Smith and Daniel Wesson patented the first successful self-contained metallic cartridge—the .22 Short rimfire.

Percussion caps were made in two types, a flanged type called the top hat for rifles (left) and a smaller type with corrugated sides normally used for handguns (right).

In 1828, elongated bullets were trialed in Vincennes, France. These and other tests conducted later in Sweden, Switzerland, Belgium, and Saxony conclusively proved the ballistic superiority of the elongated bullet over the round ball. In 1849, the French Capt. Claude Minié engraved his name in history when he developed the elongated, hollow-base bullet called the Minié ball.

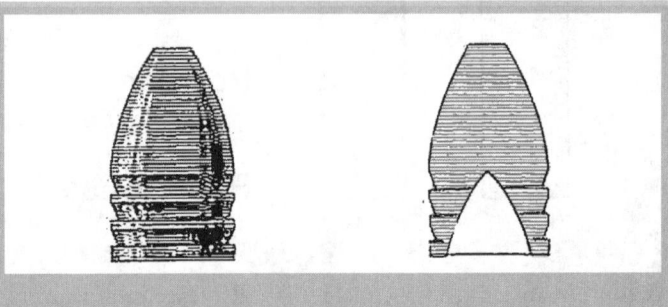

A typical .58 caliber Minié ball. Note the hollow base.

An historic event occurred in 1840 when the Prussian Army adopted the needle gun and its self-contained cartridge invented by Johann Nicholas von Dreyse. These cartridges had a 13mm diameter, 530 grain, lead bullet held in a papier-mache sabot. The bullet and 70 grain powder charge were held in a combustible paper cartridge. A small cavity in the base of the sabot held the primer. When the trigger was pulled the firing pin pierced the powder charge to strike the primer which ignited the propellant. The needle gun cartridge was a direct ancestor of today's metallic cartridge.

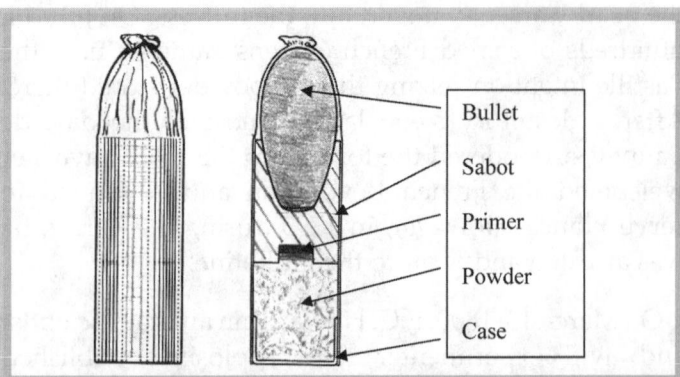

The Dreyse Needle gun cartridge was a major milestone in cartridge development. It was one of the first self-contained cartridges. The bullet was held in a paper-mache sabot with the primer in the base. The entire assembly was held in a combustible cartridge case which proved too fragile for rough use.

The period from 1855 to 1865 saw more different types of cartridges developed than any other period in history. In 1856, Smith & Wesson patented the Volcanic bullet, George W. Morse patented the inside primed cartridge, Ellis and White patented a cup-primed cartridge, and Burnside developed the first cartridge having an inside lubed bullet.

The patent race continued with Allen's lip fire, Williamson's "teat fire", and Crispin's annular rimfire.

During this period, developments in propellant chemistry occurred that would revolutionize firearms and ammunition technology. These efforts aimed to develop an entirely new form of propellant powder based on nitrated cellulose. Progress was slow. M. Braconnot in France discovered guncotton in 1832; in 1846, Christian Friedrich Schoenbein in Switzerland attempted to adapt guncotton to firearms as a propellant. His efforts proved unsuccessful as the substance was too unstable. In Italy that same year, Ascanio Sobrero nitrated glycerin to form nitroglycerin. While both of these substances were far too explosive to use as a propellant, they pointed the way forward to an energetic, hard material that could be formed into grains. In 1867, Schultze powder made of nitrated wood fiber was developed in Germany, but proved unsuccessful.

In 1885, a French chemist named Paul Vieille engraved his name in the history books by developing a way to plasticize gun cotton with collodion and solvent, which then could be extruded, cut into grains, and dried to form a non-porous white material. The result was Poudre B (for "blanche," or white, in French) in 1886, the world's first smokeless powder. Poudre B was more powerful than black powder and cleaner burning. It was to cause a revolution in firearms and ammunition design.

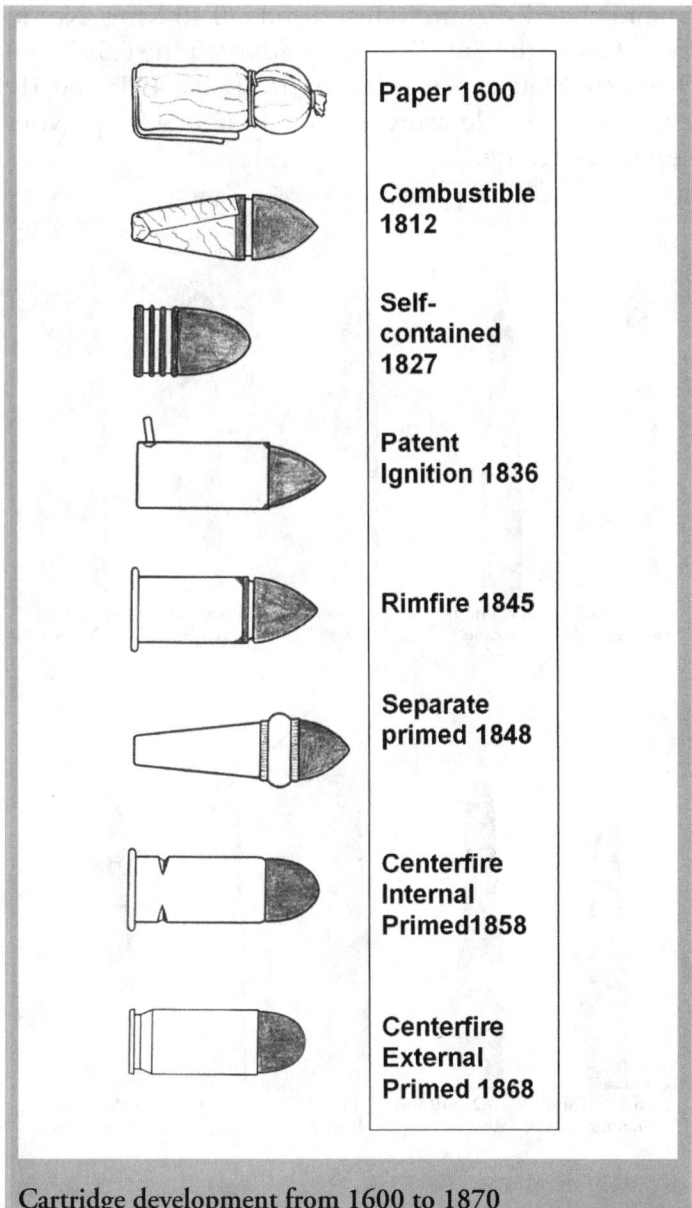

| Paper 1600 |
| Combustible 1812 |
| Self-contained 1827 |
| Patent Ignition 1836 |
| Rimfire 1845 |
| Separate primed 1848 |
| Centerfire Internal Primed 1858 |
| Centerfire External Primed 1868 |

Cartridge development from 1600 to 1870

Not to be outdone, Alfred Nobel, the inventor of dynamite and explosives king, developed and patented double-base smokeless powder in 1887. The British responded with Cordite. The race was on. In the short span of 77 years, ammunition technology progressed from the percussion cap to smokeless powder.

All the technical pieces were now in place for the firearms and ammunition we take for granted today. Firearms technology would never be the same.

SMOKELESS (1886-1913)

Everything changes overnight

Smokeless powder created a revolution overnight in firearms and ammunition design. As smokeless powders and traditional powders were not interchangeable, a clear vernacular distinction had to be made between the two types for safety reasons. In short order, the word "gunpowder"

came to refer to the new smokeless propellants while the ancient propellant formula became "black powder".

Smokeless propellant brought many ballistic advantages. It was three times more powerful than black powder, so muzzle velocity and effective range could be increased substantially. Smokeless powder was also cleaner burning, less corrosive, and less hygroscopic. Smokeless powder did produce a small amount of smoke when fired, however the amount was insignificant when compared to black powder. These ballistic advantages did not extend to muzzle loading firearms for which early smokeless powders were unsuitable.

Although cartridges designed for black powder could be loaded with smokeless propellants, cartridges designed for smokeless powders could not be loaded with black powder. For this reason, during this period sporting cartridges were divided into two categories—classic black powder calibers and modern smokeless calibers. As new smokeless powder calibers were introduced, production of many black powder calibers ended. As black powder nomenclature systems would not work for smokeless propellants, ammunition manufacturers had to create a new nomenclature system for smokeless powder cartridges.

Higher muzzle velocities offered by smokeless powder favored bottle necked cartridges with elongated bullets of smaller bore diameter. While many black powder cartridges used a bullet of .40 caliber or larger to control powder fouling, smokeless powder cartridges could be designed for bullets of six, seven, or eight millimeters in diameter. This revolutionized both firearms and ammunition design. Cartridges could now be smaller and lighter and still offer superior ballistic performance.

Smokeless powder cartridges also required new bullet designs. When unjacketed lead bullets were fired at smokeless powder velocities, rifle bores quickly fouled with lead deposits. Jacketed bullets were required to take full advantage of the high velocities offered by smokeless powders. In 1874, Lt. Col. Bode of the Prussian Army developed a rifle bullet with a lead core and a copper alloy jacket. In 1881, Col. Edouard Rubin of the Swiss Army perfected a jacketed bullet with a lead core and a clad steel jacket which was subsequently adopted for the 7.5x55mm Schmidt-Rubin cartridge. In Norway, the Norma brothers perfected the manufacture of 6.5mm jacketed rifle bullets, after which they established a new facility in Sweden.

The ballistic advantages offered by smokeless propellants were quickly appreciated by armies and sportsmen. Not surprisingly, armies were the first to get smokeless propellants and ammunition. Building on Paul Vieille's work, the French Army was the first to field smokeless powder ammunition with their 8x50Rmm Lebel cartridge in 1886. However, the 8x50Rmm Lebel was not a true smokeless powder design. To speed up the development process and save money, the French modified their existing 11mm Gras black powder cartridge case by necking it down to 8mm. This resulted in a rimmed necked cartridge with an unusually sharp double body taper. Because the 8x50Rmm Lebel cartridge and its smokeless propellant conferred a significant tactical advantage on the French Army, both were considered top secret.

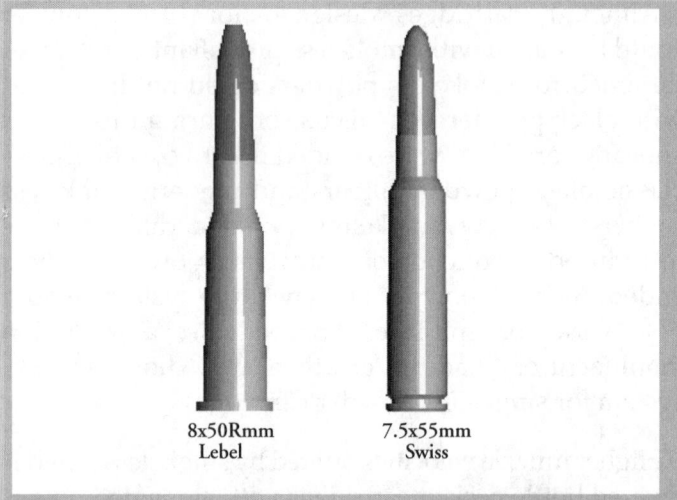

The French 8x50Rmm Lebel was the first cartridge loaded with smokeless propellant. To save money and time, the Lebel cartridge case was a modification of an earlier French black powder cartridge. The 7.5x55mm Swiss cartridge was the first cartidge intentionally designed for smokeless propellant.

Of course, Germany soon got wind of the new French cartridge and propellant. As the German Army also was working on a new smokeless powder cartridge, the French breakthrough became a matter of national security. The Germans then did the obvious; they paid a French soldier to desert and bring his new rifle and ammunition with him!

The smokeless powder military race was now on. Every army in Europe fielded new smokeless powder cartridges and infantry rifles designed to fire them as quickly as possible. Next off the mark in 1889 were the Swiss with their 7.5x55mm Schmidt-Rubin cartridge, the first to be designed from the outset for smokeless powder. By 1890, the .303 British, 8x50Rmm Austrian Mannlicher, 8x57mmJ Mauser, and the 7.65x54mm Belgian Mauser entered in service. In 1891, the 7.62x54Rmm Russian and 6.5x52mm Italian Carcano were adopted followed in 1892 by the 6.5x53Rmm

Mannlicher, 7x57mm Mauser, and .30-40 Krag. Not to be outdone, the Swedish Army adopted the 6.5x55mm Swedish Mauser cartridge in 1894. By 1905, nearly every major world army had a new smokeless powder service cartridge.

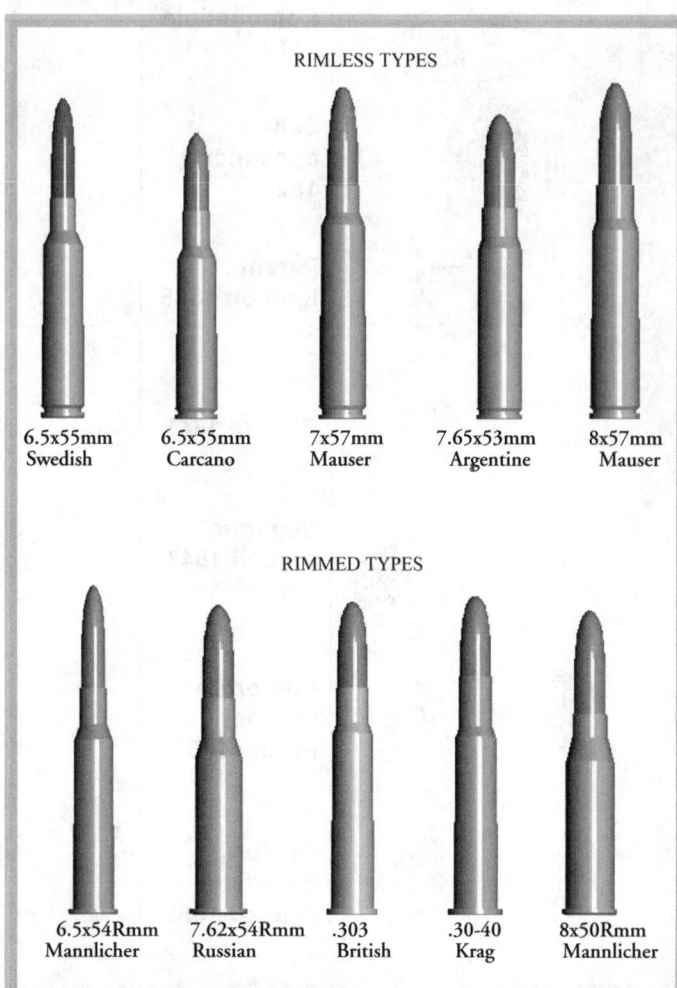

RIMLESS TYPES

| 6.5x55mm Swedish | 6.5x55mm Carcano | 7x57mm Mauser | 7.65x53mm Argentine | 8x57mm Mauser |

RIMMED TYPES

| 6.5x54Rmm Mannlicher | 7.62x54Rmm Russian | .303 British | .30-40 Krag | 8x50Rmm Mannlicher |

These calibers became the first wave of smokeless powder cartridges along with the 8x50Rmm Lebel and 7.5x55mm Swiss. The cartridges in the upper row are rimless designs while those in the lower row are rimmed types. Efforts to replace the rimmed designs with rimless types in the early 1900s were interrupted by World War I.

Most First Wave smokeless powder cartridges had heavy round nose bullets with cupro nickel-clad steel jackets.

Smokeless powder made machineguns practical for the first time. Hiram Maxim made the most of this development by designing machine guns in the new service calibers which he sold all over the world, beginning with Britain and Germany. Few military minds were able to grasp the enormity of this development before 1914.

After 1900, smokeless propellants began to enter the

commercial ammunition market in increasing quantities. Of course, first up were smokeless powder loadings for the most popular black powder cartridges. During this time, ammunition makers introduced the first commercial cartridges designed for smokeless powder. Examples of these include such stalwarts as the .30-30 Winchester, .303 Savage, .35 Remington and 7.63 Mauser.

Most of the new smokeless powder cartridges were loaded with round nose bullets having jackets of nickel-clad steel as the technology to make a pointed jacketed bullet was not mature. For example the French 8x50Rmm Lebel fired a round nose bullet weighing 231 grains and the German 8x57mmJ cartridge fired a similar bullet weighing 220 grains.

In the late 1890s, the French Army established the Gavre´ Commission to study the exterior ballistics of artillery projectiles. From this data, they ascertained that a pointed boat-tail bullet for the 8x50Rmm Lebel infantry cartridge would offer ballistic performance superior to the existing round nose type. As a jacketed bullet with a point was not yet feasible, the French adopted a swaged solid bronze bullet weighing 198 grains called the "Balle D" in 1898. The German Army followed suit in 1906 with their 152 grain "S" (spitzer) bullet with a cupro nickel-clad steel jacket. These developments quickly made round nose bullets semi-obsolete. However, many of the smaller countries were very slow in changing to a spitzer bullet despite the obvious advantages.

In the short space of 28 years, ammunition technology had been revolutionized by the introduction of smokeless powder. In turn, smokeless propellants drove advances in cartridge case design, bullet construction, metallurgy, and interior ballistics. For military service, black powder had become obsolete in the fifteen year span from 1885 to 1900. As increasing numbers of new smokeless powder sporting cartridges were introduced, it became increasingly obvious that the days of black powder-loaded sporting ammunition were numbered.

The German Navy Leads The Way

Contrary to popular perception, the famous Luger P.08 pistol was adopted by the German Navy in 1904-05, several years before the German Army followed suit in 1908.

Many people expected smokeless propellants to revolutionize military tactics as well. They were very wrong. While armies had adopted smokeless powder ammunition, as well as new rifles and machine guns, they did not adopt new tactics. In 1914, when World War I broke out, European armies still employed massed infantry tactics from the Napoleonic era. The result was a slaughter the likes of which the world had never seen.

WAR, PEACE, WAR (1914-1945)

FAST, SLOW, FAST AGAIN

By 1900, most armies realized that smokeless powder would allow them to adopt semi-automatic infantry rifles to replace their bolt-action designs. For this purpose, rimless military cartridges offered many advantages over rimmed designs. Those first wave countries which adopted smokeless powder cartridges with a rimmed configuration, namely France, England, and Austria, would need new rimless cartridge designs. Recognizing this, France and England began developing such cartridges around the turn of the century. However, progress was slow and World War I intervened before either could field such weapons. As a practical measure, they had to fight World War I with their existing cartridge designs.

The German Army replaced their round nose 8mm rifle bullets with lighter weight pointed bullets in 1906. This was a giant ballistic step forward as such bullets offered substantially flatter trajectory, higher retained velocity, and more striking energy than the blunt bullets they replaced. Britain and the U.S. quickly followed suit.

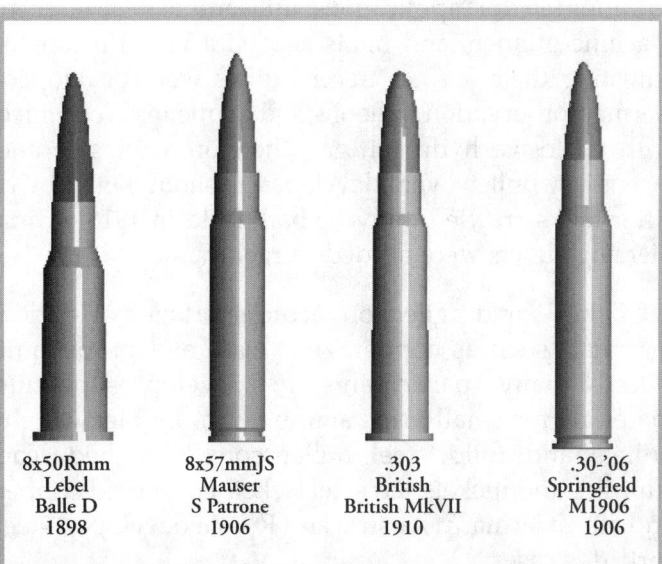

| 8x50Rmm Lebel Balle D 1898 | 8x57mmJS Mauser S Patrone 1906 | .303 British British MkVII 1910 | .30-'06 Springfield M1906 1906 |

By 1906, the rush was on to adopt pointed bullets to replace the round nose designs. The French were first with the "Balle D" in the 8x50Rmm Lebel. Next were the Germans with their 8x57mmJS and the U.S. with the .30-'06 Springfield. Others saw no immediate need to update and stuck with the round nose profile.

None of the participants were prepared for World War I. Military ammunition stocks were totally insufficient and ammunition expenditures substantially exceeded the wildest predictions. Even working three shifts per day seven days a week, government arsenals were unable to meet the demand for ammunition. Commercial manufacturers soon switched to war production. Demand still exceeded supply. In desperation, many warring nations contracted with non-combatant countries for military ammunition. The U.S. was one of these. England, France, Russia, and others let contracts to American commercial ammunition manufacturers for huge quantities of military ammunition. The U.S. stayed out of World War I until 1917. When the U.S. did enter the War, she had learned nothing from the early war contracts. The American Army was acutely short of everything, particularly ammunition. Fortunately, the French and British were able to help out at this point.

When World War I began, infantry rifles and machine guns fired full metal jacket bullets designed in accordance with guidelines agreed to during two Geneva Conventions. The purpose of such Conventions was to make war more humane. Accordingly, they banned the use of bullets designed to cause "undue human suffering". Specific examples of types to be banned in this respect were: explosive, poisonous, expanding, and incendiary.

However, the demands of war required new types of ammunition for applications unheard of before then. Machine gunners and pilots needed a visual means of adjusting their fire, so tracer bullets were developed. German observation balloons and zeppelins were filled with explosive hydrogen gas, therefore explosive and incendiary bullets were developed to shoot them down. After tanks crawled onto the battlefield in 1918, armor piercing bullets were needed—urgently.

As the War dragged on, acute shortages of critical materials such as copper, zinc, lead, and propellants forced many participants to develop substitute materials for small arms ammunition. Lighter weight bullets and mild steel bullet cores stretched lead supplies and nickel-clad steel jackets conserved copper and zinc. Germany, Austria and Russia developed steel cartridge cases.

World War I was to be "the War to end all wars". Consequently, when the fighting ended in November, 1918, France, Britain, Italy, and the U.S. quickly demobilized their armies, slashed ammunition production, closed armament plants, and stopped research and development on military weapons. Both Britain and France saw no immediate need to replace the millions of existing rifles and cartridges they had on hand. Progress toward a new military cartridge in both countries remained very slow until the mid-1930s when war loomed again. While Britain demurred, France made

a strenuous effort to develop and adopt a new military cartridge. However, it was too late.

When World War II broke out in September, 1939, shortages of small caliber ammunition staged a replay of 1914-1918. Low peacetime ammunition inventories were quickly consumed as military expenditures rose geometrically. Arsenals were placed on a wartime basis running round the clock. Commercial manufacturers switched to military production, and once again, contracts for large amounts of military ammunition were given to U.S. commercial manufacturers. War production quickly made the Depression a thing of the past.

Germany and Russia fought World War II with steel case cartridges and bullets with steel cores to conserve copper and lead. By all measures, this ammunition provided excellent performance. The Germans passed this technology along to the French during the occupation. Italy, Britain, and Japan used brass cartridge cases exclusively during the war years. In 1943, the U.S. experienced an acute shortage of copper. At this time, steel cartridge cases were developed and rushed into full production. While large quantities of steel case ammunition were made, steel case ammunition was not shipped overseas. Rather it was expended for training, practice, qualification, and function testing in the U.S.

In the early 1930s, the U.S. Army began a research program to develop a semi-automatic infantry rifle. These efforts culminated in 1936 with the adoption of the new M1 Garand rifle to replace the Springfield M1903 bolt-action rifle from World War I. Although always in short supply, the M1 Garand gave U.S. military forces a significant advantage in firepower over Axis forces. A new cartridge, the .276 Pedersen, was also developed for the Garand rifle. However, the Army Chief of Staff at the time, Gen. Douglas MacArthur, refused to accept the new cartridge, so the Garand was modified to fire the existing .30-'06 Springfield cartridge.

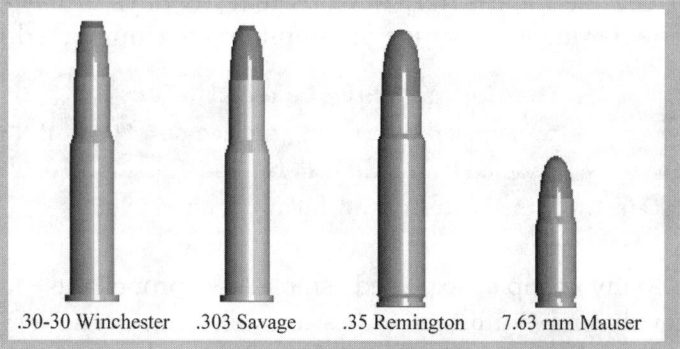

.30-30 Winchester   .303 Savage   .35 Remington   7.63 mm Mauser

The first sporting smokeless powder cartridges came out in the later 1890s. All of the above have become classics and are still in production.

Britain, France, Germany, and Russia fought World War II with the same infantry calibers of military ammunition they used in World War I. Belatedly in the late 1930s, efforts were made by Italy and Japan to adopt new military cartridges and bolt-action rifles to fire them. However, production never met demand, leaving the armed forces of these countries to make do as best they could with old equipment.

The U.S. government once again resolved to stay out of the War. However, President Roosevelt realized that the U.S. could not stand idly by while France, Britain, and other European democracies were swallowed by Germany. Accordingly, in 1940, the U.S. began tooling up production for war under the "Arsenal of Democracy" banner. Lend-Lease soon followed. In this way, the U.S. government was able to begin industrial preparations for war without actually being a combatant. However, when the U.S. entered World War II after the Japanese attack on Pearl Harbor, there were still acute shortages of all military materials including small caliber ammunition.

To ensure an adequate supply of small arms ammunition of all calibers and types, in 1941 the U.S. Army instituted a comprehensive three wave program to dramatically increase production capacity. The first wave maximized production rates at existing government facilities such as Frankford Arsenal and converted existing commercial manufacturers to war production such as Winchester, Remington, Western, Federal, and Peters. In addition, new facilities were built at Lake City, MO, St. Louis, MO, and Kings Mills, OH. The second wave constructed new plants at Des Moines, IA, New Brighton (Twin Cities), MN, and Salt Lake City, UT. The third wave built plants at Milwaukee, WI, Eau Claire, WI, Evansville, IN, Lowell, MA, and Cumberland, MD. In addition, ammunition contracts were let to Dominion Arsenal and Verdun Ordnance Works in Canada. At its peak in 1944, each plant in this massive production base could manufacture between one and two million rounds of ammunition in a 24 hour period.

Germany followed a similar program. At first, German government arsenals went on a war production schedule followed by all German commercial manufacturers and German allies such as Italy, Hungary, Romania, and Bulgaria. Ammunition manufacturers in occupied countries such as Czechoslovakia, France, Netherlands, Norway, Denmark, Belgium, and Poland were co-opted into the German production base. Finally, new ammunition plants were built in Germany and in some occupied territories. Japan expanded ammunition production in Korea and Manchuria as well as in Japan.

In 1943, the German Army began fielding a ground-breaking new military cartridge and a selective fire military rifle. The new cartridge was based on the existing 7.9x57mmJS German military cartridge reduced to 33mm in length and firing a 122 grain spitzer bullet at 2,250 fps. Recoil was substantially reduced and German soldiers could carry a larger number of these short light rounds in the field. Ballistic tests indicated the new cartridge was lethal at typical combat ranges of 500 meters or less.

The Sturmgewehr 44 assault rifle and its cartridge started a revolution in military ammunition design that continues to this day. Prior to this, the technical development of sporting and military cartridges were inseparable. From this point afterward, the development of military and sporting ammunition would follow very different paths of development.

7.92x57mmJS   7.92x33mm
Mauser   Kurz

The 7.92x33mm Kurz (right) was a shortened reduced-power version of the full-power 7.92x57mmJS Mauser cartridge (left). Developed and fielded by Germany during the latter half of World War II, the 7.92x33mm Kurz was the first assault rifle cartridge.

By the end of World War II, the amount of small caliber ammunition expended had reached dizzying numbers. The U.S. alone had manufactured approximately 45 billion rounds of small caliber ammunition. It is estimated that Britain made over 25 billion, Canada over 5 billion, Australia over 5 billion, New Zealand over 2 billion and India over 10 billion. France contributed an estimated 10 billion and Russia over 40 billion. The allied total therefore was about 140 billion rounds. Axis totals were not far behind with Germany's output estimated at 50 billion, Italy at 15 billion, Japan at 20 billion and lesser Axis allies at 15 billion for a total of at least 100 billion.

If You Can't Lick Them, Join Them

At the very end of World War II, Japanese arsenals began manufacturing a copy of the American M1 Garand rifle chambered for the Japanese 7.7x58mm service cartridge. Very few of these rifles were made and, as far as is known, these Japanese M1 rifles were never used in combat.

THE MODERN ERA (1946-2000)

POLITICS AND MARKET DYNAMICS
NOW DRIVE TECHNOLOGY

When World War II finally ended in September, 1945, the Western countries once again quickly demobilized their armies and slashed military ammunition production. However, before the peace dividend could be spent, the Cold War began in 1949 followed by the Korean War in the early 1950s and the Vietnamese War from the 1950s until the early 1970s. At various times during this period, World War II ammunition production facilities such as St. Louis, Lake City, and the Twin Cities were put back into operation.

When the western European nations formed the North Atlantic Treaty Organization (NATO) and the Soviet Union and her satellites formed the Warsaw Pact, the consolidation of military ammunition calibers was finally mandated. While NATO members agreed that a common military cartridge was badly needed, they could not agree on what caliber it should be. Following exhaustive testing, the British put forward their new .280 cartridge. The U.S. disagreed and unilaterally adopted the 7.62x51mm cartridge, a shortened .30-'06 design, leaving the other NATO members no option but to follow along. Much the same happened in the Warsaw Pact when the Soviet Union forced the adoption of their 7.62x39mm cartridge and their older 7.62x54Rmm cartridge on the other Pact members. While these developments did end the proliferation of military calibers, the process left a legacy of bad feelings in many countries.

Regarding The 7.62x39mm M43 Cartridge

"I had nothing to do with design of the 7.62x39mm M43 cartridge. One day when I was working on the AK design, they brought several such cartridges to me and said 'Make it shoot this' and I did so."

- Mikhail Kalashnikov in personal conversation with the author

---

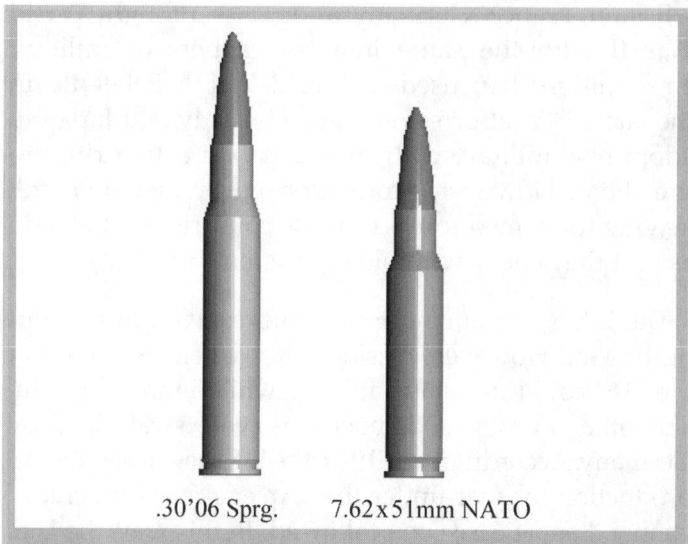

.30'06 Sprg.   7.62x51mm NATO

The 7.62x51mm NATO cartridge (right) is a shortened version of the venerable .30-'06 Spr. (left) with essentially the same ballistic performance. In the mid-1950s, the U.S. adopted the 7.62x51mm cartridge unilaterally, despite opposition from other NATO countries who had developed more modern candidate designs. Under intense U.S. pressure, the 7.62x51mm was grudgingly adopted by NATO in January 1954.

In the early 1960s, this process repeated itself in NATO when the U.S. again unilaterally adopted the 5.56x45mm cartridge while many NATO members were still converting to the 7.62x51mm caliber. After considerable political pressure, NATO grudgingly adopted the 5.56x45mm cartridge as a "second" NATO-standard caliber in the 1980s. The Soviet Union did much the same with their new 5.45x39mm cartridge in 1974.

Pent up demand for sporting ammunition in the 1950s was met by commercial ammunition manufacturers offering existing calibers which picked up where the market had left off in 1939. Shotshell tubes were made of paper. Centerfire pistol calibers were loaded with full metal jacket bullets and revolver calibers were loaded with lead bullets. Centerfire rifle cartridges were offered in pre-war calibers with soft-point hunting bullets. In the early 1960s, plastic shotshell tubes and wad columns began to replace paper and felt. By the end of the 1950s, commercial ammunition makers in the U.S. were beginning to introduce new calibers designed specifically for sporting purposes. This trend continues to this day and has recently accelerated.

However, European commercial ammunition manufacturers have not fared well since World War II. Commercial ammunition production has ended in the Netherlands, Denmark, Norway, and Austria. In Belgium, Sweden, France, and Germany, commercial ammunition production continues, but remains a shadow of former times. Only in Britain, Italy, Spain, the Czech Republic, and Serbia have commercial manufacturers prospered.

In the U.S., the commercial ammunition market matured in the 1970s and 1980s by developing premium rifle, pistol, and shotshell products with superior ballistic performance and a higher profit margin. This was done to offset the impact of low cost rimfire ammunition, light field load shotshells, and surplus military ammunition on the low price end of the U.S. ammunition market where such products have become commodities sold by mass merchants/merchandizers and importers. American ammunition makers' profits on such commodity-type ammunition is very low or nil. Yet the quantities are huge and arguably such products enable shooters on a tight budget to enter the market. For these reasons, ammunition makers must offer these products to compete. However, they must make up the lost profits with premium and other product lines. As mass merchants get out of the ammunition business, the amount of commodity-priced ammunition sold will certainly decrease.

Immediately after World War II, many war time expansion ammunition plants in the U.S. were closed, while others were placed on stand-by. As time passed, more closings eventually left only the Twin Cities and Lake City plants. The Lake City plant remained active to supply the ongoing needs of the U.S. military, while the Twin Cities plant was reactivated for the Korean War and again for the Vietnam War before being closed permanently in the 1980s. A program to maintain government-owned production equipment in commercial manufacturers' production facilities was also phased out about the time the Twin Cities plant was permanently closed.

At this time, the point of no return was reached for commercial manufacturers to produce military ammunition. The occasional low profit military contract requires a commercial manufacturer to retool its production lines at the expense of profitable commercial production. Commercial manufacturers build and hold their share of the commercial market with production machinery and products geared to these requirements. They are no longer willing or able to quickly switch production from commercial to military products. Of course, in a national emergency, commercial ammunition manufacturers would answer the call. However, the changeover to military products would require a considerable period of time.

Research and development of military ammunition has diminished at U.S. military facilities. Government owned ammunition manufacturing plants are designed for production, not research. Commercial ammunition manufacturers have no military research capability. For this reason, research, development and prototyping of military small caliber ammunition is now being done by overseas companies and by the smaller U.S. ammunition companies. Military and commercial types of ammunition are now following separate technological paths of development which may never join again.

During this 54 year period, military ammunition technology changed very little. Primers were still the familiar percussion, Boxer, or Berdan types albeit having a non-corrosive nature. Cartridge cases were still made of drawn brass alloy or steel. Bullets still had a copper alloy or clad steel jacket with a lead alloy and steel core. The only major difference was that the size of the cartridges had decreased, the bullets were lighter and smaller, and the muzzle velocity increased.

Commercial ammunition has entered a golden age in which variety, quality, and performance have increased exponentially. Today, there are more and varied types of sporting ammunition on offer than at any time in history.

During this period, anti-gun groups have made strenuous efforts to stop the technological development of ammunition and/or ban its manufacture and distribution. They have failed because they are trying to swim up a still vibrant 1,150 year old stream of technological development. History will condemn their efforts as a failure, despite their efforts to rewrite it. No one can stop the course of history because they want to opt out.

THE FUTURE (2001- 2100)

THOSE WHO DO NOT PLAN
FOR THE FUTURE WILL NOT HAVE ONE

Contrary to speculation in the popular media, the historical thread of ammunition technological development remains healthy and by no means is at an end. There remains much we do not understand and much left to discover. Gunpowder has not yet given up all its secrets!

Triple base propellants already offer improved ballistics. However, recent advances in chemical research have pointed the way toward new high energy propellants which may enable us to increase muzzle velocities by a quantum leap. This may lead to a sort of smokeless propellant redux. We can expect these new propellants to be very progressive burning so they will deliver more energy to the bullet at normal pressure levels.

Primers are already "getting the lead out". Future primers will be entirely lead-free. The Boxer primer will be with us for many years to come and will eventually replace the Berdan type in most applications. However, both may eventually be replaced by an electrically ignited primer.

Brass remains the best metal alloy for cartridge cases. However, as brass gets increasingly expensive, its use may no longer be justifiable on economic grounds. As we have seen, steel is a technologically mature alternative for cartridge cases. While steel strip is cheap and strong, the production process and tooling to convert it into cartridge cases is more expensive than the brass process.

What about aluminum? Aluminum is lightweight, but expensive and also harder to manufacture than brass. However, aluminum's major shortcoming is a phenomenon called burnout which can occur when an aluminum case head fails and high pressure gas escapes. The result is total destruction of the rifle and serious injury to the shooter. Better cross this one off the list for rifles, although it can be safely used in handgun ammunition.

OK, what about plastic? This is the holy grail of cartridge manufacture.

A cartridge case of molded plastic would be cheap, light, and easy to mold in large quantities. However, plastic will not hold a primer or bullet securely nor will a plastic rim withstand the violent forces of extraction and ejection.

The future centerfire sporting rifle cartridge case will probably be a composite using a metal head of steel or brass and a reinforced plastic body which snaps onto the head. The case neck will be molded around the bullet.

Of course, the plastic shotshell tube is a familiar product to shooters. Modern shotshells have a plastic base wad integral with the side wall and a metal head crimped on the base. The metal head serves no purpose other than to resist the violent extraction forces of semi-automatic shotguns. A completely plastic shotshell would be just fine for single-shot, double-barrel and pump-action shotguns. Perhaps the future shotshell will have a combustible paper tube and a short clad-steel head.

For military ammunition, a caseless cartridge seems the logical future choice. This technology already exists, lacking only civilian and/or government investment for it to proceed. However, military researchers predict that the familiar cartridge case has at least one more life cycle left before a caseless cartridge is adopted. Commercial ammunition will use the cartridge case well into the future.

Bullet making remains an art, albeit one that is in fast forward. In the near future, all bullets will be lead-free. This will be accomplished in sporting bullets by using homogenous bullets made of copper alloys, bullets made entirely of composites, or jacketed bullets with bismuth, tin, or composite cores. Various sophisticated ogive and interior designs will control expansion as needed. Military bullets will have copper alloy jackets with steel and bismuth cores.

Handgun bullets will be made using any of the three methods listed above for rifle bullets. A plastic jacket is also a good possibility for some handgun bullets. Military handgun bullets will have copper alloy jackets with bismuth alloy cores or they may be of sintered homogenous composite construction.

Of course new firearms will have to be developed to take maximum advantage of these new cartridges. Military cartridge design will focus on the Pk or probability of a kill of small caliber, high velocity cartridges. This includes factors such as recoil, trajectory, striking velocity, penetration, energy transfer, accuracy, and others. Commercial sporting ammunition will focus on hunting with reliable penetration, bullet expansion, and accuracy.

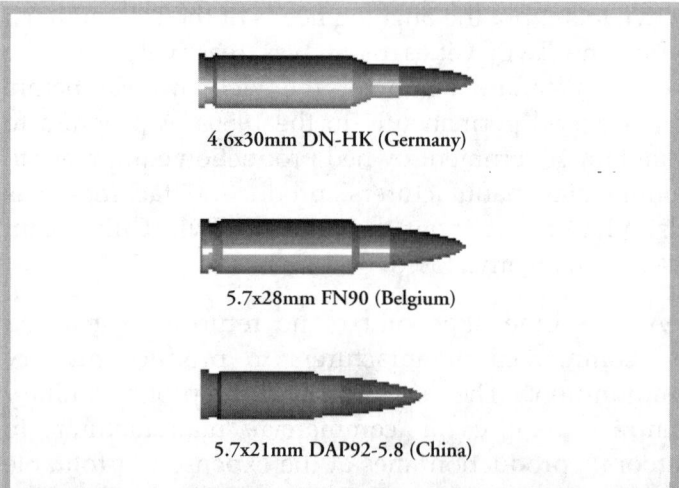

4.6x30mm DN-HK (Germany)

5.7x28mm FN90 (Belgium)

5.7x21mm DAP92-5.8 (China)

The new breed of compact high velocity military cartridge for personal defense weapons (PDW) is intended to replace pistol cartridges in military service. PDW cartridges will offer increased effective range and superior penetration than current pistol cartridges.

Perhaps no two cartridge types will change more than rimfire and shotshell. Rimfire ammunition presented a serious obstacle to the manufacturers' efforts to remove lead from the environment, because until the mid-1990s, lead primers and lead bullets were the only materials that were known to work with this type of cartridge. CCI has used non-toxic priming in its .22 rimfire industrial loads since the mid-1990s. During 2009, Winchester introduced non-toxic (both primer and bullet) .22 rimfire ammunition.

In shotshells, getting the lead out remains a difficult and expensive problem. Steel shot simply does not have the killing power or range of lead shot. Composite shot has the range and killing power of lead, but remains prohibitively expensive. The two best alternatives thus far are bismuth and polymer matrix types. Both offer acceptable killing power and range, but they are still not as good as lead shot for some types of shooting.

The 1,150 year thread of ammunition development has not been a history of accidents or chance. Nor is it a manifestation of mankind's evil intentions. Rather, this quest is driven by the human instinct to control and exploit a unique source of power for collective and personal defense. History dictates that the technological development of ammunition will continue, not only because it can, but because there is a basic human need to do so.

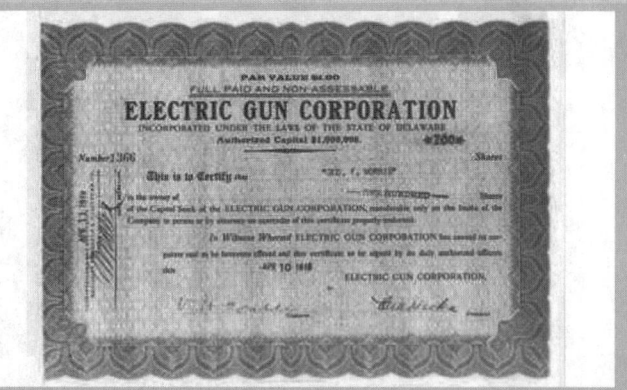

The future was clear to the owners and investors in the Electric Gun Company in 1918. Despite their vision, the technology did not exist to manufacture an electric gun at that time. In 2012, it still does not!

PROJECTILE CURIOSITIES

Over the centuries, a wide variety of items have been fired down a gun barrel. Here is an abridged listing:

Item	Purpose	Item	Purpose
Apple/orange	Muzzle loading cannon	Line throwing weight	For throwing lines to ships or over obstacles
Ballistic slug	Blunt slug for load development	Loose shot	Anti-personnel, hunting
Bean bag	Less than lethal anti-personnel (shotgun)	Marker capsule	Combat training
		Nails	Stud driver
Bird bomb	Scaring birds away from crops, airports (shotgun)	Paint ball	Marker for game
		Pepper powder	Anti-personnel
Bullet, composite	Frangible	Plastic ball	Meteorite impact simulator
Bullet, paper	Blank	Plastic pen	Advertising
Bullet, plaster	Frangible	Pop can	Muzzle loading cannon
Bullet, plastic	Short range training	Rock	Demolishing walls, sinking ships
Bullet, wood	Blank		
Canister shot	Anti-personnel	Round metal ball(s)	Anti-personnel, demolishing walls, sinking ships
Chain shot	Cutting ship rigging, anti-personnel		
		Round plastic balls	Airsoft guns
Cleaning rod	Accident	Round steel balls	BB guns (.177 in. dia. ball)
Crossbow Quarrel	Anti-personnel, piercing armor	Spark plug	Advertising
		Stacked dimes	Close range anti-personnel (shotgun)
Dummy bag	Retriever dog training		
Fireworks	Celebration (shotgun)	Stacked pennies	Close range anti-personnel (shotgun)
Flare	Signaling		
Flechette(s)	Anti-personnel, piercing armor	Steel cylinder w/edge	Fragment simulator for testing body armor
Golf ball	Amusement	Steel rod	Cutting barbed wire
Grape shot	Anti-personnel, anti-material	Tear powder	Anti-personnel

Horace Smith
1808-1893

Daniel B. Wesson
1825-1906

An Historic Partnership

When self-contained cartridges were perfected in the mid 1850s, firearm manufacturers were obliged to manufacture and sell the ammunition as well. Horace Smith and Daniel B. Wesson were experienced gunsmiths from old New England families. In 1854, they patented a revolver firing a cartridge which could be loaded into the cylinder from the rear. In 1855, they formed a partnership to manufacture both gun and ammunition. The revolver, the Model No. 1 was introduced in 1857 together with the cartridge for it—the .22 Short rimfire, the first successful self-contained cartridge in history. Both gun and ammunition were sales successes and the Smith & Wesson Company continued in the ammunition business until 1869.

Following the Company's exit from active manufacture of ammunition, S&W continued to design and introduce new cartridges in partnership with ammunition makers, a practice that continues to this day. Recent examples include: .38 S&W Special, .44 S&W Special, .357 S&W Magnum, .44 S&W Magnum, .41 S&W Magnum, .40 S&W Auto, .460 S&W Magnum, and .500 S&W Magnum.

CHAPTER 12 : PROPELLANT HISTORY

CHAPTER 12 HIGHLIGHTS:

- PRE-GUNPOWDER
- BLACK POWDER
- SMOKELESS POWDER
- EXPLOSIONS

PRE-GUNPOWDER

INCENDIARY MIXTURES CHINA 142 AD TO 1067 AD

- 142 AD China: alchemist Wei Bo-yang records a saltpeter-based mixture that will "fly and dance" in "Kinship of the Three"

- 300 AD China: alchemist Ge Hong records in "Book of the Master of the Preservation of Solidarity" the violent reaction when a mixture of saltpeter, redwood, and charcoal is heated

- 850 AD China: energetic mixtures of saltpeter, sulfur, realgar, and honey recorded in "Classified Essentials of the Mysterious Tao of the True Origin of Things" by Cheng Yin

- 904 AD China: use of saltpeter explosives recorded

- 1004 China: first mention of gunpowder in Chinese literature

- 1044 China: "Collection of the Most Important Military Techniques" by Tseng Kung-Liang records three recipes for gun powder

- 1067 China: Emperor places production of saltpeter and sulfur under state control

---

Chinese Strategic Weapon Circa 1231

"By 1231, when the Mongols attacked, (Chinese) powdermakers had devised a formula rich enough in saltpetre that its explosion could burst an iron casing. The Chin used this 'Heaven-Shaking Thunder Crash Bomb' to defend (the city of) Kaifeng against the invaders. The explosion of this blockbuster, a witness related, could be heard 33 miles away and scorched an area forty yards square. The shrapnel ripped through iron armor."

"The Mongols tried to protect their sapping trenches by using cowhide covers, but the defenders lowered a thunder crash bomb on a chain. 'The attacking soldiers were blown to bits,' an amazed chronicler noted, 'not even a trace being left behind'."

Quoted from page 12 of *Gunpowder* by Jack Kelly, ISBN 0-465-03722-4, published by Basic Books, 387 Park Avenue South, New York, NY 10016, copyright 2004.

BLACK POWDER

EARLY GUN POWDER ERA EUROPE AND MIDDLE EAST 1200 TO 1340

- Circa 1225: Marcus Graecus reveals formula for gun powder in his "Liber Ignum"

- 1234 England: Roger Bacon records formula for gun powder in his "de Nulliate Magiae"

ROGER BACON

Roger Bacon did not invent gunpowder nor did he claim to. Rather he was the first alchemist in Europe to record a formula for gunpowder.

Photo Credit: Edgar Fahs Smith Collection
University of Pennsylvania Library

- 1248 England: Roger Bacon records formula for gun powder again in "De Secretis Operibus Artis et Naturae"

- 1250 Syria, Egypt: gun powder known

- 1250 Germany: Albertus Magnus reveals gun powder formula in "De Mirabilis Mundi Ignum"

- 1267 England: Roger Bacon records ingredients for gun powder in "Opus Major"

- 1275 Germany: Albertus Magnus experiments with gun powder

- 1280 Syria: 107 recipes for gun powder described by Hasan al-Rammah in his "Book of Fighting on Horseback and with War Engines"

- 1288 China: invention of guns

- 1291 Middle East: Saracens use gun powder explosives at siege of Acre during the Crusades

- Circa 1300 England: gun powder made in Tower of London
- 1304 Middle East: al-Dimashqi records recipes for gun powder and operation of cannon
- 1313 Germany: Berthold Schwartz experiments with guns in Breisgau
- 1324 France: use of guns at battle of Metz
- 1327 England: Edward III uses guns when invading Scotland

EDWARD III & COAT OF ARMS

Edward III of Britain was the first European monarch to realize the full potential of gunpowder. He equipped the first warships with cannon and used cannon in the field for the first time against the Scots and the French.

Photo Credit: Edgar Fahs Smith Collection
University of Pennsylvania Library

EARLY GUN POWDER PRODUCTION EUROPE AND THE MIDDLE EAST 1340 TO 1627

- 1340 Germany: powder mill built in Augsburg
- Circa 1350 Middle East: Ibn Aranbugha records formula for gun powder in his military treatise "Al-Aniq fi al-manajiq"
- 1367 Spain: Moors renowned as artillerists
- 1388 Germany: first saltpetre plantation established in Frankfurt
- 1429 France: wet method of incorporation of powder introduced
- 1450 Europe: corning of gun powder developed
- 1543 England: first gun powder mill built at Rotherhilthe
- 1550 Europe: corned powder completely replaces serpentine powder
- 1561 England: first references of gun powder manufacture at Waltham Abbey
- 1578 France: eprouvette invented

- 1586 Europe: paper cartridge invented
- 1590 England: Geo. Evelyn receives license from Queen to build gun powder mills in Surrey
- 1601 France: King assumes right to make gun powder as prerogative of the crown
- 1605 England: Gunpowder plot fails to kill king

How the Globe Theater Burned Down

In 1613, a troupe called The King's Players put on their rendition of Shakespeare's play Henry VIII at the Globe theatre in London. For special effects during the play, they fired some gun powder. A spark from the discharged gun powder set fire to the thatched roof of the building which burned to the ground.

- 1612 Sweden: Gustavus Adolphus introduces paper cartridges w/ pre-measured powder charge
- 1627 England: East India Company allowed to make gun powder using saltpetre from India

SCIENCE AND REVOLUTION EUROPE AND NORTH AMERICA 1627 TO 1800

- 1627 Germany: Furtenberg invents improved powder tester
- 1652 England: Saltpetre Act

The Nature of Gunpowder

The salpetre is the Soule, the Sulphur is the Life and the Coales the Body of it.
- John Bate, *The Mysteries of Nature and Art*, Anno circa 1650

- 1665 England: Robert Hooke asserts that fire is not an element
- 1673 Netherlands: Christian Huygens proposes a gun powder fueled engine
- 1674 England: John Maynow identifies saltpetre as potassium nitrate
- 1719 England: government regulates storage and transport of gun powder, also in 1741, 1748, 1755, and 1771
- 1740 Europe: incorporation milling process for gun powder perfected
- 1772 England: stamping mills outlawed
- 1774 U.S.: Gen Thomas Gage seizes gun powder stored in Boston powder house; King bans importation of gun powder into colonies
- 1775 France: Louis XVI appoints Antoine-Laurent Lavoisier to head Gunpowder Administration

- 1775 U.S.: Gen Gage sends British Army to confiscate powder in Concord, confronts militia

- 1776 U.S.: desperately short of gun powder, American rebels import powder from France and Netherlands

- 1788 Russia: powder factory built at Kazan

- 1789 France: armed citizens seize Bastille to get gun powder stored there

---

Early Retirement

"This affair will probably save me the inconvenience of old age."
-Antoine-Laurent Lavoisier, November, 1793 during the Terror in France, on his coming appointment with the guillotine

YOUNG ELEUTHERE DU PONT BEING INSTRUCTED BY LAVOISIER IN FRANCE CIRCA 1790

Before moving to the United States in 1800, the young Eleuthere du Pont received training in chemistry from the famous French chemist Antoine Lavoisier. Eleuthere went on to found the E.I. du Pont industrial empire based on the manufacture of explosives and propellants in his new country. The du Pont Company left the propellant business in 1971.

Photo Credit: Edgar Fahs Smith Collection
University of Pennsylvania Library

INDUSTRIAL PROGRESS AND SCIENCE EUROPE AND NORTH AMERICA 1800-1855

- 1800 U.S.: Eleuthere I. du Pont emigrates from France to escape Terror

- 1804 U.S.: first du Pont gun powder mill begins operating in Delaware; du Pont installs latest equipment

- 1809 England: government purchases Waltham Abbey powder mills

- 1833 U.S.: Austin brothers establish powder mill in Akron, Ohio

- 1818 U.S.: du Pont powder works blows up, rebuilt

- 1832 France: Henri Braconnot discovers nitrated wood starch

- 1834 U.S.: Eleuthere du Pont dies, his son Alfred takes over company

- 1838 France: Theophile-Jules Pelouze discovers nitrated paper

- 1846 Switzerland: Christian Schonbein discovers gun cotton

- 1846 U.S.: Austin Powder becomes Austin and Carlton

- 1847 Italy: Ascanio Sobrero discovers nitroglycerine

- 1847 England: John Hall powder plant blows up

Second Thoughts

"When I think of all the victims killed during nitroglycerine explosions, and the terrible havoc that has been wreaked, which in all probability will continue to occur in the future, I am almost ashamed to admit to be its discoverer."
- Ascanio Sobrero, Discoverer of nitroglycerine whose face was badly scarred in a lab explosion

---

WAR AND SCIENCE EUROPE AND NORTH AMERICA 1856 TO 1870

- 1856 England: first water-driven powder mills installed

- 1857 England: first steam-driven powder mills installed

- 1857 U.S.: Lammont du Pont patents gun powder made from sodium nitrate

- 1858 U.S.: du Pont works blow up again

- 1858 India: Sepoy Mutiny

- 1859 U.S.: du Pont buys first of competitors

- 1860 England: Explosives Act passed

- 1860 U.S.: Rodman invents gauge to measure pressure of burning powder inside gun barrel; determines existing cannon powder too fine

- 1861 U.S.: du Pont supplies over half of gun powder needed by Union Army; imports saltpetre from India

- 1862: Austrian powder plant explodes

- 1863 U.S.: Confederate government builds most modern gun powder factory in the world in Augusta, Georgia; supplies all powder needs of South during Civil War

- 1863 U.S.: du Pont chemists develop method of converting sodium nitrate to potassium nitrate

- 1864 Germany: Maj. Johann F.E. Schultz perfects smokeless propellant made from wood cellulose

- 1861-1865 U.S.: du Pont works blows up eleven times during Civil War

- 1861: Austrian powder plant explosion - plant closes

- 1867 Sweden: Alfred Nobel patents dynamite

- 1868 England: Capt. Nobel invents crusher method of measuring breech pressure

SMOKELESS POWDER

*MONOPOLY EUROPE AND
NORTH AMERICA 1871 TO 1887*

- 1871 Austria: Frederick Volkmann patents Collodin smokeless powder

- 1872 U.S.: du Pont and Laflin & Rand form Gunpowder Trade Association (The Powder Trust)

- 1872 U.S.: American Powder Co. absorbs Miami Powder Co.

- 1875 England: Explosives Act regulates propellant production

- 1875 U.S.: Lammont du Pont develops progressive burning "hexagonal" black powder with grains shaped like donuts

- 1876 U.S.: du Pont buys Hazard Powder Company; Powder Trust dominates market

- 1876 England: highly compressed powder grains developed

- 1878 U.S.: Jos. King founds King's Great Western Powder Co. in King's Mill, Ohio

- 1881 England: electric lighting installed at Waltham Abbey powder mill

- 1882 Germany: compressed brown or "cocoa" powder developed

- 1884 U.S.: Lammont du Pont killed in explosion at dynamite factory

- 1884 France: Paul Vieille perfects the first smokeless powder, Poudre B

PAUL M. VIEILLE: 1854-1934

Paul Vieille was the French chemist who perfected the manufacture of smokeless powder in 1886. Vieille's discovery forever changed the world of firearms and ammunition.

Photo Credit: Edgar Fahs Smith Collection
University of Pennsylvania Library

- 1887 Sweden: Alfred Nobel patents double base powder "Ballistite"

ALFRED NOBEL: 1833-1896

Alfred Nobel was the Swedish chemist who invented Dynamite. In 1889, Nobel invented double-base propellant powders. Nobel used both inventions to build a worldwide explosive/propellant industrial empire. Parts of this empire still exist today.

Photo Credit: Edgar Fahs Smith Collection
University of Pennsylvania Library

*THE RUSH TO SMOKELESS EUROPE AND
NORTH AMERICA 1888 TO 1895*

- 1888 U.S.: du Pont begins construction of largest black powder factory in world at Keokuk, Iowa; expanded in 1892, 1900, and 1918

- 1889 England: Cordite patented by Abel and Dewar

- 1890 Europe/North America: conversion to smokeless powder begins, smokeless powder now referred to as gun powder while traditional powder called black powder

- 1890 England: Nobel builds smokeless powder plant in Ardeer

- 1890 U.S.: du Pont establishes new smokeless powder research center at Carney's Point, NJ

- 1891 England: full production of Cordite and gun cotton begins at Waltham Abbey

---

Strange Chemistry

"Chemists are a strange class of mortals, impelled by an almost insane impulse to seek their pleasure among smoke and vapor, soot and flame, poisons and poverty, yet among all these evils I seem to live so sweetly, that may I die if I would change places."
- Johann Becher

- 1891 U.S.: Miami Powder mill becomes first in U.S. to be electrified

- 1893 U.S.: du Pont makes first smokeless propellants in U.S.

- 1893 Russia: Kazan powder plant begins making smokeless powder
- 1895 U.S.: King Powder Co. begins manufacture of smokeless powder
- 1895 England: Kynoch builds Cordite plant in Arklow

EXPANSION, CONSOLIDATION AND WAR EUROPE AND NORTH AMERICA 1896 TO 1920

Choosing Sides and Types

Poudre B, Cordite, Ballistite

After Alfred Nobel's (Ballistite) patent infringement lawsuit against Frederick Abel (Cordite) failed in 1895, the major countries manufacturing smokeless propellants were divided into three groups as follows:

Poudre B single-base propellant: France, U.S., Russia

Cordite double base propellant: British Empire, Japan

Ballistite double-base propellant: Italy, Germany, Austria-Hungary, Sweden

This situation was to continue until 1945.

FREDERICK ABEL: 1827-1902

Frederick Abel invented Cordite propellants in Britain. When the British government adopted Cordite for all small arms and artillery in 1889, Alfred Nobel sued claiming infringement on his patent for double-base propellants. After many years of litigation, Nobel lost his suit. Cordite continued in use until the mid 1990s in the British Commonwealth.

- 1896 U.S.: King Powder Co. introduces semi-smokeless powder
- 1897 England: Kynoch builds Cordite plant in Kynochtown
- 1898 Cuba: U.S.S. Maine blows up in Havana harbor
- 1902 U.S.: du Pont buys Laflin & Rand, last major competitor

- 1903 England: Cordite MD introduced, replaces Cordite Mk. 1
- 1912 U.S.: federal court breaks du Pont firm into Atlas Powder Co. and Hercules Powder Co.
- 1912 U.S.: du Pont builds black powder plant in northern Louisiana
- 1913 U.S.: King Powder Co. discontinues manufacture of smokeless powder
- 1914 England: Waltham Abbey goes to war footing; large Cordite factories built at Gretna (Army) and Holton Heath (Navy)
- 1917 Russia: explosion at Kazan powder plant
- 1919 Finland: Vihtavouri established
- 1919 England: Explosives Trade group formed of Nobel, Kynoch, Eley, National, and Curtis & Harvey's; Gretna and Holton Heath military plants closed
- 1920 England: Explosives Trade Group becomes Nobel Industries
- 1920 Czechoslovakia: Powder factory built at Pardubice

EXPLOSIONS

EXPLOSIONS AND CONSOLIDATIONS THEN WAR EUROPE AND NORTH AMERICA 1920 TO 1945

- 1920 England: National Explosives Co. goes out of business
- 1921 U.S.: explosion at du Pont powder mill in Delaware, du Pont closes plant permanently
- 1921 Hungary: Hungarian Powder Factory established
- 1921 U.S.: Hercules purchases Miami Powder
- 1923 Poland: Hunting Ammunition Factory established at Pionki
- 1925 Hercules closes Miami Powder Co.
- 1927 England: powder manufacturers join ICI Metals Group
- 1928 England: Eley ends powder manufacture, goes out of business
- 1929 U.S.: Dr. Fred Olsen hired by Western Cartridge Co. invents ball powder in 1932
- 1931 Germany: RWS becomes part of Dynamit Nobel
- 1932 U.S.: King Powder Co. discontinues manufacture of semi-smokeless powder

- 1932 U.S.: Western Cartridge Co. patents process to manufacture Ball powder
- 1933 U.S.: Ball powder introduced commercial market
- 1940 U.S.: explosion at King Powder Co.
- 1940 England: Holton Heath reopened, new Cordite plants built at Caerwent (Navy), Bishopton (Army), Ranskill, and Wexham; Nobel plant at Ardeer on war footing
- 1942 England: first triple base propellants developed as Cordite N
- 1941, 1942, 1944 U.S.: explosions at King Powder Co.

Peace To The Present Europe And North America 1945 To 2011

- 1951 U.S.: explosion at King Powder Co.
- 1952 U.S.: Hodgdon Powder Co. established
- 1958 U.S.: King Powder Co. closes powder plant permanently and goes out of business
- 1968 U.S.: Daisy introduces V/L 22 caseless cartridge
- 1969 U.S.: Winchester moves Ball powder from East Alton, IL to St. Marks, FL
- 1970 U.S.: U.S. ammunition makers begin switch to piezo-electric pressure measuring system
- 1971 U.S.: du Pont leaves powder business
- 1975 U.S.: Pyrodex black powder substitute patented by Pawlak and Levenson

- 1976 U.S.: Hodgdon introduces Pyrodex
- 1977 U.S.: Explosion at Pyrodex plant
- 1983 U.S.: Hodgdon introduces improved Pyrodex
- 1991 England: Waltham Abbey plant closed
- 1991 Poland: Hunting Ammunition Factory becomes FAM-Pionki
- 1995 England: use of Cordite as propellant ceases
- 1997 Hungary: Hungarian Powder Factory becomes Nitrokemia Rt
- 2002 Czech Republic: Explosia formed at Pardubice

> *"Trust in the arm of God, but keep your powder dry."*
> - Oliver Cromwell

- 2003 Russia: Kazan powder plant becomes Federal Government Enterprise
- 2004 Europe: Eurenco formed – SNPE (France), Bofors (Sweden) and Vihtavouri (Finland)
- 2005 U.S.: Hodgdon buys IMR
- 2006 U.S.: Western Powders buys Accurate Arms
- 2006 U.S.: GOEX introduces Pinnacle black powder substitute
- 2006 U.S.: Hodgdon licenses Winchester Smokeless Propellants brand
- 2011 U.S.: St. Marks powder plant develops Hybrid powder

PAUL VIEILLE'S FORMULA FOR POUDRE B SMOKELESS PROPELLANT

68.2% insoluble nitrocellulose

29.8% soluble nitrocellulose gelatinized with ether

2% paraffin

CHAPTER 13 : BULLET HISTORY

ROUND BALLS AND ARROWS 1240-1840

- 1240 circa China: fire lances filled with metal and porcelain fragments to enhance effect

- 1250 circa China: fire lances used to launch arrows and round balls

- 1280 China: first guns firing single projectile

- 1325 Europe: Pot á Feu firing iron arrows or bolts illustrated in Walter de Milimete's "De Officiis Regum"

- 1330 Europe: first guns firing round balls of stone, or metal arrows

- 1450 circa Europe: stone balls replaced by metal balls of iron or lead

- 1600 England: metal arrows still in use

- 1827 Germany: bullet with discarding sabot developed for the Dreyse "needlegun"

- 1828 France: Delvigne experiments with elongated bullets from rifled barrels at Vincennes

POINTED LEAD BULLETS 1840-1880

- 1840 Europe, U.S.: conical (pointed) bullets coming into widespread use

- 1846 France: Capt. Claude Minié invents Minié ball

A Typical .58 Cal. American Minié Ball

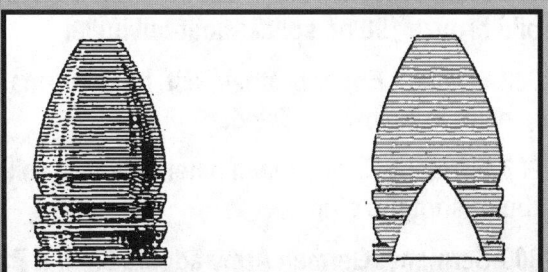

A typical .58 caliber Minié ball adopted by the U.S. Army in 1855 and used by both the North and the South during the Civil War. The ease of loading, accuracy, and range of the Minié ball changed military tactics by extending the killing range of the infantry soldier from 100 yards to over 1,000 yards. During the American Civil War, it has been estimated that approximately 200,000 men were killed by Minié balls and an equal number wounded.

Portrait of Maj. Gen. John Sedgwick, the highest ranking Union Army officer killed in combat during the Civil War. *"They couldn't hit an elephant at this distance"* - Maj. Gen. John Sedgwick, May 9, 1864 during the Battle of Spotsylvania Courthouse in Virginia seconds before he was struck under his left eye and killed instantly by a Minié ball fired by a Confederate sharpshooter over 1,000 yards away.

JACKETED BULLETS 1880-PRESENT

- 1880 Switzerland: Maj. Eduard Rubin develops metal jacketed bullet

Col. Eduard Alexander Rubin

Col. Eduard Rubin, and officer in the Swiss Army, is one of the unsung pioneers of cartridge and bullet design.

Photo Courtesy of the Swiss National Library

- 1883 U.S.: Blace patents tubular bullet

- 1886 France: French Army adopts 8x50Rmm Lebel with Balle M, 231 gr. FMJ-RN bullet

The French Balle D Bullet

In the late 1880s, the technology for drawing and forming jackets for high velocity bullets was still in its infancy. While jacketed round nose bullets could be manufactured, pointed or spitzer bullets were a problem. The French Gavré Commission tests in the late 1890s determined that the ideal rifle bullet shape was a spitzer boat-tail, but manufacture of a jacketed bullet with that profile was beyond the technology of the time. The French Army responded in 1898 by developing the solid bronze, 198 gr., spitzer boat-tail Balle D which could be made on lathes or swaged. The French Army was unique in adopting a bullet of such construction. Although expensive to manufacture, the Balle D served the French Army well during World War I where its penetration and accuracy were appreciated by French Army soldiers.

The French Balle D is historically significant because its low drag shape resulted in a quantum improvement in the exterior ballistics of rifle bullets. Almost over night, round nose bullets became obsolete for military use and the major nations quickly initiated programs to adopt spitzer bullets for their own military cartridges. Germany adopted the 8x57mmJS Patrone with a pointed bullet in 1905. The U.S. adopted the spitzer M1906 Ball for the new .30-'06 Springfield military cartridge in 1906.

But the influence of the Balle D did not stop there. During World War I, French machinegunners found the Balle D would substantially outrange the German 154 gr. S Patrone bullet (the Balle D could fly over 5,000 yards!). This led to French machineguns often being used for indirect fire much like a light field gun. The Germans reacted by developing their schwere Spitzer Geschoss, a jacketed 198 gr. spitzer boat-tail bullet which was an improved copy of the Balle D shape. The British Army followed suit with a Mk. 8Z and the U.S. Army with the 172 gr. M1 spitzer boat-tail bullet.

The Balle D highlighted the fact that machinegun fire could be effective at very long ranges in both direct and indirect tactical modes. Rifle fire from individual soldiers was effective only to approximately 200 yards. Because the individual soldier could not hit a target at long ranges, a lighter weight bullet was perfectly suitable. On the other hand, for machineguns to be effective at long ranges, they need a heavier, boat-tailed bullet. Military forces resisted this as their infantry would have to carry two different types of ammunition, one for rifles and one for machineguns. The result is that rifle caliber machineguns today are considered direct fire weapons. Indirect fire with machineguns has faded into history. However, the range dilemma, even in direct fire, has never been resolved and often resurfaces today.

- 1887 Japan: Japanese Army adopts 8x53Rmm cartridge with 235 gr. FMJ-RN bullet, Type 20

- 1888 Germany: 8x57mmJ cartridge adopted with 227 gr. FMJ-RN bullet (.318" dia.)

- 1888 Austria: 8x50Rmm cartridge adopted with 244 gr. FMJ-RN bullet

- 1889 England: British Army adopts .303 S.A. Ball cartidge with 211 gr. FMJ-RN bullet

- 1889 Norway, Sweden, Denmark: Armies adopt 8mm 237 gr. FMJ-RN bullet

- 1889 Switzerland: Swiss Army adopts 7.5x53mm cartridge with 211 gr. L-RN, capped bullet

- 1891 Italy: Italian Army adopts 6.5x52mm Mannlicher-Carcano with 162 gr. FMJ-RN bullet

- 1891 Russia: Imperial Army adopts 7.62x54Rmm cartridge with 220 gr. FMJ-RN bullet

- 1892 U.S.: U.S. Army adopts .30-40 Krag cartridge with 220 gr. FMJ-RN bullet

- 1895 U.S.: Navy adopts 6mm U.S. Navy cartridge with 112 gr. FMJ-FB bullet

- 1894 Norway: Enger brothers found the Norma ammunition company in Oslo

- 1897 Germany: Brenneke develops jacketed rifle bullet

- 1897 Japan: Japanese Army adopts 6.5mm FMJ-RN Type 30 bullet

- 1897 U.S.: Winchester patents tubular bullet

- 1898 Germany: Brenneke invents rifled shotgun slug

Wilhelm Brenneke & His Shotgun Slug

Wilhelm Brenneke revolutionized shotgun hunting with his new rifled shotgun slug (see inset) in 1898. This slug is still in production today.

Photos courtesy of Brenneke GmbH

- 1898 France: French Army adopts 8mm Balle D, a solid bronze 198 gr. spitzer boat-tail bullet

- 1902 Sweden: Enger brothers establish Norma satellite plant in Amotfors, Sweden

- 1903 Germany: Stendebach patents spin stabilized tubular shotgun slug

- 1905 Germany: German Army adopts 8mm S Patrone bullet, 154 gr. spitzer FMJ-FB (.323" dia.)

Spitzer

The word spitzer is of German origin. It means pointed. This word entered the English language in 1905 when the German Army adopted the 8x57mmJS or "S" Patrone with a pointed bullet. Today, we call a pointed bullet a spitzer bullet.

The Great Caliber Divide

The development of smokeless powder and jacketed bullets in the late 1880s allowed the caliber of military rifle bullets to be reduced. At this point there occurred a great divide as caliber preference fell into two camps: the "large bore" camp using 7.62mm and 8mm diameter bullets, and the "small bore" camp whose members preferred 6.5mm and 7mm diameter bullets. Firearms and ammunition manufacturers catered to both, of course.

Members of the large bore camp included most of the larger nations such as: the U.S. (.30-40 Krag), Britain (.303 British), Germany (8x57mmJS Mauser), France (8x50Rmm Lebel), Belgium (7.65x53mm Mauser), Russia (7.62x54Rmm Mosin-Nagant), Switzerland (7.5x55mm Swiss), Austria (8x50Rmm Austrian Mannlicher), and Japan (8mm Murata). Of course, many smaller countries took their cue from the large bore countries. These included:

1. .303 British: India, Australia, New Zealand, South Africa, Canada, Rhodesia
2. 8x57mmJS Mauser: China, Czechoslovakia, Egypt, Yugoslavia, Iran, Britain (for BESA machine guns), Luxemburg, Poland, and others
3. 8x50Rmm Lebel: Vietnam, Syria, Algeria, Morocco, and other French colonies
4. 8x50Rmm Austrian Mannlicher: Austria, Hungary, Bulgaria
5. 7.65x53mm Belgian Mauser: Argentina, Bolivia, Columbia, Peru, Paraguay, Turkey
6. 7.62x54R Russian: Finland, Mongolia

The small bore camp included many smaller nations that individually adopted calibers such as:

1. 6.5x55mm Swedish Mauser: Sweden, Norway, Denmark
2. 6.5x54Rmm Dutch Mannlicher: Netherlands, Rumania, Dutch East Indies
3. 6.5x54mm Mannlicher-Schoenauer: Greece
4. 6.5x52mm Mannlicher-Carcano: Italy
5. 6.5x50SRmm Japanese: Japan, Korea, Manchuko
6. 6.5x58mm Vergueiro: Portugal
7. 7x57mm Mauser: Brazil, Chile, Columbia, Costa Rica, Cuba, Guatemala, Honduras, Mexico, Nicaragua, El Salvador, Uruguay, Venezuela

After World War I, many members of the small bore camp switched to a larger bore in order to field more effective tracer, armor piercing, incendiary, spotting, and grenade launching versions of military ammunition. These included Japan (7.7x58mm), Italy (7.35mm), Norway (.30-'06), and Portugal (8x57mm Mauser). Only Sweden, Netherlands, and Greece retained their 6.5mm caliber military cartridges until World War II and most South American countries remained content with the 7x57mm Mauser.

What is the difference between the 8x57mmI or J and the 8x57mmJS cartridges?

The 8x57mmI cartridge was designed by the German Infantry Board at Spandau Arsenal. When the new cartridge was officially adopted in 1888, the suffix I was added to indicate it was an "Infanterie" cartridge or I Patrone. Although the German letter I is the correct designation, I was mistaken for a J, so the J suffix became the popular designation. The 8x57mmJ Patrone was loaded with a .318" diameter 226 gr. FMJ-RN bullet.

After the French Army adopted the pointed Balle D bullet in 1898, the German Army resolved to modernize their 8x57mmJ rifle bullet as well. In 1905, the German Army adopted a new .323" diameter, 154 gr. pointed (spitzer) bullet. Although the bullet diameter and the muzzle velocity increased, the cartridge case remained the same except for the neck diameter. The new cartridge was designated the 8x57mmJS Patrone—the "S" designation indicating a .323" diameter bullet. All German military rifles after 1906 were chambered for the new S Patrone cartridge.

The 8x57RmmJ and 8x57RmmJS cartridges are rimmed versions of the above made only for commercial use in combination guns.

- 1905 Germany: Brenneke introduces Ideal TUG jacketed hunting bullet
- 1905 Japan: Japanese Army adopts 6.5Sx50Rmm cartridge with 139 gr. FMJ-FB Type 38 spitzer bullet
- 1906 U.S.: U.S. Army adopts .30 M1906 Ball cartridge with 154 gr. FMJ-FB bullet
- 1907 Germany: RWS introduces jacketed hunting bullets
- 1908 Russia: Russian Army adopts 7.62mm Type L 150 gr. spitzer FMJ-FB bullet
- 1908 Denmark: Danish Army adopts 8mm 198 gr. FMJ-FB spitzer bullet
- 1910 England: British Army adopts .303 Mk. VII Ball cartridge with 174 gr. FMJ-FB bullet
- 1911 Switzerland: Swiss Army adopts 7.5x55mm cartridge with M11 Ball 174 gr. FMJ-BT bullet
- 1914 U.S.: Newton patents Protected Point Spitzer hunting bullet
- 1915 Germany: German Army adopts 8mm S.m.K. AP 178 gr. FMJ-FB bullet
- 1917 Germany: Brenneke develops the Ideal Torpedo or TIG bullet
- 1917 Germany: German Army adopts 8mm S.Pr. Incendiary cartridge with 150 gr. FMJ-FB bullet
- 1918 Germany: German Army adopts 8mm s.S. Patrone Ball cartridge with 198 gr. FMJ-BT bullet

- 1919 U.S.: Bowers patents tubular bullet

Projectile vs. Bullet

In popular usage, the words bullet and projectile are used interchangeably. To a ballistic professional, the word bullet generally is applied to a projectile below .60 caliber while the term projectile is generally applied to a bullet above .60 caliber such as those having a fuze and explosive filler.

A shotgun projectile is called a slug and a spherical bullet is properly called a ball. Most full metal jacket military bullets are called Ball bullets even though they are pointed.

There are many exceptions to the above as exemplified by the U.S. Government definition of armor piercing ammunition.

- 1920 U.S.: Halloran patents self-stabilizing shotgun slug

- 1924 U.S.: Remington patents bronze point rifle bullet

- 1924 Belgium: Belgian Army adopts 7.65mm 154 gr. FMJ-FB bullet

- 1925 U.S.: U.S. Army adopts .30-'06 M1 Ball cartridge with 172 gr. FMJ-BT bullet

- 1925 U.S.: Western Cartridge patents solid copper bullet

- 1932 U.S.: Barnes Bullets founded

- 1932 Germany: German Army standardizes 8x57JSmm s.S. Patrone 198 gr. FMJ-BT bullet with mild steel core, lead sheath, and jacket

- 1934 U.S.: Carl Foster perfects rifled shotgun slug

Faster Than a Speeding Bullet

The comic strip/TV/movie character Superman is described as being "faster than a speeding bullet". This label was applied first in the 1930s when the Superman character was developed. A rifle bullet breaks the sound barrier before exiting the muzzle, so Superman was indeed speedy.

The term "faster than a speeding bullet" has entered the lexicon as a descriptive, analogous term denoting high speed.

- 1936 Germany: H Mantle hunting bullet introduced by RWS

- 1940 Germany: D Mantle hunting bullet introduced by RWS

- 1940 U.S.: U.S. Army adopts .30-'06 M2 Ball cartridge with 152 gr. FMJ-FB bullet

- 1942 Germany: 8x33mm Kurz Ball cartridge adopted with 125 gr. FMJ-FB bullet

- 1942 U.S.: Vern Speer makes bullet jackets from fired .22 rimfire brass

- 1943 Russia: 7.62x39mm M43 Ball cartridge developed with 122 gr. FMJ-FB bullet

- 1943 U.S.: U.S. Army Air Corps adopts .30 frangible bullet ammunition to train gunners

- 1944 U.S.: Speer Bullets founded by Vern Speer

> "Whoever said the pen is mightier than the sword obviously never encountered automatic weapons."
> - Gen. Douglas MacArthur

- 1947 U.S.: Sierra Bullets founded by Joyce Hornady

- 1948 U.S.: Nosler Bullets founded, introduces Partition bullet

John Nosler

John Nosler's Partition bullet (inset) was the first of his many modern designs that revolutionized hunting bullet performance. His bullets inspired (some say forced) other bullet manufacturers and ammunition makers to upgrade their bullets' performance.

Photo and cutaway courtesy of Nosler Bullets

- 1949 U.S.: Hornady Manufacturing founded

- 1954 U.S.: Speer introduces Hot Core bullets

- 1954 U.S.: Sierra introduces MatchKing bullet

- 1958 U.S.: Olin/Winchester patents bullet jacket with internal flutes

- 1959 U.S.: Flateau patents tubular bullet

- 1960 Sweden: Norma introduces Silverflash 6.5mm 140 gr. FMJ-BT bullet

- 1964 U.S.: 5.56x45mm cartridge and M193 55 gr. FMJ-BT bullet adopted by U.S. Army

- 1961 Sweden: Norma introduces Alaska bullet

- 1972 U.S.: first shotshells w/steel shot offered

- 1974 U.S.: Randy and Coni Brooks buy Barnes Bullets

- 1974 U.S.: Burczynski patents Hydra-Shok bullet
- 1974 Russia: Soviet Army adopts 5.45x39mm cartridge with 53 gr. FMJ-BT bullet
- 1977 U.S.: Hornady introduces Interlock bullet
- 1977 Austria: Hirtenberger patents ABC bullet
- 1979 Germany: Knappworst patents Action bullet
- 1980 U.S.: Barnes introduces Solid copper bullets
- 1981 Sweden: Norma introduces Vulkan bullet
- 1982 U.S.: Speer introduces Grand Slam bullet
- 1982 U.S.: Swift Bullet Co. founded
- 1982 U.S.: Glaser Safety Slug introduced
- 1983 U.S.: Sierra introduces GameKing and Pro-Hunter bullet lines
- 1984 Australia: Woodleigh Bullets founded
- 1984 U.S.: Swift introduces A-Frame bullet
- 1984 Europe: NATO adopts 5.56x45mm cartridge with SS109/M855 62.5 gr. FMJ-BT bullet
- 1986 U.S.: Barnes introduces the X bullet
- 1987 U.S.: Burczynski patents Starfire bullet
- 1988 Australia: Woodleigh develops Weldcore bullet
- 1990 U.S.: Hornady introduces XTP bullet
- 1990 U.S.: Speer introduces African Grand Slam and African Grand Slam Tungsten Solid bullets
- 1990 U.S.: Bismuth shot patented
- 1992 U.S.: Speer introduces Gold Dot bullets
- 1992 U.S.: Bismuth Cartridge introduces shot made of bismuth alloy
- 1994 U.S.: Barnes introduces boat-tail X bullet
- 1994/95 U.S.: Olin/Winchester patents Fail Safe bullet
- 1994 U.S.: Swift introduces Scirocco bullet
- 1994 U.S.: Remington patents Core-Lokt handgun bullet

- 1995 Sweden: Norma introduces Oryx and Diamond bullets
- 1995 U.S.: Nosler patents Solid Base bullet
- 1996 U.S.: Olin/Winchester patents Black Talon bullet
- 1997 U.S.: Speer introduces Trophy Bonded Bear Claw bullet
- 1998 U.S.: Remington patents Copper Solid shotgun slug
- 1999 U.S.: Federal patents FMJ expanding bullet
- 2000 Germany: DN introduces the DK bullet
- 2001 U.S.: Bismuth Cartridge introduces bullets with bismuth alloy cores
- 2002 Nosler introduces Ballistic-Tip bullet
- 2003 U.S.: Remington introduces Hevi-Shot
- 2004 U.S.: Cor-Bon introduces Pow' R Ball bullet
- 2005 U.S.: Remington introduces Buckhammer shotgun slug
- 2006 U.S.: Barnes introduces Triple Shock X bullets and Banded Solid bullets
- 2007 U.S.: Federal offers shotshells with FS steel shot and tungsten alloy Heavyweight shot
- 2007 U.S.: Barnes introduces MRX bullet
- 2007 U.S.: Remington introduces Core-Lokt Ultra Bond bullet and Wingmaster HD shot
- 2007 U.S.: Winchester introduces E³ bullet

Bullet Points

Modern business procedures often demand that specific points of information be reduced to their core meaning and listed in order of importance to save time. The typical pattern for listing such points of information is after a series of black dots. These are called bullet points because the dots look like bullet holes in a paper target.

"The only reason I carry a .45 is they don't make a .46"
-Texas Ranger saying, no doubt based on experience, circa early 1900s.

Col. Sergei I. Mosin: 1849-1902

**Russian Army Officer, Inventor, and
Superintendent of Tula Arsenal**

Today, Col. Mosin is honored by having his name attached to the Mosin-Nagant M1891 bolt-action rifle and its cartridge, the 7.62x54Rmm Russian often called the 7.62x54Rmm Mosin-Nagant.

CHAPTER 14 : IGNITION SYSTEM HISTORY

CHAPTER 14 HIGHLIGHTS:

- SLOW MATCHES, HOT WIRES AND SPARKS 1240-1807
- SEPARATE PRIMED PERCUSSION IGNITION 1807-1854
- INSIDE PRIMED CARTRIDGES 1854-1900
- OUTSIDE PRIMED CARTRIDGES 1866-PRESENT

SLOW MATCHES, HOT WIRES AND SPARKS 1240-1807

- 1240 circa China: ignition by means of slow match, hot wire, or burning ember

- 1515 Germany: Johann Kiefuss invents the wheellock spark ignition system

- 1525 Netherlands: Snaphaunce matchlock developed

- 1570 Germany: snaplock version of matchlock developed, last of matchlock systems

- 1610 France: Marin le Bourgeoys invents flintlock ignition

"Flash in the Pan"

This popular saying is intended to convey the contextual image of a quick, strong start followed by a complete failure to make any progress.

The root of this phrase lies in the flintlock mechanism used extensively in firearms from 1610 until 1814. To fire a flintlock, the shooter first had to place a small charge of fine gunpowder in the pan to serve as a source of ignition for the main powder charge in the barrel. When the trigger was pulled, the hammer was released. As it fell, a small piece of flint mounted on the hammer struck the frizzen, producing a shower of sparks over the powder charge in the pan. If all went as intended, the sparks ignited this powder. As it burned, the powder in the pan was intended to ignite the powder in the barrel through the flash hole in the barrel. As one might surmise from such a complex, interdependent sequence of events, ignition failures were common. So much so, that "a flash in the pan" became a simile for strong start followed by much ado about nothing.

- 1663 Britain: Samuel Pepys describes fulminate of gold in his Pepys' Diary

- 1774 France: King Louis XV's physician, Dr. Bayern discovers fulminate of mercury

- 1788 France: Berthollet discovers potassium chlorate

- 1799 U.S.: E.C. Howard discovers composition of mercury fulminate

SEPARATE PRIMED PERCUSSION IGNITION 1807-1854

- 1807 Britain: Rev. Alexander Forsyth patents use of detonating substances for percussion ignition of gunpowder

REV. ALEXANDER FORSYTH: 1768-1843

Scottish clergyman, chemist, and inventor of percussion ignition

Alexander Forsyth was a member of the ancient Scottish clan of Forsyth from around Monymusk in Aberdeenshire, Scotland. This clan's heritage dates back to 1306 when King Robert The Bruce granted Osbert de Forsyth a parcel of land near Sauchie. The clan name is derived from the Gaelic word "fearsithe" which means "man of peace". The clan motto is "Instaurator ruinae" meaning "A repairer of ruin".

Alexander's father was pastor of Belhelvie Parish in Aberdeen. After graduating from seminary, Rev. Alexander Forsyth succeeded his father as pastor of Belhelvie in 1790. In his youth, Alexander Forsyth developed a keen interest in shooting, chemistry, and mechanics. Whenever his clerical duties permitted, Rev. Forsyth hunted ducks on the nearby river. During these periods, Rev. Forsyth noted that the flash from the priming pan of his flintlock frequently alerted the ducks in time for them to flare before the main powder charge of his shotgun ignited. Dr. Forsyth determined to do something about this.

Forsyth began experimenting with various explosive compositions intended to improve ignition time and reliability. He discovered that fulminate of mercury quickly and reliably ignited black powder.

Recognizing a good thing when he saw it, the Master General of Ordnance invited Rev. Forsyth to set up a laboratory in the Tower of London to conduct further experiments. However, in 1807 a new Master of Ordnance ordered Forsyth to leave. Afterward, Rev. Forsyth continued his experiments on his own and obtained a patent in that same year.

When the first percussion muskets were issued to the British Army in 1836, Her Majesty's government neglected to recognize Forsyth's work or patent. Belatedly, in 1842, Her Majesty's government elected to pay Forsyth a small grant of £200 for his work. Some four months after his death, HM's Board of Ordnance distributed £1,000 among the childless Forsyth's heirs. Earlier, Forsyth had turned down a £20,000 offer from Napoleon for his patent.

Although Rev. Alexander Forsyth discovered percussion ignition, he did not invent the percussion cap. Rather, he used loose fulminate powder in the pan of a flintlock. However, the effect on ammunition technology was revolutionary. All modern forms of percussion ignition such as percussion caps and primers are based on Forsyth's work.

Forsyth Clan Tartan

Rev. Alexander Forsyth was a member of the ancient Scottish clan Forsyth. This is their tartan.

Photo Courtesy of Rampant Scotland

- 1812 France: Jean S. Pauli develops primer for self-contained cartridge

- 1814 U.S.: Joshua Shaw invents percussion cap

- 1816 Britain: Joseph Manton develops tube ignition

- 1818 Britain: Joseph Manton patents tube lock

- 1820 France: Gevelot begins manufacture of mercury fulminate for percussion ignition

- 1821 Britain: William Westley Richards introduces the pill lock

- 1823 U.S.: Dr. Samuel Guthrie develops fulminate of mercury in pill form for percussion ignition

- 1827 Germany: Nicholas von Dreyse invents needle gun cartridge with inside primer.

- 1829 France: Pottet patents cartridge case with fulminate of mercury ignition held in case head

- 1831 Britain: Patent issued for cartridge carrying ignition cap in base

- 1836 France: Le Faucheux invents pin fire ignition system

- 1841 Britain: Hanson and Golden issued a patent for hollow base bullet with fulminate in cavity

- 1845 France: Flobert invents BB cap

- 1845 U.S.: Dr. Edward Maynard invents tape primer system

- 1846 France: M. Houllier issued patents for rimfire and centerfire ignition systems

- 1848 U.S.: W. Hunt patents hollow base bullet with fulminate in base cavity sealed by disk

- 1850 circa Britain: Needham and Lancaster shotshells with inside primers popular

- 1852 U.S.: Christian Sharps patents disk primer

Joshua Shaw: 1776-1860

Noted artist, inventor of the percussion cap

Shortly after his father died in 1783, Joshua Shaw found employment on a farm minding cattle and frightening sparrows away from the corn fields using an old flintlock musket. For the next three years, Shaw relieved the monotony by teaching himself to read, write, and draw using the sand as his writing and sketching pad. Shaw developed a passion for drawing and became proficient and thoroughly familiar with firearms. When he reached the age of ten, his stepfather trained young Joshua as a glazier after which his uncle gave him nine weeks of schooling—the only instruction he ever received.

His first break occurred when he responded to a help wanted ad in the local newspaper for an apprentice house painter. He got the job and his reputation as an artist grew quickly. Shaw moved first to London and then to Bath where his artistic gifts and abilities as a sportsman gained him entry into British high society. Despite this, Shaw frequently found himself at political odds with the aristocratic denizens of British Society. Disgusted, Shaw moved to the United States.

In 1814, Shaw used his knowledge of firearms to invent the percussion cap and cap lock. As Shaw resided in Britain at the time, he kept the details of his invention secret until he moved to the U.S. where he applied for a patent in 1822. His application was refused on a technicality, but his claim to the invention was supported after protracted investigation by the U.S. Patent Office. Despite this, he received very little compensation for his invention.

Shaw's invention revolutionized firearms by improving ignition in all types of weather conditions and speeding reloading. His invention paved the way for modern primers as we know them.

"(this) is one of the most ingenious, and one of the most useful inventions in modern times."
- U.S. Committee of Patents in their report dated February 10, 1846, regarding Joshua Shaw's application for a patent on the percussion cap.

Joshua Shaw's Percussion Cap

In 1814, Joshua Shaw's percussion cap and lock revolutionized firearm ignition and paved the way for the primers we know today. Shown above is the "top hat" version used in long arms. Handguns use a smaller type without the petals.

Photo Courtesy of the National Park Service

INSIDE PRIMED CARTRIDGES 1854-1900

- 1854 U.S.: Horace Smith and Daniel Wesson patent rimfire cartridge

PATENTS

Between 1612 and 1852, the British Patent Office issued 300 firearms related patents. In the six year period from 1852 to 1858, the British Patent Office issued approximately 600 firearms related patents!

From 1875 to 1914, firearms patents remained one of the most active categories in the U.S. Patent Office.

SECTION III – CHAPTER 14 : IGNITION SYSTEM HISTORY 99

Col. Hiram Berdan: 1824-1893

Millionaire businessman, inventor, marksman, military officer

When the Civil War began in 1861, New York City businessman, inventor, and mechanical engineer Hiram Berdan determined to offer his services to the Union. For fifteen years prior to the Civil War, Berdan had been the top marksman in the U.S. Building on this experience, Berdan proposed to raise regiments for the Union Army, each consisting of 750 trained sharpshooters. He was one of the first to recognize that trained marksmen would have an influence on the outmoded infantry tactics of the day far out of proportion to their numbers.

Using his political influence, Berdan obtained agreement from Gen. Winfield Scott, Commander-in-Chief of the Union Army, and President Abraham Lincoln, to proceed with his plan. Shooting contests were organized to find suitable marksmen. To be accepted, a man had to be able to place ten consecutive rounds in a ten inch circle at 200 yards. Within months, two regiments had been raised—the First and Second United States Sharpshooters. Berdan was appointed Colonel of the two regiments. He equipped them with Colt Revolving Rifles. Additional regiments of sharpshooters soon followed.

Berdan and his sharpshooters served with distinction in numerous battles and campaigns. For his leadership at the Battle of Chancellorsville, Berdan was brevetted to Brigadier General. Later, he was brevetted to Major General for his actions at Chancellorsville.

During his military career, Berdan was a tireless proponent of standardized ammunition, breech loading rifles, and marksmanship training.

Despite these and other accolades, Berdan was not by nature a military man. He had a reputation as an irresponsible, inept, unreliable leader. Finally, in January, 1864, Berdan resigned his Army commission and moved to Europe with his family where he continued his inventing activities.

Berdan was a prolific firearms and ammunition inventor. He designed a musket ball, repeating rifle, artillery fuze, and primer. It is the latter, the Berdan primer, invented after he arrived in Europe, that preserves his place in ammunition history.

Hiram Berdan passed away in 1893. He is buried in Arlington National Cemetery.

Gen. Hiram Berdan will be remembered as the inventor of the primer bearing his name.

Photo Courtesy of the National Archives

- 1856 U.S.: George Morse invents primer and cartridge for breech loading rifle
- 1856 U.S.: Smith and Wesson patent Volcanic cartridge with fulminate in hollow base of bullet
- 1857 U.S.: Sharp's mule ear cartridge in use
- 1858 U.S.: George Morse patents cartridge with inside anvil and perforated disk containing percussion cap

- 1859 U.S.: Dr. Edward Maynard patents separately primed metallic cartridge
- 1859 U.S.: Willard Ellis and John White patent front loaded cup primed cartridge
- 1859 U.S.: Gallager and Gladding obtain patent for inside pin fire ignition
- 1860 U.S.: Ethan Allen patents lip fire primer
- 1863 U.S.: Thomas Rodman and Silas Crispin patent separately primed brass and paper cartridge case
- 1864 U.S.: D. Williamson patents teat fire primer
- 1865 U.S.: Silas Crispin patents annular rimfire primer systems
- 1866 U.S.: Hiram Berdan patents Berdan centerfire primer
- 1866 Britain: Col. Edward Boxer invents Boxer primer

Col. Edward Boxer

Col. Edward M. Boxer is shown here in retirement seated in his garden circa the late 1880s. For over 15 years, from the early 1850s until his resignation in 1869, Col. Boxer served at the Royal Laboratory (part of Woolwich Arsenal) first as a technical officer and later as Superintendent. During that period, he played a major part in the development of the self-contained cartridge. Shooters honor Col. Boxer by the primer which bears his name – the Boxer primer in common use all over the world today.

Photo courtesy of the Royal Artillery Museum, www.firepower.org.uk

Portrait of Col. Edward M. Boxer as the Superintendent of the Royal Laboratory in the late 1860s.

Image courtesy of the Royal Artillery Museum, www.firepower.org.uk

OUTSIDE PRIMED CARTRIDGES 1866-PRESENT

- 1868 U.S.: Stephen Vincent Benet develops solid head cartridge case with inside anvil primer
- 1868 U.S.: F.A. Thuer patents outside primed centerfire tapered rimless cartridge
- 1869 U.S.: William Tribbels patents inside primed case
- 1869 U.S.: E.H. Martin patents folded head centerfire cartridge with inside primer
- 1870 U.S.: Milbank patents solid head cartridge case with rimfire primer
- 1872 U.S.: Farrington patents solid, balloon head cartridge with outside primer
- 1898 U.S.: Frankford Arsenal develops H-48 non-mercuric primer, later replaced by H-42
- 1901 Germany: RWS introduces first non-corrosive non-mercuric primer
- 1917 U.S.: U.S. Army standardizes on the K-chlorate F.A. No.70 primer in U.S. military ammunition (Winchester 35-NF)
- 1922 U.S.: Dr. Wilbert Huff publishes paper pinpointing primer chemistry's role in barrel corrosion
- 1923 Germany: Rathburg patents non-mercuric lead styphnate primer
- 1927 U.S.: Remington introduces mercuric non-corrosive "Kleanbore" primers
- 1928 U.S.: Winchester introduces "Staynless" mercuric non-corrosive primers
- 1929 U.S.: Remington purchases Rathburg and von Herz patents for non-mercuric lead styphnate primers
- 1930 U.S.: Frankford Arsenal makes test lot of non-corrosive primers for use in National Match ammunition
- 1935 U.S.: Federal Cartridge issued patent for basic lead styphnate priming compound
- 1936 U.S.: most commercial ammunition loaded with non-mercuric non-corrosive lead styphnate primers
- 1942 U.S.: .30 Carbine ammunition adopted with non-mercuric non-corrosive primer
- 1948 U.S.: K-chlorate primers replaced by LS-T (lead styphnate) primers in U.S. military ammunition
- 1950 U.S.: military ammunition begins conversion to non-corrosive lead styphnate primers
- 1960 U.S.: last military ammunition loaded with corrosive primers
- 1960 U.S.: Federal begins manufacture of magnum large rifle primer
- 1976 U.S.: Federal introduces match grade centerfire rifle primers
- 1980 Europe: Gevelot shotshell primers obsolete, replaced by No. 209 battery cup primer
- 1984 Europe: NATO countries begin conversion of military ammunition to non-corrosive primers
- 1985 Europe: IABC shotshell primer developed
- 1990 Europe/U.S.: CCI, Dynamit Nobel, Fiocchi, and Remington only remaining makers of percussion caps
- 1992 Russia: non-toxic (no heavy metals) primer developed for use in commercial ammunition
- 1992 circa U.S.: commercial ammunition makers introduce lead-free primers using diazodinitrophenol (DDNP)
- 1994 U.S.: No. 209 battery cup primers used for ignition of black powder muzzle loading guns
- 1999 U.S.: Remington introduces "EtronX" electric primer
- 2000 Germany: German Army becomes first military service to adopt a non-toxic primer (no heavy metals) for combat use

"Going Off Half Cocked"

This phrase is directly related to a "flash in the pan". Most flintlock mechanisms had a half-cock position for the hammer to facilitate safety in loading. Should the hammer accidentally be released from the half-cock position for any reason, it did not have sufficient energy to produce sparks to ignite the powder in the pan. Of course a shooter inadvertently leaving the hammer at half-cock by not paying attention was certain to experience a misfire when he pulled the trigger.

For these reasons, the phrase conveys the foolish actions of a person doomed to failure due to inadequate preparation and lack of attention to detail.

CHAPTER 15 : CARTRIDGE CASE HISTORY

CHAPTER 15 HIGHLIGHTS:

- PAPER, PLASTIC, AND COMBUSTIBLE 1586-1978
- SEPARATE PRIMED 1848-1868
- PATENT IGNITION 1835-1900
- SELF-CONTAINED RIMFIRE 1845-PRESENT
- SELF-CONTAINED CENTERFIRE 1858-PRESENT

PAPER, PLASTIC, AND COMBUSTIBLE 1586-1978

- 1586 Europe: paper cartridge invented
- 1812 Europe: combustible paper cartridge perfected
- 1812 France: Pauli invents combustible paper cartridge with metal head containing primer
- 1829 France: Pottet patents cartridge with removable metal base containing priming compound in a pocket
- 1836 France: LeFaucheux develops shotshell with paper tube and metal head
- 1840 Germany: Dreyse needle gun cartridge adopted by German Army
- 1850 Britain: Needham and Lancaster shotshells with paper tube in use
- 1857 U.S.: Smith patents rubber cartridge case
- 1867 U.S.: Crispin develops paper case with metallic head
- 1885 U.S.: shotshells with paper tubes and metal heads commercially sold
- 1896 U.S.: manufacturers discontinue paper cartridges for muzzle loading guns
- 1961 U.S.: first plastic shotshells with extruded plastic tube introduced
- 1970 U.S.: shotshells with drawn plastic tube introduced
- 1975 U.S.: shotshells with molded plastic tube introduced
- 1978 U.S.: shotshell having a molded plastic tube with head reinforced by internal metal disk introduced

SEPARATE PRIMED 1848-1868

- 1856 U.S.: first Maynard cartridge patented
- 1856 U.S.: Burnside patents tapered metallic case for Burnside rifle

- 1857 U.S.: Sharp's mule ear cartridge in production
- 1857 U.S.: Greene patents paper tube cartridge
- 1859 Britain: Whitworth patents tube cartridge
- 1859 U.S.: Dr. Edward Maynard patents separate primed metallic cartridge case

Dr. Edward Maynard

Dr. Edward Maynard (1813-1891) was a renowned dentist in Washington, D.C. who received 23 firearms and ammunition patents from 1845 to the late 1800s. Maynard rifles and cartridges were used by both sides during the Civil War. They were a favorite of Confederate cavalrymen and sharpshooters and armed four regiments in the U.S. Army.

Photo Courtesy of Library of Congress

- 1863 U.S.: Maynard patents cartridge case with "flop ear" extractor
- 1863 U.S.: Rodman and Crispin patent wrapped metal cartridge case
- 1863 U.S.: Rodman and Crispin patent metal wrapped paper cartridge case for Gallager carbine
- 1863 U.S.: Maynard patents metal cartridge case with wire extractor

PATENT IGNITION 1835-1900

- 1836 France: LeFaucheux invents the pinfire cartridge case
- 1859 U.S.: Gallager and Gladding patent inside pin fire
- 1860 U.S.: Allen patents lip fire
- 1864 U.S.: Williamson patents teat fire

- 1865 U.S.: Crispin patents annular rimfire

SELF-CONTAINED RIMFIRE 1845-PRESENT

- 1835 France: Flobert develops BB Cap from percussion cap

- 1854 U.S.: Smith and Wesson patent rimfire cartridge

SELF-CONTAINED CENTERFIRE 1858-PRESENT

- 1847 France: Houllier develops metal cartridge case with integral primer

- 1856 U.S.: Morse patents internally primed metal cartridge

- 1865 U.S.: brass shotshell developed

- 1866 Britain: British Army adopts .577 Boxer centerfire cartridge with coiled brass case

- 1868 U.S.: Col. Benet introduces solid head cartridge case with internal primer

Gen. S.V. Benet

Gen. S. V. Benet was the 8th Chief of Ordnance from 1874 until 1891. He is considered the inventor of the drawn solid-head centerfire cartridge we know today.

Photo Courtesy of Library of Congress

- 1869 U.S.: Martin patents folded head, metallic cartridge case

- 1870 U.S.: Berdan introduces cartridge case of drawn brass

- 1887 U.S.: the first solid head, semi-rimless cartridge introduced, the .50-115 Express

- 1886 France: French Army adopts first cartridge loaded with smokeless powder: 8x50Rmm Lebel

- 1889 Switzerland: Swiss Army adopts its first cartridge designed for smokeless powder: 7.5x53mm Swiss

- 1894 U.S.: first smokeless powder commercial cartridges introduced, .30-30 WCF

- 1895 U.S.: U.S. Army experiments with aluminum cases for .30-40 Krag ammunition

- 1906 U.S.: U.S. Army adopts .30-'06 cartridge

- 1912 Britain: H & H introduces the first belted rimless Magnum cartridge case, the .375 H & H Magnum

- 1914 Germany: steel case cartridges developed by German Army

- 1943 Germany: German Army adopts first assault rifle cartridge, 7.92x33mm

- 1947 Soviet Union: Red Army adopts 7.62x39mm cartridge

- 1957 U.S.: U.S. Army adopts 7.62x51mm NATO cartridge, NATO also adopted

- 1960 U.S.: U.S. Army adopts 5.56x45mm cartridge

- 1978 circa U.S.: CCI introduces Blazer aluminum cased centerfire handgun ammunition

- 1980 Europe: NATO adopts 5.56x45mm cartridge

- 2002 circa U.S.: NATEC introduces composite plastic/metal centerfire rifle cartridge case

CHAPTER 16 : CALIBER HISTORY

CHAPTER 16 HIGHLIGHTS:

- RIMFIRE
- CENTERFIRE REVOLVER
- CENTERFIRE PISTOL
- CENTERFIRE RIFLE-MILITARY
- CENTERFIRE RIFLE-COMMERCIAL

RIMFIRE

- 1845 France: BB cap (Flobert)
- 1856 U.S.: .22 Short (S&W)
- 1860 U.S.: .25 Short
- 1860 U.S.: .30 Short
- 1860 U.S.: .32 Short
- 1860 U.S.: .38 Short
- 1860 U.S.: .38 Long
- 1860 U.S.: .44 Long
- 1860 U.S.: .44 Henry Flat
- 1860 U.S.: 56-56 Spencer
- 1860 U.S.: .58 Mont Storm
- 1861 U.S.: .32 Long
- 1861 U.S.: 56-50 Spencer
- 1861 U.S.: .58 Joslyn Carbine
- 1862 U.S.: .54 Ballard
- 1862 U.S.: .58 Gatling
- 1863 U.S.: .41 Short
- 1864 U.S.: .58 Miller
- 1865 Britain: .297 British
- 1865 Britain: .442 British Revolver
- 1865 U.S.: .50 Remington Navy
- 1865 U.S.: .50 Peabody
- 1866 U.S.: 56-46 Spencer
- 1866 U.S.: 56-52 Spencer
- 1866 Denmark: 17.5x28Rmm Danish Snider
- 1867 U.S.: .52 Sharps
- 1867 Austria: 14.5mm Waenzl
- 1867 U.S.: .58 Miller/Allin
- 1868 Switzerland: 18mm Milbank-Amsler

- 1869 Switzerland: 10.4x38Rmm Swiss Vetterli M69/81 (rimfire)
- 1869 U.S.: .44 Extra Long
- 1870 Britain: .340 British
- 1870 U.S.: .38 Extra Long
- 1870 U.S.: .44 Short
- 1871 U.S.: .22 Long
- 1871 U.S.: .32 Extra Short
- 1872 Switzerland: 10.4mm Swiss Revolver
- 1873 U.S.: .30 Long
- 1873 U.S.: .41 Long
- 1873 U.S.: .46 Extra Long
- 1876 U.S.: .32 Extra Long
- 1878 U.S.: .46 Short
- 1880 U.S.: .22 Extra Long
- 1887 U.S.: .22 Long Rifle (Stevens)
- 1890 U.S.: .22 Winchester Rimfire (WRF)
- 1900 U.S.: .25 Stevens
- 1900 U.S.: .32 Long Rifle
- 1902 U.S.: .25 Stevens Short
- 1903 U.S.: .22 Winchester Automatic
- 1914 U.S.: .22 Remington Automatic
- 1920 Germany: 4mm Practice
- 1940 U.S.: .267 Remington Rimfire
- 1959 U.S.: .22 Winchester Mag. Rimfire (WMR)
- 1969 U.S.: 5mm Remington Magnum
- 1972 U.S.: .20 Wingo (Winchester)
- 1976 U.S.: .22 Stinger (ultra high velocity)
- 1987 U.S.: .22 ILARCO (Winchester)
- 1999 Mexico: .22 SSS
- 2003 U.S.: .17 Hornady Magnum Rimfire (HMR)

- 2005 U.S.: .17 Mach 2, .17 Aguila
- 2007 Switzerland: 2.34mm Swiss Minigun

CENTERFIRE REVOLVER

- 1867 U.S.: .50 Remington/M71 Army
- 1868 Britain: .44 Webley/.442 RIC
- 1868 Britain: .450 Revolver/ .450 Adams
- 1870 Britain: .320 Revolver
- 1870 Britain: .380 Short, .380 Long
- 1870 U.S.: .44 S&W Russian
- 1870 U.S.: .44 S&W American
- 1870 Austria: 11.75mm Montenegrin Rev.
- 1871 U.S.: .44 Colt
- 1873 France: 11mm French Ordnance Rev.
- 1873 U.S.: .45 Colt
- 1874 Italy: 10.4mm Italian Rev.
- 1874 U.S.: .38-40 Winchester (WCF)

> *"The .44-40 Winchester cartridge has killed more men, good and bad, than all other cartridges put together."*
> - popular saying in the Old West circa 1880

- 1874 U.S.: .44-40 Winchester (WCF)
- 1875 U.S.: .32 Short Colt, .32 Long Colt
- 1875 U.S.: .38 Short Colt, .38 Long Colt
- 1875 U.S.: .45 S&W Schofield
- 1876 Britain: .45 Webley
- 1877 U.S.: .38 S&W
- 1877 U.S.: .41 Short Colt, .41 Long Colt
- 1878 U.S.: .32 S&W
- 1879 Germany: 11mm German Service Rev.
- 1880 U.S.: .44 Bulldog
- 1881 Britain: .476 Enfield Mk. III/.476 Eley
- 1882 U.S.: .32-20 Winchester (WCF)
- 1892 Switzerland: 7.5mm Swiss Army Rev.
- 1892 France: 8mm Lebel Revolver
- 1892 Britain: .455 Revolver Mk. I/.455 Colt
- 1894 France: 5.5mm Velo Dog
- 1895 Russia: 7.62mm Nagant

- 1897 Britain: .455 Revolver Mk. II
- 1898 Austria: 8mm Rast-Gasser
- 1902 U.S.: .38 S&W Special
- 1903 U.S.: .32 S&W Long
- 1907 U.S.: .44 S&W Special
- 1920 U.S.: .45 Auto Rim
- 1935 U.S.: .357 Magnum
- 1955 U.S.: .44 Remington Magnum
- 1957 U.S.: .454 Casull
- 1961 U.S.: .22 Remington Jet Magnum
- 1961 U.S.: .401 Herter's Powermag
- 1964 U.S.: .41 Remington Magnum
- 1983 U.S.: .357 Maximum
- 1984 U.S.: .32 H&R Magnum
- 1988 U.S.: .475 Linebaugh
- 1989 U.S.: 9mm Federal
- 2001 U.S.: .480 Ruger
- 2003 U.S.: .500 S&W Magnum
- 2005 U.S.: .460 S&W Magnum
- 2005 U.S.: .500 S&W Special
- 2008 U.S.: .327 Federal

CENTERFIRE PISTOL

- 1893 U.S.: .30/7.65mm Borchardt
- 1894 Germany: 5mm and 6.5mm Bergmann
- 1896 Germany: 7.63x25mm Mauser/.30 Mauser
- 1897 Spain: 5mm Clement
- 1899 Belgium: 7.65mm Auto/.32 ACP
- 1900 Austria: 7.63mm Mannlicher
- 1900 Germany: 7.65x21mm Luger (.30 Luger)
- 1900 U.S.: .38 Automatic
- 1901 Austria: 7.65mm Roth-Sauer
- 1902 Germany: 9mm Luger/9x19mm Parabellum
- 1903 Belgium: 9mm Browning Long
- 1904 Belgium: 6.35mm Auto/.25 ACP
- 1904 Japan: 8mm Nambu
- 1905 U.S.: .45 Automatic/.45 ACP
- 1907 Austria: 8mm Roth-Steyr

- 1908 Germany: 9mm Mauser
- 1908 U.S.: .44 Marbles Game Getter
- 1910 Italy: 9mm Glisenti
- 1910 Denmark: 9mm Bergmann-Bayard Long
- 1911 U.S.: .45 ACP (Military)
- 1912 Austria: 9mm Steyr
- 1912 Belgium: .380 ACP/9x17mm Kurz
- 1912 U.S.: 9.8mm Automatic Colt
- 1912 Britain: .455 Webley Automatic
- 1913 U.S.: .35 S&W Auto
- 1914 Germany: 2.7mm Kolibri
- 1920 Germany: 4.25mm Liliput Auto
- 1920 Japan: 7mm Nambu
- 1929 U.S.: .38 Super Automatic
- 1930 Soviet Union: 7.62x25mm Tokarev
- 1935 France: 7.65mm MAS
- 1949 Soviet Union: 9mm Makarov
- 1960 U.S.: .256 Winchester Magnum
- 1963 U.S.: .221 Remington Fireball
- 1970 Soviet Union: 5.45x18mm Soviet
- 1971 U.S.: .44 Auto Mag
- 1972 Germany: 9mm Ultra (9x18mm)
- 1977 U.S.: 9mm Winchester Magnum
- 1978 U.S.: 7mm Bench Rest Remington
- 1979 U.S.: .45 Winchester Magnum
- 1983 Sweden: 10mm Automatic
- 1985 Europe: 9x21mm, .45 Auto Short
- 1986 Israel: .41 Action Express
- 1988 Israel: .50 Action Express
- 1990 U.S.: .40 S&W
- 1994 U.S.: .357 SIG
- 2003 Austria: .45 Glock Auto Pistol
- 2012 Philippines: .22 TCM

CENTERFIRE RIFLE-MILITARY

- 1866 U.S.: .50-70 Government
- 1867 Belgium: 11x50Rmm Belgian Albini M67/72

- 1867 Britain: .577 Snider
- 1867 Denmark: .45 Danish Remington
- 1867 Norway: 12.17x44Rmm Norwegian Remington
- 1867 Sweden: 12.17x42Rmm Swedish Remington
- 1867 Spain: 11.5x57Rmm Spanish Reformado
- 1868 Russia: 10.75x58Rmm Russian Berdan
- 1869 Spain: 11.15x58Rmm Spanish Remington
- 1870 Italy: 10.4x47Rmm Italian Vetterli M70
- 1870 Egypt: 11.43x50Rmm Egyptian Remington
- 1871 Germany: 11.15x60Rmm Mauser
- 1871 Netherlands: 11.3x50Rmm Beaumont M71
- 1871 Britain: .577/450 Martini-Henry
- 1873 Austria: 11.4x50Rmm Austrian Werndl M73
- 1873 U.S.: .45-70 Government
- 1874 France: 11x59Rmm French Gras
- 1874 Brazil: 11.4x50Rmm Brazilian Comblain M74
- 1874 Turkey: 11.43x55Rmm Turkish
- 1877 Austria: 11.15x58Rmm Austrian Werndl M77
- 1878 Serbia: 10.15x63Rmm Serbian Mauser
- 1878 Netherlands: 11x52Rmm Beaumont M71/78
- 1880 Japan: 11x60Rmm Japanese Murata
- 1881 Sweden, Norway: 10.16x61Rmm Jarmann M81
- 1885 Portugal: 8x60Rmm Guedes M85
- 1886 France: 8x50Rmm Lebel
- 1887 Japan: 8x53Rmm Japanese Murata
- 1887 Turkey: 9.5x60Rmm Turkish Mauser
- 1888 Germany: 7.9x57mmJ Mauser
- 1888 Britain: .303 British
- 1888 Austria: 8x50Rmm Austria Mannlicher
- 1889 Switzerland: 7.5x53mm Schmidt-Rubin
- 1889 Belgium: 7.65x53mm Belgian (Argentine) Mauser
- 1889 Denmark: 8x58Rmm Danish Krag
- 1891 Italy: 6.5x52mm Mannlicher-Carcano
- 1891 Russia: 7.62x54Rmm Russian

Oldest Military Cartridge Still in Frontline Service 2009

The oldest military cartridge still in frontline service is the venerable 7.62x54Rmm Russian. Originally adopted in 1891, it soldiers on as the standard cartridge for medium machineguns and sniper rifles in the Russian Army and People's Liberation Army in China as well as many former Warsaw Pact client states.

Although considered an anachronism by many, the 7.62x54Rmm Russian shows no signs of becoming obsolete in the near future despite being replaced officially by the 7.62x39mm Soviet cartridge for AK-47 infantry rifles and PK light machineguns.

- 1892 Netherlands, Rumania: 6.5x53Rmm Mannlicher
- 1892 U.S.: .30-40 Krag
- 1893 Spain: 7x57mm Mauser
- 1894 Sweden: 6.5x55mm Swedish Mauser
- 1895 U.S.: 6mm Lee Navy
- 1895 France: 6.5x53.5SRmm Daudeteau
- 1896 Denmark: 11.7x51Rmm Danish Remington
- 1897 Japan: 6.5x50SRmm Japanese Type 30
- 1898 Portugal: 6.5x58mm Portugese Vergueiro
- 1898 Britain: .310 Cadet/.310 Greener
- 1900 Greece: 6.5x54mm Mannlicher-Schoenauer
- 1902 Siam: 8x50Rmm Siamese Mauser Type 45
- 1903 U.S.: .30-'03 U.S. Government
- 1905 Germany: 7.9x57mmJS Mauser
- 1906 U.S.: .30-'06 Springfield
- 1911 Switzerland: 7.5x55mm Schmidt-Rubin GP11
- 1918 U.S.: .30 Pedersen
- 1918 Germany: 13x92SRmm TUF
- 1923 Siam: 8x52Rmm Siamese Type 66
- 1923 U.S.: .50 Browning Machine Gun (BMG)
- 1923 Britain: .5 Inch Vickers Mk. C (12.7x81mm)
- 1924 France: 7.5x58mm MAS M24C
- 1929 France: 7.5x54mm MAS M29C
- 1930 Soviet Union: 12.7x108mm DShK
- 1930 France: 13.2x99mm M30
- 1931 Hungary: 8x56Rmm Austrian/Hungarian Mannlicher M31
- 1932 U.S.: .276 Pedersen
- 1932 Sweden: 8x68mm Swedish

- 1934 Italy: 12.7x81mm Breda
- 1937 Italy: 8x59mm Breda
- 1937 Britain: .55 Boys W Mk. I (14x99mm)
- 1938 Italy: 7.35mm Italian Carcano
- 1939 Japan: 7.7x58mm Arisaka
- 1940 Britain: 15x104mm BESA
- 1941 U.S.: .30 M1 Carbine
- 1941 Soviet Union: 14.5x114mm KPV
- 1942 Germany: 7.92x33mm Kurz
- 1943 Soviet Union: 7.62x39mm M43
- 1952 Czechoslovakia: 7.62x45mm M52
- 1952 U.S.: 12.7x76mm Spotter
- 1957 U.S.: 7.62x51mm
- 1961 U.S.: 5.56x45mm
- 1974 Soviet Union: 5.45x39mm Soviet
- 1983 U.S./Finland: .338 Lapua Magnum
- 1987 China: 5.8x42mm DBP87
- 1988 Belgium: 5.7x28mm FN P90
- 1992 China: 5.8x21mm DAP92
- 1998 Germany: 4.6x30mm
- 2003 U.S.: 6.8x45mm SPC
- 2012 U.S.: 300 ACC Blackout

CENTERFIRE RIFLE-COMMERCIAL

- 1868 Britain: .500 Express
- 1869 U.S.: .40-60 Sharps (Necked), .44-60 Sharps
- 1870 Britain: .577 Express
- 1871 U.S.: .40-70 Sharps (Necked)
- 1872 U.S.: .50-90 Sharps
- 1873 U.S.: .45-70 Government, .40-90 Sharps (Necked), .44-90 Sharps
- 1876 U.S.: .40-60 Winchester, .40-50 Sharps (Straight), .45-60 Winchester, .45-75 Winchester, .45-90 Sharps, .45-100 Sharps, .45-110 Sharps, .50-95 Winchester
- 1877 U.S.: .40-90 Peabody, .44-95 Peabody
- 1877 Britain: .450 3¼" Black Powder Express, .577/500 No .2 Express
- 1878 U.S.: .45-120 Sharps

Everlast Cartridge Cases

In the late 1870s, brass centerfire cartridges were loaded with black powder. When fired, the corrosive residue from the powder attacked the brass case, reducing the reloading life only to a few shots. As many people at the time reloaded for practical reasons such as limited ammunition availability in remote areas, this became a real problem. Ammunition manufacturers responded by offering "everlast" cartridge cases in some popular rifle calibers. Everlast cartridge cases were thicker and heavier than standard cases to withstand the corrosive effects of black powder for increased reloading life. However, everlast cases required a special chamber and would not hold as much propellant as standard cases. For this reason, everlast cases were frequently rated for lower propellant charges than standard cases. The advent of smokeless propellants in the late 1880s ended the requirement for everlast cases and by 1900 they faded into history.

An everlast case was described in manufacturer's literature with the standard caliber nomenclature followed by the word everlast. Everlast cartridge cases were not made in shotshell gauges or in handgun calibers.

- 1881 U.S.: .40-60 Marlin
- 1882 U.S.: .32-20 Winchester (WCF)
- 1882 Britain: .297/230 Morris Short/Long
- 1884 U.S.: .32-40 Ballard, .38-55 Ballard
- 1885 U.S.: .32-35 Stevens, .40-84 Winchester
- 1885 Germany: 5.6x35Rmm Vierling
- 1886 U.S.: .45-90 Winchester
- 1887 U.S.: .38-56 Winchester, .40-65 Winchester
- 1888 U.S.: .70-150 Winchester
- 1888 Germany: 8x57mmJ Mauser, 8x51mm Mauser
- 1889 Germany: 9x57mm Mauser
- 1892 U.S.: .25-20 Winchester (WCF), .50-110 Winchester
- 1893 Germany: 6.5x57mm Mauser
- 1895 U.S.: .25-35 Winchester (WCF), .30-30 Winchester, .32 Winchester Special, .303 Savage, .25-36 Marlin, .40-72 Winchester
- 1895 Britain: .500 Nitro Express 3" and 3¼"
- 1895 Germany: 6x57mm Mauser, 8.15x46Rmm
- 1897 U.S.: .25-21 Stevens
- 1898 Britain: .450 3¼" Nitro Express
- 1900 U.S.: .28-30-120 Stevens
- 1900 Britain: .500/450 3¼" Nitro Express, .450 No. 2 Nitro Express 3½", .577 Nitro Express, .600 Nitro Express

The Meaning of Nitro Express

Many British large bore double rifle cartridges were developed in the late 1800s for hunting large heavy game in Africa or India. Such cartridges originally were loaded with black powder. With the advent of smokeless propellants in the late 1880s, loading of some (but not all) of these calibers was switched to Cordite. In doing this, considerable difficulty was often experienced in regulating the strike of the bullet to black powder standards. In some instances, new loads were developed.

To differentiate between the two propellant types, cartridges loaded with smokeless propellants were called "Nitro Express (NE)" while those loaded with black powder were called "Black Powder Express (BPE)". BPE cartridges were loaded normally with solid lead bullets while Nitro Express cartridges were loaded normally with jacketed bullets.

A good example of this process is the .577 3¼" BPE (developed circa 1866) and its modern counterpart the .577 3¼" Nitro Express (developed circa 1900).

- 1900 Germany: 9.3x57mm Mauser
- 1902 U.S.: .33 Winchester
- 1902 Britain: .400 Jeffery Nitro Express
- 1903 U.S.: .32 Ideal, .35 Winchester
- 1904 U.S.: .405 Winchester
- 1905 U.S.: .32 Winchester Self-Loading, .35 Winchester Self-Loading

What was the first belted cartridge case?

Introduced by Holland & Holland in 1905, the .400/375 Holland & Holland Belted Nitro Express was the first cartridge to have a reinforcing belt around the base of the cartridge case. Intended for hunting dangerous game in Africa, the factory load consisted of a 270 grain soft point or full metal jacket bullet at a muzzle velocity of 2771 fps. It was chambered in bolt-action rifles.

- 1905 Britain: .400/375 Belted Nitro Express Holland & Holland
- 1905 Germany: 9.3x62mm Mauser
- 1906 U.S.: .25 Remington, .30 Remington, .32 Remington, .35 Remington, .30-'06 Springfield
- 1906 Germany: 8x57mmJS Mauser

- 1906 Britain: .280 Ross
- 1907 Britain: .470 Nitro Express, .476 Nitro Express, 500/465 Nitro Express
- 1907 U.S.: .351 Winchester Self-Loading
- 1908 Austria: 8x56mm Mannlicher-Schoenauer
- 1909 Britain: .404 Jeffery, .425 Westley Richards Magnum
- 1910 Britain: .318 Westley Richards/ Rimless Nitro Express
- 1910 U.S.: .401 Winchester Self-Loading
- 1910 Germany: 8x75Rmm, 9.3x64mm Brenneke
- 1910 Austria: 9.5x57mm Mannlicher-Schoenauer, 10.75x63mm Mannlicher
- 1911 Britain: .416 Rigby, .275 Holland & Holland Belted Magnum, .505 Gibbs
- 1912 Germany: 9.3x74Rmm, 8x64mm Brenneke
- 1912 Britain: .275 Holland & Holland Magnum, .375 Holland & Holland Magnum
- 1912 U.S.: .22 Savage Hi-Power
- 1913 U.S.: .256 Newton, .30 Newton
- 1915 U.S.: .250 Savage (.250-3000), .35 Newton
- 1917 Germany: 7x64mm Brenneke
- 1920 U.S.: .300 Savage
- 1920 Germany: 8x60mmS Mauser, 11.2x60mm Mauser, 11.2x72mm Mauser, 12.5x70mm Schuler
- 1921 Britain: .240 Magnum Rimless (H&H)
- 1922 Germany: 10.75x68mm Mauser
- 1925 U.S.: .270 Winchester
- 1925 Britain: .300 Holland & Holland Magnum
- 1928 U.S.: .22 Hornet
- 1931 Germany: 7x73mm Vom Hofe (belted)
- 1932 Germany: 6.5x61mm Mauser
- 1934 U.S.: .257 Roberts
- 1934 Germany: 7x72Rmm
- 1935 U.S.: .220 Swift
- 1936 U.S.: .348 Winchester
- 1937 U.S.: .219 Zipper
- 1937 Germany: 5.6x61mm Vom Hofe Super Express
- 1938 U.S.: .218 Bee

- 1938 Germany: 6.5x68mm Schuler, 8x68mmS Magnum
- 1939 Germany: 7x75Rmm Vom Hofe Super Express
- 1943 U.S.: .270 Weatherby Magnum
- 1944 U.S.: .257 Weatherby Magnum, 7mm Weatherby Magnum, .300 Weatherby Magnum, .375 Weatherby Magnum
- 1950 U.S.: .222 Remington
- 1952 U.S.: .308 Winchester
- 1953 U.S.: .378 Weatherby Magnum, 7x61mm Sharpe & Hart Super
- 1955 U.S.: .243 Winchester, .244 Remington, .358 Winchester
- 1955 Britain: .244 Holland & Holland Magnum
- 1956 U.S.: .458 Winchester Magnum
- 1957 U.S.: .223 Remington, .280 Remington
- 1958 U.S.: .222 Remington Magnum, 264 Winchester Magnum, .338 Winchester Magnum, .460 Weatherby Magnum
- 1959 Sweden: .358 Norma Magnum
- 1960 U.S.: .256 Winchester Magnum
- 1960 Sweden: .308 Norma Magnum
- 1962 U.S.: 7mm Remington Magnum, .340 Weatherby Magnum
- 1962 Germany: 7x66mm Vom Hofe Super Express
- 1963 U.S.: .224 Weatherby Magnum, 6mm Remington, .284 Winchester, .300 Winchester Magnum
- 1964 U.S.: .225 Winchester, .444 Marlin
- 1964 Germany: 5.6x57mm RWS
- 1965 U.S.: .22-250 Remington, .350 Remington Magnum
- 1966 U.S.: 6.5mm Remington Magnum
- 1968 U.S.: .240 Weatherby Magnum
- 1968 Germany: 5.6x50Rmm Magnum
- 1969 U.S.: .25-'06 Remington
- 1971 U.S.: .17 Remington
- 1974 U.S.: .22 PPC
- 1975 U.S.: 6mm PPC
- 1977 U.S.: .495 A-Square

- 1978 U.S.: 6mm Bench Rest Remington, 8mm Remington Magnum, .375 Winchester, .338 A-Square
- 1980 U.S.: 7mm-08 Remington
- 1982 U.S.: .307 Winchester
- 1983 U.S.: .356 Winchester
- 1984 U.S.: 7-30 Waters
- 1987 U.S.: .35 Whelen, 7mm STE
- 1988 U.S.: .416 Remington Magnum, .700 Nitro Express
- 1988 Germany: 6.5x65mm RWS
- 1989 U.S.: 7mm STW, .416 Weatherby Magnum
- 1990 Germany: .30R Blaser
- 1990 U.S.: .358 Shooting Times Alaskan
- 1992 U.S.: .400 A-Square
- 1993 U.S.: .577 Tyrannosaur (A-Square)
- 1995 Britain: .450 Rigby

- 1996 U.S.: .30-378 Weatherby
- 1999 U.S.: .300 Remington Ultra Magnum, .338 Remington Ultra Magnum, .338-378 Weatherby
- 2001 U.S.: .260 Remington, .270 Winchester Short Magnum, .300 Winchester Short Magnum, 7mm Remington Ultra Magnum, .450 Marlin
- 2002 U.S.: 7mm Winchester Short Magnum, 7mm Remington Short Action Ultra Magnum, .300 Remington Short Action Ultra Magnum, .375 Remington Ultra Magnum, .458 Lott
- 2003 U.S.: .223 Winchester Super Short Magnum, .243 Winchester Super Short Magnum, 6.5 Grendel
- 2004 U.S.: .204 Ruger, .25 Winchester Super Short Magnum, 6.8mm Remington SPC, .325 Winchester Short Magnum
- 2007 U.S.: .17 Remington Fireball, .30 T/C, .308 Marlin Express, .375 Ruger, .450 Bushmaster
- 2012 U.S.: .17 Hornet

Military Rifle Cartridge Service Dates, by Nation

Nation	Caliber	Service Dates	Nation	Caliber	Service Dates
Belgium	7.65x53mm Belgian Mauser	1889-1949	Japan	10x60Rmm Murata	1880-1898
	.30-06 Springfield	1949-1956		6.5x50SRmm Arisaka	1898-1945
	7.62x51mm NATO	1953-1979		7.7x58mm Arisaka	1939-1945
	5.56x45mm NATO	1979-present		.30-06 Springfield	1945-1964
				7.62x51mm NATO	1964-present
				5.56x45mm NATO	1989-present
China	7.92x57mmJ Mauser	1888-1935	Russia	10.75x58Rmm	1869-1891
	7.92x57mmJS Mauser	1935-1952		7.62x54Rmm Russian	1891-1943
	7.62x54Rmm Russian	1953-1976		7.62x39mm Soviet	1943-1974
	7.62x39mm Soviet	1956-1995		5.45x39mm Soviet	1974-present
	5.8x42mm Chinese	1995-present			
France	11mm Chassepot	1866-1874	Spain	7x57mm Mauser	1893-1942
	11x59Rmm Gras	1874-1886		7.92x57mmJS Mauser	1942-1958
	8x50Rmm Lebel	1886-1940		7.62x51mm NATO	1958-1997
	7.5x54mm French	1936-1979		5.56x45mm NATO	2000-present
	5.56x45mm NATO	1978-present			
Germany	15.4mm Needle Gun	1848-1871	Switzerland	10.4x38Rmm RF	1869-1890
	11x60Rmm Mauser	1871-1888		7.5x55mm Schmidt-Rubin	1889-1990
	7.92x57mmJ Mauser	1888-1905		5.56x45mm G90	1990-present
	7.92x57mmJS Mauser	1905-1945			
	7.92x33mm Kurz	1943-1945	United Kingdom	.577 Snider	1866-1871
	7.62x51mm NATO	1955-1965		.577-450 Martini-Henry	1871-1888
	5.56x45mm NATO	1995-present		.303 British	1888-1956
				7.62x51mm NATO	1956-1985
East Germany	7.62x39mm Soviet	1955-1990		5.56x45mm NATO	1885-present
Israel	7.92x57mmJS Mauser	1948-1958	United States	.50-70 Gov't.	1866-1873
	7.62x51mm NATO	1955-1974		.45-70 Gov't.	1873-1886
	5.56x45mm NATO	1974-present		.30-40 Krag	1894-1903
				.30 Carbine	1941-1961
Italy	6.5x52mm Mann.-Carcano	1892-1950		.30-06 Springfield	1906-1963
	.30-06 Springfield	1945-1959		7.62x51mm NATO	1957-1961
	7.62x51mm NATO	1959-1990		5.56x45mm NATO	1961-present
	5.56x45mm NATO	1972-present			

General Manuel Mondragon

At the beginning of World War I, aircraft were used only for reconnaissance purposes and were unarmed. Inevitably, however, airmen began taking rifles, pistols and even shotguns with them on missions to shoot at enemy aircraft.

As pistols were not powerful enough and shotguns lacked sufficient range, rifles were the best choice. However, bolt-action military rifles were too cumbersome to operate while piloting an aircraft. A semi-automatic, centerfire rifle was needed, but none of the warring countries made such a rifle.

Manuel Mondragon had developed such a semi-automatic rifle before World War I. As there was no suitable manufacturer for his rifle in Mexico, Mondragon persuaded SIG, of Switzerland, to manufacture his rifle and Polte in Germany to make the cartridge. Both were available when World War I began.

The German Air Force purchased Mondragon rifles and ammunition to arm its pilots. In so doing, the 5.2x68mm Mondragon cartridge became the first rifle cartridge to be officially adopted for air combat.

SECTION IV – WORLD AMMUNITION DEVELOPMENT
CHAPTER 17 : WHAT CARTRIDGES ARE USED FOR

CHAPTER 17 HIGHLIGHTS:

- THE FIVE GENERAL USES FOR CARTRIDGES
  - SPORTING USES
- MILITARY USES
- LAW ENFORCEMENT USES
- INDUSTRIAL USES
- SCIENTIFIC USES

THE FIVE GENERAL USES FOR CARTRIDGES

1. Sporting
2. Military
3. Law enforcement
4. Industrial
5. Scientific

Cartridges may be broken down by use into five broad categories: sporting, military, law enforcement, industrial, and scientific. Within each category are numerous uses, some of which are unique and not commonly known such as signaling, line throwing, starting boat races, and removing clinkers in kilns. The sporting category is the largest with 207 different uses for 55% of the total. While the industrial and scientific categories are small, they are easily the most exotic.

In total, there are over 370 uses for cartridges!

USES FOR CARTRIDGES

	Competition	Hunting	Operations	Other	Total
SPORTING	89	104	n/a	14	207
MILITARY	52	n/a	34	n/a	86
LAW FORCEMENT	n/a	n/a	24	n/a	24
INDUSTRIAL	n/a	n/a	n/a	31	31
SCIENTIFIC	n/a	n/a	na	28	28
Total uses	141	104	58	73	376
Percentage	37.5	27.7	15.4	19.4	n/a

SPORTING USES

Sporting use of ammunition may be broken down into three sub-categories: competition, hunting, and personal defense. In turn, each sub-category contains numerous specific uses, for example there are over 89 uses for competition, 104 uses for hunting and 14 uses for personal defense. The large number of applications for competition, hunting, and personal defense effectively illustrates the wide variety and broad appeal of sporting cartridges.

1. COMPETITION (89 uses)

- **RIMFIRE COMPETITION (29 uses)**

  * Rifle (15 uses)

» Informal competition (9 uses)
- Instruction, training, practice, qualification
- Local, club, postal, intramural scholastic matches
- Plinking

PLINKING

Plinking is a uniquely American recreational past time consisting of informal target shooting using sporting guns for firing at inanimate targets of opportunity, usually not at dedicated shooting ranges.

» Formal competition (6 uses)
- Indoor 50 ft. positional
- Outdoor 50- and 100-yd positional
- Outdoor 50- and 100-meter positional
- Metallic silhouette
- Moving target
- Bench rest

* Handgun (14 uses)
» Informal competition (8 uses)
- Instruction, training, practice, qualification
- Local, club, postal
- Plinking

INSTRUCTION, TRAINING, PRACTICE, AND QUALIFICATION

Instruction: learning basic safety rules, gun handling, range etiquette, and shooting techniques as taught by a qualified instructor.

Training: concentrates on developing and mastering individual shooting skills under the guidance of a qualified shooting coach.

Practice: repetitive individual efforts to develop and refine skills.

Qualification: tests that verify mastery of shooting skills; used to rank shooters by ability and experience.

» Formal competition (6 uses)
  ¤ Indoor 50 ft.
  ¤ Outdoor bullseye
  ¤ Metallic silhouette
  ¤ Free pistol
  ¤ Turning target
  ¤ Olympic/ISU

• **CENTERFIRE COMPETITION (30 uses)**

  * Rifle (17 uses)
    » Informal competition (7 uses)
      ¤ Instruction, training, practice, qualification
      ¤ Local, club
      ¤ Plinking

INFORMAL COMPETITION

Informal competition is conducted at a club, team, or intramural level using relaxed rules dictated by competitor preferences. Friendship, relaxation, and enjoyment are the goals rather than aggressive competition.

    » Formal competition (10 uses)
      ¤ National match positional
      ¤ Classic military rifle positional
      ¤ Long range
      ¤ Service rifle positional
      ¤ Muzzle loading
      ¤ 300 Meter
      ¤ Palma
      ¤ Metallic silhouette
      ¤ Cowboy rifle
      ¤ Bench rest

FORMAL COMPETITION

Formal competition tests shooter skills in various disciplines under match conditions using a comprehensive set of rules sanctioned by a governing body as overseen by impartial referees and judges. Formal competition is normally conducted at the state, national, or international level.

---

  * Handgun (13 uses)
    » Informal competition (7 uses)
      ¤ Instruction, training, practice, qualification
      ¤ Local, club
      ¤ Plinking
    » Formal competition (6 uses)
      ¤ Indoor 50 ft.
      ¤ Outdoor National Match
      ¤ Metallic silhouette
      ¤ Turning target

¤ Cowboy action
¤ Practical pistol

• **SHOTSHELL COMPETITION (30 uses)**

  * Informal competition (23 uses)
    » Instruction, training, practice, qualification
    » Local, club matches in trap, skeet, sporting clays, five stand
    » Plinking, hand thrown targets
    » Duck Tower
    » Crazy Quail

  * Formal Competition (7 uses)
    » American trap
    » International clay pigeon
    » Live bird
    » American skeet
    » International skeet
    » Sporting clays
    » Five stand

FACTORY LOADED MATCH AMMUNITION

To make match-grade ammunition, factories use selected lots of components and special loading and handling procedures backed by extensive testing. These procedures allow factories to offer a truly superior product that most handloaders cannot duplicate. While such measures are expensive, the result is a product that provides the consistent reliable performance demanded by serious competitors

---

2. HUNTING (104 uses)

• **RIMFIRE HUNTING (20 uses)**

  * Training and qualification (2 uses)

  * Small game hunting (6 uses)
    » Rabbit
    » Squirrel
    » Opossum
    » Raccoon
    » Fox
    » Beaver

  * Varmint hunting (6 uses)
    » Prairie Dogs
    » Skunks
    » Coyote
    » Crows
    » Ground Hogs
    » Bobcat

  * Pest control (6 uses)
    » Rats
    » Chipmunks

» Squirrels
» Skunks
» Pigeons
» Nutria

• **CENTERFIRE HUNTING (57 uses)**

  * Centerfire Pistol and Revolver (14 uses)

    » Training and qualification (2 uses)

    » Small game hunting (5 uses)
       ¤ Rabbit
       ¤ Possum
       ¤ Raccoon
       ¤ Fox
       ¤ Beaver

    » Varmint hunting (4 uses)
       ¤ Coyote
       ¤ Bobcat
       ¤ Skunk
       ¤ Ground hog

    » Medium game hunting (3 uses)
       ¤ Deer
       ¤ Javelina
       ¤ Cougar

  * Centerfire Rifle (42 uses)

    » Training and qualification (2 uses)

    » Varmint hunting (6 uses)
       ¤ Prairie dog
       ¤ Skunk
       ¤ Coyote
       ¤ Crows
       ¤ Ground hog
       ¤ Bobcat

> ### VARMINT SHOOTING
> Varmints eat farm crops, dig up pastures, and attack livestock, causing serious problems for landowners, farmers, and ranchers. Many varmints are now suburbanites as they have adapted to life in close proximity to humans. As varmints reproduce at prodigious rates, they are not an endangered species and most are expanding their range. In most states, varmint hunting is always in season with no bag limits. Varmints are not considered edible.

    » Medium Game (14 uses)
       ¤ Deer
       ¤ Antelope
       ¤ Goat
       ¤ Sheep
       ¤ Boar
       ¤ African plains game (5)
       ¤ Leopard
       ¤ Reindeer

       ¤ Javelina
       ¤ Cougar

    » Large Game (8 uses)
       ¤ Elk
       ¤ Bear
       ¤ Caribou
       ¤ Musk ox
       ¤ Oryx
       ¤ Zebra
       ¤ Boar
       ¤ Wildebeest

    » Heavy Game (5 uses)
       ¤ Moose
       ¤ Eland
       ¤ Bison
       ¤ Nilgai
       ¤ Kudu

    » Dangerous game (7 uses)
       ¤ Lion
       ¤ Tiger
       ¤ Elephant
       ¤ Hippo
       ¤ Rhino
       ¤ Large bear
       ¤ Crocodile

• **SHOTSHELL HUNTING (27 uses)**

  * Training and qualification (2 uses)

  * Small game hunting (4 uses)
    » Rabbit
    » Squirrel
    » Opossum
    » Raccoon

  * Varmint hunting (2 uses)
    » Coyote
    » Crow

  * Pest control (5 uses)
    » Skunks
    » Pigeons, grackles, sparrows, magpies

  * Medium game (2 uses)
    » Deer
    » Bear

  * Large game (1 use)
    » Boar

  * Upland bird (6 uses)
    » Pheasant
    » Chukar
    » Quail
    » Dove
    » Partridge
    » Turkey

* Waterfowl (5 uses)
   » Migratory (3 uses)
      ¤ Ducks
      ¤ Geese
      ¤ Cranes
* Non-migratory (2 uses)
   » Rail
   » Snipe

THE 8-GAUGE SHOTSHELL

In the late 1800s, 8-gauge shotguns were popular for waterfowl hunting. When the U.S. government banned shotguns larger than 10-gauge for hunting migratory waterfowl in 1918, many believed this to be the death knell of the 8-gauge. Not so! The 8-gauge remains in full production to this day in its industrial role as a kiln gun cartridge.

---

3. PERSONAL DEFENSE (14 uses)

• **Rimfire (4 uses)**

* Revolver
   » Home
   » Auto
* Pistol
   » Home
   » Auto

• **Centerfire (8 uses)**

* Revolver
   » Home
   » Auto
   » Personal carry
* Pistol
   » Home
   » Auto
   » Personal carry
* Carbine
   » Home
   » Auto

• **Shotshell (2 uses)**

* Home
* Auto

MILITARY USES

Military ammunition use may be divided into two main categories: competition and operational. While military forces consume billions of rounds of operational ammunition every year in 34 different types of use, the quantity is spread over a limited number of different calibers. For example, NATO has approved only four operational military calibers: 9x19mm, 5.56x45mm, 7.62x51mm, and 12.7x99mm. Countries using Russian equipment have only seven operational cartridges to contend with: 7.62x25mm, 9x18mm, 9x19mm, 5.45x39mm, 7.62x39mm, 7.62x53.5Rmm, and 12.7x108mm. Therefore, the bulk of military ammunition used for operational purposes in the world today is spread over only 10 different calibers.

Most military organizations obtain their ammunition from government arsenals. While sporting ammunition manufacturers are capable of manufacturing military operational ammunition, retooling their production lines for this purpose would take months and cost millions. For this reason, government arsenals continue to have a place despite their high cost.

Many military forces do not participate in competition. Those that do, mostly NATO members and large countries such as Russia and China, compete in over 52 types of events. Ammunition for competition purposes is purchased from commercial manufacturers or hand loaded as required.

1. COMPETITION (52 uses)

• **Rimfire (17 uses)**

* Informal competition (5 uses)
   » Instruction, training, practice, qualification
   » Local intramural
* Formal competition (12 uses)
   » Pistol (6 uses)
      ¤ National match
      ¤ Turning target
      ¤ Free pistol
      ¤ Sport pistol
      ¤ Target pistol
   » Rifle (6 uses)
      ¤ NRA positional
      ¤ ISU/Olympic positional
      ¤ Moving target

• **Centerfire (28 uses)**

* Informal competition (5 uses)
   » Instruction, training, practice, qualification
   » Local intramural
* Formal competition
   » Pistol (23 uses)
      ¤ National Match
      ¤ Turning target
      ¤ Practical pistol

   » Rifle (16 uses)

       ¤ National Match positional
       ¤ Service rifle CMP positional
       ¤ Long range
       ¤ Inter-service
       ¤ 300 Meter
       ¤ Palma
       ¤ CISM

- **Shotshell (7 uses)**

  * Informal competition (5 uses)
    » Instruction, training, practice, qualification
    » Local intramural

  * Formal competition (2 uses)
    » International clay pigeon
    » International skeet

2. OPERATIONAL (34 uses)

- **Rimfire - no significant operational use**
- **Centerfire (24 uses)**

  * Pistol (10 uses)
    » Instruction, training, practice, qualification
    » Combat
    » Guard, security
    » Military police, criminal investigation
    » Testing

  * Rifle (14 uses)
    » Instruction, training, practice, qualification
    » Combat
    » Guard, security
    » Military police
    » Ceremony
    » Saluting
    » Signaling
    » Line throwing
    » Testing
    » Bomb disposal

- **Shotshell (10 uses)**

  * Instruction, training, practice, qualification

  * Combat

  * Guard, security

  * Military police

  * Line throwing

  * Testing

THE .45-70 GOVERNMENT CARTRIDGE STILL SERVES!

Adopted by the U.S. Army in 1873, the .45-70 Government was the military cartridge that tamed the West. It made history in the hands of Gen. George A. Custer's troopers at the Battle of the Little Big Horn and again in the hands of volunteer U.S. Army regiments during the Spanish-American War. It served in many state militias until well after 1900 followed by security duties guarding U.S. war plants during World War I. In the mid-1930s, the old warhorse began a new career in the U.S. Navy where it served as the propelling blank for line throwing guns and as the priming blank for the massive 16" guns on battleships. In both capacities, it served during World War II, Korea, and Vietnam.

When the battleship Missouri fired the opening shot of Operation Desert Storm, it was a .45-70 Gov't. caliber priming blank that sent the 16" shell on its way. Somehow, this seems appropriate. The battleships are now gone and the .45-70 has finally been retired from US military service.

LAW ENFORCEMENT USES

There are four types of law enforcement agencies in the U.S.: federal, state, local/metropolitan, and private. Federal, state, and local law enforcement agencies use large quantities of pistol ammunition for eight different operational applications. Substantially smaller quantities of shotshell and rifle ammunition are spread over 16 different operational applications. Private security agencies use very small quantities of ammunition (as compared to other law enforcement agencies).

Consumption of ammunition for all uses by law enforcement has been growing since the terrorist attacks on the World Trade Center. However, the total market for law enforcement ammunition remains at less than 12% of sporting ammunition volume. Nearly all large ammunition manufacturers offer special lines of ammunition for law enforcement purposes. Most law enforcement agencies purchase such products "off-the-shelf" from pre-qualified manufacturers. Some of the larger agencies purchase unique products made to their specifications on a bid basis.

1. OPERATIONAL (24 uses)

- **Rimfire - law enforcement is not a significant user of rimfire ammunition**

- **Centerfire**

  * Pistol (8 uses)

» Instruction, training, practice, qualification
» Operational
  ¤ Patrol
  ¤ Investigation
  ¤ Guard
  ¤ Testing

- **Rifle and Carbine (8 uses)**

  * Instruction, training, practice, qualification

  * Operational
    » Patrol
    » SWAT
    » Guard
    » Testing

- **Shotshell (8 uses)**

  * Instruction, training, practice, qualification

  * Operational
    » Patrol
    » SWAT
    » Guard
    » Testing

CARTRIDGES FOR LAW ENFORCEMENT
Today, it has been estimated that over 70% of all law enforcement pistols are chambered for the .40 S&W cartridge. The second most popular caliber in law enforcement use is the 9mm Luger cartridge.

INDUSTRIAL USES

Most shooters remain unaware of the importance of cartridges to industry. There are a wide variety of applications including the stud drivers used in building construction, the 8-gauge shotshells used for dislodging clinkers from kilns and the charges used for cutting heavy electrical and telephone cable. Other important applications include proving armor, proofing and testing firearms, and even starting races. Industrial cartridges have and will continue to serve a vital role in industry.

1. CONSTRUCTION (4 uses)

- **RIMFIRE CONSTRUCTION (3 uses)**

  * Stud driving

  * Hole punching

  * Cable cutting

- **CENTERFIRE CONSTRUCTION (1 use)**

  * Pistol and Revolver (1 use)
    ¤ Stud Driving

2. MANUFACTURING (15 uses)

- **RIMFIRE MANUFACTURING (3 uses)**

  * Testing firearms

  * Production quality control

  * Humane cattle killer

- **CENTERFIRE MANUFACTURING (8 uses)**

  * Pistol and Revolver (4 uses)
    » Proofing firearms
    » Testing firearms
    » Production quality control
    » Proving armor

  * Rifle (4 uses)
    » Proofing firearms
    » Testing firearms
    » Production quality control
    » Proving armor

- **SHOTSHELL MANUFACTURING (4 uses)**

  * Proofing firearms

  * Testing firearms

  * Production quality control

  * Removing clinkers from kilns

3. TESTING (3 uses)

- **RIMFIRE TESTING (3 uses)**

  * Developing new products

  * Proving armor with fragment simulators

  * Testing automobile brake systems

- **CENTERFIRE TESTING (no current uses)**

- **SHOTSHELL TESTING (no current uses)**

4. OTHER (9 uses)

- **RIMFIRE OTHER (2 uses)**

  * Starting races

  * Propelling charge

- **CENTERFIRE OTHER (3 uses)**

  * Pistol and Revolver
    » Starting races
    » Propelling charge
    » Humane shark killer

- **SHOTSHELL OTHER (4 uses)**

  * Starting races
  * Signalling
  * Propelling charge for line throwing
  * Humane shark killer

KILN GUNS

A kiln gun is an 8-gauge shotgun designed to remove clinkers which build up on the inside of kilns (brick ovens), by shooting them with a solid lead or zinc slug. Most kiln guns are single-shot, smooth bores using a very large, heavy Martini-Henry pivoting-block action with a muffler device to abate the sound of the muzzle blasts. As kiln guns are very heavy, they are fired from a secure mount. Normally, a kiln gun is operated by two men.

SCIENTIFIC USES

Cartridges serve an obscure but vital role in scientific research. Did you know that space vehicles are routinely tested against micrometeorite impacts using light gas guns firing plastic balls at ultra high velocities? Cartridges provide inexpensive reliable means to test advanced armor arrays, explore ballistic frontiers, and test new materials. Modern law enforcement has become a major consumer of all types of cartridges for forensic testing and analysis. Some 28 different applications exist now and new applications are being added on a regular basis.

1. FORENSICS (3 uses)
- **RIMFIRE FORENSICS (1 use)**
  * Testing
- **CENTERFIRE FORENSICS (1 use)**
  * Testing
- **SHOTSHELL FORENSICS (1 use)**
  * Testing

2. ARMOR (3 uses)
- **RIMFIRE ARMOR (2 uses)**
  * Fragment simulators
  * Testing
- **CENTERFIRE ARMOR (1 use)**
  * Armor array testing

3. PROPULSION (4 uses)
- **RIMFIRE PROPULSION (no current uses)**
- **CENTERFIRE PROPULSION (3 uses)**
  * For use in ultra-high velocity "light gas" guns
    » Meteor impact simulation, on space vehicles
    » Armor array impact testing
    » Experimental/advanced ballistics testing
- **SHOTSHELL PROPULSION (1 use)**
  * For use in ultra-high velocity "light gas" guns

4. RESEARCH AND DEVELOPMENT (18 uses)
- **RIMFIRE RESEARCH AND DEVELOPMENT (6 uses)**
  * Product and component improvement
  * New materials
  * New components
  * Interior ballistics
  * Exterior ballistics
  * Terminal ballistics
- **CENTERFIRE RESEARCH AND DEVELOPMENT (6 uses)**
  * Product and component improvement
  * New materials
  * New components
  * Interior ballistics
  * Exterior ballistics
  * Terminal ballistics
- **SHOTSHELL RESEARCH AND DEVELOPMENT (6 uses)**
  * Product and component improvement
  * New materials
  * New components
  * Interior ballistics
  * Exterior ballistics
  * Terminal ballistics

THE SIEGE OF CICERO

Hymie Weiss, head of the North Side gang in Chicago, tired of the constant turf wars with the Al Capone gang. Weiss resolved to end it by hitting Capone with everything he had. On the morning of September 20, 1926, Capone and his men were in the coffee shop of the Hawthorne Hotel, their headquarters. When gunfire broke out down the street, Capone and his men moved to the front window to see what the commotion was all about. They were confronted by a column of ten large cars that slowly cruised by the Hawthorne coffee shop as Weiss gunmen poured over 1,000 rounds of gunfire into the building. No one was killed, however the hotel building suffered heavy damage.

The Beast That Went "pooh, pooh"

The first recorded use of a machinegun in combat occurred on November 1, 1893 near the Bembezi River in Matabeleland which is now part of Zimbabwe. When the Chartered British South Africa Company sought to seize the mineral wealth of the African kingdom, King Lobengula of the Matabele ordered his 100,000 man army to resist. The first decisive battle occurred on the above date when a force of 670 British soldiers in a laager near the river were attacked on all sides by an estimated 1,700 Matabele warriors from the Imbezu and Ingubu regiments armed with rifles and spears. The British Army men also were armed with rifles– and five new, water-cooled Maxim machineguns.

The Matabele warriors were familiar with rifle fire and were prepared for it. However, they were completely unprepared for the Maxim machineguns. Repeatedly, they tried to rush the British laager over open ground, only to be met by withering fire from the Maxims. Despite their best efforts, the Matabele never got closer than 70 yards to the machineguns. It was estimated that some 1,500 Matabele warriors perished in the fight. The British suffered negligible losses.

Matabele survivors of the battle told their king they could not kill the evil spirit beast that went "pooh, pooh" which is the sound the Maxim guns made when fired.

CHAPTER 18 : AMMUNITION MANUFACTURERS

CHAPTER 18 HIGHLIGHTS:

- HOW TO CATEGORIZE MANUFACTURERS
- FULL LINE COMMERCIAL MANUFACTURER
- SHORT LINE COMMERCIAL MANUFACTURER
- PROPRIETARY PRODUCT LINE
- CUSTOM LOADER
- COMMERCIAL RELOADER
- GOVERNMENT ARSENALS
- MARKET DYNAMIC
- COMPANY PROFILES

HOW TO CATEGORIZE MANUFACTURERS

All ammunition manufacturers are not equal. Accordingly, we may categorize them into six different types: full line commercial, short line commercial, proprietary product lines, custom loaders, commercial reloaders, and government arsenals. The delineations between categories are based on three things: the number of product types offered, the number of line items, and component sources.

1. PRODUCT TYPES OFFERED

As we have seen in Chapter 2: Basic Types of Cartridges, there are three basic types of cartridges: rimfire, centerfire, and shotshell. Ammunition manufacturers can be sorted according to the basic types they offer:

- A full line manufacturer makes all three types of cartridges
- A short line manufacturer makes one or two types of cartridges
- Proprietary product lines are special products or calibers made by ammunition manufacturers but sold by an entirely different manufacturer or business
- A custom loader assembles one or two basic types of cartridge
- A commercial reloader offers remanufactured centerfire cartridges
- Government arsenals manufacture only centerfire ammunition

2. PRODUCT LINE SIZE

- Full line manufacturers offer product lines of over 400 items
- Short line manufacturers offer product lines of less than 150 items
- Proprietary product lines number less than 85 items
- Custom loaders offer less than 200 line items
- Commercial reloaders offer 50 line items or less
- Government arsenals manufacture less than 12 calibers, but many varieties of those calibers

3. COMPONENT SOURCES

- A full line manufacturer makes primers, cartridge cases, bullets, shot, wad columns, and wads
- A short line manufacturer makes cartridge cases and bullets

or wad columns
- The company marketing a proprietary product line makes no components, or bullets only
- Custom loaders purchase components, but may make some or all bullets
- A commercial reloader purchases all components including fired cases
- Government arsenals manufacture all components needed except propellants

FULL LINE COMMERCIAL MANUFACTURER

A full line commercial ammunition manufacturer makes rimfire, centerfire, and shotshell ammunition as well as the bullets, cartridge cases, primers, shot, and wad columns. A manufacturer of this type offers from 400 to 1,000 product line items marketed on a world wide basis.

A full line manufacturer must make as many component parts of a cartridge as possible to compete in the world market. Customer demand, competitor's products, and market dynamics dictate a large number of line items to maintain rough parity with competitor's product lines. In practice, this requires a product line of several hundred items. While this is a burden, large product lines allow full line manufacturers to compete with each other on a more or less equal basis. Broad product lines also limit the market share of short line manufacturers and custom loaders who compete only in profitable popular and niche markets.

Full line manufacturers market their products under one or more of their own brand names. Typically, they have three or four different brand names placed at different price levels with the cheapest consisting of military-type items. Some full line manufacturers sell bulk components such as cartridge cases with a private label headstamp to custom loaders. Full line manufacturers normally do not make or load proprietary brand ammunition.

Although they market their products world wide, all full line manufacturers maintain a strong base in one or more world markets. At present, there are ten full line manufacturers in the world. They are: Remington (U.S.), Winchester (U.S.), ATK Group (U.S.), RUAG Group (Switzerland), Fiocchi (Italy), NAMMO (Finland), CBC Group (Brazil), Poongsan Metals Corp. (Korea), Armscor (Philippines), and Industrias Technos (Mexico). Together, they offer some 4,083 line items with 1,853 (45.7%) being shotshell, 2,041 (50%) being centerfire, and 189 (4.6%) being rimfire.

markets

2. Partially privatized government arsenals selling a portion of their output in the the commercial markets

INDEPENDENT COMMERCIAL COMPANIES

As independent commercial companies cannot compete directly with full line manufacturers, they must carefully pick and choose their markets and their products. For this reason, many independent

FULL LINE MANUFACTURER PRODUCT LINE AND MARKET SUMMARY

Name of Company	Country	Base Market	Number of Items in Product Line			
			Rimfire	Centerfire	Shotshell	total
ATK Group	U.S.	U.S.	58	463	420	941
Federal, CCI, Speer, Blaser, Estate						
RUAG Group	Switzerland	Europe/U.S.	21	403	165	589
Dynamit Nobel, Norma, MFS, Swiss P						
CBC Group	Brazil	U.S., Europe	12	194	396	602
CBC, MEN, S&B, MAGTECH						
Winchester	U.S.	U.S	32	318	301	651
Remington	U.S.	U.S.	19	297	233	549
Fiocchi	Italy/U.S.	Europe/U.S.	17	194	236	447
NAMMO	Finland	Scandinavia	6	60		66
Lapua, Raufoss, Vanasverken						
PMC	Korea	Asia	1	67	98	166
Armscor	Philippines	Asia/U.S.	8	26		34
Industrias Technos	Mexico	U.S.	15	19	4	38
Total			189	2,041	1,853	4,083
Percentage			4.6	50	45.7	100
Average per company			17.2	185.5	168.5	371.2

SHORT LINE COMMERCIAL MANUFACTURER

A short line commercial ammunition manufacturer makes one or two types of ammunition, typically shotshell and centerfire types. A short line manufacturer makes the cartridge case, bullet, lead shot, and wad column. Some manufacture primers. A typical product line from such a manufacturer consists of less than 200 line items marketed on a world wide basis.

A short line manufacturer offers one or two basic ammunition types; most offer centerfire and/or shotshell. Short line manufacturers who offer centerfire or rimfire ammunition make their own cartridge cases and/or bullets. Those who offer shotshells make the hull and wad column.

There are two types of short line manufacturer:

1. Independent commercial companies marketing full-time to the commercial and/or law enforcement

commercial companies focus on regional markets where they can use their lower production costs to compete on popular items. Short line manufacturers can also develop niche markets using specialized, high quality products which are not so price sensitive. Examples of these include match grade ammunition, special police ammunition, obsolete calibers, unusual calibers, and premium hunting ammunition. Some also make proprietary brands of ammunition.

Independent short line commercial manufacturers control only a small share of the sporting and law enforcement markets. However, they are in the market for the long term and try to focus their marketing effort to that end. Although production capacity of most independent short line manufacturers is limited to small production runs, their production machinery is normally quite modern. These two factors enable them to make a profit on short production runs.

Most short line commercial manufacturers market their products world wide under their own brand names, but they lack the ability to create a strong demand via large advertising and promotion programs. On the other hand, even with limited adverstising expenditures they can depend on the enthusiast shooters in niche markets to publicize their specialized products.

Distribution can be a problem for short line commercial manufacturers. Large distributors usually decline to carry such product lines due to lack of demand and the availability of similar products from full line manufacturers. As a result, many short line manufacturers sell direct to dealers, small chains (ex. Gander Mountain, Cabela's, Bass-Pro), or mail order specialists. Product turnover in dealer stores is two or three times per year at best which is much slower than distributor turnover.

The 13 independent short line manufacturers offer some 1,620 line items of which 820 (50.6%) are centerfire, 781 (48.2%) are shotshell, and 19 (1.2%) are rimfire.

PARTIALLY PRIVATIZED GOVERNMENT ARSENALS

Government owned ammunition plants are handicapped by having little or no marketing capability and product lines geared to current centerfire military calibers. On the other hand, their overhead expense and production costs are low, their quality is acceptable, and their production capacity under-used. These factors allow them to approach the commercial market as a low cost producer using their production capacity and low price as sales tools in themselves. While such a sales strategy is short term, most government owned ammunition plants have no long term stake in the commercial market as they are not profit driven. As military orders come or go, their interest in the commercial market decreases or increases.

Most government ammunition plants have been partially privatized with up to 49% of the stock in the new company offered to private investors. Note that most governments retain 51% of the stock and therefore ownership. Although such moves are designed to

COMMERCIAL SHORT LINE MANUFACTURERS

Manufacturer Name	Country of Origin	Product Line Items			
		Rimfire	Centerfire	Shotshell	Total
Baschieri & Pellagri	Italy			160	160
Eley	Great Britain	9		260	269
Hornady	U.S.	6	286	6	298
Impala	Austria		25		25
Kynoch	Great Britain		96		96
Mesko	Poland		38		38
Nitron	Poland	3			3
PMP	South Africa		16		16
Prvi Partizan	Serbia		260		260
Sako*	Finland		89		89
Nike-Fiocchi	Hungary	1		125	126
Nobel Sport	France		10	80	90
UEE	Spain			150	150
Total		19	820	781	1,620
Percentage		1.2	50.6	48.2	100
Average		1.5	63	60	125

*Owned by Beretta

PARTIALLY PRIVATIZED GOVERNMENT ARSENALS					
Manufacturer Name	Country of Origin	Rimfire	Product Line Items		
			Centerfire	Shotshell	Total
Barnaul	Russia		36	50	86
FAM-Simadex	Poland		255		255
IMI	Israel		70		70
Igman	Bosnia		28		28
Krasnozavodsk	Russia			96	96
MKEK	Turkey		6		6
Novosibirsk	Russia	6	36		42
Raufoss	Norway		12		12
RUAG Ammotec	Switzerland		23	3	26
Uylanovsk	Russia		14		14
Wolf (Tula)	Russia	3	21	39	63
Total		9	501	188	698
Percentage		1.3	71.7	27	100
Average		.8	45.5	17	63.5

reduce the owning government's financial burden of supporting such enterprises, most lose money. Very slowly some of these companies are beginning to gain experience in the commercial market. However, the long term odds of survival are low. The 11 such companies offer 698 line items of which 501 (71.7%) are centerfire, 188 (27%) are shotshell, and 9 (1.3%) are rimfire.

As of this writing, there are some 13 independent commercial short line manufacturers and 11 government-owned short line manufacturers.

Despite the number and total production capacity of such manufacturers, their share of the commercial market is estimated at less than 15%.

PROPRIETARY PRODUCT LINE

Proprietary ammunition product lines consist of special calibers of centerfire rifle ammunition and/ or shotgun slugs loaded into standard shotshells sold under a proprietary brand name. Such ammunition is loaded for the proprietary brand by one of the short line commercial manufacturers. A typical proprietary product line consists of less than 75 line items marketed on a world wide basis.

Proprietary product lines are not manufactured by the company marketing the product. Rather their ammunition products are made for them to their specifications by an existing ammunition manufacturer. Some ammunition manufacturers welcome proprietary product business while others categorically refuse it. The major reasons for refusing such business are normally a lack of capacity, low profit margins, and the small quantities involved. In addition, tooling and separation of proprietary products can be a big problem.

PROPRIETARY AMMUNITION BRANDS					
Name of Company	Country	Rimfire	Number of Items in Product Line		
			Centerfire	Shotshell	Total
Brenneke	Germany			17	17
Lazzeroni	U.S.		25		25
Lightfield	U.S.			6	6
Weatherby	U.S.		62		62
Total			87	23	110
Percentage			79	21	100
Average			21.8	5.75	27.5

Nearly all proprietary centerfire cartridges are made in unique, non-standard rifle calibers which allegedly offer the user some type of ballistic advantage worth the added cost. In many cases, they do so. However, the small number of shooters who require the improved ballistic performance offered by proprietary calibers make this very much a niche market.

Proprietary cartridges are loaded with new brass cases and premium bullets from various existing bullet makers such as Barnes, Nosler, Sierra, Hornady, or Swift. Most proprietary cartridges are Magnums or offer Magnum performance.

A proprietary cartridge can become a victim of its own success. This happens when the sales volume increases to the point that it comes to the attention of the full line manufacturers. They then bring out their own versions of the blossoming proprietary caliber, thus splitting the market. Examples of this include the .270 Weatherby Magnum, 7mm Weatherby Magnum, and the .300 Weatherby Magnum.

The future of proprietary cartridges remains dim. Existing ammunition manufacturers do not welcome such business and will enter the market with their own products given sufficient sales volume. In addition, the cost of marketing a proprietary product line today is prohibitive.

Brenneke and Lightfield confine their products to shotgun slugs loaded in standard gauge shotshells. As the number of U.S. hunting areas which require exclusive use of shotgun slugs continues to grow, the future seems bright for these two manufacturers.

As of this writing, there are four proprietary product lines offering 110 different line items. Some 87 (79%) are centerfire and 23 (21%) are shotshell.

CUSTOM LOADER

A custom loader assembles centerfire and/or shotshell ammunition using components purchased from other manufacturers. A custom loader may make some or all of their rifle or pistol bullets. A typical custom loader offers less than 175 product line items in the most popular calibers and markets them on a regional basis.

Custom loaders may appear to be no different than many short line manufacturers in that they both offer a limited product line of the most popular items spiced with niche market specialties.

However, they are different because a short line manufacturer makes the cartridge case and the bullet while the custom loader purchases all the necessary components. Most custom loaders can offset this added expense by virtue of lower production costs, regional marketing, and low advertising and promotion expenditures. Another way custom loaders can lower cost is to offer remanufactured ammunition in selected calibers to reduce their overhead expenses. In this manner they are partially commercial reloaders as well as custom loaders.

Most distributors have no reason to stock products from custom loaders. Distributors will not sell reloaded ammunition due to product liability concerns. For this reason, custom loaders sell direct to dealers, small chains, mail order companies, and special customers of niche product.

Flexible marketing and low cost are strengths which assure custom loaders a bright future provided they do not become too large. If that should happen, then the suppliers of cartridge cases will raise prices or constrict the supply in self-defense.

Today, there are approximately 27 custom loaders offering over 1,811 line items of which 928 or 51% are shotshells and 883 or 49% are centerfire. There are no rimfire custom loaders.

COMMERCIAL RELOADER

A commercial reloader assembles centerfire ammunition using once-fired cartridge cases and new components purchased from other manufacturers. A commercial reloader may offer as many as 35 product line items depending on availability of cartridge cases. Commercially reloaded ammunition is marketed on a regional or local basis.

A commercial reloader obtains fired cartridge cases from one or more sources and reloads or remanufactures them. Traditional sources for once fired brass have been police departments, commercial shooting ranges, military organizations, and gun manufacturers.

Many custom loaders began their business life as commercial reloaders. At some point, they needed additional products to economically use their production capacity. A line of ammunition using new components was the obvious choice.

Reloaded ammunition is generally available only in those calibers for which once-fired brass is readily available in large quantities. Examples of these are: 5.56x45mm NATO, 7.62x51mm NATO, 9mm Luger, .38

			CUSTOM LOADERS		
Name of		Base	Number of Items in Product Line		
Company	Country	Market	Centerfire	Shotshell	Total
Ammo Direct	U.S.	U.S.	90		90
Black Hills	U.S.	U.S.	109		109
Buffalo Bore	U.S.	U.S.	80		80
Bullseye	U.S.	U.S.	18		18
Clever	Italy	Italy		80	80
Collins Cartridge	U.S.	U.S.	7		7
CorBon/Glaser	U.S.	U.S.	185	1	186
Dionisi	Italy	Italy		65	65
Extreme Shock	U.S.	U.S.	36		36
Gamebore	Great Britain	Great Britain		70	70
Garrett	U.S.	U.S.	8		8
Georgia Arms	U.S.	U.S.	80		80
G&L Calibers	Cyprus	Middle East		35	35
Hi-Tech Ammo	U.S.	U.S.		42	42
Hull	Great Britain	Great Britain		174	174
International Ctg Co	U.S.	U.S.	33	3	36
Kent	Great Britain	U.S.		169	169
Lyalvale	Great Britain	Great Britain		133	133
MagSafe	U.S.	U.S.	33		33
Maine Ctg Co	U.S.	U.S.	16		16
Mastercast	U.S.	U.S.	13		13
Pierce Ammo	U.S.	U.S.	23		23
Precision Cartridge	U.S.	U.S.	21		21
Saga	Spain	Spain		156	156
Ten-X	U.S.	U.S.	54		54
Ultramax	U.S.	U.S.	77		77
Total			883	928	1,811
Percentage			49	51	100
Average			34	36	70

Special, .357 Magnum, .40 S&W, and .45 ACP. On the other hand, new cartridge cases are available in any quantity required. In addition, ammunition assembled from new components has a broad appeal while many distributors, dealers, and shooters refuse to purchase or fire remanufactured ammunition.

The future of commercial reloading is cloudy. Many traditional sources of once-fired reloadable cartridge cases now insist on scrapping instead of selling them for liability reasons. In addition, many dealers will not sell remanufactured ammunition for the same reasons. Of course, full line and short line manufacturers applaud this as they want to sell these customers new ammunition. In addition, the availability of some calibers of once-fired brass such as .38 Special and .357 Magnum has dropped to shadow levels as 9mm Luger and .40 S&W availability has grown. Another problem is the on-again off-again availability of once-fired cases; a commerical reloader needs a reliable predictable supply.

Most commercial reloaders sell their products on a regional level with police departments, shooting ranges, and gun clubs being major customers.

As commercial reloaders are small companies with limited resources, they frequently go out of business, change ownership, or move to a new location. This keeps them off the ammunition radar screen, making it difficult to estimate how many commercial loaders exist. Some of the largest are listed, however there are many more.

COMMERCIAL RELOADERS	
Name of Company	Number of Centerfire Items in Product Line
Ammo Direct	42
Black Hills	26
Bullseye	37
Collins Cartridge	6
Georgia Arms	73
Mastercast	35
National Bullet	27
Precision Cartridge	28
Ultramax	34
Wagner	13
Zero	13

GOVERNMENT ARSENALS

Government arsenals manufacture centerfire rifle and pistol ammunition using components of their own manufacture. Although government arsenals make very large quantities of ammunition, the output is restricted to 6 to 10 different calibers. However, each caliber is made in many varieties such as ball, tracer, armor piercing, etc. In most cases, arsenal ammunition is produced for its owning government, or sold to foreign governments. Surplus ammunition sold on the commercial market is normally from government stocks.

Of the over 100 countries in the world, over 60 of them (60%) maintain a military ammunition manufacturing facility of some type. Of these, it is estimated that about 26 (43%) have been partially or fully privatized. The financial track record of these 26 companies remains poor as they do not understand the dynamics of commercial markets and do not have the products necessary for such markets. In addition, existing commercial markets suffer from over capacity leaving semi-privatized arsenals with very little to offer beyond low price. To develop commercial capabilities requires financial resources far beyond most governments' or arsenals' means. This makes it unlikely that other assenals will follow this path.

MARKET DYNAMIC

NORTH AMERICA

In the North American market, full line manufacturers such as Remington, Winchester, and Federal distribute their products through a three step system consisting of distributor (wholesaler), dealer, and customer. There are some 40 firearm distributors in the U.S. with the six largest doing approximately 75% of the business. Distributors sell to 8,500 licensed dealers, of which about 3,500 do over 75% of the business. These sales are supported by multi-million dollar advertising and promotion programs.

AMMUNITION DISTRIBUTIORS

Most sporting ammunition is distributed to dealer stores by specialized wholesalers (also called jobbers) and importers. Wholesalers typically carry a wide variety of products including firearms, ammunition, clothing, cutlery, reloading components, books, and accessories. A distributor often maintains tens of thousands of stock keeping units (SKUs), more than enough to fill the telephone book-sized catalog that most of them print every year. By using computer-controlled purchasing, sales, inventory, shipping, and billing, distributors maintain profit margins in a competitive market. Today, most distributors use telephone sales persons and catalogs to sell their products.

These include color catalogs, national advertising programs, co-op ad programs, special offers, new product news releases, mailings, distributor product training, gun writer seminars, attendance at trade shows, and attendance at competitive matches.

GOVERNMENT ARSENALS

NAME	COUNTRY	NAME	COUNTRY	NAME	COUNTRY
Aboukir Engineering Industries	Egypt	GIAT Industries	France	Poongsan Corporation**	Korea
Adcom Manufacturing**	Abu Dhabi	Industrias Militar	Columbia	Pova Ske Stojarne	Slovakia
Army Ammunition Plant	Indonesia	Industrias Militar	Guatemala	Prvi Partizan*	Serbia
Danish Government Arsenal	Denmark	Industrial Defence Establishment	Syria	PT Pintad	Indonesia
Australian Defence Industries	Australia	Igman Factory*	Bosnia	Government Ordnance Factories	Vietnam
BAE/Royal Ordnance Defence	Great Britain	Indian Ordnance Board	India	Greek Powder & Cartridge Co.	Greece
Bangladesh Ordnance Plant	Bangladesh	Israel Military Industries*	Israel	Republic of Philippines Arsenal	Philippines
Barnaul Cartridge Plant CSJ*	Russia	Kintex*	Bulgaria	Romtechnica*	Romania
CA Venezuelana de Industrias	Venezuela	Krasnozavodsk Chemical Plant*	Russia	Royal Thai Arsenal	Thailand
China North Industries	China	Mesko Zaklady Metalowe*	Poland	RUAG*	Switzerland
Defense Industries Organization	Iran	Mitsubishi Heavy Industries	Japan	Sako AB*	Finland
Denel Pty Ltd.*	South Africa	MKEK	Turkey	Shoubra Company	Egypt
Fabrica Nacional de Municiones	Mexico	Nammo Raufoss	Norway	SMI*	Italy
FAME	Peru	Nammo Vanasverken	Sweden	Syndikat Malaysia Explosives Ltd.	Malaysia
FAMAE	Chile	Novosibirsk LVE Plant*	Russia	Tula Cartridge Works*	Russia
FAMMAP	Argentina	Government Ordnance Factory	Nigeria	Ulyanovsk Cartridge Plant*	Russia
FN Herstal*	Belgium	Pakistan Ordnance Factories	Pakistan	Zimbabwe Defence Industries	Zimbabwe

* Partially privatized ** Fully privatized ***Now owned by RUAG Ammotec

DISTRIBUTOR SIZE

The largest distributors in the U.S. have annual sales of over $240 million each. Ammunition sales can represent about 35% of that amount.

These programs are designed to create a demand for products and/or protect existing market share. A significant point here is that such efforts are beyond the financial ability of short line commercial manufacturers, custom loaders, and commercial reloaders. Most North American distributors plan to turn over their inventory at least four to six times per year. Any product or product line which does not maintain that rate becomes a prime discontinuance candidate.

DISTRIBUTOR PRODUCT TURN

U.S. distributors expect to turnover popular ammunition product line items six to eight times per year. Product line items with fewer than four turnovers per year may not be profitable.

Another key sales tool used by large full line manufacturers is extending multi-million dollar lines of credit to distributors who fully support their product lines. Such lines of credit are of paramount importance to distributors. Smaller full line manufacturers, short line manufacturers, and custom loaders simply cannot afford to extend such lines of credit.

Mass merchants and closed distribution chains are exceptions to the three step "rule". Mass merchants (e.g. Wal-Mart) purchase only the most popular items direct from the manufacturers and do their own distribution and advertising. Closed distribution chains (Gander Mountain, Cabela's, Bass-Pro, etc.) normally buy most of the product line direct and do their own distributing. Both purchase in very large quantities at very low prices from all of the largest full line manufacturers.

Foreign full line manufacturers normally establish a wholly owned U.S. subsidiary with an office and warehouse from which they sell dealer direct on a national basis. Their product lines often contain specialized products for niche markets which the very large full line manufacturers ignore. However, their share of the North American market remains small and their advertising and promotion budgets are but a small fraction of the big three manufacturers.

OVERSEAS MARKETS

Larger countries usually have two or three distributors and smaller countries one or two. For example, there are about 25 distributors in Europe. Mass merchants in Europe do not sell ammunition, however there are several distribution chains such as Frankonia Jagd and Gresvig. European distributors plan to turnover their inventory once or twice a year which forces them to maintain high and/or increase retail prices in order to recover their higher inventory carrying costs.

The largest European markets for centerfire ammunition are in Germany, Austria, Sweden, Norway, Finland, and Switzerland. The largest European markets for shotshells are in Italy, Spain, Great Britain, and France. Of course, domestic manufacturers (if any) in those countries hold a large share of their domestic market. Most foreign ammunition manufacturers exporting ammunition to European Economic Union countries appoint a sole distributor to sell their products from a specific country with the understanding that goods can move about in the EEU without difficulty.

STRENGTHS AND WEAKNESSES

No full line manufacturer can dominate every part of the ammunition market, although they may offer products in every given segment. A variety of factors assure this. These range from the large number of market segments to the ability of the company sales department to sell products in a segment dominated by another manufacturer. The result is a combination of strengths and weaknesses in each company's marketing efforts.

Most full line ammunition manufacturers do, in fact, dominate one or more market segments. However, some manufacturers dominate no market segment, making their way profitably as second or third place competitors. As most market segments are so large, this strategy can work very well. Another important factor is that preferences and trends in a market segment frequently change, resulting in a change of market share and leadership position in that market. While full line ammunition manufacturers do monitor their market shares closely, no company can defend against every percentage point of shift in every market segment.

As a result of the above, manufacturers view the market in the context of their product lines and the share each line controls within a given segment. Most full line commercial manufacturers tend to compare and judge the success or failure of their efforts in relation to the perceived market shares held by their full line competitors. However, in some segments of the market, the shares held by short line manufacturers must be taken in account as well. In rare instances, a short line manufacturer may even dominate a given market segment.

The strengths and weaknesses of the ten full line manufacturers are summarized below.

COMPANY PROFILES

COMPANY	PRODUCT STRENGTHS	PRODUCT WEAKNESSES
Remington	Standard rimfire High velocity shotshells Field load shotshells Standard centerfire rifle Standard centerfire pistol Shotshell slugs Shotshell buckshot New products	Target shotshells Non-toxic shotshells Target rimfire Target centerfire rifle Premium centerfire rifle Target centerfire pistol Military-type centerfire Game load shotshells
Winchester	Standard rimfire Magnum shotshells Non-toxic shotshells Target shotshells Premium shotshells Standard centerfire rifle Standard centerfire pistol Premium centerfire pistol New products	Target rimfire Game load shotshells Target centerfire rifle Shotshell slugs Premium centerfire rifle Military-type centerfire Target centerfire pistol Safari centerfire rifle

ATK Group
  Federal
  Speer
  CCI
  Blaser
  Estate
	Non-toxic shotshells
	Game load shotshells
	Target shotshells
	Premium shotshells
	Shotshell slugs
	Premium centerfire rifle
	Premium centerfire pistol
	Target centerfire rifle
	Target centerfire pistol
	Safari centerfire rifle
		Target rimfire
		Military-type centerfire
		Standard centerfire pistol

NAMMO Group
  Lapua
  Raufoss
  Vanasverken
  SK-jagd
  Vihtavuori
	Target rimfire
	Target centerfire rifle
	Standard centerfire rifle
	New products
		Standard rimfire
		Shotshells-all
		Premium centerfire rifle
		Target centerfire pistol
		Premium centerfire pistol

PMC	Military-type centerfire Standard centerfire rifle Standard centerfire pistol Game load shotshells	Standard rimfire Target centerfire rifle Target centerfire pistol Magnum shotshells Premium centerfire Target shotshells

CBC Group
  CBC
  MEN
  Sellier & Bellot
  MAGTECH
	Standard centerfire rifle
	Standard centerfire pistol
	Obsolete centerfire rifle
	Obsolete centerfire pistol
	Target shotshells
	Field shotshells
	Military-type centerfire
		Target rimfire
		Non-toxic shotshells
		Premium ammunition-all
		Magnum shotshells
		Target centerfire rifle
		Target centerfire pistol
		New products

COMPANY	PRODUCT STRENGTHS	PRODUCT WEAKNESSES
Fiocchi	Target rimfire Flobert rimfire Target shotshells Field shotshells Game load shotshells Obsolete shotshells Obsolete centerfire pistol Standard centerfire pistol	Standard rimfire Magnum shotshells Shotshell slugs Standard centerfire rifle Premium ammunition Target centerfire
Armscor	Standard rimfire Field shotshells Standard centerfire pistol Military-type centerfire	Target rimfire Target shotshells Non-toxic shotshells Target centerfire Premium ammunition Standard centerfire rifle New products
Industrias Tecnos	Standard rimfire Game load shotshells Field shotshells Shotshell buckshot Standard centerfire pistol New products	Target rimfire Target shotshells Non-toxic shotshells Centerfire rifle ammunition Premium ammunition Shotshell buck shot and slug Target centerfire

RUAG Group
  Dynamit Nobel
  Norma
  MFS
  Swiss P
  Rottweil
  GECO
  Hirtenberger
  Precision Ammunition
	Target rimfire
	Standard rimfire
	Field shotshells
	Target shotshells
	Shotshell slugs (Brenneke)
	Obsolete centerfire rifle
	Premium centerfire rifle
	Flobert rimfire
		Magnum shotshells
		Non-toxic shotshells
		Game load shotshells
		Shotshell buckshot
		Target centerfire
		Standard centerfire pistol
		Target centerfire
		New products

BERGER HYBRID BULLET

Dual-ogive design combines tanget and secant ogives with hollow-point boat tail to optimize ballistic coefficient for hunting at long ranges.

After the point of first contact with the rifling, the ogive morphs into a secant curve for minimum drag

A tangent ogive from the end of the bearing to the point of first contact with the rifling allows precise control of seating depth

Bearing surface

Boat tail reduces base drag

Recently, Berger Bullets introduced their new Hybrid bullet. This very low drag (VLD), hollow-point, boat tail bullet is optimized for hunting at long ranges. Its dual-ogive design incorporates the best of both tangent and secant ogive contours. A tangent ogive begins where the bearing surface ends to allow better control of seating depth and bullet jump. Moving forward, the ogive morphs into a sharper, secant curve, which is more efficient at reducing drag. The result is claimed to be an optimum partnership between the bullet maker and the ballistican.

Berger's Hybrid bullet is a further development of their Very Low Drag (VLD) match bullet that combines a long, hollow-point secant ogive with a boat tail base. These features produce an exceptionally high ballistic coefficient for superior long range match shooting.

CHAPTER 19 : WORLD AMMUNITION MARKET SIZE

CHAPTER 19 HIGHLIGHTS:

- ROUNDS OF AMMUNITION MADE EACH YEAR
- CAPACITY VS. OUTPUT

ROUNDS OF AMMUNITION MADE EACH YEAR

How many rounds of ammunition are made in the world each year? No one knows as there is no central organization which maintains such statistics. In addition, most commercial manufacturers regard their annual production output statistics as proprietary information which they do not disclose. Government arsenals do not release production statistics for security reasons.

Ammunition is a commodity intended for mass consumption. Cartridges are fired in such numbers that individual rounds become insignificant. Some shooters fire one or two rounds per year while others may fire 50,000 rounds or more. However, all shooters intuitively know that the total number of rounds of ammunition made in the world every year is a very large number indeed—certainly well into the billions.

Here it must be noted that there is a difference between production capacity and production output.

CAPACITY VS. OUTPUT

PRODUCTION CAPACITY

Production capacity is a theoretical number consisting of the total number of rounds of ammunition a machine can load in a year if operated three shifts for 250 working days without any stoppages for any reason. Of course, this is impossible because any machine must be stopped frequently for routine maintenance, clearing jams, repair, upgrading, and component shortages. For these reasons, production capacity is a theoretical number.

PRODUCTION OUTPUT

Production output is the actual number of rounds of ammunition a machine loads in a year as governed by customer demand, inventory, raw materials, labor, transport, and many other factors. While output is an actual number, the machine may actually be capable of producing more ammunition.

In general, the two figures differ substantially. Being profit-driven, commercial manufacturers make every effort to run efficiently by reducing idle capacity and

costs. However, to survive in the marketplace, they must offer broad product lines and respond to rapidly changing market conditions, customer demands, and shifting prices. Government arsenals are not profit-driven and spend long periods on standby or run at low inefficient rates during non-emergency periods. As a result, they do not operate at the higher efficiencies of commercial manufacturers unless there is an emergency. However, arsenals manufacture a very limited number of products and must be responsive to only one customer.

ESTIMATION METHODOLOGY

As there is no central source for ammunition production statistics, we must approach the question of world ammunition capacity and output from another direction. A good way to do this involves a four part methodology based on the types and capacities of ammunition loading machines:

- **Determine the annual theoretical capacity of various types of ammunition loading machines when run for one, two, and three daily shifts (for arsenals peace, crisis, and war)**

- **Estimate the type and number of machines each manufacturer has and how many shifts each is run yearly**

- **Compute total theoretical annual capacity**

- **Apply a percentage of use factor to the theoretical total to estimate annual production output**

The world's theoretical capacity and production output for 2012, by ammunition type and by manufacturer, are detailed on the following pages of this chapter.

CONCLUSIONS

On the following pages of this chapter, we can see that there is a shortage of production in sporting ammunition of all types. This situation will continue until the expiration of military contracts.

As long as sporting ammunition production cannot meet demand, prices will remain high. While the large manufacturers focus on large military contracts, the short line manufacturers and custom loaders may gain market share.

If prices fall, this would make it harder for the short line manufacturers to compete as they lack the resources of the large manufacturers. As a result, the number of short line manufacturers would decline through closure and consolidation.

Custom loaders are especially vulnerable as they depend on the large manufacturers to supply them with cartridge cases and primers. Manufacturers selling to niche markets must carefully monitor their customer base to avoid product obsolescence in shifting markets.

Bullet manufacturers should avoid being lured into ammunition manufacture based on their reputation as bullet makers. Such niche markets do not exist outside the major manufacturers' current and intensively promoted premium product lines which use such bullets.

Manufacturers in countries with low labor costs will attempt to survive by maintaining low prices. However, another manufacturer, in order to compete, may sell something cheaper, so having a low price does not assure permanent market share needed for survival.

Many governments have fully or partially privatized inefficient arsenals. The larger arsenals will continue to sell excess capacity on the commercial market as the opportunities present themselves. However, trade barriers put in place for political reasons can be expected to limit such sales.

The Largest Commercial Ammunition Manufacturer

Who is the largest commercial ammunition manufacturer in the world? Without doubt, this would be ATK which owns Federal, CCI/Blazer/Speer, and Estate. Combined production capacity of these companies is over 5.3 billion rounds per year. In addition, ATK is the prime contractor for the Lake City Army Ammunition Plant which has a capacity of over 1.6 billion rounds per year.

Estimated world production capacity and output

Estimated Annual Production Capacity of Rimfire Loading Machines

Machine Type	Rounds/ Plate	Plates/ Minute	Rounds/ Minute	Rounds/ Shift Millions	No. Shifts	Days/ year	Rounds/ year Millions
Plate	400	3.3	3,300	1,385,000	1	250	346,250,000
					2	250	692,500,000
					3	250	1,038,750,000

Estimated 2011 World Rimfire Ammunition Production Capacity and Output

Company Name	Number of Machines	Co Cap Rounds/Year Millions	Est. Production Rounds/Year Millions	Percent of Capacity
Remington	4	4,150	3,500	85
Winchester	4	4,150	3,500	85
ATK	6	6,225	5,290	85
Fiocchi	2	2,000	1,600	80
Dynamit Nobel	2	2,000	1,400	70
Eley	2	2,000	1,700	85
CBC	1	1,000	700	70
Armscor	1	1,000	700	70
Industrias Technos	1	1,000	700	70
Lapua	1	1,000	700	70
Totals	22	24,525 Million	19,790 Million	81

Assumptions:

1. Plate loading machine capacity 1,385,000 rounds per shift
2. Three working shifts per day, seven hours per shift
3. 250 working days per year/1750 working hours per year, per shift

Estimated Annual Production Capacity of Commercial Centerfire Loading Machines

Machine Type	Rounds/ Minute	Rounds/ Shift	No. Shifts	Days/ year	Rounds/ year
Plate	120	50,000	1	250	12,500,000
			2	250	25,000,000
			3	250	37,500,000
Transfer	90	39,000	1	250	9,750,000
			2	250	19,500,000
			3	250	29,250,000
Rotary	180	75,000	1	250	18,750,000
			2	250	37,500,000
			3	250	56,250,000

Estimated 2011 World Sporting Centerfire Ammunition Production Capacity and Output

Company	Machine Type	No. of Machines	Machine Cap/Yr	Co Cap Rds/ Yr Millions	Est. 2011 Output Millions	% of Capacity
Winchester	T	30	29	870	800	92
	R	4	56	224	180	80
			Total	1,094	980	90
ATK (Federal)	T	22	29	638	520	82
	R	6	56	336	285	85
			Total	974	805	83
Remington	T	32	29	928	800	86
	R	4	56	224	180	80
			Total	1,152	980	85
PMC	T	10	29	290	195	67
	R	1	56	56	25	45
			Total	346	220	64
CBC	T	17	29	493	445	90
(Sellier & Bellot)	R	11	56	616	455	73
			Total	1109	900	81
Prvi Partizan	T	10	29	290	270	93
	R	4	56	224	215	96
			Total	514	485	94
Sako	P	2	37	74	10	14
	R	2	56	112	35	31
			Total	186	45	24
RUAG (Norma,	T	10	29	290	230	79
Dynamit Nobel)	P	1	37	37	4	11
	R	4	56	224	50	22
			Total	551	284	51
PMP	R	6	56	336	185	55

Company	Machine Type	No. of Machines	Machine Cap/Yr	Co Cap Rds/Yr Millions	Est. 2011 Output Millions	% of Capacity
Wolf	R	6	56	336	315	94
Barnaul	R	4	56	224	165	74
Novosibirsk	R	3	56	168	100	59
RUAG	R	3	56	168	145	86
Uylanovsk	R	2	56	112	80	71
Raufoss NAMMO	R	2	56	112	55	49
Igman	R	2	56	112	90	80
Lapua	T	14	29	406	330	81
Blazer/Speer	T	10	29	290	265	91
Black Hills	T	8	29	232	210	91
Hornady	T	8	29	232	220	95
Armscor	T	6	29	174	100	57
Bullseye	T	6	29	174	110	63
CorBon	T	6	29	174	110	63
Ultramax	T	6	29	174	125	73
Collins	T	4	29	116	85	73
Georgia Arms	T	4	29	116	85	73
Mastercast	T	4	29	116	85	73
Ind. Technos	T	2	29	58	50	86
Mesko	T	2	29	58	15	26
Extreme Shock	T	2	29	58	45	77
International	T	2	29	58	45	77
MagSafe	T	2	29	58	45	77
Maine Ctg	T	2	29	58	35	60
Fiocchi	T	1	29	29	20	70
Impala	T	1	29	29	12	41
Kynoch	Hand	1	.4	.4	.2	50
Totals-All Companies	N/A	298	N/A	3,842	2,942	77

Assumptions:

1. Three working shifts per day, seven hours per shift

2. 250 working days per year/1750 working hours per year, per shift

3. Machine types: P=plate, T=transfer, R=rotary

According to a 2010 study for the National Shooting Sports Foundation, 25% of U.S. modern sporting rifle owners fire over 1,056 rounds of ammunition per year enjoying their hobby.

Annual Estimated Capacity of Commercial Shotshell Loading Machines 2011

Machine Type	Rounds/ Minute	Rounds/ Shift	No. Shifts	Days/ year	Rounds/ year
Dial	60	25,000	1	250	6,250,000
			2	250	12,500,000
			3	250	18,750,000
Rotary	300	126,000	1	250	31,500,000
			2	250	63,000,000
			3	250	94,500,000
Rotary	600	252,000	1	250	63,000,000
			2	250	126,000,000
			3	250	189,000,000

Estimated 2011 World Shotshell Production Capacity and Output

Company	Machine Type	No. of Machines	Machine Cap/Yr Millions	Co Cap Rds/Yr Millions	Est. 2011 Output Millions	% of Capacity
Winchester	D	18	19	342	108	32
	R	6	189	1,134	756	67
			Total	1,476	864	58
Federal	D	18	19	342	154	45
	R	6	189	1,134	756	67
			Total	1,476	910	62
Remington	D	16	19	304	162	53
	R	4	189	756	358	47
			Total	1,060	520	49
Baschieri & Pellagri	T	4	31	124	84	68
	R	2	94	188	94	50
			Total	312	178	57
Eley	T	4	31	124	63	51
	R	1	94	94	31	33
			Total	218	94	43
Fiocchi	T	8	31	248	140	56
	R	2	94	188	94	50
			Total	436	234	54
Sellier & Bellot	T	4	31	124	42	34

Company	Machine Type	No. of Machines	Machine Cap/Yr Millions	Co Cap Rds/Yr Millions	Est. 2011 Output Millions	% of Capacity
Armscor	D	2	19	38	30	32
Ind. Technos	D	2	19	38	30	32
G&L	D	2	19	38	25	50
Hull	T	8	31	248	125	51
Kent	T	6	31	186	150	48
Lyalvale	T	6	31	186	120	59
Saga	T	8	31	248	220	58
Azot	T	2	31	62	40	64
Clever	D	4	19	76	45	46
Dionisi	D	4	19	76	40	46
Gamebore	T	4	31	124	80	56
Nike	T	4	31	124	70	44
Nobel Sport	D	4	19	76	50	39
UEE	T	6	31	186	140	54
FAM	D	6	19	114	45	39
Krasnozavodsk	D	8	19	152	70	46
Totals- All		281	N/A	7,074	4,172	59

According to a study made in 2010 for the National Shooting Sports Foundation, U. S. owners of modern sporting rifles (MSR) obtained their ammunition from the following sources:

* Hand loads 21%

* Premium factory loads 25%

* Standard factory budget/bulk ammunition 42%

* Imported ammunition 12%

Annual Estimated Capacity of Arsenal Centerfire Loading Machines

Machine Type	Rounds/ Minute	Rounds/ Shift	No. Shifts	Days/ year	Rounds/ year
Plate	250	105,000	1	250	26,250,000 (peace)
			2	250	52,500,000 (crisis)
			3	344	108,350,000 (war)
Transfer	90	36,000	1	250	9,000,000 (peace)
			2	250	18,000,000 (crisis)
			3	344	37,000,000 (war)
Rotary	180	76,000	1	250	19,000,000 (peace)
			2	250	38,000,000 (crisis)
			3	344	78,430,000 (war)
SCAMP (Sc)	1250	525,000	1	250	131,000,000 (peace)
			2	250	262,000,000 (crisis)
			3	344	542,000,000 (war)

Estimated 2011 World Arsenal Centerfire Ammunition Production Capacity and Output

Country	Machine Type	No. of Machines	Machine Cap/Yr	Co Cop Rds/Yr	Est. 2011 Output	% of Capacity
Taiwan	T	6	37	222	100	45
	Sc	1	542	542	131	24
			Total	764	231	30
USA	T	14	37	518	450	87
	P	2	108	216	180	83
	R	8	78	624	425	68
	Sc	5	542	1,710	1,600	94
			Total	3,068	2,655	86
India	T	18	37	666	144	22
	R	4	78	312	100	32
			Total	978	244	25
Israel	T	8	37	296	290	98
	R	8	78	624	600	96
	Sc	2	542	1,084	1,000	92
			Total	2,004	1,890	94
Egypt	R	6	78	468	350	75
Abu Dhabi	R	2	78	156	60	38
Australia	R	2	78	156	40	26
Great Britain	R	4	78	312	275	88
Russia	R	32	78	2,496	1,900	76
Sweden	R	2	78	156	40	26
Venezuela	R	2	78	156	40	26
Brazil	R	4	78	312	60	19
Singapore	R	2	78	156	80	51
Iran	R	4	78	312	120	38
South Africa	R	4	78	312	80	26
Belgium	R	2	78	156	25	16
France	R	4	78	312	110	35
Bosnia	R	2	78	156	80	51
Portugal	R	2	78	156	20	13
Bulgaria	R	2	78	156	25	16
Poland	R	6	78	468	80	17
Hungary	R	4	78	312	260	83
Japan	R	4	78	312	50	16
Turkey	R	4	78	312	120	38
Finland	R	4	78	312	60	19
Norway	R	2	78	156	25	16
Syria	R	2	78	156	40	26
Switzerland	R	3	78	234	220	94
Spain	R	4	78	312	170	54
Czech Rep.	R	4	78	312	290	93
Italy	R	2	78	156	60	38
Canada	R	2	78	156	30	19
Malaysia	R	2	78	156	40	26

Country	Machine Type	No. of Machines	Machine Cap/Yr	Co Cap Rds/Yr	Est. 2011 Output	% of Capacity
Serbia	R	4	78	312	295	95
China	T	60	37	2,220	1,600	73
Indonesia	T	4	37	148	30	20
Denmark	T	2	37	74	10	14
Bangladesh	T	1	37	37	10	27
Mexico	T	2	37	74	70	94
Peru	T	2	37	74	20	27
Chile	T	2	37	74	15	20
Argentina	T	2	37	74	10	14
Columbia	T	2	37	74	25	33
Guatemala	T	2	37	74	10	14
Nigeria	T	2	37	74	10	14
Pakistan	T	12	37	444	160	36
Korea	T	10	37	370	350	54
Slovakia	T	2	37	74	10	14
Vietnam	T	6	37	222	75	34
Greece	T	4	37	148	40	27
Philippines	T	4	37	148	25	17
Romania	T	4	37	148	20	14
Thailand	T	4	37	148	30	20
Zimbabwe	T	1	37	37	10	27
Burma	T	2	37	74	15	20
Algeria	T	4	37	148	50	34
Totals-All Countries		333	N/A	22,366	13,325	59

Assumptions:

1. Three working shifts per day, seven hours per shift
2. 344 working days per year/2408 working hours per year, per shift
3. Machine types: D=dial, T=transfer, R=rotary, Sc=SCAMP

Friedrich Vetterli: 1822-1882

Early Cartridge Designer

Friedrich Vetterli was a Swiss citizen who served his apprenticeship as a gunsmith at Schaffhausen, Switzerland. From there, he worked in St. Etienne, France and in London, England where he became conversant with the latest firearm and ammunition technologies. In 1865, he accepted the post of Manager of the Arms Department at the firearms factory at Neuhausen, Switzerland.

Vetterli experimented with new cartridge technologies, designing several cartridges which bear his name. He is remembered in cartridge history for developing the cupro-nickel jacket for bullets.

CHAPTER 20 : AMMUNITION GOVERNING BODIES

CHAPTER 20 HIGHLIGHTS:

- SAAMI
- CIP
- U.S. BATFE
- U.S. DIR. OF DEFENSE TRADE CONTROLS
- U.S. DEPT. OF COMMERCE
- FBI
- DOT
- AMC
- NFPA

- NRMA
- ANSI
- AFEMS
- NRA
- ATA
- NSSA
- SASS
- SPORTING CLAYS OF AMERICA
- U.S.A. SHOOTING

- USPSA
- IPSC
- IAA
- IBS
- NBRSA
- NSSF
- AFTE
- CMP
- FESAC

There are 27 governing bodies which have direct influence on the manufacture, transport, and sale of ammunition and components. Of these, five are agencies of the U.S. government. Each of these governing bodies is listed below with contact information and a short synopsis of their areas of operational authority.

(SAAMI) SPORTING ARMS AND AMMUNITION MANUFACTURERS' INSTITUTE

National Shooting Sports Foundation
Sporting Arms and Ammunition
Manufacturers' Institute
11 Mile Hill Rd.
Newtown, CT 06470
(203) 426-1320
www.saami.org

Before World War I (1914-1918), each American ammunition manufacturer used dimensional, pressure, and ballistic performance standards based on individual company practices and procedures. When the U.S. entered World War I in 1917, these multiple standards caused serious difficulties. As a result, after the War, the American firearms and ammunition industry formed the Sporting Arms and Ammunition Manufacturers' Institute to serve as a clearing house for standardized dimensions, practices, and procedures. Today, SAAMI continues this work under the National Shooting Sports Foundation (NSSF). In addition to developing standardized cartridge and chamber dimensions, interior ballistics, and exterior ballistics, SAAMI operates in the fields of metallurgy, chemistry, and engineering to help solve industry-wide problems. SAAMI also distributes safety brochures dealing with proper handling and storage of ammunition and components. Membership in SAAMI is open to all manufacturers on a voluntary basis. Why should this be of interest to the individual shooter? SAAMI's efforts are the reason cartridges of different brands in the same caliber are interchangeable and safe to fire in guns of that caliber.

(CIP) COMMISSION INTERNATIONALE PERMANENTE POUR L'EPREUVE DES ARMES À FEU PORTATIVES

Commission Internationale Permanente pour l'Epreuve
des Armes à Feu Portatives
Rue Fond des Tawes 45
Liege B-4000
Belgium
www.cip-bobp.org/home

From its headquarters in Liege, Belgium, the CIP serves much the same function as SAAMI. Dimensions, interior ballistics, and exterior ballistics are standardized so that ammunition of similar caliber is interchangeable and safe to fire in guns of that caliber. CIP dimensional, pressure, and ballistic standards are expressed in metric units of measure. In addition, some CIP measurements of pressure and velocity are not comparable or equivalent to SAAMI measurements, due to differences in methodology, test equipment, and other factors. CIP also works closely with national proof houses located in various parts of Europe including Spain, Italy, Belgium, Germany, Russia, and the U.K. Like SAAMI, corporate membership in CIP is voluntary. In fact, nearly all firearms and ammunition manufacturers in Europe are members. In recent years, SAAMI and CIP have worked closely to develop practices and procedures to assure their standards are completely compatible and safe.

(BATFE) BUREAU OF ALCOHOL, TOBACCO, FIREARMS AND EXPLOSIVES

Bureau of Alcohol, Tobacco, Firearms and Explosives
650 Massachusetts Ave. Room 8290
Washington, DC 20026
www.atf.gov

The BATFE is charged with the enforcement of Federal laws governing firearms and ammunition ownership, sale, transfer, manufacture, and licensing. The BATFE also maintains a Technical Section that determines the technical compliance of firearms and ammunition with Federal laws and regulations. For example, the Technical Section determines whether or not a given bullet design will be classed as armor piercing, explosive, etc. Their evaluations also govern the suitability of foreign ammunition for importation. While significant BATFE resources are engaged in technical evaluations and tests of various types of ammunition, the Bureau's primary focus is on enforcement of Federal laws and regulations. They do not conduct comparison tests of sporting or law enforcement ammunition.

DIRECTORATE OF DEFENSE TRADE CONTROLS

U.S. Department of State
Directorate of Defense Trade Controls
PM/DDTC, SA-1, 12th Floor
Washington, DC 20522
(202) 663-2980
www.pmddtc.state.gov

This section of the U.S. Department of State regulates export sales and transfers of firearms and ammunition manufactured in the U.S. They also regulate the importation of foreign firearms and ammunition entering the U.S. Their efforts are governed by U.S. government policies and laws as well as international treaties and conventions. In addition, the Directorate enforces the International

Traffic in Arms (ITAR) regulations which govern the transfer of controlled or restricted information from the U.S. to foreign persons, companies, and governments.

U.S. DEPARTMENT OF COMMERCE EXPORT DIVISION

U.S. Department of Commerce
Export Division
1401 Constitution Ave. NW
Washington, DC 20230
(202) 482-4811
www.commerce.gov

The U.S. Department of Commerce regulates the export of shotguns and shotshells (except shotshells loaded with slugs).

FBI

Federal Bureau of Investigation
J. Edgar Hoover Building
935 Pennsylvania Ave. NW
Washington, DC 20535-0001
(202) 324-3000
www.fbi.gov
Nationwide Instant Check System
www.fbi.gov/about-us/cjis/nics

The FBI operates the Nationwide Instant Check System (NICS). This is a computerized system containing criminal records of individuals from a wide variety of federal and state sources. This system is accessible on-line or by telephone, by Federal Firearms licensees. Using this system, a dealer can quickly obtain approval or denial of a proposed firearm sale or transfer to a customer. NICS approval is not required to purchase ammunition. Periodically, the FBI also conducts comparative tests of various calibers, types, and brands of ammunition suitable for law enforcement use. These tests utilize carefully controlled procedures to assure validity. The results of these tests are compiled and released for use by federal, state, and local law enforcement agencies. The FBI Lab assists other law enforcement agencies with forensic testing.

DOT

U.S. Department of Transportation
400 7th St. SW
Washington, DC 20590
(202) 366-4000
www.dot.gov

The U.S. Department of Transportation regulates the transport of ammunition, primers, and propellants throughout the U.S. This task includes assigning product classification codes to various ammunition products, testing and approving packaging, regulating carriers, and enforcing safety standards for transport. They also supply certificates of competent authority for export shipments.

AMC

U.S. Army Materiel Command
9301 Chapek Rd.
Fort Belvoir, VA 22060-5527
(703) 806-8010
www.amc.army.mil

The U.S. Army is charged with the procurement of all small arms ammunition for U.S. military forces. This mission is handled by the Army Materiel Command working with various government and private manufacturing facilities. To ensure quality, reliability, and interchangeability, the AMC determines and applies production and testing standards for U.S. military ammunition. The AMC also ensures that U.S. military small arms ammunition meets all NATO standards.

NFPA

National Fire Prevention Association
1 Batterymarch Park
Quincy, MA 02169-7471
(617) 770-3000
www.nfpa.org

Most state and local governments have enacted regulations governing the storage conditions and amounts of reloading components and loaded ammunition in businesses and private homes. In most cases, these regulations reflect recommendations made and published by the National Fire Prevention Association (NFPA). Local regulations governing ammunition and component storage are normally administered by the local Fire Marshal.

NRMA

National Reloading Manufacturers' Association
One Centrepointe Dr., Suite 300
Lake Oswego, OR 97035

Membership in this non-profit industry association includes most manufacturers of reloading components and machinery. It functions to assure compatibility of a member's products with SAAMI, ANSI, and CIP standards.

ANSI

American National Standards Institute
1819 L Street NW, Suite 600
Washington, DC 20036
(202) 293-8020
www.ansi.org

Membership in ANSI is comprised of manufacturers, government agencies, international bodies, academic organizations, and individuals. Founded in 1918, the mission of ANSI is to enhance the global competitiveness of U.S. business and U.S. quality of life by promoting and facilitating voluntary consensus standards and conformity assessment systems, and safeguarding their integrity. ANSI is a non-profit organization that works closely with SAAMI to establish standards for the firearms and ammunition industry. ANSI makes available booklets of cartridge and chamber dimensions for use by consumers and small businesses.

AFEMS

Association of European Manufacturers of Sporting Ammunition
Rue Th. de Cuyper 100
Brussels, Belgium B-120
www.afems.org

This is an international (European) non-governmental organization of manufacturers set up to establish dialog with decision making bodies and to provide a forum to tackle technical, scientific, and legislative challenges on behalf of its members in a competitive business environment. Currently, AFEMS has approximately 50 member companies in fifteen European countries. Member companies include those making firearms, ammunition, components, machinery, and clay targets. AFEMS was set up in 1951 and registered in Belgium in 1980. It is the successor to the International Ammunitiom Convention founded in 1898.

(NRA) NATIONAL RIFLE ASSOCIATION

11250 Waples Mill Rd.
Fairfax, VA 22230
(800) 672-3888
http://home.nra.org

The NRA is an organization of collectors, hunters, and competitive shooters of all types. In addition to watching and reporting political issues related to firearms, the NRA certifies instructors, conducts training, and publishes seven monthly magazines. The NRA also organizes the National Matches at Camp Peary, OH. Currently, there are some 3 million members of the NRA.

(ATA) AMATEUR TRAPSHOOTING ASSOCIATION

1105 East Broadway St
Sparta, IL 62286
(618) 449-2224
www.shootata.com

The ATA is the governing body of American trapshooting. In addition to organizing and hosting the Grand American of Trapshooting, the ATA also publishes a magazine and sanctions regional events.

(NSSA) NATIONAL SKEET SHOOTING ASSOCIATION

5931 Roft Road
San Antonio, TX 78253
(210) 688-3371
www.nssa-nsca.org

The NSSA is the governing body of American skeet shooting. In addition to organizing and hosting the national event, the NSSA also publishes a magazine and sanctions regional events.

(SASS) SINGLE ACTION SHOOTING SOCIETY

215 Cowboy Way
Edgewood, NM 87015
(505) 843-132
www.sassnet.com

Known as "SASS", this non-profit group promotes western-style shooting with period firearms and western dress. They also conduct regional events as well as a national event.

SPORTING CLAYS OF AMERICA

9257 Buckeye Road
Sugar Grove, OH 43155
(614) 746-8334

Sporting Clays of America is the governing body of American sporting clays shooting. This association organizes and sanctions regional and national events.

U.S.A. SHOOTING

U.S. Olympic Shooting Center
1 Olympic Plaza
Colorado Springs, CO 80909
(719) 578-4670
www.usashooting.org

This organization trains prospective U.S. Olympic shooters in all disciplines.

(USPSA) UNITED STATES PRACTICAL SHOOTING ASSOCIATION

872 North Hill Blvd
Burlington, WA 98233
Phone: (360) 855-2245
www.uspsa.org

USPSA is a non profit organization which is the organizing body for the sport in the United States. The USPSA is affiliated with the IPSC and is one of the member regions of the IPSC.

(IPSC) INTERNATIONAL PRACTICAL SHOOTING CONFEDERATION

PO Box 972,
Oakville, Ontario,
Canada L6K 0B1
www.ipsc.org

The International Practical Shooting Confederation is the organizing body for the sport of practical shooting on a world wide basis with over 67 countries as member regions. The International Practical Shooting Confederation (IPSC) was established to promote, maintain, improve and advance the sport of IPSC shooting, to safeguard its principles and to regulate its conduct worldwide in order to cultivate the safe, recreational use of firearms by persons of good character.

(IAA) INTERNATIONAL AMMUNITION ASSOCIATION, INC.

6531 Carlsbad Drive
Lincoln, NE 68510
cartridgecollectors.org

This is the organization for cartridge collectors. They publish a monthly newsletter.

(IBS) INTERNATIONAL BENCHREST SHOOTERS

Joan Borden
1231 Sheldon Hill Road
Springville, OH 18844
internationalbenchrest.com/index.php

Many benchrest shooters from the U.S, Europe, Australia, Canada, and many other countries are members of this organization. They sanction numerous matches.

(NBRSA) NATIONAL BENCH REST SHOOTERS ASSOCIATION

P.O. Box 6770
Sheridan, WY 82801
nbrsa.org

Many American and Canadian bench rest shooters are members of this group. They sanction numerous matches.

(NSSF) NATIONAL SHOOTING SPORTS FOUNDATION, INC.

11 Mile Hill Road
Newtown, CT 06470
(203) 426-1087
www.nssf.org

This is a very active industry association dedicated to promoting shooting sports of all types, representing the industry in political matters, promoting safety, and hosting SAAMI.

(AFTE) ASSOCIATION OF FIREARMS AND TOOLMARK EXAMINERS

Andy Smith
San Francisco Police Dept.
P.O. Box 34426
San Francisco, CA 94134
(415) 671-3264
www.afte.org

Membership in this organization is limited to forensic examiners and firearms experts. They maintain training and certification programs as well as information to members.

(CMP) CIVILIAN MARKSMANSHIP PROGRAM

P.O. Box 576
Camp Perry Training Facility
Port Clinton, OH
 (419) 635-2141
www.odcmp.com

A non-profit organization dedicated to promoting marksmanship training by supporting shooters and clubs with government surplus materials. They also sponsor a match during the National Matches at Camp Perry, OH.

(FESAC) FOUNDATION FOR EUROPEAN SOCIETIES OF ARMS COLLECTORS

Phoenix Building
Old Railway Road
Santa Venera SVR 9022
Malta
http://fesac.eu/

The aims of the Foundation are to: Promote the collecting, research and preservation of arms and related objects, in their original form, from all periods in history. Ensure that national and supra-national legislation protects bona-fide collectors and recognises the importance of their activity. Represent and defend the interests of European arms collector societies and their members at national and supra-national level. Support the sharing of knowledge between collectors and the diffusion of this knowledge, through member-societies' activities, among the public, the media and the authorities. Assist national and supra-national authorities in the proper identification and classification of arms as artifacts representing mankind's common heritage. Encourage strong links between member societies as well as between these societies and the authorities and media in their respective countries.

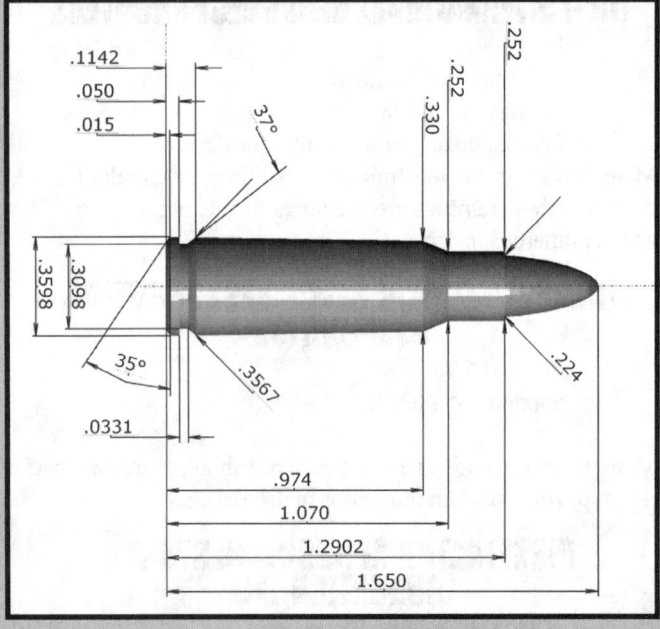

New Life for The .30 Carbine

5.7mm MMJ Spitfire

This wildcat was designed in 1963 by Col. Melvin M. Johnson of Johnson semi-automatic rifle fame. The intended purpose of this cartridge was to develop a small caliber, high-velocity cartridge which could be fired in a rebarreled M1 carbine that Johnson Guns, Inc. made and sold. The 5.7 mm Spitfire is basically a .30 Carbine cartridge necked down to hold a .224 inch diameter bullet. Indifferent sales numbers soon put an end to this project, although several other manufacturers of M1 carbines have attempted unsuccessfully to revive this cartridge since then.

Ballistic capability is modest with a 40-grain .224 inch diameter bullet at a muzzle velocity of about 2,600-2,700 fps and a muzzle energy of 647 ft-lbs. Claims of muzzle velocities in the range of 3,000 fps. should be dismissed as overly optimistic.

The .223 Rem. cartridge offers far more performance than the 5.7mm Spitfire at the same cost. However, the 5.7 mm MMJ refuses to die as long as there are M1 carbines in circulation.

CHAPTER 21 : RECENT AMMUNITION DEVELOPMENTS

MISCONCEPTIONS ABOUT THE AMMUNITION INDUSTRY

There are several misconceptions that continue to plague the ammunition industry.

Anti-gun groups base their view of the ammunition industry on, and intentionally foster misconceptions which they continue to hold despite facts to the contrary, namely:

- **The ammunition industry is run by greedy merchants of death making sinfully high profits.**

In truth, the ammunition industry is run by honest, patriotic men and women who work in the industry because they are deeply committed to responsible sport shooting, assisting law enforcement agencies and supporting the military services of their country. In short, the merchant of death image is a complete fabrication.

Ammunition industry profits are low – in an average year, most ammunition makers struggle to earn 10%. This is much lower than many other industries, making it difficult to attract investment in ammunition manufacturing.

- **Ammunition causes wars, terrorism, piracy, insurrections, drug cartels, criminals, sport hunting and self-defense.**

These old shibboleths are perpetuated by ideologues who despise hunting, would deny you the right of self-defense and believe that no one should own a gun for any reason. They include ammunition in their mindless determination to demonize firearms. These beliefs beggar common sense – ammunition causes wars, piracy and terrorism about as much as flies cause garbage.

- **Surely ammunition technology must be mature because it is over 900 years old!**

This is completely false. In fact, the pace of technological development in ammunition is accelerating as new materials, better propellants, modern manufacturing methods, optimized ballistics and improved quality control are brought to bear. Today's ammunition is the best in history and rapidly improving.

- **Hollywood stunts with guns mirror real life**

Hollywood is in the business of selling excitement. To this end, the hero/villain is shown using a single shot to blow up an automobile, blast a hole through a concrete wall, down a helicopter or shoot the pistol from the hand of an opponent at 50 yards. What's more, the hero/villain does this effortlessly, often holding the gun sideways. We know these are impossible stunts as the laws of physics do not take a vacation. However, such stunts do make for an exciting show. This raises a relevant question: "How deeply do such movie stunt images affect people's perceptions of ammunition?"

- **The ammunition industry is virtually unregulated.**

Completely and utterly false. In fact the ammunition industry is more regulated than most other industries. For example, ammunition manufacturers must comply with regulations from federal government agencies such as the DOT, EPA, BATFE, IRS, OSHA, Army Material Command, and the Department of State. In addition, numerous state and local agencies are involved, such as the local fire marshal, law enforcement agencies, insurance carriers, zoning boards, building inspectors, as well as state OSHA, EPA and DOT. Despite all this, there are calls for more regulation, increased taxes, higher license fees and customer purchase limits. As if this were not enough, the U.N. seeks to impose their control on international sales and shipment of ammunition over and above those already imposed by individual countries.

INDUSTRY OVERVIEW

COMMERCIAL MARKET

In the author's opinion, the small caliber ammunition market has entered a golden age with manufacturers offering a mind-boggling variety of high quality products. In addition, many new products have been or will be introduced, ranging from new calibers to polymer case centerfire ammunition to high energy propellants. For traditionalists and re-enactors, factory loaded ammunition in classic calibers is available from several sources. Match-grade ammunition in all calibers has set new records for consistency and accuracy. Hunting bullet designs, both lead and lead-free, are more sophisticated and capable than at any time previously. In just a few years, handgun bullets have evolved from solid, round nose designs to expanding configurations in a kaleidoscope of different configurations and capabilities.

Shotgun slugs have evolved from blunt soft lead slugs with the ballistic coefficient of a brick to sophisticated, discarding sabot projectiles with a polymer tip and lead core bonded to a copper alloy jacket. Shotshells loaded with composite, non-toxic shot offer better ballistic performance than lead shot. Shotshells loaded with buffered, copper-plated lead shot offer pattern densities only dreamt of previously.

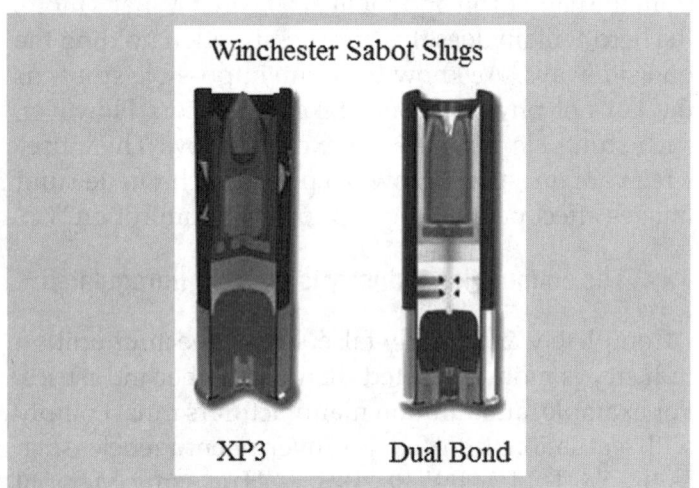

Winchester Sabot Slugs

XP3   Dual Bond

For those seeking something more exotic, there is "cold tracer" ammunition based on Cyalume chemistry, very low drag (VLD) bullets, boat tail bullets, bonded core bullets, frangible bullets, supercavitating bullets, sabot bullets, and lead-free primers. Rifle and pistol cartridges are offered with brass, steel, aluminum, polymer, and hybrid cases.

High energy ammunition in standard calibers offers substantially higher muzzle velocities at normal pressures. Going on safari? Then your choice of calibers and loads for hunting dangerous game are legendary. Indeed, the number of magnum cartridges on offer is stunning. Interested in varmint hunting? Then you will be impressed by factory loaded .22-250 Rem. ammunition with a muzzle velocity of 4,450 fps, the highest ever offered and not likely to be the last.

Dozens of ammunition manufacturers vie for your business. For example, the ATK Group offers 941 line

items, RUAG has 589 line items, and CBC Group offers 602 line items. Winchester offers 651 line items, Remington has 549, Fiocchi has 447, PMC has 166, and NAMMO offers 250+. That adds up to over 4,183 items for your shooting pleasure! These are only the larger companies; the smaller companies offer half-again as many.

GROUPS

For the past three or four years, shortages of sporting ammunition in the North American commercial market have been common. This was caused by urgent military requirements made on domestic and foreign ammunition makers in support of U.S. military operations in Iraq and Afghanistan. Such demands not only absorbed production capacity, they also caused shortages of copper and lead resulting in higher raw material prices. As these fade away, pent-up demand and election year concerns had maintained strong sales in the commercial ammunition market. This situation is likely to continue well into 2013.

Although the ammunition market is not contracting, the industry continues to undergo consolidation. This has resulted in five large corporations dominating the ammunition industry: ATK (U.S.), RUAG (Switzerland), CBC (Brazil), Freedom Group (U.S.), and NAMMO (Finland).

ATK is a large corporation with roots in the defense industry. Their extensive experience and technical expertise in a broad spectrum of ordnance fields gives them unique capabilities. Several years ago they began to diversify by purchasing Federal, CCI, Speer, Blaser, and Estate. These well-known commercial brands have enabled ATK to quickly become a major player in the commercial ammunition market. ATK/Federal is also the prime contractor for Lake City Army Ammunition Plant (LCAAP).

RUAG is based on the ordnance manufacturing facilities of the Swiss government. In a move to reduce costs in the late 1990s, the Swiss partially privatized their government ordnance manufacturing facilities. The small caliber centerpiece of the new group was the modern facility in Thun. Shortly thereafter, RUAG purchased the well-known German Dynamit Nobel facility in Furth, Germany, and Hirtenberger in Austria. This was followed in the early 2000s with the purchase of MFS, the ex-Hungarian government ammunition factory and the purchase of Precision Ammunition in Tampa, FL. Although RUAG has various large caliber divisions, it is dedicated to the commercial ammunition market.

The Freedom Group is the well-known owner of various firearms companies such as Bushmaster, H&R, Marlin, Para-USA and Remington. With their ownership of Remington, they entered the sporting ammunition market, which they have continued to pursue actively.

In the early 2000s, Freedom Group purchased Barnes Bullets to reinforce their share of the sporting ammunition market. From their ownership of Remington and Barnes Bullets, it is obvious that The Freedom Group is dedicated to the ammunition market.

Companhia Brasileira de Cartuchos (CBC) is based on the privatized Brazilian government ammunition manufacturing facilities. Following privatization in the later 1990s, CBC began actively building its export business by establishing a wholly-owned, non-manufacturing sales subsidiary in the U.S. called Magtech. In the mid-2000s, CBC purchased the German ammunition manufacturer Metallwerk Elisenhutte GmbH Nassau (MEN) followed in 2011 by Sellier & Bellot in the Czech Republic. These additions make CBC a world-class ammunition manufacturer with the technical, manufacturing, and sales capabilities to be reckoned with.

Nordic Ammunition Group (NAMMO) is a group of Scandinavian manufacturers of ammunition and ammunition components. These include Lapua (Finland), Vihtavuori (Finland), Raufoss (Norway), Bakelittefabrikken (Norway), SK-jagd und Sportmunition GmbH (Germany), Vanasverkken (Sweden) and Talley (U.S.A.). In addition to large caliber ammunition and rockets, NAMMO manufactures all types of small caliber sporting cartridges including .22 rimfire, shotshells and centerfire rifle and handgun ammunition. They also manufacture and sell components such as bullets, cartridge cases, and propellants. Their market is the customer who insists on the best quality and latest technology.

LAW ENFORCEMENT

In the not too distant past, ammunition manufacturers viewed the law enforcement market with a sharp pencil. That is to say they looked over their inventory and bid their overstock on law enforcement solicitations. For smaller accounts, the manufacturer's catalog sufficed; look the catalog over and let us know if you see anything you want. Special load requirements were not solicited, customer needs were not taken into account in sales forecasts, and service was rudimentary. After all, conventional wisdom was that the total law enforcement market amounted to about 10% of the sporting market–hardly worth making a special effort to get.

Then in the 1990s, ammunition makers discovered the law enforcement market after the federal government instituted officer certification and qualification requirements. In addition, the number of law enforcement officers at all levels increased substantially leading to large state and huge federal bid solicitations. This got the ammunition makers' attention. Today, ammunition manufacturers view law enforcement as an integral part of sales. Gone are the days of the sharp pencil.

In early 2012, the Department of Homeland Security (DHS) awarded a contract to ATK for 450 million rounds of .40 S&W ammunition and 175 million rounds of 5.56x45mm ammunition. The Treasury and Justice departments, states and large metropolitan cities also solicit bids for very large quantities. Want something special? No problem. Just ask.

MILITARY

The U.S. military has made significant efforts to develop, mature, and adopt new small arms ammunition technology. These efforts are being driven by three requirements:

1. Significantly reduce the weight a soldier must carry on field operations

2. Reduce ammunition production costs

3. Make use of new materials to achieve the above goals

Much of the ammunition technology being developed is not new. Rather, it was not technically feasible in the past for a variety of reasons. However, new materials, advanced propellants, improved ballistics, and lighter weight are now possible.

Here are two examples:

1. Improved ballistics M855A1 bullet
2. Lightweight ammunition (LWA)
    a. Short term with polymer case
    b. Long term with caseless technology.

NEW PRODUCTS

Normally, ammunition makers can be expected to develop and bring to market one or two completely new products every year along with a dozen or so new variations of existing products to flesh out imagined holes in the product line and increase the interest of writers, dealers and customers. Indeed, new products play an important part in ammunition sales. Innovation sells (at least most of the time).

In the recent past, ammunition makers have been extremely reluctant to bring a new product to market that they did not design or develop. Of course, this was the result of a boiling mixture of pride and parsimony that developed into three poisonous attitudes:

1. **The "not-invented-here" syndrome meaning if we did not think of it, you don't need it.**

2. **We are not interested in your idea no matter how good it may be and, in any case, we are unwilling to pay you for it.**

3. **When we do come up with something new, we will tell you when you need it (probably).**

This has changed dramatically in recent times as ammunition makers have awakened to the sales potential of teaming with gun makers to bring out new cartridges and guns in those calibers at the same time. However, what began as a good idea may have been stretched to the point of confusion with the proliferation of new calibers with seemingly redundant purpose and ballistic performance. For example, we now have the following tried-and-true .30 caliber extant cartridges suitable for short action length rifles: 7.62x39mm, .300 Savage, .307 Winchester and .308 Winchester. To which we must now add the following new entrants: .30 Thompson/Center, .300 Ruger Compact Magnum, .300 Remington Short-Action Ultra Magnum, .300 Winchester Short Magnum, and .308 Marlin Express.

Given the popularity of short .30 caliber cartridges for hunting, this is understandable. However, the competition in the .375 caliber market segment is no less intense and potential sales for such a large caliber cartridge are depressingly small. What's wrong with the tried-and-true .375 Holland & Holland Magnum, .378 Weatherby Magnum or the two .366 inch Mauser siblings: the 9.3x57 mm and the 9.3x62mm. Apparently, quite a lot is wrong if one is to judge from the recent .375 Winchester, .375 Ruger, .375 Remington Ultra Magnum, .376 Steyr and 9.3x66mm Sako introductions, not to mention .338 and .416 caliber proliferation.

Much the same situation exists in other calibers such as .270, 7mm, and .416. We have gone from famine to feast, but it cannot last. Many of these new cartridges are bound to suffer an ignominious, early retirement.

CONSOLIDATION

As governments close or privatize their small caliber ammunition plants and large corporations buy ammunition manufacturers to include a "national defense" segment in their portfolios, the ammunition industry has begun to consolidate. Here are some of the recent activities in this area:

ALLIANT TECHSYSTEMS (ATK)

This corporation has recently entered the small caliber ammunition business in a big way by purchasing Federal Cartridge, Speer, CCI, Blazer and Estate Cartridge. They have also won the management contract for Lake City Army Ammunition Plant.

COMPANHIA BRASILEIRA DE CARTUCHOS (CBC)

In 2007, this large manufacturer of commercial and military ammunition in Brazil established itself in Europe when it purchased the German ammunition maker Metallwerk Elisenhutte GmbH Nassau or MEN as it is popularly known. This came as a surprise to everyone. However, CBC had another surprise up its sleeve in 2009 when it announced the purchase of Sellier & Bellot in the Czech Republic.

SK JAGD

This is the former East German government-owned Ernst Thallman Ammunition Works. When East Germany fell, this plant emerged in the commercial ammunition market as SK Jagd. In 2005 SK Jagd was purchased by the Finnish company NAMMO Lapua Oy.

RUAG

RUAG began with a core small caliber ammunition production facility in Thun, Switzerland which they continue to operate for the Swiss government as well as commercial customers. In the early 2000s, RUAG purchased Dynamit Nobel (RWS) in Nuremberg, Germany and Norma Precision in Sweden. Following this, they purchased Hirtenberger Patronen in Austria. Gaining momentum, in 2009 RUAG purchased MFS2000 in Hungary and Precision Ammunition Company in the U.S.

GENERAL DYNAMICS

This corporate giant has entered the small caliber ammunition business with the purchase of SNC Technologies, well-known for its dye marking cartridges and frangible ammunition used to train law enforcement and military personnel. In 2004, they purchased Valcartier Industries of Canada, a primary supplier of small caliber ammunition to the Canadian armed forces.

NAMMO AS

This company, also known as the NAMMO Group, began as a merger in 1998 of three Nordic ammunition manufacturers: Celsius AB, Patria Induatrex Oy, and Raufoss ASA. Its five business units – Small Caliber, Medium and Large Caliber, Missile Products, Demil (Demilitarization and disposal), and NAMMO Talley – and subsidiaries are located in Norway, Sweden, Finland, Germany, Switzerland, Canada, and the U.S. Lapua Oy (Finland), Bakelittfabrikken AS (Norway), Vanasverken AB (Sweden), and Raufoss AS (Norway), develop and manufacture rimfire, centerfire, and shotgun ammunition for the civilian and military markets, as well as bullets and powders for handloading.

Nammo Group's world headquarters is located in Raufoss, Norway.

CLOSINGS

CHARTER INDUSTRIES OF SINGAPORE

Established to supply ordnance products to Singapore's military forces, this company recently ceased production of small caliber military ammunition. They continue to offer many other ordnance items.

NATEC

This small ammunition company in Plattsburg, NY was known for their innovative hybrid cartridge cases made of plastic with brass heads. They ceased operations in 2007.

OLYMPIC AMMUNITION COMPANY

This small start-up Greek ammunition maker tried very hard to establish a toe-hold in the U.S. market. Unfortunately, they were not successful and have ceased operations.

SWARTKLIP

For many years, Swartklip in South Africa was well-known for their .22 rimfire cartridges and shotshells. In the late 1990s, the corporate owner, the Denel group, directed that rimfire and shotshell production cease in order to allow Swartklip to concentrate on the flare and illumination ammunition business.

OLD WESTERN SCROUNGER (OWS)

"Dangerous Dave" has retired and sold (OWS) to Navy Arms in West Virginia.

TECHNOLOGICAL DEVELOPMENTS

PROJECTILES

Bullets, shot, and slugs continue to benefit from new technology developed by small companies.

There are seven new trends in projectiles:

1. Lead-free materials

These expanding bullets are designed for use in hunting areas where lead bullets are banned. Typical construction is copper-zinc (gilding metal) with a segmented hollow point or plastic tip design. Barnes Bullets has been the leader of this trend.

2. Frangible designs

As environmental regulations continue to reduce the levels of airborne lead in shooting ranges, the use of frangible non-toxic (lead-free) bullets continues to grow. In most instances, frangible bullets are molded from powdered metals with a polymer binding agent. No jacket is needed. Until recently, most frangible bullets have been in handgun calibers. Their use is now spreading to rifle calibers. Precision Ammunition Company has been one of the key pioneers in this market niche.

3. Bonded cores

It seems every ammunition company offers bonded core bullets these days. While the specific metal compositions and bonding processes remain proprietary, the general concept is based on heating a formed bullet which has a solder coated lead core. This works very well, frequently bonded core bullets achieve 98% retained weight.

4. Very low drag designs

The pioneer in this area was Berger Bullets which developed Dr. Louis Palmisano's concept. Initially, most VLD bullets were designed for target shooting. Now, hunting types are available such as those from Swift Bullets.

5. Plastic tips

When Nosler introduced their "Ballistic Tip" bullet over 15 years ago, none could have imagined the popularity this concept would achieve. Today, plastic tip bullets are common. We owe John Nosler a debt of gratitude for this.

6. Non-toxic shot

Several manufacturers now offer shotshells loaded with non-toxic shot pellets that are HEAVIER than lead and will not damage shotgun barrels. Downrange ballistics are BETTER than lead shot, albeit at a considerable increase in cost. But how many shells do you typically use on waterfowl every year and what percentage is this of total hunt costs?

7. Sabot Shotgun Slugs

Sabot shotgun slugs are the hot ticket these days. The ballistic performance of sabot slugs over conventional full-bore Foster types far outweighs their added cost. Mind you, a rifled barrel is required for most sabot slugs but the increased range and better accuracy are the paybacks. In the author's opinion, more work needs to be done to improve slug accuracy and range from smoothbore barrels.

CARTRIDGE CASES

Brass alloy continues to be the preferred metal for centerfire and rimfire cartridge cases. After the price of nickel skyrocketed several years ago, the popularity of "premium" nickel-plated cartridge cases faded under a cloud of cost increases.

ATK's Blazer products continue as the sole aluminum case ammunition. Many years back, the cost of aluminum and the larger number of cases yielded by a pound of metal gave aluminum cases a significant price advantage. Since then, increasing prices for aluminum have erased a good share, but not all, of this advantage.

Conventional wisdom has been that American sportsmen will not accept steel case ammunition. This myth has been thoroughly busted by Wolf and other Russian ammunition makers who sell large quantities of steel case ammunition in the North American market. .

The holy grail of centerfire ammunition is the development and mass production of a plastic which is both moldable and strong enough to be used as a cartridge case. Many have tried, but none have succeeded. NATEC came very close by solving the problems of bullet pull and shot start resistance, but failed to devise a plastic head.

Rimfire is wedged into a corner. Steel cartridge cases do not work in rimfire guns and plastic is not a suitable material. This leaves no alternative except perhaps a caseless design.

PRIMERS

Primer development continues to focus on getting the heavy metals (lead) out of priming compounds in order to meet airborne lead levels and ecological directives. Success has been slow in coming, but RWS and several Russian manufacturers have come up with suitable alternatives. The reader is referred to Chapter 27: Primer Manufacturing for further information on this topic.

What about electric primers? What happened to Remington's EtronX primers? In truth, they were a good idea that worked, only they did not solve any perceived problems for hunters or informal competitors. The lack of perceived need and high cost combined to sink Remington's efforts in short order. In the author's opinion, Remington should have pitched this primer to target shooters who can appreciate and use the super-fast ignition of these primers.

Recently, some importers have advertised ammunition as being "mildly corrosive". This is an oxymoron as primers are either corrosive or they are not.

PROPELLANTS

Although it might not be obvious, considerable advances have been made in propellant technology recently. For example, Primex has developed a new Hybrid ball propellant from which much is expected. Hornady has taken advantage of new high energy propellants to offer increased ballistic performance without the high chamber pressures. Other innovations have been based on advanced boron and synthetic substance chemistry.

Oh, and shooters have finally realized that black powder substitutes need not be smoky and sulfurous just for old time sake which has led to improved BP substitutes.

TOWARD THE FUTURE

What does the future hold for small caliber ammunition? To answer this question, we can conservatively extrapolate existing trends to develop a short range view. However, a long range view will, of necessity, require my crystal ball. So, here goes.

SHORT RANGE PREDICTIONS (WITHIN 10 YEARS)

1. **The growing differences between military and commercial small caliber ammunition will result in completely different lines of future development.**

2. **Tough economic times and the increasing cost of African hunting will reduce the number of large caliber cartridges (i.e. those with bullets over .375 inches in diameter).**

3. **Lead shot will no longer be loaded in shotshells of any type or size.**

4. **As the number of slug-only hunting areas increases, interest in and use of shotgun slugs will continue to increase.**

5. **The use of Magnum cartridges will decrease due to their high cost, heavy recoil and limited opportunities to use them.**

6. **The .40 S&W cartridge will eclipse the 9mm Luger cartridge in popularity for law enforcement and civilian applications.**

7. **The following pistol cartridges will be retired by many ammunition makers: .30 Luger, 9x21mm, .38 Super Auto, 10mm Auto, .41 AE, .45 GAP, .45 Winchester Magnum, and .476 Wildey Magnum.**

8. **Ammunition makers will retire the following revolver cartridges: .32 Short, .32 Long, .41 Magnum, .44 Special, .460 S&W Magnum and Special, and .480 Ruger.**

9. We will wave goodbye to the following rifle cartridges: .218 Bee, .223 WSSM, 6mm PPC, 6mm Rem. BR, .25 WSSM, .250 Savage, 6.5mm Grendel, 7-30 Waters, .280 Ackley Improved, 7mm Remington BR, 7mm STW, .30 R Blaser, .307 Winchester, .32 Winchester Special, .325 WSM, 8mm Rem. Magnum, .356 Winchester, .35 Whelen, .350 Remington Magnum, .375 Winchester, .376 Steyr, .458 Lott, and .460 Steyr.

10. Casualties in the rimfire lines will include: .22 BB Cap, .22 CB Cap, .22 Short, .22 Long, and .22 WRF.

11. Shotgunners will lament the passing of the 16-ga., 28-ga., and .410-bore 2 1/2" shells.

LONG RANGE PREDICTIONS (OVER 10 YEARS FROM NOW)

1. Rimfire ammunition will be replaced by caseless designs.

2. Shotshells will be either 12-ga. or 20-ga. All others will be history.

3. All shotshells will be made of molded plastic without a metal head.

4. New pistols will be made only in .380 Auto, 9mm Luger, .40 S&W, and .45 Auto.

5. New revolvers will be made only in .327 Ruger Magnum, .357 Magnum, .44 Magnum, and .454 Casull.

6. All large African rifle cartridges will be retired save the .375 H&H Magnum, .416 Rigby and the .470 NE.

7. All trap and skeet competitions will be fired with steel shot.

8. New rifle calibers made with high strength steel cartridges cases will allow increased chamber pressures to generate magnum ballistics despite their small case volumes.

9. Hunting rifle bullets will contain no lead.

10. New varmint rifle calibers will generate over 5,000 fps of muzzle velocity.

11. Military small arms will use caseless ammunition.

12. The number of sporting ammunition calibers will be reduced to 15-20.

A SAD STORY

Just before the beginning of World War II in 1939, the U.S. government implemented a four wave program to build a production base for small caliber military ammunition. The first wave included all of the major commercial manufacturers: Remington (Bridgeport, CT), Winchester (New Haven, CT), and Western (East Alton, IL) and Frankford Arsenal (Philadelphia, PA). In addition, four new plants were built: Denver, CO, Kings Mills, OH (Peters), St. Louis, MO, and Lake City, MO.

The second wave included new plants in Iowa (Des Moines), Minnesota (Twin Cities), and Utah (Salt Lake City). A planned third wave was not completed, but the the fourth wave included new plants in Cumberland, MD, Eau Claire, WI, Evansville, IN, and Lowell, MA.

At the end of World War II, the U.S. Army was operating 15 small caliber ammunition plants. The production capacity of this group was astonishing, for example the Twin Cities plant could manufacture 1 million rounds per shift, and they ran three shifts a day seven days a week! Indeed, production was so high that the U.S. government decided to cut production in 1944, only to find that ammunition expenditure increased substantially after D-Day in June 1944 forcing contracts to be let to Canadian manufacturers to avoid a shortage.

In years following World War II, Winchester (at Western in East Alton, IL) and Remington resumed production of commercial ammunition while the Peters and the Winchester (New Haven) plants were closed. All of the remaining government-owned ordnance plants were closed except Lake City Army Ammunition Plant or LCAAP in Independence, MO and Twin Cities Army Ammunition Plant or TCAAP in New Brighton, MN. In the early 1960s, Frankford Arsenal was closed.

Under a new Small Caliber Ammunition Modernization Program (SCAMP), LCAAP and TCAAP were to be modernized using the latest, high-speed, computer-controlled technology and equipment from Gulf+Western Corp. In theory, modernizing both plants with SCAMP equipment would maintain a robust small caliber production base with plenty of surge capability and requiring only a small fraction of the workers employed in the World War II plants. LCAAP was selected to continue day-to-day small caliber production operations while TCAAP would install, debug and prove the SCAMP machinery. When the machinery was deemed ready for full production, it was to be moved to LCAAP after which new machinery would be ordered for the Twin Cities plant which was to remain in mothballs as a surge capability.

However, it was not to be. Abruptly, during the late 1960s, TCAAP was ordered to ship all SCAMP machinery to LCAAP. The machinery was not fully debugged and required considerable effort by LCAAP personnel to get it running satisfactorily. No new machinery was ordered for TCAAP which was left in mothballs. Then, in the 1980s, TCAAP was ordered closed and all machinery was sold as surplus. This left LCAAP as the only small caliber military ammunition plant in the U.S. In addition, a program for keeping government-owned machinery at Federal and Winchester fully tooled and ready for an emergency was cancelled and the machinery sold.

The story gets worse. Additional SCAMP machinery was never ordered for LCAAP, leaving the .50 BMG production line antiquated and no modern capability to manufacture pistol ammunition which now has to be purchased from commercial manufacturers. Congress then cut funding for military ammunition leaving LCAAP running one shift only several days a week and the U.S. military with a dangerously low small caliber ammunition reserve. So low, in fact, that some U.S. military personnel deploying to Iraq did not have enough ammunition to zero and function test their rifles before deployment!

At this point in time, the SCAMP machinery is over 50 years old and rapidly getting long in the tooth. New manufacturing technology has rendered SCAMP obsolete and many of the parts needed to keep it in operation are no longer available. Its computer control system is now a museum artifact. New machinery is desperately needed, however, obtaining funding is unlikely.

A BRIEF HISTORY OF FRANGIBLE AMMUNITION

By Kenneth L. Alexander

Frangible ammunition first appeared in the early 20th century for use in carnival shooting galleries equipped with .22 caliber rimfire rifles. The frangible bullets were made from small particles of lead or iron lightly bonded together that broke up into small particles on impact with steel targets. Frangible ammunition offered a realistic seldom seen outside the carnival world.

Frangible military ammunition in .30-'06 caliber was developed during WWII for training aerial gunners. Trainees used frangible ammunition to fire at specially armored P-63 fighter aircraft. In theory, the frangible bullets would break up upon impact not damaging the

Commercial frangible ammunition packaging, circa 1930s

shooting experience that substantially reduced the danger of ricocheting bullets or back-splatter. The health hazards and environmental concerns associated with metallic lead were not a consideration in that era.

As frangible-bulleted, rimfire ammunition offered no advantage for sporting or hunting purposes, it was target aircraft. Experience showed otherwise, making flying such "Pin-Ball" missions very unpopular with fighter pilots. The P-63 target aircraft were wired with lights so that the gunners could observe their "hits."

Interest in frangible bulleted ammunition surged

20 CARTRIDGES
BALL, FRANGIBLE
CALIBER .30 T-44

AMMUNITION LOT L. C.

DISPOSAL OF EMPTIED CARTRIDGE CASES
MUST BE MADE AS PRESCRIBED BY A. R.

LAKE CITY ORDNANCE PLANT

WWII frangible ammo packaging

in the 1990s as the Occupational Safety and Health Administration (OSHA) began to address the health hazards of airborne lead in indoor shooting ranges. The Environmental Protection Agency (EPA) also became involved in an effort to reduce the amount of lead in the environment. Increasingly tough OSHA and EPA lead regulations forced some commercial shooting ranges to close. Law enforcement and military shooting ranges were not immune to the new regulations either and their demand drove the initial development of frangible bulleted handgun ammunition.

Materials used to develop lead-free, frangible bullets include brittle zinc alloy, polymer and metallic matrices, sintered copper-tin powder, sintered iron powder and copper alloy, and copper alloy bullet jackets filled with various materials, including tungsten powder. While there are pros and cons with each type, all are plagued by high material and production cost. In addition, many frangible bullet manufacturing processes and designs are patented. This requires ammunition manufacturers to license a patent, develop their own frangible designs, or purchase frangible bullets from an outside source. Each of these alternatives raises cost. Non-toxic, frangible bulleted ammunition must also incorporate expensive, lead-free primers to comply with government requirements.

Most frangible ammunition is sold to military and law enforcement agencies via a competitive bid process with smaller quantities sold to commercial, indoor ranges. Most frangible ammunition is made in handgun calibers. However, frangible shotshell and rifle ammunition has recently appeared. Very little frangible ammunition is sold in the sporting ammunition market.

The propellant types and charge weights employed in frangible ammunition are different than those used in the same caliber of conventional ammunition. Frangible bullets are longer than conventional bullets of the same weight because of the difference in material density.

The maximum overall length of a cartridge remains the same regardless of the type of bullet used. The extra

length of a frangible bullet must, therefore, be contained within the cartridge case, which reduces volume for the powder charge. This can cause detrimental effects upon internal ballistic factors such as pressure and velocity.

Frangible ammunition must feed and function in unmodified handguns. To accomplish this with the lightweight frangible bullets, muzzle velocities must be substantially increased. Another problem is that frangible ammunition seldom shoots to the same point of aim as lead bullet ammunition.

.40 S&W 125 gr Frangible
Copper Tin Bullet

.40 S&W 155 gr Conventional
Lead Core Bullet

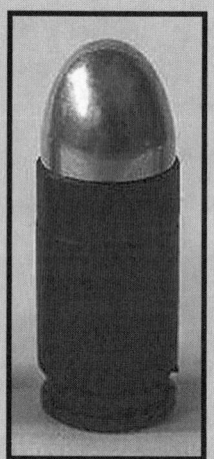

Polymer Pistol Cartridge Cases from Extreme Polymer Research

A small Spanish company called Extreme Polymer Research is developing a line of polymer cartridge cases for straight-walled pistol cartridges in calibers .380 Auto, 9mm Luger, .40 S&W and .45 Auto. Unlike other hybrid polymer cases that have a separate metal head, Extreme Polymer Research cases are molded entirely of polymer. The company selected a construction polymer used in building automotive cases for its strength and temperature stability from -40 to +150°C.

Extreme Polymer Research believes the primary benefit of their polymer cases will be low cost, light weight and consistent quality. The company plans to begin sales of their cases in 2013.

PCP Ammo To Introduce Polymer Cased Centerfire Rifle Ammunition

A small, startup company in Orlando, FL is seeking to go where others have failed–namely to manufacture and sell a polymer, center fire rifle cartridge case that is fully the equivalent of a brass cartridge case. Technically, the PCP cartridge case is a hybrid with a metal head and two piece polymer case body. A significant advantage of such a case is lighter weight than brass cartridge cases.

Based on promising initial testing, PCP announced in 2011 that they intend to begin marketing loaded ammunition using their patented polymer cartridge case in Fall 2012. Production plans begin with .308 Win. caliber ammunition with .223 Rem. added as quickly as possible. Future plans include ammunition in 6.8 SPC, .300 Win. Magnum, .338 Lapua Magnum and .50 BMG. The company plans to use Sierra, Berger and Barnes bullets.

SECTION V – MANUFACTURING
CHAPTER 22 : BULLET MANUFACTURING

CHAPTER 22 HIGHLIGHTS:

- OVERVIEW
- BULLET MAKING TECHNOLOGIES
- BULLET MAKING MACHINERY
- MATERIALS
- CRITERIA FOR A GOOD BULLET
- CRITERIA FOR THE PERFECT BULLET

All drawings by Author, unless otherwise noted.

OVERVIEW

From 1240 to 1880, most bullets were made of molded lead or lead alloy. This changed with the advent of smokeless propellants which enabled much higher muzzle velocities in 1885. Although jacketed bullets were necessary for such velocities, the manufacturing technology for drawing brass bullet jackets had not been fully developed.

Initially, jacketed rifle bullets were full metal jacketed round nose designs with a flat base as these were the easiest to manufacture. By 1900, bullet making technology had progressed to the point that jacketed spitzer (pointed) bullets could be manufactured. Early jacketed rifle bullets were made using cup and draw technology. This technology, with many improvements, remains the most common method of bullet jacket manufacture to this day.

Monolithic lead bullet and jacketed bullet core technology was not neglected either. Swaging replaced molding in most, but not all, modern lead bullet production.

Just prior to World War II, interest increased in bullets having a jacket which was built up by electro-plating on a lead core. Western was one of the first to perfect this technology. After World War II, Remington introduced their Core-Lokt bullet design with a plated jacket. Other manufacturers such as CCI have followed Remington's lead.

Today, injection molding and sintering composite bullets have become technically and commercially feasible. Although more expensive than other bullet manufacturing methods, these lead-free processes are cost-effective because they are used to make non-toxic and frangible bullets, which are more ecologically friendly than lead or lead core bullets.

Today, a bullet maker has more advanced production technologies available than at any time in the past. At last count, there were seven major technologies and numerous variations available.

Dum Dum Bullet

The term "Dum Dum" bullet comes from the British Arsenal at Dum Dum, India where Capt. Bertie-Clay invented the first expanding rifle bullet in 1890. It was developed to improve battlefield stopping power of the then-new .303 British military cartridge. In short order, British troops fighting on the northern Indian frontier applied the term "Dum Dum" to ammunition loaded with this very effective type of bullet. From this origin, the appellation entered the popular lexicon where it has remained for over 120 years.

Although expanding bullets were outlawed for military combat by the Hague Convention of 1899, the name "Dum Dum" became synonymous with expanding bullets made by cutting off the tips of full metal jacket military bullets.

The arsenal at Dum Dum, India still manufactures ammunition.

BULLET MAKING TECHNOLOGIES

There are eight major technologies for making bullets.

For monolithic bullets:

- **Casting**
- **Injection molding**
- **Sintering**
- **Swaging**
- **Turning**

For built-up or jacketed bullets:

- **Cup and draw**
- **Electro-plating**
- **Impact Extrusion**

CASTING

This is the oldest system used mainly for making lead bullets. It consists of five steps:

- **Melting the lead in a metal pot**
- **Pouring the molten lead into a two-piece model mold**

- Opening the mold to release the bullets
- Inspecting the bullet and allowing it to cool
- Sizing and lubricating the bullet

To increase output, a gang mold with multiple cavities can be used. The lead can be hardened by adding antimony or tin.

Advantages of Casting

- Cheap and simple
- Low tech - only simple equipment needed
- Can be done in the field
- Lubrication grooves can be molded on the bullet surface

Disadvantages of Casting

- Toxic fumes from melted lead
- Slow process; limited output
- Non-uniform bullet hardness and dimensions
- Bullet must be sized and lubricated

MOLDING

An injection molding process is used to manufacture frangible and lead-free bullets. While the process seems simple and straightforward, it actually incorporates a considerable amount of sophisticated technology. There are four steps in this system:

- Powdered metals are mixed with a polymer binding agent
- The mixture is heated then fed into a multi-cavity mold
- The mixture is allowed to "set" in the mold
- Finished bullets are released when the mold is opened

Advantages of Injection Molding

- Can make non-toxic and frangible bullets
- End result is a finished product
- No jacket needed
- High production rate

Disadvantages of Injection Molding

- Injection molding machinery is expensive
- Multi-cavity molds are expensive
- High cost of some metal powders and polymers
- Bullet is lighter than lead for same volume

SINTERING

Lead-Free Bullets

This is a modern process used to manufacture frangible, lead-free bullets. Although sintering is not a new technology, applying it to bullet making required considerable effort to develop suitable materials and procedures. It consists of the following four steps:

- Powdered metals are mixed together with a binding agent
- The mixture is placed in a mold and subjected to heat and pressure which fuses the metal particles together
- A finished product is released when the mold is opened
- An electro-plated copper alloy jacket can be applied if needed (except on sintered iron)

Advantages of Sintering

- Usable with a wide combination of metal powders
- End result is a finished product
- Lead-free non-toxic frangible bullet
- Can be jacketed or plated later if needed

Disadvantages of Sintering

- Expensive molds needed
- Expensive machinery needed
- Low production rate
- Some metal powders are expensive or in short supply

SWAGING

Lead Bullets

Swaging is a mature, high speed process for making monolithic lead bullets. There are two basic methods used for swaging lead bullets:

- Punch and die
- Rotating wheel

Punch and Die Systems

The punch and die system consists of six steps:

- Hot ingots of lead alloy are extruded into wire of suitable diameter and hardness then wound onto reels
- The wire is cut into suitable lengths called slugs
- A punch pushes the slug into a die to form the bullet

- Bullets are ejected from the die by an ejector pin
- Bullets are cleaned and deburred by tumbling in wood drums
- Bullets are sized and lubricated with a wax compound (and coated with graphite)

Advantages (Punch and Die)

- High production rate
- Good quality product
- Consistent bullet dimensions and weight

Disadvantages (Punch and Die)

- Machinery and tooling expensive
- Extruded wire normally out-sourced adding cost
- Bullet must be sized and lubricated

Rotating Wheel System

This system uses two rotating steel wheels with a number of half cavities cut into each rim; each half cavity being opposite halves of the bullet swaging die. As the wheels rotate, they are synchronized to bring the two halves of the die cavity together. Lead wire is fed between the wheels allowing the cavities to form the bullet.

This process consists of five steps:

- Extruding hot lead alloy ingots into wire of suitable diameter and hardness
- Forming the bullets in the cavities of the rotating wheel rims
- Deburring
- Sizing
- Lubricating and coating

Advantages of Swaging (Rotating Wheel)

- Very high production rate
- Low cost machinery and tooling
- Lead does not have to be melted

Disadvantages of Swaging (Rotating Wheel)

- Process suitable mainly for round balls, rimfire bullets, and bullet core pre-forms
- Quality not as good as punch and die system
- Extruded lead wire normally must be purchased adding cost

Bronze or Copper Alloy Bullets

This type of swaged bullet has become more popular in recent years due to environmental concerns about lead pollution. This system of making bullets dates back to the late 1880s with the French Balle D bullet.

Solid bronze bullets have no jacket, thus eliminating an entire production process and source of quality problems (jacket/core concentricity).

The swaging process is much the same as for lead bullets except several extra steps may be necessary, depending on the size and shape of the bullet. The normal steps are:

- Extruding bronze alloy metal into rods of suitable diameter
- Cutting the metal rods into appropriate lengths called slugs or pre-forms
- Forming bullet in swaging machine using punch and die, stage 1 (start)
- Forming bullet in swaging machine using punch and die, stage 2 (finish)
- Washing, deburring
- Inserting tip, or core if any
- Turning cannelures, rotating bands
- Applying coating (if any)

Advantages of Swaging (Bronze/Copper Solids)

- Finished product is high quality
- Non-toxic; (w/o lead core) no lubrication needed
- No core-jacket concentricity problems
- No core-jacket separation problems

Disadvantages of Swaging (Bronze/Copper Solids)

- Raw material is expensive
- Tooling expensive
- Machinery is expensive

TURNING

This is method of bullet production that entails high cost. It consists of four steps:

- Extruding bronze alloy metal into rods of suitable diameter
- Feeding the rods into a Swiss automatic screw ma-

chine which turns the bullet's profile on the slug, and cuts off the rod

- Washing, deburring
- Applying coating (if any)

Advantages of Turning

- Net product including cannelure, driving bands
- Close tolerances
- Few operations
- Low tooling cost, easy change overs

Disadvantages of Turning

- Machinery very expensive
- Low production rate
- High cost of raw materials

CUP AND DRAW

This method of bullet construction is by far the most common. Alloys of 95/5 or 90/10 copper/zinc are normally used. Typically, this process consists of the following steps:

Bullet jackets are formed from rolls of copper alloy strip which are fed into a multiple die path bullet jacket draw press. The press draws the jackets through a series of closely spaced die stacks. The first step is blanking to cut a disk from the strip. The disk is then drawn through the die stack to form the jacket. The result is a drawn copper alloy tube, closed at one end.

A bullet jacket draw press can have eight or more draw paths, each of which produces a drawn bullet jacket on every stroke. Following this, the jacket goes through several additional procedures:

- Jacket is washed and dried to remove draw lubricant
- Clean jacket is trimmed to desired length
- Lead wire is cut into slugs of appropriate length
- Drawn jackets and slugs fed into a multi-station bullet assembly press which:

  a. Feeds jacket and core to holding fingers in shuttle

  b. Seats core into jacket

  c. Starts forming ogive

  d. Finish forms ogive and tip

  e. Sizes bullet

  f. Ejects finished bullet from shuttle holding fingers

- Finished bullets are cannelured (if needed)
- Finished bullets are washed and dried
- Finished bullets are polished and deburred in rotating drums

STEPS IN MANUFACTURING A JACKETED RIFLE BULLET

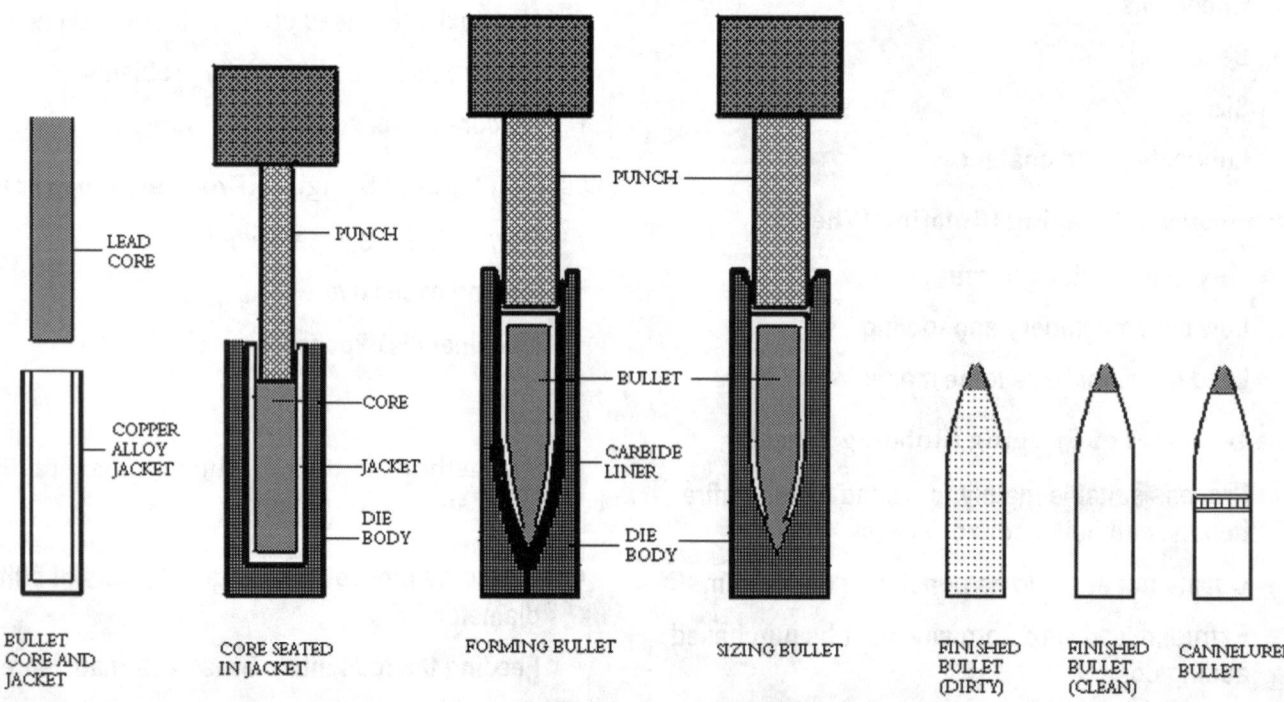

| BULLET CORE AND JACKET | CORE SEATED IN JACKET | FORMING BULLET | SIZING BULLET | FINISHED BULLET (DIRTY) | FINISHED BULLET (CLEAN) | CANNELURED BULLET |

- Bullets are coated (if required)

Advantages of Cup and Draw

- **Makes an excellent quality, accurate bullet**
- **Well established technology**
- **Low cost machinery**
- **High output at reasonable cost**

Disadvantages of Cup and Draw

- **High tooling cost**
- **Many production steps**
- **Quality brass strip often hard to get and expensive**
- **Lead subject to increasing tough regulation**

PLATING

This process was designed to produce quality bullets at reduced cost by eliminating several production steps. Basically, this is a six step process as compared to the ten step cup and draw process.

- **Core pre-form made from swaged lead alloy**
- **Core pre-form washed and dried to remove draw lube**
- **Lead pre-form immersed in high voltage electroplating tank; jacket metal accumulates on preform's surfaces**
- **Bullet with plated jacket removed from plating tank, washed and dried**
- **Bullet profiled and sized in a die**
- **Finished bullet cannelured (if needed)**

Advantages of Plating

- **Low cost, fewer production steps**
- **High output, batch manufacturing process**
- **Plating machinery inexpensive**
- **"Bonded" core and jacket**
- **Totally jacketed bullet possible**

Disadvantages of Plating

- **Difficult to control core/jacket concentricity**
- **Plating solution is a hazardous waste**
- **Plated pre-form is not a "finished product"; profiling and sizing in a die are still needed**

BULLET MAKING MACHINERY

LEAD EXTRUDERS

Before swaging a bullet, lead must first be melted, alloyed, and molded into large ingots weighing up to 1,000 lbs. each. Melting lead in an industrial setting today triggers numerous health and safety requirements. For this reason, many firms have left the lead business.

The lead ingot is extruded through a multi-die holder by a large hydraulic ram. Normally, a warm ingot is used as it requires less pressure and provides better quality wire. The extruded lead wire is wound onto metal reels for transport to the customer. The reels are recycled.

Not every bullet maker swages lead wire to make bullet cores. Many Speer bullets are made using a conventional drawn copper alloy jacket that is filled with molten lead and allowed to cool *in situ*. It is then formed and finished in a conventional manner.

CORE BONDERS

Bonding the lead core to a copper alloy jacket affords the twin advantages of greater retained weight after expansion and elimination of core/jacket separation.

As noted above, a bullet made with a plated-up jacket bonds the core and jacket by nature of the manufacturing process. The normal method of bonding the bullet core to a cup and draw jacket is to cover the lead pre-form with soldering powder. This requires several extra production steps as the lead slug must be thoroughly washed and dried to remove all lubricants prior to coating. To apply the solder coating, the clean lead cores are tumbled in drums with the solder powder. The coated slug is then seated in the jacket, formed and sized in a conventional manner. When the bullet is finished after washing and drying, it is heated just enough to melt the solder and bond the core to the jacket.

Other methods of preventing core/jacket separation include mechanical systems such as cannelures, locking rings, and dual cores.

TRIMMERS

A bullet jacket trimmer is essentially a small automatic lathe. Jackets are fed to a four finger chuck spinning at high speed. A cutter then swings down to cut off the irregular end of the drawn jacket to the specified length.

BULLET ASSEMBLY PRESSES

Most U.S. bullet and ammunition manufacturers use multi-station bullet assembly presses of horizontal-transfer design. In other words, the work (the bullet) moves horizontally in a straight line from one station to the next in sequence. Each station performs a specific task. As many of these bullet assembly machines were made by the firm of Waterbury-Ferrell, they are affectionately called simply "Waterburys." A Waterbury may be found in simplex (one bullet per stroke), duplex (two bullets per stroke), triplex (three bullets per stroke), and quadruplex (four bullets per stroke) configurations.

While each bullet manufacturer configures and operates their Waterburys with minor variations, the work performed at each station remains much the same.

These are, in order:

- **Feed jacket and lead core slug**
- **Check for presence of jacket and core (stop machine if neither is present)**
- **Seat core in jacket**
- **Form ogive and tip (two stages)**
- **Size bullet**
- **Eject finished bullet**

Each vertical stroke of the machine results in one finished bullet. On average, a well-timed Waterbury bullet assembly press can make about 75 bullets per minute. Faster running speeds are possible, but cause numerous jams. Slower speeds are often used for match bullets.

BULLET DIES AND PUNCHES

Most bullet dies contain a tungsten carbide insert for long life. Normally, the die is roughed out first using an electron discharge machine (EDM). The carbide insert is then fitted in place. A tool and die maker then polishes the inside of the die to its finished dimensions. Making bullet dies is an art that few tool makers have mastered. Consequently, bullet manufacturers make every effort to find and retain expert bullet die makers.

A bullet form die may last for 200,000 pieces or even more. A wreck on the assembly press can also ruin a good die on the first stroke. Broken carbide dies are recycled, however a new carbide forming die can easily cost over $2,500.

Punches are another perishable piece of steel tooling. Punches do not last nearly as long as dies, however they are nowhere near as expensive— $300 will buy one.

Why Most Match Rifle Bullets Are Boat Tail Hollow Point

Most match rifle bullets are boat tail hollow points for several reasons:

Manufacturing

- **Inserting the lead core into the bullet jacket from the front allows the form die to ensure the bullet's base remains square with the body and the core is securely seated**
- **The hollow point eliminates the need to deform the lead core against the ogive of the jacket**
- **The hollow point also provides an empty space for the jacket material to fold into when the ogive is formed**
- **Inserting the core from the front allows better control of core/jacket concentricity**
- **No cannelure is applied to the bullet jacket**
- **Match bullets are not crimped into the cartridge case**

Ballistics

- **The boat tail heel significantly reduces base drag for a flatter trajectory, shorter flight time, higher retained velocity, and less wind drift**
- **The hollow point shifts the center of gravity toward the rear of the bullet and closer to the center of pressure which increases accuracy**
- **A tangent ogive and hollow point tip allow maximum bearing surface, improving accuracy**

MATERIALS

BULLET JACKETS

Bullet jackets are made from an alloy containing 95/5 (95% copper, 5% zinc) or 90/10 (90% copper, 10% zinc) alloy. Of the two, 95/5 is more common. After drawing, bullet jackets are not annealed.

Most bullet jackets have walls which are not uniformly thick — they taper from greatest thickness at the base to thinnest at the nose. This helps control expansion. Notches, cuts, or striations may also be made on the ogive around the tip to pre-determine the number of petals, how far down the jacket they will open, and the final diameter of the expanded jacket.

Jackets may be thick or thin depending on their application. For example, jackets for fast expanding varmint bullets may be nearly as thin as foil, while jackets for bullets intended for heavy game may be thick with very little taper. Match bullets have very little taper, no cuts or notches on the ogive, and soft cores as they are not intended to expand.

Many bullets have a cannelure on their bearing surface to help control and retain seating depth in the cartridge case.

LEAD CORES

Although bullets intended for varmint shooting may have soft lead cores, most bullets have lead cores which are hardened to some extent. Hardening is accomplished by adding antimony to the lead in various percentages. From 1% to 3% is common for a bullet core and up to 5% may be used for some applications. Hard lead cores help retain weight and control expansion diameter. In swaged lead monolithic bullets, the hardness helps prevent leading in barrels.

COATINGS

In recent years, coatings on jacketed bullets have become a common option (many rifle bullets are offered with or without coating). Of course coated bullets are more expensive. Bullet manufacturers claim a number of advantages for coatings such as:

- **Reduced metal fouling**
- **Increased barrel life**
- **Higher muzzle velocity**
- **Higher muzzle energy**

Target shooters are attracted by the first two claims while the last two are of more interest to hunters and varmint shooters.

Nearly all jacketed bullet coatings are based on one or more variations of molybdenum. The most popular of these is molybdenum disulphide—a dry powder with a black metallic luster usually referred to simply as "moly." Moly-based lubricants are applied and then retained on bullet surfaces by lacquer, wax, or other binding agents.

One of the miracle lubricants for aerospace applications, moly lubricants work where conventional lubricants will not, such as on spacecraft, aircraft, and other low temperature, high temperature, or high vacuum applications. Molybdenum disulphide has one of the lowest coefficients of friction ever measured. In addition, molybdenum disulphide has a strong affinity for all types of steel, and iron; a weak affinity for copper; and no affinity for aluminum, titanium, or zinc.

The objective of shooting coated bullets is to coat the inside of the bore with moly. The moly in the rifle bore will reduce friction, thus increasing barrel life and muzzle velocity. Unfortunately, moly will not adhere to or penetrate steel bore surfaces by means of mechanical pressure. However, many shooters claim to have found significant advantages in moly coated bullets.

SHOT

Shotgun pellets are made by dropping, swaging, rolling, molding, or sintering. As there are many variations to each system, they are sketched here in broad form to convey the general concept employed.

Dropping

This is the classic method of making lead shot and is not suitable for making shot of other materials. Lead alloy is melted in a crucible at the top of an enclosed 200 foot tall tower and poured through a metal pan with holes of a selected size in its bottom. After it leaks through the holes in the pan, surface tension causes the lead to form drops as it falls through the tower. As they fall, air cools and solidifies the drops which end their downward journey in a water bath. Different hole sizes in the pan create different pellet diameters. This method works for shot sizes from No. 2 on down. Larger sizes must be swaged.

A variation of the drop shot method is the compact Bleimeister machine. The Bleimeister also drops the molten lead to form shot, however the drop is only about four inches. This method is suitable only for small shot sizes from No. 7 ½ to No. 9.

Swaging

Swaging is used only for lead alloy buckshot. This process begins by extruding lead ingots into thick wire. The lead wire is then fed between two stacked rotating steel wheels. The outer surfaces of each wheel have cavities which form the sides of the pellet. The swaged buckshot pellets are then tumbled in barrels to remove flashing and coated with graphite.

Rolling

Rolling is used to manufacture soft steel shot. Extruded steel wire is cut into small pieces which are then fed between two counter-rotating steel plates. The plates roll the edges off the steel pieces creating a sphere. The spheres are then heat-treated to soften them.

Molding

This method is used to make some forms of composite shot which use a polymer as a binding agent. A mixture of polymer and powdered metal particles is injected into a mold under pressure. When the mold is opened after the polymer has cured, the pellet is finished.

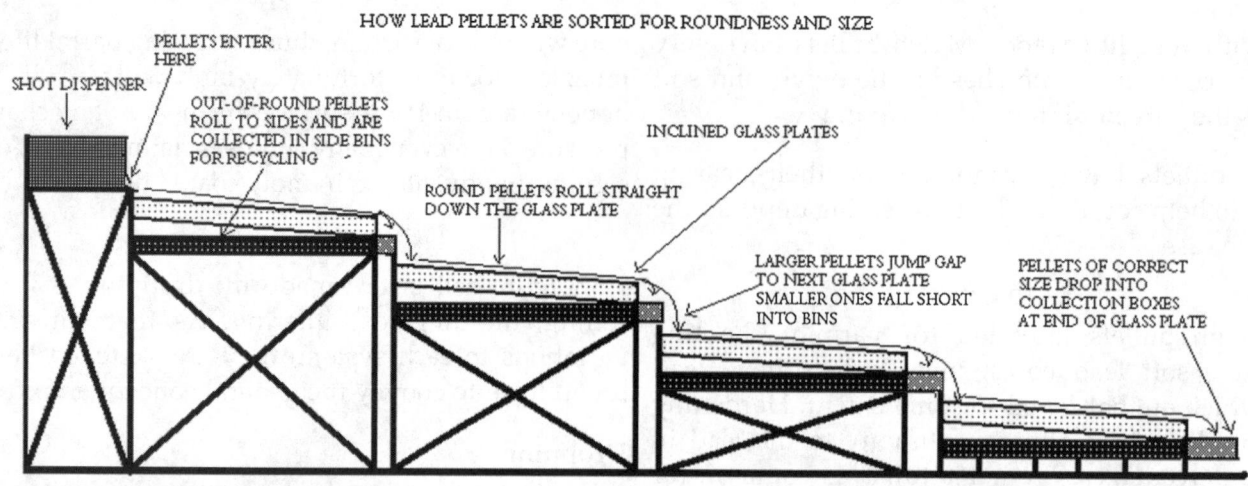

HOW LEAD PELLETS ARE SORTED FOR ROUNDNESS AND SIZE

SHOT DISPENSER

PELLETS ENTER HERE

OUT-OF-ROUND PELLETS ROLL TO SIDES AND ARE COLLECTED IN SIDE BINS FOR RECYCLING

INCLINED GLASS PLATES

ROUND PELLETS ROLL STRAIGHT DOWN THE GLASS PLATE

LARGER PELLETS JUMP GAP TO NEXT GLASS PLATE SMALLER ONES FALL SHORT INTO BINS

PELLETS OF CORRECT SIZE DROP INTO COLLECTION BOXES AT END OF GLASS PLATE

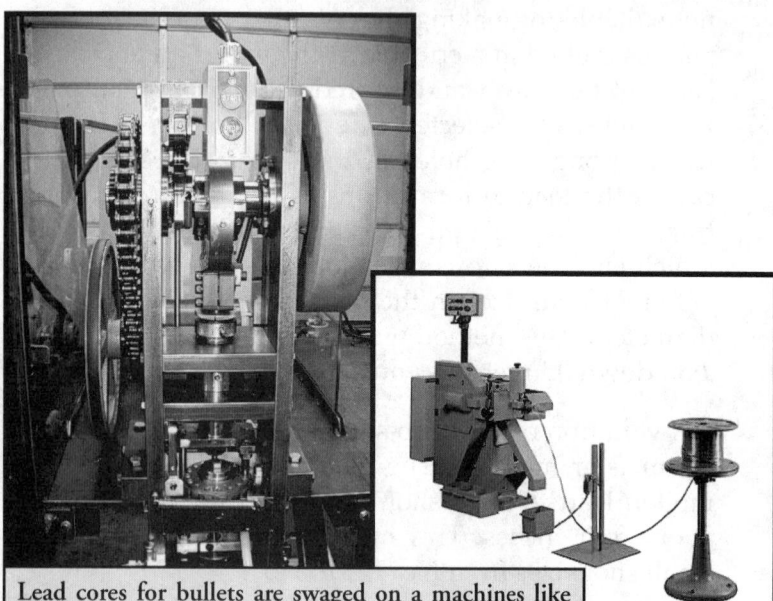

Lead cores for bullets are swaged on a machines like this AmmoLoad unit (left image) and this Lauchaussée M862 unit (right image). The lead wire is fed into a cutter that chops off a pre-form and feeds it to fingers that position it over the die. As the punch (the vertical rod) moves downward, the pre-form is swaged to the correct configuration in the die then ejected.

These ultra-modern, high speed bullet making machines do it all–and very quickly at about 240 pieces per minute! Note computer control units alongside and the multiple die stations visible through the window.

Completed bullets must be washed and dried in tumblers such as this AmmoLoad unit. The flat panels on the drum cause the bullets to mix and move. The bullets are washed in hot soapy water, rinsed, and dried in sawdust media. Crushed walnut shells can be used to polish the surfaces of the bullets if desired.

Bullets are cannelured on machines like this AmmoLoad unit. Note the bullets being rolled between the two plates-one that rotates and one that is stationary (on the right). The rotating plate has raised toothed steps on the center of its vertical edge, which engrave or impress the cannelure into the bullets as they pass between the plates.

THERE IS NO SUCH THING AS A PERFECT BULLET

WHAT THE CUSTOMER WANTED

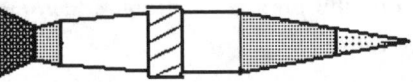

HIGH TECH, PRE-RIFLED, ULTRA LOW DRAG BULLET WITH DOUBLE BOAT TAIL AND ROCKET BOOSTER MOTOR (ANOTHER BREAKTHROUGH IDEA FROM THE ENGINEERING DEPT.)

PRE-EXPANDED BULLET THAT PIVOTS FORWARD WHEN FIRED (FROM THE ADVERTISING DEPT.)

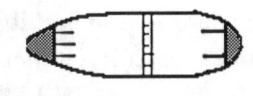

DOUBLE ENDED BULLET WITH ROUND NOSE OR SPITZER OGIVE (SUBMITTED BY THE SALES DEPT. OF COURSE)

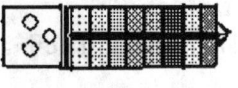

SURVIVAL BULLET WITH LIFESAVERS, TOOTHPICK AND WHISTLE (THE OWNER'S SON THOUGHT THIS ONE UP)

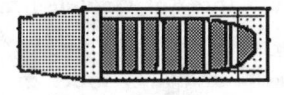

MUZZLE LOADING BULLET WITH SIX GREASE GROOVES IN A SEVEN PIECE, BOAT TAIL SABOT (FROM THE GUY WEARING BUCKSKINS ON PRESS NO 3)

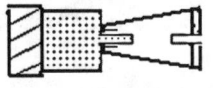

BULLET WITH INTERCHANGEABLE FRONT END--HOLLOW POINT OR FLAT NOSE (ANOTHER OUT-OF-THE-BOX IDEA FROM THE MARKETING DEPT.)

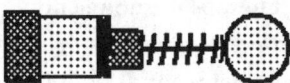

LESS-THAN-LETHAL BULLET WITH SOFT FOAM SPONGE TIP MOUNTED ON A SPRING (ANOTHER GOOD ONE FROM THE LEGAL DEPT.)

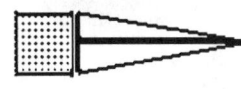

BROADHEAD BULLET FOR HUNTING WITH RIFLE DURING BOW SEASON SUBMITTED VIA CELLPHONE BY OUR FIELD REP. IN GUAM)

Sintering

Sintering is the appropriate method of making very hard and dense composite shot pellets. A suitable mixture of powdered metal ingredients and a binder is placed in a mold that subjects these ingredients to pressure and heat. This produces a finished pellet.

CRITERIA FOR A GOOD BULLET

First, it is important to note that there is no such thing as a perfect bullet. Every bullet, regardless of type, construction, or brand is a complex blend of compromises and trade-offs. For your individual requirements and expectations, some bullets may serve better than others. The experienced shooter weighs the trade-offs carefully before selecting a bullet for any given purpose.

Despite this, there are some criteria which all bullets must try to meet. Of course, some will do so better than others. With this in mind, here is an abbreviated wish list:

CRITERIA FOR THE PERFECT BULLET

MANUFACTURE

- **Use existing technology**
- **Use existing machinery**
- **Use existing production processes**
- **High profit margin**
- **Scalable (caliber/weight)**

MATERIALS

- **Low cost**
- **Unlimited availability**
- **Non-toxic**

INTERIOR BALLISTICS

- **Non-fouling**
- **Plenty of bearing surface**
- **Compatible with existing chambers and barrels**
- **Compatible with existing rifling twist rates**

EXTERIOR BALLISTICS

- **High retained velocity and energy**
- **Flat trajectory**
- **Low wind drift**

TERMINAL BALLISTICS

- **Accuracy**
- **Precision**
- **100% or greater expansion**
- **90% or greater weight retention**
- **Bonded core; no core-jacket separation**

- Reliable and consistent penetration regardless of distance to target

SALES

- Widespread availability
- Attractive, clean appearance
- Competitive price, or no other manufacturers
- Military and commercial applications

"Take your time, fast!"
- Bill Jordan on combat handgun shooting

Chicago Piano

By the early 1930s, the .45 ACP caliber Thompson sub-machine gun had become the unofficial "standard issue" among Chicago gangsters who appreciated the hitting power of the heavy 230 gr. bullet. This lead the erstwhile citizens of the city to coin the phrases "Chicago Piano," "chopper," and "Tommy Gun."

Overkill - Prohibition Style

Joe Aiello headed one of the major gangs in prohibition-era Chicago. After two of Al Capone's confederates shot-gunned a member of Aiello's gang to death on May 31, 1930, Aiello retaliated by machine-gunning three of Capone's men to death on the glass-enclosed front porch of the Fox Lake Resort Hotel. Capone's payback came on October 23, 1930, as Aiello exited the front door of his apartment building to enter a waiting taxicab. Two Thompson submachine guns and a shotgun fired from a second story window cut Aiello down. He died from fifty-nine bullet wounds - a high point in gangster marksmanship.

SHOTS OF A LIFETIME – In The Field

We took a break from hunting to shoot a Barrett .50 BMG caliber rifle from a makeshift hilltop range. On adjacent hills, the range owner setup steel B27-silhouette targets painted white for visibility. The targets were set up at various distances, the farthest being a measured 960 yards. However, no one fired at a target beyond 500 yards. When my turn came, I selected the farthest target. One of the previous shooters opined that a crosswind from left to right seemed to be worth about 10 inches at 500 yards. Taking this into account, I settled the crosshairs just inside the left center edge of the target. When the gun roared, the bullet took a second or two to reach the target. It struck dead center with a clang, leaving a hole and scorch marks as evidence. In silence, I courteously surrendered the rifle to the next shooter.

CHAPTER 23: CENTERFIRE CARTRIDGE CASE MANUFACTURING

CHAPTER 23 HIGHLIGHTS:

- MATERIALS
- MANUFACTURING CENTERFIRE CASES
- ORGANIZATION

Cartridge case manufacture is based on metal drawing technology. This technology uses a steel punch to drive a brass cup into a carbide die. As the punch fits the die very closely, the metal in the cup is reformed in a predetermined manner. To manufacture a cartridge case, the metal cup is elongated or drawn to a longer length in several steps. Before describing the process, case material must be described.

MATERIALS

BRASS

Despite nearly two centuries of experimentation, brass alloys remain the best metal for making cartridge cases. There are many reasons for this.

- **Copper and zinc are widely available, relatively inexpensive metals**

- **Manufacturing brass alloys and drawing brass cups are well-known technologies**

- **Brass alloys are easy to cup, draw, and iron the shell case walls**

- **The draw process work hardens and strengthens brass, making it spring like**

- **Springy brass returns to its original shape after firing for easy extraction**

- **The elasticity of brass allows it to conform to the chamber walls for a good gas seal**

- **Brass is non-toxic to humans and most wildlife except some types of aquatic life and will not burn**

- **Brass is light weight with fair corrosion resistance**

- **For reloading, there is no better alternative for brass**

- **Cartridge case brass is a high value recyclable**

- **Shooters prefer brass cartridge cases**

- **Other metals and materials suffer from major drawbacks**

A typical brass cartridge case today is made from either alloy of copper and zinc in the approximate ratio of 28% zinc and 72% copper (Europe) or 30% zinc and 70% copper (U.S.). However, not just any alloy will do. Cartridge brass does not tolerate a high degree of impurities. This means that recycled brass must be thoroughly refined before it is suitable for cartridge case manufacture. This is expensive and difficult. Consequently, cartridge case manufacturers prefer virgin brass certified to have a minimum of impurities.

Brass cartridge cases begin as strip from which cups are made for drawing. However, not just any strip will due. A special type called "continuously annealed brass strip" is required. It is expensive as there are few suppliers of this specialty product.

Of course, efforts have been made to find other materials for centerfire cartridge cases. Materials such as steel alloys, aluminum alloys, and plastics have been popular choices. However, all suffer from major drawbacks which limit their use for some types of centerfire cartridge case applications:

STEEL

- **Steel cases with Boxer primers can be reloaded more times than brass**

- **Must be coated to prevent corrosion**

- **Steel cases ammunition loaded with corrosive primers should not be reloaded**

- **Does not have the spring back of brass**

- **Not suitable for use in some types of revolvers**

These drawbacks have limited the use of steel cases to military applications where other concerns outweigh its shortcomings.

ALUMINUM

- **Dangerous burnout in the event of case head failure in high pressure rifle cartridge calibers**

- **Must be coated to prevent oxidation**

- **Suitable for specialized applications such as:**

  - Handgun cartridge cases (lower pressure, reduced posibility of burnout)

  - Military aircraft (light weight)

  - Shotshells (low pressure)

PLASTICS

- **Lack strength**
- **Will not hold primer or bullet securely**
- **Can not withstand rough extraction in semi- or full-auto guns**
- **Poor shot start (compromises ignition)**
- **Hybrids (metal head, plastic body) too expensive**
- **Incompatible with propellants containing nitrogen**

MANUFACTURING CENTERFIRE CASES

The basic process used to manufacture brass centerfire rifle and handgun cartridge cases is a cup and draw system, a process dating from the 19th century. A typical cup and draw production line for brass cartridge cases has thirteen steps:

Lachaussée M832 Blanking and Cupping press blanks and draws cup from strip.

BLANK AND CUP

This operation produces a shallow brass cup with thick sidewalls, a flat interior base, and a domed outer base. The exact dimensions of each cup size are specific to groups of calibers and proprietary to each manufacturer who normally owns the dies to make them. Due to the large size of cupping presses, most cartridge case manufacturers purchase cups from a specialty supplier, most of whom also make the continuously annealed strip needed for cartridge cases.

FIRST DRAW

The cups are fed individually into a large press that draws them into a short tube closed at one end. Subsequent draws increase the length of the tube. The diameter and length of each draw depends on the caliber of the cartridge case for which it is intended. For example, pistol caliber cartridge cases can normally be made in one or two draws while rifle cartridge cases may require up to four draws.

Machines such as this Lachaussée M702 Draw Press are used to draw the cups for cartridge cases.

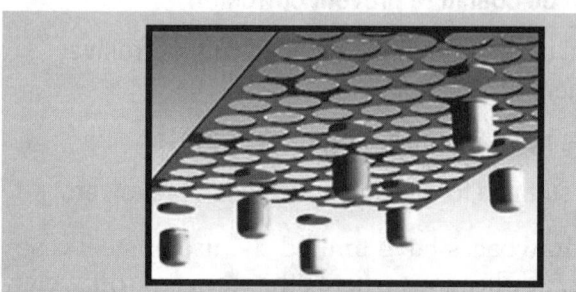

Cartridge case cups as they are blanked and drawn by the Lachaussée M832 press.

Steps in Making a Centerfire Cartridge Case

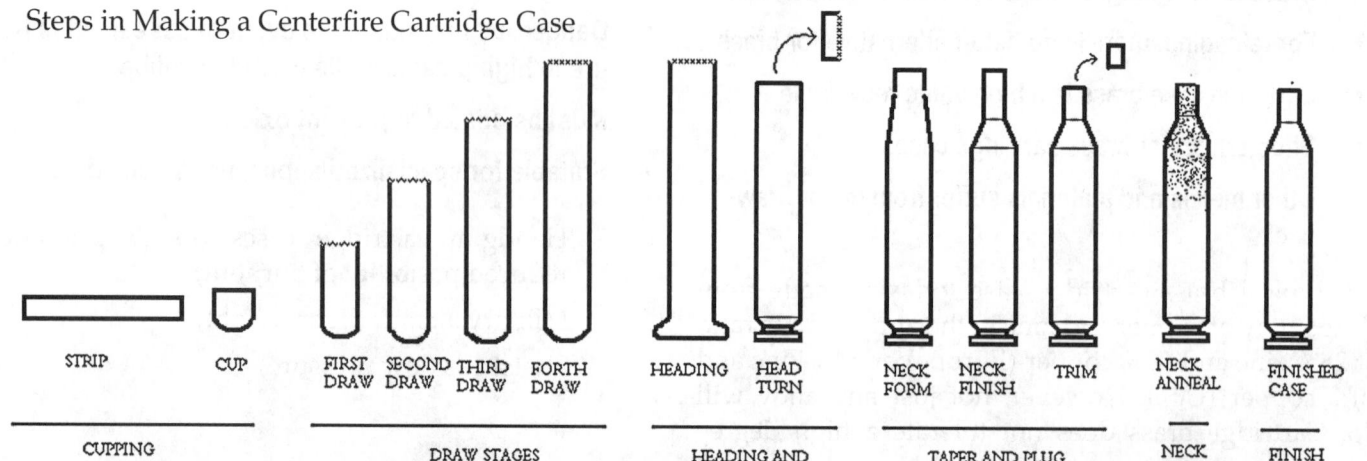

| STRIP | CUP | FIRST DRAW | SECOND DRAW | THIRD DRAW | FORTH DRAW | HEADING | HEAD TURN | NECK FORM | NECK FINISH | TRIM | NECK ANNEAL | FINISHED CASE |

| CUPPING | DRAW STAGES | HEADING AND HEAD TURN | TAPER AND PLUG | NECK ANNEAL | FINISH |

WASH

The drawn brass tubes are washed to remove the draw lubricant.

ANNEALING/STRESS RELIEVING

Each draw work-hardens the brass tube. In order to draw the tube again, it must first be annealed or stress relieved in ovens.

In between draws, cartridge case cups must be annealed using a machine like this M870 Annealing Oven.

SECOND DRAW

The three-step process described above as first draw, washing, and annealing is repeated. This is sufficient for most handgun cartridge cases and small rifle cartridge cases.

THIRD DRAW

The three-step process described above as first draw, washing, and annealing is repeated. Most rifle cartridge cases are of the correct length and diameter at this point.

FOURTH DRAW

The three-step process described above as first draw, washing, and annealing is repeated. Normally, only large magnum rifle cases require a fourth draw.

HEAD

The drawn tube is placed in a large press that upsets the closed end of the tube, rough forming the rim and fine forming the head, primer pocket, and applying the headstamp. Regardless of caliber, what is sought is a case with a hardness gradient ranging vertically from V.220 hardness at the head to relatively soft V.150 at the case mouth.

WASH AND DRY

The heading lubricant is washed off the headed case and the case dried.

HEAD TURN AND TRIM

Headed cases are fed individually into an automatic machine which cuts an extractor groove and rim in the head and trims the case at its mouth to approximate length.

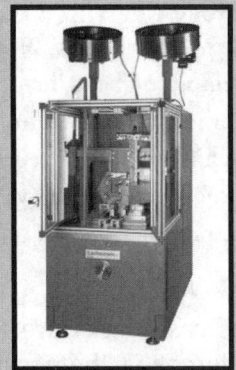

Following drawing and heading, cartridge cases must undergo head turning – a process that removes metal from the case head to form the rim and extractor groove in a machine such as this M860 Lachaussée.

TAPER AND PLUG

This is a multi-step operation performed on a single machine. The stages consist of:

- **Forming the shoulder and neck of the case bypasses through two or more dies**
- **Tapering the case sidewalls**
- **Trimming the case to the desired final length (trim at the case mouth only)**

Cartridge cases are formed in a press such as this M714 unit from Lachaussée.

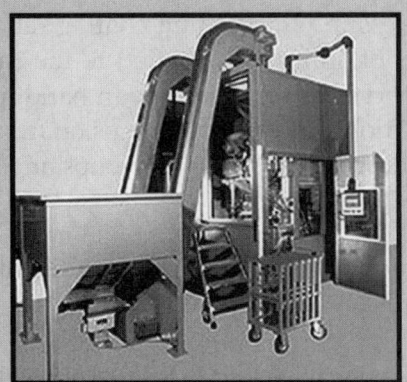

Fritz-Werner also makes Cartridge Case Forming machines such as this one.

**Why Don't Factory Cartridge Cases Have 40°
Shoulders Like Many Wildcats?**

This is a classic example of hand loaders and wildcatters being able to do something a factory cannot economically do. Case production machinery will not reliably produce a brass cartridge case with a shoulder angle above approximately 38° because the rejection rate increases to unacceptable levels.

NECK ANNEAL

At this stage, the case necks are fully formed, but work-hardened. If left as is, the necks may crack after loading. To prevent this, the necks must be annealed. This can be done in one of two ways: electric induction or flame. In either instance, the cases move down a rail approximately 18 inches long between induction coils or along a series of flame jets. This softens the necks, preventing cracking. However, this process leaves a blue-black iris on the case neck.

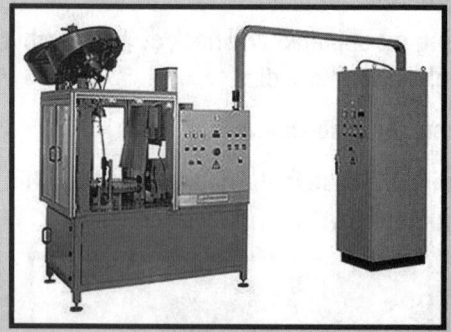

The final step in cartridge case manufacture before loading is neck annealing, which softens case necks to prevent neck cracking or splitting in subsequent manufacturing steps. This is a Lachaussée M871 Neck Anneal machine.

WASH AND POLISH

The blue-black iris left on the case neck from the annealing process is removed by washing and polishing in ground walnut shell abrasive.

NICKEL PLATING

This step is used only on selected handgun calibers and premium rifle calibers. It is an electroplating process in which a thin coating (about 3-4 ten thousandths of an inch) is applied to the case. In rifle calibers, it serves as an identifier. In handgun calibers it aids extraction and prevents corrosion from the acids present in the leather of cartridge loops and gun belts.

PRIME

This operation, performed on a multi-station rotary machine, consists of three operations:

- **Punching the flash hole in the bottom of the primer pocket of the cartridge case**

- **Inserting, seating, and crimping (optional) the primer**

- **Sealing the primer annulus with lacquer (optional)**

The case is now ready for loading.

As you might imagine, constant dimensional and visual inspections are made at each stage (save washing) to ensure quality. For example, the hardness of the cartridge case heads is checked after heading and a final visual inspection occurs after the primer has been inserted.

This Fritz-Werner Primer Insert machine performs a similar task to the Lachaussée M611 machine.

For safety reasons, wet (inert) primers are inserted in the cartridge cases, then sealed and crimped as necessary. Here is an M611 Lachaussée Primer Insert machine.

Why Should Brass Cartridge Cases Be Hard And Springy?

When a cartridge is fired, the pressure of propellant gasses inside the case irons the case body firmly against the chamber walls. As the pressure drops, a normal brass cartridge case will quickly spring back to its original dimension, making extraction easy. If the cartridge case did not spring back, extraction would be very difficult. A cartridge case turned from brass rod would not have the hardness or spring back needed.

ORGANIZATION

From the processes described above, it is evident that the manufacture of centerfire cartridge cases requires a considerable amount of handling and moving batches of in-process materials. This is inefficient and expensive. Consequently, ammunition manufacturers try to form integrated production lines where volume justifies the investment.

An integrated production line consists of ammunition production machinery grouped together for sequential automatic transfer of in-process materials between the machines. For example, an integrated production line would consist of dedicated bullet making, cartridge case making, and primer insertion machinery feeding directly into a load, assemble, and pack unit. This arrangement streamlines the handling and transfer of in-process materials, reduces tooling changeovers, and reduces labor cost.

Forensics - St. Valentine's Day Style in Chicago

Following the St. Valentine's Day Massacre in Chicago on February 14, 1929, the Chicago Police Department recovered 70 fired .45 Auto caliber cartridge cases from the scene of the crime. From this large quantity of empty brass, the police department correctly guessed the killers must have used Thompson sub-machine guns. Forensic science was still in its infancy.

IMPACT EXTRUSION SYSTEM OF MANUFACTURING CENTERFIRE CARTRIDGE CASES

By Kenneth L. Alexander

Brass centerfire cartridge cases have traditionally been manufactured using the cup, draw, and iron process developed in the mid-19th century. In this antiquated technology, a cup is produced by blanking a disk from flat strips of brass. Over one third of the raw material ends up between the disks and is known as "web scrap". The web scrap has some reclamation value, but much of the original raw material value is needlessly lost in this scrap-by-design process.

Even more of the expensive raw material is lost in sequential, subsequent trimming of the elongated parts produced by the drawing and ironing processes. This process is described in the following illustrations.

STEPS IN THE CUP AND DRAW METHOD OF MANUFACTURING A CENTERFIRE CARTRIDGE CASE

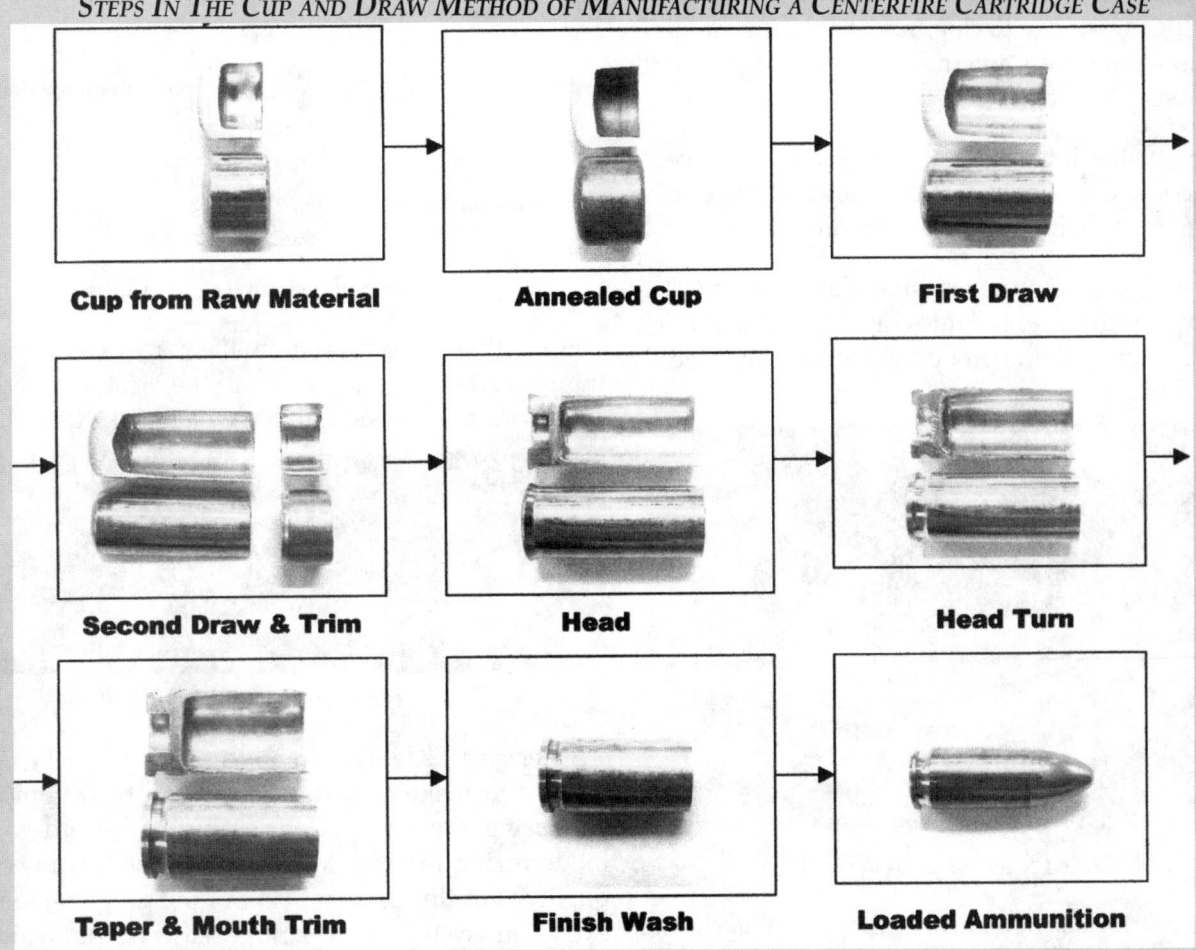

Cup from Raw Material	Annealed Cup	First Draw
Second Draw & Trim	Head	Head Turn
Taper & Mouth Trim	Finish Wash	Loaded Ammunition

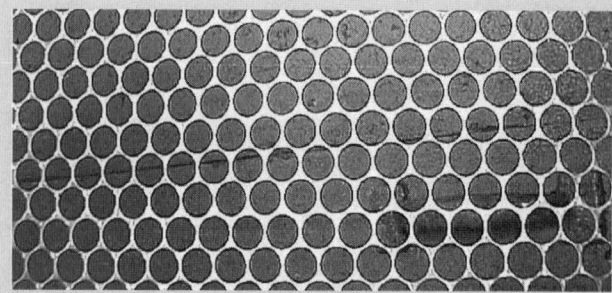

Web Scrap from the Cupping Process

In 1948, Richard Speer, who later founded CCI, instituted the impact extrusion process to manufacture brass centerfire cartridge cases. CCI refined the process decades later to produce cartridge cases from aluminum and steel as well as brass.

Compared to the old cup, draw, and iron system, impact extrusion technology has an almost 98% raw material yield. In simpler terms, 98% of the raw material ends up in the product with only 2% destined for the scrap bin by design. The reduction in needless scrap results in significant cost saving.

Progressive impact extrusion produces cartridge cases in one operation from wire coils of raw material to a finished cartridge case without the intermediate steps of heat treating, washing, drying, and trimming multiple times. Eliminating these intermediate steps significantly reduces direct labor costs.

In addition, the impact extrusion system produces a cold formed cartridge case, which is much stronger than those made by the cup, draw, and iron process.

For impact extrusion, the raw material (brass, steel, or aluminum) is purchased in large coils of wire, about 3/8 inch in diameter, with the proper temper or grain size for the product being produced.

Coiled Raw Material Wire

The material for an individual cartridge case is sheared from the wire automatically on entering the process. There are no chips from sawing or any other waste in that operation.

Designed scrap only includes the blanked flash hole, head turn, and mouth trim.

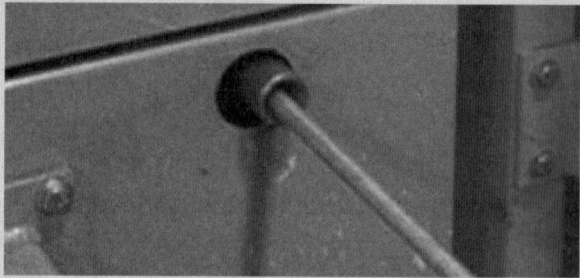

Wire Feeding Into Process

Most impact extrusion contact tooling is constructed of tungsten carbide for toughness and wear resistance.

Tremendous forces are involved in the process, forcing the raw material to flow like modeling clay.

That is an instructive analogy. Imagine the bottom half of a shot glass containing modeling clay. If you were to force your finger down into the clay, the amount of clay displaced would flow around your finger to form a cup.

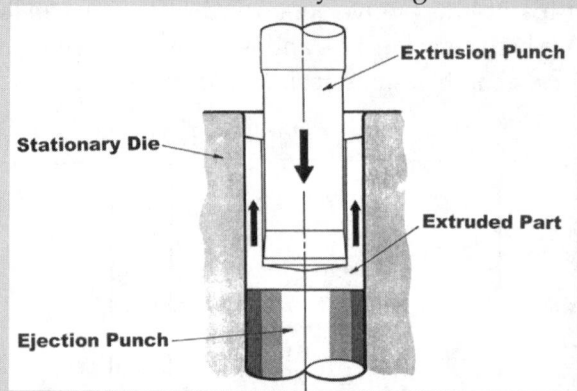

Impact Extrusion Contact Tooling

From that process station the part is automatically transferred to the next station where the cup sidewalls are drawn and ironed thinner, which make them longer.

Finished Cartridge Cases

Speer and Federal currently use the impact extrusion process to make cartridge cases. Can their competitors still using the cup and draw system afford to delay modernizing in order to remain competitive in cost and quality? For this reason, I believe the progressive impact extrusion system of cartridge case manufacture will completely replace the antiquated cup, draw, and iron system in the very near future.

CHAPTER 24: MANUFACTING RIMFIRE CARTRIDGE CASES

CHAPTER 24 HIGHLIGHTS:

- MANUFACTURING RIMFIRE CASES
- PRODUCTION STEPS
- OPTIONAL NOTES

MANUFACTURING RIMFIRE CASES

Manufacture of rimfire cartridge cases is a relatively simple four step process with an optional fifth step:

PRODUCTION STEPS

1. BLANK AND 2. CUP FROM STRIP

As they are short and thin, rimfire cases can be blanked and cupped on small machines such as this M657 Lachaussée Vertical Press.

Brass strip is fed into a multiple die draw press which blanks out up to ten disks at a time. The disks are then cupped in a sequence of dies called a die stack.

3. WASH AND DRY

The brass draws are washed to remove the draw lubricant and dried.

The clean dry draws are fed individually into a press which places the drawn cup in a die. A punch then strikes the closed end of the cup to form the head, rim, and headstamp.

DRAW, HEAD, AND FORM

Rimfire cases are drawn, headed, formed, and trimmed on machines such as this M150 Lachaussée rotary case forming machine.

4. HOAD AND TRIM

The headed case is trimmed to the correct length in an automatic trimming machine.

OPTIONAL NOTES

5. PLATING

This is an optional step: a nickel finish may be electro-plated onto the cartridge case. This is no longer common on rimfire ammunition.

The case is now ready for priming and loading.

Although rimfire cases are work-hardened by the draw process, because they are so thin and short annealing is not necessary in most instances.

Why Doesn't A Manufacturer Make Rimfire Cartridge Cases From Steel?

It Is Much Stronger Than Brass.

While steel is stronger than brass, rimfire ammunition makers have not been successful in developing a steel rimfire case which will extract reliably in some semi-automatic firearms. Steel rimfire cases do not have the spring back of brass cases, thus they cause many extraction problems in .22 rimfire semi-autos.

Steps in Making a Rimfire Cartridge Case

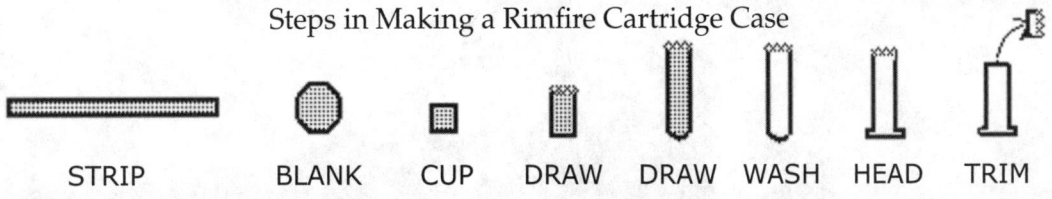

STRIP   BLANK   CUP   DRAW   DRAW   WASH   HEAD   TRIM

Oliver F. Winchester
1810-1880

Entrepreneur and Founder of
Winchester Arms Company

After gaining valuable experience in the building trade, Oliver Winchester became a successful shirt maker. In 1855, Winchester decided to enter the arms industry.

For Winchester, this was a practical business decision based on potentially high profits, not on his love of guns and shooting. While hundreds of cartridges developed by his company subsequently carried the Winchester name, not one was designed by Winchester himself.

CHAPTER 25: SHOTSHELL HULL MANUFACTURE

CHAPTER 25 HIGHLIGHTS:

- MATERIALS
- MANUFACTURING SHOTSHELL HULLS
- SHOTSHELL ASSEMBLY

MATERIALS

Compared to rimfire and centerfire ammunition, shotshells operate at very low breech pressures (see Chapter 43: Interior Ballistics). This makes them suitable for alternative cartridge case materials such as paper, plastic, aluminum, steel, and yes, brass.

As we have seen, most shotshells are built up as an assembly of three or more parts, including: tube, base wad, and metal head. Shotshell tubes have been made from metal, paper, and plastic. Metal tubes normally are made from drawn brass. However other metals have been tried with varying degrees of success and failure: aluminum (too expensive), zinc (not strong enough), and steel (corrodes or must be plated). Today, new brass shotshell hulls continue to be offered for reloading, but they are no longer loaded commercially by ammunition makers. Steel hull shotshells are offered currently by some Russian shotshell manufacturers.

For decades, paper was the ideal material for shotshell tubes. It was cheap, light, easy to roll into tubes, and provided good obturation (sealing) at low pressures. Soaking in hot wax or laquer coating gave them a degree of moisture resistance. Tightly rolled paper was also used for making base wads. However, paper shotshells remained susceptible to moisture and swelling regardless of wax, lacquer, or shellac coatings. In addition, paper tubes were made from a paper commonly used to insulate high tension electrical cables. When plastics replaced paper for electrical insulation, this special paper became rare and expensive. Today, paper shotshells remain popular only for some niche applications such as trap shooting.

In the 1950s, plastic was quickly embraced by shotshell manufacturers. Plastic proved nearly ideal for making shotshell tubes and base wads as it was cheap, tough, and easy to manufacture. This continues to this day with shotshell tubes commonly being made of extruded high-density polyethylene plastic.

A shotshell is a built-up assembly of three or more parts. These parts are prepared separately and assembled in a number of steps.

MANUFACTURING SHOTSHELL HULLS

Components and Steps in Assembling a Shotshell

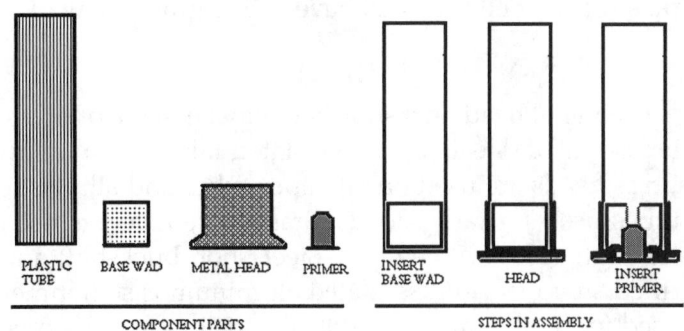

COMPONENT PARTS   STEPS IN ASSEMBLY

Tubes

Shotshell tubes are made of high-density polyethylene plastic extruded into long tubes and then cut to length. The procedure is as follows:

Extrude

White pellets of plastic are bulk-loaded into an extruder where they are heated and the desired color added. The molten plastic is then extruded through a series of water cooled dies until it emerges as 100-150 foot lengths of tubing of the desired diameter.

Trim

The plastic tubing is cut to a length slightly longer than the finished shell to allow crimping inside the head. The tubes are now ready for further assembly.

A paper shotshell tube is made by rolling layers of paper coated with glue on a steel mandrel about 24" in length. The tubes are then cut to length and placed for several days in a warm room to allow the glue to cure. Next, the cut tubes are soaked in hot wax under pressure and allowed to cool. Paper tubes are assembled into shotshells in the same manner as plastic tubes.

Base Wads

The base wad is a donut-shaped piece of material positioned inside the base end of a shotshell. It serves the same purpose as the web in a centerfire cartridge case, namely it reinforces the head of the shotshell, helps hold the primer in place, and allows the volume inside the shotshell to be adjusted. Base wads may be made of plastic, paper, or a molded composite material.

Base wads are of different thicknesses in order to vary the volume inside the hull. For example a low base wad will be used for magnums which require plenty of volume while high base wads will be used for light target loads.

If the base wad is a separate unit, it will be inserted in the tube during the heading process. If the base wad is integral, it will be made by heating one end of the plastic tube and forming it in a die. A drawn brass or plastic shotshell tube will have an integral base wad.

HEADS

The metal head on a shotshell may be made of brass, brass-plated steel, or brass-plated aluminum alloy. Brass heads are used on all paper tubes and all plastic tubes used for target loads. Brass-plated steel is used for high velocity, magnum, steel shot, buckshot, and rifled slug loads. Brass-plated aluminum is sometimes used for light game or field loads. In any case, the type of metal used for the head of a shotshell has nothing to do with strength. The metal head simply holds the primer, base wad, and tube assembly together while providing a suitable rim for extraction.

Although the height of the metal head may vary, this has no effect on the strength of the shell. Manufacturers use head height only as an indicator of the type of load. For example magnum loads have high metal heads and target loads have low metal heads. Magnum loads can be made from shotshells with low metal heads just as well as high metal heads.

Heads are manufactured in two steps.

Drawing

Metal shotshell heads are made by a drawing process similar to the process for rimfire cases, only scaled up in size. A multiple station draw press blanks, cups, and draws up to eight shell heads per stroke through a series of die stacks. The heads are not finished; as they exit the draw press they are slightly larger in diameter with oversized rims.

Washing/Drying

The metal heads are then washed and dried to remove all draw lubricant.

SHOTSHELL ASSEMBLY

The sub-assemblies for a built-up shotshell come together in the heading operation. A shotshell header is a multi-station press in which the pieces travel in a circle and dies perform various assembly steps in sequence:

Base Wad Insertion

A base wad is inserted into one end of the tube.

Heading

A metal head is placed on the base wad end of the tube and crimped into place. At the same time, this operation finishes the rim and sizes the head to the correct diameter.

Priming

A primer is inserted in a hole in the case head where it is held firmly by displacing base wad material and metal in the head.

The shotshell is now ready for loading.

Why Are Brass-Plated Steel Heads Used On Some Shotshells And Brass Heads On Others?

Brass-plated steel heads normally are used on hunting shotshells for several reasons:

- The heads rust away in three years leaving no environmental concerns
- Brass-plated steel heads are cheaper than brass heads
- Brass-plated steel heads are not subject to stress cracking
- Field hunting shells are not usually reloaded (resizing a steel head is difficult)

Brass heads are used on target loads and therefore are often reloaded. Of course, brass heads can he used on hunting ammunition if the need arises.

This situation exists in part because solvents used in extruding plastic tubes can attack brass heads, causing stress cracking.

CHAPTER 26 : PROPELLANT MANUFACTURING

CHAPTER 26 HIGHLIGHTS:

- BLACK POWDER
- SMOKELESS POWDER
- ADDITIVES
- DETERIORATION OF PROPELLANTS
- COMPONENTS OF SMOKELESS PROPELLANTS

WARNING!

Never attempt to make propellants yourself at home or elsewhere. Doing so may cause an explosion which could result in serious personal injury or death.

Good Advice

"Light fuse, retire quickly!"

-Ubiquitous warning on packs of Chinese firecrackers

BLACK POWDER

The historic formula for black powder contains the following three ingredients: potassium nitrate (73%), charcoal (17.5%), and sulfur (9.5%).

Over the centuries, manufacture of black powder has been refined into six steps:

Incorporation

The three solid ingredients are placed on a steel table on which two heavy steel rollers turn. The three ingredients are ground between the rollers and the table for several hours until they become a fine powder.

Wetting

The ground powder is mixed with a small amount of distilled water, turning it into a loaf with dough-like consistency.

Pressing

The wet loaf is loaded into a press which consolidates it into a "press cake" using over 1,000 psi. of pressure. The press cake is much smaller and denser than the loaf.

Drying

The press cake is allowed to air dry and harden.

Corning

The dry press cake is broken up into small particles which are separated by size in a sieve stack.

Coating

Sized powder batches are tumbled with graphite in wooden drums to reduce static electricity and improve resistance to moisture absorption.

SMOKELESS POWDER

As the process of manufacturing smokeless powder involves chemical reactions which change the structure of the materials, it is much more complex and more dangerous than the black powder process. Consequently, the steps listed here are abbreviated in the interest of safety and simplicity.

SINGLE BASE PROPELLANTS

Materials needed for manufacturing single base smokeless propellants include: cellulose, nitric acid, sulfuric acid, ether, alcohol, and water. This is the production process for "Poudre B" that Paul Vieille, inventor of smokeless propellants, developed in 1884:

Prepare guncotton

Make guncotton (insoluble nitrocellulose containing 13% or more nitrogen) by nitrating cotton cellulose in a hot concentrated mix consisting of 50% nitric acid and 50% sulfuric acid. Wash thoroughly with water and dry.

Prepare collodion

Make collodion (soluble nitrocellulose containing from 8-12% nitrogen) by nitrating cotton cellulose in dilute warm acids. Wash with water and dry.

Combine guncotton and collodion

Knead guncotton (insoluble nitrocellulose) and collodion (soluble nitrocellulose) together with a solvent of ether and alcohol. The collodion forms a solution which will absorb the insoluble guncotton. The result is a dough-like paste.

Roll/Extrude

Roll the paste into sheets or extrude through dies into the desired shape while still wet.

Gen. George Washington Rains C.S.A.

Gen. George Washington Rains, C.S.A. (Confederate States Army) was the designer, builder, and operator of the only public works project ever commissioned by the Confederate Government - the Confederate States Powder Works in Augusta, Georgia. Cost was $385,000.

A native of North Carolina, George Washington Rains attended West Point, graduating in 1842 at the head of his class in science. With the start of the Civil War in 1861, Rains offered his services to the Confederacy.

The Confederate Chief of Ordnance, Josiah Gorgas, assigned Rains the task of building a gun powder factory for the Confederacy. Although Gorgas gave Rains a free hand, Rains had to start from scratch. The Confederacy had no gun powder plants and Rains had never seen one. Fortunately, Rains obtained a copy of a pamphlet describing the ultra-modern powder making process in the Waltham Abbey Works in England. There were no pictures in the booklet, but the descriptions of the processes were explicit.

To find the necessary raw materials, Rains prospected all over the South. He discovered rich deposits of nitrates in limestone caves in Tennessee, Alabama, Georgia, and Arkansas. He found that the southern cottonwood tree served as an excellent source for charcoal. Sulfur was a problem until Rains located large deposits in Louisiana.

Rains selected a building site along a two mile section of canal near Augusta, Georgia to build his factory. First, he had to find the machinery needed for production. The Tredegar Iron Works in Richmond provided twelve huge circular iron plates and twenty-four five ton iron rollers for the incorporation process. From an iron plant in Tennessee, he obtained an iron drive shaft one foot thick and 300 feet long. A company in Atlanta made the sixteen foot diameter gear wheel to drive the shaft. Rains purchased a 130 hp steam engine with a fourteen ton fly wheel and had both shipped to Augusta. Iron drying pans from Tennessee, iron retorts and cylinders from Augusta, tin and zinc roofing from Alabama – materials arrived from all over the Confederacy.

The new factory was a marvel of industrial innovation. The steam engine and drive shaft operated rolling mills in separate cells with ten foot thick blast-proof walls dividing them and glass fronts in case of an explosion. Operators controlled the mills from outside the cells using levers. Above each rolling mill was a thirty gallon tank of water rigged to instantly drown the mill if there was an explosion.

Rains also improved the product and the process to manufacture it. All ingredients were carefully refined to remove all impurities. He mixed the incorporated powder into warm slush, allowing the nitrate to partially crystallize inside the charcoal before pressing. Rains even designed a new shipping box for his powders.

When it was completed in 1862, the huge complex cost the Confederate Government $385,000. However, it was the safest and most modern powder plant in the world at the time! In the next three years, the plant manufactured over 2,750,000 pounds of gunpowder. The new facility never operated at full capacity and normally ran only five days per week. However, the Confederate Army never lost a battle due to a shortage of gun powder.

When the plant was captured by Federal forces in 1865, hundreds of tons of fresh powder remained in the warehouses. These supplies were confiscated by the Federal Government and the factory closed permanently.

Solvent Removal

Dry in a vacuum to remove solvents.

Double Base Propellants

Below is the original formula for "Ballistite" double base smokeless propellant as developed and patented by its inventor Alfred Nobel in 1887.

Prepare bases

Separately prepare collodion (soluble nitrocellulose) and nitroglycerine.

Intermix

Mix the bases and camphor-benzene solvent in 45/45/10 ratio. Note: Nobel soon found that the benzene and the camphor could be eliminated as the nitroglycerine would intermix with the collodion.

Roll/Extrude

Roll or extrude the resulting dough-like paste into the desired shape.

Solvent Removal

Dry in a vacuum to remove solvents.

Why Is Smokeless Powder More Powderful Than Black Powder?

Smokeless powder contains three times more stored chemical energy than black powder. This means there is more energy available in the hot expanding gasses of smokeless propellants to accelerate the bullet down the barrel. In addition, smokeless propellant converts over 99% of its weight into gas, while black powder converts only 55% of its weight into gas, leaving the remainder as solids.

Cartridges loaded with smokeless powder are about 30% efficient while those loaded with black powder are less than 15% efficient.

Cordite Propellants

Invented by Frederick Abel and James Dewar in 1889, "Cordite" is a slightly different form of double base smokeless propellant. Here is the historic method of manufacture:

Prepare bases

Separately prepare guncotton (insoluble nitrocellulose) and nitroglycerine.

Intermix

Mix together in proportions of 58% nitroglycerine, 37% guncotton and 5% petroleum jelly using acetone as a solvent.

Shaping

Extrude resulting dough-like paste into rods while wet.

Solvent Removal

Dry in a vacuum to remove solvents.

Note that Cordite differs from Ballistite in five ways:

- **It uses guncotton (insoluble nitrocellulose) instead of collodion (soluble nitrocellulose).**

- **The percentage of nitroglycerine is much higher**

- **Cordite contains petroleum jelly instead of camphor.**

- **Cordite uses acetone as a solvent instead of benzene or ether and alcohol.**

- **Cordite is extruded into rods and loaded in that configuration while Ballistite is cut into flakes.**

BALL PROPELLANTS

Ball propellants were invented in the 1930s in the U.S. by Dr. Fred Olsen at the Western Cartridge Co. They are a type of double base propellant. The manufacturing process is as follows:

Prepare double base mix

A double base propellant mixture of the consistency of thick syrup is prepared using a solvent that is immiscible with water to dissolve nitrocellulose (as found in surplus propellants or virgin nitrocellulose).

Suspension

The syrup is suspended in water.

Agitation

When agitated, the syrup forms small spheres.

Remove solvent

The mixture is heated to drive off the solvent.

Dry/sort/coat

The spheres are then dried, sorted by size, and coated with a deterrent.

The "Crossed Cannons"

The Crossed Cannons has been a symbol of military ordnance for centuries. In the British Army, the Crossed Cannons is incorporated into the insignia of several historic formations including the Grenadier Guards, Royal Horse Artillery, and Royal Engineers.

In 1775, the young Continental Congress appointed Ezekiel Cheever as the first "Commissary General of the Artillery Stores." In 1812, an Act of Congress formally organized the Ordnance Department. The Crossed Cannons was adopted as the Ordnance Corps official insignia in 1832.

It is the oldest military insignia in the U.S. Army.

ADDITIVES

Small amounts of additives in smokeless propellants accomplish a variety of purposes. Some of the purposes and materials are:

Plasticizers to make the powder grains less brittle (0-10%)

- **Dibutyl phthalate**
- **Polyester adipate**

Binders to maintain grain shape (0-5%)

- **Rosin**
- **Ethyl acetate**

Stabilizers (Centralites) to prevent or slow decomposition (0.5-2%)

- **Diphenylamine**
- **2-nitrodiphenylamine**
- **4-nitrodiphenylamine**
- **N-nitrosodiphenylamine**
- **N-methyl-p-nitroaniline**

Decoppering additives to reduce the buildup of copper fouling in barrels (0-1.5%)

- **Tin dioxide**
- **Bismuth trioxide**
- **Bismuth nitrate**
- **Bismuth subcarbonate**
- **Bismuth antimonide**

Flash reducers (0-1.5%)

- **Potassium nitrate**
- **Potassium sulfate**

Wear reducers (0-1.5%)

- **Wax**
- **Talc**
- **Titanium dioxide**

Static electricity reducers (0.2-1%)

- **Graphite**

Acid neutralizers (0-1%)

- **Calcium carbonate**

DETERIORATION OF PROPELLANTS

Nitrocellulose deteriorates over time releasing acidic byproducts which cause further deterioration. This is the reason for the "sour" acidic smell of deteriorated powder. This process slowly releases heat and can result in self ignition of large quantities of powder.

Propellant makers add calcium carbonate to neutralize the products of decomposition. Stabilizers are added to prevent the buildup of decomposition byproducts. However, stabilizers and neutralizers are depleted over time, allowing decomposition to progress.

Single base propellants are the most susceptible to decomposition while double base and triple base propellants degrade at slower rates.

Why Not Liquid Propellants?

In theory, liquid propellants have many possible advantages. In practice, they have not proven successful – so far. In the 1970s and 1980s, the U.S. military spent millions of dollars trying to perfect liquid propellant technology for artillery. A binary system of two liquids was used, each of which was non-explosive and safe to handle. When mixed together in the barrel's chamber, they formed a propellant. However, the liquids did not mix evenly which led to pressure excursions and unacceptably high variations in muzzle velocity. With no means of correcting this problem, the program was cancelled.

COMPONENTS OF SMOKELESS PROPELLANTS

ENERGETIC SUBSTANCES

These substances provide the stored chemical energy in propellants:

1. Nitrocellulose – the main energetic substance in single-base propellants. Single-based propellants are the most common.

The Confederate Army never lost a battle due to a shortage of gunpowder. Before it was occupied and closed in 1865 by Union Army units, the Confederate States Powder Works in Augusta, Georgia manufactured 2,750,000 lbs. of gunpowder for the Confederate Army. The quality of Confederate powder was superior to the DuPont powder issued to the Union Army.

2. Nitroglycerine – an energetic component (total 3%-39%) added to single-base propellants to make double-base propellants with increased amounts of stored chemical energy. Double-base propellants are a popular choice for many handgun calibers.

3. Nitroguanidine-nitrated guano – is added to double base propellants to form triple-base propellants with increased amounts of stored chemical energy. Triple-based propellants are used mainly in military artillery and tank gun ammunition. They are rarely used in small arms.

4. Other energetic substances in small amounts that increase the level of stored chemical energy such as:

   a. bis-nitroxyethylnitramine (D1NA)

   b. tetramethylolcyclopentanone (Fivonite)

   c. di-ethylene gylcol dinitrate (DGN)

   d. acetyl cellulose

A, b, and c are uncommon as they are used mainly in artillery ammunition and seldom for small arms.

DETERRENT COATINGS

These coatings are used to slow the burning rate of the propellant:

1. Symmetrical diphenyl urea (Centralites)

2. Dibutyl phthalate

3. Asymmetrical diphenyl urea (Akardite)

4. Ortho-tolyl urethane

5. Polyester adipate

6. Graphite

In the past, camphor and dinitrotoluene were used as deterrents, but they have become obsolete. Graphite is the most common.

STABILIZERS

These additives slow decomposition of propellants:

1. Diphenylamine

2. Calcium carbonate

3. Magnesium oxide

4. Sodium bicarbonate

5. Beta-naphthol methyl ether

6. Amyl alcohol

In the past, petroleum jelly and aniline were used as stabilizers, but they have become obsolete. Diphenylamine and calcium carbonate are the most common.

DECOPPERING AGENTS

These additives are intended to reduce the buildup of copper fouling in rifle barrels:

1. Tin metal (foil) and tin compounds such as tin dioxide

2. Bismuth metal and bismuth compounds such as bismuth trioxide

Lead metal foil and lead compounds were used for this purpose in the past, but have been phased out. Bismuth compounds work best. Decoppering agents are not normally used in small arms propellants.

FLASH REDUCERS

These additives are intended to reduce the muzzle flash caused when the hot hydrogen and carbon dioxide propellant gasses mix with the oxygen in the air:

1. Potassium chloride

2. Potassium nitrate

3. Potassium sulfate

Potassium hydrogen tartarate has become obsolete for this purpose. Military and law enforcement ammunition is commonly loaded with propellants containing these additives.

WEAR REDUCING ADDITIVES

These additives are intended to reduce barrel wear by forming a cool, thin layer of gas on the bore to insulate it from the erosive effects of the hot propellant gasses:

1. Waxes

2. Talc

3. Titanium dioxide

4. Polyurethane (in the form of covers on the powder bags)

These additives are used mainly in artillery propellant applications and are seldom used for small arms ammunition. Titanium dioxide has become the most popular choice for this application.

OTHER ADDITIVES

These include solvents, binding agents, surfactants, and coloring agents.

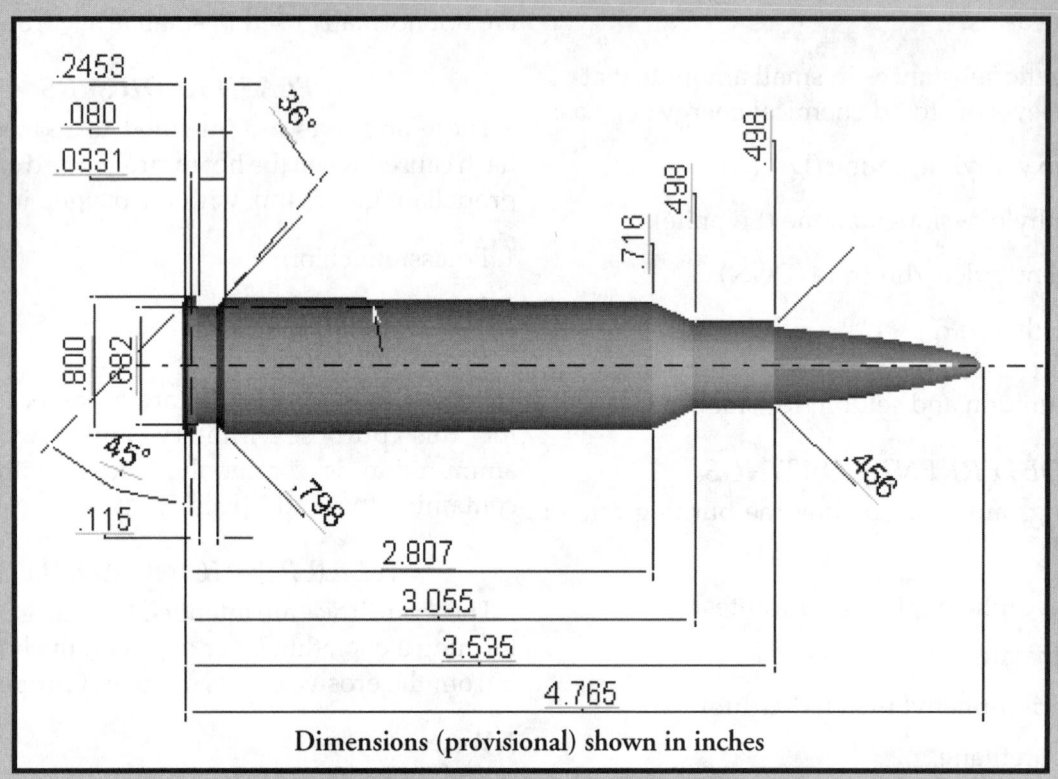

Dimensions (provisional) shown in inches

.460 STEYR

A NEW LONG RANGE CARTRIDGE

In 2006, Steyr announced the development of a new long range cartridge for law enforcement, military, and sporting applications. Based on a .50 BMG cartridge case necked down to .456 inch diameter, it uses bullets with a very low drag profile suitable for very long range shooting. Still in the developmental stage, Steyr has not announced bullet weights, muzzle velocities, or downrange ballistics. However, the ballistic performance can be expected to be substantially better that the .50 BMG.

CHAPTER 27 : PRIMER MANUFACTURING

CHAPTER 27 HIGHLIGHTS:

- OVERVIEW
- FORMING THE METAL PARTS
- MIXING THE PRIMING COMPOUND
- CHARGING
- ASSEMBLY
- TESTING SENSITIVITY

OVERVIEW

WARNING!

Never attempt to make priming compound or primers yourself at home. Doing so may cause an explosion which could result in serious personal injury or death.

Primer manufacture is one of the most complex parts of ammunition manufacture. Strict quality control must go hand-in-hand with safety. For purposes of this description, the process will be broken down into five steps:

- **Forming the metal parts**
- **Mixing priming compound**
- **Charging**
- **Assembly**
- **Testing sensitivity**

FORMING THE METAL PARTS

Centerfire primers are made of two metal parts while No. 209 shotshell primers consist of three metal parts. Centerfire primer cups and anvils are stamped and shotshell primerbattery cups drawn from brass strip. As the parts are small, the press machines used for this operation are small as well. In practice, dedicated machines produce anvils while others make cups and battery cups. After drawing, these parts are washed and dried to prepare them for charging and assembly.

MIXING PRIMING COMPOUND

As priming compound is a sensitive high explosive, it is mixed in batches inside small wooden buildings designed to easily disintegrate in the event of an explosion. The mixed priming compound remains inert as long as it is kept wet. However, these buildings are located in secure areas well away from other buildings. Access is strictly controlled and monitored.

After mixing, the wet insensitive dough-like priming compound is formed into a small loaf about the size of a brick. The loaf is then transferred in a rubber container to a specially constructed facility for charging the compound into primer cups.

CHARGING

When primers are charged, the priming compound is kept wet to render it insensitive. However, the degree of moisture content allowed is narrow. Too much moisture will kill the priming mix; too little and it will become sensitive. Controlling the moisture level enables safe handling. However, primer manufacture is no place for complacency.

Charging of primer cups (placing the priming mix into the cup) takes place in blast-proof rooms under carefully controlled operating procedures. Personnel working in charging rooms pass plates of charged primer cups through narrow slits to personnel performing subsequent operations. Inside the charging room, operators wear rubber aprons, rubber gloves, and face masks. When they leave the charging cell the apron, gloves, and mask are carefully washed with water. Their clothing is then carefully checked to make certain they have absolutely no priming compound anywhere on their person.

Charging consists of three steps: rubbing, inverting, and charging.

Rubbing

Inside the charging cell, the operator places a thin stainless steel charging plate containing approximately 500 holes in a holding fixture on a stainless steel table. He then rubs apart of the loaf of priming compound over the surface of the charging plate using a scrubbing motion. The holes in the charging plate are filled with wet priming mix.

Inverting

A matching stainless steel plate holding 500 empty primer cups is passed through the slit in the blast wall to the charge operator. He inverts this plate and slides it into the holding fixture under the charge plate holding the priming pellet. The fixture aligns the holes in both plates.

Charging

A third steel plate with pins matching those on the other plates is hinged to the holding fixture. When this plate is flipped, the pins knock the pellets of wet priming mixture into the cups. The plate with charged cups is passed back through the slit in the blast wall and the process repeated.

At the rear of each charge table is a water bath. Should the priming loaf dry out or begin to react, the operator drops it into the water bath. During handling, the operator maintains water on his gloves and all surfaces of the charging table.

ASSEMBLY

Centerfire Primers

Foiling

The plate holding the charged primer cups is placed on a small press which cuts out a paper disk and places it in the cup against the priming pellet, compressing it slightly.

Inserting the Anvil

Next, the plate is placed on a shaker table which loads an anvil into each hole. Following this, the steel plate with the anvils and charged cups is placed in a press which uses pins to seat the anvils in the cups.

Sealing

A machine with small injectors places a drop of lacquer sealer inside each primer. The finished primers are placed in plastic trays and sent to the case priming machines where they are inserted while still in a wet (insensitive) condition. Note that manufacture of Berdan primers proceeds as above with the exception that the anvil insert operation is eliminated.

Shotshell Primers

Foiling

Shotshell primer cups are foiled in a manner similar to centerfire primers.

Sealing

After foiling, shotshell primer cups are sealed in a manner similar to centerfire primers.

Covering Flash Hole

Battery cups are placed in a steel plate containing holes, each of which holds one battery cup. A paper disk is placed over the flash hole inside the battery cup.

Inserting Anvil

A shaker table is used to insert an anvil inside each battery cup. The plate is inserted in a seating press and a plate with matching pins is used to seat the anvils.

Inserting the Primer Cup

Another trip to the shaker table places a primer cup in each battery cup. With the plate once again in the seating press, the primer cups are seated firmly in position. The finished primers are packed in trays and sent to the shotshell heading machines where they are inserted while still in a wet (insensitive) condition.

Rimfire Primers

Priming a rimfire cartridge case begins with placing the cases in stainless steel charging plates having about 300 holes. The plates are passed through slits in the blast walls to the primer charge operator who follows much the same procedure as charging centerfire primer cups. The charge plate is rubbed with priming mix to charge the holes. The plate containing the rimfire cartridge cases is placed underneath and the pin plate flipped over to knock the priming pellets into the cartridge cases.

The rimfire cases must then undergo a process known as spinning. This operation consists of inserting a closely fitting steel pin rotating at some 10,000 rpm inside the rimfire case. A combination of centrifugal force and hydraulic pressure forces the priming mix into the rim. When the priming mix in the case dries, it becomes sensitized.

Primer Activation

For safety reasons, factory cartridge cases are primed with wet primers that remain inert until they dry. As the priming compound dries around the anvil, the primer becomes sensitized. Primers for reloading must be shipped dry, so insensitivity is maintained by seating the anvils out in the cup mouth so as not to touch the priming pellet. When the hand loader seats the primer in a cartridge case, the anvil is pressed home against the dry primer pellet which sensitizes the primer.

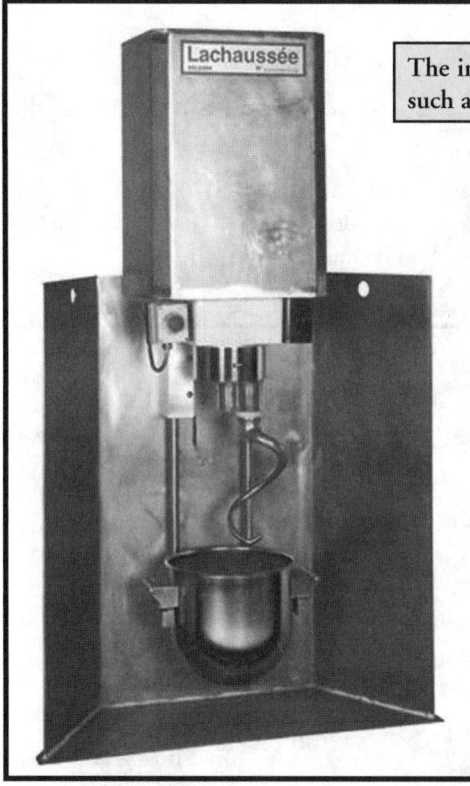

The ingredients to make priming compound are mixed in a machine such as this M743 rotary planetary primer compound mixer.

The metallic parts of a centerfire primer, such as the anvils and cups, are made in small presses such as this M798 Lachaussée machine.

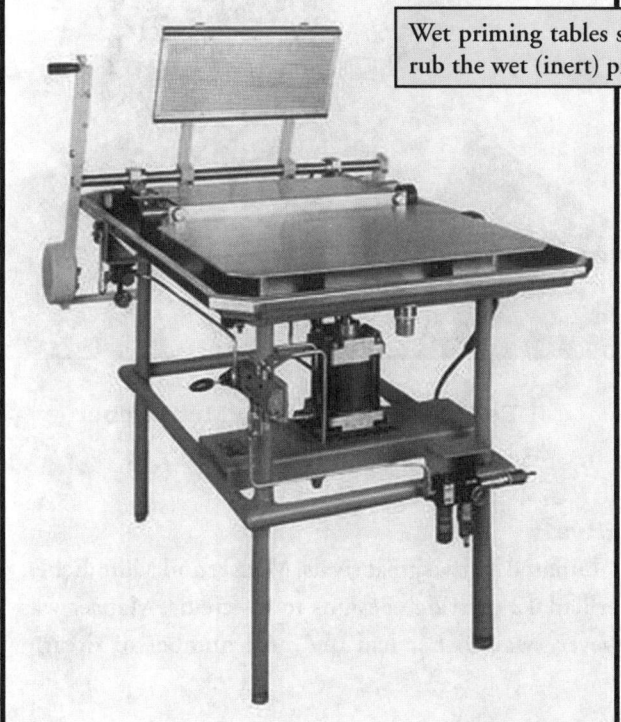

Wet priming tables such as this M569 Lachaussée model are used to rub the wet (inert) priming compound into the cups held in trays.

Once the pellets of priming compound have been rubbed into the cups, each pellet must be tamped and foiled (foiling is placing a small piece of paper over the tamped pellet to resist moisture).

Peter Paul Mauser

1833-1914

Ferdinand Ritter von Mannlicher

1848-1904

The Great Rivals

From 1880 to 1900, European cartridge development was dominated by two great rivals, Mauser and Mannlicher. Both developed dozens of cartridges. Although Mannlicher had 12 cartridge designs to his credit, Mauser was arguably the most successful with some 35 designs. However, Mannlicher had the most number of firearm patents—over 168!

CHAPTER 28 : LOADING CENTERFIRE CARTRIDGES

CHAPTER 28 HIGHLIGHTS:

- PRIMER INSERTION
- BASIC PROCEDURES
- LOADING MACHINES
- SCAMP
- PACKING

All drawings by Author, unless otherwise noted.

PRIMER INSERTION

For safety reasons, centerfire cartridge cases are primed with wet, inert primes before they are sent to the loading operation. Primer insertion consists of four steps:

- **Punch the flash hole in the bottom of the primer pocket in the cartridge case and inspect same**

- **Insert and seat the wet, insensitive primer**

- **Lacquer seal the primer annulus and/or crimp the primer in place (optional)**

- **100% Visual inspection**

BASIC PROCEDURES

Regardless of the type of machinery used, all centerfire ammunition is loaded using a general procedure called "load, assemble, and pack" or LAP. This procedure has nine steps:

- **Feed a primed, empty cartridge case into the handling mechanism of the loading machine**

- **Confirm presence of cartridge case**

- **Drop powder charge**

- **Confirm presence and correct amount of powder charge**

- **Feed and partially seat bullet**

- **Confirm presence of bullet**

- **Fully seat bullet and crimp case mouth**

- **Inspect loaded cartridge mechanically and visually**

- **Pack loaded cartridges**

Some steps may be combined to streamline the procedure; for example the presence of the bullet may be confirmed by the seating pin after feeding.

The transfer of the cartridge from work station to work station is automatic. In this connection, control of the machinery and components is vitally important. In the event of a detection station finding a fault, the machine stops and a trouble light goes on to alert the operator who may be tending several machines. In the event of a serious problem or a break-down, a set-up team of mechanics is called in to remedy the problem.

LOADING MACHINES

There are four general types of centerfire loading machines and dozens of minor variations of each. The four major types are:

- **Plate Loaders**
- **Dial Loaders**
- **Horizontal Transfer Loaders**
- **Rotary Loaders**

PLATE LOADERS

The plate loading is a system which uses a series of steel plates to hold the cartridge cases while they are loaded. Additional steel plates with matching holes are stacked as needed to measure powder, feed bullets, and seat bullets.

Early, plate-loading systems were arranged around the operators who performed a carefully choreographed sequence of actions. These plate loading systems were labor intensive as the transfer of plates between work stations in a production module was manual. Modern plate loading systems are used in comprehensively integrated production lines with automatic transfer between work stations.

Plate loading is capable of making good quantity ammunition in large quality. Plate loading systems are flexibile as changeovers from one caliber to another require a completely new set of plates and feeds. As sporting ammunition manufacturers must contend with frequent changeovers to accommodate broad product lines, plate loading remains an attractive option, especially for handgun calibers.

However, there are two exceptions: .25 Auto and .32 Auto. Both are so small, they are unsuited for horizontal transfer or rotary loading machines. Consequently, both are plate loaded.

As there is no commercial source for plate loading equipment, plate loading systems must be custom-made, usually in-house. Most ammunition manufacturers retain plate loading capability for rimfire ammunition (see Chapter 29), however it also remains popular for loading centerfire ammunition. Some government arsenals retain plate loading production capability for specialized products.

Plate loading normally proceeds in the following steps:

Fill plate

A steel plate containing approximately 500 or more holes dimensioned for a specific caliber is filled with primed, empty cartridge cases held in place by a second plate locked underneath.

Drop propellant

The plate containing the cartridge cases is moved to a second station where it slides underneath a steel powder measuring plate with holes that match the cartridge cases. A reservoir containing propellant moves across the measuring plate, filling the holes with the correct charge of powder. Removing the thin retaining plate under the powder plate allows the propellant to drop into the cartridge cases.

Position bullets

The plate of charged cartridge cases now moves to the next station where another matching plate is laid over the cases and a bullet inserted in each matching hole. So that they are aligned with the case mouths.

Seat bullets

A plate with matching steel pins then comes down to seat and crimp the bullets.

Eject cartridges

The cartridges are ejected from the holding plate into packaging machines and the cycle begins anew.

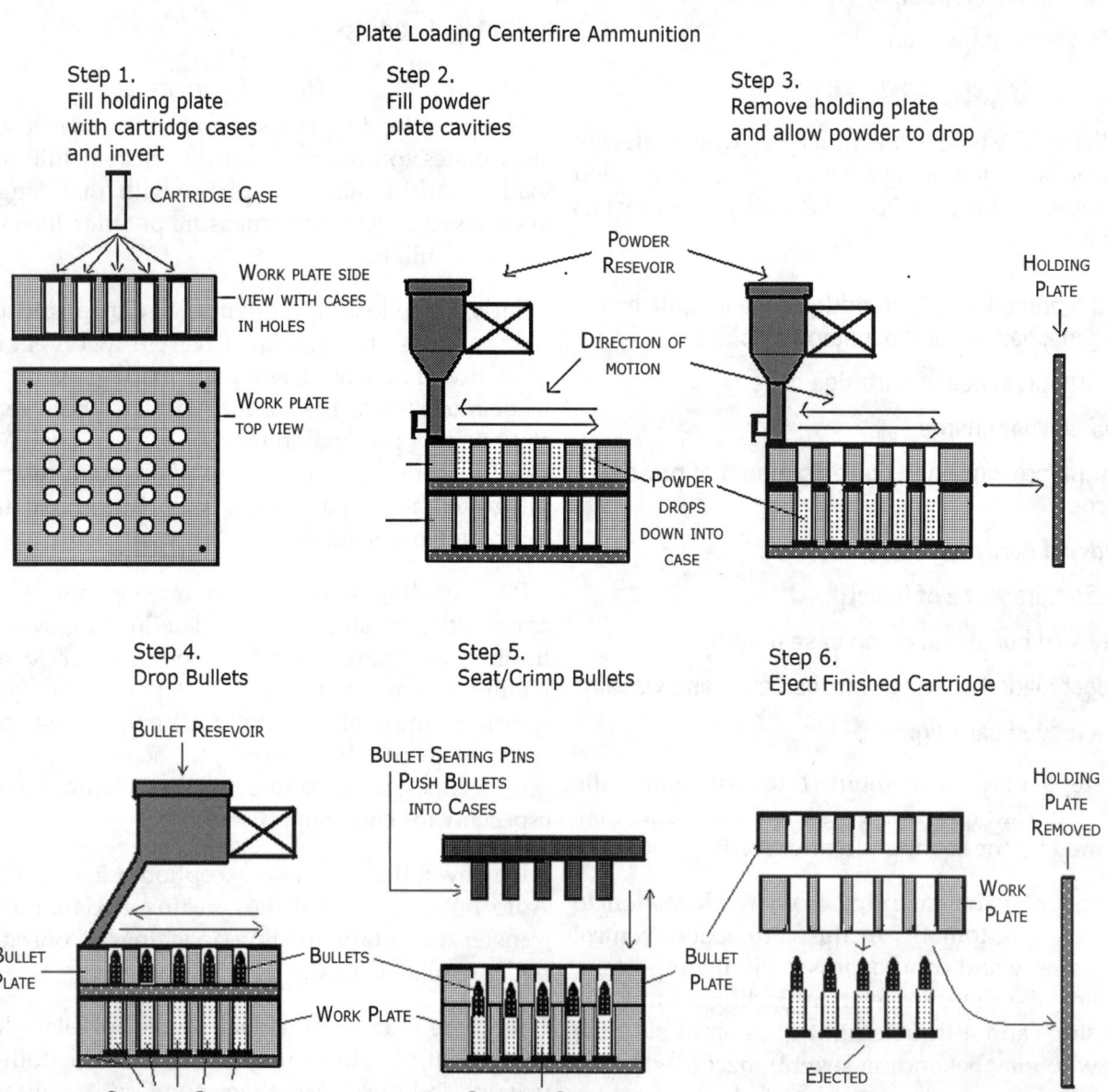

Plate Loading Centerfire Ammunition

DIAL LOADERS

A dial loader gets its name from the clock-like circular path taken by the cartridge cases as they move around the stationary tool bed. Dial loaders have work stations around the perimeter of the bed which perform the normal nine step series of operations as outlined previously. Technically, dial loaders are circular transfer machines with a vertically oriented tool holder which moves up and down. Feeds for powder and bullets may be on the tool bed or tool holder.

A big advantage of this Camdex M2500 centerfire dial loading machine is its capabilities in a compact footprint. Note computer control module.

Dial loaders are compact and relatively inexpensive, features which make them attractive for large scale handloading and semi-commercial custom loading. However, such machines are not intended for or fast enough for high volume factory applications. They may also lack the sophisticated electronic detection systems, automatic component resevoir feeds, and easily rebuildable design of factory loading machines.

Most commercial dial loaders run at a leisurely 75 rounds per minute.

Horizontal Transfer Loaders

(Left) This Camdex M2300 centerfire horizontal transfer loading machine is a popular choice for many small ammunition companies and custom loaders. Note computer control module.

(Right) The Vasini M97 centerfire horizontal transfer loading machine is another popular choice for small ammunition manufacturers and custom loaders. It features computer control.

A horizontal transfer loader gets its name from the straight line path cartridges take as they progress through the loading process. Cases are fed at one end where they are grasped by fingers on a sliding transfer bar. The bar moves back and forth, transferring the work progressively across the loader one station at a time. A vertical die holder moves up and down to perform various operations at each station and ejection pins beneath the base push the cases back onto the fingers of the transfer bar. Normally, there are seven operational stations.

Horizontal Transfer Loading Machine

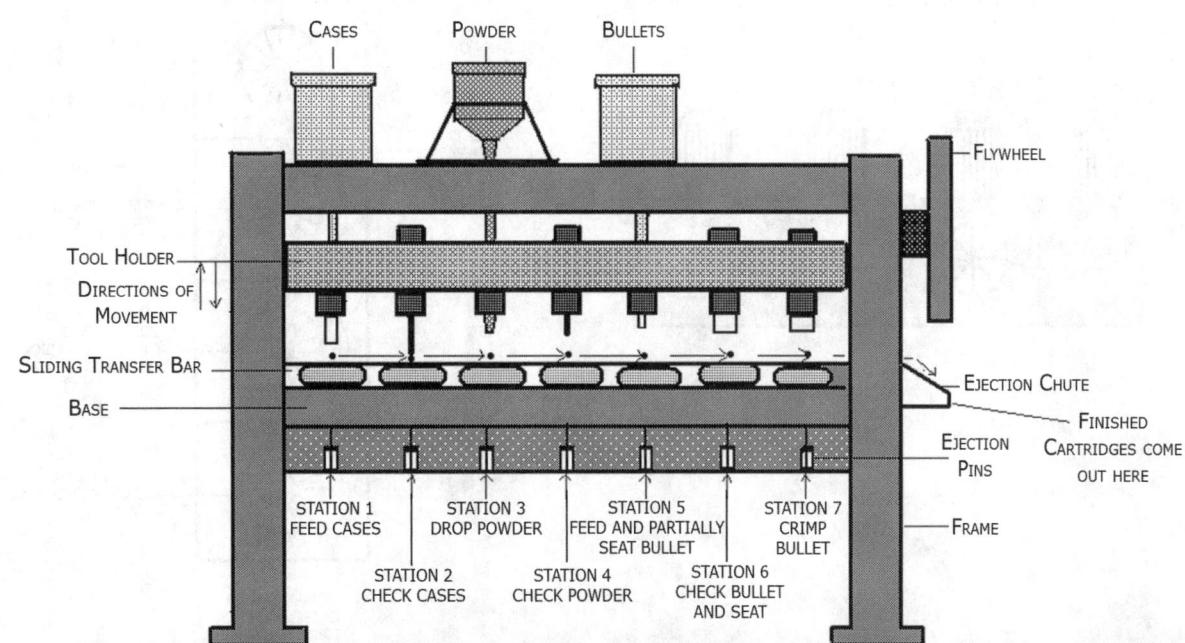

Horizontal transfer loaders are capable of loading ammunition of consistent quality in both rifle and handgun calibers.

Basically, a horizontal transfer loading machine uses 1930s technology with upgrades. Thousands of these machines were built during World War II to supply the wartime demand for small caliber ammunition. While some of these machines were upgraded after World War II, by the early 1980s they had become obsolete for production of most types of military ammunition as they were too slow and too labor intensive.

Most of these machines were expressly designed to be rebuilt as many times as needed. Consequently, when large numbers of these machines were offered on the surplus machinery market, they were eagerly purchased by commercial ammunition makers who rebuilt and upgraded them with the latest electronic detection and control systems.

Today this machine type is by far the most common sporting centerfire ammunition loader. Upgrades have reduced stoppages and associated labor costs. Changeovers are relatively easy and most tooling can be made in house. One operator can oversee several machines easily. Often, a manufacturer will configure a machine for a caliber which may be operated only once or twice a year and leave it between runs to avoid changeovers.

Horizontal transfer machines can load approximately 90 rounds per minute, meaning they can produce about 40,000 rounds per eight hour shift or some 11 million rounds per year when run for one shift per day. Here it is important to note that simply adding a second or third shift would not result in doubling or tripling the output due to bottlenecks in other areas, as well as increased maintenance and repairs.

While the horizontal transfer loader is getting long in the tooth, it remains a cost effective and flexible loading system for sporting centerfire ammunition.

ROTARY LOADERS

The M691 Lachaussée high speed rotary loading machine is an awesome device. It can load about 240 rounds of centerfire ammunition per minute. This design has become a favorite of large ammunition manufacturers and government arsenals.

Rotary centerfire loading machines are modern high-speed loaders developed in the 1960s by Lachaussée Manurhin in Belgium. Manurhin loading machines have become common in many government arsenals as well as major commercial ammunition makers.

A rotary machine gets its name from the rotating

MANURHIN HIGH SPEED ROTARY LOADING MACHINE

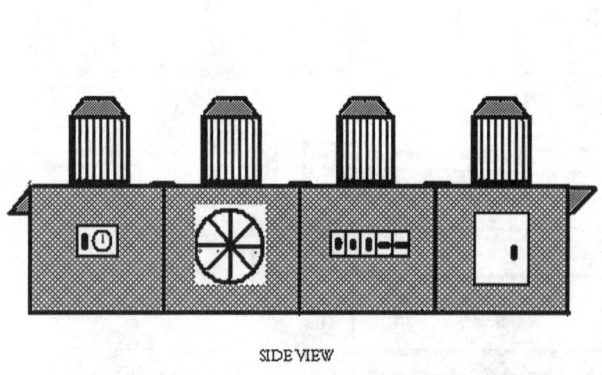

SIDE VIEW

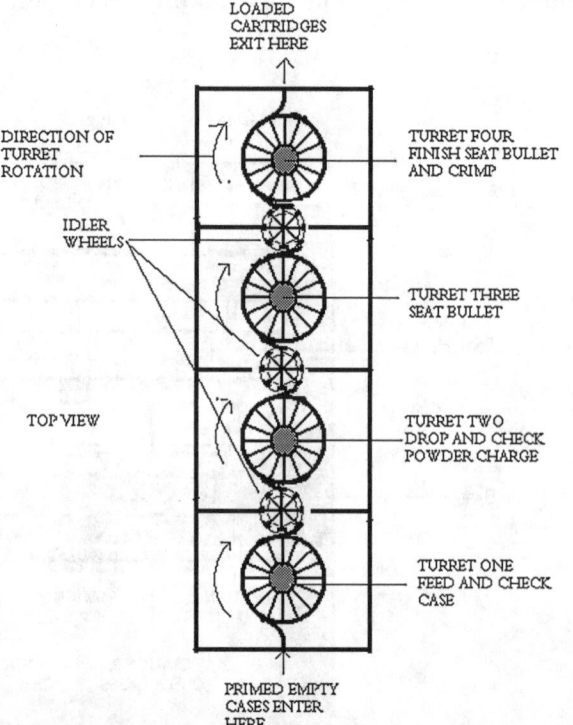

LOADED CARTRIDGES EXIT HERE

DIRECTION OF TURRET ROTATION

TURRET FOUR FINISH SEAT BULLET AND CRIMP

IDLER WHEELS

TURRET THREE SEAT BULLET

TOP VIEW

TURRET TWO DROP AND CHECK POWDER CHARGE

TURRET ONE FEED AND CHECK CASE

PRIMED EMPTY CASES ENTER HERE

modules on top of the fixed base. For loading centerfire ammunition, there are four modules about sixteen inches in diameter, all of which rotate in a clockwise direction with an idler between them. Each module contains 14 or more stations all of which perform the same function. The cartridge case is fed into the module at one end and proceeds in a series of split S motions from one module to the other (see illustration).

Rotary machines run at about 225 rounds per minute, or approximately 2.5 times faster than horizontal transfer loaders. Running for one shift per day, for one year, a rotary loader can assemble over 27 million rounds of ammunition.

However, such efficiency has its price. Rotary machines and tooling are very expensive. For this reason, they are beyond the reach of small manufacturers. Rotary machines lack flexibility as changeovers are difficult and time consuming. However they excel at making large quantities of a single caliber.

SCAMP
(Small Caliber Ammunition Modernization Project)

This was a U.S. government program, with Gulf + Western as the prime contractor, for the development of ultra-high speed technology for manufacturing small caliber ammunition at government owned plants such as Lake City Army Ammunition Plant (LCAAP) and Twin Cities Army Ammunition Plant (TCAAP). Eight modules were planned, four at each facility. The Twin Cities plant was selected for initial installation to prove the technology so as not to interrupt ongoing production at LCAAP.

After four modules had been purchased, the program was cut back, TCAAP closed, and the SCAMP machinery shipped to LCAAP. Today, LCAAP remains the sole manufacturer in the U.S. using such machinery. Other modules were sold to Israel, Australia, and Taiwan.

SCAMP production is computer-controlled and fully automatic. Brass cups, lead wire, and finished primers are the raw material for this system. SCAMP does everything else including drawing and forming the cartridge case, making the bullet, loading, packaging, and sending samples to the test range.

Large multi-station rotary modules hold tooling which can be removed and replaced quickly by hand. If a tool breaks or wears out, the computer blanks that station off and production continues. All transfers between operations are automatic with buffer magazines between most of them to allow production to continue on other operations if a machine is down for maintenance. Production rate is about 1,250 rounds per minute.

Only a small number of people are required to run the SCAMP system. For example, TCAAP had 25,000 employees during World War II who manufactured one million rounds per eight hour shift. During the Korean Conflict, TCAAP was reopened and upgraded with 12,500 employees who made one million rounds per shift. TCAAP was again reopened and upgraded during the Vietnam Conflict employing 7,500 to make one million rounds per shift.

The SCAMP machine runs with less than 20 operators per shift and can make over one million rounds during that same period of time. The SCAMP modules continue to run at LCAAP, now working to keep up with demand for U.S. overseas committments. Unfortunately, despite

What Is The Difference Between A .223 Rem And 5.56x45mm NATO Cartridge And A .308 Win. And A 7.62x51mm NATO?		
	.223 Rem./ .308 Win.	5.56x45mm/7.62x51mm NATO
Chamber dimensions	Commercial	Military
Case mouth/primer waterproofing	No	Yes
Anti-flash coating on propellant	No	Yes
Crimped primer	No	Yes
Iris on case neck and shoulder	No	Yes
Headstamp	Commerical	Military
Propellant	Commercial	Military
Bullet	Various	Military
Standards	SAAMI/CIP	Military
Packaging	Commercial	Military
Ballistics	Commercial	Military

running flat out (over 1.6 billion rounds per year) it is not enough and production contracts have been let to domestic and overseas commercial ammunition manufacturers to make up the difference.

SCAMP technology is now almost 50 years old and many of its systems need upgrading. Lachaussée AES, Indusys, and Fritz Werner are three sources of high speed centerfire loading equipment today.

PACKING

The Vasini M97 computer-controlled centerfire loading machine forms the center piece of this loading module that includes component feeders and a semi-automatic packing machine.

Until recently, packing was one of the most labor intensive operations of ammunition manufacture. This situation had to change when manufacturers started to route the output of two or more high speed loaders to a single packaging line. Human beings could simply not keep up with the avalanche of ammunition coming off such machines.

This resulted in development of automatic packing machines which count out the correct number of cartridges, put them in trays, erect the boxes, place the tray in the box, and close the box. The boxes are automatically put in cases and the cases sealed. A robot picks up the case and stacks it precisely on a shipping pallet. After the pallet has been stretch-wrapped with plastic, another robot takes the loaded pallet to the warehouse and places it in the allotted space. The entire process is computer controlled using optical scanning and bar code technology

Of course, small runs of products made infrequently are still packed by hand for reasons of economy.

SHOTS OF A LIFETIME – In the Laboratory

Measuring extreme variation (EV) in muzzle velocity is a routine quality control test by ammunition manufacturers. This test consists of firing a 20 shot string from a machine rest through a chronograph to determine the difference between the highest and the lowest velocity shots. An acceptable EV for sporting ammunition is approximately 70 fps. One day we received a sample of Ball Powder that seemed to be right on the mark .222 Rem. ammunition. As my bench rest rifle was .222 Rem. caliber, I obtained a small quantity of this propellant and used it to hand load 50 rounds of my cases. I sent these to the test range with a request to shoot these for EV to see how the propellant worked. The next day the range supervisor called to advise me that my .222 Rem. hand loads had established a company record for low EVs. The EV for the first 20 round string was 0 fps! The second string was 1 fps! Bettering this is statistically unlikely.

CHAPTER 29 : LOADING RIMFIRE CARTRIDGES

CHAPTER 29 HIGHLIGHTS:

- LOADING MACHINES
- INSPECTION/QUALITY CONTROL
- PACKING

All drawings by Author, unless otherwise noted.

LOADING MACHINES

Most large commercial ammunition companies continue to manufacture rimfire ammunition despite the fact that profits on rimfire products are thin. However, the ubiquitous .22 rimfire remains the most popular cartridge in the world. What major manufacturer would be without it?

PLATE LOADING

Nearly all manufacturers of rimfire ammunition utilize automated or semi-automated plate loading systems. The reason for this is the superior economy of plate loading for making large quantities of a single item. For example, a centerfire loading plate may contain 500 rounds while a rimfire loading plate will contain 300. This enables an automatic rimfire plate loading system to manufacture over 2 million rounds per shift. As most rimfire manufacturers have two or more rimfire production lines, the capacity truly staggers the imagination. Is it any wonder then that world production of .22 rimfire ammunition remains well into the billions.

Plate loading rimfire ammunition requires ten steps:

- **Feeding unprimed empty cases into holding plate**
- **Knocking the primer mix pellet into the case**
- **Spinning the primer mix into the rim**
- **Feeding the powder**
- **Dropping the powder**
- **Feeding the bullet**
- **Dropping and seating the bullet**
- **Ejecting the cartridges**
- **Crimping the bullet**
- **Lubricating the bullet**

Crimping a .22 rimfire cartridge case into its bullet requires that the cartridge be removed from the steel work plate and fed individually through a crimping machine. The crimped cartridges are fed into another thin steel plate which holds them vertically (bullet pointing down) and dips them in liquid bullet lubricant. Usually, the bullets are dipped twice, allowed to dry, and sent to the automatic packing machines.

The entire sequence of loading is shown on the following page, Illustrations 1, 2, 3, and 4.

DIAL LOADING

Some types of specialized .22 rimfire ammunition do not lend themselves easily to plate loading. A good example is the .22 Long Rifle shotshell with its long metal case and folded crimp closure. Such products normally are made on miniature dial loaders which transfer the cartridge case through work stations to drop the powder charge, check the powder, insert the wad column, drop the shot charge, check the shot charge, crimp the mouth closed, and place a drop of wax on the end of the crimp.

If this sounds like it is slow, it is and it is the reason for the high price of such ammunition.

INSPECTION/QUALITY CONTROL

It is not humanly possible to visually inspect every rimfire cartridge coming off a production line. The volume is simply too great. However, samples are taken at regular intervals for inspection and testing. The quality control and testing of rimfire ammunition is every bit as thorough as centerfire or shotshell ammunition.

PACKING

Automatic packing of .22 rimfire ammunition is an essential step in reducing labor costs to an acceptable level. After the bullet lubricant is dry, the cartridges in the lubrication plates are dropped into trays of 50 or 100 rounds. These trays are automatically inserted in boxes, the boxes inserted into cartons, the cartons inserted into cases, and the cases sealed. Numerous detection devices allow a few human operators to easily control and monitor the entire process.

Not everyone uses plate loaders to assemble rimfire ammunition. Lachaussée offers the M149 high speed rotary rim fire loading machine capable of loading over 240 rounds per minute or about 45 million rounds per year.

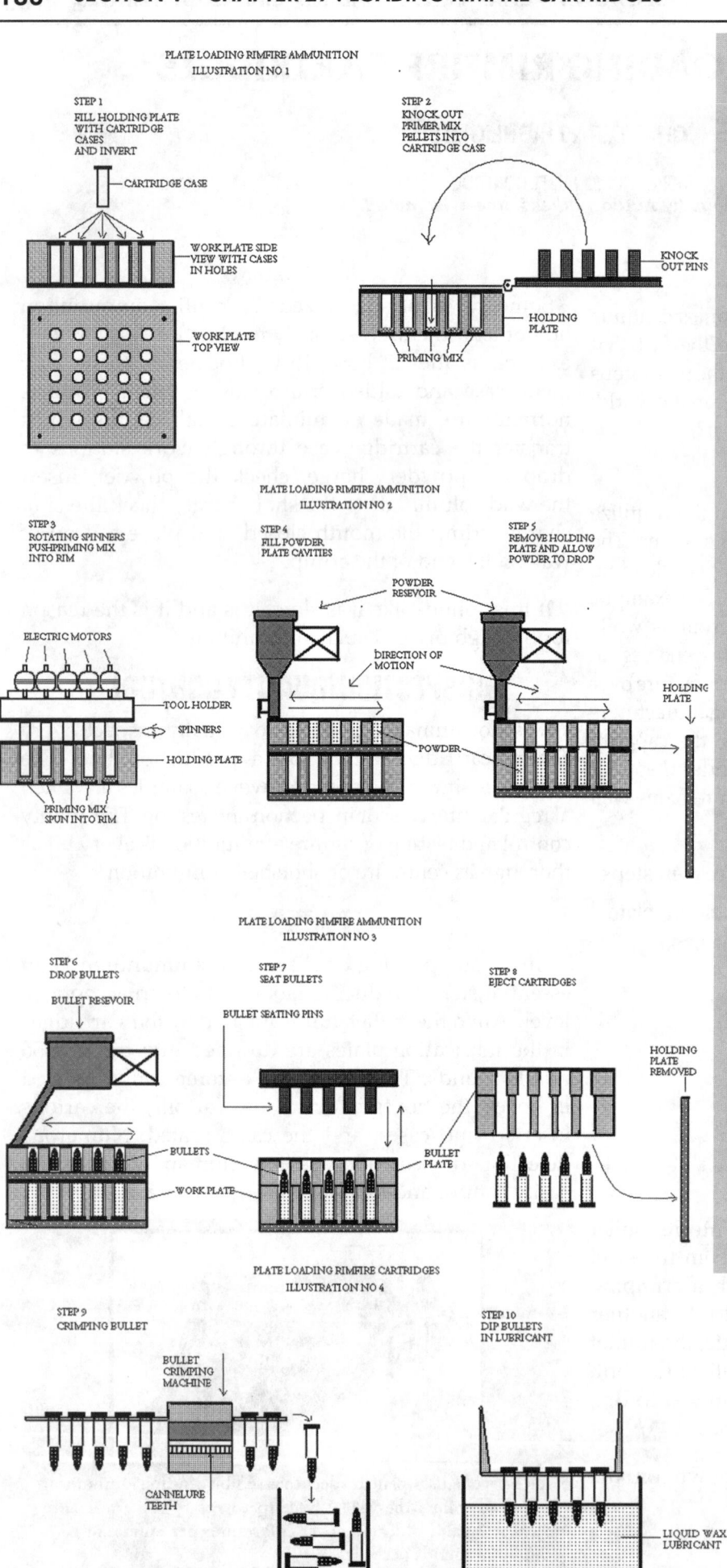

PLATE LOADING RIMFIRE AMMUNITION
ILLUSTRATION NO 1

STEP 1
FILL HOLDING PLATE
WITH CARTRIDGE
CASES
AND INVERT

CARTRIDGE CASE

WORK PLATE SIDE
VIEW WITH CASES
IN HOLES

WORK PLATE
TOP VIEW

STEP 2
KNOCK OUT
PRIMER MIX
PELLETS INTO
CARTRIDGE CASE

KNOCK
OUT PINS

HOLDING
PLATE

PRIMING MIX

PLATE LOADING RIMFIRE AMMUNITION
ILLUSTRATION NO 2

STEP 3
ROTATING SPINNERS
PUSH PRIMING MIX
INTO RIM

ELECTRIC MOTORS

TOOL HOLDER

SPINNERS

HOLDING PLATE

PRIMING MIX
SPUN INTO RIM

STEP 4
FILL POWDER
PLATE CAVITIES

POWDER
RESERVOIR

DIRECTION OF
MOTION

POWDER

STEP 5
REMOVE HOLDING
PLATE AND ALLOW
POWDER TO DROP

HOLDING
PLATE

PLATE LOADING RIMFIRE AMMUNITION
ILLUSTRATION NO 3

STEP 6
DROP BULLETS

BULLET RESERVOIR

BULLETS

WORK PLATE

STEP 7
SEAT BULLETS

BULLET SEATING PINS

BULLET
PLATE

STEP 8
EJECT CARTRIDGES

HOLDING
PLATE
REMOVED

PLATE LOADING RIMFIRE CARTRIDGES
ILLUSTRATION NO 4

STEP 9
CRIMPING BULLET

BULLET
CRIMPING
MACHINE

CANNELURE
TEETH

STEP 10
DIP BULLETS
IN LUBRICANT

LIQUID WAX
LUBRICANT

An Unlikely Success

If one set out to deliberately design a cartridge that could never be made to work, the .22 rimfire would serve nicely. Fortunately, the dark side of the .22 rimfire is something the customer never sees.

A rimfire cartridge has a thin weak case of drawn brass with a hollow rim. This limits maximum average breech pressure to 22,000 psi or less.

The rimfire priming system in the hollow rim is weak at best, leaving large quantities of the powder charge unburned. As there is no anvil in the case, ground glass must be added to the priming mix as a frictioning agent.

Shot start resistance is another chronic problem with rimfires. This requires the bullets of rimfire cartridges to be heavily crimped (mangled, actually) in order to (try to) get the propellant burning.

Rimfire bullets are a nightmare in and of themselves. The diameter of a rimfire bullet is the same as the cartridge case. This means the bullet must have an undersized heel to be held in the cartridge case and a cup base which must expand under pressure to seal the hot expanding propellant gasses. Make the bullet too hard, and the base will not seal properly. Make the bullet too soft, and it will lead the barrel. Good old American ingenuity – circa 1857.

This brings us to the slippery subject of bullet lubricant. You might expect centerfire handgun bullet lubes to work well for rimfire bullets, but you'd be wrong. Rimfire bullets require special lubricants. Even so, it remains a seesaw battle of lubricant vs. bullet to prevent barrel leading.

Those who believe that perseverance pays have an example in the ammunition engineers' diligence which has made the modern rimfire a (qualified, depending on your viewpoint) success.

CHAPTER 30 : LOADING SHOTSHELLS

BASIC LOADING PROCESS

With world demand currently at well over three billion rounds per year, shotshell manufacturers must continually modernize and upgrade their production machinery to keep costs in check and remain competitive.

All shotshells begin the loading process as a primed empty hull of a specific gauge and length. The loading operation has twelve basic steps:

- **Feed primed empty hull**
- **Check to confirm presence of hull**
- **Drop powder**
- **Check to confirm presence of powder**
- **Feed and seat wad column**
- **Check to confirm presence of wad column**
- **Drop shot charge**
- **Check to confirm presence of shot charge**
- **Start crimp**
- **Finish crimp and round nose (seal crimp optional)**
- **Print data on tube (on a different machine)**
- **Inspect and pack (on a different machine)**

LOADING MACHINES

Currently, there are three systems for loading shotshells: dial, horizontal transfer, and rotary.

DIAL LOADERS

Dial shotshell loaders are progressive rotary transfer machines with a fixed bed and an overhead tool holder which moves up and down. Most dial loaders have eight to ten work stations; transfer of work between stations is automatic.

The empty shell enters the system on its perimeter and is transferred from work station to work station where various operations are performed. Dial machine operating speeds vary from a leisurely 40 rounds per minute to a high of about 75 rounds per minute depending on the product being loaded. For example buckshot and slug loading proceed at a slow pace while loads with small shot run faster. A dial loader can load about nine million rounds per year when run one shift per day.

Although slow, dial loaders are the machine of choice for low volume specialty products such as 12-ga. slugs, buckshot, some steel shot, and some heavy magnum loads; and for 10-ga., 28-ga., and .410-bore shells.

While dial loaders are technologically old, they have been upgraded with modern electronic controllers and detection systems. In addition, they were constructed so as to be easily repaired or rebuilt as necessary. Most large shotshell manufacturers own dozens of these machines which have long ago "paid for themselves". These factors will keep dial loaders around for many years to come.

Smaller dial loading machines are compact and inexpensive making them a popular choice of small custom shotshell loaders in Europe. These loaders are designed for small companies with limited product lines and small volumes. They are not suitable for large manufacturing operations.

Hand loaders have used dial machines for many years. Most of these require manual transfer of the shell from one station to the next, although there are several semi-automatic models. These loading machines are intended to reload fired shotshells, but they can just as easily load new shells. However, the output of even the best of these is far below what would be needed for commercial manufacturing.

A top-of-the-line M97 Vasini shotshell loading machine. This versatile, computer-controlled machine is capable of loading all gauges and types of shot shells. A horizontal transfer design, it is a popular choice for many custom loaders.

HORIZONTAL TRANSFER LOADERS

Horizontal transfer loading machines for shotshells function in a manner similar to those used for loading centerfire ammunition. A fixed bed on a frame

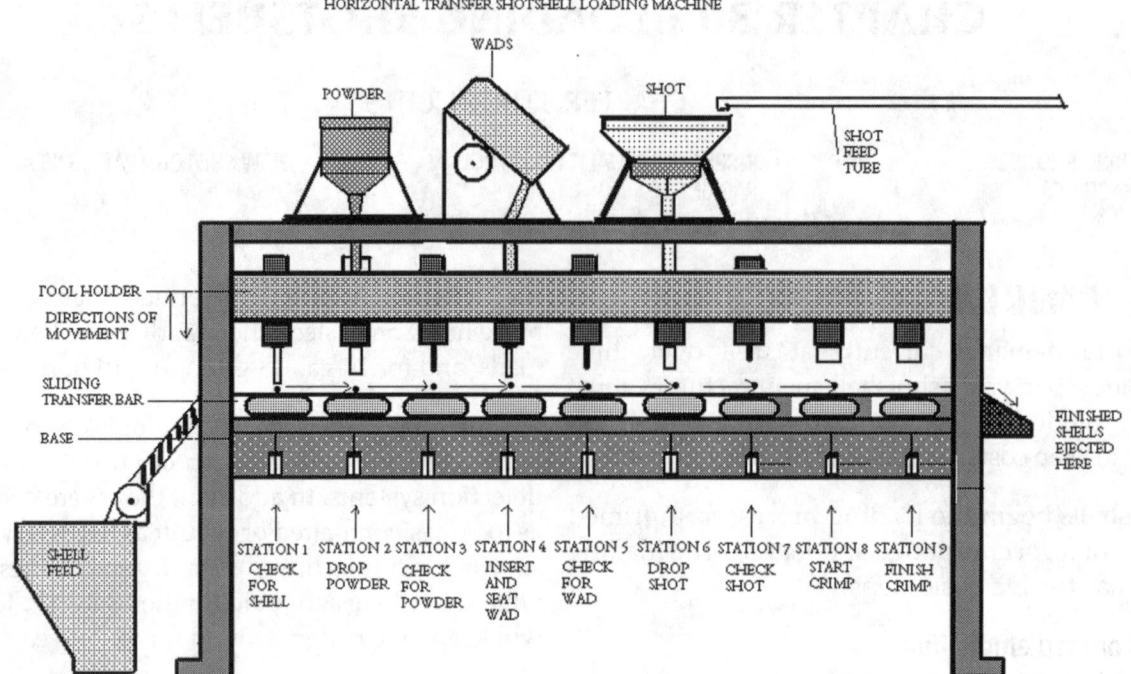

HORIZONTAL TRANSFER SHOTSHELL LOADING MACHINE

supports a sliding transfer bar which moves the shells progressively from one work station to another across the bed. A tool holder moves up and down to simultaneously perform work at each station.

When supported by automatic on-demand component feeding systems, horizontal transfer loaders such as those offered by Vasini are capable of loading 90 rounds per minute or some eleven million rounds per year.

Horizontal transfer loading machines are easily converted from one load or gauge to another, provided one purchases the proper additional tooling. They are also easy to operate, compact, and relatively inexpensive. For these reasons, they are a popular choice of custom shotshell loaders. Larger custom loaders may own several of these.

Loading machines of this type are too expensive for individual handloaders.

The BSN Kamaleon shotshell loading machine has earned an excellent reputation among custom shotshell loaders for its reliability and capability. Like most other shotshell loaders of this size and output, it is a computer-controlled, horizontal transfer design.

ROTARY LOADERS

Rotary shotshell loaders are high speed machines capable of loading well over 600 shells per minute. Often, two or more of these machines are ganged on an automatic packing module. It is fascinating to see 1,200 plus shotshells per minute (125 million or more per year!) coming off such a combination!

High speed rotary shotshell loading machines are made by the New Lachaussée Co. Ltd., a Belgian manufacturer. New Lachaussée loading machines are indeed fast, but they are also very expensive. For these reasons, ammunition manufacturers use them to load high volume popular items such as target and game loads, but they cannot economically justify acquiring such a machine for every shotshell load they produce. Most large shotshell manufacturers have eight or more of these machines. The bulk of these are 12-ga. models, although Lachaussée does make a 20-ga. version.

Lachaussée shotshell loaders are known for their smooth relatively trouble-free operation which produces a high quality product. However, set ups are complex, changeovers time consuming, and breakdowns expensive. In short, new Lachaussee loading machines lack flexibility. For these reasons, most operators set up a new Lachaussee loader for a particular high volume product and leave it that way.

New Lachaussée 12-ga. loading machines are built on a rectangular steel bed about 36" high and fifteen feet long with five rotating turrets on the bed. All turrets rotate in a clockwise direction with idlers in between and automatic component feeds. The empty shotshells are fed into a track at one end and loaded ammunition

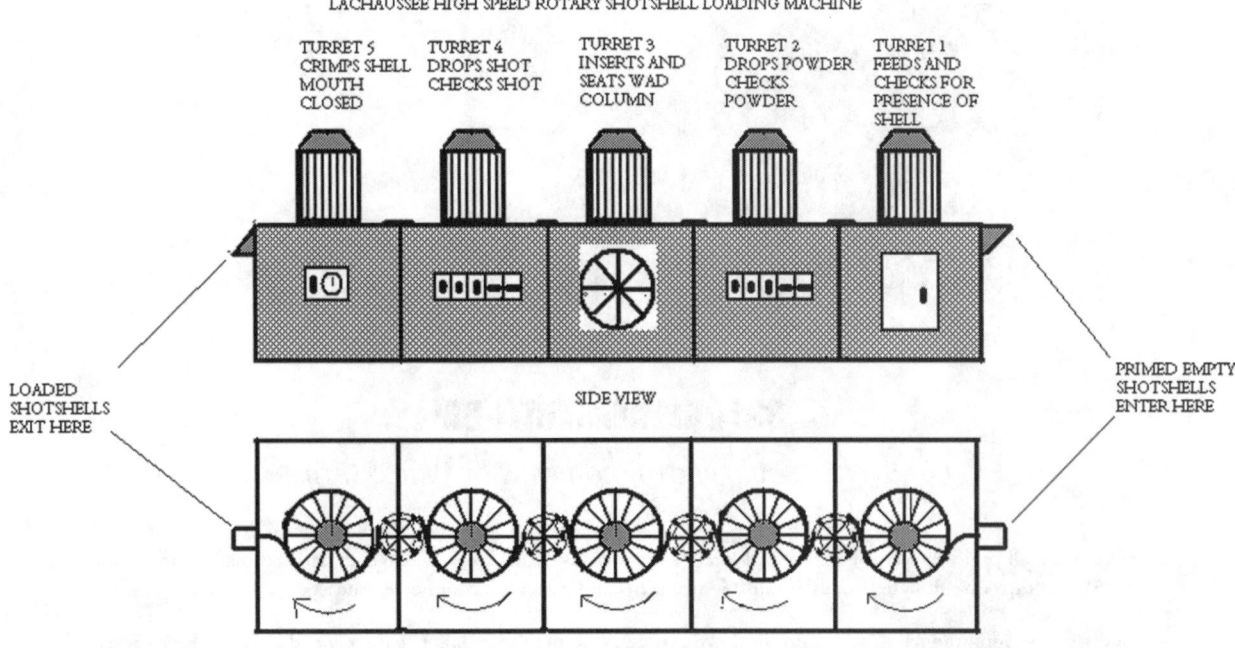

LACHAUSSEE HIGH SPEED ROTARY SHOTSHELL LOADING MACHINE

TURRET 5 CRIMPS SHELL MOUTH CLOSED | TURRET 4 DROPS SHOT CHECKS SHOT | TURRET 3 INSERTS AND SEATS WAD COLUMN | TURRET 2 DROPS POWDER CHECKS POWDER | TURRET 1 FEEDS AND CHECKS FOR PRESENCE OF SHELL

SIDE VIEW

LOADED SHOTSHELLS EXIT HERE

PRIMED EMPTY SHOTSHELLS ENTER HERE

TOP VIEW

comes out the other. In between, the path of the shells on the track describes a split S. Each turret performs a specific function. These are as follows:

- **Turret 1 Feed and confirm presence of empty shotshell**
- **Turret 2 Drop and confirm presence of powder charge**
- **Turret 3 Feed and seat wad column, confirm presence**
- **Turret 4 Drop and confirm presence of shot charge**
- **Turret 5 Crimp case mouth closed**

Whatever Happened To The Roll Crimp?

During the era of paper shotshells (1880-1960) target loads and some light field loads were often closed with a six fold crimp. High velocity and magnum loads were closed with a roll crimp.

The reason for this was simple: a folded crimp took up more length of tube than a rolled crimp. To fold crimp a shotshell required about 5-6mm of tube length while a roll crimp required about half that much. There was plenty of room inside a paper shotshell for a light target or field load, consequently a folded crimp caused no problems. A rolled crimp offered critical additional volume for the larger charges of powder and shot used in heavy loads. However, roll crimps required a top wad to close the shell. Tests showed the top wad had an adverse effect on pattern quality as well as adding extra cost to the manufacturing process. For these reasons, shotshell makers were keen to get rid of roll crimps. However, this was not possible with the card and fiber cushion wad columns of the day. The advent of plastic wad columns finally allowed folded crimps for all but the heaviest hunting load shotshells.

PACKING

Most shotshells made today are boxed by automatic packing machines. These are high speed machines which block off 25 shells at a time and align them in opposing (head to mouth) layers. The layered blocks are then inserted in a box erected by the machine which also prints the lot number inside the top flap. The box is closed, put in a case, and the case closed. A robot picks up the case, places it precisely on a shipping pallet, and stretch wraps the load with plastic. Another robot takes the pallet to the warehouse. Ammunition makers have invested large sums in these systems because they reduce cost and improve quality.

Six Fold Or Eight Fold Crimp?

Shotshells are closed with a folded crimp on the tube mouth to prevent the shot charge from leaking out. The crimp may have six folds or eight folds. Convention and marketing concerns are balanced against technical requirements in determining which crimp is used on what load.

In general, target loads have an eight fold crimp as it offers a better appearance. This is achieved by skiving (thinning) the tube mouth to allow more even folds. Many target shooters believe an eight fold crimp opens more easily with reduced adverse effect on pattern quality.

Most shotshells intended for hunting have a six fold crimp closure. Even though the tube mouth is not skived, the tube's thickness still allows for an acceptable looking crimp without skiving. Of course, skiving would make for a better looking crimp, but this is not considered necessary for hunting loads. On most shells loaded with steel shot, the center of the crimp where the folds come together is heat sealed to prevent moisture from causing rust.

All paper shotshells have a six fold crimp closure. Slug shells use a rolled crimp which exposes the nose of the projectile for easy identification.

.321 GREENER MULTI-BALL

SPECIMEN AND PHOTOS COURTESY OF PAUL SMITH

This a multiball projectile version of the .321 Greener. It was developed by W.W. Greener and was made from a modified .450-31/4" Nitro case. It dates from the mid-to-late 1920s and was not a commercial success.

The distinctive longitudinal flutes retain the 3 projectiles. Note the top 2 bullets have a coned hollow base to accept the nose of the next projectile. The rearmost projectile is retained by a stab crimp at the bottom of each flute.

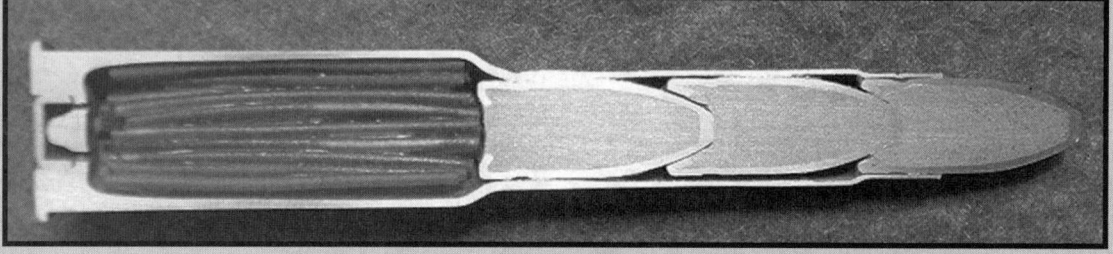

Note the use of "cordite" powder, and a "Berdan primer".

This round was not headstamped.

The single projectile version was loaded with a 155 gr. softpoint.

Reference: Hoyem, George, 1991, *The History and Development of small arms Ammunition*. Volume 3. Page 135

Courtesy International Ammunition Association, Inc. (cartridgecollectors.org)

CHAPTER 31 : AMMUNITION PACKAGING

CHAPTER 31 HIGHLIGHTS:

- WHAT IS THE PURPOSE OF AMMUNITION PACKAGING?
- WHAT IS A BOX OF AMMUNITION?
- READING A BOX OF AMMUNITION
- MILITARY AMMUNITION

Ammunition packaging is a subject often taken for granted. Most sportsmen and sportswomen pay little attention to ammunition packaging unless it affects the price, i.e. number of rounds, bulk packaging, re-usable metal or plastic, inclusion of belts or other items, etc. In practice, most shooters give the label listing the caliber cursory attention before loading and shooting.

WHAT IS THE PURPOSE OF AMMUNITION PACKAGING?

Ammunition packaging is designed to preserve the integrity, appearance and performance of the contents during shipping from the factory to the customer. The packaging must be able to withstand stacking on a skid, light impact from handling, stay closed securely during shipping, and keep dirt away from the product. In addition, the printing on the boxes and cases must withstand the rubbing effects of shipping.

Winchester Ranger packaging is designed for and aimed at the law enforcement market segment. This is a recent trend that breaks with the old practice of selling law enforcement ammunition in standard boxes. Courtesy Winchester.

The packaging must be labeled clearly so that the handler and customer knows exactly which brand, caliber, and loading is contained within. Loaded sporting ammunition is classified as 1.4S for shipping purposes. This means it can be shipped via common carrier ground services provided it is in the original packaging. To earn this classification, the packaging must pass a series of tests.

WHAT IS A BOX OF AMMUNITION?

A box of ammunition normally is the terminal packaging or container intended for use by the ultimate consumer.

A box of ammunition may contain any number of cartridges, however 50 or 100 rounds are normal for

rimfire ammunition, 5 or 25 common for shotshells, 20 rounds for centerfire rifle ammunition, and 25, 50, or 100 rounds common for handgun cartridges. There are many exceptions to these numbers. For example, ammunition may be packaged to fill a specific magazine in a specific firearm such as 30 rounds for the M-16 magazine. It may also be packed in bulk.

Here is an example of a manufacturer resurrecting an old brand for a new product line. In 1912, the Union Metallic Cartridge Company and Remington Arms Company were combined by owners Marcellus Hartley and partners forming Remington U.M.C. The head stamp REM-UMC was used on Remington centerfire and shotshell ammunition until recently. Remington has resurrected the UMC brand for their value-priced ammunition and their modern Leadless™ handgun cartridges. Courtesy Remington Catalog 2012.

Most ammunition packages contain sub-packaging materials to prevent the cartridges from banging into one another. Such materials may include paper dividers, plastic trays, foam trays, paper trays, stripper clips, belts, and cardboard spacer panels. In most instances, the interior packaging materials are expendable.

Boxes of ammunition are packed in outer containers or cases. Commercial ammunition is usually packed in cases of 200, 250, or 500 rounds. As ammunition is heavy, the number of rounds in a case is usually determined by the amount of weight a warehouse worker can safely lift by hand.

Cases of sporting ammunition may be shipped individually or on skids containing up to 50 cases or more.

READING A BOX OF AMMUNITION

There is a wealth of information on typical ammunition packaging such as the:

1. Caliber – normally this will be found on the flap and will

be abbreviated to fit the limited space available, example 30-06 Sprg.

2. Brand – the brand normally is the manufacturer, however most manufacturers offer several different product lines broken down into different types for different purposes, example Federal Gold Medal (for match shooting) and Norma's PH (Professional Hunter) product line for hunting dangerous game in Africa.

3. Bullet type – typical descriptions will include hollow point or jacketed hollow point (HP or JHP), full metal jacket (FMJ), soft point (SP), and round nose (RN). Often the bullet will be described further by assigning it to a specific product line such as Winchester Silver Tip and Remington Core-Lokt.

4. Bullet weight – normally the bullet weight will be expressed in grains.

5. Lot number – you will normally find this stamped inside one of the flaps or on the inside of the box body. However, some manufacturers now print the lot number on the back of the box if there is space.

6. Manufacturer's name and address – this will be found on the back panel of the box and is required by law.

7. Warnings – warnings about general and specific dangerous situations may be printed on the back panel.

8. Warranty – the manufacturer's warranty will be briefly explained here.

9. Muzzle velocity or load level – the load level will be inherent in the caliber designation, for example +P while the muzzle velocity may be listed on the box.

10. Special features – these include special bullets, match-grade ammunition, special loads for a specific customer, for example a law enforcement agency, a commemorative event, etc.

MILITARY AMMUNITION

Small arms ammunition loaded for military use must be packaged and labeled according to customer specifications. These specifications may differ from country to country and from one organization to another, however they do share certain features.

1. Boxes – card stock boxes containing military ammunition normally hold 20 rounds and may or may not have a paper divider inside with individual pockets for cartridges. The outside of the box is plain brown or white with black printing listing the contents in military descriptive terms.

2. Bandoliers and stripper clips – bandoliers are made of cloth with pockets holding loaded cartridges in metal stripper clips. The contents of the bandolier are clearly marked on the outside. In use, the soldier can sling the carry strap of the bandolier over his shoulder. The ammunition in the bandolier is intended to be used for refilling magazines. For that purpose, a stripper clip guide is often included in the bandolier to speed up the refilling process.

3. Clips – the M1 rifle used en-block clips holding 8 rounds of ammunition. These were issued in cloth bandoliers holding 12 clips. As the M1 rifle is no longer in military service, this type of packaging has become obsolete.

4. Belts containing cartridges held by disintegrating or refillable metal links – these are for machine guns. The disintegrating metal links are held together by the cartridges. As the cartridges are fed into the machine gun, the links disintegrate and fall away under the gun. Some metal links do not disintegrate, so they are refillable by snapping a fresh cartridge in place. Such belts usually hold 50 rounds, however any number of belts may be fastened together. In the past, fabric belts were used, but these are now obsolete. A common practice is to fill the belt with one tracer cartridge for every four ball cartridges.

5. Boxes – for many years, military ammunition has been packed in sealed, waterproof steel boxes with hinged lids. The contents may include loaded ammunition in boxes, bandoliers, or belts.

6. Wire bound crates – For shipment, the metal boxes are packed in wire bound crates containing two or more metal boxes. The contents of the metal boxes and wire bound crates are clearly marked on the outside.

Clearly, ammunition packaging is no simple matter. Considerable thought, testing, and development has been and continues to be put into this effort. For example, in order to reduce shipping weight, military services are working to develop lightweight plastic ammunition boxes to replace steel boxes.

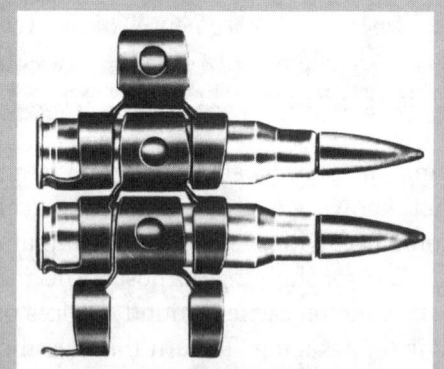

This image shows how a disintegrating metal link belt works. Each cartridge is held securely by the center of the right hand link inside the two outer rings of the left hand link. When the cartridge is withdrawn, the right hand link is released and drops away. Although links can be refilled, they are regarded as expendable. Links are made of steel.

CHAPTER 32 : QUALITY CONTROL

CHAPTER 32 HIGHLIGHTS:

- QUALITY CONTROL
- TESTING MAXIMUM AVERAGE PRESSURE AND VELOCITY
- TESTING PRIMER SENSITIVITY
- TESTING SHOTSHELL PATTERNS
- FRANGIBILITY DEFINITION AND PERFORMANCE STANDARDS

QUALITY CONTROL

STANDARDS AND SAMPLES

Ammunition manufacturers exercise stringent quality controls on all their products. This begins with a set of specifications for each piece of raw material received from suppliers. As raw material is received, it is carefully checked to see that it meets quality standards. Then a battery of continuous in-process quality checks are made until the cartridge is finished.

As the raw material works it way through the various production steps, small samples taken at regular intervals are checked to confirm that quality standards are being met. This is not done by whim, but rather by carefully prescribed procedures for ammunition quality levels (AQLs). These samples may be checked for lead hardness, brass structure and hardness, primer sensitivity, and many other criteria besides dimensional measurements. In addition, samples of completed ammunition are sent to the test range to check chamber pressure, accuracy, and functioning. Detailed computerized records are kept of every measurement, inspection, and test.

Note that quality checks run at the beginning of the operation are designed to prevent making large quantities of defective product. Quality checks made during the production run confirm that quality standards are being maintained. Failure to meet quality standards at any stage may cause the production process to stop while corrective action is taken.

INSPECTION - VISUAL

Finished ammunition coming off the loading machines is subjected to a visual inspection to cull rounds with dents, dings, debris, and other visual imperfections. Only then is the completed lot of ammunition released for packing and sales to customers. Loaded ammunition is one of the most tested and inspected products on the market today.

INSPECTION - GAUGE AND WEIGH

A gauge and weigh machine was an inspection device that weighed each cartridge and checked basic outer dimensions such as overall loaded length. In appearance, it looked like a series of spokes on a wheel hinged in the middle. On the end of each spoke was a small platform in which a cartridge was laid. A cartridge that weighed too little would allow the spoke to rise while a cartridge that was too heavy caused the spoke to sink. Rejected cartridges were knocked off the platform into separate reject bins while those passing weight testing were subjected to dimensional tests. Those failing dimensional tests were also dropped into a reject bin. Gauge and weigh machines have now become obsolete as they cannot keep up with the production rates of modern high speed manufacturing technology. They have been replaced by computerized optical inspection machines that can keep up with high production rates and also run more checks on the cartridge.

What Is A Production Lot Of Ammunition?

Ammunition is made in lots for quality control purposes. Each lot is assigned a unique number/letter code normally indicating the shift, day, year and machine number used for loading. For this reason, the correct term is lot code or day code and not lot number. Each manufacturer develops and applies their own lot coding system as there is no industry standard.

There is no set amount of ammunition in a lot, however most production lots are at least 40,000 rounds. Often, a lot code is assigned to the output of a given machine over one shift. In other instances, if the shift changes, but the loading machine continues to run, the lot code may stay the same. Each manufacturer has different procedures for determining this.

INSPECTION - OPTICAL

To keep up with high speed ammunition manufacturing technology, high speed, computer-controlled optical inspection machines have been developed. These machines function as optical comparators. Each cartridge is scanned optically to actually measure a number of characteristics such as overall loaded length, case length, head diameter, rim diameter, and shoulder diameter among other things. In addition, it checks the cartridge for blemishes, dirt, dents, holes, and folds. Variants of these machines can check primed empty cartridge cases. These sophisticated inspection machines are very capable, but also very expensive. As such, they are affordable only by large manufacturers.

TESTING MAXIMUM AVERAGE PRESSURE AND VELOCITY

Testing maximum average pressure and velocity is accomplished by taking small samples of loaded ammunition on a carefully timed basis off production machinery. These samples are then subjected to tests to determine the actual maximum average pressure and velocity. The results of these tests are carefully recorded, computerized, and retained for a number of years according to company policy. See Chapter 43: Interior Ballistics for information on testing equipment and techniques.

Here it is significant to note that sampling and testing is conducted by quality control personnel who are not members of the production department. Quality control personnel are members of a separate department and report to supervisors through an independent chain of command. In the event of poor quality coming off a given machine, the quality control department normally has the authority to stop product until the problem has been corrected.

TESTING PRIMER SENSITIVITY

Sensitivity is an extremely important characteristic of primers. If a primer is too sensitive, it may go off prematurely, before the gun has locked. If it is not sensitive enough, misfires or hang fires can result. For these reasons, industry standards have been established for primer sensitivity.

Primer sensitivity is tested in a drop test fixture. It drops a 1.94 or 3.94 ounce steel ball from a measured height onto a primer. At a given minimum height, none of the primers struck by the steel ball should fire. At a given height above this, all primers must fire. The heights for this are carefully specified based on many decades of experience. The following abridged chart summarizes this.

Height In Millimeters At Which 100% Of Primers Must Fire

Case Type	Small Rifle	Small Pistol	Large Rifle	Large Pistol
		Primer Size		
Rimmed	325	255	275	250
Rimless	335	205	305	290

Note the difference between rifle and pistol primers of similar size. The higher numbers needed for rimless cases are due to the cushioning effect of the cartridge shoulder.

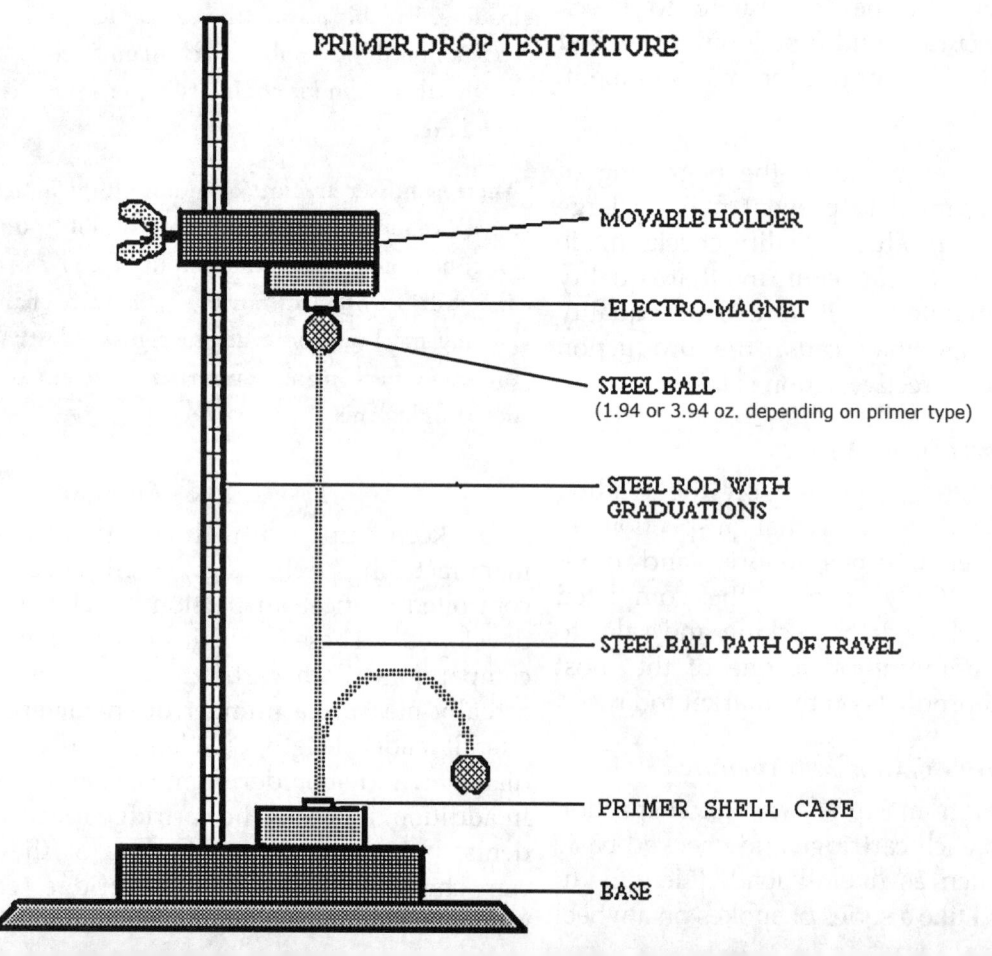

PRIMER DROP TEST FIXTURE

MOVABLE HOLDER

ELECTRO-MAGNET

STEEL BALL
(1.94 or 3.94 oz. depending on primer type)

STEEL ROD WITH GRADUATIONS

STEEL BALL PATH OF TRAVEL

PRIMER SHELL CASE

BASE

TESTING SHOTSHELL PATTERNS

Most ammunition manufacturers are especially sensitive about the quality of their shotshells. They are particularly concerned about target loads for trap, skeet, and sporting clays competition. There is a valid reason for this. Competitive shooters fire large quantities of shells. In doing so, they become keen judges of quality and tend to be outspoken opinion leaders. As competitions are heavily publicized, success or failure in quality control becomes news – fast.

In the case of hunting ammunition, poor quality control quickly circulates by word-of-mouth at gun clubs and gun stores. As hunting loads command premium prices, consistent quality control is very important to retain market share.

Of course, shotshells are subjected to many of the same batteries of inspections, testing, and firing as centerfire and rimfire ammunition. In addition, shotshells are subjected to pattern quality tests. These tests are fired at 40 yards using a full choke barrel. Quality is directly proportional to the percentage of the shotshell's total number of pellets which strike within a 30 inch circle, and how evenly those strikes are distributed throughout the circle. Visual inspection also plays an important part in target load marketing. Where necessary, ammunition makers may conduct a 100% visual inspection of certain lots to assure the quality is above reproach. For these inspections, the quality of the crimp and cleanliness are especially important.

Pattern quality is an important part of shotshell performance. Consequently, shotshell manufacturers pay considerable attention to this. Industry standard tests have been developed for pattern testing. The procedure is generally as follows:

- **Select a 25 round box of shotshells. Cut ten shotshells open and carefully count the number of pellets in each shell. Average the results.**

- **Fire ten rounds from the same box on ten large pieces of paper set up at a measured 40 yards. Mark an aiming point on the sheets before firing.**

- **With the paper sheets on a large white surface, draw a 30" diameter circle that will enclose the largest number of pellet holes.**

- **Draw a 20" diameter circle concentrically inside the 30" circle.**

- **Divide the circles evenly with one vertical line and one horizontal line to create four quadrants of two segments each inside the circles.**

- **Count the number of pellet holes in each segment and both circles. Average the results.**

- **Divide the average number of hits by the average number of pellets, per shell, to determine hit percentages.**

- **This system will allow the following aspects of a pattern to be evaluated:**
  - Hit distribution
    - Central thickening
    - Hit percentage in quadrants
    - Hit percentage in segments
  - Center of impact
  - Center of impact in relation to aiming point
  - Choke performance

Obviously, conducting pattern tests is a very labor intensive process, so shotshell manufacturers do not test the pattern performance of every lot of shotshells made. However, they do test samples on a regular basis and keep detailed records. This enables them to quickly judge the performance of any particular load without conducting daily tests.

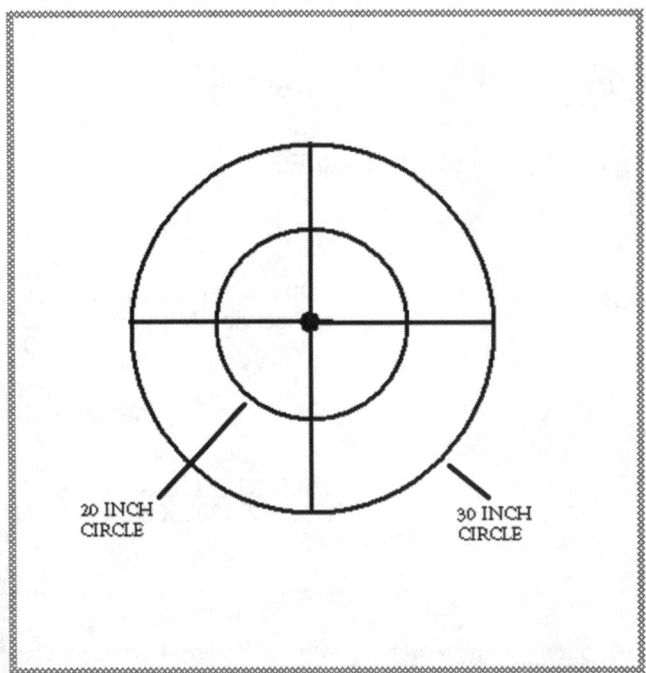

SHOTGUN PATTERN TEST DIAGRAM

20 INCH CIRCLE

30 INCH CIRCLE

FIRE AT 40 YARDS

FRANGIBILITY DEFINITION AND PERFORMANCE STANDARDS

The predominant current usage of frangible bulleted ammunition usage is by law enforcement and military, in training scenarios against steel targets that provide a much more realistic experience than traditional shooting at paper bull's eyes.

The primary goal of the ammunition is to reduce the shooter's exposure to toxic metallic lead from the projectiles and primer combustion components, as well as danger from ricocheting bullets and bullet fragments. In that regard, safety of the shooter and bystanders are held in highest regard, followed closely by protecting the environment from toxic materials. Both of those considerations are closely regulated by OSHA and EPA.

Lastly, the projectiles can not cause unacceptable damage to the steel targets or backstops. Potential damage is a function of both the bullet construction and impact velocity as well as the target material. From a practical standpoint, bullet impact velocities of over 2,800 fps will usually cause target damage regardless of the bullet materials incorporated.

In order to ensure shooter and bystander safety, performance standards have been established by the Federal Law Enforcement Training Center (FLETC) to define frangible ammunition and its performance. These standards generally have been adopted by most other federal, state, and local law enforcement agencies and the Sporting Arms and Ammunition Manufacturers Institute (SAAMI). A consolidated version, less toxicity standards, follows.

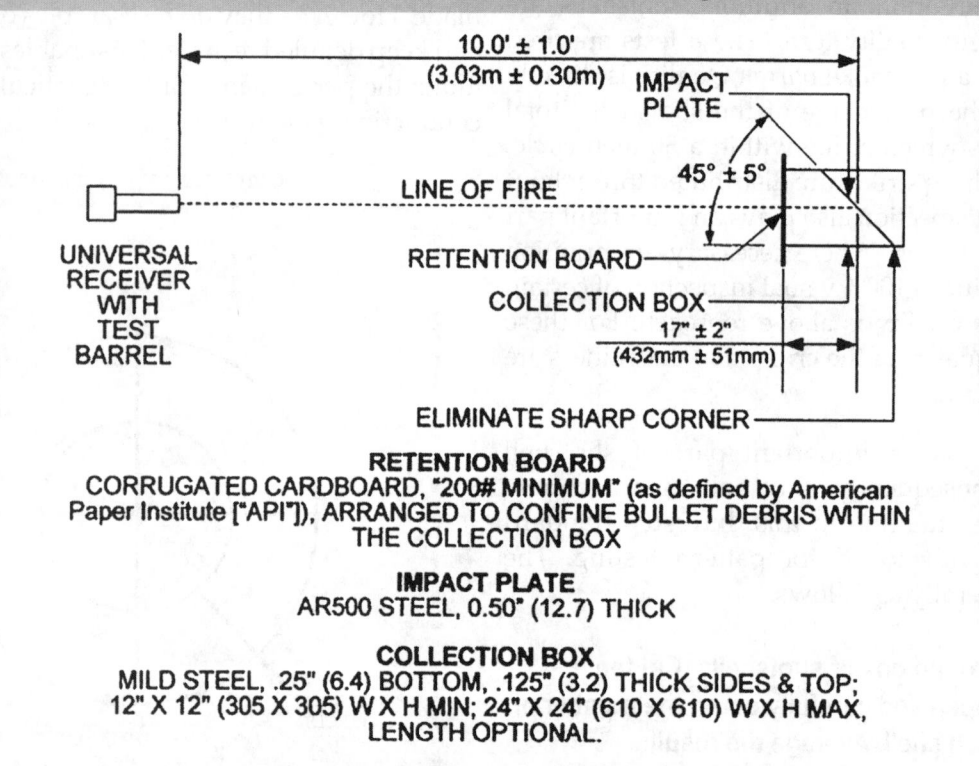

FRANGIBILITY STANDARDS
Equipment: 'Frangibility' Testing

RETENTION BOARD
CORRUGATED CARDBOARD, "200# MINIMUM" (as defined by American Paper Institute ["API"]), ARRANGED TO CONFINE BULLET DEBRIS WITHIN THE COLLECTION BOX

IMPACT PLATE
AR500 STEEL, 0.50" (12.7) THICK

COLLECTION BOX
MILD STEEL, .25" (6.4) BOTTOM, .125" (3.2) THICK SIDES & TOP; 12" X 12" (305 X 305) W X H MIN; 24" X 24" (610 X 610) W X H MAX, LENGTH OPTIONAL.

Performance Requirements: To be considered "frangible" such ammunition shall not produce any individual bullet fragments weighing more than 5% of the original nominal bullet weight when tested against AR500 steel targets as diagrammed above and as follows:

1. A sample size of ten (10) rounds shall be fired.
2. A minimum of 85% of the total nominal bullet weight shall be recovered for examination.
3. 'Splash-Back' requirements must also be satisfied.

FRANGIBILITY STANDARDS
Equipment: 'Splash-Back' Testing

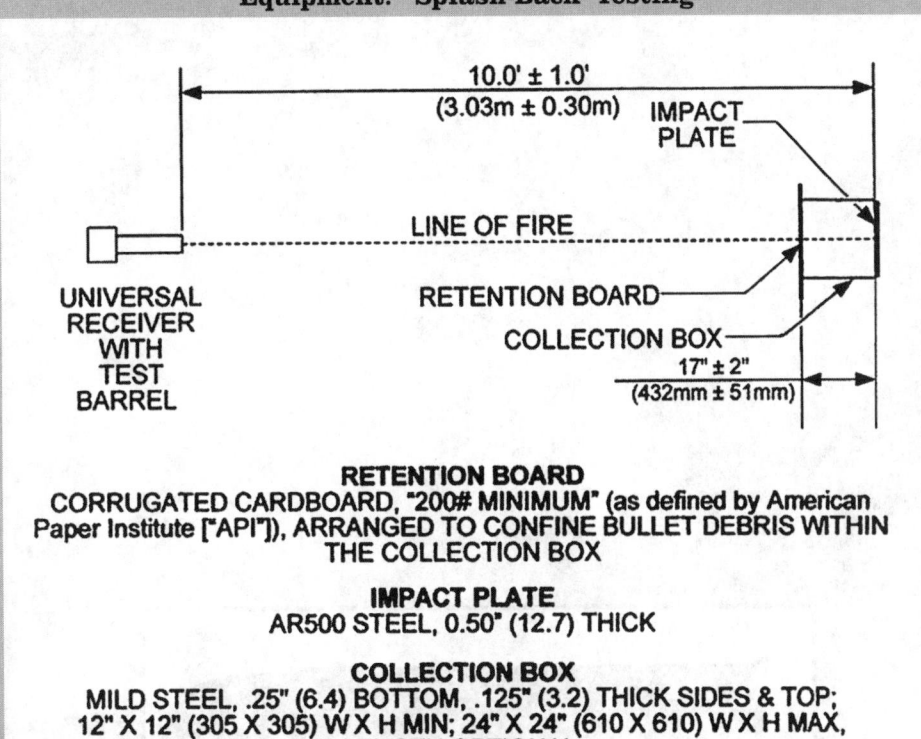

RETENTION BOARD
CORRUGATED CARDBOARD, "200# MINIMUM" (as defined by American Paper Institute ["API"]), ARRANGED TO CONFINE BULLET DEBRIS WITHIN THE COLLECTION BOX

IMPACT PLATE
AR500 STEEL, 0.50" (12.7) THICK

COLLECTION BOX
MILD STEEL, .25" (6.4) BOTTOM, .125" (3.2) THICK SIDES & TOP; 12" X 12" (305 X 305) W X H MIN; 24" X 24" (610 X 610) W X H MAX, LENGTH OPTIONAL.

Performance Requirements: To be considered safe for usage without unusual safety protection equipment worn by the shooter, "frangible" ammunition must exhibit the following characteristics when tested against AR500 steel targets as diagrammed above and as follows:

1. A sample size of ten (10) rounds shall be fired.
2. No bullet fragments shall be reflected back towards the shooter as evidenced by examination of the Retention Board after test firing.

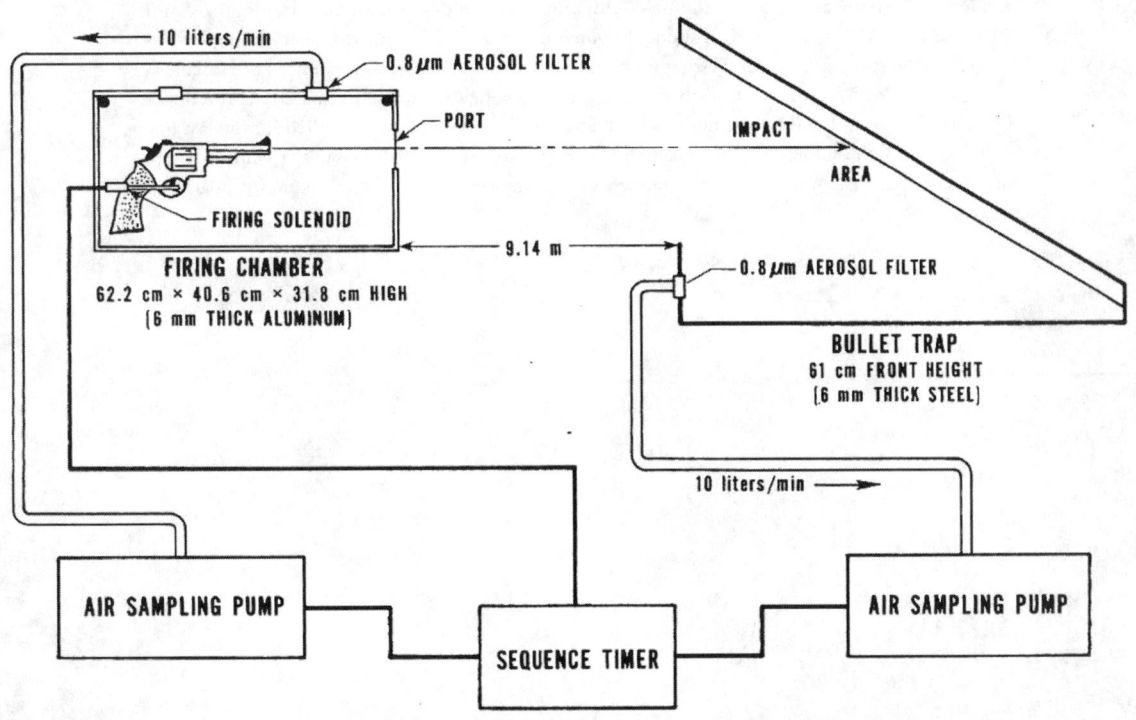

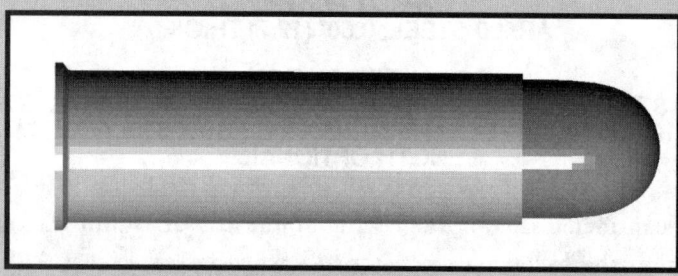

A Warm, Fuzzy Feeling in 12-gauge

.72 Paradox Shotshell

Assume for a moment you are in the field with your shotgun doing some bird hunting in South Africa or India 100 years ago when suddenly, you are attacked by a dangerous game animal. What do you do? Simply slip a pair of Westley-Richards Grouse Ejector, Kynoch Pergamoid or Holland & Holland Paradox 12-gauge 2 1/2 inch slug cartridges in your shotgun and dispatch the interloper. Of course, it was not quite that simple--a "ball and shot" shotgun barrel was rifled for the last four inches or so at the muzzle to impart a stabilizing spin to the 725-750-grain slug while having a minimal effect on shot loads. At close ranges, such slugs were considered adequate for boar, lion, tiger, and even elephant.

SECTION VI – RECOMMENDATIONS FOR USE
CHAPTER 33 : CENTERFIRE HANDGUN RECOMMENDATIONS

CHAPTER 33 HIGHLIGHTS:

- BEFORE PURCHASING A HANDGUN
- WHAT HANDGUNS ARE USED FOR
- HOW TO CHOOSE A HANDGUN CALIBER AND BULLET WEIGHT/STYLE
- HANDGUN CALIBERS RECOMMENDED FOR PERSONAL DEFENSE
- HANDGUN CALIBERS RECOMMENDED FOR HUNTING
- HANDGUN CALIBER RECOMMENDATIONS FOR TARGET SHOOTING AND COMPETITION
- HANDGUN CALIBER RECOMMENDATIONS FOR WILDERNESS SURVIVAL
- HANDGUN CALIBER RECOMMENDATIONS FOR LAW ENFORCEMENT

BEFORE PURCHASING A HANDGUN

The recommendations below are based on tradition backed by decades of experience in all parts of the world. Keep in mind that these should serve only as a guide. Your requirements may be different.

Before you purchase a handgun, check all federal, state, and local laws that apply to handgun purchase, ownership, use, transport, and storage. If you plan on interstate travel with your handgun, check the laws in each transit state as well as your destination that may apply.

WHAT HANDGUNS ARE USED FOR

Handguns serve purposes that differ considerably from long guns due to their size and weight. In general, handguns are easier to carry than long guns due to their compact dimensions and light weight. However, handguns fire cartridges and bullets of substantially less power than long guns. It is for this reason that selecting the proper caliber and bullet weight for your handgun is so important.

Here follows a list of popular tasks that handguns are normally used for:

1. **Personal defense/ home defense**
2. **Hunting small game and varmints**
3. **Backup gun for hunting big game**
4. **Target shooting/competition (informal and formal)**
5. **Wilderness survival**
6. **Training, practice, and qualification**
7. **Law enforcement**
8. **Military**

CHOOSING A HANDGUN

Handguns may be broken down into three categories:

1. **Revolvers**
   a. **Single-action only**
   b. **Double-action plus single-action**
   c. **Double-action-only**

2. **Pistols**
   a. **Single-action**
   b. **Double-action plus single-action**
   c. **Double-action-only**

3. **Other, including Derringers, single shot target guns, and miniatures**
   a. **Single shot**
   b. **Two shots**
   c. **Multi-shot**

From these choices, you must select the handgun type that meets your requirements. Once you have made this decision, you can begin the process of selecting the caliber and bullet that best meets your needs.

HOW TO CHOOSE A HANDGUN CALIBER AND BULLET WEIGHT/STYLE

Experienced handgunners use the following six-step process to make this decision:

1. **What is the primary use for the handgun?**
2. **What are your handling skills, marksmanship abilities, and sensitivity to recoil?**
3. **What will be the typical ranges and conditions when using your handgun?**
4. **Always select a caliber and bullet style/weight that best suits your primary purpose. Remember, there is no such thing as a perfect bullet for all purposes.**
5. **For defensive purposes, the object of your bullet is to incapacitate an assailant as quickly as possible. Choose a cartridge and bullet weight with enough ballistic performance to accomplish that goal.**
6. **The following series of charts has been distilled from many decades of experience. Use them to help you make your choice.**

Other Points To Keep In Mind

* Do not assume your handgun is zeroed just because it is new. Always zero your handgun before placing it into service.

* If you are recoil-sensitive, avoid Magnum calibers.
* If in doubt, err on the side of the heavier bullet or larger caliber.
* The more you shoot your handgun, the more familiar and comfortable you will be with it. Never trust a new, unfired handgun for personal defense.
* No two bullets are exactly alike, even if they are the same caliber, weight, and shape.
* After you have tested and selected a particular load, do not make last minute changes or substitutions.
* Bullet placement is more important than caliber or bullet weight and style.

HANDGUN CALIBERS RECOMMENDED FOR PERSONAL DEFENSE

The objective of any handgun cartridge selected for personal defense is to incapacitate an assailant as quickly as possible. The U.S. Army considers 58 ft.-lbs. of striking energy disabling on a human target and that 108 ft.-lbs. of striking energy will put a man down, at least temporarily.

Experts continue to debate how much striking energy and penetration from a handgun bullet is enough for immediate incapacitation of an assailant. However, there is near universal agreement that this figure is substantially higher than the Army figures quoted above. Although incapacitation measurement is not an exact science, most experts feel that a 115-gr. bullet having a striking energy of 325 ft.-lbs. at 7 yards is the minimum that can be recommended. Penetration should be from 6-8 inches with the bullet expanding to approximately twice the original diameter, retaining 90% or more of original weight and depositing all of its energy inside the target.

Evan Marshall, in his seminal book *Stopping Power*, provides the statistical results of his multi-year study of actual shooting incidents to determine the actual percentages of one shot incapacitation for various cartridges. An abridged listing is given here. For more information, the reader is referred to Marshall's comprehensive book on this subject.

HANDGUN CALIBERS RECOMMENDED FOR PERSONAL DEFENSE					
Caliber	Bullet Weight (grains)	Bullet Style	Muzzle Velocity (fps)	Muzzle Energy (ft.-lbs.)	Marshall percentage of one shot stops per Stopping Power
.25 Auto	50	FMJ	760	64	24%
.32 Auto	71	FMJ	905	129	49%
.380 Auto	90	JHP	1,000	200	69%
9mm Luger	115	JHP	1,225	383	83%
.357 SIG	125	JHP	1,350	505	92%
.40 S&W	165	JHP	1,150	396	94%
10 mm	175	JHP	1,290	647	88%
.45 Auto	230	JHP	900	415	96%
.38 Spl+P	125	JHP	945	248	72%
.357 Mag	125	JHP	1,440	575	96%
.41 Mag.	175	JHP	1,250	607	90%
.44 Spl	200	JHP	900	360	76%
.45 Colt	225	LHP	830	345	81%

Portrait of a perfectly expanded handgun bullet, in this case a Remington Golden Saber High Performance Jacket (HPJ). This bullet, designed for deep penetration, maximum expansion, and near 100% weight retention, is intended for personal defense and law enforcement use. Courtesy Remington 2012 catalog.

HANDGUN CALIBERS RECOMMENDED FOR HUNTING

The objective of any handgun cartridge selected for hunting is to kill the game as quickly and humanely as possible. That said, a handgun is a poor choice for hunting anything larger than varmints and pests. If you can, use a rifle.

Cartridges for handgun hunting fall into one of three categories that differ according to their muzzle energy and caliber.

1. Cartridges in calibers suitable for varmint and pest elimination

2. Cartridges for hunting medium and large game

3. Cartridges for use as a backup

VARMINT HUNTING AND PEST ELIMINATION

For varmint hunting and pest elimination, a pistol or revolver cartridge with an 85-125 grain JHP bullet and at least 225 ft.-lbs. of muzzle energy is a good choice. For all practical purposes, the popular calibers that can meet these requirements are:

1. 7.62x25mm Tokarev

2. .327 Federal

3. .38 Special +P

4. .357 SIG

5. 9mm Luger

As varmints and pests are small and thin skinned, there is no need for large bore magnum cartridges of .41 Magnum or above. Of course, there are a myriad of other calibers that are suitable, so if you do not see your favorite on the list, recognize that many other calibers are expensive and difficult to find.

In most states, varmint hunting and pest elimination do not require a hunting license. In addition, they are not regulated as to caliber, bullet diameter, or muzzle energy. However, check with your state fish and game department to confirm this information before going afield.

HUNTING MEDIUM GAME/LARGE THIN SKINNED GAME

For deer, antelope, and other medium game, a bullet with a diameter of .357 inches or above weighing 158 grains or more with a minimum muzzle energy of 500 ft.-lbs. is the best choice. Only a few Magnum revolver calibers meet these criteria. They are:

1. .357 Magnum

2. .41 Magnum

3. .44 Magnum

4. .454 Casull

In these calibers, recoil is manageable when fired from large, heavy revolvers with barrel lengths over six inches.

Here it must be noted that the .357 Magnum is borderline in this category. Some .357 Magnum loads with 158 grain bullets meet the criteria while some with lightweight bullets do not.

Today, many states allow handgun hunting during established hunting seasons. However, handgun hunting in some states is regulated as to caliber and muzzle energy. So, take nothing for granted–check with your local fish and game department before going afield.

BACKUP FOR BIG GAME HUNTING

As a backup caliber for big game hunting, a bullet with a diameter of .440 inches or above weighing 240 grains or more with a minimum muzzle energy of 900 ft.-lbs. is the best choice. Only a few revolver calibers meet these criteria:

1. .44 Magnum

2. .454 Casull

3. .460 S&W Magnum

4. .480 Ruger

5. .500 S&W Magnum

HANDGUN CALIBERS RECOMMENDED FOR HANDGUN HUNTING					
Caliber	Bullet Weight (grains)	Bullet Style	Muzzle Velocity (fps)	Muzzle Energy (ft.-lbs.)	Game Type
7.62x25mm Tokarev	85	JHP	1,625	511	Varmints/pests
.327 Federal	85	JHP	1,400	370	
.38 Special+P	125	JHP	945	248	
.357 SIG	125	JHP	1,350	506	
9mm Luger	115	JHP	1,225	383	
.357 Magnum	158	JHP	1,240	540	Medium Game
.41 Magnum	210	JHP	1,230	705	
.44 Magnum	240	JHP	1,230	805	
.454 Casull	250	JHP	1,530	1,300	
.44 Magnum	240	JHP	1,300	900	Backup
.454 Casull	300	JSP	1,520	1,540	
.460 S&W Mag	300	JSP	1,750	2,040	
.480 Ruger	275	JSP	1,350	1,980	
.500 S&W Mag	325	JSP	1,800	2,340	

All of these cartridges generate heavy recoil despite the fact that they are fired from large, heavyweight revolvers. But, this begs the question: "What is your life worth in an emergency?"

Carrying a large caliber revolver as a backup gun falls in a regulatory gray area in some states. Often, carrying a backup carry gun receives no mention in state hunting regulations. Here it must be noted that such a gun must be carried in plain sight and not concealed. It also must not be your primary hunting gun. Given the aforementioned stipulations, backup guns are usually acceptable.

Modern handgun hunting bullets expand reliably over a wide range of striking velocities. This is illustrated very well by this photo showing the expansion of the Swift A-Frame bullet as loaded into Federal Premium handgun ammunition. Courtesy Federal 2012 catalog.

HANDGUN CALIBER RECOMMENDATIONS FOR TARGET SHOOTING AND COMPETITION

In general, handgun calibers for target shooting may be divided into two categories: those for revolvers and those for pistols.

REVOLVERS

The most popular caliber for bullseye target shooting with a revolver is the .38 Special loaded with 148 grain lead wadcutters. Such loads are low velocity with mild recoil. The flat nose of the wadcutter bullet cuts a clean, round hole in paper targets.

For combat pistol competition, full power loads must be used in order to reliably knock down the steel targets. For this type of competition, the .357 Magnum calibers is a popular choice.

For knocking down heavy steel silhouette targets at long ranges, a big Magnum revolver cartridge must be used. The .44 Magnum and .458 Casull are popular choices.

Target shooting with revolvers has declined in recent years as pistols have supplanted revolvers in law enforcement and other types of competition.

PISTOLS

For target shooting, the .45 Auto reigns supreme. In this caliber, mild low velocity loads with FMI semi-wadcutter bullets are the most popular. For some types of competition, full power 230 grain FMJ round nose ammunition must be used.

In response to the U.S. Army adopting the 9mm Luger caliber handguns in the later 1980s, interest in target shooting with this caliber has increased. A popular load for this caliber is a 115 grain semi-wadcutter FMJ bullet.

Note that match pistol competition is dominated by semi-wadcutter FMJ bullets. This is due to the need for a short ogive to assure feeding and a sharp shoulder to cut a clean, round hole in the paper target.

For combat pistol competition, full power loads must be used to reliably knock down the steel targets. The most popular calibers for this type of competition are the 9mm Luger, .40 S&W, and .45 Auto.

HANDGUN CALIBER RECOMMENDATIONS FOR WILDERNESS SURVIVAL

For this application, you must consider a cartridge having two characteristics:

1. **A cartridge with enough power to protect yourself from dangerous game**

2. **A cartridge capable of reliably taking game for eating**

These criteria point toward a large bore Magnum cartridge in a revolver. Most experts in this area consider the .357 Magnum cartridge the minimum caliber for this application with the .44 Magnum being a safer choice.

HANDGUN CALIBER RECOMMENDATIONS FOR LAW ENFORCEMENT

At present, approximately 60% of all law enforcement agencies use the .40 S&W cartridge, with 35% using the 9mm Luger and 5% using the .45 Auto. Each law enforcement agency has adopted their cartridge of choice following a lengthy process of setting local requirements, testing, and evaluating the results.

Many people seeking a suitable cartridge for personal defense have used these statistics to help them make a choice.

CHAPTER 34 : CENTERFIRE RIFLE RECOMMENDATIONS

CHAPTER 34 HIGHLIGHTS:

- BEFORE GOING AFIELD
- HOW TO CHOOSE A RIFLE CALIBER AND BULLET
- VARMINTS, SMALL PREDATORS, RODENTS, AND PESTS
- EDIBLE SMALL GAME AND FURBEARERS
- LIGHT AND MEDIUM THIN-SKINNED GAME
- LARGE HEAVY GAME
- DANGEROUS GAME

BEFORE GOING AFIELD

The recommendations below are based on tradition and decades of hunter experience in all parts of the world. Keep in mind that these should serve only as a guide; your requirements may be different.

BEFORE you go afield, check all federal, state, and local laws in your state regarding minimum caliber and/or striking energy requirements. If you are going beyond your immediate area, check with the local guide or local authorities in that area.

HOW TO CHOOSE A RIFLE CALIBER AND BULLET

Experienced hunters use a six step process to make this decision:

- **Determine the type of game you will be hunting. If you are going to hunt two or more species of game at the same time, select a caliber adequate for both.**

- **Make an honest determination of your marksmanship abilities and sensitivity to recoil.**

- **Determine the typical conditions and ranges where you will be hunting.**

- **Select an appropriate caliber and a bullet weight for the type of game hunted from the charts provided.**

- **Zero your rifle to verify accuracy and compatibility by firing at least one box of cartridges.**

- **Determine the point blank range of your rifle and zero accordingly.**

STICK TO YOUR GUNS

The meaning of this phrase is to hold your position and defend it. It dates back to the days of muzzle loading cannon which could fire canister or grape shot to great effect. Recognizing the reluctance of enemy soldiers to attack an artillery position, the gun crews were urged to "stick to your guns" for protection.

Points To Keep In Mind

* Do not assume your rifle is zeroed just because it was zeroed last year. Always re-zero your rifle before going hunting.

* Difficult hunting conditions may require the use of a premium bullet and/or Magnum cartridge. For long ranges (beyond 200 yards), a boat tail bullet can offer a significant advantage. For tough game, a bonded core, dual core, or expanding monolithic bullet will provide an advantage.

* If you are recoil-sensitive, avoid Magnum calibers.

* If in doubt, err on the side of the heavier bullet or larger caliber.

* The more you shoot your rifle, the more familiar and comfortable you will be with it. Never take a new (to you) unfired (by you) rifle hunting.

* No two bullets are exactly alike, even if they are the same caliber, weight, and shape.

* After you have tested and selected a particular load, do not make last minute changes or substitutions.

* Bullet placement is more important than caliber or weight.

VARMINTS, SMALL PREDATORS, RODENTS, AND PESTS

This group includes: prairie dog, ground squirrel, ground hog, marmot, nutria, badger, porcupine, skunk, crow, coyote, lynx, and bobcat.

Small varmints can be difficult targets, especially on a windy day. In addition, they quickly learn the effective range of your ammunition and stay beyond it. Larger varmints are normally wary of humans, placing a premium on calling and camouflage.

Many land owners prefer that varmint hunters use lightweight bullets which disintegrate on impact to prevent ricochets. Noise is also a consideration for many landowners.

For these reasons, most hunters recommend high velocity lightweight bullets with the flattest possible trajectory for varmints. Both soft point and hollow point bullets are offered in weights ranging from 35 to 63 grains. Bullet weights of 40 and 45 grains are the most popular choice in the smaller cartridges while the larger cartridge favorites are 50 and 55 grain weights.

RAMROD

In the modern vernacular, a ramrod is a mid-level manager charged with making things happen. Of course, a ramrod also remains a gun cleaning tool as well. However, the vernacular meaning comes from muzzle loading days when a shooter needed a ramrod to seat the bullet on the powder charge. In the days of Old West cattle drives, the trail boss was called the ramrod.

VARMINT CARTRIDGE RECOMMENDATIONS

Caliber	Max Effective Range (yds.)	Prairie Dog	Skunk/ Badger	Ground Hog/ Rock Chuck	Lynx/ Bobcat	Coyote
.204 Ruger	300	X	X	X		
.22 Hornet	150	X	X			
.218 Bee	200	X	X			
.221 Fireball	200	X	X			
.222 Rem.	200	X	X	X	X	X
.223 Rem.	250	X	X	X	X	X
.223 WSSM	350	X	X	X	X	X
.22-250 Rem.	350	X	X	X	X	X
.220 Swift	400	X	X	X	X	X
.243 Win.	300		X	X	X	X
6mm Rem.	300		X	X	X	X

Points To Keep In Mind

* The smaller cartridges make substantially less noise than the large cartridges.

* On a windy day, a large high velocity cartridge is better.

* When shooting large numbers of varmints from fixed positions, the .223 Rem. and the .22-250 Rem. are the best choices because of their limited recoil. Always use a heavy barrel rifle for this application.

* Rapid firing larger cartridges can quickly overheat your barrel.

* The 6mm calibers are best for the larger varmints.

* Five hundred yards is the maximum effective range for most varmint cartridges.

* The maximum effective range of a 40 or 45 grain bullet is about 200 yards even when fired from a larger cartridge.

* Most larger .22 caliber cartridges work best with 55 grain bullets.

EDIBLE SMALL GAME AND FURBEARERS

The edible small game group includes: rabbit, raccoon, squirrel, and opossum.

The furbearer group includes: fox, mink, beaver, and muskrat.

Important considerations when hunting these species with a centerfire rifle are spoiling the meat and/or damaging the pelt. Many hunters use non-expanding, full metal jacket bullets to harvest these animals. As ranges are short and the animals relatively small, .22 caliber centerfire cartridges are preferred with FMJ bullets of 40-55 grains in weight.

Chilled Shot

Chilled shot is an obsolete term for hard lead shot. For many years, the term chilled shot was used to differentiate hard shot from soft shot. This terminology is seldom used today as nearly all lead shot is hardened to some extent.

EDIBLE SMALL GAME AND FURBEARER RECOMMENDATIONS
40 to 55 grain FMJ Bullets

Caliber	Max Effective Range (yds.)	Raccoon	Opossum	Squirrel/ Rabbit	Fox	Mink	Beaver	Muskrat
.22 Hornet	150	X	X	X	X	X	X	X
.218 Bee	200	X	X	X	X	X	X	X
.221 Fireball	200	X	X	X	X	X	X	X
.222 Rem.	200	X	X	X	X	X	X	X
.223 Rem.	250	X	X	X	X	X	X	X

LIGHT AND MEDIUM THIN-SKINNED GAME

In this group are some of the most popular game animals in the world, namely: deer, antelope, black bear, sheep, goat, caribou, and javelina.

Hunting any of these species does not require magnum calibers or heavy bullets at ranges below 300 yards. However the conditions in which they are hunted can range from a few feet (javelina, black bear) to average (deer, caribou), to relatively long ranges (antelope, sheep), to very long range (over 300 yards). For this reason, it is important to match your cartridge and bullet weight to the hunting conditions in your area (see chart).

Popular cartridges for this type of hunting are loaded with bullet weights from 100 to 350 grains. Most hunters have found that bullets weighing between 120 and 350 grains are the best choice with heavier or lighter weight bullets reserved for special circumstances such as very close ranges or light animals.

Hunters can choose among a wide range of cartridges which are suitable for this type of hunting, ranging from neo-classic to ultra-modern. Making a selection can be difficult, so recommendations have been broken down into three range classifications.

A LOOSE CANNON

This phrase dates back to the days of iron men and wooden sailing ships. Gun decks of a man o' war were crowded with heavy cannons and equipment. As the cannons weighed several tons, they were secured in place with blocks and ropes when not in use. In a rough sea, the pitch and roll of the ship could cause a cannon to break loose and uncontrollably roll around the gun deck, crushing crew members and destroying equipment.

Today, this phrase holds the same meaning of being "dangerously out of control" and a threat to everyone on the corporate gun deck.

OVER A BARREL

Most people assume this has something to do with going over Niagara Falls. Not so. This is yet another colorful phrase from the days of man o' war sailing ships. Crew members who committed serious offenses or broke naval regulations could be tied over a cannon barrel and flogged as punishment.

Today, this phrase carries the meaning of being in a hopeless, desperate personal situation. However, many traditional managers still believe that "The floggings will continue until morale improves".

LIGHT AND MEDIUM THIN-SKINNED GAME RECOMMENDATIONS

SHORT RANGE 1-100 YARDS

150 to 405 grain Soft Point Bullets
1,000 ft-lbs. Minimum Striking Energy at 100 Yards

Caliber	Javelina	Deer	Black Bear
.257 Robts	X	X	
.30-30 Win.	X	X	X
.308 Win.	X	X	X
7.62x39mm	X	X	
.32 Win. Spl	X	X	X
.338 Fed.	X	X	X
.35 Rem.	X	X	X
.375 Win.	X	X	X
.44 Mag.	X	X	
.444 Marlin	X	X	X
.450 Marlin	X	X	X
12-ga. Slug	X	X	X
.348 Win.	X	X	X
.358 Win.	X	X	X
.38-55 Win.	X	X	X
.45-70 Gov't	X	X	X

NORMAL RANGE 100-200 YARDS

100 to 405 grain Soft Point Bullets
1,300 ft.-lbs. Minimum Striking Energy at 200 Yards

Caliber	Deer	Black Bear	Caribou	Antelope	Sheep
.243 Win.	X			X	
6mm Rem.	X			X	
.25-06 Rem.	X	X		X	X
.260 Rem.	X				
6.5x55mm Swed.	X	X		X	
.270 Win.	X	X	X	X	X
7mm-08 Rem.	X	X		X	
.280 Rem.	X	X	X	X	X
7x57mm Mauser	X	X	X	X	X
7mm STW		X	X	X	X
7.62x54Rmm	X	X	X		
.30-'06 Spr.	X	X	X	X	X
.30-40 Krag	X	X		X	
.300 Savage	X	X		X	
.303 British	X	X	X	X	X
.308 Win.	X	X	X	X	X
.338 Fed.	X	X	X		
.348 Win.	X	X	X		
.358 Win.	X	X	X		
.45-70 Gov't.	X	X			

LONG RANGE 200-300 YARDS

120 to 270 grain Soft Point Bullets
1,300 ft.-lbs. Minimum Striking Energy at 300 Yards

Caliber	Deer	Black Bear	Caribou	Antelope	Sheep	Goat
.25-06 Rem.	X	X		X	X	X
.270 Win.	X	X	X	X	X	X
7x57mm Mauser	X	X		X	X	
.30-'06 Spr.	X	X	X	X	X	X
.308 Win.	X	X	X	X	X	
.30-40 Krag	X	X				
.303 British	X	X				
.25 WSSM	X			X	X	X
.270 WSM	X	X	X	X	X	X
.270 Wby. Mag.	X	X	X	X	X	X
7mm Wby. Mag.	X	X	X	X	X	X
7mm WSM	X	X	X	X	X	X
7mm Rem. Mag.	X	X	X	X	X	X
.300 H&H Mag	X	X	X	X	X	
.300 Win. Mag.	X	X	X	X	X	X
.300 WSM	X	X	X	X	X	X
.300 Wby. Mag.	X	X	X	X	X	X
.300 RSUM	X	X	X	X	X	X

VERY LONG RANGE 300-400 YARDS

130 to 180 grain Soft Point Bullets
1,300 ft.-lbs. Minimum Striking Energy at 400 Yards

Caliber	Deer	Black Bear	Caribou	Antelope	Sheep	Goat
.270 Win.	X	X	X	X	X	X
7mm STW	X	X	X	X	X	X
.30-'06 Spr.	X	X	X	X	X	X

VERY LONG RANGE 300-400 YARDS

Caliber	Deer	Black Bear	Caribou	Antelope	Sheep	Goat
.270 WSM	X	X	X	X	X	X
.270 Wby. Mag.	X	X	X	X	X	X
7mm Wby. Mag.	X	X	X	X	X	X
7mm WSM	X	X	X	X	X	X
7mm Rem. Mag.	X	X	X	X	X	X
.300 H&H Mag.	X	X	X	X	X	X
.300 Win Mag.	X	X	X	X	X	X
.300 WSM	X	X	X	X	X	X
.300 Wby. Mag.	X	X	X	X	X	X
.300 RUM	X	X	X	X	X	X

Points To Keep In Mind

* The limited performance of nearly all classic calibers restricts their effective range to 100 yards or less.

* Magnum calibers are not necessary for hunting at ranges of 200 yards or less as standard calibers offer excellent ballistic performance at such ranges.

* Magnum calibers offer a significant ballistic advantage at longer ranges – provided you can handle the recoil.

* The typical hunter will find it very difficult to hit a game animal at ranges beyond 200 yards. Never take unnecessarily long shots unless you are equipped and trained for it.

* Judging range correctly takes practice. As most hunters underestimate range, using a laser range finder decreases missed or wounding shots.

* Bullet placement is everything.

* Premium bullets are a good choice for long range shots.

> "Tracers work both ways."
>
> - *Murphy's Laws of Combat No. 27*

LARGE HEAVY GAME

The large heavy game category includes: elk, moose, bison, musk ox, water buffalo, kudu, eland, zebra, and other game weighing 750 pounds or more.

This category of game requires two different approaches to cartridge and bullet selection. The strength and bulk of these animals demand heavy bullets which strike with plenty of energy and penetrate deeply. Elk, bison, kudu, and zebra must be taken at long ranges, where big Magnums are a good choice. On the other hand, moose, musk ox, eland, and water buffalo are normally hunted at shorter ranges where some standard calibers can be used.

LARGE HEAVY GAME RECOMMENDATIONS NORMAL RANGE 100-200 YARDS

180 to 270 grain Soft Point Bullets, 2,300 ft.-lbs. Minimum Striking Energy at 200 Yards

Caliber	Moose	Musk Ox	Eland	Water Buffalo
.300 WSM	X	X	X	
.300 Win. Mag.	X	X	X	
.300 RUM	X	X	X	X
.300 Wby. Mag.	X	X	X	X
8mm Rem. Mag.	X	X	X	X
.325 WSM	X	X	X	X
.338 Win. Mag.	X	X	X	X
.338 RUM	X	X	X	X
.340 Wby. Mag	X	X	X	X
.350 Rem. Mag.	X	X	X	X
.375 H&H Mag.	X	X	X	X
.375 RUM	X	X	X	X

LONG RANGE 200-300 YARDS

180 to 300 grain Soft Point Bullets 2,300 ft.-lbs. Minimum Striking Energy at 300 Yards

Caliber	Moose	Musk Ox	Eland	Water Buffalo
.300 WSM	X	X		
.300 Win. Mag.	X	X		
.300 RUM	X	X	X	X
.300 Wby. Mag.	X	X	X	X
.30-378 Wby. Mag.	X	X	X	X
8mm Rem. Mag.	X	X	X	X
.325 WSM	X	X	X	X
.338 Win. Mag.	X	X	X	X
.338 RUM	X	X	X	X
.340 Wby. Mag	X	X	X	X
.338 Lapua Mag.	X	X	X	X
.375 H&H Mag.	X	X	X	X
.375 RUM	X	X	X	X

Points To Keep In Mind

* Some standard calibers can be used to harvest the above game at ranges of 100 yards or less provided their striking energy meets the 2,300 ft.-lb. minimum.

* Always "take enough gun", in other words a caliber big enough to do the job cleanly and effectively.
* Never hunt with more gun than you can handle.
* When in doubt, select the heavier bullet in any caliber.
* If you are uncertain about hitting the target, get closer.
* Cartridges with a bullet diameter of less than 7mm should not be used for hunting these species.
* Most African game is much "tougher" than North American or European species.
* Premium bullets are a good choice for this type of hunting.

ZEROING IN AT CLOSE RANGE

Common practice is to zero a rifle at one hundred yards. This is the reason most industry ballistic charts list a zero range at that distance.

For those shooters who do not have access to a one hundred yard range, your rifle can be sighted in at fifty yards in such a way that you will have a one hundred or two hundred yard zero. Here is the proper procedure:

* Go to the section in ballistics charts marked "Trajectory" or "Height of the Bullet Above or Below Line of Sight". Select a one hundred or two yard zero as you prefer.
* Refer to the ammunition manufacturer's catalog for "Trajectory" or "Height of the Bullet Above or Below the Line of Sight" data for your specific cartridge, bullet weight, and zero range.
* Adjust your rifle's sights so that the bullets hit above or below the aiming point the distance shown in the zero range data for 50 yards.
* Always fire five shot groups when adjusting your sights. Note that your rifle may require a small number of additional sight adjustments in the field.

DANGEROUS GAME

Any list of dangerous game must include: elephant, lion, tiger, hippopotamus, cape buffalo, rhinoceros, and large bears (grizzly, Kodiak, polar).

These species are hunted at close ranges – normally less than 100 yards. This makes a large, heavy bullet with massive striking energy mandatory. Although large bears, lions, or tigers are normally hunted with soft point bullets, the rest are taken with solids to assure penetration.

Experienced hunters nearly all agree that the minimum caliber for hunting this type of animal is the .375 H&H Magnum. They also recommend a larger caliber provided you can handle the heavy recoil.

Points To Keep In Mind
* Always hunt dangerous game with a licensed professional hunter armed with a large caliber backup rifle.
* All dangerous game cartridges have very heavy recoil. Recognize that you may not be able to handle the recoil of some of these calibers.
* These calibers are designed for short ranges only. Do not try shots over 100 yards.
* These calibers are nearly useless for any other type of hunting.

Note to Hunters Who Did Not Find Their Favorite Cartridge on Any of the Above Charts:

* It is impossible to include every potential hunting cartridge in charts such as these.
* These charts are intended only as a general guide, not an exhaustive list.

DANGEROUS GAME RECOMMENDATIONS
NORMAL RANGE 1-50 YARDS

Minimum 300 grain Full Metal Jacket Bullets
3,500 ft.-lbs. Minimum Striking Energy at 100 Yards

Caliber	Elephant	Cape Buffalo	Lion	Hippo	Rhino	Tiger	Bear
.375 H&H Mag.			X	X		X	X
.375 Wby. Mag.			X	X		X	X
.416 Rigby	X	X	X	X	X	X	X
.416 Rem. Mag.	X	X	X	X	X	X	X
.416 Wby. Mag.	X	X	X	X	X	X	X
.458 Win. Mag.	X	X	X	X	X	X	X
.458 Lott	X	X	X	X	X	X	X
.460 Wby. Mag.	X	X	X	X	X	X	X
.470 Nitro Exp.	X	X	X	X	X	X	
.577 Nitro Exp.	X	X	X	X	X		

- Hunting is not an exact science.
- The variety of cartridges and bullets available is part of the fun.
- You are entitled to your opinion.

- I am entitled to mine.
- Of course, another hunter may disagree with both of us.
- You and I are right, but that third fellow did not know what he was talking about.

A bonded core rifle bullet such as this .30 caliber Remington Core-Lokt Ultra Bonded will expand and remain intact over a wide range of striking velocities. Courtesy Remington.

Hornady .22-250 Rem. Superformance Becomes The Highest Muzzle Velocity Cartridge on the Market

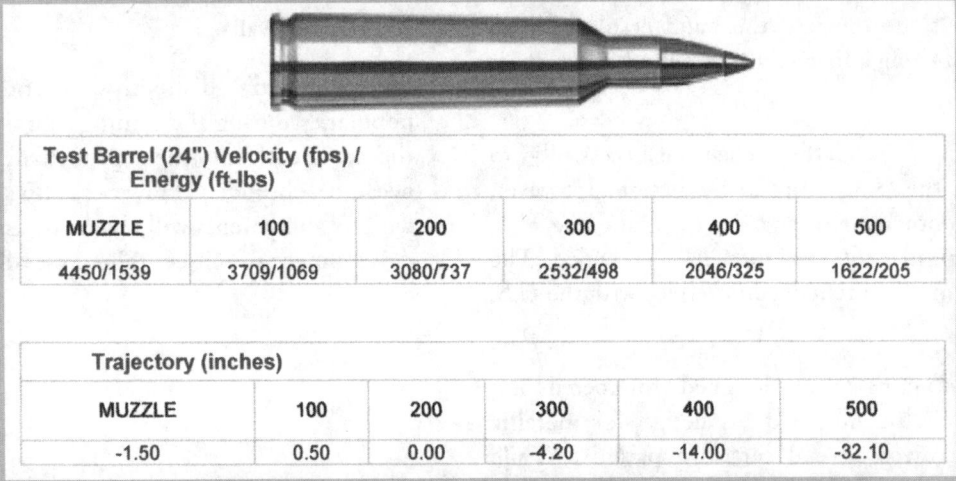

Test Barrel (24") Velocity (fps) / Energy (ft-lbs)					
MUZZLE	100	200	300	400	500
4450/1539	3709/1069	3080/737	2532/498	2046/325	1622/205

Trajectory (inches)					
MUZZLE	100	200	300	400	500
-1.50	0.50	0.00	-4.20	-14.00	-32.10

By combining new, high energy propellants with their NTX bullet technology, Hornady Manufacturing Co. developed their new Superformance line of ultra-high velocity centerfire rifle ammunition. Introduced in four popular calibers, Superformance ammunition offers muzzle velocities of 100-200 fps or more than standard loads.

Undoubtedly, the crowning example of Superformance ammunition performance is the familiar .22-250 Rem. cartridge. With a sizzling muzzle velocity of 4,450 fps, it is by far the highest muzzle velocity factory-loaded cartridge on the market!

The NTX 35 grain bullet (ballistic coefficient .170) remains supersonic to nearly 600 yards. At 200 yards, remaining velocity is 3,080 fps with a trajectory of 0 inches! Muzzle velocities in this elevated level offer increased effective range, flatter trajectory, less wind drift, and explosive expansion. Superformance .22-250 Rem. ammunition is suitable for use in all rifles factory-chambered for that caliber.

Or, hunters can choose a Superformance load in .222 Rem. (MV 3,345 fps), .223 Rem. (MV 3,465 fps), or .243 Win. (MV 3945 fps). Courtesy Hornady Manufacturing Co.

DR. RICHARD J. GATLING
1818-1903

Dentist, Cartridge Designer, and Inventor of the Multi-Barrel Gatling Gun

As a young man in his native North Carolina, Richard Gatling worked as a fisherman, court clerk, storekeeper, and teacher. He studied dentistry, but never practiced it as his real interest lay in inventing. His crowning invention was the Gatling gun; the first successful machine gun. Gatling patented his gun design in 1862 and founded the Gatling Gun Company in Indianapolis, Indiana to manufacture it. In 1897 his company merged with Colt.

Gatling's design had six barrels held in a circular frame which rotated when driven by a hand crank. As each barrel reached the bottom of its rotation, it fired. The firing rate was a then-phenomenal two hundred rounds per minute. In the later 1890s, he replaced the hand crank with an electric motor achieving a firing rate of about 3,000 rounds per minute!

During the Civil War, Gatling tried unsuccessfully to officially interest the U.S. Army in his design. However, the U.S. Navy adopted his design in 1862 and the U.S. Army followed suit in 1866 after the Civil War ended. The hand-driven Gatling Gun remained in service with the U.S. Army until 1911.

Gatling's original guns were designed for percussion chambers. In 1867, he modified his design for metallic cartridges and received several cartridge patents. While most Gatling guns were chambered for military service rifle cartridges, Gatling developed a line of powerful proprietary cartridges especially for his guns. One of the most popular of these was the 1 inch Gatling cartridge adopted by the U.S. Navy which fired a 3,500 grain lead conical bullet.

History will remember Dr. Gatling for his famous guns, not his cartridge designs. However, his cartridge designs were historically important as they were the direct predecessors of today's .50 caliber and 20mm cartridges.

DR. EDWARD MAYNARD
1813-1891

Dentist, Cartridge Designer

Dr. Edward Maynard was a renowned dentist with many patents for dental instruments and procedures still in use today. In his day, he was considered a leading scientist and received many awards. However, history remembers him more for his cartridge designs than his dentistry.

Maynard patented his signature priming system in 1845 – a rolled paper tape priming system later popular for converting flintlocks. His tape priming system was replaced by self-contained metallic cartridges in the late 1860s, however, it remains in production to this day as "ammo" for toy cap pistols. There followed a dozen or more patents on both percussion and self-contained cartridges. Maynard cartridges are readily identified by their wide rims and straight sidewalls.

Dr. Maynard's distinctive cartridges enjoyed modest popularity during the waning years of black powder. With the advent of smokeless propellants, Maynard cartridges became obsolete. However, his distinctive cartridge designs and patents will always be associated with the early development of self-contained metallic cartridges.

LOCK, STOCK, AND BARREL

In the days of flintlocks and percussion firearms, the lock, the stock, and the barrel were the three major parts of a gun. When put together, they made up a complete firearm.

The phrase entered the vernacular with the meaning of "completeness" or "the entire thing". It is still in widespread use today with the same meaning.

CHAPTER 35 : RIMFIRE RECOMMENDATIONS

CHAPTER 35 HIGHLIGHTS:

- BEFORE GOING AFIELD
- HOW TO CHOOSE A CALIBER AND BULLET
- RECOMMENDATIONS
- COPPER PLATED RIMFIRE BULLETS
- RIMFIRE HEADSTAMP CONFUSION

BEFORE GOING AFIELD

Most shooters own more than one rimfire rifle or handgun. Because there are several rimfire calibers, some not interchangeable, confirm that you have the correct caliber of .22 ammunition for the firearm you plan to use.

HOW TO CHOOSE A CALIBER AND BULLET

When hunting with rimfire ammunition, keep in mind that the maximum effective range is considerably less than centerfire ammunition. For example, the maximum effective range of .22 Long Rifle ammunition is one hundred yards while that of .22 Winchester Magnum Rimfire (WMR) ammunition is approximately one hundred fifty yards. The .17 HMR (Hornady Magnum Rimfire) offers a maximum effective range of approximately two hundred yards.

Most rimfire hunters have found the .22 Long Rifle high velocity hollow point load the most cost effective for hunting. This load is suitable for a wide variety of small game provided the shooter carefully selects his shots. Keep in mind that the .22 Long Rifle cartridge is suitable only for pests, varmints, and small game hunting. It is not powerful enough for larger game; it is also illegal to hunt any type of larger game with a .22 rimfire.

Magnum rimfire ammunition offers a maximum effective range substantially beyond that of the .22 Long Rifle ammunition – at a price. That price is a much higher cost and higher noise levels. For hunting purposes, most sportsmen have found the added cost well worth the extra range and striking energy, and the noise level remains considerably below that of centerfire rifle ammunition.

Part of the fun of rimfire shooting is trying out the various brands and loads. In fact, the rimfire shooter has more options than most centerfire users. These range from the humble BB Cap with its lead bullet to the .17 HMR with a plastic tipped spitzer boat tail bullet.

Plinking is a uniquely American activity and the .22 Long Rifle is the reigning king of plinking. Of course,

nearly any of the other .22 rimfire loads can be used for the purpose, but they are either more expensive, harder to find, or excessively powerful. In the charts below, plinking comes under the heading of "informal target shooting". For this purpose, solid bullets are best and least expensive – especially in the promotional brands.

The .22 Long Rifle standard solid bullet weight is forty grains with hollow points being somewhat lighter at thirty-five to thirty-eight grains. Lighter weight bullets with weights averaging thirty grains are used for ultra high velocity loads. The standard bullet weight for the humble .22 Short is twenty nine grains. The predominant ogive shape used for .22 Short and .22 Long Rifle ammunition is round nose or semi-round nose. Some of the ultra high velocity lightweight bullets have a broad hollow point design.

.22 caliber Winchester Magnum rimfire bullets are similar to .22 Long Rifle bullets (weight and ogive) except they are jacketed with a flat nose. Some bullets used in .22 WMR are blunt while some have semi-spitzer ogives. The new .17 calibers have sharp spitzer points with a weight of 15.5, 17, or 20 grains.

BRASS MONKEY

We have all heard the phrase "It was cold enough to freeze the balls off a brass monkey." Relax, it does not have the sexual connotation frequently ascribed to it. Actually, it is an old naval ordnance term.

In the days of wooden warships, a ready supply of iron cannon balls was kept on the gun decks. These cannon balls were held in place by a brass rack called a "monkey". Extremely cold weather often caused a brass monkey to contract enough to release the cannon balls allowing them roll around on the deck. As some of the cannon balls were fairly heavy, this could be a problem on a pitching deck in a heavy sea.

RECOMMENDATIONS

The .22 Long Rifle cartridge is loaded to four different muzzle velocity levels, each of which has a different intended purpose. These may be summarized as follows:

.22 LONG RIFLE RIMFIRE CARTRIDGE MUZZLE VELOCITY LEVELS

Load	Muzzle Velocity (fps.)	Comment
Match Velocity	1,080	Subsonic for match competition
Standard Velocity	1,150	Supersonic for plinking, training
High Velocity	1,220-1,435	Supersonic for hunting
Ultra High Velocity	1,450+	Light weight bullets for hunting

Points To Keep In Mind

* Match and Standard .22 Long Rifle ammunition will not cycle most semi-automatic guns.

* Standard velocity ammunition often is more accurate than high velocity ammunition.

* For hunting at ranges to one hundred yards, high velocity ammunition should be used.

* For hunting at ranges over fifty yards, ultra high velocity ammunition can be used.

* The 35-40 grain bullets are the most accurate.

* Bullet placement is especially important with .22 rimfire ammunition due to the limited striking energy.

CLASSIC SMALL RIMFIRE RECOMMENDATIONS

Caliber	Informal Indoor Target	Informal Outdoor Target	Plinking	Elimination of Rodents and Small Pests
.22 BB Cap	X	X		
.22 CB Cap	X	X		
.22 Short	X	X	X	X
.22 Long Z	X	X		X
.22 Shot			X	
.22 Long			X	X

Points To Keep In Mind

* The main advantages of these are low noise, limited power, and reduced range.

* They will not cycle a semi-automatic firearm, chamber for the .22 Long Rifle cartridge.

* Most will not feed through magazines and must be single-loaded by hand.

* All are subsonic with low noise levels except the .22 Long.

* Accuracy may be poor in some guns chambered for the .22 Long Rifle cartridge.

* The maximum effective range of most .22 shotshells is fifteen feet.

.22 LONG RIFLE COMPETITION RECOMMENDATIONS

Caliber/Grade	PURPOSE				COMPETITION LEVEL		
	Instruction	Practice	Training	Club	Regional	National	International
Standard Vel.	X	X	X	X			
Match/Basic	X	X	X	X			
Match/Std.			X		X		
Match/Intermed				X	X	X	
Match/Superior					X	X	X
Match/HV (Running Boar)						X	X

Points To Keep In Mind

* Match ammunition can be used for hunting, but it will not cycle semi-automatic firearms. It will also require you to re-zero your rifle as the point of impact will be very different from high velocity ammunition.

* Note that there are several intermediate quality levels of match ammunition suitable for various types of local and regional matches. Such ammunition is expensive, but well worth the price.

* For national and international competition only the very best superior match grade ammunition will do – and such ammunition is very expensive.

A Load Of Junk

On wooden warships, old rope called "junk" was collected and used as wadding for the ship's cannon. After the powder charge and cannon ball were rammed home, junk was rammed down the barrel. The junk prevented the cannon ball from rolling out of the barrel as the ship rolled and pitched during a battle.

Son Of A Gun

On many wooden warships, the gun crews were not allowed to go ashore in ports for fear of desertion. For this reason, the gun crews had to work, eat, and sleep on the cramped gun decks. Armed marines on board every ship enforced the captain's orders and naval discipline.

When in home port for extended periods, a few of the gun crew's wives sometimes were allowed to live on board. If a male child was born to one of the gun crew's wives, he was recorded as being "a son of a gun".

.22 LONG RIFLE HUNTING RECOMMENDATIONS

Load	Bullet	Rodents	Pests	Small Predators	Varmints	Furbearers	Small Game
Subsonic	HP	X	X	X			X
Std. Vel.	Solid	X	X			X	X
High Vel.	Solid			X	X	X	
High Vel.	HP			X	X		X
Ultra HV	HP	X	X	X			X

Points To Keep In Mind

* Subsonic ammunition can be a wise choice where noise may be a problem.

* Solid bullet ammunition is best for furbearers and varmints.

* Ultra high velocity ammunition is best at ranges of fifty yards or more.

* For small game hunting, solids will not anchor game and ultra high velocity loads may destroy the meat. High velocity hollow point loads are the best choice for this purpose.

.17 AND .22 MAGNUM RIMFIRE HUNTING RECOMMENDATIONS

Load	Bullet Wgt.(Grs.)	Rodents	Pests	Small Predators	Varmints	Furbearers	Small Game
.17 Mach 2	17	X	X	X	X		
.17 HRM	15.5-20	X	X	X	X		X
.22 WRF	40	X	X	X		X	X
.22 WMR	30-50	X		X	X	X	X

Points To Keep In Mind

* Magnum rimfire ammunition is not suitable (or permitted) for competition.

* Magnum ammunition costs substantially more than .22 Long Rifle ammunition, making it too expensive for plinking and informal target shooting.

* Magnum rimfire ammunition has an effective range which is 50 to 100 yards greater than .22 Long Rifle.

* .22 WMR ammunition is offered in a variety of bullet weights and types. Bullets having a very blunt profile or very light weight are performance limited to a maximum effective range of about one hundred yards.

* The .17 rimfire calibers offer the best ballistic performance as well as a very low potential for ricochets. However, they are expensive and the muzzle report is louder than .22 Long Rifle ammunition.

COPPER PLATED RIMFIRE BULLETS

A common practice for rimfire ammunition manufacturers is electroplating a very thin copper coating on selected .22 rimfire bullets. In most cases, the plating is applied to solid and hollow point bullets used in high velocity and ultra high velocity loads for identification and marketing purposes. The thin plating serves no ballistic purpose and adds expense to the production process.

Many high velocity promotional loads use an unplated bullet to reduce costs.

RIMFIRE HEADSTAMP CONFUSION

Many shooters have become confused by rimfire head stamps used by Winchester and Remington. For many years, Remington head stamped their rimfire cases with a "U" while Winchester used an "H" as their rimfire head stamp.

The "U" on the Remington cases signified the merger of Remington with the Union Metallic Cartridge Company in 1902. Remington also head stamped their centerfire ammunition for many years with "REM-UMC" for the same reason.

Winchester used the "H" headstamp on their rimfire cartridge cases to honor Benjamin Tyler Henry, a brilliant inventor and patent holder who was instrumental in early metallic cartridge and firearm development in the 1860s. Winchester worked closely with Henry to develop various rifles and cartridges and purchased many of his patents.

In modern times, the reasons to commemorate or honor the past have faded into obscurity. Today, few shooters have ever heard of Benjamin Tyler Henry or the Union Metallic Cartridge Company. As a result, Remington and Winchester no longer use "U" or "H" as rimfire headstamps.

The .22 Long Rifle Cartridge For Personal Defense Use cannot be recommended. It simply does not have the striking energy to reliably incapacitate an assailant. For example, the .22 Long Rifle high velocity loading produces about 96 ft.-lbs. of muzzle energy. Compare this to the .38 Special+P 125 grain JHP load that produces 248 ft.-lbs. of muzzle energy. The .38 Special +P loading is considered by many experts to be the minimum for personal defense.

Ultra-High Velocity .22 Long Rifle Ammunition

The major rimfire ammunition manufacturers have significantly improved their ultra-high velocity .22 Long Rifle hunting ammunition with higher muzzle velocities and new bullets.

Manufacturer	Product	Bullet Weight (grains)	Bullet Style	Muzzle Velocity (fps)	Muzzle Energy (ft.-lbs.)
CCI	Stinger®	32	CPHP	1,640	191
	Long Rifle	32	SHP	1,640	191
	Velocitor®	40	CHP	1,435	183
Winchester	VarmintLF	26	THP	1,650	157
	Xpediter	32	LHP	1,640	191
	VarmintHE	37	FHP	1,435	169
	HyperSpeed	40	LHP	1,435	183
	Super-X	37	LHP	1,330	145
Remington	Yellow Jacket	33	TCHP	1,500	165
	Viper	36	TCSolid	1,410	159
Federal	Game Shok	31	CHP	1,430	140

CHP/CPHP=copper plated hollow point

LHP=lead hollow point (copper plated)

TCHP=truncated cone hollow point

TC solid=solid lead bullet, non-expanding

SHP-segmented hollow point

THP=tin hollow point

FHP=fragmenting hollow point

CHAPTER 36 : SHOTSHELL RECOMMENDATIONS

CHAPTER 36 HIGHLIGHTS:

- BEFORE GOING AFIELD
- PATTERN AND CHOKE SELECTION
- SHOTSHELL GAUGE APPLICATIONS

- SHOTSHELL LOADS
- LOAD AND CHOKE SHOT SIZE RECOMMENDATIONS

- DOS AND DON'TS FOR STEEL SHOT

All drawings by Author, unless otherwise noted.

BEFORE GOING AFIELD

Successfully taking fast moving aerial targets demands more than "average" performance from your shotshells. Many inexperienced hunters give this requirement scant attention and select only the cheapest shotshells. Their subsequent lack of success in the field is predictable.

Faced with the multitude of shotshell gauges, loads, shot sizes, and shot materials, making the proper selection can be daunting. The following information is designed to help you make an informed decision in this respect. In the field, using the appropriate loads and shot sizes can make a world of difference.

PATTERN AND CHOKE SELECTION

Most shotgun barrels are choked – meaning there is a constriction near the muzzle. The proper choke constriction depends on the size of the shot, type of shot, and the average distance at which the game will be hunted.

Points To Keep In Mind

* Patterns expand or open up as they travel down range, rapidly losing their pellet density and killing power.

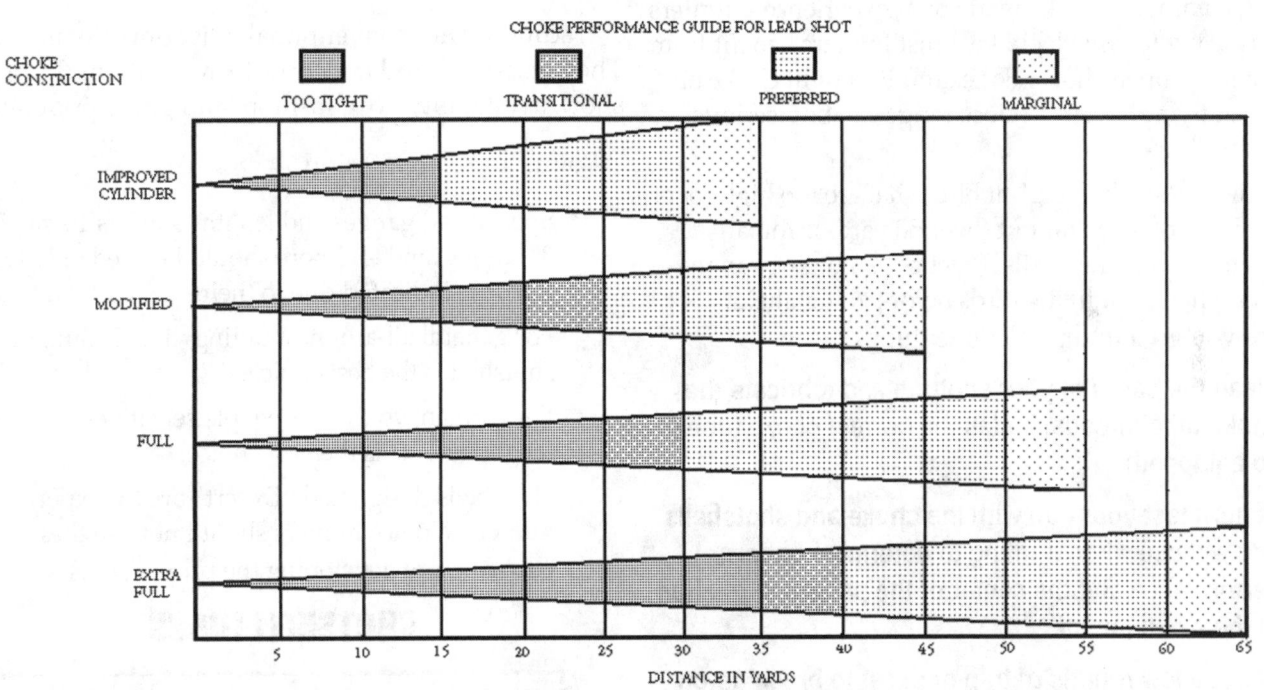

CHOKE PERFORMANCE GUIDE FOR LEAD SHOT

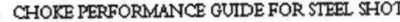

CHOKE PERFORMANCE GUIDE FOR STEEL SHOT

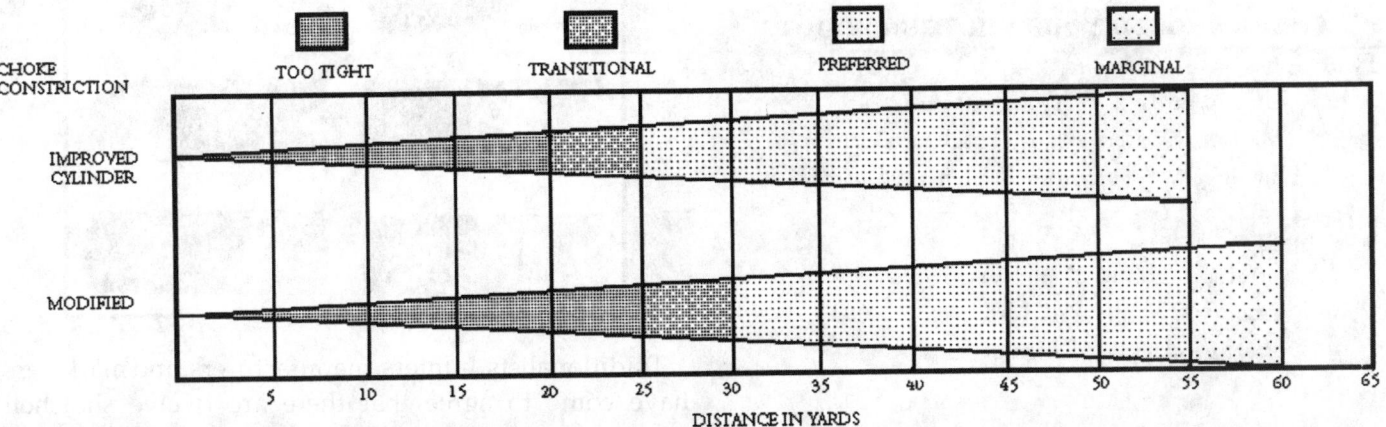

SHOTGUN CHOKE CONSTRICTIONS
EXPECTED PATTERN DENSITIES AND APPLICATION

Choke Designation	Approx. Constriction (inches)	Pattern Density @40 yds	Max. Effective Range(yds)	Typical Applications
Cylinder	none	<40%	40	Slugs, buckshot
Skeet	.005	40%	25	Skeet
Improved Cylinder	.011	50%	25	Hunting at close range
Modified	.020	60%	40	All around hunting
Improved Modified	.027	65%	40	All around hunting, live bird
Full	.036	70%	50	Trap, long range hunting
Extra Full	.040	80%	50+	Turkey, geese, handicap trap

* A full choke will hold a pattern together longer than a more open choke – select a tighter choke for longer range shooting (30 yds to 50 yds).

* For the reasons above, always select the smallest pellet size appropriate to the game as this will give you the densest pattern.

* A common mistake made by inexperienced hunters is using too much choke. Most hunters benefit from a more open choke. For example, a tight choke on fast flying targets at close range can be a serious handicap.

* Avoid "sky busting" at birds that are too high (over 150 feet) or too far out (over 50 yards). You are simply wasting shells. Practice estimating range and height of flying birds before going afield.

Before you go hunting, do three things:

• **Clean the barrel of your shotgun and lubricate the choke tube threads, install the correct choke tube (if so equipped).**

• **Pattern test your gun with the choke and shotshells you will use when hunting to determine pattern performance and the center of the pattern in relation to the aiming point.**

• **Shoot a few rounds of trap or skeet to brush up on your shooting skills.**

WHERE SHOULD YOUR SHOTGUN SHOOT?
Field Guns:

    Upland birds: 2-4" high at 40 yards

    Migratory waterfowl: 4-6" high at 40 yards

    Small game: dead on to 2" high at 25 yards

Target Guns:

    Skeet: dead on to 2" high at 25 yards

    Trap: 6-12" high at 40 yards

    Sporting clays: 2-4" high at 40 yards

SHOTSHELL GAUGE APPLICATIONS

Shotshell gauge recommendations for specific game are based on tradition, experience, and scientific analysis. Generations of hunters have accumulated valuable experience using shotshell gauges on various species of game in all types of conditions and at all ranges.

Tradition and conventional wisdom are not static. They must be updated due to regulations (non-toxic shot), availability, cost, fashion, and game population.

Points To Keep In Mind

* Specialized gauges and lengths such as 10-ga., 20-ga. 3", 28-ga., and .410 bore should be used only for the purpose indicated due to their size, cost, and recoil.

* For general all-around hunting, the 12-gauge 2 ¾" shotshell is the best choice.

* For women, youths, or people sensitive to recoil, the 20-gauge 2 ¾" is the best choice.

* Shotshells designated "Expert" are for experienced hunters. Novice hunters should not use these in any gauge before developing the proper skills.

SHOTSHELL LOADS

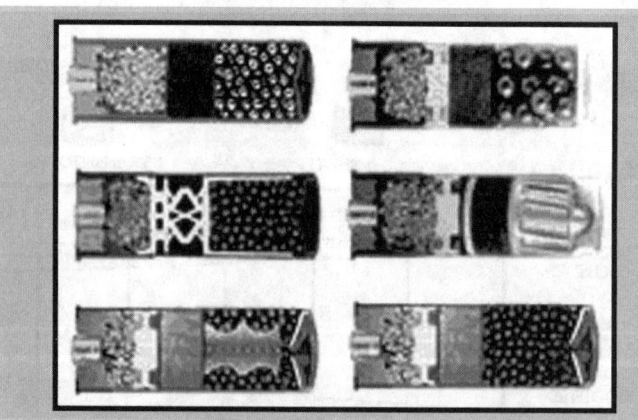

Traditionalists, hunters, manufacturers, and marketers have come to agree that there are twelve shotshell load families, each with different charge weights and velocity levels.

- **Game or Upland Loads: 12-ga. 2 3/4" 1 oz. lead shot at 1,290 fps. General all-around, women, youth.**

These inexpensive promotional shotshells are loaded with a light charge of soft lead shot in a few select sizes, normally 7 1/2 and 8. The mediocre patterns and light shot charge make these loads suitable only for close range hunting or informal target shooting. Game loads will not cycle many semi-automatic shotguns. Game loads are also offered in 16-ga. with a 1 oz. shot charge and in 20-ga. with a 7/8 oz. shot charge.

- **Light Field Loads: 12-ga. 2 3/4" 1 1/8 oz. lead shot at 1,255 fps. General all-around, women, youth.**

This is a classic field load for upland birds and small game hunting at closer ranges. It is a good combination of pattern density, muzzle velocity, and low recoil.

- **Heavy Field Loads: 12-ga. 2 3/4" 1 1/4oz. lead shot at 1,220 fps. General all-around, women, youth.**

Another classic choice for upland bird and small game, the heavier shot charge and denser patterns extend the effective range without heavy recoil. A very good choice for double guns and single barrel shotguns, these are also offered in 20- and 28-ga. with shot charges of 1 oz. and ¾ oz. respectively.

- **High Velocity/High Brass/Flyer Loads: 12-ga. 2 3/4" 1 1/4 oz. lead shot at 1,330 fps. General all-around, women, youth.**

Generations of hunters have found this classic an effective combination for large upland birds, small game, and varmint hunting at extended ranges. It is also a great choice for live bird competition. Recoil is stout, but manageable and this load will reliably cycle semi-automatic shotguns. There is also a 16-ga. 1 1/8 oz. load and a 20-ga. 2 3/4" load of this type with a 1 oz. shot charge.

- **Light Magnum/High Velocity Loads: 12-ga. 2 3/4" 1 3/8 oz. lead shot at 1,500 fps. All-around, expert.**

A combination of moderately heavy shot charge with high velocity makes these loads a popular choice for upland birds, small game, and varmints at extended ranges. The trade off is heavy recoil in light weight guns. Experienced hunters advise it is better to fire these in semi-automatic guns which mitigate perceived recoil.

- **Short Magnum Loads: 12-ga. 2 3/4" 1 1/2 oz. lead shot at 1,315 fps. All-around, expert.**

These are as good as it gets for 2 3/4" length 12-gauge shotshells. A combination of heavy shot charge and high velocity extends range to the 50 yard practical limit, although heavy recoil is the price you pay for such performance. For these reasons, experienced hunters use these sparingly on long range targets. For 20-ga. 2 3/4" shooters, there is a short magnum with 1 1/8 oz. of shot.

- **Long Magnum Loads: 10-ga. 3 1/2", 2 oz. lead shot at 1200 fps., 12-ga. 3", 1 5/8-1 3/4-1 7/8-2 oz. lead shot at 1,130-1,300 fps. Specialized.**

These big Magnums are designed for long shots at heavy birds such as turkey and varmints in difficult hunting conditions. As recoil is very heavy, most hunters prefer to fire these through semi-automatic shotguns. A mitigating factor is that most hunters do not need to fire a large number of these loads. These lead shot loads cannot be used to hunt migratory waterfowl. Shooters who prefer a 20-ga. 3" shell can select a shot charge of 1 ¼ oz.

- **Super Magnum Loads: 10-ga. 3 1/2", 2 1/4 oz. lead shot at 1,150 fps., 12-ga. 3 1/2" 2 oz. lead shot at 1,150 fps. Specialized.**

Although the muzzle velocity of these loads is low, this is not important as they are normally used for turkey or varmints on the ground. For these type of targets, a heavy shot charge is more important than high muzzle velocity. Expect heavy recoil with these loads, although you may not fire many on a typical hunt.

- **Target Loads: all gauges 2 3/4" various shot weights, various muzzle velocities. Specialized (12-ga. and 20-ga.), expert (28-ga. and .410 bore).**

In most cases, target loads are the best shotshells a manufacturer knows how to make. Most target loads are equivalent to light field loads in terms of ballistic performance albeit with better pattern densities. Some hunters use target loads in place of light field loads with excellent results. Otherwise, target loads are limited to the skeet, trap, and sporting clays fields where their performance can mean the difference between winning and losing. Target loads assembled with steel shot are also available for locations which require non-toxic ammunition.

- **Steel Shot Non-Toxic Shotshells: 10-, 12-, 16-, and 20-ga., various shot weights, various muzzle velocities. Specialized.**

Non-toxic shot is required for hunting migratory waterfowl. In a few areas, non-toxic shot is also required for other game and even target shooting. All manufacturers now offer steel shot ammunition for these purposes. Because steel is not as dense as lead, there are more steel than lead pellets in an ounce of equal sized shot; but steel shot loses velocity and striking energy more quickly than lead. Manufacturers compensate for this by increasing the muzzle velocity of steel shot shells and using light shot charge weights. In addition, hunters are advised to move up two pellet sizes above lead when shooting steel shot to maintain ballistic performance. Because of their high velocity, steel shot shells have heavy recoil. Steel shot shells can quickly damage a normal shotgun barrel. For this reason, steel shot should be fired only in shotgun barrels designed for steel shot and so marked. Steel shot is not loaded in 28-ga. or .410 bore.

- **Other Non-Toxic Shotshells: 10-, 12-, and 20-ga., various lengths, shot weights, and velocities; high density shot. Specialized.**

For hunting migratory waterfowl at extended ranges, ammunition manufacturers have developed non-toxic shot which equals or exceeds the performance of lead. In addition, this shot can be made very hard which is necessary for compact evenly distributed patterns. Such shells are very expensive, but they offer superior long range performance similar to that of lead shot. High density shot should be fired only in shotgun barrels designed for steel shot and so marked. This type of shot is offered only in high velocity and magnum loads.

Because their density is very similar to that of lead, Tungsten Matrix and Bismuth shot can be fired through any shotgun barrel without damage. Either is a good choice for hunting migratory waterfowl with older guns whose barrels were not designed for steel shot. These loads are offered in shot charge weights and muzzle velocities generally similar to lead shot loads.

- **Low Recoil Loads:**

As their name suggests, these shot shells are engineered for lower perceived recoil. For example Remington claims a reduction of 40% with their Managed-Recoil Shotshells. This is accomplished by reducing muzzle velocity, reducing peak chamber pressure, and loading a lighter shot charge. They are a good choice for shooters who are sensitive to recoil. However they may not cycle some semi-automatic shotguns. Low recoil loads are often used by skeet, trap, or sporting clays competitors to reduce fatigue during long tournaments.

WHAT MAKES A PREMIUM LEAD SHOTSHELL?

Compared to a standard shotshell, a premium shotshell has many upgraded features for improved pattern quality and greater effective range. Some of the upgrades are:

* Hard lead shot which resists deformation during acceleration for substantially better pattern density.
* Copper-plated or nickel-plated lead shot for reduced feather draw on impact.
* Granulated plastic buffer material in the shot charge to cushion pellets during acceleration.
* Higher muzzle velocity.
* Plastic wad column which fully protects shot pellets from contact with the bore surface.

Such loads produce patterns of exceptional density, often in the 95% range with a full choke. If the game is anywhere inside the dense pattern, it is killed instantly. If it is outside the pattern, you have a clean miss, instead of a crippled animal.

LOAD AND CHOKE SHOT SIZE RECOMMENDATIONS

The recommendations in this chart are the result of many years of field experience. Remember, they can only be advisory as your hunting conditions may be different than normal hunting conditions. However, no two situations, shotguns, or shooters are alike. Take all factors into account, then determine which loads and shot sizes work best for you.

Game	Load	Choke	Recommended Shot Sizes	Shot Type
Trap	Target	F	7 ½, 8, 8 ½	Lead (steel as req.)
Skeet	Target	S	8, 8 ½, 9	Lead (steel as req.)
Sporting Clays	Target	M	7 ½, 8	Lead
Live Bird	Flyer	IM	7 ½, 8	Lead
Ducks	High Vel. or Magnum	M	1, 2, 3, 4, 2, 4, 6	Steel High Density
Geese	High Vel. or Magnum	M	1, 2, BB, BBB, T, B, 2, 4	Steel High Density
Turkey	Magnum	EF	4, 5, 6	Lead
Pheasant	High Vel. or Magnum	F	4, 5, 6, 7 ½	Lead
Grouse	Field	M	6, 7 ½, 8	Lead
Partridge	Field	M	6, 7 ½, 8	Lead
Woodcock	Field	M	6, 7 ½, 8	Lead
Snipe	High Velocity	IC	4, 6	Steel
Quail	Field	IC	7 ½, 8	Lead
Dove	Field	IC	7 ½, 8, 8 ½	Lead
Rabbit	High Velocity	M	2, 4, 5, 6, 7 ½	Lead
Squirrel	Game, Field	IC	4, 5, 6	Lead
Rodents, pests	Game, Field	IC	7 ½, 8	Lead
Varmints	High Velocity	M	BB, 2, 4, 5, 6	Lead
Coyote	Magnum	M	00, 0, 4 buckshot	Lead
Personal Defense	Magnum	C	00, 0, 4 buckshot	Lead
Deer	High Vel. or Magnum	C	Slug	Lead

EF - Extra Full, F - Full, IM - Improved Modified, M - Modified, IC - Improved Cylinder, S - Steel, C - Cylinder

Efforts to improve shotshell performance continue. Recently, both Winchester and Federal introduced new types of shot designed to improve terminal performance. Both are shown below with factory descriptions of the shape and benefits of such designs.

WINCHESTER BLIND SIDE HEX SHOT

Winchester's approach is based on cube shaped (hexahedronal) steel shot that can be more densely packed inside a shotshell than round shot pellets. Basically, cube shot eliminates the spaces between round pellets allowing 15% more pellets to be loaded in the same space. Winchester claims that on impact, Blind Side™ shotshells with Hex™ steel cube shot transfers energy 250% more efficiently to the target than round pellets.

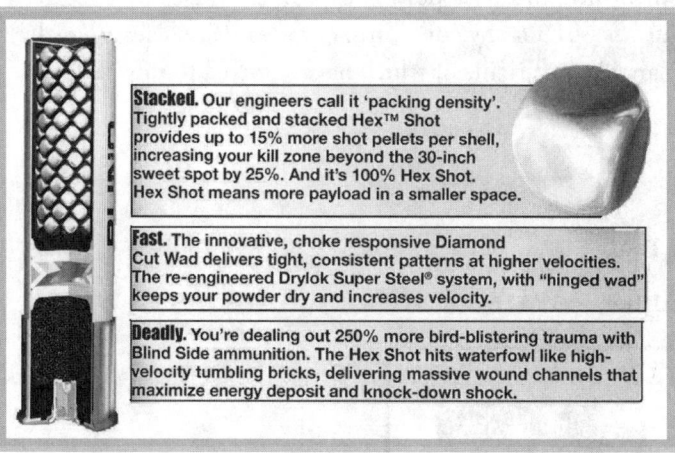

Stacked. Our engineers call it 'packing density'. Tightly packed and stacked Hex™ Shot provides up to 15% more shot pellets per shell, increasing your kill zone beyond the 30-inch sweet spot by 25%. And it's 100% Hex Shot. Hex Shot means more payload in a smaller space.

Fast. The innovative, choke responsive Diamond Cut Wad delivers tight, consistent patterns at higher velocities. The re-engineered Drylok Super Steel® system, with "hinged wad" keeps your powder dry and increases velocity.

Deadly. You're dealing out 250% more bird-blistering trauma with Blind Side ammunition. The Hex Shot hits waterfowl like high-velocity tumbling bricks, delivering massive wound channels that maximize energy deposit and knock-down shock.

FEDERAL FLIGHTSTOPPER SHOT

Federal Premium Black Cloud FS Steel shot shells are loaded with 60% round steel pellets and 40% Flightstopper or FS Steel pellets. The Flightstopper pellet design has an equator that, according to Federal, causes cutting on impact to significantly improve energy transfer to the target. In addition, both round and FS Steel pellets are layered in the shotshell (Flightstopper pellets on the bottom) so as to provide consistent edge-to-edge patterns.

REMINGTON'S HYPERSONIC STEEL

Remington's answer to these developments is their Hypersonic Steel shotshell loaded with conventional round steel shot, but at a blistering muzzle velocity of 1,700 fps*. This velocity is made possible by a new Xelerator plastic wad design with an ignition chamber on the base, combined with a hotter primer and stress concentrator notches on the wad petals. As most hunters miss their target by shooting behind, the new Remington Hypersonic Steel shotshells offer an advantage by shortening the required lead by 8 inches at 40 yds., which is the body length of a duck in flight.

* Most shotshells with steel shot are loaded to 1,400 fps with the highest being 1,500 fps.

DOS AND DON'TS FOR STEEL SHOT

Do

1. Use ONLY steel shot for hunting migratory waterfowl.

2. When selecting steel shot ammunition, move up your preferred lead shot sizes by two. In other words, if you used to use No. 4 lead shot, move up to No. 2 steel shot; if you used No. 6 lead shot, move up to No. 4 steel shot.

3. Expect some choke movement after shooting 250-300 rounds of steel shot ammunition. This is normal and is not dangerous. It does not adversely affect pattern quality or velocity. You can see choke movement by looking down the outer surface of your shotgun barrel. It will be a bulge about six inches behind the muzzle.

4. Protect your steel shot shells from moisture. Steel pellets can rust causing them to agglomerate into a single mass.

5. Your best patterns with steel shot will be from a modified choke.

6. If you want to upgrade from standard steel shot, use Winchester Blind Side, Remington Xelerator, or Federal Flightstopper loads.

Don'ts

1. Do not fire steel shot in a barrel not specifically recommend for steel. In other words, do not assume your barrel is suitable for use with steel shot unless it says so on the barrel. Using steel shot in a barrel not marked as such may void your warranty and/or damage your shotgun.

2. Just because your lead shot barrel has a cylinder, improved cylinder choke, or a chrome-lined bore does not make it suitable for use with steel shot.

3. Do not fire steel shot loads in a choke tighter than modified.

4. Do not expect steel shot to match the ballistic performance of lead shot at ranges beyond 40 yards. For shooting at longer ranges, switch to non-toxic composite shot.

5. Do not reload steel shot with wads designed for lead shot. Use wads specifically designed for steel shot.

6. Never fire steel shot against a hard target such as steel, glass, vehicles, concrete, bricks, road surfaces, or similar surfaces.

GENERAL COMMENTS ON STEEL SHOT

1. Shotshells loaded with steel shot are more expensive than those loaded with lead shot.

2. Due to their high muzzle velocity, shotshells loaded with steel shot have more recoil than equivalent lead shot loads.

3. Steel shot is not available in buckshot ammunition or with pellets smaller than No. 7 (0.100 inches in diameter).

4. Steel shot with plating (zinc, copper, nickel, or other) resists rust better than unplated pellets, but is not rust proof.

5. Before going afield, check local regulations regarding steel shot as it may be required in some areas other than typical waterfowl zones.

> " *Those who hammer their guns into plows will plow for those who do not.*"
> - Thomas Jefferson

GAUGE RIFLES—A BYGONE ERA

Prior to the introduction of smokeless propellants, African hunters often used gauge rifles to take dangerous game. Gauge rifles were side-by-side guns with heavy rifled barrels in various large shotgun gauges such as 8-gauge, 4-gauge and even 2-gauge. These rifles fired massive hard lead bullets weighing 1500 grains or more loaded into solid brass shells at muzzle velocities of approximately 1500 fps. Even though these guns typically weighed twenty-five pounds or more, recoil was extremely heavy. Hunters used porters to carry the guns until needed, then hand them the gun when the shot was set up.

Gauge rifles and shells were replaced by black powder express rifles and cartridges of smaller bore diameter in the 1880s. In their turn, the black powder express cartridges were replaced in the 1890s by the nitro express (smokeless powder) cartridges, variants of which have survived to this day.

Survival Tool

Cartridge, Shot Caliber .45 M15

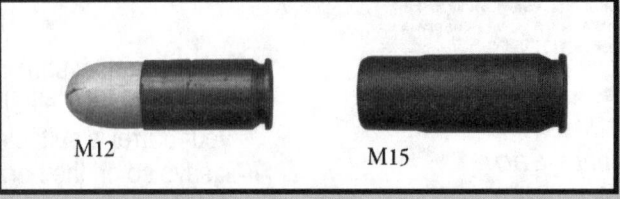

M12   M15

During World War II, the U.S. Army Air Force needed a .45 ACP caliber shotshell for packing in aircrew survival kits. The idea was for downed flyers to use such cartridges for hunting small game.

In October 1943, the Cartridge Shot Caliber .45 M12 was adopted for this purpose. The bullet was replaced with a fragile, bullet-shaped paper container holding approximately 125-131 lead alloy No. 7 1/2 pellets. It was not a success. The moisture and humidity in combat zones quickly deteriorated the paper container rendering the cartridges useless.

Following additional research, a solution to the problem was found in the form of an elongated, .45 ACP cartridge case with no bullet or shot container. Adopted by the U.S. Army in March 1944 as the Cal. .45 Shot Cartridge, M15, a waxed paper top wad sealed the case mouth and a thin fiber wad column pushed the shot charge out the barrel. The shot charge consisted of 108-118 No. 7 1/2 lead alloy pellets. Tests confirmed that the new M15 shot cartridge would place 70% of the pellets in a 30 inch circle at 30 feet.

The M15 shot cartridges would not cycle the M1911A1 pistol and had to be single-loaded. Each box of shot cartridges had the following words printed on the box in English, German, and Japanese: "Use only for Hunting Game, Do Not Use Against Enemy Troops." The M15 shot cartridge proved satisfactory in use and remained in service until aircrew survival kits were revised in the 1950s to include a folding, over-under shotgun/rifle.

SECTION VII – SAFETY
CHAPTER 37 : HANDLING SAFETY

CHAPTER 37 HIGHLIGHTS:

- PROPERTIES OF SMALL ARMS AMMUNITION
- PROPERTIES OF SMOKELESS POWDER
- PROPERTIES OF PRIMERS
- HANDLING OF PRIMERS
- TRANSPORTING SMOKELESS PROPELLANTS
- BEFORE GOING AFIELD
- IS FACTORY LOADED AMMUNITION WATERPROOF?
- SPRAY LUBRICANTS
- +P AMMUNITION

These paragraphs are meant to give everyone concerned for the shipment, storage, and handling of small arms ammunition certain basic and important facts about the properties of this widely distributed product. Such information should dispel some of the rumors and tales that persist regarding ammunition bulk safety. It also outlines recommended storage conditions, and reports the reactions of ammunition when exposed to fire or intense heat and rough or vigorous handling.

These statements and recommendations do not supersede local, state, or federal regulations. Local authorities should be consulted regarding regulations on the storage, transportation, sale, and handling of sporting ammunition in each specific community.

PROPERTIES OF SMALL ARMS AMMUNITION

All ammunition is carefully engineered and manufactured as an article of commerce. It has a specific use; if stored in a proper manner and used as intended in firearms in good condition and designed for the specific cartridge, the safety and satisfaction of the shooter should be assured.

Small arms ammunition is packed in cartons and cases as specified by the U.S. Department of Transportation. These container designs were developed in the interest of safety in transportation, storage, and marketing. Therefore, unapproved packaging should never be substituted.

Specific properties or characteristics of small arms ammunition of particular interest to shippers, warehouse operators, dealers, and users are as follows:

- **Stocks of small arms ammunition will NOT mass explode. That is to say, if one cartridge or shotshell in a carton or case is caused to fire, it will not cause other adjacent cartridges, shotshells, or their packages to explode sympathetically or in a simultaneous manner. There are no limits imposed on packaged quantities of ammunition that may be shipped, warehoused, or displayed in commercial establishments. This fact recognizes the inherently safe, non-hazardous characteristics of such ammunition in public or private storage.**

- **Small arms ammunition is not a super-sensitive item. Packages of ammunition may be dropped from any height which the packages will physically withstand, and cartridges or shotshells therein will not fire due to the shock. Properly packaged small arms ammunition will withstand all the rough handling tests of commerce such as drop tests, vibration tests, and rotating drum tests without individual cartridges or shotshells firing.**

- **Small arms ammunition, if discharged in the open without the support provided by a firearm's chamber or other close confinement, discharges inefficiently. The flights – more accurately "movement" – of projectiles or debris particles from such incidents are extremely limited in velocity, range, and energy. The small primer cups or rimfire case fragments are the missiles of highest velocity in such occurrences. Specifically, bullets and shot charges, being heavier than shell or cartridge cases in most instances, are rarely projected away from the location at which the unchambered round of ammunition was caused to ignite and discharge. However, small particles of metal or plastic from the burst case and primer cups may be propelled for short distances (usually not over 50 feet) at velocities sufficient in some instances to cause injury or discomfort.**

Insofar as the Sporting Arms and Ammunition Manufacturers' Institute has been able to determine, there have been no substantiated reports of serious or fatal injuries caused by the discharge of packaged or loose ammunition in handling or in fires, regardless of the quantity or type of cartridges or shotshells involved. SAAMI has no verified report of any fire fighter hurt by flying bullets or shot pellets in fires involving a sportsman's in-the-home personal supply of ammunition, a retail sporting goods store's stock, wholesaler's or distributor's sizable inventory, or an in-transit cargo of this product.

While blank cartridges will not mass detonate if one in a box is caused to fire, the noise of firing outside a gun will be nearly as loud as in normal use and may be harmful to hearing. The blank's "explosion" may also be rather violent due to rapidly expanding gasses released during burning. Obviously, blank cartridges deserve the same respectful handling and careful storage as other ammunition.

Retail and wholesale stocks of ammunition, not required for display, should be stored in original outer cartons or boxes exactly as supplied by the factory. When placed on basement or warehouse floors subject to moisture it would be well to stack the cartons on pallets. In some locations, police or public security regulations may prescribe the manner in which small arms ammunition stocks are displayed and the quantity that may be in sight. Check with local authorities. Packages of ammunition should not be placed in proximity to heavily trafficked aisles in the reach of children.

PROPERTIES OF SMOKELESS POWDER

Smokeless powders, or propellants, are essentially mixtures of chemicals designed to burn under controlled conditions at the proper rate to propel a projectile from a gun.

Smokeless powders are made in three forms:

1. **Thin, circular flakes or wafers**
2. **Small cylinders, both perforated and unperforated**
3. **Small spheres or flattened spheres**

Single-base smokeless powders derive their main source of energy from nitrocellulose.

The energy released from double-base smokeless powder is derived from both nitrocellulose and nitroglycerin.

All smokeless powders are extremely flammable; by design, they are intended to burn rapidly and vigorously when ignited.

Oxygen from the air is not necessary for the combustion of smokeless powders since they contain sufficient built-in oxygen to burn completely, even in an enclosed space such as the chamber of a firearm.

Ignition occurs when the powder granules are heated above their ignition temperature. This can occur by exposing the powder to:

1. **A flame such as a match or a primer flash.**
2. **An electrical spark or the sparks from welding, grinding, etc.**
3. **Heat from an electric hot plate or a fire directed against or near a closed container even if the powder itself is not exposed to the flame.**

When smokeless powder burns, a great deal of gas at high temperature is formed. If the powder is confined, this gas will create pressure in the surrounding structure. The rate of gas generation is such, however, that the pressure can be kept at a low level if sufficient space is available or if the gas can escape.

In this respect smokeless powder differs from blasting agents or high explosives such as dynamite or blasting gelatin, although powder may contain chemical ingredients common to both of these products.

Smokeless powder does not detonate like high explosives as it has a controlled rate of burn and differs considerably in its burning characteristics from common "black powder." Black powder burns at essentially the same rate out in the open (unconfined) as when in a gun.

When ignited in an unconfined state, smokeless powder burns inefficiently with an orange-colored flame. It may produce a considerable amount of light brown, noxious smelling smoke. It leaves a residue of ash and partially burned powder. The flame is hot enough to cause severe burns.

When it burns under pressure, as in a cartridge fired in a gun, smokeless powder produces very little smoke, a small glow, and leaves very little or no residue. The burning rate of smokeless powder increases with increased pressure.

If burning smokeless powder is confined, gas pressure will rise and eventually can cause the container to burst. Under such circumstances, the bursting of a strong container creates effects similar to an explosion.

PROPERTIES OF PRIMERS

Sporting ammunition primers contain carefully engineered mixtures of chemical ingredients. Primers are designed to explode and produce the heat, gas, and hot particles necessary to ignite the propellant powders in sporting ammunition when the firing pin of a firearm strikes them properly.

Properties of particular importance to the dealer and user of primers are as follows:

1. **Primers may explode if subjected to mishandling.**

Explosions may be caused by friction and by percussion, such as hammering, pounding, dropping, or bullet impact. Heating by fire, static electricity, sparks, hot tobacco ashes, or other unspecified abuses may also cause primers to explode.

2. If primers are loose or in bulk, having contact one with another, one primer exploding can, and usually will, cause a violent, sympathetic explosion of all primers so situated. In other words, one primer exploding for any reason under these circumstances will normally cause all of the primers to explode in one violent blast.

3. Primers may "dust." Small particles of priming compound may separate from the primers in the form of dust, especially when they are subjected to shaking or jolting. Accumulation of this dust in primer feed tubes, loading machines, and loading areas is extremely hazardous as it might cause explosions or fires.

4. Primers exposed to water or any organic solvent, such as paint thinner, gasoline, kerosene, oil, grease, etc. may deteriorate, resulting in misfires or poor ignition.

5. Modern sporting ammunition primers will not absorb moisture under normal or even severe conditions of atmospheric humidity. There is no advantage to be gained from air-tight containers. The factory containers in which they are packaged need only normal conditions of storage. They should be kept dry and not exposed to high temperatures (in excess of 150° F). If exposed to wet conditions or high temperatures, they may deteriorate, yielding misfires or poor ignition of the propellant powder.

HANDLING OF PRIMERS

Primers do explode. This is the purpose for which they have been designed. They demand the respect and careful handling due to any device containing explosives.

When a primer ignites, it causes the propellant to burn, which creates gases which, when under pressure in a firearm, send the bullet down the barrel. Pressure created by the propellant being burned is what discharges a bullet. As such, loose ammunition in a fire does not result in bullets being discharged because the propellant is not burning under pressure. While ammunition produces a popping sound when it burns, there is no mass detonation of the ammunition, any projectiles are of low velocity, and there is no threat to firefighters in their standard turn-out gear.

Primers should never be handled, used, or stored in bulk, since primers in bulk can explode simultaneously.

The placing of primers in tubes or columns, or using other bulk systems in which the explosion of any one primer may cause the explosion of all others, is a potentially hazardous condition. The manufacturers of primers do not recommend the use of primer feeds for reloading unless adequate protection from the hazard of explosion is provided. It is the responsibility of the manufacturers of primer handling systems to provide safety and protective features for their equipment. It is recommended that primers be handled individually unless adequate safeguards are provided and used.

Care must always be exercised in any handloading operation to avoid rough handling and undue force where a primer is involved, since the primer may fire. Any malfunction of equipment must be cleared with extreme caution. The decapping of shells or cases containing live primers is to be avoided.

Precautions should be taken to avoid buildup of static electricity on the person when handling primers or conducting handloading procedures. Loading equipment should be electrically grounded.

All loading equipment and adjacent areas must be kept scrupulously clean and free of primer dust and powder accumulations. Work areas and loading equipment must be cleaned by wiping with a damp cloth or sponge which should be thoroughly rinsed after each use. Fired primers, primer cups, anvils, or other bits of hard, abrasive material are a hazard during loading operation as contact with them may cause primers to fire.

Accidentally spilled primers should be picked up immediately as they may explode when stepped upon.

An absolute minimum of primers should be maintained at the loading operation. Only one packing tray at a time should be removed from the primer storage.

When a priming operation is completed, any remaining primers should be returned to the package in which they were originally contained. These packages have been specifically designed to protect primers during shipment and storage and also to protect the consumer.

Primers available to children, household pets, or persons not recognizing them as potentially hazardous, are an unnecessary risk to all concerned.

TRANSPORTING SMOKELESS PROPELLANTS

Quantities of smokeless propellants not exceeding 25 lb. (11.3 kg) in shipping containers approved by the U.S. Department of Transportation, may be transported in a private vehicle.

Quantities of smokeless propellants exceeding 25 lb. (11.3 kg) but not exceeding 50 lb. (22.7 kg), transported in a private vehicle, shall be transported in a portable magazine having wood walls of at least 1 in. (25.4 mm) nominal thickness.

Transportation of more than 50 lb. (22.7 kg) of smokeless propellants in a private vehicle is prohibited.

The U.S. Department of Transportation sets requirements for shipping containers for propellants and requires tests of loaded containers under actual fire conditions before approving them for use.

When smokeless powder in DOT-approved containers is ignited during such tests, the container seams split open or lids pop off to release gases and powder from confinement at low pressure.

Additional details are available in an SAAMI video "Smokeless Powder and the Fire Service."

No more than 25,000 small arms primers may be transported in a private vehicle.

The ATF also regulates the interstate transportation of small arms ammunition. A Federal Firearms License (FFL) is not required to either ship or receive small arms ammunition shipped interstate in the U.S. Basically the ATF, in 27CFR178 (specifically 27CFR178.32 & 99,) prohibits the shipment of armor piercing ammunition and prohibits the shipment of any ammunition to a person known to:

- **Be under 21 years of age**
- **Live in a state where the shipment is prohibited**
- **Be under indictment for, or, has been convicted in any court of a crime punishable by imprisonment for a term exceeding 1 year**
- **Be a fugitive from justice**
- **Be an unlawful user of or addicted to any controlled substance**
- **Have been adjudicated as a mental defective or has been committed to any mental institution**
- **Be an alien illegally or unlawfully in the United States**

If you do not know the person you are shipping the ammunition to, you may want to have the person sign a statement certifying that they meet the requirements listed above.

If you have any questions you should contact the ATF.

SHIPPING LOADED AMMUNITION IN THE UNITED STATES

LOADED AMMUNITION MAY NEVER BE SHIPPED THROUGH THE U.S. MAIL. Inert ammunition and components may be sent through the mail, but should be clearly marked as inert on a small note included inside the package to prevent a misunderstanding.

Both the United Parcel Service (UPS) and Federal Express (FedEx) will provide ground shipment of loaded small arms ammunition up through .50 caliber. For packages up to 20 pounds, the ammunition must be packed in boxes with at least a 200 pound bursting strength and be marked on the outside:

CARTRIDGES, SMALL ARMS

ORM-D

This information may be dated and you should check with the companies' hazardous materials information hotlines.

The transportation of small arms ammunition is regulated by the Federal government in 49CFR173.63. This regulation also defines packaging requirements. To determine the specific hazardous material code for ammunition (UN code) other than that which 49CFR173.63 authorized to be shipped as ORM-D, contact the Department of Transportation Hazardous Materials Hotline.

Transportation of Small Arms Ammunition in Checked Baggage on Airlines

Not all airlines allow small amounts of ammunition to be shipped with checked baggage, but the requirements vary significantly between airlines. In many cases the decision may be left to the pilot. IN ALL CASES YOU SHOULD CHECK WITH THE AIRLINES BEFORE ATTEMPTING TO CHECK BAGGAGE CONTAINING AMMUNITION. Generally there is no detail information on shipping ammunition on the airlines' web sites. You should call the toll-free number for the airline and talk to customer service. Generally, in the U.S., the requirements for the airlines that permit ammunition in checked baggage are as follows.

- **A maximum of 11 pounds (5 kg) of ammunition may be carried in a passenger's checked bags.**

- TSA Regulation requires:
- Ammunition must be packed in fiber (such as cardboard), wood or metal boxes, or other packaging that is specifically designed to carry small amounts of ammunition.
- You can't use firearm magazines/clips for packing ammunition unless they completely and securely enclose the ammunition (e.g., by securely covering the exposed portions of the magazine or by securely placing the magazine in a pouch, holder, or holster).
- You may carry the ammunition in the same hard-sided case as the firearm, as long as you pack it as described above.
- LOOSE AMMUNITION IS NOT ALLOWED. Ammunition wrapped in paper and packed in a metal can is not allowed. Plastic ammo boxes for 20-50 rounds seem acceptable to the TSA if the cartridges are wrapped in paper to keep them from rattling around in spaces intended for larger cartridges. Remember "securely" is used repeatedly by the TSA so it is wise to use tape or rubber bands to keep the ammo boxes closed.
- The bag must be locked but hard-sided bags are not required for ammunition.
- The bags must be checked at the check-in counter, and may not be checked at curbside. You have to declare the ammunition to the ticket agent, and they (or the TSA) will usually want to inspect it to ensure proper packing.
- You must declare your ammunition to the airline. Failure to do so violates U.S. Federal Law. Violators may be subject to a maximum penalty of 5 years' imprisonment and a $250,000 fine (49 U.S.C. 5124).
- Loaded ammunition may never be carried in hand-carried baggage.

BEFORE GOING AFIELD

Check to be absolutely certain that you have the correct caliber of ammunition for your firearm. If in doubt, examine the receiver, slide, or barrel; the firearm's caliber will be permanently marked on one or more. Make absolutely certain the cartridges match the caliber marked on the firearm. Check the packaging and headstamp of each cartridge to be certain they match. If in doubt consult a qualified gunsmith.

IS FACTORY LOADED AMMUNITION WATERPROOF?

Factory loaded ammunition is water resistant, but not waterproof. In other words, factory ammunition is resistant to light mist, rain, splash, and very short term immersion. Ammunition which has been fully submerged for more than a few minutes should be discarded, in a safe manner and according to local waste disposal ordinances.

Military ammunition is usually stored and shipped in watertight metal cans. Each military cartridge is sealed at the primer and case mouth and must pass a water proof test. A significant percentage of "surplus" military ammunition and metal ammunition boxes did not pass the water proof tests. As civilians generally do not need absolute reliability – except for personal defense – surplus military cartridges are sold commercially.

SPRAY LUBRICANTS

You should never spray loaded ammunition or loaded firearms with an aerosol lubricant. The penetrating oil in most aerosol lubricants will quickly seep into the primer pockets and, in a matter of hours, deactivate the primers. If the primer is sealed with lacquer around the annulus, the penetrating oil may still seep through voids in the sealer. It can also penetrate the case mouth and seep into the powder charge which is one cause of "squib loads".

+P AMMUNITION

If you plan to fire +P cartridges in a handgun it is absolutely necessary to verify that the gun has been designed to withstand the extreme pressures and mechanical stresses which are generated. If in doubt, check with the firearm manufacturer. Also be prepared for impressively greater: muzzle blast, recoil (perceived and actual), and in semi-auto pistols, ejected cartridge case velocity. Revolver shooters may encounter difficulty extracting fired cases from one, several, or all of the cylinder's chambers. The latter is more likely due to fouling and other residue from prior firing in the chamber(s) rather than the ammunition itself.

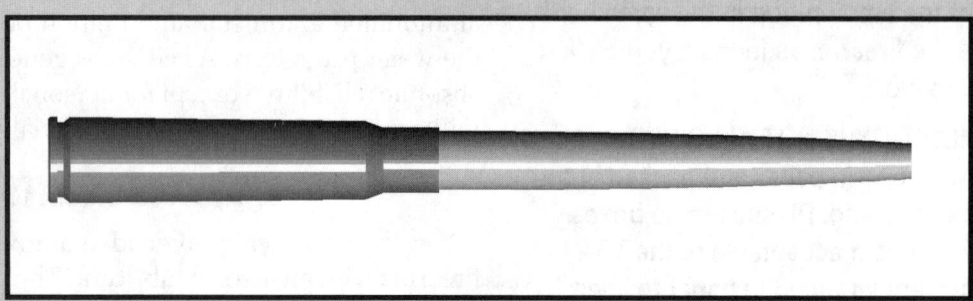

A Not-So-Sure Cure For Barbed Wire

8x57mm Wire Cutter Cartridge

Miles of barbed wire protected by the interlocking fire of multiple machineguns created a nightmare for attacking infantry during World War I. Of course, barbed wire could be cut with suitable tools, but the process was slow and machinegun fire made such work extremely dangerous (and unpopular). A quick and easy method of cutting through barbed wire was needed. German ammunition manufacturers responded with the 8x57 mm Wire Cutting Cartridge. This consisted of a steel rod loaded into a standard 8x57JS mm cartridge case. As the steel rod was less than bore diameter, the cartridge could be loaded into the standard M98 infantry rifle after the bolt was removed. Of course the steel rod was unstable in flight. This was intentional so the rod would cut barbed wire as it flew.

In practice, this concept did not work very well and the German front *soldaten* seldom used it.

CHAPTER 38 : AMMUNITION STORAGE SAFETY

CHAPTER 38 HIGHLIGHTS:

- STORAGE OF AMMUNITION
- STORAGE RECOMMENDATIONS FOR LOADED AMMUNITION
- CONSIDERATIONS FOR STORAGE OF SMOKELESS POWDER
- RECOMMENDATIONS FOR STORAGE OF SMOKELESS POWDER
- RECOMMENDATIONS FOR STORING PRIMERS
- THE PERILS OF AMMONIA
- SHELF LIFE OF AMMUNITION
- DISPOSAL OF UNSERVICEABLE AMMUNITION
- HOW TO CHECK SMOKELESS POWDER FOR DETERIORATION
- SMALL ARMS AMMUNITION IN A FIRE

STORAGE OF AMMUNITION

Small arms ammunition contains explosive ingredients including: a percussion-sensitive primer mixture and a smokeless propellant. It should be treated with respect and care in all handling, transportation, and storage.

Ammunition should be stored in the factory carton or package. The labeling and identification on the original container help to assure that future use will be in the gun for which the ammunition is intended.

Ammunition stored in the home, retail outlet, or distributor's warehouse over extended periods in factory packaging, subject to the ordinary variations of temperature and humidity ranging from tropic to Arctic conditions, can be expected to perform satisfactorily and safely in the firearms for which it was intended if such firearms are in proper working order and condition. Extreme high temperatures (over 150° F) however, should be avoided.

Ammunition should not be immersed in water or exposed to any organic solvent, paint thinner, petroleum product, ammonia, etc. Such materials may penetrate a loaded round and reach the powder or primer; and a deteriorating effect will result which may cause misfires or squib shots. The latter can result in a projectile's lodging in a gun barrel, the obstruction possibly causing serious damage or injury when another shot is fired.

Ideally, home storage of small arms ammunition is in a locked closet or cabinet out of the reach of children and uninformed or incompetent persons. Both guns and ammunition should be stored out of sight and reach of children and others not physically or mentally capable of giving them correct, proper use and respect.

Storing guns and ammunition in locked auto trunks may be convenient, or required by state or local law, during short periods when moving to and from the hunting field or target range. The possibilities of extremely high temperatures make it sensible to remove firearms and ammunition from vehicles following the trip. The passenger compartment of a closed car when exposed to the sun often develops an extreme high temperature and is thus not a desirable spot to leave ammunition.

STORAGE RECOMMENDATIONS FOR LOADED AMMUNITION

Always store ammunition in a location that is:

- **Secure**
- **Cool**
- **Dry**
- **Out of direct sunlight**
- **Away from oils, solvents, paints, and other chemicals**
- **Protected from impacts**
- **Away from electrical equipment such as fuse panels, water heaters, water softeners, furnaces, air conditioners, pumps, and shop equipment.**
- **In a locked wood or metal cabinet**
- **Away from open flames and radiators, portable heaters, fireplaces, and panel or baseboard heaters**
- **Not in direct physical contact with concrete**
- **Away from household pets and children**
- **Separately from firearms**
- **In the original packaging**

Many shooters have found that metal military ammunition cans work very well for this purpose. Be sure to label them so that you identify the contents without opening each can.

CONSIDERATIONS FOR STORAGE OF SMOKELESS POWDER

Smokeless powder is intended to function by burning, so it must be protected against accidental exposure to flame, sparks, or high temperatures.

For these reasons, storage enclosures should be made of insulating materials to protect the powder from external heat sources.

Once smokeless powder begins to burn, it will continue to burn (and generate gas pressure) until it is consumed.

DOT-approved containers are constructed to open up at low internal pressures to avoid the effects normally produced by the rupture or bursting of strong containers.

Storage enclosures for smokeless powder should be constructed in a similar manner:

1. **Of fire-resistant and heat-insulating materials to protect contents from external heat.**

2. **Sufficiently loose to vent the gaseous products of combustion satisfactorily, which would result if the quantity of smokeless powder within the enclosure accidentally ignited.**

If a small, tightly enclosed storage enclosure is loaded to capacity with containers of smokeless powder, the walls of the enclosure will expand or move outwards to release the gas pressure if the smokeless powder in storage is accidentally ignited.

Under such conditions, the effects of the release of gas pressure are similar or identical to the effects produced by an explosion. Therefore, storage of smokeless powder should be in strict compliance with all applicable regulations and recommendations of the National Fire Protection Association.

RECOMMENDATIONS FOR STORAGE OF SMOKELESS POWDER

Store smokeless powder in a cool, dry place. Be sure the storage area selected is free from any possible sources of excess heat and is isolated from open flame, furnaces, hot water heaters, etc. Do not store smokeless powder where it will be exposed to the sun's rays. Avoid storage in areas where mechanical or electrical equipment is in operation. Restrict from the storage areas heat or sparks which may result from improper, defective, or overloaded electrical circuits.

Do not store smokeless powder in the same area with solvents, flammable gases, or highly combustible materials. Store only in Department of Transportation-approved containers.

Do not transfer the smokeless powder from an approved container into one which is not approved.

Do not smoke in areas where smokeless powder is stored or used. Place appropriate "no smoking" signs in these areas.

Do not subject the storage cabinets to close confinement.

Storage cabinets should be constructed of insulating materials and with a weak wall, seams, or joints to provide an easy means of self-venting.

Do not keep old or salvaged powders. Check old powders for deterioration regularly. Destroy deteriorated powders immediately.

Obey all regulations regarding quantity and methods of storing. Do not store all your smokeless powders in one place. If you can, maintain separate storage locations. Many small containers are safer than one large container.

Keep your storage and use area clean. Clean up spilled smokeless powder promptly. Make sure the surrounding area is free of trash or other readily combustible materials.

RECOMMENDATIONS FOR STORING PRIMERS

Storage cabinets containing only primers are recommended. These cabinets should be ruggedly constructed of lumber at least 1" nominal thickness to delay or minimize the transmission of heat in the event of fire. SAAMI recommends against storing primers in sealed or pressurized containers.

Keep your storage and use area clean. Make sure the surrounding area is free of trash or other readily combustible materials.

Be sure your storage area is free from any possible sources of excessive heat and is isolated from open flame, furnaces, water heaters, etc. Do not store primers where they can be exposed to direct sunlight. Avoid storage in areas where mechanical or electrical equipment is in operation.

Do not store primers in the same area with solvents, flammable gases, or highly combustible materials. Store primers only in their original factory containers. Do not transfer the primers from their approved container into one which is not approved. The use of glass bottles, fruit jars, plastic or metal containers, or other bulk containers for primer storage is extremely hazardous.

Do not smoke in areas where primers are stored. Place appropriate "No Smoking" signs in these areas.

Do not store primers in any area where they might be exposed to gun fire, bullet impact, or ricochets.

Do not store primers with propellant powders or any other highly combustible materials so as to avoid involving primers in a fire as much as possible.

Observe all regulations regarding quantity and methods of storing primers.

Never have an open flame, source of sparks, or hot particles in the vicinity of primers or any ammunition loading operation.

Do not smoke near primers.

Safety glasses must be worn when performing any and all handloading operations. Additional protection such as face shields or machine guards are strongly recommended.

No more than 10,000 small arms primers may be stored in residences.

Smokeless propellants shall be stored in shipping containers approved by the U.S. Department of Transportation.

Smokeless propellants intended for personal use in quantities not exceeding 20 lb. (9.1 kg) shall be permitted to be stored in original containers in residences. Quantities exceeding 20 lb. (9.1 kg), but not exceeding 50 lb. (22.7 kg), shall be permitted to be stored in residences where kept in a wooden box or cabinet having walls of at least 1 in. (25.4 mm) nominal thickness.

THE PERILS OF AMMONIA

Ammonia is the arch enemy of ammunition. Even a small amount of ammonia will attack and destroy a brass cartridge case. Most household cleaning agents contain ammonia. In many instances, the typical strong odor of the ammonia has been suppressed, making it hard to detect by smell.

For this reason, all ammunition should be kept well away from household cleaning agents. Never wash once fired cases in a cleaner that has ammonia as an ingredient. If in doubt, check the label.

SHELF LIFE OF AMMUNITION

Ammunition stored under proper conditions has a shelf life measured in many decades. For example,

ammunition loaded during World War II that has been properly stored remains serviceable and capable of full ballistic performance today, more than 65 years from the date it was manufactured.

Poor storage conditions are the main enemy of ammunition shelf life. Temperature extremes, moisture, sunlight, and chemical attack are the main culprits. Very high temperatures (above 150°F) can render primers inert. Moisture can damage propellant and chemicals can attack the brass case.

Proper conditions are seldom maintained throughout long term ammunition storage. As time passes, older lots of ammunition begin to deteriorate. However, such ammunition may not show any visual symptoms of deterioration from, for example, exposure to high temperatures.

Even under the best storage conditions, ultimately the solvents in the propellant decompose, rendering the propellant useless. Fortunately, this process is very slow.

DISPOSAL OF UNSERVICEABLE AMMUNITION

Ammunition that has been in a structural fire, and has become wetted or scorched, or has been exposed to flood waters should never be returned to commercial sales channels or sold at salvage sales since it could be rendered dangerous to the shooter by such exposure. It should be scrapped.

Never dispose of ammunition by burying it or dumping it in a waterway. It may be retrieved years later, fully "live," and pose dangers to children or uninformed persons.

Under most circumstances, unserviceable ammunition may be scrapped by returning it to the manufacturer. Written permission should first be obtained from the Product Services Manager of the manufacturer before shipment is made. If the manufacturer is not known, contact SAAMI at 11 Mile Hill Rd., Newtown, CT, 06470.

HOW TO CHECK SMOKELESS POWDER FOR DETERIORATION

Although modern smokeless powders contain stabilizers and are basically free from deterioration under proper storage conditions, safe practices require recognition of the signs of deterioration and its possible effects.

Deteriorating smokeless powders produce an acidic odor and may produce a reddish brown fume. (Don't confuse this with common solvent odors such as alcohol, ether, and acetone.) Dispose of deteriorating smokeless powders immediately.

Check to make certain that smokeless powder is not exposed to extreme heat as this may cause deterioration. Such exposure produces an acidity that accelerates further reaction and has been known, because of heat generated by the reaction, to cause spontaneous combustion.

Never salvage powder from old cartridges and do not attempt to blend salvaged powder with new powder or attempt to blend two types of powder to make one.

SMALL ARMS AMMUNITION IN A FIRE

Although much has been written and rumored about the 4th of July characteristics and so-called havoc of ammunition in fires, it just isn't so. Members of fire fighting units are understandably uneasy when confronted by fires where ammunition is involved.

Several members of the Sporting Arms and Ammunition Manufacturers' Institute have undertaken extensive experiments to show what can be expected when ammunition is involved in a fire. These companies have also made careful investigations after such fires, which show that the missiles do not have sufficient energy to penetrate the garments and protective gear worn by fire fighters.

Tests also show that the whizzing sound heard in the vicinity of ammunition fires are caused by primers expelled from the burning cartridges. The "pops" and "bangs" are exploding primers; the propellant powders burn inefficiently and make little noise.

Metallic cartridges in a fire are difficult to sustain in a burning condition once the packing materials have been consumed due to the cooling effects of the metal parts and the relatively high ratio of metal weight to smokeless powder. Only a vigorous fire around metallic ammunition stocks will cause all cartridges to burn. Shotshell ammunition is difficult to ignite, but once ignited it will sustain its own burning due to the plastic or paper tubes (hulls).

Smart Paints Measure Ammunition Temperature During Transportation And Storage

Army Research and Development Command (ARDEC) engineers at Picatinny Arsenal are developing "smart" thermochromic polymers for paints that can detect if ammunition has been subjected temperatures above design limits during transport and storage. When exposed to such high temperatures, the thermochromic polymer changes wavelengths (colors) permanently, which serves as a record and a warning. In addition, by using a hand-held laser to measure the optical reflectivity of the paint, the length of exposure can be determined. The paint will cost pennies per application compared to the temperature gauges now being used.

CHAPTER 39 : SHOOTING SAFETY

AMMUNITION CHECK LIST - BEFORE GOING AFIELD

- Always verify that the cartridges you take to the field are the correct caliber and bullet weight.
- Use only fresh ammunition which has been stored properly.
- Understand the meaning of hangfire, misfire, and squib load, and the immediate action you should take in the event one of these occurs.
- Protect your ammunition in transit from direct sunlight, impact, oils, and moisture.
- Keep only ammunition for the caliber of gun you are using within your reach.
- If you are going hunting, always check the pockets of your clothing for left over ammunition from previous hunts.
- For pack trip hunts into rough country, keep your ammunition in a waterproof container.
- Never carry or ship ammunition inside your gun case.
- Always take a cleaning rod with you to the field or the range (to remove barrel obstructions).
- Understand the ballistics of your cartridges and their maximum vertical and horizontal range.

* FIREARMS SAFETY DEPENDS ON YOU

1. Always Keep the Muzzle Pointed in a Safe Direction

This is the most basic gun safety rule. If everyone handled his firearm so carefully that the muzzle never pointed at something he didn't intend to shoot, there would be virtually no firearms accidents. It's as simple as that, and it's up to you.

2. Firearms Should Be Unloaded When Not in Use

Firearms should be loaded only when you are in the field or on the target range or shooting area, ready to shoot.

3. Don't Rely on Your Gun's Safety

The safety serves as a supplement to proper gun handling, but it is not a substitute for common sense. You should never handle a gun carelessly and assume that the gun won't fire just because the "safety is on."

4. Be Sure of Your Target and What is Beyond it

Once a gun fires, you have given up all control over where the shot will go or what it will strike. Don't shoot unless you know exactly what your shot is going to strike.

5. Use Correct Ammunition

Improper or incorrect ammunition can destroy a gun and cause serious personal injury.

6. If Your Gun Fails to Fire When the Trigger Is Pulled, Handle with Care!

Occasionally, a cartridge may not fire when the trigger is pulled. If this occurs, keep the muzzle pointed in a safe direction. Keep your face away from the breech. Then, carefully open the action, unload the firearm, and dispose of the cartridge in a safe way.

7. Always Wear Eye and Ear Protection When Shooting

Exposure to shooting noise can damage hearing, and adequate vision protection is essential. Shooting glasses guard against twigs, falling shot, clay target chips, and the rare ruptured case or firearm malfunction.

8. Be Sure the Barrel is Clear of Obstructions Before Shooting

Even a small bit of mud, snow, excess lubricating oil, or grease in the bore can cause dangerously increased pressures, causing the barrel to bulge or even burst on firing, which can cause injury to the shooter and bystanders.

9. Don't Alter or Modify Your Gun, and Have Guns Serviced Regularly

Do not jeopardize your safety or the safety of others by altering the trigger, safety, or other mechanism of any firearm or allowing unqualified persons to repair or modify them.

10. Learn the Mechanical and Handling Characteristics of the Firearms You are Using

Since guns can be so different, no person should handle any firearm without first having thoroughly familiarized himself with the particular type of firearm he is using, the safe gun handling rules for loading, unloading, carrying, handling that firearm, and the rules of safe gun handling in general.

DEFINITIONS

HANGFIRE

A hangfire may be defined as a noticeable delay between the time the trigger releases the sear or striker and the ignition of the cartridge. In other words, a "click-delay-bang".

There are two major causes of hangfires: chemical and mechanical.

A mechanical hangfire is caused by a defect in the gun. A chemical hangfire is caused by a defective primer. Most chemical delays are the result of now-obsolete potassium chlorate primers in old ammunition.

Immediate Action

- Open the action of the gun and remove the fired case and any remaining cartridges.
- Carefully inspect the firearm for mechanical defects including the chamber and bore. If in doubt, have the firearm inspected by a qualified gunsmith.
- Discontinue use of the ammunition causing the hangfires.
- Dispose of such ammunition properly.

MISFIRE

This is a complete failure of the cartridge to function despite the primer being struck solidly by the firing pin.

Most misfires are caused by a light firing pin hit on the primer, or a defective or damaged primer which fails to detonate.

Immediate Action

- Assume that a hangfire is happening. Keeping the gun pointed in a safe direction, wait 60 seconds.
- If the cartridge has not fired by the end of the waiting period, carefully open the action and remove the misfired cartridge.
- Inspect the misfired cartridge for light primer indentation, contamination, damage, etc.
- Discontinue use of this particular lot of ammunition and dispose of the cartridges properly.

SQUIB LOAD

A squib load is a cartridge which produces a muzzle velocity and/or a report (sound) substantially lower than normal. In other words, it is a partial misfire in that the primer detonates, but the propellant does not ignite or only partially burns.

The force of the primer alone is often enough to drive the bullet into the barrel. In addition, unburned propellant may be left in the barrel as well.

Immediate Action

- Keeping the firearm pointed in a safe direction, open the action and remove the empty case and any remaining cartridges.
- Carefully inspect the bore for any obstruction and unburned propellant.
- Remove any unburned propellant and/or bore obstruction and carefully inspect barrel for damage, such as bulges.
- Discontinue use of any ammunition which repeatedly causes squib loads and properly dispose any remaining ammunition with the same lot code.

MAXIMUM RANGE

Every shooter should know the maximum range of his ammunition. Below is an abbreviated list of the popular calibers and maximum ranges. The reader is also referred to Chapter 96: Reference Material for a more comprehensive list.

Points To Keep In Mind

* Maximum range increases at higher altitudes, lower humidity, and higher temperatures.

* A bullet which hits the ground at maximum range may ricochet and travel further.

* A bullet descending from its maximum vertical range or striking at its maximum horizontal range may have enough remaining energy to cause serious personal injury or kill a person.

* Always make certain of your backstop and, just as important, where your bullet may impact if it misses and continues downrange.

* Maximum horizontal range requires a barrel elevation between 28° and 31° from horizontal.

* A bullet fired vertically or horizontally may impact far from the initial path of travel due to wind deflection.

MAXIMUM RANGE

Caliber	Bullet Weight (grs.)	Max. Horizontal Range (yds.)	Max. Vertical Range (ft.)
.22 Long Rifle	40	1,650	3,650
.223 Rem.	55	4,000	8,650
.30-30 Win.	150	3,000	6,800
.30-'06 Spr.	180	4,700	10,500
.300 Win. Mag.	180	5,350	12,000
9mm Luger	124	2,150	4,800
.45 ACP+P	185	2,000	4,150
.357 Mag.	158	2,500	5,400
.44 Mag.	240	2,500	5,600

Note: All ranges above are for ammunition fired at sea level, 59° F. and atmosphere pressure of 29.53 inches of Hg. All range distances are approximate.

CHAPTER 40 : WARNINGS

CHAPTER 40 HIGHLIGHTS:

- CENTERFIRE/RIMFIRE WARNINGS
- +P AMMUNITION WARNING
- SHOTSHELL WARNINGS

CENTERFIRE/RIMFIRE WARNINGS

WARNING: KEEP OUT OF REACH OF CHILDREN

1. Use these cartridges only in modern firearms in good condition marked and chambered for this cartridge.

2. Read your firearm owner's manual, contact the manufacturer if you do not have one.

3. Always wear shooting glasses to protect your eyes from flying particles and gas.

4. Always wear proper hearing protectors as repeated exposure to gun fire can damage hearing.

5. Shooting in poorly ventilated areas, cleaning firearms, or handling ammunition may result in exposure to lead, a substance known to cause birth defects, reproductive harm, and other serious physical injury.

6. Make certain you have adequate ventilation at all times.

7. Qash hands thoroughly after exposure.

8. Always be sure the barrel is free of any obstruction before shooting.

9. Never attempt to remove a barrel obstruction by shooting it out.

10. If the gun fails to fire, point the muzzle in a safe direction, wait 30 seconds, and unload carefully while avoiding exposure to the breech.

11. Discharge may occur if a primer is struck, handle with caution, do not drop.

12. Failure to comply with these warnings may cause serious injury.

+P AMMUNITION WARNING

WARNING: KEEP OUT OF REACH OF CHILDREN

1. Cartridges with a +P on the head stamp are loaded to higher maximum average pressures for greater velocity.

2. Use +P ammunition only in firearms recommended by the manufacturer for use with this type of cartridge – if in doubt, contact the manufacturer.

3. Continuous use of +P ammunition in revolvers with aluminum frames or cylinders is not recommended.

SHOTSHELL WARNINGS

WARNING: KEEP OUT OF REACH OF CHILDREN

1. Use these shotshells only in modern shotguns in good condition marked and chambered for this gauge and shell length.

2. Read your firearm owner's manual, contact the manufacturer if you do not have one.

3. Always wear shooting glasses to protect your eyes from flying particles and gas.

4. Always wear proper hearing protectors as repeated exposure to gun fire can damage hearing.

5. Do not use in shotguns with damascus or twist steel barrels or in chambers shorter than 2 3/4 inches in length.

6. It is dangerous to load 12 gauge shotshells in 10 gauge shotguns or to load 20 gauge shotshells in 12 gauge shotguns because the smaller shell will pass through the chamber and lodge in the barrel creating an obstruction.

7. Do not shoot steel shot in a barrel not designed for it.

8. Cleaning firearms or handling ammunition may result in exposure to lead, a substance known to cause birth defects, reproductive harm, and other serious physical injury.

9. Wash hands thoroughly after exposure.

10. Always be sure the barrel is free of any obstruction before shooting.

11. Never attempt to remove a barrel obstruction by shooting it out.

12. If the gun fails to fire, point the muzzle in a safe direction, wait 30 seconds, and unload carefully while avoiding exposure to the breech.

13. Discharge may occur if primer is struck, handle with caution, do not drop.

14. Failure to comply with these warnings may cause serious injury.

SHOTS OF A LIFETIME – On The Range
(Story from an unamed author)

At the annual company picnic, we opened a trap range for our employees. We provided the shotshells and clay birds free—after all we were an ammunition manufacturer. Many of our employees were regular trap shooters capable of consistently breaking 22-23 clay birds although 25 straight was rare. The President of the company and I were watching the shooting from comfortable chairs with cold drinks. Repeatedly, the employees challenged us to shoot with (against) them. While competent trap shooters, neither of us had shot trap for several years. Reluctantly, we both rose, selected completely unfamiliar shotguns from a rack behind the range, and took our positions. When all was said and done, both the president and I went 25 straight while the next highest was 22! The employees were awestruck. We reclaimed our chairs and sat on our laurels while we were ahead.

CHAPTER 41 : DANGEROUS COMBINATIONS

UNSAFE FIREARM-AMMUNITION COMBINATIONS

The discharge of ammunition in a firearm that is not designed to shoot that ammunition can be dangerous and can result in serious injury or death to the user and/or bystanders, as well as damage to the firearm. This unsafe condition is caused by an excessive build-up and/or release of high-pressure gas in a firearm's chamber, barrel, and/or action beyond which the firearm is designed to withstand. Therefore, in the interest of safety, you should use only ammunition of the caliber or gauge designated by the firearm manufacturer for use in that firearm. Markings indicating the correct caliber or gauge of ammunition to be used in a firearm are usually found on the firearm's barrel, frame, or receiver.

One way to verify that you are using the correct ammunition is to check the head stamp on the ammunition to confirm that it matches the caliber or gauge markings placed on the firearm by the firearm's manufacturer. Some types of ammunition do not have markings on the head stamp of the cartridge. In that case, check the original ammunition packaging to determine its caliber. If you have any doubt about the caliber of the ammunition, you should not use the ammunition until you have it examined by a qualified person who can determine its caliber. Remember just because a round of ammunition can fit into a firearm's chamber, barrel, or action does not mean it is safe to use that ammunition in the firearm.

Due to the availability of many different shapes and sizes of ammunition and firearms, there are countless unsafe ammunition-firearm combinations such that a comprehensive list of unsafe combinations is neither feasible, nor practical. Below is a list of some unsafe combinations that are well known because of somewhat similar chamber and ammunition dimensions.

If the caliber or gauge is not clearly marked on the firearm, or if it appears the original markings on the firearm have been altered or modified in any way, do not use the firearm as serious injury or death could result to the user and/or bystanders, as well as damage to the firearm.

Similarly, SAAMI has not published voluntary recommended practices or procedures for re-chambering of firearms. It is possible the re-chambering of a firearm may not have been done properly or may not have been properly marked on the firearm. If the caliber or gauge marking is missing or altered in any way, you should not use the firearm. You should instead have the firearm examined by a qualified person to determine what caliber or gauge ammunition can safely be used in that firearm.

RIMFIRE

In Firearms Chambered For	Do Not Use These Cartridges
5mm Rem RF Magnum	17 Precision Made Cartridge 17 Mach 2 22 BB Cap 22 CB Cap 22 Short 22 Long 22 Long Rifle 22 Long Rifle Shot 22 Winchester Automatic
17 Hornady Magnum Rimfire	17 Precision Made Cartridge 17 Mach 2 22 CB Short 22 Short 22 Long 22 Long Rifle 22 Stinger 22 CB
17 Precision Made Cartridge	22 BB Cap
22 Short	17 Mach 2 17 Precision Made cartridge
22 Long	17 Mach 2 17 Precision made Cartridge
22 Long Rifle	17 Mach 2 17 Precision Made Cartridge
22 Winchester Rimfire	17 Precision Made Cartridge 22 BB Cap 22 CB Cap 22 Short 22 Long 22 Long Rifle 22 Long Rifle Shot
22 Winchester Magnum	17 Precision Made Cartridge 22 BB Cap 22 CB Cap 22 Short 22 Long 22 Long Rifle 22 Long Rifle Shot

RIMFIRE, *CONT.*

In Firearms Chambered For	Do Not Use These Cartridges
22 Winchester Automatic	17 Precision Made Cartridge 22 BB Cap 22 CB Ca 22 Short 22 Long 22 Long Rifle 22 Long Rifle Shot
25 Stevens Long	5mm Rem RF Magnum

SHOTGUN

In Shotguns Chambered For	Do Not Use These Shells
10 Gauge	12 Gauge
12 Gauge	16 Gauge
12 Gauge	20 Gauge
16 Gauge	20 Gauge
20 Gauge	28 Gauge

In Shotguns Chambered For	Do Not Use These Centerfire Metallic Cartridges
410 Bore	Any

With any gauge, shotshells of a given nominal length should not be fired in a gun the chamber of which is shorter than the fired length, e.g. a 3" (75mm) shell fired in a 2 ¾" (70mm) chamber.

CENTERFIRE PISTOL & REVOLVER

In Firearms Chambered For	Do Not Use These Cartridges
9mm Luger (Parabellum)	9mm NATO (Military) 40 Smith & Wesson 9x18 Makarov
9mm Winchester Magnum	9x18 Makarov
9x18 Makarov	9mm Luger 38 Automatic 38 Super Automatic 380 Automatic
9x23 Winchester	38 Super Automatic 380 Automatic
32 H&R Magnum	32 Long Colt
32 Smith & Wesson	32 Automatic 32 Long Colt 32 Short Colt
32-20 Winchester Velocity	32-20 Winchester High
357 Sig	9mm Luger
38 Automatic	38 Super Automatic +P* 9mm Luger 9x18 Makarov 9x23 Winchester

CENTERFIRE PISTOL & REVOLVER, *CONT.*

In Firearms Chambered For	Do Not Use These Cartridges
38 Super Automatic +P	9mm Luger 9x18 Makarov 9x23 Winchester
38 Smith & Wesson	38 Automatic 38 Long Colt 38 Short Colt 38 Special 9x18 Makarov
38 Special	357 Magnum 380 Automatic
38-40 Winchester Velocity	38-40 Winchester High
40 Smith & Wesson	9mm Luger
44-40 Winchester Velocity	44-40 Winchester High
45 Automatic	38-40 Winchester 44 Remington Magnum 44 Special 44-40 Winchester 45 Glock Automatic Pistol
45 Colt	38-40 Winchester 44 Rem Magnum 44 S&W Special 44-40 Winchester 454 Casull
45 Winchester Magnum	45 Automatic 45 Glock Automatic Pistol 454 Casull
45 Glock Automatic Pistol	45 Automatic 45 Winchester Magnum
475 Linebaugh	45 Long Colt 44 Remington Magnum 44 S&W Special 45 Automatic Rim
480 Ruger	45 Long Colt 44 Remington Magnum 44 S&W Special 45 Automatic Rim

Note* +P ammunition is loaded to a higher pressure, as indicated by the +P marking on the cartridge case headstamp, for use only in firearms especially designed for this cartridge and so recommended by the manufacturer.

CENTERFIRE RIFLE

In Firearms Chambered For	Do Not Use These Cartridges
5.56X45 mm NATO	25-45 Sharps
6mm Remington (244 REM)	250 Savage 7.62x39
6.5mm Remington Magnum	300 Savage
6x47 Remington	25-45 Sharps

CENTERFIRE RIFLE, CONT.

In Firearms Chambered For	Do Not Use These Cartridges
6.5 Creedmore	357 Magnum 357 Remington Magnum
6.5 x 06 A-Square	7.62 x 39
6.5x55 Swedish	7mm BR Remington 7.62x39 300 Savage
7mm Express Remington	7mm Mauser (7x57) 270 Winchester 30 Remington 30-30 Winchester 300 Savage 308 Winchester 32 Remington 375 Winchester 38-55 Winchester
7mm Mauser (7x57)	7.62 x 39 300 Savage 30-30 Winchester
7mm Remington Magnum	7mm Express Remington 7mmMauser (7x57) 7mm Remington Ultra Magnum 7mm Weatherby Magnum 270 Winchester 280 Remington 300 Winchester Magnum 303 British 308 Winchester 35 Remington 350 Remington Magnum 375 Winchester 38-55 Winchester
7mm Remington Short Action Ultra Magnum	7mm-08 Remington 357 Remington Maximum 454 Casull 480 Ruger
7mm Remington Ultra Magnum	300 Winchester Magnum
7mm Shooting Times Westerner	30-06 Springfield 30-40 Krag 300 Winchester Magnum 350 Remington
7mm Weatherby Magnum	7mm Express Remington 7mm Mauser (7x57) 7mm Remington Magnum 8mm Mauser 270 Winchester 280 Remington 303 British 308 Winchester 35 Remington 350 Remington Magnum 375 Winchester 38-55 Winchester
7mm-08 Remington	7.62x39
8mm Mauser (8x57)	7mm Mauser (7x57) 35 Remington

CENTERFIRE RIFLE, CONT.

In Firearms Chambered For	Do Not Use These Cartridges
8mm Remington Magnum	338 Winchester Magnum 350 Remington Magnum 358 Norma Magnum 375 Winchester 38-55 Winchester
17 Remington	221 Remington Fireball 25-45 Sharps 30 Carbine 300 AAC Blackout
17-223 Remington	17 Remington 221 Remington Fireball 30 Carbine
204 Ruger	25-45 Sharps
220 Swift	7.62 x 39
222 Remington	25-45 Sharps 300 AAC Blackout
222 Remington Magnum	25-45 Sharps 300 AAC Blackout
223 Remington	5.56mm Military 222 Remington 25-45 Sharps 30 Carbine 300 AAC Blackout
224 Weatherby Magnum	222 Remington Magnum
240 Weatherby Magnum	220 Swift 225 Winchester
243 Winchester	7.62x39 225 Winchester 250 Savage 300 Savage
243 Winchester Super Short Magnum	30 Carbine 32-20 Winchester
25 Winchester Super Short Magnum	30 Carbine 32-20 Winchester
25-06 Remington	7mm BR Remington 7.62x39 308 Winchester
257 Roberts	7.62x39 250 Savage
257 Weatherby Magnum	25-06 Remington 25-35 Winchester 6.5mm Remington Magnum 284 Winchester 7mm-08 Remington 7mm Mauser 7.62x39 300 Savage 303 Savage 307 Winchester 308 Winchester 30-30 Winchester 32 Winchester 32-40 Winchester

CENTERFIRE RIFLE, CONT.

In Firearms Chambered For	Do Not Use These Cartridges
257 Weatherby Magnum, cont.	35 Remington
	350 Remington Magnum
	356 Winchester
	358 Winchester
	375 Winchester
	38-55 Winchester
264 Winchester Magnum	270 Winchester
	284 Winchester
	303 British
	350 Remington
	375 Winchester
	38-55 Winchester
270 Weatherby Magnum	25-06 Remington
	270 Winchester
	280 Remington
	284 Winchester
	7mm-08 Remington
	7-30 Waters
	30 Remington
	30-30 Winchester
	300 Savage
	303 Savage
	307 Winchester
	308 Winchester
	32 Winchester
	32 Winchester Special
	32-40 Winchester
	35 Remington
	35 Remington Magnum
	356 Winchester
	358 Winchester
	375 Winchester
	38-55 Winchester
270 Winchester	7m Mauser (7x57)
	7.62x39
	30 Remington
	30-30 Winchester
	300 Savage
	308 Winchester
	32 Remington
	375 Winchester
	38-55 Winchester
270 Winchester Short Magnum	7mm Remington Short Action Ultra Magnum
	32-40 Winchester
	38-40 Winchester
	44-40 Winchester
	44 Remington Magnum
	45 Colt
	454 Casull
	480 Ruger
280 Remington	7mm Mauser (7x57)
	7.62x39
	270 Winchester
	30 Remington
	30-30 Winchester
	300 Savage
	308 Winchester
	32 Remington
	375 Winchester
	38-55 Winchester
284 Winchester	7mm Mauser (7x57)
	300 Savage

CENTERFIRE RIFLE, CONT.

In Firearms Chambered For	Do Not Use These Cartridges
30 Thompson Center	41 Remington Magnum
	44 Remington Magnum
	44 Smith & Wesson Special
	45 Automatic
30-06 Springfield	7.62x39
	8mm Mauser (8x57)
	32 Remington
	35 Remington
	375 Winchester
	38-55 Winchester
30-40 Krag (30 Govt)	303 British
	303 Savage
	32 Winchester Special
30-378 Weatherby Magnum	8mm Remington Magnum
	300 Remington Ultra Magnum
	300 Weatherby Magnum
	300 Winchester Magnum
	338 Winchester Magnum
	340 Weatherby Magnum
300 Holland & Holland Magnum	8mm Mauser (8x57)
	30-06 Springfield
	30-40 Krag
	375 Winchester
	38-55 Winchester
300 Pegasus	300 Remington Ultra Magnum
300 Remington Ultra Magnum	7mm STW
	30 Weatherby Magnum
	300 H&H Magnum
	338 Winchester Magnum
300 Remington Short Action Ultra Magnum	30 Remington
	30-30 Winchester
	300 Savage
	308 Winchester
	32 Winchester Special
	357 Remington Maximum
	454 Casull
	480 Ruger
300 Savage	338 Winchester Magnum
300 Weatherby Magnum	338 Winchester Magnum
300 Winchester Magnum	8mm Mauser Rd. Nose Magnum
	303 British
	350 Remington Magnum
	375 Winchester
	38-55 Winchester
300 Winchester Short Magnum	32-40 Winchester
	38-40 Winchester
	44-40 Winchester
	44 Remington Magnum
	45 Colt
	454 Casull
	480 Ruger
303 British	30-30 Winchester
	32 Winchester Special

CENTERFIRE RIFLE, *CONT.*

In Firearms Chambered For	Do Not Use These Cartridges
303 Savage	30-30 Winchester 32 Winchester Special 32-40 Winchester
308 Marlin Express	38-40 41 Remington Magnum 44 Remington Magnum 44 Smith & Wesson Special 44-40 Winchester
308 Winchester	7.62x39 300 Savage
338 Excalibur	300 Remington Ultra Magnum
338 Lapua Magnum	444 Marlin
338 Remington Ultra Magnum	300 Weatherby Magnum 35 Whelen
338 Winchester Magnum	375 Winchester 38-55 Winchester
338-06 A-Square	35 Remington
338-378 Weatherby Magnum	338 Remington Ultra Magnum
340 Weatherby Magnum	350 Remington Magnum 375 Winchester 38-55 Winchester 416 Taylor Magnum 444 Marlin
348 Winchester	35 Remington
358 Shooting Times Alaskan	7mm Shooting Times Westerner 338 Winchester Magnum 8mm Remington 350 Remington Magnum 358 Norma Magnum 375 Winchester 38-55 Winchester 416 Taylor Magnum
375 H&H Magnum	375 Winchester 38-55 Winchester

CENTERFIRE RIFLE, *CONT.*

In Firearms Chambered For	Do Not Use These Cartridges
375 Remington Ultra Magnum	375 H&H Magnum 375 Ruger
375 Weatherby	416 Taylor Magnum
375 Winchester	38-55 Winchester 41 Long Colt
378 Weatherby Magnum	375 Remington Ultra Magnum 416 Taylor Magnum 444 Marlin 45-70 Government
38-55 Winchester	375 Winchester 41 Long Colt
405 Winchester	7x30 Waters 30-30 Winchester 30-40 Krag 303 British 375 Winchester 38-55 Winchester
416 Rigby	300 Remington Ultra Magnum 338 Remington Ultra Magnum 416 Remington 416 Ruger
416 Ruger	444 Marlin 45-75 Govt 450 Marlin 500 Smith & Wesson
416 Weatherby Magnum	416 Remington 416 Rigby 416 Ruger 45-70 Government
45-70 Government	454 Casull 475 Linebaugh 480 Ruger
460 Weatherby Magnum	458 Winchester

9MM PARABELLUM KTW

SPECIMEN AND PHOTOS COURTESY OF PAUL SMITH

In the 1960s, Dr. Paul Kopsch (an Ohio coroner), Daniel Turcos (a police sergeant), and Donald Ward (Dr. Kopsch's special investigator), began experimenting with special purpose handgun ammunition. Their objective was to develop a law enforcement round capable of improved penetration against hard targets, such as windshield glass and automobile doors. Conventional bullets, made primarily from lead, often become deformed and ineffective after striking hard targets, especially when fired at handgun velocities.

After some experimentation with steel rounds, the officers settled on a brass core with a 'lubricating' jacket of Teflon. Although a myth persists that the Teflon is there to either penetrate "bullet-proof" vests more effectively, or protect the bore of the firearm that fires it, Dr. Kopsch himself has testified that the Teflon actually reduces these bullets' penetration in Kevlar, and is only there to reduce the likelihood of ricochets. (Kopsch, Turcus, & Ward struck upon the idea of the Teflon coating after finding out that the manufacturers of canes impregnate the plastic tips of their canes with a Teflon compound; under pressure, the Teflon actually helps the bullet to "stick" momentarily, and it is this characteristic that reduces the chances of a ricochet off of the glass or metal surfaces of an automobile). The inventors named the round the 'KTW Bullet,' after their initials.(1)

This round was headstamped: KTW 9MM LUGER

Note the 2 driving bands on the brass projectile.

Lew Curtis, an advanced collector of 9mm ammunition notes:(2)

I was in Ohio when they put on their first display at the Ohio Gun Collectors show in Columbus and I spoke to one of them who was at their table. They had just started production and their big pitch at the time is that their 357 magnum shot at the back of a fleeing car would penetrate the entire car and crack the engine block stopping the car. They had photos of cars they had shot. I was a 1st Lt at the time and was impressed. I left Ohio and went back to SEA in early 1969 so this must have been 1968 they introduced the KTW ammo and began selling it because I bought a box. The cases were all reloads. In the 1970s they introduced their own headstamp. The initial production was all a steel alloy (weakly magnetic) and the name was something like Kennetite or similar I think. It was significantly later, 1981 in one source (http://www.guncite.com/gun_control_gcgvcopk.html), that the brass bullet was introduced. I think this must have been in the same time frame they left Lorain Ohio and became: NORTH AMERICAN ORDNANCE CORPORATION, Pontiac, Mighigan 48057, U.S.A.

[It is important to note...] that both a magnetic alloy bullet and later a brass bullet were produced and sold.

NOTE: Serious restrictions were placed on this ammunition by Congress after a hysterical campaign by gun control extremists branding these as "cop killer bullets".

References:
(1) Wikipedia.com
(2) email from Lew Curtis to webmaster November 26, 2006.

Courtesy International Ammunition Association, Inc. (cartridgecollectors.org)

SECTION VIII – BALLISTICS
CHAPTER 42 : BALLISTIC DEFINITIONS

CHAPTER 42 HIGHLIGHTS:

- BALLISTICS DEFINED
- WHO MAKES THESE TABLES?
- WHY THEY LOOK THE SAME

- BASIC ASSUMPTIONS
- EFFECTS

- CONTENTS OF A BALLISTIC TABLE EXPLAINED

All drawings by Author, unless otherwise noted.

BALLISTICS DEFINED

POPULAR DEFINITION

Ballistics is the study of the motion of projectiles in the gun, in flight, and in the target.

SCIENTIFIC DEFINITION

Ballistics is the collective name for the scientific study, measurement, and analysis of projectiles during three phases of movement: inside gun systems (interior ballistics), in flight (exterior ballistics), and when striking the target (terminal ballistics).

The word ballistics is derived from the Latin word "ballista" which was a military siege engine, essentially a very large crossbow, for launching either dart or spherical stone projectiles.

BALLISTIC CHARTS

Most major ammunition manufacturers' catalogs contain extensive tables listing exterior ballistic information for their products. While these tables contain a wealth of numbers, mining them for useful information can be a daunting task. Do not be intimidated by these tables. They have been designed to assist you in getting the maximum performance from your firearm. This chapter will help you understand what these tables contain and how to make maximum use of the information presented.

WHO MAKES THESE TABLES?

The exterior ballistic information published in domestic ammunition manufacturers' catalogs is generated by the Sporting Arms and Ammunition Manufacturers' Institute (SAAMI) group of the National Shooting Sports Foundation (NSSF).

WHY THEY LOOK THE SAME

The SAAMI Technical Committee developed computer software to make standardized exterior ballistic calculations. The exterior ballistic data generated by this software is used by all SAAMI member companies to generate the ballistic charts in their product catalogs.

Member companies list uniform exterior ballistic data to avoid arguments over minor variations in ballistic performance between similar products of different brands. For example, all SAAMI member companies list similar exterior ballistic performance figures for 150 grain soft point bullets in .30-'06 Sprg. caliber.

Exterior ballistic data for new products, not listed on the existing SAAMI menu, must be generated by the manufacturer introducing the new product. Manufacturer's data is only published after all members have an opportunity for comment.

Catalog exterior ballistic tables are a canvas of compromises and averages designed to cover all SAAMI members' products. While this may seem imprecise, in fact it works very well because the actual difference in ballistic performance between similar products is indeed small. This means you can trust the published charts to provide you with useful information.

Going Ballistic

This term was popularized in the 1990s. It is applied to reactive outbursts of personal behavior which are "over the top" or excessive and usually associated with anger or frustration. It also carries an element of direction or out of control motion.

"Going ballistic" is a modern example of an ordnance term entering the vernacular.

BASIC ASSUMPTIONS

Ballistic data published in company catalogs is based on a set of standard assumptions. This should be kept in mind when analyzing an exterior ballistic chart. Some of these assumptions are:

STANDARD "METRO" ATMOSPHERIC CONDITIONS

The U.S. Army and most ammunition manufacturers base their exterior ballistic calculations on standard metropolitan or "metro" conditions:

- **Altitude: sea level (0 feet)**
- **Air temperature: 59° Fahrenheit**
- **Relative humidity: 78 %**
- **Barometric pressure: 29.53 in. of Hg.**

Some manufacturers base their calculations on Standard ICAO (International Civil Aviation Organization) conditions which are:

- **Altitude: sea level (0 feet)**
- **Air temperature: 59° Fahrenheit**
- **Relative humidity: 0%**
- **Barometric pressure: 29.92 in. of Hg.**

In practical terms, the results between the two conditions are relatively minor.

Minor deviations from standard conditions will have no appreciable effect on exterior ballistic performance. For example a few degrees above or below 59° or a few percentage points difference in relative humidity are nothing to be concerned about. Likewise, minor variations in altitude and barometric pressure will have no discernible effect.

However, temperature extremes and high altitudes may have an effect. For example, temperatures below -30° F. may decrease muzzle velocity while temperatures above 120° F. may increase muzzle velocity.

Uses of Ballistic Tables

Actually, the jumble of numbers on an exterior ballistic table can provide a substantial amount of useful information which will allow you to:

- **Compare the exterior ballistic performance of various calibers to determine the one that best suits your needs.**

- **Select the bullet weight and style in your caliber so you can get maximum performance from your gun.**

- **Predict bullet path (height of trajectory) at selected distances using zero ranges of 100 yards or 200 yards.**

- **Enable you to easily zero your rifle for a specific intermediate or longer distance when you only have a short distance shooting range available.**

- **Accurately compensate for cross winds.**

- **Determine hold over for long range shots.**

- **Determine striking velocity and energy of your load at various ranges.**

EFFECT OF ALTITUDE ON BULLET PATH

As atmospheric pressure at high altitudes is lower than at sea level, the bullet encounters less air resistance. This has the effect of increasing the ballistic coefficient of the bullet which results in a flatter trajectory, higher retained velocity and higher striking energy.

At 10,000 feet altitude, the air is 70% as dense as compared to sea level. For most hunting bullets, this results in approximately one minute of angle (one inch at 100 yards) flatter trajectory. Lower altitudes will have less effect.

BARREL LENGTH

Industry ballistic calculations for rifle ammunition normally are based on the muzzle velocity achieved from a 24 inch test barrel. However, your barrel length may be different. Use this chart to determine muzzle velocity from barrels of shorter or longer lengths.

MUZZLE VELOCITY VS. BARREL LENGTH

Muzzle Velocity Range (fps)	Expected Change (in fps) Per Inch of Barrel Length
Up to 2,000	5
2,001-2,500	10
2,501-3,000	20
3,001-3,500	30
3,501-4,000	40

Subtract the indicated amount for barrels shorter than 24". Add the indicated amount for barrels longer than 24".

After you determine the muzzle velocity of your rifle, use the chart above to subtract or add the velocity difference from the published remaining velocity figures listed at each range on the ballistic table. Make certain you change the energy figures as well. Such relatively small variations in muzzle velocity will have only a minor effect on trajectory numbers.

SIGHT HEIGHT

Most ballistic tables assume the use of a telescopic sight mounted so that the line of sight is 1.5 inches above the bore line. While this is a useful assumption for many rifle/sight set-ups, there are many rifle scopes mounted at different heights. Obviously, iron sights may differ as well.

It is good practice to check the sight height on your gun to determine the difference, if any. Minor differences in sight height will have no appreciable effect at ranges of 200 yards or less. Major differences (one inch or more) should be added or subtracted from the trajectory figures. At ranges beyond 300 yards, differences from the average sight height may have a substantial effect.

NOT ALL BULLETS ARE THE SAME

Ammunition makers offer a wide variety of bullet shapes and weights loaded to different muzzle velocities. The number of brands, product lines, and product listings can be confusing. When comparing one bullet to another, it is important to make sure the bullets are similar in shape and weight. For example, do not compare a round nose bullet with a spitzer bullet even though they may be the same weight. Also, do not compare flat base bullets with boat tail bullets of similar weight.

When selecting a bullet, it is best to decide on a specific weight and style of bullet for your type of hunting first and compare the various brands before making a final choice.

EFFECT

Effect of Temperature on Muzzle Velocity

Temperature has an effect on both chamber pressure and muzzle velocity. For each degree of temperature change, muzzle velocity will change about 1.7 fps in the same direction. In practical terms, this means that for each 10° F. change, add or subtract 17 fps.

Effect of Barometeric Pressure on Remaining Velocity

Barometric pressure has an effect on the remaining velocity of bullets. At high barometric pressures, the denser air creates more resistance to the bullet. At low barometric pressure, the lower density air produces less resistance to the bullet.

For every one inch (in Hg.) change in barometric pressure, a bullet's ballistic coefficient will increase or decrease by about 3.5%. At ranges of 200 yards and less, this will have only a minimal effect and can be ignored. At longer ranges, it should be taken into account (most ballistic software can do this easily).

CONTENTS OF A BALLISTIC TABLE EXPLAINED

A typical ballistic table contains six categories of information.

Cartridge Caliber Grouping

What This Is

All loadings for a particular caliber cartridge in a product line normally are grouped together for convenience and comparison.

What You Can Do With This

This data allows you to compare the ballistic performance of various loads in each caliber as well as different calibers easily. Before doing so, confirm that the caliber you are considering is the correct one for your gun.

Bullet Weight and Style

What This Is

This information contains the bullet weights in grains and the bullet types offered in each caliber.

What You Can Do With This

Use this information to determine the most common bullet weights and types offered in each caliber which are suitable for your type of hunting.

Normally, the ballistic tables contain little or no explanation as to the intended application, features, or advantages for a particular bullet. However, you can find such information in two places in most ammunition catalogs:

- **The descriptive material explaining the characteristics of a company's bullet types**

- **Recommended use charts by game type**

Use these combined resources to make an appropriate choice of bullet weight and style before studying the various brands and product lines (see Chapter 34: Centerfire Rifle Recommendations).

Remaining Velocity in Feet per Secound (FPS) at Various Ranges

What This Is

These figures list the remaining velocity of the bullet at various ranges from the muzzle of the gun. After exiting the muzzle, bullets decelerate; they never accelerate. This chart shows you how much.

What You Can Do With This

Use these numbers to determine the aerodynamic efficiency of a particular bullet. Bullets with higher remaining velocity are more efficient. However do not use aerodynamic efficiency as the sole criteria on which you judge a particular bullet. Be aware that other characteristics such as internal construction may make a particular bullet more or less suitable for your purpose.

Speed vs. Velocity

Speed is the magnitude of velocity irrespective of direction. Speed has no vector as a direction of travel is not specified.

Velocity is the rate of change of a bullet's position along a straight line with respect to time. Velocity has a vector or a specified direction of travel.

A vector has both magnitude and direction; speed has only magnitude.

Most bullets are designed to perform best within a terminal velocity window about 500 fps wide. For example:

- **Bullets designed for magnums may not provide optimum expansion, energy transfer, or penetration in non-magnum calibers at lower velocities.**

- **Likewise, bullets intended for standard calibers may disintegrate or exhibit core-jacket separation when fired in magnum calibers at higher velocities.**

- **Bullets designed for very long range hunting (boat tail bullets for example) offer no ballistic advantage at ranges under 200 yards.**

- **Round nose or flat nose bullets work best at ranges of 100 yards or less. They are not a good choice for longer ranges due to their poor aerodynamics.**

- **Light weight bullets may not provide adequate penetration.**

- **Premium bullets are intended for hunting under extreme conditions. They are not needed for normal hunting conditions at average ranges.**

These factors require you to determine the typical ranges at which you are going to hunt then select a bullet accordingly. Never select a bullet weight or style in an effort to make up for perceived lack of ballistic performance in a particular caliber! For example, a .30-30 Winchester is not a magnum and all attempts at selecting a bullet to convert it into a magnum will be fruitless.

REMAINING ENERGY

What This Is

These numbers indicate the remaining kinetic energy of the bullet expressed in foot-pounds (ft.-lbs.). When the bullet strikes and penetrates the target, some or all of this energy will be transferred from the bullet to the target. Under ideal conditions, all bullet energy is deposited in the target.

What You Can Do With This

Remaining energy is dependent on remaining velocity and bullet weight. Given two bullets of similar caliber and weight, the bullet with higher striking velocity will also have more striking energy.

Energy goes up as the square of the velocity. In other words, a small increase in striking velocity will result in a large increase in striking energy. For example, a .30 caliber 180 grain bullet at 2,500 fps has 2,505 ft.-lbs. of striking energy while at 2,700 fps, the same bullet has 2,915 ft.-lbs. of striking energy. In this example, an 8% increase in velocity produces a 16% increase in energy.

Note that more striking energy is not necessarily better. Heavy loads in any caliber are not as accurate as more moderate loads. Heavy loads may also cause the bullet to strike outside its designed velocity window with poor penetration and erratic energy transfer.

WIND DRIFT

What This Is

Wind drift is the lateral deflection of the bullet from its original line of departure caused by crosswind. These figures quantify the effect of a 10 mph crosswind at a 90° angle to the path of bullet travel at selected ranges. Crosswinds from this angle will have the greatest effect on how much the bullet drifts horizontally from the sight line.

What You Can Do With This Information

Once you know the distance to the target, crosswind angle, and crosswind velocity you can determine how far your bullet will drift, and adjust your scope, or hold off to hit your target. There are several cardinal wind doping "rules" to consider:

- **The crosswind at the muzzle is far more important that the crosswind at the target.**

- **Use mirage, grass, flags, leaves, or other lightweight material to judge wind direction and velocity.**

- **Few crosswinds are at exactly 90° to the path of bullet travel. Crosswinds from other points of the compass will have more or less effect on the bullet.**

- **As head winds and tail winds will have a minor effect on bullet path, they may be ignored for practical purposes at typical hunting ranges.**

- **Wind deflection of a given bullet at 400 yards is not twice its deflection at 200 yards. It is more.**

- **A 20 mph crosswind will have double the deflection of a 10 mph crosswind at any given range.**

- **Aerodynamically more efficient bullets are less subject to wind drift than inefficient bullets. This is of major significance at long ranges, however typical wind drift at 100 yards amounts to less than one inch and at 200 yards less than three inches. For most practical purposes, wind drift is of minor significance at close ranges.**

- **Projectiles with higher muzzle velocity will drift less than those with lower muzzle velocity (above 1160 fps). At lower velocities, below the speed of sound (1,120 fps), different circumstances apply.**

HEIGHT OF TRAJECTORY ABOVE/BELOW LINE OF SIGHT

What This Is

Height of trajectory often is called bullet path. Consider

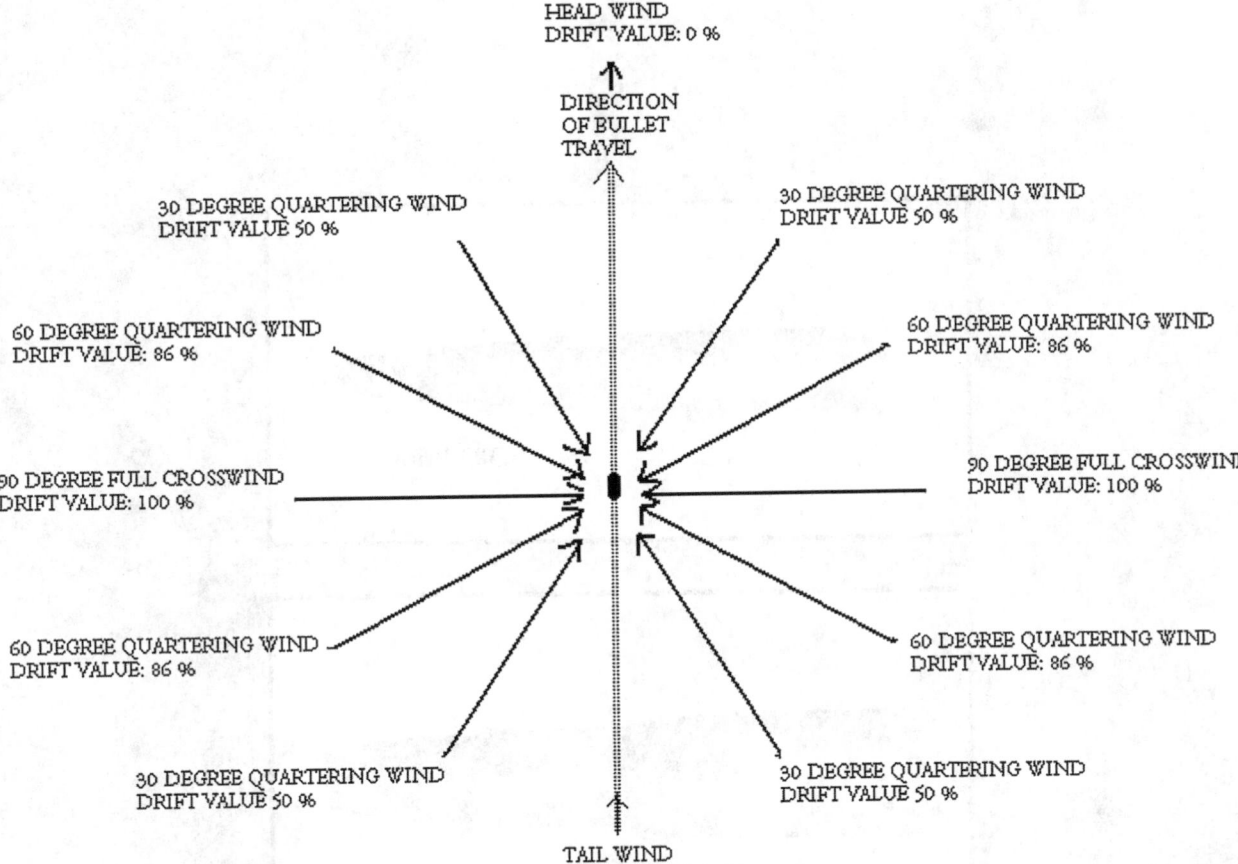

THE EFFECTS OF CROSSWINDS ON BULLET PATH FROM VARIOUS ANGLES

the numbers listed here as the height in inches above or below the line of sight at which the bullet will be, at selected ranges. Note that there are two groups of these figures – one set for a 100 yard zero and another for a 200 yard zero.

What You Can Do With This

If you zero your rifle at either range, you will know the exact path of the bullet, above or below the sight line, at any point within the usable range for that cartridge/bullet. A good practice in this regard is to write these figures on a piece of masking tape and stick it on the butt stock of your rifle in a position where you can easily read it.

If you wish to zero your rifle at another distance (say 50 yards for a short range zero), all you have to do is adjust the strike of the bullet to compensate for the height listed for that lesser range in the 100 or 200 yard bullet path tables.

Custom Tailored Ballistic Charts

Most ballistic software programs will allow you to prepare a custom ballistic table tailored to your specific rifle and load. This information should give you new confidence in the field. It is mandatory for rifles in wildcat calibers, for rifles with unusual features, or for shooting at extreme ranges. If you do not own a ballistic computer

program, most shooters who have one will be glad to prepare a custom ballistic table for you.

Loading For The 16 Inch Naval Gun

The 16 inch 50 caliber Mark 7 main guns of the now-retired Iowa class battleships have earned an almost legendary reputation. This being the case, let us take a quick look at the ballistics on which this legend is based.

Projectile Type	Projectile Weight (lbs.)	Propellant Weight (lbs.)	Muzzle Velocity (fps)	Max Range (miles)
Mk.13 HC	1900	660	2,690	23.6

The Mk. 13 HC (high explosive) shell contained 153.5 lbs. of high explosive

Mk.8 AP	2700	660	2,500	24

At 5.7 miles, the Mk. 8 Armor Piercing shell could penetrate just over 26 inches of steel armor plate or over 50 feet of reinforced concrete

Max. average chamber pressure was a modest 37,000 psi.

Muzzle energy of the Mk. 8 AP shell was 116,980 foot-TONS!

The 16 inch gun as well-known for its accuracy.

For full effect, all nine guns on the ship could be fired in a single broadside at a selected target.

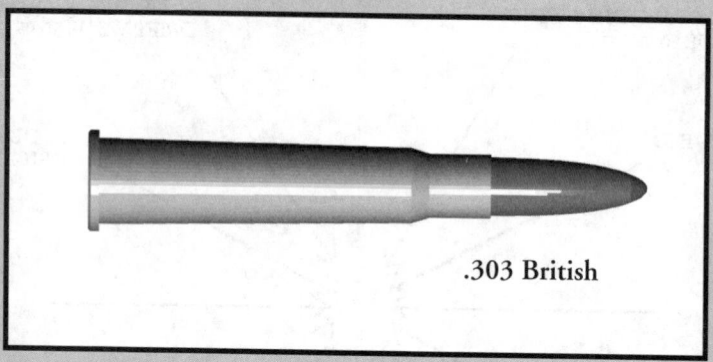

.303 British

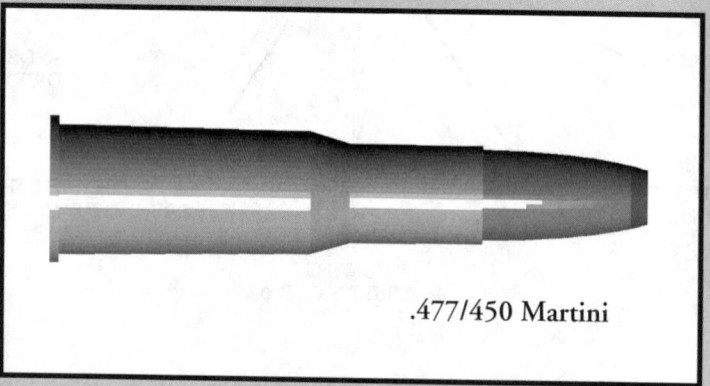

.477/450 Martini

Lessons from the Punjab circa 1880

Ignore the Lessons of History and You Are Doomed to Repeat It

During military operations against the Pathans in the Punjab border area of northern India in the late 1880s, the British Army found their new .303 British caliber Lee Enfield bolt-action repeating rifles did not have sufficient stopping power when used against these determined warriors. While British ordnance personnel sought to remedy this situation, old single-shot rifles in .577/450 Martini-Henry caliber were taken from storage and reissued to the British troops, who reported excellent results.

The .455 caliber 480-gr. soft lead bullet of the black powder .577/450 Martini-Henry cartridge exited the muzzle at only 1,350 fps carrying 1,940 ft.-lbs. of energy. However, given a fair hit anywhere on the torso, no enemy warrior could remain standing. On the other hand, the full metal jacket bullet of the .303 cartridge often passed through the target without transferring a significant amount of energy.

CHAPTER 43 : INTERIOR BALLISTICS

WHAT IS INTERIOR BALLISTICS?

Interior ballistics is the study of the processes which occur inside a firearm when it is fired. This includes the firearm as well as its ammunition. However our focus here is on the ammunition.

The Chicken or the Egg

The ordinary notion is that powder and ball are mere accessories to the gun: that the gun is the all-important and substantive thing, while the cartridge is a minor incident.

So all-pervading has this idea been in past times, that even the most expert shooters have been not only influenced by it, but sometimes governed by it. The truth is the opposite. The cartridge is primary and antecedent, the gun secondary and consequent.

- Maj. C.F. Dutton in The Ordnance Department circa 1890

For centuries, ballistics was something of a black art based mainly on observation, trial, and error. In addition, comprehension of what was observed was sketchy.

A major factor was the lack of measuring equipment. No one knew what went on inside a gun as there was no way to measure any of the parameters of interior ballistics. This situation did not change until 1861 when a young U.S. Army officer named Thomas J. Rodman invented the pressure gauge.

Today, interior ballistics is no longer a mystery as piezoelectric transducers, oscilloscopes, x-ray machines, high speed cameras, temperature probes, and closed bombs allow precision measurements of every event or condition inside a firearm during the firing sequence.

Despite this, interior ballistics remains the part of ballistics about which the average shooter knows least. Undoubtedly, this is due to the hidden nature of interior ballistics and the complex expensive measuring equipment needed to analyze it. However, there are two familiar parts of interior ballistics all shooters have experienced: recoil and muzzle blast.

TYPICAL FIRING SEQUENCE

What happens when you pull the trigger? Before plunging into interior ballistics, we must review a typical firing sequence inside a gun. There are nine steps in a typical firing sequence:

FIRING PIN ENERGIZED

The firing pin is energized in one of two ways:

- **The hammer is released and pivots forward under pressure from the mainspring until it strikes the back end of the firing pin. The stored kinetic energy in the hammer is transferred to the firing pin, causing it to move forward.**

- **The striker or firing pin is energized by the firing pin spring which is held in compression. When released, the stored energy in the firing pin spring is converted into kinetic energy, causing the firing pin to move forward.**

FIRING PIN IMPACT

The energized firing pin travels forward until its tip strikes the primer cup, deforming it and crushing the primer pellet between it and the anvil (or inner rim in the case of rimfire). Normally, firing pin travel is very short (less than 2mm) in order to keep lock time to a minimum.

PRIMER PELLET EXPLODES

As it is crushed, the primer pellet explodes sending hot expanding gasses and particles through the flash hole and into the propellant. These gasses raise the pressure and temperature inside the cartridge case, causing the propellant to begin burning.

PROPELLANT IGNITES

As it burns (deflagrates), the propellant creates a large volume of hot expanding gasses which rapidly increase temperature and pressure inside the cartridge case. This pressure irons the case walls firmly against the chamber surface. The strength of the chamber prevents further case expansion. The expanding propellant gasses cannot leak rearward because the cartridge case walls and case head act as a seal.

CHAMBER PRESSURE RISES AND PEAKS

By the time chamber pressure rises to around 10,000 psi, the bullet overcomes case neck tension holding it in place. The bullet is released and accelerates down the barrel, pushed by the expanding propellant gases.

In less than one thousandth (.001) of a second, peak pressure has been reached. By this point, the bullet or shot charge has moved approximately one inch down the barrel.

BULLET IS ACCELERATED DOWN THE BARREL

The accelerating bullet enters the chamber throat area where it contacts the rifling lands and is engraved. The bullet jacket then upsets into the grooves in the barrel, the lands grip the bullet surface, and the rifling imparts spin to the bullet as it moves down the barrel. During this process, about 5% of the energy in the propellant gasses is lost to friction. About one third of the way down the barrel, the bullet breaks the sound barrier (1,120 fps/764 mph).

AS VOLUME INCREASES GAS PRESSURE DROPS

As the bullet moves down the barrel, internal volume increases steadily, causing the chamber pressure to drop. Progressive burning propellants counter this effect to some extent, but cannot completely prevent it.

BULLET CLEARS MUZZLE

As the bullet approaches the muzzle, the column of high pressure gas behind it remains at up to 30% of peak chamber pressure. When the bullet clears the muzzle and this high pressure column of gas is released, it creates a high velocity gas jet at the muzzle (up to one and one half times the velocity of the bullet) which pushes the gun rearward and creates about 30 % of total recoil. The escaping gas also compresses the air around it creating "muzzle blast". Chemicals in the gas which were starved for oxygen flare when they encounter the air, thus causing flash.

BACK TO AMBIENT

After the initial rush of escaping gas at the muzzle, pressure inside the barrel quickly drops to ambient levels, allowing the walls of the cartridge case to contract, releasing their grip on the chamber. The case can now be extracted.

While this may sound like a complex and lengthy procedure, in fact it happens in less than .003 seconds (three thousandths of one second) on average.

BALLISTIC INQUIRY AND STUDY

The study of interior ballistics includes a wide range of subjects, many of which are completely outside the realm of everyday human experience. However, such studies are critical to understanding how a gun works and why certain events happen.

Some of these are listed below, together with descriptions of how they are measured and what has been learned.

CHAMBER PRESSURE

Measurement of chamber pressure is the major focus of most interior ballistic measurements. Such measurements

assure that a given load will remain under the maximum average pressure (MAP) safety limits established by industry standards. For this reason, ammunition makers test the chamber pressure of each lot of ammunition and carefully record the results.

For many years, measurements of chamber pressure in centerfire and rimfire calibers over 15,000 psi were made in copper units of pressure or CUP. Chamber pressures below 15,000 psi (such as in shotguns) were measured in lead units of pressure or LUP.

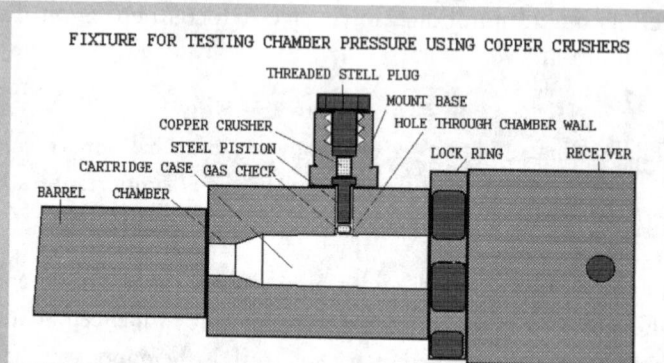

FIXTURE FOR TESTING CHAMBER PRESSURE USING COPPER CRUSHERS

FIXTURE FOR MEASURING CHAMBER PRESSURE USING PIEZOELECTRIC TRANSDUCER

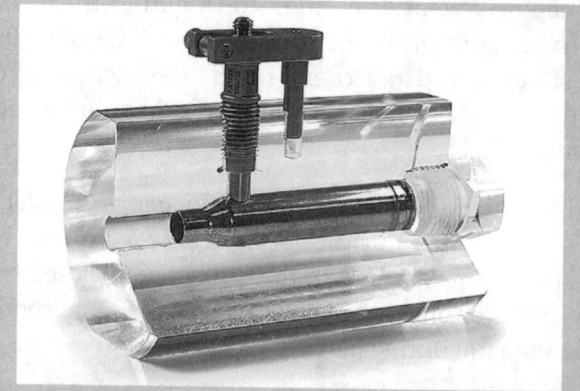

Cutaway of a PCB Mounted of a Test Barrel

This cutaway composite image shows how a PCB piezoelectric transducer conformal pressure gauge is mounted on a test barrel. The face of the conformal gauge is held against the case body through a threaded hole in the barrel. When the cartridge is fired, the expanding propellant gases force the case wall against the gauge. Image courtesy of PCB Piezotronics

CUP and LUP were holdovers from Rodman's original system (see Biography this chapter). While they did provide a benchmark for measuring chamber pressure, they suffered from a number of major drawbacks, namely:

- **The pressure measurement was about 85 % of the true chamber pressure.**
- **The only measurement provided was peak chamber pressure.**
- **Pressures were relative to copper or lead crushers, not to true pressure.**

Today, chamber pressure is measured in pounds per square inch or psi using a conformal piezoelectric transducer. This device uses a quartz crystal which generates an electric charge directly proportional to the amount of pressure applied to it. The transducer unit is mounted in a small hole in the breech of a test barrel so as to allow a portion of the case wall to press against the transducer. The minute electrical charges from the transducer are amplified and displayed on an oscilloscope in the form of a pressure-time curve which can be read directly or used to calculate the following:

- **Chamber pressure at any time**
- **The acceleration of the bullet**
- **The velocity of the bullet at any point in the barrel**
- **The gas pressure at any point along the barrel.**
- **Barrel time**

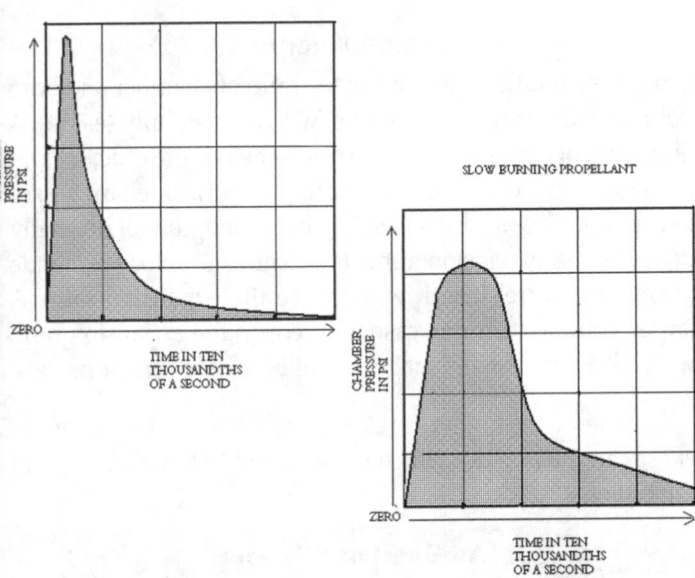

PRESSURE-TIME CURVES MADE BY A PIEZOELECTRIC TRANSDUCER

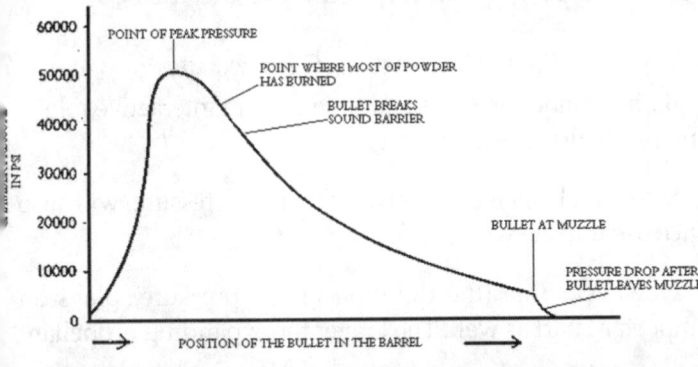

CHAMBER PRESSURE VS BULLET POSITION IN THE BARREL

Barrel Time Vs Trigger To Muzzle Time

Barrel time may be defined as the time interval from the instant the bullet (or shot charge) begins to move until it leaves the barrel. An average barrel time is between two and three thousandths (.001-.002) of a second.

Trigger to muzzle time may be defined as the time interval from the instant the trigger releases the sear to the time the bullet leaves the barrel. Normally, barrel time is less than one half of trigger to muzzle time.

In some instances, port pressure is measured in addition to chamber pressure. Port pressure is the remaining gas pressure measured at a gas port in the barrel between the muzzle and the origin of the rifling. The gas port bleeds off a small amount of gas used to cycle gas-operated self-loading guns. A minimum pressure at the gas port is necessary to reliably operate such guns.

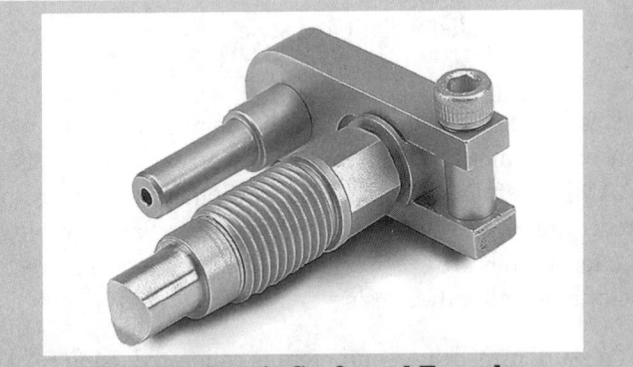

PCB Piezoelectric Conformal Transducer

A piezoelectric transducer is a solid state pressure measuring device. It consists of a metal body with a probe containing a quartz crystal that produces an electric charge when pressure is applied. The strength of the charge is proportional to the pressure applied. The amount of the charge from the transducer crystal is read by a computer that calculates a pressure-time curve of the event and displays this on a screen. Image courtesy of PCB Piezotronics

The information provided by transducers is a quantum leap forward for interior ballistics. Unlike the CUP and LUP systems, piezoelectric transducers provide a true breech pressure in psi as a function of time, and a clear picture of how a propellant behaves as it burns. This wealth of information makes it easier to select a propellant for a given purpose.

SAAMI has established industry standards for chamber pressure in psi for most caliber, bullet weight, and muzzle velocity levels. Each standard consists of two chamber pressure limits: the maximum average pressure or MAP (for ten shots) and the maximum permissible individual pressure. For example, the MAP for .30-'06 Sprg. ammunition loaded with a 150 grain bullet to a muzzle velocity of 2,900 fps. is 53,200 psi while the maximum permissible individual pressure is 61,600 psi In other words, the average chamber pressure must be lower than 53,200 psi and no individual load in the sample can exceed 61,600 psi.

Some of the variables which affect chamber pressure are:

1. Barrel wear
2. Barrel temperature (cold or overheated)
3. Metal fouling or oil in bore
4. Headspace
5. Powder position inside cartridge
6. Cartridge temperature
7. Cartridge condition
8. Flash hole diameter
9. Cartridge case material
10. Size, shape, and protrusion of firing pin
11. Striking force of firing pin
12. Powder type and charge weight
13. Bore diameter and throat dimensions
14. Calibration of equipment
15. Primer type
16. Bullet weight and style

This is a partial list, however these are some of the major concerns in measuring chamber pressure. For these reasons, SAAMI carefully specifies the equipment, practices, and procedures for testing chamber pressures. For example, no two test barrels are exactly alike, so each is given a correction factor after calibration tests.

Pressure measuring equipment is calibrated using SAAMI Standard Reference Ammunition. These special loads are carefully assembled and tested so as to be as close as possible to the exact standard for each caliber. This ammunition is then set aside under carefully controlled conditions. Each SAAMI member participates in this program by making several calibers of Reference Ammunition. Reference Ammunition is for use by SAAMI members for calibration purposes and is not sold to the public.

Chamber Pressure Vs Breech Pressure

Chamber pressure is exerted in a radial direction against the chamber walls.

Breech pressure is exerted in an axial direction against the breechblock of the firearm.

Chamber pressure is higher than breech pressure. A rough approximation of breech pressure can be obtained by dividing the chamber pressure in psi by the area of the cartridge case head in square inches.

Units of measurement

In the U.S., we measure chamber pressure in pounds per square inch (psi). In Europe, chamber pressure is measured in kilograms per square centimeter (K/cm²). Other units of measurement have been: short tons per square inch (UK), atmospheres (Europe), and pascals (Europe).

EFFICIENCY

Firearms are inefficient heat engines when it comes to converting the stored chemical energy in the propellant into kinetic energy in the bullet. On average, only 25-35% of the energy in the propellant is converted to kinetic energy in the bullet. The remainder is lost from the following causes:

- **Heat transferred to the barrel: 20-30%**
- **Friction: 5%**
- **Pressure gradient: 15-20%**
- **Expansion ratio: 20-25%**

Efficiency can be determined by two methods:

- **Thermodynamic: This is the percentage of the propellant's total energy used to accelerate the bullet.**

- **Piezometric: This is the efficiency measured by the ratio between mean effective chamber pressure and peak chamber pressure. In practical terms, this is the amount of constant push against the base of the bullet.**

These can be calculated from muzzle energy and chamber pressure-time curves (see Chapter 95: Useful Formulas).

EXPANSION RATIO

Expansion ratio is defined as the ratio of chamber and bore volume to cartridge case volume (with a bullet fully seated). A high ratio of bore volume to case volume is more efficient and preferable as it provides more space for the propellant gasses to expand. This is why increasing barrel length will normally increase the expansion ratio (and muzzle velocity), while decreasing barrel length will reduce the expansion ratio. A larger volume cartridge case will reduce the expansion ratio which is why so many magnum calibers have longer barrels.

In general, the higher the expansion ratio number, the more energy in the powder which is converted to kinetic energy in the bullet.

An Overbore Caliber

Magnum calibers which have very large case volumes in relation to bore volume are called "overbore" calibers.

BULLET CALIBER AND GAS DYNAMICS

Both chamber pressure and time play an interactive role in interior ballistic performance.

In general, increasing peak chamber pressure will also increase muzzle velocity.

However, time (the duration of the pressure) plays an important part as well. The longer the expanding propellant gasses can hold pressure against the base of the bullet, the higher the muzzle velocity. Progressive burning powders are the key here as they partially compensate for the increasing bore volume by increasing gas production as the bullet continues down the barrel. Still, all of the propellant is never burned.

In this connection, the area of the base of the bullet plays an important role.

If we assume a chamber pressure of 52,000 psi for a given cartridge with a bullet having a base area of .250 square inch, the pressure on the base of the bullet would be 13,000 psi.

If we neck this cartridge up for a bullet having a base area of .375 square inch with the same weight and chamber pressure as the previous bullet, the pressure on the base of the bullet increases to 19,000 psi and muzzle velocity will increase. In other words, the larger base area offers the expanding propellant gasses more area on which to push the bullet. This is why some large caliber cartridges can offer a higher muzzle velocity than a smaller caliber cartridge with the same bullet weight as the effective push on the bullet is directly proportional to the area of the bullet's base.

What happens if the case neck diameter is reduced to a bullet with a base area of .20 square inch, and we maintain the same bullet weight and breech pressure? Base pressure on the bullet will drop to 10,400 psi, however muzzle velocity will increase as the gas has a smaller bore volume to occupy, allowing the push on the bullet to be held for a longer time.

RECOIL

Every shooter is familiar with recoil. It is the uncomfortable "kick" on your shoulder when you fire a gun.

There are two types of recoil:

• **Perceived recoil**

• **Actual recoil**

Perceived recoil is a psychological and subjective evaluation by a shooter, influenced by his unique expectations and responses to internal and external forces. Every shooter perceives recoil in a different way and judges it accordingly. Put another way, one shooter may perceive the recoil of a particular gun as uncomfortably heavy while another shooter may perceive the recoil of the same gun to be perfectly acceptable. As perception is totally subjective, it can not be measured. But, as every shooter knows all too well, his or her perception is never wrong.

Actual recoil is completely objective, measurable, and quantified. Actual recoil is governed by Sir Isaac Newton's Three Laws of Motion:

• **A body at rest tends to stay at rest and a body in motion tends to stay in motion unless acted upon by a force.**

Practical explanation: Nothing starts or stops unless a force acts on it.

• **When a body is acted upon by a constant force, the resulting acceleration is inversely proportional to the mass of the body and directly proportional to the applied force.**

Practical explanation: Any change in motion is proportional to the total of all forces applied.

• **Whenever a body exerts a force on another, that force is equal in measure, but opposite in direction.**

Practical explanation: For each reaction, there is an equal and opposite reaction.

Actual recoil begins when the priming compound explodes and continues until the bullet has left the muzzle and the pressure inside the barrel has dropped to ambient level. The expanding propellant gas causes recoil as it accelerates the bullet down the barrel. The force is equal in both directions. Actual recoil is measured in foot-pounds of energy. This takes into consideration six factors:

• **Mass of the gun including all accessories and one loaded cartridge.**

• **Velocity of the gun during recoil**

• **Mass of the bullet**

• **Muzzle velocity of the bullet**

• **Mass of the powder charge**

• **Velocity of the propellant gasses**

The masses of bullet, powder charge, and rifle are easily determined by weighing them. The muzzle velocity of the bullet can be measured using a chronograph. Gas velocity has been found to average 4,000 fps for smokeless propellants and 2,000 fps for black powder. Using these figures, the recoil of the gun can be calculated (see Chapter 95: Useful Formulas).

There are three "comparative" scientific measures of recoil:

• **Recoil impulse**

• **Free recoil velocity of the gun**

• **Recoil energy of the gun in foot-pounds**

As the recoil impulse is based on the performance of the cartridge independent of the weight of the gun, it can be used to compare the recoil potential of various cartridges and loads without considering gun weight. Using this number, the remaining two figures can be calculated.

Free recoil velocity of the gun is simply the velocity of the weapon while it recoils. Free recoil velocity of 15 fps. or more has been found to be uncomfortable for most shooters. This is especially true for lightweight rifles where the high recoil velocity is delivered to the shoulder as a short sharp blow.

A gun's recoil energy is the figure on which most comparisons of recoil are based. Basically, it is the total amount of recoil energy transmitted by the gun. Most shooters will find the figures in the following recoil comfort chart very accurate.

Comfort Level	Total Recoil in ft.-lbs.
Very comfortable-light	14 or less
Comfortable-moderate	15-21
Uncomfortable-manageable	22-30
Very uncomfortable -manageable	30-40
Completely uncomfortable-hurts	41 or more

In this context, it becomes obvious that:

- **The heavier the gun, the lower the recoil energy.**

For example a seven pound gun weighs 49,000 grains or 327 times the weight of a 150 grain bullet while a nine pound rifle weighs 63,000 grains or 420 times the weight of a 150 grain bullet. It is obvious why the heavier rifle has less recoil.

- **A small increase in gun weight substantially reduces recoil energy.**

A 20 % increase in gun weight will decrease recoil energy by the same percentage and vice versa.

- **Recoil energy increases as the square of bullet weight. In other words bullet weight has a more substantial effect on recoil energy than gun weight.**

- **Heavier bullets in any given caliber generate more recoil energy than light bullets at the same muzzle velocity.**

- **A slow push that spreads the recoil over a longer time period will feel more comfortable than a short duration recoil impulse, even if that short impulse has less total energy than the longer impulse.**

- **Recoil energy increases as the square of muzzle velocity. This means that a 10 % increase in muzzle velocity will increase recoil energy by just over 20%.**

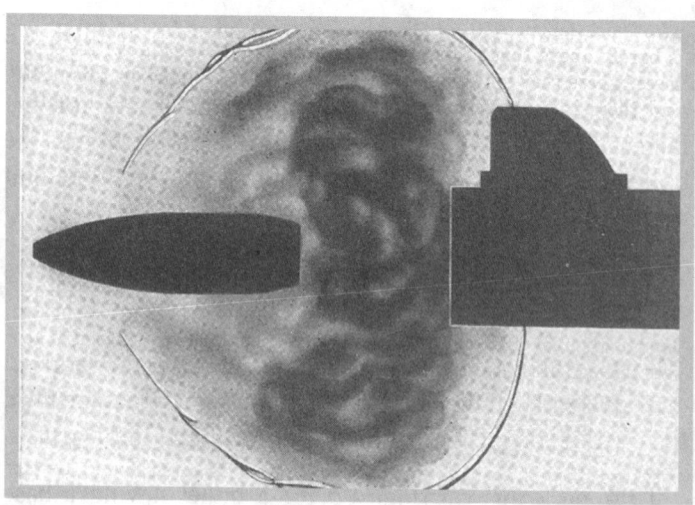

One final factor must be considered in discussing recoil-muzzle blast. From a perceived recoil perspective, muzzle blast increases the intensity of recoil and adversely affects the shooter. Considered from the technical standpoint, the high pressure gas jet at the muzzle has a rocket-like thrust effect which increases free recoil velocity. The exact amount this effect contributes to recoil energy remains in dispute, but most estimates are in the 25% range. This is the reason for muzzle devices which seek to harness or control muzzle blast to perform some useful function, such as reducing recoil. These devices include:

- **Muzzle brakes and compensators**
- **Flash hiders and flash suppressors**
- **Grenade launchers**
- **Sound suppresssors**
- **Combinations of the above**

That these devices work cannot be denied. Their popularity and repeated tests prove this. However, the efficiency of these devices varies greatly from one design to another. None are 100% efficient despite claims to the contrary.

FUNCTIONING

It is possible to load a cartridge which meets all ballistic criteria, yet fails to function properly. For this reason, samples from lots of loaded ammunition are regularly function tested at the factory to assure compatibility.

In manually operated firearms, function testing centers on feeding, chambering, extracting, and ejecting. For self-loading firearms, operation of the gun's mechanism becomes an important factor. For example, a cartridge must provide enough pressure at the gas port of gas-operated firearms to operate the mechanism. For recoil-operated firearms, the cartridge must provide enough recoil energy to cycle the

Brigadier General Thomas J. Rodman
1815-1871

Born at Salem, Indiana in 1815, young Thomas Jackson Rodman received an appointment to the United States Military Academy at West Point, NY in 1837. When he graduated in 1841, Lt. Rodman elected to join the Ordnance Department where he could best use his aptitude for engineering and math. After brief field service in the Mexican War, in 1844 Rodman began a long series of experiments aimed at improving cannon, propellants, and measurement.

Rodman's first development was a core cooling process for casting iron cannon. This substantially improved the metallurgy, strength, and durability of artillery barrels. The U.S. government ordered over 130 "Rodman Guns" during the Civil War. The largest was a huge cannon weighing 49,099 pounds with a 13 foot 9 inch long barrel and a fifteen inch bore diameter. Emplaced at Fort Monroe, it spent the Civil War protecting Washington, D.C. from Confederate attack. Nicknamed the "Lincoln Gun", this monster used 125 pounds of DuPont "Hexagonal" powder to propel a 450 pound solid iron shot to a range of over 4,600 yards (2.6 miles).

Recognizing that propellants of the day were unsuitable for large cannon, Rodman set out to improve gun powder. In this connection, he worked closely with Lamont Du Pont to develop "Mammoth" powder for cannon. "Mammoth" powder grains were over one half inch in diameter and made from hard press cake so they would burn more evenly in cannon.

In order to study propellant performance, Rodman needed to measure the chamber pressure inside a gun barrel. To do this, he invented the Rodman pressure gauge. This device was mounted over a small hole drilled into the chamber of the gun. The device held a steel rod with a chisel edge against a sheet of copper. When the gun fired, the gas pressure in the chamber forced the chisel point into the copper sheet where it made an indent. The chisel and copper sheet were removed and mounted in a holding fixture. The holding fixture, with the rod positioned against a different part of the copper sheet, was mounted in a press which forced the rod into the copper sheet. When the second indent matched that from firing the gun, the amount of force needed to do this was noted as Copper Units of Pressure (or CUP.). This system remains in limited use today, albeit with numerous improvements.

By 1864, Rodman had been promoted to Major at which time he became Superintendent of Watertown Arsenal in Massachusetts. Shortly after, Rodman was again promoted and became the Superintendent of Rock Island Arsenal in Illinois. When he passed away in 1871, Rodman was still on active duty at the Arsenal as a Brigadier General.

Gen. Rodman was one of the first soldier-technocrats in the U.S. Ordnance Department. His pressure gauge, propellant research, and metallurgical discoveries were some of the most significant ordnance developments of the 19th century. A street at Rock Island Arsenal is named in his honor.

mechanism. Given the wide variety of firearms in which the cartridge may be used, this is no small matter.

OTHER FACTORS

Interior ballistics measures many other processes and results such as:

- Bullet yaw or balloting in the barrel
- Heat transfer to barrel and barrel heat dissipation.
- Effects of various types of rifling and twist rates
- Effects of barrel length
- Barrel wear and barrel life
- Bore treatments
- Bullet lubricants
- Bullet slumping on acceleration
- Primer ignition effects
- Effect of various case shapes and sizes
- New propellants
- New primers (without heavy metals)
- Wad designs
- Shot composition
- Propellant additives

Most of these have been tested extensively and are well understood. As a substantial fund of knowledge and experience has been accumulated on the subjects above, many of these tests are not conducted on a regular basis barring some urgent need.

The "Lincoln Gun," a huge 15 inch Rodman cannon, stood guard over the approaches to Washington, D.C. at Fort Monroe in 1861-65.

The "Lincoln Gun" still on duty today at Fort Monroe.

CHAPTER 44 : EXTERIOR BALLISTICS

CHAPTER 44 HIGHLIGHTS:

- WHAT IS EXTERIOR BALLISTICS?
- A SHORT HISTORY
- TYPICAL BULLET FLIGHT PROFILE
- WHAT SUBJECTS ARE STUDIED

- FACTORS WHICH AFFECT A BULLET IN FLIGHT
- THE UNIQUE ASPECTS OF SHOTSHELLS

- MEASUREMENT EQUIPMENT AND TESTS
- MEN OF EXTERIOR BALLISTICS

All drawings by Author, unless otherwise noted.

WHAT IS EXTERIOR BALLISTICS?

Exterior ballistics is the study of the motion of projectiles in flight.

> "If the enemy is in range, so are you."
>
> *-Infantry Journal*

A SHORT HISTORY

For centuries, exterior ballistics was poorly understood. Most early gunners believed that when a projectile left the muzzle of a gun, it traveled in a straight line and, when its "natural impetus" had dissipated, simply fell to the ground. Today, we know this to be false, and recognize that the science of gunnery provided a foundation on which subsequent scientific efforts succeeded in understanding the fundamental laws of motion. In turn, this spurred development in mathematics, mechanics, thermodynamics, aerodynamics, and metallurgy.

One of the first men to challenge the straight line of travel concept was Niccolo Tartaglia who believed that cannon balls followed a curved path. In 1537, Tartaglia argued that the trajectory of a cannon ball was determined by the battle it fought with "the force" as he called it. Today, we understand that "the force" to which he referred is air resistance.

Next up was the brilliant Galileo Galilei, (yes, the man who reputedly dropped two cannon balls of different size off the Leaning Tower of Pisa) who published the results of his work in 1636. Galileo considered the effects of gravity, inertia, and muzzle velocity on the motion of projectiles.

He argued that the flight path of a cannon ball was a predictable parabolic curve regardless of the vertical angle at which the muzzle was aimed. Even though air resistance, a major factor in ballistics, was not considered by Galileo, his work was crucial in disproving the closely held theories of the past and breaking fresh ground.

> "Now it is evident…that the equable motion [of a movable object] on this plane would be perpetual if the plane were of infinite extent; but if we assume it be ended, and [elevated] on high, the movable…, driven to the end of the plane and going on further, adds on to its previous equable and indelible motion that downward tendency which it has from its own heaviness. Thus there emerges a certain motion, compounded from equable horizontal and from naturally accelerated downward [motion] which I call projection.
>
> - Galilei, *Two New Sciences,* 1638

In the late 1730s, a young Englishman named Benjamin Robins invented a device called a ballistic pendulum with which one could measure recoil and the striking velocity and energy of a bullet on a target. In 1742, Robins published his classic "New Principles of Gunnery" which became a turning point in understanding musket accuracy and exterior ballistics.

In the late 1800s, Capt. Paul-Emile Le Boulenge invented the Boulenge Chronograph which allowed accurate velocity measurements to be taken anywhere along a bullet's path of travel. This allowed accurate determination of the effects of air resistance (drag) for the first time.

About that time, the concept of a "standard bullet" was developed. Precise measurements of this bullet with its specific shape, weight, and diameter were made and all subsequent bullet shapes were compared to the standard. This eliminated the need to measure the drag characteristics of every bullet shape individually. This comparison number was called the Ballistic Coefficient and it is still used today. About 1880, Francesco Siacci developed a method which used the ballistics of a standard bullet and the ballistic coefficient of the new bullet to easily compute the ballistics of a new bullet. The Siacci Tables he made are still in use today.

A series of firing tests to determine the drag characteristics of various projectile shapes were made in the late 1800s. Krupp conducted a lengthy series of tests in 1881, followed by the Gavré Commission in France from 1873-1898. Using the Krupp data, Col. Nicholas V. Mayevski (later General of Artillery) of the Russian Army developed a mathematical model for the standard Krupp bullet. Col. James M. Ingalls of the U.S. Army Ordnance Department used Col. Mayevski's analytical model to create the Ingalls Tables in 1893; they remain in use today. In the 1930s, Wallace Coxe and Edgar Beugless developed a simplified method of determining ballistic coefficient by shape comparison which is in wide use today.

In 1965, Winchester published a set of ballistic tables developed earlier at Aberdeen Proving Ground based on four drag functions:

- **G1 For all bullets except those below**
- **G5 For boat tail bullets or tracers**
- **G6 For flat base spitzer FMJ bullets**
- **GL For HP and soft point bullets**

These are considered adequate for the majority of sporting bullets and are used today for calculating SAAMI standardized exterior ballistic tables. Here it is interesting to note that the "G" prefix for the drag function honors the work of the French Gavré Commission.

TYPICAL BULLET FLIGHT PROFILE

Consider the flight profile of a typical .30 caliber, 150 grain soft point bullet fired from a .30-'06 Sprg. cartridge at a muzzle velocity of 2,910 FPS.

Amid a cloud of hot expanding propellant gasses, the bullet emerges from the muzzle. From that instant on, the bullet begins to drop because of gravity. If the barrel of the gun was parallel to the ground, the bullet would soon strike the ground. However, the barrel of the gun is pointed upward at a slight angle, lofting the bullet above the line of sight into a parabolic path of travel. This path carries the bullet above the line of sight at

about 50 yards and then below the line of sight at a farther distance determined by the range at which the gun is zeroed. The bullet then continues its downward trajectory until it hits the ground. The shape of the path the bullet follows is not a perfect parabolic arc; it is initially flatter.

Once clear of the muzzle, the bullet has all of the velocity it will ever have. As it travels toward the target, air resistance (drag) will cause the bullet to lose velocity until it strikes the target or the ground.

As the bullet begins its journey, it is rotating at several hundred thousand revolutions per minute because of the rifling in the barrel. The rotation stabilizes the bullet, keeping it pointed forward. However, the bullet does not travel a straight path. Rather it describes a series of small helixes around the average path of travel. Initial contact with the air causes the bullet to yaw up to 5° as it ploughs forward. After traveling about one hundred yards, the bullet stabilizes into a calmer flight pattern. At supersonic velocities, shock waves form on the bullet tip and on any sharp shoulders on the ogive, however the major source of drag is the pressure of the shock wave, also called the bow wave, on the front of the bullet. The laminar air flow over the body is smooth save for the few thousandths of an inch immediately above the surface where the flow breaks up. This also has a minor effect on drag. The second major source of drag is the base of the bullet where the laminar flow breaks up abruptly, creating a partial vacuum which causes base drag.

As the bullet continues its flight, air resistance continues to force its velocity to decrease. When velocity becomes subsonic (less than 1,120 fps), there is a brief disturbance in the bullet's path of travel as drag suddenly decreases, but does not stop. By the time it has traveled 500 yards the average bullet has lost about 40-50 % of its muzzle velocity. At one thousand yards, the average bullet has shed over 70 % of its muzzle velocity.

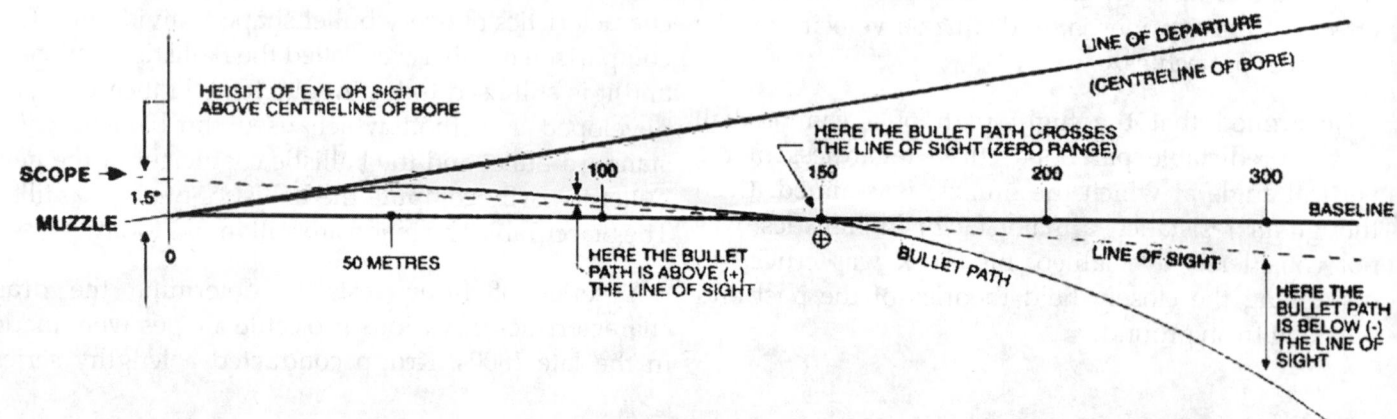

Fortunately, most hunting shots are made at about two hundred yards or less. This is good news for the bullet, as it must plow through only two hundred yards of air, shedding around 20 % of its initial velocity. Despite this velocity loss, striking energy (for effective terminal performance) and a flat trajectory (which minimizes the effects of range estimation errors) are not degraded below effective levels.

WHAT SUBJECTS ARE STUDIED

Exterior ballistics contains a lengthy list of possible subjects for study. We will discuss the most important, but only list the minor ones as space does not allow a discussion of these.

VELOCITY AND ENERGY

Muzzle Velocity

This is the estimated velocity of the bullet at the muzzle in feet per second (fps) or meters per secound (mps). For sporting rifle and handgun ammunition, the instrumental velocity is measured fifteen feet from the muzzle and muzzle velocity is computed using a numerical correction factor. For shotguns, instrumental velocity is measured at three feet at the center of mass of the shot charge and a correction factor applied to obtain muzzle velocity. These figures are of interest to sportsmen as they facilitate comparison of the potential ballistic performance of various factory loads and calibers.

For military rifle ammunition, the instrumental velocity is measured at seventy eight feet and a correction factor applied to estimate muzzle velocity.

Points To Keep In Mind

- Higher muzzle velocity is not always desirable. Check down range ballistic tables first to see how much of a difference higher muzzle velocity may make at practical ranges, if any.

- To obtain higher muzzle velocities, in many cases it will be necessary to switch to a magnum cartridge.

- Higher muzzle velocity means more recoil.

- Magnum ammunition is more expensive.

Remaining Velocity

Remaining velocity is the velocity retained by the bullet at a given distance from the muzzle. This may be estimated or measured. It is of importance to sportsmen as a tool to compare down-range efficiency of various bullets.

Points To Keep In Mind

- The more efficient the bullet, the higher the remaining velocity.

- A boat-tail bullet will have higher retained velocity at all ranges compared to a similar weight flat base bullet.

- The advantages of boat-tail bullet velocity retention at ranges below 200 yards are minimal.

Terminal Velocity

This is the remaining velocity of the bullet as it strikes the target.

Points To Keep In Mind

- For hunters, the remaining velocity shown on a ballistics table, for the range closest to that of an intended target, may be considered terminal velocity.

- For target shooters, remaining velocity is of interest mainly as a measurement of bullet efficiency.

Muzzle Energy

Muzzle energy may be defined as the amount of kinetic energy in foot-pounds or Joules of a bullet at the muzzle. Sportsmen can use this figure to compare different calibers using similar bullet weights, for example, a 150 grain bullet from a .308 Winchester and a .300 Weatherby Magnum.

Points To Keep In Mind

- Higher muzzle velocity means greater muzzle energy for bullets of the same weight, regardless of caliber.

- To obtain more muzzle energy in a given caliber, first try switching to a heavier bullet.

Remaining Energy

The energy retained by the bullet at a given range is called the remaining energy. It is expressed in foot-pounds or Joules. For sportsmen, these figures provide a useful guide to the potential ballistic performance of a bullet at a given range.

Points To Keep In Mind

- A more efficient bullet offers greater retained striking energy.

- Switching to a boat tail bullet can provide extra down range striking energy from a standard (non-magnum) cartridge.

Terminal Energy

The remaining energy as the bullet strikes the target is called terminal energy. Most sportsmen consider remaining energy to be the equivalent of terminal energy for a given distance to a target.

TRAJECTORY

Basic Factors

· Line of Departure

An imaginary straight line co-incident with the bore axis projecting through the bore to infinity The line of departure is slightly elevated so as to compensate for the parabolic path of the bullet. It is not parallel to the ground normally.

· Line of Sight

An imaginary straight line projecting from the center of the sights to the target. The line of sight does not have to be parallel to the ground (i.e. shooting uphill or downhill).

· Height of Sight Above Bore Line

This is a physical measurement of the distance between the bore axis and the sight axis. Industry ballistic calculations are based on an average of .5 inches for normal metal sights and 1.5 inches for optical sights and micrometer metal sights.

Bullet Drop

This is the distance below the line of sight at a given range at which the bullet will be if the line of departure is parallel to the ground.

Points To Keep In Mind

· Often listed in ballistic tables in the past, this measurement is of little practical value for hunters. For this reason, it is not listed in current ballistic tables.

Mid-Range Trajectory (MRT)

In most ballistic tables, handgun data is provided only for one "short range" zero because of the very limited practical range of handguns. Rifle data is usually provided for two zero ranges. Basically, MRT is the maximum height of the bullet path above the line of sight at half the distance to zero range. Such data is useful in gaining an idea of how far above the line of sight the bullet will be at close ranges if the gun is zeroed for the same zero ranges in the table. Data is also provided for ranges along the trajectory.

Points To Keep In Mind

· The total bullet drop at a given range is roughly equal to four times the mid-range height.

· The maximum mid-range height normally occurs at just over half the way to the zero range.

Wind Deflection (Drift)

The industry standard in this respect is to list the amount of wind drift in inches at a given distance assuming a 10 mph. cross wind at 90° to the bullet path.

Points To Keep In Mind

· Cross winds at angles of less than 90° to the bullet's path will reduce the effects of wind drift. At angles of about 60°, wind drift is reduced by 15%. For angles of 30° or less, the reduction is about 50%.

· Crosswinds close to the shooter have a far greater effect than cross winds at the target.

· At subsonic velocities wind drift decreases markedly.

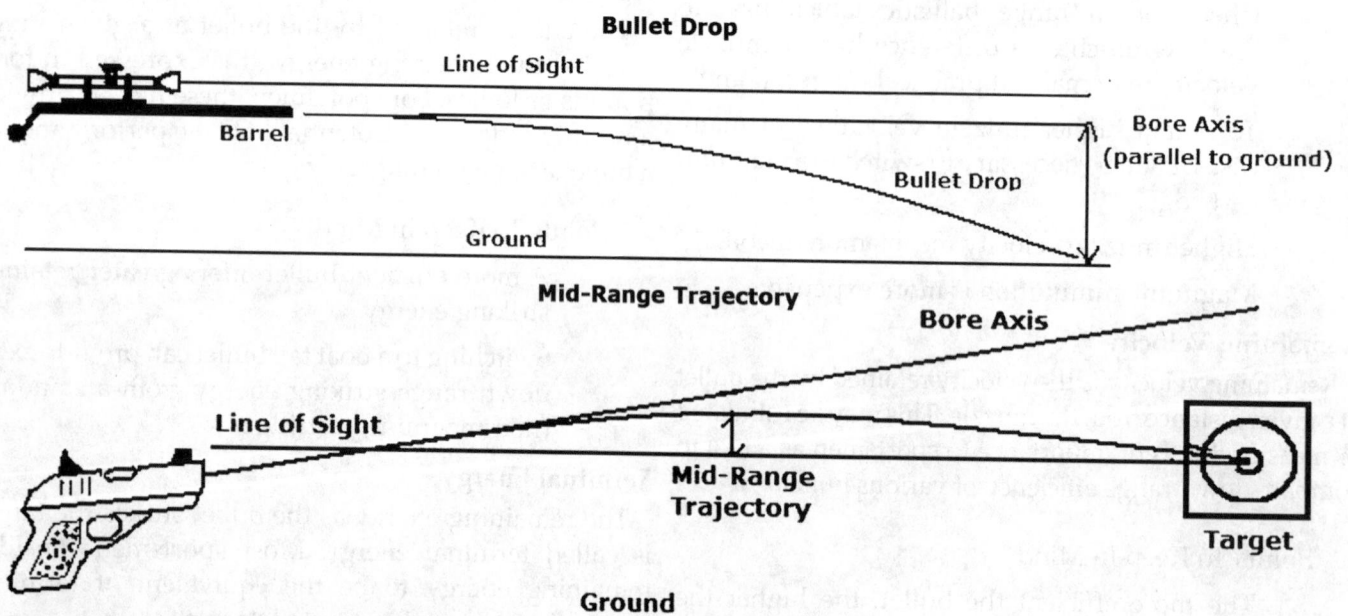

- All sight corrections for wind drift are made into the wind.
- Remember, if the range is doubled, the wind drift increases about four times – not twice.
- Bullets with a high ballistic coefficient buck crosswinds better than bullets with lower ballistic coefficients.
- Bullets with higher remaining velocity will resist cross winds better than bullets with lower remaining velocity.
- Heavy weight bullets resist cross winds better than light weight bullets in any given caliber.
- Bullets of high sectional density resist the wind better than bullets of low sectional density.

Mid-Range Height

This is an alternate term for Mid-Range Trajectory.

Points To Keep In Mind

- Use trajectory data to determine how much to hold under at ranges closer than the zero range.
- Use trajectory data to determine how much hold over will be necessary at ranges beyond the zero range.

Maximum Point Blank Range

Experienced hunters have found this to be one of the most important and useful figures in ballistics. Unfortunately, most ballistic tables do not list this. Basically, this is the maximum range at which the bullet will strike within the vital area of the target without adjusting the sights. In other words, maximum point blank range is the maximum distance at which the bullet's trajectory is always less than one-half the diameter of a pre-determined vital area, above or below the line of sight. This allows the shooter to aim at the center of the vital zone and hit the target with out adjusting the sights. For most purposes, this will be somewhere between one hundred and two hundred fifty yards. To determine this, you must know:

1. The path of the bullet.
2. The range at which the rifle is zeroed.
3. The size of the vital area of the target.

Maximum Effective Range

Unlike most other ballistic data, maximum effective range is not a fixed number. Maximum effective range may be defined as the maximum range at which an individual shooter can consistently hit the target under various conditions. This however, is the summation of a complex blend of ballistic, physical, and psychological factors.

Points To Keep In Mind

- Maximum effective range for hunting is usually 250 yards or less under most conditions.
- Before going afield, determine your approximate maximum effective range by firing from field/hunting positions at known distances.
- A good rule of thumb is to zero your rifle at your maximum effective range.
- Resist the temptation to "stretch your barrel" by taking shots at game beyond your maximum effective range.

Maximum Horizontal Range

This is the horizontal distance a projectile will travel to the point of first impact with the ground when fired from a gun at an optimum muzzle elevation angle. This is an important safety issue.

Points To Keep In Mind

- Maximum range will be obtained with a muzzle elevation between 28° and 31°.
- Remember, a muzzle elevation of just 10° is enough for the bullet to travel up to 85 % of its maximum range.
- At altitudes of 10,000 feet or more, the lower air density can increase maximum range by 30% or more from sea level conditions.

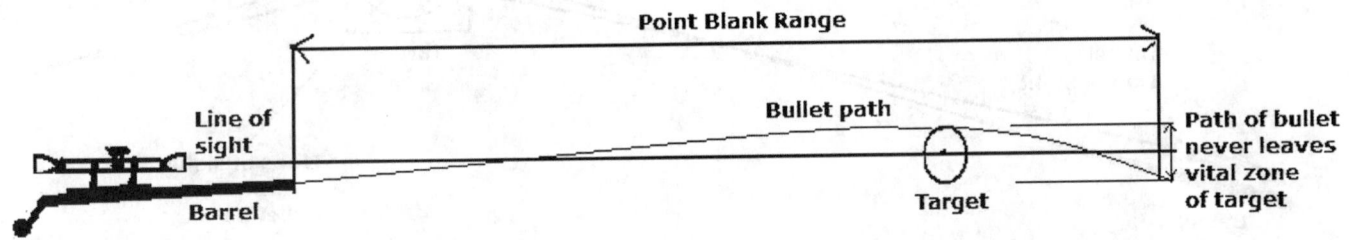

- Large caliber subsonic bullets will have a shorter maximum range than high ballistic coefficient bullets at similar velocities.

- Light weight bullets will have a shorter maximum range than heavier bullets of the same caliber.

- Remember, a 172 grain .30 caliber bullet can travel over 5,660 yards and a 40 grain .22 Long Rifle bullet can travel over 1,500 yards.

Uphill/Downhill

When shooting uphill or downhill the necessity to aim low for both applications is counter intuitive for most shooters. This is because they perceive and calculate the distance to the target along the slanted line from their shooting position to the elevated or depressed target. The path of the bullet will be high if shooters mistakenly aim /hold for the longer slant range. Instead, they should aim/hold low for the lesser horizontal "map" distance between their position and the target – the distance over which the force of gravity is acting upon trajectory.

Points To Keep In Mind

- Whether you are shooting uphill or downhill you must aim low to compensate for the shorter slant range.

- Remember, uphill or downhill, the actual horizontal range is shorter than the slant range.

- For grades of 10° or less, the correction is small enough that it can be ignored.

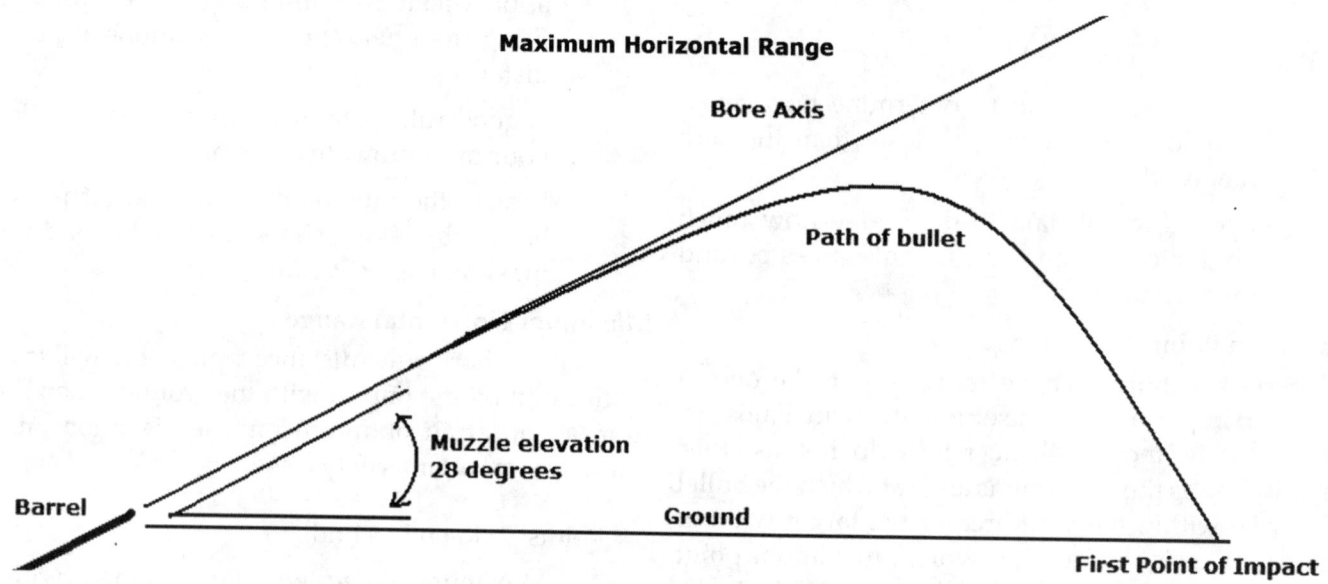

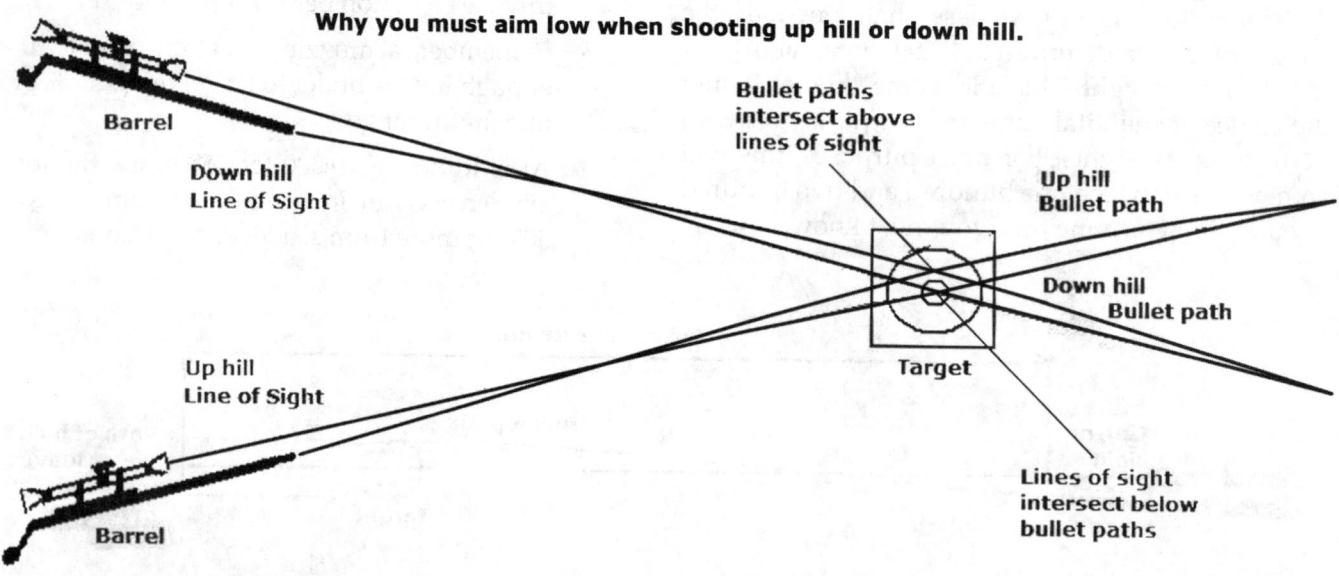

Why you must aim low when shooting up hill or down hill.

FACTORS WHICH AFFECT A BULLET IN FLIGHT

SECTIONAL DENSITY

Sectional density may be defined as the weight of the bullet in pounds divided by its cross sectional area in square inches. Basically, the sectional density describes the weight behind the diameter of a bullet (mass to cross sectional area). Sectional density is an important measure of a bullet's ability to retain velocity, penetrate the target, and resist deflection in brush.

Points To Keep In Mind

- When possible select a bullet with a high sectional density for the caliber as it will have a flatter trajectory, higher retained velocity, greater striking energy, and less wind drift than a bullet of lower sectional density.
- Heavy, long bullets of small diameter have the highest sectional densities.
- The lower the bullet weight and the larger the caliber, the lower the sectional density.
- The most efficient bullet in a given caliber is the one which is heaviest in proportion to its diameter.

COEFFICIENT OF FORM (FORM FACTOR)

This is a numerical measure of the bullet's ogive shape, body smoothness, and base configuration. Basically, the form factor is a comparison of a bullet's aerodynamic efficiency to a standard bullet listed in a specific ballistic table. This is accomplished by comparing the bullet's shape to a chart and using the multiplier number listed for it.

Points To Keep In Mind

- No two form charts or standard bullets are the same.
- Above the speed of sound (1,120 fps), the most important part of the bullet's shape is the ogive. In this context, a longer sharper point is better.
- A bullet's base shape is more important at supersonic velocity than it is at subsonic.

BALLISTIC COEFFICIENT

Ballistic coefficient is calculated by dividing the sectional density of the bullet by its coefficient of form. This produces a number comparing the ability of the bullet to cut through the air to that of a standard bullet whose ballistic performance is known.

Points To Keep In Mind

- In this connection, the important factors are bullet weight, diameter, and shape.
- The higher the ballistic coefficient, the more efficient the bullet.

Drag

Drag or air resistance affects all bullets as they fly through the air. It is drag which slows a bullet down as it flies to the target. There are three types of drag which, added together, constitute the total drag on a bullet.

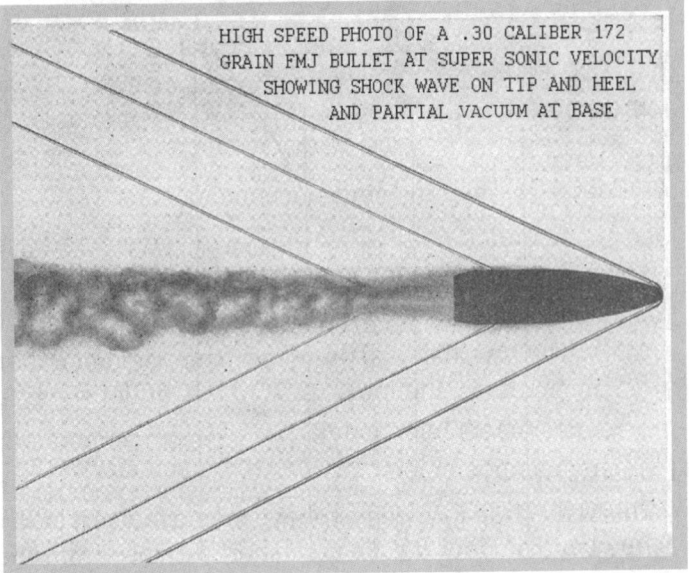

HIGH SPEED PHOTO OF A .30 CALIBER 172 GRAIN FMJ BULLET AT SUPER SONIC VELOCITY SHOWING SHOCK WAVE ON TIP AND HEEL AND PARTIAL VACUUM AT BASE

Bow Wave

The bow wave is the flow of compressed air formed around the ogive of the bullet as it pushes through the air. At subsonic velocities, the pressure wave travels in front of the bullet. At supersonic velocities, the pressure wave is deformed as the ambient air cannot move ahead/around the bullet fast enough.

Points To Keep In Mind

- The higher the drag, the more inefficient the bullet.
- A sharper point reduces bow wave drag.
- At subsonic velocities, the bow wave drag increases as the square of the velocity.
- At supersonic velocities, the bow wave drag increases at an even greater rate than its square of velocity.
- Bullet yaw and instability increase drag.

Base Drag

Base drag is caused by the partial vacuum formed at the base of the bullet where the laminar air flow along the bearing surface rips apart when it is not able to follow the acute angle formed by the base.

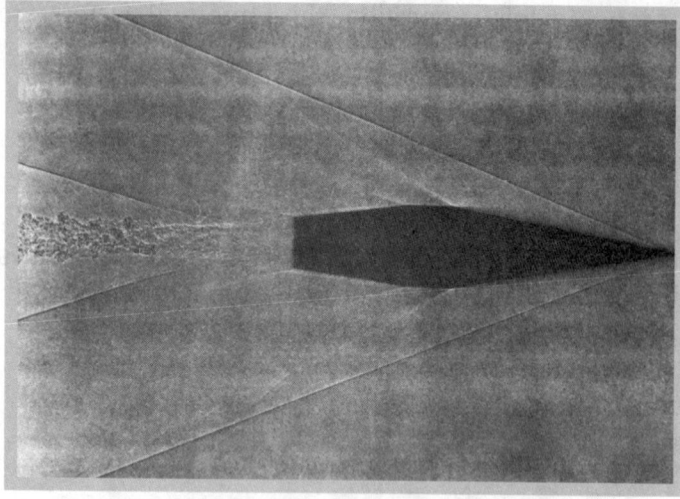

Points To Keep In Mind

- A bullet with a boat-tail will have less base drag because it has a less acute heel/base angle and a smaller diameter base.

- The partial vacuum on the base further increases the pressure on the bullet's ogive which increases drag.

Parasitic or Skin Drag

This is the drag formed just above the surface of a bullet as the laminar flow breaks up a short distance from the surface. It is the smallest contributor to bullet drag.

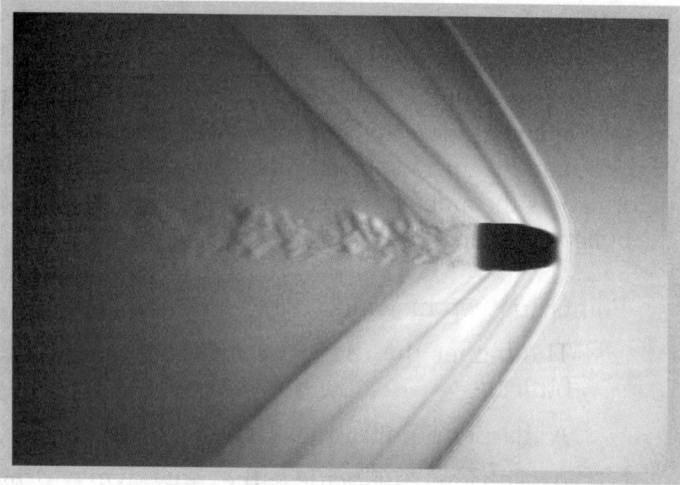

Points To Keep In Mind

- Bullet coatings do not reduce skin drag.
- Cannelures and rings increase skin drag.

Total Drag

This is the arithmetic sum of all three types of drag.

- The bow wave is the largest component of bullet drag accounting for about 60 % of the total.

- Base drag is the second highest component in total bullet drag accounting for about 30 % of the total.

- Parasitic drag is the smallest component of total drag accounting for less than 10 % of the total.

STABILITY

Stability is the ability of a rotating elongated projectile to maintain a point forward orientation along its trajectory. The most significant factor in stability is the rate of rotation because it is rotation which creates gyroscopic stability. Bullet stability depends on the following factors:

- **Diameter**
- **Length**
- **Shape**
- **Sectional density**
- **Balance**
- **Construction**
- **Velocity**
- **Rate of Rotation**

Points To Keep In Mind

- Stability is sometimes expressed as a number called the "stability factor" which may be determined in different ways, but provides a basis for comparison.

- If two bullets of the same diameter and shape are fired at the same velocity, the bullet made of the densest material will be more stable (lead vs. copper for example).

- Bullets with long ogives and boat tails are less stable than shorter bullets with a flat base.

- Bullets with hollow points, flat nose ogives, and flat bases are more stable than other configurations.

- The bullet's center of mass should be as far forward as possible, preferably in front of the center of aerodynamic pressure.

RIFLING TWIST RATE

The spiral rifling in the barrel imparts rotation or spin to the bullet. For every bullet and muzzle velocity, there is an optimum rifling twist rate. However, for practical purposes, we must make do with compromise twist rates. Over the years, experience has shown which twist rates work best for a given caliber. Firearms manufacturers have standardized on these twist rates and ammunition makers depend on them as do sportsmen. However, target shooters, varmint hunters, and big game hunters who must take very long range shots can benefit from a rifling twist rate matched to their specific load and bullet.

Points To Keep In Mind

· Rifling twist rates are normally listed in inches or millimeters per turn.

· Manufacturers use a rifling twist rate tailored to the longest heaviest bullets in a particular caliber.

· The correct rifling twist rate is a major factor in accuracy.

· A high quality barrel and bullet will improve accuracy substantially.

· When in doubt, opt for a faster twist.

· The most important factor in determining optimum rifling twist rate is bullet length.

· A pointed, flat base bullet will offer best accuracy from a slower twist rate.

· A long, pointed boat tail bullet will have best accuracy from a faster twist rate.

· A higher muzzle velocity will stabilize a bullet fired in a slower twist rate barrel than would otherwise be correct.

· Bullet stability varies as the square of the rifling twist rate. In other words, a small change in twist rate can make a big difference.

BALANCE

Although the balance of a bullet is not a factor in stability, it is an important factor in accuracy. There are two types of balance: static and dynamic.

Static Balance

This is achieved when the center of mass is located on the axis of form (centerline).

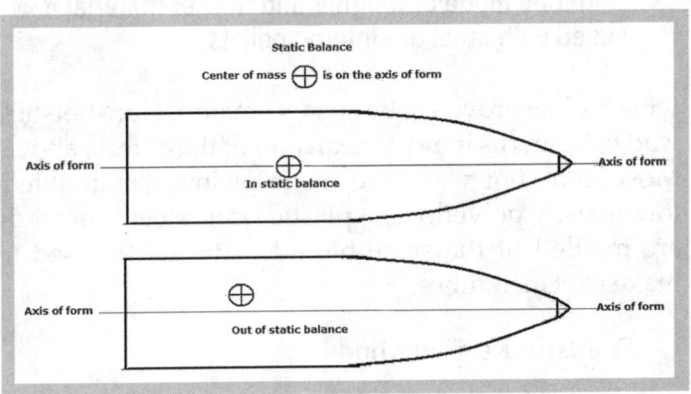

Dynamic Balance

Dynamic balance is achieved when a bullet's axis of form (centerline) is coincident with the axis of rotation.

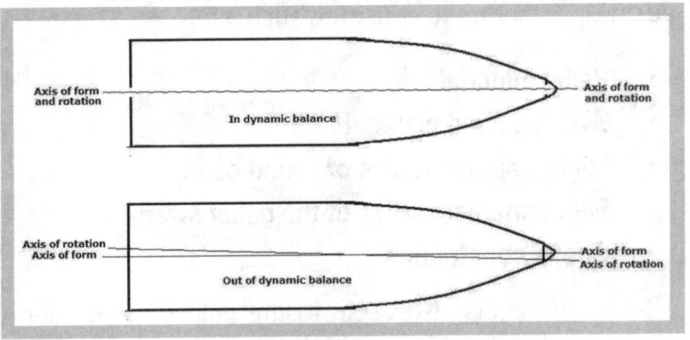

OTHER FACTORS

For most practical purposes, the following have so small an effect that they can be ignored at ranges less than 1,000 yards.

The Coriolis Effect

As the bullet travels down range, the earth turns beneath it. This is called the Coriolis effect and can amount to as much as one inch or so at 1,000 yards. North of the equator, bullets will drift to the right. South of the equator, to the left.

Vertical Drift

This is an aerodynamic effect. A crosswind in the same direction as the spin will cause drift upward while a cross wind against the direction of spin will depress the bullet's trajectory. It can amount to as much as one inch at 1,000 yards.

Lateral Jump

Some firearms (not all) displace laterally when fired. The ballistic effect of this movement or the bullet's trajectory is noticeable only at long ranges.

Long Range Wobble

As the bullet travels down range, if its spin rate decreases faster than its velocity, wobble may develop just before it becomes unstable at long range.

Gyroscopic Drift

This is the lateral deviation from the bullet's intended trajectory caused by rotation. It is in the same direction as the spin and may amount to about one and one half inches at 500 yards.

THE UNIQUE ASPECTS OF SHOTSHELLS

Shotshell pellets obey the basic laws of ballistics just like any other projectile. However there are several additional factors to consider, such as:

- **Pellet material**
- **Wad type and material**
- **Flight characteristics of round balls**
- **Flight characteristics of the pellet swarm**
- **Choke constriction**

Shotgun pellets also begin losing velocity and energy immediately after they exit the muzzle. The sectional density of a shotgun pellet is very poor. By the time they have traveled fifty yards, most pellets have lost well over half their muzzle energy.

In most cases, the pellet swarm is aimed at a moving target. Unlike a single bullet, all the pellets in the shot string will not arrive at the target at the same time. In addition, the density of the pattern has decreased with every foot of travel. From this, one can easily see why a shotgun is effective only at close ranges.

With any luck, the laws of probability will ensure that several of the pellets from the swarm will strike the target and at least one of them will hit something vital.

PELLET MATERIAL

Shotgun pellets may be made from several different materials, the oldest being lead. Many of the newer pellet materials such as steel, bismuth, and polymer-matrix pellets are not as dense as lead. Only some sintered pellets are as dense as or denser than lead.

Shotshell manufacturers compensate for some of this difference by loading non-lead pellets to a higher muzzle velocity. Even so, the down range ballistic performance of some non-lead pellets will be lower than lead by a wide margin.

Points To Keep In Mind

- In many hunting areas, use of lead shot is banned. Be sure to check local regulations before going afield.
- Use lead shot when possible for maximum down range ballistic performance.
- At ranges below forty yards, steel pellets offer acceptable ballistic performance.
- Steel pellets will have a larger number of pellets per ounce than lead.
- As steel and sintered pellets are not deformed

by acceleration, they produce excellent patterns.

- In most cases, shotshells loaded with non-lead pellets are more expensive than lead.
- Recoil with shotshells loaded to high velocities with non-lead pellets is very heavy.
- Be certain to use steel and sintered shot only in shotgun barrels designed for such loads and so marked.

WAD TYPE AND MATERIAL

Pity the poor wad column. Shooters expect it to perform numerous tasks without appreciation or thanks, and then discard it. Wad columns:

- **Seal off hot expanding propellant gasses**
- **Cushion the shot charge from the forces of acceleration**
- **Push the shot charge down the barrel**
- **Protect the shot charge from scrubbing on the bore surface**
- **Should be made of light weight material**
- **Should be made of cheap, easy to manufacture material**
- **Should be readily biodegradable**
- **Should fall away from the shot charge cleanly after exiting the muzzle**
- **Should be compatible with all existing loading machinery**
- **Should fit inside existing shotshells correctly**
- **Should be made in different gauges and lengths to accommodate various loads**
- **Must be made of tougher and thicker material if used with steel or sintered pellets**

Plastic has proven to be an ideal material for shotshell wad columns as it meets nearly all of the criteria above. Most lead shot wads are made of injection molded, low-density polyethylene plastic while steel shot wads are molded of the same high-density plastic used to make shotshell tubes.

Points To Keep In Mind

- Wad columns made up of traditional fiber cushion and nitro card wads are much heavier than plastic, which increases recoil.
- The bore of most shotguns may become fouled with plastic after many shots. Plastic fouling can be removed with specially formulated solvents.

- Wad columns without a plastic pellet protector pouch will allow lead pellets to contact the bore. This allows lead to be deposited in the bore.

- It is a good idea to inspect several spent wad columns for signs of problems such as scrub-throughs, imbedded pellets, missing parts, melting, or gas leakage.

- There is no perfect wad design and no two designs perform the same. For this reason, try several types in your shotgun before selecting one type for use.

- After exiting the muzzle, most spent wad columns will travel about twenty to thirty feet before falling harmlessly to the ground.

FLIGHT CHARACTERISTICS OF ROUND BALLS

Being spherical, a shotgun pellet has a low sectional density and a poor ballistic coefficient. The sectional density and ballistic coefficient are even lower in pellets made of most non-lead materials.

Points To Keep In Mind

- A round ball will lose velocity seven times faster than a pointed bullet of the same diameter.

- For example, the ballistic coefficient of a typical .30 caliber 125 grain bullet is about .268 while the ballistic coefficient of a .30 caliber lead ball is only .031 (see Chapter 96: Reference Material for more data).

- The lighter the pellet material, the lower the sectional density and ballistic coefficient.

FLIGHT CHARACTERISTICS OF THE PELLET SWARM

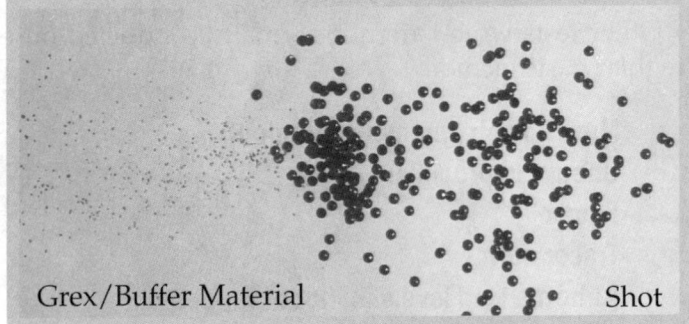

Grex/Buffer Material   Shot

While a pellet's position within the swarm is random, in general the swarm's overall dimensions and attributes are reasonably predictable and consistent. Swarm density will decrease for three reasons:

- **Round pellets will fly inside the shot swarm while pellets which are deformed or out-of-round will not remain in the shot swarm. Rather they will flare to the sides.**

- **The constricting effect of the choke in reducing swarm diameter will decrease as distance increases.**

- **The shot swarm will string out or elongate as it travels; all of the pellets will not strike the target at the same time.**

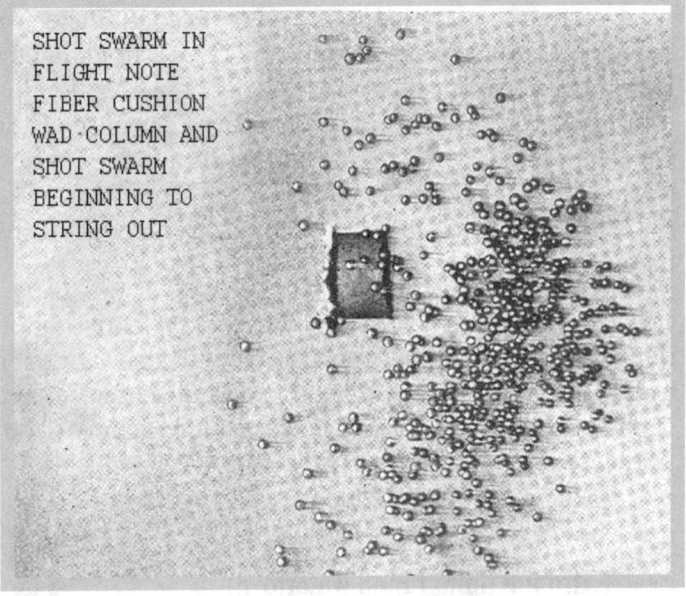

SHOT SWARM IN FLIGHT NOTE FIBER CUSHION WAD COLUMN AND SHOT SWARM BEGINNING TO STRING OUT

Typical Flight Profile For A Shot Swarm

As the shot charge and wad column exit the muzzle, the fingers of the wad are forced open by aerodynamic pressure, causing the wad column to slow quickly and fall cleanly away from the shot swarm. The spent wad column falls to the ground a few yards in front of the muzzle as the shot swarm continues on its trajectory.

The shot swarm leaves the barrel in a short cylindrical formation. As the pellets continue their travel, the forward pellets in the swarm encounter more air resistance than the rear pellets which fly in the partial vacuum of their wake. As the forward pellets slow, the rear pellets pass them to take their place at the front of the swarm. This causes the pellet swarm to become strung out.

The constriction in the choke initially reduces the diameter of the pellet swarm, holding it together for a longer time. As the swarm flies forward, some of the pellets, particularly those that have become out-of-round due to collisions, scrubbing, or slumping, will take a slightly diverging path from the swarm's main axis of travel. As these pellets go their separate ways increasing the diameter of the swarm, the density of the pattern decreases.

Of course the pellets immediately begin dropping once they leave the muzzle and they can be deflected by cross winds. The effects of pellet drop and deflection by cross winds can be ignored at ranges of less than forty yards. At longer ranges, however, their effects must be considered.

CHOKE CONSTRICTION

Most shotgun barrels are either choked or have interchangeable screw-in choke tubes. Located in the last two inches of the barrel, the choke has a shallow forcing cone leading to a parallel section of reduced diameter. As the shot swarm passes through the choke, its diameter is reduced in much the same manner as water flowing through a nozzle on a garden hose. The purpose of the choke is to maintain pattern density for a longer period thus increasing effective range. In many cases, the choke will also reduce the number of flyers at the edge of the pattern.

Chokes are made in many degrees of constriction depending upon the gun's intended use and the manufacturer's philosophy. In general, chokes have standardized names and levels of constriction (from tightest to none) as follows:

- **Turkey**
- **Extra full (long range waterfowl)**
- **Full (the most popular)**
- **Improved modified (popular for trap and sporting clays)**
- **Modified (good all-around choice)**
- **Improved cylinder (for fast, close shots in heavy woods)**
- **Skeet**
- **Cylinder (for slugs and buckshot)**

The names for each constriction are traditional and not intended to imply varying degrees of shooter competence or technical inferiority of the shotgun. For more information on chokes, see Chapter 96: Reference Material.

MEASUREMENT EQUIPMENT AND TESTS

Measurement equipment used for exterior ballistics is relatively basic.

CHRONOGRAPH

The most ubiquitous measuring device used in exterior ballistics is the chronograph. Essentially, a chronograph is a very high speed stop watch which uses two photo-electric screens (one to start the count and one to stop it) to measure the average time it takes a bullet to travel a measured distance between the screens. From this, the velocity can be easily calculated.

The screens can be positioned at any distance along the bullet's trajectory if desired.

The more recent models of these devices are chronotachs which provide a direct reading in feet per second instead of time. Radar-based chronographs can measure remaining velocity at any point (or multiple points) along a trajectory.

BALLISTIC PENDULUM

Although a ballistic pendulum can be used to determine striking velocity, they are seldom used for that purpose today. Rather, they are used to measure the total recoil of a cartridge and rifle combination. As using a ballistic pendulum is time consuming and few exist, they are employed rarely. Instead, recoil can be calculated.

YAW CARDS

Yaw cards are used to measure the amount of yaw experienced by the bullet near the muzzle before it becomes fully stabilized. After the bullet has penetrated a series of cards, the shape and dimensions of the bullet holes can be used to measure the yaw. Today, this method is seldom used as it is time consuming and the physics of bullet yaw are well understood.

SHOTGUN PATTERN TESTS

Despite the intensive labor involved, most manufacturers conduct a regular series of pattern tests to verify pattern density and quality (see Chapter 25: Shotshell Hull Manufacturing for more information, also Chapter 95: Useful Formulas for information on how to do this yourself).

OTHER TESTS

Other tests which are not normally conducted on a regular basis include:

- **Muzzle flash (intensity, duration)**
- **Unburned propellant**
- **Smoke**
- **Tracer burn**
- **Airborne lead levels in indoor ranges**
- **Sound levels**
- **Effects of cold or hot temperature extremes**

MEN OF EXTERIOR BALLISTICS

Benjamin Robins, 1707-1751

Born and raised in Bath, England, Benjamin Robins went to London to seek his fortune. He mastered several languages and mathematics on his own, became a successful tutor, and was elected a Fellow of the Royal Society in 1727.

Unhappy with being a tutor, Robins became a successful engineer going on to build several bridges, buildings, and even harbors. During this period, he became interested in fortification and gunnery. He traveled extensively on the continent studying both. In 1742, Robins published his ground breaking treatise "New Principles of Gunnery" which became the basis for subsequent scientific inquiry into artillery and projectiles.

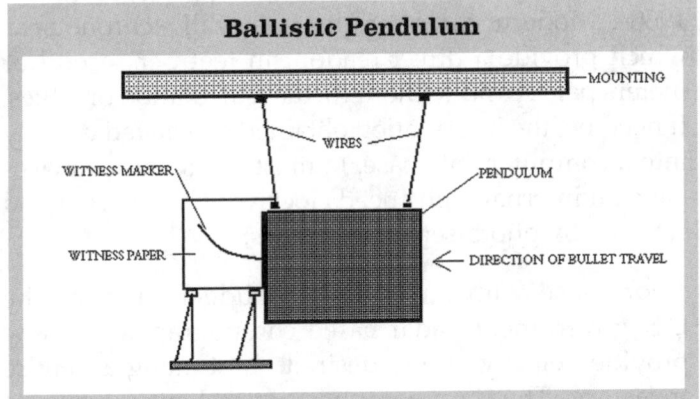

Ballistic Pendulum

It was Benjamin Robins who invented the ballistic pendulum - the first device which could measure a projectile's velocity. He also conducted experiments with smoothbore muskets to determine why they were so inaccurate and in doing so became a proponent of rifled barrels. He also experimented with rockets and published an article about them in 1750.

In 1750, Robins accepted a commission in Madras, India to design and build the fortifications there. Shortly after his arrival, he contracted a fever and died.

Even today, aspects of Robins work are still relevant. He will be remembered as a brilliant mathematician and military engineer who revolutionized the science of gunnery. His greatest legacy to 21st century shooters is the ballistic pendulum.

Niccolo Tartaglia, 1500-1557

When he was a teenager in his home town of Brescia, Italy, the French Army captured the town in 1512 and put it to the sword. Young Niccolo suffered a nearly fatal saber slash across his face. Although he survived, he could speak only with difficulty and maintained a heavy beard to cover his facial scars.

Tartaglia had an extraordinary aptitude for mathematics and was self-taught. He moved to Verona and became a math teacher and in 1534 moved to Venice to teach. He participated in numerous debates and built a reputation as a promising mathematician.

In 1537, Tartaglia wrote "Nova Scientia" on the application of mathematics to artillery fire. In this work, he put forth new ballistic concepts such as the parabolic flight of projectiles and described his new invention—the gunner's quadrant which was used to quickly determine the angle of elevation at the muzzle. Tartaglia included the first set of firing tables for artillery based on muzzle elevation.

Tartaglia passed away in 1557 in poverty. However, he remains a giant in the history of ballistics for his ground-breaking ballistic theories, gunner's quadrant, and the first set of firing tables.

Galileo Galilei, 1564-1642

Although he was enrolled in medical school at the University of Pisa, Galileo became fascinated by mathematics after he read several of Tartaglia's works. Galileo then gave up medical school and began studying and teaching mathematics. His reputation grew and he was appointed to fill the chair in mathematics at the University of Pisa in 1589. For the next three years, he taught and wrote "De Motu," a collection of essays on the theory of motion which were not published until 35 years after his death.

In "De Motu," Galileo postulated the correct law for falling bodies and determined that a projectile followed a parabolic path as it traveled through the air and not a straight line as was believed at the time. While Galileo's other discoveries earned him great fame, his "De Motu" was fundamental to the understanding of projectiles in flight. For this, Galileo secured a permanent place for himself in the history of ballistics.

Francesco Siacci, 1839-1907

When he graduated from the University of Rome in 1860, Siacci had already demonstrated an extraordinary aptitude for mathematics. At the time, Italy was experiencing a period of political upheaval so Siacci moved to Turin in 1861 where he joined the army and began teaching ballistics at the Military Academy there. In 1872, Siacci was appointed Professor of Ballistics at the Military Academy, a post he held until his retirement in 1892.

By all accounts, Siacci was an excellent instructor and published several hundred papers. In the area of ballistics, he was a master. Siacci reduced the equations of flight to four simple statements and provided tables for computing trajectory. Siacci's method was adopted by Britain, France, and Germany. In the U.S., it was adopted after modification by Col. James Ingalls. Siacci's work formed the mathematical basis for modern ballistics.

Robins, Grobert, Boulenge Measurement Pioneers

The classic formula for calculating velocity is Rate= Distance ÷ Time. If you know the distance and the time it took to cover that distance, the velocity can easily be calculated. A chronograph is a device which measures the time it takes an object to travel a known distance between two points. In other words, a chronograph can supply two parts of the equation allowing the third to be calculated.

Benjamin Robins was the first to calculate the velocity of a bullet using a ballistic pendulum. This simple device was capable of reasonably accurate measurements, but was cumbersome to use. In 1804, Col. Grobert of the French Army invented the spinning disk chronograph which utilized two spinning disks mounted on a common shaft a measured distance apart. In 1880, Capt. Paul Emile Boulenge of the Belgian Army invented a chronograph which used two electrically charged wires cut by the passage of the bullet to release two metal rods. By comparing the distance each rod dropped, a simple calculation determined velocity. Boulenge's

chronograph remained in use until the 1940s.

Alternatives to the ballistic pendulum, spinning disk, and falling rod systems were tried with varying degrees of acceptance from 1880 until about 1930 at which time electronics became sophisticated enough to determine velocity quickly, easily, and accurately. Still, such systems provided only the time of flight between two points; the operator still had to refer to a table in order to obtain velocity.

All this became obsolete almost overnight with the advent of the transistor and microprocessor in the 1960s. Modern chronographs are really chronotachs which provide a direct readout in feet per second or meters per second without further calculation or tables. If need be, the information obtained can be fed directly into a computer data base. In most cases, these devices have an internal high speed clock which is started and stopped by photo-sensitive screens.

For those with an unlimited budget, such as the U.S. government, radar based chronographs can now provide velocity at any desired point along an entire trajectory. The chronograph is an excellent example of how advances in measurement technology can affect ballistics and many other sciences.

Billy Dixon, Adobe Walls, June 27, 1874

Adobe Walls was a small settlement in the Texas panhandle some 150 miles southwest of Dodge City, Kansas. In June 1874, buffalo hunters began moving into the area to hunt the Great Central Herd using Adobe Walls as a base camp. On the morning of June 27, 1874, there were 28 people in Adobe Walls, many of them buffalo hunters. Among them were Bat Masterson and a young hunter named Billy Dixon, already well known for his shooting skills.

Led by Comanche Chief Quanah Parker, a combined force of approximately 700 Comanche, Cheyenne, and Kiowa warriors attacked the Adobe Walls settlement at dawn that day. The warriors carried their first charge to the doors and windows of the saloon, only to be repulsed by the defenders firing .44 caliber Colt and

S&W revolvers. Following this, the Indian warriors retreated and surrounded the settlement. All that day the Indian warriors were kept at a distance by accurate rifle fire from the buffalo hunters' rifles. The next morning, a group of Indian warriors rode to a nearby hill to get a better look at the settlement.

Billy Dixon took careful aim at one of the mounted Indians on the hill and fired a shot from a .50-90 Sharps buffalo rifle he borrowed from the saloon keeper. The bullet hit its intended target, knocking him from his horse and killing him. Discouraged, the warriors retreated and sought less formidable opposition.

Some two weeks after the siege was broken, a team of U.S. Army surveyors arrived to measure the actual distance of the shot. Reportedly, they determined the range as being 1,538 yards! It was a lucky shot, and Dixon knew it, as he seldom mentioned it later in life. However, the tale of Billy Dixon's long range shot has entered shooting folklore and been retold many times.

But fate and the Indians were not finished with Dixon just yet. Dixon joined the U.S. Army as a scout. Just three months after Adobe Walls, he was leading a detachment of four soldiers and another scout delivering army dispatches when they were attacked by a large band of Comanche and Kiowa warriors. Retreating to a shallow buffalo wallow, Dixon and the troopers kept up accurate rifle fire which held off the Indians all day until they became discouraged and broke off the fight late that night. Dixon and the other survivors of the Buffalo Wallow Fight were awarded the Congressional Medal of Honor.

Sadly, Dixon had to return the award as he was a civilian. Dixon later homesteaded at Adobe Walls, going on to become postmaster and then sheriff. He died in 1913 and is buried in Texline, Texas.

WOLFGANG HAACK, 1902-1994

Born in Gotha, Germany, Wolfgang Haack received his doctorate in mechanical engineering and mathematics in 1926 from Schiller University in Germany. Dr. Haack then became a teacher working at several state institutions of higher learning. During World War II, Dr. Haack worked at The Hermann Goering Aeronautical Proving Ground in Braunschweig doing research on minimum drag projectile designs.

Recognizing that ballistics and aerodynamics had much in common, Dr. Haack used his mathematical expertise to develop a new, analytical formula for projectile ogive designs that exhibit the lowest resistance to air flow. Unlike other projectiles, Haack bullet ogives are not built from geometric designs using tangent or secant curves. Rather, the Haack design formula considers only wave drag at trans-sonic and supersonic velocities. His method determines optimal projectile shape for a given i) caliber and length, ii) volume and length and iii) volume and caliber.

The German Luftwaffe immediately incorporated Dr. Haack's designs into anti-aircraft projectiles that significantly increased the maximum altitude the guns could reach. His work was kept top secret until 1947. Today, Dr. Haack's design parameters can be seen on many supersonic jet fighters such as the F-15, F-16, and F-22.

At the end of World War II, Dr. Haack returned to teaching at the university level where he earned a well-deserved reputation in mathematics, computers, and aerodynamics. Dr. Haack retired in 1968. In 1992, he was appointed an honorary member of The Society for Applied Mathematics and Mechanics.

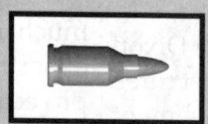

Microfun (centerfire version)

.14 Eichelberger Dart

Now, who would want to design a wildcat based on the .25 ACP cartridge? Someone had to do it and W. Eichelberger was that man. He necked down the .25 ACP cartridge to accept a .14 caliber (.144 inch diameter) bullet weighing 10-, 12-, or 13-grains. With a 13-grain bullet, Eichelberger claims muzzle velocity is 2,690 fps with a muzzle energy of 209 ft-lbs. Not too shabby for such a small cartridge! Compare this to the 3 mm Kolibri in Chapter 48.

CHAPTER 45 : TERMINAL BALLISTICS

All ballistics photos courtesy Tom Burczynski.
All drawings by Author, unless otherwise noted.

DEFINITION OF TERMINAL BALLISTICS

Terminal ballistics is the study of projectiles as they strike and penetrate various types of targets both animate and inanimate.

> "God created men. Sam Colt made them equal!"
>
> - *Popular saying in the Old West circa late 1800s.*

A SHORT HISTORY

For centuries, trial and error was the rule when it came to terminal ballistics. No one understood the scientific principles of terminal ballistics. However, medieval gunners were keen observers and quickly noted what worked and what did not. Their observations focused on two areas of interest:

- **The effects of projectiles on animate targets (humans and animals), armored or not**

- **The effects of projectiles on inanimate targets**

ANIMATE TARGETS

For example, observation and experience showed that a solid hit from a lead ball one inch in diameter or less on a human or equine target was normally fatal. In addition, the impact of the ball immediately incapacitated the target, if not killing it outright. Furthermore, it made no difference what kind of gun launched the ball. A cannon firing grapeshot or canister shot was just as effective as a musket ball.

The expensive body armor worn by the nobility in battle was designed to resist blows from swords, hammers, and lances. It was not proof against bullets. A knight could not wear enough body armor to protect himself against bullets. Of course, the knight's horse was an easy target as well. It quickly became a given that guns were very effective against animate targets of all types. For example a .775 inch diameter round ball weighing 700 grains and striking a target at 700 fps. would carry 762 ft.-lbs. of energy which is nearly twice that of a modern .45 ACP bullet.

The advent of rifled barrels and elongated bullets did not change terminal ballistic thinking. Heavy large caliber bullets of soft lead which flattened on impact were the rule as they were proven to be effective.

The development of smokeless powder in 1886 forced a quantum level change in terminal ballistic thinking. Velocities were now so high that bullets had to be jacketed to avoid stripping lead in the barrel. The higher velocity offered significantly higher striking energy, but the bullet did not upset and often bored through the target without incapacitating it. Clearly, this was a waste of energy. Something had to be done.

It was. Reports from the Northern Frontier of India were not good in the late 1800s. The new .303 British caliber cartridge did not incapacitate the tough tribesmen of the Punjab area when they were struck by its 215 grain FMJ-RN bullet. Capt. Neville S. Bertie-Clay, Superintendent of Small Arms at the Dum Dum Arsenal responded with a soft point bullet design which expanded on impact, allowing the bullet to transfer more energy to the target. The bullet was a success, but was soon made illegal by the Hague Convention in 1899.

THE HAGUE CONVENTION OF 1899

Contrary to popular folklore, it was the Hague Convention of July 29, 1899 that first addressed the subject of expanding rifle bullets in warfare. This appears in Declaration III titled "On the Use of Bullets Which Expand or Flatten Easily in the Human Body." The text itself reads: "The Contracting Parties agree to abstain from the use of bullets which expand or flatten easily in the human body, such as bullets with a hard envelope which does not entirely cover the core, or is pierced with incisions."

Obviously, this Declaration was aimed at the use of the expanding bullets designed by Capt. N.S. Bertie-Clay at the arsenal at Dum Dum, India for use in .303 British caliber rifles.

Of particular interest are the following words of the same Declaration.

"The present Declaration is only binding for the Contracting Powers in the case of a war between two or more of them."

"It shall cease to be binding from the time when, in a war between the Contracting Parties, one of the belligerents is joined by a non-Contracting Power."

"Try to look unimportant, the bad guys may be low on ammo."

- Murphy's Law of Combat No. 10

In the meantime, the U.S. Army experienced poor terminal ballistic performance of standard issue .30-40 Krag rifle and .38 revolver ammunition during the 1899-1902 Philippine Insurrection. It was about time for someone to conduct tests to find out exactly what happened when a full metal jacketed rifle or handgun bullet struck a live target. In 1904, Brig. Gen. William Crozier, Chief of Ordnance of the U.S. Army appointed Capt. John T. Thompson of the Infantry and Maj. Louis A. LaGarde of the Medical Corps to conduct a series of tests to investigate and recommend which caliber should be adopted for a new service handgun.

Their tests consisted of firing eight different handgun calibers from .30 to .45 at live cattle and human cadavers. From this they assigned a subjective value to each caliber. Not surprisingly, the .45 Colt revolver cartridge did very well. These tests served to convince the U.S. Army to adopt the M1911 semi-automatic pistol in .45 ACP caliber. The results of these tests remain controversial today.

One unexpected effect of the Thompson-LaGarde tests was to cause a great schism in terminal ballistics which continues to this day. On one side are those traditionalists who believe that a large caliber heavyweight bullet is preferable for defensive purposes. On the other side are the modernists who believe that lightweight bullets at high velocity are the best choice for defensive purposes. The controversy extends to both rifle and handgun calibers – 9mm versus the .45 ACP and the 5.56mm vs. the 7.62mm. As the argument has continued over the years, the pendulum of opinion has swung to one side, then the other many times. Opinion seems to be swinging back toward heavy bullets in light of the disappointing experience by the U.S. military forces with the 9mm and 5.56mm in Iraq and Afghanistan. The U.S. Army considered dropping the 9mm and returning to the .45ACP. At least one or two members of an infantry squad rotating to Afghanistan now carry an updated M-14 rifle in 7.62x51mm NATO caliber. The same debate goes on in the civilian realm, both for hunting and for personal defense.

"When you are in a firefight, the first time the bad guys should know is when they look down and see the exit wound!"

-good advice from a Light Weapons Instructor at the Special Forces Qualification Course

BRIGADIER GENERAL JOHN T. THOMPSON U.S. ARMY 1860-1940

By the time he was sixteen, young John Thompson had decided on a military career. He gained an appointment from his home state of Kentucky to the U.S. Military Academy at West Point, N.Y. from which he graduated in 1882. He was assigned to the Ordnance Department where he spent the remainder of his military career.

When the Spanish-American War began, Thompson (now a Lt. Colonel) became Chief Ordnance Officer for military operations in Cuba. During this period, Thompson kept his first date with destiny. Following a request from Lt. John H. Parker, Thompson organized a Gatling gun unit equipped with fifteen guns and sent them to Cuba on his own authority. They were to play a pivotal role in the Battle for San Juan Hill.

With the end of the Spanish-American War, Thompson was appointed chief of the Small Arms Division of the Ordnance Department where he kept his second appointment with destiny. Thompson played a key role in the development of the M1903 Springfield rifle and the M1911 pistol. It was during this period that he and Maj. Louis A. LaGarde conducted their (in)famous wound tests which were to become the source of so much controversy, which still continues.

Thompson retired in 1914 to become Chief Engineer for the Remington Arms Co. where he supervised construction of the Eddystone Plant which was the largest small arms plant in the world at the time. Eddystone made millions of Mosin-Nagant and Enfield rifles during World War I.

When the U.S. entered World War I in 1917, Thompson was recalled to active duty, promoted to Brigadier General, and appointed Director of Arsenals. He retired once again in 1918 after World War I ended.

During World War I, Thompson noted a new type of weapon to clear trenches. Called the MP18/1, it was the German Army developed fully automatic, compact, and chambered for a pistol cartridge impressed by a similar gun fitting designed by Commander John Blish, USN. Together, they formed the Auto Ordnance Company to manufacture the new gun and in doing so, Thompson kept his third, and most important, date with destiny. The new gun was named the "Thompson Submachine Gun", later shortened to "Tommy Gun". Much to General Thompson's chagrin, the Tommy Gun became an icon of the turbulent 1920s when it was associated with both mobsters and FBI agents. Despite this, orders were scarce and when the Auto Ordnance Company suffered a financial crisis in 1928, Thompson was replaced as head of the company.

Gen. John T. Thompson died at the age of 79 on June 21, 1940. He was buried at the U.S. Military Academy. Shortly afterward, the U.S. entered World War II and millions of "Tommy Guns" were made for the war effort. Thompson guns are still being made today.

INANIMATE TARGETS

In medieval times, gunners were much more interested in the effects their cannon balls would have on fortifications than they were about animate targets. As siege experience accumulated, the rule of thumb for firing against fortifications became: the bigger the cannon, the better. Initially, siege cannon fired stone balls. Despite the difficulty in making them, they proved effective as they usually broke up after penetrating the wall which increased the effect of the impact. The advent of cast iron cannon balls meant that cannon could easily smash stone walls in a matter of hours. On more than one occasion, only one or two shots were all that was needed.

Military engineers were quick to react, making fortifications lower (harder to hit), sloped (to deflect impacts), and covered with earth (to absorb the impacts). When high explosives and increased velocities made even this insufficient, engineers developed under ground fortifications made of concrete reinforced with steel rods and armor steel plates. Warships were armored as well.

The naval battle between the ironclads Monitor and Merrimac on March 9, 1862 proved to be a watershed event. Both ships' guns proved incapable of penetrating the armor of the other. It now became necessary to develop new types of projectiles to penetrate the new armor arrays.

Sir William Palliser, an officer in the British Army, came to the rescue with a new type of projectile designed to penetrate armor in 1863. The Palliser projectile was cast nose down using an iron mold to form the tip and a sand mold to form the body. The iron mold (later water was used) cooled the tip of the projectile much faster than the body. This hardened the tip so the projectile would penetrate armor without shattering. A small cavity in the tail held a charge of black powder which exploded after the shell penetrated the armor. As armor improved, Palliser shells were made of harder steel. By the turn of the century, the Palliser shell had become obsolete even for use in large caliber guns.

Until 1914, armor piercing (AP) projectile designs focused mainly on ships' guns. Experience during World War I indicated that many targets on a modern battlefield were protected by steel armor. For example, German machine gunners wore body armor and the machine gun was protected by an inclined steel plate which deflected normal FMJ bullets. Clearly, there was a growing need for armor piercing bullets for rifle caliber guns. This need was met by using a hardened steel insert inside a lead sleeve to form the core of an armor piercing rifle bullet. If desired, the steel core could be left unhardened so as to make a ball round of the same configuration.

During World War II, the number of hardened targets on the battlefield rose significantly. So much so, that many U.S. Army infantry units fighting in Europe in 1944-45 were issued .03-'06 M2 armor piercing ammunition routinely instead of ball.

Modern armor arrays have become even more resistant to rifle caliber bullets. Tungsten carbide is being used in the core of some modern armor piercing bullets to penetrate such arrays. And so the 750 year battle between armor and projectiles to penetrate them continues unabated.

BALLISTIC INQUIRY AND STUDY

Terminal ballistics focuses primarily on four main subjects:

- **Accuracy and precision**
- **Energy transfer**
- **Penetration**
- **Incapacitation**

ACCURACY AND PRECISION

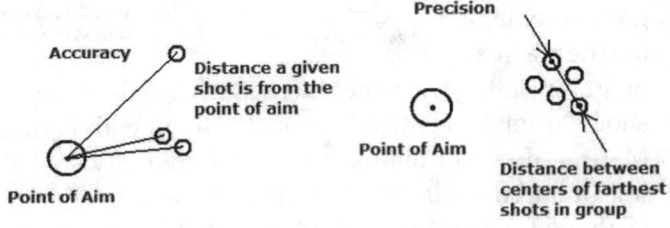

Accuracy vs Precision

Although these two terms often are used interchangeably, they are in fact different. Both are systems for evaluating bullet performance and are independent of each other.

Accuracy may be defined as the distance that a bullet strikes from its point of aim.

Precision is how close together the shots in a group may be without reference to a point of aim (remember, the sights can always be changed to compensate).

In addition to millimeters and inches, accuracy and precision may be expressed in minutes of angle (approximately 1.0472 inches at one hundred yards), or mils (100mm at 100 meters). Sportsmen generally prefer the former and military the latter.

Several different systems are used to evaluate shot groups on a target:

Extreme spread

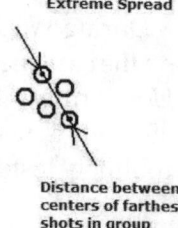

Extreme Spread

This is the distance between the two most widely separated shots. Normally, this is measured from center to center of the two bullet holes farthest apart. Extreme spread is the most popular method of evaluating a target.

Distance between centers of farthest shots in group (five or ten shots)

Figure of Merit

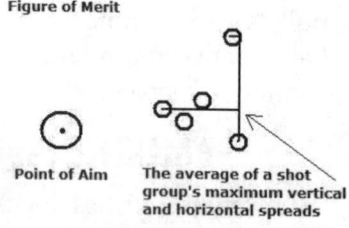

Figure of Merit

Point of Aim

The average of a shot group's maximum vertical and horizontal spreads

This is a more useful evaluation of accuracy as it takes the extreme spread method one step further. A figure of merit is the average of a shot group's maximum horizontal and vertical spreads. No consideration is given to how far the "center" of the group may be from the aiming point. Target shooters sometimes use this method to judge their groups.

Mean Radius

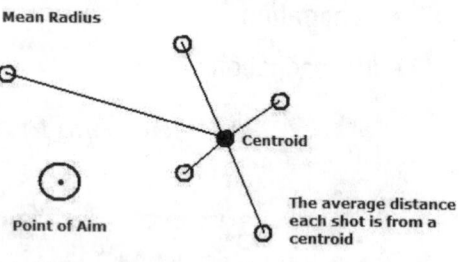

Mean Radius

Centroid

Point of Aim

The average distance each shot is from a centroid

This is a two stage computation system. The centroid of a shot group is obtained mathematically or graphically. Then the average of the distance each shot is from the centroid is calculated. As with Figure of Merit, it does not matter if the centroid and visual aiming point coincide. Military ammunition is sometimes evaluated using this method. Statistically, this is one of the best methods for comparative analysis.

There are two key concepts which relate to the use of these methods: ammunition performance is being evaluated – not the shooter's ability to hit a specific point on a target; and multiple 10-shot groups at long range must be fired.

In many instances, testing at a range of one hundred yards is the most convenient. This is adequate for most purposes and is commonly used in industry to evaluate the accuracy of production lots of ammunition. Longer distances are preferable if available. Shorter distances (fifty yards and less) are suitable for testing handguns and shotguns.

Most hunters are satisfied with a three shot group while experienced shooters opt for five shot groups. At ammunition manufacturing facilities, ten shot groups are the norm – and for good reason. They provide a greater than 95% statistical certainty that the results are valid. Groups comprised of a smaller number of shots offer a significantly lower level of statistical certainty.

As any experienced shooter will point out, in practical terms, a good ten shot group is four times harder to fire than a good five shot group.

Points To Keep In Mind

* Always fire at least five shots to form a test group. Ten shot groups are better. A three shot group is statistically useless.

* Always test rifle accuracy at a range of one hundred yards or more.

* To properly evaluate a group, use one of the methods outlined above (see also Chapter 95: Useful Formulas). The by guess and by gosh method does not work.

* Most shooters seek precision as they can always adjust the sights for accuracy.

* Precision is a key factor in determining your firearm/cartridge/bullet combination's capability for vital zone shot placement.

ENERGY TRANSFER

Energy transfer may be defined as the total amount of kinetic energy a bullet will transfer to the target from the time it strikes until it exits the target or comes to rest inside the target.

Prior to 1880, energy transfer depended on large caliber heavy weight bullets molded of soft lead which would flatten on impact. It was not scientific, but it was traditional and it worked. Smokeless powder changed this almost overnight.

Ideally, a modern bullet will transfer all of its kinetic to the target. A substantial part of the study of terminal ballistics is devoted to finding better ways to do this. There are three broad categories of bullets which will accomplish this:

Non-expanding bullets

Bullets of this type transfer energy to the target by means of their diameter, flat nose, or both. In most cases, bullets in this category retain 99% of their original weight although they may be deformed by the impact. They may bore completely through a target without depositing all their energy.

Expanding bullets

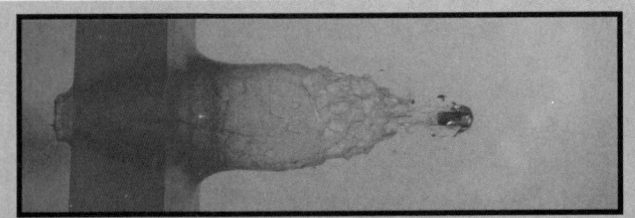

As this soft point hunting bullet exits a block of 10% ballistic gelatin, we can clearly see how the bullet has expanded. The gelatin block gives a rough indication of how much energy has been transferred to it by the bullet.

Soft point, hollow point, tipped, and capped bullets are in this category. Their primary method of energy transfer is by bullet expansion or mushrooming; some designs may expand twice or more times their original diameter. A well designed expanding bullet will retain 90% or more of its original weight upon impact. Premium bullets often retain 95%-98% of their weight while "standard" bullets make do with 60%-70% retained weight.

Bullets which break-up, tumble, or disintegrate

Many of the bullets in this category are full metal jacket military bullets. By manipulating jacket thickness and hardness, cannelure location, core size/hardness, etc. bullets of this type are intentionally designed to fragment after initial impact and transfer nearly all their energy to the target. The Russian 5.45mm military bullet is a good example. Another method is to move the bullet's center of gravity behind its aerodynamic center so that it remains stable in flight, but quickly becomes unstable on impact and begins tumbling. An example of this type is the British .303 caliber Mark VIII bullet. Now nearly complete disintegration after impact can be achieved by light weight high velocity bullets made of low strength alloys. This prevents over penetration, ricochets, and reduces maximum range in case of a miss.

Points To Keep In Mind

* Never "over drive" a bullet outside its intended performance envelope.

* Soft point bullets have the largest velocity window for terminal ballistic performance.

* Hollow point bullets normally have a narrow velocity window for terminal ballistic performance and behave like non-expanding bullets at striking velocities below that velocity window.

* Bullets that break-up or tumble are not suitable for hunting medium or large game.

* Bullets that disintegrate after penetration are suitable only for varmint hunting.

* Non-expanding bullets are illegal for hunting game in most areas of North America (except for furbearers and varmints).

PENETRATION

Animate Targets

Energy transfer is nothing without penetration. In other words, the effectiveness of energy transfer depends on where the energy is transferred inside an animate target. For example, a bullet which disintegrates on the surface may cause a superficial wound which fails to incapacitate the target. On the other hand, a bullet which bores cleanly through a target may not transfer enough energy to incapacitate it either. The ideal is for the bullet to penetrate deeply enough to reach the vital organs so as to assure incapacitation, and stop within the target.

Determining how much penetration is necessary on an animate target is not an exact science. Remember, the bullet may have to penetrate brush, leaves, dirt encrusted hide, sinew, and bone before reaching a vital organ. As there is no reliable way to test this, experience must be the guide in such cases.

The exact amount of penetration necessary depends on the physical and mental aspects of the target. For example, large heavy game may require a penetration depth of twenty-four inches or more in order to reach a vital organ. Medium game may require a bullet that expands faster with a penetration depth of twelve inches. Varmints and pests require a bullet that expands after two or three inches of penetration.

Tests have shown that a penetration of six to ten inches is optimum for most human targets. However, clothing, jewelry, and work gear can reduce penetration to the point of ineffectiveness.

Points To Keep In Mind

* Always select a bullet which will provide the penetration necessary to reliably incapacitate the intended target. For recommendations, see Chapter 33 and 34.

* The brush bucking bullet is a myth. No bullet will buck brush well.

* An expanding bullet capable of six to ten inches penetration is generally required for personal defense use.

* For personal defense, most experts recommend a bullet diameter of 9mm or larger.

Inanimate Targets

Penetration of inanimate targets can be tested and measured with excellent repeatability.

All shooters must consider penetration of inanimate objects for several reasons:

- Hunters are interested in which bullet will be least deflected by brush and foliage.

- Metallic silhouette shooters want as much energy transfer as possible (to knock down metal targets) and are not concerned with penetration.

- Gun club managers are interested in preventing penetration of baffles, berms, and dividers.

- Indoor shooting ranges want to prevent damage to armor plate backstops and other range fixtures.

- Law enforcement officers must have bullets which will penetrate commonly encountered barriers.

- Both soldiers and law enforcement officers need to know which bullets will or will not penetrate body armor.

This shotgun slug retains plenty of energy after completely penetrating two .20 inch thick spaced steel sheets.

Penetration of any inanimate object by a bullet depends on six factors:

- Impact velocity – Higher is better

- Bullet diameter – Smaller is better

- Bullet construction – Stronger is better

- Bullet weight – Heavier is better

- Angle of impact – 90° is best

- Material protecting target – Less amount is better

The ideal rifle bullet for defeating light armor, assuming a terminal velocity of 4,000 fps or more and striking the target face at a 90° angle, would be long, small diameter, and have a very hard core. Currently, there is no ammunition with these characteristics although there are cartridge/bullet designs which do

MAJOR GENERAL HENRY SHRAPNEL, ROYAL ARMY 1761-1842

In 1779, Henry Shrapnel became a cadet at the Royal Military Academy at Woolwich Arsenal in London. On graduation, Shrapnel received a commission as a Second Lt. in the Royal Artillery. During his first posting at Gibraltar, he saw the need for an effective, long range (over 1,000 yards) artillery shell to be used against massed troops. After considerable experimentation at his own expense, Shrapnel devised a thin metal shell filled with musket balls and a small powder charge ignited by a time delay fuze. Ignition of the powder charge was timed so that the shell casing was blown apart above the target, and the musket balls projected in a shotgun-like manner over a specific area.

Although his design was a ballistic break through, Shrapnel had a difficult time making anyone take notice. Finally, in 1803 the Board of Ordnance recommended adoption of Shrapnel's new shell. Reports from the field soon confirmed that Shrapnel's invention was devastatingly effective. Shrapnel became a star and was promoted to Lt. Colonel.

During the War of 1812 with the U.S., the British fleet used Shrapnel shells to bombard Ft. McHenry which protected Baltimore. The awesome bursts of the shells above the fort inspired Francis Scott Key to include the phrase "The bombs bursting in air" in his song "The Star Spangled Banner" which became our National Anthem.

Shrapnel's shell undoubtedly swung the tide in British favor during the Peninsular Wars with Napoleon. Once again, Shrapnel's Spherical Case Shot played a key role at Waterloo in defeating Napoleon. As Wellington's artillery commander put it, "No fire could be more murderous".

During this period, Shrapnel also perfected recoil mechanisms, an improved musket, an improved howitzer, and new fuzes.

In his lifetime, Shrapnel received little recognition for his invention leaving him a forgotten and bitter man. He did receive a pension of £1,200 per year in 1814 although he was passed over for promotion. Shrapnel retired in the 1830s as a Major General and passed away in 1842 at his home in Southampton. He has been described as a genius with a deadly skill and a devastating talent. He is commemorated only by a small plaque on the wall of a Sussex pub where his workshop once was.

British soldiers often adopt the name of the original manufacturer or inventor to describe a piece of equipment. In this manner, Henry Shrapnel's invention came to be called the Shrapnel Shell. From there, it entered the English lexicon (both British and American) with the generic meaning of fragments from a burst shell, bomb, or grenade. This has obscured Henry Shrapnel's accomplishments and denied him the recognition he deserves.

By the end of World War I, the Shrapnel shell had become obsolete. Amazingly, the last Spherical Case Shot was fired in 1943 by British artillery in Burma during World War II!

incorporate a few of these features such as the hard heavy core.

Recent combat action in Iraq and Afghanistan has demonstrated once again the need for armor piercing bullets which will also perform well on other targets.

Incapacitation

Perhaps no other subject in the shooting world has created more discussion, disagreement, controversy, and argument than incapacitation of animate targets. Until the 1920s, the subject of incapacitation remained in the realm of folklore based on anecdotal stories, vague historical records, and hearsay. While this may have been entertaining, it was not reliable or useful. However, this was all there was.

As recently as 1970, a reliable system for measuring the capability of a given bullet to incapacitate an animate being still remained an elusive goal. Surely this was because animate beings are complex organisms resistant to quantification (the art of the subject). Or, perhaps it was because a suitable method of measurement has not been developed yet (the science of the subject). Of course, there was general agreement on one point: a bullet striking the target should cause instant incapacitation.

INCAPACITATION AND KNOCK DOWN

As applied to terminal ballistics, incapacitation means that after a bullet strikes an animate being, the target is incapable of further activity. Incapacitation does not necessarily mean mortally wounded, or immediately dead, although it is often the result.

Knock down is a non-technical, vernacular term for the phenomenon of an animate target being knocked off its feet, from the kinetic energy of the bullet impact. However, kinetic energy is not the cause; bullet placement and the transfer of kinetic energy where it will produce the most shock are the major reasons for a bullet's knock down.

Those presently struggling with the questions of incapacitation may be categorized into two groups: the inductive logicians and the deductive logicians.

Inductive logicians approach the question of incapacitation using statistical analysis to study actual combat shooting events. To do this, they first construct a frame work of parameters which they use to filter the raw data collected from a wide variety of reliable sources. The framework is designed to organize the data into uniform categories and to remove instances of insufficient data, conflicting data, or data outside the scope of the study. A substantial body of data must be compiled, tabulated, and analyzed before a statistically valid conclusion can be made. Given enough data, statistically valid conclusions can be reached. The advantage of this approach is that it uses data from the real world to reach a conclusion.

Deductive logicians approach the question of incapacitation from the experimental standpoint. They seek to develop a series of repeatable scientific tests which can be made on any bullet to quantify its incapacitation potential. In most instances, they employ ballistic gelatin under carefully controlled conditions of temperature and humidity to test the bullets. Where appropriate, the bullets may be fired through barrier arrays such as clothing before entering the gelatin. Using such scientific methods, repeatable results can be made and compiled for comparison. While this method offers the advantage of repeatability, it remains artifically apart from real world experience.

In the past, a number of experienced shooters and government agencies have attempted unsuccessfully to codify incapacitation potential of selected bullets. This changed in the 1970s when various public and private agencies began scientific tests of police handgun ammunition. These tests have advanced the understanding of wound ballistics significantly. At the same time, however, they have provided more fuel for controversy. Examples include the effects of temporary cavities, secondary damage from fragments and shock waves, effects on the neurological system, and optimum penetration depth. The good news is that more attention is being paid to wound ballistics. Organizations are now testing before they adopt a caliber or cartridge and modifying the test procedures to suit their needs instead of relying on a "one test fits all" approach.

Significantly, nearly all recent work in incapacitation has focused on handgun calibers suitable for law enforcement use. Little or no attempt has been made to analyze the performance of hunting rifle bullets or shotgun slugs. There is plenty of work still to be done in these areas. Anyone interested?

Points To Keep In Mind

* Despite the claims, no perfect scientific method has been developed which will reliably quantify bullet incapacitation potential.

* Several of the more recent efforts to quantify bullet incapacitation potential, though still works-in-progress, contain useful material.

* Neither the inductive or deductive schools of terminal ballistic logic are right or wrong. Both are right.

* Neither the heavy bullet at low velocity school of terminal ballistic thought or the light bullet at high velocity school of terminal ballistic thought are right or wrong. Both are right.

* Select a personal defense cartridge based on the

bullet's probability of immediate incapacitation.

* Most personal defense experts advise that when in doubt, select the heavier bullet.

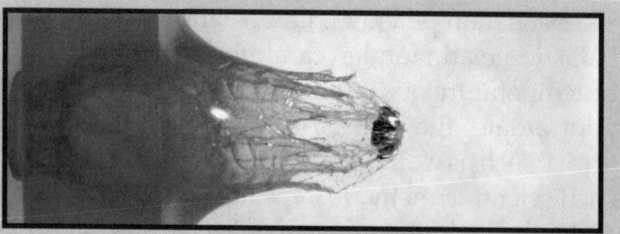

As this photo shows, a properly designed expanding pistol bullet will transfer a considerable amount of energy into an animate target.

WHERE LIES LETHALITY?

No one really knows with any degree of certainty where the non-lethal/lethal boundary lays for any combination of caliber, weight, and velocity of bullet. In fact it is probably a somewhat flexible line dependent on the physical condition and psychological outlook of the person who has been shot. This explains why one person struck by a bullet in a non-vital area dies while another struck in the same area requires only minor medical attention. The term "less-than-lethal" originated in the law enforcement community, and was used in connection with ammunition which was both non-lethal and reliably incapacitating. The term now encompasses any use-of-force option which allows an officer or soldice to subdue a suspect without resorting to deadly force.

Despite the uncertainty of the lethality boundary's lower and upper limits, there are some benchmarks. For many years the U.S. Army considered a projectile having a striking energy of 58 ft.-lbs. to be "disabling". On the other hand, the same source considers a projectile having a striking energy of 108 ft.-lbs. as the minimum to put a man down. For comparison purposes, 108 ft.-lbs. is the approximate remaining energy of a 40 grain .22 Long Rifle bullet at 50 yards.

On the definitely non-lethal side, the U.S. Army has determined that a minimum striking velocity of 170 fps is required to break unprotected human skin. Skin protected by thin summer clothing increases the minimum velocity to 200 fps. For comparison, consider that many "BB" guns have a muzzle velocity of well over 200 fps.

During the U.S. Army's fight against the Philippine Moros in the late 1800s, none of the rifle or handgun cartridges of the time were able to put these fierce warriors down when they charged. There was only one exception which worked nearly every time: 12-gauge 00 buckshot. Studies of police shootings nearly one hundred years later have found the only thing with the greatest probability of incapacitating an assailant every time is a 12-gauge slug. Some things never change.

FACTORS WHICH AFFECT A BULLET ON IMPACT

There are seven major factors that act on a bullet as it strikes the target and several minor factors. The major factors are:

STRIKING VELOCITY

Higher is better for personal defense, but not for some types of hunting.

STRIKING ENERGY

Higher is better for personal defense however hunting bullet energy should be closely matched to the game.

BULLET WEIGHT

Traditionally, heavier is better for personal defense. However, recent tests have shown that lighter weight fragmenting bullets may be better for this purpose (the battle between the heavy bullet and the light high velocity bullet continues). For hunting, bullet weight should be matched to the game.

BULLET MASS

This directly affects the size and shape of the wound channel.

CROSS SECTIONAL AREA / OGIVE SHAPE

The cross sectional area of a bullet is a good measure of its incapacitation potential, especially for non-expanding handgun bullets. The ogive shape also plays a major part. For example a flat nose design will have greater incapacitation potential than a round nose.

BULLET CONSTRUCTION

In general, for personal defense purposes expanding bullets have greater potential for incapacitation than non-expanding bullets. For hunting, expanding bullets are best for all game save large dangerous types which require FMJ bullet designs for adequate penetration.

BULLET PLACEMENT

Many feel that this is the most important of all factors, in hunting or personal defense situations.

TYPICAL BULLET IMPACT PROFILE

As a bullet strikes an animate target, the pressure on the ogive goes up dramatically. This causes the bullet to decelerate rapidly and begin transferring kinetic energy into the target. As it does so, two wounding mechanisms come into play. The first is a temporary cavity formed inside the target by hydrostatic shock. As a liquid cannot be compressed, the hydrostatic shock wave travels through surrounding tissue and may cause serious damage to vital organs not in the direct path of the bullet. The second mechanism is a permanent wound channel formed by the physical passage of the bullet through the tissue.

As the bullet continues to penetrate, the radial pressure on the ogive causes expanding bullets to mushroom or upset. This increases the frontal area which significantly improves energy transfer. Ideally, the bullet will transfer all of its energy into the target as it penetrates.

Weight retention is an important factor here to assure penetration and energy transfer. The ideal weight retention would be 98-99 % with the core and jacket of the bullet remaining firmly locked together.

Should the bullet strike bone, it may be deflected and fragments of both the bullet and bone may become secondary missiles themselves. By the time the bullet comes to rest, the temporary cavity has closed, the shock wave has dissipated, and the permanent cavity has become the primary wounding mechanism.

Points To Keep In Mind

* At striking velocities too low for bullet expansion, the cross sectional area and ogive shape of the bullet determine the incapacitation potential.

* In the majority of situations, bullet expansion dramatically improves incapacitation potential.

* A lighter weight bullet normally will not penetrate as deeply as a heavier weight bullet.

* The single most important factor for efficient incapacitation is bullet placement in a vital area.

* The second most important factor is how the bullet transfers its energy inside the target.

* Striking energy should not be the sole criteria used to judge the effectiveness of a bullet.

* Bullets of the same weight and caliber may have radically different performance. Always test before making a selection.

* A bullet selected for personal defense should expand to twice its original diameter and penetrate six to ten inches.

* Remember, there is no such thing as the perfect bullet.

> "You can get more with a kind word and a gun than you can with a kind word alone."
>
> - *Al Capone*

THE UNIQUE ASPECTS OF SHOTSHELLS

Shotshells must be considered apart from rifle and handgun bullets as they depend on a different incapacitation mechanism. In the author's opinion, the incapacitation mechanism of shotgun ammunition is the shock of multiple pellet strikes overloading the neurological system of an animate target. This opinion rests on two qualifiers: the size of the pellet is matched to the intended target, and multiple pellets strike a vital area. For example, a single No. 7 ½ lead pellet can hardly be expected to incapacitate a human, although it would incapacitate a dove.

The shot swarm and the target are players in a game of chance, with the odds stacked against the target. Given enough pellets in the swarm and a dense enough pattern, the odds strongly favor the target being struck by several pellets. In general, the closer the target, the higher the odds. At long ranges of over fifty yards, heavier pellets must be used to assure penetration, but there is a price to pay in the form of a lower number of pellets and lower odds of multiple pellets striking the target.

From this, the key role the choke plays in tailoring the pattern density becomes clear. Holding the pattern together for a longer time increases pellet density at the target and increases the probability of multiple pellet strikes. While this may sound simple, a number of factors must be taken into account such as range, choke constriction, pellet size, shot charge weight, target dimensions, target type, etc. The key point here is to select the best combination of choke, pellet size, and shot charge weight to increase the odds of multiple pellet strikes in your favor. See Chapter 96: Reference Material for more information on choke performance and pellet counts.

At this point, mention must be made of premium shotshells loaded with hard lead shot (often copper plated), granulated plastic buffer material in the shot charge, and full plastic wad columns which prevent the pellets from contacting the bore surface. Although more expensive than regular shotshells, the patterns of premium shotshells are significantly better which greatly improve the odds of multiple pellet strikes.

Selecting the best shot charge, pellet size, and choke need not be an onerous task. The recommendations published in ammunition makers' catalogs have been proven over decades of use and numerous tests. So why not take advantage of this wealth of experience? See Chapter 36: Shotshell Recommendations for more information.

Many writers recommend a shotgun loaded with nine, twelve, or fifteen 00 buckshot for home defense. This recommendation is based on solid ballistic ground. Multiple strikes of that size projectile will incapacitate a person over 98 % of the time according to statistics. Provided, of course, that the shot swarm hits the target's center of mass. Once again, in the author's opinion, neurological system overload due to the shock effect of simultaneous multiple pellet impacts is the incapacitating mechanism.

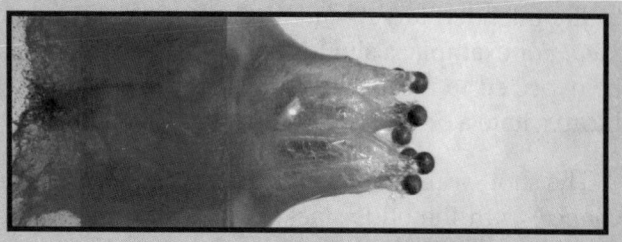

No wonder buckshot has earned such a fearsome reputation! Note the energy transferred to the block of 10 % ballistic gelatin as this swarm of OO buckshot exits.

Lastly, we come to shotgun slugs. Statistically speaking, full bore diameter shotgun slugs are the only personal defense projectile with a 99% probability of incapacitating an attacker given a hit on the torso. This is due to a number of factors, the most salient of which are the large cross sectional area of the slug, massive slug weight, and soft lead construction (enhancing expansion upon impact) which combine to create massive trauma. For example, a typical 12-gauge one ounce rifled slug has approximately 2500 ft.-lbs. of energy at close range. To put this into perspective, that is 6.75 times more energy than a .45 Auto bullet! That amount of ballistic power is why many deer hunters prefer shotgun slugs.

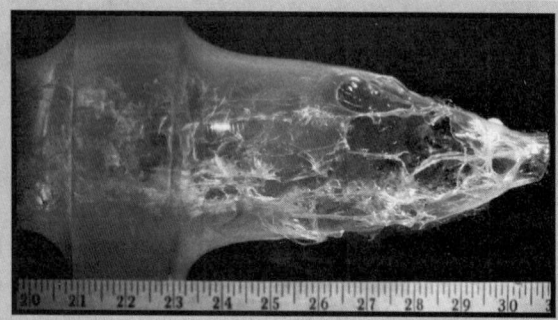

Perhaps the only more lethal projectile than buckshot on animate targets is a shotgun slug, as shown here exiting from a block of 10% ballistic gelatin.

Points To Keep In Mind

* Select a shotshell which will increase the odds of multiple hits on the target.
* Always match your choke, shot charge weight, and pellet size to the intended target.
* Recoil of buckshot and slug ammunition is very heavy, however it is normally necessary to fire only two or three shots. Reduced recoil slug and buckshot loads are also available.
* The effective range of most shotshells is about forty yards.
* Premium shotshells are more expensive, but produce significantly better patterns. Consider the higher cost against how many shells you will use.

* Select pellet size and charge weight according to ammunition manufacturers' recommendations or other qualified sources.

MEASUREMENT EQUIPMENT

Terminal ballistic research, development, and testing makes use of many types of measuring equipment, namely chronographs (to measure velocities) scales, calipers, paper targets, and normal cameras. However, terminal ballistic studies also make use of several pieces of unique equipment.

* **Materials which stop a projectile but do not deform or damage it. Normally, water tanks with white interior surfaces are used for this purpose. However, cotton batting is another common testing material.**

* **Materials which will expand bullets and allow for easy recovery and examination.**
  The general consensus is that ballistic gelatin is the best substance to duplicate an animate target. Some prefer a 10% mixture and some prefer a 20% mixture. Others use materials such as clay, paper pulp, wax, soap, wet or dry bundles of paper, and even wet or dry sand. While these substances are not as good as gelatin, they are easier to use and inexpensive.

* **Various materials for conducting penetration tests, such as .035 inch sheet steel, one inch thick soft pine boards, drywall, bricks, concrete blocks, glass, sandbags, and clothing.**

* **High speed cameras to allow visual examination of bullet dynamics during impact. As ballistic gelatin is translucent, a high speed camera can record the impact and penetration at over 10,000 frames per second for later examination.**

* **Microscopes**
  High level magnification is necessary for thoroughly analyzing expanded bullets, rifling marks, and penetration holes.

* **X-Ray Machines**
  Radiography allows non-destructive analysis of targets and projectiles inside solid targets.

"Over here, over there, everywhere,
Today, tomorrow, always,
Bad men there are,
Hate you they do,
Kill you they will,
Watch out you better."

-Shoshone Indian saying based on bitter experience

SECTION IX – BALLISTICS CHARTS & CARTRIDGE IMAGES
CHAPTER 46 - CHAPTER 64

NOTE: ALL BALLISTICS ARE APPROXIMATE

Abbreviation key:

SP = Soft Point

PT = Polymer Tip

FB = Flat Base

BT = Boat Tail

FMJ = Full Metal Jacket or solid

L = Lead

HP= Hollow Point

These ballistic tables were computer-calculated using the best available data for each load.

Trajectories are representative of the nominal behavior of each load at standard conditions:

59°F temperature, barometric pressure of 29.53 inches, and altitude at sea level.

Shooters are cautioned that actual trajectories may differ due to variations in altitude, atmospheric conditions, guns, sights, and ammunition.

In the following charts each caliber/gauge line listing is read from left to right and is separated by a black line. In the Rifle and Shotshell categories, when the information on a caliber/gauge reads continually across both pages, each line listing appears with alternating gray and white background. In the Rimfire, Revolver, and Pistol categories the information for each caliber line listing appears on one page.

These ballistic charts appear in five major categories: Rimfire, Revolver, Pistol, Centerfire Rifle, and Shotshell. The Rimfire, Revolver, and Pistol categories are broken into five fields of information, the Rifle category has six fields of information, and the Shotshell category has 16 fields of information. The Rimfire, Revolver, Pistol, and Rifle cartridge charts are organized from smallest to largest caliber. Shotshells are organized from largest to smallest gauge.

All loadings for a particular caliber/gauge cartridge are grouped together for convenience. This data allows you to compare the ballistic performance of various loads in each caliber easily.

These charts contain the bullet weights in grains and the bullet types offered in each caliber.

Each chart has bullet velocity and kinetic energy at various ranges from the muzzle of the gun.

Some of the charts list the height of trajectory, often called the bullet path.

CHAPTER 46 : SPORTING RIMFIRE - CURRENT

CALIBER	BULLET WGT-GRS	BULLET TYPE	VELOCITY IN FPS				
			MUZZLE	50 YDS.	100 YDS.	150 YDS.	200 YDS.
2.34mm Swiss	2	LRN	400	--	--	--	--
.17 Mach2	17	JHP	2,010	1,725	1,470	1,260	1,110
.17 Mach2	17	JSP	2,100	1,800	1,530	1,305	1,135
.17 HMR	17	JHP	2,550	2,210	1,900	1,620	1,380
	20	JHP	2,375	2,065	1,775	1,520	1,305
.22 BB Cap	18	LRN	780	725	675	630	585
.22 CB Short	29	LRN	710	655	605	560	515
.22 CB Long	29	LRN	710	655	605	560	515
.22 Short Match	29	LRN	650	425	270	155	55
	29	LRN	850	635	475	355	255
.22 Short SV	29	LRN	1,035	880	755	650	560
.22 Short HV	27	HP	1,105	900	780	685	605
.22 Long	29	LRN	1,215	1,020	910	830	765
.22 LR Subsonic	40	HP	1,050	960	895	840	795
.22 LR Match	40	LRN	1,080	960	880	815	760
.22 LR Std. Vel.	40	LRN	1,150	1,050	975	920	870
.22 LR High Vel.	40	LRN	1,255	1,110	1,015	945	890
.22 LR High Vel.	37	HP	1,280	1,130	1,025	955	900
.22 LR High Vel.	37	HP	1,330	1,155	1,040	960	900
.22 LR High Vel.	40	LRN	1,435	1,220	1,070	975	905
.22 LR Ultra High Vel.	31	HP	1,430	1,200	1,050	955	885
.22 LR Ultra High Vel.	32	HP	1,640	1,290	1,065	945	860
.22 LR Ultra High Vel.	33	HP	1,500	1,265	1,100	990	920
.22 LR Ultra High Vel.	36	HP	1,410	1,200	1,055	965	895
.22 Win. Rimfire	45	LRN	1,300	1,135	1,025	950	890
.22 Win. Mag. RF	30	JHP	2,200	1,775	1,420	1,155	1,000
	30	JHP	2,250	1,815	1,445	1,170	1,010
	40	JHP	1,880	1,570	1,310	1,120	1,005
	50	JHP	1,530	1,350	1,200	1,090	1,010

CHAPTER 47 : SPORTING RIMFIRE - OBSOLETE

CALIBER	BULLET WGT-GRS	BULLET TYPE	VELOCITY IN FPS				
			MUZZLE	50 YDS.	100 YDS.	150 YDS.	200 YDS.
2mm Randzunder	7.4	RB	550	235	40	30	0
4mm Ranzunder Short	5.8	RB	600	405	260	150	60
4mm Ranzunder Long	5.8	RB	600	405	260	150	60
.17 Aguila	20	JHP	1,800	1,530	1,305	1,135	1,025
5mm Rem. Rimfire Mag.	38	JHP	2,105	1,845	1,610	1,400	1,230
.22 Extra Long	40	LRN	1,050	960	895	840	795
.22 Winchester Automatic	45	LFN	880	825	780	735	695
	45	LFN	1,035	950	885	830	780
.22 Remington Automatic	45	LRN	950	890	840	795	750
.25 Stevens Short	65	LFN	935	885	840	795	760
.25 Stevens Long	65	LFN	1,115	1,020	950	895	850
.30 Short	58	LRN	700	650	605	560	520
.30 Long	75	LRN	750	705	665	625	590
.32 Extra Short	54	LRN	650	605	560	515	480
.32 Short	80	LRN	935	880	830	785	750
.32 Long	80	LRN	1,030	960	910	865	825

CHAPTER 46 : SPORTING RIMFIRE - CURRENT

	ENERGY IN FT.-LBS				BULLET PATH AT ZERO DISTANCE INDICATED			
MUZZLE	50 YDS.	100 YDS.	150 YDS.	200 YDS.	50 YDS.	100 YDS.	150 YDS.	200 YDS.
0.71	--	--	--	--	--	--	--	--
152	112	82	60	46	0	-2	-7	-18
166	122	88	64	49	0	-1	-6	-16
245	185	136	99	72	0	-1	-3	-9
250	189	140	103	76	0	-1	-4	-11
24	21	18	16	14	0	-15	-49	-105
32	28	24	20	17	0	-19	-62	-132
32	28	24	20	17	0	-19	-62	-132
27	12	5	2	0	0	-49	-173	-364
47	26	15	8	4	0	-21	-81	-210
69	50	37	27	20	0	-10	-35	-81
73	49	37	28	22	0	-9	-32	-73
95	67	53	44	38	0	-7	-24	-53
98	82	71	63	56	0	-8	-27	-58
104	82	69	59	51	0	-8	-27	-59
117	97	84	75	68	0	-6	-22	-48
140	110	92	80	71	0	-6	-19	-43
135	105	87	75	66	0	-5	-19	-42
145	110	89	76	67	0	-5	-18	-40
183	132	102	95	73	0	-4	-16	-37
141	99	76	63	54	0	-5	-17	-38
191	119	81	63	52	0	-4	-15	-36
165	117	88	72	62	0	-4	-15	-35
159	115	89	74	64	0	-5	-17	-38
169	128	105	90	79	0	-5	-19	-42
322	210	134	89	67	0	-1	-7	-20
337	220	140	91	68	0	-1	-7	-19
314	219	153	112	89	0	-2	-9	-23
260	202	160	132	114	0	-3	-13	-29

CHAPTER 47 : SPORTING RIMFIRE - OBSOLETE

	ENERGY IN FT.-LBS				BULLET PATH AT ZERO DISTANCE INDICATED			
MUZZLE	50 YDS.	100 YDS.	150 YDS.	200 YDS.	50 YDS.	100 YDS.	150 YDS.	200 YDS.
0	0	0	0	0	0	-68	0	0
5	2	1	0	0	0	-54	-184	-380
5	2	1	0	0	0	-54	-184	-380
144	104	76	57	46	0	-2	-10	-24
374	278	218	165	127	0	-1	-6	-15
98	82	71	63	56	0	-8	-27	-58
77	68	61	54	48	0	-11	-37	-78
107	90	78	69	61	0	-8	-27	-59
90	79	71	63	57	0	-10	-31	-67
126	112	101	92	83	0	-10	-32	-33
179	150	130	116	104	0	-7	-23	-28
63	54	47	41	35	0	-19	-62	-133
94	83	74	65	58	0	-16	-52	-110
51	44	37	32	27	0	-23	-73	-155
155	137	122	110	99	0	-10	-32	-69
188	165	147	133	121	0	-8	-26	-56

CALIBER	BULLET WGT-GRS	BULLET TYPE	VELOCITY IN FPS				
			MUZZLE	50 YDS.	100 YDS.	150 YDS.	200 YDS.
.32 Long Rifle	80	LRN	960	900	850	805	760
.32 Extra Long	90	LRN	1,050	980	925	875	835
.38 Short	125	LRN	725	690	650	620	590
.38 Long	150	LRN	750	725	695	675	650
.38 Extra Long	150	LRN	1,250	1,135	1,050	985	935
.41 Short	130	LRN	425	400	375	350	330
.41 Long	163	LRN	700	665	635	605	575
.44 Short	200	LRN	500	475	450	425	405
.44 Long	220	LRN	825	790	755	725	695
.44 Extra Long	220	LRN	1,250	1,120	1,025	960	910
.44 Henry Flat	200	LFN	1,125	1,015	940	880	830
.46 Extra Short	220	LRN	650	625	600	580	555
.46 Short	227	LRN	750	720	695	665	640
.46 Long	305	LRN	850	820	790	760	735
.46 Extra Long	305	LRN	1,000	950	910	870	835
.56-46 Spencer	330	LFN	1,210	1,075	990	920	865
.56-52 Spencer	386	LRN	1,200	1,090	1,010	950	905
.58 Miller	500	LRN	1,150	1,055	985	930	885

CHAPTER 48 : MILITARY RIMFIRE - OBSOLETE

CALIBER	BULLET WGT-GRS	BULLET TYPE	VELOCITY IN FPS				
			MUZZLE	50 YDS.	100 YDS.	150 YDS.	200 YDS.
.22 ILARCO	40	FMJRN	1,380	1,180	1,045	960	895
10.4x38Rmm Swiss	313	LRN	1,425	1,300	1,195	1,115	1,050
.56-50 Spencer	350	LFN	1,230	1,095	1,005	940	890
.56-56 Spencer	350	LRN	1,200	1,075	995	930	880

CHAPTER 49 : SPORTING REVOLVER - CURRENT

CALIBER	BULLET WGT-GRS	BULLET TYPE	VELOCITY in FPS			ENERGY in ft.-lbs.		
			MUZZLE	50 YDS.	100 YDS.	MUZZLE	50 YDS.	100 YDS.
.32 S&W Short	85	LRN	680	645	610	90	81	73
.32 S&W Long	98	LRN	705	670	635	115	98	88
	98	LRN	780	750	720	130	120	115
	98	WADC	780	670	570	130	95	70
	98	LRN	825	790	750	148	136	120
.32 H&R Magnum	85	JHP	1,120	1,020	950	235	195	170
.327 Federal Magnum	85	JHP	1,400	1,220	1,090	370	280	225
	100	JSP	1,500	1,320	1,180	500	390	310
.38 Special	100	FRANG	1,130	990	900	283	245	197
	110	JHP	950	890	840	220	194	172
	110	JHP	980	910	860	235	205	180
	110	JHP	1,010	940	885	249	216	191
	125	HP	830	730	640	190	145	115
	125	JSP	850	820	795	201	188	176
	125	JHP	900	855	820	225	203	185
	130	FMJ	790	765	745	173	163	153
	130	FMJ	810	780	750	190	175	160
	148	WADC	690	610	540	155	120	95

ENERGY IN FT.-LBS					BULLET PATH AT ZERO DISTANCE INDICATED			
MUZZLE	50 YDS.	100 YDS.	150 YDS.	200 YDS.	50 YDS.	100 YDS.	150 YDS.	200 YDS.
164	144	128	114	103	0	-9	-31	-65
220	91	170	153	139	0	-8	-25	-55
146	131	118	106	96	0	-17	-55	-115
187	74	162	151	140	0	-15	-48	-100
520	429	367	324	292	0	-5	-18	-40
52	46	41	36	31	0	-52	-169	-357
177	161	146	132	120	0	-18	-58	-121
111	100	90	81	72	0	-38	-119	-247
332	304	278	255	235	0	-13	-41	-85
763	611	515	451	402	0	-6	-19	-42
562	457	391	343	304	0	-7	-24	-52
206	191	177	163	151	0	-21	-65	-136
283	262	242	224	208	0	-15	-48	-102
489	453	421	392	366	0	-12	-37	-78
677	611	558	513	475	0	-8	-27	-57
1,073	848	713	621	551	0	-6	-21	-46
1,234	1,017	876	776	699	0	-6	-20	-44
1,468	1,234	1,077	962	870	0	-6	-22	-47

CHAPTER 48 : MILITARY RIMFIRE - OBSOLETE

ENERGY IN FT.-LBS					BULLET PATH AT ZERO DISTANCE INDICATED			
MUZZLE	50 YDS.	100 YDS.	150 YDS.	200 YDS.	50 YDS.	100 YDS.	150 YDS.	200 YDS.
169	123	97	82	71	0	-5	-17	-39
1,411	1,179	996	861	763	0	-4	-13	-30
1,176	935	788	688	613	0	-6	-20	-44
1,119	901	766	672	600	0	-6	-21	-45

CHAPTER 49 : SPORTING REVOLVER - CURRENT

CALIBER	BULLET WGT-GRS	BULLET TYPE	VELOCITY in FPS			ENERGY in ft.-lbs.		
			MUZZLE	50 YDS.	100 YDS.	MUZZLE	50 YDS.	100 YDS.
.38 Special, cont.	148	WADC	710	635	565	166	132	105
	148	WADC	825	685	615	224	154	124
	150	LRN	845	810	775	238	219	200
	158	LRN	755	725	690	200	183	168
	158	LRN	770	750	720	210	195	185
	158	JHP	800	765	735	199	183	168
.38 Special +P	110	JHP	995	925	870	242	210	185
	110	JHP	1,050	975	910	269	232	202
	125	JHP	945	900	860	248	224	204
	125	JHP	975	930	885	264	238	218
	129	JHP	950	900	870	260	235	215
	130	JHP	925	890	850	247	227	210
	158	LSWCHP	890	855	825	278	257	238
	158	LRN	1,035	945	900	377	313	284
.357 Magnum	100	JSP	1,450	1,220	1,000	467	330	222
	110	JSP	1,275	1,105	960	397	298	225
	110	JHP	1,295	1,095	975	410	292	232
	110	JHP	1,500	1,280	1,140	549	400	317

CALIBER	BULLET WGT–GRS	BULLET TYPE	VELOCITY in FPS			ENERGY in ft.-lbs.		
			MUZZLE	50 YDS.	100 YDS.	MUZZLE	50 YDS.	100 YDS.
.357 Magnum, cont.	125	JHP	1,220	1,095	1,010	413	333	283
	125	JSP	1,300	1,125	1,090	469	351	330
	125	JHP	1,370	1,185	1,030	506	388	294
	125	JHP	1,400	1,215	1,060	544	410	312
	125	JHP	1,440	1,240	1,100	575	425	335
	125	JHP	1,500	1,315	1,165	624	479	377
	130	JHP	1,410	1,260	1,140	575	455	373
	140	JHP	1,300	1,160	990	525	418	205
	140	JHP	1,350	1,210	1,100	566	454	376
	140	JSP	1,400	1,260	1,140	610	490	405
	140	JSP	1,440	1,275	1,145	644	504	406
	145	JHP	1,290	1,155	1,060	535	428	361
	158	JHP	1,235	1,105	1,015	535	428	361
	158	JHP	1,250	1,150	1,075	548	464	404
	158	FMJ*	1,530	1,335	1,145	821	625	460
	158	JHP*	1,615	1,405	1,205	915	692	509
	180	JHP	1,080	1,020	970	465	415	380
	180	Solid	1,130	1,060	1,000	510	450	400
	180	JSP	1,180	1,090	1,020	557	473	416
	180	JSP	1,200	1,110	1,040	576	492	432
	200	JHP	1,150	1,060	990	587	499	435
.41 Magnum	170	JHP	1,275	1,155	1,050	614	503	416
	175	JHP	1,250	1,120	1,030	607	488	412
	180	JSP	1,340	1,190	1,080	720	570	470
	210	JHP	1,230	1,120	1,040	705	585	505
	210	JSP	1,300	1,160	1,060	788	630	526
	210	JHP	1,350	1,210	1,100	850	682	564
	240	JHP	1,250	1,150	1,075	833	706	616
	250	Solid	1,160	1,090	1,030	745	655	585
	250	Solid	1,325	1,235	1,155	975	846	740
.44 Special	180	JHP	1,000	935	880	400	349	311
	200	SWCHP	870	830	790	335	305	275
	200	JHP	900	860	820	360	328	300
	200	JSP	950	910	870	401	368	336
	246	LRN	755	725	695	310	285	265
.44 Magnum	180	JHP	1,550	1,340	1,175	960	717	550
	180	JHP	1,610	1,365	1,175	1,036	745	551
	180	JHP*	1,840	1,550	1,270	1,353	960	644
.45 Colt	185	JHP	1,000	940	890	411	362	324
	225	LSWCHP	830	790	760	345	315	390
	225	JHP	920	875	840	423	384	352
	225	LSWC	960	890	830	460	395	346
	250	LRN	750	720	645	312	288	231
	255	LRN	725	690	650	298	267	240
	255	LRN	860	820	780	420	380	345
.454 Casull	240	JHP	1,450	1,230	1,030	1,121	806	565
	240	JHP	1,900	1,680	1,480	1,923	1,500	1,163
	250	JHP	1,300	1,150	1,045	938	735	608
	250	JSP	1,530	1,330	1,170	1,300	975	755
	250	JSP	1,650	1,450	1,290	1,512	1,167	923
	260	JSP	1,800	1,605	1,430	1,870	1,488	1,181

CALIBER	BULLET WGT-GRS	BULLET TYPE	VELOCITY in FPS			ENERGY in ft.-lbs.		
			MUZZLE	50 YDS.	100 YDS.	MUZZLE	50 YDS.	100 YDS.
.454 Casull, cont.	265	JHP	1,725	1,520	1,350	1,751	1,359	1,072
	285	SOLID	1,625	1,465	1,370	1,672	1,358	1,187
	300	JHP	1,650	1,490	1,350	1,813	1,480	1,210
	320	FMJ	1,550	1,400	1,230	1,708	1,392	1,145
	335	SOLID	1,550	1,400	1,270	1,788	1,458	1,198
	360	FMJ	1,300	1,195	1,110	1,351	1,140	985
.460 S&W Magnum	200	JSP	2,200	1,950	1,715	2,149	1,685	1,305
	200	JSP	2,300	2,050	1,820	2,350	1,866	1,470
	250	JHP	1,450	1,265	1,130	1,167	891	705
	260	JSP	2,000	1,790	1,595	2,309	1,849	1,470
	275	JSP	1,800	1,640	1,500	1,980	1,650	1,370
	275	JSP	1,825	1,665	1,520	2,034	1,692	1,410
	300	JSP	1,750	1,580	1,430	2,041	1,665	1,357
	325	SOLID	1,650	1,490	1,345	1,965	1,601	1,309
	395	JHP	1,525	1,410	1,305	2,040	1,744	1,498
.480 Ruger	275	JHP	1,350	1,190	1,080	1,115	870	710
	275	JSP	1,550	1,390	1,275	1,467	1,179	992
	325	JSP	1,350	1,195	1,080	1,315	1,026	839
	400	JHP	1,100	1,025	970	1,075	937	838
.500 S&W Special	275	JSP	1,250	1,080	980	954	712	586
	350	FMJ	1,100	950	840	941	701	548
	350	JHP	1,250	1,090	970	1,215	923	731
.500 S&W Magnum	275	JSP	1,665	1,490	1,370	1,688	1,355	1,146
	300	JHP	1,950	1,765	1,600	2,533	2,080	1,700
	325	JSP	1,800	1,625	1,480	2,338	1,905	1,580
	350	JHP	1,350	1,190	1,075	1,416	1,104	902
	350	JHP	1,600	1,440	1,325	1,990	1,611	1,364
	350	JSP	1,700	1,480	1,290	2,246	1,697	1,291
	375	JSP	1,725	1,575	1,435	2,477	2,061	1,713
	385	JSP	1,700	1,580	1,450	2,471	2,133	1,797
	400	JSP	1,625	1,480	1,350	2,346	1,945	1,618
	400	JHP	1,675	1,530	1,400	2,491	2,082	1,741
	440	SOLID	1,625	1,480	1,430	2,580	2,139	1,997
	500	JSP	1,300	1,180	1,085	1,876	1,543	1,310
	500	SOLID	1,500	1,400	1,310	2,499	2,175	1,904

CHAPTER 50 : SPORTING REVOLVER - OBSOLETE

CALIBER	BULLET WGT-GRS	BULLET TYPE	VELOCITY in FPS			ENERGY in ft.-lbs.		
			MUZZLE	50 YDS.	100 YDS.	MUZZLE	50 YDS.	100 YDS.
.22 Rem. Jet	40	JHP	2,460	1,900	1,710	537	321	260
.256 Win. Magnum	60	JHP	2,200	1,850	1,625	645	456	351
.32 Short Colt	80	LRN	745	665	590	100	79	62
.32 Long Colt	80	LRN	755	675	600	101	81	64
.320 Short Revolver	80	LRN	575	500	430	59	44	33
.320 Long Revolver	80	LRN	550	480	410	54	41	30
.357 Rem. Maximum	158	JHP	1,825	1655	1500	1,168	958	790
	180	JHP	1,550	1,420	1,305	960	806	680
.38 Short Colt	125	LRN	730	685	645	150	130	115
.38 Long Colt	150	LRN	770	720	685	197	173	156
.38 S&W	146	LRN	685	650	620	150	135	125

CALIBER	BULLET WGT-GRS	BULLET TYPE	VELOCITY in FPS			ENERGY in ft.-lbs.		
			MUZZLE	50 YDS.	100 YDS.	MUZZLE	50 YDS.	100 YDS.
.401 Herters Powermag	240	JSP	1,200	1,105	1,035	767	650	568
.41 Long Colt	200	LRN	730	705	680	237	220	205
.44 Webley	220	LRN	700	675	650	239	222	207
.44 Merwin & Hulbert	220	LRN	860	825	795	361	332	307
.44 Bulldog	170	LRN	460	440	420	80	72	66
.44 S&W American	205	LRN	680	655	630	210	195	182
.45 Auto Rim	230	FMJ	805	775	750	331	307	287
.45 S&W	250	LRN	710	690	670	257	242	228
.45 Webley	230	LRN	550	535	520	154	145	137

CHAPTER 52 : SPORTING PISTOL - CURRENT

CALIBER	BULLET WGT-GRS	BULLET TYPE	VELOCITY in FPS			ENERGY in ft.-lbs.		
			MUZZLE	50 YDS.	100 YDS.	MUZZLE	50 YDS.	100 YDS.
5.45x18mm Soviet	40	FMJ	1,035	970	920	95	84	75
.22 TCM	40	SP	2,100	1,840	1,435	392	270	183
.25 Auto	35	JHP	900	815	740	63	51	43
	45	JSP	815	730	655	66	53	42
	50	FMJ	760	710	660	64	56	48
	50	FMJ	790	770	755	69	66	63
.25 NAA	35	JHP	1,200	995	880	112	77	60
7.62x25mm Tokarev	85	JHP	1,710	1,400	1,175	552	373	261
	85	FMJ	1,705	1,400	1,175	552	373	261
.32 Auto	55	JSP	1,100	965	880	148	114	95
	60	JHP	970	895	835	125	107	93
	60	JHP	1,000	905	835	133	112	96
	60	JHP	1,050	960	880	147	123	103
	65	JHP	925	860	810	125	105	100
	71	FMJ	905	855	810	129	115	97
	71	FMJ	950	870	830	142	119	109
.32 NAA	60	JHP	1,200	1,025	920	192	140	113
9x19mm Luger	80	JSP	1,300	1,115	1,000	300	221	178
	85	FRANG	1,425	1,135	975	383	242	179
	105	FRANG	1,200	1,010	900	336	204	162
	115	JHP	1,135	1,025	950	329	269	231
	115	JHP	1,225	1,095	1,020	383	306	267
	115	FMJ	1,145	1,050	980	335	280	244
	115	FMJ	1,190	1,070	1,000	362	293	255
	124	JHP	1,110	1,030	970	339	292	259
	124	FMJ	1,140	1,050	990	358	303	270
	147	JHP	975	935	885	310	285	256
	147	JHP	990	945	900	320	291	264
	147	JHP	1,010	960	920	333	302	277
	147	FMJ	990	945	910	320	291	270
9x19mm Luger +P	90	JHP	1,500	1230	1070	450	302	229
	100	JHP	1,475	1,255	1,035	483	350	238
	115	JHP	1,250	1,115	1,020	399	316	265
	115	JHP	1,350	1,215	1,110	466	377	315
	124	JHP	1,200	1,095	950	396	330	248
	125	JHP	1,250	1,045	990	434	303	272
9x21mm	123	FMJ	1,160	1,060	920	367	307	231

CHAPTER 51 : CURRENT CARTRIDGE & SHOTSHELL IMAGES
CURRENT SPORTING RIMFIRE CARTRIDGES: ACTUAL SIZE

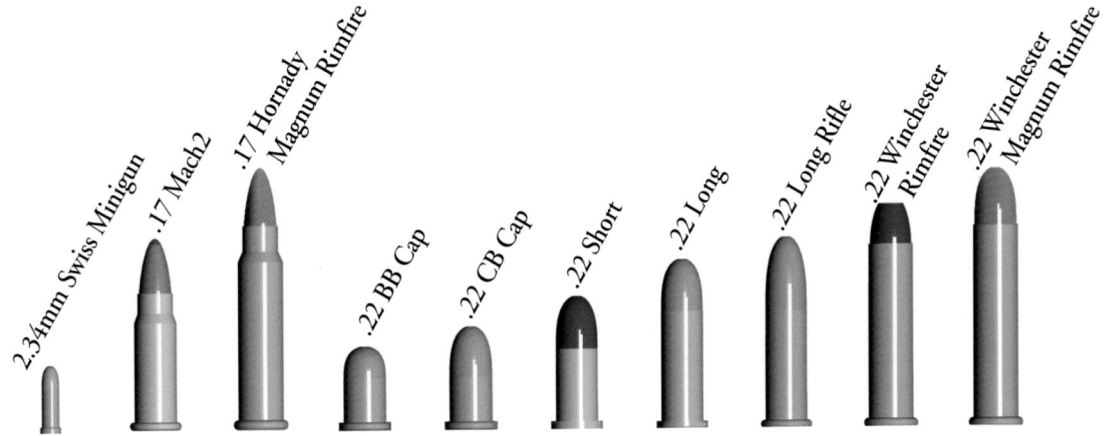

CURRENT SPORTING REVOLVER CARTRIDGES: ACTUAL SIZE

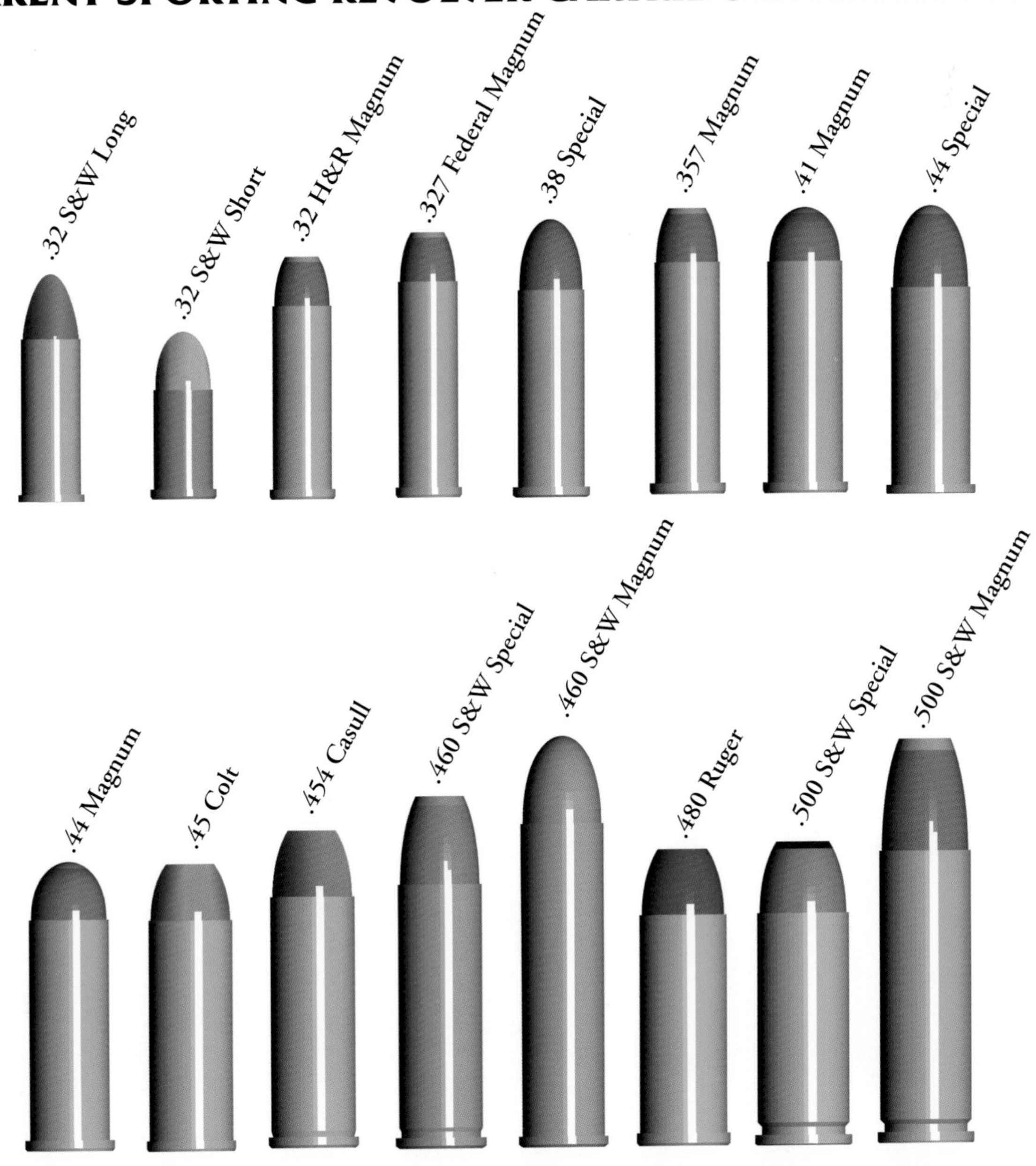

CURRENT SPORTING PISTOL CARTRIDGES: ACTUAL SIZE

5.45x18mm Soviet · .221 Fireball · .25 ACP · .25 NAA · 7.62x25mm Tokarev · .32 ACP · .32 NAA · 9mm Luger · 9x21mm · 9x23mm Winchester · .357 SIG

.38 Super Automatic +P · .380 ACP · .40 S&W Auto · .400 COR-BON · 10mm Automatic · .440 COR-BON · .45 GAP · .45 ACP · .475 Wildey Magnum · .500 Action Express

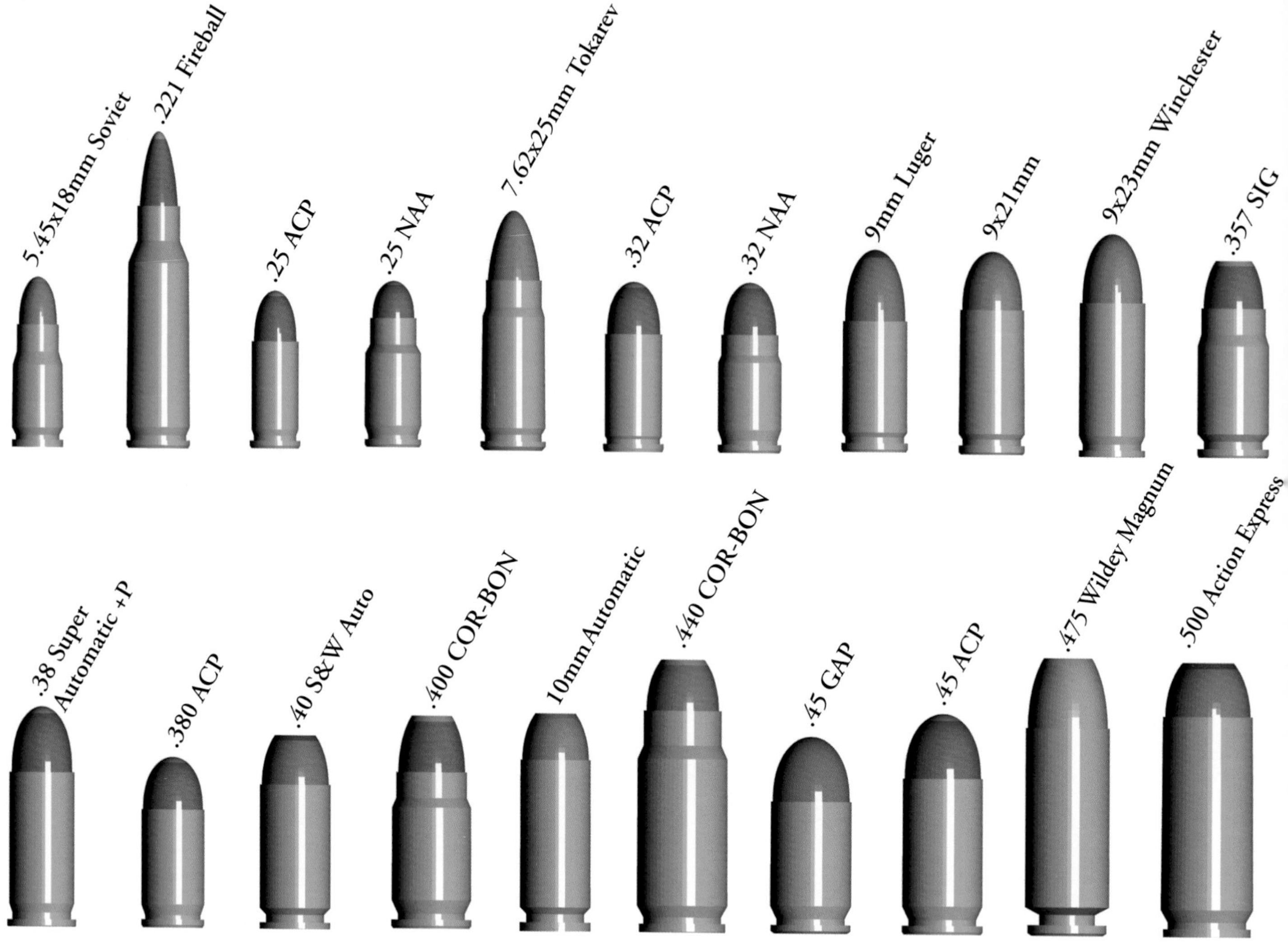

CURRENT MILITARY PISTOL CARTRIDGES: ACTUAL SIZE

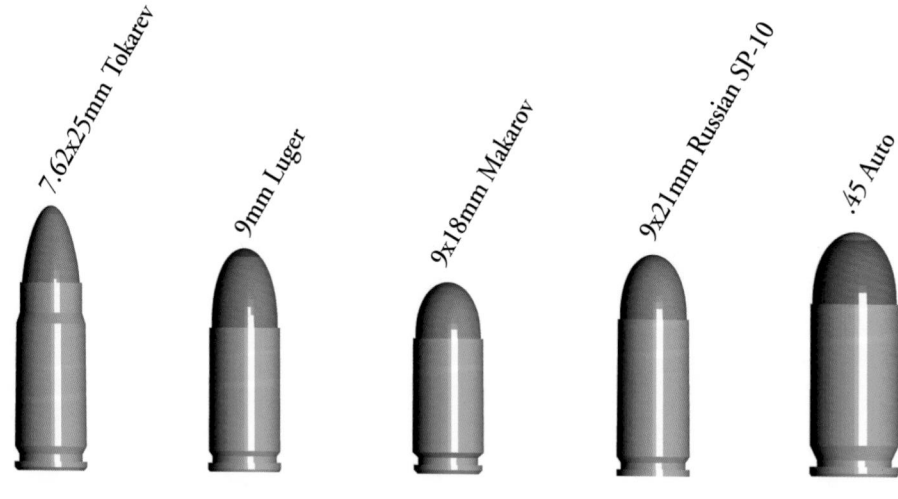

7.62x25mm Tokarev · 9mm Luger · 9x18mm Makarov · 9x21mm Russian SP-10 · .45 Auto

CURRENT CENTERFIRE SPORTING RIFLE CARTRIDGES: ACTUAL SIZE

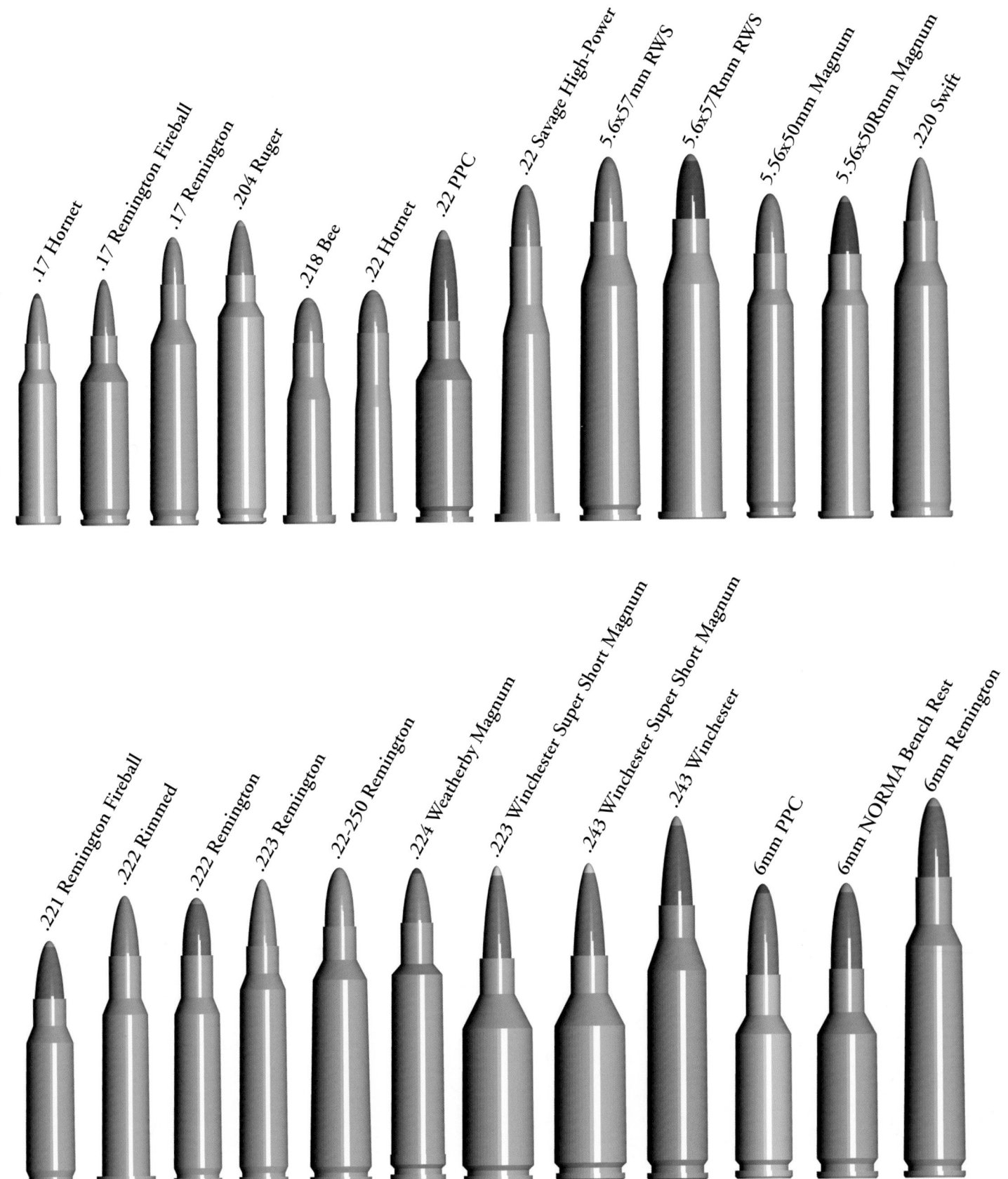

CURRENT CENTERFIRE SPORTING RIFLE CARTRIDGES: ACTUAL SIZE

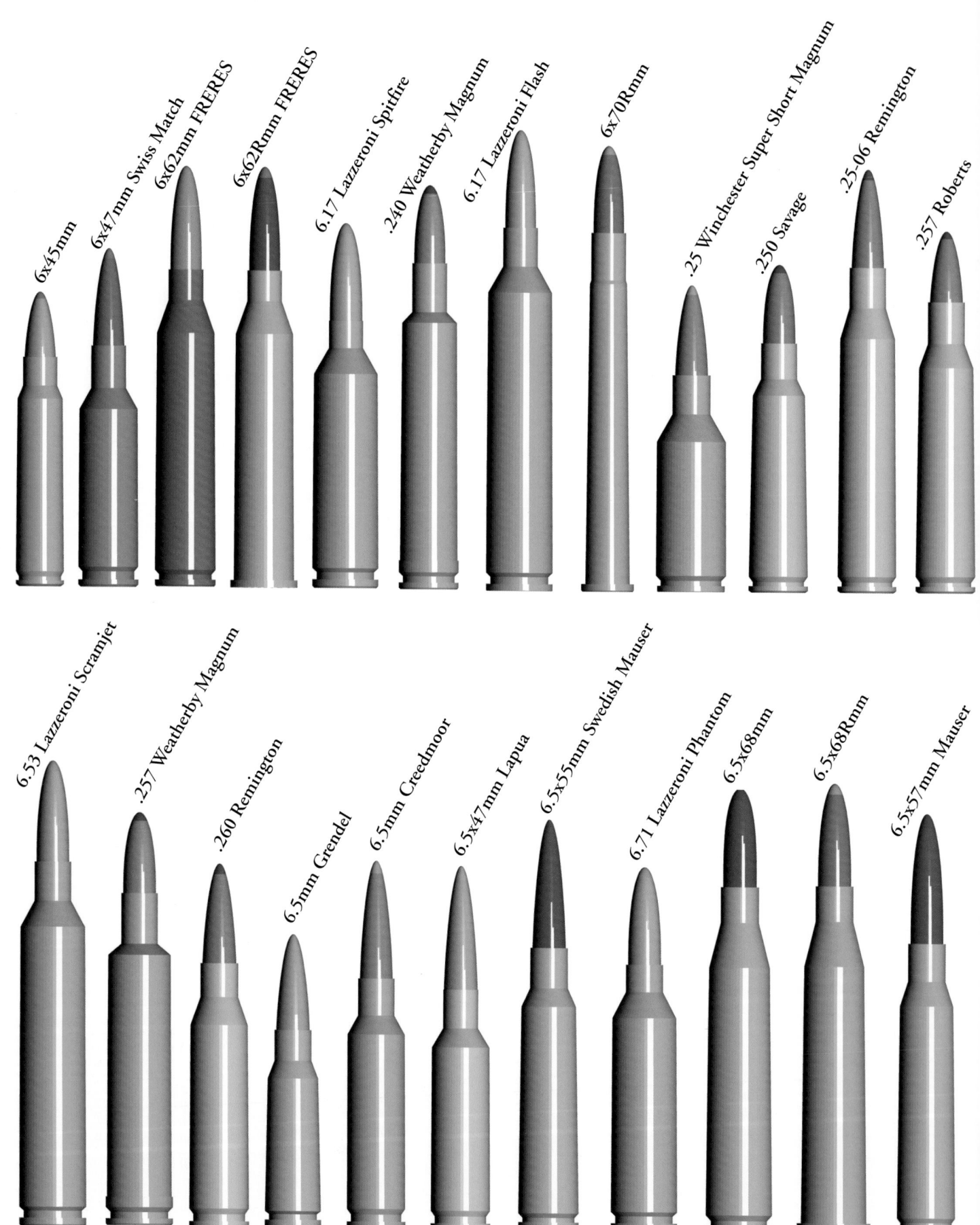

CURRENT CENTERFIRE SPORTING RIFLE CARTRIDGES: ACTUAL SIZE

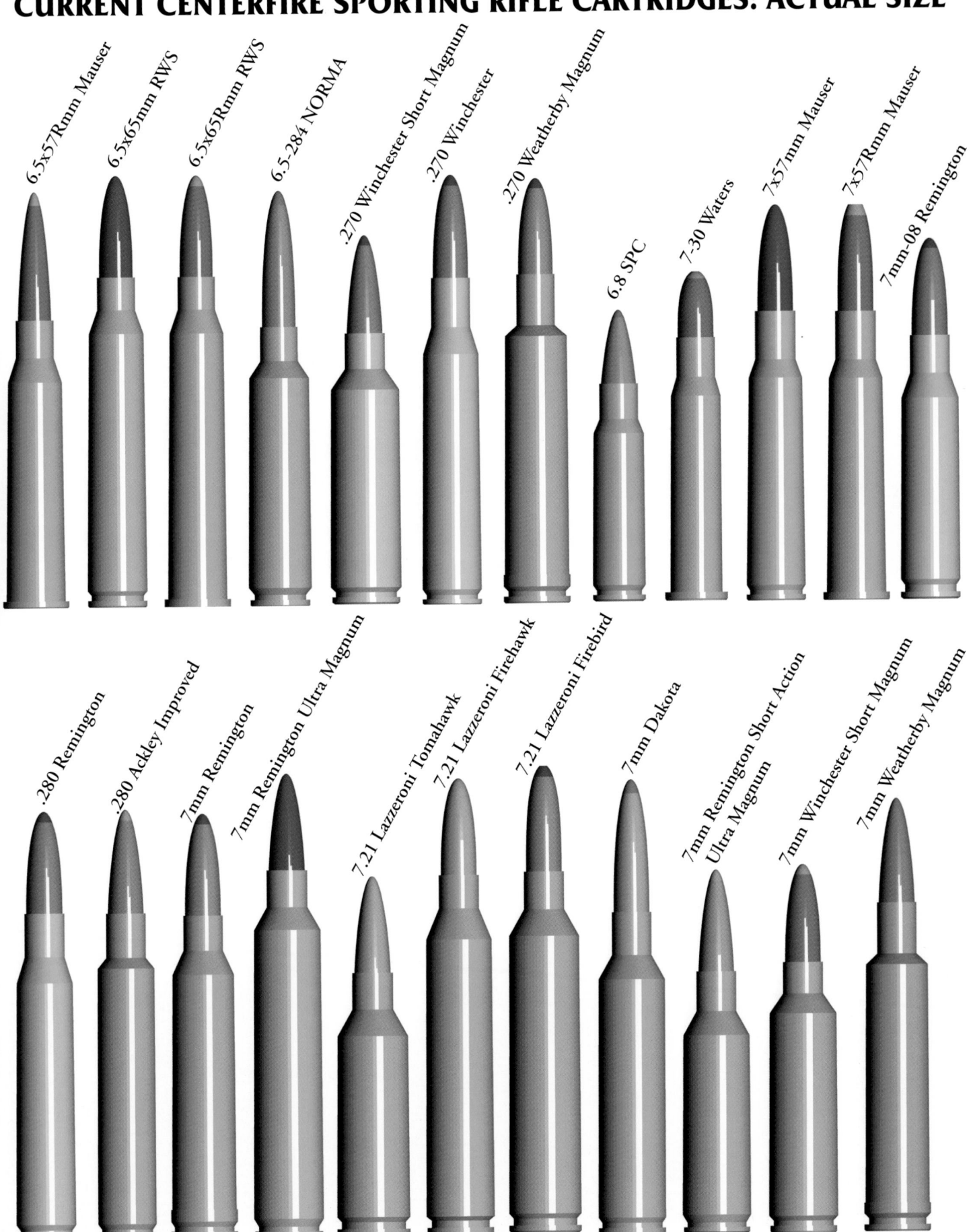

CURRENT CENTERFIRE SPORTING RIFLE CARTRIDGES: ACTUAL SIZE

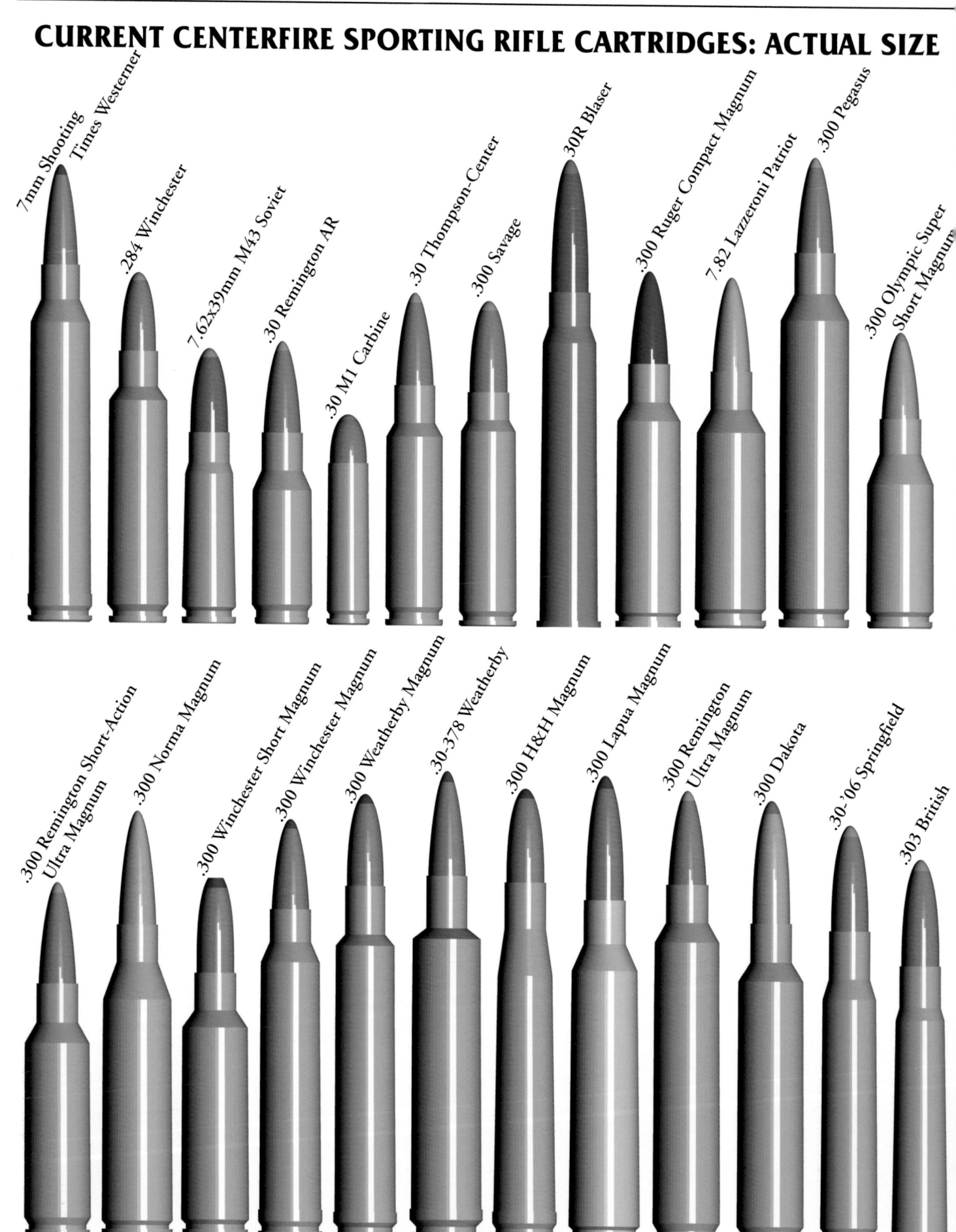

CURRENT CENTERFIRE SPORTING RIFLE CARTRIDGES: ACTUAL SIZE

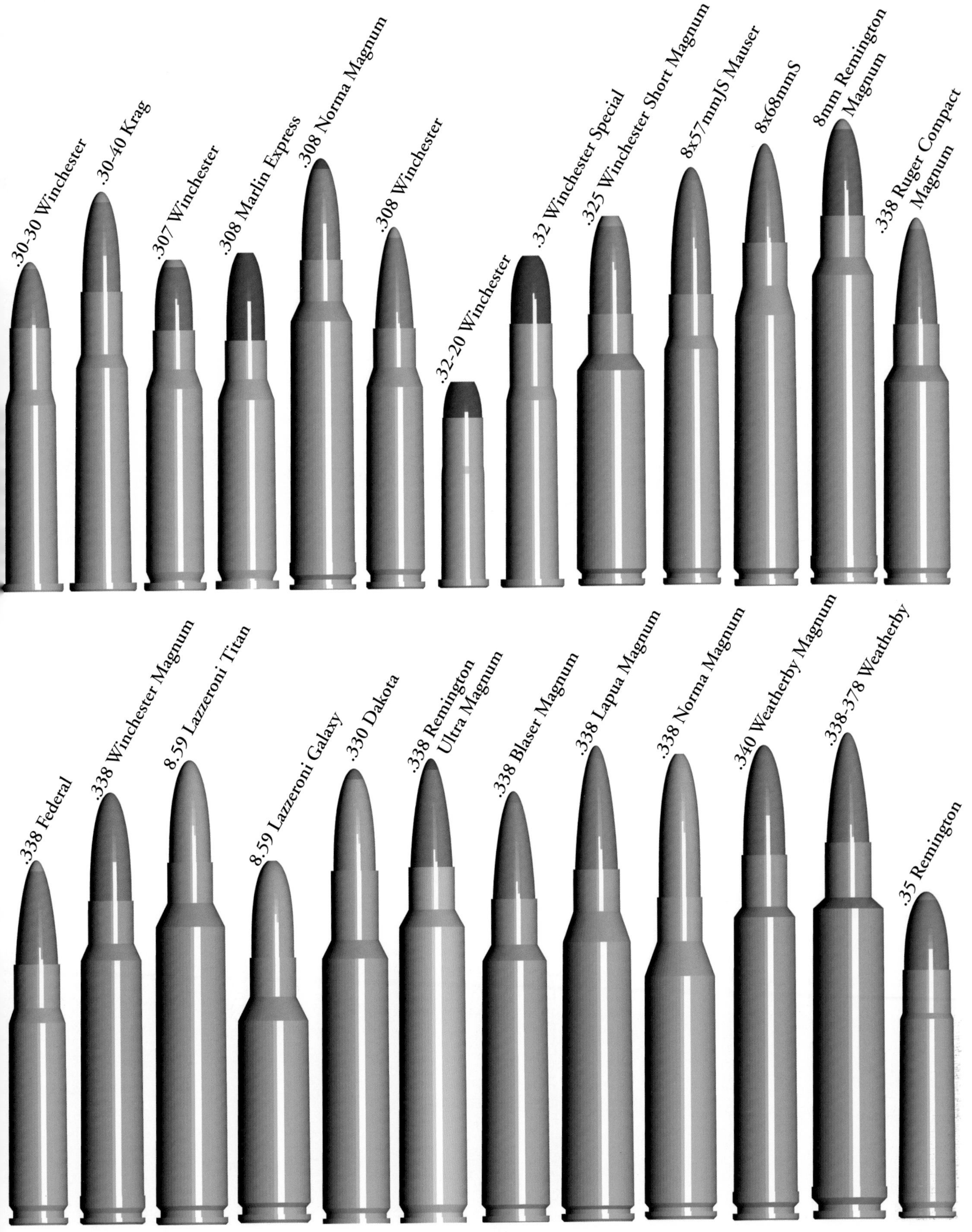

.30-30 Winchester

.30-40 Krag

.307 Winchester

.308 Marlin Express

.308 Norma Magnum

.308 Winchester

.32-20 Winchester

.32 Winchester Special

.325 Winchester Short Magnum

8x57mmJS Mauser

8x68mmS

8mm Remington Magnum

.338 Ruger Compact Magnum

.338 Federal

.338 Winchester Magnum

8.59 Lazzeroni Titan

8.59 Lazzeroni Galaxy

.330 Dakota

.338 Remington Ultra Magnum

.338 Blaser Magnum

.338 Lapua Magnum

.338 Norma Magnum

.340 Weatherby Magnum

.338-378 Weatherby

.35 Remington

CURRENT CENTERFIRE SPORTING RIFLE CARTRIDGES: ACTUAL SIZE

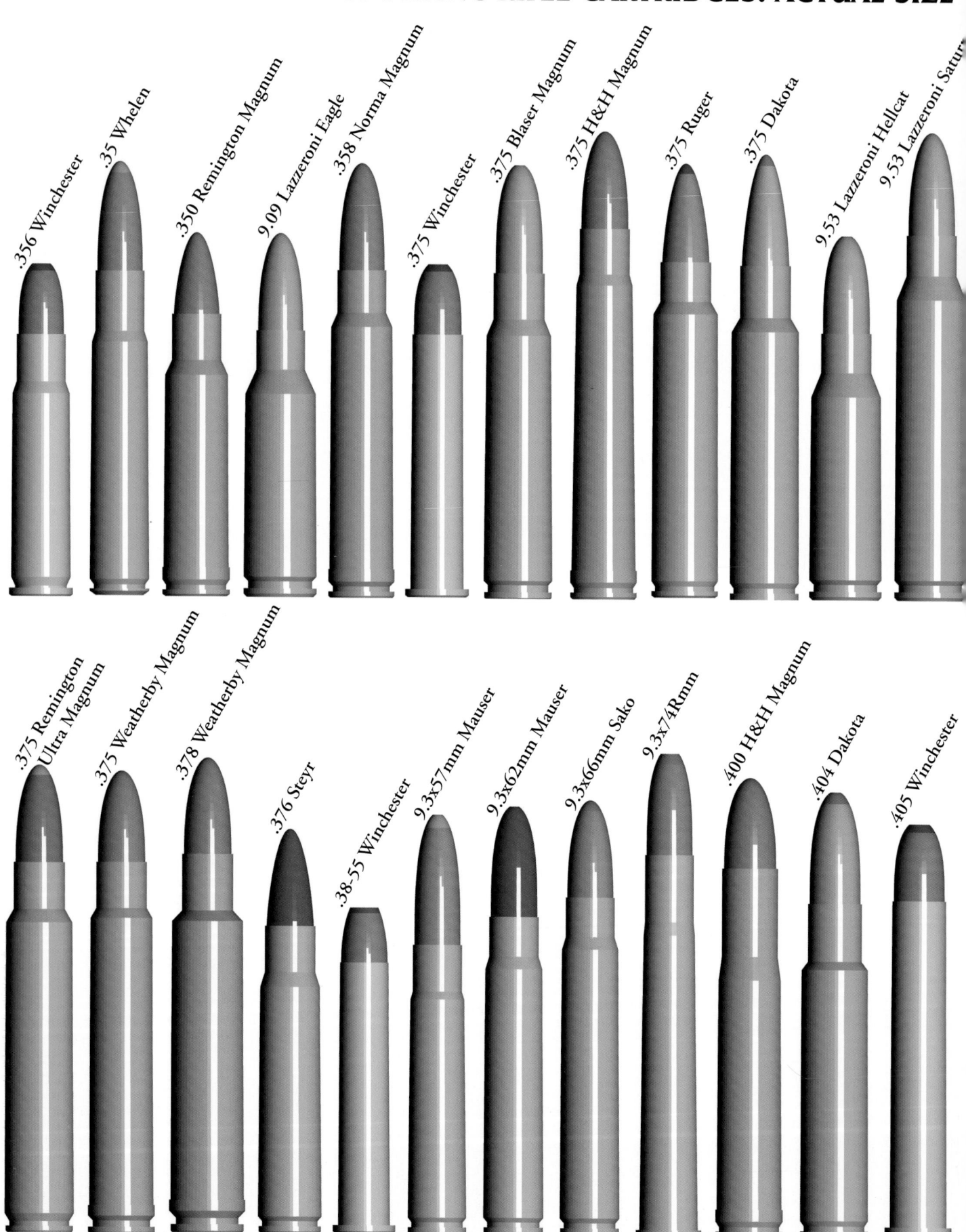

CURRENT CENTERFIRE SPORTING RIFLE CARTRIDGES: ACTUAL SIZE

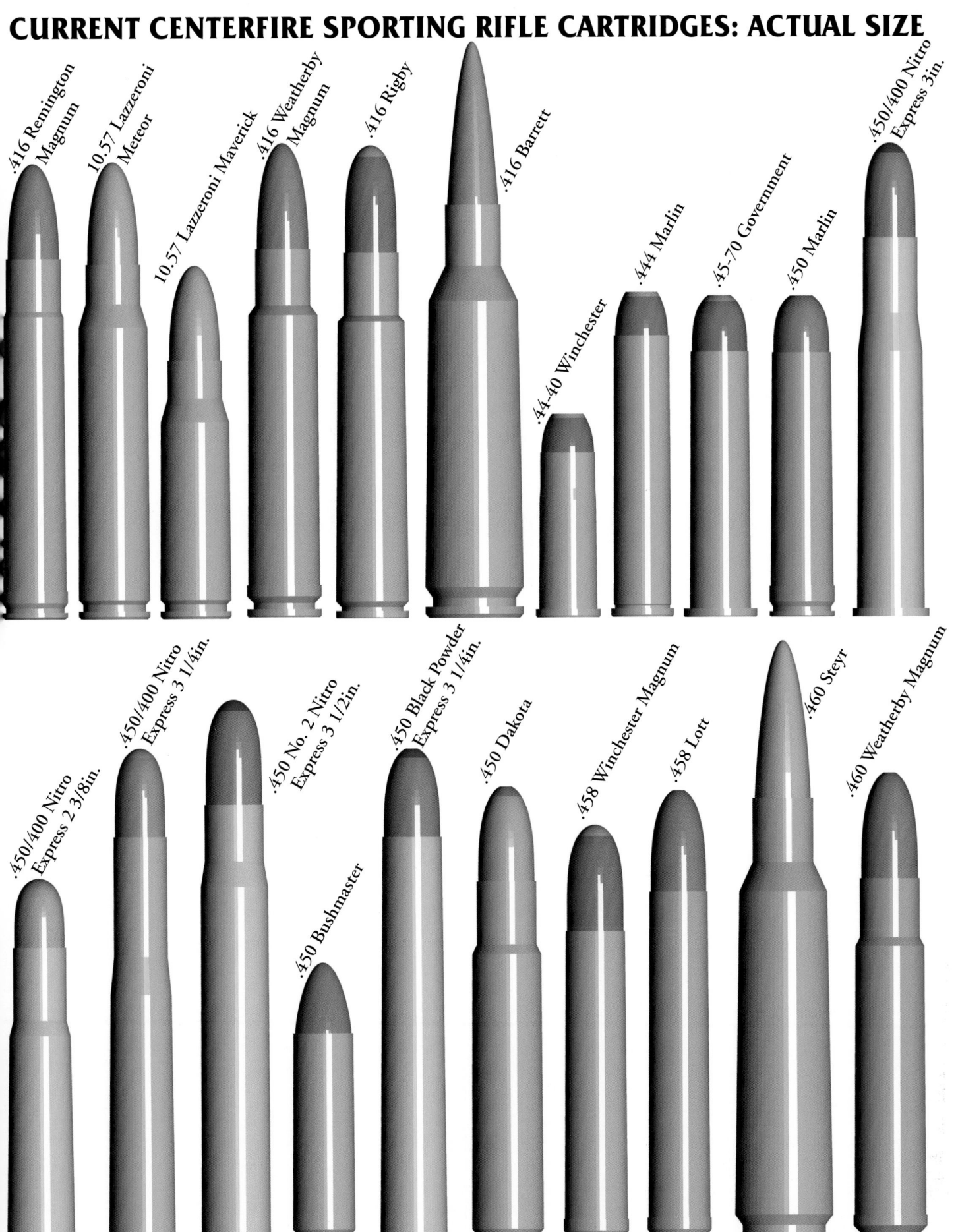

.416 Remington Magnum

10.57 Lazzeroni Meteor

10.57 Lazzeroni Maverick

.416 Weatherby Magnum

.416 Rigby

.416 Barrett

.44-40 Winchester

.444 Marlin

.45-70 Government

.450 Marlin

.450/400 Nitro Express 3in.

.450/400 Nitro Express 2 3/8in.

.450/400 Nitro Express 3 1/4in.

.450 No. 2 Nitro Express 3 1/2in.

.450 Bushmaster

.450 Black Powder Express 3 1/4in.

.450 Dakota

.458 Winchester Magnum

.458 Lott

.460 Steyr

.460 Weatherby Magnum

CURRENT CENTERFIRE SPORTING RIFLE CARTRIDGES: ACTUAL SIZE

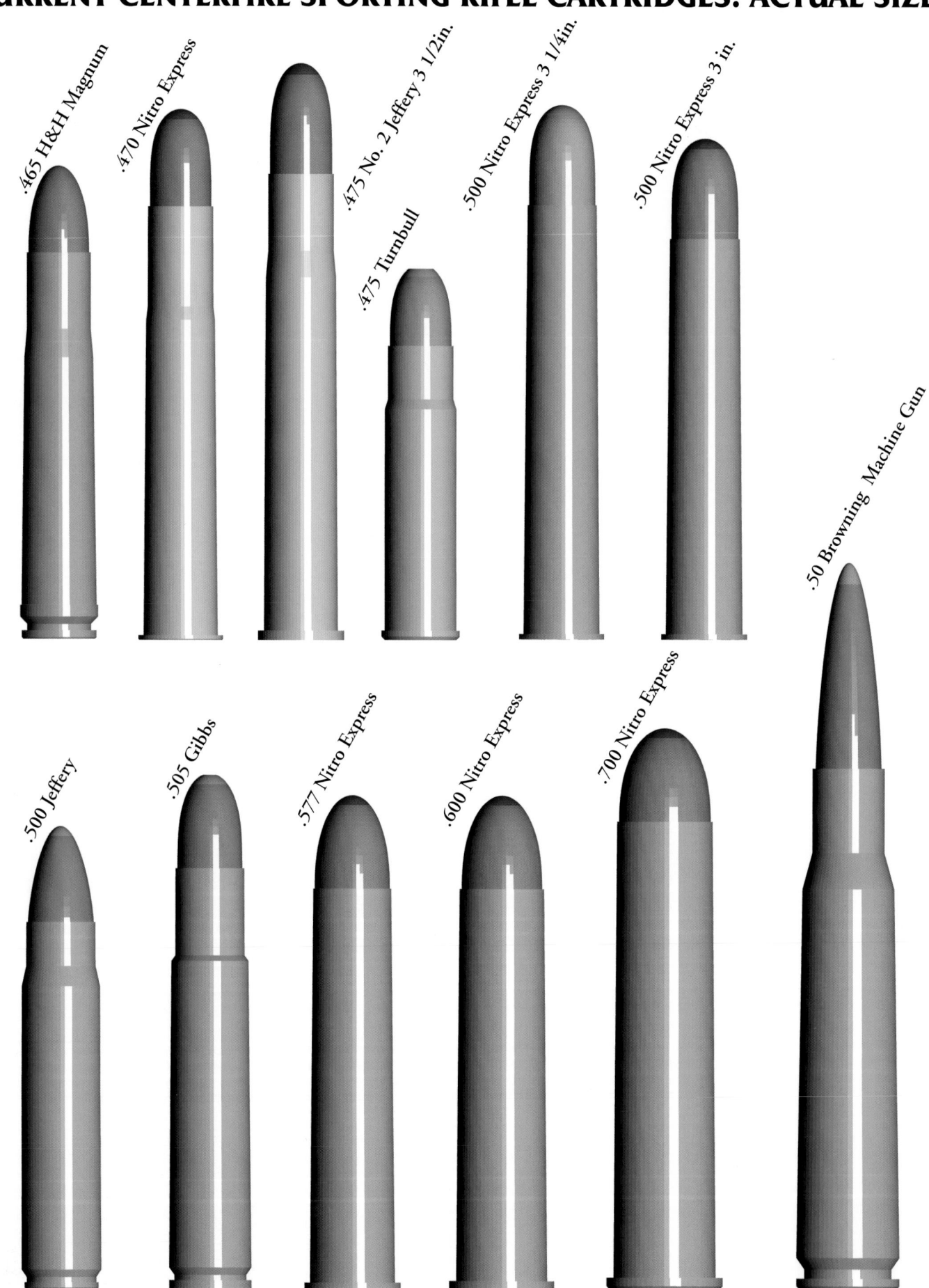

CURRENT MILITARY RIFLE CARTRIDGES: ACTUAL SIZE

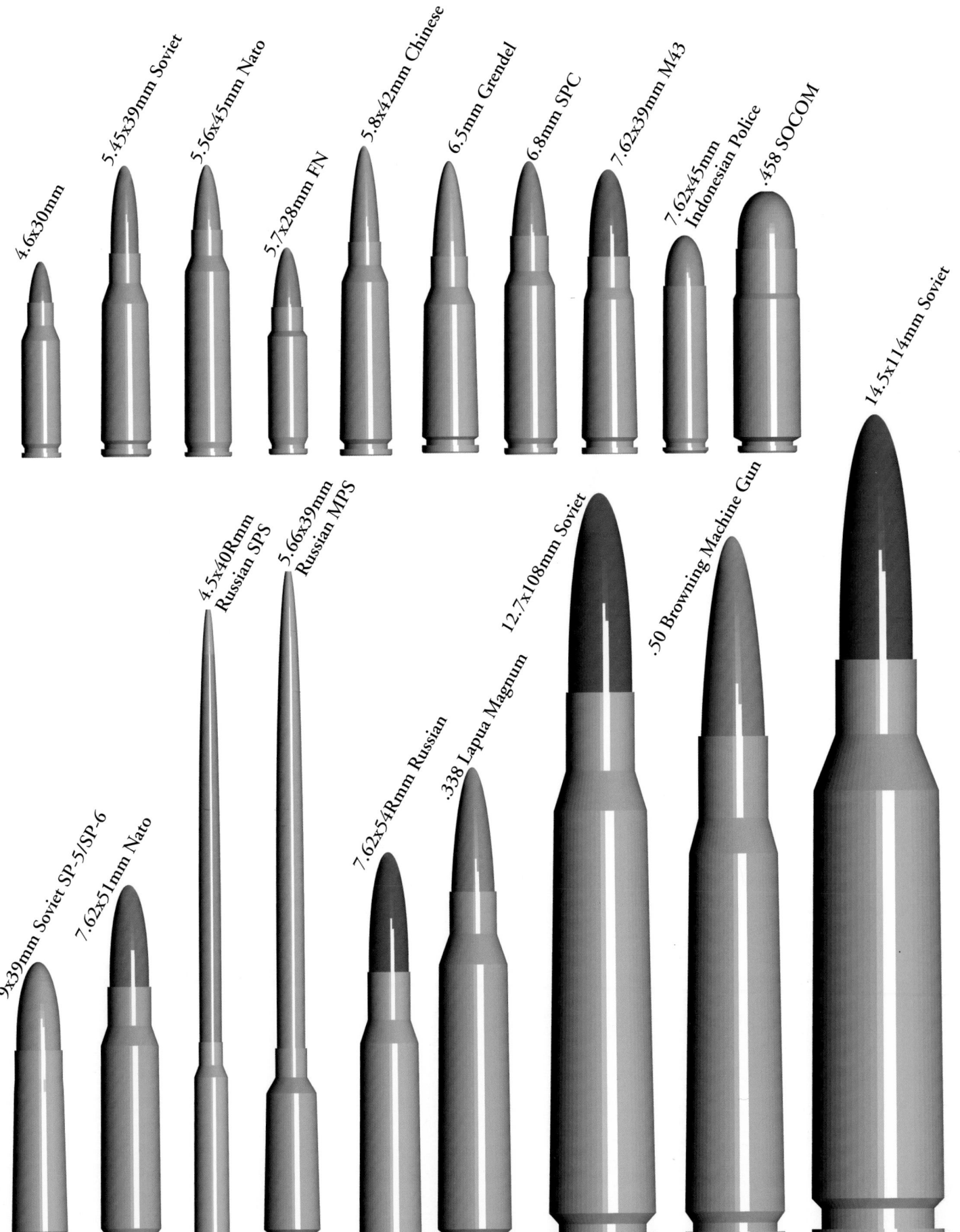

CURRENT SHOTSHELL CARTRIDGES: ACTUAL SIZE

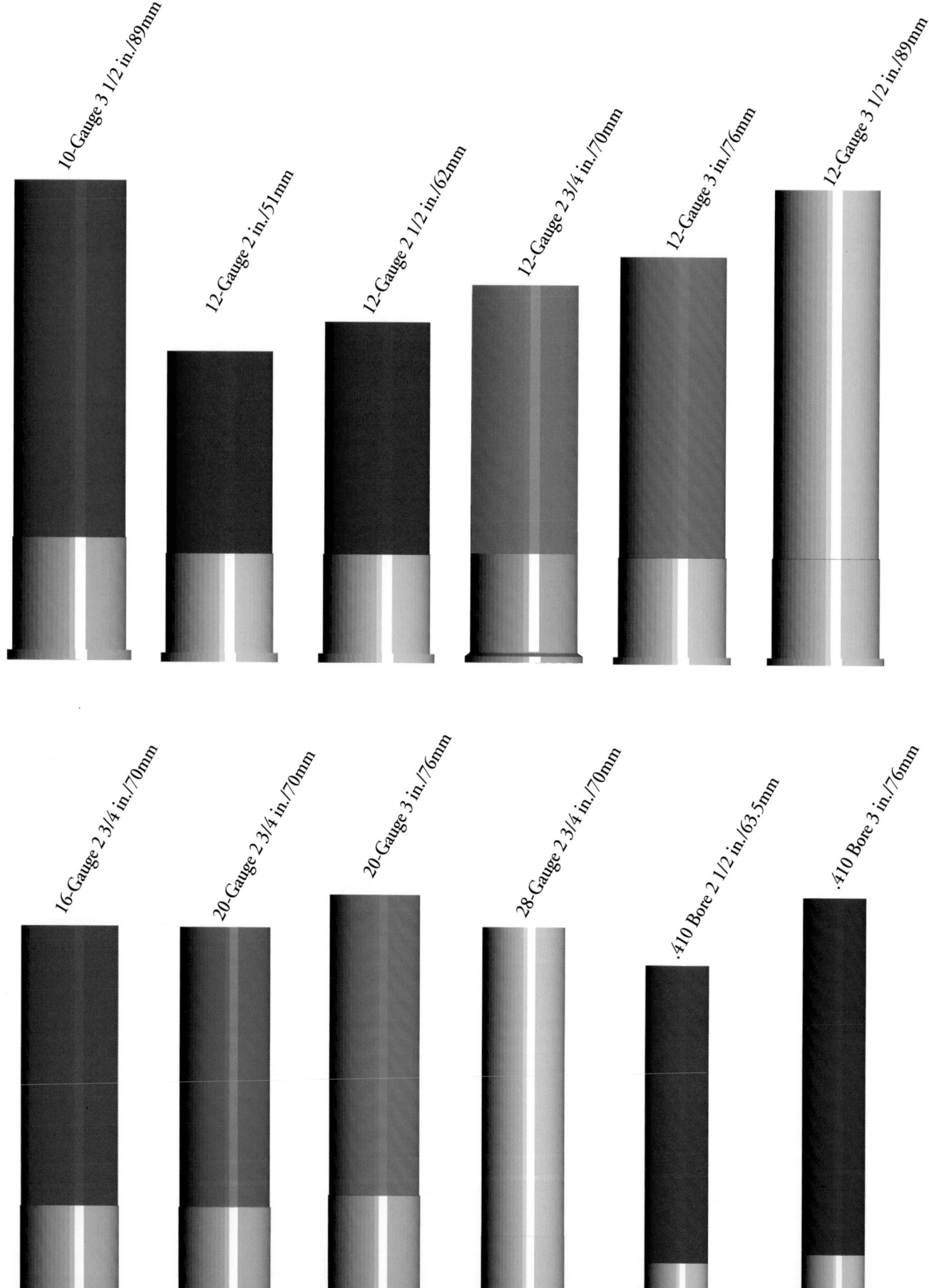

CALIBER	BULLET WGT-GRS	BULLET TYPE	VELOCITY in FPS			ENERGY in ft.-lbs.		
			MUZZLE	50 YDS.	100 YDS.	MUZZLE	50 YDS.	100 YDS.
9x23mm Winchester	100	JSP	1,600	1,380	1,160	568	423	299
	125	JHP	1,350	1,200	1,010	506	400	283
	124	JSP	1,460	1,310	1,100	587	471	333
	125	JHP	1,450	1,300	1,105	583	469	338
.357 SIG	100	FRANG	1,485	1,210	1,035	490	324	238
	100	JSP	1,600	1,380	1,160	568	423	299
	105	FRANG	1,370	1,130	990	438	297	228
	115	JHP	1,500	1,290	1,140	575	425	332
	125	JSP	1,350	1,190	1,080	505	395	325
	125	JHP	1,425	1,225	1,060	564	416	312
	147	JHP	1,225	1,240	1,070	490	422	375
.38 Super Auto +P	100	JSP	1,150	960	830	294	205	153
	115	JHP	1,425	1,265	1,130	519	408	326
	125	JHP	1,240	1,130	1,050	427	354	306
	125	JHP	1,325	1,200	1,110	487	400	342
	130	FMJ	1,215	1,100	1,015	426	348	298
.40 S&W Auto	115	FRANG	1,260	1,050	935	405	282	223
	135	JHP	1,200	1,040	940	430	325	265
	135	JSP	1,325	1,165	1,050	526	407	330
	140	JSP	1,200	1,040	920	448	336	263
	150	JHP	1,200	1,070	970	479	381	313
	155	JHP	1,140	1,030	950	445	365	315
	155	FMJ	1,160	1,040	960	465	375	320
	155	JHP	1,180	1,060	980	479	388	331
	155	JHP	1,205	1,095	1,015	499	413	356
	165	JHP	980	920	880	350	310	280
	165	FMJ	1,060	1,000	960	412	367	338
	165	JHP	1,150	1,050	1,000	485	484	366
	165	FMJ	1,130	1,040	970	470	390	340
	180	JHP	950	905	860	361	326	297
	180	JHP	990	940	900	392	363	322
	180	FMJ	1,000	950	900	400	360	325
	180	JHP	1,015	960	915	412	368	334
	190	FMJ	920	855	790	357	308	263
.400 Cor-Bon	115	JHP	1,650	1,320	1,110	816	523	371
	135	JSP	1,375	1,155	1,025	567	400	316
	135	JHP	1,450	1,205	1,055	630	435	334
	150	JHP	1,350	1,155	1,040	607	446	359
	155	JHP	1,200	1,075	990	496	397	337
	165	JHP	1,300	1,135	1,035	619	472	392
10mm Auto	135	JSP	1,400	1,240	1,120	588	461	376
	150	JHP	1,325	1,180	1,075	585	465	385
	155	JHP	1,265	1,120	1,020	551	431	358
	165	JHP	1,250	1,130	1,060	573	468	412
	175	JHP	1,290	1,140	1,035	649	506	418
	180	JHP	1,030	970	920	425	375	340
	180	JHP	1,180	1,075	1,005	556	464	403
	180	JSP	1,300	1,200	890	676	575	316
	190	FMJ	1,160	1,055	960	567	469	389
	200	JHP	1,050	995	950	490	439	399
	200	JSP	1,125	1,070	1,020	562	508	462

CALIBER	BULLET WGT-GRS	BULLET TYPE	VELOCITY in FPS MUZZLE	50 YDS.	100 YDS.	ENERGY in ft.-lbs. MUZZLE	50 YDS.	100 YDS.
10mm Auto, cont.	200	SWCHP	870	830	790	335	305	275
	200	JHP	900	860	820	360	328	300
	200	JSP	950	910	870	401	368	336
	246	LRN	755	725	695	310	285	265
.440 Cor-Bon	240	JHP	1,600	1,450	1,315	1,365	1,117	922
	260	JHP	1,650	1,505	1,375	1,572	1,310	1,095
.45 G.A.P.	160	JSP	1,075	990	910	411	348	294
	165	JSP	1,075	995	920	424	363	310
	185	JHP	1,000	940	885	411	361	323
	185	FMJ	1,090	1,010	950	490	415	365
	200	JHP	950	885	835	401	348	310
	230	JHP	880	840	800	395	363	327
	230	FMJ	850	815	795	369	338	323
	230	FMJ	875	840	805	391	360	331
.45 Auto	145	FRANG	1,160	995	895	433	319	259
	160	JSP	1,050	970	900	392	334	288
	165	JHP	1,060	980	910	475	390	335
	165	FMJ	1,150	1,030	950	475	390	335
	170	FMJ	1,050	980	855	416	364	276
	185	FMJ	770	610	540	155	120	95
	185	JHP	835	800	765	356	326	300
	185	JHP	900	830	810	333	283	269
	185	JHP	950	900	860	370	330	300
	185	JHP	970	910	860	386	340	304
	185	JHP	1,000	940	890	411	362	324
	185	JHP	1,015	950	900	423	372	332
	200	FMJ	880	815	800	344	295	284
	200	JHP	900	855	820	360	325	296
	230	FMJ	835	800	765	356	326	300
	230	FMJ	860	830	800	380	350	325
	230	JHP	850	820	790	370	345	320
	230	JHP	875	835	795	391	355	323
	230	FMJ	890	860	820	405	375	345
	230	JHP	900	870	830	415	380	355
	230	JHP	920	880	810	432	397	335
.475 Wildey Magnum	250	JHP	1,850	1,680	1,550	1,800	1,566	1,333
	300	JSP	1,610	1,440	1,310	1,727	1,381	1,143
.50 Action Express	300	JHP	1,475	1,255	1,095	1,449	1,046	799
	300	JHP	1,550	1,330	1,175	1,600	1,178	919
	325	JHP	1,400	1,240	1,080	1,414	1,109	841
.50 G.I.	275	JHP	875	830	795	467	420	386
	300	JHP	725	690	650	350	317	281

CHAPTER 53 : SPORTING PISTOL - OBSOLETE

CALIBER	BULLET WGT-GRS	BULLET TYPE	VELOCITY in FPS MUZZLE	50 YDS.	100 YDS.	ENERGY in ft.-lbs. MUZZLE	50 YDS.	100 YDS.
2.7mm Kolibri	3	RB	700	390	210	3	1	0.3
3mm Kolibri	5.4	RB	700	410	235	6	2	0.7
4mm Practice Cartridge M20	7.2	RB	655	425	275	7	3	1
4mm Practice Cartridge GECO								
4.25mm Liliput	17	FMJ	810	545	375	25	11	5

CALIBER	BULLET WGT-GRS	BULLET TYPE	VELOCITY in FPS			ENERGY in ft.-lbs.		
			MUZZLE	50 YDS.	100 YDS.	MUZZLE	50 YDS.	100 YDS.
7mm Nambu	56	FMJ	1,050	960	890	137	114	99
30 Borchardt	85	FMJ	1,280	1,095	980	309	225	181
7.63x25mm Mauser	86	FMJ	1,410	1,180	1,030	380	265	203
7.63mm Mannlicher	85	FMJ	1,025	935	865	188	156	142
7.65mm Roth-Steyr	74	FMJ	1,070	975	905	188	156	135
35 S&W Auto	76	FMJ	810	765	725	111	99	89
357 Auto Mag	110	JHP	1,900	1,625	1,400	882	646	477
	125	JHP	1,800	1,575	1,380	899	688	527
	140	JHP	1,700	1,510	1,340	898	706	557
	158	JSP	1,600	1,450	1,315	898	737	608
9mm Federal	115	JHP	1,280	1,105	995	418	313	254
9mm Ultra	123	JSP	1,070	985	920	313	265	232
9x25mm Mauser	128	FMJ	1,360	1,170	1,065	526	390	324
9mm Win. Magnum	115	FMJ	1,475	1,280	1,130	555	419	327
9x18mm Ultra	123	FMJ	1,070	995	945	313	271	243
.38 Automatic	130	FMJ	1,040	975	925	312	275	248
.41 Action Express	180	JHP	1,000	945	895	400	356	322
	200	JHP	1,000	950	905	444	400	364
.44 Auto Mag	180	JHP	1,600	1,380	1,205	1,023	763	580
	240	JHP	1,400	1,275	1,165	1,044	863	726
.45 Win. Magnum	260	JHP	1,200	1,100	1,025	831	698	607
.45 Rem./Thompson	250	FMJ	1,450	1,320	1,205	1,167	965	809

CHAPTER 54 : MILITARY REVOLVER - CURRENT

CALIBER	BULLET WGT-GRS	BULLET TYPE	VELOCITY in FPS			ENERGY in ft.-lbs.		
			MUZZLE	50 YDS.	100 YDS.	MUZZLE	50 YDS.	100 YDS.
.38 Special	158	LRN	770	750	720	210	195	185

CHAPTER 55 : MILITARY REVOLVER - OBSOLETE

CALIBER	BULLET WGT-GRS	BULLET TYPE	VELOCITY in FPS			ENERGY in ft.-lbs.		
			MUZZLE	50 YDS.	100 YDS.	MUZZLE	50 YDS.	100 YDS.
7.5mm Ord. Rev.	104	FMJ	725	695	670	121	112	104
7.62x38Rmm Nagant	98	FMJ	1,070	995	935	249	215	190
	108	FMJ	1,100	1,015	950	290	247	217
8mm Lebel Revolver	111	FMJ	845	820	795	176	165	156
8mm Rast-Gasser	125	LFN	770	750	730	165	156	148
.38 Long Colt	150	LRN	770	720	685	197	173	156
9mm Jap Revolver	149	LRN	640	620	605	135	128	121
9.4mm Danish Rev.	126	LRN	655	620	590	120	108	98
9.4mm Dutch Rev.	197	LRN	590	635	615	191	177	164
.380/200	200	FMJ	630	615	595	176	167	158
.40 Quiet Special Purpose								
10.4mm Italian Rev.	177	LRN	800	760	725	251	228	207
10.4mm Swiss Rev.	193	LRN	610	585	560	159	146	134
10.6mm Spanish Rev	250	LRN	670	645	625	249	232	216
10.6mm German Rev	255	LRN	670	640	615	254	233	214
11mm French Rev.	180	LRN	800	740	695	56	220	192
.44 S&W Russian	246	LRN	770	745	725	324	303	295
.44 Colt	210	LRN	660	630	610	203	187	173
.450 Revolver	226	LRN	650	630	610	212	199	188
.45 Colt	255	LRN	860	820	780	420	380	345

CALIBER	BULLET WGT-GRS	BULLET TYPE	VELOCITY in FPS			ENERGY in ft.-lbs.		
			MUZZLE	50 YDS.	100 YDS.	MUZZLE	50 YDS.	100 YDS.
.45 S&W	250	LRN	710	690	670	257	242	228
.455 Revolver Mk I	265	LRN	600	575	550	212	194	179
.455 Revolver Mk II	265	FMJ	600	575	550	212	194	179
11.75mm Monte. Rev	300	LRN	700	675	655	326	304	284
.476 Enfield Mk III	262	LRN	700	675	650	285	63	244
.50 Rem. Army/Navy	300	LRN	600	575	555	240	221	205

CHAPTER 56 : MILITARY PISTOL - CURRENT

CALIBER	BULLET WGT-GRS	BULLET TYPE	VELOCITY in FPS			ENERGY in ft.-lbs.		
			MUZZLE	50 YDS.	100 YDS.	MUZZLE	50 YDS.	100 YDS.
7.62x17mm Chinese	74	FMJ	525	495	470	45	41	37
	74	FMJ	1,015	935	875	169	144	126
7.62x25mm Tokarev	86	FMJ	1,380	1,160	1,020	364	256	198
	86	FMJ	1,490	1,235	1,065	424	292	217
	86	FMJ	1,655	1,365	1,150	523	356	251
	85	FMJ	1,705	1,405	1,175	549	373	261
7.62x39mm SP-3	122	FMJ	490	480	465	65	62	59
7.62x41mm SP-4	143.5	FMJ	885	865	850	250	239	230
7.62x63mm PZAM	122	FMJ	570	560	545	88	84	80
9x18mm Makarov	78	AP	1,310	1,130	1,015	297	222	179
	91	FMJ	1,035	955	895	216	184	162
	93	FMJ	1,115	1,010	935	262	215	185
	105	FMJ	995	925	870	231	200	176

CHAPTER 58 : CENTERFIRE SPORTING RIFLE - CURRENT

CALIBER	BULLET WGT-GRS	BULLET TYPE	BULLET STYLE	VELOCITY in FPS						ENERGY IN FT.-LBS.	
				MUZZLE	100 YDS.	200 YDS.	300 YDS.	400 YDS.	500 YDS.	MUZZLE	100 YDS.
.17 Hornet	20	PT	FB	1,539	3,650	3,080	2,575	2,120	1,720	1,539	1,070
.17 Fireball	20	PT	FB	4,000	3,380	2,840	2,360	1,930	1,555	710	507
	25	HP	FB	3,850	3,280	2,780	2,330	1,925	1,570	823	597
.17 Remington	20	PT	FB	4,250	3,595	3,030	2,530	2,080	1,685	802	574
	25	HP	FB	4,040	3,430	2,895	2,420	1,995	1,615	906	652
.204 Ruger	32	PT	FB	4,225	3,645	3,135	2,683	2,270	1,900	1,268	944
	40	PT	BT	3,900	3,420	3,105	2,755	2,435	2,135	1,351	1,077
	45	PT	BT	3,625	3,190	2,790	2,430	2,095	1,785	1,313	1,015
.22 Hornet	35	SP	FB	3,100	2,270	1,590	1,125	925	805	747	401
	45	SP	FB	2,690	2,040	1,500	1,130	950	840	723	417
.22 PPC	52	HP	FB	3,400	2,930	2,510	2,130	1,780	1,480	1,335	990
.22 Savage High Power	71	SP	FB	2,790	2,455	2,145	1,860	1,605	1,380	1,227	951
.22-250 Remington	40	PT	BT	4,150	3,555	3,030	2,570	2,150	1,770	1,529	1,121
	45	HP	FB	4,000	3,295	2,690	2,160	1,695	1,320	1,598	1,084
	50	PT	BT	3,800	3,340	2,925	2,545	2,200	1,880	1,603	1,238
	55	SP	FB	3,680	3,255	2,865	2,510	2,185	1,880	1,654	1,292
	60	SP	FB	3,530	3,130	2,765	2,430	2,120	1,830	1,660	1,306
	64	SP	FB	3,500	3,085	2,710	2,360	2,040	1,745	1,741	1,353
5.6x50mm Magnum	50	SP	FB	3,510	2,925	2,410	1,950	1,555	1,240	1,368	950
	64	SP	FB	3,020	2,645	2,305	1,985	1,695	1,445	1,296	996
5.6x50Rmm Magnum	55	SP	FB	3,280	2,785	2,335	1,935	1,580	1,290	1,314	946
	64	SP	FB	2,925	2,560	2,225	1,910	1,630	1,390	1,216	931
5.6x57mm RWS	74	SP	FB	3,410	3,040	2,700	2,380	2,085	1,810	1,910	1,517
5.6x57Rmm RWS	74	SP	FB	3,410	3,040	2,700	2,380	2,085	1,810	1,910	1,517

CALIBER	BULLET WGT-GRS	BULLET TYPE	VELOCITY in FPS			ENERGY in ft.-lbs.		
			MUZZLE	50 YDS.	100 YDS.	MUZZLE	50 YDS.	100 YDS.
9x18mm Makarov, cont.	106	FMJ	1,020	945	885	245	210	184
9x19mm Luger	115	FMJ	1,300	1,145	1,040	431	335	276
	115	FMJ	1,360	1,190	1,065	472	362	292
	124	FMJ	1,245	1,110	1,020	427	346	286
	124	FMJ	1,300	1,150	1,045	465	364	301
	147	FMJ	990	945	910	320	293	270
9x21mm SP-10	103	AP	1,410	1,195	1,050	455	327	253
	122	FMJ	1,280	1,135	1,035	444	349	291
.45 Auto	230	FMJ	855	820	795	373	345	321

CHAPTER 57 : MILITARY PISTOL - OBSOLETE

CALIBER	BULLET WGT-GRS	BULLET TYPE	VELOCITY in FPS			ENERGY in ft.-lbs.		
			MUZZLE	50 YDS.	100 YDS.	MUZZLE	50 YDS.	100 YDS.
7.65mm Parabellum	93	FMJ	1,220	1,110	1,040	305	255	225
7.65mm French Long	85	FMJ	1,120	1,005	930	237	192	164
8mm Nambu	102	FMJ	1,070	990	935	259	223	197
8mm Roth-Steyr	113	FMJ	1,070	1,015	975	287	259	237
9mm Browning Long	110	FMJ	1,100	1,010	940	295	248	217
9mm Steyr	116	FMJ	1,200	1,075	990	371	298	253
9mm Largo	125	FMJ	1,115	1,020	955	345	290	252
9mm Glisenti	124	FMJ	1,050	985	935	304	268	241
9.8mm Auto Colt	130	FMJ	1,150	1,060	990	382	323	283
.455 Webley Auto	224	FMJ	700	680	660	244	229	216

CHAPTER 58 : CENTERFIRE SPORTING RIFLE - CURRENT

ENERGY IN FT.-LBS.				BULLET PATH AT ZERO DISTANCE INDICATED									
200 YDS.	300 YDS.	400 YDS.	500 YDS.	100 YDS.	200 YDS.	300 YDS.	400 YDS.	500 YDS.	100 YDS.	200 YDS.	300 YDS.	400 YDS.	500 YDS.
738	499	326	205	0	-2.2	-9.8	-25.3	-53.2	1.1	0	-6.4	-20.6	-46.8
358	247	165	107	0	-2	-8	-20	-42	1	0	-5	-17	-38
429	301	206	137	0	-2	-8	-19	-44	1	0	-5	-18	-40
407	284	192	126	0	-1	-6	-17	-36	1	0	-5	-14	-33
465	325	221	145	0	-4	-12	-29	-58	2	0	-7	-22	-49
699	512	367	256	0	-1	-6	-15	-32	1	0	-4	-13	-29
855	674	526	404	0	-1	-6	-16	-32	1	0	-5	-14	-30
778	589	438	319	0	-2	-8	-21	-41	1	0	-5	-17	-36
197	99	66	51	0	-6	-26	-74	-158	3	0	-18	-62	-144
225	127	90	71	0	-9	-33	-83	-167	4	0	-20	-65	-145
730	525	367	252	0	-3	-11	-27	-54	1	0	-7	-21	-47
726	546	406	299	0	-4	-16	-38	-74	2	0	-10	-30	-63
816	585	410	278	0	-1	-6	-17	-35	1	0	-5	-14	-32
723	466	287	174	0	-2	-8	-21	-45	1	0	-5	-18	-41
949	720	536	392	0	-2	-7	-19	-37	1	0	-5	-15	-33
1,003	770	582	432	0	-2	-9	-23	-49	1	0	-6	-19	-43
1,020	787	598	447	0	-2	-9	-21	-42	1	0	-6	-17	-36
1,042	791	590	432	0	-4	-15	-39	-44	2	0	-10	-32	-74
645	423	268	171	0	-3	-11	-30	-63	1	0	-7	-24	-57
754	561	409	296	0	-4	-14	-33	-64	2	0	-8	-26	-55
666	456	304	203	0	-3	-13	-32	-65	1	0	-8	-26	-58
702	519	378	274	0	-4	-15	-36	-69	2	0	-9	-28	-60
1,195	930	714	539	0	-2	-9	-23	-44	1	0	-6	-18	-38
1,195	930	714	539	0	-2	-9	-23	-44	1	0	-6	-18	-38

CALIBER	BULLET WGT-GRS	BULLET TYPE	BULLET STYLE	VELOCITY in FPS						ENERGY IN FT.-LBS.	
				MUZZLE	100 YDS.	200 YDS.	300 YDS.	400 YDS.	500 YDS.	MUZZLE	100 YDS.
.218 Bee	46	HP	FB	2,760	2,100	1,550	1,155	960	850	778	451
.220 Swift	40	PT	FB	4,250	3,690	3,200	2,770	2,370	2,000	1,605	1,210
	50	SP	FB	3,780	3,160	2,615	2,135	1,710	1,355	1,586	1,107
	50	SP	FB	3,870	3,310	2,815	2,375	1,970	1,615	1,663	1,226
	50	SP	FB	4,020	3,395	2,850	2,370	1,940	1,565	1,794	1,279
	52	HP	FB	3,830	3,330	2,890	2,490	2,120	1,780	1,695	1,280
	55	PT	FB	3,680	3,255	2,865	2,510	2,185	1,880	1,654	1,292
	55	SP	FB	3,775	3,185	2,665	2,205	1,795	1,440	1,740	1,239
	60	HP	FB	3,530	3,140	2,785	2,455	2,150	1,865	1,660	1,314
.221 Fireball	50	PT	BT	2,995	2,605	2,245	1,918	1,620	1,370	996	753
.222 Remington	40	PT	BT	3,450	2,900	2,570	2,190	1,840	1,530	1,055	790
	40	PT	FB	3,600	3,075	2,605	2,185	1,805	1,475	1,151	839
	50	PT	BT	3,140	2,745	2,380	2,045	1,740	1,470	1,095	836
	62	SP	FB	2,885	2,465	2,080	1,730	1,430	1,195	1,148	836
.222 Rimmed Australian	50	SP	FB	3,200	2,655	2,170	1,740	1,380	1,125	1,137	782
.223 Remington	40	PT	BT	3,700	3,210	2,770	2,370	2,010	1,680	1,215	915
	40	PT	FB	3,800	3,250	2,760	2,325	1,930	1,580	1,282	937
	45	HP	FB	3,550	2,955	2,430	1,965	1,560	1,240	1,259	871
	50	PT	BT	3,425	2,900	2,430	2,005	1,635	1,325	1,302	933
	53	HP	FB	3,330	2,875	2,460	2,085	1,740	1,445	1,305	971
	55	PT	FB	3,240	2,870	2,530	2,210	1,920	1,650	1,280	1,005
	55	FMJ	BT	3,240	2,870	2,540	2,220	1,930	1,670	1,280	1,010
	55	HP	BT	3,240	2,850	2,490	2,150	1,850	1,570	1,280	990
	60	SP	FB	3,115	2,755	2,420	2,110	1,840	1,565	1,293	1,010
	62	FMJ	BT	3,020	2,710	2,430	2,160	1,900	1,670	1,255	1,015
	62	SP	FB	3,100	2,695	2,325	1,985	1,675	1,410	1,323	1,000
	64	SP	FB	3,020	2,655	2,320	2,010	1,725	1,475	1,296	1,003
	69	HP	BT	3,000	2,720	2,455	2,210	1,975	1,760	1,379	1,133
	75	HP	BT	2,790	2,560	2,345	2,135	1,940	1,755	1,296	1,092
	77	HP	BT	2,790	2,540	2,305	2,080	1,870	1,675	1,329	1,102
.223 WSSM	55	SP	FB	3,850	3,365	2,935	2,540	2,180	1,850	1,810	1,384
	64	SP	FB	3,600	3,145	2,730	2,356	2,010	1,700	1,841	1,404
.243 Winchester	55	PT	BT	3,850	3,440	3,060	2,720	2,400	2,110	1,810	1,445
	55	PT	BT	3,910	3,495	3,115	2,765	2,445	2,145	1,867	1,489
	58	PT	FB	3,750	3,310	2,910	2,545	2,205	1,895	1,811	1,409
	70	PT	BT	3,450	3,110	2,800	2,510	2,240	1,980	1,850	1,505
	75	HP	FB	3,340	2,995	2,675	2,380	2,100	1,845	1,857	1,494
	80	SP	FB	3,350	2,955	2,595	2,260	1,950	1,670	1,993	1,551
	85	HP	BT	3,300	2,980	2,680	2,410	2,140	1,900	2,055	1,675
	90	SP	BT	3,120	2,870	2,635	2,410	2,200	2,000	1,946	1,647
	95	PT	BT	3,100	2,865	2,640	2,430	2,225	2,030	2,025	1,730
	100	SP	BT	2,960	2,695	2,450	2,215	1,995	1,785	1,945	1,615
	100	SP	BT	3,100	2,860	2,635	2,420	2,215	2,020	2,133	1,817
.243 WSSM	55	PT	BT	4,060	3,630	3,235	2,880	2,550	2,245	2,013	1,607
	95	PT	BT	3,150	2,910	2,685	2,470	2,265	2,070	2,093	1,788
	100	SP	FB	3,110	2,840	2,585	2,340	2,110	1,895	2,147	1,789
6mm Remington	80	SP	FB	3,400	3,120	2,850	2,600	2,360	2,140	2,055	1,725
	85	PT	BT	3,350	3,040	2,760	2,490	2,240	2,000	2,120	1,750
	95	SP	BT	3,100	2,860	2,635	2,420	2,215	2,020	2,133	1,817
	100	SP	BT	3,100	2,860	2,635	2,420	2,215	2,020	2,133	1,817
	100	SP	BT	3,250	3,005	2,770	2,545	2,335	2,135	2,345	2,001

ENERGY IN FT.-LBS.				BULLET PATH AT ZERO DISTANCE INDICATED									
200 YDS.	300 YDS.	400 YDS.	500 YDS.	100 YDS.	200 YDS.	300 YDS.	400 YDS.	500 YDS.	100 YDS.	200 YDS.	300 YDS.	400 YDS.	500 YDS.
245	136	94	74	0	-8	-31	-78	-159	4	0	-19	-62	-139
910	680	500	355	0	-1	-6	-15	-30	1	0	-4	-12	-27
760	506	325	204	0	-2	-9	-24	-52	1	0	-6	-20	-46
881	625	432	290	0	-2	-8	-20	-42	1	0	-5	-17	-37
903	623	419	272	0	-2	-7	-20	-42	1	0	-5	-16	-38
965	715	520	365	0	-2	-9	-22	-47	1	0	-5	-16	-34
1,003	770	582	432	0	-2	-8	-20	-38	1	0	-5	-16	-34
870	594	393	253	0	-2	-9	-23	-49	1	0	-6	-19	-44
1,035	804	616	464	0	-2	-9	-21	-41	1	0	-6	-17	-36
560	408	292	208	0	-4	-14	-35	-68	2	0	-9	-27	-59
585	425	300	210	0	-2	-10	-25	-51	1	0	-7	-20	-45
603	424	289	193	0	-2	-10	-24	-51	1	0	-6	-20	-44
629	464	336	240	0	-3	-13	-30	-60	2	0	-8	-24	-52
595	413	281	197	0	-4	-17	-41	-83	2	0	-10	-33	-73
522	335	211	140	0	-4	-15	-38	-80	2	0	-9	-31	-71
680	500	360	250	0	-2	-8	-21	-43	1	0	-6	-17	-38
677	479	330	221	0	-2	-8	-21	-44	1	0	-6	-18	-39
590	385	243	154	0	-2	-11	-29	-62	1	0	-7	-24	-56
655	447	296	195	0	-3	-11	-29	-60	1	0	-7	-24	-53
712	510	537	246	0	-3	-11	-28	-57	1	0	-7	-23	-49
780	595	450	335	0	-3	-11	-26	-52	1	0	-7	-21	-45
785	605	455	340	0	-3	-11	-26	-51	1	0	-7	-21	-44
755	565	415	300	0	-3	-11	-27	-54	1	0	-7	-21	-45
780	595	443	327	0	-3	-12	-29	-57	2	0	-8	-23	-49
810	640	500	385	0	-3	-13	-32	-63	2	0	-8	-23	-48
743	541	386	273	0	-3	-13	-32	-64	2	0	-3	-25	-55
765	574	423	308	0	-4	-13	-32	-64	2	0	-8	-25	-54
925	747	598	473	0	-3	-12	-28	-54	2	0	-7	-22	-45
915	760	627	514	0	-3	-12	-27	-49	2	0	-8	-24	-49
907	740	598	480	0	-4	-14	-33	-62	2	0	-9	-25	-52
1,051	789	581	418	0	-2	-9	-18	-37	2	0	-7	-41	-96
1,061	789	574	410	0	-2	-9	-22	44	1	0	-6	-18	-39
1,145	905	705	540	0	-2	-7	-16	-32	1	0	-4	-14	-29
1,184	934	729	562	0	-1	-6	-16	-32	1	0	-4	-13	-28
1,090	833	627	463	0	-2	-8	-19	-37	1	0	-5	-15	-33
1,220	980	780	610	0	-2	-9	-21	-40	1	0	-4	-14	-29
1,193	943	736	566	0	-2	-10	-23	-44	1	0	-6	-18	-39
1,195	907	676	495	0	-2	-7	-16	-32	1	0	-7	-20	-42
1,360	1,090	870	680	0	-2	-10	-23	-44	1	0	-6	-18	-38
1,388	1,162	966	797	0	-3	-10	-24	-45	1	0	-7	-20	-40
1,471	1,245	1,044	871	0	-3	-11	-24	-45	1	0	-4	-13	-28
1,330	1,089	882	708	0	-3	-12	-29	-46	2	0	-7	-20	-42
1,514	1,299	1,087	904	0	-3	-11	-24	-45	1	0	-6	-19	-38
1,280	1,013	794	614	0	-1	-6	-14	-28	1	0	-4	-12	-26
1,521	1,287	1,083	904	0	-3	-11	-24	-45	1	0	-6	-18	-37
1,481	1,217	991	799	0	-2	-10	-23	-43	1	0	-7	-20	-41
1,445	1,200	995	815	0	-2	-9	-20	-38	1	0	-5	-16	-33
1,435	1,170	945	755	0	-2	-9	-20	-38	1	0	-6	-17	-35
1,514	1,299	1,087	904	0	-2	-11	-24	-45	1	0	-6	-19	-38
1,514	1,299	1,087	904	0	-3	-11	-24	-45	1	0	-6	-19	-38
1,702	1,440	1,211	1,011	0	-2	-9	-22	-40	1	0	-6	-17	-34

CALIBER	BULLET WGT-GRS	BULLET TYPE	BULLET STYLE	VELOCITY in FPS						ENERGY IN FT.-LBS.	
				MUZZLE	100 YDS.	200 YDS.	300 YDS.	400 YDS.	500 YDS.	MUZZLE	100 YDS.
6mm PPC	70	HP	BT	3,140	2,825	2,530	2,255	2,000	1,760	1,532	1,241
6mm Remington BR	100	HP	BT	2,550	2,310	2,085	1,870	1,670	1,490	1,444	1,185
6mm Norma BR	105	HP	BT	2,790	2,615	2,445	2,280	2,125	1,975	1,815	1,593
6x45mm	62	SP	FB	3,100	2,625	2,200	1,815	1,485	1,220	1,323	950
	70	HP	BT	3,000	2,635	2,295	1,990	1,715	1,470	1,399	1,078
	85	HP	BT	2,800	2,530	2,275	2,035	1,810	1,605	1,480	1,208
6x47mm Swiss Match	107	HP	BT	2,900	2,720	2,545	2,380	2,220	2,065	1,998	1,758
6x62mm Freres	85	SP	FB	3,460	3,055	2,685	2,345	2,025	1,740	2,259	1,761
	100	SP	BT	3,315	3,065	2,825	2,600	2,390	2,185	2,440	2,084
6x62Rmm Freres	85	SP	FB	3,460	3,055	2,685	2,345	2,025	1,740	2,259	1,761
	100	SP	BT	3,315	3,065	2,825	2,600	2,390	2,185	2,440	2,084
6x70mm	90	PT	BT	2,430	2,200	1,985	1,783	1,600	1,439	1,180	969
.250 Savage	100	SP	FB	2,820	2,465	2,140	1,840	1,570	1,340	1,765	1,351
.257 Roberts	117	SP	FB	2,650	2,290	1,960	1,665	1,405	1,200	1,824	1,363
	117	SP +P	FB	2,780	2,410	2,070	1,760	1,490	1,265	2,009	1,511
	117	PT +P	BT	2,940	2,700	2,475	2,260	2,055	1,860	2,245	1,895
.25-'06 Remington	85	PT	BT	3,470	3,155	2,865	2,590	2,330	2,090	2,273	1,880
	85	PT	BT	3,550	3,230	2,930	2,640	2,380	2,130	2,380	1,965
	100	SP	FB	3,230	2,895	2,580	2,285	2,015	1,760	2,316	1,858
	110	PT	BT	3,100	2,870	2,650	2,440	2,245	2,055	2,347	2,011
	115	SP	FB	3,000	2,750	2,515	2,995	2,080	1,880	2,298	1,933
	117	SP	BT	3,030	2,800	2,580	2,370	2,170	1,980	2,385	2,035
	117	PT	BT	3,110	2,860	2,630	2,405	2,195	1,990	2,512	2,128
	120	SP	FB	2,990	2,715	2,460	2,215	1,985	1,775	2,382	1,967
.25 WSSM	85	PT	BT	3,470	3,155	2,865	2,590	2,330	2,090	2,273	1,880
	110	PT	BT	3,100	2,870	2,651	2,442	2,243	2,053	2,347	2,011
	115	PT	BT	3,060	2,845	2,640	2,440	2,255	2,075	2,392	2,066
	120	SP	FB	2,990	2,715	2,460	2,215	1,985	1,775	2,383	1,967
.260 Remington	120	PT	BT	2,890	2,695	2,510	2,335	2,165	2,000	2,392	2,083
	120	PT	BT	2,950	2,730	2,510	2,310	2,110	1,930	2,320	1,980
	140	SP	FB	2,360	2,170	1,990	1,820	1,660	1,510	1,731	1,465
	140	PT	BT	2,750	2,555	2,365	2,185	2,015	1,850	2,351	2,027
6.5mm Grendel	110	FMJ	BT	2,755	2,565	2,395	2,230	2,075	1,925	1,854	1,609
	120	HP	BT	2,675	2,515	2,345	2,185	2,035	1,885	1,906	1,682
	123	SP	FB	2,655	2,430	2,265	2,110	1,960	1,815	1,925	1,611
6.5mm Creedmoor	120	PT	BT	2,910	2,710	2,520	2,340	2,165	2,000	2,256	1,959
	140	PT	BT	2,710	2,555	2,410	2,265	2,130	1,995	2,283	2,032
6.5x47mm Lapua	100	HP	BT	2,790	2,585	2,405	2,245	2,085	1,935	1,728	1,485
	108	PT	BT	2,950	2,755	2,565	2,395	2,230	2,075	2,087	1,818
	123	HP	BT	2,790	2,625	2,460	2,295	2,140	1,985	2,126	1,880
	139	HP	BT	2,690	2,545	2,385	2,225	2,070	1,920	2,233	1,999
6.5x55mm Swedish	100	HP	BT	2,625	2,410	2,245	2,090	1,940	1,795	1,530	1,288
	120	PT	BT	2,820	2,610	2,420	2,260	2,100	1,950	2,119	1,813
	120	FMJ	FB	2,690	2,485	2,320	2,160	2,010	1,860	1,928	1,647
	130	HP	BT	2,790	2,625	2,460	2,295	2,140	1,985	2,247	1,988
	130	HP	BT	2,985	2,810	2,645	2,485	2,320	2,160	2,572	2,282
	140	SP	FB	2,650	2,450	2,260	2,080	1,900	1,740	2,185	1,865
	140	PT	FB	2,690	2,500	2,335	2,175	2,020	1,875	2,249	1,943
	156	SP	FB	2,560	2,375	2,210	2,055	1,910	1,765	2,037	1,750
6.5x57mm Mauser	93	SP	FB	3,180	2,800	2,475	2,310	2,150	2,000	2,088	1,619
	108	SP	FB	3,000	2,695	2,445	2,280	2,125	1,970	2,158	1,742

ENERGY IN FT.-LBS.				BULLET PATH AT ZERO DISTANCE INDICATED									
200 YDS.	300 YDS.	400 YDS.	500 YDS.	100 YDS.	200 YDS.	300 YDS.	400 YDS.	500 YDS.	100 YDS.	200 YDS.	300 YDS.	400 YDS.	500 YDS.
996	792	622	482	0	-3	-11	-26	-50	1	0	-7	-21	-43
963	776	620	492	0	-5	-18	-41	-77	3	0	-10	-31	-64
1,394	1,214	1,054	910	0	-4	-13	-29	-53	2	0	-8	-22	-44
667	454	303	205	0	-4	-14	-36	-74	2	0	-9	-29	-65
817	615	457	336	0	-4	-14	-33	-64	2	0	-8	-26	-55
976	781	618	486	0	-4	-15	-34	-64	2	0	-9	-26	-54
1,542	1,345	1,169	1,011	0	-3	-12	-27	-48	2	0	7	0	-40
1,360	1,036	776	537	0	-2	-9	-23	-45	1	0	-6	-18	-39
1,774	1,503	1,266	1,059	0	-2	-9	-20	-38	1	0	-6	-16	-19
1,360	1,036	776	537	0	-2	-9	-23	-45	1	0	-6	-18	-39
1,774	1,503	1,266	1,059	0	-2	-9	-20	-38	1	0	-6	-16	-19
789	636	511	408	0	-6	-20	-46	-85	3	0	-12	-35	-71
1,017	751	547	398	0	-4	-15	-32	-58	2	0	-9	-24	-48
999	718	512	373	0	-5	-16	-35	-64	3	0	-12	-36	-78
1,115	806	576	415	0	-4	-15	-33	-60	2	0	-9	-25	-49
1,589	1,324	1,095	898	0	-3	-12	-28	-50	2	0	-7	-25	-50
1,548	1,266	1,026	823	0	-2	-8	-20	-37	1	0	-5	-16	-33
1,615	1,320	1,070	855	0	-2	-8	-19	-36	1	0	-5	-15	-31
1,478	1,161	901	689	0	-3	-11	-25	-46	1	0	-7	-20	-42
1,716	1,456	1,228	1,029	0	-3	-11	-24	-44	1	0	-6	-19	-38
1,616	1,342	1,106	903	0	-3	-12	-27	-49	2	0	-7	-21	-43
1,725	1,455	1,220	1,015	0	-3	-9	-22	-40	2	0	-7	-20	-40
1,793	1,502	1,249	1,030	0	-3	-11	-24	-45	2	0	-6	-19	-39
1,612	1,309	1,053	838	0	-3	-12	-28	-50	2	0	-7	-22	-45
1,548	1,266	1,026	823	0	-2	-8	-20	-37	1	0	-5	-16	-33
1,716	1,456	1,228	1,029	0	-3	-10	-24	-44	1	0	-6	-19	-38
1,778	1,523	1,298	1,099	0	-3	-11	-24	-45	1	0	-6	-19	-38
1,612	1,309	1,053	838	0	-3	-12	-28	-50	2	0	-7	-22	-45
1,807	1,560	1,340	1,146	0	-3	-12	-27	-50	2	0	-7	-21	-42
1,680	1,420	1,190	990	0	-3	-12	-27	-49	2	0	-7	-21	-42
1,232	1,029	856	710	0	-6	-19	-43	-79	3	0	-12	-34	-69
1,739	1,484	1,260	1,063	0	-4	-14	-31	-56	2	0	-8	-24	-48
1,399	1,216	1,053	906	0	-4	-14	-30	-55	2	0	-8	-23	-46
1,468	1,274	1,101	946	0	-4	-14	-32	-58	2	0	-8	-24	-48
1,402	1,214	1,047	898	0	-4	-16	-34	-62	2	0	-9	-25	-51
1,695	1,459	1,250	1,065	0	-3	12	27	49	2	0	-7	-21	-41
1,804	1,596	1,408	1,237	0	-4	-14	-31	-56	2	0	-8	-23	-46
1,285	1,117	967	832	0	-4	-13	-30	-54	2	0	-8	-23	-45
1,578	1,373	1,193	1,032	0	-3	-11	-26	-47	2	0	-7	-20	-40
1,654	1,440	1,249	1,078	0	-4	-13	-29	-52	-2	0	-8	-22	-43
1,757	1,527	1,321	1,137	0	-4	-14	-31	-56	2	0	-8	-23	-46
1,120	969	835	716	0	-5	-16	-35	-63	2	0	-9	-26	-52
1,561	1,358	1,176	1,013	0	-4	-13	-30	-53	2	0	-8	-22	-44
1,434	1,244	1,074	923	0	-4	-15	-33	-59	2	0	-9	-24	-49
1,749	1,523	1,320	1,139	0	-4	-13	-29	-52	2	0	-8	-22	-43
2,019	1,780	1,550	1,345	0	-3	-11	-24	-44	2	0	-6	-18	-37
1,585	1,340	1,120	935	0	-4	-15	-34	-61	2	0	-9	-26	-53
1,693	1,469	1,269	1,090	0	-4	-15	-32	-58	2	0	-9	-24	-48
1,521	1,315	1,131	969	0	-5	-17	-36	-66	2	0	-9	-27	-54
1,264	1,101	955	824	0	-3	-12	-27	-49	2	0	-7	-21	-41
1,433	1,247	1,081	932	0	-3	-12	-28	-51	2	0	-7	-22	-43

CALIBER	BULLET WGT-GRS	BULLET TYPE	BULLET STYLE	VELOCITY in FPS						ENERGY IN FT.-LBS.	
				MUZZLE	100 YDS.	200 YDS.	300 YDS.	400 YDS.	500 YDS.	MUZZLE	100 YDS.
6.5x57mm Mauser, cont.	127	SP	FB	2,855	2,600	2,400	2,240	2,085	1,935	2,298	1,908
	140	SP	FB	2,655	2,420	2,260	2,100	1,950	1,805	2,191	1,822
6.5x57Rmm Mauser	93	SP	FB	2,950	2,590	2,375	2,215	2,060	1,910	1,797	1,384
	108	SP	FB	2,855	2,560	2,370	2,205	2,050	1,905	1,955	1,572
	127	SP	FB	2,740	2,495	2,330	2,170	2,015	1,870	2,117	1,754
	140	SP	FB	2,540	2,355	2,195	2,040	1,895	1,750	2,005	1,726
6.5x65mm RWS	127	SP	FB	2,950	2,690	2,460	2,295	2,140	1,985	2,454	2,042
6.5x65Rmm RWS	127	SP	FB	2,855	2,600	2,400	2,240	2,085	1,935	2,298	1,908
6.5x68mm RWS	93	SP	FB	3,770	3,335	2,940	2,580	2,370	2,210	2,935	2,297
	127	SP	FB	3,150	2,880	2,625	2,420	2,255	2,100	2,798	2,338
6.5-.284 Norma	140	PT	FB	2,955	2,755	2,560	2,385	2,225	2,070	2,714	2,355
.270 Winchester	100	SP	FB	3,320	2,925	2,560	2,225	1,915	1,635	2,448	1,898
	110	PT	BT	3,400	3,130	2,870	2,620	2,390	2,180	2,825	2,385
	115	SP	FB	2,710	2,410	2,135	1,875	1,635	1,425	1,875	1,485
	130	PT	BT	3,050	2,830	2,620	2,420	2,230	2,045	2,685	2,311
	130	SP	BT	3,200	2,970	2,760	2,560	2,360	2,170	2,955	2,555
	140	SP	BT	2,950	2,760	2,580	2,400	2,240	2,080	2,705	2,370
	150	SP	FB	2,830	2,640	2,460	2,280	2,110	1,950	2,665	2,320
	150	PT	BT	2,950	2,765	2,585	2,410	2,245	2,085	2,898	2,542
.270 WSM	110	PT	BT	3,500	3,220	2,960	2,710	2,470	2,250	2,990	2,530
	130	PT	BT	3,275	3,045	2,825	2,614	2,415	2,225	3,096	2,673
	140	PT	BT	3,200	2,990	2,790	2,580	2,415	2,235	3,184	2,779
	150	PT	BT	3,120	2,925	2,735	2,555	2,380	2,215	3,242	2,845
6.8mm SPC	115	HP	BT	2,625	2,375	2,135	1,910	1,700	1,515	1,759	1,437
	115	SP	FB	2,625	2,330	2,060	1,805	1,575	1,372	1,759	1,389
	115	FMJ	FB	2,625	2,330	2,055	1,795	1,565	1,365	1,759	1,385
7-30 Waters	120	SP	BT	2,700	2,300	1,930	1,600	1,330	1,130	1,940	1,405
7x57mm Mauser	139	PT	BT	2,830	2,640	2,460	2,285	2,120	1,960	2,471	2,153
	140	SP	FB	2,660	2,435	2,220	2,020	1,825	1,650	2,199	1,843
	156	SP	FB	2,640	2,420	2,255	2,100	1,950	1,805	2,414	2,028
	175	SP	FB	2,390	2,090	1,810	1,560	1,350	1,180	2,220	1,695
7x57Rmm Mauser	175	SP	FB	2,390	2,090	1,810	1,560	1,350	1,180	2,220	1,695
7mm-08 Remington	120	HP	FB	3,000	2,725	2,475	2,310	2,155	2,000	2,398	1,979
	139	PT	BT	3,000	2,805	2,615	2,435	2,265	2,100	2,777	2,427
	140	SP	FB	2,360	2,200	2,045	1,895	1,755	1,620	1,731	1,504
	140	PT	BT	2,820	2,630	2,455	2,290	2,130	1,980	2,472	2,153
	150	SP	FB	2,650	2,440	2,240	2,040	1,860	1,690	2,340	1,980
.280 Remington	139	PT	BT	3,110	2,910	2,718	2,535	2,355	2,190	2,985	2,612
	140	PT	BT	3,000	2,805	2,615	2,435	2,265	2,100	2,797	2,444
	150	SP	FB	2,890	2,625	2,375	2,135	1,910	1,705	2,781	2,293
	165	SP	FB	2,820	2,510	2,220	1,950	1,700	1,480	2,913	2,308
	170	PT	FB	2,710	2,480	2,315	2,155	2,000	1,855	2,772	2,321
.280 Ackley Improved	140	Pt	BT	3,150	2,945	2,755	2,565	2,390	2,220	3,084	2,700
	160	PT	BT	2,950	2,750	2,560	2,380	2,205	2,040	3,091	2,690
.284 Winchester	150	SP	FB	2,860	2,610	2,370	2,145	1,935	1,735	2,724	2,266
7mm Rem. Magnum	85	PT	BT	3,550	3,230	2,930	2,640	2,380	2,130	2,380	1,965
	110	PT	BT	3,500	3,200	2,920	2,650	2,400	2,170	2,990	2,500
	139	PT	BT	3,250	3,045	2,845	2,655	2,475	2,300	3,259	2,857
	140	PT	BT	3,175	2,970	2,775	2,590	2,410	2,240	3,133	2,744
	150	SP	FB	3,110	2,830	2,570	2,320	2,085	1,865	3,221	2,667
	160	SP	FB	2,950	2,725	2,510	2,305	2,110	1,925	3,091	2,636
	170	PT	FB	2,955	2,690	2,460	2,295	2,135	1,985	3,296	2,732

ENERGY IN FT.-LBS.				BULLET PATH AT ZERO DISTANCE INDICATED									
200 YDS.	300 YDS.	400 YDS.	500 YDS.	100 YDS.	200 YDS.	300 YDS.	400 YDS.	500 YDS.	100 YDS.	200 YDS.	300 YDS.	400 YDS.	500 YDS.
1,627	1,415	1,224	1,054	0	-4	-13	-30	-54	2	0	-8	-23	-45
1,585	1,373	1,182	1,015	0	-4	-16	-34	-62	2	0	-9	-26	-51
1,166	1,013	876	753	0	-4	-13	-30	-54	2	0	-8	-23	-45
1,344	1,168	1,010	868	0	-4	-14	-31	-55	2	0	-8	-23	-46
1,529	1,326	1,145	984	0	-4	-15	-32	-58	2	0	-9	-24	-48
1,499	1,296	1,114	954	0	-5	-17	-38	-67	3	0	-10	-27	-55
1,709	1,488	1,290	1,114	0	-3	-12	-28	-51	2	0	-7	-21	-43
1,627	1,415	1,224	1,054	0	-4	-13	-30	-54	2	0	-8	-23	-45
1,787	1,376	1,162	1,009	0	-2	-7	-18	-35	1	0	-5	-15	-31
1,942	1,648	1,433	1,241	0	-3	-11	-24	-45	2	0	-7	-19	-38
2,036	1,768	1,537	1,330	0	-3	-12	-26	-48	2	0	-7	-20	-40
1,456	1,099	815	594	0	-3	-10	-24	-45	1	0	-7	-19	-39
2,010	1,680	1,400	1,155	0	-2	-8	-20	-37	1	0	-5	-16	-32
1,161	896	683	519	0	-4	-15	-33	-61	2	0	-9	-25	-50
1,982	1,691	1,434	1,209	0	-3	-11	-25	-45	2	0	-7	-19	-38
2,200	1,885	1,610	1,365	0	-2	-10	-22	-40	2	0	-7	-20	-39
2,065	1,795	1,555	1,340	0	-3	-12	-26	-48	2	0	-7	-20	-39
2,010	1,735	1,485	1,270	0	-4	-13	-29	-52	2	0	-8	-22	-44
2,225	1,936	1,679	1,449	0	-3	-12	-26	-48	1	0	-7	-19	-38
2,135	1,790	1,495	1,235	0	-2	-8	-18	-35	1	0	-5	-15	-30
2,301	1,973	1,683	1,427	0	-2	-9	-21	-38	1	0	-6	-16	-33
2,418	2,097	1,810	1,555	0	-3	-9	-21	-39	1	0	-6	-17	-33
2,490	2,172	1,886	1,613	0	-3	-10	-22	-41	1	0	-6	-17	-35
1,163	932	740	584	0	-5	-16	-35	-63	2	0	-10	-30	-61
1,082	832	633	481	0	-5	-16	-35	-64	3	0	-11	-32	-68
1,076	825	625	474	0	-5	-16	-35	-64	3	0	-11	-32	-68
990	685	470	340	0	-4	-16	-34	-63	2	0	-9	-26	-52
1,869	1,615	1,388	858	0	-3	-13	-28	-52	2	0	-8	-22	-44
1,533	1,266	1,037	844	0	-4	-15	-34	-61	2	0	-9	-27	-55
1,764	1,527	1,316	1,129	0	-5	-16	-35	-63	2	0	-9	-26	-52
1,275	950	705	540	0	-6	-19	-42	-76	3	0	-11	-31	-63
1,275	950	705	540	0	-6	-19	-42	-76	3	0	-11	-31	-63
1,635	1,424	1,235	1,066	0	-3	-11	-26	-47	2	0	-7	-20	-39
2,113	1,833	1,583	1,360	0	-3	-11	-25	-45	2	0	-7	-19	-38
1,300	1,120	957	815	0	-6	-19	-43	-79	3	0	-11	-32	-65
1,872	1,629	1,412	1,218	0	-4	-13	-29	-52	2	0	-8	-22	-43
1,665	1,390	1,150	950	0	-6	-19	-43	-79	3	0	-11	-32	-65
2,279	1,981	1,715	1,477	0	-3	-10	-23	-42	2	0	-6	-17	-35
2,129	1,846	1,594	1,369	0	-3	-11	-25	-45	2	0	-7	-19	-38
1,875	1,518	1,217	968	0	-4	-13	-29	-53	2	0	-8	-22	-44
1,805	1,393	1,060	801	0	-4	-14	-32	-57	2	0	-8	-24	-47
2,021	1,753	1,513	1,300	0	-4	-15	-33	-59	2	0	-9	-25	-49
2,355	2,048	1,774	1,529	0	-3	-10	-22	-40	1	0	-6	-17	-34
2,332	2,013	1,729	1,478	0	-3	-12	-27	-50	2	0	-7	-20	-40
1,872	1,533	1,244	1,001	0	-4	-13	-30	-54	2	0	-8	-23	-45
1,615	1,320	1,070	855	0	-2	-8	-19	-36	1	0	-5	-15	-31
2,075	1,720	1,410	1,145	0	-2	-8	-19	-36	1	0	-5	-15	-31
2,498	2,177	1,890	1,634	0	-2	-9	-20	-37	1	0	-6	-16	-32
2,397	2,086	1,808	1,560	0	-3	-10	-22	-40	1	0	-6	-17	-34
2,196	1,792	1,448	1,160	0	-3	-11	-25	-46	1	0	-7	-20	-39
2,237	1,887	1,581	1,315	0	-3	-12	-27	-49	2	0	-7	-21	-41
2,282	1,986	1,722	1,486	0	-3	-12	-28	-51	2	0	-7	-21	-43

CALIBER	BULLET WGT-GRS	BULLET TYPE	BULLET STYLE	VELOCITY in FPS						ENERGY IN FT.-LBS.	
				MUZZLE	100 YDS.	200 YDS.	300 YDS.	400 YDS.	500 YDS.	MUZZLE	100 YDS.
7mm Rem. Magnum, cont.	175	SP	FB	2,860	2,645	2,440	2,245	2,055	1,880	3,178	2,718
	175	SP	FB	2,750	2,530	2,320	2,120	1,930	1,750	2,940	2,485
7mm Rem, SAUM	140	SP	FB	3,175	2,935	2,705	2,490	2,285	2,085	3,133	2,676
	150	SP	FB	3,110	2,830	2,570	2,320	2,085	1,865	3,221	2,669
	160	SP	FB	2,960	2,735	2,520	2,315	2,115	1,930	3,112	2,654
7mm Win. Short Mag.	140	PT	BT	3,225	3,010	2,810	2,605	2,415	2,235	3,233	2,816
	140	PT	BT	3,310	3,100	2,900	2,700	2,520	2,340	3,405	2,985
	150	SP	FB	3,200	2,915	2,650	2,395	2,155	1,935	3,410	2,830
	160	PT	BT	3,050	2,860	2,680	2,510	2,340	2,180	3,306	2,911
7mm Rem. Ultra Mag.	140	SP	FB	3,425	3,170	2,930	2,700	2,485	2,280	3,646	3,123
	150	PT	BT	3,325	3,130	2,950	2,770	2,602	2,440	3,682	3,267
	175	SP	FB	3,025	2,830	2,645	2,465	2,295	2,210	3,555	3,114
7mm STW	140	PT	BT	3,300	3,090	2,890	2,700	2,515	2,340	3,385	2,968
	150	PT	BT	3,175	2,960	2,750	2,555	2,365	2,185	3,357	2,915
	160	PT	BT	3,100	2,920	2,740	2,570	2,410	2,250	3,415	3,020
7.62x39mm Soviet M43	125	SP	FB	2,365	2,060	1,785	1,535	1,320	1,155	1,552	1,180
.30 Remington AR	125	SP	BT	2,800	2,530	2,280	2,040	1,815	1,610	2,176	1,778
.30 M1 Carbine	110	SP	FB	1,990	1,565	1,235	1,035	925	840	967	600
.30 Thompson-Center	150	SP	BT	3,000	2,770	2,555	2,350	2,150	1,965	2,997	2,558
	165	SP	BT	2,850	2,645	2,445	2,260	2,080	1,905	2,975	2,560
.30 R Blaser	165	SP	FB	2,950	2,635	2,405	2,245	2,090	1,940	3,188	2,544
	180	SP	FB	2,820	2,565	2,375	2,215	2,060	1,910	3,178	2,625
	185	SP	FB	2,790	2,545	2,365	2,205	2,050	1,900	3,198	2,659
.30-30 Winchester	125	SP	FB	2,175	1,820	1,510	1,255	1,082	975	1,313	919
	125	HP	FB	2,570	2,080	1,660	1,310	1,080	950	1,835	1,205
	150	SP	FB	2,390	1,975	1,605	1,305	1,095	974	1,902	1,296
	170	SP	FB	2,200	1,895	1,620	1,380	1,190	1,060	1,827	1,355
.30-40 Krag	180	SP	FB	2,430	2,220	2,015	1,830	1,650	1,490	2,360	1,965
.30-'06 Springfield	125	SP	FB	3,140	2,780	2,040	1,790	1,855	1,595	2,736	2,145
	150	SP	FB	2,910	2,615	2,340	2,085	1,845	1,620	2,820	2,281
	150	PT	BT	3,100	2,865	2,645	2,435	2,235	2,040	3,200	2,736
	165	SP	FB	2,800	2,535	2,285	2,045	1,825	1,620	2,872	2,352
	165	PT	BT	3,015	2,800	2,600	2,405	2,220	2,040	3,330	2,876
	168	HP	BT	2,700	2,510	2,320	2,150	1,980	1,820	2,720	2,345
	180	SP	FB	2,700	2,350	2,025	1,725	1,465	1,250	2,913	2,203
	180	SP	BT	2,880	2,675	2,480	2,295	2,115	1,945	3,315	2,861
	220	SP	FB	2,410	2,130	1,870	1,630	1,420	1,254	2,837	2,216
.303 British	150	SP	FB	2,685	2,440	2,210	1,990	1,785	1,600	2,401	1,984
	180	SP	FB	2,460	2,235	2,020	1,815	1,630	1,460	2,418	1,993
.307 Winchester	180	SP	FB	2,510	2,180	1,875	1,600	1,365	1,175	2,518	1,897
.308 Marlin Express	160	PT	BT	2,660	2,430	2,225	2,025	1,835	1,650	2,513	2,111
.308 Winchester	110	SP	FB	3,165	2,830	2,520	2,230	1,955	1,710	2,446	1,956
	125	SP	FB	2,660	2,380	2,120	1,880	1,655	1,455	1,964	1,575
	150	SP	FB	2,820	2,535	2,265	2,010	1,775	1,560	2,648	2,137
	150	PT	BT	3,000	2,770	2,555	2,350	2,150	1,965	2,997	2,466
	165	SP	BT	2,700	2,480	2,270	2,070	1,880	1,710	2,670	2,255
	165	SP	BT	3,015	2,795	2,590	2,390	2,200	2,015	3,330	2,864
	168	HP	BT	2,680	2,485	2,295	2,120	1,950	1,785	2,680	2,303
	168	PT	BT	2,670	2,485	2,305	2,135	1,970	1,815	2,659	2,301
	180	SP	FB	2,620	2,275	1,955	1,665	1,415	1,210	2,743	2,066
	180	PT	BT	2,620	2,395	2,180	1,975	1,780	1,605	2,743	2,288

ENERGY IN FT.-LBS.				BULLET PATH AT ZERO DISTANCE INDICATED									
200 YDS.	300 YDS.	400 YDS.	500 YDS.	100 YDS.	200 YDS.	300 YDS.	400 YDS.	500 YDS.	100 YDS.	200 YDS.	300 YDS.	400 YDS.	500 YDS.
2,313	1,956	1,644	1,372	0	-3	-13	-29	-52	2	0	-8	-22	-43
2,090	1,745	1,450	1,195	0	-4	-14	-31	-57	2	0	-8	-24	-47
2,277	1,927	1,620	1,353	0	-3	-10	-23	-42	1	0	-6	-18	-36
2,197	1,793	1,450	1,161	0	-3	-11	-25	-46	1	0	-7	-20	-39
2,252	1,900	1,592	1,323	0	-3	-12	-27	-49	2	0	-7	-21	-41
2,438	2,106	1,812	1,550	0	-2	-9	-21	-39	1	0	-6	-16	-33
2,610	2,270	1,975	1,705	0	-2	-9	-20	-38	1	0	-5	-16	-32
2,335	1,911	1,550	1,245	0	-3	-10	-24	-44	1	0	-6	-18	-37
2,556	2,237	1,950	1,692	0	-3	-10	-23	-43	1	0	-6	-18	-36
2,667	2,268	1,919	1,613	0	-2	-8	-19	-35	1	0	-5	-15	-30
2,894	2,558	2,254	1,979	0	-2	-8	-19	-34	1	0	-5	-15	-29
2,718	2,364	2,047	1,764	0	-3	-11	-24	-44	1	0	-6	-18	-37
2,596	2,263	1,966	1,700	0	-2	-9	-20	-36	1	0	-5	-15	-31
2,521	2,173	1,863	1,590	0	-3	-10	-22	-41	1	0	-6	-17	-34
2,670	2,350	2,060	1,800	0	-3	-12	-27	-50	2	0	-7	-21	-41
882	652	483	370	0	-6	-19	-43	-78	3	0	-11	-32	-64
1,440	1,153	915	719	0	-4	-14	-31	-56	2	0	-8	-24	-47
373	262	208	173	0	-9	-30	-65	-117	5	0	-17	-47	-94
2,173	1,836	1,540	1,283	0	-3	-11	-26	-47	2	0	-7	-20	-40
2,193	1,868	1,582	1,331	0	-3	-13	-29	-52	2	0	-8	-22	-43
2,123	1,846	1,598	1,376	0	-4	-13	-29	-53	2	0	-8	-22	-44
2,255	1,959	1,694	1,457	0	-4	-14	-31	-55	2	0	-8	-23	-46
2,295	1,994	1,724	1,482	0	-4	-14	-31	-56	2	0	-8	-23	-46
631	437	325	264	0	-7	-24	-53	-95	3	0	-14	-39	-78
760	475	325	250	0	-5	-18	-37	-67	2	0	-10	-27	55
858	565	399	316	0	-6	-19	-42	-77	3	0	-11	-31	-63
989	720	535	425	0	-7	-23	-51	-92	3	0	-13	-38	-76
1,625	1,335	1,090	886	0	-5	-18	-40	-74	3	0	-10	-30	-60
1,662	1,269	953	706	0	-3	-12	-27	-49	1	0	-7	-21	-41
1,827	1,445	1,131	876	0	-4	-13	-30	-53	2	0	-8	-22	-45
2,330	1,973	1,660	1,387	0	-3	-11	-24	-44	1	0	-6	-18	-37
1,909	1,534	1,220	963	0	-4	-13	-30	-54	2	0	-8	-23	-45
2,474	2,118	1,803	1,526	0	-3	-11	-25	-46	2	0	-7	-19	-39
2,015	1,720	1,460	1,235	0	-4	-14	-32	-58	2	0	-9	-24	-48
1,635	1,192	859	625	0	-4	-16	-34	-62	2	0	-9	-25	-51
2,458	2,101	1,786	1,509	0	-3	-12	-28	-51	2	0	-7	-21	-42
1,708	1,301	988	758	0	-5	-19	-41	-75	3	0	-10	-30	-62
1,627	1,321	1,064	851	0	-4	-15	-34	-61	2	0	-10	-28	-58
1,628	1,320	1,060	851	0	-7	-26	-63	-126	3	0	-15	-49	-109
1,403	1,022	742	554	0	-6	-22	-51	-100	3	0	-13	-40	-86
1,761	1,457	1,197	978	0	-4	-15	-34	-61	2	0	-9	-25	-50
1,549	1,212	935	712	0	-3	-11	-26	-47	1	0	-7	-20	-40
1,249	978	759	586	0	-4	-16	-34	-62	2	0	-9	-25	-51
1,705	1,344	1,408	810	0	-4	-15	-34	-65	2	0	-9	-26	-55
2,014	1,629	1,305	1,034	0	-3	-11	-26	-47	2	0	-7	-20	-40
1,890	1,575	1,300	1,070	0	-4	-15	-33	-59	2	0	-9	-24	-49
2,453	2,090	1,771	1,490	0	-3	-11	-25	-46	2	0	-7	-19	-39
1,970	1,674	1,415	1,190	0	-4	-15	-32	-59	2	0	-9	-24	-48
1,983	1,699	1,449	1,229	0	-4	-15	-33	-59	2	0	-9	-25	-49
1,527	1,109	799	587	0	-5	-16	-35	-65	2	0	-9	-26	-53
1,896	1,557	1,269	1,028	0	-4	-16	-35	-63	2	0	-9	-26	-52

CALIBER	BULLET WGT-GRS	BULLET TYPE	BULLET STYLE	VELOCITY in FPS						ENERGY IN FT.-LBS.	
				MUZZLE	100 YDS.	200 YDS.	300 YDS.	400 YDS.	500 YDS.	MUZZLE	100 YDS.
.300 OSSM	150	SP	FB	3,045	2,735	2,445	2,170	1,915	1,685	3,088	2,490
.300 Savage	150	SP	FB	2,630	2,350	2,090	1,850	1,630	1,430	2,305	1,845
	180	SP	FB	2,350	2,140	1,930	1,750	1,570	1,410	2,205	1,825
.300 Ruger Comp. Mag.	150	SP	BT	3,300	3,050	2,825	2,605	2,395	2,200	3,627	3,110
	165	SP	BT	3,140	2,920	2,715	2,515	2,325	2,140	3,612	3,126
	180	SP	BT	3,000	2,800	2,615	2,430	2,260	2,090	3,597	3,139
.300 Remington SAUM	150	SP	FB	3,200	2,900	2,620	2,360	2,110	1,880	3,410	2,803
	165	SP	FB	3,075	2,790	2,525	2,275	2,040	1,820	3,464	2,856
	180	SP	FB	2,960	2,725	2,505	2,295	2,095	1,905	3,501	2,972
	190	HP	BT	2,900	2,725	2,555	2,395	2,240	2,090	3,547	3,133
.300 Winchester SM	130	PT	FB	3,500	3,200	2,930	2,670	2,420	2,190	3,535	2,965
	150	PT	BT	3,300	3,060	2,835	2,620	2,415	2,220	3,628	3,121
	165	SP	FB	3,130	2,910	2,710	2,510	2,320	2,140	3,590	3,110
	180	PT	BT	3,010	2,825	2,650	2,485	2,320	2,165	3,621	3,195
.300 Winchester Mag.	130	SP	BT	3,500	3,200	2,930	2,670	2,420	2,190	3,535	2,965
	150	PT	BT	3,260	3,030	2,810	2,605	2,405	2,215	3,539	3,057
	150	SP	FB	3,290	2,965	2,665	2,385	2,120	1,875	3,605	2,931
	165	PT	BT	3,050	2,800	2,560	2,340	2,120	1,920	3,410	2,870
	180	SP	FB	3,100	2,872	2,655	2,450	2,250	2,065	3,840	3,296
	190	HP	BT	2,900	2,730	2,560	2,400	2,240	2,090	3,550	3,135
	200	SP	FB	2,700	2,480	2,260	2,060	1,870	1,690	3,235	2,720
.300 Remington UM	150	PT	BT	3,450	3,210	2,980	2,760	2,555	2,360	3,964	3,427
	180	PT	BT	3,250	3,050	2,855	2,670	2,495	2,325	4,221	3,714
8x57JSmm Mauser	170	SP	FB	2,360	1,970	1,620	1,335	1,125	995	2,102	1,463
	196	SP	FB	2,525	2,270	2,030	1,800	1,595	1,410	2,774	2,240
8x57JRSmm Mauser	196	SP	FB	2,395	2,145	1,915	1,695	1,500	1,330	2,496	2,005
	196	SP	FB	2,485	2,230	1,995	1,770	1,565	1,385	2,687	2,166
8x68Smm	200	SP	FB	2,955	2,695	2,445	2,210	1,990	1,785	3,877	3,221
.32 Winchester Special	165	SP	FB	2,410	2,145	1,900	1,670	1,465	1,290	2,128	1,687
	170	SP	FB	2,250	1,920	1,625	1,370	1,175	1,045	1,911	1,393
.325 Winchester SM	180	PT	BT	3,060	2,840	2,630	2,430	2,240	2,060	3,743	3,226
	200	PT	BT	2,950	2,760	2,580	2,410	2,240	2,080	3,864	3,387
	220	SP	FB	2,840	2,605	2,380	2,170	1,970	1,780	3,941	3,316
8mm Remington Mag.	180	PT	BT	3,200	2,950	2,710	2,485	2,270	2,070	4,092	3,475
	200	SP	FB	2,900	2,625	2,360	2,115	1,885	1,670	3,734	3,054
.338 Marlin Express	200	SP	FB	2,565	2,365	2,175	1,990	1,820	1,660	2,922	2,484
.338 Ruger Comp. Mag.	200	PT	BT	2,950	2,745	2,545	2,360	2,180	2,005	3,865	3,344
	225	PT	BT	2,775	2,600	2,425	2,264	2,105	1,955	3,847	3,372
.338 Federal	180	SP	FB	2,700	2,480	2,280	2,080	1,900	1,720	3,235	2,740
	210	SP	FB	2,630	2,410	2,200	2,010	1,820	1,650	3,225	2,710
.338 Winchester Mag.	180	PT	BT	3,120	2,860	2,610	2,380	2,160	1,950	3,890	3,265
	200	SP	FB	2,960	2,660	2,375	2,110	1,860	1,635	3,890	3,137
	200	PT	BT	2,950	2,725	2,510	2,305	2,110	1,920	3,864	3,294
	225	PT	BT	2,800	2,635	2,474	2,320	2,170	2,025	3,918	3,467
	250	SP	FB	2,660	2,455	2,260	2,075	1,900	1,730	3,927	3,348
.338 Remington UM	210	SP	FB	3,050	2,810	2,580	2,370	2,160	1,970	4,335	3,685
	225	PT	BT	3,020	2,850	2,680	2,520	2,360	2,210	4,555	4,045
	250	SP	FB	2,860	2,645	2,445	2,250	2,065	1,885	4,540	3,888
.338 Lapua Magnum	250	HP	BT	2,960	2,820	2,685	2,551	2,425	2,300	4,863	4,412
.338 Norma Magnum	NA	NA	NA	NA							
.338 Blaser Magnum	230	SP	FB	2,820	2,575	2,340	2,120	1,915	1,720	4,061	3,385

ENERGY IN FT.-LBS.				BULLET PATH AT ZERO DISTANCE INDICATED									
200 YDS.	300 YDS.	400 YDS.	500 YDS.	100 YDS.	200 YDS.	300 YDS.	400 YDS.	500 YDS.	100 YDS.	200 YDS.	300 YDS.	400 YDS.	500 YDS.
1,990	1,570	1,224	944	0	-3	-12	-28	-55	2	0	-8	-22	-47
1,460	1,140	885	680	0	-5	-16	-35	-63	2	0	-9	-26	-52
1,495	1,215	985	795	0	-6	-20	-44	-80	3	0	-11	-32	-65
2,660	2,260	1,914	1,609	0	-2	-9	-21	-38	1	0	-6	-16	-33
2,697	2,316	1,979	1,681	0	-3	-10	-23	-42	1	0	-6	-18	-35
2,729	2,363	2,037	1,747	0	-3	-11	-25	-46	2	0	-7	-19	-38
2,290	1,854	1,485	1,177	0	-3	-10	-24	-45	1	0	-6	-19	-38
2,339	1,898	1,525	1,213	0	-3	-11	-26	-48	2	0	-7	-20	-40
2,509	2,105	1,753	1,449	0	-3	-12	-27	-49	2	0	-7	-21	-41
2,758	2,420	2,115	1,840	0	-3	-12	-26	-48	2	0	-7	-20	-40
2,475	2,055	1,690	1,385	0	-2	-8	-19	-36	1	0	-5	-15	-31
2,676	2,285	1,941	1,638	0	-2	-9	-20	-38	1	0	-6	-16	-32
2,680	2,305	1,970	1,675	0	-3	-10	-23	-42	1	0	-6	-18	-36
2,811	2,465	2,153	1,873	0	-3	-11	-24	-44	1	0	-6	-18	-37
2,475	2,055	1,690	1,385	0	-2	-8	-19	-36	1	0	-5	-15	-31
2,632	2,256	1,925	1,633	0	-2	-9	-21	-39	1	0	-6	-16	-33
2,366	1,893	1,496	1,168	0	-3	-10	-23	-43	1	0	-6	-18	-37
2,400	1,995	1,650	1,345	0	-3	-11	-26	-47	2	0	-7	-13	-40
2,817	2,396	2,025	1,701	0	-3	-10	-24	-44	1	0	-6	-18	-37
2,760	2,420	2,115	1,845	0	-3	-12	-26	-48	2	0	-7	-20	-40
2,275	1,885	1,550	1,265	0	-4	-15	-33	-59	2	0	-9	-25	-49
2,956	2,541	2,175	1,852	0	-2	-8	-18	-34	1	0	-5	-14	-29
3,260	2,853	2,487	2,160	0	-2	-9	-20	-37	1	0	-5	-16	-32
993	671	476	375	0	-6	-19	-43	-79	3	0	-11	-32	-65
1,790	1,414	1,110	867	0	-5	-19	-44	-82	3	0	-11	-33	-69
1,592	1,254	980	770	0	-6	-22	-50	-93	3	0	-13	-38	-78
1,728	1,363	1,069	836	0	-6	-20	-46	-85	3	0	-12	-35	-71
2,656	2,173	1,761	1,413	0	-3	-12	-29	-54	2	0	-8	-22	-46
1,319	1,023	787	611	0	-6	-22	-50	-95	3	0	-13	-38	-80
998	710	521	411	0	-8	-29	-70	-135	4	0	-17	-53	-115
2,769	2,365	2,009	1,696	0	-3	-11	-24	-45	1	0	-6	-19	-38
2,959	2,574	2,230	1,923	0	-3	-11	-26	-47	2	0	-7	-19	-39
2,772	2,300	1,893	1,547	0	-3	-12	-28	-52	2	0	-7	-21	-44
2,937	2,469	2,061	1,709	0	-3	-10	-23	-42	1	0	-6	-18	-36
2,476	1,987	1,577	1,241	0	-4	-13	-31	-59	2	0	-8	-24	-50
2,099	1,762	1,471	1,221	0	-5	-17	-38	-69	2	0	-10	-28	-57
2,881	2,471	2,108	1,787	0	-3	-12	-26	-48	2	0	-7	-20	-41
2,944	2,560	2,216	1,909	0	-4	-13	-30	-53	2	0	-8	-22	-44
2,305	1,925	1,595	1,315	0	-4	-15	-34	-63	2	0	-9	-25	-52
2,265	1,880	1,545	1,265	0	-5	-16	-36	-68	2	0	-9	-27	-56
2,730	2,265	1,865	1,520	0	-3	-11	-25	-46	1	0	-6	-19	-39
2,505	1,977	1,539	1,187	0	-3	-13	-30	-58	2	0	-8	-24	-50
2,794	2,355	1,972	1,640	0	-3	-12	-27	-50	2	0	-7	-21	-42
3,058	2,688	2,353	2,052	0	-4	-13	-28	-51	2	0	-7	-21	-43
2,837	2,389	1,999	1,663	0	-4	-15	-34	-64	2	0	-9	-26	-53
3,115	2,615	2,180	1,805	0	-3	-11	-25	-47	2	0	-7	-20	-40
3,585	3,165	2,785	2,445	0	-3	-11	-24	-43	1	0	-6	-18	-36
3,314	2,807	2,363	1,977	0	-3	-13	-29	-53	2	0	-8	-22	-44
3,996	3,613	3,259	2,932	0	-3	-11	-24	-43	2	0	-6	-18	-35
2,802	2,300	1,870	1,511	0	-4	-14	-32	-59	2	0	-8	-24	-50

CALIBER	BULLET WGT-GRS	BULLET TYPE	BULLET STYLE	VELOCITY in FPS						ENERGY IN FT.-LBS.	
				MUZZLE	100 YDS.	200 YDS.	300 YDS.	400 YDS.	500 YDS.	MUZZLE	100 YDS.
.35 Remington	150	SP	FB	2,300	1,875	1,505	1,220	1,040	935	1,762	1,169
	200	SP	FB	2,080	1,700	1,375	1,140	1,000	910	1,921	1,280
.35 Whelen	200	SP	FB	2,675	2,380	2,100	1,840	1,605	1,400	3,177	2,510
	250	SP	FB	2,400	2,195	2,005	1,825	1,650	1,495	3,197	2,680
.350 Remington Mag.	200	SP	FB	2,775	2,470	2,185	1,920	1,680	1,460	3,419	2,711
.356 Winchester	200	SP	FB	2,460	2,115	1,795	1,515	1,285	1,115	2,688	1,985
9.3x57mm Mauser	232	SP	FB	2,360	2,060	1,780	1,530	1,315	1,150	2,869	2,180
	285	SP	FB	2,065	1,860	1,665	1,490	1,335	1,205	2,698	2,183
9.3x62mm Mauser	232	SP	FB	2,625	2,305	2,005	1,730	1,485	1,280	3,549	2,731
	250	SP	FB	2,625	2,320	2,040	1,780	1,540	1,340	3,825	2,993
	285	SP	FB	2,430	2,205	1,990	1,785	1,600	1,430	3,736	3,070
	325	SP	FB	2,300	2,065	1,840	1,635	1,450	1,295	3,817	3,072
9.3x66mm Sako	286	SP	FB	2,550	2,370	2,190	2,020	1,860	1,710	4,130	3,555
9.3x74Rmm	285	PT	FB	2,360	2,135	1,925	1,725	1,545	1,385	3,524	2,888
.375 Winchester	200	SP	FB	2,200	1,840	1,525	1,270	1,090	980	2,150	1,506
.375 Ruger	270	SP	FB	2,840	2,600	2,370	2,155	1,950	1,760	4,835	4,052
	300	SP	FB	2,660	2,345	2,050	1,780	1,535	1,330	4,713	3,660
.375 H&H Magnum	270	SP	FB	2,690	2,365	2,060	1,780	1,530	1,315	4,338	3,347
	270	SP	FB	2,870	2,630	2,400	2,180	1,975	1,780	4,937	4,141
	300	SP	FB	2,520	2,280	2,050	1,835	1,635	1,460	4,238	3,462
	350	SP	FB	2,300	2,050	1,815	1,605	1,410	1,250	4,111	3,266
.375 H&H Flanged Mag.	350	SP	FB	2,200	1,960	1,730	1,525	1,340	1,200	3,761	2,973
.375 Remington UM	270	SP	FB	2,900	2,560	2,240	1,945	1,680	1,440	5,041	3,922
	300	SP	FB	2,760	2,505	2,265	2,055	1,820	1,625	5,073	4,178
.375 Blaser Magnum	300	SP	FB	2,690	2,450	2,225	2,010	1,810	1,625	4,820	4,003
.375 Norma Magnum	NA	NA	NA	NA							
.376 Steyr	225	SP	FB	2,600	2,330	2,080	1,840	1,625	1,430	3,377	2,714
	270	SP	FB	2,600	2,370	2,155	1,950	1,760	1,580	4,052	3,373
.38-55 Winchester	255	L	FB	1,320	1,190	1,090	1,020	965	915	987	802
.404 Jeffery	450	SP/FMJ	FB	2,150	1,940	1,740	1,560	1,395	1,250	4,618	3,749
.416 Ruger	400	SP	FB	2,840	2,150	1,915	1,700	1,405	1,180	5,116	4,109
.416 Rigby	400	SP	FB	2,370	2,160	1,960	1,770	1,600	1,440	4,988	4,141
.416 Remington Mag.	400	SP	FB	2,400	2,175	1,960	1,760	1,580	1,415	5,115	4,201
.416 Barrett	395	Solid	BT	3,300	3,155	3,015	2,880	2,745	2,620	9,548	8,729
.44-40 Winchester	200	SP	FB	1,190	1,005	900	820	755	700	629	449
.444 Marlin	240	SP	FB	2,350	1,815	1,375	1,085	940	845	2,942	1,755
	265	SP	FB	2,325	1,970	1,650	1,380	1,170	1,035	3,180	2,285
.45-70 Government	300	SP	FB	1,880	1,650	1,425	1,235	1,105	1,010	2,355	1,815
	405	SP	FB	1,330	1,170	1,035	975	920	870	1,590	1,227
.450 Bushmaster	250	SP	FB	2,200	1,830	1,510	1,250	1,075	965	2,686	1,860
.450 Marlin	325	SP	FB	2,225	1,885	1,585	1,330	1,140	1,020	3,572	2,567
	350	SP	FB	2,100	1,720	1,395	1,155	1,010	920	3,427	2,296
.458 Winchester Mag.	400	SP	FB	2,250	1,820	1,580	1,370	1,200	1,080	4,850	3,685
	500	SP	FB	2,140	1,880	1,645	1,430	1,250	1,120	5,084	3,926
	510	SP	FB	2,040	1,770	1,525	1,320	1,155	1,045	4,712	3,547
.458 Lott	500	PT	FB	2,280	2,090	1,900	1,730	1,560	1,420	5,770	4,835
.450/400 NE 2 3/8 in.	400	SP	FB	2,125	1,885	1,670	1,475	1,305	1,165	4,010	3,165
.450/400 Nitro Exp. 3 in.	400	SP	FB	2,100	1,845	1,610	1,405	1,230	1,105	3,917	3,016
.450 Nitro Exp. 3 1/4 in.	400	SP	FB	2,150	1,850	1,600	1,380	1,200	1,075	4,010	3,031
.450 No.2 NE 3 1/2 in.	480	SP	FB	2,175	1,905	1,660	1,440	1,260	1,120	4,201	3,224
.450 Rigby	550	SP/FMJ	FB	2,100	1,875	1,670	1,480	1,315	1,180	5,385	4,292

ENERGY IN FT.-LBS.				BULLET PATH AT ZERO DISTANCE INDICATED									
200 YDS.	300 YDS.	400 YDS.	500 YDS.	100 YDS.	200 YDS.	300 YDS.	400 YDS.	500 YDS.	100 YDS.	200 YDS.	300 YDS.	400 YDS.	500 YDS.
755	494	359	291	0	-9	-33	-81	-160	4	0	-20	-64	-139
841	577	445	369	0	-11	-40	-97	-186	5	0	-24	-75	-159
1,958	1,506	1,145	869	0	-5	-17	-41	-77	2	0	-10	-31	-65
2,230	1,844	1,515	1,242	0	-6	-20	-45	-83	3	0	-11	-34	-69
2,122	1,639	1,250	947	0	-4	-16	-37	-70	2	0	-9	-29	-60
1,434	1,022	732	550	0	-6	-24	-56	-111	3	0	-14	-44	-95
1,628	1,203	892	683	0	-7	-25	-58	-111	3	0	-15	-44	-94
1,756	1,405	1,129	920	0	-9	-30	-67	-124	4	0	-17	-49	-102
2,069	1,542	1,138	846	0	-5	-19	-45	-86	3	0	-11	-34	-74
2,310	1,756	1,323	998	0	-5	-18	-43	-82	3	0	-11	-33	-70
2,500	2,016	1,619	1,194	0	-6	-20	-46	-85	3	0	-12	-35	-71
2,445	1,934	1,521	1,206	0	-7	-24	-54	-101	3	0	-14	-41	-84
3,045	2,595	2,195	1,855	0	-5	-17	-37	-68	2	0	-10	-28	-56
2,343	1,888	1,513	1,212	0	-6	-22	-49	-91	3	0	-13	-37	-76
1,034	714	527	427	0	-9	-33	-79	-154	5	0	-20	-61	-132
3,373	2,786	2,283	1,855	0	-4	-14	-31	-57	2	0	-8	-23	-48
2,800	2,110	1,572	1,174	0	-5	-18	-42	-82	2	0	-11	-33	-69
2,543	1,900	1,403	1,039	0	-5	-18	-42	-81	2	0	-11	-33	-69
3,450	2,853	2,339	1,903	0	-4	-13	-30	-56	2	0	-8	-23	-47
2,802	2,245	1,786	1,415	0	-5	-19	-43	-80	3	0	-11	-32	-67
2,563	1,998	1,550	1,217	0	-7	-24	-55	-104	3	0	-14	-42	-87
2,327	1,807	1,407	1,116	0	-8	-27	-62	-115	4	0	-16	-46	-96
3,010	2,272	1,689	1,246	0	-4	-15	-35	-67	2	0	-9	-27	-58
3,412	2,759	2,210	1,757	0	-4	-15	-34	-64	2	0	-9	-26	-54
3,299	2,695	2,182	1,759	0	-4	-16	-36	-67	2	0	-9	-27	-56
2,157	1,694	1,319	1,023	0	-5	-18	-42	-78	3	0	-10	-32	-66
2,787	2,283	1,855	1,500	0	-5	-17	-38	-71	2	0	-10	-29	-60
674	587	525	476	0	-23	-75	-160	-282	12	0	-41	-114	-225
3,021	2,421	1,937	1,567	0	-8	-28	-61	-113	4	0	-16	-45	-93
3,264	2,568	1,757	1,238	0	-5	-18	-43	-86	2	0	-11	-34	-75
3,410	2,788	2,266	1,840	0	-6	-21	-47	-87	3	0	-12	-36	-72
3,419	2,760	2,214	1,775	0	-6	-21	-47	-87	3	0	-12	-36	-73
7,970	7,269	6,619	6,018	0	-2	-8	-18	-32	1	0	-5	-14	-28
360	300	254	217	0	-32	-107	-231	-415	16	0	-58	-167	-334
1,010	630	472	381	0	-9	-38	-95	-188	5	0	-24	-76	-164
1,606	1,120	806	630	0	-8	-28	-67	-132	4	0	-17	-52	-113
1,355	1,015	810	680	0	-12	-41	-93	-173	6	0	-23	-70	-144
1,001	858	758	679	0	-24	-79	-169	-299	12	0	-43	-121	-240
1,262	864	639	519	0	-9	-34	-81	-158	5	0	-20	-63	-135
1,814	1,278	937	748	0	-9	-31	-73	-143	4	0	-18	-56	-121
1,512	1,036	793	656	0	-10	-39	-94	-181	5	0	-23	-73	-155
2,775	2,080	1,595	1,285	0	-8	-28	-67	-128	4	0	-17	-51	-109
2,996	2,276	1,742	1,389	0	-9	-30	-69	-130	4	0	-17	-51	-108
2,640	1,970	1,516	1,239	0	-10	-35	-79	-150	5	0	-20	-60	-126
4,000	3,305	2,715	2,225	0	-6	-23	-51	-93	3	0	-13	-38	-77
2,478	1,927	1,509	1,209	0	-9	-29	-66	-124	4	0	-17	-49	-103
2,302	1,747	1,347	1,082	0	-9	-31	-71	-135	5	0	-18	-53	-112
2,267	1,687	1,282	1,028	0	-9	-31	-72	-138	5	0	-18	-55	-116
2,448	1,843	1,405	1,115	0	-8	-29	-67	-127	4	0	-17	-50	-106
3,399	2,674	2,116	1,706	0	-9	-30	-67	-124	4	0	-17	-49	-102

CALIBER	BULLET WGT-GRS	BULLET TYPE	BULLET STYLE	VELOCITY in FPS						ENERGY IN FT.-LBS.	
				MUZZLE	100 YDS.	200 YDS.	300 YDS.	400 YDS.	500 YDS.	MUZZLE	100 YDS.
.470 Nitro Express	500	SP/FMJ	FB	2,150	1,885	1,645	1,430	1,250	1,115	5,132	3,943
.475 No.2 Jeffery	500	SP/FMJ	FB	2,150	1,880	1,635	1,415	1,235	1,105	5,132	3,921
.475 Turnbull	400	HP	FB	2,150	1,895	1,665	1,460	1,285	1,145	4,105	3,197
.500/416 Nitro Express	450	SP/FMJ	FB	2,100	1,885	1,690	1,510	1,350	1,215	4,406	3,557
.500 NE 3 in.	570	SP/FMJ	FB	2,100	1,960	1,820	1,695	1,570	1,455	5,581	4,848
.500 NE 3 1/2 in	570	SP/FMJ	FB	2,150	1,880	1,635	1,420	1,240	1,105	5,850	4,479
.500 Jeffery	570	SP/FMJ	FB	2,200	1,985	1,785	1,600	1,235	1,290	6,125	4,995
.50 BMG	750	PT	BT	2,815	2,630	2,455	2,290	2,125	1,970	13,195	11,536
.505 Gibbs	600	SP/FMJ	FB	2,100	1,885	1,690	1,510	1,350	1,215	5,875	4,742
.577 Nitro Express	750	SP/FMJ	FB	2,050	1,795	1,570	1,370	1,205	1,085	6,998	5,382
.600 Nitro Express	900	FMJ	FB	1,950	1,650	1,390	1,185	1,050	960	7,598	5,438
.700 Nitro Express	1,000	SP/FMJ	FB	2,000	1,800	1,575	1,375	1,210	1,090	8,878	5,398

CHAPTER 59 : CENTERFIRE SPORTING RIFLE - OBSOLETE

CALIBER	BULLET WGT-GRS	BULLET TYPE	BULLET STYLE	VELOCITY in FPS						ENERGY IN FT.-LBS.	
				MUZZLE	100 YDS.	200 YDS.	300 YDS.	400 YDS.	500 YDS.	MUZZLE	100 YDS.
.219 Zipper	55	SP	RN	3,110	2,630	2,200	1,810	1,475	1,210	1,181	845
.22 Win. Centerfire	45	L	FN	1,540	1,075	835	695	585	490	237	115
5.6x35Rmm Vierling	39	SP	FN	1,940	1,340	1,010	860	760	675	326	155
.222 Rem. Magnum	55	HP	PTD	3,240	2,775	2,350	1,970	1,625	1,340	1,282	8,940
.225 Winchester	55	SP	PTD	3,570	3,065	2,615	2,210	1,840	1,515	1,556	1,148
5.6x33mm Rook	65	SP	RN	1,425	1,050	890	780	695	620	293	159
5.6x39mm Russian	54	SP	PTD	2,995	2,415	1,905	1,475	1,160	990	1,075	700
.242 Rimless Nitro Express	100	SP	RN	2,800	2,545	2,305	2,080	1,865	1,670	1,741	1,440
.244 Remington	75	SP	PTD	3,500	3,145	2,815	2,510	2,220	1,954	2,040	1,645
	90	SP	PTD	3,200	2,900	2,620	2,360	2,110	1,875	2,046	1,681
6x57mm Mauser	120	SP	PTD	2,700	2,465	2,240	2,030	1,830	1,645	1,942	1,618
6x58mm Forester	127	SP	PTD	2,790	2,475	2,255	2,050	1,860	1,680	2,056	1,725
.25 Remington	100	SP	PTD	2,330	2,045	1,785	1,550	1,345	1,180	1,205	931
	117	SP	RN	2,125	1,810	1,530	1,295	1,120	1,010	1,173	850
.25-20 Single Shot	86	L	FN	1,410	1,160	1,010	915	845	785	380	257
.25-20 Winchester	86	SP	FN	1,460	1,195	1,030	930	860	795	407	272
.25-35 Winchester	117	SP	FN	2,230	1,865	1,545	1,280	1,095	985	1,292	905
.25-36 Marlin	117	SP	FN	1,855	1,535	1,275	1,090	980	905	894	613
6.5mm Rem. Magnum	120	SP	PTD	3,210	2,905	2,620	2,355	2,100	1,865	2,745	2,248
6.5x54mm Mauser	119	SP	PTD	2,300	2,050	1,820	1,610	1,420	1,260	1,409	1,122
6.5x58mm Mauser	139	SP	PTD	2,775	2,540	2,315	2,110	1,905	1,720	2,377	1,992
6.5x61mm Mauser	139	SP	PTD	2,905	2,665	2,435	2,220	2,010	1,820	2,604	2,190
.26 Belted Nitro Express	110	SP	PTD	3,100	2,825	2,570	2,325	2,095	1,875	2,560	2,127
.264 Win. Magnum	140	SP	PTD	3,030	2,780	2,550	2,325	2,115	1,915	2,854	2,406
7 BR Remington	140	SP	PTD	2,215	2,010	1,820	1,644	1,480	1,335	1,525	1,259
.280 Flanged Nitro Express	140	SP	PTD	2,800	2,570	2,350	2,140	1,945	1,755	2,437	2,052
	160	HP	PTD	2,600	2,300	2,020	1,760	1,530	1,330	2,401	1,879
.280 Ross	140	SP	PTD	2,900	2,665	2,440	2,225	2,025	1,835	2,614	2,206
	160	HP	PTD	2,700	2,395	2,110	1,845	1,605	1,390	2,590	2,040
	180	SP	PTD	2,550	2,365	2,190	2,020	1,855	1,705	2,599	2,235
7x33mm Sako	78	SP	RN	2,400	1,895	1,480	1,170	1,000	895	997	620
7x61mm Sharp & Hart Super	150	JSP	PTD	3,060	2,785	2,530	2,285	2,060	1,840	3,118	2,587
7x72mm	139	JSP	FN	2,440	2,040	1,685	1,385	1,155	1,015	1,837	1,287
.297/250 Rook Rifle	56	L	RN	1,150	930	805	710	630	560	164	107
.30 Remington	170	SP	RN	2,120	1,820	1,555	1,330	1,155	1,035	1,696	1,253

ENERGY IN FT.-LBS.				BULLET PATH AT ZERO DISTANCE INDICATED									
200 YDS.	300 YDS.	400 YDS.	500 YDS.	100 YDS.	200 YDS.	300 YDS.	400 YDS.	500 YDS.	100 YDS.	200 YDS.	300 YDS.	400 YDS.	500 YDS.
3,001	2,266	1,734	1,380	0	-9	-30	-68	-130	4	0	-17	-51	-108
2,966	2,227	1,699	1,352	0	-9	-30	-69	-131	4	0	-17	-52	-110
2,468	1,890	1,461	1,144	0	-8	-29	-67	-125	4	0	-17	-50	-104
2,855	2,277	1,822	1,477	0	-9	-29	-65	-120	4	0	-16	-48	-99
4,194	3,623	3,120	2,682	0	-8	-26	-57	-101	4	0	-15	-41	-82
3,395	2,554	1,950	1,552	0	-9	-30	-69	-131	4	0	-17	-52	-109
4,036	3,247	2,600	2,102	0	-7	-26	-58	-107	4	0	-15	-43	-88
10,047	8,712	7,521	6,459	0	-4	-13	-29	-52	2	0	-8	-22	-43
3,805	3,033	2,427	1,967	0	-9	-29	-65	-120	4	0	-16	-48	-99
4,105	3,123	2,422	1,966	0	-10	-33	-75	-142	5	0	-19	-56	-118
3,857	2,811	2,203	1,849	0	-11	-41	-95	-180	6	0	-24	-73	-152
4,130	3,151	2,448	1,985	0	-10	-33	-75	-141	5	0	-19	-56	-117

CHAPTER 59 : CENTERFIRE SPORTING RIFLE - OBSOLETE

ENERGY IN FT.-LBS.				BULLET PATH AT ZERO DISTANCE INDICATED									
200 YDS.	300 YDS.	400 YDS.	500 YDS.	100 YDS.	200 YDS.	300 YDS.	400 YDS.	500 YDS.	100 YDS.	200 YDS.	300 YDS.	400 YDS.	500 YDS.
591	400	266	179	0	-4	-14	-36	-75	2	0	-9	-29	-66
70	48	34	24	0	-29	-105	-250	-493	15	0	-62	-193	-177
88	64	50	39	0	-18	-69	-163	-312	9	0	-42	-126	-266
675	475	325	220	0	-3	-13	-31	-64	2	0	-8	-25	-56
836	595	412	280	0	-2	-10	-24		1	0	-13	-31	-64
114	88	70	55	0	-29	-101	-226	-421	15	0	-57	-168	-347
436	261	162	117	0	-5	-19	-50	-108	2	0	-12	-41	-96
1,181	961	773	619	0	-4	-14	-33	-62	2	0	-9	-25	-52
1,318	1,047	822	636	0	-2	-9	-21	-39	1	0	-5	-16	-34
1,373	1,111	890	704	0	-3	-10	-24	-46	1	0	-6	-19	-39
1,337	1,096	891	720	0	-4	-15	-35	-66	2	0	-9	-26	-55
1,437	1,188	973	794	0	-4	-15	-34	-64	2	0	-9	-26	-54
708	534	402	310	0	-7	-25	-57	-109	3	0	-15	-44	-92
608	436	327	266	0	-9	-34	-79	152	5	0	-20	-60	-128
195	161	137	118	0	-24	-82	-179	-322	12	0	-46	-131	-262
203	165	141	121	0	-23	-78	-172	-310	12	0	-44	-126	-253
620	426	312	252	0	-8	-28	-66	-127	4	0	-16	-50	-107
422	310	250	212	0	-13	-48	-112	-210	7	0	-28	-85	-177
1,830	1,475	1,177	929	0	-3	-10	-24	-46	1	0	-6	-19	-39
883	690	536	422	0	-7	-24	-55	-103	3	0	-14	-42	-87
1,659	1,370	1,122	913	0	-4	-14	-32	-60	2	0	-9	-25	-51
1,830	1,520	1,250	1,020	0	-3	-13	-29	-54	2	0	-8	-22	-45
1,757	1,439	1,168	938	0	-3	-11	-26	-48	1	0	-7	-20	-41
2,018	1,682	1,389	1,139	0	-3	-11	-26	-49	2	0	-7	-20	-41
1,030	840	681	555	0	-7	-25	-55	-102	4	0	-14	-41	-84
1,716	1,425	1,174	960	0	-4	-14	-31	-58	2	0	-8	-24	-49
1,450	1,103	831	628	0	-5	-19	-44	-84	3	0	-11	-34	-71
1,850	1,542	1,274	1,044	0	-3	-13	-29	-54	2	0	-8	-22	-45
1,580	1,208	914	688	0	-5	-17	-40	-76	2	0	-10	-31	-65
1,913	1,628	1,377	1,161	0	-5	-17	-37	-68	3	0	-10	-28	-56
379	238	173	139	0	-8	-33	-83	-167	4	0	-21	-67	-145
2,132	1,742	1,410	1,130	0	-3	-11	-27	-50	2	0	-7	-21	-42
878	591	413	319	0	-7	-26	-64	-129	4	0	-16	-50	-111
81	63	50	39	0	-38	-129	-287	-529	19	0	-72	-210	-433
913	666	502	405	0	-9	-33	-76	-146	5	0	-19	-58	-123

CALIBER	BULLET WGT-GRS	BULLET TYPE	BULLET STYLE	VELOCITY in FPS						ENERGY IN FT.-LBS.	
				MUZZLE	100 YDS.	200 YDS.	300 YDS.	400 YDS.	500 YDS.	MUZZLE	100 YDS.
.300 (.295) Rook Rifle	80	L	RN	1,100	900	785	690	610	540	215	145
.300 Sherwood	140	L	RN	1,400	1,120	860	755	666	590	609	325
.303 Savage	180	SP	PTD	2,120	1,815	1,535	1,310	1,135	1,020	1,796	1,314
	190	SP	RN	1,940	1,655	1,410	1,210	1,070	980	1,588	1,158
.30-30 Wesson	165	SP	RN	1,250	1,070	965	890	830	775	572	421
8x42Rmm	157	SP	RN	1,780	1,550	1,350	1,185	1,070	990	1,104	836
8x51mm Mauser	158	SP	RN	2,300	2,025	1,770	1,540	1,340	1,180	1,856	1,438
	196	SP	RN	2,100	1,830	1,585	1,370	1,195	1,075	1,939	1,469
8x51Rmm Mauser	157	SP	RN	2,155	1,890	1,650	1,435	1,255	1,120	1,619	1,246
8x56mm Mann-Sch.	196	SP	RN	2,120	1,905	1,665	1,450	1,270	1,130	2,090	1,614
8x54mm Krag-Jorgensen	196	SP	RN	2,295	1,985	1,700	1,450	1,245	1,100	2,292	1,714
8x60mm Mauser	159	SP	RN	2,820	2,515	2,230	1,960	1,715	1,495	2,807	2,232
	196	SP	RN	2,580	2,250	1,940	1,660	1,420	1,220	2,897	2,198
8x75Rmm Brenneke	198	SP	RN	3,050	2,711	2,395	2,105	1,830	1,585	4,089	3,231
8x75Rmm Brenneke S	198	SP	RN	2,715	2,370	2,055	1,765	1,505	1,290	3,240	2,474
8.15x46Rmm	151	SP	FN	1,805	1,460	1,195	1,030	930	855	1,092	714
.32 Ideal	150	L	FN	1,250	1,060	950	875	810	755	520	375
.32 Long Centerfire	85	L	RN	850	745	635	545	470	400	136	104
.32 Remington	170	SP	RN	2,140	1,785	1,475	1,230	1,065	960	1,728	1,203
.32 Win. Self-Loading	165	SP	RN	1,400	1,175	1,005	870	765	655	718	507
.32-20 Winchester	100	L	FN	1,210	1,020	915	835	770	710	325	232
	115	L	FN	1,490	1,225	1,055	950	875	815	567	384
.32-30 Rem.-Hepburn	125	L	FN	1,380	1,130	990	895	825	765	529	354
.32-40 Rem.-Hepburn	150	L	FN	1,350	1,135	1,005	915	850	795	607	428
.32-40 Winchester	170	L	FN	1,530	1,325	1,165	1,050	975	915	883	663
.33 Winchester	200	SP	FN	2,200	1,875	1,590	1,345	1,155	1,030	2,149	1,564
.348 Winchester	200	SP	RN	2,520	2,215	1,930	1,670	1,445	1,255	2,820	2,178
.35 Win. Self-Loading	180	SP	RN	1,450	1,230	1,075	980	910	850	840	603
.35 Winchester	250	SP	RN	2,150	1,910	1,695	1,495	1,320	1,180	2,566	2,028
.351 Win. Self-Loading	180	SP	RN	1,850	1,555	1,310	1,130	1,010	935	1,368	968
.358 Winchester	200	SP	RN	2,490	2,170	1,875	1,610	1,380	1,195	2,753	2,093
	250	SP	RN	2,230	1,990	1,760	1,560	1,375	1,225	2,760	2,194
.360 Nitro Express 2 1/4 in.	300	SP	RN	1,650	1,490	1,345	1,220	1,125	1,050	1,813	1,474
.360 No.2 Nitro Express	320	SP	RN	2,200	1,985	1,780	1,590	1,420	1,275	3,439	2,793
.360 No. 5 Rook	145	L	RN	1,075	895	780	690	615	545	372	257
.369 Nitro Express Purdy	270	SP	RN	2,500	2,135	1,800	1,505	1,265	1,095	3,747	2,729
.38 Long Centerfire	145	L	RN	950	810	705	620	545	475	291	211
.38-40 Rem.-Hepburn	245	L	FN	1,200	1,075	990	925	875	830	783	628
.38-40 Winchester	180	SP	FN	1,330	1,055	920	825	750	685	707	445
.38-50 Rem-Hepburn	255	L	RN	1,320	1,155	1,045	970	910	860	986	757
.38-56 Winchester	255	L	FN	1,385	1,215	1,090	1,005	940	890	1,086	835
.38-70 Winchester	255	L	FN	1,475	1,285	1,140	1,040	970	910	1,232	938
.38-72 Winchester	275	L	FN	1,445	1,255	1,115	1,020	950	895	1,275	964
.38-90 Win. Express	217	L	FN	1,575	1,325	1,145	1,025	945	885	1,195	846
9x56mm Mann.-Schoenauer	200	SP	RN	2,110	1,820	1,560	1,340	1,165	1,045	1,977	1,472
	250	SP	RN	2,100	1,890	1,695	1,515	1,360	1,225	2,448	1,983
	280	SP	RN	1,850	1,695	1,550	1,420	1,300	1,200	2,128	1,788
9x57mm Mauser	205	SP	RN	2,425	2,114	1,825	1,570	1,345	1,170	2,677	2,034
	245	SP	RN	2,150	1,935	1,735	1,550	1,350	1,245	2,514	2,035
	281	SP	RN	1,920	1,760	1,615	1,475	1,350	1,240	2,300	1,935
9.3x72Rmm	193	SP	FN	1,950	1,560	1,255	1,055	945	865	1,629	1,046

ENERGY IN FT.-LBS.				BULLET PATH AT ZERO DISTANCE INDICATED									
200 YDS.	300 YDS.	400 YDS.	500 YDS.	100 YDS.	200 YDS.	300 YDS.	400 YDS.	500 YDS.	100 YDS.	200 YDS.	300 YDS.	400 YDS.	500 YDS.
109	85	66	52	0	-41	-137	-305	-564	21	0	-76	-224	-462
231	177	138	108	0	-31	-106	-240	-448	16	0	-60	-178	-371
946	684	514	417	0	-9	-33	-78	-150	5	0	-19	-59	-127
839	619	485	407	0	-11	-40	-93	-176	6	0	-23	-71	-148
341	290	251	220	0	-29	-94	-202	-359	14	0	-51	-145	-287
633	491	400	342	0	-13	-45	-102	-189	7	0	-26	-76	-157
1,099	833	632	490	0	-7	-25	-58	-111	4	0	-15	-44	-93
1,103	824	630	507	0	-9	-32	-74	-140	5	0	-18	-56	-117
949	718	549	437	0	-9	-30	-68	-129	4	0	-17	-51	-107
1,234	935	717	568	0	-8.3	-28.9	-66.5	-125.7	4.1	0	-16.5	-49.9	-105
1,260	916	676	524	0	-8	-27	-63	-122	4	0	-16	-48	-104
1,754	1,359	1,040	790	0	-4	-15	-35	-67	2	0	-9	-27	-57
1,638	1,203	875	648	0	-5	-20	-48	-93	3	0	-12	-37	-80
2,524	1,944	1,473	1,106	0	-3	-13	-30	-58	2	0	-8	-24	-50
1,858	1,370	998	732	0	-5	-18	-42	-82	3	0	-11	-33	-70
477	355	290	246	0	-15	-55	-126	-235	8	0	-32	-96	-197
302	254	219	190	0	-29	-96	-207	-369	14	0	-52	-149	-296
77	56	41	30	0	-62	-211	-476	-904	31	0	-118	-352	-749
821	569	426	349	0	-10	-36	-85	-164	5	0	-21	-66	-141
372	277	214	157	0	24	-81	-185	-347	12	0	-46	-138	-288
185	155	131	113	0	-32	-104	-225	-404	16	0	-57	-162	-325
284	231	196	170	0	-22	-76	-168	-305	11	0	-42	-120	-242
271	223	190	163	0	-26	-86	-188	-338	13	0	-48	-137	-274
335	281	242	211	0	-25	-85	-184	-329	13	0	-47	-133	-265
511	418	358	316	0	-18	-62	-137	-247	9	0	-35	-100	-202
1,122	801	592	473	0	-9	-31	-73	-141	4	0	-18	-56	-129
1,656	1,241	925	697	0	-6	-21	-48	-93	3	0	-12	-37	-79
462	383	330	290	0	-22	-73	-159	-286	11	0	-40	-116	-232
1,590	1,238	969	773	0	-8	-29	-64	-121	4	0	-16	-48	-100
656	508	409	348	0	-13	-46	-106	-199	7	0	-27	-81	-167
1,563	1,151	844	633	0	-6	-22	-51	-99	3	0	-13	-40	-85
1,723	1,346	1,049	832	0	-7	-26	-59	-111	4	0	-15	-44	-92
1,203	993	841	734	0	-14	-48	-105	-189	7	0	-26	-76	-153
2,248	1,800	1,436	1,157	0	-7	-26	-58	-108	4	0	-15	-43	-89
196	154	121	96	0	-42	-139	-309	-569	21	0	-77	-226	-465
1,942	1,360	961	719	0	-6	-23	-56	-111	3	0	-14	-44	-96
161	124	95	73	0	-52	-173	-383	-719	26	0	-95	-280	-582
533	467	417	375	0	-28	-92	-195	-343	14	0	-50	-138	-272
337	272	225	188	0	-29	-98	-216	-393	15	0	-55	-158	-320
618	530	467	418	0	-24	-80	-173	-306	12	0	-44	-124	-245
673	571	502	448	0	-22	-73	-158	-281	11	0	-40	-114	-226
737	612	531	471	0	-20	-66	-143	-257	10	0	-36	-104	-208
760	635	552	490	0	-21	-69	-150	-268	10	0	-38	-109	-217
631	508	432	378	0	-18	-63	-140	-253	9	0	-36	-103	-208
1,083	796	603	487	0	-9	-33	-76	-145	5	0	-19	-57	-122
1,597	1,278	1,025	833	0	-9	-29	-65	-119	4	0	-16	-48	-98
1,497	1,251	1,054	896	0	-11	-36	-78	-141	5	0	-20	-57	-114
1,518	1,120	825	625	0	-6	-23	-54	-105	3	0	-14	-42	-90
1,635	1,306	1,042	842	0	-8	-28	-62	-114	4	0	-16	-46	-94
1,623	1,356	1,138	962	0	-10	-33	-72	-131	5	0	-18	-52	-106
672	477	381	319	0	-13	-48	-114	-216	7	0	-29	-88	-184

CALIBER	BULLET WGT-GRS	BULLET TYPE	BULLET STYLE	VELOCITY in FPS						ENERGY IN FT.-LBS.	
				MUZZLE	100 YDS.	200 YDS.	300 YDS.	400 YDS.	500 YDS.	MUZZLE	100 YDS.
9.5x47Rmm	140	L	RN	1,800	1,440	1,165	1,010	910	840	1,007	642
9.5x57mm Mann.-Schoenauer	272	SP	RN	2,150	1,850	1,580	1,345	1,165	1,043	2,792	2,061
.400 Nitro Express 3in	230	SP	RN	2,050	1,650	1,320	1,095	965	880	2,146	1,389
.401 Win. Self-Loading	200	SP	RN	2,135	1,760	1,435	1,185	1,030	935	2,024	1,372
	250	SP	RN	1,870	1,585	1,340	1,155	1,030	950	1,941	1,393
.40-110 Win. Express	260	SP	FN	1,585	1,305	1,110	990	910	845	1,450	986
.405 Winchester	300	SP	FN	2,200	1,855	1,555	1,300	1,115	1,000	3,224	2,297
.40-65 Winchester	260	SP	FN	1,350	1,135	1,005	920	855	800	1,052	746
.40-60 Marlin	260	SP	FN	1,445	1,200	1,045	950	875	820	1,205	834
.40-60 Winchester	210	L	FN	1,500	1,185	1,010	910	835	765	1,049	657
.40-70 Peabody "What Cheer"	380	L	FN	1,420	1,225	1,085	995	925	870	1,701	1,266
.40-70 Winchester	330	L	FN	1,375	1,165	1,035	945	880	825	1,385	998
.40-72 Winchester	300	SP	FN	1,385	1,175	1,035	950	880	825	1,278	917
.40-82 Winchester	260	L	FN	1,350	1,135	1,005	920	855	800	1,052	746
	260	L	FN	1,475	1,225	1,060	960	885	825	1,256	866
.40-90 Peabody "What Cheer"	500	L	FN	1,250	1,150	1,075	1,015	970	930	1,735	1,472
10.5x47Rmm Stahl	298	L	FN	1,250	1,080	975	900	840	790	1,034	769
10.75x57mm Mann.-Schoenauer	350	SP	FN	1,950	1,745	1,555	1,390	1,245	1,135	2,955	2,367
10.75x63mm Mauser	347	SP	FN	2,050	1,840	1,640	1,465	1,310	1,180	3,238	2,600
10.75x68mm Mauser	347	SP	FN	2,230	2,005	1,795	1,605	1,430	1,280	3,831	3,102
.44 Evans Short	215	L	RN	850	795	730	670	615	570	345	302
.44 Evans Long	280	L	RN	1,200	1,040	940	870	810	755	895	672
.44 Wesson Extra Long	250	L	RN	1,340	1,140	1,015	930	865	810	997	720
.44-100 Rem. "Creedmoor"	520	L	RN	1,435	1,315	1,210	1,130	1,060	1,010	2,377	2,000
	550	L	RN	1,380	1,275	1,185	1,110	1,050	1,005	2,326	1,982
.44-60 Peabody "Creedmoor"	365	L	RN	1,250	1,115	1,020	955	900	855	1,266	1,007
.44-85 Wesson	390	L	RN	1,400	1,225	1,100	1,010	945	895	1,697	1,303
.44-100 Wesson	550	L	RN	1,380	1,275	1,185	1,110	1,050	1,005	2,326	1,982
.44-90 Rem. Special	550	L	RN	1,250	1,165	1,095	1,040	995	955	1,908	1,653
.44-95 Peabody "What Cheer"	550	L	RN	1,310	1,215	1,135	1,070	1,020	985	2,096	1,797
11.2x60mm Schuler	332	SP	RN	2,200	1,875	1,590	1,345	1,155	1,030	3,568	2,597
11.2x72mm Schuler	401	SP	RN	2,440	2,190	1,950	1,730	1,530	1,355	5,301	4,263
.45-60 Winchester	300	L	FN	1,315	1,130	1,010	930	870	820	1,152	849
.45-90 Winchester	300	L	FN	1,525	1,250	1,065	960	880	820	1,549	1,039
	350	L	FN	1,510	1,235	1,055	950	875	810	1,772	1,184
	405	L	FN	1,470	1,290	1,145	1,050	975	920	1,943	1,496
.45-90 Win. High Velocity	300	SP	FN	1,950	1,595	1,300	1,095	980	895	2,533	1,693
.45-100 Remington (necked)	550	L	FN	1,400	1,650	1,150	1,065	1,005	950	2,393	1,946
.45-125 Win. Express	300	SP	FN	1,680	1,370	1,140	1,005	915	845	1,880	1,247
12.5x70mm Schuler	535	SP	RN	2,400	2,220	2,045	1,880	1,725	1,580	6,842	5,851
.500 Nitro Express 3 3/4 in.	570	FMJ	RN	2,150	1,970	1,800	1,640	1,495	1,360	5,850	4,914
.500/450 Nitro Express 3 1/2 in.	480	SP	RN	2,175	1,920	1,810	1,645	1,495	1,355	5,041	4,213
.500/450 BPE 3 1/2 in.	325	L	RN	1,950	1,685	1,445	1,250	1,105	1,005	2,744	2,045
.500/450 No.1 BPE	270	L	RN	1,900	1,570	1,315	1,135	1,020	940	2,164	1,474
.500/450 No.2 BPE	340	L	RN	1,850	1,595	1,370	1,190	1,065	980	2,584	1,921
.500/450 No.1 Carbine	380	L	RN	1,300	1,145	1,035	965	905	855	1,426	1,103
.500/465 Nitro Express	480	SP	RN	2,150	1,960	1,780	1,615	1,460	1,325	4,926	4,093

ENERGY IN FT.-LBS.				BULLET PATH AT ZERO DISTANCE INDICATED									
200 YDS.	300 YDS.	400 YDS.	500 YDS.	100 YDS.	200 YDS.	300 YDS.	400 YDS.	500 YDS.	100 YDS.	200 YDS.	300 YDS.	400 YDS.	500 YDS.
424	316	258	218	0	-16	-57	-131	-243	8	0	-33	-99	-204
1,503	1,093	819	658	0	-9	-32	-74	-142	5	0	-18	-56	-120
889	611	478	397	0	-12	-43	-104	-199	6	0	-26	-81	-170
914	625	472	389	0	-10	-37	-89	-173	5	0	-22	-69	-148
996	738	590	500	0	-12	-44	-103	-192	6	0	-26	-78	-161
709	565	477	412	0	-19	-66	-147	-268	10	0	-37	-109	-221
1,607	1,126	830	668	0	-9	-32	-77	-149	5	0	-19	-59	-127
585	490	422	369	0	-25	-84	-183	-327	13	0	-46	-132	-264
631	519	44	387	0	-23	-76	-167	-302	11	0	-43	-122	-245
477	385	323	273	0	-23	-79	-175	-318	12	0	-45	-129	-260
994	832	724	641	0	-22	-73	-158	-282	11	0	-40	-115	-228
782	656	568	499	0	-24	-80	-174	-311	12	0	-44	-126	-251
715	599	518	455	0	-24	-79	-175	-308	12	0	-44	-125	-249
585	490	422	369	0	25	-84	-183	-327	13	0	-46	-132	-264
648	530	453	394	0	-22	-74	-163	-294	11	0	-41	-119	-239
1,283	1,147	1,043	958	0	-25	-79	-167	-292	12	0	-42	-118	-230
627	535	465	410	0	-28	-93	-199	-353	14	0	-50	-143	-282
1,885	1,499	1,206	997	0	-10	-34	-77	-142	5	0	-19	-57	-117
2,077	1,650	1,320	1,074	0	-9	-31	-69	-128	5	0	-17	-51	-105
2,488	1,986	1,576	1,264	0	-7	-25	-57	-106	4	0	-15	-42	-88
254	214	182	154	0	-54	-174	-372	-660	27	0	-93	-264	-525
551	470	407	357	0	-31	-99	-214	-379	15	0	-54	-153	-303
570	481	417	366	0	-25	-84	-181	-323	13	0	-46	-131	-260
1,697	1,469	1,302	1,178	0	-19	-61	-130	-230	9	0	-33	-93	-184
1,709	1,503	1,348	1,230	0	-20	-65	-138	-242	10	0	-35	-98	-192
846	739	658	593	0	-26	-86	-183	-321	13	0	-46	-130	-255
1,045	884	775	692	0	-22	-72	-156	-277	11	0	-39	-112	-223
1,709	1,503	1,348	1,230	0	-20	-65	-138	-242	10	0	-35	-98	-192
1,460	1,316	1,205	1,114	0	-24	-77	-162	-282	12	0	-41	-114	-222
1,568	1,398	1,268	1,166	0	-22	-71	-151	-263	11	0	-38	-106	-207
1,862	1,330	983	785	0	-9	-31	-73	-141	4	0	-18	-56	-120
3,390	2,670	2,088	1,636	0	-6	-21	-48	-89	3	0	-12	-36	-75
681	579	504	445	0	-26	-85	-183	-325	13	0	-46	-131	-261
757	611	517	447	0	-21	-72	-159	-289	11	0	-41	-117	-237
866	701	594	513	0	-21	-73	-162	-294	11	0	-41	-119	-241
1,184	987	857	763	0	-19	-65	-142	-255	10	0	-36	-103	-206
1,128	802	636	535	0	-12	-45	-107	-203	6	0	-27	-82	-172
1,617	1,389	1,228	1,108	0	-20	-67	-144	-254	10	0	-36	-103	-204
865	670	558	478	0	-17	-61	-138	-254	9	0	-35	-104	-211
4,976	4,203	3,540	2,970	0	-6	-19	-43	-79	3	0	-11	-32	-65
4,101	3,412	2,828	2,349	0	-8	-26	-57	-104	4	0	-15	-42	-85
3,495	2,890	2,379	1,964	0	-7	-26	-56	-103	4	0	-15	-42	-85
1,507	1,124	878	731	0	-11	-38	-89	-167	5	0	-22	-67	-140
1,037	773	623	531	0	-13	-46	-105	-196	7	0	-26	-80	-165
1,418	1,069	855	725	0	-12	-43	-99	-184	6	0	-25	-74	-154
907	782	691	619	0	-25	-82	-176	-310	13	0	-44	-126	-248
3,379	2,779	2,275	1,875	0	-8	-27	-58	-107	4	0	-15	-43	-88

CALIBER	BULLET WGT-GRS	BULLET TYPE	BULLET STYLE	VELOCITY in FPS						ENERGY IN FT.-LBS.	
				MUZZLE	100 YDS.	200 YDS.	300 YDS.	400 YDS.	500 YDS.	MUZZLE	100 YDS.
.475 Nitro Express 3 1/4 in.	480	SP	RN	2,200	2,005	1,815	1,645	1,485	1,345	5,158	4,275
.50-100 Winchester	300	SP	FN	1,580	1,270	1,065	950	870	805	1,663	1,075
	300	SP	FN	2,200	1,785	1,430	1,165	1,010	915	3,224	2,117
	450	SP	FN	1,430	1,240	1,100	1,010	940	885	2,043	1,540
.50-110 Winchester	300	SP	FN	1,605	1,290	1,080	960	875	810	1,716	1,107
	300	SP	FN	2,225	1,805	1,445	1,175	1,015	915	3,298	2,169
.50-140 Win. Express	473	L	FN	1,580	1,370	1,205	1,080	1,000	935	2,622	1,978
	700	L	FN	1,355	1,240	1,145	1,070	1,015	970	2,853	2,387
.50-95 Win. Express	300	L	FN	1,555	1,250	1,055	945	865	800	1,611	1,043
.577/500 Nitro Express 3 1/8 in.	570	FMJ	RN	2,000	1,825	1,665	1,520	1,385	1,265	5,062	4,226
.577/500 No. 2 BPE	300	L	RN	1,870	1,500	1,215	1,035	930	855	2,329	1,499
	340	L	RN	1,925	1,660	1,425	1,230	1,090	1,000	2,797	2,077
.70-140 Win.	600	L	FN	1,425	1,000	800	670	565	475	2,705	1,336

CHAPTER 60 : CENTERFIRE MILITARY RIFLE - CURRENT

CALIBER	MODEL	BULLET WGT-GRS	BULLET TYPE	BULLET STYLE	VELOCITY in FPS						ENERGY IN FT.-LBS.	
					MUZZLE	100 YDS.	200 YDS.	300 YDS.	400 YDS.	500 YDS.	MUZZLE	100 YDS.
4.6X30mm		25	Ball	FMJ	2,355	1,990	1,165	1,385	1,170	1,030	308	220
5.45x39mm Soviet	Type PS	54	Ball	FMJBT	2,950	2,730	2,515	2,305	2,105	1,910	1,043	893
5.56x45mm NATO	M193	55	Ball	FMJBT	3,250	3,030	2,815	2,610	2,407	2,211	20,211,290	1,121
	M855A1	62.5	Ball	FMJBT	3,020	2,850	2,685	2,525	2,370	2,215	1,255	1,120
5.7x28mm FN	sS109	31	Ball	FMJBT	2,325	1,690	1,215	975	850	760	372	197
5.8x21mm Chinese		46	Ball	FMJ	1,740	1,390	1,135	990	890	825	309	197
5.8x42mm Chinese	DB87P	64	Ball	FMJBT	3,050	2,855	2,660	2,475	2,290	2,115	1,322	1,156
6.5mm Grendel		123	Ball	FMJ	2,610	2,440	2,275	2,115	1,965	1,820	1,860	1,624
300 Blackout		115	SP	FB	2,295	2,000	1,725	1,445	1,280	1,125	1,245	1,020
		125	SP	FB	2,215	1,925	1,640	1,425	1,235	1,095	1,362	1,027
		220	SP	RN	1,010	945	895	850	810	775	498	437
6.8mm SPC		115		HPBT	2,625	2,485	2,345	2,210	2,080	1,950	1,759	1,576
7.62x39mm M43 Soviet	57N231S	123	Ball	FMJ	2,330	2,035	1,770	1,525	1,310	1,160	1,482	1,134
9x39mm Soviet	SP-5	247	Subsonic	FMJBT	920	900	880	860	840	820	487	465
	SP-6	259	Subsonic	FMJ	920	890	875	855	835	815	461	439
7.62x45mm Indo. Police		121	Ball	FMJRN	1,650	1,485	1,345	1,225	1,130	1,055	1,330	1,080
7.62x51mm NATO	M80/M59	150	Ball	FMJBT	2,750	2,615	2,485	2,360	2,230	2,110	2,518	2,281
	M852	168	Match	HPBT	2,550	2,425	2,300	2,180	2,060	1,935	2,425	2,192
	M118	172	Spec. Ball	FMJBT	2,640	2,525	2,410	2,300	2,190	2,085	2,661	2,435
7.62x54R mm Russian	Type LPS	147	Ball	FMJBT	2,885	2,740	2,595	2,450	2,315	2,175	2,716	2,449
	Type O	185	Ball	FMJBT	2,660	2,555	2,445	2,345	2,240	2,140	2,906	2,677
	Type CT	150	Ball	FMJBT	2,715	2,570	2,430	2,290	2,155	2,020	2,455	2,200
.458 SOCOM		450	Ball	FMJ	1,500	1,295	1,140	1,035	960	900	2,248	1,677

CHAPTER 60 : CENTERFIRE MILITARY RIFLE - CURRENT - LONG RANGE

CALIBER	MODEL	BULLET WGT-GRS	BULLET TYPE	BULLET STYLE	VELOCITY in FPS							
					MUZZLE	100 YDS.	200 YDS.	300 YDS.	400 YDS.	500 YDS.	600 Yds.	700 Yds.
.338 Lapua Magnum		300	Match	HPBT	2,800	2,745	2,685	2,630	2,575	2,515	2,460	2,410
12.7x99mm BMG	M33	660	Ball	FMJBT	2,910	2,825	2,740	2,660	2,580	2,495	2,420	2,340
.50 Browning	M1	720	Ball	FMJBT	2,810	2,730	2,655	2,580	2,505	2,430	2,355	2,280
12.7x108mm Soviet	B32	745	API	FMJ	2,625	2,550	2,475	2,400	2,325	2,255	2,180	2,110
14.5x114mm Soviet	B32	989	API	FMJ	3,200	3,130	3,060	2,990	2,925	2,855	2,790	2,725

ENERGY IN FT.-LBS.				BULLET PATH AT ZERO DISTANCE INDICATED									
200 YDS.	300 YDS.	400 YDS.	500 YDS.	100 YDS.	200 YDS.	300 YDS.	400 YDS.	500 YDS.	100 YDS.	200 YDS.	300 YDS.	400 YDS.	500 YDS.
3,516	2,880	2,348	1,922	0	-8	-25	-56	-102	4	0	-15	-41	-85
759	603	505	433	0	-20	-70	-157	-287	10	0	-40	-117	-236
1,359	903	677	555	0	-10	-37	-90	-175	5	0	-22	-70	-151
1,214	1,017	886	787	0	-21	-71	-154	-274	11	0	-39	-111	-221
774	612	511	437	0	-20	-69	-154	-281	10	0	-39	-114	-232
1,393	922	686	561	0	-9	-36	-87	-171	5	0	-22	-69	-148
1,522	1,230	1,047	920	0	-17	-58	-128	-232	9	0	-33	-94	-190
2,037	1,784	1,599	1,457	0	-21	-69	-146	-257	11	0	-37	-104	-204
744	595	500	428	0	-21	-72	-160	-292	11	0	-41	-119	-240
3,519	2,916	2,420	2,025	0	-9	-31	-67	-122	5	0	-17	-49	-99
980	714	578	487	0	-14	-52	-121	-228	7	0	-31	-93	-193
1,528	1,144	900	754	0	-11	-40	-91	-172	6	0	-23	-69	-144
858	599	423	298	0	-33	-117	-276	-541	16	0	-68	-211	-459

CHAPTER 60 : CENTERFIRE MILITARY RIFLE - CURRENT

ENERGY IN FT.-LBS.				BULLET PATH AT ZERO DISTANCE INDICATED									
200 YDS.	300 YDS.	400 YDS.	500 YDS.	100 YDS.	200 YDS.	300 YDS.	400 YDS.	500 YDS.	100 YDS.	200 YDS.	300 YDS.	400 YDS.	500 YDS.
154	106	76	59	0	-7	-27	-66	-130	4	0	-16	-51	-111
758	638	531	438	0	-3	-12	-27	-50	2	0	-7	-21	-43
969	831	707	597	0	-2	-2	-9	-21	1	0	-6	-16	-33
994	879	773	676	0	-3	-10	-23	-43	2	0	-6	-18	-36
102	66	50	40	0	-11	-46	-117	-236	6	0	-29	-95	-208
132	100	82	70	0	-17	-60	-139	-261	9	0	-35	-106	-220
1,006	869	746	635	0	-2	-6	-18	-37	2	0	-6	-18	-37
1,412	1,223	1,053	904	0	-4	-15	-34	-62	2	0	-9	-26	-51
760	561	418	384	0	-7.3	-26.4	-61.5	-118.2	3.2	0	-15.4	-46.9	-99.9
964	564	423	322	0	-8.1	-28.7	-66.8	-128	4.1	0	-16.6	-30.6	-107.8
391	353	321	293	0	-37.3	-117.8	-246.3	-426.7	18.6	0	-61.9	-171.7	-333.5
1,405	1,249	1,104	973	0	-4	-15	-32	-58	2	0	-8	-24	-47
854	636	475	366	0	-7	-25	-58	-111	4	0	-15	-44	-94
443	423	405	387	0	-42	-128	-262	-389	21	0	-66	-179	-342
419	399	381	364	0	-42	-128	-263	-390	21	0	-66	-179	-343
886	734	623	544	0	-14	-48	-104	-189	7	0	-26	-76	-152
2,058	1,852	1,659	1,481	0	-4	-13	-28	-51	2	0	-7	-21	-42
1,975	1,772	1,582	1,400	0	-4	-15	-34	-60	2	0	-9	-25	-49
2,222	2,022	1,835	1,659	0	-4	-14	-30	-54	2	0	-8	-23	-44
2,195	1,965	1,745	1,545	0	-3	-11	-26	-46	2	0	-7	-19	-38
2,460	2,256	2,063	1,882	0	-4	-13	-29	-52	2	0	-8	-22	-43
1,965	1,745	1,545	1,361	0	-4	-13	-30	-54	2	0	-8	-22	-44
1,297	1,066	918	811	0	-19	-65	-144	-260	10	0	-36	-105	-212

800 Yds.	900 Yds.	1,000 Yds.
2,355	2,300	2,245
2,260	2,185	2,110
2,210	2,135	2,065
2,040	1,970	1,902
2,660	2,595	2,530

CALIBER	ENERGY IN FT.-LBS.									
	MUZZLE	100 YDS.	200 YDS.	300 YDS.	400 YDS.	500 YDS.	600 Yds.	700 Yds.	800 Yds.	900 Yds.
.338 Lapua Magnum	5,222	5,010	4,804	4,604	4,381	4,221	4,038	3,860	3,688	3,521
12.7x99mm BMG	12,408	11,699	11,018	10,365	9,739	9,139	8,559	8,016	7,491	6,990
.50 Browning	12,622	11,930	11,264	10,625	10,010	9,421	8,856	8,314	7,795	7,298
12.7x108mm Soviet	11,397	10,745	10,120	9,519	8,944	8,392	7,864	7,359	6,876	6,417
14.5x114mm Soviet	22,256	21,295	20,363	19,459	18,584	17,737	16,917	16,123	15,356	14,614

CHAPTER 61 : CENTERFIRE MILITARY RIFLE - OBSOLETE

CALIBER	BULLET WGT-GRS	BULLET TYPE	BULLET STYLE	VELOCITY in FPS						ENERGY IN FT.-LBS.	
				MUZZLE	100 YDS.	200 YDS.	300 YDS.	400 YDS.	500 YDS.	MUZZLE	100 YDS.
4.85mm British	55	Ball	FMJBT	3,115	2,870	2,630	2,400	2,175	1,960	1,196	1,014
6mm U.S. Navy	112	Ball	FMJFB	2,550	2,285	2,035	1,800	1,590	1,400	1,617	1,297
6.5x50SRmm Arisaka	139	Ball	FMJFB	2,475	2,305	2,140	1,985	1,835	1,695	1,890	1,640
6.5x52mm Mann.-Carc.	162	Ball	FMJFB	2,295	2,015	1,755	1,520	1,320	1,160	1,894	1,457
6.5x53Rmm Mannlicher	158	Ball	FMJFB	2,220	1,945	1,690	1,465	1,275	1,130	1,707	1,308
6.5x53.5SR mm Daudeteau	150	Ball	FMJFB	2,440	2,150	1,875	1,630	1,410	1,230	1,983	1,536
6.5x54mm Mann.-Schon.	156	Ball	FMJFB	2,460	2,165	1,895	1,645	1,425	1,240	2,096	1,626
6.5x55mm Swedish	139	Ball M41	FMJBT	2,600	2,505	2,410	2,315	2,225	2,135	2,086	1,935
6.5x58mm Portugese Vergueiro	154	Ball	FMJRN	2,460	2,165	1,895	1,645	1,425	1,240	2,069	1,605
.276 Enfield Pattern 13	165	Ball	FMJBT	2,800	2,705	2,615	2,525	2,435	2,345	2,872	2,684
.276 Pedersen T-2	126	Ball T1-E20	FMJBT	2,550	2.435	2,320	2,205	2,095	1,990	1,819	1,657
.280 British	140	Ball Mk.1Z	FMJBT	2,530	2,415	2,305	2,195	2,090	1,985	1,989	1,815
7x57mm Mauser	139	Ball	FMJFB	2,660	2,435	2,225	2,020	1,830	1,655	2,183	1,832
	154	Ball	FMJFB	2,565	2,365	2,175	1,990	1,820	1,655	2,191	1,862
	173	Ball	FMJFB	2,425	2,245	2,070	1,905	1,750	1,605	2,272	1,946
7x57mm Meunier	139	Ball	FMJBT	2,790	2,670	2,550	2,435	2,320	2,210	2,402	2,200
7.36mm Italian Carcano	128	Ball	FMJFB	2,480	2,195	1,935	1,690	1,470	1,285	1,748	1,371
7.5x54mm French MAS	140	Ball	FMJBT	2,710	2,565	2,425	2,285	2,150	2,015	2,283	2,046
7.5x55mm Swiss	174	Ball GP11	FMJBT	2,560	2,445	2,335	2,225	2,115	2,010	2,532	2,312
	211	Ball GP90/03	FMJRN	1,980	1,735	1,515	1,325	1,175	1,065	1,836	1,413
7.5x57mm French M24	139	Ball	FMJBT	2,600	2,460	2,320	2,180	2,050	1,920	2,101	1,877
7.62x45mm Czech	130	Ball M52	FMJBT	2,440	2,280	2,125	1,975	1,830	1,690	1,718	1,501
.30 Pedersen	80	Ball	FMJFB	1,300	1,005	865	765	685	605	300	179
.30 Carbine	110	Ball M1	FMJFB	1,975	1,555	1,235	1,045	935	855	953	591
.30-'03 U.S.	220	Ball	FMJRN	2,200	1,990	1,790	1,605	1,450	1,315	2,364	1,930
.30-'06 Springfield	150	Ball M1906	FMJFB	2,700	2,440	2,195	1,960	1,745	1,550	2,428	1,981
	175	Ball M1	FMJBT	2,640	2,460	2,290	2,125	1,965	1,810	2,692	2,339
.30-'06 Springfield, cont.	152	Ball M2	FMJFB	2,740	2,470	2,215	1,980	1,755	1,555	2,533	2,060
.30-40 Krag	220	Ball	FMJRN	2,200	1,990	1,790	1,605	1,450	1,315	2,364	1,930
.310 Cadet	125	Ball	LRN	1,200	1,055	965	895	840	790	400	309
.303 British	215	Ball Mk II	FMJRN	1,970	1,720	1,495	1,305	1,155	1,050	1,852	1,412
	174	Ball Mk.VIII	FMJFB	2,440	2,230	2,035	1,845	1,670	1,510	2,300	1,923
	174	Ball Mk. 8Z	FMJBT	2,370	2,255	2,145	2,035	1,925	1,820	2,170	1,965
7.65x53mm Belgian Mauser	155	Ball	FMJFB	2,710	2,465	2,240	2,020	1,815	1,625	2,527	2,095
	174	Ball	FMJBT	2,460	2,345	2,230	2,120	2,010	1,900	2,338	2,123
	211	Ball	FMJRN	2,130	1,875	1,640	1,435	1,260	1,125	2,125	1,647
7.7x58mm Japanese Arisaka	181	Ball	FMJBT	2,370	2,255	2,145	2,035	1,930	1,825	2,257	2,064
	201	Ball Type 92	FMJBT	2,380	2,285	2,185	2,095	2,000	1,910	2,528	2,326
7.92x33mm Kurz	125	Ball PP 43	FMJFB	2,250	1,980	1,725	1,500	1,310	1,155	1,405	1,085
8x50Rmm Austrian Mannlicher	244	Ball	FMJRN	2,030	1,835	1,660	1,495	1,345	1,220	2,232	1,829
8x50Rmm Lebel	198	Balle D	SBT	2,300	2,195	2,090	1,985	1,885	1,790	2,325	2,115

1,000 Yds.	BULLET PATH AT ZERO DISTANCE INDICATED									
	100 YDS.	200 YDS.	300 YDS.	400 YDS.	500 YDS.	600 Yds.	700 Yds.	800 Yds.	900 Yds.	1,000 Yds.
3,360	12	20	23	20	14	0	-20	-46	-79	-120
6,512	11	18	21	20	13	0	-19	-44	-75	-114
6,823	11	20	23	21	13	0	-20	-46	-80	-121
5,982	13	23	27	24	16	0	-23	-54	-93	-141
13,897	8	14	17	15	10	0	-14	-33	-57	-86

CHAPTER 61 : CENTERFIRE MILITARY RIFLE - OBSOLETE

ENERGY IN FT.-LBS.				BULLET PATH AT ZERO DISTANCE INDICATED									
200 YDS.	300 YDS.	400 YDS.	500 YDS.	100 YDS.	200 YDS.	300 YDS.	400 YDS.	500 YDS.	100 YDS.	200 YDS.	300 YDS.	400 YDS.	500 YDS.
835	710	584	474	0	-3	-11	-24	-46	1	0	-6	-19	-39
1,029	807	627	487	0	-5	-19	-43	-82	3	0	-11	-33	-69
1,416	1,216	1,040	886	0	-5	-18	-39	-71	3	0	-10	-29	-58
1,105	830	625	485	0	-7	-26	-59	-113	4	0	-15	-45	-95
989	742	562	441	0	-8	-28	-64	-122	4	0	-16	-49	-103
1,173	884	664	505	0	-6	-22	-51	-98	3	0	-13	-39	-83
1,242	937	703	535	0	-6	-22	-50	-96	3	0	-13	-38	-81
1,791	1,655	1,526	1,404	0	-4	-14	-31	-54	2	0	-8	-23	-44
1,226	925	694	528	0	-6	-22	-50	-96	3	0	-13	-38	-81
2,505	2,334	2,171	2,016	0	-3	-12	-25	-45	2	0	-7	-19	-37
1,505	1,363	1,230	1,107	0	-4	-15	-33	-59	2	0	-9	-24	-48
1,652	1,499	1,355	1,222	0	-5	-15	-34	-60	2	0	-9	-25	-49
1,526	1,261	1,034	843	0	-4	-16	-36	-66	2	0	-9	-27	-55
1,573	1,321	1,102	914	0	-5	-17	-38	-69	2	0	-10	-28	-57
1,657	1,403	1,183	993	0	-5	-19	-42	-77	3	0	-11	-31	-63
2,009	1,830	1,663	1,506	0	-3	-12	-27	-48	2	0	-7	-20	-39
1,061	811	616	471	0	-6	-21	-48	-92	3	0	-12	-37	-77
1,826	1,625	1,435	1,640	0	-4	-14	-30	-54	2	0	-8	-22	-44
2,106	1,912	1,731	1,563	0	-4	-15	-33	-58	2	0	-9	-24	-47
1,078	826	647	532	0	-10	-35	-80	-151	5	0	-20	-60	-125
1,671	1,480	1,304	1,144	0	-4	-15	-33	-59	2	0	-9	-25	-49
1,304	1,125	965	825	0	-5	-18	-40	-72	3	0	-10	-30	-59
132	104	83	65	0	-33	-112	-252	-394	17	0	-63	-186	-383
373	266	212	178	0	-13	-49	-117	-225	7	0	-29	-91	-192
1,563	1,258	1,027	843	0	-7	-26	-57	-106	4	0	-15	-43	-87
1,602	1,282	1,015	799	0	-4	-16	-37	-69	2	0	-10	-28	-58
2,024	1,740	1,488	1,266	0	-4	-15	-34	-61	2	0	-9	-25	-51
1,659	1,321	1,042	815	0	-4	-16	-36	-67	2	0	-9	-27	-57
1,563	1,258	1,027	843	0	-7	-26	-57	-106	4	0	-15	-43	-87
257	222	195	173	0	-30	-97	-207	-367	15	0	-52	-148	-293
1,067	811	634	524	0	-10	-36	-83	-155	5	0	-21	-62	-130
1,596	1,315	1,077	879	0	-6	-19	-44	-80	8	0	-11	-33	-67
1,775	1,597	1,432	1,281	0	-5	-18	-40	-70	2	0	-10	-29	-57
1,723	1,405	1,135	911	0	-4	-15	-35	-66	2	0	-9	-27	-55
1,921	1,733	1,559	1,397	0	-5	-17	-36	-64	3	0	-9	-27	-52
1,262	962	742	592	0	-8	-30	-68	-129	4	0	-17	-51	-108
1,849	1,665	1,495	1,339	0	-5	-18	-40	-70	3	0	-10	-29	-57
2,135	1,955	1,784	1,625	0	-5	-18	-38	-67	3	0	-10	-28	-54
825	625	475	371	0	-7	-27	-61	-116	4	0	-16	-46	-98
1,489	1,208	983	809	0	-9	-30	-68	-124	5	0	-17	-50	-102
1,918	1,735	1,565	1,410	0	-6	-19	-42	-74	3	0	-11	-31	-60

CALIBER	BULLET WGT-GRS	BULLET TYPE	BULLET STYLE	VELOCITY in FPS						ENERGY IN FT.-LBS.	
				MUZZLE	100 YDS.	200 YDS.	300 YDS.	400 YDS.	500 YDS.	MUZZLE	100 YDS.
8x50Rmm Lebel, cont.	190	Balle32M	FMJBT	2,300	2,190	2,080	1,975	1,870	1,775	2,231	2,023
	231	Balle M	FMJRN	2,065	1,870	1,690	1,520	1,370	1,240	2,187	1,794
8x50Rmm Siamese Type 45	239	Type 45	FMJRN	1,840	1,690	1,550	1,415	1,300	1,205	1,797	1,514
8x52Rmm Siamese Type 66	181	Type 66	FMJFB	2,200	1,990	1,785	1,600	1,430	1,285	1,945	1,588
8x52.5Rmm Murata	238	Ball	FMJFN	1,835	1,655	1,490	1,345	1,220	1,120	1,779	1,448
8x56Rmm Austro-Hungarian Mann.	208	Ball	FMJBT	2,375	2,265	2,160	2,055	1,955	1,855	2,605	2,374
8x57Jmm Mauser	227	Ball M88	FMJRN	2,065	1,855	1,665	1,490	1,330	1,200	2,149	1,738
8x57JSmm Mauser	154	S Patrone	FMJFB	2,890	2,580	2,290	2,015	1,765	1,540	2,856	2,274
	198	sS Patrone	FMJBT	2,575	2,465	2,355	2,250	2,140	2,040	2,915	2,669
8x54Rmm Danish Krag	237	Ball	FMJRN	1,970	1,780	1,605	1,445	1,305	1,190	2,042	1,669
	196	Ball	FMJFB	2,460	2,255	2,060	1,875	1,700	1,540	2,633	2,213
8x59mm Breda	210	Ball	FMJBT	2,445	2,335	2,230	2,125	2,020	1,920	2,787	2,545
8x60Rmm Portugese Guedes	247	Ball	FMJRN	1,705	1,535	1,385	1,255	1,145	1,065	1,594	1,294
8x63mm Swedish	218	Ball	FMJBT	2,495	2,385	2,280	2,170	2,065	1,965	3,013	2,754
9.5x60Rmm Turkish Mauser	285	Ball	LRN	1,760	1,595	1,445	1,310	1,200	1,110	1,960	1,609
10.15x63Rmm Serbian Mauser	340	Ball	LRN	1,460	1,295	1,165	1,070	1,000	945	1,609	1,270
10.15x61Rmm Jarmann	337	Ball	LRN	1,625	1,440	1,280	1,155	1,060	990	1,976	1,550
10.4x47Rmm Italian Vetterli	315	Ball	LRN	1,425	1,220	1,075	985	915	860	1,420	1,041
10.6x47Rmm Russ. Berdan	370	Ball-carbine	LRN	1,060	995	940	895	855	820	923	810
10.75x58Rmm Russian Berdan	370	Ball-rifle	LRN	1,450	1,290	1,165	1,070	1,000	945	1,727	1,369
	370	Ball-carbine	LRN	1,350	1,210	1,100	1,025	965	915	1,497	1,200
11x42Rmm Belgian Comblain	386	Ball-carbine	LRN	1,100	1,035	980	935	900	865	1,037	914
11x51Rmm Belgian Comblain	386	Ball-rifle	LRN	1,445	1,310	1,195	1,105	1,035	985	1,789	1,467
11x50Rmm Belgian Comblain	386	Ball	LRN	1,370	1,245	1,145	1,065	1,005	960	1,608	1,328
11x59Rmm French Gras	388	Ball	LRN	1,495	1,355	1,230	1,135	1,060	1,000	1,925	1,576
11x60Rmm Japanese Murata	420	Ball Type 20	LRN	1,485	1,320	1,185	1,085	1,010	955	2,056	1,626
11.15x42Rmm Aust.Werndl	313	Ball-carbine	LRN	975	910	850	805	760	735	661	571
	370	Ball-carbine	LRN	1,005	955	910	870	840	810	830	746
11.15x58Rmm Aust. Werndl	370	Ball-rifle	LRN	1,435	1,275	1,155	1,065	1,000	950	1,692	1,338
11.15x58Rmm Spanish Remington	385	Ball	LRN	1,380	1,245	1,140	1,060	1,000	950	1,628	1,329
11.15x60Rmm Mauser	386	Ball	LRN	1,425	1,245	1,105	1,010	945	890	1,740	1,333
11.3x45Rmm Dutch Beaumont	300	Ball-carbine	LRN	1,200	1,060	970	900	850	800	959	748
11.3x50Rmm Dutch Beaumont	386	Ball-rifle	LRN	1,380	1,210	1,080	995	930	875	1,632	1,252
11.3x52Rmm Dutch Beau. M71/78	345	Ball-rifle	LRN	1,475	1,270	1,120	1,015	945	890	1,666	1,238
11.4x50Rmm Austrian Werndl	340	Ball	LRN	1,270	1,120	1,015	945	890	840	1,217	943
11.4x53Rmm Brazilian Comblain	486	Ball	LFN	1,310	1,190	1,095	1,025	975	930	1,852	1,527
11.43x50Rmm Egyptian	400	Ball	LRN	1,330	1,190	1,095	1,025	970	925	1,571	1,261
11.43x55Rmm Turkish	486	Ball	LRN	1,265	1,155	1,070	1,005	955	915	1,727	1,437
.45-70 Government	405	Ball-carbine	LRN	1,330	1,170	1,055	980	915	870	1,590	1,226
	500	Ball-rifle	LRN	1,100	1,010	950	895	850	815	1,343	1,138
11.5x57Rmm Spanish Reformado	395	Ball	FMJFB	1,280	1,130	1,025	955	900	850	1,437	1,119
11.7x52Rmm Danish Remington	387	Ball	LRN	1,345	1,180	1,060	980	920	870	1,554	1,196
.50 U.S. Carbine	400	Ball	LRN	1,200	1,025	925	845	785	730	1,279	934
.50-70 Government	450	Ball	LRN	1,110	995	920	860	805	760	1,231	993
.500/450 No.1 Musket	270	Ball	LRN	1,900	1,580	1,325	1,140	1,025	945	2,164	1,434
.500/450 No. 2 Musket	480	Ball	LRN	1,300	1,190	1,100	1,035	985	940	1,801	1,508
.577/450 Martini-Henry	480	Ball	LRN	1,350	1,230	1,135	1,060	1,000	956	1,942	1,612
.577 Snider	480	Ball	LRN	1,250	1,025	900	815	745	690	1,665	1,118
.58 Berdan	530	Ball-carbine	LRN	925	835	760	695	640	603	1,007	816
.58 Berdan	530	Ball-rifle	LRN	1,100	945	850	770	710	650	1,424	1,053

ENERGY IN FT.-LBS.				BULLET PATH AT ZERO DISTANCE INDICATED									
200 YDS.	300 YDS.	400 YDS.	500 YDS.	100 YDS.	200 YDS.	300 YDS.	400 YDS.	500 YDS.	100 YDS.	200 YDS.	300 YDS.	400 YDS.	500 YDS.
1,825	1,645	1,475	1,329	0	-6	-20	-43	-76	3	0	-12	-33	-62
1,460	1,186	964	792	0	-9	-29	-65	-119	4	0	-17	-48	-98
1,271	1,066	900	767	0	-11	-36	-79	-142	5	0	-20	-57	-115
1,284	1,031	824	665	0	-7	-26	-58	-107	4	0	-15	-43	-88
1,175	956	788	665	0	-11	-38	-84	-154	6	0	-21	-62	-126
2,157	1,955	1,766	1,592	0	-5	-18	-39	-69	3	0	-10	-28	-56
1,394	1,114	894	728	0	-9	-30	-67	-124	4	0	-17	-50	-102
1,790	1,391	1,066	810	0	-4	-14	-33	-63	2	0	-9	-26	-54
2,438	2,221	2,017	1,827	0	-4	-15	-32	-57	2	0	-8	-24	-47
1,635	1,357	1,101	898	0	-10	-33	-72	-132	5	0	-18	-53	-109
1,847	1,530	1,260	1,034	0	-5	-19	-42	-78	3	0	-11	-32	-65
2,317	2,103	1,904	1,718	0	-5	-17	-36	-64	3	0	-9	-27	-52
1,051	862	722	624	0	-13	-45	-98	-178	7	0	-25	-72	-145
2,511	2,282	2,069	1,869	0	-5	-16	-35	-61	2	0	-9	-25	-50
1,320	1,088	909	779	0	-12	-41	-90	-166	6	0	-23	-66	-133
1,026	862	753	673	0	-19	-64	-139	-249	10	0	-35	-101	-201
1,225	994	840	736	0	-15	-52	-115	-208	8	0	-29	-84	-170
811	676	586	518	0	-22	-27	-45	-68	11	0	-41	-118	-236
726	659	603	555	0	-34	-107	-223	-387	17	0	-56	-156	-303
1,110	936	819	733	0	-19	-65	-140	-250	10	0	-35	-101	-202
996	860	764	690	0	-22	-73	-157	-279	11	0	-40	-113	-223
823	752	693	642	0	-31	-98	-205	-355	16	0	-52	-143	-277
1,222	1,044	919	828	0	-19	-62	-134	-238	9	0	-34	-96	-191
1,120	973	867	787	0	-21	-68	-147	-259	11	0	-37	-105	-207
1,305	1,105	964	862	0	-18	-58	-126	-224	9	0	-32	-91	-180
1,310	1,096	953	850	0	-19	-62	-134	-241	9	0	-34	-97	-195
503	448	402	736	0	-41	-130	-272	-390	20	0	-68	-132	-207
680	625	577	541	0	-37	-115	-240	-388	18	0	-60	-166	-322
1,093	934	825	743	0	-20	-66	-142	-253	10	0	-36	-103	-204
1,111	960	853	772	0	-21	-68	-147	-260	10	0	-37	-105	-208
1,049	877	763	678	0	-21	-70	-153	-275	11	0	-39	-111	-223
626	542	479	426	0	-29	-96	-205	-362	15	0	-52	-146	-289
1,000	846	741	660	0	-22	-74	-161	-289	11	0	-41	-117	-233
959	792	684	605	0	-20	-68	-149	-269	10	0	-38	-109	-219
780	674	595	533	0	-26	-86	-185	-328	13	0	-47	-132	-262
1,297	1,138	1,022	931	0	-23	-75	-160	-281	12	0	-40	-114	-224
1,064	930	832	756	0	-23	-75	-160	-282	12	0	-40	-114	-225
1,235	1,094	988	903	0	-25	-79	-169	-296	12	0	-43	-119	-234
1,000	858	756	677	0	-24	-79	-171	-303	12	0	-43	-123	-244
998	892	806	733	0	-32	-103	-218	-380	16	0	-55	-153	-299
925	800	708	635	0	-26	-84	-181	-321	13	0	-46	-130	-256
967	825	725	648	0	-24	-78	-168	-300	12	0	-43	-121	-241
756	637	547	474	0	-31	-104	-224	-389	16	0	-57	-161	-323
844	736	650	578	0	-33	-108	-230	-390	17	0	-58	-163	-321
1,049	780	627	533	0	-13	-45	-104	-197	6	0	-26	-79	-165
1,295	1,144	1,032	944	0	-23	-75	-159	-278	12	0	-40	-113	-221
1,368	1,195	1,070	956	0	-22	-70	-150	-264	11	0	-38	-107	-210
866	708	590	509	0	-32	-106	-232	-389	16	0	-59	-169	-343
677	568	479	428	0	-49	-158	-339	-398	24	0	-85	-242	-395
847	701	588	497	0	-37	-123	-267	-394	19	0	-67	-192	-388

CHAPTER 61 : CENTERFIRE MILITARY RIFLE - OBSOLETE - LONG RANGE

CALIBER	BULLET WGT-GRS	BULLET TYPE	BULLET STYLE	VELOCITY in FPS						
				MUZZLE	100 YDS.	200 YDS.	300 YDS.	400 YDS.	500 YDS.	600 Yds.
7.92x94mm Panzerbuchse 318	225	AP	FMJFB	3,540	3,425	3,310	3,195	3,085	2,975	2,865
7.92x107mm Polish	197.5	AP	FMJBT	4,180	4,045	3,910	3,780	3,650	3,525	3,400
.5 in. Vickers	580	Ball	FMJFB	2,470	2,195	1,940	1,705	1,490	1,310	1,165
12.7x81SRmm Italian Breda	565	Ball	FMJFB	2,430	2,160	1,905	1,675	1,465	1,285	1,145
.50 Spotter-Tracer	827	Ball	FMJBT	1,745	1,615	1,500	1,390	1,290	1,200	1,120
13.2x99mm Hotchkiss	791	Ball	FMJFB	2,210	2,110	2,010	1,920	1,825	1,735	1,650
13x92SRmm Mauser TUF	770	AP	FMJFB	2,650	2,535	2,425	2,320	2,210	2,010	1,915
.55 Boys	926	AP Mk. I	FMJFB	2,495	2,285	2,080	1,890	1,715	1,550	1,400
	741	AP Mk. II	FMJFB	3,100	2,725	2,460	2,215	1,985	1,770	1,570
.60 Anti-tank Rifle	1,185	T-32 Ball	FMJFB	3,450	3,385	3,320	3,255	3,190	3,125	3,065

CALIBER	BULLET WGT-GRS	BULLET TYPE	BULLET STYLE	ENERNGY IN FT.-LBS.							
				MUZZLE	100 YDS.	200 YDS.	300 YDS.	400 YDS.	500 YDS.	600 YDS.	700 Yds.
7.92x94mm Panzerbuchse 318	225	AP	FMJFB	6,260	5,855	5,469	5,101	4,751	4,418	4,102	3,802
7.92x107mm Polish	197.5	AP	FMJBT	7,661	7,174	6,709	6,267	5,846	5,445	5,065	4,703
.5 in. Vickers	580	Ball	FMJFB	7,856	6,211	4,849	3,741	2,867	2,207	1,744	1,466
12.7x81SRmm Italian Breda	565	Ball	FMJFB	7,407	5,846	4,555	3,510	2,689	2,075	1,649	1,377
.50 Spotter-Tracer	827	Ball	FMJBT	5,591	4,803	4,124	3,542	3,049	2,636	2,310	2,090
13.2x99mm Hotchkiss	791	Ball	FMJFB	8,577	7,818	7,112	6,459	5,856	5,301	4,793	4,330
13x92SRmm Mauser TUF	770	AP	FMJFB	12,005	10,997	10,058	9,182	8,366	7,608	6,904	6,254
.55 Boys	926	AP Mk. I	FMJFB	12,797	10,720	8,914	7,357	6,033	4,926	4,023	3,312
	741	AP Mk. II	FMJFB	14,806	12,198	9,975	8,083	6,482	5,148	4,059	3,199
.60 Anti-tank Rifle	1,185	T-32 Ball	FMJFB	31,181	30,006	28,862	27,749	26,667	25,615	24,592	23,598

CHAPTER 62 : SHOTSHELL SLUGS FOR SMOOTHBORE BARRELS

GA.	SHELL LGT-IN.	BRAND	NAME	SLUG DESIGN	SLUG RIFLED	SLUG WGT-GRS	SLUG OGIVE	WAD MATERIAL	WAD TYPE	VELOCITY IN FPS				
										MUZZLE	50 YDS.	100 YDS.	150 YDS.	200 YDS.
10	3 1/2	Federal	Power-Shok	Full Bore	Yes	766	FN-HP	Fiber	Discarding	1,280	1,090	970	890	825
12	2 3/4	Brenneke	K.O.	Full Bore	Yes	437.5	FN	Plastic	Attached	1,600	1,195	985	870	785
12	2 3/4	Brenneke	K.O. Sabot	Subcaliber	Yes	437.5	FN	Plastic	Discarding	1,510	1,210	1,025	920	845
12	2 3/4	Brenneke	Black Magic Magnum	Full Bore	Yes	437.5	SRN	Plastic	Attached	1,510	1,210	1,025	920	845
12	2 3/4	Federal	Truball	Full Bore	Yes	437.5	FN-HP	Plastic	Attached	1,560	1,125	930	815	725
12	2 3/4	Federal	Power-Shok	Full Bore	Yes	437.5	FN-HP	Plastic	Discarding	1,600	1,180	970	855	770
12	2 3/4	Winchester	Rifled Slug	Full Bore	Yes	437.5	FN	Fiber	Discarding	1,600	1,160	955	835	745
12	2 3/4	Winchester	Power-Point	Full Bore	Yes	437.5	FN-HP	Fiber	Discarding	1,700	1,220	980	855	760
12	2 3/4	Remington	Slugger	Full Bore	Yes	437.5	FN	Fiber	Discarding	1,560	1,180	980	870	785
12	2 3/4	Remington	Slugger	Full Bore	Yes	437.5	FN	Fiber	Discarding	1,680	1,285	1,045	920	830
12	2 3/4	Remington	Slugger HV	Full Bore	Yes	383	FN	Fiber	Discarding	1,800	1,250	980	845	745
12	2 3/4	Brenneke	Classic	Full Bore	Yes	492	SRN	Felt	Attached	1,510	1,090	905	795	705
12	2 3/4	Brenneke	Emerald	Full Bore	Yes	547	SRN	Plastic	Attached	1,475	1,170	1,000	895	820
12	2 3/4	Federal	Power-Shok	Full Bore	Yes	547	FN-HP	Plastic	Discarding	1,520	1,270	1,090	985	905
12	2 3/4	Winchester	Rackmaster	Full Bore	Yes	492	FN-HP	Fiber	Discarding	1,625	1,235	1,015	895	810
12	2 3/4	Lightfield	Hybred EXF	Subcaliber	No	546	FN-HP	Plastic	Attached	1,455	1,220	1,065	965	895
12	3	Brenneke	K.O. Sabot	Subcaliber	Yes	437.5	FN	Plastic	Attached	1,675	1,325	1,090	960	870
12	3	Brenneke	Black Magic Magnum	Full Bore	Yes	601	SRN	Plastic	Attached	1,510	1,135	955	845	764
12	3	Federal	Power-Shok	Full Bore	Yes	547	FN-HP	Plastic	Discarding	1,600	1,330	1,130	1,010	925
12	3	Winchester	Rifled Slug	Full Bore	Yes	437.5	FN-HP	Plastic	Discarding	1,760	1,310	1,040	905	815
12	3	Winchester	Rackmaster	Full Bore	Yes	492	FN-HP	Plastic	Discarding	1,700	1,285	1,040	910	820

700 Yds.	800 Yds.	900 Yds.	1,000 Yds.
2,760	2,655	2,550	2,445
3,275	3,153	3,035	2,915
1,060	985	930	890
1,050	975	920	880
1,070	1,025	995	980
1,570	1,490	1,420	1,370
1,820	1,730	1,640	1,560
1,270	1,160	1,080	1,020
1,385	1,245	1,130	1,045
3,000	2,940	2,880	2,815

800 Yds.	900 Yds.	1,000 Yds.	BULLET PATH AT ZERO DISTANCE INDICATED									
			100 YDS.	200 YDS.	300 YDS.	400 YDS.	500 YDS.	600 Yds.	700 Yds.	800 Yds.	900 Yds.	1,000 Yds.
3,517	3,247	2,992	7	12	15	14	9	0	-13	-31	-53	-81
4,360	4,035	3,728	5	9	10	9	6	0	-9	-22	-37	-57
1,252	1,112	1,037	26	46	56	55	37	0	-63	-157	-287	-394
1,197	1,066	1,000	27	47	58	57	39	0	-65	-162	-295	-395
1,936	1,816	1,774	40	69	82	76	50	0	-78	-186	-327	-394
3,912	3,536	3,300	21	36	42	39	25	0	-38	-90	-158	-243
5,655	5,105	4,604	14	24	29	26	17	0	-26	-61	-107	-164
2,778	2,398	2,129	21	37	44	43	28	0	-46	-114	-208	-331
2,549	2,092	1,789	15	27	32	31	21	0	-35	-89	-164	-267
22,632	21,695	20,784	7	12	14	13	8	0	-12	-28	-47	-71

CHAPTER 62 : SHOTSHELL SLUGS FOR SMOOTHBORE BARRELS

ENERGY IN FT.-LBS.					SLUG PATH AT ZERO DISTANCE NDICATED IN INCHES			
MUZZLE	50 YDS.	100 YDS.	150 YDS.	200 YDS.	50 YDS.	100 YDS.	150 YDS.	200 YDS.
2,786	2,001	1,600	1,350	1,164	3	0	-12	-35
2,487	1,388	941	733	595	2	0	-11	-33
2,215	1,418	1,023	824	691	2	0	-10	-30
2,215	1,418	1,023	824	691	2	0	-10	-30
2,364	1,226	837	644	511	3	0	-12	-37
2,487	1,355	916	711	574	2	0	-11	-33
2,487	1,309	881	679	543	2	0	-12	-35
2,807	1,449	931	709	564	2	0	-11	-33
2,364	1,351	934	734	599	4	0	-11	-33
2,742	1,606	1,060	820	671	2	0	-10	-29
2,755	1,334	814	606	475	2	0	-11	-33
2,491	1,295	899	691	546	3	0	-13	-39
2,642	1,664	1,212	977	818	2	0	-11	-32
2,806	1,951	1,445	1,172	999	2	0	-9	
2,885	1,663	1,121	874	715	2	0	-10	-31
2,566	1,811	1,376	1,134	974	2	0	-10	-28
2,725	1,705	1,151	893	739	3	0	-9	-27
3,042	1,726	1,216	957	778	3	0	-12	-35
3,109	2,148	1,553	1,233	1,040	2	0	-9	-25
3,009	1,667	1,050	797	642	2	0	-10	-29
3,157	1,809	1,178	906	783	2	0	-10	-29

	SHELL			SLUG	SLUG	SLUG	SLUG	WAD	WAD	VELOCITY IN FPS				
GA.	LGT-IN.	BRAND	NAME	DESIGN	RIFLED	WGT-GRS	OGIVE	MATERIAL	TYPE	MUZZLE	50 YDS.	100 YDS.	150 YDS.	200 YDS.
12	3	Lightfield	Hybred EXP	Subcaliber	No	546	FN-HP	Plastic	Attached	1,730	1,440	1,210	1,055	960
12	3	Remington	Slugger	Full Bore	Yes	437.5	FN-HP	Fiber	Discarding	1,760	1,345	1,075	935	845
12	3	Remington	Slugger HV	Full Bore	Yes	383	FN-HP	Fiber	Discarding	1,875	1,300	1,000	855	755
16	2 3/4	Federal	Power-Shok	Full Bore	Yes	350	FN-HP	Fiber	Discarding	1,280	1,085	970	890	825
16	2 3/4	Brenneke	Classic	Full Bore	Yes	437.5	SRN	Fiber	Attached	1,580	1,200	995	880	795
16	2 3/4	Remington	Slugger	Full Bore	Yes	350	FN	Fiber	Discarding	1,600	1,175	965	850	765
20	2 3/4	Winchester	Rifled Slug	Full Bore	Yes	328	FN	Fiber	Discarding	1,600	1,155	950	830	740
20	2 3/4	Brenneke	Emerald	Full Bore	Yes	437.5	SRN	Plastic	Attached	1,390	1,035	880	775	690
20	2 3/4	Federal	Truball	Full Bore	Yes	325	FN-HP	Plastic	Discarding	1,600	1,220	1,010	895	810
20	2 3/4	Federal	Power-Shok	Full Bore	Yes	328	FN-HP	Fiber	Discarding	1,600	1,280	1,070	955	870
20	2 3/4	Lightfield	Hybred EXP	Subcaliber	No	385	FN-HP	Plastic	Attached	1,500	1,260	1,090	985	910
20	2 3/4	Remington	Slugger	Full Bore	Yes	273	FN-HP	Fiber	Discarding	1,580	1,240	1,035	920	840
20	2 3/4	Remington	Slugger HV	Full Bore	Yes	219	FN-HP	Fiber	Discarding	1,800	1,320	1,035	900	805
20	3	Brenneke	Magnum	Full Bore	Yes	437.5	SRN	Plastic	Attached	1,475	1,195	920	815	730
20	3	Winchester	Rifled Slug	Full Bore	Yes	328	FN	Fiber	Discarding	1,800	1,290	1,010	875	775
410	2 1/2	Federal	Power-Shok	Full Bore	Yes	109	FN-HP	Fiber	Discarding	1,775	1,335	1,060	925	830
410	2 1/2	Winchester	Rifled Slug	Full Bore	Yes	87.5	FN	Fiber	Discarding	1,830	1,320	1,025	885	785
410	2 1/2	Remington	Slugger	Full Bore	Yes	87.5	FN	Fiber	Discarding	1,830	1,335	1,040	900	805
410	3	Brenneke	Magnum	Full Bore	Yes	109	SRN	Plastic	Attached	1,755	1,180	930	800	700
410	3	Winchester	Rifled Slug	Full Bore	Yes	109	FN	Fiber	Discarding	1,800	1,280	1,000	865	770

SHOTSHELL SLUGS BALLISTICS FOR RIFLED BARRELS

	SHELL				SLUG	SLUG	OGIVE	SABOT	SABOT	STABILIZATION	WAD
GA.	LGT-IN.	BRAND	NAME	DESIGN	WGT-GRS	Construction	TYPE	TYPE	MATERIAL	SYSTEM	MATERIAL
12	2 3/4	Brenneke	SuperSabot	Subcaliber	492	Copper carrier w/ steel core	Pointed, solid	Discarding	LD Plastic	Rotation	Plastic
12	2 3/4	Federal	Barnes Sabot	Subcaliber	328	100% Copper alloy	Pointed HP	Discarding	HD Plastic	Rotation	Plastic
12	2 3/4	Federal	Barnes Sabot	Subcaliber	437.5	100% Copper alloy	Pointed HP	Discarding	HD Plastic	Rotation	Plastic
12	2 3/4	Federal	Barnes Expander	Subcaliber	325	100% Copper alloy	Polymer tip, HP	Discarding	HD Plastic	Rotation	Plastic
12	2 3/4	Winchester	BRI Sabot	Subcaliber	437.5	Lead w/wasp-waist	Flat nose	Discarding	HD Plastic	Rotation	Fiber
12	2 3/4	Winchester	Platinum Tip	Subcaliber	400	Lead core w/copper jacket	Hollow point	Discarding	HD Plastic	Rotation	Fiber
12	2 3/4	Winchester Partition Gold	Partition Gold	Subcaliber	385	Dual lead cores, copper jkt.	Hollow point	Discarding	HD Plastic	Rotation	Fiber
12	2 3/4	Winchester	Dual Bond	Subcaliber	375	Lead core bonded to copper jkt.	Hollow point	Discarding	HD Plastic	Rotation	Fiber
12	2 3/4	Winchester	XP3	Subcaliber	300	Tin core, copper alloy jacket	Polymer tip, HP	Discarding	HD Plastic	Rotation	Fiber
12	2 3/4	Remington	Buckhammer	Full Bore	547	Lead alloy	Flat nose	Attached	LD Plastic	Rotation	Plastic
12	2 3/4	Remington	Copper Solid HP	Subcaliber	437.5	100% Copper alloy	Hollow point	Discarding	HD Plastic	Rotation	Fiber
12	2 3/4	Remington	Ultra Bonded	Subcaliber	385	Lead core bonded to copper jkt.	Hollow point	Discarding	HD Plastic	Rotation	Fiber
12	2 3/4	Remington	Accutip Bonded	Subcaliber	385	Lead core bonded to copper jkt.	Polymer tip, HP	Discarding	HD Plastic	Rotation	Plastic
12	2 3/4	Sauvestre	Balle Fleche HP	Subcaliber	400	Lead with polymer fins	Hollow point	Discarding	HD Plastic	Finned	Plastic
12	2 3/4	Hornady	SST Slug	Subcaliber	300	Lead core, copper jacket	Polymer tip, HP	Discarding	HD Plastic	Rotation	Plastic
12	2 3/4	Hastings	Laser Accurate	Subcaliber	547	Lead	Hollow point	Discarding	LD Plastic	Rotation	Plastic
12	3	Brenneke	Gold Magnum	Full Bore	601	Lead, rifled body	Solid, SRN	None	NA	Rotation	Plastic
12	3	Brenneke	SuperSabot	Subcaliber	492	Copper carrier w/ steel core	Pointed, solid	Discarding	LD Plastic	Rotation	Plastic
12	3	Federal	Barnes Sabot	Subcaliber	325	100% Copper alloy	Pointed HP	Discarding	HD Plastic	Rotation	Plastic

SECTION IX – CHAPTER 62 : SHOTSHELL SLUGS FOR SMOOTHBORE BARRELS, cont. 333

ENERGY IN FT.-LBS.					SLUG PATH AT ZERO DISTANCE INDICATED IN INCHES			
MUZZLE	50 YDS.	100 YDS.	150 YDS.	200 YDS.	50 YDS.	100 YDS.	150 YDS.	200 YDS.
3,628	2,507	1,770	1,351	1,117	1	0	-7	-22
3,009	1,757	1,123	853	693	2	0	-9	-27
2,990	1,444	848	625	487	2	0	-10	-31
1,273	914	731	617	532	3	0	-12	-34
2,425	1,399	961	754	617	2	0	-10	-31
1,989	1,075	726	562	453	2	0	-11	-33
1,864	973	654	503	401	2	0	-11	-35
1,877	1,040	750	581	461	3	0	-14	-41
1,847	1,076	734	576	472	2	0	-10	-31
1,864	1,195	836	661	552	2	0	-9	-27
1,923	1,356	1,017	830	710	2	0	-9	-27
1,513	933	650	515	428	2	0	-10	-29
1,575	849	523	393	315	2	0	-9	-29
2,113	1,163	824	643	516	3	0	-12	-37
2,360	1,210	740	555	440	2	0	-10	-30
762	432	272	206	167	2	0	-9	-28
651	337	203	152	120	2	0	-9	-29
651	347	211	157	125	2	0	-9	-28
745	336	209	155	119	2	0	-12	-36
784	398	243	182	144	2	0	-10	-31

SHOTSHELL SLUGS BALLISTICS FOR RIFLED BARRELS

WAD TYPE	VELOCITY IN FPS					ENERGY IN FT.-LBS.					SLUG PATH AT ZERO DISTANCE INDICATED			
	MUZZLE	50 YDS.	100 YDS.	150 YDS.	200 YDS.	MUZZLE	50 YDS.	100 YDS.	150 YDS.	200 YDS.	50 YDS.	100 YDS.	150 YDS.	200 YDS.
Discarding	1,405	1,165	1,020	925	855	2,156	1,482	1,132	936	800	3	0	-11	-31
Discarding	1,900	1,690	1,490	1,320	1,180	2,629	2,068	1,616	1,269	1,017	1	0	-5	-14
Discarding	1,450	1,320	1,210	1,120	1,050	2,042	1,695	1,421	1,220	1,075	2	0	-8	-22
Discarding	1,900	1,745	1,600	1,465	1,345	2,605	2,198	1,848	1,549	1,304	1	0	-4	-12
Discarding	1,350	1,125	990	905	835	1,770	1,225	952	793	679	3	0	-11	-33
Discarding	1,700	1,555	1,420	1,300	1,200	2,566	2,145	1,790	1,506	1,279	1	0	-5	-16
Discarding	1,900	1,735	1,585	1,445	1,320	3,086	2,579	2,148	1,783	1,490	1	0	-4	-12
Discarding	1,800	1,630	1,470	1,330	1,210	2,698	2,210	1,800	1,476	1,223	1	0	-5	-15
Discarding	2,000	1,800	1,620	1,455	1,310	2,664	2,162	1,753	1,406	1,140	1	0	-4	-12
Attached	1,550	1,320	1,145	1,030	950	2,918	2,117	1,591	1,287	1,098	2	0	-9	-25
Discarding	1,450	1,320	1,210	1,120	1,050	2,042	1,695	1,421	1,220	1,075	2	0	-8	-22
Discarding	1,900	1,770	1,650	1,535	1,425	3,086	2,682	2,327	2,012	1,740	1	0	-4	-11
Discarding	1,850	1,610	1,400	1,225	1,100	2,926	2,222	1,677	1,288	1,032	1	0	-5	-17
Discarding	1,640	1,435	1,235	1,100	1,010	2,389	1,785	1,355	1,076	905	1	0	-7	-21
Discarding	2,000	1,810	1,640	1,480	1,340	2,664	2,188	1,790	1,458	1,190	1	0	-4	-12
Attached	1,500	1,265	1,095	990	915	2,733	1,938	1,457	1,190	1,019	2	0	-9	-27
Attached	1,500	1,135	955	850	765	3,002	1,720	1,218	961	784	2	0	-11	-34
Discarding	1,525	1,245	1,065	955	880	2,540	1,699	1,237	998	845	2	0	-9	-28
Discarding	1,530	1,390	1,270	1,170	1,090	1,689	1,396	1,164	986	856	1	0	-7	-20

	SHELL				SLUG	SLUG	OGIVE	SABOT	SABOT	STABILIZATION	WAD
GA.	LGT-IN.	BRAND	NAME	DESIGN	WGT-GRS	Construction	TYPE	TYPE	MATERIAL	SYSTEM	MATERIAL
12	3	Federal	Barnes Expander	Subcaliber	325	100% Copper alloy	Polymer tip, HP	Discarding	HD Plastic	Rotation	Plastic
12	3	Winchester	BRI Sabot	Subcaliber	437.5	Lead w/wasp-waist	Flat nose	Discarding	HD Plastic	Rotation	Fiber
12	3	Winchester	Partition Gold	Subcaliber	385	Dual lead cores, copper jkt.	Hollow point	Discarding	HD Plastic	Rotation	Fiber
12	3	Winchester	Dual Bond	Subcaliber	375	Lead core bonded to copper jkt.	Hollow point	Discarding	HD Plastic	Rotation	Fiber
12	3	Winchester	XP3 Tin Core	Subcaliber	300	Tin core, copper alloy jacket	Polymer tip, HP	Discarding	HD Plastic	Rotation	Fiber
12	3	Remington	Buckhammer	Full Bore	601	Lead alloy	Flat nose	Attached	LD Plastic	Rotation	Plastic
12	3	Remington	Copper Solid	Subcaliber	437.5	100% Copper alloy	Hollow point	Discarding	HD Plastic	Rotation	Fiber
12	3	Remington	Accutip Bonded	Subcaliber	385	Lead core bonded to copper jkt.	Polymer tip, HP	Discarding	HD Plastic	Rotation	Plastic
12	3	Hastings	Laser Accurate	Subcaliber	547	Lead	Hollow point	Discarding	LD Plastic	Rotation	Plastic
16	2 3/4	Sauvestre	Balle Fleche HP	Subcaliber	347	Lead with polymer fins	Hollow point	Discarding	HD Plastic	Finned	Plastic
16	2 3/4	Lightfield	Commander IDS	Subcaliber	385	Lead	Flat Nose HP	Attached	LD Plastic	Rotation	Plastic
20	2 3/4	Winchester	BRI Sabot	Subcaliber	275	Lead w/wasp-waist	Flat nose	Discarding	HD Plastic	Rotation	Plastic
20	2 3/4	Winchester	Partition Gold	Subcaliber	260	Dual lead cores, copper jkt.	Hollow point	Discarding	HD Plastic	Rotation	Fiber
20	2 3/4	Remington	Copper Solid	Subcaliber	273	100% Copper alloy	Hollow point	Discarding	HD Plastic	Rotation	Fiber
20	2 3/4	Hornady	SST Slug	Subcaliber	250	Lead core, copper jacket	Polymer tip, HP	Discarding	HD Plastic	Rotation	Plastic
20	2 3/4	Hastings	Laser Accurate	Subcaliber	410	Lead	Hollow point	Discarding	LD Plastic	Rotation	Plastic
20	2 3/4	Federal	Barnes Sabot	Subcaliber	275	100% Copper alloy	Pointed HP	Discarding	HD Plastic	Rotation	Plastic
20	3	Hastings	Laser Accurate	Subcaliber	410	Lead	Hollow point	Discarding	LD Plastic	Rotation	Plastic
20	3	Federal	Barnes Sabot	Subcaliber	275	100% Copper alloy	Pointed HP	Discarding	HD Plastic	Rotation	Plastic
20	3	Federal	Barnes Expander	Subcaliber	275	100% Copper alloy	Polymer tip, HP	Discarding	HD Plastic	Rotation	Plastic
20	3	Winchester	Partition Gold	Subcaliber	260	Dual lead cores, copper jkt.	Hollow point	Discarding	HD Plastic	Rotation	Fiber

CHAPTER 63 : PROPRIETARY SPORTING RIFLE - CURRENT

	BULLET	VELOCITY in FPS						ENERGY IN FT.-LBS.			
CALIBER	WGT-GRS	MUZZLE	100 YDS.	200 YDS.	300 YDS.	400 YDS.	500 YDS.	MUZZLE	100 YDS.	200 YDS.	300 YDS.
7x64mm Brenneke	150	2,905	2,685	2,480	2,280	2,090	1,910	2,811	2,403	2,044	1,729
7x64Rmm Brenneke	150	2,855	2,640	2,430	2,235	2,045	1,870	2,715	2,319	1,970	1,664
8x64Smm Brenneke	198	2,780	2,525	2,285	2,055	1,840	1,645	3,397	2,802	2,292	1,858
8x75RSmm Brenneke	198	2,715	2,465	2,225	2,000	1,790	1,600	3,240	2,668	2,177	1,760
8x75Rmm Brenneke	198	3,050	2,780	2,525	2,285	2,055	1,840	4,089	3,395	2,800	2,291
7mm Dakota	160	3,200	2,950	2,710	2,485	2,270	2,065	3,638	3,086	2,607	2,190
.300 Dakota	180	3,300	3,060	2,835	2,620	2,415	2,220	4,352	3,745	3,212	2,743
.330 Dakota	250	2,900	2,685	2,480	2,285	2,095	1,920	4,668	4,001	3,413	2,895
.375 Dakota	270	2,800	2,560	2,335	2,120	1,920	1,730	4,700	3,935	3,272	2,700
.404 Dakota	400	2,410	2,155	1,920	1,700	1,500	1,325	5,158	4,129	3,266	2,561
.450 Dakota	500	2,450	2,170	1,905	1,665	1,450	1,270	6,664	5,221	4,032	3,082
.240 Holland & Holland	100	2,900	2,655	2,425	2,210	2,000	1,810	1,867	1,568	1,308	1,083
.244 Holland & Holland	100	3,500	3,220	2,960	2,715	2,480	2,260	2,720	2,305	1,946	1,637
.275 Holland & Holland	140	2,650	2,425	2,215	2,010	1,820	1,645	2,183	1,817	1,513	1,250
.275 Holland & Holland Flanged	140	2,500	2,285	2,080	1,885	1,705	1,535	1,929	1,610	1,334	1,095

WAD TYPE	VELOCITY IN FPS					ENERGY IN FT.-LBS.					SLUG PATH AT ZERO DISTANCE INDICATED			
	MUZZLE	50 YDS.	100 YDS.	150 YDS.	200 YDS.	MUZZLE	50 YDS.	100 YDS.	150 YDS.	200 YDS.	50 YDS.	100 YDS.	150 YDS.	200 YDS.
Discarding	1,900	1,745	1,600	1,465	1,345	2,605	2,198	1,848	1,549	1,304	1	0	-3	-12
Discarding	1,400	1,155	1,005	915	845	1,904	1,292	984	813	693	3	0	-11	-32
Discarding	2,000	1,830	1,675	1,530	1,395	3,420	2,870	2,402	2,001	1,668	1	0	-3	-10
Discarding	1,850	1,690	1,545	1,410	1,290	2,850	2,382	1,982	1,648	1,820	1	0	-4	-13
Discarding	2,100	1,900	1,710	1,535	1,380	2,937	2,399	1,949	1,574	1,272	1	0	-3	-10
Attached	1,500	1,235	1,060	955	880	3,002	2,036	1,503	1,221	1,038	2	0	-9	-28
Discarding	1,550	1,380	1,240	1,130	1,045	2,334	1,856	1,494	1,236	1,063	2	0	-7	-21
Discarding	1,900	1,610	1,360	1,165	1,040	3,086	2,215	1,580	1,164	923	1	0	-5	-17
Attached	1,625	1,360	1,155	1,025	940	3,207	2,241	1,623	1,280	1,077	1	0	-8	-24
Discarding	1,560	1,285	1,090	975	900	1,875	1,268	917	735	621	2	0	-9	-26
Attached	1,630	1,360	1,155	1,025	940	2,271	1,582	1,142	899	756	2	0	-8	-24
Discarding	1,400	1,145	995	900	830	1,197	797	604	497	421	2	0	-11	-32
Discarding	1,900	1,720	1,555	1,405	1,270	2,084	1,709	1,394	1,136	935	1	0	-4	-13
Discarding	1,500	1,360	1,240	1,140	1,065	1,364	1,121	931	790	689	1	0	-7	-21
Discarding	1,800	1,630	1,470	1,330	1,210	1,798	1,471	1,200	983	815	1	0	-4	-13
Attached	1,475	1,245	1,085	985	910	1,980	1,413	1,073	882	758	2	0	-9	-24
Discarding	1,600	1,435	1,290	1,170	1,080	1,563	1,254	1,016	838	714	1	0	-6	-19
Attached	1,600	1,340	1,145	1,020	935	2,330	1,635	1,193	948	801	2	0	-8	-24
Discarding	1,900	1,710	1,530	1,370	1,235	2,204	1,780	1,429	1,149	934	1	0	-4	-13
Discarding	1,900	1,725	1,560	1,410	1,280	2,204	1,815	1,487	1,216	1,004	1	0	-4	-12
Discarding	2,000	1,810	1,640	1,480	1,340	2,309	1,896	1,552	1,264	1,034	1	0	-4	-11

CHAPTER 63 : PROPRIETARY SPORTING RIFLE - CURRENT

ENERGY IN FT.-LBS.		BULLET PATH AT ZERO DISTANCE INDICATED									
400 YDS.	500 YDS.	100 YDS.	200 YDS.	300 YDS.	400 YDS.	500 YDS.	100 YDS.	200 YDS.	300 YDS.	400 YDS.	500 YDS.
1,453	1,212	0	-3	-12	-28	-51	2	0	-7	-21	-43
1,396	1,163	0	-4	-13	-29	-54	2	0	-8	-22	-45
1,490	1,188	0	-4	-15	-33	-63	2	0	-9	-26	-53
1,409	1,122	0	-4	-10	-18	-30	2	0	-9	-27	-56
1,856	1,489	0	-3	-12	-27	-50	2	0	-7	-21	-42
1,827	1,512	0	-3	-10	-23	-42	1	0	-6	-18	-36
2,331	1,968	0	-2	-9	-20	-38	1	0	-6	-16	-33
2,440	2,042	0	-3	-12	-28	-51	2	0	-7	-21	-43
2,207	1,793	0	-4	-14	-32	-59	2	0	-8	-24	-50
1,994	1,559	0	-6	-22	-49	-93	3	0	-13	-37	-78
2,337	1,792	0	-6	-22	-50	-95	3	0	-13	-38	-80
890	725	0	-3	-13	-29	-54	2	0	-8	-22	-46
1,368	1,135	0	-2	-8	-18	-34	1	0	-5	-14	-29
1,024	836	0	-4	-16	-36	-67	2	0	-9	-27	-56
895	728	0	-5	-18	-42	-77	3	0	-10	-31	-64

CALIBER	BULLET WGT-GRS	VELOCITY in FPS						ENERGY IN FT.-LBS.			
		MUZZLE	100 YDS.	200 YDS.	300 YDS.	400 YDS.	500 YDS.	MUZZLE	100 YDS.	200 YDS.	300 YDS.
.300 Holland & Holland Magnum	180	2,750	2,540	2,335	2,145	1,960	1,790	3,022	2,576	2,184	1,840
.375 Holland & Holland Magnum	270	2,650	2,420	2,200	1,995	1,800	1,620	4,210	3,510	2,905	2,384
400/375 Holland & Holland Belted NE	270	2,175	1,970	1,775	1,595	1,435	1,295	2,836	2,325	1,890	1,530
.400 Holland & Holland Magnum	400	2,400	2,135	1,890	1,660	1,46-	1,285	5,115	4,052	3,166	2,454
500/465 H&H Nitro Express	480	2,150	1,880	1,645	1,425	1,250	1,115	4,926	3,783	2,876	2,170
.465 Holland & Holland Magnum	480	2,400	2,115	1,855	1,615	1,405	1,230	6,139	4,778	3,663	2,783
6.5x47mm Lapua	108	2,925	2,725	2,530	2,350	2,170	2,005	2,052	1,780	1,537	1,322
	139	2,690	2,535	2,385	2,245	2,105	1,970	2,233	1,985	1,758	1,553
.300 Lapua Magnum	150	3,600	3,275	2,970	2,685	2,420	2,170	4,316	3,567	2,937	2,404
	185	3,300	2,985	2,690	2,415	2,155	1,915	4,473	3,659	2,975	2,387
.338 Lapua Magnum	250	2,970	2,825	2,680	2,545	2,410	2,280	4,895	4,424	3,992	3,593
	300	2,725	2,590	2,460	2,335	2,215	2,095	4,946	4,474	4,037	3,635
6.53 Lazzeroni Scramjet Long Magnum	100	3,550	3,250	2,970	2,710	2,460	2,225	2,798	2,345	1,959	1,628
7.21 Lazzeroni Firebird Long Magnum	139	3,700	3,440	3,200	2,970	2,755	2,545	4,225	3,657	3,160	2,723
7.82 Lazzeroni Warbird Long Magnum	150	3,775	3,440	3,135	2,845	2,575	2,325	4,746	3,945	3,270	2,698
8.59 Lazzeroni Titan Long Magnum	225	3,300	3,065	2,840	2,630	2,425	2,235	5,440	4,691	4,032	3,452
10.57 Lazzeroni Meteor Long Magnum	400	2,800	2,525	2,270	2,030	1,800	1,595	6,963	5,672	4,577	3,654
6mm Norma BR	100	3,160	2,785	2,440	2,120	1,820	1,560	2,217	1,721	1,320	996
6.5-.284 Norma	156	2,790	2,530	2,285	2,055	1,840	1,640	2,696	2,220	1,812	1,465
.308 Norma Magnum	180	2,955	2,635	2,335	2,055	1,795	1,560	3,490	2,771	2,175	1,684
.358 Norma Magnum	250	2,755	2,495	2,245	2,010	1,795	1,595	4,213	3,449	2,797	2,246
.224 Weatherby Magnum	55	3,650	3,192	2,780	2,403	2,056	1,741	1,627	1,244	944	705
.240 Weatherby Magnum	100	3,405	3,135	2,880	2,640	2,415	2,200	2,576	2,183	1,844	1,550
.257 Weatherby Magnum	115	3,400	3,170	2,950	2,745	2,545	2,355	2,952	2,566	2,226	1,924
.270 Weatherby Magnum	140	3,320	3,115	2,915	2,725	2,545	2,375	3,427	3,014	2,644	2,313
7mm Weatherby Magnum	150	3,300	3,095	2,895	2,710	2,525	2,355	3,627	3,187	2,793	2,442
.300 Weatherby Magnum	180	3,250	3,050	2,860	2,675	2,505	2,335	4,223	3,721	3,271	2,868
.30-378 Weatherby Magnum	180	3,420	3,215	3,015	2,825	2,645	2,470	4,676	4,126	3,634	3,193
.340 Weatherby Magnum	250	2,940	2,745	2,555	2,370	2,200	2,030	4,801	4,176	3,618	3,120
.338-378 Weatherby Magnum	250	3,060	2,855	2,680	2,475	2,295	2,125	5,197	4,528	3,933	3,401
.375 Weatherby Magnum	300	2,800	2,570	2,365	2,140	1,963	1,760	5,224	4,408	3,696	3,076
.378 Weatherby Magnum	270	3,060	2,870	2,684	2,510	2,335	2,175	5,615	4,932	4,319	3,770
.416 Weatherby Magnum	350	2,880	2,700	2,530	2,365	2,210	2,055	6,448	5,674	4,977	4,349
.460 Weatherby Magnum	450	2,660	2,420	2,200	1,985	1,785	1,600	7,072	5,864	4,823	3,932
375/303 Westley Richards	200	2,725	2,425	2,140	1,880	1,640	1,430	3,297	2,608	2,038	1,569
.318 Westley Richards	250	2,400	2,150	1,915	1,695	1,500	1,325	3,197	2,564	2,031	1,596
400/360 Westley Richards	285	1,950	1,680	1,440	1,240	1,100	1,005	2,406	1,784	1,310	976
.425 Westley Richards	410	2,325	2,065	1,820	1,600	1,400	1,235	4,921	3,878	3,016	2,328
.476 Westley Richards	520	2,150	1,915	1,695	1,495	1,325	1,185	5,337	4,225	3,318	2,588

CHAPTER 64 : PROPRIETARY SPORTING RIFLE - OBSOLETE

CALIBER	BULLET WGT-GRS	VELOCITY in FPS						ENERGY IN FT.-LBS.			
		MUZZLE	100 YDS.	200 YDS.	300 YDS.	400 YDS.	500 YDS.	MUZZLE	100 YDS.	200 YDS.	300 YDS.
.338 A-Square	250	3,120	2,895	2,680	2,475	2,280	2,090	5,403	,4684	3,984	3,398
.375 A-Square	300	2,920	2,555	2,215	1,905	1,625	1,380	5,679	4,344	3,270	2,414
.400 A-Square DPM	400	2,400	2,145	1,910	1,690	1,490	1,320	5,115	4,094	3,236	2,537
.495 A-Square	570	2,350	2,075	1,820	1,590	1,385	1,215	6,989	5,451	4,190	3,194
.500 A-Square	600	2,470	2,205	1,955	1,725	1,515	1,335	8,127	6,475	5,096	3,968

ENERGY IN FT.-LBS.		BULLET PATH AT ZERO DISTANCE INDICATED									
400 YDS.	500 YDS.	100 YDS.	200 YDS.	300 YDS.	400 YDS.	500 YDS.	100 YDS.	200 YDS.	300 YDS.	400 YDS.	500 YDS.
1,539	1,279	0	-4	-14	-32	-59	2	0	-8	-24	-49
1,940	1,571	0	-5	-16	-36	-68	2	0	-9	-28	-57
1,234	1,004	0	-8	-26	-58	-108	4	0	-15	-43	-89
1,887	1,465	0	-6	-22	-51	-96	3	0	-13	-39	-81
1,661	1,321	0	-9	-30	-69	-130	4	0	-16	-49	-102
2,100	1,612	0	-6	-23	-53	-101	3	0	-14	-40	-85
1,131	962	0	-3	-12	-27	-49	2		-7	-20	-41
1,367	1,198	0	-4	-14	-31	-55	2	0	-8	-23	-46
1,951	1,568	0	-2	-8	-18	-35	1	0	-5	-15	-30
1,911	1,505	0	-2	-10	-23	-43	1	0	-6	-18	-37
3,226	2,890	0	-3	-11	-24	-43	1	0	-6	-18	-35
3,265	2,925	0	-4	-13	-29	-52	2	0	-8	-22	-43
1,344	1,100	0	-2	-8	-18	-34	1	0	-5	-14	-30
2,339	2,000	0	-1	-6	-15	-29	1	0	-4	-12	-25
2,212	1,797	0	-1	-6	-16	-30	1	0	-4	-13	-27
2,940	2,490	0	-2	-9	-20	-38	1	0	-6	-16	-32
2,884	2,263	0	-4	-15	-34	-64	2	0	-9	-26	-54
737	539	0	-3	-12	-29	-56	2	0	-7	-23	-49
1,172	933	0	-4	-15	-33	-63	2	0	-9	-25	-53
1,285	972	0	-4	-14	-32	-61	2	0	-8	-25	-52
1,785	1,410	0	-4	-15	-35	-66	2	0	-9	-27	-55
516	370	0	-2	-8	-21	-42	1	0	-6	-17	-37
1,294	1,073	0	-2	-8	-20	-37	1	0	-5	-15	-32
1,656	1,419	0	-2	-8	-19	-34	1	0	-5	-15	-30
2,016	1,751	0	-1	-2	-19	-35	1	0	-5	-15	-30
2,127	1,844	0	-2	-8	-20	-36	1	0	-5	-15	-31
2,505	2,179	0	-2	-9	-20	-37	1	0	-5	-16	-31
2,797	2,441	0	-2	-8	-18	-33	1	0	-5	-14	-28
2,678	2,286	0	-3	-11	-26	-47	1	0	-7	-20	-39
2,927	2,507	0	-3	-11	-24	-44	1	0	-6	-18	-37
2,541	2,084	0	-4	-14	-31	-58	2	0	-8	-24	-49
3,276	2,834	0	-3	-12	-27	-52	2	0	-7	-21	-44
3,785	3,279	0	-4	-13	-31	-58	2	0	-8	-24	-49
3,178	2,553	0	-5	-16	-37	-69	2	0	-9	-28	-57
1,196	905	0	-5	-16	-39	-74	2	0	-10	-30	-62
1,246	976	0	-6	-22	-50	-93	3	0	-13	-38	-78
763	637	0	-11	-39	-89	-168	5	0	-22	-68	-141
1,788	1,394	0	-7	-24	-55	-104	3	0	-14	-42	-87
2,027	1,619	0	-8	-29	-64	-120	4	0	-16	-48	-100

CHAPTER 64 : PROPRIETARY SPORTING RIFLE - OBSOLETE

ENERGY IN FT.-LBS.		BULLET PATH AT ZERO DISTANCE INDICATED									
400 YDS.	500 YDS.	100 YDS.	200 YDS.	300 YDS.	400 YDS.	500 YDS.	100 YDS.	200 YDS.	300 YDS.	400 YDS.	500 YDS.
2,881	2,428	0	-3	-10	-23	-43	1	0	-66	-18	-37
1,757	1,269	0	-4	-15	-25	-70	2	0	-9	-28	-60
1,975	1,545	0	-6	-22	-50	-94	3	0	-13	-38	-79
2,424	1,873	0	-7	-24	-55	-105	3	0	-14	-42	-88
3,066	2,378	0	-6	-21	-47	-89	3	0	-12	-36	-75

CALIBER	BULLET WGT-GRS	VELOCITY in FPS						ENERGY IN FT.-LBS.			
		MUZZLE	100 YDS.	200 YDS.	300 YDS.	400 YDS.	500 YDS.	MUZZLE	100 YDS.	200 YDS.	300 YDS.
.32 Ballard Extra Long	115	1,200	1,025	925	850	785	730	368	269	218	184
.32-40 Ballard/Winchester	165	1,440	1,235	1,085	990	920	865	760	557	432	359
.38 Ballard Extra Long	146	1,275	1,010	880	785	705	640	527	330	250	200
.38-50/55 Ballard	255	1,320	1,145	1,035	955	895	845	986	745	604	516
.40-70 Ballard	330	1,335	1,185	1,075	1,000	940	890	1,306	1,029	848	732
.40-90 Ballard	370	1,425	1,225	1,085	990	925	870	1,668	1,233	964	806
.44 Ballard Long	227	1,200	1,005	890	810	740	680	726	507	401	331
.44 Ballard Extra Long	265	1,320	1,100	975	895	825	770	1,025	715	562	469
.44-100 Ballard	535	1,400	1,240	1,120	1,030	965	915	2,328	1,827	1,484	1,262
.45-100 Ballard	550	1,370	1,220	1,105	1,025	965	915	2,292	1,820	1,497	1,286
.32-40 Bullard	150	1,490	1,275	1,115	1,015	940	880	739	542	416	342
.38-45 Bullard	190	1,390	1,135	990	900	830	770	815	545	414	341
.40-70 Bullard	232	1,500	1,235	1,060	955	880	820	1,159	786	580	472
.40-75 Bullard	258	1,515	1,260	1,085	980	900	840	1,315	910	674	547
.40-90 Bullard	300	1,570	1,305	1,110	995	915	850	1,642	1,131	822	658
.45-85 Bullard	290	1,600	1,290	1,080	960	880	815	1,648	1,069	750	594
.50-115 Bullard	300	1,540	1,170	980	870	785	715	1,580	913	638	503
5.6x61mm vom Hofe Super Express	77	3,710	3,345	3,010	2,695	2,405	2,135	2,353	1,912	1,547	1,244
7x66mm vom Hofe Super Express	123	3,640	3,315	3,015	2,730	2,465	2,215	3,618	3,000	2,478	2,036
7x73mm Belted vom Hofe SE	170	3,355	3,100	2,860	2,635	2,420	2,215	4,828	3,631	3,092	2,622
7x75mm vom Hofe Super Express	170	3,300	3,050	2,815	2,590	2,375	2,175	4,110	3,510	32,987	2,530
.280 Jeffery	140	3,000	2,760	2,535	2,317	2,110	1,915	2,798	2,369	1,995	1,669
.303 Jeffery Magnum	174	2,850	2,505	2,185	1,890	1,625	1,390	3,138	2,425	1,846	1,380
.333 Jeffery	250	2,500	2,305	2,115	1,940	1,770	1,615	3,469	2,946	2,487	2,085
.450/400 Jeffery	400	2,100	1,865	1,650	1,455	1,290	1,155	3,917	3,089	2,419	21,881
.404 Jeffery	450	2,600	2,365	2,140	1,925	1,730	1,550	6,754	5,579	4,571	3,708
.475 No.2 Jeffery	500	2,150	1,885	1,645	1,425	1,240	1,115	5,132	3,940	32,996	2,261
.500 Jeffery	535	2,400	2,105	1,825	1,580	1,365	1,190	6,842	5,251	3,964	2,962
.22 Newton	90	3,105	2,885	2,675	2,475	2,280	2,100	1,926	1,662	1,429	1,223
.256 Newton	123	3,105	2,875	2,660	2,455	2,255	2,065	2,633	2,260	1,932	1,643
.30 Newton	172	3,000	2,765	2,545	2,335	2,135	1,945	3,437	2,923	2,474	2,081
.33 Newton	200	3,000	2,740	2,490	2,260	2,035	1,830	3,996	3,330	2,757	2,264
.35 Newton	250	2,975	2,725	2,485	2,260	2,050	1,850	4,913	4,120	3,434	2,841
.40 Newton	301	3,040	2,665	2,320	2,000	1,710	1,450	6,176	4,743	3,589	2,669
7mm Canadian Magnum	140	3,525	3,255	23,000	2,760	2,530	2,315	3,862	3,290	2,795	2,364
.300 Canadian Magnum	180	3,425	3,180	2,945	2,725	2,515	2,315	4,688	4,039	3,470	2,971
.338 Canadian Magnum	225	3,110	2,865	2,635	2,415	2,205	2,005	4,832	4,102	3,467	32,912
.375 Canadian Magnum	270	3,000	2,750	2,515	2,290	2,080	1,880	5,395	4,538	3,794	3,150
.458 Canadian Magnum	350	2,575	2,145	1,760	1,430	1,180	1,025	5,153	3,574	2,042,403	1,585
.275 Rigby	140	3,000	2,760	2,530	2,310	2,105	1,910	2,798	2,366	21,990	1,662
400/350 Rigby	310	2,100	1,885	1,685	1,505	1,345	1,210	3,035	2,445	1,957	1,556
.350 Rigby Magnum	225	2,625	2,260	1,920	1,620	1,360	1,160	3,442	2,546	1,842	1,310
.416 Rigby	410	2,430	2,170	1,930	1,705	1,500	1,325	5,375	4,291	3,484	2,644
.450 Rigby	550	2,100	1,875	1,670	1,480	1,315	1,180	5,385	4,293	3,399	2,674

ENERGY IN FT.-LBS.		BULLET PATH AT ZERO DISTANCE INDICATED									
400 YDS.	500 YDS.	100 YDS.	200 YDS.	300 YDS.	400 YDS.	500 YDS.	100 YDS.	200 YDS.	300 YDS.	400 YDS.	500 YDS.
158	136	0	-31	-102	-221	-394	16	0	-56	-158	-316
311	274	0	-21	-72	-157	-282	11	0	-40	-114	-228
162	133	0	-32	-108	-238	-435	16	0	-60	-174	-355
453	403	0	-25	-82	-176	-312	12	0	-45	-126	-250
648	583	0	-23	-76	-164	-289	12	0	-42	-117	231
700	619	0	-22	-73	-158	-283	12	0	-40	-115	-229
277	234	0	-3	-108	-235	-422	16	0	-59	-170	-341
402	349	0	-27	-89	-194	-347	13	0	-49	-140	-280
1,110	996	0	-21	-70	-151	-268	11	0	-38	-109	-215
1,138	1,025	0	-22	-72	-154	-273	11	0	-39	-111	-219
294	259	0	-20	-68	-148	-266	10	0	-38	-108	-217
290	249	0	-25	-85	-186	-335	13	0	-47	-136	-272
401	347	0	-21	-73	-161	-292	11	0	-41	-118	-239
466	406	0	-20	-70	-155	-280	10	0	-39	-114	-229
557	483	0	-19	-66	-147	-267	10	0	-37	-109	-220
497	426	0	-20	-68	-153	-281	10	0	-39	-114	-232
412	342	0	-24	-82	-184	-339	12	0	-47	-137	-280
990	779	0	-2	-7	-17	-34	1	0	-5	-14	-30
1,660	1,341	0	-2	9	-16	-33	1	0	-5	-14	-29
2,210	1,851	0	-2	-9	-20	-37	1	0	-5	-16	-32
2,130	1,787	0	-2	-9	-21	-39	1	0	-6	-16	-33
1,386	1,142	0	-3	-12	-27	-49	2	0	-7	-20	-41
1,018	746	0	-4	-15	-37	-72	2	0	-9	-29	-61
1,738	1,445	0	-5	-18	-40	-74	3	0	-10	-30	-61
1,476	1,187	0	-9	-30	-68	-127	4	0	-17	-51	-105
2,988	2,394	0	-5	-17	-39	-73	2	0	-10	-29	-61
1,730	1,376	0	-9	-30	-69	-130	4	0	-17	-51	-108
2,206	1,682	0	-6	-23	-54	-105	3	0	-14	-42	-89
1,040	880	0	-3	-10	-24	-44	1	0	-6	-18	-37
1,389	1,167	0	-3	-10	-24	-44	1	0	-6	-18	-37
1,739	1,441	0	-3	-11	-26	-49	2	0	-7	-20	-41
1,843	1,485	0	-3	-12	-28	-51	2	0	-7	-21	-44
2,331	1,895	0	-3	-12	-28	-51	2	0	-7	-21	-43
1,947	1,406	0	-3	-13	-32	-63	2	0	-8	-25	-55
1,989	1,662	0	-2	-8	-18	-33	1	0	-5	-14	-29
2,531	2,144	0	-2	-8	-19	-35	1	0	-5	-15	-30
2,430	2,011	0	-3	-11	-24	-45	1	0	-6	-19	-38
2,595	2,118	0	-3	-12	-27	-50	2	0	-7	-21	-42
1,078	814	0	-6	-24	-59	-120	3	0	-15	-47	-104
1,378	1,133	0	-3	-12	-28	-49	2	0	-7	-21	-42
1,243	1,006	0	-9	-29	-65	-121	4	0	-16	-48	-100
925	675	0	-5	-20	-49	-97	3	0	-12	-38	-83
2,049	1,598	0	-6	-21	-49	-92	3	0	-13	-37	-77
2,117	1,707	0	-9	-30	-67	-124	4	0	-17	-49	-102

CALIBER	BULLET WGT-GRS	VELOCITY in FPS						ENERGY IN FT.-LBS.			
		MUZZLE	100 YDS.	200 YDS.	300 YDS.	400 YDS.	500 YDS.	MUZZLE	100 YDS.	200 YDS.	300 YDS.
6.5x48Rmm Sauer	126	1,155	955	840	755	685	620	373	256	199	160
6.5x58Rmm Sauer	126	2,020	1,470	1,100	930	825	740	1,141	603	339	242
8x48Rmm Sauer	196	1,665	1,420	1,220	1,080	990	920	1,206	876	648	508
8x58Rmm Sauer	196	1,690	1,440	1,235	1,090	995	925	1,243	903	666	518
8x72Rmm Sauer	227	1,900	1,625	1,385	1,195	1,065	975	1,819	1,332	968	721
9.3x72Rmm Sauer	286	1,690	1,395	1,165	1,025	935	870	1,814	1,232	865	668
.40-50 Sharps straight	265	1,410	1,190	1,050	955	890	835	1,170	836	647	539
.40-50 Sharps necked	265	1,460	1,230	1,070	970	900	845	1,254	888	675	556
.40-70 Sharps straight	330	1,260	1,120	1,025	960	905	855	1,163	921	772	672
.40-70 Sharps necked	330	1,420	1,240	1,110	1,015	950	900	1,477	1,130	901	759
.40-90 Sharps straight	370	1,385	1,230	1,115	1,030	965	915	1,576	1,245	1,018	870
.40-90 Sharps necked	370	1,475	1,305	1,170	1,070	995	940	1,787	1,401	1,122	938
.44-60 Sharps necked	396	1,250	1,110	1,020	950	895	850	1,374	1,087	911	794
.44-77 Sharps necked	365	1,250	1,100	1,005	935	880	830	1,266	985	819	709
.44-90 Sharps Special	520	1,460	1,290	1,155	1,055	985	930	2,461	1,921	1,537	1,288
.44-90 Sharps necked	520	1,270	1,140	1,045	980	925	880	1,862	1,498	1,263	1,106
.44-100 Sharps necked	520	1,380	1,225	1,105	1,025	960	910	2,199	1,730	1,412	1,207
.45-75 Sharps straight	400	1,330	1,165	1,050	970	910	860	1,571	1,203	978	838
.45-90 Sharps straight	550	1,360	1,230	1,125	1,045	990	940	2,259	1,843	1,544	1,339
.45-100 Sharps straight	550	1,435	1,290	1,175	1,085	1,015	965	2,515	2,039	1,682	1,433
.45-110 Sharps straight	550	1,510	1,355	1,225	1,120	1,045	985	2,784	2,264	1,833	1,538
.45-120 Sharps straight	500	1,520	1,350	1,210	1,100	1,025	965	2,565	2,025	1,623	1,347
.50-90 Sharps straight	473	1,350	1,170	1,050	970	905	855	1,914	1,441	1,158	984
.50-100 Sharps straight	473	1,425	1,230	1,090	995	925	870	2,133	1,584	1,241	1,038
.50-110 Sharps straight	473	1,500	1,285	1,125	1,020	945	890	2,363	1,739	1,332	1,094
.50-140 Sharps straight	700	1,355	1,225	1,125	1,050	990	945	2,854	2,341	1,971	1,713
.22-15 Stevens	60	1,150	990	895	820	760	705	176	131	107	90
.25-21 Stevens	86	1,250	1,025	910	820	750	690	298	201	157	129
.25-25 Stevens	86	1,500	1,165	985	880	800	735	430	259	185	148
.25-35 Stevens	165	1,400	1,220	1,085	1,000	935	880	718	544	433	365
.28-30 Stevens	120	1,500	1,270	1,100	995	920	865	599	428	323	264
.32-35 Stevens	165	1,400	1,215	1,080	990	925	870	718	539	427	359
.38-35 Stevens	215	1,255	1,070	965	885	825	770	752	548	442	375
.38-45 Stevens	210	1,420	1,170	1,015	920	850	790	940	635	480	395
.22-10-45 Maynard	45	1,100	905	790	695	615	550	121	82	62	48
.35-30 Maynard	250	1,280	1,115	1,010	935	875	825	909	689	564	484
.35-40 Maynard	255	1,355	1,160	1,035	950	890	835	1,039	765	607	513
.40-40 Maynard	330	1,260	1,105	1,005	930	875	825	1,163	893	737	635
.40-60 Maynard	330	1,370	1,180	1,050	965	905	850	1,375	1,021	811	686
.40-70 Maynard	270	1,645	1,400	1,200	1,065	975	910	1,622	1,171	865	681
.44-60 Maynard	430	1,200	1,085	1,000	940	890	845	1,375	1,119	957	844
.44-100 Maynard	520	1,400	1,220	1,090	1,005	940	885	2,263	1,722	1,374	1,161
.50-50 Maynard	400	1,210	1,050	955	880	825	770	1,300	981	807	691
.50-70 Maynard	400	1,400	1,170	1,030	940	870	815	1,741	1,221	940	781
.50-100 Maynard	500	1,450	1,260	1,120	1,020	950	895	2,334	1,765	1,388	1,159
.55-100 Maynard	530	1,410	1,190	1,050	955	890	835	2,339	1,672	1,293	1,077

ENERGY IN FT.-LBS.		BULLET PATH AT ZERO DISTANCE INDICATED									
400 YDS.	500 YDS.	100 YDS.	200 YDS.	300 YDS.	400 YDS.	500 YDS.	100 YDS.	200 YDS.	300 YDS.	400 YDS.	500 YDS.
130	107	0	-36	-120	-263	-480	18	0	-66	-191	-390
190	153	0	-15	-58	-139	-266	8	0	-36	-109	-228
425	369	0	-16	-55	-124	-227	8	0	-31	-92	-187
432	374	0	-15	-54	-121	221	8	0	-31	-90	-183
571	481	0	-12	-42	-96	-180	6	0	-24	-73	-151
556	478	0	-17	-59	-133	-244	8	0	-34	-100	-203
465	408	0	-23	-77	-168	-301	12	0	-43	-122	-244
477	418	0	-22	-73	-160	-288	11	0	-41	-117	-234
598	538	0	-26	85	-181	-318	13	0	-46	-129	-253
663	591	0	-21	-70	-152	-272	11	0	-39	-110	-219
768	690	0	-22	-71	-152	-271	11	0	-39	-110	-217
816	727	0	-19	-63	-138	-246	10	0	-35	-100	-199
706	635	0	-27	-86	-184	-323	13	0	-47	-131	-257
627	561	0	-27	-88	-188	-332	14	0	-48	-134	-264
1,123	1,002	0	-19	-65	-141	-252	10	0	-36	-102	-204
988	895	0	-25	-82	-175	-306	13	0	-44	-124	-243
1,065	957	0	-22	-72	-154	-274	11	0	-39	-111	-220
738	659	0	-24	-79	-171	-303	12	0	-43	-123	-242
1,193	1,081	0	-22	-71	-151	-266	11	0	-38	-108	-212
1,261	1,134	0	-19	-64	-138	-245	10	0	-35	-99	-196
1,334	1,190	0	-17	-58	-126	-225	9	0	-32	-91	-182
1,164	1,034	0	-18	-59	-129	-231	9	0	-33	-94	-187
862	767	0	-24	-79	-170	-302	12	0	-43	-122	-242
902	798	0	-22	-72	-157	-281	11	0	-40	-114	-227
941	829	0	-20	-66	-146	-262	10	0	-37	-107	-213
1,529	1,388	0	-22	-71	-151	-265	11	0	-38	-107	-211
77	66	0	-34	-110	-237	-423	17	0	-60	-170	-339
108	91	0	-31	-103	-225	-406	16	0	-57	-163	-328
122	103	0	-24	-83	-184	-336	12	0	-47	-136	-277
319	284	0	-22	-73	-158	-282	11	0	-40	-114	-227
226	198	0	-20	-69	-152	-273	10	0	-39	-111	-223
314	278	0	-22	-74	-160	-285	11	0	-41	-116	-230
324	283	0	-29	-94	-203	-360	14	0	-51	-146	-289
336	290	0	-24	-81	-177	-320	12	0	-45	-130	-260
38	30	0	-41	-136	-302	-558	20	0	-75	-221	-456
425	378	0	-26	-87	-185	-329	13	0	-47	-133	-263
447	395	0	-24	-80	-174	-310	12	0	-44	-125	-249
559	499	0	-27	-88	-188	-333	14	0	-48	-134	-266
598	530	0	-23	-78	-168	-300	12	0	-43	-122	-241
572	497	0	-16	-57	-127	-233	8	0	-32	-95	-192
757	685	0	-28	-91	-192	-336	14	0	-49	-136	-266
1,016	905	0	-22	-73	-157	-280	11	0	-40	-114	-225
602	529	0	-30	-97	-208	-369	15	0	-53	-149	-295
671	586	0	-24	-80	-174	-312	12	0	-44	-126	-253
1,007	894	0	-20	-69	-149	-267	10	0	-38	-108	-216
930	816	0	-23	-77	-168	-301	12	0	-43	-122	-244

12 GAUGE (12 BORE) EXPLORA

SPECIMEN AND PHOTOS COURTESY OF PAUL SMITH

This is a 12 ga (bore) hunting round dating from the 1920's to 1930's and used the trade name 'Explora'.

This interesting projectile was designed by Leslie Taylor and patented by Westley Richards. It weighs about 730 grains and was called the 'L.T.' Pointed bullet.

The case is brass and has 2 card board linings. The inner card board lining terminates and supports the card and fibre wads. This determines the seating depth of the projectile.

The cordite is very fine grained and mixed within is finely ground black powder.

Note how the hollow brass jacket is crimped over a second cupped piece of brass (which itself has 4 petals). Presumably the lead portion of the bullet was then cast around the assembled brass portion during manufacturing (as the brass plug portion has a reverse taper).

The headstamp is: 'star' KYNOCH 'star' No 12 Ball

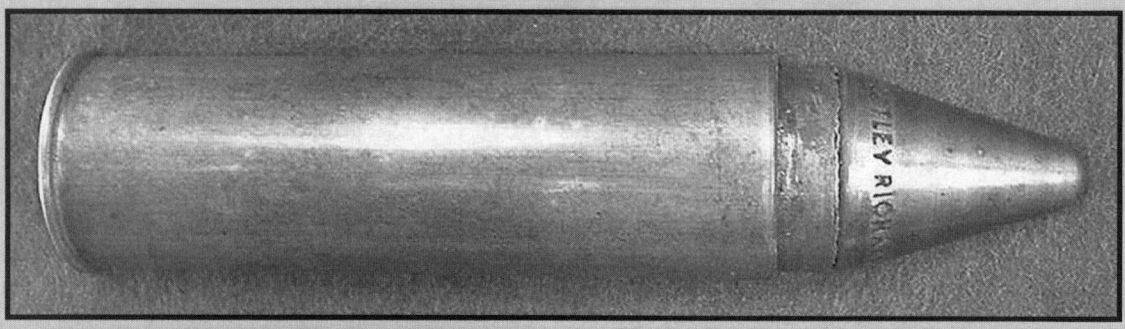

References: *The History and Development of Small Arms Ammunition*, Volume 3, by George Hoyem. Armory Publications. pp. 26-28

Courtesy International Ammunition Association, Inc. (cartridgecollectors.org)

SECTION X – CENTERFIRE RIFLE CARTRIDGE PROFILES
CHAPTER 65 : SPORTING RIFLE - CURRENT

CHAPTER 65

For Cartridge Index see Chapter 101. All drawing dimensions are approximate.

The number and variety of different sporting cartridges are both amazing and bewildering. As a man once said to me in this regard, "Why can't we reduce the total number of rifle cartridge calibers to just four or five?" While logical, such a question ignores history, technology, experience, economics, nostalgia, and customer demand among other factors. For shooters, as in other hobbies and sports, variety is the spice of life and the never-ending amount of calibers provides the spice.

At last count, there were no fewer than 18 different active cartridges firing a 7mm bullet. This number raises the question: how many different varieties of a given caliber are enough? The answer is no one knows, so the proliferation continues. Today, most major ammunition makers offer product lines numbering over 350 line items and several offer nearly 500! Of course, the bulk of these are variations on a theme in the form of various bullet weights and styles offered in a particular cartridge (the .30-'06 Spr., for example, is offered in nine different bullet weights!). However, the total remains impressive.

The main purpose of sporting rifle calibers is hunting. In this connection, most sportsmen and ammunition manufacturers break sporting cartridges into five or more categories according to the type of game normally hunted with a specific cartridge. These categories are:

- Varmint and small game – cals. from .224 - .257 using high velocity cartridges
- Medium game – cals. from .257 - .35
- Big game – cals. from .30 - .375
- Very large heavy game – cals. from .375 - .458
- Dangerous game – cals. from .45 through .70 using extremely heavy bullets

For additional information, the reader is encouraged to see Chapter 7: What Cartridges Are Used For and Chapter 45: Terminal Ballistics.

In their catalogs, most ammunition manufacturers list cartridges in ascending order of their bullet diameter or caliber designation, not power or game type. This is an arbitrary decision made only for customer's convenience, helping him/her find a particular cartridge among the many listed. Generally this pattern has been followed in this and other data chapters.

Many novice or casual shooters are confused by the wide variety of different cartridges and bullet weights. For example, why is the .30-30 Winchester cartridge such a popular number for lever-action rifles while the .22-250 Remington is not? Which is more powerful - the .243 Winchester or the 6mm Remington? How come the .35 Remington is not as potent as the .30-06 Springfield? How does one determine that the .22 Hornet, despite its racy name, is not in the same league with the .220 Swift? And finally, size may not matter, as the massive .45-70 Government is not as powerful as the smaller .375 H&H Magnum. Only from experience will a shooter learn the strengths, weaknesses, applications, and capabilities of a specific cartridge. Remember that variety is the spice in cartridge selection life.

In reviewing the data presented in this chapter, it is important to keep in mind that there is no perfect cartridge any more than one size fits all. Only experience will allow a shooter to develop his personal preferences for particular cartridges while at the same time opening new vistas offered by untried calibers. Many shooters agree that half the fun is trying as many different calibers as possible.

THE LONG AND THE SHORT OF IT – AN ANALYSIS OF SHORT, FAT CARTRIDGE CASE DESIGNS

In early 2000, Remington and Winchester began marketing new magnum rifle cartridges which had no belt on their case heads. More unusual was their shorter than normal case length in relation to their head diameter which allowed these short, fat new cartridges to be chambered in short action rifles.

According to their designers/manufacturers, the short, fat design offered a number of ballistic advantages, such as improved efficiency, lower maximum average chamber pressures, and higher muzzle velocity. All these good things were claimed to accrue because these new case designs exposed a wider ignition face at the rear of the powder column to the hot primer gases for better ignition and less unburned powder being forced down the barrel.

Most shooters accepted these claims at face value. However, exactly how much difference is there between the new short, fat cases and previously existing magnum rifle cartridges? The accompanying chart compares the length to the diameter as a ratio of the new short, fat cartridges with previous cartridges to reveal the real story.

As you look over the chart, note the following items of interest:

1. The L/D ratio of the .223 WSSM is approximately 3.00 while that of its rivals are well over 4.00. This indicates a statistical improvement in the L/D ratio of short, fat magnum cartridges of approximately 25% over existing calibers. However, note that the 3.2-3.4 L/D ratios of the .22 PPC and .22 Remington BR cartridges form a statistical half-way point as they fall in between those of the short, fat cartridges and previous designs.

2. An analysis of the .243 WSSM cartridge supports the data from the .223 WSSM above with the L/D ratio of conventional 6mm cartridges averaging well over 4.3 while the .243 WSSM falls 30% lower at 3.00. Once again, the 6mm PPC and 6mm Remington BR form a statistical half-way point.

3. When viewing the .30 caliber cartridges, note that most "standard" length belted magnum rifle cartridges have a L/D ratio of between 5.00 and 5.57 while their short magnum brothers have a L/D ratio of less than 4.00. These numbers indicate approximately a 28% improvement in the L/D ratio for the short, fat cartridges when compared to previous designs.

4. When .338 caliber short, fat magnum cartridges are reviewed, the results support those of the .300 caliber numbers. For example, the .338 WSM enjoys a 24% L/D advantage over its nearest rival. Note also the unexpectedly low L/D ratio of the .338 Winchester Magnum and the .338 Lapua Magnum.

5. Summary: This statistical analysis reveals that short, fat magnum cartridges cases have an average length/diameter ratio that is 28% lower than most previous magnum cartridges. While this is statistically significant, does it provide the claimed advantages in the real world? Company literature seems to support the claims of improved efficiency by burning less propellant at lower maximum average chamber pressures to achieve the muzzle velocities of standard magnum cartridges. However, the amount of propellant saved is small and chamber pressure excursions have plagued several of the new calibers. Does this mean that the perceived advantages of short, fat magnum cartridges are an illusion? Only time will tell.

Meet .50 Fat Mac, the king of the short, fat cartridges with a length/diameter ratio of 2.296! This is a real cartridge that will launch a .50 caliber, 750 grain Hornady A-Max bullet at a muzzle velocity of 3,425 fps with 19, 545 ft.-lbs. of muzzle energy.

CASE LENGTH TO DIAMETER RATIO COMPARISON FOR SELECTED STANDARD, MAGNUM, AND SHORT MAGNUM CARTRIDGES

CALIBER	LENGTH (IN.)	HEAD DIA. (IN.)	L/D RATIO
.222 Remington	1.70	.375	4.533
.223 Remington	1.76	.375	4.693
.22-250 Rem.	1.91	.466	4.098
.220 Swift	2.205	.445	4.955
.22 Rem. BR	1.50	.418	3.588
.22 PPC	1.505	.443	3.382
.22 WSSM	1.67	.555	3.009
.243 Winchester	2.045	.470	4.351
6mm Remington	2.233	.470	4.751
.240 Wby. Mag.	2.50	.453	5.518
6mm PPC	1.515	.443	3.419
6mm Norma BR	1.56	.469	3.326
6mm Rem. BR	1.53	.470	3.255
.243 WSSM	1.67	.555	3.009
.30-'06 Spr.	2.49	.470	5.306
.308 Win.	2.015	.470	4.287
.308 Norma Mag.	2.56	.511	5.009
.300 Win. Mag.	2.62	.511	5.127
.300 RUM	2.845	.546	5.210
.300 H&H Mag.	2.85	.511	5.577
.300 Wby. Mag.	2.825	.511	5.567
.30-378 Wby.	2.91	.582	5.000
.300 WSM	2.10	.555	3.783
.300 RSAUM	2.015	.550	3.658
.338 Win. Mag.	2.50	.513	4.873
.338 Lapua Mag.	2.72	.587	4.633
.338-378 Wby.	2.91	.582	5.005
.338 RUM	2.67	.550	5.018
.340 Wby. Mag.	2.85	.512	5.570
.338 WSM	1.96	.555	3.531
.50 Fat Mac	2.645	1.152	2.296

.17 HORNET

ALTERNATE NAME(S): 4.4x36Rmm Hornet
RELATED CALIBER(S): .22 WCF (OBSOLETE BLACK
    POWDER CARTRIDGE)

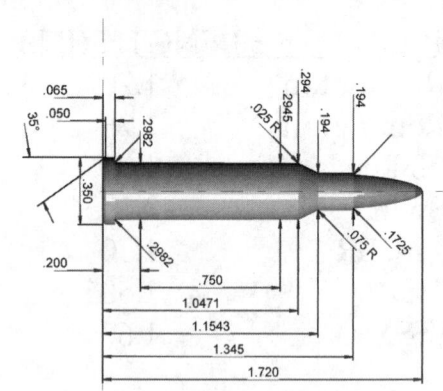

CARTRIDGE HISTORY
Year of Introduction: 2012
Country of Origin: U.S.
Designer(s): Hornady
Governing Body: SAAMI
Present Status: active

CARTRIDGE DESCRIPTION
Bullet Diameter: .172 in./4.4mm
Bullet Weight(s): 20 gr.
Rifling Twist Rate: 1 turn in 9 in.
Velocity Test Barrel Length: 24 in.
Case Type: rimmed, necked

CARTRIDGE BALLISTICS
Max. Average Breech Pressure: 47,000 C.U.P.
Max. Horizontal Range: 2,885 yds.
Max. Vertical Range: 6,550 ft.

Bullet Weight (gr.)	Bullet Type	Muzzle Velocity (fps)	Muzzle Energy (ft.-lbs.)
20	PT	3,650	592

CURRENT MANUFACTURER(S)
Hornady

GENERAL COMMENT(S)
Working at Springfield Arsenal in the late 1920s, Capt. G.L. Wotkyns, Col. Townsend Whelen, G.A. Woody, and A.L. Woodworth began their efforts to develop a modern, high velocity varmint and small game rifle cartridge. Their creation, the .22 Hornet, became one of the first, small caliber cartridges of this type and set the trend for those that would follow. Winchester became the first commercial manufacturer to offer .22 Hornet ammunition in late 1930. Winchester must have been very confidant of the .22 Hornet's sales potential as the first firearm manufacturer, Savage, did not offer a rifle in the new caliber until 1932. Come to think of it, some things never change.

Wildcatters quickly modified the .22 Hornet by necking it down to .17 caliber. There it remained until 2011 when Hornady Manufacturing Co. standardized the .17 Hornet with SAAMI then introduced it into their commercial product line.

TECHNICAL COMMENT(S)
The .17 Hornet and the .22 Hornet differ mainly in their shoulder and neck dimensions as needed to accomodate the different bullet diameters. Both cartridges share the same rim and case head dimensions with the result that chambering a rifle from .22 Hornet to .17 Hornet requires only a new barrel.

Although the .22 Hornet is getting rather long in the tooth in comparison to more modern, high velocity calibers, the .17 Hornet can hold its own with all but the most powerful modern marvels. That is to ranges of about 200 yds. or so--beyond that, the light, 17 caliber bullet falls off badly due to its light weight and modest ballistic coefficient. In this connection, it is of interest to compare the .17 Hornet with the .17 HMR rimfire cartridge.

Bullets for handloading the .17 Hornet are offered by several component bullet manufacturers including Hornady.

.17 REMINGTON FIREBALL

ALTERNATE NAME(S): .17 Rem. Fireball
RELATED CALIBER(S): .221 Remington Fireball, .222 Remington, .223 Remington

CARTRIDGE HISTORY
Year of Introduction: 2007
Country of Origin: U.S.
Designer(s): Remington
Governing Body: SAAMI
Present Status: active

CARTRIDGE DESCRIPTION
Bullet Diameter: .172 in.
Bullet Weight(s): 20 gr.
Rifling Twist Rate: 1 turn in 9 in.
Test Barrel Length: 24 in.
Case Type: rimless, necked
Case Material: brass
Primer Size: small rifle

CARTRIDGE BALLISTICS
Max. Average Breech Pressure: N/A
Max. Horizontal Range: 2,600 yds.
Max. Vertical Range: 5,800 ft.

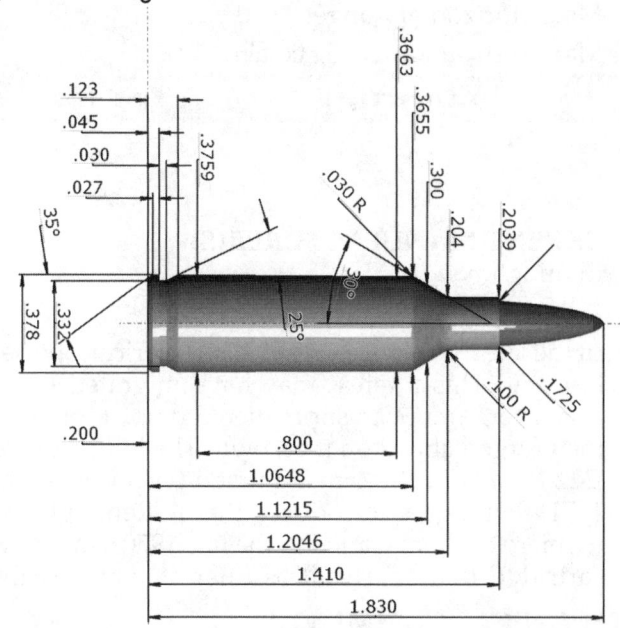

Bullet Weight (gr.)	Bullet Type	Muzzle Velocity (fps)	Muzzle Energy (ft.-lbs.)
20	JSP	4,000	710

CURRENT MANUFACTURER(S)
Remington

GENERAL COMMENT(S)
When interest in micro-caliber cartridges was rekindled in the early 2000s, Remington responded with the .17 Fireball in 2007. It is chambered in Remington's XP-100 series of handguns.

TECHNICAL COMMENT(S)
Essentially, the .17 Fireball is a .221 Fireball case necked down to .172 caliber. The diminutive, lightweight bullet achieves surprising muzzle velocities for its cartridge case volume. In turn, both Fireball cartridges are shortened versions of the .222 Remington cartridge.

.17 REMINGTON

ALTERNATE NAME(S): .17 Rem.
RELATED CALIBER(S): .204 Ruger, .222 Rem., .223 Rem.

CARTRIDGE HISTORY
Year of Introduction: 1971
Country of Origin: U.S.
Designer(s): Remington
Governing Body: SAAMI
Present Status: active

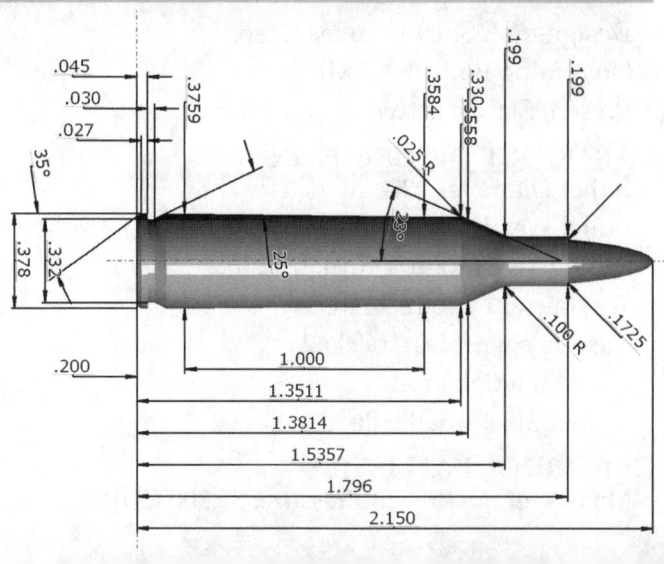

CARTRIDGE DESCRIPTION
Bullet Diameter: .172 in.
Bullet Weight(s): 20-25 gr.
Rifling Twist Rate: 1 turn in 9 in.
Test Barrel Length: 24 in.
Case Type: rimless, necked

Case Material: brass
Primer Size: small rifle

CARTRIDGE BALLISTICS
Max. Average Breech Pressure: 55,200 CUP.
Max. Horizontal Range: 2,600 yds.
Max. Vertical Range: 5,800 ft.

Bullet Weight (gr.)	Bullet Type	Muzzle Velocity (fps)	Muzzle Energy (ft.-lbs.)
20	JSP	4,250	802
25	JHP	4,040	900

CURRENT MANUFACTURER(S)
Remington

GENERAL COMMENT(S)
In the late 1960s and early 1970s, American sportsmen developed a fascination with .17 caliber rifles for varmint hunting. This interest may have migrated from Australia where .17 caliber cartridges were quite popular. However, American sportsmen did not adopt one of the Australian .17 caliber cartridges. Instead, true to form, they forged ahead on their own. The indirect results were numerous wildcats usually based on the .22 Hornet, .222 Rem., or .223 Rem. At first, none of the major domestic ammunition companies took notice. However, in 1971, Remington introduced the .17 Remington cartridge and chambered it in their M700 rifle. When interest in micro calibers waned in the late 1970s, the .17 Remington carried on alone as the smallest caliber commercial cartridge. In the early 2000s, interest in micro calibers took off once again as a result of the .204 Ruger cartridge.

TECHNICAL COMMENT(S)
By all measures, the .17 Remington is a niche cartridge suitable only for varmint and pelt hunting. Based on the .223 Rem. cartridge, the .17 Rem. can be chambered in any bolt-action or single-shot centerfire rifle capable of handling the .223 Rem. cartridge. The .17 Rem. suffers from several interior ballistic shortcomings due mainly to the small bore diameter. Barrels foul quickly and lose accuracy after a modest number of shots. The barrel must then be thoroughly cleaned which requires the shooter to carry cleaning equipment afield. In addition, throats erode quickly degrading accuracy substantially. Although the lightweight bullets offer a flat trajectory and disintegrate on impact, they are severely affected by crosswinds. In addition, the low striking energy limits the .17 Rem. to small game and fur bearers.

.204 RUGER

ALTERNATE NAME(S): none
RELATED CALIBER(S): .17 Rem., .222 Rem., .223 Rem

CARTRIDGE HISTORY
Year of Introduction: 2004
Country of Origin: U.S.
Designer(s): Sturm, Ruger & Co.
Governing Body: SAAMI
Present Status: active

CARTRIDGE DESCRIPTION
Bullet Diameter: .204 in.
Bullet Weight(s): 32-45 gr.
Rifling Twist Rate: 1 turn in 12 in.
Test Barrel Length: 24 in.
Case Type: rimless, necked
Case Material: brass
Primer Size: small rifle

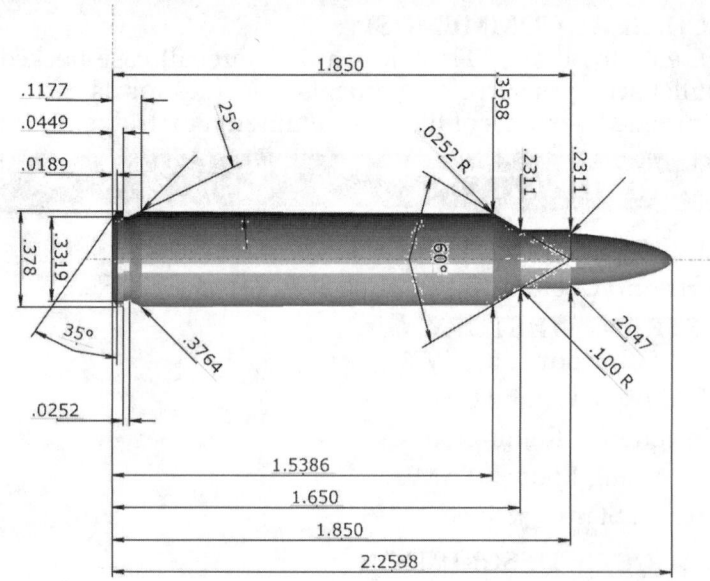

CARTRIDGE BALLISTICS
Max. Average Breech Pressure: 55,200 CUP.

Max. Horizontal Range: 4,000 yds.
Max. Vertical Range: 8,000 ft.

Bullet Weight (gr.)	Bullet Type	Muzzle Velocity (fps)	Muzzle Energy (ft.-lbs.)
32	JSP	4,030	1,155
32	JSP	4,050	1,165
32	JSP	4,225	1,268
34	JSP	4,025	1,223
35	JSP	3,100	747
39	JSP	3,750	1,220
40	JSP	3,900	1,351
45	JSP	3,625	1,313

CURRENT MANUFACTURER(S)
Hornady, Federal, Remington, Winchester

GENERAL COMMENT(S)
Although he was one of the most revered of modern American gun designers, William B. Ruger, Sr. never had a cartridge named in his honor until after his death. The .204 Ruger cartridge was the first to honor his memory. Sturm, Ruger & Co. was the first to offer rifles in this caliber; other manufacturers quickly followed.

TECHNICAL COMMENT(S)
Essentially, the .204 Ruger is either a .223 Rem. cartridge necked down to .20 caliber or a .17 Rem. cartridge necked up to .20 caliber depending on your viewpoint. Its configuration makes for easy adaptation to existing rifles, ammunition production equipment, and reloading dies.

Fresh ballistic ground is turned by the use of a .204 inch diameter bullet – the .204 Ruger being the first modern centerfire cartridge to employ this bullet diameter. While there is no ballistic magic in .204 caliber, the presumed contrast with .17 caliber and .224 caliber bullets yields rich material for gun writers, ad writers, and amateur ballisticians.

Still, the .204 Ruger cartridge does offer outstanding exterior ballistic performance provided the user keeps in mind that it is a varmint and small game cartridge – not a medium game caliber. In this connection, the .204 Ruger has earned an excellent reputation for accuracy while not requiring the shooter to carry cleaning equipment afield (as with the .17 Rem.). Component bullets for reloading are available from several of the large bullet manufacturers.

.218 BEE

ALTERNATE NAME(S): .218
RELATED CALIBER(S): .25-20 Win., .32-20 Win.

CARTRIDGE HISTORY
Year of Introduction: 1938
Country of Origin: U.S.
Designer(s): Winchester
Governing Body: SAAMI, CIP
Present Status: active

CARTRIDGE DESCRIPTION
Bullet Diameter: .225 in.
Bullet Weight(s): 46 gr.
Rifling Twist Rate: 1 turn in 16 in.
Test Barrel Length: 24 in.
Case Type: rimmed, necked
Case Material: brass
Primer Size: small rifle

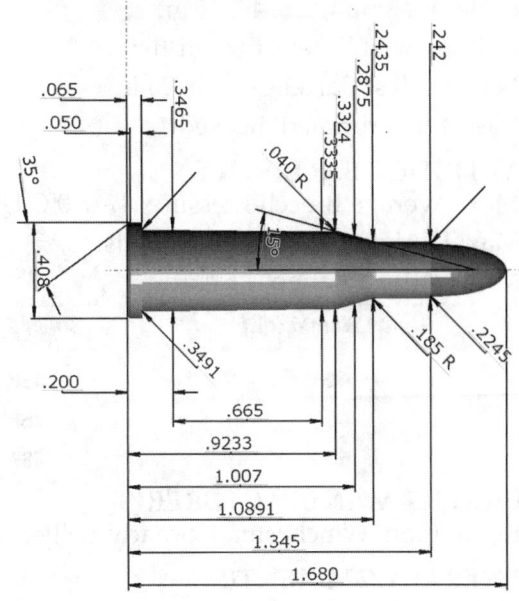

CARTRIDGE BALLISTICS
Max. Average Breech Pressure: 44,000 CUP.
Max. Horizontal Range: 2,100 yds.
Max. Vertical Range: 4,750 ft.

Bullet Weight (gr.)	Bullet Type	Muzzle Velocity (fps)	Muzzle Energy (ft.-lbs.)
46	JHP	2,760	778

CURRENT MANUFACTURER(S)
Winchester

GENERAL COMMENT(S)
The .218 Bee was introduced by Winchester in 1938 in an effort to provide a new cartridge offering improved ballistic performance over the .22 Hornet. World War II intervened and after the War the .218 Bee was eclipsed by the .222 Rem. and later the .223 Rem. The .218 Bee hangs on among shooters who feel the Hornet lacks performance and still prefer a rimmed cartridge to the rimless .222 and .223 Rem.

TECHNICAL COMMENT(S)
The .218 Bee cartridge is based on the venerable .32-20 Win. case necked down to .22 caliber. Although intended to offer improved ballistic performance over the .22 Hornet, in reality gains are modest, averaging less than 10%. Like the Hornet, the Bee is a 150 yard cartridge with factory ammunition. Unlike the Hornet, the Bee can be hand loaded to considerably higher muzzle velocities. The Bee also has a reputation for excellent accuracy and a mild report.

.22 HORNET

ALTERNATE NAME(S): 5.6x36Rmm Hornet
RELATED CALIBER(S): .22 WCF (OBSOLETE BLACK POWDER CARTRIDGE)

CARTRIDGE HISTORY
Year of Introduction: 1930
Country of Origin: U.S.
Designer(s): G.L. Wotkyns, Townsend Whelen, G.A. Woody, and A.L. Woodworth
Governing Body: SAAMI, CIP
Present Status: active

CARTRIDGE DESCRIPTION
Bullet Diameter: .224 in./5.69mm
Bullet Weight(s): 35, 40, 45 gr.
Rifling Twist Rate: 1 turn in 16 in.
Velocity Test Barrel Length: 24 in.
Case Type: rimmed, necked

CARTRIDGE BALLISTICS
Max. Average Breech Pressure: 47,000 C.U.P.
Max. Horizontal Range: 2,084 yds.
Max. Vertical Range: 4,690 ft.

Bullet Weight (gr.)	Bullet Type	Muzzle Velocity (fps)	Muzzle Energy (ft.-lbs.)
40	JSP	2,800	696
45	JSP	2,690	723
50	JSP	2,600	750

CURRENT MANUFACTURER(S)
Remington, Winchester, Hornady, Sellier & Bellot, Prvi Partizan

GENERAL COMMENT(S)
In the early 1920s, the German firm of Deutsche Waffen-und Munitionsfabriken (DWM) modernized the .22 Winchester Center Fire (WCF) black powder cartridge for use in Vierling four-barrel combination guns. Using smokeless propellant at a maximum average breech pressure of 34,800 psi and a 40 gr. jacketed bullet, muzzle velocity was a modest 1,700 fps. Called the 5.6x35Rmm Vierling, this cartridge remains popular to this day for European small game hunting and hunter rifle competition.

Working at Springfield Arsenal in the late 1920s, Capt. G.L. Wotkyns, Col. Townsend Whelen, G.A. Woody, and A.L. Woodworth began their efforts to develop a modern varmint cartridge. Like DWM, they used the venerable .22 WCF cartridge case; unlike DWM their goal was a modern high pressure, high velocity cartridge for bolt action and single-shot varmint rifles. They cobbled a .22 rimfire barrel to an M1903 Springfield bolt-action. Using smokeless propellants at a maximum average breech pressure of 47,000 psi and 40 gr. round nose bullets pulled from 5.5mm Velo-Dog revolver cartridges, they achieved the then-phenomenal muzzle velocity of 2,400 fps. Their creation, the .22 Hornet, became one of the first modern high-velocity, flat trajectory varmint cartridges.

Winchester became the first commercial manufacturer to offer .22 Hornet caliber ammunition in late 1930, despite the fact that no firearm maker offered a gun in this caliber. This changed in 1932 when Savage offered their M23-D.

TECHNICAL COMMENT(S)

The 5.6x35Rmm Vierling and the .22 Hornet differ only in minor dimensions. Although both cartridges will seat in most chambers, the .22 Hornet should not be fired in 5.6x35Rmm Vierling guns as the higher pressure may damage them.

Rifles in .22 Hornet caliber made before World War II often have .223" diameter bores. Rifles in this caliber made after World War II normally have .224" diameter bores. Component bullets are available in both diameters.

To ensure expansion at low striking velocities, Hornet bullets have a round-nose soft-point ogive, a thin jacket, and a soft lead core. Because of the slow 1 turn in 16 in. rifling twist, optimum bullet weights are 40-45 grs. While pointed bullets can be used, expansion may be unreliable due to their thick jackets.

Although the .22 Hornet is not in the same ballistic performance league as modern .22 centerfire rifle cartridges, it can hold its own out to 150 yds. Beyond that, it falls off badly due to the poor ballistic coefficient of its round nose bullet.

Manufacturers are not fans of the Hornet. Barrel makers cuss at having to make a special twist rate just for this caliber. Most bullet makers wish the old .223" bore Hornets would wear out and go away so they would not have to offer two bullet diameters. Ammunition companies abhor the .22 Hornet for its hard-to-make curved and tapered shape with no distinct shoulder or neck. Cost accountants cringe because gun makers must modify rimfire actions to chamber the .22 Hornet as standard centerfire actions are too large.

Despite this, the .22 Hornet remains a popular choice for small game and varmint hunting due to its low noise signature, limited range, and low potential for ricochet. Ammunition and components for the .22 Hornet are offered by several major manufacturers in Europe and the U.S.

.22 PPC

ALTERNATE NAME(S): .22 PPC USA
RELATED CALIBER(S): .220 Russian, 7.62X39mm Soviet

CARTRIDGE HISTORY
Year of Introduction: 1974
Country of Origin: US
Designer(s): Dr. Louis Palmisano, Ferris Pindell
Governing Body: CIP
Present Status: active

CARTRIDGE DESCRIPTION
Bullet Diameter: .224 in.
Bullet Weight(s): 40-63 gr.
Rifling Twist Rate: 1 turn in 14 in.
Test Barrel Length: 24 in.
Case Type: rimless, necked
Case Material: brass
Primer Size: small rifle

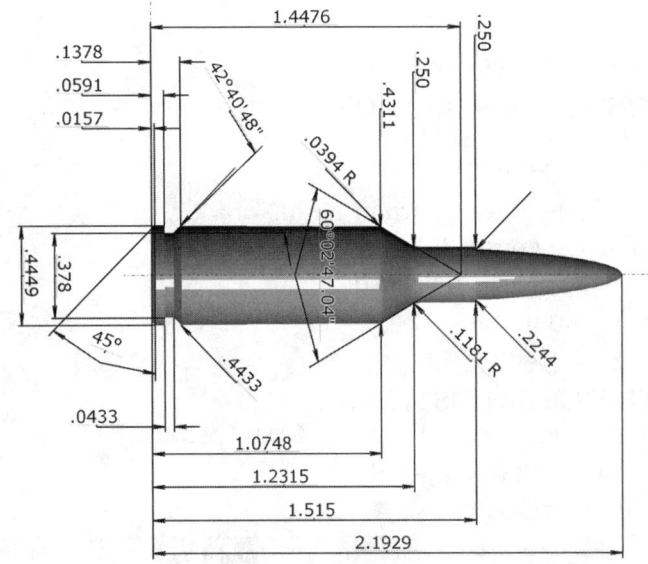

CARTRIDGE BALLISTICS
Max. Average Breech Pressure: 58,750 psi.
Max. Horizontal Range: 3,100 yds.
Max. Vertical Range: 7,200 ft.

Bullet Weight (gr.)	Bullet Type	Muzzle Velocity (fps)	Muzzle Energy (ft.-lbs.)
52	JHP	3,400	1,335

CURRENT MANUFACTURER(S)
Sako

GENERAL COMMENT(S)
In the early 1970s, two avid bench rest rifle shooters decided to design a better .22 caliber cartridge especially for bench rest competition. Dr. Louis Palmisano, an internationally noted heart surgeon, and Ferris Pindell, a master tool and die maker, teamed up to bring the new cartridge to life. They began with the .220 Russian version of the Soviet military 7.63X39mm M43 cartridge. The .220 Russian cartridge had a tapered case, so Palmisano and Pindell expanded the case wall diameter and shoulder angle to 30 degrees to increase internal capacity. A small rifle primer was specified and Sako agreed to manufacture the cases.

In 1974, both Palmisano and Pindell began competing with their new cartridge on bench rest circuits. Their success was such that many bench rest competitors switched to the new caliber. The increasing popularity of the new cartridge led Sako to offer loaded ammunition in this caliber in 1987. Although the .22 PPC cartridge never caught on as a loaded cartridge among sportsmen, it continues as a major factor in bench rest competition to this day.

Following introduction of the .22 PPC in 1974, a 6mm version, the 6mm PPC, was introduced several years later. It became so popular among the bench rest competitors that it has all but eclipsed the .22 PPC.

TECHNICAL COMMENT(S)
While the .220 Russian was a 40,000 psi chamber pressure design, the .22 PPC is a modern high pressure design intended for high velocity bench rest competition at 100 and 200 yards. For this reason, match-grade jacketed hollow point bullets of 52 to 55 grains normally are loaded in this cartridge. However, it is fully capable of firing hunting bullets weighing from 40 to 63 grains. Bench rest shooters normally develop loads combining match-grade bullets, match-grade primers and high propellant loading densities for competition. Case necks also are turned for maximum concentricity. Sako was the sole manufacturer of ammunition in this caliber.

.22 SAVAGE HIGH-POWER

ALTERNATE NAME(S): .22 Sav., .22 Savage, .22 Sav. HP, .22 Savage HP, .22 High-Power, 5.6x52Rmm, .22 Improved
RELATED CALIBER(S): .25-35 Winchester

CARTRIDGE HISTORY
Year of Introduction: 1912
Country of Origin: US
Designer(s): Charles Newton
Governing Body: CIP
Present Status: active

CARTRIDGE DESCRIPTION
Bullet Diameter: .228 in.
Bullet Weight(s): 71 gr.
Rifling Twist Rate: 1 turn in 12 in.
Test Barrel Length: 24 in.
Case Type: rimmed, necked
Case Material: brass
Primer Size: large rifle

CARTRIDGE BALLISTICS
Max. Average Breech Pressure: 40,000 psi.
Max. Horizontal Range: N/A
Max. Vertical Range: N/A

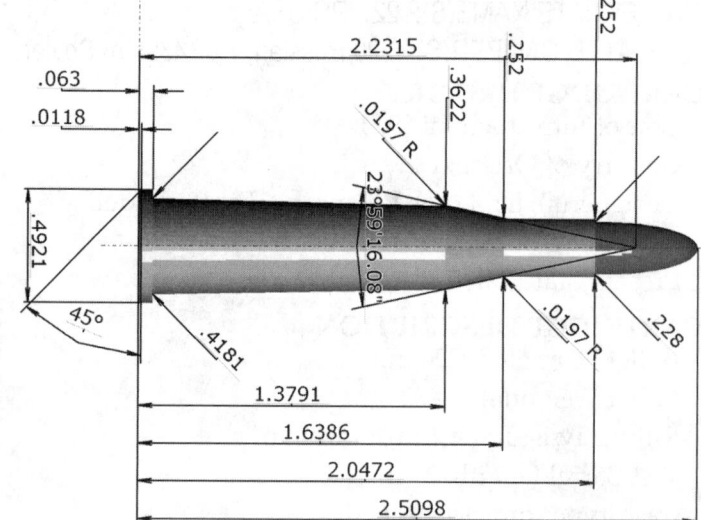

Bullet Weight (gr.)	Bullet Type	Muzzle Velocity (fps)	Muzzle Energy (ft.-lbs.)
71	JSP	2,790	1,228

CURRENT MANUFACTURER(S)
Norma

GENERAL COMMENT(S)

This was the first cartridge designed by Charles Newton who went on to become the father of the famous Newton line of proprietary caliber cartridges in the 1920s. From its introduction by Savage for their lever-action Model 99 rifle in 1912, the .22 Savage HP remained a popular caliber in the U.S. until the advent of World War II in 1938. Following the end of the War in 1945, the .22 Savage HP was replaced by more modern rimless designs better suited to bolt-action rifles. These new cartridge designs, such as the .222 Remington, fired lighter weight, (50-55gr.) bullets at higher velocities. Varmint hunters quickly adopted the new cartridges in favor of the .22 Savage HP with its heavy, 71gr. bullet which was designed more for small and medium game. By the late 1950s, most American ammunition manufacturers had dropped the .22 Savage HP cartridge.

In Europe, the .22 Savage HP, designated the 5.6x52Rmm, has remained a popular caliber by dint of the large number of break-open rifles and combination guns used for mixed bag hunts. Such guns work best with rimmed cartridges. In addition, European hunters have found the 5.6x52Rmm an excellent choice for hunting small European deer. This European demand supports Norma's continuing production of the .22 Savage HP.

TECHNICAL COMMENT(S)

Essentially, the .22 Savage HP is a necked down .25-35 Winchester cartridge case. The rimmed design of the .22 HP case makes it an excellent choice for single-shot and lever-action rifles. Surprisingly, the relatively modest breech pressure and the heavy-for-caliber bullet work against it. The low breech pressure limits ballistic performance and the .22 caliber bullet is illegal for hunting anything but small game in most states. Hand loaders must contend with the requirement for .228 inch diameter bullets that are expensive and hard to find (most modern .22 caliber center fire cartridges use .224 inch diameter bullets).

5.6x57mm RWS, 5.6x57Rmm RWS

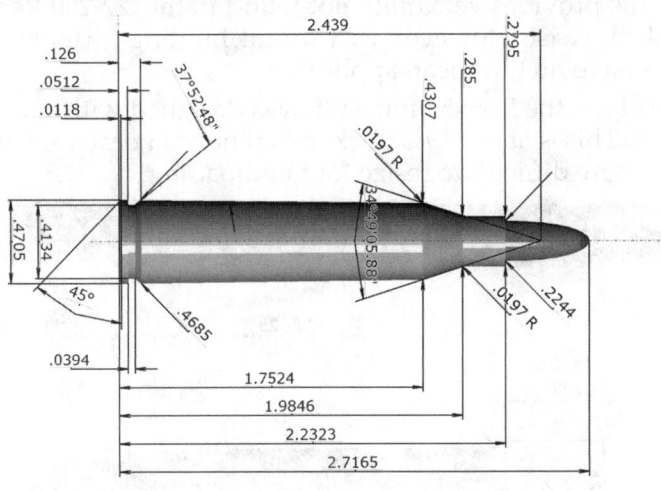 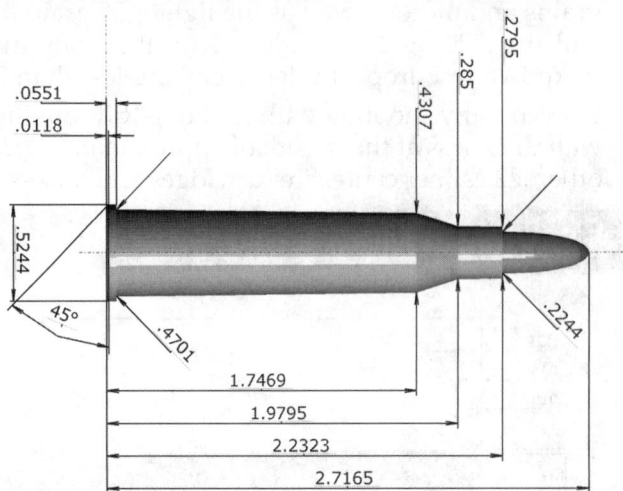

ALTERNATE NAME(S): none
RELATED CALIBER(S):6.5x57mm, 7x57mm, 8x57mm

CARTRIDGE HISTORY

Year of Introduction: 1964
Country of Origin: Germany
Designer(s): Dynamit Nobel/RWS
Governing Body: CIP
Present Status: active

CARTRIDGE DESCRIPTION

Bullet Diameter: .224 in.
Bullet Weight(s): 55-74 gr.
Rifling Twist Rate: 1 turn in10 in.
Test Barrel Length: 24 in.
Case Type: rimless, necked/rimmed, necked
Case Material: brass
Primer Size: large rifle

CARTRIDGE BALLISTICS

Max. Average Breech Pressure: 63,800 psi.

Max. Horizontal Range: 3,450 yds.

Max. Vertical Range: 7,600 ft.

Bullet Weight (gr.)	Bullet Type	Muzzle Velocity (fps)	Muzzle Energy (ft.-lbs.)
55	JSP	3,510	1,505 (obsolete)
74	JSP	3,410	1,910

CURRENT MANUFACTURER(S)

Dynamit Nobel (RUAG)

GENERAL COMMENT(S)

The 5.6x57mm cartridge was introduced by Dynamit Nobel RWS (now RUAG Ammotec) in 1964 as a new high velocity rifle cartridge for hunting deer. As European deer are small, this caliber was considered perfectly adequate, only it never really caught on. Both rimmed and rimless versions were introduced with the same ballistics. However, the rimmed version has been dropped. Hirtenberger in Austria also made this caliber with a 55 grain bullet. However, Hirtenberger has now gone out of business and this bullet weight has become obsolete. Although an excellent cartridge, the 5.6x57mm RWS never caught on in the U.S. because the .223 Rem. and .22-250 Rem. offered similar ballistic performance with the 55 grain bullets so popular for varmint hunting. In the U.S., medium game hunting with any .22 caliber centerfire caliber is illegal in most areas, leaving the 5.6x57mm with no real application.

TECHNICAL COMMENT(S)

With its one turn in 10 inch rifling twist, the 5.6x57mm RWS cartridge will stabilize long heavy bullets of 68 grains and more as well as the lighter 55 grain bullets. This provides versatility not found in the .22-250 Rem. and the .220 Swift cartridges with their one turn in 14 in. twist. However, as varmint hunting virtually is unknown in Europe, bullets weighing less than 70 grains have no European application.

For economy shooting with .22 Long Rifle auxiliary cartridges, the 5.56x57mm RWS was designed with a neck wall thickness at the mouth of approximately .0277 inches. This is about 19% thicker than normal practice with other .22 caliber centerfire cartridges and makes the case more difficult to resize for handloading.

5.56x50mm MAGNUM, 5.56x50Rmm MAGNUM

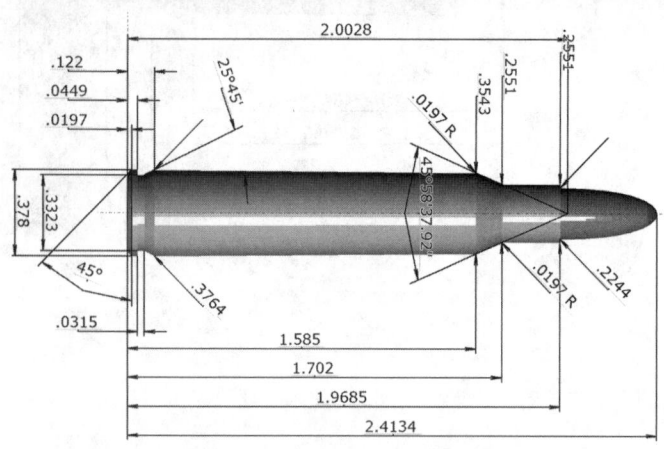 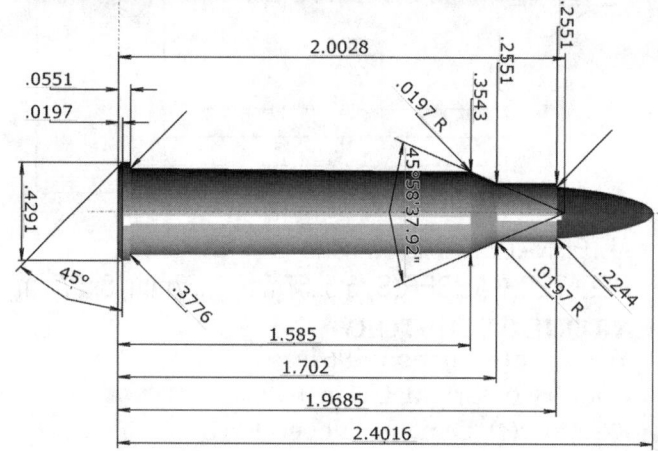

ALTERNATE NAME(S): 5.6mm Magnum DWM

RELATED CALIBER(S): .222 Rem. Mag., .223 Rem.

CARTRIDGE HISTORY

Year of Introduction: 1968

Country of Origin: Germany

Designer(s): DWM

Governing Body: CIP

Present Status: active

CARTRIDGE DESCRIPTION

Bullet Diameter: .224 in.

Bullet Weight(s): 50-63.5 gr.
Rifling Twist Rate: 1 turn in 14 in.
Test Barrel Length: 24 in.
Case Type: rimless, necked; rimmed necked
Case Material: brass
Primer Size: small rifle

CARTRIDGE BALLISTICS
Max. Average Breech Pressure: 55,100 psi. (Mag.); 49,300 psi. (R Mag.)
Max. Horizontal Range: 4,000 yds.
Max. Vertical Range: 8,750 ft.

Bullet Weight (gr.)	Bullet Type	Muzzle Velocity (fps)	Muzzle Energy (ft.-lbs.)
5.6x50mm Magnum			
50	JSP	3,510	1,368
63.5	JSP	3,020	1,285
5.6x50Rmm Magnum			
55.5	JSP	3,280	1,326
63.5	JSP	2,925	1,206

CURRENT MANUFACTURER(S)
Dynamit Nobel/RUAG, Sellier & Bellot

GENERAL COMMENT(S)
In Europe, powerful .22 center fire cartridges such as the 5.6x50mm Mag. and the 5.6x50Rmm Mag. are popular choices for hunting roe deer and similar game as most shots are taken at 100 yards or less. In addition, many owners of rifles in these calibers use them for hunter class rifle competition. By North American standards, this caliber would be considered a varmint cartridge. This is a good example of how shooters tastes in Europe differ from those in North America. These two cartridges were designed in 1969 by the famous German company Deutsche Waffen und Munitionsfabriken (DWM). It was one of the last sporting caliber cartridges DWM designed before merging with Dynamit Nobel. While the both of these cartridges are popular in Europe, they are virtually unknown in North American. Undoubtedly, this is because there already are a good number of .22 caliber center fire rifle cartridges from which to choose.

TECHNICAL COMMENT(S)
The rimless version, the 5.6x50mm Mag. is intended for use in bolt-action repeating rifles while the rimmed 5.56x50Rmm Mag. is intended for break-open drillings and single-shot rifles (lever-action rifles are not popular in Europe). As break-open rifles are not as strong as bolt-action rifles, the rimmed case is loaded to lower average chamber pressures than the rimless version.

.220 SWIFT

ALTERNATE NAME(S): none
RELATED CALIBER(S): .236 U.S. Navy, .220 Weatherby Rocket

CARTRIDGE HISTORY
Year of Introduction: 1935
Country of Origin: U.S.
Designer(s): Winchester
Governing Body: SAAMI, CIP
Present Status: active

CARTRIDGE DESCRIPTION
Bullet Diameter: .224 in.
Bullet Weight(s): 40-55 gr.
Rifling Twist Rate: 1 turn in 14 in.
Test Barrel Length: 24 in.
Case Type: semi-rimmed, necked
Case Material: brass
Primer Size: large rifle

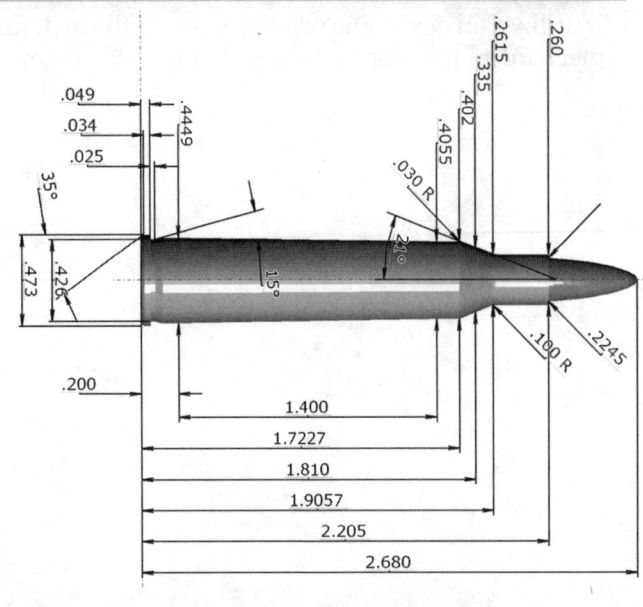

CARTRIDGE BALLISTICS

Max. Average Breech Pressure: 57,000 CUP.

Max. Horizontal Range: 3,700 yds.

Max. Vertical Range: 8,000 ft.

Bullet Weight (gr.)	Bullet Type	Muzzle Velocity (fps)	Muzzle Energy (ft.-lbs.)
40	JHP	4,050	1,457
40	JHP	4,200	1,566
40	JHP	4,250	1,605
50	JHP	3,780	1,586
50	JHP	3,850	1,645
50	JHP	4,020	1,794
52	JHP	3,830	1,695
60	JHP	3,600	1,726

CURRENT MANUFACTURER(S)

Remington, Winchester, Federal, Hornady, Norma

GENERAL COMMENT(S)

Shortly after Winchester introduced the .220 Swift cartridge in 1935, it entered the mystical realm of legend. Many were the stories of its terminal ballistics, astounding muzzle velocity, flat trajectory, and rapid barrel wear. Most of the spinners of such yarns never fired a Swift; those who had just smiled benignly. Its reputation was not unjustified – for over 70 years, the Swift had the highest published muzzle velocity of any commercial cartridge. Even today, only a few can match it and none can beat it. One reason varmint hunters liked the Swift was that the bullet often struck the target before the recoil bounced it out of the scope's field of view. No other varmint cartridge could do this.

TECHNICAL COMMENT(S)

One of the minor mysteries of history is why Winchester selected the 6mm Lee Navy cartridge case on which to base the Swift. The 6mm Lee (and the Swift) have a unique head size with a semi-rimmed configuration quite unlike any other. This makes the Swift case an orphan for commercial production and a headache to reload. Arguably, this factor alone has hampered the Swift all through its life. Until recently, bullet weights were limited. Even today, the Swift is loaded with lightweight 40-50 grain bullets. Heavier bullets are offered, but their ballistic performance is no better than the .22-250 Rem.

There is no secret to the Swift's high muzzle velocity – a lightweight bullet in front of a heavy powder charge. Likewise, the Swift possess no magic at terminal ballistics – the lightly constructed bullet penetrates a short distance and disintegrates, depositing all of its energy inside the (small) target. Surprisingly, the Swift has earned a reputation for excellent accuracy – provided you clean the barrel regularly and its throat is not shot out.

Despite all this, the Swift remains the ballistic king of the hill. Among varmint hunters, there is an old saying, "There is nothing like a Swift!"

The last new development in ths cartridge was Remington's Etronx ignition system, manufactured late 1999-2003. It utilizes an electronic primer to lower the lock time to almost zero, as opposed to a trigger utilizing a traditional mechanical transfer system to detonate the primer.

.221 REMINGTON FIREBALL

ALTERNATE NAME(S): .221 Rem. Fireball
RELATED CALIBER(S): .17 Rem. Fireball, .222 Rem.

CARTRIDGE HISTORY
Year of Introduction: 1963
Country of Origin: U.S.
Designer(s): Remington
Governing Body: SAAMI
Present Status: active

CARTRIDGE DESCRIPTION
Bullet Diameter: .224 in.
Bullet Weight(s): 50 gr.
Rifling Twist Rate: 1 turn in 14 in.
Test Barrel Length: N/A
Case Type: rimless, necked
Case Material: brass
Primer Size: small rifle

CARTRIDGE BALLISTICS
Max. Average Breech Pressure:
Max. Horizontal Range: 2,700 yds.
Max. Vertical Range: 6,100 ft.

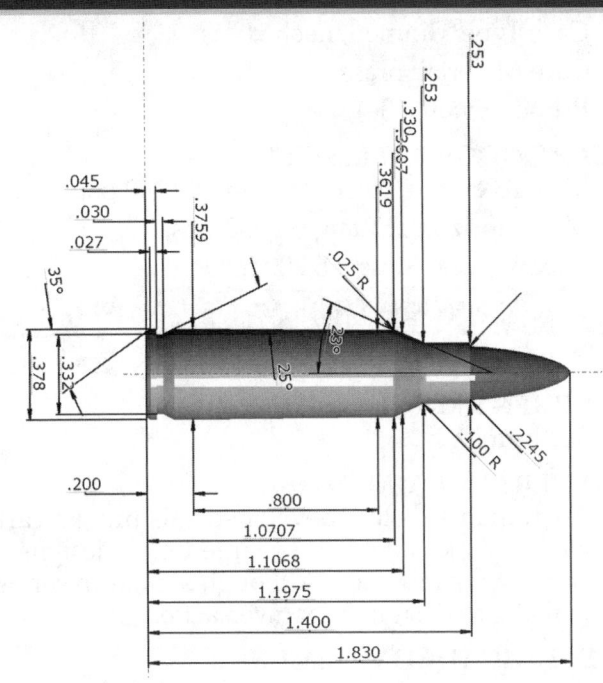

Bullet Weight (gr.)	Bullet Type	Muzzle Velocity (fps)	Muzzle Energy (ft.-lbs.)
50	JSP	2,995	996

CURRENT MANUFACTURER(S)
Remington

GENERAL COMMENT(S)
Introduced in 1963 for the Remington XP-100 bolt-action handgun, the .221 Fireball was part of a trend toward varmint hunting handguns chambered in rifle calibers. Remington has also offered rifles in this caliber and is the only manufacturer of this ammunition in this caliber.

TECHNICAL COMMENT(S)
Basically, the .221 Fireball is a shortened .222 Rem. cartridge. The reduced overall length allows it to fit in short length bolt actions to save weight. Other than its reduced length, the .221 Fireball shares head dimensions and configuration with the .222 Rem. Although the .221 Fireball is a small cartridge with limited powder, it is a high pressure rifle cartridge designed to provide excellent performance from barrels of approximately 12 inches in length.

.222 RIMMED

ALTERNATE NAME(S): .222 R., 5.56x43Rmm, .222 Australian Rimmed
RELATED CALIBER(S): .222 Rem., .223 Rem.

CARTRIDGE HISTORY
Year of Introduction: early 1960s
Country of Origin: Australia
Designer(s): Bruce Bertram
Governing Body: none
Present Status: active

CARTRIDGE DESCRIPTION
Bullet Diameter: .224 in.
Bullet Weight(s): 50 gr.

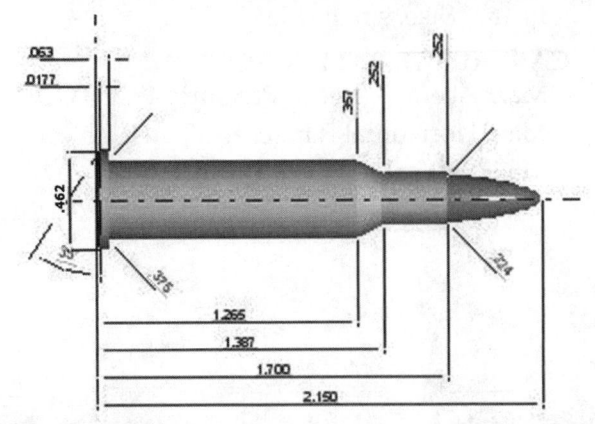

Rifling Twist Rate: 1 turn in 14 in.

Test Barrel Length: N/A

Case Type: rimmed, necked

Case Material: brass

Primer: small rifle

CARTRIDGE BALLISTICS

Max. Average Breech Pressure: 49,200 psi.

Max. Horizontal Range: 2,750 yds.

Max. Vertical Range: 6,200 ft.

Bullet Weight (gr.)	Bullet Type	Muzzle Velocity (fps)	Muzzle Energy (ft.-lbs.)
50	JSP	3,200	1,137

CURRENT MANUFACTURER(S)

Bertram

GENERAL COMMENT(S)

Australian shooters developed this unique cartridge for use in small frame Martini-Henry single shot rifles which work better with rimmed case designs. It remains an Australian specialty that is almost unknown to American sportsmen. Although similar in configuration, the .222 Rimmed is not related to the .225 Winchester which was designed for lever-action rifles.

TECHNICAL COMMENT(S)

From a technical standpoint, the .222 Rimmed is a .222 Remington case with a rim. Outside this, most other features of this cartridge are similar to those of the .222 Remington, including the ballistic capabilities.

.222 REMINGTON

ALTERNATE NAME(S): .222 Rem., 5.56x43mm, 5.6x43mm

RELATED CALIBER(S): .221 Fireball, .222 Rem. Mag., .223 Rem.

CARTRIDGE HISTORY

Year of Introduction: 1950

Country of Origin: U.S.

Designer(s): Remington, Mike Walker

Governing Body: SAAMI, CIP

Present Status: active

CARTRIDGE DESCRIPTION

Bullet Diameter: .224 in.

Bullet Weight(s): 40-55 gr.

Rifling Twist Rate: 1 turn in 14 in.

Test Barrel Length: 24 in.

Case Type: rimless, necked

Case Material: brass

Primer Size: small rifle

CARTRIDGE BALLISTICS

Max. Average Breech Pressure: 49,200 CUP.

Max. Horizontal Range: 2,750 yds.

Max. Vertical Range: 6,150 ft.

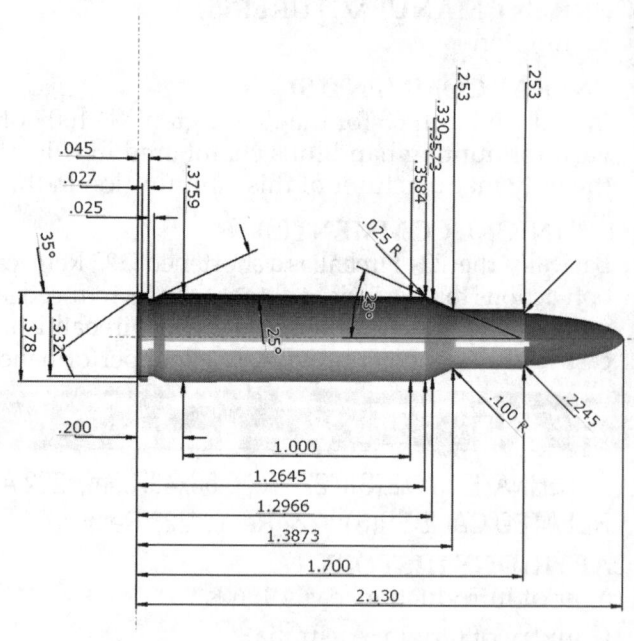

Bullet Weight (gr.)	Bullet Type	Muzzle Velocity (fps)	Muzzle Energy (ft.-lbs.)
40	JHP	3,450	1,055
50	JSP/JHP	3,140	1,095
55	FMJ-BT	3,020	1,114
62	JSP	2,885	1,148

CURRENT MANUFACTURER(S)
Federal, Hornady, Winchester, Remington, Norma, Prvi Partizan, Sellier & Bellot, PMC

GENERAL COMMENT(S)
From 1950 to 1970, the .222 Rem. was the quintessential varmint cartridge. All major ammunition manufacturers offered it and all major rifle makers chambered it. There was good reason for this. The .222 Remington's modern, rimless design and high velocity made all other small varmint cartridges obsolete.

In the early 1960s, the advent of the .223 Rem. with its higher still muzzle velocity caused a steep decline in the .222 Remington's popularity that continues to this day. By the early 2000s, the .223 Rem. had come to dominate the small caliber varmint cartridge spectrum relegating the .222 Rem. to the same status as the .218 Bee and .22 Hornet.

TECHNICAL COMMENT(S)
The .222 Rem. cartridge offers true 200 yard ballistic performance on varmints and small game. In addition, the .222 quickly earned a reputation for accuracy leading to it becoming a favorite of bench rest shooters.

Unlike the .223 Rem. cartridge which is flexible enough to extract acceptable ballistic performance from 40-69 grain bullets, the .222 works best with 40-50 grain bullet weights. It is also an efficient cartridge with powder charges filling 98% of case volume the norm for many propellants.

.223 REMINGTON

ALTERNATE NAME(S): .223 Rem., 5.56x45mm NATO
RELATED CALIBER(S): .221 Fireball, .222 Rem., .222 Rem. Mag.

CARTRIDGE HISTORY
Year of Introduction: 1964
Country of Origin: U.S.
Designer(s): Remington
Governing Body: SAAMI, CIP
Present Status: active

CARTRIDGE DESCRIPTION
Bullet Diameter: .224 in.
Bullet Weight(s): 40-75 gr.
Rifling Twist Rate: 1 turn in 12 in.
Test Barrel Length: 24 in.
Case Type: rimless, necked
Case Material: brass or steel
Primer Size: small rifle

CARTRIDGE BALLISTICS
Max. Average Breech Pressure: 55,400 CUP.
Max. Horizontal Range: 3,850 yds.
Max. Vertical Range: 8,650 ft.

Bullet Weight (gr.)	Bullet Type	Muzzle Velocity (fps)	Muzzle Energy (ft.-lbs.)
40	JHP	3,650	1,185
45	JHP	3,550	1,259
50	JSP	3,425	1,302
55	JSP/JHP	3,240	1,282
62	JHP	3,025	1,260
69	JHP	3,000	1,379
75	JHP	2,790	1,296

CURRENT MANUFACTURER(S)

Federal, Remington, Winchester, Hornady, Black Hills, IMI, Prvi Partizan, Fiocchi, PMC, PMP, MEN, Sellier & Bellot, Wolf, Lapua

GENERAL COMMENT(S)

DO NOT use 5.56x45mm NATO in a firearm chamberd for .223 Remington.

The .223 Rem. is a "civilianized" version of the 5.56x45mm cartridge adopted by the U.S. Army in 1964. Remington was the first domestic manufacturer out of the .223 starting gate and others quickly followed suit. After a tentative beginning, the .223 Rem. cartridge has come to dominate varmint hunting, bench rest competition, and law enforcement applications. This cartridge has now been authorized for U.S. National Match competition as well.

While ubiquitous in the U.S., Canada, Australia and New Zealand, the .223 Rem. has not caught on among the more traditional minded European shooters. As the popularity of the .223 Rem. continues to grow, it will eventually relegate the .22 Hornet, .218 Bee, and .222 Rem. to the history books.

TECHNICAL COMMENT(S)

A major reason for the popularity of the .223 Rem. cartridge is its ballistic performance. A true 250 yard performer, it also offers the flexibility of a wide range of bullet types and weights, near-universal availability, and excellent accuracy. The .223 Rem. was designed for 55 grain bullets, and a rifling twist rate of one turn in 12 inches. This will stabilize bullets up to 62 grains in weight. Heavier bullets require a faster twist. Another major factor in .223 Rem. popularity is the ease and economy of reloading it. The .223 happily burns a wide variety of propellant types and speeds and brass cases are readily available. And, unlike large cartridges that gulp large quantities of propellant, the .223 performs with small propellant charges.

The .223 is a high pressure cartridge which is one reason for its sterling ballistics. This places it in a completely different category from the .22 Hornet, .218 Bee, and .222 Rem. Reduced power loads do not work well in the .223; muzzle velocities are best kept above 3,000 fps. Surprisingly, the .223 has found success in single-shot handguns. Muzzle velocities are, of course, lower than in rifles. However, the muzzle velocity reduction is not as much as might be expected and trajectory remains acceptably flat according to handgun varmint shooters.

.22-250 REMINGTON

ALTERNATE NAME(S): .22-250 Rem., .22-250 Varminter
RELATED CALIBER(S): .250-3000 Savage H.P., .300 Savage

CARTRIDGE HISTORY

Year of Introduction: 1965 (entered commercial production), designed circa 1937

Country of Origin: U.S.

Designer(s): J.E. Gebby, J.B. Smith

Governing Body: SAAMI, CIP

Present Status: active

CARTRIDGE DESCRIPTION

Bullet Diameter: .224 in.

Bullet Weight(s): 40-60 gr.

Rifling Twist Rate: 1 turn in 14 in.

Test Barrel Length: 24 in.

Case Type: rimless, necked

Case Material: brass

Primer Size: large rifle

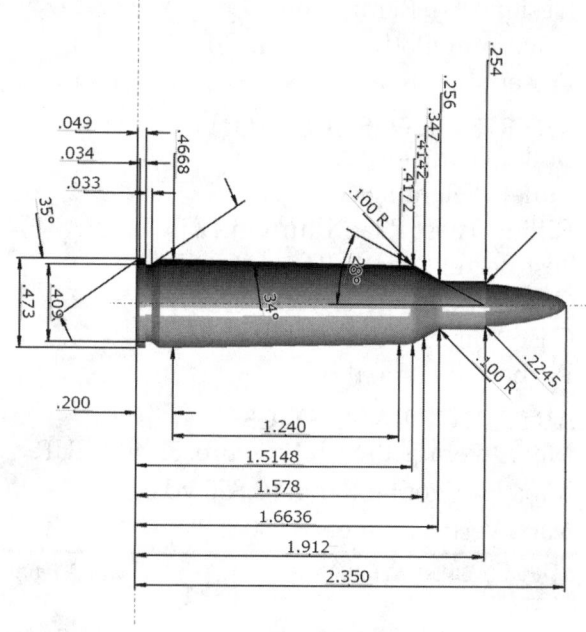

CARTRIDGE BALLISTICS

Max. Average Breech Pressure: 65,000 psi.

Max. Horizontal Range: 3,500 yds.

Max. Vertical Range: 7,900 ft.

Bullet Weight (gr.)	Bullet Type	Muzzle Velocity (fps)	Muzzle Energy (ft.-lbs.)
40	JHP	4,150	1,282
45	JHP	4,000	1,598
50	JHP	3,800	1,603
55	JSP/JHP	3,680	1,654
60	JSP/JHP	3,600	1,726

CURRENT MANUFACTURER(S)

Winchester, Remington, Federal, Hornady, Black Hills, Sellier & Bellot, Prvi Partizan, PMC

GENERAL COMMENT(S)

After the .250-3000 Savage cartridge was introduced in 1922, wildcatters immediately began experiments in necking down the parent case to .22 caliber. A number of versions were tried, however the version developed by J.E. Gebby and J.E. Smith was closest to the commercial version finally introduced by Remington in 1965. As a result, credit for the design must be given to Gebby and Smith. Gebby copyrighted the name "Varminter" for this cartridge, a name that still sticks to it although not in an "official" capacity.

Today, the .22-250 Rem. cartridge is surpassed in popularity only by the .223 Rem. Nearly every major rifle manufacturer chambers this caliber and all major domestic ammunition makers offer it. While popular in the U.S. and Canada, the .22-250 Rem. is almost unknown in Europe as varmint hunting does not exist there.

TECHNICAL COMMENT(S)

For long range varmint shooting to 300 yards and beyond, the .22-250 Rem. remains in a league of its own. Superb accuracy, light recoil, and flat trajectory form a happy combination in this cartridge which goes a long way to justifying its popularity. However, muzzle blast is heavy, barrels wear out more quickly than lesser performing cartridges, and long range is not always a requirement. The superb ballistics of the .22-250 Rem. complement the marksmanship skills required to hit a small varmint at ranges in excess of four hundred yards. With the .22-250, closer shots seem tame by comparison and longer shots are not unknown. Choose the 55 and 60 gr. bullets for long shots. Reserve the 40 and 50 gr. bullets for the closer targets to 200 yards. The last new development in ths cartridge was Remington's Etronx ignition system, manufactured late 1999-2003. It utilizes an electronic primer to lower the lock time to almost zero, as opposed to a trigger utilizing a traditional mechanical transfer system to detonate the primer.

.223 WINCHESTER SUPER SHORT MAGNUM

ALTERNATE NAME(S): .223 WSSM
RELATED CALIBER(S): .243 WSSM, .25 WSSM

CARTRIDGE HISTORY

Year of Introduction: 2002
Country of Origin: U.S.
Designer(s): Winchester
Governing Body: SAAMI
Present Status: active

CARTRIDGE DESCRIPTION

Bullet Diameter: .224 in.
Bullet Weight(s): 55-64 gr.
Rifling Twist Rate: 1 turn in 14 in.
Test Barrel Length: 24 in.
Case Type: rimless, necked
Case Material: brass
Primer Size: large rifle

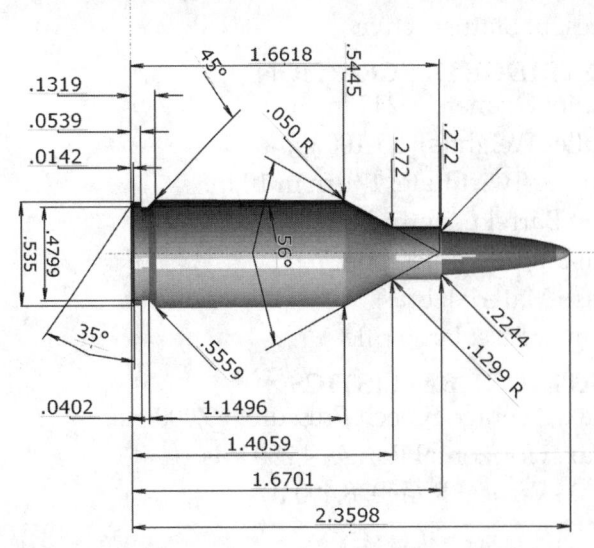

CARTRIDGE BALLISTICS

Max. Average Breech Pressure: 65,000 psi.
Max. Horizontal Range: 3,500 yds.
Max. Vertical Range: 7,900 ft.

Bullet Weight (gr.)	Bullet Type	Muzzle Velocity (fps)	Muzzle Energy (ft.-lbs.)
55	JSP	3,850	1,810
64	JSP	3,600	1,841

CURRENT MANUFACTURER(S)
Winchester

GENERAL COMMENT(S)
This was one of the last WSSM cartridges introduced before U.S. Repeating Arms ceased firearm production. Developed by Winchester, the WSSM case configuration introduced completely new interior ballistic and cartridge design concepts. The short, fat WSSM case proved less than successful in .223 caliber. While Winchester did append their name to the new cartridge, it quickly became an orphan after U.S. Repeating Arms ceased production of rifles in this caliber and other gun makers did not offer this caliber. Consequently, the future of this cartridge appears dim.

TECHNICAL COMMENT(S)
As a technical concept, the Winchester Super Short Magnum (WSSM) case design is a short, fat configuration intended for use in bolt-action rifles of ultra-short length and light weight. Case head diameter is greater than standard magnums and case length is shorter than normal. Although called a magnum, the case does not have a belt.

In contrast to larger caliber WSSM cases, the advantages of a short, fat case design in .223 caliber proved more imaginary than real. Initial efforts to build a 4,000+ fps load with a 40 grain bullet encountered unexpected interior ballistic difficulties. Winchester withdrew that bullet weight from the market leaving the .223 WSSM to march on with 55 and 64 grain bullet loads.

.243 WINCHESTER SUPER SHORT MAGNUM

ALTERNATE NAME(S): .243 WSSM
RELATED CALIBER(S): .223 WSSM, .25 WSSM

CARTRIDGE HISTORY
Year of Introduction: 2004
Country of Origin: U.S.
Designer(s): Winchester
Governing Body: SAAMI
Present Status: active

CARTRIDGE DESCRIPTION
Bullet Diameter: .243 in.
Bullet Weight(s): 55-100 gr.
Rifling Twist Rate: 1 turn in 10 in.
Test Barrel Length: 24 in.
Case Type: rimless, necked
Case Material: brass
Primer Size: large rifle

CARTRIDGE BALLISTICS
Max. Average Breech Pressure: 65,000 psi.
Max. Horizontal Range: 4,250 yds.
Max. Vertical Range: 8,400 ft.

Bullet Weight (gr.)	Bullet Type	Muzzle Velocity (fps)	Muzzle Energy (ft.-lbs.)
55	JSP	4,060	2,013
95	JSP	3,250	2,258
100	JSP	3,110	2,147

CURRENT MANUFACTURER(S)
Winchester

GENERAL COMMENT(S)

This is a member of the second wave of WSSM cartridges from Winchester which were introduced shortly before U.S. Repeating Arms terminated firearm production. Developed by Winchester, the WSSM case configuration introduced a completely new interior ballistics and cartridge design concepts. The short, fat WSSM case proved less than successful in .243 caliber. While Winchester did append their name to the new cartridge, it quickly became an orphan after U.S. Repeating Arms ceased production of rifles in this caliber and other gun makers did not offer this caliber. Consequently, the future of this cartridge appears dim.

TECHNICAL COMMENT(S)

As a technical concept, the Winchester Super Short Magnum (WSSM) case design is a short, fat configuration intended for use in bolt-action rifles of ultra-short length and light weight. Case head diameter is greater than standard magnums and case length is shorter than normal. Although called a magnum, the case does not have a belt. In contrast to larger caliber WSSM cases, the advantages of a short, fat case design in .243 caliber are more imaginary than real.

.243 WINCHESTER

ALTERNATE NAME(S): .243 Win.
RELATED CALIBER(S): .308 Win., .300 Savage, .35 Rem., .30-'06 Spr.

CARTRIDGE HISTORY
Year of Introduction: 1955
Country of Origin: U.S.
Designer(s): Winchester, Warren Page
Governing Body: SAAMI, CIP
Present Status: active

CARTRIDGE DESCRIPTION
Bullet Diameter: .243 in.
Bullet Weight(s): 55-100 gr.
Rifling Twist Rate: 1 turn in 10 in.
Test Barrel Length: 24 in.
Case Type: rimless, necked
Case Material: brass
Primer Size: large rifle

CARTRIDGE BALLISTICS
Max. Average Breech Pressure: 55,200 CUP.
Max. Horizontal Range: 4,000 yds.
Max. Vertical Range: 9,000 ft.

Bullet Weight (gr.)	Bullet Type	Muzzle Velocity (fps)	Muzzle Energy (ft.-lbs.)
55	JSP	3,910	1,867
58	JSP	3,750	1,811
75	JHP	3,400	1,925
85	JSP	3,175	1,902
95	JSP	3,100	2,027
100	JSP	3,100	2,133
100	JSP	2,960	1,945
100	JSP	2,850	1,805

CURRENT MANUFACTURER(S)
Winchester, Remington, Federal, Hornady, Black Hills, PMC, Sellier & Bellot, Norma, Prvi Partizan

GENERAL COMMENT(S)
American hunters have wholeheartedly adopted the .243 Win. as the quintessential deer cartridge. While there are many other 6mm hunting cartridges offering greater ballistic performance, the popularity of the .243 Win. eclipses all of these put together. Today, virtually every major commercial ammunition manufacturer offers this cartridge. It also serves as a good varmint cartridge, although it is not particularly popular for that purpose.

TECHNICAL COMMENT(S)

In technical terms, the .243 Win. cartridge is a .308 Win. case necked down to 6mm. The lightest 6mm bullet suitable for deer hunting is about 100 grains and this is the weight the designers selected. It combines flat trajectory, high velocity, and low recoil in a package appreciated by youthful and female hunters as well as the average male hunter. The lighter weight bullets should be reserved for varmints. The last new development in this cartridge was Remington's Etronx ignition system, manufactured late 1999-2003. It utilizes an electronic primer to lower the lock time to almost zero, as opposed to a trigger utilizing a traditional mechanical transfer system to detonate the primer.

6mm PPC

ALTERNATE NAME(S): 6 PPC
RELATED CALIBER(S): .22 PPC, 7.62x39mm Soviet

CARTRIDGE HISTORY

Year of Introduction: 1987 (commercial production)
Country of Origin: U.S.
Designer(s): Dr. Louis Palmisano, Ferris Pindell
Governing Body: CIP
Present Status: active

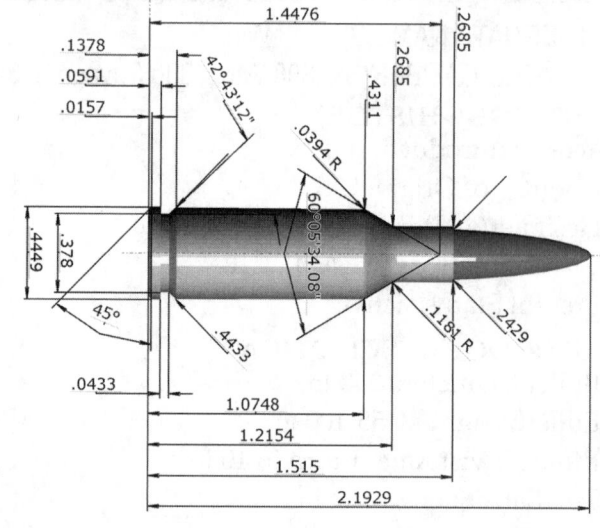

CARTRIDGE DESCRIPTION

Bullet Diameter: .243 in.
Bullet Weight(s): 60-90 gr.
Rifling Twist Rate: 1 turn in 14 in.
Test Barrel Length: 24 in.
Case Type: rimless, necked
Case Material: brass
Primer Size: small rifle

CARTRIDGE BALLISTICS

Max. Average Breech Pressure: N/A
Max. Horizontal Range: 4,100 yds.
Max. Vertical Range: 9,200 ft.

Bullet Weight (gr.)	Bullet Type	Muzzle Velocity (fps)	Muzzle Energy (ft.-lbs.)
70	JSP	3,140	1,535

CURRENT MANUFACTURER(S)

Sako, Norma

GENERAL COMMENT(S)

Dr. Louis Palmisano, a surgeon, and Ferris Pindell, a tool and die maker, combined their talents to design, develop, and introduce this cartridge in the late 1970s specifically for bench rest rifle competition. Their design showcased their belief that a shorter overall case length with a wider body diameter would be inherently more accurate than existing cartridge designs with long, narrow diameter configurations. Bench rest competitors found the 6mm PPC cartridge performed as expected and used it to establish many new bench rest records. It came to dominate bench rest competition, a position it continues to retain.

Sako began commercial manufacture in 1987. A sister cartridge, the .22 PPC did not prove as successful or popular and has since become obsolete.

TECHNICAL COMMENT(S)

The 6mm PPC cartridge is designed for efficiency and accuracy. The powder column is shorter and wider than normal cartridges and the neck longer than normal in order to hold and guide the bullet. With most loads, a nearly 100% powder fill can be achieved. The case and rifling twist rate are optimized for bullets in the 60-75 grain weight range.

6mm REMINGTON BENCH REST

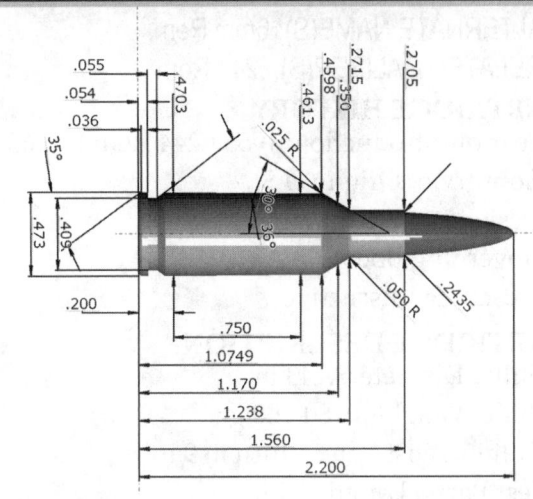

ALTERNATE NAME(S): 6mm Rem. BR, 6 BR, 6mm BR
RELATED CALIBER(S): .308 Win.

CARTRIDGE HISTORY
Year of Introduction: 1978
Country of Origin: U.S.
Designer: Mike Walker
Governing Body: SAAMI, CIP
Present Status: active

CARTRIDGE DESCRIPTION
Bullet Diameter: .243 in.
Bullet Weight(s): 68-115 gr.
Rifling Twist Rate: 1 turn in 12 in.
Test Barrel Length: 24 in.
Case Type: rimless, necked
Case Material: brass
Primer Size: small rifle

CARTRIDGE BALLISTICS
Max. Average Breech Pressure: 54,700 psi.
Max. Horizontal Range: 4,100 yds.
Max. Vertical Range: 9,500 ft.

Bullet Weight (gr.)	Bullet Type	Muzzle Velocity (fps)	Muzzle Energy (ft.-lbs.)
100	JSP	2,550	1,444
105	VLD	2,790	1,815

CURRENT MANUFACTURER(S)
Remington, Norma

GENERAL COMMENT(S)
Not to be outdone by the 6mm PPC cartridge, Remington introduced its own bench rest rifle cartridge called the 6mm BR. Despite considerable promotion by Remington, the 6mm BR cartridge never gained the popularity of the 6mm PPC in bench rest circles. Norma redesigned the cartridge for European 300 meter rifle competition at which it has been successful.

TECHNICAL COMMENT(S)
While the 6mm PPC cartridge was based on the 7.62x39mm Soviet cartridge, the 6mm Remington BR was based on a shortened .308 Win. case. Remington designed this cartridge for bench rest competition using bullets in the 60-80 grain weight range. Norma modified the throat of the chamber in order to accept longer heavier bullets in the 80-115 grain range necessary for long range rifle competition.

6mm REMINGTON

ALTERNATE NAME(S): 6mm Rem.
RELATED CALIBER(S): .244 Rem.

CARTRIDGE HISTORY
Year of Introduction: 1955 (.244 Rem.), 1963 (6mm Rem.)
Country of Origin: U.S.
Designer(s): Remington
Governing Body: SAAMI, CIP
Present Status: active

CARTRIDGE DESCRIPTION
Bullet Diameter: .243 in.
Bullet Weight(s): 80-100 gr.
Rifling Twist Rate: 1 turn in 9 in.
Test Barrel Length: 24 in.
Case Type: rimless, necked
Case Material: brass
Primer Size: large rifle

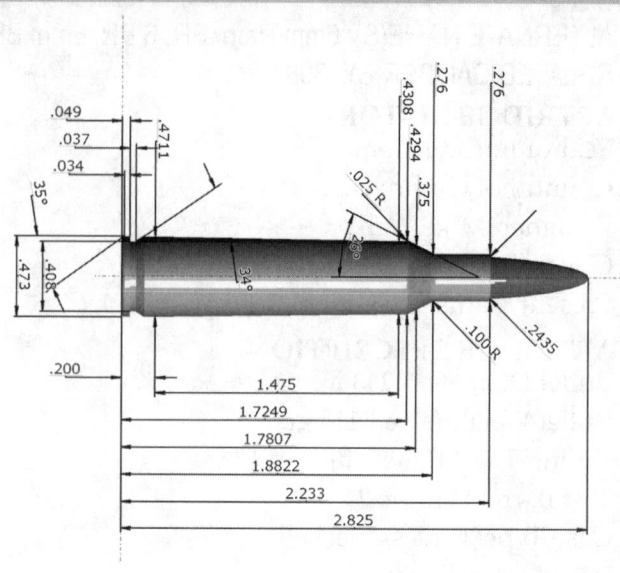

CARTRIDGE BALLISTICS
Max. Average Breech Pressure: 55,200 CUP.
Max. Horizontal Range: 4,650 yds.
Max. Vertical Range: 10,500 ft.

Bullet Weight (gr.)	Bullet Type	Muzzle Velocity (fps)	Muzzle Energy (ft.-lbs.)
80	JSP	3,470	2,139
95	JSP	3,100	2,027
100	JSP	3,250	2,345
100	JSP	3,100	2,133

CURRENT MANUFACTURER(S)
Remington, Winchester, Federal, Prvi Partizan, PMC

GENERAL COMMENT(S)
Both Remington and Winchester introduced 6mm rifle cartridges in 1955. While Winchester designed their .243 Win. cartridge for deer hunting with 100 grain bullets using a 1:10 inch rifling twist, Remington designed their .244 Rem. cartridge for varmint hunting with 60-80 grain bullets using a 1:12 inch twist. Winchester proved right and Remington had a problem as their rifling twist would not stabilize 100 grain bullets. To correct their error, in 1963 Remington revised the twist rate to 1:9 inches to stabalize the 100 grain bullets and renamed the cartridge the 6mm Remington. The .244 Rem. cartridge quickly became obsolete: the dimensions of the 6mm Rem. case are identical.

TECHNICAL COMMENT(S)
Some hunters prefer the 6mm Rem. case for its large internal volume which allows bullets to be pushed to slightly higher muzzle velocities than the .243 Win. cartridge. Otherwise, there is not much to choose between the 6mm Rem. and the .243 Win.

6x45mm

ALTERNATE NAME(S): None
RELATED CALIBER(S): .223 Rem., 6x47mm

CARTRIDGE HISTORY
Year of Introduction: 1965
Country of Origin: U.S.
Designer(s): Jim Stekl, Remington
Governing Body: SAAMI
Present Status: current

CARTRIDGE DESCRIPTION
Bullet Diameter: .429 in.
Bullet Weight(s): 62-85 gr.
Rifling Twist Rate: 1 turn in 9 in.
Test Barrel Length: 24 in.
Case Type: rimless, necked
Case Material: brass
Primer Size: small rifle

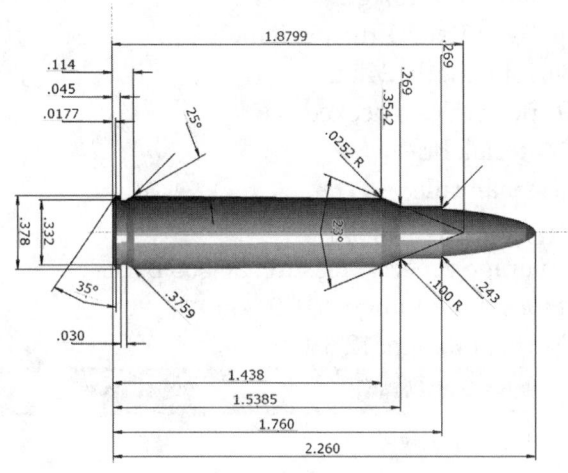

CARTRIDGE BALLISTICS
Max. Average Breech Pressure: 55,400 psi.
Max. Horizontal Range: N/A
Max. Vertical Range: N/A

Bullet Weight (gr.)	Bullet Type	Muzzle Velocity (fps)	Muzzle Energy (ft.-lbs.)
62	HP	3,100	1,399
70	HPBT	3,000	1,323
85	SP	2,800	1,480

CURRENT MANUFACTURER(S)
Cor-Bon

GENERAL COMMENT(S)
Although the 6x45mm began life as a bench rest wildcat, it has morphed into a legitimate varmint cartridge for AR15 semi-automatic rifles. Cor-Bon recently guided this cartridge through the SAAMI standardization process which will undoubtedly increase interest even further.

TECHNICAL COMMENT(S)
The 6x45mm cartridge required very little design work as it is basically a .223 Rem. cartridge necked up to 6mm without further changes. Another major advantage is that any rifle designed originally for the 5.56x45mm or .223 Rem. cartridges can be converted to the 6x45mm with very few modifications.

Many varmint hunters have come to prefer the lightweight 6mm caliber bullets in the 55-80 grain bracket for their superior down range ballistic performance when compared to the .22 caliber bullets of the 5.56x45mm and .223 Rem. cartridges.

6x47mm SWISS MATCH

ALTERNATE NAME(S): None
RELATED CALIBER(S): 6x47mm

CARTRIDGE HISTORY
Year of Introduction: 2001 (6x47mm 1974)
Country of Origin: Switzerland
Designer(s): various, incl. bench rest shooters, Federal Cartridge, author, Swiss Shooting Team
Governing Body: CIP

Present Status: active

CARTRIDGE DESCRIPTION
Bullet Diameter: .244 in.
Bullet Weight(s): 107 gr.
Rifling Twist Rate: 1 turn in 8 in.
Test Barrel Length: 24 in.
Case Type: rimless, necked
Case Material: brass
Primer: small rifle

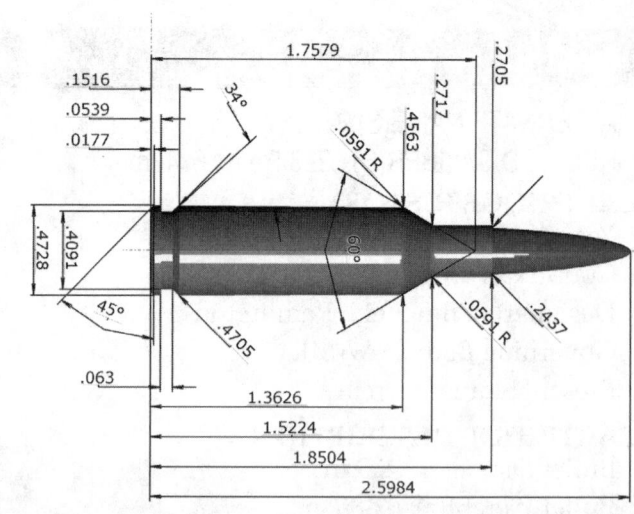

CARTRIDGE BALLISTICS
Max. Average Breech Pressure: 56,565 psi.
Max. Horizontal Range: 6,000 yds.
Max. Vertical Range: 12,650 ft.

Bullet Weight (gr.)	Bullet Type	Muzzle Velocity (fps)	Muzzle Energy (ft.-lbs.)
107	JHP-BT	2,900	1,999

CURRENT MANUFACTURER(S)
RUAG

GENERAL COMMENT(S)
The 6x47mm cartridge began life as a bench rest cartridge made by necking up a .223 Rem. case to accept .243 inch diameter bullets. As bench rest shooters compete only at 100 and 200 yards, lightweight jacketed hollow point bullets of approximately 60-75 grains were used. In Europe, the most popular types of centerfire rifle competition are fired at 300 meters using ISU rules. Until recently, popular choices for such shooting have been 6.5mm and 7.62mm cartridges with the occasional experiment using the .243 Win. or 6mm PPC cartridges.

TECHNICAL COMMENT(S)
Recently, the shooter preference in 300 meter competition has shifted from the larger more powerful cartridges to smaller calibers with less recoil. Major factors driving such interest are the nearly universal adoption of the 5.56x45mm cartridge for military purposes and the obsolescence of the larger caliber military calibers. At 300 meters, a .243 inch diameter bullet weighing less than 100 grains would be a severe handicap as it would lose too much velocity. Consequently, very low drag hollow point boat-tail bullets are used to maintain down range velocity while retaining low recoil. When the 6x47mm cartridge is loaded with very long bullets, maximum overall length of the 6x47mm cartridge is considerably longer than its 5.56x45mm parent. Consequently, the 6x47mm can not be fired in rifles originally designed for the 5.56x45mm cartridge without major modification.

6x62mm FRERES, 6x62Rmm FRERES

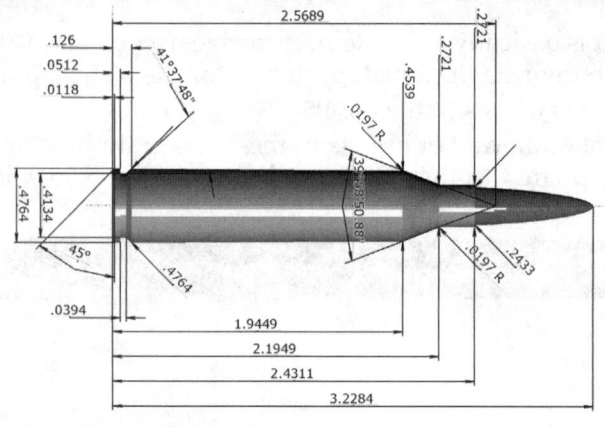

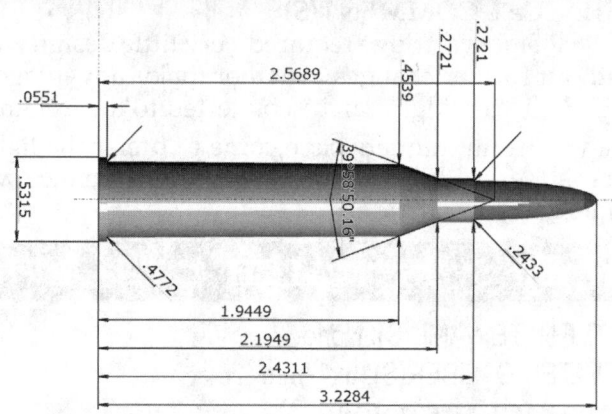

ALTERNATE NAME(S): none
RELATED CALIBER(S): 6x57mm Mauser, 6.5x57mm Mauser, 7x57mm Mauser

CARTRIDGE HISTORY
Year of Introduction: 1984; 6x62Rmm, 1992
Country of Origin: Germany

Designer(s): MEN
Governing Body: CIP
Present Status: active

CARTRIDGE DESCRIPTION
Bullet Diameter: .243 in.
Bullet Weight(s): 85-100 gr.
Rifling Twist Rate: 1 turn in 10.24 in.
Test Barrel Length: 24 in.
Case Type: rimless, necked; rimmed, necked
Case Material: brass
Primer: large rifle

CARTRIDGE BALLISTICS
Max. Average Breech Pressure: 62,366 psi. (both)
Max. Horizontal Range: 4,450 yds.
Max. Vertical Range: 9,750 ft.

Bullet Weight (gr.)	Bullet Type	Muzzle Velocity (fps)	Muzzle Energy (ft.-lbs.)
85	JSP	3,460	2,259
100	JSP	3,315	2,442

CURRENT MANUFACTURER(S)
MEN

GENERAL COMMENT(S)
These two cartridges are unique in that they are sporting cartridges introduced by the German firm of Metallwerk Elisenhutte GmbH (MEN). Historically, MEN concentrated mainly on military and law enforcement ammunition, making these cartridges something of a departure for it. In 2006, CBC of Brazil purchased MEN so perhaps more sporting cartridges are in MEN's future. Both of these cartridges are nearly unknown in the U.S. leaving a void of information about their development and market. The word "freres" in French means "brothers".

TECHNICAL COMMENT(S)
Unlike other twin cartridges having a rimless and a rimmed version, the maximum average chamber pressure is the same for both 6x62mm versions. The rimmed version is not loaded to a lower maximum average chamber pressure than the rimless cartridge. From a ballistic standpoint, the 6x62 cartridges offer performance superior to the .243 Winchester and 6mm Remington cartridges. In real terms, this amounts to 12% higher muzzle velocity and a 15% increase in muzzle energy when a 100 grain bullet is loaded. To summarize, the 6x62mm Freres cartridges are modern high performance designs intended for the European market. Given the wide selection of 6mm cartridges already offered in North America, it is unlikely either of these cartridges will be introduced to the American market.

6x70Rmm

ALTERNATE NAME(S): none
RELATED CALIBER(S): none, unique case

CARTRIDGE HISTORY
Year of Introduction: 2000
Country of Origin: Germany
Designer(s): Krieghoff, Norma
Governing Body: CIP
Present Status: active

CARTRIDGE DESCRIPTION
Bullet Diameter: .243 in.
Bullet Weight(s): 90 gr.
Rifling Twist Rate: 1 turn in 10 in.
Test Barrel Length: 24 in.

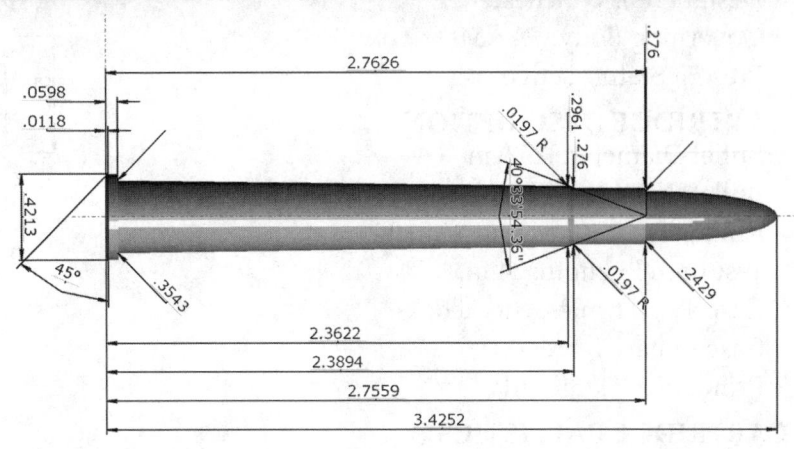

Case Type: rimmed, necked
Case Material: brass
Primer: small rifle

CARTRIDGE BALLISTICS
Max. Average Breech Pressure: 37,710 psi.
Max. Horizontal Range: N/A
Max. Vertical Range: N/A

Bullet Weight (gr.)	Bullet Type	Muzzle Velocity (fps)	Muzzle Energy (ft.-lbs.)
90	JSP-BT	2,460	1,211

CURRENT MANUFACTURER(S)
Norma

GENERAL COMMENT(S)
One might be forgiven for thinking that a new rimmed cartridge of moderate breech pressure designed for break-open drillings and single-shot rifles would be a dud idea even in the European market. However, you would be mistaken.When you carefully examine the rimmed calibers for break-open rifles, you will notice the absence of a modern 6mm cartridge firing pointed bullets. To remedy this, in 2000 Kreighoff and Norma teamed up to design and introduce just such a cartridge, the 6x70Rmm.

TECHNICAL COMMENT(S)
On seeing the rather unusual shape of the 6x70Rmm cartridge, a number of questions usually arise. For example, why is the case so long at a time when shorter and fatter is in vogue? A second question concerns its purpose, what is it used for? And one last question, why is the maximum average chamber pressure and muzzle velocity so low? The maximum average chamber pressure is maintained at its modest level as break-open rifle actions are not capable of withstanding breech pressures much over 40,000 psi. For safety reasons, the 6x70Rmm chamber pressures are kept below that level. In mixed bag hunts so popular in Europe, the hunter may encounter several types of game ranging from birds to deer to boar. A drilling accommodates all these and the 6x70Rmm is perfect for the small European deer weighing less that 40 pounds.The long slender shape of the 6x70Rmm case is dictated by the available space in the breech of a drilling. Remember, a drilling has two shotgun barrels and one or two rifle barrels. A three- or four-barrel drilling does not have a lot of space in the breech area. For this reason, the 6x70Rmm cartridge is long and thin to provide the internal volume for the powder charge. These requirements make the 6x70Rmm cartridge case unique. It is not a derivative of any other base cartridge.

.25 WINCHESTER SUPER SHORT MAGNUM

ALTERNATE NAME(S): .25 WSSM
RELATED CALIBER(S): .223 WSSM, .243 WSSM

CARTRIDGE HISTORY
Year of Introduction: 2004
Country of Origin: U.S.
Designer(s): Winchester
Governing Body: SAAMI
Present Status: active

CARTRIDGE DESCRIPTION
Bullet Diameter: .257 in.
Bullet Weight(s): 85-120 gr.
Rifling Twist Rate: 1 turn in 10 in.
Test Barrel Length: 24 in.
Case Type: rimless, necked
Case Material: brass
Primer Size: large rifle

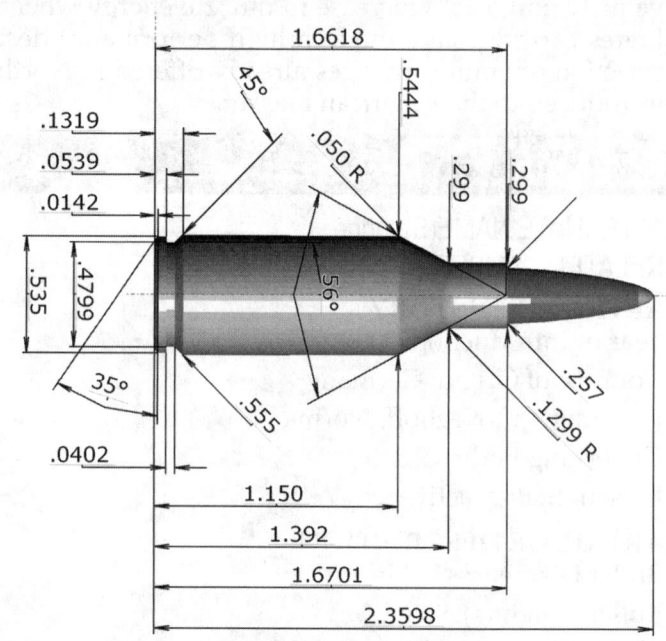

CARTRIDGE BALLISTICS
Max. Average Breech Pressure: 65,000
Max. Horizontal Range: 5,000 yds.

Max. Vertical Range: 9,900 ft.

Bullet Weight (gr.)	Bullet Type	Muzzle Velocity (fps)	Muzzle Energy (ft.-lbs.)
85	JSP	3,470	2,273
110	JSP	3,100	2,347
115	JSP	3,060	2,392
120	JSP	2,990	2,383

CURRENT MANUFACTURER(S)
Winchester

GENERAL COMMENT(S)
One of the lesser-known WSSM cartridges, the .25 WSSM faces a dim future. When U.S. Repeating Arms (USRAC) ceased production, the .25 WSSM became an orphan.

TECHNICAL COMMENT(S)
Several existing .25 caliber cartridges, in particular the .25-06 Rem., offer similar performance albeit in a long action. But, how important is the perceived weight reduction of a short action in such calibers?

.250 SAVAGE

ALTERNATE NAME(S): .250 Sav., .250-3000 Savage
RELATED CALIBER(S): .300 Savage

CARTRIDGE HISTORY
Year of Introduction: 1915
Country of Origin: U.S.
Designer(s): Charles Newton
Governing Body: SAAMI
Present Status: active

CARTRIDGE DESCRIPTION
Bullet Diameter: .257 in.
Bullet Weight(s): 87-120 gr.
Rifling Twist Rate: 1 turn in 14 in.
Test Barrel Length: 24 in.
Case Type: rimless, necked
Case Material: brass
Primer Size: large rifle

CARTRIDGE BALLISTICS
Max. Average Breech Pressure: 48,200 CUP.
Max. Horizontal Range: 3,850 yds.
Max. Vertical Range: 8,650 ft.

Bullet Weight (gr.)	Bullet Type	Muzzle Velocity (fps)	Muzzle Energy (ft.-lbs.)
87	JSP	3,030	1,770
100	JSP	2,820	1,765
120	JSP	2,645	1,865

CURRENT MANUFACTURER(S)
Remington, Winchester

GENERAL COMMENT(S)
This is another fine old cartridge designed by Charles Newton in 1915. When this cartridge was introduced, it was loaded with an 87 grain bullet at a muzzle velocity of 3,000 fps, leading to its early name of .250-3000 Savage. Some years later, heavier weight bullets were added. Today, the 87 grain and 120 grain bullets have become obsolete, leaving only the 100 grain loading. With the discontinuance of the 87 grain bullet load, the cartridge is more properly called the .250 Savage.

While an 87 grain bullet at a muzzle velocity of 3,000 fps does not raise any eyebrows today, in the 1920s it was nothing less than phenomenal and remained so until well into the 1950s. It was one of the first small bore cartridges to showcase the potential ballistics of smokeless propellants.

TECHNICAL COMMENT(S)

Many shooters believe the .250 Savage is a development of the .300 Savage, the former being a necked down version of the latter. Rather the opposite is true. The .250 Savage preceded the .300 Savage by five years and both were modern designs that pointed the way forward to the .243 Win. and .308 Win. cartridges of today.

.25-06 REMINGTON

ALTERNATE NAME(S): .25-06 Rem.
RELATED CALIBER(S): .270 Win., .30-'06 Rem.

CARTRIDGE HISTORY

Year of Introduction: 1969
Country of Origin: U.S.
Designer(s): A.O. Neidner (1920)
Governing Body: SAAMI
Present Status: active

CARTRIDGE DESCRIPTION

Bullet Diameter: .257 in.
Bullet Weight(s): 85-120 gr.
Rifling Twist Rate: 1 turn in 10 in.
Test Barrel Length: 24 in.
Case Type: rimless, necked
Case Material: brass
Primer Size: large rifle

CARTRIDGE BALLISTICS

Max. Average Breech Pressure: 56,200 CUP.
Max. Horizontal Range: 4,700 yds.
Max. Vertical Range: 10,500 ft.

Bullet Weight (gr.)	Bullet Type	Muzzle Velocity (fps)	Muzzle Energy (ft.-lbs.)
85	JSP	3,550	2,380
90	JSP	3,440	2,364
100	JSP	3,210	2,290
115	JSP	3,060	2,392
117	JSP	2,990	2,320
120	JSP	2,990	2,382

CURRENT MANUFACTURER(S)

Remington, Federal, Winchester, Hornady, Black Hills, PMC, Prvi Partizan

GENERAL COMMENT(S)

Is the .25-06 Rem. a superb deer cartridge or the ultimate varmint cartridge? From the beginning of the .25-06 Remington's production life, the answer to this question has remained an enigma. In fact, the .25-06 is

both – keeping in mind its performance and limitations. For deer at longer ranges, the .25-06 Rem. is an excellent choice. However, it is needlessly powerful for typical short and medium range deer hunting. Ditto for varmints. Most hunters find the stout recoil of the .25-06 takes the fun out of varmint shooting after 20 rounds or so. The .25-06 Rem. remains a steady seller after four decades of success.

TECHNICAL COMMENT(S)

When Remington introduced the .25-06 Rem. into commercial production, they kept A.O. Neidner's original dimensions. Basically, the reason for this was the simplicity of Neidner's design – the .25-06 Rem. is a .270 Win. necked down to accept .257 inch diameter bullets with very few other changes.

.257 ROBERTS

ALTERNATE NAME(S): .257 Rob. (+P)
RELATED CALIBER(S): 7x57mm Mauser

CARTRIDGE HISTORY
Year of Introduction: 1934
Country of Origin: U.S.
Designer(s): Ned Roberts
Governing Body: SAAMI
Present Status: active

CARTRIDGE DESCRIPTION
Bullet Diameter: .257 in.
Bullet Weight(s): 87-120 gr.
Rifling Twist Rate: 1 turn in 10 in.
Test Barrel Length: 24 in.
Case Type: rimless, necked
Case Material: brass
Primer Size: large rifle

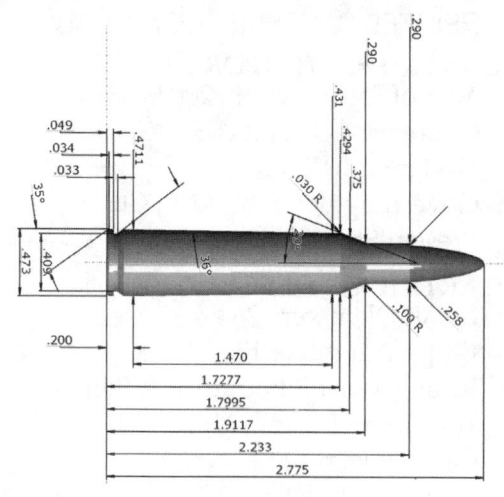

CARTRIDGE BALLISTICS
Max. Average Breech Pressure: 48,200 CUP.
Max. Horizontal Range: 3,850 yds.
Max. Vertical Range: 8,650 ft.
BALLISTICS (+P)

Bullet Weight (gr.)	Bullet Type	Muzzle Velocity (fps)	Muzzle Energy (ft.-lbs.)
87	JSP	3,200	1,980
117	JSP	2,650	1,824
117	JSP	2,780	2,009
117	JSP	2,940	2,245
120	JSP	2,780	2,060

CURRENT MANUFACTURER(S)
Federal, Remington, Winchester, Hornady

GENERAL COMMENT(S)
Introduced into commercial production by Remington in 1934, the .257 Roberts often has been billed as one of the "most versatile" centerfire rifle cartridges. However, sales of the .257 Roberts never quite lived up to this title. It became a classic example of a fine cartridge that did not sell as well as expected because ammunition makers never loaded this caliber to its full potential. Finally, in the late 1980s a +P version of the .257 Roberts was standardized by SAAMI and ballistic performance improved substantially. At this point, it may have been too late.

TECHNICAL COMMENT(S)
As a technical exercise, the .257 Roberts is a wildcat made by necking down the 7x57mm Mauser cartridge. The 20 degree shoulder angle and approximate overall length were maintained. In the field, the .257 Roberts is known for its accuracy and excellent performance on deer and other medium game.

.260 REMINGTON

ALTERNATE NAME(S): .260 Rem.
RELATED CALIBER(S): .257 Roberts

CARTRIDGE HISTORY
Year of Introduction: 2002
Country of Origin: U.S.
Designer(s): Remington
Governing Body: SAAMI, CIP
Present Status: active

CARTRIDGE DESCRIPTION
Bullet Diameter: .264 in.
Bullet Weight(s): 120-140 gr.
Rifling Twist Rate: 1 turn in 9 in.
Test Barrel Length: N/A
Case Type: rimless, necked
Case Material: brass
Primer Size: large rifle

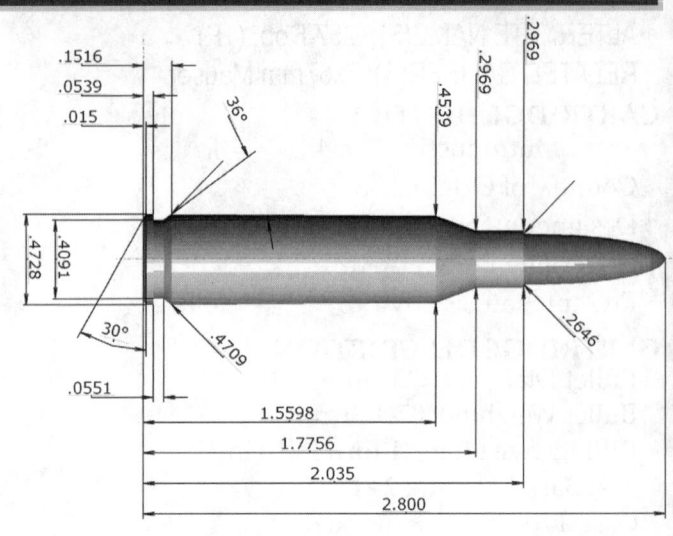

CARTRIDGE BALLISTICS
Max. Average Breech Pressure: 52,200 CUP.
Max. Horizontal Range: 4,800 yds.
Max. Vertical Range: 9,100 ft.

Bullet Weight (gr.)	Bullet Type	Muzzle Velocity (fps)	Muzzle Energy (ft.-lbs.)
120	JSP	2,890	2,392
140	JSP	2,750	2,351

CURRENT MANUFACTURER(S)
Remington, Federal

GENERAL COMMENT(S)
Historically, 6.5mm cartridges have not been popular with American sportsmen. The .260 Remington is the latest presentation in an ongoing effort to change this. Whether or not this cartridge will succeed where others have failed remains to be seen.

TECHNICAL COMMENT(S)
The .260 Rem. shares many dimensions with the venerable .257 Roberts cartridge. In every respect, the .260 Rem. is a modern high performance design with ballistics making it suitable for deer and antelope hunting.

6.5mm GRENDEL

ALTERNATE NAME(S): 6.5 Grendel
RELATED CALIBER(S): 7.62x39mm Soviet

CARTRIDGE HISTORY
Year of Introduction: 2003
Country of Origin: U.S.
Designer(s): Bill Alexander
Governing Body: SAAMI
Present Status: active

CARTRIDGE DESCRIPTION
Bullet Diameter: .264 in.
Bullet Weight(s): 123 gr.
Rifling Twist Rate: 1 turn in 9 in.
Test Barrel Length: 24 in.

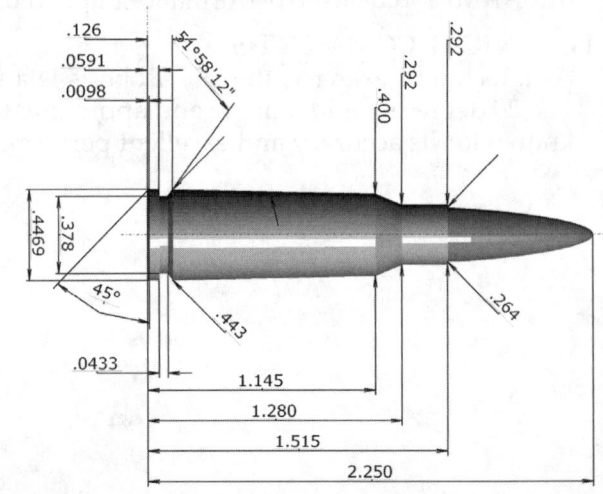

Case Type: rimless, necked
Case Material: brass
Primer Size: small rifle

CARTRIDGE BALLISTICS
Max. Average Breech Pressure: approx. 50,000 psi.
Max. Horizontal Range: 3,700 yds.
Max. Vertical Range: 7,000 ft.

Bullet Weight (gr.)	Bullet Type	Muzzle Velocity (fps)	Muzzle Energy (ft.-lbs.)
123	JSP	2,610	1,861

CURRENT MANUFACTURER(S)
Wolf

GENERAL COMMENT(S)
Developed in order to improve ballistic performance of the M-16 rifle and its variants, the 6.5mm Grendel has established a reputation for excellent accuracy and high retained energy. However, its popularity is waning in light of SOCOM's selection of the 6.8mm SPC. This cartridge is not likely to survive much longer.

TECHNICAL COMMENT(S)
The 6.5mm Grendel is a necked down 7.62x39mm Soviet case. The short tapered case of the 6.5mm Grendel allows it to feed, chamber, and extract in an M-16 style upper and lower receiver platform.

6.5mm CREEDMOOR

ALTERNATE NAME(S): 6.5x48.8mm Creedmoor
RELATED CALIBER(S): .308 Win., .260 Remington, 6.5x55mm Swedish

CARTRIDGE HISTORY
Year of Introduction: 2008
Country of Origin: U.S.
Designer(s): Dave Emary, Dennis DeMille
Governing Body: SAAMI
Present Status: active

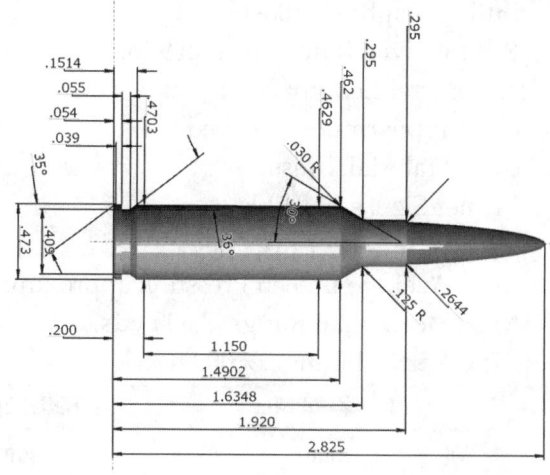

CARTRIDGE DESCRIPTION
Bullet Diameter: .264 in.
Bullet Weight(s): 120 gr.
Rifling Twist Rate: 1 turn in 10 in.
Test Barrel Length: 24 in.
Case Type: rimless, necked
Case Material: brass
Primer: large rifle

CARTRIDGE BALLISTICS
Max. Average Breech Pressure: 60,190 psi.
Max. Horizontal Range: 5,950 yds.
Max. Vertical Range: 12,400 ft.

Bullet Weight (gr.)	Bullet Type	Muzzle Velocity (fps)	Muzzle Energy (ft.-lbs.)
120	JSP-BT	3,050	2,479 (28" bbl)
140	JSP-BT	2,820	2,472 (28" bbl)

CURRENT MANUFACTURER(S)
Hornady

GENERAL COMMENT(S)
This cartridge was designed by competitive shooters for high power rifle competition. It is a modern, rimless design incorporating all the latest thinking on the ideal case and bullet diameter for high power rifle competition.

The name "Creedmoor" has a long and honorable history among American target shooters. Located on Long Island, New York, many national and international shooting competitions were held there from 1873 until 1910.

TECHNICAL COMMENT(S)

Case length of the 6.5mm Creedmoor (1.920 inches) is shorter than the .260 Remington (2.028 inches) and 6.5x55mm Swedish (2.16 inches) to assure it will fit and feed cleanly through rifles designed with short actions. A sharper than normal 30 degree shoulder provides additional case capacity and a firm seating surface on which to headspace while the aggressive body taper helps assure smooth feeding and extraction. Caliber 6.5mm bullets are known for their ideal length to diameter ratios which provides high sectional densities and high ballistic coefficients. This translates into flatter trajectory, less wind drift, and shorter flight times so important to target shooters. The 6.5mm Creedmoor is designed to provide users a slight edge in ballistic performance over the .260 Remington, 6.5x55mm Swedish, and 6.5x47mm Lapua cartridges.

6.5x47mm LAPUA

ALTERNATE NAME(S): 6.5mm Lapua
RELATED CALIBER(S): .260 Rem., .308 Win.

CARTRIDGE HISTORY

Year of Introduction: 2006
Country of Origin: Finland
Designer(s): Lapua
Governing Body: CIP
Present Status: active

CARTRIDGE DESCRIPTION

Bullet Diameter: .264 in.
Bullet Weight(s): 100-139 gr.
Rifling Twist Rate: 1 turn in 9 in.
Test Barrel Length: 24 in.
Case Type: rimless, necked
Case Material: brass
Primer Size: small rifle

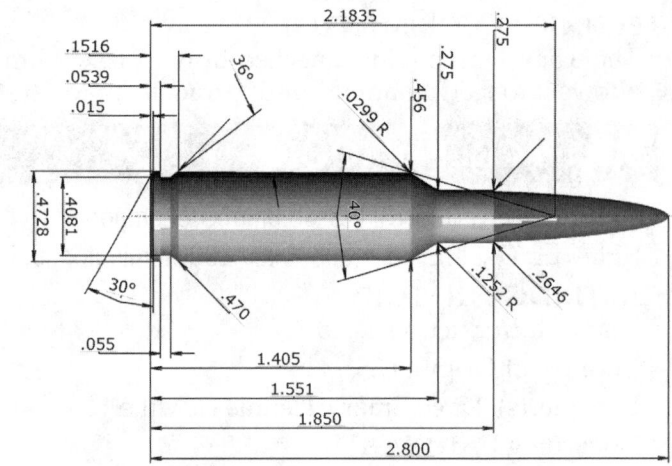

CARTRIDGE BALLISTICS

Max. Average Breech Pressure: approximately 55,000 psi.
Max. Horizontal Range: 3,600 yds.
Max. Vertical Range: 7,000 ft.

Bullet Weight (gr.)	Bullet Type	Muzzle Velocity (fps)	Muzzle Energy (ft.-lbs.)
100	JSP	2,760	1,691
108	JSP	2,925	2,050
123	JSP	2,760	2,080
139	JSP	2,665	2,191

CURRENT MANUFACTURER(S)

Lapua

GENERAL COMMENT(S)

Developed by Lapua, the primary purpose of this new cartridge is target shooting. It is designed to offer outstanding down range ballistic performance and accuracy in a small cartridge with minimum recoil.

It competes in the market with the 6.5-284 Norma and the 6.5 Grendel.

TECHNICAL COMMENT(S)

The 6.5x47mm Lapua is made from a shortened .308 Win. case but with a small rifle size primer.

6.5x55mm SWEDISH MAUSER

ALTERNATE NAME(S): 6.5x55mm Swedish
RELATED CALIBER(S): 6.5x54mm Mauser

CARTRIDGE HISTORY

Year of Introduction: 1894
Country of Origin: Sweden
Designer(s): Swedish/Norwegian Joint Military Commission
Governing Body: CIP, SAAMI
Present Status: active

CARTRIDGE DESCRIPTION

Bullet Diameter: .264 in.
Bullet Weight(s): 120-160 gr.
Rifling Twist Rate: 1 turn in 9 in.
Test Barrel Length: 24 in.
Case Type: rimless, necked
Case Material: brass
Primer Size: large rifle

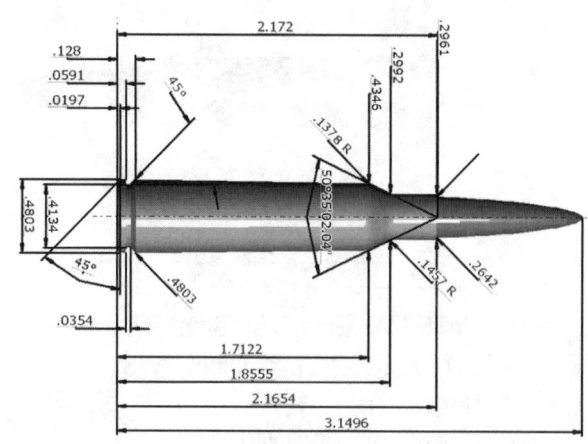

CARTRIDGE BALLISTICS

Max. Average Breech Pressure: 55,000 psi.
Max. Horizontal Range: 5,000 yds.
Max. Vertical Range: 11,000 ft.

Bullet Weight (gr.)	Bullet Type	Muzzle Velocity (fps)	Muzzle Energy (ft.-lbs.)
120	JSP	2,820	2,123
139	JSP	2,700	2,250
140	JSP	2,690	2,250
156	JSP	2,560	2,269
156	JSP	2,645	2,421

CURRENT MANUFACTURER(S)

Federal, Remington, Winchester, Hornady, Norma, Prvi Partizan, Sellier & Bellot, PMC, Lapua/NAMMO

GENERAL COMMENT(S)

Following adoption by the Swedish military in 1894, the 6.5x55mm Swedish cartridge went on to become the most popular hunting cartridge in Scandinavia, a position it continues to hold today. It is also a popular caliber for competition shooting. Until surplus military rifles in this caliber entered the U.S. in the 1950s, few American sportsmen had ever heard of the 6.5x55mm Swedish cartridge. The low cost of surplus military rifles and ammunition in this caliber persuaded many American shooters to try this Scandinavian import. They loved it. Today, the 6.5x55mm Swedish cartridge is the sole cartridge in this bore diameter which has been a commercial success in the U.S.

TECHNICAL COMMENT(S)

Ballistics of the 6.5x55mm are superb, especially with 139 grain spitzer boat-tail bullets. This bullet weight has proven a dandy choice for deer and antelope. The heavy 156 grain bullet was developed to meet a Scandinavian requirement for minimum striking energy at 100 meters for hunting moose. However, this heavy bullet is not popular in the U.S. as there are many better caliber choices for larger game.

As astute reader will note there is a similar, but not identical cartridge in this caliber: the 6.5x55mm Swedish and the 6.5x55mm SE or Super Express. A careful comparison will show the case dimensions are similar but not identical. For example, the bullet of the 6.5x55mm SE is seated farther out to free case volume for additional propellant. The SE chamber pressure is also higher.

6.5x68mm, 6.5x68Rmm

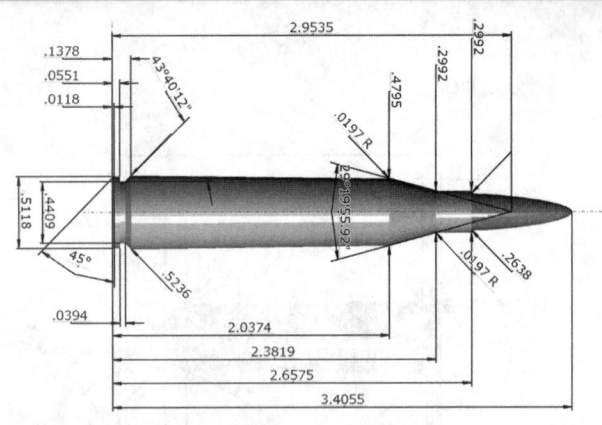 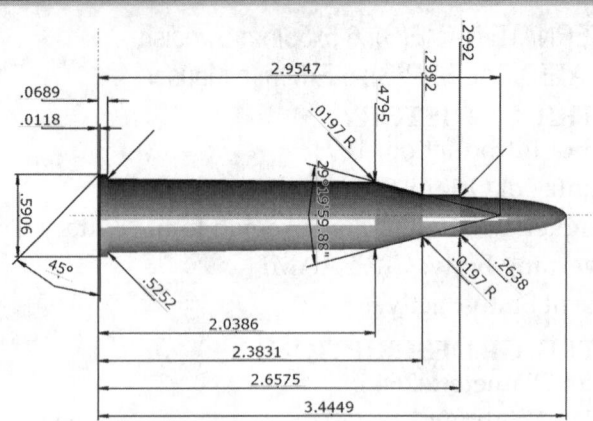

ALTERNATE NAME(S): 6.5x68mm RWS
RELATED CALIBER(S): 8x68mm RWS

CARTRIDGE HISTORY
Year of Introduction: 1940
Country of Origin: Germany
Designer(s): RWS
Governing Body: CIP
Present Status: active (6.5x68Rmm obsolete)

CARTRIDGE DESCRIPTION
Bullet Diameter: .264 in.
Bullet Weight(s): 93-127 gr.
Rifling Twist Rate: 1 turn in 9.84 in.
Test Barrel Length: 24 in.
Case Type: rimless, necked (rimmed, necked 6.5x68Rmm)
Case Material: brass
Primer: large rifle

CARTRIDGE BALLISTICS
Max. Average Breech Pressure: 63,817 psi. (6.5x68mm), 56,565 psi. (6.5x68Rmm)
Max. Horizontal Range: 4,600 yds.
Max. Vertical Range: 9,900 ft.

Bullet Weight (gr.)	Bullet Type	Muzzle Velocity (fps)	Muzzle Energy (ft.-lbs.)
93	JSP	3,770	2,935
127	JSP	3,150	2,798

CURRENT MANUFACTURER(S)
RWS/RUAG

GENERAL COMMENT(S)
Introduced during the early days of World War II, the 6.5x68mm RWS cartridge was handicapped at birth as all German commercial ammunition production was being diverted to wartime requirements. The 6.5x68mm cartridge survived World War II, only to find that it did not appeal to American sportsmen, and European sportsmen preferred the 6.5x55mm Swedish and 6.5x57mm Mauser cartridges. Although the 6.5x68Rmm cartridge has become obsolete, the 6.5x68mm remains in the RWS-RUAG product line - for now.

TECHNICAL COMMENT(S)
If you are looking for a powerful 6.5mm cartridge, look no further. Professional cartridge engineers at RWS designed this sleek-looking cartridge for hunting at long ranges. While long range hunting is rare in Europe, it is common in Africa and in the western United States. A thoroughly modern design, the 6.5x68mm is a rimless, beltless cartridge with a high maximum average chamber pressure to take full advantage of the large case volume. For years after World War II, the exterior ballistics claimed for the 6.5x68mm cartridge in RWS catalogs

are best described as "optimistic" (very). Today, the exterior ballistics claimed by RWS for this cartridge are more realistic. American sportsmen will find ammunition in this caliber expensive and hard to get as the only manufacturer has been and remains RWS (RUAG). The bullet weights and styles RWS loads in this caliber are not suited to some types of North American game. For these reasons, other 6.5mm calibers may be more attractive. However, domestic ammunition makers have discovered the hard way that American sportsmen have still not taken to the 6.5mm caliber.

6.5x57mm Mauser, 6.5x57Rmm Mauser

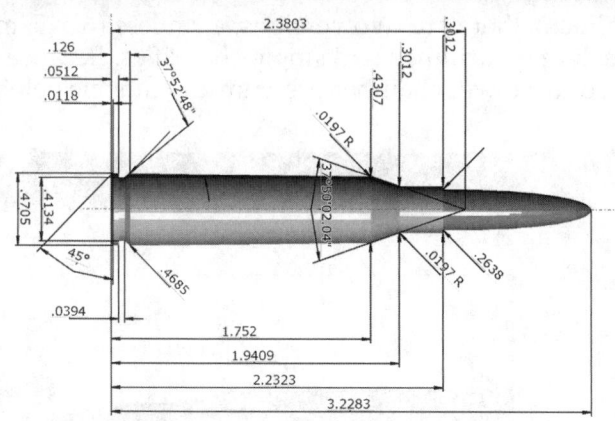 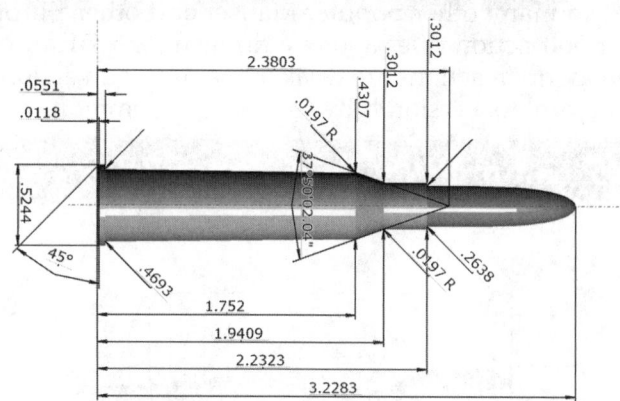

ALTERNATE NAME(S): 6.5x57mm, 6.5x57Rmm
RELATED CALIBER(S): 7x57mm Mauser, 7x57Rmm Mauser, 8x57mmJ Mauser, 8x57RmmJ Mauser

CARTRIDGE HISTORY
Year of Introduction: 1895
Country of Origin: Germany
Designer(s): Mauser
Governing Body: CIP
Present Status: active

CARTRIDGE DESCRIPTION
Bullet Diameter: .264 in.
Bullet Weight(s): 92.5-140.5 gr.
Rifling Twist Rate: 1 turn in 7.9 in.
Test Barrel Length: 24 in.
Case Type: rimless, necked
Case Material: brass
Primer: large rifle

CARTRIDGE BALLISTICS
Max. Average Chamber Pressure: 56,565 psi. (6.5x57mm), 47,860 psi. (6.5x57Rmm)
Max. Horizontal Range: 5,150 yds.
Max. Vertical Range: 11,800 ft.

Bullet Weight (gr.)	Bullet Type	Muzzle Velocity (fps)	Muzzle Energy (ft.-lbs.)
6.5x57mm			
92.5	JSP	3,315	2,257
108	JSP	3,100	2,304
126.5	JSP	2,855	2,290
140.5	JSP	2,540	2,013
6.5x57Rmm			
92.5	JSP	3,230	2,143
108	JSP	2,855	1,955
126.5	JSP	2,740	2,109
140.5	JSP	2,540	2,013

CURRENT MANUFACTURER(S)
Dynamit Nobel/RUAG, Sellier & Bellot, Prvi Partizan

GENERAL COMMENT(S)
Originally, the 6.5x57mm Mauser was intended to be a high velocity military rifle cartridge, a variant of the successful 7x57mm Mauser and 8x57mmJ Mauser cartridges. When it failed to catch on for military purposes, the 6.5x57mm Mauser found new life as a hunting cartridge among European sportsmen. It has survived in that capacity until this day. However, very few American sportsmen have heard of it.

TECHNICAL COMMENT(S)
As in many other popular Mauser and other European calibers, there are two versions, a rimless (6.5x57mm) for bolt-action rifles and one rimmed (6.5x57Rmm) for break-open drillings and single-shot rifles. Because the break-open actions are weaker, the rimmed version is loaded to a lower chamber pressure and muzzle velocity. The rimless version is by far the most common.

6.5x65mm RWS, 6.5x65Rmm RWS

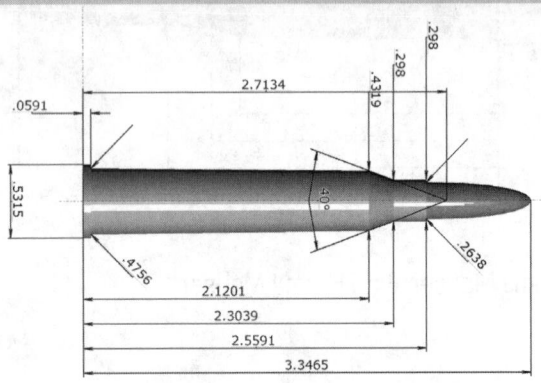
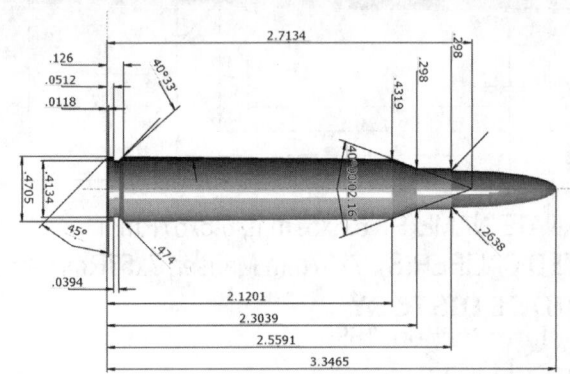

ALTERNATE NAME(S): 6.5x65mm, 6.5x65Rmm
RELATED CALIBER(S): .30-'06 Springfield

CARTRIDGE HISTORY
Year of Introduction: 1988
Country of Origin: Germany
Designer(s): RWS
Governing Body: CIP
Present Status: active

CARTRIDGE DESCRIPTION
Bullet Diameter: .264 in.
Bullet Weight(s): 108-127 gr.
Rifling Twist Rate: 1 turn in 7.87 in.
Test Barrel Length: 24 in.
Case Type: rimless, necked
Case Material: brass
Primer: large rifle

CARTRIDGE BALLISTICS
Max. Average Breech Pressure: 60,191psi. (6.5x65mm), 55,114 psi. (6.5x65Rmm)
Max. Horizontal Range: 5,400 yds.
Max. Vertical Range: 11,600 ft.

Bullet Weight (gr.)	Bullet Type	Muzzle Velocity (fps)	Muzzle Energy (ft.-lbs.)
108	JSP	3,460	2,871
127	JSP	3,315	3,099

CURRENT MANUFACTURER(S)
Dynamit Nobel/RUAG

GENERAL COMMENT(S)

For the first time in years, RWS introduced a new cartridge in 1988. The 6.5x65mm and 6.5x65Rmm were modern, high performance cartridges designed for the European market. As American sportsmen have never taken to the 6.5mm caliber for hunting, it seems certain that RWS harbored no expectations for their new cartridge in the American market. Today, both versions remain in production.

TECHNICAL COMMENT(S)

Essentially, the 6.5x65mm RWS cartridge is a .30-'06 Springfield case necked down to 6.5mm (and slightly longer). Ballistic performance is on par with the 6.5mm Remington Magnum. The 6.5x65mm RWS cartridge is a modern design and a solid performer. If American sportsmen take to any 6.5mm high performance cartridge, it should be this one.

.270 WINCHESTER SHORT MAGNUM

ALTERNATE NAME(S): .270 WSM
RELATED CALIBER(S): .300 WSM

CARTRIDGE HISTORY

Year of Introduction: 2001
Country of Origin: U.S.
Designer(s): Winchester
Governing Body: SAAMI
Present Status: active

CARTRIDGE DESCRIPTION

Bullet Diameter: .277 in.
Bullet Weight(s): 130-150 gr.
Rifling Twist Rate: 1 turn in 10 in.
Test Barrel Length: 24 in.
Case Type: rimless, necked
Case Material: brass
Primer Size: large rifle

CARTRIDGE BALLISTICS

Max. Average Breech Pressure: 65,000 psi.
Max. Horizontal Range: 5,300 yds.
Max. Vertical Range: 10,500 ft.

Bullet Weight (gr.)	Bullet Type	Muzzle Velocity (fps)	Muzzle Energy (ft.-lbs.)
130	JSP	3,275	3,096
140	JSP	3,175	3,035
150	JSP	3,020	3,037

CURRENT MANUFACTURER(S)

Winchester, Federal, Remington, Norma

GENERAL COMMENT(S)

This cartridge is part of the Winchester short, beltless magnum family. Since its introduction, most major ammunition manufacturers have added it to their product line, thus assuring its continuation even though U.S. Repeating Arms ceased manufacturing rifles in this caliber.

TECHNICAL COMMENT(S)

While it may lack the belted feature we have come to expect of a magnum cartridge, the .270 WSM lacks nothing in performance. Ballistically, it is fully equal to, and, in some instances better than, the .270 Weatherby Magnum.

.270 WINCHESTER

ALTERNATE NAME(S): .270 Win.
RELATED CALIBER(S): .30-'06 Spr., .25-06 Rem.

CARTRIDGE HISTORY
Year of Introduction: 1925
Country of Origin: U.S.
Designer(s): Winchester
Governing Body: SAAMI, CIP
Present Status: active

CARTRIDGE DESCRIPTION
Bullet Diameter: .277 in.
Bullet Weight(s): 130-150 gr.
Rifling Twist Rate: 1 turn in 10 in.
Test Barrel Length: 24 in.
Case Type: rimless, necked
Case Material: brass
Primer Size: large rifle

CARTRIDGE BALLISTICS
Max. Average Breech Pressure: 65,000 psi.
Max. Horizontal Range: 4,800 yds.
Max. Vertical Range: 11,000 ft.

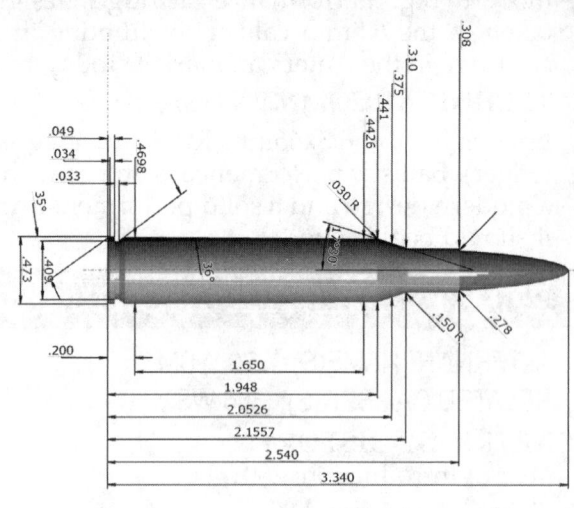

Bullet Weight (gr.)	Bullet Type	Muzzle Velocity (fps)	Muzzle Energy (ft.-lbs.)
130	JSP	3,060	2,702
140	JSP	2,925	2,659
150	JSP	2,850	2,705

CURRENT MANUFACTURER(S)
Remington, Winchester, Federal, Hornady, Black Hills, Norma, PMC, Prvi Partizan, Sellier & Bellot, IMI

GENERAL COMMENT(S)
Controversy has followed the .270 Win. cartridge since its introduction in 1925. Proponents laud its flat trajectory, high remaining velocity, and lower perceived recoil in comparison to its parent .30-'06 Spr. Opponents of the .270 deny any ballistic advantage over the .30-'06. One would expect controversy to fade after 80 years of argument and counter argument, but it has not and continues as a hot topic of conversation over many a camp fire.

Without doubt, the .270 Win. is a fine capable cartridge whose performance in the field has been proven many times over. Perennially, it ranks in the top ten most popular cartridges and production quantities remain impressive.

TECHNICAL COMMENT(S)
The whole point of the .270 Win. cartridge is a flat trajectory, high remaining velocity, and excellent long range ballistic performance. It continues to deliver these despite advancing age and newer competitive designs. It is hard to improve on a good thing – and the .270 is a good thing on deer, antelope, sheep, and goat.

6.8 SPC

ALTERNATE NAME(S): 6.8mm Special Purpose Cartridge
RELATED CALIBER(S): .30 Remington

CARTRIDGE HISTORY

Year of Introduction: 2003
Country of Origin: U.S.
Designer(s): U.S. Army Special Operations Command
Governing Body: SAAMI
Present Status: active

CARTRIDGE DESCRIPTION

Bullet Diameter: .277 in.
Bullet Weight(s): 70-115 gr.
Rifling Twist Rate: 1 turn in 10 in.
Test Barrel Length: 28 in.
Case Type: rimless, necked
Case Material: brass
Primer Size: large rifle originally; subsequently
changed to small rifle

CARTRIDGE BALLISTICS

Max. Average Breech Pressure: 50,000 CUP.
Max. Horizontal Range: 3,400 yds.
Max. Vertical Range: 6,750 ft.

Bullet Weight (gr.)	Bullet Type	Muzzle Velocity (fps)	Muzzle Energy (ft.-lbs.)
115	JHP	2,625	1,759

CURRENT MANUFACTURER(S)

Remington, Federal, Hornady, Black Hills, Silver State

GENERAL COMMENT(S)

This cartridge was designed by members of the U.S. Special Operations Command (SOCOM) in response to the need for increased striking energy over the 5.56x45mm M855A1 cartridge issued to U.S. military forces. The operational concept was simple: replace the entire upper assembly of M16 rifles with a new one chambered for a new cartridge firing a heavier bullet. For initial production, SOCOM turned to Black Hills Ammunition Company. Subsequent production has been made by both Black Hills and Remington. In 2005, this caliber became a commercial Remington offering. The 6.8mm SPC is designed to work in AR-15 rifles to provide a caliber suitable for hunting deer and small game.

TECHNICAL COMMENT(S)

To achieve the increased muzzle velocity and energy sought, a larger cartridge case was needed. The solution was a modified .30 Remington cartridge (an obsolete design from the early 1900s) firing a 115 grain .277 inch diameter bullet at a muzzle velocity of 2,625 fps.

On paper, the new cartridge offered 37% more muzzle energy than the 5.56x45mm M855A1 cartridge. Field testing proved the heavier bullets of the 6.8mm did improve energy transfer, but not as much as expected or hoped.

The new cartridge was named the 6.8mm Special purpose Cartridge (SPC). Limited military use by SOCOM and further experiments in bullet weights and velocity combinations continue.

7-30 WATERS

ALTERNATE NAME(S): none
RELATED CALIBER(S): .30-30 Winchester

CARTRIDGE HISTORY
Year of Introduction: 1984
Country of Origin: U.S.
Designer(s): Ken Waters
Governing Body: SAAMI
Present Status: active

CARTRIDGE DESCRIPTION
Bullet Diameter: .284 in.
Bullet Weight(s): 120 gr.
Rifling Twist Rate: 1 turn in 9.5 in.
Test Barrel Length: 24 in.
Case Type: rimmed, necked
Case Material: brass
Primer Size: large rifle

CARTRIDGE BALLISTICS
Max. Average Breech Pressure: 45,000 psi.
Max. Horizontal Range: 3,900 yds.
Max. Vertical Range: 9,000 ft.

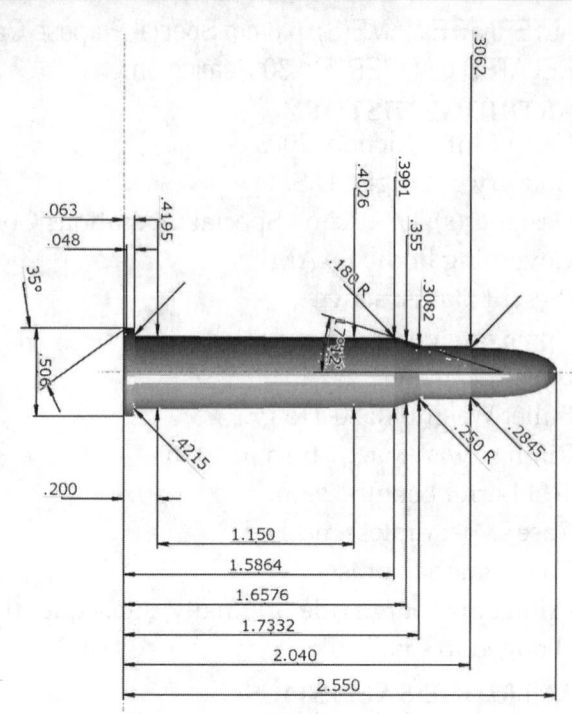

Bullet Weight (gr.)	Bullet Type	Muzzle Velocity (fps)	Muzzle Energy (ft.-lbs.)
120	JSP	2,700	1,940

CURRENT MANUFACTURER(S)
Federal

GENERAL COMMENT(S)
Ken Waters, a prominent gun writer, designed this cartridge to provide lever-action rifles with improved ballistic performance over the flat-nosed bullets normally used in such rifles. Winchester brought out a Model 94 rifle in this caliber. Federal helped develop the cartridge and remains the sole manufacturer. By all measures, this cartridge has not been a commercial best seller, consequently, its days are numbered.

TECHNICAL COMMENT(S)
This cartridge is yet another attempt to improve the ballistic performance of lever-action rifles using a modified .30-30 Winchester cartridge case. None has been very successful. The 7-30 Waters, with pointed bullets, should not be used in tubular magazines.

7x57mm MAUSER/ 7x57Rmm MAUSER

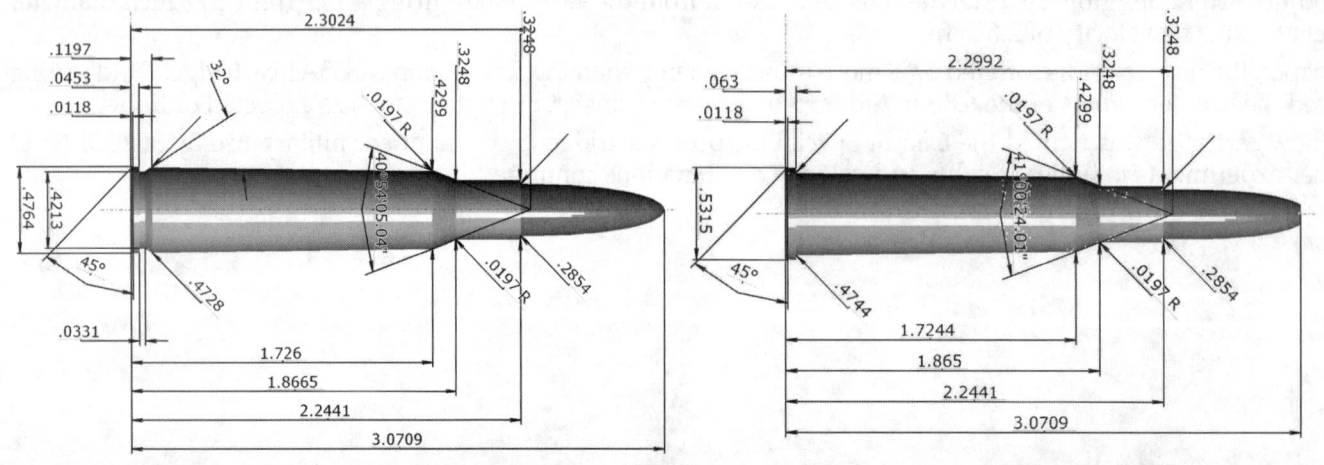

ALTERNATE NAME(S): 7x 57mm Mau.
RELATED CALIBER(S): 8x57mm Mauser

CARTRIDGE HISTORY
Year of Introduction: 1892
Country of Origin: Germany
Designer(s): Peter Paul Mauser
Governing Body: CIP, SAAMI
Present Status: active

CARTRIDGE DESCRIPTION
Bullet Diameter: .284 in.
Bullet Weight(s): 139-175 gr.
Rifling Twist Rate: 1 turn in 8.75 in.
Test Barrel Length: 24 in.
Case Type: rimless, necked
Case Material: brass
Primer Size: large rifle

CARTRIDGE BALLISTICS
Max. Average Breech Pressure: 51,000 psi.
Max. Horizontal Range: 4,200 yds.
Max. Vertical Range: 9,500 ft.

Bullet Weight (gr.)	Bullet Type	Muzzle Velocity (fps)	Muzzle Energy (ft.-lbs.)
139	JSP	2,830	2,471
139	JSP	2,790	2,417
140	JSP	2,660	2,200
145	JSP	2,660	2,279
150	JSP	2,690	2,411
156	JSP	2,640	2,417
173	JSP	2,380	2,171
175	JSP	2,440	2,315

CURRENT MANUFACTURER(S)
Federal, Winchester, Remington, Hornady, Sellier & Bellot, DN, PMC, Norma

GENERAL COMMENT(S)
This is the grand old man of 7mm cartridges. Although developed as a military cartridge in 1892, the 7x57mm also caught on as a sporting cartridge, especially with European hunters. Its commercial career began in the U.S. in the early 1900s, but its popularity with American sportsmen has always been modest. Most domestic rifle manufacturers offer one or more models in 7x57mm if not on a regular basis, then in special runs. The result is a steady if limited supply of rifled carbines which sustains ammunition manufacture. However, most ammunition makers limit their 7x57mm production to a single loading. Hornady is the exception, offering a variety of loads, similar to European ammo makers' product lines.

TECHNICAL COMMENT(S)
Mauser based the 7x57mm cartridge on their existing 8x57mm cartridge. The 7x57mm was one of the first variants, but certainly not the last, to be based on the 8x57mm case. Although the 7x57mm offers excellent performance with 139 grain bullets, most ammunition manufacturers load this caliber with 150-175 grain bullets today. This is a great choice for hunting deer and antelope as well as other medium game. The 7x57mm is well known for its accuracy and mild recoil.

7mm-08 REMINGTON

ALTERNATE NAME(S): 7mm-08 Rem., 7mm-08
RELATED CALIBER(S): .308 Winchester, .243 Winchester

CARTRIDGE HISTORY
Year of Introduction: 1980
Country of Origin: U.S.
Designer(s): Remington
Governing Body: SAAMI, CIP
Present Status: active

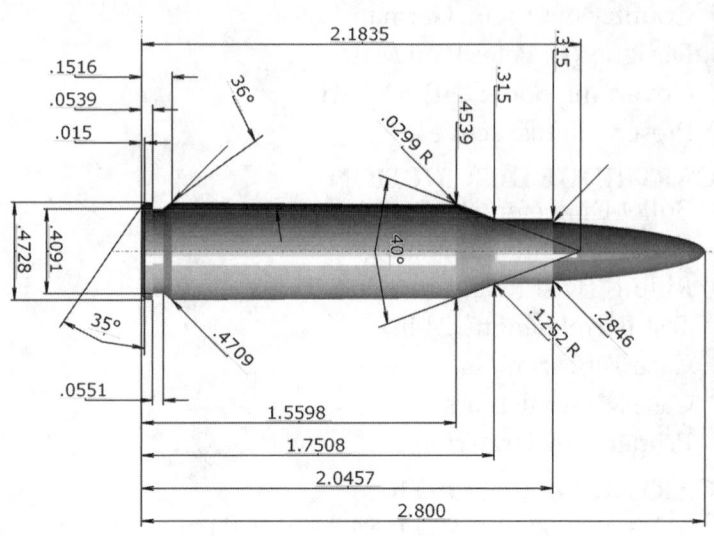

CARTRIDGE DESCRIPTION
Bullet Diameter: .284 in.
Bullet Weight(s): 120-140 gr.
Rifling Twist Rate: 1 turn in 9.5 in.
Test Barrel Length: 24 in.
Case Type: rimless, necked
Case Material: brass
Primer Size: large rifle

CARTRIDGE BALLISTICS
Max. Average Breech Pressure: 61,000 psi.
Max. Horizontal Range: 4,400 yds.
Max. Vertical Range: 8,700 ft.

Bullet Weight (gr.)	Bullet Type	Muzzle Velocity (fps)	Muzzle Energy (ft.-lbs.)
120	JSP	3,000	2,398
139	JSP	3,000	2,777
140	JSP	2,860	2,542

CURRENT MANUFACTURER(S)
Hornady, Winchester, Remington, Federal, PMC, Norma

GENERAL COMMENT(S)
Metallic silhouette competitors were the first to appreciate the efficiency and accuracy of this cartridge as a wildcat. As its popularity grew, Remington decided to commercialize this cartridge in 1980. Since then, its popularity has spread quickly as sportsmen have come to appreciate its performance in the field on deer and antelope. Today, nearly all domestic ammunition manufacturers offer this caliber, which remains a popular choice for competition as well as hunting.

TECHNICAL COMMENT(S)
Easy is always better and the 7mm-08 was easy to design. It is nothing more than a .308 Winchester cartridge necked down to seat .284 inch diameter bullets. Although the 7mm Rem. cannot handle as wide a range of bullet weights as its parent .308, the 120 and 140 grain bullets work extremely well for most purposes.

Mild recoil and excellent accuracy are attributes appreciated by 7mm-08 Rem. shooters. The short overall length allows chambering in a wide range of rifle models.

.280 REMINGTON

ALTERNATE NAME(S): 7mm Express Remington
RELATED CALIBER(S): .30-'06 Springfield

CARTRIDGE HISTORY
Year of Introduction: 1957
Country of Origin: U.S.
Designer(s): Remington
Governing Body: SAAMI, CIP
Present Status: active

CARTRIDGE DESCRIPTION
Bullet Diameter: .284 in.
Bullet Weight(s): 120-165 gr.
Rifling Twist Rate: 1 turn in10 in.
Test Barrel Length: 24 in.
Case Type: rimless, necked
Case Material: brass
Primer Size: large rifle

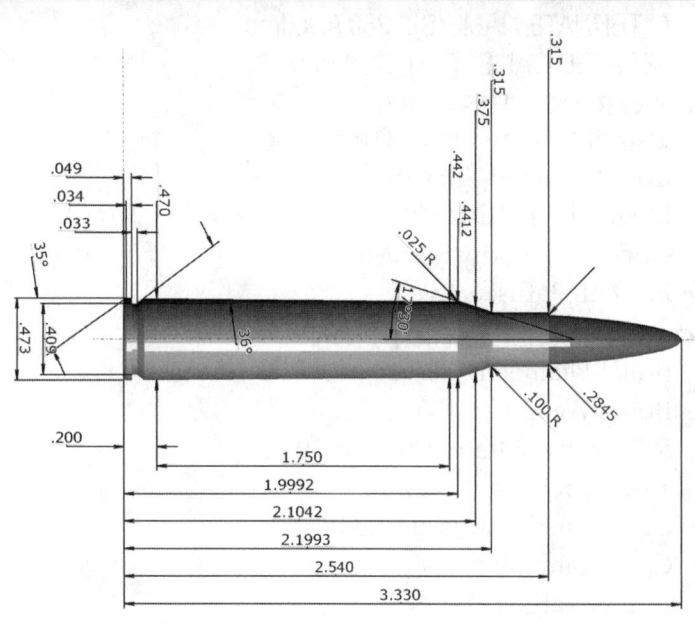

CARTRIDGE BALLISTICS
Max. Average Breech Pressure: 60,000 psi.
Max. Horizontal Range: 4,500 yds.
Max. Vertical Range: 10,000 ft.

Bullet Weight (gr.)	Bullet Type	Muzzle Velocity (fps)	Muzzle Energy (ft.-lbs.)
139	JSP	3,110	2,985
139	JSP	3,030	2,855
140	JSP	2,990	2,780
150	JSP	2,890	2,781
160	JSP	2,800	2,785
170	JSP	2,705	2,767

CURRENT MANUFACTURER(S)
Remington, Federal, Winchester, Hornady, Norma

GENERAL COMMENT(S)
In response to a growing interest in 7mm cartridges, Remington introduced the .280 Remington in 1957. Since then, it has achieved only moderate acceptance, although it remains an excellent cartridge. After Remington introduced the 7mm Remington Magnum in 1962, the .280 Rem. was reduced to also-ran status. This cartridge remains an excellent choice for all North American medium game.

TECHNICAL COMMENT(S)
The .280 Rem. cartridge is essentially a .30-'06 Springfield case necked down to 7mm. This allows compatibility with any rifle originally designed for cartridges of that length and head dimension. The case is not belted and this is not a magnum cartridge. The .280 Rem. is not as powerful as the 7mm Rem. Magnum and many of the other recent 7mm magnums. While the big magnums can fire 175 grain bullets, the .280 Rem. is limited to 150 grain bullets.

.280 ACKLEY IMPROVED

ALTERNATE NAME(S): .280 Ack. Imp.
RELATED CALIBER(S): .280 Rem.

CARTRIDGE HISTORY

Year of Introduction: 2008 (Nosler)
Country of Origin: U.S.
Designer(s): P.O. Ackley
Governing Body: SAAMI
Present Status: active

CARTRIDGE DESCRIPTION

Bullet Diameter: .284 in.
Bullet Weight(s): 130-175 gr.
Rifling Twist Rate: 1 turn in 10 in.
Test Barrel Length: 24 in.
Case Type: rimless, necked
Case Material: brass
Primer: large rifle

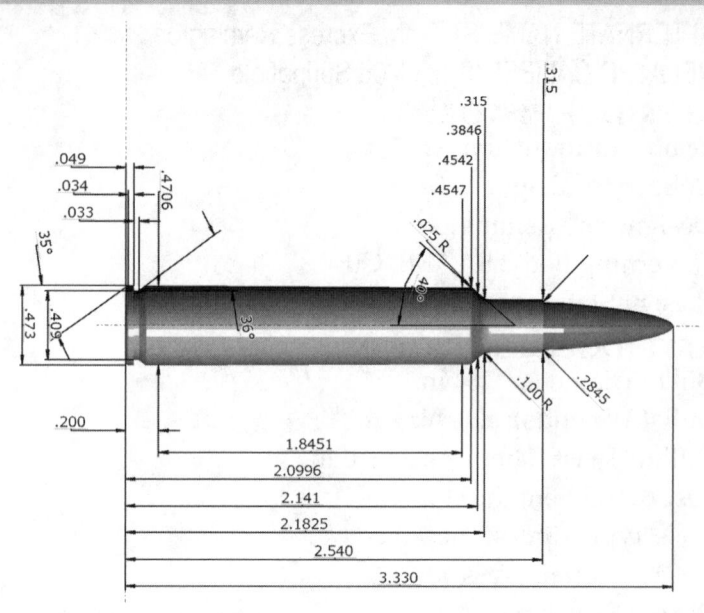

CARTRIDGE BALLISTICS

Max. Average Breech Pressure: 60,000 psi.
Max. Horizontal Range: 5,000 yds.
Max. Vertical Range: 10,600 ft.

Bullet Weight (gr.)	Bullet Type	Muzzle Velocity (fps)	Muzzle Energy (ft.-lbs.)
130	JSP	3,100	2,774
140	JSP	3,100	2,987
150	JSP	3,000	2,997
160	JSP	2,950	3,091
175	JSP	2,800	3,046

CURRENT MANUFACTURER(S)

Nosler

GENERAL COMMENT(S)

As the popularity of the 7mm caliber grows, the number of 7mm cartridges has increased exponentially with well over 20 at last count. Nosler's reintroduction of the .280 Ackley Improved is the latest. Although not really a new cartridge in the classic sense, the .280 Ackley Improved is one of P.O. Ackley's wildcats which has been domesticated. Given the large number of existing 7mm cartridges, the .280 Ackley Improved must be considered as a limited volume niche market offering.

TECHNICAL COMMENT(S)

Ballistic performance of the .280 Ackley Improved cartridge compares favorably with the popular 7mm Remington Magnum. However, in the modern market, that is yesterday's news. Perhaps of more interest is that the .280 Ackley Imp. makes an impressive ballistic statement without the benefit of a belted case and with only minor modifications to the standard .280 Remington case. This raises the question, "Should the .280 Remington have been the .280 Ackley Improved?" Probably not, as very few of P.O. Ackley's wildcats have made it into commercial production.

7mm REMINGTON MAGNUM

ALTERNATE NAME(S): 7mm Rem. Mag.
RELATED CALIBER(S): .300 Winchester Magnum

CARTRIDGE HISTORY
Year of Introduction: 1962
Country of Origin: U.S.
Designer(s): Remington
Governing Body: SAAMI, CIP
Present Status: active

CARTRIDGE DESCRIPTION
Bullet Diameter: .284 in.
Bullet Weight(s): 140-175 gr.
Rifling Twist Rate: 1 turn in 9.5 in.
Test Barrel Length: 24 in.
Case Type: rimless, belted, necked
Case Material: brass
Primer Size: large rifle

CARTRIDGE BALLISTICS
Max. Average Breech Pressure: 61,000 psi.
Max. Horizontal Range: 7,000 yds.
Max. Vertical Range: 16,700 ft.

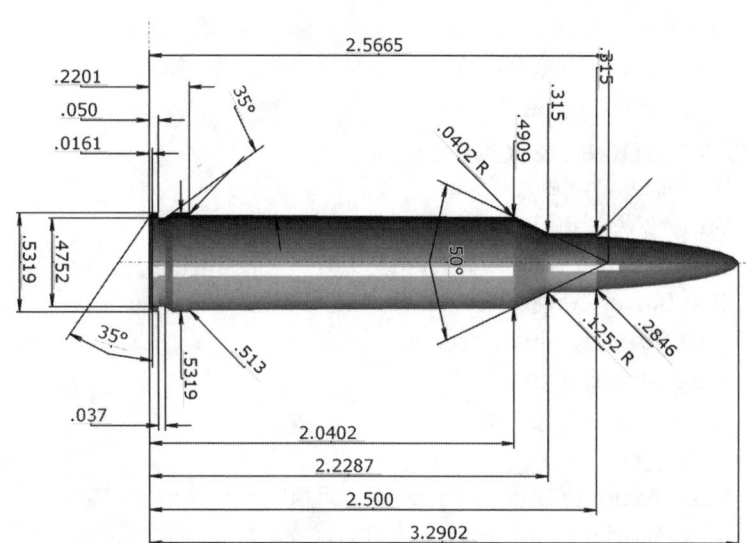

Bullet Weight (gr.)	Bullet Type	Muzzle Velocity (fps)	Muzzle Energy (ft.-lbs.)
139	JSP	3,250	3,259
140	JSP	3,150	3,085
150	JSP	3,110	3,221
154	JSP	3,035	3,149
160	JSP	2,950	3,090
165	JSP	2,950	3,190
170	JSP	2,955	3,293
175	JSP	2,860	3,178

CURRENT MANUFACTURER(S)
Federal, Remington, Winchester, Hornady, Black Hills, PMC, Norma, Prvi Partizan

GENERAL COMMENT(S)
Remington hit a home run when they introduced this cartridge in 1962. The 7mm Remington Magnum quickly became the most popular 7mm cartridge on the market; a position it continues to hold to this day.

Sportsmen appreciated its flat trajectory, wide choice of bullet weights, and high striking energy. With the right bullet, the 7mm Rem. Mag. is suitable for any North American game except large bear. However, it is needlessly powerful for deer hunting at ranges of less than 200 yards.

TECHNICAL COMMENT(S)
Remington modeled their 7mm Rem. Mag. on a shortened .300 H&H Magnum case with a 25 degree shoulder angle. The 2.50 inch case length allowed the large volume cartridge case to fit in standard length rifle actions. As recoil can be heavy with this caliber, a recoil pad is recommended and a muzzle brake should be considered as well.

Like most 7mm magnums, the accuracy of the 7mm Remington Magnum is especially sensitive to bullet quality. This is particularly true for long range shots where the 160-165 grain bullets offer the best combination of accuracy and ballistic performance. Many shooters have noted also that the 7mm Rem. Mag. is sensitive to bore fouling, so for best accuracy the bore should be cleaned regularly.

7mm REMINGTON ULTRA MAGNUM

ALTERNATE NAME(S): 7mm RUM
RELATED CALIBER(S): .300 Remington Ultra Magnum

CARTRIDGE HISTORY
Year of Introduction: 2000
Country of Origin: U.S.
Designer(s): Remington
Governing Body: SAAMI, CIP
Present Status: active

CARTRIDGE DESCRIPTION
Bullet Diameter: .284 in.
Bullet Weight(s): 140-160 gr.
Rifling Twist Rate: 1 turn in 9.5 in.
Test Barrel Length: 24 in.
Case Type: rimless, necked
Case Material: brass
Primer Size: large rifle

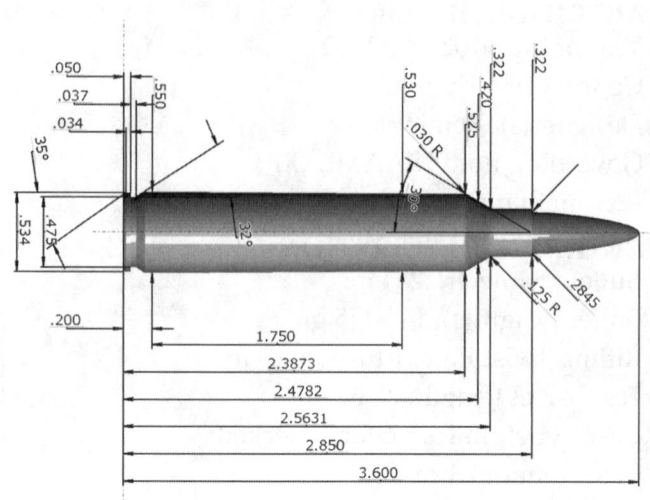

CARTRIDGE BALLISTICS
Max. Average Breech Pressure: 65,000 psi.
Max. Horizontal Range: 5,500 yds.
Max. Vertical Range: 10,500 ft.

Bullet Weight (gr.)	Bullet Type	Muzzle Velocity (fps)	Muzzle Energy (ft.-lbs.)
140	JSP	3,425	3,646
160	JSP	3,200	3,637
175	JSP	3,025	3,555

CURRENT MANUFACTURER(S)
Remington

GENERAL COMMENT(S)
With this new cartridge, Remington sought to offer the most powerful commercial 7mm cartridge available. By all measures, they succeeded. The 7mm RUM is even more powerful than the legendary 7mm Weatherby Magnum. For long range hunting, the 7mm RUM cartridge offers superior ballistic performance over nearly any other cartridge in its class. To date, other ammunition manufacturers have not offered this cartridge.

TECHNICAL COMMENT(S)
The 7mm RUM uses a full length 2.50 inch beltless case with a .535 inch diameter body to achieve a very large case volume. The heavy powder charges enable the 7mm RUM to offer muzzle velocities on order of magnitude higher than the 7mm Weatherby Magnum.

Beltless cartridge cases have become popular as they are easier to manufacture and offer strength equivalent to belted designs. The 7mm RUM is an excellent example of this trend.

7mm REMINGTON SHORT-ACTION ULTRA MAGNUM

ALTERNATE NAME(S): 7mm RSUM
RELATED CALIBER(S): 7mm Remington Ultra Magnum

CARTRIDGE HISTORY
Year of Introduction: 2001
Country of Origin: U.S.
Designer(s): Remington

Governing Body: SAAMI
Present Status: active

CARTRIDGE DESCRIPTION
Bullet Diameter: .284 in.
Bullet Weight(s): 140-160 gr.
Rifling Twist Rate: 1 turn in 9.5 in.
Test Barrel Length: 24 in.
Case Type: rimless, necked
Case Material: brass
Primer Size: large rifle

CARTRIDGE BALLISTICS
Max. Average Breech Pressure: 65,000 psi.
Max. Horizontal Range: 5,300 yds.
Max. Vertical Range: 10,500 ft.

Bullet Weight (gr.)	Bullet Type	Muzzle Velocity (fps)	Muzzle Energy (ft.-lbs.)
140	JSP	3,175	3,133
150	JSP	3,110	3,221
160	JSP	2,960	3,112

CURRENT MANUFACTURER(S)
Remington

GENERAL COMMENT(S)
Remington introduced the 7mm Remington Short-Action Ultra Magnum (RSUM) cartridge in 2002. The design objective was to bring 7mm magnum performance in short-action rifles. The 7mm RSUM does this, however it has close competition from several similar cartridges vying for the sportsmen's attention. Sportsmen report the 7mm RSUM offers excellent performance on most North American medium game.

TECHNICAL COMMENT(S)
The 7mm Remington Short-Action Ultra Magnum cartridge (case length 2.035 inches) is best viewed as a 7mm RUM cartridge (case length 2.850 inches) with a shorter length. Despite this, it is a very efficient cartridge with ballistics fully equal to older 7mm cartridges such as the 7mm Remington Magnum.

7mm WINCHESTER SHORT MAGNUM

ALTERNATE NAME(S): 7mm WSM
RELATED CALIBER(S): .300 Winchester Short Magnum

CARTRIDGE HISTORY
Year of Introduction: 2002
Country of Origin: U.S.
Designer(s): Winchester
Governing Body: SAAMI, CIP
Present Status: active

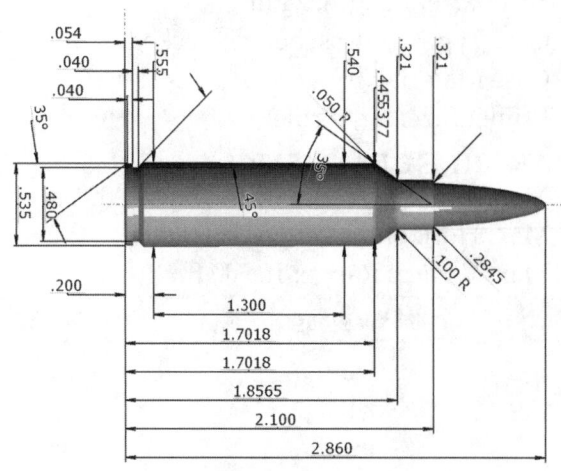

CARTRIDGE DESCRIPTION
Bullet Diameter: .284 in.
Bullet Weight(s): 140-160 gr.
Rifling Twist Rate: 1 turn in 10 in.
Test Barrel Length: 24 in.
Case Type: rimless, necked
Case Material: brass
Primer Size: large rifle

CARTRIDGE BALLISTICS
Max. Average Breech Pressure: 65,000 psi.
Max. Horizontal Range: 5,000 yds.
Max. Vertical Range: 9,900 ft.

Bullet Weight (gr.)	Bullet Type	Muzzle Velocity (fps)	Muzzle Energy (ft.-lbs.)
140	JSP	3,225	3,233
150	JSP	3,225	3,410
160	JSP	3,050	3,306

CURRENT MANUFACTURER(S)
Winchester, Federal

GENERAL COMMENT(S)
To bring 7mm magnum performance to short-action rifles, Winchester introduced the 7mm Winchester Short Magnum in 2002. It is comparable to the 7mm RSUM, but not interchangeable.

It is too soon to determine whether the Winchester or the Remington short action concept will prevail. Other ammunition manufacturers have introduced the 7mm Winchester WSM, but not the 7mm RSUM.

TECHNICAL COMMENT(S)
This beltless design has a magnum head diameter for maximum case volume and a case length of 2.10 inches so as to fit in short-action rifles. This allows a sufficiently large powder change which generates exterior ballistics fully equal to many belted magnum cartridges. The 7mm WSM is suitable for all North American medium game.

7mm SHOOTING TIMES WESTERNER

ALTERNATE NAME(S): 7mm STW
RELATED CALIBER(S): 8mm Remington Magnum

CARTRIDGE HISTORY
Year of Introduction: 1996
Country of Origin: U.S.
Designer(s): Layne Simpson
Governing Body: SAAMI
Present Status: active

CARTRIDGE DESCRIPTION
Bullet Diameter: .284 in.
Bullet Weight(s): 140-160 gr.
Rifling Twist Rate: 1 turn in 10 in.
Test Barrel Length: 24 in.
Case Type: rimless, belted, necked
Case Material: brass
Primer Size: large rifle

CARTRIDGE BALLISTICS
Max. Average Breech Pressure: 65,000 psi.
Max. Horizontal Range: 5,500 yds.
Max. Vertical Range: 10,500 ft.

Bullet Weight (gr.)	Bullet Type	Muzzle Velocity (fps)	Muzzle Energy (ft.-lbs.)
140	JSP	3,325	3,436
150	JSP	3,280	3,583
160	JSP	3,200	3,640

CURRENT MANUFACTURER(S)
Winchester, Federal, Remington

GENERAL COMMENT(S)

This cartridge was the creation of a noted gun writer and experimenter named Layne Simpson who decided to create a new 7mm magnum cartridge offering superior performance compared to those available at the time. Following considerable fanfare in shooting magazines, including Shooting Times for which Simpson wrote, the major ammunition companies were persuaded to introduce the new cartridge in 1996.

The 7mm STW was ahead of its time and an anachronism. It served as the precursor of the new 7mm magnums such as the 7mm RUM. It was out-of-date in that it is a belted case design. There was also a Shooting Times Easterner cartridge, but it did not catch on.

TECHNICAL COMMENT(S)

Simpson began with an 8mm Remington Magnum case so as to provide more case volume than the 7mm Wby. Mag. cartridge. A 25 degree neck angle and straight case walls achieved this end. Using 140 or 150 grain bullets, ballistic performance proved excellent. The 7mm STW is excellent for medium North American game at long ranges.

.284 WINCHESTER

ALTERNATE NAME(S): .284 Win.
RELATED CALIBER(S): None

CARTRIDGE HISTORY

Year of Introduction: 1963
Country of Origin: U.S.
Designer(s): Winchester
Governing Body: SAAMI
Present Status: active

CARTRIDGE DESCRIPTION

Bullet Diameter: .284 in.
Bullet Weight(s): 140-150 gr.
Rifling Twist Rate: 1 turn in 10 in.
Test Barrel Length: 24 in.
Case Type: rebated rim, necked
Case Material: brass
Primer Size: large rifle

CARTRIDGE BALLISTICS

Max. Average Breech Pressure: 56,000 psi.
Max. Horizontal Range: 4,500 yds.
Max. Vertical Range: 8,800 ft.

Bullet Weight (gr.)	Bullet Type	Muzzle Velocity (fps)	Muzzle Energy (ft.-lbs.)
150	JSP	2,860	2,724

CURRENT MANUFACTURER(S)

Winchester

GENERAL COMMENT(S)

Winchester's modern Model 88 and Model 100 rifles needed a powerful cartridge, but could not be modified to handle belted magnum calibers. Winchester's solution was a new cartridge with .30-06 head dimensions and a magnum diameter body. The result was a new caliber with a rebated rim – a first for an American ammunition manufacturer. This case design allowed Winchester to chamber both rifles in this powerful cartridge, however they did not prove a commercial success and were both discontinued. This left the .284 Win. cartridge an orphan. Despite this, the .284 refuses to die. Its high capacity case is the basis for a number of successful wildcats.

TECHNICAL COMMENT(S)

The .284 Win. cartridge with its rebated rim and beltless magnum body must be considered as one of the more uniquely specialized 7mm cartridge designs. However, despite its potential, it never caught on and no guns are currently being made in this caliber.

7.62x39mm M43 SOVIET

ALTERNATE NAME(S): 7.62x39mm Russian
RELATED CALIBER(S): 5.54x39mm Soviet

CARTRIDGE HISTORY

Year of Introduction: 1943
Country of Origin: Soviet Union
Designer(s): Soviet arsenals
Governing Body: CIP, SAAMI
Present Status: active

CARTRIDGE DESCRIPTION

Bullet Diameter: .309-.311 in.
Bullet Weight(s): 123-125 gr.
Rifling Twist Rate: 1 turn in 9.45 in.
Test Barrel Length: 20 in.
Case Type: rimless, necked
Case Material: steel or brass
Primer Size: small rifle

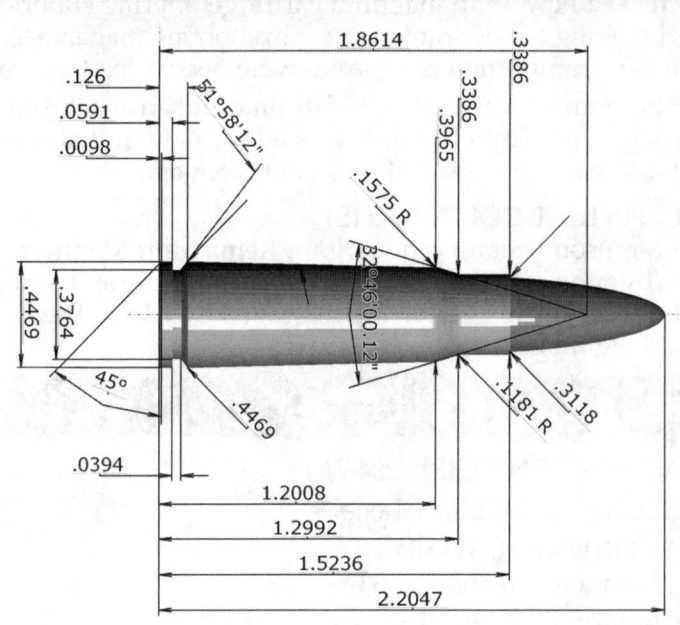

CARTRIDGE BALLISTICS

Max. Average Breech Pressure: 45,000 psi.
Max. Horizontal Range: 4,400 yds.
Max. Vertical Range: 10,000 ft.

Bullet Weight (gr.)	Bullet Type	Muzzle Velocity (fps)	Muzzle Energy (ft.-lbs.)
123	JSP	2,440	1,629
123	JSP	2,365	1,527
123	JSP	2,300	1,445
150	JSP	2,300	1,762

CURRENT MANUFACTURER(S)

Remington, Winchester, Federal, Cor-Bon, Wolf, Barnaul, Sellier & Bellot, IMI, Prvi Partizan, PMC, Norinco, Novosibirsk, Arsenal, Romtechnica.

GENERAL COMMENT(S)

As civilian variants of the SKS and AK-47 began entering the U.S. in the 1980s, the 7.62x39mm Soviet cartridge reached popular status among American sportsmen. At first, the main use for the 7.62x39mm cartridge was for plinking and informal target shooting. However, it was not long before American sportsmen found the 7.62x39mm cartridge to be ideal for hunting deer. Female and youth hunters especially appreciated the low recoil. Today, the 7.62x39mm has become firmly embedded in the minds of American sportsmen as a popular, multi-purpose cartridge. All major domestic ammunition makers offer this caliber.

TECHNICAL COMMENT(S)

Like all Soviet cartridge of the 1940s, chamber pressure of the 7.62x39mm was kept at lower levels than western practices. This limits the effectiveness of this cartridge to hunting varmints and medium game at ranges under 200 yards. Many owners of rifles in this caliber also regard this cartridge as being eminently suitable for home defense.

.30 REMINGTON AR

ALTERNATE NAME(S): .30 RAR, 30 Rem. AR
RELATED CALIBER(S): .308 Win.

CARTRIDGE HISTORY

Year of Introduction: 2008

Country of Origin: U.S.

Designer(s): John Fink (Remington) and Randy Luth (DPMS)

Governing Body: SAAMI Present

Status: active

CARTRIDGE DESCRIPTION

Bullet Diameter: .308 in.

Bullet Weight(s): 125 gr.

Rifling Twist Rate: 1 turn in 10 in.

Test Barrel Length: 24 in.

Case Type: rimless, necked

Case Material: brass

Primer Size: large rifle.

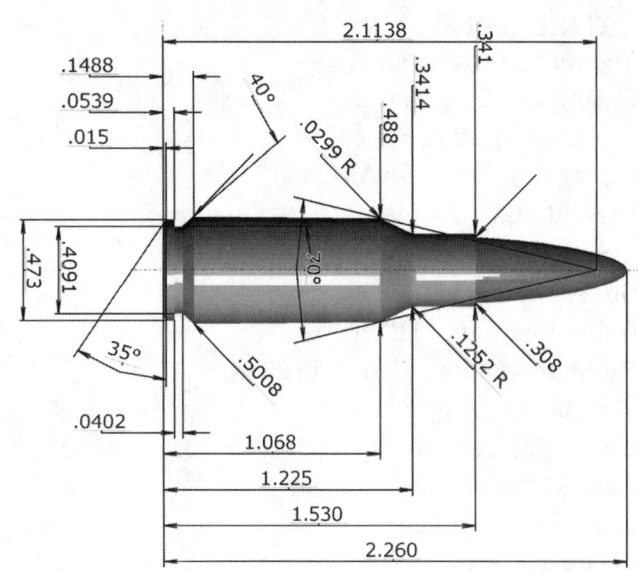

CARTRIDGE BALLISTICS

Max. Average Breech Pressure: 55,000 psi.

Max. Horizontal Range: 4,700 yds.

Max. Vertical Range: 10,500 ft.

Bullet Weight (gr.)	Bullet Type	Muzzle Velocity (fps)	Muzzle Energy (ft.-lbs.)
125	JSP-BT	2,800	2,176

CURRENT MANUFACTURER(S)

Remington

GENERAL COMMENT(S)

According to the designers of this cartridge, their objective was to increase the ballistic performance of AR-type rifles to make them suitable for hunting deer, antelope, and other medium game. To reach this goal, a new cartridge firing a .30 caliber bullet would be needed. A limiting factor was the magazine well of AR-style rifles. An optimal new cartridge would be the largest which could fit within in the dimensional constraints imposed by the magazine well. So far, Remington has been the only manufacturer of this caliber of ammunition. Remington must be congratulated for their pioneering effort in this respect. However, reaction from the targeted customers has been lukewarm at best. Perhaps Remington miscalculated and medium game hunters do not want to use an AR rifle, or they use a more powerful caliber when they do.

TECHNICAL COMMENT(S)

Performance requirements and dimensional limitations dictated a .473 in. (.308 Win.) rebated rim and a .5008 in. body to maximize case capacity at 44 gr. of water. While test barrels are 24 inches long, AR barrels are typically 22 inches or less. For a 20 inch barrel, muzzle velocity would be approximately 40 to 80 fps slower than test barrel results. The published ballistics for the .30 Remington AR cartridge indicate it will offer 34% more muzzle energy than the 7.62x39mm Soviet cartridge and about 19% more than the venerable .30-30 Winchester with 125 gr. bullets. These numbers indicate that the .30 RAR cartridge should be an adequate and effective deer cartridge, albeit only barely.

.30 M1 CARBINE

ALTERNATE NAME(S): .30 Carb.
RELATED CALIBER(S): .32 Winchester Self-Loading

CARTRIDGE HISTORY
Year of Introduction: 1941
Country of Origin: U.S.
Designer(s): Winchester
Governing Body: SAAMI, CIP
Present Status: active

CARTRIDGE DESCRIPTION
Bullet Diameter: .308 in.
Bullet Weight(s): 110 gr.
Rifling Twist Rate: 1 turn in 20 in.
Test Barrel Length: 20 in.
Case Type: rimless, tapered
Case Material: brass or steel
Primer Size: small rifle

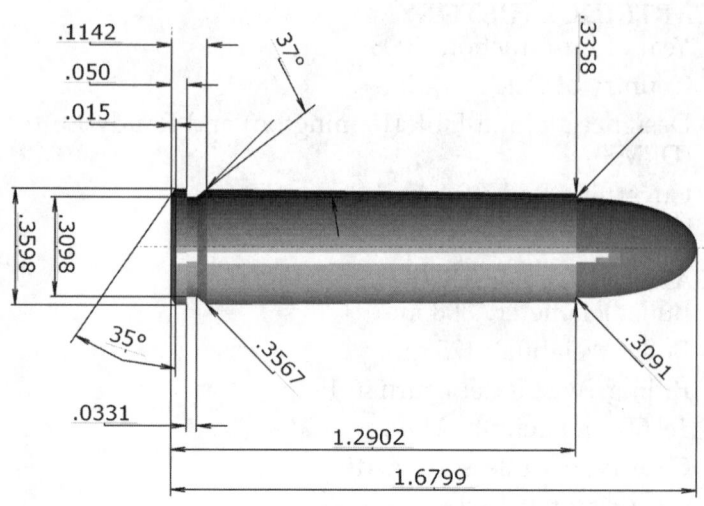

CARTRIDGE BALLISTICS
Max. Average Breech Pressure: 40,000 psi.
Max. Horizontal Range: 2,600 yds.
Max. Vertical Range: 5,800 ft.

Bullet Weight (gr.)	Bullet Type	Muzzle Velocity (fps)	Muzzle Energy (ft.-lbs.)
110	JSP/FMJ	1,990	965

CURRENT MANUFACTURER(S)
Winchester, Remington, Federal, Sellier & Bellot, PMC, IMI, Industrios Technos, CBC, PMP, Wolf, Prvi Partizan

GENERAL COMMENT(S)
Following World War II, many returning American GIs retained a fond memory of the lightweight, low-recoil M1 Carbine they had carried during the War. This assured a place for the .30 Carbine in the post War sporting arms and ammunition market. The .30 Carbine still remains one of the most popular cartridges in any ammunition maker's product line. Why is this? The secret seems two-fold. The limited power, low recoil, and light weight of the .30 Carbine and its cartridge appeal to many shooters who enjoy the "fun factor" of shooting. Often neglected is the home defense aspect of the .30 Carbine cartridge which at close ranges exceeds the striking energy of the .357 Magnum. The .30 Carbine is useless for hunting anything except small game and varmints (indeed it is illegal for hunting in many states). The end of cheap surplus ammunition in this caliber effectively ended plinking with the Carbine in the 1970s.

TECHNICAL COMMENT(S)
By any measure, the .30 Carbine cartridge is a short-range, low powered caliber of limited performance. The possibilities of ballistic improvement of this cartridge are nil, although it has been necked down to accept .224 inch diameter bullets in the cartridge known as the 5.7mm Spitfire. Commercial factory ammunition is loaded with a slightly heavier full metal jacket or hollow point bullet at a somewhat higher muzzle velocity than the military load.

.30 THOMPSON-CENTER

ALTERNATE NAME(S): .30 T/C
RELATED CALIBER(S): .308 Win.

CARTRIDGE HISTORY
Year of Introduction: 2007
Country of Origin: U.S.
Designer(s): Thompson/Center, Hornady

Governing Body: SAAMI
Present Status: active

CARTRIDGE DESCRIPTION
Bullet Diameter: .308 in.
Bullet Weight(s): 150 - 165gr.
Rifling Twist Rate: 1 turn in 10 in.
Test Barrel Length: 24 in.
Case Type: rimless, necked
Case Material: brass
Primer: large rifle

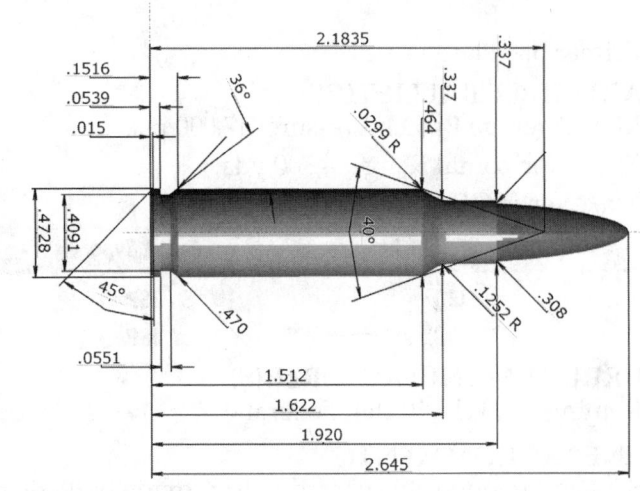

CARTRIDGE BALLISTICS
Max. Average Breech Pressure: 60,000 psi.
Max. Horizontal Range: 5,200 yds.
Max. Vertical Range: 11,000 ft.

Bullet Weight (gr.)	Bullet Type	Muzzle Velocity (fps)	Muzzle Energy (ft.-lbs.)
150	SJ-BT	3,000	2,997
165	SJ-BT	2,850	2,975

CURRENT MANUFACTURER(S)
Hornady

GENERAL COMMENT(S)
A key concept in this design was balance. Basically, this required the cartridge design process to operate in reverse of the normal procedure. Previously, most cartridge designs were finalized first and the ballisticians had to find a way to make them work. Balancing meant that the desired ballistic performance requirements were established first and the cartridge designers optimized their design to achieve the performance specified. We can expect to see more of this type of development in the future.

TECHNICAL COMMENT(S)
Ballistic performance specifications for this new cartridge were challenging: muzzle velocities exceeding that of the .30-'06 Springfield from a case smaller than a .308 Winchester and a 20 inch rifle barrel. The designers began with a case having the rim and head dimensions of the .308 Winchester. From there, they shortened the case length and increased the body taper to assure smooth extraction. Next, they increased the shoulder angle from 20 to 29 degrees to maintain case capacity and provide a solid shoulder to maintain headspace. The .30 T/C has a case capacity about 3.5% less than a .308 Winchester. A high-energy, double-base propellant allowed muzzle velocities to be increased without exceeding normal maximum average chamber pressures and bullets with a high ballistic coefficient assured superior down range performance.

.300 SAVAGE

ALTERNATE NAME(S): .300 Sav.
RELATED CALIBER(S): .250 Savage
CARTRIDGE HISTORY
Year of Introduction: 1920
Country of Origin: U.S.
Designer(s): Savage
Governing Body: SAAMI, CIP
Present Status: active

CARTRIDGE DESCRIPTION
Bullet Diameter: .308 in.
Bullet Weight(s): 150-180 gr.
Rifling Twist Rate: 1 turn in 12 in.
Test Barrel Length: 24 in.
Case Type: rimless, necked
Case Material: brass

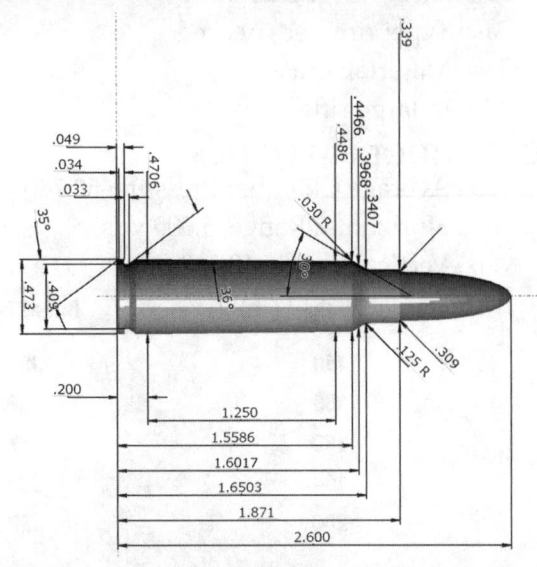

Primer Size: large rifle

CARTRIDGE BALLISTICS

Max. Average Breech Pressure: 47,000 psi.

Max. Horizontal Range: 4,700 yds.

Max. Vertical Range: 10,500 ft.

Bullet Weight (gr.)	Bullet Type	Muzzle Velocity (fps)	Muzzle Energy (ft.-lbs.)
150	JSP	2,630	2,303
180	JSP	2,350	2,207

CURRENT MANUFACTURER(S)

Remington, Winchester, Federal

GENERAL COMMENT(S)

Savage intended this cartridge to provide ballistic performance similar to the .30-'06 Springfield from a short action. In this they succeeded and the .300 Sav. became a popular choice for medium game hunting. And so it remained until 1952 when the .308 Win. cartridge began pushing the Savage into semi-retirement. The major domestic ammunition companies still offer .300 Savage caliber ammunition. As its popularity fades, this caliber may not be around much longer.

TECHNICAL COMMENT(S)

Because the Savage 99 lever-action rifle was chambered for the .300 Savage, chamber pressure had to be kept at a modest 47,000 psi. This limited ballistic performance, although the .300 Savage proved an excellent cartridge in the field.

30R BLASER

ALTERNATE NAME(S): none

RELATED CALIBER(S): 6.5x61Rmm Mauser, 6.5x65Rmm RWS

CARTRIDGE HISTORY

Year of Introduction: 1990

Country of Origin: Germany

Designer(s): Dynamit Nobel

Governing Body: CIP

Present Status: active

CARTRIDGE DESCRIPTION

Bullet Diameter: .308 in.

Bullet Weight(s): 150 - 180 gr.

Rifling Twist Rate: 1 turn in 12 in.

Test Barrel Length: 24 in.

Case Type: rimmed, necked

Case Material: brass

Primer: large rifle

CARTRIDGE BALLISTICS

Max. Average Chamber Pressure: 58,740 psi.

Max. Horizontal Range: 5,000 yds.

Max. Vertical Range: 10,560 ft.

Bullet Weight (gr.)	Bullet Type	Muzzle Velocity (fps)	Muzzle Energy (ft.-lbs.)
150	JSP	3,085	3,165
165	JSP	2,925	3,134
180	JSP	2,820	3,190
184	JSP	2,790	3,180
200	JSP	2,625	3,060

CURRENT MANUFACTURER(S)
Norma, Dynamit Nobel/RUAG

GENERAL COMMENT(S)
The 30R Blaser is a thoroughly modern cartridge designed for use in break-open combination guns or drillings so popular for mixed bag hunts in Europe. The 30R Blaser is one of the few new cartridges developed in Europe in recent years. Undoubtedly, this is because of the shrinking ammunition market due to the proliferation of regulations imposed on the private ownership of firearms throughout Europe. One would assume that there are plenty of rimmed versions of popular rimless calibers to choose from already for a drilling. You would be wrong as most choices until now have not included a rimmed .30 caliber cartridge. In this respect, the 30R Blaser is ground breaking. While the 30R Blaser cartridge has much to offer, it is virtually unknown to American sportsmen.

TECHNICAL COMMENT(S)
Modern drillings are designed for high pressure cartridges and the 30R Blaser takes full advantage of this with maximum average chamber pressure levels similar to high pressure bolt-action rifle cartridges. Still, the 30R Blaser cannot be considered a magnum cartridge. In ballistic performance, the 30R Blaser lies a cut above the .30-'06 Springfield but a cut below the .300 Winchester Magnum.

.300 RUGER COMPACT MAGNUM

ALTERNATE NAME(S): .300 RCM
RELATED CALIBER(S): .300 Remington Short-Action
  Ultra Mag (RSUM), .300 Winchester Short Magnum
  (WSM)

CARTRIDGE HISTORY
Year of Introduction: 2008
Country of Origin: U.S.
Designer(s): Hornady
Governing Body: SAAMI
Present Status: active

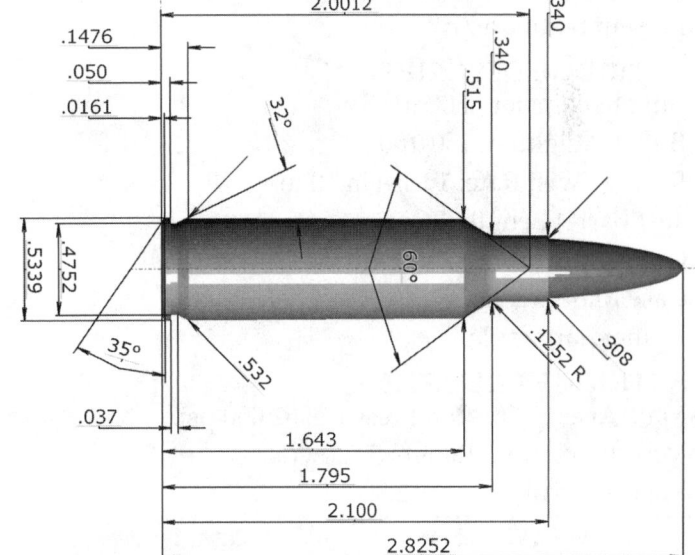

CARTRIDGE DESCRIPTION
Bullet Diameter: .308 in.
Bullet Weight(s): 150 - 180 gr.
Rifling Twist Rate: 1 turn in 10 in.
Test Barrel Length: 24 in.
Case Type: rimless, necked
Case Material: brass
Primer: large rifle

CARTRIDGE BALLISTICS
Max. Average Breech Pressure: N/A
Max. Horizontal Range: 5,450 yds.
Max. Vertical Range: 11,500 ft.

Bullet Weight (gr.)	Bullet Type	Muzzle Velocity (fps)	Muzzle Energy (ft.-lbs.)
150	JSP-BT	3,170	3,347
165	JSP-BT	3,030	3,363
180	JSP-BT	2,900	3,361

CURRENT MANUFACTURER(S)
Hornady

GENERAL COMMENT(S)
Here is one of the latest of the new compact magnum rifle cartridges that are designed for hunting and can be chambered in most rifles with short-action lengths (cartridges having an overall loaded length of 2.85 inches or less). As a class, all of the modern short magnums share a similar configuration, namely a rimless beltless case with a base diameter between .532 and .555 inches and a case length of between 2.03 and 2.10 inches. Ballistics are also similar.

TECHNICAL COMMENT(S)

The short fat case geometry of these beltless compact magnums is claimed to deliver higher muzzle velocity than equivalent cartridges of "standard" configuration while burning 10-15% less propellant. Additional claims include longer barrel life, less muzzle flash, less muzzle blast, and lower recoil. Undoubtedly, these claims are based on empirical evidence that the short, fat case configuration allows a smaller amount of unburned propellant to be driven up the barrel behind the bullet. This results in higher efficiency allowing a smaller propellant charge and a shorter barrel. In general, cartridges with a lower length to diameter ratio are considered to be more accurate. Of course, there are many other factors involved which will have a major effect on the performance of these short cartridges.

.300 PEGASUS

ALTERNATE NAME(S): .300 Pegasus A-Square
RELATED CALIBER(S): 7.82mm Lazzeroni Warbird, 8.59mm Lazzeroni Titan etc.

CARTRIDGE HISTORY

Year of Introduction: 1994
Country of Origin: U.S.
Designer(s): Art Alphin
Governing Body: none
Present Status: active

CARTRIDGE DESCRIPTION

Bullet Diameter: .308 in.
Bullet Weight(s): 150-180 gr.
Rifling Twist Rate: 1 turn in 10 in.
Test Barrel Length: 26 in.
Case Type: rimless, necked
Case Material: brass
Primer: large rifle

CARTRIDGE BALLISTICS

Max. Average Breech Pressure: 62,000 psi.
Max. Horizontal Range: 5,800 yds.
Max. Vertical Range: 12,500 ft.

Bullet Weight (gr.)	Bullet Type	Muzzle Velocity (fps)	Muzzle Energy (ft.-lbs.)
150	JSP	3,780	4,760
180	JSP	3,525	4,966

CURRENT MANUFACTURER(S)

A-Square

GENERAL COMMENT(S)

This cartridge design from A-Square is a worthy entry into the ".300 caliber super magnum" category of modern cartridges. It is intended for very long range hunting under difficult conditions.

TECHNICAL COMMENT(S)

Like many modern cartridge designs, the .300 Pegasus eschews belts in favor of a beltless head configuration. In addition, A-Square has specified an extra-large case head diameter in order to increase case volume (borrowed from the Lazzeroni product line). As in many modern case designs, the shoulder is kept fairly short to maximize case volume. However, a reasonable neck length is maintained to provide an adequate hold on the bullet. The result is a large, modern, sleek looking cartridge that, if looks could kill, would be the king of the .30 caliber mountain. Burning the heavy powder charges used in this cartridge will certainly cause short barrel life. Such is the price for performance and a price many sportsmen are only too willing to pay.

.300 OLYMPIC SUPER SHORT MAGNUM

ALTERNATE NAME(S): .300 OSSM
RELATED CALIBER(S): none

CARTRIDGE HISTORY
Year of Introduction: 2010
Country of Origin: U.S.
Designer(s): Olympic Arms
Governing Body: SAAMI
Present Status: current

CARTRIDGE DESCRIPTION
Bullet Diameter: .308 in.
Bullet Weight(s):150 gr.
Rifling Twist Rate: 1 turn in 12 in.
Test Barrel Length: 24 in.
Case Type: rimless, beltless, necked
Case Material: brass
Primer Size: large rifle

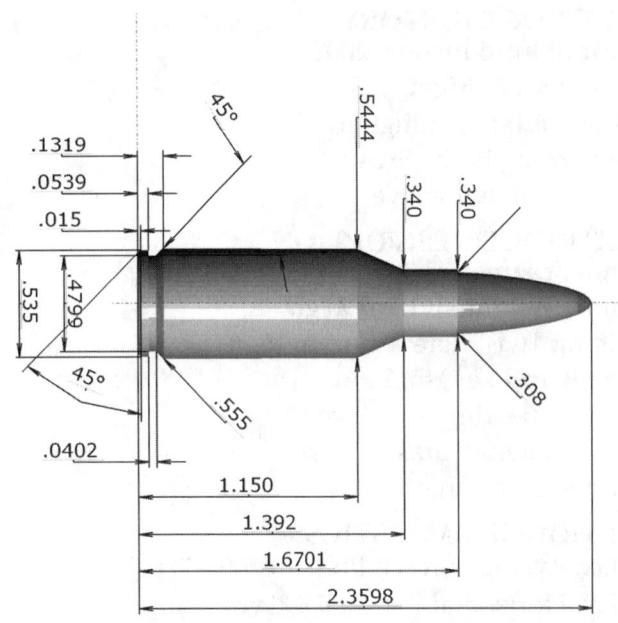

CARTRIDGE BALLISTICS
Max. Average Breech Pressure: 55,000 psi.
Max. Horizontal Range: 5,200 yds.
Max. Vertical Range: 11,000 ft.

Bullet Weight (gr.)	Bullet Type	Muzzle Velocity (fps)	Muzzle Energy (ft.-lbs.)
150	SP	3,045	3,087

CURRENT MANUFACTURER(S)
Cor-Bon

GENERAL COMMENT(S)
With the rapidly growing use of semi-automatic AR15-type rifles for hunting medium game, the need for a suitable cartridge became acute. Most of these rifles are chambered for the 5.56x45mm NATO cartridge which is unsuitable (and in some jurisdiction illegal) for use on deer and other medium game. The new short and super-short magnums for bolt-action rifles are too large to fit in actions designed for the 5.56x45mm cartridge. The 6.5mm Grendel and 6.8mm SPC offer a marginal improvement for hunting. Thus far, the .30 Remington AR has been the best (and only) choice. However, its 115 gr. bullet lacks ballistic performance for hunting.

What was needed was a hunting cartridge using a .30 caliber bullet that would offer ballistic performance suited for use in the field. Actually, a .300 Winchester or Remington Super Short Magnum was needed, but manufacturers did not answer the call. The .300 Olympic Super Short Magnum is the answer and it is now a standard SAAMI caliber made by Cor-Bon.

TECHNICAL COMMENT(S)
When it comes to AR rifles, most .30 cartridges with .479 in. case head diameter are too long. Traditional belted magnums are too wide. Calibers with small diameter case heads such as the 6.8mm SPC lack sufficient case volume. To answer these shortcomings requires many compromises, but it can be done and the .300 OSSM is proof. The .300 OSSM uses a modern, beltless case with a .535 in. diameter head to provide sufficient case volume. Its short 2.25 in. length assures it will fit in the magazine wells of AR15 rifles. These two features allow ballistics suitable for hunting medium game.

.300 REMINGTON SHORT-ACTION ULTRA MAGNUM

ALTERNATE NAME(S): .300 RSUM
RELATED CALIBER(S): .300 RUM, .300 WSM

CARTRIDGE HISTORY
Year of Introduction: 2002
Country of Origin: U.S.
Designer(s): Remington
Governing Body: SAAMI
Present Status: active

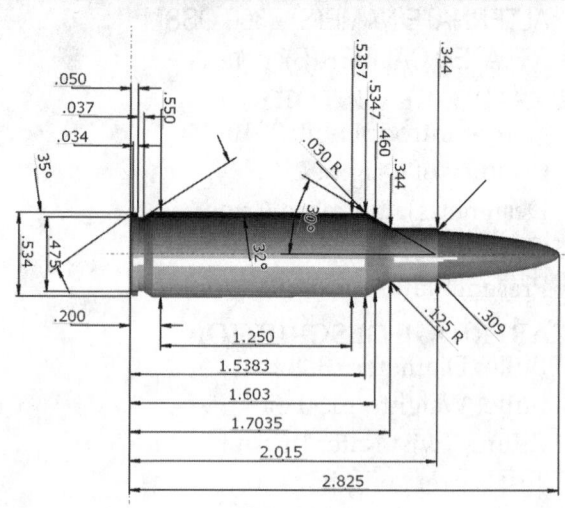

CARTRIDGE DESCRIPTION
Bullet Diameter: .308 in.
Bullet Weight(s): 150-190 gr.
Rifling Twist Rate: 1 turn in 10 in.
Test Barrel Length: 24 in.
Case Type: rimless, necked
Case Material: brass
Primer Size: large rifle

CARTRIDGE BALLISTICS
Max. Average Breech Pressure: 65,000 psi.
Max. Horizontal Range: 5,800 yds.
Max. Vertical Range: 11,500 ft.

Bullet Weight (gr.)	Bullet Type	Muzzle Velocity (fps)	Muzzle Energy (ft.-lbs.)
150	JSP	3,200	3,410
165	JSP	3,075	3,464
180	JSP	2,960	3,501
190	JHP	2,900	3,547

CURRENT MANUFACTURER(S)
Remington

GENERAL COMMENT(S)
This is another Remington magnum cartridge for short-action rifles. Introduced in 2002, other ammunition manufacturers have not added a comparable cartridge to their product lines.

TECHNICAL COMMENT(S)
The .300 RSUM combines magnum head dimensions with a beltless short cartridge length. Ballistic performance is on par with classic belted magnums of standard length.

.300 WINCHESTER SHORT MAGNUM

ALTERNATE NAME(S): .300 WSM
RELATED CALIBER(S): .300 RSUM

CARTRIDGE HISTORY
Year of Introduction: 2001
Country of Origin: U.S.
Designer(s): Winchester
Governing Body: SAAMI, CIP
Present Status: active

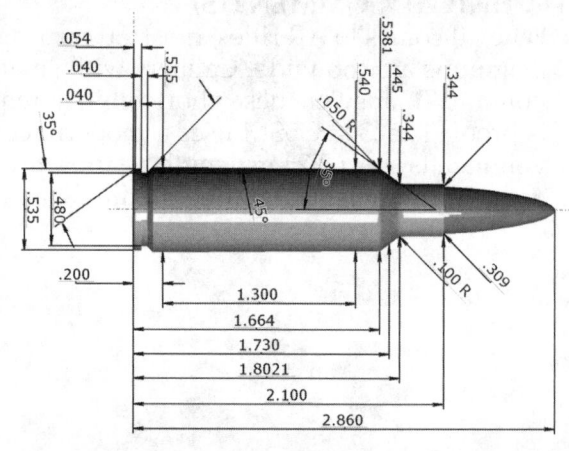

CARTRIDGE DESCRIPTION
Bullet Diameter: .308 in.
Bullet Weight(s): 150-180 gr.
Rifling Twist Rate: 1 turn in 10 in.

Test Barrel Length: 24 in.
Case Type: rimless, necked
Case Material: brass
Primer Size: large rifle

CARTRIDGE BALLISTICS
Max. Average Breech Pressure: 65,000 psi.
Max. Horizontal Range: 5,800 yds.
Max. Vertical Range: 11,500 ft.

Bullet Weight (gr.)	Bullet Type	Muzzle Velocity (fps)	Muzzle Energy (ft.-lbs.)
150	JSP	3,300	3,628
150	JSP	3,200	3,410
165	JSP	3,130	3,590
180	JSP	2,980	3,535

CURRENT MANUFACTURER(S)
Winchester, Federal, Black Hills, Remington

GENERAL COMMENT(S)
This cartridge is Winchester's entry into the short beltless magnum field. Unlike the Remington Short-Action Ultra Magnum, the .300 WSM seems to have caught on and is now being offered by several major ammunition makers.

TECHNICAL COMMENT(S)
Although nearly identical in dimension and ballistics, the .300 Winchester Short Magnum and the .300 RSUM are not interchangeable.

The .300 WSM is another high pressure, short magnum case for use in short-action rifles. As such, it has magnum head dimensions without a belt to maximize case volume.

.300 WINCHESTER MAGNUM

ALTERNATE NAME(S): .300 Win. Mag.
RELATED CALIBER(S): .338 Winchester Magnum

CARTRIDGE HISTORY
Year of Introduction: 1963
Country of Origin: U.S.
Designer(s): Winchester
Governing Body: SAAMI, CIP
Present Status: active

CARTRIDGE DESCRIPTION
Bullet Diameter: .308 in.
Bullet Weight(s): 150-190 gr.
Rifling Twist Rate: 1 turn in 10 in.
Test Barrel Length: 24 in.
Case Type: rimless, belted, necked
Case Material: brass
Primer Size: large rifle

CARTRIDGE BALLISTICS
Max. Average Breech Pressure: 64,000 psi.
Max. Horizontal Range: 5,800 yds.
Max. Vertical Range: 11,500 ft.

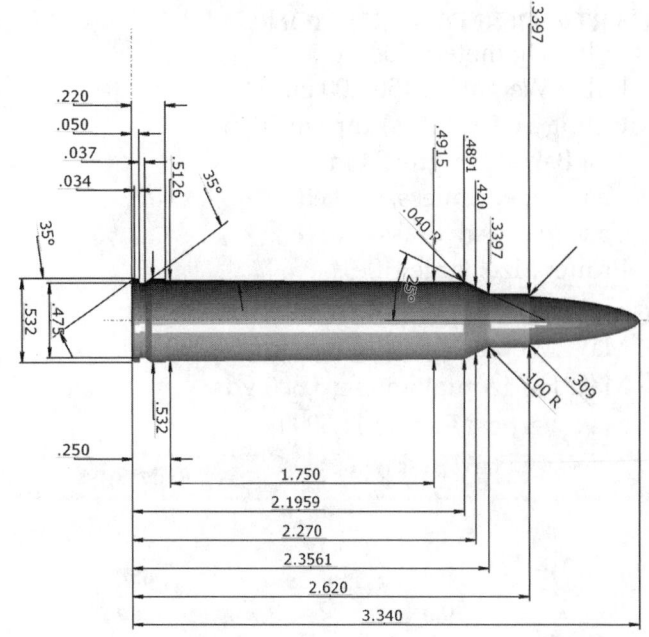

Bullet Weight (gr.)	Bullet Type	Muzzle Velocity (fps)	Muzzle Energy (ft.-lbs.)
150	JSP	3,290	3,570
165	JSP	3,140	3,610
180	JSP	3,100	3,840
180	JSP	3,000	3,597
190	JSP	2,900	3,547

CURRENT MANUFACTURER(S)

Federal, Winchester, Remington, Hornady, Black Hills, PMC, Prvi Partizan, Sellier & Bellot, Norma

GENERAL COMMENT(S)

In the 45 years since its introduction, the .300 Winchester Magnum has become the most popular .300 magnum rifle cartridge in the world. Every major ammunition maker offers this caliber. The .300 Win. Mag. is suitable for all types of North American game and many species of African plains game. It has also been used successfully for 1,000 yard rifle competition.

TECHNICAL COMMENT(S)

The .300 Winchester Magnum cartridge is a direct descendent of the venerable .300 H&H Magnum with a modern 25 degree shoulder angle, a shortened case, and higher chamber pressure. Although offered with 150-190 grain bullets, the 165 and 180 grain bullets perform best in this cartridge. For long range hunting, the .300 Win. Magnum remains an excellent choice.

.300 REMINGTON ULTRA MAGNUM

ALTERNATE NAME(S): .300 RUM

RELATED CALIBER(S): 7mm Remington Ultra Magnum

CARTRIDGE HISTORY

Year of Introduction: 1999
Country of Origin: U.S.
Designer(s): Remington
Governing Body: SAAMI
Present Status: active

CARTRIDGE DESCRIPTION

Bullet Diameter: .308 in.
Bullet Weight(s): 150-200 gr.
Rifling Twist Rate: 1 turn in 10 in.
Test Barrel Length: 24 in.
Case Type: rimless, necked
Case Material: brass
Primer Size: large rifle

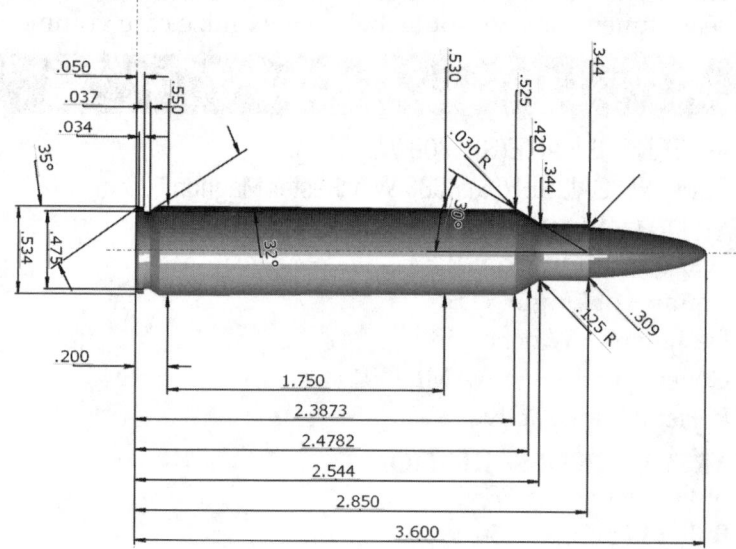

CARTRIDGE BALLISTICS

Max. Average Breech Pressure: 65,000 psi.
Max. Horizontal Range: 5,800 yds.
Max. Vertical Range: 11,500 ft.

Bullet Weight (gr.)	Bullet Type	Muzzle Velocity (fps)	Muzzle Energy (ft.-lbs.)
150	JSP	3,450	3,964 Level I
180	JSP	2,960	3,501 Level II
180	JSP	3,250	4,221 Level III
200	JSP	3,025	4,063 Level III

CURRENT MANUFACTURER(S)

Remington

GENERAL COMMENT(S)

Remington kicked off the new trend toward beltless, magnum calibers with this cartridge. Other Remington

Ultra Magnum cartridges have followed, including both the short and the long action versions. At this time, Remington is the only manufacturer of this cartridge.

TECHNICAL COMMENT(S)

The lack of a belt does not make the .300 RUM cartridge case weaker or require a lower chamber pressure. It makes manufacture of the case much easier, however. The head diameter and length of this case allows substantial internal volume for the heavy powder charges needed to achieve the specified muzzle velocities. Ballistically, the .300 RUM rivals the classic .300 Weatherby Magnum. In an innovative touch, Remington offers the .300 RUM cartridge loaded to three different velocity levels allowing the user to match his load to the game.

.30-'06 SPRINGFIELD

ALTERNATE NAME(S):. 30-'06 Spr., .30-'06 Spfld., 7.62x63mm, .30 Government, .30 M1, .30 M2
RELATED CALIBER(S): .270 Winchester, .25-06 Remington, .280 Remington

CARTRIDGE HISTORY

Year of Introduction: 1906

Country of Origin: U.S.

Designer(s): Springfield Armory

Governing Body: SAAMI, CIP

Present Status: active

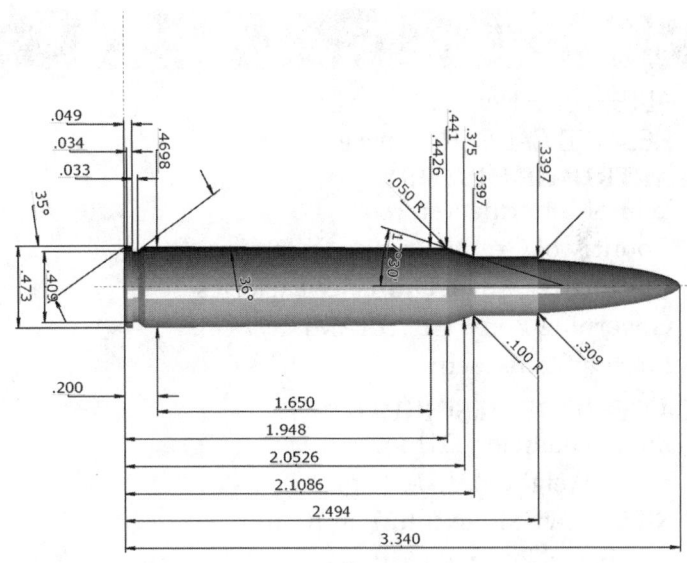

CARTRIDGE DESCRIPTION

Bullet Diameter: .308 in.

Bullet Weight(s): 125-220 gr.

Rifling Twist Rate: 1 turn in 10 in.

Test Barrel Length: 24 in.

Case Type: rimless, necked

Case Material: brass or steel

Primer Size: large rifle

CARTRIDGE BALLISTICS

Max. Average Breech Pressure: 60,000 psi.

Max. Horizontal Range: 6,200 yds.

Max. Vertical Range: 14,000 ft.

Bullet Weight (gr.)	Bullet Type	Muzzle Velocity (fps)	Muzzle Energy (ft.-lbs.)
125	JSP	3,140	2,735
150	JSP	3,100	3,200
150	JSP	3,050	3,089
150	JSP	2,960	2,919
150	JSP	2,910	2,820
165	JSP	3,015	3,330
165	JSP	2,800	2,872
168	JHP	2,700	2,970
180	JSP	2,900	3,361
180	JSP	2,700	2,914
200	JSP	2,625	3,061
220	JSP	2,410	2,837

CURRENT MANUFACTURER(S)

Remington, Winchester, Federal, Hornady, Black Hills, PMC, Sellier & Bellot, Wolf, Prvi Partizan, IMI, PMP, DN

GENERAL COMMENT(S)

When the .30-'06 Springfield cartridge was introduced to American sportsmen in 1906, they eagerly embraced its sterling ballistic performance and accuracy. Today, over 100 years later, the now-venerable .30-'06 Spr. cartridge remains the most popular sporting caliber in the world. It is an excellent choice for any game in

North America and many species of African game as well. For deer and medium game hunting, only the .30-30 Win. is more popular.

A wide range of bullet weights allows flexibility seldom found in other calibers. Although its days as a premier match cartridge are behind it, the .30-'06 Spr. remains a sturdy and classic competitor on the range. Its popularity and ballistic performance have kept the .30-'06 Spr. at the top of the charts for over a century. It shows no sign of fading. Every major ammunition manufacturer in the world offers this caliber. Although its military career ended in the late 1950s, the .30-'06 Spr. shows no sign of fading in the commercial market.

TECHNICAL COMMENT(S)

Choose a .30-'06 Spr. for hunting and you cannot go wrong. Excellent ballistic performance assures effectiveness on a wide range of game at any reasonable distance. Even large bears can be hunted with the .30-'06.

The one turn in ten inch rifling twist allows a wide range of bullet weights to be used and the large case capacity allows sufficient propellant to achieve effective muzzle velocities. For ballistic flexibility, the .30-'06 remains unmatched. The .30-'06 has also been the godfather of several other classic cartridges such as the .270 Win., .280 Rem., .25-06 Rem., and .35 Whelen.

.303 BRITISH

ALTERNATE NAME(S): .303 Brit.
RELATED CALIBER(S): none

CARTRIDGE HISTORY
Year of Introduction: 1888
Country of Origin: Britain
Designer(s): Royal Ordnance Factories
Governing Body: CIP, SAAMI
Present Status: active

CARTRIDGE DESCRIPTION
Bullet Diameter: .311 in.
Bullet Weight(s): 150-215 gr.
Rifling Twist Rate: 1 turn in 10 in.
Test Barrel Length: 24 in.
Case Type: rimmed, necked
Case Material: brass
Primer Size: large rifle

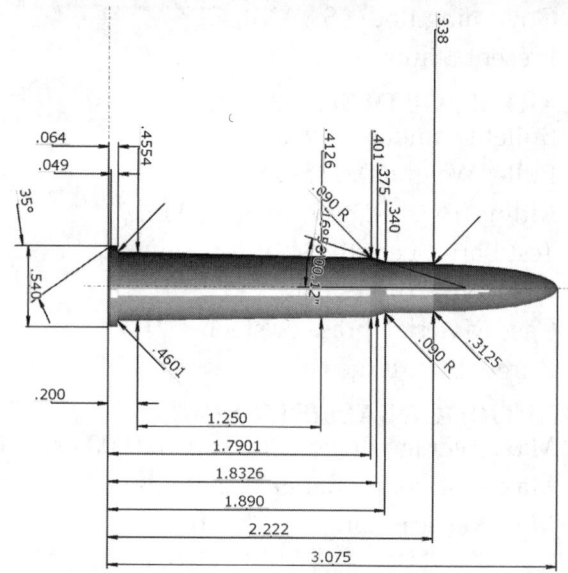

CARTRIDGE BALLISTICS
Max. Average Breech Pressure: 46,400 psi.
Max. Horizontal Range: 3,000 yds.
Max. Vertical Range: 6,500 ft.

Bullet Weight (gr.)	Bullet Type	Muzzle Velocity (fps)	Muzzle Energy (ft.-lbs.)
150	JSP	2,690	2,400
180	JSP	2,460	2,420
215	JSP	2,180	2,270

CURRENT MANUFACTURER(S)
Federal, Remington, Winchester, Sellier & Bellot, Prvi Partizan, PMC

GENERAL COMMENT(S)
With the end of World War II, a flood of surplus British Short Magazine Lee-Enfield rifles reached U.S. shores. These quickly became popular for informal target shooting and hunting. American ammunition manufacturers have offered .303 British caliber ammunition since the early 1900s. Although the .303 British has been loaded with bullets from 150-215 grains for hunting, American manufacturers presently offer only a 180 grain bullet.

Throughout the British Empire, the .303 British was the caliber of choice for normal hunting purposes due to its broad availability. This caliber also served for target shooting with great success.

With the formation of NATO in the early 1950s, the .303 British cartridge became obsolete in British and

Commonwealth service. It remains a popular hunting caliber in those countries, however its use in the U.S. has been dropping as it becomes semi-obsolete.

TECHNICAL COMMENT(S)

The .303 British cartridge is loaded to more moderate chamber pressures than modern cartridges. As a result, muzzle velocities are lower than contemporaries such as the .30-'06 Spr. The .303 also uses .311 inch diameter bullets.

Military surplus ammunition in this caliber is normally loaded with corrosive Berdan primers. Sporting ammunition in .303 British caliber is loader with non-corrosive Boxer primers. For deer and medium game hunting, the .303 British is an excellent choice.

.30-30 WINCHESTER

ALTERNATE NAME(S): .30-30 Win., .30 Win., .30-30 WCF, 7.62x51Rmm
RELATED CALIBER(S): .225 Winchester, .25-35 Winchester, 7-30 Waters, .32 Winchester Special, .38-55 Winchester

CARTRIDGE HISTORY

Year of Introduction: 1895
Country of Origin: U.S.
Designer(s): Winchester
Governing Body: SAAMI, CIP
Present Status: active

CARTRIDGE DESCRIPTION

Bullet Diameter: .308 in.
Bullet Weight(s): 125-170 gr.
Rifling Twist Rate: 1 turn in 12 in.
Test Barrel Length: 24 in.
Case Type: rimmed, necked
Case Material: brass
Primer Size: large rifle

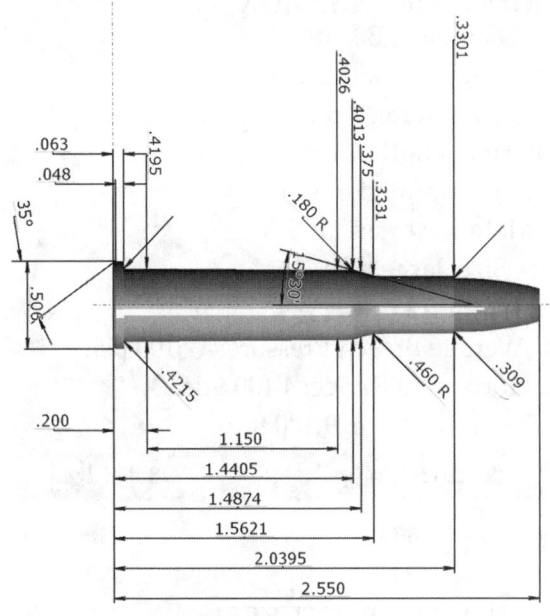

CARTRIDGE BALLISTICS

Max. Average Breech Pressure: 42,000 psi.
Max. Horizontal Range: 3,100 yds.
Max. Vertical Range: 7,000 ft.

Bullet Weight (gr.)	Bullet Type	Muzzle Velocity (fps)	Muzzle Energy (ft.-lbs.)
125	JHP	2,570	1,830
150	JSP	2,480	2,049
150	JSP	2,390	1,900
150	JSP	2,300	1,762
170	JSP	2,200	1,827

CURRENT MANUFACTURER(S)

Winchester, Remington, Federal, PMC, Sellier & Bellot, Prvi Partizan

GENERAL COMMENT(S)

For over 100 years, the .30-30 Winchester has been the quintessential deer cartridge for American sportsmen. Probably more deer have been harvested with a .30-30 Win. than all other rifle cartridges combined. Even today, the .30-30 Win. still has no rivals when it comes to deer hunting. The .30-30 Win. must be considered unsuitable for larger game. Chambered in the popular, lightweight Winchester and Marlin lever-action carbines, the .30-30 Win. cartridge provides excellent ballistic performance to ranges of 200 yards. While capable of excellent inherent accuracy, the short barrels and crude iron sights of rifles normally chambered for this cartridge handicap precision shooting. Every major ammunition maker offers this cartridge.

TECHNICAL COMMENT(S)

Chamber pressures must be kept moderate for use in lever-action rifles with actions not strong enough for higher pressures. This limits muzzle velocities to relatively modest levels. Flat nose bullets must be used in the

.30-30 Win. to prevent magazine tube explosions which could be caused by a pointed bullet striking the primer of the cartridge above it. Flat nose bullets are not the ballistic handicap they seem, as effective range of the .30-30 Win. is limited. Approximately 70 % of hunters select the 150 grain bullet.

.30-40 KRAG

ALTERNATE NAME(S): .30-40, .30 U.S. Army
RELATED CALIBER(S): none

CARTRIDGE HISTORY
Year of Introduction: 1892
Country of Origin: U.S.
Designer(s): Herman Ole Krag
Governing Body: SAAMI, CIP
Present Status: active

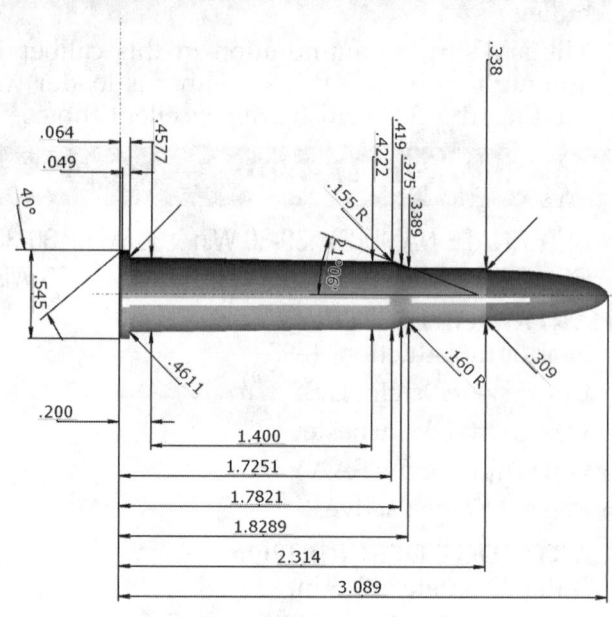

CARTRIDGE DESCRIPTION
Bullet Diameter: .308 in.
Bullet Weight(s): 150-220 gr.
Rifling Twist Rate: 1 turn in 10 in.
Test Barrel Length: 24 in.
Case Type: rimmed, necked
Case Material: brass
Primer Size: large rifle

CARTRIDGE BALLISTICS
Max. Average Breech Pressure: 47,100 psi.
Max. Horizontal Range: 4,100 yds.
Max. Vertical Range: 9,100 ft.

Bullet Weight (gr.)	Bullet Type	Muzzle Velocity (fps)	Muzzle Energy (ft.-lbs.)
180	JSP	2,430	2,360
220	JSP	2,200	2,360

CURRENT MANUFACTURER(S)
Remington, Winchester

GENERAL COMMENT(S)
From 1892 until the adoption of the .30-03 Springfield cartridge in 1903, the .30-40 Krag was the official service caliber of the U.S. Army. As such, it became popular for a time with American sportsmen for hunting. However, its tenure was short, being cut off by the advent of the far superior .30-'06 Spr. cartridge. After 1906, the .30-40 Krag faded quickly to semi-obsolete status where it remains today. Only the popularity of the Ruger No.1 Single Shot rifles in this chambering has kept the .30-40 Krag from full retirement.

TECHNICAL COMMENT(S)
Original military ammunition for the .30-40 Krag cartridge was loaded with black powder. A quick transition to smokeless propellant was made in the mid-1890s. As the military load was a 220 grain round nose bullet, a soft point bullet of the same weight was introduced for commercial loading of the .30-40 Krag. However, sportsmen soon found that the .30-40 Krag performed very well with 180 grain bullets. Consequently, the 220 grain bullets soon faded from popular use in the hunting fields. Today, the .30-40 Krag has become an historical footnote with only Remington and Winchester continuing limited production of the 180 grain bullet load.

.307 WINCHESTER

ALTERNATE NAME(S): .307 Win.
RELATED CALIBER(S): .308 Win.

CARTRIDGE HISTORY
Year of Introduction: 1982
Country of Origin: U.S.
Designer(s): Winchester
Governing Body: SAAMI
Present Status: active

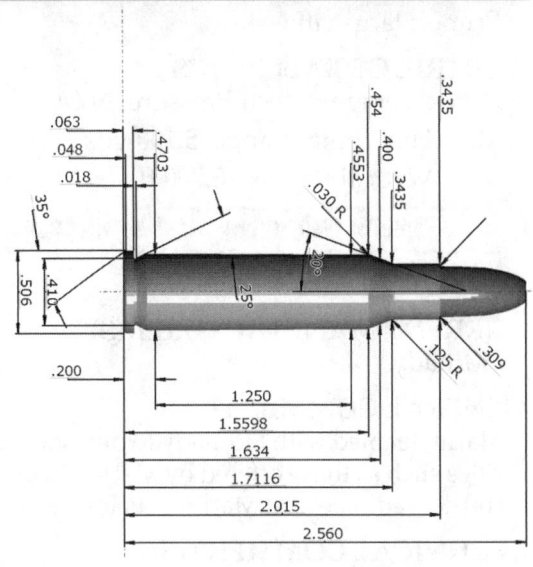

CARTRIDGE DESCRIPTION
Bullet Diameter: .308 in.
Bullet Weight(s): 150-180 gr.
Rifling Twist Rate: 1 turn in 12 in.
Test Barrel Length: 24 in.
Case Type: rimmed, necked
Case Material: brass
Primer Size: large rifle

CARTRIDGE BALLISTICS
Max. Average Breech Pressure: 52,000 CUP.
Max. Horizontal Range: 4,700 yds.
Max. Vertical Range: 10,500 ft.

Bullet Weight (gr.)	Bullet Type	Muzzle Velocity (fps)	Muzzle Energy (ft.-lbs.)
150	JSP	2,760	2,538
180	JSP	2,510	2,519

CURRENT MANUFACTURER(S)
Winchester

GENERAL COMMENT(S)
The purpose of this cartridge was to provide modern ammunition for the Winchester Angle-Eject lever-action rifle. It was not a commercial success and today hangs precariously to life supported by the few rifles in the field.

TECHNICAL COMMENT(S)
The .307 Winchester is a rimmed .308 Winchester cartridge for use in lever-action rifles. Ballistics are similar to the .308 Win. although fewer bullet weights are offered.

.308 MARLIN EXPRESS

ALTERNATE NAME(S): .308 Marlin
RELATED CALIBER(S): .307 Win., .444 Marlin

CARTRIDGE HISTORY
Year of Introduction: 2007
Country of Origin: U.S.
Designer(s): Marlin, Hornady
Governing Body: SAAMI
Present Status: active

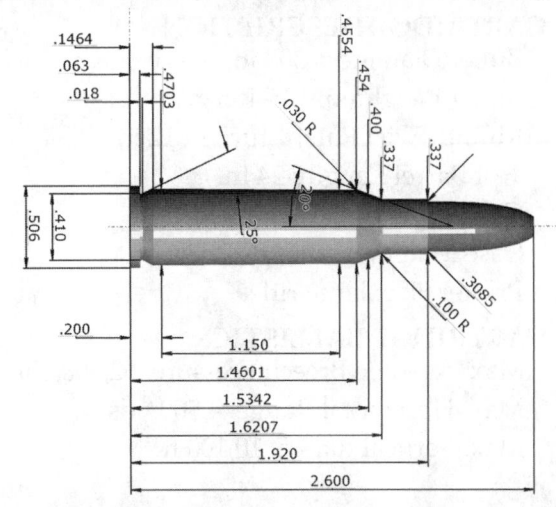

CARTRIDGE DESCRIPTION
Bullet Diameter: .308 in.
Bullet Weight(s): 160 gr.
Rifling Twist Rate: N/A
Test Barrel Length: 24 in.

Case Type: rimmed, necked
Case Material: brass
Primer: large rifle

CARTRIDGE BALLISTICS
Max. Average Breech Pressure: N/A
Max. Horizontal Range: 5,100 yds.
Max. Vertical Range: 10,700 ft.

Bullet Weight (gr.)	Bullet Type	Muzzle Velocity (fps)	Muzzle Energy (ft.-lbs.)
160	FMJ-PSP	2,660	2,513

CURRENT MANUFACTURER(S)
Hornady

GENERAL COMMENT(S)
Marlin teamed with Hornady to develop and market this new cartridge in 2007. It is intended for modern lever-action rifles such as those offered by Marlin. In order to optimize it for this purpose, all aspects of the cartridge were carefully considered. The .308 Marlin develops ballistics similar to the .308 Winchester, but burns less powder doing so.

TECHNICAL COMMENT(S)
Lever-action rifles work best with rimmed cartridge cases. Accordingly, Hornady used a rimmed design, but with a modern, under-cut extractor groove. Compared to the seminal .308 Winchester case, the .308 Marlin has a slightly smaller base diameter and an increased case taper to aid extraction. Case length was shortened slightly to allow a shorter lever throw and assure smooth feeding and chambering. Essentially, the .308 Marlin has a .30-30 Winchester rim diameter mated to the base of a .22-250 Remington. Case capacity was reduced about 8% compared to the .308 Win. This did not prove to be a handicap as the difference was more than made up by using new propellants which generated .308 Win. ballistics. Hornady developed a new pointed bullet for this application which plays a major role in its performance. Normally, the tubular magazines of lever-action rifles require flat nose bullets to prevent magazine tube explosions. Hornady developed an elastomer flexible bullet tip which prevents magazine tube explosions while significantly increasing the ballistic coefficient of the new bullet in comparison to the flat nose designs of old. The result is substantially improved down range ballistic performance.

.308 WINCHESTER

ALTERNATE NAME(S): .308 Win.
RELATED CALIBER(S): .243 Win.

CARTRIDGE HISTORY
Year of Introduction: 1952
Country of Origin: U.S.
Designer(s): Winchester
Governing Body: SAAMI, CIP
Present Status: active

CARTRIDGE DESCRIPTION
Bullet Diameter: .308 in.
Bullet Weight(s): 125-185 gr.
Rifling Twist Rate: 1 turn in 12 in.
Test Barrel Length: 24 in.
Case Type: rimless, necked
Case Material: brass or steel
Primer Size: large rifle

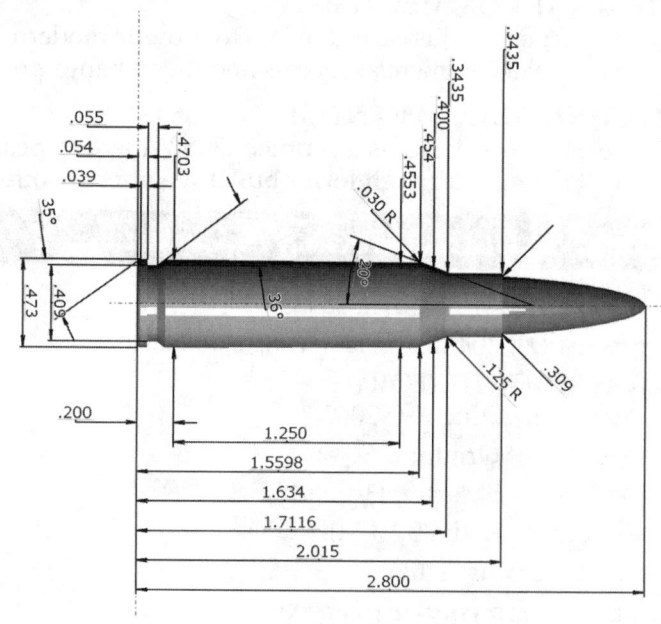

CARTRIDGE BALLISTICS
Max. Average Breech Pressure: 62,000 psi.
Max. Horizontal Range: 4,500 yds.
Max. Vertical Range: 10,100 ft.

Bullet Weight (gr.)	Bullet Type	Muzzle Velocity (fps)	Muzzle Energy (ft.-lbs.)
125	JSP	2,660	1,964
150	JSP	3,000	2,997
150	JSP	2,900	2,802
150	JSP	2,820	2,648
150	JSP	2,750	2,519
165	JSP	2,700	2,670
168	JHP	2,700	2,719
175	JHP	2,600	2,627
180	JSP	2,620	2,745
180	JSP	2,450	2,414
185	JSP	2,510	2,589

CURRENT MANUFACTURER(S)

Federal, Winchester, Remington, Hornady, Black Hills, Cor-Bon, PMC, Prvi Partizan, IMI, PMP, Wolf, MEN, DN

GENERAL COMMENT(S)

When it was introduced in 1952, the .308 Winchester cartridge immediately captured the market for short-action rifles. Its ballistic performance proved suitable for hunting all but the heaviest game. Its inherent accuracy soon allowed it to dominate competitive rifle shooting of all types. From its hopeful start over 50 years ago, the .308 Win. has become the most ubiquitous and popular hunting cartridge in the world. Every major ammunition manufacturer offers this cartridge, even Russian ammunition makers.

TECHNICAL COMMENT(S)

A major reason for the popularity of the .308 Win. cartridge is its balance of efficiency, inherent accuracy, flexibility, and length. Bullet weights from 125 to 185 grains can be used. The small case volume and modest charges of propellant are efficient and provide long barrel life (10,000 rounds is not uncommon). Accuracy remains superb, especially with match-grade bullets. And, the short overall length enables the .308 Win. to be chambered in short-action rifles.

.32-20 WINCHESTER

ALTERNATE NAME(S): .32-20 Win., .32-20 WCF, .32 CLMR
RELATED CALIBER(S): .25-20 Winchester

CARTRIDGE HISTORY

Year of Introduction: 1882
Country of Origin: U.S.
Designer(s): Winchester
Governing Body: SAAMI, CIP
Present Status: active

CARTRIDGE DESCRIPTION

Bullet Diameter: .312 in.
Bullet Weight(s): 100 gr.
Rifling Twist Rate: 1 turn in 20 in.
Test Barrel Length: 24 in.
Case Type: rimmed, necked
Case Material: brass
Primer Size: small rifle

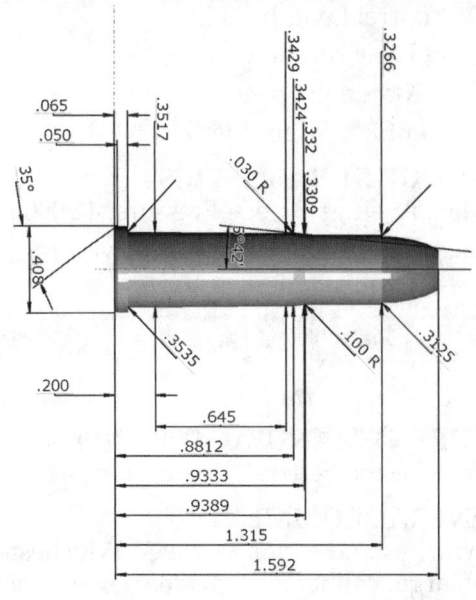

CARTRIDGE BALLISTICS

Max. Average Breech Pressure: 16,000 CUP.
Max. Horizontal Range: 2,000 yds.
Max. Vertical Range: 3,800 ft.

Bullet Weight (gr.)	Bullet Type	Muzzle Velocity (fps)	Muzzle Energy (ft.-lbs.)
100	L - FN	1,210	325

CURRENT MANUFACTURER(S)
Winchester, Remington

GENERAL COMMENT(S)
This old favorite has been chambered in a wide variety of lever-action, slide-action, and single-shot rifles over the years. In recent times, it has been re-popularized by cowboy action shooters for both revolver and rifle use.

In the late 1880s, the .32-20 WCF was considered a suitable caliber for small and medium game. Today, the .32-20 is considered completely unsuitable for hunting medium game such as deer.

TECHNICAL COMMENT(S)
Designed for and loaded to low chamber pressure, the .32-20 WCF offers very modest ballistic performance. Any possible improvement immediately comes up against the small case volume and low chamber pressure limits.

The .32-20 WCF is truly a relic from another era; it survives today mainly on nostalgia. At one time, an 80 grain bullet was loaded to 2,100 fps muzzle velocity. Today, the 100 grain loading is the only one still offered.

.32 WINCHESTER SPECIAL

ALTERNATE NAME(S): .32 Win. Spl., .32 Special
RELATED CALIBER(S): .30-30 Winchester

CARTRIDGE HISTORY
Year of Introduction: 1902
Country of Origin: U.S.
Designer(s): Winchester
Governing Body: SAAMI
Present Status: active

CARTRIDGE DESCRIPTION
Bullet Diameter: .321 in.
Bullet Weight(s): 170 gr.
Rifling Twist Rate: 1 turn in 16 in.
Test Barrel Length: 24 in.
Case Type: rimmed, necked
Case Material: brass
Primer Size: large rifle

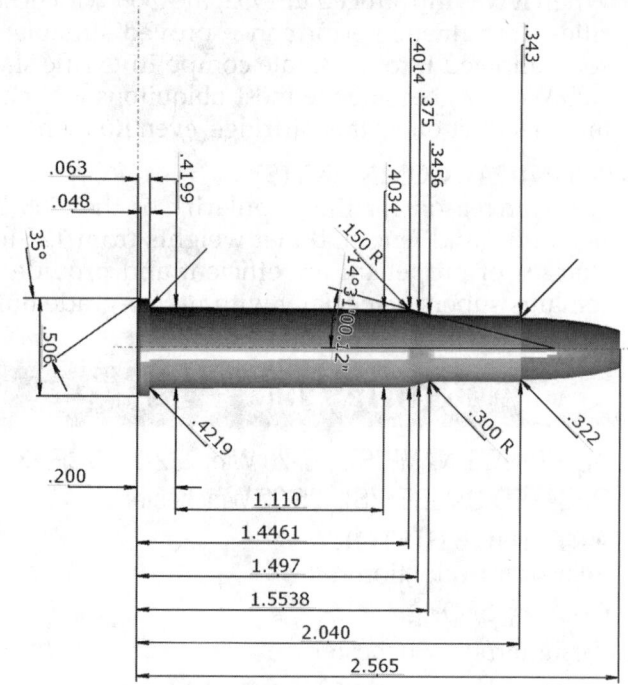

CARTRIDGE BALLISTICS
Max. Average Breech Pressure: 42,000 psi.
Max. Horizontal Range: 3,400 yds.
Max. Vertical Range: 7,500 ft.

Bullet Weight (gr.)	Bullet Type	Muzzle Velocity (fps)	Muzzle Energy (ft.-lbs.)
170	JSP	2,250	1,910

CURRENT MANUFACTURER(S)
Winchester, Federal, Remington

GENERAL COMMENT(S)
Winchester developed the .32 Winchester Special in 1902 in response to requests for a lever-action rifle cartridge of larger caliber and greater power than the .30-30 Winchester introduced in 1894. For many years, the .32 Win. Special was offered in lever-action rifles by Marlin and Winchester. Rifles in this caliber are no longer offered and the .32 Win. Special is fading away although all major domestic ammunition makers offer it.

TECHNICAL COMMENT(S)
The .32 Win. Special is basically a .30-30 Win. cartridge necked up to accept .321 inch diameter bullets as compared to the .308 inch diameter bullets of the .30-30 Win. The ballistic improvement offered by the .32 Win.

Special over the .30-30 Win. averages about 10-12%; not much by any standards. Although designed from the outset for smokeless propellants, the .32 Win. Special is constrained by the same case volume and modest chamber pressures of the .30-30 Win. cartridge. Introduction of the .32 Win. Special began a dispute over the value of the ballistic improvement that continues to this day.

.325 WINCHESTER SHORT MAGNUM

ALTERNATE NAME(S): .325 WSM
RELATED CALIBER(S): .300 WSM

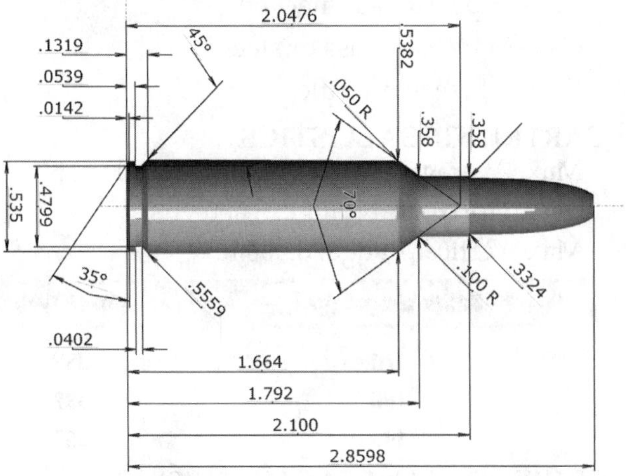

CARTRIDGE HISTORY
Year of Introduction: 2004
Country of Origin: U.S.
Designer(s): Winchester
Governing Body: SAAMI
Present Status: active

CARTRIDGE DESCRIPTION
Bullet Diameter: .323 in.

Bullet Weight(s): 180-220 gr.

Rifling Twist Rate: 1 turn in 10 in.

Test Barrel Length: 24 in.

Case Type: rimless, necked

Case Material: brass

Primer Size: large rifle

CARTRIDGE BALLISTICS
Max. Average Breech Pressure: 65,000 psi.

Max. Horizontal Range: 3,500 yds.

Max. Vertical Range: 7,000 ft.

Bullet Weight (gr.)	Bullet Type	Muzzle Velocity (fps)	Muzzle Energy (ft.-lbs.)
180	JSP	3,060	3,743
200	JSP	2,950	3,866
220	JSP	2,840	3,941

CURRENT MANUFACTURER(S)
Winchester

GENERAL COMMENT(S)
In naming this new cartridge, Winchester avoided the traditional American prejudice against 8mm cartridges by calling it the .325 WSM. Of course, a .323 inch diameter bullet is an 8mm bullet. One wonders what ballistic gap this new cartridge is intended to fill.

TECHNICAL COMMENT(S)
This cartridge is yet another in the series of Short Magnum cartridges from Winchester. Ballistic performance is on par with the .338 Win. Mag. and considerably better than the .35 Whelen and .350 Rem. Magnum.

8x57mmJS MAUSER

ALTERNATE NAME(S): 8x57mmJS, 8mm Mauser, 7.9x57mmJS Mauser
RELATED CALIBER(S): 8x57RmmJS, .30-'06 Spr., .308 Winchester

CARTRIDGE HISTORY
Year of Introduction: 1888 (J), 1905 (JS)

Country of Origin: Germany

Designer(s): German Military Commission

Governing Body: CIP, SAAMI

Present Status: active

CARTRIDGE DESCRIPTION
Bullet Diameter: .318 (J), .323 (JS) in.

Bullet Weight(s): 170-200 gr.

Rifling Twist Rate: 1 turn in 9.5 in.

Test Barrel Length: 24 in.

Case Type: rimless, necked

Case Material: brass or steel

Primer Size: large rifle

CARTRIDGE BALLISTICS
Max. Average Breech Pressure: 53,000 psi.

Max. Horizontal Range: 3,000 yds.

Max. Vertical Range: 8,500 ft.

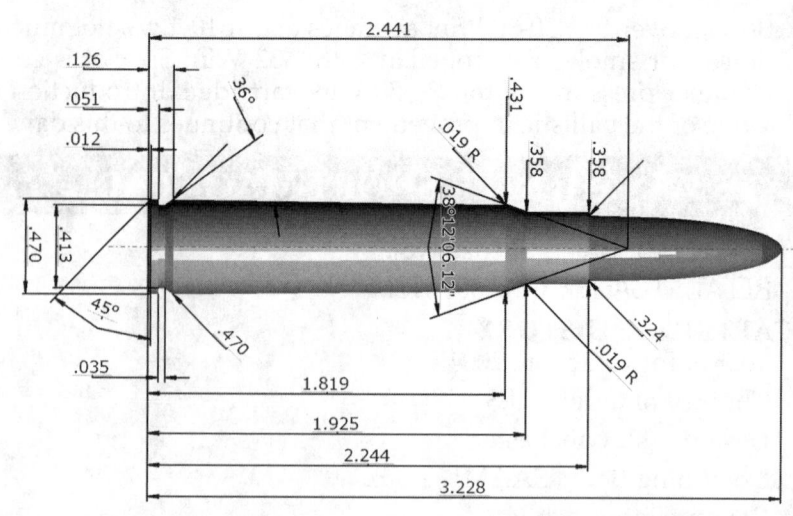

Bullet Weight (gr.)	Bullet Type	Muzzle Velocity (fps)	Muzzle Energy (ft.-lbs.)
170	JSP	2,360	2,102
180	JSP	2,625	2,755
196	JSP	2,595	2,871

CURRENT MANUFACTURER(S)
Remington, Winchester, Federal, Hornady, PMC, Sellier & Bellot, Prvi Partizan, Norma, DN

GENERAL COMMENT(S)
Without doubt, the 8x57mmJS Mauser cartridge is the grandfather of many modern cartridge that share head dimensions with it. These include the .30-'06 Spr., .308 Win., .300 Savage, and all their derivatives.

In Europe, the 8x57mmJS Mauser is the single most popular hunting cartridge. This is due to its suitability for any game in Europe including boar and moose. Many U.S. sportsmen have come to appreciate the game-getting qualities of the 8x57mmJS Mauser as well, due to the thousands of surplus Mauser M98 rifles imported into the country and sporterized into hunting rifles.

TECHNICAL COMMENT(S)
Domestic ammunition makers load the 8x57mmJS to a lower chamber pressure and muzzle velocity than do European ammunition makers. This is due to the product liability dangers inherent in firing a JS cartridge with a .323 inch diameter bullet in a J chamber for a .318 inch diameter bullet. U.S. ammunition makers also offer only a 170 grain bullet weight in this caliber.

8x68mmS

ALTERNATE NAME(S): 8x68mmS Magnum

RELATED CALIBER(S): 7x66mm vom Hofe Super Express

CARTRIDGE HISTORY
Year of Introduction: 1940

Country of Origin: Germany

Designer(s): RWS

Governing Body: CIP

Present Status: active

CARTRIDGE DESCRIPTION
Bullet Diameter: .323 in.

Bullet Weight(s): 180-234 gr.

Rifling Twist Rate: 1 turn in 11 in.

Test Barrel Length: 24 in.

Case Type: rimless, necked

Case Material: brass

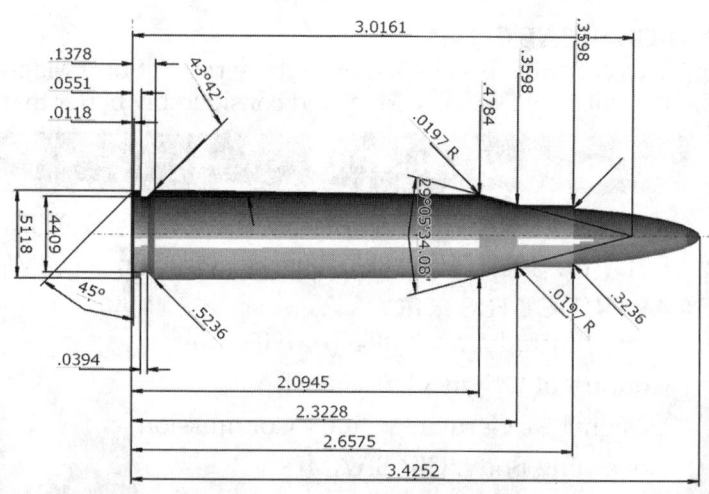

Primer Size: large rifle

CARTRIDGE BALLISTICS

Max. Average Breech Pressure: 63,800 psi.

Max. Horizontal Range: 4,850 yds.

Max. Vertical Range: 11,000 ft.

Bullet Weight (gr.)	Bullet Type	Muzzle Velocity (fps)	Muzzle Energy (ft.-lbs.)
180	JSP	3,100	3,841
180	JSP	3,250	4,221
187	JSP	3,150	4,120
200	JSP	3,000	3,996
224	JSP	2,850	4,040

CURRENT MANUFACTURER(S)

Dynamit Nobel/RUAG

GENERAL COMMENT(S)

Many cartridge historians ascribe the design of the 8x68mmS to E.A. vom Hofe, a prolific German cartridge designer of high velocity rifle cartridges active from the late 1930s until the mid-1960s. Undoubtedly, this is due to the fact that the head dimensions of the 8x68mmS are nearly identical to another vom Hofe cartridge, the 7x66mm vom Hofe Super Express. As 8mm cartridges have never been popular with American hunters, the 8x68mmS cartridge is almost unknown in North America. Despite this, it offers sufficient striking energy for any North American game, if you can find the ammunition.

TECHNICAL COMMENT(S)

Although it is a high pressure magnum cartridge, the 8x68mmS does not have a belted case. This makes it much easier to headspace and the case is just as strong as belted types. The 8x68mmS offers ballistics similar to the 8mm Rem. Magnum cartridge, however, it offers a greater variety of bullet weights than does the 8mm Rem. Mag. The "S" designates the cartridge's use of .323 inch diameter bullets.

8mm REMINGTON MAGNUM

ALTERNATE NAME(S): 8mm Rem. Mag.

RELATED CALIBER(S): .375 H&H Magnum

CARTRIDGE HISTORY

Year of Introduction: 1978

Country of Origin: U.S.

Designer(s): Remington

Governing Body: SAAMI

Present Status: active

CARTRIDGE DESCRIPTION

Bullet Diameter: .323 in.

Bullet Weight(s): 200 gr.

Rifling Twist Rate: 1 turn in 9.5 in.

Test Barrel Length: 24 in.

Case Type: rimless, belted, necked

Case Material: brass

Primer Size: large rifle

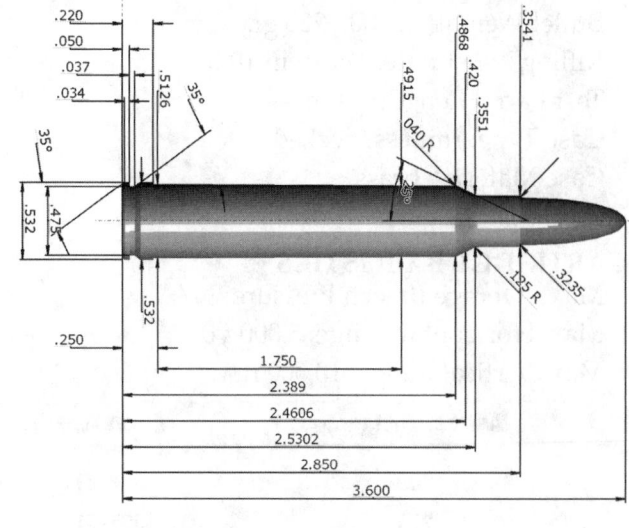

CARTRIDGE BALLISTICS

Max. Average Breech Pressure: 65,000 psi.

Max. Horizontal Range: 4,900 yds.

Max. Vertical Range: 11,000 ft.

Bullet Weight (gr.)	Bullet Type	Muzzle Velocity (fps)	Muzzle Energy (ft.-lbs.)
200	JSP	2,900	3,734

CURRENT MANUFACTURER(S)
Remington

GENERAL COMMENT(S)
When Remington introduced this cartridge in 1978, they became the first American ammunition maker to introduce an 8mm cartridge of their own design. Based on the full-length .375 H&H Magnum case, the 8mm Rem. Magnum also departed from Remington practice and preference for cartridges which fit in standard length rifle actions. Despite the fanfare at introduction, the 8mm Rem. Magnum has suffered from an old American malady; 8mm cartridges do not appeal to American shooters. Consequently, the 8mm Rem. Magnum has not been a best seller.

TECHNICAL COMMENT(S)
Many shooters feel the 8mm Rem. Magnum serves no ballistic purpose. Sandwiched between the various .300 magnum cartridges and the growing number of .338 magnum cartridges, the 8mm Rem. Mag. seems superfluous. European sportsmen have their well-established 8x68mmS cartridge which accomplishes the same purpose.

Remington offers only one bullet weight in this caliber. Does this predict imminent obsolescence? Time will tell.

.338 RUGER COMPACT MAGNUM

ALTERNATE NAME(S): .338 RCM
RELATED CALIBER(S): .300 RCM, .300 RSUM, .300 WSM

CARTRIDGE HISTORY
Year of Introduction: 2008
Country of Origin: U.S.
Designer(s): Hornady
Governing Body: SAAMI
Present Status: active

CARTRIDGE DESCRIPTION
Bullet Diameter: .338 in.
Bullet Weight(s): 200 - 225 gr.
Rifling Twist Rate: 1 turn in 10 in.
Test Barrel Length: 24 in.
Case Type: rimless, necked
Case Material: brass
Primer: large rifle

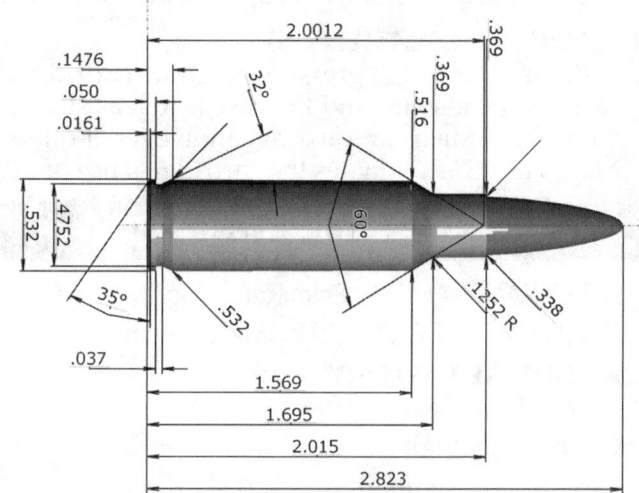

CARTRIDGE BALLISTICS
Max. Average Breech Pressure: N/A
Max. Horizontal Range: 5,000 yds.
Max. Vertical Range: 10,500 ft.

Bullet Weight (gr.)	Bullet Type	Muzzle Velocity (fps)	Muzzle Energy (ft.-lbs.)
200	JSP-BT	2,850	3,607
225	JSP-BT	2,710	3,669

CURRENT MANUFACTURER(S)
Hornady

GENERAL COMMENT(S)
Here is one of the latest new compact magnum rifle cartridges which are designed for hunting and can be chambered in most rifles with short action lengths (cartridges having an overall loaded length of 2.85 inches or less). As a class, all of the modern short magnums share a similar configurations, namely a rimless beltless case with a base diameter between .532 and .555 inches and a case length of between 2.03 and 2.10 inches. To date, .338 RCM is the only short magnum in .338 caliber.

TECHNICAL COMMENT(S)

The short fat case geometry of these beltless compact magnums is claimed to deliver higher muzzle velocity than equivalent cartridges of "standard" configuration while burning 10-15% less propellant. Additional claims include longer barrel life, less muzzle flash, less muzzle blast, and lower recoil. Undoubtedly, these claims are based on empirical evidence that this configuration allows a smaller amount of unburned propellant to be driven up the barrel behind the bullet. This results in higher efficiency allowing a smaller propellant charge and a shorter barrel.

.338 FEDERAL

ALTERNATE NAME(S): .338 Fed.
RELATED CALIBER(S): .308 Win.

CARTRIDGE HISTORY

Year of Introduction: 2005
Country of Origin: U.S.
Designer(s): Federal
Governing Body: SAAMI
Present Status: active

CARTRIDGE DESCRIPTION

Bullet Diameter: .338 in.
Bullet Weight(s): 180-210 gr.
Rifling Twist Rate: 1 turn in 12 in.
Test Barrel Length: 24 in.
Case Type: rimless, necked
Case Material: brass
Primer Size: large rifle

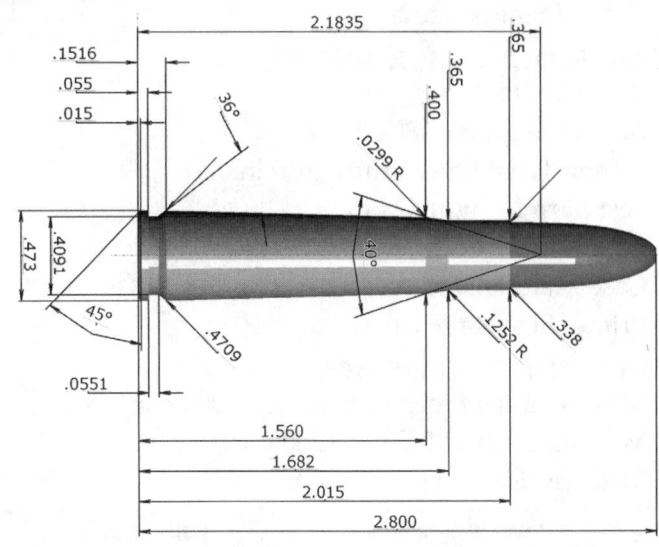

CARTRIDGE BALLISTICS

Max. Average Breech Pressure: N/A
Max. Horizontal Range: 3,800 yds.
Max. Vertical Range: 8,800 ft.

Bullet Weight (gr.)	Bullet Type	Muzzle Velocity (fps)	Muzzle Energy (ft.-lbs.)
180	JSP	2,830	3,200
185	JSP	2,750	3,105
210	JSP	2,630	3,225

CURRENT MANUFACTURER(S)

Federal

GENERAL COMMENT(S)

This is the first rifle cartridge to have Federal's name on it. Jointly developed with Sako, the .338 Federal is the first .338 caliber non-magnum rifle cartridge.

TECHNICAL COMMENT(S)

We may consider this cartridge as a .308 Win. case necked up to accept .338 inch diameter bullets. As this cartridge fits in short length rifle actions, it provides large caliber high performance capability in short actions for the first time. Federal claims the remaining energy levels are on par with the 7mm Rem. Magnum.

.338 WINCHESTER MAGNUM

ALTERNATE NAME(S): .338 Win. Mag.
RELATED CALIBER(S): .300 Winchester Magnum

CARTRIDGE HISTORY
Year of Introduction: 1958
Country of Origin: U.S.
Designer(s): Winchester
Governing Body: SAAMI, CIP
Present Status: active

CARTRIDGE DESCRIPTION
Bullet Diameter: .338 in.
Bullet Weight(s): 180-250 gr.
Rifling Twist Rate: 1 turn in 10 in.
Test Barrel Length: 24 in.
Case Type: rimless, belted, necked
Case Material: brass
Primer Size: large rifle

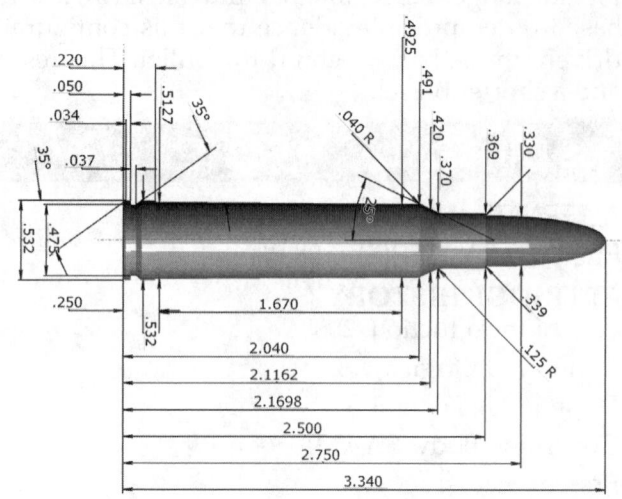

CARTRIDGE BALLISTICS
Max. Average Breech Pressure: 64,000 psi.
Max. Horizontal Range: 5,200 yds.
Max. Vertical Range: 11,700 ft.

Bullet Weight (gr.)	Bullet Type	Muzzle Velocity (fps)	Muzzle Energy (ft.-lbs.)
180	JSP	3,120	3,890
200	JSP	2,960	3,890
210	JSP	2,830	3,735
225	JSP	2,940	4,320
225	JSP	2,800	3,915
225	JSP	2,600	3,377
250	JSP	2,800	4,350
250	JSP	2,660	3,927

CURRENT MANUFACTURER(S)
Winchester, Federal, Remington, Hornady, Norma

GENERAL COMMENT(S)
After its introduction in 1958, the .338 Win. Magnum struggled to find an identity and purpose. In the minds of many shooters, hunting calibers went directly from .30 caliber to .375 caliber. Anything in between was an oddity. The advantages of the .338 caliber were simply not appreciated, which was undoubtedly due to lack of experience. So there it remained until 2000 when a sudden awakening to the usefulness of the .338 occurred for reasons not yet understood. Regardless, the .338 Win. Mag. entered this wave of interest from its position as an established cartridge of proven performance. Sales of this cartridge have risen steadily ever since.

It is very likely that American sportsmen have come to appreciate the value of the 200-250 grain bullets in the .338 caliber in lieu of bullets of the same weight in .358 caliber. One possible reason is the higher ballistic coefficient of the .338 diameter bullets. Another is the historical disinterest in large .358 caliber cartridges by American sportsmen.

TECHNICAL COMMENT(S)
As a .300 Winchester Magnum cartridge necked up to .338 caliber, the .338 Win. Magnum fits in standard length rifle actions. Despite the heavy weight of the .338 caliber bullets, they offer excellent ballistic performance due to their high ballistic coefficient. The .338 Win. Mag. may be considered the largest caliber suitable for long range hunting and target shooting.

.338 REMINGTON ULTRA MAGNUM

ALTERNATE NAME(S): .338 RUM
RELATED CALIBER(S): .300 RUM

CARTRIDGE HISTORY
Year of Introduction: 1999
Country of Origin: U.S.
Designer(s): Remington
Governing Body: SAAMI
Present Status: active

CARTRIDGE DESCRIPTION
Bullet Diameter: .338 in.
Bullet Weight(s): 180-250 gr.
Rifling Twist Rate: 1 turn in 9 in.
Test Barrel Length: 24 in.
Case Type: rimless, necked
Case Material: brass
Primer Size: large rifle

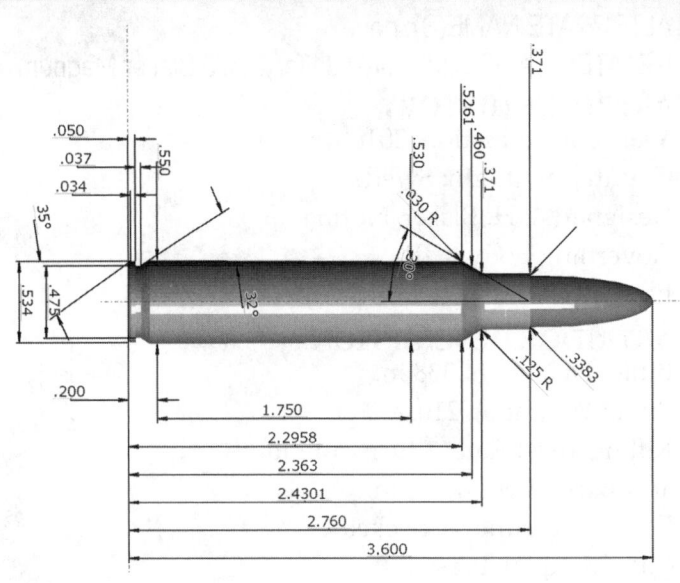

CARTRIDGE BALLISTICS
Max. Average Breech Pressure: 52,000 CUP.
Max. Horizontal Range: 7,000 yds.
Max. Vertical Range: 14,000 ft.

Bullet Weight (gr.)	Bullet Type	Muzzle Velocity (fps)	Muzzle Energy (ft.-lbs.)
180	JSP	3,280	4,300
210	JSP	3,030	4,280
225	JSP	3,020	4,555
250	JSP	2,860	4,540

CURRENT MANUFACTURER(S)
Remington, Federal

GENERAL COMMENT(S)
The .338 Remington Ultra Magnum cartridge is part of the Ultra Magnum series which was initially introduced in 1999 with .300 Rem. Ultra Magnum. That Remington would offer a .338 caliber in their Ultra Magnum cartridge line speaks loudly of the growing popularity of the .338 caliber. Sportsmen have discovered the .338 caliber to be an excellent choice for hunting large game at long ranges.

TECHNICAL COMMENT(S)
The .338 RUM cartridge is based on the parent .300 RUM cartridge necked up to accept .338 inch diameter bullets. Its overall length restricts it to chambering only in long-action rifles. The ballistic improvement of the .338 RUM over the .338 Win. Mag. is less than 10%.

.338 BLASER MAGNUM

ALTERNATE NAME(S): none
RELATED CALIBER(S): .404 Jeffery, .375 Blaser Magnum

CARTRIDGE HISTORY

Year of Introduction: 2010
Country of Origin: Sweden
Designer(s): H. Blaser, Norma
Governing Body: CIP
Present Status: current

CARTRIDGE DESCRIPTION

Bullet Diameter: .338 in.
Bullet Weight(s): 210-230 gr.
Rifling Twist Rate: 1 turn in 12 in.
Test Barrel Length: 24 in.
Case Type: rimless, necked
Case Material: brass
Primer Size: large rifle

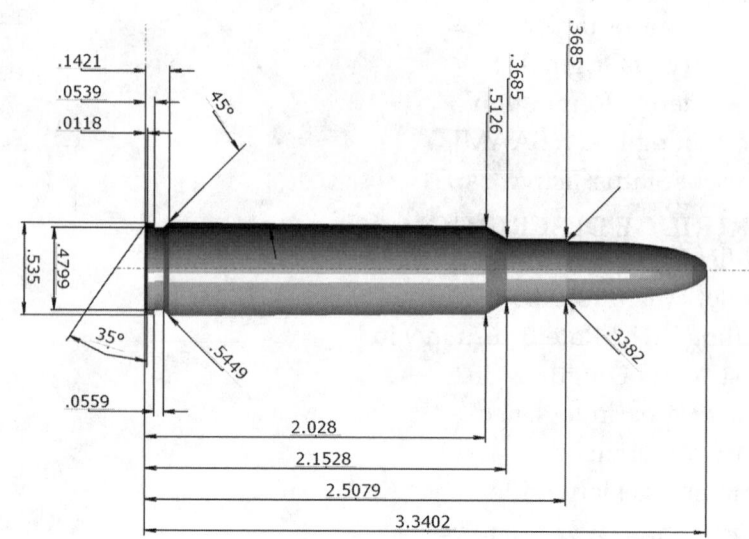

CARTRIDGE BALLISTICS

Max. Average Breech Pressure: 60,900 psi.
Max. Horizontal Range: 4,630 yds.
Max. Vertical Range: 10,050 ft.

Bullet Weight (gr.)	Bullet Type	Muzzle Velocity (fps)	Muzzle Energy (ft.-lbs.)
200	SP	3,050	4,130
210	SP	2,950	4,056
230	SP	2,820	4,068

CURRENT MANUFACTURER(S)

Norma

GENERAL COMMENT(S)

In the mid-2000s, the firearms and ammunition industry began a surge in the development of new cartridges with rimless, beltless cases designed to fit standard length rifle actions. This is an example of one of the recent European entries in this effort. It was designed by Horst Blaser, a noted gun designer, in cooperation with Norma, a division of RUAG. At this time, Norma is the sole manufacturer of ammunition in this caliber. Both Blaser and Norma will sell ammunition.

With the possible exception of the .338 Winchester Magnum, previous .338 caliber cartridges have not been outstanding marketing successes as they were considered too powerful for North American game. However, this may be about to change.

TECHNICAL COMMENT(S)

Based on the venerable .404 Jeffery cartridge, a classic rimless magnum design from 1909, the .338 Blaser Magnum slots slightly above the .338 Winchester Magnum and below the .338 Remington Ultra Magnum. The .338 Blaser Magnum offers approximately 15% more muzzle energy than the .338 Ruger Compact Magnum and 26% more than the .338 Federal. Will the .338 Blaser Magnum be too powerful for North American hunting conditions? You decide.

.35 REMINGTON

ALTERNATE NAME(S): .35 Rem.
RELATED CALIBER(S): .30-'06 Spr., .308 Win.

CARTRIDGE HISTORY
Year of Introduction: 1908
Country of Origin: U.S.
Designer(s): Remington
Governing Body: SAAMI
Present Status: active

CARTRIDGE DESCRIPTION
Bullet Diameter: .358 in.
Bullet Weight(s): 150-200 gr.
Rifling Twist Rate: 1 turn in 16 in.
Test Barrel Length: 24 in.
Case Type: rimless, necked
Case Material: brass
Primer Size: large rifle

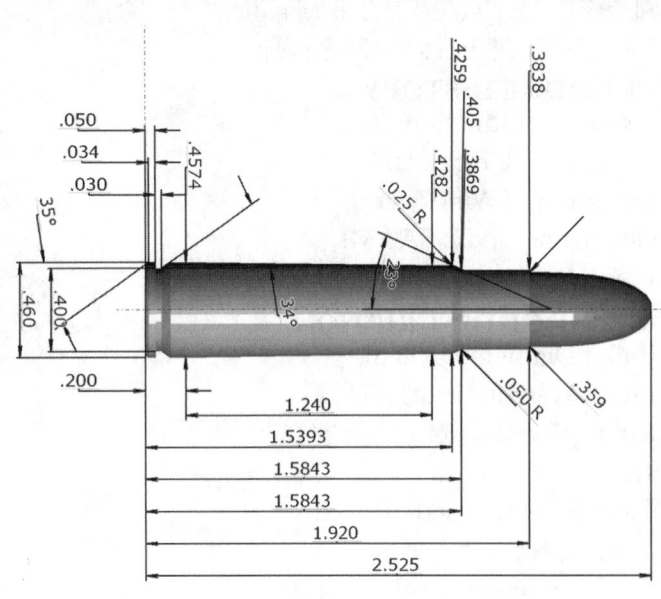

CARTRIDGE BALLISTICS
Max. Average Breech Pressure: 33,500 psi.
Max. Horizontal Range: 2,700 yds.
Max. Vertical Range: 6,000 ft.

Bullet Weight (gr.)	Bullet Type	Muzzle Velocity (fps)	Muzzle Energy (ft.-lbs.)
150	JSP	2,300	1,762
200	JSP	2,080	1,921

CURRENT MANUFACTURER(S)
Remington, Winchester, Federal, Hornady

GENERAL COMMENT(S)
Introduced in 1906 as part of a Remington product line of new rimless cartridges, the .35 Rem. is the only one of these calibers still in production. Its modest chamber pressures make it a suitable caliber for slide- and lever-action rifles. All major domestic ammunition makers offer this caliber. Many sportsmen prefer the .35 Rem. with its heavy bullet over the .30-30 Win. for hunting at close ranges in heavy brush.

TECHNICAL COMMENT(S)
Historically, the .35 Remington has been loaded with a 200 grain round nose bullet at the modest muzzle velocity of 2,080 fps. This is the same load offered by domestic ammunition makers today in deference to the tubular magazines used in rifles of this caliber. Only Remington offers a 150 grain semi-pointed bullet in this caliber.

Muzzle energy of the .35 Rem. cartridge is a 5% improvement over the .30-30 Win. with a 170 grain bullet. However, this modest advantage disappears at 100 yards where the .30-30 Win. retains 1,355 ft.-lbs. of energy compared to the .35 Remington with 1,280 ft.-lbs. Perhaps this is the reason for the declining popularity of the .35 Rem.

.356 WINCHESTER

ALTERNATE NAME(S): .356 Win.
RELATED CALIBER(S): .30-30 Win.

CARTRIDGE HISTORY
Year of Introduction: 1983
Country of Origin: U.S.
Designer(s): Winchester
Governing Body: SAAMI
Present Status: active

CARTRIDGE DESCRIPTION
Bullet Diameter: .358 in.
Bullet Weight(s): 200-250 gr.
Rifling Twist Rate: 1 turn in 12 in.
Test Barrel Length: 24 in.
Case Type: rimmed, necked
Case Material: brass
Primer Size: large rifle

CARTRIDGE BALLISTICS
Max. Average Breech Pressure: 52,000 CUP.
Max. Horizontal Range: 3,500 yds.
Max. Vertical Range: 7,000 ft.

Bullet Weight (gr.)	Bullet Type	Muzzle Velocity (fps)	Muzzle Energy (ft.-lbs.)
200	JSP	2,460	2,688
250	JSP	2,160	2,591

CURRENT MANUFACTURER(S)
Winchester

GENERAL COMMENT(S)
Winchester introduced this cartridge in 1983 in order to offer a modern large bore cartridge for lever-action rifles based on the .30-30 Win. cartridge. While this concept had merit, it did not find acceptance with American sportsmen. Guns in this caliber are no longer made and obsolescence seems just around the corner for this cartridge.

TECHNICAL COMMENT(S)
Think of the .356 Win. cartridge as a .30-30 Win. cartridge necked up to accept .358 inch diameter bullets at higher chamber pressures. As a result of the higher chamber pressures, ballistics of the .356 Win. are substantially better than the venerable .35 Rem.

.35 WHELEN

ALTERNATE NAME(S): .35 Whe.
RELATED CALIBER(S): .30-'06 Springfield

CARTRIDGE HISTORY
Year of Introduction: 1987
Country of Origin: U.S.
Designer(s): Col. Townsend Whelen
Governing Body: SAAMI
Present Status: active

CARTRIDGE DESCRIPTION
Bullet Diameter: .358 in.
Bullet Weight(s): 200-250 gr.

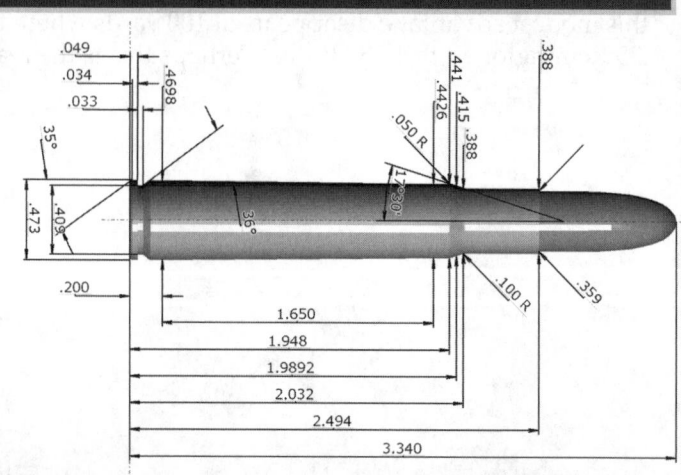

Rifling Twist Rate: 1 turn in 12 in.

Test Barrel Length: 24 in.

Case Type: rimless, necked

Case Material: brass

Primer Size: large rifle

CARTRIDGE BALLISTICS

Max. Average Breech Pressure: 52,000 CUP.

Max. Horizontal Range: 3,500 yds.

Max. Vertical Range: 7,000 ft.

Bullet Weight (gr.)	Bullet Type	Muzzle Velocity (fps)	Muzzle Energy (ft.-lbs.)
200	JSP	2,675	3,177
250	JSP	2,400	3,197

CURRENT MANUFACTURER(S)

Remington

GENERAL COMMENT(S)

Although Col. Townsend Whelen's name is appended to this cartridge, he worked together with James Howe to develop it. Their goal was a new cartridge for hunting large game based on the .30-'06 Spr. case. To accomplish this, they necked the .30-'06 Spr. case up to accept .358 inch diameter bullets. For over 65 years, the .35 Whelen remained a (much) respected wildcat cartridge until Remington introduced it into commercial production in 1987. Never a big seller, this cartridge may be headed for obsolescence very soon. Remington remains the sole manufacturer.

TECHNICAL COMMENT(S)

Although not a magnum, the .35 Whelen cartridge offers ballistic performance considerably better than the .30-'06 Spr., .35 Rem., and .444 Marlin cartridges. Consider the .35 Whelen a "semi-magnum" that fits into all standard length rifle actions and offers sufficient performance for all North American game.

.350 REMINGTON MAGNUM

ALTERNATE NAME(S): .350 Rem. Mag.

RELATED CALIBER(S): .300 H&H Magnum, 7mm Remington Magnum

CARTRIDGE HISTORY

Year of Introduction: 1965

Country of Origin: U.S.

Designer(s): Remington

Governing Body: SAAMI

Present Status: active

CARTRIDGE DESCRIPTION

Bullet Diameter: .358 in.

Bullet Weight(s): 200 gr.

Rifling Twist Rate: 1 turn in 16 in.

Test Barrel Length: 24 in.

Case Type: rimless, belted, necked

Case Material: brass

Primer Size: large rifle

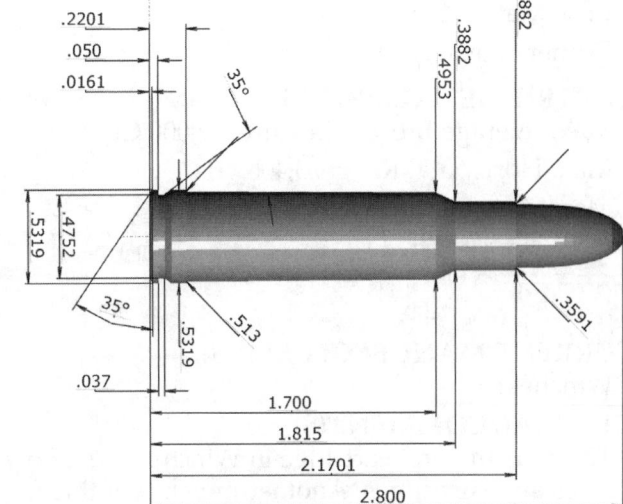

CARTRIDGE BALLISTICS

Max. Average Breech Pressure: 53,000 CUP.

Max. Horizontal Range: 3,500 yds.

Max. Vertical Range: 7,000 ft.

Bullet Weight (gr.)	Bullet Type	Muzzle Velocity (fps)	Muzzle Energy (ft.-lbs.)
200	JSP	2,775	3,419

CURRENT MANUFACTURER(S)
Remington

GENERAL COMMENT(S)
Before Remington made the .35 Whelen its own, there was the .358 Remington Magnum. A true belted magnum cartridge, a variety of Remington rifles including the M600 Carbine were chambered for this cartridge. However, the .35 Rem. Mag. never caught on with American sportsmen and the cartridge entered obsolescence. Then in 2007, Remington reintroduced the caliber to an appreciative press, sales took off, and oblivion was avoided.

Remington has been, and remains, the sole manufacturer.

TECHNICAL COMMENT(S)
The early failure of the .350 Rem. Mag. can be attributed to heavy recoil and the ballistic black hole of .358 inch bullets. When the .350 Rem. Mag. was fired from the lightweight M600 carbine, recoil proved brutally unpleasant. This caused the cartridge to earn a reputation as a "kicker" which contributed heavily toward its unpopularity.

In performance, the .350 Rem. Mag. fell in the very narrow ballistic gap between the .300 magnums and the .338 magnums. In practice, this left the .350 Rem. Mag. with no readily apparent application.

.375 WINCHESTER

ALTERNATE NAME(S): .375 Win.
RELATED CALIBER(S): .30-30 Win., .356 Win.

CARTRIDGE HISTORY
Year of Introduction: 1978
Country of Origin: U.S.
Designer(s): Winchester
Governing Body: SAAMI
Present Status: active

CARTRIDGE DESCRIPTION
Bullet Diameter: .375 in.
Bullet Weight(s): 200 gr.
Rifling Twist Rate: 1 turn in 12 in.
Test Barrel Length: 24 in.
Case Type: rimmed, tapered
Case Material: brass
Primer Size: large rifle

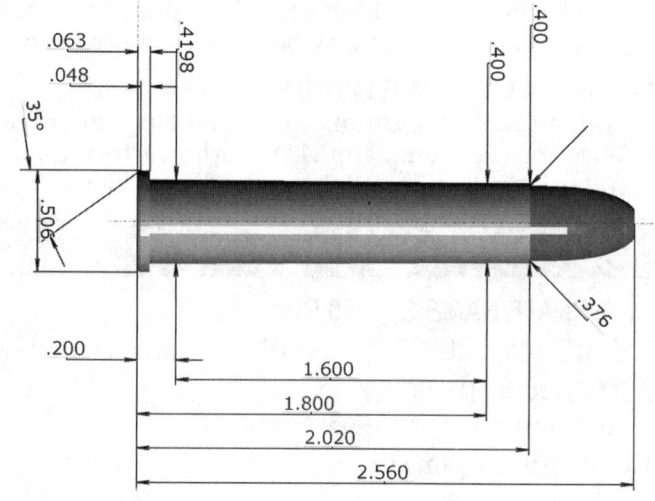

CARTRIDGE BALLISTICS
Max. Average Breech Pressure: 52,000 CUP.
Max. Horizontal Range: 3,400 yds.
Max. Vertical Range: 6,500 ft.

Bullet Weight (gr.)	Bullet Type	Muzzle Velocity (fps)	Muzzle Energy (ft.-lbs.)
200	JSP	2,200	2,150

CURRENT MANUFACTURER(S)
Winchester

GENERAL COMMENT(S)
This was the first cartridge in Winchester's effort to increase the variety and performance of their lever-action rifles and cartridges. Another member of this family was the .356 Win. which came along later. Much like the .356 Win., the .375 Winchester proved a market failure which did not strike a responsive cord with American hunters. Guns are no longer made in this caliber leaving one to consider that obsolescence for this cartridge is but a few short years off.

TECHNICAL COMMENT(S)
Like the .356 Win., the .375 Win. cartridge is based on a .30-30 Win. case necked up to accept .375 inch diameter bullets. The slight ballistic advantage offered by this cartridge was not sufficiently better than the .30-30 Win. to warrant purchase of a new rifle by most hunters.

.375 BLASER MAGNUM

ALTERNATE NAME(S): none
RELATED CALIBER(S): .404 Jeffery, .338 Blaser Magnum

CARTRIDGE HISTORY
Year of Introduction: 2010
Country of Origin: Sweden
Designer(s): H. Blaser, Norma
Governing Body: CIP
Present Status: current

CARTRIDGE DESCRIPTION
Bullet Diameter: .375 in.
Bullet Weight(s): 270-300 gr.
Rifling Twist Rate: 1 turn in 12 in.
Test Barrel Length: 24 in.
Case Type: rimless, necked
Case Material: brass
Primer Size: large rifle

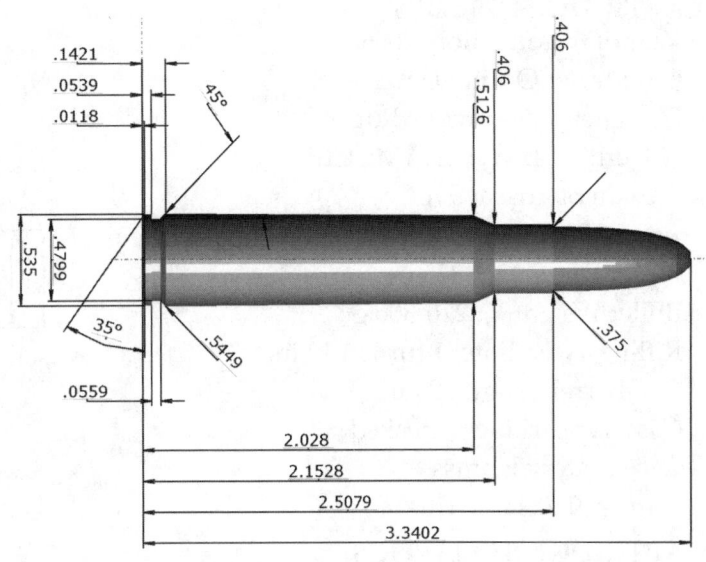

CARTRIDGE BALLISTICS
Max. Average Breech Pressure: 60,900 psi.
Max. Horizontal Range: N/A
Max. Vertical Range: N/A

Bullet Weight (gr.)	Bullet Type	Muzzle Velocity (fps)	Muzzle Energy (ft.-lbs.)
270	SP	2,760	4,565
300	SP	2,690	4,818

CURRENT MANUFACTURER(S)
Norma

GENERAL COMMENT(S)
In the mid-2000s, the firearms and ammunition industry began a surge in the development of new cartridges with rimless, beltless cases designed to fit standard length rifle actions. This is another example of the recent European entries in this effort. It was designed by Horst Blaser, a noted gun designer, in cooperation with Norma, a division of RUAG. At this time, Norma is the sole manufacturer of ammunition in this caliber. Both Blaser and Norma will sell ammunition.

With the exception of the .375 H&H Magnum and the .378 Weatherby Magnum, previous .375 caliber cartridges have not been outstanding marketing successes as they required magnum length rifle actions and were considered too powerful for North American game. However, this may be about to change.

TECHNICAL COMMENT(S)
Based on the venerable .404 Jeffery cartridge, a classic rimless magnum design from 1909, ballistics of the .375 Blaser Magnum are quite similar to the .375 Ruger cartridge. In muzzle energy, it slots above the .375 H&H Magnum and below the .375 Remington Ultra Magnum. Too powerful for most North American game? As with the .338 Blaser Magnum, the answer will be determined by individual hunters.

.375 RUGER

ALTERNATE NAME(S): none
RELATED CALIBER(S): .300 Remington Ultra Magnum

CARTRIDGE HISTORY
Year of Introduction: 2006
Country of Origin: U.S.
Designer(s): Hornady, Ruger
Governing Body: SAAMI, CIP
Present Status: active

CARTRIDGE DESCRIPTION
Bullet Diameter: .375 in.
Bullet Weight(s): 270-300 gr.
Rifling Twist Rate: 1 turn in 12 in.
Test Barrel Length: 24 in.
Case Type: rimless, necked
Case Material: brass
Primer Size: large rifle

CARTRIDGE BALLISTICS
Max. Average Breech Pressure: 65,000
Max. Horizontal Range: 4,500 yds.
Max. Vertical Range: 8,800 ft.

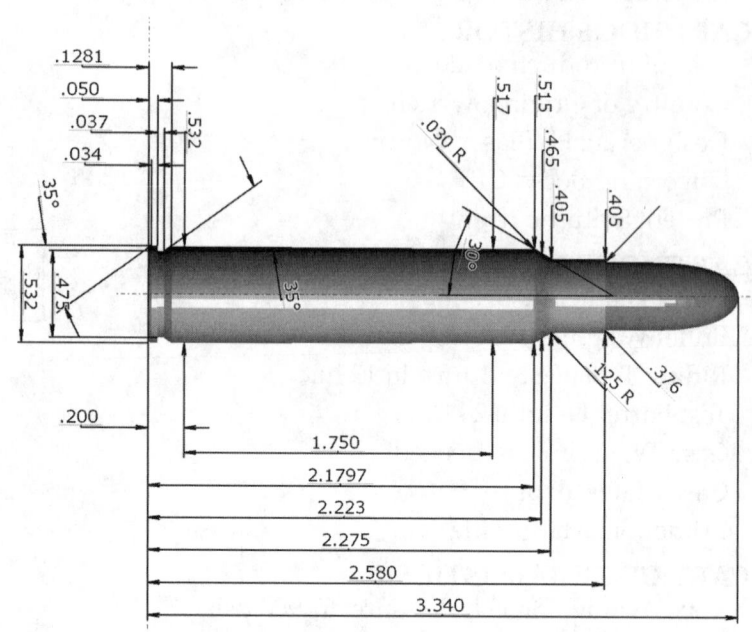

Bullet Weight (gr.)	Bullet Type	Muzzle Velocity (fps)	Muzzle Energy (ft.-lbs.)
270	JSP	2,870	4,937
300	JSP	2,705	4,873

CURRENT MANUFACTURER(S)
Hornady

GENERAL COMMENT(S)
Developed by Hornady and Ruger, this is the first cartridge to have Ruger's name on it. Hornady is the sole manufacturer of ammunition in this caliber.

TECHNICAL COMMENT(S)
The .375 Ruger is a beltless design which shares many key dimensions with the Remington Ultra Magnum series of cartridges. Unlike the Remington Ultra Magnum cartridges, the .375 Ruger is short enough to fit in a standard length rifle action. Ballistic performance of the .375 Ruger is approximately the same as the .375 H&H Magnum and the .376 Steyr.

.375 REMINGTON ULTRA MAGNUM

ALTERNATE NAME(S): .375 RUM
RELATED CALIBER(S): .300 Remington Ultra Magnum

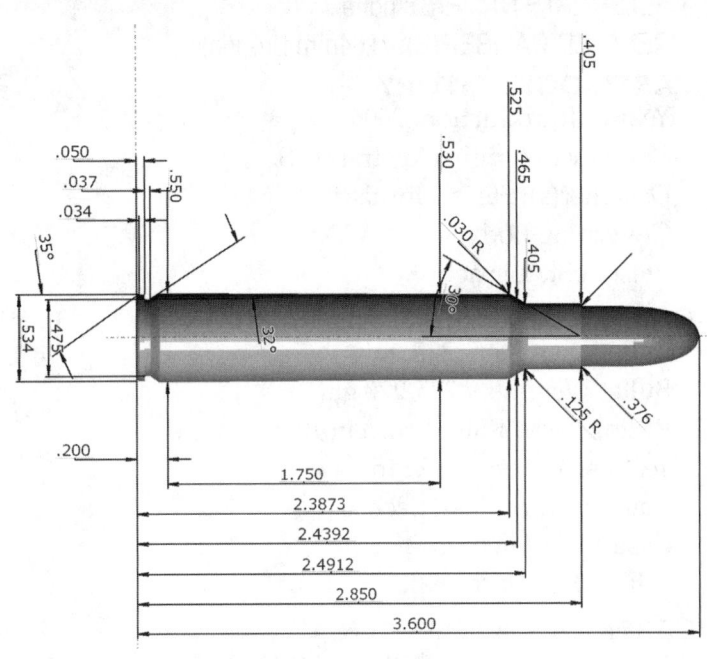

CARTRIDGE HISTORY
Year of Introduction: 2002
Country of Origin: U.S.
Designer(s): Remington
Governing Body: SAAMI, CIP
Present Status: active

CARTRIDGE DESCRIPTION
Bullet Diameter: .375 in.
Bullet Weight(s): 270-300 gr.
Rifling Twist Rate: 1 turn in 12 in.
Test Barrel Length: 24 in.
Case Type: rimless, necked
Case Material: brass
Primer Size: large rifle

CARTRIDGE BALLISTICS
Max. Average Breech Pressure: 65,000
Max. Horizontal Range: 4,500 yds.
Max. Vertical Range: 8,800 ft.

Bullet Weight (gr.)	Bullet Type	Muzzle Velocity (fps)	Muzzle Energy (ft.-lbs.)
270	JSP	2,900	5,041
300	JSP	2,760	5,073

CURRENT MANUFACTURER(S)
Remington

GENERAL COMMENT(S)
The Ultra Magnums are a new class of Remington cartridges. Introduced in 2002, the .375 RUM cartridge (and its sibling the .338 RUM) are based on the .300 RUM beltless magnum case.

TECHNICAL COMMENT(S)
Despite its imposing name, the .375 RUM is not in the same league as the powerful proprietary magnums such as those from A-Square, Weatherby, and Dakota. However, the .375 RUM does offer better ballistic performance than the classic .375 H&H Magnum.

.376 STEYR

ALTERNATE NAME(S): none
RELATED CALIBER(S): 7x64mm Brenneke

CARTRIDGE HISTORY
Year of Introduction: 2000
Country of Origin: Austria/U.S.
Designer(s): Steyr, Hornady
Governing Body: CIP, SAAMI
Present Status: active

CARTRIDGE DESCRIPTION
Bullet Diameter: .375 in.
Bullet Weight(s): 225-270 gr.
Rifling Twist Rate: 1 turn in 12 in.
Test Barrel Length: 24 in.
Case Type: rimless, necked
Case Material: brass
Primer Size: large rifle

CARTRIDGE BALLISTICS
Max. Average Breech Pressure: N/A
Max. Horizontal Range: N/A
Max. Vertical Range: N/A

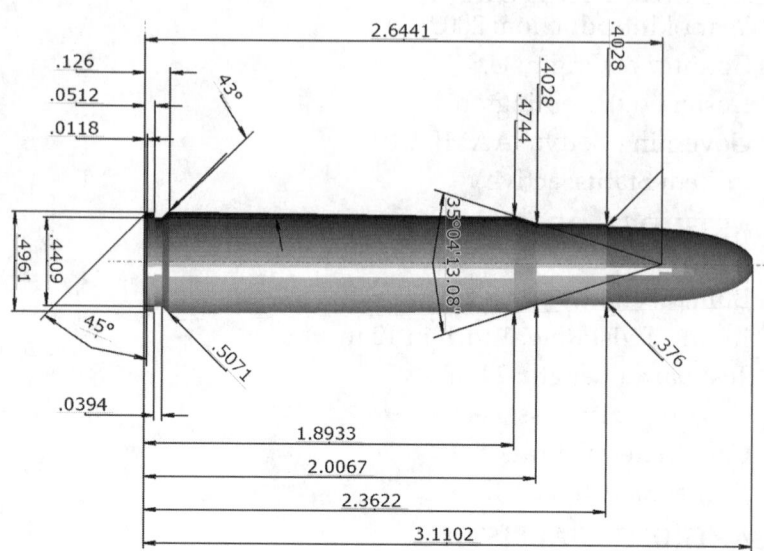

Bullet Weight (gr.)	Bullet Type	Muzzle Velocity (fps)	Muzzle Energy (ft.-lbs.)
225	JSP	2,600	3,377
270	JSP	2,600	4,052

CURRENT MANUFACTURER(S)
Hornady

GENERAL COMMENT(S)
This cartridge came as something of a surprise as it was the first new cartridge from Steyr in decades. Announced in 2000, it was developed by a triumvirate consisting of Steyr, Hornady, and Jeff Cooper. The stated application of this cartridge was for hunting cape buffalo and other dangerous game using Jeff Cooper's Scout Rifle. Steyr made the rifles and Hornady the ammunition. With Cooper's death, much of the steam seems to have gone out of this development.

TECHNICAL COMMENT(S)
The .376 Steyr cartridge is based on the 7x64mm Brenneke case necked up to accept a .375 inch diameter bullet. Although ballistic performance exceeds most non-magnum calibers, the .376 Steyr can not be considered a magnum.

.38-55 WINCHESTER

ALTERNATE NAME(S): .38-55 Win., .38-55 Ballard
RELATED CALIBER(S): N/A
CARTRIDGE HISTORY
Year of Introduction: 1884
Country of Origin: U.S.
Designer(s): Winchester, Ballard
Governing Body: SAAMI
Present Status: active

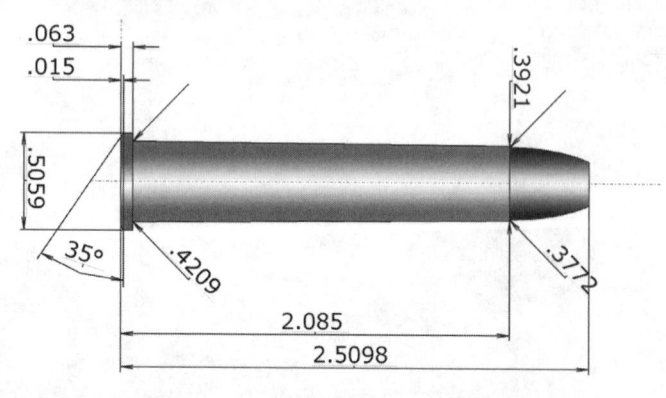

CARTRIDGE DESCRIPTION
Bullet Diameter: .379 in.
Bullet Weight(s): 255 gr.

Rifling Twist Rate: 1 turn in 18 in.
Test Barrel Length: 24 in.
Case Type: rimmed, straight
Case Material: brass
Primer Size: large rifle

CARTRIDGE BALLISTICS
Max. Average Breech Pressure: 30,000 CUP.
Max. Horizontal Range: 2,800 yds.
Max. Vertical Range: 6,500 ft.

Bullet Weight (gr.)	Bullet Type	Muzzle Velocity (fps)	Muzzle Energy (ft.-lbs.)
255	L, FN	1,320	987

CURRENT MANUFACTURER(S)
Winchester

GENERAL COMMENT(S)
This is a grand old cartridge originally developed by Ballard as a black powder target cartridge. Winchester, Marlin, and others chambered this cartridge in a wide variety of lever-action, slide-action, and single-shot rifles. The last new rifle for this caliber was made in 1940 with a few special runs in this caliber from Winchester in the 1990s.

Dead, but for the cowboy action crowd, the .38-55 continues life based on nostalgia. However, it remains historically important as the grandfather of the .22 Savage Hi-Power and .30-30 Winchester cartridges. Some tradition-minded sportsmen hunt deer with this cartridge, however it is barely adequate for the purpose.

TECHNICAL COMMENT(S)
Constrained by low chamber pressures, ballistics of the .38-55 Winchester cartridge are anemic. Even though it was designed for target shooting, ballistic performance of the .38-55 Win. belongs to an earlier age when heavy bullets, low muzzle velocities, and black powder were the norm.

9.3x57mm MAUSER

ALTERNATE NAME(S): 9.3x57mm
RELATED CALIBER(S): 8x57mm Mauser, 9x57mm Mauser

CARTRIDGE HISTORY
Year of Introduction: 1900
Country of Origin: Sweden
Designer(s): N/A
Governing Body: CIP
Present Status: active

CARTRIDGE DESCRIPTION
Bullet Diameter: .365 in.
Bullet Weight(s): 232-286 gr.
Rifling Twist Rate: 1 turn in 14.2 in.
Test Barrel Length: 24 in.
Case Type: rimless, necked
Case Material: brass
Primer: large rifle

CARTRIDGE BALLISTICS
Max. Average Breech Pressure: 37,710 CUP.
Max. Horizontal Range: 3,500 yds.
Max. Vertical Range: 7,000 ft.

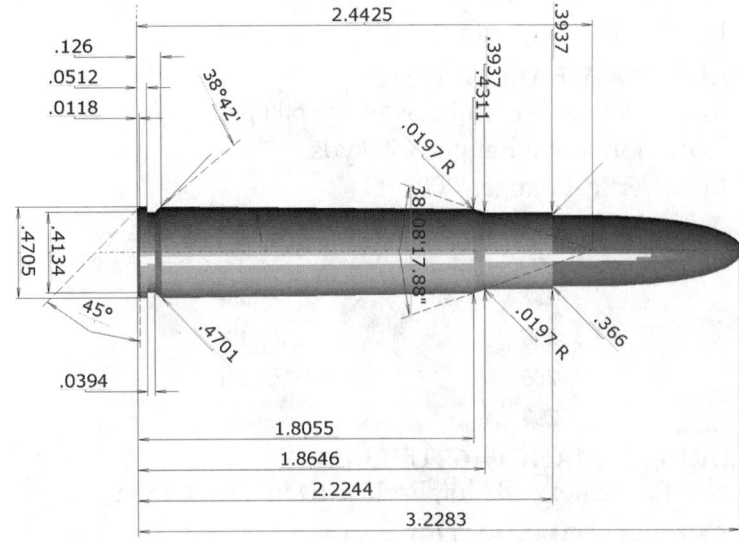

Bullet Weight (gr.)	Bullet Type	Muzzle Velocity (fps)	Muzzle Energy (ft.-lbs.)
232	JSP	2,360	2,875
286	JSP	2,065	2,714

CURRENT MANUFACTURER(S)
Norma

GENERAL COMMENT(S)
Immediately following the adoption of the 8x57mmJ Mauser cartridge in the late 1880s, Mauser set about developing a family of hunting cartridges based upon its case.

TECHNICAL COMMENT(S)
Using the existing basic cartridge saved time and money. In addition, the new cartridge would fit in the standard length Mauser rifle actions with few modifications. The 9.3x57mm cartridge with its large heavy 9.3mm bullet was an excellent choice for the German hunter looking for a cartridge with more power than the 8x57mm for hunting big game (but not dangerous game) in Africa. For European hunting, the 9.3x57mm Mauser found the shooter comfortably over-gunned. This cartridge gained an excellent reputation and continues to appeal to a tenth generation of hunters. This is very much a European cartridge. Most American sportsmen are unfamiliar with the 9.3x57mm Mauser.

9.3x62mm MAUSER

ALTERNATE NAME(S): 9.3x62mm
RELATED CALIBER(S): 8x57mm Mauser

CARTRIDGE HISTORY
Year of Introduction: 1905
Country of Origin: Germany
Designer(s): Otto Bock
Governing Body: CIP
Present Status: active

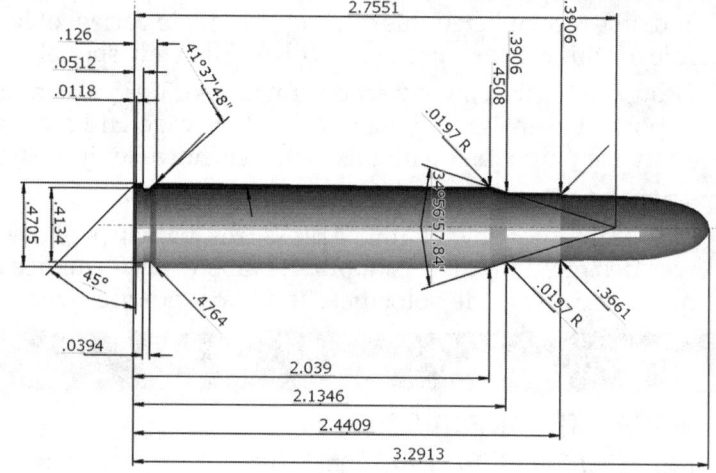

CARTRIDGE DESCRIPTION
Bullet Diameter: .366 in.
Bullet Weight(s): 232-293 gr.
Rifling Twist Rate: 1 turn in 14 in.
Test Barrel Length: 24 in.
Case Type: rimless, necked
Case Material: brass
Primer Size: large rifle

CARTRIDGE BALLISTICS
Max. Average Breech Pressure: 56,600 psi.
Max. Horizontal Range: 3,500 yds.
Max. Vertical Range: 7,000 ft.

Bullet Weight (gr.)	Bullet Type	Muzzle Velocity (fps)	Muzzle Energy (ft.-lbs.)
232	JSP	2,625	3,548
256	JSP	2,560	3,726
286	JSP	2,360	3,544
293	JSP	2,430	3,842

CURRENT MANUFACTURER(S)
Norma, Sellier & Bellot, Prvi Partizan, DN, Lapua

GENERAL COMMENT(S)
Developed in Germany, this cartridge quickly became a favorite of European sportsmen for large European game as well as African plains game. The 9.3x62mm held this position until the 1960s when the new magnums began to supplant it. Today, it remains in widespread use in Europe and many other countries as it is a non-military, purely sporting caliber. Among American sportsmen, this caliber remains nearly unknown.

TECHNICAL COMMENT(S)
Like so many other cartridges, the grandfather of the 9.3x63mm is the venerable 8x57mm Mauser. With an overall loaded length of 3.29 inches, the 9.3x62mm cartridge will fit in standard length rifle actions.

9.3x66mm SAKO

ALTERNATE NAME(S): 9.3x66mm
RELATED CALIBER(S): .30-'06 Springfield

CARTRIDGE HISTORY
Year of Introduction: 2002
Country of Origin: Finland
Designer(s): Sako
Governing Body: CIP
Present Status: active

CARTRIDGE DESCRIPTION
Bullet Diameter: .366 in.
Bullet Weight(s): 250-286 gr.
Rifling Twist Rate: 1 turn in 14 in.
Test Barrel Length: 24 in.
Case Type: rimless, necked
Case Material: brass
Primer Size: large rifle

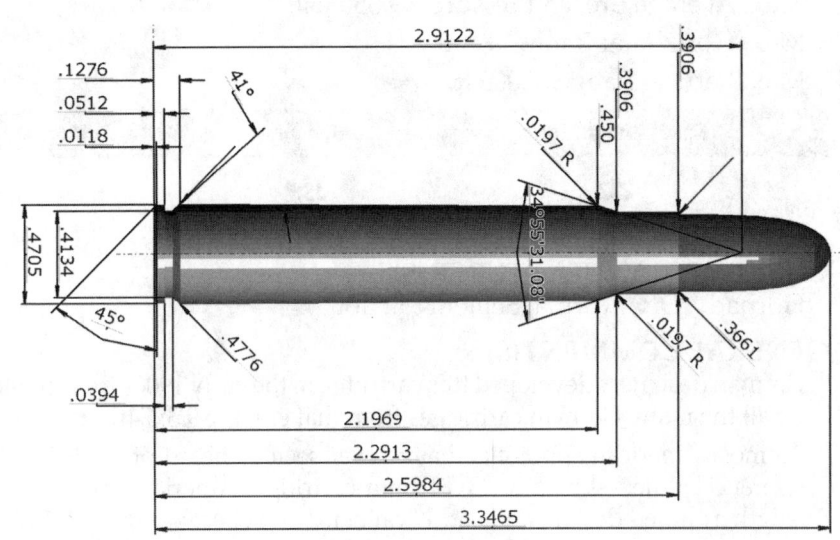

CARTRIDGE BALLISTICS
Max. Average Breech Pressure: 60,200 psi.
Max. Horizontal Range: 3,500 yds.
Max. Vertical Range: 7,000 ft.

Bullet Weight (gr.)	Bullet Type	Muzzle Velocity (fps)	Muzzle Energy (ft.-lbs.)
250	JSP	2,755	4,210
286	JSP	2,560	4,147

CURRENT MANUFACTURER(S)
Sako

GENERAL COMMENT(S)
This cartridge is unique in that it is a new design from a European source – in this case Finland. With its 9.6mm bullet, this cartridge is obviously aimed at the European market.

TECHNICAL COMMENT(S)
Although a modern design, ballistics of the new 9.3x66mm Sako cartridge are not substantially better than that of the well-established 9.3x62mm Mauser cartridge. This leaves one wondering why the 9.3x66mm Sako was developed.

9.3x74Rmm

ALTERNATE NAME(S): none
RELATED CALIBER(S): 9.3x72Rmm Sauer

CARTRIDGE HISTORY
Year of Introduction: circa 1900
Country of Origin: Germany
Designer(s): N/A
Governing Body: CIP
Present Status: active

CARTRIDGE DESCRIPTION
Bullet Diameter: .366 in.
Bullet Weight(s): 232-286 gr.
Rifling Twist Rate: 1 turn in 14 in.
Test Barrel Length: 24 in.
Case Type: rimmed, necked

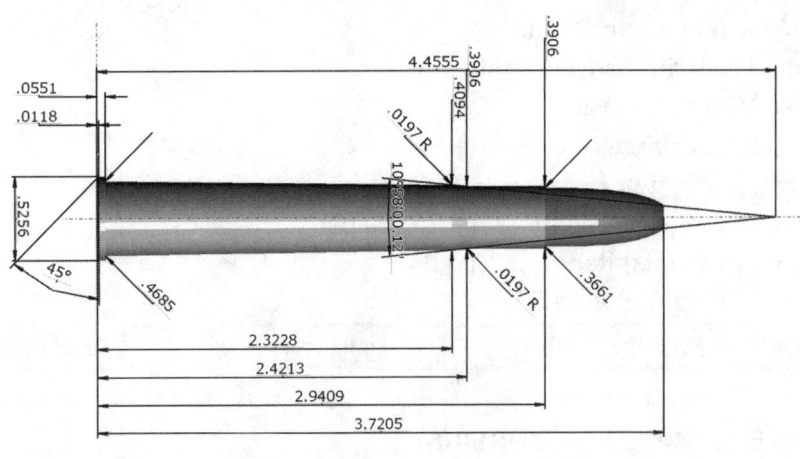

Case Material: brass

Primer Size: large rifle

CARTRIDGE BALLISTICS

Max. Average Breech Pressure: 49,350 psi.

Max. Horizontal Range: 3,500 yds.

Max. Vertical Range: 7,000 ft.

Bullet Weight (gr.)	Bullet Type	Muzzle Velocity (fps)	Muzzle Energy (ft.-lbs.)
232	JSP	2,560	3,374
286	JSP	2,360	3,530

CURRENT MANUFACTURER(S)

Hornady, DN, Norma, Sellier & Bellot

GENERAL COMMENT(S)

German designers developed this cartridge in the early 1900s to compete with the British 400/360 Nitro Express cartridge. Of all the many German cartridges from that era, the 9.3x74Rmm is one of the few remaining in production.

As most American sportsmen have never seen or heard of the 9.3x74Rmm cartridge, it remains beyond their frame of reference. When shown a 9.3x74Rmm cartridge, American hunters find it difficult to fathom the reason for the long length, rimmed design, and "odd" caliber. This is because the 9.3x74Rmm cartridge was designed for use in break-open combination guns used on mixed bag hunts, both concepts being completely unfamiliar to U.S. hunters.

TECHNICAL COMMENT(S)

Ballistically, the 9.3x74Rmm cartridge compares favorably with the .300 Win. Mag., the .35 Whelen and the .350 Rem. Mag. Its rimmed design precludes its use in repeating rifles while its length prevents use in most lever-action rifles. The 9.3x74Rmm is an effective choice for all North American game as well as all European game.

.405 WINCHESTER

ALTERNATE NAME(S): .405 WCF, 10.5x65Rmm

RELATED CALIBER(S): .35 Winchester

CARTRIDGE HISTORY

Year of Introduction: 1904

Country of Origin: U.S.

Designer(s): Winchester

Governing Body: SAAMI

Present Status: active

CARTRIDGE DESCRIPTION

Bullet Diameter: .411 in.

Bullet Weight(s): 300 gr.

Rifling Twist Rate: 1 turn in 14 in.

Test Barrel Length: 24 in.

Case Type: rimmed, straight

Case Material: brass

Primer Size: large rifle

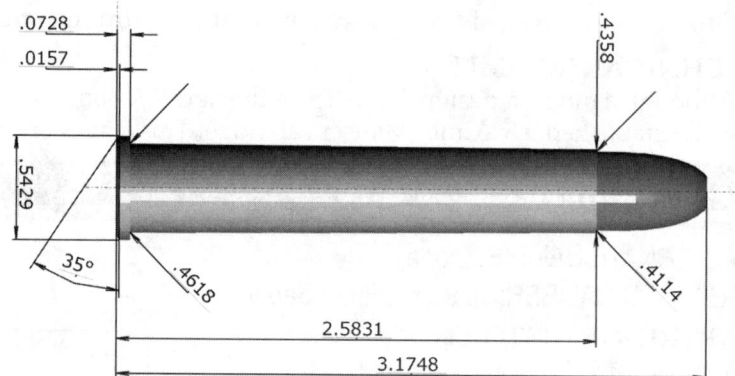

CARTRIDGE BALLISTICS

Max. Average Breech Pressure: 35,500 psi.

Max. Horizontal Range: 2,200 yds.

Max. Vertical Range: 4,500 ft.

Bullet Weight (gr.)	Bullet Type	Muzzle Velocity (fps)	Muzzle Energy (ft.-lbs.)
300	JSP	2,200	3,224

CURRENT MANUFACTURER(S)

Hornady, Winchester

GENERAL COMMENT(S)

Shortly after its introduction in the early 1900s, Teddy Roosevelt took a Winchester M1895 lever-action rifle with him to hunt African big game. After using the cartridge successfully on several species of game, Roosevelt pronounced the .405 cartridge "big medicine"– a phrase which still follows this cartridge today. More experienced African hunters did not share Roosevelt's enthusiasm for the .405 Win. Back in North America, the .405 Win. quickly gained a reputation for very heavy recoil.

Production life of the .405 Win. cartridge was short and quantities were always small. By 1940 the .405 Win. cartridge had become legendary and obsolete. Then, in 2002, the .405 Win. came back from the dead when Browning made limited runs of M1895 lever-action rifles in this caliber. Hornady made the ammunition.

TECHNICAL COMMENT(S)

While lacking the bullet weight, striking energy, and penetration for dangerous African game, the .405 Win. is an excellent caliber for North American game. Muzzle velocity and energy are constrained by the modest chamber pressures. This limits the effective range of the .405 Win. cartridge to about 100-150 yards.

.416 REMINGTON MAGNUM

ALTERNATE NAME(S): .416 Rem. Mag.
RELATED CALIBER(S): .300 H&H Magnum, .375 H&H Magnum

CARTRIDGE HISTORY

Year of Introduction: 1988
Country of Origin: U.S.
Designer(s): Remington
Governing Body: SAAMI, CIP
Present Status: active

CARTRIDGE DESCRIPTION

Bullet Diameter: .416 in.
Bullet Weight(s): 400 gr.
Rifling Twist Rate: 1 turn in 14 in.
Test Barrel Length: 24 in.
Case Type: rimless, belted, necked
Case Material: brass
Primer Size: large rifle

CARTRIDGE BALLISTICS

Max. Average Breech Pressure: 62,400
Max. Horizontal Range: 2,500 yds.
Max. Vertical Range: 5,000 ft.

Bullet Weight (gr.)	Bullet Type	Muzzle Velocity (fps)	Muzzle Energy (ft.-lbs.)
400	SP	2,400	5,115

CURRENT MANUFACTURER(S)

Remington, Norma

GENERAL COMMENT(S)

A sudden spark of interest in .416 caliber cartridges swept through American sportsmen in the late 1980s and early 1990s. One of the results was the new .416 Remington Magnum cartridge.

This new cartridge was aimed squarely at the African safari market due, no doubt, to rapidly increasing interest from a new generation of affluent hunters. The attraction of this cartridge was that it could successfully take any African game, so the hunter need take only one rifle with him. In fact, this concept had been around for many years in the form of the .416 Rigby cartridge.

TECHNICAL COMMENT(S)

While the large internal volume .416 Rigby cartridge is loaded to relatively modest chamber pressures, the .416 Rem. Mag. is a modern high pressure cartridge which uses chamber pressure to compensate for its smaller case volume. The .416 Rigby was loaded to moderate chamber pressures in order to compensate for the sensitivity of early smokeless propellants to high temperatures. With modern propellants, the .416 Rem. Mag. does not suffer from such a handicap. Both approaches seem to provide equally effective ballistics on paper. However, the higher chamber pressure of the .416 Rem. Mag. seems to produce greater perceived recoil.

.416 RIGBY

ALTERNATE NAME(S): 10.5x74mm
RELATED CALIBER(S): none

CARTRIDGE HISTORY
Year of Introduction: 1911
Country of Origin: Britain
Designer(s): John Rigby
Governing Body: CIP, SAAMI
Present Status: active

CARTRIDGE DESCRIPTION
Bullet Diameter: .416 in.
Bullet Weight(s): 410 gr.
Rifling Twist Rate: 1 turn in 16.5 in.
Test Barrel Length: 26 in.
Case Type: rimless, necked
Case Material: brass
Primer Size: large rifle

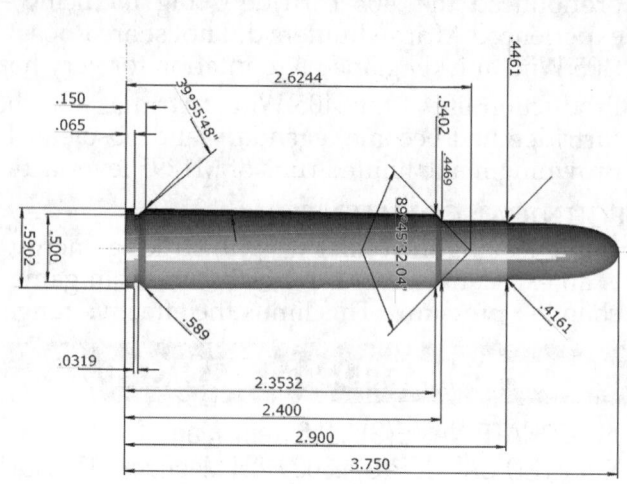

CARTRIDGE BALLISTICS
Max. Average Breech Pressure: 47,100 psi.
Max. Horizontal Range: 2,500 yds.
Max. Vertical Range: 5,000 ft.

Bullet Weight (gr.)	Bullet Type	Muzzle Velocity (fps)	Muzzle Energy (ft.-lbs.)
410	JSP/FMJ	2,370	4,990

CURRENT MANUFACTURER(S)
Federal, Hornady, Kynoch

GENERAL COMMENT(S)
John Rigby created a classic when he designed the .416 Rigby cartridge shortly after the turn of the 20th century. His brainchild was a fortunate blend of accuracy, reliability, and low perceived recoil, all at moderate chamber pressure. Word spread, and Rigby's new cartridge became a popular choice for hunting dangerous game with a bolt-action rifle.

Experienced African hunters advise that the .416 Rigby is the one caliber capable of reliably taking all species of dangerous African game. As they point out, an African safari with a .416 Rigby is a one-rifle hunt.

Today, modern hunters have rediscovered the .416 Rigby and rifles and factory ammunition in this caliber has to become available once again. Ammunition factories loading the .416 Rigby cartridge have resisted the urge to increase muzzle velocity and energy. The existing load is so well balanced, it needs no improvement.

Despite this, the .416 Rigby remains something of a rarity. Since its first sale, the number of rifles manufactured in this caliber total less than 12,000 units although many remain in service despite their age.

Undoubtedly, the .416 Rigby will remain the classic African cartridge as long as there is hunting in Africa.

TECHNICAL COMMENT(S)
Some of the features many hunters like about the .416 Rigby cartridge include the beltless case design, huge case volume, and low recoil (a big, soft push). The .416 Rigby cartridge case has served as the basis for countless wildcats, experimental designs, and proprietary cartridges. Here it is interesting to note that despite its noteworthy ballistic capabilities, the .416 Rigby is not a magnum cartridge and is not labeled as such.

.416 BARRETT

ALTERNATE NAME(S): .416 Bar.
RELATED CALIBER(S): .50 BMG

CARTRIDGE HISTORY
Year of Introduction: 2007
Country of Origin: U.S.
Designer(s): Chris Barrett
Governing Body: N/A
Present Status: active

CARTRIDGE DESCRIPTION
Bullet Diameter: .416 in.
Bullet Weight(s): 395 gr.
Rifling Twist Rate: 1 turn in 12 in.
Test Barrel Length: 32 in.
Case Type: rimless, belted
Case Material: brass
Primer Size: No. 35

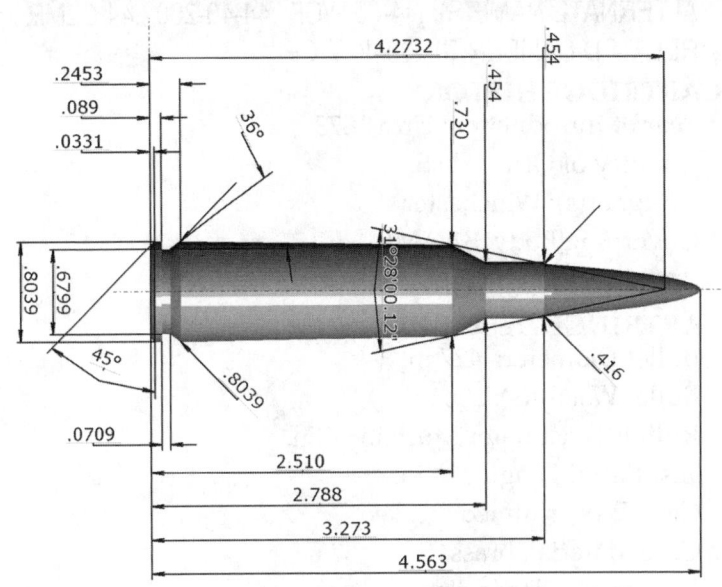

CARTRIDGE BALLISTICS
Max. Average Breech Pressure: 58,000 psi.
Max. Horizontal Range: 7,800 yds.
Max. Vertical Range: 17,500 ft.

Bullet Weight (gr.)	Bullet Type	Muzzle Velocity (fps)	Muzzle Energy (ft.-lbs.)
395	VLD Solid	3,300	9,551

CURRENT MANUFACTURER(S)
Barrett

GENERAL COMMENT(S)
The .416 Barrett was developed for use in areas where ownership of a .50 BMG caliber rifle is not allowed.

TECHNICAL COMMENT(S)
Developed exclusively for the Barrett series of large high performance rifles, the .416 Barrett cartridge is unusual in that it is based on the .50 BMG cartridge case shortened and necked down to accept .416 inch diameter bullets. Very few wildcatters work with a case this large due to the expense of the oversized press and dies.

To provide extraordinary down range ballistic performance, it is loaded with a solid brass very low drag spitzer boat-tail bullet weighing 395 grains. Approximately 204 grains of propellant launch this bullet at a muzzle velocity of 3,300 fps and 9,551 ft.-lbs. of energy. The .416 Barrett provides true 2,000+ meter ballistic performance, but it is not for the faint of heart!

.44-40 WINCHESTER

ALTERNATE NAME(S): .44-40 WCF, .44-40-200, .44 CLMR
RELATED CALIBER(S): .38-40 WCF

CARTRIDGE HISTORY
Year of Introduction: circa 1873
Country of Origin: U.S.
Designer(s): Winchester
Governing Body: SAAMI
Present Status: active

CARTRIDGE DESCRIPTION
Bullet Diameter: .427 in.
Bullet Weight(s): 200 gr.
Rifling Twist Rate: 1 turn in 36 in.
Test Barrel Length: 24 in.
Case Type: rimmed, necked
Case Material: brass
Primer Size: large pistol

CARTRIDGE BALLISTICS
Max. Average Breech Pressure: 16,000 psi.
Max. Horizontal Range: 2,200 yds.
Max. Vertical Range: 4,500 ft.

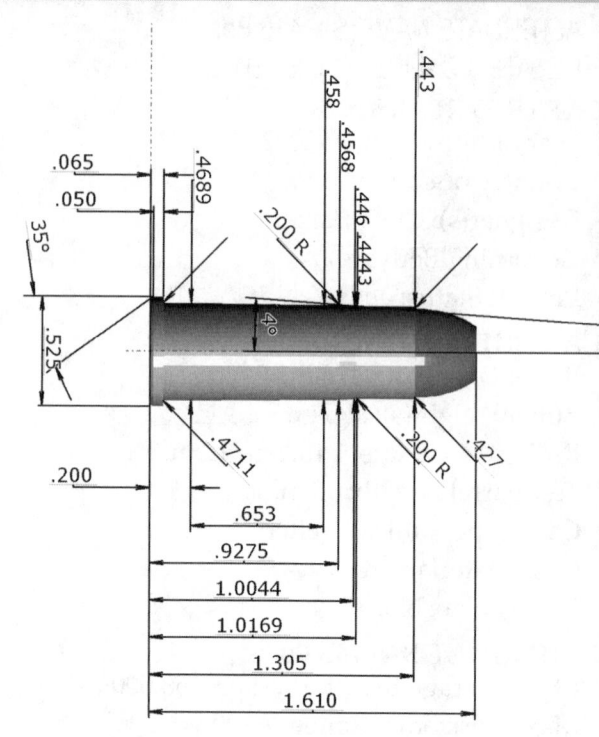

Bullet Weight (gr.)	Bullet Type	Muzzle Velocity (fps)	Muzzle Energy (ft.-lbs.)
200	JSP	1,190	629

CURRENT MANUFACTURER(S)
Winchester, Black Hills, Remington

GENERAL COMMENT(S)
This is the cartridge that won the West in the late 1800s. Rifles and revolvers were chambered for this cartridge so hunters, cowboys, and lawmen could fire the same caliber of ammunition in both guns. It has been said that the .44-40 WCF cartridge has killed more men, good and bad, than any other cartridge. While this is undoubtedly a legend, at close range the .44-40 Win. is indeed a reliable man stopper. Today, the .44-40 Win. cartridge has become overshadowed by the .45 Colt used by re-enactors, cowboy action shooters, and small game hunters.

TECHNICAL COMMENT(S)
While the .45 Colt has a straight-sided case, the .44-40 Win. has a shallow neck. Both cartridges offer broadly similar ballistics with the .45 Colt slightly better from revolvers and the .44-40 Win. better from rifles. Originally, the .44-40 WCF was a black powder cartridge loaded with 40 grains of powder and a flat nose lead bullet. Modern .44-40 Win. ammunition is loaded with smokeless propellant and a jacketed soft point bullet.

By modern standards the .44-40 Win. cartridge offers acceptable performance from a revolver but dismal ballistics from a rifle which makes it suitable only for small game hunting at best.

.444 MARLIN

ALTERNATE NAME(S): .444 Mar.
RELATED CALIBER(S): .38-55 Winchester, .30-40 Krag

CARTRIDGE HISTORY
Year of Introduction: 1964
Country of Origin: U.S.
Designer(s): Marlin, Remington
Governing Body: SAAMI, CIP
Present Status: active

CARTRIDGE DESCRIPTION

Bullet Diameter: .430 in.

Bullet Weight(s): 240 gr.

Rifling Twist Rate: 1 turn in 38 in.

Test Barrel Length: 24 in.

Case Type: rimmed, straight

Case Material: brass

Primer Size: large rifle

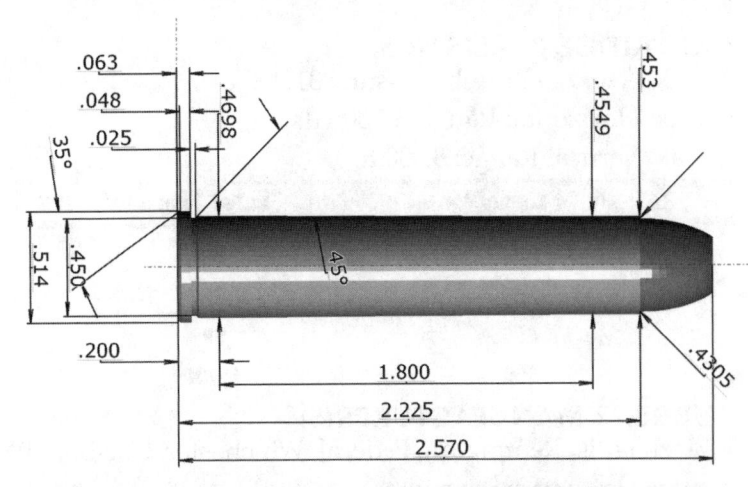

CARTRIDGE BALLISTICS

Max. Average Breech Pressure: 51,000 psi.

Max. Horizontal Range: 2,300 yds.

Max. Vertical Range: 5,000 ft.

Bullet Weight (gr.)	Bullet Type	Muzzle Velocity (fps)	Muzzle Energy (ft.-lbs.)
240	JSP	2,330	2,942

CURRENT MANUFACTURER(S)

Remington

GENERAL COMMENT(S)

By the mid-1960s, hunters discovered that the popular .44 Magnum caliber carbines lacked the power for taking deer and other medium game. As .44 caliber bullets were so popular, something needed to be done to improve ballistic performance of these bullets in rifles to make them suitable for hunting medium game. Such an opportunity presented itself in 1964 when Marlin reintroduced their M1895 lever-action rifle.

Teaming with Remington, the two companies designed a new cartridge to provide the improved performance required. Unfortunately, the devotion to .44 caliber bullets did not run as deep as expected and the .444 Marlin never reached its predicted sale potential. As a result, today it has become something of an anachronism.

TECHNICAL COMMENT(S)

Looking at a .444 Marlin, one is immediately struck by its similarity to the .45-70 Gov't. cartridge. However, the two cartridges are different and not interchangeable. Maximum average chamber pressure of the .444 Marlin is 51,500 psi while that of the .45-70 Gov't. is 32,000 psi. The .444 Marlin also is loaded with a much lighter bullet than the .45-70 Gov't. In fact, the bullet used is very similar to the one used in the .44 Magnum cartridge.

For hunting deer and medium game, the .444 Marlin is far more powerful than the .30-30 Win., .35 Rem., and .45-70 Gov't.

.45-70 GOVERNMENT

ALTERNATE NAME(S): .45 U.S. Army M73, .45 Trapdoor, .45-70-405, .45-70-500, 11.4x53Rmm

RELATED CALIBER(S): .38-56 Winchester, .44-100 Ballard, and etc.

CARTRIDGE HISTORY

Year of Introduction: 1873

Country of Origin: U.S.

Designer(s): Springfield Armory

Governing Body: SAAMI, CIP

Present Status: active

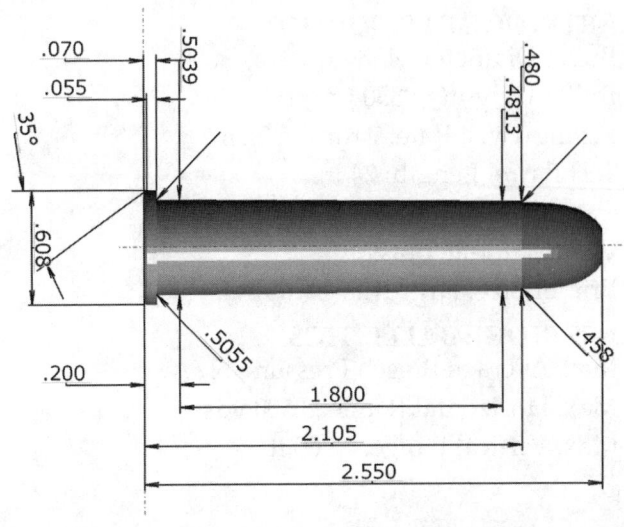

CARTRIDGE DESCRIPTION

Bullet Diameter: .458 in.

Bullet Weight(s): 300-500 gr.

Rifling Twist Rate: 1 turn in 20 in.

Test Barrel Length: 24 in.

Case Type: rimmed, straight

Case Material: brass

Primer Size: large rifle

CARTRIDGE BALLISTICS
Max. Average Breech Pressure: 31,900 psi.
Max. Horizontal Range: 3,500 yds.
Max. Vertical Range: 8,000 ft.

Bullet Weight (gr.)	Bullet Type	Muzzle Velocity (fps)	Muzzle Energy (ft.-lbs.)
300	HP	1,880	2,355
350	SP	1,800	2,519
405	SP	1,330	1,590
500	L, RN	1,150	1,468

CURRENT MANUFACTURER(S)
Black Hills, Remington, Federal, Winchester, Cor-Bon, PMC

GENERAL COMMENT(S)
In the late 19th and early 20th centuries, cartridges in military service often became popular calibers for hunting and target shooting. Such was the case for the .45-70 Gov't. Adopted by the U.S. Army in 1873, it continues in commercial production supported by innumerable deer hunters who appreciate its close range stopping power. As of the publication of this book, the .45-70 cartridge has long since entered iconic status as it celebrates its 137th birthday.

In the early 1900s, hunters discovered the .45-70 cartridge performed even better when the standard factory 405 grain bullet was replaced by a 300 or 330 grain expanding bullet. Military ammunition in this caliber had a tin-plated case.

TECHNICAL COMMENT(S)
While the .45-70 Gov't. cartridge itself remains a sturdy design, chamber pressures and ballistic performance must be governed by the weakest firearm in that caliber – in this case the "trapdoor" Springfield rifles and carbines. If one removes the trapdoor rifles from the equation, the .45-70 Gov't. could be loaded to .458 Winchester Magnum levels! But, such is not the case and the .45-70 is constrained by low chamber pressures, modest muzzle velocity, and rainbow trajectory. In its element at ranges of 100 yards and less, the .45-70 is an outstanding performer with manageable recoil and amazing terminal ballistic performance.

.450 MARLIN

ALTERNATE NAME(S): .450 Mar.
RELATED CALIBER(S): .458 Win. Mag., .300 Win. Mag.

CARTRIDGE HISTORY
Year of Introduction: 2000
Country of Origin: U.S.
Designer(s): Marlin, Hornady
Governing Body: SAAMI
Present Status: active

CARTRIDGE DESCRIPTION
Bullet Diameter: .458 in.
Bullet Weight(s): 350 gr.
Rifling Twist Rate: 1 turn in 22 in.
Test Barrel Length: 24 in.
Case Type: rimless, belted, straight
Case Material: brass
Primer Size: large rifle

CARTRIDGE BALLISTICS
Max. Average Breech Pressure: N/A
Max. Horizontal Range: 3,500 yds.
Max. Vertical Range: 7,200 ft.

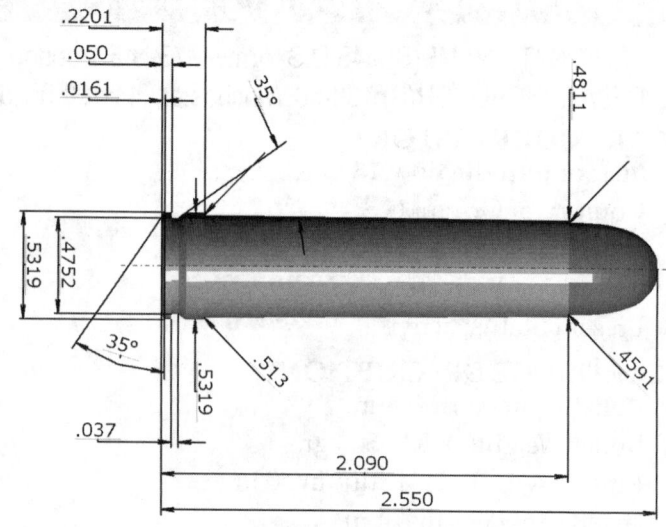

Bullet Weight (gr.)	Bullet Type	Muzzle Velocity (fps)	Muzzle Energy (ft.-lbs.)
350	SP	2,100	3,427

CURRENT MANUFACTURER(S)
Hornady

GENERAL COMMENT(S)
Enter Marlin once again, this time teamed with Hornady for another go at designing a high performance big bore cartridge for lever-action rifles such as Marlin's M1895. Introduced in 2000, Marlin (and Hornady) got it right this time. The .450 Marlin is a true high performance, big bore cartridge suitable for hunting all North American big game. As the new kid on the block, the jury remains out on hunter acceptance of this new caliber.

TECHNICAL COMMENT(S)
Consider the .450 Marlin as a short .458 Win. Magnum – nearly half an inch shorter to be exact. Of course with less case volume, the .450 Marlin does not have the ballistic potential of the .458. By way of compensating for this, the .450 Marlin is loaded with a lighter 350 grain bullet which restores muzzle velocity and energy.

A solid, modern design, however, does not guarantee commercial success or hunter acceptance. The track record of new cartridges designed to improve the modest ballistics of lever-action rifles can only be characterized as dismal. The .450 Marlin does not deserve such a fate.

.450/400 NITRO EXPRESS 3 INCH

ALTERNATE NAME(S): .400 Jeffery Nitro Express, .450/400 NE 3-in.
RELATED CALIBER(S): 450/400 Nitro Express 2 3/8-in., 450/400 Nitro Express 3 1/4-in., .475 Nitro Express 3 1/4-in.

CARTRIDGE HISTORY
Year of Introduction: 1902
Country of Origin: Britain
Designer(s): Jeffery
Governing Body: CIP
Present Status: active

CARTRIDGE DESCRIPTION
Bullet Diameter: .411 in.
Bullet Weight(s): 400 gr.
Rifling Twist Rate: 1 turn in 15 in.
Test Barrel Length: 24 in.
Case Type: rimmed, necked
Case Material: brass
Primer: large rifle

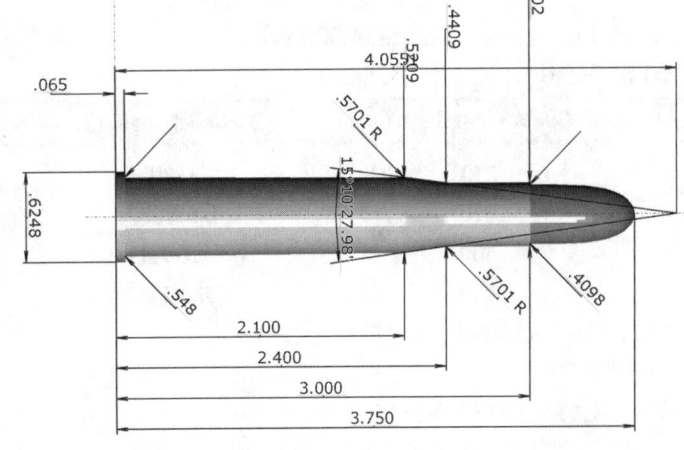

CARTRIDGE BALLISTICS
Max. Average Breech Pressure: 40,600 psi.
Max. Horizontal Range: 3,700 yds.
Max. Vertical Range: 7,850 ft.

Bullet Weight (gr.)	Bullet Type	Muzzle Velocity (fps)	Muzzle Energy (ft.-lbs.)
400	SP/FMJ	2,100	3,920

CURRENT MANUFACTURER(S)
Hornady, A-Square, Kynoch

GENERAL COMMENT(S)
W.J. Jeffery & Co. developed the .450/400 Nitro Express 3 inch after reports that the .450/400 Nitro Express 2 3/8-in. length cartridges cases suffered from extraction problems in the field. This cartridge quickly became a popular choice for hunting all types of dangerous game. It remains so to this day.

TECHNICAL COMMENT(S)
Unlike many other nitro express cartridges, the .450 Jeffrey Nitro Express 3 inch was not converted from black powder as it was designed for and loaded with smokeless propellant from the outset. Manufacturers of this cartridge take great pains to assure that their ammunition shoots to the point of aim for the regulated sights of the double-barrel rifles chambered for this cartridge.

.450/400 NITRO EXPRESS 2 3/8 IN., .450/400 BLACK POWDER EXPRESS (BPE) 2 3/8 IN.

ALTERNATE NAME(S): .450/400 Nitro for Black 2 3/8 in.
RELATED CALIBER(S): .450 BPE 3 1/4 in.

CARTRIDGE HISTORY
Year of Introduction: 1880 (black powder), 1899 (smokeless)
Country of Origin: Britain
Designer(s): N/A
Governing Body: none
Present Status: active

CARTRIDGE DESCRIPTION
Bullet Diameter: .407 in.
Bullet Weight(s): 210-400 gr.
Rifling Twist Rate: N/A
Test Barrel Length: 24 in.
Case Type: rimmed, necked
Case Material: brass
Primer: large rifle

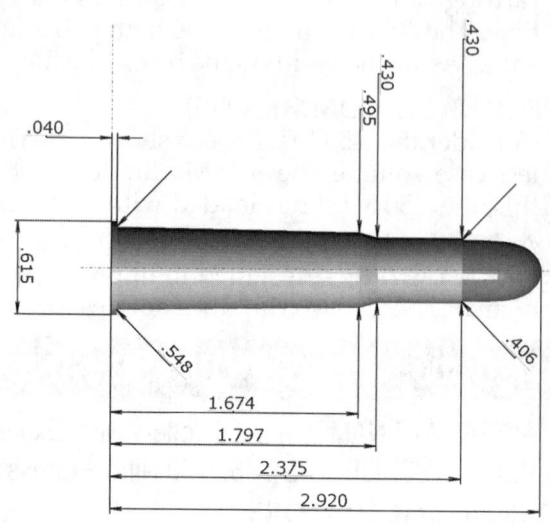

CARTRIDGE BALLISTICS
Max. Average Breech Pressure: 32,000 psi.
Max. Horizontal Range: 4,300 yds.
Max. Vertical Range: 8,950 ft.

Bullet Weight (gr.)	Bullet Type	Muzzle Velocity (fps)	Muzzle Energy (ft.-lbs.)
210	L-RN	1,800	1,511 (BP-est.)
270	L-RN/JSP	1,650	1,630 (Nitro for Black)
300	JSP-FMJ	2,200	3,224 (Nitro)
400	JSP-FMJ	2,125	4,011 (Nitro-Kynamco)

CURRENT MANUFACTURER(S)
Kynamco

GENERAL COMMENT(S)
These cartridges were intended for hunting dangerous African game. By modern standards, they appear underpowered for such a task, however, they were considered very effective by the standards of the 1880s when they were designed. They achieved a modest popular following, but were eclipsed by their more powerful brethren.

TECHNICAL COMMENT(S)
The .450/400 2 3/8-in. cartridge case was the shortest of the .450/400 series. Basically, it is the .450 3 1/4-in. BPE case shortened and necked down. Originally loaded with black powder, in the late 1890s the .450/400 2 2/8-in. cartridge transitioned to smokeless propellants. When this was done, bullet weights were increased. Even with smokeless propellants, maximum average chamber pressures were kept very low.

.450/400 NITRO EXPRESS 3 1/4 IN., .450/400 BLACK POWDER EXPRESS 3 1/4 IN.

ALTERNATE NAME(S):.450/400 Nitro for Black Express 3 1/4 in.
RELATED CALIBER(S): .450 Nitro
    Express 3 1/4 in.

CARTRIDGE HISTORY
Year of Introduction: circa late 1800s
Country of Origin: Britain
Designer(s): N/A
Governing Body: none
Present Status: active

CARTRIDGE DESCRIPTION
Bullet Diameter:. 405 in.
Bullet Weight(s): 400 gr.
Rifling Twist Rate: 1 turn in 15 in.
Test Barrel Length: 24 in.
Case Type: rimmed, necked
Case Material: brass
Primer: large rifle

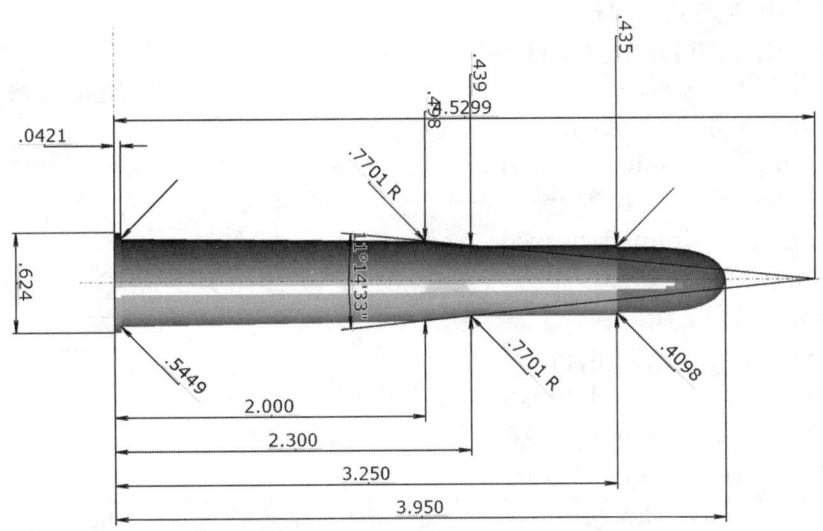

CARTRIDGE BALLISTICS
Max. Average Breech Pressure: 22,000 psi. (black powder), 33,000 psi. (smokeless powder)
Max. Horizontal Range: 4,300 yds.
Max. Vertical Range: 9,000 ft.

Bullet Weight (gr.)	Bullet Type	Muzzle Velocity (fps)	Muzzle Energy (ft.-lbs.)
270	JSP	1,975	2,340 (BP)
310	L-RN	1,800	2,240 (BP)
325	JSP	1,775	2,280 (BP)
365	L-RN	1,700	2,340 (BP)
400	JSP/FMJ	2,150	4,100 (Nitro)

CURRENT MANUFACTURER(S)
Kynamco

GENERAL COMMENT(S)
This was another large bore hunting cartridge which developed sticking cases and hard extraction problems when it transitioned to smokeless propellants. Later variants, such as the .400 Jeffery, had redesigned cases and thickened rims among other changes to resolve extraction problems. Eventually, using thicker harder brass for such cartridges was able to solve this nagging problem.The .450-400 NE 3 1/4 in. survives in the Kynamco product line.

TECHNICAL COMMENT(S)
Many experienced African hunters preferred this cartridge with FMJ bullets as they reliably penetrated dangerous game. Not so with the copper tube jacketed bullets. These were not liked because of their weak construction and lack of reliable penetration. The soft-point bullets used in nitro express loads were much-improved and more reliable. An important point in using these calibers is to match the cartridge to the barrel of your rifle. Rifles designed for black powder express loads with lead bullets had deeper rifling grooves in the barrel, while rifles designed for nitro express cartridges had shallower grooves.

.450 No. 2 NITRO EXPRESS 3 1/2 IN.

ALTERNATE NAME(S): .450 No. NE
RELATED CALIBER(S): .360 No.2 Nitro Express, .470 Nitro Express, .475 No.2 Nitro Express, .500/450 Magnum
    Express

CARTRIDGE HISTORY
Year of Introduction: 1900
Country of Origin: Britain
Designer(s): Eley
Governing Body: none
Present Status: active

CARTRIDGE DESCRIPTION
Bullet Diameter: .458 in.
Bullet Weight(s): 480 gr.
Rifling Twist Rate: 1 turn in 15 in.
Test Barrel Length: 24 in.
Case Type: rimmed, necked
Case Material: brass
Primer: large rifle

CARTRIDGE BALLISTICS
Max. Average Breech Pressure: 26,000 psi.
Max. Horizontal Range: 4,600 yds.
Max. Vertical Range: 9,500 ft.

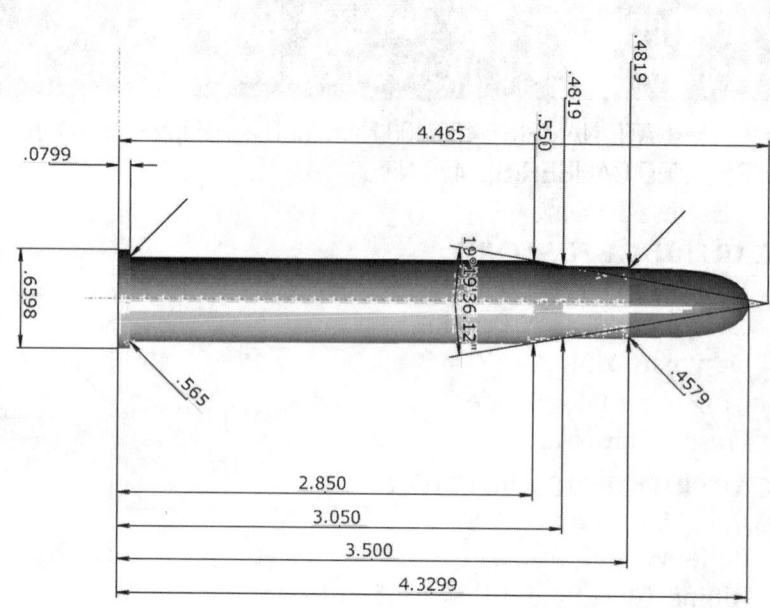

Bullet Weight (gr.)	Bullet Type	Muzzle Velocity (fps)	Muzzle Energy (ft.-lbs.)
480	JSP/FMJ	2,175	5,050

CURRENT MANUFACTURER(S)
Kynamco

GENERAL COMMENT(S)
Smokeless powder was still new and case technology still developing when the .450 No.2 NE 3 1/2 in. cartridge was designed. Earlier, problems had been encountered with nitro express cartridges sticking in the chamber and causing hard extraction in double rifles. Naturally, this was an unpleasant and potentially dangerous occurrence in the field.

TECHNICAL COMMENT(S)
Eley took several steps with this cartridge to solve the sticking case problem that occurred with other nitro express calibers. First, they reduced the chamber pressure by extending the .500/450 BPE case .50 inches to increase case volume. Second, they increased the rim thickness and shoulder angle to aid extraction. Third (and later), they increased the thickness and hardness of the case. Otherwise, ballistics of the .450 No. 2 NE were significantly better than the .500/450 BPE and the same as the .500/450 Nitro Express 3 1/4 in. (H&H), although the two cartridges were not interchangeable.

.450 BUSHMASTER

ALTERNATE NAME(S): 11.5x57mm
RELATED CALIBER(S): .308 Win.

CARTRIDGE HISTORY
Year of Introduction: 2008
Country of Origin: U.S.
Designer(s): Tom LeGendre
Governing Body: SAAMI
Present Status: active

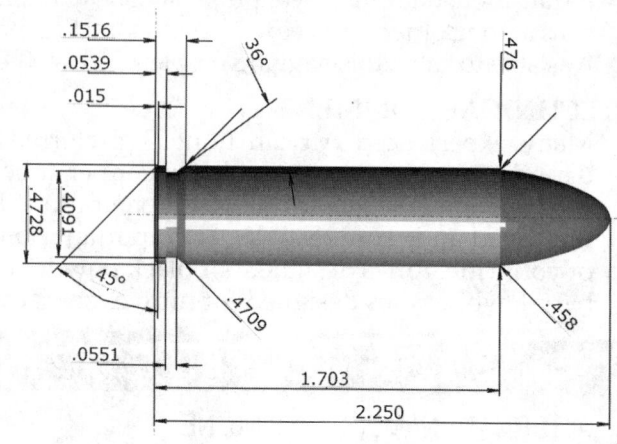

CARTRIDGE DESCRIPTION
Bullet Diameter: .452 in.
Bullet Weight(s): 250 gr.
Rifling Twist Rate: N/A
Test Barrel Length: 20 in.

Case Type: rebated rimless, tapered
Case Material: brass

CARTRIDGE BALLISTICS
Max. Average Breech Pressure: N/A
Max. Horizontal Range: 3,200 yds.
Max. Vertical Range: 6,000 ft.

Bullet Weight (gr.)	Bullet Type	Muzzle Velocity (fps)	Muzzle Energy (ft.-lbs.)
250	FIX FMJ	2,200	2,686

CURRENT MANUFACTURER(S)
Hornady

GENERAL COMMENT(S)
A recent addition to Hornady's product line, the .450 Bushmaster cartridge brings big bore hunting performance to the AR-15. Nicknamed "The Thumper," the .450 Bushmaster is capable to taking any North American game. It has proven an especially good choice for bear.

TECHNICAL COMMENT(S)
A rebated rim and 2.250 inch overall length allows the .450 Bushmaster to cycle through an AR-15 rifle action and feed through modified 5.56x45mm magazines.

.450 BLACK POWDER EXPRESS 3 1/4 IN., .450 NITRO EXPRESS 3 1/4 IN.

ALTERNATE NAME(S): .450 Nitro Express for Black Powder 3 1/4 in. .450/400 Magnum Nitro Express 3 1/4 in.
RELATED CALIBER(S): .369 Purdey, .450/400 Nitro Express 3 1/4 in., .400 Jeffery

CARTRIDGE HISTORY
Year of Introduction: 1898 (Nitro Express)
Country of Origin: Britain
Designer(s): John Rigby
Governing Body: CIP
Present Status: active

CARTRIDGE DESCRIPTION
Bullet Diameter: .458 in.
Bullet Weight(s): 480 gr.
Rifling Twist Rate: N/A
Test Barrel Length: 24 in.
Case Type: rimmed, straight
Case Material: brass
Primer: large rifle

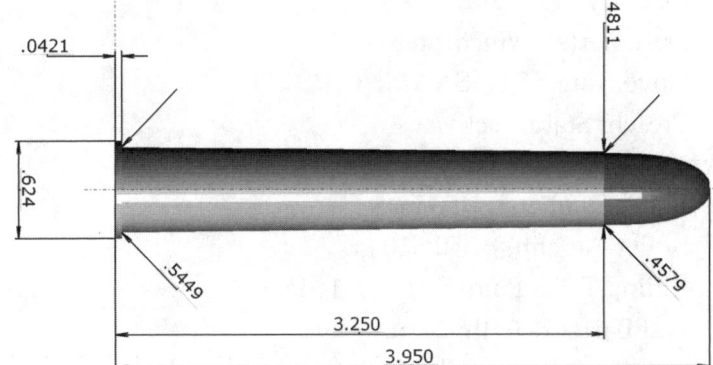

CARTRIDGE BALLISTICS
Max. Average Breech Pressure: 34,000 psi.
Max. Horizontal Range: 4,600 yds.
Max. Vertical Range: 9,500 ft.

Bullet Weight (gr.)	Bullet Type	Muzzle Velocity (fps)	Muzzle Energy (ft.-lbs.)
480	JSP/FMJ	2,150	4,926 (Nitro)
365	JSP	2,100	3,574 (Nitro for BP)
365	L-RN	1,700	2,240 (BP)

CURRENT MANUFACTURER(S)
Kynamco

GENERAL COMMENT(S)
Black powder cartridges with coiled brass cases in this caliber can be traced back to 1871. Drawn brass cases were introduced circa 1877. Various case lengths were offered ranging from approximately 1.30 inches to 3.25 inches. Depending on case length, up to 150 grains of black powder could be loaded. Then, the introduction of smokeless propellants changed everything.

TECHNICAL COMMENT(S)
As smokeless propellants began to replace black powder, John Rigby saw an opportunity to significantly upgrade this caliber's ballistic performance. Accordingly, beginning with the longest case (3 1/4 in.), he developed smokeless powder loads with heavier jacketed bullets at a higher muzzle velocity. The significantly improved ballistic performance boosted the .450 Nitro Express 3 1/4 in. cartridge into the forefront of dangerous game hunting. But why?

Part of the answer is that the .450 Nitro Express was an excellent balance between bullet weight (for penetration), muzzle velocity (adequate, but not excessive), and striking energy (over 100% higher than the black powder loads). When fired from a proper double rifle, recoil was manageable and terminal ballistic performance was adequate for any dangerous game given a fair hit. But, there were two other reasons for the popularity of this caliber. The first was that double rifles in this caliber were lighter so that the hunter could, if desired, carry the rifle himself without the need for a gun bearer. The second was the "sporting" aspect. Most hunters preferred to use "enough gun", but never excessively powerful calibers, to harvest game. The .450 Nitro Express' reputation for reliability promoted this. It was for these reasons that the .450 Nitro Express shortly became one of the most popular calibers for hunting dangerous game of all types. Ammunition in this caliber is still made today..

.458 WINCHESTER MAGNUM

ALTERNATE NAME(S): .458 Win. Mag.
RELATED CALIBER(S): .375 H&H Mag., .300 Win. Mag.

CARTRIDGE HISTORY
Year of Introduction: 1956
Country of Origin: U.S.
Designer(s): Winchester
Governing Body: SAAMI, CIP
Present Status: active

CARTRIDGE DESCRIPTION
Bullet Diameter: .458 in.
Bullet Weight(s): 350-510 gr.
Rifling Twist Rate: 1 turn in 14 in.
Test Barrel Length: 24 in.
Case Type: rimless, belted, straight
Case Material: brass
Primer Size: large rifle

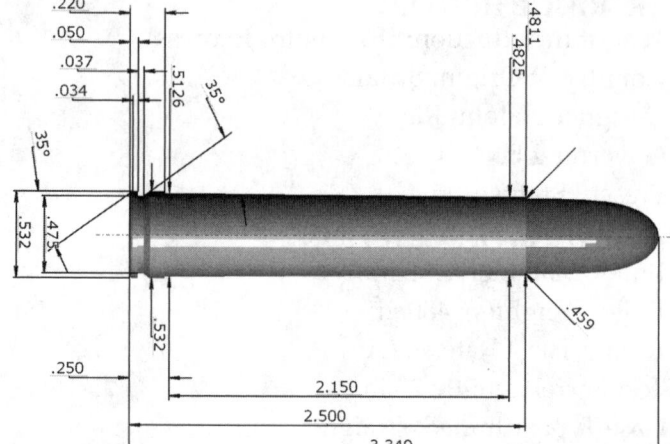

CARTRIDGE BALLISTICS
Max. Average Breech Pressure: 62,400 psi.
Max. Horizontal Range: 4,300 yds.
Max. Vertical Range: 9,600 ft.

Bullet Weight (gr.)	Bullet Type	Muzzle Velocity (fps)	Muzzle Energy (ft.-lbs.)
350	JSP	2,470	4,740
500	JSP	2,040	4,620
510	FMJ	2,040	4,712

CURRENT MANUFACTURER(S)
Federal, Winchester, Hornady, Norma, Kynoch

GENERAL COMMENT(S)
For kids growing up in the 1950s and 1960s, the .458 Winchester Magnum was the very essence of a powerful

African cartridge. Just to see a .458 Win. Mag. cartridge was a rare privilege. Many were the legends surrounding the recoil and ballistic performance of this cartridge. A chance to shoot a .458 earned bragging rights for the "lucky" young hunter. Of course, in reality, few shooters had ever seen a .458 much less fired one.

As time went by and the limited demand for this cartridge was fulfilled, its popularity began to fade. Introduction of the many modern magnums in the 1980s and 1990s which offered better ballistic performance accelerated the decline. Today, the .458 Win. Mag. has become yesterday's news.

TECHNICAL COMMENT(S)

While its ballistics look impressive on paper, the .458 Win. Magnum's ballistic performance is severely constrained by limited case volume which is, in turn, governed by the maximum allowable cartridge length that will fit in a standard rifle action. Add a long, heavy bullet which consumes more volume and you have difficulty meeting even a modest muzzle velocity. In short, the .458 Win. Mag. is a difficult cartridge to manufacture even given the modest muzzle velocity. In the field, the .458 Win. Mag. proved adequate-nothing more. Classic calibers such as the .416 Rigby and .470 Nitro Express were better suited to Africa despite their age.

.458 LOTT

ALTERNATE NAME(S): none
RELATED CALIBER(S): .458 Win. Mag.

CARTRIDGE HISTORY
Year of Introduction: 2002
Country of Origin: U.S.
Designer(s): Jack Lott, Hornady
Governing Body: SAAMI
Present Status: active

CARTRIDGE DESCRIPTION
Bullet Diameter: .458 in.
Bullet Weight(s): 500 gr.
Rifling Twist Rate: 1 turn in 10 in.
Test Barrel Length: 24 in.
Case Type: rimless, belted, straight
Case Material: brass
Primer Size: large rifle

CARTRIDGE BALLISTICS
Max. Average Breech Pressure: 62,400 psi.
Max. Horizontal Range: 4,500 yds.
Max. Vertical Range: 9,000 ft.

Bullet Weight (gr.)	Bullet Type	Muzzle Velocity (fps)	Muzzle Energy (ft.-lbs.)
500	JSP/FMJ	2,100/2,300	4,897/5,872

CURRENT MANUFACTURER(S)
Hornady, Federal, Norma

GENERAL COMMENT(S)
Normally, an ammunition maker decides to offer a new cartridge, then lobbies gun makers to chamber the new caliber. In the case of the .458 Lott, the reverse is true – Ruger wanted to chamber the cartridge (a popular wildcat) and lobbied the ammunition makers to produce it. Hornady agreed and Federal followed. Of course, Ruger had a magnum-length rifle action to chamber it in as well as a suitable single-shot rifle. To date, no other major firearm manufacturer has followed Ruger's lead.

TECHNICAL COMMENT(S)
Consider the .458 Lott as a longer .458 Winchester Magnum. By extending the case length over one-quarter of an inch, the .458 Lott gains enough case volume to completely eliminate the volume-induced restrictions holding back the .458 Win. Mag. Of course the penalty is that the .458 Lott is too long to fit in standard-length rifle actions and must be chambered in a magnum-length rifle action.

The .458 Lott is what the .458 Winchester Magnum should have been.

.460 STEYR

ALTERNATE NAME(S): 11.6x90mm Steyr
RELATED CALIBER(S): .50 BMG

CARTRIDGE HISTORY
Year of Introduction: early 2000s
Country of Origin: Austria
Designer(s): Horst Grillmayr
Governing Body: CIP
Present Status: active

CARTRIDGE DESCRIPTION
Bullet Diameter: .458 in.
Bullet Weight(s): 565 gr.
Rifling Twist Rate: 1 turn in 15 in.
Test Barrel Length: 24 in.
Case Type: rimless, necked
Case Material: brass
Primer: No. 35

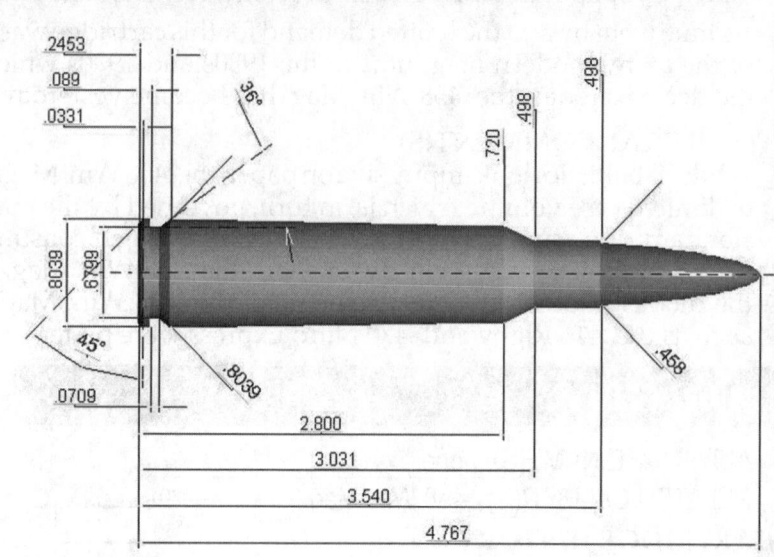

CARTRIDGE BALLISTICS
Max. Average Breech Pressure: 57,327 psi.
Max. Horizontal Range: 5,800 yds.
Max. Vertical Range: 12,250 ft.

Bullet Weight (gr.)	Bullet Type	Muzzle Velocity (fps)	Muzzle Energy (ft.-lbs.)
565	JHP	3,000	11,290

CURRENT MANUFACTURER(S)
None

GENERAL COMMENT(S)
Horst Grillmayr designed this new cartridge specifically for Steyr to provide a high performance, long range, tactical cartridge capable of effective terminal ballistic effects at ranges to 2,000 meters. Development of this cartridge continues with current efforts concentrated on developing suitable low drag bullets.

TECHNICAL COMMENT(S)
Essentially, the .460 Steyr is a .50 BMG case necked down to accept .458 inch diameter bullets. This assures commonality with all .50 BMG caliber firearm action lengths. Design muzzle velocity was 3,000 fps or better using a 600 grain bullet. However, as no suitable tactical bullets of this caliber or weight exist, design has now focused on a 560 grain bullet of a secant ogive boat-tail design. This cartridge has great potential and it will be interesting to see what eventually becomes available.

.470 NITRO EXPRESS

ALTERNATE NAME(S): .470 NE
RELATED CALIBER(S): .500/465 Nitro Express, .500/450 NE

CARTRIDGE HISTORY
Year of Introduction: 1907
Country of Origin: Britain
Designer(s): unknown
Governing Body: CIP, SAAMI
Present Status: active

CARTRIDGE DESCRIPTION
Bullet Diameter: .474 in.
Bullet Weight(s): 500 gr.
Rifling Twist Rate: 1 turn in 21 in.
Test Barrel Length: 24 in.
Case Type: rimmed, necked
Case Material: brass
Primer Size: large rifle

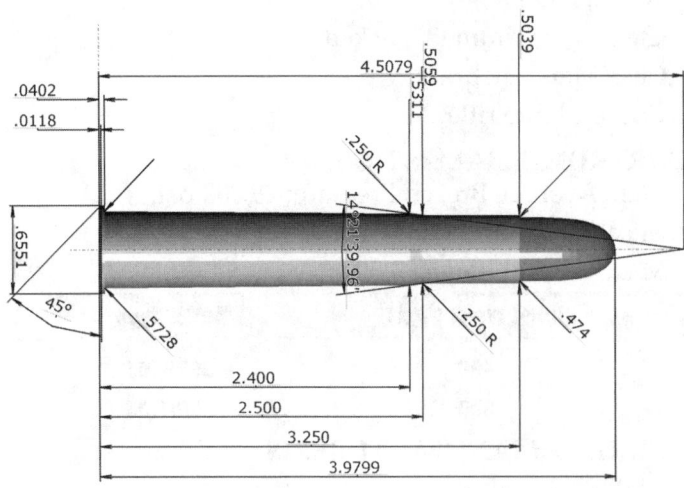

CARTRIDGE BALLISTICS
Max. Average Breech Pressure: 39,200 psi.
Max. Horizontal Range: 4,800 yds.
Max. Vertical Range: 10,000 ft.

Bullet Weight (gr.)	Bullet Type	Muzzle Velocity (fps)	Muzzle Energy (ft.-lbs.)
500	JSP/FMJ	2,150	5,130

CURRENT MANUFACTURER(S)
Federal, Kynoch, Norma

GENERAL COMMENT(S)
One of the most popular of the nitro express cartridges, the .470 Nitro Express owes its longevity to a balance of effective ballistic performance on dangerous game, moderate recoil, and cartridge dimensions which allow a light weight and compact double rifle. A hunter can use this caliber effectively on all species of dangerous African game without being under gunned. The .470 Nitro Express is one of the very few British cartridges of this type made by a domestic ammunition manufacturer (Federal).

TECHNICAL COMMENT(S)
Most nitro express cartridges are rimmed designs intended for use in double rifles where a long cartridge case is no handicap. The .470 NE is such a design, however the larger nitro express calibers require a heavy rifle to tame the recoil. While recoil of the .470 NE is heavy, it is substantially less than most of the larger nitro express calibers.

Like other nitro express calibers, chamber pressures and muzzle velocity are modest. However, the large diameter 500 grain bullet carries substantial striking energy and penetrative power despite the low muzzle velocity.

.475 No. 2 JEFFERY 3 1/2 in.

ALTERNATE NAME(S):.475 Nitro Express, .475 No.2 Jeffery Nitro Express
RELATED CALIBER(S): .500 Nitro Express 3 in, .500 Nitro Express 3 1/4 in.

CARTRIDGE HISTORY
Year of Introduction: circa 1907
Country of Origin: Britain
Designer(s): Jeffery
Governing Body: CIP
Present Status: active

CARTRIDGE DESCRIPTION
Bullet Diameter: .489 in.
Bullet Weight(s): 480-500 gr.
Rifling Twist Rate: 1 turn in 18 in.
Test Barrel Length: 24 in.
Case Type: rimmed, necked
Case Material: brass
Primer: large rifle

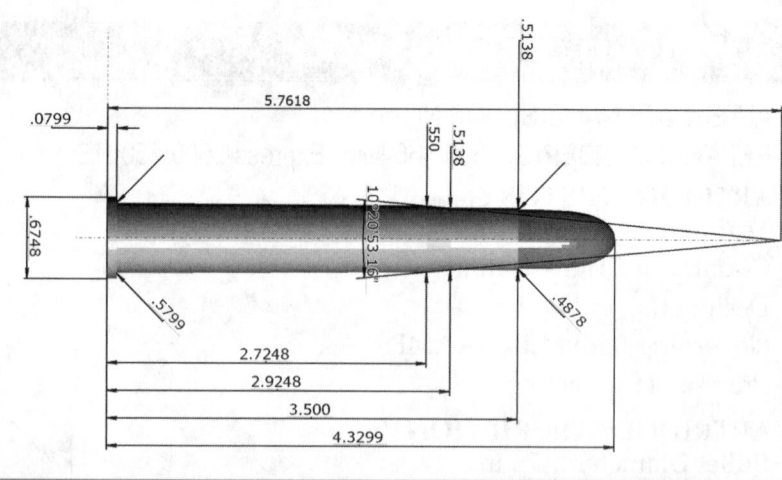

CARTRIDGE BALLISTICS
Max. Average Breech Pressure: 28,000 psi.
Max. Horizontal Range: 4,600 yds.
Max. Vertical Range: 9,500 ft.

Bullet Weight (gr.)	Bullet Type	Muzzle Velocity (fps)	Muzzle Energy (ft.-lbs.)
480	JSP/FMJ	2,200	5,170
500	JSP/FMJ	2,150	5,132 (Jeffery)

CURRENT MANUFACTURER(S)
Kynamco

GENERAL COMMENT(S)
This is another cartridge that was introduced in response to the British government banning certain popular hunting calibers in Sudan and India in an effort to quash insurgencies in both countries. This cartridge was intended to replace the .450 No. 2 Nitro Express which was on the banned list. Field reports gave the .475 No. 2 NE cartridge high marks. It is still offered by Kynamco.

TECHNICAL COMMENT(S)
Jeffery loaded this cartridge with a heavier than standard bullet at a slightly lower muzzle velocity. The reason for this was to lower chamber pressure. As Cordite could substantially increase chamber pressure at high temperatures, Jeffery offered special loads for such applications with lighter propellant charges to compensate. Note the thick rim on this cartridge case to assist in removing stuck cartridge cases.

.475 TURNBULL

ALTERNATE NAME(S): none
RELATED CALIBER(S): .50-110 Winchester

CARTRIDGE HISTORY
Year of Introduction: 2010
Country of Origin: U.S.
Designer(s): Doug Turnbull
Governing Body: SAAMI
Present Status: current

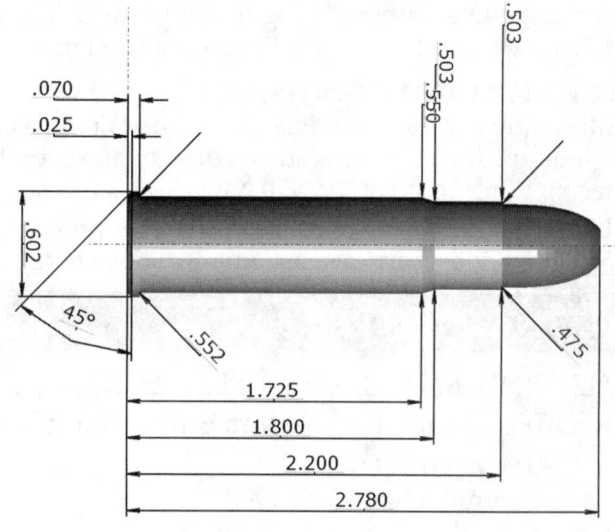

CARTRIDGE DESCRIPTION
Bullet Diameter: .475 in.
Bullet Weight(s): 400 grs.
Rifling Twist Rate: N/A
Test Barrel Length: 26 in.
Case Type: rimmed, necked
Case Material: brass
Primer Size: large rifle

CARTRIDGE BALLISTICS
Max. Average Breech Pressure: N/A
Max. Horizontal Range: 2,570 yds.
Max. Vertical Range: 5,670 ft.

Bullet Weight (gr.)	Bullet Type	Muzzle Velocity (fps)	Muzzle Energy (ft.-lbs.)
400	SP	2,150	4,107

CURRENT MANUFACTURER(S)
Cor-Bon

GENERAL COMMENT(S)
For many years the designer of this cartridge, Doug Turnbull, has been a well-known source for restoring vintage Winchester Model 1873 and 1886 lever-action rifles. This modern cartridge has been designed especially for these restored rifles. Although this is a niche market, shooters undoubtedly will find this cartridge an attractive choice for other models and types of rifles.

TECHNICAL COMMENT(S)
Unlike many other cartridges of this type, the .475 Turnbull will be fully standardized by SAAMI through the efforts of Cor-Bon which will serve also as the manufacturer. The .475 Turnbull is based on the .50-110 Winchester cartridge case – one of the largest ever offered by Winchester, shortened from 2.4 inches to 2.2 inches and necked down to take .475 caliber bullets. The ballistics of the .475 Turnbull are optimized for ranges of 100 yards or less where the terminal energy of its large diameter bullet will be very effective on large, heavy game. Recoil of the .475 Turnbull when fired in a lightweight rifle is not for the faint-hearted.

.50 BROWNING MACHINE GUN

ALTERNATE NAME(S): 12.7x99mm BMG, .50 BMG
RELATED CALIBER(S): 12.7x76mm M48

CARTRIDGE HISTORY
Year of Introduction: 1918
Country of Origin: U.S.
Designer(s): John Browning
Governing Body: SAAMI, CIP
Present Status: active

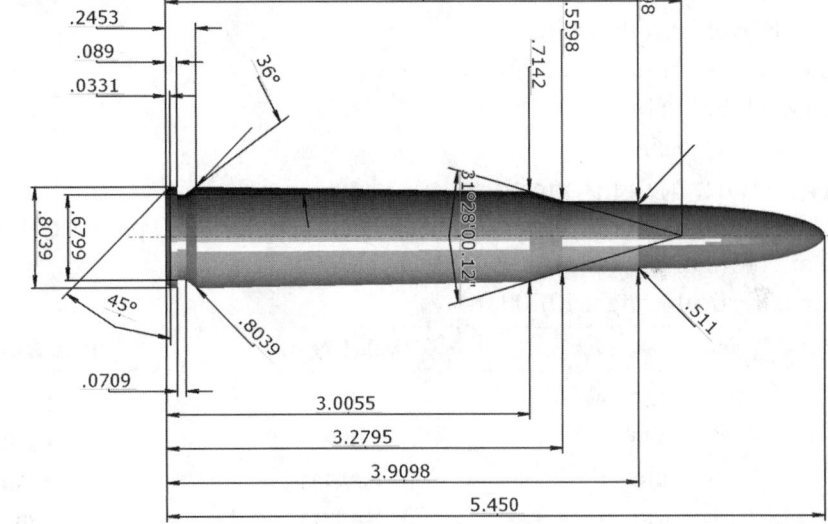

CARTRIDGE DESCRIPTION
Bullet Diameter: .510 in.
Bullet Weight(s): 661 gr.
Rifling Twist Rate: 1 turn in 15 in.
Test Barrel Length: 40 in.
Case Type: rimless, necked
Case Material: brass
Primer Size: No. 35

CARTRIDGE BALLISTICS
Max. Average Breech Pressure: 60,000 psi.
Max. Horizontal Range: 7,300 yds.
Max. Vertical Range: 16,400 ft.

Bullet Weight (gr.)	Bullet Type	Muzzle Velocity (fps)	Muzzle Energy (ft.-lbs.)
661	FMJ-BT	2,710	10,778

CURRENT MANUFACTURER(S)
Winchester, PMC, CBC, IMI, DN, PMP, PPU, Igman, Pyrkal, Raufoss

GENERAL COMMENT(S)
Despite its well-earned military reputation, only recently have American sportsmen warmed to the .50 BMG cartridge for hunting and long range target competition. Much of this growth has been the result of Ronnie Barrett's rifle designs and his promotions. The absence of suitable hunting and match bullets has caused numerous difficulties, a shortcoming that has only recently been addressed. Consequently, the potential of the .50 BMG cartridge for long range hunting and target competition are still unknown. In some countries (and states), private ownership of a rifle chambered for the .50 BMG is illegal. In this connection, the reader may wish to review the data on the new .416 Barrett cartridge in this chapter. This new cartridge is legal in nearly all states.

TECHNICAL COMMENT(S)

What are the proper bullet weights and muzzle velocities for hunting with a .50 BMG caliber rifle? At the moment, this remains a work in progress. Still, some facts have emerged. The .50 BMG works best with bullet weights between 600 and 750 grain. From this, one can assume the weight of a soft-point or hollow-point hunting bullet for this caliber would certainly fall into this bracket. With its slow rifling twist rate, large case capacity, new bullet designs and updated powders, much remains to be done in load development for the .50 BMG .

.500 NITRO EXPRESS 3 1/4 IN., .500 NITRO EXPRESS 3 in., .500 BLACK POWDER EXPRESS 3 1/4 in.

ALTERNATE NAME(S): .500 NE 3 in., .500 NE 3 1/4 in., ,500 BPE 3 1/4 in., 12.7x76Rmm
RELATED CALIBER(S): .475 No. 2 Nitro Express

CARTRIDGE HISTORY

Year of Introduction: circa1868 (3 in.), circa 1895 (3 1/4 in.)

Country of Origin: Britain

Designer(s): N/A

Governing Body: CIP

Present Status: active

CARTRIDGE DESCRIPTION

Bullet Diameter: .510 in.

Bullet Weight(s): 440-570 gr.

Rifling Twist Rate: 1 turn in 15 in.

Test Barrel Length: 24 in.

Case Type: rimmed, straight

Case Material: brass

Primer: large rifle

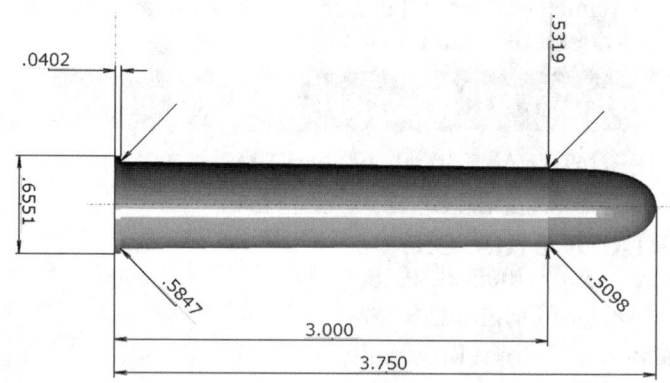

CARTRIDGE BALLISTICS

Max. Average Breech Pressure: 32,000 psi. (3 in.), 31,000 psi. (3 1/4 in.)

Max. Horizontal Range: 4,950 yds.

Max. Vertical Range: 10,200 ft.

Bullet Weight (gr.)	Bullet Type	Muzzle Velocity (fps)	Muzzle Energy (ft.-lbs.)
440	JSP	1,925	3,620 (BP)
440	JSP	1,900	3,527 (Nitro for Black)
570	JSP/FMJ	2,150	5,850 (Nitro-3 in.)
570	JSP/FMJ	2,100	5,583 (Nitro-3 in.)
570	JSP/FMJ	2,125	5,720 (Nitro-3 1/4 in.)

CURRENT MANUFACTURER(S)

Kynamco, Norma

GENERAL COMMENT(S)

In black powder form, this cartridge was a popular choice in India, but seldom seen in Africa as it did poorly on dangerous game. This all changed with the advent of smokeless propellants and better bullets in the 1890s after which the .500 Nitro Express swiftly became an African favorite. It remains so to this day. Experienced hunters report that this caliber is fully capable of reliably taking any species of dangerous game. Kynamco offers .500 Nitro Express loaded ammunition in both 3 in. and 3 1/4 in. case lengths.

TECHNICAL COMMENT(S)

Many readers will question why the 3 in. case and the 3 1/4 in. case offer the same ballistics. After all, should not the longer case offer higher velocity? The answer is the longer case was introduced as a means of reducing chamber pressure in order to eliminate extraction problems. Caution! Recoil of this caliber is very heavy despite the weight of the double rifle.

.500 JEFFERY

ALTERNATE NAME(S): 12.7x70mm Schuler
RELATED CALIBER(S):

CARTRIDGE HISTORY

Year of Introduction: circa 1909
Country of Origin: Germany
Designer(s): Schuler
Governing Body: CIP
Present Status: active

CARTRIDGE DESCRIPTION

Bullet Diameter: .510 in.
Bullet Weight(s): 535 gr.
Rifling Twist Rate: 1 turn in 20 in.
Test Barrel Length: 24 in.
Case Type: rebated, beltless, necked
Case Material: brass
Primer Size: large rifle

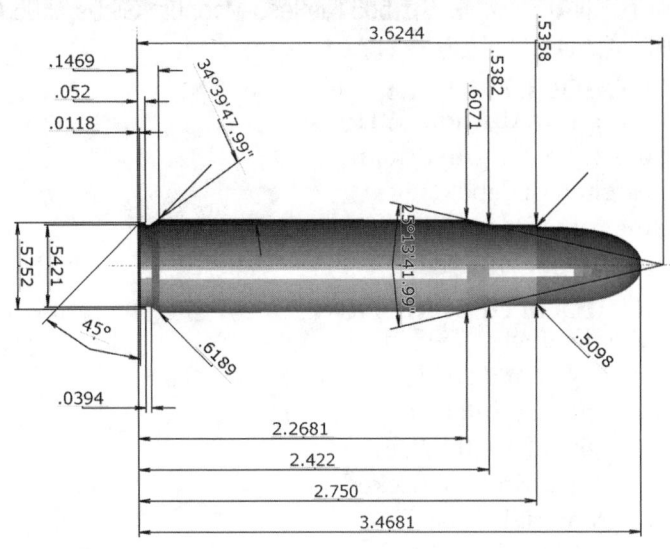

CARTRIDGE BALLISTICS

Max. Average Breech Pressure: 47,900 psi.
Max. Horizontal Range: 4,500 yds.
Max. Vertical Range: 9,000 ft.

Bullet Weight (gr.)	Bullet Type	Muzzle Velocity (fps)	Muzzle Energy (ft.-lbs.)
535	JSP/FMJ	2,400	6,800

CURRENT MANUFACTURER(S)

Kynoch, Norma

GENERAL COMMENT(S)

Despite its British name, the .500 Jeffery was designed by Schuler in Germany where it was called the 12.7x70mm Schuler. Jeffery chambered his bolt-action rifles in this caliber and called it the .500 Jeffery. Both names are correct, however Jeffery has become the most common name for this cartridge. Compared to the .505 Gibbs, the .500 Jeffery offers higher muzzle velocity and energy. Despite this, the .505 Gibbs seems to have been the more popular of the two in North America, although this is not saying much as most American sportsmen are not familiar with either of them. The .500 Jeffery soldiers in Britain where bolt-action rifles are still being chambered for this caliber, albeit on a custom basis.

TECHNICAL COMMENT(S)

The 12.7x70mm Schuler was designed for use in bolt-action repeating rifles preferred by German and American sportsmen. To accommodate this, the rim of the 12.7x70mm Schuler is rebated so as to fit the standard bolt face of the Mauser M98 rifle. Overall cartridge length is also held to under 3.50 inches so as to fit in standard-length rifle actions.

For many years after its introduction, the 12.7x70mm Schuler cum .500 Jeffery was the most powerful bolt-action rifle cartridge available. It earned a reputation for heavy, but manageable, recoil that was undoubtedly due in large measure to the stock design of the bolt-action rifles chambered for it. But, it also earned a reputation for accuracy that double rifles simply could not match. Over the years, the .500 Jeffery cartridge case has been the basis for numerous wildcats and proprietary cartridges.

.505 GIBBS

ALTERNATE NAME(S): .505 Rimless Magnum Gibbs, .505 Magnum Gibbs, .505 Gibbs Magnum
RELATED CALIBER(S): N/A

CARTRIDGE HISTORY
Year of Introduction: 1911
Country of Origin: Britain
Designer(s): Gibbs
Governing Body: CIP
Present Status: active

CARTRIDGE DESCRIPTION
Bullet Diameter: .505 in.
Bullet Weight(s): 525 gr.
Rifling Twist Rate: 1 turn in 16 in.
Test Barrel Length: 24 in.
Case Type: rimless, necked
Case Material: brass
Primer Size: large rifle

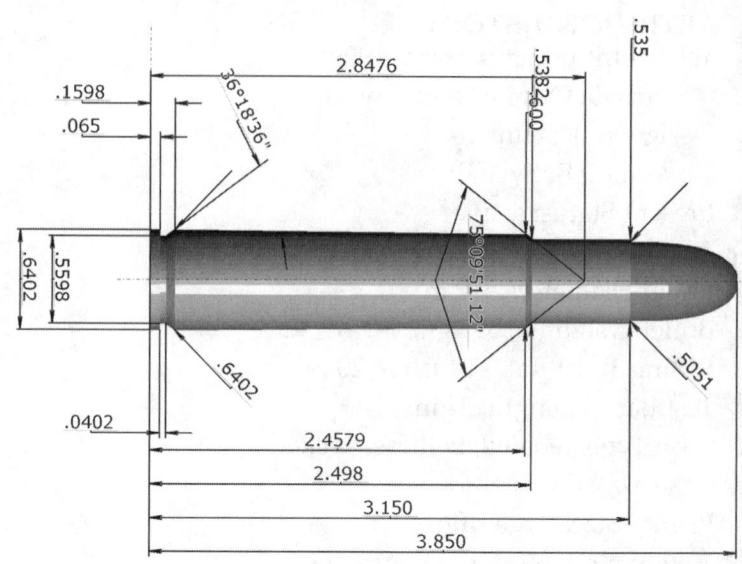

CARTRIDGE BALLISTICS
Max. Average Breech Pressure: 39,200 psi.
Max. Horizontal Range: 4,500 yds.
Max. Vertical Range: 9,000 ft.

Bullet Weight (gr.)	Bullet Type	Muzzle Velocity (fps)	Muzzle Energy (ft.-lbs.)
525	JSP/FMJ	2,300	6,190
660	SP/FMJ	2,100	5,877

CURRENT MANUFACTURER(S)
Kynoch, Norma

GENERAL COMMENT(S)
Introduced in 1911, the .505 Gibbs was designed by a British gunsmith named Gibbs. It was one of the early attempts to design a smokeless powder cartridge for a bolt-action rifle suitable for dangerous African game. Sales were moderate but steady and the .505 Gibbs remains in limited production today.

TECHNICAL COMMENT(S)
Unlike the .500 Jeffery, the .505 Gibbs has a normal rimless necked configuration, although the 3.80 inch overall length and .640 inch rim diameter requires a magnum length rifle action. Here it is interesting to note that the .500 Jeffery cartridge will fit in a standard-length rifle action.

Despite the greater length of the .505 Gibbs, the shorter .500 Jeffery offers the higher muzzle velocity and energy of the two. The .505 Gibbs has served as a basis of numerous wildcats and proprietary cartridges.

.577 NITRO EXPRESS

ALTERNATE NAME(S): .577 NE, .577 Nitro Express 3 in., 14.8x76Rmm
RELATED CALIBER(S): .577 Snider

CARTRIDGE HISTORY
Year of Introduction: circa 1900
Country of Origin: Britain
Designer(s): N/A
Governing Body: CIP
Present Status: active

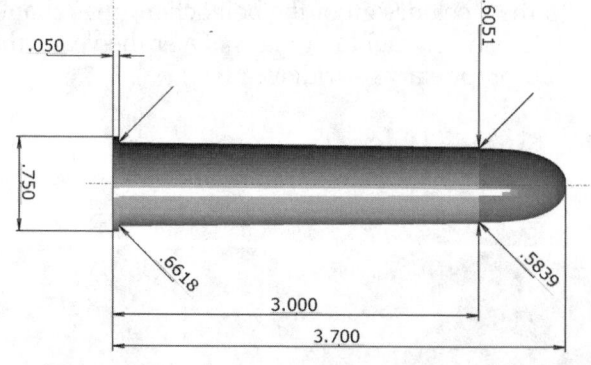

CARTRIDGE DESCRIPTION
Bullet Diameter: .584 in.

Bullet Weight(s): 750 gr.

Rifling Twist Rate: 1 turn in 30 in.

Test Barrel Length: 24 in.

Case Type: rimmed, straight

Case Material: brass

Primer Size: large rifle

CARTRIDGE BALLISTICS

Max. Average Breech Pressure: 35,500 psi.

Max. Horizontal Range: 4,500 yds.

Max. Vertical Range: 9,600 ft.

Bullet Weight (gr.)	Bullet Type	Muzzle Velocity (fps)	Muzzle Energy (ft.-lbs.)
750	JSP/FMJ	2,050	7,010

CURRENT MANUFACTURER(S)

Kynoch

GENERAL COMMENT(S)

Now here is a classic dangerous game cartridge with full performance credentials that has withstood the test of time. Because of this, the .577 NE remains one of the most popular of the nitro express cartridges– especially among guides, professional hunters, and game wardens. They recognize that when the chips are down against dangerous game of all species, the .577 NE is a powerful, proven killer.

Interestingly, the .577 NE does not live in the shadow of its larger brother, the .600 Nitro Express. Rather the opposite is true. Experienced African hunters have found the .577 NE a flexible, manageable caliber while the .600 NE is very specialized making it suitable for only the heaviest game. In fact, only a handful of .600 NE rifles have even been built, while thousands of .577 NE caliber rifles have been sold.

TECHNICAL COMMENT(S)

Do not be fooled by the leisurely 2,050 fps muzzle velocity of the .577 NE. The 750 grain bullet packs 7,010 ft.-lbs. of muzzle energy. Both soft-point and full metal jacket designs are available. Obviously, the key element in the kill mechanism is bullet weight and penetration. In particular, the full metal jacket bullets in this caliber have a long, successful record of bringing down dangerous game. Often, a single shot is all that is needed. Now you know why many professional hunters prefer to carry rifles in this caliber.

One drawback is certainly the weight of a double rifle in .577 NE caliber. The weight is needed to tame the recoil, but a heavy double rifle is tiring to carry and hard to shoulder and aim. A gun bearer who follows the hunter is the normal solution to this problem. And, I have never found a hunter who remembered the recoil of his .577 NE when taking a shot at dangerous game.

The .577 NE has been made with case lengths of 2 3/4", 3", and 3 1/4". The 3" length is the most common.

.600 NITRO EXPRESS

ALTERNATE NAME(S): .600 NE 3 in., 15.2x76Rmm

RELATED CALIBER(S): N/A

CARTRIDGE HISTORY

Year of Introduction: 1899

Country of Origin: Britain

Designer(s): Jeffery

Governing Body: CIP

Present Status: active

CARTRIDGE DESCRIPTION

Bullet Diameter: .620 in.

Bullet Weight(s): 900 gr.

Rifling Twist Rate: 1 turn in 30 in.

Test Barrel Length: 24 in.

Case Type: rimmed, straight

Case Material: brass

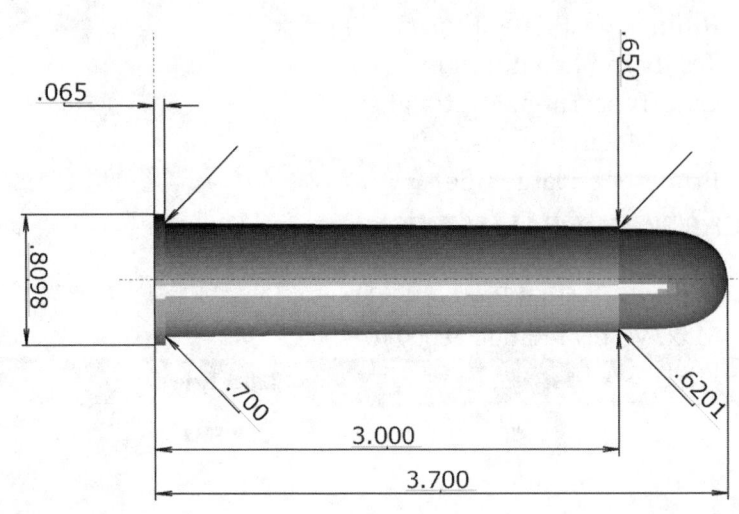

Primer Size: large rifle

CARTRIDGE BALLISTICS

Max. Average Breech Pressure: 35,500 psi.

Max. Horizontal Range: 4,600 yds.

Max. Vertical Range: 9,600 ft.

Bullet Weight (gr.)	Bullet Type	Muzzle Velocity (fps)	Muzzle Energy (ft.-lbs.)
900	FMJ	1,950	7,600

CURRENT MANUFACTURER(S)

Kynoch

GENERAL COMMENT(S)

For over 88 years, the .600 Nitro Express cartridge was the biggest, most powerful hunting cartridge on the planet. Its name was mentioned with reverential familiarity by those who had never seen one, much less fired one. This was not unusual as only a handful of rifles in this caliber were ever made and most of the cartridges ended up as souvenirs or in cartridge collections.

The legend of the .600 NE was concocted of equal parts recoil, bullet weight, size, and striking power. And, they were true. In reality, most owners of a rifle in .600 Nitro Express seldom or never fired them. Rather, they purchased such guns for the bragging rights and pride of ownership conferred by such rifles.

TECHNICAL COMMENT(S)

By any measure, the .600 Nitro Express is a very specialized cartridge designed for stopping very large, dangerous game at close range. The heavy bullets needed to do this generated legendary levels of recoil. Consequently, .600 NE caliber rifles were exceptionally heavy making a sturdy gun bearer (hopefully one with nerves of steel) a vital accessory. Legends aside, in the field the 900 grain bullets of the .600 NE performed as advertised. The only problem was the limited number of scenarios in which rifles of this caliber could be used.

.700 NITRO EXPRESS

ALTERNATE NAME(S): .700 NE
RELATED CALIBER(S): .600 Nitro Express

CARTRIDGE HISTORY

Year of Introduction: 1988

Country of Origin: U.S.

Designer(s): William Feldstein, Jim Bell

Governing Body: CIP

Present Status: active

CARTRIDGE DESCRIPTION

Bullet Diameter: .700 in.

Bullet Weight(s): 1,000 gr.

Rifling Twist Rate: 1 turn in 29 in.

Test Barrel Length: 24 in.

Case Type: rimmed, straight

Case Material: brass

Primer Size: large rifle

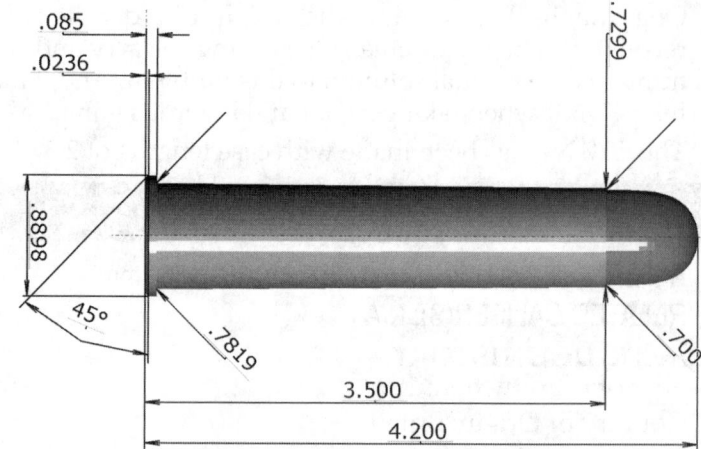

CARTRIDGE BALLISTICS

Max. Average Breech Pressure: 39,900 psi.

Max. Horizontal Range: 4,500 yds.

Max. Vertical Range: 9,000 ft.

Bullet Weight (gr.)	Bullet Type	Muzzle Velocity (fps)	Muzzle Energy (ft.-lbs.)
1,000	JSP/FMJ	2,000	8,900

CURRENT MANUFACTURER(S)
Kynoch

GENERAL COMMENT(S)
When you are the big dog on the porch, someone always wants to knock you off your pedestal. In this case the cartridge on the pedestal was the .600 Nitro Express and Mr. William Feldstein was the man who knocked it off. For this purpose, he engaged the technical services of Jim Bell. Together they designed and built a new NE plus ultra cartridge in 1988 – the .700 Nitro Express.

Holland & Holland built the first .700 Nitro Express rifles for the project and Bell made the first cartridges. A series of additional rifles in this caliber followed, after which H&H added this chambering to their product line. Today, the .600 NE no longer reigns supreme over lesser cartridges and souvenir .700 Nitro Express cartridges go for $125 each.

TECHNICAL COMMENT(S)
The .700 Nitro Express is an assembly of ballistic superlatives. Launched at 2,000 fps, the 1,000 grain full metal jacket or soft-point bullets carry 8,900 ft.-lbs. of muzzle energy, easily making the .700 Nitro Express the most powerful sporting cartridge in the world. For comparison, this is 17% more muzzle energy than the .600 Nitro Express, 27% more than the .577 Nitro Express, and 305% more than the .30-'06 Spr.

Obviously, the .700 NE is enough gun for any species of dangerous game on the planet. But is it practical? That is not the point!

.45-70 MULTIBALL CARTRIDGE

SPECIMEN AND PHOTOS COURTESY OF PAUL SMITH

Starting in 1901, Frankford Arsenal began loading multiball loadings for use in federal prisons. The first 1,000 rounds were loaded for guards at federal prisons. An additional 29,060 rounds were made in 1902.

Beginning in 1902 production of multiball cartridges (in both .45 and .30 cal) was increased because of an order from Washington requiring each post to keep on hand 10 rounds per soldier for use in case of riot. Commercial cases were used and as a result, mixed headstamps can be found within the same box.

During WW1 it was necessary to guard military installations. Two million rounds were manufactured by Remington for this purpose.

This sectioned round is likely from the 1903 and onwards production run as the headstamp is UMC 45-70. It is assumed that the 1917 production was probably headstamped REM-UMC.

This round has a smooth cannelure ca. 0.7" below the case mouth.

Unfortunately the powder charge was not weighted. It is thought that this may help indicate when the round was manufactured.

References: *History of Modern U.S. Military Small Arms Ammunition*, Vol. 1 (revised), Hackely, Woodin and Scranton. p. 215 and the IAA discussion forum (with thanks to Lee R., Randy Hedeen, Ray Meketa, Ron Merchant and John Moss).

Courtesy International Ammunition Association, Inc. (cartridgecollectors.org)

CHAPTER 66 : CENTERFIRE SPORTING RIFLE - OBSOLETE

CHAPTER 66

For Cartridge Index see Chapter 101. All drawing dimensions are approximate.

This chapter should be regarded as a resource rather than a mausoleum. The cartridges listed offer a rich and colorful tale of development, design, technological milestones, what worked, what did not, and what calibers were in vogue in certain eras. Such information is of inestimable value to the experienced shooter. It also provides a perspective on history not found in any textbook. Here you will find the creations of Winchester, Remington, Ross, Sharps, Savage, Holland & Holland, Jeffrey, Mauser, Mannlicher, and others.

As the reader peruses the cartridges in this chapter, it may appear that Winchester had an inordinate number of flops. This is simply not the case. Rather, in the late 1800s Winchester was the undisputed king of new cartridge development and introduction. Obviously, because Winchester took more chances on new cartridge introductions, their number of failures increased proportionately.

The reader also must beware of developing the impression that the cartridges listed in this chapter were all failures. This is most emphatically not the case. In fact, many of the cartridges listed in this chapter were extremely popular in their day and had long-term production life spans. As guns chambered for these calibers began to wear out and demand for the cartridges started to wane, production of these calibers gradually ceased.

A great many of these cartridges were designed originally for black powder. Many of them made the transition to smokeless propellants only to be eclipsed by cartridges designed specifically for the new propellants. In other words, many of the black powder cartridges did not make the transition to smokeless propellants primarily due to the low permissible chamber pressures in black powder rifles. As the corrosive effects of black powder and mercuric priming wore out black powder guns quickly, many cartridges which survived the transition enjoyed a very short life span. Nearly all black powder cartridges that did not make the transition to smokeless propellants were quickly discontinued after the turn of the century, a good example being the Sharps calibers.

In the case of cartridges, death is not always permanent. Nostalgia, marketing, and demand can sometimes combine to bring an "oldie" back to production life, if only on a limited basis. A good example of this is the .405 Winchester which recently sprang back to limited production after a long period of discontinuance.

Enjoy the following calibers, be proud of them, and above all, learn from them.

NOTE:

The following obsolete rifle cartridges are listed in Chapter 68: Proprietary Sporting Rifle - Obsolete, by brand name.

A-Square	North American Shooting Systems
Ballard	Rigby
Brenneke, Wilhelm	Sauer
Bullard	Sharps
Jeffery	Stevens
Maynard	vom Hofe, E.A.
Newton	Westley Richards

.219 ZIPPER

ALTERNATE NAME(S): none
RELATED CALIBER(S): .25-35 Win., .30-30 Win.

CARTRIDGE HISTORY
Year of Introduction: 1937
Country of Origin: U.S.
Designer(s): Winchester
Governing Body: SAAMI
Present Status: obsolete

CARTRIDGE DESCRIPTION
Bullet Diameter: .224 in.
Bullet Weight(s): 55 gr.
Rifling Twist Rate: 1 turn in 16 in.
Test Barrel Length: N/A
Case Type: rimmed, necked, tapered
Case Material: brass
Primer Size: large rifle

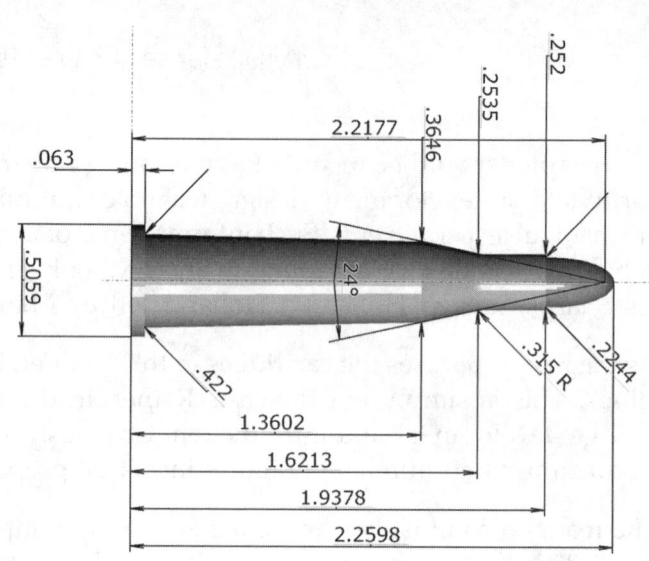

CARTRIDGE BALLISTICS
Max. Average Breech Pressure: 46,400 psi.
Max. Horizontal Range: 3,800 yds.
Max. Vertical Range: 8,600 ft.

Bullet Weight (gr.)	Bullet Type	Muzzle Velocity (fps)	Muzzle Energy (ft.-lbs.)
55	JSP	3,110	1,200

CURRENT MANUFACTURER(S)
None

GENERAL COMMENT(S)
Introduced by Winchester for their M64 lever-action rifle, the .219 Zipper never really caught on. It was obsolete by the early 1960s.

TECHNICAL COMMENT(S)
The .219 Zipper was an excellent varmint cartridge which was hindered by the inherent lack of accuracy of most lever-action rifles.

.22 WINCHESTER CENTERFIRE

ALTERNATE NAME(S): .22 WCF
RELATED CALIBER(S): .22 Hornet, 5.6x35Rmm Vierling

CARTRIDGE HISTORY
Year of Introduction: 1885
Country of Origin: U.S.
Designer(s): Winchester
Governing Body: SAAMI
Present Status: obsolete

CARTRIDGE DESCRIPTION
Bullet Diameter: .228 in.
Bullet Weight(s): 45 gr.
Rifling Twist Rate: 1 turn in 16 in.
Test Barrel Length: 24 in.
Case Type: rimmed, necked

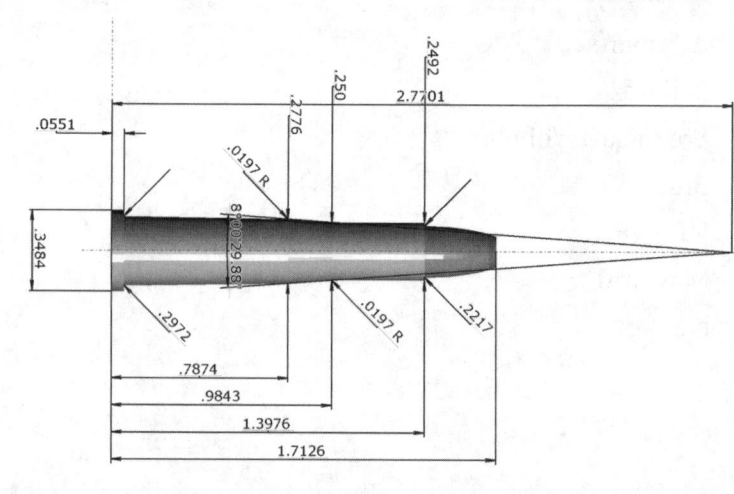

Case Material: brass
Primer: Small rifle

CARTRIDGE BALLISTICS

Max. Average Breech Pressure: N/A

Max. Horizontal Range: 2,700 yds.

Max. Vertical Range: 5,900 ft.

Bullet Weight (gr.)	Bullet Type	Muzzle Velocity (fps)	Muzzle Energy (ft.-lbs.)
45	L-FN	1,540	237 (W.C.F.)
46	JSP	2,030	418 (Vierling)

CURRENT MANUFACTURER(S)

None

GENERAL COMMENT(S)

Winchester introduced this cartridge in 1885 for their single-shot rifles and it was later offered in the Winchester Model 1873 lever-action rifle. This cartridge was quite popular as a small game, varmint and target cartridge in the U.S. until the mid-1920s. It was dropped from Winchester's product line in 1936 and disappeared from the U.S. market. But that is not the end of the story! In the late 1920s, three experimenters at Springfield Arsenal developed a new wildcat cartridge based on the .22 WCF called the .22 Hornet. Winchester added the Hornet to their product line in 1930 and the .22 Hornet remains a staple of ammunition maker product lines to this day. But the story is still not over. European sportsmen took to the .22 WCF cartridge immediately after its introduction. They found the .22 WCF perfect for chambering in drillings where space was tight as well as for single-shot and bolt-action rifles. Around 1900, European ammunition makers transitioned the .22 WCF to smokeless propellants. At that time, they increased muzzle velocity to well over 2,000 fps. and christened it the 5.6x35Rmm Vierling. By 1970, its popularity faded as it was replaced by the .22 Hornet and .222 Rem. Today, the 5.6x35Rmm is obsolete. The .22 WCF is an historically significant cartridge as the direct predecessor of the .22 Hornet and 5.6x35Rmm Vierling.

TECHNICAL COMMENT(S)

The compact size, accuracy and performance on small game and varmints were always the attractions of the .22 WCF. However, when smokeless powder allowed the .22 WCF to morph into the high velocity 5.6x35Rmm Vierling, it only set the stage for the .22 Hornet.

.222 REMINGTON MAGNUM

ALTERNATE NAME(S): .222 Rem. Mag.

RELATED CALIBER(S): .221 Fireball, .222 Rem., .223 Rem.

CARTRIDGE HISTORY

Year of Introduction: 1958

Country of Origin: U.S.

Designer(s): Remington

Governing Body: SAAMI

Present Status: obsolete

CARTRIDGE DESCRIPTION

Bullet Diameter: .224 in.

Bullet Weight(s): 55 gr.

Rifling Twist Rate: 1 turn in 14 ins.

Test Barrel Length: 24 in.

Case Type: rimless, necked

Case Material: brass

Primer Size: small rifle

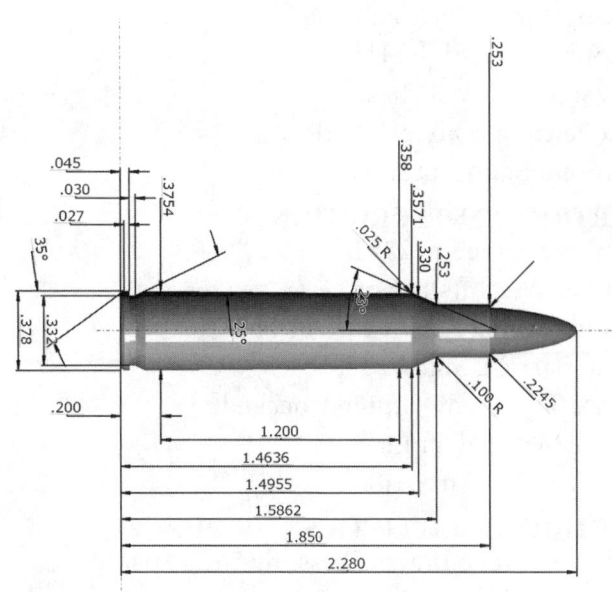

CARTRIDGE BALLISTICS

Max. Average Breech Pressure: 55,400 psi.

Max. Horizontal Range: 3,850 yds.

Max. Vertical Range: 8,650 ft.

Bullet Weight (gr.)	Bullet Type	Muzzle Velocity (fps)	Muzzle Energy (ft.-lbs.)
55	JSP	3,240	1,282

CURRENT MANUFACTURER(S)

None

GENERAL COMMENT(S)

Originally designed by Remington under U.S. Army contract, this cartridge was intended to be the standard military cartridge for the new M16 rifle. However, weapons designers found the cartridge capable of slightly more muzzle velocity than was wanted by the military. As a result, James Sullivan, an engineer on the M16 project, was assigned the job of revising the existing cartridge to obtain the same ballistic performance from a slightly smaller, more compact cartridge. Sullivan reduced the case length from 1.850 inches to 1.760 inches and the overall loaded cartridge length from 2.280 to 2.210. The result was the 5.56x45mm M193 military cartridge. In an effort to salvage something from their development efforts, in 1958 Remington introduced the .222 Rem. Mag. into the commercial market. Although it gained a modest popularity with some bench rest shooters and varmint hunters, the .222 Rem. Mag. gained market share very slowly with mainstream sportsmen. When the 5.56x45mm cartridge became the standard U.S. Army combat cartridge in 1964, it sealed the fate of the .222 Rem Mag. The market quickly became infatuated with the new 5.56x45mm cartridge which offered essentially identical ballistic performance to the .222 Rem. Mag. Bowing to the inevitable, Remington introduced a commercial version of the 5.56x45mm cartridge called the .223 Remington in 1965. From then on, the .222 Rem. Mag. steadily lost market share to the .223 Rem. until it was finally retired in the early 1980s. Today, the .222 Rem. Magnum cartridge has become a forgotten footnote in the history of high velocity military cartridge development.

TECHNICAL COMMENT(S)

Although the .222 Rem. Mag. has approximately 5 % more case volume than the .223 Rem., the difference in ballistic performance is nil. Basically, the .223 Rem. cartridge can do anything the .222 Rem. Mag. cartridge can do. Today, the .223 Rem. has become far more flexibile than the .222 Rem. Mag. ever was due to an amazing range of bullet weights from 40 grains to 77 grains. Following its military debut in 1964, the 5.56x45mm/.223 Rem. has moved on to NATO adoption status, a growing law enforcement market, a bench rest favorite and the accepted standard for varmint hunting.

.225 WINCHESTER

ALTERNATE NAME(S): .225 Win., 5.6x49Rmm
RELATED CALIBER(S): .30-30 Win.

CARTRIDGE HISTORY

Year of Introduction: 1964
Country of Origin: U.S.
Designer(s): Winchester
Governing Body: SAAMI
Present Status: obsolete

CARTRIDGE DESCRIPTION

Bullet Diameter: .224 in.
Bullet Weight(s): 55 gr.
Rifling Twist Rate: 1 turn in 14 in.
Test Barrel Length: 24 in.
Case Type: semi-rimmed, necked
Case Material: brass
Primer Size: large rifle

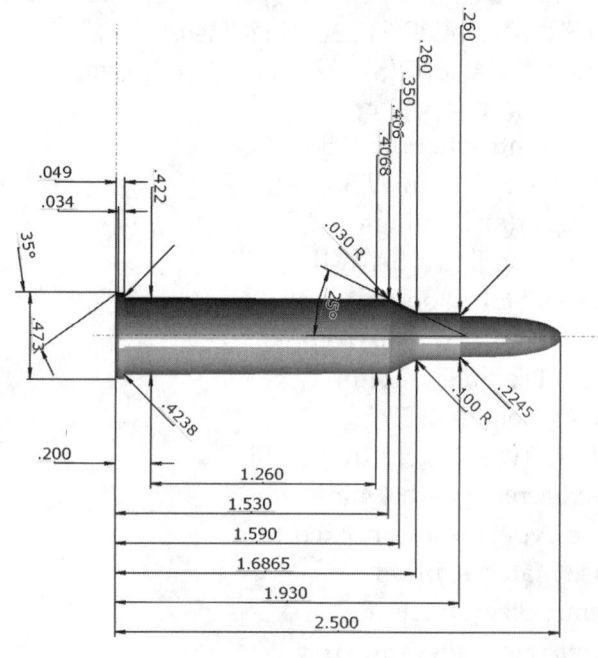

CARTRIDGE BALLISTICS

Max. Average Breech Pressure: 56,560 psi.
Max. Horizontal Range: 3,500 yds.
Max. Vertical Range: 7,800 ft.

Bullet Weight (gr.)	Bullet Type	Muzzle Velocity (fps)	Muzzle Energy (ft.-lbs.)
55	JSP	3,570	1,556

CURRENT MANUFACTURER(S)
Winchester

GENERAL COMMENT(S)
The advent of the popular rimless .22-250 Rem. cartridge in 1965 sealed the fate of the semi-rimmed .225 Win. cartridge. Winchester still offers ammunition in .225 Win. caliber, however new rifles have not been made since 1972 so its days are numbered.

TECHNICAL COMMENT(S)
From a technical standpoint, the .225 Win. is a sound design. However, its semi-rimmed design limited its market appeal and no other firearm maker offered rifles in this caliber.

5.6x33mm ROOK, 5.6x33Rmm ROOK

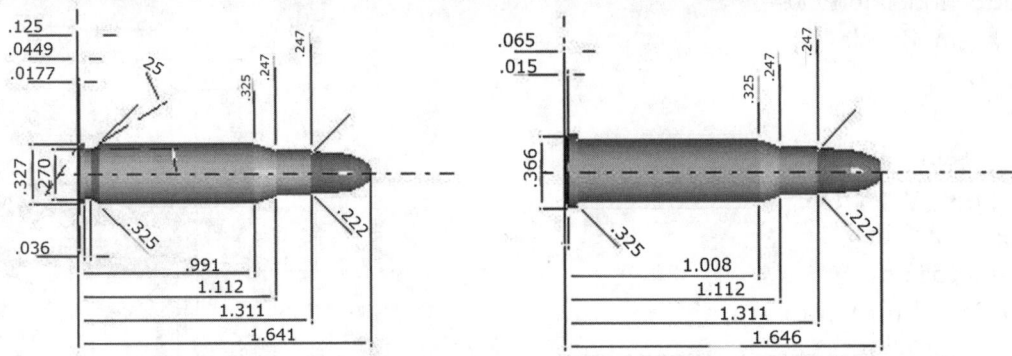

ALTERNATE NAME(S): 5.6x33mm, 5.6x33Rmm
RELATED CALIBER(S): 5.6x35Rmm Vierling

CARTRIDGE HISTORY
Year of Introduction: 1900
Country of Origin: Germany
Designer(s): N/A
Governing Body: none
Present Status: obsolete

CARTRIDGE DESCRIPTION
Bullet Diameter: .222 in.
Bullet Weight(s): 65 gr.
Rifling Twist Rate: N/A
Test Barrel Length: N/A
Case Type: rimless, necked; rimmed, necked
Case Material: brass
Primer: small rifle

CARTRIDGE BALLISTICS
Max. Average Breech Pressure: N/A
Max. Horizontal Range: 2,300 yds.
Max. Vertical Range: 5,000 ft.

Bullet Weight (gr.)	Bullet Type	Muzzle Velocity (fps)	Muzzle Energy (ft.-lbs.)
65	JSP	1,425	293 (est.)

CURRENT MANUFACTURER(S)
None

GENERAL COMMENT(S)

Like British and American sportsmen, German hunters also developed small caliber, low power rifle cartridges for pest control and small game hunting. The 5.6x33mm Rook was one of these German cartridges, popular in Germany but unknown in the U.S. and vaguely familiar in Britain. It went obsolete in the mid-1930s.

TECHNICAL COMMENT(S)

The rimmed version was intended for use in drillings while the rimless version was for use in bolt-action rifles. Born as black powder cartridges, German sportsmen were eager to convert these to smokeless propellants. As these were low powered cartridges, the change in propellants did not significantly affect ballistic performance. Within their limits, these were fine cartridges.

5.6x39mm RUSSIAN

ALTERNATE NAME(S): 5.6x39mm Vostok, .220 Russian
RELATED CALIBER(S): 7.62x39mm Soviet, .22 PPC

CARTRIDGE HISTORY

Year of Introduction: late 1950s

Country of Origin: Russia

Designer(s): N/A

Governing Body: CIP

Present Status: semi-obsolete

CARTRIDGE DESCRIPTION

Bullet Diameter: .220 in.

Bullet Weight(s): 54 gr.

Rifling Twist Rate: 1 turn in 16.5 in.

Test Barrel Length: 24 in.

Case Type: rimless, necked

Case Material: steel (Russian manufacture), brass (Lapua or Sako, Finland manufacture)

Primer Size: small rifle

CARTRIDGE BALLISTICS

Max. Average Breech Pressure: 50,763psi.

Max. Horizontal Range: 3,700 yds.

Max. Vertical Range: 8,500 ft.

Bullet Weight (gr.)	Bullet Type	Muzzle Velocity (fps)	Muzzle Energy (ft.-lbs.)
54	SP	2,993	1,075

CURRENT MANUFACTURER(S)

Wolf

GENERAL COMMENT(S)

The 5.6x39mm Russian cartridge was designed for competition use in the Olympic Running Deer events. While other Olympic rifle and pistol shooting events that are limited to .22 rimfire, the Running Deer event required a rifle firing a center fire cartridge. Caliber was not specified, however the event placed a premium on rapid firing and fast recovery time. This required a low recoil cartridge firing a light weight bullet at high velocity. However, the last Running Deer competition was fired in 1956 at the Melbourne, Australia Olympics. Many potential host countries did not have a suitable venue for the Running deer event and, in any case, interest in the event dwindled quickly. As a result, the Running deer event was dropped from the Olympics and further attempts to revive it were unsuccessful.

In the 1970s, Dr. Louis Palmisano and Mr. Ferris Pindell used the 5.6x39mm Russian cartridge as the basis for their PPC series of cartridges which have been so successful in bench rest and other types of rifle competition. Never much of a hunting cartridge and upstaged by the PPC series of cases for competition use, the 5.6x39mm Russian quietly slipped into obscurity in the U.S. although it is still made and used in Russia for hunting.

TECHNICAL COMMENT(S)

To create the 5.6x39mm cartridge, the ever-practical Russians simply necked down their 7.62x39mm M43 service cartridge to 5.6mm. Russian ammunition in 5.6x39mm caliber was and is made with steel cartridge cases. Later, the Finnish companies Sako and Lapua made conventional brass cases for this caliber.

.242 RIMLESS NITRO EXPRESS

ALTERNATE NAME(S): .242 Rimless NE
RELATED CALIBER(S): .30-'06 Springfield, 8x57mm Mauser

CARTRIDGE HISTORY

Year of Introduction: 1923
Country of Origin: Britain
Designer(s): Manton & Co.
Governing Body: CIP
Present Status: obsolete

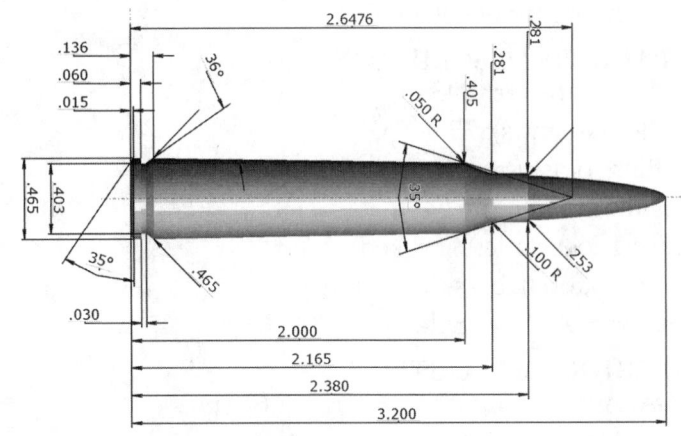

CARTRIDGE DESCRIPTION

Bullet Diameter: 253 in.
Bullet Weight(s): 100 gr.
Rifling Twist Rate: N/A
Test Barrel Length: 24 in.
Case Type: rimless, necked
Case Material: brass
Primer: large rifle

CARTRIDGE BALLISTICS

Max. Average Breech Pressure: N/A
Max. Horizontal Range: 4,600 yds.
Max. Vertical Range: 9,850 ft.

Bullet Weight (gr.)	Bullet Type	Muzzle Velocity (fps)	Muzzle Energy (ft.-lbs.)
100	JSP	2,800	1740

CURRENT MANUFACTURER(S)

None

GENERAL COMMENT(S)

A unique twist in the history of this cartridge is that it was developed by Kynoch in Britain for Manton & Co. in Calcutta, India. Undoubtedly, Manton was responding to a strong, local requirement for a small bore, high velocity cartridge for light weight, bolt-action rifles. What would one hunt in India using such a cartridge? Various types of medium game were undoubtedly the perceived market as this caliber was far too small for big game hunting. It seems this cartridge with the grand nomenclature struck a cord with Commonwealth hunters as the .242 Rimless NE remained in production until well after World War II.

TECHNICAL COMMENT(S)

Ballistics of the .242 Rimless NE were approximately 11% inferior to the present .243 Winchester. For example, the .242 Rimless NE generated 1,740 ft.-lbs. of muzzle energy compared to the .243 Winchesters 1,945 ft.-lbs. And, a 100 grain bullet was the only one offered. The .242 Rimless NE case is based on the venerable .30-'06 Springfield, one of the few British cartridges to do so. However, despite its shortcomings, the .242 Rimless Nitro Express remains one of the best of the British .243 caliber cartridges.

.244 REMINGTON

ALTERNATE NAME(S): .244 Rem.
RELATED CALIBER(S): 6mm Rem.

CARTRIDGE HISTORY

Year of Introduction: 1955
Country of Origin: U.S.
Designer(s): Remington
Governing Body: SAAMI
Present Status: obsolete

CARTRIDGE DESCRIPTION

Bullet Diameter: .243 in.
Bullet Weight(s): 75-90 gr.
Rifling Twist Rate: 1 turn in 12 in.
Test Barrel Length: 24 in.
Case Type: rimless, necked
Case Material: brass
Primer Size: large rifle

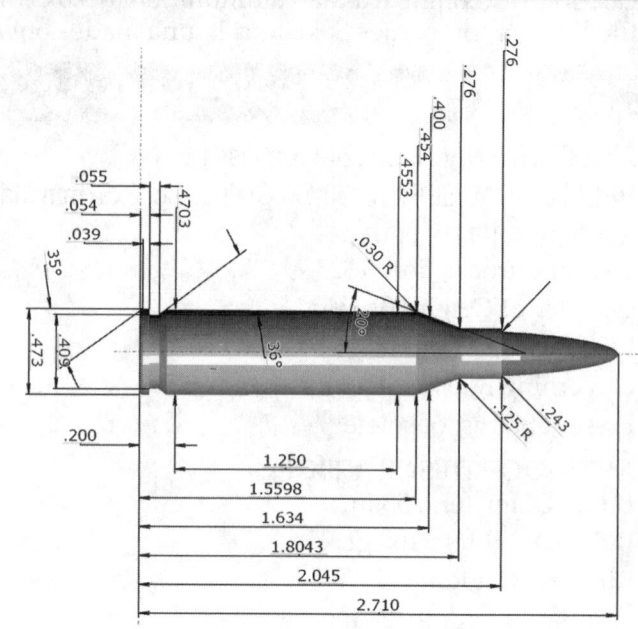

CARTRIDGE BALLISTICS

Max. Average Breech Pressure: 61,640 psi.
Max. Horizontal Range: 4,000 yds.
Max. Vertical Range: 9,000 ft.

Bullet Weight (gr.)	Bullet Type	Muzzle Velocity (fps)	Muzzle Energy (ft.-lbs.)
75	JSP	3,500	2,040
90	JSP	3,200	2,050

CURRENT MANUFACTURER(S)

GENERAL COMMENT(S)

When interest in 6mm rifles bloomed in the mid-1950s, both Remington and Winchester developed new cartridges to meet this demand.

TECHNICAL COMMENT(S)

Winchester designed their cartridge for deer hunting with a 100 grain bullet and a rifling twist rate of 1:10 inches for such a long bullet. Remington believed the new 6mm calibers were for varmint hunting and used a rifling twist rate of 1:12 inch suited for their 75 and 90 grain bullets. Remington's approach proved wrong and the .244 Rem. cartridge was a marketing failure. It was soon replaced by the 6mm Rem. cartridge with an appropriate rifling twist rate of 1 turn in 10 inches.

6x57mm MAUSER

ALTERNATE NAME(S): none
RELATED CALIBER(S): 6.5x57mm Mauser, 7x57mm Mauser, 6mm Remington

CARTRIDGE HISTORY

Year of Introduction: 1895
Country of Origin: Germany
Designer(s): Peter Paul Mauser
Governing Body: none
Present Status: obsolete

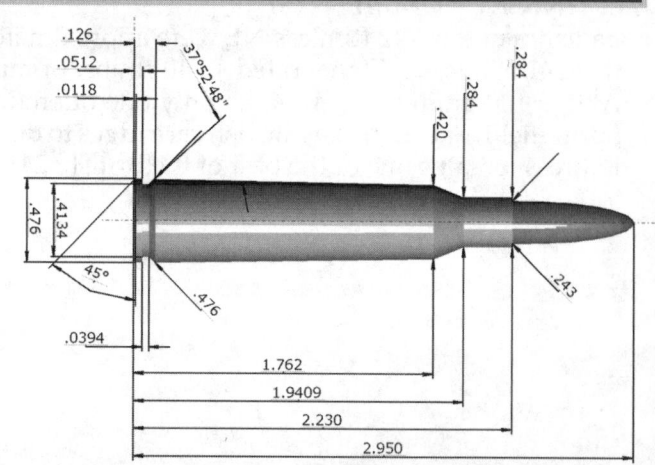

CARTRIDGE DESCRIPTION

Bullet Diameter: .243 in.

Bullet Weight(s): 120 gr.
Rifling Twist Rate: N/A
Test Barrel Length: N/A
Case Type: rimless, necked
Case Material: brass
Primer: large rifle

CARTRIDGE BALLISTICS
Max. Average Breech Pressure: N/A
Max. Horizontal Range: 4,550 yds.
Max. Vertical Range: 9,700 ft.

Bullet Weight (gr.)	Bullet Type	Muzzle Velocity (fps)	Muzzle Energy (ft.-lbs.)
120	JSP	2,700	1,942 (est.)

CURRENT MANUFACTURER(S)
None

GENERAL COMMENT(S)
While the 6x57mm Mauser is an uncommon cartridge, it is included here as it was the smallest caliber in the Mauser 57mm case product line. The 6x57mm Mauser cartridge never gained the acceptance of the other 57mm length members of the Mauser cartridge family. Undoubtedly, this was due to the bad reputation for rapid bore erosion in other 6mm cartridges.

TECHNICAL COMMENT(S)
The 6x57mm Mauser is essentially a 6.5x57mm Mauser case necked down to 6mm. To place this in a more modern perspective, the 6x57mm Mauser and the present 6mm Remington cartridges have much in common! German ammunition makers loaded this cartridge with 120 grain bullets. By today's standard, this is a significantly heavier bullet than we load today. Part of this is due to the intended market for the 6x75mm being Europe where a heavy bullet was preferred. American hunters prefer lighter bullets with higher muzzle velocity in this caliber.

6x58mm FORSTER, 6x58Rmm FORSTER

ALTERNATE NAME(S): none
RELATED CALIBER(S): 6.5x57mm Mauser, 6.5x57Rmm Mauser

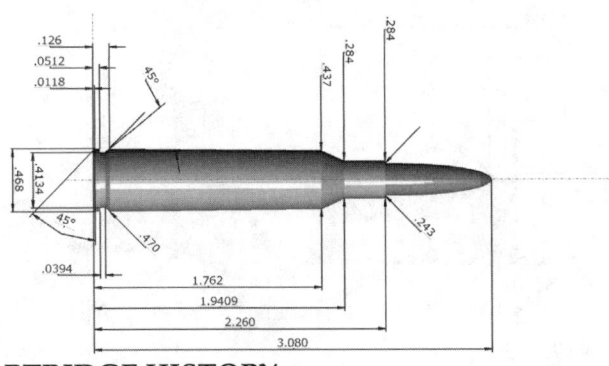
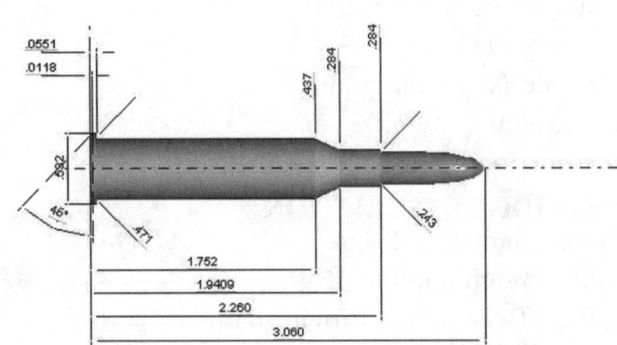

CARTRIDGE HISTORY
Year of Introduction: 1904
Country of Origin: Germany
Designer(s): N/A
Governing Body: none
Present Status: obsolete

CARTRIDGE DESCRIPTION
Bullet Diameter: .243 in.
Bullet Weight(s): 127 gr.
Rifling Twist Rate: N/A

Test Barrel Length: N/A
Case Type: rimless, necked
Case Material: brass
Primer: large rifle

CARTRIDGE BALLISTICS
Max. Average Breech Pressure: N/A
Max. Horizontal Range: 4,250 yds.
Max. Vertical Range: 9,150 ft.

Bullet Weight (gr.)	Bullet Type	Muzzle Velocity (fps)	Muzzle Energy (ft.-lbs.)
127	JSP	2,790	2,195

CURRENT MANUFACTURER(S)
None

GENERAL COMMENT(S)
In German, the word "forster" means a man (a forester) who professionally manages the game on a large property. A forster becomes intimately familiar with every inch of the property he manages as he is constantly outside working. It may be assumed that such a man is an accomplished hunter himself who appreciates a light handy rifle as a tool for his work. As a large caliber was not needed, the Forster cartridges were designed for this purpose, presumably with the expectation that expert word-of-mouth would build sales. It did not work that way and the Forster cartridges did not last long.

TECHNICAL COMMENT(S)
From a design standpoint, the Forster cartridges are simple modifications of the 6.5x57mm/6.5x57Rmm Mauser cartridges made by necking these down to 6mm. While the Forster cartridges did not break fresh design ground, early, small caliber, smokeless rifle cartridges received a bad reputation for bore erosion. Whether or not this applied to the Forster cartridges did not matter. Small bore diameter cartridges as a group did not recover from their bad reputation until better smokeless propellants came along many years later.

.25 REMINGTON

ALTERNATE NAME(S): .25 Rem.
RELATED CALIBER(S): .25-35 Winchester, .30 Remington, .32 Remington

CARTRIDGE HISTORY
Year of Introduction: 1906
Country of Origin: U.S.
Designer(s): Remington
Governing Body: CIP
Present Status: obsolete

CARTRIDGE DESCRIPTION
Bullet Diameter: .259 in.
Bullet Weight(s): 100-117 gr.
Rifling Twist Rate: 1 turn in 10 in.
Test Barrel Length: 24 in.
Case Type: rimless, necked
Case Material: brass
Primer Size: large rifle

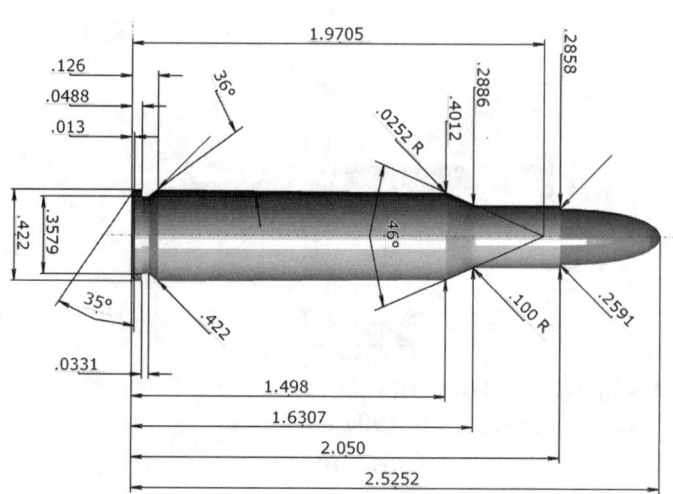

CARTRIDGE BALLISTICS
Max. Average Breech Pressure: 35,500 psi.
Max. Horizontal Range: 4,200 yds.
Max. Vertical Range: 8,850 ft.

Bullet Weight (gr.)	Bullet Type	Muzzle Velocity (fps)	Muzzle Energy (ft.-lbs.)
100	JSP-RN	2,330	1,216
117	JSP-RN	2,125	1,175

CURRENT MANUFACTURER(S)

None

GENERAL COMMENT(S)

Remington did not cut Winchester any slack in the race to offer the first semi-automatic sporting rifles in the early 1900s. Winchester was first with their Model 1905 rifle chambered for the relatively weak .32 WSL and .35 WSL cartridges. Remington entered the semi-automatic sporting rifle sweepstakes with their Model 8 rifle chambered for three new calibers – .25 Remington, .30 Remington, and .32 Remington. While the .30 Remington achieved popular acceptance, its siblings never really achieved critical mass. Production of both the .25 Remington and .32 Remington was stopped in the early 1950s. Surprisingly, the .30 Remington remained in production by Remington until the early 2000s.

TECHNICAL COMMENT(S)

These Remington cartridges are rimless versions of popular rimmed cartridges. For example, the .25 Remington is a rimless version of the .25-35 Winchester; the .30 Remington a rimless version of the venerable .30-30 Winchester, and the .32 Remington a rimless version of the .32 Winchester Special. The Winchester cartridges were rimmed as they were designed for lever-action and single-shot rifles while the Remington cartridges were modern, rimless designs for bolt-action and semi-automatic actions. Bullet weight, muzzle velocity and muzzle energy of the Remington cartridges were in the same general class as their rimmed Winchester counterparts noted above. While the flat nose bullets used in the Winchester calibers were launched at slightly higher muzzle velocities than the Remington cartridges, the round nose bullets used in the Remington calibers made up for this by slightly more retained velocity and energy down range. Despite their modern, rimless design, these Remington calibers were not high pressure cartridges. Maximum average chamber pressure was a very modest 35,000-40,000 psi. This, in turn, limited their muzzle velocity.

.25-20 SINGLE SHOT

ALTERNATE NAME(S): .25-20 SS
RELATED CALIBER(S): None

CARTRIDGE HISTORY

Year of Introduction: 1882
Country of Origin: U.S.
Designer(s): J. Francis Rabbeth
Governing Body: none
Present Status: obsolete

CARTRIDGE DESCRIPTION

Bullet Diameter: .257 in.
Bullet Weight(s): 86 gr.
Rifling Twist Rate: 1 turn in 12 in.
Test Barrel Length: N/A
Case Type: rimmed, necked
Case Material: brass
Primer: small rifle

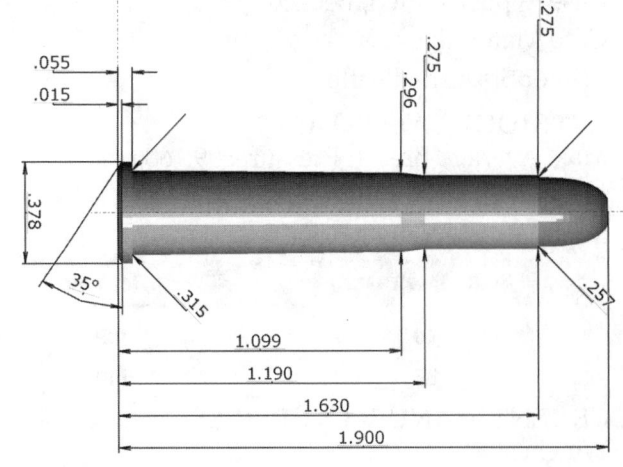

CARTRIDGE BALLISTICS

Max. Average Breech Pressure: N/A
Max. Horizontal Range: 2,450 yds.
Max. Vertical Range: 5,500 ft.

Bullet Weight (gr.)	Bullet Type	Muzzle Velocity (fps)	Muzzle Energy (ft.-lbs.)
86	L-FN	1,410	380

CURRENT MANUFACTURER(S)
None

GENERAL COMMENT(S)
Before it was adopted for mass production by Remington in 1882, the .25-20 Single Shot was one of the first centerfire rifle wildcat cartridges. It survived into the 1930s. J. Francis Rabbeth, the 19th century gun writer who designed this cartridge, would have been proud.

TECHNICAL COMMENT(S)
A major drawback of the .25-20 SS cartridge was that its length was too long for it to fit in most lever-action rifles. This situation consigned the .25-20 SS to single-shot rifles where it gained a well-earned reputation for excellent accuracy. This was a blessing in disguise as the dedicated target shooters propped up .25-20 SS ammunition production for the next several decades. As the .25-20 SS was not much of a field cartridge, hunters would not have been so kind.

.25-20 WINCHESTER

ALTERNATE NAME(S): .25-20 WCF, 6.5x33Rmm
RELATED CALIBER(S): .32-20 WCF

CARTRIDGE HISTORY
Year of Introduction: 1893
Country of Origin: U.S.
Designer(s): Winchester
Governing Body: SAAMI
Present Status: obsolete

CARTRIDGE DESCRIPTION
Bullet Diameter: .257 in.
Bullet Weight(s): 60-86 gr.
Rifling Twist Rate: 1 turn in 14 in.
Test Barrel Length: 24 in.
Case Type: rimmed, necked
Case Material: brass
Primer Size: small rifle

CARTRIDGE BALLISTICS
Max. Average Breech Pressure: 39,160 psi.
Max. Horizontal Range: 2,500 yds.
Max. Vertical Range: 5,500 ft.

Bullet Weight (gr.)	Bullet Type	Muzzle Velocity (fps)	Muzzle Energy (ft.-lbs.)
60	JSP	2,250	675
86	JSP	1,460	407

CURRENT MANUFACTURER(S)
Winchester

GENERAL COMMENT(S)
Prior to the development of the .22 Hornet and .218 Bee cartridges, the .25-20 Win. cartridge was a popular choice for varmint and small game hunting. Special runs of rifles in this caliber are still made occasionally and Winchester still offers ammunition in this caliber.

TECHNICAL COMMENT(S)
The 60 grain bullet loading is more effective for most hunting purposes than the 86 grain.

.25-35 WINCHESTER

ALTERNATE NAME(S): .25-35 WCF, 6.5x52Rmm
RELATED CALIBER(S): .30-30 Win.

CARTRIDGE HISTORY
Year of Introduction:1895
Country of Origin: U.S.
Designer(s): Winchester
Governing Body: SAAMI
Present Status: obsolete

CARTRIDGE DESCRIPTION
Bullet Diameter: .257 in.
Bullet Weight(s): 117 gr.
Rifling Twist Rate: 1 turn in 8 in.
Test Barrel Length: 24 in.
Case Type: rimmed, necked
Case Material: brass
Primer Size: large rifle

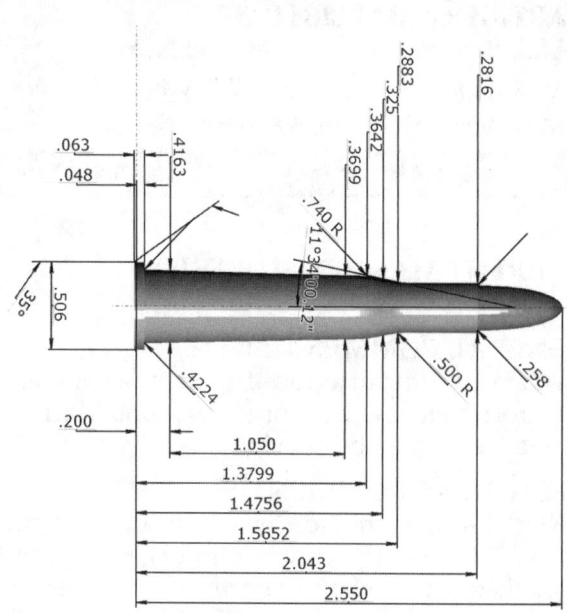

CARTRIDGE BALLISTICS
Max. Average Breech Pressure: 44,230 psi.
Max. Horizontal Range: 3,200 yds.
Max. Vertical Range: 7,200 ft.

Bullet Weight (gr.)	Bullet Type	Muzzle Velocity (fps)	Muzzle Energy (ft.-lbs.)
117	JSP	2,230	1,292

CURRENT MANUFACTURER(S)
Winchester

GENERAL COMMENT(S)
Introduced with the .30-30 Winchester cartridge in 1895, the .25-35 Win. was the first small-bore sporting cartridge designed for smokeless propellants in the U.S.

TECHNICAL COMMENT(S)
The .25-35 Win. cartridge shares head dimensions with its big brother, the .30-30 Win. Ballistic performance of the .25-35 Win. cartridge is outdated.

.25-36 MARLIN

ALTERNATE NAME(S): none
RELATED CALIBER(S): .25-37, .25-35 WCF

CARTRIDGE HISTORY
Year of Introduction: 1895
Country of Origin: U.S.
Designer(s): William Lowe
Governing Body: none
Present Status: obsolete

CARTRIDGE DESCRIPTION
Bullet Diameter: .257 in.
Bullet Weight(s): 117 gr.
Rifling Twist Rate: 1 turn in 9 in.
Test Barrel Length: N/A
Case Type: rimmed, necked

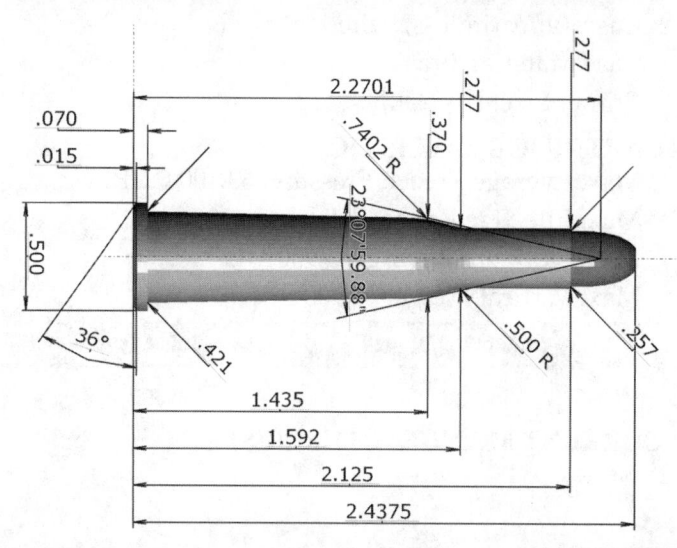

Case Material: brass
Primer: large rifle

CARTRIDGE BALLISTICS

Max. Average Breech Pressure: N/A
Max. Horizontal Range: 3,200 yds.
Max. Vertical Range: 6,800 ft.

Bullet Weight (gr.)	Bullet Type	Muzzle Velocity (fps)	Muzzle Energy (ft.-lbs.)
117	JSP	1,855	894

CURRENT MANUFACTURER(S)

None

GENERAL COMMENT(S)

When Marlin introduced their new Model 1895 rifle, the .25-36 Marlin cartridge was introduced as well. Unfortunately, after sportsmen found Marlin's new cartridge offered less than sterling accuracy, it faded quickly away and was obsolete by the early 1920s.

TECHNICAL COMMENT(S)

Marlin's new creation was basically a slightly shortened version of an obscure, earlier cartridge called the .25-37. Originally loaded with black powder, the ammunition manufacturers transitioned the .25-36 Marlin to smokeless propellants shortly after its introduction. Surely, Marlin hoped this would improve its accuracy, but apparently it did not. The .25-36 Marlin and the .25-37 cartridges are not interchangeable. Ballistics of the .25-36 Marlin are inferior to the .25-35 WCF leaving the .25-36 useless for anything but small game hunting.

6.5mm REMINGTON MAGNUM

ALTERNATE NAME(S): 6.5 Rem. Mag.
RELATED CALIBER(S): 7mm Rem. Mag.

CARTRIDGE HISTORY

Year of Introduction: 1966
Country of Origin: U.S.
Designer(s): Remington
Governing Body: SAAMI
Present Status: obsolete

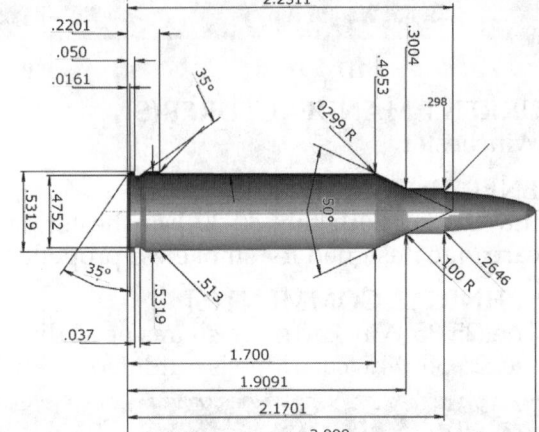

CARTRIDGE DESCRIPTION

Bullet Diameter: .264 in.
Bullet Weight(s): 120 gr.
Rifling Twist Rate: 1 turn in 9 in.
Test Barrel Length: 24 in.
Case Type: rimless, belted, necked
Case Material: brass
Primer Size: large rifle

CARTRIDGE BALLISTICS

Max. Average Breech Pressure: 63,100 CUP.
Max. Effective Range: 300 yds.
Max. Horizontal Range: 4,900 yds.
Max. Vertical Range: 10,900 ft.

Bullet Weight (gr.)	Bullet Type	Muzzle Velocity (fps)	Muzzle Energy (ft.-lbs.)
120	JSP	3,210	2,745

CURRENT MANUFACTURER(S)

None

GENERAL COMMENT(S)
Here is yet another excellent 6.5mm cartridge that did not catch on with American shooters.

TECHNICAL COMMENT(S)
The 6.5mm Rem. Mag. cartridge is based on the 7mm Rem. Mag. cartridge case necked down to 6.5mm. The 6.5mm Rem. Mag. was loaded with lighter weight bullets than the .264 Win. Mag. This may explain its quick demise.

6.5x54mm MAUSER

ALTERNATE NAME(S): None
RELATED CALIBER(S): None

CARTRIDGE HISTORY
Year of Introduction: 1900
Country of Origin: Germany
Designer(s): Peter Paul Mauser
Governing Body: none
Present Status: obsolete

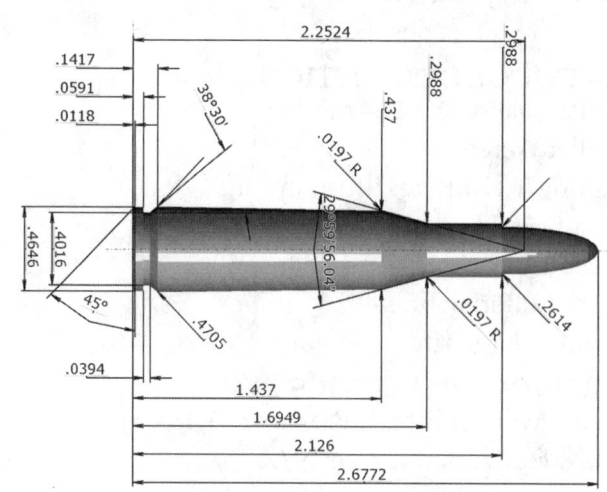

CARTRIDGE DESCRIPTION
Bullet Diameter: .264 in.
Bullet Weight(s): 119 gr.
Rifling Twist Rate: N/A
Test Barrel Length: N/A
Case Type: rimless, necked
Case Material: brass
Primer: large rifle

CARTRIDGE BALLISTICS
Max. Average Breech Pressure: N/A
Max. Horizontal Range: 4,900 yds.
Max. Vertical Range: 10,200 ft.

Bullet Weight (gr.)	Bullet Type	Muzzle Velocity (fps)	Muzzle Energy (ft.-lbs.)
119	JSP	2,360	1,468

CURRENT MANUFACTURER(S)
None

GENERAL COMMENT(S)
The 6.5x54mm Mannlicher-Schoenauer cartridge and the 6.5x54mm Mauser cartridge looked very similar and offered equivalent ballistic performance. The 6.5x54mm M-S caught on and remains popular to this day while the 6.5x57mm Mauser did not and faded away.

TECHNICAL COMMENT(S)
From a technical standpoint, the 6.5x54mm is the smallest caliber in the Mauser 8x54mm short case family of cartridges. Lackluster ballistics of the 6.5x57mm Mauser cartridge certainly made a major contribution to its demise.

6.5x58mm MAUSER

ALTERNATE NAME(S): 6.5x58mm Mauser (P), 6.5x58mm Portuguese Mauser, 6.5x58mm Portuguese Vergueiro
RELATED CALIBER(S): 6.5x57mm Mauser, 7x57mm Mauser

CARTRIDGE HISTORY

Year of Introduction: 1904
Country of Origin: Germany
Designer(s): Peter Paul Mauser
Governing Body: none
Present Status: obsolete

CARTRIDGE DESCRIPTION

Bullet Diameter: .264 in.
Bullet Weight(s): 126 gr.
Rifling Twist Rate: 1 turn in 8 in.
Test Barrel Length: 24 in.
Case Type: rimless, necked
Case Material: brass
Primer: large rifle

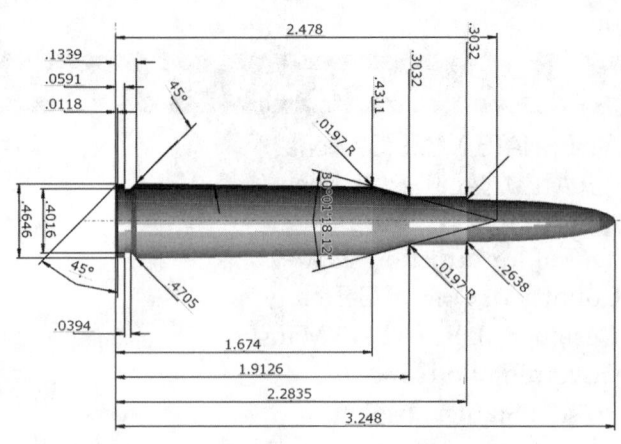

CARTRIDGE BALLISTICS

Max. Average Breech Pressure: 51,488 psi.
Max. Horizontal Range: N/A
Max. Vertical Range: N/A

Bullet Weight (gr.)	Bullet Type	Muzzle Velocity (fps)	Muzzle Energy (ft.-lbs.)
139	JSP	2,775	2,372
157	JSP	2,570	2,292

CURRENT MANUFACTURER(S)

None

GENERAL COMMENT(S)

This cartridge is a sporting version of the 6.5x58mm Portuguese Vergueiro service rifle cartridge. As one of the early 6.5mm military cartridges, it developed a modest following in the sporting market until other 6.5mm cartridges entered the fray. In many instances, the first cartridge to develop a sporting market segment retains a major share of that segment when competitors enter. This held true for the 6.5x58mm Portuguese Mauser in that it took several decades for competing 6.5 caliber cartridges such as the 6.5x55mm Swedish and 6.5x57mm Mauser to wear away the market dominance of the 6.5x58mm Portuguese Mauser cartridge. By the mid-1930s, this process was nearly complete when Portugal adopted the 8x57Smm Mauser cartridge and rebarreled their remaining Vergueiro rifles to the new caliber. The 6.5x58mm Portuguese cartridge in sporting livery was made in Britain and Germany.

TECHNICAL COMMENT(S)

The 6.5x58mm cartridge is basically a 6.5x57mm cartridge necked down and with a 1mm longer case. Rim and head dimensions correspond with other Mauser cartridges such as the 6.5x57mm, 7x57mm, 8x57mm, and etc. (Parenthetically, one wonders just how many variations on a common rim/case head dimension Mauser could develop? Apparently, quite a few! In any case, Mauser had all the important bases covered in this regard.) It seems being first trumps being best every time! It had to be in this case as the ballistics and bullet weights of the 6.5x58mm Portuguese cartridge were nearly identical to those of the 6.5x55mm Swedish Mauser and 6.5x57mm Mauser cartridges.

6.5x61mm MAUSER, 6.5x61Rmm MAUSER

ALTERNATE NAME(S): 6.5x62mm
RELATED CALIBER(S): .256 Newton, 6.5x57mm Mauser, 7x57mm Mauser, 8x57mmJS Mauser

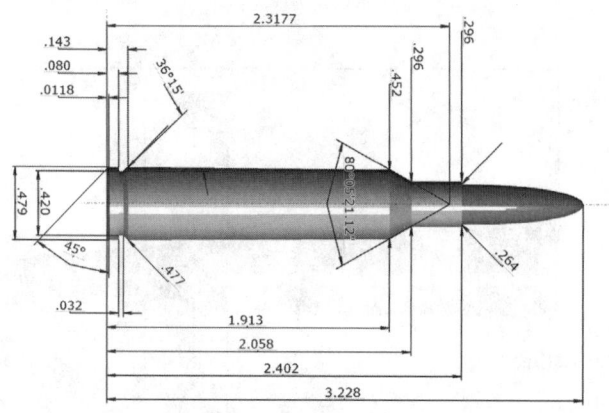
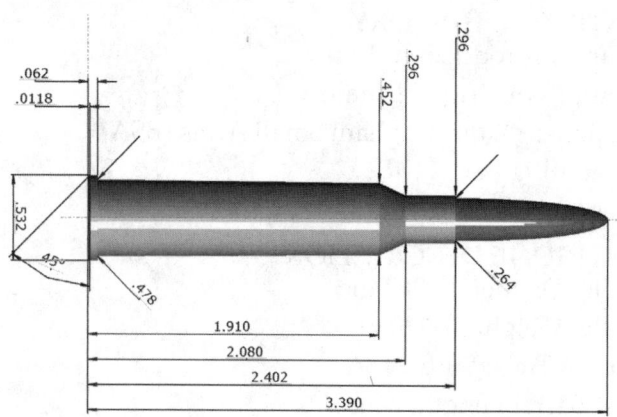

CARTRIDGE HISTORY
Year of Introduction: 1930
Country of Origin: Germany
Designer(s): DWM
Governing Body: none
Present Status: obsolete

CARTRIDGE DESCRIPTION
Bullet Diameter: .264 in.
Bullet Weight(s): 120-157 gr.
Rifling Twist Rate: 1 turn in 7.87 in.
Test Barrel Length: 24 in.
Case Type: rimless, necked; rimmed, necked
Case Material: brass
Primer: large rifle

CARTRIDGE BALLISTICS
Max. Average Breech Pressure: 56,000 psi. 6.5x61; 47,000 psi. 6.5x61R
Max. Horizontal Range: 5,350 yds.
Max. Vertical Range: 11,300 ft.

Bullet Weight (gr.)	Bullet Type	Muzzle Velocity (fps)	Muzzle Energy (ft.-lbs.)
119	JSP	3,090	2,510
139	JSP	2,905	2,604
157	JSP	2,750	2,636
139	JSP	2,550	2,007 (6.5x61R est.)

CURRENT MANUFACTURER(S)
None

GENERAL COMMENT(S)
This was one of the last cartridges introduced with the Mauser name. Unfortunately, its production life was short as World War II intervened a few years after its introduction. Following the end of the War, production of this caliber was not resumed.

TECHNICAL COMMENT(S)
Judging from the design features and published ballistics, the 6.5x61mm Mauser cartridge was an attempt to design a more powerful cartridge than was possible on the 6.5x57mm Mauser cartridge case. For manufacturing economy, the 6.5x61mm Mauser shares the rim and head dimensions with its 57mm siblings, but with a 4mm longer case to provide more volume for a heavier powder charge. The down side of this is an overall loaded length that requires a long rifle action. This concept succeeds from a ballistic performance standpoint, but following the War, sportsmen were not interested in a new 6.5mm cartridge.

.26 BELTED RIMLESS NITRO EXPRESS (BSA)

ALTERNATE NAME(S): .26 BSA, .26 Rimless Belted NE (BSA)
RELATED CALIBER(S): .300 H&H Magnum, .275 H&H Magnum

CARTRIDGE HISTORY

Year of Introduction: 1921
Country of Origin: Britain
Designer(s): Birmingham Small Arms (BSA)
Governing Body: CIP
Present Status: obsolete

CARTRIDGE DESCRIPTION

Bullet Diameter: .267 in.
Bullet Weight(s): 110 gr.
Rifling Twist Rate: N/A
Test Barrel Length: 24 in.
Case Type: rimless, belted, necked
Case Material: brass
Primer: large rifle

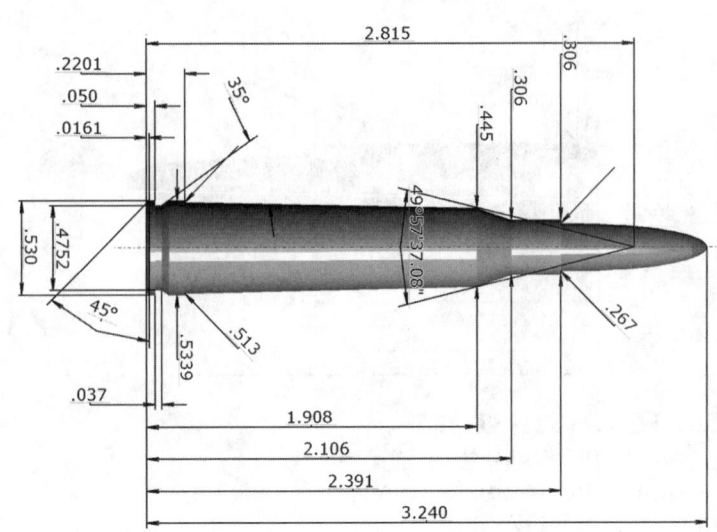

CARTRIDGE BALLISTICS

Max. Average Breech Pressure: 60,000 psi.
Max. Horizontal Range: 4,550 yds.
Max. Vertical Range: 9,800 ft.

Bullet Weight (gr.)	Bullet Type	Muzzle Velocity (fps)	Muzzle Energy (ft.-lbs.)
110	JSP	3,100	2,345

CURRENT MANUFACTURER(S)

None

GENERAL COMMENT(S)

The .26 Rimless Belted Nitro Express (BSA) is a 6.5mm cartridge by another (peculiarly British) name. It was one of the few British cartridges of this caliber, but was no more successful than the others.

TECHNICAL COMMENT(S)

Unlike many other high performance, or magnum, 6.5mm cartridges, the .26 BSA cartridge case is a belted design based on the .300 H&H Magnum cartridge. Arguably, the belted design did nothing to enhance the appeal of this cartridge in the market. A major handicap proved to be the selection of a bullet that was too light and too fragile for hunting medium game, leaving the .26 BSA with no real advantage over the numerous other 6.5mm cartridges firing heavier more robust bullets. British ammunition manufacturers did not seem to understand this and did nothing to correct the problem with predictable results, oblivion.

.264 WINCHESTER MAGNUM

ALTERNATE NAME(S): .264 Win. Mag.
RELATED CALIBER(S): .300 Win. Mag.

CARTRIDGE HISTORY
Year of Introduction: 1958
Country of Origin: U.S.
Designer(s): Winchester
Governing Body: SAAMI
Present Status: obsolete

CARTRIDGE DESCRIPTION
Bullet Diameter: .264 in.
Bullet Weight(s): 140 gr.
Rifling Twist Rate: 1 turn in 9 in.
Test Barrel Length: 24 in.
Case Type: rimless, belted, necked
Case Material: brass
Primer Size: large rifle

CARTRIDGE BALLISTICS
Max. Average Breech Pressure: 57,200 CUP.
Max. Horizontal Range: 4,900 yds.
Max. Vertical Range: 10,900 ft.

Bullet Weight (gr.)	Bullet Type	Muzzle Velocity (fps)	Muzzle Energy (ft.-lbs.)
140	JSP	3,030	2,854

CURRENT MANUFACTURER(S)
Winchester

GENERAL COMMENT(S)
With the sole exception of the 6.5x55mm Swedish cartridge, 6.5mm/.264 in. caliber cartridges have never been popular in the U.S. This is not for lack of trying as the ammunition manufacturers have developed several very good 6.5mm designs. All have proven to be a marketing failure – the .264 Win. Mag. is a good example of this.

TECHNICAL COMMENT(S)
The .264 Win. Mag. cartridge is based on the .300 Win. Mag. with which it shares head configuration and dimensions.

7mm BR REMINGTON

ALTERNATE NAME(S): 7mm BR
RELATED CALIBER(S): 6mm BR, .308 Winchester

CARTRIDGE HISTORY
Year of Introduction: 1978
Country of Origin: U.S.
Designer(s): Mike Walker
Governing Body: SAAMI, CIP
Present Status: obsolete

CARTRIDGE DESCRIPTION
Bullet Diameter: .284 in.
Bullet Weight(s): 140 gr.
Rifling Twist Rate: 1 turn in 9.5 in.
Test Barrel Length: 24 in.
Case Type: rimless, necked
Case Material: brass

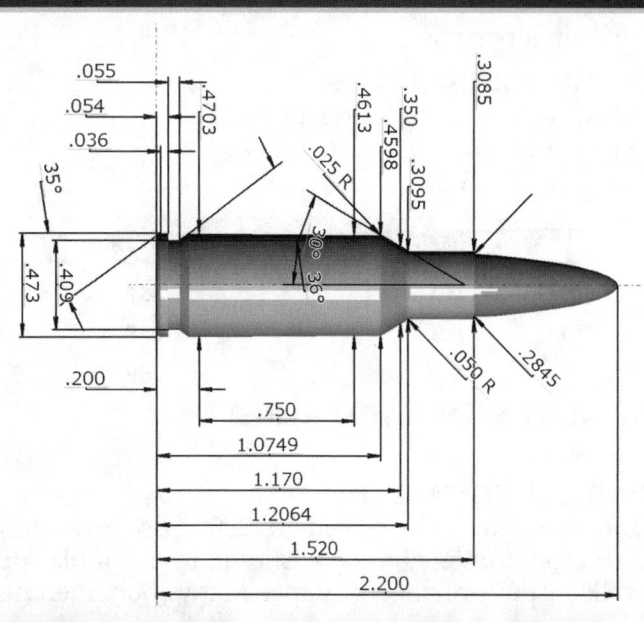

Primer: small rifle

CARTRIDGE BALLISTICS
Max. Average Breech Pressure: 58,740 psi.
Max. Horizontal Range: 4,400 yds.
Max. Vertical Range: 8,700 ft.

Bullet Weight (gr.)	Bullet Type	Muzzle Velocity (fps)	Muzzle Energy (ft.-lbs.)
140	JHP	2,215	1,525

CURRENT MANUFACTURER(S)
None

GENERAL COMMENT(S)
In 1978, Remington announced a new family of cartridges designed specifically for bench rest and silhouette shooting. The 7mm BR Remington cartridge was the largest caliber of this product line. It was declared obsolete in the early 2000s.

TECHNICAL COMMENT(S)
Essentially, the 7mm BR is a shortened .308 Winchester case necked down to .284 in. The shorter case allows powder charges of nearly 100% density for efficiency. An interesting feature is the use of a small rifle primer as that size is believed to enhance accuracy in a short large diameter cartridge.

.280 FLANGED NITRO EXPRESS

ALTERNATE NAME(S): .280 Lancaster
RELATED CALIBER(S): .280 Ross

CARTRIDGE HISTORY
Year of Introduction: 1906
Country of Origin: Britain
Designer(s): Lancaster
Governing Body: none
Present Status: obsolete

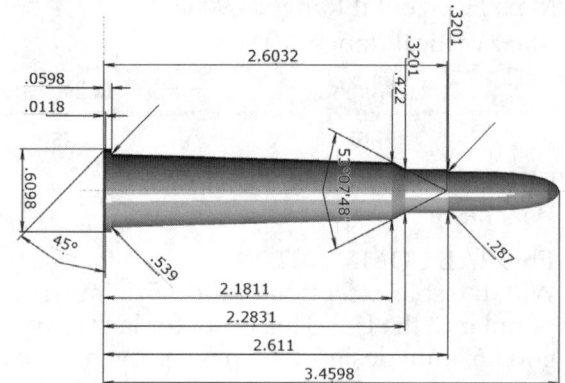

CARTRIDGE DESCRIPTION
Bullet Diameter: .288 in.
Bullet Weight(s): 140-180 gr.
Rifling Twist Rate: 1 turn in 10 in.
Test Barrel Length: 24 in.
Case Type: rimmed, necked
Case Material: brass
Primer: large rifle

CARTRIDGE BALLISTICS
Max. Average Breech Pressure: 42,786 psi.
Max. Horizontal Range: 5,000 yds.
Max. Vertical Range: 10,500 ft.

Bullet Weight (gr.)	Bullet Type	Muzzle Velocity (fps)	Muzzle Energy (ft.-lbs.)
140	JSP	2,800	2,440
160	JSP	2,600	2,400
180	JSP	2,400	2,300

CURRENT MANUFACTURER(S)
None

GENERAL COMMENT(S)
Introduction of the Canadian .280 Ross cartridge in 1906 created quite a stir among sporting shooters still used to thinking about ballistics in terms of black powder. The .280 Ross offered a quantum level increase in ballistic performance, on paper. Many sportsmen rushed to try the new .280 Ross on all sorts of game, including

African. However, bullets used in the Ross were designed only for medium plains game.

TECHNICAL COMMENT(S)

The .280 Ross cartridge was a rimless design suitable for bolt-action rifles. What was wanted by many sportsmen was a rimmed version for use in single-shot rifles and drillings. The British Lancaster firm developed such a cartridge in 1906 on the heels of the .280 Ross. Called the .280 Flanged, the new cartridge enjoyed a brief surge of interest before sportsmen became disillusioned with all things .280.

.280 ROSS

ALTERNATE NAME(S): .280 Rimless
RELATED CALIBER(S): .280 Halger Magnum

CARTRIDGE HISTORY

Year of Introduction: 1906
Country of Origin: Britain
Designer(s): Sir Charles Ross and F.W. Jones
Governing Body: CIP
Present Status: obsolete

CARTRIDGE DESCRIPTION

Bullet Diameter: .287 in.
Bullet Weight(s): 140-180 gr.
Rifling Twist Rate: 1 turn in 8.66 in.
Test Barrel Length: 24 in.
Case Type: semi-rimmed, necked
Case Material: brass
Primer Size: large rifle

CARTRIDGE BALLISTICS

Max. Average Breech Pressure: 47,140 psi.
Max. Horizontal Range: 4,500 yds.
Max. Vertical Range: 8,800 ft.

Bullet Weight (gr.)	Bullet Type	Muzzle Velocity (fps)	Muzzle Energy (ft.-lbs.)
140	JSP	2,900	2,620
150	JSP	2,800	2,610
160	JSP	2,700	2,600
180	JSP	2,550	2,600

CURRENT MANUFACTURER(S)

None

GENERAL COMMENT(S)

Originally designed as a military cartridge for the Canadian Army before World War I (but not adopted), the .280 Ross found modest acceptance as a sporting cartridge by virtue of it being one of the first small bore, high velocity cartridges. Although a popular choice of Canadian hunters, the .280 Ross remained rather an oddity to American hunters who preferred the 7x57mm Mauser cartridge. As a result, domestic ammunition manufacturers ceased making .280 Ross ammunition in the mid-1930s.

TECHNICAL COMMENT(S)

When it was first introduced, the killing power of the high velocity, fast-expanding Ross bullets seemed revolutionary. On medium game such as deer, the .280 Ross reliably delivered clean, one-shot kills. This did not translate to large, heavy game however where the lightly constructed bullet did not penetrate deeply enough.

7x33mm SAKO

ALTERNATE NAME(S): 7x33mm Finnish
RELATED CALIBER(S): 9mm Luger, 7.62x25mm Tokarev, 7.63mm Mauser

CARTRIDGE HISTORY
Year of Introduction: 1942
Country of Origin: Finland
Designer(s): Sako
Governing Body: CIP
Present Status: obsolete

CARTRIDGE DESCRIPTION
Bullet Diameter: .2858 in.
Bullet Weight(s): 78 gr.
Rifling Twist Rate: 1 turn in 15.8 in.
Test Barrel Length: 24 in.
Case Type: rimless, necked
Case Material: brass
Primer: small rifle

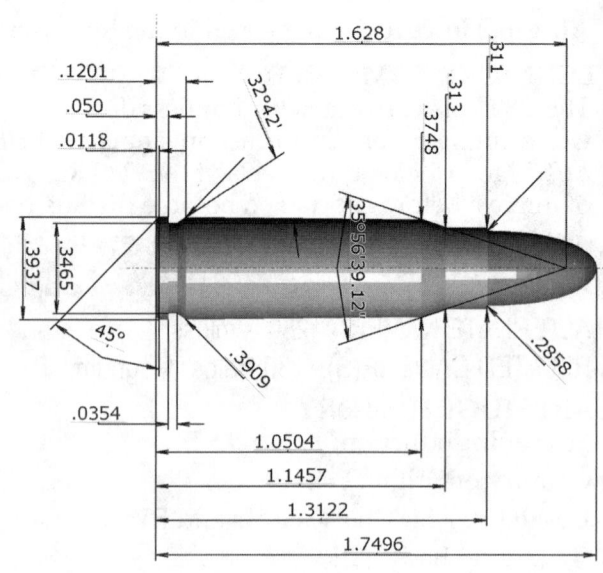

CARTRIDGE BALLISTICS
Max. Average Breech Pressure: 40,611 psi.
Max. Horizontal Range: 2,400 yds.
Max. Vertical Range: 5,300 ft.

Bullet Weight (gr.)	Bullet Type	Muzzle Velocity (fps)	Muzzle Energy (ft.-lbs.)
78	JSP/ FMJ	2,400	998

CURRENT MANUFACTURER(S)
None

GENERAL COMMENT(S)
In Finland, large birds such as capercaillie and grouse are hunted with a center fire rifle. A large bore, high velocity caliber is not needed as most shots are taken at ranges of 150 yards or less. In addition, high velocity bullets destroy the meat and/or the trophy. These requirements led Sako to develop a rifle cartridge in 1942 specifically for this purpose of hunting small game. Use of this cartridge was limited to Scandinavia. Sako declared the 7x33mm Sako cartridge obsolete in the early 1960s and dropped it from their product line. It has now become a collector's item. Sako was the only manufacturer.

TECHNICAL COMMENT(S)
Design of the 7x33mm Sako cartridge was an interesting exercise in the art of the possible in response to a self-developing need rather than a marketing decision or government requirement. Of course, the need developed first. Remember that the World War II years were hard times for the Finns. They fought two bitter campaigns against Russian invasions which cost them dearly, but preserved their independence. During that era, the Finns were short of everything and a world at war could provide little help. Food was rationed, so Finnish hunters harvested game to supplement their ration. As military cartridges were unsuitable for hunting, a cartridge that could be developed quickly and easily for hunting applications was needed. In 1942, Sako was busy manufacturing large quantities of 9mm Luger ammunition for the Finnish military. Lacking the tooling or raw materials for another caliber or cartridge, Sako elected to use the longest possible 9mm Luger case their machinery could make, and neck the case to 7mm. Using a 78 grain bullet, the new cartridge proved a success and survived long after World War II ended.

7x61mm SHARPE & HART SUPER

ALTERNATE NAME(S): 7x61mm S&H, 7x61mm S&H Super
RELATED CALIBER(S): none

CARTRIDGE HISTORY
Year of Introduction: 1953
Country of Origin: U.S.
Designer(s): Phil Sharpe and Richard Hart
Governing Body: CIP
Present Status: obsolete

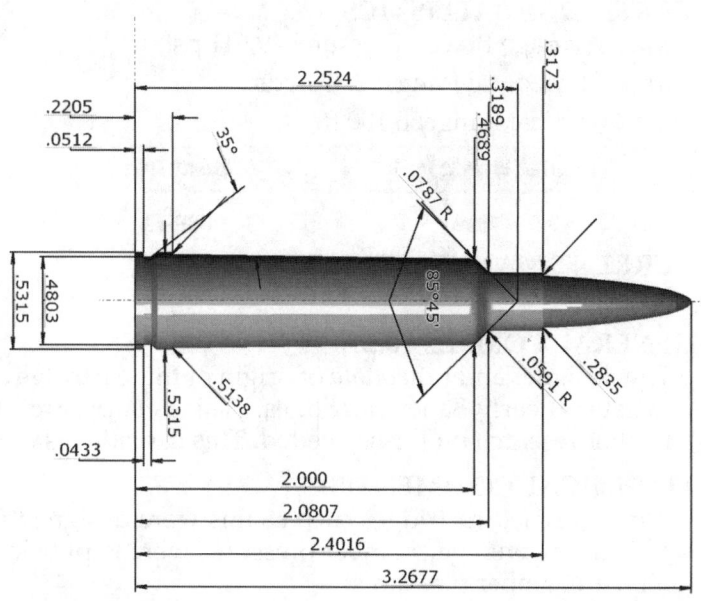

CARTRIDGE DESCRIPTION
Bullet Diameter: .284 in.
Bullet Weight(s): 160 gr.
Rifling Twist Rate: 1 turn in 9 in.
Test Barrel Length: 24 in.
Case Type: rimless, belted, necked
Case Material: brass
Primer Size: large rifle

CARTRIDGE BALLISTICS
Max. Average Breech Pressure: 58,140 psi.
Max. Effective Range: 400 yds.
Max. Horizontal Range: 7,000 yds.
Max. Vertical Range: 15,700 ft.

Bullet Weight (gr.)	Bullet Type	Muzzle Velocity (fps)	Muzzle Energy (ft.-lbs.)
154	JSP	3,060	3,200

CURRENT MANUFACTURER(S)
None

GENERAL COMMENT(S)
For most of its 50 year production life, this cartridge was loaded by Norma. As the designers copyrighted their design, the large American firearm and ammunition makers remained uninterested in this cartridge. The amazing thing was that it lasted as long as it did. The 7x61mm S&H was one of the first post-war high velocity sporting cartridges in 7mm caliber. As such, it must be considered a modern prototype for the present large 7mm magnum cartridges of today.

TECHNICAL COMMENT(S)
Original examples of the 7mm S&H did not have a belted case. Later examples with a belted case were called 7mm S&H Super to differentiate them from the earlier design.

7x72Rmm

ALTERNATE NAME(S): none
RELATED CALIBER(S): 8x72Rmm Sauer, 9.3x72Rmm Sauer

CARTRIDGE HISTORY
Year of Introduction: N/A
Country of Origin: Germany
Designer(s): N/A
Governing Body: CIP
Present Status: obsolete

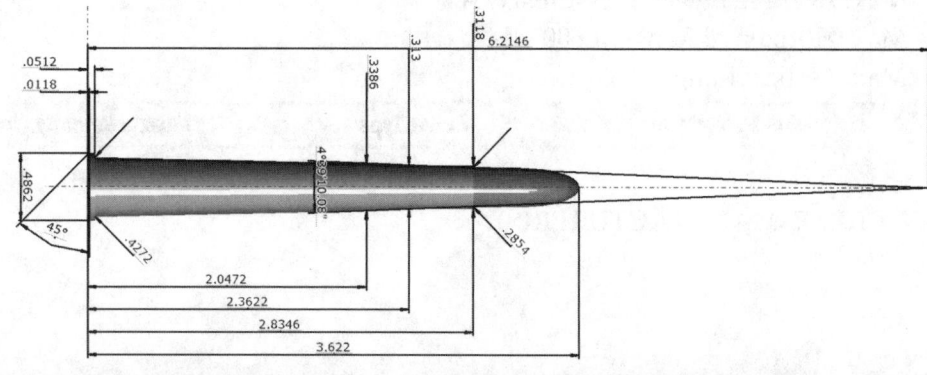

CARTRIDGE DESCRIPTION
Bullet Diameter: .284 in.
Bullet Weight(s): 139 gr.
Rifling Twist Rate: 1 turn in 8.66 in.

Test Barrel Length: 24 in.
Case Type: rimmed, tapered w/slight neck
Case Material: brass
Primer: large rifle

CARTRIDGE BALLISTICS
Max. Average Breech Pressure: 49,611 psi.
Max. Horizontal Range: 2,800 yds.
Max. Vertical Range: 6,100 ft.

Bullet Weight (gr.)	Bullet Type	Muzzle Velocity (fps)	Muzzle Energy (ft.-lbs.)
139	JSP-FN	2,440	1,837

CURRENT MANUFACTURER(S)
None

GENERAL COMMENT(S)
The designer and exact date of origin of this cartridge are not firmly established. It bears a striking resemblance to several early Sauer cartridges. This is supported by the fact it has an original DWM number. However, further research on this is needed. This cartridge is now obsolete.

TECHNICAL COMMENT(S)
Long, rimmed cartridges such as this were designed for use in drillings where breech space is at a premium. Maximum average chamber pressures were kept below 50,000 psi. as break-open actions could not withstand higher chamber pressures.

.297/250 ROOK RIFLE

ALTERNATE NAME(S): .297/250 H&H Rook Rifle
RELATED CALIBER(S): .297/230 Morris Short and Long

CARTRIDGE HISTORY
Year of Introduction: circa late 1870s
Country of Origin: Britain
Designer(s): Holland & Holland
Governing Body: none
Present Status: obsolete

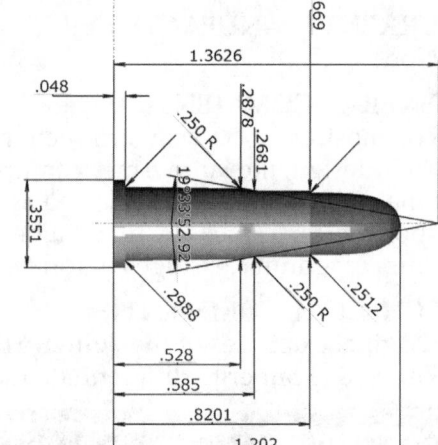

CARTRIDGE DESCRIPTION
Bullet Diameter: .250 in.
Bullet Weight(s): 56 gr.
Rifling Twist Rate: 1 turn in 10 in.
Test Barrel Length: N/A
Case Type: rimmed, necked
Case Material: brass
Primer: small rifle

CARTRIDGE BALLISTICS
Max. Average Breech Pressure: N/A
Max. Horizontal Range: 1,600 yds.
Max. Vertical Range: 3,550 ft.

Bullet Weight (gr.)	Bullet Type	Muzzle Velocity (fps)	Muzzle Energy (ft.-lbs.)
56	L-RN	1,150	164

CURRENT MANUFACTURER(S)
None

GENERAL COMMENT(S)

A rook is a large, black bird similar to a North American raven or crow. In the early years of the 20th century, British farmers used small caliber, low-powdered rifle cartridges to shoot rooks in order to keep them away from crops. As cost was an issue, rook cartridges were center fire designs that could be reloaded. A number of different diminutive cartridges were developed for this purpose. The .297/250 Rook is one of them. Holland & Holland designed the .297/250 Rook cartridge. Not to be outdone, Jeffery (.255 Jeffery Rook), Westley Richards (.300 Sherwood), Greener (.310 Greener), Lancaster (.297/230 Sporting), and other British firms offered rook cartridges as well. Many of the rook calibers survived into the late 1930s, a handful held on until the early 1960s. Eley was a primary manufacturer of these calibers. The .22 Long Rifle rimfire cartridge proved to be the cause of their demise. Today, rook shooting in Britain has all but ended.

TECHNICAL COMMENT(S)

As a group, the smaller rook cartridges were necked, while most of the larger cartridges had a straight sidewall case. All were rimmed designs used only in single-shot rifles and a few revolvers. The exterior ballistic performance of most rook cartridges scarcely exceeds that of some modern .22 Long Rifle loads. But, that misses the point. In densely populated Britain, rooks were shot at close ranges, so a reduced maximum range was more important than a long effective range. For this reason, the ballistic performance of rook cartridges must not be judged by modern standards. Most rook cartridges began as black powder designs that were subsequently loaded with smokeless propellants. Typical bullets were plain lead round-nose designs although some were loaded with jacketed hollow- or soft-point bullets.

.30 REMINGTON

ALTERNATE NAME(S): .30 Rem., 7.62x52mm
RELATED CALIBER(S): .30-30 Win., .25 Rem., 32. Rem., .25-35 Win., .32 Win. Spl.

CARTRIDGE HISTORY

Year of Introduction: 1906
Country of Origin: U.S.
Designer(s): Remington
Governing Body: CIP
Present Status: obsolete

CARTRIDGE DESCRIPTION

Bullet Diameter: .308 in.
Bullet Weight(s): 160-170 gr.
Rifling Twist Rate: 1 turn in 12 in.
Test Barrel Length: 24 in.
Case Type: rimless, necked
Case Material: brass
Primer Size: large rifle

CARTRIDGE BALLISTICS

Max. Average Breech Pressure: 40,600 psi.
Max. Horizontal Range: 2,800 yds.
Max. Vertical Range: 6,000 ft.

Bullet Weight (gr.)	Bullet Type	Muzzle Velocity (fps)	Muzzle Energy (ft.-lbs.)
160	JSP-RN	2,220	1,750
170	JSP-RN	2,120	1,695

CURRENT MANUFACTURER(S)

None

GENERAL COMMENT(S)

Remington did not cut Winchester any slack in the race to offer the first semi-automatic sporting rifles in the early 1900s. Winchester was first with their Model 1905 rifle chambered for the relatively weak .32 W.S.L. and .35 W.S.L. cartridges. Remington entered the semi-automatic sporting rifle sweepstakes with their Model 8 rifle chambered for three new calibers – .25 Remington, .30 Remington, and .32 Remington. While the .30 Remington achieved popular acceptance, its siblings never really achieved critical mass. Production of both the .25 Remington and .32

Remington was stopped in the early 1950s. Surprisingly, the .30 Remington remained in production by Remington until the early 2000s. At approximately the time Remington dropped this old hunter, the U.S. military began experimenting with the 6.8mm SPC which is derived from the .30 Rem. case with a small rifle primer.

TECHNICAL COMMENT(S)

The .25, .30, and .32 Remington cartridges are rimless versions of popular rimmed cartridges. For example, the .25 Remington is a rimless version of the .25-35 Winchester, the .30 Remington a rimless version of the venerable .30-30 Winchester, and the .32 Remington a rimless version of the .32 Winchester Special. The Winchester cartridges were rimmed as they were designed for lever-action and single-shot rifles while the Remington cartridges were modern, rimless designs for bolt-action and semi-automatic actions. Bullet weight, muzzle velocity, and muzzle energy of the Remington cartridges were in the same general class as their rimmed Winchester counterparts noted above. While the flat nose bullets used in the Winchester calibers were launched at slightly higher muzzle velocities than the Remington cartridges, the round nose bullets used in the Remington calibers made up for this by slightly more retained velocity and energy down range. Despite their modern, rimless design, these Remington calibers were not high pressure cartridges. Maximum average chamber pressure was a very modest 35,000-40,000 psi. This, in turn, limited their muzzle velocity.

.300 (295) ROOK RIFLE

ALTERNATE NAME(S): .300 Rook, .300 Long C.F., 7.5x30mm, .300 Long Revolver, .300 C.F. Long
RELATED CALIBER(S): .32 Extra Long

CARTRIDGE HISTORY

Year of Introduction: circa early 1870s

Country of Origin: Britain

Designer(s): N/A

Governing Body: none

Present Status: obsolete

CARTRIDGE DESCRIPTION

Bullet Diameter: .300 in.

Bullet Weight(s): 80 gr.

Rifling Twist Rate: 1 turn in 20 in.

Test Barrel Length: 24 in.

Case Type: rimmed, straight

Case Material: brass

Primer: small rifle

CARTRIDGE BALLISTICS

Max. Average Breech Pressure: 17,450 psi.

Max. Horizontal Range: 1,850 yds.

Max. Vertical Range: 4,000 ft.

Bullet Weight (gr.)	Bullet Type	Muzzle Velocity (fps)	Muzzle Energy (ft.-lbs.)
80	L-RN	1,100	215

CURRENT MANUFACTURER(S)

None

GENERAL COMMENT(S)

Many British farms kept a small caliber rifle on hand for dispatching predators, pests, and wounded farm animals. For these purposes, a cartridge of great power or long range was not needed or wanted. A large number of small, centerfire cartridges of this type were developed in Britain, however their popularity did not extend to the U.S. As a group, these cartridges were called "Rook" cartridges. Many were short-lived and obscure. This was one of the more popular and successful numbers that remained in production until the early 1960s.

TECHNICAL COMMENT(S)

Like most of its brethren, the .300 (295) Rook cartridge began life as a black powder cartridge, then transitioned to smokeless. Simple, lead round-nose bullets were the norm at very modest muzzle velocities and energies due to the very low maximum average chamber pressures.

.300 SHERWOOD

ALTERNATE NAME(S): none
RELATED CALIBER(S): .300 (.295) Rook, .32 Extra Long Ballard, .310 Cadet

CARTRIDGE HISTORY
Year of Introduction: 1901
Country of Origin: Britain
Designer(s): Westley Richards
Governing Body: CIP
Present Status: obsolete

CARTRIDGE DESCRIPTION
Bullet Diameter: .300 in.
Bullet Weight(s): 140 gr.
Rifling Twist Rate: 1 turn in 20 in.
Test Barrel Length: 24 in.
Case Type: rimmed, straight
Case Material: brass
Primer: small rifle

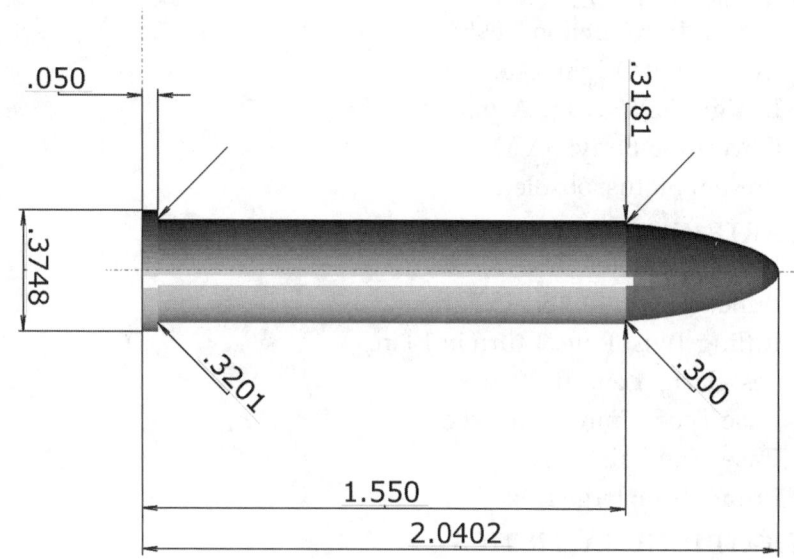

CARTRIDGE BALLISTICS
Max. Average Breech Pressure: 20,305 psi.
Max. Horizontal Range: 3,000 yds.
Max. Vertical Range: 6,250 ft.

Bullet Weight (gr.)	Bullet Type	Muzzle Velocity (fps)	Muzzle Energy (ft.-lbs.)
140	JHP	1,400	610

CURRENT MANUFACTURER(S)
None

GENERAL COMMENT(S)
One year after Greener introduced their .310 Greener (Cadet) cartridge, Westley Richards responded with their .300 Sherwood cartridge. While the .310 Greener cartridge was aimed at the military cadet market which required low cost training and target ammunition, the new Westley Richards cartridge was aimed at the sporting market for small game hunting. Accordingly, the .300 Sherwood was loaded with a jacketed, expanding bullet. History has judged Westley Richards wrong on the .300 Sherwood. Cartridges such as these worked well for training and target shooting, but lacked sufficient power for hunting. The .310 Greener cartridge survived, the .300 Sherwood did not.

TECHNICAL COMMENT(S)
Both the .310 Cadet and the .300 Sherwood were basic designs with a rim and a straight walled case. The .300 Sherwood case was about .42 inches longer than the .310 Cadet with a correspondingly greater internal volume. These two rivals differed slightly in ballistic performance. The .310 Cadet cartridge fired a 125 grain bullet at a muzzle velocity of 1,200 fps.; the .300 Sherwood offered a 140 grain bullet at a muzzle velocity of 1,400 fps. Certainly, the .300 Sherwood was the more powerful of the two, but it really did not matter as the main purpose of these cartridges was training and competition. Neither cartridge was useful for hunting anything other than small game.

.303 SAVAGE

ALTERNATE NAME(S): .301 Savage
RELATED CALIBER(S): .30-30 Win.

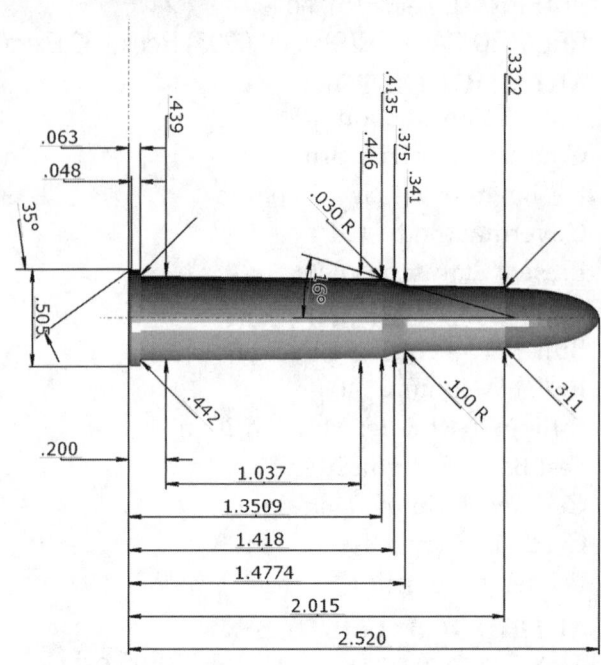

CARTRIDGE HISTORY
Year of Introduction: 1895
Country of Origin: U.S.
Designer(s): Savage Arms Co.
Governing Body: SAAMI
Present Status: obsolete

CARTRIDGE DESCRIPTION
Bullet Diameter: .308-.310 in.
Bullet Weight(s): 180-190 gr.
Rifling Twist Rate: 1 turn in 10 in.
Test Barrel Length: 20 in.
Case Type: rimmed, necked
Case Material: brass
Primer Size: large rifle

CARTRIDGE BALLISTICS
Max. Average Breech Pressure: 37,200 CUP.
Max. Horizontal Range: 4,200 yds.
Max. Vertical Range: 8,000 ft.

Bullet Weight (gr.)	Bullet Type	Muzzle Velocity (fps)	Muzzle Energy (ft.-lbs.)
180	JSP	2,140	1,830
190	JSP	1,890	1,507

CURRENT MANUFACTURER(S)
None

GENERAL COMMENT(S)
This old timer has been obsolete since before World War II. Developed originally as a potential military cartridge but not adopted, it was later redesigned for sporting use where it enjoyed only modest popularity. Here is a classic case of a cartridge developed for one purpose attempting to gain production life in another - unsuccessfully.

TECHNICAL COMMENT(S)
There is very little to recommend this cartridge. It offers ballistic performance similar to the .30-30 Win., .32 Win. Spl., and .38-55 Win. cartridges and no advantages over any of them.

.30-30 WESSON

ALTERNATE NAME(S): none
RELATED CALIBER(S): .38 Extra Long Ballard

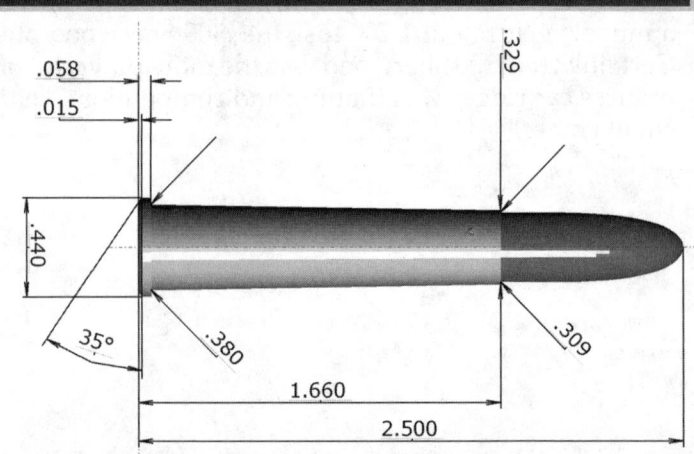

CARTRIDGE HISTORY
Year of Introduction: circa 1880
Country of Origin: U.S.
Designer(s): Frank Wesson
Governing Body: none
Present Status: obsolete

CARTRIDGE DESCRIPTION
Bullet Diameter: .308 in.
Bullet Weight(s): 165 gr.

Rifling Twist Rate: 1 turn in 12 in.
Test Barrel Length: N/A
Case Type: rimmed, straight (tapered)
Case Material: brass
Primer: large rifle

CARTRIDGE BALLISTICS
Max. Average Breech Pressure: N/A
Max. Horizontal Range: 2,800 yds.
Max. Vertical Range: 5,850 ft.

Bullet Weight (gr.)	Bullet Type	Muzzle Velocity (fps)	Muzzle Energy (ft.-lbs.)
165	L-RN	1,250	572

CURRENT MANUFACTURER(S)
None

GENERAL COMMENT(S)
In the late 1800s, low cost, single-shot rifles in medium calibers became very popular. Companies that made such rifles included Ballard, Wesson, Stevens and Maynard as well as Winchester and Remington. Frank Wesson, the brother of Daniel B. Wesson of Smith & Wesson fame, was a gun designer in his own right. In the early 1860s, he founded a company to manufacture his single-shot rifle designs. By 1870, Wesson rifles were a recognized name, although the company was small. As was the custom at the time, Frank Wesson designed several cartridges for his single-shot rifles. The .30-30 Wesson was one of the smallest in caliber. Wesson rifles were chambered for a wide variety of cartridges other than those of Frank Wesson. Most of these cartridges were loaded with lead bullets of flat-nose or round-nose profile. A few used paper-patched bullets. Such cartridges had the advantages of low cost, reduced recoil and sufficient power for small game and deer hunting at close ranges. They were also popular for formal and informal target shooting at close ranges. Remington, Winchester and United States Cartridge Co. manufactured ammunition in this caliber for a short time.

TECHNICAL COMMENT(S)
Unfortunately, the .30-30 Wesson did not prove to be popular in an era of large bore, black powder cartridges. Today, it is a rare cartridge. One must resist the urge to claim the .30-30 Wesson is the progenitor of the .30-30 Winchester cartridge introduced in 1894. Such is most certainly not the case, the common designations being nothing more than chance. The designs are quite different and have nothing in common.

8x42Rmm

ALTERNATE NAME(S): none
RELATED CALIBER(S): 8x51Rmm Mauser, .32-40 WCF

CARTRIDGE HISTORY
Year of Introduction: 1888
Country of Origin: Germany
Designer(s): Peter Paul Mauser
Governing Body: none
Present Status: obsolete

CARTRIDGE DESCRIPTION
Bullet Diameter: .318 in.
Bullet Weight(s): 157 gr.
Rifling Twist Rate: N/A
Test Barrel Length: N/A
Case Type: rimmed, necked
Case Material: brass
Primer: large rifle

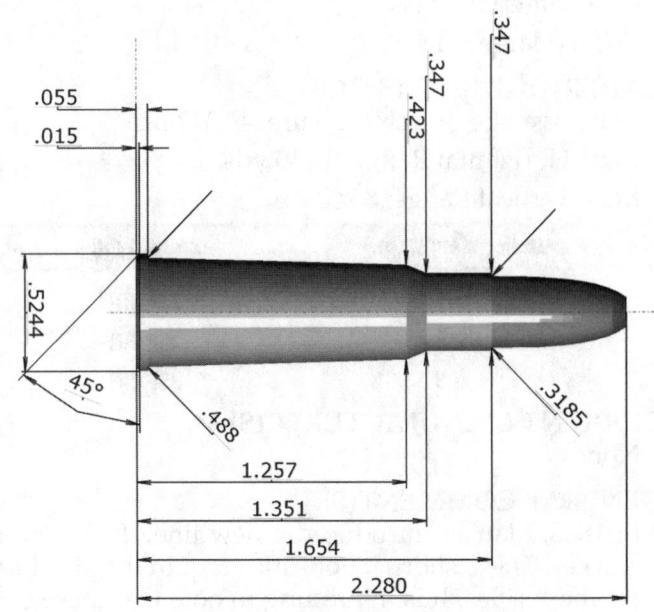

CARTRIDGE BALLISTICS
Max. Average Breech Pressure: N/A
Max. Horizontal Range: 3,800 yds.

Max. Vertical Range: 7,900 ft.

Bullet Weight (gr.)	Bullet Type	Muzzle Velocity (fps)	Muzzle Energy (ft.-lbs.)
157	JSP	1,780	1,110

CURRENT MANUFACTURER(S)
None

GENERAL COMMENT(S)
Although this cartridge looks very similar to many German *"schutzen"* target cartridges, in fact it was designed exclusively for hunting. The market segment this cartridge was intended to appeal to has been lost to history. However, its ballistics limit the possible applications to small game hunting. It was never very popular and disappeared early in the 20th century.

TECHNICAL COMMENT(S)
The only load offered in the 8x42Rmm cartridge was a 157 grain JSP hunting bullet. Here it is important to note that this bullet was the same .318 inch diameter as the 8x57mmJ Mauser cartridge. When the German Army switched to .323 inch diameter bullets for the 8x57mmJS cartridge in 1905, the 8x42Rmm cartridge got stuck with an obsolete bullet diameter.

8x51mm MAUSER, 8x51Rmm MAUSER

ALTERNATE NAME(S): 8x51mm Kurz, 8x51mm Mauser K, 8mm Mauser Kurz
RELATED CALIBER(S): 8x57mmJ Mauser, 8x57Rmm Mauser

CARTRIDGE HISTORY
Year of Introduction: 1888
Country of Origin: Germany
Designer(s): Mauser
Governing Body: none
Present Status: obsolete

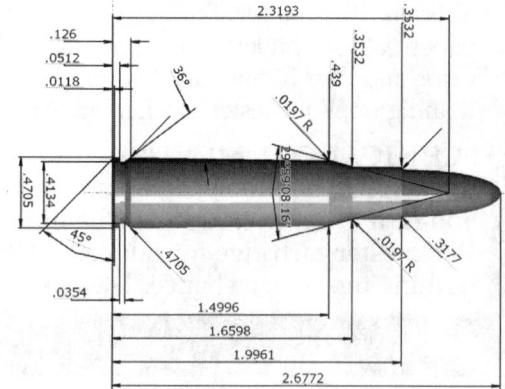

CARTRIDGE DESCRIPTION
Bullet Diameter: .318 in.
Bullet Weight(s): 157-196 gr.
Rifling Twist Rate: 1 turn in 9.45 in.
Test Barrel Length: 24 in.
Case Type: rimless, necked
Case Material: brass
Primer: large rifle

CARTRIDGE BALLISTICS
Max. Average Breech Pressure: 49,313 psi.
Max. Horizontal Range: 4,150 yds.
Max. Vertical Range: 8,700 ft.

Bullet Weight (gr.)	Bullet Type	Muzzle Velocity (fps)	Muzzle Energy (ft.-lbs.)
157	JSP-RN	2,155	1,619 (8x52R)
158	JSP-RN	2,380	1,927
196	JSP-RN	2,100	2,302

CURRENT MANUFACTURER(S)
None

GENERAL COMMENT(S)
In 1888, Mauser introduced a new line of "K" model (K for kurz or short) bolt-action rifles for the sporting market. These short-action rifles required a short cartridge and the 8x51mm series was developed especially for these rifles. It is interesting to note that these cartridges pre-dated the 7.62x51mm (.308 Win.) cartridge by 66 years.

TECHNICAL COMMENT(S)
This modern-looking, rimless, smokeless powder cartridge was developed for the sporting market. For bolt-action rifles, there was the rimless version. A second, rimmed version for break-open drillings was loaded to a lower muzzle velocity and chamber pressure.

8x54mm KRAG-JORGENSEN

ALTERNATE NAME(S): 8x54mm Krag
RELATED CALIBER(S): 6.5x55mm Swedish Mauser

CARTRIDGE HISTORY
Year of Introduction: circa 1898
Country of Origin: Norway
Designer(s): N/A
Governing Body: none
Present Status: obsolete

CARTRIDGE DESCRIPTION
Bullet Diameter: .323 in.
Bullet Weight(s): 196 gr.
Rifling Twist Rate: 1 turn in 10 in.
Test Barrel Length: 24 in.
Case Type: rimless, necked
Case Material: brass
Primer: large rifle

CARTRIDGE BALLISTICS
Max. Average Breech Pressure: 46,000 CUP.
Max. Horizontal Range: 4,300 yds.
Max. Vertical Range: 9,000 ft.

Bullet Weight (gr.)	Bullet Type	Muzzle Velocity (fps)	Muzzle Energy (ft.-lbs.)
196	FMJ-RN	2,295	2,292

CURRENT MANUFACTURER(S)
None

GENERAL COMMENT(S)
In 1889, Denmark, Norway and Sweden adopted a new, rimmed cartridge for their Krag rifles called the 8x58Rmm Krag-Jorgensen. Its service life proved short as it was replaced in Norwegian and Swedish service by the 6.5x55mm Swedish Mauser cartridge in 1896.

TECHNICAL COMMENT(S)
In short order, this created a dilemma as Norwegian target shooters preferred the 8mm caliber bullet. As their Norwegian Krag rifles fired the rimless 6.5x55mm Mauser cartridge, the earlier rimmed 8x58Rmm case could not be used. An expedient 8mm cartridge was the answer, and it was created by necking up the 6.5x55mm Mauser cartridge to 8mm.This cartridge is an excellent example of an early expedient cartridge developed for a narrow market as it was used only in Norway.

8x56mm MANNLICHER-SCHOENAUER

ALTERNATE NAME(S): 8x56 M-Sch., 8.2x56 M-Sch.
RELATED CALIBER(S): 6.5x54mm Mannlicher-Schoenauer, 8x57mmJS Mauser

CARTRIDGE HISTORY
Year of Introduction: 1908
Country of Origin: Austria
Designer(s): von Mannlicher
Governing Body: CIP
Present Status: obsolete

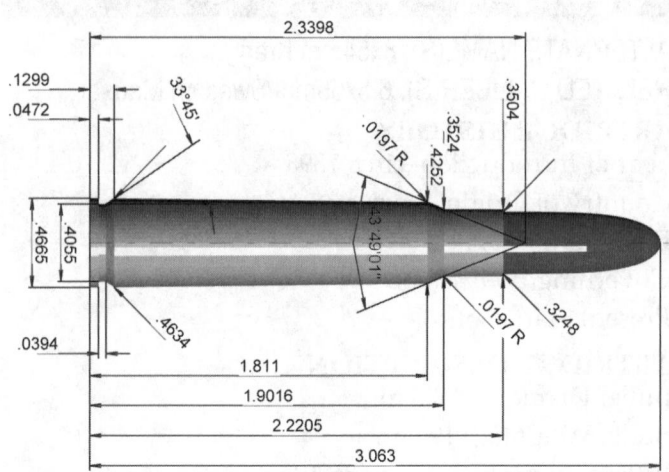

CARTRIDGE DESCRIPTION
Bullet Diameter: .3248 in.
Bullet Weight(s): 200 gr.
Rifling Twist Rate: 1 turn in 9.84 in.
Test Barrel Length: 24 in.
Case Type: rimless, necked
Case Material: brass
Primer Size: large rifle

CARTRIDGE BALLISTICS
Max. Average Breech Pressure: 46,400 psi.
Max. Horizontal Range: 3,600 yds.
Max. Vertical Range: 7,550 ft.

Bullet Weight (gr.)	Bullet Type	Muzzle Velocity (fps)	Muzzle Energy (ft.-lbs.)
200	SP	2,170	2,113

CURRENT MANUFACTURER(S)
none

GENERAL COMMENT(S)
For many years after its introduction circa 1908 along with the Mannlicher Model 1908 bolt-action rifle, the 8x56mm Mannlicher-Schoenauer cartridge was a moderately popular choice for hunting by European sportsmen. Over the years, most large European ammunition makers offered this caliber although none do so today as it has become obsolete. The 8x56mm M-Sch. cartridge remained almost unknown in the U.S. market.

TECHNICAL COMMENT(S)
Despite its relatively large case volume, the 8x56mm M-Sch. cartridge offered mediocre ballistic performance in comparison to its rivals such as the 8x57JS mm Mauser. Much of this was undoubtedly due to its modest chamber pressure combined with a heavy bullet.

8x60mmJ MAUSER, 8x60RmmJ MAUSER, 8x60mmS MAUSER, 8x60RmmS MAUSER

ALTERNATE NAME(S): 8x60mm Magnum, 8x60Rmm Magnum
RELATED CALIBER(S): 8x57mmJ Mauser, 8x57mmS Mauser

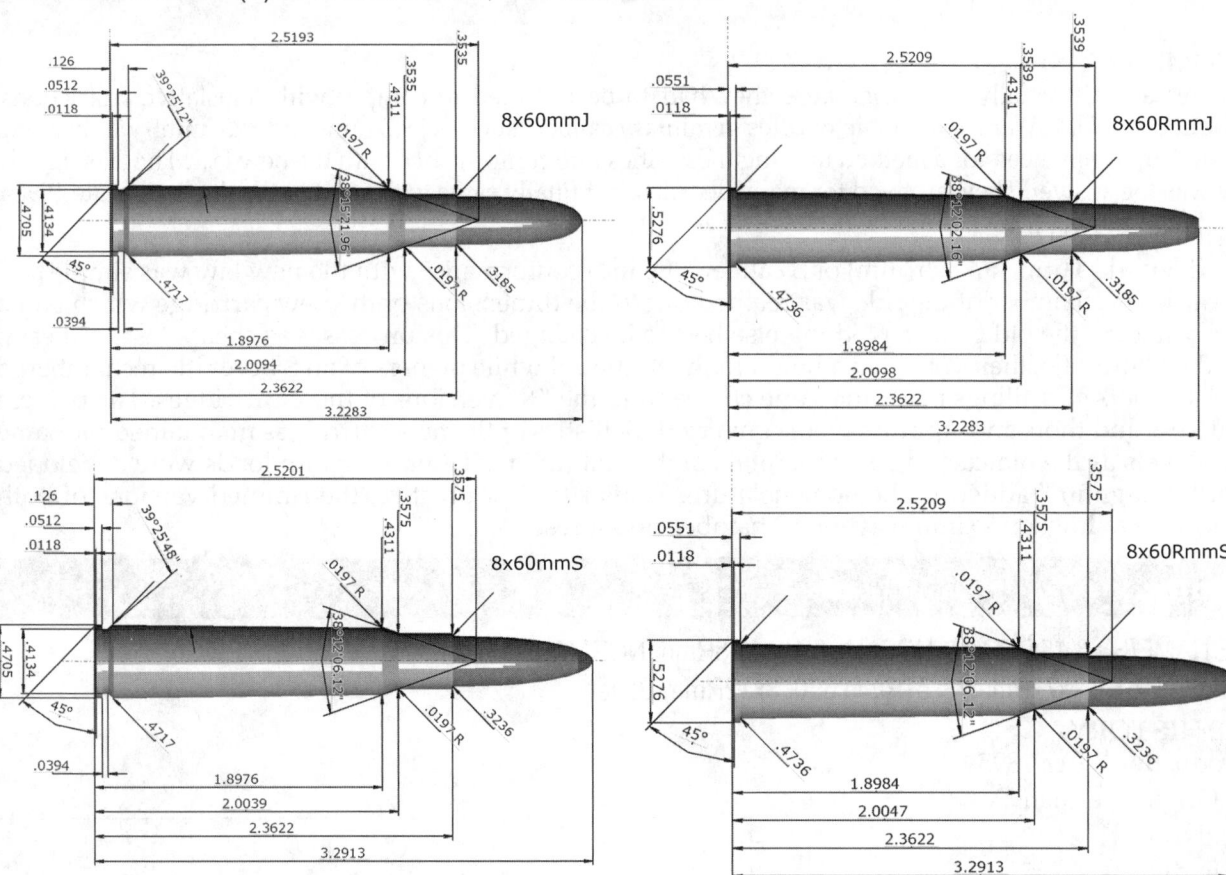

CARTRIDGE HISTORY

Year of Introduction: 1919
Country of Origin: Germany
Designer(s): N/A
Governing Body: CIP
Present Status: obsolete

CARTRIDGE DESCRIPTION

Bullet Diameter: .318 in. (J, RJ), .323 in. (S, RS)
Bullet Weight(s): 159-196 gr.
Rifling Twist Rate: I turn in 9.45 in.
Test Barrel Length: 24 in.
Case Type: rimless, necked; rimmed, necked
Case Material: brass
Primer: large rifle

CARTRIDGE BALLISTICS

Max. Average Breech Pressure: 58,740 psi.; 49,313 psi. in R cartridges
Max. Horizontal Range: 4,400 yds.
Max. Vertical Range: 9,400 ft.

Bullet Weight (gr.)	Bullet Type	Muzzle Velocity (fps)	Muzzle Energy (ft.-lbs.)
159	JSP	2,820	2,805
187	JSP	2,810	3,275
196	JSP	2,580	2,890

CURRENT MANUFACTURER(S)
None

GENERAL COMMENT(S)
These cartridges are historically unique because they had to be invented to comply with legislative restrictions. Following the end of World War I, ownership of rifles in military calibers such as 8x57mmJ and 8x57mmS was banned. This ban created an urgent need for a method to bring these rifles into conformance with the new law. The 8x60 family of cartridges was the answer. They survived for many decades, but finally came to the end of the line in the late 1990s.

TECHNICAL COMMENT(S)
The method devised to bring an 8x57mmJ or S caliber rifle into conformance with the new law was simple and straightforward. The chamber of the rifle was reamed out to the dimensions of the new cartridge which had a 3mm longer case than the old caliber. Nothing else had to be changed. This process was cheap, fast, and easy. If you owned a J bore rifle, then you rechambered to the 8x60mmJ while owners of an S bore rifle rechambered to 8x60mmS. Owners of drillings made the same choice from the "R" versions of these cartridges. The process was a big success and thousands of rifles were converted. Ballistics of the new cartridges maintained the same performance levels as the old cartridges to maintain sight calibrations. Later, magnum loads were developed and the word "Magnum" added to the nomenclature. Similar to past practice, the rimmed versions of both types were loaded to lower maximum average chamber pressures.

8.15x46Rmm

ALTERNATE NAME(S): 8.15x46Rmm NORMA, 8.15x46.5Rmm NORMA
RELATED CALIBER(S): 7x72Rmm, 8x57Rmm 360, 8x72Rmm Sauer

CARTRIDGE HISTORY
Year of Introduction: circa 1895
Country of Origin: Germany
Designer(s): Frohn
Governing Body: CIP
Present Status: obsolete

CARTRIDGE DESCRIPTION
Bullet Diameter: .330 in.
Bullet Weight(s): 151 gr.
Rifling Twist Rate: 1 turn in 14.17 in.
Test Barrel Length: 24 in.
Case Type: rimmed, necked
Case Material: brass
Primer: large rifle

CARTRIDGE BALLISTICS
Max. Average Breech Pressure: 23,931 psi.
Max. Horizontal Range: 2,900 yds.
Max. Vertical Range: 6,200 ft.

Bullet Weight (gr.)	Bullet Type	Muzzle Velocity (fps)	Muzzle Energy (ft.-lbs.)
151	JSP-FN	1,805	1,092

CURRENT MANUFACTURER(S)
None

GENERAL COMMENT(S)
This old veteran was designed as a black powder target cartridge for use in single-shot rifles and drillings. In Europe, it was a popular choice for 200 meter off hand competition until World War II. It survived in the RWS catalog until very recently, however it is now obsolete.

TECHNICAL COMMENT(S)

Characteristics of this cartridge are carefully balanced to the requirements of rifle target shooting. Its rimmed and necked configuration is perfect for single-shot rifles. The long neck assures excellent bullet retention and alignment while bullet diameter (caliber) is large enough to cope with black powder fouling if need be. Case volume will hold a black powder charge of nearly 100 percent density to eliminate variations in muzzle velocity due to powder position. Muzzle velocity is more than adequate for 200 meter target shooting while keeping recoil within manageable limits. As ammunition in this caliber was loaded with bullets designed for target shooting, it is not suitable for hunting unless reloaded with appropriate bullets. In short, the 8.15x46Rmm is an excellent example of the tradeoffs necessary to design a good target cartridge.

.32 IDEAL

ALTERNATE NAME(S): .32-25-150 Ideal
RELATED CALIBER(S): .25-21 Marlin, .32-20 Marlin, .28-30 Stevens

CARTRIDGE HISTORY

Year of Introduction: 1903
Country of Origin: U.S.
Designer(s): N/A
Governing Body: SAAMI
Present Status: obsolete

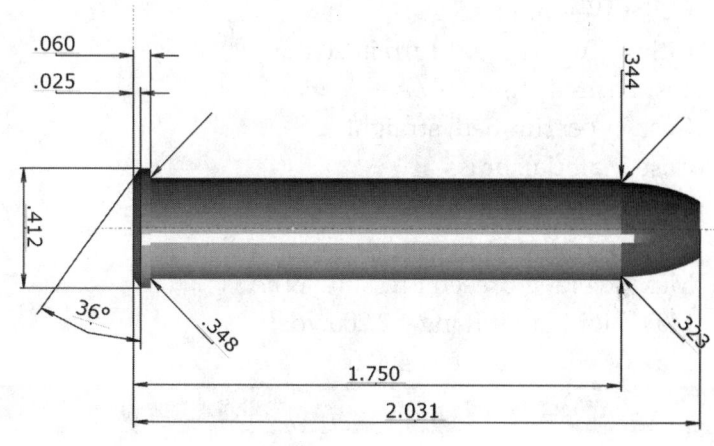

CARTRIDGE DESCRIPTION

Bullet Diameter: .323 in.
Bullet Weight(s): 150 gr.
Rifling Twist Rate: 1 turn in 18 in.
Test Barrel Length: 24 in.
Case Type: rimmed, straight
Case Material: brass
Primer: large rifle

CARTRIDGE BALLISTICS

Max. Average Breech Pressure: N/A
Max. Horizontal Range: 2,650 yds.
Max. Vertical Range: 5,500 ft.

Bullet Weight (gr.)	Bullet Type	Muzzle Velocity (fps)	Muzzle Energy (ft.-lbs.)
150	L-FN	1,250	520

CURRENT MANUFACTURER(S)

None

GENERAL COMMENT(S)

In the early 1900s, low cost, single-shot rifles in a variety of low power calibers from .30 to .44 caliber were very popular. Companies that made such rifles included Stevens, Winchester, Remington, and many others. These cartridges normally had a rimmed, straight case design holding a maximum of 40 grains of black powder. Plain lead bullets of flat-nose or round-nose profile were the norm. A few used paper-patched bullets. Such cartridges had the advantages of low cost, reduced recoil and sufficient power for small game and hunting at close ranges. They were also popular for formal and informal target shooting at close ranges.

TECHNICAL COMMENT(S)

The .32 Ideal is one of the smaller caliber cartridges outlined above. In keeping with common practice, rim and case head dimensions are very similar to those of one or more other cartridges, in this case the .28-30 Stevens and the .32-20 Marlin. Despite this, these two cartridges are not interchangeable with the .32 Ideal. Keeping the cost of shooting as low as possible was a key factor in designing the .32 Ideal. The light weight bullet conserved lead and the modest powder charge stretched the number of loads per can of black powder substantially. As a rough estimate, the cost of powder and bullets for the .32 Ideal were half those of the larger calibers. Of course, a price had to be paid for all this economy, and in this case the bottom line was weak ballistic performance. Muzzle energy of the .32 Ideal was hardly more than many handgun cartridges, constraining its use to small game hunting and target shooting. However, these were large markets and the .32 Ideal remained a popular choice well into the 1920s.

.32 LONG CENTER FIRE

ALTERNATE NAME(S): .32 Long CF
RELATED CALIBER(S): .32 Extra Long Ballard, .32-20 WCF

CARTRIDGE HISTORY
Year of Introduction: 1875
Country of Origin: U.S.
Designer(s): Marlin
Governing Body: none
Present Status: obsolete

CARTRIDGE DESCRIPTION
Bullet Diameter: .317 in.
Bullet Weight(s): 85 gr.
Rifling Twist Rate: 1 turn in 20 in.
Test Barrel Length: N/A
Case Type: rimmed, straight
Case Material: brass
Primer: small rifle

CARTRIDGE BALLISTICS
Max. Average Breech Pressure: N/A
Max. Horizontal Range: 2,200 yds.
Max. Vertical Range: 4,400 ft.

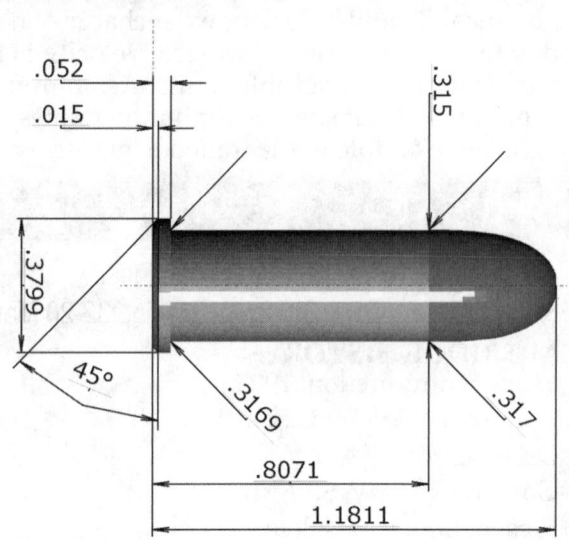

Bullet Weight (gr.)	Bullet Type	Muzzle Velocity (fps)	Muzzle Energy (ft.-lbs.)
85	L-RN	850	136

CURRENT MANUFACTURER(S)
None

GENERAL COMMENT(S)
In the 1870s, a number of companies including Ballard, Stevens, and Remington offered small, single-shot rifles with the dual capability of firing either rimfire or center fire cartridges of similar caliber. All that was required was a simple adjustment or part(s) replacement to make the changeover. The .32 Long Center Fire cartridge is the center fire brother of the .32 Long rimfire. The .32 Long C.F. was considered obsolete by 1900, however the .32 Long Rimfire cartridge plodded on until 1936.

TECHNICAL COMMENT(S)
Ammunition in this caliber had to be loaded for the weakest link in the chain, rimfire cartridges. This required that maximum average chamber pressure be maintained at modest levels for safety which removed any advantage the stronger case of a center fire cartridge may have offered. Therefore, the advantage of the dual cartridge capability offered by such rifles was purely convenience. The .32 Long Center Fire was a rifle cartridge firing .317 inch diameter bullets from a rifle barrel. It should not be confused with the .32 Long Colt or .32 S&W handgun cartridges with their .313 inch diameter bullets. From any viewpoint, ballistic performance of the .32 Long C.F. cartridge is anemic at best. Muzzle velocity and muzzle energy are scarcely better than many handgun cartridges of that day, leaving the .32 Long C.F. suitable only for small game hunting. In addition, the rainbow trajectory of the .32 Long limits its practical effective range to 50 yards or less. For these reasons, it was replaced in short order by the .32 Extra Long Ballard. Considered from a dimensional standpoint, the .32 Long C.F. cartridge will chamber and fire in most .32 S&W Long and .32 Long Colt guns, but not vice-versa. In any case, .32 Long C.F. cartridges are now collectors items and far too expensive to fire.

.32 REMINGTON

ALTERNATE NAME(S): .32 Rem.
RELATED CALIBER(S): .32 Win. Spl., .25 Rem., .30 Rem., .30-30 Win., .25-35 Win.

CARTRIDGE HISTORY
Year of Introduction: 1906
Country of Origin: U.S.
Designer(s): Remington
Governing Body: SAAMI
Present Status: obsolete

CARTRIDGE DESCRIPTION
Bullet Diameter: .320 in.
Bullet Weight(s): 170 gr.
Rifling Twist Rate: 1 turn in 14 in.
Test Barrel Length: 24 in.
Case Type: rimless, necked
Case Material: brass
Primer Size: large rifle

CARTRIDGE BALLISTICS
Max. Average Breech Pressure: 40,200 CUP.
Max. Horizontal Range: 2,900 yds.
Max. Vertical Range: 6,400 ft.

Bullet Weight (gr.)	Bullet Type	Muzzle Velocity (fps)	Muzzle Energy (ft.-lbs.)
170	JSP-RN	2,220	1,860

CURRENT MANUFACTURER(S)
None

GENERAL COMMENT(S)
Remington did not cut Winchester any slack in the race to offer the first semi-automatic sporting rifles in the early 1900s. Winchester was first with their Model 1905 rifle chambered for the relatively weak .32 W.S.L. and .35 W.S.L. cartridges. Remington entered the semi-automatic sporting rifle sweepstakes with their Model 8 rifle chambered for three new calibers – .25 Remington, .30 Remington, and .32 Remington. While the .30 Remington achieved popular acceptance, its siblings never really achieved critical mass. Production of both the .25 Remington and .32 Remington was stopped in the early 1950s. The .32 Remington was the least popular of these Remington calibers. Surprisingly, the .30 Remington remained in production by Remington until the early 2000s.

TECHNICAL COMMENT(S)
These Remington cartridges are rimless versions of popular rimmed cartridges. For example, the .25 Remington is a rimless version of the .25-35 Winchester, the .30 Remington a rimless version of the venerable .30-30 Winchester, and the .32 Remington a rimless version of the .32 Winchester Special. The Winchester cartridges were rimmed as they were designed for lever-action and single-shot rifles while the Remington cartridges were modern, rimless designs for bolt-action and semi-automatic actions. Bullet weight, muzzle velocity and muzzle energy of the Remington cartridges was in the same general class as their rimmed Winchester counterparts noted above. While the flat nose bullets used in the Winchester calibers were launched at slightly higher muzzle velocities than the Remington cartridges, the round nose bullets used in the Remington calibers made up for this by slightly more retained velocity and energy down range. Despite their modern, rimless design, these Remington calibers were not high pressure cartridges. Maximum average chamber pressure was a very modest 35,000-40,000 psi. This, in turn, limited their muzzle velocity.

.32 WINCHESTER SELF-LOADING

ALTERNATE NAME(S): .32 WSL
RELATED CALIBER(S): .30 M1 Carbine, .35 WSL

CARTRIDGE HISTORY
Year of Introduction: 1905
Country of Origin: U.S.
Designer(s): Winchester
Governing Body: CIP
Present Status: obsolete

CARTRIDGE DESCRIPTION
Bullet Diameter: .322 in.
Bullet Weight(s): 165 gr.
Rifling Twist Rate: 1 turn in 16 in.
Test Barrel Length: 24 in.
Case Type: semi-rimmed, straight
Case Material: brass
Primer: small rifle

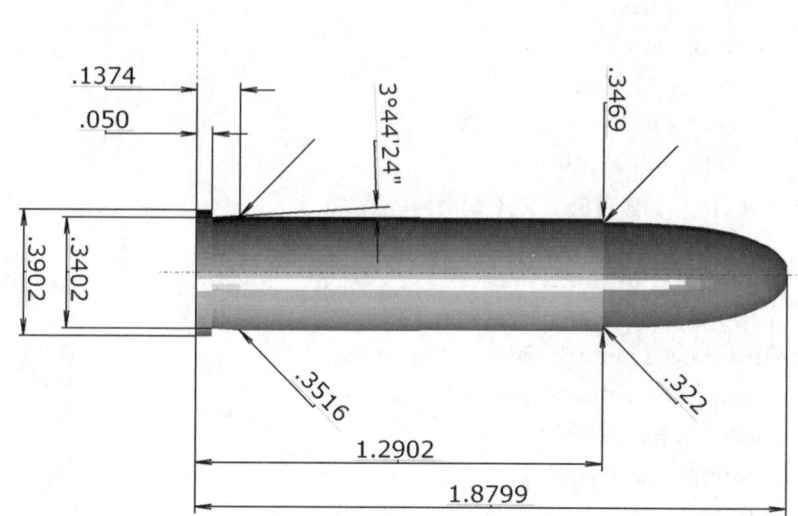

CARTRIDGE BALLISTICS
Max. Average Breech Pressure: 22,480 psi.
Max. Horizontal Range: 2,900 yds.
Max. Vertical Range: 6,000 ft.

Bullet Weight (gr.)	Bullet Type	Muzzle Velocity (fps)	Muzzle Energy (ft.-lbs.)
165	JSP-FN	1,400	760

CURRENT MANUFACTURER(S)
None

GENERAL COMMENT(S)
In 1905, Winchester introduced their first semi-automatic hunting rifle, the Model 05, chambered for their new .32 W.S.L. and .35 W.S.L. cartridges. Reaction from Winchester's customers to the anemic ballistic performance of these cartridges, especially the .32 W.S.L., was so bad that Winchester hurriedly began a crash program of improvement. The improved .35 caliber cartridge, called the .351 W.S.L., was introduced in 1907 along with the Model 07 rifle. No attempt was made to improve the .32 W.S.L. cartridge which was summarily dropped. Both the unlamented .32 W.S.L. and .35 W.S.L. cartridges faded quickly to obsolescence. Our story might have ended here, but the outbreak of World War II in 1939 changed everything. In response to a military requirement for a light, handy carbine firing a reduced power cartridge, Winchester dusted off their trusty .32 W.S.L. cartridge. A few minimal changes to speed development included going to a rimless head, a higher average chamber pressure and increased case taper to handle the smaller, lighter .308 inch diameter bullet. The result was the famous .30 M1 Carbine cartridge so popular still today. Few modern sportsmen realize that the .30 Carbine's DNA contains a marketing mistake by Winchester in 1905!

TECHNICAL COMMENT(S)
By any measure, the ballistic performance of the .32 W.S.L. was poor. This became very apparent when sportsmen compared the ballistic performance of the .32 W.S.L. to those of the .32 Winchester Special and new .32 Remington cartridge. One wonders what Winchester was thinking when they introduced this cartridge!

.32-20 WINCHESTER

ALTERNATE NAME(S): .32-20 WCF, .32 CLMR
RELATED CALIBER(S): .25-20 WCF

CARTRIDGE HISTORY
Year of Introduction: 1882
Country of Origin: U.S.
Designer(s): Winchester
Governing Body: SAAMI
Present Status: obsolete

CARTRIDGE DESCRIPTION
Bullet Diameter: .312 in.
Bullet Weight(s): 80-100 gr.
Rifling Twist Rate: 1 turn in 20 in.
Test Barrel Length: 20 in.
Case Type: rimmed, necked
Case Material: brass
Primer Size: small rifle

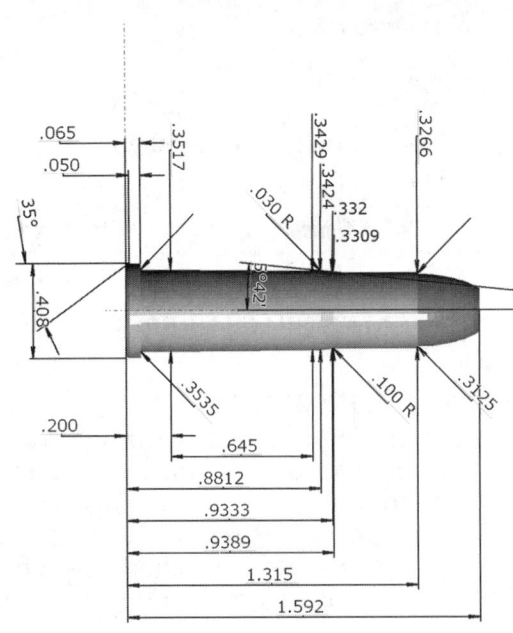

CARTRIDGE BALLISTICS
Max. Average Breech Pressure: 17,700 CUP.
Max. Effective Range: 100 yds.
Max. Horizontal Range: 2,500 yds.
Max. Vertical Range: 5,100 ft.

Bullet Weight (gr.)	Bullet Type	Muzzle Velocity (fps)	Muzzle Energy (ft.-lbs.)
80	JSP	2,100	780
100	JSP	1,210	325

CURRENT MANUFACTURER(S)
Winchester

GENERAL COMMENT(S)
Prior to the introduction of high velocity, .22 caliber, center fire cartridges, the .32-20 Win. cartridge was a popular choice for small game and varmint hunting. However, time has passed this old number by leaving it mainly for cowboy action competition and shooting old lever guns. Winchester still offers the 100 grain load.

TECHNICAL COMMENT(S)
Ballistics of the .32-20 Win. are poor even by 19th century standards.

.32-30 REMINGTON-HEPBURN

ALTERNATE NAME(S): .32-30 Rem., .32-30 Remington
RELATED CALIBER(S): .30-30 Wesson, .38 Extra Long Ballard, .357 Maximum

CARTRIDGE HISTORY
Year of Introduction: 1884
Country of Origin: U.S.
Designer(s): Remington
Governing Body: none
Present Status: obsolete

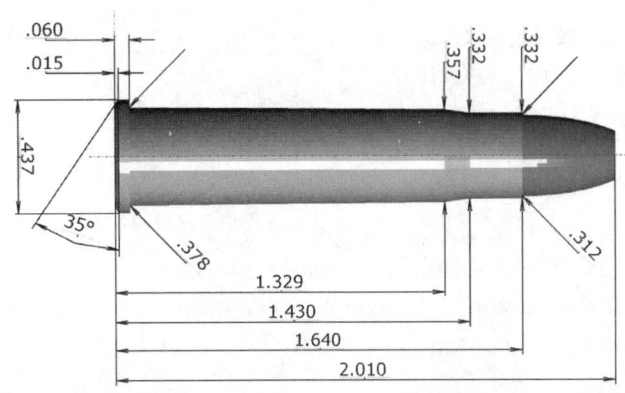

CARTRIDGE DESCRIPTION
Bullet Diameter: .312 in.
Bullet Weight(s): 125 gr.
Rifling Twist Rate: 1 turn in 16 in.
Test Barrel Length: N/A

Case Type: rimmed, slightly necked
Case Material: brass
Primer: large rifle

CARTRIDGE BALLISTICS
Max. Average Breech Pressure: N/A
Max. Horizontal Range: 2,150 yds.
Max. Vertical Range: 4,650 ft.

Bullet Weight (gr.)	Bullet Type	Muzzle Velocity (fps)	Muzzle Energy (ft.-lbs.)
125	L-FN	1,380	535

CURRENT MANUFACTURER(S)
None

GENERAL COMMENT(S)
Remington announced this cartridge in 1880 for the Remington-Hepburn No. 3 single-shot target rifle. However, for reasons unknown, production of ammunition in this caliber did not begin until 1884. Remington's marketing department described this cartridge as being adapted for long range hunting and target shooting. It was good for neither and this was quite obvious to all and sundry. Another handicap was that the .32-30 Rem. cartridge was too long for the lever-action repeating rifles that were rapidly increasing in popularity. Predictably, the .32-30 Remington-Hepburn cartridge was a marketing dud leading Remington to drop it in 1912.

TECHNICAL COMMENT(S)
Despite its marketing shortcomings, the .32-30 Remington cartridge is interesting from the design standpoint for its unusual case configuration. The body of the case may best be described as necked, however the neck is shallow and elongated to the point it is hard to determine where it begins and ends. In this respect, it is very similar to the German Sauer series of cartridges. In order to hold the bullet, the case becomes parallel at the mouth. The reason Remington selected this case configuration has been lost to history. However, it was very likely an attempt at a compromise cartridge design that would satisfy proponents of both straight and necked cartridge cases. As with most such compromises, it satisfied neither group. Plain lead bullets with a flat nose were used in .32-30 ammunition.

.32-40 REMINGTON-HEPBURN

ALTERNATE NAME(S): .32-40 Rem.
RELATED CALIBER(S): .35 Winchester, .38-50 Remington-Hepburn, .405 Winchester, .40-60 Maynard

CARTRIDGE HISTORY
Year of Introduction: 1872
Country of Origin: U.S.
Designer(s): Remington
Governing Body: none
Present Status: obsolete

CARTRIDGE DESCRIPTION
Bullet Diameter: .308 in.
Bullet Weight(s): 150 gr.
Rifling Twist Rate: 1 turn in 16 in.
Test Barrel Length: N/A
Case Type: rimmed, necked
Case Material: brass
Primer: large rifle

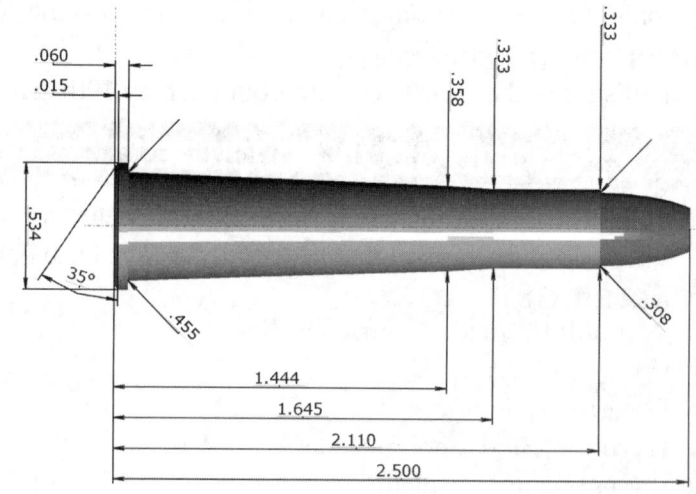

CARTRIDGE BALLISTICS
Max. Average Breech Pressure: N/A
Max. Horizontal Range: 2,200 yds.
Max. Vertical Range: 4,750 ft.

Bullet Weight (gr.)	Bullet Type	Muzzle Velocity (fps)	Muzzle Energy (ft.-lbs.)
150	L-FN	1,350	607

CURRENT MANUFACTURER(S)
None

GENERAL COMMENT(S)
Remington announced the .32-40 Remington cartridge in 1874 for their rolling-block series of single-shot rifles. It was intended as a dual purpose hunting and target cartridge.

TECHNICAL COMMENT(S)
The .32-40 Remington cartridge is interesting from the design standpoint for its unusual case configuration. The body of the case may best be described as necked, however the neck is shallow and elongated to the point it is hard to determine where it begins and ends. In this respect, it is very similar to the German Sauer series of cartridges. In order to hold the bullet, the case becomes parallel at the mouth. The reason Remington selected this case configuration has been lost to history. Plain lead bullets with a flat nose were used in .32-40 ammunition. One is tempted to point out the relationship of the .32-40 Remington and .32-30 Remington-Hepburn cartridges, only none seems to exist beyond the maker's name. The rim, head and bullet diameter of these two cartridges are very different and obviously made from different base cases. The .32-40 Remington preceded the .32-30 Remington by twelve years and is not a true Hepburn cartridge, although later it was chambered in Hepburn rifles. After 1884, the .32-40 Remington cartridge had to compete with the .32-40 Ballard/Winchester in the marketplace. It lost.

.32-40 WINCHESTER

ALTERNATE NAME(S): .32-40 Ballard, .32-40 Marlin, 7.65x54Rmm
RELATED CALIBER(S): None

CARTRIDGE HISTORY
Year of Introduction: 1884
Country of Origin: U.S.
Designer(s): Ballard
Governing Body: SAAMI, CIP
Present Status: obsolete

CARTRIDGE DESCRIPTION
Bullet Diameter: .321 in.
Bullet Weight(s): 165 gr.
Rifling Twist Rate: 1 turn in 16 in.
Test Barrel Length: 24 in.
Case Type: rimmed, tapered
Case Material: brass
Primer Size: large rifle

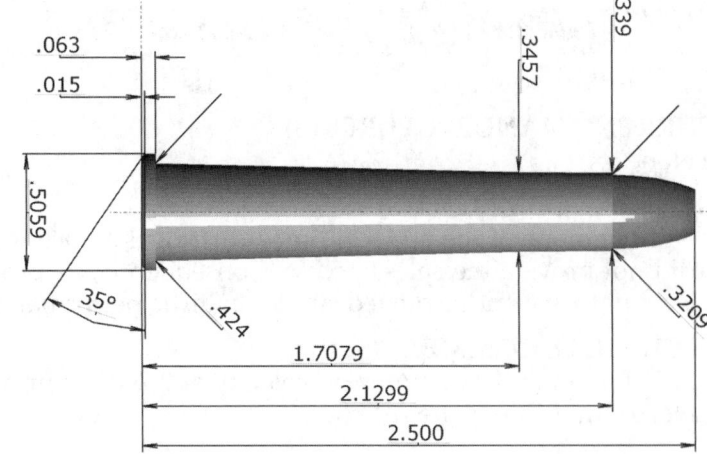

CARTRIDGE BALLISTICS
Max. Average Breech Pressure: 34,100 psi.
Max. Horizontal Range: 3,000 yds.
Max. Vertical Range: 6,500 ft.

Bullet Weight (gr.)	Bullet Type	Muzzle Velocity (fps)	Muzzle Energy (ft.-lbs.)
165	L-FN	1,440	760
165	L-FN	1,750	1,125

CURRENT MANUFACTURER(S)
Winchester

GENERAL COMMENT(S)
Ballard designed this cartridge for competition. Its success in that field caused Winchester to introduce it in 1886. Loaded with nostalgia, this cartridge still sells out occasional limited runs by Winchester.

TECHNICAL COMMENT(S)

Although the .32-40 Win. cartridge offers nothing out of the ordinary for the smokeless powder shooter, with black powder this cartridge comes into its own. It is a nice balance between a moderate powder charge, mild recoil and accuracy. Would that many modern cartridges should be this good!

.33 WINCHESTER

ALTERNATE NAME(S): .33 WCF, 8x53Rmm
RELATED CALIBER(S): .45-70 Gov't.

CARTRIDGE HISTORY
Year of Introduction: 1902
Country of Origin: U.S.
Designer(s): Winchester
Governing Body: SAAMI, CIP
Present Status: obsolete

CARTRIDGE DESCRIPTION
Bullet Diameter: .3385 in.
Bullet Weight(s): 200 gr.
Rifling Twist Rate: 1 turn in 12 in.
Test Barrel Length: 24 in.
Case Type: rimmed, tapered, necked
Case Material: brass
Primer Size: large rifle

CARTRIDGE BALLISTICS
Max. Average Breech Pressure: 44,200 psi.
Max. Horizontal Range: 3,600 yds.
Max. Vertical Range: 8,200 ft.

Bullet Weight (gr.)	Bullet Type	Muzzle Velocity (fps)	Muzzle Energy (ft.-lbs.)
200	JSP	2,200	2,150

CURRENT MANUFACTURER(S)
None

GENERAL COMMENT(S)
Although one of the better rimmed cartridges Winchester developed for their lever-action rifles, the .33 Win. did not prove a big sales success. Consequently, its production life lasted only from 1902 until 1940. The .35 Remington cartridge offered similar ballistic performance in a modern, rimless cartridge design.

TECHNICAL COMMENT(S)
A 200 grain bullet at a muzzle velocity of 2,200 fps proved a very effective combination on all types of large, North American game.

.348 WINCHESTER

ALTERNATE NAME(S): .348 Win.
RELATED CALIBER(S): None

CARTRIDGE HISTORY
Year of Introduction: 1936
Country of Origin: U.S.
Designer(s): Winchester
Governing Body: SAAMI
Present Status: obsolete

CARTRIDGE DESCRIPTION
Bullet Diameter: .3495 in.
Bullet Weight(s): 200-250 gr.
Rifling Twist Rate: 1 turn in 12 in.
Test Barrel Length: 20 in.
Case Type: rimmed, necked
Case Material: brass
Primer Size: large rifle

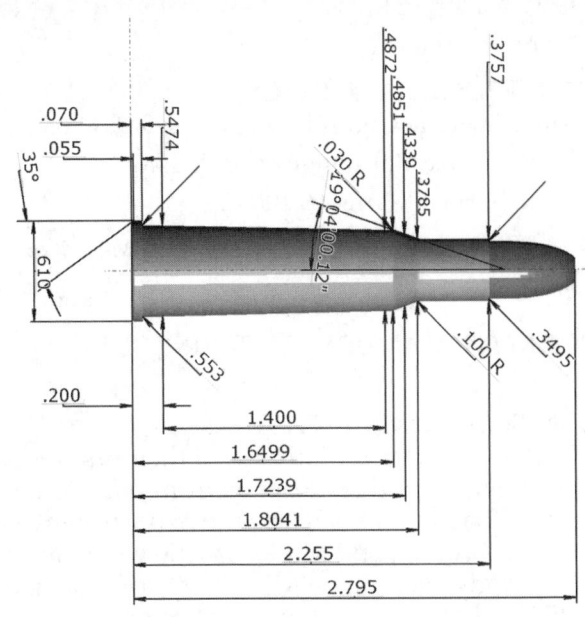

CARTRIDGE BALLISTICS
Max. Average Breech Pressure: 43,200 psi.
Max. Horizontal Range: 4,000 yds.
Max. Vertical Range: 9,000 ft.

Bullet Weight (gr.)	Bullet Type	Muzzle Velocity (fps)	Muzzle Energy (ft.-lbs.)
200	JSP	2,520	2,820
250	JSP	2,350	3,060

CURRENT MANUFACTURER(S)
Winchester

GENERAL COMMENT(S)
Here is another lever-gun cartridge from Winchester that never seemed to catch on with American shooters. Winchester still offers ammunition in this caliber although rifles have not been made for it since the late 1950s. You have got to hand it to Winchester - when it comes to lever-gun cartridges, they just keep trying.

TECHNICAL COMMENT(S)
The .348 Win. is a competent cartridge for the field, however, it offers nothing ballistically speaking that several other cartridges do not offer. Basically, the .348 Win. is a cartridge in search of a purpose. It never found one.

.35 WINCHESTER SELF-LOADING

ALTERNATE NAME(S): .35 WSL, 8.5x29.9SRmm, 9x29mm
RELATED CALIBER(S): .351 WSL

CARTRIDGE HISTORY
Year of Introduction: 1905
Country of Origin: U.S.
Designer(s): Winchester
Governing Body: CIP
Present Status: obsolete

CARTRIDGE DESCRIPTION
Bullet Diameter: .351 in.
Bullet Weight(s): 180 gr.
Rifling Twist Rate: 1 turn in 16 in.

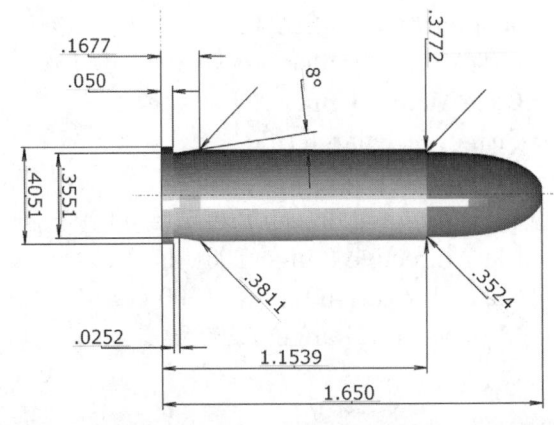

Test Barrel Length: 24 in.
Case Type: semi-rimmed, straight
Case Material: brass
Primer: large rifle

CARTRIDGE BALLISTICS
Max. Average Chamber Pressure: 34,800 psi.
Max. Horizontal Range: 2,900 yds.
Max. Vertical Range: 6,100 ft.

Bullet Weight (gr.)	Bullet Type	Muzzle Velocity (fps)	Muzzle Energy (ft.-lbs.)
180	JSP-RN	1,450	842

CURRENT MANUFACTURER(S)
None

GENERAL COMMENT(S)
In 1905, Winchester introduced their first semi-automatic hunting rifle, the Model 05, chambered for their new .35 W.S.L. cartridge. Reaction from Winchester's customers to the anemic ballistic performance of this cartridge was so bad that Winchester hurriedly began a crash program to improve it. When the improved cartridge, called the .351 W.S.L., and Model 07 rifle were introduced in 1907, both received a lukewarm reception. Despite this, the handy, well-made Model 1907 rifle carried the indifferent .351 W.S.L. onward until 1957. The unlamented .35 W.S.L. faded quickly into obsolescence.

TECHNICAL COMMENT(S)
By any measure, the ballistic performance of the .35 W.S.L. was poor. This became very apparent when sportsmen compared the ballistic performance of the .35 W.S.L. to that of the new .32 Remington cartridge. One wonders what Winchester was thinking when they introduced this cartridge. Although limited by the blow-back action of their rifle design, Winchester elected to cut their losses and redesign the .35 W.S.L. cartridge to significantly improve ballistic performance. The result was the new .351 W.S.L. cartridge introduced in 1907.

.35 WINCHESTER

ALTERNATE NAME(S):.35 Win., .35 Winchester M1895, 8.5x61Rmm, 9x62Rmm
RELATED CALIBER(S): .38-72 Win., .40-72 Win., .405 Win.

CARTRIDGE HISTORY
Year of Introduction: 1903
Country of Origin: U.S.
Designer(s): Winchester
Governing Body: CIP
Present Status: obsolete

CARTRIDGE DESCRIPTION
Bullet Diameter: .359 in.
Bullet Weight(s): 250 gr.
Rifling Twist Rate: 1 turn in 14 in.
Test Barrel Length: 24 in.
Case Type: rimmed, necked
Case Material: brass
Primer Size: large rifle

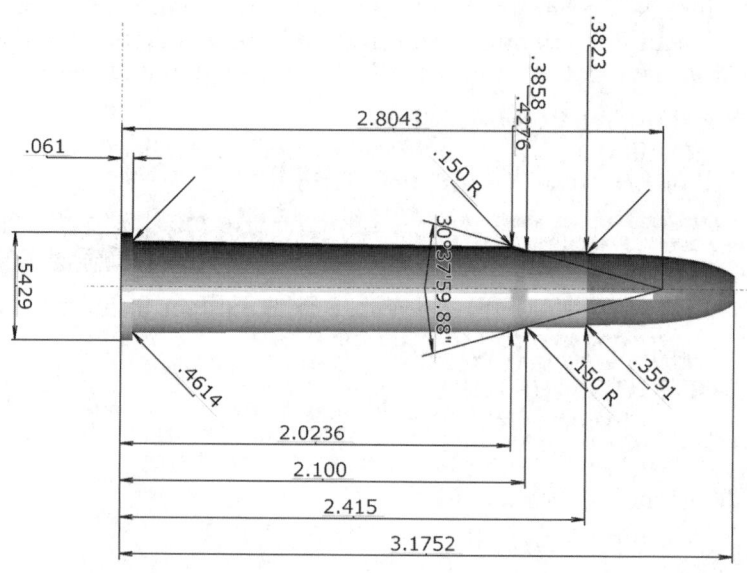

CARTRIDGE BALLISTICS
Max. Average Breech Pressure: 44,200 psi.
Max. Effective Range: 200 yds.
Max. Horizontal Range: 3,300 yds.
Max. Vertical Range: 7,250 ft.

Bullet Weight (gr.)	Bullet Type	Muzzle Velocity (fps)	Muzzle Energy (ft.-lbs.)
250	JSP-RN	2,150	2,567

CURRENT MANUFACTURER(S)
None

GENERAL COMMENT(S)
With the emergence of bolt-action rifles firing high-pressure cartridges in the late 1880s and early 1890s, Winchester lever-action rifles were becoming outclassed as they could not handle the high maximum average chamber pressures generated by the new cartridges. In an effort to defend their share of the rifle market, Winchester developed a new lever-action rifle, the Model 1895, for its new family of high pressure cartridges. By adopting a box magazine and a stronger action, Winchester was able to chamber their new Model 1895 lever-action rifle for high-pressure cartridges firing round nose bullets. Winchester's new cartridge family included the .35 Winchester, .38-72 Win., .40-72 Win., and .405 Win. None of these calibers gained a popular following and all were dropped from the Winchester product line in 1936 and quickly faded into obscurity.

TECHNICAL COMMENT(S)
Winchester designed all four of these new cartridges on a common .460 inch diameter base and .539 inch diameter rim with only minor variations. Maximum average chamber pressures of approximately 44,000 psi were high for a lever-action rifle but Winchester's M1895 had been designed for such pressures.Despite these improvements, the new cartridges remained old-school, namely blunt, heavy bullets at moderate muzzle velocities. The trend was toward lighter, pointed bullets at high muzzle velocities offering superior down-range ballistic performance. The 250 grain bullet was the only weight offered.

.351 WINCHESTER SELF-LOADING

ALTERNATE NAME(S): .351 SL, .351 WIN. SL, .351 WSL
RELATED CALIBER(S): .35 WINCHESTER SELF-LOADING

CARTRIDGE HISTORY
Year of Introduction: 1907
Country of Origin: U.S.
Designer(s): Winchester
Governing Body: SAAMI
Present Status: obsolete

CARTRIDGE DESCRIPTION
Bullet Diameter: .352 in.
Bullet Weight(s): 180 gr.
Rifling Twist Rate: 1 turn in 16 in.
Test Barrel Length: 24 in.
Case Type: semi-rimmed, straight
Case Material: brass
Primer Size: small rifle

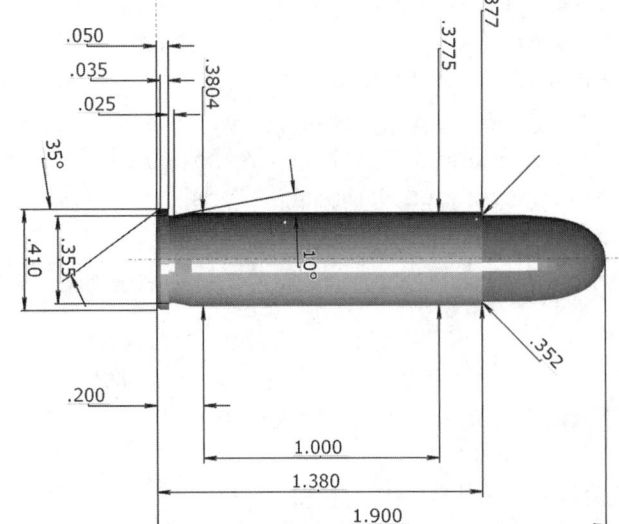

CARTRIDGE BALLISTICS
Max. Average Breech Pressure: 48,200 CUP.
Max. Effective Range: 100 yds.
Max. Horizontal Range: 2,600 yds.
Max. Vertical Range: 6,000 ft.

Bullet Weight (gr.)	Bullet Type	Muzzle Velocity (fps)	Muzzle Energy (ft.-lbs.)
180	JSP	1,850	1,370

CURRENT MANUFACTURER(S)
None

GENERAL COMMENT(S)
Winchester's first effort in 1905 at a semi-automatic rifle cartridge, the .35 Winchester Self-Loading was a

marketing failure as it was too weak. In 1907, the cartridge case was lengthened 0.24 inches, the chamber pressure increased to improve ballistic performance and the nomenclature changed to .351 Winchester Self-Loading. The .351 W.S.L. cartridge remained in production until the late 1980s although new firearms in this caliber were discontinued in 1957.

TECHNICAL COMMENT(S)

The .351 W.S.L. cartridge fell into a ballistic black hole that limited its market acceptance for the remainder of its production life. Too weak for deer or medium game, it was too powerful for small game and lacked the muzzle velocity for varmint shooting. The .351 W.S.L. was at its best for hunting light game at close ranges and for law enforcement use. Even in these roles, it was quickly outclassed by other calibers. It remained a cartridge in search of a purpose throughout its life.

.358 WINCHESTER

ALTERNATE NAME(S): .358 Win., 8.8x51mm
RELATED CALIBER(S): .308 Win.

CARTRIDGE HISTORY

Year of Introduction: 1955
Country of Origin: U.S.
Designer(s): Winchester
Governing Body: SAAMI
Present Status: semi-obsolete

CARTRIDGE DESCRIPTION

Bullet Diameter: .358 in.
Bullet Weight(s): 200-250 gr.
Rifling Twist Rate: 1 turn in 12 in.
Test Barrel Length: 24 in.
Case Type: rimless, necked
Case Material: brass
Primer Size: large rifle

CARTRIDGE BALLISTICS

Max. Average Breech Pressure: 55,300 CUP.
Max. Horizontal Range: 4,000 yds.
Max. Vertical Range: 9,000 ft.

Bullet Weight (gr.)	Bullet Type	Muzzle Velocity (fps)	Muzzle Energy (ft.-lbs.)
200	JSP	2,490	2,753
250	JSP	2,250	2,810

CURRENT MANUFACTURER(S)

Winchester

GENERAL COMMENT(S)

Conventional wisdom has it that American sportsmen have never taken to .35 caliber rifle cartridges. A few notable examples in the graveyard of calibers include the .35 Newton, .350 Remington Magnum, .35 Winchester and .351 W.S.L. And then there is the .35 Remington. Since its introduction in 1906, it has puttered along never becoming a super seller, but never fading completely away. Undoubtedly, this is due, rightly or wrongly, to the belief that this caliber bucks brush better than the .30-30 Win. cartridge. By 1955, Winchester believed the time had come for a modern, powerful .35 caliber cartridge that would, hopefully, finally capture the hearts of American sportsmen once and for all. To this end, they introduced the .358 Winchester in 1955. The market accepted this new caliber only fractionally, leaving it to putter along with its .35 Rem. alter ego. In short, the improved ballistic performance failed to shortstop the American sportsman's lack of interest in .35 caliber cartridges, save for a few brush busters.

TECHNICAL COMMENT(S)

Winchester created the .358 Win. cartridge by necking up the .308 Win. case to accept a .358 caliber bullet. Although it was designed for lever-action rifles, the .358 Win. will feed smoothly in almost any rifle originally designed for the .308 Win. cartridge. Despite this, the .358 Win. remains an exclusively lever-action caliber in sportsmen's minds. For those hunters seeking a better brush buster, the .358 Win. offers 156% more striking energy than the .35 Rem. with a similar bullet weight. The .358 Win. accomplishes this with a stronger cartridge case permitting higher chamber pressures. The .358 Win. is an analog to the .35 Whelen (both derived from a necked up .30 caliber case) in design, but not in performance. With its .30-'06 Spr. case capacity, the .35 Whelen is simply a quantum level higher in performance.

.360 NITRO EXPRESS 2 1/4 in.

ALTERNATE NAME(S): .360 Nitro Express, .360 Black Powder Express 2 1/4 in., .360 Nitro for Black
RELATED CALIBER(S): none

CARTRIDGE HISTORY
Year of Introduction: circa 1873
Country of Origin: Britain
Designer(s): N/A
Governing Body: none
Present Status: obsolete

CARTRIDGE DESCRIPTION
Bullet Diameter: .365 in.
Bullet Weight(s): 134-300 gr.
Rifling Twist Rate: 1 turn in 20 in.
Test Barrel Length: 24 in.
Case Type: rimmed, straight
Case Material: brass
Primer: large rifle

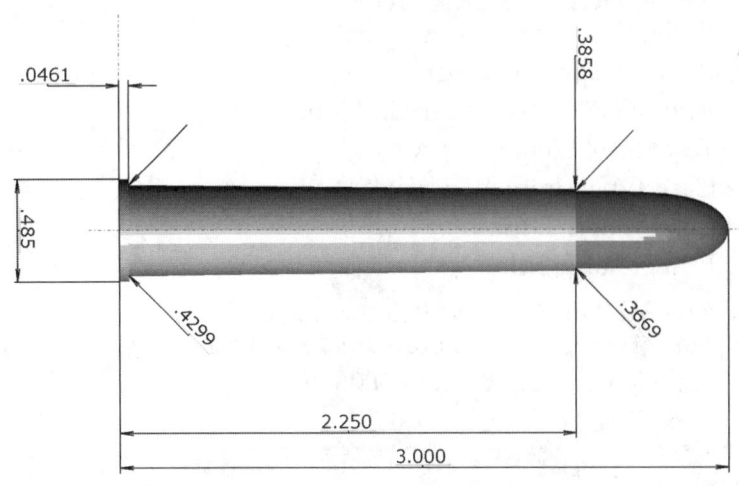

CARTRIDGE BALLISTICS
Max. Average Breech Pressure: 35,534 psi.
Max. Horizontal Range: 4,000 yds.
Max. Vertical Range: 8,150 ft.

Bullet Weight (gr.)	Bullet Type	Muzzle Velocity (fps)	Muzzle Energy (ft.-lbs.)
134	L-FN	1,025	312 (BP)
190	JSP	1,700	1,222 (Nitro for Black)
300	JSP	1,650	1,820 (Nitro)

CURRENT MANUFACTURER(S)
None

GENERAL COMMENT(S)
Do not be fooled by the words "nitro express" in the nomenclature of this cartridge. It was most certainly not intended for hunting dangerous or even big game. Rather, the term simply denotes that this cartridge had completed the transition from black powder to smokeless propellants (Cordite). This cartridge was suitable only for hunting thin-skinned medium game.

TECHNICAL COMMENT(S)
However, we should not write this cartridge off just yet. Because of its small dimensions, a double rifle in this caliber could be relatively light with good handling and low recoil. At close ranges in brush or woods with limited visibility, such a rifle was very effective. Like most well balanced cartridges, the .360 Nitro Express had its niche.

.360 No. 2 NITRO EXPRESS

ALTERNATE NAME(S):.360 No. 2 NE
RELATED CALIBER(S): .450 Nitro Express 3 1/4 in.

CARTRIDGE HISTORY
Year of Introduction: 1905
Country of Origin: Britain
Designer(s): Eley
Governing Body: none
Present Status: obsolete

CARTRIDGE DESCRIPTION
Bullet Diameter: .367 in.
Bullet Weight(s): 320 gr.
Rifling Twist Rate: 1 turn in 16 in.
Test Barrel Length: N/A
Case Type: rimmed, necked
Case Material: brass
Primer: large rifle

CARTRIDGE BALLISTICS
Max. Average Breech Pressure: 29,400 psi.
Max. Horizontal Range: 4,300 yds.
Max. Vertical Range: 9,000 ft.

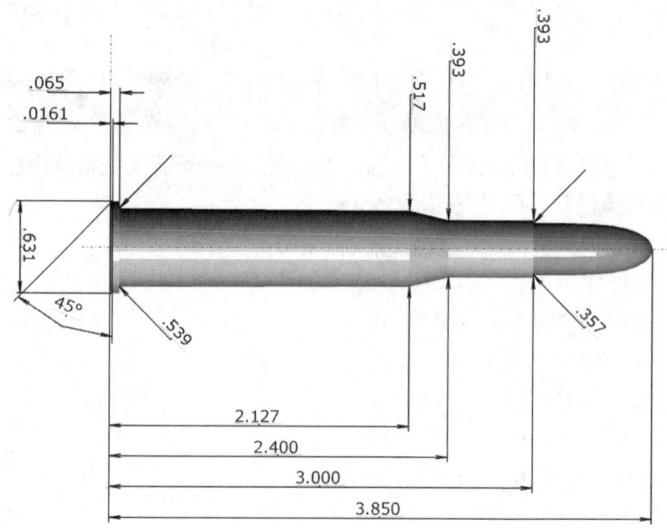

Bullet Weight (gr.)	Bullet Type	Muzzle Velocity (fps)	Muzzle Energy (ft.-lbs.)
320	JSP	2,200	3,442

CURRENT MANUFACTURER(S)
None

GENERAL COMMENT(S)
Just six years after Eley developed the .360 No. 2 Nitro Express cartridge, Holland & Holland introduced their legendary .375 H&H Magnum and .375 Flanged Magnum cartridges. As these two cartridges rapidly gained acceptance, the .360 No. 2 NE cartridge faced an uphill fight almost from the start. Despite a brief flush of popularity, the .360 No. 2 NE cartridge could not compete with Holland & Holland's creations and faded away quickly.

TECHNICAL COMMENT(S)
Technically speaking, there is nothing wrong with the .360 No. 2 NE cartridge. Ballistic performance was on par with the .375 Flanged H&H Magnum. However, the .360 No.2 NE had no rimless counterpart to do battle with the .375 H&H Magnum which was by far the driving force in this market segment. Another handicap was that H&H endowed their .375 Flanged Magnum with bullet weights ranging from 235 grains to 300 grains, whereas the .360 No. 2 NE was never developed beyond a single 320 grain bullet loading.

.360 No. 5 ROOK

ALTERNATE NAME(S): .360 Rook
RELATED CALIBER(S): .380 Long, .38 Long Colt

CARTRIDGE HISTORY
Year of Introduction: circa 1875
Country of Origin: Britain
Designer(s): N/A
Governing Body: none
Present Status: obsolete

CARTRIDGE DESCRIPTION
Bullet Diameter: .362 in.

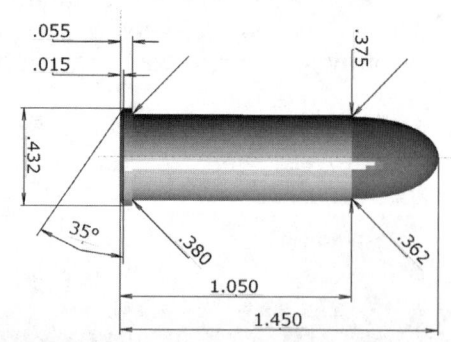

Bullet Weight(s): 125-145 gr.
Rifling Twist Rate: N/A
Test Barrel Length: N/A
Case Type: rimmed, straight
Case Material: brass
Primer: small rifle

CARTRIDGE BALLISTICS
Max. Average Breech Pressure: N/A
Max. Horizontal Range: 2,050 yds.
Max. Vertical Range: 4,400 ft.

Bullet Weight (gr.)	Bullet Type	Muzzle Velocity (fps)	Muzzle Energy (ft.-lbs.)
125	L-RN	1,050	310
134	L-RN	1,025	312
145	L-RN	1,075	373

CURRENT MANUFACTURER(S)
None

GENERAL COMMENT(S)
Many British farms kept a small caliber rifle on hand for dispatching predators, pests, and wounded farm animals. For these purposes, a cartridge of great power or long range was not needed or wanted. A large number of small, centerfire cartridges of this type were developed in Britain, however their popularity did not extend to the U.S. As a group, these cartridges were called "Rook" cartridges. Many were short-lived and obscure. This was one of the more popular and successful numbers that remained in production until the late 1930s.

TECHNICAL COMMENT(S)
Like most of its brethren, the .360 No. 5 Rook cartridge began life as a black powder cartridge, then transitioned to smokeless. Simple, lead round-nose bullets were the norm at very modest muzzle velocities and energies due to the very low maximum average chamber pressures. Unlike the longer rook cartridges, the .360 Rook was short enough to allow revolvers to be chambered for it and several were. Ballistics listed are from a rifle barrel.

.369 NITRO EXPRESS PURDEY

ALTERNATE NAME(S): .369 NE Purdey
RELATED CALIBER(S): .450/400 2 3/8 in., .400 Jeffery, .450/400 Nitro Express 3 1/4 in.

CARTRIDGE HISTORY
Year of Introduction: 1923
Country of Origin: Britain
Designer(s): Purdey
Governing Body: CIP
Present Status: obsolete

CARTRIDGE DESCRIPTION
Bullet Diameter: .375 in.
Bullet Weight(s): 270 gr.
Rifling Twist Rate: 1 turn in 16 in.
Test Barrel Length: 24 in.
Case Type: rimmed, necked
Case Material: brass
Primer: large rifle

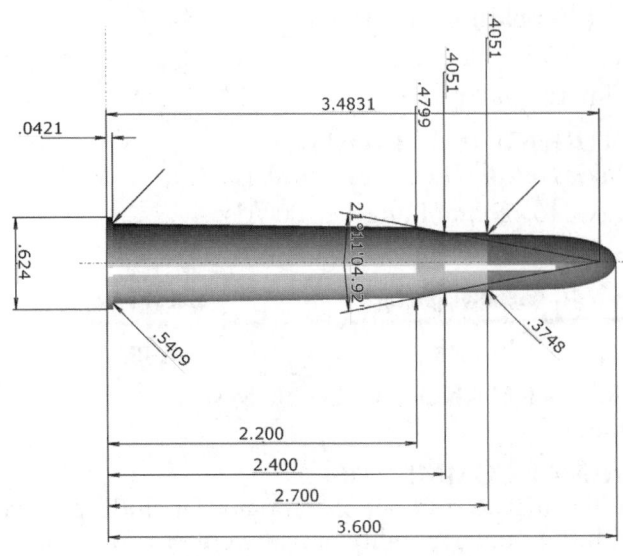

CARTRIDGE BALLISTICS
Max. Average Breech Pressure: 44,236 psi.
Max. Horizontal Range: 3,800 yds.
Max. Vertical Range: 8,200 ft.

Bullet Weight (gr.)	Bullet Type	Muzzle Velocity (fps)	Muzzle Energy (ft.-lbs.)
270	JSP	2,500	3,760

CURRENT MANUFACTURER(S)
None

GENERAL COMMENT(S)
Purdey introduced this cartridge in 1923. Their intended market seems to have been the hunter seeking better ballistic performance than the .360 Nitro Express could offer while retaining as much of the positive handling characteristics of a light weight double rifle as possible. Yes, the new cartridge met those goals, however, it did not catch on. Hard economic times (the Great Depression) were ahead that virtually erased much of the demand in the fine rifle market. Many hunters had come to prefer and rely on the .375 H&H Magnum, reducing the need for the .369 Purdey cartridge. And, lastly, the golden age of big game hunting nearly was over in India and waning fast in Africa.

TECHNICAL COMMENT(S)
There is nothing wrong with the .369 Nitro Express Purdey cartridge. It offers over twice the muzzle energy of the .360 Nitro Express cartridge in a compact (but not quite as compact as the .360 NE) package. In a light double rifle, the .369 Nitro Express offered a quantum level improvement in ballistic performance while maintaining a relatively light weight rifle.

.38 LONG CENTER FIRE

ALTERNATE NAME(S): .38 Long CF
RELATED CALIBER(S): .38 Long Rimfire

CARTRIDGE HISTORY
Year of Introduction: 1875
Country of Origin: U.S.
Designer(s): N/A
Governing Body: none
Present Status: obsolete

CARTRIDGE DESCRIPTION
Bullet Diameter: .376 in.
Bullet Weight(s): 145 gr.
Rifling Twist Rate: 1 turn in 36 in.
Test Barrel Length: N/A
Case Type: rimmed, straight
Case Material: brass
Primer: small rifle

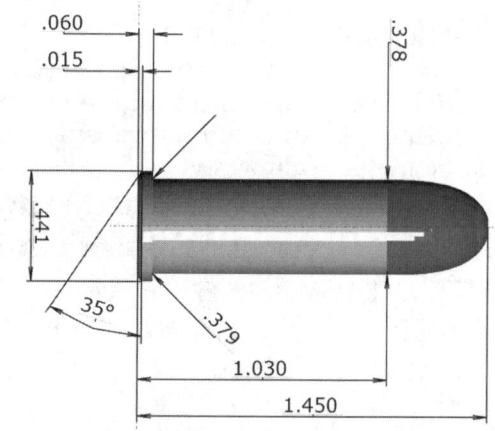

CARTRIDGE BALLISTICS
Max. Average Breech Pressure: N/A
Max. Horizontal Range: 1,300 yds.
Max. Vertical Range: 2,850 ft.

Bullet Weight (gr.)	Bullet Type	Muzzle Velocity (fps)	Muzzle Energy (ft.-lbs.)
145	L-RN	950	291

CURRENT MANUFACTURER(S)
None

GENERAL COMMENT(S)
In the 1870s, a number of companies including Ballard, Stevens and Remington offered small, single-shot rifles with the dual capability of firing either rimfire or center fire cartridges of similar caliber. All that was required was a simple adjustment or part(s) replacement to make the changeover. The .38 Long Center Fire cartridge is the center fire brother of the .38 Long rimfire. The .38 Long C.F. was considered obsolete by 1900, however the .38 Long Rimfire cartridge plodded on for many years afterward.

TECHNICAL COMMENT(S)

Ammunition in this caliber had to be loaded for the weakest link in the chain, rimfire cartridges. This required that maximum average chamber pressure be maintained at modest levels for safety which removed any advantage the stronger case of a center fire cartridge may have offered. Therefore, the advantage offered by dual cartridge capability rifles was purely convenience. The .38 Long Center Fire was a rifle cartridge firing .376 inch diameter bullets from a rifle barrel. It should not be confused with the .38 Long Colt or .38 Special revolver cartridges with their .358 inch diameter bullets. From any viewpoint, ballistic performance of the .38 Long C.F. cartridge is anemic at best. Muzzle velocity and muzzle energy are scarcely better than many revolver cartridges of that day, leaving the .38 Long C.F. suitable only for small game hunting In addition, the rainbow trajectory of the .38 Long limits its practical effective range to 100 yards or less. Still, this was certainly the reason for its success. Its limited range, negligible recoil, modest sound report, and low cost made it a handy tool around a farm, stable, or warehouse.

.38-40 REMINGTON-HEPBURN

ALTERNATE NAME(S): .38-40 Remington
RELATED CALIBER(S): .38-50 Remington-Hepburn, .40-50 Sharps (Straight), .40-85 Ballard, .40-90 Sharps (Straight)

CARTRIDGE HISTORY

Year of Introduction: 1873 (.38-40 Rem.), 1875 (.38-40 Rem.-Hepburn)
Country of Origin: U.S.
Designer(s): Remington
Governing Body: none
Present Status: obsolete

CARTRIDGE DESCRIPTION

Bullet Diameter: .376 in.
Bullet Weight(s): 245 gr.
Rifling Twist Rate: 1 turn in 16 in.
Test Barrel Length: N/A
Case Type: rimmed, straight
Case Material: brass
Primer: large rifle

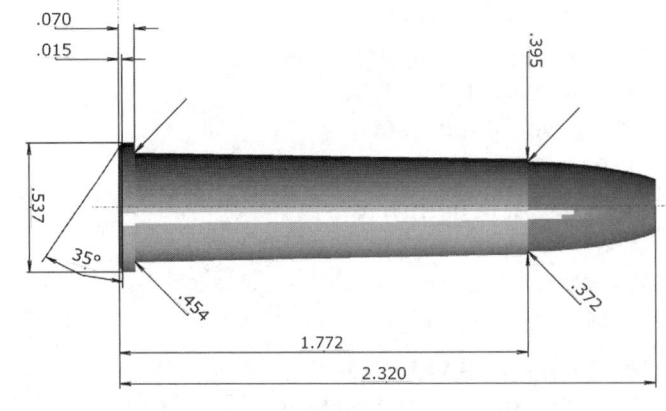

CARTRIDGE BALLISTICS

Max. Average Breech Pressure: N/A
Max. Horizontal Range: 3,300 yds.
Max. Vertical Range: 6,700 ft.

Bullet Weight (gr.)	Bullet Type	Muzzle Velocity (fps)	Muzzle Energy (ft.-lbs.)
245	L-FN	1,200	783

CURRENT MANUFACTURER(S)

None

GENERAL COMMENT(S)

Remington introduced their .38-40 Remington cartridge in 1873 for their rolling-block rifle. It was set to become just another .38 caliber rifle cartridge in the herd of such cartridges. Then, in 1871, Lewis L. Hepburn became Superintendent of the sporting arms production line at Remington Arms Co. in Ilion, N.Y. Shortly after the Creedmoor shooting range opened on Long Island, N.Y. in 1873, the Irish shooting team challenged American shooters to a long range match. This match was fired on September 26, 1873 at the Creedmoor range. Hepburn was a member of the American shooting team that won the match. Hepburn's Remington single-shot rolling block rifle was handmade with many modifications. Seeing this, shooters pressed Remington to offer such a rifle. The result was the Remington-Hepburn "Creedmoor" rifle chambered for the .38-40 Rem. and, later, for the .38-50 Remington-Hepburn cartridges. For a few bright years in the early life of the Creedmoor shooting range, the Remington-Hepburn cartridge made quite an impression based largely on Hepburn's rifles. In short order, however, it became obvious that a Hepburn cartridge with a heavier propellant charge and increased muzzle velocity would be needed. The result was the .38-50 Remington-Hepburn cartridge. Both Remington-Hepburn cartridges proved good performers and both made the transition to smokeless propellants. The .38-40 Remington-Hepburn cartridges remained in Remington's product line until the mid-1930s.

TECHNICAL COMMENT(S)

As designed, the .38-40 Remington was a medium capacity cartridge having a case of rimmed, straight configuration firing a 245 grain lead bullet at the very modest muzzle velocity of 1,200 fps. Recognizing a good marketing opportunity when they saw one, Remington jumped on the Creedmoor bandwagon using Hepburn's success. For good measure, the .38-40 Remington cartridge was renamed the .38-40 Remington-Hepburn and slotted in the Remington product line as a target cartridge. By 1883, it became obvious that a more powerful cartridge would be needed to complement the existing .38-40. To speed up development, Remington decided to create the new cartridge on the cheap by making minor modifications to the existing .38-40 Remington case. Accordingly, Remington increased the case length .46 inches to provide increased powder capacity and upped the bullet weight 10 grains to create the new .38-50 Remington-Hepburn cartridge.

.38-40 WINCHESTER

ALTERNATE NAME(S): .38-40 WCF, .38 CLMR
RELATED CALIBER(S): .44-40 WCF

CARTRIDGE HISTORY

Year of Introduction: 1874
Country of Origin: U.S.
Designer(s): Winchester
Governing Body: SAAMI
Present Status: obsolete

CARTRIDGE DESCRIPTION

Bullet Diameter: .400 in.
Bullet Weight(s): 180 gr.
Rifling Twist Rate: 1 turn in 36 in.
Test Barrel Length: 6 in.
Case Type: rimmed, necked
Case Material: brass
Primer Size: large pistol

CARTRIDGE BALLISTICS

Max. Average Breech Pressure: 15,700 CUP.
Max. Horizontal Range: 1,900 yds.
Max. Vertical Range: 4,300 ft.

Bullet Weight (gr.)	Bullet Type	Muzzle Velocity (fps)	Muzzle Energy (ft.-lbs.)
180	JSP	1,160	538

CURRENT MANUFACTURER(S)

Black Hills

GENERAL COMMENT(S)

Designed as a cartridge for lever-action rifles, the .38-40 Win. cartridge was also used in revolvers. It became a popular cartridge in the 1870s and 1880s, although it always lived in the shadow of its parent .44-40 Win. cartridge. Until recently, no new guns had been made in this caliber since before World War II. The advent of cowboy action competition changed all this and new guns chambered for the .38-40 Win. are reappearing.

TECHNICAL COMMENT(S)

Regardless of the nomenclature, the .38-40 Win. uses .400 inch diameter bullets and was often loaded with 38 grains of black powder. At close range, the striking energy of the 180 grain bullet was more than adequate for personal defense against man or animal. For any other use, its range was too limited.

.38-50 REMINGTON-HEPBURN

ALTERNATE NAME(S): .38-50 Hepburn
RELATED CALIBER(S): .38-40 Remington-Hepburn, .40-50 Sharps (Straight), .40-85 Ballard, .40-90 Sharps (Straight)

CARTRIDGE HISTORY
Year of Introduction: 1883
Country of Origin: U.S.
Designer(s): Lewis L. Hepburn/Remington
Governing Body: none
Present Status: obsolete

CARTRIDGE DESCRIPTION
Bullet Diameter: .376 in.
Bullet Weight(s): 255 gr.
Rifling Twist Rate: 1 turn in 16 in.
Test Barrel Length: N/A
Case Type: rimmed, straight
Case Material: brass
Primer: large rifle

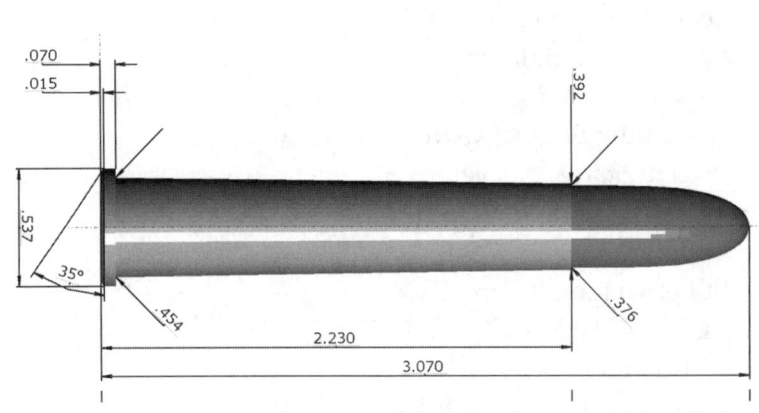

CARTRIDGE BALLISTICS
Max. Average Breech Pressure: N/A
Max. Horizontal Range: 3,400 yds.
Max. Vertical Range: 6,900 ft.

Bullet Weight (gr.)	Bullet Type	Muzzle Velocity (fps)	Muzzle Energy (ft.-lbs.)
255	L-FN	1,320	986

CURRENT MANUFACTURER(S)
None

GENERAL COMMENT(S)
Lewis L. Hepburn (1832-1914) became interested in firearms at an early age. He worked for some years as a blacksmith and a gunsmith, earning a reputation for making excellent rifles. In 1871, Hepburn became Superintendent of the sporting arms production line at Remington Arms Co. in Ilion, N.Y. Shortly after the Creedmoor shooting range opened on Long Island, N.Y. in 1873, the Irish shooting team challenged American shooters to a long range match. This match was fired on September 26, 1873 and Hepburn was a member of the American team that won the match. Many of the American competitors used Remington single-shot rolling block rifles in the match. Hepburn's rifle was handmade with many modifications. Seeing this, shooters pressed Remington to offer such a rifle. The result was the Remington-Hepburn No. 3 "Creedmoor" rifle and .38-50 Remington-Hepburn cartridge. For a few bright years in the early life of the Creedmoor shooting range, the Remington-Hepburn cartridge made quite an impression based largely on Hepburn's rifles. In short order, however, the Hepburn cartridges were replaced in the limelight by larger caliber cartridges with heavier bullets and substantially heavier powder charges. These were, in turn, made redundant by the advent of smokeless propellants. However, the .38-50 Remington-Hepburn cartridge proved such a good performer, it made the transition to smokeless propellants and remained in Remington's product line until the mid-1930s.

TECHNICAL COMMENT(S)
Designed specifically for target shooting using black powder, the .38-50 Remington-Hepburn case was of rimmed, straight design as preferred by target shooters of the day. A 255 grain, lead bullet with a flat meplat was the only style offered. Muzzle velocity was a leisurely 1,320 fps. Remington dusted off an older cartridge of their own design, the .38-40 Remington from 1873, to serve as the basis of the new .38-50 cartridge. The .38-40 case was made .46 inches longer so as to provide increased powder capacity and the bullet weight increased 10 grains to 255 grains. Driven by 10 additional grains of black powder, muzzle velocity increased approximately 120 fps. Today these seem minor improvements, but by the standards of the time, they were considered significant.

.38-56 WINCHESTER

ALTERNATE NAME(S): .38-56 Win.
RELATED CALIBER(S): .38-55 Ballard/Winchester

CARTRIDGE HISTORY
Year of Introduction: 1887
Country of Origin: U.S.
Designer(s): Winchester
Governing Body: SAAMI
Present Status: obsolete

CARTRIDGE DESCRIPTION
Bullet Diameter: .376 in.
Bullet Weight(s): 255 gr.
Rifling Twist Rate: 1 turn in 20 in.
Test Barrel Length: 26 in.
Case Type: rimmed, bottlenecked
Case Material: brass
Primer: large rifle

CARTRIDGE BALLISTICS
Max. Average Breech Pressure: N/A
Max. Horizontal Range: 3,450 yds.
Max. Vertical Range: 7,050 ft.

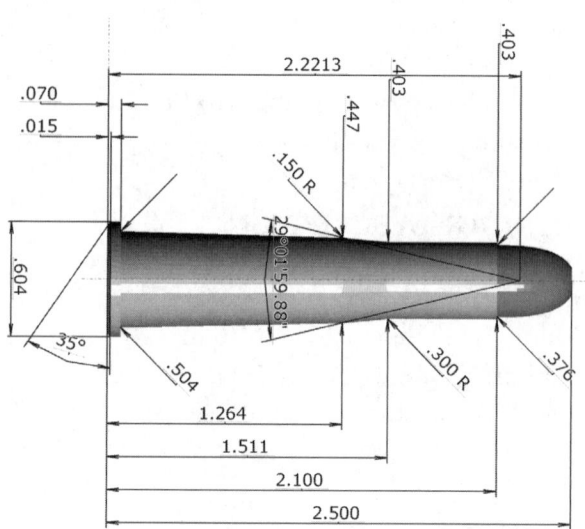

Bullet Weight (gr.)	Bullet Type	Muzzle Velocity (fps)	Muzzle Energy (ft.-lbs.)
255	JSP	1385	1,086

CURRENT MANUFACTURER(S)
None

GENERAL COMMENT(S)
This was one of the cartridges Winchester introduced with their Model 1886 lever-action rifle. It was intended to supplement the earlier .38-55 Ballard/Winchester cartridge with one having higher muzzle velocity.

TECHNICAL COMMENT(S)
Unlike the .38-55 Ballard/Winchester straight case cartridge introduced in 1884, the .38-56 Winchester was a bottle necked design intended to provide additional case volume without increasing case length. With its heavier charge of black powder, muzzle velocity of the .38-56 would be higher than the .38-55 cartridge. Both cartridges have the same case length and overall loaded length, but they are not interchangeable. The rapidly spreading introduction of smokeless propellants made such plans redundant, so Winchester transitioned both the .38-55 and the .38-56 cartridges to smokeless propellants. In doing so, any ballistic advantage the .38-56 Win. cartridge might have had was lost due to chamber pressure limitations for black powder firearms. For these reasons, the .38-56 cartridge gradually lost its market. Winchester doggedly kept the .38-56 Win. cartridge in their product line until the mid-1930s leaving the popular .38-55 Ballard/Winchester cartridge to soldier on alone.

.38-70 WINCHESTER

ALTERNATE NAME(S): .38-70 Win.

RELATED CALIBER(S): .38-56 Winchester, .40-70 Winchester, .40-90 Sharps (Necked), .40-75 Bullard

CARTRIDGE HISTORY
Year of Introduction: 1894
Country of Origin: U.S.
Designer(s): Winchester
Governing Body: none
Present Status: obsolete

CARTRIDGE DESCRIPTION
Bullet Diameter: .376 in.
Bullet Weight(s): 255 gr.
Rifling Twist Rate: 1 turn in 24 in.
Test Barrel Length: 26 in.
Case Type: rimmed, necked
Case Material: brass
Primer: large rifle

CARTRIDGE BALLISTICS
Max. Average Breech Pressure: N/A
Max. Horizontal Range: 3,500 yds.
Max. Vertical Range: 7,200 ft.

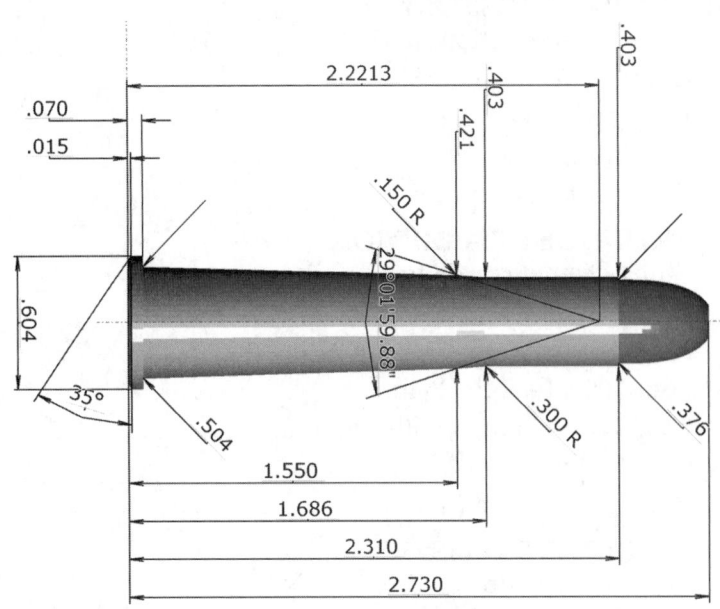

Bullet Weight (gr.)	Bullet Type	Muzzle Velocity (fps)	Muzzle Energy (ft.-lbs.)
255	JSP	1,475	1,232

CURRENT MANUFACTURER(S)
None

GENERAL COMMENT(S)
This was another Winchester cartridge belatedly introduced in 1894 for the Model 1886 lever-action rifle. This cartridge was introduced in the twilight years of black powder at a time when sportsmen were expecting smokeless powder cartridges. In addition, there were already plenty of .38 caliber rifle cartridges to choose from that duplicated the ballistic performance of the .38-70. Indeed, three of the competing cartridges carried the Winchester name! Winchester was competing with itself. Inherently, the market understood this, even if Winchester did not, and the .38-70 Win. cartridge failed to garner any market interest and quickly faded away.

TECHNICAL COMMENT(S)
The rim and case head dimensions of the .38-70 Win. cartridge were shared with the .38-56 Win., .40-70 Win. and .40-82 Win. as well as several non-Winchester calibers. Any possible ballistic advantage of the .38-70 Win. cartridge was ephemeral. Muzzle velocity was less than 100 fps higher than the .38-56 Win. and 15 fps. higher than the .38-72 Win. with the same or nearly the same bullet weight.

.38-72 WINCHESTER

ALTERNATE NAME(S): .38-72 Win.
RELATED CALIBER(S): .35 Win., .40-72 Win., .405 Win.

CARTRIDGE HISTORY
Year of Introduction: 1895
Country of Origin: U.S.
Designer(s): Winchester
Governing Body: none
Present Status: obsolete

CARTRIDGE DESCRIPTION
Bullet Diameter: .378 in.
Bullet Weight(s): 275 gr.
Rifling Twist Rate: 1 turn in 22 in.
Test Barrel Length: 26 in.
Case Type: rimmed with slight neck
Case Material: brass
Primer Size: large rifle

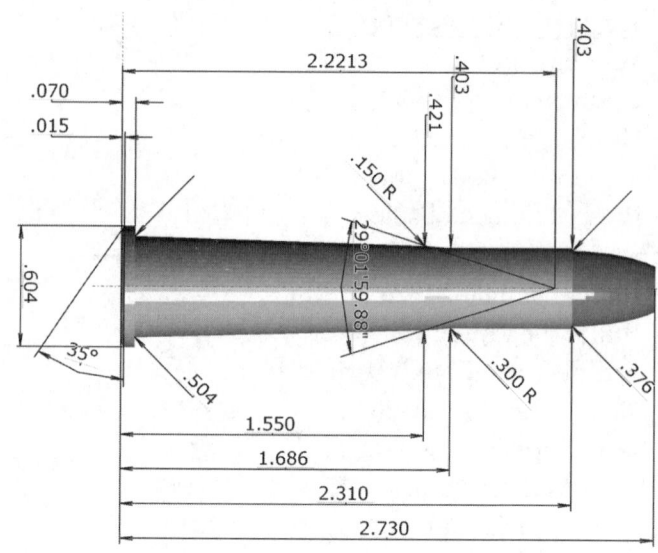

CARTRIDGE BALLISTICS
Max. Average Breech Pressure: N/A
Max. Horizontal Range: 3,000 yds.
Max. Vertical Range: 6,200 ft.

Bullet Weight (gr.)	Bullet Type	Muzzle Velocity (fps)	Muzzle Energy (ft.-lbs.)
275	FMJ-RN	1,445	1,293

CURRENT MANUFACTURER(S)
None

GENERAL COMMENT(S)
With the emergence of bolt-action rifles firing high-pressure cartridges in the late 1880s and early 1890s, Winchester lever-action rifles were becoming outclassed as they could not handle the high maximum average chamber pressures generated by the new cartridges. In an effort to defend their share of the rifle market, Winchester developed a new lever-action rifle, the Model 1895, for its new family of high pressure cartridges. By adopting a box magazine and a stronger action, the Model 1895 used high-pressure cartridges firing round nose and pointed bullets. The new family began with the .38-72 Win. and the .40-72 Win. which were introduced with the new rifle in 1895. The .35 Winchester and the .405 Winchester followed on 1903 and 1904 respectively. None of these calibers gained a popular following and all were dropped from the Winchester product line in 1936 and quickly faded into obscurity.

TECHNICAL COMMENT(S)
Winchester designed all four of these new cartridges on a common .460 inch diameter base and .539 inch diameter rim with only minor variations. Despite the capabilities of the new M1895 rifle, the first two new cartridges Winchester introduced for it had modest chamber pressures and heavy bullets at moderate muzzle velocity. As both the .38-72 Win. and .40-72 Win. cartridges were offered in smokeless powder and black powder loadings, the old black powder nomenclature was used. In response to the demand for higher muzzle velocities, Winchester introduced two, new high pressure cartridges, the .38-72 Winchester in 1903 and the .405 Winchester in 1904. As both of these cartridges were loaded only with smokeless propellants, the new nomenclature without the propellant weight was used.

.38-90 WINCHESTER EXPRESS

ALTERNATE NAME(S): .38-90 Win. Exp.

RELATED CALIBER(S): .40-63 Ballard, .40-90 Sharps (Straight), .40-110 Winchester Express, .45-125 Winchester Express, .50-140 Winchester Express

CARTRIDGE HISTORY

Year of Introduction: 1886

Country of Origin: U.S.

Designer(s): Winchester

Governing Body: none

Present Status: obsolete

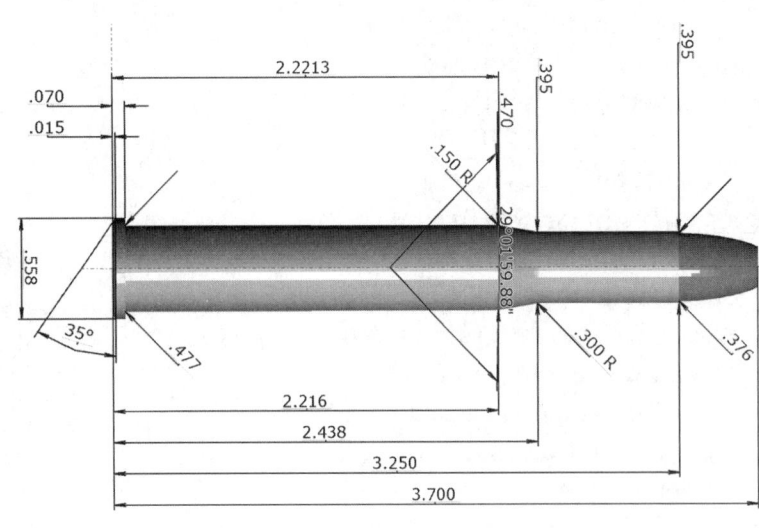

CARTRIDGE DESCRIPTION

Bullet Diameter: .376 in.

Bullet Weight(s): 217 gr.

Rifling Twist Rate: 1 turn in 26 in.

Test Barrel Length: 30 in.

Case Type: rimmed, necked

Case Material: brass

Primer: large rifle

CARTRIDGE BALLISTICS

Max. Average Breech Pressure: N/A

Max. Horizontal Range: 3,550 yds.

Max. Vertical Range: 7,350 ft.

Bullet Weight (gr.)	Bullet Type	Muzzle Velocity (fps)	Muzzle Energy (ft.-lbs.)
217	L-FN	1,575	1,195

CURRENT MANUFACTURER(S)

None

GENERAL COMMENT(S)

Between 1880 and 1886, Winchester introduced four massive black powder rifle cartridges with a case length of 3.25 inches and overall loaded lengths of almost four inches. These four were: .50-140 Winchester Express, .45-125 Winchester Express, .40-110 Winchester Express and the .38-90 Winchester Express. These cartridges were intended to compete with the largest Sharps cartridges for hunting big game. Winchester called these "Express" cartridges, a label they placed on no other caliber. As a group, these cartridges were obsolete when they were introduced as the advent of smokeless propellants made such massive cartridges ballistically unnecessary. By 1914, most of them had faded away.

TECHNICAL COMMENT(S)

The .38-90 Winchester Express is the runt of the family. It used a light weight 217 grain bullet instead of the normal 255 grain for this caliber in order to increase muzzle velocity. However, muzzle energy was the same or less than other Winchester cartridges of this caliber. As a result, the .38-90 cartridge offered no ballistic reason for choosing it. While the case length was 3.25 inches, the .38-90 case had a rim and case head of semi-unique dimensions shared with only three other cartridges, all of them Winchester. As a result, the .38-90 was an orphan with no market. By 1904, it was no longer offered by Winchester.

9x56mm MANNLICHER-SCHOENAUER

ALTERNATE NAME(S): 9x56mm M-S
RELATED CALIBER(S): 8x56mm M-S, 9.5x56mm M-S, 10.75x57mm M-S

CARTRIDGE HISTORY
Year of Introduction: circa 1900
Country of Origin: Austria
Designer(s): Mannlicher
Governing Body: CIP
Present Status: obsolete

CARTRIDGE DESCRIPTION
Bullet Diameter: .3575 in.
Bullet Weight(s): 200-280 gr.
Rifling Twist Rate: 1 turn in 11 in.
Test Barrel Length: 24 in.
Case Type: rimless, necked
Case Material: brass
Primer: large rifle

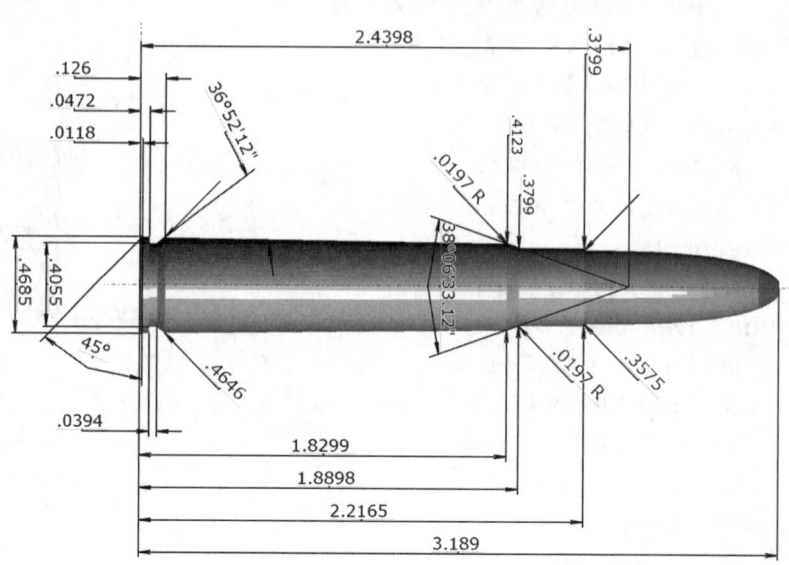

CARTRIDGE BALLISTICS
Max. Average Chamber Pressure: 30,168 psi.
Max. Horizontal Range: 3,500 yds.
Max. Vertical Range: 8,000 ft.

Bullet Weight (gr.)	Bullet Type	Muzzle Velocity (fps)	Muzzle Energy (ft.-lbs.)
200	JSP	2,110	1,980
250	JSP	2,100	2,448
280	JSP	1,850	2,128

CURRENT MANUFACTURER(S)
None

GENERAL COMMENT(S)
Here we have a member of the original family of Mannlicher sporting rifle calibers introduced around the turn of the 20th century. The 8x56mm M-S was the smallest calliber of the family with brethren up to 10.75x57mm. The M-S sporting rifle cartridges never achieved the popularity of the Mauser calibers which benefitted from their military acceptance and higher ballistic performance.

TECHNICAL COMMENT(S)
Although the Mannlicher sporting cartridges were designed from the beginning for smokeless propellants, they were very much creatures of traditional thinking, namely heavy bullets at moderate muzzle velocities from relatively low chamber pressures. Undoubtedly, this contributed to the lack of acceptance of these M-S calibers as they did not stand up well in comparison to the light bullets and high muzzle velocities made possible by the higher chamber pressures of the newer Mauser calibers.

9x57mm MAUSER, 9x57Rmm MAUSER

ALTERNATE NAME(S): 9x57mm , 9x57Rmm
RELATED CALIBER(S): 8x57mm Mauser , 9.3x57mm Mauser

CARTRIDGE HISTORY
Year of Introduction: 1888
Country of Origin: Germany
Designer(s): Peter Paul Mauser
Governing Body: none
Present Status: obsolete

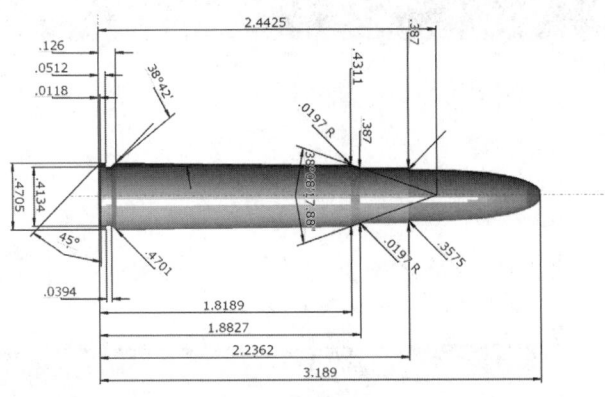 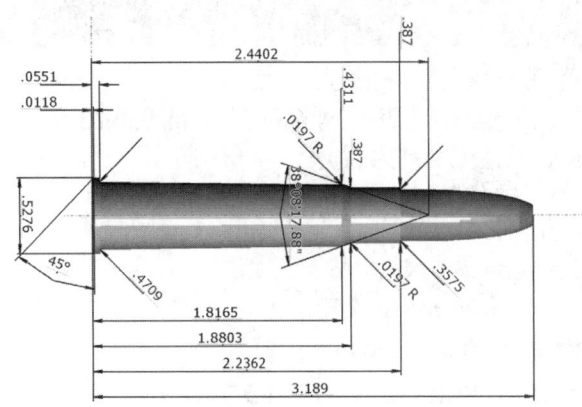

CARTRIDGE DESCRIPTION

Bullet Diameter: .356 in.

Bullet Weight(s): 205-281 gr.

Rifling Twist Rate: 1 turn in 14.2 in.

Test Barrel Length: N/A

Case Type: rimless, necked

Case Material: brass

Primer: large rifle

CARTRIDGE BALLISTICS

Max. Average Breech Pressure: 40,611 psi.

Max. Horizontal Range: 2,800 yds.

Max. Vertical Range: 6,500 ft.

Bullet Weight (gr.)	Bullet Type	Muzzle Velocity (fps)	Muzzle Energy (ft.-lbs.)
205	JSP	2,425	2,682
245	JSP	2,150	2,520
281	JSP	1,920	2,285

CURRENT MANUFACTURER(S)

None

GENERAL COMMENT(S)

Immediately following the adoption of the 8x57mmJ Mauser cartridge in the late 1880s, Mauser set about developing a family of hunting cartridges based on the 8x57 cartridge case. The 9x57mm Mauser cartridges were two of the first.

TECHNICAL COMMENT(S)

Using the existing cartridge saved time and money. In addition, the new cartridge would fit in the standard length Mauser rifle actions with few modifications. The 9x57mm cartridge with its large, heavy 9mm bullet was an excellent choice for the German hunter looking for slightly more power than the 8x57mm. And here was the sleight of hand, because the 9x57mm cartridges did not produce significantly more muzzle energy than the 8x57mm cartridge. In any case, neither was intended for hunting dangerous game, but they performed very well on medium and thin-skinned large game. Even some American ammunition makers loaded it until the mid-1930s.

9.3x72Rmm

ALTERNATE NAME(S): none
RELATED CALIBER(S): 9.3x57Rmm, 9.3x70Rmm

CARTRIDGE HISTORY
Year of Introduction: N/A
Country of Origin: Germany
Designer(s): N/A
Governing Body: CIP
Present Status: obsolete

CARTRIDGE DESCRIPTION
Bullet Diameter: .3768 in.
Bullet Weight(s): 193 gr.
Rifling Twist Rate: 1 turn in 16.5 in.
Test Barrel Length: 24 in.
Case Type: rimmed, straight
Case Material: brass
Primer: large rifle

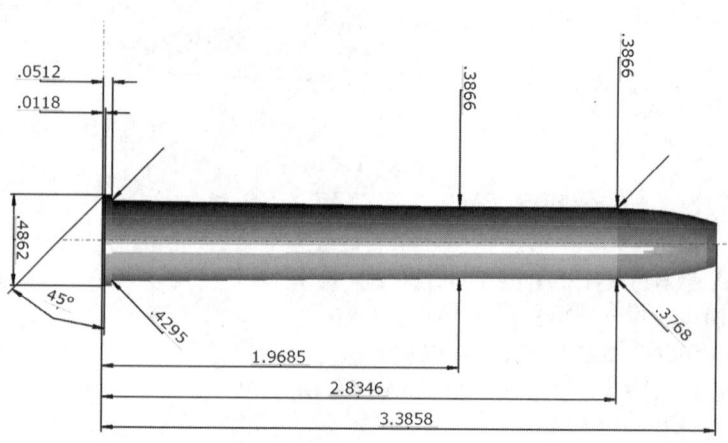

CARTRIDGE BALLISTICS
Max. Average Chamber Pressure: 29,000 psi.
Max. Horizontal Range: 2,800 yds.
Max. Vertical Range: 6,000 ft.

Bullet Weight (gr.)	Bullet Type	Muzzle Velocity (fps)	Muzzle Energy (ft.-lbs.)
193	JSP-FN	1,950	1,629

CURRENT MANUFACTURER(S)
Dynamit Nobel/RUAG, Sellier & Bellot

GENERAL COMMENT(S)
The designer and date of introduction of this old hunter have been lost to history. However, it was a popular caliber in drillings for many years due to its low chamber pressure and rimmed case. Now long in the tooth, it tenuously clings to life, but the end is very near as its popularity is fading quickly. The 9.3x74Rmm which replaced it is a better cartridge.

TECHNICAL COMMENT(S)
This old cartridge should not be confused with the 9.3x72Rmm Sauer which has larger head and rim dimensions as well as a .365 inch diameter bullet. It is easy to differentiate between the two in that the 9.3x72Rmm Sauer has a slightly necked case while the 9.3x72Rmm has a straight case. While the smaller dimensioned 9.3x72Rmm will chamber and fire in some rifles of 9.3x72Rmm Sauer caliber, this practice can not be recommended.

9.5x47Rmm

ALTERNATE NAME(S): Schuetzen cartridges
RELATED CALIBER(S): various black powder target cartridges

CARTRIDGE HISTORY
Year of Introduction: 1880s
Country of Origin: Germany
Designer(s): N/A
Governing Body: none
Present Status: obsolete

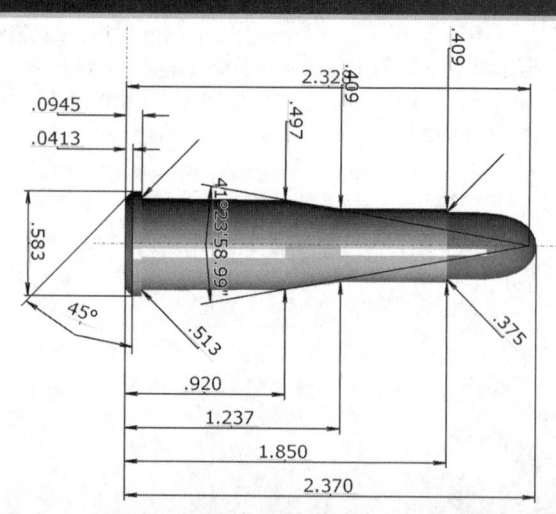

CARTRIDGE DESCRIPTION
Bullet Diameter: .375 in. (in general .335-.512 in.)
Bullet Weight(s): 211 gr. (in general 140-385 grs.)
Rifling Twist Rate: N/A

Test Barrel Length: N/A
Case Type: rimmed, necked (or straight)
Case Material: brass
Primer: large rifle

CARTRIDGE BALLISTICS
Max. Average Breech Pressure: N/A
Max. Horizontal Range: N/A
Max. Vertical Range: N/A

Bullet Weight (gr.)	Bullet Type	Muzzle Velocity (fps)	Muzzle Energy (ft.-lbs.)
140	L-RN	1,800	1,007

CURRENT MANUFACTURER(S)
None

GENERAL COMMENT(S)
In the 1880s, a new class of black powder rifle cartridges was developed in Germany and Austria. Optimized for target shooting at ranges to 200 meters, these were called "schuetzen" cartridges. They were used in single-shot target rifles of various designs. The 9.5x47Rmm cartridge is typical of the breed. Cartridges of this type remained popular for many years with some designs lasting well into the 1930s. As a class, they are now obsolete, having been replaced by small caliber cartridges such as the 5.6x35Rmm Vierling for hunting rifle competition at 100 meters.

TECHNICAL COMMENT(S)
This class of cartridges rapidly developed into dozens of variations ranging in caliber from 8.1mm (.335 in.) to 13mm (.512 in.). An astute reader will note that the Mauser-type base was a popular design characteristic. Calibers under .335 in. were impractical due to black powder fouling. Many of these target/schuetzen calibers used smokeless propellant as it became available. As these cartridges were designed for target shooting and not hunting, bullet weights were kept light for caliber, propellant charges were kept as small as possible and muzzle velocities were modest. These combined to provide good accuracy with reduced recoil and low cost. Most bullets were lead round-nose or flat-nose designs.

9.5x57mm MANNLICHER-SCHOENAUER

ALTERNATE NAME(S): 9.5x57mm M-S, 9.5x56mm Mannlicher-Schoenauer, 9.5x56.7mm Mannlicher-Schoenauer, .375 Nitro Express Rimless
RELATED CALIBER(S): None

CARTRIDGE HISTORY
Year of Introduction: 1910
Country of Origin: Austria
Designer(s): Ferdinand von Mannlicher
Governing Body: none
Present Status: obsolete

CARTRIDGE DESCRIPTION
Bullet Diameter: .375 in.
Bullet Weight(s): 272 gr.
Rifling Twist Rate: N/A
Test Barrel Length: 24
Case Type: rimless, necked
Case Material: brass
Primer: large rifle

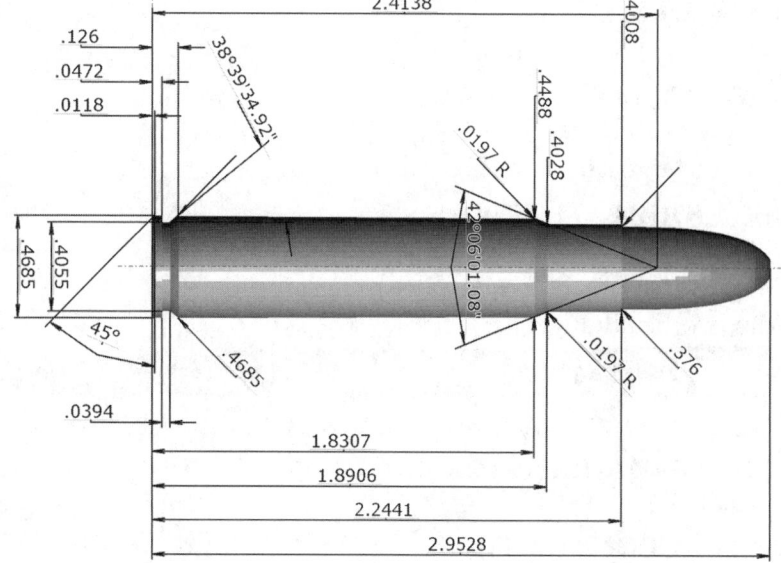

CARTRIDGE BALLISTICS
Max. Average Breech Pressure: 55,114 psi.
Max. Horizontal Range: 3,250 yds.
Max. Vertical Range: 7,000 ft.

Bullet Weight (gr.)	Bullet Type	Muzzle Velocity (fps)	Muzzle Energy (ft.-lbs.)
272	JSP-RN	2,150	2,792

CURRENT MANUFACTURER(S)

None

GENERAL COMMENT(S)

Intended as a sporting cartridge, the 9.5x57mm M-S is not in the same league as the .375 H&H Magnum despite both using the same bullet diameter and weight. In fact, the 9.5x57mm M-S offers less than half the muzzle energy of the .375 H&H Magnum, leaving it suitable only for thin-skinned, medium game at ranges under 200 yards. Ammunition in this caliber was manufactured in Britain by Kynoch, Germany by RWS, and Austria by Roth.

TECHNICAL COMMENT(S)

This old sporting cartridge is based on the 8x57mm case necked up to accept a .375 inch diameter bullet. One reason for selecting the 8x57mm cartridge as a base was that the case head configuration and dimensions were fully compatible with the bolt face of standard length M88/M98 Mauser bolt-action rifles. Another reason is that the overall loaded length of this cartridge allowed it to feed through the magazine of the above-mentioned Mauser rifles. Like other cartridges of this type, difficulty was experienced controlling headspace on the diminutive shoulder. Another drawback was that the muzzle energy of this cartridge was the same as the common 8x57mmJS Mauser cartridge leaving the 9.5x57mm M-S with no clear ballistic advantage.

.400 NITRO EXPRESS 3 in.

ALTERNATE NAME(S): .400 Straight 3 in., .400 Purdey 3 in. Light Express, 10.2x76Rmm
RELATED CALIBER(S): .400/350 Rigby, .350 No. 2 Rigby

CARTRIDGE HISTORY

Year of Introduction: pre-1870
Country of Origin: Britain
Designer(s): N/A
Governing Body: none
Present Status: obsolete

CARTRIDGE DESCRIPTION

Bullet Diameter: .405 in.
Bullet Weight(s): 230 gr.
Rifling Twist Rate: N/A
Test Barrel Length: 24 in.
Case Type: rimmed, straight
Case Material: brass
Primer: large rifle

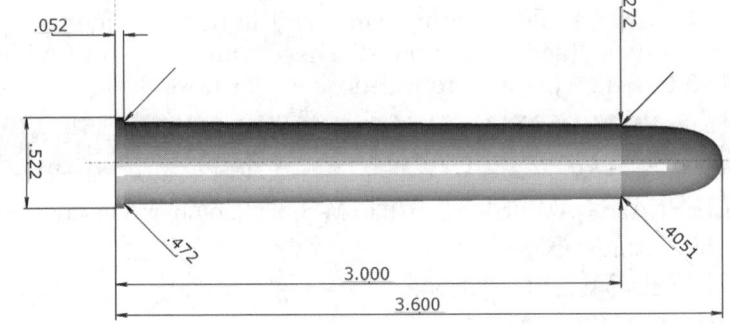

CARTRIDGE BALLISTICS

Max. Average Breech Pressure: 28,000 psi.
Max. Horizontal Range: 2,550 yds.
Max. Vertical Range: 5,500 ft.

Bullet Weight (gr.)	Bullet Type	Muzzle Velocity (fps)	Muzzle Energy (ft.-lbs.)
230	L-RN	2,050	2,148

CURRENT MANUFACTURER(S)

Kynamco

GENERAL COMMENT(S)

This old hunter began life as a black powder cartridge with a case made of paper, then coiled brass, and finally drawn brass. By the time it made the transition to smokeless propellants, it was already several decades old. Many British hunters preferred this caliber for hunting medium size game such as deer, springbok and the like. One of the reasons for this was that double rifles in this caliber were light and handy with low recoil. Kynamco still offers loaded ammunition in this caliber.

TECHNICAL COMMENT(S)

For smokeless propellants, this case is hopelessly long. However, smokeless powder ammunition in this caliber loaded in Britain used Cordite, because a modest charge of granulated propellant sloshing around in all that volume would have caused erratic ignition. Plain lead bullets were the norm. Muzzle velocity was high enough to generate well over 2,000 ft.-lbs. of muzzle energy placing the .400 NE well above many other highly regarded cartridges without causing excessive recoil. The .400 NE was a well balanced cartridge despite its excessive length.

.401 WINCHESTER SELF-LOADING

ALTERNATE NAME(S): .401 WSL, .401 SL, 10x38mm, 10.3x38mm
RELATED CALIBER(S): .35 WSL, .351 WSL

CARTRIDGE HISTORY

Year of Introduction: 1910
Country of Origin: U.S.
Designer(s): Winchester
Governing Body: CIP
Present Status: obsolete

CARTRIDGE DESCRIPTION

Bullet Diameter: .407 in.
Bullet Weight(s): 200-250 gr.
Rifling Twist Rate: 1 turn in 16 in.
Test Barrel Length: 24 in.
Case Type: rimless, straight
Case Material: brass
Primer Size: large rifle

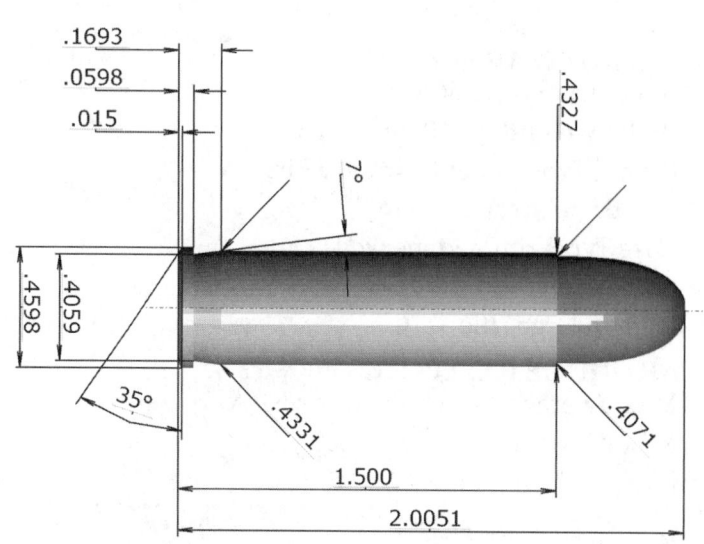

CARTRIDGE BALLISTICS

Max. Average Breech Pressure: 35,500 psi.
Max. Effective Range: 100 yds.
Max. Horizontal Range: 2,000 yds.
Max. Vertical Range: 8,000 ft.

Bullet Weight (gr.)	Bullet Type	Muzzle Velocity (fps)	Muzzle Energy (ft.-lbs.)
200	JSP	2,135	2,020
250	JSP	1,870	1,940

CURRENT MANUFACTURER(S)

None

GENERAL COMMENT(S)

In 1907, Winchester introduced their first semi-automatic rifle and cartridge, the M1907 rifle chambered for the .35 Win. Self-Loading cartridge. In response to complaints about the underpowered .35 W.S.L. cartridge, Winchester introduced a new rifle and cartridge in 1910, the M1910 rifle chambered for the improved .351 W.S.L. cartridge. While an improvement over the original .35 W.S.L. cartridge, the .351 W.S.L. remained marginal and still left many hunters underwhelmed. At the same time, Winchester introduced a Model 1910 rifle chambered for a much more powerful cartridge, the .401 Winchester Self-Loading. Finally, Winchester had a semi-automatic rifle firing a cartridge offering sufficient power for hunting medium game. Despite this, the .401 S.L. achieved only modest popularity as a short-range deer caliber for use in heavy brush. In 1936, Winchester gave up on the .401 W.S.L. and dropped the cartridge from their catalog. Few hunters lamented their action.

TECHNICAL COMMENT(S)

From a modern perspective, the .401 W.S.L. is an interesting piece of Winchester Americana, i.e. a large caliber heavy bullet at very modest muzzle velocity. While this limited the effective range to about 100 yards, recoil was mild and the rifles were short and well balanced. The .401 W.S.L. is fun to shoot from a nostalgic view point, if you can find the ammunition. Note the maximum average chamber pressure is a rather modest 35,500 psi due to the rifle's blow-back operation. Note also the long undercut at a shallow angle on the case head in front of the extractor groove. Although SAAMI has long since dropped the .401 W.S.L. from their active cartridge listings, it continues to be listed in CIP despite the fact that no company loads it.

.40-110 WINCHESTER EXPRESS

ALTERNATE NAME(S): .40-110 Express, .40-110 Win. Exp.

RELATED CALIBER(S): .38-90 Winchester Express, .45-125 Winchester Express, .50-140 Winchester Express, .40-90 Sharps (Straight)

CARTRIDGE HISTORY

Year of Introduction: 1886

Country of Origin: U.S.

Designer(s): Winchester

Governing Body: none

Present Status: obsolete

CARTRIDGE DESCRIPTION

Bullet Diameter: .403 in.

Bullet Weight(s): 260 gr.

Rifling Twist Rate: 1 turn in 28 in.

Test Barrel Length: 30 in.

Case Type: rimmed, necked

Case Material: brass

Primer: large rifle

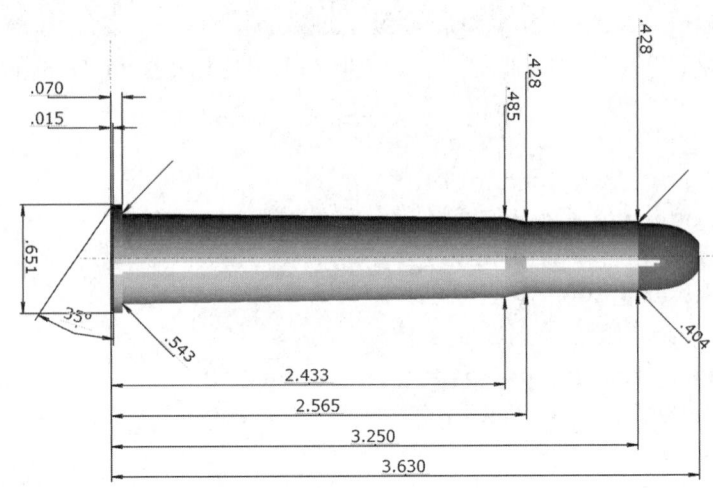

CARTRIDGE BALLISTICS

Max. Average Breech Pressure: N/A

Max. Horizontal Range: 3,000 yds.

Max. Vertical Range: 6,350 ft.

Bullet Weight (gr.)	Bullet Type	Muzzle Velocity (fps)	Muzzle Energy (ft.-lbs.)
260	JSP	1,585	1,450

CURRENT MANUFACTURER(S)

None

GENERAL COMMENT(S)

Between 1880 and 1886, Winchester introduced four massive black powder rifle cartridges with a case length of 3.25 inches and overall loaded lengths of almost four inches. These four were: .50-140 Winchester Express, .45-125 Winchester Express, .40-110 Winchester Express and the .38-90 Winchester Express. These cartridges were intended to compete with the largest Sharps cartridges for hunting big game. Winchester called these "Express" cartridges, a label they placed on no other caliber. As a group, these cartridges were obsolete when they were introduced as the advent of smokeless propellants made such massive cartridges ballistically unnecessary. By 1914, most of them had faded away.

TECHNICAL COMMENT(S)

While most large-capacity .40 caliber black powder cartridges (i.e. Sharps) were loaded with a 370 grain bullet, Winchester specified a light weight, 260 grain bullet for the .40-110 Winchester Express in order to increase muzzle velocity. Despite this, muzzle energy was the same or less than several other Winchester cartridges of this caliber. As a result, the .40-110 cartridge offered no ballistic reason for choosing it. While the case length was 3.25 inches, the .40-110 case had unique rim and case head dimensions shared with no other cartridges. As a result, the .40-110 was an orphan with no market.

.40-60 MARLIN, .40-65 WINCHESTER

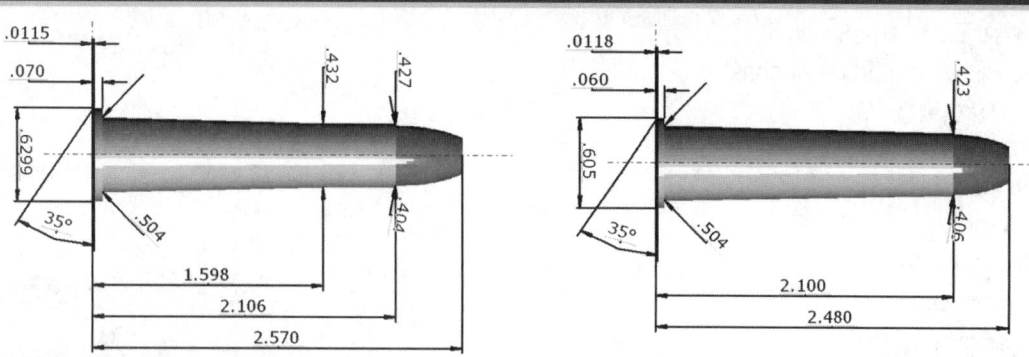

ALTERNATE NAME(S): .40-60 Colt
RELATED CALIBER(S): .38-56 Winchester, .40-90 Sharps (Straight), .40-72 Winchester, .38-70 Winchester, .40-70 Winchester

CARTRIDGE HISTORY
Year of Introduction: 1881 Marlin, 1887 Winchester
Country of Origin: U.S.
Designer(s): Marlin
Governing Body: none
Present Status: obsolete

CARTRIDGE DESCRIPTION
Bullet Diameter: .403-.406 in.
Bullet Weight(s): 260 gr.
Rifling Twist Rate: 1 turn in 20 in.
Test Barrel Length: 28 in.
Case Type: rimmed, straight
Case Material: brass
Primer: large rifle

CARTRIDGE BALLISTICS
Max. Average Breech Pressure: N/A
Max. Horizontal Range: 3,000 yds.
Max. Vertical Range: 6,250 ft.

Bullet Weight (gr.)	Bullet Type	Muzzle Velocity (fps)	Muzzle Energy (ft.-lbs.)
260 (.40-65 Win.)	L-FN	1,350	1,052
260 (.40-60 Marlin)	L-FN	1,445	1,205

CURRENT MANUFACTURER(S)
None

GENERAL COMMENT(S)
Marlin lever-action rifles were quite popular in the late 1800s. To complement their rifles, Marlin introduced several cartridges of their own design and the .40-60 Marlin was one of the most popular. About six years after the .40-60 Marlin was introduced, Winchester brought out their version. It was a common practice in the late 1800s for each ammunition manufacturer to apply his own brand name on a cartridge even if it was only a different loading of an existing cartridge. For this reason, the .40-60 Marlin, the .40-60 Colt and the .40-65 Winchester were actually different loads for the same cartridge and the three are interchangeable.

TECHNICAL COMMENT(S)
Designed as a black powder hunting cartridge for the Marlin Models 1881 and 1895, the .40-60 Marlin cartridge proved capable of reliably taking all but the largest game. Winchester confirmed its popularity when it added this cartridge to its product line in 1887. The .40-60 Marlin became the progenitor of many other cartridges (see list of related cartridges above) but it is important to note that the .40-60 Winchester was NOT one of them. Its popularity carried the .40-60 Marlin through the transition to smokeless propellants in the early 1900s. It held a solid place in the Winchester product line until the mid-1930s.

.40-60 WINCHESTER

ALTERNATE NAME(S): .40-60 Win.
RELATED CALIBER(S): .45-60 Winchester

CARTRIDGE HISTORY
Year of Introduction: 1876
Country of Origin: U.S.
Designer(s): Winchester
Governing Body: none
Present Status: obsolete

CARTRIDGE DESCRIPTION
Bullet Diameter: .404 in.
Bullet Weight(s): 210 gr.
Rifling Twist Rate: 1 turn in 40 in.
Test Barrel Length: 28 in.
Case Type: rimmed, necked
Case Material: brass
Primer: large rifle

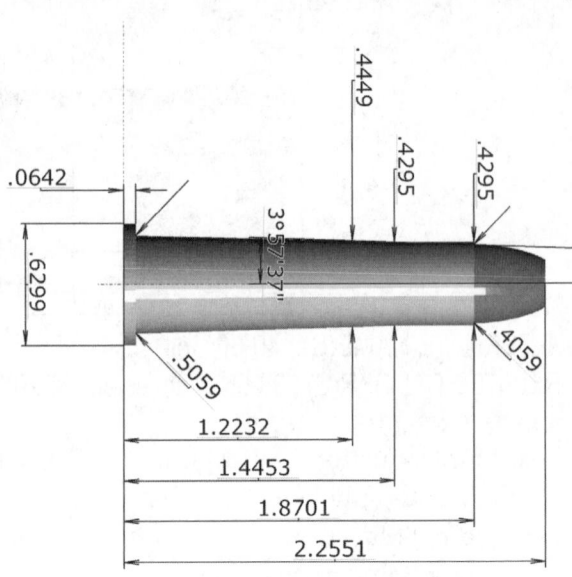

CARTRIDGE BALLISTICS
Max. Average Breech Pressure: N/A
Max. Horizontal Range: 2,100 yds.
Max. Vertical Range: 4,600 ft.

Bullet Weight (gr.)	Bullet Type	Muzzle Velocity (fps)	Muzzle Energy (ft.-lbs.)
210	L-FN	1,500	1,049

CURRENT MANUFACTURER(S)
None

GENERAL COMMENT(S)
The .40-60 Winchester is an old cartridge originally designed for and introduced with the Winchester Model 1876 lever-action rifle. During its 58 year life (1876-1934), it achieved popularity well before many of the other .40 caliber cartridges entered the market, successfully made the jump to smokeless propellants and held its place in the Winchester product line long after many of the other .40 caliber cartridges were put out to pasture.

TECHNICAL COMMENT(S)
Outwardly, the .40-60 Winchester ploughed no new technical ground. The rimmed, straight cartridge case configuration, lead flat-nose bullet and ballistic performance were conventional and unremarkable for the time. By using a lighter than normal bullet, muzzle velocity was higher than some other .40 caliber cartridges, however muzzle energy was equivalent. The .40-60 Marlin and the .40-60 Winchester are not interchangeable, so how to tell the difference? First, the .40-60 Winchester case is necked (albeit slightly) while that of the .40-60 Marlin is straight. Second, the .40-60 Winchester case and overall loaded length are noticeably shorter. This advice is offered as many older cartridges from this era carried no headstamp or no caliber markings.

.40-70 PEABODY "WHAT CHEER"

ALTERNATE NAME(S): .40-70 Peabody
RELATED CALIBER(S): .40-90 Peabody, .44-95 Peabody

CARTRIDGE HISTORY
Year of Introduction: 1877
Country of Origin: U.S.
Designer(s): H.L. Peabody
Governing Body: none
Present Status: obsolete

CARTRIDGE DESCRIPTION

Bullet Diameter: .408 in.

Bullet Weight(s): 380 gr.

Rifling Twist Rate: 1 turn in 18 in.

Test Barrel Length: N/A

Case Type: rimmed, necked

Case Material: brass

Primer: large rifle

CARTRIDGE BALLISTICS

Max. Average Breech Pressure: N/A

Max. Horizontal Range: 3,000 yds.

Max. Vertical Range: 6,200 ft.

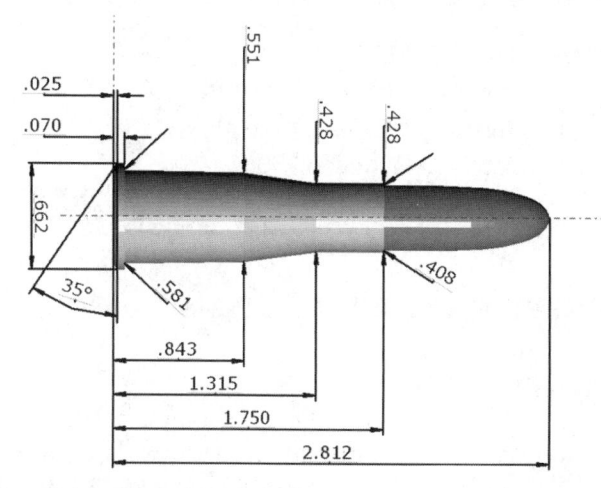

Bullet Weight (gr.)	Bullet Type	Muzzle Velocity (fps)	Muzzle Energy (ft.-lbs.)
380	L-FN	1,420	1,701

CURRENT MANUFACTURER(S)

None

GENERAL COMMENT(S)

A new shooting range was opened near Providence, R.I. in 1875. The new range was called "What Cheer" after a greeting the pilgrims once exchanged with the local Native Americans. The Creedmoor range in Long Island, N.Y. was opened about the same time. As interest in long range shooting increased, ammunition makers hastened to design cartridges for such purposes and name them after one of these ranges. Some companies, such as Peabody, used both. The .40-70 Peabody "What Cheer" was one of the Peabody target cartridges for the Peabody "Creedmoor" rifle. Peabody target cartridge designs enjoyed a short life as smokeless propellants made large-bore, black powder cartridges obsolete by the early 1900s.

TECHNICAL COMMENT(S)

From a technical standpoint, the .40-70 Peabody "What Cheer" cartridge is a typical Peabody rimmed design with plenty of case volume for heavy powder charges and a long neck to assure bullet retention. We consider such a configuration normal today, but in the 1880s most long range competitors came to prefer straight case designs. This handicapped Peabody target cartridges as all of them were necked. All Peabody target cartridges had larger rim and head diameters than most other cartridges. This made them difficult and expensive to manufacture. Both Union Metallic Cartridge and Winchester manufactured ammunition in Peabody calibers. Weighing 380 grains, the lead, paper-patched, round-nose bullet was optimized for long range shooting and not intended for hunting.

.40-70 WINCHESTER

ALTERNATE NAME(S): .40-70 Win.

RELATED CALIBER(S): .40-65 Winchester, .40-82 Winchester

CARTRIDGE HISTORY

Year of Introduction: 1894

Country of Origin: U.S.

Designer(s): Winchester

Governing Body: none

Present Status: obsolete

CARTRIDGE DESCRIPTION

Bullet Diameter: .405 in.

Bullet Weight(s): 330 gr.

Rifling Twist Rate: 1 turn in 20 in.

Test Barrel Length: 26 in.

Case Type: rimmed, necked

Case Material: brass

Primer: large rifle

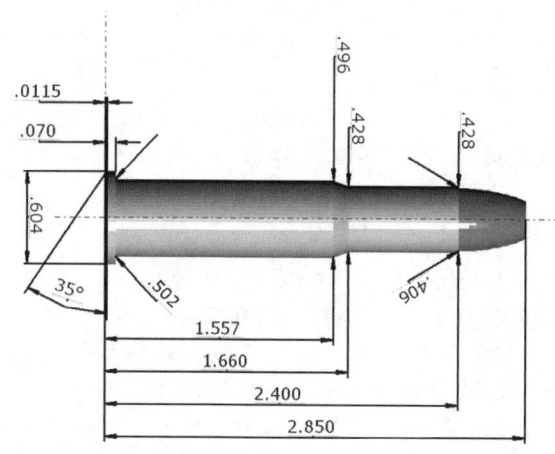

CARTRIDGE BALLISTICS
Max. Average Breech Pressure: N/A

Max. Horizontal Range: 3,000 yds.

Max. Vertical Range: 6,300 ft.

Bullet Weight (gr.)	Bullet Type	Muzzle Velocity (fps)	Muzzle Energy (ft.-lbs.)
330	L-FN	1,375	1,385

CURRENT MANUFACTURER(S)
None

GENERAL COMMENT(S)
When it comes to .40 caliber black powder cartridges, Winchester certainly had all the bases covered with no less than six different cartridges. There was the: .40-60, .40-65, .40-70, .40-72, .40-82 and .40-110. Sorting all these out at Winchester must have been quite a job, not to mention the confusion for the customer. The .40-70 Winchester is one of the lesser-known Winchester .40 caliber cartridges. Introduced in 1894, for the Winchester Model 1886 lever-action rifle, this cartridge seems to have got lost in the shuffle and failed to achieve popularity. Nonetheless, it was still listed in the 1906 Winchester catalog.

TECHNICAL COMMENT(S)
This is how the fruit salad of Winchester .40 caliber cartridges shakes out. The .40-70 shares its rim and head dimensions with the .40-65 and .40-82 Winchester as well as the .40-60 Marlin cartridges. The .40-72 is related to its own family of Winchester cartridges and the .40-60 Winchester and .40-110 Winchester are unique orphans. The .40-65 and .40-82 Winchester cartridges have straight (tapered) sidewalls, but all other Winchester .40 caliber cartridges are necked. While .40 caliber Winchester cartridges offer broadly similar ballistic performance, none are interchangeable. And, the .40-60 Winchester is not interchangeable with the .40-60 Marlin nor is the .40-70 Winchester interchangeable with the .40-70 Remington or .40-70 Sharps necked. However, the .40-65 Winchester is interchangeable with the .40-60 Marlin! The .40-65, .40-70 and .40-82 were chambered in the Model 1886 lever-action rifle. In view of the ballistic duplication, one wonders how some of these cartridges remained in the Winchester product line as long as they did. All of these calibers, including the .40-60 Marlin and .40-70 Sharps (Necked), were still listed in the 1906 Winchester catalog!

.40-72 WINCHESTER

ALTERNATE NAME(S): .40-72 Win.

RELATED CALIBER(S): .35 Win., .38-72 Win., .405 Win.

CARTRIDGE HISTORY
Year of Introduction: 1895

Country of Origin: U.S.

Designer(s): Winchester

Governing Body: none

Present Status: obsolete

CARTRIDGE DESCRIPTION
Bullet Diameter: .406 in.

Bullet Weight(s): 300 gr.

Rifling Twist Rate: 1 turn in 22 in.

Test Barrel Length: 26 in.

Case Type: rimmed, straight

Case Material: brass

Primer Size: large rifle

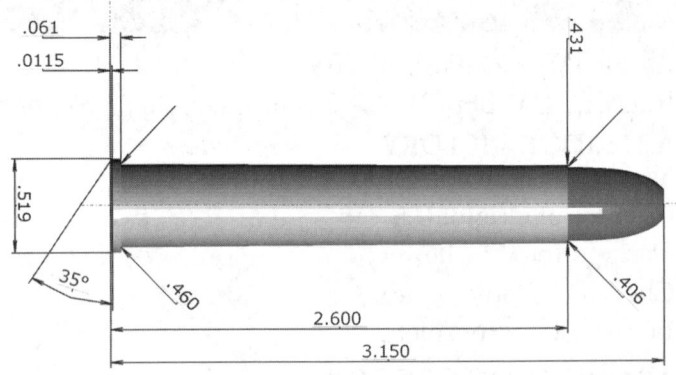

CARTRIDGE BALLISTICS
Max. Average Breech Pressure: N/A

Max Horizontal Range: 2,900 yds.

Max. Vertical Range: 6,000 ft.

Bullet Weight (gr.)	Bullet Type	Muzzle Velocity (fps)	Muzzle Energy (ft.-lbs.)
300	L-RN	1,385	1,307

CURRENT MANUFACTURER(S)

None

GENERAL COMMENT(S)

With the emergence of bolt-action rifles firing high-pressure cartridges in the late 1880s and early 1890s, Winchester lever-action rifles were becoming outclassed as they could not handle the high maximum average chamber pressures generated by the new cartridges. In an effort to defend their share of the rifle market, Winchester developed a new lever-action rifle, the Model 1895, for its new family of high pressure cartridges. By adopting a box magazine and a stronger action, the Model 1895 lever-action rifle used high-pressure cartridges firing round nose and pointed bullets. The new family began with the .38-72 Win. and the .40-72 Win. which were introduced with the new rifle in 1895. The .35 Winchester and the .405 Winchester followed in 1903 and 1904 respectively. None of these calibers gained a popular following and all were dropped from the Winchester product line in 1936 and quickly faded into obscurity.

TECHNICAL COMMENT(S)

Winchester designed all four of these cartridges on a common .460 inch diameter base and .539 inch diameter rim with only minor variations. Winchester's new M1895 rifle had been designed for high chamber pressures and pointed bullets. Despite the capabilities of the new rifle, the first two new cartridges Winchester introduced for it generated modest chamber pressures and had heavy bullets with moderate muzzle velocity. As both the .38-72 Win. and .40-72 Win. cartridges were offered in smokeless powder and black powder loadings, the old black powder nomenclature was used.

.40-82 WINCHESTER

ALTERNATE NAME(S): .40–75 Win. to .40–82 Win.
RELATED CALIBER(S): .45-82 Winchester

CARTRIDGE HISTORY

Year of Introduction: 1885
Country of Origin: U.S.
Designer(s): Winchester
Governing Body: none
Present Status: obsolete

CARTRIDGE DESCRIPTION

Bullet Diameter: .406 in.
Bullet Weight(s): 260 gr.
Rifling Twist Rate: 1 turn in 28 in.
Test Barrel Length: 26 in.
Case Type: rimmed, necked
Case Material: brass
Primer: large rifle

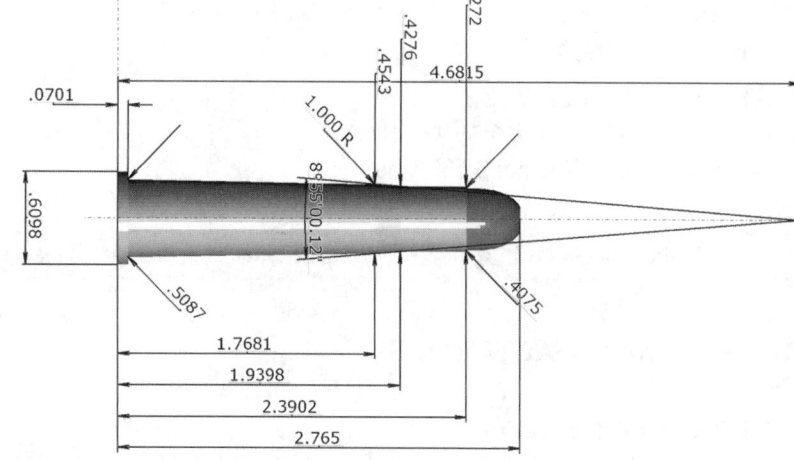

CARTRIDGE BALLISTICS

Max. Average Breech Pressure: N/A
Max. Horizontal Range: 3,000 yds.
Max. Vertical Range: 6,300 ft.

Bullet Weight (gr.)	Bullet Type	Muzzle Velocity (fps)	Muzzle Energy (ft.-lbs.)
260	L-FN	1,475	1,256
260 (Black Powder)	L-FN	1,350	1,052 (est.)

CURRENT MANUFACTURER(S)

None

GENERAL COMMENT(S)

Designed as a black powder hunting cartridge, the .40-82 Winchester was first chambered in the Winchester Model 1886 lever-action rifle. By all accounts, it was a popular and effective hunting cartridge capable of reliably taking most large game. This reputation and the Winchester name combined to keep this cartridge in the Winchester product line until the mid-1930s.

TECHNICAL COMMENT(S)

This case shares its rim and head dimensions with the .45-82/85/90 series of Winchester cartridges. The .40-82 is the smallest of the lot and arguably less popular than its .45 caliber brothers. Like all black powder cartridges of this type, to survive, it had to successfully transition to smokeless propellants. The .40-82 did so buoyed by its hunting prowess, fading away gracefully in the 1930s.

.40-90 PEABODY "WHAT CHEER"

ALTERNATE NAME(S): .40-90 Peabody
RELATED CALIBER(S): .40-70 Peabody, .44-95 Peabody

CARTRIDGE HISTORY

Year of Introduction: 1877
Country of Origin: U.S.
Designer(s): H.L. Peabody
Governing Body: none
Present Status: obsolete

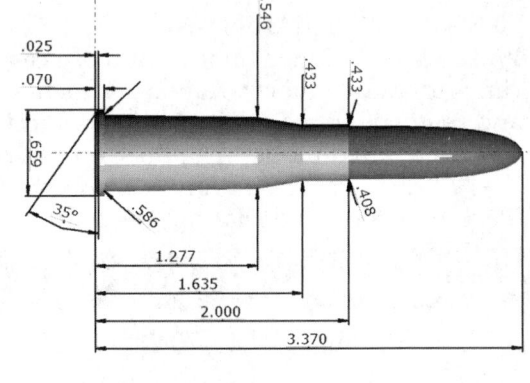

CARTRIDGE DESCRIPTION

Bullet Diameter: .408 in.
Bullet Weight(s): 500 gr.
Rifling Twist Rate: N/A
Test Barrel Length: N/A
Case Type: rimmed, necked
Case Material: brass
Primer: large rifle

CARTRIDGE BALLISTICS

Max. Average Breech Pressure: N/A
Max. Horizontal Range: 3,600 yds.
Max. Vertical Range: 7,600 ft.

Bullet Weight (gr.)	Bullet Type	Muzzle Velocity (fps)	Muzzle Energy (ft.-lbs.)
500	L-RN	1,250	1,735

CURRENT MANUFACTURER(S)

None

GENERAL COMMENT(S)

A new shooting range was opened near Providence, R.I. in 1875. The new range was called "What Cheer" after a greeting the pilgrims once exchanged with the local Native Americans. The Creedmoor range in Long Island, N.Y. was opened about the same time. As interest in long range shooting increased, ammunition makers hastened to design cartridges for such purposes and name them after one of these ranges. Some companies, such as Peabody, used both. The .40-90 Peabody "What Cheer" was one of the Peabody target cartridges chambered in the Peabody "Creedmoor" rifle. Peabody target cartridge designs enjoyed a short life as smokeless propellants made large-bore, black powder cartridges obsolete by the early 1900s.

TECHNICAL COMMENT(S)

From a technical standpoint, the .40-90 Peabody "What Cheer" cartridge is a typical Peabody rimmed design with plenty of case volume for heavy powder charges and a long neck to assure bullet retention. We consider such a configuration normal today, but in the 1880s most long range competitors came to prefer straight case designs. This handicapped Peabody target cartridges as all of them were necked. All Peabody target cartridges had larger rim and head diameters than most other cartridges. This made them difficult and expensive to manufacture. Both Union Metallic Cartridge and Winchester manufactured ammunition in Peabody calibers. A noteworthy feature of this cartridge was the abnormally long heavy bullet for the caliber. Weighing 500 grains, the lead, paper-patched, round-nose bullet was optimized for long range shooting and not intended for hunting.

10.5x47Rmm STAHL

ALTERNATE NAME(S): none
RELATED CALIBER(S): "*Schutzen*" cartridges

CARTRIDGE HISTORY
Year of Introduction: circa late 1800s
Country of Origin: Austria
Designer(s): Stahl
Governing Body: none
Present Status: obsolete

CARTRIDGE DESCRIPTION
Bullet Diameter: .411 in.
Bullet Weight(s): 298 gr.
Rifling Twist Rate: N/A
Test Barrel Length: N/A
Case Type: rimmed, necked
Case Material: brass
Primer: large rifle

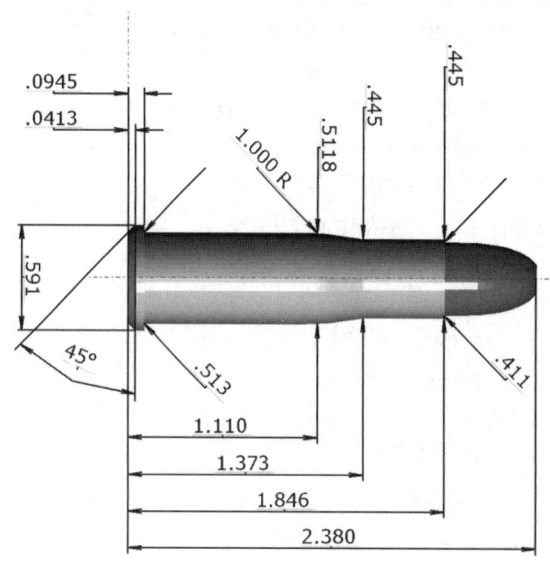

CARTRIDGE BALLISTICS
Max. Average Breech Pressure: N/A
Max. Horizontal Range: N/A yds.
Max. Vertical Range: N/A ft.

Bullet Weight (gr.)	Bullet Type	Muzzle Velocity (fps)	Muzzle Energy (ft.-lbs.)
298	L-FN	N/A	N/A

CURRENT MANUFACTURER(S)
None

GENERAL COMMENT(S)
In the 1880s, a new class of black powder rifle cartridges was developed in Germany and Austria. Optimized for target shooting at ranges to 200 meters, these were called "*schutzen*" cartridges. They were adapted to single-shot target rifles of various designs. The 10.5x47Rmm Stahl cartridge is typical of the breed. For further examples of this class of cartridges, the reader is referred to the 8.15x46Rmm and 9.5x47Rmm cartridge listings in this chapter. Cartridges of this type remained popular for many years with some designs lasting well into the 1930s. As a class, they are now obsolete, having been replaced by small caliber cartridges such as the 5.6x35Rmm Vierling for hunting rifle competition at 100 meters.

TECHNICAL COMMENT(S)
This class of cartridges rapidly developed into dozens of variations ranging in caliber from 8.1mm (.335 in.) to 13mm (.512 in.). An astute reader will note that the Mauser-type base was a popular design characteristic. When smokeless propellants became available, many of these calibers transitioned to such powders. As these cartridges were designed for target shooting and not hunting, bullet weights were kept light for their caliber, propellant charges were kept as small as possible and muzzle velocities were modest. These combined to provide good accuracy with reduced recoil and low cost. Most bullets were lead round-nose or flat-nose designs.

10.75x57mm MANNLICHER-SCHOENAUER

ALTERNATE NAME(S): 10.75x57mm
RELATED CALIBER(S): 8x57mmJ Mauser, 9.5x57mm M-S

CARTRIDGE HISTORY
Year of Introduction: circa 1900
Country of Origin: Austria
Designer(s): Ferdinand von Mannlicher
Governing Body: none
Present Status: obsolete

CARTRIDGE DESCRIPTION
Bullet Diameter: .424 in.
Bullet Weight(s): 350 gr.
Rifling Twist Rate: N/A
Test Barrel Length: N/A
Case Type: rimless, necked slightly
Case Material: brass
Primer: large rifle

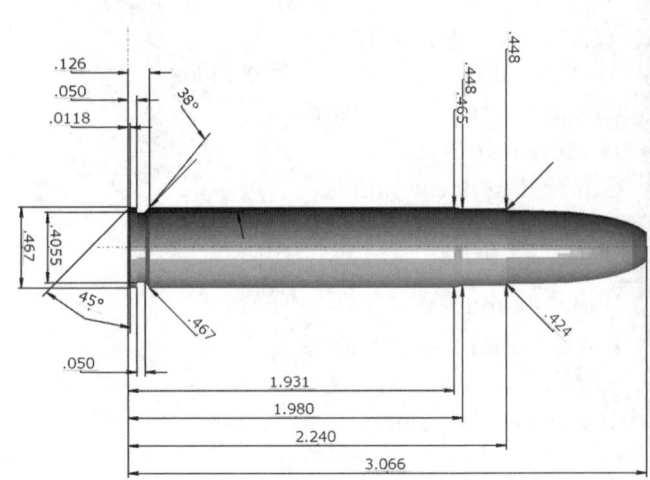

CARTRIDGE BALLISTICS
Max. Average Breech Pressure: 55,114 psi.
Max. Horizontal Range: 3,100 yds.
Max. Vertical Range: 6,600 ft.

Bullet Weight (gr.)	Bullet Type	Muzzle Velocity (fps)	Muzzle Energy (ft.-lbs.)
350	JSP-FN	1,950	2,955

CURRENT MANUFACTURER(S)
None

GENERAL COMMENT(S)
Created by Ferdinand von Mannlicher, this cartridge did not prove popular and faded away rather quickly. It was intended for hunting large, heavy game with a bolt-action rifle. Both Roth and RWS manufactured ammunition in this caliber.

TECHNICAL COMMENT(S)
This old sporting cartridge is based on the 8x57mmJ cartridge case necked up to accept a .424 inch diameter bullet, the largest diameter the case could accomodate. One reason for selecting the 8x57mmJ cartridge as a base was that the case head configuration and dimensions were fully compatible with the bolt face of standard length M88/M98 Mauser bolt-action rifles. Another reason is that the overall loaded length of this cartridge allowed it to feed through the magazine of the above-mentioned Mauser rifles. One possible reason for the lack of acceptance of this cartridge may have been the difficulty controlling headspace on the diminutive shoulder. Another likely reason is that the muzzle energy of this cartridge was the same as the 8x57mmJS Mauser cartridge leaving the 10.75x57mm M-S with no clear ballistic advantage and several possible disadvantages. To maximize bullet weight, a semi-round nose design with large, flat meplat was used.

10.75x63mm MAUSER

ALTERNATE NAME(S): 10.75x63mm
RELATED CALIBER(S): 10.75x68mm Mauser

CARTRIDGE HISTORY
Year of Introduction: 1910
Country of Origin: Germany
Designer(s): Mauser
Governing Body: none
Present Status: obsolete

CARTRIDGE DESCRIPTION

Bullet Diameter: .424 in.

Bullet Weight(s): 347 gr.

Rifling Twist Rate: N/A

Test Barrel Length: N/A

Case Type: rebated rim, slightly necked

Case Material: brass

Primer: large rifle

CARTRIDGE BALLISTICS

Max. Average Breech Pressure: 47,862 psi.

Max. Horizontal Range: 3,100 yds.

Max. Vertical Range: 3,800 ft.

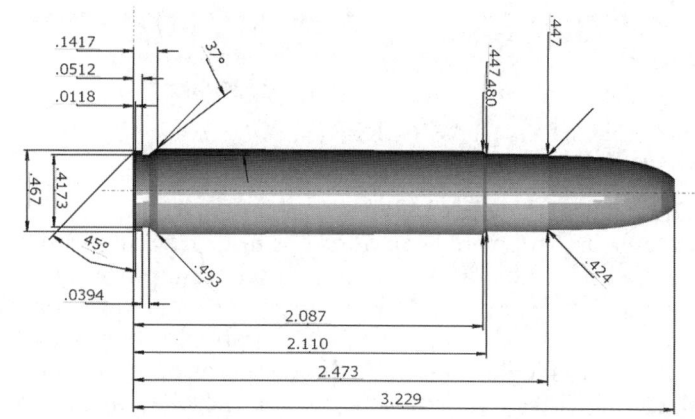

Bullet Weight (gr.)	Bullet Type	Muzzle Velocity (fps)	Muzzle Energy (ft.-lbs.)
347	JSP-RN	2,050	3,238 (est.)

CURRENT MANUFACTURER(S)

None

GENERAL COMMENT(S)

Not a lot is known about this cartridge. Some historians ascribe the design to Mannlicher while others insist on Mauser as the design source. In my opinion, the Mauser roots are plain, so the Mauser name has been added to the nomenclature. Obviously, the 10.75x63mm Mauser cartridge was designed for hunting large, heavy game. Beyond that, published ballistics have proven hard to find, so they have been estimated using the 10.75x68mm Mauser as a guide. RWS seems to have been the sole manufacturer (another point in Mauser's favor over Mannlicher as designer).

TECHNICAL COMMENT(S)

Structurally, the 10.75x63mm cartridge appears to be a shortened version of the 10.75x68mm cartridge. The 10.75x63mm cartridge appeared about 10 years before the 10.75x68mm indicating the latter is a lengthened version of the former. Due to its size, the 10.75x63mm Mauser cartridge required a magnum-length rifle action.

10.75x68mm MAUSER

ALTERNATE NAME(S): 10.75x68mm , 10.75mm Mauser, .423 Mauser

RELATED CALIBER(S): none

CARTRIDGE HISTORY

Year of Introduction: 1920

Country of Origin: Germany

Designer(s): Mauser

Governing Body: CIP

Present Status: obsolete

CARTRIDGE DESCRIPTION

Bullet Diameter: .424 in.

Bullet Weight(s): 347 gr.

Rifling Twist Rate: 1 turn in 16.54 in.

Test Barrel Length: 24 in.

Case Type: rimless, slightly necked

Case Material: brass

Primer: large rifle

CARTRIDGE BALLISTICS

Max. Average Breech Pressure: 47,862 psi.

Max. Horizontal Range: 3,200 yds.

Max. Vertical Range: 3,850 ft.

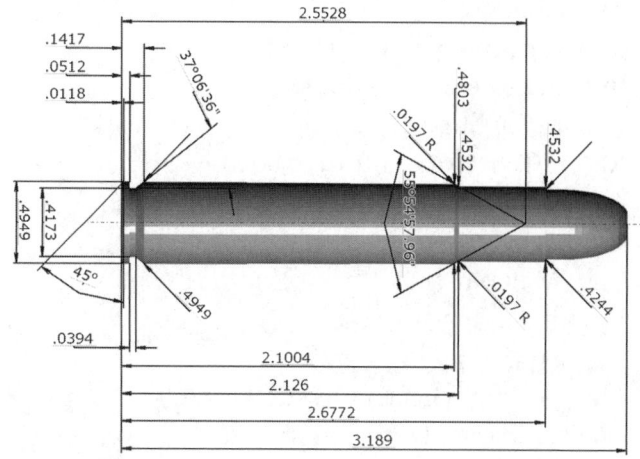

Bullet Weight (gr.)	Bullet Type	Muzzle Velocity (fps)	Muzzle Energy (ft.-lbs.)
347	JSP-RN	2,230	3,831

CURRENT MANUFACTURER(S)
None

GENERAL COMMENT(S)
Mauser designed this cartridge for hunting dangerous African game. It enjoyed considerable popularity with European hunters in Africa, India and other places such as the arctic and South East Asia. Experienced hunters felt the 10.75x68mm Mauser cartridge could not match the general purpose capabilities of the .375 H&H Magnum. In addition, it was not suitable for elephant and marginal for other heavy game in some situations. Some of this feeling must be dismissed as being part of the general prejudice against bolt-action rifles in favor of double-rifles which were considered "safer" as they provided two quick shots without having to manipulate the bolt. Loaded ammunition in this caliber was made by RWS in Germany and Kynoch in Britain.

TECHNICAL COMMENT(S)
The length of the 10.75x68mm Mauser cartridge required a magnum-length action as it was too long and too wide for a standard-length action. The rimless design of the 10.75x68mm Mauser cartridge made it unsuitable for use in double-rifles which worked best with rimmed case designs. Reportedly, the German-made soft-point bullets loaded in the 10.75x68mm ammunition would not always hold together or penetrate sufficiently. Kynoch in England loaded ammunition in this caliber based on their considerable experience in Africa hunting. One reason the 10.75x68mm cartridge failed to measure up to the .375 H&H Magnum as a jack-of-all-trades was bullet selection. The .375 H&H Magnum was offered with bullets weighing from 235 grains to 300 grains. Selecting a lighter or heavier bullet allowed the hunter to tailor his load to the game. The 10.75x68mm offered no such flexibility. When the ballistics of the 10.75x68mm Mauser cartridge are compared with proven, African favorites such as the .404 Jeffery and .416 Rigby, it seems plain that the 10.75x68mm Mauser cartridge lacked the striking energy of these stalwarts. This restricted the killing power of the 10.75x68mm cartridge on large, dangerous game (ie. elephant) and, undoubtedly, was the source of the advice against using this caliber on such game. As controlling headspace on the diminutive shoulder of this cartridge alone would have been difficult, the rim was extended approximately .04 inches above the base similar to semi-rimmed cases.

.44 EVANS SHORT

ALTERNATE NAME(S): .44 Evans (Old Model)
RELATED CALIBER(S): .44 Evans Long, .44 Extra Long Ballard

CARTRIDGE HISTORY
Year of Introduction: 1875
Country of Origin: U.S.
Designer(s): Warren R. Evans
Governing Body: none
Present Status: obsolete

CARTRIDGE DESCRIPTION
Bullet Diameter: .419 in.
Bullet Weight(s): 215 gr.
Rifling Twist Rate: 1 turn in 36 in.
Test Barrel Length: N/A
Case Type: rimmed, straight
Case Material: brass
Primer: large pistol

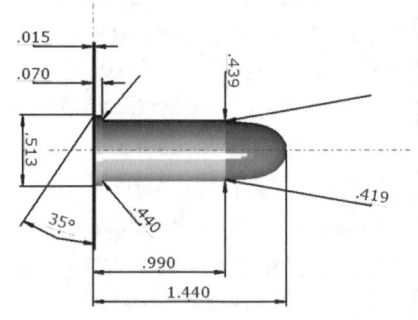

CARTRIDGE BALLISTICS
Max. Average Breech Pressure: N/A
Max. Horizontal Range: 1,750 yds.
Max. Vertical Range: 3,600 ft.

Bullet Weight (gr.)	Bullet Type	Muzzle Velocity (fps)	Muzzle Energy (ft.-lbs.)
215	L-FN	850	345

CURRENT MANUFACTURER(S)
None

GENERAL COMMENT(S)
Warren R. Evans and his brother George Evans founded the Evans Repeating Rifle Company in 1873 in order to manufacture lever-action rifles of their patented design. The Evans rifle was very unusual in that it had a rotary magazine in the stock that held 34 rounds of ammunition! In order for the magazine to hold this number of cartridges, Warren Evans designed the .44 Evans Short cartridge. In short order, Warren Evans left the company to pursue his profession in dentistry leaving George to run the company and improve the design of the rifle. Loaded ammunition in .44 Evans Short was offered by Winchester until the mid-1920s.

TECHNICAL COMMENT(S)
Warren Evans designed the .44 Evans Short cartridge for military applications, but the U.S. Army was not interested. The Evans Repeating Rifle Co. then began selling their rifle on the commercial market. By any standard of measure, the .44 Evans Short cartridge was totally unsuited for any type of hunting and too anemic for military applications. Nonetheless, the rifles (and cartridges) sold fairly well based on their amazing magazine capacity alone. Recognizing the limiting nature of the .44 Evans Short cartridge, a new, more powerful cartridge called the .44 Evans Long was introduced in 1876 with the improved rifle. Although obsolete, the .44 Evans Short cartridge was available until the mid-1920s.

.44 EVANS LONG

ALTERNATE NAME(S): .44 Evans (New Model)
RELATED CALIBER(S): .44 Evans Short. 44 Extra Long Ballard

CARTRIDGE HISTORY
Year of Introduction: 1876
Country of Origin: U.S.
Designer(s): George Evans
Governing Body: none
Present Status: obsolete

CARTRIDGE DESCRIPTION
Bullet Diameter: .419in.
Bullet Weight(s): 275-300 gr.
Rifling Twist Rate: 1 turn in 36 in.
Test Barrel Length: N/A
Case Type: rimmed, straight
Case Material: brass
Primer: large rifle

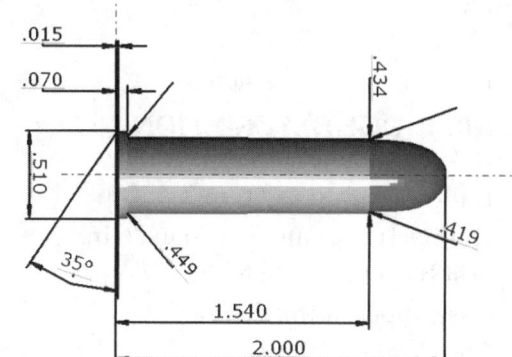

CARTRIDGE BALLISTICS
Max. Average Breech Pressure: N/A
Max. Horizontal Range: 2,500 yds.
Max. Vertical Range: 5,350 ft.

Bullet Weight (gr.)	Bullet Type	Muzzle Velocity (fps)	Muzzle Energy (ft.-lbs.)
280	L-FN	1,200	895

CURRENT MANUFACTURER(S)
None

GENERAL COMMENT(S)
Warren R. Evans and his brother George Evans founded the Evans Repeating Rifle Company in 1873 in order to manufacture lever-action rifles of their patented design. The Evans rifle was very unusual in that it had a rotary magazine in the stock that held 34 rounds of ammunition! In order for the magazine to hold this number of

cartridges, Warren Evans designed the .44 Evans Short cartridge. In short order, Warren Evans left the company to pursue his profession in dentistry leaving George to run the company and improve the design of the rifle. In 1876, the Evans Repeating Rifle Co. introduced a significantly improved rifle that held 28 rounds of the new .44 Evans Long (New Model) cartridges. The new cartridge was longer and more powerful than the .44 Short (Old Model). Loaded ammunition in .44 Evans Short and .44 Evans Long was offered by Winchester until the mid-1920s.

TECHNICAL COMMENT(S)

George Evans designed the .44 Evans Long to improve the anemic ballistics of the .44 Evans Short that kept Evans rifles from selling in larger numbers. The new, more powerful .44 Evans Long was introduced in 1876 with the improved rifle. However, the new cartridge also had limitations imposed by the maximum cartridge length the rifle action could accept. Then there was the consideration of magazine capacity, a major selling point of the first model Evans rifle. The first model Evans rifle held 34 rounds in its magazine while the new model chambered for the .44 Evans Long cartridge "only" held 28 rounds. In the end, magazine capacity took a back seat to continued anemic ballistic performance. Without doubt, the new .44 Evans Long cartridge was significantly more powerful than the earlier .44 Evans Short. But, this was not saying much as both cartridges could only be considered anemic. In the end, the Evans rifle could not be sold only relying on the novelty of its large magazine capacity. As it was useless for any real purpose, it had no market.

.44 WESSON EXTRA LONG

ALTERNATE NAME(S): none

RELATED CALIBER(S): .44 Extra Long Ballard, .303 Savage

CARTRIDGE HISTORY

Year of Introduction: circa 1876

Country of Origin: U.S.

Designer(s): Frank Wesson

Governing Body: none

Present Status: obsolete

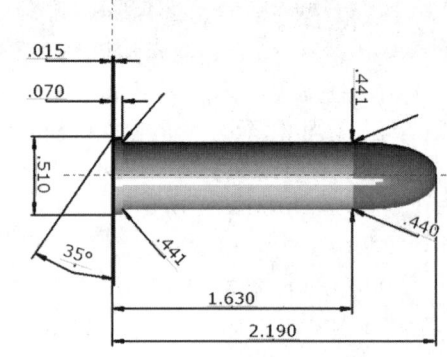

CARTRIDGE DESCRIPTION

Bullet Diameter: .440 in.

Bullet Weight(s): 250 gr.

Rifling Twist Rate: 1 turn in 36 in.

Test Barrel Length: N/A

Case Type: rimmed, straight

Case Material: brass

Primer: large rifle

CARTRIDGE BALLISTICS

Max. Average Breech Pressure: N/A

Max. Horizontal Range: 1,600 yds.

Max. Vertical Range: 3,600 ft.

Bullet Weight (gr.)	Bullet Type	Muzzle Velocity (fps)	Muzzle Energy (ft.-lbs.)
250	Lead-Semi-RN	1,340	997

CURRENT MANUFACTURER(S)

None

GENERAL COMMENT(S)

In the late 1800s, low cost, single-shot rifles in medium calibers were very popular. Companies that made such rifles included Ballard, Wesson, Stevens and Maynard as well as Winchester and Remington. They were chambered for a wide variety of low powered cartridges with a rimmed, straight case design. Most of these cartridges were .44 caliber or less and held a maximum of 40 grains of black powder. Plain lead bullets with flat-nose or round-nose profiles were the norm. A few used paper-patched bullets. This cartridge type had the advantages of low cost, reduced recoil and sufficient power for small game and deer hunting at close ranges. This type was also popular for formal and informal target shooting at close ranges.

TECHNICAL COMMENT(S)

The .44 Wesson Extra Long is one of the larger caliber cartridges outlined above. In keeping with a common practice at the time, case dimensions and ballistics of the .44 Wesson Extra Long are nearly identical to those of the .44 Ballard Extra Long. The two cartridges are interchangeable, differing only in bullet weight and shape. These minor differences allowed manufacturers to affix their name on a different load for the same cartridge.

.44-100 REMINGTON "CREEDMOOR"

ALTERNATE NAME(S): .44-90 Remington Straight, .44-2.6 inch Remington Straight
RELATED CALIBER(S): .44-2.4 inch Remington Straight

CARTRIDGE HISTORY

Year of Introduction: 1880
Country of Origin: U.S.
Designer(s): Remington
Governing Body: none
Present Status: obsolete

CARTRIDGE DESCRIPTION

Bullet Diameter: .442 in.
Bullet Weight(s): 520-550 gr.
Rifling Twist Rate: 1 turn in 26 in.
Test Barrel Length: N/A
Case Type: rimmed, straight
Case Material: brass
Primer: large rifle

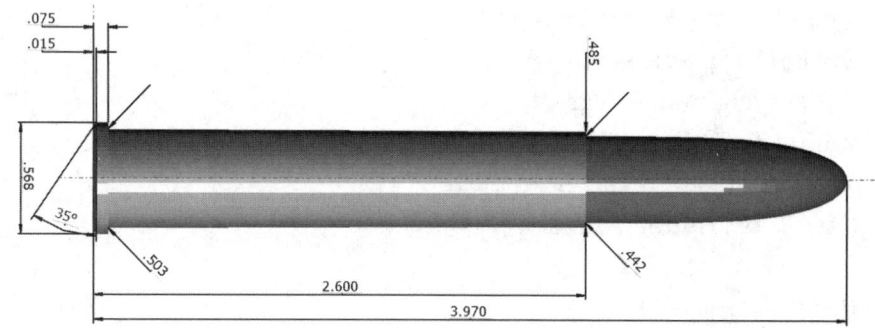

CARTRIDGE BALLISTICS

Max. Average Breech Pressure: N/A
Max. Horizontal Range: 4,050 yds.
Max. Vertical Range: 8,150 ft.

Bullet Weight (gr.)	Bullet Type	Muzzle Velocity (fps)	Muzzle Energy (ft.-lbs.)
520	L-RN	1,435	2,377
550	L-RN	1,380	2,326

CURRENT MANUFACTURER(S)

None

GENERAL COMMENT(S)

Unlike many other cartridges designed by Remington for hunting, this cartridge was designed explicitly for long range target shooting at 1,000 yards and more. In 1873, the new NRA shooting range at Creedmoor on Long Island, New York opened. By 1880, long range rifle matches were held there to popular acclaim. The .44-100 Remington cartridge was an attempt by Remington to focus the Creedmoor limelight on their products. In that effort, Remington applied the "Creedmoor" and also the "Creedmore" moniker to several cartridges, including some that had nothing to do with competitive shooting. Remington was not the only ammunition maker to try this. In any case, the .44-100 Remington Creedmoor's market base was very narrow as it was aimed exclusively at competitive shooters (and long range shooters at that). As a result, the .44-100 Remington Creedmoor was never very popular as Winchester also offered this cartridge which split the already narrow market base. The dawn of the smokeless powder age soon put and end to massive, black powder rifle cartridges such as this. By 1900, nearly all cartridges of this type had faded into history.

TECHNICAL COMMENT(S)

By the standards and technology of that day, the .44-100 Remington Creedmoor cartridge was cutting edge modern. It employed a .442 inch diameter, paper-patched, lead bullet that was extremely heavy for its caliber. This provided a high sectional density (SD). The SD of the 520 grain bullet was .378 and that of the 550 grain bullet .400! Of course, the round-nose bullet offset some of the advantage conferred by the high sectional density. However, the long, heavy bullet spent much of its flight below the speed of sound where the low muzzle velocity and round-nose bullet profile were not such a handicap. In order to achieve the leisurely muzzle velocity claimed, 100 grains of black powder had to be burned. Very likely recoil was not a problem due to the heavy rifles employed and the low muzzle velocity resolving the recoil impulse into a sustained push rather than a sharp hit.

.44-60 PEABODY "CREEDMOOR"

ALTERNATE NAME(S): .44-60 Winchester, .44-60-1.875 inch Sharps Necked, .44-60 Remington
RELATED CALIBER(S): various .40 and .45 black powder rifle cartridges offered by Remington, Winchester, Ballard and others.

CARTRIDGE HISTORY
Year of Introduction: 1869

Country of Origin: U.S.

Designer(s): Remington

Governing Body: none

Present Status: obsolete

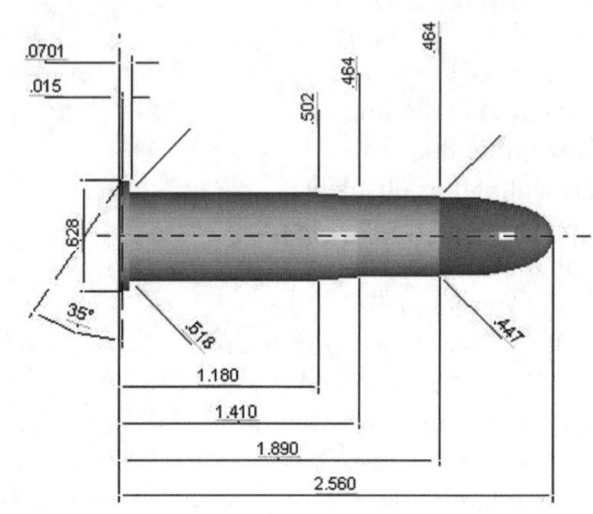

CARTRIDGE DESCRIPTION
Bullet Diameter: .447 in.

Bullet Weight(s): 365 gr.

Rifling Twist Rate: N/A

Test Barrel Length: N/A

Case Type: rimmed, necked

Case Material: brass

Primer: large rifle

CARTRIDGE BALLISTICS
Max. Average Breech Pressure: N/A

Max. Horizontal Range: 2,300 yds.

Max. Vertical Range: 4,900 ft.

Bullet Weight (gr.)	Bullet Type	Muzzle Velocity (fps)	Muzzle Energy (ft.-lbs.)
365	L-RN	1,250	1,266

CURRENT MANUFACTURER(S)
None

GENERAL COMMENT(S)
Remington introduced this cartridge in 1869 as a general purpose hunting cartridge. When the Creedmoor shooting range opened in Long Island, New York in 1873, the long range rifle matches held there attracted popular interest. Never one to miss a marketing opportunity, Remington pasted the Creedmoor name on the .44-60 cartridge in an effort to open a new market. Others, such as Peabody, followed suit. History has not recorded how successful these efforts were. However, by the late 1880s, the Creedmoor range had passed its prime and went dormant in 1890. Given the narrow market base of competitive shooters (certainly less than 10% of all shooters), the .44-60 Peabody cartridge did not survive long after 1890. The dawn of the smokeless powder age soon put paid to the fate of large, black powder rifle cartridges such as this. By 1900, nearly all cartridges of this type had faded into history.

TECHNICAL COMMENT(S)
The .44-60 Peabody cartridge must be considered a prototypical member of the first wave of large caliber, centerfire rifle cartridges introduced shortly after the end of the Civil War. In that era, ammunition technology was advancing by leaps and bounds and no one could predict where the new technology would take them. Ballistic performance of a typical cartridge of this era was modest, although it was a quantum leap ahead of the earlier rimfire cartridges. Round-nose, lead bullets in calibers from .35 to .45 and weighing from 250 to 390 grains were the norm. A typical muzzle velocity was about 1,350 fps. and from 40-80 grains of black powder had to be burned to achieve it. No doubt the .44-60 Remington/Winchester/Sharps/Peabody cartridge was effective for hunting. However, when Remington and Peabody tried to market the .44-60 cartridge for competition, it was a failure.

.44-85 WESSON, .44-100 WESSON

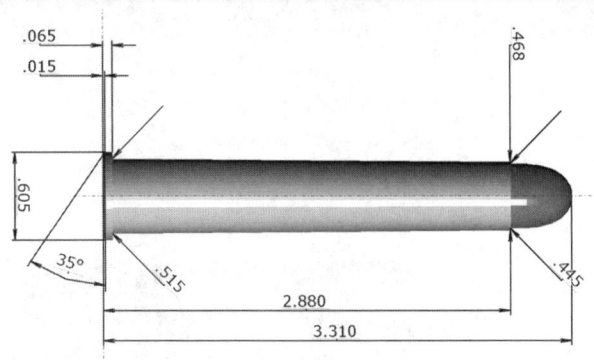
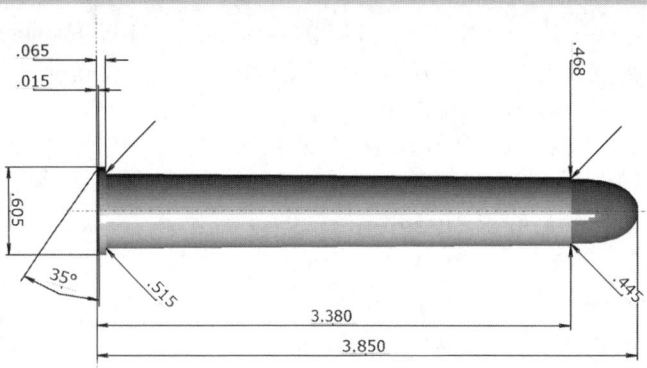

ALTERNATE NAME(S): .44-85 Wesson
RELATED CALIBER(S): .44-70 Maynard, .44-100 Ballard

CARTRIDGE HISTORY
Year of Introduction: circa 1882
Country of Origin: U.S.
Designer(s): Frank Wesson
Governing Body: none
Present Status: obsolete

CARTRIDGE DESCRIPTION
Bullet Diameter: .446 in.
Bullet Weight(s): 390 gr. (.44-85), 550 gr. (.44-100)
Rifling Twist Rate: 1 turn in 20 in. (est.)
Test Barrel Length: N/A
Case Type: rimmed, straight
Case Material: brass
Primer: large rifle

CARTRIDGE BALLISTICS
Max. Average Breech Pressure: N/A
Max. Horizontal Range: 3,750 yds. (.44-100)
Max. Vertical Range: 7,550 ft. (.44-100)

Bullet Weight (gr.)	Bullet Type	Muzzle Velocity (fps)	Muzzle Energy (ft.-lbs.)
390	L-RN	1,400	1,697 (est. .44-85)
550	L-RN	1,380	2,326 (est. .44-100)

CURRENT MANUFACTURER(S)
None

GENERAL COMMENT(S)
These two obscure cartridges are related. Both were designed by Frank Wesson, a noted gun designer of the time and relative of Daniel B. Wesson of Smith & Wesson. From their design, it seems clear that both cartridges were intended for Creedmoor competition. At the time, some competitors preferred straight cases, while others preferred necked cases. These Wesson cartridges would appeal to the former. What little we know about these two Wesson cartridges was found in an 1881-1882 United States Cartridge Company broad sheet.

TECHNICAL COMMENT(S)
The .44-100 Wesson cartridge is simply a .44-85 Wesson made .50 inches longer. Both cartridges exceed 3.25 inches in overall loaded length making them suitable only for use in single-shot rifles. As facts about these cartridges are scarce, ballistics were estimated based on the performance of similar cartridges. Both of these cartridges were loaded with paper-patched, lead, round-nose bullets.

.44-90 REMINGTON SPECIAL

ALTERNATE NAME(S): .44-90 Remington, .44-90 Remington Creedmoor
RELATED CALIBER(S): .44-60 Sharps, .44-90 Sharps

CARTRIDGE HISTORY
Year of Introduction: 1873
Country of Origin: U.S.
Designer(s): Remington
Governing Body: none
Present Status: obsolete

CARTRIDGE DESCRIPTION
Bullet Diameter: .442 in.
Bullet Weight(s): 550 gr.
Rifling Twist Rate: 1 turn in 22 in.
Test Barrel Length: N/A
Case Type: rimmed, necked
Case Material: brass
Primer: large rifle

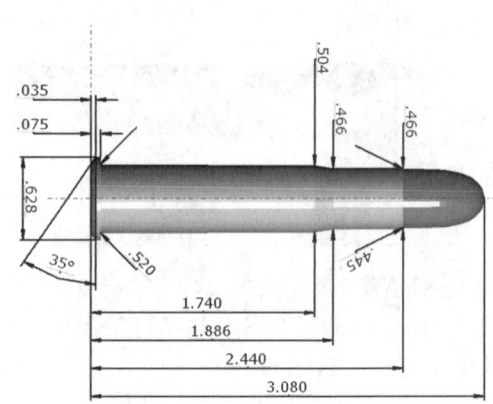

CARTRIDGE BALLISTICS
Max. Average Breech Pressure: N/A
Max. Horizontal Range: 3,600 yds.
Max. Vertical Range: 7,300 ft.

Bullet Weight (gr.)	Bullet Type	Muzzle Velocity (fps)	Muzzle Energy (ft.-lbs.)
550	L-RN	1,250	1,908

CURRENT MANUFACTURER(S)
None

GENERAL COMMENT(S)
Introduction of the .44-90 Remington Special was coordinated with the opening of the new Creedmoor shooting range in 1873. The new range spurred the large ammunition makers to introduce new cartridges specifically designed for competition at ranges of 1,000 yards and beyond. The .44-90 Remington Special was one of these cartridges. By the turn of the century (1900), interest in long range competitive shooting declined and Creedmoor range was closed, effectively ending the market for such cartridges. Smokeless powder soon made large caliber black powder cartridges such as the .44-90 Remington Special obsolete. By 1910, it was no longer listed in Remington catalogs.

TECHNICAL COMMENT(S)
In keeping with the precepts of that era for long range shooting, the .44-90 Remington Special cartridge was designed for a massive 550 grain lead, round-nose, paper-patched bullet backed by a 90 grain charge of black powder. Muzzle velocity was a modest 1,250 fps. The .44-90 Remington Special was always considered a match cartridge, a categorization that greatly limited its appeal for other purposes such as hunting. In part, this was due to the massively heavy bullet which was not suitable for hunting.

.44-95 PEABODY "WHAT CHEER"

ALTERNATE NAME(S):.44-95 Peabody, .44-100 Peabody
RELATED CALIBER(S): .40-70 Peabody, .40-90 Peabody

CARTRIDGE HISTORY
Year of Introduction: 1877
Country of Origin: U.S.
Designer(s): H.L. Peabody
Governing Body: none
Present Status: obsolete

CARTRIDGE DESCRIPTION
Bullet Diameter: .443 in.
Bullet Weight(s): 550 gr.
Rifling Twist Rate: 1 turn in 20 in.
Test Barrel Length: N/A
Case Type: rimmed, necked
Case Material: brass
Primer: large rifle

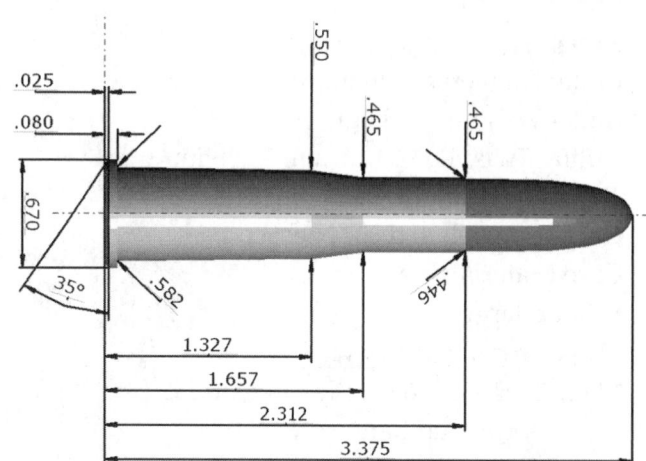

CARTRIDGE BALLISTICS
Max. Average Breech Pressure: N/A
Max. Horizontal Range: 3,700 yds.
Max. Vertical Range: 7,500 ft.

Bullet Weight (gr.)	Bullet Type	Muzzle Velocity (fps)	Muzzle Energy (ft.-lbs.)
550	L-RN	1,310	2,096

CURRENT MANUFACTURER(S)
None

GENERAL COMMENT(S)
A new shooting range was opened near Providence, R.I. in 1875 called "What Cheer" after a greeting the pilgrims once exchanged with the local Native Americans. The Creedmoor range in Long Island, N.Y. was opened about the same time. As interest in long range shooting increased, ammunition makers hastened to design cartridges for competition and named them after one of these ranges. Some companies, such as Peabody, used both. The .44-95 Peabody "What Cheer" was the largest of the Peabody target cartridges and also the first. Peabody target cartridge designs enjoyed a short life as smokeless propellants made large-bore, black powder cartridges obsolete by the early 1900s.

TECHNICAL COMMENT(S)
From a technical standpoint, the .44-95/100 Peabody "What Cheer" cartridge seems a well-balanced design with plenty of case volume for heavy powder charges and a long neck to assure bullet retention. It is a rimmed design as were all of the Peabody cartridges of this type. However, the .44-95 Peabody cartridge was necked. We consider such a configuration normal today, but in the 1880s most long range competitors came to prefer straight case designs. This handicapped Peabody target cartridges as all of them were necked. All Peabody target cartridges had larger rim and head diameters than most other cartridges. This made them difficult and expensive to manufacture. Both a 95 grain and a 100 grain load were offered in the same case with the same bullet. A lead, paper-patched, round-nose bullet weighing 550 grains was the only one offered as this cartridge was optimized for long range shooting and not intended for hunting. The Union Metallic Cartridge Co. manufactured Peabody cartridges.

11.2x60mm SCHULER

ALTERNATE NAME(S): 11.2x60mm Mauser, 11.15x59.8mm Schuler
RELATED CALIBER(S): 11x60Rmm Mauser

CARTRIDGE HISTORY
Year of Introduction: circa early 1900s
Country of Origin: Germany
Designer(s): August Schuler
Governing Body: none
Present Status: obsolete

CARTRIDGE DESCRIPTION
Bullet Diameter: .440 in.
Bullet Weight(s): 332 gr.
Rifling Twist Rate: 1 turn in 13.78 in.
Test Barrel Length: 24 in.
Case Type: rebated rim, necked
Case Material: brass
Primer: large rifle

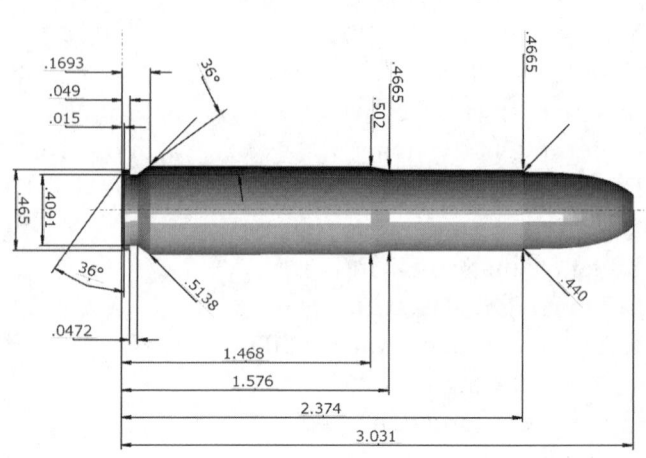

CARTRIDGE BALLISTICS
Max. Average Breech Pressure: 36,259 psi.
Max. Horizontal Range: N/A
Max. Vertical Range: N/A

Bullet Weight (gr.)	Bullet Type	Muzzle Velocity (fps)	Muzzle Energy (ft.-lbs.)
332	JSP	2,200	3,568

CURRENT MANUFACTURER(S)
None

GENERAL COMMENT(S)
This cartridge is very likely one of the first of August Schuler's designs. When his 11.2x60mm cartridge did not prove successful due to the lack of performance, Schuler developed the improved (and more powerful) 11.2x72mm and 12.5x70mm cartridges. The 11.2x60mm Schuler then faded away quietly.

TECHNICAL COMMENT(S)
In order to create his 11.2x60mm cartridge, Schuler began with the rimmed 11x60Rmm Mauser military cartridge. As the rim was too large to fit the standard Model 98 Mauser rifle bolt face, Schuler reduced the diameter to fit while retaining the body diameter to assure case volume. The long neck so beloved of black powder cartridges was retained for expediency. The result was, arguably, one of the better looking large-bore, hunting cartridges for bolt-action rifles. Why did the 11.2x60RBmm Schuler cartridge fail in the field? The stock answer is to blame the weakly constructed German bullets. However, the lighter than normal bullets loaded had poor sectional density in addition to weak construction, very likely due to German inexperience in hunting African game. Schuler's subsequent cartridge designs crept up on a solution to these problems, but never entirely resolved them.

11.2x72mm SCHULER

ALTERNATE NAME(S): 11.2x72mm Mauser,
RELATED CALIBER(S): 11.2x60mm Schuler/Mauser

CARTRIDGE HISTORY
Year of Introduction: circa 1910
Country of Origin: Germany
Designer(s): August Schuler
Governing Body: none
Present Status: obsolete

CARTRIDGE DESCRIPTION

Bullet Diameter: .440 in.

Bullet Weight(s): 401 gr.

Rifling Twist Rate: 1 turn in 13.78 in.

Test Barrel Length: 24

Case Type: rebated rim, necked

Case Material: brass

Primer: large rifle

CARTRIDGE BALLISTICS

Max. Average Breech Pressure: N/A

Max. Horizontal Range: 4,300 yds.

Max. Vertical Range: 9,000 ft.

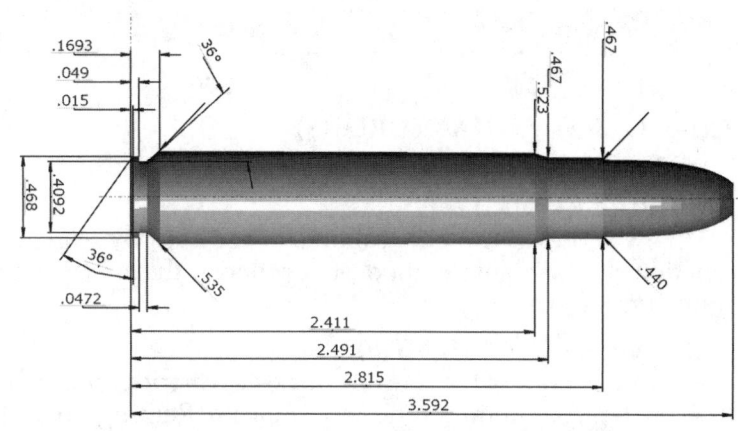

Bullet Weight (gr.)	Bullet Type	Muzzle Velocity (fps)	Muzzle Energy (ft.-lbs.)
401	JSP-FN	2,440	5,301

CURRENT MANUFACTURER(S)

None

GENERAL COMMENT(S)

This is another design by August Schuler of Suhl, Germany that appeared about the same time as the 12.5x70mm Schuler cartridge. It did not gain a significant following due to the need for an expensive magnum rifle action, weak bullet construction and lack of choice in bullet weights. Made only in Germany, manufacture was not resumed after World War II.

TECHNICAL COMMENT(S)

A rebated rim was necessary to achieve both the required case volume and standard bolt face dimensions. The .440 inch diameter bullet is seated deeply in the case mouth. Published muzzle energy levels place the 11.2x70mm Schuler cartridge in the same league as the .470 Nitro Express. While on paper this may be true, in the field, the 11.2x70mm was handicapped by poor bullet construction.

.45-60 WINCHESTER

ALTERNATE NAME(S): .45-60 Win.

RELATED CALIBER(S): .44-60 Sharps/Remington, .44-77 Sharps/Remington, .44-90 Sharps

CARTRIDGE HISTORY

Year of Introduction:1876

Country of Origin: U.S.

Designer(s): Winchester

Governing Body: none

Present Status: obsolete

CARTRIDGE DESCRIPTION

Bullet Diameter: .454 in.

Bullet Weight(s): 300 gr.

Rifling Twist Rate: 1 turn in 20 in.

Test Barrel Length: 30 in.

Case Type: rimmed, straight

Case Material: brass

Primer: large rifle

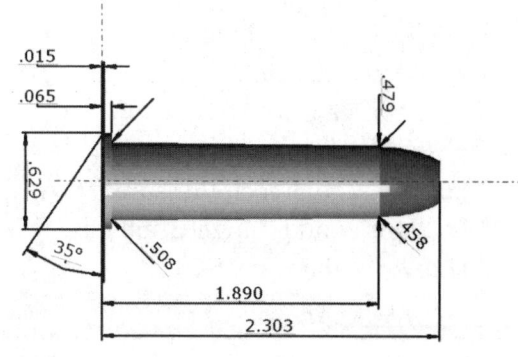

CARTRIDGE BALLISTICS

Max. Average Breech Pressure: N/A

Max. Horizontal Range: 2,450 yds.

Max. Vertical Range: 5,200 ft.

Bullet Weight (gr.)	Bullet Type	Muzzle Velocity (fps)	Muzzle Energy (ft.-lbs.)
300	L-FN	1,315	1,152

CURRENT MANUFACTURER(S)
None

GENERAL COMMENT(S)
This was one of the new calibers introduced by Winchester in 1876 with their Model 1876 Centennial lever-action rifle. Achieving modest popularity, the .45-60 Winchester cartridge remained in the Winchester product line until the mid-1930s.

TECHNICAL COMMENT(S)
The dimensions of the .44-60 Winchester cartridge were influenced by several earlier short cartridges, namely the .44-60 Sharps/Remington, .44-77 Sharps/Remington and the .44-90 Sharps. However, all of these were necked designs while the .45-60 Winchester had a straight case. As with other new Winchester calibers introduced with the Model 1876 Centennial rifle, the overall loaded length of the cartridge was dictated by the medium length of the rifle action. One of Winchester's goals in developing the .45-60 cartridge was to offer improved ballistic performance over the .44-40 Winchester cartridge used in the Model 73 Winchester lever-action rifle. In this, the new cartridge succeeded, but not by much. Ballistics of the .45-60 cartridge could only be described as "adequate" for medium game and unsuitable for large game.

.45-75 WINCHESTER CENTENNIAL

ALTERNATE NAME(S): .45-75 Winchester
RELATED CALIBER(S): .348 Win.

CARTRIDGE HISTORY
Year of Introduction: 1876
Country of Origin: U.S.
Designer(s): Winchester
Governing Body: none
Present Status: obsolete

CARTRIDGE DESCRIPTION
Bullet Diameter: .454 in.
Bullet Weight(s): 350 gr.
Rifling Twist Rate: 1 turn in 20 in.
Test Barrel Length: 30 in.
Case Type: rimmed, necked
Case Material: brass
Primer: large rifle

CARTRIDGE BALLISTICS
Max. Average Breech Pressure: N/A
Max. Horizontal Range: 2,450 yds.
Max. Vertical Range: 5,200 ft.

Bullet Weight (gr.)	Bullet Type	Muzzle Velocity (fps)	Muzzle Energy (ft.-lbs.)
350	L-FN	1,380	1,480

CURRENT MANUFACTURER(S)
None

GENERAL COMMENT(S)
To celebrate the 100th anniversary of the Declaration of Independence, the Centennial International Exhibition was held in 1876 in Philadelphia. Essentially, it was a world's fair, the first held on American soil. Over 10 million people attended the exhibits from all over the world. Winchester introduced their new Model 1886 Centennial lever-action rifle chambered for the new .45-75 Winchester cartridge at the Exhibition. To honor the occasion, Winchester appended the name "Centennial" to both the rifle and cartridge. Winchester intended

their new centennial rifle and cartridge to compete with the Sharps cartridges for hunting large, heavy game. Obviously, Winchester felt their lever-action repeating rifle would be more attractive to sportsmen than the Sharps single-shot designs. This cartridge is historically significant for two reasons. First, its 1876 Centennial International Exhibition introduction; and second, the Winchester Model 1876 rifle and .45-75 cartridge was adopted by the Royal Canadian Mounted Police and retained for 27 years.

TECHNICAL COMMENT(S)

The .45-75 Winchester Centennial cartridge was designed specifically for the Winchester Model 1876 lever-action rifle which was not capable of handling a loaded cartridge over 2.25 inches in length. To accommodate this, the .45-75 Winchester Centennial cartridge case dimensions are unique. The .45-75 Centennial cartridge made the transition to smokeless propellants and remained in the Winchester product line until the mid-1930s.

.45-82 WINCHESTER, .45-85 WINCHESTER, .45-90 WINCHESTER, .45-90 WINCHESTER HIGH VELOCITY

ALTERNATE NAME(S): none
RELATED CALIBER(S): .45-70 Gov't.

CARTRIDGE HISTORY

Year of Introduction: 1886
Country of Origin: U.S.
Designer(s): Winchester
Governing Body: none
Present Status: obsolete

CARTRIDGE DESCRIPTION

Bullet Diameter: .458 in.
Bullet Weight(s): 300-405 gr.
Rifling Twist Rate: 1 turn in 32 in.
Test Barrel Length: 26 in.
Case Type: rimmed, straight
Case Material: brass
Primer: large rifle

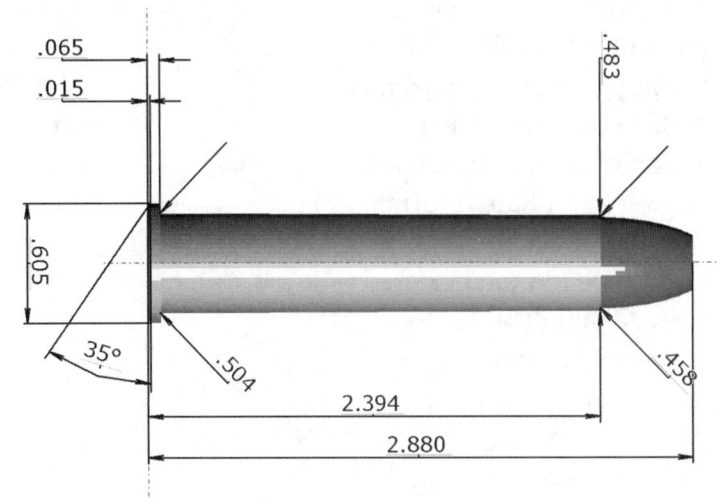

CARTRIDGE BALLISTICS

Max. Average Breech Pressure: N/A
Max. Horizontal Range: 2,650 yds.
Max. Vertical Range: 5,800 ft.

Bullet Weight (gr.)	Bullet Type	Muzzle Velocity (fps)	Muzzle Energy (ft.-lbs.)
300 HV	L-RN	2,000	2,663
300	L-RN	1,555	1,609
300 (.45-90)	L-FN	1,525	1,549
300 (.45-90 High Vel.)	JSP	1,950	2,533
350	L-FN	1,510	1,775
405	L-FN	1,470	1,938/1,943

CURRENT MANUFACTURER(S)

None, but unprimed brass available from Huntington and other sources

GENERAL COMMENT(S)

The .45-90 Winchester cartridge was introduced in 1886 for Winchester's new Model 1886 lever-action rifle. It was also chambered in some single-shot rifles. Winchester obviously intended this cartridge for hunting large, heavy game. For this reason, a variety of bullet weights were offered.

TECHNICAL COMMENT(S)

Originally designed for black powder, Winchester transitioned the .45-90 cartridge to smokeless propellants circa 1895. During the transition, Winchester also did something to the .45-90 cartridge they seldom did for other black powder hold-over calibers, they updated it with a 300 grain High Velocity load. The High Velocity loading boosted the muzzle energy 63.5% over the standard load. When fired in light-weight rifles, recoil of the High Velocity load must have been legendary. Despite the nomenclature, the 82, 85, and 90 grain loads share the same case dimensions. The .45-90 cartridge is essentially a .45-70 case lengthened by .30 inches. This cartridge appealed to a broad market, became quite popular and survived in Winchester's product line until 1936. New rifles in this caliber are available to this day.

.45-100 REMINGTON (NECKED)

ALTERNATE NAME(S): none
RELATED CALIBER(S): .44-90 Remington Special

CARTRIDGE HISTORY
Year of Introduction: 1880
Country of Origin: U.S.
Designer(s): Remington
Governing Body: none
Present Status: obsolete

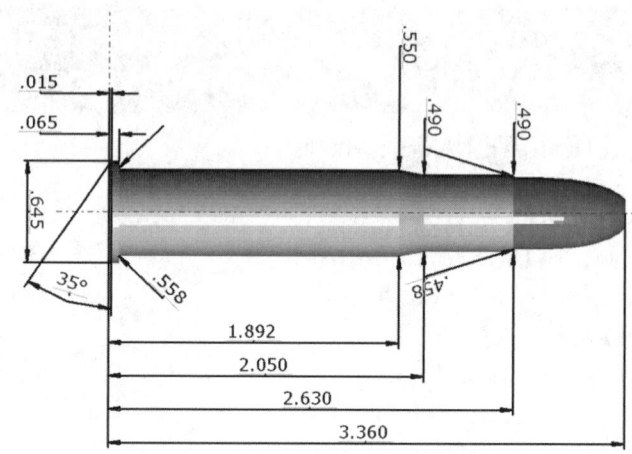

CARTRIDGE DESCRIPTION
Bullet Diameter: .458 in.
Bullet Weight(s): 550 gr. (est.)
Rifling Twist Rate: 1 turn in 20 in.
Test Barrel Length: N/A
Case Type: rimmed, necked
Case Material: brass
Primer: large rifle

CARTRIDGE BALLISTICS
Max. Average Breech Pressure: N/A
Max. Horizontal Range: 3,750 yds.
Max. Vertical Range: 7,600 ft.

Bullet Weight (gr.)	Bullet Type	Muzzle Velocity (fps)	Muzzle Energy (ft.-lbs.)
550	L-FN	1,400 (est.)	2,393

CURRENT MANUFACTURER(S)
None

GENERAL COMMENT(S)
As a special order only caliber for Sharps (and other single-shot) rifles, this cartridge was obscure with a very limited following. The U.S. Cartridge Company listed loaded ammunition in this caliber in their 1880-1881 catalog. It disappeared shortly after.

TECHNICAL COMMENT(S)
In configuration, this cartridge seems to be a big brother to the .44-90 Remington Special. It is of similar shape with a larger rim, wider base and longer neck. The .45-100 Remington is a large cartridge case designed to hold a heavy charge of black powder. These characteristics and the date of its appearance indicate that it was intended for long range target shooting. While no ballistics for this cartridge are available, its ballistic parameters have been estimated based on those of similar cartridges. Long range target shooters of that era fell into two camps: one preferred straight cases and the other preferred necked cases. The .45-100 Remington, therefore, was produced for the latter. Rim and head dimensions for this cartridge are unique.

.45-125 WINCHESTER EXPRESS

ALTERNATE NAME(S): .45-125 Win.
RELATED CALIBER(S): .45-90 Winchester

CARTRIDGE HISTORY
Year of Introduction: 1886
Country of Origin: U.S.
Designer(s): Winchester
Governing Body: none
Present Status: obsolete

CARTRIDGE DESCRIPTION
Bullet Diameter: .458 in.
Bullet Weight(s): 300 gr.
Rifling Twist Rate: 1 turn in 18 in.
Test Barrel Length: 30 in.
Case Type: rimmed, straight
Case Material: brass
Primer: large rifle

CARTRIDGE BALLISTICS
Max. Average Breech Pressure: N/A
Max. Horizontal Range: 2,550 yds.
Max. Vertical Range: 5,550 ft.

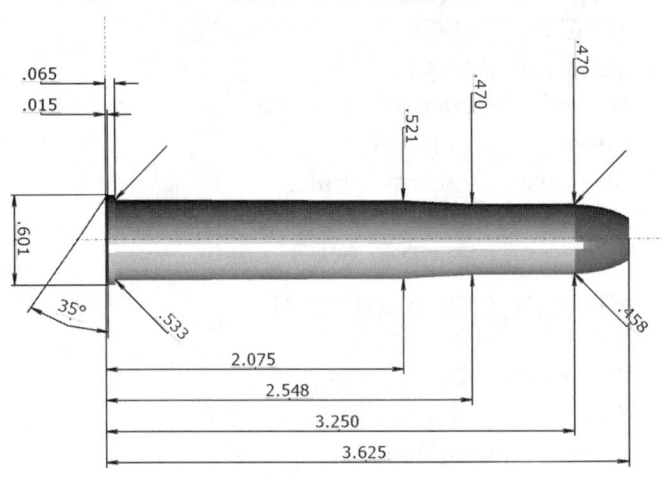

Bullet Weight (gr.)	Bullet Type	Muzzle Velocity (fps)	Muzzle Energy (ft.-lbs.)
300	JSP	1,680	1,880

CURRENT MANUFACTURER(S)
None

GENERAL COMMENT(S)
For their new lever-action Model 1886 rifle, Winchester developed a set of black powder cartridges and introduced them concurrently with the rifle. The .45-125 Winchester Express was one of these cartridges, but available only on special order. Although it was quite powerful, the era of large caliber black powder cartridges was fading away and the .45-125 Winchester Express never became popular. Winchester dropped this caliber from their product line in 1916.

TECHNICAL COMMENT(S)
Essentially, the .45-125 Winchester Express cartridge is a .45-90 Winchester case lengthened .85 inches to create more volume for the heavier powder charge. Despite the significantly heavier powder charge, ballistic performance was not significantly better than the .45-90 Winchester cartridge. Both cartridges were fully capable of generating over 1,900 ft.-lbs. of muzzle energy (the .45-90 using a 405 grain bullet and the .45-125 using a 300 grain bullet), however .45-90 Winchester ammunition was cheaper, easier to get and offered in various bullet weights. For most hunters, the decision on which cartridge to use was an easy one. The .45-125 Winchester Express is historically significant because, at 4.19 inches in length, it was the longest, American, black-powder sporting cartridge.

12.5x70mm SCHULER

ALTERNATE NAME(S): .500 Jeffery
RELATED CALIBER(S): 11.2x72mm Schuler

CARTRIDGE HISTORY
Year of Introduction: circa 1910
Country of Origin: Germany
Designer(s): August Schuler
Governing Body: none
Present Status: obsolete

CARTRIDGE DESCRIPTION
Bullet Diameter: .510 in.
Bullet Weight(s): 535 gr.
Rifling Twist Rate: N/A
Test Barrel Length: N/A
Case Type: rebated rim, necked
Case Material: brass
Primer: large rifle

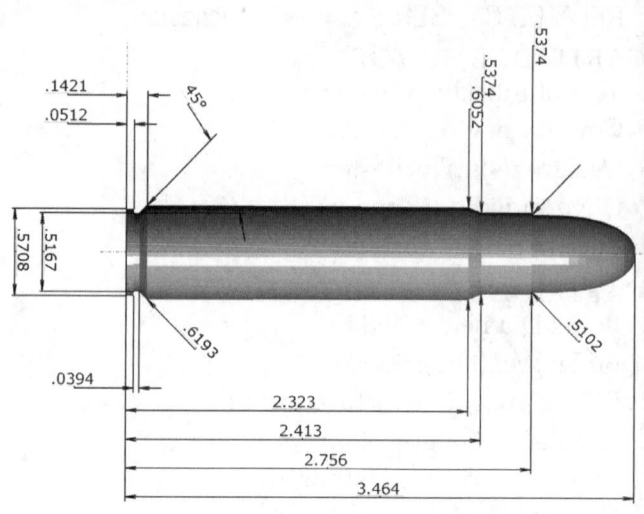

CARTRIDGE BALLISTICS
Max. Average Breech Pressure: N/A
Max. Horizontal Range: 2,200 yds.
Max. Vertical Range: 5,000 ft.

Bullet Weight (gr.)	Bullet Type	Muzzle Velocity (fps)	Muzzle Energy (ft.-lbs.)
535	JSP/FMJ	2,400	6,842

CURRENT MANUFACTURER(S)
None

GENERAL COMMENT(S)
With the introduction of the 12.5x70mm Schuler, European hunters finally had a powerful, dangerous game cartridge for bolt-action rifles capable of competing with the British large bore, nitro express cartridges. For nearly 40 years, the 12.7x70mm Schuler reigned supreme as the most powerful cartridge available for bolt-action rifles. In 1958, the .460 Weatherby Magnum replaced the 12.5x70mm Schuler on the throne of bolt-action power. In the field, however, the German bullets did not prove to be as tough as the British designs. The 12.5x70mm Schuler was loaded only in Germany and production was not resumed after World War II. Today, 12.5x70mm Schuler ammunition cannot be imported due to its bullet diameter being over .500 inches.

TECHNICAL COMMENT(S)
In Britain, Jeffery offered an identical cartridge called the .500 Jeffery. The Jeffery and the Schuler cartridges are interchangeable. To achieve the ballistic goals for the 12.5x70mm cartridge, it proved necessary to tailor virtually every dimension toward this goal. The case rim, head and body diameters were all substantially larger than other bolt-action rifle cartridges, however they remained well within the capabilities of magnum rifle actions. Of course, the bullet was larger as well. Esthetics may be a strange measure of a cartridge, but the 12.5x70mm Schuler created a purposeful impression when viewed.

.500 NITRO EXPRESS-3 3/4

ALTERNATE NAME(S): .500 NE, .500 Nitro Express 3 1/4 in.
RELATED CALIBER(S): none

CARTRIDGE HISTORY
Year of Introduction: mid-1890s
Country of Origin: Britain
Designer(s): N/A
Governing Body: CIP
Present Status: obsolete

CARTRIDGE DESCRIPTION

Bullet Diameter: .509 in.
Bullet Weight(s): 570 gr.
Rifling Twist Rate: 1 turn in 15 in.
Test Barrel Length: 24 in.
Case Type: rimmed, straight
Case Material: brass
Primer Size: large rifle

CARTRIDGE BALLISTICS

Max. Average Breech Pressure: 40,160 psi.
Max. Horizontal Range: 4,700 yds.
Max. Vertical Range: 9,500 ft.

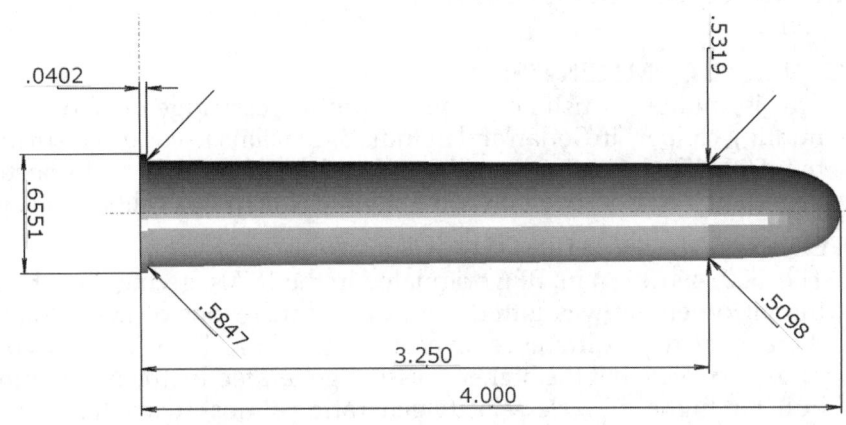

Bullet Weight (gr.)	Bullet Type	Muzzle Velocity (fps)	Muzzle Energy (ft.-lbs.)
570	JSP/FMJ	2,150	5,850

CURRENT MANUFACTURER(S)

Kynoch

GENERAL COMMENT(S)

Professional hunters regard this as one of the best all around calibers for African game of all types.

TECHNICAL COMMENT(S)

The heavy bullet and striking energy of the .500 Nitro Express 3 1/4 in. cartridge is an excellent balance for dangerous game. However, its ballistic performance is much the same as the present .470 Nitro Express cartridge.

.500/450 NITRO EXPRESS 3 1/2 in., .500/450 BLACK POWDER EXPRESS 3 1/2 in. (BPE)

ALTERNATE NAME(S): .500/450 NE
RELATED CALIBER(S): .500/465 Nitro Express

CARTRIDGE HISTORY

Year of Introduction: circa 1870s
Country of Origin: Britain
Designer(s): Holland & Holland
Governing Body: none
Present Status: obsolete

CARTRIDGE DESCRIPTION

Bullet Diameter: .458 in.
Bullet Weight(s): 325-480 gr.
Rifling Twist Rate: N/A
Test Barrel Length: N/A
Case Type: rimmed, slight neck
Case Material: brass
Primer: large rifle

CARTRIDGE BALLISTICS

Max. Average Breech Pressure: 31,000 psi.
Max. Horizontal Range: 5,100 yds.
Max. Vertical Range: 10,000 ft.

Bullet Weight (gr.)	Bullet Type	Muzzle Velocity (fps)	Muzzle Energy (ft.-lbs.)
325	L-RN	1,950	2,745 (BP)
365	L-RN	1,875	2,850 (Nitro for Black)
480	JSP-RN	2,175	5,080 (Nitro)

CURRENT MANUFACTURER(S)
Kynamco

GENERAL COMMENT(S)
This is another British large caliber hunting cartridge developed as a consequence of the banning of selected hunting calibers in Sudan and in India as a means to control insurrections. Despite this slightly tawdry purpose, the .500/450 3 1/4 in. cartridge proved itself reliable and effective on all species of dangerous game. U.S. President T.R. Roosevelt owned a double rifle in this caliber and spoke well of its performance.

TECHNICAL COMMENT(S)
The .500/450 3 1/4 in. BPE originated in the 1870s, giving it nearly two decades of experience in the field when the nitro version was introduced. Case dimensions of the BPE and Nitro versions were identical. However, there were major differences in chamber pressure between the two (hint: the nitro version was higher). Another difference was that the higher pressure generated by the NE loading allowed it to drive a substantially heavier bullet at higher muzzle velocity generating almost twice the striking energy of the BPE.

.500/450 No. 1 BLACK POWDER EXPRESS, .500/450 No. 2 BLACK POWDER EXPRESS

ALTERNATE NAME(S): .500/450 No.1 BPE, .500/450 No. 2 BPE, .500/450 No. 1 Express, .500/450 No. 2 Express
RELATED CALIBER(S): .500/450 No. 2 Musket

CARTRIDGE HISTORY
Year of Introduction: circa 1875
Country of Origin: Britain
Designer(s): Westley Richards
Governing Body: none
Present Status: obsolete

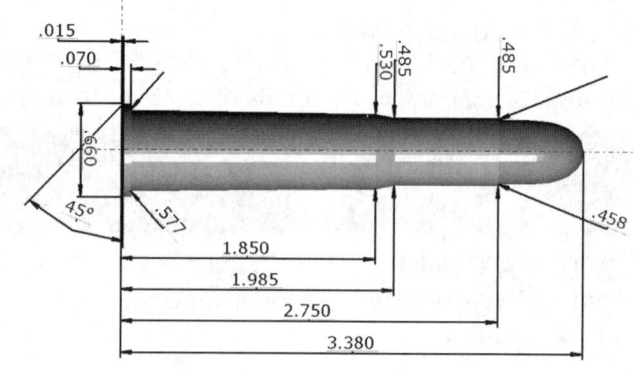

CARTRIDGE DESCRIPTION
Bullet Diameter: .458 in.
Bullet Weight(s): 270-340 gr.
Rifling Twist Rate: N/A
Test Barrel Length: N/A
Case Type: rimmed, necked
Case Material: brass
Primer: large rifle

CARTRIDGE BALLISTICS
Max. Average Breech Pressure: 20,000 psi.
Max. Horizontal Range: 3,550 yds.
Max. Vertical Range: 7,500 ft.

Bullet Weight (gr.)	Bullet Type	Muzzle Velocity (fps)	Muzzle Energy (ft.-lbs.)
270	L-RN	1,900	2,162 (No. 1 Exp.)
340	L-RN	1,850	2,581 (No. 2 Exp.)

CURRENT MANUFACTURER(S)
None

GENERAL COMMENT(S)
These two black powder sporting cartridges are historically significant in that they were among the first center fire cartridge with cases made from drawn brass. They began life as coiled brass case designs however. Westley Richards has been credited with designing these cartridges, although his name is not included in the nomenclature.

TECHNICAL COMMENT(S)
The .500/450 No. 1 and No. 2 Black Powder Express (BPE) cartridges share rim and head dimensions with the .500/450 No. 1 and 2 musket military cartridges. However, the BPE cartridges have a .39 inch longer case to hold a heavier charge of propellant. Both .500/450 BPE sporting cartridges took advantage of their extra case volume to drive lighter bullets to higher muzzle velocities than the military musket loads. Lead round nose bullets were normally loaded.

.500/450 No. 1 CARBINE

ALTERNATE NAME(S): none
RELATED CALIBER(S): none

CARTRIDGE HISTORY
Year of Introduction: circa 1872
Country of Origin: Britain
Designer(s): Westley Richards
Governing Body: none
Present Status: obsolete

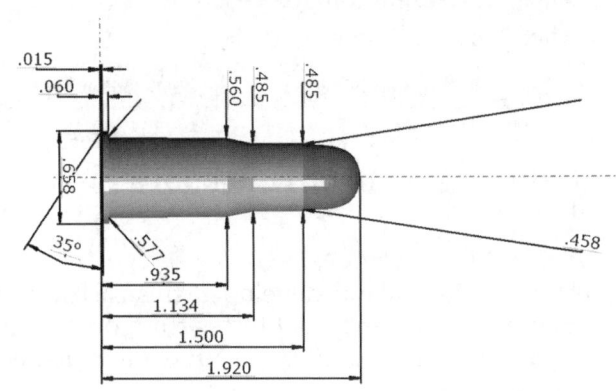

CARTRIDGE DESCRIPTION
Bullet Diameter: 458 in.
Bullet Weight(s): 380 gr.
Rifling Twist Rate: N/A
Test Barrel Length: N/A
Case Type: rimmed, necked
Case Material: brass
Primer: large rifle

CARTRIDGE BALLISTICS
Max. Average Breech Pressure: N/A
Max. Horizontal Range: 3,250 yds.
Max. Vertical Range: 6,650 ft.

Bullet Weight (gr.)	Bullet Type	Muzzle Velocity (fps)	Muzzle Energy (ft.-lbs.)
380	L-RN	1,300	1,424

CURRENT MANUFACTURER(S)
None

GENERAL COMMENT(S)
This is the carbine version of the British .500/450 No. 2 Musket cartridge with a shorter case and reduced powder charge. This cartridge is historically significant in that it was the first drawn brass cartridge case perfected by Westley Richards and introduced in 1879.

TECHNICAL COMMENT(S)
Carbines with their reduced power cartridges were issued to cavalry, artillery, and engineer troops.

.500/465 NITRO EXPRESS

ALTERNATE NAME(S): .500/465 NE
RELATED CALIBER(S): .500 Nitro Express 3 1/4 in.

CARTRIDGE HISTORY
Year of Introduction: 1907
Country of Origin: Britain
Designer(s): Holland & Holland
Governing Body: CIP
Present Status: obsolete

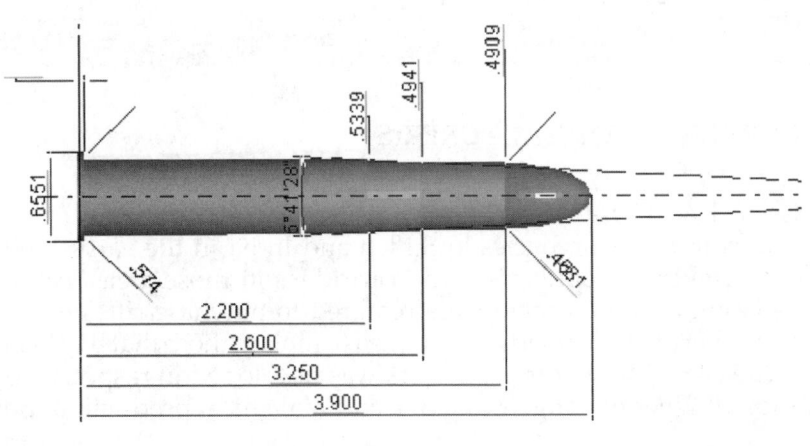

CARTRIDGE DESCRIPTION
Bullet Diameter: .468 in.
Bullet Weight(s): 480 gr.
Rifling Twist Rate: 1 turn in 28 in.
Test Barrel Length: 24 in.
Case Type: rimmed, necked
Case Material: brass
Primer Size: large rifle

CARTRIDGE BALLISTICS
Max. Average Breech Pressure: 35,550 psi.
Max. Horizontal Range: 3,600 yds.
Max. Vertical Range: 7,100 ft.

Bullet Weight (gr.)	Bullet Type	Muzzle Velocity (fps)	Muzzle Energy (ft.-lbs.)
480	JSP/FMJ	2,150	4,930

CURRENT MANUFACTURER(S)
Kynoch

GENERAL COMMENT(S)
Holland & Holland developed this cartridge as a result of the British government outlawing the .450 Nitro Express to prevent rebel forces from obtaining ammunition and loading components which could be used in military rifles. The .500/465 NE went on to become a popular and effective sporting caliber in its own right.

TECHNICAL COMMENT(S)
Despite its politically motivated beginnings, hunters found the .500/465 NE to be an excellent general purpose caliber for dangerous African game.

.475 NITRO EXPRESS 3 1/4 in.

ALTERNATE NAME(S): none
RELATED CALIBER(S): .450 3 1/4 in. Nitro Express, .400 Jeffery

CARTRIDGE HISTORY
Year of Introduction: 1900
Country of Origin: Britain
Designer(s): N/A
Governing Body: none
Present Status: obsolete

CARTRIDGE DESCRIPTION
Bullet Diameter: .483 in.
Bullet Weight(s): 480 gr.
Rifling Twist Rate: N/A
Test Barrel Length: 24 in.
Case Type: rimmed, straight
Case Material: brass
Primer: large rifle

CARTRIDGE BALLISTICS
Max. Average Breech Pressure: 30,000 psi.
Max. Horizontal Range: 4,450 yds.
Max. Vertical Range: 9,250 ft.

Bullet Weight (gr.)	Bullet Type	Muzzle Velocity (fps)	Muzzle Energy (ft.-lbs.)
480	JSP	2,175	5,042

CURRENT MANUFACTURER(S)
Kynamco

GENERAL COMMENT(S)
To counter insurgencies in Sudan and India in the early 1900s, the British government outlawed the sale of a number of popular hunting cartridges in those areas. As these areas offered excellent hunting, sportsmen planning to hunt there were required to purchase rifles in a caliber which was not banned. This spawned a number of new cartridges designed to replace those that had been banned while offering equivalent performance. The .475 Nitro Express 3 1/4 in. was developed in response to the ban. It soon gained respect and acceptance for all types of dangerous game and remains in production today.

TECHNICAL COMMENT(S)

The designers of this "new" cartridge followed tradition. They selected a large rimmed straight case with plenty of volume to keep breech pressures low. A heavy bullet was launched at slightly higher muzzle velocity than many other cartridges of this type in order to keep muzzle energy above 5,000 ft.-lbs. The combination was a success.

.50-100 WINCHESTER

ALTERNATE NAME(S): .50-105 Winchester, .50-110 Winchester, .50-110 Winchester High Velocity
RELATED CALIBER(S): .45-75 Winchester Centennial, .348 Winchester

CARTRIDGE HISTORY

Year of Introduction: 1887
Country of Origin: U.S.
Designer(s): Winchester
Governing Body: SAAMI
Present Status: obsolete

CARTRIDGE DESCRIPTION

Bullet Diameter: .512 in.
Bullet Weight(s): 300 gr.
Rifling Twist Rate: 1 turn in 54 in.
Test Barrel Length: 26 in.
Case Type: rimmed, straight
Case Material: brass
Primer: large rifle

CARTRIDGE BALLISTICS

Max. Average Breech Pressure: N/A
Max. Horizontal Range: 2,300 yds. (high velocity load)
Max. Vertical Range: 5,050 ft. (high velocity load)

Bullet Weight (gr.)	Bullet Type	Muzzle Velocity (fps)	Muzzle Energy (ft.-lbs.)
300	JSP	1,580	1,663
300 HV	JSP	2,200	3,224
450	JSP	1,430	2,043

CURRENT MANUFACTURER(S)

None

GENERAL COMMENT(S)

The .50-100 Winchester series of cartridges was introduced in 1887 for Winchester's new Model 1886 lever-action rifle. It was also chambered in some single-shot rifles. Winchester obviously intended this cartridge for hunting large, heavy game. However, buffalo hunting was over when this cartridge was introduced and the Sharps Rifle Co. had closed its doors five years earlier. For these reasons, Winchester marketing efforts undoubtedly were focused on competing with the .50-115 Bullard and .55-100 Maynard cartridges.

TECHNICAL COMMENT(S)

Originally designed for black powder, Winchester transitioned the .50-100 cartridge to smokeless propellants circa 1895. Following the transition, Winchester also did something to the .50-100 cartridge they seldom did for other black powder hold-over calibers, they updated it. For the initial transition, a 450 grain bullet load was added. Then around 1910, a High Velocity load with a 300 grain bullet was added. The High Velocity loading boosted the muzzle energy of the .50-100 Winchester cartridge into the realm of the British African calibers. When fired in light-weight rifles, recoil must have been very impressive. Despite the nomenclature, the 100, 105, and 110 grain loads share the same case dimensions. This cartridge appealed only to a very small, specialized, niche market. Contrary to what might be expected, the .50-100 Winchester remained in production until 1935.

.50-110 WINCHESTER

ALTERNATE NAME(S): none
RELATED CALIBER(S): .50-100 Win., .50-105 Win.

CARTRIDGE HISTORY
Year of Introduction: 1887
Country of Origin: U.S.
Designer(s): Winchester
Governing Body: N/A
Present Status: obsolete

CARTRIDGE DESCRIPTION
Bullet Diameter: .512 in.
Bullet Weight(s): 300 gr.
Rifling Twist Rate: 1 turn in 54 in.
Test Barrel Length: N/A
Case Type: rimmed, straight
Case Material: brass
Primer Size: large rifle

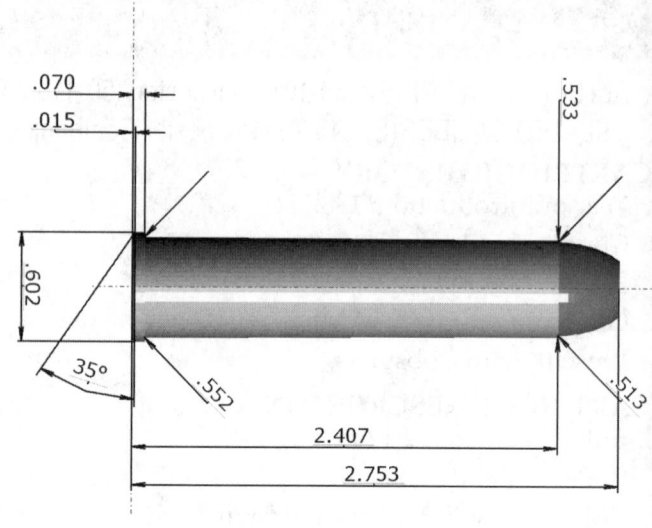

CARTRIDGE BALLISTICS
Max. Average Breech Pressure: N/A
Max. Effective Range: 300 yds.
Max. Horizontal Range: 3,800 yds.
Max. Vertical Range: 8,000 ft.

Bullet Weight (gr.)	Bullet Type	Muzzle Velocity (fps)	Muzzle Energy (ft.-lbs.)
300	L-RN	1,605	1,720
300 HV	L-RN	2,225	3,298

CURRENT MANUFACTURER(S)
None

GENERAL COMMENT(S)
This family of .50 caliber Winchester cartridges should not be confused with the Sharps family of .50 caliber cartridges. In fact, the Winchester .50 caliber cartridges were introduced long after buffalo hunting had ended. Rather these Winchester cartridges were intended for hunting large, heavy North American game. They remained in production until 1935.

TECHNICAL COMMENT(S)
Like the .50 Sharps cartridges, the .50 Winchester cartridges all share the same case length - the difference being entirely the powder charge weight. These are powerful cartridges from a time when big bore, black powder rifles were the norm. The .50 Win. cartridges made the transition to smokeless propellants in the late 1890s. The high velocity load was introduced at that time.

.50-140 WINCHESTER EXPRESS

ALTERNATE NAME(S): .50-140 Sharps
RELATED CALIBER(S): .50-90/100/110 Sharps

CARTRIDGE HISTORY
Year of Introduction: 1880
Country of Origin: U.S.
Designer(s): Winchester
Governing Body: none
Present Status: obsolete

CARTRIDGE DESCRIPTION
Bullet Diameter: .512 in.
Bullet Weight(s): 473-700 gr.
Rifling Twist Rate: 1 turn in 54 in.
Test Barrel Length: N/A
Case Type: rimmed, straight
Case Material: brass
Primer: large rifle

CARTRIDGE BALLISTICS
Max. Average Breech Pressure: N/A
Max. Horizontal Range: 2,400 yds.
Max. Vertical Range: 5,200 ft.

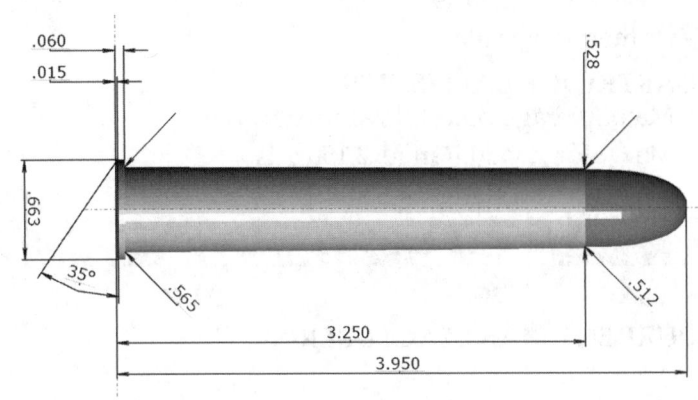

Bullet Weight (gr.)	Bullet Type	Muzzle Velocity (fps)	Muzzle Energy (ft.-lbs.)
473	L-FN	1,580	2,622
700	L-FN	1,355	2,854

CURRENT MANUFACTURER(S)
None

GENERAL COMMENT(S)
The .50-140 Winchester Express cartridge remains something of an enigma. It was introduced in 1880 shortly before the Sharps Rifle Co. closed its doors for good in 1881. Sharps never offered ammunition with a 3 1/4 inch case length. Reportedly, late Sharps brochures and price lists offered rifles chambered for this cartridge only on special order. Very few could have been made in the one year before Sharps closed. Although Winchester offered this cartridge, it was introduced with the Sharps name in an obvious attempt to garner some of the fame of Sharps cartridges. When Sharps went out of business, Winchester carried on with their own name on the cartridge. When the last buffalo herd was exterminated in 1884, the market for a large, powerful, black powder cartridge such as this evaporated and the .50-140 Sharps/Winchester cartridge never made the transition to smokeless propellants.

TECHNICAL COMMENT(S)
Comparing the .50-140 Winchester Express case with the classic .50-90 Sharps indicates they share all major dimensions save case length and bullet diameter (Sharps .509 inches; Winchester .512 inches). Of course, one might assume the ballistics of the .50-140 Winchester to be considerably improved over those of the .50-90 Sharps. Both were loaded with a 473 grain, lead, paper-patched, flat-nose bullet; the .50-90 achieved 1,350 fps. and the .50-140 reached 1,580 fps. However, the difference is unexpectedly small leading one to conjecture whether the enormous increase in recoil with the .50-140 would have been worth it.

.50-95 WINCHESTER EXPRESS

ALTERNATE NAME(S): .50 WCF
RELATED CALIBER(S): .50-70 Gov't., .50-90 Sharps, .348 Winchester

CARTRIDGE HISTORY
Year of Introduction: 1876
Country of Origin: U.S.
Designer(s): Winchester
Governing Body: none
Present Status: obsolete

CARTRIDGE DESCRIPTION
Bullet Diameter: .513 in.
Bullet Weight(s): 300 gr.
Rifling Twist Rate: 1 turn in 60 in.
Test Barrel Length: 30 in.
Case Type: rimmed, slight neck

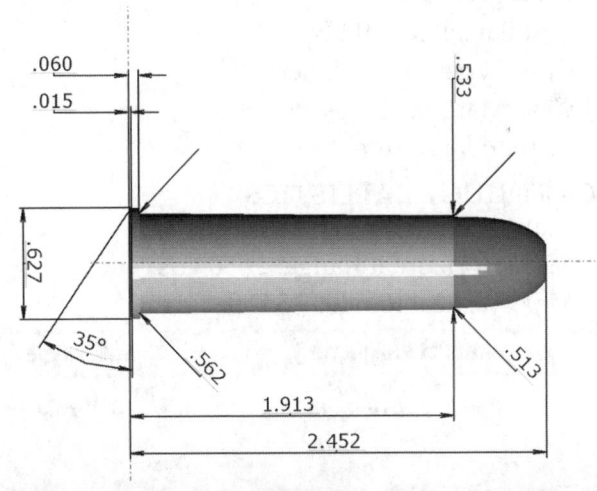

Case Material: brass
Primer: large rifle

CARTRIDGE BALLISTICS
Max. Average Breech Pressure: N/A
Max. Horizontal Range: 2,150 yds.
Max. Vertical Range: 4,650 ft.

Bullet Weight (gr.)	Bullet Type	Muzzle Velocity (fps)	Muzzle Energy (ft.-lbs.)
300	L-FN	1,555	1,611

CURRENT MANUFACTURER(S)
None

GENERAL COMMENT(S)
In 1876, Winchester introduced their new Model 1876 Centennial lever-action rifle. For this rifle, Winchester introduced a number of new cartridges; the .50-95 was the largest of the group, but did not prove as popular as the new smaller caliber cartridges.

TECHNICAL COMMENT(S)
Basically, the .50-95 Winchester Express is a slightly updated .50-70 Gov't. cartridge. Changes included a slight neck, 0.2 inch longer case and a 0.033 smaller diameter rim. These minor changes were intended to make the new cartridge more compatible with the M1876 rifle. By using a lighter, 300 grain bullet, muzzle velocity of the .50-95 Winchester Express could be increased 23% above that of the .50-70 Gov't. cartridge (1,555 fps. vs. 1,260 fps). This provided a corresponding 8.5% increase in muzzle energy. Yet, despite these ballistic improvements, the .50-95 Winchester Express was significantly less powerful than the "poison slinger" .50-90 Sharps cartridge. In effect, the .50-95 Winchester Express was a specialized cartridge for hunting large, heavy game. This limited its appeal in other markets. In its chosen niche market, it could not overcome the widespread acceptance of the .50-90 Sharps.

.577/500 NITRO EXPRESS 3 1/8 in.

ALTERNATE NAME(S): 12.9x79.3Rmm
RELATED CALIBER(S): 577/500 No. 2 Nitro Express

CARTRIDGE HISTORY
Year of Introduction: circa late 1800s
Country of Origin: Britain
Designer(s): N/A
Governing Body: none
Present Status: obsolete

CARTRIDGE DESCRIPTION
Bullet Diameter: .508 in.
Bullet Weight(s): 570 gr
Rifling Twist Rate: N/A
Test Barrel Length: N/A
Case Type: rimmed, necked
Case Material: brass
Primer: large rifle

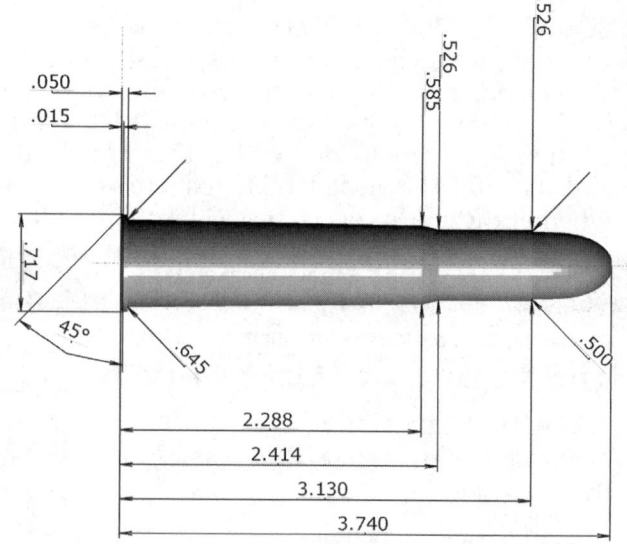

CARTRIDGE BALLISTICS
Max. Average Breech Pressure: N/A
Max. Horizontal Range: 2,550 yds.
Max. Vertical Range: 5,550 ft.

Bullet Weight (gr.)	Bullet Type	Muzzle Velocity (fps)	Muzzle Energy (ft.-lbs.)
570	JSP-FMJ	2,000	5,062 (est.)

CURRENT MANUFACTURER(S)
None

GENERAL COMMENT(S)
Like the 577/500 No. 2 BPE, the 577/500 3 1/8 in. Nitro Express began life as a black powder cartridge. However, the two cartridges are not related, not the same and not interchangeable! The 577/500 3 1/8 in. Nitro Express cartridge gained a loyal following among British expatriates in India, but it was not popular for African hunting.

TECHNICAL COMMENT(S)
Following the transition to smokeless propellants, the 577/500 Nitro Express was upgraded by replacing the 440 grain lead with a 570 grain full metal jacket bullet. This significantly improved ballistic performance (read penetration) on dangerous game and prolonged its useful service life. However, there were better nitro express cartridges available and these eventually captured the market.

.577/500 No. 2 BLACK POWDER EXPRESS

ALTERNATE NAME(S): 12.7mm British No. 2
RELATED CALIBER(S): none

CARTRIDGE HISTORY
Year of Introduction: circa 1878
Country of Origin: Britain
Designer(s): N/A
Governing Body: none
Present Status: obsolete

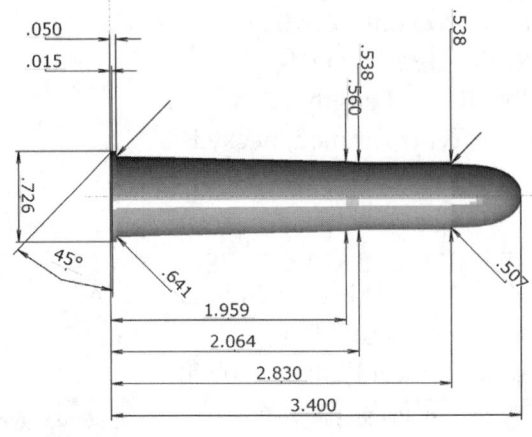

CARTRIDGE DESCRIPTION
Bullet Diameter: .507 in.
Bullet Weight(s): 300-340 gr.
Rifling Twist Rate: N/A
Test Barrel Length: N/A
Case Type: rimmed, necked
Case Material: brass
Primer: large rifle

CARTRIDGE BALLISTICS
Max. Average Breech Pressure: N/A
Max. Horizontal Range: 2,100 yds.
Max. Vertical Range: 4,650 ft.

Bullet Weight (gr.)	Bullet Type	Muzzle Velocity (fps)	Muzzle Energy (ft.-lbs.)
300	L-RN	1,870	2,340
340	L-RN	1,925	2,800

CURRENT MANUFACTURER(S)
None

GENERAL COMMENT(S)
In the late 1800s, black powder was having its last hurrah in the form of large caliber, high volume cartridges capable of holding very heavy charges of propellant. In Britain, such cartridges often were called "Express" cartridges, a moniker adopted by Winchester in the U.S. for some of their own large, black powder cartridges. In the U.S., they were offered by Sharps, Bullard, Ballard, Winchester and Remington for use on buffalo, moose and bear in single-shot rifles. However, the British calibers were used in Africa, India and other far corners of the Empire on heavy (but not dangerous) game. The 577/500 No. 2 Black Powder Express (BPE) is a typical British cartridge of this type.

TECHNICAL COMMENT(S)
Ballistic performance of British BPE cartridges compares favorably with the American Sharps, Ballard and Winchester calibers. The 577/500 No. 2 BPE was loaded with lead, round-nose bullets of 300-340 grains suitable for non-dangerous game. For dangerous game, British sportsmen upped caliber to one of the Nitro Express cartridges. American sportsmen did not need such performance. A noteworthy feature of the 577/500 No. 2

BPE cartridge is the massive, .726 inch diameter rim which is bested only by the .577/500 NE, .600 NE, and .700 NE cartridges.

.70-140 WINCHESTER

ALTERNATE NAME(S): .70-140-600 Winchester
RELATED CALIBER(S): 12-gauge 2 3/4 inch shotshell

CARTRIDGE HISTORY
Year of Introduction: 1888
Country of Origin: U.S.
Designer(s): Winchester
Governing Body: none
Present Status: obsolete

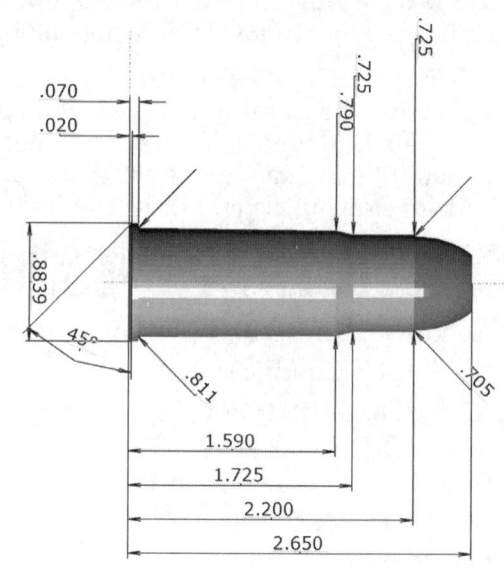

CARTRIDGE DESCRIPTION
Bullet Diameter: .705 in.
Bullet Weight(s): 600 gr.
Rifling Twist Rate: N/A
Test Barrel Length: N/A
Case Type: rimmed, necked
Case Material: brass
Primer: large rifle

CARTRIDGE BALLISTICS
Max. Average Breech Pressure: N/A
Max. Horizontal Range: 1,300 yds.
Max. Vertical Range: 2,800 ft.

Bullet Weight (gr.)	Bullet Type	Muzzle Velocity (fps)	Muzzle Energy (ft.-lbs.)
600	L-FN	1,425	2,705 (est.)

CURRENT MANUFACTURER(S)
None

GENERAL COMMENT(S)
The .70-140 Winchester cartridge has been and continues to be an enigma. It appeared on a Winchester cartridge display board issued circa 1888, however no ballistics or further information are available. Some historians have asserted this cartridge may have been an advertising novelty, however this is unlikely as Winchester did not make a practice of doing such a thing with their other cartridge boards. Other researchers have asserted that it was designed for a Winchester Model 1887 shotgun with a rifled barrel that never got past the experimental stage. This seems more likely as Winchester would not have included this cartridge on their display board unless they had serious plans to introduce it. This cartridge is historically significant as it was the largest caliber sporting rifle cartridge of the black powder era.

TECHNICAL COMMENT(S)
Technically, the .70-140 Winchester is a brass 12-gauge 2 3/4 inch shotshell, shortened .12 inches with a shallow neck. However, it is not a slug load as the bullet was intended to be spin-stabilized by rifling in the barrel. The flat-nose, lead bullet is in keeping with the practice of that era. Unfortunately, due to its historic value and rarity, no example has been disassembled for component measurement. Consequently, the actual weight of the bullet can only be estimated with 600 to 900 grains being quoted. Given the practices of that era and comparing this cartridge with the bullet weights of other, large-caliber Winchester cartridges, 600 grains seems to be the most likely weight. The exact amount of black powder propellant Winchester proposed to load in this cartridge case is not known. Almost certainly, the large case would hold 150 grains of black powder as no wad column was needed. However, it is more likely that Winchester would take a conservative approach and use a lighter powder charge of, say, 140 grains. As a conservative estimate, a 140 grain charge might offer a muzzle velocity of approximately 1,425 fps. as the proposed firearm was a shotgun. Here, it must be noted that the .70-140-600 Winchester rifle cartridge is not the same as a shotgun slug which is fired from a smoothbore barrel. Nor is it the same as a "Paradox" shotshell slug using a wad column and designed to be fired from a partially rifled barrel.

CHAPTER 67 : PROPRIETARY CARTRIDGES - CURRENT

CHAPTER 67

For Cartridge Index see Chapter 101. All drawing dimensions are approximate.

A proprietary cartridge may be defined as a unique caliber (or calibers) made under contract by an ammunition manufacturer exclusively for the owner of a private label brand and distributed by the same. Here it is important to draw a distinction between a proprietary cartridge and a private label cartridge. In both instances, the owner of the private label is a sales organization, not an ammunition manufacturer. A proprietary cartridge combines both unique caliber and private label brand name, while a private label cartridge is in a standard, non-unique caliber.

A proprietary caliber cartridge carries its private label brand name as part of its nomenclatural designation, for example the .460 Weatherby Magnum. For non-proprietary cartridges, the cartridge nomenclature does not include the private label name, for example ammunition such as .45 Colt or .300 Savage manufactured by Federal for the private label.

Cartridges carrying in their nomenclature the brand name of a major ammunition or firearms manufacturer are not considered proprietary calibers. The reason for this is that other ammunition manufacturers who may join in the production of popular calibers do not want the nomenclature and the brand linked or restricted, for example .243 Winchester ammunition as made by Remington, Federal, or even Winchester itself.

For a proprietary caliber cartridge to become a commercial success and retain its market share, its private label brand name must be jealously protected and its distribution closely controlled by the brand owner as these are the only defenses against encroachments by other ammunition makers. Non-proprietary ammunition brands are distributed through general unrestricted channels of distribution.

A proprietary caliber can become a victim of its own success. When this happens, a proprietary cartridge can lose its private label protection and become a standard caliber. There is nothing to prevent this. For example, this is precisely what happened to the .300 Weatherby Magnum and the .375 Holland & Holland Magnum – their popularity grew to the point that their sales volume attracted the attention of major ammunition manufacturers who then offered cartridges in this caliber under their own brand name. For most proprietary caliber cartridges, sales volume remains "well below the radar" of the major manufacturers, thus insulating them from capture.

Exactly what does a proprietary caliber cartridge offer? In most cases, higher muzzle velocity, greater striking energy, and flatter trajectory than normal calibers, which the user perceives as ballistically advantageous. For example, it was on precisely such grounds that Roy Weatherby earned the sobriquet "The high priest of high velocity." Case shape and size, bullet construction or weight, and perceived applicability are lesser factors.

DAKOTA CALIBERS

ALTERNATE NAME(S): none
RELATED CALIBER(S): .404 Jeffery, .416 Rigby (.450 Dakota only)

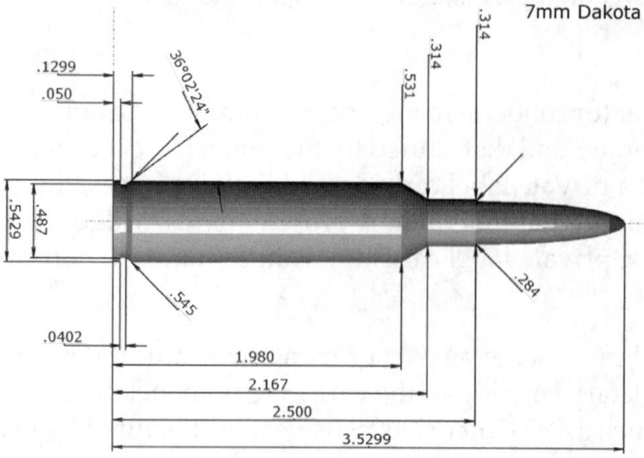

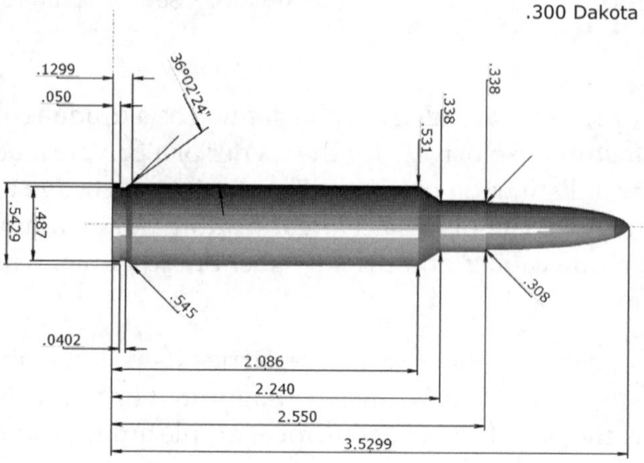

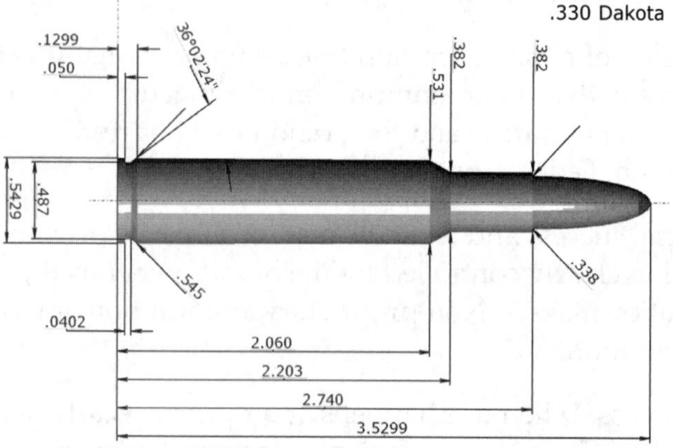

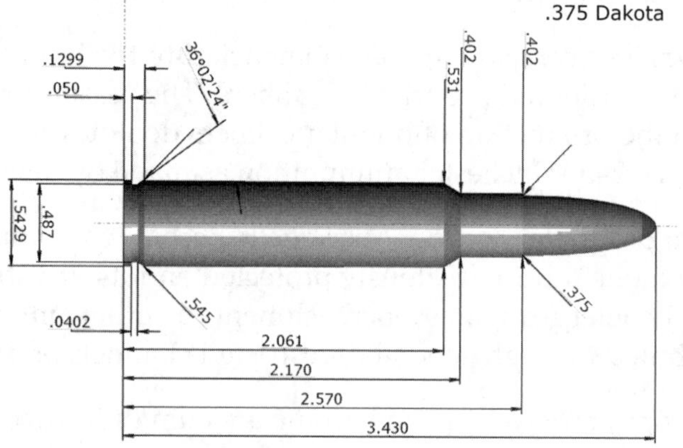

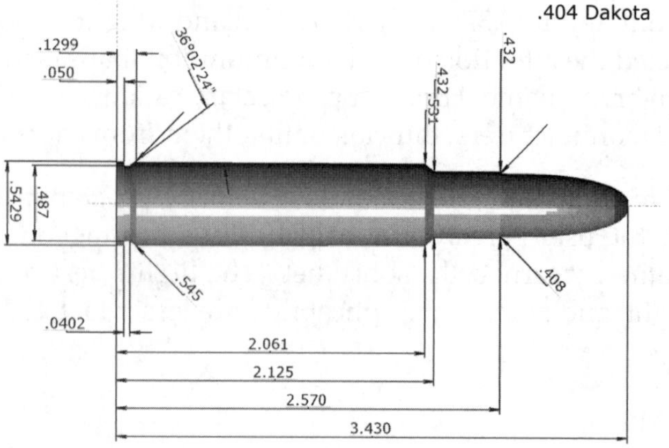

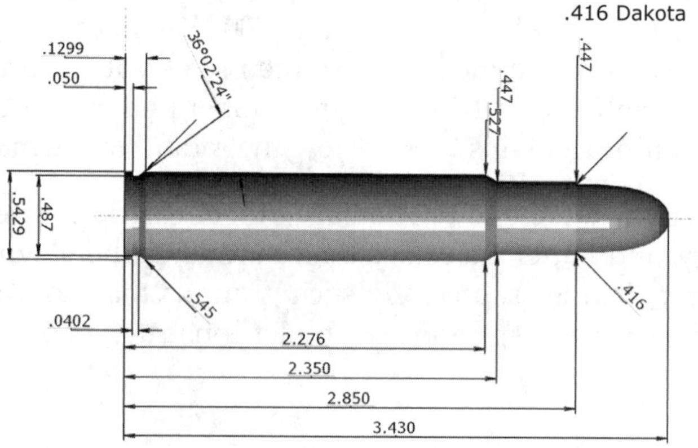

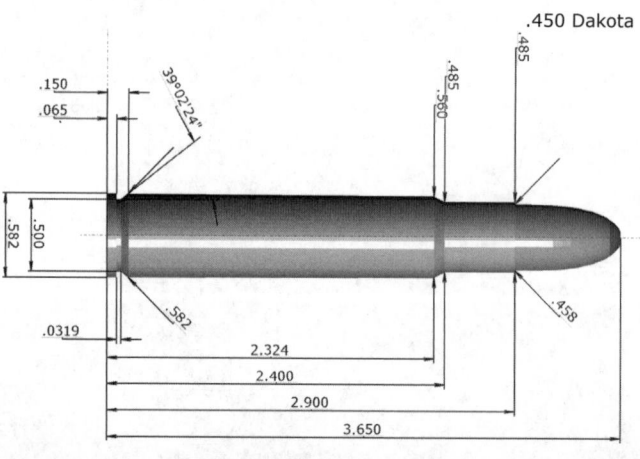

CARTRIDGE HISTORY

Year of Introduction: circa mid-1980s
Country of Origin: U.S.
Designer(s): Don Allen
Governing Body: none
Present Status: active

CARTRIDGE DESCRIPTION

Test Barrel Length: 26 in.
Case Type: rimless, necked
Case Material: brass
Primer Size: large rifle

CARTRIDGE BALLISTICS
Max. Average Breech Pressure: N/A

Caliber	Bullet Diameter (in.)	Bullet Weight (gr.)	Rifling Twist 1 turn in (in.)	Max Horizontal Range (yd.)	Max Veritical Range (ft.)	Muzzle Velocity (fps)	Muzzle Energy (ft.-lbs.)
7 MM Dakota	0.284	140	10	5,500	10,000	3,400	3,593
.300 Dakota	0.308	150	10	5,800	11,500	3,300	3,626
.330 Dakota	0.338	250	10	5,200	11,700	2,900	4,668
.375 Dakota	0.375	270	10	4,400	8,800	2,800	4,680
.404 Dakota	0.408	400	10	2,500	5,000	2,400	5,115
.416 Dakota	0.416	400	10	2,500	5,100	2,450	5,330
.450 Dakota	0.458	500	10	4,500	8,800	2,450	6,663

CURRENT MANUFACTURER(S)
Dakota Arms, currently owned by Remington

GENERAL COMMENT(S)
Dakota Arms was the brainchild of Don Allen who saw the need for a line of very high quality big game rifles chambered for modern, high performance cartridges which would outperform standard sporting calibers. Allen based all of his Dakota cartridges (except for the .450 Dakota) on the .404 Jeffery cartridge as its rimless, short case made it ideal for bolt-action rifles. Hunters reported excellent results with Dakota cartridges.

TECHNICAL COMMENT(S)
Dakota cartridges do not have a belt which makes it easier to control their headspace. An interesting design point on Dakota calibers is the shoulder length decreases and the shoulder angle increases as the caliber goes up. This is necessary to provide maximum case volume. It indicates the cartridge designer's dilemma as to how to maintain or increase case volume for a given case length.

HOLLAND & HOLLAND CALIBERS

ALTERNATE NAME(S): H&H Magnum, H&H Mag., H&H Rimless Nitro
RELATED CALIBER(S): all belted magnum cartridges

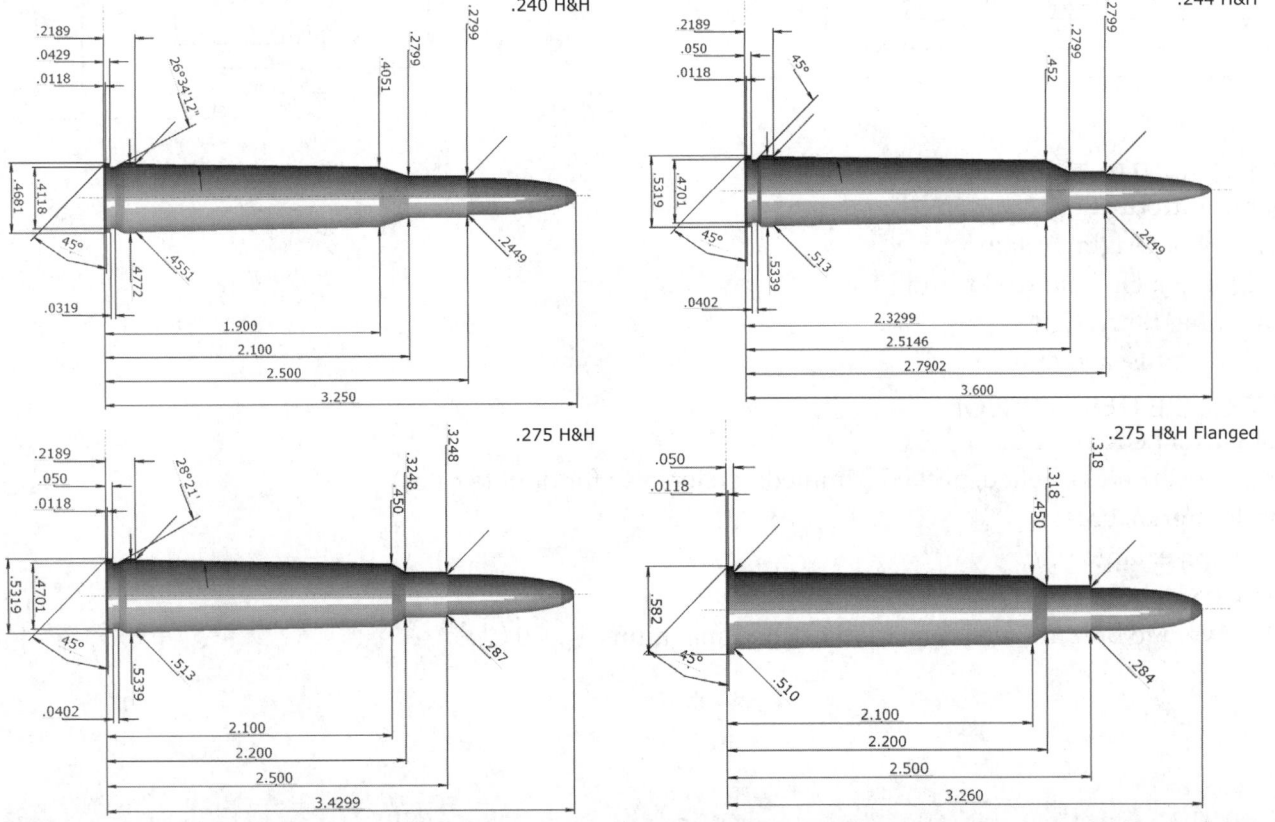

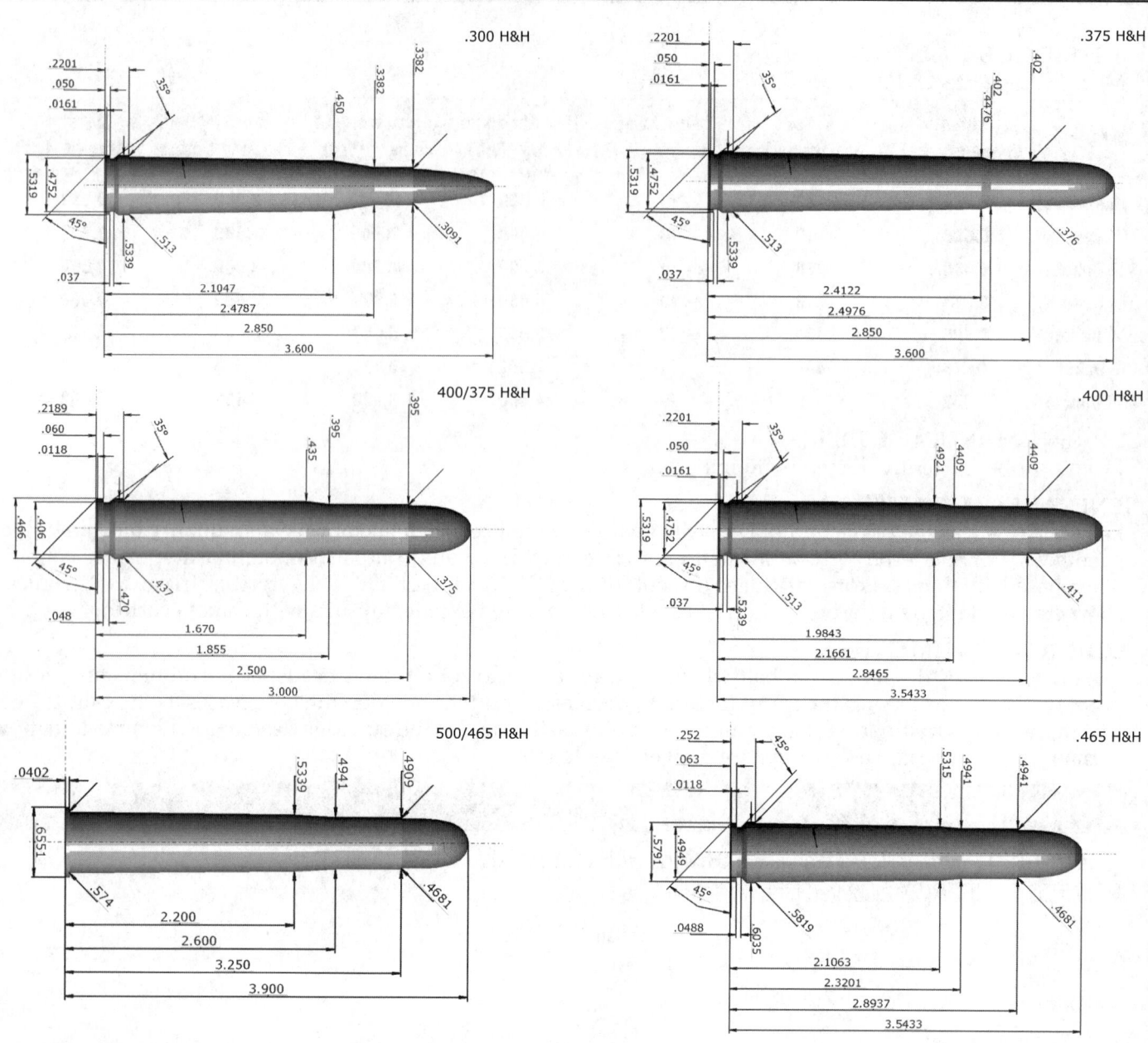

CARTRIDGE HISTORY
Year of Introduction: N/A
Country of Origin: Britain
Designer(s): Holland & Holland
Governing Body: CIP
Present Status: active

CARTRIDGE DESCRIPTION
Test Barrel Length: 24 in.
Case Type: rimless, belted, necked (rimmed version also for double rifles)
Case Material: brass
Primer Size: large rifle

CARTRIDGE BALLISTICS
Max. Average Breech Pressure: various, belted magnums 54,000 CUP.

Caliber	Bullet Diameter (in.)	Bullet Weight (gr.)	Rifling Twist 1 turn in (in.)	Max Horizontal Range (yd.)	Max Veritical Range (ft.)	Muzzle Velocity (fps)	Muzzle Energy (ft.-lbs.)
.240 H&H							
Magnum (Apex)	0.245	100	8	4,000	9,000	2,900	1,865
.244 H&H Magnum	0.245	100	8	4,900	11,000	3,500	2,720
.275 H&H Magnum	0.284	140	10	4,200	9,500	2,650	2,184
.300 H&H Magnum	0.308	180	10	5,200	11,800	2,750	3,020
.375 H&H Magnum	0.375	270	12	4,400	9,600	2,650	4,160
400/375 H&H							
Belted Nitro	0.375	270	12	4,000	9,200	2,175	2,840
.400 H&H Magnum	0.416	400	14	3,500	5,000	2,400	5,115
500/465 H&H							
Nitro Express	0.466	480	28	3,000	4,000	2,150	4,930
.465 H&H Magnum	0.465	480	N/A	4,400	8,700	2,400	6,138

CURRENT MANUFACTURER(S)

Federal, Remington, Winchester (.300 H&H and .375 H&H only), Kynoch, Holland & Holland

GENERAL COMMENT(S)

Although well known for their superior quality rifles, for over a century Holland & Holland has developed a steady stream of innovative sporting rifle cartridges. Their efforts include what many experienced hunters consider the best large caliber of all time, the .375 H&H Magnum. And, it was Holland & Holland who introduced the first belted cartridge case (the .400/375 H&H) as well as the classic .300 H&H Magnum, the father of all modern .300 magnum cartridges. Lately, H&H has begun developing a new series of modern cartridges for big game hunting.

TECHNICAL COMMENT(S)

Some cartridge designs prove to be so well-balanced that they become classics. All Holland & Holland cartridges are noted for their accuracy, ballistic performance, low recoil and moderate chamber pressures. Arguably, the belt on the case head is technically unnecessary. However, the H&H belt has become a magnum icon copied many times over, regardless of need. A magnum rifle cartridge must have a belt, if only to satisfy the traditionalists.

LAPUA CALIBERS

ALTERNATE NAME(S): Lapua Mag., Lapua Magnum
RELATED CALIBER(S): .416 Rigby, 223 Rem.

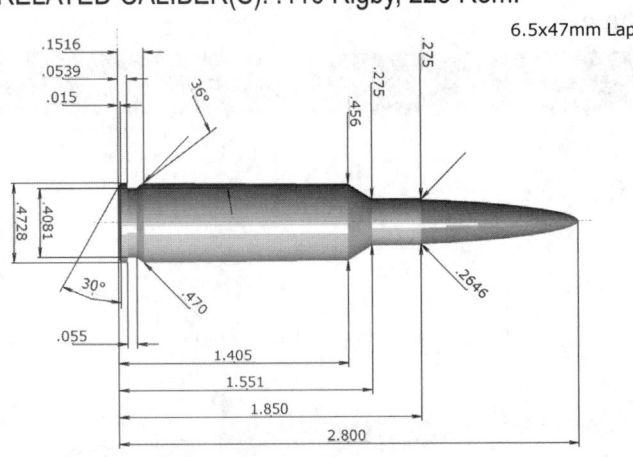

6.5x47mm Lapua

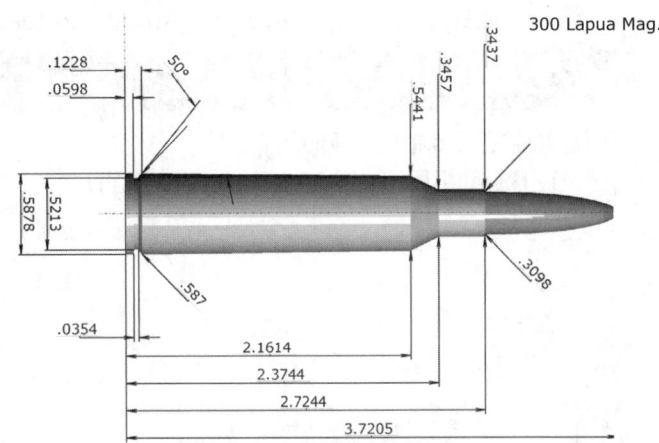

300 Lapua Mag.

CARTRIDGE HISTORY

Year of Introduction:

Country of Origin: Finland

Designer(s): Lapua

Governing Body: CIP

Present Status: N/A

CARTRIDGE DESCRIPTION
Bullet Diameter: .264, .308, .338 in.
Bullet Weight(s): 154-216 gr.
Rifling Twist Rate: 1 turn in 9.45 in.
Test Barrel Length: 27 in.
Case Type: rimless, necked
Case Material: brass
Primer: large rifle

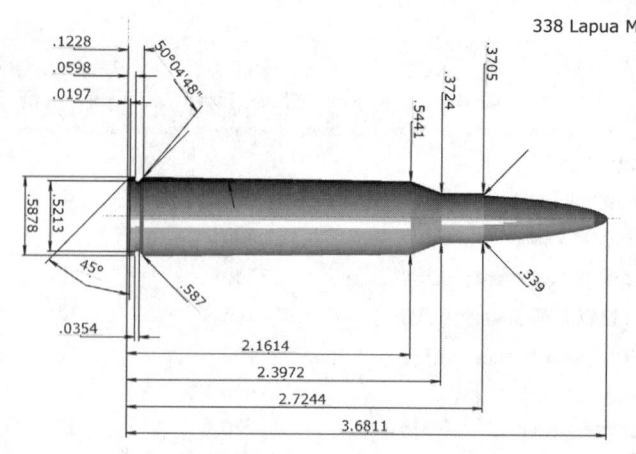

338 Lapua Mag

CARTRIDGE BALLISTICS
Max. Average Breech Pressure: 68,168 psi.
Max. Horizontal Range: 5,950 yds.
Max. Vertical Range: 12,700 ft.

Bullet Weight (gr.)		Bullet Type	Muzzle Velocity (fps)	Muzzle Energy (ft.-lbs.)
6.5x47 Lapua	108	JSP	2,925	2,050
	139	JSP	2,665	2,191
300 Lapua Mag.	154	JSP	3,600	4,445
	185	JSP	3,300	4,525
338 IAPUA mAG.	250	JSP	2,970	4,895
	300	JSP	2,800	5,224

CURRENT MANUFACTURER(S)
None

GENERAL COMMENT(S)
In recent years, Lapua has developed several new cartridges for hunting. Those include the 6.5x47mm, .300 Lapua Magnum, and .338 Lapua Magnum. The .300 Lapua Magnum is a specialized, long range target cartridge developed by Lapua in 1989 and registered with CIP. However, no production was undertaken and the cartridge was never listed in the Lapua product catalog. Its future remains uncertain, but production is now very unlikely. On the other hand, the .338 Lapua Magnum has been adopted by many law enforcement agencies and military units for sniper/counter-sniper applications.

TECHNICAL COMMENT(S)
Although magnums, the Lapua cartridges are not belted and no rimmed versions have been developed. Lapua magnum cartridges have a very large internal volume to allow heavy powder charges sufficient to drive .308 and .338 bullets at exceptionally high muzzle velocities. Unlike its big brothers, the 6.5x47mm is an efficient, small capacity cartridge for hunting small and medium game.

LAZZERONI CALIBERS

ALTERNATE NAME(S): None
RELATED CALIBER(S): .404 Jeffery, .416 Rigby

6.17 Spitfire

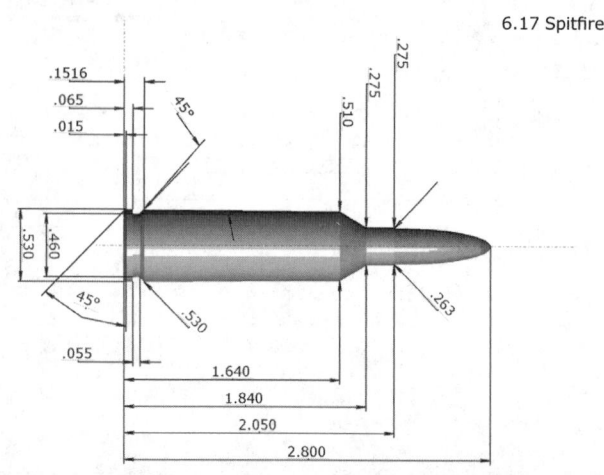

6.17 Flash

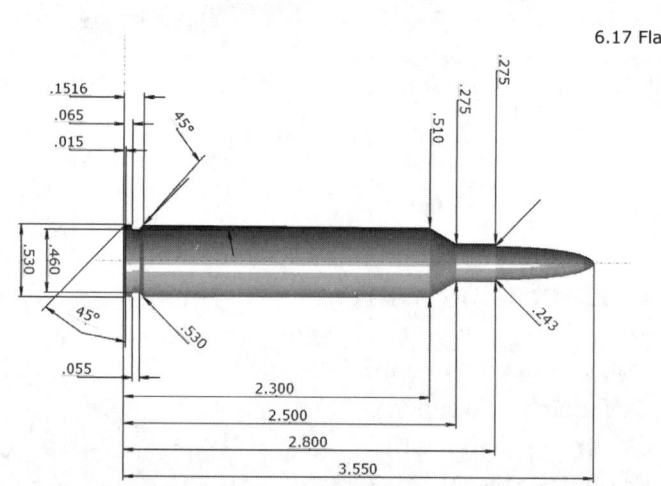

6.53 Scramjet

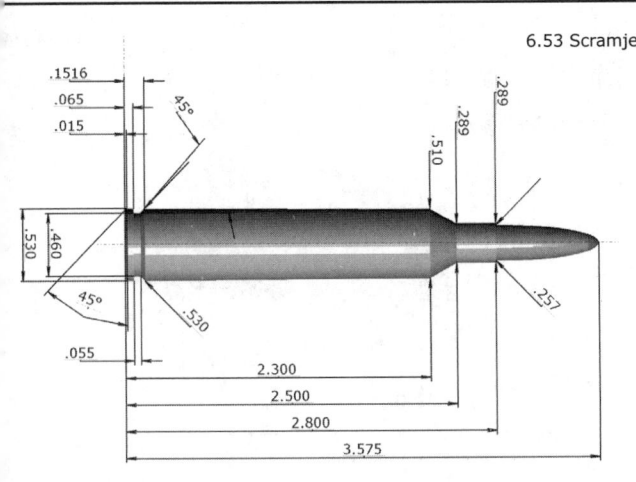

6.71 Phantom

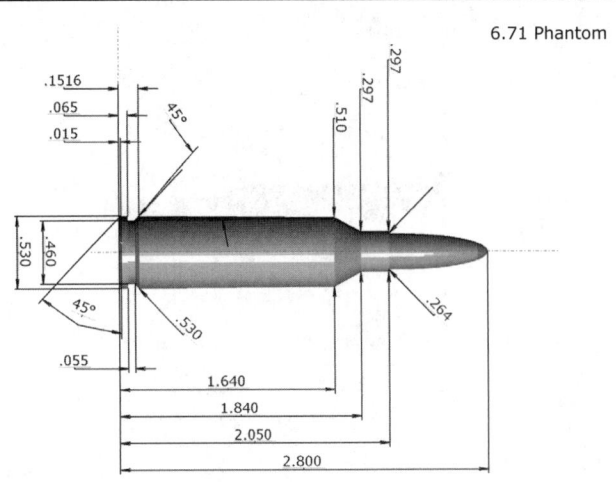

6.71 Blackbird

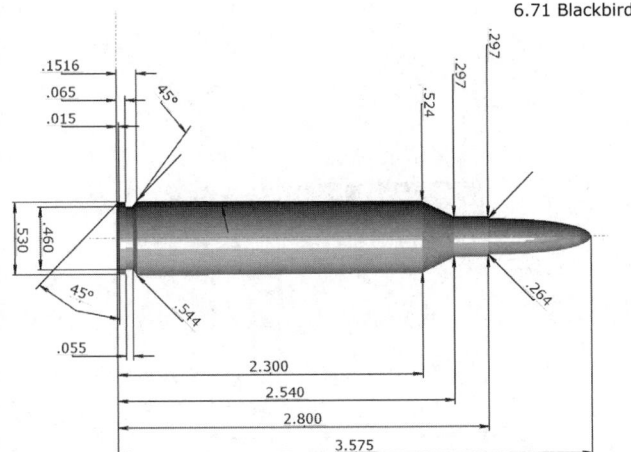

7.21 Tomahawk

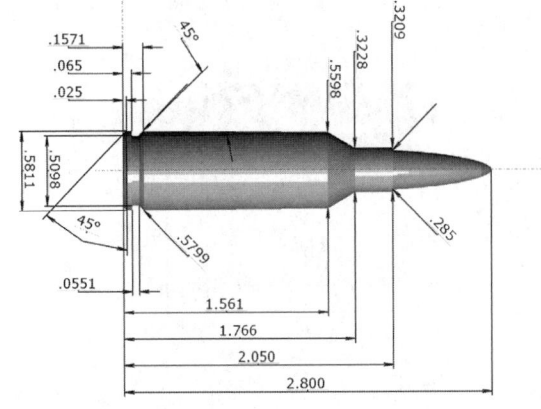

7.21 Firehawk

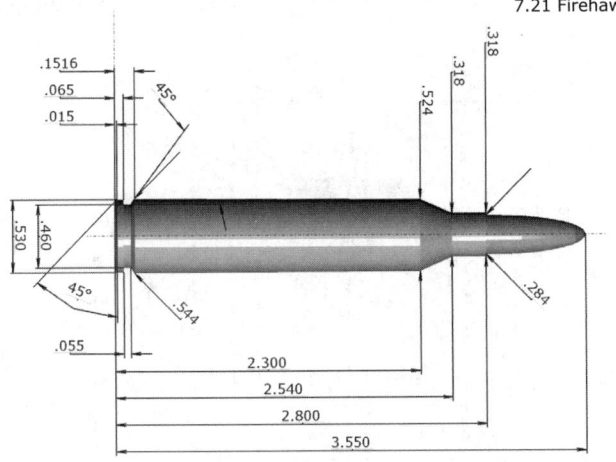

7.21 Firebird

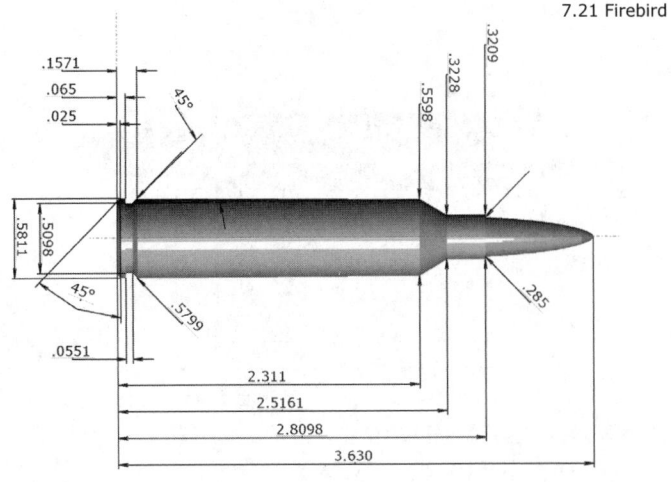

7.82 Warbird

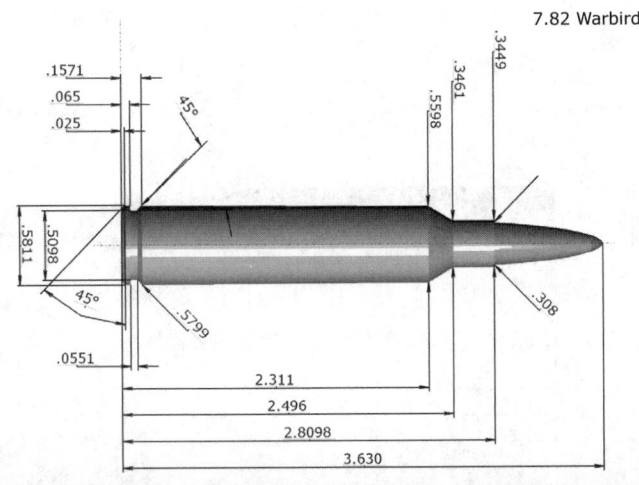

7.82 Patriot

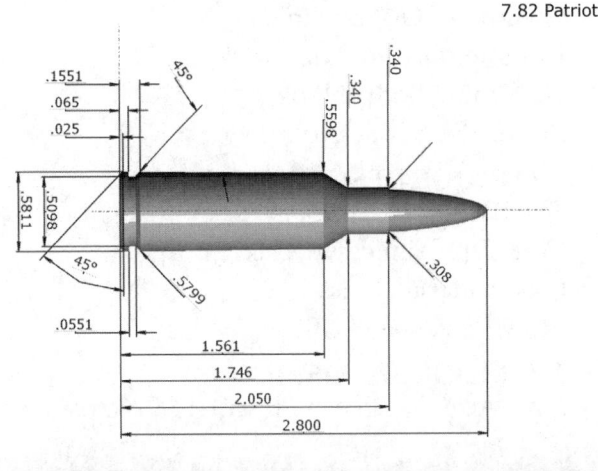

8.59 Galaxy

8.59 Titan

9.09 Eagle

9.53 Hellcat

9.53 Saturm

10.57 Maverick

10.57 Meteor

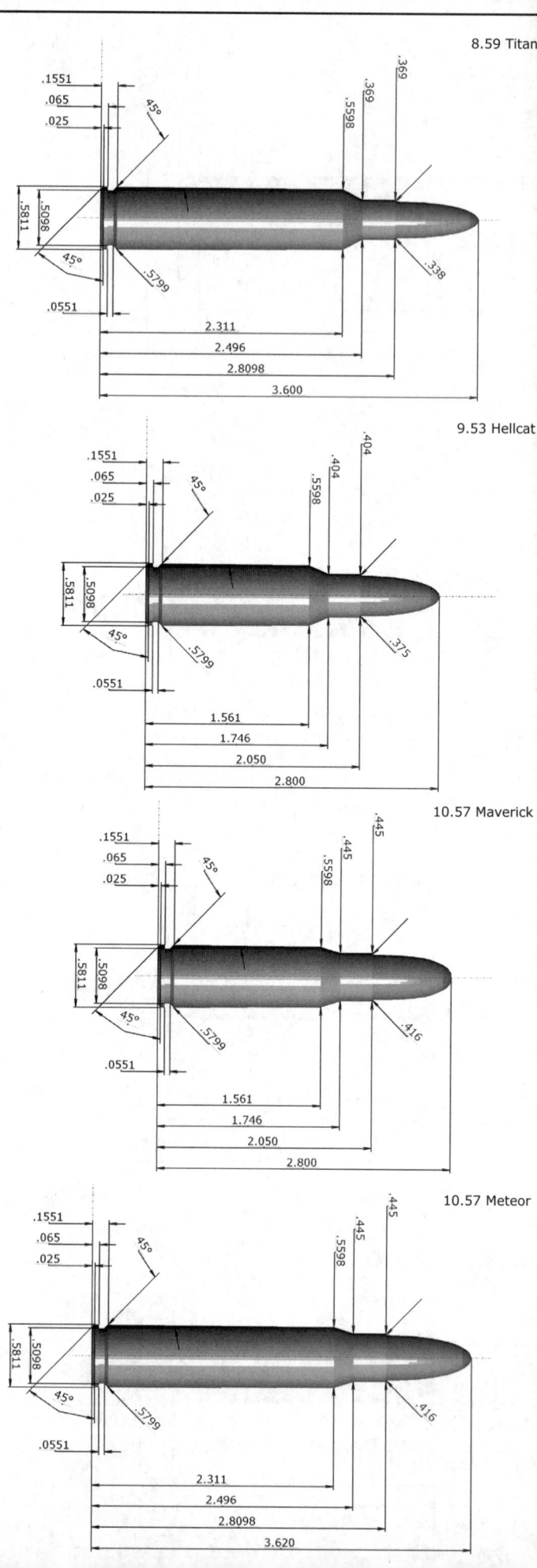

CARTRIDGE HISTORY

Year of Introduction: N/A

Country of Origin: Finland

Designer(s): John Lazzeroni

Governing Body: None

Present Status: active

CARTRIDGE DESCRIPTION

Test Barrel Length: 24 in.

Case Type: rimless, necked

Case Material: brass

Primer Size: large rifle

CARTRIDGE BALLISTICS

Max. Average Breech Pressure: 66,700 psi.

Caliber	Bullet Diameter (in.)	Bullet Weight (gr.)	Rifling Twist 1 turn in (in.)	Max Horizontal Range (yd.)	Max Veritical Range (ft.)	Muzzle Velocity (fps)	Muzzle Energy (ft.-lbs.)
6.17 Spitfire	0.243	100	10	4,400	8,500	3,350	2,493
6.17 Flash	0.243	100	10	5,700	11,000	3,700	3,041
6.53 Scramjet	0.257	100	12	5,400	10,700	3,550	3,219
6.71 Phantom	0.264	140	10	5,000	10,000	3,250	2,815
6.71 Blackbird	0.264	140	10	5,600	11,000	3,750	3,123
7.21 Tomahawk	0.284	140	12	5,400	10,500	3,650	4,435
7.21 Firehawk	0.284	160	10	5,900	11,100	3,200	3,412
7.21 Firebird	0.284	160	12	5,000	10,000	3,650	4,435
7.82 Warbird	0.308	150	12	5,000	10,000	3,775	4,747
7.82 Patriot	0.308	150	12	4,800	9,600	3,550	5,038
8.59 Galaxy	0.338	250	12	4,400	8,700	3,300	3,628
8.59 Titan	0.338	250	14	5,300	11,000	2,750	4,199
9.09 Eagle	0.358	250	12	3,900	8,700	3,150	5,510
9.53 Hellcat	0.375	300	10	4,100	9,200	2,850	4,510
9.53 Saturn	0.375	300	14	5,000	9,600	2,600	4,500
10.57 Maverick	0.416	400	14	2,500	5,000	3,010	6,035
10.57 Meteor	0.416	400	14	3,000	6,000	2,400	5,117

CURRENT MANUFACTURER(S)
Lazzeroni

GENERAL COMMENT(S)
Lazzeroni cartridges are very much a work in progress. As older cartridges are dropped, new ones are introduced in their place. Many of the Lazzeroni cartridges listed above are now obsolete. However, obsolete calibers are retained in the Lazzeroni cartridge line although new rifles are no longer offered. Here is an example of one man's vision for a line of cartridges that offer even more ballistic performance than most Weatherby calibers. However, Lazzeroni would certainly agree that the financial cost of introducing such a product line into the modern market place is enormous.

TECHNICAL COMMENT(S)
Lazzeroni caliber nomenclature is unique, but somewhat confusing. The three numbers describing each caliber are the actual bullet diameter expressed in millimeters followed by the somewhat whimsical surnames. Lazzeroni cartridges are magnums, but none are labeled as such. All Lazzeroni cartridges are based on one of three different head diameters and most are (were) offered in two case lengths: 2.05 inches and 2.80 inches. Another interesting point in opposites is that, unlike Weatherby calibers, Lazzeroni cartridges are all magnums, but do not have belts.

NORMA CALIBERS

ALTERNATE NAME(S): 6mm Norma BR, 6.5-284 Norma, .308 Norma Mag., .358 Norma Mag.
RELATED CALIBER(S): 6mm Rem. BR, .284 Win., .300 H&H Mag.

6mm

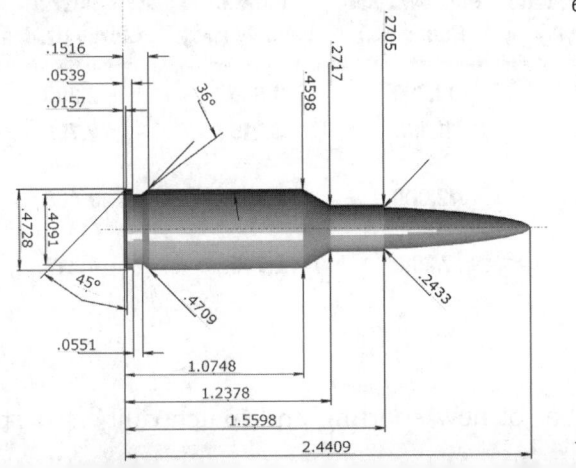

6.5-284

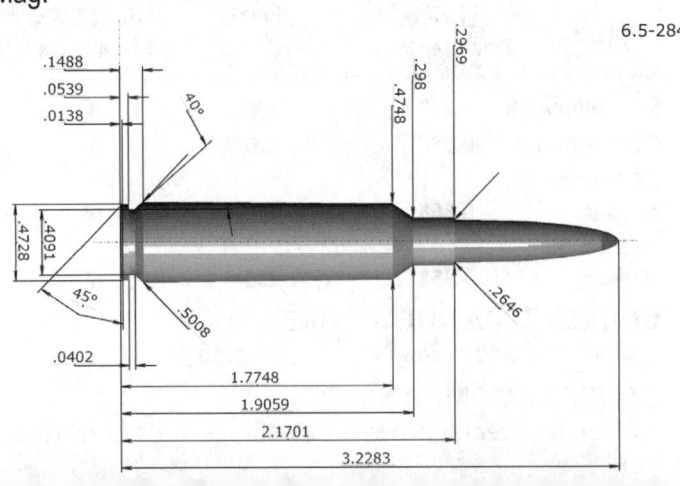

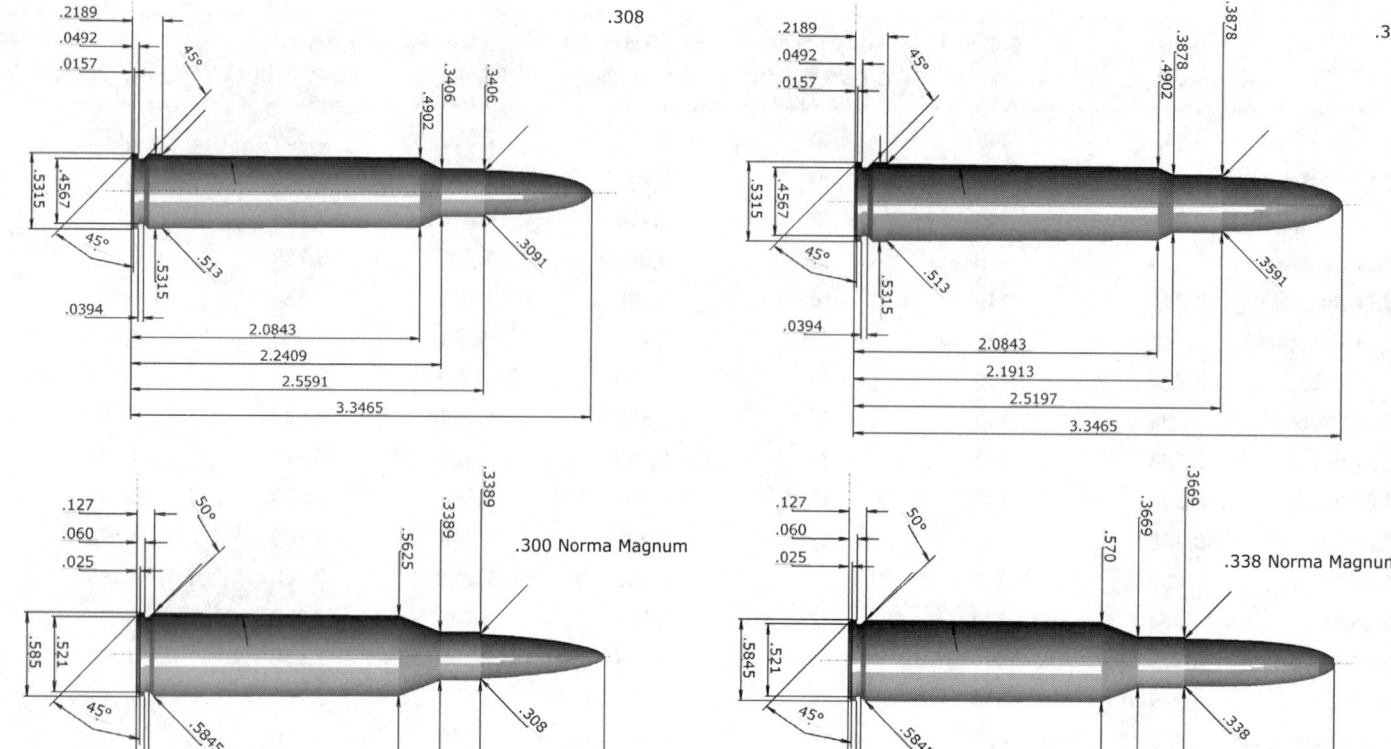

CARTRIDGE HISTORY

Year of Introduction: 1959 (.358 Norma Mag.), 1960 (.308 Norma Mag.), 1996 (6mm Norma BR), 2002 (6.5-284 Norma)
Country of Origin: Sweden
Designer(s): Nils Kvale, others
Governing Body: CIP
Present Status: active

CARTRIDGE DESCRIPTION

Test Barrel Length: 24 in.
Case Type: rimless, necked – 6mm Norma BR
rimless, rebated, necked – 6.5-284 Norma
rimless, belted, necked – Norma Magnums
Case Material: brass
Primer Size: large rifle (6mm Norma BR – small rifle)

CARTRIDGE BALLISTICS

Max. Average Breech Pressure: 63,800 psi.

Caliber	Bullet Diameter (in.)	Bullet Weight (gr.)	Rifling Twist 1 turn in (in.)	Max Horizontal Range (yd.)	Max Veritical Range (ft.)	Muzzle Velocity (fps)	Muzzle Energy (ft.-lbs.)
6mm Norma BR	0.243	105	8	4,800	10,700	3,045	2,203
6.5-284 Norma	0.264	120	8	5,000	11,100	3,215	2,755
.308 Norma Magnum	0.308	180	10	5,300	12,000	2,955	3,486
.358 Norma Magnum	0.358	250	12	3,800	7,200	2,755	4,217

CURRENT MANUFACTURER(S)

Black Hills (6.5-284 Norma), Norma

GENERAL COMMENT(S)

Over the years, Norma has successfully introduced a number of new sporting and match calibers despite the fact that they do not manufacture firearms. Additional new calibers can be expected in the future. Norma calibers are aimed primarily at the U.S. market.

TECHNICAL COMMENT(S)

The Norma Magnum calibers were designed to fit in standard length (eg. .30-'06 Spr.) rifle actions. In the 40 years since its introduction, the .308 Norma Mag. has become somewhat dated as numerous new .300 magnum cartridges have been introduced. No manufacturer is chambering new rifles in this caliber. While the .358 Norma Mag. has sufficient ballistic performance for many types of African game, American hunters have not taken strongly to .358 caliber cartridges.

WEATHERBY CALIBERS

ALTERNATE NAME(S): Wby. Magnum, Wby. Mag.
RELATED CALIBER(S): .300 H&H Magnum, .416 Rigby

CARTRIDGE HISTORY

Year of Introduction: N/A
Country of Origin: U.S.
Designer(s): Roy Weatherby
Governing Body: CIP
Present Status: active

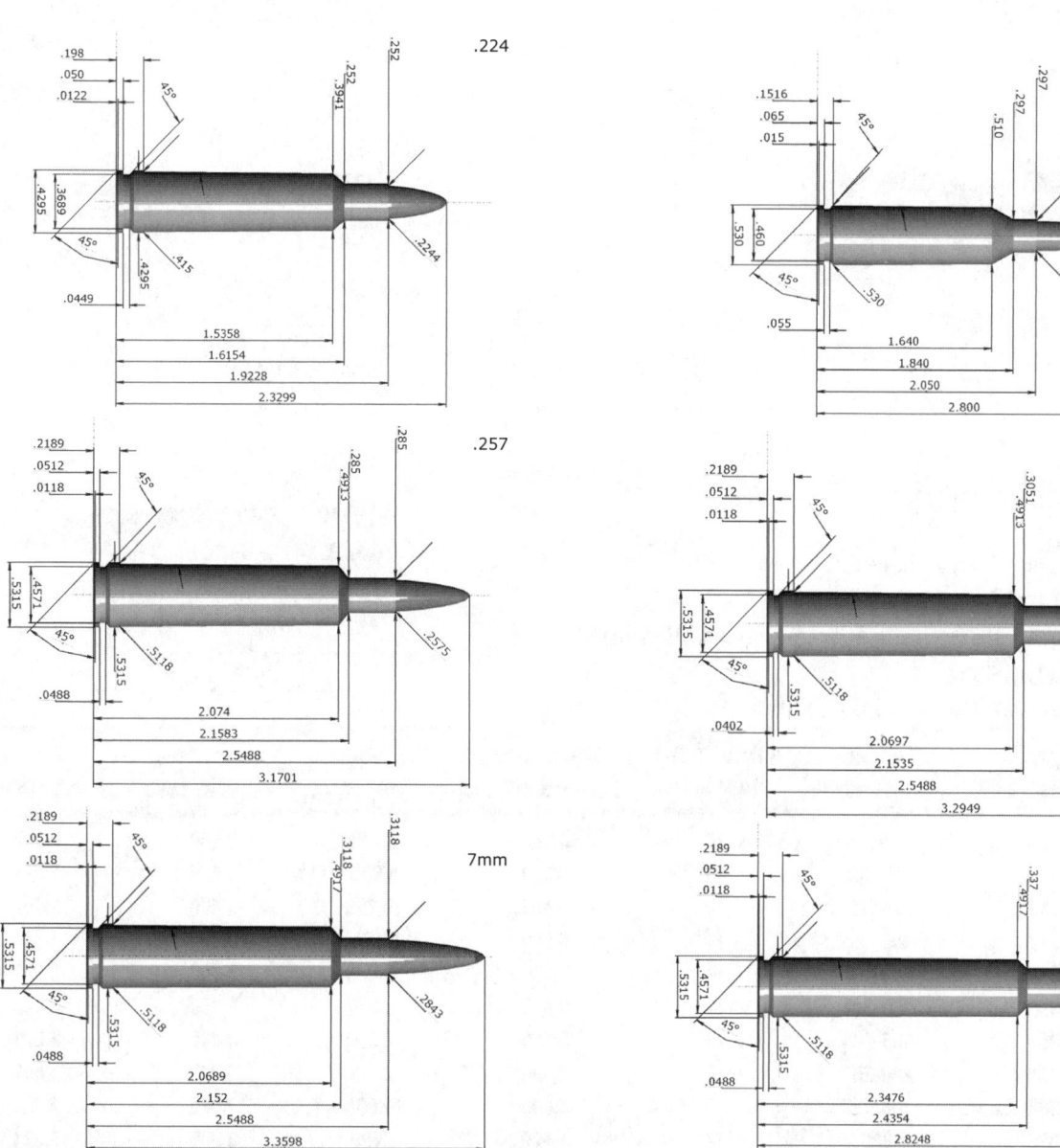

.30-378

.340

.338-378

.375

.375

.416

.460

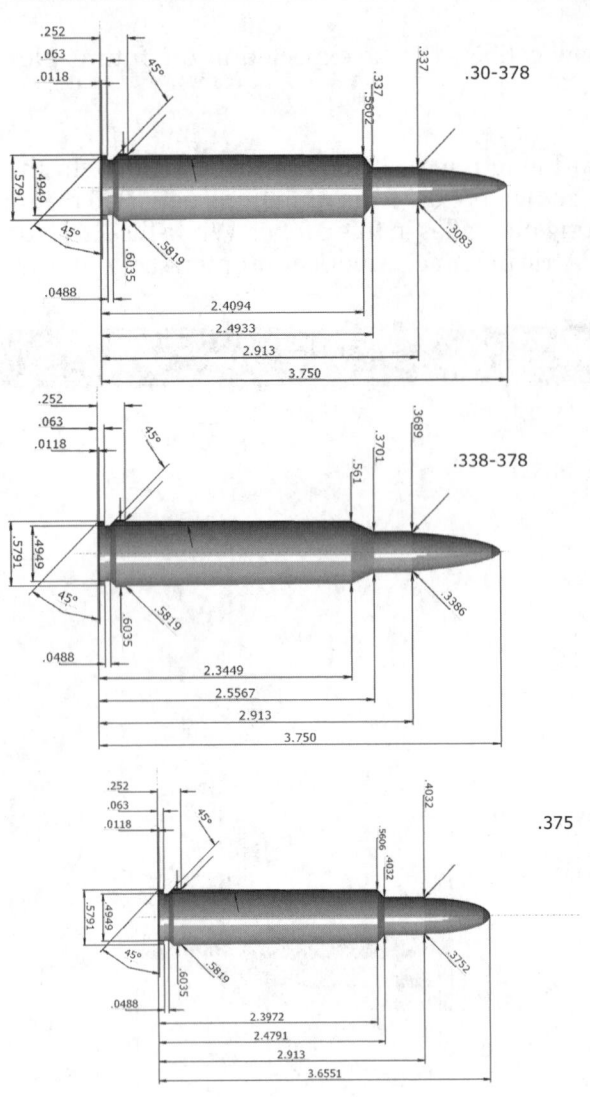

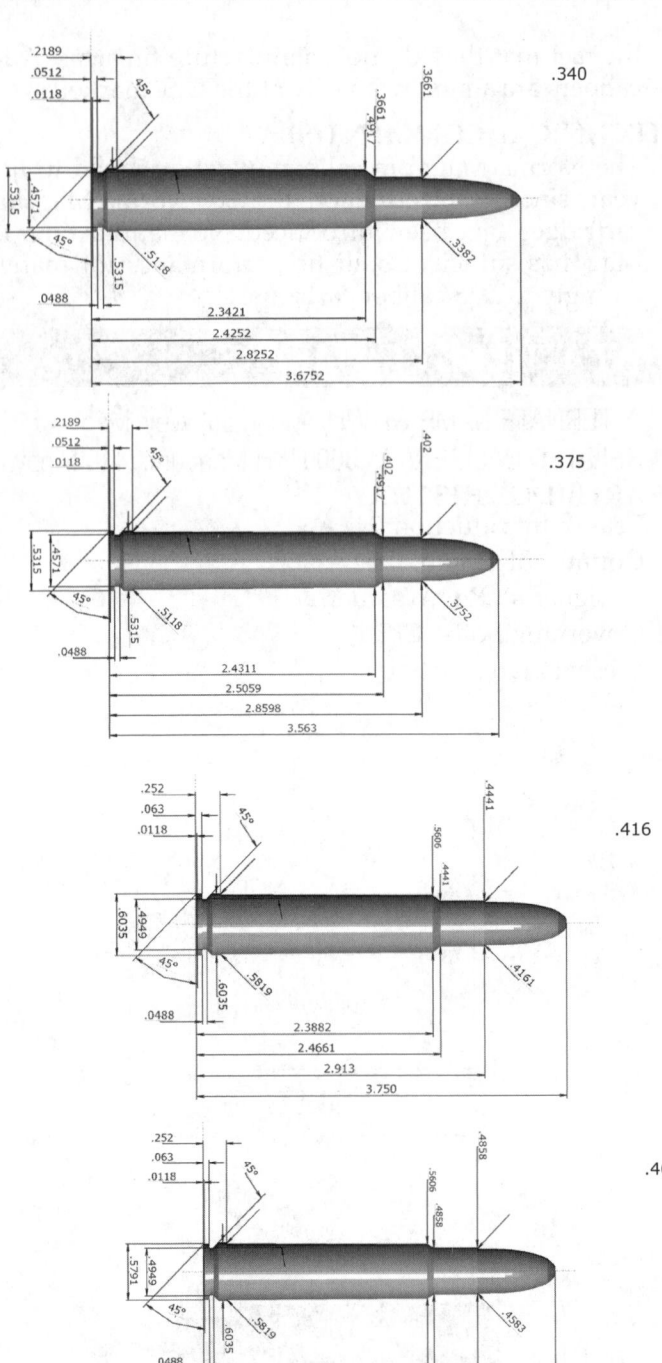

CARTRIDGE DESCRIPTION

Test Barrel Length: 26 in.
Case Type: rimless, belted, necked
Case Material: brass
Primer Size: large rifle (ex. .224 Wby. Mag. small rifle)

CARTRIDGE BALLISTICS

Max. Average Breech Pressure: 65,000 psi.

Caliber	Bullet Diameter (in.)	Bullet Weight (gr.)	Rifling Twist 1 turn in (in.)	Max Horizontal Range (yd.)	Max Veritical Range (ft.)	Muzzle Velocity (fps)	Muzzle Energy (ft.-lbs.)
.224 Wby. Magnum	0.224	55	14	3,500	7,900	3,650	1,627
.240 Wby. Magnum	0.243	87-100	10	4,600	8,800	3,405	2,576
.257 Wby. Magnum	0.257	87-120	10	5,400	10,700	3,400	2,952
.270 Wby. Magnum	0.277	100-150	10	5,000	9,900	3,300	3,385
7 mm Wby. Magnum	0.284	139-175	10	5,000	10,000	3,300	3,627
.300 Wby. Magnum	0.308	150-220	10	5,800	11,500	3,250	4,223
.30-378 Wby.	0.308	165-200	10	6,100	12,000	3,420	4,676
.340 Wby. Magnum	0.338	200-250	10	4,400	8,700	3,220	4,607
.338-378 Wby.	0.338	200-250	10	5,600	10,000	3,060	5,197
.375 Wby. Magnum	0.375	300	12	4,400	8,700	2,800	5,224

Caliber	Bullet Diameter (in.)	Bullet Weight (gr.)	Rifling Twist 1 turn in (in.)	Max Horizontal Range (yd.)	Max Veritical Range (ft.)	Muzzle Velocity (fps)	Muzzle Energy (ft.-lbs.)
.378 Wby. Magnum	0.375	270-300	12	4,500	8,800	2,925	5,699
.416 Wby. Magnum	0.416	350-400	14	3,000	5,800	2,700	6,474
.460 Wby. Magnum	0.458	450-500	16	4,700	9,300	2,600	7,504

CURRENT MANUFACTURER(S)

Selected calibers only – Federal, Remington, Winchester. All calibers – Norma

GENERAL COMMENT(S)

When Roy Weatherby began experimenting with different cartridges in the mid-1940s, he noticed that bullets driven at high velocities killed game more reliably than bullets at low velocity. Of such are empires made. Weatherby quickly became known as the "high priest of high velocity", and he built his company on this premise. Today, there are 13 different Weatherby rifle cartridges in the Weatherby product line, all of them magnums. They cover the field from varmint cartridges with the .224 Wby. Mag. to large, dangerous game with the .460 Wby. Mag. The most popular are the .300 Wby. Mag., 7 mm Wby. Mag. and .270 Wby. Mag. Weatherby ammunition is made to their specifications by Norma in Sweden. However, the growing popularity of the three most popular Weatherby calibers mentioned above has made Weatherby a victim of their own success in that Remington, Winchester, and Federal have added some of these to their product lines.

TECHNICAL COMMENT(S)

All Weatherby cartridges are high velocity magnums with rimless, belted cartridge cases. Weatherby calibers of .340 Wby. Mag. and below are based on the .300 H&H Magnum case head dimensions while Weatherby calibers of .338-378 Weatherby and above are based on a .416 Rigby case head with a belt added. All Weatherby cartridges are known for their high velocity and flat trajectory as well as for their heavy recoil and high cost. Performance hath its cost, and Weatherby cartridges deliver such performance. Muzzle velocity figures for all Weatherby cartridges are measured from a 26 inch barrel.

A Look at the Big Boys' Ballistics

Caliber	Bullet Weight (grains)	Muzzle Velocity (fps.)	Muzzle Energy ft.-lbs.)
12.7x76mm M48 Spotter	827	1,745	5,591
12.7x81mm Breda	565	2,430	7,407
.5 in. Vickers (12.7x81mm)	580	2,470	7,856
12.7x99mm Browning MG	661	2,910	12,427
12.7x108mm Soviet	745	2,755	12,554
13x92SRmm TUF	770	2,650	12,005
13.2x99mm Hotchkiss	791	2,210	8,578
.55 Boys	926	2,495	12,798
14.5x114mm Soviet	979	3,200	22,258

CHAPTER 68 : PROPRIETARY CARTRIDGES - OBSOLETE

CHAPTER 68
For Cartridge Index see Chapter 101. All drawing dimensions are approximate.

In many ways, we must classify this chapter as a field of broken dreams - the dreams of cartridge pioneers such as Charles Newton, W.J. Jeffery, Westley Richards, E. A. vom Hofe, Art Alphin (A-Square), and Wilhelm Brenneke. These visionaries were ahead of their time, and their creations were mostly unappreciated and unsuccessful during their lives. Only later did the extent of their influence on cartridge development come to be fully appreciated, but still seldom acknowledged. While success did not elude them entirely, its rewards were parsimonious.

The history lesson here is that the proprietary ammunition market is a difficult one in which too few achieve commercial success. However, although these men sought commercial success, they did so in a field of endeavor in which they sincerely believed - firearms and ammunition.

Today's shooters owe them a debt of gratitude for their vision and technical developments from which we now benefit. I believe this is the legacy for which they would most want to be remembered.

A-SQUARE CALIBERS

ALTERNATE NAME(S): none
RELATED CALIBER(S): .378 Wby. Mag., .460 Wby. Mag.

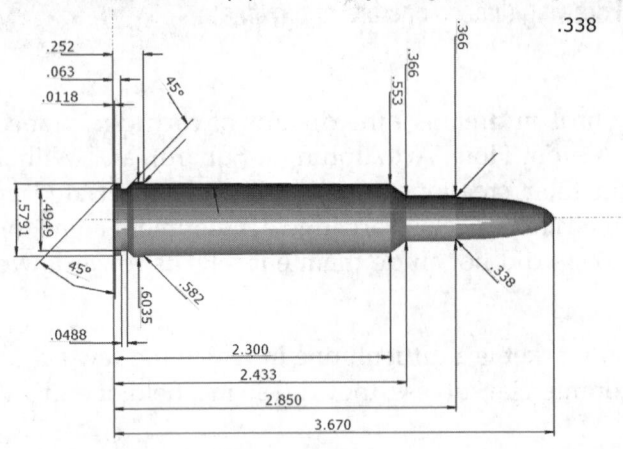

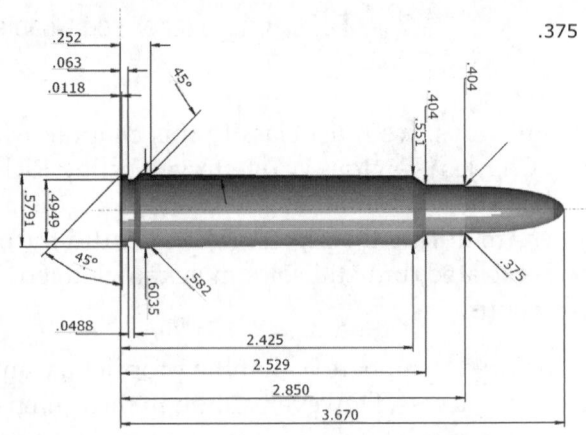

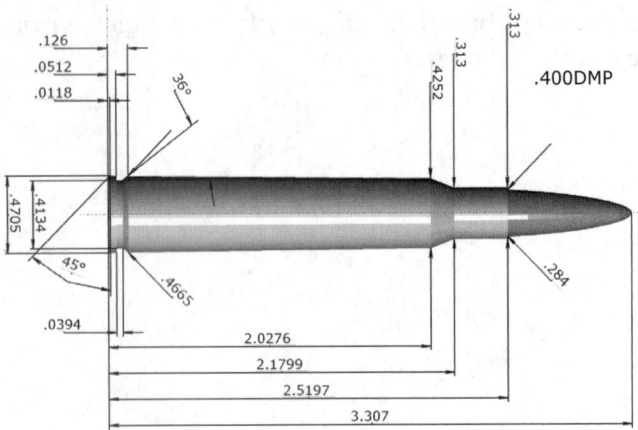

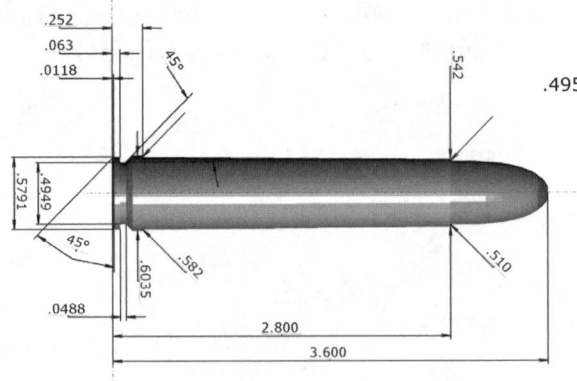

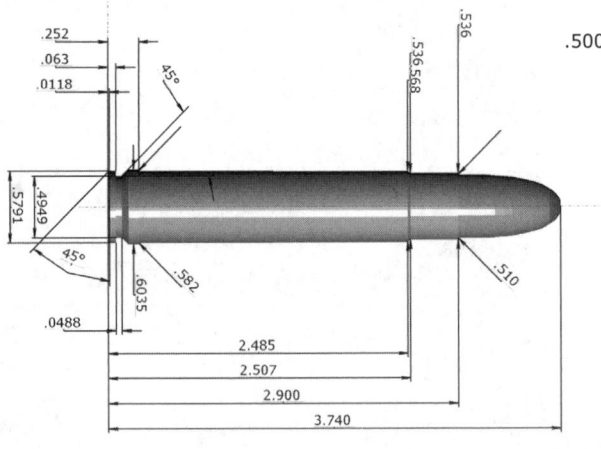

CARTRIDGE HISTORY
Country of Origin: U.S.
Designer(s): Arthur Alphin
Governing Body: SAAMI
Present Status: semi-active

CARTRIDGE DESCRIPTION
Test Barrel Length: 26 in.
Case Type: rimless, belted, necked
Case Material: brass
Primer Size: large rifle

CARTRIDGE BALLISTICS
Max. Average Breech Pressure: 60,000 psi.

Caliber	Bullet Diameter (in.)	Bullet Weight (gr.)	Rifling Twist 1 turn in (in.)	Max Horizontal Range (yd.)	Max Veritical Range (ft.)	Muzzle Velocity (fps)	Muzzle Energy (ft.-lbs.)
.338 A-Square	.338	200-250	10	5,500	12,500	3,120	5,403
.375 A-Square	.375	300	10	5,000	9,800	2,920	5,679
.400 A-Square DPM	.410	400	10	3,000	6,200	2,400	5,116
.495 A-Square	.510	570	10	5,000	10,000	2,350	6,989
.500 A-Square	.510	600	10	5,300	10,600	2,470	8,127

CURRENT MANUFACTURER(S)
A-Square

GENERAL COMMENT(S)
After retiring from a career as an Army officer, Col. Alphin set out to improve the ballistics of big game cartridges and sell rifles and ammunition to discerning customers. He started the A-Square company in order to accomplish this. A-Square cartridges are siblings of the .460 Weatherby Magnum cartridge case. In the matter of ballistics, A-Square cartridges are designed to improve on Weatherby ballistic performance and by all measures, they do so. For this reason, many hunters of heavy or dangerous game prefer A-Square cartridges.   In much the same manner as Weatherby calibers, A-Square cartridges are designed for bolt-action rifles. In recent years, A-Square has encountered serious difficulties that have adversely affected production and sales, but not quality.

TECHNICAL COMMENT(S)
Nothing has been invented that can not be improved. This is the whole point of A-Square calibers, to go Weatherby one better in ballistic performance. Of course, Weatherby cartridges are well known for their ballistic performance in the field, so they do not leave much room for improvement. Despite this, A-Square has succeeded in improving on Weatherby ballistic performance.

BALLARD CALIBERS

ALTERNATE NAME(S): none

RELATED CALIBER(S): .32-40 Winchester (.32-40 Ballard), .30-30 Winchester (.38-50 Ballard), .38-90 Winchester and .40-90 Sharps (.40-70 Ballard), .44-70 Maynard and .44-100 Wesson (.44-100 Ballard and .45-100 Ballard)

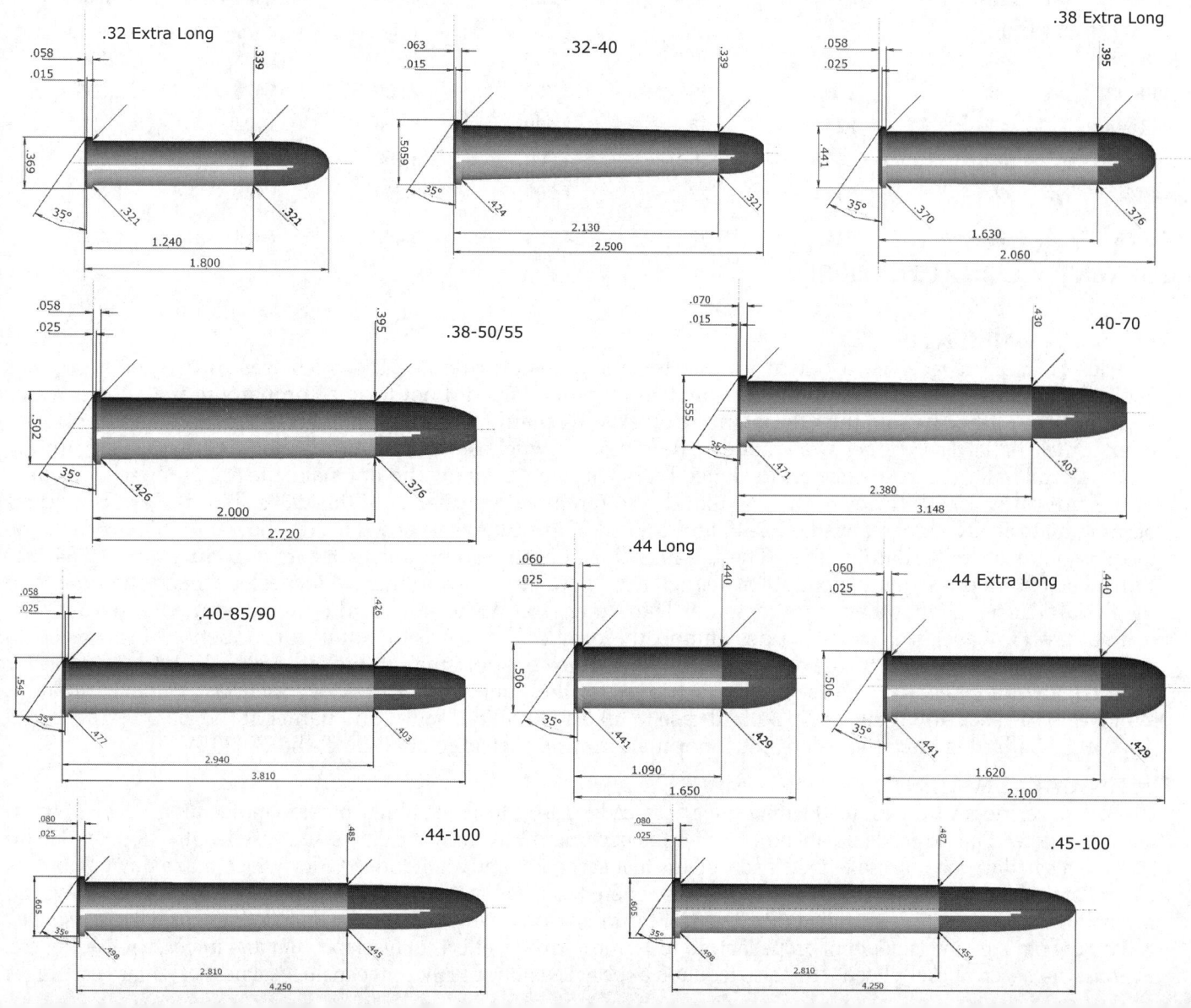

CARTRIDGE HISTORY
Country of Origin: U.S.
Designer(s): Charles H. Ballard
Governing Body: none
Present Status: obsolete

CARTRIDGE DESCRIPTION
Test Barrel Length: N/A
Case Type: rimmed, straight
Case Material: brass
Primer Size: large rifle

CARTRIDGE BALLISTICS
Max. Average Breech Pressure: N/A

Caliber	Bullet Diameter (in.)	Bullet Weight (gr.)	Rifling Twist 1 turn in (in.)	Max Horizontal Range (yd.)	Max Veritical Range (ft.)	Muzzle Velocity (fps)	Muzzle Energy (ft.-lbs.)
32 Extra Long	.317	115	22	2,900	6,100	1,200	368
.32-40 (Win.)	.32	165	16	2,600	5,500	1,440	760
.38 Extra Long	.375	146	36	2,650	5,600	1,275	527
.38-50/55	.375	255	20	3,200	6,550	1,320	986
.40-70 (.40-63/65/70 Ballard)	.403	330	18	3,700	7,550	1,335	1,306
.40-85/90	.403	370	18	3,900	7,800	1,425	1,668
.44 Long	.439	227	36	2,400	5,100	1,200	726
.44 Extra Long	.439	265	36	1,600	5,300	1,320	1,025
.44-100	.445	535	20	4,300	8,500	1,400	2,328
.45-100	.454	550	20	4,200	8,400	1,370	2,292

CURRENT MANUFACTURER(S)
None

GENERAL COMMENT(S)
Charles H. Ballard received a patent in 1861 for a single-shot rifle design which was to become a popular choice of target shooters and hunters for some 40 years. Ballard did not form a company to make firearms or ammunition. Rather, he sold the rifle patents to an existing manufacturer. From there, it was sold and purchased many times. Ballard cartridges were made by Remington, Winchester, and Union Metallic Cartridge Co. among others. As all Ballard cartridges were designed for black powder, many did not make the transition to smokeless propellants after 1890. However, the few that did so remained on offer until the 1930s. Two Ballard cartridges became historically significant, the .32-40 and the .38-50. In the black powder era, the .40-90 Ballard was the most popular of the Ballard calibers.The .32-40 Ballard became so popular after its introduction in 1884 that Winchester started making it a couple of years later. As was the custom then, Winchester affixed their name to the Ballard cartridge that they manufactured. The Winchester name stuck and remains on the .32-40 cartridge to this day. However it is a Ballard design and the only Ballard cartridge still in production. Introduced in 1876, the .38-50 Ballard cartridge became a popular choice of sportsmen in the late 1800s. In 1891, Winchester began developing new smokeless powder cartridges for their new Model 1894 lever-action carbine. Ultimately, Winchester necked down the .38-50 Ballard case to take a .30 caliber bullet and named it the .30-30 Winchester! The .38-50 Ballard is the father of the most popular hunting cartridge of all time, the .30-30 WCF.

TECHNICAL COMMENT(S)
All Ballard cartridges were rimmed with a straight cartridge case. However, unlike other manufacturers such as Sharps and Winchester, Ballard made no attempt to offer the bewildering variety of calibers and case lengths. Rather, Ballard stuck to a small variety of case lengths and calibers that earned a reputation for accuracy which made them a popular choice for competition. Many Ballard cartridges were offered as "Everlast" calibers designed especially for reloading and normally sold as an empty, unprimed case. Everlast cartridge cases were substantially thicker than normal cases so they could not hold the same amount of propellant. To resist the corrosive effects of black powder and increase reloading life, Everlast cases were nickel-plated. They also required a special chamber. Perhaps the main weakness of Ballard cartridges

was that Ballard rifles were never made by Ballard. Rather, they were made and/or marketed by others who were uninterested in cartridge development. Compounding the problem, most ammunition makers also made firearms, so they were less than enthusiastic about promoting Ballard cartridges. This separation of rifle production from ammunition production left neither with an interested manufacturer support base for the pending change to smokeless propellants.

BULLARD CALIBERS

ALTERNATE NAME(S): none
RELATED CALIBER(S): .303 Savage (.32-40 Bullard); .40-65 Ballard and .40-60 Colt (.40-75 Bullard); .45-75 Winchester Centennial (.40-90 Bullard); .50-70 Gov't (.50-115 Bullard)

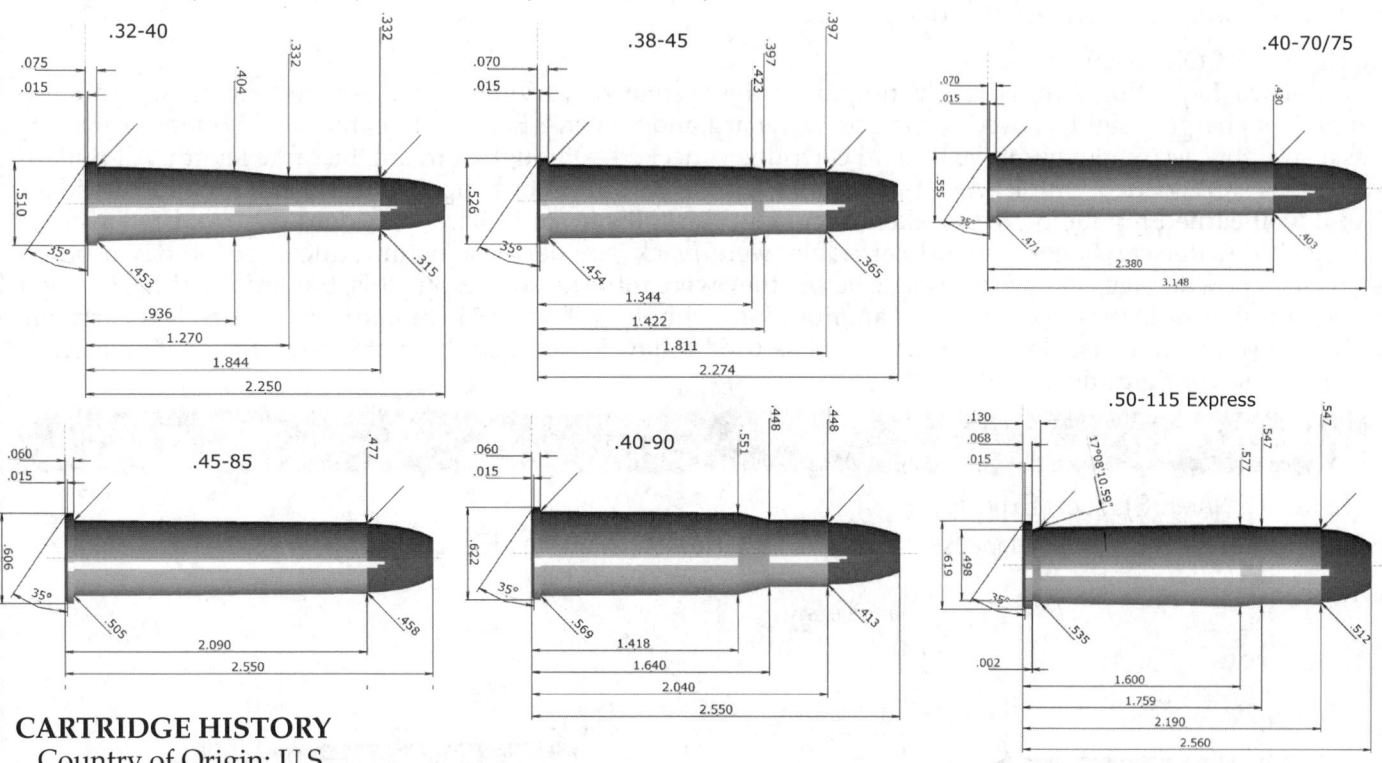

CARTRIDGE HISTORY
Country of Origin: U.S.
Designer(s): James H. Bullard
Governing Body: none
Present Status: obsolete

CARTRIDGE DESCRIPTION
Test Barrel Length: N/A
Case Types: see above
Case Material: brass
Primer Size: large rifle

CARTRIDGE BALLISTICS
Max. Average Breech Pressure: N/A

Caliber	Bullet Diameter (in.)	Bullet Weight (gr.)	Rifling Twist 1 turn in (in.)	Max Horizontal Range (yd.)	Max Veritical Range (ft.)	Muzzle Velocity (fps)	Muzzle Energy (ft.-lbs.)
.32-40	.315	150	16	3,050	6,350	1,490	739
.38-45	.365	190	18	2,800	5,900	1,390	815
.40-70	.413	232	20	2,600	5,600	1,500	1,159
.40-75	.413	258	20	2,600	5,600	1,515	1,315
.40-90	.413	300	18	2,100	4,600	1,570	1,642
.45-85	.458	290	22	2,100	4,600	1,600	1,648
.50-115	.512	300	54	2,300	4,900	1,540	1,580

CURRENT MANUFACTURER(S)

None

GENERAL COMMENT(S)

For several years, James Bullard worked for S&W. In 1881, Bullard received a patent for a new lever-action rifle and in 1885 he founded the Bullard Repeating Arms Co. to manufacture his rifle. The Bullard Repeating Arms Co. struggled for four years trying to compete with Winchester and Marlin. During this time, Bullard manufactured approximately 2,800 rifles which had a reputation for very high quality. In an effort to bolster sales of their rifles, Bullard Repeating Arms Co. introduced seven new Bullard cartridges in 1886-1887 to an indifferent and saturated market. The Bullard cartridges never really caught on, although Remington and Winchester offered some of them for a time. Buffalo Bill owned a Bullard rifle as did Teddy Roosevelt. By the early 1900s, Bullard cartridges had disappeared.

TECHNICAL COMMENT(S)

The Bullard Repeating Arms Co. did not adopt the system of varying cartridge case lengths according to propellant charge weight as used by Sharps, Maynard and Stevens. For example, the .40-75 Bullard cartridge has a straight case while the .40-90 Bullard cartridge is necked, although both are the same length. All Bullard cartridges were loaded with lead, flat-nose bullets, jacketed bullets or copper tube bullets. Bullard cartridges had a well-earned reputation for excellent accuracy. The ballistics of Bullard cartridges were, at best, average for black powder cartridges. Bullard cartridges were black powder designs introduced at the dawn of the smokeless powder age, and were obsolete before they were introduced. Despite this, Bullard cartridges occupy an historical niche in the development of ammunition technology. The .50-115 Bullard was the first U.S. cartridge to have a solid head case design similar to those used today. It was also the first U.S. cartridge with a semi-rimmed case configuration.

E. A. VOM HOFE CALIBERS

ALTERNATE NAME(S): Super Express
RELATED CALIBER(S): 8x60mm Mauser (5.6x61 SE), .30 Newton (7x66mm SE)

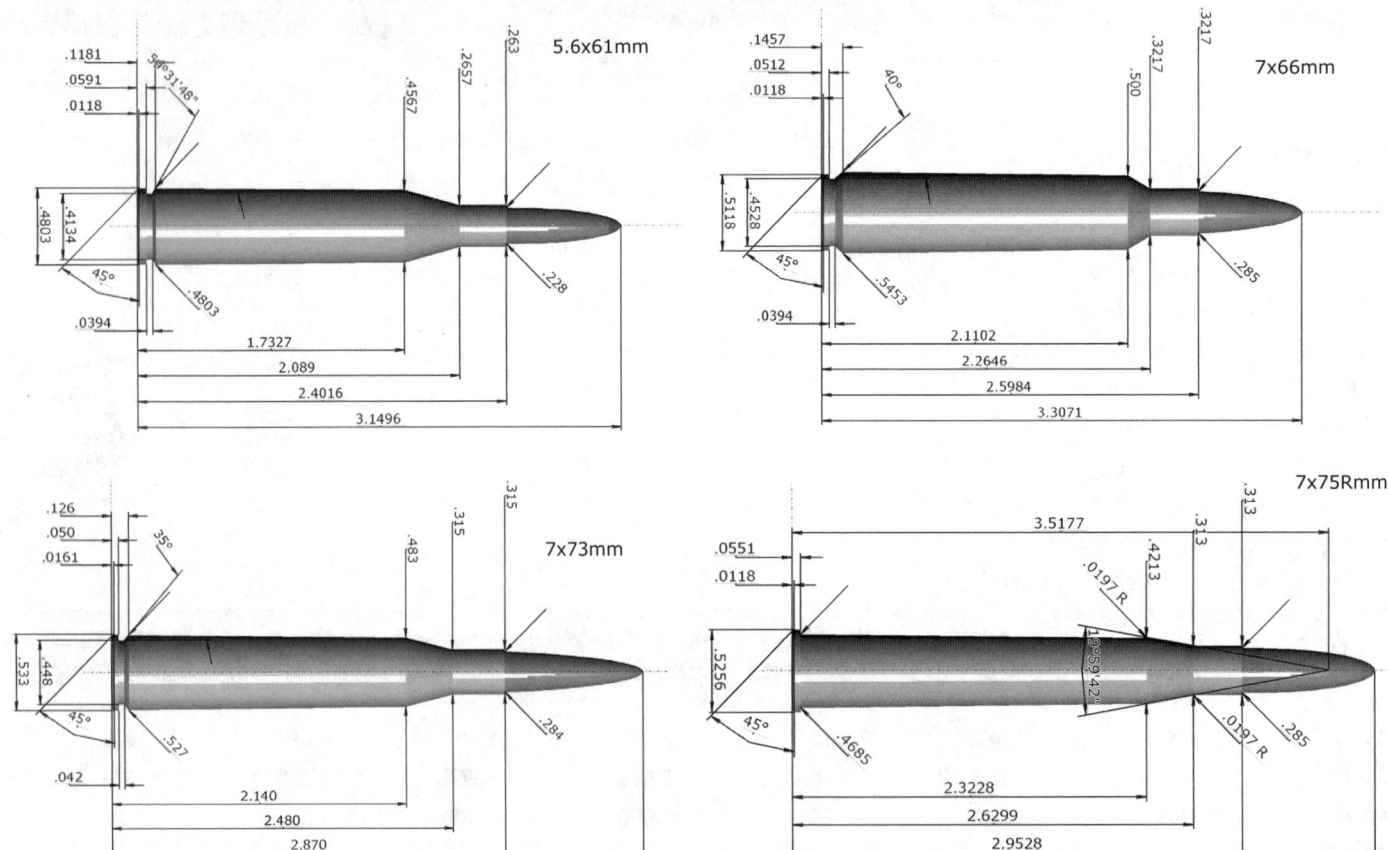

CARTRIDGE HISTORY
Country of Origin: Germany
Designer(s): E.A. vom Hofe
Governing Body: CIP
Present Status: semi-active

CARTRIDGE DESCRIPTION
Test Barrel Length: 24 in.
Case Type: various, necked
Case Material: brass
Primer Size: large rifle

CARTRIDGE BALLISTICS
Max. Average Breech Pressure:
5.6x61mm SE – 55,100 psi.
7x66mm SE – N/A
7x73mm Belted – N/A
7x75Rmm SE – 60,190 psi.

Caliber	Bullet Diameter (in.)	Bullet Weight (gr.)	Rifling Twist 1 turn in (in.)	Max Horizontal Range (yd.)	Max Veritical Range (ft.)	Muzzle Velocity (fps)	Muzzle Energy (ft.-lbs.)
5.6x61mm SE	.227	77	8.6	4,800	11,100	3,710	2,351
7x66mm SE	.284	123	9.5	5,500	11,200	3,640	3,620
7x73mm Belted	.284	170	9.5	5,300	11,000	3,355	3,500
7x75Rmm SE	.284	170	9.5	5,300	11,000	3,300	4,056

CURRENT MANUFACTURER(S)
Gehmann

GENERAL COMMENT(S)
The cartridge design career of Ernest August vom Hofe spanned the 1930s, World War II, and the modern era. Unlike so many other calibers and designs, the vom Hofe products survived the war years and two of them remain in production to this day. In some ways, vom Hofe was a European Weatherby who believed very high muzzle velocities resulted in superior terminal ballistic performance. However, due to the limitations of European hunting opportunities, he never got beyond the 7mm. Vom Hofe was a believer in the 7mm undoubtedly because of the ballistic gains possible with its long slender bullet. In this, we can easily see he was correct; just consider the number and variety of 7mm magnum cartridges today.

TECHNICAL COMMENT(S)
Vom Hofe achieved his muzzle velocities the old fashioned way, he used heavy charges of propellant in long, somewhat slender cases. No belts or short shoulders at acute angles here. Instead, beltless designs with long shoulders at shallow angles. If nothing else, vom Hofe cartridges certainly look the part. Their case length, long neck, sharply pointed bullets and size are impressive and create an image of modern performance.

JEFFERY CALIBERS

ALTERNATE NAME(S): none
RELATED CALIBER(S): variations of the .404 Jeffery

CARTRIDGE HISTORY
Country of Origin: Britain
Designer(s): W. J. Jeffery
Governing Body: CIP
Present Status: semi-obsolete

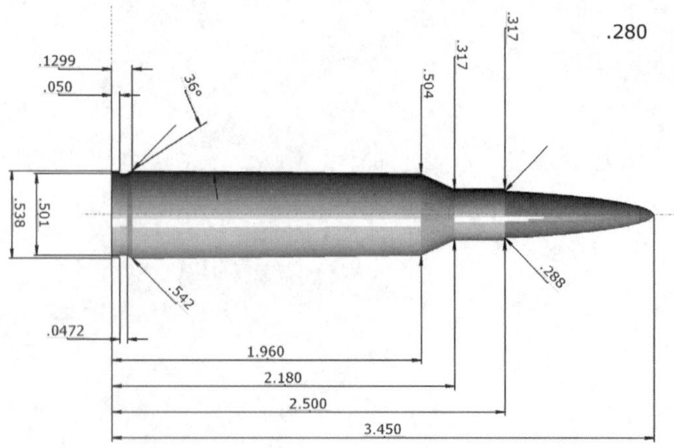

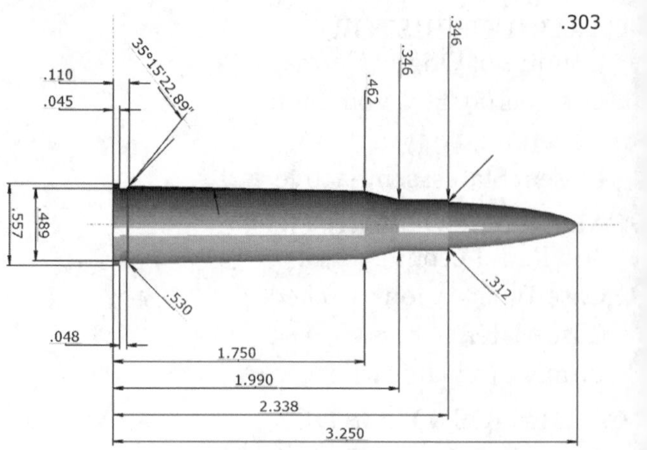

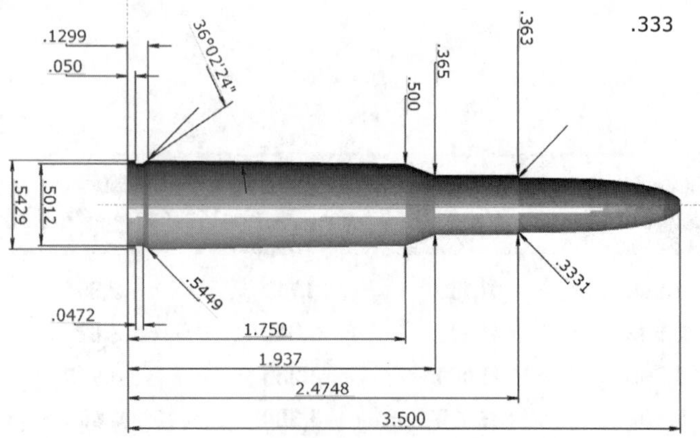

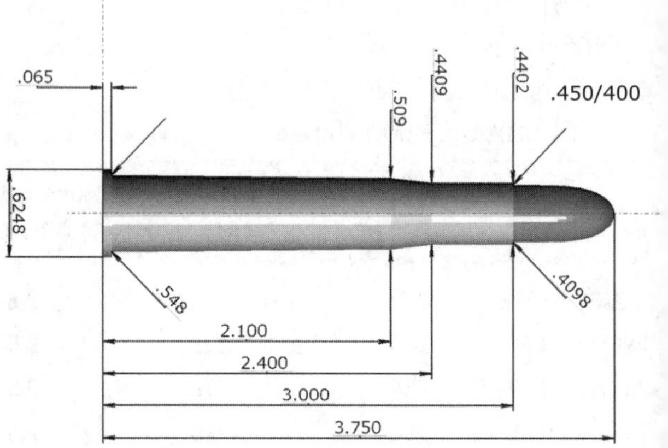

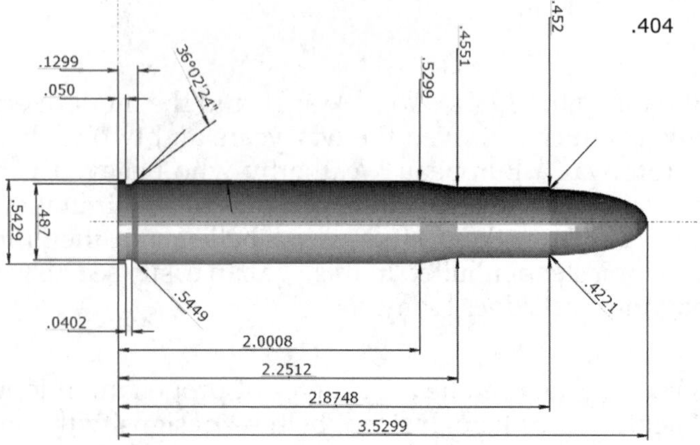

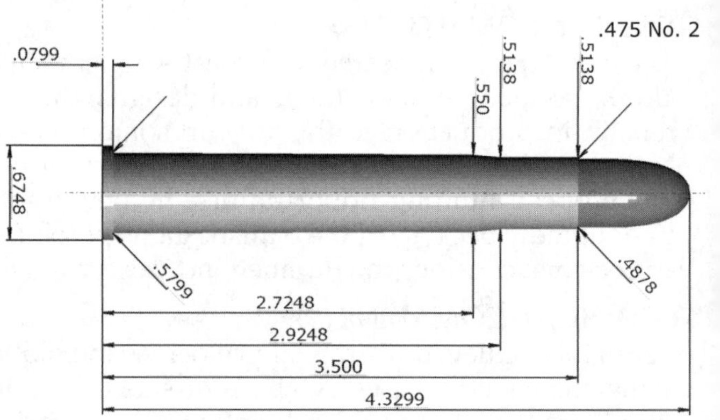

.280

.303

.333

.450/400

.404

.475 No. 2

CARTRIDGE DESCRIPTION

Test Barrel Length: 24 in.

Case Type: various

Case Material: brass

Primer Size: large rifle

CARTRIDGE BALLISTICS

Max. Average Breech Pressure:

.333 Jeffery - 47,860 psi.

.400 Jeffery - 40,600 psi.

.404 Jeffery - 52,900 psi.

.475 Jeffery - 39,880 psi.

.500 Jeffery - 47,800 psi.

.500

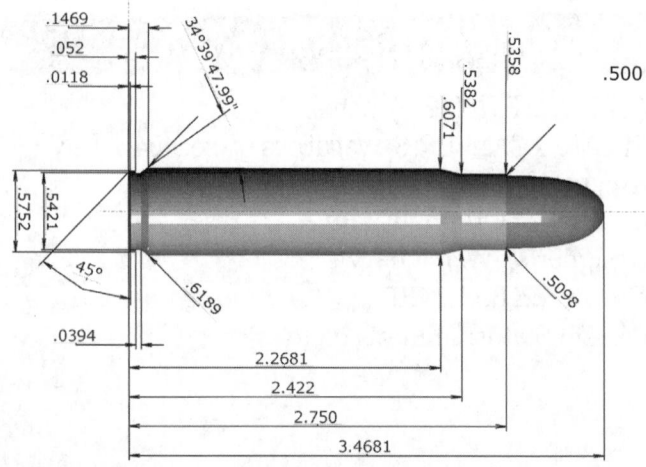

Caliber	Bullet Diameter (in.)	Bullet Weight (gr.)	Rifling Twist 1 turn in (in.)	Max Horizontal Range (yd.)	Max Veritical Range (ft.)	Muzzle Velocity (fps)	Muzzle Energy (ft.-lbs.)
.280 Jeffery	.288	140	na	4,600	8,900	3,000	2,800
.303 Magnum	.312	174	na	6,000	13,200	2,850	3,050
.333 Jeffery	.333	250	na	4,400	9,800	2,500	3,480
.450/400 Jeffery	.410	400	15	2,100	4,500	2,100	3,920
.404 Jeffery	.422	300	16.54	2,500	4,700	2,600	4,500
.404 Jeffery	.422	450	16.54	2,150	4,700	2,600	4,620
.475 No. 2 Jeffery	.489	500	18	4,100	9,300	2,150	5,140
.500 Jeffery	.510	535	20	4,600	9,000	2,400	6,800

CURRENT MANUFACTURER(S)
Kynoch, Norma (.405 and .500)

GENERAL COMMENT(S)
Just after the turn of the 20th century, W. J. Jeffery introduced a number of new cartridges. Several were designed for smokeless propellants and bolt-action, repeating rifles. His .280 Jeffery, .303 Magnum and .333 Jeffery were not a commercial hat trick. However, his .404 Jeffery cartridge was to become a big game classic which still serves as the basis for many modern cartridges such as the Dakota and Canadian Magnum series. The .404 Jeffery earned its place in history as one of the first rimless cartridges powerful enough for dangerous African and Indian game. This allowed hunters to take bolt-action, repeating rifles to Africa instead of expensive double rifles. Jeffery's .404 cartridge developed a strong following among German hunters who called it the 10.75x73mm. In 1920, Schuler-Krieghoff introduced a new rimless cartridge for hunting dangerous game with bolt-action rifles called the 12.5x70mm Schuler. Today, although W.J. Jeffery has long gone to his reward, his legacy remains the Jeffery cartridges that have become milestones in the history of cartridge development.

TECHNICAL COMMENT(S)
Early bolt-action sporting rifles did not feed reliably. While this was not a problem for most hunting conditions, it was a serious problem when hunting dangerous game. Rimless cartridges feed more reliably through bolt-action rifles than rimmed designs, so Jeffery incorporated a rimless head configuration in his classic .404 cartridge. He also kept overall loaded length short enough to fit into bolt rifle actions and wide enough to hold a heavy charge of propellant.

MAYNARD CALIBERS

ALTERNATE NAME(S): 1873 or 1882 often added after name to designate model
RELATED CALIBER(S): none

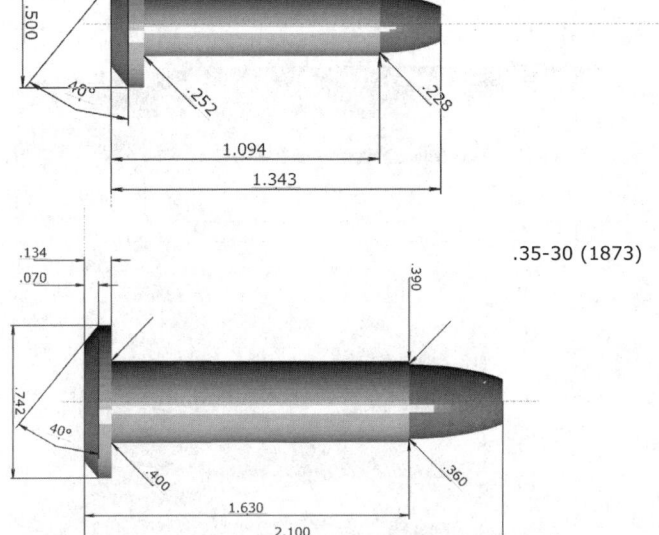

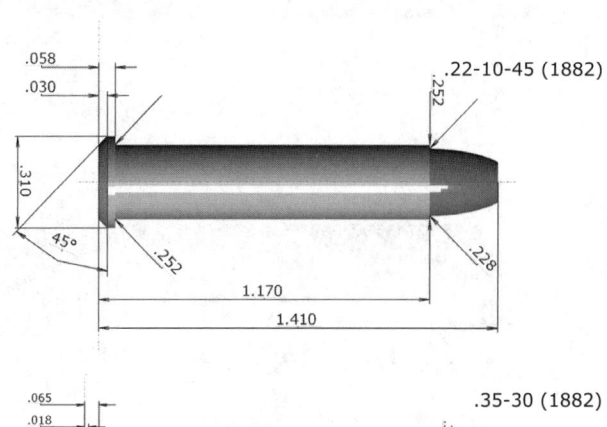

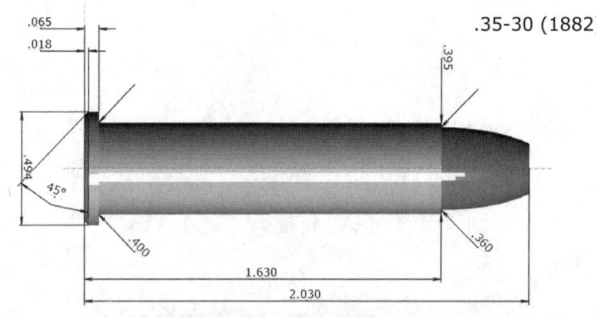

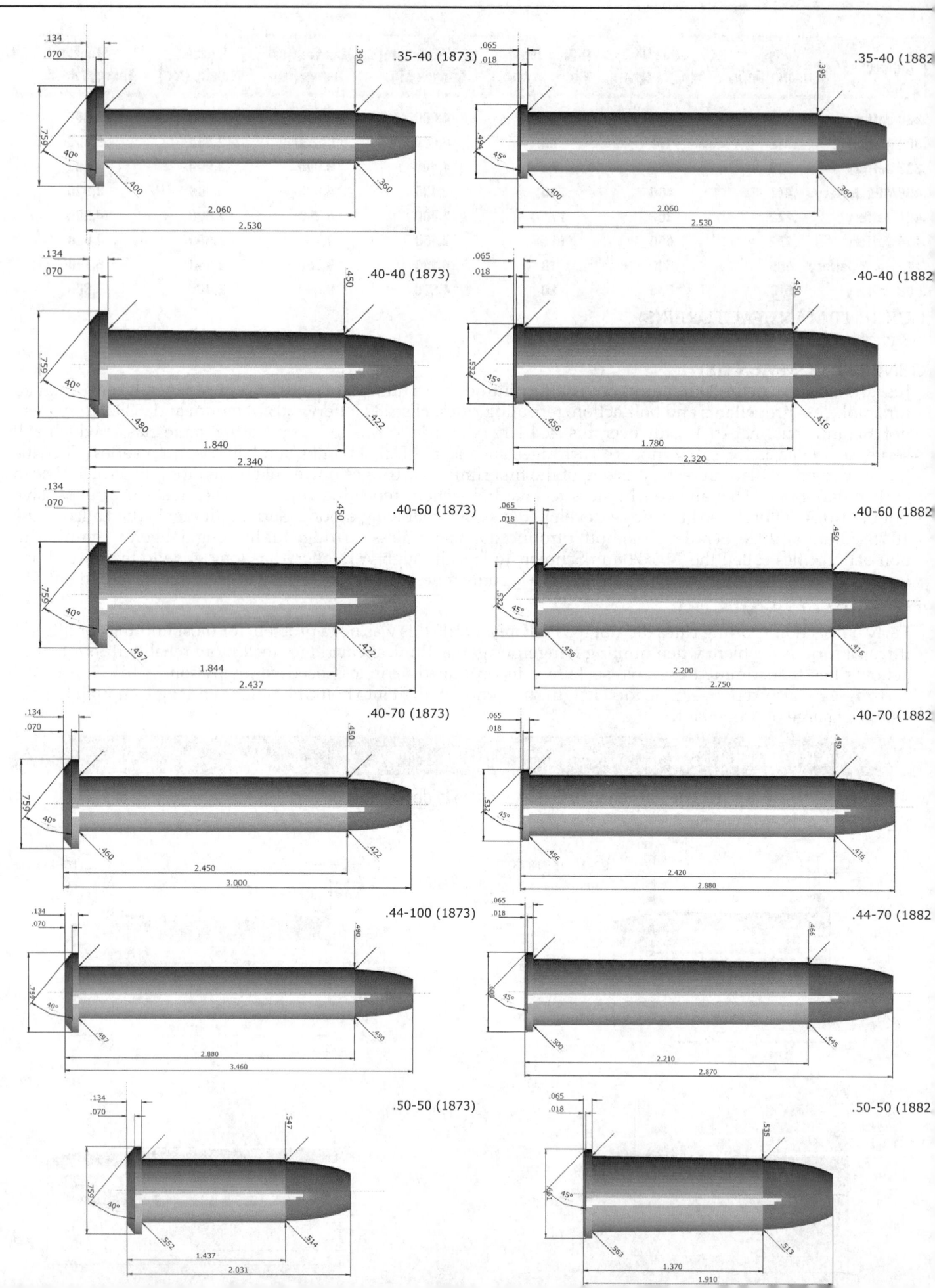

.35-40 (1873)

.35-40 (1882)

.40-40 (1873)

.40-40 (1882)

.40-60 (1873)

.40-60 (1882)

.40-70 (1873)

.40-70 (1882)

.44-100 (1873)

.44-70 (1882)

.50-50 (1873)

.50-50 (1882)

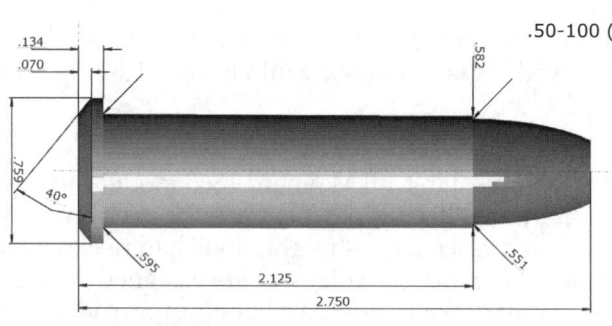

.50-100 (1873)

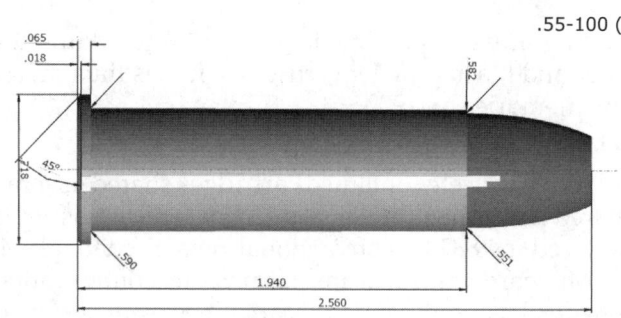

.55-100 (1882)

CARTRIDGE HISTORY
Country of Origin: U.S.
Designer(s): Dr. Edward Maynard
Governing Body: none
Present Status: obsolete

CARTRIDGE DESCRIPTION
Test Barrel Length: N/A
Case Type: rimmed, straight
Case Material: brass
Primer Size: large rifle

CARTRIDGE BALLISTICS
Max. Average Breech Pressure: N/A

Caliber	Bullet Diameter (in.)	Bullet Weight (gr.)	Rifling Twist 1 turn in (in.)	Max Horizontal Range (yd.)	Max Veritical Range (ft.)	Muzzle Velocity (fps)	Muzzle Energy (ft.-lbs.)
22-10-45 Maynard	.228	45	16	2,000	4,200	1,100	121
.35-30 Maynard	.36	250	16-18	3,050	6,300	1,280	909
.35-40 Maynard	.375	255	16-18	2,700	5,800	1,355	1,019
.40-40 Maynard	.417	270-330	18-20	2,200	4,750	1,260	1,163
.40-60 Maynard	.417	330	18-20	2,400	5,100	1,370	1,375
.40-70 Maynard	.417	270	18-20	2,400	5,100	1,645	1,622
.44-60 Maynard	.445	430	na	2,000	4,600	1,200	1,375
.44-100 Maynard	.445	520	na	2,500	5,200	1,400	2,263
.50-50 Maynard	.513	400	42	1,800	4,800	1,210	1,300
.50-70 Maynard	.513	400	42	2,000	5,000	1,400	1,741
.50-100 Maynard	.513	500	na	2,400	5,400	1,450	2,334
.55-100 Maynard	.551	530	na	2,200	5,000	1,410	2,339

CURRENT MANUFACTURER(S)
None

GENERAL COMMENT(S)
Dr. Edward Maynard (1813-1891) was a dentist and a prolific inventor who held 23 patents for cartridges and priming systems. He began in 1845 with his first patent for a tape priming system for military applications. During the Civil War, Maynard separate-primed, metallic cartridges and breech-loading rifles were used extensively by Union and Confederate troops. Maynard's uncomplicated, brass cartridge cases were manufactured in both the North and the South. With the conclusion of the Civil War in 1865, Dr. Maynard turned his attention to designing sporting cartridges. His first designs were introduced in 1865 to an indifferent market. They were replaced by a new series in 1873 and again in 1882. None were particularly successful, but Dr. Maynard kept trying. Maynard's 1865 designs were handicapped by having a bizarre, large diameter rim that proved unnecessary. His 1873 cartridge designs reduced the rim diameter, but made them twice as thick, the purpose being to help extraction from fouled barrels. When this design proved equally unpopular, Maynard gave up and used normal rims for his cartridges. Maynard cartridges now looked conventional, but this became the problem. Why would a sportsman buy a Maynard cartridge when the market was already saturated with dozens of conventional cartridges in a wide variety of calibers? Unfortunately for Dr. Maynard, they did not. In the late 1880s, smokeless powder made self-

loading firearms possible for the first time. With these two attractions on the horizon, no one wanted single-shot rifles and black powder cartridges. It was thus that Maynard cartridges faded quickly into history leaving only a few memories by 1900.

TECHNICAL COMMENT(S)

All Maynard self-contained cartridges shared several consistent features. First, all Maynard 1865 model cartridges shared the wide "dinner plate" rim which was replaced in 1873 by the "frying pan" extra thick rim. Both were replaced in 1882 by conventional rims. Second, all Maynard cartridge cases were straight, none had necks. Third, all Maynard bullets were flat-nose in configuration. Fourth, all Maynard cartridges were designed for black powder. Lastly, all Maynard cartridges were designed for rifles; Maynard never offered a handgun cartridge. Most shooters remember Maynard cartridges for one key feature, the "frying pan" rim of the 1873 designs. "What was the purpose?" is a question asked by modern shooters. The answer is that the thick rim provides a strong surface for the extractor to act upon in order to remove a sticking cartridge case from a fouled chamber (remember, black powder was dirty and quickly fouled barrels). The rim also provides a large surface for grasping while loading or unloading. Another feature of the 1873 rim is the prominent, curved chamfer under the rim. This was included to allow the extractor to easily override the rim when loading a cartridge into the chamber. Ballistics of Maynard cartridges were competitive for their era, but otherwise unremarkable. As far as is known, no Maynard cartridges were transitioned to smokeless propellants. Dr. Maynard's legacy to shooters includes his tape priming system, some of the very first separate primed metallic cartridge cases, and 23 patents in the ammunition arts.

NEWTON CALIBERS

ALTERNATE NAME(S): none
RELATED CALIBER(S): .30-'06 Spr. (.256 Newton), others unique

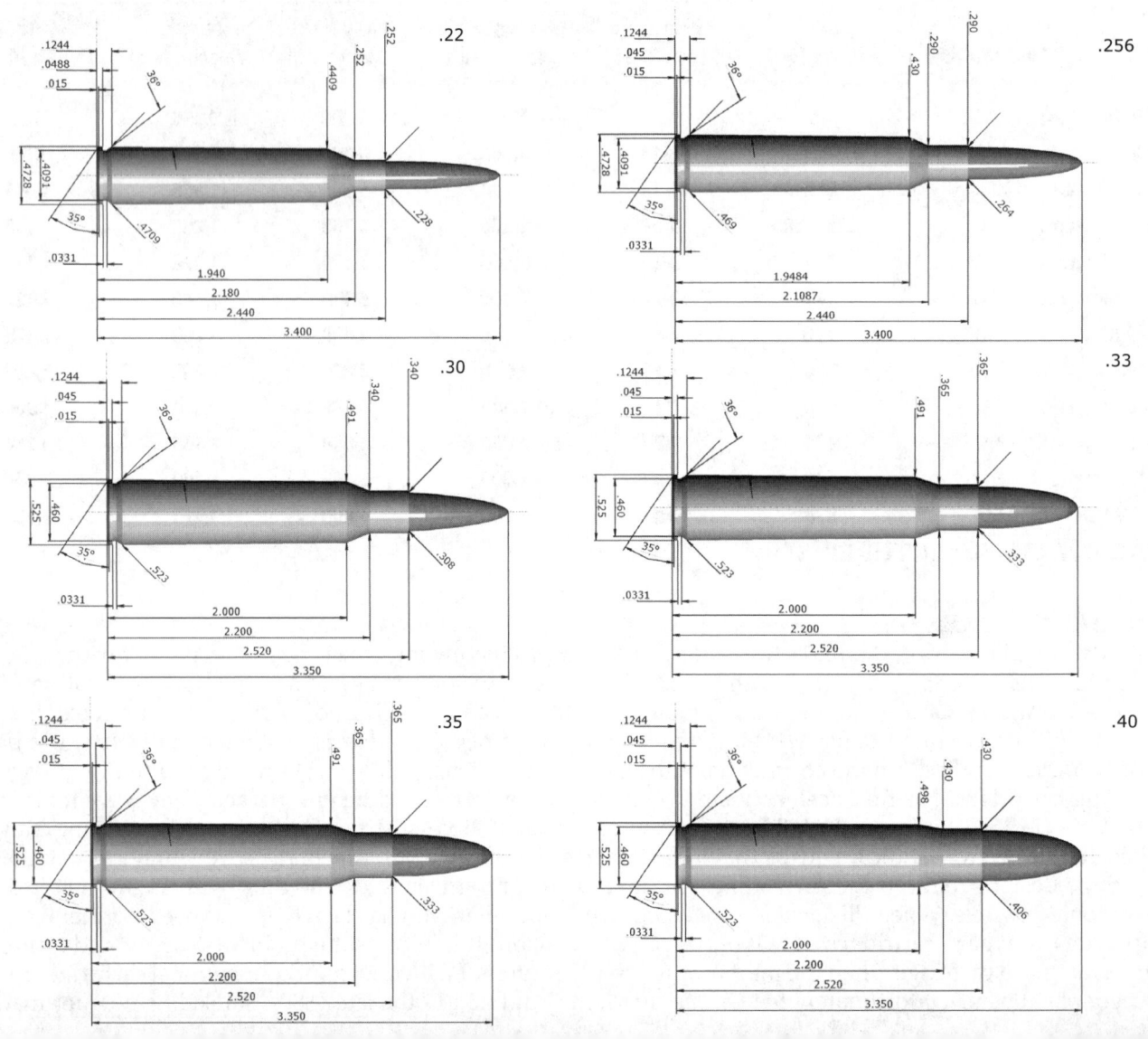

CARTRIDGE HISTORY
Country of Origin: U.S.
Designer(s): Charles Newton
Governing Body: none
Present Status: obsolete

CARTRIDGE DESCRIPTION
Test Barrel Length:
Case Type: rimless, necked
Case Material: brass
Primer Size: large rifle

CARTRIDGE BALLISTICS
Max. Average Breech Pressure: N/A

Caliber	Bullet Diameter (in.)	Bullet Weight (gr.)	Rifling Twist 1 turn in (in.)	Max Horizontal Range (yd.)	Max Veritical Range (ft.)	Muzzle Velocity (fps)	Muzzle Energy (ft.-lbs.)
.22 Newton	.228	90	N/A	4,300	8,500	3,105	1,921
.256 Newton	.264	123	10	4,900	11,000	3,105	2,632
.30 Newton	.308	172	10	5,400	12,000	3,000	3,440
.33 Newton	.333	200	N/A	5,200	11,700	3,000	4,000
.35 Newton	.358	250	12	4,400	9,200	2,975	4,925
.40 Newton	.405	301	N/A	3,500	6,800	3,040	6,180

CURRENT MANUFACTURER(S)
None

GENERAL COMMENT(S)
Charles Newton was not the first cartridge designer to offer a line of proprietary cartridges, but he was the first to sell the benefits of high velocity. He and his cartridges were ahead of the times and his company had financial difficulties that could never be overcome. Western Cartridge Co. loaded several Newton calibers until the mid-1930s. Undoubtedly, Newton influenced Weatherby and others. Today, high velocity cartridges are taken for granted.

TECHNICAL COMMENT(S)
Newton cartridges were all rimless, necked designs without a belt. Head dimensions were unique and larger than the .30-'06 Spr. in order to gain case capacity. Essentially, Newton cartridges were non-belted magnums. Interestingly, Newton never labeled any of his cartridges as "magnums". Today, only one of Newton's cartridges remains in production, the .22 Savage Hi-Power. Newton designed this cartridge, but it is not commonly associated with his name. Although listed in the Newton company catalog, the .40 Newton never entered full production and is quite rare today.

NORTH AMERICAN SHOOTING SYSTEMS CANADIAN MAGNUM CALIBERS

ALTERNATE NAME(S): NASS, Canadian Magnum
RELATED CALIBER(S): .404 Jeffery

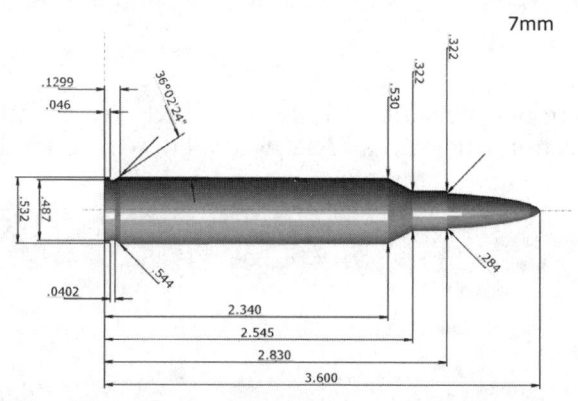

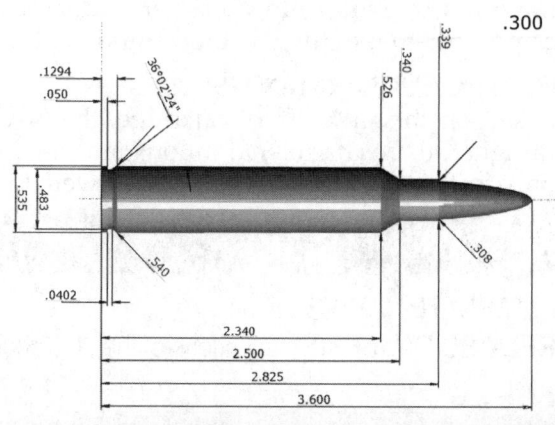

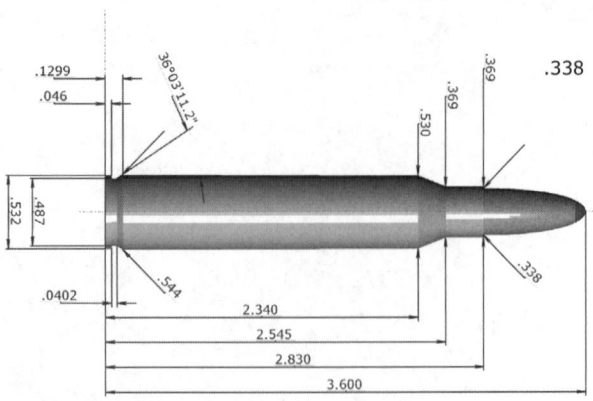

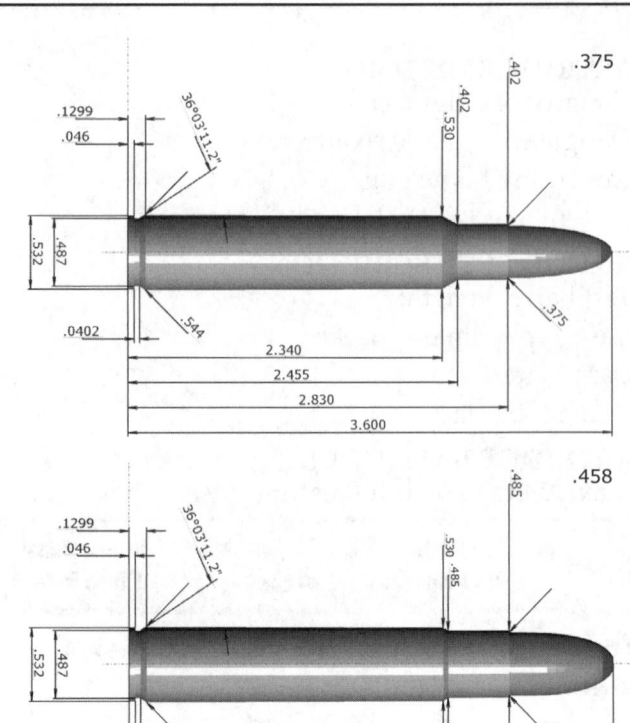

CARTRIDGE HISTORY
Country of Origin: Canada
Designer(s): North American Shooting Systems
Governing Body: SAAMI
Present Status: obsolete

CARTRIDGE DESCRIPTION
Test Barrel Length: 24 in.
Case Type: rimless, rebated, necked
Case Material: brass
Primer Size: large rifle

CARTRIDGE BALLISTICS
Max. Average Breech Pressure: N/A

Caliber	Bullet Diameter (in.)	Bullet Weight (gr.)	Rifling Twist 1 turn in (in.)	Max Horizontal Range (yd.)	Max Veritical Range (ft.)	Muzzle Velocity (fps)	Muzzle Energy (ft.-lbs.)
7mm Canadian Magnum	.284	140	12	5,300	10,300	3,525	3,862
.300 Canadian Magnum	.308	180	10	5,700	13,000	3,425	4,685
.338 Canadian Magnum	.338	225	10	5,300	12,000	3,110	4,830
.375 Canadian Magnum	.375	270	10	4,500	9,000	3,000	5,395
.458 Canadian Magnum	.458	350	10	4,000	8,500	2,575	5,150

CURRENT MANUFACTURER(S)
None

GENERAL COMMENT(S)
The North American Shooting Systems (NASS) cartridges were an attempt to resurrect the older Imperial Magnum calibers from Canadian Industries Limited. Ballistic performance of all NASS calibers essentially duplicated that of the Weatherby and the Dakota calibers.

TECHNICAL COMMENT(S)
Based on the .404 Jeffery cartridge, the NASS cartridges were all of rebated, rimless, necked configuration designed to be chambered in long and magnum length bolt action rifles. As all NASS calibers were intended only for North American game, they were loaded only with light-weight bullets.

RIGBY CALIBERS

ALTERNATE NAME(S): none
RELATED CALIBER(S): variations of the .416 Rigby

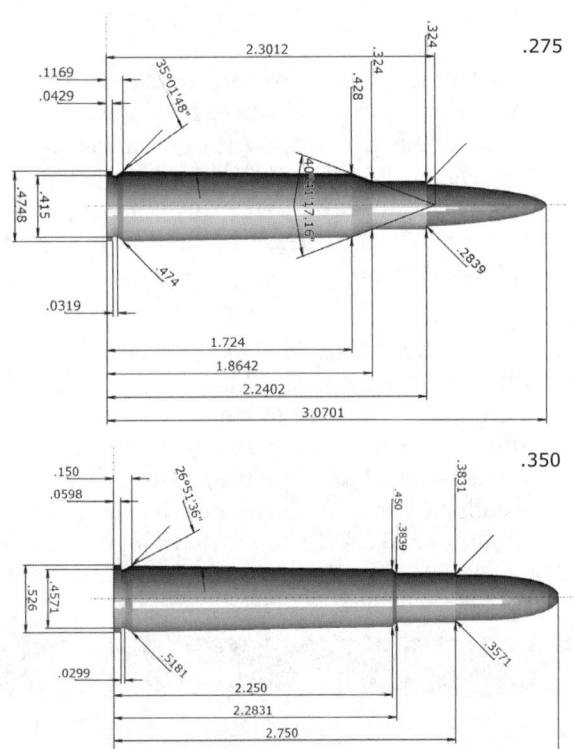

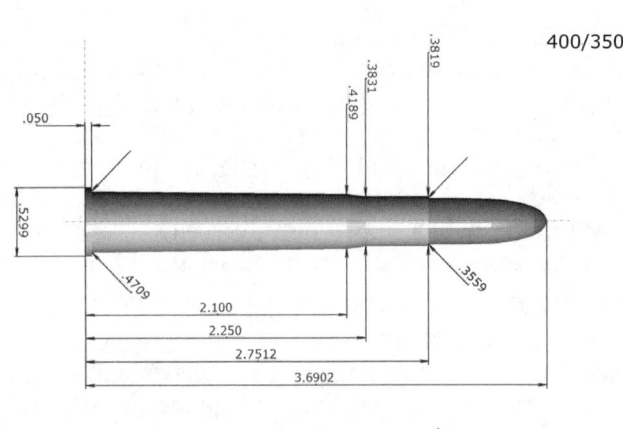

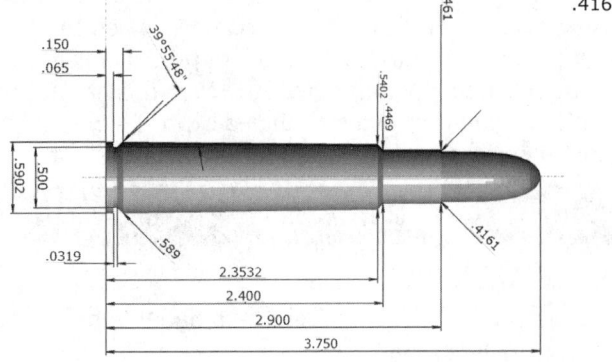

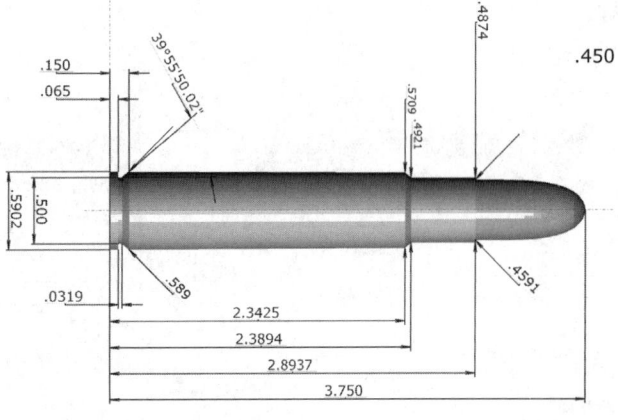

CARTRIDGE HISTORY
Country of Origin: Britain
Designer(s): John Rigby
Governing Body: CIP
Present Status: semi-obsolete

CARTRIDGE DESCRIPTION
Test Barrel Length: 24 in.
Case Type: various, all necked
Case Material: brass
Primer Size: large rifle

CARTRIDGE BALLISTICS

Max. Average Breech Pressure:	Date of Introduction
.275 Rigby - 46,400 psi.	1899
.400/350 Rigby - 47,800 psi.	1899
.350 Rigby - 44,900 psi.	1908
.416 Rigby - 47,100 psi.	1912
.450 Rigby - 58,000 psi.	1995

Caliber	Bullet Diameter (in.)	Bullet Weight (gr.)	Rifling Twist 1 turn in (in.)	Max Horizontal Range (yd.)	Max Veritical Range (ft.)	Muzzle Velocity (fps)	Muzzle Energy (ft.-lbs.)
.275 Rigby	.284	140	10	4,500	8,900	3,000	2,800
400/350 Rigby	.358	310	12	2,200	4,100	2,100	3,035
.350 Rigby Magnum	.358	225	16.5	4,200	7,000	2,625	3,440
.416 Rigby	.416	400-410	16.5	2,400	4,800	2,430	5,245
.450 Rigby	.458	480	16.5	4,400	8,700	2,350	5,887
.450 Rigby	.458	550	16.5	2,400	8,700	2,100	5,387

CURRENT MANUFACTURER(S)
Federal (.416 only), Kynoch, Norma (.416 and .450)

GENERAL COMMENT(S)

As a contemporary of Jeffery, Holland & Holland and Brenneke, Rigby concentrated on rimless cartridge designs for bolt-action, repeating rifles. His first design in 1908, the .350 Rigby Magnum was a commercial non-event. However, Rigby hit a home run in 1911 with his .416 Rigby cartridge. This cartridge became one of the classic African/dangerous game calibers. With the .416 Rigby cartridge, a hunter can take any of the African big five dangerous game without being under gunned. The .416 Rigby remains a popular African caliber to this day and has become the base for many other large caliber cartridges. In 1927, Rigby introduced the .275 Rigby cartridge. This was the 7x57mm Mauser by another name. Rigby's attempt to affix his name to the popular 7x57mm Mauser cartridge was not successful.

TECHNICAL COMMENT(S)

Rigby's .350 and .416 cartridge designs were rimless, but not belted like the emerging Holland & Holland magnum cartridges. An interesting point here is while the .350 Rigby's nomenclature includes the word "Magnum," the .416 Rigby does not. Both the .350 Rigby Magnum and the .416 Rigby cartridges are loaded to very moderate chamber pressure levels by modern standards. This was done in order to prevent the Cordite propellants from reaching excessive chamber pressures at high summer temperatures. When the .416 Rigby is loaded with single-base stick propellants, this becomes unnecessary. Of course, with modern propellants and modern steels, the ballistic performance of the .416 Rigby cartridge can be substantially improved. However, this has not been done by ammunition makers for two reasons: higher velocities would not conform to the regulated express sights on .416 Rigby caliber rifles, and the .416 Rigby cartridge has more than enough performance in its current state of development.

SAUER CALIBERS

ALTERNATE NAME(S): none
RELATED CALIBER(S): 6.5x48Rmm Sauer (6.5x58Rmm Sauer), 8x48Rmm Sauer (8x58Rmm Sauer), 9.3x72Rmm Sauer (9.3x74Rmm)

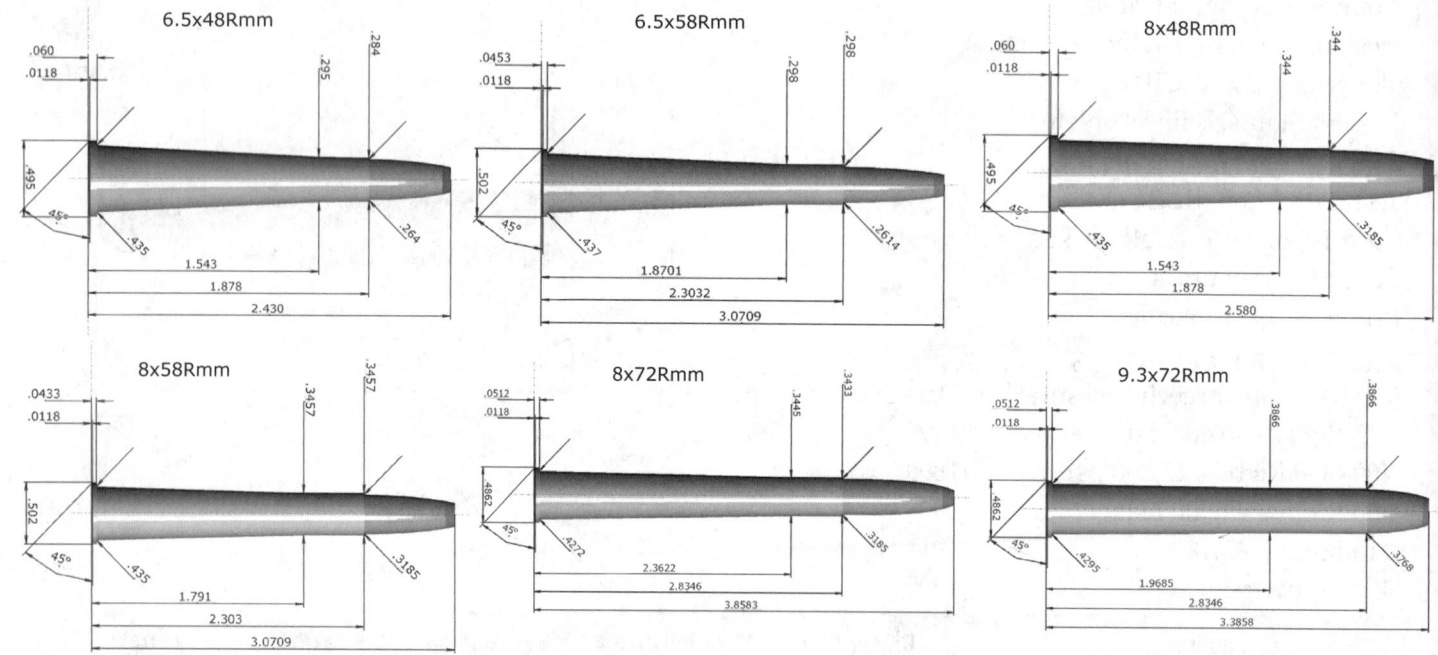

CARTRIDGE HISTORY

Country of Origin: Germany
Designer(s): J.P. Sauer & Sohn
Governing Body: CIP
Present Status: obsolete

CARTRIDGE DESCRIPTION

Test Barrel Length: N/A
Case Type: rimmed, straight
Case Material: brass
Primer Size: large rifle

Caliber	Bullet Diameter (in.)	Bullet Weight (gr.)	Rifling Twist 1 turn in (in.)	Max Horizontal Range (yd.)	Max Veritical Range (ft.)	Muzzle Velocity (fps)	Muzzle Energy (ft.-lbs.)
6.5x48Rmm Sauer .264	.264	126	8	4,500	9,350	1,155	373
6.5x58Rmm Sauer .264	.264	126	8	3,350	7,050	2,020	1,151
8x48Rmm Sauer .318	.318	196	9.45	4,300	8,850	1,665	1,206
8x58Rmm Sauer .318	.318	196	9.45	3,850	7,900	1,690	1,243
8x72Rmm Sauer .318	.318	227	9.45	4,000	8,000	1,900	1,819
9.3x72Rmm Sauer .365	.365	286	16.5	4,000	8,200	1,690	1,814

CURRENT MANUFACTURER(S)
None

GENERAL COMMENT(S)
J.P. Sauer & Sohn has been making firearms in Germany since 1751. By the late 1800s, a major part of their product line consisted of high quality shotguns and drillings. As many of the black powder cartridges of that era were unsuitable for drillings due to their configuration, Sauer designed a series of black powder cartridges specifically for drillings. Sauer did not actually manufacture cartridges, they left that to the large ammunition makers such as DWM and Roth. As most of the Sauer cartridges were quite popular in Europe, many of them made the transition to smokeless propellants around the turn of the century (1900). However, as smokeless powder cartridge designs spread, the need for "updated" black powder cartridges loaded with smokeless propellants faded away. By the late 1920s, most Sauer cartridges had become obsolete in Europe.Sauer cartridges always were unknown in the U.S. market. The last Sauer cartridge remaining in production was the 9.3x72Rmm which was listed in the RWS catalog into the 1980s.

TECHNICAL COMMENT(S)
Sauer cartridges are readily identified by their long length and unique, wedge-like configuration. They are rimmed with a sharply tapered body leading to a faint neck with no shoulder. This was a specialized design developed for break-open single-shot rifles and drillings. Sauer cartridges were unsuitable for bolt-action repeating rifles due to their shape and length. As black powder designs, they have plenty of interior volume which is unnecessary for smokeless propellants. Sauer cartridges were loaded with flat-nose or round-nose lead or jacketed bullets. The ballistics of Sauer cartridges could best be described as quite modest by modern standards, but they were competitive for their era. Today, Sauer cartridges are collector's items showing the ingenuity and breadth of cartridge design in the twilight of the black powder era.

SHARPS CALIBERS

ALTERNATE NAME(S): none
RELATED CALIBER(S): .45-70 Gov't.

NECKED

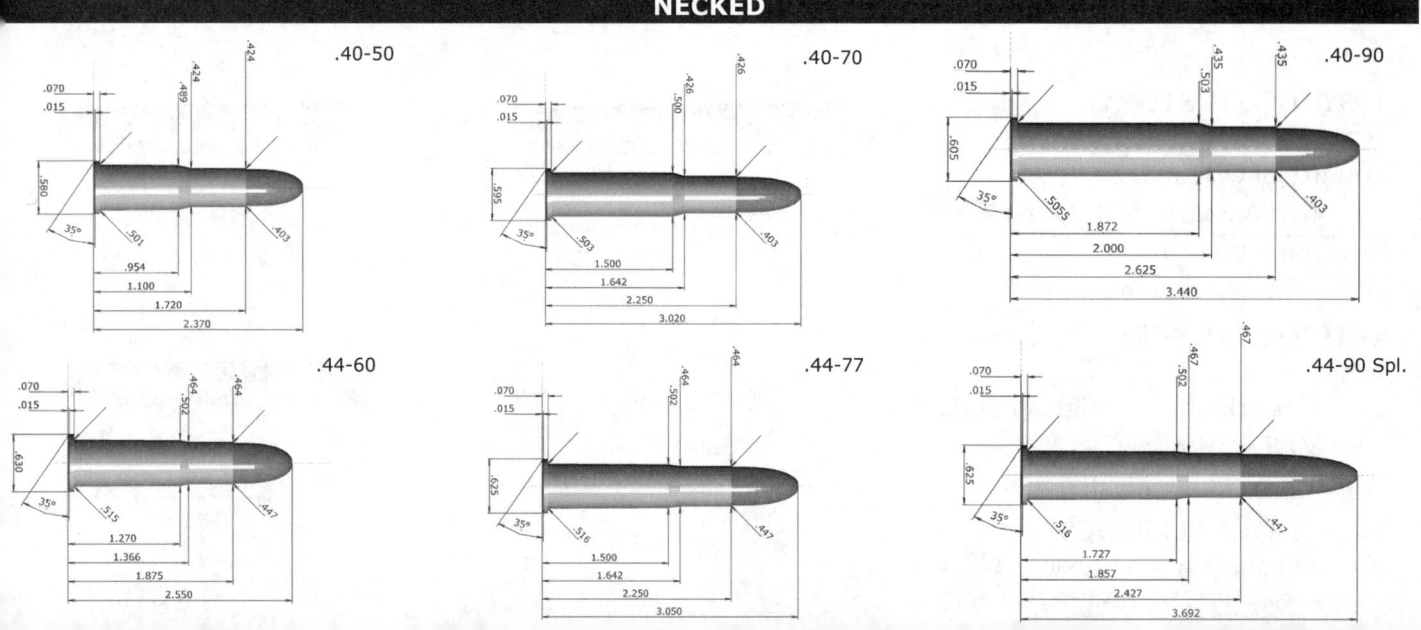

NECKED

.44-90
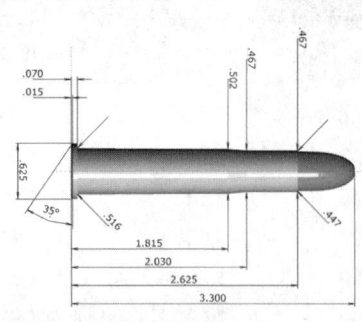

.44-100
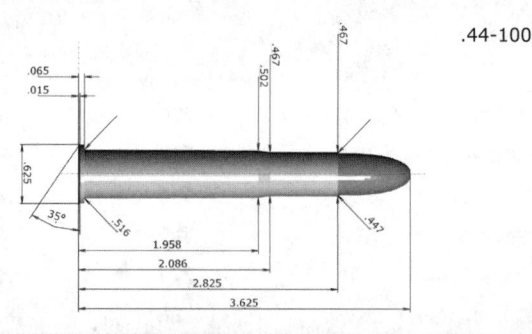

STRAIGHT

.40-50
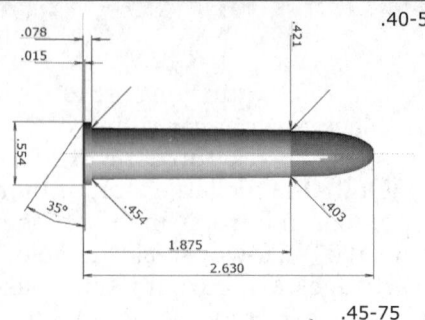

.40-70
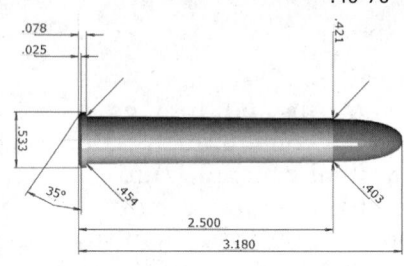

.40-90
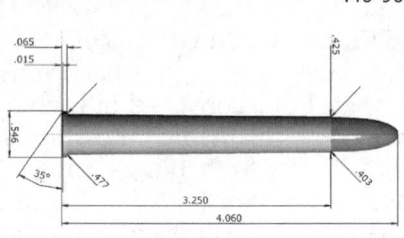

.45-75
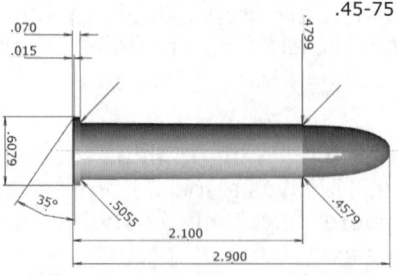

.45-100
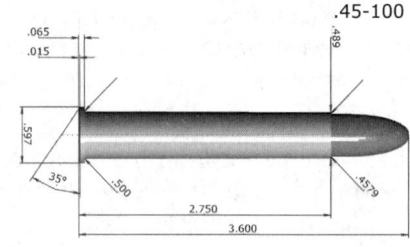

.45-90
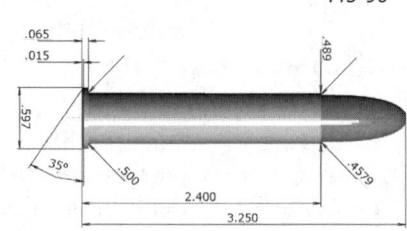

.45-110
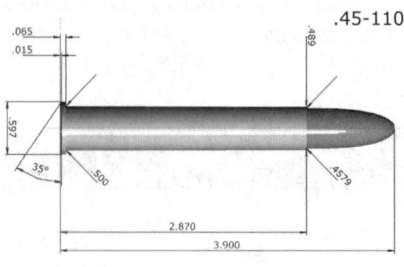

.45-120
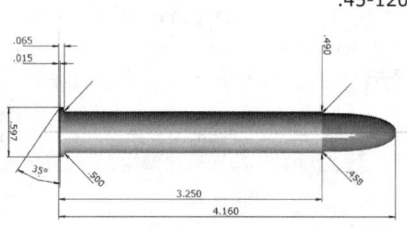

.50-90
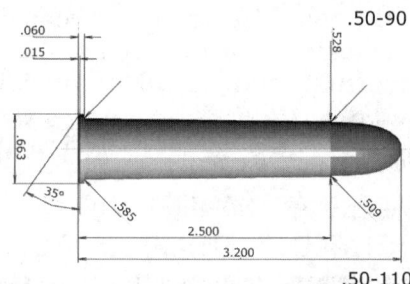

.50-100
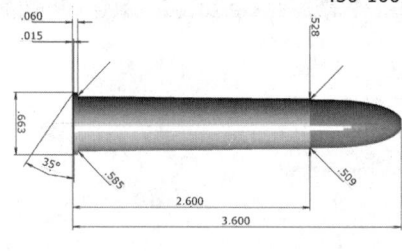

.50-110
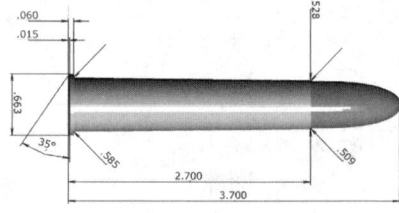

.50-140
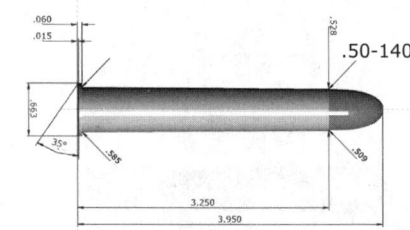

CARTRIDGE HISTORY
Year of Introduction: 1869-1885
Country of Origin: U.S.
Designer(s): Sharps Rifle Mfg. Co.
Governing Body: none
Present Status: obsolete

CARTRIDGE DESCRIPTION
Test Barrel Length: N/A
Case Type: rimmed, straight or necked
Case Material: brass
Primer Size: large rifle

CARTRIDGE BALLISTICS
Max. Average Breech Pressure: N/A

Caliber	Bullet Diameter (in.)	Bullet Weight (gr.)	Rifling Twist 1 turn in (in.)	Max Horizontal Range (yd.)	Max Veritical Range (ft.)	Muzzle Velocity (fps)	Muzzle Energy (ft.-lbs.)
.40-50 Sharps (straight)	.403	265	18-20	3,150	6,550	1,410	1,170
.40-50 Sharps (necked)	.403	265	18-20	3,150	6,550	1,460	1,254
.40-70 Sharps (straight)	.403	330	18-20	3,150	6,550	1,260	1,163
.40-70 Sharps (necked)	.403	330	18-20	3,150	6,550	1,420	1,477
.40-90 Sharps (straight)	.403	370	18-20	3,100	6,500	1,385	1,582
.40-90 Sharps (necked)	.403	370	18-20	6,150	6,550	1,475	1,787
.44-60 Sharps (necked)	.447	396	18-20	3,750	7,600	1,250	1,375
.44-77 Sharps (necked)	.447	365	18-20	3,750	7,600	1,250	1,374
.44-90 Sharps Spl. (necked)	.447	N/A	18-20	3,750	7,600	1,460	1,727
.44-90 Sharps (necked)	.447	520	18-20	3,750	7,600	1,270	1,862
.44-100 Sharps (necked)	.447	520	18-20	3,750	7,600	1,380	2,199
.45-75 Sharps (straight)	.457	400	18-20	3,800	7,800	1,330	1,571
.45-90 Sharps (straight)	.457	550	18-20	3,800	7,800	1,360	2,259
.45-100 Sharps (straight)	.457	550	18-20	3,800	7,800	1,435	2,515
.45-110 Sharps (straight)	.457	550	18-20	3,800	7,800	1,510	2,784
.45-120 Sharps (straight)	.457	500	18	3,800	7,800	1520	2561
.50-90 Sharps (straight)	.509	473	N/A	3,900	7,900	1,350	1,914
.50-100 Sharps (straight)	.509	473	N/A	3,900	7,900	1,425	2,133
.50-110 Sharps (straight)	.509	473	N/A	3,900	7,900	1,500	2,363
.50-140 Sharps (straight)	.509	700	N/A	4,400	8,000	1,355	2,850

CURRENT MANUFACTURER(S)
None

GENERAL COMMENT(S)
Sharps cartridges occupy a unique place in American history. They served during the Civil War with Union sharpshooters, fought Indians in the West and exterminated the buffalo herds. Sharps cartridges also earned a sterling reputation at long range rifle shooting competitions at Creedmoor and other venues that continues to this day. The historical reputation of Sharps cartridges is built on our image of the rough-and-tumble buffalo hunter with his "Big Fifty" Sharps rifle capable of hitting targets at 1,000 yards and beyond. This is essentially

correct as the .50-90 Sharps "poison slinger" was designed specifically for buffalo hunting and the single most popular Sharps cartridge. Sharps developed more cartridges than the 18 shown here, however, the other Sharps cartridges were minor variations or experimental. Sharps cartridges were made by the Sharps Rifle Manufacturing Co. (1851-1881) and by many of the major ammunition manufacturers such as Union Metallic Cartridge Co., Remington and Winchester. From 1869 to 1880, Sharps rifles and metallic cartridges were at the height of their popularity. But it did not last and the end came quickly. By the late 1870s, with the end of buffalo hunting and the decline in rifle competition, the market for Sharps rifles and cartridges had nearly disappeared. The Sharps Rifle Manufacturing Co. closed in 1881. In short order, smokeless propellants made large caliber black powder cartridges obsolete and most of the Sharps cartridges quickly faded away. By 1910, only a few remained on offer and by the beginning of World War I in 1914, they were gone.

TECHNICAL COMMENT(S)

Sharps made cartridges only in calibers .40, .44, .45 and .50. When Sharps standardized on .45 caliber cartridges in the late 1870s, they discontinued making rifles in the other Sharps calibers except on special order. Besides the famous .50-90 Sharps, the most popular Sharps calibers for hunting were the .40-90 (necked) and .45-90 (straight). For target shooting, the most popular Sharps calibers were the .40-70 (necked), .44-77 and .44-90. In addition to the 20 Sharps cartridges covered here, a number of other cartridges carried the Sharps name, but were not, in fact, Sharps cartridges. One example is the .40-90 "Sharps" (straight) which was designed and manufactured by Remington. It followed that a good number of Sharps rifles were made in this caliber which is probably why the Sharps name stuck. Other prominent examples are the .45 and .50 caliber "Sharps" cartridges with 3.25 inch length cartridges cases. The Sharps Rifle Mfg. Co. never made a cartridge of that length. Rather, these extra-long "Sharps" cartridges were designed and introduced by ammunition makers who used the Sharps name in hopes of promoting sales. By the time they did this, however, Sharps metallic cartridges were already fading into history and smokeless propellants were making them obsolete. Sharps made each caliber in one or more basic case lengths that increased proportionately in length to hold heavier powder charges. For example, the .45-110 had a longer case than the .45-90. All Sharps cartridges were designed for black powder propellants. Due to their size and obsolescence, most Sharps cartridges did not transition to smokeless propellants. Most factory loaded Sharps cartridges were assembled with round-nose, lead, paper-patched bullets. Today, Sharps cartridges are enjoying a revival as many black powder shooters discover the fun and the challenge of turning the cartridge clock back 125 years.

STEVENS CALIBERS

ALTERNATE NAME(S): none

RELATED CALIBER(S): .32 Ex. Long Ballard (.25-25 Stevens), .32 Ideal (.28-30 Stevens), .32-40 Ballard/Winchester (.32-35 Stevens), .35-40 Maynard 1882 (.38-35 Stevens)

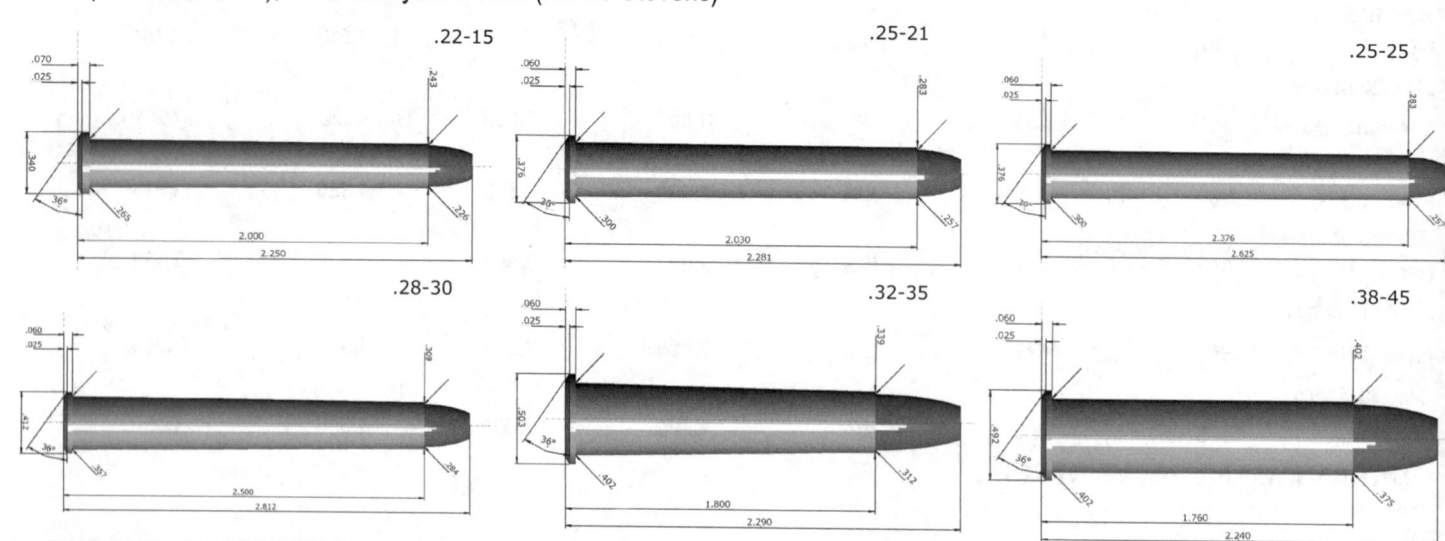

CARTRIDGE HISTORY

Country of Origin: U.S.

Designer(s): Charles W. Herrick, Cpt. W.L. Carpenter,

J. Stevens Arms & Tool Co.

Governing Body: none

Present Status: obsolete

CARTRIDGE DESCRIPTION

Test Barrel Length: N/A

Case Type: rimmed, straight or necked

Case Material: brass

Primer Size: large rifle

CARTRIDGE BALLISTICS

Max. Average Breech Pressure: N/A

Bullet Weight (gr.)	Bullet Type	Muzzle Velocity (fps)	Muzzle Energy (ft.-lbs.)
.22-15 Stevens	60	1,150	176
.25-21 Stevens	86	1,250	298
.25-25 Stevens	86	1,500	430
.25-35 Stevens	165	1,400	718
.28-30 Stevens	120	1,500	599
.32-35 Stevens Everlast	165	1,400	718
.38-35 Stevens Everlast	215	1,255	752
.38-45 Stevens Everlast	210	1,420	940

CURRENT MANUFACTURER(S)

None

GENERAL COMMENT(S)

If Sharps cartridges were for the long range hunter and competitor, then Stevens cartridges were for everyman. Sharps did not offer a cartridge smaller than .40 caliber and Stevens did not offer a cartridge above .38 caliber. Stevens cartridges were intended for hunting small and medium game and for short range target shooting. Low cost reloading was a major factor in the Stevens cartridge philosophy. Stevens did not manufacture loaded ammunition. They contracted production out to various ammunition makers, some of whom incorporated Stevens cartridges into their own product lines. Development of the Stevens cartridge line began in 1875, but proceeded more slowly than those of competitors. New Stevens black powder cartridges were still being introduced as late as 1900. However, the life of Stevens cartridges was cut short by the widespread appeal of smokeless propellants in the early 1900s. Few Stevens cartridges remained on offer by 1918.

TECHNICAL COMMENT(S)

Stevens cartridges are all of rimmed, straight configuration. In fact, the smaller calibers are easily recognized by their exceptionally long overall length for their caliber, frequently being compared to pencils. For example, the .25-35 Stevens cartridge is over 2.6 inches in length. The lack of a neck makes for easy reloading and Everlast cases were offered for some Stevens calibers. Ballistics of Stevens cartridges are unremarkable beyond noting they were competitive for their era. Only flat-nose, lead bullets were used in factory loaded Stevens ammunition. Stevens cartridges made one very significant contribution to cartridge development. The first 7mm center fire rifle cartridge in the U.S. was the .28-30 Stevens. As a black powder cartridge, the .28-30 Stevens could not take full advantage of smokeless propellants like more modern cartridge designs such as the 7x57mm Mauser. However, the .28-30 Stevens introduced the 7mm caliber to U.S. sportsmen.

WESTLEY RICHARDS CALIBERS

ALTERNATE NAME(S): W-R
RELATED CALIBER(S): none

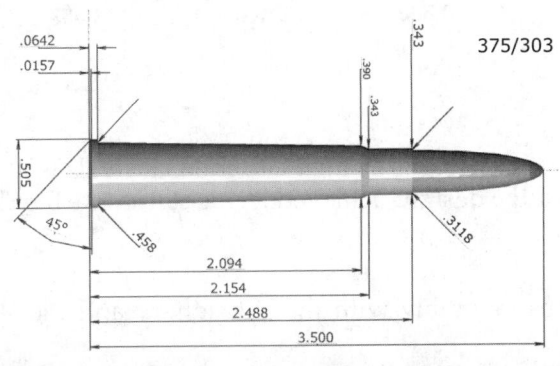

375/303

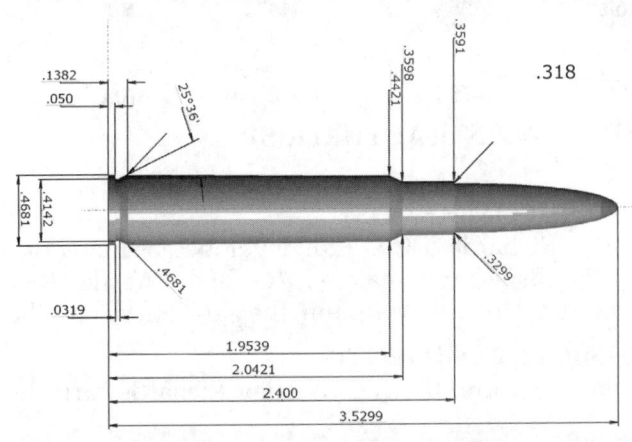

.318

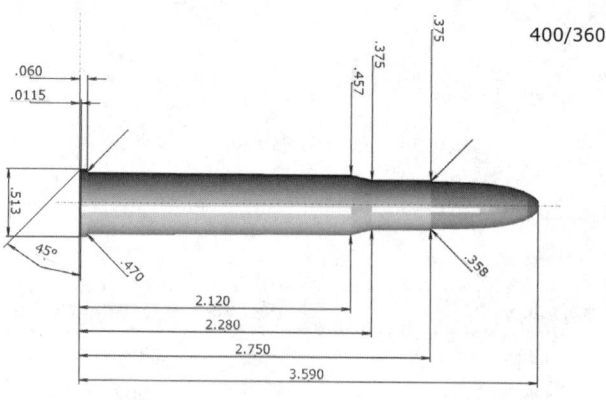

400/360

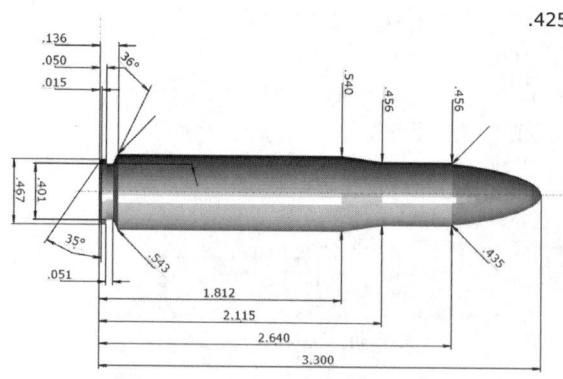

.425

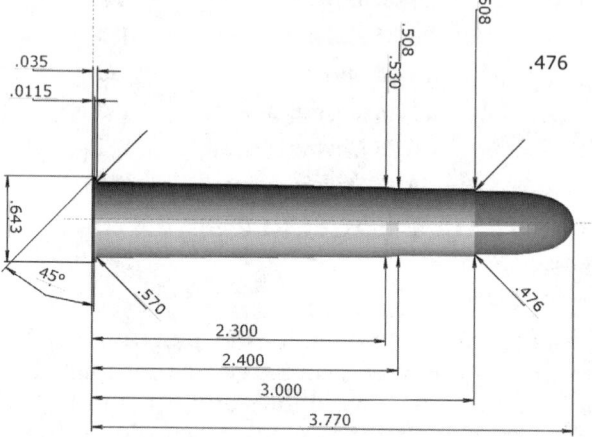

.476

CARTRIDGE HISTORY
Country of Origin: Britain
Designer(s): Westley Richards & Co., Ltd.
Governing Body: CIP
Present Status: semi-obsolete

CARTRIDGE DESCRIPTION
Test Barrel Length: 24 in.
Case Type: various
Case Material: brass
Primer Size: large rifle

CARTRIDGE BALLISTICS
Max. Average Breech Pressure:
375/303 Westley Richards – N/A
.318 Westley Richards – 47,800 psi.
400/360 Westley Richards – N/A
.425 Westley Richards – N/A
.476 Westley Richards – N/A

Caliber	Bullet Diameter (in.)	Bullet Weight (gr.)	Rifling Twist 1 turn in (in.)	Max Horizontal Range (yd.)	Max Veritical Range (ft.)	Muzzle Velocity (fps)	Muzzle Energy (ft.-lbs.)
375/303 Westley Richards	.312	200	10	6,300	14,300	2,725	2,980
.318 Westley Richards	.330	250	12	3,500	7,000	2,400	3,200
400/360 Westley Richards	.358	314	12	2,000	4,000	1,900	1,500
.425 Westley Richards	.435	410	N/A	2,500	4,900	2,350	5,028
.476 Westley Richards	.476	520	N/A	4,300	9,800	2,100	5,093

CURRENT MANUFACTURER(S)
Kynoch

GENERAL COMMENT(S)
Westley Richards & Co., Ltd. developed as many or more cartridge designs as their commercial rivals. Unlike the other British gun makers, none of the Westley Richards cartridge designs achieved iconic status like the .375 Holland & Holland Magnum, the .404 Jeffery and the .416 Rigby.

TECHNICAL COMMENT(S)
By any measure, the .425 Westley Richards cartridge compares favorably with the .404 Jeffery and the .416

Rigby. For example, the .425 W-R offers better ballistic performance than the .404 Jeffery and only slightly inferior ballistic performance to the .416 Rigby. And, very likely this was why the .425 W-R never really caught on, it was caught in a ballistic black hole between the .404 Jeffery and the .416 Rigby. Note that the .425 Westley Richards cartridge has a rebated rim to allow it to fit standard Mauser 8x57mm bolt faces with only minor modification.

WILHELM BRENNEKE CALIBERS

ALTERNATE NAME(S): none
RELATED CALIBER(S): 8x57mm Mauser, .30-'06 Spr.

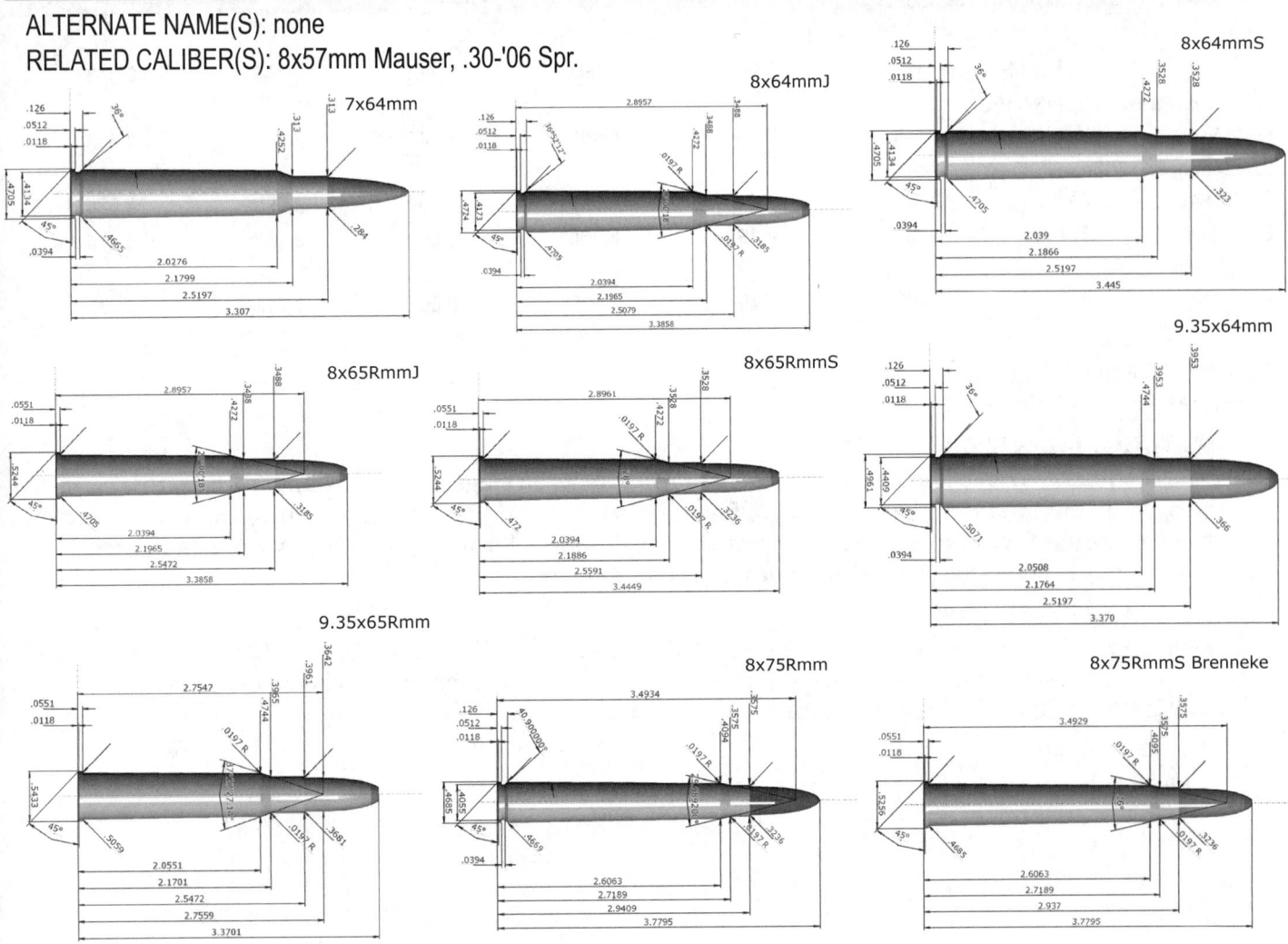

CARTRIDGE HISTORY

Year of Introduction: 1910 (9.3x64mm), 1912 (8x64mm), 1917 (7x64mm)

Country of Origin: Germany

Designer(s): Wilhelm Brenneke

Governing Body: CIP

Present Status: active

CARTRIDGE DESCRIPTION

Test Barrel Length: 24 in.

Case Type: rimless, necked; rimmed, necked

Case Material: brass

Primer Size: large rifle

CARTRIDGE BALLISTICS

Max. Average Breech Pressure:

7x64mm – 60,200 psi.

8x64mmS – 58,750 psi.

9.3x64mm – 63,800 psi.

8x75Rmm – 55,114 psi.

8x75RmmS Brenneke – 63,817 psi.

Caliber	Bullet Diameter (in.)	Bullet Weight (gr.)	Rifling Twist 1 turn in (in.)	Max Horizontal Range (yd.)	Max Veritical Range (ft.)	Muzzle Velocity (fps)	Muzzle Energy (ft.-lbs.)
7x64mm Brenneke	.284	170	8.66	6,900	15,400	2,780	2,965
8x64mmS, 8x64Rmm, 8x64mmJ Brenneke	.323	185	9.45	4,400	10,000	2,890	3,432
9.3x64mm, 9.3x65Rmm Brenneke	.365	285	12	4,300	9,500	2,690	4,580
8x75Rmm	.323	196	9.45	3,950	8,600	3,050	4,079
8x75RmmS Brenneke	.323	196	9.45	3,950	8,600	2,715	3,232

CURRENT MANUFACTURER(S)
Federal, Dynamit Nobel

GENERAL COMMENT(S)
Wilhelm Brenneke is remembered as the pioneer of rifled shotgun slugs. Less well known are his rifle cartridge designs. A contemporary of Charles Newton, Brenneke's rifle cartridge designs have proven the more durable of the two. While Brenneke focused his products on Europe, Newton's cartridges were wholly American. Brenneke's most successful and enduring design is the 7x64mm.

TECHNICAL COMMENT(S)
All Brenneke rifle cartridge designs are based on the standard 8x57mm Mauser case head dimensions with longer case lengths to provide increased volume. In this respect, the Brenneke calibers are more like the .30-06 Spr. (7.62x63mm) than the 8x57mm Mauser.

CHAPTER 69 : MILITARY RIFLE CARTRIDGES - CURRENT

CHAPTER 69

For Cartridge Index see Chapter 101. All drawing dimensions are approximate.

Modern military cartridge development and usage have shown a continuous progression to smaller (case lenth and bullet diameter) calibers since WWI. A milestone of sorts was reached in 1943 with the adoption of new "assault rifle" cartridges by Germany (7.9x33mm) and the Soviet Union (7.62x39mm). For reasons of wartime expediency, both of these cartridges were not of smaller caliber than their predecessors so much as shorter, lighter, and reduced power versions. Over considerable opposition from member nations with well-developed small caliber experimental military cartridges, the U.S. forced NATO members to adopt the 7.62x51mm cartridge in the early 1950s. This was not to last.

In 1963, the U.S. Army adopted the 5.56x45mm cartridge. Almost overnight, the paradigm for a modern military cartridge changed. Other nations rushed to develop their own small calibers (such as the Soviet 5.45x39mm) and the members of military alliances such as NATO adopted them (reluctantly) to establish interchangeability. This process continues with the latest proposed military cartridges from Germany in the 4.6mm (.18 caliber) range. To date, none of these "micro" calibers has been adopted by the military forces of major nations. However, many military ordnance experts believe these smaller calibers may be the prototypes for future military cartridges and contracts. What happened to caseless military cartridges? After several expensive development programs in the U.S. and other nations, the difficulties and drawbacks of caseless military cartridges were reduced, but not completely resolved. Still, the potential advantages of caseless cartridges for military service eventually led Germany to make a serious effort to perfect such ammunition in the 1980s. By most measures, they succeeded, only to shelve the project for economic reasons with the end of the Cold War. Today, much of the German expertise in caseless ammunition remains dormant for lack of demand. Most military ordnance experts believe the self-contained cartridge has enough potential remaining to carry it through one or two more developmental generations before it can be widely adopted. Development will focus on high energy, insensitive propellants, new case materials, ignition systems, and modernization of production technology.

Dissecting MIL SPEC Nomenclature

MIL SPEC cartridge nomenclature systems are used by the armed forces of individual nations to precisely identify their military ammunition. Today, the armed foces of most countries adhere in whole or in part to the MIL SPEC nomenclature systems developed by treaty organizations such as NATO and the ex-Warsaw Pact to ensure interoperability.

These systems use metric units of measure beginning with one to three numbers to indicate the caliber in millimeters (mm) followed by an "x" and two or three numbers indicating the case length in mm. Following this is the name of the country that first adopted the cartridge or the treaty organization writing the MIL SPEC. Modern examples of such systems include: 5.56x45mm NATO, 7.62x51mm NATO, and 7.62x39mm Soviet. Following this, the year of adoption is sometimes indicated such as 7.62mm Soviet M43.

From this point, modern MIL SPEC nomenclature systems further identify the nature and variant of the cartridge. Examples of the nature may include ball, tracer, armor piercing, blank, match, subsonic, proof, incendiary, grenade launching, etc. Lastly, a series of numbers and/or letters identifies variants, for example: 7.62x51mm NATO Ball M80, 7.62x39mm Soviet Ball M43 Type XXX, or 5.56x45mm NATO Ball M855A1.

Prior to 1950, most nations used individual MIL SPEC systems which were confusing and often complicated. These systems used English or metric measurement units to define caliber followed by a dizzying array of unique systems to express nature, variants, and models. In some countries, several different systems were in use at the same time as new calibers were introduced but old calibers remained in service. Examples include: .303 British Mark 8z, .30-'06 Ball M2, 7.62x54Rmm Russian Type LPS, and 7.9x57mmJS Mauser sS Geschoss Eisenkern.

4.5x40Rmm RUSSIAN SPS

ALTERNATE NAME(S): 4.5x40Rmm SPS
RELATED CALIBER(S): .22 Hornet

CARTRIDGE HISTORY
Year of Introduction: 1968
Country of Origin: Soviet Union
Designer(s): N/A
Governing Body: none
Present Status: active

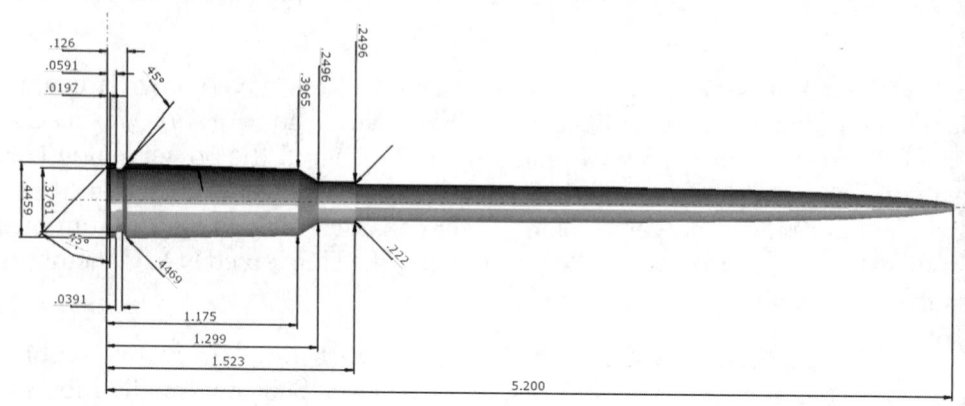

CARTRIDGE DESCRIPTION
Bullet Diameter: .177 in.
Bullet Weight(s): 203.7 gr.
Rifling Twist Rate: smooth bore
Test Barrel Length: N/A
Case Type: rimmed, necked
Case Material: brass
Primer: small rifle

CARTRIDGE BALLISTICS
Max. Average Breech Pressure: N/A
Max. Horizontal Range: 150 yds. in air
Max. Vertical Range: 450 ft. in air

Bullet Weight (gr.)	Bullet Type	Muzzle Velocity (fps)	Muzzle Energy (ft.-lbs.)
203.7	Ball-Steel rod	820 (in air)	304

CURRENT MANUFACTURER(S)
Russian State Arsenals

GENERAL COMMENT(S)
This is a unique and specialized Russian Navy cartridge for offensive or defensive under water combat, although it can also be fired in air. Russia offers both the pistol and its ammunition for export. No other country makes this cartridge.

TECHNICAL COMMENT(S)
The 4.5x40Rmm SPS cartridge was designed especially for the SPP-1 and SPP-1M under water handguns. A flat metal clip holding four rounds facilitates loading and unloading. This cartridge is not a variant of any other cartridge in Russian military service. The rimmed, necked case is a unique design somewhat similar to an elongated .22 Hornet. In a departure from normal Russian practice, the cartridge case is brass, not steel. The projectile is a 4.13 inch long steel rod weighing 203.7 grains. As water is many times more dense than air, under water muzzle velocity is considerably lower. In fact, it depends on the depth. The barrels of the SPP under water handguns are smoothbore. The rods are drag-stabilized under water. Maximum effective range under water depends on the depth as well as visibility. However, the effective ballistic range under water is estimated to be 30 feet. In air, the rods are unstable, but capable of reliably hitting a target at very close range.

4.6x30mm

ALTERNATE NAME(S): 4.6x30mm H&K
RELATED CALIBER(S): 5.7x28mm FN

CARTRIDGE HISTORY
Year of Introduction: late 1990s
Country of Origin: Germany
Designer(s): H&K
Governing Body: CIP
Present Status: active

CARTRIDGE DESCRIPTION
Bullet Diameter: .183 in.
Bullet Weight(s): 25 gr.
Rifling Twist Rate: N/A
Test Barrel Length: N/A
Case Type: rimless, necked
Case Material: brass
Primer Size: small rifle

CARTRIDGE BALLISTICS
Max. Average Breech Pressure: N/A
Max. Horizontal Range: 3,000 yds.
Max. Vertical Range: 6,000 ft.

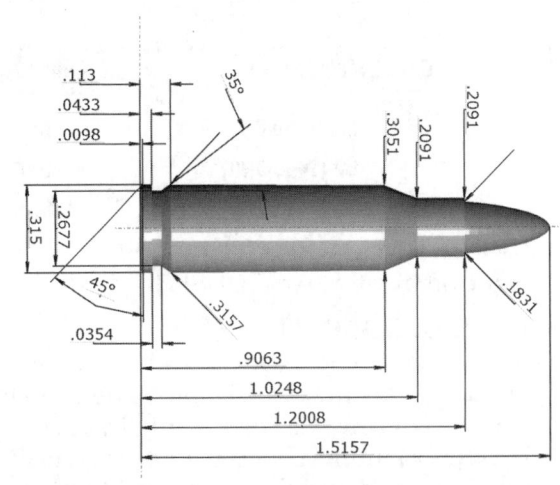

Bullet Weight (gr.)	Bullet Type	Muzzle Velocity (fps)	Muzzle Energy (ft.-lbs.)
25	FMJ	2,355	308

CURRENT MANUFACTURER(S)
ROF, DN

GENERAL COMMENT(S)
This is a contemporary personal defense weapon (PDW) cartridge very similar to the 5.7x28mm FN. Designed by Heckler & Koch for their new H&K PDW currently being marketed as a competitor to the FN P90.

TECHNICAL COMMENT(S)
The small bore diameter, light weight bullet, and relatively low muzzle velocity all work against this cartridge. Given the recent stopping power failures of the 5.56x45mm M855A1 cartridge in Iraq and Afghanistan, it seems very unlikely that a military organization will adopt such a small caliber.

5.45x39mm SOVIET

ALTERNATE NAME(S): 5.45x39mm Russian, 5.45x39mm Kalashnikov, 5.45mm M74, 5.45x39.5mm
RELATED CALIBER(S): 7.62x39mm M43

CARTRIDGE HISTORY
Year of Introduction: 1974
Country of Origin: Soviet Union
Designer(s): N/A
Governing Body: CIP
Present Status: active

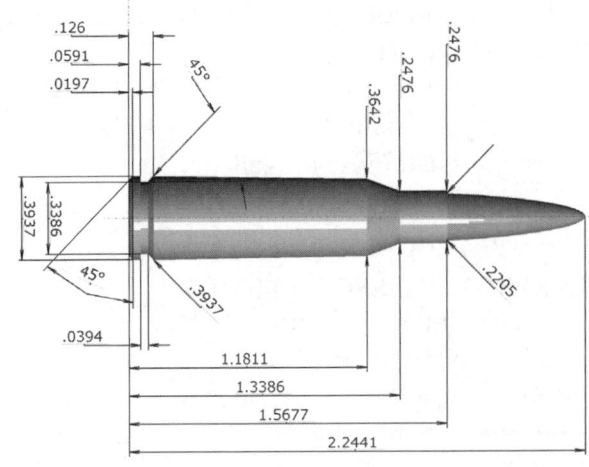

CARTRIDGE DESCRIPTION
Bullet Diameter: .220 in.
Bullet Weight(s): 50-60 gr.
Rifling Twist Rate: 1 turn in 10 in.
Test Barrel Length: 24 in.
Case Type: rimless, necked
Case Material: steel
Primer Size: small rifle

CARTRIDGE BALLISTICS
Max. Average Breech Pressure: 55,114 psi.
Max. Horizontal Range: 4,100 yds.
Max. Vertical Range: 9,200 ft.

Bullet Weight (gr.)	Bullet Type	Muzzle Velocity (fps)	Muzzle Energy (ft.-lbs.)
54 (Type PS)	Ball	2,950	1,045
52 (Type 7N6)	Ball	2,890	964
79.5	Subsonic	985	171

CURRENT MANUFACTURER(S)

Neutron, Kintex, Arsenal, SK Jagd, Mesko, Romtechnica, Barnaul, Lugansk, Tula, Ulyanovsk, Prvi Partizan

GENERAL COMMENT(S)

In 1974, the Soviet Army introduced a new assault rifle and cartridge. The new rifle was the AK-74 and the new cartridge was the 5.45x39mm Soviet. Mikhail Kalashnikov designed the rifle, but not the cartridge. While the new AK-74 rifle was a substantially revised AK-47, the 5.45x39mm cartridge was a completely new design. The U.S. 5.56x45mm M193 cartridge obviously exerted a considerable influence on the designers of the new Soviet cartridge. The new Soviet cartridge fires a small caliber, lightweight bullet at high muzzle velocity much like its U.S. predecessor. Combat in Afghanistan proved the effectiveness of the new cartridge. Since then, a new military rifle has been adopted by the Russian Army. It too is chambered for the 5.45x39mm Soviet cartridge. While many Warsaw Pact satellite nations officially adopted the 5.45x39mm cartridge, they were slow to field it because of the expense. By the time the Iron Curtain came down, many former Warsaw Pact nations had still not begun production. Significantly, China (P.R.C.) did not adopt the 5.45x39mm Soviet cartridge electing instead to develop a new military cartridge of their own.

TECHNICAL COMMENT(S)

The 5.45x39mm Soviet cartridge is not merely a necked down 7.62x39mm M43 cartridge. The case head diameter of the 5.45x39mm case is smaller than that of the 7.62x39mm. In addition, the 5.45x39mm breaks with Russian military tradition in that it is loaded to a substantially higher chamber pressure than the 7.62x39mm. The very low drag, full metal jacket boat-tail bullet is a three-piece design with a copper alloy jacket, lead core and steel penetrator. There is a hollow cavity under the tip. This bullet is analogous to the SS109/M855A1 bullet for the 5.56x45mm NATO round in that it is designed to penetrate body armor. In addition to the Ball round, tracer and other types have been developed. For the commercial market, hollow point and FMJBT bullets without the steel penetrator are offered.

5.56x45mm NATO

ALTERNATE NAME(S): 5.56x45mm, 5.56x45mm M193, 5.56x45mm M855A1, 5.56mm NATO, 5.56mm
RELATED CALIBER(S): .222 Rem., .222 Rem. Mag., .223 Rem.

CARTRIDGE HISTORY

Year of Introduction: 1964 (U.S.) 1980 (NATO)

Country of Origin: U.S.

Designer(s): James Sullivan

Governing Body: SAAMI, CIP

Present Status: active

CARTRIDGE DESCRIPTION

Bullet Diameter: .224 in.

Bullet Weight(s): 55-64 gr.

Rifling Twist Rate: 1 turn in 7 in.

Test Barrel Length: 24 in.

Case Type: rimless, necked

Case Material: brass or steel

Primer Size: small rifle

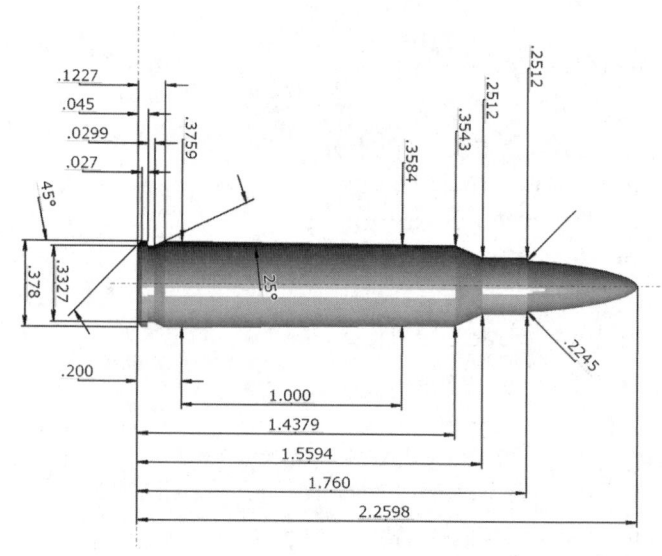

CARTRIDGE BALLISTICS

Max. Average Breech Pressure: 52,000 psi.

Max. Horizontal Range: 4,100 yds.

Max. Vertical Range: 9,200 ft.

Bullet Weight (gr.)	Bullet Type	Muzzle Velocity (fps)	Muzzle Energy (ft.-lbs.)
55 (M193)	Ball	3,250	1,290
62.5 (M855A1)	Ball	3,020	1,265

CURRENT MANUFACTURER(S)
Federal, Remington, Winchester, Wolf, Prvi Partizan, Igman, IMI, PMP, PMC, Sellier & Bellot, Singapore Tech, RUAG, many government arsenals

GENERAL COMMENT(S)
The M-16 rifle was designed by Eugene Stoner and the 5.56x45mm cartridge by James Sullivan who worked with Stoner. Both rifle and cartridge were complementary parts of a single weapon system concept. In the early 1960s, the U.S. Air Force under Gen. Curtis LeMay adopted the M-16 rifle and 5.56x45mm M193 cartridge for U.S. airbase defense teams. The light weight, minimal recoil and flat trajectory were appreciated by airbase personnel who were not trained as front line infantry. Special Forces personnel in Vietnam also preferred the M-16 and 5.56x45mm cartridge. Bowing to the inevitable, the U.S. Army officially adopted the M-16 rifle and 5.56x45mm M193 cartridge in 1964. Other NATO members were not happy with the new U.S. cartridge as they had only recently had the 7.62x51mm cartridge shoved down their throats, spending millions to convert their military forces in the process. They viewed the 5.56x45mm cartridge as lacking in stopping power, penetration and long range performance. In answer to these objections, FN in Belgium developed the 5.56mm SS109, a 62.5 grain FMJBT design with a steel penetrator, substantially improved penetration, and longer effective range. NATO adopted the 5.56x45mm cartridge in 1980.

TECHNICAL COMMENT(S)
The original M193 load with a 55 grain FMJBT bullet was designed for optimum ballistic performance at ranges of approximately 200 yards or less to meet airbase defense requirements. This bullet proved effective at the close ranges in Vietnam as well, although penetration of dense foliage was minimal. The M193 loading has been replaced in U.S. military service by the M855A1 loaded with a 62.5 grain penetrator bullet that meets all NATO requirements. However, combat experience in Iraq has shown that penetrator bullets do not offer the desired level of stopping power against unprotected targets. Another lesson learned in Iraq is that the 5.56x45mm bullet will not penetrate the concrete walls that predominate in many parts of the world where wood is scarce. U.S. military personnel in Iraq have compensated by using 7.62x51mm and .50 BMG caliber weapons to defeat concrete walls. As a quick fix to the lack of stopping power, U.S. special forces have developed a heavy 77 grain bullet for the 5.56x45mm. They also developed a new 6.8mm cartridge which has a 115 grain bullet. Original M-16 rifles had a rifling twist of 1 turn in 14 inches. When it was found that the bullets would not stabilize at very cold temperatures, the rifling twist rate was increased to 1 turn in 12 inches. The adoption of the heavy 62.5 grain NATO bullet required yet another change in the rifling twist rate, this time to 1 turn in 7 inches. Actually, a twist rate of 1 turn in 9 inches is sufficient to stabilize the M855A1 Ball cartridge; the 1 turn in 7 inch twist was adopted to stabilize the M856A1 Tracer cartridge. Here it is important to note that the commercial .223 Rem. cartridge is NOT the same as the 5.56x45mm NATO cartridge and they are NOT interchangeable.

5.66x39mm RUSSIAN MPS

ALTERNATE NAME(S): 5.66x39mm MPS
RELATED CALIBER(S): 5.45x39mm M74, 4.5x40Rmm SPS

CARTRIDGE HISTORY
Year of Introduction: 1975
Country of Origin: Soviet Union
Designer(s): N/A
Governing Body: none
Present Status: active

CARTRIDGE DESCRIPTION
Bullet Diameter: .222 in.
Bullet Weight(s): 232 gr.
Rifling Twist Rate: smoothbore
Test Barrel Length: N/A
Case Type: rimless, necked, under water type

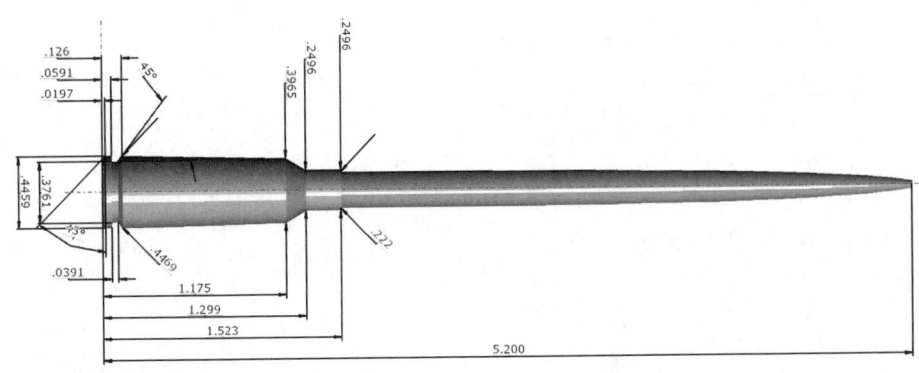

Case Material: steel
Primer: small rifle

CARTRIDGE BALLISTICS
Max. Average Breech Pressure: 55,114 psi.

Max. Horizontal Range: 150 yds. in air

Max. Vertical Range: 450 ft. in air

Bullet Weight (gr.)	Bullet Type	Muzzle Velocity (fps)	Muzzle Energy (ft.-lbs.)
232	Ball-Steel rod	1,180 (in air)	717

CURRENT MANUFACTURER(S)
Russian State Arsenals

GENERAL COMMENT(S)
This is a unique and specialized cartridge for under water combat, although it can be fired in air. It is designed to be fired in the APS underwater assault rifle used by combat divers in the Russian Navy in offensive or defensive modes. Russia offers both the rifle and ammunition for export. No other country makes this cartridge.

TECHNICAL COMMENT(S)
This cartridge is a technological first and a credit to those who designed it. The 5.66x39mm MPS is the first military cartridge designed from the outset for use under water. The APS assault rifle, which is a special variant of the seminal AK-47, is chambered and modified for this cartridge. The steel cartridge case is a standard 7.62x39mm M43 case necked down to accept a pointed, 4.37 inch long steel rod weighing 232 grains. Muzzle velocity in air is 1,180 fps. As water is many times more dense than air, under water muzzle velocity is considerably lower and depends on the depth. The barrel of the APS under water assault rifle is smoothbore. The rods are drag-stabilized under water. Maximum effective range under water depends on the depth as well as visibility. However, the effective ballistic range under water is estimated to be 60 feet. In air, the rods are unstable, but capable of reliably hitting a target at very close range. Modifications to the cartridge case are minimal beyond the expected close attention to waterproofing. The case is simply necked down to accept the 5.66mm caliber rod. Identifying a 5.66x39mm under water cartridge is quite easy given the unusual length and projectile.

5.7x28mm FN

ALTERNATE NAME(S): 5.7x28mm, 5.7 P90, 5.7x28mm FN P90
RELATED CALIBER(S): none

CARTRIDGE HISTORY
Year of Introduction: 1993

Country of Origin: Belgium

Designer(s): FN

Governing Body: CIP

Present Status: active

CARTRIDGE DESCRIPTION
Bullet Diameter: .224 in.

Bullet Weight(s): 23-30 gr.

Rifling Twist Rate: 1 turn in 9 in.

Test Barrel Length: 4.9 in.

Case Type: rimless, necked

Case Material: brass

Primer Size: small rifle

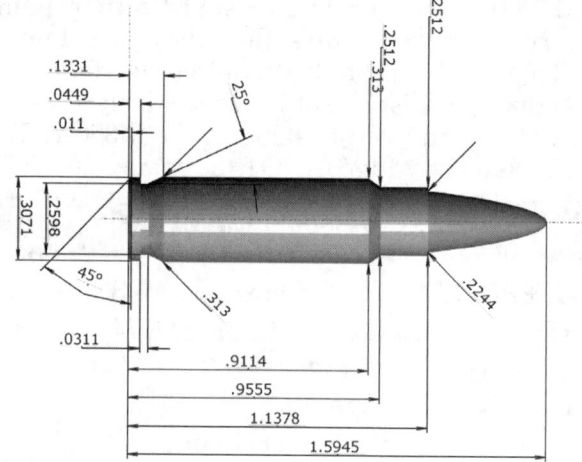

CARTRIDGE BALLISTICS
Max. Average Breech Pressure: 50,038 psi.

Max. Horizontal Range: 3,400 yds.

Max. Vertical Range: 8,000 ft.

Bullet Weight (gr.)	Bullet Type	Muzzle Velocity (fps)	Muzzle Energy (ft.-lbs.)
31 (SS 190)	Ball	2,325	372
55.5 (Sb 193)	Subsonic	975	117

CURRENT MANUFACTURER(S)
Hornady, FN, Elite Ammunition, Federal

GENERAL COMMENT(S)
In the late 1980s, FN pioneered a new concept, the "personal defense weapon" (PDW). The PDW was not a pistol, sub-machinegun or carbine. Rather it was a compact, selective fire weapon with an integrated sighting system designated the P90. It fired a new, small centerfire cartridge with a bullet designed to provide optimum performance against enemy personnel wearing body armor out to a distance of 200 meters. It was intended for technical personnel, drivers, artillery crews, signal specialists and guards, not front line infantry. FN also offers a semi-automatic pistol in this caliber. FN has endeavored to sell their P90 PDW to security forces, gendarmeries, and law enforcement agencies as well as to military organizations. As always, militaries are slow to adopt new ideas, so FN has a difficult job in this connection. H&K has introduced a similar concept firing a different cartridge.

TECHNICAL COMMENT(S)
Despite its small size and limited case volume, the 5.7x28mm FN offers equivalent or substantially better ballistic performance than most handgun cartridges at ranges of 25 meters. At ranges beyond 25 meters it is far superior to most military pistol cartridges. The FN bullet will also pierce body armor while most handgun bullets will not. The compact design, ergonomic grips and sighting system of the P90 are far easier to use than any handgun and more accurate. Recoil impulse from the lightweight bullet is minimal. As a result of experiences in Iraq, U.S. military organizations have begun to question the stopping power of the 5.56x45mm cartridge with the M855A1 bullet. This does not bode well for the P90 with its lighter bullet at lower muzzle velocity.

5.8x21mm CHINESE

ALTERNATE NAME(S): 5.8x21mm Chinese PDW, 5.8x21mm DAP-92
RELATED CALIBER(S): 5.8x42mm Chinese, 5.7x28mm FN

CARTRIDGE HISTORY
Year of Introduction: circa 2000
Country of Origin: China (P.R.C.)
Designer(s): N/A
Governing Body: N/A
Present Status: active

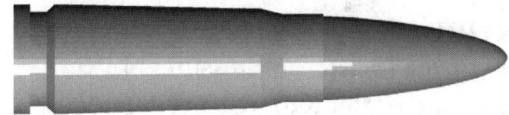

No dimensions available at this time.

CARTRIDGE DESCRIPTION
Bullet Diameter: .228 in.
Bullet Weight(s): 46 gr., 123 gr.
Rifling Twist Rate: N/A
Test Barrel Length: N/A
Case Type: rimless, necked
Case Material: steel with copper wash
Primer Size: small rifle

CARTRIDGE BALLISTICS
Max. Average Breech Pressure: N/A
Max. Horizontal Range: 3,000 yds.
Max. Vertical Range: 7,500 ft.

Bullet Weight (gr.)	Bullet Type	Muzzle Velocity (fps)	Muzzle Energy (ft.-lbs.)
46	Ball	1,740	309
123	FMJ	1,000	N/A

CURRENT MANUFACTURER(S)
Norinco

GENERAL COMMENT(S)

The Chinese military calls this new round of ammunition a "compact submachine gun" (CSG) cartridge. Western military nomenclature would classify this new round as a "personal defense weapon" (PDW) cartridge such as the 5.7x28mm FN or 4.6x30mm H&K. Reportedly, the Chinese military is now fielding this new cartridge along with their new 5.8x42mm service cartridge. The heavier bullet is subsonic for use with suppressors.

TECHNICAL COMMENT(S)

The Chinese 5.8x 21mm CSG cartridge employs a different ballistic approach than its western PDW counterparts such as the 5.7x28mm FN cartridge. While western designs use a lightweight bullet at high muzzle velocities, the Chinese 5.8x21mm uses a heavier bullet at a substantially lower muzzle velocity to achieve an equivalent striking energy. The ball bullet used in the 5.8x21mm cartridge has a hardened steel penetrator capable of piercing most body armor at 100 meters.

5.8x42mm CHINESE

ALTERNATE NAME(S): 5.8mm M95
RELATED CALIBER(S): 5.56x45mm , 5.45x39mm, 7.62x39mm

CARTRIDGE HISTORY
Year of Introduction: 1995
Country of Origin: China (P.R.C.)
Designer(s): N/A
Governing Body: N/A
Present Status: active

CARTRIDGE DESCRIPTION
Bullet Diameter: .228 in.
Bullet Weight(s): 64 gr.
Rifling Twist Rate: N/A
Test Barrel Length: N/A
Case Type: rimless, necked
Case Material: steel
Primer Size: small rifle

CARTRIDGE BALLISTICS
Max. Average Breech Pressure: N/A
Max. Horizontal Range: N/A
Max. Vertical Range: N/A

Bullet Weight (gr.)	Bullet Type	Muzzle Velocity (fps)	Muzzle Energy (ft.-lbs.)
64 (DBP87)	Ball	3,050	1,321

CURRENT MANUFACTURER(S)
Norinco

GENERAL COMMENT(S)

In the late 1970s, Chinese ordnance engineers began designing a replacement for their standard 7.62x39mm M43 military cartridge. Although the Soviet 5.45x39mm M74 cartridge had been introduced in 1974, the Chinese military preferred a domestic design. The result is the 5.8x42mm cartridge fired from the new Type 95 assault rifle. Unlike the 5.45x39mm M74 and 5.56x45mm M855A1 cartridges, the new Chinese 5.8x42mm cartridge is intended to be a universal replacement for the 7.62x39mm and 7.62x54Rmm cartridges in the infantry rifle, squad machinegun, and general purpose machinegun roles as well as for snipers and designated marksmen. To fill all these requirements, a variety of different loadings are being developed including tracer, heavy ball, and armor-piercing variants. Although officially adopted in 1995, this new cartridge is only now being fielded in quantity.

TECHNICAL COMMENT(S)

An important requirement for the new Chinese 5.8x42mm service cartridge was penetration of body armor. To this end, the 64 grain DBP87 Ball bullet has a 22.6 grain hardened steel penetrator. Reportedly, this bullet is able to penetrate 10mm of steel armor at 310 meters and 3.5mm of steel armor at 700 meters. A heavy Ball and a Heavy Ball Sniper loading are reportedly under development.

6.5mm GRENDEL

ALTERNATE NAME(S): 6.5 Grendel
RELATED CALIBER(S): 7.62x39mm Soviet

CARTRIDGE HISTORY
Year of Introduction: 2003
Country of Origin: U.S.
Designer(s): Bill Alexander
Governing Body: SAAMI
Present Status: active

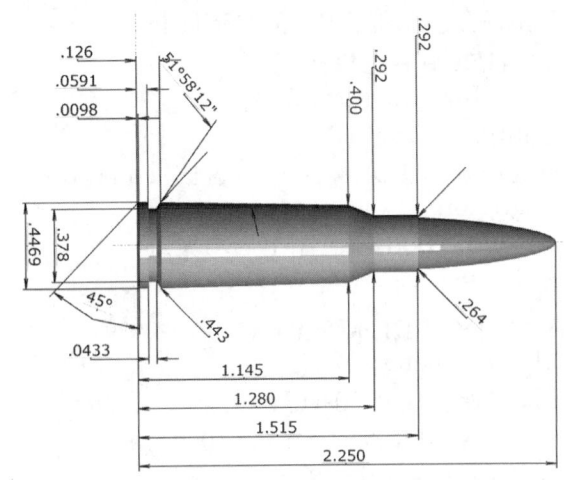

CARTRIDGE DESCRIPTION
Bullet Diameter: .264 in.
Bullet Weight(s): 123 gr.
Rifling Twist Rate: 1 turn in 9 in.
Test Barrel Length: 24 in.
Case Type: rimless, necked
Case Material: brass
Primer Size: small rifle

CARTRIDGE BALLISTICS
Max. Average Breech Pressure: approx. 50,000 psi.
Max. Horizontal Range: 3,700 yds.
Max. Vertical Range: 7,000 ft.

Bullet Weight (gr.)	Bullet Type	Muzzle Velocity (fps)	Muzzle Energy (ft.-lbs.)
123	JSP	2,610	1,861

CURRENT MANUFACTURER(S)
Wolf

GENERAL COMMENT(S)
Ever since its adoption in 1964, military pundits have consistently criticized the (perceived) lack of stopping power of the 5.56x45mm NATO cartridge. When reports from Iraq and Afghanistan also indicated the 5.56x45mm lacked stopping power, fresh fuel was added to the fires of criticism. Obviously, the U.S. military is not interested in adopting a new service cartridge in the middle of a war, and with ammunition shortages in existing calibers. In addition, research and development money is lacking. A number of prescient independent experimenters, intent on upholding historical precedent, have designed 5.56x45mm replacements. The Grendel cartridge is one of those replacement candidates.

Given its intended purpose, the 6.5mm Grendel cartridge has a dim future. The U.S. military is unlikely to adopt a new service caliber any time soon and American hunters already have a wide choice of 6.5mm cartridges. Domestic ammunition manufacturers have shown little or no interest in the 6.5 Grendel. Indeed, Remington has thrown the advantage to the 6.8mm SPC by placing it in mass production and standardizing it in SAAMI.

TECHNICAL COMMENT(S)
Any attempt to improve the terminal ballistics of the present 5.56x45mm NATO cartridge founder on two rocky obstacles: the laws of physics and the laws of geometry. In the latter, the new cartridge must fit within the constrictions of the M16 rifle's magazine well. In the former, barring a radical break-through in existing components, the choice is simply one of various trade-offs between muzzle velocity, bullet caliber, and bullet weight. All trade-offs result in roughly the same performance level, which has been substantiated by limited field testing. The 6.5mm Grendel cartridge uses a necked-down 7.62x39mm Soviet case.

6.8mm SPC

ALTERNATE NAME(S): 6.8mm Special Purpose Cartridge, 6.8mm Remington SPC
RELATED CALIBER(S): .30 Remington

CARTRIDGE HISTORY
Year of Introduction: 2003
Country of Origin: U.S.
Designer(s): U.S. Army Special Operations Command, Remington
Governing Body: SAAMI
Present Status: active

CARTRIDGE DESCRIPTION
Bullet Diameter: .277 in.
Bullet Weight(s): 70-115 gr.
Rifling Twist Rate: 1 turn in 10 in.
Test Barrel Length: 28 in.
Case Type: rimless, necked
Case Material: brass
Primer Size: large rifle originally; subsequently changed to small rifle

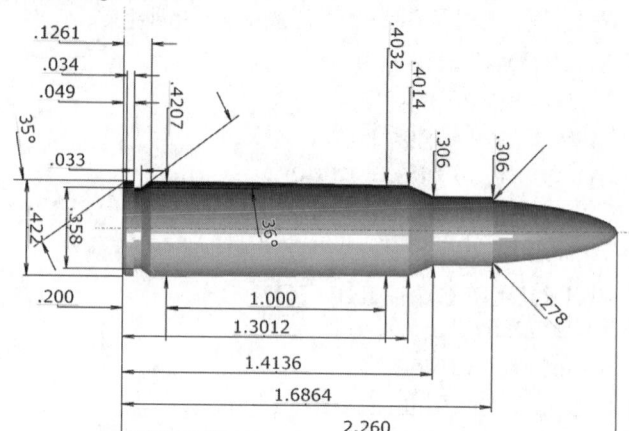

CARTRIDGE BALLISTICS
Max. Average Breech Pressure: 50,000 CUP.
Max. Horizontal Range: 3,400 yds.
Max. Vertical Range: 6,750 ft.

Bullet Weight (gr.)	Bullet Type	Muzzle Velocity (fps)	Muzzle Energy (ft.-lbs.)
115	JHP	2,625	1,759

CURRENT MANUFACTURER(S)
Remington, Cor-Bon

GENERAL COMMENT(S)
This cartridge was designed by the Special Operations Command (SOCOM) following receipt of field reports critical of the terminal ballistic performance of the 5.56x45mm NATO cartridge in Iraq and Afghanistan combat. The objective of this effort was to increase the striking energy and transfer of that energy inside the target. Two major criteria had to be met - the new cartridge must fit in the existing magazine well of the AR16 rifle, and the terminal ballistics had to be significantly better. To solve the first problem, the plan was to replace the entire upper receiver assembly of the rifle with a new one designed for the larger cartridge. The laws of physics made the second requirement very difficult to achieve.

For prototype production, SOCOM turned to Black Hills Ammunition Company. Subsequent production has been made by Black Hills, Remington, and Cor-Bon. In 2005, this caliber became a commercial Remington offering. The 6.8mm SPC is designed to work in civilian AR-15 rifles. Remington markets this new cartridge for hunting deer, varmints, and small game. However, the jury remains out on the success of this as few hunters employ the AR15 platform for this purpose. U.S. military operations in Afghanistan and Iraq, lack of official interest (outside SOCOM), and a shortage of funds make it very unlikely that the U.S. military will adopt a new service rifle cartridge anytime soon.

TECHNICAL COMMENT(S)
To achieve the increased muzzle velocity and energy sought, a larger cartridge case was needed. The solution adopted was a modified .30 Remington cartridge, an obsolete design from the early 1900s. On paper, the 6.8 SPC offered 37% more muzzle energy than the 5.56x45mm M855A1 with a 62.5 grain bullet. Field testing revealed that the heavier bullets of the 6.8mm SPC did improve energy transfer, but not as much as expected or hoped.

For deja vu purposes, the reader is referred to the .276 Pedersen listed in Chapter 43: Centerfire Military Rifle Cartridges - Obsolete.

.300 AAC BLACKOUT

ALTERNATE NAME(S): .300 AAC, .300 Blackout, .300 Blk
RELATED CALIBER(S): .223 Remington

CARTRIDGE HISTORY
Year of Introduction: 2011
Country of Origin: U.S.
Designer(s): Robert Silvers
Governing Body: SAAMI
Present Status: active

CARTRIDGE DESCRIPTION
Bullet Diameter: .308 in.
Bullet Weight(s): 115-220 gr.
Rifling Twist Rate: 1 turn in 7 in.
Test Barrel Length: 16 in.
Case Type: rimless, necked
Case Material: brass
Primer Size: small rifle

CARTRIDGE BALLISTICS
Max. Average Breech Pressure: 55,000 psi.
Max. Horizontal Range: 3,370 yds.
Max. Vertical Range: 7,250 ft.

Bullet Weight (gr.)	Bullet Type	Muzzle Velocity (fps)	Muzzle Energy (ft.-lbs.)
115	JSP	2,295	1,344
125	JSP	2,215	1,360
220	JSP	1,010	498

CURRENT MANUFACTURER(S)
AAC

GENERAL COMMENT(S)
The .300 AAC Blackout is a new center fire rifle cartridge designed to offer flexible ballistic performance for the modern soldier. There were three goals in developing this new cartridge: it must offer subsonic terminal ballistic performance superior to the 9mm Luger cartridge, it must offer supersonic terminal ballistic performance as good as or better than existing 7.62x39mm ammunition, and it must fit in M 16 magazines and rifles with minimal modification. AAC believes they have achieved these goals. As AAC is a major manufacturer of silencers and suppressors, a key objective was assuring full compatibility with these devices. As such, the .300 AAC Blackout is the first cartridge optimized for use with such devices that has been standardized by SAAMI.

To date, no military organization has adopted this concept. However, tests and demonstrations continue and AAC is optimistic about success in this effort.

7.62x39mm M43

ALTERNATE NAME(S): 7.62x39mm, 7.62x39mm Kalashnikov, 7.62x39mm Soviet, 7.62x39mm Russian, 7.62mm Type 56
RELATED CALIBER(S): 7.92x33mm Kurz

CARTRIDGE HISTORY
Year of Introduction: 1943
Country of Origin: Soviet Union
Designer(s): N.M. Elizarov and B.V. Semin
Governing Body: CIP, SAAMI
Present Status: active

CARTRIDGE DESCRIPTION
Bullet Diameter: .312 in.
Bullet Weight(s): 122-123 gr.
Rifling Twist Rate: 1 turn in 9.45 in.
Test Barrel Length: 24 in.
Case Type: rimless, necked
Case Material: steel or brass
Primer Size: small rifle

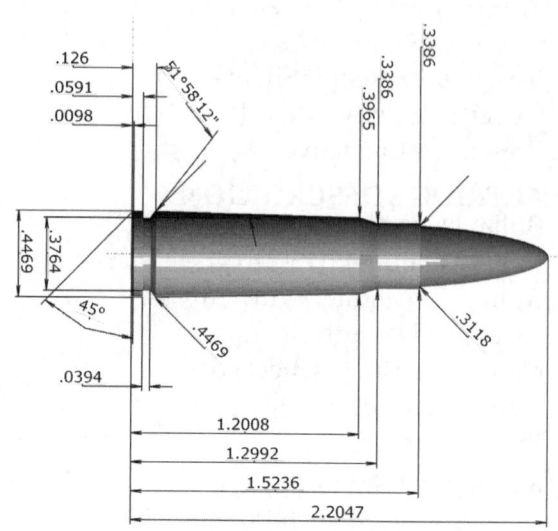

CARTRIDGE BALLISTICS
Max. Average Breech Pressure: 51,488 psi.
Max. Horizontal Range: 3,200 yds.
Max. Vertical Range: 6,600 ft.

Bullet Weight (gr.)	Bullet Type	Muzzle Velocity (fps)	Muzzle Energy (ft.-lbs.)
122 (57-N-231S)	Ball	2,330	1,470

CURRENT MANUFACTURER(S)
Federal, Remington, Winchester, LCAAP, Arsenal, Kintex, Neutrol, Sellier & Bellot, MFS, Norinco, AEI, PMC, Prvi Partizan, NAMMO, IMI, Romtechnica, Mesko, Barnaul, Ulyanovsk, Novosibirsk, Tula, PMP

GENERAL COMMENT(S)
When examples of the new German "machine carbine" and its reduced-power cartridge were captured near Cholm in 1942, Soviet weapons designers studied them carefully. They were fully aware of earlier German feasibility studies and technical designs along these lines and the captured examples proved the concept worked. The 7.9x33mm Kurz cartridge fired in the new German machine carbine was a departure from all earlier designs in that it was short and loaded with a light, 123 grain bullet at a muzzle velocity of approximately 2,250 fps which limited effective tactical range to 300 meters. Reduced recoil, lighter weight, selective-fire controllability and fewer raw materials were additional advantages of the concept. Earlier German experiments had included a 7.62mm short cartridge, the details of which the Russians were fully informed. When the new 7.9x33mm Kurz German cartridge was fielded, Russian weapons designers quickly realized they needed to catch up with the new German technology despite the shortages and difficulties imposed by the War. To save time, the details of the earlier German experiments were reviewed. By 1943, a new 7.62x39mm cartridge was designed and the SKS carbine chambered for it. Later, when the AK-47 appeared, it too was chambered for the new cartridge. Mikhail Kalashnikov did not design the 7.62x39mm M43 cartridge. Rather, he was given the design and told to make his new gun fire that cartridge. The 7.62x39mm M43 cartridge was replaced officially in Soviet military service in 1974. However, it continues in front line service with numerous other countries around the world and shows no signs of obsolescence despite its age.

TECHNICAL COMMENT(S)
German studies of World War I clearly indicated that an infantryman in combat could not reliably hit a target beyond 300 meters. For this reason, the long effective range of powerful military cartridges was wasted on individual infantrymen. What an infantryman needed, they concluded, was a small, lightweight, reduced-power cartridge with a low recoil impulse that was combat-effective at 300 meters. This would allow an infantryman to carry more ammunition, control his sector of the battle field and allow controlled full-automatic fire to clear trenches and buildings. In the 1930s when the aforementioned studies were made, this new ammunition concept was called the machine carbine cartridge. Later it became known as an assault rifle cartridge after Adolf Hitler reclassified the machine carbine as an assault rifle to rebuild morale during World War II. These criteria remain valid today. The 7.62x39mm M43 cartridge is the most successful and famous example of this.

7.62x45mm INDONESIAN POLICE

ALTERNATE NAME(S): 7.62x45mm I.P.
RELATED CALIBER(S): .30 Carbine

CARTRIDGE HISTORY
Year of Introduction: early 1990s
Country of Origin: Indonesia
Designer(s): Pindad
Governing Body: none
Present Status: current

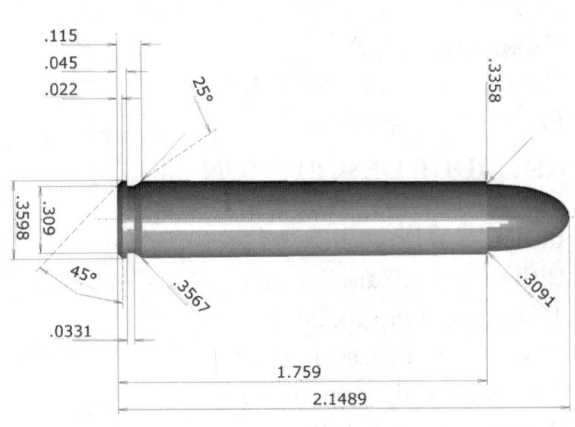

CARTRIDGE DESCRIPTION
Bullet Diameter: .308 in.
Bullet Weight(s): 121 grs.
Rifling Twist Rate: 1 turn in 16 in.
Test Barrel Length: 24 in.
Case Type: rimless, straight
Case Material: brass
Primer Size: small rifle

CARTRIDGE BALLISTICS
Max. Average Breech Pressure: 22,750 psi.
Max. Horizontal Range: 3,120 yds.
Max. Vertical Range: 6,610 ft.

Bullet Weight (gr.)	Bullet Type	Muzzle Velocity (fps)	Muzzle Energy (ft.-lbs.)
121	FMJRN	1,649	723

CURRENT MANUFACTURER(S)
PT Pindad

GENERAL COMMENT(S)
This is a unique cartridge in that it was designed and manufactured in Indonesia to satisfy local requirements for a law enforcement only, but limited power, carbine-specific cartridge. It is used in the gas-operated V-1 and V-2 Sabhara Police Rifles, which are licensed-made variants of the FNC rifle. No other country uses this rifle or its unique cartridge. This cartridge should not be confused with the Czech 7.62x45mm M52 military cartridge.

TECHNICAL COMMENT(S)
The 7.62x45mm cartridge is based on a .30 Carbine case with length increased from 1.29 to 1.759 inches. Breech pressure of the 7.62x45mm cartridge is substantially lower than that of the .30 Carbine (22,750 psi vs. 40,000 psi) and a 10% heavier 121 gr. bullet is used. As a result, muzzle velocity is 16% lower and muzzle energy is 25% lower than the .30 Carbine.

It can be argued that these characteristics make the 7.62x45mm cartridge an ideal choice for law enforcement in urban environments.

7.62x51mm NATO

ALTERNATE NAME(S): 7.62mm, 7.62x51mm, 7.62 NATO
RELATED CALIBER(S): .30-'06 Springfield, .300 Savage

CARTRIDGE HISTORY
Year of Introduction: 1957
Country of Origin: U.S.
Designer(s): N/A
Governing Body: SAAMI, CIP
Present Status: active

CARTRIDGE DESCRIPTION
Bullet Diameter: .308 in.
Bullet Weight(s): 142-175 gr.
Rifling Twist Rate: 1 turn in 12 in.
Test Barrel Length: 24 in.
Case Type: rimless, necked
Case Material: brass or steel
Primer Size: large rifle

CARTRIDGE BALLISTICS
Max. Average Breech Pressure: 50,000 psi
Max. Horizontal Range: 5,500 yds.
Max. Vertical Range: 12,350 ft.

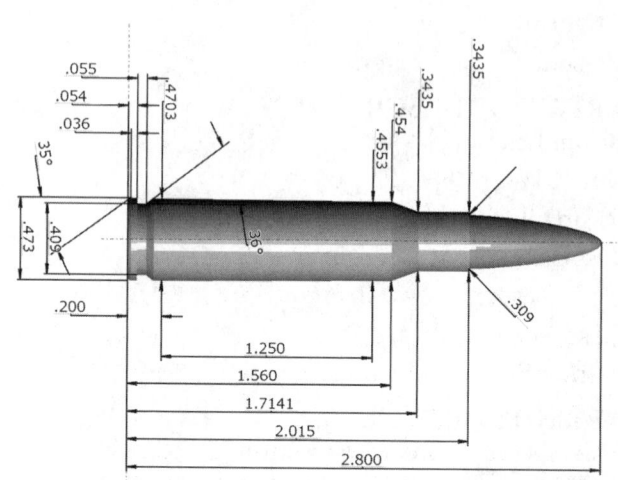

Bullet Weight (gr.)	Bullet Type	Muzzle Velocity (fps)	Muzzle Energy (ft.-lbs.)
150 (M80)	FMJBT Ball	2,750	2,518
168 (M852)	JHPBT Match	2,550	2,424
172 (M118)	FMJBT Match	2,640	2,660
170 (2@85) (M198)	FMJ Duplex	2,750	1,426 each bullet

CURRENT MANUFACTURER(S)
Federal, Remington, Winchester, Adcom, DGFM, FAMAE, FN, PMC, Singapore Tech, CBC, PMP, RUAG, IMI, MKEK, NAMMO, Wolf, Sellier & Bellot, POF, Pyrkal, Igman, DN, MEN, GIAT, INDEP, Barnaul, Novosibirsk, Santa Barbara, IOF, Prvi Partizan, various government arsenals

GENERAL COMMENT(S)
After World War II ended, all European nations recognized the urgent need to replace their outdated military cartridges with new, more modern designs. Several technically advanced candidates were put forward by Belgium and Britain, while the U.S. advocated a 7.62x51mm cartridge which was a .30-06 Springfield cartridge with the case length shortened from 63mm to 51mm. Of the candidates, the U.S. proposal was the least sophisticated and broke no new technological ground. However, the U.S. exercised its influence to get NATO to adopt their candidate cartridge in 1957. The 7.62x51mm NATO cartridge remains a NATO standard to this day. While its use in infantry rifles has deferred to the 5.56x45mm NATO cartridge, the 7.62x51mm cartridge remains supreme for use in machine guns. Here it is important to note that the military 7.62x51mm NATO cartridge and the commercial .308 Win. cartridge are NOT the same. They differ in many minor ways, but are considered interchangeable for most applications.

TECHNICAL COMMENT(S)
Despite its shorter length and reduced case volume, for military applications, the 7.62x51mm cartridge is the full ballistic equal of its parent, the venerable .30-'06 Springfield. Ball, tracer, armor piercing, frangible, grenade launching, blank, match, and proof loads have been developed for the 7.62x51mm. For competition shooting, the reduced case volume has proven to be a significant factor in the outstanding accuracy of 7.62x51mm match ammunition. For sniper applications, the 7.62x51mm cartridge is regarded as suitable for targets out to 1,000 meters. Nearly every NATO nation and many other nations manufacture the 7.62x51mm cartridge ensuring widespread availability and interchangeability. The 7.62x51mm cartridge has approximately twice the striking energy of the 5.56x45mm cartridge. The 7.62x51mm will easily penetrate body armor, most urban barrier materials, automobile bodies, and field fortifications. This capability ensures its place in military service for many years to come.

7.62x54Rmm RUSSIAN

ALTERNATE NAME(S): 7.62x54mm Mosin-Nagant, 7.62mm Russian Long/M91
RELATED CALIBER(S): 11.15x60Rmm Mauser

CARTRIDGE HISTORY
Year of Introduction:1891
Country of Origin: Russia
Designer(s): Col. S.J. Mosin
Governing Body: CIP
Present Status: active

CARTRIDGE DESCRIPTION
Bullet Diameter: .312 in.

Bullet Weight(s): 147-200 gr.

Rifling Twist Rate: 1 turn in 9.45 in.

Test Barrel Length: 24 in.

Case Type: rimmed, necked

Case Material: steel or brass

Primer Size: large rifle

CARTRIDGE BALLISTICS
Max. Average Breech Pressure: 56,565 psi.

Max. Effective Range: 1,000 yds.

Max. Horizontal Range: 5,500 yds.

Max. Vertical Range: 12,400 ft.

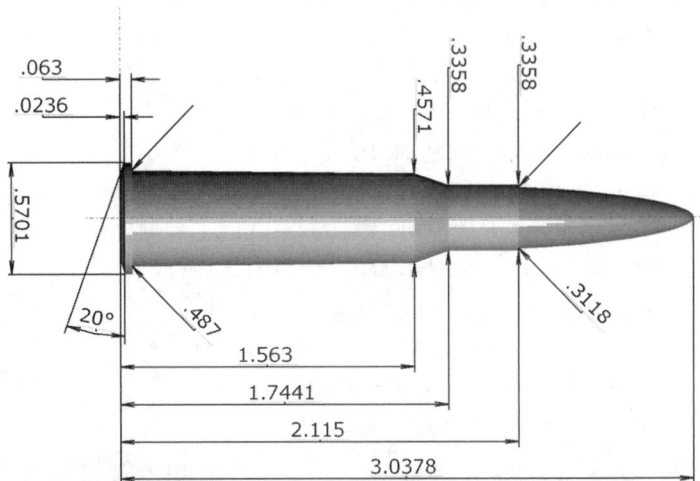

Bullet Weight (gr.)	Bullet Type	Muzzle Velocity (fps)	Muzzle Energy (ft.-lbs.)
147 (Type LPS)	Ball	2,885	2,727
185 (Type O)	Ball	2,660	2,910
150 (Type CT)	Ball	2,715	2,454
151 (Type 7N14)	Sniper	2,715	2,454

CURRENT MANUFACTURER(S)
Barnaul, Novosibirsk, Sellier & Bellot, MFS, Norinco, NAMMO, Prvi Partizan, Kintex, Mesko, Romtechnica, AEI, Arsenal

GENERAL COMMENT(S)
This is one old soldier that will not die. Adopted in 1891 for Russian military service along with the M1891 Mosin-Nagant bolt-action rifle, the 7.62x54Rmm was the standard service cartridge of the Russian military forces during both World Wars. This veteran is now over 117 years old and still active. Today, it is used in heavy machine guns and sniper rifles in Russian and Chinese military service and in numerous other military organizations around the world. During World War I, American ammunition manufacturers made millions of rounds of this caliber under contract for the Russian government.

TECHNICAL COMMENT(S)
While many dismiss the 7.62x54Rmm Russian cartridge as an anachronism, it remains an effective military cartridge that serves essentially the same purpose as the 7.62x51mm NATO cartridge, namely as a machine gun and sniper cartridge.The rimmed case of the 7.62x54Rmm cartridge does pose some difficulties in stacking and feeding from detachable box magazines and machine gun belts. However, these minor problems were solved many years ago so the future of this old war horse seems secure.

.338 LAPUA MAGNUM

ALTERNATE NAME(S): .338 Lapua Mag., 8.58x71mm Lapua
RELATED CALIBER(S): .416 Rigby

CARTRIDGE HISTORY
Year of Introduction: 1983
Country of Origin: U.S., Finland
Designer(s): Armament Research Co.
Governing Body: CIP, SAAMI
Present Status: active

CARTRIDGE DESCRIPTION
Bullet Diameter: .338 in.
Bullet Weight(s): 250-300 gr.
Rifling Twist Rate: 1 turn in 10 in.
Test Barrel Length: 24 in.
Case Type: rimless, necked
Case Material: brass
Primer Size: large rifle (magnum)

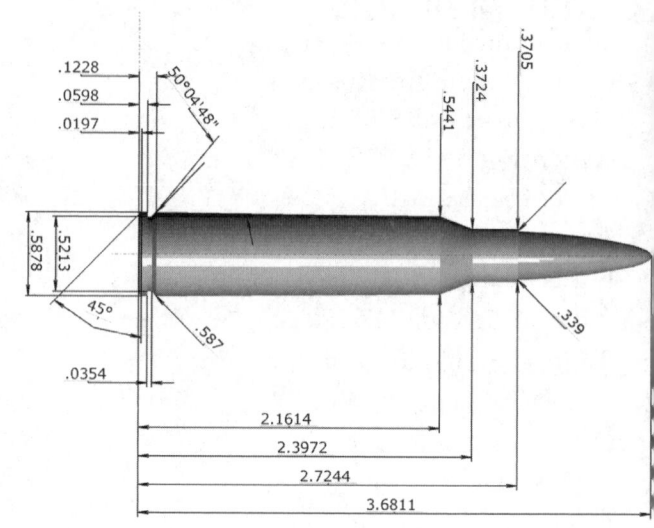

CARTRIDGE BALLISTICS
Max. Average Breech Pressure: 60,900
Max. Horizontal Range: 7,000 yds.
Max. Vertical Range: 14,000 ft.

Bullet Weight (gr.)	Bullet Type	Muzzle Velocity (fps)	Muzzle Energy (ft.-lbs.)
250	HP	2,970	4,895
275	HPBT	2,690	4,415
300	HPBT	2,800	5,224

CURRENT MANUFACTURER(S)
Lapua, Norma, Prvi Partisan, RUAG

GENERAL COMMENT(S)
This cartridge is unique in several respects. First, it was designed by an American company as a long range sniper cartridge with no thought for its hunting capability. Second, it was introduced into commercial production by Lapua of Finland. Third, its case is a beltless magnum design based on the .416 Rigby cartridge, which requires a magnum length rifle action. After a slow start, adoption by some European law enforcement agencies has helped build a base of demand for this caliber. For United States law enforcement service the .338 Lapua Magnum is considered much too powerful, as police agencies generally do not allow shots over 200 yards. Many military services, such as the U.S. Marines, are considering adoption of the .338 Lapua Magnum for Intermediate Range (1,000-1,800 yds.) sniping. Semi-automatic rifles in this caliber are being developed for that application also.

The future of the .338 Lapua Magnum looks bright based on its acceptance by European law enforcement agencies and military services. Its general usefulness for hunting remains constrained because its overall length leaves it suited mainly for African dangerous game rifles. It is far too powerful for U.S. and European game.

TECHNICAL COMMENT(S)
The most useful characteristic of the .338 Lapua Magnum is its ballistic performance at ranges between 1,000 and 1,800 yards. It provides a more effective alternative to the 7.62x51mm NATO cartridge, and a more efficient alternative to the .50 BMG, for Intermediate Range targets. European law enforcement and military groups prefer the .338 Lapua cartridge with a 250 grain bullet and a 10 inch rifling twist. However, others such as the U.S. Marine Corps, prefer a 300 grain bullet with a faster rifling twist rate.

9x39mm SOVIET SP-5/SP-6

ALTERNATE NAME(S): 9x39mm SP-5
RELATED CALIBER(S): 7.62x39mm Soviet M43

CARTRIDGE HISTORY
Year of Introduction: circa late 1980s
Country of Origin: Soviet Union
Designer(s): Nicolai Zabelin (SP-5), Yuri Folov (SP-6)
Governing Body: none
Present Status: active

CARTRIDGE DESCRIPTION
Bullet Diameter: .355 in.
Bullet Weight(s): 247-260 gr.
Rifling Twist Rate: N/A
Test Barrel Length: 24 in.
Case Type: rimless, necked
Case Material: steel
Primer: N/A

CARTRIDGE BALLISTICS
Max. Average Breech Pressure: 51,500 psi.
Max. Horizontal Range: 3,400 yds.
Max. Vertical Range: 6,400 ft.

Bullet Weight (gr.)	Bullet Type	Muzzle Velocity (fps)	Muzzle Energy (ft.-lbs.)
259 (SP-5)	FMJ-BT	920	488
245 (SP-6)	FMJ-BT	920	464

CURRENT MANUFACTURER(S)
CIS (Russian) Arsenals

GENERAL COMMENT(S)
This cartridge was developed at the request of the Soviet Army Spetsnaz (special forces) and reconnaissance units who needed subsonic ammunition for their suppressed assault rifles. However, the cartridge had to be effective to ranges of 440 yards against body armor. Russian designers responded with the 9x39mm SP-5/6 cartridges. Later, additional weapons for this cartridge were developed for the Ministry of Internal Affairs and police. The only user and manufacturer of this cartridge is the Commonwealth of Independent States. Two rifles with integral suppressors were developed for this new cartridge, the VSS sniper rifle and the AS assault rifle.

TECHNICAL COMMENT(S)
Basically, the 9x39mm SP-5/6 cartridge is a standard 7.62x39mm M43 cartridge necked up to accept a 9mm (.355 inch) diameter bullet. This was done in order to provide a combat assault rifle cartridge that would be fully compatible with suppressors to reduce sound levels, yet still be capable of penetrating body armor at 440 yards. This was accomplished by trading off muzzle velocity for a heavier weight bullet. If muzzle velocity must be kept below the speed of sound (1,150 fps), a heavier bullet will hold its velocity and energy further down range than a light weight bullet. Both a ball and an AP bullet are available.

.458 SOCOM

ALTERNATE NAME(S): 11.6x40mm, 11.6mm SOCOM
RELATED CALIBER(S): .450 Bushmaster, .500 Linebaugh, .50 Beowulf, .425 Westley-Richards

CARTRIDGE HISTORY
Year of Introduction: circa late 1990s
Country of Origin: U.S.
Designer(s): Marty ter Weeme
Governing Body: none
Present Status: active

CARTRIDGE DESCRIPTION
Bullet Diameter: .458 in.
Bullet Weight(s): 300-600 grs.
Rifling Twist Rate: 1 turn in 14 in. (light bullets), 1 turn in 18 in. (heavy bullets)
Test Barrel Length: 16 in.
Case Type: rebated rim, necked
Case Material: brass
Primer: large rifle

CARTRIDGE BALLISTICS
Max. Average Breech Pressure: N/A
Max. Horizontal Range: N/A
Max. Vertical Range: N/A

Bullet Weight (gr.)	Bullet Type	Muzzle Velocity (fps)	Muzzle Energy (ft.-lbs.)
250	JSP	2,000	2,938
300	JHP	1,900	2,405
450	SLD-RN	1,500	2,249
600	JSP	950	1,203

CURRENT MANUFACTURER(S)
CorBon

GENERAL COMMENT(S)
SOCOM is an abbreviation for the Special Operations Command of the U.S. Army. The .458 SOCOM is a civilian design intended for use in modified M16 rifles with suppressors. The 600 grain bullet load with its subsonic muzzle velocity is used in the suppressed weapons; the supersonic loads are for hunting.

TECHNICAL COMMENT(S)
The .458 SOCOM is one of the modern, high-efficiency cartridges that are compact enough to be fired from modified M16 and similar rifles. Using small propellant charges to drive the heavy bullets at moderate muzzle velocities, the striking energy of the heavy bullet weight compensates for the low muzzle velocity. These compact cartridges are easily loaded to subsonic muzzle velocities for use in suppressed rifles. In order to make this cartridge compatible with military rifles designed for 7.62x51mm NATO ammunition, the rim of the .458 SOCOM has been rebated and dimensioned to fit a 7.62x51mm bolt face. Despite its name, the .458 SOCOM has not been adopted by the U.S. Army. Maximum effective range is approximately 150 yards.

12.7x108mm SOVIET

ALTERNATE NAME(S): 12.7x108mm Soviet, 12.7x108mm Russian DShK
RELATED CALIBER(S): 12.7x99mm Browning, .5 in. Vickers, 12.7x81SRmm Breda, 13x92SRmm Mauser

CARTRIDGE HISTORY
Year of Introduction: 1930
Country of Origin: Soviet Union
Designer(s): N/A
Governing Body: CIP
Present Status: active

CARTRIDGE DESCRIPTION
Bullet Diameter: .512 in.
Bullet Weight(s): 680-745 gr.
Rifling Twist Rate: 1 turn in 15 in.
Test Barrel Length: 39.4 in.
Case Type: rimless, necked
Case Material: steel
Primer: No. 35

CARTRIDGE BALLISTICS
Max. Average Breech Pressure: 60,915 psi.
Max. Horizontal Range: 8,100 yds.
Max. Vertical Range: 16,400 ft.

Bullet Weight (gr.)	Bullet Type	Muzzle Velocity (fps)	Muzzle Energy (ft.-lbs.)
745	AP-I (B32)	2,625	11, 394
681	AP-I-T (BZT44)	2,705	11,060

CURRENT MANUFACTURER(S)
Novosibirsk M.P. (Russia), Norinco, Egypt, Poland, Syria, North Korea, India

GENERAL COMMENT(S)
After World War I, the major powers took a lesson from the German 13x92SRmm Mauser anti-tank cartridge and the 12.7x99mm Browning Machine Gun (BMG) cartridge developed in the U.S. Both were intended originally as anti-tank and anti-aircraft heavy machine guns. The German 13x92SRmm cartridge saw only limited service in World War I as an anti-tank rifle and further development as a heavy machine gun cartridge ended with the conclusion of World War I in 1918. However, the 12.7x99mm BMG cartridge was standardized by the U.S. Army in 1923 and the race was on. Most major powers then began developing heavy machine gun/anti-tank rifle cartridges of their own. In the Soviet Union, the 12.7x108mm cartridge was adopted in 1930 and Britain followed suit in 1934 with the Cartridge SA Ball .5 in. Mk I.z. Vickers cartridge. Not to be left out, the Italian Army developed the 12.7x81SRmm Breda cartridge in the mid-1930s which was adopted by Italy, Spain, Japan and Hungary. Of course, the French Army was in the forefront of such developments, adopting the 13.2x99mm Hotchkiss cartridge in 1930. Following the French lead, China, Italy, Japan, and Poland also adopted this cartridge. By and large, these cartridges served their masters well through World War II following which a shakeout occurred. The first to go were the .5 in. Vickers and the 12.7x81SRmm Breda. The 13.2x99mm Hotchkiss and Breda cartridges soldiered on into the early 1960s after which they were replaced by the 12.7x99mm BMG in NATO service. The Soviet 12.7x108mm remains in front-line military service in the Russian Army.

TECHNICAL COMMENT(S)
Both the U.S. 12.7x99mm BMG and the Soviet 12.7x108mm cartridges were developed for the same purpose and offer comparable ballistic performance. However, despite their similarity, the two cartridges are not interchangeable. In the 1970s and 1980s, the Soviet 12.7x108mm cartridge underwent a modernization of sorts with the development of several innovative AP tungsten alloy penetrator bullets. At the same time, many of the older bullet types were declared obsolete. Today, only one ammunition factory in Russia produces this cartridge.

.50 BROWNING MACHINE GUN

ALTERNATE NAME(S): 12.7x99mm, 12.7x99mm Browning, .50 BMG, .50 Browning
RELATED CALIBER(S): 13mm German TUF

CARTRIDGE HISTORY

Year of Introduction: 1923

Country of Origin: U.S.

Designer(s): John Browning

Governing Body: SAAMI, CIP

Present Status: active

CARTRIDGE DESCRIPTION

Bullet Diameter: .511 in.

Bullet Weight(s): 360-750 gr.

Rifling Twist Rate: 1 turn in 15 in.

Test Barrel Length: 40 in.

Case Type: rimless, necked

Case Material: brass

Primer Size: No. 35

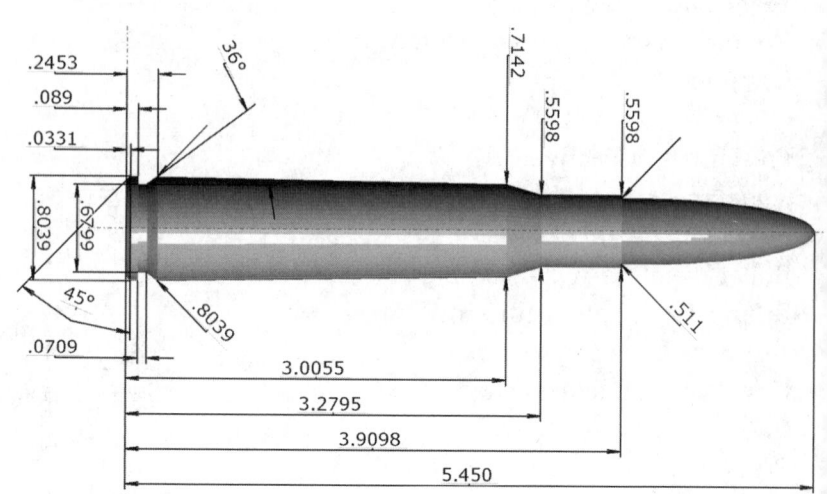

CARTRIDGE BALLISTICS

Max. Average Breech Pressure: 53,664

Max. Horizontal Range: 7,300 yds.

Max. Vertical Range: 16,400 ft.

Bullet Weight (gr.)	Bullet Type	Muzzle Velocity (fps)	Muzzle Energy (ft.-lbs.)
720 (M2)	Ball	2,810	12,600
668 (M33)	Ball	2,910	12,550

CURRENT MANUFACTURER(S)

Winchester, IMI, CBC, PMP, PMC, Igman, Singapore Technology, NAMMO, various government arsenals

GENERAL COMMENT(S)

During World War I, the German Army developed the 13mm TUF cartridge for use against tanks and aircraft. S impressive was this powerful cartridge, the U.S. Army began developing a similar cartridge in 1918. John Browning was selected for the task and the new cartridge and heavy machine gun were adopted in 1923. The main task for the new gun and cartridge was placing direct fire on ground and air targets. However, it is interesting to note that the U.S Army also viewed the .50 BMG cal. heavy machine guns as fast-firing light artillery capable of laying down indirect area suppressive fires against enemy personnel at ranges far beyond the limit of infantry rifle caliber machine guns For this purpose, a water cooling jacket for the barrel and a search and traverse aiming mechanism were added to the gun. During World War II, the .50 BMG came into its own as the primary gun on U.S. military aircraft and secondar armament on tanks. It was also used extensively on light naval craft, trucks and fixed installations. A wide variety o loadings were developed including ball, armor-piercing, incendiary, tracer, armor-piercing-incendiary and armor piercing-incendiary-tracer. Caliber .50 BMG ammunition was so important to the U.S. war effort that it was made in huge quantities by multiple sources. By the end of World War II, conventional wisdom was that the .50 BMG had become outmoded for aerial combat, anti-aircraft duties and naval warfare. Some studies even showed the .50 BMG should be replaced for ground warfare. However, someone forgot to tell the soldiers, sailors and marines who swea by the .50 BMG and have continually found new uses for it. Its future seems secure.

TECHNICAL COMMENT(S)

While traditional .50 BMG loadings continue to offer sterling military service, they are getting long in the tooth. In fact most current .50 BMG bullets were developed before or during World War II! Fortunately, new bullet designs for the .50 BMG have become available in recent years. For example, the Norwegian firm of Raufoss has developed an explosiv bullet for the .50 BMG which has entered service with many NATO countries including the U.S. Another example is the Winchester-developed, saboted light armor piercing (SLAP) round which has a sub-caliber, armor piercing projectil launched at very high velocity using a discarding sabot. In addition, several companies have developed new, full-bore armor-piercing bullets with tungsten carbide cores for the .50 BMG. While special ammunition of these types remains very expensive, they prove that the .50 BMG still has plenty of room for future ballistic development.

14.5x114mm SOVIET

ALTERNATE NAME(S): 14.5mm KPV, 14.5mm Type 56, 14.5mm Russian, 14.5mm Soviet
RELATED CALIBER(S): U.S. Cal. .60, 13x92SRmm Mauser

CARTRIDGE HISTORY
Year of Introduction: 1941
Country of Origin: Soviet Union
Designer(s): N/A
Governing Body: none
Present Status: active

CARTRIDGE DESCRIPTION
Bullet Diameter: .5858 in.
Bullet Weight(s): 920-994 gr.
Rifling Twist Rate: N/A
Test Barrel Length: 54.7 in.
Case Type: rimless, necked
Case Material: brass or steel
Primer: No. 35

CARTRIDGE BALLISTICS
Max. Average Breech Pressure: 59,560 psi.
Max. Horizontal Range: 7,100 yds.
Max. Vertical Range: 15,000 ft.

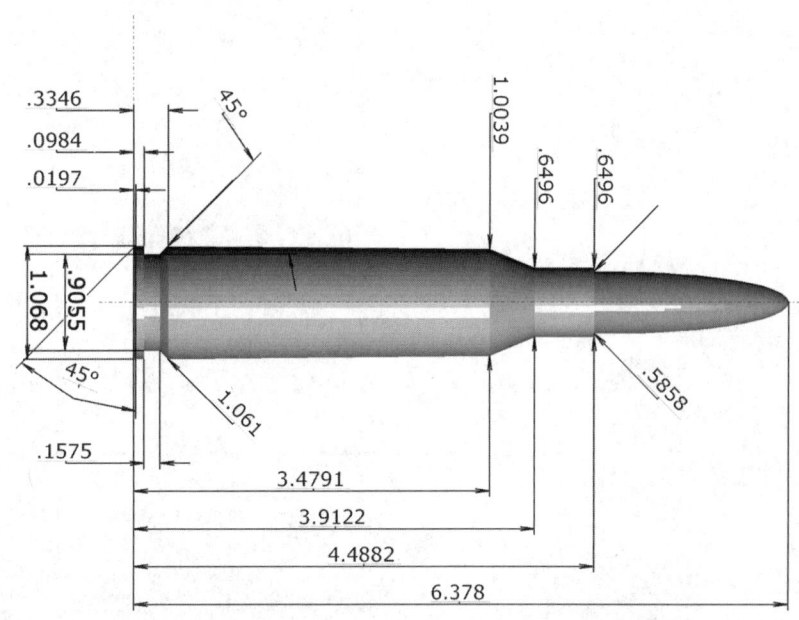

Bullet Weight (gr.)	Bullet Type	Muzzle Velocity (fps)	Muzzle Energy (ft.-lbs.)
979	AP-I Type B-32	3,200	22,258

CURRENT MANUFACTURER(S)
Norinco, Novosibirsk

GENERAL COMMENT(S)
In the late 1930s, the Soviet Union began development of a new infantry anti-tank rifle and cartridge. By 1941, this program resulted in the adoption of the 14.5x114mm Soviet cartridge and the PTRS and PTRD anti-tank rifles to fire them. Like other infantry anti-tank rifles, they were obsolete before adoption. However, when Germany invaded the Soviet Union in 1941, the Russian Army had to make do with these rifles as they were the only thing available. Later, when effective anti-tank guns became available, the 14.5mm rifles were relegated to use against soft-skinned vehicles, armored cars and pillboxes. At the end of World War II in 1945, the 14.5x114mm Soviet cartridge seemed obsolete. Then, in 1949, a Russian gun designer named Vladimirov designed a new heavy machine gun around the 14.5x114mm cartridge. Called the KPV, the new machine gun gave the old warhorse cartridge a completely new tactical life for use against aircraft, light armored vehicles and field fortifications, especially in dual and quad mountings. The 14.5x114mm Soviet cartridge continues in that capacity today.

TECHNICAL COMMENT(S)
Arguably, the 14.5x114mm Soviet cartridge is the most successful and most effective, but not the most powerful, of the infantry anti-tank guns. When adopted in 1941, the 14.5x114mm cartridge was a remarkable achievement, but not a technical break through. It defeated armor with brute force rather than technical finesse. Still, it had one significant advantage, it retained enough development capability to be upgraded. In short order, operational necessity required more armor piercing capability. The Type B-32 AP-I bullet was one of the first used. Its hardened steel core could penetrate 38mm (1.5 inches) of armor at 100 meters and approximately 35mm at 300 meters. Later bullets with tungsten alloy penetrators increased this by approximately 50%.

.30-06 MARSH COULTER FLARE

SPECIMEN AND PHOTOS COURTESY OF PAUL SMITH

Marshall Coulter, of Tecumseh, Michigan, patented this flare shell in ca. 1960 and they were sold at the retail level for many years. They were still being advertised in the 1970's.

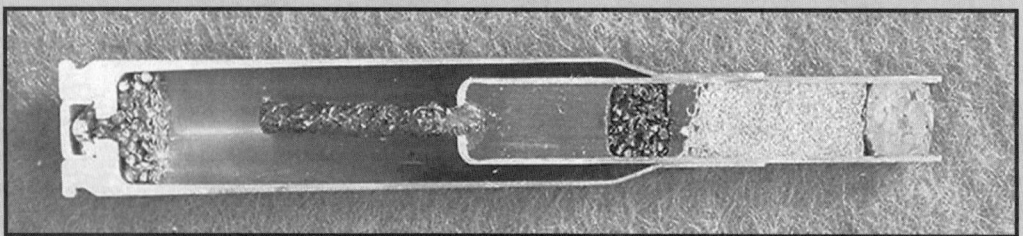

The projectile consists of a brass tube which is closed at one end. A piece of cannon fuse is lit upon firing and ignites the flare material which burns until it reaches a small charge of black powder. The black powder is designed to either rupture the brass tube or expel a secondary igniter and flare charge which burns brightly. The brass tube is sealed with a piece of cork and has a red sealant overtop of this. The flare has a maximum altitude of about 500 feet.

This round did not have a headstamp.

This flare was loaded for a variety of rounds in both .30 and .35 calibers.

References: *.30-06* by Chris Punnett. Page 271

Courtesy International Ammunition Association, Inc. (cartridgecollectors.org)

CHAPTER 70 : MILITARY RIFLE CARTRIDGES - OBSOLETE

CHAPTER 70

For Cartridge Index see Chapter 101. All drawing dimensions are approximate.

When Gen. Douglas MacArthur said, "Old soldiers never die, they just fade away," he did not have obsolete military cartridges in mind. However, the adage certainly applies as obsolete military cartridges often remain in production long after they have been retired from active military service. Consider the .45-70 Government, the 8x57mm Mauser, and the .30-'06 Springfield as examples.

A major reason for this longevity is the large number of surplus but serviceable ex-military rifles and ammunition readily available on the civilian/commercial market. Informal target shooting and basic marksmanship instruction with these rifles provide low cost shooting enjoyment, as long as cheap surplus ammunition is available. Once surplus ammo starts drying up however, the cost of shooting a "military surplus" rifle increases, but still may remain a bargain in comparison to a currently manufactured rifle and ammunition.

As many surplus military rifles were suitable for hunting, sportsmen often took them afield with soft-point ammunition. Sales volume of all hunting ammunition was such that Norma AB of Sweden allocated a substantial part of their production capacity to hunting ammunition in military calibers. Most sportsmen agree that the era of inexpensive surplus military rifles and ammunition is ending as nations complete the disposal of their emergency war reserve stocks. Fortunately, commercial ammunition makers have started filling this void with new production ammunition and Norma soldiers on.

In the past, the threads of military and sporting firearms' development were identical, or closely intertwined. Such is not the case today as military and sporting arms and ammunition development has diverged dramatically and permanently. For sportsmen, this means future military ammunition calibers are not likely to have a commercial application and surplus lots of military ammunition are likely to be destroyed rather than sold.

The good news is that there are tens of thousands of surplus military rifles in existence which will create a viable demand for ammunition in their calibers for many years to come. This has not escaped the notice of ammunition makers.

As you read this chapter, it will become obvious that the caliber/bullet diameter of military cartridges has been steadily decreasing for the last 150 years. For example, in the late 1800s, military cartridges for infantry rifles normally were of .40-.45 caliber to alleviate black powder fouling. The advent of smokeless propellants in the late 1890s created a window of opportunity. Smokeless propellants had demonstrated the feasibility of substantially reducing the caliber of military cartridges. Quickly, the major military powers of the day reduced the caliber of their infantry rifles to 7-8mm. However, the same powers soon realized that their first efforts at smokeless powder cartridges were less than perfect, leading several to initiate broad development programs for new cartridges of even smaller caliber. Two World Wars prevented this from happening, but the military forces of the major nations never lost sight of the smaller caliber goal and continued their experimental efforts.

Eclectic Tastes

Before and during World War II, Japanese military arsenals and private companies loaded large quantities of .25 ACP, .380 ACP, .30 Luger, .30 Mauser, and .44 S&W Russian ammunition. This ammunition was made for Japanese Army and Navy officers who often purchased foreign pistols (usually of German or Belgian origin) instead of the standard Japanese military Nambu series of pistols in 8mm Nambu caliber. Surprisingly, pistols in 9x19mm Luger and .45 ACP caliber were not popular choices.

4.85mm BRITISH

ALTERNATE NAME(S): 4.85x49mm British, 4.85mm, 4.85mm British
RELATED CALIBER(S): 5.56x45mm NATO

CARTRIDGE HISTORY
Year of Introduction: proposed 1976
Country of Origin: Britain
Designer(s): Royal Ordnance
Governing Body: none
Present Status: obsolete

CARTRIDGE DESCRIPTION
Bullet Diameter: .197 in.
Bullet Weight(s): 55.3 gr.
Rifling Twist Rate: 1 turn in 8 in.
Test Barrel Length: N/A
Case Type: rimless, necked
Case Material: brass
Primer: small rifle

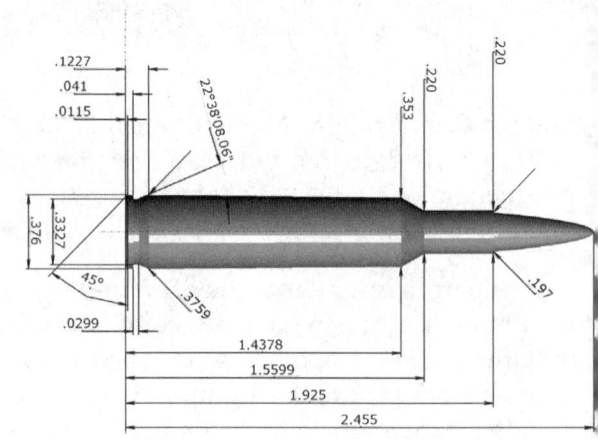

CARTRIDGE BALLISTICS
Max. Average Breech Pressure: 52,000 psi.
Max. Horizontal Range: 3,600 yds.
Max. Vertical Range: 7,900 ft.

Bullet Weight (gr.)	Bullet Type	Muzzle Velocity (fps)	Muzzle Energy (ft.-lbs.)
55.3	FMJ-BT	3,115	1,210

CURRENT MANUFACTURER(S)
None

GENERAL COMMENT(S)
Before you read these comments, review the history of the .280 British cartridge in this chapter. After strong arming the other NATO members into adopting the 7.62x51mm NATO cartridge in the early 1950s, the U.S. adopted the 5.56x45mm cartridge in 1964. This catapulted the U.S. Army to the forefront of assault rifle cartridge development, but greatly upset the other NATO members who had just replaced their entire military ammunition infrastructure to support the 7.62x51mm NATO cartridge. As a result, the other NATO members resisted adoption of the 5.56x45mm cartridge for NATO service. From 1977-1979, NATO conducted a series of Small Arms Trials to determine the next generation of small arms ammunition. Obviously, this meant a smaller caliber, more compact cartridge with a light weight bullet. The "second" wave of post-war assault rifle cartridge development had begun. Once again, the British jumped into the breech, entering their new 4.85mm cartridge in the NATO trials. While the 4.85mm British cartridge proved more efficient and more accurate with better long range penetration, the 5.56x45mm cartridge was selected along with the FN-designed SS109 bullet. The 4.85mm British cartridge was abandoned.

TECHNICAL COMMENT(S)
British engineers took a long look at reality before they began designing the 4.85mm British cartridge. This led them to base their new cartridge on the same head and rim dimensions as the 5.56x45mm cartridge along with the same maximum average chamber pressure. Essentially, the 4.85mm British cartridge was a slightly longer 5.56mm cartridge case with a smaller diameter bullet. This ensured that machinery and tooling designed to manufacture 5.56x45mm ammunition could be cheaply and easily converted to 4.85mm production. Ball, armor-piercing and tracer bullets were developed and small lots of ball and tracer ammunition were made for the NATO Trials. But it was not to be. When NATO officially adopted the 5.56x45mm cartridge in 1980, the British accepted the inevitable and abandoned further development of the 4.85mm British cartridge. However, the 4.85mm British cartridge secured a place in history as the smallest caliber cartridge ever seriously considered for general military use.

6mm U.S. NAVY

ALTERNATE NAME(S): 6mm Lee Navy, .236 U.S.N
RELATED CALIBER(S): .220 Swift, 6.5x52mm Mannlicher-Carcano, 7.35mm Carcano, .276 Pedersen

CARTRIDGE HISTORY
Year of Introduction: 1895
Country of Origin: U.S.
Designer(s): Winchester, Union Metallic Cartridge
Governing Body: SAAMI
Present Status: obsolete

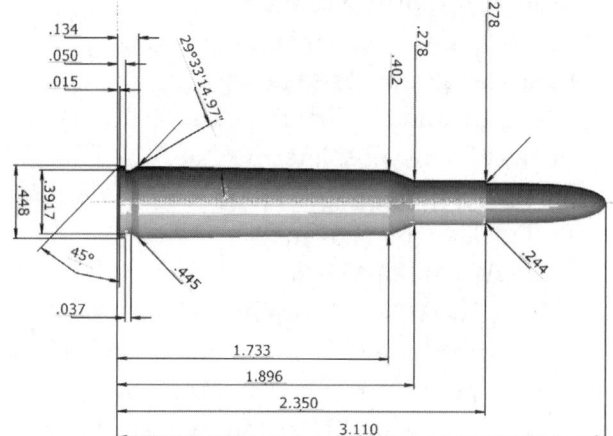

CARTRIDGE DESCRIPTION
Bullet Diameter: .244 in.
Bullet Weight(s): 112 gr.
Rifling Twist Rate: 1 turn in 7 in.
Test Barrel Length: 24 in.
Case Type: rimless, necked
Case Material: brass
Primer: large rifle

CARTRIDGE BALLISTICS
Max. Average Breech Pressure: 43,000 psi.
Max. Horizontal Range: N/A
Max. Vertical Range: N/A

Bullet Weight (gr.)	Bullet Type	Muzzle Velocity (fps)	Muzzle Energy (ft.-lbs.)
112	FMJ-RN	2,550	1,617

CURRENT MANUFACTURER(S)
None

GENERAL COMMENT(S)
From 1895-1901, this was the standard small caliber rifle cartridge of the U.S. Navy and U.S. Marine Corps. It was chambered in the Lee M1895 straight-pull rifle, Colt "potato digger" machine gun and some Gatling guns. This cartridge was the one used by the U.S. Marine detachment in China to break the siege of the legations in Peking during the Boxer Rebellion. It was also used during the Spanish-American War. According to Winchester, the 6mm U.S. Navy was the first rimless cartridge made in the U.S. Until the adoption of the 5.56x45mm cartridge in 1963, the 6mm U.S. Navy remained the smallest caliber military rifle cartridge ever used.

TECHNICAL COMMENT(S)
Winchester's original proposal for this cartridge was a rimmed design called the .236 U.S. Navy. However, the Navy Bureau of Ordnance solicited a rimless design from Winchester which was adopted in 1895 as the "6mm U.S. Navy ball cartridge". Union Metallic Cartridge and Winchester shared the first government order for 500,000 rounds. A 136 grain FMJ round nose bullet with a nickel-plated steel jacket and lead core was proposed by Winchester, but rejected in favor of a 112 grain FMJ round nose bullet with a copper alloy jacket and lead core that reduced bore wear and increased muzzle velocity. Maximum average chamber pressure was high for that era, leading to complaints from both Winchester and Union Metallic Cartridge who found it difficult to control the interior ballistics. A fatal blow was dealt the 6mm U.S. Navy cartridge when it was determined that the propellant deteriorated quickly during shipboard storage making the ammunition unfit for military service. Most of the ammunition in inventory had to be destroyed. These problems led the Navy Ordnance Bureau to begin phasing out the 6mm U.S. Navy cartridge in 1900. Shortly after, the U.S. Navy adopting the .30-40 Krag cartridge and rifle of the U.S. Army. But the brief, meteoric career of the 6mm U.S. Navy cartridge did not end there. Winchester continued manufacturing this cartridge for sporting use until the mid-1930s. When the U.S. Army began efforts to replace the .30-06 Springfield cartridge with one of a smaller caliber in 1923, the resultant .276 Pedersen cartridge bore a strong resemblance to the 6mm Lee Navy. Again in the 1970s, the 6mm SAW machinegun cartridge developed for the U.S. Army reflected the strong influence of the 6mm U.S. Navy. Once again in the early 2000s in response to complaints about the weak stopping power of the 5.56x45mm NATO cartridge have led to the 6.8mm SPC cartridge, another inheritor of the legacy of the 6mm U.S. Navy cartridge.

6.5x50SRmm ARISAKA

ALTERNATE NAME(S): 6.5mm Jap, 6.5x50mm Japanese, .256 Jap, 6.5mm Arisaka
RELATED CALIBER(S): 6.5x64mm M-S, 6.5x53Rmm Mannlicher, 6.5x55mm Swedish, 6.5x52mm Mannlicher-Carcano

CARTRIDGE HISTORY

Year of Introduction:1897
Country of Origin: Japan
Designer(s): Col. Arisaka
Governing Body: CIP
Present Status: obsolete

CARTRIDGE DESCRIPTION

Bullet Diameter: .261 in.
Bullet Weight(s): 139 gr.
Rifling Twist Rate: 1 turn in 7.87 in.
Test Barrel Length: 24 in.
Case Type: semi-rimmed, necked
Case Material: brass (Japanese) or steel (Chinese)
Primer Size: large rifle

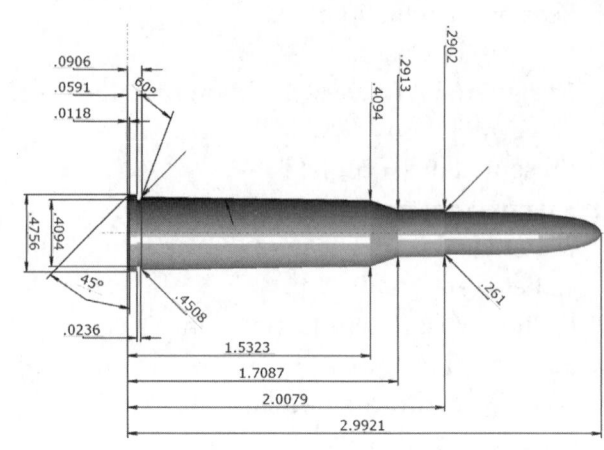

CARTRIDGE BALLISTICS

Max. Average Breech Pressure: 42,786 psi.
Max. Horizontal Range: 4,200 yds.
Max. Vertical Range: 9,500 ft.

Bullet Weight (gr.)	Bullet Type	Muzzle Velocity (fps)	Muzzle Energy (ft.-lbs.)
139	Ball	2,475	1,890

CURRENT MANUFACTURER(S)

Norma, Prvi Partizan, Norinco

GENERAL COMMENT(S)

From 1897 until 1939, the 6.5x50SRmm Arisaka was the standard Japanese military service rifle cartridge. In 1939, it was replaced by the 7.7x58mm Arisaka cartridge as its larger, heavier bullet made tracer, incendiary, high explosive and armor piercing types more effective. Due to the late start in manufacturing the new cartridge, demand never caught up with supply so the venerable 6.5x50SRmm cartridge soldiered on until the end in 1945. U.S. and Allied military forces encountered the 6.5x50SRmm cartridge throughout the World War II Pacific campaigns where it quickly gained respect despite its small diameter bullet. Following the end of World War II, China (P.R.C.) issued captured Japanese rifles to Chinese reserve and militia troops. To support these, Chinese arsenals restarted production of 6.5x50 SRmm ammunition.

TECHNICAL COMMENT(S)

The 6.5x50 SRmm cartridge is a typical example of 1890s technology with a maximum average chamber pressure in the low 40,000 psi range. Of all the 6.5mm military cartridges from that era, the 6.5x50mm Japanese is the shortest with the smallest case volume. When adopted, the 6.5mm Arisaka was loaded with a round nose FMJ bullet. A pointed, flat base FMJ bullet was adopted in the early 1900s. American soldiers quickly found that the long barrel of the Japanese 6.5x50SRmm rifles allowed nearly all of the propellant to be consumed before the bullet exited the muzzle. As a result, Japanese 6.5mm Arisaka rifles produced no muzzle flash making them difficult to spot during night operations. Light machine guns were also chambered for this cartridge.

6.5x52mm MANNLICHER-CARCANO

ALTERNATE NAME(S): 6.5x52mm Italian, 6.5 Italian, 6.5mm Italian, 6.5mm M1891
RELATED CALIBER(S): 6.5x50SR Arisaka, 6.5x55mm Swedish, 6.5x54mm, 6.5x54mm M-S

CARTRIDGE HISTORY
Year of Introduction: 1891
Country of Origin: Italy
Designer(s): N/A
Governing Body: CIP
Present Status: obsolete

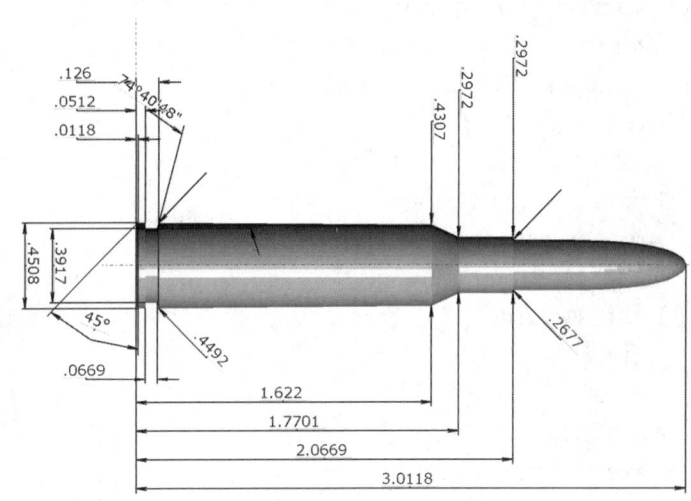

CARTRIDGE DESCRIPTION
Bullet Diameter: .261 in.
Bullet Weight(s): 139 gr.
Rifling Twist Rate: 1 turn in 19.3-8.3 gain twist
Test Barrel Length: 24 in.
Case Type: rimless, necked
Case Material: brass
Primer Size: large rifle

CARTRIDGE BALLISTICS
Max. Average Breech Pressure: 4,336
Max. Effective Range: 500 yds.
Max. Horizontal Range: 3,900 yds.
Max. Vertical Range: 9,000 ft.

Bullet Weight (gr.)	Bullet Type	Muzzle Velocity (fps)	Muzzle Energy (ft.-lbs.)
162	Ball	2,295	1902

CURRENT MANUFACTURER(S)
Prvi Partzan, Hornady

GENERAL COMMENT(S)
The 6.5x52mm cartridge was the standard Italian military service cartridge from 1891 until 1938. It was replaced in that year by the 7.35mm Italian Carcano with its larger, heavier bullet. However, rifles and ammunition in 7.35mm were in short supply all during World War II, so most Italian troops kept their 6.5mm rifles. Students of ordnance history quickly will recognize Ritter von Mannlicher's name on this cartridge. Carcano was an Italian Arsenal where a considerable amount of research and development work with cartridges was carried out. The 6.5x52mm M-C cartridge had/has a negative reputation due to the rough workmanship on many of the Carcano rifles. However, both rifle and ammunition gave good service during both World War I and World War II. Unfortunately, the 6.5x52mm M-C cartridge earned an infamous place in history when it was used to assassinate President John Kennedy. This cloud has followed it ever since.

TECHNICAL COMMENT(S)
The 6.5x52mm Mannlicher-Carcano is another late 1890s cartridge with a chamber pressure in the low 40,000 psi range. Although the Italian Army adopted a spitzer-pointed bullet in the 1930s, the round nose bullet remained the dominant type due to production shortages. This cartridge was obsolete with the end of World War II, however some countries and revolutionary groups used captured Italian rifles until well into the 1970s firing remaining stocks of Italian war time ammunition.

6.5x53Rmm MANNLICHER (DUTCH & ROMANIAN)

ALTERNATE NAME(S): 6.5mm Dutch, 6.5mm Romanian, 6.5mm Mannlicher M/93
RELATED CALIBER(S): 6.5x54mm M-S

CARTRIDGE HISTORY
Year of Introduction: 1892
Country of Origin: Austria
Designer(s): Steyr
Governing Body: N/A
Present Status: obsolete

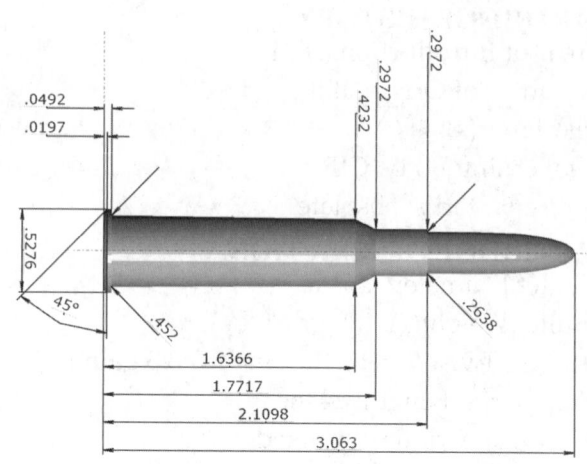

CARTRIDGE DESCRIPTION
Bullet Diameter: .264 in.
Bullet Weight(s): 156 gr.
Rifling Twist Rate: 1 turn in 7.87 in.
Test Barrel Length: 24 in.
Case Type: rimmed, necked
Case Material: brass
Primer Size: large rifle

CARTRIDGE BALLISTICS
Max. Average Breech Pressure: 40,700 psi.
Max. Horizontal Range: 3,900 yds.
Max. Vertical Range: 9,000 ft.

Bullet Weight (gr.)	Bullet Type	Muzzle Velocity (fps)	Muzzle Energy (ft.-lbs.)
156	Ball	2,220	1,706

CURRENT MANUFACTURER(S)
None

GENERAL COMMENT(S)
Both the Netherlands and Romania adopted this cartridge in 1892. The 6.5x53Rmm Mannlicher cartridge remained in front line military service in each country until the end of World War II. Obsolescent at the beginning of World War II, by the end of the war both were obsolete and slid into obscurity. They are not well known by American shooters.

TECHNICAL COMMENT(S)
No effort was made by either country to update the 6.5x53Rmm Mannlicher cartridge with a pointed bullet of lighter weight. Basically, the 6.5x53mm Mannlicher cartridge is a rimmed version of the 6.5x54mm M-S cartridge.

6.5x53.5SRmm DAUDETEAU

ALTERNATE NAME(S): 6.5x53.5SRmm , 6.5mm Daudeteau No. 12
RELATED CALIBER(S): none

CARTRIDGE HISTORY
Year of Introduction: 1895
Country of Origin: France
Designer(s): Maj. Louis d'Audeteau
Governing Body: none
Present Status: obsolete

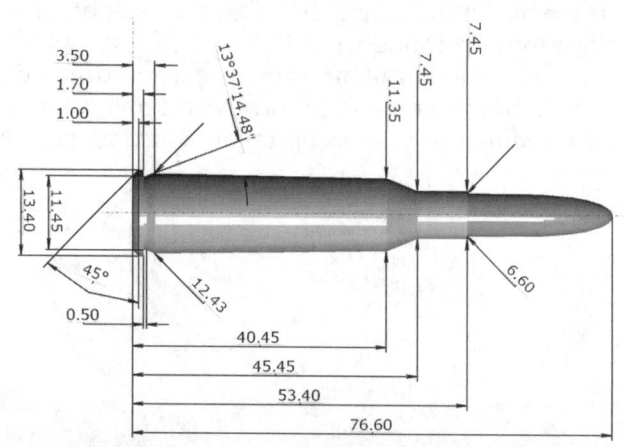

CARTRIDGE DESCRIPTION
Bullet Diameter: .263 in.
Bullet Weight(s): 150 gr.
Rifling Twist Rate: N/A
Test Barrel Length: N/A

Case Type: semi-rimmed, necked
Case Material: brass
Primer: large rifle

CARTRIDGE BALLISTICS
Max. Average Breech Pressure: N/A
Max. Horizontal Range: 3,500 yds.
Max. Vertical Range: 7,600 ft.

Bullet Weight (gr.)	Bullet Type	Muzzle Velocity (fps)	Muzzle Energy (ft.-lbs.)
150	FMJ-RN	2,440	1,983

CURRENT MANUFACTURER(S)
None

GENERAL COMMENT(S)
This cartridge was adopted by the French Navy in 1895, but replaced three years later. It was also used by the Uruguayan armed forces from 1895-1898.

TECHNICAL COMMENT(S)
One of the estimated 10 different experimental rifle cartridges developed between 1886 and 1902 by Maj. Louis d'Audeteau of the French Army, it was the only one of his cartridges to be adopted for military service.

6.5x54mm MANNLICHER-SCHOENAUER

ALTERNATE NAME(S): 6.5x54mm Greek Mannlicher
RELATED CALIBER(S): 6.5x53R Mannlicher, 6.5x55mm Swedish, 6.5x52mm Mannlicher-Carcano

CARTRIDGE HISTORY
Year of Introduction: 1900
Country of Origin: Austria
Designer(s): von Mannlicher
Governing Body: none
Present Status: obsolete

CARTRIDGE DESCRIPTION
Bullet Diameter: .264 in.
Bullet Weight(s): 156 gr.
Rifling Twist Rate: 1 turn in 7.8 in.
Test Barrel Length: 24 in.
Case Type: rimless, necked
Case Material: brass
Primer Size: large rifle

CARTRIDGE BALLISTICS
Max. Average Breech Pressure: 40,700 psi.
Max. Horizontal Range: 3,900 yds.
Max. Vertical Range: 9,000 ft.

Bullet Weight (gr.)	Bullet Type	Muzzle Velocity (fps)	Muzzle Energy (ft.-lbs.)
156	Ball	2,460	2,100

CURRENT MANUFACTURER(S)
Dynamit Nobel

GENERAL COMMENT(S)
Adopted by the Greek Army in 1903, the 6.5x54mm Mannlicher-Schoenauer cartridge remained in Greek military service until the German Occupation in 1941. This cartridge became obsolete at the end of World War II. Greece was the only country to take this cartridge into military service. Arguably a flop for military service, this cartridge did enjoy a limited popularity among sportsmen that continues to this day.

TECHNICAL COMMENT(S)

Despite its large case volume, the 6.5x54mm Mannlicher-Schoenauer cartridge offered mediocre ballistic performance in comparison to other military 6.5mm cartridges. Part of this is due to the relatively low chamber pressure. Another factor is that the 6.5x54mm M-S cartridge was never updated with a lighter weight pointed bullet.

6.5x55mm SWEDISH MAUSER

ALTERNATE NAME(S): 6.5mm Swedish, 6.5x55mm Swedish
RELATED CALIBER(S): 6.5x53Rmm Mannlicher, 6.5x54mm M-S, 6.5x52mm Mannlicher-Carcano

CARTRIDGE HISTORY

Year of Introduction: 1894

Country of Origin: Sweden

Designer(s): Swedish/Norwegian Joint Military Commission

Governing Body: CIP, SAAMI

Present Status: obsolete

CARTRIDGE DESCRIPTION

Bullet Diameter: .264 in.

Bullet Weight(s): 139, 144, 156 gr.

Rifling Twist Rate: 1 turn in 7.9 in.

Test Barrel Length: 24 in.

Case Type: rimless, necked

Case Material: brass

Primer Size: large rifle

CARTRIDGE BALLISTICS

Max. Average Breech Pressure: 55,000 psi.

Max. Horizontal Range: 4,000 yds.

Max. Vertical Range: 10,000 ft.

Bullet Weight (gr.)	Bullet Type	Muzzle Velocity (fps)	Muzzle Energy (ft.-lbs.)
139 (M41)	Ball	2,600	2,085

CURRENT MANUFACTURER(S)

Federal, Remington, Winchester, NAMMO, Prvi Partizan, Sellier & Bellot, INDEP

GENERAL COMMENT(S)

From 1894 until the early 1970s, the 6.5x55mm Swedish Mauser cartridge remained in front line military service in Sweden. Norway also adopted this caliber albeit with a 144 grain bullet. The Swedes replaced the 6.5x55mm cartridge with the 7.62x51mm NATO cartridge in the 1970s. In the early 1990s, the Swedes adopted the 5.56x45mm NATO cartridge for front line military service.

TECHNICAL COMMENT(S)

The 6.5x55mm Swedish Mauser cartridge is considered by most shooters as the best 6.5mm caliber cartridge ever designed. It is deservedly well known for its accuracy and excellent ballistic performance. The original round nose bullet was updated to a sharply pointed boat-tail design in the late-1930s to become the M41. Maximum average chamber pressure of the 6.5mm Swedish is also higher than other 6.5mm military cartridges.

6.5x58mm PORTUGUESE VERGUEIRO

ALTERNATE NAME(S): 6.5mm Mauser Vergueiro, 6.5x58mm , 6.5mm Vergueiro, 6.5mm Portuguese
RELATED CALIBER(S): 6.5x57mm Mauser

CARTRIDGE HISTORY
Year of Introduction: 1904
Country of Origin: Germany
Designer(s): Mauser
Governing Body: none
Present Status: obsolete

CARTRIDGE DESCRIPTION
Bullet Diameter: .264 in.
Bullet Weight(s): 154 gr.
Rifling Twist Rate: 1 turn in 7.8 in.
Test Barrel Length: N/A
Case Type: rimless, necked
Case Material: brass
Primer: large rifle

CARTRIDGE BALLISTICS
Max. Average Breech Pressure: N/A
Max. Horizontal Range: N/A
Max. Vertical Range: N/A

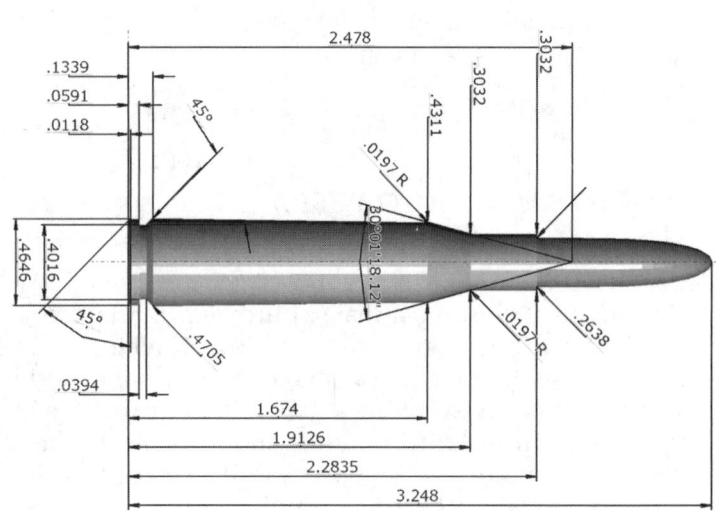

Bullet Weight (gr.)	Bullet Type	Muzzle Velocity (fps)	Muzzle Energy (ft.-lbs.)
154	FWJ-RN	2,460	2,069

CURRENT MANUFACTURER(S)
None

GENERAL COMMENT(S)
Adopted by Portugal in 1904, the 6.5x58mm served until replaced by the 7.9x57mm Mauser cartridge in 1937. In European commercial markets, it achieved a limited following. No other country adopted this cartridge for military service.

TECHNICAL COMMENT(S)
This cartridge is very similar to the 6.5x57mm Mauser in dimension but had lower ballistic performance.

.276 ENFIELD PATTERN 13

ALTERNATE NAME(S): .276 Pattern 13, .276 Mark I, 7x60mm
RELATED CALIBER(S): .280 Ross, 7x57mm Meunier

CARTRIDGE HISTORY
Year of Introduction: 1913
Country of Origin: Britain
Designer(s): Royal Laboratories-Woolwich
Governing Body: none
Present Status: obsolete

CARTRIDGE DESCRIPTION
Bullet Diameter: .284 in.
Bullet Weight(s): 165 gr.
Rifling Twist Rate: 1 turn in 9 in.
Test Barrel Length: N/A

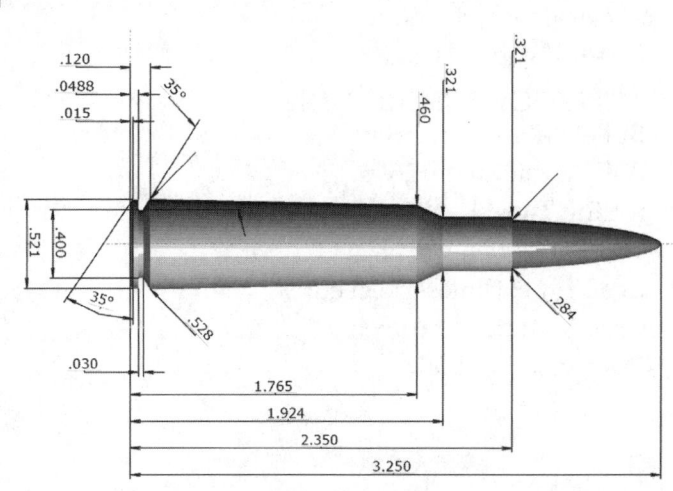

Case Type: rimless, necked
Case Material: brass
Primer: large rifle

CARTRIDGE BALLISTICS
Max. Average Chamber Pressure: N/A
Max. Horizontal Range: 6,500 yds.
Max. Vertical Range: 13,500 ft.

Bullet Weight (gr.)	Bullet Type	Muzzle Velocity (fps)	Muzzle Energy (ft.-lbs.)
165	FMJ-BT	2,800	2,881

CURRENT MANUFACTURER(S)
None

GENERAL COMMENT(S)
By the late 1890s, most major European military organizations realized that the first military cartridges for smokeless propellants were becoming obsolete. Generally, it was recognized that this would lead to a rimless, necked case design using a smaller caliber bullet and higher maximum average chamber pressure. The British War Office began studying a new military cartridge in 1908 to replace the .303 British cartridge then in service with the British Army. Studies and tests led to the .276 Enfield cartridge for the new Pattern 13 rifle. Both completed successful troop trials in 1913-1914. Official adoption was just around the corner when World War I broke out in late 1914. The beginning of the War forced all new military rifle and cartridge projects in Britain to be postponed for the duration. With the end of World War I in 1918, fiscal cut backs and war exhaustion ended further development for many years. In 1929-1930, the British Army tested the American Pedersen rifle and its .276 Pedersen cartridge. Ammunition for these tests was manufactured in Britain. The British Army did not adopt the .275 Pedersen rifle or cartridge. This cartridge was not produced commercially.

TECHNICAL COMMENT(S)
Certainly the .276 Enfield was ahead of its time in a variety of ways. First, it was a rimless design with plenty of volume for a large propellant charge. Second, it was designed from the outset for smokeless propellants and high maximum average chamber pressures. Lastly, it used a small caliber, streamlined (boat-tail) bullet launched at high muzzle velocity. Both ball and armor piercing bullets were developed. No further production of this caliber was undertaken following the conclusion of the combat tests.

.276 PEDERSEN

ALTERNATE NAME(S): .276 T-2, .276 Pedersen T2, .276 M1929, 7x51mm Pedersen
RELATED CALIBER(S): .30-'06 Springfield, 7x57mm Mauser

CARTRIDGE HISTORY
Year of Introduction: 1932
Country of Origin: U.S.
Designer(s): J.D. Pedersen
Governing Body: none
Present Status: obsolete

CARTRIDGE DESCRIPTION
Bullet Diameter: .283 in.
Bullet Weight(s): 126 gr.
Rifling Twist Rate: 1 turn in 9 in.
Test Barrel Length: N/A
Case Type: rimless, necked
Case Material: brass
Primer: large rifle

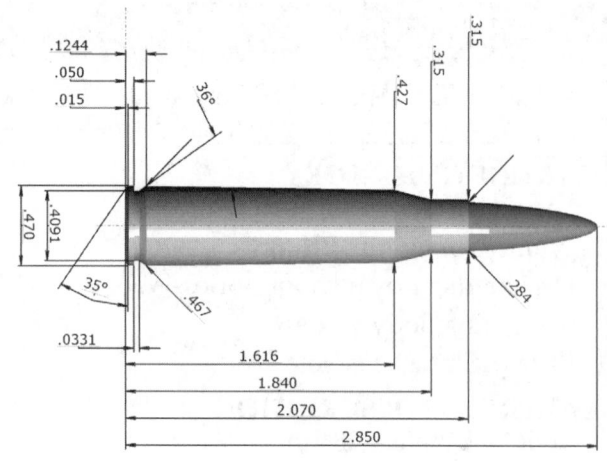

CARTRIDGE BALLISTICS

Max. Average Breech Pressure: 40,000-45,000 psi.

Max. Horizontal Range: 4,450 yds.

Max. Vertical Range: 9,350 ft.

Bullet Weight (gr.)	Bullet Type	Muzzle Velocity (fps)	Muzzle Energy (ft.-lbs.)
126	FMJ-BT/T-2	2,550	1,819

CURRENT MANUFACTURER(S)

None

GENERAL COMMENT(S)

In 1906, the U.S. Army adopted the .30-'06 Springfield cartridge for military service. In so doing, the U.S. Army traded in the rimmed .30-40 Krag cartridge with its heavy round nose bullet for a modern, rimless case designed from the outset for smokeless propellants and pointed bullets. Inspiration for this undoubtedly came from the German 8x57mmJS cartridge adopted by the German Army in 1905. Adoption of the new .30-'06 Sprg. cartridge catapulted the U.S. Army to the forefront of military cartridge development, albeit on the shoulders of the German Army. However, this technical edge was not exploited due to the leisurely pace of peace time funding and manufacture. When the U.S. finally entered World War I in 1917, the U.S. armed forces were woefully short of both Springfield rifles and .30-'06 ammunition. With the end of World War I in 1918, the U.S. Ordnance Department recognized the advantage of developing a semi-automatic infantry rifle firing a lighter, smaller caliber cartridge. Certainly the Ordnance Department personnel were well aware of the British .276 Enfield and the French 7x57mm Meunier cartridges developed for the same reasons. In 1923, the U.S. Ordnance Department gave the go-ahead for a development program proposed by J.D. Pedersen, a well known and successful firearms designer, working at Springfield Armory. Frankford Arsenal was to develop and manufacture the cartridges while Springfield Armory concentrated on the rifle. Pedersen developed a toggle-bolt, semi-automatic rifle for the .276 Pedersen cartridge. Both were demonstrated in the U.K. to the British War Office in 1929-1930 using .276 Pedersen ammunition made in Britain. The British were not impressed. A fortunate event occurred in 1929 when John Garand finished his gas-operated rifle design, soon to become the famous M1 Garand rifle. As development on the .276 Pedersen cartridge was well along at the time, Garand designed and chambered his prototype M1 rifles in .276 Pedersen caliber. Ultimately, Garand's rifle design was selected for adoption and both it and the .276 Pedersen cartridge were submitted to the U.S. Army Chief of Staff, General Douglas MacArthur, for final approval in 1932. General MacArthur was not impressed. He disapproved the adoption of the .276 Pedersen cartridge and directed that Garand redesign his rifle to fire the existing .30-'06 Springfield cartridge. Work was then halted permanently on the .276 Pedersen cartridge. This cartridge was not produced commercially.

TECHNICAL COMMENT(S)

Some ten variations of .276 case and bullet configuration were tried before the final T2 design was selected in 1929. To lower manufacturing cost, the .276 Pedersen used the head dimensions of the existing .30-'06 Springfield cartridge. This meant that the draw and heading operations for the .30-'06 Spr. could be used with virtually no changes so that only taper and plug tooling would be needed to make the .276 cartridge case. Both small rifle and large rifle primer were tested before finalizing on the existing large rifle primer used in the .30-'06 Spr. Ball, armor-piercing and tracer bullets were developed. The ball bullet was a 126 grain, spitzer boat-tail design with a copper alloy jacket and a lead core. Armor-piercing and tracer bullets were spitzer flat base designs. Ballistic performance was mediocre as maximum average chamber pressures were kept at a very conservative level with the result that muzzle velocity was a modest 2,550 fps. With further ballistic development, the .276 Pedersen cartridge could have catapulted the U.S. Army once again into the forefront of military cartridge design. However, it was not to be, leaving the .276 Pedersen as a footnote in U.S. military history.

.280 BRITISH

ALTERNATE NAME(S): .280 Enfield, .280 NATO, .280 UK, .280 Short, 7x43mm British, .280/30 British, 7mm High Velocity, 7x49mm, 7mm Intermediate

RELATED CALIBER(S): .30-'06 Springfield, 7.62x51mm NATO, 9mm Japanese

CARTRIDGE HISTORY
Year of Introduction: 1947
Country of Origin: Britain
Designer(s): Royal Ordnance
Governing Body: none
Present Status: obsolete

CARTRIDGE DESCRIPTION
Bullet Diameter: .284 in.
Bullet Weight(s): 130 - 140 gr.
Rifling Twist Rate: N/A
Test Barrel Length: N/A
Case Type: rimless, necked
Case Material: brass
Primer: large rifle

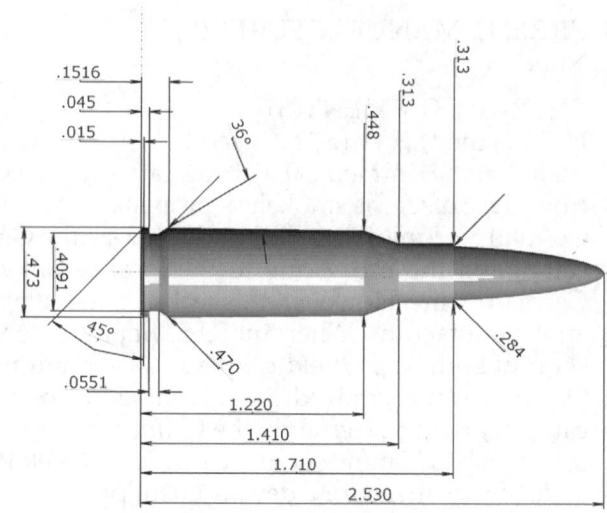

CARTRIDGE BALLISTICS
Max. Average Breech Pressure: N/A
Max. Horizontal Range: 5,300 yds.
Max. Vertical Range: 11,000 ft.

Bullet Weight (gr.)	Bullet Type	Muzzle Velocity (fps)	Muzzle Energy (ft.-lbs.)
140	FMJ-BT	2,530	1,990 (Imp.)

CURRENT MANUFACTURER(S)
None

GENERAL COMMENT(S)
Following the conclusion of World War II in 1945, the British Army immediately started a program to replace the obsolescent .303 British rifle cartridge. They did not simply pick up where they left off in 1913 with the .276 Enfield, although they stuck with a 7mm bullet diameter doubtless after studying the results of German efforts along this line in the 1930s. A major effort was made to draw on the German wartime experiences in developing assault rifles. This meant a lighter, less powerful but more compact cartridge with low recoil. Subsequently, the British developed a 7x44mm rimless cartridge with ballistics similar to the German 7.92x33mm Kurz. The British also developed the EM series of bullpup assault rifles for their new cartridge. Many other European countries did much the same with the result that there were several well tested examples of such cartridges, but no general agreement on a common dimension or interchangeability. The advent of NATO changed that. At that time, the U.S. military got the same message, but interpreted it differently. They developed the 7.62x51mm (civilian version in the .308 Winchester) cartridge which was essentially a shortened .30-'06 Springfield with nearly the same ballistic performance. The U.S. government urged the NATO countries to adopt the 7.62x51mm cartridge. When they proved reluctant to do so, the U.S. strong-armed the other NATO members to finally get the 7.62x51mm cartridge adopted. To meet U.S. military objections of the .280 British cartridge lacking power, the British adapted the .280 cartridge case to use a .308 in diameter bullet, the hybrid being dubbed the .280/30. When the .280/30 concept went nowhere, the British revised the .280 cartridge to hold more propellant by increasing the case length from 44mm to 49mm. The new cartridge was called the 7mm High Velocity or 7mm Medium. When the new British 7x49mm HV was rejected by NATO, the British government abandoned the project. But, Fabrique Nationale in Belgium, who worked with the British on .280 ammunition development, did not end efforts to sell the 7x49mm cartridge. Eventually, they succeeded in selling the 7x49mm High Velocity cartridge together with a suitably chambered FAL rifle to the Venezuelan Army who ended up being the sole customer.

TECHNICAL COMMENT(S)
The .280 British is a well thought-out example of the "first" wave of potential new military rifle cartridges designed immediately after World War II. While these cartridges incorporated many modern features such as

a short, compact, rimless case and reduced bullet weight, lower muzzle velocity and lower recoil, they were not, in fact, assault rifle cartridges. Rather, they were an interim development step more along the concept of an intermediate power cartridge, too long and powerful to be an assault rifle cartridge, but substantially more compact and less powerful than the traditional infantry rifle cartridges they proposed to replace. For this reason, most of them remained experimental, except the .280 British which became the "Cartridge, Small Arm, Ball, 7mm Mark IZ". However, despite its official designation and exhaustive testing, it was never officially fielded. Nearly two decades later, there would be a "second" wave of assault rifle cartridges of even smaller caliber closer to the original German concept.

7x57mm MAUSER

ALTERNATE NAME(S): 7mm Mauser, 7x57mm , 7x57mm M93, 7mm Chilean Mauser, 7mm Spanish Mauser
RELATED CALIBER(S): 8x57mm

CARTRIDGE HISTORY
Year of Introduction: 1893
Country of Origin: Germany
Designer(s): Mauser
Governing Body: CIP, SAAMI
Present Status: obsolete

CARTRIDGE DESCRIPTION
Bullet Diameter: .286 in.
Bullet Weight(s): 139-173 gr.
Rifling Twist Rate: 1 turn in 8.66 in.
Test Barrel Length: 24 in.
Case Type: rimless, necked
Case Material: brass
Primer Size: large rifle

CARTRIDGE BALLISTICS
Max. Average Breech Pressure: 56,600 psi.
Max. Horizontal Range: 4,500 yds.
Max. Vertical Range: 9,500 ft.

Bullet Weight (gr.)	Bullet Type	Muzzle Velocity (fps)	Muzzle Energy (ft.-lbs.)
139	Ball	2,660	2,183
150	Ball	2,565	2,190
174	Ball	2,425	2,271

CURRENT MANUFACTURER(S)
Federal, Remington, Winchester, DN, Prvi Partizan, Sellier & Bellot, NAMMO, Hornady

GENERAL COMMENT(S)
After the Spanish Army adopted the 7x57mm cartridge in 1893, it quickly became a popular military cartridge in South America. It was adopted for military service in Mexico, Columbia, Brazil, Chile, and Uruguay and remained in front line service until the 1960s in many of them. The 7x57mm Mauser cartridge became headline news at the turn of the 19th century when Spanish Army troops used it to defend San Juan Hill in Cuba during the Spanish-American War. American soldiers were very impressed by the range and ballistic performance of the 7x57mm. As a military cartridge, the 7x57mm Mauser was seldom put to the test with the exception of the historical footnote of San Juan Hill. South American countries seldom went to war with the exception of several border disputes. As a result, the 7x57mm never earned the military reputation of its older brother, the 8x57mm Mauser.

TECHNICAL COMMENT(S)
The Spanish-American War made the ballistic reputation of the 7x57mm Mauser cartridge and that reputation was well-deserved. When loaded with a spitzer, boat-tail bullet, the 7x57mm offers high retained velocity, great striking energy, and a flat trajectory.

7x57mm MEUNIER

ALTERNATE NAME(S): 7x59mm Meunier, 7mm Meunier
RELATED CALIBER(S): .280 Ross, .276 Enfield

CARTRIDGE HISTORY
Year of Introduction: 1910
Country of Origin: France
Designer(s): Etienne Meunier
Governing Body: none
Present Status: obsolete

CARTRIDGE DESCRIPTION
Bullet Diameter: .284 in.
Bullet Weight(s): 139 gr.
Rifling Twist Rate: 1 turn in 8.66 in.
Test Barrel Length: N/A
Case Type: rimless, necked
Case Material: brass
Primer: large rifle

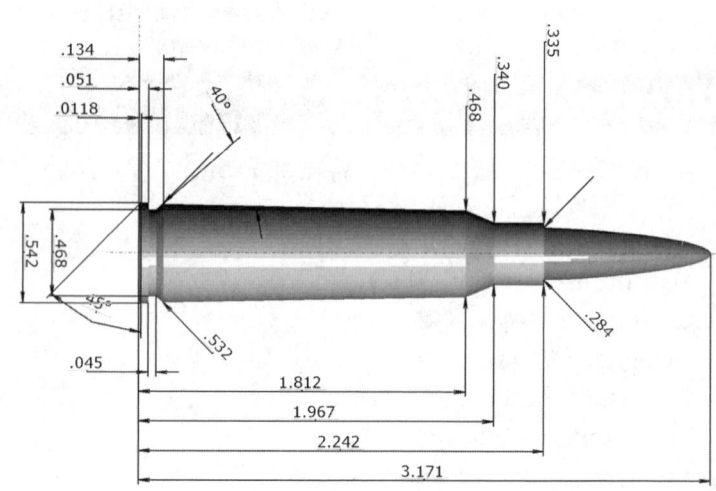

CARTRIDGE BALLISTICS
Max. Average Breech Pressure: 59,740 psi.
Max. Horizontal Range: 5,450 yds.
Max. Vertical Range: 11,450 ft.

Bullet Weight (gr.)	Bullet Type	Muzzle Velocity (fps)	Muzzle Energy (ft.-lbs.)
139	FMJ	2,790	2,402

CURRENT MANUFACTURER(S)
None

GENERAL COMMENT(S)
By the late 1890s, most major European military organizations realized that the first military cartridges using smokeless propellants were becoming obsolete. Generally, it was recognized that this would lead to a rimless, necked case design using a smaller caliber bullet and higher maximum average chamber pressure. France was determined to take the lead on this by beginning a series of studies and tests in 1894 to replace the rapidly aging 8x50Rmm Lebel cartridge. By 1900, these studies produced several ultra-modern cartridges in calibers 6mm, 6.5mm and 7mm. However, none were adopted as the emphasis had shifted to development of a semi-automatic military rifle in 1900. In 1905, the French Small Arms Commission drafted the specifications for the new rifle and cartridge and the French Supreme War Council made it official in 1909 by announcing a program of development. Minimum caliber was to be 6.5mm with a maximum average chamber pressure of 59,740 psi. In 1910, the long-recoil Meunier A6 semi-automatic rifle firing the 7x57mm Meunier cartridge was officially adopted. Surprisingly, a decision to begin mass production was not taken until 1913, but the beginning of World War I in 1914 forced all new projects to be postponed for the duration. However, in 1916, the project was revived and 1,000 Meunier A6 rifles were manufactured in 1917 together with a short run of 7x57mm Meunier ammunition from Puteaux Arsenal. Some 843 A6 Meunier rifles were issued to French Army sharpshooters in the front lines. It was thus that the Meunier A6 rifle and its 7x57mm Meunier cartridge became the first semi-automatic military rifle and purpose-designed cartridge to enter military service.

TECHNICAL COMMENT(S)
Certainly the 7x57mm Meunier cartridge was ahead of its time in a variety of ways. First, it was a rimless design with plenty of volume for a large propellant charge. Second, it was designed from the outset for smokeless propellants and high maximum average chamber pressures. Lastly, it used a small caliber, light weight bullet launched at high muzzle velocity. Only ball-type bullets were developed. No further production of this caliber was undertaken following the conclusion of the combat tests.

7.35mm ITALIAN CARCANO

ALTERNATE NAME(S): 7.35mm Italian
RELATED CALIBER(S): 8x57mm Mauser, 7.5x54mm French, .303 British, .30-'06 Springfield

CARTRIDGE HISTORY
Year of Introduction: 1938
Country of Origin: Italy
Designer(s): N/A
Governing Body: none
Present Status: obsolete

CARTRIDGE DESCRIPTION
Bullet Diameter: .298 in.
Bullet Weight(s): 128 gr.
Rifling Twist Rate: 1 turn in 10 in.
Test Barrel Length: N/A
Case Type: rimless, necked
Case Material: brass
Primer Size: large rifle

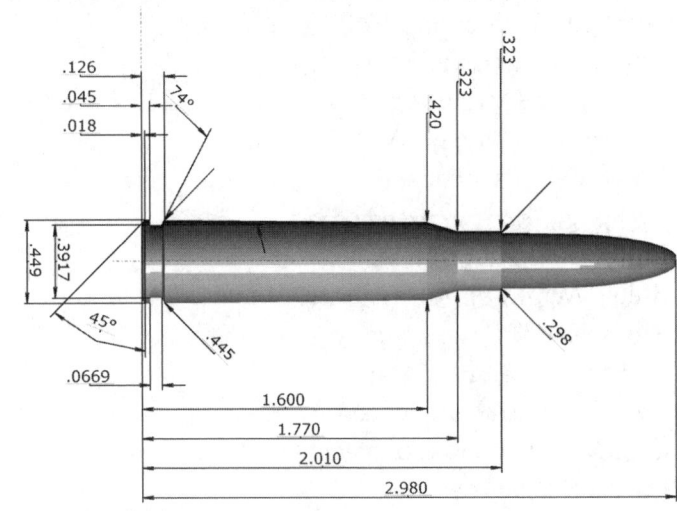

CARTRIDGE BALLISTICS
Max. Average Breech Pressure: approximately 38,000 psi.
Max. Horizontal Range: 3,000 yds.
Max. Vertical Range: 7,000 ft.

Bullet Weight (gr.)	Bullet Type	Muzzle Velocity (fps)	Muzzle Energy (ft.-lbs.)
128	Ball	2,480	1,749

CURRENT MANUFACTURER(S)
None

GENERAL COMMENT(S)
In the mid-1930s, the Italian Army realized their 6.5x52mm Mannlicher-Carcano cartridge was fast becoming obsolete. Bowing to the inevitable while taking careful note of developments in other countries, the Italian Army adopted a new 7.35mm Carcano cartridge in 1938. However, it was too late as production had scarcely begun when World War II broke out. The urgency of supplying a large army led the Italian military to withdraw the 7.35mm rifles and ammunition for the duration so as to increase production capacity for 6.5x53mm Mannlicher-Carcano ammunition and reduce supply line complications. Toward the end of World War II, many Italian military units were reequipped with German weapons in 8x57mm Mauser caliber. Some Italian military rifles were converted to that caliber as well. Most of the remaining 7.35mm rifles and ammunition were sold to Finland where they were used with success against the Russians during the First Russo-Finnish War in the early 1940s. Following World War II, remaining stocks of 7.35mm rifles and ammunition were quickly sold off on the surplus market. As this cartridge was not adopted by any other nation, it quickly faded into history.

TECHNICAL COMMENT(S)
The 7.35mm Italian cartridge is something of an odd duck among military cartridges. Although it shares many case dimensions with the 6.5x53mm Carcano cartridge, it is unique in that it uses a bullet of unusual diameter and ogive shape that is relatively light weight for its size. This gives the 7.35mm cartridge a distinctive appearance. As the Finns proved, the 7.35mm cartridge performed satisfactorily on the battle field. However, its exterior ballistics were nothing more than barely adequate at best.

7.5x54mm FRENCH MAS

ALTERNATE NAME(S): 7.5x54mm , 7.5mm French, 7.5mm MAS, 7.5x54mm MAS
RELATED CALIBER(S): 8x57mm Mauser, .30-'06 Springfield, 7.62x51mm NATO

CARTRIDGE HISTORY
Year of Introduction: 1929
Country of Origin: France
Designer(s): Manufacture d'Armes de St. Etienne
Governing Body: N/A
Present Status: obsolete

CARTRIDGE DESCRIPTION
Bullet Diameter: .308 in.
Bullet Weight(s): 140 gr.
Rifling Twist Rate: 1 turn in 10 in.
Test Barrel Length: 24 in.
Case Type: rimless, necked
Case Material: brass or steel
Primer Size: large rifle

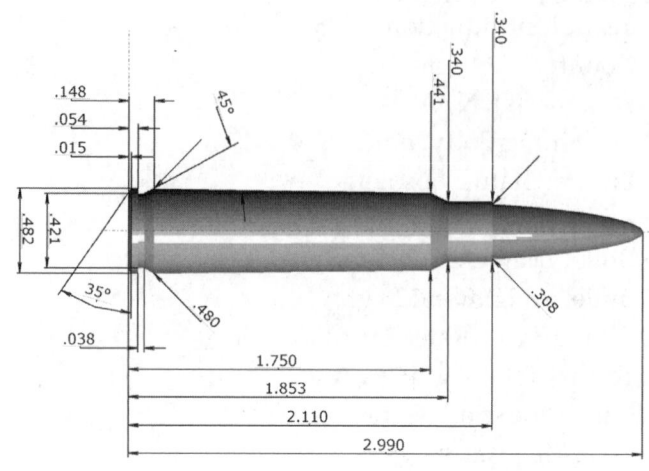

CARTRIDGE BALLISTICS
Max. Average Breech Pressure: approx. 45,000 psi.
Max. Horizontal Range: 3,400 yds.
Max. Vertical Range: 7,800 ft.

Bullet Weight (gr.)	Bullet Type	Muzzle Velocity (fps)	Muzzle Energy (ft.-lbs.)
140 (M1933)	Ball	2,710	2,282
143 (Ord.)	Ball	2,680	2,280

CURRENT MANUFACTURER(S)
Prvi Partizan

GENERAL COMMENT(S)
In the early 1900s, the French Army recognized the need to replace the obsolete 8x50Rmm Lebel cartridge. Toward this end, a series of studies was initiated to design a new military cartridge. World War I interrupted this effort, but work was resumed in the early 1920s. By 1924, a suitable design had been developed and was adopted as the 7.5x58mm MLE 1924C. However, the new cartridge was short lived. In 1929 it was replaced with a similar, but 4mm shorter, cartridge designated the 7.5x54mm MLE 1929C. This cartridge remained in front line service in the French Army until NATO was formed in the early 1950s. It continued in reserve status until the late 1980s when the French military services adopted the 5.56x45mm NATO cartridge.

TECHNICAL COMMENT(S)
The dimensions of the 7.5x54mm MLE 1929C cartridge are very similar to the .30-'06 Springfield and 8x57mm Mauser. In fact, it was the inability to easily distinguish the earlier 7.5x57mm MLE 1924C from the German 8x57mm Mauser which caused the French to shorten the case 4mm and adopt a new cartridge. The French philosophy for military cartridge ballistics differs from many other nations and the 7.5x54mm MAS cartridge shows this. An example is the bullet weight which is lower than other military cartridges of similar caliber. In addition, the maximum average breech pressure is lower than many of the newer military cartridges of the time such as the 8x57mm Mauser and .30-'06 Springfield. However, the French bullet does have a more efficient ballistic profile than the .30-'06 Spr. M2 bullet and the lighter weight and lower muzzle velocity reduce recoil. No other country adopted this cartridge for military service although the local military forces of a number of small African nations were given rifles and ammunition in this caliber after World War II.

The 7.5x54mm MAS cartridge saw extensive combat in Vietnam during the 1950s.

7.5x55mm SWISS GP11

ALTERNATE NAME(S): 7.5x55mm Swiss
RELATED CALIBER(S): 7.5x53.5mm Swiss GP90 and GP90/03; 7.5x54.5mm Swiss GP90/23

CARTRIDGE HISTORY
Year of Introduction: 1911
Country of Origin: Switzerland
Designer(s): Maj. Eduard Rubin
Governing Body: CIP
Present Status: obsolete

CARTRIDGE DESCRIPTION
Bullet Diameter: .308 in.
Bullet Weight(s): 174 grs.
Rifling Twist Rate: 1 turn in 10.63 in.
Test Barrel Length: 24 in.
Case Type: rimless, necked
Case Material: brass or rarely aluminum
Primer Size: large rifle

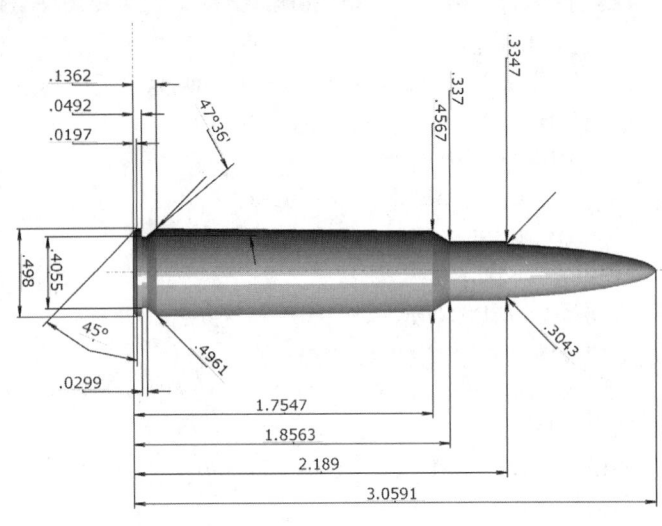

CARTRIDGE BALLISTICS
Max. Average Breech Pressure: 45,500 psi.
Max. Horizontal Range: 6,926 yds.
Max. Vertical Range: 14,625 ft.

Bullet Weight (gr.)	Bullet Type	Muzzle Velocity (fps)	Muzzle Energy (ft.-lbs.)
174 (GP11)	Ball	2,560	2,533

CURRENT MANUFACTURER(S)
RUAG, Norma, Prvi Partizan, INDEP

GENERAL COMMENT(S)
The 7.5x55mm Swiss GP11 service cartridge is a direct descendent of the 7.5x53.5mm GP90 and GP90/03 cartridges. It remained in front line Swiss Army service until the mid-1980s when it was finally replaced by the 5.56x45mm M90 cartridge. Although considered superannuated, the 7.5x55mm GP11 cartridge continues to serve in Swiss Army reserve forces and in fortress machineguns.

By the early 1900s, the first and second waves of infantry cartridges designed in the mid- to late 1880s were getting long in the tooth and scheduled for replacement. These included the 8x50Rmm Lebel (France), the .303 British (UK), the 8x57mm Mauser M88 (Germany), and the 7.5x53.5mm GP90-90/03 (Switzerland). While France and Britain struggled to develop completely new infantry cartridges, Germany and Switzerland saved money and time by updating their existing infantry cartridges. The result was the 8x57mm Mauser S Patrone in 1905 and the Swiss 7.5x55mm GP11 in 1911.

TECHNICAL COMMENT(S)
In 1903, the GP90 was upgraded with a less corrosive primer and a 31 gr. powder charge that increased muzzle velocity to 1,980 fps. The upgraded cartridge was designated GP90/03.

In the early 1900s, many European armies updated their service cartridge by replacing the heavy round nose bullet with a lighter weight spitzer (pointed) bullet at a higher muzzle velocity. Before the 7.5x53.5mm GP90/03 cartridge could be updated, the Schmidt-Rubin rifle had to be strengthened in order to withstand higher average breech pressures. These measures were completed during the 1911-1913 time frame. The new 7.5x55mm Swiss GP11 cartridge was loaded to a maximum average breech pressure to 45,500 psi. using a charge of 49.35 gr. of smokeless propellant. A new 174 gr. FMJBT bullet allowed muzzle velocity to be increased to 2,560 fps and non-corrosive primers were used exclusively. The case length was increased to 55mm to prevent it from being fired in the older rifles.

The result was a thoroughly modern cartridge with internationally competitive ballistic performance. In addition to the 174 gr. FMJBT ball bullet, armor piercing, tracer, dummy, and match loads were developed. Swiss government arsenals at Dornach, Altdorf, and Thun produced this cartridge.

The designation 7.5mm instead of 7.62mm for a .308 inch diameter bullet is due to the fact that, at the time, the Swiss expressed the bore diameter as measured across the top of the lands, not across the grooves as many other military services did.

7.5x53.5mm SWISS GP1890

ALTERNATE NAME(S): 7.5x53.5mm GP90, 7.5x53.5mm GP90/03
RELATED CALIBER(S): 7.5x53.5mm Swiss GP90/23, 7.5x55mm Swiss GP11

CARTRIDGE HISTORY
Year of Introduction: 1890
Country of Origin: Switzerland
Designer(s): Maj. Eduard Rubin
Governing Body: CIP
Present Status: obsolete

CARTRIDGE DESCRIPTION
Bullet Diameter: .308 in. (.3208 in. w/paper patch)
Bullet Weight(s): 211 grs.
Rifling Twist Rate: 1 turn in 10.63 in.
Test Barrel Length: 24 in.
Case Type: rimless, necked
Case Material: brass
Primer Size: large rifle

CARTRIDGE BALLISTICS
Max. Average Breech Pressure: 36,970 psi.
Max. Horizontal Range: 4,385 yds.
Max. Vertical Range: 9,120 ft.

Bullet Weight (gr.)		Bullet Type	Muzzle Velocity (fps)	Muzzle Energy (ft.-lbs.)
GP90	211	Ball	1,968	1,819
GP90/03	211	Ball	1,980	1,837

CURRENT MANUFACTURER(S)
None

GENERAL COMMENT(S)
As adopted, the GP90 cartridge was loaded with a 211 gr. round nose, paper-patched lead bullet with a steel cap on its ogive. Using a propellant charge of approximately 29 gr. of semi-smokeless powder, muzzle velocity was 1,968 fps with a maximum average breech pressure of 36,970 psi.

In 1903, the GP90 was upgraded with a less corrosive primer and a 31 gr. powder charge that provided a muzzle velocity of 1,980 fps. The upgraded cartridge was designated GP90/03.

By 1913, the Schmidt-Rubin rifle had been modified to increase its strength which in turn allowed use of a more powerful cartridge. In order to take advantage of the improved ballistic performance offered by the new rifle, the cartridge was again updated by increasing maximum average breech pressure to 45,500 psi. and increasing case length to 55mm. Using a charge of 49.35 gr. of smokeless propellant and a new 174 gr. FMJBT bullet allowed muzzle velocity to be increased to 2,560 fps. The new cartridge, adopted in 1911, was designated the 7.5x55mm GP11.

But, what to do with the many older Schmidt-Rubin rifles still chambered for the GP90 and GP90/03 cartridges? It would be dangerous to fire the new higher pressure GP11 ammunition in these older rifles. A solution to this problem was found by updating the GP90/03 cartridge again in 1923. The cartridge case length was increased to 54.5 mm and maximum average breech pressure was increased to 38,390 psi. The paper-patched lead bullets were replaced by a lighter 190 gr. cupro-nickel jacketed round nose design. These changes allowed muzzle velocity to be increased to 2,050 fps using a 33.7 gr. charge of smokeless propellant. The newly updated cartridge was designated the 7.5x54.5mm GP90/23. Many serviceable Schmidt-Rubin rifles of early vintage were modified to fire this new cartridge.

7.5x57mm FRENCH M1924

ALTERNATE NAME(S): 7.5mm M1924
RELATED CALIBER(S): 7.5x54mm M1929, 8x57mmJS Mauser

CARTRIDGE HISTORY
Year of Introduction: 1924
Country of Origin: France
Designer(s): Manufacture d'Armes St. Etienne (MAS)
Governing Body: none
Present Status: obsolete

CARTRIDGE DESCRIPTION
Bullet Diameter: .308 in.
Bullet Weight(s): 139 gr.
Rifling Twist Rate: 1 turn in 10 in.
Test Barrel Length: N/A
Case Type: rimless, necked
Case Material: brass
Primer: large rifle

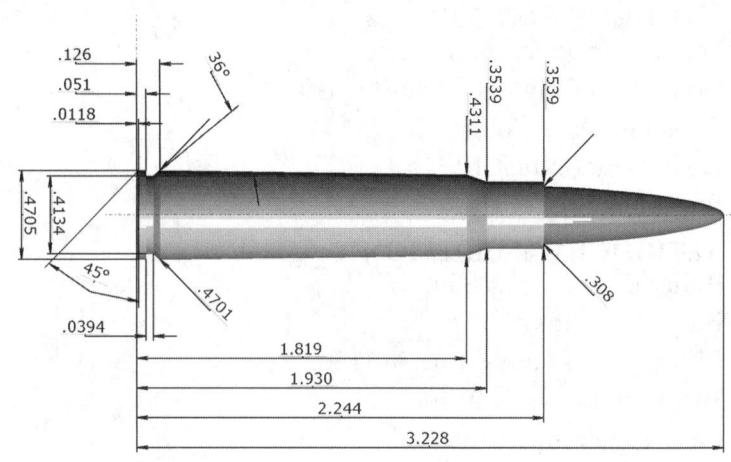

CARTRIDGE BALLISTICS
Max. Average Chamber Pressure: 45,000 psi.
Max. Horizontal Range: 3,400 yds.
Max. Vertical Range: 7,800 ft.

Bullet Weight (gr.)	Bullet Type	Muzzle Velocity (fps)	Muzzle Energy (ft.-lbs.)
139	FMJ	2,600	2,100

CURRENT MANUFACTURER(S)
None

GENERAL COMMENT(S)
Following the end of World War I in 1918, France restarted efforts to replace the 8x50Rmm Lebel cartridge with a more modern, rimless design. These efforts began in 1920 and culminated in 1924 with the adoption of the 7.5x57mm Model 1924 cartridge. France had been given thousands of German Maxim machine guns, M98 Mauser rifles and millions of rounds of 8x57JSmm Mauser ammunition as reparations after World War I. These guns and ammunition were used for training French front line troops and equipping reserves. As the German 8x57JSmm Mauser and the French 7.5x57mm M1924 cartridges looked very much alike, French troops having both available frequently got them mixed up with disastrous results. Something had to be done and in 1929 the French Army declared the 7.5x57mm M1924 cartridge obsolete and replaced it with the 7.5x54mm M1929 cartridge. As a result of the change over, the French Army was only just beginning to field the M1929 cartridge when World War II began in 1939. Fielding the M1929 cartridge resumed after World War II ended in 1945. The M1929 cartridge was to remain in French front line service until the 1990s when France adopted the 5.56x45mm NATO cartridge. In addition to France, the 7.5x54mm M1929 cartridge has been used by Vietnam, Cambodia, Algeria and many other ex-French colonial countries. The 7.5x57mm M1924 became a small footnote in military history as an excellent example of a serious and costly mistake.

TECHNICAL COMMENT(S)
The 7.5x57 M1924 cartridge and its shorter, younger sibling the 7.5x54mm M1929 cartridge share similar head and base dimensions as well as ball bullet caliber and weight. Both are loaded to a maximum average chamber pressure of 45,000 psi. Otherwise, the only major difference is in the case and overall cartridge length. Ballistic performance of both is modestly adequate, but not up to the same standard as the German 8x57JSmm Mauser or American .30-'06 Springfield. Only ball ammunition was manufactured. No commercial manufacture was undertaken.

7.62x45mm CZECH

ALTERNATE NAME(S): 7.62 Vz.52, 7.62mm M52
RELATED CALIBER(S): 7.62x39mm Soviet, 6.5x52mm Carcano, 7.35mm Carcano

CARTRIDGE HISTORY
Year of Introduction: 1952
Country of Origin: Czechoslovakia
Designer(s): N/A
Governing Body: CIP
Present Status: obsolete

CARTRIDGE DESCRIPTION
Bullet Diameter: .308 in.
Bullet Weight(s): 130 gr.
Rifling Twist Rate: 1 turn in 11 in.
Test Barrel Length: 24 in.
Case Type: rimless, necked
Case Material: brass or steel
Primer Size: large rifle

CARTRIDGE BALLISTICS
Max. Average Breech Pressure: 62,400 psi.
Max. Effective Range: 300 yds.
Max. Horizontal Range: 3,700 yds
Max. Vertical Range: 8,000 ft.

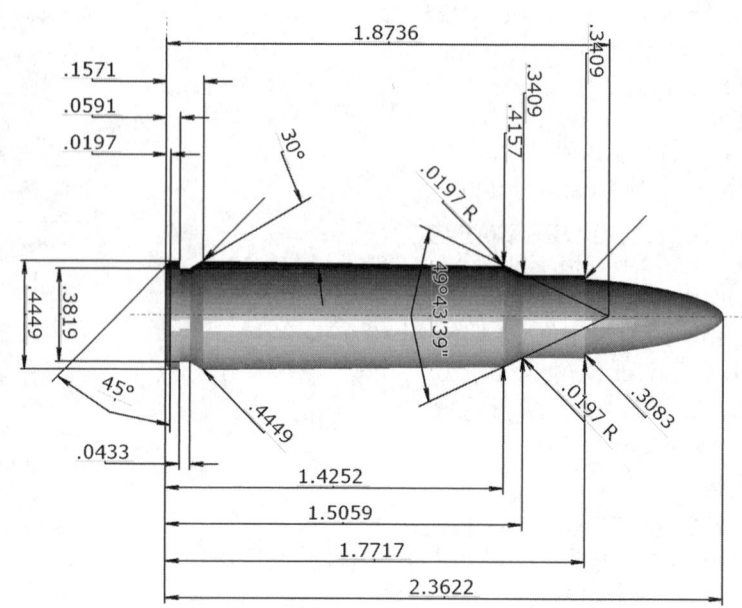

Bullet Weight (gr.)	Bullet Type	Muzzle Velocity (fps)	Muzzle Energy (ft.-lbs.)
130	FMJBT	2,440	1,718

CURRENT MANUFACTURER(S)
None

GENERAL COMMENT(S)
Czechoslovakia has always been a vibrant center of independent firearm and ammunition design. This tradition of independence continued after the end of World War II in 1945 with Czech designers quickly capitalizing on the trend toward assault rifles firing low power ammunition. In this effort, they drew on their wartime experience working on the German 7.9x33mm Kurz cartridge and studied the new Russian 7.62x39mm M43 cartridge. The result was the adoption of a Simonov-style, semi-automatic carbine firing a new 7.62x45mm cartridge in 1952.

After Czechoslovakia joined the Warsaw Pact, for standardization reasons, they adopted the Soviet 7.62x39mm M43 cartridge. The 7.62x45mm cartridge was then declared obsolete and production ceased.

No other country adopted or manufactured this cartridge.

TECHNICAL COMMENT(S)
The rim and case head dimensions of the 7.62x45mm Czech Vz52 are very similar to those of the 7.62x39mm Soviet M43 cartridge leading many to believe the Czech Vz52 is merely a long 7.62x39mm M43. However, both share rim and case head dimensions with the 6.5x52mm Italian Mannlicher-Carcano cartridge, so both can be looked upon as derivatives of that cartridge.

From a ballistic standpoint, the 7.62x45mm Czech cartridge offers broadly similar performance to the ubiquitous Soviet 7.62x39mm M43 cartridge as it fires a bullet of similar diameter and slightly heavier weight at approximately 100 fps. higher muzzle velocity. However, the 7.62mm M52 cartridge has a maximum average chamber pressure 21% higher to achieve this small advantage. While on paper the Czech M52 offers 17% more muzzle energy, this is not a significant enough improvement to recommend it over the 7.62x39mm cartridge. Both ball and tracer types were made.

.30-40 KRAG

ALTERNATE NAME(S): .30 U.S. Army, .30 Service (Krag) Model 1898, 7.62x59Rmm, .30 Krag-Jorgensen
RELATED CALIBER(S): .303 British, 8x50Rmm Austrian

CARTRIDGE HISTORY
Year of Introduction: 1892
Country of Origin: U.S.
Designer(s): Springfield Armory
Governing Body: SAAMI
Present Status: obsolete

CARTRIDGE DESCRIPTION
Bullet Diameter: .308 in.
Bullet Weight(s): 220 gr.
Rifling Twist Rate: 1 turn in 10 in.
Test Barrel Length: 24 in.
Case Type: rimmed, necked
Case Material: brass
Primer Size: large rifle

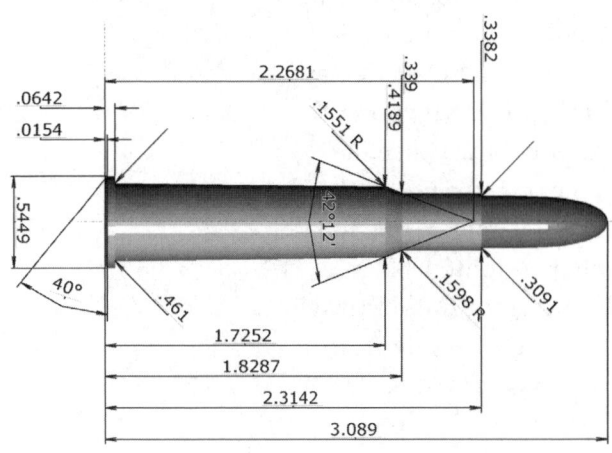

CARTRIDGE BALLISTICS
Max. Average Breech Pressure: 47,100 psi.
Max. Horizontal Range: 9,100 ft.
Max. Vertical Range: 4,100 yds.

Bullet Weight (gr.)	Bullet Type	Muzzle Velocity (fps)	Muzzle Energy (ft.-lbs.)
220 (1892)	FMJRN	2,000	1,953
220 (1899)	FMJRN	2,200	2,365

CURRENT MANUFACTURER(S)
Winchester, Remington

GENERAL COMMENT(S)
In the mid-1880s, the major European powers began crash programs to develop new military rifle cartridges for smokeless propellants. The U.S Army took careful note of this and began a similar program at Springfield Arsenal in the same time frame. Many technical problems had to be solved and Frankford Arsenal soon joined the program.

In 1892, the U.S. Army adopted the Krag bolt-action rifle and the new .30-40 U.S. Army cartridge along with it. The first production lot of .30 U.S. Army ammunition was made at Frankford Arsenal in October, 1893. After the standardization of the .30-'03 cartridge in 1903, the official designation of the Krag cartridge was changed to "Cal. .30 Service (Krag) Cartridge Model 1898" to avoid confusion.

TECHNICAL COMMENT(S)
After testing various cartridge designs including the 7.5x53.5mm Swiss GP90 and 7.65x53mm Belgian Mauser cartridges, in 1890 the Small Arms Board selected a rimmed case design loaded with a .308 inch diameter 220 grain full metal jacket round nose bullet. The Small Arms Board had selected a rimmed cartridge design similar to many contemporaries such as the .303 British, 8mm Lebel and 8x50Rmm Austrian.

Although initial tests were conducted using black powder (capacity was between 38-49 gr.), the intention always was to use smokeless propellants and the .30 U.S. Army cartridge production runs were loaded with the same. Muzzle velocity was a leisurely 2,000 fps using the 220 bullet. In 1899 this was increased to 2,200 fps.

By any measure, the .30 U.S. Army cartridge was obsolescent when adopted and no attempt was made to update it with a lighter weight pointed bullet at a higher velocity. For that reason, it remained in U.S. Army front line service only until 1903 when the M1903 Springfield rifle and its .30-'03 cartridge were adopted. Interestingly, the .30-'03 was loaded with the Krag 220 gr. FMJRN bullet. By World War I (1914-18), the Krag rifle and its .30 U.S. Army cartridge were obsolete, both being relegated to training and guard duty. The U.S. Navy adopted the Krag Rifle and .30 U.S. Army cartridge in 1900 to replace their .236 U.S. Navy caliber Lee rifles. Ever conservative, the U.S. Navy held the Krag rifle and cartridge in reserve service until 1931.

.30 PEDERSEN

ALTERNATE NAME(S): Cal. 30 Automatic Pistol Ball Cartridge, Model of 1918
RELATED CALIBER(S): 7.65mm French MAS

CARTRIDGE HISTORY
Year of Introduction: 1918
Country of Origin: U.S.
Designer(s): J.D. Pedersen
Governing Body: none
Present Status: obsolete

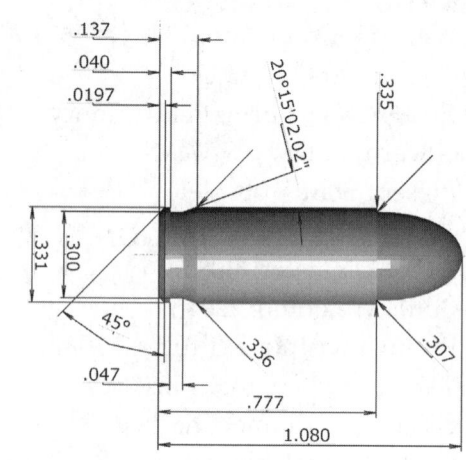

CARTRIDGE DESCRIPTION
Bullet Diameter: .307 in.
Bullet Weight(s): 80 gr.
Rifling Twist Rate: 1 turn in 12 in.
Test Barrel Length: 24 in.
Case Type: rimless, straight
Case Material: brass
Primer: small pistol

CARTRIDGE BALLISTICS
Max. Average Breech Pressure: 40,000 psi.
Max. Horizontal Range: 1,650 yds.
Max. Vertical Range: 3,600 ft.

Bullet Weight (gr.)	Bullet Type	Muzzle Velocity (fps)	Muzzle Energy (ft.-lbs.)
80	FMJ	1,300	300

CURRENT MANUFACTURER(S)
None

GENERAL COMMENT(S)
During World War I (1914-1918), infantry soldiers were armed with slow-firing, bolt-action rifles. Some method of increasing the fire power of the infantry was needed urgently and a semiautomatic infantry rifle was the obvious answer. In 1917, J.D. Pedersen of Remington Arms demonstrated a novel device for quickly converting existing, bolt-action M1903 Springfield rifles to semi-automatic fire in the field. Pedersen's device fired a short, reduced-power, .30 cartridge from a blow-back operated assembly that a soldier could insert quickly and easily in the action of his Springfield rifle after removing the bolt. The only modification required on the Springfield M1903 rifle was a rectangular cut on the left side of the receiver for the 40 round Pedersen magazine. Following several demonstrations, the U.S. War Department ordered 500,000 Pedersen devices for the Springfield rifle and 800 million rounds of Cal. .30 Automatic Pistol Ball Cartridge, Model of 1918 ammunition for delivery as quickly as possible. With the end of World War I in 1918, the order was scaled back to 65,000 Pedersen Devices and 65 million rounds of ammunition. The 65,000 Pedersen Devices manufactured were placed in storage and scrapped in 1931.

TECHNICAL COMMENT(S)
For his device, Pedersen designed a new cartridge seemingly more appropriate for a pistol than a rifle. While it appeared to be a long .32 ACP cartridge, the Pedersen case was actually a rimless design. It fired an 80 grain full metal jacket semi-pointed bullet at a muzzle velocity of approximately 1,300 fps from a Springfield rifle barrel. Of course the .30 "Pedersen" cartridge was substantially weaker than the standard .30-06 Springfield cartridge. Despite its ballistic handicap, the maximum effective range of the .30 Pedersen cartridge was officially put at 350 yards. Following official adoption, efforts were made to improve the ballistics of the .30 Pedersen cartridge using heavier powder charges, longer cases and heavier bullets. None were adopted and remaining stocks of Cal. .30 Automatic Pistol Ball Cartridges were scrapped in the early 1930s along with the Pedersen Devices. In 1935, the French Army adopted a new pistol (the MAS M1935A) chambered for a new cartridge called the 7.65mm French Long. This cartridge had nearly identical dimensions and ballistics as the .30 Pedersen, but are not, in fact, interchangeable as the 7.65mm MAS has a longer case and loaded length.

.30 CARBINE

ALTERNATE NAME(S): .30 M1 Carbine, 7.62x33mm
RELATED CALIBER(S): .32 WSL

CARTRIDGE HISTORY
Year of Introduction: 1941
Country of Origin: U.S.
Designer(s): Winchester
Governing Body: SAAMI, CIP
Present Status: obsolete

CARTRIDGE DESCRIPTION
Bullet Diameter: .308 in.
Bullet Weight(s): 110 gr.
Rifling Twist Rate: 1 turn in 16 in.
Test Barrel Length: N/A
Case Type: rimless, tapered
Case Material: brass or steel
Primer Size: small rifle

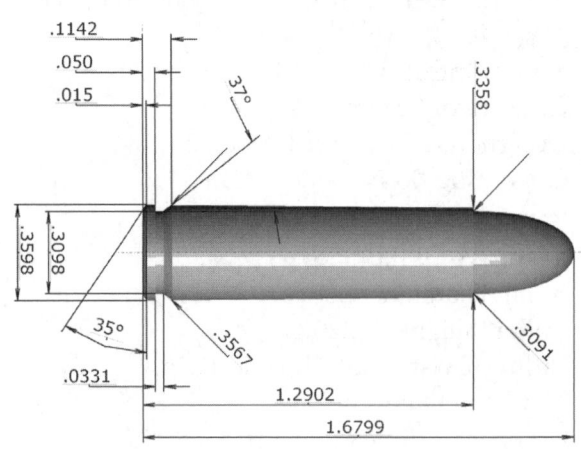

CARTRIDGE BALLISTICS
Max. Average Breech Pressure: 40,000 psi.
Max. Horizontal Range: 2,600 yds.
Max. Vertical Range: 5,800 ft.

Bullet Weight (gr.)	Bullet Type	Muzzle Velocity (fps)	Muzzle Energy (ft.-lbs.)
110 (M1)	Ball	1,975	955

CURRENT MANUFACTURER(S)
Federal, Remington, Winchester, PMC, Sellier & Bellot, Industrias Technos, Wolf, Prvi Partizan, IMI, CBC, PMP

GENERAL COMMENT(S)
Winchester's design for a lightweight carbine cartridge (to replace the .45 ACP pistol cartridge)was adopted in 1941, a relatively brief time after the U.S. Army had requested proposals from manufacturers. It was based on the .32 Winchester Self-Loading cartridge of 1906. The purpose of the .30 M1 Carbine and its new cartridge was to provide a light weight, short rifle for officers, artillerymen, signal corps personnel and the like. Few could have predicted the success of this cartridge. Despite the original intent, the short, handy, light weight carbine quickly became a popular choice for all types of U.S. soldiers including infantrymen who overlooked its limited power and range. The .30 Carbine went on to serve in Korea in the 1950s, but was declared obsolete when the 7.62x51mm NATO cartridge was adopted by the U.S. Army in 1957. Remaining stocks of M1 Carbines were issued in large quantities to the Army of Viet Nam in the 1960 and 1970s. Production of M1 Carbines and .30 Carbine ammunition continues for the commercial market.

TECHNICAL COMMENT(S)
By any measure, the .30 Carbine cartridge lacks range and striking energy. Maximum effective range is considered to be 200 yards and even that is optimistic. In power, the .30 Carbine falls into the same category as the .357 Magnum. For this reason, the .30 Carbine is an excellent choice for home and personal defense by virtue of its limited range, low recoil and limited power.

Commercial ammunition companies offer soft-point ammunition for personal defense. The .30 Carbine is illegal for hunting in most states (except for varmints).

.30-'03 U.S.

ALTERNATE NAME(S): Cal. .30 Ball Cartridge Model of 1903, .30-'03 Springfield, .30 Government Model 03, 7.62x65mm
RELATED CALIBER(S): .30-01 Springfield, .30-'06 Springfield, 8x57mmJS Mauser

CARTRIDGE HISTORY
Year of Introduction: 1903
Country of Origin: U.S.
Designer(s): Frankford Arsenal
Governing Body: none
Present Status: obsolete

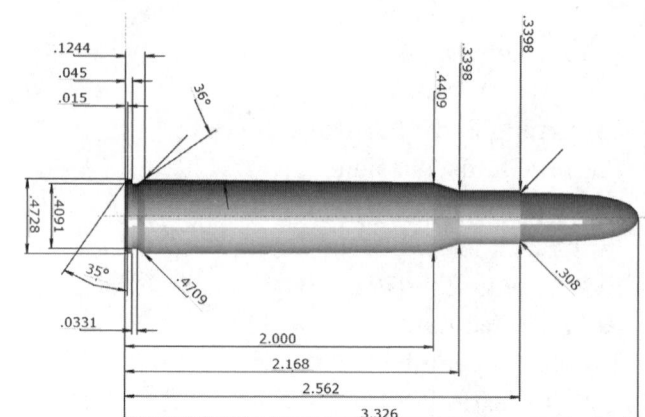

CARTRIDGE DESCRIPTION
Bullet Diameter: .308 in.
Bullet Weight(s): 220 gr.
Rifling Twist Rate: 1 turn in 10 in.
Test Barrel Length: N/A
Case Type: rimless, necked
Case Material: brass
Primer: large rifle

CARTRIDGE BALLISTICS
Max. Average Breech Pressure: 49,000 psi.
Max. Horizontal Range: 3,700 yds.
Max. Vertical Range: 7,900 ft.

Bullet Weight (gr.)	Bullet Type	Muzzle Velocity (fps)	Muzzle Energy (ft.-lbs.)
220	FMJ-RN	2,300	2,583 (early)
220	FMJ-RN	2,200	2,364 (late)

CURRENT MANUFACTURER(S)
None

GENERAL COMMENT(S)
Recognizing the need for a new military rifle cartridge capable of a higher maximum average chamber pressure and muzzle velocity, from 1897 to 1900 the U.S. Ordnance Department experimented with various ways of reaching these goals using the existing .30-40 Krag cartridge. However, as a suitable powder was not available, the Ordnance Department cancelled the program in 1900. In 1901, the program was restarted using the 8x57mmJ Mauser cartridge for inspiration. Unlike the earlier experiments, this new cartridge was a modern, rimless design fully capable of handling the specified chamber pressures. The same 220 grain FMJ round nose ball bullet from the .30-40 Krag bullet was used. After a variety of tests, the .30 Ball Cartridge, Model of 1901 was deemed worthy for adoption.

TECHNICAL COMMENT(S)
Technically speaking, the .30-01 and .30-'03 Springfield cartridges were old news from 1900 on. When the Model of 1901 cartridge was finally deemed ready for adoption in 1903, a change in the rim thickness from .060 inches to .045 inches resulted in the nomenclature being changed to Model 1903. Otherwise, there was no difference between these two cartridges. However, everything changed when the German Army replaced their heavy round nose bullet in the 8x57mmJ Mauser with the lighter spitzer "S" type in 1905. A new era had begun and the U.S. could not afford to fall behind. As a result, the Ordnance Bureau sent the engineers back to work to modify the Model of 1903 cartridge for a modern, light weight, spitzer bullet. To prevent interchangeability, the case of the Model 1903 cartridge was lengthened slightly. The resulting new cartridge was adopted as the Cal. .30 Ball Cartridge, Model of 1906 or .30-'06 Springfield. The Cal. .30 Ball Cartridge Model of 1903 was the U.S. military standard rifle cartridge for only three years. For this reason, production was limited and the remaining stocks of Model 1903 cartridges were destroyed when the Model of 1906 cartridge was adopted. The Model 1903 is a classic example of the cost of failing to anticipate developments in the immediate future that will render a new product obsolete before it is adopted.

.30-'06 SPRINGFIELD

ALTERNATE NAME(S): .30 U.S. Government, 7.62x63mm .30 Browning, .30 M1, .30 M2
RELATED CALIBER(S): 8x57mm Mauser, 7.5x45mm French MAS, 7.7x58mm Japanese Arisaka, 7.62x51mm NATO

CARTRIDGE HISTORY
Year of Introduction: 1906
Country of Origin: U.S.
Designer(s): Springfield Armory
Governing Body: SAAMI, CIP
Present Status: obsolete

CARTRIDGE DESCRIPTION
Bullet Diameter: .308 in.
Bullet Weight(s): 150-172 gr.
Rifling Twist Rate: 1 turn in 10 in.
Test Barrel Length: 24 in.
Case Type: rimless, necked
Case Material: brass or steel
Primer Size: large rifle

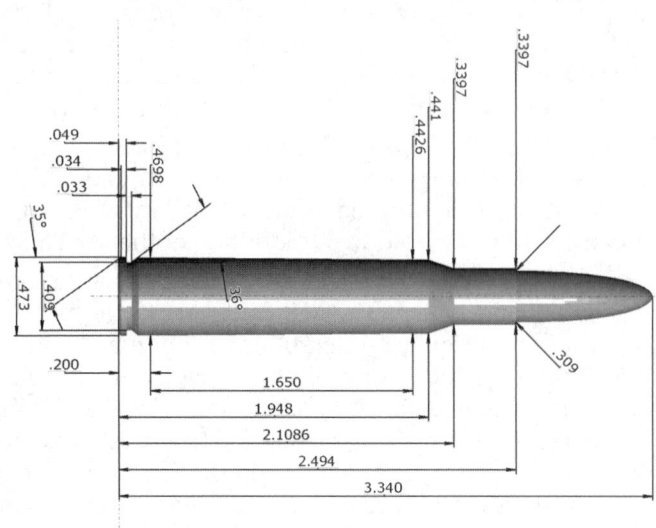

CARTRIDGE BALLISTICS
Max. Average Breech Pressure: 50,000 psi.
Max. Horizontal Range: 5,500 yds.
Max. Vertical Range: 12,400 ft.

Bullet Weight (gr.)	Bullet Type	Muzzle Velocity (fps)	Muzzle Energy (ft.-lbs.)
150 (M1906)	Ball	2,700	2,428
175 (M1)	Ball	2,640	2,707
152 (M2)	Ball	2,740	2,533
108 (M22)	Frangible	1,320	417
175 (M72)	Match	2,640	2,707

CURRENT MANUFACTURER(S)
Federal, Winchester, Remington, PMC, Wolf, Prvi Partizan, IMI, PMP, CBC, NAMMO, Sellier & Bellot

GENERAL COMMENT(S)
The .30-'06 Spr. cartridge is a direct descendant, contemporary, and rival of the German 7.9x57mm Mauser military cartridge adopted in 1888. Both cartridges share similar case head dimensions, case configuration, and military concept.

When the .30-40 Krag cartridge was standardized for U.S. military service in 1892, the cartridge was already semi-obsolete. European military services were rapidly taking full advantage of smokeless propellants to develop new high velocity military cartridges. As the .30-40 Krag rifle and cartridge could not be adapted to the higher pressure, the U.S Army began to develop a new cartridge and rifle. In 1903, the U.S. Army adopted the M1903 Springfield rifle and the .30-'03 cartridge loaded with the 220 gr. FMJ round nose Krag bullet at a muzzle velocity of 2,400 fps.

In the late 1890s, many European military services began replacing their heavy round nose service bullets with lighter, pointed bullets of significantly better exterior ballistics. A major turning point was reached in 1898 when the French Army adopted the pointed 198 gr. "Balle D" bullet for their 8x50Rmm Lebel cartridge.

The German Army followed suit in 1905 with the 7.9x57mm JS Mauser "S Patrone" high velocity military cartridge with a 154 gr. spitzer (pointed bullet). These developments sent U.S designers back to the drawing board to improve the M1903 cartridge. The result was a modified cartridge case with a .07 inch shorter neck and a 150 gr. pointed bullet at a muzzle velocity of 2,700 fps. The new cartridge was adopted in 1906 as the "Cartridge, caliber .30, Model of 1906." In use, the name and date are generally contracted into .30-'06 Springfield.

In 1932 following almost 10 years of development, the U.S. Army proposed to adopt the new .276 Pedersen infantry cartridge along with John Garand's new M1 semi-automatic rifle. Gen. Douglas MacArthur, the U.S. Army Chief of Staff at the time, disagreed and Garand was forced to redesign his rifle for the .30-'06 cartridge.

During World War II, U.S. ordnance plants manufactured over 23 billion rounds of .30-'06 ammunition. Production dropped substantially when World War II ended in 1945, only to be ramped up once again for the Korean War in the early 1950s. Manufacture of this caliber in U.S. government facilities ended in the late 1950s.

However, Lake City Army Ammunition Plant has been manufacturing (for several years) M1909 .30 caliber Blank ammunition for use at funerals, salutes and other patriotic events. As a military cartridge, the .30-'06 Spr. must be ranked as one of the most successful of the 20th century.

TECHNICAL COMMENT(S)

The .30-'03 and .30-'06 cartridges were the first high pressure (50,000 psi) military rifle cartridges standardized by the U.S. Army. All .30-'06 ammunition manufactured for or by the U.S. military services had a Boxer primer and brass cartridge case. Corrosive primers were standard until 1952. During World War II, ammunition in this caliber loaded with a steel cartridge case was used for practice and training, but not sent overseas.

During World War I, the M1906 150 gr. spitzer flat base bullet was found to offer insufficient maximum effective range for use in machine guns. Accordingly, a 172 gr. spitzer boat-tail bullet that offered substantially improved long range performance was adopted as the M1 Ball in 1926, but recoil was found to be excessive when the M1 Ball was fired in infantry rifles. This led to the adoption of the M2 Ball cartridge with a 152 gr. spitzer flat-base bullet in 1940.

Many special types of bullet were developed for the .30-'06 cartridge including armor piercing (AP), tracer, incendiary, frangible, and match. The M1 Tracer cartridge has a red trace from the muzzle to 900 yds. Tests found that tracer ignition at the muzzle often blinded the gunner and that an orange-colored trace was more visible than red. The result was the M25 Tracer with an orange trace from 75 yds to 900 yds. Armor piercing, incendiary and frangible loadings were developed for aircraft use. When .30 caliber machine guns proved useless for aerial combat, they were relegated to training duties which led to a substantial decrease in demand for .30 caliber armor piercing and incendiary ammunition. In 1943, operations in the European Theater indicated that M2 Ball ammunition was inadequate for the numerous resistant targets such as armored vehicles and personnel behind concrete barriers. As a result, .30-'06 M2 Ball ammunition production quickly switched to M2 armor piercing for general issue in that theater.

Combat veterans speak appreciatively of the terminal ballistic effectiveness, superior penetration and long range of the .30-'06 cartridge. Enemy personnel struck squarely with .30 caliber bullets were usually knocked down and immediately incapacitated. The M2 Ball and particularly the M2 AP bullets would readily penetrate barriers with enough remaining energy to incapacitate enemy personnel behind them. Even at ranges of 1,000 yards, terminal ballistic ability of the .30-'06 proved remarkable.

The .30-'06 Spr. cartridge successfully served the U.S. military well for over 51 years through two World Wars and numerous lesser actions. However, technology, weight and cost eventually caught up with the .30-'06. By modern standards, the .30-'06 is needlessly powerful, too heavy and uses an excessive amount of strategic materials. For these reasons it was replaced in 1957 by the 7.62x51mm NATO cartridge in U.S. military service. This ended the era of aimed fire from bolt-action infantry rifles chambered for powerful, .30 caliber cartridges. The future lay in selective-fire assault rifles in smaller, less powerful calibers with large magazine capacities. By 1970, other countries had also relegated the .30-'06 to war reserve or obsolete status. Perhaps the last front line users of the .30-'06 were the military forces of The Republic of South Africa who continued to use .30-'06 in Browning machineguns until well into the 1980s.

.310 CADET

ALTERNATE NAME(S): .310 Greener
RELATED CALIBER(S): 7.5mm Swedish Nagant revolver, 7.5mm Swiss revolver

CARTRIDGE HISTORY

Year of Introduction: 1900

Country of Origin: Britain

Designer(s): W.W. Greener

Governing Body: CIP

Present Status: obsolete

CARTRIDGE DESCRIPTION

Bullet Diameter: .311 in.

Bullet Weight(s): 84-125 gr.

Rifling Twist Rate: 1 turn in 20 in.

Test Barrel Length: 24 in.

Case Type: rimmed, straight

Case Material: brass

Primer: small rifle

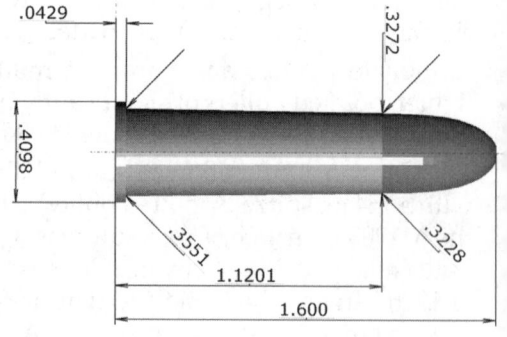

CARTRIDGE BALLISTICS

Max. Average Breech Pressure: 15,954 psi.

Max. Horizontal Range: 2,600 yds.

Max. Vertical Range: 5,400 ft.

Bullet Weight (gr.)	Bullet Type	Muzzle Velocity (fps)	Muzzle Energy (ft.-lbs.)
125	L-RN	1,200	400

CURRENT MANUFACTURER(S)

None

GENERAL COMMENT(S)

In turn of the century England, small, single-shot rifles with Martini actions were a popular choice for training military cadets. For these rifles, an accurate, low cost, limited-power cartridge was needed. W.W. Greener designed the .310 Cadet cartridge for this purpose. Martini cadet rifles remained in active military service in some countries until well after World War II. During the early years of World War II, the Japanese threatened to invade Australia. There were simply not enough SMLE military rifle to equip the Australian home guard, so the Martini cadet rifle were pressed back into emergency Australian military service. .310 cadet lead with an FMJ bullet was developed for these. In the 1950s, many of these rifles used by the Australian Army were released for sale as surplus military equipment. Most American and Australian sportsmen who purchased one of these rifles converted it to a more suitable caliber for hunting. For this reason, most Martini rifles of this type encountered today are no longer chambered for the .310 Cadet cartridge. Today, the .310 Cadet cartridge has become a fading memory. This caliber was never manufactured in the U.S.

TECHNICAL COMMENT(S)

Design of the .310 Cadet cartridge was conservative to keep costs down and use the least amount of raw materials. The case is rimmed with straight sidewalls to complement the strengths of the Martini action. Case volume is sufficient to hold 6 grains of black powder (later changed to smokeless propellants). A round-nose, lead bullet was the most common bullet used, although jacketed types were made as well.The normal ballistic considerations for a hunting cartridge (to provide high muzzle velocity and the greatest possible striking energy) did not apply to the .310 Cadet cartridge. Rather, the opposite is true. Accuracy, limited power and low cost were the factors that drove the ballistics of the .310 Cadet cartridge. In essence, the .310 Cadet cartridge served the same military training and match functions assigned to the .22 Long Rifle cartridge today.

.303 BRITISH

ALTERNATE NAME(S): 7.9x56Rmm, .303 Lee Metford, .303 Vickers, .303 Lee Enfield

RELATED CALIBER(S): 8x56Rmm Hungarian, 8x50Rmm Lebel, 7.62x54Rmm Mosin-Nagant, .30-40 Krag

CARTRIDGE HISTORY

Year of Introduction:1888

Country of Origin: Britain

Designer(s): N/A

Governing Body: CIP, SAAMI

Present Status: obsolete

CARTRIDGE DESCRIPTION

Bullet Diameter: .311 in.

Bullet Weight(s): 174-215 gr.

Rifling Twist Rate: 1 turn in 10 in.

Test Barrel Length: 24 in.

Case Type: rimmed, necked, tapered

Case Material: brass

Primer Size: large rifle

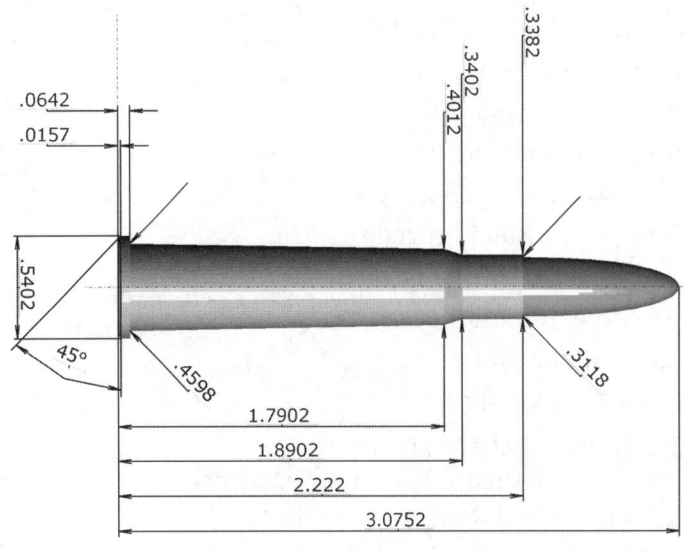

CARTRIDGE BALLISTICS

Max. Average Breech Pressure: 52,939 psi.

Max. Horizontal Range: 5,500 yds.

Max. Vertical Range: 12,400 ft.

Bullet Weight (gr.)	Bullet Type	Muzzle Velocity (fps)	Muzzle Energy (ft.-lbs.)
174 (Mk 7)	Ball	2,440	2,310
174 (Mk 8)	Ball	2,370	2,169
215 (Mk 2)	Ball	1,970	1,850

CURRENT MANUFACTURER(S)

Federal, Remington, Winchester, AEI, Pyrkal, POF, NAMMO, PMP, INDEP, Prvi Partizan

GENERAL COMMENT(S)

It was said that the sun never set on the British Empire and the .303 British cartridge helped keep it that way for nearly three-quarters of a century. This cartridge was also adopted as the standard military cartridge of most members of the Commonwealth including Canada, Australia, New Zealand, India and South Africa as well as many others. It served with distinction until replaced in British military service by the 7.62x51mm NATO cartridge in the late 1950s.

Conceived and adopted at the dawn of smokeless propellants, the .303 British began life with a compressed charge of black powder. It became one of the first military cartridges to be loaded with Cordite propellant and continued to be so loaded for most of its service life. The .303 British cartridge saw combat in all parts of the world from Flanders Fields to New Guinea to Egypt to Normandy and was never found wanting.

TECHNICAL COMMENT(S)

A number of different bullets were tried beginning with a 215 grain round nose. When this bullet failed to produce satisfactory results, a soft-point, expanding bullet made at Dum Dum Arsenal in India was briefly adopted, then dropped due to restrictions agreed to in the Hague Convention. The subsequent Mark VII bullet was then adopted and remained standard for most of the remainder of its service life. The Mark VII was a three piece, 174 grain flat base bullet consisting of a copper alloy jacket, a light compressed material filling a hollow under the nose, and a lead core in the tail. Stable in air, the Mark VII bullet was quite unstable in any other medium.

Some of the very first explosive and incendiary bullets were designed for the .303 British in 1916-1918. These were the (in)famous Buckingham and Pomeroy bullets designed to combat Zeppelin dirigible airship attacks on Britain, by igniting the volatile hydrogen gas in the airships' gas envelopes.

7.65x53mm MAUSER

ALTERNATE NAME(S): 7.65x53mm Belgian Mauser, 7.65x53mm Argentine Mauser
RELATED CALIBER(S): 8x57mm Mauser, .30-'06 Springfield, 7.62x51mm NATO

CARTRIDGE HISTORY

Year of Introduction: 1889

Country of Origin: Germany

Designer(s): Peter Paul Mauser

Governing Body: CIP, SAAMI

Present Status: obsolete

CARTRIDGE DESCRIPTION

Bullet Diameter: .313 in.

Bullet Weight(s): 155-211 gr.

Rifling Twist Rate: 1 turn in 11.02 in.

Test Barrel Length: 24 in.

Case Type: rimless, necked

Case Material: brass

Primer Size: large rifle

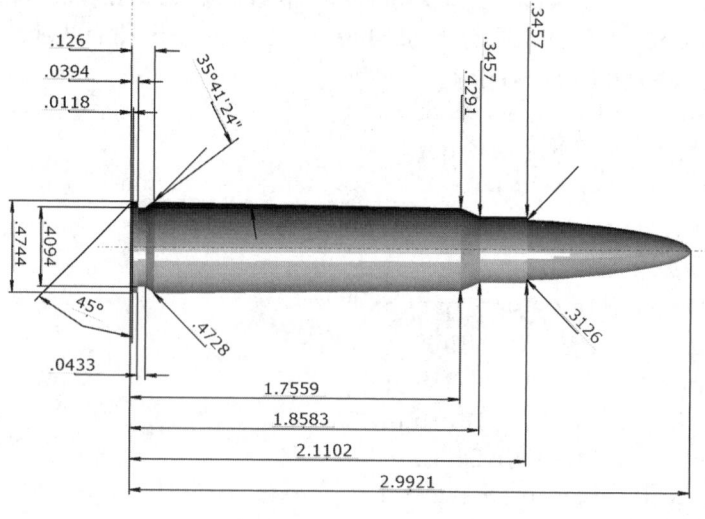

CARTRIDGE BALLISTICS

Max. Average Breech Pressure: 56,565 psi.

Max. Horizontal Range: 3,500 yds.

Max. Vertical Range: 7,900 ft.

Bullet Weight (gr.)	Bullet Type	Muzzle Velocity (fps)	Muzzle Energy (ft.-lbs.)
155	Ball	2,710	2,530
174	Ball	2,460	2,340
211	Ball	2,130	2,150

CURRENT MANUFACTURER(S)
NAMMO, Prvi Partizan

GENERAL COMMENT(S)
The 7.62x51mm NATO and the 7.65x53mm Belgian/Argentine Mauser had the same design criteria, namely a shorter, lighter cartridge with the full power of the longer types. However, the 7.65x53mm cartridge (designed in 1899) preceded the 7.62x51mm by 58 years! Belgium, Argentina, Columbia, Bolivia, Ecuador, Peru, and Turkey found the 7.65x53mm cartridge served them well in military service. Belgium adopted the 7.62x51mm NATO cartridge in the late 1950s along with other NATO nations. The 7.65x53mm Belgian Mauser was ahead of its time.

TECHNICAL COMMENT(S)
The short case of the 7.65x53mm cartridge results in a very efficient, compact, light weight design. The reduced length of the cartridge allows a shorter bolt travel and lighter rifle. Both 155 and 174 grain bullets were used. The heavier bullet provided longer range for use in machine guns.

7.7x58mm JAPANESE ARISAKA, 7.7x58SRmm JAPANESE ARISAKA

ALTERNATE NAME(S): 7.7mm Japanese, 7.7x58mm Japanese, .31 Japanese
RELATED CALIBER(S): 8x57mm Mauser, 7.5x54mm French MAS, .30-'06 Springfield

CARTRIDGE HISTORY
Year of Introduction: 1939
Country of Origin: Japan
Designer(s): N/A
Governing Body: CIP
Present Status: obsolete

CARTRIDGE DESCRIPTION
Bullet Diameter: .311 in.
Bullet Weight(s): 181-201 gr.
Rifling Twist Rate: 1 turn in 9.8 in.
Test Barrel Length: N/A
Case Type: semi-rimmed, necked (SR), rimless, necked
Case Material: brass
Primer Size: large rifle

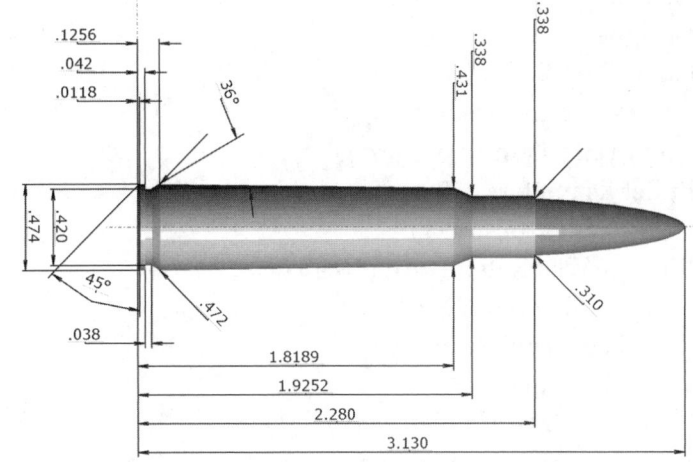

CARTRIDGE BALLISTICS
Max. Average Breech Pressure:
Max. Horizontal Range: 5,500 yds.
Max. Vertical Range: 12,600 ft.

Bullet Weight (gr.)	Bullet Type	Muzzle Velocity (fps)	Muzzle Energy (ft.-lbs.)
181	Ball	2,370	2,256
201 (SR)	Ball	2,380	2,527

CURRENT MANUFACTURER(S)
NAMMO, Prvi Partizan, Norinco

GENERAL COMMENT(S)
With World War II on the horizon, the Imperial JapaneseArmy and Navy finally recognized the need for a new, more modern service cartridge. The 7.7x58mm Japanese Arisaka, adopted in 1939, was the result. However,

production shortages never allowed the 7.7x58mm cartridge to fully replace the 6.5x50SRmm cartridge, so Japan fought World War II with both. In the initial stages of the War, Allied forces encountered 6.5x50SRmm caliber small arms almost exclusively. It was not until the later stages of the War that American, Australian, New Zealand and British forces came against the 7.7x58mm in any quantity. This was not because the Japanese gave priority for new equipment to their forces in China. The 6.5x50SRmm cartridge was felt adequate for the rifle and light machine guns for island campaigns supplemented by the 7.7x58SRmm cartridge fired from heavy machine guns. This did not hold true for the Japanese Army or Navy Air Forces who quickly adopted the 7.7x58SRmm cartridge from the first.

No other country adopted either of these calibers. However, the Chinese captured huge stocks of rifles and machine guns in these calibers which they issued to reserves and local militia. To support these forces, China (P.R.C.) had to put these Japanese cartridges back into production.

TECHNICAL COMMENT(S)

Without regard for manufacturing and logistical complications, the Japanese military adopted two 7.7x58mm cartridges – one rimless for rifles and one semi-rimmed for machine guns. The 7.7x58SRmm cartridge could be single-loaded and fired in a rifle, but would not feed through the magazine. The 181 grain ball bullet was intended to be fired mainly in rifles; the 201 grain ball was for use in machine guns. In addition, tracer, armor piercing, incendiary and explosive variants were developed and issued. At the very end of the War, the Japanese Army even began manufacturing a copy of the M1 Garand rifle in 7.7x58mm caliber.

7.92x33mm KURZ

ALTERNATE NAME(S): Pist. Patr. 43, Pist. Patr. 43mE, 8mm Kurz, 7.9mm M43, 7.9mm Infanterie Kurz Patron (1941)
RELATED CALIBER(S): 8x57mmJS Mauser

CARTRIDGE HISTORY
Year of Introduction: 1943
Country of Origin: Germany
Designer(s): Polte
Governing Body: CIP
Present Status: obsolete

CARTRIDGE DESCRIPTION
Bullet Diameter: .323 in.
Bullet Weight(s): 125 gr.
Rifling Twist Rate: 1 turn in 9.45 in.
Test Barrel Length: N/A
Case Type: rimless, necked
Case Material: steel
Primer Size: large rifle

CARTRIDGE BALLISTICS
Max. Average Breech Pressure: 49,313 psi.
Max. Horizontal Range: 3,000 yds.
Max. Vertical Range: 6,000 ft.

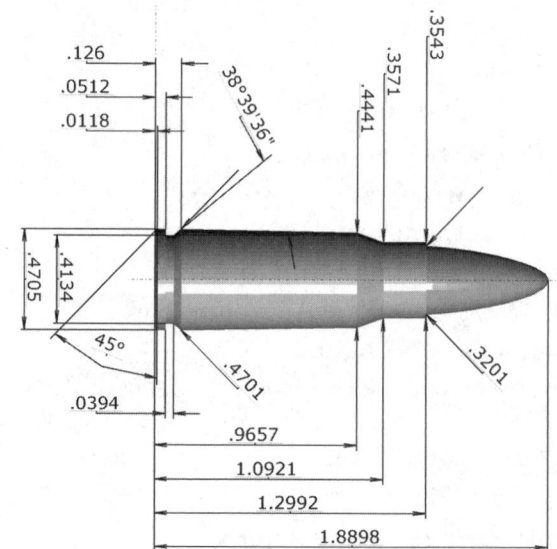

Bullet Weight (gr.)	Bullet Type	Muzzle Velocity (fps)	Muzzle Energy (ft.-lbs.)
125	Ball	2,250	1,404

CURRENT MANUFACTURER(S)
Prvi Partizan

GENERAL COMMENT(S)
This is the real thing – the first assault rifle cartridge in the world. It was developed in Germany in the 1930s based on studies of World War I that showed an infantryman could not reliably hit a target beyond 300 meters in combat. For this reason, high powered long-range cartridges were useless. What was wanted was a reduced power cartridge that provided satisfactory lethality at 300 meters, a small size to reduce weight, and lower velocity with a light weight bullet to reduce recoil. The new machine carbine would be selective fire.

After many studies and experimentation, the 7.9mm Infanterie Kurz Patron was adopted in 1941.

Interestingly, Hitler disapproved of the concept when it was first shown to him in about 1941. He forbade further development, however work went forward anyway. When Hitler again was shown the concept, he again forbade further development which again went forward in spite of his instructions. In order to disguise the project, the cartridge was given the name Pist. Patr. 43 (pistol cartridge 43) ostensibly for a submachine gun. The third time Hitler was shown the rifle and cartridge, he approved and dubbed it the "assault rifle" in hopes the moniker would boost the sagging morale of the German troops. However, the StG44/45 and 7.92x33mm were not enough to stave off defeat.

TECHNICAL COMMENT(S)

The base and neck of this cartridge as well as the bullet construction and diameter were taken from the 7.9x57mmJS cartridge so that the new cartridge could be made on the same machinery as the longer cartridge. Like the 7.9x57mm cartridge, the 7.92x33mm Kurz cartridge case was also made of steel.

The light weight 125 grain bullet and low muzzle velocity of 2,250 fps developed a low recoil impulse while providing sufficient lethality at ranges to 300 yards. The main problem was that the German Army could never get enough of the StG44 rifles or Pistol Patron 43mE ammunition. While it was planned to equip most German infantry squads with this rifle and cartridge, only some 550,000 "assault rifles" were produced before the surrender in 1945. Consequently, the StG44 and its cartridge were issued to only a select few.

7.92x94mm PANZERBUCHSE

ALTERNATE NAME(S): 7.92mm Panzerbuchse, 7.92x94mm, 7.92mm Patr. 318 SmKH.RsL "Spur"
RELATED CALIBER(S): 13x92SRmm Mauser

CARTRIDGE HISTORY

Year of Introduction: 1938
Country of Origin: Germany
Designer(s): N/A
Governing Body: none
Present Status: obsolete

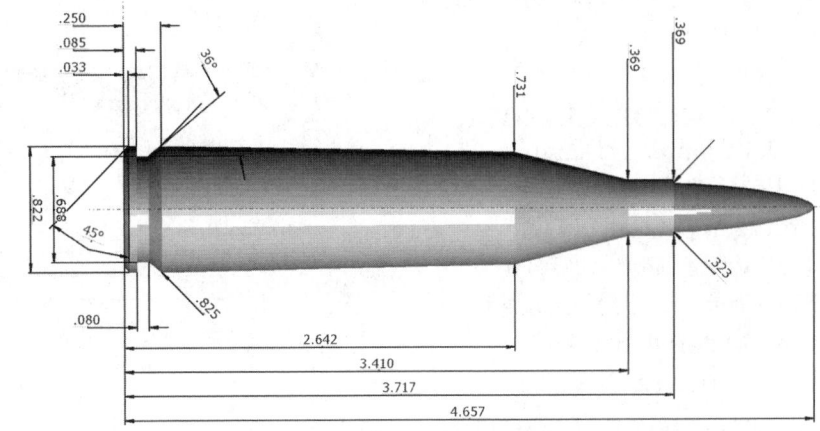

CARTRIDGE DESCRIPTION

Bullet Diameter: .323 in.
Bullet Weight(s): 225 gr.
Rifling Twist Rate: N/A
Test Barrel Length: 50.9 in.
Case Type: rimless, necked
Case Material: brass or steel
Primer: N/A

CARTRIDGE BALLISTICS

Max. Average Breech Pressure: N/A
Max. Horizontal Range: 6,150 yds.
Max. Vertical Range: 13,400 ft.

Bullet Weight (gr.)	Bullet Type	Muzzle Velocity (fps)	Muzzle Energy (ft.-lbs.)
225	AP-L-T	3,540	6,258

CURRENT MANUFACTURER(S)

None

GENERAL COMMENT(S)

With Adolf Hitler's ascent to power in Germany in the early 1930s, German ordnance technicians resumed development of the 13x92SRmm infantry anti-tank rifle concept where they left off at the end of World War I. By 1939, a new, infantry, anti-tank rifle and cartridge were introduced into German Army service, the 7.92x94mm Panzerbuchse. To maintain the secrecy of the new cartridge, all training was conducted using a substitute cartridge called the 13x94mm Panzerbuchse. Both cartridges were fired from a PzB38 (and various later models) anti-tank rifle carried by a two-man team. The armor-piercing bullets used with the 7.92x94mm rifle would be able, or so it was thought, to penetrate the relatively thin armor on tanks of the era. During the German campaigns in Poland and France in 1940, this assumption proved incorrect as larger, more heavily armored tanks were rapidly entering service in most European armies. This situation became acute at the start of the Russian campaign when German infantry units encountered the heavily armored Russian T-34 and KV-1 tanks, against which they were defenseless. Most of the PzB38/39 anti-tank rifles were converted to grenade throwers, but the problem of how German infantry could protect themselves against tanks was not solved until German engineers developed the Panzerfaust anti-tank weapon late in the War.

TECHNICAL COMMENT(S)

To penetrate armor, the 7.92x94mm cartridge combined high muzzle velocity with a 7.92mm bullet having a tungsten carbide penetrator inside a clad steel jacket. For good measure, a small lachrymatory (tear gas) pellet and a tracer were included as well. By early 1930s standards, penetration performance of this bullet was outstanding. It was capable of penetrating 30mm (1.18 inches) of armor steel inclined at a 60 degree angle at 100 meters and 25mm (1 inch) of steel armor at the same angle of inclination at 300 meters. In order to achieve the highest possible muzzle velocity, a large cartridge case capable of holding heavy powder charges was needed. The 7.92x94mm case certainly provided the needed volume. Although the 7.92x94mm Model 1939 rifles remained serviceable against armored cars, pillboxes and soft targets, by 1942 infantry anti-tank rifles had become obsolete. The British and Russian armies shared the same unhappy experience with their infantry anti-tank rifles.

7.92x107mm POLISH

ALTERNATE NAME(S): 7.92x107mm Maroszek, 8x107mm , 8mm Maroszek, Patrone 318 (P)
RELATED CALIBER(S): none

CARTRIDGE HISTORY
Year of Introduction: 1935
Country of Origin: Poland
Designer(s): Jan Maroszek
Governing Body: none
Present Status: obsolete

CARTRIDGE DESCRIPTION
Bullet Diameter: .323 in.
Bullet Weight(s): 197.5 gr.
Rifling Twist Rate: N/A
Test Barrel Length: 47.3 in.
Case Type: rimless, necked
Case Material: brass
Primer: not available

CARTRIDGE BALLISTICS
Max. Average Breech Pressure: N/A
Max. Horizontal Range: 5,900 yds.
Max. Vertical Range: 13,000 ft.

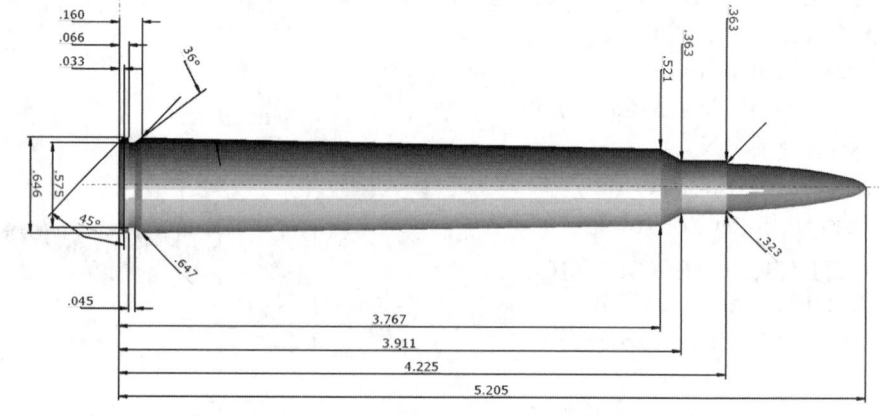

Bullet Weight (gr.)	Bullet Type	Muzzle Velocity (fps)	Muzzle Energy (ft.-lbs.)
197.5	AP	4,180	7,659

CURRENT MANUFACTURER(S)
None

GENERAL COMMENT(S)
In 1935, The Committee for Development of Weapons and Related Equipment (KSUS) in Poland was instructed to develop a one-man anti-tank rifle post-haste. By the late 1930s, the fruits of their work were the Korabin wz. 35 Anti-Tank Rifle chambered for the 7.92x107mm Maroszek cartridge. The cartridge was named in honor of the head of the committee. Production of 1,000 rifles and a suitable quantity of ammunition was begun immediately and additional orders soon followed. When the German Army finally occupied Poland, they captured 2,000 Polish rifles and a large quantity of ammunition. By that time, the Germans realized that the effectiveness of infantry anti-tank rifles was past, so the rifles were passed on to the Italian Army and production of 7.92x107mm was undertaken in Germany. The Maroszek cartridge was never chambered in any other gun.

TECHNICAL COMMENT(S)
The Maroszek cartridge is unique in design due to its unusually long, thin cartridge case. Although it is a

7.92mm caliber cartridge, its case length is nearly the same as the Soviet 12.7x107mm heavy machine gun cartridge. Development philosophy of the 7.92x107mm cartridge proceeded along similar lines to the German 7.92x94mm cartridge – a small caliber, armor-piercing bullet launched the highest possible muzzle velocity. As the Polish bullet used a penetrator core of hardened steel instead of tungsten carbide, its penetrative capabilities were approximately half that of its German counterpart, namely 15mm (.59 inches) of armor steel inclined at an angle of 60 degrees at 100 meters. Despite this, the Polish Maroszek rifles served the Italian Army well in various minor theaters of operation.The Germans were able to significantly improve the penetrating power of the 7.92x107mm cartridge by loading their own tungsten carbide core bullet in lieu of the Polish bullet – that is until German industry until ran out of tungsten by which time most 7.92mm anti-tank rifles were no longer in front-line service. The 7.92x107mm Maroszek cartridge is historically significant for its unique case configuration, for its very high muzzle velocity, and for being one of the last of its breed.

8x50Rmm AUSTRIAN MANNLICHER

ALTERNATE NAME(S): 8mm Steyr, 8x50Rmm Austrian-Mannlicher M93, 8mm Bulgarian Mannlicher
RELATED CALIBER(S): 8x56Rmm Hungarian

CARTRIDGE HISTORY

Year of Introduction: 1888

Country of Origin: Austria

Designer(s): Mannlicher

Governing Body: CIP

Present Status: obsolete

CARTRIDGE DESCRIPTION

Bullet Diameter: .323 in.

Bullet Weight(s): 244 gr.

Rifling Twist Rate: 1 turn in 9.84 in.

Test Barrel Length: 24 in.

Case Type: rimmed. necked

Case Material: brass

Primer Size: large rifle

CARTRIDGE BALLISTICS

Max. Average Breech Pressure: 51,488 psi.

Max. Horizontal Range: 4,200 yds.

Max. Vertical Range: 9,400 ft.

Bullet Weight (gr.)	Bullet Type	Muzzle Velocity (fps)	Muzzle Energy (ft.-lbs.)
244	FMJ	2,030	2,240

CURRENT MANUFACTURER(S)

None

GENERAL COMMENT(S)

Austria-Hungary fought World War I with this cartridge. While it provided satisfactory service, the Austro-Hungarian Army fought mainly on secondary fronts where ballistic performance was not so important. This resulted in Hungary delaying updating this cartridge until 1931. Following World War II, the 8x56mm cartridge became obsolete as Hungary adopted Soviet military weapons and ammunition.

TECHNICAL COMMENT(S)

By all measures, the 8x50Rmm cartridge was obsolete in World War I and obsolete by World War II. When the Austrian Army was absorbed into the German Army just before World War II, they were re-equipped with 8x57mm Mauser weapons. The 8x50Rmm weapons were issued to police and reserve units.

8x50Rmm LEBEL

ALTERNATE NAME(S): 8mm MLE 1886M
RELATED CALIBER(S): 11mm French Gras

CARTRIDGE HISTORY

Year of Introduction: 1886
Country of Origin: France
Designer(s): French Army Committee
Governing Body: CIP
Present Status: obsolete

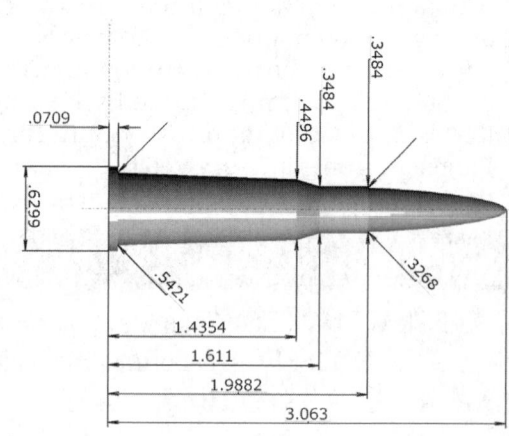

CARTRIDGE DESCRIPTION

Bullet Diameter: .323 in.

Bullet Weight(s): 170-198 gr.

Rifling Twist Rate: 1 turn in 9.84 in.

Test Barrel Length: 24 in.

Case Type: rimmed, necked, tapered

Case Material: brass of steel

Primer Size: large rifle

CARTRIDGE BALLISTICS

Max. Average Breech Pressure: 50,563 psi.

Max. Horizontal Range: 5,600 yds.

Max. Vertical Range: 12,500 ft.

Bullet Weight (gr.)	Bullet Type	Muzzle Velocity (fps)	Muzzle Energy (ft.-lbs.)
198 (Balle D)	Ball	2,300	2,325
190 (Balle 32M)	Ball	2,300	2,231
231 (Balle M)	AP	2,065	2,187

CURRENT MANUFACTURER(S)

Prvi Partizan

GENERAL COMMENT(S)

This was the first cartridge to be adapted for smokeless propellant by reforming and necking down the 11mm Gras cartridge case. Adopted in 1886, the 8x50Rmm Lebel served the French Army into the mid-1930s. It remained in service during World War II; during the Occupation, the Germans issued rifles in this caliber to allies and police units and restarted ammunition production.

By the early 1900s, the French Army realized that the 8x50Rmm cartridge was obsolete. It was unsuited to automatic weapons. A search for a new military service cartridge ensued but was not completed before the beginning of World War I. As a result, the 8x50Rmm Lebel cartridge soldiered on through the War. With the end of World War I, the French Army renewed efforts to find a new military cartridge. A long period of testing and one false start delayed introduction of the new 7.5x54mm French MAS cartridge until the late 1930s. As a result, the French Army entered World War II with obsolete World War I vintage rifles and ammunition.

TECHNICAL COMMENT(S)

Initially, the 8x50Rmm Lebel cartridge was loaded with a 232 grain Balle M round nose bullet. This was updated in 1898 to the famous Balle D – a 198 grain spitzer boat-tail of solid bronze. During World War I, American ammunition manufacturers were enlisted to make 8x50Rmm Lebel ammunition for the French. A 170 grain spitzer flat base bullet with a lead core and copper jacket was used. In 1932, the French Army updated this veteran with a 198 grain spitzer boat-tail bullet with a lead core and cupro-nickel clad steel jacket. The shape of the 8x50Rmm Lebel cartridge makes it nearly impossible for it to be fed reliably from a detachable box magazine. It is also difficult to feed from an internal rifle magazine. However, despite its physical shortcomings, the 8x50Rmm Lebel cartridge was ballistically efficient and served the French Army well during its 51 year service life.

8x50Rmm SIAMESE Type 45

ALTERNATE NAME(S): 8x50Rmm Siamese, 8mm Siamese
RELATED CALIBER(S): 8x52.5Rmm Murata, 8x52Rmm Siamese Type 66

CARTRIDGE HISTORY
Year of Introduction: 1902
Country of Origin: Japan
Designer(s): unknown
Governing Body: none
Present Status: obsolete

CARTRIDGE DESCRIPTION
Bullet Diameter: .323 in.
Bullet Weight(s): 239 grs.
Rifling Twist Rate: 1 turn in 13 in.
Test Barrel Length: N/A
Case Type: rimmed, necked
Case Material:
Primer Size: large rifle

CARTRIDGE BALLISTICS
Max. Average Breech Pressure: N/A
Max. Horizontal Range: 4,740 yds.
Max. Vertical Range: 9,730 ft.

Bullet Weight (gr.)	Bullet Type	Muzzle Velocity (fps)	Muzzle Energy (ft.-lbs.)
239	Ball	1,840	1,797

CURRENT MANUFACTURER(S)
None

GENERAL COMMENT(S)
In the late 1800s, Siam (Thailand today) was being squeezed between British and French colonial ambitions to dominate Southeast Asia. Although Siam remained an independent nation, King Chulalongkorn (1868-1910) recognized the vulnerable position of his country and the need to modernize the Siamese Army.

After Britain and France refused to help in this endeavor, the King approached Germany and Japan for assistance. From Germany, Siam was able to purchase the rights to manufacture a modern hybrid M96/M98 bolt-action Mauser rifle. The Japanese also designed a new 8x50Rmm cartridge for the Siamese rifle based on the 8x52.5Rmm Murata. The Siamese Army adopted the new cartridge in 1902 as the 8x50Rmm Type 45.

As Siam had no capability for ammunition production, contracts for Type 45 ammunition were initially given to Germany and Japan. Today, Type 45 cartridges are collector's items as supplies have long since run out. As there were less than 40,000 rifles made for this cartridge, it is unlikely that ammunition in this caliber will be mass produced again. To fill this gap, some custom loaders can provide limited quantities of ammunition in this caliber.

TECHNICAL COMMENT(S)
The 8x50Rmm Siamese Type 45 cartridge was obsolescent when it was adopted in 1902. Early ammunition was loaded with black powder. Although the switch to smokeless powder was quickly made, the new propellant could not improve the anemic ballistic performance of the Type 45 cartridge.

With the end of World War I in 1918, it quickly became painfully obvious that the Type 45 cartridge was outdated and should be replaced as quickly as possible. The Type 45 cartridge remained in front line service in the Siamese military until the Royal Siamese Arsenal developed an updated cartridge adopted in 1923 as the 8x52Rmm Type 66 (see following listing).

Despite its shortcomings, the 8x50Rmm Type 45 cartridge has one claim to fame –it and the 8x52Rmm type 66 remain the only rimmed military cartridges adopted for a Mauser bolt-action rifle.

8x52Rmm SIAMESE Type 66

ALTERNATE NAME(S): 8x52Rmm Siamese, 8mm Siamese Type 66
RELATED CALIBER(S): 8x52.5Rmm Murata, 8x50Rmm Siamese Type 45

CARTRIDGE HISTORY
Year of Introduction: 1923
Country of Origin: Siam
Designer(s): Royal Arsenal
Governing Body: none
Present Status: obsolete

CARTRIDGE DESCRIPTION
Bullet Diameter: .323 in.

Bullet Weight(s): 181 grs.

Rifling Twist Rate: 1 turn in 13 in.

Test Barrel Length: N/A

Case Type: rimmed, necked

Case Material: brass

Primer Size: large rifle

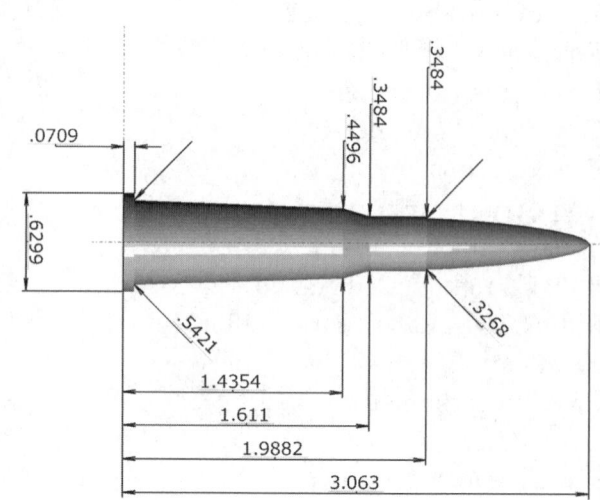

CARTRIDGE BALLISTICS
Max. Average Breech Pressure: N/A

Max. Horizontal Range: 4,270 yds.

Max. Vertical Range: 9,065 ft.

Bullet Weight (gr.)	Bullet Type	Muzzle Velocity (fps)	Muzzle Energy (ft.-lbs.)
181	Ball, Spitzer	2,200	1,946

CURRENT MANUFACTURER(S)
None

GENERAL COMMENT(S)
Although the 8x50Rmm Type 45 cartridge had been adopted by the Siamese military in 1902, by 1923 it had become obsolete. For Siam (present day Thailand), a small country with limited funding for military modernization, a completely new military cartridge and rifle was not affordable. Consequently, a low cost upgrade program was initiated.

The existing 8x50Rmm Type 45 cartridge was upgraded in such a manner as to allow it to be fired from existing Siamese Mauser rifles that had been suitably modified. In addition, all work on the rifle and ammunition projects was performed "in-country" by the Royal Siamese Arsenal.

The new cartridge was designated the 8x52Rmm Type 66. It was to remain in front line military service in the Thai Army until well into the 1960s. Thailand was the only country to adopt the Type 45 or Type 66.

TECHNICAL COMMENT(S)
A major goal of the upgrade effort was to increase muzzle velocity and improve downrange ballistic performance. As construction of the Siamese Mauser rifle did not allow an increase in breech pressure, muzzle velocity was increased by the simple expedient of replacing the 239 gr. bullet of the Type 45 cartridge with a lighter 181 gr. bullet. This change allowed muzzle velocity to be increased from 1,840 fps. to 2,200 fps. While this was still not competitive with other 8mm military cartridges, it was a cost-effective solution sufficient for the conditions in Siam. Downrange ballistic performance was enhanced by replacing the blunt round-nose bullet of the Type 45 cartridge with a pointed bullet. The length of the new Type 66 cartridge was increased to assure it could not be fired in a 50mm Type 45 chamber. However, both cartridges had the same overall loaded length to eliminate the need to modify the magazine of the rifles.

8x52.5Rmm MURATA

ALTERNATE NAME(S): 8x53Rmm, 8mm Type 20, 8x52.5Rmm
RELATED CALIBER(S): 8x50Rmm Austrian, 8x56Rmm Hungarian

CARTRIDGE HISTORY
Year of Introduction: 1887
Country of Origin: Japan
Designer(s): Maj. Murata
Governing Body: none
Present Status: obsolete

CARTRIDGE DESCRIPTION
Bullet Diameter: .329 in.
Bullet Weight(s): 238 gr.
Rifling Twist Rate: N/A
Test Barrel Length: N/A
Case Type: rimmed, necked
Case Material: brass
Primer: large rifle

CARTRIDGE BALLISTICS
Max. Average Breech Pressure: N/A
Max. Horizontal Range: 4,500 yds.
Max. Vertical Range: 9,000 ft.

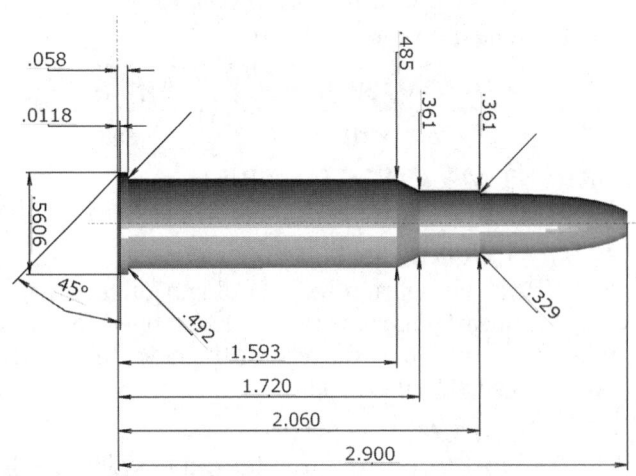

Bullet Weight (gr.)	Bullet Type	Muzzle Velocity (fps)	Muzzle Energy (ft.-lbs.)
238	FMJ-FN	1,835	1,779

CURRENT MANUFACTURER(S)
None

GENERAL COMMENT(S)
The 8x52.5Rmm Murata was the first small caliber rifle cartridge adopted by the Japanese Army in 1887. At the same time, they adopted the Type 20 Murata bolt-action, repeating rifle. This cartridge was replaced in 1897 by the 6.5x50SRmm Arisaka cartridge in 1897.

TECHNICAL COMMENT(S)
The 8x52.5Rmm Murata was loaded with a flat nose copper jacketed bullet to prevent primer ignition of catridges in the Type 20 rifle's tubular magazine. With its smokeless propellant, its ballistics were typical of the era.

8x56Rmm AUSTRO-HUNGARIAN MANNLICHER

ALTERNATE NAME(S): 8x56Rmm Hungarian, 8x56Rmm Hungarian M31
RELATED CALIBER(S): 8x50Rmm Austrian Mannlicher

CARTRIDGE HISTORY
Year of Introduction: 1931
Country of Origin: Switzerland
Designer(s): Solothurn
Governing Body: CIP
Present Status: obsolete

CARTRIDGE DESCRIPTION
Bullet Diameter: .330 in.
Bullet Weight(s): 206 gr.
Rifling Twist Rate: 1 turn in 8.84 in.
Test Barrel Length: 24 in.
Case Type: rimmed. Necked, tapered

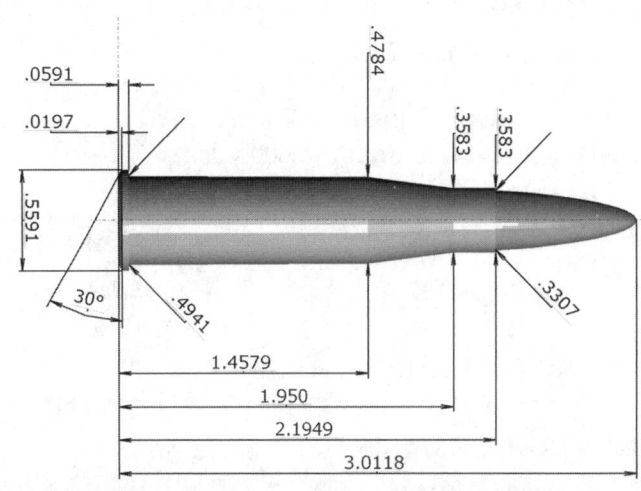

Case Material: brass or steel
Primer Size: large rifle

CARTRIDGE BALLISTICS
Max. Average Breech Pressure: 51,488 psi.
Max. Horizontal Range: 5,100 yds.
Max. Vertical Range: 10,500 ft.

Bullet Weight (gr.)	Bullet Type	Muzzle Velocity (fps)	Muzzle Energy (ft.-lbs.)
208 (M31)	Ball	2,375	2,604

CURRENT MANUFACTURER(S)
Hornady, Prvi Partizan

GENERAL COMMENT(S)
By 1930, the Hungarian Army could no longer postpone updating the 8x50Rmm cartridge. To save money, the existing 8x50Rmm cartridge was simply lengthened to 56mm and the bullet diameter changed to .330 inches. Existing rifles were fitted with new barrels for the new caliber. This was the cartridge which the Hungarian Army used in World War II as an ally of Germany.

TECHNICAL COMMENT(S)
Unlike most updated cartridges, the 8x56mm Hungarian proved to be an excellent compromise. In ballistic performance, the 8x56mm Hungarian cartridge was fully the equal of the German 8x57mm Mauser. However, outside eastern Europe, the 8x56mm cartridge is relatively unknown.

Tracer and AP variants were developed in addition to the Ball bullet.

8x57mm MAUSER

ALTERNATE NAME(S): 7.92x57mmJS Mauser , 8mm Mauser, 8mm S Mauser, 8x57mmJS Mauser, 8x57mmJS
RELATED CALIBER(S): 8x57mmJ, .30-06 Springfield, 7.5x54mm French MAS, 7.62x51mm NATO

CARTRIDGE HISTORY
Year of Introduction: 1888 (J Patrone), 1905 (S Patrone)
Country of Origin: Germany
Designer(s): 1888 Military Commission (J Patrone)
Governing Body: CIP, SAAMI
Present Status: obsolete

CARTRIDGE DESCRIPTION
Bullet Diameter: .323 (S Patrone) in.
Bullet Weight(s): 152-200 gr.
Rifling Twist Rate: 1 turn in 9.45 in.
Test Barrel Length: 24 in.
Case Type: rimless, necked
Case Material: steel or brass
Primer Size: large rifle

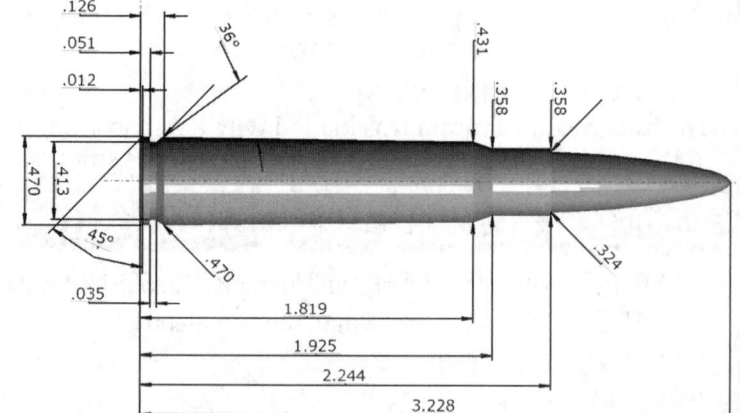

CARTRIDGE BALLISTICS
Max. Average Breech Pressure: 56,565 psi.
Max. Effective Range: 1,000 yds.
Max. Horizontal Range: 5,600 yds.
Max. Vertical Range: 12,500 ft.

Bullet Weight (gr.)	Bullet Type	Muzzle Velocity (fps)	Muzzle Energy (ft.-lbs.)
198	sS Ball	2,575	N/A
154	S Ball	2,890	N/A

CURRENT MANUFACTURER(S)
Federal, Remington, Winchester, Prvi Partizan, DN, NAMMO, Sellier & Bellot

GENERAL COMMENT(S)

Undoubtedly, the 8x57mm Mauser is the most famous military cartridge in history. It was adopted for military service by dozens of countries throughout the world and served with distinction through two World Wars.

Perhaps more important, it was the founding father of a cartridge dynasty which includes such military calibers as the .30-'06 Springfield, 7.5x54mm French MAS, 7.65x53mm Belgian Mauser, 7x57mm Mauser, and 7.7x58mm Japanese Arisaka. Indeed, the 7.62x51mm NATO cartridge of today is a direct lineal descendent of the 8x57mm Mauser cartridge. And, this is not to mention the dozens of sporting calibers based on the 8x57mm cartridge. With the end of World War II in 1945, the 8x57mm Mauser cartridge quickly slipped from world military service, but remains entrenched in current sporting applications.

TECHNICAL COMMENT(S)

The German Army entered World War I with the 8x57mm cartridge loaded with a 152 grain spitzer flat base bullet. This load proved less than satisfactory for machine gun use as the French Balle D bullet outranged the German bullet by a substantial margin. German infantry also disliked the flash, muzzle blast and recoil of the 152 grain load. In response, the German Army developed the schwere spitzergeschoss (sS) bullet – a 198 grain spitzer boat-tail with excellent long range performance.

The sS bullet was the standard issue Ball bullet in German military service throughout World War II. It was manufactured in a wide variety with steel cores, iron cores, lead cores and combinations of these. Amazingly, all were effective and interchangeable. German infantrymen disliked the heavy recoil impulse of the sS patrone ammunition. However, Hitler, who had served in the trenches during World War I, insisted that this bullet remain standard issue.

8x58Rmm DANISH KRAG

ALTERNATE NAME(S): 8x58R, 8x58R Danish, 8mm Danish Krag
RELATED CALIBER(S): 11.7mm Danish Remington

CARTRIDGE HISTORY
Year of Introduction: 1889
Country of Origin: Denmark
Designer(s): N/A
Governing Body: none
Present Status: obsolete

CARTRIDGE DESCRIPTION
Bullet Diameter: .323 in.
Bullet Weight(s): 196-237 gr.
Rifling Twist Rate: 1 turn in 12 in.
Test Barrel Length: N/A
Case Type: rimmed, necked
Case Material: brass
Primer: large rifle

CARTRIDGE BALLISTICS
Max. Average Breech Pressure: 42,000 psi.
Max. Horizontal Range: 4,700 yds.
Max. Vertical Range: 9,800 ft.

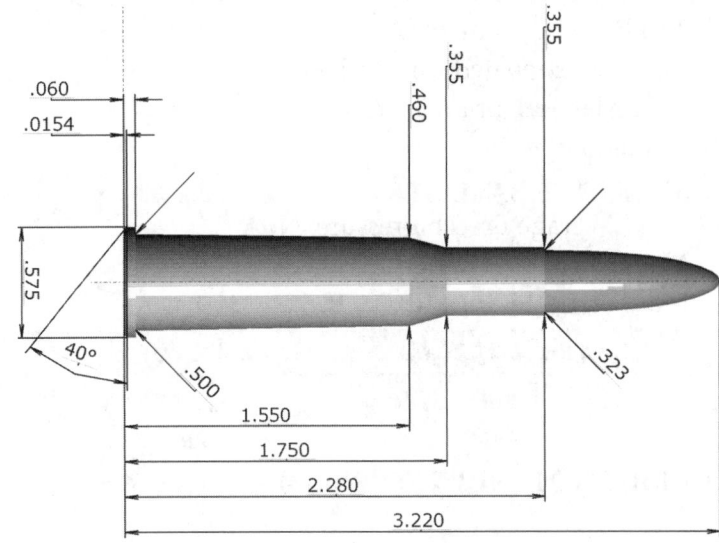

Bullet Weight (gr.)	Bullet Type	Muzzle Velocity (fps)	Muzzle Energy (ft.-lbs.)
196	FMJ-Spitzer	2,460	2,633
237	FMJ-RN	1,970	2,039

CURRENT MANUFACTURER(S)
None

GENERAL COMMENT(S)
Adopted by the Danish Army in 1889, this cartridge remained in front line military service until 1945. The 8x58R cartridge became a popular caliber for hunting and target shooting where its reputation for accuracy was appreciated.

TECHNICAL COMMENT(S)
The original military bullet was a 237 grain FMJ round nose. In 1908, the round nose bullet was replaced with the 196 grain spitzer that also allowed an increase in muzzle velocity. In many ways, the 8x58R Danish cartridge is typical of those designed around 1890. It is a rimmed, necked design of moderate chamber pressure and a relatively heavy bullet at modest muzzle velocity.

8x59mm BREDA

ALTERNATE NAME(S): 8mm Breda M1935, 8mm Italian Breda, 8mm Fiat, 8mm Model 35, Patrone 204(i)
RELATED CALIBER(S): 8x63mm Swedish

CARTRIDGE HISTORY
Year of Introduction: 1935
Country of Origin: Italy
Designer(s): N/A
Governing Body: none
Present Status: obsolete

CARTRIDGE DESCRIPTION
Bullet Diameter: .323 in.
Bullet Weight(s): 210 gr.
Rifling Twist Rate: N/A
Test Barrel Length: N/A
Case Type: rebated rim, necked
Case Material: brass or steel
Primer: large rifle

CARTRIDGE BALLISTICS
Max. Average Breech Pressure: N/A
Max. Horizontal Range: 5,250 yds.
Max. Vertical Range: 11,000 ft.

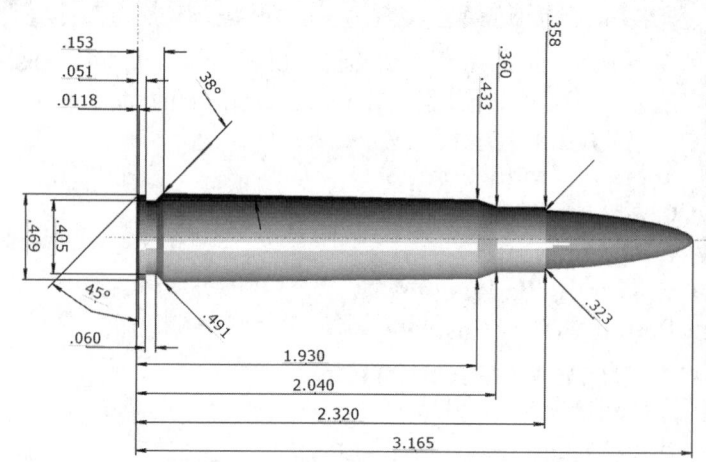

Bullet Weight (gr.)	Bullet Type	Muzzle Velocity (fps)	Muzzle Energy (ft.-lbs.)
210	FMJ-BT	2,445	2,787
193	AP	2,525	2,731

CURRENT MANUFACTURER(S)
None

GENERAL COMMENT(S)
Recognizing the shortcomings of their existing 6.5x52mm Carcano rifle cartridge for medium machine gun use, the Italian Army began a program to develop a new, more powerful cartridge for that purpose along with a new machine gun in the early 1920s. In 1935, the new 8x59mm Breda M1935 cartridge was officially standardized for Italian military service. Shortly after, the Breda M37 and M38 machineguns in the new caliber were adopted. Both the 8mm Breda cartridge and the Breda machine guns were retained in Italian military service until the late 1950s. Ammunition in this caliber was manufactured until the early 1960s. Italy was the only country to take this cartridge into military service. It was never offered for sporting use.

TECHNICAL COMMENT(S)
The 8mm Breda cartridge is one of the few infantry machine gun cartridges with a rebated rim. Otherwise, it is conventional in design with an "S" or .323 inch diameter bullet. Despite its longer case and greater interior volume, the 8x59mm Breda cartridge offers ballistic performance similar to the German 8x57mmJ military cartridge.

8x60Rmm PORTUGUESE GUEDES M86

ALTERNATE NAME(S): 8mm Guedes, 8x60Rmm, 8x60Rmm Portuguese, 8.2x59.5mm Portuguese M86
RELATED CALIBER(S): 8x60Rmm Kropatschek (1st model)

CARTRIDGE HISTORY
Year of Introduction: 1886
Country of Origin: Austria
Designer(s): G. Roth
Governing Body: none
Present Status: obsolete

CARTRIDGE DESCRIPTION
Bullet Diameter: .326 in.
Bullet Weight(s): 247 gr.
Rifling Twist Rate: 1 turn in 11 in.
Test Barrel Length: N/A
Case Type: rimmed, necked
Case Material: brass
Primer: large rifle

CARTRIDGE BALLISTICS
Max. Average Breech Pressure: N/A
Max. Horizontal Range: 4,300 yds.
Max. Vertical Range: 8,800 ft.

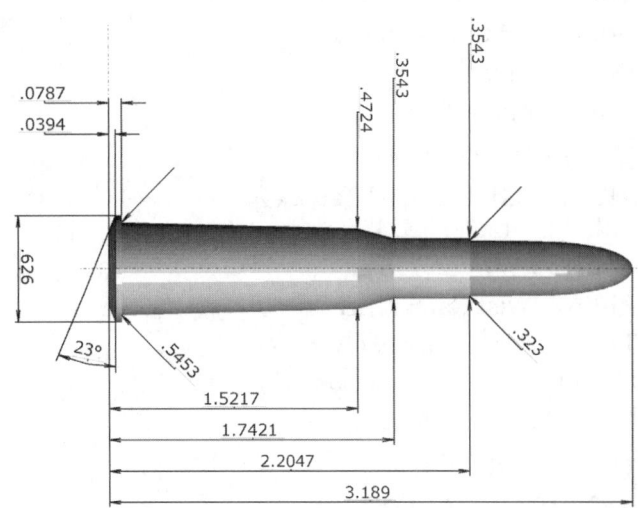

Bullet Weight (gr.)	Bullet Type	Muzzle Velocity (fps)	Muzzle Energy (ft.-lbs.)
247	FMJ-RN	1,705	1,605

CURRENT MANUFACTURER(S)
None

GENERAL COMMENT(S)
When it was adopted in 1886, the 8x60Rmm Guedes cartridge was the first small caliber military cartridge taken into Portuguese military service. It was designed for a Martini-Henry single-shot rifle adopted at the same time. Unfortunately, both rifle and cartridge were already obsolete. The 8x60Rmm cartridge was loaded with black powder and a paper-patched bullet and single-shot rifles, which were being replaced with bolt-action repeaters in most armies. In 1886, the Portuguese military finally adopted a new, bolt-action repeating rifle designed by Kropatschek in Austria. At the same time, the Austrian firm of G. Roth introduced the 8x60Rmm Kropatschek cartridge which was interchangeable with the earlier 8x60Rmm Guedes cartridge. A later version of the Kropatschek cartridge had a shorter 56mm case length. Portugal was the only country that took this cartridge into military service. It was replaced by the 6.5x58mm Portuguese Vergueiro cartridge in 1904. Neither the Guedes or Kropatschek cartridges were sold for sporting use.

TECHNICAL COMMENT(S)
Even by the ballistic criteria of that era, the 8x60Rmm cartridge offers weak military performance. Muzzle velocity and energy are no better than many of the large-bore, black-powder cartridges it replaced. When Roth introduced the 8x60Rmm Kropatschek cartridge in 1896, they modernized the bullet by replacing the earlier paper-patched version with one having a lead core with a cupro-nickel steel jacket. Undoubtedly, the propellant was changed to smokeless at about that time as well.

8x63mm SWEDISH

ALTERNATE NAME(S): 8mm Swedish Service, 8mm Browning, 8mm sk ptr m/32, 8mm Bofors
RELATED CALIBER(S): 8x59mm Breda

CARTRIDGE HISTORY
Year of Introduction: 1932
Country of Origin: Sweden
Designer(s): N/A
Governing Body: none
Present Status: obsolete

CARTRIDGE DESCRIPTION
Bullet Diameter: .323 in.
Bullet Weight(s): 218 gr.
Rifling Twist Rate: N/A
Test Barrel Length: N/A
Case Type: rimless, necked
Case Material: brass or steel
Primer: large rifle

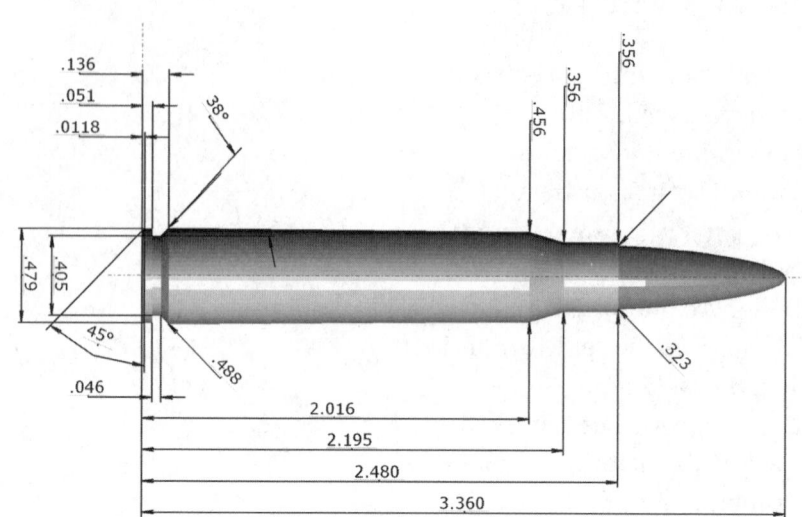

CARTRIDGE BALLISTICS
Max. Average Breech Pressure: N/A
Max. Horizontal Range: 5,300 yds.
Max. Vertical Range: 11,000 ft.

Bullet Weight (gr.)	Bullet Type	Muzzle Velocity (fps)	Muzzle Energy (ft.-lbs.)
218	FMJ-BT	2,495	3,013

CURRENT MANUFACTURER(S)
None

GENERAL COMMENT(S)
Recognizing the ballistic shortcomings of their existing 6.5x55mm Swedish Mauser rifle cartridge for military use (especially in machine guns), the Swedish Army began a program to develop a new, more powerful 8mm cartridge for that purpose in the early 1930s. In 1932, the Swedish Army adopted the 8x63mm Swedish cartridge for military service. Initially, the new cartridge was used in Browning m/36, m/42 and m/42B machine guns introduced in 1936. Originally, the Swedish Army planned to replace infantry rifles chambered for the old 6.5x55mm Swedish cartridge with a completely new, bolt-action infantry rifle in the new 8x63mm Swedish caliber. A small number of Mauser rifles were purchased from Germany in 1939 for that purpose and rebarrelled in the new caliber for testing. When recoil proved too heavy in these rifles, the 8x63mm Swedish cartridge was used exclusively for machine guns and the infantry rifles left in 6.5x55mm Swedish caliber. The 8x63mm Swedish cartridge remained in front line military service in Sweden until the 1960s when it was replaced by the 7.62x51mm NATO cartridge.

TECHNICAL COMMENT(S)
The 8x63mm Swedish cartridge is one of most powerful infantry cartridges ever adopted. It is more powerful than the German 8x57mmJ cartridge against which it was compared. Contrary to its appearance, the 8x63mm Swedish is not a .30-'06 Springfield cartridge (7.62x63mm) necked up to 8mm. The base and rim are wider. The two cartridges are not interchangeable. It is unsafe to fire .30-'06 Springfield ammunition in firearms chambered for 8x63mm Swedish. Doing so may cause serious personal injury.

9.5x60Rmm TURKISH MAUSER

ALTERNATE NAME(S): 9.5x60Rmm Turkish
RELATED CALIBER(S): 11.15x60Rmm Mauser

CARTRIDGE HISTORY
Year of Introduction: 1887
Country of Origin: Germany
Designer(s): Peter Paul Mauser
Governing Body: none
Present Status: obsolete

CARTRIDGE DESCRIPTION
Bullet Diameter: .389 in.
Bullet Weight(s): 285 gr.
Rifling Twist Rate: 1 turn in 20 in.
Test Barrel Length: N/A
Case Type: rimmed, necked
Case Material: brass
Primer: large rifle

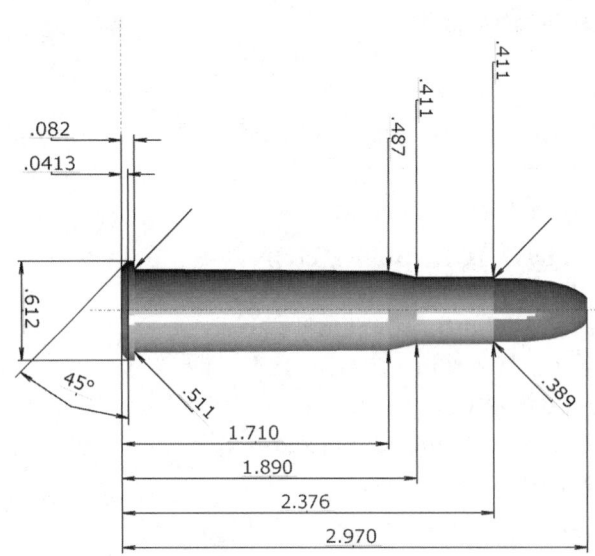

CARTRIDGE BALLISTICS
Max. Average Breech Pressure: N/A
Max. Horizontal Range: 3,100 yds.
Max. Vertical Range: 6,600 ft.

Bullet Weight (gr.)	Bullet Type	Muzzle Velocity (fps)	Muzzle Energy (ft.-lbs.)
285	L-RN	1,760	1,960

CURRENT MANUFACTURER(S)
None

GENERAL COMMENT(S)
The 9.5x60Rmm Turkish Mauser cartridge is historically significant because it was the last black powder cartridge designed by Peter Paul Mauser. Turkey lagged behind the other powers in military technology in the late 1800s. This is evident from their adoption of a new black powder cartridge at a time when other European armies were quickly adopting smokeless powder cartridges. For this reason, the service life of the 9.5x60Rmm Turkish Mauser cartridge was very short – it was declared obsolete in 1890, just three years after adoption. It was replaced by the smokeless powder 7.65mm Mauser cartridge as the Turkish Army continued to modernize. Following the sudden demise of its military career, this cartridge never developed a significant share of the sporting market and disappeared by 1900.

TECHNICAL COMMENT(S)
As a technical exercise, the 9.5x60Rmm is one of the most efficient black powder cartridge ever designed. When Mauser set pen to paper, the trend in military cartridges was already moving toward smaller bore diameters, lighter bullet weights and increased muzzle velocity. Mauser incorporated all these trends in his design. Note that the bullet is about 15% lighter than earlier designs, the bullet diameter is significantly smaller and the muzzle velocity is 15-20% higher on average. For these reasons, the 9.5x60Rmm Turkish Mauser cartridge must be regarded as the pinnacle of black powder military cartridge development.

10.15x61Rmm JARMANN

ALTERNATE NAME(S): 10.15x61Rmm Swedish
RELATED CALIBER(S): None

CARTRIDGE HISTORY
Year of Introduction: 1884
Country of Origin: Sweden
Designer(s): Norwegian-Swedish Rifle Committee
Governing Body: none
Present Status: obsolete

CARTRIDGE DESCRIPTION
Bullet Diameter: .403 in.
Bullet Weight(s): 337 gr.
Rifling Twist Rate: 1 turn in 22 in.
Test Barrel Length: N/A
Case Type: rimmed, necked
Case Material: brass
Primer: large rifle

CARTRIDGE BALLISTICS
Max. Average Breech Pressure: N/A
Max. Horizontal Range: 3,100 yds.
Max. Vertical Range: 6,600 ft.

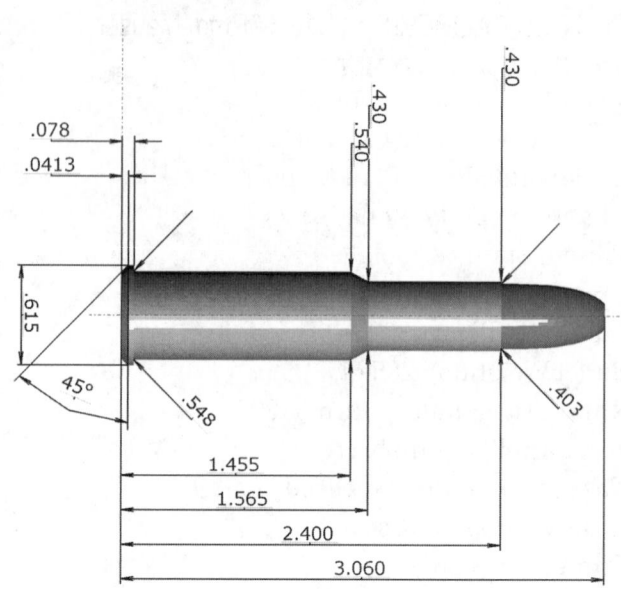

Bullet Weight (gr.)	Bullet Type	Muzzle Velocity (fps)	Muzzle Energy (ft.-lbs.)
337	L-RN	1,625	1,976

CURRENT MANUFACTURER(S)
None

GENERAL COMMENT(S)
The Jarmann 10.15x61Rmm cartridge was designed by a Norwegian-Swedish Rifle Committee charged with getting the new Jarmann M1884 rifle into military service. The 10.15x61Rmm Jarmann began life as a black powder cartridge and made the transition to smokeless propellants. It remained in Swedish and Norwegian military service until 1900 after which it was relegated to reserve status. However, that was not the end of the Jarmann cartridge story by any means. In 1928, Kongsberg Vapenfabrikk had thousands of M1884 Jarmann rifles in reserve storage with no future military use. Seeing an opportunity in the commercial fishing market, Kongsberg started rebuilding Jarmann rifles as M28 harpoon guns! This program continued until 1952. Some 1,911 Jarmann rifles were converted. When Norway was occupied by the German Army in 1940, thousands of Jarmann rifles remained in reserve storage. As these rifles were obsolete, they were of no military interest. However, the Germans did not want to leave them lying around, so they melted most of them down. To support the users of the M28 harpoon guns, manufacture of 10.15x61Rmm harpoon propelling blank ammunition continued into the 1970s.

TECHNICAL COMMENT(S)
When the 10.15x61Rmm Jarmann was adopted, it was loaded with black powder and a paper-patched lead bullet. With the transition to smokeless propellant, a steel jacketed bullet was used. The Jarmann rifle and cartridge were well known for their accuracy. The 10.15x61Rmm Jarmann cartridge was loaded to approximately 17% higher muzzle velocity than other military cartridges of the time. Jarmann bulleted cartridges can be safely fired in the M28 harpoon gun. Harpoon blanks can be identified by the lack of a bullet and crimp closure on the case mouth, while military blanks were loaded with a wood bullet.

10.15x63Rmm SERBIAN MAUSER

ALTERNATE NAME(S): 10.15x63Rmm
RELATED CALIBER(S): 9.5x60Rmm Turkish Mauser, 11.15x60Rmm Mauser

CARTRIDGE HISTORY
Year of Introduction: 1878
Country of Origin: Germany
Designer(s): Peter Paul Mauser
Governing Body: none
Present Status: obsolete

CARTRIDGE DESCRIPTION
Bullet Diameter: .411 in.
Bullet Weight(s): 340 gr.
Rifling Twist Rate: 1 turn in 22 in.
Test Barrel Length: N/A
Case Type: rimmed, necked
Case Material: brass
Primer: large rifle

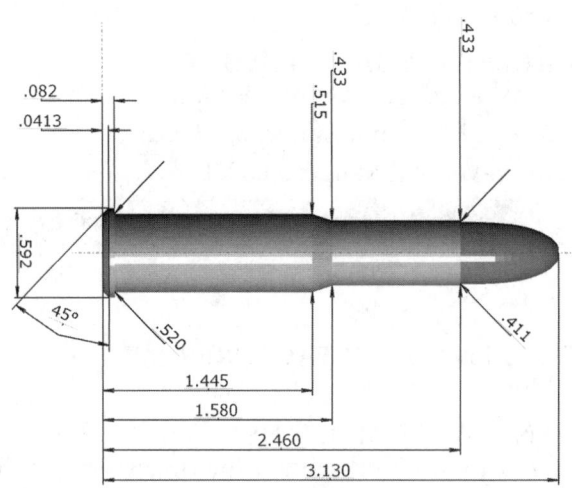

CARTRIDGE BALLISTICS
Max. Average Breech Pressure: N/A
Max. Horizontal Range: 2,400 yds.
Max. Vertical Range: 5,200 ft.

Bullet Weight (gr.)	Bullet Type	Muzzle Velocity (fps)	Muzzle Energy (ft.-lbs.)
340	L-RN	1460	1,609

CURRENT MANUFACTURER(S)
None

GENERAL COMMENT(S)
Serbia adopted this cartridge for military service in 1878 for their Mauser M78/80 single-shot rifle. Mauser designed both the rifle and cartridge. DWM and other European cartridge makers supplied the ammunition. In the Balkans, old soldiers never die. After they occupied the area in 1940 during World War II, the German Army encountered M78/80 rifles firing the 10.15x63Rmm Serbian Mauser cartridge in the hands of the partisans. Of course, both the rifle and cartridge were long-obsolete, but the partisans used what they had at hand. As black powder is very hard on firearms, it is very likely that most rifles and ammunition in this caliber are worn out and been discarded.

TECHNICAL COMMENT(S)
Designed for black powder, the 10.15x63Rmm cartridge was a typical cartridge for its time-a large diameter, heavy, paper-patched, lead bullet; rimmed, necked brass case, and a prototypical Mauser case head. However, this was the twilight of the black powder era and the 10.15x63Rmm Serbian cartridge became obsolete by the time the Serbian Army began receiving their new rifles and ammunition in the early 1880s.

10.4x47Rmm ITALIAN VETTERLI M70

ALTERNATE NAME(S): 10.65x47Rmm Italian M71, 10.4x47Rmm, 10.8x48Rmm, 10.35x47Rmm
RELATED CALIBER(S): 10.3x39.5Rmm Swiss

CARTRIDGE HISTORY
Year of Introduction: 1871
Country of Origin: Switzerland
Designer(s): Friedrich Vetterli
Governing Body: none
Present Status: obsolete

CARTRIDGE DESCRIPTION
Bullet Diameter: .425 in.
Bullet Weight(s): 315 gr.
Rifling Twist Rate: 1 turn in 26 in.
Test Barrel Length: N/A
Case Type: rimmed, necked

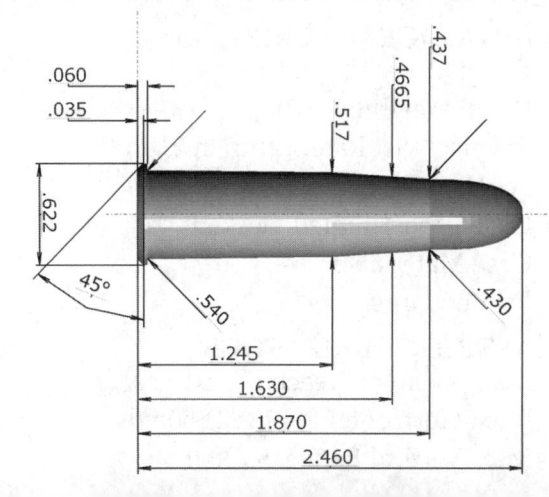

Case Material: copper or brass
Primer: large rifle

CARTRIDGE BALLISTICS
Max. Average Breech Pressure: N/A
Max. Horizontal Range: 6,300 yds.
Max. Vertical Range: 3,000 ft.

Bullet Weight (gr.)	Bullet Type	Muzzle Velocity (fps)	Muzzle Energy (ft.-lbs.)
315	FMJ	1,345	1,257
315	L-RN	1,425	1,420

CURRENT MANUFACTURER(S)
None

GENERAL COMMENT(S)
Friedrich Vetterli joined the Swiss firm of SIG in 1864. He immediately set about designing a new rifle and cartridge for the Swiss Army. Later, Vetterli became Superintendent of the Bern Arsenal in Switzerland. Vetterli's cartridge for the Swiss Army was a rimfire design. The Italian version, adopted in 1871 along with his rifle, was a centerfire type. The 10.4x47Rmm Italian cartridge was originally a black powder load with the customary lead, round-nose bullet at a muzzle velocity of about 1,350 fps. Later, the 10.4x47Rmm cartridge transitioned to smokeless propellant, and in so doing, became one of the first military cartridges to be loaded with a full metal jacketed bullet. Although the Italian Vetterli cartridge was made obsolete by 1891 with the Italian Army's adoption of the 6.5x52mm Mannlicher-Carcano cartridge, the 10.4x47Rmm continued to serve in reserve and law enforcement for several more decades.

TECHNICAL COMMENT(S)
The 10.4x47Rmm Italian Vetterli cartridge is a compact, necked design which was considered quite advanced for its time. Muzzle velocity is slightly higher than many of its contemporaries; however its bullet is also considerably lighter. All things considered, ballistic performance of the 10.4x47Rmm cartridge is only average, but typical of the era. Note the difference in muzzle velocity of the lead bullet and the jacketed bullet loads. This is very likely due to the transition to smokeless propellant for the jacketed bullet. So, why did it serve so long? The answer is very likely the balance consisting of its compactness and efficient, though average, ballistic performance. An additional factor was certainly the high order of workmanship of the Vetterli rifles.

10.6x47Rmm RUSSIAN BERDAN CAR.

ALTERNATE NAME(S):10.6x47Rmm Russian Carbine, .42 Russian Carbine
RELATED CALIBER(S): 10.6x57.5Rmm Russian Berdan (rifle)

CARTRIDGE HISTORY
Year of Introduction: 1870
Country of Origin: U.S.
Designer(s): Hiram Berdan
Governing Body: none
Present Status: obsolete

CARTRIDGE DESCRIPTION
Bullet Diameter: .426 in.
Bullet Weight(s): 370 gr.
Rifling Twist Rate: 1 turn in 21 in.
Test Barrel Length: N/A
Case Type: rimmed, necked
Case Material: brass
Primer: large rifle

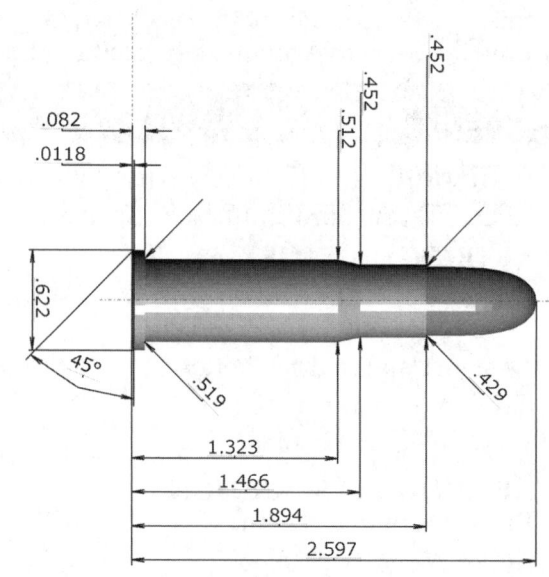

CARTRIDGE BALLISTICS
Max. Average Breech Pressure: N/A
Max. Horizontal Range: 2,850 yds.
Max. Vertical Range: 5,750 ft.

Bullet Weight (gr.)	Bullet Type	Muzzle Velocity (fps)	Muzzle Energy (ft.-lbs.)
370	L-RN	1,060 (est.)	923

CURRENT MANUFACTURER(S)
None

GENERAL COMMENT(S)
The Russian Army adopted this cartridge for cavalry use in 1870, one year after they adopted the 10.75x58Rmm Russian Berdan rifle cartridge.

TECHNICAL COMMENT(S)
Like other carbine cartridges of that era, the 10.6x47Rmm Russian Berdan Carbine cartridge was basically a shortened standard rifle cartridge loaded with the same lead, round-nose bullet at a lower muzzle velocity.

10.75x58Rmm RUSSIAN BERDAN

ALTERNATE NAME(S): .43 Berdan, .43 Russian Berdan, 10.75x58Rmm Berdan, 10.75x58Rmm Russian, .42 Berdan, 4.2 Line Berdan (a line is a unit of Russian linear measurement).

RELATED CALIBER(S): 11x60Rmm Murata

CARTRIDGE HISTORY
Year of Introduction: 1868
Country of Origin: U.S.
Designer(s): Hiram Berdan, Lt. Col. Gorloff (Russia)
Governing Body: none
Present Status: obsolete

CARTRIDGE DESCRIPTION
Bullet Diameter: .430 in.
Bullet Weight(s): 370 gr.
Rifling Twist Rate: 1 turn in 21 in.
Test Barrel Length: N/A
Case Type: rimmed, necked
Case Material: brass
Primer: large rifle

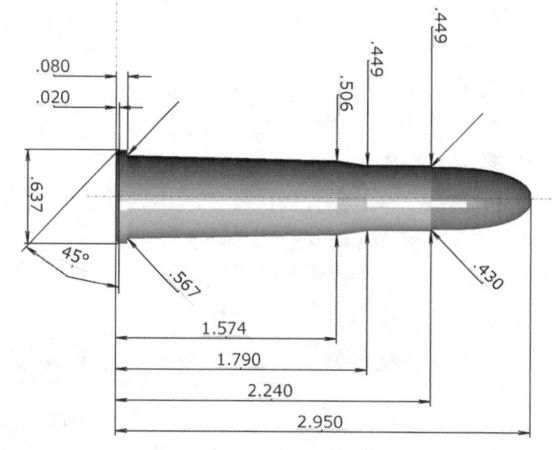

CARTRIDGE BALLISTICS
Max. Average Breech Pressure: N/A
Max. Horizontal Range: 3,000 yds.
Max. Vertical Range: 6,500 ft.

Bullet Weight (gr.)	Bullet Type	Muzzle Velocity (fps)	Muzzle Energy (ft.-lbs.)
370	L-RN	1,450	1,727(rifle load)
370	L-RN	1,350	1,497(cav. load)

CURRENT MANUFACTURER(S)
None

GENERAL COMMENT(S)
From 1869 to 1897, the 10.75x58Rmm Berdan was the official Russian military rifle cartridge. It was replaced in 1897 by the 7.62x54Rmm Russian cartridge which remains in front line service to date. Despite its replacement in 1897, the 10.75x58Rmm Berdan cartridge saw extensive service during World Wars I and II as well as during the Bolshevik Revolution in 1917. The 10.17x58Rmm Russian remained in production as a hunting cartridge until the mid-1930s.

TECHNICAL COMMENT(S)
The 10.75x58Rmm cartridge is historically significant as it was the first metallic cartridge to use the Berdan primer. Large quantities of this cartridge were made in the U.S. by Remington and Winchester for the Russian government. From a technical point of view, the 10.75x58Rmm cartridge was a conservative, black powder design using a paper-patched lead bullet. During its service life, the .43 Berdan was known for its power and accuracy. There were two loadings that used the same 370 grain paper-patched bullet – the standard rifle loading with a muzzle velocity of 1,450 fps, and a cavalry load with a 10% lighter powder charge.

11x42Rmm BELGIAN ALBINI-COMBLAIN CARBINE M71

ALTERNATE NAME(S): 11x42Rmm Belgian M71, 11mm Comblain Carbine M71, 11mm Belgian Albini-Comblain, 11x42Rmm Comblain Carbine

RELATED CALIBER(S): 11x51Rmm Belgian Comblain M71, 11.4x50Rmm Brazilian Comblain

CARTRIDGE HISTORY

Year of Introduction: 1871

Country of Origin: Belgium

Designer(s): Hubert-Joseph Comblain

Governing Body: none

Present Status: obsolete

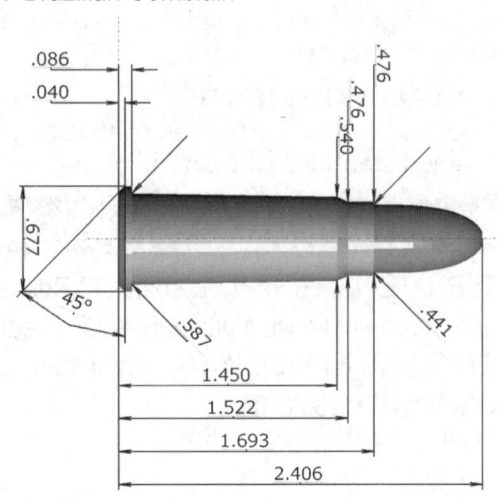

CARTRIDGE DESCRIPTION

Bullet Diameter: .448 in.

Bullet Weight(s): 386 gr.

Rifling Twist Rate: 1 turn in 22 in.

Test Barrel Length: N/A

Case Type: rimmed, necked

Case Material: brass

Primer: large rifle

CARTRIDGE BALLISTICS

Max. Average Breech Pressure: N/A

Max. Horizontal Range: 2,900 yds.

Max. Vertical Range: 5,900 ft.

Bullet Weight (gr.)	Bullet Type	Muzzle Velocity (fps)	Muzzle Energy (ft.-lbs.)
386	L-RN	1,100	1,037 (M76 carbine)

CURRENT MANUFACTURER(S)

None

GENERAL COMMENT(S)

In 1867, the Belgian Army began trials to replace their rimfire Comblain No.1 rifle. Many different rifles were submitted, but the trials concluded without a clear winner in 1869. As firearms technology was advancing by leaps and bounds at the time, the Belgian Army elected to forego a selection pending further consideration. In 1870, the Comblain M70 rifle in caliber 11x51Rmm Belgian Comblain (tested in the earlier trials in the Comblain No. 2 rifle) was adopted for service for the Belgian Guarde Civique (army reserves). Then, in 1871, the Belgian Army adopted the 11x42Rmm Belgian Albini Carbine cartridge, leaving the question of a Belgian Army rifle and cartridge still undecided.

TECHNICAL COMMENT(S)

All of the 11x50Rmm and 11x51Rmm rifle cartridges and the 11x42Rmm carbine cartridge fired the same 386 grain, paper-patched lead bullet. However, the muzzle velocity and muzzle energy produced by the carbine cartridge are substantially lower. Both cartridge types are typical in design and performance for the black powder cartridge era.

11x51Rmm BELGIAN COMBLAIN M71

ALTERNATE NAME(S): 11x51Rmm, 11mm Comblain M71 Comblain

RELATED CALIBER(S): 11x51Rmm Belgian Comblain M71, 11.4x50Rmm Brazilian Comblain

CARTRIDGE HISTORY

Year of Introduction: 1871

Country of Origin: Belgium

Designer(s): Hubert-Joseph Comblain

Governing Body: none

Present Status: obsolete

CARTRIDGE DESCRIPTION
Bullet Diameter: .441 in.

Bullet Weight(s): 386 gr.

Rifling Twist Rate: 1 turn in 22 in.

Test Barrel Length: N/A

Case Type: rimmed, necked

Case Material: brass

Primer: large rifle

CARTRIDGE BALLISTICS
Max. Average Breech Pressure: N/A

Max. Horizontal Range: 3,100 yds.

Max. Vertical Range: 6,500 ft.

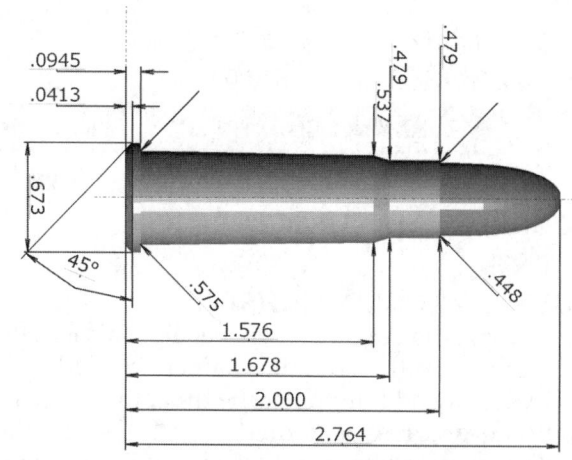

Bullet Weight (gr.)	Bullet Type	Muzzle Velocity (fps)	Muzzle Energy (ft.-lbs.)
386	L-RN	1,445	1,789

CURRENT MANUFACTURER(S)
None

GENERAL COMMENT(S)
In 1867, the Belgian Army began trials to replace their rimfire Comblain No. 1 military rifle. Many different rifles were submitted, but the trials concluded without a clear winner in 1869. As firearms technology was advancing by leaps and bounds at the time, the Belgian Army elected to forego a selection pending further consideration. Some progress was made in 1871 when the 11x51Rmm Belgian Comblain M71 cartridge was adopted for service in the Belgian Guarde Civique (army reserves). However, the Belgian Army continued to make do with reworked rifles in caliber 11x50Rmm M70. Finally, in 1882 the Belgian Army adopted the M82 Comblain Rifle chambered for the 11x50Rmm M81 cartridge, a slightly modified and interchangeable version of the M71 and M76 11x50Rmm cartridges. Service life of the 11x51Rmm M71 cartridge was brief as it was not as popular as the Belgian Army's (then) use of the 11x50Rmm cartridge. Following another series of trials from 1884-1889, the Belgian Army adopted the ultra-modern 7.65x53mm Belgian Mauser cartridge in 1889.

TECHNICAL COMMENT(S)
All 11x51Rmm cartridges fire the same 386 grain, paper-patched, lead, round-nose bullet as the 11x50Rmm cartridge, but at a higher muzzle velocity. The 11x51Rmm cartridge is NOT interchangeable with the 11x50Rmm cartridges. All models of this cartridge are typical in design and performance of the final era of black powder cartridges.

11x50Rmm BELGIAN ALBINI-COMBLAIN M70/76

ALTERNATE NAME(S): 11x50Rmm, 11mm Belgian Comblain M70/76

RELATED CALIBER(S): 11x51Rmm Belgian Comblain M71, 11.4x50Rmm Brazilian Comblain

CARTRIDGE HISTORY
Year of Introduction: 1872

Country of Origin: Belgium

Designer(s): Hubert-Joseph Comblain

Governing Body: none

Present Status: obsolete

CARTRIDGE DESCRIPTION
Bullet Diameter: .448 in.

Bullet Weight(s): 386 gr.

Rifling Twist Rate: 1 turn in 22 in.

Test Barrel Length: N/A

Case Type: rimmed, necked

Case Material: brass

Primer: large rifle

CARTRIDGE BALLISTICS
Max. Average Breech Pressure: N/A

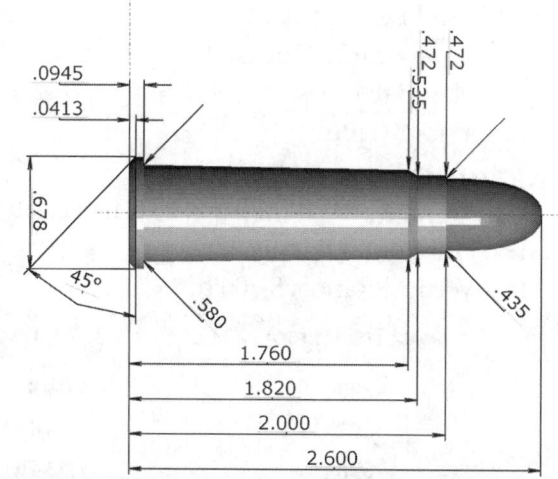

Max. Horizontal Range: 3,200 yds.
Max. Vertical Range: 6,400 ft.

Bullet Weight (gr.)	Bullet Type	Muzzle Velocity (fps)	Muzzle Energy (ft.-lbs.)
386	L-RN	1,370	1,609

CURRENT MANUFACTURER(S)
None

GENERAL COMMENT(S)
In 1867, the Belgian Army began trials to replace their rimfire Comblain No.1 military rifle. Many different rifles were submitted, but the trials concluded without a clear winner in 1869. As firearms technology was advancing by leaps and bounds at the time, the Belgian Army elected to forego a selection pending further consideration. Some progress was made in 1871 when the 11x51Rmm Belgian Comblain M71 cartridge was adopted for service in the Belgian Guarde Civique (army reserves). However, the Belgian Army continued to make do with reworked rifles in caliber 11x50Rmm M70. Finally, in 1882 the Belgian Army adopted the M82 Comblain Rifle chambered for the 11x50Rmm M81 cartridge, a slightly modified and interchangeable version of the M70 and M76 11x50Rmm cartridges. Service life of the 11x50Rmm M81 cartridge was brief as it was already obsolescent when adopted. Following another series of trials from 1884-1889, the Belgian Army adopted the ultra-modern 7.65x53mm Belgian Mauser cartridge in 1889. A popular caliber in Belgium, the 11x50Rmm cartridge remained in production until 1913.

TECHNICAL COMMENT(S)
All 11x51Rmm cartridges fire the same 386 grain, lead, round-nose bullet at the same muzzle velocity. The M71 used a paper-patched bullet while the M76 was loaded with a plain lead bullet. The M81 reverted to a paper-patched bullet. All models of the 11x50Rmm Belgian Comblain cartridge were interchangeable despite minor variations in case configuration and construction. The 11x51Rmm cartridge is NOT interchangeable with the 11x50Rmm cartridges. All models of this cartridge are typical designs of the final black powder cartridges era.

11x59Rmm FRENCH GRAS

ALTERNATE NAME(S): 11x59Rmm Vickers, 11mm Gras-Vickers, .433 Gras
RELATED CALIBER(S): 11.15x60Rmm Mauser, 8x50Rmm Lebel

CARTRIDGE HISTORY
Year of Introduction: 1874
Country of Origin: France
Designer(s): Col. Basile Gras
Governing Body: none
Present Status: obsolete

CARTRIDGE DESCRIPTION
Bullet Diameter: .445 in.
Bullet Weight(s): 388 gr.
Rifling Twist Rate: 1 turn in 22 in.
Test Barrel Length: 24 in.
Case Type: rimmed, necked
Case Material: brass
Primer: large rifle

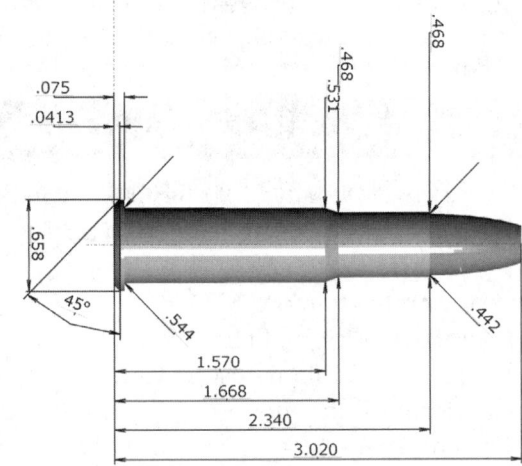

CARTRIDGE BALLISTICS
Max. Average Breech Pressure: 26,000 psi., later 30,000 psi. (+P), later 35,000psi. (+P+) with stronger cartridge case
Max. Horizontal Range: 4,000 yds.
Max. Vertical Range: 8,200 ft.

Bullet Weight (gr.)	Bullet Type	Muzzle Velocity (fps)	Muzzle Energy (ft.-lbs.)
388	L-RN	1,495	1,925 (original)
387	L-FN	1,495	1,920 (M79)
398	FMJ-FN	1,850	3,024 (1918)

CURRENT MANUFACTURER(S)
None

GENERAL COMMENT(S)

When adopted in 1874, the 11x59Rmm Gras was the first self-contained, metallic cartridge taken into French military service. It remained the standard French Army infantry cartridge until the 8x50Rmm Lebel cartridge loaded with smokeless propellant was adopted in 1886. Designed by Col. Basile Gras, the 11x59Rmm cartridge was a typical black powder cartridge of the 1870s with a heavy, round-nose, lead bullet, a rimmed and necked case and a modest muzzle velocity of 1,495 fps. Like many other black powder military rifle cartridges, the 11mm Gras cartridge's fate seemed to be sealed when smokeless powder was developed in the early 1880s. But fate decreed otherwise. The 11mm Gras cartridge served as the parent for the first smokeless powder cartridge – the 8x50Rmm Lebel which was basically an 11mm Gras case necked to 8mm. So, the Gras was to live on through its 8mm sibling. However, the saga still was not over. When World War I began in 1914, the German Army used tethered balloons for adjusting artillery fire and for observation. Allied fighter pilots often attacked these balloons, but they were hard to shoot down with ball bullets. Enter the concept of the anti-balloon gun which was a large caliber, ground-mounted Hotchkiss or Vickers machine gun. Wartime requirements being what they were, there was no time to develop a completely new cartridge for this purpose, so the ordnance engineers used what they had – the 11mm Gras cartridge. It served the purpose well. Following experiments, incendiary-tracer, armor-piercing, spotting and high explosive variants were developed. Production of this cartridge spread from France to the U.S. (Western Cartridge Co. and Frankford Arsenal). After the end of World War I in 1918, the 11mm Gras continued in service as a reserve until 1931 when the U.S. Ordnance Department scrapped the remaining stocks of this ammunition. The 11mm Gras cartridge continued in French military service in many colonial areas until the 1950s. The last production run of 11mm Gras ammunition was made in the mid 1950s for Yemen.

TECHNICAL COMMENT(S)

When first adopted for military service, the 11mm Gras cartridge case had a balloon head. This did not matter as maximum average chamber pressures were in the 25,000 psi. range with black powder propellant. When the 11mm Gras cartridge transitioned to smokeless propellants in the 1890s, the maximum average chamber pressure was maintained at approximately 25,000 psi. There it stayed until World War I when its new role as an anti-balloon gun cartridge demanded an increase in muzzle velocity and the maximum average chamber pressure to achieve it. This proceeded in two stages. First, the chamber pressure was simply increased to approximately 30,000 psi. This allowed the muzzle velocity to be safely increased to about 24% to 1,850 fps. This still was not sufficient, so a further increase in maximum average chamber pressure to 35,000 psi. was tried. At this point, the balloon head cartridge case design failed, so a stronger case with a solid head had to be designed. The new case provided enough strength to allow the chamber pressure to be increased to the desired level of 35,000 psi. In turn, this allowed muzzle velocity to be increased to 2,000 fps and then 2,350 fps. At the beginning of World War I, the 11mm Gras cartridge had only a ball bullet available. For its new application in the role of an anti-balloon gun, incendiary-tracer, spotting, high explosive and armor-piercing bullets were developed. In the end, the role as a heavy machine gun cartridge proved too much for the 11mm Gras. It was simply an outmoded design with no further development potential. The introduction of the Browning .50 caliber machine gun and cartridge finally sealed the fate of the 11mm Gras. French cartridge cases in this caliber are about .0625 inches shorter than those made in the U.S.

11x60Rmm JAPANESE MURATA

ALTERNATE NAME(S): 11x60Rmm Japanese, 11mm Murata
RELATED CALIBER(S): 10.15x60Rmm Mauser, 11x59Rmm Gras, 8x53Rmm Murata

CARTRIDGE HISTORY

Year of Introduction: 1880

Country of Origin: Japan

Designer(s): Maj. Gen. Tsuneyoshi Murata (1838-1921)

Governing Body: none

Present Status: obsolete

CARTRIDGE DESCRIPTION

Bullet Diameter: .432 in.

Bullet Weight(s): 420 gr.

Rifling Twist Rate: 1 turn in 20 in.

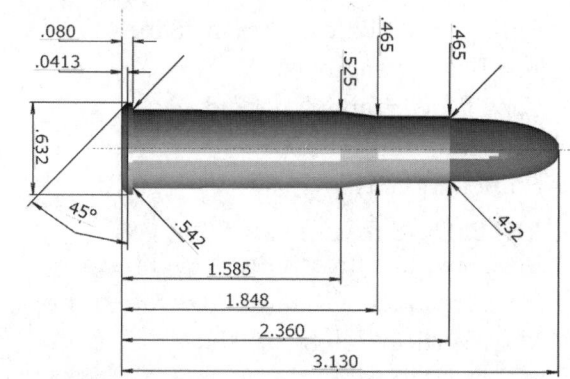

Test Barrel Length: N/A

Case Type: rimmed, necked

Case Material: brass

Primer: large rifle

CARTRIDGE BALLISTICS

Max. Average Breech Pressure: N/A

Max. Horizontal Range: 3,700 yds.

Max. Vertical Range: 7,500 ft.

Bullet Weight (gr.)	Bullet Type	Muzzle Velocity (fps)	Muzzle Energy (ft.-lbs.)
420	L-RN	1,485	2,056

CURRENT MANUFACTURER(S)

None

GENERAL COMMENT(S)

As a young 2nd lieutenant, Tsuneyoshi Murata visited Europe in 1875 to study gunnery and weapons design. When he returned to Japan, he designed the first modern Japanese rifle, the Model 1880 Murata and its cartridge, the 11x60Rmm Murata. Undoubtedly, Lt. Murata visited Germany and France during his European trip as his 11x60Rmm Murata cartridge bears a strong resemblance to the 11.15x60Rmm Mauser and the 11x59Rmm Gras. Murata is also credited with the design of the 8x53Rmm Murata cartridge in 1887. Murata continued his work at the Tokyo Arsenal until his transfer to the reserves in the early 1890s.

TECHNICAL COMMENT(S)

The 11x60Rmm Murata cartridge was obsolete when it was introduced as it was a conservative design using established technology based on black powder propellants and paper-patched lead bullets. European countries were quickly moving on to smokeless powder propellants and cartridges. Therefore, the 11x60Rmm Murata remained in Japanese military service for just seven years. The 8x53Rmm Murata cartridge which replaced it in 1887 was an intermediate design using a jacketed, smaller caliber bullet and smokeless propellant with increased muzzle velocity. However, it too was obsolete when it was adopted.Both Murata cartridges were replaced by the 6.5x50SRmm Arisaka cartridge in 1897.

11.15x42Rmm AUS. WERNDL CAR. M67/77

ALTERNATE NAME(S): 11.15x42Rmm, 11.15x42Rmm Austrian M67
RELATED CALIBER(S): 11.15x58Rmm Austrian Werndl M77

CARTRIDGE HISTORY

Year of Introduction: 1867

Country of Origin: Austria

Designer(s): Josef Werndl

Governing Body: none

Present Status: obsolete

CARTRIDGE DESCRIPTION

Bullet Diameter: .452 in.

Bullet Weight(s): 370 gr.

Rifling Twist Rate: 1 turn in 28 in.

Test Barrel Length: N/A

Case Type: rimmed, necked

Case Material: brass

Primer: large rifle

CARTRIDGE BALLISTICS

Max. Average Breech Pressure: N/A

Max. Horizontal Range: 3,100 yds.

Max. Vertical Range: 6,500 ft.

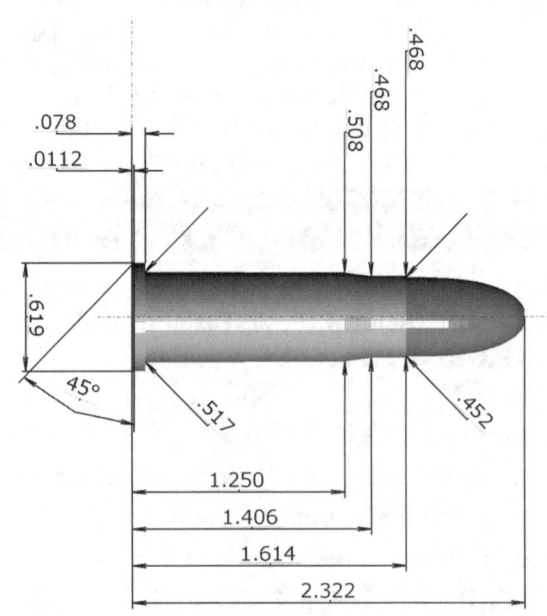

Bullet Weight (gr.)	Bullet Type	Muzzle Velocity (fps)	Muzzle Energy (ft.-lbs.)
313	L-RN	975	661 (M67)
370	L-RN	1,005	830 (M77)

CURRENT MANUFACTURER(S)
None

GENERAL COMMENT(S)
From 1867 until 1886, the 11.15x42Rmm Austrian Werndl Carbine cartridge was the standard military rifle cartridge for the Austro-Hungarian Cavalry and Combat Engineers. It was fired in a single-shot carbine designed by Josef Werndl. This cartridge was replaced in Austro-Hungarian military service by the 8x50Rmm Austrian Mannlicher cartridge in 1886.

TECHNICAL COMMENT(S)
The 11.15x42Rmm Werndl is a typical black powder cavalry cartridge in that it is a shortened version of the standard rifle cartridge with the same bullet. Of course, the muzzle velocity is lower to reduce recoil. Like its contemporaries, it fires a large caliber, round-nose, lead bullet at a muzzle velocity of approximately 1,000 fps. Also like its contemporaries, it became obsolete with the advent of smokeless powder. The 11.15x42Rmm Werndl carbine cartridge remained in front-line service with the Austro-Hungarian cavalry for 19 years from 1867 until 1886.

11.15x58Rmm AUSTRIAN WERNDL M77

ALTERNATE NAME(S): 11.15x58Rmm, 11.15x58Rmm Austrian M77
RELATED CALIBER(S): 11.15x58Rmm Austrian Werndl M77

CARTRIDGE HISTORY
Year of Introduction: 1877
Country of Origin: Austria
Designer(s): Josef Werndl
Governing Body: none
Present Status: obsolete

CARTRIDGE DESCRIPTION
Bullet Diameter: .452 in.
Bullet Weight(s): 370 gr.
Rifling Twist Rate: 1 turn in 28 in.
Test Barrel Length: N/A
Case Type: rimmed, necked
Case Material: brass
Primer: large rifle

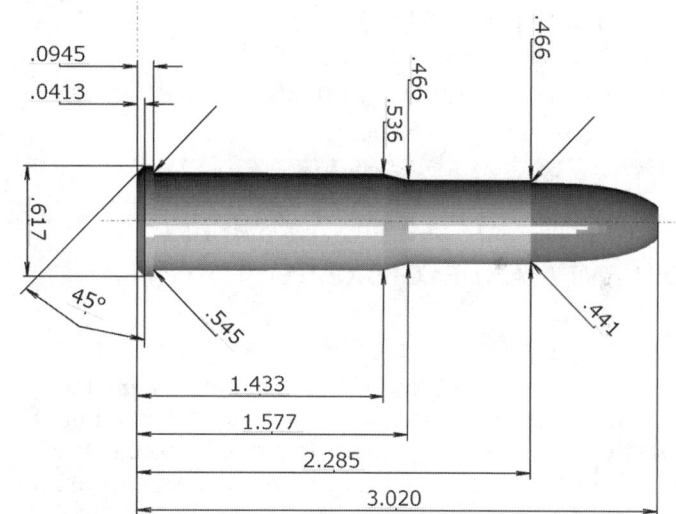

CARTRIDGE BALLISTICS
Max. Average Breech Pressure: N/A
Max. Horizontal Range: 3,100 yds.
Max. Vertical Range: 6,500 ft.

Bullet Weight (gr.)	Bullet Type	Muzzle Velocity (fps)	Muzzle Energy (ft.-lbs.)
370	L-RN	1,435	1,692

CURRENT MANUFACTURER(S)
None

GENERAL COMMENT(S)
From 1877 until 1886, the 11.15x58Rmm Austrian Werndl M77 cartridge was the standard military rifle cartridge for the Austro-Hungarian Army. It was fired in a single-shot rifle designed by Josef Werndl. This cartridge was replaced in Austro-Hungarian military service by the 8x50Rmm Austrian Mannlicher cartridge in 1886.

TECHNICAL COMMENT(S)
The 11.15x58Rmm Werndl is a typical black powder cartridge of the late 1870s. Like its contemporaries, it fired a large caliber, round-nose, lead bullet at a muzzle velocity of approximately 1,400 fps. Also like its contemporaries,

its service life was short as it was adopted in the twilight of black powder cartridges just before smokeless powder changed everything. The 11.4x50Rmm cartridge was obsolete after just nine years of service.

11.15x58Rmm SPANISH REMINGTON

ALTERNATE NAME(S): .43 Spanish, .433 Spanish, 11mm Spanish, 11x57Rmm
RELATED CALIBER(S): 11.5x57Rmm Reformado

CARTRIDGE HISTORY
Year of Introduction: 1867
Country of Origin: U.S.
Designer(s): Remington
Governing Body: none
Present Status: obsolete

CARTRIDGE DESCRIPTION
Bullet Diameter: .439 in.
Bullet Weight(s): 375 gr.
Rifling Twist Rate: 1 turn in 20 in.
Test Barrel Length: N/A
Case Type: rimmed, necked
Case Material: brass
Primer: large rifle

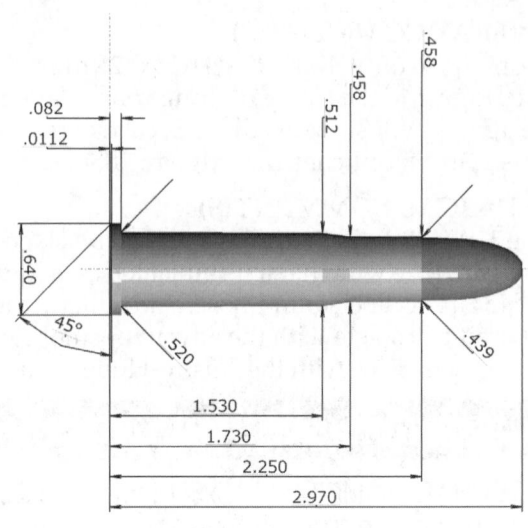

CARTRIDGE BALLISTICS
Max. Average Breech Pressure: N/A
Max. Horizontal Range: 3,100 yds.
Max. Vertical Range: 6,400 ft.

Bullet Weight (gr.)	Bullet Type	Muzzle Velocity (fps)	Muzzle Energy (ft.-lbs.)
387	L-RN	1,380	1,636

CURRENT MANUFACTURER(S)
None

GENERAL COMMENT(S)
Recognizing the need to quickly modernize their infantry rifle and cartridge in 1867, the Spanish Army purchased Remington rolling-block, single-shot rifles and ammunition in 11.15x58Rmm Spanish Remington caliber as a stopgap measure. Meanwhile, Spanish Ordnance personnel began working on the specifications for a new cartridge called the 11.5x57Rmm Reformado. They completed their work in 1871 and the new cartridge was adopted as the M1871 11.5x58Rmm Reformado. The Reformado cartridge was replaced in Spanish military service by the 7x57mm Mauser in 1893.

TECHNICAL COMMENT(S)
The 11.15x58Rmm Spanish Remington cartridge can be identified by its necked case and 387 grain, .439 inch diameter, round-nose lead bullet. Caliber 11.5x57Rmm Reformado cartridges have no neck and a 395 grain, .454 in diameter, semi-pointed, flat-nose bullet. Reformado bullets are jacketed. The 11.15x58Rmm Spanish Remington can be fired in 11.5x57Rmm Reformado chambers, but not vice versa.

11.15x60Rmm MAUSER

ALTERNATE NAME(S): 11.15x60Rmm, .43 Mauser
RELATED CALIBER(S): 9.5x60Rmm Turkish Mauser, 11.15x63Rmm Serbian Mauser

CARTRIDGE HISTORY
Year of Introduction: 1871
Country of Origin: Germany
Designer(s): Peter Paul Mauser
Governing Body: none
Present Status: obsolete

CARTRIDGE DESCRIPTION
Bullet Diameter: .446 in.
Bullet Weight(s): 386 gr.
Rifling Twist Rate: 1 turn in 22 in.
Test Barrel Length: N/A
Case Type: rimmed, necked
Case Material: brass
Primer: large rifle

CARTRIDGE BALLISTICS
Max. Average Breech Pressure: N/A
Max. Horizontal Range: 2,500 yds.
Max. Vertical Range: 5,400 ft.

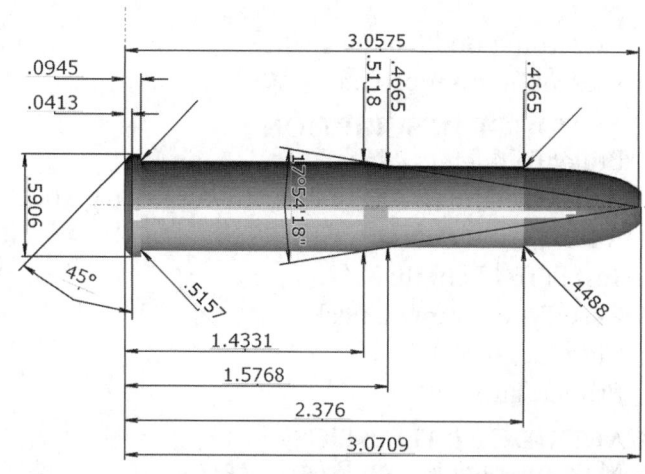

Bullet Weight (gr.)	Bullet Type	Muzzle Velocity (fps)	Muzzle Energy (ft.-lbs.)
386	L-RN	1,425	1,740

CURRENT MANUFACTURER(S)
None

GENERAL COMMENT(S)
Of historical note, this is the first cartridge designed by Peter Paul Mauser. It would influence many of Mauser's future cartridge designs and be followed by a long line of Mauser calibers. This cartridge was a black powder design for the German M71/84 single-shot, bolt-action rifle adopted by the German Army in 1871. The .43 Mauser spawned many imitations by Werndl, Beaumont, Gras, and Remington. The .43 Mauser went on to a distinguished military career and became a popular sporting cartridge as well. In sporting form, it made the transition to smokeless propellants, but its military career was over by 1890.

TECHNICAL COMMENT(S)
This cartridge is typical of Mauser black powder cartridges with a particularly long neck, shallow shoulder and heavily chamfered rim. The purpose of the heavy rim chamfer was to give the residue from the black powder a place to go so as not to jam the action. Bullets used were typical of the time; a lead or paper-patched lead round nose bullet weighing well over 350 grains. Muzzle velocity was modest by today's standards, but typical of its era.

11.3x46Rmm DUTCH BEAUMONT CARBINE, 11.3x50Rmm DUTCH BEAUMONT RIFLE M71, 11.3x52Rmm DUTCH BEAUMONT M71/78

ALTERNATE NAME(S): 11x50Rmm Beaumont, 11mm Dutch, 11.3x51Rmm, 11x51Rmm
RELATED CALIBER(S): .43 Egyptian

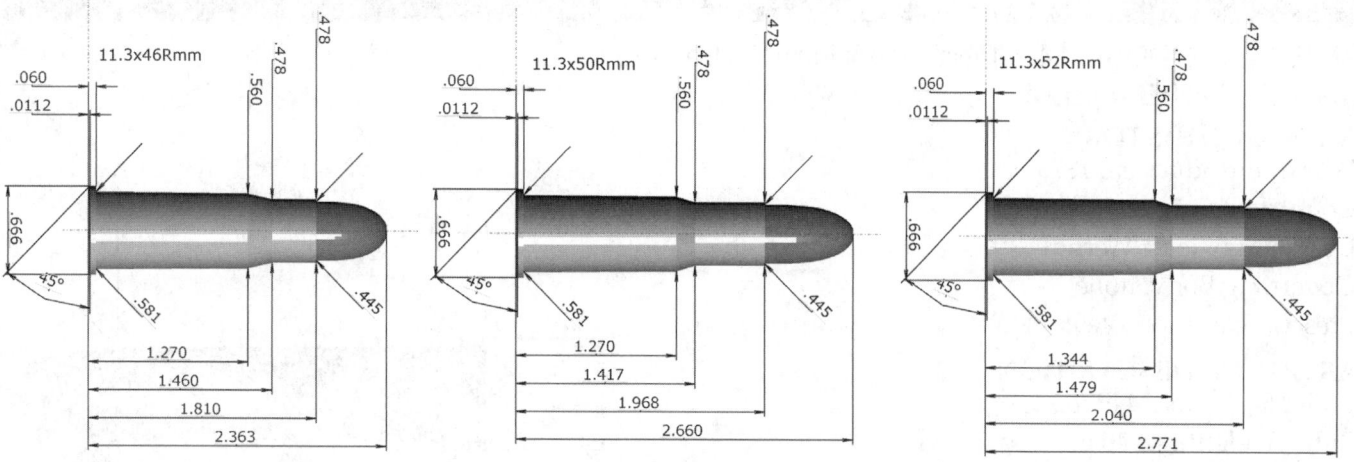

CARTRIDGE HISTORY
Year of Introduction: 1871
Country of Origin: Netherlands
Designer(s): Edouard de Beaumont

Governing Body: none
Present Status: obsolete

CARTRIDGE DESCRIPTION
Bullet Diameter: .445 in.
Bullet Weight(s): 300 gr. (carbine-est.), 386 gr. (M71), 345 gr. (M71/78)
Rifling Twist Rate: 1 turn in 29 in.
Test Barrel Length: N/A
Case Type: rimmed, necked
Case Material: brass
Primer: large rifle

CARTRIDGE BALLISTICS
Max. Average Breech Pressure: N/A
Max. Horizontal Range: 3,000 yds. (carbine), 3,100 yds (M71 and M71/78)
Max. Vertical Range: 5,900 ft. (carbine), 6,400 ft. (M71 and M71/78)

Bullet Weight (gr.)	Bullet Type	Muzzle Velocity (fps)	Muzzle Energy (ft.-lbs.)
386	L-RN	1,380	1,632 (M71)
300	L-RN	1,200 (est.)	959 (carbine-est.)
345	L-RN	1,475	1,666 (M71/78)

CURRENT MANUFACTURER(S)
None

GENERAL COMMENT(S)
When the Dutch Army adopted the Beaumont turn-bolt, single shot rifle in 1871, the 11.3x50Rmm was the cartridge adopted with it. At the same time, the Dutch Army adopted the 11.3x46Rmm Dutch Beaumont M71 Carbine cartridge. In 1888, when the Beaumont rifle was converted to a tubular magazine repeater, the 11x50Rmm cartridge was modified by lengthening the case 2mm and reducing bullet weight to 345 grains. The result was the 11.3x52Rmm Beaumont M71/78 cartridge. Beaumont cartridges in Dutch military service were replaced by the 6.5x53Rmm Mannlicher cartridge in 1892.

TECHNICAL COMMENT(S)
Both the 11x50Rmm and 11.3x52Rmm Beaumont cartridges are easily mistaken for the .43 Egyptian. In fact, the Beaumont and Egyptian cartridges are not the same. However, .43 Egyptian cartridges can be fired in both 11x50Rmm and 11.3x52Rmm Beaumont chambers. In addition, the older, shorter 11x50Rmm M71 Beaumont cartridge can be fired in the 11.3x52Rmm M71/78 Beaumont caliber rifles, but not the reverse.

11.4x50Rmm AUSTRIAN WERNDL M73

ALTERNATE NAME(S): 11.4x50Rmm, 11.4x50Rmm Austrian M73
RELATED CALIBER(S): none

CARTRIDGE HISTORY
Year of Introduction: 1873
Country of Origin: Austria
Designer(s): Josef Werndl
Governing Body: none
Present Status: obsolete

CARTRIDGE DESCRIPTION
Bullet Diameter: .449 in.
Bullet Weight(s): 340 gr.
Rifling Twist Rate: 1 turn in 29 in.
Test Barrel Length: N/A
Case Type: rimmed, straight
Case Material: brass

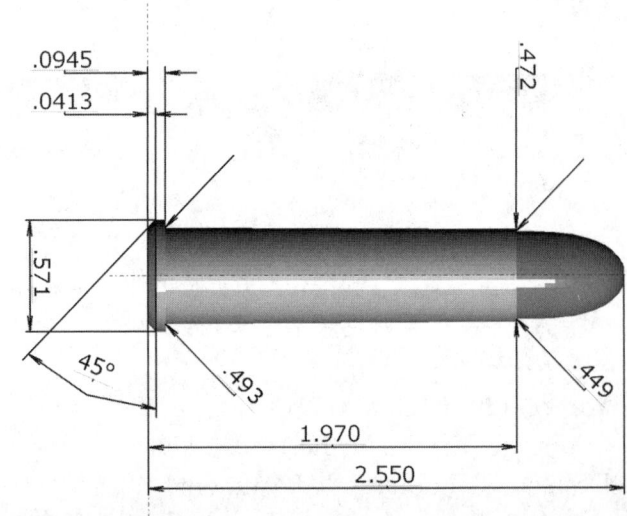

Primer: large rifle

CARTRIDGE BALLISTICS
Max. Average Breech Pressure: N/A
Max. Horizontal Range: 2,950 yds.
Max. Vertical Range: 6,100 ft.

Bullet Weight (gr.)	Bullet Type	Muzzle Velocity (fps)	Muzzle Energy (ft.-lbs.)
340	L-RN	1,270	1,218

CURRENT MANUFACTURER(S)
None

GENERAL COMMENT(S)
From 1873 until 1877, the 11.4x50Rmm Austrian Werndl M73 cartridge was the standard military rifle cartridge for the Austro-Hungarian Army. It was fired in a single-shot rifle designed by Josef Werndl. This cartridge was replaced in Austro-Hungarian military service by the 11.15x58Rmm Werndl cartridge in 1877.

TECHNICAL COMMENT(S)
The 11x50Rmm Werndl is a typical black powder cartridge of the late 1860s and early 1870s. Like its contemporaries, it fires a large caliber, round-nose, lead bullet at a moderate muzzle velocity. Also like its contemporaries, its service life was short. Before smokeless powder changed everything, there was time for one more generation of black powder cartridges with slightly improved ballistic performance.

11.4x53Rmm BRAZILIAN COMBLAIN M89

ALTERNATE NAME(S): 11.3x53Rmm Brazilian, 11.4x53Rmm Brazilian M89, 11.4x53Rmm Comblain
RELATED CALIBER(S): 11x50Rmm Belgian Comblain M81

CARTRIDGE HISTORY
Year of Introduction:1874
Country of Origin: Belgium
Designer(s): Hubert-Josef Comblain
Governing Body: none
Present Status: obsolete

CARTRIDGE DESCRIPTION
Bullet Diameter: .452 in.
Bullet Weight(s): 486 gr.
Rifling Twist Rate: 1 turn in 22 in.
Test Barrel Length: N/A
Case Type: rimmed, necked
Case Material: brass
Primer: large rifle

CARTRIDGE BALLISTICS
Max. Average Breech Pressure: N/A
Max. Horizontal Range: 3,750 yds.
Max. Vertical Range: 7,500 ft.

Bullet Weight (gr.)	Bullet Type	Muzzle Velocity (fps)	Muzzle Energy (ft.-lbs.)
486	L-FN	1,310	1,852

CURRENT MANUFACTURER(S)
None

GENERAL COMMENT(S)
In 1873, the Brazilian military adopted two Belgian Comblain cartridges: the 11x42Rmm carbine and the 11x50Rmm rifle. These were identical to those used by the Belgian Army. Both cartridges remained in front-line Brazilian military service until replaced by the 7x57mm Mauser cartridge in 1894. The Brazilian Army purchased additional Comblain rifles in 1889 chambered for the 11.4x53Rmm Comblain cartridge. The new

cartridge did not prove satisfactory and was quickly discarded. However, the manufacture of 11x50Rmm Comblain ammunition continued in Brazil into the 1920s and the Brazilian police continued using Comblain rifles and ammunition until 1930.

TECHNICAL COMMENT(S)

The Brazilian 11.4x53Rmm cartridge looks very similar to the Belgian 11x50Rmm cartridge, but the two are not interchangeable.

11.43x50Rmm EGYPTIAN

ALTERNATE NAME(S): .43 Egyptian, .43 Egyptian Remington
RELATED CALIBER(S): 11.43x55Rmm Turkish, 11x52Rmm Netherlands Beaumont

CARTRIDGE HISTORY

Year of Introduction: 1870

Country of Origin: U.S.

Designer(s): Remington

Governing Body: none

Present Status: obsolete

CARTRIDGE DESCRIPTION

Bullet Diameter: .448 in.

Bullet Weight(s): 400 gr.

Rifling Twist Rate: 1 turn in 20 in.

Test Barrel Length: N/A

Case Type: rimmed, necked

Case Material: brass

Primer: large rifle

CARTRIDGE BALLISTICS

Max. Average Breech Pressure: N/A

Max. Horizontal Range: 3,600 yds.

Max. Vertical Range: 7,400 ft.

Bullet Weight (gr.)	Bullet Type	Muzzle Velocity (fps)	Muzzle Energy (ft.-lbs.)
400	L-FN	1,330	1,571

CURRENT MANUFACTURER(S)

None

GENERAL COMMENT(S)

In 1870, Remington succeeded in selling their rolling-block, single-shot rifle chambered for this cartridge to the Egyptian Army. Some idea of the value of the Egyptian government order can be gauged from their purchase of 60,000 rifles from 1870 to 1876. To support these rifles in Egyptian military service, Remington loaded an estimated 90 million rounds of this cartridge.

TECHNICAL COMMENT(S)

In appearance, the .43 Egyptian looks very much like the .43 Spanish and 11x52Rmm Netherlands Beaumont. In the case of the Netherlands Beaumont, the similarity goes much deeper as both cartridges are interchangeable. Design of the .43 Egyptian cartridge case follows typical black powder practice – a rimmed, very long necked case, and a paper-patched round-nose lead bullet. Muzzle velocity is comparable to the .43 Spanish (also a Remington design) but about 7% lower than the German .43 Mauser cartridge. The .43 Egyptian cartridge made the transition to smokeless powder, but as a commercial cartridge for hunting.

11.43x55Rmm TURKISH

ALTERNATE NAME(S): .45 Peabody-Martini, .450 Turkish Peabody-Martini, 11.45mm Turkish
RELATED CALIBER(S): .43 Egyptian, 11mm Beaumont M71

CARTRIDGE HISTORY
Year of Introduction: 1874
Country of Origin: Britain
Designer(s): N/A
Governing Body: none
Present Status: obsolete

CARTRIDGE DESCRIPTION
Bullet Diameter: .447 in.
Bullet Weight(s): 486 gr.
Rifling Twist Rate: 1 turn in 22 in.
Test Barrel Length: N/A
Case Type: brass
Case Material: rimmed, necked
Primer: large rifle

CARTRIDGE BALLISTICS
Max. Average Breech Pressure: N/A
Max. Horizontal Range: 3,600 yds.
Max. Vertical Range: 7,400 ft.

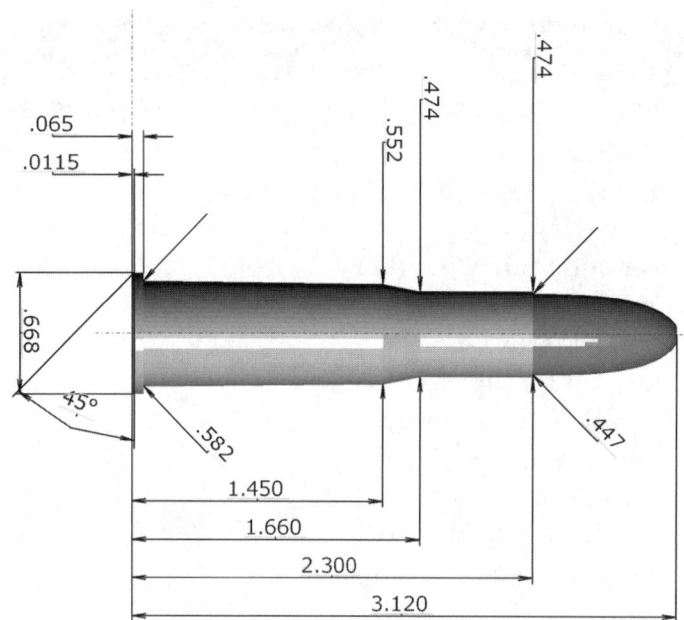

Bullet Weight (gr.)	Bullet Type	Muzzle Velocity (fps)	Muzzle Energy (ft.-lbs.)
486	L-RN or FMJ	1,265	1,727

CURRENT MANUFACTURER(S)
None

GENERAL COMMENT(S)
In 1874, the Turkish Army adopted the single-shot, falling-block, Peabody-Martini rifle together with the new 11.43x55Rmm Turkish cartridge. Thus did fate set the stage for the first battle in history where quick-firing rifles chambered for self-contained, metallic cartridges changed infantry tactics forever. By 1877, Turkey was at war with Russia and Romania. The war was not going well for Turkey when Osman Pasha established a defense line at Plevna, about 70 miles south of Bucharest in Romania. The Turks dug in and set up their range markers in 100 yard increments out to some 3,000 yards. When the Russians launched a massive attack on July 30th, they were met by massed plunging fire from the Peabody-Martini rifles beginning at 3,000 yards. At 2,000 yards the Russian casualties began to mount much more quickly. At 1,000 yards, the Turkish rifle fire devastated the Russian ranks to the point that at 600 yards they began to break up into smaller groups. Still they came on. At 200 yards, the Turkish rifleman put down their Peabody-Martini rifles and picked up their new .44 caliber Winchester Model 66 lever action rifles. With these, they poured fire into the Russian ranks before withdrawing to their second line of defense where the entire process began all over again. The Russian Army lost over 7,300 men before their attack broke down and they retreated under harassing fire once again from the Peabody-Martini rifles. On September 11th, the Russian Army together with their Romanian allies launched a second, even more massive attack, on the Turkish positions. The Turkish riflemen followed their earlier tactics. By the end of the day, the Russians lost 12,800 men and the Romanians another 2,550. The next day, another Russian attack resulted in a further 8,000 men killed. The battles at Plevna cost the Russian and Romanian armies over 33,500 men. However, Plevna proved only a delay and Turkey lost the war in 1878. But not before the Turkish Army ordered 140,000 more Winchester M66 rifles. The lesson of Plevna was not lost on military staffs throughout the world. The combined technology of self-contained, metallic cartridges and quick-firing rifles capable of firing accurately at long ranges had clearly put an end to Napoleonic tactics of massed ranks of infantry. The Turkish Army eventually retired their trusty 11.43x55Rmm in 1887 when they adopted the German 9.5x60Rmm Turkish Mauser cartridge.

TECHNICAL COMMENT(S)
The 11.43x55Rmm Turkish was a typical black powder cartridge of that era with a rimmed, necked case and a heavy, paper-patched, round-nose, lead bullet. However, at 486 grains, the bullet was heavier than normal, which gave it a range of over 3,000 yards using plunging fire. In addition, it was quite accurate in direct fire to 700 yards. A soldier was quite capable of firing 17 aimed shots per minute with this cartridge. However, it was not the ballistic properties of the cartridge which counted so much as its tactical advantage which the Turks exploited.

.45-70 GOVERNMENT

ALTERNATE NAME(S): .45-70, .45-70 Gov., .45-70-405, .45-70-500, .45 U.S. Army M73, .45 Springfield, .45 Trapdoor, 11.4x53.5Rmm
RELATED CALIBER(S): .50-70 Government

CARTRIDGE HISTORY
Year of Introduction: 1873
Country of Origin: U.S.
Designer(s): N/A
Governing Body: SAAMI
Present Status: obsolete

CARTRIDGE DESCRIPTION
Bullet Diameter: .458 in.
Bullet Weight(s): 405-500 gr.
Rifling Twist Rate: 1 turn in 20 in.
Test Barrel Length: N/A
Case Type: rimmed, straight
Case Material: brass, tin plated
Primer Size: large rifle

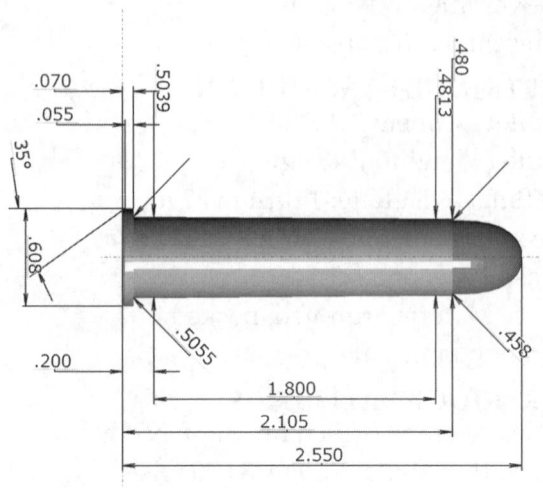

CARTRIDGE BALLISTICS
Max. Average Breech Pressure: 31,908 psi.
Max. Horizontal Range: 3,500 yds.
Max. Vertical Range: 7,900 ft.

Bullet Weight (gr.)	Bullet Type	Muzzle Velocity (fps)	Muzzle Energy (ft.-lbs.)
405 (Carbine)	LRN	1,330	1,590
500 (Rifle)	LRN	1,100	1,342

CURRENT MANUFACTURER(S)
Federal, Remington, Winchester, Cor-Bon, PMC

GENERAL COMMENT(S)
This was the cartridge that, in the hands of the U.S. Army, tamed the American West in the 1870s. It was standard issue to cavalry units such as Gen. George Custer's at the battle of the Little Big Horn. By 1892, the .45-70 was obsolete. It was replaced in front line U.S. Army service by the .30-40 Krag and the .45-70 relegated to the reserves and state national guard units. However, during the Spanish-American War, many American troops sent to Cuba were armed with .45-70 caliber rifles. They found themselves uncomfortably outranged by the 7x57mm Mauser rifles of the Spanish Army.

TECHNICAL COMMENT(S)
The .45-70 cartridge was loaded with 70 grains of black powder. The 405 grain bullet was intended for use in cavalry carbines to reduce the recoil. The 500 grain bullet was issued to infantry units. Both bullets were lead round nose designs that were well-known for their knock-down power given a fair hit on the target. Ammunition in this caliber for government use had a tin-plated brass cartridge case to prevent damage to the brass by black powder.

11.5x57Rmm SPANISH REFORMADO

ALTERNATE NAME(S): 11.5x57Rmm Spanish, 11.5x57Rmm Reformado
RELATED CALIBER(S): 11.15x58Rmm Spanish Remington

CARTRIDGE HISTORY
Year of Introduction: 1871
Country of Origin: Spain
Designer(s): N/A

Governing Body: none
Present Status: obsolete

CARTRIDGE DESCRIPTION
Bullet Diameter: .454 in.
Bullet Weight(s): 395 gr.
Rifling Twist Rate: 1 turn in 20 in.
Test Barrel Length: N/A
Case Type: rimmed, double tapered body
Case Material: brass
Primer: large rifle

CARTRIDGE BALLISTICS
Max. Average Breech Pressure: N/A
Max. Horizontal Range: 3,700 yds.
Max. Vertical Range: 7,600 ft.

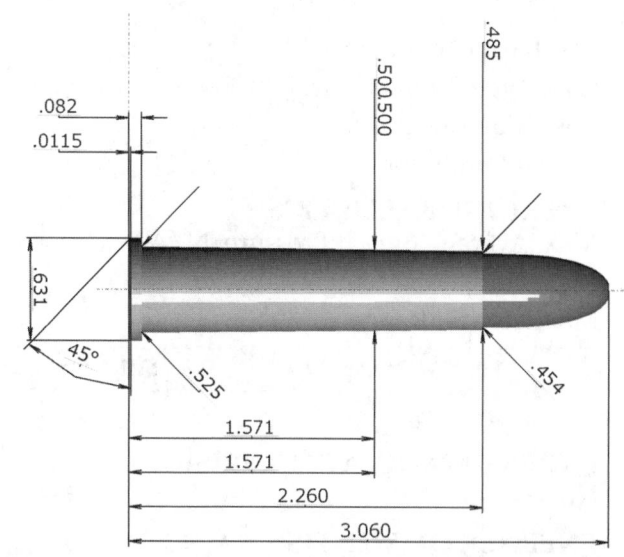

Bullet Weight (gr.)	Bullet Type	Muzzle Velocity (fps)	Muzzle Energy (ft.-lbs.)
395	FMJ-semi-pointed	1,280	1,437

CURRENT MANUFACTURER(S)
None

GENERAL COMMENT(S)
Recognizing the need to quickly modernize their infantry rifle and cartridge in 1867, the Spanish Army purchased Remington rolling-block, single-shot rifles and ammunition in 11.15x57Rmm Spanish Remington caliber as a stopgap measure. Meanwhile, Spanish Ordnance personnel began working on the specifications for a new cartridge called the 11.5x57Rmm Reformado. They completed their work in 1871 and the new cartridge was adopted as the M1871 11.5x57Rmm Reformado. The Reformado cartridge was replaced in Spanish military service by the 7x57mm Mauser in 1893. During the Spanish-American War, U.S. troops captured reserve stores of rifles and Reformado ammunition in Cuba. Many U.S. soldiers thought this ammunition was loaded with poisoned bullets due to the green verdigris on the bullets cause by the hot, humid climate.

TECHNICAL COMMENT(S)
The new cartridge was similar to the old in that it had a rimmed case of approximately the same length and caliber. However, the Reformado case was loaded with a .454 in. diameter bullet while the 11.15x57Rmm Remington used a .439 inch diameter bullet. The Reformado case was 1mm shorter and had no neck, although it did have a double taper. The case mouth, base and rim of the Reformado were slightly larger in diameter than the Remington. While the 11.15x58Rmm Remington was loaded with a lead, round-nose bullet, the Reformado was loaded with a jacketed semi-pointed, flat tip bullet. If necessary, the 11.15x58Rmm Remington ammunition could be fired in the Reformado chamber, but not vice versa.

11.7x51Rmm DANISH REMINGTON

ALTERNATE NAME(S): 11.7x51Rmm Danish M67/96, 11.7mm Danish Remington Centerfire, 11.43mm Danish Remington M/67/96

RELATED CALIBER(S): .45-70 Gov't.

CARTRIDGE HISTORY
Year of Introduction: 1896 (centerfire version)
Country of Origin: U.S.
Designer(s): Remington
Governing Body: none
Present Status: obsolete

CARTRIDGE DESCRIPTION
Bullet Diameter: .455 in.
Bullet Weight(s): 387 gr.
Rifling Twist Rate: 1 turn in 29.5 in.

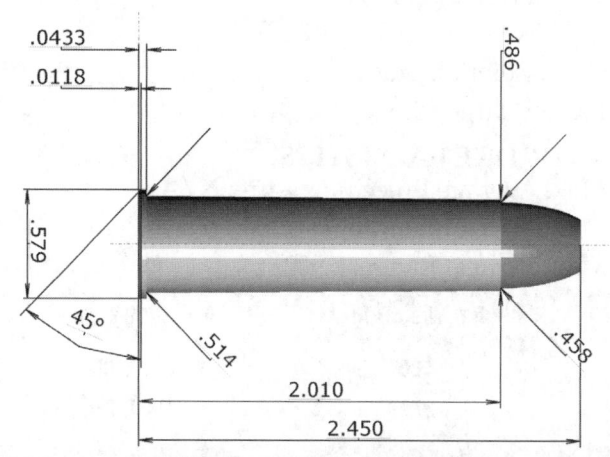

Test Barrel Length: N/A
Case Type: rimmed, straight
Case Material: brass
Primer: large rifle

CARTRIDGE BALLISTICS
Max. Average Breech Pressure: N/A
Max. Horizontal Range: 3,050 yds.
Max. Vertical Range: 6,350 ft.

Bullet Weight (gr.)	Bullet Type	Muzzle Velocity (fps)	Muzzle Energy (ft.-lbs.)
387	L-RN	1,345	1,554

CURRENT MANUFACTURER(S)
None

GENERAL COMMENT(S)
In 1867, the Danish Army adopted the Remington rolling-block, single-shot rifle in 11.7x42Rmm rimfire. In 1896, the thrifty Danes altered their obsolete Remington rolling-block rimfire rifles to fire this centerfire version of the cartridge.

TECHNICAL COMMENT(S)
When the 11.7x42Rmm Danish Remington rimfire cartridge was taken into Danish military service it was a competitive design offering average ballistic performance for the time. However, by 1896, both the rifle and cartridge were badly obsolete and altering an obsolete rimfire rifle for a centerfire cartridge with inadequate ballistic performance did nothing to change the situation. The 11.7mm Danish rimfire cartridge was loaded with black powder and a lead bullet while the centerfire cartridge was loaded with smokeless propellant and a jacketed bullet.

.500/450 No. 1 and No. 2 MUSKET

ALTERNATE NAME(S): none
RELATED CALIBER(S):.500/450 No. 1 and No. 2 Express

CARTRIDGE HISTORY
Year of Introduction: circa 1875
Country of Origin: Britain
Designer(s): N/A
Governing Body: none
Present Status: obsolete

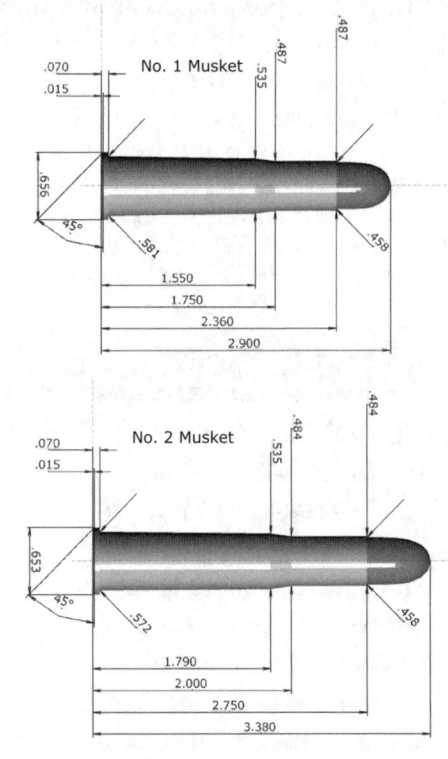

CARTRIDGE DESCRIPTION
Bullet Diameter: .458 in.
Bullet Weight(s): 480 gr.
Rifling Twist Rate: N/A
Test Barrel Length: N/A
Case Type: rimmed, necked
Case Material: brass
Primer: large rifle

CARTRIDGE BALLISTICS
Max. Average Breech Pressure: N/A
Max. Horizontal Range: 4,000 yds.
Max. Vertical Range: 7,900 ft.

Bullet Weight (gr.)	Bullet Type	Muzzle Velocity (fps)	Muzzle Energy (ft.-lbs.)
480	L-RN	1,300	1,799 (No. 2 Musket)
270	L-RN	1,900	2,165 (No. 1 Express)

CURRENT MANUFACTURER(S)
None

GENERAL COMMENT(S)
The .500/450 No. 1 and No. 2 military cartridges were made in Britain by Eley and others for the export market. Over the years, a large number of case lengths and loads were offered in confusing variety. Westley Richards has been credited with designing both of the above which were the most common.

TECHNICAL COMMENT(S)
As military cartridges loaded with military service bullets, these cartridges were not effective for most types of hunting. For this reason, Westley Richards designed two cartridges based on them with sporting bullets and improved ballistic performance.

.5 in. VICKERS

ALTERNATE NAME(S): 12.7x80mm, .5 in. Vickers Mark C
RELATED CALIBER(S): 13.2x99Rmm Breda

CARTRIDGE HISTORY
Year of Introduction: 1922

Country of Origin: Britain

Designer(s): Vickers-Armstrong

Governing Body: N/A

Present Status: obsolete

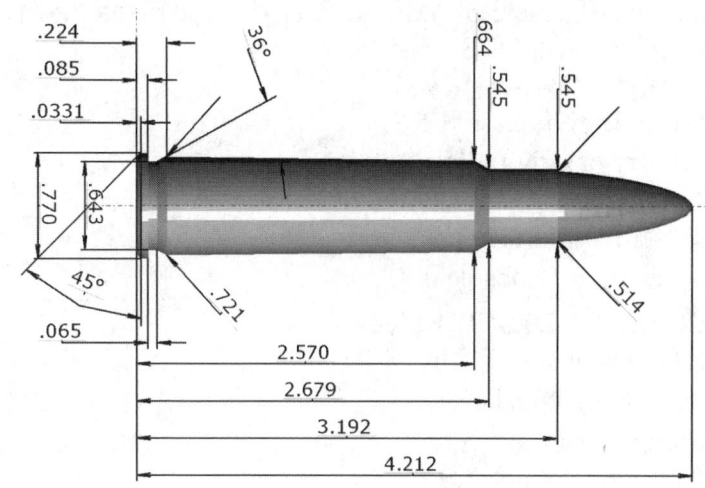

CARTRIDGE DESCRIPTION
Bullet Diameter: .514 in.

Bullet Weight(s): 580 gr.

Rifling Twist Rate: N/A

Test Barrel Length: N/A

Case Type: rimless, necked

Case Material: brass

Primer: 12.7mm Berdan

CARTRIDGE BALLISTICS
Max. Average Breech Pressure: N/A

Max. Horizontal Range: 3,400 yds.

Max. Vertical Range: 6,750 ft.

Bullet Weight (gr.)	Bullet Type	Muzzle Velocity (fps)	Muzzle Energy (ft.-lbs.)
580	FMJ-Ball	2,470	7,856

CURRENT MANUFACTURER(S)
None

GENERAL COMMENT(S)
With the conclusion of World War I in November, 1918, the battlefield potential of the German 13x92SRmm TUF cartridge as an infantry anti-tank cartridge and heavy machine gun cartridge was not lost on the participant nations. Development programs were begun immediately in the U.S., France, Italy, Russia and Britain. In the early 1920s, the U.S. adopted the .50 Browning Machine Gun (BMG) cartridge and France the 13.2x99mm Hotchkiss. Meanwhile, Italy adopted the 12.7x81SRmm Breda cartridge along with Spain, Hungary and Japan. The Soviet Union caught up in 1930 with their 12.7x108mm DShK.

Britain did not neglect this area of development either. In 1922, they adopted the .5 in. Vickers cartridge which was a rimless variant of the later Italian 12.7x81SRmm Breda. The .5 in. Vickers remained in British military service until the early 1950s when it was replaced by the .50 BMG when NATO adopted the same. While the British Army and Royal Navy used the .5 in. Vickers, the Royal Air Force remained uninterested.

TECHNICAL COMMENT(S)
Ballistic performance of the .5 in. Vickers cartridge is not in the same league as the .50 BMG, 13.2x99mm or

12.7x108mm cartridges. The bullet is substantially lighter and the muzzle velocity lower. This made it unsuitable as an infantry anti-tank cartridge, forcing the British Army to adopt the .55 Boys cartridge for that purpose. For ground combat applications, especially when mounted on vehicles or ships, it provided barely adequate performance. While the Royal Air Force refused it for air combat, the Italian and Japanese air forces found the 12.7x81SRmm version effective for that purpose.

Four different bullets were developed for the .5 in. Vickers Class "C" machine guns: Ball, Tracer, Armor-Piercing Tracer, and Incendiary.

Recognizing the lack of ballistic performance, Vickers introduced a new, more powerful cartridge in the early 1930s. This new, larger cartridge was designated the .5 in. Vickers V/664 or 12.7x120mm. While it was loaded with bullets of similar weight to those of the .50 BMG, muzzle velocity remained lower and the new cartridge was not taken into British military service.

12.7x81SRmm ITALIAN BREDA

ALTERNATE NAME(S): 12.7x81SRmm, 12.7mm Breda, 12.7mm Type 1, 12.7mm M36, 12.7mm Japanese
RELATED CALIBER(S): .5 in. Vickers

CARTRIDGE HISTORY
Year of Introduction: 1936
Country of Origin: Italy
Designer(s): Breda
Governing Body: none
Present Status: obsolete

CARTRIDGE DESCRIPTION
Bullet Diameter: .512 in.
Bullet Weight(s): 565 gr.
Rifling Twist Rate: N/A
Test Barrel Length: N/A
Case Type: semi-rimmed, necked
Case Material: brass or steel
Primer: N/A

CARTRIDGE BALLISTICS
Max. Average Breech Pressure: N/A
Max. Horizontal Range: 3,900 yds.
Max. Vertical Range: 8,200 ft.

Bullet Weight (gr.)	Bullet Type	Muzzle Velocity (fps)	Muzzle Energy (ft.-lbs.)
565	Ball	2,430	7,407

CURRENT MANUFACTURER(S)
None

GENERAL COMMENT(S)
This cartridge was adopted by the armed forces of Italy, Japan, Spain and Hungary just prior to World War II. Judging from user reports, it gave them satisfactory service throughout that conflict. During its service life, a wide variety of loadings were developed including ball, armor-piercing, observation, incendiary, explosive and tracer as well as various combination types such as API-T, I-T, AP-I. With the end of the War in 1945, this cartridge quickly disappeared as it was significantly inferior in ballistic performance to both the .50 BMG and the Soviet 12.7x108mm.

TECHNICAL COMMENT(S)
From a design standpoint, the 12.7x81SRmm Breda cartridge was a .5 in. Vickers cartridge case with a semi-rimmed head. However, the two cartridges are not interchangeable. If anything, the 12.7x81SRmm Breda cartridge offered even lower ballistic performance than that of the notoriously poor .5 in. Vickers. Like its Britannic cousin, this was due entirely to its relatively low maximum average chamber pressure. However, its limited case volume and designs of guns chambering it prevented any attempt at product improvement.

.50 U.S. CARBINE

ALTERNATE NAME(S): none
RELATED CALIBER(S): none

CARTRIDGE HISTORY
Year of Introduction: 1866
Country of Origin: U.S.
Designer(s): N/A
Governing Body: none
Present Status: obsolete

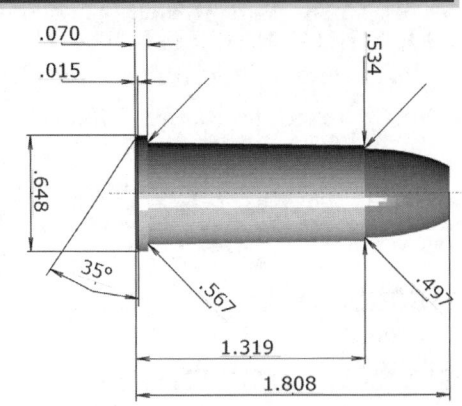

CARTRIDGE DESCRIPTION
Bullet Diameter: .515 in.
Bullet Weight(s): 400 gr.
Rifling Twist Rate: N/A
Test Barrel Length: N/A
Case Type: rimmed, straight
Case Material: brass
Primer: large rifle

CARTRIDGE BALLISTICS
Max. Average Breech Pressure: N/A
Max. Horizontal Range: 3,350 yds.
Max. Vertical Range: 6,800 ft.

Bullet Weight (gr.)	Bullet Type	Muzzle Velocity (fps)	Muzzle Energy (ft.-lbs.)
400	L-FN	1,200	1,279 (est.)

CURRENT MANUFACTURER(S)
None

GENERAL COMMENT(S)
This is the carbine version of the .50-70 Government cartridge with a shorter case and reduced powder charge. It was used in Remington rolling-block carbines in the early 1870s.

TECHNICAL COMMENT(S)
As many other black powder military carbine cartridges, the .50 U.S. Carbine shares the rim and case head dimensions with the .50-70 service rifle cartridge, but its case is .59 inches shorter. The carbine and its reduced power cartridge were issued to cavalry, artillery and engineer troops.

.50 SPOTTER-TRACER M48A1

ALTERNATE NAME(S): 12.7x76mm Spotter M48A1, 12.7mm Spotter M48A1, 12.7mm Spotter-Tracer, .50 BAT
RELATED CALIBER(S): 12.7x99mm BMG

CARTRIDGE HISTORY
Year of Introduction: early 1950s
Country of Origin: U.S.
Designer(s): Frankford Arsenal
Governing Body: none
Present Status: obsolete

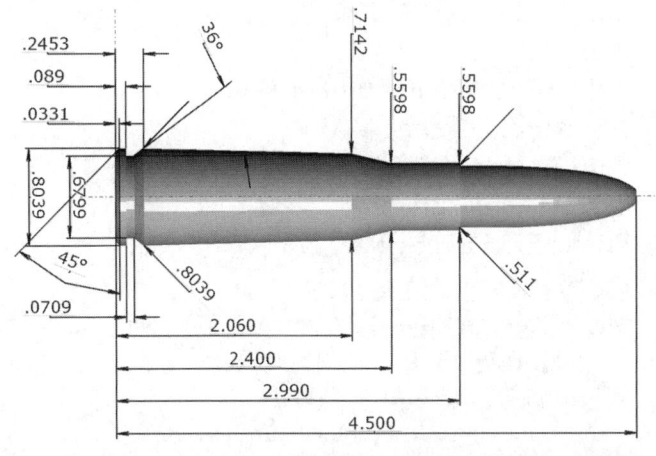

CARTRIDGE DESCRIPTION
Bullet Diameter: .510 in.
Bullet Weight(s): 827 gr.
Rifling Twist Rate: 1 turn in 15 in.
Test Barrel Length: 40
Case Type: rimless, necked

Case Material: brass
Primer: No. 35

CARTRIDGE BALLISTICS

Max. Average Breech Pressure: 55,660 psi.

Max. Horizontal Range: 7,450 yds.

Max. Vertical Range: 14,250 ft.

Bullet Weight (gr.)	Bullet Type	Muzzle Velocity (fps)	Muzzle Energy (ft.-lbs.)
827	Spotter-Tracer	1,745	5,591

CURRENT MANUFACTURER(S)

None

GENERAL COMMENT(S)

The .50 Spotter-Tracer was fired from the semi-automatic M8 Spotting Rifle mounted on top of the 106mm recoilless rifle. The M48A1 bullet duplicated the trajectory of the 106mm projectile. When the .50 Spotter-Tracer bullet was fired, the gunner followed the trajectory by watching the tracer. When the bullet struck the target, it made a bright flash and a puff of smoke. This told the 106mm gunner he was on target and could fire the main weapon with a good chance of hitting the target. The M8 Spotting rifle was not intended for anti-personnel use. Both the .50 Spotter-Tracer and the 106mm recoilless rifle are now obsolete.

TECHNICAL COMMENT(S)

The M48A1 bullet is a complex assembly consisting of a gilding metal jacket with an ignitor and two tracer elements held in a lead filler in the base. In front of the lead base is a steel core with an aluminum nose holding 31.6 grains of incendiary/smoke powder. A detonator crimped into the nose of the bullet exploded on contact with the target setting off, in turn, the incendiary/smoke powder. The tracer element was visible to 1,650 yards. The M48A1 bullet was the only one used in the .50 Spotter-Tracer cartridge. Essentially, the 12.7x77mm cartridge case was a 12.7x99mm BMG case shortened about one inch. The same head, rim, and primer were used in both. The muzzle velocity of the M48A1 Spotter-Tracer bullet was about 40% less than the .50 BMG cartridge. The maximum average chamber pressure of the .50 Spotter-Tracer cartridge was reduced about 10% compared to the .50 BMG cartridge.

.50-70 GOVERNMENT

ALTERNATE NAME(S): .50-70 Musket
RELATED CALIBER(S): .50-60-400 Joslyn rimfire

CARTRIDGE HISTORY

Year of Introduction: 1866

Country of Origin: U.S.

Designer(s): N/A

Governing Body: none

Present Status: obsolete

CARTRIDGE DESCRIPTION

Bullet Diameter: .515 in.

Bullet Weight(s): 450 gr.

Rifling Twist Rate: 1 turn in 24 in.

Test Barrel Length: N/A

Case Type: rimmed, straight

Case Material: brass

Primer Size: large rifle

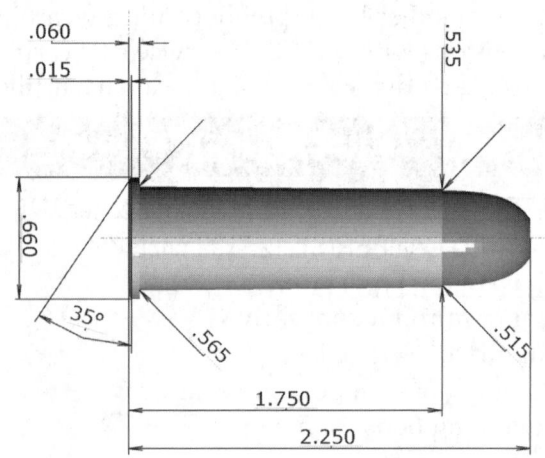

CARTRIDGE BALLISTICS

Max. Average Breech Pressure: 25,000 psi (est.)

Max. Horizontal Range: 3,500 yds.

Max. Vertical Range: 7,500 ft.

Bullet Weight (gr.)	Bullet Type	Muzzle Velocity (fps)	Muzzle Energy (ft.-lbs.)
450	L-RN	1,110	1,230

CURRENT MANUFACTURER(S)
None

GENERAL COMMENT(S)
From 1866 to 1873, this was the standard military service cartridge of the U.S. Army. It was replaced by the .45-70 Government cartridge in 1873. The .50-70 was fired in various single-shot rifles.

TECHNICAL COMMENT(S)
The 450 grain lead, round nose bullet of the .50-70 was felt to be very effective on buffalo and other heavy game as well as human targets. With the end of its short military career, the .50-70 remained a sporting cartridge until well into the 20th century.

13.2x99mm HOTCHKISS

ALTERNATE NAME(S): 13.2mm Hotchkiss Long, 13.2mm Model 1930, 13.2mm Breda, 13.2mm Type 93
RELATED CALIBER(S): .50 BMG, 12.7x108mm Soviet, 13x92SRmm Mauser

CARTRIDGE HISTORY
Year of Introduction: 1930
Country of Origin: France
Designer(s): Hotchkiss
Governing Body: none
Present Status: obsolete

CARTRIDGE DESCRIPTION
Bullet Diameter: .531 in.
Bullet Weight(s): 791 gr.
Rifling Twist Rate: N/A
Test Barrel Length: N/A
Case Type: rimless, necked
Case Material: brass
Primer: N/A

CARTRIDGE BALLISTICS
Max. Average Breech Pressure: N/A
Max. Horizontal Range: 8,000 yds.
Max. Vertical Range: 16,000 ft.

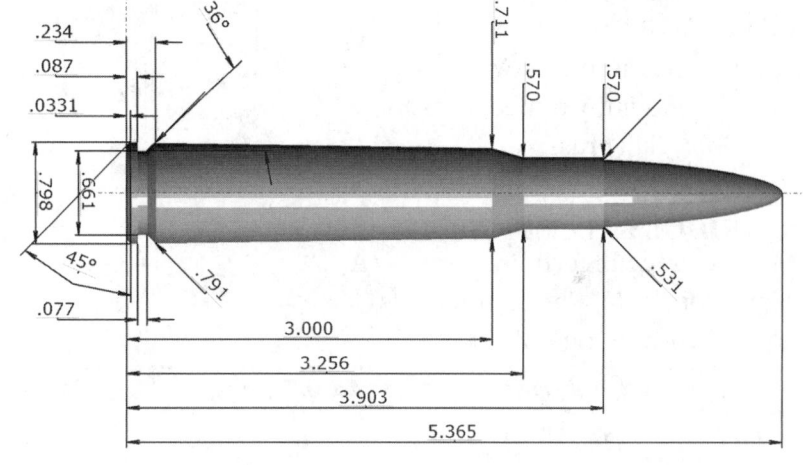

Bullet Weight (gr.)	Bullet Type	Muzzle Velocity (fps)	Muzzle Energy (ft.-lbs.)
791	FMJ BT	2,210	8,578

CURRENT MANUFACTURER(S)
None

GENERAL COMMENT(S)
This was the heavy machine gun cartridge developed for the French Army after World War I in response to the German wartime development of the 13x92SRmm Mauser (TUF). Although Hotchkiss completed development in the early 1920s, it was not adopted by the French Army until 1930. Following the French lead, it was adopted shortly thereafter by the armies of Italy, Japan, China and others. The 13.2x99mm Hotchkiss cartridge enjoyed a notably undistinguished career during World War II and disappeared quickly after the War ended in 1945.

TECHNICAL COMMENT(S)
There was nothing wrong with the basic design of the 13.2x99mm Hotchkiss cartridge. The case was a modern, rimless, necked design similar to the .50 BMG. And, the 13.2mm bullets were of similar weight and variety to other cartridges in this class. In addition, several countries, such as Japan, used this cartridge in Browning machine guns similar to the American M2 which was chambered for the .50 BMG. With all these things going for it, why must the 13.2x99mm Hotchkiss cartridge be judged a failure? The main reason seems to be the lack

of ballistic performance in comparison to the 12.7x99mm BMG. For example, the .50 BMG fired its 720 grain, M2, Ball bullet at a muzzle velocity of 2,810 fps. in the process generating 12,600 ft.-lbs. of muzzle energy. While the 791 grain ball bullet of the 13.2x99mm Hotchkiss cartridge exited the muzzle at a leisurely 2,210 fps. generating 8,578 ft.-lbs. of muzzle energy. In other words, the 13.2x99mm cartridge offered 21% lower muzzle velocity and 32% less muzzle energy than the .50 BMG. During a war, ballistic handicaps are seldom tolerated quietly by the users. Obviously, the 13.2x99mm cartridge was loaded to a much lower maximum average chamber pressure than the .50 BMG cartridge. This handicap prevented the 13.2x99mm cartridge from reaching its full ballistic potential, sealing its doom.

13x92SRmm MAUSER ANTI-TANK (TUF)

ALTERNATE NAME(S): 13x92SRmm, 13mm TUF, 13mm T-Patrone
RELATED CALIBER(S): .50 BMG, 13.2x99mm Hotchkiss, 7.92x94mm Panzerbuchse

CARTRIDGE HISTORY
Year of Introduction: 1917
Country of Origin: Germany
Designer(s): Mauser
Governing Body: none
Present Status: obsolete

CARTRIDGE DESCRIPTION
Bullet Diameter: .522 in.
Bullet Weight(s): 770 gr.
Rifling Twist Rate: N/A
Test Barrel Length: N/A
Case Type: semi-rimmed, necked
Case Material: brass
Primer: N/A

CARTRIDGE BALLISTICS
Max. Average Breech Pressure: N/A
Max. Horizontal Range: 8,200 yds.
Max. Vertical Range: 17,000 ft.

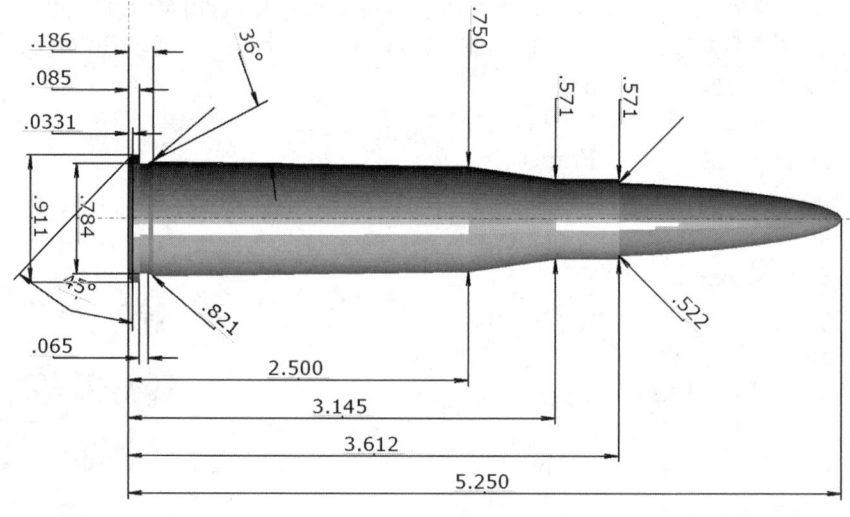

Bullet Weight (gr.)	Bullet Type	Muzzle Velocity (fps)	Muzzle Energy (ft.-lbs.)
770	AP	2,650	12,005

CURRENT MANUFACTURER(S)
None

GENERAL COMMENT(S)
By 1917, trench warfare brought World War I to a stalemate. To break this impasse, the British and French introduced the first tanks onto the battlefield in 1917. Although armor-piercing ammunition in infantry rifle calibers was available, the new tanks were immune to infantry rifle and machine gun fire, even with armor piercing ammunition. The German Army desperately needed a new infantry weapon to counter the new tanks. The problem was put in the hands of Mauser on November 27, 1917 and just six days later drawings for the new 13x92SRmm Mauser cartridge were shown to the German General Staff. Testing began in January, 1918 followed by full-scale production in May of the same year. A new heavy machine gun firing the new 13x92SRmm Mauser cartridge was put into accelerated development. Called the 13x92SRmm "Tank und Flieger" (TUF) maschinengeweher (machine gun), it was intended for the dual role of anti-tank and anti-aircraft fire. While the new TUF machine gun was being developed, as a stopgap measure to meet the urgent need, Mauser scaled up their seminal M98 bolt-action rifle to accept the new cartridge. While the new rifle seemed ungainly at first, it worked, and the German troops in the trenches could never get enough of them. The 13x92SRmm Mauser is historically significant for four reasons. First, it created a new class of infantry heavy machine gun. Second, it served as the inspiration and benchmark for the development of the .50 BMG, 13x99mm Hotchkiss and 12.7x108mm Soviet cartridges for the new heavy machine guns. Third, it created a new class of infantry anti-tank cartridges such as the 7.92x94mm Panzerbuchs, 7.92x107 Polish ATR, .55 Boys ATR and Soviet 14.5x114mm PTRD/PTRS. Fourth, it renewed interest in and further development of small caliber armor-piercing bullets. These four trends continue to this day.

TECHNICAL COMMENT(S)

The 770 grain spitzer boat-tail bullet of the 13x92SRmm Mauser cartridge was capable of penetrating 22mm (.866 inches) of steel armor at an impact angle of 0 degrees (dead on) at 100 meters. The bullet was a conventional design, with a gilding metal jacket, lead filler and hardened steel core penetrator. While not a sophisticated, state-of-the-art design, it did the job. In addition to bullet weight and core hardness, impact velocity plays a major part in the ability of a bullet to penetrate armor. In the case of the 13x92SRmm cartridge, muzzle velocity was a respectable, but not spectacular, 2,650 fps.

.55 BOYS

ALTERNATE NAME(S): 14x99mm, .55 Boys Mk I or Mk II,
RELATED CALIBER(S): 13x92SRmm Mauser

CARTRIDGE HISTORY

Year of Introduction: 1937
Country of Origin: Britain
Designer(s): Capt. Boys
Governing Body: none
Present Status: obsolete

CARTRIDGE DESCRIPTION

Bullet Diameter: .562 in.
Bullet Weight(s): 926 gr.
Rifling Twist Rate: N/A
Test Barrel Length: 36 in.
Case Type: rimless, belted, necked
Case Material: brass
Primer: N/A

CARTRIDGE BALLISTICS

Max. Average Breech Pressure: N/A
Max. Horizontal Range: 8,450 yds.
Max. Vertical Range: 17,450 ft.

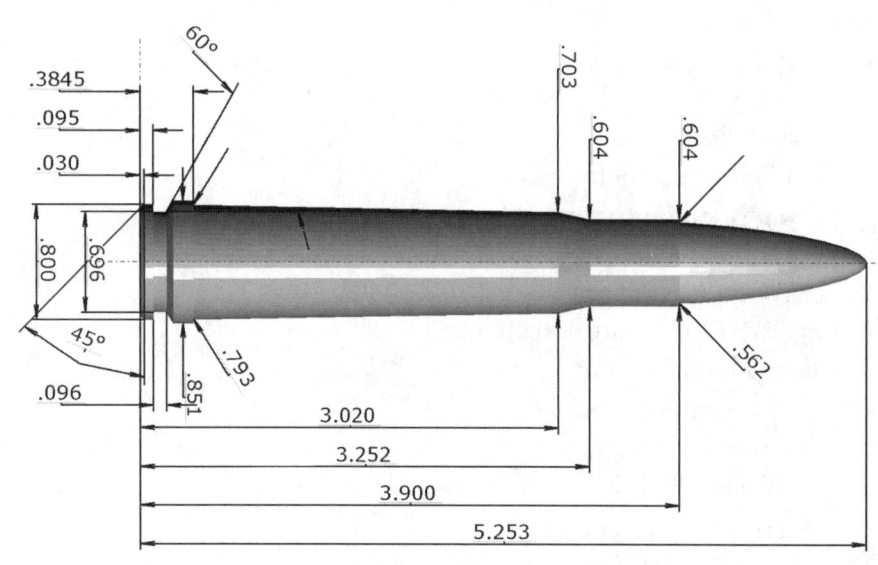

Bullet Weight (gr.)	Bullet Type	Muzzle Velocity (fps)	Muzzle Energy (ft.-lbs.)
926	Ball or AP Mk I	2,495	12,794
741	AP Mk. II	3,000	14,802

CURRENT MANUFACTURER(S)

None

GENERAL COMMENT(S)

By the end of World War II, the British Boys anti-tank rifle had been used all over the world ranging from issue to Home Guard units in 1940 Britain when a German invasion was expected, to Chinese troops fighting the Japanese in the heartland of China. Some U.S. Marine Corps units even used them for short periods. The Boys rifle and its .55 Boys cartridge served throughout World War II, despite its being obsolete by any standard of measure. The existence of the Boys rifle and cartridge goes back to the early 1930s when infantry anti-tank rifles were considered effective against tanks. Capt. Boys, a British officer, determined that the British Army should have such a rifle and cartridge. Accordingly, he designed both which were accepted for British military service in 1937. When World War II broke out in 1939, it became obvious very quickly that the Boys rifle and cartridge were obsolete. In addition, the heavy Boys rifle (weighing nearly 40 pounds!) and its daunting recoil made it unpopular with British troops. By 1943, use of the Boys rifle and cartridge in front-line British Army service in the European theater of operations had become quite limited, however it continued to serve effectively in other areas until the end of World War II in 1945.

TECHNICAL COMMENT(S)

In the early 1930s, the configuration and anticipated tactical use of infantry anti-tank rifle cartridges were rooted in German experience from World War I with their 13x92SRmm Mauser (TUF) cartridge. The .55 Boys cartridge was prototypical of such thinking, in that it used a cartridge case with enough volume to hold a propellant charge capable of driving a large caliber, armor-piercing bullet to a muzzle velocity of approximately 2,600 fps. However, the .55 Boys cartridge case had a unique design feature, it was belted. A variety of different bullets were developed, including armor-piercing (two Marks), ball, tracer and practice ball with a reduced propellant charge. All Boys bullets were of flat base configuration and assembled with cupro-nickel clad, steel jackets. Both the ball and armor-piercing bullets had a steel core in a lead sleeve, the armor-piercing core was hardened. At an impact angle of 60 degrees, the Boys Mark I AP bullet was capable of penetrating 12mm (.47 inches) of armor plate at 100 meters and 10mm (.39 inches) of armor plate at 300 meters. In comparison to other infantry anti-tank cartridges of the time, penetration capabilities of the Boys bullet was about half that of German and Russian designs. A lighter Mark II AP bullet increased muzzle velocity, but it was too little too late to keep the .55 Boys from obsolete.

.577/450 MARTINI-HENRY

ALTERNATE NAME(S): 11.4x59Rmm, 11.43x60Rmm, M.1873
RELATED CALIBER(S): .577 Snider

CARTRIDGE HISTORY
Year of Introduction: 1871
Country of Origin: Britain
Designer(s): N/A
Governing Body: CIP
Present Status: obsolete

CARTRIDGE DESCRIPTION
Bullet Diameter: .465 in.
Bullet Weight(s): 480 gr.
Rifling Twist Rate: 1 turn in 20 in.
Test Barrel Length: 24 in.
Case Type: rimmed, necked
Case Material: brass
Primer Size: large rifle

CARTRIDGE BALLISTICS
Max. Average Breech Pressure: 25,382 psi.
Max. Horizontal Range: 3,500 yds.
Max. Vertical Range: 7,900 ft.

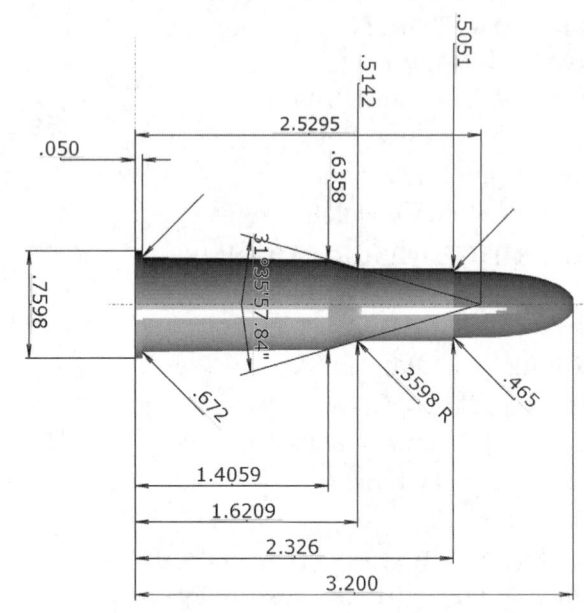

Bullet Weight (gr.)	Bullet Type	Muzzle Velocity (fps)	Muzzle Energy (ft.-lbs.)
480	LRN	1,350	1,940

CURRENT MANUFACTURER(S)
Kynoch

GENERAL COMMENT(S)
On January 22-23, 1879, the .577/450 Martini-Henry entered history from the cartridge boxes of B Company, 24th Regiment of the British Army. During those two days, Lt. John Chard and Lt. Gonville Bromhead with some 140 men defended a remote outpost named Rorke's Drift in Natal, South Africa from a Zulu Army of over 4,000 men. This battle became one of the classic stands of a small, but determined, group of soldiers against overwhelming odds. When the battle was over, some 20,000 rounds of .577/450 M-H had been expended by the defenders.

The .577/450 M-H again entered the headlines in the late 1800s when the British Army took their new .303 British caliber rifles to the Punjab on the northern Indian frontier. To their dismay, they found the .303 caliber bullets would not incapacitate the Pushtun fighters unless struck multiple times. Something had to be done-and fast. As a temporary solution, single-shot rifles in .577/450 M-H caliber were taken from storage and reissued. Problem solved.

TECHNICAL COMMENT(S)
While the .577/450 cartridge did not offer high muzzle velocity, the 480 grain lead bullet had 1,940 ft.-lbs. of energy at the muzzle. Effective range was about 200 yards. Even at that distance, the 480 grain lead bullets were renowned for their knock-down power given a fair hit. All .577/450 M-H ammunition was loaded with black powder. This cartridge did not make the transition to smokeless propellants as it was already obsolete by that time.

.577 SNIDER

ALTERNATE NAME(S): .57 Snider, .577 Snider Mk I, .577 Solid Snider 2 in., 14.7x50Rmm Snider
RELATED CALIBER(S): 577/450 M-H

CARTRIDGE HISTORY

Year of Introduction: 1867

Country of Origin: Britain

Designer(s): Joseph Snider

Governing Body: CIP

Present Status: obsolete

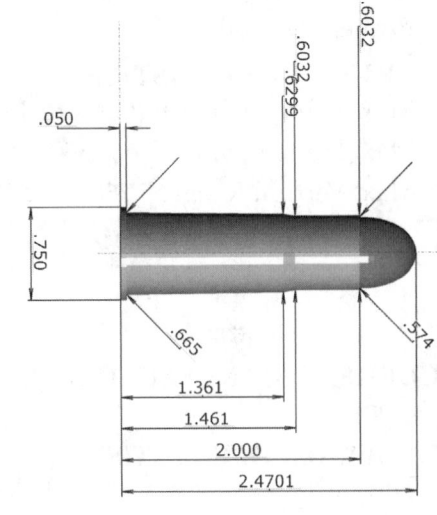

CARTRIDGE DESCRIPTION

Bullet Diameter: .570 in.

Bullet Weight(s): 480 gr.

Rifling Twist Rate: 1 turn in 20 in.

Test Barrel Length: 24 in.

Case Type: rimmed, straight

Case Material: brass

Primer Size: large rifle

CARTRIDGE BALLISTICS

Max. Average Breech Pressure: 21,756 psi.

Max. Horizontal Range: 3,500 yds.

Max. Vertical Range: 7,500 ft.

Bullet Weight (gr.)	Bullet Type	Muzzle Velocity (fps)	Muzzle Energy (ft.-lbs.)
480	LRN	1,250	1,664

CURRENT MANUFACTURER(S)

Kynoch

GENERAL COMMENT(S)

The .577 Snider was the standard British Army rifle cartridge from 1867 until 1871. It was fired in various single-shot rifles including the Martini-Henry. It was replaced in British military service by the .577/450 Martini-Henry cartridge.

TECHNICAL COMMENT(S)

Original .577 Snider cartridges had a paper case with a metal head. Col. Boxer developed a coiled brass case to replace these. Later, a solid drawn brass case was developed and adopted. The massive 480 grain .570 caliber bullet was devastating at ranges of 150 yards or less. Despite this, the .577 Snider cartridge did not prove popular with hunters as many other better cartridges were available.

.58 BERDAN MUSKET, .58 BERDAN CARBINE

ALTERNATE NAME(S): .58 Musket (Berdan), .58 Carbine (Berdan)
RELATED CALIBER(S): none

CARTRIDGE HISTORY

Year of Introduction: 1869

Country of Origin: U.S.

Designer(s): Hiram Berdan

Governing Body: none

Present Status: obsolete

CARTRIDGE DESCRIPTION

Bullet Diameter: .585 in.

Bullet Weight(s): 530 gr.

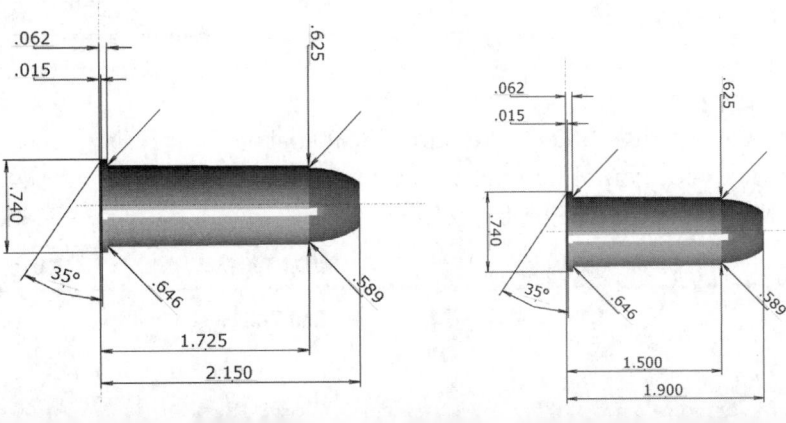

Rifling Twist Rate: N/A

Test Barrel Length: N/A

Case Type: rimmed, straight

Case Material: brass

Primer: large rifle

CARTRIDGE BALLISTICS

Max. Average Breech Pressure: N/A

Max. Horizontal Range: 2,850 yds.

Max. Vertical Range: 5,750 ft.

Bullet Weight (gr.)	Bullet Type	Muzzle Velocity (fps)	Muzzle Energy (ft.-lbs.)
530	L-RN	925	1,012 (carbine)
530	L-RN	1,100	1,420 (musket)

CURRENT MANUFACTURER(S)

None

GENERAL COMMENT(S)

The carbine version of the .58 U.S Musket cartridge with a .656 inch shorter case held half the black powder charge of the Musket version. Both cartridges were used in Colt Berdan muskets and carbines.

TECHNICAL COMMENT(S)

As many other black powder military carbine cartridges, the .58 Berdan Carbine shared the rim and case head dimensions of the .58 Berdan musket cartridge.The carbine and its reduced power cartridge were issued to cavalry, artillery and engineer troops.

.60 ANTI-TANK RIFLE CARTRIDGE

ALTERNATE NAME(S): .60 Machine Gun, 15.2x114mm
RELATED CALIBER(S): 14.5x114mm Soviet

CARTRIDGE HISTORY

Year of Introduction: requirement issued in 1939

Country of Origin: U.S.

Designer(s): Winchester, Frankford Arsenal

Governing Body: none

Present Status: obsolete

CARTRIDGE DESCRIPTION

Bullet Diameter: .6055 in.

Bullet Weight(s): 1,185 gr.

Rifling Twist Rate: 1 turn in 18 in.

Test Barrel Length: 56 in.

Case Type: rimless, necked

Case Material: brass

Primer: No. 35

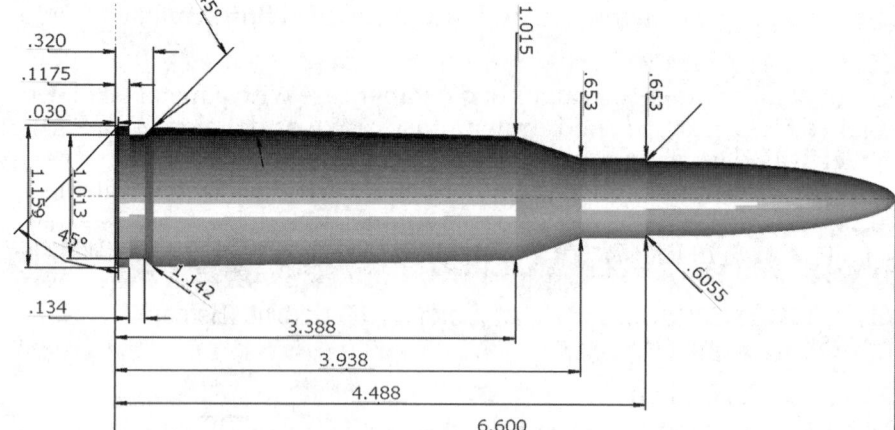

CARTRIDGE BALLISTICS

Max. Average Breech Pressure: 58,000 psi.

Max. Horizontal Range: 7,300 yds.

Max. Vertical Range: 15,500 ft.

Bullet Weight (gr.)	Bullet Type	Muzzle Velocity (fps)	Muzzle Energy (ft.-lbs.)
1,185	Ball T-32	3,450	31,306

CURRENT MANUFACTURER(S)
None

GENERAL COMMENT(S)
Better late than never, the U.S. Army Ordnance Committee approved development of an infantry anti-tank rifle firing a new .60 caliber cartridge in 1939. Ballistic requirements called for a muzzle velocity of approximately 3,500 fps. and a 1,200 grain, armor piercing bullet capable of penetrating 31.75mm (1.25 inches) of armor plate at 100 yards (later increased to 500 yards). Accordingly, a contract was given immediately to Winchester to develop a suitable cartridge case and Frankford Arsenal began developing a suitable bullet. In May, 1943 all work on the .60 caliber anti-tank rifle cartridge was stopped when it was realized that the entire concept of an infantry anti-tank rifle was made obsolete by the development of rocket launchers and recoilless rifles. Work to develop a .60 caliber heavy machine gun cartridge continued into the early 1950s. After manufacture of nearly 3.5 million rounds, this project too was cancelled.

TECHNICAL COMMENT(S)
At the time it was issued, the ballistic requirements for a .60 caliber infantry anti-tank rifle and cartridge set by the U.S. Army Ordnance Committee were at the upper edge of available technology. This required considerable experimentation by Winchester to develop a cartridge case and Frankford Arsenal to develop a bullet. By early 1942, Frankford Arsenal had developed a suitable AP bullet for the T32 cartridge. This bullet had a hardened, manganese-molybdenum steel core with a soft steel ballistic cap and a gilding metal cup base. It could penetrate 1.25 inches of armor plate at 500 yards. This was as far as the Cal. 60 anti-tank rifle cartridge project got before work was stopped and efforts were refocused exclusively on developing a Cal. .60 machine gun cartridge. In retrospect, the U.S. Cal. .60 ATR concept was obsolete before it was started and the efforts to develop this cartridge and bullet were wasted. However had the Cal. .60 cartridge entered U.S. military service, it would have been one of the most powerful infantry anti-tank cartridges in existence.

A Look at the Big Boys' Ballistics

Caliber	Bullet Weight (grains)	Muzzle Velocity (fps.)	Muzzle Energy ft.-lbs.)
12.7x76mm M48 Spotter	827	1,745	5,591
12.7x81mm Breda	565	2,430	7,407
.5 in. Vickers (12.7x81mm)	580	2,470	7,856
12.7x99mm Browning MG	661	2,910	12,427
12.7x108mm Soviet	745	2,755	12,554
13x92SRmm TUF	770	2,650	12,005
13.2x99mm Hotchkiss	791	2,210	8,578
.55 Boys	926	2,495	12,798
14.5x114mm Soviet	979	3,200	22,258

SECTION XI – CENTERFIRE HANDGUN CARTRIDGE PROFILES
CHAPTER 71 : SPORTING REVOLVER - CURRENT

CHAPTER 71

For Cartridge Index see Chapter 101. All drawing dimensions are approximate.

Cartridges for semi-automatic pistols are limited in power by the strength and operation of the gun system as well as the cartridge design. In contrast, revolvers can easily handle heavy calibers as their operation does not depend on the gun system, cartridge feeding, or cartridge power level.

While revolvers have fallen out of favor for personal defense, the powerful new cartridges now offered for revolvers have proven a boon to hunters. Handgun hunting is permitted now in many states. In other areas, hunters carry large caliber magnum revolvers to dispatch downed game and as personal protection from dangerous game at close ranges.

These requirements make the choice of a revolver cartridge clear: it must be powerful enough to cleanly and reliably kill medium game to ranges of 100 yards as well as offer enough close range stopping power for backup applications. This translates into high striking energy that can only be delivered by a large caliber heavy bullet at high muzzle velocity. As the reader can see, such a requirement quickly eliminates handgun cartridges of .38 caliber or less.

Aggressive marketing by ammunition manufacturers has touched off a race to offer increasingly powerful revolver cartridges for hunting. The generally agreed upon lower limit for such applications is the venerable .41 Magnum. The new upper limit for revolvers is the .500 S&W Magnum, which offers more muzzle energy than many rifle cartridges. In between are numerous entries in .44, .45, and .476 caliber. U.S. federal statutes and regulations limit handguns to a maximum of .50 caliber. For this reason, this race may have run its course.

Most smaller caliber revolver cartridges continue to soldier on in their original configuration. One bright spot, however, is the .327 Federal Magnum cartridge, which has shown that the moribund .32 caliber revolver cartridge can really be a useful caliber for personal defense.

.32 S&W SHORT, .32 S&W LONG

ALTERNATE NAME(S): .32 Smith & Wesson Short, .32 Colt New Police
RELATED CALIBER(S): .32 Short Colt, .32 Long Colt, .380 Revolver

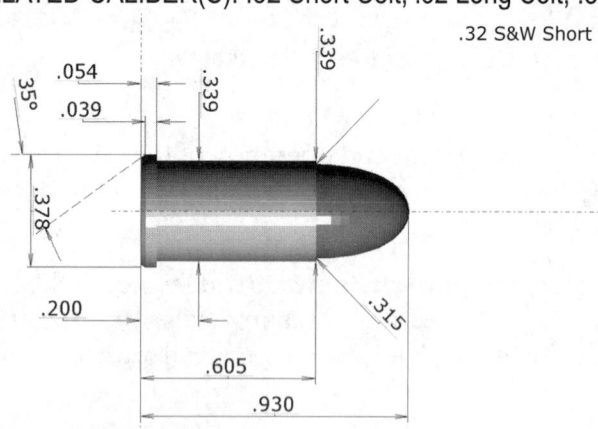

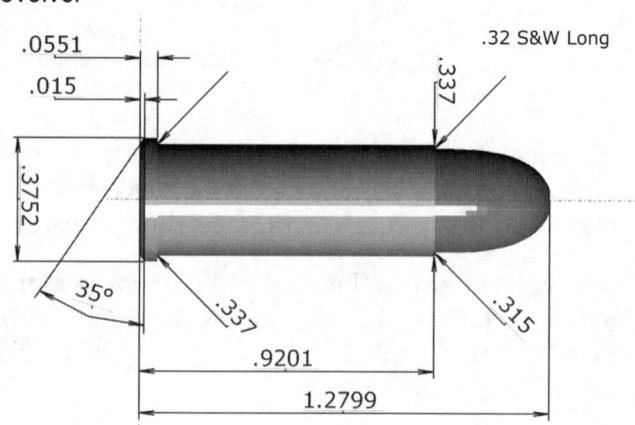

CARTRIDGE HISTORY
Year of Introduction: 1875 (Short), 1903 (Long)
Country of Origin: U.S.
Designer(s): Smith & Wesson
Governing Body: SAAMI, CIP
Present Status: active

CARTRIDGE DESCRIPTION
Bullet Diameter: .315 in.
Bullet Weight(s): 85-100 gr.
Rifling Twist Rate: 1 turn in 18.75 in. (Long)
Test Barrel Length: 4 in.
Case Type: rimmed, straight
Case Material: brass
Primer Type: small pistol

CARTRIDGE BALLISTICS
Max. Average Breech Pressure: 15,000 psi (Long)
Max. Effective Range: 10 yds.
Max. Horizontal Range: 1,550 yds.
Max. Vertical Range: 3,100 ft.

Bullet Weight (gr.)	Bullet Type	Muzzle Velocity (fps)	Muzzle Energy (ft.-lbs.)
Short 85	L-RN	680	87
Long 98	L-RN	705	108

CURRENT MANUFACTURER(S)
Federal, Remington, Winchester, Fiocchi, NAMMO, PMC, Sellier & Bellot, CBC, Industrias Technos, RUAG

GENERAL COMMENT(S)
In 1870, British ammunition makers introduced the .320 Revolver cartridge. Colt answered this with their .32 Short Colt and .32 Long Colt cartridges in 1875. Not to be left behind, S&W introduced their .32 S&W Short in 1878 followed by their .32 S&W Long in 1902. As was the custom in those days, none of these cartridges were interchangeable.

These cartridges were a popular choice for women, drivers, bank tellers and store owners who appreciated the small size of the revolvers and light recoil of the cartridges. Ballistic performance was not a consideration. Size and concealment were. Many thousands of small revolvers in .32 S&W Short and Long were made and sold over the years and it is this ownership base that has kept both in production for over 100 years.

The small, cheap revolvers chambered for these cartridges have often been called "Saturday night specials". Undoubtedly, this is because such small revolvers can easily be concealed inside a coat pocket or purse when the owner goes out on Saturday evening. Such small revolvers have also been called "Suicide specials" as they are sometimes used by despondent individuals to end their lives. Both labels are merely derisive inventions of anti-gun groups.

In recent years, the .32 S&W Long found limited use in international pistol competition. A major boost came with the introduction of the .32 H&R Magnum and .327 Federal Magnum in which the .32 S&W Short and Long can safely be fired. The future seems secure.

TECHNICAL COMMENT(S)

Even by the standards of the late 1900s, the ballistic performance of the .32 S&W Short and .32 S&W Long were anemic. The muzzle energy (90 ft.-lbs.) of the .32 S&W Short were no better than the lowly .22 Long Rifle rim fire cartridge! With 135 ft.-lbs. of muzzle energy, the .32 S&W Long was hardly much better. On the other hand recoil was mild, noise levels low and maximum range in case of a miss less than 1550 yds.

However, it would be wrong to sell the .32 S&W cartridge short. Ballistic potential was there and in 1983 that potential was realized with the introduction of the .32 H&R Magnum (muzzle energy 230 ft.-lbs.) followed by the .327 Federal Magnum (muzzle energy 435 ft.-lbs.) in 2007.

.32 H&R MAGNUM

ALTERNATE NAME(S): .32 Colt New Police
RELATED CALIBER(S): .32 S&W Short

CARTRIDGE HISTORY
Year of Introduction: 1983 Magnum
Country of Origin: U.S.
Designer(s): Harrington & Richardson
Governing Body: SAAMI, CIP
Present Status: active

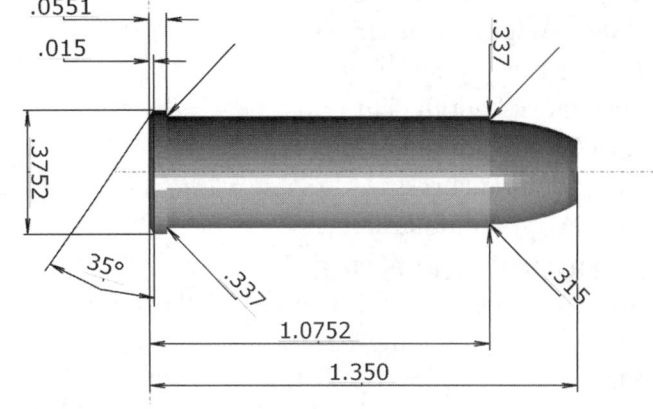

CARTRIDGE DESCRIPTION
Bullet Diameter: .315 in.
Bullet Weight(s): 85-100 gr.
Rifling Twist Rate: 1 turn in 16 in. Magnum
Test Barrel Length: 4 in.
Case Type: rimmed, straight
Case Material: brass
Primer Type: small pistol

CARTRIDGE BALLISTICS
Max. Average Breech Pressure: 21,000 psi Magnum
Max. Effective Range: 10 yds.
Max. Horizontal Range: 1,800 yds.
Max. Vertical Range: 3,600 ft.

Bullet Weight (gr.)	Bullet Type	Muzzle Velocity (fps)	Muzzle Energy (ft.-lbs.)
Mag 85	JHP	1,100	230
Mag 95	L-WC	1,030	225

CURRENT MANUFACTURER(S)
Federal, Remington, Winchester, Fiocchi, NAMMO, PMC, Sellier & Bellot, CBC, Industrias Technos, RUAG

GENERAL COMMENT(S)
The .32 Long has been a favorite for small revolvers since its introduction in 1903. It was never as popular as its big brother, the .38 Special, but the small size of the revolvers and the light recoil appealed to many people who were not regular shooters, in particular women, drivers and tellers. Most revolver manufacturers have offered one or more of their models in .32 Long because of this. Then along came H&R with a new cartridge called the .32 H&R Magnum in 1983. This new .32 caliber cartridge offered a substantially higher level of ballistic performance. In many countries, the .32 Long cartridge loaded with wadcutter bullets is a popular caliber for world-class pistol competion.

TECHNICAL COMMENT(S)
The high-pressure .32 H&R Magnum cartridge has a longer cartridge case to prevent firing it in a revolver chambered for the .32 Long. Because both cartridges share similar head dimensions, low-pressure .32 Long ammunition can

be safely fired in all revolvers chambered for the .32 Magnum. This is analogous to firing .38 Special ammunition in .357 Magnum revolvers. The .32 H&R Mag. Cartridge effectively puts its higher chamber pressure to work by offering muzzle energy levels about twice that of the .32 Long. This significantly increases the usefulness of the .32 Magnum for hunting varmints and small game while using .32 Long ammunition for informal target shooting.

.327 FEDERAL MAGNUM

ALTERNATE NAME(S): .327 Fed. Mag.
RELATED CALIBER(S): .32 S&W, .32 S&W Long, .32 H&R Magnum

CARTRIDGE HISTORY
Year of Introduction: 2007
Country of Origin: U.S.
Designer(s): Larry Head
Governing Body: SAAMI
Present Status: active

CARTRIDGE DESCRIPTION
Bullet Diameter: .312 in.
Bullet Weight(s): 86-115 gr.
Rifling Twist Rate: 1 turn in 16 in.
Test Barrel Length: 5 in.
Case Type: rimmed, straight
Case Material: brass
Primer Type: small rifle

CARTRIDGE BALLISTICS
Max. Average Breech Pressure: 46,000 psi.
Max. Horizontal Range: 2,000 yds.
Max. Vertical Range: 3,700 ft.

Bullet Weight (gr.)	Bullet Type	Muzzle Velocity (fps)	Muzzle Energy (ft.-lbs.)
86	JHP	1,330	338
100	JSP	1,400	435
115	JHP	1,300	431

CURRENT MANUFACTURER(S)
Federal

GENERAL COMMENT(S)
The .327 Federal Magnum cartridge can trace its roots back to 1878 when the .32 S&W cartridge was introduced. When shooters found its ballistic performance lacking, the more powerful .32 S&W Long cartridge was introduced in 1896. In 1984, the .32 H&R Magnum cartridge raised the performance of this caliber yet again, but not enough as it turns out. Enter Federal in 2007 with their new .327 Federal Magnum cartridge that finally puts some starch into this venerable caliber.

TECHNICAL COMMENT(S)
The story of the .32 caliber pistol cartridge family is rooted in case length and maximum average chamber pressure. These statistics have been summarized as follows:

Caliber	Case Length (in.)	Max. Avg. Breech Pressure
.32 S&W Short	.610	15,000 psi.
.32 S&W Long	.920	15,000 psi.
.32 H&R Magnum	1.075	21,000 psi.
.327 Federal Magnum	1.200	46,000 psi.

By increasing the case length and volume as well as increasing the maximum average allowable chamber pressure, ballistic performance rivaling the .357 Magnum can be obtained from a very short 3 1/16 in. revolver barrel!

.38 SPECIAL, .38 SPECIAL +P

ALTERNATE NAME(S): .38 Spl., .38 S&W Special, .38 Colt Special, .38 Special +P
RELATED CALIBER(S): .38 Long Colt, .357 Mag

CARTRIDGE HISTORY
Year of Introduction: 1902
Country of Origin: U.S.
Designer(s): S&W
Governing Body: SAAMI, CIP
Present Status: active

CARTRIDGE DESCRIPTION
Bullet Diameter: .357 in.
Bullet Weight(s): 110-200 gr.
Rifling Twist Rate: 1 turn in 18.75 in.
Test Barrel Length: 4 in.
Case Type: rimmed, straight
Case Material: brass
Primer Type: small pistol

CARTRIDGE BALLISTICS
Max. Average Breech Pressure: 17,000 psi (Special), 18,500 psi (Special +P)
Max. Effective Range: 50 yds.
Max. Horizontal Range: 1,805 yds. (+P)
Max. Vertical Range: 3,820 ft. (+P)

Bullet Weight (gr.)	Bullet Type	Muzzle Velocity (fps)	Muzzle Energy (ft.-lbs.)
110	JHP	950	220
125	JHP	950	251
140	JHP	825	212
148	L-WC	710	166
158	L-RN	755	200
158	L-RN	800	225
+P 110	JHP	1,000	245
+P 125	JHP	950	250
+P 158	SJHP-SWC	890	278

CURRENT MANUFACTURER(S)
Federal, Remington, Winchester, Cor-Bon, Black Hills, Hornady, NAMMO, PMC, CBC, Industrias Tecnos, Fiocchi, IMI, Prvi Partizan

GENERAL COMMENT(S)
In 1892, the U.S. Army replaced their .45 caliber service revolvers and cartridges with a new, revolver chambered for the already dated and anemic .38 Long Colt cartridge. They soon learned to regret this decision when the .38 Long Colt was found severely wanting against the Moro rebels during the Philippine Insurrection. However, bureaucratic inertia carried the .38 Long Colt cartridge along as the U.S. Army service handgun service cartridge from 1892 until 1911 when it was finally replaced by the .45 caliber M1911 cartridge.

By 1902, the major ammunition and handgun manufacturers began to pitch the .38 Long Colt cartridge to U.S. police departments. Lest the anemic ballistic performance of the .38 Long Colt scuttle the marketing concept, a "new" cartridge with a 0.120 inch longer case and increased maximum average pressure (from 13,000 psi to 17,000 psi) was introduced. Called the .38 Special, the new cartridge was a marketing success and quickly came to dominate law enforcement handgun ammunition sales. It retained this dominance until the 1990s when it was replaced by the 9mm Luger and .40 S&W calibers. It remains a staple of sportsmen and for undercover law enforcement agents carrying snub-nosed revolvers.

.38 Long Colt ammunition remains in production and can safely be fired in all .38 Special caliber revolvers, but who cares? Under no circumstances should you fire .38 Special ammunition in .38 Long Colt caliber revolvers.

TECHNICAL COMMENT(S)

The .38 Special cartridge is versatile and accurate. It is an excellent blend of performance and handling with mild recoil. By present standards, the anemia of the .38 Long Colt cartridge seems to have caught up with the .38 Special as it is now considered a marginal choice for personal defense.

This did not go unnoticed however. In the late 1960s an effort to increase the muzzle velocity of the .38 Special was made by increasing maximum average pressure from 17,000 psi to 18,500 psi. While this did not give much room for improvement, it was possible to raise muzzle velocity of a typical 158 grain bullet from 800 fps to 890 fps. To identify the heavier loads, a "+P" was added to the head stamp and the packaging. Most steel frame revolvers could handle the new loads without difficulty. However, aluminum frame revolvers could not withstand the higher pressures so manufacturers of those revolvers were forced to warn against the use of +P ammunition in such guns.

The advent of +P ammunition satisfied the demand for improved performance temporarily (actually approximately 20 years). By the late 1980s, the day of the revolver for front line law enforcement quickly passed to semi-automatic pistols and with it the .38 Special cartridge.

.357 MAGNUM

ALTERNATE NAME(S): .357 S&W Magnum, .357 Mag.
RELATED CALIBER(S): .38 Long Colt, .38 Special

CARTRIDGE HISTORY
Year of Introduction: 1935
Country of Origin: U.S.
Designer(s): S&W
Governing Body: SAAMI, CIP
Present Status: active

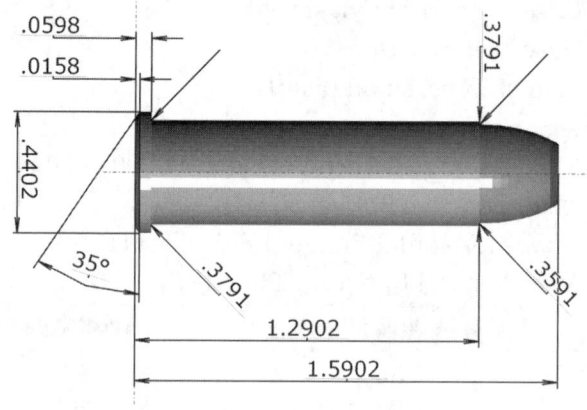

CARTRIDGE DESCRIPTION
Bullet Diameter: .357 in.
Bullet Weight(s): 110-158 gr.
Rifling Twist Rate: 1 turn in 18.75 in.
Test Barrel Length: 4 in.
Case Type: rimmed, straight
Case Material: brass
Primer Type: small pistol

CARTRIDGE BALLISTICS
Max. Average Breech Pressure: 35,000 psi
Max. Effective Range: 50 yds.
Max. Horizontal Range: 2,040 yds.
Max. Vertical Range: 4,450 ft.

Bullet Weight (gr.)	Bullet Type	Muzzle Velocity (fps)	Muzzle Energy (ft.-lbs.)
110	JHP	950	220
125	JHP	950	251
140	JHP	825	212
158	JSP	1,235	535

CURRENT MANUFACTURER(S)
Federal, Remington, Winchester, Cor-Bon, Black Hills, Hornady, NAMMO, PMC, CBC, Industrias Tecnos, Fiocchi, IMI, Prvi Partizan

GENERAL COMMENT(S)
By the early 1930s, it had become obvious that the stalwart and popular .38 S&W Special cartridge was in need of a ballistic update. The 158 grain lead round nose bullet at a leisurely 755fps simply did not produce enough muzzle energy (225 ft.-lbs.) for reliable personal defense. For example, the .44 S&W Special offered 38% more muzzle energy and the .45 Colt 32% more at similar muzzle velocities. Clearly, something needed to be done to modernize the .38 Special. It fell to S&W to improve "their"--an activity at which they had considerable experience.

In 1935, S&W introduced their new .357 S&W Magnum cartridge to favorable reviews. The new cartridge became the first magnum handgun cartridge. Production had hardly gotten under weigh when World War II intervened.

All production .357 S&W Magnum guns and ammunition were curtailed by the war effort. Still, a few notable personalities did obtain .357 Magnum revolvers and ammunition such as Gen. George S. Patton. One of the ivory handled revolvers he was famous for carrying during the War was a .357 Magnum. On occasions, the cartoon character Dick Tracy carried one as well.

With the end of World War II, manufacture of .357 Magnum guns and ammunition resumed and quickly regained the growing popularity it had enjoyed in the 1930s. Today, the .357 magnum has become a staple--doesn't every shooter have one?

TECHNICAL COMMENT(S)

In order to generate the muzzle velocities and muzzle energies required, S&W found it necessary to more than double the maximum average pressure (MAP) of the .38 Special from 17,000 psi to 35,000 psi in the .357 Magnum. This made it necessary to assure the new .357 Magnum cartridge could not be chambered in .38 Special revolvers for obvious safety reasons. S&W accomplished this by lengthening the .357 cartridge case by approximately 0.135 inches. Of course, .38 Special ammunition could safely be fired in revolvers chambered for the .357 Magnum cartridge.

The additional MAP allowed muzzle velocity of the .357 Magnum to be 1,235 fps with a muzzle energy of 536 ft.-lbs. from a 4 inch barrel. In 1935, this was a sensational level of revolver performance. Initially, a solid lead, 158 grain, semi-wadcutter bullet was loaded; expanding, jacketed bullets were added much later. While recoil is substantially higher than the .38 Special, most shooters can master this with training and practice.

.41 MAGNUM

ALTERNATE NAME(S): .41 Remington Magnum, .41 S&W Magnum
RELATED CALIBER(S): .41 Long Colt

CARTRIDGE HISTORY
Year of Introduction: 1964
Country of Origin: U.S.
Designer(s): Elmer Keith
Governing Body: SAAMI
Present Status: active

CARTRIDGE DESCRIPTION
Bullet Diameter: .400 in.
Bullet Weight(s): 175-250 gr.
Rifling Twist Rate: 1 turn in 18.75 in.
Test Barrel Length: 4 in.
Case Type: rimmed, straight
Case Material: brass
Primer Type: large pistol

CARTRIDGE BALLISTICS
Max. Average Breech Pressure: 36,000 psi.
Max. Effective Range: 50 yds.
Max. Horizontal Range: 2,300 yds.
Max. Vertical Range: 5,000 ft.

Bullet Weight (gr.)	Bullet Type	Muzzle Velocity (fps)	Muzzle Energy (ft.-lbs.)
175	JHP	1,250	607
210	JHP	1,300	790
250	L	1,250	865

CURRENT MANUFACTURER(S)
Federal, Remington, Winchester, Cor-Bon, PMC

GENERAL COMMENT(S)
The .41 Magnum cartridge has always lived in the shadow of its older, more powerful brother, the .44 Magnum. For this reason, the .41 Magnum cartridge is far less popular and occupies more of a specialty market position than the broad market appeal of the .44 Magnum. Because of its specialty market niche, the .41 Magnum has never been the focal point of intense ballistic load development like the .44 Magnum.

TECHNICAL COMMENT(S)

Ballistically, the .41 Magnum offers no advantage over the .44 Magnum. Revolvers chambered for either caliber are virtually the same weight, leaving the .41 Magnum no advantage in that area. Perceived recoil of the .41 Mag. is lower than that of the .44 Magnum, but not by a wide margin in the opinion of most shooters. In areas where handgun hunting is legal, the .41 Magnum is fully capable of taking deer-sized game at close ranges. For personal defense, it is too large and powerful.

.44 SPECIAL

ALTERNATE NAME(S): .44 S&W Special, .44 Spl., .44 Remington Magnum, .44 Mag.
RELATED CALIBER(S): .45 Colt

CARTRIDGE HISTORY

Year of Introduction: 1907
Country of Origin: U.S.
Designer(s): S&W, Elmer Keith
Governing Body: SAAMI, CIP
Present Status: active

CARTRIDGE DESCRIPTION

Bullet Diameter: .429 in.
Bullet Weight(s): 180-300 gr.
Rifling Twist Rate: 1 turn in 20 in.
Test Barrel Length: 4 in.
Case Type: rimmed, straight
Case Material: brass
Primer Type: large pistol

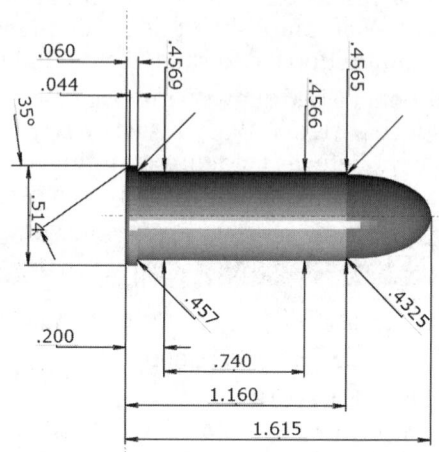

CARTRIDGE BALLISTICS

Max. Average Breech Pressure: 15,500 psi
Max. Effective Range: 50 yds.
Max. Horizontal Range: 1,750 yds.
Max. Vertical Range: 3,725 ft.

Bullet Weight (gr.)	Bullet Type	Muzzle Velocity (fps)	Muzzle Energy (ft.-lbs.)
180	JHP	1,000	400
200	JHP	920	376
246	L-RN	755	310

CURRENT MANUFACTURER(S)

Federal, Remington, Winchester, Cor-Bon, Black Hills, Hornady, PMC, IMI, CBC, Fiocchi, NAMMO, Prvi Partizan

GENERAL COMMENT(S)

The .44 Special cartridge has a long and impeccable pedigree dating back to the dawn of the self-contained cartridge. Its grandfather is the .44 S&W Russian cartridge introduced in 1870 and offered by Colt in their seminal Single-Action revolver as well as their Bisley target models. Contemporaries such as the .44 Colt (1870), .44 S&W American (1870) and .44 Merwin & Hulbert (1882) fell by the wayside to became obscure curiosities today.

 The popularity of the .44 Russian cartridge with shooters of the day was founded on its combination of accuracy with sufficient power for personal defense if needed (although with 24% less muzzle energy it was not as powerful as the .45 Colt). The .44 Russian was the preferred cartridge for many prominent western personalities such as Buffalo Bill Cody.

Although the .44 Special has had to live in the shadow of the seminal .45 Colt cartridge all its life, it has survived due to a loyal corps of followers who appreciate its excellent accuracy.

TECHNICAL COMMENT(S)

Designed for black powder, the .44 Russian did not fare well during the transition to smokeless propellants at the turn of the century in 1900. The bulk smokeless propellants of that era required more case volume than the .44 Russian offered. Clearly, a new cartridge case with more volume was needed to meet the demand for a modern .44 caliber cartridge. In 1907, S&W introduced the .44 (S&W) Special cartridge with a case length approximately O.19 inches longer than the .44 Russian and with approximately 27 % more volume.

The .44 Russian with its shorter case length could safely be fired in a .44 Special revolver (and also the .44 Magnum that came much later).

.44 MAGNUM

ALTERNATE NAME(S): .44 Remington Magnum, .44 Mag., .44 Rem. Mag.
RELATED CALIBER(S):.45 Colt

CARTRIDGE HISTORY
Year of Introduction: 1955
Country of Origin: U.S.
Designer(s): Remington, Elmer Keith
Governing Body: SAAMI, CIP
Present Status: active

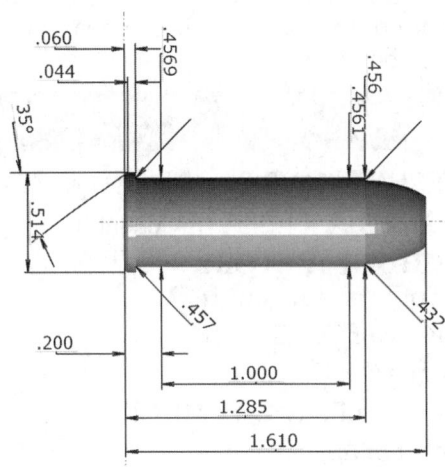

CARTRIDGE DESCRIPTION
Bullet Diameter: .429 in.
Bullet Weight(s): 180-300 gr.
Rifling Twist Rate: 1 turn in 20 in.
Test Barrel Length: 4 in.
Case Type: rimmed, straight
Case Material: brass
Primer Type: large pistol

CARTRIDGE BALLISTICS
Max. Average Breech Pressure: 36,000 psi
Max. Effective Range: 50 yds.
Max. Horizontal Range: 2,600 yds.
Max. Vertical Range: 5,600 ft.

Bullet Weight (gr.)	Bullet Type	Muzzle Velocity (fps)	Muzzle Energy (ft.-lbs.)
180	JSP	1,610	1,036
200	JHP	1,500	999
210	JHP	1,450	980
240	JSP	1,180	741
240	JHP	1,300	900
250	JHP	1,250	867
300	L	1,250	1,126

CURRENT MANUFACTURER(S)
Federal, Remington, Winchester, Cor-Bon, Black Hills, Hornady, PMC, IMI, CBC, Fiocchi, NAMMO, Prvi Partizan

GENERAL COMMENT(S)
It was cowboy, lawman and gun writer Elmer Keith who appreciated the need for a modern, powerful, large bore revolver cartridge as a backup for large game hunting, for taking medium game and for personal defense. Keith liked the classic .44 Special cartridge so he selected it as the basis for his concept. Essentially, Keith's idea was to increase the maximum average pressure of the .44 Special cartridge in order to achieve a substantial increase in muzzle velocity and muzzle energy.

Obviously, a stronger cartridge case would be needed to handle the increased pressure. Keith contacted his friends at Remington who immediately saw the market potential of such a new cartridge. Working together, they developed the .44 Remington Magnum cartridge which was introduced in 1955. At the same time, S&W introduced a revolver designed for the new cartridge.

While the new cartridge proved a marketing success on its own merits, sales really went through the roof following release of the movie "Dirty Harry" whose character, Detective Harry Callahan, carried a .44 Magnum which was dramatic overkill for law enforcement use. Several movies starring the same character followed. No one could have predicted the success of the .44 Magnum concept. Elmer had it right and the popularity of the .44 Magnum cartridge continues to this day.

TECHNICAL COMMENT(S)

The .44 Special is a low pressure cartridge (MAP 15,500 psi) and the .44 Magnum a high pressure cartridge (MAP 36,000 psi). With twice the maximum average pressure of the .44 Special, the .44 Magnum required a reinforced cartridge case to handle the increased pressure. Of course it would be unsafe to fire the .44 Magnum in revolvers chambered for the .44 Special. To prevent that, the .44 Magnum cartridge case was made 0.125 inches longer so it could not be chambered in .44 Special guns.

The .44 Magnum generates sufficient striking energy to hunt medium game and some species of large game. It is a popular choice for metallic silhouette competition, and, yes it is a good choice for personal defense provided you can handle the heavy recoil. There seems to be nothing the .44 Magnum cannot do well. Elmer would be proud.

.45 COLT

ALTERNATE NAME(S): .45 Long Colt, .45 Colt Long, .45 Colt Army
RELATED CALIBER(S): .44 Magnum

CARTRIDGE HISTORY

Year of Introduction: 1873
Country of Origin: U.S.
Designer(s): Colt
Governing Body: SAAMI, CIP
Present Status: active

CARTRIDGE DESCRIPTION

Bullet Diameter: .454 in.
Bullet Weight(s): 200-260 gr.
Rifling Twist Rate: 1 turn in 16 in.
Test Barrel Length: 4 in.
Case Type: rimmed, straight
Case Material: brass
Primer Type: large pistol

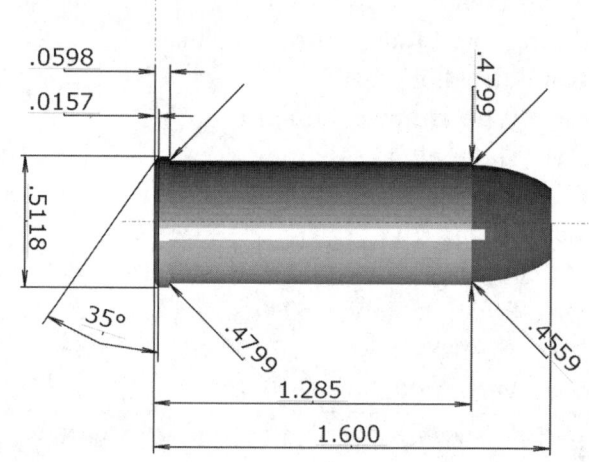

CARTRIDGE BALLISTICS

Max. Average Breech Pressure: 14,000 psi
Max. Effective Range: 50 yds.
Max. Horizontal Range: 1,660 yds.
Max. Vertical Range: 3,500 ft.

Bullet Weight (gr.)	Bullet Type	Muzzle Velocity (fps)	Muzzle Energy (ft.-lbs.)
200	JHP	1,000	444
225	JHP	900	405
255	LRN	860	420
255	LRN	725	298

CURRENT MANUFACTURER(S)

Federal, Remington, Winchester, Cor-Bon, Hornady, PMC

GENERAL COMMENT(S)

In most western movies, the hero (he is the one wearing the white hat) nearly always uses a Colt Single-Action Army revolver--sometimes two--nickel-plated. When this revolver was introduced in 1871, the .45 Colt cartridge was introduced along with it. Both quickly became icons to the extent that the combination was preferred by the well-equipped "shootist" and law enforcement officer alike. From 1871 to approximately 1900, the Colt Single-Action Army revolver and its .45 Colt cartridge helped mold American history while playing a major part in winning the west.

Today, some 140 years after its introduction, the .45 Colt cartridge remains in production by nearly all major ammunition manufacturers. It survival is not based solely on nostalgia, it remains an effective caliber for personal defense By the way, have you ever noticed that the movie hero/bad guys may be equipped with a .45 Colt revolver, but the cartridges in the gun belt loops or bandoliers are not of this caliber?

TECHNICAL COMMENT(S)

The .45 Colt cartridge is one of the truly great cartridges in history, but to look at it you would never believe this. By modern standards, it seems overly large and too long for its purpose. Actually, it looks old fashioned. And, rightly so as it was designed originally for black powder which required a large volume cartridge case. It survived the transition to smokeless propellants, however the case volume is needlessly large for such a requirement which explains its old fashioned appearance.

Did someone forget to put the rim on the case? And that blunt lead bullet looks as if someone pushed it too far down inside the cartridge case. So, on what is its reputation built? Despite its ungainly appearance, the .45 Colt cartridge is a very effective blend of bullet diameter, weight and shape at a modest muzzle velocity. The .45 Colt cartridge is a classic example of the large diameter, heavy bullet at low velocity school of handgun performance thinking. In reality, the .45 Colt is a very efficient man-killer that earned its reputation the hard way.

The low maximum average pressures (MAP) of the .45 Colt cartridge preclude all but the most incremental efforts at a ballistic upgrade. Although some companies sell a .45 Colt +P cartridge, SAAMI has not standardized such a load.

.454 CASULL

ALTERNATE NAME(S): .45 Cas.
RELATED CALIBER(S): .44 Magnum, 45 Colt

CARTRIDGE HISTORY
Year of Introduction: 1957
Country of Origin: U.S.
Designer(s): Dick Casull, Jack Fulmer
Governing Body: SAAMI
Present Status: active

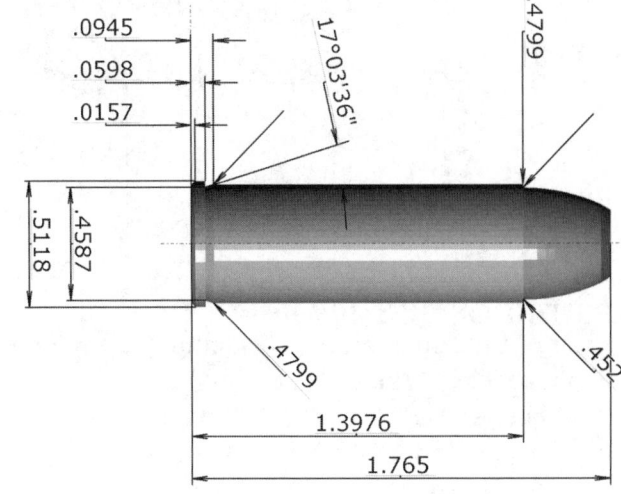

CARTRIDGE DESCRIPTION
Bullet Diameter: .452 in.
Bullet Weight(s): 250-300 gr.
Rifling Twist Rate: 1 turn in 20 in.
Test Barrel Length: 6 in.
Case Type: rimmed, straight
Case Material: brass
Primer Type: large pistol

CARTRIDGE BALLISTICS
Max. Average Breech Pressure: 56,600 psi
Max. Effective Range: 50 yds.
Max. Horizontal Range: 2,375 yds.
Max. Vertical Range: 5,150 ft.

Bullet Weight (gr.)	Bullet Type	Muzzle Velocity (fps)	Muzzle Energy (ft.-lbs.)
250	JSP	1,300	938
260	JSP	1,800	1,870
300	JHP	1,650	1,813

CURRENT MANUFACTURER(S)
Federal, Remington, Winchester, Cor-Bon, Hornady, PMC

GENERAL COMMENT(S)
Many handgun hunters and metallic silhouette competitors found the .44 Magnum did not offer sufficient muzzle energy as a hunting, backup or silhouette cartridge. Something more powerful was needed, however the choices were limited by the cartridge cases available. The iconic .45 Colt cartridge had potential, but it was doomed to low maximum average pressures (MAP) by the weakness of the guns chambered for it. But what if the case could be lengthened so it would not fit in .45 Colt chambers? This would allow the chamber pressure to be increased and the new cartridge chambered in guns designed for it. For years, Dick Casull promoted his idea while the industry ignored him. Finally, in the late 1980s, Casull had built enough momentum for the major manufacturers to take notice.

TECHNICAL COMMENT(S)

The .454 Casull cartridge case differs from the .45 Colt in that it is 0.165 inches longer to prevent it being chamber in guns of the latter caliber. Of course, .45 Colt ammunition can be safely fired in a gun chambered for the .454 Casull, but who cares? In addition, the web of the .454 Casull case is substantially thicker and harder than the .45 Colt. Here it is interesting to note that the .45 Colt cartridge has a large pistol primer pocket while the .454 Casull cartridge has a small pistol cartridge primer pocket. However, the Casull cartridge is loaded with a small rifle primer due to the high MAP.

As a handgun hunting and backup cartridge, the .454 Casull had no peer until recently when more power handgun carkidge yet have been introduced.

.460 S&W SPECIAL, .460 S&W MAGNUM

ALTERNATE NAME(S): .460 S&W Spl., .460 S&W Mag.
RELATED CALIBER(S): .45 S&W Schofield

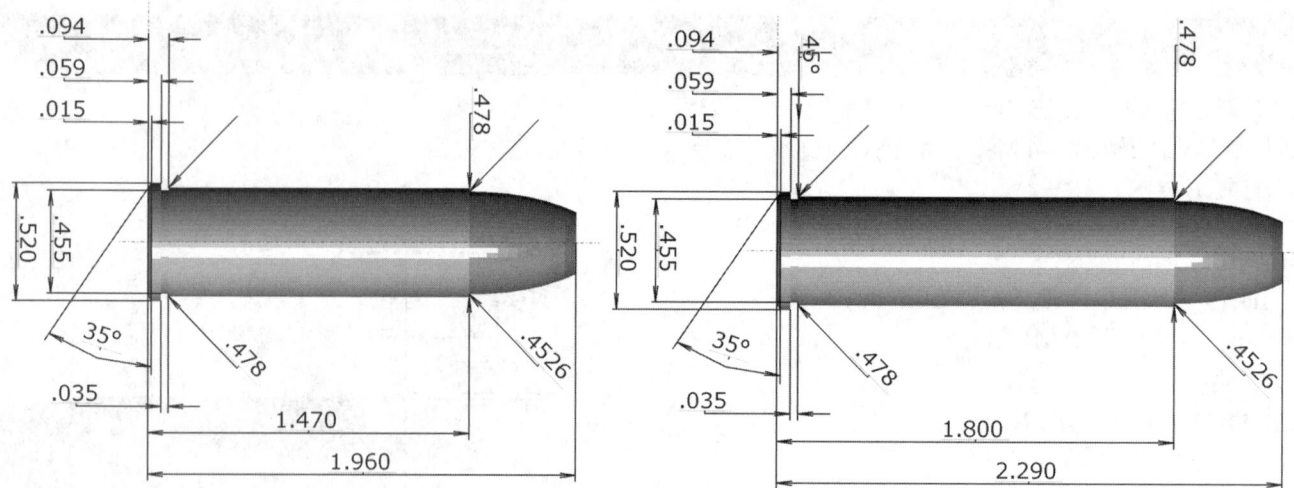

CARTRIDGE HISTORY

Year of Introduction: 2006 (Magnum), 2006 (Special)
Country of Origin: U.S.
Designer(s): S&W
Governing Body: SAAMI
Present Status: active

CARTRIDGE DESCRIPTION

Bullet Diameter: .4525 in.
Bullet Weight(s): 200-395 gr.
Rifling Twist Rate: 1 turn in 20 in.
Test Barrel Length: 10 in.
Case Type: rimmed, straight
Case Material: brass
Primer Type: large pistol

CARTRIDGE BALLISTICS

Max. Average Breech Pressure: N/A
Max. Effective Range: 50 yds.
Max. Horizontal Range: 2,600 yds.
Max. Vertical Range: 5,700 ft.

Bullet Weight (gr.)	Bullet Type	Muzzle Velocity (fps)	Muzzle Energy (ft.-lbs.)
275	JHP	1,800	1,980
260	JHP	2,000	2,309

CURRENT MANUFACTURER(S)

Hornady, Federal, Winchester, Con-Bon

GENERAL COMMENT(S)

With these two cartridges, S&W has helped build a recent trend toward very powerful, large caliber revolver cartridges for big game hunting. At this time, no one is certain how large or deep this market niche may be. However, it certainly has produced several interesting new cartridges.

TECHNICAL COMMENT(S)

From published literature, it appears that the .460 Special is loaded to a lower maximum average chamber pressure than the .460 Magnum. Both cartridges share similar case head dimensions and bullet diameters; the .460 Magnum has a longer cartridge case. Apparently, this is intentional. The heavy recoil and high striking energy of both the Special and Magnum limit their use in handguns by experienced hunters only.

.480 RUGER

ALTERNATE NAME(S): none
RELATED CALIBER(S): .475 Linebaugh

CARTRIDGE HISTORY

Year of Introduction: 2005
Country of Origin: U.S.
Designer(s): Ruger/Hornady
Governing Body: SAAMI, CIP
Present Status: active

CARTRIDGE DESCRIPTION

Bullet Diameter: .475 in.
Bullet Weight(s): 275-400 gr.
Rifling Twist Rate: 1 turn in 18 in.
Test Barrel Length: 7.5 in.
Case Type: rimmed, straight
Case Material: brass
Primer Type: large pistol

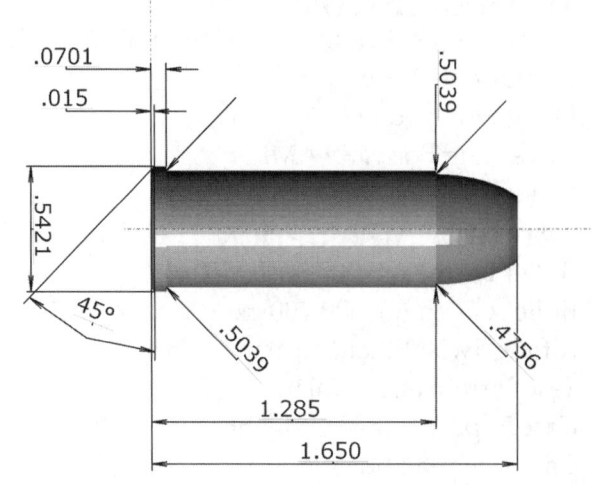

CARTRIDGE BALLISTICS

Max. Average Breech Pressure: 47,860 psi.
Max. Effective Range: 50 yds.
Max. Horizontal Range: 2,500 yds.
Max. Vertical Range: 5,600 ft.

Bullet Weight (gr.)	Bullet Type	Muzzle Velocity (fps)	Muzzle Energy (ft.-lbs.)
275	JHP	1,350	1,115
325	JHP	1,350	1,315
400	JHP	1,100	1,075

CURRENT MANUFACTURER(S)

Hornady, Federal

GENERAL COMMENT(S)

Like the .460 S&W Magnum, the .480 Ruger is intended for big game hunting by experienced handgunners, but the two cartrdiges are NOT interchangeable. The .480 Ruger fires a .475 caliber bullet that will be new to most shooters. Not since the .476 Enfield Mark III cartridge in British military service in the 1890s have shooters been offered a handgun cartridge using bullets of this diameter. Note that the .480 Ruger offers magnum performance, but is not labeled a magnum. The .480 Ruger is the first handgun cartridge to bear the Ruger name.

TECHNICAL COMMENT(S)

A review of the .480 Ruger's ballistics reveals that it was designed to avoid being over-powered. Unlike many other modern, large caliber handgun cartridges that try to one-up each other in power, the .480 Ruger avoids trying to be the biggest and most powerful, leaving that to the .476 Linebaugh cartridge. Powerful it certainly is, however the power is restrained. For example, all .480 Ruger loads offer muzzle energies in the 1,100 ft.-lb. range. This is more than sufficient for hunting big game while keeping recoil within limits that the average person can handle.

.500 S&W SPECIAL, .500 S&W MAGNUM

ALTERNATE NAME(S): .500 S&W Spl., .500 S&W Mag.
RELATED CALIBER(S): .460 S&W Spl., .460 S&W Mag.

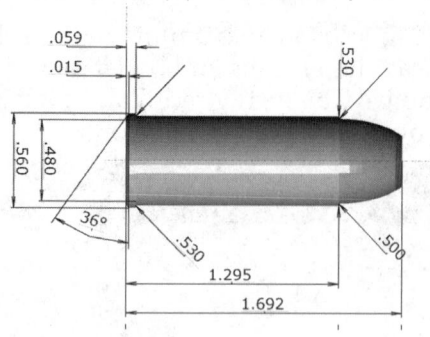
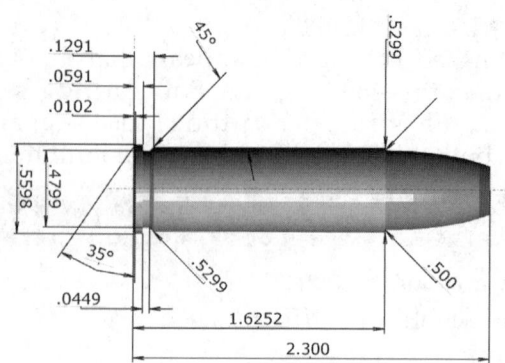

CARTRIDGE HISTORY
Year of Introduction: 2003 (Magnum), 2004 (Special)
Country of Origin: U.S.
Designer(s): S&W
Governing Body: SAAMI
Present Status: active

CARTRIDGE DESCRIPTION
Bullet Diameter: .500 in.
Bullet Weight(s): 300-500 gr.
Rifling Twist Rate: 1 turn in 18.75 in.
Test Barrel Length: 10 in.
Case Type: rimmed, straight
Case Material: brass
Primer Type: large pistol

CARTRIDGE BALLISTICS
Max. Average Breech Pressure: N/A
Max. Effective Range: 50 yds.
Max. Horizontal Range: 2,500 yds.
Max. Vertical Range: 5,200 ft.

Bullet Weight (gr.)	Bullet Type	Muzzle Velocity (fps)	Muzzle Energy (ft.-lbs.)
350 (Spl)	JHP	1,400	1,523
275 (Spl)	JHP	1,660	1,680
300 (Mag)	JHP	2,075	2,868
350 (Mag)	JHP	1,900	2,805
500 (Mag)	JHP	1,425	2,254

CURRENT MANUFACTURER(S)
Federal, Winchester, Cor-Bon

GENERAL COMMENT(S)
In designing the .460 and .500 S&W Special and Magnum cartridges, and the new "X-Frame™" revolvers Smith & Wesson restored its status as teh manufacturer of "the most powerful production revolver in the world" (.500); and "the highest muzzle velocity of any production revolver on earth" (.460). While there are custom or limited availability cartridges and guns that have more muzzle energy or velocity, both S&W cartridges and revolvers are standard catalog "factory" products readily available at retail.

TECHNICAL COMMENT(S)
The .460 and .500 S&W Magnums are the dual monarchs of magnum handgun cartridges– heavy large diameter bullets, extreme muzzle velocities, and copious amounts of muzzle energy. Only experienced shooters and hunters need apply.

CHAPTER 72 : SPORTING REVOLVER - OBSOLETE

CHAPTER 72

For Cartridge Index see Chapter 101. All drawing dimensions are approximate.

The menu of obsolete revolver cartridges contains a colorful mixture of cowboys, outlaws, western movies, inventors, the British Empire, and the taming of the West. Throw in the transition from black powder to smokeless starting in the 1890s along with two World Wars and numerous lesser conflicts, and you have something of interest for nearly everyone.

Today, a shooter can indulge his old west revolver fantasies to a greater degree than ever before due to SASS (the Single Action Shooting Society), which sponsors numerous cowboy action competitions. Authentic gear, period single-action revolvers, and appropriate ammunition are required. Thanks to SASS, classic revolver calibers such as the .32-20, .38-40, .44-40, and .44 Russian have survived. The SASS benefits even extend to unlikely calibers such as the .41 Colt.

The reader is encouraged not to view this chapter as a mausoleum for deceased revolver cartridges. Consider it rather as a box full of human history documenting both the good and the bad of life, commercial successes and failures, and eras passed– or so we thought.

.22 REMINGTON JET MAGNUM

ALTERNATE NAME(S): .22 Jet, .22 Remington Jet, .22 Center Fire Magnum
RELATED CALIBER(S): .357 Magnum

CARTRIDGE HISTORY
Year of Introduction: 1961
Country of Origin: U.S.
Designer(s): S&W and Remington
Governing Body: SAAMI
Present Status: obsolete

CARTRIDGE DESCRIPTION
Bullet Diameter: .223 in.
Bullet Weight(s): 40-50 gr.
Rifling Twist Rate: 1 turn in 10 in.
Test Barrel Length: 8 in.
Case Type: rimmed, tapered
Case Material: brass
Primer Type: small rifle

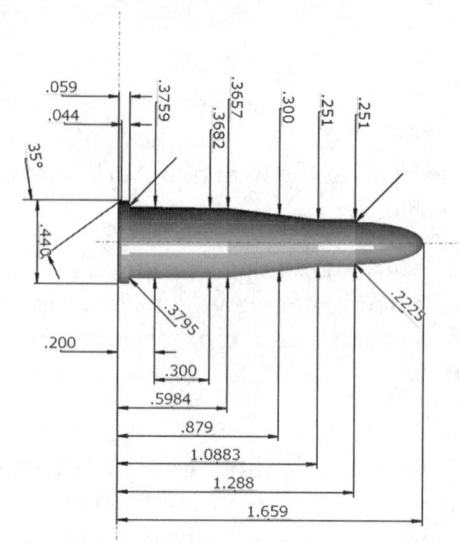

CARTRIDGE BALLISTICS
Max. Average Breech Pressure: 40,000 CUP.
Max. Effective Range: 200 yds.
Max. Horizontal Range: 2,100 yds.
Max. Vertical Range: 4,800 ft.

Bullet Weight (gr.)	Bullet Type	Muzzle Velocity (fps)	Muzzle Energy (ft.-lbs.)
40	JHP	2,460	535

CURRENT MANUFACTURER(S)
Prvi Partizan

GENERAL COMMENT(S)
As a marketing concept, the .22 Jet was an attempt to offer a high velocity, centerfire, .22 caliber cartridge for a revolver. It did not work very well. As the cartridge was fired, the delete case was forced back against the recoil plate on the revolver's frame. Chamber pressure expanded the case against the tapered chamber walls, causing the case head to remain pressed against the recoil plate. The "jammed" case made it difficult or impossible to rotate the cylinder.

TECHNICAL COMMENT(S)
No technical unknowns here. Radically tapered or necked cartridge cases loaded to high chamber pressures simply cannot be made to stay in the chamber and off the recoil plate of a revolver. Here is a classic case of a good marketing idea that technology could not make work properly.

.256 WINCHESTER MAGNUM

ALTERNATE NAME(S): .256 Win. Mag
RELATED CALIBER(S): .357 Magnum

CARTRIDGE HISTORY
Year of Introduction: 1960
Country of Origin: U.S.
Designer(s): Winchester
Governing Body: SAAMI
Present Status: obsolete

CARTRIDGE DESCRIPTION
Bullet Diameter: .257 in.
Bullet Weight(s): 60 gr.
Rifling Twist Rate: 1 turn in 14 in.
Test Barrel Length: 24 in.
Case Type: rimmed, necked
Case Material: brass
Primer Type: small rifle

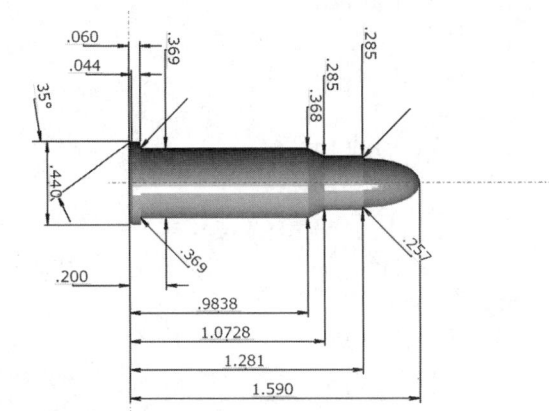

CARTRIDGE BALLISTICS
Max. Average Breech Pressure: 43,000 CUP.
Max. Effective Range: 200 yds.
Max. Horizontal Range: 2,600 yds.
Max. Vertical Range: 5,600 ft.

Bullet Weight (gr.)	Bullet Type	Muzzle Velocity (fps)	Muzzle Energy (ft.-lbs.)
60	JHP	2,200	650

CURRENT MANUFACTURER(S)
Winchester

GENERAL COMMENT(S)
American sportsmen have had a long-running love affair with .22 caliber centerfire varmint calibers ever since the .22 Hornet was developed. However, there was no room in American shooters' hearts for a .257 caliber varmint cartridge and the .256 Win. Mag. quietly disappeared.

TECHNICAL COMMENT(S)
Technically speaking, there was nothing wrong with the .256 Win. Mag. except the bullet diameter.

.32 SHORT COLT, .32 LONG COLT

ALTERNATE NAME(S): none
RELATED CALIBER(S): .320 Short, .32 S&W

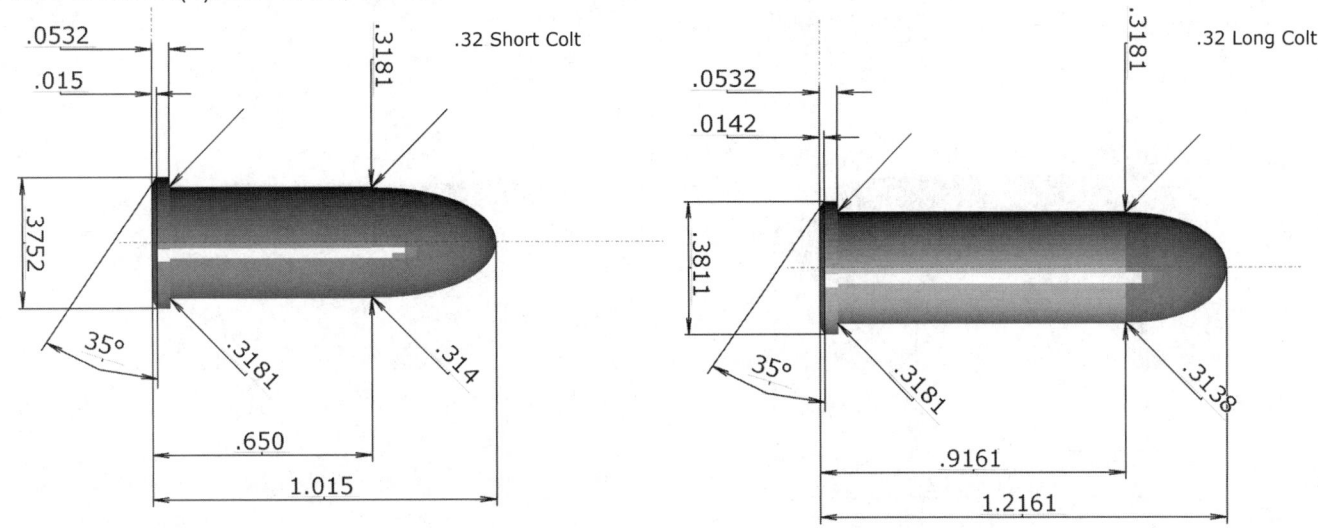

CARTRIDGE HISTORY
Year of Introduction: 1875
Country of Origin: U.S.
Designer(s): Colt
Governing Body: CIP
Present Status: obsolete

CARTRIDGE DESCRIPTION
Bullet Diameter: .314 in.

Bullet Weight(s): 80-82 gr.
Rifling Twist Rate: 1 turn in 16 in.
Test Barrel Length: 4.9 in.
Case Type: rimmed, straight
Case Material: brass
Primer: small pistol

CARTRIDGE BALLISTICS
Max. Average Breech Pressure: 14,500 psi.
Max. Horizontal Range: 1,550 yds.
Max. Vertical Range: 3,100 ft.

Bullet Weight (gr.)	Bullet Type	Muzzle Velocity (fps)	Muzzle Energy (ft.-lbs.)
80	L-RN	745	100 (Short)
80	L-RN	755	104 (Long)

CURRENT MANUFACTURER(S)
None

GENERAL COMMENT(S)
In 1870, British ammunition makers introduced their .320 Revolver cartridge. Colt followed with their .32 Short and .32 Long Colt in 1875 and Smith & Wesson in 1878 with their .32 S&W. As was the custom in those days, none of these cartridges were interchangeable. However, they were popular and remained in production until the early 2000s in support of the large number of small, cheap revolvers chambered for these calibers.

TECHNICAL COMMENT(S)
Both of the .32 Colt cartridges offer similar ballistic performance to their rival .32 S&W and .320 Revolver cartridges. However, all of them have substantially less striking energy than a typical .22 Long Rifle rimfire cartridge.

.320 SHORT REVOLVER, .320 LONG REVOLVER

ALTERNATE NAME(S): none
RELATED CALIBER(S): .32 Short Colt, .32 Long Colt

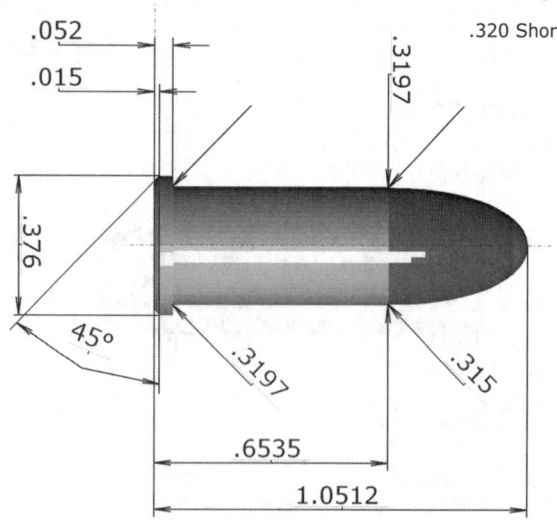

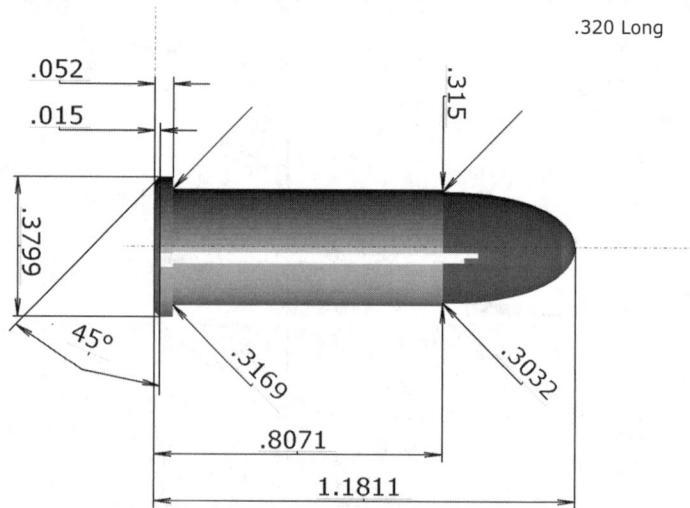

CARTRIDGE HISTORY
Year of Introduction: 1870
Country of Origin: Britain
Designer(s): Webley
Governing Body: CIP
Present Status: obsolete

CARTRIDGE DESCRIPTION
Bullet Diameter: .313 in.

Bullet Weight(s): 80 gr.
Rifling Twist Rate: 1 turn in 22 in.
Test Barrel Length: 4.9 in.
Case Type: rimmed, straight
Case Material: brass
Primer: small pistol

CARTRIDGE BALLISTICS

Max. Average Breech Pressure: 17,405 psi. (Short), 14,504 psi. (Long)
Max. Horizontal Range: 1,400 yds.
Max. Vertical Range: 2,900 ft.

Bullet Weight (gr.)	Bullet Type	Muzzle Velocity (fps)	Muzzle Energy (ft.-lbs.)
80	L-RN	575	59 (Short)
80	L-RN	550	54 (Long est.)

CURRENT MANUFACTURER(S)

Fiocchi

GENERAL COMMENT(S)

Webley used the .32 Short and Long Colt as inspiration for the design of these cartridges in 1870. Many small revolvers in Europe were chambered for these cartridges. The .320 Short was made by U.S. ammunition makers until 1930. Today, Fiocchi is the sole remaining manufacturer.

TECHNICAL COMMENT(S)

When studying the ballistics of these cartridges, one can not help but wonder what they were good for. A .22 Long Rifle cartridge has more striking energy. In all honesty, the .320 Revolver cartridge is a good nominee for "The Most Useless Cartridge" in the under .38 caliber category.

.357 REMINGTON MAXIMUM

ALTERNATE NAME(S): .357 Maximum
RELATED CALIBER(S): .38 Special, .357 Magnum

CARTRIDGE HISTORY

Year of Introduction: 1983
Country of Origin: U.S.
Designer(s): Remington and Ruger
Governing Body: SAAMI
Present Status: obsolete

CARTRIDGE DESCRIPTION

Bullet Diameter: .357 in.
Bullet Weight(s): 158-180 gr.
Rifling Twist Rate: 1 turn in 18.75 in.
Test Barrel Length: 6 in.
Case Type: rimmed, straight
Case Material: brass
Primer Type: small pistol

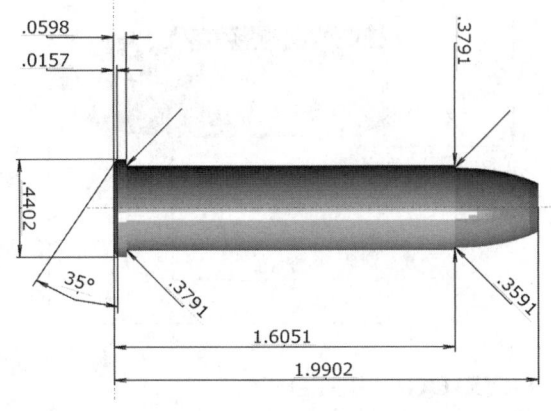

CARTRIDGE BALLISTICS

Max. Average Breech Pressure: 44,962 psi.
Max. Effective Range: 100 yds.
Max. Horizontal Range: 3,000 yds.
Max. Vertical Range: 5,900 ft.

Bullet Weight (gr.)	Bullet Type	Muzzle Velocity (fps)	Muzzle Energy (ft.-lbs.)
158	JHP	1,825	1,168
180	JHP	1,550	960

CURRENT MANUFACTURER(S)

None

GENERAL COMMENT(S)

Shortly after this cartridge was introduced, extended testing indicated unacceptable gas erosion on the inside of the top strap of revolvers chambered for this cartridge. After efforts to solve this problem were unsuccessful, gun manufacturers stopped making firearms in this caliber. Demand for .357 Maximum ammunition subsequently dropped and by the early 2000s, ammunition makers had ceased production as well.

TECHNICAL COMMENT(S)

The .357 Maximum is one of the most powerful .357 caliber revolver cartridge ever made. Muzzle velocities of the .357 Maximum using 158 grain bullets were 48% higher than .357 Magnum ammunition loaded with the same bullet. Design of the .357 Maximum cartridge was straightforward, a lengthened .357 Magnum cartridge case to hold more powder together with a higher maximum average chamber pressure. Bullets designed for the .357 Magnum could be used. And, both the .38 Special and the .357 Magnum cartridges, by virtue of their shorter cartridge case length and lower chamber pressure, could be fired safely in .357 Maximum caliber guns. But, it was not quite that simple. The heavy charges of fast burning powder in factory loaded .357 Maximum ammunition caused gas cutting problems on revolver top straps after just 1,000 rounds of ammunition had been fired. This was unacceptable and could not be remedied at reasonable cost, leading the gun makers to discontinue production of .357 Maximum revolvers. It was thus that the .357 Maximum cartridge was sent to Valhalla.

.38 SHORT COLT, .38 LONG COLT

ALTERNATE NAME(S): none

RELATED CALIBER(S): .38 Special, .38 S&W

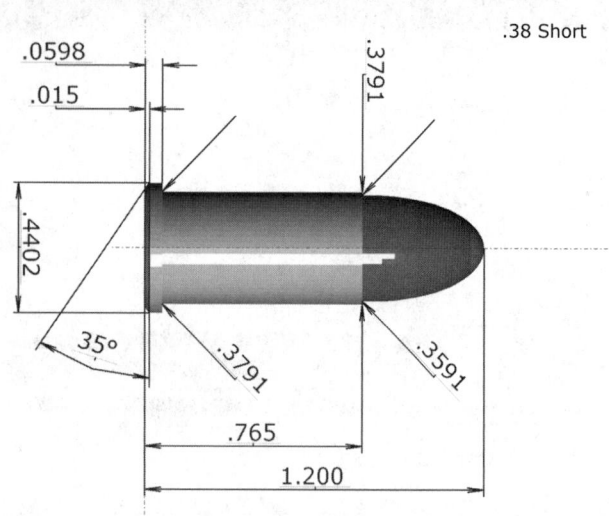

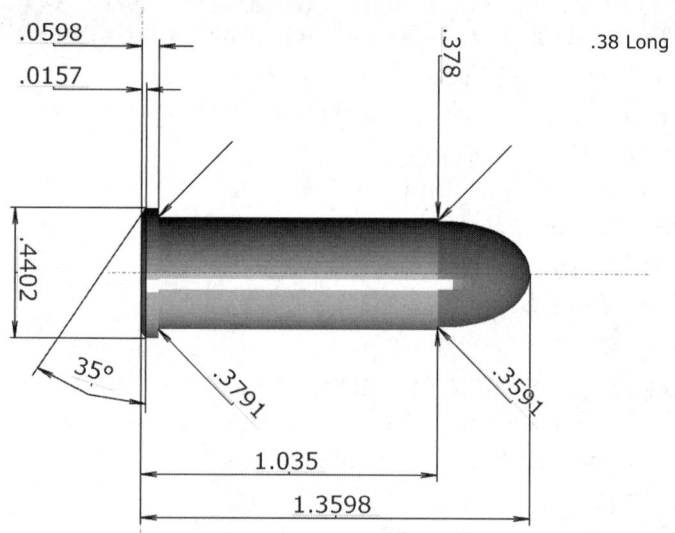

CARTRIDGE HISTORY

Year of Introduction: 1875

Country of Origin: U.S.

Designer(s): Colt

Governing Body: SAAMI, CIP

Present Status: active

CARTRIDGE DESCRIPTION

Bullet Diameter: .357 in.

Bullet Weight(s): 125-150 gr.

Rifling Twist Rate: 1 turn in 16 in.

Test Barrel Length: 4.9 in.

Case Type: rimmed, straight
Case Material: brass
Primer: small pistol

CARTRIDGE BALLISTICS

Max. Average Breech Pressure: 13,053 psi.
Max. Horizontal Range: 1,750 yds.
Max. Vertical Range: 3,900 ft.

Bullet Weight (gr.)	Bullet Type	Muzzle Velocity (fps)	Muzzle Energy (ft.-lbs.)
125	L-RN	730	149 (Short)
150	L-RN	770	195 (Long)

CURRENT MANUFACTURER(S)

Remington, Black Hills

GENERAL COMMENT(S)

From 1892 until 1911, the .38 Long Colt was the standard U.S. Army service revolver cartridge. Experience in the field during the Philippine Insurrection clearly indicated that the .38 Long Colt lacked sufficient striking energy for military service. It was replaced in U.S. military service in 1911 by the .45 ACP.

TECHNICAL COMMENT(S)

Most mid-caliber, black powder revolver cartridges in military service during the late 1800s provided anemic ballistic performance. Much of this was due to the revolver being regarded as a military officer's badge of rank, rather than the expectation of actually having to stop an adversary in his tracks. Of course, low maximum average chamber pressures were another handicap. The U.S. Army soon found this concept faulty and went back to a .45 caliber handgun. After all, if low chamber pressure was preferred, better to use it to drive a large caliber, heavy bullet (the .45 Colt comes to mind here). However, the .38 Long Colt "soldiered" on in the commercial market until this day.

.38 SMITH & WESSON

ALTERNATE NAME(S): .38 S&W, .38 S&W Super Police
RELATED CALIBER(S): .380/200, .38 S&W Spl.

CARTRIDGE HISTORY

Year of Introduction: circa 1877
Country of Origin: U.S.
Designer(s): Smith & Wesson
Governing Body: SAAMI, CIP
Present Status: obsolete

CARTRIDGE DESCRIPTION

Bullet Diameter: .361 in.
Bullet Weight(s): 145-200 gr.
Rifling Twist Rate: 1 turn in 18.75 in.
Test Barrel Length: 5 in.
Case Type: rimmed, straight
Case Material: brass
Primer Type: small pistol

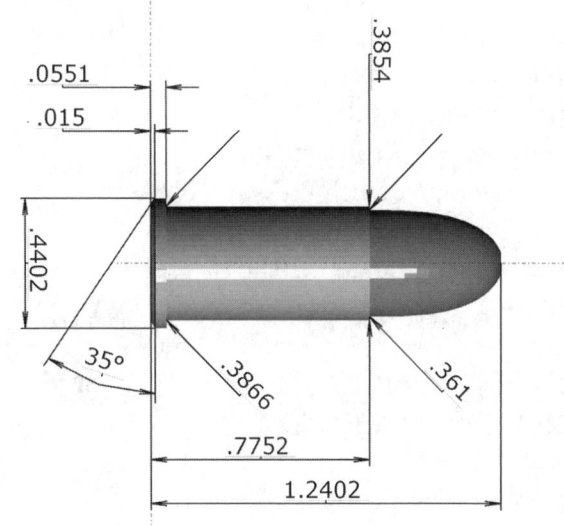

CARTRIDGE BALLISTICS

Max. Average Breech Pressure: 17,450 psi.
Max. Effective Range: 25 yds.
Max. Horizontal Range: 1,400 yds.
Max. Vertical Range: 3,200 ft.

Bullet Weight (gr.)	Bullet Type	Muzzle Velocity (fps)	Muzzle Energy (ft.-lbs.)
145	LRN	685	150
200	FMJ	630	176

CURRENT MANUFACTURER(S)
Remington, Winchester, Fiocchi

GENERAL COMMENT(S)
Thousands of old revolvers in this classic caliber help maintain a limited, but steady, demand that supports continued production. However, no new handguns in this caliber have been manufactured for many years. The .380/200 was adopted as the service bullet for the British Army just before World War II. In law enforcement service, the 200 grain lead bullet was known as the .38 S&W Super Police.

TECHNICAL COMMENT(S)
Here is another heritage caliber that offers fairly snappy ballistic performance by 19th century standards, but is hopelessly outclassed by modern standards of handgun cartridge performance. But who says a cartridge has to be modern to remain effective? The very low chamber pressure precludes any creative attempts at performance upgrades.

.401 HERTERS POWERMAG

ALTERNATE NAME(S): .401 PowerMag
RELATED CALIBER(S): .41 Rem. Magnum

CARTRIDGE HISTORY
Year of Introduction: 1961
Country of Origin: Germany
Designer(s): DWM
Governing Body: none
Present Status: obsolete

CARTRIDGE DESCRIPTION
Bullet Diameter: .403 in.
Bullet Weight(s): 240 gr.
Rifling Twist Rate: N/A
Test Barrel Length: 5.9 in.
Case Type: rimmed, straight
Case Material: brass
Primer: large pistol

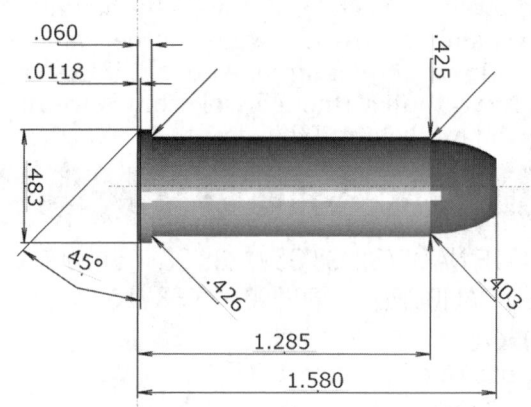

CARTRIDGE BALLISTICS
Max. Average Breech Pressure: N/A
Max. Horizontal Range: 2,450 yds.
Max. Vertical Range: 5,100 ft.

Bullet Weight (gr.)	Bullet Type	Muzzle Velocity (fps)	Muzzle Energy (ft.-lbs.)
240	JSP	1,200	767

CURRENT MANUFACTURER(S)
None

GENERAL COMMENT(S)
Herter's of Waseca, MN was active in the mail order business from the late 1950s until the early 1970s. One of Herter's specialties was firearms and ammunition. In the late 1950s, Herter's correctly foresaw the growing interest in single-action revolvers chambered for modern, large-bore, magnum cartridges. Accordingly, Herter's contracted with Sauer & Sohn in Germany to make a copy of the classic, Colt Single-Action Army revolver chambered for a new cartridge called the .401 Herter's PowerMag. The revolver and cartridge quickly became popular. So much so, that three years later Remington introduced their .41 Remington Magnum cartridge with similar proportions and ballistics.

TECHNICAL COMMENT(S)

Herter's .401 PowerMag cartridge was unique at the time. It was more powerful than the .357 Magnum, but less of a handful than the .44 Remington Magnum. Herter's success with the .401 PowerMag ended in the 1970s when the company ceased operations. Manufacture of .401 PowerMag ammunition was not taken up by any of the major ammunition makers. Today, .401 Herter's PowerMag cartridges are collector's items.

.41 LONG COLT

ALTERNATE NAME(S): .41 LC
RELATED CALIBER(S): none

CARTRIDGE HISTORY

Year of Introduction: 1877
Country of Origin: U.S.
Designer(s): Colt
Governing Body: none
Present Status: obsolete

CARTRIDGE DESCRIPTION

Bullet Diameter: .401 in.
Bullet Weight(s): 200 gr.
Rifling Twist Rate: 1 turn in 16 in.
Test Barrel Length: 6 in.
Case Type: rimmed, straight
Case Material: brass
Primer Type: large pistol

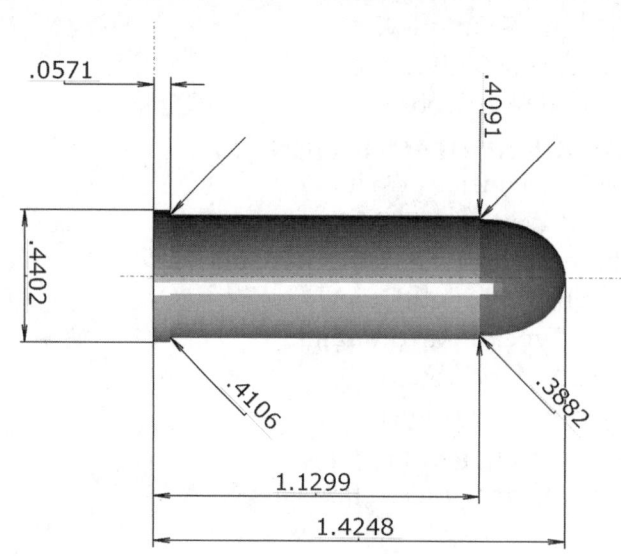

CARTRIDGE BALLISTICS

Max. Average Breech Pressure: 13,053 psi.
Max. Effective Range: 25 yds.
Max. Horizontal Range: 1,900 yds.
Max. Vertical Range: 4,200 ft.

Bullet Weight (gr.)	Bullet Type	Muzzle Velocity (fps)	Muzzle Energy (ft.-lbs.)
200	L-RN	730	235

CURRENT MANUFACTURER(S)

None

GENERAL COMMENT(S)

This cartridge was introduced in 1877 for the new Colt Lightning double-action revolver. At that time, double-action revolvers were new so the .41 Long Colt cartridge gained a market foot hold by means of the new revolver. Later, the .41 Long Colt was chambered in other revolvers such as the Colt Single-action Army. Although long obsolete, the .41 Long Colt has enjoyed a modest revival recently with the growing popularity of cowboy action competition.

TECHNICAL COMMENT(S)

The .41 Long Colt cartridge began life as a black powder number and made the transition to smokeless propellant. When it did so, the outside-lubricated, .401 inch diameter bullet of the black powder loading was changed to an inside-lubricated, hollow-base bullet of approximately .387 inch diameter. At close range, the blunt, heavy bullet of the .41 Long Colt had a good reputation for stopping power. Muzzle energy was only 65% of its big brother, the .45 Colt, however recoil was lower and the Colt Lightning double-action mechanism allowed very fast follow-up shots.

.44 WEBLEY

ALTERNATE NAME(S): .442 Royal Irish Constabulary (RIC), 10.5x17Rmm, .442 Kurz
RELATED CALIBER(S): .44 Bulldog, .45 Webley

CARTRIDGE HISTORY
Year of Introduction: 1868
Country of Origin: Britain
Designer(s): Webley
Governing Body: none
Present Status: obsolete

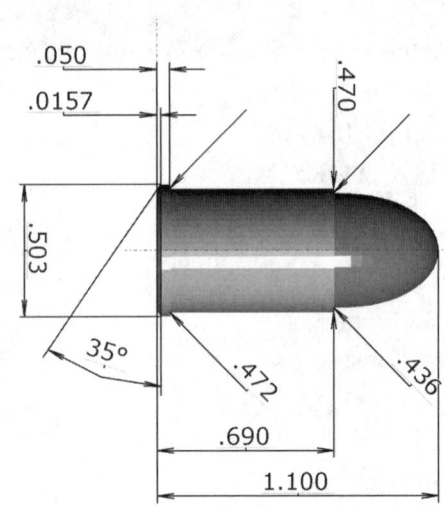

CARTRIDGE DESCRIPTION
Bullet Diameter: .436 in.
Bullet Weight(s): 200-220 gr.
Rifling Twist Rate: 1 turn in 20 in.
Test Barrel Length: N/A
Case Type: rimmed, straight
Case Material: brass
Primer: large pistol

CARTRIDGE BALLISTICS
Max. Average Breech Pressure: N/A
Max. Horizontal Range: 1,600 yds.
Max. Vertical Range: 3,150 ft.

Bullet Weight (gr.)	Bullet Type	Muzzle Velocity (fps)	Muzzle Energy (ft.-lbs.)
200	L-RN	715	230
220	L-RN	700	239

CURRENT MANUFACTURER(S)
None

GENERAL COMMENT(S)
This cartridge was developed by Webley in 1868 for the Royal Irish Constabulary or RIC in Northern Ireland. In civilian form, this cartridge was called the .44 Webley and became a favorite caliber for small, personal defense revolvers. Production life of this cartridge extended to the beginning of World War II in 1939.

TECHNICAL COMMENT(S)
The .442 RIC/.44 Webley is a typical, low-powered revolver cartridge of its era suitable only for personal defense at close ranges. Originally loaded with black powder, it made the transition to smokeless propellants around 1900. The .44 Webley case served as the basis for the later .45 Webley cartridge.

.44 MERWIN & HULBERT

ALTERNATE NAME(S): .44 M&H
RELATED CALIBER(S): .44 S&W American, .44 Webley

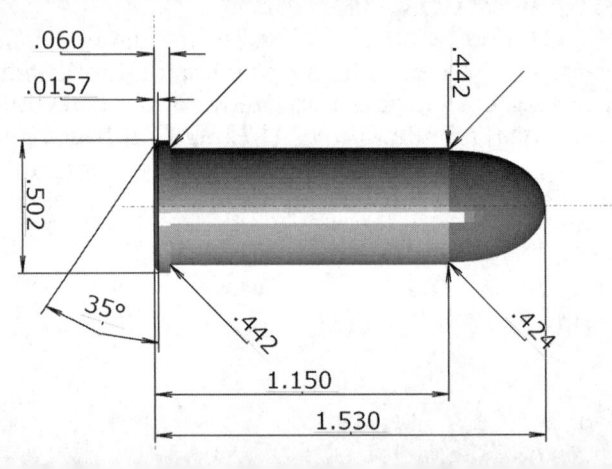

CARTRIDGE HISTORY
Year of Introduction: circa 1882
Country of Origin: U.S.
Designer(s): Merwin & Hulbert
Governing Body: none
Present Status: obsolete

CARTRIDGE DESCRIPTION
Bullet Diameter: .424 in.
Bullet Weight(s): 220 gr.
Rifling Twist Rate: 1 turn in 20 in.

Test Barrel Length: N/A
Case Type: rimmed, straight
Case Material: brass
Primer: large pistol

CARTRIDGE BALLISTICS
Max. Average Breech Pressure: N/A
Max. Horizontal Range: 1,900 yds.
Max. Vertical Range: 3,850 ft.

Bullet Weight (gr.)	Bullet Type	Muzzle Velocity (fps)	Muzzle Energy (ft.-lbs.)
220	L-RN	860	350

CURRENT MANUFACTURER(S)
None

GENERAL COMMENT(S)
By the time the .44 Merwin & Hulbert cartridge appeared around 1882, the .44-40 Winchester and .45 Colt cartridges had already been around for almost ten years. During that time, both established an enviable reputation as reliable personal defense cartridges. Enter Merwin & Hulbert with their well-regarded revolver chambered for their new .44 Merwin & Hulbert cartridge. From the beginning, it was clear that the revolver would have to carry the cartridge in the market. It was unable to do so and the .44 M&H cartridge had become history by 1920.

TECHNICAL COMMENT(S)
Merwin & Hulbert based their new cartridge on a .44 S&W American case. Head dimensions of the two were nearly identical, but the .44 M&H cartridge had a 0.24 inch longer body offering 20% more case volume. While its ballistics were inferior to the .44-40 Win. and .45 Colt, they were far superior to the .41 Long Colt, .44 Russian and .44 S&W American.

.44 BULLDOG

ALTERNATE NAME(S): .44 Webley Bulldog
RELATED CALIBER(S): .44 Webley, .45 Webley

CARTRIDGE HISTORY
Year of Introduction: circa 1880
Country of Origin: Britain
Designer(s): Webley
Governing Body: none
Present Status: obsolete

CARTRIDGE DESCRIPTION
Bullet Diameter: .440 in.
Bullet Weight(s): 170 gr.
Rifling Twist Rate: 1 turn in 21 in.
Test Barrel Length: N/A
Case Type: rimmed, straight
Case Material: brass
Primer: N/A

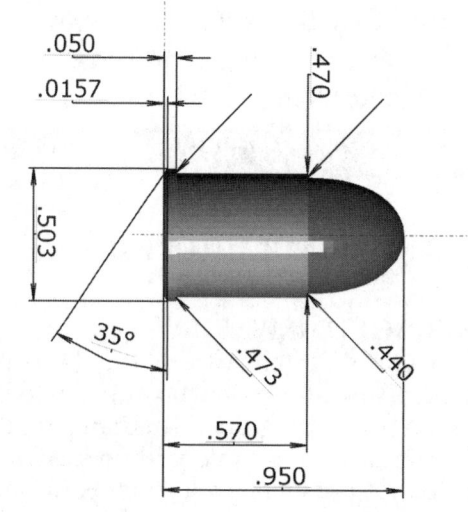

CARTRIDGE BALLISTICS
Max. Average Breech Pressure: N/A
Max. Horizontal Range: 1,000 yds.
Max. Vertical Range: 1,750 ft.

Bullet Weight (gr.)	Bullet Type	Muzzle Velocity (fps)	Muzzle Energy (ft.-lbs.)
170	L-RN	460	80

CURRENT MANUFACTURER(S)
None

GENERAL COMMENT(S)
By 1880, many city dwellers routinely carried a small revolver for personal defense. Prior to that time, most handguns of this type were chambered for one of the weak rimfire calibers. In the early 1880s, the fashion in low-powered revolvers for this purpose shifted from rimfire to centerfire cartridges such as the .44 Bulldog.

TECHNICAL COMMENT(S)
To modern minds, a 170 grain .44 caliber bullet with less striking energy than a typical .22 Long Rifle rimfire cartridge seems ludicrous. However, at very close ranges, the .44 Bulldog cartridge was perfectly capable of inflicting a serious wound which was the goal of this class of cartridges.

.44 SMITH & WESSON AMERICAN

ALTERNATE NAME(S): .44 S&W American, .44 American
RELATED CALIBER(S): .44 Merwin & Hulbert, .44 Russian, .44 S&W Special

CARTRIDGE HISTORY
Year of Introduction: circa 1869
Country of Origin: U.S.
Designer(s): Smith & Wesson
Governing Body: none
Present Status: obsolete

CARTRIDGE DESCRIPTION
Bullet Diameter: .434 in.
Bullet Weight(s): 205 gr.
Rifling Twist Rate: 1 turn in 20 in.
Test Barrel Length: N/A
Case Type: rimmed, straight
Case Material: brass
Primer: large pistol

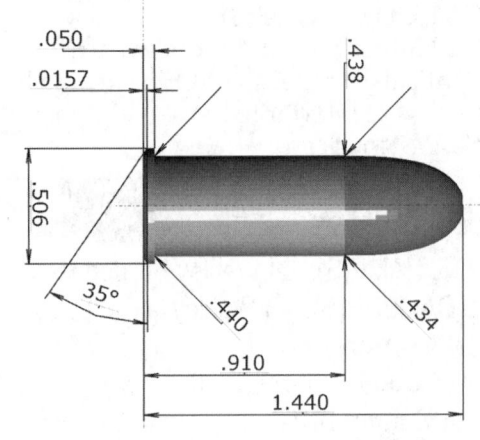

CARTRIDGE BALLISTICS
Max. Average Breech Pressure: N/A
Max. Horizontal Range: 1,550 yds.
Max. Vertical Range: 3,100 ft.

Bullet Weight (gr.)	Bullet Type	Muzzle Velocity (fps)	Muzzle Energy (ft.-lbs.)
205	L-RN	680	212

CURRENT MANUFACTURER(S)
None

GENERAL COMMENT(S)
In the Old West (circa 1870), the .44 S&W American cartridge became a popular choice among knowledgeable shooters and shootists who appreciated the knock-down power and accuracy of this caliber. During this time, Buffalo Bill Cody guided Russian Grand Duke Alexis on a hunting trip in the western states. It is recorded that the Grand Duke was very impressed with the .44 S&W Army Revolver in .44 S&W American caliber that Bill carried for personal protection. For a short time (1871-1873), the U.S. Army adopted this cartridge for military use. Both Smith & Wesson and Merwin & Hulbert made revolvers in this caliber.More powerful cartridges such as the .44-40 Winchester and .45 Colt soon eclipsed the .44 S&W American in ballistic performance. However, the .44 American held its own until the late 1890s, then made the transition to smokeless propellants. It remained in production until 1940.

TECHNICAL COMMENT(S)
From the ballistic standpoint of the time, the .44 American cartridge offered a good balance of case capacity (for black powder), bullet weight, muzzle velocity and moderate recoil. More powerful cartridges generated greater striking energy, but they also increased recoil, cost and weight. These were more important considerations in those days than now.

.45 AUTO RIM

ALTERNATE NAME(S): .45 A.R.
RELATED CALIBER(S): .45 ACP

CARTRIDGE HISTORY
Year of Introduction: 1920
Country of Origin: U.S.
Designer(s): Peters Cartridge Co.
Governing Body: SAAMI
Present Status: obsolete

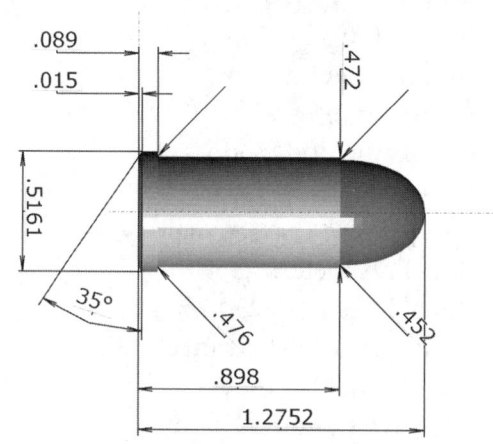

CARTRIDGE DESCRIPTION
Bullet Diameter: .452 in.
Bullet Weight(s): 230 gr.
Rifling Twist Rate: 1 turn in 16 in.
Test Barrel Length: 6 in.
Case Type: rimmed, straight
Case Material: brass
Primer Type: large pistol

CARTRIDGE BALLISTICS
Max. Average Breech Pressure: 16,900 CUP.
Max. Effective Range: 25 yds.
Max. Horizontal Range: 1,650 yds.
Max. Vertical Range: 3,700 ft.

Bullet Weight (gr.)	Bullet Type	Muzzle Velocity (fps)	Muzzle Energy (ft.-lbs.)
230	LRN	805	331

CURRENT MANUFACTURER(S)
PMC, Cor-Bon, Black Hills

GENERAL COMMENT(S)
At first sight, most people are confounded by this odd cartridge. Its unusually thick rim appears to serve no obvious purpose. But the .45 Auto Rim has two purposes, specifically in relation to World War I Model 1917 and modern revolvers chambered for the .45 ACP cartridge. Those revolvers require the use of "half-moon" or "full-moon" clips (which are snapped into the .45 ACP case extractor groove) to maintain headspace, and to act as a rim so the revolver's extractor can be used to remove all fired cases simultaneously. Without "moon clips," misfires are likely, and each .45 ACP case has to be manually pushed out of each chamber. The .45 Auto Rim cartridge does not requre "moon clips," and provides versatility of energy, velocity, projectile weight/shape/type, and cartridge overall length not available with .45 ACP loads intended for semi-auto pistol use.

TECHNICAL COMMENT(S)
The .45 Auto Rim was/is a clever design that works very well, but only in revolvers specifically designed to chamber .45 ACP cartridges with "moon clips." It can be reloaded using standard .45 ACP dies, but a unique shellholder is required. High performance loads are currently available for use in short barrel self-defense revolvers.

.45 SMITH & WESSON

ALTERNATE NAME(S): .45 S&W Schofield, .45 Schofield
RELATED CALIBER(S): .45 Colt

CARTRIDGE HISTORY
Year of Introduction: 1875
Country of Origin: U.S.
Designer(s): S&W
Governing Body: none
Present Status: obsolete

CARTRIDGE DESCRIPTION
Bullet Diameter: .4559 in.
Bullet Weight(s): 230-250 gr.
Rifling Twist Rate: 1 turn in 16 in.
Test Barrel Length: 6 in.
Case Type: rimmed, straight
Case Material: brass
Primer Type: large pistol

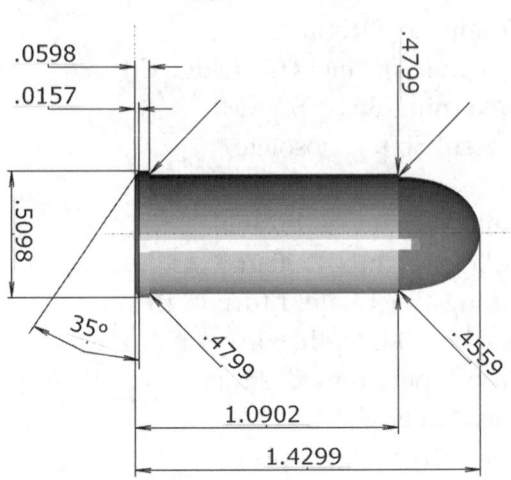

CARTRIDGE BALLISTICS
Max. Average Breech Pressure: 14,504 psi.
Max. Effective Range: 25 yds.
Max. Horizontal Range: 1,860 yds.
Max. Vertical Range: 4,175 ft.

Bullet Weight (gr.)	Bullet Type	Muzzle Velocity (fps)	Muzzle Energy (ft.-lbs.)
230	L-RN	730	276
250	L-RN	710	283

CURRENT MANUFACTURER(S)
Black Hills

GENERAL COMMENT(S)
Shortly after the U.S. Army adopted the .45 Colt cartridge for use in Colt Single-Action Army revolvers, they also adopted the .45 S&W cartridge for use in S&W Schofield revolvers. The .45 S&W remained in service until 1892 when it was replaced by the .38 Long Colt.

TECHNICAL COMMENT(S)
As the Schofield revolver's cylinder was not long enough for the .45 Colt cartridge, it had to make do with the shorter, less-powerful .45 S&W. This cartridge did not have the terminal ballistic performance of its service brother, the .45 Colt. While the .45 Colt offered 490 ft.-lbs. of muzzle energy, the .45 S&W had just 58% of the Colt's energy. This substantial difference was compensated for, in part, by the top-break extractor design of the Schofield revolver which made reloading much faster.

.45 WEBLEY

ALTERNATE NAME(S): .45 Webley Bulldog
RELATED CALIBER(S): .44 Bulldog, .44 Webley, .450 Revolver

CARTRIDGE HISTORY
Year of Introduction: circa 1875
Country of Origin: Britain
Designer(s): Webley
Governing Body: none
Present Status: obsolete

CARTRIDGE DESCRIPTION
Bullet Diameter: 452 in.
Bullet Weight(s): 230 gr.
Rifling Twist Rate: 1 turn in 16 in.
Test Barrel Length: N/A
Case Type: rimmed, straight
Case Material: brass
Primer: large pistol

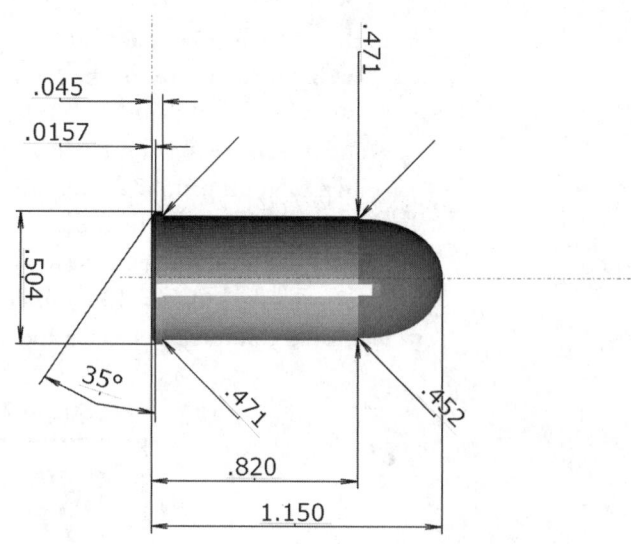

CARTRIDGE BALLISTICS
Max. Average Breech Pressure: N/A
Max. Horizontal Range: 1,400 yds.
Max. Vertical Range: 2,600 ft.

Bullet Weight (gr.)	Bullet Type	Muzzle Velocity (fps)	Muzzle Energy (ft.-lbs.)
230	L-RN	550	150

CURRENT MANUFACTURER(S)
None

GENERAL COMMENT(S)
Webley introduced this cartridge for their popular Bulldog series of revolvers in the late 1870s. When it became a popular chambering, American manufacturers also made it until the advent of World War II in 1939.

TECHNICAL COMMENT(S)
When the .45 Webley cartridge was introduced, the .450 Revolver cartridge was in the sunset of its British military service. To simplify cost, the .45 Webley cartridge used the same case head dimensions as the .450 Revolver. The two cartridges were interchangeable in most guns. Although both cartridges were loaded with lead bullets of nearly the same caliber and weight, the muzzle velocity of the Webley cartridge was 100-150 fps lower than the .450 Revolver cartridge. At very close ranges, this did not matter. At longer ranges, bullets from the two cartridges had substantially different points of impact. To put the ballistic performance of these two cartridges into perspective, a major reason the .450 Revolver cartridge was replaced in British military service in 1880 was its poor ballistic performance. The .45 Webley was substantially less powerful than the .450 Revolver cartridge!

Not Lost, Just Unpopular

Where Are All The 6.5 mm Pistol Cartridges?

Have you noticed that pistol cartridges between .25 and .30 caliber are few and far between? In 1896, the German firm of Theo. Bergmann thought so too and introduced their 6.5 mm Bergmann cartridge. Not to be outdone, Mauser and Deutsche Waffen-und Munition Fabriken AG (DWM) developed their own 6.5 mm pistol cartridges in the early 1900s using existing cartridge cases with 6.5 mm (.264 inch diameter) bullets. Unlike Bergmann, these cartridges remained experimental, however the observer must admit they look modern for cartridges almost 100 years old. The 6.5 mm Bergmann cartridge enjoyed limited commercial success and was discontinued in the early 1930s.

6.35 mm Mauser (.250 caliber)

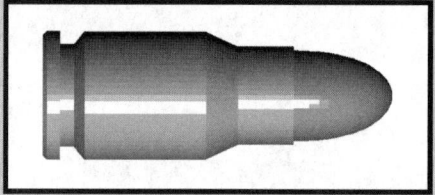

6.5 mm Parabellum

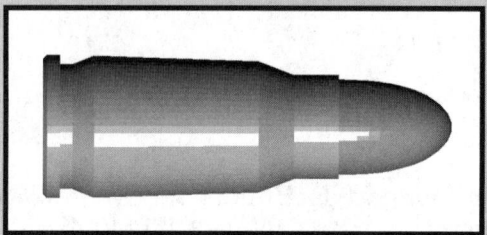

6.5 mm Mauser

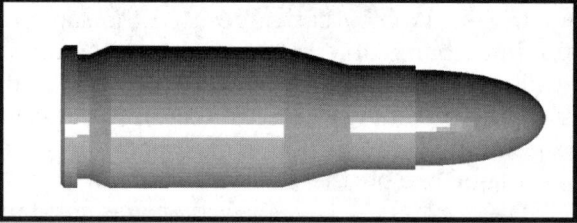

6.5 mm Bergmann

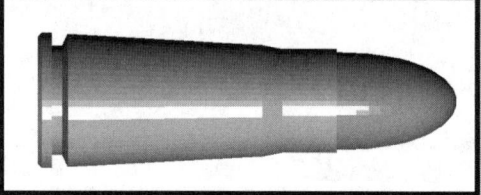

CHAPTER 73 : SPORTING PISTOL - CURRENT

CHAPTER 73

For Cartridge Index see Chapter 101. All drawing dimensions are approximate.

When it comes to cartridges for personal defense, there are two schools of thought: one recommends heavy, large caliber (.40 or larger) bullets at muzzle velocities up to 1,000 FPS while the other advocates small caliber (.38 or less) lightweight bullets at muzzle velocities over 1,100 FPS. Both agree that the goal of a self-defense cartridge is to instantly incapacitate an assailant by means of efficient energy transfer. They differ on how to achieve this. Heavy bullet advocates believe bullet diameter and mass are the keys while the lightweight bullet crowd prefers high striking velocity and expanding bullets. This argument has been raging back and forth for over 100 years with no compromise in sight. Readers should keep this dichotomy in mind when reviewing the following cartridge data as it provides an insight into the development of calibers such as the .357 SIG and the .40 S&W Auto, and expanding handgun bullets.

Most ballistic pundits quickly dismiss any handgun cartridge smaller than the .380 ACP as unacceptable for personal defense. Normally included on this list are all the .25 .30, .32, and .380 caliber cartridges. However, this short-sighted view ignores several key points. First, these small caliber cartridges are intended to be used at very close ranges where their lower ballistic capabilities are of less importance. Second, the ability to conceal a small handgun may be more important than a small cartridge's ballistic performance. In an emergency, it is still better having a small caliber handgun than no gun at all.

Target shooters are a special breed. Their numbers are small, yet they fire large amounts of ammunition. This gives them an influence on the ammunition industry that is out of proportion with their relatively small numbers. Handgun competitors participate in a wide variety of disciplines, including bulls eye, metallic silhouette, and combat. However, common to all types of handgun competition is the requirement for ammunition of superior, or match grade, accuracy. Match ammunition is more expensive than standard grades of ammunition, but absolutely necessary for experienced competitors. The reader will note a variety of match loads in several calibers listed, many with wadcutter or semi-wadcutter bullets.

Innovation sells, and for this reason ammunition manufacturers are constantly developing new handgun calibers with which they hope to start a new wave of shooter interest and, of course, profitable sales. Historically, the seeds of innovative handgun cartridges have been sown in the fertile ground of handgunners' continuing demand for such products. However, many new handgun calibers never catch on and are quickly put to rest. Readers interested in moribund calibers are directed to Chapter 74: Sporting Pistol - Obsolete.

As you review the following data, it seems appropriate to quote an old adage regarding handgun cartridges:

"The only reason I didn't buy a .65 Super Magnum +P is they do not make one!" Perhaps, but remember you can buy more gun than you can handle!

5.45x18mm SOVIET

ALTERNATE NAME(S): 5.45x18mm , 5.45x18mm Auto
RELATED CALIBER(S): Unique

CARTRIDGE HISTORY
Year of Introduction: late 1970s
Country of Origin: Soviet Union
Designer(s): N/A
Governing Body: CIP
Present Status: active

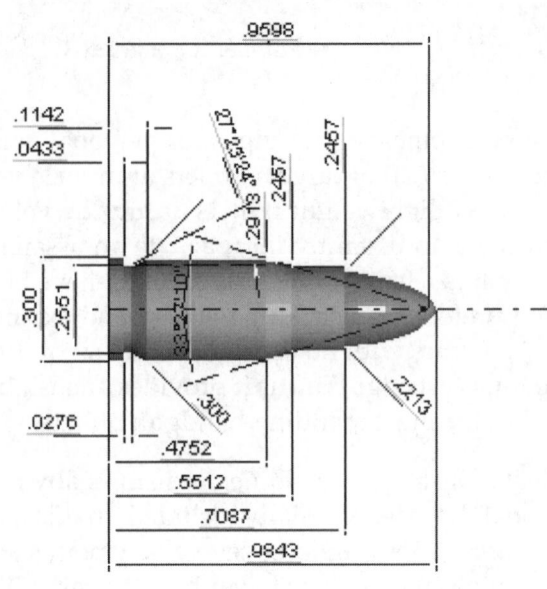

CARTRIDGE DESCRIPTION
Bullet Diameter: .221 in.
Bullet Weight(s): 40 gr.
Rifling Twist Rate: 1 turn in 18.75 in.
Test Barrel Length: 24 in.
Case Type: rimless, necked
Case Material: steel
Primer Type: small pistol

CARTRIDGE BALLISTICS
Max. Average Breech Pressure: 25,382 psi.
Max. Effective Range: 15 yds.
Max. Horizontal Range: 1,985 yds.
Max. Vertical Range: 4,210 ft.

Bullet Weight (gr.)	Bullet Type	Muzzle Velocity (fps)	Muzzle Energy (ft.-lbs.)
40	FMJ	1,035	95

CURRENT MANUFACTURER(S)
Russian companies, Prvi Partizan

GENERAL COMMENT(S)
This diminutive cartridge was developed in the Soviet Union in the 1970s for an ultra-slim, small automatic pistol called the PSM. The 5.45x18mm Soviet was not adopted by the Soviet military and the PSM is the only known pistol chambered for this cartridge. For these reasons, it appears this cartridge was designed for personal defense and undercover law enforcement. This is confirmed by the use of this pistol and cartridge for VIP security.

TECHNICAL COMMENT(S)
With a muzzle energy of only 95 ft.-lbs., it is easy to dismiss this cartridge as nothing more than a glorified .22 Long Rifle cartridge. This is not true. The.22 Long Rifle cartridge with the solid lead bullet is well known for its penetration ability. While the striking energy of the .22 L.R. is not high, it is concentrated. The 5.45x18mm cartridge is very similar in this respect with the added advantage of a steel penetrator under the bullet tip to allow penetration of body armor.

.221 FIREBALL

ALTERNATE NAME(S): .221 Remington Fireball
RELATED CALIBER(S): .222 Rem., .223 Rem.

CARTRIDGE HISTORY
Year of Introduction: 1963
Country of Origin: U.S.
Designer(s): Remington
Governing Body: SAAMI
Present Status: active

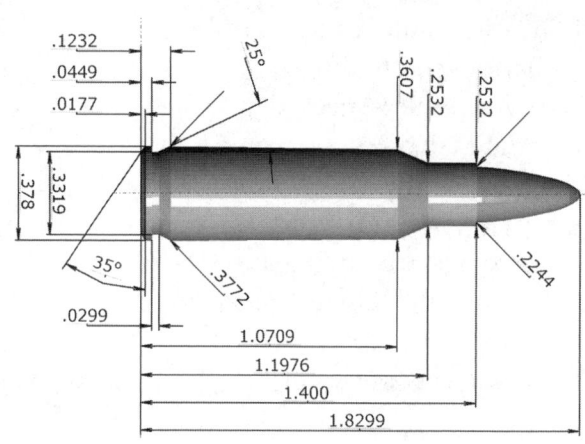

CARTRIDGE DESCRIPTION
Bullet Diameter: .224 in.
Bullet Weight(s): 50 gr.
Rifling Twist Rate: 1 turn in 12 in.
Test Barrel Length: 24 in.
Case Type: rimless, necked
Case Material: brass
Primer Type: small rifle

CARTRIDGE BALLISTICS
Max. Average Breech Pressure: 55,500 psi.
Max. Effective Range: 200 yds.
Max. Horizontal Range: 2,500 yds.
Max. Vertical Range: 6,000 ft.

Bullet Weight (gr.)	Bullet Type	Muzzle Velocity (fps)	Muzzle Energy (ft.-lbs.)
50	JSP	2,650	780

CURRENT MANUFACTURER(S)
Remington

GENERAL COMMENT(S)
The .221 Fireball is not really a handgun cartridge by any classic measure. Rather it is a rifle cartridge adapted for use in a long-barreled handgun typically using a single-shot rifle bolt-action. Cartridges used in such handguns have rifle-class chamber pressures that substantially exceed those of most other handgun cartridges.   Such handguns are designed to be fired from a rest normally for hunting varmints and small game. Examples in standard rifle calibers have been developed for hunting medium and even large game. Designed by Remington in 1963, the .221 Fireball was the first of this type.

TECHNICAL COMMENT(S)
Mike Walker's classic .222 Rem. cartridge served as the basis for the .221 Fireball. Both have the same head and rim dimensions and use bullets of the same caliber. However, the .221 Fireball uses a shorter case of smaller capacity for improved efficiency in the shorter barrel of handguns. Bullets of 50 grains or less work best in the Fireball.

.22 TUASON CRAIG MICROMAGNUM

ALTERNATE NAME(S): .22 TCM
RELATED CALIBER(S): .223 Rem., 9mm Luger

CARTRIDGE HISTORY
Year of Introduction: circa 2011
Country of Origin: Philippines
Designer(s): Fred Craig
Governing Body: None
Present Status: active

CARTRIDGE DESCRIPTION
Bullet Diameter: .2245 in.

Bullet Weight(s): 40 gr.

Rifling Twist Rate: 1 turn in 12 in.

Test Barrel Length: 5 in.

Case Type: rimless, necked

Case Material: brass

Primer Type: rifle

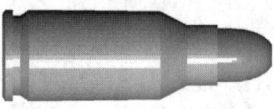

Dimesions are not available.

CARTRIDGE BALLISTICS
Max. Average Breech Pressure: 35,000 psi.

Max. Horizontal Range: 1,660 yds.

Max. Vertical Range: 3,800 ft.

Bullet Weight (gr.)	Bullet Type	Muzzle Velocity (fps)	Muzzle Energy (ft.-lbs.)
40	SP	2,100	392

CURRENT MANUFACTURER(S)
Armscor

GENERAL COMMENT(S)
This is the first cartridge designed in the Philippines. Armscor of the Philippines, the manufacturer, chambers this new cartridge in a number of their popular M1911 semi-automatic pistols. The company will load this, and many other rifle and pistol calibers, in a new ammunition plant in Stevensville, MT.

TECHNICAL COMMENT(S)
The .22 TCM cartridge is a new concept that uses a small caliber, high velocity bullet in a semi-automatic pistol. Based on a shortened and necked down .223 Rem. cartridge case with an overall loaded length of approximately 1.16 inches, the .22 TCM fits in most 9mm Luger caliber M1911 pistols and magazines with a minimum of modification.

By using a 40 grain jacketed soft point bullet, Armscor states that the .22 TCM cartridge develops a muzzle velocity of 2,100 fps and 392 ft.-lbs. of muzzle energy from a 5 inch barrel. Recoil is claimed to be mild and terminal performance of the small bullet impressive.

.25 AUTO

ALTERNATE NAME(S): .25 ACP, 6.35mm ACP, 6.35mm Browning, 6.35x15.5mm
RELATED CALIBER(S): .32 ACP, .380 ACP

CARTRIDGE HISTORY
Year of Introduction: circa 1900

Country of Origin: Belgium

Designer(s): John Browning

Governing Body: CIP, SAAMI

Present Status: active

CARTRIDGE DESCRIPTION
Bullet Diameter: .251 in.

Bullet Weight(s): 40 gr.

Rifling Twist Rate: 1 turn in 10 in.

Test Barrel Length: 3 in.

Case Type: semi-rimmed, straight

Case Material: brass

Primer Type: small pistol

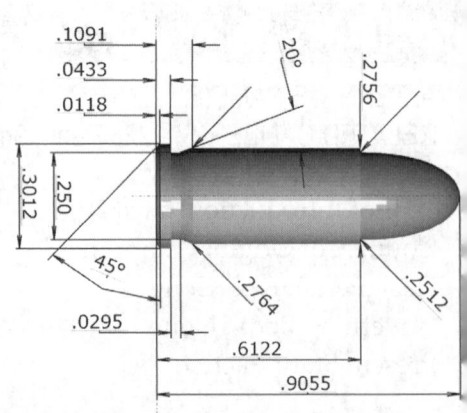

CARTRIDGE BALLISTICS
Max. Average Breech Pressure: 25,000 psi.

Max. Effective Range: 7 yds.

Max. Horizontal Range: 1,200 yds.
Max. Vertical Range: 2,700 ft.

Bullet Weight (gr.)	Bullet Type	Muzzle Velocity (fps)	Muzzle Energy (ft.-lbs.)
35	JHP	900	63
45	JSP	815	66
59	FMJ	760	64

CURRENT MANUFACTURER(S)

Federal, Remington, Winchester, Cor-Bon, Hornady, CBC, Fiocchi, Sellier & Bellot, PMC, Industrias Technos, Speer, CCI

GENERAL COMMENT(S)

Ballistic concepts of suitable cartridges for personal defense were very different in the late 1890s and early 1900s than they are today. Small, low powered cartridges chambered in small revolvers or derringers were the norm. Such guns and cartridges were designed more to dissuade than to incapacitate, although they could, and frequently did, kill the person struck. Enter the semi-automatic pistol about 1900. Smokeless powder and improved metallurgy made such handguns feasible. Into this mix stepped John Browning with a radical for the time ultra-small semi-automatic pistol that one could carry discretely in their vest pocket. Indeed, this was the very name of the pistol. The new pistol needed a new cartridge suitable for semi-automatic handguns and detachable magazines. The .25 ACP was his answer.

TECHNICAL COMMENT(S)

A normal powder charge used in this diminutive cartridge case is about one grain making the .25 ACP essentially a primer-powered cartridge. Indeed, individual cartridges with little or no powder can normally work a gun. Although muzzle energy of the .25 ACP is in the .22 Long Rifle class, the .25 Auto bullet is heavier and jacketed allowing it to penetrate more deeply than the lead bullets of the .22 L.R. Regardless, the continued popularity of the .25 ACP is not based on its ballistics. Rather, the main reason for the long lasting popularity of the .25 ACP is intimidation of an attacker. Ammunition companies do not like the .25 ACP as this centerfire cartridge is so small, it must be made on rimfire machinery.

.25 NAA

ALTERNATE NAME(S): .25 North American Arms
RELATED CALIBER(S): .32 Auto

CARTRIDGE HISTORY

Year of Introduction: 1999
Country of Origin: U.S.
Designer(s): J.B. Wood
Governing Body: SAAMI
Present Status: active

CARTRIDGE DESCRIPTION

Bullet Diameter: .251 in.
Bullet Weight(s): 35 gr.
Rifling Twist Rate: 1 turn in 16 in.
Test Barrel Length: 3 in.
Case Type: rimless, necked
Case Material: brass
Primer Type: small pistol

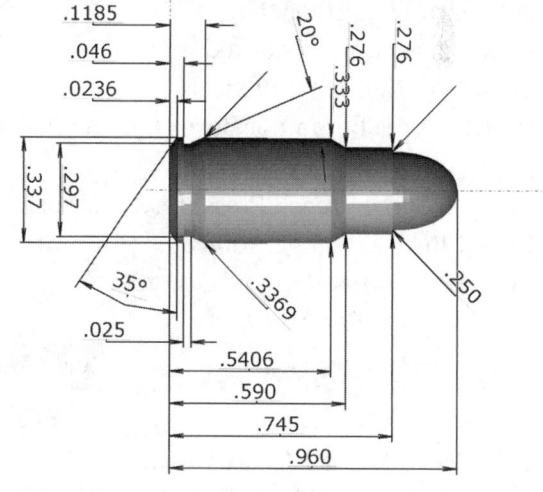

CARTRIDGE BALLISTICS

Max. Average Breech Pressure: 20,500
Max. Effective Range: 10 yds.
Max. Horizontal Range: 1,600 yds.
Max. Vertical Range: 3,000 ft.

Bullet Weight (gr.)	Bullet Type	Muzzle Velocity (fps)	Muzzle Energy (ft.-lbs.)
35	JHP	1,200	112

CURRENT MANUFACTURER(S)
Cor-Bon

GENERAL COMMENT(S)
Called affectionately the "Mighty Mouse", the .25 NAA is an effort to upgrade the ballistic performance of small, concealable handguns of .25 caliber. In this, J.B. Wood has been successful. Undercover law enforcement officers who have tested this cartridge gave it the nickname.

TECHNICAL COMMENT(S)
Although the bullet used in the .25 NAA cartridge is substantially lighter than the .25 ACP, it is an expanding design to more effectively transfer the striking energy which is approximately double than of the .25 ACP. The .25 NAA is based on a necked down .32 ACP cartridge case.

7.62x25mm TOKAREV

ALTERNATE NAME(S): 7.62mm Tokarev, 7.62 M38/40, 7.62 M40, 7.62 Type P, 7.62 Type 50, 7.62x24.6mm, Pist. Patr. 2601

RELATED CALIBER(S): 7.65mm Mauser (.30 Mauser)

CARTRIDGE HISTORY
Year of Introduction: 1930
Country of Origin: Soviet Union
Designer(s): Fedor V. Tokarev
Governing Body: CIP
Present Status: active

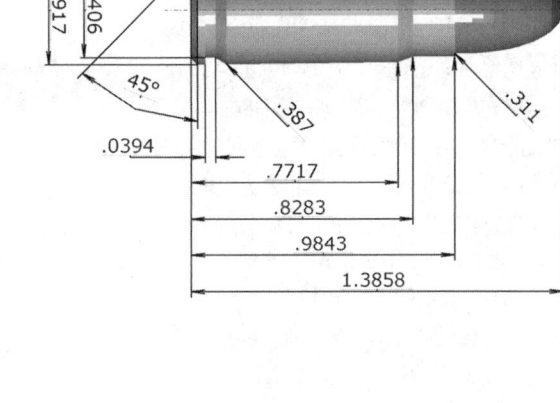

CARTRIDGE DESCRIPTION
Bullet Diameter: .308 in.
Bullet Weight(s): 85-87 gr.
Rifling Twist Rate: 1 turn in 9.45 in.
Test Barrel Length: 5.9 in.
Case Type: rimless, necked
Case Material: brass or steel
Primer Type: Berdan or Boxer (small pistol)

CARTRIDGE BALLISTICS
Max. Average Breech Pressure: 35,750 psi.
Max. Effective Range: 150 yds.
Max. Horizontal Range: 2,500 yds.
Max. Vertical Range: 5,500 ft.

Bullet Weight (gr.)	Bullet Type	Muzzle Velocity (fps)	Muzzle Energy (ft.-lbs.)
87	FMJ	1,390	365

CURRENT MANUFACTURER(S)
Norinco, Wolf, Prvi Partizan, Romtechnica, Sellier & Bellot, Arsenal (Bulgaria), MFS

GENERAL COMMENT(S)
This cartridge was once standard issue in the military services of Warsaw Pact countries .As this cartridge has become obsolescent in military service, large quantities of guns and ammunition in this caliber have been sold on the surplus market. American shooters have always been open to the low cost shooting potential offered by

military surplus cartridges and firearms. For that reason the once obscure 7.62x25mm Tokarev cartridge has become a popular staple of modern recreational shooting. Several manufacturers now offer soft point bullets in this caliber and handloading components and tested reloading data are now readily available.

TECHNICAL COMMENT(S)

The 7.62x25mm Tokarev and the 7.62mm Mauser cartridges are very similar, but not identical. The Tokarev cartridge has a slightly longer overall loaded length, a slightly shorter cartridge case length and a smaller diameter body than the Mauser cartridge. In addition, the shoulder angle of the Mauser cartridge is 34.5 degrees while the shoulder angle of the Tokarev cartridge is 38 degrees. However, despite these differences the two cartridges are considered to be interchangeable. Both are normally loaded to similar chamber pressures with the Tokarev having been converted to piezoelectric transducer readings and the older obsolete Mauser remaining with CUP readings. Despite this, firing Tokarev caliber ammunition in Mauser pistols cannot be recommended. The reason is that some 7.62x25mm ammunition was made with a 20% overload for use in submachine guns. While the Tokarev pistol can be fired safely with such loads, Mauser pistols were not designed to withstand the higher chamber pressure developed by 7.62x25mm SMG cartridges.

.32 AUTO

ALTERNATE NAME(S): .32 ACP, 7.65mm Browning, 7.65mm ACP, 7.65 Browning M1897, 7.8x17.5mm
RELATED CALIBER(S): .25 Auto, .380 Auto

CARTRIDGE HISTORY

Year of Introduction: 1897
Country of Origin: Belgium
Designer(s): John Browning
Governing Body: CIP, SAAMI
Present Status: active

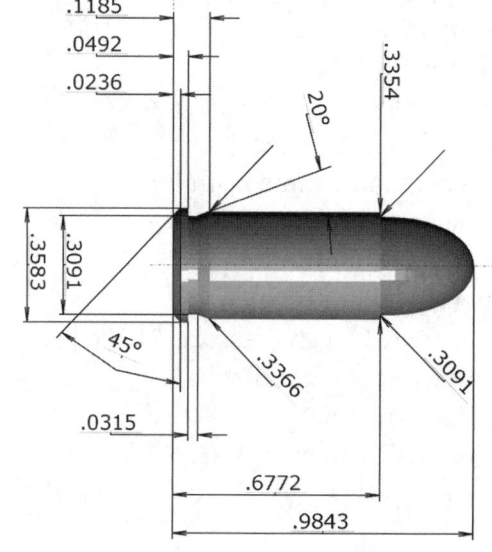

CARTRIDGE DESCRIPTION

Bullet Diameter: .309 in.
Bullet Weight(s): 60-74 gr.
Rifling Twist Rate: 1 turn in 9.84 in.
Test Barrel Length: 4 in.
Case Type: semi-rimmed, straight
Case Material: brass or steel
Primer Type: small pistol

CARTRIDGE BALLISTICS

Max. Average Breech Pressure: 20,500 psi.
Max. Effective Range: 10 yds.
Max. Horizontal Range: 1,550 yds.
Max. Vertical Range: 3,400 ft.

Bullet Weight (gr.)	Bullet Type	Muzzle Velocity (fps)	Muzzle Energy (ft.-lbs.)
60	JHP	1,000	133
65	JHP	950	130
71	FMJ	905	129

CURRENT MANUFACTURER(S)

Federal, Remington, Winchester, Hornady, Cor-Bon, Sellier & Bellot, Fiocchi, CBC, PMC, Industrias Technos

GENERAL COMMENT(S)

This is another of John Browning's classic cartridges from the early 1900s. It was designed especially for small, concealable, semi-automatic pistols. Like its siblings, the .25 Auto and the .380 Auto, the .32 Auto continues to be very popular for discrete carry. In many world law enforcement agencies, .32 Auto pistols are standard issue. Many American law enforcement officers carry a .32 Auto caliber pistol for a back-up gun.

TECHNICAL COMMENT(S)

While many gun writers and ballistic pundits have decried the .32 Auto as being next to useless for personal defense, this is certainly not the case. Unlike its junior sibling the .25 Auto, the .32 Auto has a bite to back-up its growl. The 71 grain FMJ bullet strikes with over twice the remaining energy of the .25 Auto with excellent penetration. For those who prefer faster energy transfer, the 60 grain JHP loads offer additional striking energy as well. Most pistols of this type and size are offered in both .32 Auto and .380 Auto. If given a choice, select the .380 Auto model.

.32 NAA

ALTERNATE NAME(S): .32 North American Arms
RELATED CALIBER(S): .32 Auto, .380 Auto

CARTRIDGE HISTORY

Year of Introduction: 2003
Country of Origin: U.S.
Designer(s): Ed Sanow and North American Arms
Governing Body: SAAMI
Present Status: active

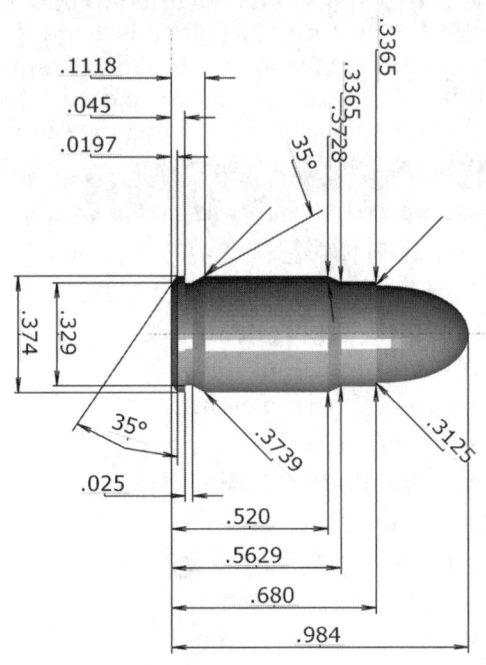

CARTRIDGE DESCRIPTION

Bullet Diameter: .312 in.
Bullet Weight(s): 60 gr.
Rifling Twist Rate: 1 turn in 16 in.
Test Barrel Length: 4 in.
Case Type: semi-rimmed, straight
Case Material: brass
Primer Type: small pistol

CARTRIDGE BALLISTICS

Max. Average Breech Pressure: 21,500 psi.
Max. Effective Range: 10 yds.
Max. Horizontal Range: 1,800 yds.
Max. Vertical Range: 3,500 ft.

Bullet Weight (gr.)	Bullet Type	Muzzle Velocity (fps)	Muzzle Energy (ft.-lbs.)
60	JHP	1,200	192

CURRENT MANUFACTURER(S)

Cor-Bon

GENERAL COMMENT(S)

This cartridge was designed for improved ballistic performance over the .32 Auto in compact pistols typically used by law enforcement officers for back-up and undercover work.

TECHNICAL COMMENT(S)

The .32 NAA offers 35% more muzzle energy than a typical .32 Auto cartridge and an expanding bullet to more efficiently transfer the striking energy. This cartridge is based on the .380 Auto case necked down to .32 caliber.

9mm LUGER

ALTERNATE NAME(S): 9x19mm Luger, 9x19mm Parabellum, 9x19mm P08, 9 Para.
RELATED CALIBER(S): 7.62mm Mauser, 7.65mm Luger, .380 Auto

CARTRIDGE HISTORY

Year of Introduction: 1903
Country of Origin: Germany
Designer(s): Georg Luger
Governing Body: CIP, SAAMI
Present Status: active

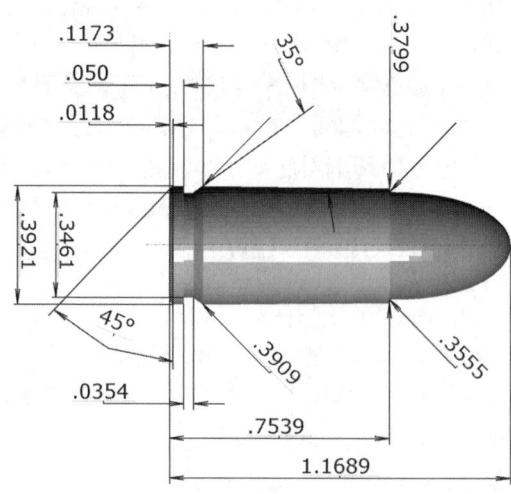

CARTRIDGE DESCRIPTION

Bullet Diameter: .355 in.
Bullet Weight(s): 90-147 gr.
Rifling Twist Rate: 1 turn in 10 in.
Test Barrel Length: 4 in.
Case Type: rimless, tapered
Case Material: brass or steel
Primer Type: small pistol

CARTRIDGE BALLISTICS

Max. Average Breech Pressure: 35,000 psi.
Max. Effective Range: 50 yds.
Max. Horizontal Range: 2,350 yds.
Max. Vertical Range: 5,300 ft.

Bullet Weight (gr.)	Bullet Type	Muzzle Velocity (fps)	Muzzle Energy (ft.-lbs.)
95	JHP	1,250	330
105	JSP	1,200	336
115	JHP	1,160	345
124	JHP	1,120	345
135	JHP	1,050	330
147	JHP	1,010	333
+P 90	JHP	1,500	450
+P 115	JHP	1,250	399
+P 124	JHP	1,250	430

CURRENT MANUFACTURER(S)

Federal, Remington, Winchester, Cor-Bon, Hornady, PMC, Fiocchi, CBC, PMP, Sellier & Bellot, NAMMO, Wolf, Prvi Partizan, IMI, Singapore Tech, MKEK, RUAG

GENERAL COMMENT(S)

Despite its sterling military service in two world wars and numerous smaller operations, the popularity of the 9x19mm Luger cartridge in the U.S. was road-blocked by the ubiquitous domestic preference for the .45 ACP cartridge. This was due in large part by experiences with large caliber bullets in the old West, the Philippine Insurrection (against the Moros) and World Wars I and II. Such remained the situation until the late 1970s when American law enforcement agencies decided to replace their revolvers. Given the additional training required to master the .45 ACP as well as increased numbers of females and male recruits unfamiliar with firearms joining such agencies, the 9mm Luger caliber seemed the obvious choice. The changeover came quickly; just ten years later, over half of American law enforcement agencies had switched to the 9mm Luger cartridge.Following several high profile failures of the 9mm cartridge to stop criminal assailants, the .40 S&W came into existence as a compromise between the 9mm Luger and the .45 ACP. Today, the majority of American law enforcement agencies use the .40 S&W cartridge, leaving the 9mm Luger for undercover and detective use.The 9mm has undergone a strong resurgence of interest in international law enforcement circles leading many agencies to upgrade their .32 ACP handguns to 9mm Luger. These developments have led the 9mm Luger to become the most popular pistol cartridge in the North American market. It is suitable for personal defense, small game and varmint hunting, but has not become popular with traditionalist-minded target shooters.

TECHNICAL COMMENT(S)

The 9mm Luger cartridge operates at a substantially higher chamber pressure than the .45 ACP. Despite this, the 9mm Luger cartridge is volume-limited in performance as only small charges of fast burning propellant can be loaded in the case. In other words, if you could find a way to get more propellant (or enough slow-burning propellant) in the case, you could increase muzzle velocity without reaching maximum average chamber pressure. This effectively prevents double charges, but not squib loads. The tapered case also makes it difficult to load heavy bullets as they can not be seated deeply enough without causing a bulge. Bullet pull and push must be addressed by "gluing" the uncannelured bullet into the case mouth using a lacquer sealer.

9x21mm

ALTERNATE NAME(S): 9mmx21, 9x21mm IMI, 9mm IMI, 9mm IMI/Jaeger
RELATED CALIBER(S): 9x19mm Luger, 9mm Steyr

CARTRIDGE HISTORY

Year of Introduction: 1984
Country of Origin: Israel
Designer(s): IMI
Governing Body: CIP
Present Status: obsolete

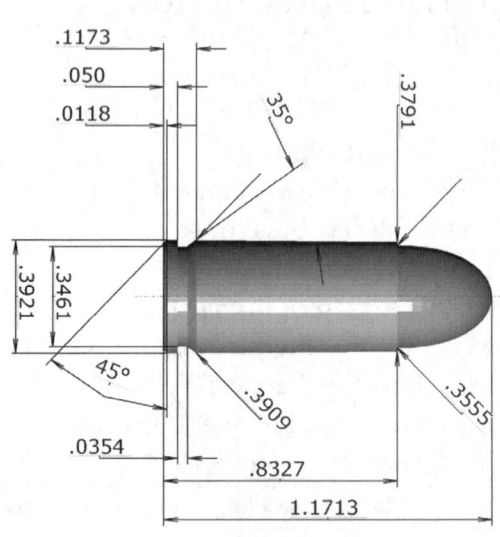

CARTRIDGE DESCRIPTION

Bullet Diameter: .355 in.
Bullet Weight(s): 124 gr.
Rifling Twist Rate: 1 turn in 10 in.
Test Barrel Length: 5.9 in.
Case Type: rimless, tapered
Case Material: brass
Primer: small pistol

CARTRIDGE BALLISTICS

Max. Average Breech Pressure: 34,084 psi.
Max. Horizontal Range: 1,900 yds.
Max. Vertical Range: 4,100 ft.

Bullet Weight (gr.)	Bullet Type	Muzzle Velocity (fps)	Muzzle Energy (ft.-lbs.)
115	FMJ	1,205	371
124	FMJ	1,110	340
124	FMJ	1,180	383

CURRENT MANUFACTURER(S)

Fiocchi, Sellier & Bellot, IMI, Prvi Partizan

GENERAL COMMENT(S)

In many countries of the world, ownership of handguns in military calibers is prohibited, although handguns in sporting calibers may be allowed. The prohibition against military handgun calibers normally includes any military handgun caliber, obsolete or modern. Consequently, in such countries large caliber revolvers are popular as are semi-automatic pistols in .38 Super Auto, provided you can obtain the ammunition. However, shooters in such countries wanted a 9mm non-military cartridge they could use. Ammunition and firearm makers answered this need with the 9x21mm sporting cartridge. Sales were always modest, but the laws were not broken.With the coming of the European Union, an effort was made to harmonize firearms ownership law among member countries. As a result, the prohibition against ownership of handguns in military calibers was dropped throughout Europe. This ended the need for the 9x21mm cartridge in that market. However, it did not end the demand for such a cartridge in other markets such as Central and South America where the prohibition against ownership of handguns in military calibers continues.

TECHNICAL COMMENT(S)

Basically, the 9x21mm cartridge is a 9x19mm Luger case made longer by 2mm. Both the 9x19mm Luger and the 9x21mm share the same bullet and maximum average chamber pressure. The muzzle velocity and energy of both cartridges are similar as well. The added length of the 9x21mm prevents it from being fired in handguns chambered for the 9x19mm Luger cartridge, which is exactly the point. History must regard the 9x21mm cartridge as an adaption made for a very limited purpose that ended in the 1990s. As such, the 9x21mm developed no significant market base of its own. Although presently offered by several ammunition manufacturers, very likely it will soon become obsolete.

9x23mm WINCHESTER

ALTERNATE NAME(S): 9x23mm , 9x23mm Win.
RELATED CALIBER(S): 9x19mm Luger, 9x21mm

CARTRIDGE HISTORY
Year of Introduction: 1996
Country of Origin: U.S.
Designer(s): Winchester
Governing Body: SAAMI
Present Status: active

CARTRIDGE DESCRIPTION
Bullet Diameter: .355 in.
Bullet Weight(s): 125 gr.
Rifling Twist Rate: 1 turn in 10 in.
Test Barrel Length: 6 in.
Case Type: rimless, straight
Case Material: brass
Primer: small pistol

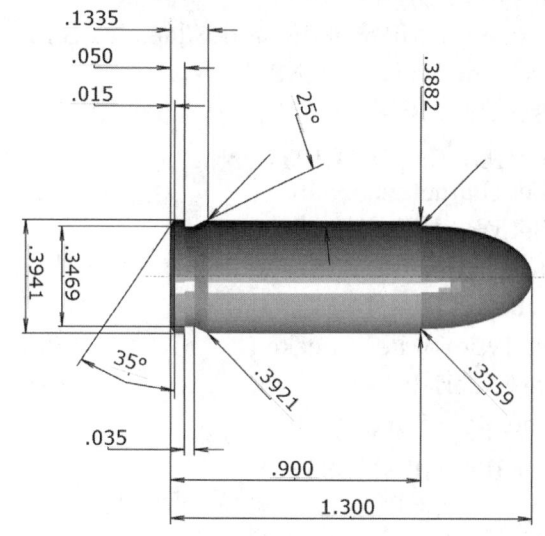

CARTRIDGE BALLISTICS
Max. Average Breech Pressure: 42,000 psi. (estimated)
Max. Horizontal Range: 2,000 yds.
Max. Vertical Range: 4,350 ft.

Bullet Weight (gr.)	Bullet Type	Muzzle Velocity (fps)	Muzzle Energy (ft.-lbs.)
125	JHP	1,450	583

CURRENT MANUFACTURER(S)
Winchester

GENERAL COMMENT(S)
This cartridge was designed by Winchester to meet the requirements of the International Practical Shooting Confederation (IPSC) rules for combat pistol competition. As all IPSC competition is fired against falling steel plates, a caliber selected for such competition must be powerful enough to consistently knock the plates down; any plate that fails to fall results in a penalty for the competitor. For this reason, large caliber cartridges are favored that can meet the IPSC requirement for a classification as a "major cartridge". This classification is determined by multiplying the bullet weight in grains times the muzzle velocity in feet-per-second and dividing by 1,000. Any cartridge that generates a score of 175 power units or more is classed as a major cartridge. Consequently, the 9mm and .45 caliber pistol cartridges are the well-considered favorites for IPSC competition. Although designed as a target cartridge, the 9x23mm Winchester has considerable, though unappreciated, potential as a self-defense caliber.

TECHNICAL COMMENT(S)
For IPSC competition, a cartridge must deliver high striking energy and low recoil. There is only one way to do this, increase muzzle velocity using a light bullet. Most existing pistol cartridges are limited by maximum average chamber pressures of 35,000 psi. or less. Since the only way to increase muzzle velocity is to increase the maximum average chamber pressure, two additional requirements need to be met: a cartridge case with enough interior volume to hold a heavy powder charge, and a case of heavier construction to contain the higher chamber pressure. The 9x23mm Winchester fulfills all of these requirements while the 9x19mm Luger cannot.

.357 SIG

ALTERNATE NAME(S): None
RELATED CALIBER(S): .40 S&W Auto, 9mm Luger

CARTRIDGE HISTORY
Year of Introduction: 1994
Country of Origin: U.S.
Designer(s): Michael Bussard, Alan Newcomb
Governing Body: SAAMI
Present Status: active

CARTRIDGE DESCRIPTION
Bullet Diameter: .355 in.
Bullet Weight(s): 115-150 gr.
Rifling Twist Rate: 1 turn in 16 in.
Test Barrel Length: 4 in.
Case Type: rimless, necked
Case Material: brass
Primer Type: small pistol

CARTRIDGE BALLISTICS
Max. Average Breech Pressure: 35,000 psi.
Max. Effective Range: 50 yds.
Max. Horizontal Range: 2,200 yds.
Max. Vertical Range: 4,400 ft.

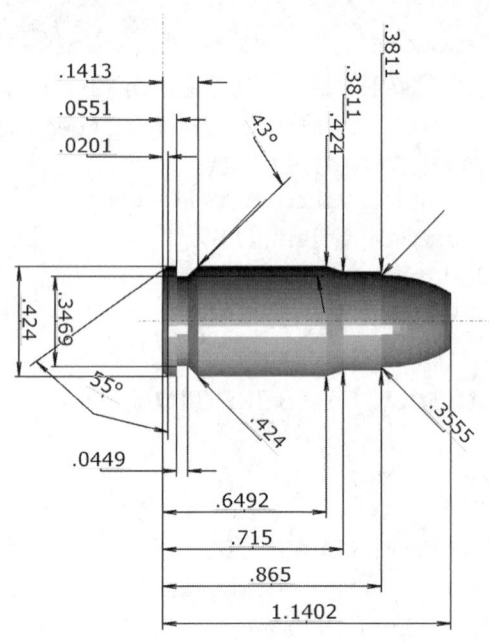

Bullet Weight (gr.)	Bullet Type	Muzzle Velocity (fps)	Muzzle Energy (ft.-lbs.)
115	JHP	1,500	575
125	JHP	1,350	506
150	JHP	1,130	420

CURRENT MANUFACTURER(S)
Federal, Remington, Winchester, Cor-Bon, Black Hills, PMC

GENERAL COMMENT(S)
When American law enforcement agencies found the 9mm Luger lacking in ballistic performance, this cartridge was conceived by the designers as a quick, easy solution to the problem. While several large law enforcement agencies use this cartridge, it remains something of a police specialty and has not become popular with sportsmen.

TECHNICAL COMMENT(S)
The .357 SIG is a .40 S&W cartridge case necked down to 9mm. This provides the additional internal volume for heavier powder charges and higher muzzle velocities than the classic 9mm Luger. Normally, the .357 SIG is loaded with 124-125 grain bullets. Despite its nomenclature, the .357 SIG uses 9mm/.355 inch diameter bullets.

.38 SUPER AUTOMATIC +P

ALTERNATE NAME(S): .38 Super Auto, .38 Super Auto Colt, .38 Super +P
RELATED CALIBER(S): .38 Automatic, 9mm Bergmann-Bayard, 9mm Luger

CARTRIDGE HISTORY

Year of Introduction: 1929
Country of Origin: U.S.
Designer(s): Colt
Governing Body: SAAMI
Present Status: active

CARTRIDGE DESCRIPTION

Bullet Diameter: .355 in.
Bullet Weight(s): 115-130 gr.
Rifling Twist Rate: 1 turn in 16 in.
Test Barrel Length: 5 in.
Case Type: semi-rimmed, straight
Case Material: brass
Primer Type: small pistol

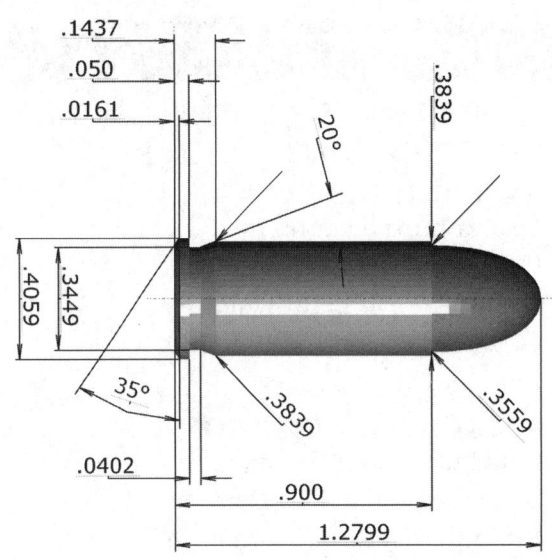

CARTRIDGE BALLISTICS

Max. Average Breech Pressure: 36,500 psi.
Max. Effective Range: 50 yds.
Max. Horizontal Range: 2,500 yds.
Max. Vertical Range: 5,400 ft.

Bullet Weight (gr.)	Bullet Type	Muzzle Velocity (fps)	Muzzle Energy (ft.-lbs.)
115	JHP	1,300	431
125	JHP	1,240	427
130	FMJ	1,215	426

CURRENT MANUFACTURER(S)

Remington, Federal, Winchester, Cor-Bon, PMC, Industrias Tecnos

GENERAL COMMENT(S)

When the .38 Automatic cartridge was introduced in 1900, it was one of the first, successful semi-automatic pistol cartridges and predated the 9 mm Luger cartridge by several years. However, by 1929, the ballistic performance of the .38 Automatic cartridge needed improvement and updating. This process resulted in the .38 Super Auto cartridge in the same year.

The U.S. was intended to be the main market for the updated cartridge. However, it did not prove to be a big seller and so became a good candidate for obsolescence. Then, a new and unforeseen overseas market developed--in countries where handguns in military calibers were banned, the .38 Super Auto was allowed as it was not a military cartridge. Mexico became an especially good market for .38 Super Auto handguns and ammunition for that reason.

When most countries rescinded such laws, the .38 Super Auto became an unwanted child yet again. Enter the competitors in combat pistol shooting who fire at falling metal targets. Turns out the .38 Super Auto is one of this minimum calibers that reliably knocks these targets down. Saved once again.

The .38 Super Auto cartridge has always had to live in the shadow of its popular big brother, the .45 Auto. However, reports of the death of the .38 Super Auto cartridge are premature.

TECHNICAL COMMENT(S)

By increasing the maximum average pressure from 33,360 psi in the .38 Automatic to 36,500 psi in the .38 Super Automatic, muzzle velocity of the 130 grain FMJ bullet was increased 175 fps from 1,040 fps to 1,215 fps. Muzzle energy also increased from 312 ft.-lbs. to 426 ft.-lbs., pushing the .38 Super Auto in to acceptable levels for effective personal defense Of course, modifications to the gun were necessary to accomodate the additional stresses incurred.

The .38 Super Auto cartridge suffers from two major technical drawbacks. The first is its semi-rimmed case head which is hard to feed from magazines due to the rim protruding beyond the case body. The second problem is that the length of the .38 Super cartridge will not allow it to fit in a pistol originally designed for the shorter, ubiquitous .45 Auto cartridge. In short, pistols for the .38 Super Auto cartridge require a longer (and therefore unique) frame.

Another major problem for the .38 Super Auto cartridge is that it shares exterior dimensions with the earlier .38 Automatic cartridge. In other words, the .38 Super Auto cartridge can be fired in pistols chambered for the older .38 Automatic cartridge--an unsafe combination often with disastrous results. For this reason, all .38 Super Auto ammunition bears a "+P" on the head stamp as well as warnings on all packaging. So, be aware--be safe.

.380 AUTO

ALTERNATE NAME(S): .380 ACP, 9mm Browning court/corto/kurz, 9x17mm
RELATED CALIBER(S): 9mm Luger

CARTRIDGE HISTORY
Year of Introduction:1908
Country of Origin: Belgium
Designer(s): John Browning
Governing Body: CIP, SAAMI
Present Status: active

CARTRIDGE DESCRIPTION
Bullet Diameter: .355 in.
Bullet Weight(s): 77-102 gr.
Rifling Twist Rate: 1 turn in 16 in.
Test Barrel Length: 3.75 in.
Case Type: rimless, straight
Case Material: brass
Primer Type: small pistol

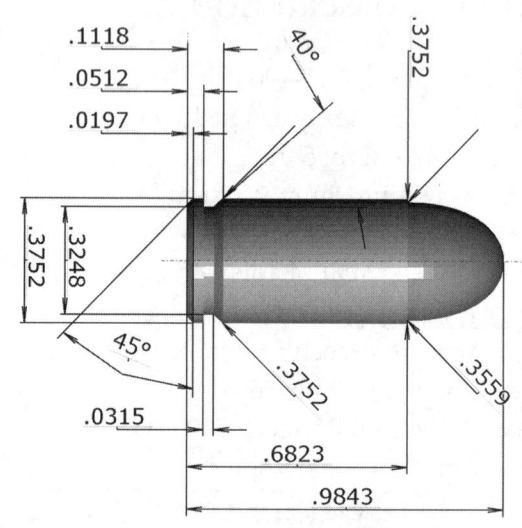

CARTRIDGE BALLISTICS
Max. Average Breech Pressure: 21,500 psi.
Max. Effective Range: 15 yds.
Max. Horizontal Range: 2,150 yds.
Max. Vertical Range: 4,800 ft.

Bullet Weight (gr.)	Bullet Type	Muzzle Velocity (fps)	Muzzle Energy (ft.-lbs.)
77	JHP	1,100	207
85	JHP	1,000	189
90	JHP	1,000	200
95	JHP	955	190

CURRENT MANUFACTURER(S)
Federal, Remington, Winchester, Cor-Bon, Fiocchi, PMC, CBC, Industrios Tecnos, Prvi Partizan, Sellier & Bellot, IMI

GENERAL COMMENT(S)
Arguably, the .380 Auto is the best of John Browning's creations for small pistols. It is certainly the most popular. Ballistic pundits opine that "Old John B." finally got it right with this design, as it is the least caliber pistol cartridge suitable for personal defense. As many small pistols of equal size are offered in either .32 Auto or .380 Auto, for the pundits, the choice is obvious– take the .380 Auto, please. Many law enforcement officers use the .380 Auto as a back-up, undercover or off-duty caliber. It is also a very popular cartridge for personal defense.

TECHNICAL COMMENT(S)
The .380 Auto shares basic rim and head dimensions with its big brother, the 9x19mm Luger cartridge. Basically, the .380 ACP is a 9mm Luger with a 17mm case length and reduced volume. For this reason, the power of the .380 Auto is volume-limited. To compensate, lighter weight 90 grain bullets must be used rather than the 115 and 124 grain bullets of the 9mm Luger. The short length of .380 Auto bullets leaves precious little bearing surface, which makes the .380 ACP unsuitable for competition. Nearly all pistols chambered for the .380 ACP are straight blow-back in operation.

.40 S&W

ALTERNATE NAME(S): .40 S&W, .40 Auto
RELATED CALIBER(S): .357 SIG, 10mm Automatic

CARTRIDGE HISTORY

Year of Introduction: 1990

Country of Origin: U.S.

Designer(s): Robert M. Klunk Jr. (Winchester)

Governing Body: SAAMI

Present Status: active

CARTRIDGE DESCRIPTION

Bullet Diameter: .400 in.

Bullet Weight(s): 135-180 gr.

Rifling Twist Rate: 1 turn in 16 in.

Test Barrel Length: 4 in.

Case Type: rimless, straight

Case Material: brass

Primer Type: small pistol

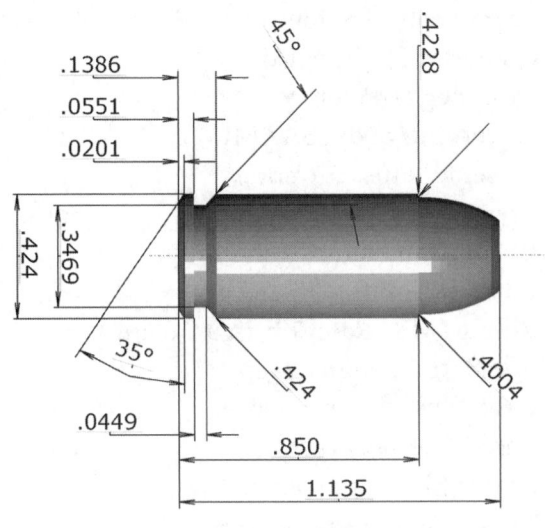

CARTRIDGE BALLISTICS

Max. Average Breech Pressure: 35,000 psi.

Max. Effective Range: 50 yds.

Max. Horizontal Range: 2,200 yds.

Max. Vertical Range: 4,400 ft.

Bullet Weight (gr.)	Bullet Type	Muzzle Velocity (fps)	Muzzle Energy (ft.-lbs.)
135	JHP	1,190	420
155	JHP	1,205	499
165	JHP	1,150	485
180	JHP	1,015	412

CURRENT MANUFACTURER(S)

Federal, Remington, Winchester, Cor-Bon, Black Hills, Hornady, Fiocchi, PMC, Sellier & Bellot, CBC, Industrias Tecnos

GENERAL COMMENT(S)

This became the law enforcement "go to" cartridge when the 9x19mm Luger was found wanting in ballistic performance. Today, the majority of American law enforcement agencies use this cartridge. Its rise has been meteoric, in the commercial was well as law enforcement markets.

TECHNICAL COMMENT(S)

The .40 S&W Auto is a compromise: recoil and bullet weight are lower than the .45 ACP, but higher than the 9mm. Most law enforcement officers can quickly master the .40 S&W for these reasons. In addition, most pistols originally designed for the 9x19mm Luger cartridge can quickly and easily be converted to take the .40 S&W.

.400 COR-BON

ALTERNATE NAME(S): .400 C-B
RELATED CALIBER(S): none

CARTRIDGE HISTORY
Year of Introduction: 1995
Country of Origin: U.S.
Designer(s): Peter Pi
Governing Body: SAAMI
Present Status: current

CARTRIDGE DESCRIPTION
Bullet Diameter: .401 in.
Bullet Weight(s):115-165 gr.
Rifling Twist Rate: 1 turn in 16 in.
Test Barrel Length: 24 in.
Case Type: rimless, necked
Case Material: brass
Primer Size: large pistol

CARTRIDGE BALLISTICS
Max. Average Breech Pressure: 37,500 psi.
Max. Horizontal Range: N/A
Max. Vertical Range: N/A

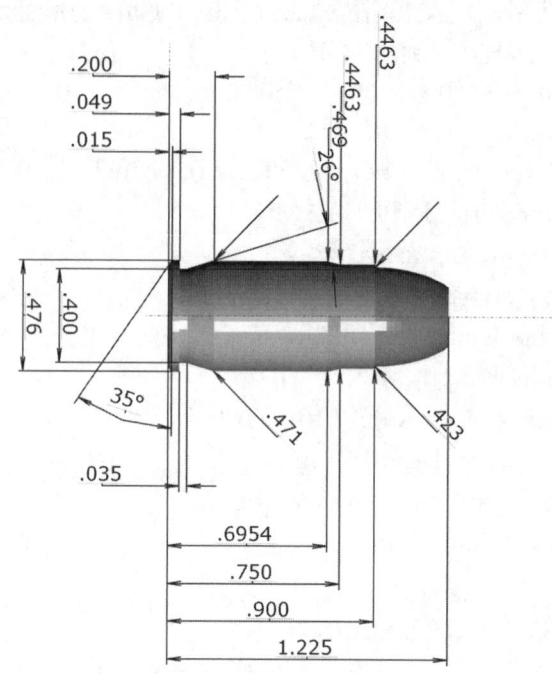

Bullet Weight (gr.)	Bullet Type	Muzzle Velocity (fps)	Muzzle Energy (ft.-lbs.)
115	JHP	1,650	695
135	JSP	1,375	567
135	JHP	1,450	630
150	JHP	1,350	607
155	JHP	1,200	496
165	JHP	1,300	619

CURRENT MANUFACTURER(S)
Cor-Bon

GENERAL COMMENT(S)
The .400 Cor-Bon cartridge is aimed squarely at the rapidly expanding personal defense market and the legions of M1911 shooters seeking a cartridge offering improved ballistic performance over the .45 Auto cartridge. While the .400 Cor-Bon serves very well in this role, no major firearm manufacturer has introduced a factory-made pistol in this caliber. However, the new cartridge can be fired in most M1911 pistols using only a new barrel and recoil spring which the shooter can easily install himself.

TECHNICAL COMMENT(S)
Technically speaking, the .400 Cor-Bon is a .45 Auto cartridge case necked down to accept .40 caliber/10mm bullets. Unlike the 10mm Auto cartridge that is too long for .45 caliber dimensioned M1911 pistols, the configuration of the .400 Cor-Bon offers a reasonably large case capacity and it will function in all .45 caliber M1911 pistols.

A major problem with necking down short cartridge cases such as the .45 Auto is ensuring that the case neck is long enough to reliably secure the bullet. Although Cor-Bon succeeded in this, arguably the case neck of the .400 Cor-Bon is minimal.

While the .400 Cor-Bon offers muzzle energy broadly similar to the 10mm Auto, it does so using lighter weight bullets driven at higher velocities. Cor-Bon claims that the lighter bullets reduce perceived recoil. For members of the "light bullet at high muzzle velocity" school of personal defense, the .400 Cor-Bon will be an excellent and cost-effective choice.

10mm AUTOMATIC

ALTERNATE NAME(S): 10mm Auto, Bren 10,
RELATED CALIBER(S): .40 S&W, .357 SIG

CARTRIDGE HISTORY

Year of Introduction: 1983
Country of Origin: U.S.
Designer(s): Jeff Cooper
Governing Body: SAAMI, CIP
Present Status: active

CARTRIDGE DESCRIPTION

Bullet Diameter: .400 in.
Bullet Weight(s): 135-200 gr.
Rifling Twist Rate: 1 turn in 16 in.
Test Barrel Length: 5 in.
Case Type: rimless, straight
Case Material: brass
Primer Type: large pistol

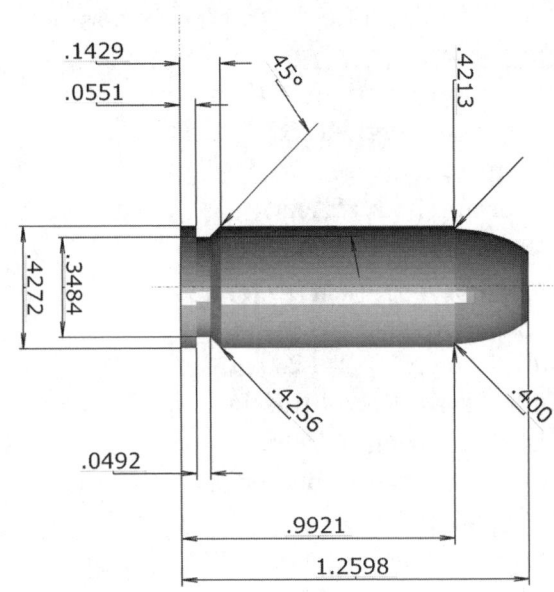

CARTRIDGE BALLISTICS

Max. Average Breech Pressure: 37,500 psi.
Max. Effective Range: 50 yds.
Max. Horizontal Range: 2,100 yds.
Max. Vertical Range: 4,100 ft.

Bullet Weight (gr.)	Bullet Type	Muzzle Velocity (fps)	Muzzle Energy (ft.-lbs.)
135	JHP	1,400	588
155	JHP	1,330	605
165	JHP	1,250	573
180	JHP	1,030	425
200	JHP	1,050	490

CURRENT MANUFACTURER(S)

Federal, Remington, Winchester, Hornady, Cor-Bon, PMC

GENERAL COMMENT(S)

For many years, Jeff Cooper studied the ballistic performance of handguns. The culmination of his work was the 10mm Auto cartridge that incorporated all the features Cooper believed necessary for a law enforcement cartridge. Following its introduction in 1983 along with the Bren 10 pistol, a flurry of interest enticed Norma, Federal and several other ammunition makers to add this caliber to their product lines. However, the anticipated ground wave of interest never developed. Today, the 10mm Auto cartridge is near extinction.

TECHNICAL COMMENT(S)

The heavy recoil impulse of the 10mm Auto cartridge quickly discouraged most law enforcement agencies. An exception, however, was the FBI which was looking for a new handgun cartridge at the time. They, too, found the 10mm Auto too much of a handful for the average agent, so they specified a reduced -power load. This cartridge enjoyed a very short tenure and was replaced by the .40 S&W shortly after.

A continuing problem with the 10mm Auto is that most M1911 handguns can not withstand the heavy recoil impulse for long without breakage. In addition, a special model is required with a longer action stroke to accommodate the longer cartridge. Needless to say, pistol manufacturers have not been keen to develop such guns in the face of low market demand.

.440 COR-BON

ALTERNATE NAME(S): .440 C-B
RELATED CALIBER(S): .50 Action Express

CARTRIDGE HISTORY
Year of Introduction: 1997
Country of Origin: U.S.
Designer(s): Peter Pi
Governing Body: SAAMI
Present Status: current

CARTRIDGE DESCRIPTION
Bullet Diameter: .429 in.
Bullet Weight(s): 240-260 gr.
Rifling Twist Rate: 1 turn in 18 in.
Test Barrel Length: 24 in.
Case Type: rimless, necked
Case Material: brass
Primer Size: large pistol

CARTRIDGE BALLISTICS
Max. Average Breech Pressure: 40,000 psi.
Max. Horizontal Range: N/A
Max. Vertical Range: N/A

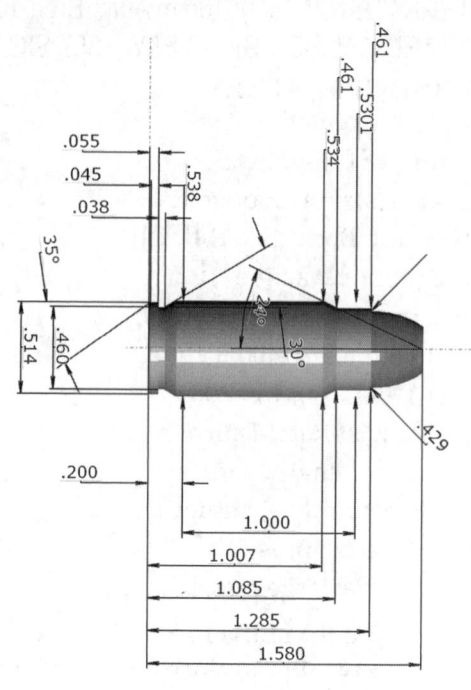

Bullet Weight (gr.)	Bullet Type	Muzzle Velocity (fps)	Muzzle Energy (ft.-lbs.)
240	JHP	1,600	1,365
260	JHP	1,650	1,214

CURRENT MANUFACTURER(S)
Cor-Bon

GENERAL COMMENT(S)
By all measures, the .440 Cor-Bon cartridge occupies a niche market –and a narrow one at that. Its large dimensions remove it from consideration in any "standard" pistol. Still, the interest in such calibers by shooters seeking something different remains strong enough to support a steady, but small demand.

TECHNICAL COMMENT(S)
To design the .440 Cor-Bon cartridge, Peter Pi began with a .50 Action Express cartridge and necked it down to .44 caliber. One advantage of beginning with the .50 A.E. cartridge case is its length which allows the .440 Cor-Bon to have a reasonable neck length. Of course case volume is another major plus.

The lighter bullets used in the .440 cartridge offer a flatter trajectory and a modest increase in striking energy over the .50 A.E. Cor-Bon also claims the .440 Cor-Bon cartridge offers lower perceived recoil than the .50 A.E. by virtue of the lighter bullets used.

The large head diameter of the .50 A.E. and .440 Cor-Bon effectively eliminates their use in most pistols. Large frame pistols, such as the Desert Eagle, which are suitable for the .440 Cor-Bon, are expensive and require conversion by a gunsmith.

.45 G.A.P.

ALTERNATE NAME(S): .45 Glock Automatic Pistol
RELATED CALIBER(S): .45 Auto, .45 Short

CARTRIDGE HISTORY
Year of Introduction: 2003
Country of Origin: Austria, United States

Designer(s): Ernest Durham(CIP)

Governing Body: CIP

Present Status: active

CARTRIDGE DESCRIPTION

Bullet Diameter: .452 in.

Bullet Weight(s): 185-230 gr.

Rifling Twist Rate: 1 turn in 16 in.

Test Barrel Length: 5 in.

Case Type: rimless, straight

Case Material: brass

Primer Type: small pistol

CARTRIDGE BALLISTICS

Max. Average Breech Pressure: 23,000 psi. (Same as .45 Auto +P)

Max. Effective Range: 50 yds.

Max. Horizontal Range: 1,700 yds.

Max. Vertical Range: 3,700 ft.

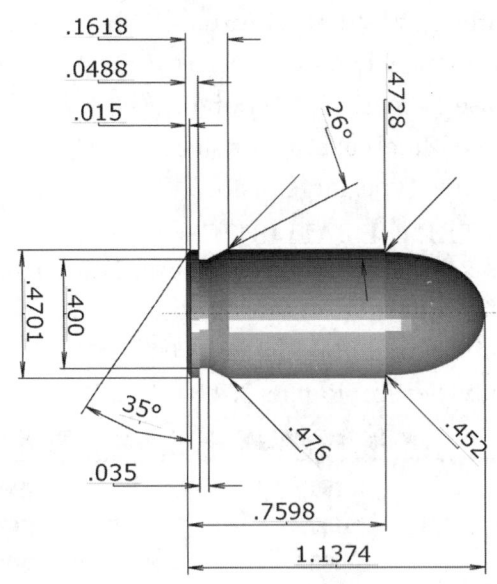

Bullet Weight (gr.)	Bullet Type	Muzzle Velocity (fps)	Muzzle Energy (ft.-lbs.)
185	JHP	1,090	488
200	JHP	950	401
230	JHP/FMJ	880	395
230	JHP	1,020	462

CURRENT MANUFACTURER(S)

Federal, Remington, Winchester, Cor-Bon

GENERAL COMMENT(S)

The concept behind this new cartridge is to offer ballistic performance equivalent to the .45 ACP in a shorter cartridge length that, in turn, allows a more compact pistol. Although named for Glock, domestic pistol manufacturers quickly added this caliber to their product lines. In the opinion of many this is a good idea. Others dismiss this concept as hardly worth the effort as the size and weight of pistols chambered for the .45 G.A.P. cartridge are not significantly lighter or more compact.

TECHNICAL COMMENT(S)

From a design standpoint, the .45 G.A.P. cartridge has more in common with the .45 Auto +P than with the .45 Auto. Maximun average pressures are the same (higher than the .45 Auto) and the inner contour of the case, and the extactor groove differ from the .45 Auto. The .45 G.A.P. uses the small pistol primer while the .45 Auto and .45 Autoo +P use a large pistol primer.

.45 AUTO

ALTERNATE NAME(S): .45 ACP, .45 Ball M1911, .45 Auto Colt Gov't Model

RELATED CALIBER(S): .45 Win. Mag., .45 G.A.P., .45 Auto +P

CARTRIDGE HISTORY

Year of Introduction: 1911

Country of Origin: U.S.

Designer(s): John Browning, U.S. Army

Governing Body: SAAMI, CIP

Present Status: active

CARTRIDGE DESCRIPTION

Bullet Diameter: .452 in.

Bullet Weight(s): 185-230 gr.

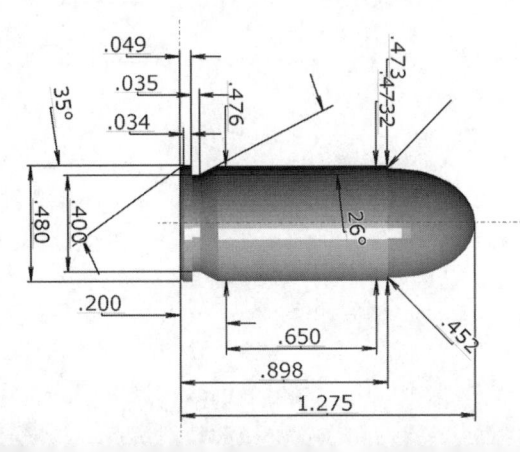

Rifling Twist Rate: 1 turn in 16 in.

Test Barrel Length: 5 in.

Case Type: rimless, straight

Case Material: brass or steel

Primer Type: large pistol

CARTRIDGE BALLISTICS

Max. Average Breech Pressure: 21,000 psi.

Max. Effective Range: 50 yds.

Max. Horizontal Range: 1,700 yds.

Max. Vertical Range: 3,700 ft.

Bullet Weight (gr.)	Bullet Type	Muzzle Velocity (fps)	Muzzle Energy (ft.-lbs.)
165	JHP	1,060	410
185	JHP	1,000	411
185	JHP	950	370
185	FMJ	780	245
200	JHP	900	358
230	JHP/FMJ	850	370
230	FMJ	780	310

CURRENT MANUFACTURER(S)

Federal, Remington, Winchester, Cor-Bon, Hornady, Black Hills, PMC, IMI, Prvi Partizan, CBC, Wolf

GENERAL COMMENT(S)

This John Browning creation has become an icon for personal defense. This is because it works better for this purpose than nearly any other pistol cartridge. Given a fair hit in the torso, the .45 Auto will incapacitate the target with great reliability.

American experience in taming the old West, fighting Indians on the frontiers and battling Moros in the Philippines established a civilian and military preference for large caliber handgun bullets at modest muzzle velocities. Quantifying this, we find a bullet of .44 caliber or larger weighing at least 250 grains with a muzzle velocity of 700-800 fps. In other words, we get the .45 Colt cartridge. This experience served as the basic framework of thought in designing a cartridge for a new pistol in 1911. Of course, a new pistol cartridge had to be rimless to feed properly and the case need not be so long due to the use of smokeless propellants. A jacketed, round nose bullet was a given. Browning proposed a 200 grain design; Springfield Armory increased this to 230 grains. A classic was born– the .45 Auto.

TECHNICAL COMMENT(S)

Like its black powder forefathers, the .45 Auto is a low pressure cartridge that depends on its large caliber, heavyweight bullet for terminal ballistic effectiveness. Modern attempts to improve on this formula using 185 grain JHP bullet at higher muzzle velocities have not been entirely successful. One modern formula has proven the exception– a 230 JHP bullet at a muzzle velocity of 850 fps. Basically, this is the low velocity, large caliber, heavy weight bullet with the added ballistic effect of bullet expansion for improved energy transfer. It works very well. While the cartridge case of the .45 Auto can safely withstand greater chamber pressure than allowed, the M1911 pistols cannot. This limits potential ballistic upgrades to incremental improvements such as the recent development of +P .45 Auto ammunition. For personal defense purposes, the .45 Auto is an ideal choice.

.45 AUTO +P

ALTERNATE NAME(S): .45 Automatic +P
RELATED CALIBER(S): .45 Win. Mag., .45 G.A.P., .45 Auto

CARTRIDGE HISTORY

Year of Introduction: 1911

Country of Origin: U.S.

Designer(s): Remington

Governing Body: SAAMI

Present Status: active

CARTRIDGE DESCRIPTION

Bullet Diameter: .452 in.

Bullet Weight(s): 185-230 gr.

Rifling Twist Rate: 1 turn in 16 in.

Test Barrel Length: 5 in.

Case Type: rimless, straight

Case Material: brass

Primer Type: large pistol

CARTRIDGE BALLISTICS

Max. Average Breech Pressure: 23,000 psi.

Max. Effective Range: 50 yds.

Max. Horizontal Range: 1,700 yds.

Max. Vertical Range: 3,700 ft.

Bullet Weight (gr.)	Bullet Type	Muzzle Velocity (fps)	Muzzle Energy (ft.-lbs.)
185	JHP	1,140	534
200	JHP	1,050	490
230	JHP	950	460

CURRENT MANUFACTURER(S)

Remington, Cor-Bon, Hornady

GENERAL COMMENT(S)

When Remington introduced this new .45 Auto +P "cartridge", fans of the .45 Auto were delighted. It was high time that a major ammunition manufacturer updated the venerable .45 Auto to higher muzzle velocity and greater striking energy than existing factory ammunition in that caliber. However, the tradeoff for using .45 Auto +P ammunition is increased recoil which significantly increases wear and tear on the guns. This was a price that many shooters refused to pay.

Those who read the ballistic charts found that the increase in muzzle velocity over the .45 Auto cartridge was more modest than anticipated although the striking energy was significantly higher. The tradeoffs necessary for increased ballistic performance did not appeal to many shooters. In short, the .45 Auto +P is not for everyone. In practice, it is favored mainly by experienced shooters and for the ammunition makers it is a niche market.

Following Remington's lead, Hornady and Cor-Bon introduced .45 Auto +P ammunition. To date, however, other manufacturers have not followed suit.

TECHNICAL COMMENT(S)

In order to increase muzzle velocity and energy for the .45 Auto +P, the 21,000 psi maximum average pressure (MAP) of the .45 Auto had to be increased. However, the limits of the gun system strength allowed only a 2,000 psi MAP increase (to 23,000 psi). While this may not seem like much, it is sufficient to allow an increase in the muzzle velocity of the 185 grain JHP bullet from 950 fps in the .45 Auto to 1,140 fps in the .45 Auto +P.

Aside from the different MAP levels, the internal taper of the .45 Auto +P cartridge case differs from those of the .45 Auto. All .45 Auto +P ammunition can be identified by the "45 Auto +P" on the head stamp.

In his seminal book "Street Stoppers" author Evan Marshall notes that statistics show the probability of a single shot incapacitating an assailant of the .45 Auto cartridge 230 grain FMJ is 62% while that of a .45 Auto +P 185 grain JHP is 92%.

.475 WILDEY MAGNUM

ALTERNATE NAME(S): .475 Wildey
RELATED CALIBER(S): .284 Win.,

CARTRIDGE HISTORY
Year of Introduction: circa late 1980s
Country of Origin: U.S.
Designer(s): Wildey Moore
Governing Body: none
Present Status: active

CARTRIDGE DESCRIPTION
Bullet Diameter: .475 in.
Bullet Weight(s): 250-300 gr.
Rifling Twist Rate: N/A
Test Barrel Length: N/A
Case Type: rebated rimless, straight
Case Material: brass
Primer: large pistol

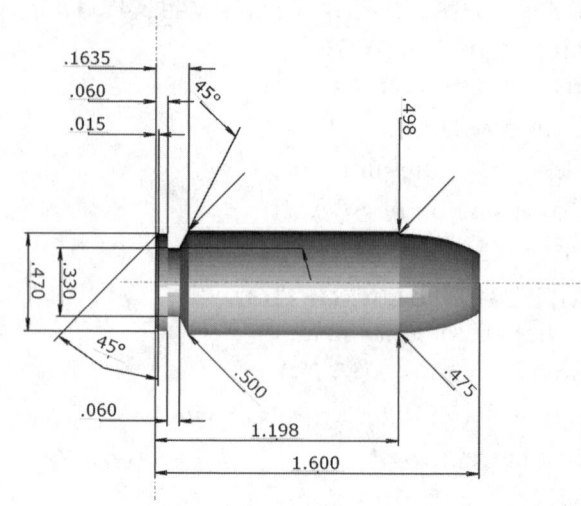

CARTRIDGE BALLISTICS
Max. Average Breech Pressure: 48,000 psi.
Max. Horizontal Range: 2,050 yds.
Max. Vertical Range: 4,500 ft.

Bullet Weight (gr.)	Bullet Type	Muzzle Velocity (fps)	Muzzle Energy (ft.-lbs.)
250	JHP	1,850	1,900
300	JSP	1,610	1,727

CURRENT MANUFACTURER(S)
Wildey Arms

GENERAL COMMENT(S)
Wildey Moore designed this powerful handgun cartridge for a gas-operated, semi-automatic pistol of his own design and manufacture. It is intended for hunting large game and as a backup handgun for hunting dangerous game. This cartridge is not the only one from the drawing board of Wildey Moore. He has also designed the .30 Wildey Mag., .357 W.M., .41 W.M., .44 W.M., and .45 W.M. as well as the .475 W.M. However, the other calibers have remained wildcats while the .475 W.M. has been offered in the form of loaded ammunition.

TECHNICAL COMMENT(S)
To make the .475 Wildey Magnum cartridge case, a .284 Win. cartridge case is cut off and inside-reamed to the correct diameter. This is necessary as a rifle case head is needed to stand up to the chamber pressures which are in the rifle category. The pistol has a gas regulator that allows the user to adjust functioning for different loads.

50 GI

ALTERNATE NAME(S): .50 Auto
RELATED CALIBER(S): .45 ACP

CARTRIDGE HISTORY

Year of Introduction: 2004
Country of Origin: U.S.
Designer(s): Vic Tibbets, Alex Zimmermann
Governing Body: none
Present Status: active

CARTRIDGE DESCRIPTION

Bullet Diameter: .515 in.
Bullet Weight(s): 275-300 gr.
Rifling Twist Rate: N/A
Test Barrel Length: 6 in.
Case Type: rebated, straight
Case Material: brass
Primer Type: large pistol

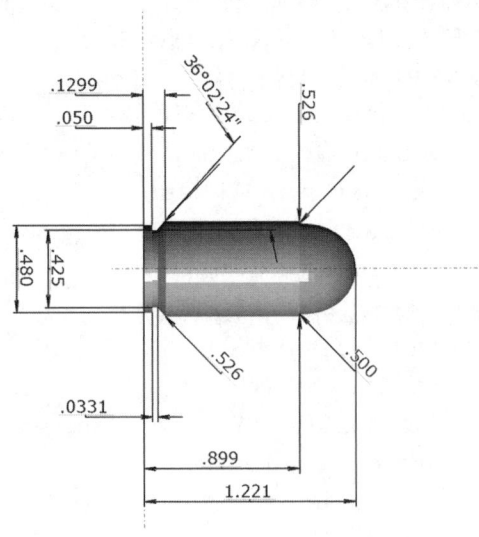

CARTRIDGE BALLISTICS

Max. Average Breech Pressure: 21,000 psi.
Max. Effective Range: 50 yds.
Max. Horizontal Range: 2,200 yds.
Max. Vertical Range: 4,800 ft.

Bullet Weight (gr.)	Bullet Type	Muzzle Velocity (fps)	Muzzle Energy (ft.-lbs.)
275	JHP	875	467
300	JHP	725	350

CURRENT MANUFACTURER(S)

Guncrafter Industries

GENERAL COMMENT(S)

This cartridge was designed to fit in a modified M1911A1 pistol offered by Guncrafter Industries, which is owned by the two designers of this cartridge. They offer a controllable M1911A1 style pistol with substantially improved terminal ballistic performance by using a very heavy bullet (for the size of the weapon) at low velocity. The .50 GI represents the maximum size cartridge which can be contained within and and function in a modified M1911A1 action.

TECHNICAL COMMENT(S)

Note than the rim of the .50 GI case must be rebated to the dimensions of the M1911A1 breech face to assure operating cycle reliability. Cases are formed from one of the .300 Winchester Magnum family of cartridges. This makes for a strong case, however, the M1911A1 pistol is not designed to handle centerfire rifle chamber pressures which limits any potential ballistic improvement. For example, the 275 grain bullet at 875 fps delivers 467 ft.-lbs. of muzzle energy. A standard .45 ACP cartridge with a 230 grain bullet offers 356-405 ft.-lbs. of muzzle energy depending on the loading. Therefore, the .50 GI yields an energy increase of between 15 and 31% over the standard .45 ACP. The 300 grain bullet is on the lee side of the pressure curve and simply overmatches the available chamber pressure. We have all heard it said that "The only reason I do not carry a .50 caliber M1911 is they do not make one!" Well, now you have no excuse. Guncrafter Industries makes the ammunition and the gun.

.50 ACTION EXPRESS

ALTERNATE NAME(S): .50 AE
RELATED CALIBER(S): none

CARTRIDGE HISTORY
Year of Introduction: 1991
Country of Origin: Israel
Designer(s): Evan Whildin
Governing Body: SAAMI
Present Status: active

CARTRIDGE DESCRIPTION
Bullet Diameter: .500 in.
Bullet Weight(s): 300-325 gr.
Rifling Twist Rate: 1 turn in 20 in.
Test Barrel Length: 6 in.
Case Type: rimless, straight
Case Material: brass
Primer Type: large pistol

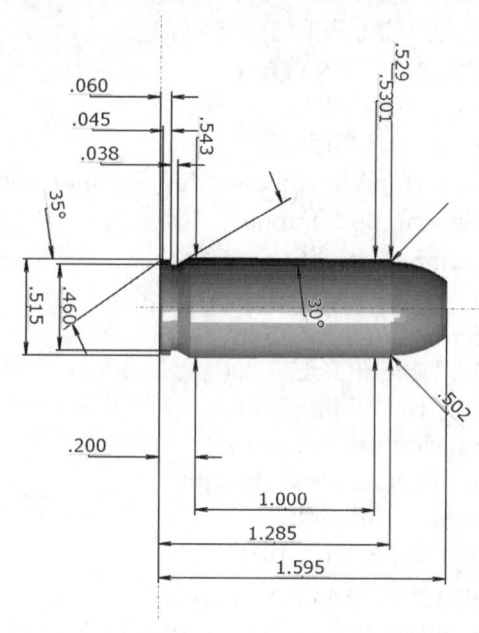

CARTRIDGE BALLISTICS
Max. Average Breech Pressure: 35,000 psi.
Max. Effective Range: 50 yds.
Max. Horizontal Range: 2,200 yds.
Max. Vertical Range: 4,800 ft.

Bullet Weight (gr.)	Bullet Type	Muzzle Velocity (fps)	Muzzle Energy (ft.-lbs.)
300	JHP	1,550	1,600
325	JHP	1,400	1,414

CURRENT MANUFACTURER(S)
Speer, IMI

GENERAL COMMENT(S)
This cartridge was designed to be the most powerful "production" handgun cartridge when it was introduced. It succeeded until it was eclipsed by the .460 and .500 S&W Magnums. Some would argue that certain limited edition handguns in niche calibers are more powerful. In response, one can only say that such pistols are rare, expensive and usually out of production. On the other hand, the .50 AE continues to remain in production with both guns and ammunition easily available. It takes a big pistol to fire the .50 AE cartridge and the gas-operated Desert Eagle pistol certainly meets this criteria. Although it is a powerful cartridge, the .50 AE differs from other large caliber handgun cartridges in that it does not take an expert to fire it. The gas-operation of the Desert Eagle pistol significantly reduces perceived recoil.

TECHNICAL COMMENT(S)
Yes, the .50 AE has been successfully used for personal defense on a number of occasions. However, the .50 AE cartridge is too powerful for such applications. Rather it is a good choice for hunting medium game in areas where handgun hunting is legal. The .50 AE cartridge case is unique as is its bullet diameter. Speer makes the bullets and IMI manufactures the cartridge case.

CHAPTER 74 : SPORTING PISTOL - OBSOLETE

CHAPTER 74

For Cartridge Index see Chapter 101. All drawing dimensions are approximate.

Why do some pistol cartridges fail to gain and hold critical mass in the marketplace? From a mathematical perspective, the odds favor failure over success when it comes to a long-lasting caliber. Many of the cartridges listed in this section are testimony to the fact that for every new pistol cartridge introduced, a greater number fail.

There are two types of obsolete pistol cartridges. First, there are the classic cartridges that enjoyed a successful commercial career and when active production ended, they aged gracefully into a specialty product status and remained in limited production. Examples include the 7.63mm Mauser (AKA .30 Mauser) and the .44 Auto Mag. Next, we have the failed newer calibers such as the 9mm Winchester Magnum and the .45 Winchester Magnum. After brief, unsuccessful production careers they were unceremoniously dropped in the discontinued SKU bin. As they have no nostalgic credentials, they have not (yet) become a specialty product.

A specialty product is an obsolete classic cartridge that has been re-introduced in limited production quantity only, usually by a small ammunition manufacturer set up to make such small quantities. While no longer in mass production, limited production supports the nostalgic, niche markets for such cartridges. Examples include the 7.65mm Luger (AKA .30 Luger) and the .38 Automatic. Obsolete modern cartridges enjoy no such support. Any ammunition available in such calibers comes from remaining stocks in distributor or dealer inventories, with some ammunition collectors also providing a limited inventory. Rarely, a major manufacturer may make special short runs of such calibers.

On occasion, an obsolete pistol cartridge will regain critical mass to such an extent that it goes back into mass production. Examples of this include the .38 Super Auto+P and the 9mm Browning Long.

The reader is encouraged not to view this chapter as a cemetery for deceased cartridges, but rather as a jewelry box full of useful history, containing trinkets, baubles, and a few gems.

2.7mm KOLIBRI AUTO

ALTERNATE NAME(S): 2.7mm Kolibri
RELATED CALIBER(S): 3mm Kolibri

CARTRIDGE HISTORY
Year of Introduction: 1914
Country of Origin: Germany
Designer(s): Kolibri
Governing Body: none
Present Status: obsolete

CARTRIDGE DESCRIPTION
Bullet Diameter: .107 in.
Bullet Weight(s): 3 gr.
Rifling Twist Rate: N/A
Test Barrel Length: N/A
Case Type: rimless, straight
Case Material: brass
Primer Type: special Berdan type

CARTRIDGE BALLISTICS
Max. Average Breech Pressure: N/A
Max. Effective Range: 0 yds.
Max. Horizontal Range: N/A
Max. Vertical Range: N/A

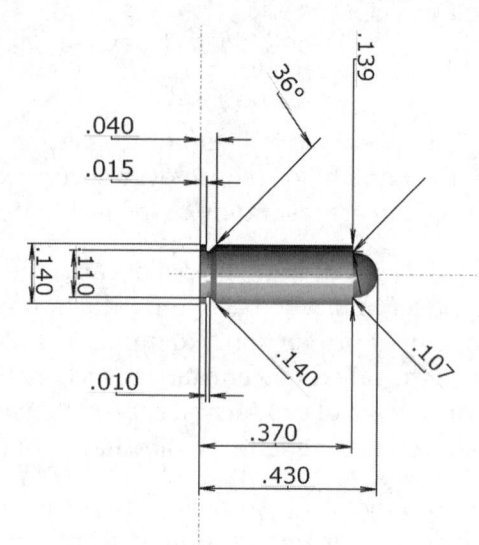

Bullet Weight (gr.)	Bullet Type	Muzzle Velocity (fps)	Muzzle Energy (ft.-lbs.)
3	FMJ	700 (est.)	3

CURRENT MANUFACTURER(S)
GENERAL COMMENT(S)
While unusual, this cartridge is included here as it is the smallest semi-automatic pistol cartridge ever made.

TECHNICAL COMMENT(S)
While small and weak, the 2.7mm Kolibri cartridge is not a toy. At close range the Lilliputian bullet of this pipsqueak cartridge is capable of inflicting a serious wound. For those of you seeking more stopping power, you may wish to consider the 2.7mm Kolibri's big brother, the 3mm Kolibri with an estimated 6 ft.-lbs. of muzzle energy.

3mm KOLIBRI

ALTERNATE NAME(S): 3mm Kolibri, 3mm Kolibri Pistol, 3x8mm Kolibri
RELATED CALIBER(S): 2.7mm Kolibri

CARTRIDGE HISTORY
Year of Introduction: 1914
Country of Origin: Austria
Designer(s): Georg Grabner
Governing Body: none
Present Status: obsolete

CARTRIDGE DESCRIPTION
Bullet Diameter: .122 in.
Bullet Weight(s): 5.4 gr.
Rifling Twist Rate: N/A
Test Barrel Length: N/A

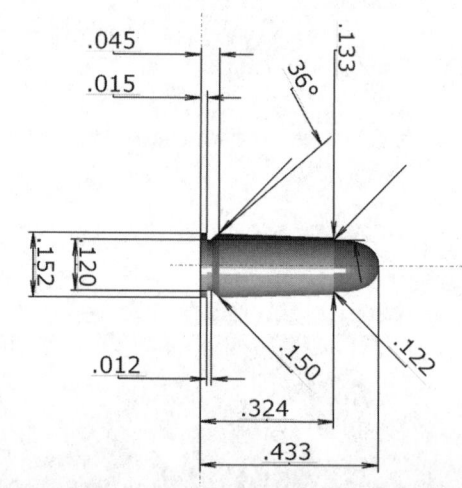

Case Type: rimless, straight
Case Material: brass
Primer: special Berdan

CARTRIDGE BALLISTICS
Max. Average Breech Pressure: N/A
Max. Horizontal Range: 500 yds.
Max. Vertical Range: 260 ft.

Bullet Weight (gr.)	Bullet Type	Muzzle Velocity (fps)	Muzzle Energy (ft.-lbs.)
5.4	L-RN	700	5.9

CURRENT MANUFACTURER(S)
none

GENERAL COMMENT(S)
When the 2mm (2.7mm) Kolibri cartridge failed to sell, a new, more powerful cartridge was developed to replace it. Called the 3mm Kolibri, these cartridges were made at the Franz Pfannl arms and ammunition factory in Krems, Austria. When the 3mm Kolibri did nothing to improve sales, both cartridges were dropped at the beginning of World War I in 1914.

TECHNICAL COMMENT(S)
The 3mm Kolibri cartridge was intended to be a more powerful cartridge than its sibling, the 2.7mm Kolibri. Accordingly, while the diameter of the case was enlarged, case length had to be shortened to keep overall loaded length with the elongated round nose bullet at .433 inches. This was the same loaded length as the 2.7mm Kolibri because the Kolibri pistol could not handle a cartridge with a loaded length exceeding .433 inches. As the barrel was rifled, a round nose lead bullet of .122 inch diameter replaced the lead round ball of the 2.7mm cartridge and smokeless powder was used exclusively. With muzzle velocity estimated at 700 fps, muzzle energy nearly doubled. While all this may have sounded good, in reality, both cartridges remained ineffective and virtually useless. This was not lost on potential customers and the 3mm Kolibri cartridge suffered the same fate as the 2.7mm.

4mm PRACTICE CARTRIDGE M20, 4mm PRACTICE CARTRIDGE GECO

ALTERNATE NAME(S): 4mm Ubungsmunition, 4mm Practice Cartridge RWS
RELATED CALIBER(S): 4mm Randzunder

CARTRIDGE HISTORY
Year of Introduction: 1920 (GECO), 1921 (M20)
Country of Origin: Germany
Designer(s): Gustav Genschow (GECO), Karl Weiss (M20)
Governing Body: CIP
Present Status: obsolete

CARTRIDGE DESCRIPTION
Bullet Diameter: .177 in.
Bullet Weight(s): 7.2 gr.
Rifling Twist Rate: N/A
Test Barrel Length: N/A
Case Type: rimmed, necked
Case Material: brass
Primer: GECO rimfire and centerfire, M20 inside

CARTRIDGE BALLISTICS
Max. Average Breech Pressure: N/A
Max. Horizontal Range: 200 yds.
Max. Vertical Range: 600 ft.

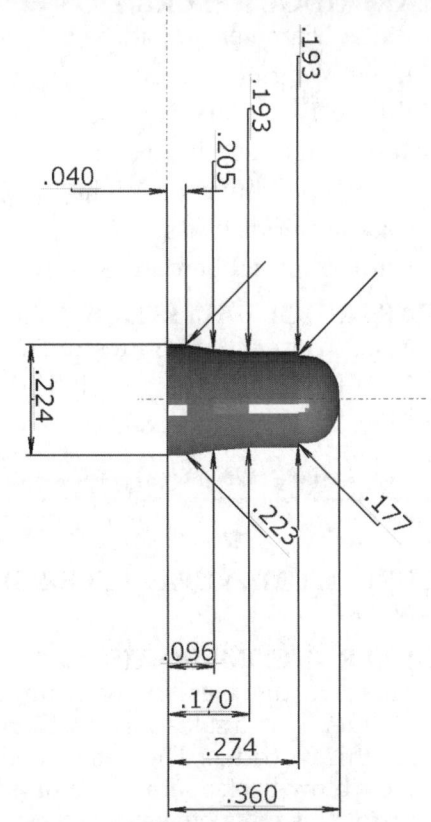

Bullet Weight (gr.)	Bullet Type	Muzzle Velocity (fps)	Muzzle Energy (ft.-lbs.)
7.2	L-RN	655	7

CURRENT MANUFACTURER(S)
RWS

GENERAL COMMENT(S)
How do you practice shooting indoors at close range when you cannot shoot full power ammunition? The answer is a barrel insert chambered for a small caliber bullet launched at low velocity for safety. The 4mm Ubungsmunition cartridges were designed for this purpose. Both were introduced at about the same time, but the GECO version was soon replaced by the RWS M20.

TECHNICAL COMMENT(S)
Although similar in concept, the GECO and the M20 differed in detail. The M20 had an inside primer compatible with most center fire handguns. With the insert in the barrel, the M20 cartridge could be single-loaded into its chamber and fired. Of course the M20 cartridge was too weak to cycle the action so the pistol had to be reloaded manually. The GECO cartridge used a rimfire and center fire priming system, thus making it compatible with rim fire or center fire guns. As both cartridges have no propellant, the primer serves to power the bullet. The two types of cartridge are not interchangeable. The GECO type can be identified by its rimmed, necked case. The M20 case has a bulge at the base rather than a rim.

4.25mm LILIPUT

ALTERNATE NAME(S): 4.25mm Erika Pistol, 4.25mm Menz-Liliput, 4.25x10.5mm Liliput
RELATED CALIBER(S): none

CARTRIDGE HISTORY
Year of Introduction: 1914
Country of Origin: Austria
Designer(s): Franz Pfannl
Governing Body: none
Present Status: obsolete

CARTRIDGE DESCRIPTION
Bullet Diameter: .167 in.
Bullet Weight(s): 17 gr.
Rifling Twist Rate: N/A
Test Barrel Length: 1.66 in.
Case Type: rimless, straight
Case Material: brass
Primer: special Berdan centerfire

CARTRIDGE BALLISTICS
Max. Average Breech Pressure: N/A
Max. Horizontal Range: 1,100 yds.
Max. Vertical Range: 800 ft.

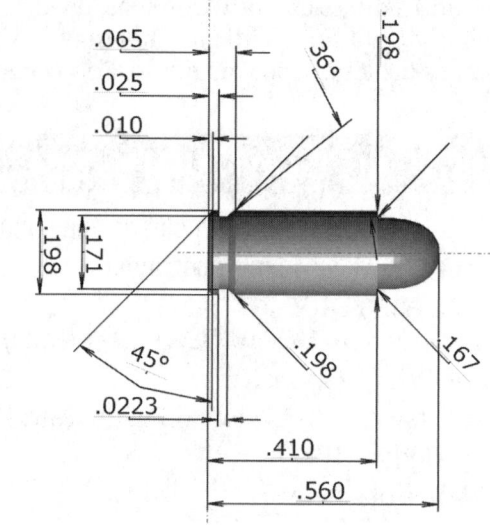

Bullet Weight (gr.)	Bullet Type	Muzzle Velocity (fps)	Muzzle Energy (ft.-lbs.)
17	JRN	810	22.4

CURRENT MANUFACTURER(S)
None

GENERAL COMMENT(S)
This cartridge was originally introduced in 1914 by Franz Pfannl, an Austrian watchmaker, for the Erika pistol. Neither were a sales success, then in 1920 Waffenfabrik August Menz in Germany introduced the Liliput pistol for this cartridge. The name stuck and it is now called the 4.25mm Liliput. Both the Liliput and Erika pistols were blow-back operated, semi-auto designs. Unfortunately, for Waffenfabrik August Menz, the 4.25mm Liliput pistol was not a big sales success. By the late 1920s, both had disappeared.

TECHNICAL COMMENT(S)

Despite its diminutive size, the 4.25mm cartridge is quite capable of inflicting a serious wound, especially if the target is struck by several of these bullets. However, effective range would be only 10-15 feet. The 4.25mm Liliput cartridge was loaded with smokeless propellant and a jacketed bullet. A special, small diameter, centerfire Berdan primer was used. This cartridge was made only in Europe.

7mm NAMBU

ALTERNATE NAME(S): 7x19.8mm Nambu
RELATED CALIBER(S): 8mm Nambu

CARTRIDGE HISTORY

Year of Introduction: 1919
Country of Origin: Japan
Designer(s): Col. Kijiro Nambu
Governing Body: none
Present Status: obsolete

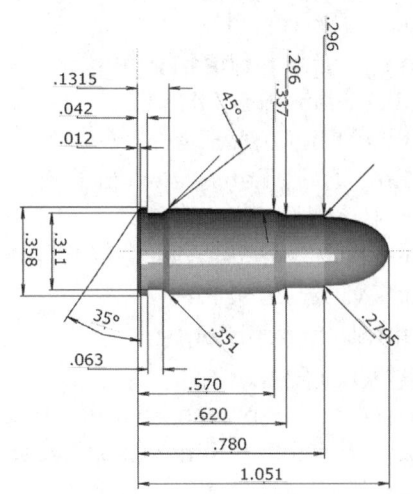

CARTRIDGE DESCRIPTION

Bullet Diameter: .280 in.
Bullet Weight(s): 56 gr.
Rifling Twist Rate: 1 turn in 12.5 in.
Test Barrel Length: N/A
Case Type: rimless, necked
Case Material: brass
Primer Type: small pistol

CARTRIDGE BALLISTICS

Max. Average Breech Pressure: N/A
Max. Effective Range: 10 yds.
Max. Horizontal Range: 2,600 yds.
Max. Vertical Range: 5,600 ft.

Bullet Weight (gr.)	Bullet Type	Muzzle Velocity (fps)	Muzzle Energy (ft.-lbs.)
56	FMJ	1,050	137

CURRENT MANUFACTURER(S)

GENERAL COMMENT(S)

For personal carry, many high-ranking Japanese military officers purchased a scaled down version of the standard 8mm Nambu pistol. This very well made pistol was chambered for a unique 7mm Nambu cartridge which was also a smaller version of the standard Japanese 8mm Nambu cartridge. Very few of the pistols were made and they are rare. The cartridges are also rare collector's items.

TECHNICAL COMMENT(S)

The 7mm Nambu cartridge is unique in that it is one of the very few handgun cartridges designed with a 7mm caliber bullet. BALLISTICS of the 7mm Nambu are unremarkable and rather poor by western standards.

.30 BORCHARDT

ALTERNATE NAME(S): 7.65mm Borchardt
RELATED CALIBER(S): 7.63mm Mauser, 7.62x25mm Tokarev

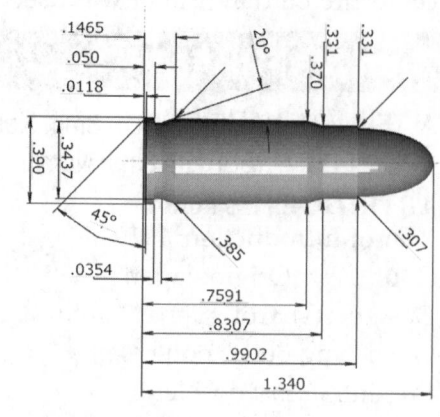

CARTRIDGE HISTORY
Year of Introduction: 1893
Country of Origin: U.S.
Designer(s): Hugo Borchardt
Governing Body: none
Present Status: obsolete

CARTRIDGE DESCRIPTION
Bullet Diameter: .307 in.
Bullet Weight(s): 85 gr.
Rifling Twist Rate: 1 turn in 12 in.
Test Barrel Length: N/A
Case Type: rimless, necked
Case Material: brass
Primer: small pistol

CARTRIDGE BALLISTICS
Max. Average Breech Pressure: N/A
Max. Horizontal Range: 1,650 yds.
Max. Vertical Range: 3,600 ft.

Bullet Weight (gr.)	Bullet Type	Muzzle Velocity (fps)	Muzzle Energy (ft.-lbs.)
85	FMJ	1,280	312

CURRENT MANUFACTURER(S)
None

GENERAL COMMENT(S)
Hugo Borchardt has the distinction of designing and introducing the first successful semi-automatic pistol, the Borchardt Model 1893. This is the cartridge that Borchardt designed for his pistol. Although the cartridge in its original loading was not commercially successful, with a few minor improvements it was to become the grand daddy of all semi-automatic pistol cartridges in the form of the 7.63mm/.30 Mauser pistol cartridge. Mauser copied the Borchardt cartridge for his "broom handle" Mauser pistol introduced in 1897. While the dimensions remainded similar, the maximum average chamber pressure and muzzle velocity were substantially increased. In fact, the 7.63mm Mauser pistol cartridge was the most powerful handgun cartridge in the world until the .357 Magnum was introduced in 1935. From 1917 until the mid-1920s, the C96 Mauser pistol in 7.63mm Mauser with a shortened barrel was a favorite of the Russian Bolshevik revolutionaries, thus the term "Bolo" Mauser pistol. Subsequently, the Soviet Army adopted the 7.62x25mm Tokarev cartridge which remained in front line service well into the 1950s.

TECHNICAL COMMENT(S)
While the 7.65mm Borchardt and the 7.63mm Mauser and 7.62x25mm Tokarev share generally similar dimensions and are loaded with bullets of approximately the same weight, the Mauser and the Tokarev are loaded to a much higher maximum average chamber pressure. As a result, they must not be fired in Borchardt pistols as they will damage the gun. The 7.65mm Borchardt was the first handgun cartridge with a light weight bullet at a high muzzle velocity. Thus began the debate between the heavy bullet at low velocity and the light bullet at high velocity groups, still going on today.

7.63x25mm MAUSER

ALTERNATE NAME(S): .30 Mauser, 7.63mm Mauser
RELATED CALIBER(S): .30 Borchardt

CARTRIDGE HISTORY
Year of Introduction: 1896
Country of Origin: Germany
Designer(s): Hugo Borchardt
Governing Body: CIP, SAAMI
Present Status: obsolete

CARTRIDGE DESCRIPTION
Bullet Diameter: .308 in.
Bullet Weight(s): 85 gr.
Rifling Twist Rate: 1 turn in 7.9 in.
Test Barrel Length: N/A
Case Type: rimless, necked
Case Material: brass or steel
Primer Type: small pistol

CARTRIDGE BALLISTICS
Max. Average Breech Pressure: N/A
Max. Effective Range: 50 yds.
Max. Horizontal Range: 2,500 yds.
Max. Vertical Range: 5,600 ft.

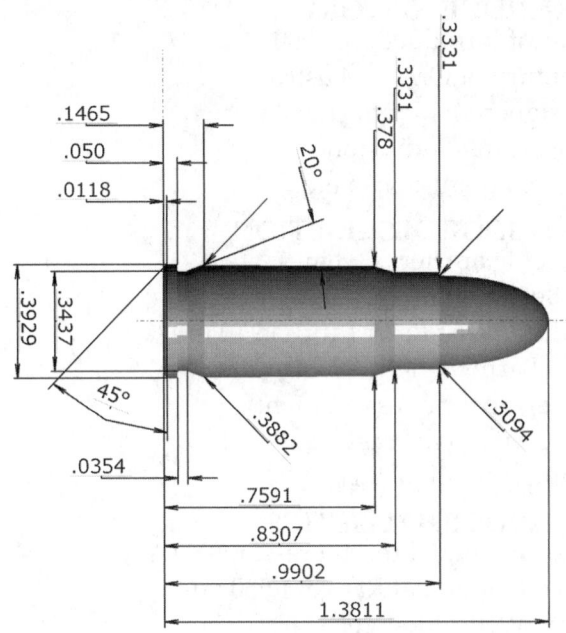

Bullet Weight (gr.)	Bullet Type	Muzzle Velocity (fps)	Muzzle Energy (ft.-lbs.)
86	FMJ	1,410	375

CURRENT MANUFACTURER(S)
Fiocchi, Prvi Partizan

GENERAL COMMENT(S)
This is one of the most historically significant handgun cartridges in history. Mauser introduced his C96 Military Model pistol in 1896 for the 7.63x25mm Mauser cartridge. The C96 pistol was affectionately called the "broomhandle" Mauser after its stubby grip. It became a great favorite of Russian Bolsheviks revolutionaries, Chinese warlords, Arab bedouins, and Pashto tribesman. Winston Churchill carried one during his years as a news correspondent in the Sudan where he had several opportunities to use it. Although the 7.63mm Mauser cartridge was never officially adopted by any country for military use, it was used extensively in both World Wars and in law enforcement service. Production of C96 pistols ended in the mid 1930s.

TECHNICAL COMMENT(S)
From 1896 until 1935 when the .357 Magnum cartridge was introduced, the 7.63mm Mauser cartridge was the most powerful handgun cartridge in the world. The 7.63mm Mauser cartridge was one of the very first handgun cartridges designed from the start for smokeless propellants. In turn, the 7.63mm Mauser cartridge made a semi-automatic pistol feasible and the C96 Mauser was one of the first. Today, reports of the demise of the 7.63mm Mauser cartridge are premature. Most major ammunition makers have given up on it. However, a steady, if small demand persists that Fiocchi and Prvi Partizan fill.

7.63mm MANNLICHER

ALTERNATE NAME(S): none
RELATED CALIBER(S): 7.65mm MAS, .30 Pedersen, 7.65mm Roth-Sauer

CARTRIDGE HISTORY
Year of Introduction: 1900
Country of Origin: Austria
Designer(s): Mannlicher
Governing Body: none
Present Status: obsolete

CARTRIDGE DESCRIPTION
Bullet Diameter: .308 in.
Bullet Weight(s): 85 gr.
Rifling Twist Rate: 1 turn in 10 in.
Test Barrel Length: N/A
Case Type: rimless, straight
Case Material: brass
Primer: small pistol

CARTRIDGE BALLISTICS
Max. Average Breech Pressure: N/A
Max. Horizontal Range: 1,550 yds.
Max. Vertical Range: 3,350 ft.

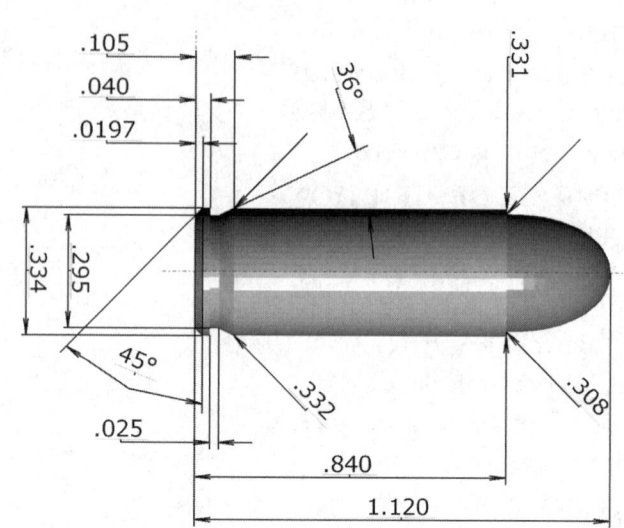

Bullet Weight (gr.)	Bullet Type	Muzzle Velocity (fps)	Muzzle Energy (ft.-lbs.)
85	FMJ	1,025	201

CURRENT MANUFACTURER(S)
None

GENERAL COMMENT(S)
Judging from the date of introduction and ballistics, the 7.63mm Mannlicher cartridge was conceived as a slightly more powerful contemporary of John Browning's .32 ACP. In the early 1930s, the French Army began efforts to develop a new service pistol and cartridge. In 1935, they adopted the new SACM M1935A pistol chambered for the new 7.65mm French Long which was nearly identical with the earlier 7.63 Mannlicher and .30 Pedersen.

TECHNICAL COMMENT(S)
From a ballistic standpoint, the 7.63 Mannlicher/.30 Pedersen/7.65 MAS cartridges must be considered weak for military service and marginal for self-defense. Their ballistic performance is a relic of turn-of-the-century thinking with light weight bullets at moderate muzzle velocities. In other words, stopping power was not a major factor in their design. All three are loaded to relatively modest maximum average chamber pressures (approximately 24,000 psi.) leaving no margin of reserve performance. In addition, the FMJ round nose bullets used in these cartridges did nothing to enhance their stopping power.

7.65mm ROTH-SAUER

ALTERNATE NAME(S): 7.65mm Roth
RELATED CALIBER(S): 7.63mm Mannlicher, 7.65mm MAS

CARTRIDGE HISTORY
Year of Introduction: 1901
Country of Origin: Austria
Designer(s): Roth
Governing Body: none
Present Status: obsolete

CARTRIDGE DESCRIPTION
Bullet Diameter: .301 in.
Bullet Weight(s): 70 -74 gr.
Rifling Twist Rate: 1 turn in 14 in.
Test Barrel Length: N/A
Case Type: rimless, straight
Case Material: brass
Primer: small pistol

CARTRIDGE BALLISTICS
Max. Average Breech Pressure: N/A
Max. Horizontal Range: 1,600 yds.
Max. Vertical Range: 3,500 ft.

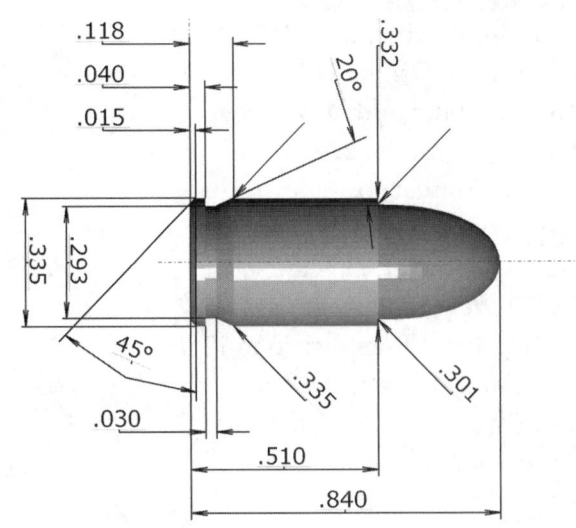

Bullet Weight (gr.)	Bullet Type	Muzzle Velocity (fps)	Muzzle Energy (ft.-lbs.)
74	FMJ	1,070	188

CURRENT MANUFACTURER(S)
None

GENERAL COMMENT(S)
It seems very likely that the 7.65mm Roth cartridge was a "me too" copy of the Browning .32 ACP cartridge introduced two years earlier. The popularity of the compact Sauer Model 1905 pistol chambered for this cartridge was such that the name of the cartridge itself merged with the pistol to become the 7.65mm Roth-Sauer. However, Sauer had nothing to do with the design of the cartridge. By 1930, the 7.65mm Roth-Sauer cartridge had fallen victim to the .32 ACP cartridge's popularity and faded quietly away.

TECHNICAL COMMENT(S)
From its case dimensions, the 7.65mm Roth cartridge appears to have been designed by the simple expedient of shortening a 7.63mm Mannlicher cartridge case. The .32 ACP and the 7.65mm Roth-Sauer cartridges are of similar size, caliber and appearance however the .32 ACP has a semi-rimmed case while the 7.65mm case is a rimless design. Bullet diameter, bullet weight, muzzle velocity and muzzle energy are equivalent leading to the conclusion that maximum average chamber pressures must have been very similar.

.35 SMITH & WESSON AUTOMATIC

ALTERNATE NAME(S): .35 Automatic, .35 S&W Auto
RELATED CALIBER(S): .32 ACP

CARTRIDGE HISTORY
Year of Introduction: 1913
Country of Origin: U.S.
Designer(s): Smith & Wesson
Governing Body: SAAMI
Present Status: obsolete

CARTRIDGE DESCRIPTION
Bullet Diameter: .309 in.
Bullet Weight(s): 76 gr.
Rifling Twist Rate: 1 turn in 12 in.
Test Barrel Length: N/A
Case Type: semi-rimmed, straight
Case Material: brass
Primer: small pistol

CARTRIDGE BALLISTICS
Max. Average Breech Pressure: N/A
Max. Horizontal Range: 1,400 yds.
Max. Vertical Range: 3,000 ft.

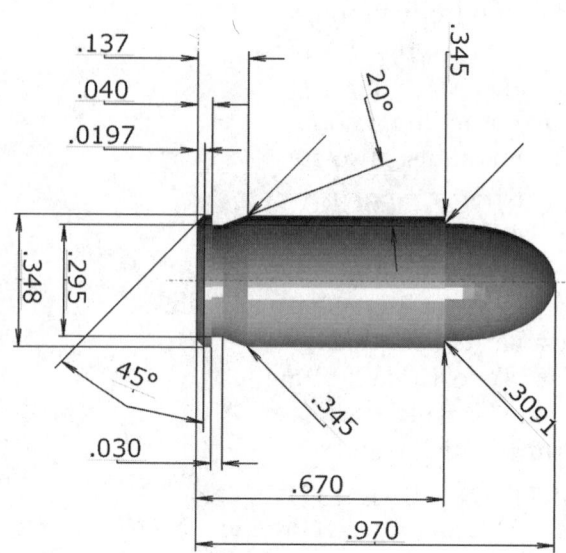

Bullet Weight (gr.)	Bullet Type	Muzzle Velocity (fps)	Muzzle Energy (ft.-lbs.)
76	FMJ	810	110

CURRENT MANUFACTURER(S)
None

GENERAL COMMENT(S)
Smith & Wesson must have been dimly cognizant of the Browning-designed .32 ACP/7.65mm cartridge introduced in 1899 by FN in Belgium. All this changed in 1903 when Colt introduced their M1903 pistol chambered for the new Browning cartridge, both of which quickly became a commercial success. This must have been quite a blow to Smith & Wesson's ego. After all, S&W had been the originators of dozens of handgun cartridges in the past and this turn of events was a challenge to their technical prowess and market position. In response, S&W introduced their own small caliber pistol chambered for a new cartridge in 1913.

TECHNICAL COMMENT(S)
Called the .35 Smith & Wesson Automatic (to eliminate any confusion with the Browning cartridge), the new cartridge looked very similar to the .32 ACP, used a similar bullet weight and offered comparable muzzle velocity and striking energy. Despite the nomenclatural designation, the .35 S&W Auto used a .308 inch diameter bullet identical to the .32 ACP. The major difference was the .32 ACP was a semi-rimmed design while the .35 S&W was rimless and arguably the more modern of the two. In addition, the base diameter of the .35 S&W cartridge was 0.010 inch larger than the .32 ACP, so the two cartridges were not interchangeable. Smith & Wesson slowly recognized that the .32 ACP train had already left the station, leaving them to play catch-up. Sales of the S&W pistol in their new caliber proved very slow as all the other handgun makers jumped on the .32 ACP band wagon.

Finally, bowing to the inevitable, S&W discontinued pistols in this caliber in 1921, although ammunition makers continued to offer the cartridge until 1940. The .35 S&W Auto cartridge remains an example of the danger of allowing a corporate ego to dictate marketing decisions.

.357 AUTO MAG

ALTERNATE NAME(S): .357 A.M.
RELATED CALIBER(S): .44 Auto Mag

CARTRIDGE HISTORY

Year of Introduction: 1973
Country of Origin: U.S.
Designer(s): Auto Mag
Governing Body: CIP
Present Status: obsolete

CARTRIDGE DESCRIPTION

Bullet Diameter: .359 in.
Bullet Weight(s): 110-158 gr.
Rifling Twist Rate: 1 turn in 18 in.
Test Barrel Length: 5.9 in.
Case Type: rimless, necked
Case Material: brass
Primer: small pistol

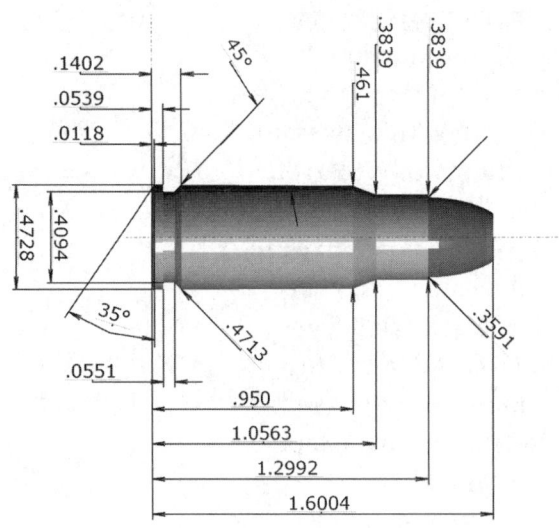

CARTRIDGE BALLISTICS

Max. Average Breech Pressure: 36,965 psi.
Max. Horizontal Range: 2,200 yds.
Max. Vertical Range: 4,700 ft.

Bullet Weight (gr.)	Bullet Type	Muzzle Velocity (fps)	Muzzle Energy (ft.-lbs.)
110	JHP	1,900	882
125	JHP	1,800	899
140	JHP	1,700	898
158	JSP	1,600	898

CURRENT MANUFACTURER(S)

None

GENERAL COMMENT(S)

The .357 Auto Mag was introduced several years after the .44 Auto Mag, but never achieved the popularity of the latter. Consequently, its production life was short leaving it obscure in the shadow of its big brother. It was chambered in the massive, semi-automatic Auto Mag pistol. This handgun and cartridge were suitable only for hunting large varmints and medium game where handgun hunting was legal. And this was its Achilles heel, it was too specialized for most shooters.

TECHNICAL COMMENT(S)

In its day, the .357 Auto Mag was considered a high pressure, high velocity pistol cartridge with striking energy that very few other handgun cartridges could match. However, by today's performance standards with many magnum handgun cartridges now having chamber pressures nearly the same as many rifle cartridges, .357 Auto Mag chamber pressures are moderate and, in fact, nearly the same as the 9mm Luger. As one would expect when shooting a cartridge of this type, muzzle blast and recoil are very heavy. The .357 Auto Mag case is basically a .44 Auto Mag cartridge case necked down for .357 inch diameter bullets. Nearly any jacketed bullet designed for the .38 Special or the .357 Magnum is suitable, although the 158 grain bullets are best for hunting medium game such as deer and javelina. Flat nose bullets can be used, but round nose or semi-round nose designs will feed more reliably.

9mm FEDERAL

ALTERNATE NAME(S): 9 Fed.
RELATED CALIBER(S): 9X19mm Luger

CARTRIDGE HISTORY
Year of Introduction: 1989
Country of Origin: U.S.
Designer(s): Mike Bussard, Alan Newcomb
Governing Body: SAAMI
Present Status: obsolete

CARTRIDGE DESCRIPTION
Bullet Diameter: .355 in.
Bullet Weight(s): 115 gr.
Rifling Twist Rate: 1 turn in 9 in.
Test Barrel Length: 4 in.
Case Type: rimmed, tapered
Case Material: brass
Primer Type: small pistol

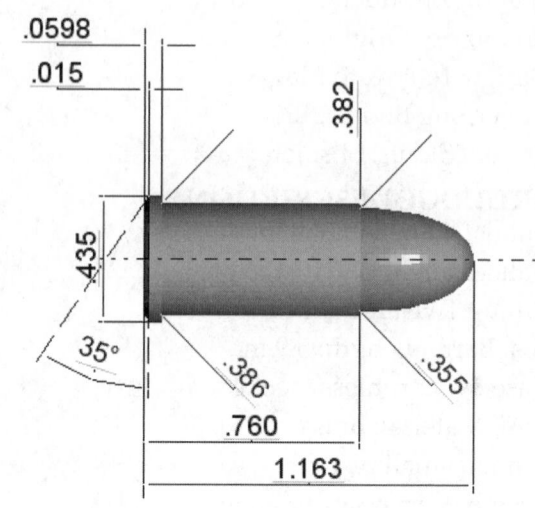

CARTRIDGE BALLISTICS
Max. Average Breech Pressure: 35,000 psi.
Max. Effective Range: 25 yds.
Max. Horizontal Range: 2,150 yds.
Max. Vertical Range: 4,800 ft.

Bullet Weight (gr.)	Bullet Type	Muzzle Velocity (fps)	Muzzle Energy (ft.-lbs.)
115	JHP	1,280	420

CURRENT MANUFACTURER(S)
None

GENERAL COMMENT(S)
In the late 1980s, the standard issue handgun of the Quebec City Police Department (QCPD) was a .38 caliber revolver. As they were unhappy with the ballistic performance of the .38 Special cartridge, the QCPD sought to replace the .38 Special with a more powerful caliber. During that time, many law enforcement agencies were switching to Luger caliber pistols. The QCPD desired to retain a revolver as their standard issue handgun. While the 9mm Luger was a popular choice, existing revolvers required a rimmed cartridge case and the 9mm Luger was a rimless design. Federal's solution to this problem was a rimmed case. Charter Arms and several other revolver makers brought out guns in this caliber. After a few years, the QCPD retired their revolvers and adopted a semi-automatic pistol. The 9mm Federal cartridge no longer had a reason to exist and was quietly retired in the early 2000s.

TECHNICAL COMMENT(S)
Basically, the 9mm Federal is a rimmed 9x19mm Luger cartridge intended for a revolver. In other words, the 9mm Federal is a 9x19mm cartridge with the approximate rimmed head dimensions of a .38 Special case. Bullets of 9mm and maximum average chamber pressures are similar. Unlike the .45 Auto Rim cartridge, the 9mm Federal does not have an extra-thick rim. Interestingly, 9x19mm cartridges can be safely fired in a 9mm Federal chamber, although fired cases may protrude sufficiently from the rear of the cylinder to drag on the recoil plate making cylinder rotation and extraction difficult. A dangerous interchange situation exists in that 9mm Federal ammunition will chamber and fire in .38 S&W caliber revolvers. This could damage such a revolver and cause serious personal injury. Older revolvers in .38 S&W are not designed to handle the chamber pressures of the 9mm Federal. Conversely, some brands of .38 S&W ammunition may chamber and fire in 9mm Federal caliber revolvers. Such a practice can not be recommended as the lead bullets of the .38 S&W cartridge may cause heavy lead buildup in the bore.

9mm ULTRA

ALTERNATE NAME(S): None
RELATED CALIBER(S): 9x19mm Luger, .380 ACP

CARTRIDGE HISTORY
Year of Introduction: 1936
Country of Origin: Germany
Designer(s): Carl Walther G.m.b.H.
Governing Body: CIP
Present Status: obsolete

CARTRIDGE DESCRIPTION
Bullet Diameter: .355 in.
Bullet Weight(s): 123 gr.
Rifling Twist Rate: N/A
Test Barrel Length: N/A
Case Type: rimless, straight
Case Material: brass
Primer Type: small pistol

CARTRIDGE BALLISTICS
Max. Average Breech Pressure: N/A
Max. Effective Range: 25 yds. (est.)
Max. Horizontal Range: 2,200 yds. (est.)
Max. Vertical Range: 5,100 ft. (est.)

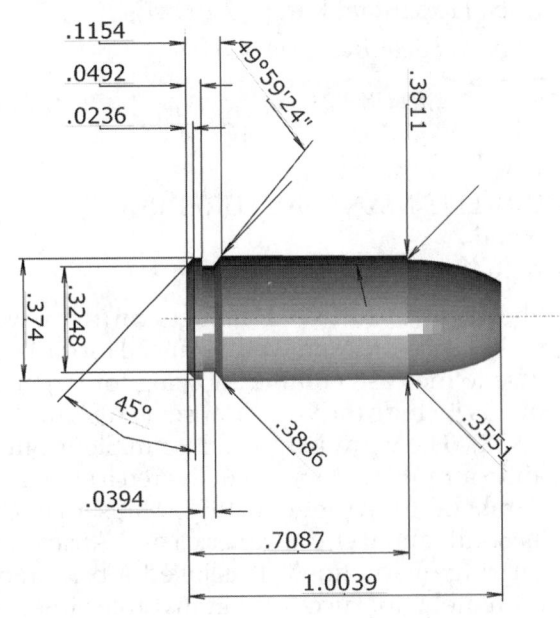

Bullet Weight (gr.)	Bullet Type	Muzzle Velocity (fps)	Muzzle Energy (ft.-lbs.)
123	JSP	1,070 (est.)	312 (est.)

CURRENT MANUFACTURER(S)
None

GENERAL COMMENT(S)
Designed in 1936 for the German Luftwaffe, it was never officially adopted. It is not identical to the DWM 9mm Ultra/9x18mm Ultra introduced in 1972.

TECHNICAL COMMENT(S)
N/A

9mm MAUSER

ALTERNATE NAME(S): 9x25mm, 9mm Mauser Export
RELATED CALIBER(S): 9x19mm Luger, 9mm Steyr, 9mm Largo

CARTRIDGE HISTORY
Year of Introduction: 1908
Country of Origin: Germany
Designer(s): Mauser
Governing Body: none
Present Status: obsolete

CARTRIDGE DESCRIPTION
Bullet Diameter: .355 in.
Bullet Weight(s): 128 gr.
Rifling Twist Rate: 1 turn in 12 in.
Test Barrel Length: N/A

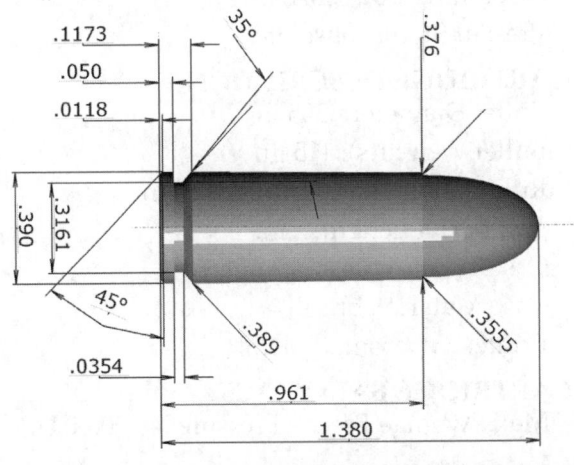

Case Type: rimless, straight
Case Material: brass
Primer: small pistol

CARTRIDGE BALLISTICS
Max. Average Breech Pressure: N/A
Max. Horizontal Range: 2,250 yds.
Max. Vertical Range: 4,800 ft.

Bullet Weight (gr.)	Bullet Type	Muzzle Velocity (fps)	Muzzle Energy (ft.-lbs.)
128	FMJ	1,360	534

CURRENT MANUFACTURER(S)
None

GENERAL COMMENT(S)
Shortly after the 9x19mm Luger cartridge was introduced in 1902, various companies started trying to improve on its successful and well-balanced formula. Most of these efforts consisted of lengthening the 9x19mm cartridge case to increase volume allowing for larger powder charges to increase muzzle velocity and energy. Examples of this include the 9mm Mauser (1908), the 9mm Largo (1910), 9mm Steyr (1912) and 9mm Winchester Magnum (1988). The 9mm Largo and 9mm Steyr offered only marginal ballistic improvements while the 9mm Mauser and 9mm Win. Magnum delivered a substantial improvement. As the German Army had adopted the 9x19mm Parabellum cartridge in 1908, Mauser concentrated on selling their 9mm cartridge in overseas markets such as South and Central America and Africa. They had little success and by 1920 production of the 9mm Mauser cartridge had ended. It enjoyed a brief reprieve in the mid-1930s as a submachine gun cartridge, but was ultimately not successful in that role either.

TECHNICAL COMMENT(S)
All of these long 9mm cartridges have become obsolete. Why? For the simple reason they are predicated on the false assumption that the 9mm Luger cartridge lacks ballistic performance. In practice, the 9x19mm Luger cartridge is an excellent balance of ballistic factors. It is compact, efficient and powerful enough for a wide variety of applications including military, law enforcement and personal defense. It is also made by nearly all major ammunition manufacturers so it is common and available all over the world. This is a tough combination to beat. Here it is interesting to note that nearly all of the long 9mm cartridges, such as the 9mm Mauser, are loaded with a 124 grain bullet to take advantage of the increased case capacity.

9mm WINCHESTER MAGNUM

ALTERNATE NAME(S): 9mm Win. Mag., 9x29.5mm Win. Mag.
RELATED CALIBER(S): 9mm Bergmann-Bayard, 9mm Luger

CARTRIDGE HISTORY
Year of Introduction: circa 1977
Country of Origin: U.S.
Designer(s): Winchester
Governing Body: SAAMI
Present Status: obsolete

CARTRIDGE DESCRIPTION
Bullet Diameter: .355 in.
Bullet Weight(s): 115 gr.
Rifling Twist Rate: 1 turn in 10 in.
Test Barrel Length: 5 in.
Case Type: rimless, straight
Case Material: brass
Primer Type: small pistol

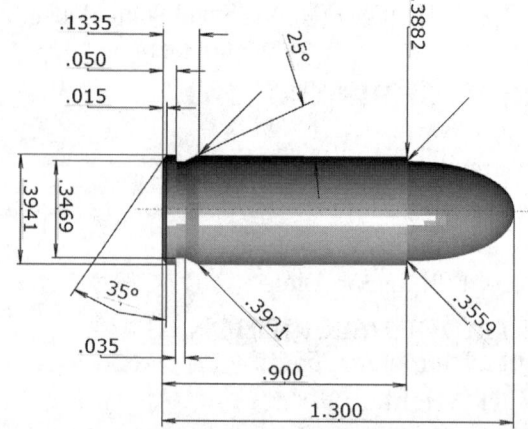

CARTRIDGE BALLISTICS
Max. Average Breech Pressure: 48,500 CUP.

Max. Effective Range: 50 yds.
Max. Horizontal Range: 2,850 yds.
Max. Vertical Range: 4,900 ft.

Bullet Weight (gr.)	Bullet Type	Muzzle Velocity (fps)	Muzzle Energy (ft.-lbs.)
115	FMJ	1,475	556

CURRENT MANUFACTURER(S)

None

GENERAL COMMENT(S)

Developed by Winchester for the Wildey pistol, Winchester was left holding the bag when Wildey ran into financial difficulties. To their credit, Winchester kept the cartridge in the product line for approximately 10 years in hopes a gun maker would bring out a pistol in this caliber. None did. After this decent interval, Winchester killed off the 9mm Win. Mag. and it became but a short footnote in cartridge history.

TECHNICAL COMMENT(S)

The 9mm Win. Mag. is one of the most powerful 9mm cartridge ever made. It was intended as a hunting cartridge and for metallic silhouette competition. In the event, silhouette shooters and handgun hunters preferred larger caliber revolver cartridges.

9x18mm POLICE

ALTERNATE NAME(S): 9x18 Police, 9mm Super
RELATED CALIBER(S): 9mm Kurz (9x17mm), 9x19mm Luger, 9mm Makarov, 9mm Ultra (1936)

CARTRIDGE HISTORY

Year of Introduction: 1972
Country of Origin: Germany
Designer(s): Carl Walther G.m.b.H.
Governing Body: CIP
Present Status: obsolete

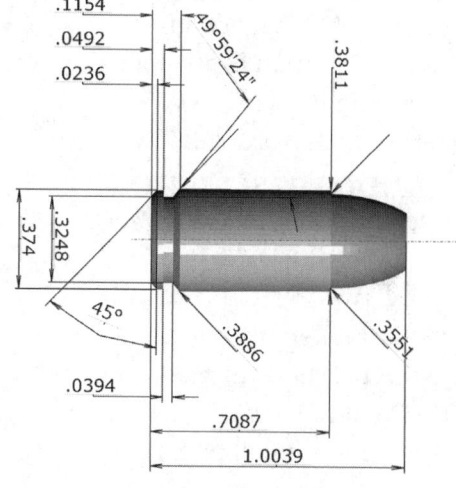

CARTRIDGE DESCRIPTION

Bullet Diameter: .355 in.
Bullet Weight(s): 100-124 gr.
Rifling Twist Rate: 1 turn in 9.8 in.
Test Barrel Length: 5.9 in.
Case Type: rebated rimless, tapered
Case Material: brass
Primer: small pistol

CARTRIDGE BALLISTICS

Max. Average Breech Pressure: 26,100 psi.
Max. Horizontal Range: 1,600 yds.
Max. Vertical Range: 3,400 ft.

Bullet Weight (gr.)	Bullet Type	Muzzle Velocity (fps)	Muzzle Energy (ft.-lbs.)
94	FMJ-FN	1,055	232
100	FMJ-FN	1,065	250
123	FMJ-FN	1,070	350
124	FMJ-FN	1,050	308

CURRENT MANUFACTURER(S)

GENERAL COMMENT(S)

In the early 1970s, the growing terrorist threat convinced many European law enforcement agencies to adopt a handgun cartridge more powerful than the .32 ACP and .380 ACP. Being conservative, these agencies viewed the

9x19mm Luger cartridge as too powerful; something in-between was wanted that was exclusively for law enforcement. The result was the 9x18mm Ultra cartridge with a ballistic performance in-between the .380 ACP and the 9x19mm Luger. This cartridge's name was previously used in a 1936 German program to design a new pistol cartridge for the Luftwaffe. Although it was never adopted, the 9mm Ultra circa 1936 went on to influence development of the 9mm Makarov as well as the 9x18mm Police. The 1972 9x18mm cartridge had a short life. Slowly, it was realized that distribution of 9x18mm Ultra ammunition could not be restricted to law enforcement agencies only. In addition, its ballistics proved inadequate as the nature of the terrorist threat evolved. By the mid-1990s, most European law enforcement agencies had adopted the 9x19mm Luger cartridge and the 9x18mm Ultra quickly disappeared.

TECHNICAL COMMENT(S)

Basically, the 9x18mm Ultra is either a 9x17mm Kurz case made longer or a 9x19mm Luger case made shorter depending on how you look at it. However, while the body diameter of the 9x18mm case is the same, the rim of the 9x18mm case is slightly rebated in comparison to its siblings. Here we must consider the relatively small case capacity of the 9x17mm Kurz cartridge. This restricts the propellant charge and bullet weight and, consequently, muzzle velocity and striking energy. The 9x18mm Ultra cartridge case is 1mm longer to provide increased case volume. However, when we consider that the 9x19mm Luger cartridge case is also volume-limited, the limited benefit of the 9x18mm case comes into focus. An astute observer will notice that the 9x18mm Ultra bears a striking resemblance to the Russian 9mm Makarov cartridge. Both share a 9x18mm nomenclature and ballistic performance is similar. However, the two cartridges differ in other dimensions and are not interchangeable.

.38 AUTOMATIC

ALTERNATE NAME(S): .38 Auto, .38 ACP, .38 Colt Automatic
RELATED CALIBER(S): .38 Super Auto, .38 Super Auto +P

CARTRIDGE HISTORY
Year of Introduction: 1900
Country of Origin: Belgium
Designer(s): John Browning
Governing Body: SAAMI
Present Status: obsolete

CARTRIDGE DESCRIPTION
Bullet Diameter: .355 in.
Bullet Weight(s): 130 gr.
Rifling Twist Rate: 1 turn in 16 in.
Test Barrel Length: 5 in.
Case Type: semi-rimmed, straight
Case Material: brass
Primer Type: small pistol

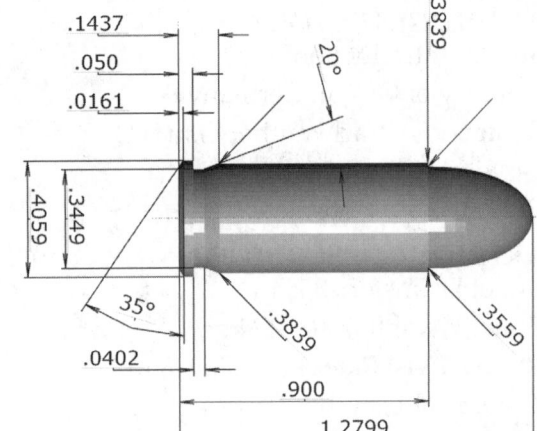

CARTRIDGE BALLISTICS
Max. Average Breech Pressure: 33,359 psi.
Max. Effective Range: 25 yds.
Max. Horizontal Range: 2,150 yds.
Max. Vertical Range: 4,800 ft.

Bullet Weight (gr.)	Bullet Type	Muzzle Velocity (fps)	Muzzle Energy (ft.-lbs.)
130	FMJ	1,040	312

CURRENT MANUFACTURER(S)
None

GENERAL COMMENT(S)
The .38 Auto was superseded by the higher pressure, more powerful .38 Super Automatic in 1929. Made semi-obsolete by the new loading, the .38 Auto cartridge began a slow decline in sales that finally ended in the 1990s by which time all major manufacturers had dropped it in favor of the .38 Super Auto. You know demand for a cartridge must be very low when even Fiocchi does not make it.

TECHNICAL COMMENT(S)

Although both the .38 Auto and the .38 Super Auto share similar case dimensions and will chamber in either pistol, they are not interchangeable. The modern high pressure .38 Super Auto +P cartridge must not be fired in older pistols chambered for the .38 Auto cartridge. While the older .38 Auto cartridge can safely be fired in pistols designed for the .38 Super Auto or +P cartridge, it will not reliably cycle those pistols' actions.

.41 ACTION EXPRESS

ALTERNATE NAME(S): .41 A.E.
RELATED CALIBER(S): 9mm Luger, .40 S&W Auto

CARTRIDGE HISTORY

Year of Introduction: 1986
Country of Origin: U.S.
Designer(s): Evan Whildin
Governing Body: CIP
Present Status: obsolete

CARTRIDGE DESCRIPTION

Bullet Diameter: .411 in.
Bullet Weight(s): 180-200 gr.
Rifling Twist Rate: 1 turn in 18.75 in.
Test Barrel Length: 6 in.
Case Type: rimless, rebated, straight
Case Material: brass
Primer Type: small pistol

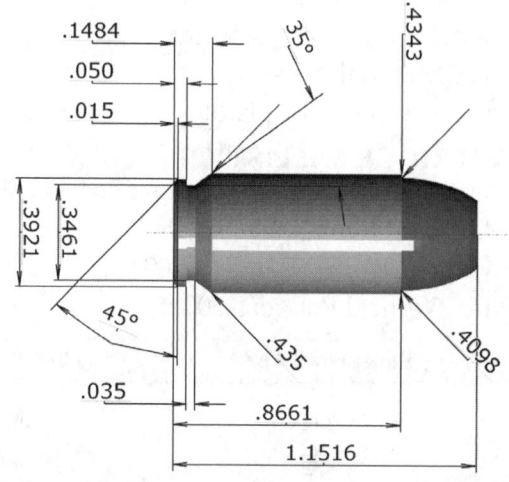

CARTRIDGE BALLISTICS

Max. Average Breech Pressure: 35,700 CUP.
Max. Effective Range: 25 yds.
Max. Horizontal Range: 2,200 yds.
Max. Vertical Range: 4,400 ft.

Bullet Weight (gr.)	Bullet Type	Muzzle Velocity (fps)	Muzzle Energy (ft.-lbs.)
180	JHP	1,000	400
200	JHP	1,000	448

CURRENT MANUFACTURER(S)

IMI

GENERAL COMMENT(S)

The purpose of this cartridge was to obtain the improved termincal ballistics of a larger diameter bullet while using 9mm Luger caliber guns without having to completely redesign the frame and slide. This was accomplished by grafting a 9mm Luger rim and extraction groove onto a larger diameter (.434 inch) case body giving the cartridge a rebated rim. While the new case was longer than the 9mm Luger, the overall loaded length remains the same by using a blunt bullet.The .41 A.E. worked and enjoyed a modest popularity from the mid-1980s until the mid-1990s. When Action Arms closed its doors, the .41 A.E. cartridge became an unwanted orphan.

TECHNICAL COMMENT(S)

Arguably, the .41 A.E. cartridge accomplished its purpose. However, the improvement was modest, about 21% more muzzle energy than a 9mm Luger cartridge.   The fate of the .41 A.E. cartridge was sealed in the early 1990s with the introduction of 9mm Luger +P ammunition that offered the same muzzle energy.

.44 AUTO MAG

ALTERNATE NAME(S): .44 Automatic Magnum
RELATED CALIBER(S): .44 Magnum

CARTRIDGE HISTORY
Year of Introduction: 1971
Country of Origin: U.S.
Designer(s): Harry Sanford
Governing Body: CIP
Present Status: obsolete

CARTRIDGE DESCRIPTION
Bullet Diameter: .429 in.
Bullet Weight(s): 180-240 gr.
Rifling Twist Rate: 1 turn in 18 in.
Test Barrel Length: 6 in.
Case Type: rimless, straight
Case Material: brass
Primer Type: large pistol

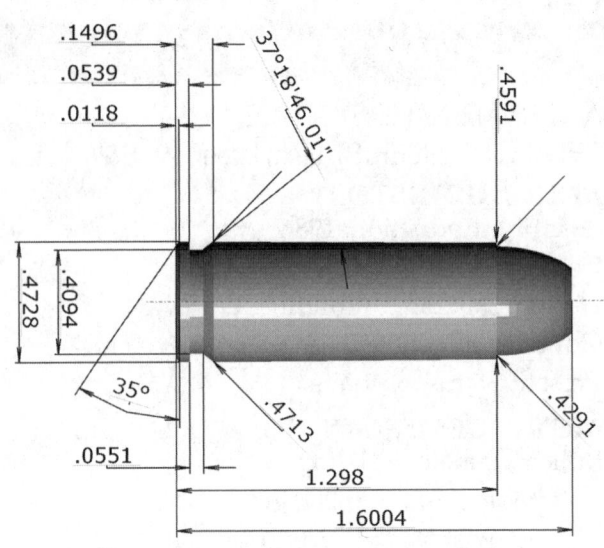

CARTRIDGE BALLISTICS
Max. Average Breech Pressure: 36,985 psi.
Max. Effective Range: 50 yds.
Max. Horizontal Range: 2,500 yds.
Max. Vertical Range: 5,600 ft.

Bullet Weight (gr.)	Bullet Type	Muzzle Velocity (fps)	Muzzle Energy (ft.-lbs.)
180	JHP	1,600	1,024
240	JHP	1,400	1,045

CURRENT MANUFACTURER(S)
None

GENERAL COMMENT(S)
The .44 Auto Mag was designed for the semi-automatic pistol of the same name. This pistol and cartridge were an early 1970s attempt to develop a powerful, large bore, semi-auto pistol. Norma made loaded ammunition in this caliber and Cartuchos Deportivos made empty brass. Both pistol and cartridge were dogged by numerous financial, manufacturing and mechanical trials and tribulations during their short production life. Both pistol and cartridge faded away in the late 1980s.

TECHNICAL COMMENT(S)
Basically, the .44 Auto Mag cartridge is a rimless .44 Magnum for use in semi-auto pistols. BALLISTICS are similar and both use the same .429 inch diameter jacketed bullets. Case head dimensions of the .44 Auto Mag are similar to the .308 Win. or .30-'06 Springfield cartridges.

.45 WINCHESTER MAGNUM

ALTERNATE NAME(S): .45 Win. Mag.
RELATED CALIBER(S): .45 ACP

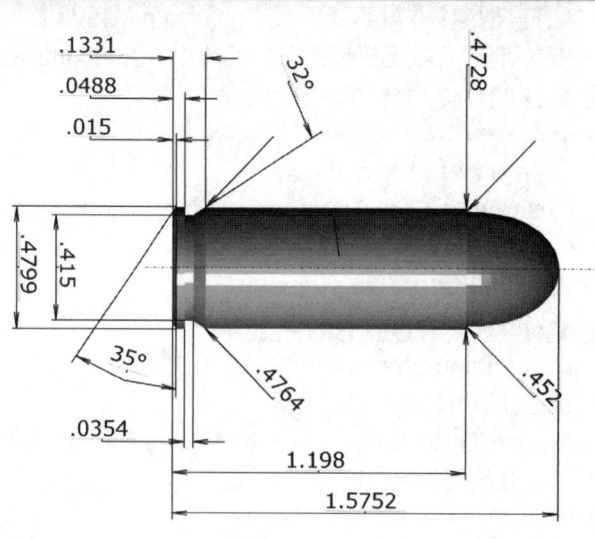

CARTRIDGE HISTORY
Year of Introduction: 1979
Country of Origin: U.S.
Designer(s): Winchester
Governing Body: SAAMI
Present Status: active

CARTRIDGE DESCRIPTION
Bullet Diameter: .452 in.
Bullet Weight(s): 200-320 gr.
Rifling Twist Rate: 1 turn in 16 in.
Test Barrel Length: 5 in.
Case Type: rimless, straight
Case Material: brass
Primer Type: large pistol

CARTRIDGE BALLISTICS
Max. Average Breech Pressure: 40,000 CUP.
Max. Effective Range: 50 yds.
Max. Horizontal Range: 2,100 yds.
Max. Vertical Range: 4,600 ft.

Bullet Weight (gr.)	Bullet Type	Muzzle Velocity (fps)	Muzzle Energy (ft.-lbs.)
260	JSP	1,200	831
320	FMJ	1,150	940

CURRENT MANUFACTURER(S)
none

GENERAL COMMENT(S)
This is an example of the true potential of the .45 ACP cartridge. In a unique historic twist, Winchester introduced this ammunition before a gun was available to shoot it (the Wildey pistol for which the cartridge was originally designed having run into financial problems). Following this, handgun makers have been reluctant to design new pistols for this cartridge given the unproven market demand for such a product. Recent developments in large-bore revolver cartridges may change this. Winchester dropped this cartridge in 2011.

TECHNICAL COMMENT(S)
The muzzle energy and recoil impulse of the cartridge place it in the "for experts only" category. It is too powerful for personal defense, however, it is suitable for hunting medium game where legal. Maximum average breech pressure of the .45 Winchester Auto cartridge is approximately double that of the .45 ACP and equivalent to the 9mm Luger and .357 Magnum. To take advantage of the full potential of this cartridge, 250 grain bullets must be used.

.45 REMINGTON-THOMPSON

ALTERNATE NAME(S): .45 Thompson M1923
RELATED CALIBER(S): .45 ACP, .30-'06 Springfield, .45 Winchester Magnum

CARTRIDGE HISTORY
Year of Introduction: 1923
Country of Origin: U.S.
Designer(s): Auto Ordnance/Remington
Governing Body: none (SAAMI)
Present Status: obsolete

CARTRIDGE DESCRIPTION
Bullet Diameter: .447 in.
Bullet Weight(s): 250 gr.
Rifling Twist Rate: 1 turn in 16 in.
Test Barrel Length: N/A
Case Type: rimless, straight
Case Material: brass
Primer: large rifle

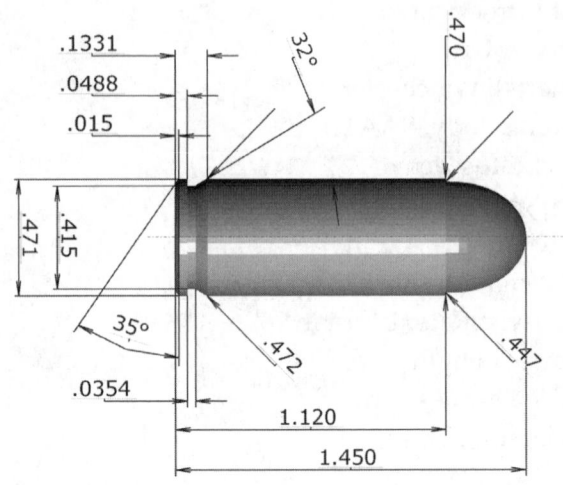

CARTRIDGE BALLISTICS
Max. Average Breech Pressure: N/A
Max. Horizontal Range: 2,100 yds.
Max. Vertical Range: 4,500 ft.

Bullet Weight (gr.)	Bullet Type	Muzzle Velocity (fps)	Muzzle Energy (ft.-lbs.)
250	FMJ-RN	1,450	1,165

CURRENT MANUFACTURER(S)
None

GENERAL COMMENT(S)
In 1923 the Auto Ordnance Company, manufacturer of the famous Thompson submachine gun, developed a new version with a longer barrel, the M-1923 Military Model. In an effort to increase muzzle velocity and striking energy, a new cartridge was developed for the gun called the .45 Thompson M1923 or .45 Remington-Thompson. Remington manufactured a short run of ammunition in this caliber for test and development. When little or no interest was shown by prospective customers, the gun and cartridge were summarily dropped.

TECHNICAL COMMENT(S)
While the new cartridge appeared to be made from an elongated .45 ACP case, in fact the .45 Thompson case head dimensions were taken from the .30-'06 Spr. cartridge for added strength. Advertised ballistics claimed a muzzle velocity of 1,450 fps generating an impressive 1,167 ft.-lbs. of muzzle energy using a 250 grain FMJ bullet. Now, fast forward to 1979 when Winchester introduced their .45 Winchester Magnum cartridge with similar case dimensions, but inferior ballistics. The .45 Winchester Automatic cartridge also did not achieve military or commercial success.

CHAPTER 75 : MILITARY REVOLVER - CURRENT

CHAPTER 75

For Cartridge Index see Chapter 101. All drawing dimensions are approximate.

In the modern world, military arms are designed to enable soldiers to achieve firepower superiority over an opponent. For this reason, military rifles are selective fire and military pistols have magazines containing as many as 15 rounds. For many strategists, these requirements have consigned the military revolver to the dustbin of history. However, reports of its demise may be premature.

The military revolver remains in U.S. military service. It remains in full or limited use for some military police functions, for clandestine operations, and for plant guards. In addition, some aircrew carry revolvers and some ground force soldiers carry revolvers, which they purchase themselves for backup purposes – officially or unofficially. In some countries, revolvers are issued to paramilitary units and held in reserve for emergency purposes.

Historically, the U.S. has had to resort to purchasing and issuing revolvers when wartime demands for M1911A1 pistols far outstripped production capacity. Should this happen yet again, it is comforting to know that suitable double-action revolvers remain in full production by several major manufacturers here in the U.S. to meet civilian demand.

All U.S. military revolvers are chambered for the Caliber .38, Ball M41, or PGU/12B cartridge. This is a .38 Special cartridge in appearance and performance. Military .38 M41or PGU/12B ammunition can be fired safely in any .38 Special caliber sporting revolver in good condition.

Is there a future for the military revolver? Maybe, for specialized applications. A revolver's capability to fire magnum ammunition loaded with suitable bullets that will penetrate body armor may well enable it to stage a limited comeback.

.38 SPECIAL

ALTERNATE NAME(S): .38 Spl., .38 S&W Special, .38 Special,
RELATED CALIBER(S): .38 Long Colt

CARTRIDGE HISTORY
Year of Introduction: 1902
Country of Origin: U.S.
Designer(s): S&W
Governing Body: U.S. Army
Present Status: obsolete

CARTRIDGE DESCRIPTION
Bullet Diameter: .357 in.
Bullet Weight(s): 130-158 gr.
Rifling Twist Rate: 1 turn in 18.75 in.
Test Barrel Length: 4 in.
Case Type: rimmed, straight
Case Material: brass
Primer Type: small pistol

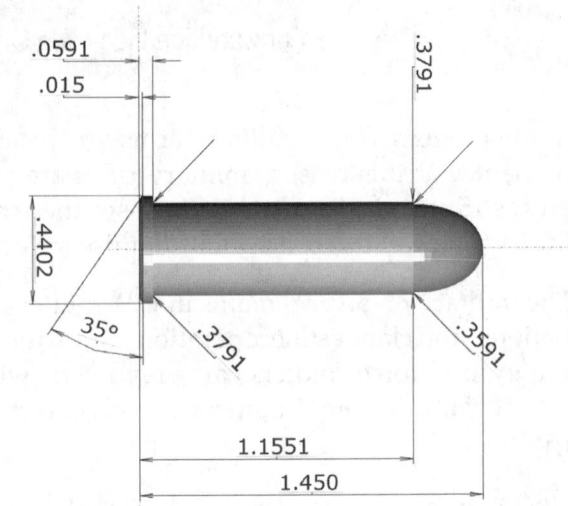

CARTRIDGE BALLISTICS
Max. Average Breech Pressure: 13,000 psi (M41), 16,000 psi (M41 Special), 20,000 psi (PGU/12B)
Max. Effective Range: 50 yds.
Max. Horizontal Range: 1,890 yds.
Max. Vertical Range: 4,000 ft.

Bullet Weight (gr.)	Bullet Type	Muzzle Velocity (fps)	Muzzle Energy (ft.-lbs.)
158	FMJ	725	184
130 M41	FMJ	750	162
130 PGU/12	FMJ	950	260

CURRENT MANUFACTURER(S)
none

GENERAL COMMENT(S)
Faced with a severe shortage of .45 M1911 pistols, in the early part of 1943, the U.S. Army decided to purchase revolvers chambered for the standard commercial .38 Special cartridge for issue to aircrew, military police and guards. To supply these revolvers with ammunition, the Army let a contract to Remington to develop a .38 Special Ball cartridge with a full metal jacket bullet. Remington responded with a 158 grain full metal jacketed bullet with a gilding metal-clad steel jacket. Following extensive tests at Springfield Armory, the Remington cartridge was approved by the Ordnance Committee for use by the U.S. Navy to arm its aircrew and shore patrol personnel. In 1944, the cartridge was approved for issue to U.S. Army aircrew and ground forces. Large contracts for this cartridge were placed with Remington. At the end of World War II, Remington had manufactured over 50 million rounds of .38 Special Ball ammunition for the U.S. government. Some 6 million rounds of this total were sent to allied military forces.

Following World War II, the .38 Special Ball cartridges remain in U.S. military service with aircrew, military police, guards and other units. Ammunition was contracted to various commercial manufacturers, but never made in a military ammunition plant.

TECHNICAL COMMENT(S)
To speed development and production, the Cartridge, .38 Special, Ball partridge case was made to commercial dimensions and specifications. By using a standard l58 grain weight bullet and commercial loading practices and procedures, a muzzle velocity of 725 fps at 25 ft. was achieved--again standard commercial practice. While ballistic performance of the Cartridge, .38 Special, Ball could muster 39% less muzzle energy than the venerable Cartridge, Ball, .45 M1911, its ballistic performance was perfectly acceptable for its purpose.

Late in World War II, Remington developed a .38 Special cartridge loaded with a red tracer bullet that traced for 350 yards. Its purpose was to enable downed aircrew to signal rescuers. Some 5 million rounds were manufactured all of which went to the U.S. Navy.

In 1956, the U.S. Air Force adopted the Cartridge, Caliber .38, Ball M41 with a peculiar 130 "FMJ" bullet having a metal nose covering and a lead bearing surface. Due to its poor ballistic performance, this load proved unsatisfactory. This led to the adoption in 1961 of the Cartridge, Caliber.38, Ball M41 Special with slightly improved (but still unsatisfactory) ballistic performance. As pressure to improve this cartridge increased, the Cartridge, Caliber.38, Ball PGU/12B was adopted having a muzzle velocity of 950 fps with the same 130 grain capped bullet.

CHAPTER 76 : MILITARY REVOLVER - OBSOLETE

CHAPTER 76

For Cartridge Index see Chapter 101. All drawing dimensions are approximate.

As you look over these old calibers, several points will come to mind. First, many were designed for black powder (note especially the various Nagant calibers and the British .455 Webley). Also, revolvers have been obsolete in military applications for almost 100 years. Second, perceptions of adequate ballistic performance (stopping power) when these cartridge were designed differs substantially from country to country as well as from modern handgun performance concepts.

Most military revolver cartridges became obsolete with the advent of smokeless propellants. Of course smokeless powder loads in these calibers were developed in a vain effort to stave off inevitable obsolescence. However, by the end of World War I in 1918, revolvers had been replaced in military service in nearly all large, modern countries except Britain. While most countries retained modest stocks of obsolete military revolvers as a last ditch reserve, large numbers of these revolvers passed through surplus markets in backwater areas of the world. In any case, the corrosive effects of neglect, climate, mercuric primers, and black powder quickly rendered many such handguns unserviceable.

Most European armies viewed the military revolver as a badge of rank for officers and as a backup weapon for cavalry and artillery troops. Such views were directly related to experiences with Napoleonic mass infantry tactics. For this form of warfare, stopping power was not important. Rather a military revolver cartridge was deemed acceptable if it merely wounded the intended target. Both Britain and the United States were exceptions. Based on British military experience in creating and maintaining an empire and American experiences during the Indian Wars and Philippine Insurrection, stopping power was the first and foremost consideration. As a result, both preferred .45 caliber revolvers firing a heavy bullet at modest muzzle velocities such as the .455 Webley and .45 Colt. European military services preferred 9-, 10-, or 11mm calibers firing lighter weight bullets.

7.5mm SWISS ORDNANCE REVOLVER, 7.5mm SWEDISH NAGANT REVOLVER

ALTERNATE NAME(S): 7.5mm Schweizer Ordonnanz Revolver M.82, 7.5mm Schweizer Ordonnanz, 7.7x22.8mm Schweizer Ordonnanz, 7.72x23.10 Kal. 7.5mm Schweiz, 7.5mm Nagant Schweiz, 7.5mm Schwedisch Nagant Mod.87, 7.5mm Nagant revolver (Norwegian), 7.5mm Nagant (.295) Schwedisch, 7.5mm Norwegian Nagant, 7.55mm Luxemburg Officers Revolver, 8mm Luxemburg (Officers Revolver)

RELATED CALIBER(S): 11MM French Ordnance Revolver, 11mm German Service Revolver, 476 Enfield Mk III, 11.4mm Italian Ordnance Revolver

CARTRIDGE HISTORY

Year of Introduction: 1882 Swiss, 1887 Swedish

Country of Origin: Belgium

Designer(s): Emile Nagant

Governing Body: CIP

Present Status: obsolete

CARTRIDGE DESCRIPTION

Bullet Diameter: .315 Swiss, .325 Swedish in.

Bullet Weight(s): 104 gr.

Rifling Twist Rate: 1 turn in 13.78 in.

Test Barrel Length: 5.9 in.

Case Type: rimmed, straight

Case Material: brass

Primer Type: small pistol

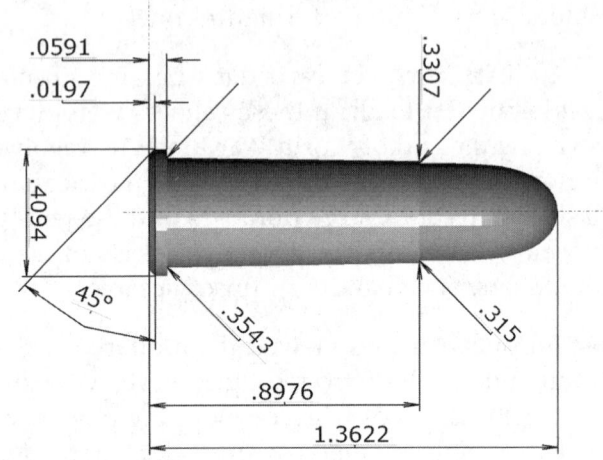

CARTRIDGE BALLISTICS

Max. Average Breech Pressure: 26,830 psi.

Max. Effective Range: 25 yds.

Max. Horizontal Range: 1,050 yds.

Max. Vertical Range: 2,300 ft.

Bullet Weight (gr.)	Bullet Type	Muzzle Velocity (fps)	Muzzle Energy (ft.-lbs.)
104	L-RN or FMJ	725	123

CURRENT MANUFACTURER(S)

Fiocchi

GENERAL COMMENT(S)

Switzerland adopted the 7.5mm cartridge in 1882. Sweden and Norway followed suit in 1887. Luxembourg also adopted this caliber for military service. By 1900, both of these cartridges were obsolete and both were replaced in 1903, the Swiss adopting the 7.65mm Luger cartridge and the Swedes the 9mm Browning Long. Both of these cartridges remained in production for many years after to support existing guns. Some are still being used today. Military production of ammunition in this caliber has long since ended. However, Fiocchi still makes the Swiss version.

TECHNICAL COMMENT(S)

The 7.5mm Swiss and the 7.5mm Swedish Nagant cartridges are interchangeable. Both were originally black powder cartridges later updated to smokeless propellants. Both lead and full metal jacket bullets will be encountered. Swedish ammunition has an outside-lubricated lead bullet while Swiss ammunition has an inside-lubricated bullet. Neither of the cartridges can be considered suitable for personal defense by modern standards.

7.62x38Rmm NAGANT

ALTERNATE NAME(S): 7.62mm Russian Nagant, 7.62mm Revolver Patr. 2602 (r.), 7.62x38Rmm Nagant Revolver
RELATED CALIBER(S): none

CARTRIDGE HISTORY
Year of Introduction: 1895
Country of Origin: Russia (Belgium)
Designer(s): Emile Peiper
Governing Body: CIP
Present Status: obsolete

CARTRIDGE DESCRIPTION
Bullet Diameter: .307-.311 in.
Bullet Weight(s): 100-110 gr.
Rifling Twist Rate: 1 turn in 9.84 in.
Test Barrel Length: 5.9 in.
Case Type: rimmed, necked, internal bullet
Case Material: brass
Primer Type: small pistol

CARTRIDGE BALLISTICS
Max. Average Breech Pressure: 12,330 CUP.
Max. Effective Range: 25 yds.
Max. Horizontal Range: 2,200 yds.
Max. Vertical Range: 5,100 ft.

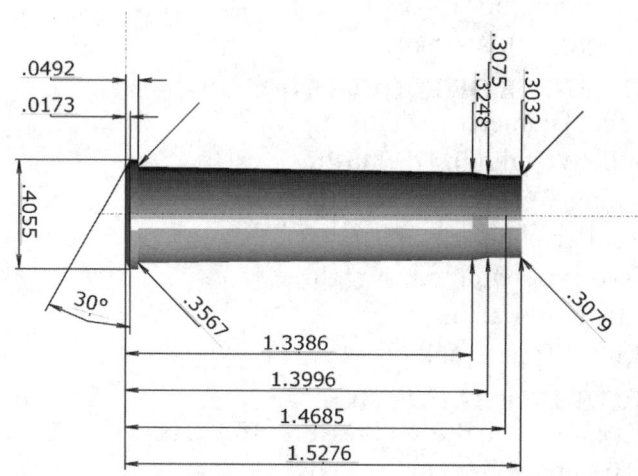

Bullet Weight (gr.)	Bullet Type	Muzzle Velocity (fps)	Muzzle Energy (ft.-lbs.)
108	FMJ	1,100	290
98	FMJ	1,070	249

CURRENT MANUFACTURER(S)
Fiocchi

GENERAL COMMENT(S)
Emile Peiper designed this unusual cartridge for his gas-sealing Nagant revolver circa 1895. This revolver sealed the gasses that normally would escape from the gap between the cylinder and barrel by pushing the cylinder forward so that the front end of the cartridge case entered the rear of the barrel. This required the bullet to be held completely inside the cartridge case. While a clever design, it attempted to solve a minor problem and did not prove popular. However, the Russian government adopted the handgun and the cartridge for military service in 1895. It continued in Russian military service officially until 1930 when it was replaced by the 7.62x25mm Tokarev cartridge. Many thousands of Nagant revolvers were still in use during World War II. Surprisingly, this revolver and cartridge continue in commercial production for inexpensive target practice.

TECHNICAL COMMENT(S)
A common question is whether the gas sealing design offers any real ballistic advantage making it worth all the effort. In absolute terms, the sealing design probably does improve muzzle velocity slightly. However, in real terms it hardly seems worth the effort as muzzle energy is only 290 ft.-lbs. which placed the 7.62mm Nagant in the marginal category for military use. Reloading Russian ammunition in this caliber is difficult as most have corrosive, Berdan primers. Commercial Fiocchi ammunition in this caliber is loaded with non-corrosive, Boxer primers.

8mm LEBEL REVOLVER

ALTERNATE NAME(S): 8mm Reglementaire M. 1892, 8mm Revolver M. 1892, 8.3x27.5 Lebel Revolver
RELATED CALIBER(S): 10.4mm Italian Ordnance Revolver, .455 Webley Revolver Mk II,
   10.4mm German Ordnance Revolver

CARTRIDGE HISTORY
Year of Introduction: 1892
Country of Origin: France
Designer(s): Col. Nicolas Lebel
Governing Body: CIP
Present Status: obsolete

CARTRIDGE DESCRIPTION
Bullet Diameter: .323 in.
Bullet Weight(s): 117-148 gr.
Rifling Twist Rate: 1 turn in 9.45 in.
Test Barrel Length: 5.9 in.
Case Type: rimmed, straight
Case Material: brass
Primer Type: small pistol

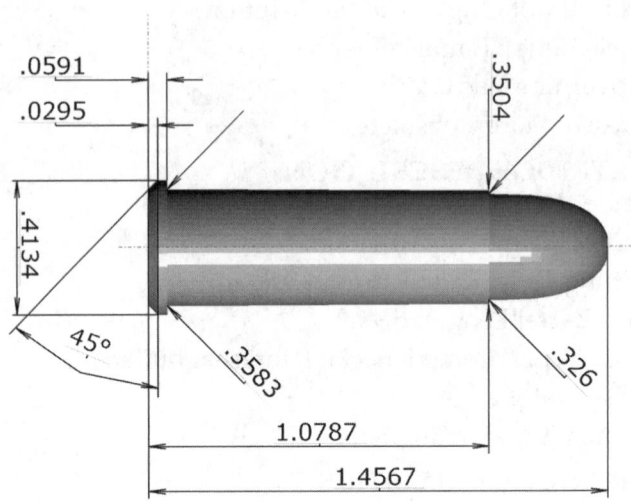

CARTRIDGE BALLISTICS
Max. Average Breech Pressure: 18,130 psi.
Max. Effective Range: 25 yds.
Max. Horizontal Range: 1,600 yds.
Max. Vertical Range: 3,800 ft.

Bullet Weight (gr.)	Bullet Type	Muzzle Velocity (fps)	Muzzle Energy (ft.-lbs.)
111	FMJ-RN	845	176

CURRENT MANUFACTURER(S)
Fiocchi

GENERAL COMMENT(S)
Adopted by the French Army in 1892 after several years of tests, this cartridge replaced the 11mm French Ordnance Revolver cartridge in French military service. It was originally loaded with black powder and a lead, round nose bullet. After adoption, a FMJRN bullet was used. Ammunition in this caliber was made only in France and is long since obsolete. Fiocchi still offers this cartridge on the commercial market with smokeless powder and a Boxer primer.

TECHNICAL COMMENT(S)
Although the revolvers that fired this cartridge were well-made, its ballistic performance was disappointing as it offered substantially less muzzle energy than the cartridge it replaced. Effectively, the 8mm Lebel Revolver cartridge was semi-obsolete by the time it was adopted. However, it continued in French Military service until well after World War I.

8mm RAST-GASSER

ALTERNATE NAME(S): 8mm Gasser
RELATED CALIBER(S): .32 S&W Long

CARTRIDGE HISTORY
Year of Introduction: 1898
Country of Origin: Belgium
Designer(s): Gasser
Governing Body: CIP
Present Status: obsolete

CARTRIDGE DESCRIPTION
Bullet Diameter: .320 in.

Bullet Weight(s): 125 gr.

Rifling Twist Rate: N/A

Test Barrel Length: 5.9 in.

Case Type: rimmed, straight

Case Material: brass

Primer: small pistol

CARTRIDGE BALLISTICS
Max. Average Breech Pressure: 14,500 psi.

Max. Horizontal Range: 2,100 yds.

Max. Vertical Range: 4,100 ft.

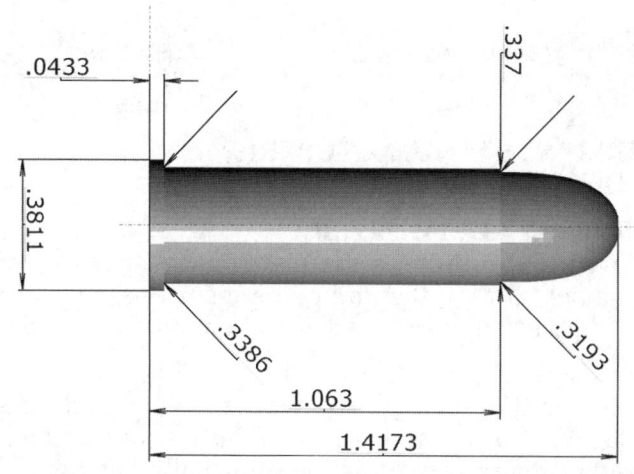

Bullet Weight (gr.)	Bullet Type	Muzzle Velocity (fps)	Muzzle Energy (ft.-lbs.)
125	L-FN	770	165

CURRENT MANUFACTURER(S)
Fiocchi

GENERAL COMMENT(S)
When this revolver cartridge was introduced in 1898, it was intended for military service in Rast-Gasser revolvers. However, revolvers were quickly being replaced in major world military services with semi-automatic pistols, leaving the 8mm Rast-Gasser cartridge with a bleak future. Accordingly, the cartridge and its revolver were marketed to the military services of smaller countries that tended to be more conservative. They also held on to their Rast-Gasser revolvers long after other countries had adopted semi-automatic pistols. For this reason, the 8mm Rast-Gasser cartridge remained in production for longer than anyone would have predicted. This cartridge has been made only in Europe, and it remains in production to this day.

TECHNICAL COMMENT(S)
Even by 19th century standards, the 8mm Rast-Gasser cartridge had poor ballistic performance. Fortunately, ballistic performance was not high on the list of reasons for adoption in smaller countries.

.38 LONG COLT

ALTERNATE NAME(S): none

RELATED CALIBER(S): .38 Special, .38 S&W

CARTRIDGE HISTORY
Year of Introduction: 1875

Country of Origin: U.S.

Designer(s): Colt

Governing Body: SAAMI, CIP

Present Status: active

CARTRIDGE DESCRIPTION
Bullet Diameter: .357 in.

Bullet Weight(s): 125-150 gr.

Rifling Twist Rate: 1 turn in 16 in.

Test Barrel Length: 4.9 in.

Case Type: rimmed, straight

Case Material: brass

Primer: small pistol

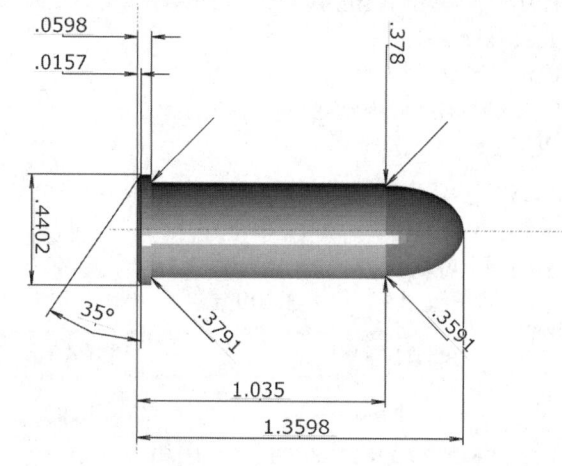

CARTRIDGE BALLISTICS
Max. Average Breech Pressure: 13,053 psi.

Max. Horizontal Range: 1,750 yds.

Max. Vertical Range: 3,900 ft.

Bullet Weight (gr.)	Bullet Type	Muzzle Velocity (fps)	Muzzle Energy (ft.-lbs.)
150	L-RN	770	195 (Long)

CURRENT MANUFACTURER(S)
Remington, Black Hills

GENERAL COMMENT(S)
From 1892 until 1911, the .38 Long Colt was the standard U.S. Army service revolver cartridge. Experience in the field during the Philippine Insurrection clearly indicated that the .38 Long Colt lacked sufficient striking energy for military service. It was replaced in U.S. military service in 1911 by the .45 ACP.

TECHNICAL COMMENT(S)
Most mid-caliber, black powder revolver cartridges in military service during the late 1800s provided anemic ballistic performance. Much of this was due to the revolver being regarded as a military officer's badge of rank, rather than the expectation of actually having to stop an adversary in his tracks. Of course, low maximum average chamber pressures were another handicap. The U.S. Army soon found this concept faulty and went back to a .45 caliber handgun. After all, if low chamber pressure was preferred, better to use it to drive a large caliber, heavy bullet (the .45 Colt comes to mind here). However, the .38 Long Colt "soldiered" on in the commercial market until this day.

9mm JAPANESE REVOLVER TYPE 26

ALTERNATE NAME(S): 9mm Japanese
RELATED CALIBER(S): .380 Revolver

CARTRIDGE HISTORY
Year of Introduction: 1893
Country of Origin: Japan
Designer(s): N/A
Governing Body: none
Present Status: obsolete

CARTRIDGE DESCRIPTION
Bullet Diameter: .354 in.
Bullet Weight(s): 149 gr.
Rifling Twist Rate: N/A
Test Barrel Length: 4.7 in.
Case Type: rimmed, straight
Case Material: brass
Primer: small pistol

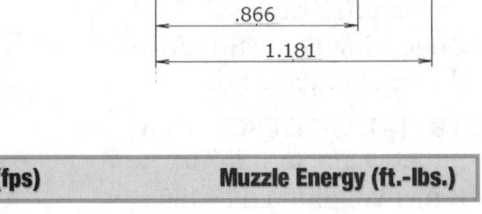

CARTRIDGE BALLISTICS
Max. Average Breech Pressure: 7,000 psi.
Max. Horizontal Range: 1,650 yds.
Max. Vertical Range: 3,200 ft.

Bullet Weight (gr.)	Bullet Type	Muzzle Velocity (fps)	Muzzle Energy (ft.-lbs.)
149	L-RN	640	135

CURRENT MANUFACTURER(S)
None

GENERAL COMMENT(S)
This is the cartridge adopted by the Japanese Army in 1893 for their Type 26 double-action-only revolver. Although the Type 26 revolver became obsolete when the Nambu semi-automatic pistol was adopted in 1904, the Type 26 continued in reserve status until 1945. As a consequence, ammunition in this caliber continued in production until 1945. Japan was the only country to use this caliber cartridge.

TECHNICAL COMMENT(S)
This rimmed revolver cartridge is distinguished by its thin rim, straight case body and round nose lead bullet. BALLISTICS, by any measure, are poor.

9.4mm DANISH ARMY REVOLVER

ALTERNATE NAME(S): 9.4mm Dutch Hembrug, 9.4mm Hembrug, 9.4mm Dutch Revolver M1873-1874-1912, 10mm Luxembourg Revolver, .380 Dutch

RELATED CALIBER(S): .380 Long

CARTRIDGE HISTORY
Year of Introduction: 1901
Country of Origin: Denmark
Designer(s): Haerens Ammunitionsarsenalet-Denmark
Governing Body: none
Present Status: obsolete

CARTRIDGE DESCRIPTION
Bullet Diameter: .375 in.
Bullet Weight(s): 124 gr.
Rifling Twist Rate: N/A
Test Barrel Length: N/A
Case Type: rimmed, straight
Case Material: brass
Primer Type: small pistol

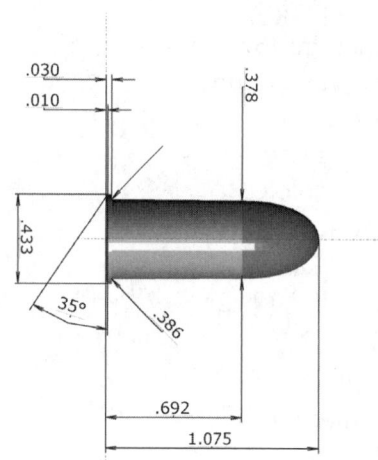

CARTRIDGE BALLISTICS
Max. Average Breech Pressure: N/A
Max. Effective Range: 25 yds.
Max. Horizontal Range: 1,600 yds.
Max. Vertical Range: 3,500 ft.

Bullet Weight (gr.)	Bullet Type	Muzzle Velocity (fps)	Muzzle Energy (ft.-lbs.)
124	L-RN	655	118

CURRENT MANUFACTURER(S)
None

GENERAL COMMENT(S)
This cartridge was adopted by the Danish Army in 1901 for their M1891 revolver. It remained in Dutch Army service through World War II. Postwar to date it was replaced by the 9mm Luger cartridge as Denmark is a member of NATO. As no other country used this cartridge and production ended over 65 years ago, examples are are now collector's items.

TECHNICAL COMMENT(S)
Initially loaded with black powder, the 9.4mm was quickly switched to smokeless propellant. The bullet was an ogival unjacketed lead design. By the time the Danish Army adopted this cartridge, its terminal ballistics were already semi-obsolete for military purposes. The low muzzle velocity and light bullet weight combined to produce only 118 ft.-lbs. of energy at the muzzle. To put this into perspective, this is less that the .22 Long Rifle rimfire cartridge (135 ft.-lbs. at the muzzle)!

9.4mm DUTCH REVOLVER

ALTERNATE NAME(S): 9.4 Hembrug Revolver, 9.4mm Netherlands Revolver Model 1873-1874-1912, 10mm Beaumont Revolver, 10mm Luxembourg Revolver, .380 Dutch, 10x20mm Dutch
RELATED CALIBER(S): .41 Rem. Mag.

CARTRIDGE HISTORY
Year of Introduction: 1873
Country of Origin: Belgium
Designer(s): N/A
Governing Body: none
Present Status: obsolete

CARTRIDGE DESCRIPTION
Bullet Diameter: .400 in.
Bullet Weight(s): 177-199 gr.
Rifling Twist Rate: N/A
Test Barrel Length: N/A
Case Type: rimmed, straight
Case Material: brass
Primer: N/A

CARTRIDGE BALLISTICS
Max. Average Breech Pressure: N/A
Max. Horizontal Range: 1,500 yds.
Max. Vertical Range: 2,800 ft.

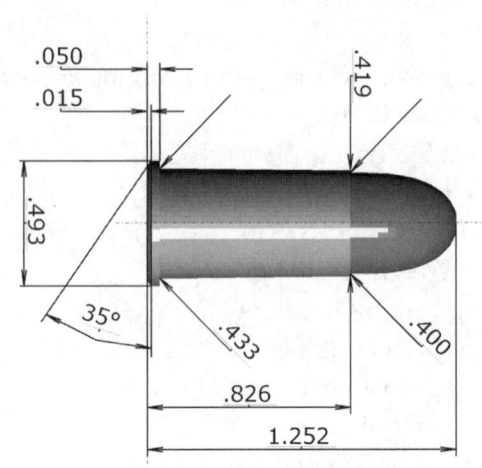

Bullet Weight (gr.)	Bullet Type	Muzzle Velocity (fps)	Muzzle Energy (ft.-lbs.)
197	L-RN	590	152

CURRENT MANUFACTURER(S)
None

GENERAL COMMENT(S)
When European armies moved to adopt new revolvers in the 1870s, this was one of the cartridges swept in on the tide. Both the Netherlands and Luxembourg used this cartridge in military and police service.

TECHNICAL COMMENT(S)
Ballistically speaking, this is yet another anemic black powder revolver cartridge common in European military service during the 1870s and 1880s.This cartridge was used only in the Netherlands and Luxembourg. Manufacture of ammunition in this caliber ceased in the early 1930s. It shares rim and head dimensions with the modern .41 Rem. Magnum cartridge, but is substantially shorter.

.380/200

ALTERNATE NAME(S): .38 S&W, .38 S&W Super Police
RELATED CALIBER(S): .38 Special

CARTRIDGE HISTORY
Year of Introduction: 1877 (late 1930s in British military service)
Country of Origin: U.S.
Designer(s): S&W
Governing Body: SAAMI
Present Status: obsolete

CARTRIDGE DESCRIPTION
Bullet Diameter: .361 in.
Bullet Weight(s): 200 gr.
Rifling Twist Rate: 1 turn in 18.75 in.

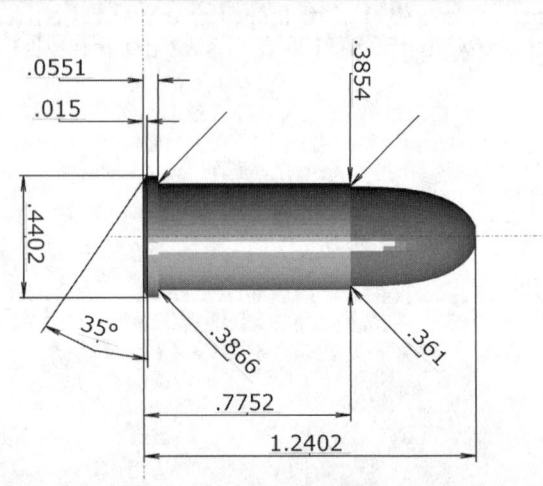

Test Barrel Length: 4.9 in.

Case Type: rimmed, straight

Case Material: brass

Primer Type: small pistol

CARTRIDGE BALLISTICS

Max. Average Breech Pressure: 17,450 psi.

Max. Effective Range: 25 yds.

Max. Horizontal Range: 1,500 yds.

Max. Vertical Range: 3,200 ft.

Bullet Weight (gr.)	Bullet Type	Muzzle Velocity (fps)	Muzzle Energy (ft.-lbs.)
200	FMJ	630	176

CURRENT MANUFACTURER(S)
None

GENERAL COMMENT(S)
Just before the beginning of World War II, the British Army adopted the .380/200 cartridge and a new Webley revolver to fire it. The intent was to replace the existing .455 Revolver Mk II and its ammunition with the new smaller cartridge and smaller, lighter revolver. However, World War II intervened before the new cartridge and revolver were fully fielded and the British Army muddled through the War with both cartridges. Both were declared obsolete in the mid-1950s.

TECHNICAL COMMENT(S)
Even by European standards, the .380/200 cartridge lacks lethality. It was a poor choice for military use and British troops disliked it, preferring instead the .455 Revolver Mk II when available. In practice, the .380/200 was a stopgap measure that was better than nothing. In the early days of World War II, when the British Army was short on everything, except determination, the .380/200 did its part when the going was rough.

.40 QUIET SPECIAL PURPOSE REVOLVER

ALTERNATE NAME(S): .40 QSPR, 10x40.6mm QSPR
RELATED CALIBER(S): various special Russian cartridges

CARTRIDGE HISTORY
Year of Introduction: 1969

Country of Origin: U.S.

Designer(s): AAI Corporation

Governing Body: none

Present Status: obsolete

CARTRIDGE DESCRIPTION
Bullet Diameter: 15 tungsten alloy balls in plastic sabot

Bullet Weight(s): 7.5 gr. each, total 112.5 gr.

Rifling Twist Rate: smoothbore

Test Barrel Length: 1.375 in.

Case Type: rimmed, straight

Case Material: machined steel

Primer: Boxer type, internally mounted

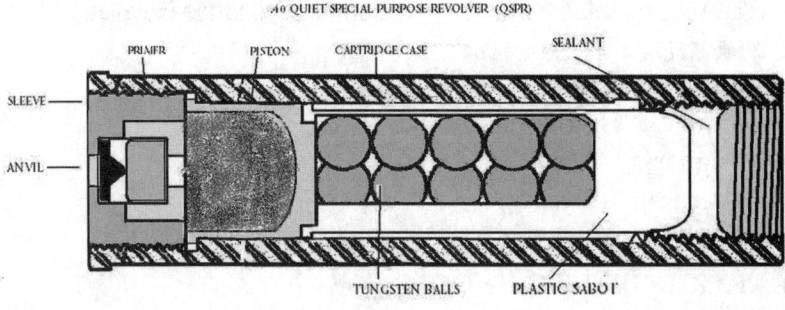

.40 QUIET SPECIAL PURPOSE REVOLVER (QSPR)

CARTRIDGE BALLISTICS
Max. Average Breech Pressure: N/A

Max. Horizontal Range: N/A

Max. Vertical Range: N/A

Bullet Weight (gr.)	Bullet Type	Muzzle Velocity (fps)	Muzzle Energy (ft.-lbs.)
112.5	15 tungsten balls	730	133 (8.86 Ft-lbs each)

CURRENT MANUFACTURER(S)
None

GENERAL COMMENT(S)
AAI Corporation developed the .40 Quiet Special Purpose Revolver (QSPR) cartridge in response to a U.S. government requirement for a handgun cartridge that had a lower noise level than a .22 Long Rifle cartridge fired from a suppressed pistol. Essentially, what was wanted was a silent handgun cartridge that did not need a suppressor on the end of the barrel. This requirement was for U.S. Army "tunnel exploration personnel" in Vietnam who urgently needed a handgun for use in the confines of the Viet Cong tunnel system. AAI responded with the .40 QSPR fired in a S&W Model 29 revolver with a 1.375 inch smoothbore barrel.

TECHNICAL COMMENT(S)
In appearance, the .40 QSPR cartridge looked like a .410-bore metal shotshell. The cartridge was rimmed with a straight body made of machined steel. Inside the case head, a separate threaded steel insert held the primer with a separate anvil and cover to transfer the blow of the firing pin to the primer cap. The front interior walls of the cartridge case were coarsely threaded from the mouth extending downward for about 25% of its length. A U-shaped metal piston inside the cartridge case held the propellant charge against the primer flash hole. In front of the piston was a plastic sabot containing 15 tungsten balls. The case mouth was sealed with a plug. When the cartridge was fired, the expanding propellant gases drove the piston forward pushing the sabot and tungsten balls from the case. When the sabot and its payload of tungsten balls cleared the case mouth, the piston's forward travel was arrested by the threads inside the case mouth. By so doing, the piston sealed the propellant gases inside the cartridge case, thus eliminating all muzzle blast and flash. Sound levels were reduced to just 110 decibels. Technically, such cartridges are called " internally silenced ammunition". In some instances, this type of cartridge can be used in unmodified weapons. Examples include the .45 ACP, 40mm Grenade launcher and .38 Special. However, a serious drawback of such ammunition is substantially reduced muzzle velocity. While the concept of an internally silenced cartridge is not new, the technology to make it work did not become available until the 1950s. The Soviet Union was one of the first to adopt this type of ammunition. It must be noted that the Bureau of Alcohol, Tobacco, Firearms, and Explosives (BATFE) regards EACH unfired cartridge of this type as a suppressor that must be registered.

10.4mm ITALIAN ORDNANCE REVOLVER

ALTERNATE NAME(S): 10.35mm Bodego, 10.35mm Glisenti M. 1889, 10.4mm Ital. Ordonnanz Rev. Mod. 1894
RELATED CALIBER(S): 10.6mm German Ordnance Revolver, 11mm French Ordnance Revolver

CARTRIDGE HISTORY
Year of Introduction: 1874
Country of Origin: Italy
Designer(s): N/A
Governing Body: N/A
Present Status: obsolete

CARTRIDGE DESCRIPTION
Bullet Diameter: .420 in.
Bullet Weight(s): 170 gr.
Rifling Twist Rate: 1 turn in 10 in.
Test Barrel Length: N/A
Case Type: rimmed, necked
Case Material: brass
Primer Type: large pistol

CARTRIDGE BALLISTICS
Max. Average Breech Pressure: N/A
Max. Effective Range: 25 yds.
Max. Horizontal Range: 1,900 yds.

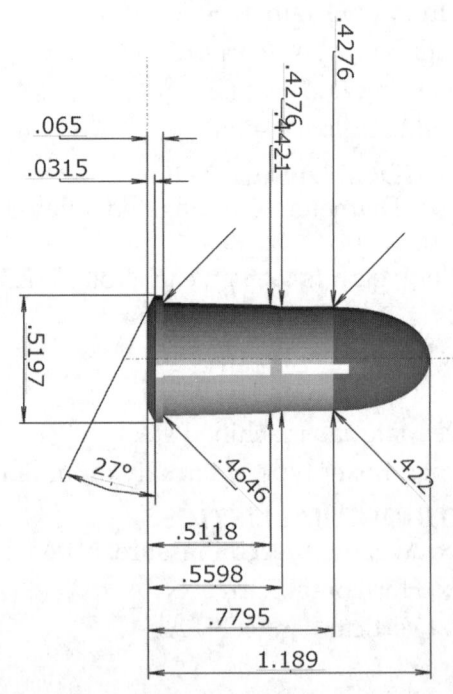

Max. Vertical Range: 4,200 ft.

Bullet Weight (gr.)	Bullet Type	Muzzle Velocity (fps)	Muzzle Energy (ft.-lbs.)
177	L-RN	800	240

CURRENT MANUFACTURER(S)
Fiocchi

GENERAL COMMENT(S)
The 10.4mm Italian Ordnance Revolver cartridge was taken into Italian Army service in 1874. It remained in Italian military service until replaced by the 9mm Glisenti cartridge in 1910.

TECHNICAL COMMENT(S)
This is another typical black powder military revolver cartridge of the late 1800s. Unlike its contemporaries, it has a slight neck. In addition, a longer overall cartridge length (1.25 inches) was used when loading a lead bullet and a shorter case with jacketed bullets (1.17 inches).

10.4mm SWISS ORDNANCE REVOLVER

ALTERNATE NAME(S): 10.4mm Swiss Ordnance Revolver M1872/78
RELATED CALIBER(S): .44 Henry Flat rimfire

CARTRIDGE HISTORY
Year of Introduction: 1878
Country of Origin: Switzerland
Designer(s): Col. Rudolf Schmidt
Governing Body: none
Present Status: obsolete

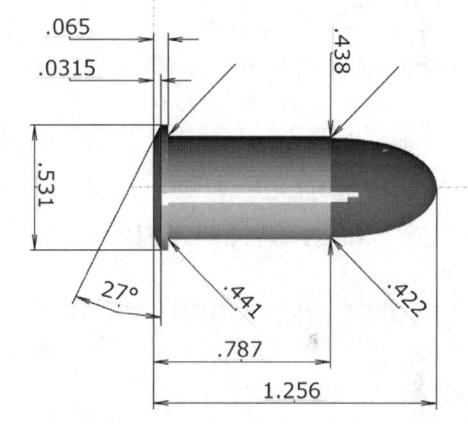

CARTRIDGE DESCRIPTION
Bullet Diameter: .425 in.
Bullet Weight(s): 193 gr.
Rifling Twist Rate: N/A
Test Barrel Length: N/A
Case Type: rimmed, straight
Case Material: brass
Primer: large pistol

CARTRIDGE BALLISTICS
Max. Average Breech Pressure: N/A
Max. Horizontal Range: 1,400 yds.
Max. Vertical Range: 2,700 ft.

Bullet Weight (gr.)	Bullet Type	Muzzle Velocity (fps)	Muzzle Energy (ft.-lbs.)
193	L-RN	610	159

CURRENT MANUFACTURER(S)
None

GENERAL COMMENT(S)
When the Swiss Army adopted the 10.4mm M1872 Revolver cartridge, it replaced a Swiss rimfire cartridge of the same caliber and very similar to the .44 Henry Flat rimfire. To save money, the Swiss rimfire revolvers were converted to fire this new centerfire cartridge. However, the service life of the 10.4mm Swiss Ordnance cartridge was cut short in 1882 with the adoption of the 7.5mm Swiss Ordnance revolver and cartridge.

TECHNICAL COMMENT(S)
Like most black powder military cartridge of this type, the ballistic performance of the 10.4mm Swiss Ordnance cartridge was anemic. Unlike other black powder cartridges of this type, the 10.4mm Swiss Ordnance cartridge did not share similar dimensions with any other centerfire cartridge. It was used and manufactured only in Switzerland.

10.6mm SPANISH REVOLVER

ALTERNATE NAME(S): 10.6mm Spanish Ordnance Revolver, 10.6mm Revolver M1884
RELATED CALIBER(S): .44 Special, .44 Russian, 10.6mm German Ordnance Revolver

CARTRIDGE HISTORY
Year of Introduction: 1884
Country of Origin: Germany
Designer(s): Mauser
Governing Body: none
Present Status: obsolete

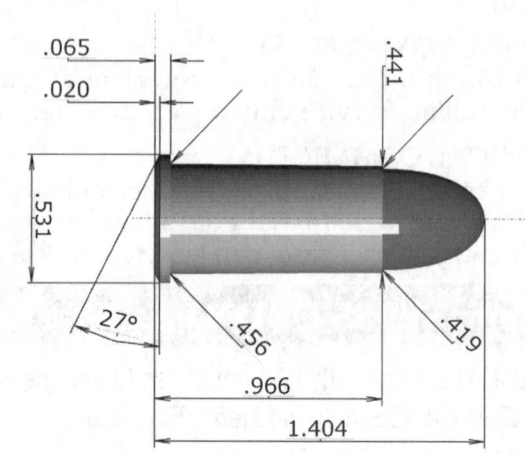

CARTRIDGE DESCRIPTION
Bullet Diameter: .418 in.
Bullet Weight(s): 250 gr.
Rifling Twist Rate: 1 turn in 23 in.
Test Barrel Length: N/A
Case Type: rimmed, straight
Case Material: brass
Primer: large pistol

CARTRIDGE BALLISTICS
Max. Average Breech Pressure: N/A
Max. Horizontal Range: 1,600 yds.
Max. Vertical Range: 3,100 ft.

Bullet Weight (gr.)	Bullet Type	Muzzle Velocity (fps)	Muzzle Energy (ft.-lbs.)
250	L-RN	670	249

CURRENT MANUFACTURER(S)
None

GENERAL COMMENT(S)
This cartridge was adopted by the Spanish Army in 1884 along with the Model 1884 revolver.

TECHNICAL COMMENT(S)
The 10.4mm Spanish Ordnance Revolver cartridge shares similar dimensions and ballistics with the 10.6mm German Ordnance Revolver. In most revolvers, the two cartridges are interchangeable.

10.6mm GERMAN ORDNANCE REVOLVER

ALTERNATE NAME(S): 10.6x25Rmm, 10.85x25Rmm, 10.6mm Offiziers revolver M. 1884, 10.6mm Deutscher Ordonnanz revolver M. 1879 & 83, 10.85x24.90mm Revolver M. 79 & 83, 11mm German Ordnance Revolver
RELATED CALIBER(S): 11mm French Ordnance Revolver, 10.4mm Italian Ordnance Revolver

CARTRIDGE HISTORY
Year of Introduction: 1879
Country of Origin: Germany
Designer(s): N/A
Governing Body: N/A
Present Status: obsolete

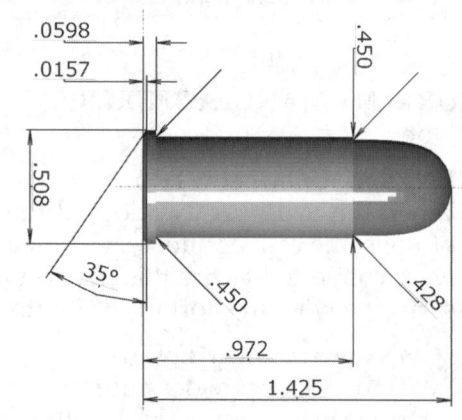

CARTRIDGE DESCRIPTION
Bullet Diameter: .451 in.
Bullet Weight(s): 250-260 gr.
Rifling Twist Rate: 1 turn in 23 in.
Test Barrel Length: N/A
Case Type: rimmed, straight
Case Material: brass
Primer Type: large pistol

CARTRIDGE BALLISTICS
Max. Average Breech Pressure: N/A
Max. Effective Range: 25 yds.
Max. Horizontal Range: 1,900 yds.
Max. Vertical Range: 4,200 ft.

Bullet Weight (gr.)	Bullet Type	Muzzle Velocity (fps)	Muzzle Energy (ft.-lbs.)
255	L-RN	670	256

CURRENT MANUFACTURER(S)
None

GENERAL COMMENT(S)
Adopted by the German Army in 1879, the 10.6mm Ordnance revolver remained in service until the end of World War I. It was replaced by the 9mm Luger cartridge in 1908.

TECHNICAL COMMENT(S)
This is a typical large caliber, black powder military cartridge at the end of the black powder era. These are characterized by low muzzle velocities and heavy lead bullets. While they were effective in service, they were replaced in the early 1900s by smokeless powder cartridges.

11mm FRENCH ORDNANCE REVOLVER

ALTERNATE NAME(S): none
RELATED CALIBER(S): 11mm German Ordnance Revolver, 10.4mm Italian Ordnance Revolver, .41 Colt

CARTRIDGE HISTORY
Year of Introduction: 1873
Country of Origin: France
Designer(s): N/A
Governing Body: N/A
Present Status: obsolete

CARTRIDGE DESCRIPTION
Bullet Diameter: .451 in.
Bullet Weight(s): 180 gr.
Rifling Twist Rate: 1 turn in 16 in.
Test Barrel Length: N/A
Case Type: rimmed, straight
Case Material: brass
Primer Type: large pistol

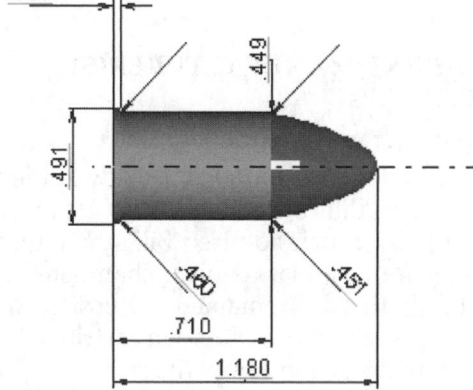

CARTRIDGE BALLISTICS
Max. Average Breech Pressure: N/A
Max. Effective Range: 25 yds.
Max. Horizontal Range: 2,000 yds.
Max. Vertical Range: 4,200 ft.

Bullet Weight (gr.)	Bullet Type	Muzzle Velocity (fps)	Muzzle Energy (ft.-lbs.)
180	L-RN	800	253

CURRENT MANUFACTURER(S)
None

GENERAL COMMENT(S)
This cartridge was the standard French Army revolver cartridge from 1873 until it was replaced by the 8mm Lebel Revolver cartridge in 1892. The French Army was the only military service to adopt this cartridge.

TECHNICAL COMMENT(S)
This cartridge was loaded with an odd, pointed lead bullet weighing approximately 170 grains. Otherwise, it is yet another military black powder revolver cartridge of modest ballistic performance.

.44 SMITH & WESSON RUSSIAN

ALTERNATE NAME(S): .44 Russian
RELATED CALIBER(S): .44 S&W Special, .44 S&W American, .44 Magnum

CARTRIDGE HISTORY
Year of Introduction: 1870
Country of Origin: U.S.
Designer(s): Smith & Wesson
Governing Body: CIP
Present Status: obsolete

CARTRIDGE DESCRIPTION
Bullet Diameter: .4323 in.
Bullet Weight(s): 206-246 gr.
Rifling Twist Rate: 1 turn in 20 in.
Test Barrel Length: 5.9 in.
Case Type: rimmed, straight
Case Material: brass
Primer: large pistol

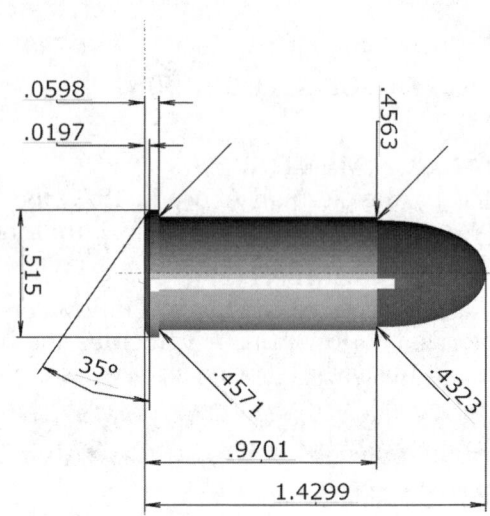

CARTRIDGE BALLISTICS
Max. Average Breech Pressure: 14,500 psi.
Max. Horizontal Range: 1,900 yds.
Max. Vertical Range: 3,800 ft.

Bullet Weight (gr.)	Bullet Type	Muzzle Velocity (fps)	Muzzle Energy (ft.-lbs.)
246	L-RN	770	324

CURRENT MANUFACTURER(S)
Black Hills

GENERAL COMMENT(S)
In the late 1860s, Buffalo Bill Cody guided Russian Grand Duke Alexis on a hunting trip in the western states. During the hunt, Bill carried a .44 S&W Army Revolver in .44 S&W American caliber for personal protection. Reportedly, the Duke much admired Bill's handgun with the result that the Russian government placed a large order with S&W for a similar revolver chambered for a somewhat more powerful new cartridge called the .44 S&W Russian. The .44 Russian remained in Russian Army service until 1895 when the 7.62mm Nagant revolver was adopted. In recent years, the .44 Russian cartridge has its second life based on a resurgence of interest in the burgeoning sport of cowboy action competition. New reproduction revolvers in this caliber are now being made.

TECHNICAL COMMENT(S)
Back in the days of the Old West, the .44 American and .44 Russian became a popular choice among knowledgeable shooters and shootists who appreciated the knock-down power and accuracy of these calibers. From a ballistic standpoint, both cartridges were a good balance of case capacity (from a black powder standpoint), bullet weight, muzzle velocity and moderate recoil. Of course, original ammunition in both calibers was loaded with black powder and a lead, round nose bullet weighing from 206-246 grains and offering plenty of bearing surface which explains their accuracy. Because of this, both became a popular choice among target shooters. Users reported excellent accuracy to 200 yards! By 1900, both had transitioned successfully to smokeless propellants. Both remained in production until 1940.

.44 COLT

ALTERNATE NAME(S): none
RELATED CALIBER(S): .44 Russian, 11mm French Ordnance Revolver

CARTRIDGE HISTORY

Year of Introduction: 1871

Country of Origin: U.S.

Designer(s): Colt

Governing Body: CIP

Present Status: obsolete

CARTRIDGE DESCRIPTION

Bullet Diameter: .443 in.

Bullet Weight(s): 210-230 gr.

Rifling Twist Rate: 1 turn in 20 in.

Test Barrel Length: 5.9 in.

Case Type: rimmed, straight

Case Material: brass

Primer: large pistol

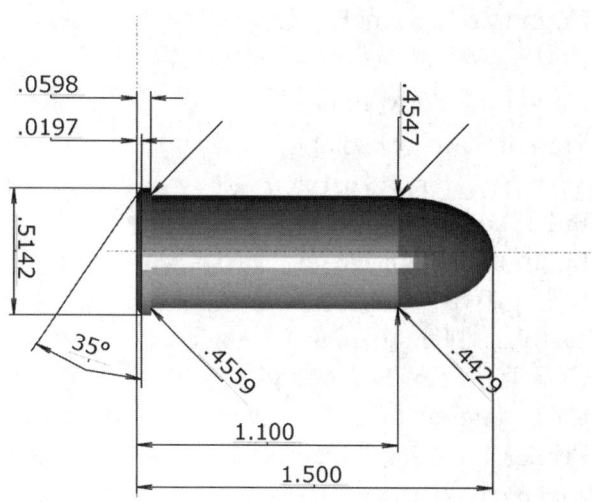

CARTRIDGE BALLISTICS

Max. Average Breech Pressure: 14,500 psi.

Max. Horizontal Range: 1,600 yds.

Max. Vertical Range: 3,200 ft.

Bullet Weight (gr.)	Bullet Type	Muzzle Velocity (fps)	Muzzle Energy (ft.-lbs.)
210	L-RN	660	206
225	L-RN	640	207
230	L-RN	730	272 (BH load)

CURRENT MANUFACTURER(S)

Black Hills

GENERAL COMMENT(S)

Most shooters are surprised to find the .44 Colt cartridge listed in the chapter on obsolete military handgun cartridges. This is not a mistake; the .44 Colt cartridge was used by the U.S. Army from 1871 until 1873 in conversions of Colt percussion revolvers after which it was replaced in U.S. Army service in 1875 by the .45 Colt cartridge. This old caliber ended its production life in 1940. However, Black Hills has recently revived it due to demand from cowboy action shooters.

TECHNICAL COMMENT(S)

BALLISTICS of the .44 Colt cartridge are comparable to the .44 S&W American, but considerably inferior to the .44 Russian, .44 S&W Special and .45 Colt. From a ballistic standpoint, the .44 Colt has nothing to recommend it other than nostalgia.

.450 REVOLVER

ALTERNATE NAME(S): .450 Adams, .450 Short, .450 Short Colt
RELATED CALIBER(S): .45 Webley, .45 Long Colt

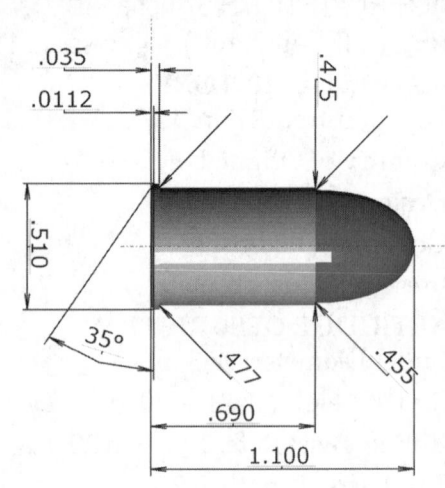

CARTRIDGE HISTORY
Year of Introduction: 1868
Country of Origin: Britain
Designer(s): N/A
Governing Body: none
Present Status: obsolete

CARTRIDGE DESCRIPTION
Bullet Diameter: .450 in.
Bullet Weight(s): 226 gr.
Rifling Twist Rate: 1 turn in 16 in.
Test Barrel Length: 6 in.
Case Type: rimmed, straight
Case Material: brass
Primer Type: small pistol

CARTRIDGE BALLISTICS
Max. Average Breech Pressure: N/A
Max. Effective Range: 25 yds.
Max. Horizontal Range: 1,600 yds.
Max. Vertical Range: 3,800 ft.

Bullet Weight (gr.)	Bullet Type	Muzzle Velocity (fps)	Muzzle Energy (ft.-lbs.)
226	L-RN	650	211

CURRENT MANUFACTURER(S)
Fiocchi

GENERAL COMMENT(S)
This was the first center fire cartridge to be adopted by the British Army. It served until 1880 when it and the Adams revolver were replaced by the Webley revolver and the .455 Mark I cartridge.

TECHNICAL COMMENT(S)
Initially loaded with approximately 13 grains of black powder, smokeless propellant loads were made in the last years of its service. By any measure, the terminal ballistics of the .450 Revolver cartridge were minimal, limiting its effectiveness to very short range only. However, the British Army did not seem to regard this as a handicap when they replaced it in 1880 with the .455 Mark I cartridge which offered no significant increase in terminal performance.

.45 COLT

ALTERNATE NAME(S): .45 Long Colt, .45 Colt Army, .45 Colt USA
RELATED CALIBER(S): .45 S&W Schofield, .45 S&W American

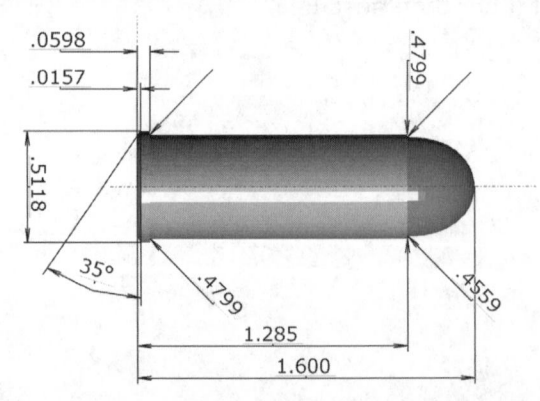

CARTRIDGE HISTORY
Year of Introduction: 1875
Country of Origin: U.S.
Designer(s): Colt
Governing Body: SAAMI, CIP
Present Status: obsolete in military service

CARTRIDGE DESCRIPTION
Bullet Diameter: .454 in.
Bullet Weight(s): 225-260 gr.

Rifling Twist Rate: 1 turn in 16 in.

Test Barrel Length: 5.9 in.

Case Type: rimmed, straight

Case Material: brass

Primer Type: large pistol

CARTRIDGE BALLISTICS

Max. Average Breech Pressure: 15,954 psi.

Max. Effective Range: 25 yds.

Max. Horizontal Range: 1,860 yds.

Max. Vertical Range: 4,200 ft.

Bullet Weight (gr.)	Bullet Type	Muzzle Velocity (fps)	Muzzle Energy (ft.-lbs.)
255	L-RN	860	420

CURRENT MANUFACTURER(S)

CCI/Speer, Federal, Remington, Winchester, Black Hills, Cor-Bon, PMC

GENERAL COMMENT(S)

In 1875, the U.S. Army adopted the .45 Colt cartridge for general military service along with the .45 Schofield, .45 S&W American and .45 Colt Government (an unsuccessful compromise cartridge to fit all). The .45 Colt served until 1892 when it was replaced by the .38 Long Colt. The .45 Colt was the revolver cartridge that tamed the Old West and entered legend in so doing. The stopping power of the massive lead bullet is still spoken of in reverent terms as a baseline on which all other handgun cartridges should be measured. Books, films, and TV have perpetuated this legend helping the .45 Colt cartridge to secure a firm place in U.S. history. Although long retired from military service, the .45 Colt continues to be a popular caliber for sportsmen, cowboy action competition and even personal defense.

TECHNICAL COMMENT(S)

The .45 Colt is the buckle on the gun belt of the heavy bullet at low velocity proponents versus the light bullet at high velocity crowd for personal defense. Interestingly, nearly all the data regarding the stopping power of the .45 Colt is anecdotal, but not invalid. Such material makes interesting reading, especially when written by someone who was actually involved. Of such material is the legend the .45 Colt made. Here it is important to remember that the fearsome reputation of the .45 Colt's stopping power was earned, not created with smoke and mirrors. Many other cartridges are fully the equal of the .45 Colt in stopping power (eg. the .44-40 Win.) and played an equally important role in winning the West. However, none have the historical recognition that the .45 Colt has.

11.75mm MONTENEGRIN REVOLVER

ALTERNATE NAME(S): 11mm Austrian Gasser, 11.25x36mm Montenegrin

RELATED CALIBER(S): none

CARTRIDGE HISTORY

Year of Introduction: 1870

Country of Origin: Austria-Hungary

Designer(s): Gasser, Roth

Governing Body: none

Present Status: obsolete

CARTRIDGE DESCRIPTION

Bullet Diameter: .445 in.

Bullet Weight(s): 280-320 gr.

Rifling Twist Rate: 1 turn in 20 in.

Test Barrel Length: N/A

Case Type: rimmed, straight

Case Material: brass

Primer: large pistol

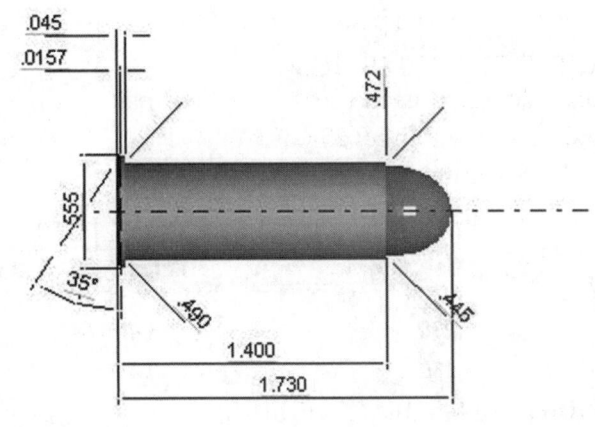

CARTRIDGE BALLISTICS
Max. Average Breech Pressure: N/A
Max. Horizontal Range: 2,000 yds.
Max. Vertical Range: 3,700 ft.

Bullet Weight (gr.)	Bullet Type	Muzzle Velocity (fps)	Muzzle Energy (ft.-lbs.)
300	L-RN	700	326

CURRENT MANUFACTURER(S)
none

GENERAL COMMENT(S)
This cartridge was developed for a massive, tip-up revolver designed by Gasser circa 1870. It remained popular in many of the Balkan countries until the mid-20th century. This cartridge is virtually unknown outside the Balkans.

TECHNICAL COMMENT(S)
The 11.75mm cartridge is unique in that it did not share head dimensions with any other cartridge. Both the rim and head diameter are substantially larger than other .44 caliber revolver cartridges. At about 300 grains, the round nose lead bullet used in the 11.75mm Montenegrin cartridge was heavier than bullets used in most other .44 caliber cartridges. However, the low muzzle velocity limited muzzle energy to .44 Merwin & Hulbert, .44 Special, and .44 Russian levels.

.45 SMITH & WESSON

ALTERNATE NAME(S): .45 S&W Schofield, .45 Schofield
RELATED CALIBER(S): .45 Colt

CARTRIDGE HISTORY
Year of Introduction: 1875
Country of Origin: U.S.
Designer(s): S&W
Governing Body: none
Present Status: obsolete

CARTRIDGE DESCRIPTION
Bullet Diameter: .4559 in.
Bullet Weight(s): 230-250 gr.
Rifling Twist Rate: 1 turn in 16 in.
Test Barrel Length: 6 in.
Case Type: rimmed, straight
Case Material: brass
Primer Type: large pistol

CARTRIDGE BALLISTICS
Max. Average Breech Pressure: 14,504 psi.
Max. Effective Range: 25 yds.
Max. Horizontal Range: 1,860 yds.
Max. Vertical Range: 4,175 ft.

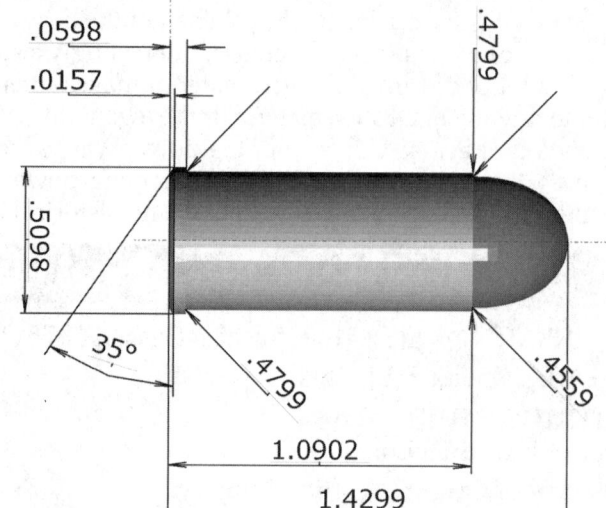

Bullet Weight (gr.)	Bullet Type	Muzzle Velocity (fps)	Muzzle Energy (ft.-lbs.)
230	L-RN	730	276
250	L-RN	710	283

CURRENT MANUFACTURER(S)
Black Hills

GENERAL COMMENT(S)
Shortly after the U.S. Army adopted the .45 Colt cartridge for use in Colt Single-Action Army revolvers, they also adopted the .45 S&W cartridge for use in S&W Schofield revolvers. The .45 S&W remained in service until

1892 when it was replaced by the .38 Long Colt.

TECHNICAL COMMENT(S)

As the Schofield revolver's cylinder was not long enough for the .45 Colt cartridge, it had to make do with the shorter, less-powerful .45 S&W. This cartridge did not have the terminal ballistic performance of its service brother, the .45 Colt. While the .45 Colt offered 490 ft.-lbs. of muzzle energy, the .45 S&W had just 58% of the Colt's energy. This substantial difference was compensated for, in part, by the top-break extractor design of the Schofield revolver which made reloading much faster.

.450 REVOLVER/.450 ADAMS

ALTERNATE NAME(S): .450 Rev., .450 Short, .450 Colt, .450 Adams, .450 Boxer Mk1
RELATED CALIBER(S): .455 Webley

CARTRIDGE HISTORY

Year of Introduction: 1868
Country of Origin: Britain
Designer(s): N/A
Governing Body: CIP
Present Status: obsolete

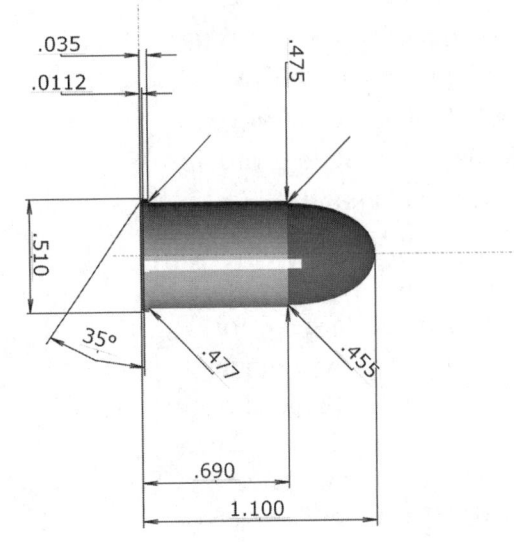

CARTRIDGE DESCRIPTION

Bullet Diameter: .455 in.
Bullet Weight(s): 225 gr.
Rifling Twist Rate: 1 turn in 16 in.
Test Barrel Length: N/A
Case Type: rimmed, straight
Case Material: brass
Primer Size: large pistol

CARTRIDGE BALLISTICS

Max. Average Breech Pressure: 16,000 psi.
Max. Horizontal Range: 2,000 yds.
Max. Vertical Range: 4,400 ft.

Bullet Weight (gr.)	Bullet Type	Muzzle Velocity (fps)	Muzzle Energy (ft.-lbs.)
225	LRN	650	211 (black powder)
225	LRN	700	245 (smokeless)

CURRENT MANUFACTURER(S)

Fiocchi

GENERAL COMMENT(S)

When adopted in November of 1868, the .450 Revolver cartridge became the first center fire revolver cartridge to enter British military service. However, its ballistic performance, anemic even by the standards of that time, was a major reason it was replaced by the .476 Enfield in 1880. Despite its poor military performance, the .450 Revolver cartridge did gain a marginal level of acceptance in the U.S. commercial market, which supported production until 1940.

The .450 Revolver cartridge is sometimes called the .450 Adams after the Adams military revolver. In the commercial market, the .450 Revolver cartridge was sometimes called the .450 Colt for the same reason. Other major revolver manufacturers such as Webley, and S&W offered guns in this caliber as well.

TECHNICAL COMMENT(S)

When adopted, the .450 Revolver cartridge was loaded with black powder. Later, it was loaded with smokeless propellants which allowed a small increase in muzzle velocity and energy. However, such modest increases were not enough to improve its marginal ballistic performance. For example, the .45 Colt cartridge, a popular contemporary, offered 46% more muzzle energy!

The .450 cartridge can be fired in any revolver chambered for .455 Webley ammunition.

.455 REVOLVER MK I

ALTERNATE NAME(S): .455 Colt, .455 Enfield
RELATED CALIBER(S): .45 Colt

CARTRIDGE HISTORY
Year of Introduction: 1892
Country of Origin: Britain
Designer(s): N/A
Governing Body: N/A
Present Status: obsolete

CARTRIDGE DESCRIPTION
Bullet Diameter: .455 in.
Bullet Weight(s): 265 gr.
Rifling Twist Rate: 1 turn in 16 in. (est.)
Test Barrel Length: N/A
Case Type: rimmed, straight
Case Material: brass
Primer Type: large pistol

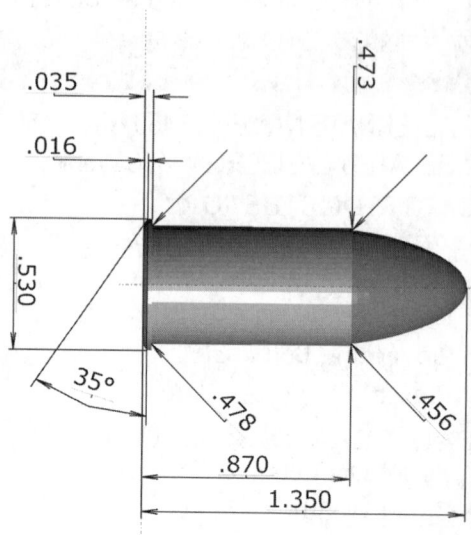

CARTRIDGE BALLISTICS
Max. Average Breech Pressure: N/A
Max. Effective Range: 25 yds.
Max. Horizontal Range: 1,800 yds.
Max. Vertical Range: 4,000 ft.

Bullet Weight (gr.)	Bullet Type	Muzzle Velocity (fps)	Muzzle Energy (ft.-lbs.)
265	L-RN	700 (black powder)	289
265	L-RN	600 (Cordite)	212

CURRENT MANUFACTURER(S)
None

GENERAL COMMENT(S)
In 1892, the British Army adopted the .455 Revolver Mk I cartridge to replace the 476 Webley Revolver cartridge. The .455 Revolver Mk I enjoyed a short service life. It was replaced by the .455 Revolver Mk II cartridge in 1897.

TECHNICAL COMMENT(S)
Originally a black powder cartridge, in 1894 the propellant for the .455 Revolver Mk I cartridge was switched to Cordite and in 1897 the case was shortened to make the .455 Revolver MK II cartridge. A version of this cartridge was made in the U.S. as the .455 Colt cartridge. The .455 Mk I, .455 Mk II, .455 Colt and the .476 Revolver cartridges are all interchangeable.

.455 REVOLVER MK II

ALTERNATE NAME(S): .455 Webley Revolver Mk II
RELATED CALIBER(S): none

CARTRIDGE HISTORY
Year of Introduction: 1897
Country of Origin: Britain
Designer(s): N/A
Governing Body: N/A
Present Status: obsolete

CARTRIDGE DESCRIPTION

Bullet Diameter: .455 in.

Bullet Weight(s): 265 gr.

Rifling Twist Rate: 1 turn in 16 in.

Test Barrel Length: N/A

Case Type: rimmed, straight

Case Material: brass

Primer Type: large pistol

CARTRIDGE BALLISTICS

Max. Average Breech Pressure: N/A

Max. Effective Range: 25 yds.

Max. Horizontal Range: 1,800 yds.

Max. Vertical Range: 4,000 ft.

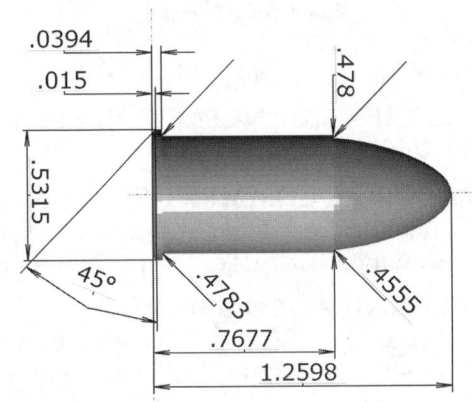

Bullet Weight (gr.)	Bullet Type	Muzzle Velocity (fps)	Muzzle Energy (ft.-lbs.)	
265	FMJ	600	212	Military
262	L-RN	845	415	Fiocchi

CURRENT MANUFACTURER(S)

Fiocchi

GENERAL COMMENT(S)

Adopted into British Army service in 1897, the .455 Revolver Mk II remained in front line service until just after World War II. It was finally replaced by the 9mm Luger cartridge as part of NATO standardization in the 1950s. Although obsolete for military service, the .455 Revolver Mk II cartridge remains in commercial production by Fiocchi.

TECHNICAL COMMENT(S)

The .455 Revolver Mk II cartridge has a shorter case than the Mk I to more efficiently burn Cordite propellant. The original Mk II Revolver bullet was a lead round nose design. In 1939, a jacketed bullet was adopted as the Mk VI.

.476 ENFIELD MK III

ALTERNATE NAME(S): .476 Eley, .455/476

RELATED CALIBER(S): .45 Colt, .44 S&W American

CARTRIDGE HISTORY

Year of Introduction: 1881

Country of Origin: Britain

Designer(s): Eley

Governing Body: N/A

Present Status: obsolete

CARTRIDGE DESCRIPTION

Bullet Diameter: .472 in.

Bullet Weight(s): 262 gr.

Rifling Twist Rate: 1 turn in 10 in. (est.)

Test Barrel Length: N/A

Case Type: rimmed, straight

Case Material: brass

Primer Type: large pistol

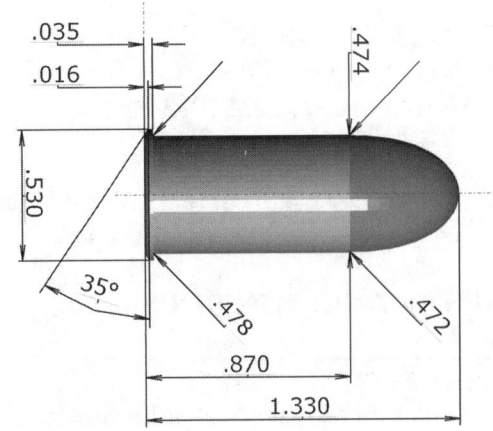

CARTRIDGE BALLISTICS

Max. Average Breech Pressure: N/A

Max. Effective Range: 25 yds.

Max. Horizontal Range: 1,800 yds.

Max. Vertical Range: 4,000 ft.

Bullet Weight (gr.)	Bullet Type	Muzzle Velocity (fps)	Muzzle Energy (ft.-lbs.)
262	L-RN	700	285

CURRENT MANUFACTURER(S)
None

GENERAL COMMENT(S)
Taken into military service by the British Army from 1881 until 1891, the .476 Enfield Mk II replaced the .450 Revolver cartridge. The .476 Enfield cartridge was replaced in 1891 by the .455 Webley Mk I cartridge.

TECHNICAL COMMENT(S)
When the .476 Enfield cartridge was introduced, it was loaded with a hollow base lead bullet called the Mk I. In short order, this bullet was replaced by one having a clay plug in the base and called the Mk III. Although muzzle velocity was low, the heavy, large caliber lead bullet of the .476 Enfield proved to be very effective in the field. Stopping power of the .476 cartridge was very similar to the .45 Colt cartridge.

.50 REMINGTON M71 ARMY, .50 REMINGTON NAVY

ALTERNATE NAME(S): .50 Navy, .50 Army, 12.9x22Rmm
RELATED CALIBER(S): .50-70 Government

CARTRIDGE HISTORY
Year of Introduction: 1867 (Navy), 1871 (Army)
Country of Origin: U.S.
Designer(s): Remington
Governing Body: none
Present Status: obsolete

CARTRIDGE DESCRIPTION
Bullet Diameter: .508 in.
Bullet Weight(s): 300 gr.
Rifling Twist Rate: N/A
Test Barrel Length: N/A
Case Type: rimmed, tapered
Case Material: brass
Primer: large pistol

CARTRIDGE BALLISTICS
Max. Average Breech Pressure: N/A
Max. Horizontal Range: 1,200 yds.
Max. Vertical Range: 2,300 ft.

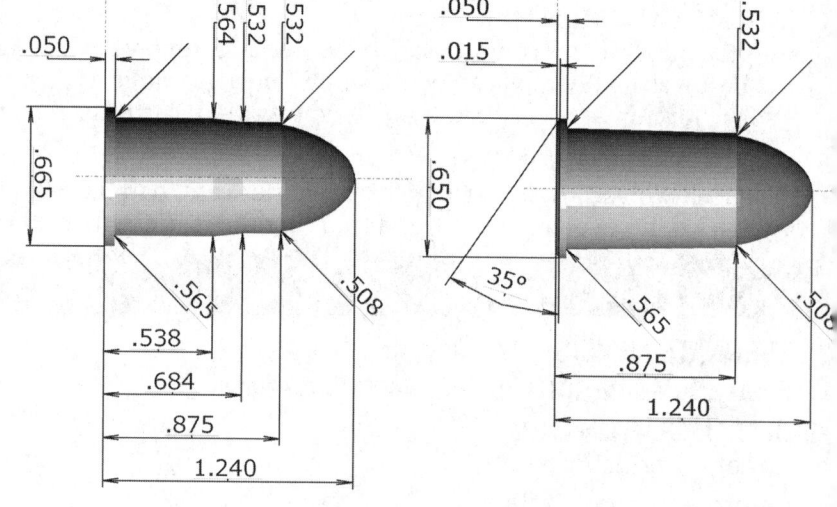

Bullet Weight (gr.)	Bullet Type	Muzzle Velocity (fps)	Muzzle Energy (ft.-lbs.)
300	L-RN	600	240

CURRENT MANUFACTURER(S)
None

GENERAL COMMENT(S)
The .50 Navy cartridge was adopted by the Bureau of Naval Ordnance in 1867 along with the Remington single shot, rolling block pistol. The U.S. Army adopted the pistol a few years later, but with a slightly modified cartridge case. In 1871, when the U.S. Army adopted a centerfire revolver, the brief era of the single shot pistols in U.S. military service was over.

TECHNICAL COMMENT(S)
The .50 Navy and .50 Army cartridge cases differ slightly. The Army case has a slight bottle neck while the Navy case has a continuous taper. The Army case has a larger rim diameter that prevents it from chambering in Navy pistols. However, the Navy cartridge will chamber and fire in either pistol. Commercial ammunition, available until around 1920, and used the Navy-pattern case.

CHAPTER 77 : MILITARY PISTOL - CURRENT

CHAPTER 77

For Cartridge Index see Chapter 101. All drawing dimensions are approximate.

In the last 50 years, the number of military pistol calibers has shrunk substantially with the near-universal winner being the ubiquitous 9x19mm Luger. There are several reasons for this train of events: interchangeability among military services, the decline of the pistol and submachine gun in military doctrine, the drive for ever lighter weapons in smaller calibers, and the widespread acceptance of the 9x19mm (if you can't beat 'em, join them). Yet despite the juggernaut 9x19mm Luger bandwagon, a few military organizations, namely the special operations communities, retain the .45 ACP for its proven stopping power. As the litany goes, "The magazine of a 9x19mm Luger caliber pistol holds more rounds of ammunition than the .45 ACP, and you will need every one of them to stop an adversary!"

Viewed historically, what we have here is the classic argument between those who favor heavy bullets at modest muzzle velocities versus those who prefer light weight bullets at higher muzzle velocities. This controversy has been going on now for nearly a century. Today, the light weight bullet at higher velocity school of thought is ascendant in most military circles. Just a few years ago before the U.S. Army adopted the 9x19mm Luger cartridge, the heavy bullet school was in session.

Recently, FN and H&K have developed a new concept called a Personal Defense Weapon (PDW). Each company has developed a new cartridge for their PDW - FN offers a 5.7x28mm cartridge and H&K a 4.6x30mm cartridge. A PDW is a not a handgun and does not fire a pistol cartridge. Rather, it is a compact, select-fire shoulder weapon akin to a carbine and fires a small caliber rifle cartridge designed to penetrate body armor at 100 meters. Both manufacturers claim their PDW is more accurate, more effective, and easier to use than any pistol. To date, very few military services have bought into this concept as 5.56x45mm carbines such as the M4 version of the M16 serve the same purpose without requiring a new weapon or cartridge. Those readers interested in the PDW concept are referred to Chapter 69: Military Rifle-Current for more information on both cartridges.

Many theorists believe the military pistol and its cartridge are obsolete. Nearly all of these pundits have never been in a combat situation and have never bothered to ask those who have for their opinion. If the military pistol and its cartridge indeed are obsolete, no one told the combat infantryman who continues to carry a pistol despite the added weight, short effective range, and inability to penetrate body armor. This writer suggests that the pundits have forgotten the positive, human mindset carrying a pistol offers to those going in harm's way.

7.62x17mm TYPE 64

ALTERNATE NAME(S): 7.62x17mm Type 64
RELATED CALIBER(S): .32 ACP

CARTRIDGE HISTORY

Year of Introduction: N/A
Country of Origin: Peoples' Republic of China (PRC)
Designer(s): N/A
Governing Body: Chinese military
Present Status: active

CARTRIDGE DESCRIPTION

Bullet Diameter: .307 in.
Bullet Weight(s): 74 gr.
Rifling Twist Rate: N/A
Test Barrel Length: N/A
Case Type: rimless, straight
Case Material: steel
Primer: small pistol

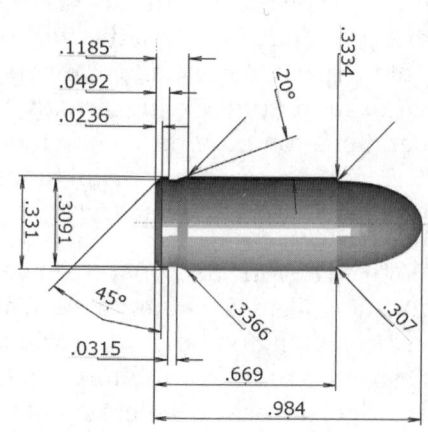

CARTRIDGE BALLISTICS

Max. Average Breech Pressure: N/A
Max. Horizontal Range: 1,600 yds.
Max. Vertical Range: 3,410 ft.

Bullet Weight (gr.)	Bullet Type	Muzzle Velocity (fps)	Muzzle Energy (ft.-lbs.)
46	AP	655	44
74	FMJ	525	45
74	FMJ	1,015	N/A

CURRENT MANUFACTURER(S)

PRC State Arsenals

GENERAL COMMENT(S)

This is a special cartridge designed and manufactured in the People's Republic of China for use in the Type 64 and Type 67 silenced pistols.

TECHNICAL COMMENT(S)

Although the case bears a strong resemblance to the .32 ACP, in fact the 7.65x17mm is rimless while the .32 ACP is semi-rimmed. The two cartridges are not interchangeable. Muzzle velocity of the 7.65mm Type 64 ammunition is kept well below the speed of sound (approx. 1,160 fps) to prevent any telltale supersonic "crack" during the bullet's flight.

7.62x25mm TOKAREV

ALTERNATE NAME(S): 7.62mm Tokarev, 7.62 M38/40, 7.62 M40, 7.62 Type P, 7.62 Type 50,
   7.62x24.6mm , Pist. Patr. 2601

RELATED CALIBER(S): 7.65mm Mauser (.30 Mauser)

CARTRIDGE HISTORY

Year of Introduction: 1930

Country of Origin: Soviet Union

Designer(s): Fedor V. Tokarev

Governing Body: CIP

Present Status: current in China, many third world countries, obsolete in Russia but still being manufactured for existing guns

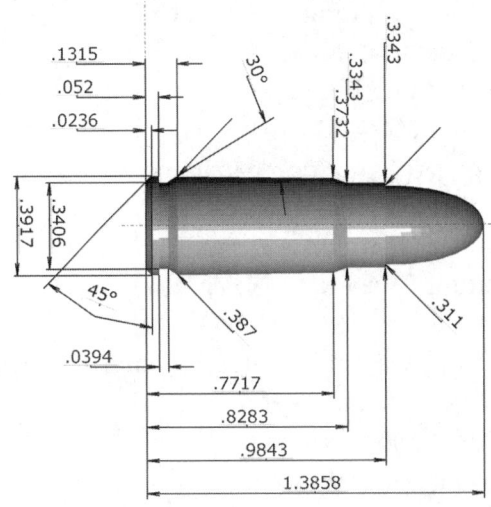

CARTRIDGE DESCRIPTION

Bullet Diameter: .311 in.

Bullet Weight(s): 85-87 gr.

Rifling Twist Rate: 1 turn in 9.45 in.

Test Barrel Length: 5.9 in.

Case Type: rimless, necked

Case Material: brass or steel

Primer Type: Berdan or Boxer (small pistol)

CARTRIDGE BALLISTICS

Max. Average Breech Pressure: 35,750 psi.

Max. Effective Range: 150 yds.

Max. Horizontal Range: 1,620 yds.

Max. Vertical Range: 3,625 ft.

Bullet Weight (gr.)	Bullet Type	Muzzle Velocity (fps)	Muzzle Energy (ft.-lbs.)
87	FMJ	1,705	552

CURRENT MANUFACTURER(S)

Norinco, Wolf, Prvi Partizan, Romtecnica, Sellier & Bellot, Arsenal (Bulgaria), MFS, Vietnam Gov't Arsenals

GENERAL COMMENT(S)

From 1917 on, the C96 "Broomhandle" 7.62mm (.30) Mauser pistol was a favorite handgun of the Bolshevik revolutionaries in Russia. When it came time for the new Red Army to adopt a new military handgun in 1930, the tried and true 7.62mm Mauser cartridge was selected in slightly modified form along with a new TT30 pistol that was a close copy of a Browning design. Called the 7.62x25mm Tokarev, this cartridge served the Soviet armed forces well into the 1950s and Warsaw pact satellite nations for many years after that. Indeed, the 7.62x25mm Tokarev cartridge continues in front line service in many third world countries. Only recently, China began replacing its 7.62x25mm handguns. In recent years, large numbers of surplus handguns and ammunition in this caliber have been imported into the U.S.

TECHNICAL COMMENT(S)

The 7.62x25mm Tokarev and the 7.62mm Mauser cartridges are very similar, but not identical. The Tokarev cartridge has a slightly longer overall loaded length, a slightly shorter cartridge case length and a smaller diameter body than the Mauser cartridge. In addition, the shoulder angle of the Mauser cartridge is 34 1/2 degrees while the shoulder angle of the Tokarev cartridge is 38 degrees. In spite of differences, they are considered to be interchangeable. Both cartridges normally are loaded to similar chamber pressures with the Tokarev having been converted to piezoelectric transducer readings and the older, obsolete Mauser remaining with CUP readings. Despite this, firing Tokarev caliber ammunition cannot be recommended in Mauser pistols. The reason is that some 7.62x25mm ammunition was made with a 20% overload for use in submachine guns. While the Tokarev pistol can be fired safely with such loads, the higher chamber pressure developed by such loadings are unsafe to fire in the Mauser pistol.

7.62x38mm RUSSIAN SP-3

ALTERNATE NAME(S): 7.62x38mm
RELATED CALIBER(S): 7.62x39mm Soviet, 7.62x41mm SP-4, 7.62x63mm PZAM

CARTRIDGE HISTORY
Year of Introduction: 1972
Country of Origin: Soviet Union
Designer(s): N/A
Governing Body: none
Present Status: active

CARTRIDGE DESCRIPTION
Bullet Diameter: .311 in.
Bullet Weight(s): 122 gr.
Rifling Twist Rate: N/A
Test Barrel Length: 2.6 in.
Case Type: rimless, necked, internally silenced
Case Material: steel
Primer: small rifle

CARTRIDGE BALLISTICS
Max. Average Breech Pressure: 51,500 psi.
Max. Horizontal Range: 1,360 yds.
Max. Vertical Range: 2,450 ft.

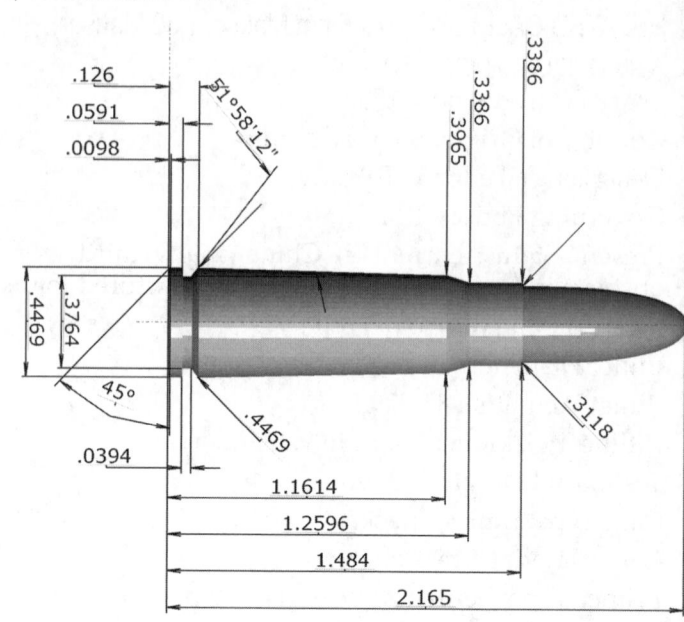

Bullet Weight (gr.)	Bullet Type	Muzzle Velocity (fps)	Muzzle Energy (ft.-lbs.)
122	FMJ-BT	490	66

CURRENT MANUFACTURER(S)
Russian State Arsenals

GENERAL COMMENT(S)
For nearly 100 years, the concept of an internally silenced cartridge was understood, but remained beyond the technical capability of ammunition makers. In the 1960s, this changed when Russian ammunition engineers introduced the first successful internally silenced cartridge, the 7.62x39mm SP-2. Improvements that followed significantly improved the performance and reduced the cost of such cartridges. Introduced in 1972, the SP-3 cartridge discussed here is a product-improved, second generation version of the original SP-2 cartridge. And, the parade of Russian-designed, internally silenced cartridges continues through the third generation 7.62x63mm PZAM and the fourth generation 7.62x41mm SP-4. The 7.62x38mm SP-3 cartridge is used in the MSP two-shot, over-under, derringer pistol and the NRS-1 combat shooting knife. Ballistic performance could best be described as "barely adequate even at close range". As far as is known, the Russian Army and Ministry of Internal Affairs are the only current users.

TECHNICAL COMMENT(S)
An internally silenced cartridge case contains a pusher-type pistons. When the cartridge is fired, the hot expanding propellant gases push the piston forward. The piston contacts the bullet and slaps it down the barrel. The propellant gases never touch the bullet. At the end of its travel inside the case, the piston is brought to rest so that it seals the propellant gas inside the case. When an internally silenced cartridge is fired, muzzle blast and flash are completely eliminated. For this reason, no bulky silencer or suppressor on the end of the barrel is needed. Indeed, an internally silenced cartridge can be fired in a standard gun. Internally silenced cartridges suffer from a number of drawbacks. First, their muzzle velocity is very low which significantly reduces their maximum effective range. Second, internally silenced cartridges are complex assemblies that are much more expensive than standard ammunition. Third, after an internally silenced cartridge has been fired, the piston and/or push rod protrudes from the case mouth which interferes with ejection. The SP-3 cartridge is loaded with a standard 7.62mm, 122 grain ball bullet seated in a normal position in the case mouth. From the outside, a loaded SP-3 cartridge looks like an ordinary 7.62x39mm ball cartridge.

7.62x41mm RUSSIAN SP-4

ALTERNATE NAME(S): 7.62x38mm SP-4
RELATED CALIBER(S): 7.62x39mm M43, 7.62x38mm SP-3

CARTRIDGE HISTORY
Year of Introduction: 1980
Country of Origin: Soviet Union
Designer(s): N/A
Governing Body: none
Present Status: active

CARTRIDGE DESCRIPTION
Bullet Diameter: .311 in.
Bullet Weight(s): 143.5 gr.
Rifling Twist Rate: N/A
Test Barrel Length: N/A
Case Type: rimless, necked, internally silenced
Case Material: steel
Primer: small rifle

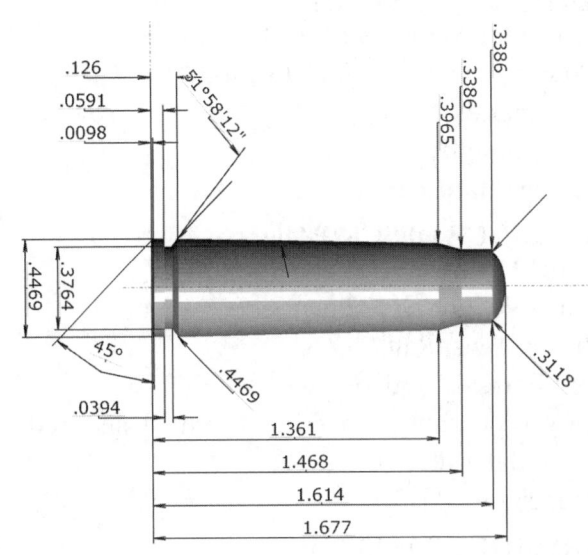

CARTRIDGE BALLISTICS
Max. Average Breech Pressure: 51,500 psi.
Max. Horizontal Range: 1,400 yds.
Max. Vertical Range: 2,800 ft.

Bullet Weight (gr.)	Bullet Type	Muzzle Velocity (fps)	Muzzle Energy (ft.-lbs.)
143.5	Ball-Flat Nose	885	250

CURRENT MANUFACTURER(S)
Russian State Arsenals

GENERAL COMMENT(S)
Following the development and fielding of the SP-2, SP-3 and PZAM internally silenced cartridges, Russian engineers continued improving this technology. Introduced in 1980, the 7.62x41mm SP-4 cartridge became the fourth generation of internally silenced Russian cartridges.

TECHNICAL COMMENT(S)
For nearly 100 years, the concept of an internally silenced cartridge was understood, but remained beyond the technical capability of ammunition makers. In the 1960s, this changed when Russian ammunition engineers introduced the first successful internally silenced cartridge, the 7.62x39mm SP-2. Improvements that followed significantly improved the performance and reduced the cost of such cartridges. Introduced in 1980, the 7.62x41mm SP-4 cartridge discussed here is a fourth generation version of the original SP-2 cartridge. The SP-4 cartridge is loaded with a flat nose cylindrical steel bullet seated flush with the case mouth. Note the vestigial shoulder and neck intended to provide additional interior room for the piston. When the SP-4 cartridge is fired, the single-stage piston does not project from the case mouth. This makes it much easier to design a semi-automatic firearm for this cartridge. A 55% increase in muzzle velocity over its nearest sibling finally produced an internally silenced cartridge with enough striking energy for serious combat at close ranges. From the outside, a loaded SP-4 cartridge looks like it has been fired as there is nothing visible in the case mouth.

7.62x63mm RUSSIAN PZAM

ALTERNATE NAME(S): 7.62x63mm PZAM
RELATED CALIBER(S): 7.62x38mm M43, 7.62x38 SP-3, 7.62x41mm SP-4

CARTRIDGE HISTORY
Year of Introduction: 1965
Country of Origin: Soviet Union
Designer(s): N/A
Governing Body: none
Present Status: active

CARTRIDGE DESCRIPTION
Bullet Diameter: .311 in.
Bullet Weight(s): 122 gr.
Rifling Twist Rate: N/A
Test Barrel Length: N/A
Case Type: rimless, necked, internally silenced
Case Material: steel
Primer: small rifle

CARTRIDGE BALLISTICS
Max. Average Breech Pressure: 51,500 psi.
Max. Horizontal Range: 1,650 yds.
Max. Vertical Range: 3,000 ft.

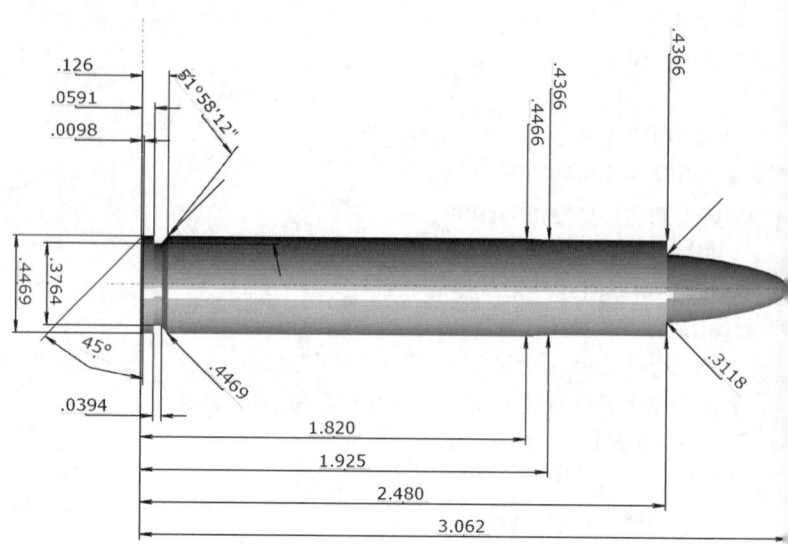

Bullet Weight (gr.)	Bullet Type	Muzzle Velocity (fps)	Muzzle Energy (ft.-lbs.)
122	FMJ-BT	570	90

CURRENT MANUFACTURER(S)
Russian State Arsenals

GENERAL COMMENT(S)
The S-4M "Groza" two-barrel, over-under derringer and PSS blow-back operated, six-shot, semi-automatic pistols are chambered for this cartridge. The Russian Army and Ministry of Internal Affairs are the only current users.

TECHNICAL COMMENT(S)
In the 1960s, Russian ammunition engineers introduced the first successful internally silenced cartridge, the 7.62x39mm SP-2. Introduced in 1965, the 7.62x63mm PZAM cartridge discussed here is a third generation version of the original SP-2 cartridge. Certainly the 7.62x63mm PZAM is an odd looking cartridge with a vestigial shoulder and neck diameter too large for the bullet. In order to create more internal space for the piston, push rod and propellant charge, the standard 39mm cartridge case has been lengthened to 63mm (the same length as a .30-'06 Spr.!). Muzzle velocity also increased 16%. Despite this improvement, ballistic performance is suitable only for very close range. The PZAM cartridge is loaded with a standard 7.62mm, 122 grain ball bullet. Note: protruding, two-stage piston and push rod are still present on fired cartridges of this type.

9x18mm MAKAROV

ALTERNATE NAME(S): 9mm Makarov
RELATED CALIBER(S): 9mm Kurz/.380 ACP, 9x18mm Ultra

CARTRIDGE HISTORY

Year of Introduction: circa late 1940s
Country of Origin: Soviet Union
Designer(s): N/A
Governing Body: CIP
Present Status: active

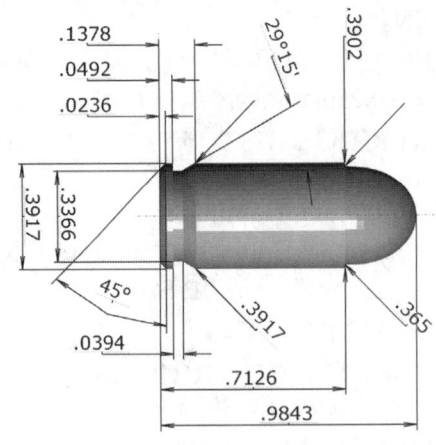

CARTRIDGE DESCRIPTION

Bullet Diameter: .365 in.
Bullet Weight(s): 95 gr.
Rifling Twist Rate: 1 turn in 9.45 in.
Test Barrel Length: 5.9 in.
Case Type: rimless, straight
Case Material: steel or brass
Primer Type: small pistol

CARTRIDGE BALLISTICS

Max. Average Breech Pressure: 26,700 psi.
Max. Effective Range: 25 yds.
Max. Horizontal Range: 1,250 yds.
Max. Vertical Range: 2,650 ft.

Bullet Weight (gr.)	Bullet Type	Muzzle Velocity (fps)	Muzzle Energy (ft.-lbs.)
86	AP	1,345	345
93	FMJ	1,115	262
106	FMJ	1,020	245

CURRENT MANUFACTURER(S)

CCI, Federal, Hornady, Winchester, Fiocchi, Prvi Partizan, Sellier & Bellot, Wolf, MFS, Norinco

GENERAL COMMENT(S)

The 9mm Makarov cartridge was introduced into Soviet military service just after the end of World War II along with the new blow-back operated Makarov pistol. Although Makarov designed the pistol and not the cartridge, he was honored by the standard Soviet practice of appending his name to both. The new cartridge was to replace the 7.62x25mm Tokarev cartridge while the new pistol replaced the Tokarev TT30 series in Soviet military service. The later Stechkin pistol was also chambered for the 9mm Makarov cartridge. The Makarov pistol was a somewhat modified copy of the German Walther PPK. In like manner, the 9mm Makarov cartridge was a modified version of the German experimental 9mm Ultra cartridge. In 2005, the 9mm Makarov cartridge was replaced in Russian military service by the ubiquitous 9x19mm Luger cartridge. A new 9x19mm service pistol called the "Grach" was introduced at the same time.The Makarov cartridge will remain in production for many years to come in order to service existing pistols. However, very few new Makarov pistols are being made today and the design is considered obsolescent in Russia for military service.

TECHNICAL COMMENT(S)

Ballistically, the 9mm Makarov is similar to the familiar .380 ACP/9mm Kurz cartridge. Bullet weight and muzzle velocity are very similar. In Russian military service, the 9mm Makarov cartridge proved a disappointment as it lacked stopping power for serious tactical use. For law enforcement and security use, it offered marginal, but acceptable terminal ballistics by Russian standards. In the 1980s and 1990s, the Soviet military made an effort to upgrade the performance of the 9mm Makarov cartridge with new high velocity, armor piercing and other special purpose loads. These did not work well due to the inherent limitations of the case volume and strength of the pistol.

9x19mm LUGER

ALTERNATE NAME(S): 9x19mm, 9mm Luger, 9mm NATO, 9mm Parabellum, 9x19mm Parabellum, 9mm Para., 9x19mm 7N21

RELATED CALIBER(S): 9mm Steyr, 9mm Browning Long, 9mm Glisenti, .38 Super, 9mm Largo, 7.62x25mm Tokarev, .45 ACP

CARTRIDGE HISTORY

Year of Introduction: 1902
Country of Origin: Germany
Designer(s): Deutsche Waffen und Munitionsfabriken AG
Governing Body: CIP, SAAMI
Present Status: active

CARTRIDGE DESCRIPTION

Bullet Diameter: .355 in.
Bullet Weight(s): 77-147 gr.
Rifling Twist Rate: 1 turn in 9.84 in.
Test Barrel Length: 5.9 in.
Case Type: rimless, tapered
Case Material: brass, steel, aluminum
Primer Type: small pistol

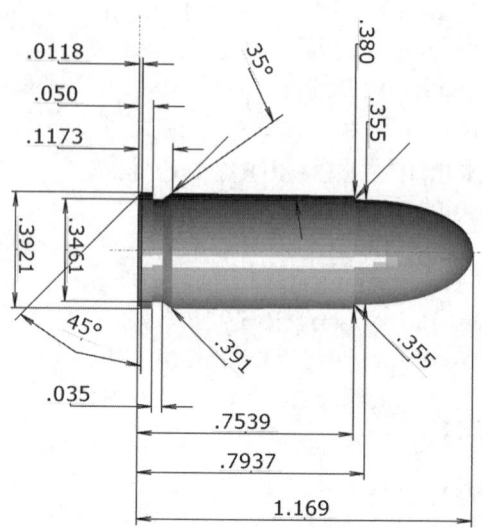

CARTRIDGE BALLISTICS

Max. Average Breech Pressure: 34,100 psi.
Max. Effective Range: 50 yds.
Max. Horizontal Range: 1,960 yds.
Max. Vertical Range: 4,250 ft.

Bullet Weight (gr.)	Bullet Type	Muzzle Velocity (fps)	Muzzle Energy (ft.-lbs.)
77	Frangible	1,350	312
100	Frangible	1,230	335
115	FMJ	1,160	344
115	FMJ	1,300	431
115	FMJ	1,360	472
124	FMJ	1,150	364
124	FMJ	1,245	427
124	FMJ	1,300	465
147	FMJ	990	320

CURRENT MANUFACTURER(S)

CCI/Speer, Federal, Hornady, Remington, Winchester, PMP, IMI, RUAG, Fiocchi, Sellier & Bellot, Lapua, Wolf, CBC, PMC, Prvi Partizan, MKEK, POF, Industrias Tecnos

GENERAL COMMENT(S)

If there is such a thing as a universal military cartridge, it is the 9mm Luger. Adopted by the German Navy in 1904 and the German Army in 1908, the 9x19mm Parabellum cartridge served Germany well through two world wars. Today, it is the standard military pistol caliber for NATO nations (including the U.S.) and serves with dozens of military and law enforcement agencies in other countries from Afghanistan to Zimbabwe.

As a result, 9mm Luger ammunition is manufactured in large quantities in government arsenals and commercial factories all over the globe.

Sportsmen were slow to take up the 9mm Luger cartridge. Prior to 1975, it was considered underpowered for hunting except for small game. Target shooters felt it was inaccurate. "Experts" advised against it for personal defense (too weak). Reloading components were hard to find. In some countries, civilian ownership of 9mm

Luger caliber handguns was prohibited. Most law enforcement agencies in the U.S. used revolvers while those in Europe used .32 ACP or .380 ACP caliber guns.

Despite these hurdles, the 9mm Luger cartridge now has become the most popular handgun cartridge in the world. These days, it is considered suitable for personal defense, hunting and target shooting. Many countries have dropped their restrictions on 9mm handgun ownership and world law enforcement agencies have made a massive switch to 9mm Luger caliber service pistols. Reloading components are plentiful and all major ammunition makers include numerous 9mm Luger loads in their product lines.

TECHNICAL COMMENT(S)

For over 100 years a controversy has endured between those who favor the 9mm Luger cartridge for all types of military, law enforcement and personal defense needs and those who feel the .45 ACP cartridge is best for these purposes. No end to this dispute is in sight. In fact both cartridges offer suitable terminal ballistic performance provided the user recognizes their limits and advantages. For example the 9mm Luger is better at penetrating body armor, produces less recoil, allows the user to carry more rounds of ammunition and has a flatter trajectory than the .45 ACP. On the other hand, the .45 ACP transfers energy more efficiently to unprotected, animate targets (allowing the user to carry FEWER rounds), offers better accuracy for competitive shooting and generates recoil energies most shooters can easily handle with practice.

American shooters' doctrine and experience has led them to prefer the .45 ACP cartridge, while European theories and experience have led them to prefer the 9mm Luger. History has shown both are right and neither is a bad choice.

9x21mm RUSSIAN SP-10

ALTERNATE NAME(S): 9x21mm SP-10, 9x21mm SP-11, 9x21mm SP-12
RELATED CALIBER(S): 9x19mm Luger, 9x21mm

CARTRIDGE HISTORY
Year of Introduction: circa late 1990s
Country of Origin: Russia
Designer(s): N/A
Governing Body: none
Present Status: active

CARTRIDGE DESCRIPTION
Bullet Diameter: .355 in.
Bullet Weight(s): 103-122 gr.
Rifling Twist Rate: 1 turn in 9 in.
Test Barrel Length: N/A
Case Type: rimless, straight
Case Material: steel
Primer: small pistol

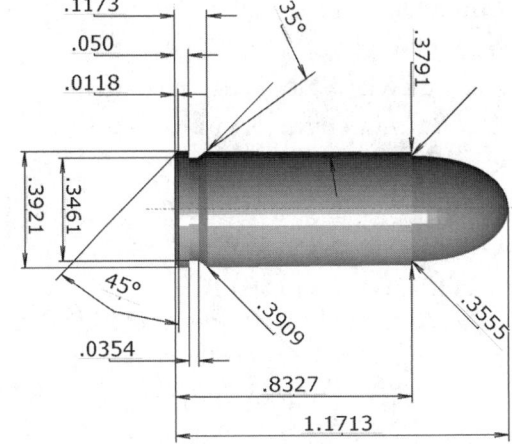

CARTRIDGE BALLISTICS
Max. Average Breech Pressure: 40,000 psi.
Max. Horizontal Range: 1,950 yds.
Max. Vertical Range: 4,250 ft.

Bullet Weight (gr.)	Bullet Type	Muzzle Velocity (fps)	Muzzle Energy (ft.-lbs.)
103	FMJ-AP	1,410	455
122	FMJ-RN	1,280	444

CURRENT MANUFACTURER(S)
Russian State Arsenals

GENERAL COMMENT(S)
In 1994, the Russian Army adopted the 9x19mm Luger cartridge. Shortly after, a similar, but more powerful pistol cartridge, the 9x21mm SP-10/11/12, was adopted by the Russian Federal Security Bureau (FSB) for use in their SR-1 "Gyurza" pistol and SR-2 " Veresk" submachine guns. Dimensions of this cartridge are similar to the

9x21mm cartridge on the American and European commercial market. However, in Russia its ballistic potential is used for law enforcement and security while in the U.S. it is used for IPSC competition. The designation "SP" is an abbreviation for "spetsialnyi patron" or special cartridge.

TECHNICAL COMMENT(S)

In configuration, the 9x21mm SP-10/11/12 is basically a 9x19mm Luger cartridge case made 2mm longer. Head and rim dimensions of both cartridges are similar and the bullets used are identical. Russian ammunition factories routinely load 9x19mm Luger ammunition to maximum average chamber pressures approximately 14% higher than SAAMI and CIP normal levels. In the U.S., such heavily loaded cartridges are classified as +P loads. The additional volume in the 9x21mm SP cartridge case provides room for even heavier powder charges than the 9x19mm Luger. As a direct result, the 9x21mm cartridge has a substantially higher muzzle velocity. Both lead core ball and steel core AP bullets are available. Curiously, an expanding bullet is not offered.

.45 AUTO

ALTERNATE NAME(S): .45, .45 Auto, .45 Automatic Colt Pistol, 11.25mm Colt, 11.25mm Pist. Patr. 632 (n)
RELATED CALIBER(S): .455 Webley Revolver Mk.II, .455 Webley Automatic, 7.65mm Luger, 8mm Nambu, 9mm Largo, 9mm Steyr, 9mm Browning Long

CARTRIDGE HISTORY

Year of Introduction: 1905 (Civilian), 1911 (Military)

Country of Origin: U.S.

Designer(s): John M. Browning

Governing Body: SAAMI, CIP

Present Status: active

CARTRIDGE DESCRIPTION

Bullet Diameter: .452 in.

Bullet Weight(s): 145-230 gr.

Rifling Twist Rate: 1 turn in 16 in.

Test Barrel Length: 5.9 in.

Case Type: rimless, straight

Case Material: brass or steel

Primer Type: large pistol

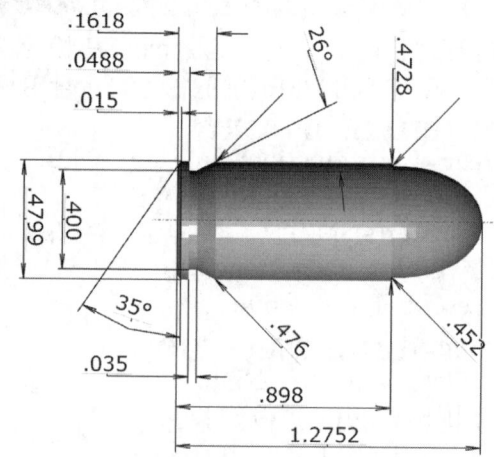

CARTRIDGE BALLISTICS

Max. Average Breech Pressure: 21,000 psi.

Max. Effective Range: 50 yds.

Max. Horizontal Range: 1,650 yds.

Max. Vertical Range: 3,700 ft.

Bullet Weight (gr.)	Bullet Type	Muzzle Velocity (fps)	Muzzle Energy (ft.-lbs.)
230	FMJ	855	373

CURRENT MANUFACTURER(S)

CCI/Speer, Cor-Bon, Federal, Hornady, Black Hills, Remington, Winchester, Fiocchi, Sellier & Bellot, IMI, Wolf, CBC, PMC, Industrias Technos

GENERAL COMMENT(S)

The U.S. Army adopted the .45 ACP cartridge as the Cartridge, caliber .45 Model 1911 in that same year. This cartridge remained in U.S. military service until 1985 when it was replaced by the 9mm Luger. It has been noted that old soldiers never die and the .45 ACP is no exception. Based on numerous instances in Iraq and Afghanistan of poor terminal ballistic performance by the 9mm Luger, a movement has started to bring the good old .45 ACP back into U.S. military service. While such a move may be doubtful, the controversy between the two old rivals, the 9mm Luger and the .45 ACP, is far from over.

On the civilian side, there was never any doubt, the .45 ACP was clearly superior to the 9mm Luger in stopping power. Nearly all ballistic "experts" and gun makers agreed on this and the American love affair with the .45 ACP cartridge has continued to grow. Most combat action competitions now favor the .45 ACP and penalize 9mm Luger caliber guns. Law enforcement SWAT teams and specialist agencies have always used .45 ACP handguns and continue to do so. Today, about 10% of U.S. law enforcement personnel carry a .45 ACP caliber handgun. However, most rank and file law enforcement officers dislike the heavy recoil, weight and size of .45 ACP pistols. When the chips are down, many shooters feel strongly that there is nothing like a .45 ACP. The reason is mostly mental. The proven terminal ballistic performance of the .45 ACP builds and backs user confidence, something few other calibers can do.

TECHNICAL COMMENT(S)

John Browning designed the .45 ACP cartridge in 1905 with a 200 grain FMJ-RN bullet at 900 fps muzzle velocity. As a result of historical experience and various tests, the U.S. Government increased the bullet weight to 230 grains and lowered the muzzle velocity to about 850 fps before adopting this cartridge for military service.

The 185 grain bullet serves two purposes: as a match loading in FMJ form and as a personal defense loading in JHP configuration. Many shooters still prefer the 230 grain FMJ-RN for personal defense. Chamber pressures of the .45 ACP are lower than many modern handgun cartridges such as the 9mm Luger and .44 Magnum. This limits the possibility of increasing muzzle velocity. Regardless, many American ammunition makers have introduced +P ammunition in .45 ACP caliber with relatively small increases in muzzle velocity.

Tests have shown that firing a .45 ACP cartridge in a carbine with a barrel 16 inches in length increases muzzle velocity over 20%. The .45 ACP cartridge is easy to reload and there are multiple sources for components. However, do not try to reload steel cartridge cases as they may scratch your dies rendering them useless.

John Moses Browning: 1855-1926
A Prolific Designer of Both Guns and Cartridges

Arguably the most famous gun designer in history, John M. Browning also designed many popular cartridges still in production today. Among those cartridges are the: .25 ACP, .32 ACP, .380 ACP, .45 ACP, and 9mm Browning Long.

CHAPTER 78 : MILITARY PISTOL - OBSOLETE

CHAPTER 78

For Cartridge Index see Chapter 101. All drawing dimensions are approximate.

It has been said that old soldiers never die. Perhaps there is no better example of this than obsolete military pistol cartridges Some were finally retired after decades of faithful service, witness the 7.62x25mm Tokarev in Russian military service. Others never found acceptance outside their homeland such as the Japanese 8mm Nambu. Lastly, there are those that simply were not a good idea in the beginning and declined from there such as the 7.65mm French MAS and the 9x19mm Glisenti.

Yet another factor was the rise of NATO and the Warsaw Pact during the Cold War. Ammunition interchangeability among member states was important, so all members of the group agreed to field a common pistol (and rifle) caliber. In the case of NATO, this was the 9x19mm Luger cartridge for which the British gave up their .455 Webley, the French their 7.65mm MAS, and the United States their .45 ACP (eventually).

Many of these obsolete calibers have survived because thousands of surplus pistols and revolvers in these calibers have been sold as surplus on the commercial market. In most cases, these relics (or derelicts depending on your point of view), provide low cost shooting for sportsmen on a tight budget even when ammunition in such calibers increases sharply in price.

7.65mm PARABELLUM

ALTERNATE NAME(S): 7.65x21mm Luger, 7.65 Luger, 7.65x21mm, .30 Luger Parabellum, 7.65mm Borchardt-Luger M1900, 7.65mm Luger-Borchardt, 7.65mm Parabellum Pistole
RELATED CALIBER(S): .30 Mauser

CARTRIDGE HISTORY
Year of Introduction: 1900
Country of Origin: Germany
Designer(s): Georg Luger/Deutsche Waffen und Munitions Fabriken
Governing Body: CIP, SAAMI
Present Status: obsolete

CARTRIDGE DESCRIPTION
Bullet Diameter: .308 in.
Bullet Weight(s): 93 gr.
Rifling Twist Rate: 1 turn in 10.83 in.
Test Barrel Length: 5.9 in.
Case Type: rimless, necked
Case Material: brass or aluminum
Primer Type: small pistol

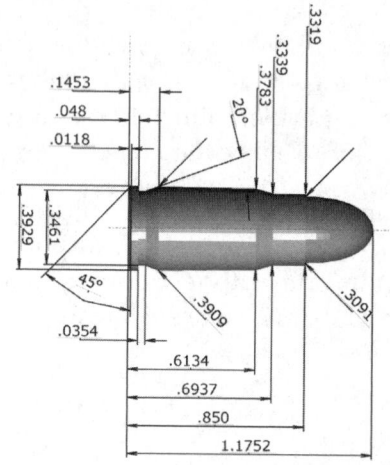

CARTRIDGE BALLISTICS
Max. Average Breech Pressure: 34,100 psi.
Max. Effective Range: 50 yds.
Max. Horizontal Range: 2,300 yds.
Max. Vertical Range: 5,150 ft.

Bullet Weight (gr.)	Bullet Type	Muzzle Velocity (fps)	Muzzle Energy (ft.-lbs.)
93	FMJ	1,220	305

CURRENT MANUFACTURER(S)
Winchester, Fiocchi, RUAG

GENERAL COMMENT(S)
Georg Luger designed and patented this cartridge in 1900 while working as an engineer at DWM. He based his design on the earlier Borchardt 7.62mm cartridge for the Borchardt 1893 pistol. It was listed in DWM catalogs as cartridge case number 471. Despite its designation as being 7.65mm, the bullet diameter is actually 7.62mm or .308 inches. The 7.65mm nomenclature was adopted to differentiate the .30 Luger cartridge from the .30 Mauser. Adopted for military service by the Swiss Army in 1903, Brazil, Bulgaria and Portugal later followed suit. The U.S. Army also tested the .30 Luger cartridge in the "American Eagle Luger" pistol during trials prior to adopting the John Browning designed M1911 .45 ACP caliber pistol. The 7.65mm cartridge was felt to be too under powered by the U.S. military. With the widespread adoption of another of Georg Luger's creations, the 9x19mm Luger cartridge, in 1908, the 7.65mm Luger has lived in the shadow of its more popular sibling. Although obsolete in military service, it remains a staple of commercial ammunition production.

TECHNICAL COMMENT(S)
The 7.65mm Luger cartridge is one of the high velocity, bottle neck pistol cartridges designed in the 1890s and 1900s. Smokeless propellants made such handgun cartridges and semi-automatic pistols feasible for the first time. At the time, lightweight, .30 caliber bullets at high velocity were a popular trend. These cartridges also set the stage for the still-brewing controversy between high velocity, light weight bullets and heavy weight bullets at low velocities for personal defense. The .30 Luger cartridge is not the same as the .30 Mauser cartridge. Although the two are contemporaries and use a .308 caliber bullet, they are not interchangeable. The .30 Luger uses a slightly heavier bullet (93 grains) than the .30 Mauser (86 grains), but the Mauser offers higher muzzle velocity and greater muzzle energy. The .30 Luger and the 9mm Luger cartridge have the same head dimensions and overall loaded length allowing guns in one caliber to be easily modified for the other. Early .30 Luger ammunition was loaded with a truncated cone bullet. Later, a round nose bullet was adopted. Ammunition in this caliber having a blackened case is for carbines and should not be fired in handguns.

7.65mm FRENCH LONG

ALTERNATE NAME(S): 7.65mm MAS, 7.65mm L Pour Pistolet, 7.65x19.7mm
RELATED CALIBER(S): .30 Pedersen, 9mm Luger, .45 ACP

CARTRIDGE HISTORY
Year of Introduction: 1935
Country of Origin: France
Designer(s): French Arsenals
Governing Body: CIP
Present Status: obsolete

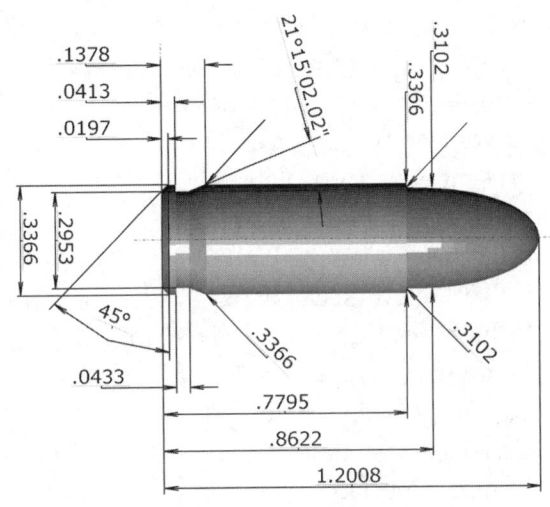

CARTRIDGE DESCRIPTION
Bullet Diameter: .308 in.
Bullet Weight(s): 85 gr.
Rifling Twist Rate: 1 turn in 10 in.
Test Barrel Length: 5.9 in.
Case Type: rimless, straight
Case Material: steel or brass
Primer Type: small pistol

CARTRIDGE BALLISTICS
Max. Average Breech Pressure: 24,570 psi.
Max. Effective Range: 25 yds.
Max. Horizontal Range: 1,800 yds.
Max. Vertical Range: 3,600 ft.

Bullet Weight (gr.)	Bullet Type	Muzzle Velocity (fps)	Muzzle Energy (ft.-lbs.)
85	FMJ	1,120	240

CURRENT MANUFACTURER(S)
None

GENERAL COMMENT(S)
From 1935 until 1950, the 7.65mm French Long was the official military pistol cartridge of the French military forces for pistols and sub-machineguns. France was the only country to adopt this cartridge for military service. It was manufactured only in France and in Vietnam.

TECHNICAL COMMENT(S)
By most standards, the ballistics of this cartridge are mediocre. With just 240 ft.-lbs. of muzzle energy, the 7.65mm MAS must be regarded as marginal for tactical use. Despite this, the 7.65mm MAS cartridge served the French military well for fifteen turbulent years. While the nomenclature is 7.65mm, bullet diameter is actually .308 inches. The 7.65mm MAS cartridge is very similar to the U.S. .30 Pedersen cartridge of the 1920s.

8mm NAMBU

ALTERNATE NAME(S): 8mm Japanese Nambu, 8x21.5mm Nambu
RELATED CALIBER(S): .30 Luger, .30 Mauser, 7mm Nambu, 9mm Luger, .45 ACP

CARTRIDGE HISTORY
Year of Introduction: 1904
Country of Origin: Japan
Designer(s): Col. Kijiro Nambu
Governing Body: none
Present Status: obsolete

CARTRIDGE DESCRIPTION
Bullet Diameter: .320 in.
Bullet Weight(s): 99-103 gr.
Rifling Twist Rate: 1 turn in 11 in.
Test Barrel Length: N/A
Case Type: rimless, necked
Case Material: brass
Primer Type: small pistol

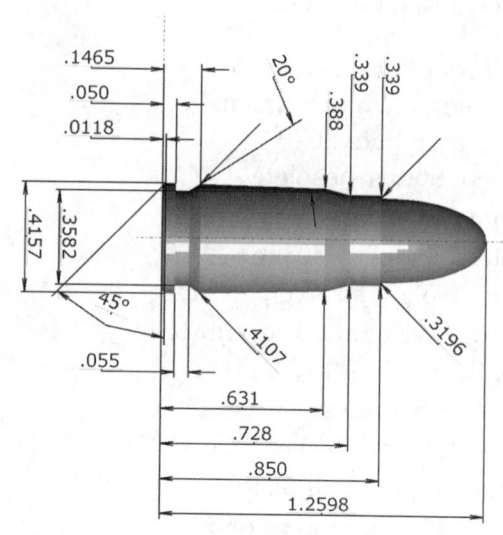

CARTRIDGE BALLISTICS
Max. Average Breech Pressure: 28,000 psi (estimated)
Max. Effective Range: 25 yds.
Max. Horizontal Range: 2,000 yds.
Max. Vertical Range: 3,700 ft.

Bullet Weight (gr.)	Bullet Type	Muzzle Velocity (fps)	Muzzle Energy (ft.-lbs.)
102	FMJ	1070	253

CURRENT MANUFACTURER(S)
None

GENERAL COMMENT(S)
Col. Kijiro Nambu was a prolific firearms and ammunition designer. It was he who designed the Nambu pistol and the 8mm Nambu cartridge. While the Nambu pistol went through several improved models, the 8mm Nambu cartridge served the Imperial Japanese military forces essentially unchanged from 1904 until 1945. Japan and its satellite Manchukuo were the only countries to take this cartridge into military service. After World War II, thousands of Nambu pistols came to the U.S. with returning GIs. Ammunition for these guns quickly disappeared leaving many Nambu pistols found today in unfired condition. Several U.S. companies have manufactured 8mm Nambu ammunition in limited quantities. However, ammunition in this caliber is expensive and hard to find.

TECHNICAL COMMENT(S)
By U.S. military standards, the 8mm Nambu cartridge offers mediocre ballistic performance for tactical use. However, one must judge the 8mm Nambu cartridge ballistic performance against its intended purpose. It was quite modern when designed and was intended for commissioned officers to use for self-defense at close ranges. The Japanese military, in concert with other military services around the world, considered the military pistol more a badge of office than a tactical weapon. Measured by these standards, the 8mm Nambu cartridge must be considered successful. By the late 1930s, it was obvious that the 8mm Nambu cartridge was fast becoming obsolete. However, the Japanese military made no effort to replace it with a more powerful cartridge.

8mm ROTH-STEYR

ALTERNATE NAME(S): 8mm Steyr Armeepistole Mod. 7, 8.2mm Roth Mod. 7, 8.2x18.8 Roth Mod. 7,
   8mm Repetierpistole M. 7
RELATED CALIBER(S): 9mm Luger, .45 ACP, .30 Mauser, .30 Luger, 8mm Nambu

CARTRIDGE HISTORY
Year of Introduction: 1907
Country of Origin: Austria
Designer(s): Karel Krnka
Governing Body: none
Present Status: obsolete

CARTRIDGE DESCRIPTION
Bullet Diameter: .329 in.
Bullet Weight(s): 110 gr.
Rifling Twist Rate: 1 turn in 10 in.
Test Barrel Length: N/A
Case Type: rimless, straight
Case Material: brass
Primer Type: small pistol

CARTRIDGE BALLISTICS
Max. Average Breech Pressure:
Max. Effective Range: 25 yds.
Max. Horizontal Range: 1,900 yds.
Max. Vertical Range: 3,800 ft.

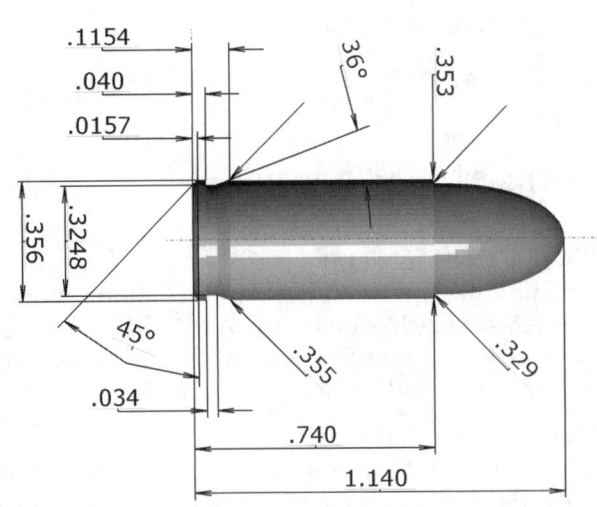

Bullet Weight (gr.)	Bullet Type	Muzzle Velocity (fps)	Muzzle Energy (ft.-lbs.)
113	FMJ	1,070	287

CURRENT MANUFACTURER(S)
Fiocchi

GENERAL COMMENT(S)
Adopted in 1907 for the Austro-Hungarian army, this cartridge remained in front line service until the advent of World War II. It was not adopted by any other country for military service. Although obsolete, Fiocchi still offers this caliber.

TECHNICAL COMMENT(S)
Despite its small caliber, this cartridge offers modestly effective ballistic performance. Still it is by no means a suitable tactical cartridge by modern standards.

9mm BROWNING LONG

ALTERNATE NAME(S): 9mm Long, 9mm Swedish M.07, 9mm Armee-Long
RELATED CALIBER(S): 9mm Luger, .380 ACP

CARTRIDGE HISTORY
Year of Introduction: 1903
Country of Origin: Belgium
Designer(s): John M. Browning
Governing Body: CIP
Present Status: obsolete

CARTRIDGE DESCRIPTION
Bullet Diameter: .355 in.
Bullet Weight(s): 110 gr.
Rifling Twist Rate: 1 turn in 15.75 in.
Test Barrel Length: 4.9 in.

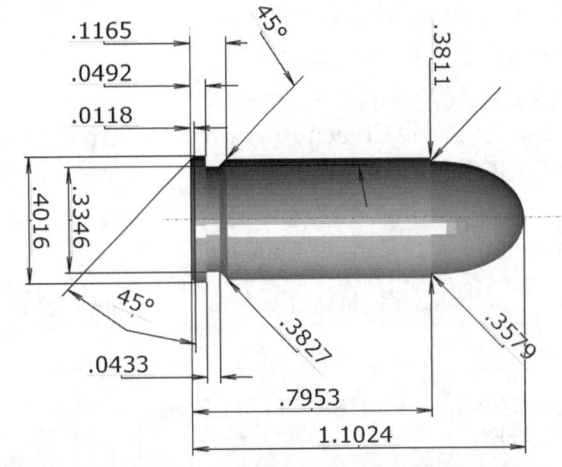

Case Type: rimless, straight
Case Material: brass
Primer Type: small pistol

CARTRIDGE BALLISTICS
Max. Average Breech Pressure: 23,930 psi.
Max. Effective Range: 25 yds.
Max. Horizontal Range: 2,000 yds.
Max. Vertical Range: 4,650 ft.

Bullet Weight (gr.)	Bullet Type	Muzzle Velocity (fps)	Muzzle Energy (ft.-lbs.)
110	FMJ	1,100	295

CURRENT MANUFACTURER(S)
None

GENERAL COMMENT(S)
Adopted by the Swedish Army in 1907 along with the Browning M1904 pistol, this cartridge became obsolete in Swedish service before World War II. The 9mm Browning Long also enjoyed a limited commercial following and was made at one time or another by every ammunition maker in Europe. It is now completely out of production, although quantities of surplus ammunition are still available.

TECHNICAL COMMENT(S)
Although similar to and a contemporary of the 9mm Luger cartridge, the 9mm Browning Long offers no practical ballistic advantage over the 9mm Luger cartridge. The maximum average chamber pressure of the 9mm Browning Long is substantially lower than the 9mm Luger.

9mm STEYR M1911

ALTERNATE NAME(S): 9mm Mannlicher, 9mm Steyr-Hahn, 9 M 12, 9x23mm
RELATED CALIBER(S): .45 ACP, 9mm Luger, .455 Webley Revolver Mk II, 9mm Largo

CARTRIDGE HISTORY
Year of Introduction: 1911
Country of Origin: Austria
Designer(s): Steyr
Governing Body: CIP
Present Status: obsolete

CARTRIDGE DESCRIPTION
Bullet Diameter: .355 in.
Bullet Weight(s): 116 gr.
Rifling Twist Rate: 1 turn in 9.84 in.
Test Barrel Length: 5.9 in.
Case Type: rimless, straight
Case Material: brass
Primer Type: small pistol

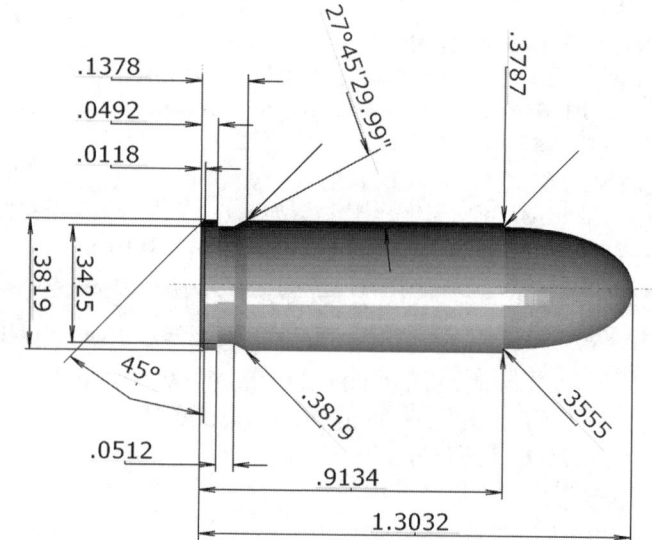

CARTRIDGE BALLISTICS
Max. Average Breech Pressure: 19,500 psi.
Max. Effective Range: 25 yds.
Max. Horizontal Range: 2,000 yds.
Max. Vertical Range: 4,500 ft.

Bullet Weight (gr.)	Bullet Type	Muzzle Velocity (fps)	Muzzle Energy (ft.-lbs.)
116	FMJ	1,200	370

CURRENT MANUFACTURER(S)
Fiocchi

GENERAL COMMENT(S)

Adopted for front line service in the Austro-Hungarian Army in 1912, the Romanian Army and the Chilean Army followed suit shortly after. These three countries were the only military services to adopt this cartridge. During World War II, Germany issued many of the Steyr-Hahn M1911 pistols to satellite countries. Ammunition production also continued. The 9mm Steyr cartridge became obsolete at the end of World War II. Today, Fiocchi is the only remaining manufacturer.

TECHNICAL COMMENT(S)

Although it is a large, impressive cartridge, the 9mm Steyr is constrained by a substantially lower maximum average breech pressure than the 9mm Luger. Despite this, it still manages to produce a respectable muzzle velocity and muzzle energy. Unfortunately, the 9mm Luger does everything the 9mm Steyr can do and more. As a result, the 9mm Steyr has become obsolete.

9mm LARGO

ALTERNATE NAME(S): 9mm Bergmann-Bayard, 9mm Bergmann 1910/21, 9mm Bayard, 9mm Astra M 21, 9mm Star S.P.
RELATED CALIBER(S): 9mm Luger, 9mm Steyr, .45 ACP, .455 Webley Revolver Mk II, 7.62mm Nagant

CARTRIDGE HISTORY

Year of Introduction: 1903

Country of Origin: Belgium

Designer(s): T. Bergmann

Governing Body: CIP

Present Status: obsolete

CARTRIDGE DESCRIPTION

Bullet Diameter: .355 in.

Bullet Weight(s): 125 gr.

Rifling Twist Rate: 1 turn in 10 in. (est.)

Test Barrel Length: N/A

Case Type: rimless, straight

Case Material: brass

Primer Type: small pistol

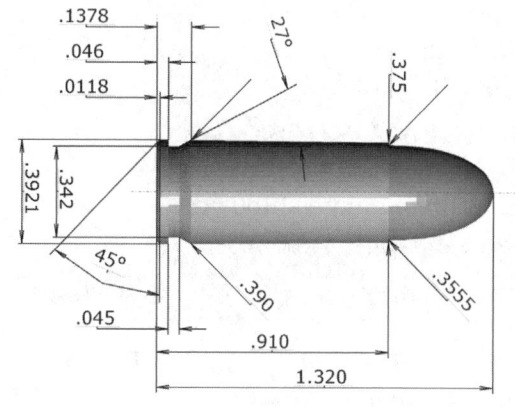

CARTRIDGE BALLISTICS

Max. Average Breech Pressure: N/A

Max. Effective Range: 50 yds.

Max. Horizontal Range: 2,150 yds.

Max. Vertical Range: 4,800 ft.

Bullet Weight (gr.)	Bullet Type	Muzzle Velocity (fps)	Muzzle Energy (ft.-lbs.)
125	FMJ	1,115	375

CURRENT MANUFACTURER(S)

None

GENERAL COMMENT(S)

Taken into military service by the Danish Army (in 1910 as the 9mm Bergmann-Bayard) the 9mm Largo was the service caliber for the Spanish Army until the 1950s. Ammunition in this caliber is no longer being manufactured. However, CCI/Speer made it until 2004.

TECHNICAL COMMENT(S)

This is another of the long 9mm cartridges developed just after 1900. While very similar to the 9mm Steyr, the 9mm Largo cartridge is loaded to higher chamber pressure with a heavier bullet. Although the .38 Automatic cartridge has a slightly shorter case, it can be safely fired in pistols chambered for the 9mm Largo. The 9mm Largo is a powerful cartridge in the same category of ballistic performance as the .38 Super Auto and 9mm Luger. It is suitable for personal defense if JHP bullets are used.

9mm GLISENTI

ALTERNATE NAME(S): 9x19mm Glisenti, 9mm Italian Glisenti
RELATED CALIBER(S): 9x19mm Luger

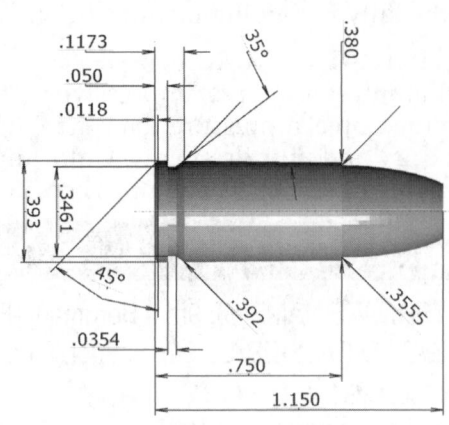

CARTRIDGE HISTORY
Year of Introduction: 1910
Country of Origin: Italy
Designer(s): Abiel Bethel Revelli
Governing Body: none
Present Status: obsolete

CARTRIDGE DESCRIPTION
Bullet Diameter: .355 in.
Bullet Weight(s): 124 gr.
Rifling Twist Rate: 1 turn in 10 in.
Test Barrel Length: N/A
Case Type: rimless, tapered
Case Material: brass
Primer: small pistol

CARTRIDGE BALLISTICS
Max. Average Breech Pressure: N/A
Max. Horizontal Range: 2,100 yds.
Max. Vertical Range: 4,400 ft.

Bullet Weight (gr.)	Bullet Type	Muzzle Velocity (fps)	Muzzle Energy (ft.-lbs.)
124	FMJ-FN	1,050	308

CURRENT MANUFACTURER(S)
None

GENERAL COMMENT(S)
Shortly after the German Army adopted the 9x19mm Parabellum cartridge in 1908, the Italian Army followed suit with their 9mm Glisenti cartridge in 1910. The 9mm Glisenti cartridge was to remain in active service with the Italian Army until the end of World War II in 1945. Both pistols and submachine guns were chambered for this cartridge.

TECHNICAL COMMENT(S)
The 9mm Glisenti looks identical to the 9x19mm Parabellum cartridge and uses the same bullet. In fact the 9mm Glisenti is dimensionally almost identical to the 9x19mm Parabellum cartridge so it will chamber and fire in most 9x19mm Luger caliber pistols, but may not function them reliably. This is because the 9mm Glisenti is loaded to a lower maximum average chamber pressure than the 9x19mm Luger. As a result, muzzle velocity is about 100 fps. lower than 9x19mm Luger ammunition. For this reason, 9x19mm Luger ammunition must not be fired in 9mm Glisenti pistols.

9.8mm AUTOMATIC COLT

ALTERNATE NAME(S): 9.65mm Browning Automatic Colt, 9.8mm Auto-Colt, 9.8mm Colt, 9.8mm Colt Auto Pistol
RELATED CALIBER(S): .38 Automatic, 9mm Browning Long

CARTRIDGE HISTORY
Year of Introduction: 1912
Country of Origin: U.S.
Designer(s): Colt
Governing Body: none
Present Status: obsolete

CARTRIDGE DESCRIPTION
Bullet Diameter: .378 in.
Bullet Weight(s): 130 gr.
Rifling Twist Rate: N/A
Test Barrel Length: N/A
Case Type: rimless, straight
Case Material: brass
Primer: small pistol

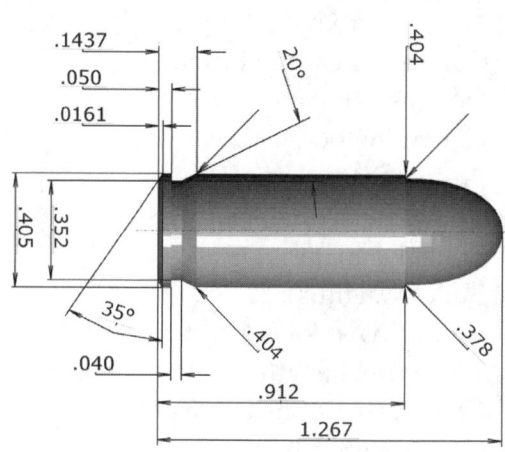

CARTRIDGE BALLISTICS
Max. Average Breech Pressure: N/A
Max. Horizontal Range: 2,100 yds.
Max. Vertical Range: 4,400 ft.

Bullet Weight (gr.)	Bullet Type	Muzzle Velocity (fps)	Muzzle Energy (ft.-lbs.)
130	FMJ-RN	1,150 (est.)	382

CURRENT MANUFACTURER(S)
None

GENERAL COMMENT(S)
This cartridge had a brief life around 1912 as part of a Colt Firearms Co. effort to sell overseas customers the new M1911 pistol. As most potential overseas customers felt the .45 ACP cartridge was too powerful, Colt developed the 9.8mm Automatic Colt cartridge. When this effort failed, the cartridge was dropped ignominiously.

TECHNICAL COMMENT(S)
A cursory review of the 9.8mm Auto Colt cartridge ballistics shows why this cartridge died at birth. A light bullet and moderate muzzle velocity combined to offer less muzzle energy than the 9mm Luger cartridge. These ballistics were already obsolete before the cartridge was introduced.

.455 WEBLEY AUTOMATIC

ALTERNATE NAME(S): none
RELATED CALIBER(S): .45 ACP, .455 Revolver Mk II, 9mm Luger

CARTRIDGE HISTORY
Year of Introduction: 1912
Country of Origin: Britain
Designer(s): Webley
Governing Body: N/A
Present Status: obsolete

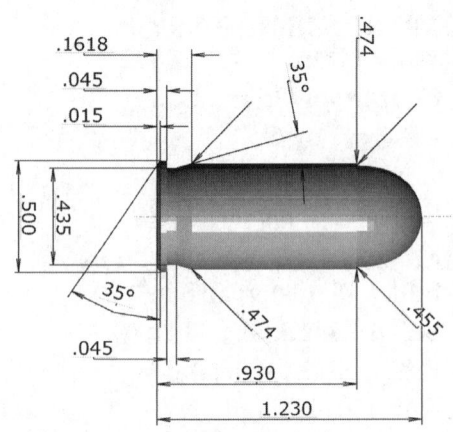

CARTRIDGE DESCRIPTION
Bullet Diameter: .455 in.
Bullet Weight(s): 224 gr.
Rifling Twist Rate: 1 turn in 10 in.
Test Barrel Length: N/A
Case Type: rimmed, straight
Case Material: brass
Primer Type: large pistol

CARTRIDGE BALLISTICS
Max. Average Breech Pressure: N/A
Max. Effective Range: 25 yds.
Max. Horizontal Range: 1,500 yds.
Max. Vertical Range: 3,500 ft.

Bullet Weight (gr.)	Bullet Type	Muzzle Velocity (fps)	Muzzle Energy (ft.-lbs.)
224	FMJ	700	247

CURRENT MANUFACTURER(S)
None

GENERAL COMMENT(S)
Adopted by the British Royal Navy in 1912, the .455 Webley Automatic was declared obsolete following the end of World War I. During World War II, the .455 Webley self-loading pistols and remaining stocks of these cartridges were reissued as a stopgap measure.

TECHNICAL COMMENT(S)
Contrary to opinions expressed by some writers, the .455 Webley Automatic cartridge is not a copy of the .45 ACP. While the bullet diameter and weight are very similar, the .455 Webley Auto cartridge is rimmed while the .45 ACP is rimless. The .455 Webley Auto also has a slightly longer case together with a longer overall loaded length than the .45 ACP. In fact, the .455 Webley Automatic seems based more on the .455 Revolver Mk I cartridge than on the .45 ACP. The .455 Webley Automatic and the .45 ACP cartridges are not interchangeable.

SECTION XII – RIMFIRE CARTRIDGE PROFILES
CHAPTER 79 : SPORTING RIMFIRE - CURRENT

CHAPTER 79

For Cartridge Index see Chapter 101. All drawing dimensions are approximate.

Any discussion of rimfire ammunition must pay homage to the king of rimfire calibers– the .22 Long Rifle cartridge. It succeeded where others failed due largely to its happy combination of low cost, versatility, and effective ballistic performance.

From its humble beginning, the .22 Long Rifle was always sold as a low price product. However, shooters and manufacturers viewed the .22 Long Rifle as just another cartridge, albeit a low price one. Customers purchased and used .22 rimfire ammunition sparingly as times were frequently tough and money short. Such was the condition of the .22 Long Rifle cartridge until the advent of mass merchandising in the 1960s.

Mass merchants purchased only the most popular items in multiple truck load quantities from the manufacturers and sold them directly to customers at a discount. Their emphasis was on large volumes, existing brand identification and low prices. These conditions were perfect for the .22 Long Rifle. They accelerated the sales volume of .22 Long Rifle ammunition to unheard of levels and forced rimfire manufacturers to lower costs by upgrading their machinery. Perhaps more important, mass merchants changed the mindset of rimfire customers and manufacturers from viewing the .22 Long Rifle as not just another "regular" cartridge, but now a cheap bulk commodity.

This had serious consequences. Firearm dealers could not compete with mass merchants and deemphasized rimfire ammunition altogether. Development of new rimfire calibers was blocked by lack of mass merchant interest and the costly machinery upgrades. Ammunition manufacturers routinely lost money on rimfire sales and had to make up the difference from the profits on other products.

By the 1990s, the largest mass merchants begin to reduce their sales of rimfire ammunition for political reasons. As the market for rimfire ammunition began to change (and contract), rimfire manufacturers responded with innovative new calibers offering superior ballistic performance and, incidentally, injecting some profit back into rimfire sales.

Here, then, are the victors– the old rimfire calibers still standing and the new wave of rimfire calibers leading the charge into the 21st century.

2.34mm SWISS MINIGUN

ALTERNATE NAME(S): 2.34mm Rimfire
RELATED CALIBER(S): none

CARTRIDGE HISTORY
Year of Introduction: 2007
Country of Origin: Switzerland
Designer(s): Swiss MiniGun Co.
Governing Body: none
Present Status: active

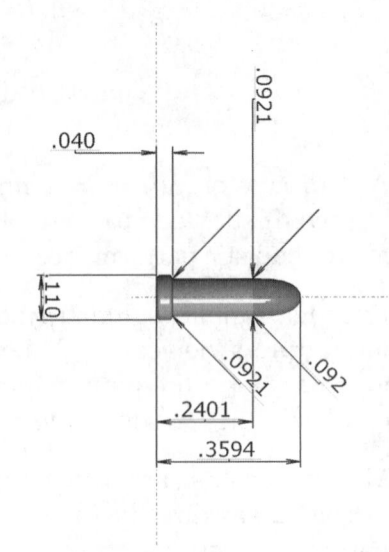

CARTRIDGE DESCRIPTION
Bullet Diameter: .092 in.
Bullet Weight(s): 1.975 gr.
Rifling Twist Rate: N/A
Test Barrel Length: N/A
Case Type: rimmed, straight
Case Material: brass

CARTRIDGE BALLISTICS
Max. Average Breech Pressure: 28,000 psi.
Max. Horizontal Range: 205 yds.
Max. Vertical Range: 400 ft.

Bullet Weight (gr.)	Bullet Type	Muzzle Velocity (fps)	Muzzle Energy (ft.-lbs.)
1.975	L-RN	400	.715

CURRENT MANUFACTURER(S)
Swiss MiniGun Co.

GENERAL COMMENT(S)
This interesting new rimfire cartridge was developed by the Swiss MiniGun company for their miniature six-shot, double-action revolver which is just under two inches long! This cartridge is the smallest rimfire caliber ever offered!

TECHNICAL COMMENT(S)
Parameters of this cartridge were driven by two factors: the size of the revolver, and the maximum amount of muzzle energy allowed by European firearms regulations. By any measure, the ballistic performance of the 2.34mm rimfire cartridge is less than that of most BB guns and far less than all air rifles. Obviously, the 2.34mm cartridge is not intended for any tactical application. Rather it is an example of fine workmanship and attention to detail that can actually be fired.

.17 MACH2

ALTERNATE NAME(S): .17 M2
RELATED CALIBER(S): .22 Long, .22 Long Rifle

CARTRIDGE HISTORY
Year of Introduction: 2004
Country of Origin: U.S.
Designer(s): Hornady, CCI/Federal
Governing Body: SAAMI
Present Status: active

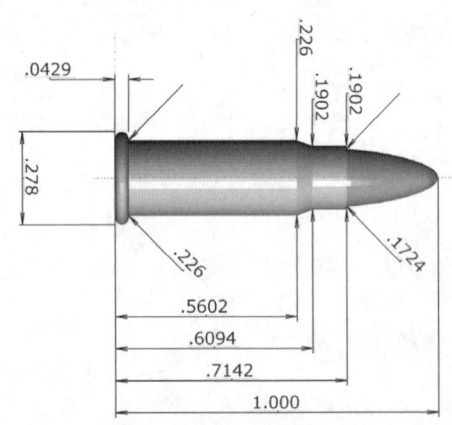

CARTRIDGE DESCRIPTION
Bullet Diameter: .171 in.
Bullet Weight(s): 17-20 gr.
Rifling Twist Rate: N/A

Test Barrel Length: 24 in.
Case Type: rimmed, necked
Case Material: brass

CARTRIDGE BALLISTICS
Max. Average Breech Pressure: 24,000 psi.
Max. Horizontal Range: 2,200 yds.
Max. Vertical Range: 4,400 ft.

Bullet Weight (gr.)	Bullet Type	Muzzle Velocity (fps)	Muzzle Energy (ft.-lbs.)
17	JSP	2010	152
17	JSP	2100	166
20	FMJ	1800	144

CURRENT MANUFACTURER(S)
CCI, Hornady, Remington, Eley, Fiocchi

GENERAL COMMENT(S)
Conceptual design work on this cartridge began at Federal Cartridge in 1989 in an effort to dramatically improve rimfire exterior ballistics and enhance safety by reducing the potential for ricochets. Basically, the concept was for a .22 Long Rifle cartridge case necked down to accept a 17-18 grain .171" caliber bullet at a proposed muzzle velocity of 2,000 fps. However, development stalled due to lack of suitable bullets and propellants.Fast forward to 2004 and things changed. Hornady developed a suitable bullet and propellant makers came up with a suitable powder. These made the .17 Mach2 possible. Not surprisingly, the case dimensions, bullet weights and ballistic performance are nearly identical to those proposed in 1989.

TECHNICAL COMMENT(S)
The .17 Mach2 cartridge has been a sales success as firearms manufacturers need only to change the barrel caliber on most models. This has allowed the consumer a wide choice of models quickly and at low cost. However, development of a reliable semi-automatic rifle in this caliber has proven difficult. The exterior ballistics of the .17 Mach2 are far superior to any version of the .22 Long Rifle. Unlike the .22 Long Rifle, the .17 Mach2 is a true 150 yard hunting cartridge. Cost remains a problem for the .17 Mach2 as retail prices are substantially higher compared to .22 Long Rifle ammunition. For hunting, the higher price is not significant although .17 Mach2 ammunition remains too expensive for plinking and informal target shooting.

.17 HORNADY MAGNUM RIMFIRE

ALTERNATE NAME(S): .17 HMR
RELATED CALIBER(S): .22 WMR

CARTRIDGE HISTORY
Year of Introduction: 2002
Country of Origin: U.S.
Designer(s): CCI/Federal (Alliant) and Hornady
Governing Body: SAAMI
Present Status: active

CARTRIDGE DESCRIPTION
Bullet Diameter: .1725 in.
Bullet Weight(s): 15.5-20 gr.
Rifling Twist Rate: N/A
Test Barrel Length: 24 in.
Case Type: rimmed, necked
Case Material: brass

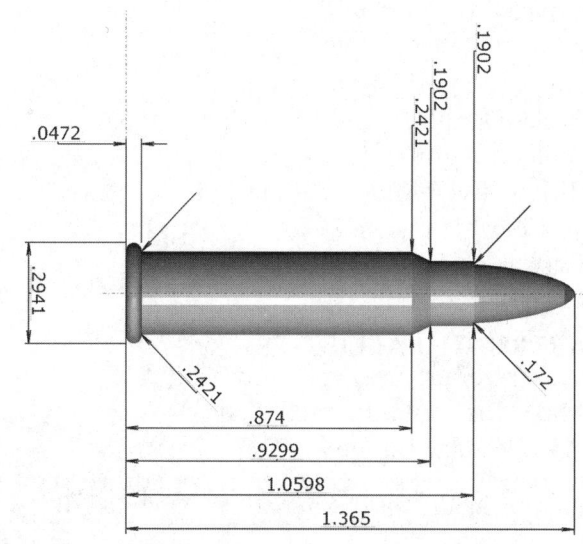

CARTRIDGE BALLISTICS
Max. Average Breech Pressure: 26,000
Max. Horizontal Range: 2,500 yds.
Max. Vertical Range: 5,000 ft.

Bullet Weight (gr.)	Bullet Type	Muzzle Velocity (fps)	Muzzle Energy (ft.-lbs.)
17	JSP/JHP	2,530	240
17	JSP/JHP	2,550	245
20	JSP	2,375	250
20	FMJ	2,375	250

CURRENT MANUFACTURER(S)

CCI, Federal, Hornady, Remington, Winchester

GENERAL COMMENT(S)

Preliminary design work on this cartridge began at Federal Cartridge in 1989 based on earlier work by Steve Chernicky. The concept was to dramatically improve rimfire magnum exterior ballistics and enhance safety by reducing the potential for ricochets. This could be achieved by using a .22 WMR cartridge case necked down to accept a 17-18 grain .171" caliber bullet at a proposed muzzle velocity of 2,650 fps. However, development stalled due to lack of suitable bullets and propellants. Fast forward to 2004 and things changed. Hornady developed a suitable bullet and propellant makers came up with a suitable powder. These made the .17 HMR possible. Not surprisingly, the case dimensions, bullet weights and ballistic performance are nearly identical to those proposed in 1989.

TECHNICAL COMMENT(S)

The flat trajectory, high remaining velocity and substantial remaining energy make the .17 HMR a true 200 yard rimfire hunting cartridge. The light bullets buck cross winds surprisingly well and recoil is minimal making recovery for a second shot very quick. For those who feel the 17 grain bullet is too light, the 20 grain bullet should offer satisfaction. In either case, the bullets disintegrate soon after penetration making them well suited for pest elimination, pelt hunting and varmint shooting. For small game, these bullets may spoil too much meat. The light weight and lack of penetration this cartridge unsuitable for hunting predators. The .17 HMR puts the fun back into rimfire hunting, but at a price. Ammunition in this caliber is expensive, but unlike the .22 WMR, the improved ballistic performance is worth the price.

Safety Notice from Federal Premium Product Services http://www.federalpremium.com
Do not use .17 HMR ammunition in semi-automatic firearms without consulting with your firearms manufacturer. Use of .17 HMR ammunition in semi-automatic firearms may result in serious personal injury or property damage.

.22 BB CAP

ALTERNATE NAME(S): .22 Bulleted Breech Cap
RELATED CALIBER(S): Flobert rimfire cartridges

CARTRIDGE HISTORY

Year of Introduction: 1845
Country of Origin: France
Designer(s): Flobert
Governing Body: CIP
Present Status: active

CARTRIDGE DESCRIPTION

Bullet Diameter: .225 in.
Bullet Weight(s): 16-20 gr.
Rifling Twist Rate: 1 turn in 16 in.
Test Barrel Length: 24 in.
Case Type: rimmed, straight
Case Material: brass

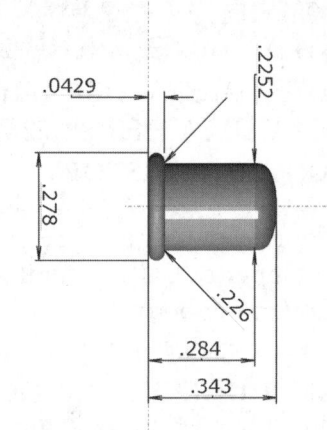

CARTRIDGE BALLISTICS

Max. Average Breech Pressure: N/A
Max. Horizontal Range: 1,000 yds.
Max. Vertical Range: 1,000 ft.

Bullet Weight (gr.)	Bullet Type	Muzzle Velocity (fps)	Muzzle Energy (ft.-lbs.)
18	L-FN	780	24

CURRENT MANUFACTURER(S)

Dynamit Nobel

GENERAL COMMENT(S)

This humble (very) "cartridge" was designed by a French gunsmith in Paris. Originally, it consisted of a flanged rifle percussion cap modified to hold a small, lead round ball in the front end. There was no powder charge, the sole means of propulsion being the primer. Flobert ammunition was the forefather of the modern .22 rimfire cartridges of today. True rimfire cartridges were designed by Horace Smith and Daniel Wesson in 1856. Following this development, Flobert cartridges evolved to become rimfire designs. At one time, nearly all domestic rimfire manufacturers made .22 BB Cap ammunition. Today, Dynamit Nobel is the only remaining manufacturer.

TECHNICAL COMMENT(S)

The low noise and limited velocity of the .22 BB Cap makes it an ideal cartridge for indoor shooting at ranges to 50 feet. These characteristics also make the .22 BB Cap a good load for eliminating pests and rodents. BB Cap ammunition is loaded in cartridge cases substantially shorter than the .22 Short case. Because of its very short length, the .22 BB Cap must be single-loaded in all firearms save revolvers. When fired in .22 Long Rifle chambers, leading may build up at the forward portion of the chambers.

.22 CB CAP

ALTERNATE NAME(S): .22 Conical Ball Cap, .22 CB Short, .22 CB Long, .22 Long Z
RELATED CALIBER(S): Flobert rimfire cartridges

CARTRIDGE HISTORY
Year of Introduction: circa 1888
Country of Origin: U.S.
Designer(s): unknown
Governing Body: SAAMI
Present Status: active

CARTRIDGE DESCRIPTION
Bullet Diameter: .225 in.
Bullet Weight(s): 20-29 gr.
Rifling Twist Rate: 1 turn in 16 in.
Test Barrel Length: 24 in.
Case Type: rimmed, straight
Case Material: brass

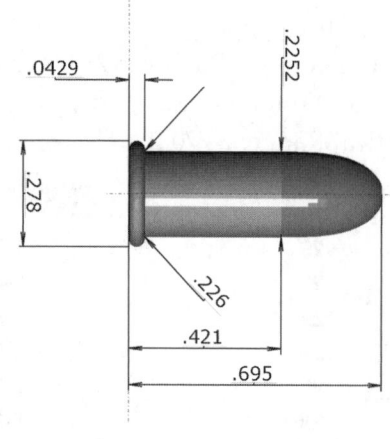

CARTRIDGE BALLISTICS
Max. Average Breech Pressure: 21,000
Max. Horizontal Range: 1,000 yds.
Max. Vertical Range: 1,600 ft.

Bullet Weight (gr.)	Bullet Type	Muzzle Velocity (fps)	Muzzle Energy (ft.-lbs.)	
29	L-RN	710	32	Short
20	L-RN	590	15	Colibri
29	L-RN	710	32	Long

CURRENT MANUFACTURER(S)
CCI, Dynamit Nobel, Industrias Tecnos

GENERAL COMMENT(S)
The .22 CB Cap was developed to provide reduced noise and lower muzzle energy than standard .22 rimfire ammunition while maintaining accuracy. It was intended to supplement the BB Cap, not replace it. While many would say one useless cartridge replaced another, this is not true. The CB Cap offers improved accuracy and increased power over the BB Cap. It is an excellent choice for indoor target shooting and eliminating pests and rodents.

TECHNICAL COMMENT(S)
The CB Cap differs from its BB Cap brother in two ways: it is loaded with a conical bullet; and it may contain a very small powder charge. Still, the major energy source for propelling the bullet is the primer. CB Cap cartridges normally are loaded in .22 Short cases. Modern CB Caps are offered in two varieties: CB Short and CB Long. Both are assembled with the same 29 grain, solid lead bullet and both have the same 710 fps muzzle velocity. The difference is in the case length. While the CB Short may leave lead deposits in .22 Long Rifle chambers, the CB Long will eliminate this problem.

.22 SHORT

ALTERNATE NAME(S): none
RELATED CALIBER(S): .22 CB Cap, .22 Long, .22 Long Rifle

CARTRIDGE HISTORY
Year of Introduction: 1856
Country of Origin: U.S.
Designer(s): Horace Smith and Daniel Wesson
Governing Body: SAAMI
Present Status: active

CARTRIDGE DESCRIPTION
Bullet Diameter: .225 in.
Bullet Weight(s): 27-29 gr.
Rifling Twist Rate: 1 turn in 24 in.
Test Barrel Length: 24 in.
Case Type: rimmed, straight
Case Material: brass

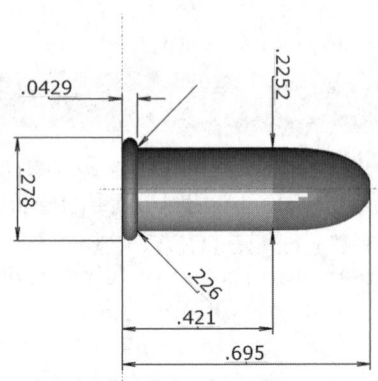

CARTRIDGE BALLISTICS
Max. Average Breech Pressure: 21,000 psi.
Max. Horizontal Range: 1,231 yds.
Max. Vertical Range: 2,770 ft.

Bullet Weight (gr.)	Bullet Type	Muzzle Velocity (fps)	Muzzle Energy (ft.-lbs.)	
29	L-RN	1035	58	Std Vel
29	L-RN	1080	75	Hi Vel
29	L-RN	1095	77	Hi Vel
29	L-RN	830	44	Match
29	L-RN	850	46	Match
29	L-RN	650	23	Match
27	L-HP	1105	73	Hi Vel

CURRENT MANUFACTURER(S)
CCI, Remington, Winchester, Eley, Dynamit Nobel, Fiocchi, Industrias Tecnos

GENERAL COMMENT(S)
Now over 150 years old, the humble .22 Short is the oldest, self-contained cartridge still in production. Handguns in .22 Short were carried by soldiers during the Civil War. Today the Short soldiers on as a specialized target cartridge for world-class competition in rapid fire events. For many years, the .22 Short was the popular choice for plinking due to its lower cost. As the cost difference has disappeared, the Short has faded in popularity for plinking and small game hunting. However, it still excels at pest elimination.

TECHNICAL COMMENT(S)
For rapid fire pistol competition where as much recoil as possible must be eliminated to speed recovery between shots, the .22 Short remains the best choice. The high velocity hollow point loads are a good choice for pest elimination and many types of small game. Today, the .22 Short is made from trimmed .22 Long Rifle cases to reduce costs. Due to low production volumes, the .22 Short is made on older modules rather than modern high speed machinery. This increases cost which further reduces the popularity of the Short. The standard velocity load is clearly intended for target competition, while the high velocity load remains the choice for hunting and plinking. This ammunition will not cycle in semi-automatic rifles or pistols designed to fire .22 Long Rifle ammunition. It must be single loaded into some pump, lever and bolt-action rifles as well. While it is safe to fire Short ammunition in Long Rifle chambers, accuracy may be poor. In addition, lead may build up in the front of the chamber requiring cleaning before shooting with .22 Long Rifle ammunition can resume.

.22 LONG

ALTERNATE NAME(S): .22 L
RELATED CALIBER(S): .22 Short, .22 Long Rifle

CARTRIDGE HISTORY
Year of Introduction: 1871
Country of Origin: U.S.
Designer(s): Great Western Gun Works
Governing Body: SAAMI
Present Status: active

CARTRIDGE DESCRIPTION
Bullet Diameter: .225 in.
Bullet Weight(s): 29 gr.
Rifling Twist Rate: 1 turn in 16 in.
Test Barrel Length: 24 in.
Case Type: rimmed, straight
Case Material: brass

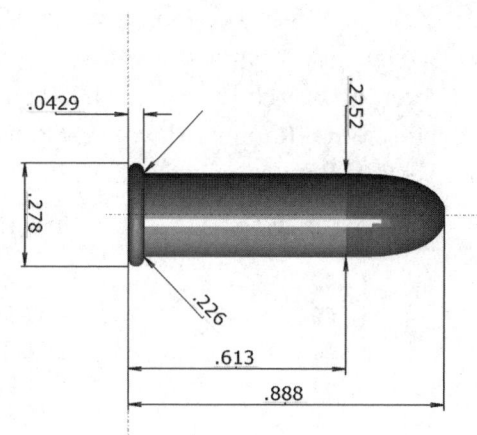

CARTRIDGE BALLISTICS
Max. Average Breech Pressure: 24,000 psi.
Max. Horizontal Range: 1,500 yds.
Max. Vertical Range: 3,000 ft.

Bullet Weight (gr.)	Bullet Type	Muzzle Velocity (fps)	Muzzle Energy (ft.-lbs.)	
29	L-RN	1,215	95	Hi Vel

CURRENT MANUFACTURER(S)
CCI

GENERAL COMMENT(S)
The .22 Long was introduced in 1871, some 15 years before the .22 Long Rifle cartridge. This cartridge made the transition to smokeless powder in the 1890s and is now over 135 years old. During its lengthy production life, the .22 Long has been offered in standard velocity, high velocity and shot loadings. The high velocity load is the only survivor. Until the late 1950s, the .22 Long was regarded as a kind of intermediate load between the .22 Short and the .22 Long Rifle as its muzzle velocity and price fell into that category. All major domestic rimfire manufacturers made the .22 Long. By all measures today, the .22 Long cartridge is obsolete, only CCI still manufactures it.

TECHNICAL COMMENT(S)
While many shooters regard the .22 Long as being a 29 grain Short bullet loaded into a .22 Long Rifle cartridge case, such is not the case. As the .22 Long preceded the .22 Long Rifle by 15 years, it is very likely that the .22 Long cartridge case length played a key role in the design of the .22 Long Rifle cartridge. Although .22 Long ammunition will not cycle semi-automatic rifles and pistols, it will usually function in manually operated firearms. The ultra high velocity range of .22 rimfire cartridges were inspired by the .22 Long, namely a light weight bullet at high velocity. However, the success of the UHV Long Rifle loads has sounded the death knell of the .22 Long.

.22 LONG RIFLE

ALTERNATE NAME(S): .22 L.R., .22 LR, 5.6mm
RELATED CALIBER(S): .17 Mach2, .17 Aguila, .22 Short, .22 Long,
.22 Ultra High Velocity, .22 LR Match, .22 SSS

CARTRIDGE HISTORY
Year of Introduction: 1887
Country of Origin: U.S
Designer(s): J. Stevens Arms & Tool Co.
Governing Body: SAAMI, CIP
Present Status: active

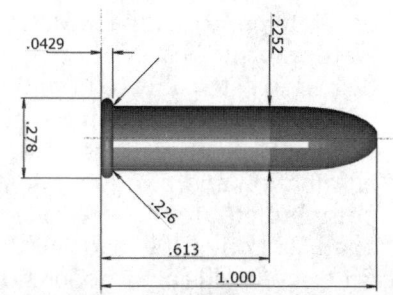

CARTRIDGE DESCRIPTION
Bullet Diameter: .225 in.

Bullet Weight(s): 31-40 gr.
Rifling Twist Rate: 1 turn in 16 in.
Test Barrel Length: 24 in.
Case Type: rimmed, straight
Case Material: brass, occasionally steel (Russian)

CARTRIDGE BALLISTICS
Max. Average Breech Pressure: 24,000 psi.
Max. Horizontal Range: std. vel. 1,588, high vel. 1,622, ultra high vel. 1,458 yds.
Max. Vertical Range: std. vel. 3,505, high vel. 3,650, ultra high vel. 3,280 ft.

Bullet Weight (gr.)	Bullet Type	Muzzle Velocity (fps)	Muzzle Energy (ft.-lbs.)	
40	L-RN	1025	93	Sub
40	L-RN	1080	105	Match
40	L-RN	1150	117	Std Vel
40	L-RN	1200	130	Std Vel
40	L-RN	1240	135	Hi Vel
36	L-RN	1410	159	UHV
40	L-HP	1470	192	UHV
38	L-HP	1025	89	Sub
38	L-HP	1050	93	Sub
38	L-HP	1260	135	Hi Vel
38	L-HP	1280	138	Hi Vel
37	L-HP	1280	135	Hi Vel
36	L-HP	1280	131	Hi Vel
36	L-HP	1260	125	Hi Vel
36	L-HP	1220	122	Hi Vel
33	L-HP	1500	165	UHV
32	L-HP	1640	191	UHV
31	L-HP	1430	140	UHV
30	L-HP	1700	192	UHV
31	#12 shot	1000	---	Shot

CURRENT MANUFACTURER(S)
CCI, Federal, Remington, Winchester, Eley, Fiocchi, Lapua, Dynamit Nobel, PMC, Industrias Tecnos

GENERAL COMMENT(S)
The .22 Long Rifle cartridge was loaded with black powder until the late 1890s when smokeless powders became available. Most small game hunters quickly preferred smokeless powder loads although match shooters clung to black powder and semi-smokeless powder loads until the early 1930s. Early .22 Long Rifle black powder cartridges were loaded to a muzzle velocity of about 950 fps with an uncrimped bullet. Smokeless powder loads increased muzzle velocity to around 1,100 fps and required a crimped bullet. In 1930, Remington introduced the first .22 Long Rifle high velocity cartridges loaded to supersonic muzzle velocity. CCI introduced the first ultra high velocity .22 Long Rifle loading, the Stinger, in 1977. Today, .22 Long Rifle match ammunition remains popular for all types of competition from club matches to the Olympics. Although it is now over 120 years old, the .22 Long Rifle remains the single most popular sporting cartridge in the world with well over five billion rounds being loaded every year.

TECHNICAL COMMENT(S)
Match Long Rifle ammunition is loaded to subsonic velocities (below 1,135 fps) to assure that all rounds remain below the speed of sound so as to strike the same point of impact. Rounds above the speed of sound will have a different point of impact. Match ammunition is offered in a number of different grades depending on performance. Naturally, the best quality match ammunition is very expensive. The base of some .22 Long Rifle ammunition is dished in ostensibly to improve interior ballistics. Standard velocity, subsonic and match ammunition normally will not operate semi-automatic firearms. Many hunters prefer these loads for their reduced noise levels and excellent accuracy. High velocity .22 Long Rifle ammunition is a popular choice for hunting small game, pest elimination and plinking. Most shooters prefer solid bullets for plinking and informal target shooting. Hollow point bullets are the recommended choice for hunting. When fired in pistols and revolvers, the muzzle velocity of all .22 Long Rifle loads will be reduced considerably. For pest elimination at ranges of 15 feet or less, .22 Long Rifle shot shells are a good choice. Use hollow point bullets at longer ranges.

.22 WINCHESTER RIMFIRE

ALTERNATE NAME(S): .22 WRF, .22 Remington Special
RELATED CALIBER(S): .22 WMR

CARTRIDGE HISTORY
Year of Introduction: 1890
Country of Origin: U.S.
Designer(s): Winchester
Governing Body: SAAMI
Present Status: Active

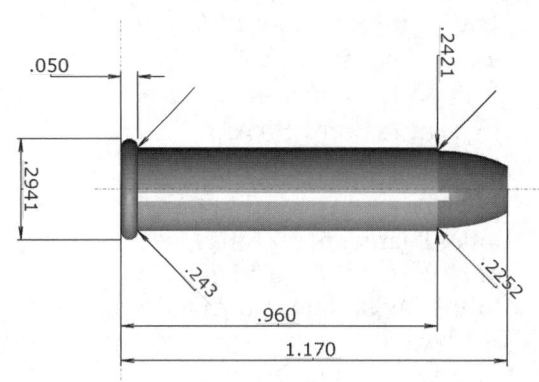

CARTRIDGE DESCRIPTION
Bullet Diameter: .224 in.
Bullet Weight(s): 40 gr.
Rifling Twist Rate: 1 turn in 16 in.
Test Barrel Length: 24 in.
Case Type: rimmed, straight
Case Material: brass

CARTRIDGE BALLISTICS
Max. Average Breech Pressure: 20,000 psi.
Max. Horizontal Range: 1,700 yds.
Max. Vertical Range: 3,800 ft.

Bullet Weight (gr.)	Bullet Type	Muzzle Velocity (fps)	Muzzle Energy (ft.-lbs.)
45	L-FN	1300	169

CURRENT MANUFACTURER(S)
CCI, Winchester

GENERAL COMMENT(S)
The .22 WRF is a good example of how a cartridge long ago consigned to obsolete status can come back from the dead to be listed in modern manufacturers' product lines. Introduced by Winchester in 1890, the .22 WRF enjoyed production status until World War II. By 1950, the .22 WRF had been consigned to historical oblivion. Then, in 1986, Winchester made a special production run of .22 WRF to meet market demand. Another production run followed in 1995. Following this, the .22 WRF has been added to the Winchester and the CCI product lines.

TECHNICAL COMMENT(S)
The .22 WRF must be considered as the predecessor of the .22 WMR. Both cartridges share many similar dimensions and both are designed for a full caliber bullet. However, the .22 WRF has a shorter cartridge case and is loaded with a lead bullet to a lower chamber pressure. The .22 WRF can be safely fired in most .22 WMR caliber firearms except revolvers. Because of this, many shooters seem to have determined that the venerable .22 WRF is a type of lower powered .22 WMR which may explain its sudden popularity. For small game hunting and varmint shooting the .22 WRF is a better ballistic choice than the .22 Long Rifle at ranges beyond 100 yards. The high price of .22 WRF ammunition precludes plinking and informal target shooting.

.22 WINCHESTER MAGNUM RIMFIRE

ALTERNATE NAME(S): .22 WMR
RELATED CALIBER(S): .17 HMR, .22 WRF

CARTRIDGE HISTORY
Year of Introduction: 1959
Country of Origin: U.S.
Designer(s): Winchester
Governing Body: SAAMI
Present Status: Active

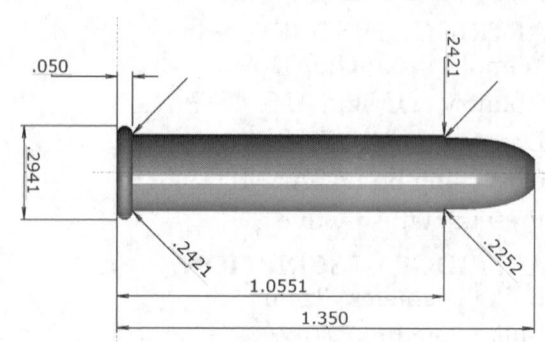

CARTRIDGE DESCRIPTION
Bullet Diameter: .224 in.
Bullet Weight(s): 30-50 gr.
Rifling Twist Rate: 1 turn in 16 in.
Test Barrel Length: 24 in.
Case Type: rimmed, straight
Case Material: brass

CARTRIDGE BALLISTICS
Max. Average Breech Pressure: 24,000 psi.
Max. Horizontal Range: 1,715 yds.
Max. Vertical Range: 3,860 ft.

Bullet Weight (gr.)	Bullet Type	Muzzle Velocity (fps)	Muzzle Energy (ft.-lbs.)
50	JHP	1530	260
45	JHP	1550	240
40	FMJ	1875	312
40	FMJ	1880	315
40	FMJ	1910	324
40	JHP	1875	312
40	JHP	1910	312
30	JHP	2200	322
30	JHP	2250	337
34	JHP	2120	338
52	#12 Shot	1000	N/A

CURRENT MANUFACTURER(S)
CCI, Federal, Remington, Winchester, Dynamit Nobel, Fiocchi, PMC

GENERAL COMMENT(S)
Introduced to popular acclaim by Winchester in 1959, the .22 Winchester Magnum Rimfire was an attempt to improve rimfire hunting performance. For this purpose, a new stronger and longer cartridge case was developed. It proved very effective on small game and varmints out to 100 yards and soon became a staple in most domestic rimfire manufacturers' product lines. It did not catch on in Europe, however. The improved ballistic performance of the .22 WMR has always come at a high price. Ammunition in this caliber has always been three or four times more expensive than .22 Long Rifle ammunition without a commensurate ballistic performance. This has always limited the appeal of the .22 WMR and continues to do so.

TECHNICAL COMMENT(S)
The .22 WMR is not simply a longer .22 Long Rifle case. Rather it is designed to accept a full diameter jacketed bullet. In addition, it is a stronger case with different dimensions in order to withstand increased chamber pressures. The .22 WMR shares many case dimensions with its predecessor, the .22 Winchester Rim Fire (.22 WRF) cartridge. Although the two cartridges are not identical, the .22 WRF can be fired in .22 WMR chambers.Throughout its life, the .22 WMR has been plagued by flat nose bullets of poor quality with rainbow trajectories and poor accuracy. This was due to efforts to reduce production costs by plating the jacket on a lead core. This changed recently with the introduction of cup-and-draw jackets with spitzer point bullets. Due to its case length and inherently weak rimfire design, it has proven difficult to make the .22 WMR cycle reliably in semi-automatic rifles. Several makers have offered rifles in this caliber with indifferent success. Ultra high velocity loadings that significantly improve short range ballistics have entered the market in the last few years. The higher muzzle velocities are achieved by using lightweight bullets. As such bullets are, of necessity, blunt they have poor ballistics at ranges over 150 yards.

CHAPTER 80 : SPORTING RIMFIRE - OBSOLETE

CHAPTER 80

For Cartridge Index see Chapter 101. All drawing dimensions are approximate.

Note: No "Primer" data is shown under CARTRIDGE DESCRIPTION in this chapter, as all cartridges have rimfire priming.

For a brief and shining moment in history (circa 1855-1870), rimfire designs were the predominant system of self-contained cartridges. As a result, a large number of different rimfire cartridges were developed, ranging from .22- to .58 caliber. After 1875, however, the inherent weakness of its case design and ignition system began to work against the rimfire. Various central ignition systems allowed a stronger cartridge case, higher chamber pressures, and improved ballistic performance. The rimfire could not compete.

Many rimfire calibers did not make the cut for conversion to smokeless propellants in the late 1890s. In addition, hard use and the corrosive effects of mercuric priming and black powder retired many rimfire guns, effectively ending demand for many classic rimfire calibers.

By the turn of the century, it was soon realized that one area in which the rimfire cartridge could compete effectively with central-fire designs was in smaller calibers such as .22 and .25. In these small calibers, low cost trumped limited ballistic performance and demand for these calibers grew.

After World War I (1914-1918), many older rimfire calibers that had survived the conversion to smokeless propellants faded away and were dropped. The final cut for many of the remaining old rimfire calibers was made in World War II (1939-1945) when production of all non-essential calibers was suspended for the duration. When civilian production resumed in 1946, commercial ammunition manufacturers took the opportunity to weed out many of the remaining rimfire calibers for which demand no longer existed.

Between 1946 and 1985, a few isolated efforts to develop new rimfire calibers were made by various ammunition makers. Virtually none were successful. Here then is the graveyard of rimfire cartridges. RIP.

2mm RANDZUNDER

ALTERNATE NAME(S): 2mm Kolibri Rimfire
RELATED CALIBER(S): 2mm Rimfire Blank

CARTRIDGE HISTORY
Year of Introduction: circa 1930s
Country of Origin: Austria
Designer(s): Kolibri
Governing Body: none
Present Status: obsolete

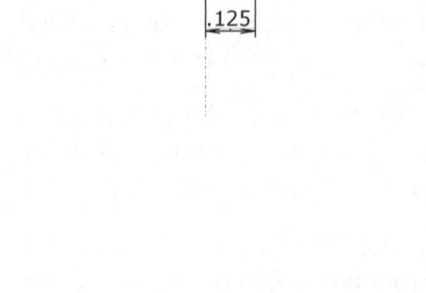

CARTRIDGE DESCRIPTION
Bullet Diameter: .0787 in. (approx. No. 9 1/2 shot pellet)
Bullet Weight(s): .78 gr.
Rifling Twist Rate: smoothbore
Test Barrel Length: N/A
Case Type: rimmed, straight
Case Material: copper

CARTRIDGE BALLISTICS
Max. Average Breech Pressure: N/A
Max. Horizontal Range: 235 yds.
Max. Vertical Range: 540 ft.

Bullet Weight (gr.)	Bullet Type	Muzzle Velocity (fps)	Muzzle Energy (ft.-lbs.)
7.8	L-RB	550	.52

CURRENT MANUFACTURER(S)
None

GENERAL COMMENT(S)
These diminutive rimfire cartridges were chambered in miniature revolvers and single-shot pistols designed to be carried on key chains. Cartridges and pistols in this caliber were made in Germany and Austria. Both guns and ammunition were imported into the U.S. in the 1950s by Stoeger. Cartridges in this caliber are now obsolete.

TECHNICAL COMMENT(S)
There were two versions of 2mm cartridges: rimfire ball and blank. The blank version was the more common of the two. These cartridges must be regarded as technical novelties as they had no practical use. However, they were capable of causing personal injury and must be treated with all normal safety precautions due firearms.

4mm RANDZUNDER SHORT, 4mm RANDZUNDER LONG

ALTERNATE NAME(S): 4mm Zimmerstutzen
RELATED CALIBER(S): .22 Rimfire

CARTRIDGE HISTORY
Year of Introduction: 1921
Country of Origin: Germany
Designer(s): G. Genschow Co.
Governing Body: CIP
Present Status: active

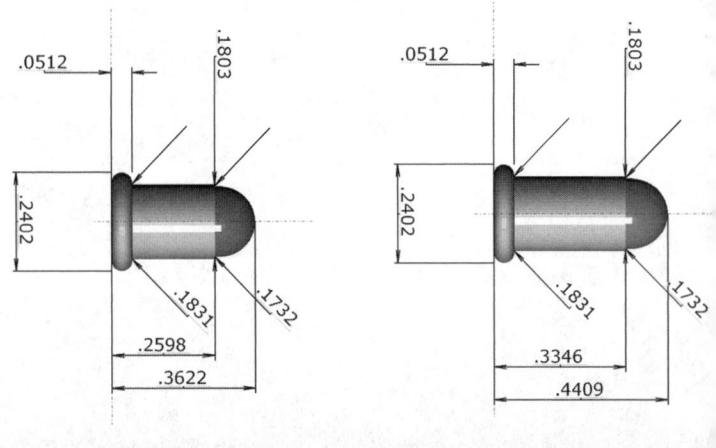

CARTRIDGE DESCRIPTION
Bullet Diameter: .177 in.
Bullet Weight(s): 7 gr.
Rifling Twist Rate: 1 turn in 17.7 in.
Test Barrel Length: 17.3 in.

Case Type: rimmed, straight
Case Material: brass, copper

CARTRIDGE BALLISTICS
Max. Average Breech Pressure: N/A
Max. Horizontal Range: N/A
Max. Vertical Range: N/A

Bullet Weight (gr.)	Bullet Type	Muzzle Velocity (fps)	Muzzle Energy (ft.-lbs.)
7	L-RB	600	5.6

CURRENT MANUFACTURER(S)
RWS (RUAG)

GENERAL COMMENT(S)
Zimmerstutzen ("room shooter") rifles were intended for inexpensive, indoor shooting at home for practice and informal competition. The rifles looked very similar to a .22 rimfire target rifle. Today, air rifles have replaced Zimmerstutzen rifles for indoor home shooting as they are more accurate and cheaper to shoot. Ammunition in 4mm caliber is no longer being made.

TECHNICAL COMMENT(S)
The 4mm rimfire cartridge has no propellant. The priming charge serves that purpose in much the same manner as .22 BB caps. The "bullet" is a lead shotgun pellet. While ballistic performance is puny, it must be remembered that this cartridge is designed for indoor shooting on paper targets, so sound, muzzle velocity and energy must be kept to safe levels. Both a short and a long version of this cartridge exist. Ballistic performance is the same; the long cartridge is easier to handle and load.

.17 AGUILA

ALTERNATE NAME(S): .17 PMC, .17 Precision Made Cartridge
RELATED CALIBER(S): .17 Mach2, .22 Long, .22 Long Rifle

CARTRIDGE HISTORY
Year of Introduction: 2003
Country of Origin: U.S.
Designer(s): PMC
Governing Body: SAAMI
Present Status: Obsolete

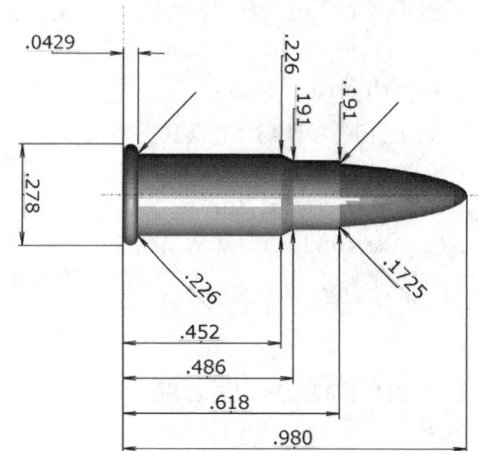

CARTRIDGE DESCRIPTION
Bullet Diameter: .1725 in.
Bullet Weight(s): 20 gr.
Rifling Twist Rate: 1 turn in 8 in.
Test Barrel Length: 24 in.
Case Type: rimmed, necked
Case Material: brass

CARTRIDGE BALLISTICS
Max. Average Breech Pressure: 26,000 psi.
Max. Horizontal Range: 2,100 yds.
Max. Vertical Range: 4,300 ft.

Bullet Weight (gr.)	Bullet Type	Muzzle Velocity (fps)	Muzzle Energy (ft.-lbs.)
20	JSP	1800	144

CURRENT MANUFACTURER(S)
None

GENERAL COMMENT(S)

This cartridge was an effort by PMC/El Dorado Cartridge to offer a high performance rimfire cartridge based on the .22 Long Rifle case necked to .17 caliber. This effort preceded the .17 Mach2 cartridge, but was not a sales success. The ammunition was manufactured by Industrias Tecnos in Mexico who also sold ammunition in this caliber as the .17 Aguila. The .17 PMC/.17 Aguila became obsolete with the introduction of the .17 Mach2. It is a classic case of the innovator being unable to gain critical acceptance in the market for their new product only to have competitors introduce a similar product to wide acclaim and market acceptance.

TECHNICAL COMMENT(S)

The .17 PMC/.17 Aguila cartridge is slightly shorter with a shallower neck than the .17 Mach2. The .17 PMC/.17 Aguila should not be fired in the .17 Mach2 chamber, doing so is a dangerous combination that should be avoided. Muzzle velocity is also lower than the .17 Mach2 due to the heavier bullet. Other ballistic performance parameters are similar to the .17 Mach2.

5mm REMINGTON RIMFIRE MAGNUM

ALTERNATE NAME(S): 5mm RRM, 5mm Remington Magnum
RELATED CALIBER(S): .25 Stevens, Hilti Power Tool Ctg.

CARTRIDGE HISTORY

Year of Introduction: 1970
Country of Origin: U.S.
Designer(s): Remington Arms Company
Governing Body: SAAMI
Present Status: obsolete

CARTRIDGE DESCRIPTION

Bullet Diameter: .2045 in.
Bullet Weight(s): 38 gr.
Rifling Twist Rate: N/A
Test Barrel Length: 24 in.
Case Type: rimmed, necked
Case Material: brass

CARTRIDGE BALLISTICS

Max. Average Breech Pressure: 28,000 psi.
Max. Horizontal Range: 3,500 yds.
Max. Vertical Range: 6,500 ft.

Bullet Weight (gr.)	Bullet Type	Muzzle Velocity (fps)	Muzzle Energy (ft.-lbs.)
38	JHP	2,105	374

CURRENT MANUFACTURER(S)

CBC

GENERAL COMMENT(S)

The 5mm Remington Rimfire Magnum was Remington's answer to the .22 Winchester Magnum Rimfire introduced at the same time. The .22 WMR caught on, albeit slowly, while the 5mm Remington Rimfire Magnum did not. The Remington was the more innovative of the two and offered superior ballistic performance. Why it did not catch on is something of a mystery. Perhaps the 5mm Remington Rimfire Magnum was before its time. Some 35 years later, a similar concept in the .17 HRM was to prove a commercial success.

TECHNICAL COMMENT(S)

The 5mm Remington Rimfire Magnum is based on a power tool cartridge case that Remington was making for Hilti at the time. The 26mm long case was the longest in the Hilti product line and similar in dimensions to the old .25 Stevens cartridge case. Unlike the .22 WMR, the large base diameter of the 5mm Remington Rimfire Magnum required a major redesign of existing rimfire rifles. In addition, bullets and rifle barrels in 5mm caliber were hard to get. As a result, the new 5mm RRM cartridge did not receive the commercial support from other manufacturers of rifles and ammunition that the .22 WMR did. A few years later, Hilti discontinued the 26mm long power tool cartridge and the case became an obsolete orphan, sealing its fate. This technical heritage remains the main obstacle to manufacturing the cartridge until CBC offered it.

.22 EXTRA LONG

ALTERNATE NAME(S): none
RELATED CALIBER(S): .22 Short, .22 Long, .22 Long Rifle

CARTRIDGE HISTORY
Year of Introduction: circs 1880
Country of Origin: U.S.
Designer(s): N/A
Governing Body: SAAMI
Present Status: obsolete

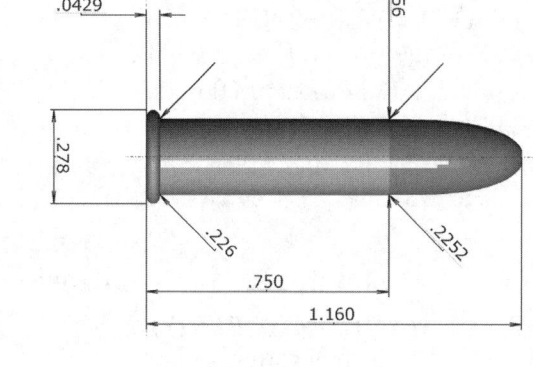

CARTRIDGE DESCRIPTION
Bullet Diameter: .225 in.
Bullet Weight(s): 40 gr.
Rifling Twist Rate: 1 turn in 16 in.
Test Barrel Length: 24 in.
Case Type: rimmed, straight
Case Material: brass

CARTRIDGE BALLISTICS
Max. Average Breech Pressure: N/A
Max. Horizontal Range: 1,600 yds.
Max. Vertical Range: 3,500 ft.

Bullet Weight (gr.)	Bullet Type	Muzzle Velocity (fps)	Muzzle Energy (ft.-lbs.)
40	L-RN	1050	97

CURRENT MANUFACTURER(S)
None

GENERAL COMMENT(S)
When it was introduced in the 1880s, the .22 Extra Long was intended as a more powerful cartridge than the .22 Long Rifle. However, shooters found that in the field, any ballistic advantage of the .22 Extra Long over the .22 Long Rifle proved minor. However, the .22 Extra Long continued in production as demand was maintained by the large number of rifles and revolvers made for it.

TECHNICAL COMMENT(S)
The .22 Extra Long cartridge case could hold more black powder than the shorter .22 Long Rifle case, although both cartridges used the same 40 grain bullet. The additional powder in the .22 Extra Long added about 100 fps higher muzzle velocity which proved insignificant to most shooters. The .22 Extra Long made the transition to smokeless powder and was listed in domestic ammunition manufacturers' catalogs until 1935. As modern, high velocity .22 Long Rifle ammunition developed in the 1930s offered the same ballistic performance as the .22 Extra Long, this caliber lost its reason to be and faded into history.

.22 WINCHESTER AUTOMATIC

ALTERNATE NAME(S): .22 Win. Auto
RELATED CALIBER(S): none

CARTRIDGE HISTORY
Year of Introduction: circa 1903
Country of Origin: U.S.
Designer(s): Winchester
Governing Body: SAAMI
Present Status: obsolete

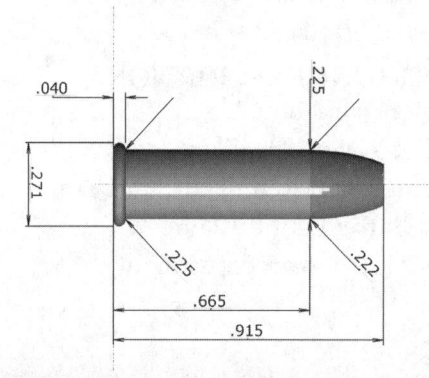

CARTRIDGE DESCRIPTION
Bullet Diameter: .222 in.

Bullet Weight(s): 45 gr.

Rifling Twist Rate: 1 turn in 16 in.

Test Barrel Length: 24 in.

Case Type: rimmed, straight

Case Material: brass

CARTRIDGE BALLISTICS

Max. Average Breech Pressure: 23,000 psi.

Max. Horizontal Range: 1,700 yds.

Max. Vertical Range: 3,900 ft.

Bullet Weight (gr.)	Bullet Type	Muzzle Velocity (fps)	Muzzle Energy (ft.-lbs.)
45	L-FN	880	77
45	L-FN	1035	107

CURRENT MANUFACTURER(S)

CBC (Old Western Scrounger)

GENERAL COMMENT(S)

The original purpose for this cartridge was to prevent the use of black powder ammunition which would quickly foul the action of semi-automatic rifles. To this end, the .22 Winchester Automatic cartridge was loaded only with smokeless propellant. However, such exclusivity was expensive and .22 Winchester Automatic ammunition always cost more than .22 Long Rifle ammunition. As .22 Long Rifle ammunition loaded with smokeless propellants began to dominate the rimfire market, by 1935 the .22 Winchester Automatic cartridge had lost any reason for existence. It soldiered on based on the large number of existing guns chambered for it until the 1970s when Winchester finally dropped it. However, the .22 Winchester Automatic was not yet ready for the historical scrap heap. In 2003, Old Western Scrounger (now owned by Navy Arms) imported shooting quantities of new ammunition in this caliber.

TECHNICAL COMMENT(S)

A unique feature of this cartridge was the .222 inch diameter, inside lubricated bullet. Unlike the .22 Long Rifle, the bullet of the .22 Winchester Automatic was smaller than the outside case diameter. Muzzle velocity of the original .22 Win. Automatic loading was an anemic 880 fps. Later, it was increased to a more respectable 1,055 fps. Still, field performance was no better than the .22 Long Rifle. .22 Winchester Automatic ammunition cannot be fired in firearms chambered for .22 Long Rifle. Conversely, .22 Long Rifle ammunition cannot be used in firearms chambered for the .22 Win. Automatic. A similar round, the .22 Remington Automatic is also not interchangeable with either the .22 L.R. or the .22 Win. Auto.

.22 REMINGTON AUTOMATIC

ALTERNATE NAME(S): .22 Rem. Automatic, .22 Rem. Auto.

RELATED CALIBER(S): none

CARTRIDGE HISTORY

Year of Introduction: 1914

Country of Origin: U.S.

Designer(s): Remington Arms Company

Governing Body: SAAMI

Present Status: obsolete

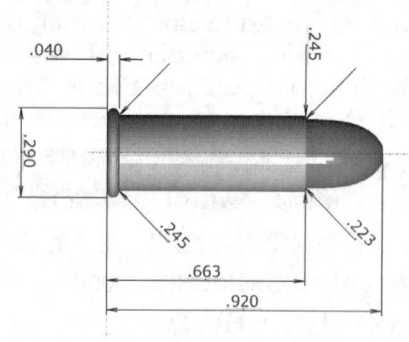

CARTRIDGE DESCRIPTION

Bullet Diameter: .223 in.

Bullet Weight(s): 45 gr.

Rifling Twist Rate: 1 turn in 16 in.

Test Barrel Length: 24 in.

Case Type: rimmed, straight

Case Material: brass

CARTRIDGE BALLISTICS
Max. Average Breech Pressure: 23,000 psi.
Max. Horizontal Range: 1,500 yds.
Max. Vertical Range: 3,300 ft.

Bullet Weight (gr.)	Bullet Type	Muzzle Velocity (fps)	Muzzle Energy (ft.-lbs.)
45	L-RN/HP	950	89

CURRENT MANUFACTURER(S)
None

GENERAL COMMENT(S)
The .22 Remington Automatic was introduced in 1914 for the same reason as the .22 Winchester Automatic, namely to prevent use of black powder cartridges in semi-automatic rifles. This concept did not prove successful as .22 Long Rifle ammunition loaded with smokeless propellants came to dominate the market thus eliminating any need for such calibers. By 1928, the .22 Remington Automatic was obsolete.

TECHNICAL COMMENT(S)
In similar manner to its rival the .22 Winchester Automatic, the .22 Remington Automatic used an inside lubricated bullet of smaller diameter than the outside diameter of the cartridge case. Unlike the Winchester cartridge loaded with a flat nose bullet, the .22 Remington Automatic was loaded with a round nose bullet at a slightly higher muzzle velocity of 950 fps. Both solid and hollow point types were offered. The .22 Remington Automatic is a unique design that is not interchangeable with any other rimfire cartridge including the .22 Winchester Automatic.

.25 STEVENS SHORT, .25 STEVENS

ALTERNATE NAME(S): .25 Stevens Rimfire, .25 Stevens Rimfire Short
RELATED CALIBER(S): none

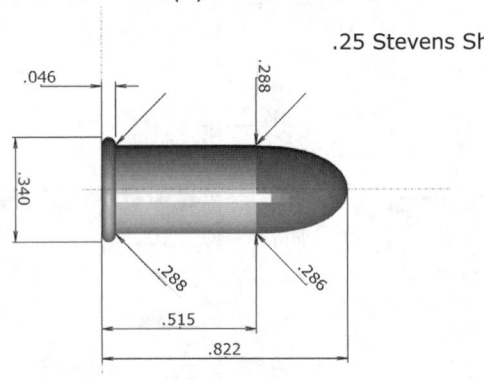

.25 Stevens Short

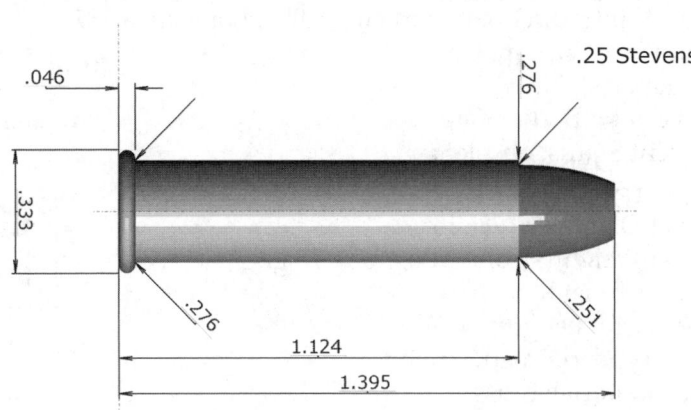

.25 Stevens

CARTRIDGE HISTORY
Year of Introduction: 1900 (Short 1902)
Country of Origin: U.S.
Designer(s): Peters Cartridge Co.
Governing Body: SAAMI
Present Status: obsolete

CARTRIDGE DESCRIPTION
Bullet Diameter: .251 in.
Bullet Weight(s): 65 (Short 43) gr.
Rifling Twist Rate: N/A
Test Barrel Length: 24 in.
Case Type: rimmed, straight
Case Material: brass

CARTRIDGE BALLISTICS
Max. Average Breech Pressure: 23,000 psi.
Max. Horizontal Range: 1,700 yds.
Max. Vertical Range: 3,800 ft.

Bullet Weight (gr.)	Bullet Type	Muzzle Velocity (fps)	Muzzle Energy (ft.-lbs.)
65 (Short)	L-FN	935	126
65	L-FN	1,115	179

CURRENT MANUFACTURER(S)
None

GENERAL COMMENT(S)
The .25 Stevens was a popular cartridge for hunting small game and pests as it had more power than the .22 Long Rifle. Firearms in this caliber were made from 1900 until about 1935. After World War II, production of rifles or ammunition in this caliber was not resumed. The .25 Stevens Short was intended as a lower powered (and lower priced) version of the .25 Stevens to compete with the .22 Short. The concept did not catch on and the .25 Short was never popular. Commercial production of both calibers was discontinued in 1942.

TECHNICAL COMMENT(S)
Originally a black powder cartridge, the .25 Stevens made the transition to smokeless propellants. By modern standards, the ballistic performance of the .25 Stevens cartridge is mediocre and the bullet trajectory high. However, at ranges of less than 100 yards, the .25 Stevens is good field cartridge. In the 1930s, many shooters felt the .25 Stevens had considerable remaining potential for increased muzzle velocity using new smokeless propellants. In response to this, Remington began working on a new rimfire cartridge reportedly called the .267 Remington Rimfire loaded with a 67 grain bullet at a muzzle velocity of 1,400 fps. World War II intervened and all work on the .267 Remington Rimfire ceased in 1942.

.30 SHORT, .30 LONG

ALTERNATE NAME(S): .30 RF Short, .30 RF Long
RELATED CALIBER(S): none, Short developed first

CARTRIDGE HISTORY
Year of Introduction: Short circa 1860, Long circa 1873
Country of Origin: U.S.
Designer(s): N/A
Governing Body: none
Present Status: obsolete

CARTRIDGE DESCRIPTION
Bullet Diameter: .286 in.
Bullet Weight(s): Short 58, Long 75 gr.
Rifling Twist Rate: N/A
Test Barrel Length: N/A
Case Type: rimmed, straight
Case Material: brass

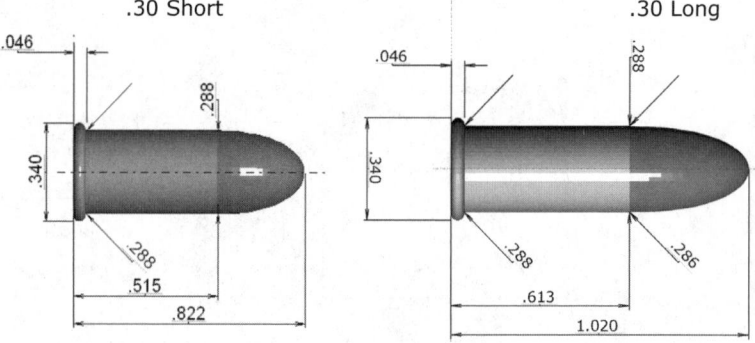

CARTRIDGE BALLISTICS
Max. Average Breech Pressure: 23,000 psi.
Max. Horizontal Range: 1,100 yds.
Max. Vertical Range: 2,400 ft.

Bullet Weight (gr.)	Bullet Type	Muzzle Velocity (fps)	Muzzle Energy (ft.-lbs.)
58 (Short)	L-RN	700	62
75 (Long)	L-RN	750	81

CURRENT MANUFACTURER(S)
None

GENERAL COMMENT(S)
Typically, these two black powder cartridges were chambered in cheap revolvers which kept them in production even though more powerful calibers were available. Both had become obsolete by 1920.

TECHNICAL COMMENT(S)
Even by the low ballistic expectations of the late 19th century, both of these cartridges were considered underpowered and nearly useless for personal defense.

.32 EXTRA SHORT, .32 SHORT, .32 LONG, .32 LONG RIFLE, .32 EXTRA LONG

ALTERNATE NAME(S): .32 Rimfire Short and etc.
RELATED CALIBER(S): to each other, the .32 Short was the first

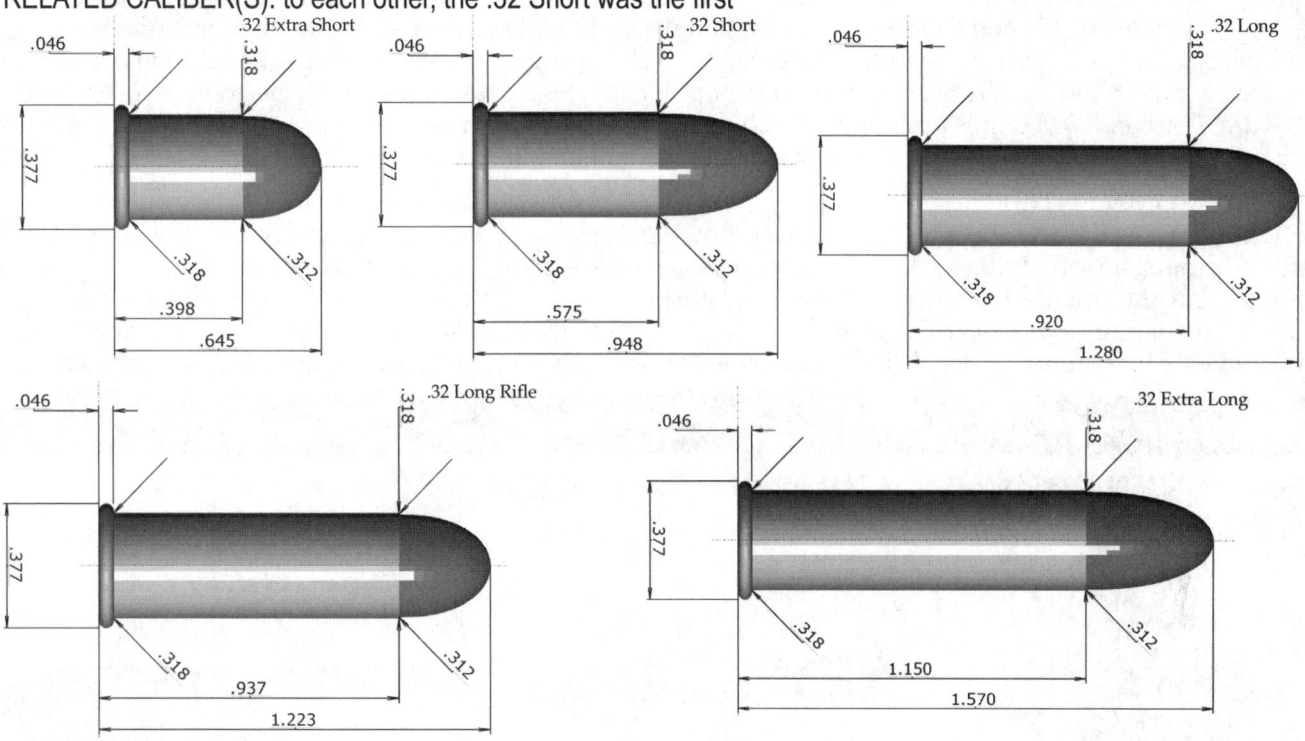

CARTRIDGE HISTORY

Year of Introduction: .32 Extra Short 1871, .32 Short 1860, .32 Long 1861, .32 Long Rifle 1900, .32 Extra Long 1875
Country of Origin: U.S.
Designer(s): Smith & Wesson (.32 Short)
Governing Body: SAAMI
Present Status: obsolete

CARTRIDGE DESCRIPTION

Bullet Diameter: .32 Long Rifle .312 in., remainder .316 in.
Bullet Weight(s): 54-90 gr.
Rifling Twist Rate: N/A
Test Barrel Length: N/A
Case Type: rimmed, straight
Case Material: brass

CARTRIDGE BALLISTICS

Max. Average Breech Pressure: N/A
Max. Horizontal Range: 1,800 yds.
Max. Vertical Range: 3,600 ft.

Bullet Weight (gr.)	Bullet Type	Muzzle Velocity (fps)	Muzzle Energy (ft.-lbs.)
54 (Extra Short)	L-RN	650	51
80 (Short)	L-RN	935	155
80 (Long)	L-RN	1.030	188
80 (Long Rifle)	L-RN	960	186
90 (Extra Long)	L-RN	1,050	221

CURRENT MANUFACTURER(S)
None

GENERAL COMMENT(S)
The .32 Short was the first cartridge of this series appearing in 1860. It was based on the Smith & Wesson patent that also served as the basis for the .22 Short. The .32 Short, .32 Extra Short and .32 Long were originally designed for revolvers while the .32 Long Rifle and .32 Extra Long were intended for rifles. Many rifles and revolvers were made in these calibers by nearly every firearms maker. Many of these may still be encountered today. In the late 1800s, the .32 Extra Short and .32 Short rimfire were popular choices for hunting small game and pests. Production of .32 Extra Short and .32 Long Rifle ended in 1920. However, the .32 Short and .32 Long remained in production until the 1970s. In 1990, Navy Arms imported new ammunition in both calibers made in Brazil by CBC.

TECHNICAL COMMENT(S)
The .32 rimfire family delete began life as black powder cartridges, but successfully made the transition to smokeless propellants. In doing so, their ballistic performance was only maintained, not improved. They never benefited from the intense ballistic development lavished on the .22 Long Rifle. By modern standards, the ballistic performance of these cartridges must be judged inadequate. However, in their day, they offered high perceived value by giving reasonable ballistic performance at low cost. Seen in this light, they were successful.

.38 SHORT, .38 LONG, .38 EXTRA LONG

ALTERNATE NAME(S): .38 Rimfire Short, .38 Rimfire Long, .38 Rimfire Extra Long
RELATED CALIBER(S): to each other

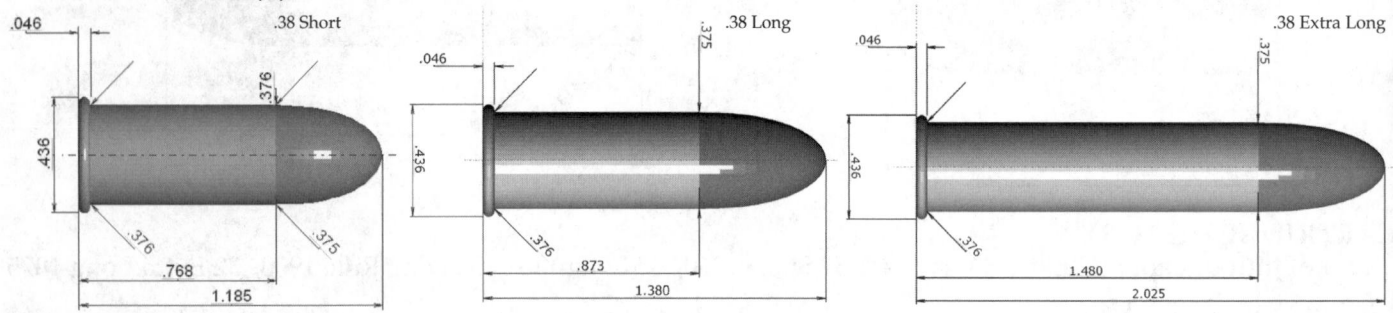

CARTRIDGE HISTORY
Year of Introduction: circa 1860, Extra Long 1870
Country of Origin: U.S.
Designer(s): N/A
Governing Body: SAAMI
Present Status: obsolete

CARTRIDGE DESCRIPTION
Bullet Diameter: .375 in.
Bullet Weight(s): 125-150 gr.
Rifling Twist Rate: 1 turn in 18 3/4 in.
Test Barrel Length: N/A
Case Type: rimmed, straight
Case Material: brass

CARTRIDGE BALLISTICS
Max. Average Breech Pressure: N/A
Max. Horizontal Range: 1,500 yds.
Max. Vertical Range: 3,300 ft.
(Data for revolvers)

Bullet Weight (gr.)	Bullet Type	Muzzle Velocity (fps)	Muzzle Energy (ft.-lbs.)
125 (Short)	L-RN	725	150
150 (Long)	L-RN	750	190
150 (Extra Long)	L-RN	1,250	526

CURRENT MANUFACTURER(S)
None

GENERAL COMMENT(S)
Both the .38 Short and .38 Long are based on the same Smith & Wesson rimfire patents that covered the .22 Short. They were introduced just before the Civil War and gained popularity during that conflict. A major factor in the popularity of these cartridges was in rimfire conversions of .38 caliber cap-and-ball revolvers. Later, both were chambered in new revolvers of many brands and types. After the Civil War, rifles were also made in .38 Long caliber, however, the .38 Short remained a revolver cartridge. Although the .38 Long was discontinued in 1920, the .38 Short survived until 1940. Introduced in 1870 as a rifle cartridge, the .38 Extra Long could not compete with reloadable centerfire cartridges of the same caliber and was retired by 1918.

TECHNICAL COMMENT(S)
As revolver cartridges, the .38 Short and .38 Long offered marginal performance by modern standards. However, they did match the performance of the cap-and-ball revolvers of their era of which many were converted to .32 Short. This led to their continued existence as chamberings for new revolvers. Both retained the 1 turn in 18 3/4″ rifling twist of the .38 cap-and-ball revolvers. Firearms manufacturers continue using this rifling twist rate in .38 Special and .357 Magnum revolvers to this day. However, few know why.

.41 SHORT, .41 LONG

ALTERNATE NAME(S): .41 Rimfire Short, .41 Rimfire Long
RELATED CALIBER(S): none

CARTRIDGE HISTORY
Year of Introduction: Short 1863, Long 1873
Country of Origin: U.S.
Designer(s): N/A
Governing Body: SAAMI
Present Status: obsolete

CARTRIDGE DESCRIPTION
Bullet Diameter: .405 in.
Bullet Weight(s): Short 130, Long 163 gr.
Rifling Twist Rate: N/A
Test Barrel Length: N/A
Case Type: rimmed, straight
Case Material: brass

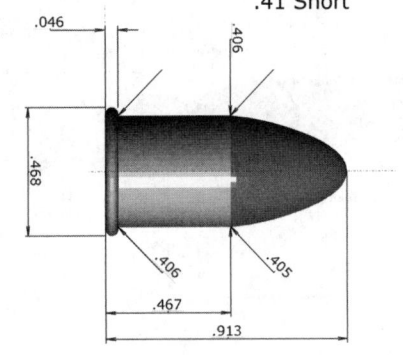

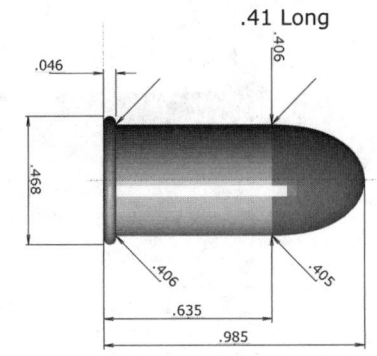

CARTRIDGE BALLISTICS
Max. Average Breech Pressure: N/A
Max. Horizontal Range: 1,700 yds.
Max. Vertical Range: 3,800 ft.

Bullet Weight (gr.)	Bullet Type	Muzzle Velocity (fps)	Muzzle Energy (ft.-lbs.)
130 (Short)	L-RN	425	52
163 (Long)	L-RN	700	180

CURRENT MANUFACTURER(S)
None

GENERAL COMMENT(S)
While the .41 Long remains obscure, the .41 Short is undeservedly well known. If it were not for the Colt, Remington

and other brands of derringers that were chambered for it, the .41 Short would long ago have been consigned to the historical scrap heap of useless cartridges. Regardless of its anemic ballistics, the .41 Short has retained its popularity to this day based on the derringers. At one time or another, all major ammunition manufacturers have offered the .41 Short. Although considered obsolete since before World War II, small runs of ammunition in this caliber have been made by CBC on special order into the 1980s. The .41 Long became obsolete by 1920.

TECHNICAL COMMENT(S)

Anemic is the best word to describe the ballistics of the .41 Short. Indeed it has such poor ballistics that it can be said to be nothing more than a morale builder. It is outclassed in striking energy by even the .22 Short! While the .41 Short is capable of inflicting a serious wound at close ranges in dangerous situations, it cannot be recommended for personal defense and is useless for any type of hunting or even pest control. The amazing thing is that it has lasted as long as it has.

.44 SHORT, .44 LONG, .44 EXTRA LONG, .44 HENRY FLAT

ALTERNATE NAME(S): .44 Rimfire Short, .44 Rimfire Long, .44 Rimfire Extra Long Ballard, .44 Henry
RELATED CALIBER(S): original cartridge was .44 Henry Flat

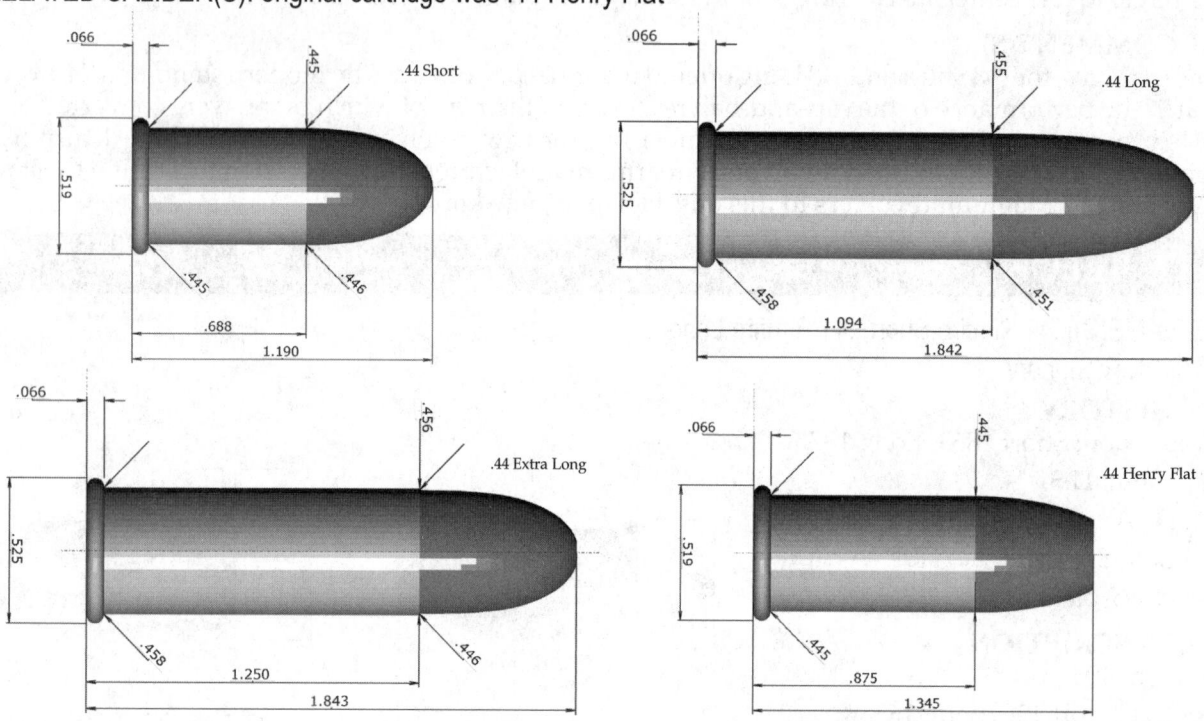

CARTRIDGE HISTORY

Year of Introduction: Henry circa 1860, Short 1870, Long 1860, Extra Long 1869
Country of Origin: U.S.
Designer(s): B. Tyler Henry
Governing Body: SAAMI
Present Status: obsolete

CARTRIDGE DESCRIPTION

Bullet Diameter: Short, Extra Long, and Henry Flat .446 in., Long .451 in.
Bullet Weight(s): 200-220 gr.
Rifling Twist Rate: N/A
Test Barrel Length: N/A
Case Type: rimmed, straight
Case Material: brass

CARTRIDGE BALLISTICS

Max. Average Breech Pressure: N/A
Max. Horizontal Range: 1,800 yds.
Max. Vertical Range: 4,200 ft.

Bullet Weight (gr.)	Bullet Type	Muzzle Velocity (fps)	Muzzle Energy (ft.-lbs.)
200 (Short)	L-RN	500	112
220 (Long)	L-RN	825	332
220 (Extra Long)	L-RN	1,250	763
200 (Henry)	L-FN	1,125	568

CURRENT MANUFACTURER(S)

None

GENERAL COMMENT(S)

Despite its humble appearance, the .44 Henry is historically significant as it was one of the first self-contained metallic cartridges as well as the first cartridge to be chambered in the Henry lever-action rifle in 1860. Following successful, if limited, service in the Civil War, the Henry became the forerunner of the long line of Winchester lever-action rifles. It was the Henry rifle that became the favorite firearm of settlers heading west after the Civil War and the rifle of choice for miners during the California gold rush. As such, the Henry rifle and cartridge enjoy a secure position in U.S. history. Because of its 15 shot magazine capacity, the Henry rifle was called "The rifle you load on Sunday and shoot all week". Production of the .44 Henry cartridge continued until 1934. The .44 Extra Long passed on to obsolescence in 1880 and the .44 Short and Long ceased production in the early 1920s.

TECHNICAL COMMENT(S)

While none of the .44 rimfire cartridges offer outstanding ballistics, they are adequate for hunting small and medium game at close ranges and for personal defense at close ranges. Originally loaded with a pointed bullet, the .44 Henry bullet was changed to a flat nose design in 1863 to provide more "stopping" power. This is the origin of its designation as the .44 Henry Flat. All of the .44 rimfire cartridges began life as black powder designs. The .44 Henry Flat was the only member of the family to successfully make the transition to smokeless powder.

.46 EXTRA SHORT, .46 SHORT, .46 LONG, .46 EXTRA LONG

ALTERNATE NAME(S): .46 Rimfire Extra Short, .46 Rimfire Short, .46 Rimfire Long
RELATED CALIBER(S): to each other

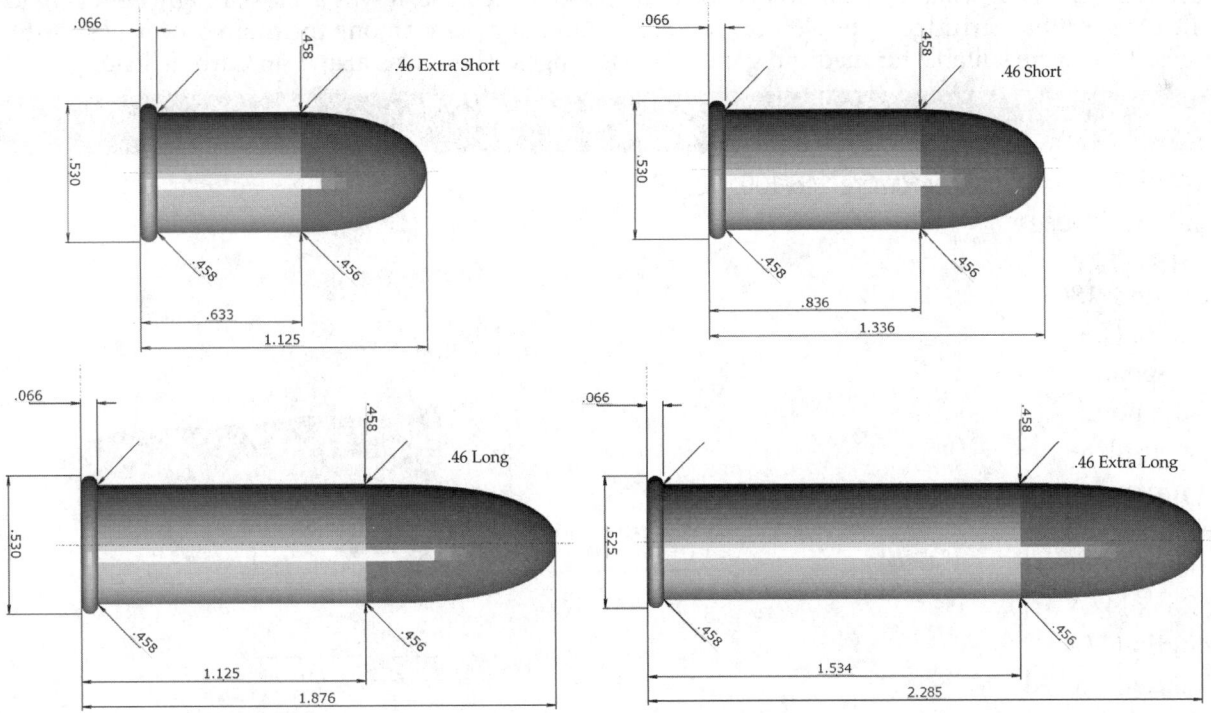

CARTRIDGE HISTORY

Year of Introduction: circa 1870
Country of Origin: U.S.
Designer(s): N/A
Governing Body: SAAMI
Present Status: obsolete

CARTRIDGE DESCRIPTION

Bullet Diameter: .46 Long .454 in., others .456 in.

Bullet Weight(s): .220-305 gr.

Rifling Twist Rate: N/A

Test Barrel Length: N/A

Case Type: rimmed, straight

Case Material: brass

CARTRIDGE BALLISTICS

Max. Average Breech Pressure: N/A

Max. Horizontal Range: 1,800 yds.

Max. Vertical Range: 4,100 ft.

Bullet Weight (gr.)	Bullet Type	Muzzle Velocity (fps)	Muzzle Energy (ft.-lbs.)
220 (Extra Short)	L-RH	650	206
227 (Short)	L-RN	750	274
305 (Long)	L-RN	850	489
305 (Extra Long)	L-RN	1,000	677

CURRENT MANUFACTURER(S)

None

GENERAL COMMENT(S)

While the .46 Extra Short and .46 Short were revolver cartridges (the Short was chambered in the Colt Single Action Army revolver), the .46 Long and .46 Extra Long were chambered only in rifles such as those made by Remington and Ballard. All of the .46 rimfire cartridges were discontinued after World War I. Remington was the only manufacturer of the .46 Extra Long.

TECHNICAL COMMENT(S)

While the .46 Short should be considered a minimal choice for personal defense, it was a substantially better choice than most of the other rimfire cartridges. The .46 Long and .46 Extra Long were among the more powerful sporting rimfire cartridges. They were suitable for medium game at close ranges. There was also a .46 Carbine load.

56-46 SPENCER

ALTERNATE NAME(S): 56-46 Spencer Rimfire, .46/100, No. 46

RELATED CALIBER(S): none

CARTRIDGE HISTORY

Year of Introduction: 1866

Country of Origin: U.S.

Designer(s): C. Spencer

Governing Body: none

Present Status: obsolete

CARTRIDGE DESCRIPTION

Bullet Diameter: .465 in.

Bullet Weight(s): 330 gr.

Rifling Twist Rate: N/A

Test Barrel Length: N/A

Case Type: rimmed, necked

Case Material: brass

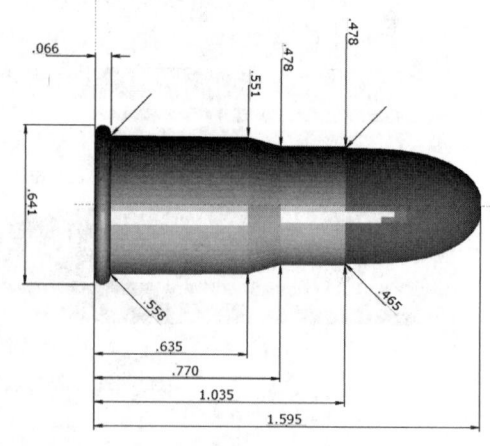

CARTRIDGE BALLISTICS

Max. Average Breech Pressure: N/A

Max. Horizontal Range: 3,200 yds.

Max. Vertical Range: 7,400 ft.

Bullet Weight (gr.)	Bullet Type	Muzzle Velocity (fps)	Muzzle Energy (ft.-lbs.)
330	L-RN	1,210	1,080

CURRENT MANUFACTURER(S)
None

GENERAL COMMENT(S)
This sporting cartridge entered the commercial market in 1866 just after the end of the Civil War. It was chambered in Spencer lever-action rifles until 1872. Remington, Sharps, Peabody, and others made rifles for these cartridges also. Sportsmen of that era who preferred lever-action rifles were drawn to the Spencer caliber because it was among the most powerful rimfire cartridges of that day. By 1880 when centerfire caliber lever-action rifles entered production the 56-46 Spencer faded away. Manufacture of 56-46 Spencer ammunition was discontinued in 1919.

TECHNICAL COMMENT(S)
For hunting medium game at close ranges, the 56-46 Spencer was a popular choice from 1879 until 1890. It was considerably more powerful than most other rimfire cartridges of that era.

56-52 SPENCER RIFLE

ALTERNATE NAME(S): 56-52 Spencer Rimfire
RELATED CALIBER(S): 56-50 Spencer Rimfire, 56-56 Spencer

CARTRIDGE HISTORY
Year of Introduction: 1866
Country of Origin: U.S.
Designer(s): C. Spencer
Governing Body: none
Present Status: obsolete

CARTRIDGE DESCRIPTION
Bullet Diameter: .512 in.
Bullet Weight(s): 340-400 gr.
Rifling Twist Rate: N/A
Test Barrel Length: N/A
Case Type: rimmed, tapered or slightly necked
Case Material: brass

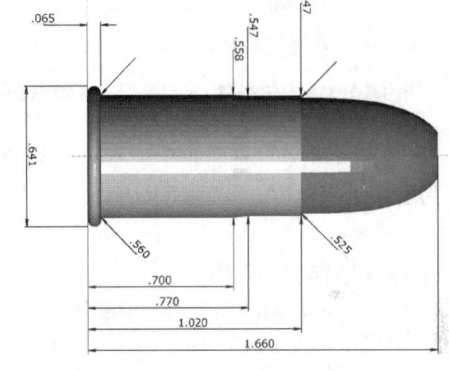

CARTRIDGE BALLISTICS
Max. Average Breech Pressure: N/A
Max. Horizontal Range: 3,300 yds.
Max. Vertical Range: 5,800 ft.

Bullet Weight (gr.)	Bullet Type	Muzzle Velocity (fps)	Muzzle Energy (ft.-lbs.)
386	L-RN	1,200	1,234

CURRENT MANUFACTURER(S)
None

GENERAL COMMENT(S)
Designed by Springfield Armory in 1861, the 56-50 Spencer eventually entered U.S. military service in 1865 after the end of the Civil War. The Model 1865 Spencer Carbine and the 56-50 Spencer cartridge saw extensive military service fighting Indians and taming the West in the late 1860s. Production of 56-50 Spencer ammunition ceased in 1920.

TECHNICAL COMMENT(S)
Christopher Spencer felt the crimp on the 56-50 Spencer cartridge was much too heavy, so he replaced it for sporting applications with the 56-52 that had a shallow bottle neck and a lighter crimp. As many manufacturers omitted the bottle neck, the two cartridges are interchangeable and otherwise indistinguishable. Although effective on medium game at close ranges, most hunters of the day preferred one of the larger, more powerful calibers available in many single-shot rifles.

.58 MILLER

ALTERNATE NAME(S): .585 Springfield, .58 Musket, .58 Allin, .58 Ball
RELATED CALIBER(S): none

CARTRIDGE HISTORY
Year of Introduction: 1864
Country of Origin: U.S.
Designer(s): N/A
Governing Body: none
Present Status: obsolete

CARTRIDGE DESCRIPTION
Bullet Diameter: .585 in.
Bullet Weight(s): 500 gr.
Rifling Twist Rate: N/A
Test Barrel Length: N/A
Case Type: rimmed, straight
Case Material: brass

CARTRIDGE BALLISTICS
Max Average Breech Pressure: N/A
Max. Horizontal Range: 3,400 yds.
Max. Vertical Range: 7,700 ft.

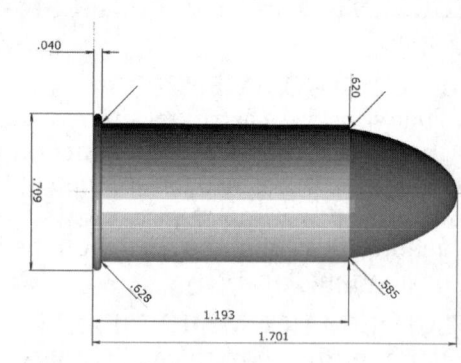

Bullet Weight (gr.)	Bullet Type	Muzzle Velocity (fps)	Muzzle Energy (ft.-lbs.)
500	L-RN	1,150	1,468

CURRENT MANUFACTURER(S)
None

GENERAL COMMENT(S)
This cartridge was developed for the Miller and Allin conversions of the muzzle loading Springfield muskets left over from the Civil War. The concept was not popular, although a large number of conversions were made by government arsenals. Shortly after, most of these conversions were sold on the commercial market at very low prices. Many must have been carried by settlers heading west. This created a demand for .58 Miller ammunition. However, after hard use, the conversions quickly became unserviceable thus contributing to the demise of the cartridge. The .58 Miller cartridge then quickly faded into history and by 1910 it had become only a memory.

TECHNICAL COMMENT(S)
The .58 Miller cartridge is quite capable of taking medium game at close ranges, although the highly curved trajectory is a handicap. Other than musket conversions, no other rifles were made in this caliber.

CHAPTER 81 : MILITARY RIMFIRE - OBSOLETE

CHAPTER 81

For Cartridge Index see Chapter 101. All drawing dimensions are approximate.

Note: No "Primer" data is shown under CARTRIDGE DESCRIPTION in this chapter, as all cartridges have rimfire priming.

From 1855-1870, rimfire designs were the predominant system of self-contained cartridges. As a result, a large number of different rimfire cartridges were developed, ranging from .22- to .58 caliber. The American Civil War provided the stage for the introduction of the first self-contained cartridge (in the form of rimfire) for warfare. It revolutionized military tactics. Although many high ranking officers failed to understand the impact the rimfire cartridge would have on military tactics, individual soldiers and entire units on both sides eagerly acquired rimfire firearms and ammunition by any means possible.

Firepower began to dominate the battlefield and rimfire ammunition and firearms allowed this to be achieved with significantly fewer soldiers. As usual, the soldiers described it best: "rimfire rifles can be loaded on Sunday and shot all week!" Many muzzle loading rifles were converted to fire rimfire ammunition developed specifically for the purpose. In most cases, these efforts were not entirely successful.

After 1875, however, the inherent weakness of its case design and ignition system began to work against the rimfire. Various central ignition systems allowed a stronger cartridge case, higher chamber pressures, and improved ballistic performance. The rimfire could not compete, except in Switzerland, where the .41 Swiss rimfire cartridge soldiered on well into the 1890s.

4.5x26RFmm INTERDYNAMICS

ALTERNATE NAME(S): 4.5x26RFmm , 4.5mm Interdynamics
RELATED CALIBER(S): .22 WMR

CARTRIDGE HISTORY
Year of Introduction: 1978
Country of Origin: Sweden
Designer(s): Interdynamics Forsknings AB
Governing Body: none
Present Status: obsolete

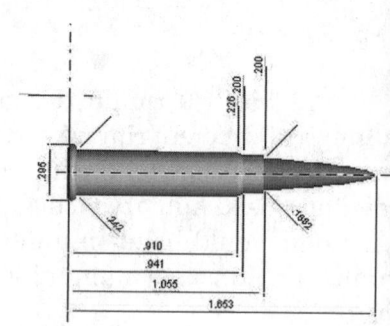

CARTRIDGE DESCRIPTION
Bullet Diameter: .177 in.
Bullet Weight(s): 24.5-30 gr.
Rifling Twist Rate: 1 turn in 7.4 in.
Test Barrel Length: N/A
Case Type: rimmed, necked
Case Material: brass
Primer: rimfire

CARTRIDGE BALLISTICS
Max. Average Breech Pressure: 28,000 psi.
Max. Horizontal Range: 2,850 yds.
Max. Vertical Range: 6,400 ft.

Bullet Weight (gr.)	Bullet Type	Muzzle Velocity (fps)	Muzzle Energy (ft.-lbs.)
24.5	FMJ	3,280	585

CURRENT MANUFACTURER(S)
None

GENERAL COMMENT(S)
Introduced in 1978 for the MKR assault rifle designed by the same company, this cartridge is a unique approach to the small caliber, personal defense weapon or PDW concept in that it is a rimfire cartridge. As such, it is one of the very few rimfire cartridges intended for military applications designed in the last century. While it was never adopted by a military organization, it remains a viable and interesting concept.

TECHNICAL COMMENT(S)
As with most rimfire cartridges, maximum average chamber pressure is limited to 28,000 psi. This limits bullet weight and muzzle velocity. To make up for this, the 4.5 Interdynamics cartridge combines a very low drag bullet to maximize down range velocity and striking energy together with solid copper construction to provide penetration. Various bullet weights up to approximately 30 grains are possible as are different configurations and construction to achieve the desired terminal ballistic effects. A major consideration of such a cartridge would be the low cost as compared to center fire cartridges.

.22 ILARCO

ALTERNATE NAME(S): .22 Short Magnum Rimfire, .22 Illinois Arms Company
RELATED CALIBER(S): .22 WMR

CARTRIDGE HISTORY
Year of Introduction: 1987
Country of Origin: U.S.
Designer(s): Winchester
Governing Body: none
Present Status: obsolete

CARTRIDGE DESCRIPTION
Bullet Diameter: .224 in.
Bullet Weight(s): 40 gr.
Rifling Twist Rate: 1 turn in 16 in.
Test Barrel Length: 24 in.
Case Type: rimmed, straight
Case Material: brass

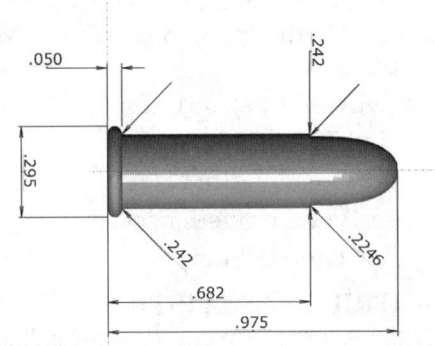

CARTRIDGE BALLISTICS
Max. Average Breech Pressure: 28,000 psi.
Max. Horizontal Range: 1,715 yds.
Max. Vertical Range: 3,860 ft.

Bullet Weight (gr.)	Bullet Type	Muzzle Velocity (fps)	Muzzle Energy (ft.-lbs.)
40	FMJ-RN	1,380	168

CURRENT MANUFACTURER(S)
None

GENERAL COMMENT(S)
When Illinois Arms Co. brought out their .22 Long Rifle caliber Model 180 rifle, they soon found that the outside lubricated bullets on these cartridges picked up and held debris that caused malfunctions in their rifle and its 165-round drum magazine. Something had to be done about this problem. There were no easy solutions. As the action of the Model 180 had been designed for the .22 Long Rifle cartridge, it was too short for the .22 Winchester Magnum Rimfire cartridge with its jacketed bullet. Winchester offered a solution, a short .22 WMR cartridge with a jacketed bullet.

TECHNICAL COMMENT(S)
Beginning with the standard .22 WMR cartridge case, Winchester shortened the case so that its overall loaded cartridge length was approximately .975 inches, also the overall length of the .22 Long Rifle cartridge. The new cartridge, called the .22 ILARCO, would feed through Model 180 rifles and magazines and the full metal jacket would not pick up or hold debris. Winchester loaded experimental lots of .22 ILARCO ammunition. However, shortly after they did so, Illinois Arms Co. was sold and work on the .22 ILARCO cartridge abandoned.

10.4x38Rmm SWISS M1867 AND M1867-71/78

ALTERNATE NAME(S): .41 Swiss
RELATED CALIBER(S): 10.4x38Rmm centerfire

CARTRIDGE HISTORY
Year of Introduction: 1867
Country of Origin: Switzerland
Designer(s): N/A
Governing Body: Swiss Army
Present Status: obsolete

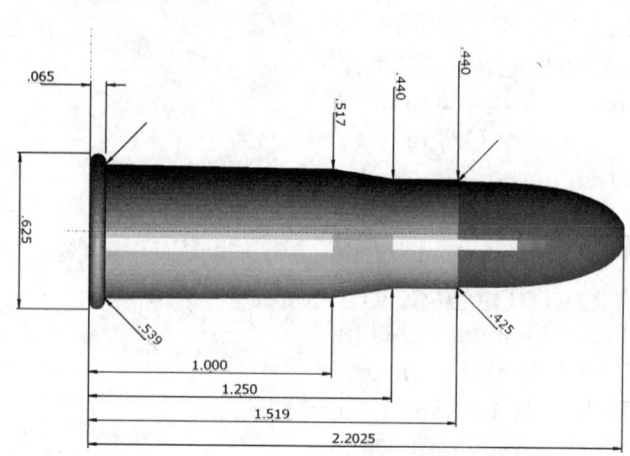

CARTRIDGE DESCRIPTION
Bullet Diameter: M1867 .425 in.; M1871/78 .419 in. plus paper patch
Bullet Weight(s): 334 gr.
Rifling Twist Rate: N/A
Test Barrel Length: N/A
Case Type: rimmed, necked
Case Material: brass

CARTRIDGE BALLISTICS
Max. Average Breech Pressure: 20,000 psi.
Max. Horizontal Range: 3,800 yds.
Max. Vertical Range: 8,000 ft.

Bullet Weight (gr.)	Bullet Type	Muzzle Velocity (fps)	Muzzle Energy (ft.-lbs.)
313	L-RN	1,425	1,401

CURRENT MANUFACTURER(S)
None

GENERAL COMMENT(S)
From 1869 through 1889 the 10.4x38Rmm was the standard military cartridge for the Swiss Army. It remains one of the few rimfire cartridges adopted for official military service. Many surplus, Swiss Vetterli rifles in this caliber were sold in the U.S. prompting a demand for ammunition in this caliber. Domestic manufacturers responded by offering .41 Swiss ammunition until 1942. Always ready to appreciate a bargin when they see one, American sportsman soon found the .41 Swiss cartridge to be reasonably effective on deer and other medium game at close ranges. When production of .41 Swiss ammunition was not resumed by domestic manufacturers after World War II, most of the Swiss Vetterli rifles became wall decorations for lack of ammunition.

TECHNICAL COMMENT(S)
The original bullet was a plain lead round nose design of .425" dia. In 1871 and again in 1878, the bullet was improved by reducing the diameter to .419" and adding a paper patch to bring the diameter up to .425". Jacketed bullets were developed later as well. Early 10.4x38Rmm caliber ammunition was loaded with black powder. Later ammunition was loaded with semi-smokeless: all .41 Swiss caliber ammunition made in the U.S. was loaded with smokeless propellant. Although replaced in Swiss military service by the centerfire 7.5x55mm Swiss cartridge in 1890, the rimfire 10.4x38Rmm cartridge continued to serve in Swiss reserve organizations until well into the 20th century.

56-50 SPENCER CARBINE

ALTERNATE NAME(S): 56-50 Spencer Rimfire
RELATED CALIBER(S): 56-56 Spencer, 56-52 Spencer Rimfire

CARTRIDGE HISTORY
Year of Introduction: 1861
Country of Origin: U.S.
Designer(s): C. Spencer
Governing Body: none
Present Status: obsolete

CARTRIDGE DESCRIPTION
Bullet Diameter: .512 in.
Bullet Weight(s): 350 gr.
Rifling Twist Rate: N/A
Test Barrel Length: N/A
Case Type: rimmed, tapered or slightly necked
Case Material: brass

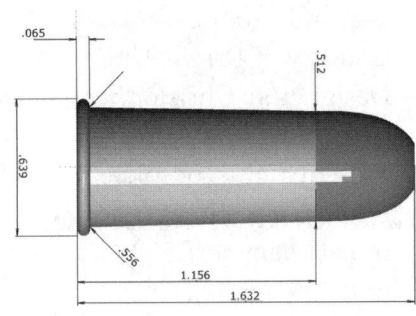

CARTRIDGE BALLISTICS
Max. Average Breech Pressure: N/A
Max. Horizontal Range: 3,300 yds.
Max. Vertical Range: 5,800 ft.

Bullet Weight (gr.)	Bullet Type	Muzzle Velocity (fps)	Muzzle Energy (ft.-lbs.)
350	L-RN	1,230	1,175

CURRENT MANUFACTURER(S)
None

GENERAL COMMENT(S)
Designed by Springfield Armory in 1861, the 56-50 Spencer eventually entered U.S. military service in 1865 after the end of the Civil War. The Model 1865 Spencer Carbine and the 56-50 Spencer cartridge saw extensive military service fighting Indians and taming the West in the late 1860s. Production of 56-50 Spencer ammunition ceased in 1920.

TECHNICAL COMMENT(S)
Christopher Spencer felt the crimp on the 56-50 Spencer cartridge was much too heavy, so he replaced it for sporting applications with the 56-52 that had a shallow bottle neck and a lighter crimp. As many manufacturers omitted the bottle neck, the two cartridges are interchangeable and otherwise indistinguishable. Although effective on medium game at close ranges, most hunters of the day preferred one of the larger, more powerful calibers available in many single-shot rifles.

56-56 SPENCER

ALTERNATE NAME(S): none
RELATED CALIBER(S): 56-46 Spencer, 56-50 Spencer, 56-52 Spencer

CARTRIDGE HISTORY
Year of Introduction: 1860
Country of Origin: U.S.
Designer(s): Christopher Spencer
Governing Body: none
Present Status: obsolete

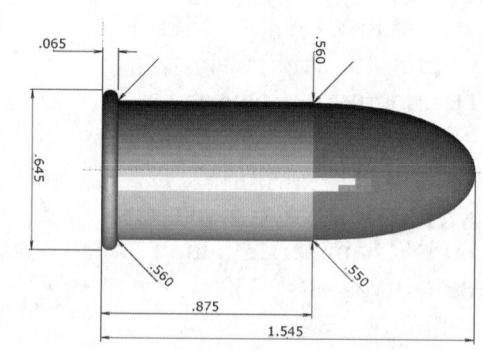

CARTRIDGE DESCRIPTION
Bullet Diameter: .550 in.
Bullet Weight(s): 350 gr.
Rifling Twist Rate: N/A
Test Barrel Length: N/A
Case Type: rimmed, necked
Case Material: brass

CARTRIDGE BALLISTICS
Max. Average Breech Pressure: N/A
Max. Horizontal Range: 3,300 yds.
Max. Vertical Range: 5,800 ft.

Bullet Weight (gr.)	Bullet Type	Muzzle Velocity (fps)	Muzzle Energy (ft.-lbs.)
350	L-RN	1,200	1,119

CURRENT MANUFACTURER(S)
None

GENERAL COMMENT(S)
This cartridge is the original designed by Christopher Spencer. It saw extensive U.S. military service during the Civil War after President Lincoln personally test fired the Spencer rifle and ammunition. Production finally ceased in 1920.

TECHNICAL COMMENT(S)
As a military cartridge, the 56-56 Spencer was a success. As a hunting cartridge, it was quite capable of taking medium size game at close range.

SECTION XIII – SHOTSHELL PROFILES
CHAPTER 82 : SPORTING SHOTSHELL - CURRENT

CHAPTER 82

For Cartridge Index see Chapter 101. All drawing dimensions are approximate.

Technical development of shotshells has always been driven by materials. Monolithic cases of solid metal (brass, zinc, or steel) and built up cases of paper with a brass head were the norm until the early 1960s. Metal shells were expensive, hard to close, and required over-sized wad columns. Built up paper shotshells frequently swelled as they absorbed moisture and offered a very short reloading life. Efforts to remedy these shortcomings met with limited success. Clearly, something better was needed.

Something better came along in the early 1960s in the form of extruded, high density polyethylene plastic tubing. It was cheap, strong, and easy to manufacture. Shotshell makers scrambled to incorporate this new material into their shotshells and by 1970, plastic had replaced paper and metal shotshells in all but a few specialized applications. However, solvents in some plastics attacked brass heads, so manufacturers switched to brass-plated steel heads, which were stronger and cheaper as well as impervious to attack by solvents.

Two types of plastic shotshells were developed—a monolithic tube of drawn plastic with an integral base and separate brass head, and a built-up shell using an extruded plastic tube and a paper, plastic, or composite base wad with a brass-plated steel head. Although they were more expensive than built-up shells, drawn shells were preferred by target shooters for their long reloading life. On the other hand, the less-expensive built-up shell type became the norm for hunting shotshells. Such was the case for approximately 20 years until the drawn plastic shell became prohibitively expensive and was replaced by built-up designs in the early 1990s.

From the beginning of plastic shotshell manufacture, the holy grail of shotshell design has been a monolithic shotshell molded of high density plastic with no metal head. Many have tried; none have succeeded. While a molded shotshell works well enough in break-open and pump-action shotguns, their plastic rims cannot withstand the violent extraction of semi-automatic shotguns. Clearly, much work remains to be done on molded shotshells.

Perhaps plastic's greatest contribution to shotshell design is in wad construction and manufacture. Plastic is nearly ideal for such applications; it is lightweight, cheap, tough, and moldable. With careful design, the shot charge can be cushioned on acceleration and protected from scrubbing on bore surfaces during its travel down the barrel. Plastic wads seal propellant gases far better than the older card and fiber cushion wads and fall cleanly away on exit from the muzzle. It is no exaggeration to say that plastic wad columns have revolutionized wad design and performance.

Recent increases in the cost of plastics, brass, lead, labor, and transport have forced significant increases in shotshell manufacturing costs that are certain to adversely impact sales volume. Manufacturers have responded by offering cheaper loads with lighter shot charges and packaging containing fewer shells. However, there is only so much a manufacturer can do to cut costs.

Environmental concerns and regulations have become another significant factor in shotshell design and manufacture. For example, empty paper shotshells quickly degrade gracefully in an outdoor environment while plastic is significantly longer-lived. This has caused the development of more environmentally friendly plastics. Spent lead shot in wetlands has become another environmental concern. This led to the development of non-toxic shot made of steel, bismuth, and various composites for use in such areas. Here we should note that non-toxic shot is substantially more expensive to manufacture and load than lead shot.

A word or two about lead shot is appropriate here. Regardless of environmental concerns, the deposit of lead shot in nonwetlands has little or no adverse impact. For this reason, lead shot is likely to be with us for some time to come. However, all lead shot is not equal. Lead pellets hardened with up to six percent antimony produce superior patterns compared to soft lead shot. Copper plating lead pellets reduce feather-draw and increase penetration. Granulated plastic filler (called grex) in the shot charge adds a significant cushion for the pellets on acceleration. Taken together in a plastic shell with a plastic wad column, one has the current epitome of shotshell performance.

Shooter preference combined with technical advances, economics, and environmental factors have greatly favored the 12-gauge and to a lesser degree the 20-gauge to the extent that 10-,16-, and 28-gauge shotshells and the .410 bore may shortly become extinct. The small-gauge shells offer less performance than 12- or 20-gauge shotshells and cost the same or even more. The 10-gauge is too specialized and too expensive. Today, 12-gauge shotshells amount to over 95% of all shotshells made.

Today, there is a bewildering variety of shotshell loads with labels that frequently do not convey their best application. Suggested load and shot size application charts offered by the shotshell manufacturers frequently disagree, leaving the shooter confused. Experience and recommendations from seasoned shooters are recommended in such instances. Caveat emptor!

10-GAUGE 3 1/2 in./89mm

ALTERNATE NAME(S): 10-Gauge Magnum, 10-ga., 10-ga. 3 1/2
RELATED SHOTSHELL(S): 10-ga. 2 9/16, 10-ga. 2 5/8, 10-ga. 2 7/8

SHOTSHELL HISTORY

Year of Introduction: circa 1930
Country of Origin: various European, U.S.
Designer(s): N/A
Governing Body: SAAMI, CIP
Present Status: active

SHOTSHELL DESCRIPTION

Bore Diameter: .775 in.
Case Type: rimmed, straight
Case Material: plastic or paper
Head Material: brass, brass-plated steel
Basewad Type: separate
Basewad Material: paper or composite
Wad Column Type: plastic or fiber combination
Crimp Closure: six fold
Primer Type: No. 209

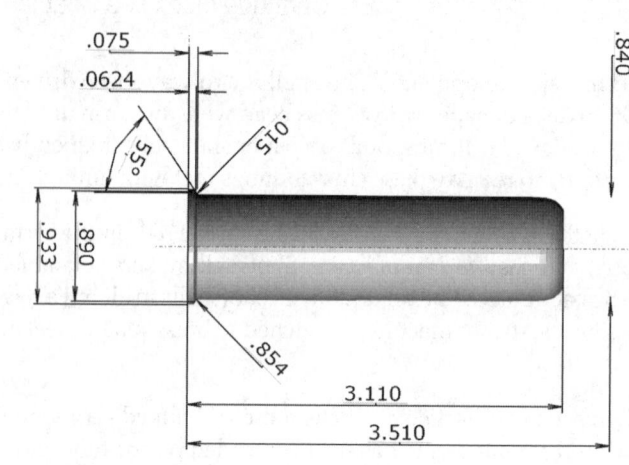

SHOTSHELL BALLISTICS

Max. Average Breech Pressure: 12,500 psi.
Test Barrel Length: 32 in.
Shot Charge Weight Range: 1 1/2-2 1/4 oz.

Shot Charge Weight (ozs)	Shell Length (in.)	Shot Type	Muzzle Velocity (fps)	Type
2 1/4	3 1/2	lead	1,210	Turkey
2	3 1/2	lead	1,300	High Vel
1 3/4	3 1/2	non-toxic	1,300	Waterfowl
1 5/8	3 1/2	steel	1,450	Waterfowl
1 1/2	3 1/2	steel	1,450	Waterfowl
1 3/8	3 1/2	steel	1,500	Waterfowl
18 pellets 00 buck	3 1/2	lead	1,100	Buckshot
1 3/4	3 1/2	lead	1,280	Foster slug

CURRENT MANUFACTURER(S)

Federal, Remington, Winchester, Eley, Gamebore

GENERAL COMMENT(S)

The 10-ga. was very popular among hunters and law enforcement personnel in the black powder era because its large shell volume that could hold heavy charges of black powder and shot. In the late 1880s, the popularity of the 10-ga. began to drop with the advent of smokeless powder and introduction of the slide-action shotgun. Smokeless propellants enabled the 12-ga. to rival the 10-ga. in ballistic performance. The 10-ga. remained bound in heavy single-and double-barrel shotguns, while the 12-ga. moved on to the lighter slide-action and semi-auto models. The end of market hunting in the late 1890s also contributed to the drop in 10-ga. popularity. By 1950, the 10-ga. was barely being kept alive by a small number of stubborn waterfowl hunters who preferred it for long range pass shooting. However, ammunition manufacturers did not expend any effort to modernize their 10-ga. product line as they did for 12-ga. As a result, 10-ga. shotshells were among the last to be converted to plastic tubes and wad columns. The advent of steel shot for waterfowl hunting gave the 10-ga. a new lease on life. Once again, the large interior volume of the 10-ga. shotshell became of critical importance because it could hold large amounts of steel shot. Today, the 10-ga. has found another niche market with turkey hunters who prefer the heavy shot charges that the 10-ga. can offer. In modern times the mighty 10 continues production life as a specialized gauge for hunting migratory waterfowl and turkey. It is the largest gauge legal for hunting migratory waterfowl in the U.S.

TECHNICAL COMMENT(S)

Efforts to improve the ballistic performance of the 12-ga. to 10-ga. levels have been less than successful. For some ballistic applications, there simply is no substitute for the internal volume of a 10-ga. 3 1/2 inch shotshell. In the 1980s, ammunition manufacturers modernized the 10-ga. with plastic tubes, folded crimps and plastic mono wad columns. These improved the pattern performance of the 10-ga. substantially. One manufacturer now offers a slug load and a buckshot load for the 10-ga. demonstrating that it is more versatile than many believed. Contrary to popular belief, the maximum average chamber pressure of the 10-ga. (12,500 psi.) is not higher than the 12-ga. (13,000 psi). The short 10-ga. shotshells are now obsolete.

12-GAUGE 2 in./51mm, 12-GAUGE 2 1/2 in./62mm, 12-GAUGE 2 3/4 in./70mm, 12-GAUGE 3 in./76mm, 12-GAUGE 3 1/2 in./89mm

---

ALTERNATE NAME(S): 12-ga., 12-ga. 2, 12-ga. 2 1/2, 12-ga. 2 3/4, 12-ga. 3, 12-ga. 3 1/2
RELATED SHOTSHELL(S): to each other

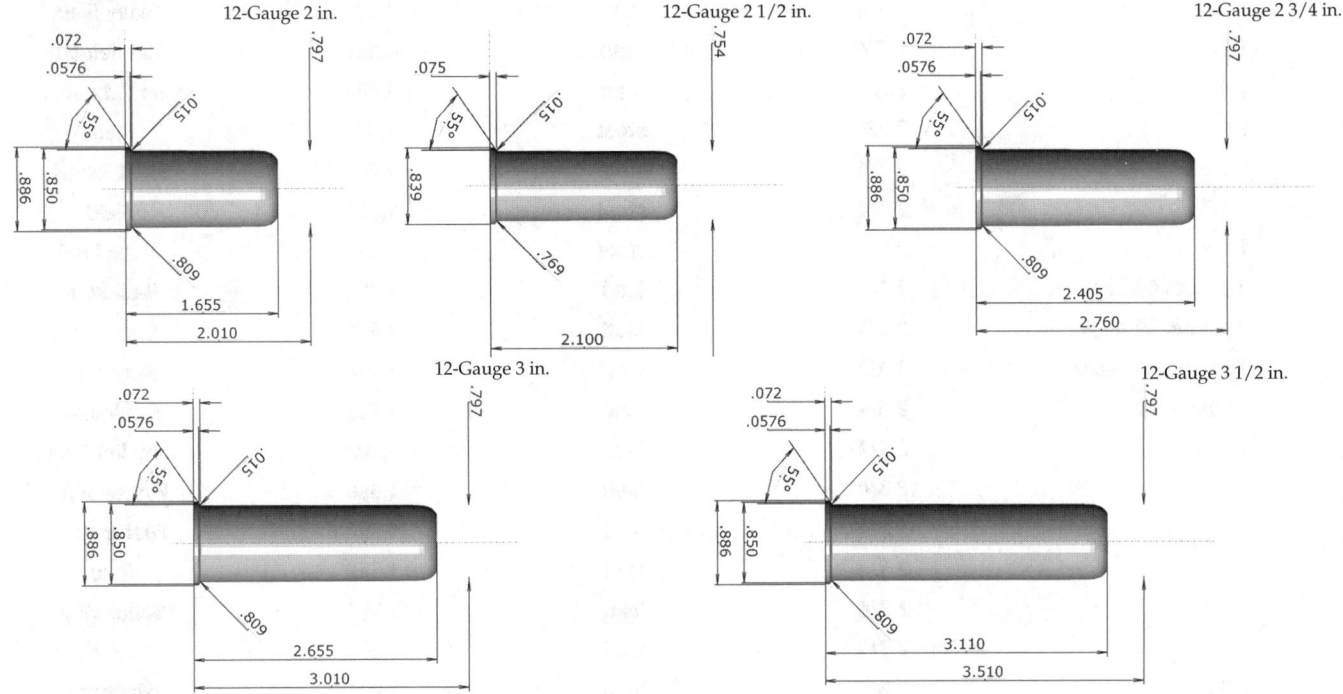

SHOTSHELL HISTORY

Year of Introduction: circa 1860

Country of Origin: various European, U.S.

Designer(s): various

Governing Body: SAAMI, CIP

Present Status: active

SHOTSHELL DESCRIPTION

Bore Diameter: .729 in.

Case Lengths: 2 in./51mm, 2 1/2 in./63.5mm, 2 3/4 in./70mm, 3/76mm, 3 1/2 in./89mm

Case Types: rimmed, straight

Case Materials: plastic, paper or metal

Head Materials: brass, brass-plated steel, brass-plated aluminum, plastic

Basewad Types: separate, integral

Basewad Materials: wound paper, plastic, composite

Wad Column Types: plastic, paper or felt

Crimp Closure: six segment fold for all field, high velocity, magnums and paper shells; eight segment fold for target loads; roll crimp for slugs; top wad for brass shells

Primer Type: No. 209

SHOTSHELL BALLISTICS
Max. Average Breech Pressure: 13,000 psi.
Test Barrel Length: 30 in.
Shot Charge Weight Range: 7/8-2 oz.

Shot Charge Weight (ozs)	Shell Length (in.)	Shot Type	Muzzle Velocity (fps)	Type
7/8	2 3/4	lead	1,250	Ultra Light
1	2 3/4	lead	1,200	Ultra Light
1 1/8	2 3/4	lead	1,150	Light Target
1 1/8	2 3/4	lead	1,200	Heavy Target
1	2 3/4	lead	1,290	Game Load
1 1/8	2 3/4	lead	1,255	Light Field
1 1/4	2 3/4	lead	1,220	Heavy Field
1 1/4	2 3/4	lead	1,330	High Velocity
1 1/2	2 3/4	lead	1,260	Short Magnum
1	2 3/4	steel	1,375	Field
1 1/8	2 3/4	steel	1,200	Steel Target
1 1/8	2 3/4	steel	1,365	Field
1 1/4	2 3/4	steel	1,375	Waterfowl
9 pellets 00 buck	2 3/4	lead	1,325	Buckshot
9 pellets 00 buck	2 3/4	lead	1,450	Buckshot
12 pellets 00 buck	2 3/4	lead	1,290	Buckshot
27 pellets 4 buck	2 3/4	lead	1,325	Buckshot
1	2 3/4	lead	1,200	Low Vel Slug
1	2 3/4	lead	1,600	Foster slug
1	2 3/4	lead	1,800	Foster slug
1 1/4	2 3/4	lead	1,550	Slug
1	2 3/4	lead	1,350	Sabot slug
1 1/8	2 3/4	lead	1,900	Sabot slug
1 3/8	3	lead	1,295	Magnum
1 5/8	3	lead	1,280	Magnum
1 7/8	3	lead	1,210	Magnum
2	3	lead	1,175	Magnum
1 1/8	3	steel	1,550	Magnum
1 3/8	3	steel	1,300	Magnum
1 1/4	3	steel	1,450	Magnum
12 pellets 00 buck	3	lead	1,450	Buckshot
15 pellets 00 buck	3	lead	1,225	Buckshot
41 pellets 4 buck	3	lead	1,225	Buckshot
1 1/4	3	lead	1,600	Foster Slug
1 3/8	3	lead	1,500	Slug
1	3	lead	1,760	Foster slug
7/8	3	lead	1,875	Foster slug
1	3	lead	1,530	Sabot slug
2	3 1/2	lead	1,300	Turkey
2 1/4	3 1/2	lead	1,150	Turkey
1 3/8	3 1/2	steel	1,550	Magnum

Shot Charge Weight (ozs)	Shell Length (in.)	Shot Type	Muzzle Velocity (fps)	Type
1 1/2	3 1/2	steel	1,500	Magnum
1 5/8	3 1/2	steel	1,350	Magnum
1 9/16	3 1/2	steel	1,300	Magnum
18 pellets 00 buck	3 1/2	lead	1,125	Buckshot
54 pellets 4 buck	3 1/2	lead	1,150	Buckshot

CURRENT MANUFACTURER(S)

Federal, Remington, Winchester, Estate, Fiocchi, Kent, Fiocchi, Saga, Sellier & Bellot, SK, UEE, Azot, Dynamit Nobel, Cheddite, Eley, Kent, Baschieri & Pellagri, Pionki, Industrias Tecnos

GENERAL COMMENT(S)

The first, self-contained shotshells that appeared circa 1860 were made of brass. A few years later, shotshells with built-up paper tubes and brass heads appeared. Shotshells were available with smokeless Schultz propellants from the middle of the 1860s– well before centerfire rifle and pistol ammunition was offered with smokeless propellants. However, black powder shotshells continued to be made until well into the 20th century. Shotshells made with plastic tubes appeared in the late 1950s. Plastic tube shotshells were far superior to paper shells and substantially cheaper than brass shells. As a result, plastic tube shotshells rapidly replaced both types for most types of shooting. In fact, 12-ga. shotshells account for over 90% of all shotshells sold. There is a good reason for this. The 12-ga. shotshell offers a nearly ideal combination of flexibility, performance and size at a reasonable cost.

TECHNICAL COMMENT(S)

Shotshells may be loaded with hard or soft lead shot. Hard shot is desirable as it produces denser, more even patterns. Copper-plated lead shot offers less feather draw on impact for increased penetration. Buffered loads with granulated plastic in the shot charge cushion the pellets on acceleration to produce the best patterns of all. Non-toxic shot such as steel, high density composites or sintered pellets must be used to hunt migratory waterfowl. When using steel shot, select a pellet size two sizes larger than your preferred lead shot size. High density shot sizes can be selected like lead shot. Target loads have an eight-fold crimp while hunting loads and paper shells have a six-fold crimp. A roll crimp will be found on some buckshot and most slug loads. The interior volume of shotshells often varies, even among those of the same brand. Manufacturers vary the height of the base wad to compensate for different loadings. The shells often look the same, but have different volumes. The height of the metal head on shotshells has no effect on the strength of the hull. Rather it is a method of differentiating target and game loads (low head height) from magnum, buckshot and slug loads (high head height). All modern shotshells are designed for the No. 209 battery cup primer except all-metal brass shotshells that are designed for Boxer rifle primers. Brass shotshells use wad columns one gauge larger in diameter than the shell they are loaded in. Brass shells also require a top wad to seal the case mouth.

16-GAUGE 2 3/4 in./70mm

ALTERNATE NAME(S): Sweet 16, 16-ga., 16-ga. 2 3/4
RELATED SHOTSHELL(S): 14-Gauge, Roper 16-ga., 16-ga. 2 1/2

SHOTSHELL HISTORY

Year of Introduction: late 1800s
Country of Origin: various European, U.S.
Designer(s): N/A
Governing Body: SAAMI, CIP
Present Status: active

SHOTSHELL DESCRIPTION

Bore Diameter: .665 in.
Case Type: rimmed, straight
Case Material: plastic or paper
Head Material: brass or brass-plated steel
Basewad Type: separate
Basewad Material: paper, plastic or composite
Wad Column Type: plastic
Crimp Closure: six fold or rolled (slug)
Primer Type: No. 209

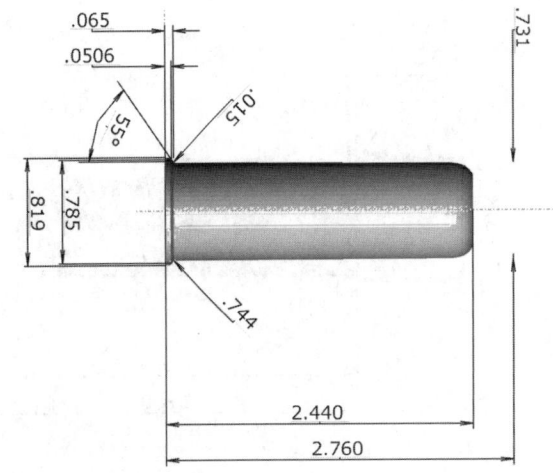

SHOTSHELL BALLISTICS

Max. Average Breech Pressure: 13,000 psi.

Test Barrel Length: 28 in.

Shot Charge Weight Range: 15/16-1 1/4 oz.

Shot Charge Weight (ozs)	Shell Length (in.)	Shot Type	Muzzle Velocity (fps)	Type
1 1/4	2 3/4	lead	1,260	Magnum
1 1/8	2 3/4	lead	1,295	Field
1	2 3/4	lead	1,165	Game
15/16	2 3/4	steel	1,350	Waterfowl
12 pellets 1 buck	2 3/4	lead	1,225	Buckshot
4/5	2 3/4	lead	1,600	Foster slug

CURRENT MANUFACTURER(S)

Federal, Remington, Winchester, Fiocchi, Eley, Dynamit Nobel, Sellier & Bellot, UEE, Baschieri & Pellagri, Gamebore, Kent

GENERAL COMMENT(S)

The 16-ga. remains far more popular in Europe than it does in the U.S. This is due to the fact that European hunters prefer double-barrel shotguns and lighter loads. A double-barrel shotgun can be made much lighter with better handling in 16-ga. than in 12-ga. In Europe, magnum shotshell loads are not popular. In the U.S., for many years those who preferred the 16-ga. were generally upland bird hunters seeking a compromise between the 12-ga. and the 20-ga. The 16-ga. was seen as offering increased ballistic performance over the 20-ga. together with a lighter gun than the 12-ga. Modern hunters seek no such compromise as the reasons for doing so have faded with the development of lighter 12-ga. shotguns and 12-ga. field loads offered identical performance to 16-ga. shotshells. With the advent of steel shot, many experts predicted the demise of the 16-ga. They were wrong, as very few hunters use the 16-ga. on waterfowl. As a result, the steel shot issue had little effect on sales of 16-ga. shotshells. Rather, shotgun manufacturers offered limited runs of 16-ga. guns and found themselves quickly sold out. In fact, the 16-ga. was never as popular as the 12-ga. or the 20-ga. Demand for the 16-ga. has faded, but it has always lived in the shadow of the other gauges and will continue to do so. Most sporting goods stores still stock the 16-ga. and domestic manufacturers have no urgent reason to discontinue it.

TECHNICAL COMMENT(S)

Shotshell manufacturers offer 16-ga. steel shot, lead buckshot and rifled slug loads. However, these seem almost beside the point as do the 1 1/4 oz. 16-ga. magnum loads. The real purpose of the 16-ga. is upland game hunting where shot charges of 1 or 1 1/8 oz. are a near-perfect combination with a lightweight shotgun. Modern 16-ga. shotshells have been upgraded with plastic tubes and wad columns so they give away nothing to their 12-ga. or 20-ga. rivals.

20-GAUGE 2 3/4 in./70mm , 20-GAUGE 3 in./76mm

ALTERNATE NAME(S): 20-ga., 20-ga 2 3/4, 20-ga. 3, 20-ga. 3 in. Magnum

RELATED SHOTSHELL(S): to each other

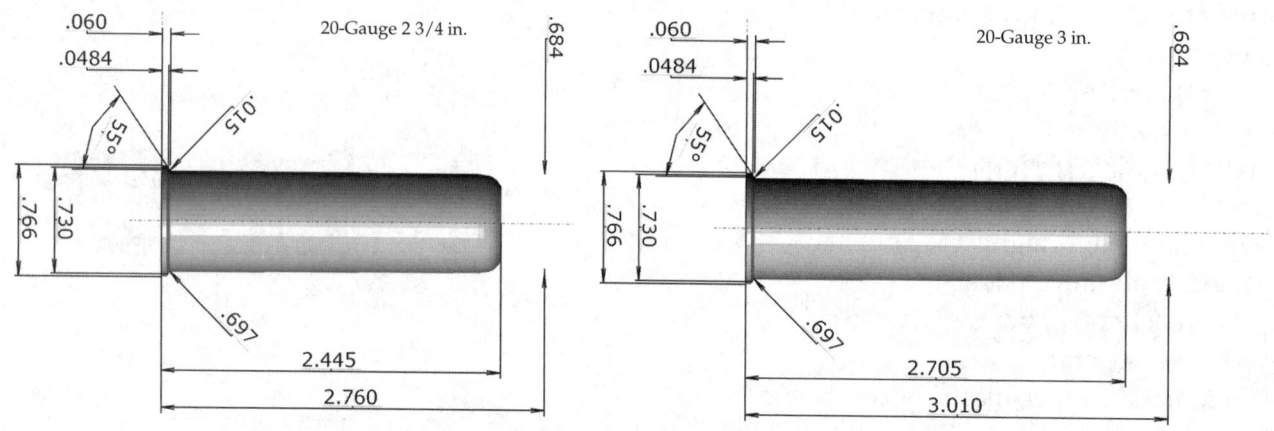

SHOTSHELL HISTORY
Year of Introduction: circa late 1800s
Country of Origin: various European, U.S.
Designer(s): N/A
Governing Body: SAAMI, CIP
Present Status: active

SHOTSHELL DESCRIPTION
Bore Diameter: .615 in.
Case Type: rimmed, straight
Case Material: plastic, paper or brass
Head Material: brass or brass-plated steel
Basewad Type: integral or separate
Basewad Material: plastic or paper
Wad Column Type: plastic or fiber combo
Crimp Closure: six fold (hunting loads), eight-fold (target loads) or rolled (slugs)
Primer Type: No. 209

SHOTSHELL BALLISTICS
Max. Average Breech Pressure: 13,500 psi.
Test Barrel Length: 26 in.
Shot Charge Weight Range: 3/4-1 5/16 oz.

Shot Charge Weight (ozs)	Shell Length (in.)	Shot Type	Muzzle Velocity (fps)	Type
1 1/8	2 3/4	lead	1,175	Magnum
1	2 3/4	lead	1,350	High Vel
1	2 3/4	lead	1,165	Upland
7/8	2 3/4	lead	1,300	Sport
7/8	2 3/4	lead	1,225	Game load
7/8	2 3/4	lead	1,200	Target load
7/8	2 3/4	lead	980	Lite target
3/4	2 3/4	steel	1,300	Waterfowl
3/4	2 3/4	steel	1,450	Waterfowl
20 pellets 3 buck	2 3/4	lead	1,175	Buckshot
3/4	2 3/4	lead	1,600	Foster slug
1	2 3/4	lead	1,500	Slug
5/8	2 3/4	lead	1,600	Sabot slug
1/2	2 3/4	lead	1,800	HV Slug
1 1/8	3	non-toxic	1,225	Turkey
1 1/4	3	lead	1,300	Magnum
1 5/16	3	lead	1,200	Magnum
7/8	3	steel	1,500	Waterfowl
1	3	steel	1,350	Waterfowl
18 pellets 2 buck	3	lead	1,175	Buckshot
5/8	3	lead	1,900	Sabot slug
1	3	lead	1,550	Slug

CURRENT MANUFACTURER(S)
Federal, Remington, Winchester, Estate, Kent, Fiocchi, Eley, Fiocchi, Dynamit Nobel, SK, Sellier & Bellot, UEE, Baschieri & Pellagri, Gamebore, Kent, Azot, Saga

GENERAL COMMENT(S)

The 20-ga. remains the second most popular choice after the 12-ga. In recent years, the 20 has led a resurgence of interest in the smaller gauges. Although often dismissed as an expert's gauge, this is not true as the 20-ga. is a good choice for beginners and those sensitive to recoil. In the upland bird fields, 20-ga. guns are preferred for their light weight and fast handling. Skeet shooting with the 20-ga. is an especially challenging sport for experienced shooters. Shotshells in 20-ga. are universally available in wide variety second only to 12-ga.

TECHNICAL COMMENT(S)

Although small, the 20-ga. is capable of effective performance in most types of shotgun activity except waterfowl pass shooting, turkey hunting and law enforcement duties. Technical advances such as plastic tubes and wads have increased the versatility and ballistic performance of the 20-ga. to the point that many 20-ga. loads can duplicate the performance of some 12-ga. loads. Today, the 20-ga. shooter need not give away any performance to advantage to hunting partners with 12-ga. shotguns.

28-GAUGE 2 3/4 in./70mm

ALTERNATE NAME(S): 28-ga., 28-ga. 2 3/4
RELATED SHOTSHELL(S): 24-ga., 28-ga. 2 1/2, 32-ga.

SHOTSHELL HISTORY

Year of Introduction: late 1800s
Country of Origin: various European, U.S.
Designer(s): N/A
Governing Body: SAAMI, CIP
Present Status: active

SHOTSHELL DESCRIPTION

Bore Diameter: .545 in.
Case Type: straight, rimmed
Case Material: plastic or paper
Head Material: brass or brass-plated steel
Basewad Type: integral or separate
Basewad Material: plastic or paper
Wad Column Type: plastic
Crimp Closure: six fold (hunting loads) eight fold (target loads)
Primer Type: No. 209

SHOTSHELL BALLISTICS

Max. Average Breech Pressure: 14,000 psi.
Test Barrel Length: 26 in.
Shot Charge Weight Range: 5/8-1 oz.

Shot Charge Weight (ozs)	Shell Length (in.)	Shot Type	Muzzle Velocity (fps)	Type
3/4	2 3/4	lead	1,300	Upland
3/4	2 3/4	lead	1,230	Target load
7/8	2 3/4	lead	1,200	Target load
1	2 3/4	lead	1,205	Field load

CURRENT MANUFACTURER(S)

Federal, Remington, Winchester, Fiocchi, Kent, Eley, Kent, Gamebore, Sellier & Bellot, UEE

GENERAL COMMENT(S)

By all measure, the 28-ga. is the most specialized of the active shotshell gauges. Basically, its market niche is for hunting upland birds over dogs. For this reason, most shotgunners regard the diminutive 28-ga. as a "gentleman's" gauge for experienced hunters. Shotshells in 28-ga. are normally not found on the shelves of local sporting goods stores as the demand is small and the shells expensive. However, skeet competitions normally feature a 28-ga. event so target shells in that gauge commonly are available at gun clubs. Although small production quantities have increased the price of 28-ga. shotshells, most shooters who use the 28-ga. are willing to pay the added cost.

TECHNICAL COMMENT(S)

Because of its small size and limited internal volume, the 28-ga. is unsuitable for steel shot, buckshot and magnum loads. Rifled slug loads are not offered as they are not compatible with many upland shotguns. However, plastic tubes and wad columns have substantially improved the ballistic performance of this small gauge with lead shot field and target loads. A major reason for selecting the 28-ga. is the reduced recoil and the light weight shotgun combine to offer lively handling and reduced fatigue during long hunts. Shooting over dogs allows the hunter to get set for the flush of birds and select only shots that experience has shown are inside the range of the shotgun. For this reason, most 28-ga. field loads contain No. 7 1/2 or 8 shot. Target loads contain No. 9 shot.

.410 BORE 2 1/2 in./63.5mm, .410 BORE 3 in./76mm

ALTERNATE NAME(S): .410-ga., .410 Magnum, 36-ga., 36-Gauge
RELATED SHOTSHELL(S): .45-70 Gov't., 32-ga.

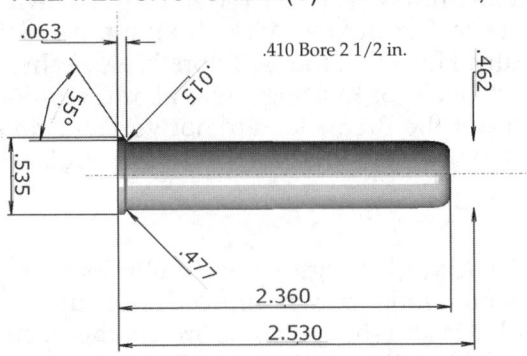
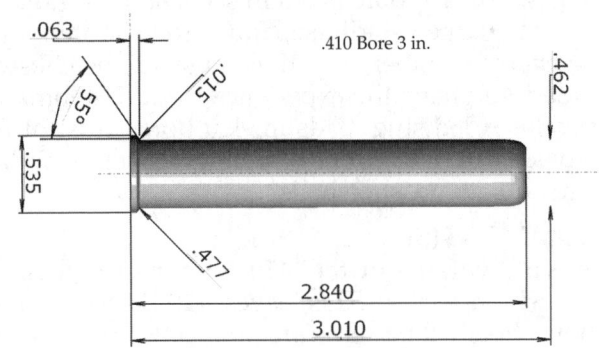

SHOTSHELL HISTORY

Year of Introduction: early 1900s (est.)
Country of Origin: U.S.
Designer(s): N/A
Governing Body: SAAMI
Present Status: active

SHOTSHELL DESCRIPTION

Bore Diameter: .410 in.
Case Type: rimmed, straight
Case Material: plastic
Head Material: brass or brass-plated steel
Basewad Type: separate
Basewad Material: plastic or paper
Wad Column Type: plastic
Crimp Closure: six fold
Primer Type: No. 209

SHOTSHELL BALLISTICS

Max. Average Breech Pressure: 14,000 psi. (2 1/2"), 15,000 psi. (3")
Test Barrel Length: 26 in.
Shot Charge Weight Range: 1/4-5/8 oz.

Shot Charge Weight (ozs)	Shell Length (in.)	Shot Type	Muzzle Velocity (fps)	Type
1/2	2 1/2	lead	1,230	Target load
3 pellets 000	2 1/2	lead	1,300	Buckshot
1/4	2 1/2	lead	1,830	Slug
5/8	3	lead	1,135	Field
3/4	3	lead	1,100	Field
5 pellets 000	3	lead	1,135	Buckshot
1/4	3	lead	1,800	Slug

CURRENT MANUFACTURER(S)

Federal, Remington, Winchester, Fiocchi, Fiocchi, Eley, Kent, Sellier & Bellot, Azot

GENERAL COMMENT(S)

In the late 1880s, U.S. Army foragers were issued .45-70 Gov't. ammunition loaded with lead shot for taking birds and small game. Ammunition companies also offered various calibers of centerfire and rimfire rifle and pistol ammunition loaded with shot. By the early 1900s, small shotguns were being chambered for the .44 XL cartridge which was a centerfire design with a brass case and extended paper nose containing lead shot. This cartridge was based on a .44 caliber centerfire revolver case for a .425 inch bore diameter. These cartridges served as the fore-runners of the .410 Bore shotshell we know today. While the .410 Bore has always been a popular choice for beginners, most experts now feel this is a bad choice. The very small shot charge makes it very hard to hit a moving target thus discouraging the novice shooter. The 20-ga. is a far better choice for instruction and training of this type. The .410 Bore is a good choice for eliminating pests and for small game hunting. There is also a .410 Bore event in skeet shooting that is normally fun to watch as the small gauge with its diminutive shot charge rapidly separates the shooters by experience. For upland game hunting, the .410 Bore is truly an expert's caliber and shots must still be chosen carefully. However, the .410 Bore is a delight in the field, provided you have the experience for it. Use only the 3 inch shell for hunting. Several ammunition manufacturers offer rifled slug loads in .410 Bore. Most of these, except the Brenneke, are not very effective and should be passed up in favor of a larger gauge slug. Today, the .410 Bore remains No. 3 in sales popularity behind the 12-ga. and 20-ga. shotshells.

TECHNICAL COMMENT(S)

The limited internal volume of the .410 Bore shotshell restricts plastic wad design so as to eliminate any possibility of a cushion section. This leaves .410 Bore plastic wads as little more than reinforced shot cups. As a result, .410 Bore shotshell patterns are poor unless hard shot is loaded in the shell. Crimps are another focus area of .410 Bore problems. The small diameter of the shell makes folded crimps difficult. For this reason, some ammunition makers continue to use a rolled crimp and top wad on .410 Bore shells. Crimp blow-offs occur frequently in .410 Bore shells. As the .410 Bore is similar in many ways to a rifle cartridge, slow burning propellants are the norm. Maximum average chamber pressures higher than other shotshells reflect this.

CHAPTER 83 : SPORTING SHOTSHELL - OBSOLETE

CHAPTER 83

For Cartridge Index see Chapter 101. All drawing dimensions are approximate.

There is no perfect shotshell gauge. This graveyard of departed gauges is eloquent testimony to that fact. At one time or another, nearly every gauge of shotshell has been tried, ranging from the gigantic letter gauges to the micro-caliber bores. Here it is interesting to note that in each instance, someone thought he saw a useful application for a failed gauge, only to find it was not so.

Of course, market forces determine which gauges succeed and which gauges fail. However, there is no fixed point of failure as shooter preferences, economic currents, and government regulations conspire to move the goal posts about on a regular basis. Just when you think a particular gauge has become extinct, events combine to bring it back to life. A good example is the regulatory introduction of non-toxic shot that brought the 10-gauge back from the edge of oblivion. Then there is the 8-gauge. When hunting migratory waterfowl with 8-ga. shotguns was outlawed in 1918, many pundits confidently predicted the demise of the big 8. Not so! It found a secure home in the industrial sector and soldiers on to this day in kiln gun applications.

Some failed gauges are very useful such as the 14-gauge and 24-gauge. For many years, the 14-gauge and 16-gauge as well as the 24-gauge and 28-gauge competed for the hunter's favor. The 14- and 24-gauges lost, although this is no reflection on their performance so much as their proximity to other gauges.

Modern-day shooters will find these failed gauges interesting, especially in their all-brass metal shell form.

Most will be found with a paper tube in a wide variety of colors, a rolled crimp, and a fiber cushion wad column as plastic did not exist prior to their demise. The presently ubiquitous No. 209 shotshell primer is also notably absent.

Failed gauges are the end of an era. Resurrection of a failed gauge in the modern market is extremely unlikely. In fact, several existing gauges such as the 16- and 28-gauge as well as the .410 bore are likely to join the ranks of the departed in the near future. Very likely, the 16-gauge will expire first.

Why this group suicide? Simply put, shotshell manufacturers can duplicate the performance of virtually any failed shotshell gauge by varying the length, shot charge weight, and muzzle velocity of existing 12-gauge and 20-gauge shotshells. There is simply no longer a need for a large number of different gauges today.

Of course, nostalgia may support several of these obsolescent gauges well beyond their time. Let us hope they age gracefully.

4-GAUGE

ALTERNATE NAME(S): 4-ga., 4-ga. 4 1/4, 4-ga. 4 1/4 in.
RELATED SHOTSHELL(S): 4-ga. 2-4 in.

SHOTSHELL HISTORY

Year of Introduction: late 1880s
Country of Origin: various European, U.S.
Designer(s): N/A
Governing Body: none-never standardized
Present Status: obsolete

SHOTSHELL DESCRIPTION

Bore Diameter: 1.052 in.
Case Type: rimmed, straight
Case Material: brass or paper
Head Material: brass or steel
Basewad Type: separate
Basewad Material: paper
Wad Column Type: fiber
Crimp Closure: rolled
Primer Type: centerfire rifle

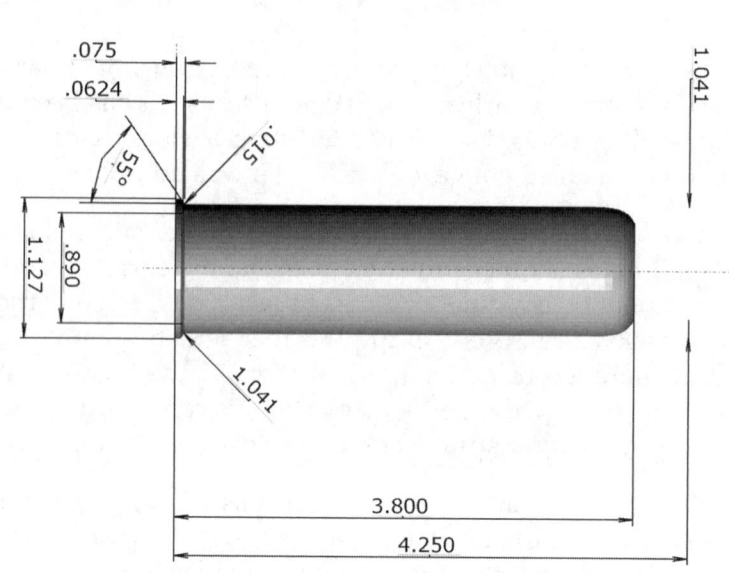

SHOTSHELL BALLISTICS

Max. Average Breech Pressure: not standardized
Test Barrel Length: not standardized
Shot Charge Weight Range: approx. 3+ oz.

Shot Charge Weight (ozs)	Shell Length (in.)	Shot Type	Muzzle Velocity (fps)	Type
3+	4 1/4	lead	unknown	Shot or slug

CURRENT MANUFACTURER(S)

None

GENERAL COMMENT(S)

Large gauge shotshells such as this were sometimes used by market hunters in the late 1880s. Use of such gauges for hunting migratory waterfowl was outlawed in 1918. In any case, the large, heavy shotguns chambered for 4-ga. shells were very difficult to fire from the shoulder. Recoil must have been heavy. For these reasons, shotguns in 4-ga. were not popular or common.

TECHNICAL COMMENT(S)

A normal shot charge for the 4-ga. shell would be about 3 ozs. or more. Shotshells of this gauge were also loaded with slugs. As these were mostly black powder shells, muzzle velocity was probably about 1,000 fps. Production of such large gauge shotshells ended early in the 20th century in the U.S. Consequently, most 4-ga. shotshells were made of brass or paper with a rolled crimp. Shotshells of this size were never standardized as they preceded SAAMI and CIP. As a result, chamber dimensions and shell lengths vary.

8-GAUGE

ALTERNATE NAME(S): 8-ga., 8-ga. 4, 8-ga. 4 in.
RELATED SHOTSHELL(S): kiln gun shells, 8-ga. 2 3/4-3 3/4 in.

SHOTSHELL HISTORY

Year of Introduction: late 1880s

Country of Origin: various European, U.S.

Designer(s): N/A

Governing Body: SAAMI

Present Status: obsolete for sporting, active for industrial

SHOTSHELL DESCRIPTION

Bore Diameter: .835 in.

Case Type: rimmed, straight

Case Material: brass, paper or plastic

Head Material: brass or brass-plated steel

Basewad Type: separate

Basewad Material: paper

Wad Column Type: fiber

Crimp Closure: rolled

Primer Type: centerfire rifle (brass), No. 209 (plastic)

Dimensions shown on diagram: .075, .0624, 55°, .015, .902, .998, .890, .913, 3.600, 4.000

SHOTSHELL BALLISTICS

Max. Average Breech Pressure: N/A

Test Barrel Length: N/A

Shot Charge Weight Range: 1 3/4-2 1/4 oz.

Shot Charge Weight (ozs)	Shell Length (in.)	Shot Type	Muzzle Velocity (fps)	Type
2 1/4	3 1/4	lead	1,200	Shot

CURRENT MANUFACTURER(S)

Remington, Winchester, Gamebore

GENERAL COMMENT(S)

Prior to 1918 when shotshells larger than 10-ga. were outlawed in the U.S. for hunting migratory waterfowl, the 8-ga. enjoyed modest popularity for such hunting. Shells were offered by all the major domestic ammunition makers. The 8-ga. was the magnum of its day for long range pass shooting at waterfowl. Although technically the 8-ga. is legal for hunting birds other than migratory waterfowl, few have bothered and shotguns in this gauge have not been commonly available for many years. Many shooters are surprised to learn that the 8-ga. shotshell remains alive and well in full production by two domestic ammunition makers and several overseas manufacturers. This gauge is very popular for kiln guns to shoot the clinkers off kilns using heavy lead or zinc slugs. Modern 8-ga. shells have a plastic tube and a brass-plated steel head reinforced inside with a second steel cup. They are loaded only with slugs and not reloaded.

TECHNICAL COMMENT(S)

A heavy shotgun was required to fire 8-ga. shotshells in order to tame the recoil. Such shotguns had poor handling characteristics and were very expensive. Of course, a modern 8-ga. shotshell could easily be developed, however there would be no ballistic justification for such a shell. Modern 10-ga. and 12-ga. shotshells offer ballistics making an 8-ga. shell unnecessary.

14-GAUGE

ALTERNATE NAME(S): 14-ga., 14-ga. 2 1/2, 14-ga. 2 1/2 in.
RELATED SHOTSHELL(S): 14-ga. 1 3/4-2 9/16

SHOTSHELL HISTORY

Year of Introduction: late 1880s
Country of Origin: various European, U.S.
Designer(s): N/A
Governing Body: SAAMI, CIP
Present Status: obsolete

SHOTSHELL DESCRIPTION

Bore Diameter: .693 in.
Case Type: rimmed, straight
Case Material: brass or paper
Head Material: brass
Basewad Type: separate
Basewad Material: paper
Wad Column Type: fiber
Crimp Closure: rolled
Primer Type: centerfire rifle

SHOTSHELL BALLISTICS

Max. Average Breech Pressure: 12,500 psi.
Test Barrel Length: 28-30 in.
Shot Charge Weight Range: 1 oz.

Shot Charge Weight (ozs)	Shell Length (in.)	Shot Type	Muzzle Velocity (fps)	Type
1	2 1/2	lead	1,250 approx.	Field

CURRENT MANUFACTURER(S)

None

GENERAL COMMENT(S)

The last production of 14-ga. shotshells occurred in Europe in the early 1970s.

TECHNICAL COMMENT(S)

As an attempted compromise between the 12-ga. and the 16-ga., the 14-ga. had modest success in the black powder era and a failure in the smokeless era. The ballistic development of the 12-ga. sealed the fate of the 14-ga., it lost its reason to be and faded away.

24-GAUGE

ALTERNATE NAME(S): 24-ga., 24-ga. 2 1/2, 24-ga. 2 1/2 in./62mm
RELATED SHOTSHELL(S): 20-ga., 24-ga. 2, 28-ga.

SHOTSHELL HISTORY
Year of Introduction: late 1880s
Country of Origin: various European, U.S.
Designer(s): N/A
Governing Body: SAAMI (obsolete), CIP (active)
Present Status: obsolete

SHOTSHELL DESCRIPTION
Bore Diameter: .580 in.
Case Type: rimmed, straight
Case Material: brass, paper or plastic
Head Material: brass
Basewad Type: separate
Basewad Material: plastic or paper
Wad Column Type: fiber
Crimp Closure: six fold
Primer Type: centerfire rifle (brass), No. 209 (plastic)

SHOTSHELL BALLISTICS
Max. Average Breech Pressure: 12,500 psi.
Test Barrel Length: 26 in.
Shot Charge Weight Range: 3/4 oz.

Shot Charge Weight (ozs)	Shell Length (in.)	Shot Type	Muzzle Velocity (fps)	Type
3/4	2 1/2	lead	1,285	Field

CURRENT MANUFACTURER(S)
Fiocchi

GENERAL COMMENT(S)
Shotguns in this gauge are still made occasionally in Europe and Fiocchi is the sole remaining manufacturer of shotshells in this gauge. Fiocchi offers only one loading with a choice of shot sizes.

TECHNICAL COMMENT(S)
The 24-ga. was another compromise gauge that tried to split the ballistic difference between the 20-ga. and the 28-ga. In this endeavor it failed. At the end of the 1930s, ballistic development of the 20-ga. made the 24-ga. superfluous. In the U.S., manufacture of 24-ga. shotshells was not resumed after World War II. In Europe, the 24-ga. hung on much longer, but is now all but dead in that market as well.

32-GAUGE

ALTERNATE NAME(S): 32-ga., 32-ga. 2 1/2, 32-ga. 2 1/2 in., 32-ga. 2 1/2 in./62mm
RELATED SHOTSHELL(S): 28-ga., 32-ga. 2 1/4, .410 Bore

SHOTSHELL HISTORY

Year of Introduction: late 1880s

Country of Origin: various European, U.S.

Designer(s): N/A

Governing Body: SAAMI (obsolete), CIP (active)

Present Status: obsolete

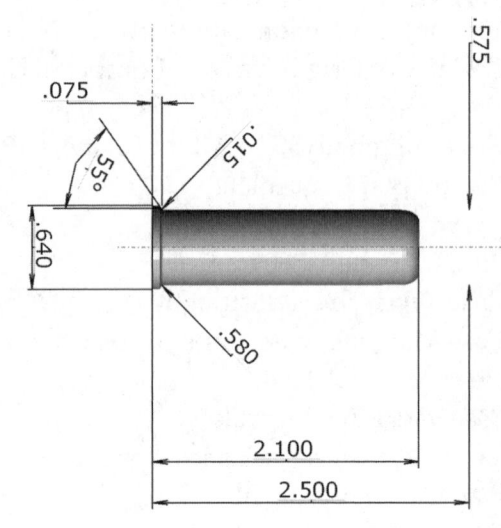

SHOTSHELL DESCRIPTION

Bore Diameter: .526 in.

Case Type: rimmed, straight

Case Material: brass, paper or plastic

Head Material: brass

Basewad Type: separate

Basewad Material: paper

Wad Column Type: plastic

Crimp Closure: six fold

Primer Type: centerfire rifle (brass), No. 209 (plastic)

SHOTSHELL BALLISTICS

Max. Average Breech Pressure: 13,000 psi. (est.)

Test Barrel Length: 26 in.

Shot Charge Weight Range: 1/2 oz.

Shot Charge Weight (ozs)	Shell Length (in.)	Shot Type	Muzzle Velocity (fps)	Type
1/2	2 1/2	lead	1,285	Field

CURRENT MANUFACTURER(S)

Fiocchi, UEE

GENERAL COMMENT(S)

Manufacture of 32-ga. shotshells in the U.S. ended with World War II. It remains in production in Europe with two manufacturers offering shells in this gauge.

TECHNICAL COMMENT(S)

The 32-ga. is yet another attempted ballistic compromise, in this instance between the 28-ga. and the .410 Bore. Ballistic development of the .410 Bore made the 32-ga. unnecessary.

CHAPTER 84 : CENTERFIRE SHOTSHELL - CURRENT

CHAPTER 84

For Cartridge Index see Chapter 101. All drawing dimensions are approximate.

Centerfire handgun shooters have always felt the need for a shot loading in the most popular calibers for close range dispatch of rodents, pests, and snakes. Although the market for such loads is modest, ammunition manufacturers have tried to meet this demand with varying degrees of success.

Centerfire handgun cartridges loaded with shot pose several thorny technical problems.

The first is how to securely hold the shot charge.

The large volume of many large caliber revolver cartridges allows the shot charge to be held securely inside a standard cartridge case. However, the space required for the pusher wad and the top wad leaves little space for a useful shot charge. The short length of most pistol cartridges makes it impossible to hold a shot charge inside the case.

Of course, a longer cartridge case could be used to gain more volume, but this would require a special case design and specific tooling, which further increases cost.

The ideal solution would be to find a means to hold the shot in a bullet-like container that could be loaded into the case mouth like a bullet. Over the years, various materials have been tried for this purpose including wood, paper, and plastic. Plastic has proven to be ideal and is the basis for the popular CCI Speer shotshells.

9mm LUGER SHOT

ALTERNATE NAME(S): 9x19mm, 9x19mm Luger, 9mm Parabellum, 9x19mm Parabellum
RELATED CALIBER(S): 9mm Steyr, 9mm Browning Long, 9mm Glisenti, .38 Super, 9mm Largo, 7.62x25mm Tokarev, .45 ACP

CARTRIDGE HISTORY
Year of Introduction: 1902
Country of Origin: Germany
Designer(s): Deutsche Waffen und Munitionsfabriken AG
Governing Body: CIP, SAAMI
Present Status: active

CARTRIDGE DESCRIPTION
Bullet Diameter: .355 in.
Bullet Weight(s): 53 gr.
Rifling Twist Rate: 1 turn in 9.84 in.
Test Barrel Length: 5.9 in.
Case Type: rimless, tapered
Case Material: brass, aluminum
Primer Type: small pistol

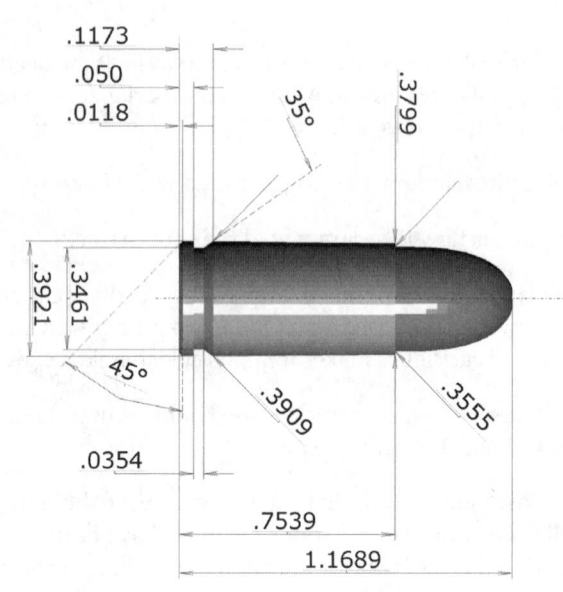

CARTRIDGE BALLISTICS
Max. Average Breech Pressure: 34,100 psi.
Max. Effective Range: 15 ft.
Max. Horizontal Range: 100 yds.
Max. Vertical Range: 400 ft.

Bullet Weight (gr.)	Bullet Type	Muzzle Velocity (fps)	Muzzle Energy (ft.-lbs.)
53	No. 12 Lead Shot	1,000	-

CURRENT MANUFACTURER(S)
CCI

GENERAL COMMENT(S)
This type of 9mm Luger shot cartridge with a plastic nose capsule containing the shot pellets was developed by CCI in the early 1960s. This design has replaced most other types of shot carriers such as wood, paper and metal which had consistently proven unsatisfactory. CCI has comfortably dominated this niche market ever since; the limited volume of this market will not support more than one major manufacturer.

A major reason for CCI's success is that the product looks attractive. CCI packaging supports this with a flat, plastic, 10 round box with a clear plastic cover and a white tray that accentuates their appearance. While the per round price is double that of conventional 9mm Luger ammunition, most customer requirements are fully satisfied by 10 rounds.

Shooters have a tendency to expect too much of 9mm Luger shot cartridges. Remember, although the cartridge is large and the bore diameter substantial, the shot charge weight is small and the No. 12 lead pellets will not penetrate deeply. Patterns are poor as the rifling adversely affects pattern quality. In fact, their effective range is only 15 ft.

TECHNICAL COMMENT(S)
This shot cartridge design has several well designed technical features. It uses a standard 9mm Luger cartridge case that requires no special tooling. In this instance, CCI uses their aluminum cartridge case. The plastic nose capsule holds the shot charge. On exiting the muzzle, the plastic nose capsule disintegrates minimizing pellet deformation.

Remember, 9mm Luger shot cartridges must be manually fed one at a time into the chamber of semi-automatic pistols as feeding them through the magazine may break the plastic nose capsule. These cartridges will NOT function semi-automatic pistols or rifles. They should NOT be fired in 9mm Luger caliber revolvers.

.38 SPECIAL

ALTERNATE NAME(S): .38 S&WSpecial,.38 Colt Special, .38 Spl., .38-44 HV
RELATED CALIBER(S): .38 Long Colt

CARTRIDGE HISTORY
Year of Introduction: 1902
Country of Origin: U.S.
Designer(s): S&W
Governing Body: SAAMI, CIP
Present Status: active

CARTRIDGE DESCRIPTION
Bullet Diameter: .357 in.
Bullet Weight(s): 100 gr.
Rifling Twist Rate: 1 turn in 18.75 in.
Test Barrel Length: 4 in.
Case Type: rimmed, straight
Case Material: brass
Primer Type: small pistol

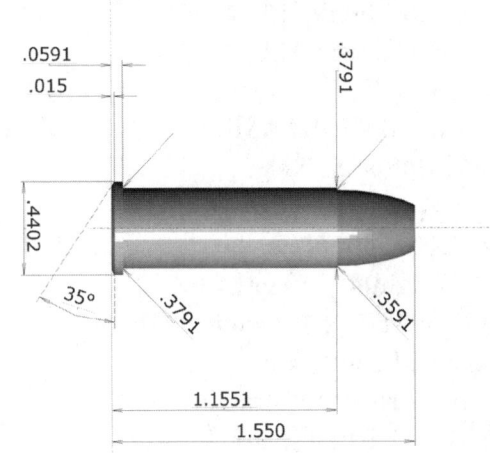

CARTRIDGE BALLISTICS
Max. Average Breech Pressure: 17,000 psi.
Max. Effective Range: 15 ft.
Max. Horizontal Range: 100 yds.
Max. Vertical Range: 400 ft.

Bullet Weight (gr.)	Bullet Type	Muzzle Velocity (fps)	Muzzle Energy (ft.-lbs.)
100	No. 12 Lead Shot	1,000	-

CURRENT MANUFACTURER(S)
CCI

GENERAL COMMENT(S)
This type of .38 Special shot cartridge with a plastic nose capsule containing the shot pellets was developed by CCI in the early 1960s. This design has replaced most other types of shot carriers such as wood, paper and metal. CCI has comfortably dominated this niche market ever since; the limited volume of this market will not support more than one major manufacturer.

A major reason for CCI's success is that the product looks attractive. CCI packaging supports this with a flat, plastic, 10 round box with a clear plastic cover and a white tray that accentuates their appearance. While the per round price is double that of conventional .38 Special ammunition, most customer requirements are fully satisfied by 10 rounds.

Shooters have a tendency to expect too much of .38 Special shot cartridges. Remember, the shot charge weights are very small and the No. 12 lead pellets will not penetrate deeply. Patterns are poor as the rifling adversely affects pattern quality. In fact, their effective range is only 15 ft.

TECHNICAL COMMENT(S)
This shot cartridge design has several well designed technical features. It uses a standard .38 Special cartridge case that requires no special tooling. In this instance, CCI uses their aluminum cartridge case. The plastic nose capsule holds the shot charge. On exiting the muzzle, the plastic nose capsule disintegrates minimizing pellet deformation.

Remember, .38 Special shot cartridges can be used in .357 Magnum caliber revolvers. Shot cartridges can be fired in all revolvers in a normal manner.

.44 MAGNUM

ALTERNATE NAME(S): .44 Remington Magnum, .44 Mag.
RELATED CALIBER(S): .45 Colt

CARTRIDGE HISTORY
Year of Introduction: 1955
Country of Origin: U.S.
Designer(s): CCI
Governing Body: SAAMI
Present Status: active

CARTRIDGE DESCRIPTION
Bullet Diameter: none
Bullet Weight(s): 150 gr.
Rifling Twist Rate: 1 turn in 20 in.
Test Barrel Length: 4 in.
Case Type: rimmed, straight
Case Material: brass, aluminum
Primer Type: large pistol

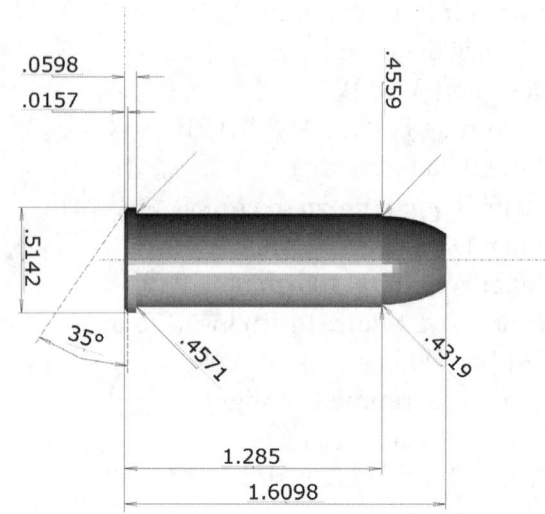

CARTRIDGE BALLISTICS
Max. Average Breech Pressure: 36, 000 psi.
Max. Effective Range: 15 ft.
Max. Horizontal Range: 100 yds.
Max. Vertical Range: 400 ft.

Bullet Weight (gr.)	Bullet Type	Muzzle Velocity (fps)	Muzzle Energy (ft.-lbs.)
150	No. 12 Lead Shot	1,000	-

CURRENT MANUFACTURER(S)
CCI

GENERAL COMMENT(S)
This type of .44 Magnum shot cartridge with a plastic nose capsule containing the shot pellets was developed by CCI in the early 1960s. This design has replaced most other types of shot carriers such as wood, paper and metal which had consistently proven unsatisfactory. CCI has comfortably dominated this niche market ever since; the limited volume of this market will not support more than one major manufacturer.

A major reason for CCI's success is that the product looks attractive. CCI packaging supports this with a flat, plastic, 10 round box with a clear plastic cover and a white tray that accentuates their appearance. While the per round price is double that of conventional .44 Magnum ammunition, most customer requirements are fully satisfied by 10 rounds.

Shooters have a tendency to expect too much of .44 Magnum shot cartridges. Remember, although the cartridge is large and the bore diameter substantial, the shot charge weight is small and the No. 12 lead pellets will not penetrate deeply. Patterns are poor as the rifling adversely affects pattern quality. In fact, their effective range is only 15 ft.

TECHNICAL COMMENT(S)
This shot cartridge design has several well designed technical features. It uses a standard .44 Magnum cartridge case that requires no special tooling. In this instance, CCI uses their aluminum cartridge case. The plastic nose capsule holds the shot charge. On exiting the muzzle, the plastic nose capsule disintegrates minimizing pellet deformation.

Remember, .44 Magnum shot cartridges will work normally through revolvers, but may NOT function in many rifles.

.45 AUTO SHOT (PLASTIC)

ALTERNATE NAME(S): .45 Automatic, .45 ACP (Obsolete)
RELATED CALIBER(S): .45 Win. Mag., .45 G.A.P.

CARTRIDGE HISTORY
Year of Introduction: 1905, 1911 (Military)
Country of Origin: U.S.
Designer(s): John Browning
Governing Body: SAAMI, CIP
Present Status: active

CARTRIDGE DESCRIPTION
Bullet Diameter: .452 in.
Bullet Weight(s): 120 gr.
Rifling Twist Rate: 1 turn in 16 in.
Test Barrel Length: 5 in.
Case Type: rimless, straight
Case Material: brass or aluminum
Primer Type: large pistol

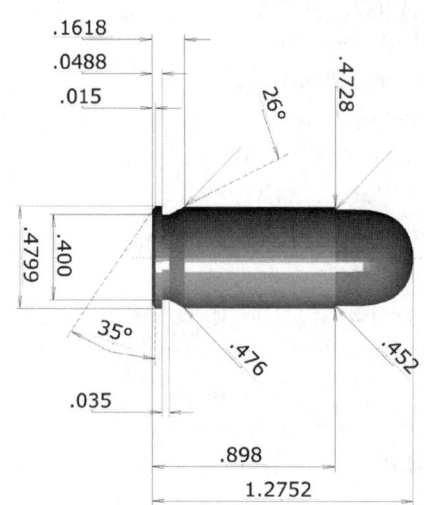

CARTRIDGE BALLISTICS
Max. Average Breech Pressure: 21,000 psi.
Max. Effective Range: 15 ft.
Max. Horizontal Range: 100 yds.
Max. Vertical Range: 400 ft.

Bullet Weight (gr.)	Bullet Type	Muzzle Velocity (fps)	Muzzle Energy (ft.-lbs.)
120	No. 12 Lead Shot	1,000	-

CURRENT MANUFACTURER(S)
CCI

GENERAL COMMENT(S)
This type of .45 Auto shot cartridge with a plastic nose capsule containing the shot pellets was developed by CCI in the early 1960s. This design has replaced most other types of shot carriers such as wood, paper and metal which had consistently proven unsatisfactory. CCI has comfortably dominated this niche market ever since; the limited volume of this market will not support more than one major manufacturer.

A major reason for CCI's success is that the product looks attractive. CCI packaging supports this with a flat, plastic, 10 round box with a clear plastic cover and a white tray that accentuates their appearance. While the per round price is double that of conventional .45 Auto ammunition, most customer requirements are fully satisfied by 10 rounds.

Shooters have a tendency to expect too much of .45 Auto shot cartridges. Remember, although the cartridge is large and the bore diameter substantial, the shot charge weight is small and the No. 12 lead pellets will not penetrate deeply. Patterns are poor as the rifling adversely affects pattern quality. In fact, their effective range is only 15 ft.

TECHNICAL COMMENT(S)
This shot cartridge design has several well designed technical features. It uses a standard .45 Auto cartridge case that requires no special tooling. In this instance, CCI uses their aluminum cartridge case. The plastic nose capsule holds the shot charge. On exiting the muzzle, the plastic nose capsule disintegrates minimizing pellet deformation.

Remember, .45 Auto shot cartridges must be manually fed one at a time into the chamber of semi-automatic pistols as feeding them through the magazine may break the plastic nose capsule. These cartridges will NOT function semi-automatic pistols or rifles. They should NOT be fired in .45 Auto caliber revolvers.

.45 COLT SHOT

ALTERNATE NAME(S): .45 Long Colt, .45 Colt Long, .45 Colt Army
RELATED CALIBER(S): .45 Magnum

CARTRIDGE HISTORY
Year of Introduction: 1873
Country of Origin: U.S.
Designer(s): Colt
Governing Body: SAAMI
Present Status: active

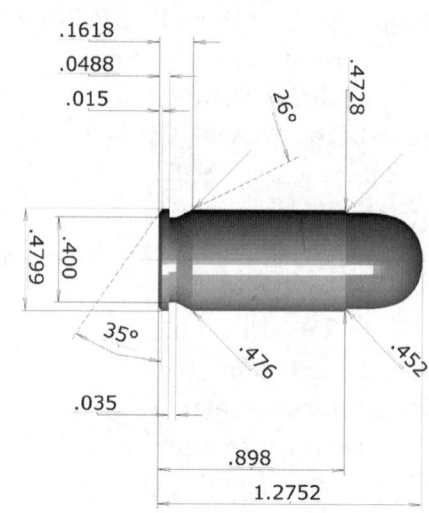

CARTRIDGE DESCRIPTION
Bullet Diameter: .454 in.
Bullet Weight(s): 150 gr.
Rifling Twist Rate: 1 turn in 16 in.
Test Barrel Length: 4 in.
Case Type: rimmed, straight
Case Material: brass
Primer Type: large pistol

CARTRIDGE BALLISTICS
Max. Average Breech Pressure: 14,000 psi.
Max. Effective Range: 15 ft.
Max. Horizontal Range: 100 yds.
Max. Vertical Range: 400 ft.

Bullet Weight (gr.)	Bullet Type	Muzzle Velocity (fps)	Muzzle Energy (ft.-lbs.)
150	No. 12 Lead Shot	1,000	-

CURRENT MANUFACTURER(S)
CCI

GENERAL COMMENT(S)
This type of .45 Colt shot cartridge with a plastic nose capsule containing the shot pellets was developed by CCI in the early 1960s. This design has replaced most other types of shot carriers such as wood, paper and metal which had consistently proven unsatisfactory. CCI has comfortably dominated this niche market ever since; the limited volume of this market will not support more than one major manufacturer.

A major reason for CCI's success is that the product looks attractive. CCI packaging supports this with a flat, plastic, 10 round box with a clear plastic cover and a white tray that accentuates their appearance. While the per round price is double that of conventional .45 Colt ammunition, most customer requirements are fully satisfied by 10 rounds.

Shooters have a tendency to expect too much of .45 Colt shot cartridges. Remember, although the cartridge is large and the bore diameter substantial, the shot charge weight is small and the No. 12 lead pellets will not penetrate deeply. Patterns are poor as the rifling adversely affects pattern quality. In fact, their effective range is only 15 ft.

TECHNICAL COMMENT(S)
This shot cartridge design has several well designed technical features. It uses a standard .45 Colt cartridge case that requires no special tooling. In this instance, CCI uses their aluminum cartridge case. The plastic nose capsule holds the shot charge. On exiting the muzzle, the plastic nose capsule disintegrates minimizing pellet deformation.

Remember, .45 Colt shot cartridges will work normally through revolvers, but may NOT function in many rifles.

CHAPTER 85 : CENTERFIRE SHOTSHELL - OBSOLETE

CHAPTER 85

For Cartridge Index see Chapter 101. All drawing dimensions are approximate.

These include the unsuccessful shot load designs with wood or paper containers or lengthened cases sold by various manufacturers over the 20th century. Some are even of fairly recent vintage. The one thing all these have in common is that they did not sell well enough to remain in production long.

.44 XL CENTERFIRE SHOTSHELL

ALTERNATE NAME(S): .44 XL Shotshell
RELATED SHOTSHELL(S): none

SHOTSHELL HISTORY

Year of Introduction: circa 1900
Country of Origin: U.S.
Designer(s): N/A
Governing Body: none
Present Status: obsolete

SHOTSHELL DESCRIPTION

Bore Diameter: .425 in. (61-gauge)
Case Type: rimmed, straight
Case Material: brass, paper
Head Material: brass
Basewad Type: integral
Basewad Material: brass
Wad Column Type: fiber
Crimp Closure: paper container
Primer: large rifle

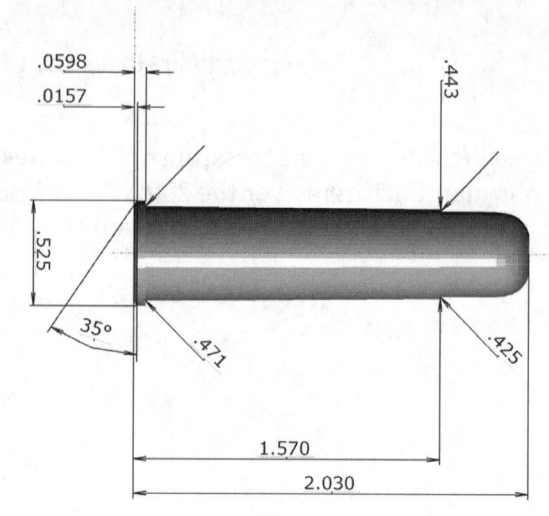

SHOTSHELL BALLISTICS

Max. Average Breech Pressure: 12,000 psi.
Test Barrel Length: N/A
Shot Charge Weight Range: 5/16 - 3/8 oz.

Shot Charge Weight (ozs)	Shell Length (in.)	Shot Type	Muzzle Velocity (fps)	Type
3/8	1.281	No. 8 lead	950 (est.)	Field

CURRENT MANUFACTURER(S)

None

GENERAL COMMENT(S)

The .44 XL was one of the predecessors of the .410 bore shotshell introduced in 1911. Prior to that time, small shotshells based on a version of the ubiquitous .44-40 WCF cartridge with a straight case were offered in a variety of configurations. One of the most popular of these was loaded with a waxed paper container in the mouth holding a charge of lead shot. As other varieties held less shot, "XL" meaning extra long was added to the nomenclature. Popular firearms for .44 shotshells included the Marble's Game Getter, Stevens Pocket Shotgun and smoothbore versions of Winchester lever-action rifles and Colt Lightning slide-action rifles. Most owners of these small shotguns used them as a working tool to eradicate rodents and pests and to harvest small game as the opportunity presented itself. These shotshells were used by many of the exhibition shooters in Buffalo Bill's Wild West Show. Famous shooters such as Annie Oakley used them in special, smoothbore rifles to break glass balls and other objects tossed into the air. With the introduction of the .410 bore shotshell, the need for .44 shotshells ended and manufacture ended in the 1930s.

TECHNICAL COMMENT(S)

All .44 Shotshells were versions of the same basic .44-40 WCF cartridge made with a straight case instead of a necked case. A variety of different methods were used to hold the shot including internally with paper top wad, extended length cases and wood containers holding the shot. The XL was one of the most popular as it held the heaviest shot charge but its length prevented it from being fired in lever-action or slide-action rifles.Development of the .410 bore shotshell was based on .44 shotshell dimensions and ballistics. This extended to the point that .44 Shotshells could be fired in .410-bore shotguns. Although various sizes of lead shot were offered, No. 8 was the most popular. A load with a single, 115 grain, lead round ball was a popular item as well.

.45 AUTO SHOT (METAL)

ALTERNATE NAME(S): .45 Automatic, .45 ACP (Obsolete)
RELATED CALIBER(S): .45 Win. Mag., .45 G.A.P.

CARTRIDGE HISTORY
Year of Introduction: 1943
Country of Origin: U.S.
Designer(s): Remington
Governing Body: SAAMI
Present Status: obsolete

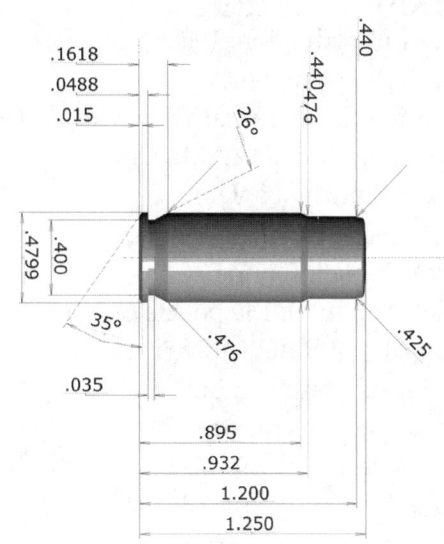

CARTRIDGE DESCRIPTION
Bullet Diameter: none
Bullet Weight(s): 120 gr.
Rifling Twist Rate: 1 turn in 16 in.
Test Barrel Length: 5 in.
Case Type: rimless, straight
Case Material: brass
Primer Type: large pistol

CARTRIDGE BALLISTICS
Max. Average Breech Pressure: 21,000 psi.
Max. Effective Range: 15 ft.
Max. Horizontal Range: 100 yds.
Max. Vertical Range: 400 ft.

Bullet Weight (gr.)	Bullet Type	Muzzle Velocity (fps)	Muzzle Energy (ft.-lbs.)
120	No. 12 Lead Shot	1,000	-

CURRENT MANUFACTURER(S)
None

GENERAL COMMENT(S)
N/A

TECHNICAL COMMENT(S)
N/A

.45 AUTO SHOT (PAPER)

ALTERNATE NAME(S): .45 Automatic, .45 ACP (Obsolete)
RELATED CALIBER(S): .45 Win. Mag., .45 G.A.P.

CARTRIDGE HISTORY
Year of Introduction: 1922
Country of Origin: U.S.
Designer(s): Peters Cartridge Co.
Governing Body: SAAMI, CIP
Present Status: obsolete

CARTRIDGE DESCRIPTION
Bullet Diameter: none
Bullet Weight(s): 130 pellets of No. 7 1/2 Lead Shot
Rifling Twist Rate: 1 turn in 16 in.
Test Barrel Length: 5 in.
Case Type: rimless, straight
Case Material: brass
Primer Type: large pistol

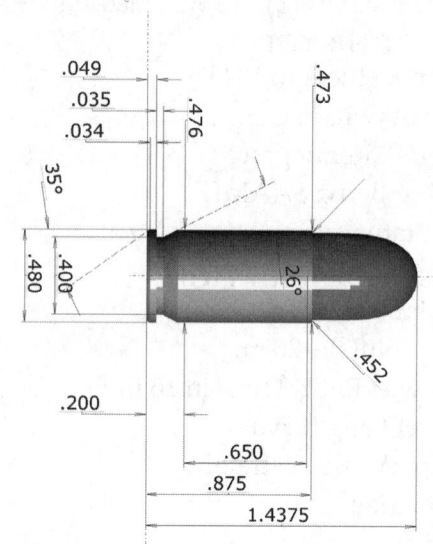

CARTRIDGE BALLISTICS
Max. Average Breech Pressure: 21,000 psi.
Max. Effective Range: 50 yds.
Max. Horizontal Range: 100 yds.
Max. Vertical Range: 400 ft.

Bullet Weight (gr.)	Bullet Type	Muzzle Velocity (fps)	Muzzle Energy (ft.-lbs.)
165 gr (130 Pellets)	No. 12 Lead Shot	1,000	-

CURRENT MANUFACTURER(S)
None

GENERAL COMMENT(S)
This type of .45 Auto shot cartridge loaded with a paper bullet holding lead shot pellets is typical of the early 20th century. This example was designed and introduced in 1922 by Peters Cartridge Co. specifically for the Thompson submachinegun. To quote Peters Cartridge Co. literature of 1922, "This cartridge has been developed by the Peters Cartridge Company specifically for the Thompson Gun, to reduce the range of the gun for safe use in public thoroughfares and places where the welfare of bystanders must be taken into chief consideration. These cartridges contain about 130 pellets of No.7 1/2 shot and are effective up to 50 yards." Law enforcement agencies of the time did not buy into this philosophy and the .45 Auto Shot cartridge for the Thompson Gun faded into history.

TECHNICAL COMMENT(S)
Peters Cartridge engineers designed this shot cartridge with a shorter case and a normal overall loaded length in order to make space for a heavier shot charge. The paper bullet body was extremely fragile, so much so that a special magazine was required to fire them in the gun.

Unlike other shot cartridges, the Peters .45 Auto shot cartridges DID function the Thompson Gun.

CHAPTER 86 : RIMFIRE SHOTSHELL - CURRENT

CHAPTER 86
For Cartridge Index see Chapter 101. All drawing dimensions are approximate.

There are two distinct markets for rimfire shotshells– American and European. While both are based on rimfire designs, the American centers on the .22 Long Rifle and .22 WMR while the European centers on the 9mm shotshell.

American shooters view rimfire shotshells as a safe alternate to bulleted ammunition for killing rodents, pests, and snakes around and inside buildings. Until recent times, American rimfire shotshells were made with elongated cartridge cases closed with a rosette crimp. Today, only Federal makes such shotshells. CCI has developed a shotshell with a plastic, bullet shaped container that is loaded into a standard length cartridge case. Pattern performance of such ammunition is poor due to the adverse effect the rifling in the barrel has on pattern quality. In addition, the miniscule amount of small-size shot (generally, No. 11 or 12 lead) in such loads reduces their effective range to 15 feet or less. American rimfire rifle makers have offered special, smoothbore models for rimfire shotshells on an on and off basis.

The European approach to rimfire shotshells is centered on the "garden gun" concept. A garden gun is an inexpensive shotgun designed specifically for rimfire shotshells– usually of 9mm caliber. The concept for such a gun is to dispatch winged pests over gardens, orchards, and grape vines. Such guns make very little noise and the small pellets do not carry very far. In addition, ownership restrictions are minimal.

This mixed bag of requirements results in an interesting array of designs.

.22 LONG RIFLE SHOT (METAL)

ALTERNATE NAME(S): .22 L.R., .22 LR, 5.6mm
RELATED CALIBER(S): .17 Mach2, .17 Aguila, .22 Hort, .22 Long, .22 Ultra High Velocity, .22 LR Match, .22 SSS

CARTRIDGE HISTORY

Year of Introduction: 1887
Country of Origin: U.S.
Designer(s): J. Stevens Arms & Tool Co.
Governing Body: SAAMI, CIP
Present Status: active

CARTRIDGE DESCRIPTION

Bullet Diameter: .225 in.
Bullet Weight(s): 25 gr.
Rifling Twist Rate: 1 turn in 16 in.
Test Barrel Length: 24 in.
Case Type: rimmed, straight
Case Material: brass

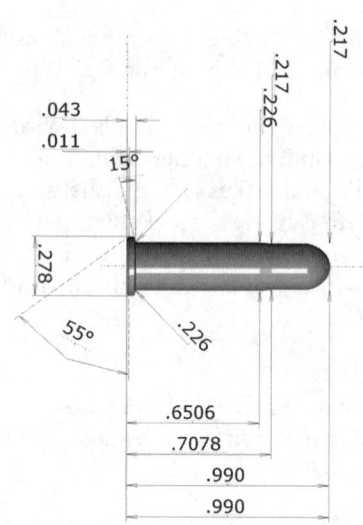

CARTRIDGE BALLISTICS

Max. Average Breech Pressure: 24,000psi.
Max. Effective Range: 15 ft.
Max. Horizontal Range: 100 yds.
Max. Vertical Range: 100 ft.

Bullet Weight (gr.)	Bullet Type	Muzzle Velocity (fps)	Muzzle Energy (ft.-lbs.)
25	No. 12 Lead Shot	1,000	-

CURRENT MANUFACTURER(S)

Federal

GENERAL COMMENT(S)

This type of all-metal .22 rimfire shot cartridge was the norm for many years. It was offered by Winchester, Remington and others. Today, Federal is the only remaining manufacturer. Although originally intended for dispatching rodents, pests and snakes at close range, this type of cartridge has been used for miniature trap systems such as Moskito Trap as well as various shooting games. Variations of this design containing heavier shot loads have been made for such types of activities on a limited basis.

Shooters have a tendency to expect too much of .22 shot cartridges. Remember, the shot charge weights are very small and the No. 12 lead pellets will not penetrate deeply. Patterns are poor as the rifling adversely affects pattern quality. In fact, their effective range is only 15 ft.

TECHNICAL COMMENT(S)

This shot cartridge design has several technical flaws. It uses a longer cartridge case that requires special tooling and loading machinery. The case configuration severely limits the shot charge weight and the shot pellets are deformed by forcing open the metal crimp petals. In many instances, the opened crimp petals stick in the throat of the barrel making for hard extraction. Lastly, .22 shot cartridge will NOT function in semi-automatic firearms.

Typically, .22 Long Rifle shot cartridges cost twice that of .22 Long Rifle bulleted ammunition.

.22 LONG RIFLE SHOT (PLASTIC)

ALTERNATE NAME(S): .22 L.R., .22 LR, 5.6mm
RELATED CALIBER(S): .17 Mach2, .17 Aguila, .22 Hort, .22 Long, .22 Ultra High Velocity, .22 LR Match, .22 SSS

CARTRIDGE HISTORY
Year of Introduction: 1887
Country of Origin: U.S.
Designer(s): J. Stevens Arms & Tool Co.
Governing Body: SAAMI, CIP
Present Status: active

CARTRIDGE DESCRIPTION
Bullet Diameter: .225 in.
Bullet Weight(s): 31 gr.
Rifling Twist Rate: 1 turn in 16 in.
Test Barrel Length: 24 in.
Case Type: rimmed, straight
Case Material: brass

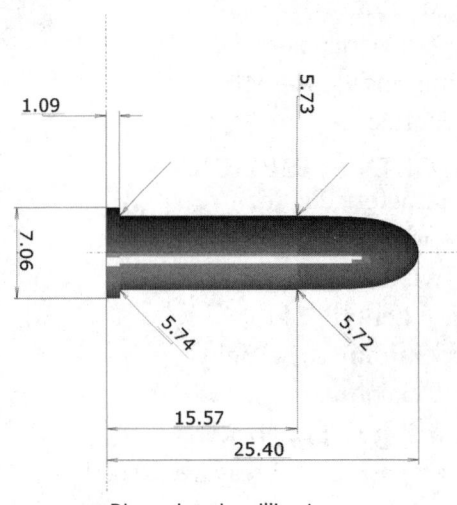

Dimensions in millimeters

CARTRIDGE BALLISTICS
Max. Average Breech Pressure: 24,000psi.
Max. Effective Range: 15 ft.
Max. Horizontal Range: 100 yds.
Max. Vertical Range: 100 ft.

Bullet Weight (gr.)	Bullet Type	Muzzle Velocity (fps)	Muzzle Energy (ft.-lbs.)
31	No. 12 Lead Shot	1,000	-

CURRENT MANUFACTURER(S)
CCI

GENERAL COMMENT(S)
This type of .22 rimfire shot cartridge with a plastic nose capsule containing the shot pellets was developed by CCI in the early 1960s. CCI has comfortably dominated this niche market ever since; the limited volume of this market will not support more than one major manufacturer. A major reason for CCI's success is that the product looks attractive. CCI packaging supports this with a flat, plastic, 20 round box with a clear plastic cover and a white tray that accentuates their appearance. While the per round price is double that of conventional .22 Long Rifle ammunition, most customer requirements are fully satisfied by 20 rounds.

Shooters have a tendency to expect too much of .22 shot cartridges. Remember, the shot charge weights are very small and the No. 12 lead pellets will not penetrate deeply. Patterns are poor as the rifling adversely affects pattern quality. In fact, their effective range is only 15 ft.

TECHNICAL COMMENT(S)
This shot cartridge design has several well designed technical features. It uses a standard .22 Long Rifle cartridge case that requires no special tooling. The plastic nose capsule holds a 24% heavier shot charge than all-metal .22 shot cartridges. On exiting the muzzle, the plastic nose capsule disintegrates minimizing pellet deformation. Fired CCI shot cartridge cases will not stick in the chambers of firearms. However, in similar manner to other shot cartridges, they will NOT function in semi-automatic firearms.

.22 WINCHESTER RIMFIRE

ALTERNATE NAME(S): .22 WRF, .22 Remington Special
RELATED CALIBER(S): .22 WMR

CARTRIDGE HISTORY
Year of Introduction: 1890
Country of Origin: U.S.
Designer(s): Winchester
Governing Body: SAAMI
Present Status: Active

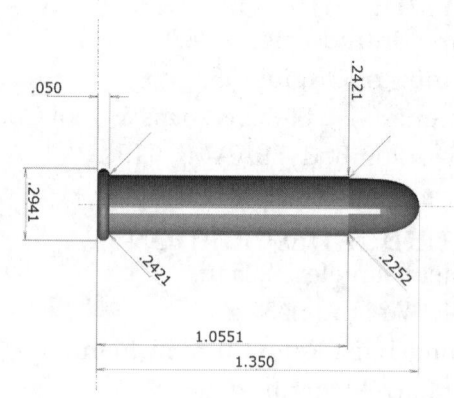

CARTRIDGE DESCRIPTION
Bullet Diameter: .224 in.
Bullet Weight(s): 52 gr.
Rifling Twist Rate: 1 turn in 16 in.
Test Barrel Length: 24 in.
Case Type: rimmed, straight
Case Material: brass

CARTRIDGE BALLISTICS
Max. Average Breech Pressure: 20,000 psi.
Max. Effective Range: 15 ft.
Max. Horizontal Range: 100 yds.
Max. Vertical Range: 100 ft.

Bullet Weight (gr.)	Bullet Type	Muzzle Velocity (fps)	Muzzle Energy (ft.-lbs.)
52	No. 12 Lead Shot	1,000	-

CURRENT MANUFACTURERS
CCI

GENERAL COMMENT(S)
This type of .2 WMR shot cartridge with a plastic nose capsule containing the shot pellets was developed by CCI in the early 1960s. This design has replaced most other types of shot carriers such as wood, paper and metal. CCI has comfortably dominated this niche market ever since; the limited volume of this market will not support more than one major manufacturer.

A major reason for CCI's success is that the product looks attractive. CCI packaging supports this with a flat, plastic, 20 round box with a clear plastic cover and a white tray that accentuates their appearance. While the per round price is double that of conventional .22 WMR ammunition, most customer requirements are fully satisfied by 20 rounds.

Shooters have a tendency to expect too much of .22 WMR shot cartridges. Remember, the shot charge weights are very small and the No. 12 lead pellets will not penetrate deeply. Patterns are poor as the rifling adversely affects pattern quality. In fact, their effective range is only 15 ft.

TECHNICAL COMMENT(S)
This shot cartridge design has several well designed technical features. It uses a standard .22 WMR cartridge case that requires no special tooling. The plastic nose capsule holds the shot charge. On exiting the muzzle, the plastic nose capsule disintegrates minimizing pellet deformation.

The .22 WMR Shot cartridges can be fired in all revolvers and manually operated rifles in a normal manner. However, they will NOT function in semi-automatic guns.

CHAPTER 87 : RIMFIRE SHOTSHELL - OBSOLETE

CHAPTER 87

For Cartridge Index see Chapter 101. All drawing dimensions are approximate.

Arguably, this is a small scrapheap of ammunition history. The obscure, limited market and short production life of most of the cartridges (or loadings) led to their unremarked demise. However, from a technical standpoint, they are a record of attempts to solve a difficult problem with a solution that had to wait for the development of suitable materials (i.e. plastic). Their variety is impressive despite their ignominy.

9mm RIMFIRE SHOTSHELL

ALTERNATE NAME(S): 9mm Rimfire
RELATED SHOTSHELL(S): 9mm Winchester R.F.

SHOTSHELL HISTORY

Year of Introduction: N/A
Country of Origin: Europe
Designer(s): N/A
Governing Body: none
Present Status: active

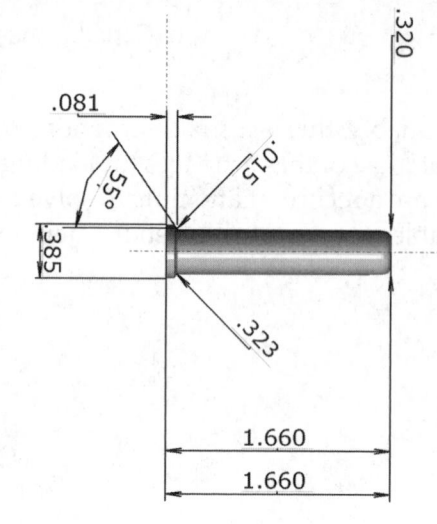

SHOTSHELL DESCRIPTION

Bore Diameter: .355 in.
Case Type: rimmed
Case Material: brass and paper
Head Material: brass
Basewad Type: integral
Basewad Material: brass
Wad Column Type: paper
Crimp Closure: rolled
Primer: rimfire

SHOTSHELL BALLISTICS

Max. Average Breech Pressure: N/A
Test Barrel Length: N/A
Shot Charge Weight Range: 109.6 grains single charge, 220 grains double charge

Shot Charge Weight (ozs)	Shell Length (in.)	Shot Type	Muzzle Velocity (fps)	Type
1/3	1.125	lead	600	paper, brass head

CURRENT MANUFACTURER(S)

Fiocchi

GENERAL COMMENT(S)

These diminutive shotshells are used in cheap, single-barrel and over/under shotguns called "garden guns" in Europe. Their low cost, light report and limited range have been carefully adjusted for this purpose. The main application of these shotshells is rodent, pest, and varmint control in orchards, vineyards, gardens, and buildings. In many European countries, the firearms license requirements for such shotguns are substantially more relaxed than for regular shotguns.

TECHNICAL COMMENT(S)

These shotshells are loaded with lead shot of various charge weights and pellet diameters. For example, there are loadings with a single and also a double shot charge. Loadings with a single lead round ball are offered as well. These shells are a close range only proposition as the barrels of the shotguns are not choked. With the single charge of shot, effective range is approximately 15-20 yards. Note that these shells and shotguns are not toys and are quite capable of inflicting a serious injury. Rimfire shotshells of this type are not reloadable.

9mm FLOBERT

ALTERNATE NAME(S): none
RELATED SHOTSHELL(S): 9mm Centerfire, .360 Centerfire

SHOTSHELL HISTORY

Year of Introduction: mid-1800s

Country of Origin: France

Designer(s): Flobert

Governing Body: CIP

Present Status: obsolete

SHOTSHELL DESCRIPTION

Bore Diameter: .355 in.

Case Type: rimmed, straight

Case Material: brass

Head Material: brass

Basewad Type: none

Basewad Material: N/A

Wad Column Type: fiber

Crimp Closure: rolled with top wad

Primer Type: rimfire

SHOTSHELL BALLISTICS

Max. Average Breech Pressure: 23,000 psi. (est.)

Test Barrel Length: N/A

Shot Charge Weight Range: approx. 1/4 oz.

Shot Charge Weight (ozs)	Shell Length (in.)	Shot Type	Muzzle Velocity (fps)	Type
1/4	1.45 (approx)	lead	1,000 (est)	Rimfire

CURRENT MANUFACTURER(S)

(Winchester 1920-27), Fiocchi

GENERAL COMMENT(S)

In Europe, these small rimfire shotshells are used to eliminate pests in vineyards and to hunt small, edible birds in populated areas. These shells and the smoothbore shotguns chambered for them are particularly popular in Italy and France. In the field, these shells are quiet and of limited range. An attractive point is that both the guns and the ammunition are relatively inexpensive.

TECHNICAL COMMENT(S)

These shotshells are effective only at close ranges due to the small shot charge. However, they are more effective than the .22 Long Rifle shotshells so popular in the U.S. In the past, both a short and a long version of the 9mm shotshell were offered with a metal head and paper tube. Time has winnowed the line to the long version only in a full-length brass case, albeit with a double shot charge in six shot sizes plus a single conical ball. Fiocchi remains the sole manufacturer.

.32 RIMFIRE SHOTSHELL

ALTERNATE NAME(S): .32 R.F. Shotshell
RELATED SHOTSHELL(S): .22 Long Rifle Shotshell

SHOTSHELL HISTORY
Year of Introduction: circa mid-1860s
Country of Origin: U.S.
Designer(s): Smith & Wesson
Governing Body: none
Present Status: obsolete

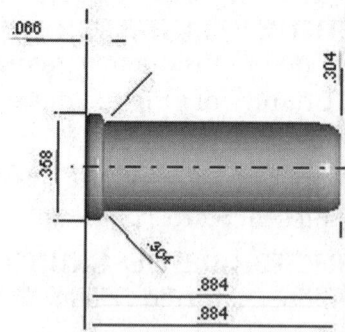

SHOTSHELL DESCRIPTION
Bore Diameter: .312 in.
Case Type: rimmed, straight
Case Material: brass
Head Material: brass
Basewad Type: integral
Basewad Material: brass
Wad Column Type: fiber
Crimp Closure: rolled with paper top wad, or extended wood container
Primer: rimfire

SHOTSHELL BALLISTICS
Max. Average Breech Pressure: N/A
Test Barrel Length: N/A
Shot Charge Weight Range: appox. 1/4-1/3 oz.

Shot Charge Weight (ozs)	Shell Length (in.)	Shot Type	Muzzle Velocity (fps)	Type
1/4-1/3	.884-1.215	lead	850 (est.)	Rimfire

CURRENT MANUFACTURER(S)
None

GENERAL COMMENT(S)
These were standard .32 Long rimfire cartridge cases with a shot load instead of a bullet. Such loads were used on .32 Long rifles and revolvers for killing rodents and pests at close ranges (15 feet or less).

TECHNICAL COMMENT(S)
There were two types of .32 Long shot cartridges. The first held the shot charge internally with a paper top wad and rolled crimp to hold it in place. This was considered a general-purpose load and held the smallest shot charge. The second type held the shot charge in an extended wood container that was held in the case mouth in place of the bullet. This arrangement held a heavier shot charge and helped minimize the effects of the rifling spinning the shot charge.

.310 REMINGTON

ALTERNATE NAME(S): .310 Remington Rimfire, .310 Shotshell
RELATED SHOTSHELL(S): .32 Long Rimfire, .32 Extra Long Rimfire

SHOTSHELL HISTORY

Year of Introduction: circa early 1960s

Country of Origin: U.S.

Designer(s): Remington

Governing Body: SAAMI

Present Status: obsolete

SHOTSHELL DESCRIPTION

Bore Diameter: .310 in.

Case Type: rimmed, straight

Case Material: brass

Head Material: brass

Basewad Type: integral

Basewad Material: brass

Wad Column Type: fiber

Crimp Closure: rolled with top wad

Primer Type: rimfire

SHOTSHELL BALLISTICS

Max. Average Breech Pressure: 23,000 psi.

Test Barrel Length: 24 in.

Shot Charge Weight Range: approx 1/4 oz.

Shot Charge Weight (ozs)	Shell Length (in.)	Shot Type	Muzzle Velocity (fps)	Type
1/4	1.06	lead	1,000 (est)	Moskeeto

CURRENT MANUFACTURER(S)

None

GENERAL COMMENT(S)

This cartridge was developed in the 1960s by Remington for a miniature clay bird shooting system. A small, spring-powered trap, which threw the clay, was mounted under the barrel of a smoothbore bolt action gun. The trap could be released by the shooter. While the concept was sound, it did not strike a responsive note with shooters. Remington then dropped the project. Production of .310 Remington ammunition was limited; .310 Remington cartridges are now collector's items.

TECHNICAL COMMENT(S)

The .310 Remington Rimfire shotshell shares many dimensions with the .32 Long Rimfire such as rim diameter and body diameter. Case length of the .310 Remington cartridge is longer than the .32 Long, but shorter than the .32 Extra Long. The shot charge contains approximately 100 grains of fine lead shot sealed with a paper top wad held in place by a rolled crimp on the case mouth.

.20 WINGO RIMFIRE

ALTERNATE NAME(S): .20 Caliber Wingo
RELATED SHOTSHELL(S): .22 Long Rifle

SHOTSHELL HISTORY
Year of Introduction: early 1970s
Country of Origin: U.S.
Designer(s): Winchester
Governing Body: SAAMI
Present Status: obsolete

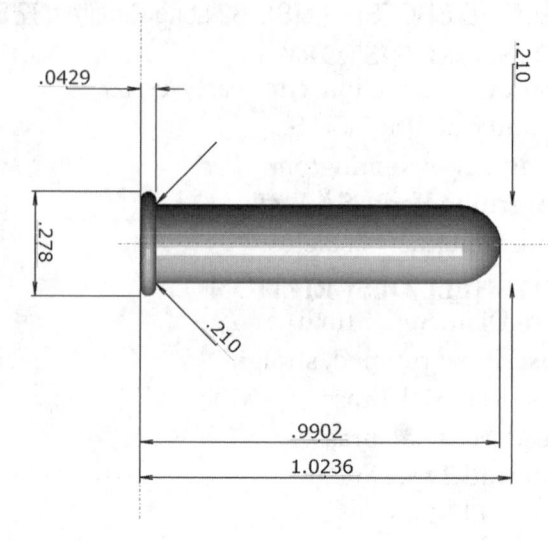

SHOTSHELL DESCRIPTION
Bore Diameter: .200 in.
Case Type: rimmed
Case Material: brass
Head Material: brass
Basewad Type: integral
Basewad Material: brass
Wad Column Type: fiber
Crimp Closure: rosette fold on case mouth
Primer Type: rimfire

SHOTSHELL BALLISTICS
Max. Average Breech Pressure: 23,000 psi.
Test Barrel Length: 24 in.
Shot Charge: approx. 115 pellets of No. 12 lead shot

Shot Charge Weight (ozs)	Shell Length (in.)	Shot Type	Muzzle Velocity (fps)	Type
115 pellets No. 12	1.02	lead	1,000 (est)	Wingo

CURRENT MANUFACTURER(S)
None

GENERAL COMMENT(S)
Now it was Winchester's turn to try something new. Unlike the Remington miniature clay bird system that placed priority on informal competition outdoors, Winchester's Wingo was an indoor sport where competitors fired at hollow ice balls pneumatically launched from tubes. A smoothbore, Martini type action gun was used. After considerable time and effort promoting this new, urban sport, Winchester realized the concept was not attracting the investors necessary to build the indoor facilities. The Wingo project then was quietly cancelled. Today, Wingo cartridges have become collector's items.

TECHNICAL COMMENT(S)
Basically, the Wingo cartridge consists of a .20 caliber brass body with a .22 caliber rim and head. This combination prevented someone from chambering and firing a .22 Long Rifle cartridge. The small charge of No. 12 lead shot was sufficient to break the hollow ice balls given a fair hit.

SECTION XIV – WILDCATS CARTRIDGE PROFILES
CHAPTER 88 : WILDCATS THAT MADE IT

CHAPTER 88 HIGHLIGHTS:

- Famous Designers
- Center Fire Rifle Wildcats
- Center Fire Handgun Wildcats
- Profile: P.O. Ackley
- Profile: J.D. Jones

Although it was not possible to include comprehensive coverage of wildcat cartridges in this book, the following abbreviated list is offered to provide the reader with a basic idea of this very broad field of innovation and invention. The reader will note immediately that the number of rifle caliber wildcats far exceeds those in rim fire and handgun calibers. We may attribute this to a larger basic field of calibers from which to begin as well as ease of modification.

In the field of wildcats, two individuals stand out: P.O. Ackley (deceased) and J.D. Jones (alive and well last time I saw him). Both of these men have established a well-earned reputation for excellence and quantity in this field. As a result, their creations are listed separately.

Technical details cannot be provided here. However, the reader certainly will enjoy the colorful names of the inventions.

FAMOUS WILDCAT CARTRIDGE DESIGNERS AND THEIR CREATIONS

NAME	INVENTION(S)
Parker O. Ackley	Numerous wildcat rifle cartridges
Don Allen	Dakota family of rifle cartridges
Art Alphin	A-Square family of rifle cartridges
Bill Atkinson	A&M cartridges
Frank C. Barnes	Barnes series of rifle caliber wildcats
James Calhoon	Various micro calibers
Jim Carmichel	.22 Cheetah rifle cartridge
Harvey Donaldson	R-2 Lovell, .219 Donaldson Wasp
W. Eichelberger	Various micro calibers
Elgin Gates	IHMSA rifle cartridges, many pistol cartridges
Jerry Gebby	.22-250 Varminter (.22-250 Rem.)
R.E. Gibbs	.25 Gibbs, 6.5 Gibbs, .270 Gibbs etc.
Jim Harvey	Harvey Kay-Chuk cartridge
Steve Herrett	Herrett family of handgun cartridges
George Hoffman	.458 Hoffman
Cameron Hopkins	.425 Express
Don Hopkins	.333 OKH, .334 OKH, .475 OKH
Ken Howell	.425 Express Howell African
Alton Jones	.14 Alton Jones Express, other micro calibers
J.D. Jones	Master wildcatter, over 400 designs
Elmer Keith	.333 OKN, .334 OKN, .475 OKH
Lysle Kilbourn	K-Hornet series
John Lazzeroni	Lazzeroni family of rifle cartridges
John Linebaugh	Linebaugh handgun cartridges
Jacque P. Lott	.458 Lott

NAME	INVENTION(S)
Hervey Lovell	.22 Lovell
A.E. Mashburn	.218 Mashburn Bee, 7mm-06 Mashburn
Paul Middlestead	.22-243 Middlestead rifle cartridge series
Wildey Moore	Wildey magnum pistol cartridges
Charles O'Neil	.333 OKH, .334 OKH, .475 OKH
Peter Pi	.400 and .440 Cor-Bon pistol cartridges
Dr. Louis Palmisano	PPC cartridge family, Pindell-Palmisano Cartridge
Ferris Pindell	PPC cartridge family, Pindell-Palmisano Cartridge
Harry Sanford	Auto-Mag family of pistol cartridges
Ross Seyfried	.585 Nyati
Layne Simpson	Shooting Times family of rifle cartridges
Jim Stekl	Remington BR series of rifle cartridges
Jon Sundra	JRS family of rifle cartridges
Skip Talbot	Talbot long range rifle cartridges
Robert Chatfield-Taylor	.416 Taylor
Wes Ugalde	TCU family of rifle cartridges
Townsend Whelen	Whelen cartridges
Evan Whildin	Action Express pistol cartridges
L.E. Wilson	.220 Wotkyns-Wilson Arrow rifle cartridge
J.B. Wood	North American Arms pistol cartridges
Grosvenor Wotkyns	.220 Wotkyns-Wilson Arrow rifle cartridge

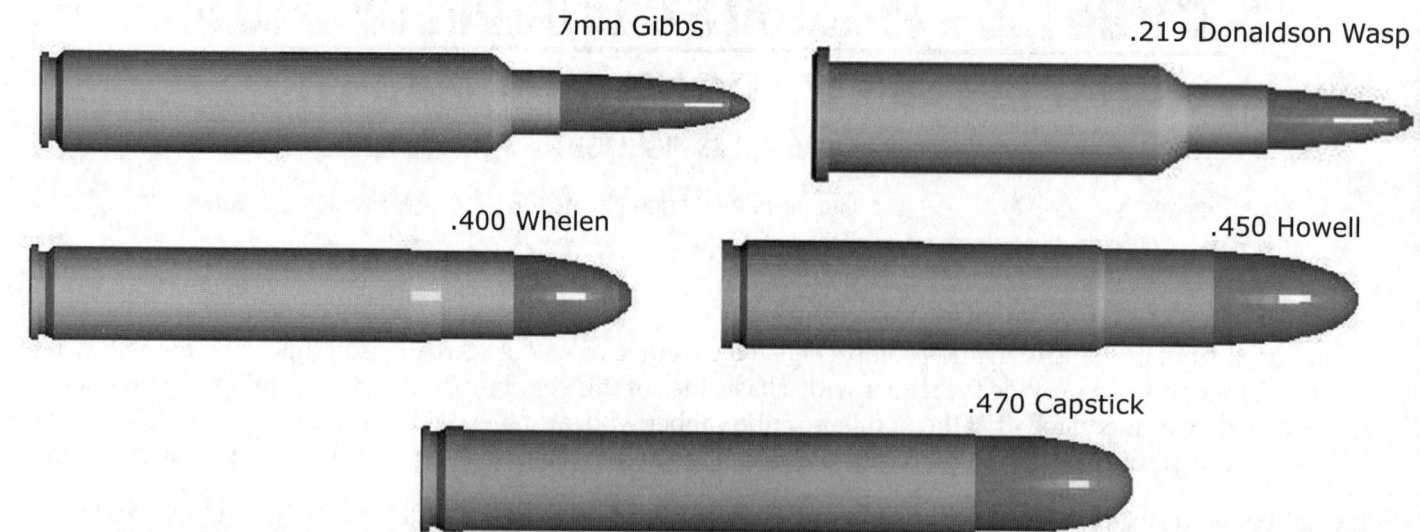

7mm Gibbs

.219 Donaldson Wasp

.400 Whelen

.450 Howell

.470 Capstick

CENTER FIRE RIFLE WILDCATS

.10 Eichelberger Dart
.10 Eichelberger Long Rifle (RF)
.10 Eichelberger Pup
.10 Squirrel
.12 Cooper (CCM)
.12 Eichelberger Carbine
.12 Eichelberger Long Rifle (RF)
.12 Eichelberger WMR (RF)
.12 Squirrel
.12 Viper
.14 Alton Jones Express (RF)
.14 Cooper (CCM)
.14 Eichelberger Bee
.14 Eichelberger Dart
.14 Jet Junior
.14 Walker Hornet
.14/221 Walker Fireball
.14/222
.14/222 Eichelberger
.14/222 Eichelberger Mag
.17 Bumblebee
.17 Cooper Magnum
.17 Hornet
.17 Javelina
.17 Libra
.17 Mach IV (CF)
.17-222
.17-22-250
.17-223

.17-224
.17-225
.17-357 RG
.19 Badger
.19 Calhoon (Hornet)
.19-221
.19-223 Calhoon
.20 BR
.20 Hornet BRD
.20 PPC
.20 Practical
.20 Tactical
.20 Var-Targ
.20 Var-Targ Turbo
.20-20 BDR
.20-222
.20-222 Magnum
.22 Dasher
.22 Newton
.22 Spitfire (MMJ-5.7mm)
.22 Super Jet
.22-303
5mm-223 Forker
5mm Epperson Cricket
5mm Craig
5mm EV
5mm Hornet Short
.218 Mashburn Bee
.219 Donaldson Wasp
.22 BR Remington
.22 CHeetah
.22 Cooper Magnum
.22 K-Hornet

.22 Maximum Lovell
.22 MDK
.22 Picra
.22 R-2 Lovell
.22 Reed Express
.22 Taranah Hornet
.22 Waldog
.220 Howell
.220 Wby Rocket
.220 Wotkyns-Wilson Arrow
.222 Rimmed
.22-243 Middlestead
.22-3000
.224 BOZ
.224 Clark
.224 Harvey Kay-Chuk
.224 R-C Maximum
.224 Texas Trophy Hunter
.224-284 ALS
5.56x42mm Harrison DMR
5.6x50Rmm Bellm
.240 Cobra
.240 Gibbs
.240 Hawk
.240 Howell
.240 Incinerator
.240 Madame
.240 Page Pooper
.240 Super Varminter
6-08 Liles
6BRBS

6mm BR Improved
6mm BRDX
6mm BRX
6mm CHeetah
6mm Dasher
6mm International (6mm-250)
6mm SPC
6mm TCU
6mm Thermos Bottle
6mm XC
6mm/30-30 Improved
6mm-03 Epps
6mm-06
6mm-284
6mmBR UBL
6x45mm (6mm-223 Remington)
6x47mm
6x47mm ATZL
6x51mm ATZL
6x52Rmm Bretschneider
.25 Gibbs
.25 Krag
.25 TCU
.250 Howell
.250 Humdinger
.25-08/25 Souper
.25-222 Copperhead
.25-284
.256 Ferret
.257 DEL Challenger
.257 Kimber

57 Shooting Times
Westerner
5 Gibbs
5 Jonson
5 Shooting Times West-
erner
5/06 (.256/06)
5mm Leopard
5mm TCU
5mm-257
5x40Rmm Fuller
5x52mm American
5x63mm Messner Mag-
num
5mm Harrison Reaper
50 Howell
60 Picra
64 Hawk
64 Leroy Nitro Express
64 RLB
70 Gibbs
70 H&S Echo
70 Hawk
70 Howell
70 IHMSA
70 REN
70 Titus Savage
70/303 Sportco
77 GS
GNR
mm Bellm
nm Gibbs
nm Hawk
mm Holy Grail
mm IHMSA
mm JRS (Jon R. Sundra)
mm KM
mm MK Super
mm SGLC
mm Shooting Times
Easterner
mm Shooting Times
Westerner
mm Super Magnum

7mm TCU
7mm Ultimate Silhouette
7mm YRM
7mm-06 Mashburn
7x23mm Penna
7x28mm Penna
7x49mm GJW
.280 Howell
.30 American
.30 Apache
.30 Cody
.30 Gibbs
.30 H&S
.30 Herrett
.30 Kurz
.30 PICRA
.300 GNR
.300 Howell
.300 ICL Tornado
.300 LBFM
.300 Phoenix
.30-06 Court Carty
.30-284 Winchester
.30-338 Winchester Mag-
num
.30-357 Paxton
.308 Baer
.308 EH
.30-8mm Remington
.308x1 1/2 in. Barnes
7.62 UKM
8mm-06
.32 Pueblo
.328 Mitchell
.33-08
.333 OKH
.334 OKH
.338 Canadian KCG
.338 Clipper
.338 Edge
.338 Nicholson
.338 Spectre
.338 Wyatt
.338 Xtreme

.338/50 Talbot
.338-223 Straight
.340 Jaden
.35 Sambar
.35-284 McPherson
.35-30/30
.357 Atomic
.358 Shooting Times
　Alaskan
.358 Ultra Mag Towsley
.360 Kestrel
.366 DGW
.374 Epstein
.375 JRS Magnum (Jon R.
　Sundra)
.375 Ras
.375 Super Swede
.375 Tyrvaa
.375 Van Horn
.375 Whelen
.375-284 McPherson
.395 Tayanka
.400 Tembo
.400 Whelen
.411 Express
.411 Hawk
.416 Aagard
.416 A-Square Rimmed
.416 B&M
.416 Barnes
.416 BGA
.416 Chatsfield-Taylor
.416 Hoffman
.416 Howell
.416 Prairie Gun Works
.416 Taylor
.416-284 McPherson
.425 Express
.425 Fossdal
.45 Blaser
.45-70 Elko Magnum
.450 Watts
.450 Bonecrusher
.450 Alaskan

.450 Howell
.450 KNR
.450 Watts Magnum
.450 Assegai
.450 GNR
.452 JBX
.458x1 1/2 in. Barnes
.458x2 in. American
.458 Alpine
.458 Lott
.460 Alliance
.460 A-Square Short
.460 G&A Special
.470 Capstick
.475 Jurras
.475 OKH
.475 A&M Magnum
12.04 Bibamufu
.50 Alaskan
.50 American Eagle
.50 B&M
.50 Martin
.50 McMillan Fat Mac
.50 McMurdo
.50 Peacekeeper
.500 Belted Magnum
.500 Mbogo
.500 Wyoming Express
.505/530 Woodleigh
.510 DTC-Europ
.510 GNR
.510 Kodiak Express
.510 McMurdo
.510 Nitro Express
.577 Tyrannosaur
.585 Belted Hubel Express
.585 Nyati
.600 Overkill
.666 Teufel
.700 AHR
.700 Hubel Express
.729 Jongmans

CENTER FIRE HANDGUN WILDCATS

8.5mm Mars
9mm Mars
9mm Action Express

9x22mm MJR
9x25mm Dillon
9x25mm Super Auto G

.300 GNR
.357 Aut. Mag.
.357 Herrett

.357/44 B&D
.38 Casull
.38/45 Safestop
.38-45 Auto/Clerke
.38-45 Hard Head
.40 Super
.401 Bobcat
.41 Avenger

.41 Special
.445 Super Magnum
.45 Mars Long Case
.45 Mars Short Case
.45 Silhouette
.45 Super
.45 Wildey Magnum
.450 GNR

.451 Detonics
.460 Rowland
.475 Linebaugh
.475 Linebaugh.38 AMU
.475 Wildey Magnum
.500 Linebaugh
.510 GNR

PROFILE : PARKER OTTO ACKLEY - 1903-1989

By any measure, P.O. Ackley was a renaissance man in the world of shooting. He held a college degree in engineering and was a trained gunsmith who authored several popular books on shooting and reloading. In addition, he was on the teaching staff at Trinidad State Junior College in Trinidad, CO and served on the staff of Guns & Ammo and Shooting Times magazines. He owned and operated his own custom gun shop, first in Oregon and later in Trinidad, CO, moving eventually to Salt Lake City, UT.

Ackley is warmly remembered for all these activities, however we remember him here as a prolific ballistic experimenter and developer of dozens of wildcat cartridges. Ackley called his cartridges "Ackley" or "Ackley Improved" as they were designed to improve ballistic performance by increasing powder capacity. Most were based on standard caliber cartridges modified to his concepts. Experienced shooters appreciated that Ackley Improved cartridges offered several key design features.

Ackley's preferred method of increasing the powder capacity of a case was to blow out the sides to eliminate the taper and increase the shoulder angle. Converting a rifle to an Ackley caliber normally required only rechambering the existing barrel on the rifle - an inexpensive process. Ackley cartridge cases could be formed by simply firing standard cartridges in the rechambered barrel. If necessary, standard ammunition could be fired safely in most Ackley chambered barrels. For these reasons, none of Ackley's wildcat cartridge designs were adopted by a large ammunition manufacturer.

Notable Ackley accomplishments include developing the first .17 caliber cartridges and the first short magnum cartridges. Here then is an abridged list of Ackley wildcat cartridges.

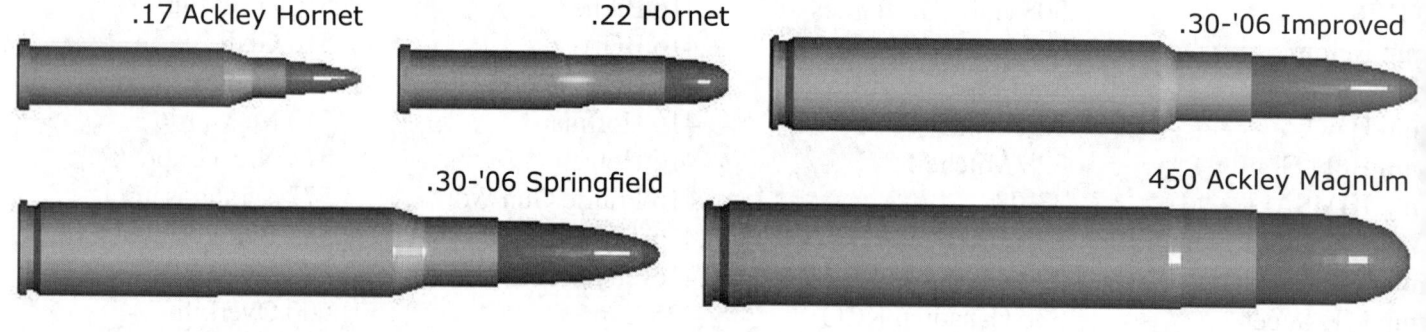

.17 Ackley Hornet   .22 Hornet   .30-'06 Improved

.30-'06 Springfield   450 Ackley Magnum

ACKLEY WILDCATS

.17 Ackley Hornet
.17 Ackley Improved Bee
.17/221
.19 Ackley Bee
.20 Ackley Bee
.22 Ackley Improved Hornet
.218 Ackley Improved Bee
.220 Swift Ackley Improved

.22-250 Ackley Improved
.223 Ackley Improved
.22-30/30 Ackley Improved
.22 Jet Ackley Improved
.22 Hi-Power Ackley Improved
.228 Ackley Magnum
.243 Ackley Improved
6mm/30-30 Ackley Improved

6mm-06 Ackley Improved
6mm 30/40 Ackley Improved
.25 Short Ackley Krag
.25-35 Ackley Improved
.25 Ackley Improved Krag
.250-3000 Ackley Improved
.257 Ackley Improved
6.5mm-06 Ackley Improved

.25-06 Ackley Improved

.270 Ackley Improved Savage

.280 Ackley Improved

.30 Ackley Short Magnum No. 1
  and No. 2

.30/348 Ackley Improved

.30-30 Ackley Improved

.30-06 Ackley Improved

.300 Ackley Improved Magnum

.303 Ackley Improved

.35 Ackley Short Magnum No. 1
  and No. 2

.35 Ackley Improved Whelen

.375 Akley Improved Whelen

.375 Ackley Improved

.450 Ackley Magnum

.475 Ackley Magnum

PROFILE : J.D. JONES

By any measure, J.D. Jones is the master of wildcat cartridges– to date, he has designed over 400 and is still active! In the early 1980s, J.D. founded SSK Industries to turn his hobby into a business. How, you might well ask, can anyone make a living at designing wildcats? J.D. can, and has.

Modern life leaves many of us with little time to do the things we really want, for example, developing a new cartridge, building a rifle in a wildcat caliber, or working up loads for an existing rifle. J.D. can help by bringing his expertise to your projects and getting them done for you. These activities keep J.D. very busy, but in between jobs, he is a well-known gun writer and author of several books on shooting. Oh yes, did I mention he is an avid hunter himself?

JDJ cartridges are hard to categorize as they vary so widely. Among them are subsonic cartridges for use with suppressors in special operations, African rifle cartridges, handgun cartridges, hunting cartridges, and target cartridges. He has them all.

J.D. Jones is one of the few people in this world who works at something he loves. This makes going to work in the morning a pleasure and it shows. Everyone in the shooting industry knows and respects J.D. Jones for his friendly demeanor, courtesy and knowledge.

A PARTIAL LIST OF J.D. JONES CARTRIDGES

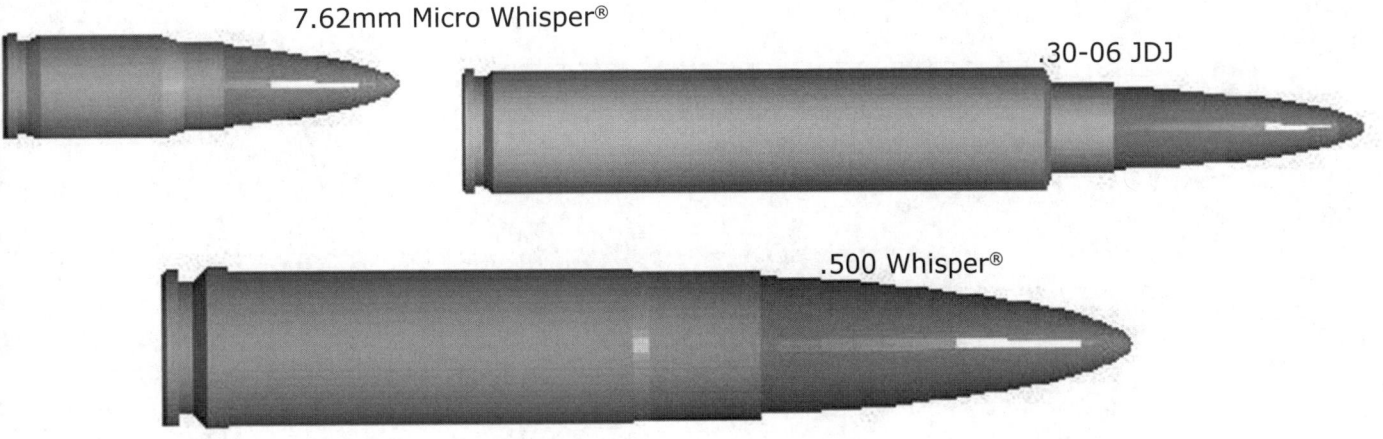

7.62mm Micro Whisper®

.30-06 JDJ

.500 Whisper®

.226 JDJ

6mm Whisper®

6mm JDJ

.257 JDJ

.25/06 JDJ

.257 JDJ Mini Dreadnaught

6.5mm Whisper®

6.5mm JDJ

6.5mm JDJx30

6.5 Mini Dreadnaught

6.5mm JDJ No. 2

6.5/270 JDJ

.270 JDJ

.270 JDJ No. 2

7mm Whisper®

7mm JDJ

7mm-30 JDJ

7mm JDJ No. 2

.280 JDJ

7.62 Micro-Whisper®

7.63 Mini-Whisper®

.300 Whisper®

.302 Whisper®

.309 JDJ

.30-'06 JDJ

8mm JDJ

.338 Whisper®

.338 JDJ

.338 Woodswalker

.338-06 JDJ

.358 JDJ

.35-06 JDJ

9.3mm JDJ

.375 Whisper®

.375 JDJ

.375-06 JDJ

.375/454 Woodswalker

.40-44 Woodswalker

.40-454 JDJ

.411 JDJ

.416 JDJ

.416-06 JDJ

.44/454 Woodswalker

.458 Whisper®

.475 JDJ

.50 American Eagle

.50 Peacekeeper

.500 Whisper®

.510 Whisper®

14.5mm Whisper®

14.5mm JDJ

.600/577 JDJ

.620 JDJ

.700 JDJ

.950 JDJ

Master wildcatter J.D. Jones take aim with one of his newest creations, the .620 JDJ cartridge. No shrinking violet, the .620 JDJ launches a 1,100 grain .620 inch diameter bullet at a muzzle velocity of 1,100 fps from a 10 inch barrel!

SECTION XV – EXOTIC CARTRIDGE PROFILES
CHAPTER 89 : EXOTIC CARTRIDGES

CHAPTER 89 HIGHLIGHTS:

- Exotic Cartridges
- Exotic Centerfire Cartridges
- Exotic Shotshells

EXOTIC CARTRIDGES

Efforts to improve ammunition technology have not always followed conventional paths of development. Rather, the bewildering variety of cartridge designs and technologies explored over the centuries are a vivid testimony to mankind's inventiveness. A common thread through these efforts is forward thinking retarded by immature technology. However, all things change, technology advances, and what was impossible yesterday may become commonplace tomorrow.

Here, then, are a few of the more exotic cartridge designs that have been tried in the past with indifferent results.

1. 3.8x28.5mm MINIATURE MAUSER

No miniature firearm is complete without appropriate ammunition. While most craftsmen are content to provide dummy cartridges for their creations, in some instances miniature cartridges actually capable of being fired in the gun are also made. The example pictured here is a one-half scale 7x57mm Mauser cartridge made for a miniature Mauser rifle presented to a Mexican general officer by the Mauser Company. This miniature cartridge is typical of the detail in such cartridges.

2. 5.2x68mm MONDRAGON CARTRIDGE

Gen. Manuel Mondragon was a prolific Mexican firearms and ammunition designer who believed that pistons inside cartridge cases would provide a greater surface for the expanding gasses to push against thus increasing muzzle velocity and efficiency. Accordingly, Mondragon cases were made with unusually long bodies and short necks to accommodate an internal piston which was located by the cannelure on the case body. This example cartridge was capable of launching a 102 grain .204 inch diameter bullet at 2,650 fps. Mondragon's interior ballistic piston theories did not hold up and ammunition of his design was too expensive. However it was made briefly in Europe prior to World War I where it was used in one of the first semi-automatic rifles in commercial production. Mondragon's rifles and ammunition entered history when they became the first firearms purchased for aerial combat in World War I (purchased by Germany from SIG in Switzerland in 1914).

3. THE ACCELERATOR OR DISCARDING SABOT CONCEPT AND RABBETH'S SABOT

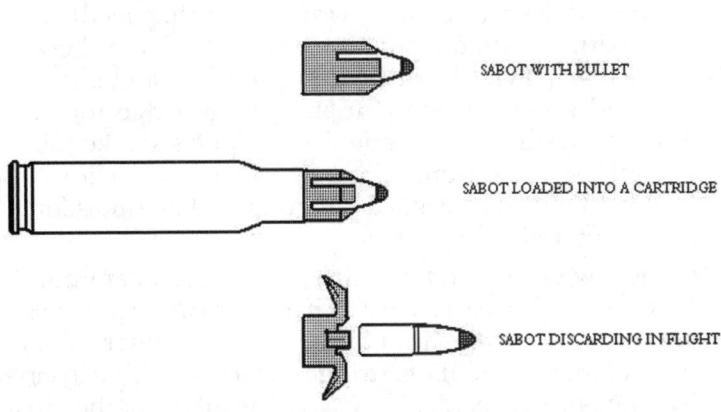

SABOT WITH BULLET

SABOT LOADED INTO A CARTRIDGE

SABOT DISCARDING IN FLIGHT

The concept of launching a sub-caliber bullet through a larger caliber barrel using a carrier or "sabot" is a very old one. The basis of the concept is that the full-bore diameter sabot will provide a larger area for the expanding propellant gasses to push against, thus propeling the light weight bullet at high muzzle velocity. This concept is not only sound, it works. However, designing a light weight sabot which will launch the bullet accurately and separate cleanly at the muzzle is no mean feat. Such a design was patented in the 1880s by Rabbeth (see drawing above), but sabot design was poorly understood and suitable materials did not exist to make the idea work properly.

Enter Remington in 1977 with their Accelerator loads in .30-30 Win., .308 Win., and .30-'06 Spr. These .30 caliber cartridges use a plastic sabot to launch 55 grain .224 inch diameter bullets at muzzle velocities up to 4,080 fps. These work reasonably well enough to have remained in production for over 30 years. However, Remington has not expanded this concept to other calibers of their product line.

4. XM645 5.77mm SPIW FLECHETTE CARTRIDGE

Beginning in the late 1950s, the U.S. government funded a series of development programs aimed at providing a modern lightweight individual combat weapon with minimal recoil capable of engaging both point and area targets with high lethality. One of the concepts studied was a finned steel flechette weighing 10.3 grains and .071 inches in diameter. A segmented fiberglass puller sabot launched the flechette at a muzzle velocity of 4,600 fps from a smooth bore barrel.

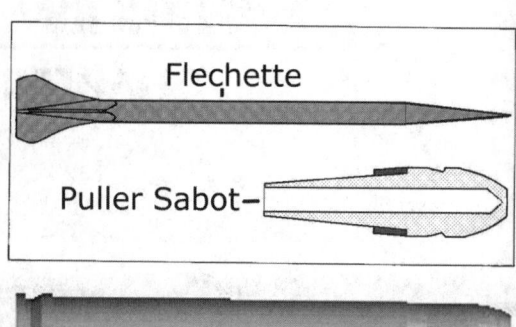

Despite considerable engineering efforts, accuracy proved poor and the flechettes were easily deflected by crosswinds, raindrops, and foliage. The concept was later adapted successfully for tank guns; however efforts at developing it for small arms have ended.

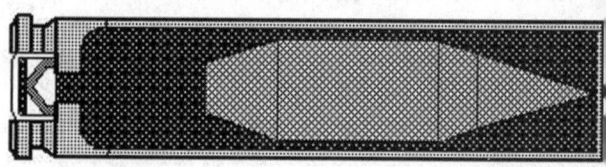

5. CASED TELESCOPED CARTRIDGE

If the overall loaded length of a cartridge can be reduced, the amount of space required for storage and packaging can be reduced accordingly. Cartridges of this type are called cased telescoped cartridges. However, this configuration requires that a number of interior ballistic problems be solved such as placement of the propellant, variable burn rates, ignition and shot start. Considerable work has been done on cased

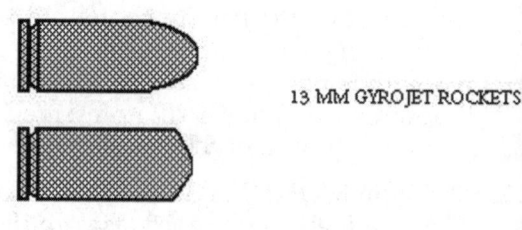

telescoped ammunition with promising results. However, to date, no ammunition of this type has been fielded as the benefits of such ammunition are closely tied to the cost of adopting new gun systems to fire them.

6. GYROJET MINIATURE ROCKETS

In the early 1960s, MBAssociates introduced a new handgun (and carbine) which fired 13mm (.511 inch diameter) miniature rockets made by the same firm. The technology for this was based on government research contracts the company had received in the past. The rocket weighed 185 grains and was propelled by a compressed charge of double-base propellant ignited by a conventional primer in the base. Four angled exhaust nozzles in the base provided the thrust to accelerate

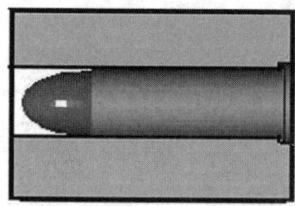

13 MM GYROJET ROCKETS

the rocket as well as the spin to stabilize it. Thrust was only 7.5 pounds, but the thrust-to-weight ratio was 284:1! This allowed a burn of just one tenth of a second to accelerate the rocket to a velocity of 1,250 fps. at 60 feet with 700 ft.-lbs. of energy at that distance. Recoil was nil, but so was muzzle velocity and energy as the rocket exited the muzzle while still accelerating. Accuracy was poor as was reliability - a misfire rate of 20% or more was common. These shortcomings spelled the end for the Gyrojet pistol. However, as all of these shortcomings can be solved, the future for this concept looks bright.

7. TROUND

TROUND LOADED WITH .38 SPECIAL CARTRIDGE

The tround was developed for fast firing gun systems for military applications. A major problem in such systems is control of the cartridges during feeding, chambering, extraction, and ejection. To solve these problems, David Dardick designed a chamberless gun and a new "tround" triangular cartridge for it. The feed system for this gun was designed to take full advantage of the tround's configuration to provide a feed path which controlled the trounds at all times for maximum reliability.

EMPTY TROUND

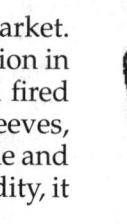

There was no need for such a gun or tround ammunition in the commercial market. However, in the early 1960s, a handgun of Dardick design and tround ammunition in various calibers was introduced in the commercial market. The Dardick pistol fired normal round metallic cartridges which had to be inserted into tround shaped sleeves, leaving one to consider if it was worth all the bother. In addition, the cumbersome and somewhat bulky pistol operated like a double-action revolver. As a technical oddity, it was a success. As a commercial venture it was a failure.

3. FOLDED CARTRIDGES

What if you could significantly decrease the length of a loaded cartridge? Perhaps by folding it over into a "U" shape? Sound preposterous? Then meet the folded cartridge, the brainchild of Mr. Andrew Grandy. Molded of low cost plastic, the upper chamber holds the propellant while the lower contains the bullet. Very little unburned propellant follows the bullet down the barrel, magazines hold stacks of these cartridges very neatly, and the distances moved and time taken to move by the gun's operating components can be very short. Extraction is by means of a simple rod which pushes the fired case out from the front of the chamber.

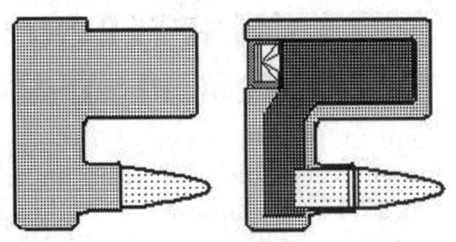

At this time, the folded cartridge is a proven concept in search of an application.

EXOTIC CENTERFIRE CARTRIDGES

.22 BR
.220 Russian
.244 Halger Magnum
.246 Purdey
.255 Jeffery Rook
.256 Gibbs Mag.
.33 BSA (.33 Belted Rimless/330 BSA)
.45-50 Peabody
.45-70 Van Choate
6x29.5Rmm Stahl
6.5x40Rmm

6.5x57mm Chinese
6.5x58 Krag
8x71mm Peterlongo
9x45mm
9x71mm Peterlongo
9.1x40Rmm
9.3x53mm Swiss
9.3x53Rmm Swiss
9.5x65Rmm Collath this s/b
   9.3x65Rmm Collath
9.5x73mm Miller-Greiss Magnum
10.75x65Rmm Collath

.30 USA
.308 Cor-Bon
.408 Chey-Tac
.41 Action Express
.445 Super Mag. – and other Elgin Gates Cartridges
5mm Bergmann
5mm Clement Auto
.54 Morse
.55 Morse
6.5mm Bergmann
7.65mm Brev.

EXOTIC SHOTSHELLS

SPC 12 gauge Military
Clucas Hatton Breaching Rounds and others (for defeating door locks, door hinges and other structural barriers)

Clucas Hatton (RIPS) and other anti-personnel rounds
Pyrotechnic – Dragons Breath and other incendiary rounds
Flechette Rounds

Collath Shotshells in special Collath gauges 0, 1, 3, 4, 5, 6, 7, and 8
Morse Shotshells
6mm Shotshell
7mm Shotshell
9mm Centerfire Shotshell
9.1x40mm Shotshell

CHAPTER 90 : MODERN MILITARY EXPERIMENTALS

ARRIVAL OF THE SELF-GUIDING BULLET

For more than eleven centuries, gunners dreamed of a bullet that would steer itself unerringly to the intended target. The technology to build such a bullet did not exist until now. Recently, Red Jones and Brian Kast, two engineers working at the Sandia National Labs in Albuquerque, NM, designed and built a 12mm/.472 inch diameter bullet that will guide itself to a designated target.

For simplicity, they used an aerodynamically stable design with its center of gravity forward of the center of pressure in much the same manner as a Foster shotgun slug. Four movable fins maintain slow rotation and make course corrections. Launch is from a smooth-bore barrel using a discarding sabot.

A laser seeker in the nose detects a laser beam on the target. The seeker sends information to an 8-bit central processing unit that uses algorithms developed by Kast and Jones to control the electromagnetic actuators for the fins. The processor makes course corrections 30 times per second in sync with the 30 hertz per second of the bullet's natural frequency of pitch and yaw so that corrections do not have to be as precise. To reduce costs, off-the-shelf electrical components were used.

High speed photos have shown that as the projectile flies down range, accuracy at long ranges is excellent. How excellent? In a real world situation at 1,000 yards, an unguided bullet could miss a target by nearly 30 feet. A guided projectile under the same conditions at the same range could get within 8 inches.

Further development is planned and Sandia National Labs is seeking an industrial partner for this purpose. The first use for the self-guided bullet is expected to be for military snipers.

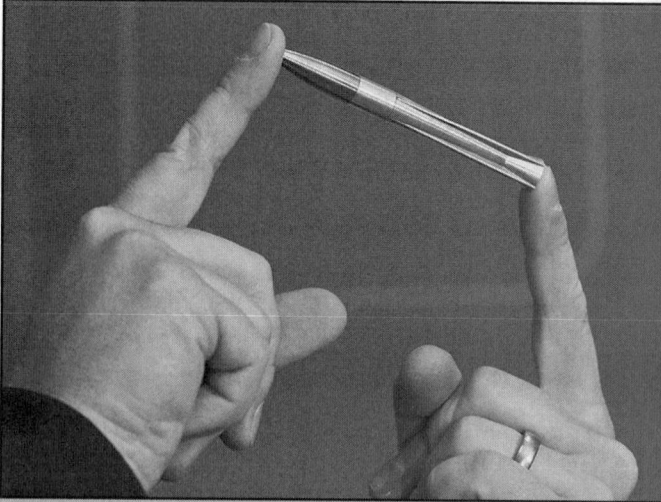

Developed by Red Jones and Brian Kast at Sandia National Labs, the world's first self-guided bullet is just four inches in length, fin stabilized, and laser guided.

A light emitting diode on the tail of the Sandia National Labs self-guided bullet shows the curving path of travel during this night shot.

LIGHTWEIGHT .50 BMG AMMUNITION

Few cartridges are so beloved by U.S. soldiers as the venerable .50 Browning Machine Gun cartridge. For many years, the U.S. Army tried to phase this caliber out in the belief it was obsolescent. The users would not hear of this and the .50 BMG continues to serve in Iraq and Afghanistan where its range and penetrating power are constantly appreciated.

If the .50 BMG has a drawback, it is that the ammunition is HEAVY. The U.S. Navy resolved to do something about this. To this end, the Naval Surface Weapons Command at Crane, Indiana has developed a hybrid metal/polymer .50 BMG cartridge case that allows a substantial

The Naval Surface Warfare Center has developed a lightweight, hybrid, metal/polymer cartridge case for the venerable .50 BMG. It is shown here with a conventional, metal cased cartridge. Note the transparent case body allowing the user to see the propellant powder charge.

The U.S. Army has developed two new types of lightweight ammunition for the U.S. soldier. The upper machinegun belt is loaded with 5.56mm caseless ammunition; the lower belt is filled with 5.56mm polymer cased, telescoped ammunition. The latter will soon enter troop trials while the former awaits the future.

This impromptu display compares the lightweight, cased telescoped ammunition with conventional 5.56x45mm ammunition. Note the cutaway cartridges in the box and the large, transparent display cartridge.

Often, one can learn more from a fired cartridge case than a loaded one. The fired, telescoped empties shown here provide a clear understanding of their construction.

decrease in weight. While the sailors and Marines will undoubtedly appreciate this, the case is easier to manufacture and load than conventional metal cased ammunition.

The new, lightweight .50 BMG ammunition has another unique feature--the case body is transparent allowing the user to see the propellant powder charge! Testing continues at an advanced level.

U. S. ARMY TRIALS
LIGHTWEIGHT 5.56MM AMMUNITION

Asx any soldier–ammunition is HEAVY. The U.S. Army Research and Engineering Development Command (ARDEC) at Picatinny Arsenal is determined to do something about this. Two types of 5.56mm lightweight ammunition have been developed and thoroughly tested. The first is a cased, telescoped cartridge with a molded plastic body, metal head insert and a conventional 5.56mm M855 bullet. The short length and lighter weight allows this type of ammunition to be approximately 25% lighter than conventional 5.56x45mm cartridges with a metal case. All the materials and technology to manufacture this cartridge already exist. Troop trials are scheduled to begin soon.

With a somewhat longer time frame of adoption in mind, ARDEC has developed and tested a caseless cartridge with a conventional 5.56mm M855 bullet. Caseless ammunition is significantly lighter (approximately 20%) than the plastic cased telescoped cartridge above which further lightens the soldier's load. Or allows him to carry more ammunition for the same weight–which do you think he will choose?

SUPERCAVITATING PROJECTILES

When conventional bullets enter water, 70% of the drag becomes skin friction caused by the water density and 30% becomes blockage or pressure drag. Supercavitation projectile designs allow much higher velocity through water by accelerating the fluid over a sharp edge on the nose so that the pressure drops below the vapor pressure of the water. This creates an air cavity or bubble in which the projectile can travel before it collapses. As the cavitator is the only part of the projectile in constant contact with the water, drag is reduced allowing higher velocities. This concept works with conventional bullets and with fin stabilized, long rod projectiles provided they have a cavitator tip. Tests have shown the concept works in air as well.

Under a program called the Rapid Airborne Mine Clearance System (RAMICS), the U.S. Navy is developing a 30mm cannon firing supercavitating MK 258 Armor Piercing, Fin Stabilized, Discarding Sabot-Tracer (APFSDS-T) ammunition capable of penetrating 140 feet of water to neutralize mines. The projectile can also be fired at surface targets.

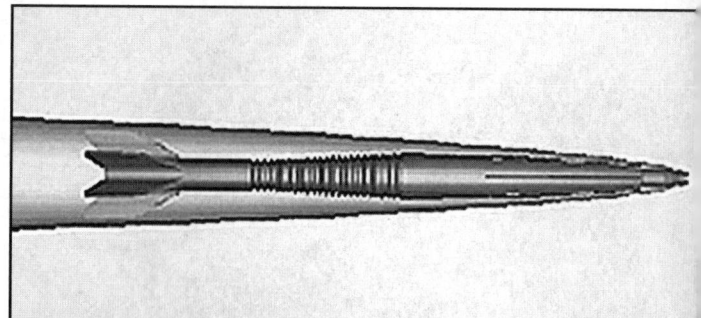

This cutaway shows the 30mm MK 268 Mod 1 cartridge loaded with its APFSDS supercavitating projectile optimized for neutralizing underwater mines. Note the cavitator on the tip of the projectile.

A supercavitating projectile such as the MK 268 Mod 1 utilizes a cavitator on its tip to form a bubble in water through which the projectile can travel with substantially increased velocity.

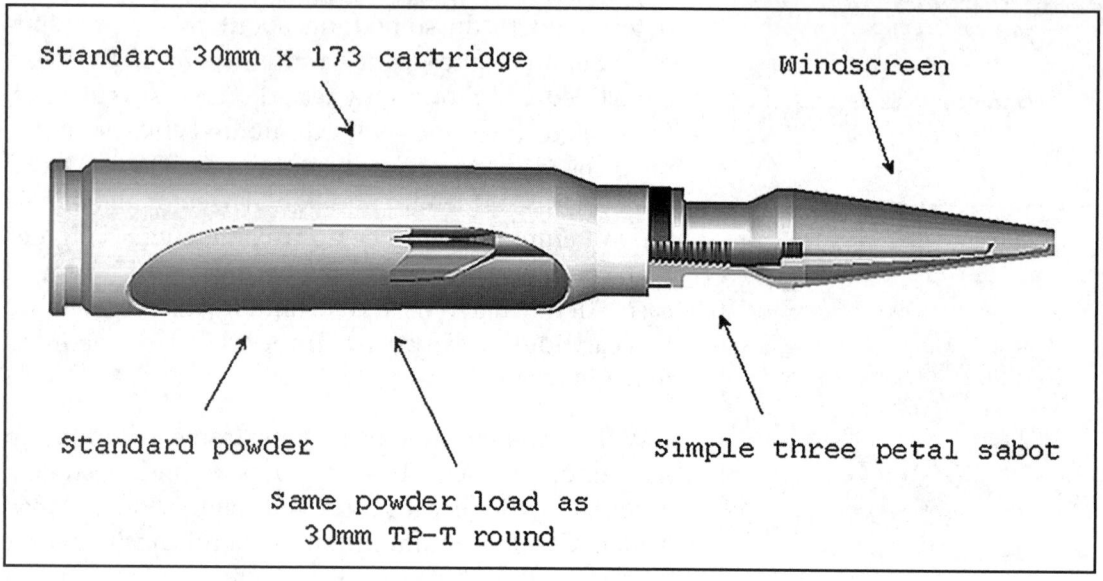

Standard 30mm x 173 cartridge

Windscreen

Standard powder

Same powder load as 30mm TP-T round

Simple three petal sabot

SECTION XVI – AIR RIFLE PELLETS
CHAPTER 91 : CALIBER, TYPE, AND BALLISTICS

CHAPTER 91 HIGHLIGHTS:

- AIR RIFLE PELLET OR SHOTGUN PELLET?
- WHAT IS THE "BB" GUN/AIR RIFLE SHOT CONFUSION
- WHAT THE DEVIL IS THE MEANING OF "DIABOLO"?
- HOW TO CHOOSE AN AIR RIFLE CALIBER

Although many airgun manufacturers list pellets in their product catalog under "ammunition", technically this is incorrect as airgun pellets are akin to component bullets. Airgun pellets are NOT loaded ammunition in that they do not have a cartridge case, propellant, or primer. For this reason, they are not subject to the many restrictions on packaging, shipping, storing, and purchase that apply to loaded ammunition.

Most airguns are technically *air rifles* in that their barrels are rifled and their pellets are designed to be fired from rifled barrels as they are spin stabilized (except round balls and bolts). Historically, airgun pellets have been swaged from lead alloys, infrequently copper plated to enhance their appearance. Recently, as a result of various initiatives to get lead out of the environment, air rifle pellets made of other metal alloys such as tin and non-metals such as polymers have appeared, although they have not completely replaced lead types. An interesting development in this vein are new hybrid designs combining colored polymers and metals such as steel, aluminum, and tin.

AIR RIFLE PELLET OR SHOTGUN PELLET?

Round lead, steel, or composite balls used to load shotshells are called "pellets".

WHAT IS THE "BB" GUN/AIR RIFLE SHOT CONFUSION

Generations of American shooters have grown up shooting inexpensive BB guns such as those made by Daisy and others. A BB gun has a smooth bore that accepts a .175 inch diameter copper-plated, steel round ball weighing about 5.6 grains. Muzzle velocities range from about 225 fps to 325 fps. (substantially lower than air rifles) for safety. Although called a BB gun, the term has been applied loosely as the diameter of a true BB shot is .180 inches which prevents it from being used in a BB gun. For this reason, the industry uses the term "air rifle shot" to describe the balls used in BB guns. There are approximately 78 steel air rifle shot per ounce; the number of lead pellets of "air rifle shot" diameter (.175 in.) is 55.

Air rifle pellets come in four popular calibers: .177/4.5mm, .20/5mm, .22/5.5mm, and .25/6.3mm. Of these, by far the most popular is the .177-4.5mm that accounts for approximately 80% of sales. Next in order of popularity is the .22/5.5mm followed by the .20/5mm and the .25/6.3mm. Current trends favor growth of the other calibers at the expense of the .177/4.5mm.

There are geographic differences as well. European air rifle shooters favor the .177 caliber by a wide margin as they use their air rifles indoors for target competition. Laws in European countries restrict air rifle pellet striking energies to reducing potential lethality without curtailing competition activities. An air rifle that exceeds established striking energy limits must be registered as a firearm.

In the U.S. air rifles are used outdoors mainly for plinking, elimination of rodents and pests, and for small game hunting. While air rifle competition is growing, it remains only a very small percentage of air rifle activity. There are no restrictions as to air rifle pellet weights, muzzle velocity, or striking energy in the U.S. Here it must be pointed out that, for the above reasons, U.S. shooters prefer .20 and .22 caliber air rifles with high muzzle velocities and striking energies as these are more effective for hunting and pest elimination.

WHAT THE DEVIL IS THE MEANING OF "DIABOLO"?

The diabolo is named after the "diabolo" a device used by jugglers. In appearance, a diabolo looks like two identical bowls fastened together at the base in a figure 8 configuration (an air rifle pellet looks similar). The two bowls are free to rotate independently allowing the juggler to impart spin to produce gyroscopic effects.

The diabolo pellet design was introduced by the Birmingham Small Arms Co. (BSA) in 1905.

Although air rifle pellets are designed to be spin stabilized, they differ from bullets for firearms in several ways:

- They are substantially lighter than bullets.
  This is necessary because the propulsion systems used by air rifles are weak in comparison to the capabilities of gun powder firearms. Lighter pellets make it possible for the compressed gas systems of air guns to develop higher muzzle velocities.

- Interior ballistic design criteria for air gun pellets designs are quite different from bullets.

These include engraving surfaces, sealing skirts, reduction of bore friction, slumping, center of mass location, and weight distribution among others.

- Exterior ballistic design criteria for air gun pellet designs also differ from bullets.

Pellets are designed to produce drag, not reduce it, in order to help stabilize the short length of a typical pellet; an additional benefit is to reduce maximum horizontal and vertical ranges for safety. The center of mass must be in front of the center of pressure to provide additional stabilization much like a Forster shotgun slug.

- Terminal ballistic design criteria for air rifle pellets was minimal to rudimentary until recently when considerably more attention has been devoted on this area. Today, there are a growing number of expanding pellet designs–mostly of the hollow point type.

- Muzzle velocities are much lower than cartridge ammunition.

This has been driven mainly by legal and safety considerations rather than technical capabilities. In fact, air rifles are quite capable of producing muzzle velocities equal to many .22 Long Rifle loads, and even more. These restrictions are quickly dissolving as many of the air rifle manufacturers have entered into a race to see who can market an air rifle with the highest muzzle velocity.

AIR RIFLE PELLETS ARE MADE IN FOUR BASIC CONFIGURATIONS:

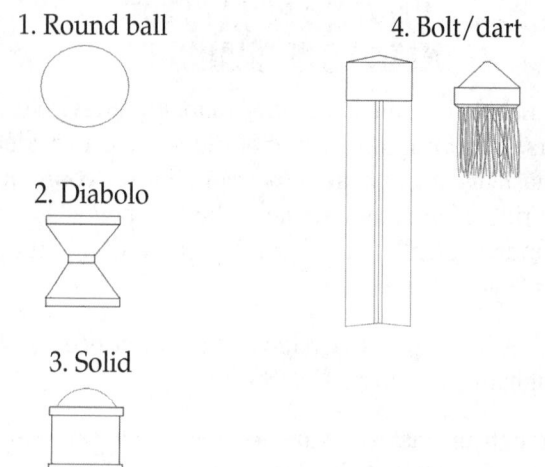

1. Round ball
2. Diabolo
3. Solid
4. Bolt/dart

Most diabolo and solid pellet types have a hollow base to more effectively seal the expanding gasses. In addition, their bodies are land diameter with groove diameter rotating bands at the front and/or base to grip the rifling. Beyond this, the variations are endless and most have been tried.

The bolt or dart is unique to airguns. They are fin-stabilized so as to allow firing from a smooth bore barrel. Compared to an air rifle pellet, they are substantially heavier and so are driven at lower velocities. These types of "pellets" are suited mainly for plinking; they are also expensive in comparison to lead pellets.

In addition, the diabolo and solid pellet types are available with the following ogive configurations:

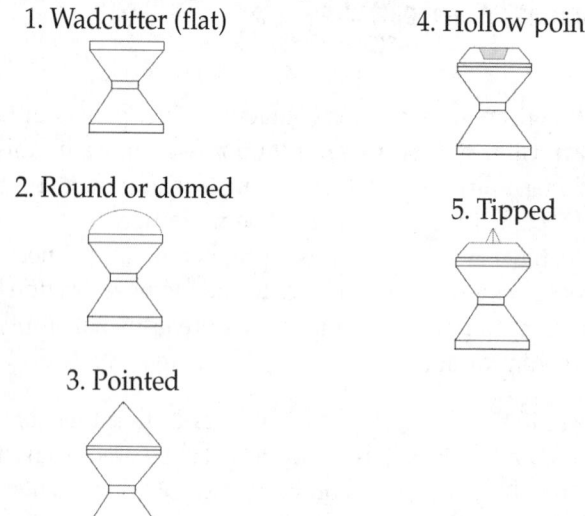

1. Wadcutter (flat)
2. Round or domed
3. Pointed
4. Hollow point
5. Tipped

The variety, shape, and style of air rifle pellet ogives is truly astonishing. There are cone tips, full wadcutters, semi-wadcutters, large radius domes, shallow domes, hollow points, tipped hollow points, and steel tips.

The wadcutter design is the jack-of-all-trades as it is the most accurate and serves as well for competition as for hunting and plinking. Domed designs are for small game hunting and pest elimination. The pointed pellet designs are a popular choice for longer ranges. The hollow point designs are intended for hunting, but they are particularly effective for rodent and pest elimination. The tipped designs are the most modern. They incorporate sharp tips to reduce drag and assist expansion for superior long range performance.

Air rifle pellets are marketed in grades–especially the diabolo types. The highest quality pellets are for world class competition. These pellets are high precision products made to strict, no expense spared specifications, so be prepared for price sticker shock! However, the accuracy of these pellets in a match-quality air rifle can easily beat the best firearms!

At the opposite end of the spectrum are the pellets for hunting and plinking. These are reasonably priced and generally of excellent quality, without the sticker shock.

HOW TO CHOOSE AN AIR RIFLE CALIBER

Purpose	Recommended Caliber
Match competition	.177/4.5mm
Informal target shooting	.177/4.5mm
Plinking	.177/4.5mm, .22/5.5mm
Pest/rodent elimination	.20/5mm, .22/5.5mm
Small game hunting	.22/5.5mm, .25/6.3mm

SECTION XVII – REFERENCE

CHAPTER 92 : COLLECTING & PRESERVING OLDER AMMUNITION – WHAT YOU NEED TO KNOW by S.P. Fjestad

CHAPTER 92 HIGHLIGHTS:

- A Brief History of Cartridge Collecting
- Why Collect Cartridges?
- How to Get Started
- Is Ammunition/Cartridge Collecting Expensive?
- What Type of Equipment Do I Need For Cartridge Collecting?
- How Do I Learn More or Get Information About the Field of Interest I've Chosen?

- Where Can I Buy Collectible Ammunition and Related Items?
- What Should I Look For When Buying Collectible Ammo and Related Items?
- Determining Condition on Ammo and Related Items
- Proper Maintenance/Storage, Care, and Safety – How It Relates to Ammunition Collecting
- Is Cartridge/Ammunition Collecting a Good Investment?

am•mu•ni•tion (ăm´yə-nĭsh´ən) – *noun.* **All projectiles, such as bullets or shot, together with their fuses and primers that can be fired from guns or otherwise propelled.[1]**

car•tridge (kär´trĭj) – *noun.* **A completely assembled and self-contained round of ammunition, consisting at minimum of a primer, propellant, and bullet/shot. In muzzle loading, refers to a container holding a pre-measured charge of black powder and a conical bullet or round ball.**

These two definitions sound simple enough, but things can quickly become complicated. Millions of man hours have been expended designing, developing, and manufacturing an almost infinite amount of ammunition, and as a result, the amount and variety of new cartridges introduced over the centuries is staggering.

In comparison to the thousands of gun collectors scattered around the world with a wide variety of firearms, cartridge collectors are a much smaller fraternity, but equally as dedicated. From a collector's viewpoint, the guns I've managed to assemble over the years don't qualify as a collection since they do not follow a centralized theme, compared to my cartridge collection. So why is this? Perhaps because I never planned on being a gun collector, so my assortment is comprised of a little bit of everything. Being a hunter, hunting firearms were my primary consideration for many years, but then I started buying various guns that were outside this realm, especially handguns.

At the time, it never occurred to me that I should develop an orderly gun collection focused on a specific area of interest. As a result, there's no consistency or central element to my firearms acquisitions.

Fortunately, this disarray of wood and metal didn't overflow into my cartridge collection. Why? Because I got some good advice from several experienced cartridge collectors and dealers before getting started. Initially, I bought a few .22 cal. rimfire boxes because they were neat and didn't take up a lot of space. After finding out there were over 7,000 different variations on this single caliber alone, I quickly decided this was too large of an area for me. Being primarily a duck and upland game hunter, I decided to collect older shotshell

Alvin Olson, long time member of the MWCA (Minnesota Weapons Collectors Association), is also a keen ammunition collector and dealer. In that capacity, he has been displaying at the various MWCA and NRA Shows for decades and continues to be a significant contributing editor for this publication on older ammunition. If you see a red coat and a white hat at a gun show, the British aren't coming – it 's simply Alvin Olson in his trademark attire, going about business as usual.

1. Definitions courtesy of the American Heritage Dictionary

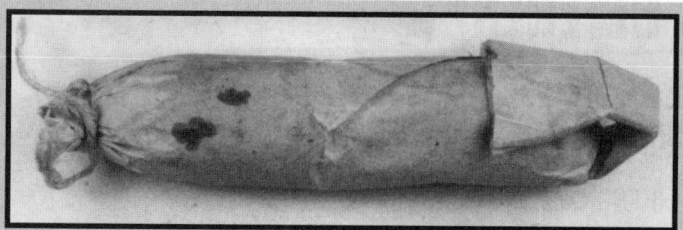

What appears to be a vintage wrapped tobacco plug is actually a .58 caliber Model 1855 musket paper cartridge. This buff paper wrapped cartridge, complete with powder and ball, was used in the Civil War and shot through the Springfield Models 1855, 1861, 1863, and 1864 rifles and muskets. Condition: Very Good. 1994 auction price: $43. Current value range: $60-$80, and has virtually disappeared in today's marketplace.

boxes, but only if they were full of original cartridges. Focusing on a particular area of cartridge collecting was the best thing that happened to me, initially. It centered my concentration on this specified area of interest, and then came the fun of trying to complete sets by gauges/cartridge lengths from older shotgun shell manufacturers.

A BRIEF HISTORY
OF CARTRIDGE COLLECTING

Col. Sam Colt was one of the first gun collectors in the U.S., and most of his collection is still on display at the Wadsworth Atheneum in Hartford, CT. History has not recorded much in the way of ammunition collectors – probably because there were very few until after WWII. Virtually all ammo purchased until then was intended to be shot over time, not put aside as a potential future collectible. Some gun collectors wanted token cartridges and perhaps a box or two of a specific caliber/gauge to complement their antiques, but this didn't qualify as ammunition collecting. Unfortunately, many cartridges and ammunition were improperly cached during long term storage. Much of it was damaged and/or ruined, then scrapped or destroyed. There has been a lot of attrition in stockpiled

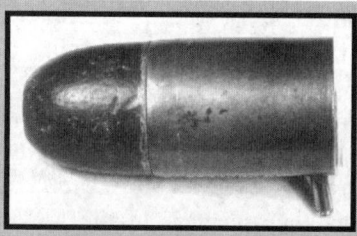

15mm pinfire cartridge. Factory loaded pinfire with lead bullet, with headstamp marking "15 FIOCCHI". Invented by Casimir LeFaucheux in 1836, pinfire cartridges bridged the gap between percussion ignition and rimfire/centerfire, and quickly became obsolete after the invention of the self-contained rimfire metallic cartridge, invented by Horace Smith and Daniel Wesson in 1854. Condition: Very Good. 1994 auction price: $35. Current value range: $35-$45.

Understanding Cartridge Condition Factors

The following grading factors and descriptions will help you to understand each cartridge's unique condition factor. Percentages refer to the percentage of original condition remaining, with 100% being New, and 0% meaning no original condition remaining.

New = 100%. Must be new in every respect with no problems (including color fading or brass deterioration), regardless of when manufactured. This condition is mostly encountered in newer cartridges/ammunition.

Mint = 98% - 99%. Close to new condition, with light scratching due to slight handling use. Will not be found in a drawer with other loose cartridges. Infrequently encountered in pre-WWII cartridges.

Excellent = 85% - 97%. Cartridge shows very little wear or damage, which detracts only slightly from overall appearance. No dents or major problems. Most ammunition collectors prefer to collect this condition factor or better, if possible.

Very Good = 70% - approx. 84%. Usually exhibits some wear, damage, brass frosting/pitting, paper deterioration, and/or color fading. Acceptable overall appearance, and must be 100% original. Check for possible over cleaning and/or alterations.

Good = 50% - approx. 69%. Includes moderate wear, damage (including storage), corrosion, brass erosion, serious paper deterioration, color fading, and normal nicks and handling marks. Not more than one dent. Check for possible over cleaning and/or alterations. Must be 100% original.

Fair = 35% - approx. 49%. Item will show significant wear, possible storage damage, and/or multiple dents. May not be all original.

Poor = 0% - 34%. Overall bad condition, possible repairs, alterations or reloaded, brass will have major corrosion and/or pitting, paper will be dark in color due to handling and possible bad storage conditions. Normally not collectible unless rarity precludes condition factors.

Some dealers may use "+" (plus) and "–" (minus) designations following a particular condition factor listed above. For instance Good++ would indicate a cartridge that is in the upper end of that factor's percentage range. Excellent– would indicate condition that is in the lowest end of the percentage range, and possibly even under a little bit.

.44 cal. Henry flat cartridge. Copper cased flat twin rimfire cartridge with "D" headstamp, indicating Dominion manufacture. Most older lead bullets had a coating on the outside that could have been either cleaned off in error or worn off in a hunting jacket. This creates a lead oxide, which is white colored and helps explain the originality of this cartridge. Condition: Very Good. 1994 auction price: $16. Current value range: $35-$50.

This was made at Frankford Arsenal and was to be used as a training aid for Gatling Gunner Instruction. It has the same dimensions as the loaded service round. As most of the service ammunition of the 1870s thru 1880s it is of the "Inside Primed" type, and has no visible center fire primer. The "Wood Stick" is inside the dummy to avoid having the bullet 'telescope' back into the case, since black powder loads were "Full Case", with the bullet seated against the powder. The holes in the cartridge case were to indicate an inert round. The bullet shows the gray lead oxide because its protective coating had been removed. It is a very rare cartridge that most collectors never acquire. Condition: Very Good. 1994 auction price: approx. $1,750. Current value range: $1,900 - $2,200.

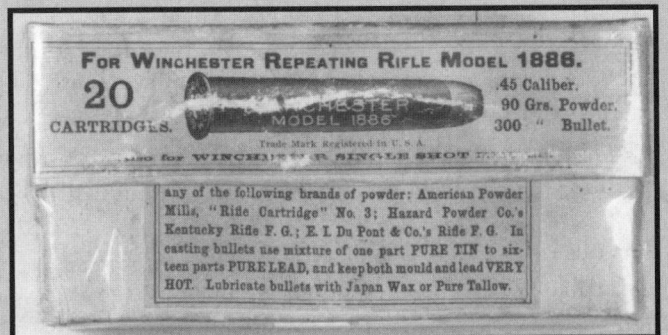

Winchester Repeating Arms Co. .45-90-300 caliber rifle box. Full two-piece buff box with light green label. Box states "Cartridges for Model 1886." Note minor scuffing on bullet. Any full box of early Winchester centerfire ammo specifically manufactured for the lever action Models 1866, 1873, 1876, 1886, 1892, 1894, and 1895 in this condition or better is very desirable and expensive. If the box is described as full but opened, check to make sure all cartridges are original to box. Condition: Very Good. 1994 auction price: $110. Current value range: $250-$500.

or stored ammunition over the centuries, and improper storage conditions (wet and damp) have always been the major problem.

Cartridge collecting finally matured in the 1960s, mostly due to gun collectors deciding that correct period ammunition and related advertising/promotional material would be the perfect accessories to complement their gun collections. This additional demand element from many well-heeled gun collectors quickly raised prices and brought lots of good collectible ammunition out of the attics and basements. Older cartridge collectors will tell you that they didn't like the new, richer blood that transformed the sleepy cartridge marketplace into a vibrant industry now running high on energy drinks. Interestingly, most gun collectors with a lot of collectible ammo to complement their gun collections do not consider themselves ammo collectors.

The 1990s started bringing the collectible cartridge marketplace out of the gun shows and into the auction arenas. Classic Sporting Collectibles, a division of Blue Book Publications, Inc., put on four auctions in 1994-95. Thousands of lots were auctioned off, covering every conceivable type of ammunition, components, and related advertising/promotional items.

WHY COLLECT CARTRIDGES?

Just as your laptop can't run without software, neither can a gun be used for shooting without ammunition. The development of cartridges has a very long and colorful history, and even though the firearms command the attention of more collectors, studying ammunition will be of great value to further understand the history of firearms. Cartridge/ammo collecting is educational, rewarding, and is relatively inexpensive, not requiring special equipment, vault storage, licensing, fire permits, or large amounts of space. It is also a great way of getting to know other knowledgeable people within your field of interest(s). Finding your treasures may also take awhile longer than filling out a firearms wish list.

HOW TO GET STARTED

Remember, every gun is designed to shoot a particular cartridge(s). Paper cartridges were introduced circa 1586, and metallic rimfire ammunition was patented in 1854, so there are centuries of cartridge manufacture and almost an infinite number of ways to create a collection. Cartridges can be collected by type of ignition (i.e., pinfire, rimfire, centerfire, etc.), groups of ammo used by various firearms configurations (i.e., handguns, rifles, and shotguns), caliber or gauge, boxed or single round, individual manufacturers/trademarks, commercial, military, or industrial, head

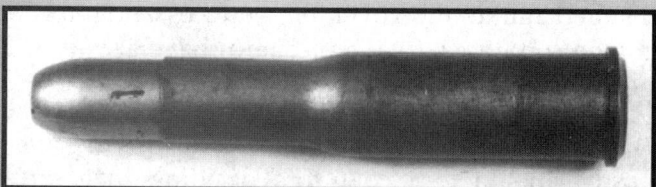

10.15x61R Jarmann cartridge. Brass primer with flat cupro nickel full jacketed bullet. Headstamp "X". Adopted in 1887 by Norway and Sweden for the Jarmann turn-bolt, tube magazine repeating rifle. Condition: Very Good. 1994 auction price: $20. Current value range: $25-$35. Moral to the story? There are much fewer metric cartridge collectors in the U.S. than in Europe, so value hasn't changed much.

stamp markings, and even by color! As a result, ammunition collecting is a much bigger field than it appears, so getting focused on a particular area of interest is important before beginning.

My advice would be to find a particular area of interest and go from there. If you're a longtime deer hunter, you're probably not going to want to start out buying centerfire pistol cartridges. The whole point is that there are so many ways to collect cartridges. So carving out a domain before starting is absolutely critical. Doing so will guarantee that your experience in cartridge collecting will be a lot more manageable.

IS AMMUNITION/CARTRIDGE COLLECTING EXPENSIVE?

Like any other collectible, a budget should be established initially, which may also help determine what area you want to get involved with. Collecting single cartridges is probably the least expensive way to go, but again, there are so many variations and types that specialization is important. While many single cartridges can be bought for under $15, a hundred count box of original Henry rifle rimfire ammunition can exceed $10,000 if the condition is high. In many cases, ammunition for many collectible guns is much rarer than the guns themselves. Yet, prices for rare ammo are a fraction of the value of the guns for which they were chambered.

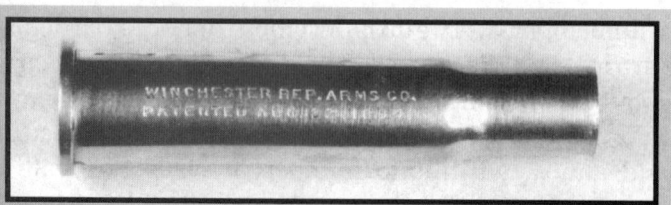

Winchester supplemental chamber for .30 Army (.30-40 Krag). Nickeled chamber marked "Winchester Rep. Arms Co. Patented Aug. 22, 1899. .30 Caliber – Army. Use .32 S&W Smokeless." Condition: Excellent. 1994 auction price: $17. Current value range: $25-$30 (must be nice and clean).

Boxed Ammunition Grading

The following grading factors and descriptions will help you to determine each box's unique condition factor. Percentages refer to the percentage of original condition remaining, with 100% being New, and 0% meaning no original condition remaining.

New Condition = 100%. New from factory with cartridges. No observable wear of any type. Should be plastic wrapped to ensure this condition factor.

Mint Condition = 98% - 99%. Near perfect condition. No tears, frays, rips, or edge wear. If box has color, the color(s) should be sharply defined, vibrant, and bright with no fading, blotching, or color/hue deterioration. All markings and lettering should be factory original. With or without cartridges.

Excellent Condition = 85% - up to 97%. Slight wear on edges and corners, colors (if any) still sharp, bright, and vibrant. No rips, tears, major creases, or other defects. Must be intact – with or without cartridges. Minor scuffing possible.

Very Good Condition = 70% - up to 84%. Noticeable wear (mostly handling), on edges, sides, and label. Colors faded somewhat, but still sharp overall. Could have creases, small tears, and other minor problems. Must be intact – with or without cartridges.

Good Condition = 50% - up to 69%. More noticeable wear including some tears, rips, possible edge splitting, and other visible signs of deterioration. Colors more faded with box soiling possible. Scuffing and non-handling wear observable throughout. Should be intact unless described otherwise – with or without cartridges.

Fair Condition = 35% - up to 49%. Major problems observable including serious rips, tears, creases, label damage, and color loss. Major wear on all surfaces. May have repairs or alterations. Probably not intact – with or without cartridges.

Cartridge boxes in less than Fair condition are generally not collectible or valuable. Exceptions are those boxes so rare and infrequently offered for sale that collector demand is the sole determinant of value.

Some dealers may use "+" (plus) and "–" (minus) designations following a particular condition factor listed above. For instance Good++ would indicate a cartridge that's in the upper range of the description. Excellent– would indicate condition that's somewhat lower than the condition's description.

1969 Speer "Wells Fargo" bullet board. Bullet and cartridge boards have always been some of the more collectible (and expensive) items in ammo collecting. Older 19th century cartridge boards, particularly from Winchester and Remington-UMC, have always been very desirable, and Winchester's famous "Double W" can sell for over $15,000, if complete and original! Condition: Excellent. 1994 auction price: $180. Current value range: $150-$200 (must be complete or sizable discount applies).

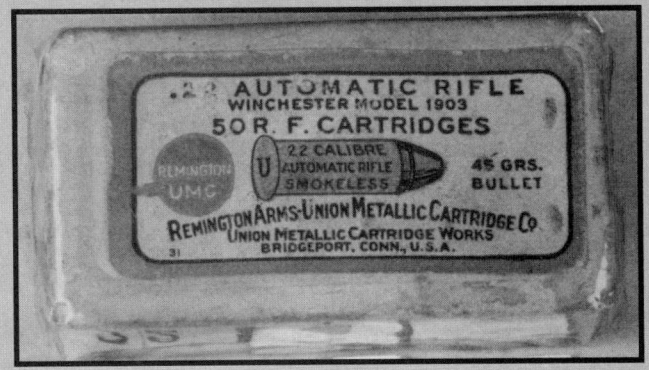

Remington Arms 22 Automatic Model 1903 box, circa 1911. Full two-piece buff box with green label and black print, showing normal wear with one end label partially missing. Box code: 31. Dunn REM-2 WA-1. Label states "Specially Adapted for .22 Winchester Model 1903." Although Remington never made a gun chambered for the .22 Auto cartridge, it still made ammo for its competitor's gun. Condition: Good. 1994 auction price: $45. Current value range: $125-$175.

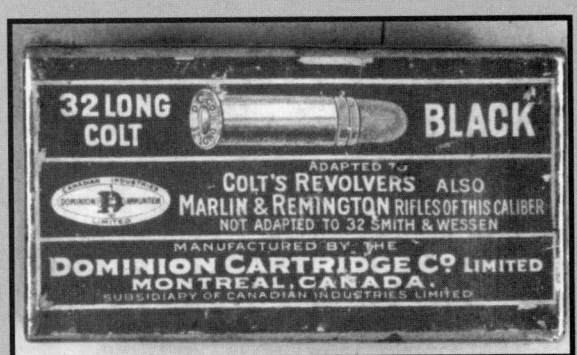

Dominion Cartridge Co. .32 Long Colt "Black Powder" box. Full buff box with red wrap around label with white print. Label states "Adapted to Colt's Revolvers Also Marlin & Remington Rifles of this Caliber. Not Adapted to .32 Smith & Wesson." Early bent "D" box. Condition: Very Good. 1994 auction price: $30. Current value range: $65-$85.

WHAT TYPE OF EQUIPMENT DO I NEED FOR CARTRIDGE COLLECTING?

The following is a listing of items need for cartridge collecting, and as a collection develops, more items might be needed:

- A lockable metal or wood cabinet with multiple shallow drawers and roller guides.
- Cardboard panels to line the drawers so cartridges will not shift.
- A vernier caliper or micrometer caliper.
- A good magnifying glass.
- A strong desk light.
- One pair of thin cloth gloves.
- Small quantity of fine steel wool for cleaning.
- A permanent marker pen with a fine point and black ink.
- Index cards with storage box to retain data on each cartridge.
- Books on the type of cartridge you have elected to collect.

HOW DO I LEARN MORE OR GET INFORMATION ABOUT THE FIELD OF INTEREST I'VE CHOSEN?

As opposed to gun collecting, there are not that many cartridge experts since it is a much smaller field. Additionally, there are quite a few dealers who specialize in older ammunition and related memorabilia, and it is highly recommended to learn as much as you can about your particular area of cartridge collecting. The Internet has certainly become the major driving force in today's collectible ammo marketplace, which makes much of the information readily available. But don't take everything you read on the Internet as gospel or you will be very disappointed.

Unfortunately, there is much less historical information (published or otherwise) available on cartridges than on firearms. While my firearms reference library consists of 11 seven-foot book cabinets that are filled to capacity, I have less than 36 inches of shelf space devoted to ammunition publications.

The International Ammunition Association is also an excellent resource for information on cartridge collecting. Many useful resources and hotlinks are provided on a wide variety of cartridges and ammunition. Please visit them at: www.cartridgecollectors.org

When the anti-gun administration took over after the last election, new ammunition (and tactical firearms)

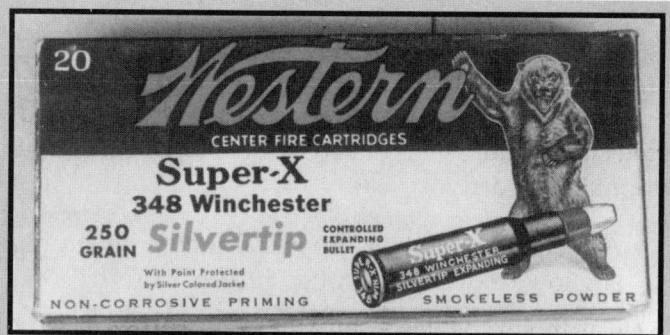

Western Cartridge Co. .348 Winchester "Bear" box. Full blue and yellow box with red and blue print and picturing a standing bear. Western & Winchester bear boxes (both rifle and handgun) were made circa late 1930s, and are some of the most collectible of all Western boxed ammo, especially in rare calibers like this. Condition: Very Good. 1994 auction price: $85. Current value range: $125-$175. Have gone up in value a lot recently.

sales went ballistic since many gun owners believed that ammunition would become hard to get, and that certain firearm configurations would be banned. Many shooters bought ammo to hoard rather than to shoot, which spiked prices and also created a major shortage worldwide. Coupled with a near depletion of military stockpiles/surplus, there has been an unprecedented shortage of both civilian and military ammunition over the past several years. Between January and October of 2009, over 215 million .22 caliber rimfire cartridges were imported into the U.S. – that's one rimfire caliber (no centerfire or shotshells) and no domestic production! This recent feeding frenzy on new ammunition has not affected the higher values on collectible ammunition, but it has raised the floor price of shooting ammunition.

WHERE CAN I BUY COLLECTIBLE AMMUNITION AND RELATED ITEMS?

Most desirable collectible ammunition is now being sold at auction houses, and three of today's largest

Winchester .22 Long Rifle "Precision 200" box, circa 1933. Full blue, red, and white box with red and white print. This is a very scarce box and tough to find in this type of superior condition. Note the spelling of "Lesmok." Traditional spelling was altered by the powder company to create a catchy trademark. Dunn: WRA-53 LR-11(f). Condition: Excellent. 1994 auction price: $110. Current value range: $150-$200.

Grading for Ammo Related Items

The following grading factors and descriptions will help you to understand each item's unique condition factor.

New = must be new in every respect with no problems, (including color fading or deterioration), regardless of when manufactured.

Mint = near perfect, no observable wear, colors (if any) bright and vibrant, sharp edges on corners. A tick away from new condition.

Excellent = slight observable wear without rips, tears, major fading, or noticeable problems areas and/or blemishes.

Very Good = some observable wear including paint chips, minor nicking and scratching, colors or printing (if any) somewhat faded. May or may not be intact.

Good = major observable wear including dings, scratching, chipping, dents, tears, rips, fading, and other areas of deterioration.

Fair = overall condition has greatly deteriorated. Without rarity factor, could be a garage sale item – check your local dumpster or landfill for possible inventory. Probably not intact.

Winchester Boy Scout 75th Anniversary .22 Long Rifle brick. Full brick (500 rounds) of a beautiful box done by Winchester in 1985 to commemorate the 75th Anniversary of the Boy Scouts. Most of the reasons why this brick is so expensive are because it was made to complement the Model 9422 Boy/Eagle Scouts 75th Anniversary Commemoratives manufactured in two variations during 1985. With the Eagle Scout variation selling for $6,000+ currently, this ammo brick is the best accessory to complement the rifle. Condition: Very Good. 1994 auction price: $75. Current value range: $150, and it's a lot easier and faster to split up the brick and sell at $15 a box than trying to get $150 for a complete brick.

Savage 12 Gauge paper shotshell. Factory loaded shell with tan paper case. Headstamp: "BPD 12 12 ROMA". The case wall has an Indianhead and is marked "SAVAGE SHELLS". Savage sued this Italian company, and therefore ceased production, making this shell very scarce. Condition: Excellent. 1994 auction price: $25. Current value range: $25-$30.

Winchester Shotshell Powder Cutaway sample shell. Six inch overall length on this tan case wall shell displaying the various types of powder used by Winchester in the following shotshells: Leader, Repeater, Metal Lined, and Pigeon, and displays 12 different powder types. Headstamp is: "Winchester No. 12 Leader". Cutaway or window shells were also manufactured by various companies for standard ammo to show components and inside construction. Condition: Very Good. 1994 auction price: $65. Current value range: $125-$150.

Eley 8 Gauge shotshell. Factory loaded shell with red paper case, 3 in. shell length. Headstamp: 'ELEY-KYNOCH 8. TW: BB". Case wall print: "Eley 8 Gauge Cartridge Eley Loaded With A Noble Smokeless Powder." Made in Great Britain. Condition: Very Good. 1994 auction price: $26. Current value range: $35-$50.

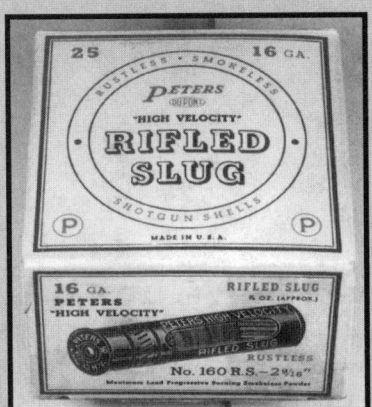

Peters 16 Gauge "Rifled Slug" shotshell box. White box with blue and red print. The box contains one original shell. Each end pictures a rifled slug window shell. Condition: Very Good. 1994 auction price: $20. Current value range: $150, and hard to sell. Secret to selling? This box contains five individual five-packs of slugs that can be easily sold at $25 a pack. The empty box will bring another $25!

ammunition and sporting collectibles auction houses are Ward's Auctions (www.wardscollectibles.com), Sold USA (www.soldusa.com), and Past Tyme Pleasures (www.pasttyme1.com). Reviewing their listings and asked bid/prices realized might be one of the better ways to get information and current values for your field of interest.

Larger gun shows usually have several exhibitors that specialize in older ammunition and related memorabilia, and they can be very helpful. There is also the annual International Cartridge show, and for more information, please check the website of the International Ammunition Association: www.cartridgecollectors.org

WHAT SHOULD I LOOK FOR WHEN BUYING COLLECTIBLE AMMO AND RELATED ITEMS?

As in gun collecting, major manufacturers/trademarks, superior original condition, and rarity are the three primary factors to consider. Rare variations will typically command higher prices, and some manufacturers/brands existed for a very short time, making their ammunition very hard to find. Also, ammunition tied in to a specific make/model, especially a major trademark, will always bring a premium.

Fortunately, there are not a lot of fakes and counterfeits in cartridge collecting, unlike some popular firearms today. Boxed ammunition should always be inspected for possible repairs/alterations, correct markings, and color to make sure the condition is all original.

It might be a good thing that eBay® does not allow ammunition, cartridges, or individual shooting components to be sold on its site. However, empty ammunition boxes/crates, advertising posters, calendars, die cuts, catalogs and brochures, and other sporting collectibles are allowed. One dealer mentioned he had seen more than a few "fantasy" factory catalogs and brochures listed on eBay® that were outright fakes – the manufacturer never had them printed. Also on boxed ammo, carefully check for possible repairs such as replaced flaps, recent color image glued to a side panel or bottom, etc. On individual cartridges, check for older cleaning, possible reloading, and any other alterations that will lower the value.

DETERMINING CONDITION ON AMMO AND RELATED ITEMS

Surprisingly, there is almost nothing written on how to evaluate cartridges, ammunition, and related items for condition, and even less on condition factors. Please refer to the sidebars for current grading criteria, definitions, and more information on individual cartridges, boxed ammo, and ammo memorabilia.

Australian 12 Gauge "Nudie" shotshell box. Q: What happens when you put this $75 box next to a $60,000 Holland & Holland Royal Hammerless Ejector shotgun? A: The shotgun initially gets no respect! An authentic box from Down Under with a full color picture of a semi-nude female holding a SxS shotgun. Boxes like this are more of a novelty item than anything else. Condition: Excellent. 1994 auction price: $75. Current value range: $50-$75, if you find the right buyer who likes a little porn in his gun room (hidden or exposed!).

PROPER MAINTENANCE/STORAGE, CARE, AND SAFETY – HOW IT RELATES TO AMMUNITION COLLECTING

Two primary factors have been responsible for damage to cartridges and ammunition when long term storage is involved. The first is obvious – moisture and humidity. Think musty basements, wet floors, damp cellars, and extreme temperature and humidity variations. Ammunition using paper in its construction (typically shotshells) tends to take on moisture and swell up. Brass and other metals will also tarnish and corrode. Boxes tend to deteriorate quickly, and sometimes fall apart because of the weight and pressure of the shells inside. Always store ammunition in a cool and dry place.

The other major factor is ultraviolet ray exposure from unfiltered sunlight (direct or indirect). Over time, a lack of UV protection in windows, doors, and even skylights will create major color deterioration, especially on boxes that have a lot of bright colors. I intentionally left a mint box of Federal Monarch shotshells with vivid greens and oranges in my office without UV protection, but not in direct sunlight. After two years, the box's colors had changed from hunter green and bright orange to aqua and dull pumpkin. As a result of this color deterioration, this box has now lost 50% of its value, despite all 25 original cartridges being in mint condition. Which brings up an interesting point – the values for many older and rarer boxes are the same with or without original cartridges.

Wrapping shotshell, pistol, and rifle ammunition boxes with protective plastic is highly recommended to prevent scuffing and the cartridges from blowing out

Peters 20 Gauge High Velocity "Blue Winged Teal" box. A full two-piece buff box that is still sealed, with blue and white label picturing a blue winged teal in flight. Loading: 2 3/4 -5/8-BALL. Label shows only handling wear. If this box was empty, the value wouldn't change that much, and many shotshell box collectors prefer empty boxes, as they are not prone to damage created by the pressure of the full cartridges blowing out the side walls, and top/bottom flaps. Condition: Very Good. 1994 auction price: $225. Current value range: $300-$400. Original, sealed two-piece shotshell boxes in excellent original condition are the top of the food chain for shotshell collectors and are priced accordingly. As with any other collectible, values for mediocre, poor condition have not changed that much. Most appreciation has occurred in full sealed boxes in better than average condition.

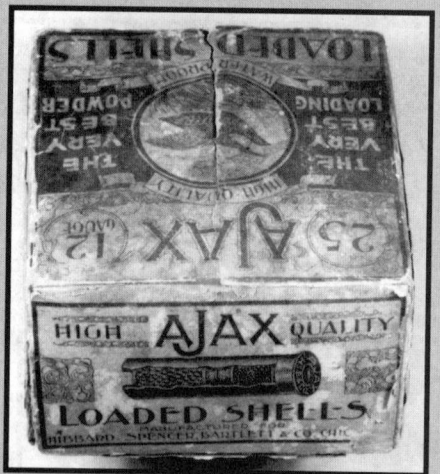

Hibbard, Spencer, Bartlett & co. 12 Gauge "AJAX" shotshell box. Empty two-piece box with purple and white label and printing. Loading: 4-1 1/8-5 BUCK. Box is solid and labels intact, except for a split along the top label. This is a good example of what happens to value when rarity overrules the condition factor (see sidebar for explanation of condition factors). Even most advanced shotshell collectors have never seen nor heard of this box. Condition: Fair-Good. 1994 auction price: $820. Current value range: $1,500+. On older and rare boxes like this one, check for possible repairs, alterations, and touch ups.

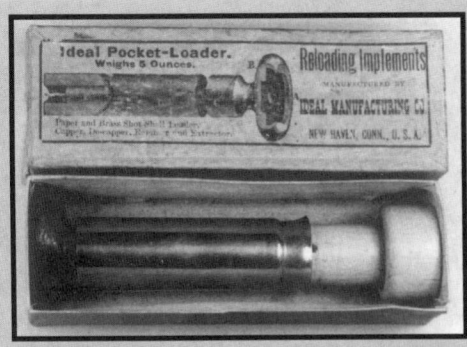

Ideal 12 Gauge shotshell "Pocket Reloader." Pocket reloader by Ideal in buff box with yellow label and black print. Label states "Paper and Brass Shot Shell Loader. Capper, De-Capper, Rammer, and Extractor." Unusual in that it has a threaded type primer seater. Ammunition collecting involves more than just cartridges – reloading kits like this one, powder tins, box components, and primers are also very desirable, as only a few survived in this type of original condition. Condition: Very Good. 1994 auction price: $48. Current value range: $45-$75. Clue: the box is worth as much as the reloader. Also, if this was a Parker Bros. shotshell reloader, pricing would start at $200.

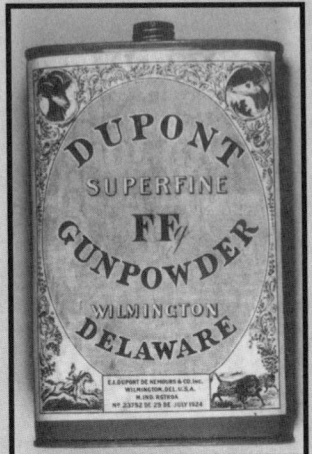

Dupont Superfine FFg gunpowder tin. Red, one pound oval tin with white and black label picturing a game scene in each corner. Tin is dated July 1924. The Dupont trademark on gun powder is world-renowned, and many ammunition collectors like to have a tin like this to accent their collections. Most older black powder tins like this are now empty, and gun shows no longer allow black powder onto show premises. Condition: Very Good. 1994 auction price: $43. Current value range: $75.

April 1919 issue of *Dupont Magazine*. 9x12 in. magazine full of wonderful advertisements of the period. The cover pictures a well-heeled woman negotiating with a Native American for a colorful blanket. Anything with Dupont on it is collectible, and this cover image is very unusual. The more colorful the image, the more collectible the item. Condition: Very Good. 1994 auction price: $15. Current value range: $30-$40.

requires TLC, and never stack too many heavy boxes on top of each other, or put an empty box at the bottom of a container. Transporting collectible ammunition properly is much more difficult than transporting firearms.

Another consideration is handling. Allowing individual metallic cartridges to be handled requires that they be wiped down afterwards. The normal acids and salts found on human hands can cause indelible fingerprinting, pitting, and possibly serious corrosion. Boxed ammunition must be carefully opened, closed, and resealed so as not to rip the corners of the outside flaps or inside lips.

When collecting ammunition in older metric calibers, be very careful if you plan to shoot them. Many drillings, Schuetzens, combination guns, and stalking rifles have non-standard metric calibers. Even though the caliber of the ammunition may appear to be correct for a specific firearm, have a competent gunsmith perform a chamber check on the gun you want to shoot and then double check the ammunition to make sure it is compatible. On rifles, pay attention to the chamber caliber, which is stamped on the barrel. Also, pay close attention when interchanging ammunition. On shotguns, while there are only six current major gauges in use, there have been many different chamber lengths, so never shoot a shotshell that is longer than the chamber length indicated on the barrel.

Remember, even though some ammunition might be 100 years old, treat every cartridge like it can still be fired and handle/store accordingly. A longtime local cartridge dealer likes to tell the story of how one collector had some old S&W No. 1 cartridges (predecessor to the .22 Short), and wondered about the powder used in them. Before attempting to disassemble the cartridges, he wondered if they would still fire. He put a round into a revolver and pulled the trigger – and promptly shot a .22 inch diameter hole through his work bench. The cartridge was more than 100 years old, so never forget that older black powder cartridges are very dangerous when exposed to extreme heat or fire.

Please go through the following check list to make sure everything possible has been done to maintain safe storage and proper handling:

STORING & HANDLING CHECKLIST

- Always wear safety glasses when handling cartridges.
- Always assume a cartridge is live and handle it with respect.
- Store your collection in a clean, dry, secure place.

- Keep cartridges away from children and other unauthorized personnel at all times.

- Store cartridges away from acids, solvents, cleaning agents, paint, oils, and gasoline.

- Do not store your cartridges in direct sunlight, next to heat sources, or in places where temperatures exceed 100° F.

- Do not store your cartridges where they are exposed to damage from impact, moisture, or fire.

- Never allow products containing ammonia to come into contact with cartridges.

- Handle your specimens only while wearing gloves.

- Do not attempt to disassemble specimens.

Interestingly, the older smokeless powder, which quickly took over the marketplace from black powder in the late 19th century, typically deteriorates much faster than its predecessor black powder equivalent. The new smokeless propellant has a tendency to react chemically with the brass and paper case and over time, the propellant changes color and becomes almost inert. The introduction of non-corrosive primers and improved smokeless propellants solved much of those problems, but regardless, treat every loaded cartridge like it could be fired in a gun.

The ultimate bad explosives/ammunition tragedy occurred on December 6, 1917, in the harbor of Halifax, Nova Scotia. A freighter called the *Mont Blanc*, loaded with 3,000 tons of TNT, caught fire after a collision with the Belgian steamer *Imo* and the flames quickly spread into the cargo hold. The entire crew immediately took to the lifeboats, but probably already knew they were rowing on borrowed time. Moments later, a catastrophic detonation occurred, devastating the entire northern part of the city. Most of the 1,600 who died were killed instantly by the initial blast, and there was some $50 million in property damage.

IS CARTRIDGE/AMMUNITION COLLECTING A GOOD INVESTMENT?

If you are a shooter who has a box of miscellaneous cartridges next to your reloading bench in the basement, the answer is probably no, since most recent and common ammunition is not collectible. The bottom line on any cartridge recently manufactured is its current shooting value. However, if you have a good complete collection of Peters shotshell boxes, then the answer is yes, but it certainly shouldn't be compared to such traditional investments as gold and silver. I'll guarantee however, that good collectible ammo/cartridges have definitely outperformed most

"Doc Peters" shotshell advertising brochure. This beautiful but common fold out brochure from Peters is dated 1948 – cover pictures two hunters with dogs and the inside pictures, in full color, the Peters "Mallard" and "Victor Field Loads" shotshell boxes along with game animals. Ammunition advertising brochures like this and related promotional materials are very collectible, and in many cases, are more expensive than the ammo they depict, especially if pre-WWII. Condition: Excellent. 1994 auction price: $40. Current value range: $30-$40. Since eBay users can sell ammo-related memorabilia only, a lot of this type of merchandise has come out of the woodwork. But watch out, as there are quite a few fakes and non-original items.

Winchester Repeating Arms Co. "Bird Busters" posters. These posters were done in the early 1980s to promote Winchester's famous AA trap shells. This is a complete unsigned set, which is worth more than if the gals would have signed them with a Sharpie. Condition: Excellent. 1994 auction price: $150. Current value range: $125-$150. Again, not an easy sell, and must find the right victim.

Union Metallic Cartridge Co. 10 Gauge "CLUB" wood ammo box, circa late 1920s. Very nice early box joint (not dovetailed) UMC crate in 10 gauge, marked #7 shot and Laflin & Rand. Later wooden crates were not dovetailed, and the sides were nailed together. Any older 10 gauge shotshell box or wooden crate is very collectible. Premiums are also paid for .410 bore and 28 gauge crates, as 12, 16, or 20 gauge are the most commonly encountered. Condition: Very Good. 1994 auction price: $125. Current value range: $100-$125.

Hercules Powder Company 1927 "Pals" calendar. 13 x 30 in. calendar named "Pals" by artist William Eaton depicting a man with his pipe and dog. Background pictures a shotgun, shotshells, and game laws hanging on the wall. Any older calendar with all 12 months intact is very collectible, and since Hercules has always been one of the biggest and most important names in powder manufacturing, this usually turbo charges the price tag. Older rare ammo and firearms calendars like this with striking artwork in superior original condition and bright colors typically sell in the $1,750 - $5,000+ range. Condition: Excellent. 1994: $275. Current value range: $350-$700, depending on condition.

Winchester Cardboard Counter Top "Super Speed" fold out die cut. 14x18 in., dated 1953, picturing a full color Super Speed shotshell and advertising its positive points with bright colors. Background has sharp image of a father, dog, and son shooting a SxS shotgun. The father is pointing, and it is entitled "His First Duck." In-store ammunition advertising materials in this type of superior condition are ultra rare, as most were discarded after a new product was introduced, and/or have severe color fading due to UV damage from sunlight after months/years in store windows. Condition: Excellent. 1994 framed value: $240. Current value range: $175-$300.

Union Metallic Cartridge Co. ammunition broadsheet. 23x35 in. ammunition broadsheet from the 1800s shows everything from .22 cal. to one inch Gatling. Also shows shotshells including the Sturtevant Patent Movable Anvil shotshell. Has one small tear and some thumbtack holes, but is otherwise nice and bright. Older artwork with period information is extremely valuable, as in many cases it may be the only source of what a company offered at the time. Condition: Very Good. 1994 auction price: $310. Current value range: $200-$300. Caveat emptor: most of these are recent reproductions. How can you tell if it's original? Check the paper for shininess – older original broadsheets used the cheapest pulpwood paper available at the time, and today's reproductions usually use a brighter semi-gloss paper.

real estate and 401K programs over the last two years. I've never run into an "ammunition investor."

Like firearms, always buy as much original condition as you can afford. Please study the images in this chapter to find out more about condition factors that are normally described as Mint, Excellent, Very Good, Good, and Fair. Like every other collectible, condition is the most important overall factor, unless extreme rarity overrides the condition factor.

Unlike guns, some extremely rare cartridges are almost impossible to find, let alone buy. I've talked to ammo dealers/collectors who, after thirty years of diligent searching, have still not located the specific item(s) they are looking for. Also unlike guns, rare manufacturers/trademarks usually equate to higher prices, as some companies/trademarks were only in existence for a few years.

Savvy ammo dealers and collectors know exactly what they are looking for, always buy as much original condition as inexpensively as possible, and usually sell only when they can get top dollar. At a Wanenmacher Tulsa gun show, a dealer friend of mine came by on Saturday morning, reached inside his black bag, and took out a tattered Peters shotshell box that I had never seen before. After telling him this, he said, "Don't feel bad, I've only seen one other like this, and it's in my collection." Quickly asking what he paid for it, his response was "Ten bucks." My immediate response was, "How much is it worth?", and his upshot reply was, "I think I can get $1,000 for it." That's what

patience, perseverance, a little luck, and walking thousands of miles by gun show tables can do for you.

Keeping track of your ammo collection and related items is very important, and it is always easier if you start keeping records after your first purchase. This can be done in a multitude of ways, but it is highly recommended that the inventory is done on a computer. It can be done on standard word processing programs or spreadsheets. Most advanced boxed ammo collectors have a notebook filled with color images they've made from putting their shell boxes on top of a copier and then copying all sides. The more detailed your ammo inventory records, the more manageable your collection will be over the years. Homeowner rider insurance policies are usually available for your ammo collection. Please contact your insurance agent for availability and rates.

Liquidity in today's marketplace typically involves auctions, as the ones that specialize in collectible ammunition have a much larger audience than a gun show where maybe only two or three people might be interested, and usually, for a sizable discount.

Another consideration is when a large surplus military ammo cache is located and finds its way into the ammo-crazed U.S. marketplace. In many cases like this, ammo prices for that particular caliber/configuration go down to a lower price point, followed by stabilized prices after more normal supply/demand economics take over.

Ammunition/cartridge collecting can be lot of fun, and it is usually a longer treasure hunt than gun collecting. Do your homework, get to know the right people, obtain as much information as you can (remember, not everything you read will be true, especially online), and have a defined area of interest. While ammunition collecting might not get as much respect as gun collecting, it's just as fun and educational, takes up a lot less space, plus it can be done for a fraction of the cost of most collectible firearms.

Publisher's note: The Publisher would like to express his thanks to Mr. Patrick McKune, Mr. Alvin Olson, and Mr. Bruce Hart, all longtime ammunition and shooting collectibles dealers. You are encouraged to visit Pat's website: www.sportingcollectibles.com to view his extensive line of ammunition and related items. Alvin can be reached at: cartal@hickorytech.net.

Peters Cartridge Co. No. 2 primer tin. Partially full darkened green tin with side sealing label mostly gone but top label is nice. Primer tins like this are another example of individual ammo components also being collectible. Condition: Good. 1994 auction price: $36. Current value range: $30-$35.

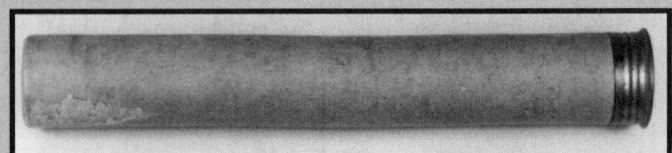

Winchester 10 Gauge paper shotshell. If you're thinking this is a hell of a goose load, and wondering what kind of shotgun fires such a monster round, you'll be disappointed to learn that this is a 5¾ in. factory loaded shell for practice bombing WWII pilots would drop practice bombs while training and could judge accuracy by the pyrotechnic flash/smoke payload emitted upon impact. Headstamp: 'WINCHESTER NO. 10 NUBLACK Made in USA". Condition: Good. 1994 auction price: $15. Current value range: $20-$25.

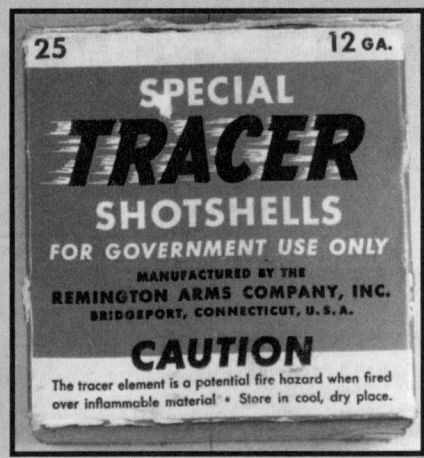

Remington Arms Company 12 Gauge "Special Tracer" shotshell box. Any time an older ammunition box is marked "For Government Use Only," the price usually goes up. The first place the U.S. Army took aspiring WWII aerial gunners was to the trap range, and what better way of showing them how to adequately lead a flying object than with tracer rounds. Obviously, these were never meant to get into the commercial marketplace. Full red and white box with white and black print. Loading: 3-1 1/8 TRACER. Condition: Very Good. 1994 auction price: $21. Current value range: $35-$50.

CHAPTER 93 : GLOSSARY

A

ACCURACY
The ability to hit a given aiming point on the target; a measurement of the dispersion of shots fired from a rifle, handgun or shotgun slug at a given range. A typical system used is extreme spread. Also see PRECISION.

ACCURACY LIFE
The number of rounds that can be fired from a rifle barrel before it loses its ability to produce an acceptable measurement of dispersion.

ACTION
An assembly consisting of the receiver or frame and the mechanism by which a firearm is loaded, fired, and unloaded.

AERODYNAMIC LIFT
The force perpendicular to the bullet's trajectory tending to pull the bullet in the direction the nose is pointed.

AERODYNAMIC STABILITY
The stability due to the bullet's shape and how the shape disrupts or assists airflow over the point, meplat, ogive, bearing surface, heel, and base.

AIMING POINT
The point on the target on which the sights of the firearm are aligned.

AIR GUN
A gun (not a firearm) with a rifled barrel which uses compressed air or CO_2 to propel a pellet.

AIR RESISTANCE
The resistance of air to the passage of the bullet in flight.

AIR RIFLE
See AIR GUN.

AIR SPACE
The volume inside a rifle or pistol cartridge not occupied by the propellant or bullet.

AIR SPIRAL
See BULLET TIPPING.

ALTITUDE
The elevation above mean sea level, normally expressed in feet.

ALTITUDE EFFECT
The change in bullet velocity and trajectory due to changes in air density. As altitude increases air density decreases. As air density decreases, aerodynamic drag on a projectile decreases. However, the effect is so negligible that it can be disregarded by most shooters and hunters.

AMMUNITION
One or more loaded cartridges or shotshells.

ANGLE OF DEPARTURE
The angle formed by a line from the gun muzzle to the target and the bore axis, when the bullet exits the muzzle.

ANGLE OF ELEVATION
The angle formed by the line from the gun muzzle to the target and the bore axis, prior to firing the gun.

ANGLE OF FALL
The angle between a line tangent to the bullet's trajectory at its level point and the line from the muzzle to the target.

ANGLE OF IMPACT
The angle formed by the bullet's path of travel and the ground when the bullet strikes the ground.

ANNEAL, ANNEALING
The process of softening metal normally using controlled exposure to heat and slow cooling. Brass is an exception - it must be cooled rapidly.

ANTIMONY
A metallic element (Sb) used as an alloy to harden lead.

ANVIL
An internal metallic component of a primer assembly. The firing pin crushes the primer mix between the anvil and cup to initiate the explosion of the primer mix.

ARMOR PIERCING
A type of military bullet having a hardened steel or tungsten alloy core designed to penetrate resistant targets.

ASCENDING BRANCH
A projectile's trajectory from muzzle to the highest point along the trajectory.

AUTOMATIC
A term popularly used to describe (incorrectly) self-loading firearms.

AUXILIARY CARTRIDGE
A device which allows a smaller cartridge but of the same bullet diameter to be fired in a larger chambered firearm. While not technically a cartridge, it usually consists of an assembly with a steel body and a firing pin that can inserted in the firearms' chamber. Also see SUBCALIBER BARREL.

B

BACK STOP
A structure, material(s), or device designed to safely stop a bullet on impact.

BACK THRUST
See BOLT THRUST.

BALL
A round lead ball for a muzzle loading firearm; a full metal jacket military bullet with a lead, mild steel, or composite core.

BALL AMMUNITION
Ammunition in military calibers loaded to military specifications, with a full metal jacket bullet. Also see MILITARY AMMUNITION.

BALL CARTRIDGE
See BALL AMMUNITION.

BALLED SHOT
A portion of the shot charge which has slumped together, instead of dispersing after exiting the muzzle. Also see FUSED SHOT.

BALLISTIC COEFFICIENT
A numerical expression of a bullet's ability to overcome air resistance in flight compared to a standard reference bullet.

BALLISTIC PENDULUM
A measuring device which functions like a pendulum; used to calculate a bullet's impact velocity and striking energy.

BALLISTIC TABLE
A numerical summary in chart form of a bullet's exterior ballistic performance.

BALLISTICS
The study of projectiles in motion.

BALLOON HEAD CASE
An obsolete cartridge design that appears to be solid head case, but is not. Also called a folded head case, a balloon head case is structurally weak and should not be fired.

BARREL
A smooth bore or rifled acceleration tube attached to a firearm through which the bullet or shot charge is accelerated by the expanding powder gasses, compressed gas, or other propulsion methods.

BARREL EROSION
The physical deterioration of the bore and throat of a barrel caused by hot powder gasses.

BARREL FOULING
Propellant residue, metal (lead, copper, or nickel stripped off the bullet), or other materials deposited in the bore during firing.

BARREL LENGTH
The distance between the rear portion of the barrel where it contacts the breech face or bolt and the muzzle. Revolvers are an exception as their barrel lengths do not include their cylinder lengths.

BARREL LIFE
The number of rounds which can be fired through a barrel until it may be considered worn out.

BARREL TIME
The time taken by a projectile to move through the barrel, starting when the projectile first moves in the cartridge, and ending as it exits the muzzle.

BARREL VIBRATION

Motion along a barrel's length created by the passage of the bullet, propellant gas pressure, jump, and barrel whip (which is localized at the muzzle end of the barrel).

BARREL WHIP

A vertical displacement of the barrel's muzzle and after a fired projectile leaves the muzzle. This effect is more pronounced in lightweight barrels.

BASE DRAG

The resistance associated with the partial vacuum which forms at and extends behind the bullet's base. Also see DRAG, PARASITIC DRAG, and WAVE DRAG.

BASE WAD

An interior base configuration in a shotshell in which the base wad is separate and not integral with the tube.

BATTERY CUP PRIMER

A five piece primer for shotshells consisting of a drawn brass battery cup, anvil, primer cup, primer pellet, and paper disk.

BB

A steel ball of .177 inch diameter called air rifle shot designed to be fired from a BB gun. Also a specific diameter of shotgun pellet, namely .180 inches.

BB GUN

A generic term for an inexpensive smoothbore airgun, usually spring powered.

BEARING SURFACE

That part of a bullet, also called the shank, which contacts the bore and is engraved by the lands and grooves of the rifling.

BELTED CARTRIDGE

A type of centerfire cartridge with a raised belt at the junction of the case body and extractor groove. Introduced in 1912 by Holland and Holland for their magnum ammunition, these cartridges headspace on their belts rather than their shoulders or mouths.

BERDAN PRIMER

A type of centerfire rifle and handgun percussion primer with two components - the primer cup and primer pellet. The anvil is an integral part of the primer pocket in the cartridge case. A Berdan primed case may have up to three flash holes. Named after its developer and patentee, Col. Hiram Berdan, U.S. Army.

BIG BORE

A centerfire cartridge for firearms having a bore diameter over .300 inches (and over .450 inches in England).

BLACK POWDER

A physical mixture of potassium nitrate, sulfur, and charcoal; the classic and only propellant for over 1,000 years.

BLANK AMMUNITION

Cartridges without normal bullets. Blanks are used for starting races, signaling, saluting, in motion picture productions, re-enacting, line throwing, and grenade launching.

BLANKS

See BLANK AMMUNITION.

BLOWBACK

The flow of expanding powder gasses out of and rearward past the cartridge case. Excessive blowback is caused by defective primers, case splits, or case ruptures.

BLOWBACK ACTION

A semi-automatic or automatic firearm operating design which uses expanding propellant gasses to push a heavy unlocked breechbolt open, and which relies upon the inertia of its moving parts to keep the action closed until the bullet has exited the muzzle and pressure has decreased to a safe level.

BLOWN PATTERN

An uneven erratically distributed shotgun pattern. Most often due to excessive choke or propellant gases which have escaped around the shotshell wad and entered the shot column.

BLOWN PRIMER

A primer which has ruptured or been completely expelled from the primer pocket; normally due to excessive pressure.

BOAT-TAIL

A bullet with a tapering transition from its bearing surface to a smaller diameter base, which reduces base drag.

BODY SPLIT

A length-wise crack or spilt in a cartridge case sidewall; a very dangerous condition because it allows high pressure gas to escape into the firearm's breech, action, receiver, or frame. Also see RUPTURE.

BOLT THRUST

The pressure on the breech face or bolt face when a cartridge is fired. The pressure is transmitted by the head of the cartridge case; the source is propellant gas. It is equal to the maximum chamber pressure in pounds per square inch divided by cartridge head area in square inches. Also called back thrust.

BORE

The interior surface of the barrel forward of the chamber.

BORE AXIS

An imaginary line through the center of the bore. Also called line of bore or bore line.

BORE DIAMETER

The distance across the grooves or lands inside a rifled barrel in front of the throat; the distance across the inner barrel surfaces in front of the chamber for shotshells. Land diameter is the caliber dimension for rifled barrels.

BORE LINE

See BORE AXIS.

BORE SCOPE

A small optical device which allows its user to see inside the bore.

BOXER PRIMER

A type of centerfire rifle and handgun percussion primer in which the anvil is held by the primer cup and pressed against the primer pellet when the assembly is seated in the primer pocket of the case head. This three piece design was invented by Col. Edward Boxer, of the Royal Artillery in Great Britain.

BRASS

An alloy of copper and zinc, normally 90/10 or 95/5.

BREECH

The rear end of a barrel where a cartridge is chambered. Also commonly used in reference to the entire chamber, breech, and receiver of long guns.

BRISANCE

A term describing the shattering power of high explosives.

BROACHED RIFLING

Rifling grooves made by removing metal from the bore using a cutting tool which cuts all of the grooves simultaneously. Each groove is cut by a series of stepped cutting edges which progressively remove metal rather than by one full-depth cutting edge.

BROWN POWDER

A physical mixture of potassium nitrate and charcoal with a much smaller amount of sulfur than black powder (less than 3%); so called after its color.

BUCKSHOT

Shotshell pellets having a diameter of .20 inches or larger.

BULLET

An elongated projectile for use in rifled barrels.

BULLET CORE

The interior portion of a bullet.

BULLET DIAMETER

A measurement of the diameter of a bullet taken across its widest cylindrical section.

BULLET DROP

The vertical distance a bullet has fallen below the bore line, at any point along its trajectory.

BULLET JUMP

The distance the bullet must travel from its seated position in the chambered cartridge case to the first point at which it starts to be engraved by the rifling in the bore. Also see JUMP (firearm motion caused by recoil).

BULLET JACKET

See JACKET.

BULLET OGIVE

See OGIVE.

BULLET PATH

The bullet's curved trajectory above or below the line of sight. Also see TRAJECTORY.

ULLET PENETRATION
The distance a bullet travels inside the target after striking it.

ULLET PULL
The amount of force needed to pull a bullet from an unfired cartridge case.

ULLET PUSH
The amount of force needed to push a bullet inside an unfired cartridge case.

ULLET ROTATION
The spin imparted to the bullet by the rifling in the barrel. See RATE OF SPIN, SPIN, and GYROSCOPIC STABILITY.

ULLET SLIPPAGE
The failure of a projectile to fully engage the rifling as it travels down the bore. Also see BULLET STRIPPING.

ULLET STRIPPING
An internal ballistic problem in which jacket metal is removed as the bullet travels down the bore, due to the bullet not properly engaging the rifling. Also see BULLET SLIPPAGE.

ULLET TIPPING
The corkscrew-like trajectory of an unstable bullet which yaws uncontrollably and does not travel point first. Also called air spiraling.

ULLET TRAP
A structure designed and built to safely decelerate and stop bullets, and prevent ricochets of the bullet or fragments.

ULLET UPSET
The expansion of a bullet inside a target during its terminal ballistic phase; also the bullet's expansion and distortion as the propellant gasses force it into the lands and grooves of the barrel's rifling. See OBTURATION.

ULLET WEAR
Barrel bore surface wear caused by the bullet and hot propellant as they travel down the barrel. Also see EROSION.

ULLET WOBBLE
See WOBBLE.

URNING RATE
The rate at which a given propellant burns in comparison with other propellants.

UTTON RIFLING
Rifling grooves made by displacing metal in the bore with a carbide button pushed or pulled through the barrel.

C

ALIBER
An alpha-numeric expression or name of the specific cartridge for which a firearm is chambered; the approximate land diameter of the barrel; a numeric term used to describe the approximate bullet diameter.

ANNELURE
A circumferential groove cut or impressed into the surface of a bullet to control seating depth, bullet pull, and bullet push.

ARD WAD
A paper disk in various thicknesses used as a spacer, powder gas seal, and top wad (under a rolled crimp to hold the shot pellets in the shell).

ARTRIDGE
A completely assembled and self-contained round of ammunition, consisting at minimum of a primer, propellant, cartridge case, and bullet.

ARTRIDGE BODY
The portion of the cartridge case above its head or base.

ARTRIDGE CASE
The body of a cartridge which holds the other components and serves as a gas seal in the chamber.

ASE
See CARTRIDGE CASE.

ASE CAPACITY
The volume available for propellant inside a cartridge case with a properly seated bullet.

ASE LIFE
The number of times a cartridge case can be reloaded and fired before becoming unserviceable.

ASE SEPARATION
The partial or complete breakage of a cartridge case, forward of its head, upon firing. Also called a rupture.

CASE SPLITS
A condition in which splits or cracks occur in a brass cartridge case. See BODY SPLIT, NECK SPLIT, and SEASON CRACKING.

CASE STRETCHING
The elongation of a cartridge case caused by the chamber pressure generated when the cartridge is fired.

CASELESS AMMUNITION
Ammunition without a traditional metallic cartridge case. Its propellant is molded in a "chamber" shape which contains the projectile and primer.

CAST BULLET
An elongated projectile made by casting melted metal alloy.

CATION RIFLING
Rifling grooves made by removing metal from the bore using a chemical erosion process.

CENTER OF IMPACT
The center of a shot pattern or bullet group on a target.

CENTERFIRE AMMUNITION
Rifle, handgun, and shotgun ammunition with primers in the center of the cartridge case heads.

CENTERFIRE CARTRIDGE
A round of centerfire ammunition, with Berdan or Boxer primers in metallic cartridges and battery cup primers in shotshells. See CENTERFIRE AMMUNITION.

CHAMBER
The rear or breech end of a barrel which has been machined to secure a cartridge and align it with the firing pin and bore.

CHAMBER PRESSURE
The force acting on the chamber walls of the barrel by the expanding propellant gasses.

CHAMFER
The process of removing small amounts of metal from the inside or outside of the case mouth or primer pocket to remove burrs and sharp edges.

CHILLED SHOT
Lead shot hardened by alloying it with antimony or other metals.

CHOKE
The constriction of the bore at the muzzle of a shotgun barrel designed to control the shot pattern.

CHRONOGRAPH
An electronic instrument which measures the time a projectile takes to traverse a carefully measured distance between two sensors and then converts that time to a velocity.

COEFFICIENT OF FORM
A numerical indication of the bullet's profile which is used in calculating the bullet's ballistic coefficient.

COMBUSTION
Rapid oxidation which produces heat and flame. An explosion is oxidation at an extremely rapid rate.

COMPENSATOR
Slots, vents, or ports machined into a firearm's barrel near its muzzle, or a muzzle device, which allow propellant gasses to escape upwards and partially reduce muzzle jump.

COMPONENTS
The various parts of a cartridge.

CONCUSSION
The localized air blast effect of an explosion.

COOK OFF
A cartridge will cook off - fire without operation of the fire control system - when sufficient heat has built up in the firearm's chamber to detonate the priming mixture and/or ignite the powder. This also occurs when unchambered cartridges are exposed to intense heat.

COPPER UNITS OF PRESSURE
A relative measure of chamber pressure generated by rifle and handgun ammunition; determined by how much a copper crusher cylinder is compressed when a cartridge is fired in a dedicated barrel test fixture. This method is semi-obsolete. Also see PRESSURE GAUGE and PRESSURE TESTING BARREL.

CORDITE
A British double base smokeless propellant; so called because of its resemblance to lengths of cord.

CORROSIVE PRIMER

An obsolete primer type. Its priming compound contains potassium chlorate, mercury, or both. When fired it leaves a moisture attracting salt residue in the bore; causing corrosion.

CRATERED PRIMER

An indication of above normal pressure, a fired primer with a small ridge of primer cup metal surrounding the firing pin indentation. Also caused by an enlarged firing pin hole or excess firing pin protrusion.

CRIMP

A method of closing the mouth of a shotshell using folds or top wads to prevent the shot charge from leaking out; a constriction placed on the case mouth of rimfire and centerfire cartridges to control bullet pull and push, as well as overall loaded length.

CRISPIN CARTRIDGE

A Civil War era rimfire cartridge, named after its inventor, Captain Silas Crispin. The rim which contained the primer was approximately in the middle of the case body.

CUSHION WAD

A thick soft wad used for separating the shot charge from the powder gasses and for cushioning the shot during acceleration.

CUT RIFLING

Rifling grooves made by removing metal from the bore with a hook shaped cutting tool.

D

DEFLAGRATION

A rapid exothermic reaction propagated at subsonic velocity by heat transfer through the reactants. Reaction products (hot gasses and flame) flow in a direction opposite to the direction of combustion propagation.

DEFLECTION

The lateral distance a bullet diverges from its intended or predicted flight path, due primarily to crosswinds and to a lesser extent, ammunition variations, firearm motion, and target motion. Also called lateral deflection.

DESCENDING BRANCH

A projectiles trajectory from its highest point to its impact point.

DETERRENT COATING

A chemical coating applied to the outer surface of propellant grains, to help control burning rate.

DETONATION

An extremely rapid exothermic reaction propagated at supersonic velocity through the reactants. Reaction products flow in the same direction as the propagation.

DEVIATION

The distance, angular or linear, between the point of aim and the point of impact for one shot.

DISCHARGE

The firing of a gun.

DISPERSION

The scattered distribution of hits on a target; also the most distance between any two bullet holes in the target, on both the horizontal and vertical axes of the target. See HORIZONTAL DISPERSION and VERTICAL DISPERSION.

DOUBLE-BASE PROPELLANT

Single-base nitrocellulose smokeless propellant enhanced by the addition of up to 49% nitroglycerine.

DRAG

The resistance a bullet (or any other object) encounters as it flies through air. Also see BASE DRAG, PARASITIC DRAG, AND WAVE DRAG.

DRAM EQUIVALENT

A method of comparing the ballistic efficiency and muzzle velocity of shotshells loaded with smokeless powder to the muzzle velocity of a "standard reference" shotshell loaded with 3 drams of black powder and 1 1/8 ounce of lead shot generating a muzzle velocity of 1,200 fps. All smokeless powder shotshells with dram equivalent information are comparing themselves to this "standard reference", i.e. their velocity is either less, equal to, or greater than 1,200 fps. This measurement is now obsolete.

DRIFT

A bullet's in-flight lateral movement off the bore line, due to gyroscopic precession.

DUMMY CARTRIDGE

A cartridge without propellant but with an actual or replica bullet, and deactivated or fired primer. Used for functional testing and training.

DUPLEX CARTRIDGE

A cartridge with two projectiles; or with two or more propellants wit different burning rates. Also called a multiplex cartridge.

E

EFFECTIVE RANGE

The maximum range at which a bullet retains sufficient energy for effectiv terminal ballistic performance.

EJECTA

All components which exit the muzzle when a firearm is discharged. Th weight of ejecta is an important consideration in determining a powde charge.

EJECTION

That part of the firing cycle where the fired cartridge case is thrown fro the firearm. Also see EXTRACTION, which occurs prior to ejection.

ENERGY

The kinetic energy of a bullet expressed in foot-pounds, joules, or kilogram meters.

ENGRAVING

The marks left on the bullet's outer surface by the lands and grooves the rifling.

EROSION

See BARREL EROSION.

ERROR

The distance between the point of impact of one shot and the center of th impact for a group of shots.

EXPANDING POINT BULLET

A projectile with a point purposely designed to expand on impact. Expose lead tip, split tip, flat point, hollow point, and other point designs ar examples.

EXPLOSION

An extremely rapid combustion. The slower explosion of propellant called deflagration; instantaneous explosions are detonations.

EXPLOSIVE (VS PROPELLANT)

1. Both are chemical compounds containing nitrogen and oxygen so th neither requires air to deflagrate.
2. Both require some type of initiator to begin deflagration.
3. Explosives contain substantially more chemical energy than propellant
4. Explosives are not intended to be confined in order to deflagrat properly, propellants are.
5. Explosives deflagrate at substantially higher speeds than propellants.

EXPRESS CARTRIDGE

Of British origin, a cartridge with a heavier powder charge and a lighte weight bullet, as compared to the normal or standard weight for tha cartridge, with increased velocity.

EXTERNAL BALLISTICS

The study of a projectile's motion in its flight from the muzzle to the targe

EXTRACTION

That part of the firing cycle in which the fired cartridge case is pulled out the chamber by the extractor. Also see EJECTION, which follows extractio

EXTRACTOR

A firearm component part which removes a live cartridge or a fire cartridge case from the chamber.

EXTRACTOR GROOVE

A circumferential groove cut into the outer surface of a cartridge case jus in front of the base which provides a gripping surface for the firearm extractor.

EXTREME SPREAD

The maximum distance on a target between the centers of any two bulle holes of a group.

F

FEET PER SECOND

A measurement used to express the velocity of a bullet in flight.

FIXED AMMUNITON

A round of ammunition completely assembled and ready as is to be loade and fired.

AKE POWDER
Smokeless powder with its kernels in the form of thin flakes of various shapes and configurations.

ASH HIDER
See FLASH SUPPRESSOR.

ASH HOLE
A small hole in the bottom of the primer pocket which allows flame and hot expanding gasses to flow into the case body and ignite the powder charge.

ASH INHIBITOR
See FLASH SUPPRESSANT.

ASH SUPPRESSANT
A chemical compound which may be added to smokeless propellants to reduce muzzle flash.

ASH SUPPRESSOR
A muzzle attachment which mechanically disrupts and reduces muzzle flash. It does not reduce muzzle blast or recoil.

ATTENED PRIMER
A fired primer with its normally rounded edge completely displaced to the level of the case head by excessive pressure.

ECHETTE
A small, metal, fin-stabilized arrow or dart fired from a gun barrel instead of a bullet.

YER
A bullet, fired with others in the same conditions and in the same time frame, which markedly strikes the target outside the main group.

LDED HEAD CASE
See BALLOON HEAD CASE.

OT POUNDS
A unit of measurement used to express the amount of a bullet's kinetic energy.

RM FACTOR
A correction factor used in calculating a bullet's ballistic coefficient; it adjusts for meplat, nose, ogive, and base shape variations from a standard reference bullet.

ULING
Propellant gas, plastic, and metal residues deposited in the barrel when a gun is fired.

ANGIBLE BULLET
A monolithic bullet made of compressed metallic powder and binding agents which safely disintegrates on impact with a hard surface.

EE BORE
The un-tapered and un-rifled portion of the barrel between the throat and the start of the rifling. Free bore decreases the rate at which chamber pressure increases and allows the bullet to enter the rifling after pressure has peaked. Technically considered to be part of the throat. See THROAT.

ICTION
The resistance to relative motion of bodies in contact.

LL METAL JACKET
A bullet having a metal jacket covering its outer surfaces, except the base.

LL PATCH BULLET
An obsolete term for a full metal jacket bullet.

SED SHOT
Shot which has been partially melted and formed into masses by high temperature propellant gas leaking into the shot charge. See also BALLED SHOT.

G

AIN TWIST RIFLING
See PROGRESSIVE RIFLING.

ALLERY PRACTICE AMMUNITION
Reduced power or small caliber ammunition optimized for use in indoor or enclosed ranges.

AS
The hot expanding material created by the burning propellant.

AS CHECK
A short metal cup crimped on the base of a lead bullet; it acts as a seal to prevent excessive leading of the bore and distortion of the bullet's base.

GAS CUTTING
Erosion of the bore by the hot propellant gasses; erosion of jacket material by hot propellant gasses flowing around an undersized (in relation to the bore dimensions) bullet for that specific barrel.

GAS PORT
A small opening in the barrel of a gas operated firearm which allows high pressure gas to flow into the gas system's components. Also an escape vent in a firearm's receiver, a safety feature.

GAS SEAL WAD
A thin plastic cup wad placed directly over a shotshell's propellant charge.

GAUGE
The traditional method of measuring and expressing the bore diameter of a shotgun. A gauge number is equal to the number of pure lead balls, each the same diameter as the bore in question, which can be cast from one pound of lead. For example, the bore diameter of a 12-ga. shotgun barrel is equal to the diameter of a pure lead ball weighing precisely 1/12th of a pound.

GAVRE COMMISSION
A military commission of French National Artillery technical officers who conducted bullet drag tests from 1873 to 1898; modern drag functions are expressed with a "G" followed by a number in recognition of their contributions to the science of aeroballistics.

GILDING METAL
An alloy of copper and zinc used for bullet jackets; alloys of 90 % copper and 10% zinc (90/10), and 95% copper and 5% zinc (95/5) are the most common.

GRAIN
A unit of Avoirdupois weight measurement; grains are normally used to express bullet, powder charge, and other cartridge related weights. Also a kernel of propellant.

GRAM
A unit of metric weight measurement; grams are normally used to express bullet, powder charge, and other cartridge related weights. There are 15.432 grains in one gram and 453.6 grams in one pound.

GREASE GROOVE
A shallow circumferential depression in the bearing surface of a lead bullet. The groove is filled with bullet lube to decrease bore leading. A grease groove is not a cannelure.

GROOVES
The spiral depressions of the rifling in a barrel bore; created by cutting, swaging, broaching, hammering, cation action, or other methods. Also see LANDS and RIFLING.

GROOVE DIAMETER
The diameter of a major circle circumscribed by the bottom of the grooves in a rifled barrel.

GROUP
A given number of consecutive shots fired at the same aiming point on a target.

GUARD AMMUNITION
Military ammunition with reduced effective and maximum ranges; for use by security personnel.

GUN COTTON
Nitrated wood or cotton cellulose. See NITROCELLULOSE.

GUN POWDER
A popular generic term for firearm propellants of all types.

GYROSCOPIC STABILITY
Bullet stability in flight due to a high rate of rotation about its long axis; created by the barrel rifling. The optimal rate of rotation prevents tumbling and/or yawing but does not compromise structural integrity. Also see AERODYNAMIC STABILITY and STABILIZE.

H

HAMMER FORGED RIFLING
Rifling grooves made by compressing the barrel around a rifling mandrel (a metal rod with a "negative" of the grooves) using a series of hammers.

HANDLOADING
The manual process of assembling ammunition - using fired cartridge cases and new primers, propellants, and bullets - for personal non-commercial use. Also called reloading. Also see REMANUFACTURING.

HANGFIRE
A ten or less millisecond delay of cartridge ignition after the primer has been struck by the firing pin or striker. Also see MISFIRE.

HARDBALL
A popular slang term among pistol competitors for a full metal jacket pistol bullet.

HEAD
The base of a cartridge case including the primer pocket, rim, extractor groove, and web.

HEAD CLEARANCE
See HEADSPACE.

HEADSPACE
The distance from the breech face with the action closed to a given surface in the chamber where the cartridge rim, belt, shoulder, or case mouth seats.

HEADSPACE GAUGE
A metal gauge which is inserted in the chamber of a firearm to determine if the headspace is correct; normally three gauges are used: go, no-go, and field.

HEADSTAMP
A combination of numbers, letters, or symbols stamped into the base of a cartridge case around the primer which may denote information such as the caliber of the cartridge, the manufacturer, the date of manufacture, or other information. A cartridge may also have no headstamp.

HEEL
The part of a bullet's body where it transitions to its base. Boat-tail bullets are sometimes described as having a tapered or tapering heel.

HIGH BASE
A reference to the relative height of the base wad inside a shotshell. Often erroneously used instead of the term high brass to describe the height of the metal sleeve surrounding the lower part of a shotshell body. Also see LOW BASE.

HIGH BRASS
A subjective reference to the height of the metal head on a shotshell. There is no standard height, but high brass heads are markedly longer than low brass heads. Usually found on magnum, high velocity, buckshot, or slug loads.

HIGH VELOCITY AMMUNITION
Metallic cartridges or shotshells loaded to a higher than normal muzzle velocity for their caliber or gauge.

HIGH VELOCITY CARTRIDGE
See HIGH VELOCITY AMMUNITION.

HOLD-OFF
A method of aiming to overcome wind and other sources of deflection. The sight picture is moved off the target and into the wind. Also see HOLD-OVER.

HOLD-OVER/UNDER
The distance to be aimed above or below a target to hit it when the firearm's zero range and the target's range do not coincide. Also see HOLD-OFF.

HOLLOW POINT
A cavity in the nose of an expanding bullet; it allows greater energy transfer to the target compared to a solid bullet. In match rifle bullets, it moves the center of balance toward the base for greater accuracy. Also incorrectly substituted for "hollow point bullet" or "hollow point ammunition".

HOMOGENOUS BULLET
See MONOLITHIC BULLET.

HORIZONTAL DISPERSION
The maximum horizontal distance across the target between vertical parallel lines through the furthest left and right bullet holes in a group. Also call horizontal spread. Also see DISPERSION, and VERTICAL DISPERSION.

HORIZONTAL SPREAD
See DISPERSION, HORIZONTAL DISPERSION, and VERTICAL DISPERSION.

HULL
A popular term for an empty shotshell.

HUNTING AMMUNITION
Ammunition loaded with bullets or shot suitable for hunting game. Normally a hunting bullet is designed to expand on impact, but non-expanding full metal jacket or solid bullets may be used for some applications.

HUNTING CARTRIDGE
See HUNTING AMMUNITION.

HYDROSTATIC SHOCK
A destructive shock wave caused by the passage of a high velocity bul through living tissue.

HYGROSCOPIC POWDER
A smokeless propellant that readily absorbs moisture; all black powder hygroscopic.

HYPERVELOCITY
Muzzle velocity equal to or greater than 4,500 feet per second – sm arms ammunition.

I

IGNITION
The initiation of propellant deflagration by the hot primer gasses.

IGNITION TIME
The time elapsed from primer detonation to initial movement of the bul within the cartridge case.

INERTIA
The tendency of a body to resist acceleration; i.e. a body at rest will rema at rest, and a body in motion will stay in motion in a straight line unle disturbed or acted upon by an external force.

INCENDIARY
A type of military bullet containing a mixture inside designed to igni flammable substances after it penetrates a target.

INCENDIARY BULLET
A projectile which has a chemical payload. Upon impact the payload dispersed and generates heat sufficient to cause ignition.

INFRA-RED TRACER
A military bullet that emits infra-red light from its base during flight. contrast to regular tracers, it has a short ignition time for easy detecti and is designed to be visible only through an infra-red night vision devi (NVD).

INGALLS TABLES
A set of ballistic tables computed by Col. James Ingalls using material fro Col. Francesco Siacci (Italy), Col. Mayevski (Russia), and the 1875-188 Krupp ballistic tests at Meppen, Germany; the Ingalls tables remain in u today for estimating the coefficient of form and ballistic coefficient for given bullet shape.

INHIBITOR
A chemical compound which slows or prevents the breakdown of smokele propellant. Also called a stabilizer, or a deterrent coating.

INTEGRAL BASE WAD
An interior base configuration of a shotshell in which the base wad permanently attached to or integrally formed with the tube.

INTERNAL BALLISTICS
The study of a projectile's motion within a gun barrel.

INTERNALLY SILENCED AMMUNITION
Centerfire ammunition which eliminates muzzle blast and flash b containing them entirely within the cartridge case by means of a flexib internal component.

INSTRUMENTAL VELOCITY
The velocity of a bullet, shot swarm, or slug recorded by instrumentatio at a selected distance from the muzzle.

J

JACKET
The metal alloy cover surrounding the bullet's core.

JACKETED BULLET
A bullet which has a metal alloy cover over its core.

JACKETED HOLLOW POINT
An expanding bullet with its jacket open at the front end, exposing a co cavity designed to increase expansion on impact.

JACKETED SOFT POINT
An expanding bullet with its jacket open at the front end, exposing sc core material designed to increase expansion on impact.

JUMP
The horizontal, vertical, and rotating motion of a firearm when fire Rotation is caused by the passage of the projectile; horizontal and vertic motion by recoil forces pushing the firearm along a path of least resistanc Also see BULLET JUMP.

K

KERNEL
A single particle or grain of gunpowder; shapes include balls, flattened balls, tubes, rods, and flakes.

KEYHOLE
An oval or oblong hole in a target made by an unstable or "keyholing" bullet.

L

LANDS
The uncut surface of a rifle bore; the raised portion of the rifling.

LAND DIAMETER
One of two bore diameters; the diameter of a major circle circumscribing the top of the lands. Also see BORE, GROOVE, GROOVE DIAMETER, and RIFLING.

LATERAL DEFLECTION
See DEFLECTION.

LATERAL JUMP
See JUMP.

LEAD UNITS OF PRESSURE
A relative measure of shotgun chamber pressure determined by the use of lead crusher cylinders; this method is semi-obsolete and only used for shotshells.

LEADING
The deposit of lead fouling in a gun barrel caused by an unjacketed bullet or shot charge coming into contact with the bore surface.

LEVEL POINT
The point on the descending portion of its trajectory where the projectile is at the same level as the muzzle. Also called point of fall. Also see LINE OF FALL, and TIME OF FALL.

LINE OF BORE
See BORE AXIS.

LINE OF DEPARTURE
The bore axis line extended to infinity at the precise moment the bullet leaves the muzzle; also called the tangent to the trajectory at the muzzle. Also see ANGLE OF DEPARTURE and ANGLE OF ELEVATION.

LINE OF FALL
A line tangent to the trajectory curve at the bullet's level point. Also see ANGLE OF FALL, LEVEL POINT, and TIME OF FALL.

LINE OF FIRE
A horizontal straight line from the muzzle of a gun extending in the direction of a projectile fired from that gun.

LINE OF IMPACT
A line tangent to the trajectory curve at the bullet's point of impact. Also see ANGLE OF IMPACT, and POINT OF IMPACT.

LINE OF SIGHT
An imaginary straight line to infinity passing through the sights and coincident with the point of aim.

LIPFIRE
An obsolete rimfire primer and cartridge design.

LIVE AMMUNITION
Loaded metallic cartridges or shotshells capable of being fired.

LIVE CARTRIDGE
See LIVE AMMUNITION.

LOAD
The combination of components used to assemble a complete cartridge or shotshell; including a primer, propellant, cartridge case or hull, bullet or shot charge, and wad column.

LOAD DENSITY
The ratio of propellant volume to available case volume, expressed as a percentage.

LOCK TIME
The time between sear release and priming compound detonation.

LOW BASE
A reference to the relative height of the base wad inside a shotshell. Often erroneously used instead of the term low brass to describe the height of the metal sleeve surrounding the lower part of a shotshell body. Also see HIGH BASE.

LOW BRASS
A subjective reference to the height of the metal head on a shotshell. There is no standard height, but low brass heads are markedly shorter than high brass heads.

M

MACH NUMBER
The ratio of a bullet's speed in air to the speed of sound in air.

MAGNUM AMMUNITION
A term first used by Holland & Holland in 1912 for their .375 H & H Magnum cartridge. The term has now been applied to rimfire, centerfire, or shotshell cartridges having a larger cartridge case, heavier shot charge, or higher muzzle velocity than standard cartridges or shotshells of a given caliber or gauge. Most magnum rifle cartridges are belted designs.

MAGNUM CARTRIDGE
See MAGNUM AMMUNITION.

MAGNUS FORCE
Side force; unequal pressures on opposite sides of an axially rotating bullet caused by the viscous interaction between the air and the bullet's surface. This force acts upon the bullet's center of pressure in a direction perpendicular to the plane of yaw. Discovered by German physicist Hienrich G. Magnus (died 1870).

MAGNUS MOMENT
A positive or negative coefficient of moment acting upon the bullet's center of gravity in direction perpendicular to the bullet's longitudinal axis. Bullet shape, center of gravity location, yaw, and in-flight Mach number have an effect on this phenomenon. Magnus Force and Moment have a very large influence on projectile dynamic stability.

MATCH AMMUNITION
Centerfire or rimfire ammunition manufactured with selected bullets, propellants, primers, cartridge cases, and with higher precision and consistency, to reduce levels of dispersion compared to standard ammunition. Match ammunition is more expensive than standard ammunition.

MATCH CARTRIDGE
See MATCH AMMUNITION.

MAXIMUM AVERAGE BREECH PRESSURE
The maximum arithmetic mean pressure allowable for a test lot of ammunition.

MAXIMUM CHARGE
The heaviest charge of a given propellant which may safely be loaded into a specific cartridge without exceeding the maximum allowable chamber pressure.

MAXIMUM HORIZONTAL RANGE
The longest horizontal distance a bullet may travel to the point of first impact with the ground, with the muzzle elevated at the optimum angle when the firearm is discharged. "Maximum range" is often substituted for this range term.

MAXIMUM ORDINATE
The vertical distance between a firearm's muzzle and the highest point on the trajectory of a bullet fired from that firearm.

MAXIMUM POINT BLANK RANGE
See POINT BLANK RANGE.

MAXIMUM VERTICAL RANGE
The greatest elevation a bullet will reach when fired from a vertically oriented barrel.

MEAN DEVIATION
The average of the deviation of a number of shots.

MEAN ERROR
The average distance between impact points and the center of impact for a group of shots.

MEAN RADIUS
The arithmetic average of the distances from the center of each shot to the group center.

MEAN RANGE
The average distance which a group of shots has travelled.

MEAN TRAJECTORY
The trajectory, for a group of shots, which intersects the group's impact center.

MEPLAT

The small flat surface on the tip of a bullet.

MEPPEN TESTS

A series of bullet drag tests conducted by Krupp at their Meppen Proving Grounds between 1875 and 1881.

METAL FOULING

Lead, nickel, copper, or other alloy deposits left in the bore after firing; fouling adversely affects accuracy.

METALLIC AMMUNITION

One or more rounds of rimfire or centerfire ammunition with cases made of metal, usually brass.

METALLIC CARTRIDGE

See METALLIC AMMUNITION.

MID RANGE TRAJECTORY

The point in a trajectory which is half the distance between the firearm's muzzle and the target. Also a term for the bullet's height above the line of sight at the same distance. Also see MID RANGE TRAJECTORY HEIGHT.

MID RANGE TRAJECTORY HEIGHT

The maximum height above the line of sight, from muzzle to zero range, for a specific combination of ammunition, sights, firearm, and zero distance. Also see MID RANGE TRAJECTORY.

MIL

The angle subtended by one unit of length at a distance of 1,000 units of length.

MILITARY AMMUNITION

Centerfire rifle, shotgun, or pistol ammunition in calibers used by a military service; may be loaded with specialized bullets for military applications.

MILITARY CARTRIDGE

See MILITARY AMMUNITION.

MINIE BALL

An obsolete ogival-cylindrical lead bullet with a conical base cavity which obturates under the propellant gas pressure to form a gas seal, even in rifled barrels.

MINIMUM CARTRIDGE

A statutory, regulatory, or administrative lower limit criteria for cartridges which must be used when hunting specified game animals. The criteria may be one or more of the following: bullet diameter, bullet weight, muzzle energy, case dimensions, or overall cartridge dimensions.

MINUTE OF ANGLE

1/60th of a degree; subtending 1.047 inches at 100 yards; normally taken as 1.00 inch at 100 yards.

MIRAGE

The shimmering effect caused by heated air refracting light; often used to estimate the velocity and variability of crosswinds.

MISFIRE

Failure of the primer to detonate after being struck a normal blow by the firing pin; failure of a properly initiated primer to ignite the propellant powder.

MONOLITHIC BULLET

A cast, swaged, molded, sintered, extruded, or turned bullet made from a single material; it is not jacketed but may be plated with a thin layer of copper, nickel, zinc, or other material such as molybdenum disolphide. Lead monolithic bullets may have a coating of lubricant. Alternatively described as a homogenous bullet.

MOUTH

The front open end of a cartridge case.

MULTI ENVIRONMENT AMMUNITION

Rifle cartridges with supercavitating projectiles designed specifically for tactical firing underwater, or from air into water, or from water into air.

MULTIPLEX CARTRIDGE

See DUPLEX CARTRIDGE.

MUSHROOM

A commonly used non-technical term describing the expansion of a bullet as it impacts and/or traverses through a target.

MUZZLE

The front end of a gun barrel.

MUZZLE BLAST

The high decibel audible report caused by the column of high pressure and high temperature propellant gases exiting the muzzle along with the bullet. Also called powder blast. Also see MUZZLE FLASH and MUZZLE WAVE.

MUZZLE BRAKE

A muzzle device (permanent or removable) or barrel modification which reduces muzzle jump and recoil by diverting propellant gasses sideways or to the rear. Not to be confused with a flash hider or a flash suppressor. Also see COMPENSATOR.

MUZZLE ENERGY

The kinetic energy of the bullet at the muzzle, normally expressed in foot-pounds or joules.

MUZZLE FLASH

The brief burst of light at the muzzle caused by burning particles of propellant and gas ejected from the barrel which have mixed with oxygen in the air. Also see MUZZLE BLAST and MUZZLE WAVE.

MUZZLE JUMP

See JUMP.

MUZZLE VELOCITY

The velocity of a bullet as it exits the muzzle: usually expressed in feet per second or meters per second.

MUZZLE WAVE

The circumferentially expanding wave of compressed air which starts at a gun's muzzle when a cartridge has been fired. Also see MUZZLE BLAST and MUZZLE FLASH.

N

NECK

The front portion of a cartridge case from the mouth to the shoulder.

NECK RADIUS

The small curvature at the junction of the case neck and shoulder.

NECK SPLIT

A crack in the neck or mouth of a cartridge case, most often a season crack attributable to improper annealing. Also caused by improper and or multiple sizings.

NECK TENSION

The force exerted by the case neck or mouth which holds the projectile at its proper seating depth.

NITRO CARD WAD

A stiff paper wad of various thicknesses used to seal propellant gasses, spacing, or sealing the tube mouth.

NITROCELLULOSE

Nitrated cotton or wood cellulose used to make single-base smokeless propellants.

NITROGLYCERINE

Glyceryl nitrate or nitric ester of glycerine; used to make double-base smokeless propellants.

NON-CORROSIVE

A term describing priming compounds which do not cause corrosion or rust in gun barrels.

NON-HYGROSCOPIC POWDER

A smokeless propellant which does not tend to absorb moisture.

NOSE

The forward portion of the bullet's ogive, or its point.

O

OBTURATION

The expansion of the cartridge case body against the chamber walls which acts as a seal to prevent rearward flow of the hot high pressure propellant gases. Also used to describe the deformation of the bullet as it is forced into the lands and grooves of the barrel rifling. See BULLET UPSET.

OGIVE

The rounded, curved, pointed, or tapered portion of a bullet forward of the bearing surface.

OUTSIDE LUBED BULLET

A bullet with a grease groove intentionally located so that it is not enclosed by the cartridge case.

OVERALL LENGTH

The maximum length of a loaded cartridge from base to meplat.

VER-IGNITION
Caused by the use of a primer more powerful than necessary, the propellant charge burns too fast. Also see UNDER-IGNITION.

VER BORE CAPACITY
A cartridge loaded with more propellant than can be burned efficiently in a given bore diameter, barrel length, and bore volume. Typically, magnum calibers are over bore capacity.

VER SHOT WAD
A thin nitro card or plastic wad placed over the shot charge to prevent shot pellets from falling out of a rolled crimp shotshell.

P

PER PATCHED BULLET
An obsolete bullet type; a land diameter lead bullet wrapped in paper until it was at groove diameter. The paper engaged the rifling, acted as a gas seal, and reduced leading.

RTITION BULLET
A jacketed bullet with its core in two separate inner compartments; ideally the rear compartment remains intact while the forward compartment expands on impact.

TTERN
For shotguns - the distribution of shotgun pellets in a swarm at a given range; and the distribution and number of pellets which hit within the thirty inch diameter circle of a pattern test target at 40 yards. In general, the distribution of multiple shots on a single target, all fired in a single session in the same manner under the same conditions.

AK PRESSURE
The maximum chamber pressure an individual cartridge reaches when fired; not an average.

LLET
An individual round ball in a shot charge; a diabolo-shaped projectile for an air rifle.

RCUSSION CAP
A thin metal container (resembling a cap or hat) which holds a small charge of priming mixture; used for igniting muzzle-loading firearms.

ERCED PRIMER
A primer which has been pierced by the firing pin. This allows some propellant gasses to escape rearward rather than exiting at the muzzle.

EZOELECTRIC TRANSDUCER
A pressure measuring device which uses a calibrated quartz crystal that releases an electric current proportional to the pressure applied on it; normally expressed in pounds per square inch or psi.

NFIRE
An obsolete ignition system that held the primer inside the case with a small firing pin protruding from the rear sidewall of the case.

US P/PLUS P PLUS AMMUNITION
Handgun ammunition loaded to higher, or very high pressure levels; originally developed for military and law enforcement use. Offered by many manufacturers for self-defense or personal protection use. Warning: to be used only in firearms which the manufacturer has designated as capable of safely firing this type of ammunition. Specifically identified as such by "+P" or "+P+" labeling on boxes or containers and on the cartridge case headstamp.

OINT BLANK RANGE
The maximum distance from the muzzle at which the bullet's vertical path is never above or below the target's vital zone. For hunters this is an advantage as there is no need for hold-over or sight adjustment.

OINT OF AIM
The specific point on the target where the shooter aligns the sights of a firearm.

OINT OF FALL
See LEVEL POINT.

OINT OF IMPACT
The location or point where a bullet in flight first strikes the target.

ORT PRESSURE
The pressure at the location of a barrel's gas port. Also see GAS PORT.

OWDER
Propellant, both smokeless and black.

POWDER BURNING RATE
The speed at which a given powder deflagrates or burns compared to other powders.

POWDER CHARGE
The weight of propellant loaded into a cartridge; usually expressed in grains avoirdupois.

POWDER DETERIORATION
The partial or full decomposition of smokeless powder.

POWDER FOULING
A solid residue remaining in a gun barrel after a cartridge has been fired through it.

PRECISION
The ability to tightly cluster all shots into a small group on the target regardless of where the center of impact of the group is located on the target; the ultimate precision would be all bullets striking in one hole.

PRESSURE
The force exerted by the expanding propellant gasses on the chamber, barrel, bolt, and receiver of a firearm.

PRESSURE CURVE
A graphical presentation of the relationship of chamber pressure to time when a cartridge is fired.

PRESSURE GAUGE
A device, also called a strain gauge, for measuring the pressure in the chamber or barrel of a firearm; utilizing copper or lead crushers to measure Copper Units of Pressure (CUP) and Lead Units of Pressure (LUP). Piezoelectric transducers are used to measure pressure in pounds per square inch (psi). Also see COPPER UNITS OF PRESSURE, LEAD UNITS OF PRESSURE, PIEZOELECTRIC TRANSDUCER, and PRESSURE TESTING BARREL.

PRESSURE TESTING BARREL
A barrel specifically designed and calibrated to measure chamber pressure by means of collars and holes which accept piezoelectric transducers and/or crusher cylinders. These barrels are designed for and used only in special test fixtures.

PRIMER
A percussion device designed to ignite the propellant charge of a centerfire cartridge or shotshell by generating flame and high temperature expanding gasses.

PRIMER CUP
The small metallic cup into which the priming compound is placed. Also see PERCUSSION CAP.

PRIMER DROP TEST
A test of primer sensitivity using a measuring device which drops a steel ball from calibrated heights onto a primer fixture. Also see PRIMER SENSITIVITY.

PRIMER INDENT
The small indentation made by the tip of the firing pin when it strikes the primer cap or cup.

PRIMER LEAK
The escape of propellant gas around the outside edge of a primer, evidenced by dark residue on the case head around the primer. Generally due to oversize primer pockets or excessive pressure.

PRIMER MIXTURE
An explosive chemical mixture, a component part of percussion caps, battery cup primers, Berdan primers, Boxer primers, and rimfire priming.

PRIMER SENSITIVITY
A comparative measure of the firing pin energy needed to ignite a primer.

PROGRESSIVE BURNING POWDER
A smokeless propellant with a burning rate which increases as pressure within the cartridge or shotshell decreases. Burning rate can be controlled by: modifying kernel shape, chemical energy content, deterrent coatings, or other means.

PROGRESSIVE RIFLING
A type of rifling with an increasing rate of twist from throat to muzzle, also called gain twist rifling.

PROOF AMMUNITION
Ammunition loaded to approximately 125% of normal pressure levels for testing the strength and safety of new or repaired firearms and barrels.

PROOF CARTRIDGE
See PROOF AMMUNITION and PROOF TEST.

PROOF TEST

A test which subjects a firearm to approximately 125% of the pressure generated by standard cartridges. Also see PROOF AMMUNITION.

PROPELLANT

The powdered energetic material in a cartridge case which deflagrates when ignited, producing a large volume of hot expanding gas which propels the bullet down the barrel.

PROPRIETARY AMMUNITION

Ammunition which was not manufactured by the organization or business selling it.

PROPRIETARY CARTRIDGE

See PROPRIETARY AMMUNITION.

PROTRUDING PRIMER

A primer which protrudes above the base surface of the case head. Also called an extruded primer.

R

RANGE

The horizontal distance from the muzzle to the target.

RATE OF SPIN

A bullet's rate of rotation when fired from a rifled barrel; usually expressed in revolutions per minute (rpm).

RATE OF TWIST

The distance in which rifling makes one complete revolution; normally expressed as one turn in a specific number of inches or millimeters. Also called rifling pitch.

REBATED CASE

A cartridge case with a rim diameter smaller than its body diameter.

RECOIL

The energy imparted to the shooter's shoulder by the rearward movement of the firearm when it is fired.

REFERENCE AMMUNITION

Specially made calibration ammunition of tested uniformity used by manufacturers to confirm the veracity of their chronographs, pressure guns, and other measurement equipment. The measurement results from firing the calibrated ammunition are compared to industry specifications for that caliber and loading.

REFERENCE CARTRIDGE

See REFERENCE AMMUNITION.

RELOADING

See HANDLOADING and REMANUFACTURING.

REMAINING ENERGY

The residual energy of a bullet at a given range from the muzzle.

REMAINING VELOCITY

The residual velocity of a bullet at a given range from the muzzle.

REMANUFACTURING

Commercial reloading of fired cartridge cases, in very large quantity compared to handloading by individuals.

RESIDUAL PRESSURE

The pressure still in the chamber at the instant the bullet exits the muzzle.

RETICLE

The lines, shapes, and reference marks visible when looking through an optical sight; used for aiming, range estimation, or other purposes.

RICOCHET

A projectile which strikes a hard surface without penetrating and continues on a new but erratic and reduced velocity trajectory.

RIFLED SLUG

A single conical shotshell projectile which has parallel spiral grooves on its body.

RIFLING

The spiral grooves in the bore of a firearm or air gun barrel that impart rotation to the projectile as it travels down the barrel. Also see GROOVES, LANDS, and RATE OF TWIST.

RIFLING PITCH

See RATE OF TWIST.

RIM

The flange on the base of a cartridge which provides a gripping surface for the extractor.

RIMFIRE AMMUNITION

Metallic ammunition in which the priming mixture is held inside the hollow rim of the case head.

RIMFIRE CARTRIDGE

See RIMFIRE AMMUNITION.

RIMFIRE PRIMER/PRIMING

A metallic cartridge priming system where the priming compound located inside of and around the hollow rim of the case.

ROUND

A cartridge containing all components necessary to assemble and fire or shot. A round of ammunition, i.e. a cartridge, consists of a case, primer powder, and bullet completely assembled and self-contained.

RUPTURE

See CASE SEPARATION.

S

SAAMI

The Sporting Arms and Ammunition Manufacturers' Institute; a branch the National Shooting Sports Foundation.

SABOT

A lightweight groove diameter carrier which holds a sub-caliber bullet; is discarded shortly after exiting the muzzle allowing the sub-caliber bull to fly to the target.

SEASON CRACKING

Fine cracks in brass cartridge case heads, necks, or mouths. Caused b age, defective brass, or chemical action of the propellant. Often called ag cracking or stress cracking.

SEATING DEPTH

The longitudinal position of a bullet, primer, or wad column in a cartridg case.

SECANT OGIVE

A bullet having an ogive slope not tangent to the bearing surface; relatively sharp point.

SECTIONAL DENSITY

The ratio of the bullet's weight in pounds to the square of its diameter inches.

SEPARATE-LOADING AMMUNITION

See ROUND.

SEMI-RIMMED CASE

A cartridge case having a rim slightly larger in diameter than the ca body.

SEMI-WADCUTTER BULLET

A lead or jacketed pistol or revolver bullet with a truncated cone ogive an a sharp outer shoulder to cut clean round holes which aid spotting an scoring hits on paper targets. With appropriate core and jacket materi also suitable for some types of personal defense and hunting.

SERVICE AMMUNITION

See BALL AMMUNITION and MILITARY AMMUNITION.

SERVICE CARTRIDGE

See BALL AMMUNITION and MILITARY AMMUNITION.

SETBACK PRIMER

A loose or partially dislocated primer; an indication of excessive pressur defective cartridge case, or a problem with the firearm's bolt or chambe

SHANK

See BEARING SURFACE.

SHOCKING POWER

A popular non-technical term loosely rating the ability of a bullet to depos kinetic energy inside a target.

SHOCK WAVE

Compression of the air in front of a bullet in flight forms shock waves whic create air disturbances surrounding the ogive, bearing surface, and base the bullet. Also see DRAG, and WAVE DRAG.

SHORT ROUND

A cartridge which has its bullet seated too far into the case.

SHOT

Small spherical metal or metal composite pellets used as shotshe projectiles.

OT COLLAR
A plastic pouch which holds the shot charge; usually formed integrally with the wad column. It prevents pellets from contacting the bore surface, thereby improving the shot pattern. Also see SHOT PROTECTOR WAD.

OT COLUMN
The space occupied by the shot charge inside a shotshell.

OT PROTECTOR WAD
A type of wad column which incorporates a shot collar pouch at its front end for holding the shot charge and preventing the shot pellets from contacting the bore surface.

OT SIZE
The diameter of shot pellets, in inches or millimeters.

OT STRING
The radially expanding and lengthening shot column, or shot swarm, in flight. See PATTERN.

OT TOWER
A tall narrow structure for making lead shot. Molten shot alloy is dropped from the top level, forming into spherical droplets during its descent and ands in a water bath.

OT SWARM
See SHOT STRING, PATTERN.

OTSHELL
An assembly consisting of a rimmed metal head, paper or plastic base wad, 209 battery cup primer, and paper or plastic body. A shotshell cartridge is a shotshell loaded with propellant, wad column, and shot charge or a single large diameter slug.

OULDER
The sloping portion of the cartridge case between the case body and the neck.

OULDER RADIUS
The small curvature at the junction of the shoulder and the case body.

GHT ELEVATION
Vertical movement of an adjustable sight to compensate for the vertical displacement of bullet impact points from the aiming point.

GNAL CARTRIDGE
A cartridge with a pyrotechnic projectile (a flare) which burns intensely, similar to the common Roman candle firework. Used for signaling by the military and civilians.

LENCER
See SUPPRESSOR.

NGLE-BASE POWDER
A propellant with nitrocellulose as its primary content.

ZING
The mechanical compression of a fired cartridge case to restore its as-manufactured dimensions; a step in the handloading process. Also performed on cast lead bullets to meet dimensional and concentricity requirements.

IN FRICTION DRAG
See PARASITIC DRAG.

UG
A slang term describing any single projectile (other than shot) regardless of size, construction, or use.

MALL ARMS AMMUNITION
The military designation for all ammunition for firearms having a bore diameter of .500 inch or less.

MALL BORE CARTRIDGE
A colloquial term for a .22 rimfire cartridge.

MOKELESS POWDER
A chemical mixture made of a base of nitrocellulose with a variety of additives, coatings, and enhancements.

OLID HEAD CASE
The modern metallic centerfire case, most often drawn from brass; developed by Col. Hiram Berdan. Also see BERDAN PRIMER and BOXER PRIMER.

UND SUPPRESSOR
See SUPPRESSOR.

EED OF ROTATION
See RATE OF SPIN.

SPIN
The stabilizing rotation of a bullet about its longitudinal axis, created by rifling as the bullet is propelled down the barrel. Also see RATE OF SPIN.

SPIN DAMPING MOMENT
The force which opposes and reduces the bullet's rate of spin.

SPITZER BULLET
A sharply pointed bullet; more aerodynamically and ballistically efficient than round or flat nose bullets.

SPIRE POINT BULLET
See SPITZER BULLET.

SPLIT, SPLITS
See BODY SPLIT, CASE SPLITS, NECK SPLIT, SEASON CRACKING.

STABILITY
Resistance to change, dislodgement, or diversion. See AERODYNAMIC STABILITY, GYROSCOPIC STABILITY, STABILIZED BULLET.

STABILIZED BULLET
A bullet in flight with sufficient rate of spin and velocity to maintain it in a point first attitude along its trajectory. Also see AERODYNAMIC STABILITY and GYROSCOPIC STABILITY.

STABILIZER
See DETERRENT COATING.

STANDARD DEVIATION
A statistical analysis concept, a measure quantifying the dispersion of various samples around the mean of a set of data.

STANDARD VELOCITY
A designation applied to rimfire ammunition loaded to a maximum of 1,155 fps to distinguish it from high velocity rimfire ammunition loaded to muzzle velocities over 1,160 fps.

STRIKING ENERGY
The kinetic energy of the bullet when it strikes the target.

STRIKING VELOCITY
The retained velocity of a bullet at the point of striking the target.

STRIPPING
See BULLET STRIPPING.

SUBCALIBER BARREL
An insert consisting of a barrel with a chamber or fixture, usually designed for rifles, which allows firing a smaller caliber/dimension cartridge. Widely used by the military for training and weapon familiarization.

SUBSONIC AMMUNITION
Ammunition loaded to a muzzle velocity of less than 1,120 fps (the nominal speed of sound at standard conditions).

SUBSONIC CARTRIDGE
See SUBSONIC AMMUNITION.

SUBSONIC VELOCITY
A muzzle velocity below the speed of sound; 1,120 fps at standard conditions.

SUMMIT VELOCITY
Projectile velocity at the apex of its trajectory.

SUPPRESSOR
A mechanical device, usually cylindrical and detachable, which alters and decreases muzzle blast and noise. Commonly referred to, in error, as a silencer, it acts only on the sound of the firearm's discharge – it does not have any effect on the sounds generated by: the firearm's moving parts, a supersonic bullet in flight, or the bullet's impact.

SWAGE
Working or forming cold metal by pushing it through one or more dies.

T

TANGENT OGIVE
A bullet having an ogive slope tangent to the bearing surface, a very effective and popular design.

TAPE PRIMER
An obsolete priming system developed by Dr. Edward Maynard. Instead of loose individual percussion caps, priming pellets were secured between two strips of paper. The "tape" was wound into a roll, which was mechanically advanced for each shot.

TARAGE TABLE

A table of numerical values which quantify the relationship between the compressed length of a lead or copper crusher cylinder, and peak chamber pressure. See PRESSURE TESTING BARREL.

TEATFIRE CARTRIDGE

A rimless tapered body cartridge with a round body terminating in a small teat which contained the primer compound. A very specialized design as it was loaded through the front end of a Moore and Williamson patent revolver's cylinder.

TEMPERATURE EFFECT

The increase or decrease in projectile velocity due to an increase or decrease in propellant temperature; 1.7 feet per second per degree change from 59 degrees F (the standard performance testing and reference temperature).

TEMPERATURE OF IGNITION

The lowest temperature to which the surface of a material (propellant) must be raised to initiate self-sustaining combustion.

TERMINAL BALLISTICS

The study of the projectile's accuracy and effect on the target.

TERMINAL VELOCITY

The remaining velocity of a bullet at the point on its descending trajectory where it is on the same level as the muzzle of the firearm from which it was fired. Also see LEVEL POINT, and POINT OF FALL.

THROAT

The tapering section of the barrel from the end of the chamber to the point where the bullet first contacts the rifling. The forward portion that is un-tapered is known as free bore. Also called leade. See FREE BORE.

TIME OF FALL

The flight time for a projectile to reach its level point. Also see ANGLE OF FALL, LEVEL POINT, LINE OF FALL, and TERMINAL VELOCITY.

TIME OF FLIGHT

The total elapsed time, normally expressed in seconds, for a bullet to travel a given distance from the muzzle.

TORQUE

The force which causes a rifled firearm to counter-rotate when a projectile travels down its bore.

TRACER

A type of military bullet that emits a colored flame from its base when fired allowing the gunner to adjust his fire onto a target.

TRAJECTORY

The curved flight path of a bullet from muzzle to target; resembling but not a true parabolic arc.

TRAJECTORY TABLE

A numerical table of computed data summarizing the down range trajectory of a bullet, shot pellet, or shotgun slug.

TRIPLE-BASE POWDER

A double-base propellant further enhanced by the addition of nitroguanadine.

TUMBLING BULLET

A bullet turning end over end during its flight or after impact.

TURNED BULLET

A bullet made by turning metal alloy bar stock on a Swiss screw machine. Also called a monolithic or homogenous bullet.

U

UNDER-IGNITION

An incomplete ignition of the propellant charge, usually due to a defective primer or contaminated powder which fails to produce enough brisance, contaminated propellant or a light propellant change. Under-ignition causes erratic velocity, hangfires, and degraded accuracy. Also see OVER-IGNITION.

UNIVERSAL RECEIVER

A test equipment fixture which functions as a receiver for interchangeable pressure testing barrels. Used for firing ammunition being tested for chamber pressure.

V

VELOCITY

The speed of a projectile at a given point along its path of trave normally expressed in feet per second or meters per second. Also s INSTRUMENTAL VELOCITY.

VELOCITY TEST BARREL

A special barrel calibrated for testing velocity and accuracy.

VERTICAL DISPERSION

The maximum vertical distance across the target between horizon parallel lines through the furthest upper and lower bullet holes in a grou Also called vertical spread. Also see DISPERSION, and HORIZONT/ DISPERSION.

VERTICAL JUMP

See JUMP.

VERTICAL SPREAD

See DISPERSION, VERTICAL DISPERSION, and HORIZONTAL DISPERSIO

VISCOUS DRAG

See PARASITIC DRAG.

W

WAD

A unitary or multi-piece spacer and cushion between the powder charg and the shot charge; it also acts as a powder gas seal. When assemble from multiple components it is more correctly called a wad column.

WAD COLUMN

An assembly of paper and plastic components which act as a cushi between the powder charge and the shot charge and also seal off powd gasses.

WAD SEATING PRESSURE

The number of pounds required to seat a given wad; plastic wad colum are normally seated with 15 pounds of pressure while cushion and ca wad columns are seated with as much as 100 pounds of pressure.

WADCUTTER BULLET

A lead target bullet for revolvers having a flat nose and a sharp outer edg or shoulder which will cut clean holes in paper targets to aid in spottin and scoring.

WAVE DRAG

The resistance associated with the compression and displacement of air t the bullet's ogive. Also see DRAG, and SHOCK WAVE.

WILDCAT CARTRIDGE

An experimental or non-standard cartridge, not commerciall manufactured, often using a standard cartridge case which has bee significantly modified.

WINDAGE

The deflection of a projectile from its trajectory due to wind. Als adjustment of a firearm's sight(s) to compensate for the deflection.

WIND DRIFT

See DEFLECTION.

WOBBLE

Bullet yaw (side to side motion) during flight. Caused by manufacturin defects or damage which unbalances the bullet. Alternately spelle wabble. Also see AERODYNAMIC STABILITY, GYROSCOPIC STABILITY, an TUMBLING.

X, Y, Z

YAW

The angle between the longitudinal axis of a bullet and the trajectory alon which it is traveling; a large yaw reduces stability and therefore accuracy

ZERO

The procedure of adjusting a firearm's sight(s) so that the point of ai coincides with the bullet's point of impact at a selected range.

CHAPTER 94 : ABBREVIATIONS

A.E.	Action Express
ACP	Automatic Colt Pistol
AEI	AEI Systems Ltd.
AJHP	Aluminum Jacketed Hollow Point
AMC	Army Material Command
ANSI	American National Standards Institute
AP	Armor-Piercing
APFSDS	Armor Piercing Fin-Stabilized Discarding Sabot
API	Armor Piercing Incendiary
APIT	Armor Piercing Incendiary Tracer
AP-S	Armor Piercing Super
Arg.	Argentine
ATA	Amateur Trap Association
ATK	Alliant Techsystems Inc.
Auto	Automatic
Avg.	Average
Bal.	Ballard
BATFE	Bureau of Alcohol, Tobacco, Firearms and Explosives
BB	Bulleted Breech
Bbl	Barrel
BBWC	Bevel Base Wadcutter
BEB	Brass Enclosed Base/Bullet
BHP	Bonded Hollow Point
BJHP	Brass Jacketed Hollow Point
BPE	Black Powder Express
BR	Bench Rest
Bren.	Brenneke
BMG	Browning Machine Gun
BRPT	Bronze Point
Br., Brit.	British
BSA	Birmingham Small Arms
BST	Ballistic Silvertip
BT	Boat-Tail
Bul.	Bullard
Cal	Caliber
Car.	Carcano
Carb.	Carbine
Cas.	Casull
CB	Conical Breech
CBC	Companhia Brazileira de Cartuchos
CC	Copper Coated
CCI	Cascade Cartridge Inc.
CDM	Cartuchos Deportivos de Mexico
CEP	Circular Error Probability
CEPP	Controlled Effect Police Projectile
CF	Centerfire
CIP	Commission Internationale Permanente des Armes A Feu
CL	Core-Lokt
COL	Cartridge Overall Length
CP	Copper Plated
CTC	Center to Center
Ctg.	Cartridge
CUP	Copper Units of Pressure
CZ	Ceska Zbrojovka a.s.
DA	Double action
DCM	Director of Civilian Markmanship
DEN	Denver Army Ammunition Plant
DEWC	Double Ended Wadcutter
DGFM	Direccion General de Fabricaciones Militares, Argentina
DN	Dynamit Nobel
DS	Discarding Sabot
DWM	Deutsche Waffen und Munitions Fabriken
EFMJ	Expanding Full Metal Jacket
E0	Muzzle energy
EP	Expanding Point
ERBT	Extended Range Boat-Tail
EV	Extreme variation
Exp.	Express
FA	Frankford Arsenal
FAMAE	Fabricas y Maestranzas del Ejerito (owned by the government of Chile)
FBI	Federal Bureau of Investigation
FC, Fed.	Federal Cartridge Corp.
FFL	Federal Firearms License
FL	Factory Load
FMC	Full Metal Case
FMJ	Full Metal Jacket
FMJBT	Full Metal Jacket Boat-Tail
FMJE	Full Metal Jacket Encapsulated
FMJLP	Full Metal Jacket Limited Penetration
FMJSWC	Full Metal Jacket Semi-Wad Cutter
FN	Flat Nose, Fabrique Nationale
FNH	Fabrique Nationale Herstal
FNSP	Flat Nose Soft Point
FP	Flat Point, Full Patch (FMJ)
FPJ	Flat Point Jacketed
fps	feet per second
ft.	feet
ft-lbs	Foot-pounds
FTX	Flex Tip Expanding
FRAN	Frangible
g.	gram
Ga.	gauge
GAP	Glock Automatic Pistol
GC	Gas Check
GDHP	Gold Dot Hollow Point
GECO	Gustav Genschow & co.
GFL	Giulio Fiocchi-Lecco Fiocchi Munzioni Spa
GIAT	Groupment Industrial d'Armament Terrestre
Gov., govt.	Government
grs.	Grains
GS	Grand Slam
H	Henry
HBWC	Hollow Base Wadcutter
HE	WWII German Incendiary Explosive Bullet
H.E.	High Energy
H & H	Holland & Holland
HK	Heckler und Koch
H & K	Heckler und Koch
H.M.	Heavy Magnum
HMR	Hornady Magnum Rimfire
HP	Hollow Point
H-P	Hi-Power
HPBT	Hollow Point Boat-Tail
HPE	Hollow Point Expanding
HPL	Hollow Point Lead
HPS	High Performance Sniper
HSHK	Hydra-Shok
HSP	Hollow Soft Point
HV	High Velocity
I	Incendiary
IMI	Israel Military Industries
IMR	Improved Military Rifle Powder
in.	inches
INDEP	Industrias Nacionais de Defensa, EP (Public corporation owned by the government of Portugal)
IOF	Indian Ordnance Factory
IRT	Infra Red Tracer/Indoor Range Training
ISSF	International Shooting Sports Federation
Ital.	Italian
J	Jacket, Jacketed
Jap.	Japanese
JFP	Jacketed Flat Point
JHC	Jacketed Hollow Cavity
JHP	Jacketed Hollow Point
JSP	Jacketed Soft Point
JSZ	Jacketed Stranded Zinc
JTC	Jacketed Truncated Cone
L	Lead or Long, Lachrimatory (tear gas)
LC	Long Colt
LCAAP	Lake City Army Ammunition Plant
L.M.	Light Magnum
LP	Limited Penetration
LR	Long Rifle
LRN	Lead Round Nose
LSWC	Lead Semi-Wadcutter
LSWCHP	Lead Semi-Wadcutter Hollow Point
LUP	Lead Units of Pressure
M.	Magnum
MAB	Manuf. d'Armes de Bayonne
Mag.	Magnum, Magazine
Mak.	Makarov
Mar.	Marlin
MAS	Manut. d'Armes de St. Etienne
Mau.	Mauser

Max	Maximum
MB	Multi Ball
MC	Metal Case, aka FMJ
MCOPE	Metal Case Open Point Expanding
MCWC	Metal Cased Wad Cutter
ME	Muzzle Energy
MEA	Multi Environment Ammunition
MEN	Metallwerk Elisenhutte GmbH Nassau
MFS	MFS 2000 Inc. (Hungary)
M-H	Martini-Henry
M & H	Merwin & Hulbert
MIL SPEC	Military Specification(s)
MK	Match King, Mark (version, variation)
MKEK	Makina ve Kimya Endustrisi Kurumu (Mechanical and Chemical Industries Corp., Turkey)
mm	millimeter
MOA	Minute of Angle
MOLY	Moly Coated
MP	Multipurpose (cartridge)
mps	meters per second
MR	Mean Radius
M.R.	Managed-Recoil
MRT	Mid Range Trajectory
M-S	Mannlicher-Schoenauer
MTCH	Match
MV	Muzzle Velocity
N/A, n/a	not applicable or not available
Nag.	Nagant
NAMMO	Nordic Ammunition Manufacturer's Organization
NATO	North Atlantic Treaty Organization
NBT	Nosler Ballistic Tip
NE	Nitro Express
NFPA	National Fire Prevention Association
NP	Nosler Partition
NRA	National Rifle Association
NRMA	National Reloading Manufacturer's Association
NSSA	National Skeet Shooting Association
NSSF	National Shooting Sports Foundation
NT	Non-Toxic
OAL	Overall Length
OPE	Open Point Expanding
OTM	Open Tip Match
Para.	Parabellum
Patr.	Patrone (Cartridge)
PCC	Peters Cartridge Company
PDW	Personal Defense Weapon
PEP	Positive Expanding Point
PPC	Pindell-Palmisano Cartridge
POF	Pakistan Ordnance Factory
psi, PSI	pounds per square inch
PG	Partition Gold
PL	Power-Lokt

PMC	Poongsan Metals Corp.
PMP	Pretoria Metal Pressings
PP	Power-Point
PSP & PTDSP	Pointed Soft Point
P-SRTA	Plastic Short Range Training Ammunition
PTHP	Platinum Tipped Hollow Point
PWCP	Pointed Wadcutter
R	Rimmed
RAR	Remington Automatic Rifle
RB	Round Ball
RCM	Ruger Compact Magnum
Rem.	Remington
RF	Rimfire
RFM	Rimfire Magnum
RN	Round Nose
ROF	Royal Ordnance Factory (England)
RR	Reduced Range
RRM	Remington Rimfire Magnum
RSUM, RSAUM	Remington Short-Action Ultra Magnum
RUM	Remington Ultra Magnum
Rus.	Russian
RWS	Rheinsch-Westfalische Sprengstoff Fabriken
S	Short
SA	Springfield Arsenal
SA	Single action
SAAMI	Sporting Arms and Ammunition Manufacturer's Institute
Sav.	Savage
S & B	Sellier and Bellot
SBK	Sierra Blitz King
SBT	Spitzer Ballistic Tip
SE	Super Express
SFS	Supreme Fail Safe
SG	Special Grade (cartridge)
S & H	Sharpe & Hart
SIG	Schweizerische Industrie-Gesellschaft
SJHP	Semi-Jacketed Hollow Point
SJSP	Semi-Jacketed Soft Point
SJWC	Semi-Jacket, Wad Cutter
SL	Self-Loading or St. Louis Army Ammunition Plant
SLAP	Saboted Light Armor Piercing
SLC	Salt Lake City Army Ammunition Plant
SLD	Solid
SMG	Submachine Gun
SMP	Semi-Pointed
SOCOM	Special Operations Command, U.S. Army
Sov.	Soviet
SP	Soft Point
SPC	Special Purpose Cartridge
SPCE	Soft Point Cutting Edge
SPCL	Soft Point Core-Lokt
Spl.	Special
Sprg., Spr.	Springfield

SPT	Spitzer
SR	Semi-Rimmed
SRC	Short Range Cartridge
sS	Schwere Spitzergeschoss
SS	Subsonic
SST	Super Shock Tipped
ST	Silvertip
STA	Shooting Times Alaskan
STE	Shooting Times Easterner
Stev.	Stevens
STHP	Silvertip Hollow Point
STW	Shooting Times Westerner
SV	Standard Velocity
S & W	Smith & Wesson
SWC/SW	Semi-Wadcutter
SWCHP	Semi Wad Cutter Hollow Point
SWCL	Semi-Wad Cutter Lead
Swe.	Swedish
SXT	Supreme Expansion Technology
T	Tracer or Tungsten, Tungsten Carbide Penetrator
TAP	Tactical Application Police
TC	Truncated Cone
TCHP	Truncated Cone Hollow Point
TCSB	Truncated Cone Solid Bullet
TMJ	Total Metal Jacket
TMWC	Targetmaster Wadcutter
Tok.	Tokarev
TSX	Triple Shock Extreme
TW	Twin Cities Army Ammunition Plant
UIT	Union International de Tir.
UMC	Union Metallic Cartridge Company
VEL	Velocity
VLD	Very Low Drag
VMax	Varmint Express Ballistic Tip
WC	Wadcutter
WCC	Winchester Cartridge Company
WCF	Winchester Centerfire
Wea., Wby.	Weatherby
West.	Western Cartridge
Win., Winch.	Winchester
WMR	Winchester Magnum Rimfire
WRA	Winchester Repeating Arms
WRF	Winchester Rimfire
WSL	Winchester Self-Loading
WSM	Winchester Short Magnum
WSSM	Winchester Super Short Magnum
W-W	Winchester-Western
yds.	yards
XTP	Extreme Terminal Performance

CHAPTER 95 : FORMULAS

INTERIOR BALLISTICS

RECOIL

The recoil energy of a gun in foot-pounds

Step 1. Calculate the recoil impulse of the gun

$$I = \frac{(WB \times MV + 4{,}000 \times WP)}{225{,}400}$$

I = Recoil impulse of gun in foot-pounds

WB = Bullet weight in grains

MV = Muzzle velocity in feet per second

WP = Weight of powder charge in grains

Step 2. Calculate the recoil velocity of the gun

$$RV = \frac{32.2 \times I}{G}$$

RV = Recoil velocity of gun in feet per second

I = Recoil impulse of gun in foot-pounds (see Step 1)

G = Weight of gun in pounds (including all accessories and a magazine of ammo)

Step 3. Calculate free recoil energy of gun

$$E = \frac{G \times V^2}{64.4}$$

E = Free recoil energy of gun

G = Weight of gun in pounds

V = Recoil velocity of gun in feet per second (see Step 2)

In general, most shooters rate perceived recoil in the following categories:

Mild	10 foot-pounds or less
Moderate	11-20 foot-pounds
Heavy	21-35 foot-pounds
Very heavy	36 or more foot-pounds

GREENHILL'S FORMULA FOR PROPER RIFLING TWIST RATE

$$T = 150 \times \frac{BD^2}{BL}$$

T = Rifling twist rate in inches per turn

BD = Diameter of bullet in inches

BL = Bullet length in inches

EXPANSION RATIO

Ratio of Bore Volume to Cartridge Case Volume

Step 1. Calculate bore volume in cubic inches

$$BV = L \times D \times .773$$

BV = Bore volume in cubic inches

L = Distance in inches from the base of the bullet, in a chambered cartridge, to the muzzle

D = Groove diameter in inches

Step 2. Calculate expansion ratio

$$ER = \frac{BV + PV}{PV}$$

ER = Expansion ratio

BV = Bore volume in cubic inches

PV = Powder chamber volume in cubic inches

CHAMBER PRESSURES

Pressure Conversions

	Bar	Atmosphere	Kg/cm²	PSI
Bar	1	0.9869	1.0197	14.890
Atmospheres (Tech)	1.0132	1	1.0332	14.696
Kg/cm²	0.9806	0.9678	1	14.223
Pounds per Square Inch	14.890	14.696	14.223	1

Note: A pressure of approximately 65,000 PSI is needed to deform the "average" brass cartridge case.

EFFICIENCY

How efficiently stored energy is converted to kinetic energy

Step 1. Calculate muzzle energy

$$ME = \frac{W \times MV^2}{450,400}$$

ME = Muzzle energy in foot pounds
W = Bullet weight in grains
MV = Muzzle velocity in feet per second

Step 2. Calculate potential energy

$$P = WP \times 180$$

P = Potential energy in foot-pounds
WP = Powder weight in grains
180 = average potential in one grain of smokeless propellant

Step 3. Calculate cartridge efficiency in percent

$$CE = \frac{ME}{P}$$

CE = Efficiency percentage
ME = Muzzle energy in foot-pounds
P = Potential energy in foot-pounds

STANDARD DEVIATION (SD)

The variation from the average

Step 1. Calculate average velocity of shots

$$A = \frac{\sum (MV)}{N}$$

A = Average velocity
MV = Velocity of each shot
N = Number of shots
$\sum$ = Add velocities of all shots

Step 2. Calculate the difference between each shot and the average using the following formula:

$$S = \frac{\sum (A-MV)^2}{N-1}$$

S = Step 2 result
A = Average velocity from step 1
MV = Velocity of each shot
N = Number of shots
$\sum$ = Sum of the differences for each shot

Step 3. Calculate square root of the results from step 2 using the following formula:

$$SD = \sqrt{S}$$

S = Result from step 2
SD = Standard deviation

EXTERIOR BALLISTICS

BULLET STRIKING ENERGY IN FOOT-POUNDS (FT.-LBS.)

$$E = \frac{W \times V^2}{450,400}$$

E = Striking energy of the bullet in ft.-lbs.
W = Bullet weight in grains
V = Remaining velocity of bullet in feet per second (FPS)

BULLET STRIKING MOMENTUM (IMPETUS) IN POUND-SECONDS (LB.-SEC.)

$$E = \frac{W \times V}{225,200}$$

E = Striking energy in lb.-sec.
W = Bullet weight in grains
V = Bullet striking velocity in feet per second

BULLET MASS (AS RELATED TO INERTIA)

$$M = \frac{W \times 7000}{32.17}$$

M = Mass of the bullet
W = Weight of the bullet in grains

SECTIONAL DENSITY OF A BULLET (SD)

$$SD = \frac{W}{7,000 \; BD^2}$$

SD = Sectional density of the bullet
W = Bullet weight in grains
BD = Diameter of the bullet in inches

BALLISTIC COEFFICIENT OF A BULLET (BC)

$$BC = \frac{W}{7,000 \times F \times BD^2}$$

BC = Ballistic coefficient of the bullet
W = Bullet weight in grains
BD = Bullet diameter in inches
F = Form factor (use chart below)

APPROXIMATE FORM FACTORS

Profile of Bullet Ogive	Form Factor
Very sharp	.60
Moderately sharp (secant)	.70
Sharp (tangent)	.85
Semi-round nose	1.00
Round or flat nose	1.20

APPROXIMATE FORM FACTORS, CONT.

Profile of Bullet Ogive	Form Factor
For boat tail base subtract	.06
For small meplat tip add	.07
For large, blunt meplat add	.20

BULLET TIME OF FLIGHT IN AIR

$$TA = \frac{2R}{MV + VR}$$

TA = Time of flight in seconds in air
R = Range to target in feet
MV = Muzzle velocity in feet per second
VR = Remaining velocity at target in feet per second

BULLET TIME OF FLIGHT IN A VACUUM

$$TV = \frac{R}{MV}$$

TV = Time of flight in a vacuum in seconds
R = Range to target in feet
MV = Muzzle velocity in feet per second

BULLET WIND DRIFT IN 90 DEGREE CROSSWIND

$$WD = CV (TA - TV)$$

WD = Wind deflection in feet
CV = Cross wind velocity in feet per second
TA = Bullet time of flight to target in air (see above)
TV = Bullet time of flight to target in a vacuum (see above)

BULLET ROTATIONAL SPEED

$$RS = \frac{MV \times 60 \times 12}{T}$$

RS = Bullet rotational speed in revolutions per minute
MV = Muzzle velocity in feet per second
T = Rifling twist rate in inches per turn

JOURNEE'S FORMULA

Estimated maximum horizontal range of spherical lead shot pellets

$$MR = PD \times 2,200$$

MR = Estimated maximum range in yards
PD = Diameter of pellet in inches

ZERO AT SHORT RANGE

$$RC = \frac{RZ \times H}{DB}$$

RC = Close range at which you will fire for zero
RZ = Range at which you wish the rifle to be zeroed
H = Height of sight above the bore line
DB = Bullet drop in inches

TERMINAL BALLISTICS

EXTREME SPREAD OF SHOTS

$$ES = MD - BD$$

ES = Extreme spread of shots in inches
MD = Maximum distance in inches between two most widely separated shots
BD = Bullet diameter in inches

MEAN VERTICAL OR HORIZONTAL DEVIATION OF SHOTS

$$AM = \frac{\sum (DH \text{ or } DV)}{N}$$

AM = Arithmetic mean measure of central tendency
DH = Horizontal distance of each shot from center of group
DV = Vertical distance of each shot from center of group
N = Number of shots in group
$\sum$ = Sum of the horizontal or vertical distances for all shots

MAXIMUM MEAN RADIUS OF SHOTS

$$MR = \frac{\sum (DC)}{N}$$

MR = Maximum mean radius of shots
DC = Distance of each shot from center of group
N = Number of shots in group
$\sum$ = Sum of the distances of each shot from center of group

POWER FACTOR – NRA

$$PF = MV \times W$$

PF = NRA Power factor (must be 120,000 or more)
W = Bullet weight in grains
MV = Muzzle velocity of bullet in feet per second

POWER FACTOR - IPSC

$$PF = \frac{W \times MV^2}{1,000}$$

PF = IPSC Power factor (major caliber must be 175 or more)
W = Bullet weight in grains
MV = Muzzle velocity in feet per second

HATCHER'S FORMULA FOR RELATIVE STOPPING POWER FOR HANDGUN BULLETS

$$MB \times SB \times C = RSP$$

RSP = Relative stopping power
MB = Momentum of bullet
SB = Shape of bullet multiplier (see chart below)
C = Cross sectional area of bullet (radius squared x 3.1416)

COEFFICIENT OF FORM (SB) MULTIPLIERS

Bullet Construction/Shape	Multiplier
Jacketed round nose	.90
Jacketed flat nose	1.00
Lead round nose	1.00
Lead blunt round nose	1.05
Lead flat nose	1.10
Lead wadcutter	1.25

Caliber	Cross Sectional Area in sq. inches
.22	.039
.25	.049
.30	.075
.32	.077
9 mm	.098
.357/.38	.101
.41	.129
.44	.144
.45	.159
.50	.196

TAYLOR'S KNOCK OUT INDEX

$$TKO = W \times V \times BD$$

TKO = Taylor's Knock Out index number
W = Bullet weight in pounds (bullet weight in grains divided by 7,000)
V = Striking velocity in feet per second
BD = Bullet diameter in inches

CONVERSION FORMULAS

VELOCITY CONVERSIONS

1. Feet per second (fps) to meters per second (mps) — MPS = FPS x 0.3048
2. Meters per second to feet per second — FPS = MPS x 3.2808
3. Feet per second to miles per hour (MPH) — MPH = FPS x 0.6818
4. Feet per second to Mach Number (M) — $M = \frac{FPS}{1,117}$
5. Velocity in feet per second to knots (K) — K = FPS x 1.6878

ENERGY CONVERSIONS

1. Energy in foot-pounds to energy in Joules — EJ = EFP x 1.3558
2. Energy in Joules (EJ) to energy in foot-pounds (EFP) — EFP = EJ x 0.7375

LINEAR CONVERSIONS

1. Inches to millimeters — MM = I x 25.4
2. Millimeters to inches — I = MM x 0.0394
3. Meters to yards — Y = M x 1.0936
4. Yards to meters — M = Y x 0.9144

WEIGHT CONVERSIONS

1. Grains to grams — Grams = grains x 0.0648
2. Grams to grains — Grains = grams x 15.4323
3. Kilograms to pounds — Pounds = kilograms x 2.2046
4. Pounds to kilograms — Kilograms = pounds x 0.4535
5. Dram equivalent — 1 dram = 27.3 grains of black powder

Note: a Dram Equivalent is NOT a unit of measurement, NOT a conversion factor, and NOT to be used to determine the charge weight for a smokeless powder shotshell. It is a method of comparing the ballistic efficiency of smokeless powder shotshells to black powder shotshells, expressed as a quantity, in drams, of black powder. A dram is a unit of apothecary weight, equal to 27.4 grains and to 1.771 grams.

PRESSURE CONVERSIONS

1. Physical atmospheres (ATM) to pounds per square inch (PSI) — PSI = ATM x 14.696
2. Technical atmospheres (AT) to pounds per square inch (PSI) — PSI = AT x 14.223
3. Short tons per square foot (ST) to pounds per square inch — PSI = ST x 13.8888
4. Pounds per square inch to kilograms per square centimeter — Kg/cm² = PSI x 0.0703
5. Kilograms per square centimeter to pounds per square inch — PSI = Kg/cm² x 14.223

TEMPERATURE CONVERSIONS

1. Centigrade to Fahrenheit
$$F = \frac{9 \times C}{5} + 32$$

2. Fahrenheit to Centigrade
$$C = \frac{5 \times (F - 32)}{9}$$

CHAPTER 96 : REFERENCE MATERIAL

CHAPTER 96 HIGHLIGHTS:

- INTERIOR BALLISTICS
- EXTERIOR BALLISTICS

- TERMINAL BALLISTICS

INTERIOR BALLISTICS

STANDARD CONDITIONS FOR SPORTING AMMUNITION

Altitude: sea level or 0 feet
Temperature: 59° Fahrenheit/15° Centigrade
Relative Humidity: 78 %
Barometric pressure: 29.58″ of Hg.

TEMPERATURE VS. MUZZLE VELOCITY

For every 1° F. below 59° F. at standard conditions, deduct 1.7 fps (to -40° F.)

For every 1° F. above 59° F. at standard conditions, add 1.7 fps (to +160° F.)

A temperature increase of 17° F. will have the same effect as increasing altitude by 1,000 feet.

AIR DENSITY VS. ALTITUDE

Elevation (ft.)	Percent (%) of Sea Level Density
above Sea Level	100%
2,000	94%
4,000	88%
6,000	83%
8,000	78%
10,000	73%

LOADING DENSITY

This is a dimensionless ratio between the powder charge weight and the weight of water needed to fill the inside of the cartridge case. Loading density is related to chamber pressure. It does NOT matter how much propellant is inside the cartridge case. This number is a comparison of weights.

Bulk density is the ratio between the total amount of propellant that can be put in a cartridge case and the weight of water that will occupy the same space. This number is a comparison of capacities.

AVERAGE ENERGY EXPENDITURES BREAKDOWN OF PROPELLANTS

Unburned propellant	2%
Friction	3%
Heat to barrel	30%
Energy to push hot gas	30%
Energy used to accelerate bullet	35%

EMISSIONS FROM BURNING PROPELLANTS
(IN POUNDS OF GAS PER TON OF POWDER BURNED)

Product Emitted	Propellant Type			
	Blackpowder	Single-Base	Double-Base	Triple-Base
Carbon monoxide	0	798	327	794
Carbon dioxide	844	758	1,137	143
Nitrogen	205	240	297	0
Water	0	147	163	481
Hydrogen	0	46	26.5	43
Carbon	19	0	0	0
Methane	0	10	14.5	14
Ammonia	0	.03	0	3
Hydrogen cyanide	0	0	0	2
Potassium	274	0	0	0
Carbon oxisulphide	330	0	0	0
Sulphur	1	0	0	0
Carbon disulphide	26	0	0	0
Total Emissions	1,698	1,999	1965	1,480

POWDER COMPOSITION

Powder Type	Main Ingredients
Black	potassium nitrate, charcoal, sulfur
Brown	potassium nitrate, charcoal, sulfur (2% or less)
Semi-smokeless	mixture of black powder and smokeless
Single-base smokeless	nitrocellulose
Double-base smokeless	nitrocellulose, nitroglycerin (2-39%)
Triple-base smokeless	nitrocellulose, nitroglycerin, nitro-guanidine

PRIMERS DIMENSIONS

Boxer Primer Dimensions

Size	Diameter in Inches/mm	Height in Inches/mm
Small Pistol	0.175/4.44	0.122/3.09
Small Rifle	0.175/4.44	0.123/3.12
Large pistol	0.210/5.33	0.123/3.12
Large Rifle	0.210/5.33	0.130/3.30

Berdan Primer Dimensions

Primer Size	Diameter in Inches/mm	Height in Inches/mm
Pistol	0.180/4.57	0.0866/2.20
Pistol	0.180/4.57	0.0906/2.30
Pistol	0.200/5.08	0.0866/2.20
Rifle	0.180/4.57	0.0827/2.10
Rifle	0.220/5.59	0.1102/2.78
Rifle	0.220/5.59	0.1043/2.65
Rifle	0.240/6.10	0.1339/3.40
Rifle	0.250/6.35	0.0925/2.35
Rifle	0.250/6.35	0.1161/2.95

SHOTSHELL CHAMBER PRESSURES

Gauge	Length in Inches	Maximum Average Chamber Pressure in Pounds per Square Inch
10	3 ½	11,000
12	3 ½	14,000
12	3	11,500
12	2 ¾	11,500
16	2 ¾	11,500
20	3	12,000
20	2 ¾	12,000
28	2 ¾	12,500
.410 bore	3	13,500
.410 bore	2 ½	12,500

REVOLVER CALIBER CHAMBER PRESSURES

Maximum Average Chamber Pressure

Caliber	Copper Units of pressure (CUP)	Pounds per Square Inch (psi)
.32 Long	12,000	15,000
.32 H&R Mag.	21,000	
.32-20 Win.	16,000	
.357 Mag.		35,000
.357 Maximum	48,000	
.38 S&W	13,000	14,500
.38 Special		17,000
.38 Special +P		18,500
.38-40 Win.	14,000	
.41 Mag.	40,000	36,000
.44 Mag.	40,000	36,000
.44-40 Win.	13,000	
.45 Colt	14,000	
.454 Casull	50,000	
.460 S&W Mag.		36,000
.480 Ruger		36,000
.500 S&W Mag.		36,000

PISTOL CALIBER CHAMBER PRESSURES

| Caliber | Maximum Average Chamber Pressure | |
	Copper Units of Pressure (CUP)	Pounds per Square Inch (psi)
.25 ACP	25,000	
.30 Luger	28,000	
.32 ACP	20,500	
.380 ACP	23,000	21,500
.38 Auto	23,000	
.38 Super Auto +P	33,000	
.40 S&W Auto	35,000	
.41 AE	35,000	
.45 ACP	21,000	21,000
.45 Win. Mag.	40,000	
.50 AE	36,000	
9x18mm Makarov	24,100	
9mm Luger	33,000	35,000
10mm Auto	37,500	

STANDARD RIFLE CALIBER CHAMBER PRESSURES

| Caliber | Maximum Average Chamber Pressure | |
	Copper Units of Pressure (CUP)	Pounds per Square Inch (psi)
.25-20 Win.	28,000	
.45-70 Govt.	32,000	
.32-40 Win.	30,000	
.38-55 Win.	30,000	
.303 Savage	34,000	
.30 Rem.	35,000	
.35 Rem.	33,500	
.470 Nitro express	33,500	
.25-35 Win.	37,000	
.32 Rem.	40,200	
8x57mmJS Mauser	35,000	
.30-30 Win.	38,000	42,000
.32 Win. Special		42,000
.218 Bee	40,000	
7-30 Waters	45,000	
.30 Carbine	40,000	
.30-40 Krag		47,100
.348 Win.		42,300
416 Rigby	42,000	47,100
.22 Hornet	47,000	
.256 Win. Mag.	43,000	
.444 Marlin	44,000	42,000
.250 Savage	45,000	
.257 Roberts	54,000	
7.62x39mm Soviet	45,000	45,000
.303 British	45,000	49,000
.351 Win. SL	48,200	
.222 Rem.	46,000	
6.5x55mm Swe.		46,000

STANDARD RIFLE CALIBER CHAMBER PRESSURES, CONT.

| Caliber | Maximum Average Chamber Pressure | |
	Copper Units of Pressure (CUP)	Pounds per Square Inch (psi)
7x57mm Mauser		56,600
.300 Savage	47,000	
.225 Win.	50,000	
.257 Roberts +P	54,000	
.280 Rem.	60,000	
.30-06 Spr.	60,000	
.17 Rem.	52,000	
.221 Fireball		55,500
.223 Rem.	55,000	
.243 Win.	60,000	
6mm Rem.	65,000	
.270 Win.	65,000	
7mm-08	61,000	
.307 Win.	52,000	
.308 Win.	62,000	
.356 Win.	52,000	
.358 Win.	55,300	
.35 Whelen	52,000	
.375 Win.	52,000	
.22-250	53,000	65,000
.25-06 Rem.	63,000	
.220 Swift	54,000	
.284 Win.	56,000	

MAGNUM RIFLE CALIBER CHAMBER PRESSURES

| Caliber | Maximum Average Chamber Pressure | |
	Copper Units of Pressure (CUP)	Pounds per Square Inch (psi)
7mm Rem. Mag.	52,000	61,000
6.5mm Rem. Mag	53,000	65,000
.375 H&H Mag.		62,400
.458 Win. Mag.	62,400	
.264 Win. Mag.	54,000	64,000
.300 H&H Mag.	57,200	
.300 Win. Mag.	64,000	
8mm Rem. Mag.	65,000	
.338 Win. Mag.	64,000	
.416 Rem. Mag.	65,000	
.240 Wby. Mag.		55,100
.270 Wby. Mag.		55,100
.308 Norma Mag.		55,100
.350 Rem. Mag.	56,200	
7mm Wby. Mag.	65,000	
.300 Wby. Mag.		65,000

Muzzle Velocity vs. Rifle Barrel Length

Muzzle Velocity Range in fps	Expected Change in Muzzle Velocity fps per Inch Change in Barrel Length
Up to 2,000	5
2,001 to 2,500	10
2,501 to 3,000	20
3,001 to 3,500	30
3,501 to 4,000+	40

Barrel Lengths

Barrel Length In Inches	Barrel Length In Millimeters
2	51
2.5	63.5
3	76.2
4	101.6
5	127
6	152.4
7.5	190.5
8	203.2
10	254
12	304.8
14	355.6
16	406.4
16.5	419.1
18	457.2
18.5	469.9
20	508

Barrel Lengths, cont.

Barrel Length In Inches	Barrel Length In Millimeters
20.5	520
22	558.8
24	609.6
25	635
26	660.4
28	711.2
30	762
32	812.8
34	863.6
36	914.4

EXTERIOR BALLISTICS

Ballistic Coefficient of Selected Sizes of Lead Pellets (4% Antimony)

Pellet Size	Diameter in Inches	Ballistic Coefficient
9	.08	.008
8	.09	.009
7 ½	.095	.0095
6	.11	.011
4	.13	.013
2	.15	.015
BB	.18	.018
4 Buck	.24	.025
1 Buck	.30	.031
00 Buck	.33	.034

Sectional Density of Shotgun Pellets

Shot Size	Diameter in Inches	Shot Material and Sectional Intensity				
		Steel	Bismuth	Tung./Iron	Lead	Hevi-Shot
9	.08	.0119	.0147	.0157	.0168	.0181
8	.090	.0134	.0165	.0177	.0189	.0204
7 ½	.095	.0141	.0174	.0187	.0199	.0215
6	.110	.0164	.0202	.0216	.0231	.0249
5	.120	.0178	.0220	.0236	.0252	.0278
4	.130	.0193	.0238	.0255	.0273	.0297
3	.140	.0208	.0257	.0275	.0294	.0320
2	.150	.0223	.0275	.0295	.0315	.0346
1	.160	.0238	.0293	.0314	.0336	.0368
B	.170	.0253	.0312	.0334	.0357	.0391
BB	.180	.0268	.0330	.0353	.0378	.0419
BBB	.190	.0283	.0348	.0373	.0399	.0437
T	.200	.0297	.0367	.0393	.0420	.0471
TT	.210	.0312	.0385	.0412	.0441	.0497
F	.220	.0327	.0403	.0432	.0462	.0520
FF	.230	.0342	.0421	.0452	.0483	.0535

THEORETICAL PELLET COUNT PER OUNCE FOR VARIOUS MATERIALS

Shot Size	Diameter in Inches	Lead – Antimony %				Steel	Bi	T/M	T/I	TE	TIH
		½ %	2 %	4 %	6 %						
9	.080	576	579	589	599	821	664	620	729	536	432
8 ½	.085	480	483	491	500	685	554	517	608	447	360
8	.090	404	407	414	421	577	466	435	512	376	304
7 ½	.095	344	346	352	358	490	397	370	435	320	258
7	.100	295	296	302	307	420	340	318	372	275	220
6	.110	221	222	226	230	316	255	238	280	207	166
5	.120	170	171	174	177	243	196	183	215	159	128
4	.130	134	135	137	139	191	155	144	169	125	100
3	.140	107	108	110	111	153	123	115	136	99	80
2	.150	87	87	89	91	125	100	94	108	85	66
1	.160	72	72	73	74	103	83	78	91	67	54
B	.170	60	60	61	62	86	69	65	76	56	45
BB	.180	50	50	51	52	72	58	54	63	47	38
BBB	.190	43	43	44	44	61	50	46	54	40	32
T	.200	36	37	37	38	53	42	39	55	34	28
TT	.210	31	32	32	33	45	36	33	39	29	24
F	.220	27	27	28	28	39	31	29	34	25	21
FF	.230	24	24	24	25	35	28	26	31	22	18

Shot Material Density; grams per cc

Lead = 11.1

Steel = 7.9

Bi = Bismuth alloy, 9.4

T/M = Tungsten matrix, 10.4

T/I = Tungsten iron, 10.2

TE = Tungsten extended range, Hevi-Shot, 12

TIH = Tungsten/iron heavy weight high density, 15

THEORETICAL BUCKSHOT PELLET COUNTS PER POUND

Size	Diameter in Inches	Lead-Antimony %		Steel	Bi	T/M	T/I	T/E	TIH
		½ %	6 %						
No.4	.24	338	352	479	390	364	436	319	252
No.3	.25	299	311	424	345	322	386	282	223
No.2	.27	238	248	337	275	256	307	225	178
No.1	.30	173	180	245	200	186	223	163	129
O	.32	143	149	203	165	154	185	135	107
OO	.33	130	135	184	150	140	168	123	97
OOO	.36	100	104	142	115	100	129	94	75

Shot Material Density; grams per cc

Steel = 7.9

T/M = Tungsten matrix, 10.4

Bi = Bismuth alloy, 9.7

T/I = Tungsten iron, 10.2

Lead = 11.1

TE = Tungsten extended range Hevi-Shot, 12

TIH = Tungsten/iron heavy weight, high density, 15

SHOT CHARGE WEIGHT CONVERSION CHART

Grains	Ounces	Grams
220	½	14.2
328	¾	21.3
385	7/8	24.8
437.5	1	28.3
465	1 1/16	30.1
600	1 3/8	39
655	1 ½	42.5
710	1 5/8	46.1
765	1 ¾	49.6
820	1 7/8	53.1
875	2	56.7
984	2 ¼	63.8

TERMINAL BALLISTICS

SHOTGUN CHOKES AND EXPECTED PERFORMANCE

Choke	Abbreviation	Average Constriction	Percentage of Pellets in 30″ Circle at 40 Yards
Cylinder	C	None	up to 40 %
Skeet	S	.005″	40 %
Improved Cylinder	IC	.011″	50 %
Modified	M	.020″	60 %
Improved Modified	IM	.027″	65 %
Full	F	.036″	70 %
Extra Full	EF	.040″ +	80+ %

SHOTSHELL GAUGES

Bore Diameter

Gauge	Weight of Round Ball		
	In Inches	In mm	in Grains
A	2.00	50.8	
C	1.875	47.62	
E	1.750	44.45	
1	1.669	42.39	7,000 (one pound)
J	1.563	39.7	
L	1.438	36.52	
2	1.325	33.65	3,500
3	1.157	29.38	
4	1.052	26.72	
6	0.919	23.34	
8	0.835	21.20	
10	0.775	19.68	700

SHOTSHELL GAUGES, CONT.

Bore Diameter

Gauge	Weight of Round Ball		
	In Inches	In mm	in Grains
11	0.751	19.07	
12	0.729	18.51	583.3
14	0.693	17.60	
16	0.662	16.81	437.5 (one ounce)
18	0.637	16.17	
20	0.615	15.62	350
22	0.596	15.13	
24	0.579	14.70	
26	0.564	14.32	
28	0.550	13.97	250
30	0.537	13.63	
32	0.526	13.36	
34	0.515	13.08	
36	0.506	12.85	
48	0.459	11.66	
50	0.453	11.50	
68	0.410	10.41	(.410 bore shotshell)

PENETRATION BY .30-06 CALIBER M2 152 GRAIN FMJ BULLET

Material	Penetration (in Inches)
Concrete	7
Dry sand	24
Wet sand	36
Oak	40
Earth, plowed	56
Earth, compacted	52
Earth, hard packed	48

MAXIMUM HORIZONTAL AND VERTICAL RANGES – RIMFIRE RIFLE CALIBERS

Caliber	Muzzle Velocity (fps)	Bullet Wgt. (gr.)	Maximum Ranges Horz. (yds.)	Maximum Ranges Vert. (ft.)
.17 Mach2	2,100	17	2,200	4,400
.17 HMR	2,550	17	2,500	5,000
.22 Short HV	1,130	29	1,230	2,770
.22 L.R. SV	1,145	40	1,600	3,500
.22 L.R. HV	1,255	40	1,650	3,650
.22 L.R. UHV	1,640	33	1,460	3,300
.22 WMR	2,000	40	1,725	3,860

MAXIMUM HORIZONTAL AND VERTICAL RANGES – CENTERFIRE REVOLVER CALIBERS

Caliber	Muzzle Velocity (fps)	Bullet Wgt. (gr.)	Maximum Ranges Horz. (yds.)	Maximum Ranges Vert. (ft.)
.32 Short Colt	745	80	1,050	2,325
.32 S&W Short	680	85	1,200	2,700
.32 S&W Long	705	98	1,300	2,875
.32 H&R Mag.	1,100	85	1,800	3,600
.38 Short Colt	730	125	1,440	3,230
.38 S&W	685	145	1,425	3,200
.38 Special	755	158	1,750	3,925
.38 Special +P	945	125	2,260	5,100
.357 Mag.	1,235	158	2,400	5,400
.41 Mag.	1,300	210	2,100	4,725
.44 Special	755	246	1,880	4,230
.44 Mag.	1,350	240	2,480	5,580
.45 Colt	860	250	1,855	4,170

MAXIMUM HORIZONTAL AND VERTICAL RANGES – CENTERFIRE PISTOL CALIBERS

Caliber	Muzzle Velocity (fps)	Bullet Wgt. (gr.)	Maximum Ranges Horz. (yds.)	Maximum Ranges Vert. (ft.)
.25 ACP	745	50	1,200	2,700
.30 Luger	1,220	93	2,300	5,150
.32 ACP	905	71	1,510	3,400
.380 ACP	970	95	1,100	2,460
.357 SIG	1,350	124	2,200	4,400
9mm Luger	1,140	124	2,130	4,800
.38 Super +P	1,215	130	2,300	5,165
.40 S&W	990	180	2,200	4,400
10mm Auto	1,290	155	2,230	5,025
.45 ACP +P	1,140	185	1,840	4,150
.45 Win. Mag.	1,200	260	2,055	4,625

MAXIMUM HORIZONTAL AND VERTICAL RANGES – VARMINT CENTERFIRE RIFLE CALIBERS

Caliber	Muzzle Velocity (fps)	Bullet Wgt. (gr.)	Maximum Ranges Horz. (yds.)	Maximum Ranges Vert. (ft.)
.17 Rem.	4,040	25	2,655	5,775
.204 Ruger	3,900	40	4,000	8,000
.218 Bee	2,760	46	2,100	4,715
.22 Hornet	2,690	46	2,100	4,700
.222 Rem.	3,140	50	2,750	6,150
.223 Rem.	3,240	55	3,850	8,650
.225 Win.	3,570	55	3,215	7.225
.22-250 Rem.	3,680	55	3,500	7,880
.25-20 Win.	1,460	86	2,450	5,500

MAXIMUM HORIZONTAL AND VERTICAL RANGES – STANDARD CENTERFIRE RIFLE CALIBERS

Caliber	Muzzle Velocity (fps)	Bullet Wgt. (gr.)	Maximum Ranges Horz. (yds.)	Vert. (ft.)
.243 Win.	2,906	100	4,000	9,000
6mm Rem.	3,100	100	4,650	10,460
.25-35 Win.	2,230	117	3,185	7,165
.250 Sav.	2,820	100	3,840	8,635
.25-06 Rem.	2,990	117	4,660	10,470
6.8 Rem. SPC	2,625	115	3,400	6,750
.270 Win.	3,050	130	4,800	10,790
7mm-08	2,875	140	4,400	8,700
7x57mm	2,660	139	4,200	9,450
.280 Rem.	2,890	150	4,450	10,000
.284 Win.	2,860	150	4,425	9,950
.30-30 Win.	2,200	170	3,310	7,450
.308 Win.	2,620	180	4,655	10,450
.30-06 Spr.	2,700	180	4,170	9,400
.30-06 Spr.	2,600	200	6,200	13,950
.30-40 Krag	2,430	180	4,550	10,250
.300 Sav.	2,350	180	4,510	10,150
8x5mmJS	2,871	170	2,870	6,460
.348 Win.	2,520	200	3,635	8,175
.35 Rem.	2,020	200	2,650	6,000
.35 Whelen	2,400	250	3,500	7,000
.358 Win.	2,490	250	3,965	8,900
.405 Win.	2,200	300	2,000	4,000
.444 Marlin	2,350	240	2,220	5,000
.45-70 Govt.	1,315	405	3,500	7,900
.450 Marlin	2,225	325	3,500	7,000

MAXIMUM HORIZONTAL AND VERTICAL RANGES – MAGNUM CENTERFIRE RIFLE CALIBERS

Caliber	Muzzle Velocity (fps)	Bullet Wgt. (gr.)	Maximum Ranges Horz. (yds.)	Vert. (ft.)
.243 WSSM	3,250	95	4,250	8,400
.25 WSSM	3,060	115	5,000	9,900
.257 Wby. Mag.	3,400	115	5,400	10,700
.264 Win. Mag.	3,030	140	4,875	11,000
.270 Wby. Mag.	3,280	130	5,000	9,900
7mm Rem. Mag.	2,950	165	7,000	15,650
7mm RUM	3,325	150	5,000	9,900
.300 Win. Mag.	2,960	180	5,315	12,000
.300 RUM	3,450	150	4,700	9,300
.300 RSUM	2,900	190	5,800	11,500
.300 WSM	3,010	180	5,700	11,300
.300 Wby. Mag.	3,110	180	5,800	11,500
.325 WSM	3,060	180	5,000	9,900
8mm Rem. Mag.	2,900	200	4,850	11,000
.338 Win Mag.	2,960	225	5,200	11,700
.338 Lapua	2,940	250	7,000	14,000
.340 Wby. Mag.	2,900	225	4,400	8,700
.350 Rem. Mag.	2,710	200	3,900	8,750
.375 H&H Mag.	2,530	300	4,100	9,200
.375 RUM	2,760	300	4,400	8,700
.416 Rigby	2,440	400	2,400	4,800
.416 Rem. Mag.	2,400	400	2,400	4,800
.416 Wby. Mag.	2,850	350	2,900	5,800
.458 Win. Mag.	2,040	500	4,250	9,600
.458 Lott	2,300	500	4,400	8,700
.460 Wby. Mag.	2,700	450	4,700	9,300

Maximum Horizontal and Vertical Ranges – Military Ammunition

Caliber	Muzzle Velocity (fps)	Bullet Wgt. (gr.)	Maximum Ranges Horz. (yds.)	Vert. (ft.)
5.56x45mm M193	3,240	55	3,850	8,650
5.56x45mm M855A1	3,050	62.5	4,100	9,200
.30 Carbine	1,970	111	2,560	5,750
7.62x51mm M80	2,780	150	4,470	10,100
7.62x51mm M118	2,640	175	5,500	12,400
7.62x51mm M852	2,550	168	4,760	10,700
.30-06 M1	2,640	172	5,500	12,400
.30-06 M2	2,780	152	3,500	7,900
.30-40 Krag	2,000	220	4,100	9,150
.50 BMG M2	2,810	709	7,300	16,400
9x19mm M882	1,276	124	2,350	5,300
.45 ACP M1911	825	230	1,650	3,700

Maximum Horizontal and Vertical Ranges – Shot Pellets

Size	Shot Material	Muzzle Velocity (fps)	Maximum Ranges Horz. (yds.)	Vert. (ft.)
F	Steel	1,350	360	860
T	Steel	1,500	335	820
BBB	Steel	1,500	325	800
	Tungsten-Iron	1,450	400	960
BB	Steel	1,500	320	800
	Lead	1,330	400	960
	Bismuth	1,330	360	860
	Tungsten-Iron	1,450	380	920
1	Steel	1,500	280	685
	Tungsten-Iron	1,450	330	800
	Tungsten-Matrix	1,375	350	830
2	Steel	1,500	265	650
	Lead	1,330	345	830
	Bismuth	1,330	310	750
	Tungsten-Iron	1,450	330	800
	Hevi-shot	1,300	360	870
4	Steel	1,500	235	500
	Lead	1,400	310	750
	Bismuth	1,330	275	665
	Tungsten-Iron	1,400	300	710
	Hevi-Shot	1,325	325	780
5	Lead	1,400	290	710
	Bismuth	1,330	260	625
	Tungsten-Matrix	1,400	280	675
	Tungsten-Iron	1,400	275	665
	Hevi-Shot	1,300	285	700
6	Steel	1,450	205	500
	Lead	1,400	270	705
	Bismuth	1,330	240	590
	Tungsten-matrix	1,400	260	630
	Hevi-Shot	1,325	285	605
7	Steel	1,300	185	460
7 ½	Lead	1,400	240	590
	Bismuth	1,330	215	520
	Hevi-Shot	1,325	250	605
8	Lead	1,295	225	550
8 ½	Lead	1,325	215	520
9	Lead	1,230	200	490

MAXIMUM HORIZONTAL AND VERTICAL RANGES – FULL BORE RIFLED SLUGS

Gauge	Muzzle Velocity (fps)	Slug Wgt. (gr.)	Maximum Ranges Horz. (yds.)	Vert. (ft.)
10	1,280	766	1,350	3,100
12	1,600	547	1,300	3,000
12	1,610	437.5	1,260	2,850
16	1,600	350	1,270	2,860
20	1,680	328	1,050	2,350
.410 bore	1,775	109	920	2,100

MAXIMUM HORIZONTAL AND VERTICAL RANGES – BUCKSHOT

Size	Muzzle Velocity (fps)	Maximum Ranges Horz. (yds.)	Vert. (ft.)
000	1,325	700	1,650
00	1,325	650	1,550
0	1,275	630	1,500
No. 1	1,250	600	1,400
No. 2	1,200	540	1,250
No. 3	1,200	510	1,200
No. 4	1,325	510	1,200

HIGHEST MUZZLE VELOCITY
(USING SMOKELESS PROPELLANTS)

Highest efficient muzzle velocity: approximately 4,500-5,000 fps.

Highest practical muzzle velocity: approx. 6,500 fps.

Highest experimental (laboratory conditions) muzzle velocity: approx. 8,600 fps.

Highest theoretical muzzle velocity: approx. 11,000 fps.

Highest muzzle velocity using black powder: approx. 1,700 fps.

Highest muzzle velocity using a light gas gun: approx. 13,500 fps.

Highest muzzle velocity using an electromagnetic rail gun: approx. 28,000 fps

ENERGY CONVERSIONS

	Joules	Kilogram-meters	Foot-pounds
Joules	1	0.102	0.7373
Kilogram-meters	9.81	1	7.233
Foot-pounds	1.356	1.1383	1

MIL vs. MOA

Measure	mm @ 100 Meters	Inches @ 100 Yards
1 MIL	100	3.60
1 MOA	34.38	1.047

CHAPTER 97 : ADDRESSES, TRADEMARKS, AND BRANDS

NAME AND ADDRESS		TRADEMARK/BRAND NAMES
AAA Arms & Ammo 14717 Industrial Road Omaha, NE 68144 www.aaa-ammo.com		AAA Ammunition, AAA M2, AAA AP, Dominator-X, Dominator-XPE, AAA .460 Steyr, Harlow (a projectile), Semi-Bore-Rider
ALS Technologies, Inc. 1103 Central Blvd. Bull Shoals, AR 72619 www.lesslethal.com		Bore Thunder, Acrial Pest, Power Punch, Hydrorenitic, Tri-Dent, Hornets Nest, Pen-Prevent, Triton Tail Stabilized, Rubber Fin Rocket
Alexander Arms US Army, Radford Arsenal P.O. Box 1 Radford, VA 24143 www.alexanderarms.com		.50 Beowulf, 6.5 Grendel
Alliance Armament 1077 Mt. Gilead Road Boonville, IN 47601 http://www.alliancearmament.com		.460 Alliance
Armas y Cartuchos Del Sur S.L. Ctra. HU-4403 Km. 1,200 Alosno (Huelva), E-21520 Spain www.delsur.es		Mancha, Voelo, Prestigio, Novecento, Amargord
Arms Corporation of the Philippines 6th Floor, Strata 100 Bldg. Emerald Avenue Ortigas Center Pasig City, 1600 Philippines www.armscor.com.ph		ARMSCOR, Strike 3
Atlanta Arms and Ammo 721 Vine Circle Social Circle, GA 30025 www.atlantaarmsandammo.com		
Azot 1 Rdultovskogo Square Krasnozavodsk 141321 Russia www.azot-patron.ru		Azot, AZ, Joker, Rex, CSB

NAME AND ADDRESS		TRADEMARK/BRAND NAMES
Barnes Bullets P.O. Box 620 Monda, UT 84645 www.barnesbullets.com	BARNES Unleaded. Unfailing. Unbeatable.™	Triple-Shock, X-Bullet, XLC, Varmint Grenade, XPB, TMZ, Spit-Fire MZ, Banded Solids, Expander MZ, MRX, Barnes Originals
Barnaul Machine Tool Plant 28 Kulagina St. Barnaul 656002 Russia www.ab.ru/~stanok	Barnaul CARTRIDGE PLANT	Barnaul, Brown Bear, Silver Bear
Baschieri & Pellagri S.p.A. Via frullo 26 Marano di Castenasco (BO) I-40055 Italy www.bascheri-pellagri.com	B&P	B&P, Gordon System, Gigante, Tricolor, Super Star, Dual-Pigeon, Allodola
Bitteroot Valley Ammo & Components 3616 Eastside Highway Stevensville, MT 59870 www.bvac-ammo.com	BVAC AMMUNITION & COMPONENTS	
Black Hills Ammunition P.O. Box 3090 Rapid City, SD 57709-3090 www.black-hills.com	The Power of BLACK HILLS Performance	Black Hills, Black Hills Gold
Bornaghi s.r.l. Via dei Livelli Snc 24047 Treviglio (Bg) Italy www.bornaghi.it	FRANCO BORNAGHI FTB TREVIGLIO	Bornaghi, FTB, GM 3, S 4, BIOR
Brenneke GmbH Postfach 1646 30837 Langenhagen Germany www.brenneke.de	ORIGINAL BRENNEKE USA★	Brenneke, Original Brenneke, SuperSabot, K.O., K.O. Sabot, Black Magic, B.E.T.
Buffalo Bore Ammunition www.buffalobore.com	BUFFALO BORE	

NAME AND ADDRESS		TRADEMARK/BRAND NAMES
Bumar sp. z.o.o. ZPS Pionki Ul. Zakladowa 7 26-670 Pionki Poland www.bumar.com		MESKO
Cartuchos Saga S.A. Caparrella, s/n 25192 Lleida Spain www.saga.es		Saga, Diana, Munysur, Export, Sur, Partida de la Sierra, Ansar
CCC Ammo 1713 Meridian Court Conroe, TX 77301 www.cccammo.com		
CCI Ammunition 2299 Snake River Ave. Lewiston, ID 83501 www.cci-ammunition.com	Division of ATK	CCI, STINGER, GREEN TAG, MINI-MAG, VELOCITOR, MAXI-MAG, MAXI-MAG TMJ, APS, TNT, Mag-Tip, Plinker, TMJ, GAMEPOINT, SGB, SELECT, POLY-TIP V-MAX, TNT Green, Pistol Match, Short Range Green
Cesaroni Technology Incorporated P.O. Box 246 2561 Stouffville Rd. Gormley, Ontario L0H 1G0 www.cesaronitech.com		
Cheddite France S.A. Route de Lyon, 99/Box 112 Bourg-Les-Valence, F-26500 France www.cheddite.com		
Cheddite Italy Via del Giaggiolo 189 Livorno, I-5700 Italy www.chedditeitaly.com		
CheyTac, LLC 303 Sunset Drive, P.O. Box 822 Arco, ID 83213 www.cheytac.com		

NAME AND ADDRESS		TRADEMARK/BRAND NAMES
Clever Mirage S.r.L. Via A. De Legnago No. 9 37141 Ponte Florio Montorio (VR) Italy www.clevervr.com		Clever, Mirage
Companhia Brasileira de Cartuchos Av. Humberto de Campos, 3220 CEP 09426-900 Guapituba Ribeiro Pires/SP Brasil www.cbc.com.br		CBC, Magtech, MAGTECH First Defense, Guardian Gold, Shootin' Size, CleanRange, Featherweight
Concho Cartridge Company, Inc. P.O. Box 1430 San Angelo, TX 76902 www.conchocartridge.com		
Conley Precision Cartridge Co. 207 E. Oak Av. Como, MS 38619 www.cpcartridge.com		
Cor-Bon/Glaser 1311 Industry Rd. Sturgis, SD 57785 www.corbon.com		CorBon, CorBon/Glaser, DPX, Pow'R Ball, Glaser Safety Slug, Thunder Ranch, Corbon Hunter, U.S. Cavalry Cowboy Action
Custom Cartridge, Inc. 5878 Hollister Av. Goleta, CA 93117 www.customcartridge.com		Hush, SoftShot, Supercharged, The Legend, Orion, Legend, Hunter
DDupleks Ltd. Brivibas Gatve 197 Riga, LV-1039 Latvia www.ddupleks.lv		
DOUBLE TAP AMMUNITION 646 S. Main St., #333 Cedar City, UT 84720 www.doubletapammo.com		

NAME AND ADDRESS		TRADEMARK/BRAND NAMES
Dynamic Research Tech. 405 N. Lyon Street Grant City, MO 64456 www.drtammo.com		DRT, Terminal Shock
Eley Limited Selco Way Minworth Industrial Estate Sutton, Coldfield West Midlands B76 1BA England www.eleyammunition.com		ELEY, Tenex, Match EPS, Club Xtra, Practice 100, Ultimate EPS, Pistol Xtra, Silhouex, Biathlon Match EPS
Eley Hawk Ltd. Selco Way, First Ave. Minworth Industrial Estate Sutton Coldfield West Midlands B76 1BA England www.eleyhawk.com		Hawk, FIRST, Blue, VIP, Superb, Impax, Hi Flyer, Hymax, Fourlong, Alphamax, Grand Prix, Black Feather, ELEY, Superb Competition, Competition Trap, VIP Sporting, Trainer, HUSH POWER, Grand Prix, Maximum, Alphamax, Alphamax Magnum, Classic Game, Fausteen, Fourlong, Extra Long, VIP Game, HB Pigeon, HI-FLYER, HYMAX, CT GAME, Grand Prix Steel, First Steel, Grand Prix HV, Saluting Blanks, Winchester Cannon Blanks, REALTREE PIGEON
Elite Enterprises Inc. DBA Elite Ammunition P.O. Box 639 Harvard, IL 60033 www.eliteammunition.net		Trident Tactucal, PenetraTOR, ProtecTOR, QuieTOR, SinTOR, VarminTOR, X-TerminaTOR
Engel Ballistic Research, Inc. 544 Alum Creek Road, Unit A Smithville, TX 78957 www.ebr-inc.net		Ultra Stealth Match Subsomic, Thumper Subsonic, Precision Bonded Subsonic, Jackhammer Subsonic, Limited Penetration, Facility Protection Frangible, Anti-Ricochet
Environ-Metal Inc. 1307 Clark Mill Rd. Sweet Home, OR 97386 www.hevishot.com		HEVI-SHOT, HEVI-SHOT Classic Doubles, HEVI-STEEL, HEVI-13, DEAD COYOTE!
Estate Cartridge, Inc. 900 Ehlen Dr. Anoka, MN 55303 www.estatecartridge.com	Division of ATK	ESTATE CARTRIDGE INC.
Extreme Shock USA Rt. 2, Box 304-N Clintwood, VA 24228 www.extremeshockusa.com		Extreme Shock, Tungsten Nytrillium, Allegiance Ammunition

NAME AND ADDRESS		TRADEMARK/BRAND NAMES
FAM - PIONKI LLC Ul. Zakladowa 7 Pionki PL-26-670 Poland www.fam-pionki.pl		ROJ, BAK, CHRABASZCZ 20/30/50, LFT 6.8, W8MP, Olympic, PR-PIK 94/94M/98, SAK, FAM, FAM Plus, W-8 (slug), FS (slug), Dzik (slug), Atut (slug), ONS 2000, CS 94/94M/98
Federal Premium Ammunition 900 Ehlen Dr. Anoka, MN 55303 www.federalpremium.com	FEDERAL PREMIUM AMMUNITION Division of ATK	Premium, V-Shok, Vital-Shok, Cape-Shok, Gold Medal, Personal Defense, Ultra-Shok, Black Cloud, Mag-Shok, High Density, Heavyweight, Wing-Shok, Federal, American Eagle, Champion, Hi-Power, Game-Shok, Power-Shok, Strut-Shok, Top Gun, Speed-Shok, Flitecontrol, Flitestopper, TruBall, Hydra-Shok, EFMJ, Spitfire, Prairie Storm, FS Lead, FS Steel, Bonded, Tru, BallistiClean, Classic, Toxic-Metal Free, HST, RHT, Hi-Shok, Tactical, Triple Plus
Fiocchi Munizioni S.p.A. Via Santa Barbara 4 23900 Lecco Italy www.fiocchigfl.it	FIOCCHI	Extrema, Exacta, Shooting Dynamics, Shooting Dynamics Target, Aero Slugs, Golden Pheasant, MAXAC, Helice, X-Low Recoil, White Rino, Super Crusher, Little Rino, Interceptor, Spreader, Power Spreader, Super Match Competition, Golden Goose, Golden Turkey, Rhino 16, Speed Steel, Golden Waterfowl, Golden Trap Evo, Official Trap Evo, Official Skeet Evo, Official Double Evo, PL 32/34, HV 36, GFL 16/20/24/28/32/36/410, TRADITIONAL 34 DISP, TRADITIONAL, BECCACCIA DISP/38 DISP, 12 HV, NOVA SLUG, TRIO A PALLA, NOVA, NOVA BIOR, NOVALLODOLLA, ELLE, EFFE, GI, JK6, CANE, TOP DEFENSE, BLACK MAMBA, TOP TARGET, SUPER MATCH 300/320, BIATHLON S.M. 340, RAPID FIRE S.M. 280, MAXAC SOFT, RAPID FIRE MAXAC, LONG Z, ULTRASONIC, SHORT SUP. MATCH 200, SHORT MATCH 200, 9 P.A. KNALL 9x22
G&L Calibers LTD P.O. Box 22198 Nicosia, 1518 Cyprus www.victorycom.com	Victory Quality Ammunition	Victory, Baby Victory, Starlight, Lucky, Mini Magnum, Challenger Game, Rocket, Europa
Gamebore Cartridge Co. Ltd. Great Union St. GB-Hull HU9 1AR England www.gamebore.com	Gamebore	Tradition, Clear Pigeon, Buffalo, Mammoth, Pure Gold, White Gold, Gamebore, Super XLR, White Gold XLR, Blue Diamond, Kent Champion, White Gold F2, White Gold Extreme, Patriot F2, Super Competition, XLR Subsonic, Black Gold, SuperSteel, Super Game Extreme, Pigeon Extreme, Super Game, Mammoth Magnum, Super Game High Bird, Traditional Game, Traditional Hunting, Impact, Impact Mallard, Impact Multi-Shot, Steel-Fibre Game & Wetland Steel
Garrett's Cartridge, Inc. 1004 Long Road Centralia, WA 98531 www.garrettcartridges.com	GARRETT CARTRIDGES INC.	Hammerhead, SuperJack, Exciter, Defender

NAME AND ADDRESS		TRADEMARK/BRAND NAMES
Georgia Arms P.O. Box 238 15 Industrial Court E. Villa Rica, GA 30180 www.georgia-arms.com		
GOEX Inc. P.O. Box 659 Doyline, LA 71023 www.goexpowder.com	GOEX BLACK POWDER — THE TRADITION CONTINUES —	GOEX, Black Dawge Cartridges, GOEX Pinnacle, E-Z Loads, GOEX Pinnacle Replica Black Powder, GOEX Express
Grizzly Cartridge Co. - see Rintoul Enterprises, LLC		
Gyttorp AB Malmvagen 1 Nora, SE-71330 Sweden www.gyttorp.com	GYTTORP Precision by Tradition	Centurion, Roda, Wetland, Fasan, Steel Max
HS Munitions, Inc. 4406 Rathbun Lane Stevensville, MT 59870 www.thehuntingshack.com	HSM	HSM, HSM Trophy Gold, HSM Varmint Gold, Urban, COPper, Hunting Shack
Hornady Manufacturing Co. P.O. Box 1848 Grand Island, NE 68802 www.hornady.com	Hornady Accurate. Deadly. Dependable.	Hornady, Frontier, LEVERevolution, For Personal Defense, FPD, TAP, SST, HMR, Varmint Express, V-Max, Custom, InterBond, A-Max, XTP, Evolution, SST Shotgun Slug, Buckshot Light Mag, SST-ML, Lock-N-Load Speed Sabot, FPB, XTP MAG, PowerBelt, Great Plains, SST Interlock, Dangerous Game Series, DGS (Dangerous Game Solid), DGX (Dangerous Game eXpanding), Interlock, Flex-Tip, LIGHT/HEAVY MAG, LIGHT/HEAVY MAG INTERBOND, LIGHT/HEAVY MAG SST, LIGHT MAG, CUSTOM IB, CUSTOM Shot, HAP (Hornady Action Pistol), .17 Mach 2, .17 HMR
Hull Cartridge Co. Ltd. Bontoft Ave., National Ave. Hull, England HU5 4HZ www.hullcartridge.co.uk	HULL CARTRIDGE	Sovereign, Elite, Sterling, Imperial, Three Crowns, Hulmax, Solway, Sovereign FITASC, Sovereign Fibre, PRO ONE, PRO ONE DTL300, PRO FIBRE, PRO TWENTY, PROSTEEL, INTERCOMP, CHEVRON, SUBSONIC, SUBSONIC 20, STEEL CLAY, HIGH PHEASANT, ULTRAMAX, SPECIAL PIGEON, GAME & CLAY, STEEL GAME

NAME AND ADDRESS		TRADEMARK/BRAND NAMES
Igman d.d. Donje Polje 42 88400 Konjic Bosnia-Herzegovina www.igman.co.ba		Igman, Hot Shot
Impala Europa Dr. Karl Renner Str. 2b Guntramsdorf A-2353 Austria www.impalabullets.at		Impala
Industrias Tecnos S.A. de C.V. Km. 6 carretera Cuernavaca a Tepoztlan Cuernavaca, Mor. Mexico C.P. 62000 www.itecnos.com.mx		Aguila, Colibri, Interceptor, Super Maximum, Sniper Subsonic SSS, Super Colibri, IQ
International Cartridge Corp. 2273 Route 310 Reynoldsville, PA 15851 www.internationalcartridge.com		Green Elite TR, Green Elite HP Duty, Green Elite SD, Green Elite FR, Green Elite NT
ISRAEL MILITARY INDUSTRIES LTD (IMI) Ramat Hasharon 47100 Israel www.imi-israel.com		IMI, Action Express
JSC Novosibirsk LVE Plant (JSC Novosibirsk Cartridge Plant) Stantsionnaya 30A Novosibirsk 630108 Russia www.lveplant.ru		Junior, Sobol, Extra, Korostel, Surok, Kosach
James Calhoon 4343 U.S. Hwy. 87 Havre, MT 59501 www.jamescalhoon.com		Slick Silver, ST/Saber Tip, DHP (Double Hollow Point), 19 BADGER, 19 Calhoon, 19-223 Calhoon
Jamison International V LLC 3551 Mayer Av. Sturgis, SD 57785		
Kent Cartridge P.O. Box 849 Kearneysville, WV 25430 www.kentgamebore.com		Kent, Tungsten Matrix, Fasteel, Precision Steel, Diamond Shot, Velocity, Ultimate Upland, Ultimate Gamebore, White Gold, Blue Diamond, Bio-Wad, Protrial, All-Purpose Diamond Shot, Pure Gold, Traditional Game, Black Gold, Impact

NAME AND ADDRESS		TRADEMARK/BRAND NAMES
Krasnozavodsk Chemical Factory Moscow Region Krasnovavodsk RUSS-141321 Russia www.khz-record.ru	*Record*	Record, Strela, Caban, Poleva, Tandem
Kynamco Ltd. The Old Railway Station, Station Road Mildenhall, Suffolk IP28 7DT England www.kynochammunition.co.uk	KYNOCH TRADE MARK	Kynoch
KYRGIAS M.G. S.A. 1 klm. Neochorouda turn Neochorouda Thessaloniki, GR-54500 Greece	M.G. KIRGIAS S.A.	
Lazzeroni Arms Company P.O. Box 26696 Tucson, AZ 85726 www.lazzeroni.com	LAZZERONI®	Scramjet, Phantom, Firebird, Patriot, Warbird, Titan, Meteor, Tomahawk, Galaxy, Hellcat, Spitfire, Maverick, Lilmufu, Eagle, Saturn, Bibamufu
Lightfield Ammunition Corp. P.O. Box 162 Adelphia, NJ 07710 www.lightfieldslugs.com	LIGHTFIELD	Hybred EXP, Commander IDS Lightfield Lites, Hybred-Elite, Lightfield, Star Lite, Alpha Gold 300, Super Star
Lyalvale Express Ltd. Express Estate Fisherwick Nr. Whittington Lichfield WS13 8XA England www.lyalvaleexpress.com	LYALVALE EXPRESS	Pro-Fibre, Superfelt, H.V. Fibre, Pro-Comp, Pro-Game, Excel, World Cup, Fibre-Comp, Lyalvale
MFS 2000 INC. Magyar Loszergyarto ZRt. 3332 Sirok, Pf. 9 Hungary www.mfs2000.hu	MFS Division of RUAG Ammotec	MFS, MFS 2000

NAME AND ADDRESS		TRADEMARK/BRAND NAMES
MagSafe Ammo, Inc. 4700 So. U.S. Hwy. 17-92 Casselberry, FL 32707 www.magsafeonline.com	**MagSafe Ammo**	SWAT, Defender, Stealth, Agent, Special Ops, MagSafe, X-Load
Magtech Ammunition 248 Apollo Dr. #180 Lino Lakes, MN 55014 www.magtechammunition.com	MAGTECH Technologically Advanced	CleanRange, FIRST DEFENSE, GUARDIAN GOLD, MAGTECH, SHOOTIN' SIZE
Mast Technology Inc. P.O. Box 1026 Blue Springs, MO 64013 www.masttechnology.com	MAST TECHNOLOGY INC	
Mastercast Bullet Company 292 Anderson Road Enon Valley, PA 16120 www.mastercast.net		
MAXAM Outdoors S.A. Avenida del Partenon, 16 bajo Madrid, E-28042 Spain www.ueec.es/	MAXAM Outdoors	
Mesko S.A. Zaklady Metalowe Ul. Legionow 122 Skarzysko-Kamienna PL-26111 Poland	Division of Bumar	
Metallwerk Elisenhutte GmbH Nassau (MEN) 10 Elisenhutte Nassau/Lahn D-56377 Germany Men-info@elisenhuette.de www.elisenhuette.de	MEN Division of CBC	QD PEP, QD 1, QD 2, PTP, DK, SFC, MEN
NAMMO Lapua Oy P.O. Box 5 Lapua FIN-62101 Finland www.lapua.com	L LAPUA	Lapua, Scenar, Midas, Master, Pistol King, Polar Biathlon, D4G, Speed Ace, Rapid Pistol, Mira, SK, Lock Base, Naturalis, CEPP, Hubertus, X-ACT, Midas +, Center-X, Pistol OSP, Bullex-N, Naturalis Long Range, Vihtavuor

NAME AND ADDRESS		TRADEMARK/BRAND NAMES
Nike Fiocchi Sporting Ammunition Ltd. Lajos Street 78 H-1036 Budapest Hungary www.nike-fiocchi.hu	NIKE FIOCCHI nf	NF, NIKE, NIKE-FIOCCHI, NIKE sport skeet, NIKE sport trap, NIKE Tracer, NIKE Parcours, NIKE extra, NIKE Mini Magnum, NIKE stren, NIKE Magnum, NIKE Industrial 8 Gauge, NIKE Signal Alarm, NIKE Double Alarm, NIKE Rubber Ball(s), NIKE Voice, NIKE Signal (4-ga.), MONDIAL
Nitro Ammunition Company 7560 Newkirk road Mountain Grove, MO 65711 www.nitrocompany.com		Destroyer Series Defense Loads
Nitron S.A. Zaklady Tworzyw Sztucznych Krupski Mlyn PL-42693 Poland	NITRON	
Nobel Sport S. A. 57 Rue Pierre Charron Paris F-75181 France www.nobelsport.fr	NOBELSPORT	
NOBEL SPORT ESPANA S.A. Apartado 428 Villacil (Leon), E-24080 Spain www.excopesa.com/nobel	NOBELSPORT ESPAÑA	
Nobel Sport Italia S.r.l. Via di Palazzetto 7/11 San Giuliano (PI) I-56017 Italy www.nobelsport.it	nsi NOBELSPORTITALIA	Prestige, Migration
Norma Precision AB Jagargatan SE-67040 Amotfors Sweden www.norma.cc	norma Division of RUAG Ammotec	norma, Oryx, Vulkan, Alaska, Plastic Point, Diamond Line, Golden Target, Jaktmatch
Nosler, Inc. 107 SW Columbia St. Bend, OR 97702 www.nosler.com	Nosler®	Nosler, Partition-HG, E-Tip, Nosler Custom, Partition, AccuBond, Ballistic Tip, CT Ballistic Silver Tip, Nosler Solid, Custom Competition, Sporting Handgun, Solid Base

NAME AND ADDRESS		TRADEMARK/BRAND NAMES
OJSC "The Tula Cartridge Works" 47-b Marata Tula, 300004 Russia www.wolfammo.ru	**WOLF**	Wolf, Wolf Gold, Wolf Military Classic, Polyperformance, Wolf Performance Ammunition
Old Western Scounger/ Navy Arms 219 Lawn St. Martinsburg, WV 25401 www.ows-ammunition.com		
P. Gavrielides Ltd P.O. Box 40217,6302 Larnaka, CYPRUS www.olympia.com.cy	OLYMPIA	Fibre, Scatter 31/35, Shock, Big Olympia Cartridges, Alfa, Gem, Minimax Fibre, Gem 30 Fibre, Super Game Fibre, Special Game, Copper 32/34, Nickel 32/36, Competition 28, Competition Fibre, Minimax Sporting, Minimax Game, Baby Game, Super Game, Quick, Mini Magnum
Pinnacle Ammunition 111 W. Port Plaza #600 St. Louis, MO 63146 www.pinnacleammo.com	PINNACLE	AeroSteel, BIS-Maxx
Polyshok, Inc. 2702 Woodmere Drive Panama City, FL 32405 www.polyshok.com		POLYSHOK I.R.P. (Impact Reactive Projectile)
Polywad, Inc. P.O. Box 396 Roberta, GA 31078 www.polywad.com	POLYWA INCORPORATED	Spred-R, Polymag, Gram Crak-R, Vintager, DoubleWide, GreenLite, Quik-Shok
Poongsan Metals Corp. (PMC) Keuk Dong Bldg. 60-1 Chungmuro Chung-ku Seoul 100-705 Korea www.poongsan.co.kr/www.pmcammo.com	PMC	PMC, Starfire, eRange, Gold Line, Bronze Line, Zapper, Predator, PMC X-TAC, Cowboy Action Line, Precision Line, Precision Made Cartridges, Frangible
Precision Cartridge, Inc. 940 Georgiana St. Hobart, IN 46342		
Precision Delta Corporation P.O. Box 128 Ruleville, MS 38771 www.precisiondelta.com	PRECISION DELTA	Precision Delta

NAME AND ADDRESS		TRADEMARK/BRAND NAMES
Pretoria Metal Pressings (PMP) Div. of Denel Ltd. Private Bag X334 Pretoria, 0001 Republic of South Africa		
Prvi Partizan Milosa Obrenovica 2 Uzice YU-31000 Serbia www.privipartizan.com		Prvi Partizan, PPU, Hotshot, GROM
Quality Cartridge P.O. Box 445 Hollywood, MD 20636 www.qual-cart.com		
RBCD Performance Plus 1538 SE Military Drive, Suite 206 San Antonio, TX 78214 www.rbcd.net		Performance Plus, Performance Plus TFSP, Performance Plus Platinum, Predator
Remington Arms Co. P.O. Box 700 Madison, NC 27025 www.remington.com	**REMINGTON**®	Accelerator, AccuTip/AccuTip-V, Bronze Point, Buckhammer, CBEE 22, Copper-Lokt, Copper Solid, Cyclone, Disintegrator, DriLube, Driving Band, Duplex, ETA, EtronX, Express, Express-Steel, Fireball, Genesis, Golden Saber, Gun Club, Ideal, Hi-Speed, Kleanbore, Lead-Lokt, Core-Lokt, Managed-Recoil, Nitro 27, Nitro CLP, Nitro Mag, Nitro Turkey, Nitro Steel, Peters, Power Level, Power-Lokt, Power Piston, Power Port, R-P, Premier, Rem-Lite, Remington, Remington Leadless, Rustless, Scirocco, Sportsman, ShurShot, Slugger, STS, Subsonic, Super Magnum, Swift-Lokt, Targetmaster, Thunderbolt, UMC, UMC Leadless, Ultra Mag, Viper, VLS, Vortex, Wetproof, Wingmaster HD, Nitro Pheasant, Yellow Jacket, Gold Box, Short-Action Ultra Mag, Drop Dead Better, Ultra Bonded, Unibody, Zulu, A-Frame, Disintegrator CTF, Golden Bullet, Hypersonic Steel
Rintoul Enterprises, LLC Grizzly Cartridge Co. 30201 Carmel Road P.O. Box 1466 Rainier, OR 97048 www.grizzlycartridge.com		
RUAG USA 5402 East Diana St. Tampa, FL 33610 www.ruag-usa.com	**RUAG**	Copper-Matrix NTF

NAME AND ADDRESS		TRADEMARK/BRAND NAMES
RUAG Ammotec AG (RWS, norma, Dynamit Nobel, Hirtenberger, GECO, Rottweil, SWISS MATCH) Uttigenstrasse 67 CH-3602 Thun Switzerland www.ruag.com		Dynamit Nobel, DN, RWS, Geco, Rottweil, R50, R25, FP50, DE-EVOLUTION, T-Mantel, KS GESCHOSS, ID Classic, UNI Classic, H-Mantel, DK GESCHOSS, V-Mantel, MJ MATCHJAGD, FS GESCHOSS, TMS/TMR GESCHOSS, BIONIC BLACK, BIONIC YELLOW, RWS PREMIUM LINE, RWS PROFESSIONAL LINE, RIFLE MATCH S, RIFLE MATCH, PISTOL MATCH SUPER CLEAN, PISTOL MATCH, PISTOL C 25, RWS SPORT LINE, TARGET RIFLE, TARGET PISTOL, CLUB, RWS FIELD LINE, Z-LANG, SUBSONIC, MAGNUM FMJ, MAGNUM SP, SINOXID, SINTOX, norma, Hirtenberger, Swiss Match, R25, R50, R100, SUPER PISTOL 250, ACTION, GREEN POWER, PENETRATOR, SPECIAL MATCH RUAG, Sintox, Swiss P, Action 1, Action 3, Action 4, Action 5, SeCa, Self, Styx Action
SBR Ammunition 1118 Glynn Park Rd. Brunswick, GA 31525 www.sbrammunition.com		GreenMatch, LaserMatch
SNC Technologies 5 Montee des Arsenaux Le Gardeur Quebec J5Z 2P4 Canada www.snctec.com		Greenshield, Short Stop, CQT, FX, Simunition, Dragonfly, SecuriBlank, Sniper Elite
Sage Control Ordnance 3391 E. Eberhardt St. Oscoda, MI 48750 www.sageinternationalltd.com		
Scharch Mfg. Inc. 10325 County Road 120 Salida, CO 81201		TopBrass, Lions Cartridge
Sellier & Bellot JSC Licicka 667 Vlasim CZ-25813 Czech Republic www.sellier-bellot.cz	Division of CBC	Lord, Fortuna, Mark III, Corona, Junior, Favorit, Tortorella, Black Star, Nontox
Silver State Armory P.O. Box 962 Packwood, WA 98361 www.ssarmory.com		
SOTIRIOS NAFPLIOTIS A.B.E.E. P.O. Box 8- Eleon Thiva, GR-32200 Greece		

NAME AND ADDRESS		TRADEMARK/BRAND NAMES
Speer 2299 Snake River Ave. Lewiston, ID 83501 www.speer-bullets.com.	*speer* Division of ATK	Clean-Fire, Lawman, Speer, Gold Dot, Nitrex, Grand Slam, TMJ, TNT, Uni-Cor, Mag-Tip, Hot-Cor Trophy Bonded, Bear Claw, Lawman RHT, Blazer Clean Fire, Blazer, Flitecontrol, DeepCurl, Plinker, Short Barrel, TNT Green
Superior Ammunition, Inc. 20788 Mossy Oak Place Sturgis, SD 57785 www.superiorammo.com		
Superior Ballistics, Inc. c/o Mic McPherson 10725 Road 24.4 Loop Cortez, CO 81321 www.superiorballistics.com		SMc Cartridges
Swift Bullet Company 201 Main Street Quinter, KS 67752 www.swiftbullets.com	*Swift* BULLET COMPANY	
TTI Armory 14884 Heritagecrest Way Bluffdale, UT 84065 www.ttiarmory.com	TTI·ARMORY	
Ten-X Ammunition 5650 Arrow Highway Montclair, CA 91763 www.tenxammo.com		
Thifan Industrie S.a.r.l. 275 Rue de Malitorne, B.P. 61 18230 St. Doulchard France www.sauvestre.com	BALLE FLECHE **Sauvestre**®	Balle Fleche Sauvestre, FIP
Trust Eibarres S.A. Murrategui 9 (Azitain) Apartado 32 Eibar ES-20600 Spain www.trust-eibarres.com	**TRUST**	Trust, Super Halcon, Caza, Galgo Verde, Impulsor, Super Star, Halcon, Semi-Magnum, Caza Slug, Magnum Slug, F-uno, Ujeo Perdiz, Galgo Verde Ecofieltro, Halcon Ecofieltro, Semi-Magnum Ecofieltro, Magnum Ecofieltro, Caza/Bala Star, Pequenos, Sepiol
UEE Cartucheria Deportiva S.A. Avda. del Partenon, 16 bajo 28042 Madrid - Espana Spain www.ueec.es	UEE	Rio, Royal, Royal Steel, Starteam, Rio Ammunition

NAME AND ADDRESS		TRADEMARK/BRAND NAMES
Ultramax Ammunition 2112 Elk Vale Rd. Rapid City, SD 57701 www.ultramaxammunition.com	**ULTRAMAX**	Ultramax
Ulyanovsk Machinery Plant SUE, PA 2 Metallistov St. Ulyanovsk RUSS-32007 Russia www.ulmash.narod.ru		
Weatherby, Inc. 1605 Commerce Way Paso Robles, CA 93446 www.weatherby.com	*Weatherby*	Weatherby
Winchester Div. Olin Corp. Shamrock St. East Alton, IL 62024 www.winchester.com	**WINCHESTER**	AA, Black Talon, BRI, CXP, Double A, Double X, Drylok Hi-Velocity, Drylok Super Steel, Dynapoint, Fail Safe, Hi-Impact, Lubalox, Lubaloy, Platinum Tip, Popper-Load, Power-Point, Ranger, Silvertip, Super-Handicap, Super-Lite, Super Match, Super Pigeon, Super Steel, Super Unleaded, Super-X, Supreme, SXT, T22, W, Western, Wildcat, Winchester, Xpert, XP3, Xtended Range, Xtra-Lite, XX, Superclean NT, Controlled Expansion Performance, Power-Point Plus, Upland, Winclean, Winlite, Rackmaster, Winglide, Mark 5, E-Tip, AccuBond CT, SRTA (Short Range Training Ammunition), Ranger Law Enforcement, Supreme Elite, Partition Gold, Ranger T-Series, Super Speed, Supersport, USA, Olin, XP^3, Platinum Tip, Dual Bond, Super Pheasant, Super-Target, USA, Bonded PDX1, PHP Bonded, Power Max Bonded, Pointed Soft Point TIN Lead Free Projectiles, Ballistic Silvertip, Xpediter, SXT Design, Power-Point Plus, Super-Target, Stop The Threat, Explosive Technology, Ringblaster, 333 Rounds, 555 Rounds
WOLF Performance Ammunition P.O. Box 757 Placentia, CA 92871 www.wolfammo.com	**WOLF**	Wolf Performance Ammunition, Wolf Polyperformance, Wolf Gold, Wolf Military Classic
YAVASCALAR A.S. Ataturk Mah. Badirma Cad N 49 Balikesir, TR-10100 Turkey www.yavascalar.com	YAVAŞÇALAR A.Ş.	
ZERO AMMUNITION CO. INC P.O. box 1188 Cullman, AL 35056 www.zerobullets.com		ZERO

CHAPTER 98 : FALLEN FLAGS

CHAPTER 98 HIGHLIGHTS:

- **DOMESTIC**
- **FOREIGN**

DOMESTIC

Company Name	Location	Products	Approx. Dates
Action Ammo Ltd	Philadelphia, PA	Private label	1985-1990
Activ	Kearneysville, WV	Shotshells	1985-1996
Alcan Co. Inc.	Alton, IL	See Note 7	1951-1972
Allegheny Ordnance Plant	Cumberland, MD	Military	1942-1943
American Ballistics	Marietta, GA	Metallic	1976-1986
American Ammunition Co.	Oak Park, IL	Shotshells	1910-1922
American Cartridge Co.	Kansas City, MO	See Note 8	N/A -1924
American Buckle & Cartridge Co.	Kansas City, MO	Shotshells	1884-N/A
American Metallic Ammunition Co.	New York, NY	Metallic	1867-1898
Amron Inc.	Waukesha, WI	Metallic	1956-1979
Anderson Munitions Inc	Cardova, TN	Military	1996-1998
Austin Cartridge Co.	Cleveland, OH	Private label	1895-1909
Bingham Ltd.	Atlanta, GA	Metallic	1972-1994
Bismuth Cartridge Co.	No. Hollywood, CA	Shotshell	1992-2007
Brass Extrusion Labs Ltd	Bensenville, IL	Metallic	1976-1988
Browning Arms Co.	Morgan, UT	Private label	1976-1980
Burnside Rifle Co.	Providence, RI	Metallic	circa 1870
Central Cartridge Co.	Kansas City, MO	Shotshells	1921-1925
Chamberlain Cartridge & Target Co.	Cleveland, OH	Shotshells	1883-1932
Clinton Cartridge Co.	East Alton, IL	See Note 5	1909-1934
Connecticut Cartridge Co.	N/A	Metallic	circa 1970
Creedmore Cartridge Co.	Barberton, OH	Metallic	1890-1892
Crittenden & Tribbals Mfg. Co.	So. Coventry, CT	See Note 1	1862-1866
Denver Ordnance Plant	Denver, CO	Military	1941-1944
Des Moines Ordnance Plant	Des Moines, IA	Military	1941-1945
Delaware Cartridge Co.	Wilmington, DE	Shotshells	1860-1888
B.C. English	Springfield, MA	Maynards	circa 1860s
Eau Claire Ordnance Plant	Eau Claire, WI	Military	1942-1943
Eclipse Cartridge Co.	Texas	Shotshells	1980-1985
El Dorado Cartridge Co.	Henderson, NV	Metallic	1988-2007
Ethan Allen & Co.	Worcester, MA	See Note 2	1856-1871
Evansville Ordnance Plant	Evansville, IN	Military	1942-1944
Federal Primer Corp.	North Arlington, NJ	Metallic	1916-1918
Forehand & Wadsworth	Worcester, MA	Metallic	1871-1890
Forehand Arms Co.	Worcester, MA	Metallic	1890-1898
Frankford Arsenal	Philadelphia, PA	Military	1816-1977
Gamble-Skogmo Inc.	Minneapolis, MN	Private label	1956-1978
Hall & Hubbard	Springfield, MA	Metallic	1869-1874
Hastings	Clay Center, KS	N/A	N/A
Herter's Inc.	Waseca, MN	Metallic	1959-1982
H. W. Mason & Co.	South Coventry, CT	Metallic	1870-1874
Holiday Stores	Minneapolis, MN	Private label	1971-1975
Hoxie Ammunition Co.	Chicago, IL	Metallic	1908-1920
KTW, Inc.	Lorain, OH	Metallic	1978-1998
Kilgore Co. LLC.	Toone, TN	Metallic	2011-2011
Kings Mills Ordnance Plant	Kings Mills, OH	Military	1942-1944
Independent Cartridge Co.	N/A	Shotshells	1910-1913
Liberty Cartridge Co.	Mount Carmel, CT	Shotshells	1908-1917
C.D. Leet	Springfield, MA	See Note 1	1860-1875
Lowell Ordnance Plant	Lowell, MA	Military	1942-1943
Maxim Munitions Corp.	Watertown, NY	Metallic	1915-1918
Massachusetts Arms Co.	Chicopee Falls, MA	Metallic	1849-1930
Meriden Firearms Mfg. Co.	Meriden, CT	Shotshells	1863-1868
Merwin & Hulbert	South Coventry, CT	Metallic	1860-1891
Milwaukee Ordnance Plant	Milwaukee, WI	Military	1942-1943
Montgomery Ward & Co.	Chicago, IL	Private label	ended 1977
NATEC, Inc.	Plattsburg, NY	Metallic	2004-2006
National Cartridge Co.	St. Louis, MO	See Note 4	1908-1909
Nevins Ammunition Co.	Boise, ID	Metallic	1982-1984
New Haven Arms Co.	New Haven, CT	See Note 9	1858-1867
New York Metallic Powder Co.	New York, NY	Metallic	1865-1867

Company Name	Location	Products	Approx. Dates
National Projectile Works	Grand Rapids, MI	N/A	N/A
Newton Arms Co.	Buffalo, NY	Metallic	1918-1926
Peters Cartridge Co.	Kings Mills, OH	All	1887-1934
Phoenix Cartridge Co.	So. Coventry, CT	Metallic	1874-1891
Robin Hood Ammunition Co.	Swanton, VT	See Note 3	1887-1916
Sage Ammunition Works	Middletown, CT	Metallic	1864-1866
Sandia Die and Cartridge	Albuquerque, NM	Metallic	circa 1978
Sears, Roebuck & Co.	Chicago, IL	Private label	1875-1976
Smiths Graphited Cartridge Co.	Washington, D.C.	Metallics	1916-N/A
Southern Cartridge Co.	Houston, TX	Private label	1923-1929
Southern Cartridge Co.	Savannah, GA	Shotshells	1909-1914
St. Louis Ordnance Plant	St. Louis, MO	Military	1941-1945
Standard Cartridge Co.	Pinale, CA	N/A	N/A
Smith & Wesson	Springfield, MA	Metallic	1857-1860
C. Sharps & Co.	Philadelphia, PA	Metallic	1858-1861
Sharps & Hankins	Philadelphia, PA	Metallic	1862-1867
Super-Vel	Shelbyville, IN	Metallic	1972-1980
Triton Cartridge Co.	Wappingers Falls, NY	Metallic	1984-2000
Twin Cities Ordnance Plant	New Brighton, MN	Military	1941-1990
Union Cap & Chemical Co.	East Alton, IL	Metallic	1905-1908
Union Metallic Cartridge & Cap Co.	Bridgeport, CT	See Note 3	1866-1867
Union Metallic Cartridge Co.	Bridgeport, CT	See Note 3	1867-1916
U.S. Cartridge Co.	Lowell, MA	See Note 6	1864-1938
Volcanic Repeating Arms Co.	New Haven, CT	N/A	1855-1860
Wanda Cartridge Co.	Houston, TX	Shotshells	1965-1972
Western Auto Stores	N/A	Private label	1955-1977
Western Cartridge Co.	East Alton, IL	Winchester	1898-1932
Worcester Metallic Cartridge Co.	Worcester, MA	Private label	1885-N/A
Utah Ordnance Plant	Ogden, UT	Military	1941-1943

Notes:
1. UMC was founded by Schuyler, Hartley, Graham & Co. in 1866 by purchasing Crittenden & Tribbals as well as C.D. Leet.
2. Ethan Allen became Forehand & Wadsworth in 1871 and Forehand Arms Co. from 1871 until 1898. The company became Hopkins & Allen in 1902.
3. Union Metallic Cartridge Co., Remington Arms & Ammunition, and Robin Hood Ammunition Co. merged in 1916 to form Remington Arms-Union Metallic Cartridge Co. Inc.
4. Purchased by Western Cartridge in 1909.
5. A trade name of Western Cartridge Co. on products made for Sears. Western Cartridge purchased Winchester in 1931.
6. Owner National Lead Co. sold company to Winchester in 1926.
7. Alcan became Smith & Wesson Ammunition Co. in 1972.
8. Purchased by Federal in 1924.
9. Acquired by Winchester in 1866.

FOREIGN

Company Name	Location	Products	Approx. Dates
Canadian Arsenals Ltd.	Quebec, Canada	Military	1945-1986
Chartered Industries	Singapore	see Note 1	1980-2006
Colonial Ammunition Co.	Auckland, NZ	Metallic	closed 1975
Deutsche Waffen und Munitionsfabriken	Berlin, Germany	Metallic	1896-1949
Dominion Arsenal	Quebec, Canada	Military	1882-1945
Dominion Cartridge Co. Ltd.	Brownsburg, Canada	Metallic	1886-1976
Gustav Genschow	Berlin, Germany	Metallic	1887-1959
Halger Arms Co.	Kiel, Germany	Private Label	N/A -1939
Hingston Smith Arms Co.	Winnipeg, Canada	Shotshells	1879-1920
Hirtenberger (purchased by RUAG)	Hirtenberg, Austria	Metallic	1860-2004
Kynoch Cartridge Co. (now Kynamco)	Birmingham, England	Metallic	1870-1970
Myra Sports Stores	Broken Hill, Australia	Metallic	circa 1970
Olympic Arms & Ammunition S.A.	Kilkis, Greece	Metallic	N/A-2006
Pegorano Sport S.r.l.	Dolo, Italy	N/A	N/A
Ross Rifle Co.	Quebec, Canada	Metallic	circa 1910
G. Roth	Roth, Austria	Metallic	N/A
SK Jagd (sold to Lapua)	Schonebeck, Germany	Metallic	1829-2003
Societe Francaise des Munitions Gevelot	Paris, France	See Note 2	1883-1982
Super Cartridge Pty. Ltd.	Victoria, Australia	Metallic	circa 1970
Svenska Metallwerk	Blikstorp, Sweden	Metallic	1954-1965
Swartklip	Cape Town, South Africa	Metallic	N/A - 2001
Valcartier Industries Inc. (I.V.I.)	Courcellette, Canada	See Note 3	1940s-1980
West Can Industries	Okotoks, Canada	Shotshells	1959-1966

Notes:
1. Military small caliber ammunition production terminated, still producing other ordnance.
2. Purchased by Cheddite S.r.l. of Italy
3. Purchased by General Dynamics in 1980; when GD purchased Canadian Arsenals Ltd. in 1986, IVI and CAL became General Dynamics Ordnance and Tactical Systems-Canada Inc.

CHAPTER 99 : CARTRIDGE IDENTIFICATION CHARTS

To identify an unknown cartridge, simply match the cartridge type with a provided labeled drawing, go to the appropriate labeled chart, and with the use of a precision measuring tool (caliper) match the dimensions in the order they are provided.

RIMMED STRAIGHT CARTRIDGE CASE DIMENSIONS

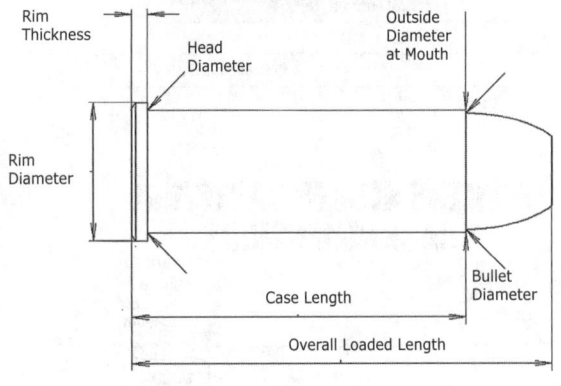

RIMMED NECKED CARTRIDGE CASE DIMENSIONS

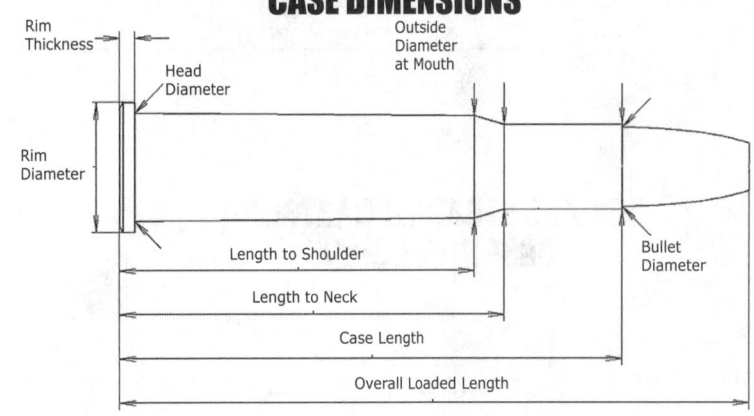

SEMI-RIMMED STRAIGHT CARTRIDGE CASE DIMENSIONS

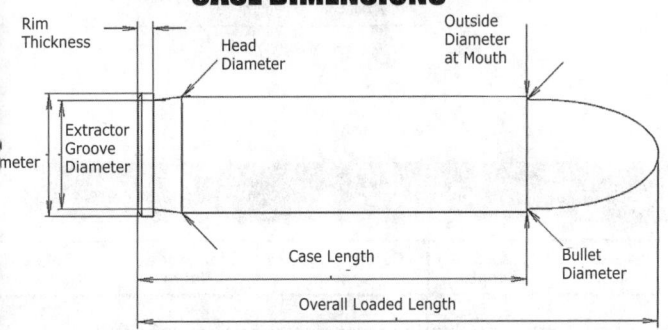

SEMI-RIMMED NECKED CARTRIDGE CASE DIMENSIONS

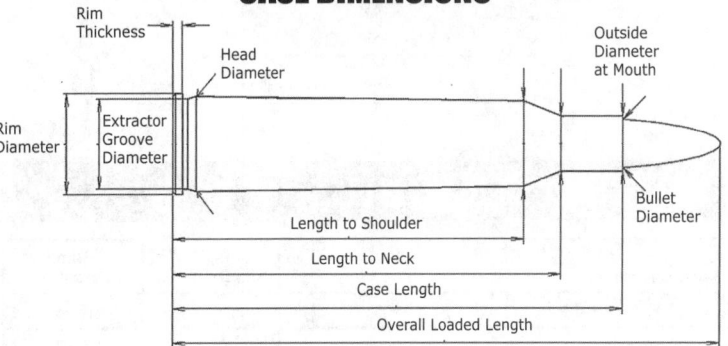

REBATED STRAIGHT CARTRIDGE CASE DIMENSIONS

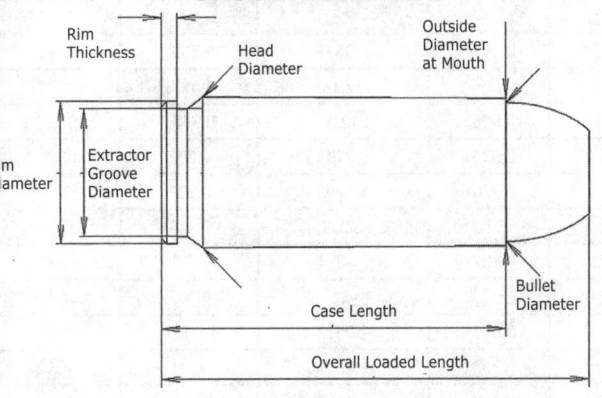

REBATED NECKED CARTRIDGE CASE DIMENSIONS

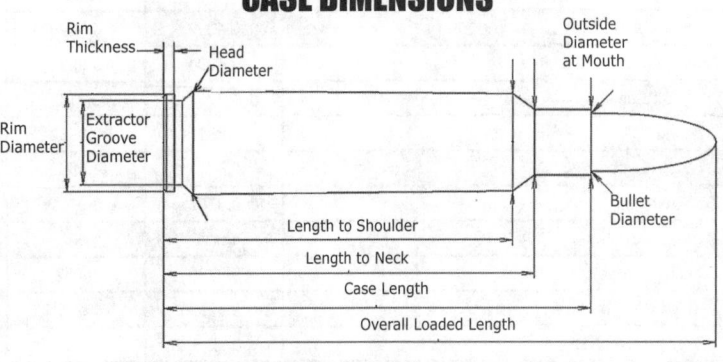

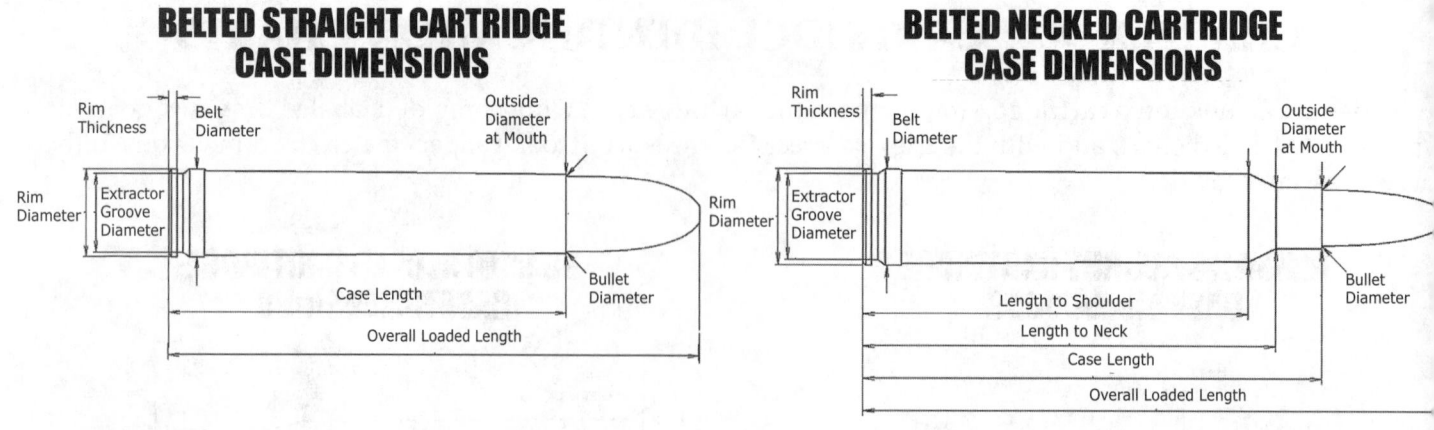

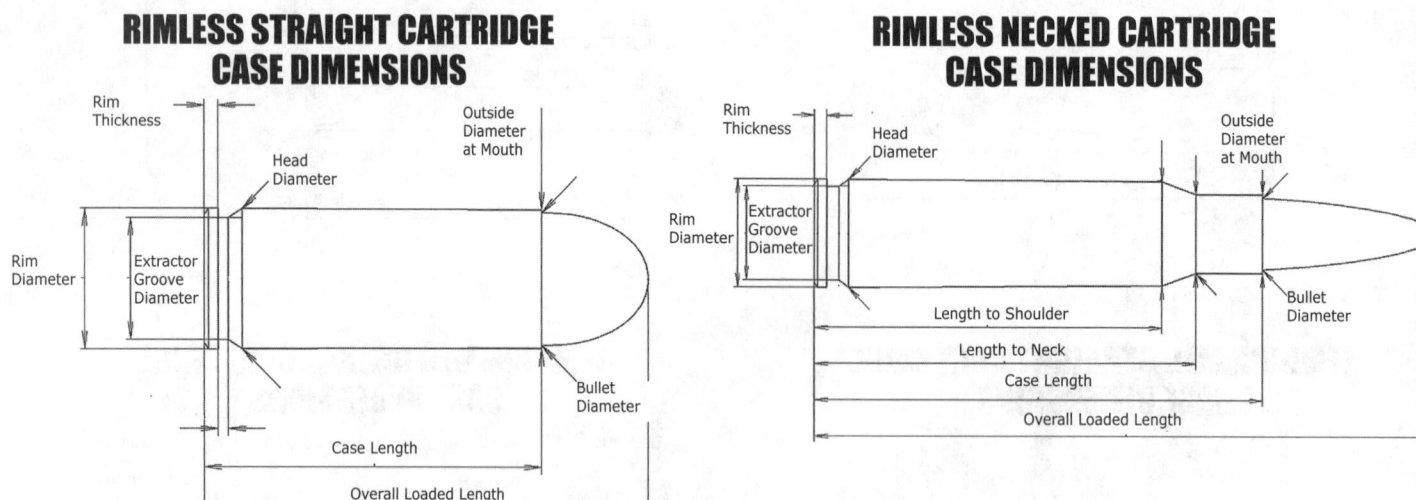

RIMMED STRAIGHT

Cartridge Name	Rim Diameter	Rim Thickness	Head Diameter	Case Length	Overall Loaded Length	Diameter at Mouth	Bullet Diameter
.22-10-45 Maynard	0.31	0.58	0.252	1.17	1.41	0.252	0.228
.22-15 Stevens	0.34	0.07	0.265	2	2.25	0.243	0.226
.25-21 Stevens	0.376	0.06	0.3	2.03	2.281	0.283	0.257
.25-25 Stevens	0.376	0.06	0.3	2.376	2.625	0.283	0.257
.28-30 Stevens	0.412	0.06	0.357	2.5	2.812	0.309	0.284
.300 (295) Rook Rifle	0.3748	0.0449	0.3189	1.1524	1.45	0.3181	0.3012
.300 Sherwood	0.3748	0.05	0.3201	1.55	2.0402	0.3181	0.3
.30-30 Wesson	0.44	0.058	0.38	1.66	2.5	0.329	0.309
.310 Cadet	0.4098	0.0429	0.3551	1.12	1.6	0.3271	0.323
7.5mm Swiss/Swedish Rev	0.4094	0.0591	0.3543	0.8976	1.3622	0.3307	0.315
.32 Short Colt	0.3752	0.0532	0.3181	0.65	1.015	0.3181	0.314
.32 Long Colt	0.3811	0.0532	0.3181	0.9161	0.12161	0.3181	0.3138
.32 S&W Short	0.3752	0.0551	0.337	0.9201	1.2799	0.337	0.315
.32 S&W Long	0.3752	0.0551	0.337	0.9201	1.2799	0.337	0.315
.32 Ideal	0.412	0.06	0.348	1.75	2.031	0.344	0.323
.32 Long Centerfire	0.3799	0.052	0.3169	0.8071	1.1811	0.335	0.317
.32 H&R Magnum	0.3752	0.0551	0.337	1.0752	1.35	0.337	0.315
.320 Short Revolver	0.376	0.052	0.3197	0.6535	1.0512	0.3197	0.315
.320 Long Revolver	0.3799	0.052	0.3169	0.8071	1.1811	0.315	0.3032
8mm Lebel Rev	0.4134	0.0591	0.3583	1.0787	1.4567	0.3504	0.326

Cartridge Name	Rim Diameter	Rim Thickness	Head Diameter	Case Length	Overall Loaded Length	Diameter at Mouth	Bullet Diameter
8mm Rast-Gasser	0.3811	0.0433	0.3386	1.063	1.4173	0.337	0.3193
.327 Federal Magnum	0.3752	0.055	0.337	1.2	1.475	0.337	0.312
.32-35 Stevens	0.503	0.06	0.402	1.8	2.29	0.339	0.312
.32-40 Winchester	0.5059	0.063	0.424	2.1299	2.5	0.339	0.3209
.32 Ballard Extra Long	0.369	0.058	0.321	1.24	1.8	0.339	0.321
.32-40 Ballard	0.5059	0.063	0.424	2.13	2.5	0.339	0.321
9mm Japanese Rev T26	0.4409	0.0394	0.38	0.866	1.181	0.379	0.3555
9mm Federal	0.435	0.0598	0.386	0.76	1.163	0.382	0.355
.35 S&W Auto	0.348	0.04	0.345	0.67	0.97	0.345	0.3091
.35-30 Maynard	0.494	0.065	0.4	1.63	2.03	0.395	0.36
.35-40 Maynard	0.494	0.065	0.4	2.06	2.53	0.395	0.36
.35-55 Winchester	0.5059	0.063	0.4209	2.085	2.5098	0.3921	0.3772
.357 Magnum	0.4402	0.0598	0.3791	1.2902	1.5902	0.3791	0.3591
.357 Rem Maximum	0.4402	0.0598	0.3791	1.6051	1.9902	0.3791	0.3591
.360 Nitro Express	0.485	0.0461	0.4299	2.25	3	0.3858	0.3669
.360 No.5 Rook	0.432	0.055	0.38	1.05	1.45	0.375	0.362
.375 Winchester	0.506	0.063	0.4198	2.02	2.56	0.4	0.376
.38 Short Colt	0.4402	0.0598	0.3791	0.765	1.2	0.3791	0.3591
.38 Long Colt	0.4402	0.0598	0.3791	1.035	1.3598	0.378	0.3591
.38 S&W	0.4402	0.0551	0.3866	0.7752	1.2402	0.3854	0.361
.38 Long Centerfire	0.441	0.06	0.379	1.03	1.45	0.378	0.376
.38 Ballard Extra Long	0.441	0.058	0.37	1.63	2.06	0.395	0.376
.38-35 Stevens	0.492	0.06	0.402	1.76	2.24	0.402	0.375
.38-40 Remington Hepburn	0.537	0.07	0.454	1.772	2.32	0.395	0.372
.38-50/55 Ballard	0.502	0.058	0.426	2	2.72	0.395	0.376
.38-50 Remington Hepburn	0.537	0.07	0.454	2.23	3.07	0.392	0.376
.38 Special	0.4402	0.0591	0.3791	1.1551	1.55	0.3791	0.3591
.380-200	0.4402	0.0551	0.3866	0.7752	1.2402	0.3854	0.361
9.4mm Danish rev	0.433	0.03	0.386	0.692	1.075	0.378	0.375
9.4mm Dutch Rev	0.493	0.05	0.433	0.826	1.252	0.419	0.4
.40-40 Maynard	0.494	0.065	0.456	1.78	2.32	0.45	0.416
.40-50 Sharps straight	0.544	0.078	0.454	1.875	2.63	0.421	0.403
.40-60 Maynard	0.532	0.065	0.456	2.2	2.75	0.45	0.416
.40-70 Maynard	0.532	0.065	0.456	2.42	2.88	0.45	0.416
.40-70 Sharps straight	0.533	0.078	0.454	2.5	3.18	0.421	0.403
.40-70/75 Bullard	0.555	0.07	0.471	2.38	3.148	0.43	0.403
.40-70 Ballard	0.555	0.07	0.471	2.38	3.148	0.426	0.403
.40-72 Winchester	0.519	0.061	0.46	2.6	3.15	0.431	0.406
.40-85/90 Ballard	0.555	0.058	0.471	2.94	3.81	0.426	0.403
.40-90 Sharps straight	0.546	0.065	0.477	3.25	4.06	0.425	0.403
.401 Herters Powermag	0.483	0.06	0.426	1.285	1.58	0.425	0.403
.405 Winchester	0.5429	0.0728	0.4618	2.5831	3.1748	0.4358	0.4114
.41 Magnum	0.492	0.059	0.435	1.29	1.59	0.434	0.41
.41 Long Colt	0.4402	0.0571	0.4106	1.1299	1.4248	0.4091	0.3882
10.4mm Swiss Rev	0.531	0.065	0.441	0.787	1.256	0.438	0.422
10.6mm Spanish Rev	0.531	0.065	0.456	0.966	1.404	0.441	0.419
10.6mm German Rev	0.508	0.598	0.45	0.972	1.425	0.45	0.428
.44 Ballard Long	0.506	0.06	0.441	1.09	1.65	0.44	0.439
.44 Ballard Extra Long	0.506	0.06	0.441	1.62	2.1	0.44	0.439
.44 Evans Short	0.513	0.07	0.44	0.99	1.44	0.439	0.419
.44 Evans Long	0.51	0.07	0.449	1.54	2	0.434	0.419
.44 Wesson Extra Long	0.51	0.07	0.441	1.63	2.19	0.441	0.44

Cartridge Name	Rim Diameter	Rim Thickness	Head Diameter	Case Length	Overall Loaded Length	Diameter at Mouth	Bullet Diameter
.44 Special	0.514	0.06	0.457	1.16	1.615	0.4565	0.4325
.44 Magnum	0.514	0.06	0.457	1.285	1.61	0.456	0.432
.44 Webley	0.503	0.05	0.472	0.69	1.1	0.47	0.436
.44 Bulldog	0.503	0.05	0.473	0.57	0.95	0.47	0.44
.44 Merwin&Hulbert	0.502	0.06	0.442	1.15	1.53	0.442	0.424
.44 S&W American	0.506	0.05	0.44	0.91	1.44	0.438	0.434
.44 S&W Russian	0.515	0.0598	0.4571	0.9701	1.4299	0.4563	0.4323
.44 Colt	0.5142	0.0598	0.4559	1.1	1.5	0.4547	0.4429
.44-70 Maynard	0.6	0.065	0.5	2.21	2.87	0.466	0.445
.44-100 Ballard	0.605	0.08	0.498	2.81	4.25	0.485	0.445
11mm French rev	0.491	0.035	0.46	0.71	1.18	0.449	0.451
.444 Marlin	0.514	0.063	0.4698	2.225	2.57	0.453	0.4305
.45-60 Winchester	0.629	0.065	0.508	1.89	2.303	0.479	0.458
.45-'70 Government	0.608	0.07	0.5055	2.105	2.55	0.48	0.458
.45-75 Sharps straight	0.6079	0.07	0.5055	2.1	2.9	0.4799	0.4579
.45-82/85 Winchester	0.605	0.065	0.504	2.394	2.88	0.483	0.458
.45-85 Bullard	0.606	0.06	0.505	2.09	2.55	0.477	0.458
.45-90 Win. High Velocity	0.605	0.065	0.504	2.394	2.88	0.483	0.458
.45-90 Sharps straight	0.597	0.065	0.5	2.4	3.25	0.489	0.4579
.45-100 Sharps straight	0.597	0.065	0.5	2.75	3.6	0.489	0.4579
.45-100 Ballard	0.605	0.08	0.498	2.81	4.25	0.487	0.454
.45-110 Sharps straight	0.597	0.065	0.5	2.87	3.9	0.489	0.4579
.45-120 Sharps straight	0.597	0.065	0.5	3.25	4.16	0.49	0.458
.45 Colt	0.5118	0.0598	0.4799	1.285	1.6	0.4799	0.4559
.45 S&W	0.5098	0.0598	0.4799	1.0902	1.4299	0.4799	0.4559
.45 Auto Rim	0.5161	0.089	0.476	0.898	1.2752	0.472	0.452
.45 Webley	0.504	0.045	0.471	0.82	1.15	0.471	0.452
.450 Nitro Express 3 1/4 in	0.624	0.0421	0.5449	3.25	3.95	0.4811	0.4579
500/450 Nitro Express 3 1/2 in	0.644	0.05	0.57	3.25	3.91	0.479	0.458
.450 Rev	0.51	0.035	0.477	0.69	1.1	0.475	0.455
.454 Casull	0.5118	0.0598	0.4799	1.3976	1.765	0.4799	0.452
.455 Rev. Mk I	0.53	0.035	0.478	0.87	1.35	0.473	0.456
.455 Rev. Mk II	0.5315	0.0394	0.4783	0.7677	1.2598	0.478	0.4555
.460 S&W Special	0.52	0.059	0.478	1.47	1.96	0.478	0.4526
.460 S&W Magnum	0.52	0.059	0.478	1.8	2.29	0.478	0.4526
11.4x50Rmm Aus Werndl M73	0.571	0.0945	0.493	1.97	2.55	0.472	0.449
11.5x57Rmm Spanish Ref.	0.631	0.082	0.525	2.26	3.06	0.485	0.454
11.7x51Rmm Danish Rem	0.579	0.0433	0.514	2.01	2.45	0.486	0.458
11.75mm Montenegrin Rev	0.555	0.045	0.49	1.4	1.73	0.472	0.445
.475 Nitro Express 3 1/4 in	0.621	0.0402	0.545	3.296	4	0.502	0.453
.476 Enfield Mk III	0.53	0.035	0.478	0.87	1.33	0.474	0.472
.480 Ruger	0.5421	0.0701	0.5039	1.285	1.65	0.5039	0.4756
.50 Rem Navy	0.65	0.05	0.565	0.875	1.24	0.532	0.508
.50 U.S. Carbine	0.648	0.07	0.567	1.319	1.808	0.534	0.497
.50-50 Maynard	0.661	0.065	0.563	1.37	1.91	0.535	0.512
.50-'70 Government	0.66	0.06	0.565	1.75	2.25	0.535	0.515
.50-90 Sharps straight	0.663	0.06	0.585	2.5	3.2	0.528	0.509
.50-95 Winchester Express	0.627	0.06	0.562	1.913	2.452	0.533	0.513
.50-100 Sharps straight	0.663	0.06	0.585	2.6	3.6	0.528	0.509
.50-100 Winchester	0.602	0.07	0.552	2.407	2.753	0.533	0.513
.50-110 Sharps straight	0.663	0.06	0.585	2.7	3.7	0.528	0.509
.50-110 Winchester	0.602	0.07	0.552	2.407	2.753	0.533	0.513

Cartridge Name	Rim Diameter	Rim Thickness	Head Diameter	Case Length	Overall Loaded Length	Diameter at Mouth	Bullet Diameter
50-140 Sharps straight	0.663	0.06	0.585	3.25	3.95	0.528	0.509
50-140 Winchester Express	0.663	0.06	0.565	3.25	3.95	0.528	0.512
500 S&W Special	0.56	0.059	0.53	1.295	1.692	0.53	0.5
500 S&W Magnum	0.56	0.059	0.53	1.6252	2.3	0.53	0.5
500 Nitro Express 3 in	0.6551	0.0402	0.5847	3	3.75	0.5319	0.5098
500 Nitro Express 3 1/4 in	0.6551	0.0402	0.5847	3	3.75	0.5319	0.5098
500 Nitro Express 3 3/4 in	0.6551	0.0402	0.5847	3.25	4	0.5319	0.5098
55-100 Maynard	0.718	0.065	0.59	1.94	2.5	0.582	0.551
577 Nitro Express	0.75	0.05	0.6618	3	3.7	0.6051	0.5839
58 Berdan Carbine	0.74	0.062	0.646	1.5	1.9	0.625	0.589
58 Berdan Musket	0.74	0.062	0.646	1.725	2.15	0.625	0.589
600 Nitro Express	0.8098	0.065	0.7	3	3.7	0.65	0.6201
700 Nitro Express	0.8898	0.085	0.7819	3.5	4.2	0.7299	0.7

RIMMED NECKED

Cartridge Name	Rim Diameter	Rim Thickness	Head Diameter	Length to Shoulder	Length to Neck	Case Length	Overall Loaded	Diameter at Mouth	Bullet Diameter
4.5x40Rmm Russian SPS	0.4459	0.0591	0.4469	1.175	1.299	1.523	5.2	0.2496	0.222
17 Hornet	0.35	0.065	0.2982	1.0471	1.1543	1.345	1.72	0.194	0.1725
218 Bee	0.408	0.065	0.3491	0.9233	1.0891	1.345	1.68	0.242	0.2245
219 Zipper	0.5059	0.063	0.422	1.36	1.621	1.937	2.259	0.252	0.2245
22 Winchester Centerfire	0.3484	0.0551	0.2972	0.7871	0.9843	1.3976	1.7126	0.2492	0.2217
22 Rem Jet Magnum	0.44	0.059	0.3795	0.5984	1.0883	1.288	1.659	0.251	0.2225
22 Hornet	0.35	0.065	0.2989	0.8527	1.0173	1.403	1.723	0.2425	0.2245
22 Savage Hi-Power	0.4921	0.063	4181	1.3791	1.6386	2.0472	2.5098	0.252	0.228
5.56X50Rmm Magnum	0.429	0.0551	0.3776	1.585	1.702	1.9685	2.4016	0.2551	0.2244
5.6x57mm RWS	0.5244	0.0551	0.4701	1.7469	1.9795	2.2323	2.7165	0.2795	0.2244
222 Rimmed	0.462	0.063	0.375	1.265	1.387	1.7	2.15	0.252	0.224
225 Winchester	0.473	0.049	0.4238	1.53	1.6865	1.93	2.5	0.26	0.2245
5.6x33Rmm Rook	0.366	0.065	0.325	1.008	1.112	1.311	1.646	0.247	0.222
6x58Rmm Forster	0.532	0.0551	0.471	1.752	1.9409	2.26	3.06	0.284	0.243
297/250 Rook Rifle	0.3551	0.048	0.2988	0.528	0.585	0.8201	1.202	0.2669	0.2512
25-20 Single Shot	0.378	0.055	0.315	1.099	1.19	1.63	1.9	0.275	0.257
25-20 Winchester	0.408	0.065	0.3492	0.8573	0.9527	1.33	1.592	0.2738	0.258
25-35 Winchester	0.506	0.063	0.4224	1.3799	1.5652	2.043	2.55	0.2816	0.258
25-36 Marlin	0.5	0.07	0.421	1.435	1.592	2.125	2.4375	0.277	0.257
256 Winchester Mag	0.44	0.06	0.369	0.9838	1.0728	1.281	1.59	0.285	0.257
6.5x48Rmm Sauer	0.495	0.06	0.435	N/A	1.543	1.878	2.43	0.284	0.264
6.5x53Rmm Mannlicher	0.5276	0.0492	0.452	1.6366	1.7717	2.1098	3.063	0.2972	0.2638
6.5x57Rmm Mauser	0.5244	0.0551	0.4693	1.752	1.9409	2.2323	3.2283	0.3012	0.2638
6.5x58Rmm Sauer	0.502	0.0453	0.437	N/A	1.8701	2.3032	3.07	0.298	0.2614
6.5x61Rmm Mauser	0.532	0.062	0.478	1.91	2.08	2.402	3.39	0.296	0.264
6.5x65Rmm RWS	0.5315	0.0591	0.4756	2.1201	2.3039	2.5591	3.3465	0.298	0.2638
6.5x68Rmm	0.5906	0.0689	0.5252	2.0386	2.3831	2.6575	3.4449	0.2992	0.2638
7-30 Waters	0.506	0.063	0.4215	1.5864	1.7332	2.04	2.55	0.3062	0.2845
7x57Rmm Mauser	0.5315	0.063	0.4744	1.7244	1.865	2.2441	3.0709	0.3248	0.2854
7x72Rmm	0.4862	0.0512	0.4272	2.0472	2.3622	2.8346	3.622	0.3118	0.2854
7x75Rmm Super Exp	not available at this time								
280 Flanged Nitro Express	0.6098	0.0598	0.539	2.1811	2.2831	2.611	3.4598	0.3201	0.287
30R Blaser	0.5315	0.0551	0.4803	2.2744	2.4079	2.6772	3.7402	0.3437	0.3091
30-30 Winchester	0.506	0.063	0.4215	1.4405	1.5621	2.0395	2.55	0.3301	0.309
30-40 Krag	0.545	0.064	0.4611	1.7251	1.8289	2.314	3.089	0.338	0.309

Cartridge Name	Rim Diameter	Rim Thickness	Head Diameter	Length to Shoulder	Length to Neck	Case Length	Overall Loaded	Diameter at Mouth	Bullet Diameter
.307 Winchester	0.506	0.063	0.4703	1.5598	1.7116	2.015	2.56	0.3435	0.309
.308 Marlin Express	0.506	0.063	0.4703	1.4601	1.6207	1.92	2.6	0.337	0.3085
.303 Savage	0.505	0.063	0.442	1.3509	1.4774	2.015	2.52	0.3322	0.311
.303 British	0.54	0.064	0.4601	1.7901	1.89	2.222	3.075	0.338	0.3125
375/303 Westley Richards	0.505	0.0642	0.458	2.094	2.154	2.488	3.5	0.343	0.3118
7.62x38Rmm Rev	0.4055	0.0492	0.3567	1.3386	1.3996	1.5276	1.5276	0.3032	0.3079
7.62x54Rmm Russian	0.5701	0.063	0.487	1.563	1.7441	2.115	3.0378	0.3358	0.3118
.32-20 Winchester	0.408	0.065	0.3535	0.8812	0.9389	1.315	1.592	0.3266	0.3125
.32 Winchester Special	0.506	0.063	0.4219	1.4461	1.5538	2.04	2.565	0.343	0.322
.32-20 Winchester	0.408	0.065	0.3535	0.8812	0.9389	1.315	1.592	0.3266	0.3125
.32-30 Remington Hepburn	0.437	0.06	0.378	1.329	1.43	1.64	2.01	0.332	0.312
.32-40 Remington Hepburn	0.534	0.06	0.455	1.444	1.645	2.11	2.5	0.333	0.308
.32-40 Bullard	0.51	0.075	0.453	0.936	1.27	1.844	2.25	0.332	0.315
8x48Rmm Sauer	0.495	0.06	0.435	N/A	1.543	1.878	2.58	0.344	0.3185
8x50Rmm Austrian Mann	0.5606	0.0551	0.4941	1.5032	1.7384	1.9882	2.9921	0.3512	0.3236
8x50Rmm Lebel	0.6299	0.0709	0.5421	1.4354	1.611	1.9882	3.063	0.3484	0.3268
8x50Rmm Siamese	0.552	0.07	0.491	1.454	1.614	1.973	2.968	0.349	0.3236
8x51Rmm Mauser	not available at this time								
8x52Rmm Siamese	0.6299	0.0709	0.5421	1.4354	1.611	1.9882	3.063	0.3484	0.3268
8.52.5Rmm Murata	0.5606	0.058	0.492	1.593	1.72	2.06	2.9	0.361	0.329
8x54Rmm Krag-Jorgensen	not available at this time								
8x56Rmm Hungarian M31	0.5591	0.0591	0.4941	1.4579	1.95	2.1949	3.0118	0.3583	0.3307
8x58Rmm Sauer	0.502	0.0433	4.35	N/A	1.791	2.303	3.709	0.3457	0.3185
8x60Rmm Port Guedes M86	0.626	0.0787	0.5453	1.5217	1.7421	2.2047	3.189	0.3543	0.323
8x60RJmm Mauser	0.5276	0.0551	0.4736	1.8984	2.0098	2.3622	3.2283	0.3539	0.3185
8x60RSmm Mauser	0.5276	0.0551	0.4736	1.8984	2.0047	2.3622	3.2913	0.3575	0.3236
8x65RJmm Brenneke	0.5244	0.0551	0.4705	2.0394	2.1965	2.5472	3.3858	0.3488	0.3185
8x65RSmm Brenneke	0.5244	0.0551	0.472	2.0394	2.1886	2.5591	3.449	0.3528	0.3236
8x72Rmm Sauer	0.4862	0.0512	0.4272	N/A	2.3622	2.8346	3.8583	0.3433	0.3185
8x75RSmm Brenneke	0.5256	0.0551	0.4685	2.6063	2.7189	2.937	3.7795	0.3575	0.3236
.33 Winchester	0.6098	0.0701	0.5079	1.6126	1.7362	2.1051	2.7949	0.3657	0.3386
.348 Winchester	0.61	0.07	0.553	1.6499	1.8041	2.255	2.795	0.3757	0.3495
.35 Winchester	0.5429	0.061	0.4614	2.0236	2.1	2.415	3.1752	0.3823	0.3591
.356 Winchester	0.506	0.063	N/A	1.5598	1.6505	2.015	2.56	0.388	0.3585
.38-40 Winchester	0.525	0.065	0.4695	0.9224	1.074	1.305	1.592	0.4167	0.4005
.38-45 Bullard	0.536	0.07	0.454	1.344	1.422	1.811	2.274	0.397	0.365
.38-56 Winchester	0.604	0.07	0.504	1.264	1.511	2.1	2.5	0.403	0.376
.38-70 Winchester	0.604	0.07	0.504	1.55	1.686	2.31	2.73	0.403	0.376
.38-72 Winchester	0.604	0.07	0.504	1.55	1.686	2.31	2.73	0.403	0.376
.38-90 Winchester Express	0.558	0.07	0.477	2.216	2.438	3.25	3.7	0.395	0.376
.360 No. 2 Nitro Express	0.631	0.065	0.539	2.127	2.4	3	3.85	0.393	0.357
9x57Rmm Mauser	0.5276	0.0551	0.4709	1.8165	1.8803	2.2362	3.189	0.387	0.3575
9.3x60Rmm Turkish Mauser	0.4862	0.0512	0.4295	N/A	1.9685	2.8346	3.3858	0.3866	0.3768
9.3x72Rmm Sauer	0.5256	0.0551	0.4685	2.3228	2.4213	2.9409	3.7205	0.3906	0.3661
9.3x74Rmm	0.5433	0.0551	0.5059	2.0551	2.1701	2.5472	3.3701	0.3961	0.3681
9.35x65Rmm Brenneke	0.624	0.0421	0.5409	2.2	2.4	2.7	3.6	0.4051	0.3748
.369 Nitro Express Purdey	0.583	0.0945	0.513	0.92	1.237	1.85	2.37	0.409	0.375
9.5x47Rmm	0.612	0.082	0.511	1.71	1.89	2.376	2.97	0.411	0.389
.40-50 Sharps necked	0.58	0.07	0.501	0.954	1.1	1.72	2.37	0.424	0.403
.40-60 Marlin	not available at this time								
.40-65 Winchester	not available at this time								
.40-60 Winchester	0.6299	0.0642	0.5059	1.2232	1.4453	1.8701	2.2551	0.4295	0.4059

rtridge Name	Rim Diameter	Rim Thickness	Head Diameter	Length to Shoulder	Length to Neck	Case Length	Overall Loaded	Diameter at Mouth	Bullet Diameter
)-70 Sharps necked	0.595	0.07	0.503	1.5	1.642	2.25	3.02	0.426	0.403
-70 Peabody What Cheer	0.662	0.07	0.581	0.843	1.315	1.75	2.812	0.428	0.408
)-70 Winchester	0.604	0.07	0.502	1.557	1.66	2.4	2.85	0.428	0.406
)-82 Winchester	0.6098	0.0701	0.5087	1.7681	1.9398	2.3902	2.765	0.4272	0.4075
)-90 Peabody What Cheer	0.659	0.07	0.586	1.277	1.635	2	3.37	0.433	0.408
)-90 Bullard	0.622	0.06	0.569	1.418	1.64	2.04	2.55	0.448	0.413
)-110 Winchester Express	0.651	0.07	0.543	2.433	2.565	3.25	3.63	0.428	0.404
0/350 Rigby	0.5299	0.05	0.4709	2.1	2.25	2.7512	3.6902	0.3819	0.3559
0-360 Westley Richards	0.513	0.06	0.47	2.12	2.28	2.75	3.59	0.375	0.358
.15x61Rmm Jarmann	0.615	0.078	0.548	1.455	1.565	2.4	3.06	0.43	0.403
.15x63Rmm Serbian Mauser	0.592	0.082	0.52	1.445	1.58	2.46	3.13	0.433	0.411
.4mm Italian Rev	0.5197	0.065	0.4646	0.5118	0.5598	0.7795	1.189	0.4276	0.422
.4x47Rmm Ital Vetterli M70	0.622	0.06	0.54	1.245	1.63	1.87	2.46	0.437	0.43
.5x47Rmm Stahl	0.591	0.0945	0.513	1.11	1.373	1.846	2.38	0.445	0.411
.6x47Rmm Russ Berdan Car	0.622	0.082	0.519	1.323	1.466	1.894	2.597	0.452	0.429
.75x58Rmm Russ. Berdan	0.637	0.08	0.567	1.574	1.79	2.24	2.95	0.449	0.43
.75x63mm Mauser	0.467	0.0512	0.493	2.087	2.11	2.473	3.229	0.447	0.424
4-40 Winchester	0.525	0.065	0.4711	0.9275	1.0169	1.305	1.61	0.443	0.427
4-60 Sharps necked	0.63	0.07	0.515	1.27	1.366	1.875	2.55	0.464	0.447
4-77 Sharps necked	0.625	0.07	0.516	1.5	1.642	2.25	3.05	0.464	0.447
4-90 Remington Special	0.628	0.075	0.52	1.74	1.886	2.44	3.08	0.466	0.445
4-90 Peabody What Cheer	0.67	0.08	0.582	1.327	1.657	2.312	3.375	0.465	0.446
4-90 Sharps Special necked	0.625	0.07	0.516	1.727	1.857	2.427	3.692	0.467	0.447
4-90 Sharps necked	0.625	0.07	0.516	1.815	2.03	2.0625	3.3	0.467	0.447
4-100 Sharps necked	0.625	0.065	0.516	1.958	2.086	2.825	3.625	0.467	0.447
x42Rmm Bel Albini Carb M71	0.677	0.086	0.587	1.45	1.522	1.693	2.406	0.476	0.441
x50Rmm Bel Albini M70/76	0.678	0.0945	0.58	1.76	1.82	2	2.6	0.472	0.435
x51Rmm Bel Comblain M71	0.673	0.0945	0.575	1.576	1.678	2	2.764	0.479	0.448
x59Rmm French Gras	0.658	0.075	0.544	1.57	1.668	2.34	3.02	0.458	0.442
x60Rmm Murata	0.632	0.08	0.542	1.585	1.848	2.36	3.13	0.465	0.432
.15x42Rmm Aus Werndl Car	0.619	0.078	0.517	1.25	1.406	1.614	2.322	0.468	0.452
.15x58Rmm Aus Werndl M77	0.617	0.0945	0.545	1.433	1.577	2.285	3.02	0.466	0.441
.15x58Rmm Spanish Rem	0.64	0.082	0.52	1.53	1.73	2.25	2.97	0.458	0.439
.15x60Rmm Mauser	0.5906	0.0945	0.5157	1.4331	1.5768	2.376	3.0709	0.4665	0.4488
.3x46Rmm Dutch Beaumont Car	0.666	0.06	0.581	1.27	1.46	1.81	2.363	0.478	0.445
.3x50Rmm Dutch Beaumont M71	0.666	0.06	0.581	1.27	1.417	1.968	2.66	0.478	0.445
.3x52Rmm Dutch Beaumont M71/78	0.666	0.06	0.581	1.344	1.479	2.04	2.771	0.478	0.445
.4x53Rmm Brazilian Comblain M89	0.683	0.0945	0.587	1.791	1.922	2.13	2.66	0.494	0.452
.43x50Rmm Egyptian	0.666	0.065	0.581	1.2	1.31	1.94	2.73	0.479	0.448
.43x55Rmm Turkish	0.668	0.065	0.582	1.45	1.66	2.3	3.12	0.474	0.447
5-75 Winchester Centennial	0.624	0.065	0.562	1.104	1.27	1.882	2.283	0.479	0.458
5-100 Remington (necked)	0.645	0.065	0.558	1.892	2.05	2.63	3.36	0.49	0.458
5-125 Winchester Express	0.601	0.065	0.533	2.075	2.548	3.25	3.625	0.47	0.458
50/400 Nitro Express 2 3/8 in	0.615	0.04	0.548	1.674	1.797	2.375	2.92	0.43	0.406
50/400 Nitro Express 3 in	0.6248	0.065	0.548	2.1	2.4	3	3.75	0.4402	0.4098
50/400 Nitro Express 3 1/4 in	0.624	0.421	0.5449	2	2.3	3.25	3.95	0.435	0.4098
50/400 Jeffery	0.6248	0.065	0.548	2.1	2.4	3	3.75	0.4402	0.4098
50 No.2 Nitro Express 3 1/2 in	0.6598	0.0799	0.565	2.85	3.05	3.5	4.3299	0.4819	0.4579
00/450 No.1/2 Black Pdr Express	0.66	0.07	0.577	1.85	1.985	2.75	3.38	0.485	0.458
77/450 Martini Henry	0.7598	0.05	0.672	1.4059	1.6209	2.326	3.2	0.5051	0.465
00/465 Nitro Express	0.6551	N/A	0.574	2.2	2.6	3.25	3.9	0.4909	0.4681
70 Nitro Express	0.6551	0.0402	0.5728	2.4	2.5	3.25	3.9799	0.5039	0.474

Cartridge Name	Rim Diameter	Rim Thickness	Head Diameter	Length to Shoulder	Length to Neck	Case Length	Overall Loaded	Diameter at Mouth	Bullet Diameter
.475 Turnbull	0.602	0.07	0.552	1.725	1.8	2.2	2.78	0.503	0.475
.475 No.2 Jeffery 3 1/2 in	0.6748	0.0799	0.5799	2.7248	2.9248	3.5	4.3299	0.5138	0.4878
.476 Westley Richards	0.643	0.035	0.57	2.3	2.4	3	3.77	0.508	0.476
.50 Rem Army	0.665	0.05	0.565	0.538	0.684	0.875	1.24	0.532	0.508
.50-115 Bullard Express	0.619	0.068	0.535	1.6	1.759	2.19	2.56	0.547	0.512
577/500 Nitro Express 3 1/8 in	0.717	0.05	0.645	2.288	2.414	3.13	3.74	0.526	0.5
577/500 No.2 Black Pdr Express	0.726	0.05	0.641	1.959	2.064	2.83	3.4	0.538	0.507
.577 Snider	0.75	0.05	0.665	1.361	1.461	2	2.4701	0.6032	0.574
.70-140 Winchester	0.8839	0.07	0.811	1.59	1.725	2.2	2.65	0.725	0.705

SEMI-RIMMED STRAIGHT

Cartridge Name	Rim Diameter	Rim Thickness	Extractor Groove Diameter	Head Diameter	Case Length	Overall Loaded Length	Outside Diameter at Mouth	Bullet Diameter
.25 Auto	0.3012	0.043	0.25	0.2764	0.6122	0.9055	0.2756	0.251
.32 Auto	0.3583	0.05	0.3091	0.3366	0.6772	0.9843	0.3354	0.312
.32 Winchester Self-Loading	0.3902	0.05	0.3402	0.3516	1.2902	1.8799	0.3469	0.322
.38 Auto	0.4059	0.05	0.3449	0.3839	0.9	1.2799	0.3839	0.356
.38 Super Auto	0.4059	0.05	0.3449	0.3839	0.9	1.2799	0.3839	0.356
.35 Winchester Self-Loading	0.4051	0.05	0.3551	0.3811	1.1539	1.65	0.3772	0.352
.351 Winchester Self-Loading	0.41	0.035	0.355	0.3804	1	1.9	0.377	0.352
.401 Winchester Self-Loading	0.4598	0.06	0.4059	0.4331	1.5	2.0051	0.4327	0.407

SEMI-RIMMED NECKED

Cartridge Name	Rim Diameter	Rim Thickness	Extractor Groove Diameter	Head Diameter	Length to Shoulder	Length to Neck	Case Length	Overall Loaded Length	Outside Diameter at Mouth	Bullet Diameter
.220 Swift	0.473	0.034	0.426	0.449	1.7227	1.9057	2.205	2.68	0.26	0.224
.25 NAA	0.337	0.046	0.297	0.3369	0.5406	0.59	0.745	0.96	0.276	0.251
6.5x50SRmm Arisaka	0.4756	0.059	0.4094	0.4508	1.5323	1.7087	2.0079	2.9921	0.2902	0.261
6.5x53.5SRmm Daudeteau	0.5275	0.066	0.4507	0.4893	1.592	1.789	2.1	3.015	0.293	0.26
.280 Ross	0.5598	0.06	0.4902	0.535	2.1811	2.283	2.611	3.4598	0.3201	0.287
.32 NAA	0.374	0.045	0.329	0.3739	0.52	0.5629	0.68	0.984	0.3365	0.312
7.7x58SRmm Arisaka	0.5	0.042	0.42	0.472	1.818	1.925	2.28	3.338	0.34	0.313
12.7x81SRmm Breda	0.77	0.085	0.643	0.722	2.57	2.679	3.184	4.226	0.545	0.514
13x92SRmm Mauser TUF	0.911	0.085	0.784	0.821	2.5	3.145	3.612	5.25	0.571	0.522

REBATED STRAIGHT

Cartridge Name	Rim Diameter	Rim Thickness	Extractor Groove Diameter	Head Diameter	Case Length	Overall Loaded Length	Outside Diameter at Mouth	Bullet Diameter
.41 AE	0.3921	0.05	0.3461	0.435	0.8661	1.151	0.4343	0.41
50AE	0.515	0.045	0.46	0.543	1.285	1.595	0.529	0.502

REBATED RIM NECKED

Cartridge Name	Rim Diameter	Rim Thickness	Extractor Groove Diameter	Head Diameter	Length to Shoulder	Length to Neck	Case Length	Overall Loaded Length	Outside Diameter at Mouth	Bullet Diameter
6.5-.284 Norma	0.4728	0.054	0.4091	0.5008	1.774	1.905	2.17	3.228	0.2969	0.264
.284 Winchester	0.4728	0.054	0.4091	0.5008	1.7748	1.885	2.17	2.8	0.3201	0.284
10.75x63mm Mauser	0.467	0.051	0.4173	0.493	2.087	2.11	2.473	3.229	0.447	0.424
.425 Westley Richards	0.467	0.05	0.401	0.543	1.812	2.115	2.64	3.3	0.456	0.435

Cartridge Name	Rim Diameter	Rim Thickness	Extractor Groove Diameter	Head Diameter	Length to Shoulder	Length to Neck	Case Length	Overall Loaded Length	Outside Diameter at Mouth	Bullet Diameter
.440 Cor-Bon	0.514	0.045	0.46	0.538	1	1.007	1.285	1.58	0.461	0.429
11.2x60mm Schuler	0.465	0.05	0.4091	0.5138	1.468	1.576	2.374	3.031	0.4665	0.44
11.2x72mm Schuler	0.468	0.05	0.4092	0.535	2.411	2.491	2.815	3.592	0.467	0.44
.458 SOCOM	0.473	0.054	0.4091	0.538	1.187	1.23	1.575	2.015	0.486	0.458
.500 Jeffery	0.5752	0.052	0.5421	0.6189	2.268	2.422	2.75	3.468	0.5358	0.5098
12.5x70mm Schuler	0.5708	0.051	0.5167	0.6193	2.323	2.413	2.756	3.464	0.5374	0.51

BELTED STRAIGHT

Cartridge Name	Rim Diameter	Rim Thickness	Extractor Groove Diameter	Head Diameter	Case Length	Overall Loaded Length	Outside Diameter at Mouth	Bullet Diameter
.450 Marlin	0.5319	0.05	0.4752	0.5319	2.09	2.55	0.4811	0.458
.458 Winchester Magnum	0.532	0.05	0.475	0.532	2.5	3.34	0.4811	0.458
.458 Lott	0.5319	0.05	0.475	0.532	2.8	3.6	0.4811	0.458
.495 A-Square	0.5791	0.063	0.4949	0.6035	2.8	3.6	0.542	0.51

BELTED NECKED

Cartridge Name	Rim Diameter	Rim Thickness	Extractor Groove Diameter	Head Diameter	Length to Shoulder	Length to Neck	Case Length	Overall Loaded Length	Outside Diameter at Mouth	Bullet Diameter
.224 Weatherby Magnum	0.4295	0.05	0.3689	0.4295	1.5358	1.6154	1.9228	2.3299	0.252	0.224
.240 Weatherby Magnum	0.5315	0.065	0.46	0.53	1.64	1.84	2.05	2.8	0.252	0.224
.240 H&H Magnum	0.4681	0.043	0.4118	0.4772	1.9	2.1	2.5	3.25	0.2799	0.2449
.244 H&H Magnum	0.5319	0.05	0.4701	0.5339	2.33	2.51	2.79	3.6	0.2799	0.2449
.257 Weatherby Magnum	0.5315	0.051	0.04571	0.5315	2.074	2.153	2.549	3.17	0.285	0.257
6.5mm Remington Magnum	0.5319	0.05	0.4752	0.5319	1.7	1.91	2.17	2.8	0.298	0.264
.26 Belted Rimless NE (BSA)	0.53	0.05	0.4752	0.5339	1.91	2.106	2.39	3.24	0.306	0.267
.264 Winchester Magnum	0.532	0.05	0.475	0.532	2.04	2.25	2.5	3.34	0.298	0.264
.270 Weatherby Magnum	0.5315	0.051	0.4571	0.5118	2.074	2.153	2.549	3.29	0.3051	0.277
7x61 S&H Super	0.5315	0.051	0.4803	0.5315	2	0.208	2.4	3.27	0.3173	0.284
7mm Weatherby Magnum	0.5315	0.051	0.4571	0.5118	2.069	2.152	2.549	3.36	0.3118	0.284
7mm Remington Magnum	0.5319	0.05	0.4752	0.5319	2.04	2.23	2.5	3.29	0.315	0.284
7mm Shooting Times Western	0.5319	0.05	0.4752	0.5319	2.39	2.57	2.85	3.65	0.3169	0.284
.275 H&H Magnum	0.5319	0.05	0.4701	0.5339	2.1	2.2	2.5	3.43	0.3248	0.287
.300 H&H Magnum	0.5319	0.05	0.4752	0.5339	2.105	2.48	2.85	3.6	0.3382	0.309
.300 Winchester Magnum	0.532	0.05	0.475	0.532	2.196	2.365	2.62	3.34	0.3397	0.308
.300 Weatherby Magnum	0.5315	0.051	0.4571	0.5118	2.347	2.435	2.825	3.56	0.337	0.308
.30-378 Weatherby Magnum	0.5791	0.063	0.4949	0.6035	2.409	2.493	2.913	3.75	0.337	0.308
8mm Remington Magnum	0.5319	0.05	0.4752	0.5319	2.389	2.53	2.85	3.6	0.3541	0.323
.338 Winchester Magnum	0.532	0.05	0.475	0.532	2.04	2.17	2.5	3.34	0.369	0.338
.338 A-Square	0.5791	0.063	0.4949	0.6035	2.3	2.433	2.85	3.67	0.366	0.338
.338-378 Weatherby Magnum	0.5791	0.063	0.4949	0.6035	2.345	2.557	2.913	3.75	0.3689	0.338
.340 Weatherby Magnum	0.5315	0.051	0.4571	0.5315	2.431	2.505	2.859	3.563	0.402	0.375
.350 Remington Magnum	0.5319	0.05	0.4752	0.5319	1.7	1.815	2.17	2.8	0.3882	0.358
.375 Holland & Holland Magnum	0.5319	0.05	0.4752	0.5339	2.41	2.497	2.85	3.6	0.402	0.375
.375 A-Square	0.5791	0.063	0.4949	0.6035	2.425	2.529	2.85	3.67	0.404	0.375
.375 Weatherby Magnum	0.5315	0.051	0.4571	0.5315	2.431	2.506	2.856	3.563	0.402	0.375
400/375 H&H Magnum	0.466	0.06	0.406	0.47	1.67	1.855	2.5	3	0.395	0.375
.378 Weatherby Magnum	0.5791	0.063	0.4949	0.6035	2.4	2.48	2.913	3.655	0.4032	0.375
.400 H&H Magnum	0.5319	0.05	0.4752	0.5339	1.98	2.166	2.846	3.543	0.4409	0.411
.416 Weatherby Magnum	0.6035	0.063	0.4949	0.6035	2.388	2.466	2.913	3.75	0.4441	0.416

Cartridge Name	Rim Diameter	Rim Thickness	Extractor Groove Diameter	Head Diameter	Length to Shoulder	Length to Neck	Case Length	Overall Loaded Length	Outside Diameter at Mouth	Bullet Diameter
.416 Remington Magnum	0.532	0.05	0.475	0.532	2.389	2.41	2.85	3.6	0.447	0.416
.460 Weatherby Magnum	0.5791	0.063	0.4949	0.6035	2.378	2.448	2.913	3.75	0.4858	0.458
.465 H&H Magnum	0.5791	0.063	0.4949	0.6035	2.106	2.32	2.897	3.543	0.4941	0.468
.500 A-Square	0.5791	0.063	0.4949	0.6035	2.485	2.507	2.9	3.74	0.526	0.51

RIMLESS STRAIGHT

Cartridge Name	Rim Diameter	Rim Thickness	Extractor Groove Diameter	Head Diameter	Case Length	Overall Loaded Length	Outside Diameter at Mouth	Bullet Diameter
2.7mm Kolibri Auto	0.14	0.015	0.11	0.14	0.37	0.43	0.139	0.107
3mm Kolibri	0.152	0.015	0.12	0.15	0.324	0.433	0.133	0.122
4.25mm Liliput	0.198	0.025	0.171	0.198	0.47	0.56	0.198	0.167
.30 Pedersen	0.311	0.04	0.3	0.336	0.777	1.08	0.335	0.307
.30 Carbine	0.3598	0.05	0.3098	0.3567	1.2902	1.6799	0.3358	0.0309
7.62x17mm Type 64	0.331	0.049	0.3091	0.3366	0.669	0.984	0.3334	0.307
7.62x45mm Indo Police	0.3598	0.05	0.3098	0.3567	1.759	2.1489	0.3358	0.309
7.63mm Mannlicher	0.334	0.04	0.295	0.332	0.84	1.12	0.331	0.308
7.65mm Roth-Steyr	0.335	0.04	0.293	0.335	0.51	0.84	0.332	0.301
7.65mm French Long	0.3366	0.41	0.2953	0.3366	0.7795	1.2	0.3102	0.31
8mm Roth-Steyr	0.356	0.04	0.3248	0.355	0.74	1.14	0.353	0.329
.35 S&W Auto	0.348	0.04	0.295	0.345	0.67	0.97	0.345	0.309
.380 Auto	0.3752	0.05	0.3248	0.3752	0.6823	0.9843	0.3752	0.355
9x18mm Police	0.374	0.049	0.3248	0.3886	0.7087	1	0.3811	0.355
9mm Ultra	0.374	0.049	0.3248	0.3886	0.7087	1	0.3811	0.355
9mm Luger	0.3921	0.05	0.3461	0.3909	0.7539	1.1689	0.3799	0.355
9mm Steyr	0.3819	0.049	0.3425	0.3819	0.9134	1.303	0.3787	0.355
9mm Glisenti	0.393	0.05	0.3461	0.392	0.75	1.15	0.38	0.355
9x21mm	0.3921	0.05	0.3461	0.3909	0.8327	1.1713	0.3791	0.355
9x21mm Russian SP-10	0.3921	0.05	0.3461	0.3909	0.8327	1.1713	0.3791	0.355
9x23mm Winchester	0.3941	0.05	0.3469	0.3921	0.9	1.3	0.3882	0.355
9mm Largo	0.3921	0.046	0.342	0.39	0.91	1.32	0.375	0.355
9mm Mauser	0.39	0.05	0.3161	0.389	0.961	1.38	0.376	0.355
9mm Winchester Mag	0.3941	0.05	0.3469	0.3921	0.9	1.3	0.3882	0.355
9mm Browning Long	0.4016	0.049	0.3346	0.3827	0.7953	1.1024	0.3811	0.3579
9x18mm Makarov	0.3917	0.049	0.3366	0.3917	0.7126	0.9843	0.3902	0.365
9.8mm Auto Colt	0.405	0.05	0.352	0.404	0.912	0.267	0.404	0.375
.40 S&W	0.424	0.055	0.3469	0.424	0.85	1.135	0.4228	0.4
10mm Auto	0.4272	0.055	0.3484	0.4256	0.9921	1.2598	0.4213	0.4
.44 Auto Mag	0.4728	0.054	0.4094	0.4713	1.298	1.6	0.4591	0.4291
.45 GAP	0.4701	0.0488	0.4	0.476	0.7598	1.1374	0.4728	0.452
.45 Auto	0.48	0.035	0.4	0.476	0.65	1.275	0.473	0.452
.45 Winchester Mag	0.4799	0.0488	0.415	0.4764	1.198	1.5752	0.4728	0.452
.45 Rem Thompson	0.471	0.049	0.415	0.472	1.12	1.45	0.47	0.452
.450 Bushmaster	0.4728	0.054	0.4091	0.4709	1.703	2.25	0.476	0.458
.455 Webley Auto	0.5	0.045	0.435	0.474	0.93	1.23	0.474	0.455
.475 Wildey Mag	0.47	0.06	0.33	0.5	1.198	1.6	0.498	0.475
.50 GI	0.48	0.05	0.425	0.526	0.899	1.221	0.526	0.5

RIMLESS NECKED

Cartridge Name	Rim Diameter	Rim Thickness	Extractor Groove Diameter	Head Diameter	Length to Shoulder	Length to Neck	Case Length	Overall Loaded Length	Outside Diameter at Mouth	Bullet Diameter
.6x30mm	0.315	0.043	0.2677	0.3157	0.9063	1.025	1.2	1.5157	0.2091	0.1831
17 Fireball	0.378	0.045	0.332	0.3759	1.065	1.204	1.41	1.83	0.2039	0.1725
17 Remington	0.378	0.045	0.332	0.3759	1.3511	1.535	1.796	2.15	0.199	0.1725
.85mm British	0.376	0.041	0.3327	0.3759	1.438	1.56	1.925	2.455	0.22	0.197
204 Ruger	0.378	0.045	0.332	0.3764	1.538	1.65	1.85	2.26	0.2311	0.2047
.45x18mm Soviet	0.3	0.043	0.2551	0.3	0.4752	0.5512	0.7087	0.9843	0.2457	0.2213
.45x39mm Soviet	0.3937	0.06	0.3386	0.3937	1.181	1.338	1.568	2.244	0.2476	0.2205
.66x39mm Russian MPS	0.4459	0.059	0.3761	0.4469	1.175	1.299	1.523	5.2	0.2496	0.222
22 PPC	0.4449	0.059	0.378	0.4433	1.074	1.23	1.515	2.19	0.25	0.224
.6x33mm Rook	0.327	0.036	0.27	0.325	0.991	1.11	1.311	1.646	0.247	0.222
.6x39mm Russian	0.4469	0.06	0.3764	0.4469	1.063	1.267	1.52	1.917	0.2476	0.223
.56x50mm Magnum	0.378	0.045	0.3323	0.3764	1.585	1.702	1.97	2.413	0.2551	0.2245
.6x57mm RWS	0.4705	0.051	0.4134	0.4685	1.752	1.984	2.232	2.716	0.2795	0.2245
.6x61mm vom Hofe SE	0.4803	0.059	0.4134	0.4803	1.732	2.089	2.401	3.149	0.263	0.228
221 Fireball	0.378	0.045	0.332	0.3759	1.07	1.197	1.4	1.83	0.253	0.224
222 Remingtom	0.378	0.045	0.332	0.3759	1.26	1.387	1.7	2.13	0.253	0.224
222 Remington Magnum	0.378	0.045	0.332	0.3754	1.46	1.586	1.85	2.28	0.253	0.224
223 Remington	0.378	0.049	0.332	0.3754	1.438	1.557	1.76	2.26	0.253	0.224
.56x45mm NATO	0.378	0.045	0.3327	0.3759	1.4379	1.5594	1.76	2.2598	0.2512	0.224
.7x28mm FN	0.3071	0.05	0.2598	0.313	0.9114	0.9555	1.1378	1.5945	0.2512	0.224
.8x21mm Chinese					not available at this time					0.228
.8x42mm Chinese	0.411	0.056	0.3402	0.411	1.345	1.475	1.655	2.396	0.2579	0.228
22-250 Remington	0.473	0.034	0.409	0.4668	1.514	1.663	1.912	2.35	0.254	0.224
223 Winchester Short Mag	0.5311	0.054	0.4799	0.5559	1.15	1.405	1.67	2.36	0.272	0.224
236 U.S. Navy	0.448	0.05	0.3917	0.445	1.733	1.896	2.35	3.11	0.278	0.244
242 Rimless Nitro Express	0.465	0.06	0.403	0.465	2	2.165	2.38	3.2	0.281	0.253
243 Winchester	0.472	0.054	0.409	0.4703	1.56	1.8	2.045	2.71	0.275	0.243
243 Winchester Short Mag	0.5311	0.054	0.4799	0.5559	1.15	1.39	1.67	2.359	0.287	0.243
244 Remington	0.473	0.054	0.409	0.4703	1.559	1.8	2.045	2.71	0.276	0.243
6mm PPC	0.4449	0.059	0.378	0.4433	1.074	1.21	1.515	2.19	0.2685	0.243
6mm Remington Bench Rest	0.473	0.054	0.409	0.4703	1.075	1.24	1.5	2.2	0.2705	0.243
6mm Norma Bench Rest	0.4728	0.054	0.409	0.4709	1.075	1.24	1.56	2.44	0.2705	0.243
6 mm Remington	0.473	0.037	0.408	0.4711	1.725	1.88	2.233	2.825	0.276	0.243
6x45mm	0.378	0.045	0.322	0.3759	1.438	1.538	1.76	2.26	0.269	0.243
6x47mm Swiss Match	0.4728	0.054	0.4091	0.4705	1.36	1.52	1.85	2.6	0.2705	0.243
6x57mm Mauser	0.476	0.051	0.4134	0.476	1.762	1.94	2.23	2.95	0.284	0.243
6x58mm Forster	0.468	0.051	0.4134	0.47	1.762	1.94	2.26	3.08	0.284	0.243
25 Remington	0.422	0.05	0.3579	0.422	1.498	1.63	2.05	2.525	0.2858	0.259
25 Winchester Super Short Mag	0.535	0.054	0.4799	0.555	1.15	1.39	1.67	2.36	0.299	0.257
250 Savage	0.473	0.049	0.409	0.4668	1.511	1.6377	1.912	2.515	0.2856	0.258
25-'06 Remington	0.473	0.049	0.409	0.4698	1.948	2,186	2.494	3.25	0.29	0.257
257 Roberts	0.473	0.049	0.409	0.4711	1.73	1.91	2.233	2.775	0.29	0.257
.53 Lazzeroni Scramjet	0.53	0.065	0.46	0.53	2.3	2.5	2.8	3.575	0.289	0.257
.260 Remington	0.4728	0.054	0.409	0.4709	1.56	1.77	2.035	2.8	0.2969	0.264
6.5mm Grendel	0.4469	0.059	0.378	0.443	1.145	1.28	1.515	2.25	0.292	0.264
6.5mm Creedmoor	0.473	0.055	0.409	0.4703	1.49	1.634	1.92	2.825	0.295	0.264
6.5x47mm Lapua	0.4728	0.054	0.4081	0.47	1.405	1.551	1.85	2.8	0.275	0.264
6.5x52mm Mann. Carcano	0.4508	0.051	0.3917	0.4492	1.622	1.7701	2.067	3.0118	0.2972	0.2677
6.5x54mm Mann Schoenauer	0.4535	0.041	0.3819	0.4516	1.645	1.795	2.112	3.063	0.2949	0.2638

Cartridge Name	Rim Diameter	Rim Thickness	Extractor Groove Diameter	Head Diameter	Length to Shoulder	Length to Neck	Case Length	Overall Loaded Length	Outside Diameter at Mouth	Bullet Diameter
6.5x54mm Mauser	0.4646	0.06	0.4016	0.4705	1.437	1.69	1.126	2.677	0.2988	0.264
6.5x55mm Swedish Mauser	0.4803	0.059	0.4134	0.4803	1.71	1.855	2.165	3.149	0.296	0.264
6.5x57mm Mauser	0.4705	0.051	0.4134	0.4685	1.75	1.94	2.23	3.228	0.3012	0.264
6.5x58mm Mauser	0.4646	0.6	0.4016	0.4705	1.674	1.912	2.28	3.248	0.3032	0.264
6.5x58mm Port. Vergueiro	0.4646	0.059	0.4016	0.4705	1.674	1.912	2.283	3.248	0.3032	0.2638
6.5x61mm Mauser	0.479	0.08	0.42	0.477	1.913	2.058	2.402	3.228	0.296	0.264
6.5x65mm RWS	0.4705	0.051	0.4134	0.474	2.12	2.303	2.559	3.346	0.298	0.264
6.5x68mm	0.5118	0.055	0.4409	0.5236	2.037	2.38	2.657	3.405	0.2992	0.264
.270 Winchester	0.473	0.049	0.409	0.4698	1.948	2.155	2.54	3.34	0.308	0.277
.270 Winchester Short Magnum	0.535	0.054	0.48	0.555	1.664	1.823	2.1	2.86	0.314	0.277
6.8mm SPC	0.422	0.049	0.358	0.4207	1.3	1.41	1.686	2.26	0.306	0.277
.275 Rigby	0.4748	0.043	0.415	0.474	1.724	1.864	2.24	3.07	0.324	0.284
.276 Enfield Pattern 13	0.521	0.049	0.4	0.528	1.765	1.924	2.35	3.25	0.321	0.284
.276 Pedersen	0.47	0.05	0.4091	0.467	1.616	1.84	2.07	2.85	0.315	0.284
.280 British	0.473	0.045	0.4091	0.47	1.22	1.41	1.71	2.53	0.313	0.284
7mm BR Remington	0.473	0.054	0.409	0.4703	1.075	1.206	1.52	2.2	0.3085	0.284
7x57mm Meunier	0.542	0.051	0.468	0.532	1.812	1.967	2.242	3.171	0.335	0.284
7x57mm Mauser	0.4764	0.045	0.4213	0.4728	1.726	1.866	2.244	3.07	0.3248	0.284
7x64mm Brenneke	0.4705	0.051	0.4134	0.4665	2.027	2.1799	2.519	3.307	0.313	0.284
7x66mm vom Hofe SE	0.5118	0.051	0.4528	0.5453	2.11	2.264	2.598	3.3071	0.3217	0.284
7x73mm vom Hofe SE	0.533	0.05	0.448	0.527	2.14	2.48	2.87	3.88	0.315	0.284
7mm-08 Remington	0.4728	0.054	0.4091	0.4709	1.56	1.75	2.04	2.8	0.315	0.284
7mm Nambu	0.358	0.042	0.311	0.351	0.57	0.62	0.78	1.051	0.296	0.2795
7mm Dakota	0.5429	0.05	0.487	0.545	1.98	2.167	2.5	3.5299	0.314	0.284
.280 Jeffery	0.538	0.05	0.501	0.542	1.96	2.18	2.5	3.45	0.317	0.288
.280 Remington	0.473	0.049	0.409	0.47	1.999	2.199	2.54	3.33	0.315	0.284
.280 Ackley Improved	0.473	0.049	0.409	0.47	2.099	2.182	2.54	3.33	0.315	0.284
7mm Winchester Short Magnum	0.535	0.054	0.48	0.555	1.701	1.8565	2.1	2.86	0.321	0.284
7mm Rem. Short Action U.M.	0.5339	0.05	0.4752	0.5512	1.538	1.724	2.035	2.825	0.3201	0.284
7mm Remington Ultra Magnum	0.534	0.05	0.475	0.55	2.387	2.563	2.85	3.6	0.322	0.284
7mm Canadian Mag	0.532	0.05	0.487	0.544	2.34	2.545	2.83	3.6	0.322	0.284
7.21 Lazzeroni Firebird	0.5811	0.065	0.5098	0.5799	2.311	2.516	2.809	3.63	0.3209	0.284
.400 DMP	0.4705	0.051	0.4134	0.4665	2.027	2.1799	2.519	3.307	0.313	0.284
7x33mm Sako	0.3937	0.05	0.3465	0.3909	1.05	1.145	1.31	1.749	0.311	0.284
7.62x39mm Russian SP-3	0.4469	0.059	0.3764	0.4449	1.161	1.295	1.484	2.165	0.3386	0.312
7.62x41 Russian SP-4	0.4469	0.059	0.3764	0.4449	1.361	1.468	1.614	1.677	0.3386	0.312
7.62x63mm Russian PZAM	0.4469	0.051	0.3764	0.4469	1.82	1.925	2.48	3.062	0.4366	0.312
7.65mm Luger	0.3929	0.048	0.3461	0.3909	0.6134	0.6937	0.85	1.175	0.3319	0.309
7.35mm Italian Carcano	0.449	0.045	0.3917	0.445	1.6	1.77	2.01	2.98	0.323	0.298
7.5x54mm French MAS	0.482	0.054	0.421	0.48	1.75	1.853	2.11	2.99	0.34	0.308
7.5x55mm Swiss GP11	0.498	0.049	0.4055	0.4961	1.7547	1.856	2.189	3.0591	0.3347	0.3043
7.5x53.5mm Swiss GP1890	0.5276	0.067	0.4508	0.4894	1.592	1.789	2.102	3.0157	0.2933	0.2598
7.5x57mm French M1924	0.4705	0.051	0.4134	0.4701	1.819	1.93	2.244	3.228	0.3539	0.308
7.62x25mm Tokarev	0.3917	0.052	0.3406	0.387	0.7717	0.8283	0.9843	1.385	0.3343	0.311
7.62x39mm Soviet	0.4469	0.059	0.3764	0.4469	1.2	1.299	1.523	2.2	0.3386	0.312
7.62x45mm Czech	0.4449	0.059	0.3819	0.4449	1.425	1.505	1.771	2.362	0.3409	0.308
7.62x51mm NATO	0.473	0.054	0.409	0.4703	1.56	1.714	2.015	2.8	0.3435	0.309
7.63x25mm Mauser	0.3929	0.05	0.3437	0.3882	0.7591	0.8307	0.9902	1.3811	0.3331	0.309
7.65x53mm Mauser	0.4744	0.04	0.4094	0.4728	1.7559	1.858	2.11	2.992	0.3457	0.312
7.7x58mm Arisaka	0.474	0.042	0.42	0.472	1.818	1.925	2.28	3.13	0.338	0.31
7.82 Lazzeroni Warbird	0.5811	0.065	0.5098	0.5799	2.311	2.496	2.809	3.63	0.3449	0.308
.30 Borchardt	0.39	0.05	0.3437	0.385	0.7591	0.8307	0.9902	1.34	0.331	0.307

Cartridge Name	Rim Diameter	Rim Thickness	Extractor Groove Diameter	Head Diameter	Length to Shoulder	Length to Neck	Case Length	Overall Loaded Length	Outside Diameter at Mouth	Bullet Diameter
Remington	0.422	0.049	0.358	0.4207	1.498	1.578	2.05	2.525	0.3317	0.307
Remington AR	0.473	0.054	0.4091	0.5008	1.068	1.225	1.53	2.26	0.341	0.308
Thompson/Center	0.4728	0.054	0.4091	0.47	1.512	1.622	1.92	2.645	0.337	0.308
'03 U.S.	0.4728	0.045	0.4091	0.4709	2	2.168	2.562	3.326	0.3398	0.308
-'06 Springfield	0.473	0.049	0.409	0.4698	1.948	2.108	2.494	3.34	0.3397	0.308
8 Winchester	0.473	0.054	0.409	0.4703	1.5598	1.711	2.015	2.8	0.3435	0.308
0 Savage	0.473	0.049	0.409	0.4706	1.558	1.65	1.87	2.6	0.339	0.309
0 Ruger Compact Magnum	0.5339	0.05	0.4752	0.532	1.643	1.795	2.1	2.825	0.34	0.308
0 Pegasus	0.58	0.055	0.5	0.5797	2.45	2.66	2.99	3.75	0.338	0.308
0 Olympic Super Short Mag	0.535	0.054	0.4799	0.555	1.15	1.392	1.67	2.359	0.34	0.308
0 Rem. Super Short U.M.	0.534	0.05	0.475	0.55	1.538	1.703	2.015	2.825	0.344	0.308
0 Canadian Mag	0.535	0.05	0.483	0.54	2.34	2.5	2.825	3.6	0.339	0.308
0 Winchester Short Magnum	0.535	0.054	0.48	0.555	1.664	1.821	2.1	2.86	0.344	0.308
0 Norma Magnum	0.585	0.06	0.521	0.5845	1.892	2.191	2.492	3.4	0.3389	0.308
0 Remington Ultra Mag	0.534	0.05	0.475	0.55	2.387	2.544	2.85	3.6	0.344	0.309
0 Dakota	0.5429	0.05	0.487	0.545	2.086	2.24	2.55	3.5299	0.338	0.308
0 Lapua Magnum	0.5878	0.06	0.5213	0.587	22.16	2.374	2.724	3.72	0.3437	0.31
03 Jeffery	0.557	0.045	0.489	0.53	1.75	1.99	2.338	3.25	0.346	0.312
8 Westley Richards	0.4681	0.05	0.4142	0.4681	1.953	2.042	2.4	3.5299	0.3591	0.3299
2 Remington	0.422	0.049	0.358	0.4207	1.498	1.569	2.05	2.525	0.3477	0.321
25 Winchester Short Magnum	0.535	0.054	0.4799	0.5559	1.664	1.792	2.1	2.86	0.358	0.3324
92x33mm Kurz	0.4705	0.051	0.4134	0.4701	0.9657	1.092	1.299	1.8898	0.3543	0.323
92x94mm Panzerbuschse	0.822	0.085	0.658	0.825	2.642	3.41	3.717	4.657	0.369	0.323
92x107mm Polish	0.646	0.066	0.575	0.647	3.767	3.911	4.225	5.205	0.363	0.323
51mm Mauser	0.4705	0.051	0.4134	0.4705	1.499	1.659	1.996	2.677	0.3532	0.319
56mm Mann-Schoenauer	0.4685	0.047	0.4055	0.4634	1.811	1.901	2.22	3.063	0.3504	0.3307
57JSmm Mauser	0.4705	0.051	0.4134	0.4717	1.897	2.003	2.36	3.29	0.3575	0.323
59mm Breda	0.469	0.051	0.405	0.491	1.93	2.04	2.32	3.165	0.358	0.323
60Jmm Mauser	0.4705	0.051	0.4134	0.4717	1.897	2	2.36	3.228	0.3535	0.3185
60Smm Mauser	0.4705	0.051	0.4134	0.4717	1.897	2	2.362	3.291	0.3575	0.323
63mm Swedish	0.479	0.051	0.405	0.488	2.016	2.195	2.48	3.36	0.356	0.323
64Jmm Brenneke	0.4724	0.051	0.4173	0.4075	2.039	0.219	0.2507	3.385	0.3488	0.3185
64Smm Brenneke	0.4724	0.051	0.4173	0.4705	2.039	2.18	2.519	3.445	0.3528	0.323
68Smm	0.5118	0.055	0.4409	0.5236	2.094	2.322	2.657	3.425	0.3598	0.323
nm Nambu	0.4157	0.05	0.3582	0.4107	0.631	0.728	0.85	1.2598	0.339	0.3196
30 Dakota	0.5429	0.05	0.487	0.545	2.06	2.203	2.74	3.5299	0.382	0.338
59 Lazzeroni Titan	0.5811	0.065	0.5098	0.5799	2.311	2.496	2.809	3.6	0.369	0.338
38 Canadian Mag	0.532	0.045	0.487	0.544	2.34	2.545	2.83	3.6	0.369	0.338
38 Ruger Compact Mag	0.532	0.05	0.4752	0.532	1.569	1.695	2.015	2.823	0.369	0.338
38 Federal	0.473	0.055	0.4091	0.4709	1.56	1.682	2.015	2.8	0.365	0.338
38 Remington Ultra Magnum	0.534	0.05	0.475	0.55	2.296	2.43	2.76	3.6	0.371	0.338
38 Blaser Magnum	0.535	0.054	0.4799	0.5449	2.028	2.153	2.501	3.34	0.3685	0.338
38 Lapua Magnum	0.5878	0.06	0.5213	0.587	2.16	2.397	2.72	3.68	0.3705	0.338
38 Norma Magnum	0.5845	0.06	0.521	0.5845	1.88	2.15	2.49	3.6	0.3669	0.338
5 Whelen	0.473	0.05	0.409	0.4698	1.948	2.032	2.494	3.34	0.388	0.358
5 Remington	0.46	0.05	0.4	0.4574	1.539	1.584	1.92	2.525	0.3838	0.358
58 Winchester	0.473	0.054	0.409	0.4703	1.56	1.65	2.015	2.78	0.388	0.358
3x57mm Mauser	0.4705	0.051	0.4134	0.4701	1.805	1.864	2.224	3.228	0.3937	0.366
3x62mm Mauser	0.4705	0.051	0.4134	0.4764	2.039	2.134	2.4409	3.29	3.906	0.366
3x66 Sako	0.4705	0.051	0.4134	0.4776	2.197	2.291	2.598	3.346	0.3906	0.366
75 Canadian Magnum	0.532	0.045	0.487	0.544	2.34	2.455	2.83	3.6	0.402	0.375
75 Blaser Magnum	0.535	0.053	0.4799	0.5449	2.028	2.153	2.508	3.34	0.406	0.375

Cartridge Name	Rim Diameter	Rim Thickness	Extractor Groove Diameter	Head Diameter	Length to Shoulder	Length to Neck	Case Length	Overall Loaded Length	Outside Diameter at Mouth	Bullet Diameter
.375 Ruger	0.532	0.05	0.475	0.532	2.18	2.275	2.58	3.34	0.405	0.375
.375 Remington Ultra Magnum	0.534	0.5	0.475	0.55	2.387	2.49	2.85	3.6	0.405	0.375
.375 Dakota	0.5429	0.05	0.487	0.545	2.061	2.17	2.57	3.43	0.402	0.375
.376 Steyr	0.4961	0.5	0.4409	0.5071	1.893	2.006	2.362	3.11	0.4028	0.375
.404 Dakota	0.5429	0.05	0.487	0.545	2.061	2.125	2.57	3.43	0.432	0.408
10.57 Lazzeroni Meteor	0.5811	0.065	0.5098	0.5799	2.311	2.496	2.809	3.62	0.445	0.416
.416 Rigby	0.5902	0.065	0.5	0.589	2.353	2.4	2.9	3.75	0.4461	0.416
.416 Barrett	0.8039	0.089	0.6799	0.8039	2.51	2.788	3.273	4.563	0.454	0.416
.416 Dakota	0.5429	0.05	0.487	0.545	2.276	2.35	2.85	3.43	0.447	0.416
.404 Jeffery	0.5429	0.05	0.482	0.5449	2	2.251	2.875	3.5299	0.452	0.422
10.75x68mm Mauser	0.4949	0.061	0.4173	0.4949	2.1	2.126	2.677	3.189	0.4352	0.422
10.75x57mm Mann-Schoenauer	0.467	0.05	0.4055	0.467	1.931	1.98	2.24	3.066	0.448	0.424
.450 Dakota	0.582	0.065	0.5	0.582	2.324	2.4	2.9	3.65	0.485	0.458
.450 Rigby	0.5902	0.065	0.5	0.589	2.342	2.389	2.893	3.75	0.4874	0.458
.458 Canadian Mag	0.532	0.045	0.487	0.544	2.34	2.378	2.83	3.6	0.485	0.458
.460 Steyr	0.8039	0.089	0.6799	0.8039	2.8	3.03	3.54	4.787	0.498	0.458
.505 Gibbs	0.6402	0.065	0.5598	0.6402	2.457	2.498	3.15	3.85	0.535	0.505
.50 Spotter/Tracer	0.8039	0.089	0.6799	0.8039	2.06	2.4	2.99	4.5	0.5598	0.511
.50 BMG	0.8039	0.09	0.6799	0.8039	3	3.279	3.91	5.45	0.5598	0.511
12.7x108mm Soviet	0.8583	0.079	0.7087	0.8602	3.338	3.645	4.252	5.787	0.5484	0.511
.5 in Vickers	0.77	0.085	0.643	0.721	2.57	2.68	3.192	4.212	0.545	0.514
13.2x99mm Hotchkiss	0.798	0.087	0.661	0.791	3	3.256	3.903	5.365	0.57	0.531
14.5x114mm Soviet	1.061	0.098	0.9055	1.061	3.479	3.912	4.488	6.378	0.6496	0.5858
.60 ATR	1.159	0.1175	1.013	1.142	3.388	3.938	4.488	6.6	0.653	0.6055

CHAPTER 100 : BIBLIOGRAPHY

Barnes, Frank. 2003. *Cartridges of the World (10th.edition)*. (*Each edition is significantly different in specialized articles*). Krause Publications, Iola, WI. 526p

Barnes, Frank. 2006. *Cartridges of the World (11th.edition)*. Krause Publications. Iola, WI. 552p

Barnes, Frank. 2009. *Cartridges of the World (12th.edition)*. Krause Publications. Iola, WI. 567p

Bearse, Ray. 1966. *Centerfire American Rifle Cartridges, 1892-1963*. Barnes. Brunswick, New Jersey. 198p

Brandt, Jakob and Erlmeier, Hans. 1998. *Handbuch der Pistolen und Revolver Patronen - Manual of Pistol and Revolver Cartridges* (Originally three separate volumes, updated and now bound as one). Journal Verlag Schwend. Schwäbisch Hall, Germany. 706p (Text in German and English) ISBN: 3935210086

Brandt, Jakob and Hamann, Horst. 1986. *Die Militärpatronen Kaliber 7,62 x 51 mm NATO, ihre Entwicklung und Abarten - The Military Cartridges Calibre 7,62 x 51 mm NATO, Their Development and Variants* (Text in German and English). Journal-Verlag Schwend. Schwäbisch Hall, Germany. 314p

Brandt, Jakob and Hamann, Horst. 1972. *Identifizierung von Handfeuerwaffen-Munition*. Journal-Verlag Schwend. Schwäbisch Hall, Germany. 228p

Brandt, Jakob and Hamann, Horst. 1972. *Identifizierung von Patronenmunition*. Wiesbaden, Germany. 334p ISBN: 3925969012

Brandt, Jakob and Hamann, Horst and Dr.Windisch, Erik. 1981. *Die Militärpatronen Kaliber 7,9mm: Ihre Vorlaufer und Abarten*. Journal-Verlag Schwend. Schwabisch Hall, Germany. 314p

Datig, Fred. 1963. *Cartridges for Collectors. Vol. 1 Centerfire, Metric, British & American Cartridges*. Borden Publishing. Los Angeles, California. (1983 Fadco. Beverly Hills, California.) 176p

Datig, Fred. 1980. *Cartridges for Collectors. Vol. 2 Centerfire, Rimfire, Patent Ignition*. Borden Publishing. Los Angeles, California. (1983 Fadco. Beverly Hills, California.) 176p ISBN: 0875050972

Datig, Fred. 1967. *Cartridges for Collectors. Vol 3 Centerfire, Rimfire, Plastic*. Borden Publishing. Los Angeles, California. (1983 Fadco. Beverly Hills, California .) 176p

Datig, Fred. 1983. *Cartridges for Collectors. Vol 4 CenterfireRimfire, Patent Ignition*. Borden Publishing. Los Angeles, California . (1983 Fadco. Beverly Hills, California.) 283p

Datig, Fred. *The History and Development of Imperial and Soviet Russian Military Small Arms and Ammunition 1700 - 1986: Volume 16, Soviet Russian Postwar Military Pistols and Cartridges 1945-1986* (1988 Handgun Press. Glenview, IL.) 152p

Dixon, Brad. 1997. *European Sporting Cartridges Vol. 1 German and Austrian Cartridges*. Armory Publications. Bellingham, Washington. 247p ISBN: 0939683105

Dixon, Brad. 2000. *European Sporting Cartridges Vol. 2 Switzerland, Norway, Sweden, Denmark, Finland, Czechoslovakia, France, Belgium, Russia, Hungary, Italy, Netherlands, Poland and Spain : 1870 to 1998*. Armory Publications. Bellingham, Washington. 346p ISBN: 0939683180

Fleming, Bill. 1993. *British Sporting Rifle Cartridges: A Summary of Case Types, Headstamps, Bullets and Charge Variations*. Armory Publications. Tacoma . 311p ISBN: 0939683113

Hackley, Frank and Woodin, William and Scranton, Eugene. 1967-78. *History of Modern U.S. Military Small Arms Ammunition Vol. 1 1880-1939*. Macmillan. New York, U.S.A. 328p ISBN: 1577470338

Hackley, Frank and Woodin, William and Scranton, Eugene. 1967-78. *History of Modern U.S. Military Small Arms Ammunition Vol. 2 1940-1945*. Macmillan. New York, U.S.A. 297p ISBN: 0882270079

Hedlund, Dale. 2000. *Kynoch: George Kynoch and the 100 Year History of the Company*. Armory Publications. Tacoma. 132p ISBN: 0939683202

Hogg, Ian. 1982. The *Cartridge Guide*. Stackpole Books. Harrisburg. 192p ISBN: 0811710483

Hogg, Ian. 1985. *Jane's Directory of Military Small Arms Ammunition*. Jane's Information Group. London, U.K. 124p ISBN 0710603312

Hoyem, George. 1981. *History and Development of Small Arms Ammunition Vol. 1 Martial Long Arms: Flintlock through Rimfire* Armory Publications. Tacoma. 230p ISBN: 0960498281 (ISBN: 0960498206. set)

Hoyem, George. 1982. *History and Development of Small Arms Ammunition Vol. 2 American Sporting Black Powder Centerfire Cartridges and their Rifles, ca 1812 to 1890*. Armory Publications. Tacoma. 303p ISBN: 096049829X (ISBN: 0960498206. set)

Hoyem, George. 1982 *History and Development of Small Arms Ammunition Vol. 3 British Sporting Rifle*. Armory Publications Tacoma. 220p ISBN: 0960498273 (ISBN: 0960498206. set)

Hoyem, George. 1999. *History and Development of Small Arms Ammunition Vol 4 Martial Long Arms: Black Powder Centerfire Cartridges and their Rifles ca 1812 to 1890*. Armory Publications. Tacoma. 224p ISBN: 096049829X (ISBN: 0960498206. set)

Huon, Jean. 1988. *Military Rifle and Machine Gun Cartridges*. Alexandria . Ironside International Publishers. 378p ISBN: 093555405X

Johnson, Melvin and Haven, Charles. 1943. *Ammunition, Its History, Development and Use, 1600 to 1943, .22 BB Cap to the 20mm Shell*. Morrow. New York, U.S.A. 374p

Kent, Daniel. 1990. *German 7.9mm Military Ammunition, 1888-1945*. Daniel W. Kent. Ann Arbor, Michigan. 232p

Labbett, Peter. 1993. *British Small Arms Ammunition, 1864-1938 (Other than .303 Inch)*. Labbett. London, U.K. 358p ISBN: 0952056704

Labbett, Peter. 1988. *.303 Inch: A History of the .303 inch Cartridge in British Service*. London, U.K. 258p ISBN: 095129220X

Logan, Herschel. 1948. *Cartridges: A Pictorial Digest of Small Arms Ammunition*. Standard Publications. Huntington, U.S.A. 204p

Pople-Crump, John. 2004. *A History of British Small Arms Ammunition - Part One - The Royal Laboratory, Woolwich*. Gloucestershire, U.K. 69p

Punnett, Chris. 1997. *.30-06*. CTG Publishing. Chadds Ford , Pennsylvania . 382p

Richards, James. 1992. *British Cartridge Guide*. Z-Towne Images. Zelienople , Pennsylvania . 150p

Shuey, Daniel. 1999. *WRACo Headstamped Cartridges and Their Variations, Vol. 1*. WCF Publications. Rockford, Illinois. 360p

Suydam, Charles. 1982. *The American Cartridge, An Illustrated Study of the Rimfire Cartridge in the United States*. Borden Publishing. 184p ISBN: 0875051065

Suydam, Charles. 1977. *U.S. Cartridges and their Handguns 1795-1975*. Beinfield Publications. North Hollywood, California. 333p ISBN: 0917714040

Taylor, John. *African Rifles & Cartridges*. The Gun Room Press. Highland Park. New Jersey.

Thomas, Dean and Thomas, James. *A Handbook of Civil War Bullets and Cartridges*. Thomas Publications. Gettysburg, Pennsylvania. 75p ISBN: 0939631946

White, Henry and Munhall, Burton . 1977. *Cartridge Headstamp Guide* (revised). H. P. White Laboratory. Bel Air, Maryland . 261p

SECTION XVIII – INDEXES
CHAPTER 101 : CARTRIDGE INDEX

SHOTSHELLS

CHAPTER 102 : GENERAL INDEX

P.S. : CAN A GUN FIRE A SATELLITE INTO ORBIT?

Gerald Bull thought so when he proposed HARP (High Altitude Research Programme) based on his concept of using a large gun to fire probes into the upper atmosphere. Later, he proposed firing rocket boosted satellites with 50 pound payloads into low earth orbit. Initial support came from the Space Research Institute at McGill University. Later, the U.S. Army entered the project. HARP was built near the runway of the Seawell International Airport in Barbados.

The installation of a heavy, specially designed concrete firing stand allowed firing at vertical elevations. The U.S. Army supplied a naval 16 inch 45 caliber gun breech and barrel. Later, the barrel was extended to 86 calibers in length by welding a second barrel on top of the first. The bore of the barrel was made smooth by boring it out to 16.5 inches to remove the rifling. The gun fired discarding sabot, fin stabilized, 5 inch diameter "darts" weighing 185 pounds at muzzle velocities of up to 7,000 fps. To achieve such performance, the HARP gun was loaded with up to 960 pounds of propellant! The highest altitude reached was 591,000 feet (112 miles) with a Martlet 2C projectile. Between 1961 and 1969 when the project was ended, HARP personnel fired 572 shots at a cost of just $10 million. The last shot was fired in late 1969.

The HARP gun occupies a unique place in the history of gunnery. It contradicts the generally accepted view that gunnery is a dead technology by showing how much potential remains to be discovered. Will history record the HARP gun as the last large caliber gun to be fired? Let us hope not.

View of the HARP gun firing a missile into the upper atmosphere from Barbados.